American Casebook Series
Hornbook Series and Basic Legal Texts
Nutshell Series

of

WEST PUBLISHING COMPANY
P.O. Box 3526
St. Paul, Minnesota 55165
February, 1982

ACCOUNTING

Fiflis and Kripke's Teaching Materials on Accounting for Business Lawyers, 2nd Ed., 684 pages, 1977 (Casebook)

ADMINISTRATIVE LAW

Davis' Cases, Text and Problems on Administrative Law, 6th Ed., 683 pages, 1977 (Casebook)

Davis' Basic Text on Administrative Law, 3rd Ed., 617 pages, 1972 (Text)

Davis' Police Discretion, 176 pages, 1975 (Text)

Gellhorn and Boyer's Administrative Law and Process in a Nutshell, 2nd Ed., 445 pages, 1981 (Text)

Mashaw and Merrill's Introduction to the American Public Law System, 1095 pages, 1975, with 1980 Supplement (Casebook)

Robinson, Gellhorn and Bruff's The Administrative Process, 2nd Ed., 959 pages, 1980 (Casebook)

ADMIRALTY

Healy and Sharpe's Cases and Materials on Admiralty, 875 pages, 1974 (Casebook)

AGENCY—PARTNERSHIP

Crane and Bromberg's Hornbook on Partnership, 695 pages, 1968 (text)

Fessler's Alternatives to Incorporation for Persons in Quest of Profit, 258 pages, 1980 (Casebook)

AGENCY—PARTNERSHIP—Continued

Henn's Cases and Materials on Agency, Partnership and Other Unincorporated Business Enterprises, 396 pages, 1972 (Casebook)

Reuschlein and Gregory's Hornbook on the Law of Agency and Partnership, 625 pages, 1979, with 1981 pocket part (Text)

Seavey's Hornbook on Agency, 329 pages, 1964 (Text)

Seavey and Hall's Cases on Agency, 431 pages, 1956 (Casebook)

Seavey, Reuschlein and Hall's Cases on Agency and Partnership, 599 pages, 1962 (Casebook)

Selected Corporation and Partnership Statutes and Forms, 777 pages, 1980

Steffen and Kerr's Cases and Materials on Agency-Partnership, 4th Ed., 859 pages, 1980 (Casebook)

Steffen's Agency-Partnership in a Nutshell, 364 pages, 1977 (Text)

AMERICAN INDIAN LAW

Canby's American Indian Law in a Nutshell, 288 pages, 1981 (Text)

Getches, Rosenfelt and Wilkinson's Cases on Federal Indian Law, 660 pages, 1979 (Casebook)

ANTITRUST LAW

Gellhorn's Antitrust Law and Economics in a Nutshell, 2nd Ed., 425 pages, 1981 (Text)

Oppenheim, Weston and McCarthy's Cases and Comments on Federal Antitrust Laws, 4th Ed., 1168 pages, 1981 (Casebook)

ANTITRUST LAW—Continued

Posner and Easterbrook's Cases and Economic Notes on Antitrust, 2nd Ed., 1077 pages, 1981 (Casebook)

Sullivan's Hornbook of the Law of Antitrust, 886 pages, 1977 (Text)

See also Regulated Industries, Trade Regulation

BANKING LAW

See Regulated Industries

BUSINESS PLANNING

Epstein and Scheinfeld's Teaching Materials on Business Reorganization Under the Bankruptcy Code, 216 pages, 1980 (Casebook)

Painter's Problems and Materials in Business Planning, 791 pages, 1975, with 1980 Supplement (Casebook)

CIVIL PROCEDURE

Casad's Res Judicata in a Nutshell, 310 pages, 1976 (text)

Cound, Friedenthal and Miller's Cases and Materials on Civil Procedure, 3rd Ed., 1147 pages, 1980 with 1980 Supplement (Casebook)

Cound, Friedenthal and Miller's Cases on Pleading, Joinder and Discovery, 643 pages, 1968 (Casebook)

Ehrenzweig, Louisell and Hazard's Jurisdiction in a Nutshell, 4th Ed., 232 pages, 1980 (Text)

Federal Rules of Civil-Appellate-Criminal Procedure—West Law School Edition, 344 pages, 1981

Hodges, Jones and Elliott's Cases and Materials on Texas Trial and Appellate Procedure, 2nd Ed., 745 pages, 1974 (Casebook)

Hodges, Jones and Elliott's Cases and Materials on the Judicial Process Prior to Trial in Texas, 2nd Ed., 871 pages, 1977 (Casebook)

Kane's Civil Procedure in a Nutshell, 271 pages, 1979 (Text)

Karlen's Procedure Before Trial in a Nutshell, 258 pages, 1972 (Text)

Karlen and Joiner's Cases and Materials on Trials and Appeals, 536 pages, 1971 (Casebook)

Karlen, Meisenholder, Stevens and Vestal's Cases on Civil Procedure, 923 pages, 1975 (Casebook)

Koffler and Reppy's Hornbook on Common Law Pleading, 663 pages, 1969 (Text)

McBaine's Cases on Introduction to Civil Procedure, 399 pages, 1950 (Casebook)

CIVIL PROCEDURE—Continued

McCoid's Cases on Civil Procedure, 823 pages, 1974 (Casebook)

Park's Computer-Aided Exercises on Civil Procedure, 118 pages, 1976 (Coursebook)

Shipman's Hornbook on Common-Law Pleading, 3rd Ed., 644 pages, 1923 (Text)

Siegel's Hornbook on New York Practice, 1011 pages, 1978 with 1979–80 Pocket Part (Text)

See also Federal Jurisdiction and Procedure

CIVIL RIGHTS

Abernathy's Cases and Materials on Civil Rights, 660 pages, 1980 (Casebook)

Cohen's Cases on the Law of Deprivation of Liberty: A Study in Social Control, 755 pages, 1980 (Casebook)

Lockhart, Kamisar and Choper's Cases on Constitutional Rights and Liberties, 5th Ed., 1298 pages plus Appendix, 1981, with 1981 Supplement (Casebook)—reprint from Lockhart, et al. Cases on Constitutional Law, 5th Ed., 1980

Vieira's Civil Rights in a Nutshell, 279 pages, 1978 (Text)

COMMERCIAL LAW

Bailey's Secured Transactions in a Nutshell, 2nd Ed., 391 pages, 1981 (Text)

Epstein and Martin's Basic Uniform Commercial Code Teaching Materials, 599 pages, 1977 (Casebook)

Henson's Hornbook on Secured Transactions Under the U.C.C., 2nd Ed., 504 pages, 1979 with 1979 P.P. (Text)

Murray's Commercial Law, Problems and Materials, 366 pages, 1975 (Coursebook)

Nordstrom and Clovis' Problems and Materials on Commercial Paper, 458 pages, 1972 (Casebook)

Nordstrom and Lattin's Problems and Materials on Sales and Secured Transactions, 809 pages, 1968 (Casebook)

Nordstrom, Murray and Clovis' Problems and Materials on Sales, 515 pages, 1982 (Casebook)

Nordstrom's Hornbook on Sales, 600 pages, 1970 (Text)

Selected Commercial Statutes, 1367 pages, 1981

Speidel, Summers and White's Teaching Materials on Commercial and Consumer Law, 3rd Ed., 1490 pages, 1981 (Casebook)

Stockton's Sales in a Nutshell, 2nd Ed., 370 pages, 1981 (Text)

COMMERCIAL LAW—Continued

Stone's Uniform Commercial Code in a Nutshell, 507 pages, 1975 (Text)

Uniform Commercial Code, Official Text with Comments, 994 pages, 1978

UCC Article 8, 1977 Amendments, 249 pages, 1978

UCC Article 9, Reprint from 1962 Code, 128 pages, 1976

UCC Article 9, 1972 Amendments, 304 pages, 1978

Weber and Speidel's Commercial Paper in a Nutshell, 3rd Ed., approximately 425 pages, 1982 (Text)

White and Summers' Hornbook on the Uniform Commercial Code, 2nd Ed., 1250 pages, 1980 (Text)

COMMUNITY PROPERTY

Huie's Texas Cases and Materials on Marital Property Rights, 681 pages, 1966 (Casebook)

Verrall's Cases and Materials on California Community Property, 3rd Ed., 547 pages, 1977 (Casebook)

COMPARATIVE LAW

Gordon, Osakwe and Glendon's Comparative Legal Traditions in a Nutshell, approximately 400 pages, 1982 (Text)

Langbein's Comparative Criminal Procedure: Germany, 172 pages, 1977 (Casebook)

CONFLICT OF LAWS

Cramton, Currie and Kay's Cases-Comments-Questions on Conflict of Laws, 3rd Ed., 1026 pages, 1981 (Casebook)

Ehrenzweig's Conflicts in a Nutshell, 3rd Ed., 432 pages, 1974 (Text)

Scoles and Weintraub's Cases and Materials on Conflict of Laws, 2nd Ed., 966 pages, 1972, with 1978 Supplement (Casebook)

Siegel's Conflicts in a Nutshell, approximately 450 pages, 1982 (Text)

CONSTITUTIONAL LAW

Engdahl's Constitutional Power in a Nutshell: Federal and State, 411 pages, 1974 (Text)

Lockhart, Kamisar and Choper's Cases-Comments-Questions on Constitutional Law, 5th Ed., 1705 pages plus Appendix, 1980, with 1981 Supplement (Casebook)

CONSTITUTIONAL LAW—Continued

Lockhart, Kamisar and Choper's Cases-Comments-Questions on the American Constitution, 5th Ed., 1185 pages plus Appendix, 1981, with 1981 Supplement (Casebook)—reprint from Lockhart, et al. Cases on Constitutional Law, 5th Ed., 1980

Manning's The Law of Church-State Relations in a Nutshell, 305 pages, 1981 (Text)

Miller's Presidential Power in a Nutshell, 328 pages, 1977 (Text)

Nowak, Rotunda and Young's Handbook on Constitutional Law, 974 pages, 1978, with 1979 pocket part (Text)

Rotunda's Modern Constitutional Law: Cases and Notes, 1034 pages, 1981, with 1981 Supplement (Casebook)

Williams' Constitutional Analysis in a Nutshell, 388 pages, 1979 (Text)

See also Civil Rights

CONSUMER LAW

Epstein and Nickles' Consumer Law in a Nutshell, 2nd Ed., 418 pages, 1981 (Text)

McCall's Consumer Protection, Cases, Notes and Materials, 594 pages, 1977, with 1977 Statutory Supplement (Casebook)

Schrag's Cases and Materials on Consumer Protection, 2nd Ed., 197 pages, 1973 (Casebook)—reprint from Cooper, et al. Cases on Law and Poverty, 2nd Ed., 1973

Selected Commercial Statutes, 1367 pages, 1981

Spanogle and Rohner's Cases and Materials on Consumer Law, 693 pages, 1979 (Casebook)

See also Commercial Law

CONTRACTS

Calamari & Perillo's Cases and Problems on Contracts, 1061 pages, 1978 (Casebook)

Calamari and Perillo's Hornbook on Contracts, 2nd Ed., 878 pages, 1977 (Text)

Corbin's Text on Contracts, One Volume Student Edition, 1224 pages, 1952 (Text)

Freedman's Cases and Materials on Contracts, 658 pages, 1973 (Casebook)

Friedman's Contract Remedies in a Nutshell, 323 pages, 1981 (Text)

Fuller and Eisenberg's Cases on Basic Contract Law, 4th Ed., 1203 pages, 1981 (Casebook)

Jackson and Bollinger's Cases on Contract Law in Modern Society, 2nd Ed., 1329 pages, 1980 (Casebook)

CONTRACTS—Continued

Keyes' Government Contracts in a Nutshell, 423 pages, 1979 (Text)

Reitz's Cases on Contracts as Basic Commercial Law, 763 pages, 1975 (Casebook)

Schaber and Rohwer's Contracts in a Nutshell, 307 pages, 1975 (Text)

Simpson's Hornbook on Contracts, 2nd Ed., 510 pages, 1965 (Text)

COPYRIGHT

Nimmer's Cases and Materials on Copyright and Other Aspects of Law Pertaining to Literary, Musical and Artistic Works, Illustrated, 2nd Ed., 1023 pages, 1979 (Casebook)

See also Patent Law

CORPORATIONS

Hamilton's Cases on Corporations—Including Partnerships and Limited Partnerships, 2nd Ed., 1108 pages, 1981, with 1981 Statutory Supplement (Casebook)

Hamilton's Law of Corporations in a Nutshell, 379 pages, 1980 (Text)

Henn's Cases on Corporations, 1279 pages, 1974, with 1980 Supplement (Casebook)

Henn's Hornbook on Corporations, 2nd Ed., 956 pages, 1970 (Text)

Jennings and Buxbaum's Cases and Materials on Corporations, 5th Ed., 1180 pages, 1979 (Casebook)

Selected Corporation and Partnership Statutes, Regulations and Forms, 777 pages, 1980

CORRECTIONS

Krantz's Cases and Materials on the Law of Corrections and Prisoners' Rights, 2nd Ed., 735 pages, 1981 (Casebook)

Krantz's Law of Corrections and Prisoners' Rights in a Nutshell, 353 pages, 1976 (Text)

Model Rules and Regulations on Prisoners' Rights and Responsibilities, 212 pages, 1973

Popper's Post-Conviction Remedies in a Nutshell, 360 pages, 1978 (Text)

Robbins' Cases and Materials on Post Conviction Remedies, approximately 400 pages, April 1982 (Casebook)

Rubin's Law of Criminal Corrections, 2nd Ed., 873 pages, 1973, with 1978 Supplement (Text)

CREDITOR'S RIGHTS

Epstein's Debtor-Creditor Law in a Nutshell, 2nd Ed., 324 pages, 1980 (Text)

CREDITOR'S RIGHTS—Continued

Epstein and Landers' Debtors and Creditors: Cases and Materials, 722 pages, 1978, with 1979 Supplement (Casebook)

Epstein and Sheinfeld's Teaching Materials on Business Reorganization Under the Bankruptcy Code, 216 pages, 1980 (Casebook)

Riesenfeld's Cases and Materials on Creditors' Remedies and Debtors' Protection, 3rd Ed., 810 pages, 1979 with 1979 Statutory Supplement and 1981 Case Supplement (Casebook)

Selected Bankruptcy Statutes, 351 pages, 1979

CRIMINAL LAW AND CRIMINAL PROCEDURE

Cohen and Gobert's Problems in Criminal Law, 297 pages, 1976 (Problem book)

Davis' Police Discretion, 176 pages, 1975 (Text)

Dix and Sharlot's Cases and Materials on Criminal Law, 2nd Ed., 771 pages, 1979 (Casebook)

Federal Rules of Civil-Appellate-Criminal Procedure—West Law School Edition, 344 pages, 1981

Grano's Problems in Criminal Procedure, 2nd Ed., 176 pages, 1981 (Problem book)

Heymann and Kenety's The Murder Trial of Wilbur Jackson: A Homicide in the Family, 340 pages, 1975 (Case Study)

Israel and LaFave's Criminal Procedure in a Nutshell, 3rd Ed., 438 pages, 1980 (Text)

Johnson's Cases, Materials and Text on Substantive Criminal Law in its Procedural Context, 2nd Ed., 956 pages, 1980 (Casebook)

Kamisar, LaFave and Israel's Cases, Comments and Questions on Modern Criminal Procedure, 5th ed., 1635 pages plus Appendix, 1980 with 1981 Supplement (Casebook)

Kamisar, LaFave and Israel's Cases, Comments and Questions on Basic Criminal Procedure, 5th Ed., 869 pages, 1980 with 1981 Supplement (Casebook)—reprint from Kamisar, et al. Modern Criminal Procedure, 5th ed., 1980

LaFave's Modern Criminal Law: Cases, Comments and Questions, 789 pages, 1978 (Casebook)

LaFave and Scott's Hornbook on Criminal Law, 763 pages, 1972 (Text)

CRIMINAL LAW AND CRIMINAL PROCEDURE—Continued

Langbein's Comparative Criminal Procedure: Germany, 172 pages, 1977 (Casebook)

Loewy's Criminal Law in a Nutshell, 302 pages, 1975 (Text)

Saltzburg's American Criminal Procedure, Cases and Commentary, 1253 pages, 1980 with 1981 Supplement (Casebook)

Saltzburg's Introduction to American Criminal Procedure, 702 pages, 1980 with 1981 Supplement (Casebook)—reprint from Saltzburg's American Criminal Procedure, 1980

Uviller's The Processes of Criminal Justice: Investigation and Adjudication, 2nd Ed., 1384 pages, 1979 with 1979 Statutory Supplement and 1980 Update (Casebook)

Uviller's The Processes of Criminal Justice: Adjudication, 2nd Ed., 730 pages, 1979. Soft-cover reprint from Uviller's The Processes of Criminal Justice: Investigation and Adjudication, 2nd Ed. (Casebook)

Uviller's The Processes of Criminal Justice: Investigation, 2nd Ed., 655 pages, 1979. Soft-cover reprint from Uviller's The Processes of Criminal Justice: Investigation and Adjudication, 2nd Ed. (Casebook)

Vorenberg's Cases on Criminal Law and Procedure, 2nd Ed., 1088 pages, 1981 (Casebook)

See also Corrections, Juvenile Justice

DECEDENTS ESTATES

See Trusts and Estates

DOMESTIC RELATIONS

Clark's Cases and Problems on Domestic Relations, 3rd Ed., 1153 pages, 1980 (Casebook)

Clark's Hornbook on Domestic Relations, 754 pages, 1968 (Text)

Krause's Cases and Materials on Family Law, 1132 pages, 1976, with 1978 Supplement (Casebook)

Krause's Family Law in a Nutshell, 400 pages, 1977 (Text)

EDUCATION LAW

Morris' The Constitution and American Education, 2nd Ed., 992 pages, 1980 (Casebook)

EMPLOYMENT DISCRIMINATION

Cooper, Rabb and Rubin's Fair Employment Litigation: Text and Materials for Student and Practitioner, 590 pages, 1975 (Coursebook)

Player's Cases and Materials on Employment Discrimination Law, 878 pages, 1980 with 1982 Supplement (Casebook)

Player's Federal Law of Employment Discrimination in a Nutshell, 2nd Ed., 402 pages, 1981 (Text)

Sovern's Cases and Materials on Racial Discrimination in Employment, 2nd Ed., 167 pages, 1973 (Casebook)—reprint from Cooper et al. Cases on Law and Poverty, 2nd Ed., 1973

See also Women and the Law

ENERGY AND NATURAL RESOURCES LAW

Rodgers' Cases and Materials on Energy and Natural Resources Law, 995 pages, 1979 (Casebook)

Selected Environmental Law Statutes, 681 pages, 1981

Tomain's Energy Law in a Nutshell, 338 pages, 1981 (Text)

See also Environmental Law, Oil and Gas, Water Law

ENVIRONMENTAL LAW

Currie's Cases and Materials on Pollution, 715 pages, 1975 (Casebook)

Federal Environmental Law, 1600 pages, 1974 (Text)

Findley and Farber's Cases and Materials on Environmental Law, 738 pages, 1981 (Casebook)

Hanks, Tarlock and Hanks' Cases on Environmental Law and Policy, 1242 pages, 1974, with 1976 Supplement (Casebook)

Rodgers' Hornbook on Environmental Law, 956 pages, 1977 (Text)

Selected Environmental Law Statutes, 681 pages, 1981

See also Energy and Natural Resources Law, Water Law

EQUITY

See Remedies

ESTATES

See Trusts and Estates

ESTATE PLANNING

Casner and Stein's Estate Planning under the Tax Reform Act of 1976, 2nd Ed., 456 pages, 1978 (Coursebook)

JUDICIAL ADMINISTRATION

Carrington, Meador and Rosenberg's Justice on Appeal, 263 pages, 1976 (Casebook)

Leflar's Appellate Judicial Opinions, 343 pages, 1974 (Text)

Nelson's Cases and Materials on Judicial Administration and the Administration of Justice, 1032 pages, 1974 (Casebook)

JURISPRUDENCE

Christie's Text and Readings on Jurisprudence—The Philosophy of Law, 1056 pages, 1973 (Casebook)

JUVENILE JUSTICE

Fox's Cases and Materials on Modern Juvenile Justice, 2nd Ed., 960 pages, 1981 (Casebook)

Fox's Juvenile Courts in a Nutshell, 2nd Ed., 275 pages, 1977 (Text)

LABOR LAW

Gorman's Basic Text on Labor Law-Unionization and Collective Bargaining, 914 pages, 1976 (Text)

Leslie's Labor Law in a Nutshell, 403 pages, 1979 (Text)

Nolan's Labor Arbitration Law and Practice in a Nutshell, 358 pages, 1979 (Text)

Oberer, Hanslowe and Andersen's Cases and Materials on Labor Law—Collective Bargaining in a Free Society, 2nd Ed., 1168 pages, 1979, with 1979 Statutory Supplement (Casebook)

See also Employment Discrimination, Social Legislation

LAND FINANCE

See Real Estate Transactions

LAND USE

Hagman's Cases on Public Planning and Control of Urban and Land Development, 2nd Ed., 1301 pages, 1980 (Casebook)

Hagman's Hornbook on Urban Planning and Land Development Control Law, 706 pages, 1971 (Text)

Wright and Gitelman's Cases and Materials on Land Use, 3rd Ed., 1300 pages, 1982 (Casebook)

Wright and Webber's Land Use in a Nutshell, 316 pages, 1978 (Text)

See also Housing and Urban Development

LAW AND ECONOMICS

Manne's The Economics of Legal Relationships—Readings in the Theory of Property Rights, 660 pages, 1975 (Text)

See also Antitrust, Regulated Industries

LAW AND MEDICINE—PSYCHIATRY

Cohen's Cases and Materials on the Law of Deprivation of Liberty: A Study in Social Control, 755 pages, 1980 (Casebook)

King's The Law of Medical Malpractice in a Nutshell, 340 pages, 1977 (Text)

Shapiro and Spece's Problems, Cases and Materials on Bioethics and Law, 892 pages, 1981 (Casebook)

Sharpe, Fiscina and Head's Cases on Law and Medicine, 882 pages, 1978 (Casebook)

LEGAL CLINICS

See Office Practice

LEGAL HISTORY

Presser and Zainaldin's Cases on Law and American History, 855 pages, 1980 (Casebook)

See also Legal Method and Legal System

LEGAL METHOD AND LEGAL SYSTEM

Aldisert's Readings, Materials and Cases in the Judicial Process, 948 pages, 1976 (Casebook)

Bodenheimer, Oakley and Love's Readings and Cases on an Introduction to the Anglo-American Legal System, 161 pages, 1980 (Casebook)

Davies and Lawry's Institutions and Methods of the Law—Introductory Teaching Materials, approximately 550 pages, 1982 (Casebook)

Dvorkin, Himmelstein and Lesnick's Becoming a Lawyer: A Humanistic Perspective on Legal Education and Professionalism, 211 pages, 1981 (Text)

Fryer and Orentlicher's Cases and Materials on Legal Method and Legal System, 1043 pages, 1967 (Casebook)

Greenberg's Judicial Process and Social Change, 666 pages, 1977 (Coursebook)

Kempin's Historical Introduction to Anglo-American Law in a Nutshell, 2nd Ed., 280 pages, 1973 (Text)

Kimball's Historical Introduction to the Legal System, 610 pages, 1966 (Casebook)

LAW SCHOOL PUBLICATIONS—Continued

LEGAL METHOD AND LEGAL SYSTEM—Continued

Mashaw and Merrill's Introduction to the American Public Law System, 1095 pages, 1975, with 1980 Supplement (Casebook)

Murphy's Cases and Materials on Introduction to Law—Legal Process and Procedure, 772 pages, 1977 (Casebook)

Reynolds' Judicial Process in a Nutshell, 292 pages, 1980 (Text)

See also Legal Research and Writing

LEGAL PROFESSION

Aronson's Problems in Professional Responsibility, 280 pages, 1978 (Problem book)

Aronson and Weckstein's Professional Responsibility in a Nutshell, 399 pages, 1980 (Text)

Mellinkoff's The Conscience of a Lawyer, 304 pages, 1973 (Text)

Mellinkoff's Lawyers and the System of Justice, 983 pages, 1976 (Casebook)

Pirsig and Kirwin's Cases and Materials on Professional Responsibility, 3rd Ed., 667 pages, 1976, with 1981 Supplement (Casebook)

Smith's Preventing Legal Malpractice, 142 pages, 1981 (Text)

LEGAL RESEARCH AND WRITING

Cohen's Legal Research in a Nutshell, 3rd Ed., 415 pages, 1978 (Text)

Dickerson's Materials on Legal Drafting, 425 pages, 1981 (Casebook)

Felsenfeld and Siegel's Writing Contracts in Plain English, 290 pages, 1981 (Text)

Gopen's Writing From a Legal Perspective, 225 pages, 1981 (Text)

How to Find the Law With Special Chapters on Legal Writing, 7th Ed., 542 pages, 1976. Problem book available (Coursebook)

Mellinkoff's Legal Writing Sense and Nonsense, 242 pages, 1982 (Text)

Rombauer's Legal Problem Solving—Analysis, Research and Writing, 3rd Ed., 352 pages, 1978 (Coursebook)

Statsky's Legislative Analysis: How to Use Statutes and Regulations, 216 pages, 1975 (Text)

Statsky and Wernet's Case Analysis and Fundamentals of Legal Writing, 576 pages, 1977 (Text)

Weihofen's Legal Writing Style, 2nd Ed., 332 pages, 1980 (Text)

LEGISLATION

Davies' Legislative Law and Process in a Nutshell, 279 pages, 1975 (Text)

LEGISLATION—Continued

Nutting and Dickerson's Cases and Materials on Legislation, 5th Ed., 744 pages, 1978 (Casebook)

Statsky's Legislative Analysis: How to Use Statutes and Regulations, 216 pages, 1975 (Text)

LOCAL GOVERNMENT

McCarthy's Local Government Law in a Nutshell, 386 pages, 1975 (Text)

Michelman and Sandalow's Cases-Comments-Questions on Government in Urban Areas, 1216 pages, 1970, with 1972 Supplement (Casebook)

Stason and Kauper's Cases and Materials on Municipal Corporations, 3rd Ed., 692 pages, 1959 (Casebook)

Valente's Cases and Materials on Local Government Law, 2nd Ed., 980 pages, 1980 (Casebook)

MASS COMMUNICATION LAW

Gillmor and Barron's Cases and Comment on Mass Communication Law, 3rd Ed., 1008 pages, 1979 (Casebook)

Ginsburg's Regulation of Broadcasting: Law and Policy Towards Radio, Television and Cable Communications, 741 pages, 1979 (Casebook)

Zuckman and Gayne's Mass Communications Law in a Nutshell, 431 pages, 1977 (Text)

MILITARY LAW

Shanor and Terrell's Military Law in a Nutshell, 378 pages, 1980 (Text)

MORTGAGES

See Real Estate Transactions

NATURAL RESOURCES LAW

See Energy and Natural Resources Law, Environmental Law, Oil and Gas, Water Law

OFFICE PRACTICE

Binder and Price's Legal Interviewing and Counseling: A Client-Centered Approach, 232 pages, 1977 (Text)

Edwards and White's Problems, Readings and Materials on the Lawyer as a Negotiator, 484 pages, 1977 (Casebook)

Hegland's Trial and Practice Skills in a Nutshell, 346 pages, 1978 (Text)

Shaffer's Legal Interviewing and Counseling in a Nutshell, 353 pages, 1976 (Text)

Strong and Clark's Law Office Management, 424 pages, 1974 (Casebook)

OIL AND GAS

Hemingway's Hornbook on Oil and Gas, 486 pages, 1971, with 1979 pocket part (Text)

Huie, Woodward and Smith's Cases and Materials on Oil and Gas, 2nd Ed., 955 pages, 1972 (Casebook)

See also Energy and Natural Resources Law

PARTNERSHIP

See Agency—Partnership

PATENT LAW

Choate and Francis' Cases and Materials on Patent Law, 2nd Ed., 1110 pages, 1981 (Casebook)

See also Copyright

POVERTY LAW

Brudno's Poverty, Inequality, and the Law: Cases-Commentary-Analysis, 934 pages, 1976 (Casebook)

Cooper, Dodyk, Berger, Paulsen, Schrag and Sovern's Cases and Materials on Law and Poverty, 2nd Ed., 1208 pages, 1973 (Casebook)

LaFrance, Schroeder, Bennett and Boyd's Hornbook on Law of the Poor, 558 pages, 1973 (Text)

See also Social Legislation

PRODUCTS LIABILITY

Noel and Phillips' Cases on Products Liability, 2nd Ed., approximately 822 pages, 1982 (Casebook)

Noel and Phillips' Products Liability in a Nutshell, 2nd Ed., 341 pages, 1981 (Text)

PROPERTY

Aigler, Smith and Tefft's Cases on Property, 2 volumes, 1339 pages, 1960 (Casebook)

Bernhardt's Real Property in a Nutshell, 2nd Ed., 448 pages, 1981 (Text)

Boyer's Survey of the Law of Property, 766 pages, 1981 (Text)

Browder, Cunningham, Julin and Smith's Cases on Basic Property Law, 3rd Ed., 1447 pages, 1979 (Casebook)

Burby's Hornbook on Real Property, 3rd Ed., 490 pages, 1965 (Text)

Chused's A Modern Approach to Property: Cases-Notes-Materials, 1069 pages, 1978 with 1980 Supplement (Casebook)

Cohen's Materials for a Basic Course in Property, 526 pages, 1978 (Casebook)

Donahue, Kauper and Martin's Cases on Property, 1501 pages, 1974 (Casebook)

PROPERTY—Continued

Hill's Landlord and Tenant Law in a Nutshell, 319 pages, 1979 (Text)

Moynihan's Introduction to Real Property, 254 pages, 1962 (Text)

Phipps' Titles in a Nutshell, 277 pages, 1968 (Text)

Uniform Land Transactions Act, Uniform Simplification of Land Transfers Act, Uniform Condominium Act, 1977 Official Text with Comments, 462 pages, 1978

See also Housing and Urban Development, Real Estate Transactions, Land Use

REAL ESTATE TRANSACTIONS

Bruce's Real Estate Finance in a Nutshell, 292 pages, 1979 (Text)

Maxwell, Riesenfeld, Hetland and Warren's Cases on California Security Transactions in Land, 2nd Ed., 584 pages, 1975 (Casebook)

Nelson and Whitman's Cases on Real Estate Transfer, Finance and Development, 2nd Ed., 1114 pages, 1981 (Casebook)

Osborne's Cases and Materials on Secured Transactions, 559 pages, 1967 (Casebook)

Osborne, Nelson and Whitman's Hornbook on Real Estate Finance Law, 3rd Ed., 885 pages, 1979 (Text)

REGULATED INDUSTRIES

Gellhorn and Pierce's Regulated Industries in a Nutshell, approximately 400 pages, 1982 (Text)

Morgan's Cases and Materials on Economic Regulation of Business, 830 pages, 1976, with 1978 Supplement (Casebook)

Pozen's Financial Institutions: Cases, Materials and Problems on Investment Management, 844 pages, 1978 (Casebook)

White's Teaching Materials on Banking Law, 1058 pages, 1976, with 1980 Case and Statutory Supplement (Casebook)

See also Mass Communication Law

REMEDIES

Cribbet's Cases and Materials on Judicial Remedies, 762 pages, 1954 (Casebook)

Dobbs' Hornbook on Remedies, 1067 pages, 1973 (Text)

Dobbs' Problems in Remedies, 137 pages, 1974 (Problem book)

Dobbyn's Injunctions in a Nutshell, 264 pages, 1974 (Text)

LAW SCHOOL PUBLICATIONS—Continued

REMEDIES—Continued

Friedman's Contract Remedies in a Nutshell, 323 pages, 1981 (Text)

Leavell, Love and Nelson's Cases and Materials on Equitable Remedies and Restitution, 3rd Ed., 704 pages, 1980 (Casebook)

McClintock's Hornbook on Equity, 2nd Ed., 643 pages, 1948 (Text)

McCormick's Hornbook on Damages, 811 pages, 1935 (Text)

O'Connell's Remedies in a Nutshell, 364 pages, 1977 (Text)

York and Bauman's Cases and Materials on Remedies, 3rd Ed., 1250 pages, 1979 (Casebook)

REVIEW MATERIALS

Ballantine's Problems

Black Letter Series

Smith's Review Series

West's Review Covering Multistate Subjects

SECURITIES REGULATION

Ratner's Securities Regulation: Materials for a Basic Course, 2nd Ed., 1050 pages, 1980 with 1980 Statutory Supplement (Casebook)

Ratner's Securities Regulation in a Nutshell, 300 pages, 1978 (Text)

SOCIAL LEGISLATION

Brudno's Income Redistribution Theories and Programs: Cases-Commentary-Analyses, 480 pages, 1977 (Casebook)—reprint from Brudno's Poverty, Inequality and the Law, 1976

LaFrance's Welfare Law: Structure and Entitlement in a Nutshell, 455 pages, 1979 (Text)

Malone, Plant and Little's Cases on Workers' Compensation and Employment Rights, 2nd Ed., 951 pages, 1980 (Casebook)

See also Poverty Law

TAXATION

Chommie's Hornbook on Federal Income Taxation, 2nd Ed., 1051 pages, 1973 (Text)

Dodge's Federal Taxation of Estates, Trusts and Gifts: Principles and Planning, 771 pages, 1981 (Casebook)

Garbis and Struntz' Cases and Materials on Tax Procedure and Tax Fraud, 829 pages, 1982 (Casebook)

Gunn's Cases and Materials on Federal Income Taxation of Individuals, 785 pages, 1981 (Casebook)

TAXATION—Continued

Hellerstein and Hellerstein's Cases on State and Local Taxation, 4th Ed., 1041 pages, 1978 (Casebook)

Kahn's Handbook on Basic Corporate Taxation, 3rd Ed., Student Ed., 614 pages, 1981 (Text)

Kahn and Gann's Corporate Taxation and Taxation of Partnerships and Partners, 1107 pages, 1979, with 1981 Supplement (Casebook)

Kragen and McNulty's Cases and Materials on Federal Income Taxation, Vol. I: Taxation of Individuals, 3rd Ed., 1283 pages, 1979 (Casebook)

Kragen and McNulty's Cases and Materials on Federal Income Taxation, Vol. II: Taxation of Corporations, Shareholders, Partnerships and Partners, 3rd Ed., 989 pages, 1981 (Casebook)

Kramer and McCord's Problems for Federal Estate and Gift Taxes, 206 pages, 1976 (Problem book)

Lowndes, Kramer and McCord's Hornbook on Federal Estate and Gift Taxes, 3rd Ed., 1099 pages, 1974 (Text)

McCord's 1976 Estate and Gift Tax Reform-Analysis, Explanation and Commentary, 377 pages, 1977 (Text)

McNulty's Federal Estate and Gift Taxation in a Nutshell, 2nd Ed., 488 pages, 1979 (Text)

McNulty's Federal Income Taxation of Individuals in a Nutshell, 2nd Ed., 422 pages, 1978 (Text)

Rice's Problems and Materials in Federal Estate and Gift Taxation, 3rd Ed., 474 pages, 1978 (Casebook)

Rice and Solomon's Problems and Materials in Federal Income Taxation, 3rd Ed., 670 pages, 1979 (Casebook)

Rose and Raskind's Advanced Federal Income Taxation: Corporate Transactions—Cases, Materials and Problems, 955 pages, 1978 (Casebook)

Selected Federal Taxation Statutes and Regulations, 1307 pages, 1981 with 1981 Economic Recovery Tax Act Supplement

Soboleff and Weidenbruch's Federal Income Taxation of Corporations and Stockholders in a Nutshell, 362 pages, 1981 (Text)

TORTS

Green, Pedrick, Rahl, Thode, Hawkins, Smith and Treece's Cases and Materials on Torts, 2nd Ed., 1360 pages, 1977 (Casebook)

TORTS—Continued

Green, Pedrick, Rahl, Thode, Hawkins, Smith, and Treece's Advanced Torts: Injuries to Business, Political and Family Interests, 2nd Ed., 544 pages, 1977 (Casebook)—reprint from Green, et al. Cases and Materials on Torts, 2nd Ed., 1977

Keeton's Computer-Aided and Workbook Exercises on Tort Law, 164 pages, 1976 (Coursebook)

Keeton and Keeton's Cases and Materials on Torts, 2nd Ed., 1200 pages, 1977, with 1981 Supplement (Casebook)

Kionka's Torts in a Nutshell: Injuries to Persons and Property, 434 pages, 1977 (Text)

Malone's Torts in a Nutshell: Injuries to Family, Social and Trade Relations, 358 pages, 1979 (Text)

Prosser's Hornbook on Torts, 4th Ed., 1208 pages, 1971 (Text)

Shapo's Cases on Tort and Compensation Law, 1244 pages, 1976 (Casebook)

See also Products Liability

TRADE REGULATION

Oppenheim and Weston's Cases and Materials on Unfair Trade Practices and Consumer Protection, 3rd Ed., 1065 pages, 1974, with 1981 Supplement (Casebook)

See also Antitrust, Regulated Industries

TRIAL AND APPELLATE ADVOCACY

Appellate Advocacy, Handbook of, 249 pages, 1980 (Text)

Bergman's Trial Advocacy in a Nutshell, 402 pages, 1979 (Text)

Hegland's Trial and Practice Skills in a Nutshell, 346 pages, 1978 (Text)

Jeans' Handbook on Trial Advocacy, Student Ed., 473 pages, 1975 (Text)

McElhaney's Effective Litigation, 457 pages, 1974 (Casebook)

Nolan's Cases and Materials on Trial Practice, 518 pages, 1981 (Casebook)

TRUSTS AND ESTATES

Atkinson's Hornbook on Wills, 2nd Ed., 975 pages, 1953 (Text)

Averill's Uniform Probate Code in a Nutshell, 425 pages, 1978 (Text)

TRUSTS AND ESTATES—Continued

Bogert's Hornbook on Trusts, 5th Ed., 726 pages, 1973 (Text)

Clark, Lusky and Murphy's Cases and Materials on Gratuitous Transfers, 2nd Ed., 1102 pages, 1977 (Casebook)

Gulliver's Cases and Materials on Future Interests, 624 pages, 1959 (Casebook)

Gulliver's Introduction to the Law of Future Interests, 87 pages, 1959 (Casebook)—reprint from Gulliver's Cases and Materials on Future Interests, 1959

Halbach (Editor)—Death, Taxes, and Family Property: Essays and American Assembly Report, 189 pages, 1977 (Text)

Mennell's Cases and Materials on California Decedent's Estates, 566 pages, 1973 (Casebook)

Mennell's Wills and Trusts in a Nutshell, 392 pages, 1979 (Text)

Powell's The Law of Future Interests in California, 91 pages, 1980 (Text)

Simes' Hornbook on Future Interests, 2nd Ed., 355 pages, 1966 (Text)

Turrentine's Cases and Text on Wills and Administration, 2nd Ed., 483 pages, 1962 (Casebook)

Uniform Probate Code, 5th Ed., Official Text With Comments, 384 pages, 1977

Waggoner's Future Interests in a Nutshell, 361 pages, 1981 (Text)

WATER LAW

Trelease's Cases and Materials on Water Law, 3rd Ed., 833 pages, 1979 (Casebook)

See also Energy and Natural Resources Law, Environmental Law

WILLS

See Trusts and Estates

WOMEN AND THE LAW

Kay's Text, Cases and Materials on Sex-Based Discrimination, 2nd Ed., 1045 pages, 1981 (Casebook)

See also Employment Discrimination

WORKMEN'S COMPENSATION

See Social Legislation

XII

HANDBOOK

OF

THE LAW OF TORTS

By

WILLIAM L. PROSSER
Professor of Law
Hastings College of the Law

FOURTH EDITION

HORNBOOK SERIES

ST. PAUL, MINN.
WEST PUBLISHING CO.
1971

Prosser Torts 4th Ed. HB
12th Reprint—1982

To Thomas Lovett Prosser

PREFACE

The first edition of this book, which was published in 1941, proposed only to make, within the limits permitted by available space, some reasonable selection of the law of torts which seemed particularly significant in the light of the problems of the middle of the century. The text was to be kept relatively brief and simple throughout, in order that it might be intelligible to the student making his first contact with the law in a first-year course; and the footnote material was to be developed beyond what is usual in a short text, in order to provide a convenient reference to other sources from which more information might be obtained than it was possible to set forth in so limited a number of pages. Cases decided within the last decade or two were to be preferred, not because they were necessarily better cases, or necessarily more important ones, but because they tended to show the present state of the law, and themselves, in many instances at least, adequately reviewed what had gone before.

Thirty years later this fourth edition can do no more than adhere to the original plan. The volume of decisions in the field of torts has grown by geometrical progression, even since 1941. There have been many changes to report—some of them fully accomplished, recognized, and well accepted by now, others in midstream and still a matter of some controversy, and still others merely incipient, with a case or two here or there, and an outlook for the future upon the basis of which one might venture a prediction. The shift on the whole has been heavily toward the side of the plaintiff, with expanded liability in nearly every area. The outstanding exception has been the recognition of the constitutional privilege in the fields of defamation and privacy, which must rank as the greatest victory for the defendants in this century. The current agitation in favor of compulsory automobile insurance and compensation plans has begun to bear fruit, and it may be that we are about to enter a new era in which legislation will take over and adopt the approach of the workmen's compensation acts, at least so far as automobile drivers, and conceivably that of other defendants, may be concerned. Such a book as this can at most report the arguments which have been going on, and the perhaps fleeting present state of the law.

The writer can only deplore the limitations of space that compel the condensation of so vast an amount of material into so limited a number of pages. As before, he must express his gratitude, together with his apologies, to the dozens of other able and distinguished writers whose ideas he has unblushingly appropriated. A packrat is at best a collector, and no heroic figure; and the most that can be said for him is that he sometimes chooses well.

WILLIAM L. PROSSER

San Francisco, California
April 1, 1971

•

XI

SUMMARY OF CONTENTS

TABLE OF CONTENTS

CHAPTER 1. INTRODUCTION

CHAPTER 2. INTENTIONAL INTERFERENCE WITH THE PERSON

CHAPTER 3. INTENTIONAL INTERFERENCE WITH PROPERTY

CHAPTER 4. DEFENSES TO INTENTIONAL INTERFERENCE WITH PERSON OR PROPERTY

TABLE OF CONTENTS

CHAPTER 5. NEGLIGENCE: STANDARD OF CONDUCT

CHAPTER 6. NEGLIGENCE: PROOF

CHAPTER 7. PROXIMATE CAUSE

CHAPTER 8. JOINT TORTFEASORS

CHAPTER 9. LIMITED DUTY

TABLE OF CONTENTS

CHAPTER 10. OWNERS AND OCCUPIERS OF LAND

CHAPTER 11. NEGLIGENCE: DEFENSES

CHAPTER 12. IMPUTED NEGLIGENCE

CHAPTER 13. STRICT LIABILITY

CHAPTER 14. LIABILITY INSURANCE

TABLE OF CONTENTS

CHAPTER 15. NUISANCE

CHAPTER 16. TORT AND CONTRACT

CHAPTER 17. PRODUCTS LIABILITY

CHAPTER 18. MISREPRESENTATION

CHAPTER 19. DEFAMATION

TABLE OF CONTENTS

CHAPTER 20. PRIVACY

CHAPTER 21. CONSTITUTIONAL PRIVILEGE

CHAPTER 22. MISUSE OF LEGAL PROCEDURE

CHAPTER 23. DOMESTIC RELATIONS

CHAPTER 24. SURVIVAL AND WRONGFUL DEATH

CHAPTER 25. ECONOMIC RELATIONS

CHAPTER 26. IMMUNITIES

*

HANDBOOK

OF

THE LAW OF TORTS

CHAPTER 1

INTRODUCTION

1. Function of the Law of Torts.
2. Tort and Crime.
3. "Social Engineering".
4.. Factors Affecting Tort Liability.
5. Motive.
6. General Plan.

1. FUNCTION OF THE LAW OF TORTS

A really satisfactory definition of a tort has yet to be found.[1] The numerous at-tempts which have been made to define the term[2] have succeeded only in achieving lan-

---

1. "No such definition of a tort can be offered. A tort, in English law, can only be defined in terms which really tell us nothing. A tort is a breach of a duty (other than a contractual or quasi-con-tractual duty) which gives rise to an action for damages. That is, obviously, a merely procedural definition, of no value to the layman. The latter wants to know the nature of those breaches of duty which give rise to an action for damages. And the only answer that can be given to him is: 'Read this and the preceding volume.' To put it briefly, there is no English Law of Tort; there is merely an English Law of Torts, i. e., a list of acts and omissions which, in certain conditions, are action-able. Any attempt to generalize further, however interesting from a speculative standpoint, would be profoundly unsafe as a practical guide." Miles, Digest of English Civil Law, 1910, Book II, pp. xiv, xv.

"The definition of a tort may be said to have baffled the text-book writers not so much on account of the inherent difficulty of the conception as because of the implication of the conception in questions of jurisdiction. It is a creation of the common law, a fact which rules out on the one side personal, rights created by equity, and on the other, rights created by ecclesiastical or admiralty law. Fur-ther, it is usual to exclude from the definition most

if not all of the rights and duties arising out of the family relation—that is, as regards the imme-diate parties. Again, a tort is usually defined nega-tively in such terms as to distinguish it from breach of contract, and sometimes also from the breach of duties, vaguely described as quasi-contractual. Perhaps none of the text-books succeeds in intro-ducing all of these limitations into its definition." Lee, Torts and Delicts, 1918, 27 Yale L.J. 721, 723.

2. " * * * an act or omission, not a mere breach of contract, and producing injury to another, in the absence of any existing lawful relation of which such act or omission is a natural outgrowth or in-cident." Cooke, A Proposed New Definition of a Tort, 1899, 12 Harv.L.Rev. 335, 336.

"Tortious liability arises from the breach of a duty primarily fixed by the laws; such duty is toward persons generally, and its breach is redressible by an action for unliquidated damages." Winfield, Province of the Law of Tort, 1931, 32.

"A civil wrong for which the remedy is a common law action for unliquidated damages, and which is not exclusively the breach of a contract or the breach of a trust or other merely equitable obliga-tion." Salmond, Law of Torts, 10th Ed.1945, 13.

" * * * an injury inflicted otherwise than by a mere breach of contract; or, to be more nicely ac-curate, one's disturbance of another in rights which the law has created, either in the absence of con-tract, or in consequence of a relation which a con-

1

guage so broad that it includes other matters than torts, or else so narrow that it leaves out some torts themselves. The word is derived from the Latin "tortus" or "twisted." [3] The metaphor is apparent: a tort is conduct which is twisted, or crooked, not straight. "Tort" is found in the French language, and was at one time in common use in English as a general synonym for "wrong." [4] When it faded out of common speech, it remained in the law, and gradually acquired a technical meaning. Broadly speaking, a tort is a civil wrong, other than breach of contract, for which the court will provide a remedy in the form of an action for damages. This, of course, says nothing more than that a tort is one kind of legal wrong, for which the law will give a particular redress. But even this vague statement is inaccurate in one respect, since one important form of remedy for a tort is an injunction, granted in a court of

equity, before any damage occurs, while another is the restitution of what has been wrongfully taken, and still another is self-help by the injured party. But the availability of all such remedies will depend in the first instance upon the possibility that an action for damages would lie for the wrong thus averted, and so the statement made is sufficiently accurate to serve the purpose.[5]

It might be possible to define a tort by enumerating the things that it is not. It is not crime, it is not breach of contract, it is not necessarily concerned with property rights or problems of government, but is the occupant of a large residuary field remaining if these are taken out of the law. But this again is illusory, and the conception of a sort of legal garbage-can to hold what can be put nowhere else is of no help. In the first place, tort is a field which pervades the entire law, and is so interlocked at every point with property, contract and other accepted classifications that, as the student of law soon discovers, the categories are quite arbitrary and there is no virtue in them. In the second, there is a central theme, or basis or idea, running through the cases of what are called torts, which, while it is difficult to put into words, does distinguish them in a greater or less degree from other types of cases.

Included under the head of torts are a miscellaneous group of civil wrongs, ranging from simple, direct interferences with the person, such as assault, battery and false imprisonment, or with property, as in the case of trespass or conversion, up through various

---

tract has established between the parties." Bishop, Non-Contract Law, 1889, 4.

"A tort is an act or omission which unlawfully violates a person's right created by the law, and for which the appropriate remedy is a common law action for damages by the injured person." Burdick, Torts, 3d Ed.1913, 12.

"Never did a Name so obstruct a true understanding of the Thing. To such a plight has it brought us that a favorite mode of defining a Tort is to declare merely that it is not a Contract. As if a man were to define Chemistry by pointing out that it is not Physics or Mathematics." 1 Wigmore, Select Cases on the Law of Torts, 1912, vii.

Dozens of similar passages might be cited, but they would add nothing to the foregoing. See Louisville & Nashville R. Co. v. Spinks, 1898, 104 Ga. 692, 30 S.E. 968; Smith, Tort and Absolute Liability—Suggested Changes in Classification, 1917, 30 Harv.L.Rev. 241, 319, 409.

3. "'Tort,' from the Latin 'tortus,' a French word for injury or wrong, as 'de son tort demesne,' in his own wrong." Jacob's Law Dictionary, 1811, vol. 6, p. 251. Similarly, "wrong" is derived from "wrung."

4. For example, it is found frequently in Spencer's "Faerie Queene," as in the following passage in the fourth book:

"The lyon did with the lamb consort
And eke the dove safe by the faulcons side;
No each of other feared fraud or tort
But did in safe security abide."

5. "Although an action for damages is the essential remedy for a tort, there may be and often are other remedies also. In an action for a private nuisance an injunction may be obtained in addition to damages. In an action for detention of a chattel an order for specific restitution may be obtained in certain cases instead of judgment for its value. In an action by a plaintiff dispossessed of his land he recovers the land itself, in addition to damages for the loss suffered during the period of his dispossession. But in all such cases it is solely by virtue of the right to damages that the wrong complained of is to be classed as a tort." Salmond, Law of Torts, 12th Ed. 1957, 9.

forms of negligence, to disturbances of intangible interests, such as those in good reputation, or commercial or social advantage. These wrongs have little in common and appear at first glance to be entirely unrelated to one another, except perhaps by the accident of historical development; and it is not easy to discover any general principle upon which they may all be based, unless it is the obvious one that injuries are to be compensated, and anti-social behavior is to be discouraged. This led Sir John Salmond, one of the greatest writers on the subject, to contend [6] as late as 1928 that there is no such thing as a law of Tort, but only a law of particular unconnected torts—that is, a set of pigeon-holes, each bearing a name, into which the act or omission of the defendant must be fitted before the law will take cognizance of it and afford a remedy.

This view has been rejected by many other writers,[7] who have felt that tort law is broader than any named categories, and that some more or less vague general principles run through it, however difficult they may be to formulate.[8] There is no necessity whatever

that a tort must have a name.[9] New and nameless torts are being recognized constantly, and the progress of the common law is marked by many cases of first impression, in which the court has struck out boldly to create a new cause of action, where none had been recognized before. The intentional infliction of mental suffering,[10] the obstruction of the plaintiff's right to go where he likes,[11] the invasion of his right of privacy,[12] the denial of his right to vote,[13] the conveyance of land to defeat a title,[14] the infliction of prenatal injuries,[15] the alienation of the affections of a parent,[16] and injury to a man's reputation by entering him in a rigged television contest,[17] to name only a few instances, could not be fitted into any accepted classifications when they first arose, but nevertheless have been held to be torts. The law of torts is anything but static, and the limits of its development are never set. When it becomes clear that the plaintiff's interests are entitled to legal protection against the conduct of the defendant, the mere fact that

---

6. Salmond, Law of Torts, 7th Ed. 1928, § 2, subsec. 3. To the same effect are Goodhart, The Foundation of Tortious Liability, 1938, 2 Mod.L.Rev. 1; Bradshaw, The Foundation of Tortious Liability, 1938, 1 Res Judicatae 320; Williams, The Foundation of Tortious Liability, 1938, 7 Camb.L.J. 111; James, Tort Law in Midstream: Its Challenge to the Judicial Process, 1959, 8 Buff.L.Rev. 315.

It is to be noted that Dr. Stallybrass, the learned editor of later editions of Salmond, somewhat retreated from this view, saying that "although we have not yet discovered any general principle of liability, the law is slowly but surely moving in that direction." Salmond, Law of Torts, 10th Ed. 1945, 17.

7. Pollock, Law of Torts, 14th Ed. 1939, 16–18; Winfield, The Foundation of Liability in Tort, 1927, 27 Col.L.Rev. 1; Winfield, Province of the Law of Tort, 1931, ch. III; Harper, Law of Torts, 1933, ch. 1; Wigmore, The Tripartite Division of Torts, 1894, 8 Harv.L.Rev. 200; Ward, The Tort Cause of Action, 1956, 42 Corn.L.Q. 28.

8. See, attempting to state very broad principles, Seavey, Principles of Torts, 1942, 56 Harv.L.Rev. 72, 22 Neb.L.B. 177, 21 Can.Bar Rev. 265; Fleming, Introduction to the Law of Torts, 1967.

9. Smith, Torts Without Particular Names, 1921, 69 U.Pa.L.Rev. 91.

10. See infra, § 12.

11. Cullen v. Dickinson, 1913, 33 S.D. 27, 144 N.W. 656.

12. See infra, ch. 20.

13. Ashby v. White, 1703, 2 Ld.Raym. 938, 92 Eng. Rep. 126. A famous case, if only because of Chief Justice Holt's declaration that for every interference with a recognized legal right the law will provide a remedy. Accord: Nixon v. Herndon, 1927, 273 U.S. 536; Valdez v. Gonzales, 1946, 50 N.M. 281, 176 P.2d 173; Lane v. Mitchell, 1911, 153 Iowa 139, 133 N.W. 381.

See also Morningstar v. Lafayette Hotel Co., 1914, 211 N.Y. 465, 105 N.E. 656, to the effect that the triviality of the right is all the more reason for allowing the action.

14. Ring v. Ogden, 1878, 45 Wis. 303.

15. See infra, § 55.

16. See infra, p. 887.

17. Morrison v. National Broadcasting Co., 1965, 24 A.D.2d 284, 266 N.Y.S.2d 406, reversed 19 N.Y.2d 453, 280 N.Y.S.2d 641, 227 N.E.2d 572.

the claim is novel will not of itself operate as a bar to the remedy.[18]

At the opposite extreme is the bold attempt [19] to reduce the entire law of torts to a single broad principle, that any harm done to another is a wrong, and calls for redress, unless "justification" for it can be shown. In its form such a statement is objectionable, since there are some torts, such as malicious prosecution,[20] as to which proof of the absence of justification is an indispensable part of the plaintiff's case, and others, such as libel or slander,[21] where it is the defendant who must justify his conduct, and lose if he does not. But even with allowance made for the difficulty of wording it, the rule does not tell us what the law will recognize as "harm" to another, or as "justification" for it. There are many interferences with the plaintiff's interests, such as negligently causing him mere mental suffering without physical consequences [22] or depriving him of the benefit of a contract,[23] for which the law will give no remedy, although the defendant has been clearly at fault. On the other hand, the "justification" may be something quite different from the moral exoneration which absolves the defendant in his own eyes and those of his neighbors.[24] Not only may a morally innocent man be held liable for the damage he has done, but many a scoundrel has been guilty of moral outrages, such as base ingratitude, without committing any tort. It is *legal* justification which must be looked to: the law will hold the defendant responsible for what the law regards as unjustified—and so stated, the broad rule means little, or nothing.

Characteristics of a Tort

Abandoning the attempt to find a definition, which, "strictly speaking, is nothing but an abbreviation in which the user of the term defined may please himself," [25] efforts have been made to discover certain characteristics common to all torts, which might throw some light upon their nature.[26] As has already been said,[27] a wrong is called a tort only if the harm which has resulted, or is about to result from it, is capable of being compensated in an action at law for damages, although other remedies may also be available. Beyond this, it has been said that torts consist of the breach of duties fixed and imposed upon the parties by the law itself, without regard to their consent to assume them, or their efforts to evade them. That is to say, that no man need enter into the obligation of a contract with another save by his own free will; but when he drives an automobile down the street, the law imposes upon him an obligation to all persons

18. Well stated in Kujok v. Goldman, 1896, 150 N.Y. 176, 44 N.E. 773. See also Bishop v. Byrne, S.D. W.Va.1967, 265 F.Supp. 460, and Custodio v. Bauer, 1967, 251 Cal.App.2d 303, 59 Cal.Rptr. 463, both involving damages for the birth of a child following negligent sterilization. See Smith, Torts Without Particular Names, 1921, 69 U.Pa.L.Rev. 91; Albertsworth, Recognition of New Interests in the Law of Torts, 1922, 10 Cal.L.Rev. 461; Malone, Ruminations on a New Tort, 1942, 4 La.L.Rev. 309; Heindl, A Remedy for All Injuries? 1946, 25 Chi. Kent L.Rev. 90.

See also Seidel v. Greenberg, 1969, 108 N.J.Super. 248, 260 A.2d 863.

See, however, Zepeda v. Zepeda, 1963, 41 Ill.App.2d 240, 190 N.E.2d 849, cert. denied 1964, 379 U.S. 945, where a son sued his father for causing him to be born a bastard. This was said to be a tort; but the action was not allowed, on the basis that such a sweeping change in the existing law should be for the legislature. In accord as to the conclusion is Williams v. State, 1966, 18 N.Y.2d 481, 223 N.E.2d 343, 276 N.Y.S.2d 885, reversing 1965, 46 Misc.2d 824, 260 N.Y.S.2d 953.

19. Winfield, Law of Tort, 5th Ed.1950, § 7.

20. See infra, § 119.

21. See infra, ch. 19.

22. See infra, § 54.

23. See infra, p. 938.

24. See infra, p. 16.

25. Pollock, Review of Winfield, Province of the Law of Tort, 1931, 47 L.Q.Rev. 588.

26. Winfield, Law of Tort, 5th Ed.1950, §§ 2–6. Cf. Radin, A Speculative Inquiry Into the Nature of Torts, 1943, 21 Tex.L.Rev. 697; Stone, Touchstones of Tort Liability, 1950, 2 Stan.L.Rev. 259; Seavey, Cogitations on Torts, 1954.

27. Supra, p. 2.

in the highway, to drive it with reasonable care for their safety—and this without his consent or understanding, and if necessary over his vigorous protest. If he does not do so, and injures another, it is a tort.

But this, however superficially attractive it may be, is an illusory distinction.[28] All legal duties are of course imposed by the law, and it is the modern rule that the maker of a contract is held to assume the obligation, not because of his intention or consent to do so, but because the law attaches such consequences to his manifested conduct; and that he assumes it nevertheless when he has no intention at all of doing so. Quasi-contractual duties are likewise imposed by the law, without regard to the consent of the defendant. In the same sense, the tort duty of care in driving the car is assumed because the law attaches that result to what has been done voluntarily. Furthermore, such tort obligations of conduct are imposed by reason of the relation in which the parties stand toward one another; and in determining that relation, the law will often take into account what has been agreed between them, either to increase the actor's responsibility [29] or to lessen it,[30] so that the tort duty finally fixed may coincide with that set by a contract, and for its breach either a contract or a tort action will lie. To say that the one obligation is voluntarily assumed in such a case, while the other is not, is to resort to abstract fictions.

Again, it has been said [31] that tort duties are owed to persons generally, or toward general classes of persons. Or in other words, that the automobile driver is under a tort obligation of care to everyone in his path whom he may injure, and is not free, as he is when he makes a contract or accepts a trust, to single out one person only toward whom he will be bound. Certainly the distinction holds good in many cases: a common carrier, for example, may make a different contract with each single passenger, varying in its terms as to fare and the length of transportation, but the tort duty of reasonable care for their safety extends to every person toward whom it stands in the relation of carrier and passenger, including those who have not contracted at all, but are riding free.[32] But again the classification cannot be carried through. The tort liability of a servant to his master, or of a bailee to his bailor, or of a converter of goods to their owner rests upon a duty owed to one person, and one only; and it can be called general only in the same sense that everyone is under a general obligation to perform all of his contracts. Liability in tort is based upon the relations of men with another; and those relations may arise generally, with large groups or classes of persons, or singly, with an individual.

Enough has been said to indicate that definition or description of a tort in terms of generalities distinguishing it from other branches of the law is difficult, or impossible. It is somewhat easier to consider the function and purpose of the law of torts.[33] Contract liability is imposed by the law for the protection of a single, limited interest, that of having the promises of others performed. Quasi-contractual liability is created for the prevention of unjust enrichment of one man at the expense of another, and the restitution of benefits which in good conscience belong to the plaintiff. The criminal law is concerned with the protection of interests common to the public at large, as they are represented by the entity which we call the state; and it accomplishes its ends by

28. Seavey, Review of Winfield, Province of the Law of Tort, 1931, 45 Harv.L.Rev. 209.

29. See infra, § 92.

30. See infra, p. 442.

31. Winfield, Province of the Law of Tort, 5th Ed. 1950, § 4.

32. Cf. Philadelphia & R. R. Co. v. Derby, 1852, 55 U. S., 14 How., 468; Southern R. Co. v. Lee, 1907, 30 Ky.L.Rep. 1360, 101 S.W. 307; Littlejohn v. Fitchburg R. Co., 1889, 148 Mass. 478, 20 N.E. 103.

33. Seavey, Review of Winfield, Province of the Law of Tort, 1931, 45 Harv.L.Rev. 209.

exacting a penalty from the wrongdoer. There remains a body of law which is directed toward the compensation of individuals, rather than the public, for losses which they have suffered in respect of all their legally recognized interests, rather than one interest only, where the law considers that compensation is required. This is the law of torts.

The law of torts, then, is concerned with the allocation of losses arising out of human activities; and since these cover a wide scope, so does this branch of the law. "Arising out of the various and ever-increasing clashes of the activities of persons living in a common society, carrying on business in competition with fellow members of that society, owning property which may in any of a thousand ways affect the persons or property of others—in short, doing all the things that constitute modern living—there must of necessity be losses, or injuries of many kinds sustained as a result of the activities of others. The purpose of the law of torts is to adjust these losses, and to afford compensation for injuries sustained by one person as the result of the conduct of another." [34]

In so broad a field, where so many different types of individual interests are involved, and they may be invaded by so many kinds of conduct, it is not easy to find any single guilding principle which determines when such compensation is to be paid. So far as there is one, it would seem that liability must be based upon conduct which is socially unreasonable. The common thread woven into all torts is the idea of unreasonable interference with the interests of others. In many cases, of course, what is socially unreasonable will depend upon what is unreasonable from the point of view of the individual. The tort-feasor usually is held liable because he has acted with an unreasonable intention, or because he has departed from a reasonable standard of care. The endeavor to find

some standard of reasonable intention,[35] of the conduct of a reasonable man under the circumstances,[36] of the reasonable use of one's own land,[37] of reasonable reliance upon representations made,[38] of risks and inconveniences which others may reasonably be required to endure at the hands of the defendant— [39] in short, to strike some reasonable balance between the plaintiff's claim to protection against damage and the defendant's claim to freedom of action for his own ends, occupies a very large part of the tort opinions.

But socially unreasonable conduct is broader than this, and the law looks beyond the defendant's own state of mind and the appearances which his own conduct presented, or should have presented to him. It must measure his acts, and the harm he has done, by an objective, disinterested and social standard. It may consider that his behavior, although entirely reasonable in itself from the point of view of any man in his position, has created a risk or has resulted in harm to his neighbors which is so far unreasonable that he should nevertheless pay for what he breaks. Sometimes it must range rather far afield, and look primarily to the social consequences which will follow. The purchaser in good faith of a stolen horse, or the man who trespasses on the land of another in an entirely reasonable belief that it is his own, may have acted only as any reasonable man would act in his place; but the property rights of every owner would be threatened if such acts could be done with impunity, and as against the claim to exclusive possession, they are regarded as a socially unreasonable interference.[40] The innocent publisher of words which turn out to be

34. Wright, Introduction to the Law of Torts, 1944, 8 Camb.L.J. 238.

35. See infra, chs. 2, 3.

36. See infra, ch. 4.

37. See infra, chs. 10, 15.

38. See infra, § 108.

39. See infra, ch. 15.

40. See infra, p. 99.

libel may have behaved quite reasonably so far as his personal conduct is concerned, but as against the helpless victim whose reputation is blasted, his act has been regarded, whether rightly or not, as a social menace, and so unreasonable in itself.[41] It is worthy of note that such cases of liability for personally reasonable acts have not gone unchallenged, and that they represent a field of present controversy. So far as they can be rationalized, it must be on the ground that it is acts which are unreasonable, or socially harmful, from the point of view of the community as a whole, rather than the sole matter of individually questionable conduct, with which the law of torts is concerned.

2. TORT AND CRIME

A tort is not the same thing as a crime, although the two sometimes have many features in common. The distinction between them lies in the interests affected and the remedy afforded by the law.[42] A crime is an offense against the public at large, for which the state, as the representative of the public, will bring proceedings in the form of a criminal prosecution. The purpose of such a proceeding is to protect and vindicate the interests of the public as a whole, by punishing the offender or eliminating him from society, either permanently or for a limited time, by reforming him or teaching him not to repeat the offense, and by deterring others from imitating him.[43] A criminal prosecution is not concerned in any way with compensation of the injured individual against whom the crime is committed, and his only part in it is that of an accuser and a witness for the state. So far as the criminal law is concerned, he will leave the courtroom empty-handed.

The civil action for a tort, on the other hand, is commenced and maintained by the injured person himself, and its purpose is to compensate him for the damage he has suffered, at the expense of the wrongdoer. If he is successful, he receives a judgment for a sum of money, which he may enforce by collecting it from the defendant. The state never can sue in tort in its political or governmental capacity, although as the owner of property it may resort to the same tort actions as any individual proprietor to recover for injuries to the property,[44] or to recover the property itself.[45] It has been held, for example, that the state as a government has no cause of action against an escaped convict for the expenses incurred in recapturing him.[46]

The same act may be both a crime against the state and a tort against an individual. In such a case, since the interests invaded are not the same, and the objects to be accomplished by the two suits are different, there may be both a civil tort action and a criminal prosecution for the same offense. The two may be conducted successively, or at the same time,[47] and a decision for or against the defendant in one is not conclusive as to the other.[48] It is the prevailing view,

41. See infra, p. 772.

42. Winfield, Province of the Law of Tort, 1931, ch. 8; Hall, Interrelation of Criminal Law and Torts, 1943, 43 Col.L.Rev. 753, 967.

43. Kenny, Outlines of Criminal Law, 15th Ed. 1936, ch. 1.

44. State v. Ohio Oil Co., 1898, 150 Ind. 21, 49 N.E. 809; State v. F. W. Fitch Co., 1945, 236 Iowa 208, 17 N.W.2d 380. The same is true of a municipal corporation. Cf. Daly City v. Holbrook, 1918, 39 Cal. App. 326, 178 P. 725; City of Milwaukee v. Meyer, 1931, 204 Wis. 350, 235 N.W. 768; Mayor of Paterson v. Erie R. Co., 1910, 78 N.J.L. 592, 75 A. 922.

45. State v. Delesdenier, 1851, 7 Tex. 76.

46. State Highway & Public Works Comm. v. Cobb, 1939, 215 N.C. 556, 2 S.E.2d 565.

47. Williams v. Dickenson, 1891, 28 Fla. 90, 9 So. 847; White v. Fort, 1821, 10 N.C. 251; Ballew v. Alexander, 1846, 6 Humph., Tenn., 433; Austin v. Carswell, 1893, 67 Hun 579, 22 N.Y.S. 478. It is not an abuse of discretion to refuse to stay the tort action. Pettingill v. Rideout, 1833, 6 N.H. 454; Poston v. Home Ins. Co., 1939, 191 S.C. 314, 4 S.E.2d 261; State v. Schauenberg, 1924, 197 Iowa 445, 197 N.W. 295.

48. Williams v. Dickenson, 1891, 28 Fla. 90, 9 So. 847; Bundy v. Maginess, 1888, 76 Cal. 532, 18 P. 668.

with which a few courts have disagreed,[49] that a conviction[50] or an acquittal[51] in the criminal case is not even admissible in evidence in the tort action. If the crime is a felony, it was the law in England that the tort is so far "merged" in the crime[52] that the civil action must be suspended or stayed until the criminal one had been completed,[53] apparently on the basis of some notion of a policy of compelling the injured party to prefer criminal charges and bring major offenders to justice. Early American decisions[54] took over the rule, but it has now been almost entirely discarded in the United States.[55]

Originally the two remedies were administered by the same court, and in the same action. Tort damages were at first awarded to the injured individual as an incident to a criminal prosecution; and as late as 1694 the defendant to a writ of trespass was still theoretically liable to a criminal fine and imprisonment.[56] Because of this common origin, it is not unusual for a tort and a crime to bear the same name, such as "assault," "battery," "trespass," or "libel," and often enough such terms will refer to the same conduct. But tort and criminal law have developed along different lines, with different ends in view, and so it does not necessarily follow that the term has the same meaning in both. Thus it is entirely possible that an act may be a tort, but not a crime of the same name,[57] or that it may amount to the

---

49. Almost entirely in insurance cases, where the crime is set up as a defense. Eagle, S. & B. D. Ins. Co. v. Heller, 1927, 149 Va. 82, 140 S.E. 314; Schindler v. Royal Ins. Co., 1932, 258 N.Y. 310, 179 N.E. 711; North River Ins. Co. v. Militello, 1937, 100 Colo. 343, 67 P.2d 625; Fidelity-Phenix Fire Ins. Co. v. Murphy, 1933, 226 Ala. 226, 146 So. 387.

50. Interstate Dry Goods Stores v. Williamson, 1922, 91 W.Va. 156, 112 S.E. 301; Blackman v. Coffin, 1938, 300 Mass. 432, 15 N.E.2d 469; Sklebar v. Downey, 1926, 220 Mo.App. 5, 285 S.W. 148; General Exchange Ins. Corp. v. Sherby, 1933, 165 Md. 1, 165 A. 809.

Some qualifications of this are called for however— as for example that a plea of guilty is admissible in the civil action as an admission by the accused, and that some courts apply a doctrine of collateral estoppel as to particular facts in issue. See for example Newman v. Larsen, 1964, 225 Cal.App.2d 22, 36 Cal.Rptr. 883.

51. Shires v. Boggess, 1913, 72 W.Va. 109, 97 S.E. 542; Bray-Robinson Clothing Co. v. Higgins, 1925, 210 Ky. 432, 276 S.W. 129; Id. 1929, 219 Ky. 293, 293 S.W. 151; Hampton v. Westover, 1940, 137 Neb. 695, 291 N.W. 93; Harper v. Blasi, 1944, 112 Colo. 518, 151 P.2d 760.

See, generally, Griffis, Evidence of Disposition of Related Criminal Case in Subsequent Damage Suit, 1958, 25 Ins.Couns.J. 480; Note, 1941, 50 Yale L.J. 499. Cases on both conviction and acquittal are collected in the annotation in 1951, 18 A.L.R.2d 1287.

52. Crosby v. Leng, 1810, 12 East 409, 104 Eng.Rep. 160; Gimson v. Woodfull, 1825, 2 C. & P. 41, 172 Eng. Rep. 19. The origin of the rule probably lay in the fact that a felon's lands were forfeited to the crown, which thus had the prior claim against them. 3 Holdsworth, History of English Law, 3d Ed. 1923, 331–333; White v. Fort, 1821, 10 N.C. 251.

53. Wells v. Abrahams, 1872, L.R. 7 Q.B. 554; Smith v. Selwyn, [1914] 3 K.B. 98.

54. Cross v. Guthery, 1794, 2 Root, Conn. 90; Boardman v. Gore, 1819, 15 Mass. 331.

The rule still survives in New Jersey. Leeman v. Public Service R. Co., 1909, 77 N.J.L. 420, 72 A. 8. In Horby v. King, 1951, 13 N.J.Super. 395, 80 A.2d 476, the court evaded it by finding an estoppel, but showed no disposition to change it.

There are other states in which cases have not been overruled, but there has been no decision since 1875. Bell's Adm'r v. Troy, 1859, 35 Ala. 184; Chick v. Southwestern R. Co., 1875, 57 Ga. 357; Hutchinson v. Merchants' & Mechanics' Bank, 1861, 41 Pa.St. 42.

55. Fidelity & Deposit Co. v. Grand Nat. Bank, 8 Cir. 1934, 69 F.2d 177; Pearl Assur. Co., Ltd. v. National Ins. Agency, Inc., 1942, 150 Pa.Super. 265, 28 A.2d 334, affirmed 1943, 151 Pa.Super. 146, 30 A.2d 333; Quimby v. Blackey, 1884, 63 N.H. 77; Howk v. Minnick, 1869, 19 Ohio St. 462; Note, 1952, 5 Okl.L.Rev. 242. Likewise the fact that the prosecuting witness has brought suit in tort does not bar criminal prosecution. Foster v. Commonwealth, 1824, 8 Watts & S., Pa., 77.

56. Pollock, Law of Torts, 15th Ed. 1951, 150; Stat. 5 & 6 W. & M., ch. 12.

57. Compare the following cases, in which the same type of act was held to be a tort but not a crime: Beach v. Hancock, 1853, 27 N.H. 223, with Chapman v. State, 1884, 78 Ala. 463 (assault); Malcom v. Spoor, 1847, 12 Metc., Mass., 279, with Milton v. State, 1898, 40 Fla. 251, 24 So. 60 (trespass ab initio); Basely v. Clarkson, 1681, 3 Lev. 37, 83 Eng.Rep. 565 with Garrett v. State, 1906, 49 Tex. Cr.R. 235, 91 S.W. 577.

crime and not the tort.[58] Criminal cases may be useful as guides to the type of conduct which the law will condemn or excuse, and the existence of a criminal statute may indicate a legislative policy which the courts will further by creating tort liability.[59] But such conclusions do not always follow, and the criminal law must be regarded as a very unreliable analogy to the law of torts.

Punitive Damages

The idea of punishment, or of discouraging other offenses, usually does not enter into tort law, except in so far as it may lead the courts to weight the scales somewhat in favor of the plaintiff's interests in determining that a tort has been committed in the first place.[60] In one rather anomalous respect, however, the ideas underlying the criminal law have invaded the field of torts. Where the defendant's wrongdoing has been intentional and deliberate, and has the character of outrage frequently associated with crime, all but a few courts [61] have permitted

the jury to award in the tort action "punitive" or "exemplary" damages, or what is sometimes called "smart money." Such damages are given to the plaintiff over and above the full compensation for his injuries, for the purpose of punishing the defendant, of teaching him not to do it again, and of deterring others from following his example.[62] Occasional decisions [63] have mentioned the additional purpose of reimbursing the plaintiff for elements of damage which are not legally compensable, such as his wounded feelings or the expenses of suit.

Something more than the mere commission of a tort is always required for punitive damages. There must be circumstances of aggravation or outrage,[64] such as spite or "mal-

---

58. Compare Deaton v. State, 1908, 53 Tex.Cr.R. 393, 110 S.W. 69, with Robertson v. Edelstein, 1899, 104 Wis. 440, 80 N.W. 724 (abusive but not defamatory language). See Rubin, May a Person be Convicted of a Felony and Yet Escape Civil Liability Therefor, 1926, 10 Marq.L.Rev. 113.

59. See infra, § 36.

60. See infra, p. 12.

61. Four states reject punitive damages entirely. Moore v. Blanchard, 1949, 216 La. 253, 43 So.2d 599; Boott Mills v. Boston & Me. R. Co., 1914, 218 Mass. 582, 106 N.E. 680; Wilfong v. Omaha & Council Bluffs St. R. Co., 1935, 129 Neb. 600, 262 N.W. 537; Anderson v. Dalton, 1952, 40 Wash.2d 894, 246 P.2d 853. England has recently done away with them except where they could serve a "useful purpose," by penalizing oppressive, arbitrary and unconstitutional action by government servants, conduct calculated to make a profit for the actor, and the like. Rookes v. Barnard, [1964] A.C. 1129.

New Hampshire and Michigan allow such damages, but regard them as extra compensation for injured feelings or sense of outrage rather than as punishment. Bixby v. Dunlap, 1876, 56 N.H. 456; Wise v. Daniel, 1922, 221 Mich. 229, 190 N.W. 746. Connecticut limits punitive damages to the expenses of

litigation, which must be proved. Tedesco v. Maryland Cas. Co., 1941, 127 Conn. 533, 18 A.2d 357.

62. Scott v. Donald, 1896, 165 U.S. 58; Gostkowski v. Roman Catholic Church, 1933, 262 N.Y. 320, 186 N.E. 798; Gill v. Selling, 1928, 125 Or. 587, 267 P. 812, second opinion, 1928, 126 Or. 584, 270 P. 411; Kirschbaum v. Lowrey, 1925, 165 Minn. 233, 206 N.W. 171. See McCormick, Damages, 1935, § 278; Notes, 1957, 70 Harv.L.Rev. 517; 1962, 26 Albany L.J. 288.

63. Battle v. Kilcrease, 1936, 54 Ga.App. 808, 189 S.E. 573; Wright Titus, Inc. v. Swafford, Tex.Civ.App. 1939, 133 S.W.2d 287, error dismissed, judgment correct; Brewer v. Home-Stake Production Co. (1967) 200 Kan. 96, 434 P.2d 828.

64. Chiles v. Drake, 1859, 2 Metc., Ky., 146; Birmingham Waterworks Co. v. Brooks, 1917, 16 Ala. App. 209, 76 So. 515, cert. denied 200 Ala. 697, 76 So. 995. Cf. Battle v. Kilcrease, 1936, 54 Ga.App. 808, 189 S.E. 573 (hit-and-run driver); Miller v. Blanton, 1948, 213 Ark. 246, 210 S.W.2d 293 (intoxication); Bucher v. Krause, 7 Cir.1952, 200 F.2d 576, cert. denied Krause v. Bucher, 1953, 345 U.S. 997, rehearing denied 346 U.S. 842 (cover-up activities of police).

"The jury must find that he acted with actual malice (in the sense of ill will) or conscious disregard of consequences to others. The jury may infer this from circumstances of aggravation surrounding the tortious conduct." Kelite Products, Inc. v. Binzel, 5 Cir.1955, 224 F.2d 131, 143. See also Diapulse Corp. of America v. Birtcher Corp., 2 Cir. 1966, 362 F.2d 736, cert. dismissed 385 U.S. 801; Mills v. Levine, 1956, 98 U.S.App.D.C. 137, 233 F.2d 16, cert. denied 352 U.S. 858.

ice," [65] or a fraudulent [66] or evil [67] motive on the part of the defendant, or such a conscious and deliberate disregard of the interests of others that his conduct may be called wilful or wanton.[68] Lacking this element, there is general agreement that mere negligence is not enough,[69] even though it is so extreme in degree as to be characterized as "gross," [70]

an unhappy term of ill-defined content,[71] which occasionally, in a few jurisdictions, has been stretched to include the element of conscious indifference to consequences, and so to justify punitive damages.[72] Still less, of course, can such damages be charged against one who acts under an innocent mistake in engaging in conduct that nevertheless constitutes a tort.[73]

Typical of the torts for which such damages may be awarded are assault and battery,[74] libel and slander,[75] deceit,[76] seduction,[77] alienation of affections,[78] malicious prosecution,[79] and intentional interferences with

65. This includes a deliberate wrongful act known to be injurious to another. Cherry-Burrell Co. v. Thatcher, 9 Cir. 1940, 107 F.2d 65; Jones v. West Side Buick Co., 1936, 231 Mo.App. 187, 93 S.W.2d 1083; Morgan v. French, 1945, 70 Cal.App.2d 785, 161 P.2d 800; Bourne v. Pratt & Whitney Aircraft Corp., Mo.App.1948, 207 S.W.2d 533.

It does not include the "legal malice" implied in such torts as defamation. Corrigan v. Bobbs-Merrill Co., 1920, 228 N.Y. 58, 126 N.E. 260; Neeb v. Hope, 1886, 111 Pa.St. 145, 2 A. 568; Fields v. Bynum, 1911, 156 N.C. 413, 72 S.E. 449; Cottle v. Johnson, 1920, 179 N.C. 426, 102 S.E. 769 (alienation of affections).

As to the necessity of "actual" rather than "implied" malice, see Waters v. Novak, 1953, 94 Ohio App. 347, 115 N.E.2d 420.

66. Prince v. State Mut. Life Ins. Co., 1907, 77 S.C. 187, 57 S.E. 766; Treesh v. Stone, 1921, 51 Cal. App. 708, 197 P. 425.

67. Eshelman v. Rawalt, 1921, 298 Ill. 192, 131 N.E. 675 (criminal conversation); Cobb v. Atlantic C. L. R. Co., 1918, 175 N.C. 130, 95 S.E. 92 (blasting); Gamble v. Keyes, 1917, 39 S.D. 592, 166 N.W. 134; Hintz v. Roberts, 1923, 98 N.J.L. 768, 121 A. 711.

68. Sebastian v. Wood, 1954, 246 Iowa 94, 66 N.W. 2d 841 (drunken driving); Dorn v. Wilmarth, 1969, —— Or. ——, 458 P.2d 942 (same); Brooks v. Wootton, 2 Cir. 1966, 355 F.2d 177 (same); Allman v. Bird, 1960, 186 Kan. 802, 353 P.2d 216; Toole v. Richardson-Merrell, Inc., 1967, 251 Cal.App.2d 689, 60 Cal.Rptr. 398 (withholding vital information in sale of drug).

69. Greyhound Corp. v. Townsend, 1959, 234 Miss. 839, 108 So.2d 208, suggestion of error sustained 234 Miss. 839, 108 So.2d 853; Wright v. Everett, 1956, 197 Va. 608, 90 S.E.2d 855; Spackman v. Ralph M. Parsons Co., 1966, 147 Mont. 500, 414 P.2d 918; Sheffield Division Armco Steel Corp. v. Jones, 1964, Tex., 376 S.W.2d 825.

70. Milwaukee & St. Paul R. Co. v. Arms, 1875, 91 U.S. 489; Moore v. Wilson, 1929, 180 Ark. 41, 20 S.W.2d 310; Hicks v. McCandlish, 1952, 221 S.C. 410, 70 S.E.2d 629; Eatley v. Mayer, 1931, 9 N.J. Misc. 918, 154 A. 10, affirmed 1932, 10 N.J.Misc. 219, 158 A. 411.

See, however, Arnold v. Frigid Feed Express Co., 1969, 9 Ariz.App. 472, 453 P.2d 983 (driving car at top

speed through dust storm; enough that the conduct involves a risk "substantially greater than that which is necessary to make his conduct negligent.")

71. See infra, p. 183.

72. Cf. Texas Pac. Coal & Oil Co. v. Robertson, 1935, 125 Tex. 4, 79 S.W.2d 830; Teche Lines v. Pope, 1936, 175 Miss. 393, 166 So. 539; Sebastian v. Wood, 1954, 246 Iowa 94, 66 N.W.2d 841.

73. Thomas v. Commercial Credit Corp., Mo.App.1960, 335 S.W.2d 703 (repossession of wrong automobile); Calhoun v. Universal Credit Co., 1944, 106 Utah 166, 146 P.2d 284 (repossession where no default); Winn & Lovett Grocery Co. v. Archer, 1936, 126 Fla. 308, 171 So. 214 (detention of suspect in store). See also De Marasse v. Wolf, Sup.Ct.1955, 140 N. Y.S.2d 235.

74. Trogden v. Terry, 1916, 172 N.C. 540, 90 S.E. 583; Bannister v. Mitchell, 1920, 127 Va. 578, 104 S.E. 800; Maxa v. Neidlein, 1932, 163 Md. 366, 163 A. 202.

75. Reynolds v. Pegler, 2 Cir. 1955, 223 F.2d 429, cert. denied 350 U.S. 846; Rogers v. Florence Printing Co., 1958, 233 S.C. 567, 106 S.E.2d 258; Coffin v. Brown, 1901, 94 Md. 190, 50 A. 567; Loftsgaarden v. Reiling, 1964, 267 Minn. 181, 126 N.W.2d 154, cert. denied 379 U.S. 845.

76. Walker v. Sheldon, 1961, 10 N.Y.2d 401, 223 N.Y. S.2d 488, 179 N.E.2d 497; J. Truett Payne Co. v. Jackson, 1967, 281 Ala. 426, 203 So.2d 443; Saberton v. Greenwald, 1946, 146 Ohio St. 414, 66 N.E.2d 224. See Note, 1962, 26 Alb.L.J. 288.

77. Reutkemeier v. Nolte, 1917, 179 Iowa 342, 161 N.W. 290.

78. Scott v. O'Brien, 1908, 129 Ky. 1, 110 S.W. 260.

79. Jackson v. American Tel. & Tel. Co., 1905, 139 N. C. 347, 51 S.E. 1015; Brown v. McBride, 1898, 24 Misc. 235, 52 N.Y.S. 620. Cf. Seidel v. Greenberg, 1969, 108 N.J.Super. 248, 260 A.2d 863.

property such as trespass,[80] private nuisance,[81] and conversion.[82] But it is not so much the particular tort committed as the defendant's motives and conduct in committing it [83] which will be important as the basis of the award. Statutes in most states have provided punitive damages for particular torts, as in the case of multiple damages for trespass.[84]

The policy of giving punitive damages has been a subject of much controversy. They have been condemned [85] as undue compensa-tion of the plaintiff beyond his just deserts in the form of a criminal fine which should be paid to the state, if anyone, with the amount fixed only by the caprice of the jury and imposed without the usual safeguards thrown about criminal procedure, such as proof of guilt beyond a reasonable doubt, the privilege against self-incrimination, and even the rule against double jeopardy—since the defendant may still be prosecuted for the crime after he has been mulcted in the tort action.[86] They have been defended as a salutary method of discouraging evil motives, as a partial remedy for the defect in American civil procedure which denies compensation for actual expenses of litigation, such as counsel fees, and as an incentive to bring into court and redress a long array of petty cases of outrage and oppression which in practice escape the notice of prosecuting attorneys occupied with serious crime, and which a private individual would otherwise find not worth the trouble and expense of a lawsuit.[87] At any rate, they are an established part of our legal system, and there is no indication of any present desire or tendency to abandon them.

80. Oden v. Russell, 1952, 207 Okl. 570, 251 P.2d 184; Huling v. Henderson, 1894, 161 Pa. 553, 29 A. 276; Singer Mfg. Co. v. Holdfodt, 1877, 86 Ill. 455.

81. Ruppel v. Ralston Purina Co., Mo.1968, 423 S.W. 2d 752; Lutz v. Independent Const. Co., 1958, 183 Kan. 798, 332 P.2d 269; Corwine v. Maracaibo Oil Exploration Corp., 1959, 184 Kan. 151, 334 P.2d 419; Yazoo & M. V. R. Co. v. Sanders, 1906, 87 Miss. 607, 40 So. 163; Schumacher v. Shawhan Distillery Co., 1914, 178 Mo.App. 361, 165 S.W. 1142 (pollution of stream continued in defiance of injunction).

82. Watkins v. Layton, 1958, 182 Kan. 702, 324 P.2d 130; Lindgren Plumbing Co. v. Doral Country Club, Inc., Fla.App.1967, 196 So.2d 242; Jones v. Fisher, 1969, 42 Wis.2d 209, 166 N.W.2d 175 (forcible removal of dental plate as security for loan).

83. Thus punitive damages may be awarded against only one of two joint tortfeasors for the same tort. Kim v. Chinn, 1943, 56 Cal.App.2d 857, 133 P.2d 677; Hotel Riviera, Inc. v. Short, 1964, 80 Nev. 505, 396 P.2d 855; Mauk v. Brundage, 1903, 68 Ohio St. 89, 67 N.E. 152; Nelson v. Halvorsen, 1912, 177 Minn. 255, 135 N.W. 818.

Cf. Heinze v. Murphy, 1942, 180 Md. 423, 24 A.2d 917 (no punitive damages for false arrest in good faith); American Oil Co. v. Colonial Oil Co., 4 Cir. 1942, 130 F.2d 72, cert. denied 317 U.S. 679 (same as to trespass).

But punitive damages are not minimized by the value to the community of defendant's activity and its general contribution to the locality. Lampert v. Reynolds Metals Co., 9 Cir. 1967, 372 F.2d 245.

84. See for example Kelly v. Fine, 1958, 354 Mich. 384, 92 N.W.2d 511; Clark v. Sheriff, 1956, 247 Iowa 509, 74 N.W.2d 569; Louis Pizitz Dry Goods Co. v. Yeldell, 1927, 274 U.S. 112; and the cases collected in 1937, 111 A.L.R. 91.

85. Willis, Measure of Damages When Property is Wrongfully Taken by a Private Individual, 1909, 22 Harv.L.Rev. 419, 420; Walther, Punitive Damages— A Critical Analysis, 1965, 49 Marq.L.Rev. 369; Duffy, Punitive Damages: A Doctrine Which Should be Abolished, [1969] Def. Research Inst. 4; Note, 1966, 41 N.Y.U.L.Rev. 1158. See also Fay v. Parker, 1872, 53 N.H. 342; Murphy v. Hobbs, 1884, 7 Colo. 541, 5 P. 119; Spokane Truck & Dray Co. v. Hoefer, 1891, 2 Wash. 45, 25 P. 1072.

86. Morris v. McNab, 1957, 25 N.J. 271, 135 A.2d 657; Pratt v. Duck, 1945, 28 Tenn.App. 502, 191 S.W.2d 562; Dubois v. Roby, 1911, 84 Vt. 465, 80 A. 150; Irby v. Wilde, 1908, 155 Ala. 388, 46 So. 454. Contra, Borkenstein v. Schrack, 1903, 31 Ind.App. 220, 67 N.E. 547. See Aldridge, The Indiana Doctrine of Exemplary Damages and Double Jeopardy, 1945, 20 Ind.L.J. 124.

Some courts permit the defendant to show in mitigation of punitive damages that he has been criminally punished for the same wrong. Saunders v. Gilbert, 1911, 156 N.C. 463, 72 S.E. 610; Wirsing v. Smith, 1908, 222 Pa. 8, 70 A. 906.

87. Sedgwick, Damages, 9th Ed. 1912, § 354; 1 Street, Foundations of Legal Liability, 1906, ch. XXXII; McCormick, Damages, 1935, § 77; Morris, Punitive Damages in Tort Cases, 1931, 44 Harv.L.Rev. 1173. See also Morris, Rough Justice and Some Utopian Ideas, 1930, 24 Ill.L.Rev. 730.

Perhaps the chief among the various controversies which have surrounded punitive damages has been over whether they may be awarded against an employer vicariously liable for the tort of his servant,[88] where he has neither authorized nor ratified it.[89] Following a leading federal case,[90] a considerable minority of the courts have held that they can not,[91] laying stress upon the injustice of a punishment inflicted upon one who has been entirely innocent throughout. This is of course particularly true where the employer is a corporation, and the pocket which is hit is that of the blameless stockholders, whom

no one wants to punish. The Restatement of Torts [92] has taken this position.

The majority of the courts, however, have held that the vicarious liability of the master for acts within the scope of the employment extends to punitive as well as compensatory damages, even in the absence of approval or ratification,[93] and that this is true especially in the case of corporations, who can only act through their agents.[94] They have been concerned primarily with the deterrent effect of the award of exemplary damages, and have said often enough that if such damages will encourage employers to exercise closer control over their servants for the prevention of outrageous torts, that is sufficient ground for awarding them.[95]

A related problem, on which there is surprisingly little case law, is that of whether punitive damages awarded against one who is insured against liability are to be paid by his insurer.[96] This involves not only construc-

---

88. See Morris, Punitive Damages in Personal Injury Cases, 1960, 21 Ohio St. L.J. 216, Notes, 1961, 70 Yale L.J. 1296; 1967, 19 Syr.L.Rev. 189.

89. The employer's liability for punitive damages is of course clear where he has authorized the employee's misconduct, or where he has participated in it. He may, however, become liable for such damages by "ratification," when, with knowledge of the tort, he fails to take action expressing his disapproval of it, as by retaining the offending servant in his employment. Haines v. Schultz, 1888, 50 N.J.L. 481, 14 A. 488; Farvour v. Geltis, 1949, 91 Cal.App.2d 603, 205 P.2d 424; Will v. Hughes, 1951, 172 Kan. 45, 238 P. 478; Donivan v. Manhattan R. Co., 1893, 1 Misc. 368, 21 N.Y.S. 457; Security Alum. Window Mfg. Corp. v. Lehman Associates, Inc., 1970, 108 N.J.Super. 137, 260 A.2d 248.

90. Lake Shore & M. S. R. Co. v. Prentice, 1893, 147 U.S. 101. See, however, General Motors Acc. Corp. v. Froelich, 1959, 106 U.S.App.D.C. 357, 273 F.2d 92, where the misconduct of the employees was neither directed, authorized, nor ratified, but responsibility was attributed to the corporation on the basis of its general policies.

91. Emmke v. De Silva, 8 Cir.1923, 293 F. 17; Gates v. St. James Operating Co., 1939, 122 N.J.L. 610, 7 A.2d 632; Curtis v. Siebrand Bros. Circus & Carnival Co., 1948, 68 Idaho, 285, 194 P.2d 281; Rickman v. Safeway Stores, Inc., 1951, 124 Mont. 451, 227 P.2d 607; Parris v. St. Johnsbury Trucking Co., 2 Cir. 1968, 395 F.2d 543.

Almost without exception, this is the position taken as to the liability of municipal corporations. Fisher v. City of Miami, Fla.1965, 172 So.2d 455; Desforge v. City of West St. Paul, 1950, 231 Minn. 205, 42 N.W. 2d 633; Rascoe v. Town of Farmington, 1956, 62 N.M. 51, 304 P.2d 575; Clarke v. City of Greer, 1957, 231 S.C. 327, 98 S.E.2d 751. See Note, 1965, 22 Wash. & Lee L.Rev. 126.

92. § 909.

93. Miller v. Blanton, 1948, 213 Ark. 246, 210 S.W.2d 293; Eaddy v. Greensboro-Fayetteville Bus Lines, 1939, 191 S.C. 538, 5 S.E.2d 281; Atlantic Greyhound Corp. v. Austin, 1945, 72 Ga.App. 289, 33 S.E.2d 718; Western Coach Corp. v. Vaughn, 1969, 9 Ariz. App. 336, 452 P.2d 117; Clemmons v. Life Ins. Co. of Georgia, 1968, 274 N.C. 416, 163 S.E.2d 761. See Notes, 1942, 30 Geo.L.J. 294; 1961, 70 Yale L.J. 1296.

94. Occasional courts have distinguished between corporate and individual employers, holding the latter not liable for punitive damages in the absence of approval or ratification. State ex rel. United Factories v. Hostetter, 1939, 344 Mo. 386, 126 S.W.2d 1173. Most courts make no such distinction. See State ex rel. Coffelt v. Hartford Acc. & Ind. Co., 1958, 44 Tenn.App. 405, 314 S.W.2d 161, holding a sheriff liable for punitive damages for the tort of his deputy.

95. The classic diatribe to this effect is in Goddard v. Grand Trunk Ry. of Canada, 1869, 57 Me. 202.

96. See Morris, Punitive Damages in Personal Injury Cases, 1960, 21 Ohio St.L.J. 216; Long, Insurance Protection Against Punitive Damages, 1965, 32 Tenn. L.Rev. 573; Brin, Punitive Damages and Liability Insurance, 1964, 31 Ins. Couns. J. 265; Marks, Automobile Insurance Coverage for Punitive Damages, [1966] Ins. L.J. 480; Notes, 1966, 20 U. Miami L.Rev. 192; 1966, 39 Temp.L.Q. 459; 1966, 25 Md.L.Rev. 326.

tion of the terms of the contract of insurance,[97] but also the question whether the purposes of punishment and deterrence underlying the damages themselves are not only not accomplished when the insured is allowed to shift the penalty to the shoulders of an innocent party, but are actually frustrated when he is thus afforded protection against what is essentially a criminal punishment imposed by the law. If punitive damages are supported by any sound policy, that policy would appear to demand that they shall not be covered by liability insurance.[98] Most of the small number of decided cases, however, possibly having in mind the supposed function of punitive damages in providing a substitute for attorney's fees, have held that the liability contract effectively covers such damages.[99] A few cases have held to the contrary.[1] A compromise position appears to be emerging, under which the insurance will be effective to protect the insured against any liability which is purely vicarious, but not where he is to be charged with any wrong of his own.[2] This may be the ultimate solution.

A recent problem which has arisen to haunt the courts concerns the "mass disaster"[3] litigation, in which the defendant, as for example by putting a drug on the market, has caused injury to a very large number of consumers. How often is such a defendant to be punished? Is there no limiting rule analogous to double jeopardy? And is there any order of priority among the claimants? Confronted with this problem, in Roginsky v. Richardson-Merrell, Inc.,[4] Judge Friendly, refused, in the absence of controlling authority in the New York cases, to find a basis for punitive damages at all in the misconduct of the defendants. The question might well lead to a re-examination of the whole basis and policy of awarding punitive damages.[5]

It is generally agreed that punitive damages are a windfall to the plaintiff and not a matter of right, and that it is always within the discretion of the jury to withhold them.[6] The greater number of courts have said that they are limited to cases in which actual compensatory damages are found by

---

97. Thus in Abbott v. Western Nat. Ind. Co., 1958, 165 Cal.App.2d 302, 331 P.2d 997, a policy excluding liability for intentional misconduct was held not to cover punitive damages for assault and battery.

98. It was so held in Northwestern Nat. Cas. Co. v. McNulty, 5 Cir. 1962, 307 F.2d 432; Nicholson v. American Fire & Cas. Ins. Co., Fla.App.1965, 177 So.2d 52; Lo Rocco v. New Jersey Mfrs. Ind. Ins. Co., 1964, 82 N.J.Super. 323, 197 A.2d 591, aff'd memo, 42 N.J. 144, 199 A.2d 655; Crull v. Gleb, Mo. App.1964, 382 S.W.2d 17; American Sur. Co. of New York v. Gold, 10 Cir. 1966, 375 F.2d 523.

99. Lazenby v. Universal Underwriters Ins. Co., 1964, 214 Tenn. 639, 383 S.W.2d 1; Southern Farm Bureau Cas. Ins. Co. v. Daniel, 1969, 246 Ark. 813, 440 S.W. 2d 582; Carroway v. Johnson, 1965, 245 S.C. 200, 139 S.E.2d 908; Pennsylvania Threshermen & Farmers Mut. Cas. Ins. Co. v. Thornton, 4 Cir. 1957, 244 F.2d 823; General Cas. Co. of America v. Woodby, 6 Cir. 1956, 238 F.2d 452.

1. See supra, note 96.

2. Commercial Union Ins. Co. of New York v. Reichard, S.D.Fla.1967, 273 F.Supp. 952; Sterling Ins. Co. v. Hughes, Fla.App.1966, 187 So.2d 898; Ohio Cas. Ins. Co. v. Welfare Finance Co., 8 Cir. 1934, 75 F.2d 58, cert. denied 295 U.S. 734.

See Long, Insurance Protection Against Punitive Damages, 1965, 32 Tenn.L.Rev. 573; Notes, 1966, 39 Temp.L.Q. 459; 1965, 25 Md.L.Rev. 326; 1969, 22 Sw.L.Rev. 433.

3. See the account of one such disaster in Rheingold, The MER/29 Story—An Instance of Successful Mass Disaster Litigation, 1968, 56 Cal.L.Rev. 116. The total claims for punitive damages alone ran to a total of hundreds of millions of dollars.

4. 2 Cir. 1967, 378 F.2d 832.

5. See Rice, Exemplary Damages in Private Consumer Actions, 1969, 55 Iowa L.Rev. 307; Notes, 1966, 41 N.Y.U.L.Rev. 1158; 1967, 34 U. Chi.L.Rev. 408.

6. Hodges v. Hall, 1916, 172 N.C. 29, 89 S.E. 802; Louisville & N. R. Co. v. Logan's Adm'x, 1917, 178 Ky. 29, 198 S.W. 537; Petrey v. Liuzzi, 1945, 76 Ohio App. 19, 61 N.E.2d 158; Luke v. Mercantile Acc. Corp., 1952, 111 Cal.App.2d 431, 244 P.2d 764. Contra, Sample v. Gulf Refining Co., 1937, 183 S.C. 399, 191 S.E. 209.

In Security Aluminium Window Mfg. Corp. v. Lehman Associates, Inc., 1970, 108 N.J.Super. 137, 260 A.2d 248, "discretionary" was held to mean legal discretion as to a judge sitting without a jury, and an abuse was found in the failure to award punitive damages.

the jury. Sometimes this obviously means only that without a finding of such damages there is no cause of action at all, and nothing to support the award;[7] but some of these courts have gone further and have held that punitive damages cannot be sustained where a cause of action is found but only nominal damages are awarded.[8] Since it is precisely in the cases of nominal damages that the policy of providing an incentive for plaintiffs to bring petty outrages into court comes into play, the view very much to be preferred appears to be that of the minority which have held that there is sufficient support for punitive damages.[9]

It frequently is said [10] also that punitive damages must bear some reasonable proportion, or at least some undefined kind of relation, to the actual damages found, so that a very small award of compensation will not support a very large penalty. Apparently, however, this has meant little more than that under the particular circumstances these courts do not like the size of some verdicts; and where the enormity of the defendant's outrage calls for it, very large awards of punitive damages, ranging far out of all conceivable proportion to the amount found by way of compensation, have been sustained.[11] A few courts have begun to repudiate outright the necessity of any ratio or relation.[12] Most courts agree that evidence of the defendant's wealth may be received as bearing on the question of the amount which will adequately punish him for his conduct.[13]

3. "SOCIAL ENGINEERING"

Perhaps more than any other branch of the law, the law of torts is a battleground of

7. See for example Schippel v. Norton, 1888, 38 Kan. 567, 16 P. 804; Hoagland v. Forest Park Highlands Amusement Co., 1902, 170 Mo. 335, 70 S.W. 878.

8. Richard v. Hunter, 1949, 151 Ohio St. 185, 85 N.E. 2d 109; Kroeger Groc. & Baking Co. v. Reeves, 1946, 210 Ark. 178, 194 S.W.2d 876; Ennis v. Brawley, 1946, 129 W.Va. 621, 41 S.E.2d 680; Behymer v. Milgram Food Stores, 1940, 151 Kan. 921, 101 P.2d 912; Suflas v. Cleveland Wrecking Co., E.D.Pa. 1963, 218 F.Supp. 289.

9. Wardman-Justice Motors v. Petrie, 1930, 59 App. D.C. 262, 39 F.2d 512; Edwards v. Nulsen, 1941, 347 Mo. 1077, 152 S.W.2d 28; Crystal Dome Oil & Gas Co. v. Savic, 1931, 51 Idaho 409, 6 P.2d 155; Barber v. Hohl, 1956, 40 N.J.Super. 526, 123 A.2d 785; Scalise v. National Utility Service, 5 Cir.1941, 120 F.2d 938 (Florida law).

This has been carried so far as to sustain punitive damages where it is clear that there is a cause of action, but no other damages are found by the jury. Clark v. McClurg, 1932, 215 Cal. 279, 9 P.2d 505 (no finding); Fauver v. Wilkoske, 1949, 123 Mont. 228, 211 P.2d 420 (finding of no actual damages).

10. Mitchell v. Randal, 1927, 288 Pa. 518, 137 A. 171; Cotton v. Cooper, Tex.Com.App.1919, 209 S.W. 135; Luke v. Mercantile Acc. Corp., 1952, 111 Cal.App.2d 431, 244 P.2d 764. In Wehrman v. Liberty Petroleum Co., Mo.App.1964, 382 S.W.2d 56, it was said that punitive damages must bear some relation to the injury, but need not as to damages allowed by way of compensation.

The rule resulted in setting aside such verdicts as $100 actual and $14,900 punitive damages in Bangert v. Hubbard, 1955, 127 Ind.App. 579, 126 N.E.2d 778, and $1,250 actual and $25,000 punitive in Hall Oil Co. v. Barquin, 1925, 33 Wyo. 92, 237 P. 255.

11. Reynolds v. Pegler, S.D.N.Y.1954, 123 F.Supp. 36, affirmed 2 Cir. 1954, 223 F.2d 429, cert. denied 350 U.S. 846 (outrageous libel; nominal damages and $175,000 punitive); Toomey v. Farley, 1956, 2 N.Y. 2d 71, 156 N.Y.S.2d 840, 138 N.E.2d 221 (libel; six cents actual and $5,000 punitive); Livesey v. Stock, 1929, 208 Cal. 315, 281 P. 70 (battery; $750 actual and $10,000 punitive); Seaman v. Dexter, 1921, 96 Conn. 334, 114 A. 75 ($318 actual and $5,000 punitive); Pelton v. General Motors Acc. Corp., 1932, 139 Or. 198, 7 P.2d 263, rehearing denied 9 P.2d 128 ($225 actual, $5,000 punitive).

12. Finney v. Lockhart, 1950, 35 Cal.2d 161, 217 P.2d 19 (unfair competition; $1 actual, $2,000 punitive); Edwards v. Nulsen, 1941, 347 Mo. 1077, 152 S.W.2d 28 (libel; $1 actual, $25,000 punitive); Malco, Inc. v. Midwest Aluminum Sales, Inc., 1961, 14 Wis.2d 57, 109 N.W.2d 516 (no arbitrary rule that punitive damages cannot be 15 times actual damages); Wegner v. Rodeo Cowboys Ass'n, D.Colo.1968, 290 F. Supp. 369; Foster v. Floyd, 1964, 276 Ala. 428, 163 So.2d 213.

13. Phelan v. Beswick, 1958, 213 Or. 612, 326 P.2d 1034; Wilson v. Oldroyd, 1954, 1 Utah 2d 362, 267 P.2d 759; Allen v. Rossi, 1929, 128 Me. 201, 146 A. 692; Johnson v. Horn, 1930, 86 Mont. 314, 283 P. 427; Charles v. Texas Co., 1942, 199 S.C. 156, 18 S.E.2d 719. Contra: Texas Pub. Utilities Corp. v. Edwards, Tex.Civ.App.1936, 99 S.W.2d 420, error dismissed; Blackman v. Honer, 1925, 119 Kan. 404, 239 P. 750; Taulborg v. Andresen, 1930, 119 Neb. 273, 228 N.W. 528. See Notes, 1965, 19 Ark.L.Rev. 189; 1966, 20 U.Miami L.Rev. 465.

social theory. Its primary purpose, of course, is to make a fair adjustment of the conflicting claims of the litigating parties. But the twentieth century has brought an increasing realization of the fact that the interests of society in general may be involved in disputes in which the parties are private litigants.[14] The notion of "public policy" involved in private cases is not by any means new to tort law,[15] and doubtless has been with us ever since the troops of the sovereign first intervened in a brawl to keep the peace; but it is only in recent decades that it has played a predominant part. Society has some concern even with the single dispute involved in a particular case; but far more important than this is the system of precedent on which the entire common law is based, under which a rule once laid down is to be followed until the courts find good reason to depart from it, so that others now living and even those yet unborn may be affected by a decision made today. There is good reason, therefore, to make a conscious effort to direct the law along lines which will achieve a desirable social result, both for the present and for the future.

Individuals have many interests for which they claim protection from the law, and which the law will recognize as worthy of protection. Various interesting attempts have been made [16] to classify these interests into categories, which of course have no virtue in themselves, and only serve to suggest the wide extent to which the law is concerned with human welfare. Men wish to be secure in their persons against harm and interference, not only as to their physical integrity, but as to their freedom to move about and their peace of mind. They want food and clothing, homes and land and goods, money, automobiles and entertainment, and they want to be secure and free from disturbance in the right to have these things, or to acquire them if they can. They want freedom to work and deal with others, and protection against interference with their private lives, their family relations, and their honor and reputation. They are concerned with freedom of thought and action, with opportunities for economic gain, and with pleasant and advantageous relations with their fellow men. The catalogue of their interests might be as long as the list of legitimate human desires; and not the least of them is the desire to do what they please, without restraint and without undue consideration for the interests and claims of others.

In any society, it is inevitable that these interests shall come into confict. When they do, the primitive man determines who shall prevail with sword and club and tomahawk; and there is recent melancholy evidence that the law of the jungle is not yet departed from the affairs of nations. But in a civilized community, it is the law which is called upon to act as arbiter. The administration of the law becomes a process of weighing the interests for which the plaintiff demands protection against the defendant's claim to untrammeled freedom in the furtherance of his own desires, together with the importance of those desires themselves. When the interest of the public is thrown into the scale and allowed to swing the balance for or against the plaintiff, the result is a form of "social engineering" [17] that deliberately seeks to use the law as an instrument to promote that "greatest happiness of the greatest number," [18] which by common consent is the object of society. This process of "balancing

14. Bohlen, Fifty Years of Torts, 1937, 50 Harv.L.Rev. 725.

15. Winfield, Public Policy and the English Common Law, 1928, 42 Harv.L.Rev. 76.

16. The classic catalogue of the interests protected by the law is that of Pound, Outlines of Lectures on Jurisprudence, 1928, 60–71. See also Pound, Theory of Social Interests, 1920, 4 Pub.Am.Soc.Society 15; Pound, Interests of Personality, 1915, 28 Harv.L. Rev. 343, 445; Bowman, Introduction to the Common Law, 1932, ch. 5; Harper, Law of Torts, 1933, 5; Green, Judge and Jury, 1930, ch. 1.

17. Pound, Theory of Social Interests, 1920, 4 Pub. Am.Soc.Society 15.

18. Jeremy Bentham's phrase, although an acknowledged translation from an Italian source.

the interests" is by no means peculiar to the law of torts, but it has been carried to its greatest lengths and has received its most general conscious recognition in this field.

The process is not a simple one, and the problems which arise are complex, and seldom easy of solution. It is usually far easier to describe what has been done than to give a clear reason for it, and harder still to predict what the future may hold. It is a simple matter to say that the interests of individuals are to be balanced against one another in the light of those of the general public, but far more difficult to say where the public interest may lie. Most of the writers who have pointed out the process have stopped short of telling us how it is to be done. It is easy to say that the law will require of every man reasonable conduct [19] not unduly harmful to his neighbors; but what is reasonable, and what is undue harm? In determining the limits of the protection to be afforded by the law, the courts have been pulled and hauled by many conflicting considerations,[20] some of them ill defined and seldom expressed at all, no one of which can be said always to control. Often they have had

chiefly in mind the justice of the individual case, which may not coincide with the social interest in the long run.[21] If we are to have

19. See supra, p. 6.

20. See infra, § 4. An amusing but quite profound discussion is Cowan, The Victim of the Law of Torts, 1939, 33 Ill.L.Rev. 532. See also Williams, The Aims of the Law of Tort, 1951, 4 Curr.Leg. Prob. 137.

21. One very interesting illustration is the case of Rasmussen v. Benson, 1937, 133 Neb. 449, 275 N.W. 674, affirmed 1938, 135 Neb. 232, 280 N.W. 890, where recovery was permitted for illness and death caused by mental distress at the negligent poisoning of the decedent's cows and fear that poisoned milk had been sold to customers. It may be suggested that the decision is just and right; but even the Nebraska court recoils from the idea of any general rule permitting recovery for mental suffering at the loss of property, or at the peril of strangers. "If the facts are different than presented in this case, different reasoning and a different conclusion might be necessary." 135 Neb. 239, 280 N.W. 893.

general rules, and the law is to have no favorites, occasional injustice is inevitable to someone who does not fit into the rule; and the constant struggle is to make the rule sufficiently flexible to allow for the particular circumstances, and yet so rigid that lawyers may predict what the decision may be, and men may guide their conduct by that prediction. It is only by a slow, halting, confused, and often painful progress that any agreement is reached as to the best general rule. Ultimately the law must coincide with public opinion, and cannot stand against it; but when that opinion is in a state of division and flux, it is not surprising that the courts' decisions reflect the battle which is raging about them.

Without any pretense of comprehensiveness, mention may be made, in the following pages, of some of the factors which are to be thrown into the balance in this process of evaluating conflicting interests.

4. FACTORS AFFECTING TORT LIABILITY

Among the many considerations affecting the decision as to which of the conflicting interests is to prevail, a few may be singled out for special mention, with the repeated caution that no one of them is of such supervening importance that it will control the decision of every case in which it appears.

Moral Aspect of Defendant's Conduct

One such factor is the moral aspect of the defendant's conduct—or in other words, the moral guilt or blame to be attached in the eyes of society to his acts, his motives, and his state of mind. Personal morals are of course a matter on which there may be differences of opinion; but it may be assumed that in every community there are certain acts and motives which are generally regarded as morally right, and others which are considered morally wrong. Of course such public opinion has its effect upon the decisions of the courts. The oppressor, the perpetrator of outrage, the knave, the liar, the scandal-monger, the man who does spiteful harm for its own sake, the egotist who deliberately disregards and overrides the interests of his neighbors, may expect to find that the courts of society condemn him no less than the opinion of society itself. In a very vague general way, the law of torts reflects current ideas of morality, and when such ideas have changed, the law has kept pace with them.

This has not always been true. Historians have differed as to how the law began. There is one theory that it originated with liability based upon "actual intent and actual personal culpability," with a strong moral tinge, and slowly formulated external standards which took less account of personal fault.[22] It seems quite likely that the most flagrant wrongs would be the first to receive redress. Another, and more generally accepted theory, is that the law began by making a man act at his peril, and gradually developed toward the acceptance of moral standards as the basis of liability.[23] It has been suggested that there has been no steady progression, and the law has moved erratically, with the pendulum swinging slowly between "unmoral" periods and those in which stress has been laid upon moral fault.[24]

Certainly at one time the law was not concerned very much with the moral responsibility of the defendant. "The thought of man shall not be tried," said Chief Justice Brian, "for the devil himself knoweth not the thought of man."[25] The courts were interested primarily in keeping the peace between individuals by providing a substitute for private vengeance,[26] and the party injured was quite as likely to take the law into his own hands when the injury was an innocent one. The man who hurt another by pure accident[27] or in self-defense[28] was required to make good the damage inflicted. "In all civil acts," it was said, "the law doth not so much regard the intent of the actor, as the loss and damage of the party suffering."[29] Even then, however, there was an undercurrent of feeling that legal liability should coincide with moral blame; and it is not accurate to say that it was ever the law of England that one acts at his peril, and is responsible for any harm that may result.[30] Liability was commonly imposed, however, without regard to the moral innocence of the defendant. From this point of view the law has moved forward toward the recognition of moral responsibility as one basis of the remedy, and at least a partial identification of tort liability with the immoral conduct which would not be expected of a good citizen.[31] Toward the close of the nineteenth

22. Holmes, The Common Law, 1881, Lecture I.

23. Wigmore, Responsibility for Tortious Acts: Its History, 1894, 7 Harv.L.Rev. 315, 383, 441; Ames, Law and Morals, 1908, 22 Harv.L.Rev. 97; 3 Holdsworth, History of English Law, 3d Ed.1923, 375–377; 8 Holdsworth, History of English Law, 3d Ed.1923, 446–459.

24. Isaacs, Fault and Liability, 1918, 31 Harv.L.Rev. 954, 966.

25. Y.B. 7 Edw. IV, f. 2, pl. 2.

26. Holmes, The Common Law, 1881, 2, 3.

27. "Although the defendant's intent was good, still the intent is not material, though in felony it is; as where one is shooting at butts and kills a man, it is not felony. * * * But when one shooting at butts wounds a man unintentionally, he shall be called a trespasser against his will." 1506, Y.B. 21 Hen. VII, 27, 5. See also, 1466, Y.B.Edw. IV, 7, pl. 18; Wigmore, Responsibility for Tortious Acts: Its History, 1894, 7 Harv.L.Rev. 315, 383, 441; Smith, Tort and Absolute Liability, 1917, 30 Harv.L.Rev. 241, 248; 1 Street, Foundations of Legal Liability, 1906, 76.

28. 1319, Y.B. 12 Edw. II, 381.

29. Lambert v. Bessey, 1681, T.Raym. 421, 88 Eng. Rep. 220.

30. "Such a proposition is merely ridiculous. Life would not be worth living on such terms. Life never has been lived on such terms in any age or in any country. If a man always acted at his peril, the whole community would be in gaol but for three obstacles. No one could legally build the gaol, no one could legally send people to it, and no one could legally keep them there." Winfield, The Myth of Absolute Liability, 1926, 42 L.Q.Rev. 37, 38. See also Isaacs, Fault and Liability, 1918, 31 Harv.L. Rev. 954.

31. Ames, Law and Morals, 1908, 22 Harv.L.Rev. 97.

century this tendency was so marked, that efforts were made by noted writers to construct a consistent theory of tort law upon the basic principle that there should be no liability without "fault," involving a large element of personal blame.[32]

Today we have retreated from this position. It is now more or less generally recognized that the "fault" upon which liability may rest is social fault, which may but does not necessarily coincide with personal immorality. The law finds "fault" in a failure to live up to an ideal standard of conduct which may be beyond the knowledge or capacity of the individual,[33] and in acts which are normal and usual in the community, and without moral reproach in its eyes.[34] It will impose liability for good intentions and for innocent mistakes.[35] One who trespasses upon the land of another in the honest, reasonable belief that it is his own,[36] or buys stolen chattels in good faith,[37] or innocently publishes a statement which proves to be a libel of another,[38] is held liable without any personal guilt, because his conduct, while innocent, is still so far anti-social that the law considers that he should pay for the harm he does. In the legal sense, "fault" has come to mean no more than a departure from the conduct required of a man by society for the protection of others,[39] and it is the public and social interest which determines what is required. The twentieth century has seen the develop-

ment of entire fields of liability in which the defendants are held liable for well-intentioned and entirely moral and reasonable conduct, because it is considered to be good social policy that their enterprises should pay their way by bearing the loss they inflict.[40] In the larger sense, there is no less of a moral point of view in the rule that one who quite innocently causes loss should make it good; but it is social morality, and not personal blame, which is involved. The individual may be in no way to blame, and subject to no personal reproach whatever, because he is out of line with what society requires of him; but he is none the less out of line, and treated accordingly by the law.

On the other hand, there are still many immoral acts which do not amount to torts, and the law has not yet enacted the golden rule. It is impossible to afford a lawsuit for every deed of unkindness or betrayal, and there is much evil in the world which must necessarily be left to other agencies of social control. The basest ingratitude is not a tort, nor is a cruel refusal of kindness or courtesy, or a denial of aid. The rich man is under no compulsion to feed his starving neighbor, and it is still the law that the owner of a boat who sees another drowning before his eyes may rest on his oars and let him drown [41]—although perhaps in so extreme a case it is a reproach to the law that it is so. Petty insults, threats, abuse and lacerated feelings must be endured in a society not many centuries removed from the law of the club.[42] To what extent the moral ideas of a future day may yet create new torts to deal with such misconduct, it is now impossible to say.

In short, it is undoubtedly true that in the great majority of the cases liability in tort rests upon some moral delinquency on the

---

32. Holmes, The Common Law, 1881, 144–163; Smith, Tort and Absolute Liability, 1917, 30 Harv.L.Rev. 241, 319, 409; Salmond, Law of Torts, 7th Ed.1924, 11, 12.

33. See infra, § 32.

34. See infra, p. 166.

35. See infra, § 17.

36. Lowenburg v. Rosenthal, 1899, 18 Or. 178, 22 P. 601; Hazelton v. Week, 1880, 49 Wis. 661, 6 N.W. 309; Perry v. Jefferies, 1901, 61 S.C. 292, 39 S.E. 515.

37. See infra, p. 84.

38. See infra, § 113.

39. Seavey, Speculations as to "Respondeat Superior," Harvard Legal Essays, 1934, 433, 442.

40. See infra, ch. 13.

41. See infra, § 56; Ames, Law and Morals, 1908, 22 Harv.L.Rev. 97, 112; Bohlen, The Moral Duty to Aid Others as a Basis of Tort Liability, 1908, 56 U.Pa.L.Rev. 217, 316; Bruce, Humanity and the Law, 1911, 73 Cent.L.J. 335.

42. See infra, p. 52.

part of the individual. But quite often it is based upon considerations of public policy which have little connection with private morals. The ethical principles which underlie the law are "not the moral code of popular speech, but an artificial and somewhat sublimated morality, which is formulated by the law and is called morality only by a use of that term which is almost metaphorical." [43]

The last three decades have witnessed much more willingness on the part of the courts to discard, as an absolute requirement for liability, even legal, as distinguished from moral "fault," and at least to consider and entertain the contention that the law is, or should be, primarily a question of which interest is to prevail even where no one is at "fault;" or in other words, of where society is going, and what the courts are trying to do. As a result there has been a recrudescence of the older "strict" liability, "without fault," in several areas, where new and modern ideas of policy have developed to support it; there has been legislation, and proposals for a great deal more; and the availability of liability insurance as a means of distributing a loss which might otherwise be ruinous for the individual has become a subject of much discussion. Consideration of these matters must be left to a later chapter.[44]

Historical Development

The shadow of the past still lies rather heavily on the law of torts. When the common law first emerged, its forms of procedure were rigidly prescribed, and the plaintiff could have no cause of action unless he could fit his claim into the form of some existing and recognized writ. These "forms of action we have buried, but they still rule us from their graves." [45] At the beginning of the nineteenth century they still existed, although somewhat blurred in their outlines, as the core of common law procedure. By the middle of the century they began to be modified, liberalized, and at last replaced to a great extent by the modern procedural codes. The old attitude still persisted, however, that the substance of the plaintiff's right is determined and limited by the possibility of a remedy under the common law forms. Thus even today we find courts holding that blasting operations which cast rocks onto the plaintiff's land may be actionable where those which merely shake his house to pieces are not,[46] on the basis of the old distinction between the action of trespass and the action on the case.[47] Added to this is the devotion to precedent and the distrust of new ideas, which is by no means peculiar to the law but for which it often is reproached, and which has made it change slowly. There are not many rules in tort law as to which one may say that there is no better reason for their existence than that they were laid down by Lord Mildew three centuries since, at a time when the world was a very different place,[48] but they do exist.[49]

Nevertheless, change and development have come, as social ideas have altered, and they are constantly going on. The law of deceit has progressed from a point where it was assumed as a matter of course that every seller of goods will lie; [50] the law of slander at one time held that mere "brabling words" imputing harlotry to a woman were not actionable; [51] and the same evolution is to be

46. See infra, p. 65.

47. See infra, § 7.

48. The phrase is borrowed from A. P. Herbert, Uncommon Law, 1936, 85.

49. As instances, one may mention the distinction between libel and slander, infra, § 112, and the law as to trespass ab initio, infra, p. 129.

50. See Chandelor v. Lopus, 1625, Cro.Jac. 4, 79 Eng. Rep. 3; infra, § 100.

51. See infra, p. 759.

43. Keigwin, Cases on Torts, 1929, 19; Vold, The Functional Perspective for the Law of Torts, 1936, 14 Neb.L.B. 217.

44. See infra, ch. 14.

45. Maitland, Forms of Action, 1936, 296. See Wilson, Writs v. Rights: An Unended Contest, 1920, 18 Mich. L.Rev. 255.

traced in the law of seduction,[52] the right of privacy,[53] and interference with contractual relations.[54] More recently[55] courts have recognized for the first time an action for prenatal injuries,[56] a recovery by a wife for personal injury at the hands of her husband,[57] new tort liabilities of municipal corporations,[58] and a whole new field of actions for nervous shock and mental suffering.[59] This process of development, of course, is not ended, and continues every year.

It was not until yesterday, as legal generations go, that there was any recognition of torts as a distinct branch of the law, or any attempt to treat it as a unified whole. The first treatise in English on Torts was published in 1859 by Francis Hilliard of Cambridge, Massachusetts, who was followed a year later by Addison in England. Even as late as 1871, the leading American legal periodical said that "We are inclined to think that Torts is not a proper subject for a law book."[60]

Since that day there have appeared the excellent treatises of Pollock, Salmond, Winfield, Clerk and Lindsell, and Street in England. These have been followed by the very thoughtful Australian text of Fleming—the

last edition of which, in the opinion of this writer at least, must rank as the best text extant upon the law of Torts. In the United States there flourished for a season a whole set of now largely forgotten short texts, such as Bigelow, Hale, Jaggard, and Burdick, as well as professor Harper's first short exposition of tort theory. The latest, longest, and most complete treatise in the whole field is that of Harper and James, which is more or less frankly partisan, and devoted to the proposition that there should be liability, and compensation of the plaintiff's injury, in virtually every situation in which one may seek to recover for harm done to him by another. In addition, there are numerous texts on particular torts, which may throw valuable light on different phases of the law.

The influence of these text writers upon the courts has been very great; and perhaps even more influential has been the constant discussion of tort problems in the law reviews. The most complete, penetrating and helpful writing on torts is found in the periodical literature. Within the past thirty years there has been a very significant attempt at a searching and exhaustive analysis of the entire field in the American Law Institute's Restatement of the Law of Torts, which was begun in 1923, and finally completed in 1939. Some of the most eminent legal scholars of that day took part in the work, with the assistance of numerous judges and lawyers. The form of the Restatement is perhaps unfortunate, in that it seeks to reduce the law to a definite set of blackletter rules or principles, ignoring all contrary authority—since the law of torts in its present stage of development does not lend itself at all readily to such treatment. There is room for suspicion that the courts have tended to cite the Restatement when they are already in agreement with it, and to ignore it when they are not, so that the impressive list of references to it in the cases may be somewhat misleading; and there are those who have disagreed with many of its conclu-

---

52. See infra, p. 884.

53. See infra, ch. 20.

54. See infra, § 129.

55. See Albertsworth, Recognition of New Interests in the Law of Torts, 1922, 10 Cal.L.Rev. 461.

56. See infra, § 55.

57. See infra, § 122.

58. See Feezer, Capacity to Bear Loss as a Factor in the Decision of Certain Types of Tort Cases, 1930, 78 U.Pa.L.Rev. 805, 815; Albertsworth, Recognition of New Interests in the Law of Torts, 1922, 10 Cal. L.Rev. 461, 480; infra, § 131.

59. See infra, § 12.

60. 1871, 5 Am.L.Rev. 341. In 1853, when Mr. Joel Bishop proposed to write a book on the law of torts, he was assured by all the publishers that there was no call for a work on such a subject, and that "if the book were written by the most eminent and prominent author that ever lived, not a dozen copies a year could be sold." Bishop, Non-Contract Law, 1889, 2.

sions, and even denounced the whole project.[61]

It is also unfortunate that much of the immensely valuable work which was done in its preparation, together with all of the cases on which it has relied, are buried in Tentative Drafts which remain unpublished for general circulation. Nevertheless it unquestionably represents the most complete and thorough consideration which tort law ever has received; and only the most hopelessly biased would be disposed to question its importance as an influence upon the courts. At the present writing the American Law Institute is in process of reconsideration and revision of the Restatement of Torts, at the hands of a different drafting and study group, which will lead to the publication of a Second Restatement. The first two volumes of this, covering much the same ground as the first dozen chapters of this book, were published in 1965; but completion of the whole work probably still lies several years ahead.

This flood of comment and discussion, of analysis and efforts to synthesize and unify the law, has greatly speeded up its development, and the opinion may be ventured that more progress has been made in the tort field in the last two decades than in a century or two preceding.

Convenience of Administration

It does not lie within the power of any judicial system to remedy all human wrongs. The obvious limitations upon the time of the courts, the difficulty in many cases of ascertaining the real facts or of providing any effective remedy, have meant that there must be some selection of those more serious injuries which have the prior claim to redress and are dealt with most easily. Trivialities must be left to other means of settlement, and many wrongs which in themselves are

flagrant—ingratitude, avarice, broken faith, brutal words, and heartless disregard of the feelings of others—are beyond any effective legal remedy, and any practical administration of the law.

The courts always have stood more or less in dread of a "flood of litigation" involving problems which they are not prepared to deal with.[62] At one time they refused to permit any inquiry as to the state of a man's knowledge, or his belief or intentions, upon the ground that "they cannot be known." [63] For many years they denied all recovery in cases of "mental suffering" involving fright or shock without physical impact, for fear that it would "open a wide door for unjust claims, which cannot successfully be met." [64] The refusal to extend the obligation of a contract to third parties was based upon the "infinity of actions" and the "most absurd and outrageous consequences" which might ensue,[65] and this is still the chief obstacle to holding some contractors liable to third persons.[66]

The reluctance of many courts for so many years to recognize the so-called "right of privacy" rested upon the same objection,[67] and

---

61. See for example Green, The Torts Restatement, 1935, 29 Ill.L.Rev. 582. Also Milner, Restatement: The Failure of a Legal Experiment, 1959, 20 U. Pitt.L.Rev. 794.

62. Green, Judge and Jury, 1930, 77–96.

63. "Upon this the plaintiff demurred and had judgment, for it appears that the fact was voluntary, and his intention and knowledge are not traversable; they cannot be known." Basely v. Clarkson, 1681, 3 Lev. 37, 83 Eng.Rep. 565.

64. Spade v. Lynn & Boston R. Co., 1897, 168 Mass. 285, 288, 47 N.E. 88, 89. "If the right of recovery in this class of cases should be once established, it would naturally result in a flood of litigation in cases where the injury complained of may be easily feigned without detection." Mitchell v. Rochester R. Co., 1896, 151 N.Y. 107, 110, 45 N.E. 354.
This is re-echoed, as to mental distress at injury to the plaintiff's child, in Amaya v. Home Ice, Fuel & Supply Co., 1963, 59 Cal.2d 295, 29 Cal.Rptr. 33, 379 P.2d 513, where the "administrative factor" is singled out by name as the reason for the decision.

65. Winterbottom v. Wright, 1842, 10 M. & W. 109, 152 Eng.Rep. 402.

66. See H. R. Moch Co. v. Rensselaer Water Co., 1928, 247 N.Y. 160, 159 N.E. 896.

67. "If such a principle be incorporated into the body of the law through the instrumentality of a

many similar instances of hesitation in the face of an expected deluge of questionable claims or troublesome problems of proof might be mentioned. Such difficulties of administration are perhaps most significant in new developments of the law, and are overcome slowly as the courts find some workable method of affording redress where it is clearly merited and justified as a matter of policy.[68]

Capacity to Bear Loss

Another factor to which the courts have given weight in balancing the interests before them is the relative ability of the respective parties to bear the loss which must necessarily fall upon one or the other.[69] This is not so much a matter of their respective wealth, although certainly juries, and sometimes judges, are not indisposed to favor the poor against the rich. Rather it is a matter of their capacity to absorb the loss or avoid it. The defendants in tort cases are to a large extent public utilities, industrial corporations, commercial enterprises, automobile owners, and others [70] who by means of rates, prices, taxes or insurance are best able to distribute to the public at large the risks and losses which are inevitable in a complex civilization. Rather than leave the loss on the shoulders of the individual plaintiff, who may be ruined by it, the courts have tended to find reasons to shift it to the defendants. Probably no small part of the general extension of the tort law to permit more frequent recovery in recent years has been due to this attitude. The development of the doctrine of strict liability "without fault" for dangerous conditions and activities has rested to some extent on this basis,[71] as has that of vicarious liability for the torts of a servant;[72] and the extension of the liability of a manufacturer to the ultimate consumer of his product has been favored by the feeling that he is best able to bear the loss.[73] The same principle, of course, underlies such statutes as the workmen's compensation acts.[74]

But there are obvious limitations upon the power of a defendant to shift the loss to the public,[75] and the courts frequently have been reluctant to saddle an industry with the entire burden of the harm it may cause, for fear that it may prove ruinously heavy.[76] This is particularly true where the liability may extend to an unlimited number of un-

court of equity, the attempts to logically apply the principle will necessarily result, not only in a vast amount of litigation, but in litigation bordering upon the absurd. * * *" Roberson v. Rochester Folding-Box Co., 1902, 171 N.Y. 538, 64 N.E. 442.

68. Green, Judge and Jury, 1930, 96.

69. Green, Judge and Jury, 1930, ch. 4; Feezer, Capacity to Bear Loss as a Factor in the Decision of Certain Types of Tort Cases, 1930, 78 U.Pa.L.Rev. 805, 1931, 79 U.Pa.L.Rev. 742; Morris, Hazardous Enterprises and Risk Bearing Capacity, 1952, 61 Yale L.J. 1172; Green, The Thrust of Tort Law: The Influence of Environment, 1961, 64 W.Va.L. Rev. 1.

70. Thus a count of 672 California cases bearing on the issue of "proximate cause," made in 1950, disclosed the following list of defendants: railways, street railways and other carriers 137; other public utilities 68; automobile drivers 127; manufacturers, industrial concerns and sellers of goods 78; owners and occupiers of land 75; employers 31; municipal and other government corporations 24; contractors 39; physicians and surgeons 22; notaries and other bonded officers 13; steamship companies 8; other defendants, including several who might well have carried liability insurance, 48. See Prosser, Proximate Cause in California, 1950, 38 Cal.L.Rev. 369, 397.

71. See Pound, The End of Law as Developed in Legal Rules and Doctrines, 1914, 27 Harv.L.Rev. 195, 233; infra, ch. 13.

72. See Seavey, Speculations, as to "Respondeat Superior," Harvard Legal Essays, 1934, 433, 450; infra, § 70.

73. Feezer, Social Justice in the Field of Torts, 1926, 11 Minn.L.Rev. 313, 323. See Traynor, J., concurring in Escola v. Coca Cola Bottling Co., 1944, 24 Cal.2d 453, 150 P.2d 436.

74. Bohlen, The Drafting of Workmen's Compensation Acts, 1912, 25 Harv.L.Rev. 544; Smith, Sequel to Workmen's Compensation Acts, 1914, 27 Harv.L. Rev. 235; see infra, § 80.

75. Douglas, Vicarious Liability and the Administration of Risk, 1928, 38 Yale L.J. 584, 720.

76. See H. R. Moch Co. v. Rensselaer Water Co., 1928, 247 N.Y. 160, 159 N.E. 896.

known persons, and is incapable of being estimated or insured against in advance.[77] It is also likely to be true as to a new industry, which may be unduly hampered in its development, as is illustrated by the controversy over the liability of the aviation industry for damage to persons or property on the ground, which used to turn primarily on the policy of imposing such a burden upon a new enterprise.[78]

Prevention and Punishment

The "prophylactic" factor of preventing future harm has been quite important in the field of torts. The courts are concerned not only with compensation of the victim, but with admonition of the wrongdoer. When the decisions of the courts become known, and defendants realize that they may be held liable, there is of course a strong incentive to prevent the occurrence of the harm. Not infrequently one reason for imposing liability is the deliberate purpose of providing that incentive. The rule of vicarious liability is intended, among other things, to result in greater care in the selection and instruction of servants than would otherwise be the case;[79] the carrier which is held to the "highest practicable degree of care" toward its passengers will tend to observe it for their safety; the manufacturer who is made liable to the consumer for defects in his product

will do what he can to see that there are no such defects. While the idea of prevention is seldom controlling, it very often has weight as a reason for holding the defendant responsible.[80]

This idea of prevention shades into that of punishment of the offender for what he has already done, since one admitted purpose of punishment itself is to prevent repetition of the offense. There are those who believe [81] that punishment or retaliation is an important and proper aim of the law in assessing damages, since what is paid to the plaintiff is taken away from the defendant. However this may be, it is not often mentioned in the award of compensatory damages, which usually are treated by the courts as a mere adjustment of the loss which has occurred in accordance with responsibility. To the extent that punitive damages [82] are given, however, both prevention and retaliation become accepted objects of the administration of the law of torts.[83]

5. MOTIVE

The motive or purpose underlying the defendant's conduct frequently plays a rather important part in the determination of tort liability. When an act is done, there are nearly always a number of different objectives and motivations behind it. A rather shadowy line has been drawn by the courts between the more immediate objective, which is called the actor's intent, and the more remote ends, which are designated as his motive or purpose. In the case of as-

---

77. See for example the court's solicitude for the defendant's industry in Ryan v. New York Central R. Co., 1866, 35 N.Y. 210; Palsgraf v. Long Island R. Co., 1928, 248 N.Y. 339, 162 N.E. 99; and the case cited in the preceding footnote.

78. See Bohlen, Aviation under the Common Law, 1934, 48 Harv.L.Rev. 216; Sweeney, Adjusting the Conflicting Interests of Landowner and Aviator in Anglo-American Law, 1932, 3 J.Air Law 329, 531; Kingsley and Maugham, The Correlative Interests of the Landowner and Airman, 1932, 3 J.Air Law 374; Ewing, The Ground Rule of Torts by Aircraft at the American Law Institute, 1934, 5 Air L.Rev. 323; Proceedings of American Law Institute, vol. 11, 543–579.

79. Seavey, Speculations as to "Respondeat Superior," Harvard Legal Essays, 1934, 433, 448, 462, note 36.

80. There is a detailed analytical consideration of how far present rules of tort liability are consistent with a basis of deterrence, in Williams, The Aims of the Law of Tort, 1951, 4 Curr.Leg.Prob. 137.

81. Salmond, Jurisprudence, 7th Ed. 1924, 132, 424, 441; 1 Street, Foundations of Legal Liability, 1906, 477; Morris, Rough Justice and Some Utopian Ideas, 1930, 24 Ill.L.Rev. 730; Morris, Punitive Damages in Tort Cases, 1931, 44 Harv.L.Rev. 1173.

82. See supra, p. 9.

83. See for example Goddard v. Grand Trunk Ry. Co., 1869, 57 Me. 202.

sault and battery we say that the defendant intends to strike the plaintiff, or even to kill him, but that his motive is one of revenge, or the gratification of his rage, or self-defense, or defense of his country. Similarly, if he acts to induce a third person to break a contract with the plaintiff, it is said that his intent is to interfere with the contract relation, while his motive may be one of pure spite, business competition, or protection of the interests of a labor union.

The early common law, which was willing to hold the defendant liable for accidental injuries that were not even intended, took little or no account of his motives. It was only by a slow process and at a later date that such justifiable purposes as self-defense were recognized, and then they were accepted as defenses to acts long since established as wrongful. Conversely, a bad motive, while it might aggravate the damages, was considered of no significance unless a tort could be made out without it; and it was not until the beginning of the eighteenth century [84] that such a motive was first held to be sufficient in itself to determine liability.

Out of this older law there has survived the statement, repeated frequently by the courts,[85] and accepted even by so able a writer as Judge Cooley,[86] that "Malicious motives make a bad case worse, but they cannot make that wrong which is in its essence lawful." This of course merely begs the question, since unless motive is to be eliminated altogether, it must be taken into account in determining whether the act is "in its essence lawful" in the first place.[87] Equally empty is the assertion that an unlawful act resulting in damage to another is actionable unless it is "justified" by its purpose,[88] since it is the legality of the act in the light of the purpose that we seek to determine.

It is undoubtedly true that there are many questions of tortious conduct where the defendant's motive is entirely immaterial. That is because over the passage of centuries, and with the approval of custom and public opinion, the rights and privileges of the parties in the particular situation have become crystallized, standardized, definite or "absolute," so that the law looks at them with a purely objective view and applies fixed rules. Thus a defendant may use all reasonable force to exclude others from his land,[89] to eject a trespasser [90] or remove an encroachment,[91] or may revoke a license,[92] or resort to legal process to collect a valid debt [93] or to

---

84. The leading case is Keeble v. Hickeringill, 1707, 11 East 574, note, 11 Mod.Rep. 14, 130, 3 Salk. 9, Holt 14, 103 Eng.Rep. 1127, where the defendant repeatedly fired guns to frighten away wild fowl from the plaintiff's decoy pond, and was held liable because the act was "malicious" rather than intended to further any legitimate interest.

85. Apparently first said in Jenkins v. Fowler, 1855, 24 Pa. 308, 310, with the pious addition that "As long as a man keeps himself within the law by doing no *act* which violates it, we must leave his motives to Him who searches the heart." See also Bourlier Bros. v. Macauley, 1891, 91 Ky. 135, 15 S.W. 60; Boyson v. Thorn, 1893, 98 Cal. 578, 33 P. 492; Bohn Mfg. Co. v. Hollis, 1893, 54 Minn. 223, 55 N.W. 1119.

See the defense of this antiquated view in Ormsby, Malice in the Law of Torts, 1892, 8 L.Q.Rev. 140.

86. Cooley, Torts, 1st Ed. 1888, 497.

87. See Ames, How Far an Act May be a Tort Because of the Wrongful Motive of the Actor, 1905, 18 Harv.L.Rev. 411. Cf. Boggs v. Duncan-Schell Furn. Co., 1913, 163 Iowa 106, 143 N.W. 482.

88. See Raycroft v. Tayntor, 1896, 68 Vt. 219, 35 A. 53; London Guarantee & Acc. Co. v. Horn, 1904, 206 Ill. 493, 69 N.E. 526.

89. Rader v. Davis, 1912, 154 Iowa 306, 134 N.W. 849.

90. Kiff v. Youmans, 1881, 86 N.Y. 324; Brothers v. Morris, 1877, 49 Vt. 460. On the same basis, of course, an unprivileged trespasser is not excused by good motives. Ketcham v. Cohn, 1893, 2 Misc. 427, 22 N.Y.S. 181; Bruch v. Carter, 1867, 32 N.J.L. 554; Cubit v. O'Dett, 1883, 51 Mich. 347, 16 N.W. 679.

91. Smith v. Johnson, 1874, 76 Pa. 191. Cf. Jenkins v. Fowler, 1855, 24 Pa. 308; Clinton v. Myers, 1871, 46 N.Y. 511.

92. Marshfield Land & Lumber Co. v. John Week Lbr. Co., 1900, 108 Wis. 268, 84 N.W. 434.

93. Morris v. Tuthill, 1878, 72 Hun, N.Y., 573; Sullivan v. Collins, 1900, 107 Wis. 291, 83 N.W. 310;

recover from a tortfeasor,[94] or he may publish defamatory truth,[95] or refuse entirely to deal with one to whom he is not under contract,[96] all in the worst possible spirit of malevolent vindictiveness, and still claim immunity from all liability.

When the more modern law began to inquire into the character of the defendant's conduct, however, and to base liability upon his immediate intent to interfere with the interest of the plaintiff, it was inevitable that his underlying motives should be called into play. With recognition that the interests of the parties are to be weighed against one another has come a realization that the actor's state of mind may be an important factor in the scale. Accordingly, in many situations where the interests involved are more nicely balanced, and the rights and privileges of the parties are not fixed by definite rule but are interdependent and relative, the defendant's motive or purpose may in itself determine whether he is to be held liable.[97]

One conspicuous example of this is found in the field of nuisance,[98] where the reasonableness of an interference with the plaintiff's use or enjoyment of his land may depend upon the defendant's motive in causing it. Thus the erection of a spite fence, with no other purpose than the vindictive one of shutting off the plaintiff's view, or his light and air, is now held by most courts [99] to be actionable as a nuisance, where the same fence serving some useful end would not. Quite in line with such cases are the modern decisions holding defendants liable for accumulating checks drawn on the plaintiff and presenting them all at once for payment,[1] or buying up his note and transferring it to a bona fide purchaser who can enforce it against him,[2] where the sole motive is to ruin him financially. The part played by motive where abuse of a qualified privilege is in question, in cases of defamation,[3] malicious prosecution,[4] and alienation of affections,[5] is very much the same. In actions for interference with economic relations, it is now generally recognized that the defendant's motive or purpose is frequently the determining factor as to liability,[6] and sometimes it is said that bad motive is the gist of the action.[7]

Stevenson v. Newnham, 1853, 13 C.B. 285, 138 Eng. Rep. 1208; Hamilton v. Windolf, 1872, 36 Md. 301.

94. Jacobson v. Van Boening, 1896, 48 Neb. 80, 66 N.W. 993.

95. See infra, p. 796.

96. McCune v. Norwich City Gas Co., 1862, 30 Conn. 521 (shutting off plaintiff's gas); Kelly v. Chicago, M. & St. P. R. Co., 1895, 93 Iowa 436, 61 N.W. 957 (refusal of free service afforded to others); see Elmore v. Atlantic C. L. R. Co., 1926, 191 N.C. 182, 131 S.E. 633 (discharge of conductor).

97. Terry, Malicious Torts, 1904, 20 L.Q.Rev. 10; Ames, How Far an Act may be a Tort Because of the Wrongful Motive of the Actor, 1905, 18 Harv. L.Rev. 411; Lewis, Should the Motive of the Defendant Affect the Question of His Liability, 1905, 5 Col.L.Rev. 107; Lawrence, Motive as an Element in Tort, 1919, 12 Maine L.Rev. 47; Eliot, Malice in Tort, 1919, 4 St. Louis L.Rev. 50; Duport, Disinterested Malevolence as an Actionable Wrong, 1953, 22 Ford L.Rev. 185; Fridman, Malice in the Law of Torts, 1958, 21 Mod.L.Rev. 484.

For comparison with the similar principles of the civil law, see Walton, Motive as an Element in Torts in the Common and in the Civil Law, 1909, 22 Harv.L.Rev. 501; Jenks, Theories of Tort in Modern Law, 1903, 19 L.Q.Rev. 19.

98. See infra, p. 596.

99. See infra, p. 598.

1. American Bank & Trust Co. v. Federal Reserve Bank, 1921, 256 U.S. 350.

2. Silliman v. Dobner, 1925, 165 Minn. 87, 205 N.W. 696. Cf. St. Charles Mercantile Co. v. Armour & Co., 1930, 156 S.C. 397, 153 S.E. 473 (alteration and premature presentation of postdated check).

3. See infra, p. 794.

4. See infra, p. 847.

5. See infra, § 124.

6. See infra, § 129.

7. West Virginia Transp. Co. v. Standard Oil Co., 1902, 50 W.Va. 611, 40 S.E. 591; Wheeler-Stenzel Co. v. American Window Glass Co., 1909, 202 Mass. 471, 89 N.E. 28; Globe & Rutgers Fire Ins. Co. v. Firemen's Fund Fire Ins. Co., 1910, 97 Miss. 148, 52 So. 454; S. C. Posner Co. v. Jackson, 1918, 223 N.Y. 325, 119 N.E. 573.

Out of all this a number of courts [8] have developed a "prima facie tort" doctrine, the classic statement of which [9] is that "intentionally to do that which is calculated in the ordinary course of events to damage, and which does, in fact, damage another in that person's property or trade, is actionable if done without just cause or excuse." This, of course, is no more than a form of words emphasizing the importance of motive; and the real problem underlying the question of motive remains the same one of balancing the conflicting interests of the parties, and determining whether the defendant's objective should prevail at the expense of the damage to the plaintiff. Whether the social value of that objective is sufficient to outweigh the gravity of the interference often becomes the question of deciding significance. It is in the cases where motive is called into question that it becomes most clearly apparent that the law of torts is a battlefield of the conflict between capital and labor, between business competitors, and others who have conflicting claims in the economic struggle.

6. GENERAL PLAN

There are many possible approaches to the law of torts, and many different arrangements of the material to be considered have been attempted. Other than mere convenience in discussion, there is of course no inherent merit in any of them. By some odd coincidence, the classifications usually have gone by threes, and nearly everyone has found some "tripartite division." Dean Wigmore [10] arranged torts under the three general heads of the "Damage Element" (did the plaintiff suffer legal harm, or what loss or damage is actionable); the "Causation Element" (who is answerable, or was the defendant responsible for the damage); and the "Excuse Element" (what is sufficient justification or excuse for an apparent wrong). No doubt it is difficult to improve upon this as a matter of tort theory and the ultimate reasons underlying the law, but it does not assemble in any one place the questions likely to be considered by a court at the same time. Sir Frederick Pollock,[11] who has been followed by most of the text writers, classified tort into personal wrongs, wrongs to possession and property, and wrongs to person, estate and property generally. Dean Green,[12] in addition to setting forth an elaborate alignment of fact situations, has divided torts into "physical harms," "harms of appropriation," and "harms to relational interests." There are certainly many other possible categories into which the law of torts might be separated, according to the particular theory or purpose of the writer.

For no other reason than that the author finds it most convenient for what he has to say, the general plan of this book is the same as that adopted by the Restatement of Torts. The fundamental basis of tort liability may first be divided into three parts—not because that number is traditional, but because every case in which such liability has been imposed has rested upon one of three, and only three, grounds for imposing it. These are:

1. Intent of the defendant to interfere with the plaintiff's interests.

2. Negligence.

---

8. See for example Al Raschid v. News Syndicate Co., 1934, 265 N.Y. 1, 191 N.E. 713; Aikens v. Wisconsin, 1904, 195 U.S. 194; Imperial Ice Co. v. Rossier, 1941, 18 Cal.2d 33, 112 P.2d 631; Wilkinson v. Powe, 1942, 300 Mich. 275, 1 N.W.2d 539; Louis Kamm, Inc. v. Flink, 1934, 113 N.J.L. 582, 175 A. 62. See Halpern, Intentional Torts and the Restatement, 1957, 7 Buff.L.Rev. 7; Notes, 1951, 51 Col.L.Rev. 398; 1952, 52 Col.L.Rev. 503; 1958, 32 St. Johns L. Rev. 282; 1958, 10 Syr.L.Rev. 53.

9. By Lord Bowen, in Mogul Steamship Co. v. McGregor, Gow & Co., 1889, 23 Q.B.D. 598, 613.

10. Wigmore, The Tripartite Division of Torts, 1894, 8 Harv.L.Rev. 200; Wigmore, A General Analysis of Tort Relations, 1895, 8 Harv.L.Rev. 377; Wigmore, Select Cases on the Law of Torts, 2 vols. 1912.

11. Pollock, Law of Torts, 15th Ed. 1951, 6, 7.

12. Green, Judge and Jury, 1930, 9–13.

3. Strict liability, "without fault," where the defendant is held liable in the absence of any intent which the law finds wrongful, or any negligence, very often for reasons of policy.

These will be considered in order, and in connection with each there will be discussed those "torts," or invasions of the plaintiff's interests, which have been more or less exclusively identified with each, together with the defenses available against them.

This will carry the reader through Chapter 13. The remainder of the volume is devoted to a consideration of particular fields of liability which are of sufficient importance to warrant separate treatment. Usually, as in the case of liability for Nuisance, for Misrepresentation, or that of Owners and Occupiers of Land and Suppliers of Chattels, these cannot be assigned to any one ground of intent, negligence or strict liability, but recovery may rest upon any of the three. The principal reason for such separate treatment, however, is not so much any difficulty of separating out the grounds of liability as the presence of problems peculiar to the particular interest invaded, which makes it desirable to consider them together.

The effort has been, wherever possible, to adhere to the terminology and the concepts which are in use in the courts, and so generally familiar to the bar. Sometimes these are not the most accurate or desirable ones that might be found, and from a theoretical point of view it might perhaps be better to refer, for example, to a "harm of appropriation" rather than to "conversion;" but any attorney approaching a court with such language would receive no very warm reception, and there are obvious advantages in preserving so far as possible the language in which lawyers must talk, even though there must necessarily be a good deal of inquiry as to its meaning.

CHAPTER 2

INTENTIONAL INTERFERENCE WITH
THE PERSON

7. HISTORY: TRESPASS AND CASE

The origins of the law of torts are "secreted in the interstices of procedure." [1] The ghosts of ancient common law forms of action, long since obsolete, still walk through our courts. "In earlier days they filled the law with formalism and fiction, confusion and complexity, and though most of the mischief which they did has been buried with them, some portion of it remains inherent in the law of the present day." [2]

In the early English law, remedies for wrongs were dependent upon the issuance of writs to bring the defendant into court. No one could bring an action in the King's common law courts without the King's writ. The number of such writs available was very limited, and their forms were strictly prescribed; and unless the plaintiff's cause of action could be fitted into the form of some recognized writ, he was without a remedy. The result was a highly formal and artificial system of procedure, which governed and controlled the law as to the substance of wrongs which might be remedied. The writs which were available for remedies that were purely tortious in character were two—that for the action of trespass, and that for the action of trespass on the case. [3]

The action of trespass, which first emerged in the thirteenth century, had a basic criminal character. It was directed at serious and forcible breaches of the King's peace, and it was upon this basis that the royal courts assumed jurisdiction over the wrong. They were concerned primarily with punishment of the crime; and when the defendant was convicted of trespass, he was fined, and was subject to imprisonment if the fine was not paid. It was in connection with this criminal proceeding that damages first came to be awarded incidentally to the injured plaintiff. [4] What similarity remains between tort and crime is to be traced to this common beginning.

Trespass was the remedy for all forcible, direct and immediate injuries, whether to person or to property—or in other words, for the kind of conduct likely to lead to a breach of the peace by provoking immediate retaliation. Trespass on the case, or the action on the case, as it came to be called, developed somewhat later, [5] as a supplement to the

wrongful detention of property, were not purely delictual in character. Trover, which developed later, was a specialized form of the action on the case, modeled after detinue. 3 Street, Foundations of Legal Liability, 1906, 223.

4. Woodbine, The Origin of the Action of Trespass, 1923, 33 Yale L.J. 799, 1934, 34 Yale L.J. 343; Deiser, The Development of Principle in Trespass, 1917, 27 Yale L.J. 220; Fifoot, History and Sources of the Common Law, 1949, ch. 3.

5. Kiralfy, The Action on the Case, 1951, ch. 1; Fifoot, History and Sources of the Common Law,

1. Maine, Early Law and Custom, 1883, 389.

2. Salmond, Observations on Trover and Conversion, 1905, 21 L.Q.Rev. 43.

3. Salmond, Law of Torts, 10th Ed. 1945, 3–4. The actions of detinue and replevin, which lay for the

parent action of trespass, designed to afford a remedy for obviously wrongful conduct resulting in injuries which were not forcible or not direct. The distinction between the two lay in the immediate application of force to the person or property of the plaintiff, as distinguished from injury through some obvious and visible secondary cause. The classic illustration of the difference between trespass and case is that of a log thrown into the highway. A person struck by the log as it fell could maintain trespass against the thrower, since the injury was direct; but one who was hurt by stumbling over it as it lay in the road could maintain, not trespass, but an action on the case.[6]

The distinction was not one between intentional and negligent conduct. The emphasis was upon the causal sequence, rather than the character of the defendant's wrong. Trespass would lie for all direct injuries, even though they were not intended,[7] and the action on the case might be maintained for those which were intended but indirect.[8] There were, however, two significant points of difference between the two actions. Trespass, perhaps because of its criminal origin, required no proof of any actual damage, since the invasion of the plaintiff's rights was regarded as a tort in itself; while in the action on the case, which developed purely as a tort remedy, there could ordinarily be no

liability unless actual damage was proved.[9] Also, in its earlier stages trespass was identified with the view that liability might be imposed without regard to the defendant's fault,[10] while case from the beginning required proof of either a wrongful intent or negligence.[11]

Transition to Intent and Negligence

The procedural distinction between trespass and case has long been antiquated, although some vestige of it still survives in a few states which retain common law pleading in a modified form. Modern law has almost completely abandoned the artificial classification of injuries as direct or indirect, and looks instead to the intent of the wrongdoer, or to his negligence. The first step was taken when the action on the case was extended to include injuries which were not intended but were merely negligent, and were inflicted directly and immediately.[12] Because of the greater convenience of the action, it came to be used quite generally in all cases of negligence,[13] while trespass remained as the remedy for the greater number of intentional wrongs. Terms such as battery, assault and false imprisonment, which were varieties of trespass, came to be associated with intent,

1949, ch. 4; Plucknett, Case and the Statute of Westminster II, 1931, 31 Col.L.Rev. 778; Dix, The Origins of the Action of Trespass on the Case, 1937, 46 Yale L.J. 1142.

6. Reynolds v. Clarke, 1725, 1 Strange 634, 2 Ld. Raym. 1399, 92 Eng.Rep. 410; Leame v. Bray, 1802, 3 East 593, 102 Eng.Rep. 724.

Cf. Dodson v. Mock, 1838, 20 N.C. 282 (giving poison to a dog is trespass, but leaving it for him to find is case); Fleming v. Lockwood, 1907, 36 Mont. 384, 92 P. 962 (compares opening of floodgates and ditch giving way).

7. Day v. Edwards, 1794, 5 Term Rep. 649, 101 Eng. Rep. 361; Leame v. Bray, 1803, 3 East 593, 102 Eng. Rep. 724; Welch v. Durand, 1869, 36 Conn. 182; Edmands v. Olson, 1939, 64 R.I. 39, 9 A.2d 860.

8. Reynolds v. Clarke, 1725, 1 Stra. 634, 2 Ld.Raym. 1399, 92 Eng.Rep. 410.

9. Shipman, Common Law Pleading, 3d Ed. 1922, 211, 223.

10. 1 Street, Foundations of Legal Liability, 1906, 74–77.

11. Shipman, Common Law Pleading, 3d Ed. 1923, 216.

12. Williams v. Holland, 1833, 10 Bing. 112, 131 Eng. Rep. 848; Blin v. Campbell, 1817, 14 Johns., N.Y., 432; Schuer v. Veeder, 1845, 7 Blackf. Ind., 342; Clafin v. Wilcox, 1846, 18 Vt. 605.

13. The story of the change in the law is narrated in Goodhart and Winfield, Trespass and Negligence, 1933, 49 L.Q.Rev. 358, 365; Prichard, Trespass, Case, and the Rule in Williams v. Holland, [1964] Camb. L.J. 234; Millner, The Retreat of Trespass, 1965, 18 Curr.Leg.Prob. 20; Malone, Ruminatious on the Role of Fault in the History of Torts, 1970, 31 La. L.Rev. 1, Gregory, Trespass to Negligence to Absolute Liability, 1951, 37 Va.L.Rev. 359; Roberts, Negligence: Blackstone to Shaw to ? 1965, 50 Corn. L.Q. 191.

and negligence emerged as a separate tort.[14] The shift was a gradual one, and the courts seem to have been quite unconscious of it. When, in the nineteenth century, the old forms of action were replaced in most jurisdictions by the modern code procedure, the new classification remained. There is still some occasional confusion, and some talk of a negligent "assault and battery," [15] but in general these terms are restricted to cases of intent.[16]

This transition was accompanied by a growing recognition that, regardless of the form of the action, there should be no liability for pure accident, and that the defendant must be found to be at fault, in the sense of being chargeable with a wrongful intent, or with negligence. With rare exceptions, actions for injuries to the person, or to tangible property, now require proof of an intent to inflict them, or of failure to exercise proper care. As to the necessity of proving actual damage, the courts have continued the distinctions found in the older actions of trespass and case; and whether such damage is essential to the existence of a cause of action for a particular tort may depend very largely upon its ancestry in terms of the old procedure.[17]

More Extensive Liability for Intent

There is a definite tendency to impose greater responsibility upon a defendant whose conduct has been intended to do harm, or morally wrong.[18] More liberal rules are applied as to the consequences for which he will be held liable,[19] the certainty of proof required,[20] and the type of damage for which recovery is to be permitted,[21] as well as the measure of compensation.[22] The defendant's

---

14. Winfield, History of Negligence in the Law of Torts, 1926, 42 L.Q.Rev. 184.

15. See for example Anderson v. Arnold's Ex'r, 1881, 79 Ky. 370, where it was alleged that defendant's testator negligently and recklessly, but not intentionally, wounded plaintiff with a pistol, and it was held that the action was for "assault and battery" and so did not survive the death of the wrongdoer. Cf. Perkins v. Stein & Co., 1893, 94 Ky. 433, 22 S.W. 649, holding, without reference to the earlier case, that "to constitute an assault and battery * * * the act complained of must be done with a hostile intent."

See also Kendall v. Drake, 1892, 67 N.H. 592, 30 A. 524; Conway v. Reed, 1877, 66 Mo. 346 (allegation of assault held supported by proof of negligence). A later example of this use of an outmoded terminology is Honeycutt v. Louis Pizitz Dry Goods Co., 1938, 235 Ala. 507, 180 So. 91, which finds assault and battery where plaintiff was negligently, but not intentionally, struck by a lollipop.

16. Donner v. Graap, 1908, 134 Wis. 523, 115 N.W. 125, 126; Hackenberger v. Travelers Mut. Cas. Co., 1936, 144 Kan. 607, 62 P.2d 545; Ott v. Great Northern R. Co., 1897, 70 Minn. 50, 72 N.W. 833; Baran v. Silverman, 1912, 34 R.I. 279, 83 A. 263.

"The intention to do harm, or an unlawful intent, is of the very essence of an assault, and without it there can be none." Raefeldt v. Koenig, 1912, 152 Wis. 459, 140 N.W. 56.

17. Thus in assault and battery, false imprisonment, and trespass to land, which were derived from trespass, the action may be maintained without proof of damage. In negligence and deceit, which are descended from the action on the case, damage is the gist of the action.

18. Bauer, The Degree of Moral Fault as Affecting Defendant's Liability, 1933, 81 U.Pa.L.Rev. 586; Note, 1962, 14 Stan.L.Rev. 362.

19. "For an intended injury the law is astute to discover even very remote causation. For one which the defendant merely ought to have anticipated it has often stopped at an earlier stage of the investigation of causal connection. And as to those where there was neither knowledge nor duty to foresee, it has usually limited accountability to direct and immediate results. This is not because the defendant's act was a more immediate cause in one case than in the others, but because it has been felt to be just and reasonable that liability should extend to results further removed when certain elements of fault are present." Derosier v. New England Telephone & Telegraph Co., 1925, 81 N.H. 451, 463, 130 A. 145, 152. See infra, p. 263.

See Green, Rationale of Proximate Cause, 1925, 170 ff.

20. Cases are Collected in Bauer, The Degree of Moral Fault as Affecting Defendant's Liability, 1933, 81 U.Pa.L.Rev. 586, 592–596.

21. Thus damages for mental disturbance, whether or not it results in physical injury, are more readily held to be recoverable where the wrong is intentional. See infra, §§ 12, 54.

22. Cases are collected in Bauer, The Degree of Defendant's Fault as Affecting the Administration of the Law of Excessive Compensatory Damages, 1934,

interests have been accorded substantially less weight in opposition to the plaintiff's claim to protection when moral iniquity is thrown into the balance. Apparently the courts have more or less unconsciously worked out an irregular and poorly defined sliding scale, by which the defendant's liability is least where his conduct is merely inadvertent, greater when he acts in disregard of consequences increasingly likely to follow, greater still when he intentionally invades the rights of another under a mistaken belief that he is committing no wrong, and greatest of all where his motive is a malevolent desire to do harm.

8. MEANING OF INTENT

The intent with which tort liability is concerned is not necessarily a hostile intent, or a desire to do any harm.[23] Rather it is an intent to bring about a result which will invade the interests of another in a way that the law will not sanction. The defendant may be liable although he has meant nothing more than a good-natured practical joke,[24] or has honestly believed that he would not injure the plaintiff,[25] or even where he was seeking the plaintiff's own good.[26]

To result in liability, the defendant's act must be a voluntary one.[27] But a voluntary act, reduced to its lowest terms, is a contraction of the muscles, and nothing else.[28] The movement of the finger which fires a gun is the same, whether it takes place in a crowded city, or in the solitude of the Mojave Desert. Its legal character must depend upon the actor's surroundings, and his state of mind with respect to them. His state of mind may involve many things: he may intend to move his finger, for the purpose of pulling the trigger, for the purpose of causing the bullet to strike a man, for the purpose of killing the man, for the purpose of revenge, of defending his country, or of protecting himself against attack. "Intent" is the word commonly used to describe the desire to bring about the physical consequences, up to and including the death; the more remote objective which inspires the act is called "motive."[29] The one is merely a step less removed from the muscular contraction than the other. Each has its own importance in the law of torts, and a justifiable motive, such as that of self-defense, may avoid liability for the intent to kill.

Intent, however, is broader than a desire to bring about physical results. It must extend not only to those consequences which are desired, but also to those which the actor believes are substantially certain to follow from what he does. An anarchist who throws a bomb into the royal carriage may actually wish to kill no one but the king; but since he knows that the death of others in the carriage is a necessary and almost inevitable incident to that end, and neverthe-

---

82 U.Pa.L.Rev. 583. See for example the rules applied to innocent and wilful trespassers who remove timber or minerals from land, as to the value of the property converted "in place" or after removal. McCormick, Damages, 1935, 492–496.

23. Baldinger v. Banks, 1960, 26 Misc.2d 1086, 201 N.Y.S.2d 629; Restatement of Torts, § 13, Comment e.

24. Reynolds v. Pierson, 1902, 29 Ind.App. 273, 64 N.E. 484; State v. Monroe, 1897, 121 N.C. 677, 28 S.E. 547.

25. Vosburg v. Putney, 1891, 80 Wis. 523, 50 N.W. 403; Craker v. Chicago & N. W. R. Co., 1875, 36 Wis. 657.

26. Clayton v. New Dreamland Roller Skating Rink, 1951, 14 N.J.Super. 390, 82 A.2d 458 (plaintiff fell and broke her arm; over her protest defendant proceeded to manipulate the arm in order to set it); Johnson v. McConnel, 1878, 15 Hun, N.Y., 293 (defendant intervened in a scuffle to protect plaintiff and broke plaintiff's leg); Maxwell v. Maxwell, 1920, 189 Iowa 7, 177 N.W. 541, (arrest of insane person for his own protection).

27. Slattery v. Haley, [1923] 3 Dom.L.Rep. 156, 25 Ont.L.Rep. 95; Stokes v. Carlson, 1951, 362 Mo. 93, 240 S.W.2d 132; Wishone v. Yellow Cab Co., 1936, 20 Tenn.App. 229, 97 S.W.2d 452; see infra, p. 140.

28. Holmes, The Common Law, 1881, 91; Cook, Act, Intention and Motive in the Criminal Law, 1917, 26 Yale L.J. 644.

29. Cook, Act, Intention and Motive in the Criminal Law, 1917, 26 Yale L.J. 644; Walton, Motive as an Element in Torts in the Common and in the Civil Law, 1909, 22 Harv.L.Rev. 501.

less goes ahead with the deed, it must be said that he intends to kill them.[30] The man who fires a bullet into a dense crowd may fervently pray that he will hit no one, but since he must believe and know that he cannot avoid doing so, he intends it. The practical application of this principle has meant that where a reasonable man in the defendant's position would believe that a particular result was substantially certain to follow, he will be dealt with by the jury, or even by the court, as though he had intended it. The driver who whips up his horses with a loud yell while passing a neighbor's team will not be credited when he denies that he intended to cause a runaway;[31] and the defendant on a bicycle who rides down a man in full view on a sidewalk where there is ample room to pass may find the court unwilling to accept his statement that he did not mean to do it.[32]

On the other hand, the mere knowledge and appreciation of a risk, short of substantial certainty, is not the equivalent of intent. The defendant who acts in the belief or consciousness that he is causing an appreciable risk of harm to another may be negligent, and if the risk is great his conduct may be characterized as reckless or wanton,[33] but it is not classed as an intentional wrong. In such cases the distinction between intent and negligence obviously is a matter of degree. Apparently the line has been drawn by the courts at the point where the known danger ceases to be only a foreseeable risk which a reasonable man would avoid, and becomes a substantial certainty.[34]

"Transferred" Intent

One definite area in which there is more extensive liability for intent than for negligence is that covered by the curious surviving fiction of "transferred intent." If the defendant shoots or strikes at A, intending to wound or kill him, and unforeseeably hits B instead, he is held liable to B for an intentional tort.[35] The intent to commit a battery upon A is pieced together with the resulting injury to B; it is "transferred" from A to B. "The intention follows the bullet."[36]

This peculiar idea appeared first in criminal cases[37] at a time when tort and crime were still merged in the old trespass form of action. It represents an established rule of the criminal law, in cases in which shooting, striking, throwing a missile or poisoning has resulted in unexpected injury to the wrong man.[38] The criminal cases have been under-

---

30. Salmond, Jurisprudence, 4th Ed. 1913, 337.

Thus in Garratt v. Dailey, 1955, 46 Wash.2d 197, 279 P.2d 1091, second appeal, 1956, 49 Wash.2d 499, 304 P.2d 681, a boy who pulled away a chair just as plaintiff was about to sit down was held liable for battery because he knew that she was substantially certain to suffer a forcible seating on the ground. Cf. Burr v. Adam Eidemiller, Inc., 1956, 386 Pa. 416, 126 A.2d 403 (contamination of plaintiff's underground water supply by run-off water from slag); Jost v. Dairyland Power Co-op., 1969, 45 Wis.2d 164, 172 N.W.2d 647 (damaging crops by sulphur dioxide).

31. Lambrecht v. Schreyer, 1915, 129 Minn. 271, 152 N.W. 645. See also Land v. Bachman, 1921, 223 Ill. App. 473.

32. Mercer v. Corbin, 1889, 117 Ind. 450, 20 N.E. 132. Cf. Commonwealth v. Raspa, 1939, 138 Pa.Super. 26, 9 A.2d 925.

33. See infra, p. 184.

34. Hackenberger v. Travelers Mut. Cas. Co., 1936, 144 Kan. 607, 62 P.2d 545; Cook v. Kinzua Pine Mills Co., 1956, 207 Or. 34, 293 P.2d 717. See Restatement of Torts, § 13, Comment d; Note, 1962, 34 Rock Mt.L.Rev. 268; De Muth, A Comparison of the Conduct Required in Trespass to Chattels and Negligence, 1961, 33 Rocky Mt.L.Rev. 323.

"If the manifest probability of harm is very great, and the harm follows, we say that it is done maliciously or intentionally; if not so great, but still considerable, we say that the harm is done negligently; if there is no apparent danger, we call it mischance." Holmes, Privilege, Malice and Intent, 1894, 8 Harv. L.Rev. 1.

35. Prosser, Transferred Intent, 1967, 45 Tex.L.Rev. 650.

36. State v. Batson, 1936, 339 Mo. 298, 305, 96 S.W.2d 384, 389.

37. Regina v. Salisbury, 1553, 1 Plowd. 100, 75 Eng. Rep. 158; Queen v. Saunders and Archer, 1576, 2 Plowd. 473, 75 Eng.Rep. 706.

38. Dunaway v. People, 1884, 110 Ill. 333; State v. Williams, 1904, 122 Iowa 115, 97 N.W. 992; State v.

standably preoccupied with moral guilt, and the obvious fact that if the defendant is not convicted there is no one to hold liable for the crime. But the same rule was applied to tort cases arising in trespass.[39] This may possibly have been due to a considered feeling that the defendant could not sustain his burden of proof that he was free from fault when he had at least intended to injure another person.[40] But a better explanation may lie in nothing more than the mere proximity of the criminal law to the trespass action, with its criminal tradition and the similarity of the fact situations. It is quite probable, however, that the persistence of the principle has been due to a definite feeling that the defendant is at fault, and should make good the damage. His act is characterized as "wrongful," and his fault is regarded as absolute toward all the world, rather than relative to any one person. Having departed from the social standard of conduct, he is liable for the harm which follows from his act, although he did not intend it.

The rule has been applied in a considerable number of American cases that have held the defendant liable for accidental battery to an unintended person by shooting,[41] strik-ing,[42] or throwing,[43] where the intent was commit a battery upon a third person. It is not, however, limited to cases of intended or resulting battery. The action of trespass was the progenitor not only of battery, but also of assault, false imprisonment, trespass to land and trespass to chattels; and it seems fairly clear that when the defendant intends any one of the five, his intent will be "transferred" to make him liable for any of the five, provided that the harm is direct and immediate.[44] Thus one who intends an assault, as where he shoots to frighten another, is liable for battery when the bullet unexpectedly hits a stranger;[45] and one who intends a trespass to a chattel, as where he shoots at somebody's dog, is liable for battery when he hits a man.[46] There has been some incidental extension of the principal in cases involving damages ensuing from trespass to land, which is best considered in connection with that tort.[47] On the other hand, where the case

McKey, La.App.1964, 167 So.2d 416, writ refused 246 La. 910, 914, 168 So.2d 822, 823.

42. Carnes v. Thompson, Mo.1932, 48 S.W.2d 903; Davis v. Collins, 1904, 69 S.C. 460, 48 S.E. 469; Bannister v. Mitchell, 1920, 127 Va. 578, 104 S.E. 800.

43. Singer v. Marx, 1956, 144 Cal.App.2d 637, 301 P. 2d 440; Peterson v. Haffner, 1877, 59 Ind. 130; Talmage v. Smith, 1894, 101 Mich. 370, 59 N.W. 656; Keel v. Hainline, Okl.1958, 331 P.2d 397.

44. Battery-trespass to chattel: People v. Washington, 1966, 18 N.Y.2d 366, 275 N.Y.S.2d 508, 222 N.E.2d 378 (dictum). Trespass to land-battery: Schmitt v. Kurrus, 1908, 234 Ill. 578, 85 N.E. 261.

45. Randall v. Ridgley, La.App.1939, 185 So. 632; Brown v. Martinez, 1961, 68 N.M. 271, 361 P.2d 152; Weisbart v. Flohr, 1968, 260 Cal.App.2d 281, 67 Cal. Rptr. 114; Daingerfield v. Thompson, 1880, 33 Gratt. 136, 74 Va. 136.

Accord, as to resulting assault: Jeppsen v. Jensen, 1916, 47 Utah 536, 155 P. 429. As to damage to chattel, Vandenburgh v. Truax, 1847, 4 Denio, N.Y., 464.

46. Corn v. Sheppard, 1930, 179 Minn. 490, 229 N.W. 869; Osborne v. Van Dyke, 1901, 113 Iowa 557, 85 N.W. 784; State ex rel. Harbin v. Dunn, 1943, 39 Tenn.App. 190, 282 S.W.2d 203; Isham v. Dow's Estate, 1898, 70 Vt. 588, 41 A. 585. Contra, Belk v. Boyce, 1964, 263 N.C. 24, 138 S.E.2d 789, which rather misses the point.

47. See infra, p. 67.

Ochoa, 1956, 61 N.M. 225, 297 P.2d 1053; People v. Aranda, 1938, 12 Cal.2d 307, 83 P.2d 928; Coston v. State, 1939, 139 Fla. 250, 190 So. 520.

39. Scott v. Shepherd, 1773, 2 Wm.Bl. 892, 96 Eng. Rep. 525; James v. Campbell, 1832, 5 C. & P. 372, 172 Eng.Rep. 1015.

40. "Originally a defendant whose act had caused bodily harm to another was prima facie liable as a trespasser unless he could exculpate himself by showing that the harm resulted from inevitable accident. To do this, he was required to show that he was innocent of fault, and it would be natural to regard it as impossible for him to do this if his conduct was intended to inflict upon even a third party an injury the same as or closely similar to that which the plaintiff had suffered." Restatement of Torts, Tentative Draft 1935, Commentary to § 10(1).

41. Lopez v. Surchia, 1952, 112 Cal.App.2d 314, 246 P.2d 111; Smith v. Moran, 1963, 43 Ill.App.2d 373, 193 N.E.2d 466; Anderson v. Arnold's Ex'r, 1881, 79 Ky. 370; Morrow v. Flores, Tex.Civ. App. 1948, 225 S.W.2d 621, refused n. r. e.; Davis v.

does not fit within the scope of the old writ of trespass, the "transfer" of intent is not applied. This is true where the injury is not direct and immediate, but consequential; [48] and where the plaintiff's interest which is invaded, as for example by causing him pecuniary loss,[49] was one not protected by the old trespass writ. Since mental disturbance was protected only to the extent of allowing recovery for an assault, it has followed that where that tort cannot be made out, intent is not "transferred" to allow recovery for such consequences.[50]

As will be seen hereafter,[51] where the defendant's conduct is merely negligent, many courts refuse to hold him liable unless his neligence can be found to be relative to the particular plaintiff, in the sense that the foreseeable risk of harm created extends to him. The broader liability in the case of an intentional invasion of another's rights is an illustration of the general attitude of the courts as to the imposition of greater responsibility upon an intentional wrongdoer.

9. BATTERY

The interest in freedom from intentional and unpermitted contacts with the plaintiff's person is protected by an action for the tort commonly called battery. The protection extends to any part of the body,[52] or to anything which is attached to it and practically identified with it.[53] Thus contact with the plaintiff's clothing,[54] or with a cane,[55] a paper,[56] or any other object held in his hand,[57] will be sufficient; and the same is true of the chair in which he sits,[58] the horse [59] or the car [60] which he is riding or driving, or the person against whom he is leaning.[61] His interest in the integrity of his person includes all those things which are in contact or connected with it.

Since the disappearance of the distinction between trespass and case, it is no longer important that the contact is not brought about by a direct application of force such as a

48. Oklahoma Gas & Elec. Co. v. Hofrichter, 1938, 196 Ark. 1, 116 S.W.2d 599; Commonwealth v. Campbell, 1863, 7 Allen 541, 89 Mass. 541; People v. Rockwell, 1878, 39 Mich. 503.

49. See, as to misrepresentation, infra, p. ——. Also Mobile Life Ins. Co. v. Brame, 1877, 95 U.S. 754; Rockingham Mut. Fire Ins. Co. v. Bosher, 1855, 39 Me. 253; Anthony v. Slaid, 1846, 11 Met. 290, 52 Mass. 290; Clark v. Gay, 1901, 112 Ga. 777, 38 S.E. 81.

50. See infra, p. 60.

51. See infra, p. 254.

52. Cole v. Turner, 1704, 6 Mod.Rep. 149, 90 Eng.Rep. 958; Mailand v. Mailand, 1901, 83 Minn. 453, 86 N. W. 445.

53. "* * * anything so closely attached thereto that it is customarily regarded as a part thereof." Restatement of Torts, § 18.

54. United States v. Ortega, 3 Cir., 1825, Fed.Cas.No. 15,971, 4 Wash.C.C. 531; Geraty v. Stern, 1883, 30 Hun, N.Y., 426; Piggly-Wiggly Alabama Co. v. Rickles, 1925, 212 Ala. 585, 103 So. 860 (attempted search of pockets).

55. Respublica v. De Longchamps, 1784, 1 Dall., Pa., 111, 1 L.Ed. 59.

56. Dyk v. De Young, 1889, 35 Ill.App. 138; S. H. Kress & Co. v. Brashier, Tex.Civ.App.1932, 50 S.W. 2d 922.

57. Fisher v. Carrousel Motor Hotel, Inc., Tex.1967, 424 S.W.2d 627 (plate held in hand); Morgan v. Loyacomo, 1941, 190 Miss. 656, 1 So.2d 510 (package); Brodsky v. Rieser, 1921, 195 App.Div. 557, 186 N.Y.S. 841 (starting automobile of which plaintiff had hold); Wilson v. Orr, 1923, 210 Ala. 93, 97 So. 133 (opening and putting hand in box held by plaintiff); Kirkpatrick v. Crutchfield, 1919, 178 N.C. 348, 100 S.E. 602.

58. Hopper v. Reeve, 1817, 7 Taunt. 698, 129 Eng.Rep. 278. Cf. Interstate Life & Acc. Ins. Co. v. Brewer, 1937, 56 Ga.App. 599, 193 S.E. 458 (bed); Singer Sewing Mach. Co. v. Phipps, 1911, 49 Ind.App. 116, 94 N.E. 793 (sewing machine).

59. Riding: Dodwell v. Burford, 1669, 1 Mod.Rep. 24, 86 Eng.Rep. 703. Attached to carriage in which plaintiff riding: Clark v. Downing, 1882, 55 Vt. 259; Bull v. Colton, 1856, 22 Barb., N.Y., 94.

60. Crossman v. Thurlow, 1957, 336 Mass. 252, 143 N.E.2d 814; United States v. Anderson, D.Md.1961, 190 F.Supp. 589; Farm Bureau Mut. Auto Ins. Co. v. Hammer, 4 Cir.1949, 177 F.2d 793.

61. Reynolds v. Pierson, 1902, 29 Ind.App. 273, 64 N. E. 484. Cf. State v. Davis, 1833, 1 Hill, S.C., 46 (slave roped to plaintiff).

blow, and it is enough that the defendant sets a force in motion which ultimately produces the result,[62] as by setting out food for the plaintiff to eat which contains a poison,[63] or digging a pitfall in the path on which he is to walk. It is not essential that the plaintiff should be conscious of the contact at the time it occurs. Interest in personal integrity still is entitled to protection, although the plaintiff is asleep or under an anaesthetic,[64] or otherwise unaware of what is going on.[65] The invasion is equally great; and the girl who is kissed in her sleep is likely to be affronted quite as much, and perhaps more, when she discovers it after the event, as when she knows it at the time.[66] Proof of the technical invasion of the integrity of the plaintiff's person by even an entirely harmless, but offensive, contact entitles him to vindication of his legal right by an award of nominal damages,[67] and the establishment of the tort cause of action entitles him also to compensation for the mental disturbance inflicted upon him, such as fright or humilia-

tion.[68] The defendant's liability for the harm resulting from his conduct extends, as in most other cases of intentional torts, to consequences which he did not intend, and could not reasonably have foreseen,[69] upon the obvious basis that it is better for unexpected losses to fall upon the intentional wrongdoer than upon the innocent victim. Since battery usually is a matter of the worst kind of intentions, it is a tort which frequently justifies punitive damages;[70] but in the comparatively infrequent case where the defendant has acted in good faith under a mistake of fact, but still has committed the tort, punitive damages are not allowed.[71]

Character of Defendant's Act

In order to be liable for battery, the defendant must have done some positive and affirmative act; mere passive obstruction of the plaintiff's passage, while it may perhaps constitute another tort,[72] does not amount to a battery.[73] The act must cause, and must be intended to cause, an unpermitted contact. Mere negligence, or even recklessness, which creates only a risk that the contact will result, may afford a distinct cause of action

62. Mooney v. Carter, 1945, 114 Colo. 267, 160 P.2d 390 (operating car so as to throw plaintiff from running board); Schmitt v. Kurrus, 1908, 234 Ill. 578, 85 N.E. 261 (striking glass door, plaintiff hit with fragments); Thomas v. Dunne, 1955, 131 Colo. 20, 279 P.2d 427 (seating plaintiff on electrified bench); Garratt v. Dailey, 1955, 46 Wash.2d 197, 279 P.2d 1091, second appeal, 1956, 49 Wash.2d 499, 304 P.2d 681 (removing chair in which plaintiff was about to sit down). Cf. Restatement of Torts, § 18, Comment *d* (daubing filth on towel plaintiff expected to use, or pulling away the chair in which he is about to sit).

63. Commonwealth v. Stratton, 1873, 114 Mass. 303 (cantharides); State v. Monroe, 1897, 121 N.C. 677, 28 S.E. 547 (croton oil).

64. Mohr v. Williams, 1905, 95 Minn. 261, 104 N.W. 12; Hively v. Higgs, 1927, 120 Or. 588, 253 P. 363. See infra, p. 104.

65. Vosburg v. Putney, 1891, 80 Wis. 523, 50 N.W. 403.

66. Second Restatement of Torts, § 18, Comment *d*.

67. Mason v. Wrightson, 1954, 205 Md. 481, 109 A.2d 128; Bumgart v. Bailey, 1963, 247 Miss. 604, 156 So. 2d 823; Rullis v. Jacobi, 1963, 79 N.J.Super. 525, 192 A.2d 186; Marble v. Jensen, 1919, 53 Utah 226, 178 P. 66.

68. Smith v. Hubbard, 1958, 253 Minn. 215, 91 N.W. 2d 756; Mecham v. Foley, 1951, 120 Utah 416, 235 P.2d 497; Glickstein v. Setzer, Fla.1955, 78 So.2d 374; Lamb v. Woodry, 1936, 154 Or. 30, 58 P.2d 1257.

69. Vosburg v. Putney, 1891, 80 Wis. 523, 50 N.W. 403; Watson v. Rinderknecht, 1901, 82 Minn. 235, 84 N.W. 798; Trousil v. Bayer, 1909, 85 Neb. 431, 123 N.W. 445; Harris v. Hindman, 1929, 130 Or. 15, 278 P. 954; Ware v. Garvey, D.Mass.1956, 139 F.Supp. 71.

70. See for example Rodgers v. Bryan, 1957, 82 Ariz. 143, 309 P.2d 773; Deevy v. Tassi, 1942, 21 Cal.2d 109, 130 P.2d 389; May v. Baron, 1938, 329 Pa. 65, 196 A. 866; Vaughn v. Mesch, 1939, 107 Mont. 498, 87 P.2d 177; Schlessman v. Brainard, 1939, 104 Colo. 514, 92 P.2d 749.

71. See for example Heinze v. Murphy, 1942, 180 Md. 423, 24 A.2d 917.

72. Cullen v. Dickinson, 1913, 33 S.D. 27, 144 N.W. 656; and see infra, p. 44.

73. Innes v. Wylie, 1844, 1 Car. & K. 257, 174 Eng. Rep. 800.

in itself, but under modern usage of the term it is not enough for battery.[74]

The original purpose of the courts in providing the action for battery undoubtedly was to keep the peace by affording a substitute for private retribution.[75] The element of personal indignity involved always has been given considerable weight. Consequently, the defendant is liable not only for contacts which do actual physical harm, but also for those relatively trivial ones which are merely offensive and insulting.[76] Spitting in the face is a battery,[77] as is forcibly removing the plaintiff's hat,[78] or any other contact brought about in a rude and insolent manner.[79] "The least touching of another in anger," said

Chief Justice Holt, "is a battery;"[80] and no harm or actual damage of any kind is required.[81] The plaintiff is entitled to demand that the defendant keep his hands to himself, although the contact results in no visible injury.

The gist of the action[82] for battery is not the hostile intent of the defendant, but rather the absence of consent to the contact on the part of the plaintiff.[83]

The defendant may be liable where he has intended only a joke,[84] or even a compliment, as where an unappreciative woman is kissed without her consent,[85] or a misguided effort

---

74. Cook v. Kinzua Pine Mills Co., 1956, 207 Or. 34, 293 P.2d 717; Hackenberger v. Travelers Mut. Cas. Co., 1936, 144 Kan. 607, 62 P.2d 545. As to the persistence, in one or two states, of reference to a negligent "battery," even in criminal cases, see Note, 1942, 30 Ky.L.J. 418; supra, p. 30.

75. "As to the assault, this is, perhaps, one of the kind in which the insult is more to be considered than the actual damage; for, though no great bodily pain is suffered by a blow on the palm of the hand, or the skirt of the coat, yet these are clearly within the legal definition of assault and battery, and among gentlemen too often induce duelling and terminate in murder." McKean, C. J., in Respublica v. De Longchamps, 1784, 1 Dall., Pa., 111, 114, 1 L. Ed. 59.

76. Harrigan v. Rosich, La.App.1965, 173 So.2d 880 (pushing with finger, "Go home, old man"), People v. Martinez, 1970, 3 Cal.App.3d 886, 83 Cal.Rptr. 914 (barefooted defendant kicked police officer protected by motorcycle boots); Wilson v. Orr, 1923, 210 Ala. 93, 97 So. 133; Masters v. Becker, 1964, 22 A.D. 2d 118, 254 N.Y.S.2d 633.

77. Alcorn v. Mitchell, 1872, 63 Ill. 553; Draper v. Baker, 1884, 61 Wis. 450, 21 N.W. 527.

78. Seigel v. Long, 1910, 169 Ala. 79, 53 So. 753; Hull v. Bartlett, 1887, 49 Conn. 64. Cf. Piggly-Wiggly Alabama Co. v. Rickles, 1925, 212 Ala. 585, 103 So. 860 (attempted search of pockets); Forde v. Skinner, 1830, 4 C. & P. 239, 172 Eng.Rep. 687 (cutting plaintiff's hair).

79. United States v. Ortega, 3 Cir.1825, Fed.Cas.No. 15,971, 4 Wash. C.C. 531; Crosswhite v. Barnes, 1924, 139 Va. 471, 124 S.E. 242; Singer Sewing Machine Co. v. Methvin, 1913, 184 Ala. 554, 63 So. 997; Baldinger v. Banks, 1960, 26 Misc.2d 1086, 201 N.Y.S.2d 629; Rullis v. Jacobi, 1963, 79 N.J.Super. 525, 192 A.2d 186.

80. Cole v. Turner, 1704, 6 Mod.Rep. 149, 90 Eng. 958. Cf. Mailand v. Mailand, 1901, 83 Minn. 453, 86 N.W. 445; Interstate Life & Accident Co. v. Brewer, 1937, 56 Ga.App. 599, 193 S.E. 458; Fort Wayne & Northern Indiana Traction Co. v. Ridenour, 1919, 71 Ind. App. 263, 123 N.E. 720.

81. "If Gibbs kicked plaintiff with his foot, it cannot be said as a matter of law, that there was no physical injury to him. In a legal sense, it was a physical injury, though it may have caused no physical suffering, and though the sensation resulting therefrom may have lasted but for a moment." South Brilliant Coal Co. v. Williams, 1921, 206 Ala. 637, 638, 91 So. 589, 590.

82. In Illinois, under a statute permitting imprisonment of the defendant in a civil suit where "malice is the gist of the action," it has been held that there may be such imprisonment for assault and battery. In re Murphy, 1884, 109 Ill. 31; In re Bobzin, 1921, 220 Ill.App. 470. This seems wrong, since an intent to do harm is not essential to the action. See Note, 1922, 4 Ill.L.Q. 211; Galvan v. Torres, 1956, 8 Ill. App.2d 227, 131 N.E.2d 367.

83. Clerk and Lindsell, Law of Torts, 8th Ed. 1929, 173.

84. Newman v. Christensen, 1948, 149 Neb. 471, 31 N.W.2d 417; Moore v. El Paso Chamber of Commerce, Tex.Civ.App.1929, 220 S.W.2d 327 (rodeo day horseplay); Markley v. Whitman, 1893, 95 Mich. 236, 54 N.W. 763; Reynolds v. Pierson, 1902, 29 Ind. App. 273, 64 N.E. 484; Keel v. Hainline, Okl.1958, 331 P.2d 397.

85. Ragsdale v. Ezell, 1899, 49 S.W. 775, 20 Ky.L.Rep. 1567; Liljegren v. United Rys. Co. of St. Louis, Mo. App.1921, 227 S.W. 925; Craker v. Chicago & N. W. R. Co., 1875, 36 Wis. 657, 17 Am.Rep. 504.

Taking indecent liberties with a woman without her consent is of course a battery. Hatchett v. Blacketer, 1915, 162 Ky. 266, 172 S.W. 533; Hough v. Iderhoff, 1914, 69 Or. 568, 139 P. 931; Martin v. Jansen,

is made to render assistance.[86] The plaintiff is entitled to protection according to the usages of decent society, and hostile contacts, or those which are contrary to all good manners, need not be tolerated. At the same time, in a crowded world, a certain amount of personal contact is inevitable, and must be accepted. Consent is assumed to all those ordinary contacts which are customary and reasonably necessary to the common intercourse of life, such as a tap on the shoulder to attract attention,[87] a friendly grasp of the arm,[88] or a casual jostling to make a passage.[89] There is as yet no very satisfactory authority[90] as to whether even such innocuous and generally permitted contacts can become tortious if they are inflicted with knowledge that the individual plaintiff objects to them and refuses to permit them. Although where there is any doubt at all the plaintiff's expressed wishes may very well turn the scale as to what is reasonable, it may be questioned whether any individual can be permitted, by his own fiat, to erect a glass cage around himself, and to announce that all physical contact with his person is at the expense of liability.

The time and place,[91] and the circumstances under which the act is done,[92] will necessarily affect its unpermitted character, and so will the relations between the parties. A stranger is not to be expected to tolerate liberties which would be allowed by an intimate friend.[93] But unless the defendant has special reason to believe that more or less will be permitted by the individual plaintiff, the test is what would be offensive to an ordinary person not unduly sensitive as to his dignity.[94] The intent required is only the intent to bring about such a contact; and given that, liability will depend upon whether there is a privilege, because of the plaintiff's individual consent, or otherwise.[95]

10. ASSAULT

The interest in freedom from apprehension of a harmful or offensive contact with the person, as distinguished from the contact itself, is protected by an action for the tort known as assault. No actual contact is necessary to it, and the plaintiff is protected

---

1920, 113 Wash. 290, 193 P. 674, affirmed 1921, 198 P. 393; Skousen v. Nidy, 1961, 90 Ariz. 215, 367 P.2d 248. Cf. Gates v. State, 1964, 110 Ga.App. 303, 138 S.E.2d 473 (slapping on buttocks).

86. Clayton v. New Dreamland Roller Skating Rink, 1951, 14 N.J.Super. 390, 82 A.2d 458 (attempt to manipulate broken arm to set it); Johnson v. McConnel, 1878, 15 Hun, N.Y., 293 (intervening in scuffle to protect plaintiff).

87. Wiffin v. Kincard, 1807, 2 Bos. & P. N. R. 471, 126 Eng.Rep. 1391; Coward v. Baddeley, 1859, 4 H. & N. 478, 157 Eng.Rep. 927.

88. See United States v. Ortega, 3 Cir.1825, Fed.Cas. No.15,971, 4 Wash.C.C. 531; Courtney v. Kneib, 1908, 131 Mo.App. 204, 110 N.W. 665. Cf. Steinman v. Baltimore Antiseptic Steam Laundry Co., 1908, 109 Md. 62, 71 A. 517 (accidental contact); State v. Hemphill, 1913, 162 N.C. 632, 78 S.E. 167 (taking hold of child to persuade); Hoffman v. Eppers, 1866, 41 Wis. 251 (assistance to an intoxicated person); Noble v. Louisville Taxicab & Transfer Co., Ky.1952, 255 S.W.2d 493 (taking hold of sick child to help).

89. Cole v. Turner, 1704, 6 Mod.Rep. 149, 90 Eng.Rep. 958.

90. The Restatement of Torts, § 19, leaves the question open in a Caveat. The only case approaching the matter is Richmond v. Fiske, 1893, 160 Mass. 34, 35 N.E. 103, where defendant, in violation of express instructions, entered plaintiff's room, touched him, and woke him up to present a milk bill. This was held to be a battery. It would appear, however, that this might be classified as offensive to a reasonable man, even in the absence of the instructions. See Carpenter, Intentional Invasion of Interest of Personality, 1934, 13 Or.L.Rev. 227, 231.

91. Thus horseplay which would be permissible upon the playground is out of order in the schoolroom. Vosburg v. Putney, 1891, 80 Wis. 523, 50 N.W. 403.

92. In Crawford v. Bergen, 1894, 91 Iowa 675, 60 N.W. 205, defendant, suspecting that plaintiff had set fire to a granary, touched him on the shoulder, and said, "Did you feel better after you set the fire?" It was held a question for the jury whether this was a battery. Cf. McDonald v. Franchere, 1897, 102 Iowa 496, 71 N.W. 427.

93. Reynolds v. Pierson, 1902, 29 Ind.App. 273, 64 N.E. 484. Cf. Nicholls v. Colwell, 1903, 113 Ill.App. 219.

94. Restatement of Torts, § 19.

95. See the discussion of consent, infra, § 18, and mistake, infra, § 17.

against a purely mental disturbance of his personal integrity. This action, which developed very early as a form of trespass,[96] is the first recognition of a mental, as distinct from a physical, injury. There is "a touching of the mind, if not of the body." [97] The explanation of its early appearance lies in the obvious likelihood that assaults will result in breaches of the peace, against which the action of trespass was created to enforce the criminal law.[98]

Since assault, as distinguished from battery, is essentially a mental rather than a physical invasion, it follows that the damages recoverable for it are those for the plaintiff's mental disturbance,[99] including fright, humiliation and the like, as well as any physical illness which may result from them. The establishment of the technical cause of action, even without proof of any harm, entitles the plaintiff to vindication of his legal right by an award of nominal damages.[1] Like battery, assault frequently arises out of the worst intentions, and therefore is an appro-

priate tort for punitive damages,[2] except in those cases where it is committed because of an innocent mistake.

Apprehension

Any act of such a nature as to excite an apprehension of a battery may constitute an assault. It is an assault to shake a fist under another's nose,[3] to aim or strike at him with a weapon,[4] or to hold it in a threatening position,[5] to rise or advance to strike another,[6] to surround him with a display of force,[7] to chase him in a hostile manner,[8] or to lean over a woman's bed and make indecent proposals, in such a way as to put her in fear.[9]

Since the interest involved is the mental one of apprehension of contact, it should follow that the plaintiff must be aware of the

---

96. I de S et ux. v. W de S, 1348, Y.B.Lib.Assis. f. 99, pl. 60; 1366, Y.B. 40 Edw. III 40, pl. 19; Smith v. Newsam, 1674, 3 Keb. 283, 34 Eng.Rep. 722.

97. Kline v. Kline, 1902, 158 Ind. 602, 64 N.E. 9.

98. Carpenter, Intentional Invasion of Interest of Personality, 1934, 13 Or.L.Rev. 227, 237; Restatement of Torts, § 24, Comment *c.*

"The law regards these acts as breaches of the peace, because they *directly* invade that personal security, which the law guarantees to every citizen. They do not excite an apprehension that his person may be attacked on a future occasion, and thus authorize a resort to cautionary remedies against it; but they are the beginnings of an attack, excite terror of immediate personal harm or disgrace, and justify a resort to actual violence to repel the impending injury and insult." State v. Morgan, 1842, 3 Ired., N.C., 186.

99. Kline v. Kline, 1902, 158 Ind. 602, 64 N.E. 9; Ross v. Michael, 1923, 246 Mass. 126, 140 N.E. 292; Brown v. Crawford, 1944, 296 Ky. 249, 177 S.W.2d 1; Hrnicek v. Chicago, M. & St. P. R. Co., 1919, 187 Iowa 1145, 175 N.W. 30; John R. Thompson Co. v. Vildibill, 1924, 211 Ala. 199, 100 So. 139.

1. Walker v. L. B. Price Mercantile Co., 1932, 203 N.C. 511, 166 S.E. 391.

2. Trogden v. Terry, 1916, 172 N.C. 540, 90 S.E. 583.

3. United States v. Myers, C.C.D.C.1806, Fed.Cas.No. 15,845, 1 Cranch C.C. 310; Plonty v. Murphy, 1901, 82 Minn. 268, 84 N.W. 1005; Howell v. Winters, 1910, 58 Wash. 436, 108 P. 1077; Stockwell v. Gee, 1926, 121 Okl. 207, 249 P. 389.

4. Kline v. Kline, 1902, 158 Ind. 602, 64 N.E. 9. Cf. Nielson v. Eiler, 1929, 248 Mich. 545, 227 N.W. 688 (shooting at plaintiff); In re Cuykendalls' Estate, 1937, 223 Iowa 526, 273 N.W. 117 (same); Holdorf v. Holdorf, 1918, 185 Iowa 838, 169 N.W. 737 (threatening gesture with a club).

5. United States v. Richardson, C.C.D.C.1837, Fed. Cas.No.16,155, 5 Cranch C.C. 348; State v. Church, 1868, 63 N.C. 15; Trogdon v. Terry, 1916, 172 N.C. 540, 90 S.E. 583.

6. Stephens v. Myers, 1830, 4 C. & P. 349, 172 Eng. Rep. 735; Bishop v. Ranney, 1887, 59 Vt. 316, 7 A. 820; State v. Davis, 1840, 23 N.C. (1 Ired.) 125; Hrnicek v. Chicago, M. & St. P. R. Co., 1919, 187 Iowa 1145, 175 N.W. 30 (advancing on plaintiff with poker and threats).

7. Read v. Coker, 1853, 13 C.B. 850, 138 Eng.Rep. 1437.

8. Mortin v. Shoppee, 1823, 3 C. & P. 373, 172 Eng. Rep. 462; State v. Neely, 1876, 74 N.C. 425; State v. Martin, 1881, 85 N.C. 508; Townsdin v. Nutt, 1877, 19 Kan. 282 (riding toward plaintiff with intent to run her down).

9. Newell v. Whitcher, 1880, 53 Vt. 589. Cf. State v. Allen, 1956, 245 N.C. 185, 95 S.E.2d 526, where defendant stopped his car close to plaintiff, stared at her, and moved the lower part of his body in a "lustful" manner.

defendant's act at the time, and that it is not an assault to aim a gun at one who is unaware of it.[10] Apprehension is not the same thing as fear, and the plaintiff is not deprived of his action merely because he is too courageous to be frightened or intimidated.[11] It would seem, however, that he need not be aware that the threatened danger proceeds from a hostile human being, and that if a concealed defendant sets off an explosion which puts the plaintiff in fear of his life or safety, the same interest is invaded, and in substantially the same manner, as when a visible defendant shoots at him with a gun.

At the same time, the courts have been reluctant to protect extremely timid individuals from exaggerated fears of contact, and seem to have required quite uniformly that the apprehension be one which would normally be aroused in the mind of a reasonable person. Perhaps if the defendant has knowledge of the plaintiff's peculiar and abnormal timidity, and intends to act upon it, there should be a right to recover;[12] but there are no assault cases, and the remedy apparently has been left to the more modern tort of the infliction of mental distress.[13] But at least in the absence of such knowledge on the part of the defendant, there is no assault. It usual-

ly is held that the defendant's act must amount to an offer to use force,[14] and there must be an apparent ability and opportunity to carry out the threat immediately. There is no assault where the defendant is too far away to do any harm,[15] or in mere preparation, as in bringing a gun along to an interview; [16] it is when the defendant presents the weapon in such a condition or manner as to indicate that it may immediately be made ready for use, as where all that is necessary is to cock it, that the threat becomes sufficiently imminent to constitute an assault.[17]

It is probably upon the same basis that mere words, however violent, are held not to amount to an assault.[18] Apparently the ori-

10. State v. Barry, 1912, 45 Mont. 598, 124 P. 775; Restatement of Torts, § 22. To the contrary are State v. Baker, 1897, 20 R.I. 275, 38 A. 653; People v. Pape, 1885, 66 Cal. 366, 5 P. 621; and see People v. Lilley, 1880, 43 Mich. 521, 5 N.W. 982. These cases are to be explained as involving criminal, rather than civil assault, in jurisdictions in which the crime is defined as an attempted battery. This is an aberration to which legislatures are prone. Thus Cal. Penal Code, § 240: "An assault is an unlawful attempt, coupled with a present ability, to commit a violent injury upon the person of another."

See Notes, 1909, 57 U.Pa.L.Rev. 249; 1937, 21 Minn.L. Rev. 213; 1939, 11 Rocky Mt.L.Rev. 104; 1945, 33 Ky.L.J. 189.

11. Restatement of Torts, § 24, Comment *b*; Brady v. Schatzel, [1911] Q.S.R. 206.

12. The Second Restatement of Torts, § 27, takes the position that intended apprehension is always enough for an assault, even though it is unreasonable. Apparently there are no cases.

13. See infra, § 12.

14. State v. Daniel, 1904, 136 N.C. 571, 48 S.E. 544; Haupt v. Swenson, 1905, 125 Iowa 694, 101 N.W. 520; Alexander v. Pacholek, 1923, 222 Mich. 157, 192 N.W. 652. In Nelson v. Crawford, 1899, 122 Mich. 466, 81 N.W. 335, the defendant, known to be a harmless eccentric, appeared at plaintiff's door, dressed in woman's clothing, and followed her into the house. It was held there was no assault.

In Stearns v. Sampson, 1871, 59 Me. 568, it was held that causing physical discomfort, by removing plaintiff's doors and windows, was not an assault. Contra, Wood v. Young, 1899, 50 S.W. 541, 20 Ky. Law Rep. 1931.

15. State v. Davis, 1840, 23 N.C. (1 Ired.) 125; Fuller v. State, 1903, 44 Tex.Cr.R. 463, 72 S.W. 184 (kissing gesture at girl); Bowles v. May, 1932, 159 Va. 419, 166 S.E. 550 (shaking finger at plaintiff); Western Union Tel. Co. v. Hill, 1933, 25 Ala.App. 540, 150 So. 709, cert. denied 1933, 227 Ala. 469, 150 So. 711 (across counter). Cf. State v. Ingram, 1953, 237 N.C. 197, 74 S.E.2d 532 ("leering" at plaintiff not enough).

16. State v. Painter, 1877, 67 Mo. 84; Restatement of Torts, § 29. Cf. Lawson v. State, 1857, 30 Ala. 14 (drawing pistol without presenting it); Penny v. State, 1901, 114 Ga. 77, 39 S.E. 871 (holding rocks in hands); Lawrence v. Womack, Mo.App.1930, 23 S.W. 2d 190 (picking up stick); Cucinotti v. Ortmann, 1960, 399 Pa. 26, 159 A.2d 216 (exhibiting blackjacks).

17. Osborn v. Veitch, 1858, 1 F. & F. 317, 175 Eng. Rep. 744; State v. Church, 1868, 63 N.C. 15. Contra, Woodruff v. Woodruff, 1857, 22 Ga. 237.

18. Kaufman v. Kansas Power & Light Co., 1936, 144 Kan. 283, 58 P.2d 1055; State v. Daniel, 1904, 136 N.C. 571, 48 S.E. 544; Gelhaus v. Eastern Air Lines, 5 Cir. 1952, 194 F.2d 774; Hixson v. Slocum, 1913, 156 Ky. 487, 161 S.W. 522; Republic Iron & Steel Co. v. Self, 1915, 192 Ala. 403, 68 So. 328; Second Restatement of Torts, § 31.

gin of this rule lay in nothing more than the fact that in the early days the King's courts had their hands full when they intervened at the first threatening gesture, or in other words, when the fight was about to start; and taking cognizance of all of the belligerent language which the foul mouths of merrie England could dispense was simply beyond their capacity. Threats for the future,[19] and insults for the present,[20] are simply not present breaches of the peace, and so never have fallen within the narrow boundaries of this rather antiquated tort.

It would appear, however, that too much emphasis has been placed by the courts upon the idea of motion or gesture, usually described as "some overt act." The only valid reason that mere words do not amount to an assault is that ordinarily they create no reasonable apprehension of immediate contact. But they may do so; and when they do, there should be no less of an assault than when the defendant shakes his fist. It may be suggested that a perfectly motionless highwayman, standing with his pistol pointed and his finger on the trigger, who cries "Stand and deliver!" or even merely appears to the plaintiff's view, commits an assault. It is the immediate physical threat which is important, rather than the manner in which it is conveyed.[21]

Words may, however, give character to an act. A movement inoffensive in itself may be preceded or accompanied by words which give it a hostile color, as where one who has been making verbal threats of violence reaches for his pocket, so that the words and the act together create an apprehension that might otherwise be unreasonable.[22] Likewise, the words may so far explain away the apparent intent to attack that immediate apprehension is not justified, as where they indicate that the defendant is offering a blow in jest, or that the threat is solely for the future. "Were you not an old man, I would knock you down," so far negatives the threatening gesture that there is no assault.[23] But the defendant is not free to compel the plaintiff to buy his safety by compliance with a condition which there is no legal right to impose. "Your money or your life," whether or not it does anything to allay the anxiety of the plaintiff, is an obvious invasion of his rights, and will not prevent an actionable assault.[24] And even a lawful demand may be made in such a violent manner, and with such a display of excessive and unreasonable force, that there may be recovery on the basis of assault.[25]

Intent

To be held liable for assault, the defendant must have intended to interfere with the

19. Cucinotti v. Ortmann, 1960, 399 Pa. 26, 159 A.2d 216; Kramer v. Ricksmeier, 1913, 159 Iowa 48, 139 N.W. 1091; Brooker v. Silverthorne, 1918, 111 S.C. 553, 99 S.E. 350.

20. Thus the mere solicitation of illicit intercourse from a woman is quite uniformly held not to amount to an assault. Prince v. Ridge, 1900, 32 Misc. 666, 66 N.Y.S. 454; Reed v. Maley, 1903, 115 Ky. 816, 74 S.W. 1079; Davis v. Richardson, 1905, 76 Ark. 348, 89 S.W. 318; Bennett v. McIntire, 1889, 121 Ind. 231, 23 N.E. 78.

21. See Seavey, Threats Inducing Emotional Reactions, 1960, 39 N.C.L.Rev. 74.

22. Hulse v. Tollman, 1893, 49 Ill.App. 490; Keep v. Quallman, 1887, 68 Wis. 451, 32 N.W. 233; Fogden v. Wade, [1945] N.Z.L.Rep. 724 (immoral suggestion to girl followed by advancing towards her).

23. State v. Crow, 1841, 1 Ired., N.C., 375; Tuberville v. Savage, 1669, 1 Mod.Rep. 3, 86 Eng.Rep. 684 ("If it were not assize time, I would not take such language from you"); Commonwealth v. Eyre, 1815, 1 Serg. & R., Pa., 347 ("If it were not for your gray hairs, I would tear your heart out"). In State v. Hampton, 1868, 63 N.C. 13, "I have a great mind to hit you" was held not to prevent the existence of an assault.

24. Keefe v. State, 1857, 19 Ark. 190; United States v. Allison Richardson, C.C.D.C.1837, Fed.Cas.No.16,-155, 5 Cranch C.C. 348; State v. Church, 1868, 63 N.C. 15; Trogdon v. Terry, 1916, 172 N.C. 540, 90 S.E. 583.

25. Ross v. Michael, 1923, 246 Mass. 126, 140 N.E. 292 (plaintiff ordered out of defendant's house with violent words and a revolver); Ansteth v. Buffalo R. Co., 1895, 145 N.Y. 210, 39 N.E. 708 (conductor frightened boy off of street car).

plaintiff's personal integrity—which is to say that he must have intended to bring about an assault, a battery, or an imprisonment. There is, properly speaking, no such thing as a negligent assault.[26] But the intent need not necessarily be to inflict physical injury, and it is enough that there is an intent to arouse apprehension.[27] Thus it is an assault to fire a gun not aimed at the plaintiff for the purpose of frightening him,[28] or to point it at him when the defendant knows that it is unloaded, and the plaintiff does not.[29] "It is not the secret intent of the assaulting party, nor the undisclosed fact of his ability or inability to commit a battery that is material; but what his conduct and the attending circumstances denote at the time to the party assaulted."[30] Once the apprehension has been intentionally created, it is no defense that the defendant changed his mind, and desisted or withdrew without doing physical harm.[31] The tort is complete with the invasion of the plaintiff's mental peace, and the failure to carry it through to battery will not prevent liability.

Assault and Battery

Assault and battery go together like ham and eggs. The difference between them is that between physical contact and the mere apprehension of it. One may exist without the other. It is a battery to strike a man while he is asleep, although he does not discover it until afterward; it is an assault to shoot at him, frighten him and miss him. Except for this difference in the character of the invasion of the plaintiff's interests, the two are in all respects identical, and there is no apparent reason why the rules applied to battery, including the fiction of "transferred intent",[32] should not also apply to assault. In the ordinary case, both assault and battery are present; it is an assault when the defendant swings his fist to strike the plaintiff, and the plaintiff sees the movement, a battery when the fist comes in contact with the plaintiff's nose. The two terms are so closely associated in common usage that they are generally used together, or regarded as more or less synonymous.[33] Loosely drawn criminal statutes, which make use of "assault" to include attempted battery, or even battery itself, have assisted in obscuring the distinction. It is not accurate to say that "every battery includes an assault,"[34] but in practice the difference between the two is often entirely ignored.

26. White v. Sander, 1897, 168 Mass. 296, 47 N.E. 90; Atchison, T. & S. F. R. Co. v. McGinnis, 1891, 46 Kan. 109, 26 P. 453; Eckerd v. Weve, 1911, 85 Kan. 752, 118 P. 870; Second Restatement of Torts, § 21. As to the occasional use of the term "assault" to include negligence, see supra, p. 30.

27. Second Restatement of Torts, § 32.

28. State v. Baker, 1897, 20 R.I. 275, 38 A. 653; State v. Triplett, 1894, 52 Kan. 678, 35 P. 815; Nelson v. State, 1955, 92 Ga.App. 738, 90 S.E.2d 38; State v. Newton, 1959, 251 N.C. 151, 110 S.E.2d 810; Burgess v. Commonwealth, 1923, 136 Va. 697, 118 S.E. 273. Contra, Degenhardt v. Heller, 1896, 93 Wis. 662, 68 N.W. 411, relying upon the criminal law definition of assault as an attempted battery (see supra, p. 39). The case is criticized in 1897, 10 Harv.L.Rev. 252.

29. Beach v. Hancock, 1853, 27 N.H. 223; Allen v. Hannaford, 1926, 138 Wash. 423, 244 P. 700; Burge v. Forbes, 1928, 23 Ala.App. 67, 120 So. 577, certiorari denied, 1929, 219 Ala. 700, 121 So. 915 (displaying gun); Commonwealth v. Henson, Mass.1970, 259 N.E.2d 769.

Criminal statutes frequently define assault as an attempted battery, requiring present ability. See supra, p. 39. This was the original criminal law meaning of assault. Under such a definition it is often held, as in People v. Sylva, 1904, 143 Cal. 62, 76 P. 814, that pointing an unloaded gun is not an assault. See the full discussion in Perkins, An Analysis of Assault and Attempts to Assault, 1962, 47 Minn.L.Rev. 71; Notes, 1945, 33 Ky.L.J. 189; 1951, 30 Tex.L.Rev. 120; 1939, 11 Rocky Mt.L.Rev. 104. Such statutes will ordinarily have no application to tort liability. Lowry v. Standard Oil Co., 1944, 63 Cal.App.2d 1, 146 P.2d 57.

30. Commonwealth v. White, 1872, 110 Mass. 407, 409.

31. Handy v. Johnson, 1854, 5 Md. 450; Brister v. State, 1899, 40 Tex.Cr.R. 505, 51 S.W. 393.

32. See supra, p. 32.

33. See Mailand v. Mailand, 1901, 83 Minn. 453, 86 N.W. 445; Perkins v. Stein & Co., 1893, 94 Ky. 433, 22 S.W. 649.

34. As in Wood v. Commonwealth, 1927, 149 Va. 401, 140 S.E. 114; Greenman v. Smith, 1874, 20 Minn. 418. See Note, 1928, 12 Minn.L.Rev. 405.

11. FALSE IMPRISONMENT

The action for the tort of false imprisonment, sometimes called false arrest, is another lineal descendant of the old action of trespass. It protects the personal interest in freedom from restraint of movement. "Imprisonment," while it seems originally to have meant stone walls and iron bars, no longer signifies incarceration;[35] the plaintiff may be imprisoned when his movements are restrained in the open street,[36] or in a travelling automobile,[37] or when he is confined to an entire city,[38] or is compelled to go along with the defendant.[39] The older idea of confinement has persisted, however, in the requirement that the restraint be a total one, rather than a mere obstruction of the right to go where the plaintiff pleases. Thus it is not imprisonment to block the plaintiff's passage in one direction only,[40] or to shut him in a room with a reasonable exit open.[41] But it seems clear that too much emphasis has been placed upon the technical name of the tort; such interferences may invade a right which is entitled to protection, and an action may lie for them, though it is not that of false imprisonment.[42] If there is any distinction, it is that false imprisonment, being derived from the action of trespass, may be maintained without proof of actual damage, while in such other actions, proof of some damage may be required.

Since the interest is in a sense a mental one, resembling the apprehension of contact in the assault cases, the Restatement of Torts[43] has taken the position that there can be no imprisonment unless the plaintiff is aware of it at the time, arguing that the right is one of freedom to go where he pleases, and until he is aware of restraint there is no real interference with it; and that the mere dig-

---

35. It does, however, include it. St. Louis, I. M. & S. R. Co. v. Wilson, 1902, 70 Ark. 136, 66 S.W. 661 (locking plaintiff in a room); Reese v. Julia Sport Wear, 1940, 260 App.Div. 263, 21 N.Y.S.2d 99 (locking employee in a store).

36. Lukas v. J. C. Penney Co., 1963, 233 Or. 345, 378 P.2d 717. Determined as long ago as, 1348, Y.B.Lib. Assis., f. 104, pl. 85. Cf. C. N. Robinson & Co. v. Greene, 1906, 148 Ala. 434, 43 So. 797 (island).

37. Cieplinski v. Severn, 1929, 269 Mass. 261, 168 N.E. 722; Jacobson v. Sorenson, 1931, 183 Minn. 425, 236 N.W. 922. Cf. Ward v. Egan, 1935, 64 Can.C.C. 21 (moving train); Turney v. Rhodes, 1930, 42 Ga.App. 104, 155 S.E. 112 (elevator); Regina v. Macquarie, N.S.W.1875, 13 S.C.Rep. 264 (adrift in a boat).

38. Allen v. Fromme, 1910, 141 App.Div. 362, 126 N.Y.S. 520. Cases of confinement within a state, or within the United States, as by wrongful refusal of a passport, have not arisen. One may speculate that, although this may be a tort, it is not false imprisonment, since the line must obviously be drawn somewhere short of confinement to the hemisphere.

39. Brushaber v. Stegemann, 1871, 22 Mich. 266; Goodell v. Tower, 1904, 77 Vt. 61, 58 A. 790; cf. Fotheringham v. Adams Express Co., C.C.Mo.1888, 36 F. 252.

40. Bird v. Jones, 1845, 7 Ad. & El. 742, 115 Eng. Rep. 668 (obstruction of highway); Crossett v. Campbell, 1908, 122 La. 659, 48 So. 141 (expulsion from premises); Great A. & P. Tea Co. v. Billups, 1934, 253 Ky. 126, 69 S.W.2d 5 (stopping plaintiff); Martin v. Lincoln Park West Corp., 7 Cir. 1955, 219

F.2d 622 (locking him out of his room); Marrone v. Washington Jockey Club, 1910, 35 U.S.App.D.C. 82, affirmed 1913, 227 U.S. 633 (refusal of admission to race track); Second Restatement of Torts, § 36.

41. Wright v. Wilson, 1699, 1 Ld. Raym. 739, 91 Eng. Rep. 1394; Davis & Alcott Co. v. Boozer, 1926, 215 Ala. 116, 110 So. 28; Furlong v. German-American Press Ass'n, Mo.1916, 189 S.W. 385, 389 ("if a way of escape is left open which is available without peril of life or limb, no imprisonment"). The Second Restatement of Torts, § 36, Comment a, regards the means of escape as unreasonable if it involves exposure of the person, material harm to the clothing, or danger of substantial harm to another.

Of course a means of escape is not a reasonable one if it is unknown to the plaintiff. Talcott v. National Exhibition Co., 1911, 144 App.Div. 337, 128 N.Y.S. 1059.

42. Both Holt, C. J., in Wright v. Wilson, 1699, 1 Ld. Raym. 739, 91 Eng.Rep. 1394, and Patterson, J., in Bird v. Jones, 1845, 7 Ad. & El. 742, 115 Eng.Rep. 668, said that an action on the case might be maintained. Recovery was allowed in Cullen v. Dickinson, 1913, 33 S.D. 27, 144 N.W. 656, where plaintiff was prevented from entering a dance hall. Civil rights statutes have been held to afford a cause of action, as in Amos v. Prom, Inc., N.D.Iowa 1953, 115 F.Supp. 127, where a Negro was excluded from a ballroom.

43. Second Restatement of Torts, § 42. See Note, 1920, 68 U.Pa.L.Rev. 360.

nitary interest in freedom from unconscious confinement is not worthy of redress. One English case [44] supports this position; but there is a later English dictum to the contrary,[45] as well as three American decisions in cases of children and an idiot [46] where there was imprisonment, apparently without consciousness of it. Although very few cases ever have considered the point, it would appear that the Restatement is wrong, at least in any case where, as is certainly possible, substantial damage results to the plaintiff from a confinement of which he is unaware at the time.[47] It is at least settled that the imprisonment need not be for more than an appreciable length of time, and that it is not necessary that any damage result from it other than the confinement itself,[48] since the tort is complete with even a brief restraint of the plaintiff's freedom.

As in the case of other torts derived from the old action of trespass, the fact that there has been false imprisonment at all establishes a cause of action for at least nominal damages.[49]

The plaintiff is entitled to compensation [50] for his loss of time,[51] for physical discomfort or inconvenience,[52] and for any resulting physical illness or injury to his health.[53] Since the injury is in large part a mental one, he is entitled to damages for his mental suffering, humiliation, and the like.[54] The recoverable damages range further afield, and extend also to the interruption of the plaintiff's business,[55] the harm to his reputation or credit,[56] loss of the company of his family during imprisonment,[57] and expenses, such as attorney's fees, to which he has been put by

---

7 P.2d 981; Noce v. Ritchie, 1930, 109 W.Va. 391, 155 S.E. 127.

50. There are good general statements of the elements of compensatory damages in Duggan v. Baltimore & O. R. Co., 1893, 159 Pa. 248, 28 A. 182; Beckwith v. Bean, 1878, 98 U.S. 266; Gold v. Campbell, 1909, 54 Tex.Civ.App. 269, 117 S.W. 463; Oliver v. Kessler, Mo.App.1936, 95 S.W.2d 1226.

51. Goodell v. Tower, 1904, 77 Vt. 61, 58 A. 790; Young v. Gormley, 1903, 120 Iowa 372, 94 N.W. 922; Hewlett v. George, 1891, 68 Miss. 703, 9 So. 885.

52. Margaret Ann Super Markets v. Dent, Fla.1953, 64 So.2d 291; Jacques v. Parks, 1902, 96 Me. 268, 52 A. 763; Fox v. McCurnin, 1928, 205 Iowa 752, 218 N.W. 499; Paine v. Kelley, 1907, 197 Mass. 22, 83 N.E. 8.

53. Tierney v. State, 1943, 266 App.Div. 434, 42 N.Y. S.2d 877, affirmed 1943, 292 N.Y. 523, 54 N.E.2d 207; Van Dorn v. Kimball, 1916, 100 Neb. 590, 160 N.W. 953; Bailey v. Warner, 10 Cir. 1902, 118 F. 395 (nervous prostration).

54. Boies v. Raynor, 1961, 89 Ariz. 257, 361 P.2d 1; Schanafelt v. Seaboard Finance Co., 1951, 108 Cal. App.2d 420, 239 P.2d 42; Great A. & P. Tea Co. v. Smith, 1940, 281 Ky. 583, 136 S.W.2d 759; Burke v. Robinson, Mo.App.1925, 271 S.W. 1005; Jones v. Hebdo, 1921, 88 W.Va. 386, 106 S.E. 898.

55. Allen v. Fromme, 1910, 141 App.Div. 362, 126 N.Y. S. 520. Or the loss of particular business opportunities. Bailey v. Warner, 10 Cir. 1902, 118 F. 395; Kenyon v. Hartford Acc. & Indem. Co., 1927, 86 Cal. App. 266, 260 P. 954; Gariety v. Fleming, 1926, 121 Kan. 42, 245 P. 1054.

56. Thompson v. St. Louis-S. F. R. Co., Mo.App.1928, 3 S.W.2d 1033; Hayes v. Hutchinson & Shields, 1914, 81 Wash. 394, 142 P. 865; Margaret Ann Super Markets v. Dent, Fla.1953, 64 So.2d 291.

57. Walling v. Fields, 1923, 209 Ala. 389, 96 So. 471; cf. Gariety v. Fleming, 1926, 121 Kan. 42, 245 P. 1054.

---

44. Herring v. Boyle, 1834, 1 Cr. M. & R. 377, 149 Eng.Rep. 1126.

45. In the opinion of Atkin, L. J., in Meering v. Grahame-White Aviation Co., C.A.1919, 122 L.T.R. 44, 55.

46. Barker v. Washburn, 1911, 200 N.Y. 280, 93 N.E. 958; Commonwealth v. Nickerson, 1861, 5 Allen, 87 Mass. 518; Robalina v. Armstrong, 1852, 15 Barb., N.Y. 247.

47. See Prosser, False Imprisonment: Consciousness of Confinement, 1955, 55 Col.L.Rev. 847. Suppose a baby one month old is locked in a bank vault for three days, and suffers serious illness, or even dies, as a result. Is there no tort merely because the child is unaware of the confinement? And if there is a tort, what else but false imprisonment?

48. Strain v. Irwin, 1915, 195 Ala. 414, 70 So. 734 (momentary); Callahan v. Searles, 1894, 78 Hun 238, 28 N.Y.S. 904 (few minutes); Miller v. Ashcraft, 1895, 98 Ky. 314, 32 S.W. 1085, 17 Ky.Law Rep. 894; Moore v. Thompson, 1892, 92 Mich. 498, 52 N.W. 1000; Restatement of Torts, § 35.

49. Palmer v. Maine Central R. Co., 1899, 92 Me. 399, 42 A. 800; Butcher v. Adams, 1949, 310 Ky. 205, 220 S.W.2d 398; Mason v. Wrightson, 1954, 205 Md. 481, 109 A.2d 128; McLean v. Sanders, 1932, 139 Or. 144,

reason of a false arrest.[58] There may also be such special and unusual consequential damages as the theft of the plaintiff's automobile when the arrest compels him to leave it unguarded.[59] Because of the malevolent intentions which usually accompany false imprisonment, or at least the reckless disregard of the plaintiff's interests, it is usually a proper case for the award of punitive damages;[60] but where any such element of bad intent or wanton misconduct is lacking, and the imprisonment is the result of a mere mistake, either as to identity of the party or as to the propriety of arrest or imprisonment, punitive damages are denied.[61]

Character of Defendant's Act

The restraint may be by means of physical barriers,[62] or by threats of force which intimidate the plaintiff into compliance with orders.[63] It is sufficient that he submits to an apprehension of force reasonably to be understood from the conduct of the defendant, although no force is used or even expressly

threatened.[64] The plaintiff is not required to incur the risk of personal violence by resisting until it actually is used.[65] It is essential, however, that the restraint be against the plaintiff's will; and if he agrees of his own free choice to surrender his freedom of motion, as by remaining in a room or accompanying the defendant voluntarily, to clear himself of suspicion or to accommodate the desires of another,[66] rather than yielding to the constraint of a threat, then there is no imprisonment.[67] This gives rise, in borderline cases, to questions of fact, turning upon the details of the testimony, as to what was reasonably to be understood and implied from the defendant's conduct, tone of voice and the like, which seldom can be reflected accurately in an appellate record, and normally are for the jury.[68]

---

58. Worden v. Davis, 1909, 195 N.Y. 391, 88 N.E. 745; Nelson v. Kellogg, 1912, 162 Cal. 621, 123 P. 1115; Bolton v. Vellines, 1897, 94 Va. 393, 26 S.E. 847.

59. Whitehead v. Stringer, 1919, 106 Wash. 501, 180 P. 486.

60. Atkinson v. Dixie Greyhound Lines, 5 Cir. 1944, 143 F.2d 477, cert. denied 323 U.S. 758; Lindquist v. Friedman's, 1937, 366 Ill. 232, 8 N.E.2d 625; Sternberg v. Hogg, 1934, 254 Ky. 761, 72 S.W.2d 421; Parrott v. Bank of America Nat. Trust & Sav. Assn., 1950, 97 Cal.App.2d 14, 217 P.2d 89; McAleer v. Good, 1907, 216 Pa. 473, 65 A. 934.

61. Kroger Grocery & Baking Co. v. Waller, 1945, 208 Ark. 1063, 189 S.W.2d 361; Walker v. Tucker, 1955, 131 Colo. 198, 280 P.2d 649; S. H. Kress & Co. v. Powell, 1938, 132 Fla. 471, 180 So. 797; Shelton v. Barry, 1946, 328 Ill.App. 497, 66 N.E.2d 697; Heinze v. Murphy, 1942, 180 Md. 423, 24 A.2d 917.

62. Salisbury v. Poulson, 1918, 51 Utah 552, 172 P. 315; cf. Cieplinski v. Severn, 1929, 269 Mass. 261, 168 N.E. 722 (refusal to stop moving automobile).

63. Meints v. Huntington, 8 Cir. 1921, 276 F. 245; Mahan v. Adam, 1924, 144 Md. 355, 124 A. 901; Garnier v. Squires, 1900, 62 Kan. 321, 62 P. 1005; Second Restatement of Torts, § 40.

64. Stevens v. O'Neill, 1900, 51 App.Div. 364, 64 N.Y. S. 663, affirmed 1900, 169 N.Y. 375, 62 N.E. 424; Hales v. McCrory-McLellan Corp., 1963, 260 N.C. 568, 133 S.E.2d 225; W. T. Grant Co. v. Owens, 1928, 149 Va. 906, 141 S.E. 860; Sinclair Refining Co. v. Meek, 1940, 62 Ga.App. 850, 10 S.E.2d 76; Panisko v. Dreibelbis, 1942, 113 Mont. 310, 124 P.2d 997.

The fact that the plaintiff considers that he is being restrained is not sufficient unless there is reasonable ground to apprehend force upon an attempt to assert his liberty. Hoffman v. Clinic Hospital, 1938, 213 N.C. 669, 197 S.E. 161.

65. Brushaber v. Stegemann, 1871, 22 Mich. 266; Meints v. Huntington, 8 Cir. 1921, 276 F. 245; Halliburton-Abbott Co. v. Hodge, 1935, 172 Okl. 175, 44 P.2d 122; and see cases cited in the preceding note.

66. State for Use of Powell v. Moore, 1965, 252 Miss. 471, 174 So.2d 352; Meinecke v. Skaggs, 1950, 123 Mont. 308, 213 P.2d 237; Hunter v. Laurent, 1925, 158 La. 874, 104 So. 747; James v. MacDougall & Southwick Co., 1925, 134 Wash. 314, 235 P. 812. Cf. Great A. & P. Tea Co. v. Billups, 1934, 253 Ky. 126, 69 S.W.2d 5.

67. Payson v. Macomber, 1861, 3 Allen, Mass., 69; Sweeney v. F. W. Woolworth Co., 1924, 247 Mass. 277, 142 N.E. 50; Knowlton v. Ross, 1915, 114 Me. 18, 95 A. 281; see Powell v. Champion Fiber Co., 1908, 150 N.C. 12, 63 S.E. 159.

68. Compare Durgin v. Cohen, 1926, 168 Minn. 77, 209 N.W. 532; Lester v. Albers Super Markets, 1952, 94 Ohio App. 313, 114 N.E.2d 529; and Swetman v. F. W. Woolworth Co., 1957, 83 Ariz. 189, 318 P.2d 364, where it was held that no implied threat of force was to be found, with Garner v. Mears, 1958,

A substantial number of cases in recent years have found false imprisonment where the plaintiff surrendered his freedom of motion because of force directed against his valuable property, as where a woman remained in a store because her purse was taken,[69] or left a train because her suitcase was removed from it.[70] Beyond this the tort has not been extended, probably because of the confining scope of its origin as a branch of the action of trespass, which required direct and immediate interference with person or property, and the absence of any great necessity for the change. Moral pressure, as where the plaintiff remains with the defendant to clear himself of suspicion of theft,[71] or to avoid a scene on the street,[72] is not enough; nor, as in the case of assault, are threats for the future, as for example, to call the police and have the plaintiff arrested.[73] Any remedy

for such wrongs must lie with the more modern tort of the intentional infliction of mental distress.[74] It is for such reasons that the action for false imprisonment has remained relatively ineffective as a remedy, particularly for the violation of individual rights by the police.[75]

The restraint upon the plaintiff's freedom may also be imposed by the assertion of legal authority. If the plaintiff submits,[76] or if there is even a momentary taking into the custody of the law,[77] there is an arrest; and

87 Ga.App. 506, 103 S.E.2d 610, and Jacques v. Childs Dining Hall Co., 1923, 244 Mass. 438, 138 N.E. 843, where the jury were permitted to find it. Also compare, upon almost identical facts, the opposite conclusions in Weiler v. Herzfeld-Phillipson Co., 1926, 189 Wis. 554, 208 N.W. 599 (also Safeway Stores, Inc. v. Amburn, Tex.Civ.App.1965, 388 S.W. 2d 443), and Dillon v. Sears-Roebuck, Inc., 1934, 126 Neb. 357, 253 N.W. 331.

69. Ashland Dry Goods Co. v. Wages, 1946, 302 Ky. 577, 195 S.W.2d 312. Compare the cases where plaintiff remained with his automobile rather than leave it: National Bond & Investment Co. v. Whithorn, 1938, 276 Ky. 204, 123 S.W.2d 263; Cordell v. Standard Oil Co., 1930, 131 Kan. 221, 289 P. 472; see Verstraelen v. Kellog, 1962, 60 Wash.2d 115, 372 P.2d 543. Also Schanafelt v. Seaboard Finance Co., 1951, 108 Cal.App.2d 420, 239 P.2d 42; Harnik v. Levine, Mun.Ct.N.Y.1951, 106 N.Y.S.2d 460, affirmed 1952, 202 Misc. 648, 115 N.Y.S.2d 25, reversed 1953, 281 App. Div. 878, 120 N.Y.S.2d 62, appeal denied 282 App. Div. 684, 122 N.Y.S.2d 817.

70. Griffin v. Clark, 1935, 55 Idaho 364, 42 P.2d 297.

71. Hershey v. O'Neill, C.C.N.Y.1888, 36 F. 168; Hunter v. Laurent, 1925, 158 La. 874, 104 So. 747; James v. MacDougall & Southwick Co., 1925, 134 Wash. 314, 235 P. 812.

72. Fitscher v. Rollman & Sons Co., 1929, 31 Ohio App. 340, 167 N.E. 469. But in Lopez v. Wigwam Dept. Stores No. 10, 1966, 49 Haw. 416, 421 P.2d 289 this, under the circumstances, was held sufficient.

73. See supra, p. 39. Such threats for the future were held not to constitute imprisonment in Knowl-

ton v. Ross, 1915, 114 Me. 18, 95 A. 281; Sweeney v. F. W. Woolworth Co., 1924, 247 Mass. 277, 142 N.E. 50; Priddy v. Bunton, Tex.Civ.App.1943, 177 S.W.2d 805, error refused; Safeway Stores, Inc. v. Amburn, Tex.Civ.App.1965, 388 S.W.2d 443; Blumenfeld v. Harris, 1957, 3 App.Div.2d 219, 159 N.Y.S.2d 561, affirmed 1957, 3 N.Y.2d 905, 167 N.Y.S.2d 925, 145 N.E.2d 871, cert. denied 356 U.S. 930. The case last cited also involved a threat of civil process.

74. Infra, § 12.

75. Foote, Tort Remedies for Police Violations of Individual Rights, 1955, 39 Minn.L.Rev. 493.

76. Boies v. Raynor, 1961, 89 Ariz. 257, 361 P.2d 1; Martin v. Houck, 1906, 141 N.C. 317, 54 S.E. 291; Pike v. Hanson, 1838, 9 N.H. 491; Hebrew v. Pulis, 1906, 73 N.J.L. 621, 64 A. 121; Lyons v. Worley, 1931, 152 Okl. 57, 4 P.2d 3.

77. It has been held that an arrest by a police officer is complete when the officer lays his hand on the prisoner, although the latter resists and succeeds in escaping. See Genner v. Sparkes, 1704, 1 Salk. 79, 91 Eng.Rep. 74; Whithead v. Keyes, 1862, 3 Allen, Mass., 495. In Weissengoff v. Davis, 4 Cir. 1919, 260 F. 16, cert. denied 250 U.S. 674, a sheriff, with a warrant for the arrest of the defendant, stepped on the running board of his automobile, informed the defendant that he was under arrest, and directed him to stop. It was held that this was as complete an arrest as if the sheriff had touched his person.

There is no arrest where the defendant does not purport to take the plaintiff presently into custody, but merely directs him to appear in court at a future date. Chrestman v. State, 1927, 148 Miss. 673, 114 So. 748; Hart v. Herzig, 1955, 131 Colo. 458, 283 P.2d 177 (invalid summons for violation of game law); City of Toledo v. Lowenberg, 1955, 99 Ohio App. 165, 131 N.E.2d 682 (citation for traffic violation).

Nor is there any arrest when the plaintiff merely goes voluntarily with the officer to the police station, to clear the matter up. Pollack v. City of Newark, D. N.J.1956, 147 F.Supp. 35, affirmed 1957, 248 F.2d 543, cert. denied 355 U.S. 964, rehearing denied 362

if it is without proper legal authority, it is a false arrest, and so false imprisonment.

It is not necessary that the defendant have a warrant,[78] or even that he be an officer,[79] so long as he asserts the legal power to detain the plaintiff, and the plaintiff believes that the authority exists, and yields to it against his will.[80] The submission may be by words only,[81] although it may be gathered from the cases that the authority must at least be asserted in the plaintiff's presence, and that a mere submission over the telephone is not enough.[82] Whether the defendant's conduct reasonably implies a claim of legal authority, and an intent to detain the plaintiff under it, is of course entirely a matter of the circumstances of the particular case. The presence of a policeman who questions the plaintiff,[83] or the bare assertion that authority to arrest exists in the defendant, without purporting to exercise it by taking the plaintiff into custody,[84] is not imprisonment, so long as no present restraint of liberty is to be implied. And if the plaintiff does not submit, but seeks

to resist or escape, actual force must be used before the arrest is complete.[85]

The restraint may consist in the intentional breach of a duty to take active steps to release the plaintiff from a confinement in which he has already properly been placed—as, for example, a failure to let him out at the end of his sentence to a term in jail,[86] or to produce him in court promptly after an arrest.[87] Such a duty has been found in one case where the confinement was entered into voluntarily upon an assurance of release,[88] and in another where it was caused by the innocent acts of the defendant himself.[89] It seems reasonable to say that whenever a legal duty to

U.S. 907; Foulke v. New York Consol. R. Co., 1917, 180 App.Div. 848, 168 N.Y.S. 72, affirmed 1920, 228 N.Y. 269, 127 N.E. 237.

78. Wood v. Lane, 1834, 6 C. & P. 774, 172 Eng.Rep. 1458.

79. Whitman v. Atchison, T. & S. F. R. Co., 1911, 85 Kan. 150, 116 P. 234 (railroad conductor detaining plaintiff by assertion that he had authority to require a statement as to an accident); Daniel v. Phillips Petroleum Co., 1934, 229 Mo.App. 150, 73 S.W.2d 355 (filling station attendant).

80. Pike v. Hanson, 1838, 9 N.H. 491; Hebrew v. Pulis, 1906, 73 N.J.L. 621, 64 A. 121; Worden v. Davis, 1909, 195 N.Y. 391, 88 N.E. 745; Johnson v. Norfolk & W. R. Co., 1918, 82 W.Va. 692, 97 S.E. 189; Lyons v. Worley, 1931, 152 Okl. 57, 4 P.2d 3.

81. Haskins v. Young, 1837, 19 N.C. 527; Jones v. Jones, 1852, 35 N.C. 448.

82. Second Restatement of Torts, § 41, Comment f.

83. Knowlton v. Ross, 1915, 114 Me. 18, 95 A. 281; Durgin v. Cohen, 1926, 168 Minn. 77, 209 N.W. 532; State ex rel. Sovine v. Stone, 1965, 149 W.Va. 310, 140 S.E.2d 801.

84. Hill v. Taylor, 1883, 50 Mich. 549, 15 N.W. 899; Simpson v. Hill, 1793, 1 Esp. 431, 170 Eng.Rep. 409.

85. Genner v. Sparkes, 1704, 1 Salk. 79, 91 Eng.Rep. 74; Russen v. Lucas, 1824, 1 Car. & P. 153, 171 Eng. Rep. 1141. Cf. Horner v. Battyn, Buller N.P. 62.

86. Withers v. Henley, 1614, Cro.Jac. 379, 79 Eng.Rep. 392; Weigel v. McCloskey, 1914, 113 Ark. 1, 166 S.W. 944; Birdsall v. Lewis, 1936, 246 App.Div. 132, 285 N.Y.S. 146, affirmed 1936, 271 N.Y. 592, 3 N.E.2d 200 (one day over sentence); Shakespeare v. City of Pasadena, 1964, 230 Cal.App.2d 387, 40 Cal.Rptr. 863 (admitted to bail); Whirl v. Kern, 5 Cir. 1969, 407 F.2d 781.

Cf. Geddes v. Daughters of Charity of St. Vincent de Paul, 5 Cir. 1965, 348 F.2d 144 (failure to release mental patient).

87. Thurston v. Leno, 1964, 124 Vt. 298, 204 A.2d 106; Ames v. Strain, Okl.1956, 301 P.2d 641; Lincoln v. Grazer, 1958, 163 Cal.App.2d 758, 329 P.2d 928; Doherty v. Shea, 1946, 320 Mass. 173, 68 N.E.2d 707; Kleidon v. Glascock, 1943, 215 Minn. 417, 10 N.W.2d 394. Cf. Hall v. State ex rel. Freeman, 1944, 114 Ind.App. 328, 52 N.E.2d 370 (taking to distant jail); Matovina v. Hult, 1955, 125 Ind.App. 236, 123 N.E. 2d 893 (delay in obtaining warrant for further detention).

The unlawful imprisonment is a continuing trespass, and a new cause of action arises with each moment of it. Bennett v. Austro-Americana S.S. Co., 1914, 161 App.Div. 753, 147 N.Y.S. 193; Brush v. Lindsay, 1924, 210 App.Div. 361, 206 N.Y.S. 304; Note, 1925, 25 Col.L.Rev. 505.

88. Whittaker v. Sandford, 1912, 110 Me. 77, 85 A. 399; Second Restatement of Torts, § 45. Cf. Cieplinski v. Severn, 1929, 269 Mass. 261, 168 N.E. 722; C. N. Robinson & Co. v. Greene, 1906, 148 Ala. 434, 43 So. 797.

89. Talcott v. National Exhibition Co., 1911, 144 App. Div. 337, 128 N.Y.S. 1059 (baseball park failing to inform business visitor of exit, after main entrance closed because of crowd).

release another from confinement can be made out, an intentional refusal to do so is sufficient for false imprisonment;[90] but of course without such a duty there is no such tort.[91] Recovery has been denied in several cases where the plaintiff had good reason to know, when he voluntarily entered the confinement, that the defendant did not intend to assist him to escape.[92] For example, a workman who goes down in a mine with the understanding that he is not to return to the surface until a definite hour, cannot complain, in the absence of some emergency that would alter the terms of his bargain, when the hoist is not operated sooner to bring him up.[93]

One who participates in an unlawful arrest,[94] or procures or instigates the making of one without proper authority,[95] will be lia-ble for the consequences; but the defendant must have taken some active part in bringing about the unlawful arrest itself, by some "affirmative direction, persuasion, request or voluntary participation."[96] There is no liability for merely giving information to legal authorities, who are left entirely free to use their own judgment,[97] or for identifying the plaintiff as the person wanted,[98] or requesting a proper arrest when an officer makes an improper one instead,[99] or swearing to a complaint before a magistrate who turns out not to have jurisdiction.[1] The remedy in such cases, if any, is by an action for malicious prosecution.[2]

---

90. As, for example, where an invitee in a department store is accidentally locked in the washroom.

91. Schichowski v. Hoffmann, 1933, 261 N.Y. 389, 185 N.E. 676 affirmed 1933, 236 App.Div. 653, 257 N.Y.S. 920 (refusal to produce corporate books to obtain plaintiff's release from confinement for contempt). See Notes, 1934, 7 So.Cal.L.Rev. 102; 1914, 23 Yale L.J. 607.

92. Spoor v. Spooner, 1847, 12 Metc., Mass. 281 (plaintiff went on boat about to sail); Moses v. Dubois, 1838, Dud., S.C., 209 (same); Balmain New Ferry Co. v. Robertson, Aust.1905, 4 Comm.L.Rep. 379 (entering ferry wharf with notice no exit until payment); Burns v. Johnston, [1916] 2 Ir.Rep. 444, affirmed [1917] 2 Ir.Rep. 137 (going to work in factory with notice no exit during working hours). Cf. Timmons v. Fulton Bag & Cotton Mills, 1932, 45 Ga.App. 670, 166 S.E. 40.

93. Herd v. Weardale Steel, Coal & Coke Co., [1913] 3 K.B. 771, [1915] A.C. 67. See Amos, Contractual Restraint of Liberty, 1928, 44 L.Q.Rev. 464.

94. Cook v. Hastings, 1907, 150 Mich. 289, 114 N.W. 71; Parker v. Roberts, 1925, 99 Vt. 219, 131 A. 21; Howard v. Burton, 1953, 338 Mich. 178, 61 N.W.2d 77; Kearley v. Cowan, 1928, 217 Ala. 295, 116 So. 145; Monk v. Ehret, 1923, 192 Cal. 186, 219 P. 452. As to participation in the detention of the mentally ill, see Note, [1966] Wash.U.L.Q. 193.

95. Minor v. Seliga, 1958, 168 Ohio St. 1, 150 N.E.2d 852; Jillson v. Caprio, 1950, 86 U.S.App.D.C. 168, 181 F.2d 523; McDermott v. W. T. Grant Co., 1943, 313 Mass. 736, 49 N.E.2d 115; Winters v. Campbell, 1964, 148 W.Va. 710, 137 S.E.2d 188; Knupp v. Esslinger, Mo.1962, 363 S.W.2d 210; Second Restatement of Torts, § 45A.

Cf. Kettelhut v. Edwards, 1919, 65 Colo. 506, 177 P. 961 (ratification); Leon's Shoe Stores v. Hornsby, Tex.Civ.App.1957, 306 S.W.2d 402 (failure to disclose facts). See Note, 1959, 35 Ind.L.J. 80.

96. Edgar v. Omaha Public Power District, 1958, 166 Neb. 452, 89 N.W.2d 238.

97. Burlington Transp. Co. v. Josephson, 8 Cir. 1946, 153 F.2d 372; Ingo v. Koch, 2 Cir. 1942, 127 F.2d 667; Gogue v. MacDonald, 1950, 35 Cal.2d 482, 218 P.2d 542; Gooch v. Wachowiak, 1958, 352 Mich. 347, 89 N.W.2d 496; Hoock v. S. S. Kresge Co., Mo.1950, 230 S.W.2d 758.

But one who knowingly gives false information to a police officer becomes liable for the false arrest. Jensen v. Barnett, 1965, 178 Neb. 429, 134 N.W.2d 53; Wehrman v. Liberty Petroleum Co., Mo.App. 1964, 382 S.W.2d 56.

98. Miller v. Fano, 1901, 134 Cal. 103, 66 P. 183; Bisgaard v. Duvall, 1915, 169 Iowa 711, 151 N.W. 1051; Turner v. Mellon, 1953, 41 Cal.2d 45, 257 P.2d 15; Heinold v. Muntz T. V., Inc., Mo.1953, 262 S.W. 2d 32.

99. Lemmon v. King, 1915, 95 Kan. 524, 148 P. 750; Central Motor Co. v. Roberson, Tex.Civ.App.1941, 154 S.W.2d 180, affirmed 1941, Burton v. Roberson, 139 Tex. 562, 164 S.W.2d 524.

1. Gifford v. Wiggins, 1892, 50 Minn. 401, 52 N.W. 904; Smith v. Clark, 1910, 37 Utah 116, 106 P. 653. Otherwise if the defendant knows or should know of the lack of jurisdiction. Pomeranz v. Class, 1927, 82 Colo. 173, 257 P. 1086; Tiede v. Fuhr, 1915, 264 Mo. 622, 175 S.W. 910.

2. See infra, § 119.

Intent and Motive

There is no false imprisonment unless the defendant intends to cause a confinement.[3] There may, however, be liability for any negligence in such a case, if actual damage results.[4] It has been held that a mere incidental confinement due to acts directed at another purpose—as, for instance, locking the door with the plaintiff inside for the sole purpose of keeping others out—[5] is not a sufficiently important invasion of the plaintiff's interests to require the protection of the law. Since in such a case the defendant is aware that his conduct is certain to result in the confinement, it can scarcely be said that he did not intend it; and the real justification would appear to lie not in any lack of intent, but in a privilege to proceed reasonably about the defendant's own affairs.[6]

Although intent to confine the individual is necessary, it need not be with knowledge of who he is; and, as in the case of other intentional interferences with person or property,[7] an innocent, and quite reasonable, mistake as to his identity will not avoid liability.[8]

Although intent is necessary, malice, in the sense of ill will or a desire to injure, is not.[9] There may be liability although the defendant believed in good faith that the arrest was justified,[10] or that he was acting for the plaintiff's own good.[11] The presence or absence of malice may, however, be shown in aggravation [12] or mitigation [13] of damages. Nor is probable cause a defense,[14] except in so far as it may serve to validate the arrest itself,[15] or to justify a defense of person or property.[16] The defendant, merely because he believes that an arrest is called for or warranted, is not permitted to take the law into his own hands, but must resort to proper legal measures.[17] Once the fact of imprison-

---

3. Second Restatement of Torts, § 35; also § 43, approving the rule as to transferred intent found in the battery cases, where the intent is to imprison a third person. There are no decisions.

4. Restatement of Torts, § 35, Comment *h.* Compare, as to negligence causing arrest: Mouse v. Central Savings & Trust Co., 1929, 120 Ohio St. 599, 167 N.E. 868; Weaver v. Bank of America Nat. Trust & Savings, Inc., 1963, 59 Cal.2d 428, 30 Cal.Rptr. 4, 380 P.2d 644; Collins v. City Nat. Bank & Trust Co. of Danbury, 1944, 131 Conn. 167, 38 A.2d 582.

5. Wood v. Cummings, 1908, 197 Mass. 80, 83 N.E. 318. Cf. Williams v. Powell, 1869, 101 Mass. 467; Spoor v. Spooner, 1847, 12 Metc., Mass., 281; Moses v. Dubois, 1838, Dud., S.C., 209.

6. Suppose a janitor, whose duty it is to lock up a library at 10 o'clock to keep people out, decides to lock it up at 9 o'clock instead, and locks in those who refuse to leave. Is there any doubt that it is false imprisonment?

7. See pp. 74, 77, 83, 100.

8. Holmes v. Blyler, 1890, 80 Iowa 365, 45 N.W. 756; West v. Cabell, 1893, 153 U.S. 78. Cf. Garvin v. Muir, Ky.1957, 306 S.W.2d 256 (jailor confining plaintiff without knowledge of absence of valid order).

9. Colter v. Lower, 1871, 35 Ind. 285; Garnier v. Squires, 1900, 62 Kan. 321, 62 P. 1005; Casserly v. Wheeler, 9 Cir. 1922, 282 F. 389; Wilson v. Lapham, 1923, 196 Iowa 745, 195 N.W. 235; Hall v. Rice, 1929, 117 Neb. 813, 223 N.W. 4. See Ashton, Motive as an Essential Element in the Crime of False Imprisonment, 1934, 38 Dick.L.Rev. 184, 187.

10. West v. Cabell, 1893, 153 U.S. 78; Holmes v. Blyler, 1890, 80 Iowa 365, 45 N.W. 756; Oxford v. Berry, 1918, 204 Mich. 197, 170 N.W. 83; Johnson v. Norfolk & W. R. Co., 1918, 82 W.Va. 692, 97 S.E. 189.

11. Maxwell v. Maxwell, 1920, 189 Iowa 7, 177 N.W. 541; Keleher v. Putnam, 1880, 60 N.H. 30.

12. Phillips v. Morrow, 1923, 210 Ala. 34, 97 So. 130; Bolton v. Vellines, 1897, 94 Va. 393, 26 S.E. 847; Jones v. Hebdo, 1921, 88 W.Va. 386, 106 S.E. 898; Nappi v. Wilson, 1926, 22 Ohio App. 520, 155 N.E. 151; Note, 1927, 1 U.Cin.L.Rev. 364.

13. Roth v. Smith, 1870, 54 Ill. 431; Beckwith v. Bean, 1878, 98 U.S. 266; Landrum v. Wells, 1894, 7 Tex.Civ.App. 625, 26 S.W. 1001; Holmes v. Blyler, 1890, 80 Iowa 365, 45 N.W. 756.

14. Nelson v. Kellogg, 1912, 162 Cal. 621, 123 P. 1115; Lewis v. Montgomery Ward & Co., 1936, 144 Kan. 656, 62 P.2d 875; Titus v. Montgomery Ward & Co., 1938, 232 Mo.App. 987, 123 S.W.2d 574; Hostettler v. Carter, 1918, 73 Okl. 125, 175 P. 244; Fleischer v. Ensminger, 1922, 140 Md. 604, 118 A. 153.

15. See infra, § 26.

16. See infra, §§ 19–21.

17. Kroeger v. Passmore, 1908, 36 Mont. 504, 93 P. 805; Salisbury v. Poulson, 1918, 51 Utah 552, 172 P. 315.

ment is established, the burden is upon the defendant to show legal justification.[18]

Distinguished from Malicious Prosecution

The kindred action of malicious prosecution protects interests closely related to those involved in false imprisonment,[19] and sometimes the two are confused by the courts.[20] Malicious prosecution is the groundless institution of criminal proceedings against the plaintiff. False imprisonment fell within the action of trespass, as a direct interference with the plaintiff's person, while malicious prosecution was regarded as more indirect, and the remedy for it was an action on the case.[21] The distinction between the two lies in the existence of valid legal authority for the restraint imposed. If the defendant complies with the formal requirements of the law, as by swearing out a valid warrant, so that the arrest of the plaintiff is legally authorized, the court and its officers are not his agents to make the arrest, and their acts are those of the law and the state, and not to be imputed to him.[22] He is therefore liable, if at all, only for a misuse of legal process to effect a valid arrest for an improper purpose. The action must be for malicious prosecution, upon proof of malice and want of probable cause,[23] as well as termination of the

proceeding in favor of the plaintiff.[24] The weight of modern authority is that where the defendant has attempted to comply with legal requirements, and has failed to do so through no fault of his own, false imprisonment will not lie, and the remedy is malicious prosecution.[25] The policy is to give the defendant the privilege of making reasonable efforts to bring his case properly before the court, without liability unless his ultimate purpose is an improper one.[26]

12. INFLICTION OF MENTAL DISTRESS

Notwithstanding its early recognition in the assault cases, the law has been slow to accept the interest in peace of mind as entitled to independent legal protection, even as against intentional invasions. It is not until comparatively recent years that there has been any general admission that the inflic-

18. Snead v. Bonnoil, 1901, 166 N.Y. 325, 59 N.E. 899; Joseph v. Meier & Frank Co., 1926, 120 Or. 117, 250 P. 739.

19. See Harper, Malicious Prosecution, False Imprisonment and Defamation, 1937, 15 Tex.L.Rev. 157; and see, as to malicious prosecution, infra, § 119.

20. See for example Neall v. Hart, 1886, 115 Pa. 347, 8 A. 628; Stewart v. Cooley, 1877, 23 Minn. 347. The frequency of such confusion is pointed out in Rich v. McInerny, 1894, 103 Ala. 345, 15 So. 663.

21. 1 Street, Foundations of Legal Liability, 1906, 12; Kramer v. Lott, 1865, 50 Pa. 495, 498; Colter v. Lower, 1871, 35 Ind. 285.

22. Brown v. Chapman, 1848, 6 C.B. 365, 136 Eng.Rep. 1292; Sheppard v. Furniss, 1851, 19 Ala. 760; Damilitis v. Kerjas Lunch Corp., 1937, 165 Misc. 186, 300 N.Y.S. 574.

23. Nesmith v. Alford, 5 Cir.1963, 318 F.2d 110, rehearing denied 319 F.2d 859, cert. denied 1964, 375 U. S. 975; Genito v. Rabinowitz, 1966, 93 N.J.Super., 225, 225 A.2d 590; S. H. Kress & Co. v. Powell, 1938,

132 Fla. 471, 180 So. 757; Riegel v. Hygrade Seed Co., W.D. N.Y.1942, 47 F.Supp. 290; Wilson v. Lapham, 1923, 196 Iowa 745, 195 N.W. 235. But in the event of an improper arrest and other proceedings, both actions may lie. Young v. Andrews Hardwood Co., 1931, 200 N.C. 310, 156 S.E. 501.

24. Frisbie v. Morris, 1903, 75 Conn. 637, 55 A. 9; Lowe v. Wartman, 1885, 47 N.J.L. 413, 1 A. 489. Such proof is not necessary in a false imprisonment action. Boesch v. Kick, 1922, 98 N.J.L. 183, 119 A. 1; Davis v. Johnson, 1900, 42 C.C.A. 111, 101 F. 952; Barry v. Third Ave. R. Co., 1900, 51 App.Div. 385, 64 N.Y.S. 615. See Note, 1923, 21 Mich.L.Rev. 704.

25. Langford v. Boston & A. R. Co., 1887, 144 Mass. 431, 11 N.E. 697; Utz v. Mayes, Mo.App.1925, 267 S.W. 59, cert. quashed, 1925, 287 S.W. 606; Nelson v. Hill, 1924, 30 N.M. 288, 232 P. 526. Contra: Krause v. Spiegel, 1892, 94 Cal. 370, 29 P. 707; Satilla Mfg. Co. v. Cason, 1895, 98 Ga. 14, 25 S.E. 909. See Notes, 1925, 34 Yale L.J. 908; 1927, 11 Minn.L.Rev. 678.

26. "This exemption of the litigant from any liability for false imprisonment extends even to cases in which the court ordering the imprisonment has acted without jurisdiction. It is the right of every litigant to bring his case before the court, and it is for the court to know the limits of its own jurisdiction and to keep within them." Salmond, Law of Torts, 13th Ed. 1961, 309, citing Carratt v. Morley, 1841, 1 Q.B. 18; West v. Smallwood, 1838, 3 M. & W. 418, 150 Eng.Rep. 1208; Brown v. Chapman, 1848, 6 C.B. 365, 136 Eng.Rep. 1292.

tion of mental distress, standing alone, may serve as the basis of an action, apart from any other tort. In this respect, the law is clearly in a process of growth, the ultimate limits of which cannot as yet be determined.[27]

Various reasons have been advanced for this reluctance to redress mental injuries. One is the difficulty of proof, or of measurement of the damages.[28] "Mental pain or anxiety," said Lord Wensleydale in a famous English case, "the law cannot value, and does not pretend to redress, when the unlawful act causes that alone." [29] It was regarded as something "metaphysical," "too subtle and speculative to be capable of admeasurement by any standard known to the law." [30] But

mental suffering is scarcely more difficult of proof, and certainly no harder to estimate in terms of money, than the physical pain of a broken leg, which never has been denied compensation; [31] and the courts have been quite willing to allow large sums as damages for such "mental anguish" itself, where it accompanies a slight physical injury.[32]

Again, it has been said that mental consequences are so evanescent, intangible, and peculiar, and vary to such an extent with the individual concerned, that they cannot be anticipated, and so lie outside the boundaries of any reasonable "proximate" connection with the act of the defendant.[33] It is not difficult to discover in the earlier opinions a distinctly masculine astonishment that any woman should ever be so silly as to allow herself to be frightened or shocked into a miscarriage. But medical science has recognized long since that not only fright and shock, but also grief, anxiety, rage and shame, are in themselves "physical" injuries, in the sense that

27. The progress of the law may be traced in the following series of articles: Bohlen, Right to Recover for Injury Resulting from Negligence Without Impact, 1902, 41 Am.L.Reg.,N.S., 141; Throckmorton, Damages for Fright, 1921, 34 Harv.L.Rev. 260, 57 Am.L.Rev. 828, 153 L.T. 24, 89; Goodrich, Emotional Disturbance as Legal Damage, 1922, 20 Mich.L.Rev. 497; Bohlen and Polikoff, Liability in Pennsylvania for Physical Effects of Fright, 1932, 80 U.Pa.L.Rev. 627; Bohlen and Polikoff, Liability in New York for the Physical Consequences of Emotional Disturbance, 1932, 32 Col.L.Rev. 409; Hallen, Damages for Physical Injuries Resulting from Fright or Shock, 1933, 19 Va.L.Rev. 253; Hallen, Hill v. Kimball—A Milepost in the Law, 1933, 12 Tex.L.Rev. 1; Green, "Fright" Cases, 1933, 27 Ill.L.Rev. 761, 873; Magruder, Mental and Emotional Disturbance in the Law of Torts, 1936, 49 Harv.L.Rev. 1033; Harper and McNeely, A Re-examination of the Basis for Liability for Emotional Disturbance, [1938] Wis.L.Rev. 426. See also the excellent summary in the Report of the New York State Law Revision Commission, Study Relating to Liability for Injuries Resulting from Fright or Shock, 1936, Legislative Doc.No.65(E).

28. Bohlen, Right to Recover for Injury Resulting from Negligence Without Impact, 1902, 41 Am.L.Reg., N.S., 141, 143, attributes this in part to the early rule that the parties themselves were not competent witnesses.

29. Lynch v. Knight, 1861, 9 H.L.C. 577, 598, 11 Eng. Rep. 854, continuing: "Though where a material damage occurs, and is connected with it, it is impossible a jury, in estimating it, should altogether overlook the feelings of the party interested."

30. Mitchell v. Rochester R. Co., 1896, 151 N.Y. 107, 45 N.E. 354; Cleveland, C. C. & St. L. R. Co. v. Stew-

art, 1899, 24 Ind.App. 374, 56 N.E. 917; Chicago, B. & Q. R. Co. v. Gelvin, 8 Cir. 1916, 238 F. 14.

31. McCormick, Damages, 1935, 315, 316; Pennsylvania R. Co. v. Allen, 1866, 53 Pa. 276; Fry v. Dubuque & S. W. R. Co., 1877, 45 Iowa 416. "As all pain is mental and centers in the brain, it follows that as an element of damage for personal injury the injured party is allowed to recover for actual suffering of mind and body when they are the immediate and necessary consequence of the negligent injury." Hargis v. Knoxville Power Co., 1917, 175 N.C. 31, 94 S.E. 702, 703. As to the difficulty of distinguishing the two, see Nashville, C. & St. L. R. Co. v. Miller, 1904, 120 Ga. 453, 47 S.E. 959.

32. Craker v. Chicago & N. W. R. Co., 1875, 36 Wis. 657 ($1,000 to school teacher who was kissed for "terror and anguish, her outraged feeling and insulted virtue, her mental humiliation and suffering"); Draper v. Baker, 1884, 61 Wis. 450, 21 N.W. 527 ($1,200 for spitting in the face). "A lusty hug and kiss were priced at $700 in Ragsdale v. Ezell, 1899, 99 Ky. 236, 49 S.W. 775." Magruder, Mental and Emotional Disturbance in the Law of Torts, 1936, 49 Harv.L.Rev. 1033, 1034.

33. See Victorian Ry. Comm'rs v. Coultas, 1888, 13 App.Cas. 222; Mitchell v. Rochester R. Co., 1896, 151 N.Y. 107, 45 N.E. 354; Braun v. Craven, 1898, 175 Ill. 401, 51 N.E. 657; Chittick v. Philadelphia Rapid Trans. Co., 1909, 224 Pa. 13, 73 A. 4.

they produce well marked changes in the body, and symptoms that are readily visible to the professional eye.[34] Such consequences are the normal, rather than the unusual, result of a threat of physical harm, and of many other types of conduct; and, in any case, nearly all courts have discarded foreseeability as the sole criterion of legal cause.[35]

The most valid objection to the protection of such interests lies in the "wide door" which might be opened, not only to fictitious claims, but to litigation in the field of trivialities and mere bad manners.[36] It would be absurd for the law to seek to secure universal peace of mind, and many interferences with it must of necessity be left to other agencies of social control. "Against a large part of the frictions and irritations and clashing of temperaments incident to participation in a community life, a certain toughening of the mental hide is a better protection than the law could ever be."[37] But this is a poor reason for denying recovery for any genuine, serious mental injury. It is the business of the law to remedy wrongs that deserve it, even at the expense of a "flood of litigation," and it is a pitiful confession of in-

competence on the part of any court of justice to deny relief on such grounds.[38] "And it is no objection to say, that it will occasion multiplicity of actions; for if men will multiply injuries, actions must be multiplied; for every man that is injured ought to have his recompense."[39] So far as distinguishing true claims from false ones is concerned, what is required is rather a careful scrutiny of the evidence supporting the claim;[40] and the elimination of trivialities calls for nothing more than the same common sense which has distinguished serious from trifling injuries in other fields of the law.[41]

Type of Injury Redressed

The early cases refused all remedy for mental injury, unless it could be brought within the scope of some already recognized tort. Thus it was held that mere words, however violent, threatening or insulting, did not constitute an assault, and hence afforded no ground for redress.[42] It might well be in-

34. See Goodrich, Emotional Disturbance as Legal Damage, 1922, 20 Mich.L.Rev. 497, listing, upon medical authority, a variety of physical symptoms, from accelerated pulse to pyorrhea; Tibbetts, Neurasthenia, the Result of Nervous Shock, as a Ground for Damages, 1904, 59 Cent.L.J. 83; Earengey, The Legal Consequences of Shock, 1934, 2 Medico-Legal & Crim. Rec. 14; Crile, The Origin and Nature of the Emotions, 1915; Chiuchiolo v. New England Wholesale Tailors, 1930, 84 N.H. 329, 150 A. 540.

35. Throckmorton, Damages for Fright, 1921, 34 Harv.L.Rev. 260, 270, 57 Am.L.Rev. 828, 153 L.T. 24, 89; and see infra, § 43.

36. Mitchell v. Rochester R. Co., 1896, 151 N.Y. 107, 45 N.E. 354; Spade v. Lynn & Boston R. Co., 1897, 168 Mass. 285, 288, 47 N.E. 88, 89; Huston v. Freemansburg Borough, 1905, 212 Pa. 548, 61 A. 1022; Ward v. West Jersey & S. R. Co., 1900, 65 N.J.L. 383, 47 A. 561. See Throckmorton, Damages for Fright, 1921, 34 Harv.L.Rev. 260, 276, 57 Am.L.Rev. 828, 153 L.T. 24, 89.

37. Magruder, Mental and Emotional Disturbance in the Law of Torts, 1936, 49 Harv.L.Rev. 1033, 1035.

38. Simone v. Rhode Island Co., 1907, 28 R.I. 186, 195, 66 A. 202; Kenney v. Wong Len, 1925, 81 N.H. 427, 128 A. 343; Green v. T. A. Shoemaker & Co., 1909, 111 Md. 69, 73 A. 688; Alabama Fuel & Iron Co. v. Baladoni, 1916, 15 Ala.App. 316, 73 So. 205.

39. Holt, C. J., in Ashby v. White, 1703, 2 Ld.Raym. 938, 955, 92 Eng.Rep. 126.

40. Compare the holding that substantial verdicts for personal injuries will not be sustained where the evidence consists entirely of subjective testimony on the part of the plaintiff. Johnson v. Great Northern R. Co., 1909, 107 Minn. 285, 119 N.W. 1061; Sprogis v. Butler, 1919, 40 Cal.App. 647, 181 P. 246; Paderas v. Stauffer, 1929, 10 La.App. 50, 119 So. 757, 120 So. 886; City of Pawhuska v. Crutchfield, 1932, 155 Okl. 222, 8 P.2d 685. And see Johnson v. Sampson, 1926, 167 Minn. 203, 207, 208 N.W. 814.

41. Goodrich, Emotional Disturbance as Legal Damage, 1922, 20 Mich.L.Rev. 497, 512. Compare Rogers v. Elliott, 1888, 146 Mass. 349, 15 N.E. 768, holding that a church bell is not a nuisance, even though it throws plaintiff into convulsions; and similar cases cited infra, p. 578.

42. State v. Daniel, 1904, 136 N.C. 571, 48 S.E. 544; Grayson v. St. Louis Transit Co., 1903, 100 Mo.App. 60, 71 S.W. 730; Hixson v. Slocum, 1913, 156 Ky. 487, 161 S.W. 522; Kramer v. Ricksmeier, 1913, 159 Iowa 48, 139 N.W. 1091; Brooker v. Silverthorne, 1918, 111 S.C. 553, 99 S.E. 350.

quired why the trespass action for assault, which was a remedy designed to keep the peace, never was extended to words which were more insulting, unendurable, and generally provocative than blows. Perhaps it was the proximity of the criminal law, with its fixed notion that assault must always be something in the nature of an attempted battery. In any event, the result was a rule which permitted recovery for a gesture that might frighten the plaintiff for a moment, and denied it for menacing words which kept him in terror of his life for a month. But if some independent tort, such as assault,[43] battery,[44] false imprisonment,[45] or seduction[46] could be made out, the cause of action served as a peg upon which to hang the mental damages, and recovery was freely permitted. Such "parasitic" damages were the entering wedge.[47]

It has gradually become recognized that there is no magic inherent in the name given to a tort, or in any arbitrary classification,[48] and that the infliction of mental injury may be a cause of action in itself. Its limits are

as yet ill defined, but it has been extended to its greatest length in the case of intentional[49] acts of a flagrant character, whose enormity adds especial weight to the plaintiff's claim, and is in itself an important guarantee that the mental disturbance which follows is serious and not feigned.[50]

Insult and Indignity

The earliest appearance of anything like a separate cause of action for the intentional infliction of mental suffering was in cases holding a common carrier liable for insulting a passenger.[51] The justification first advanced was that of breach of an "implied contract" to be polite;[52] but the liability was soon imposed where a prospective passenger had not yet bought a ticket,[53] and the later

43. Trogdon v. Terry, 1916, 172 N.C. 540, 90 S.E. 583; Kline v. Kline, 1902, 158 Ind. 602, 64 N.E. 9; Holdorf v. Holdorf, 1918, 185 Iowa 838, 169 N.W. 737; Allen v. Hannaford, 1926, 138 Wash. 423, 244 P. 700.

44. Williams v. Underhill, 1901, 63 App.Div. 223, 71 N.Y.S. 291; Draper v. Baker, 1884, 61 Wis. 450, 21 N.W. 527.

45. Gadsden General Hospital v. Hamilton, 1925, 212 Ala. 531, 103 So. 553; Fisher v. Rumler, 1927, 239 Mich. 224, 214 N.W. 310.

46. Anthony v. Norton, 1899, 60 Kan. 341, 56 P. 529; Haeissig v. Decker, 1918, 139 Minn. 422, 166 N.W. 1085.

47. "The treatment of any element of damages as a parasitic factor belongs essentially to a transitory stage of legal evolution. A factor which is today recognized as parasitic will, forsooth, tomorrow be recognized as an independent basis of liability. It is merely a question of social, economic and industrial needs as those needs are reflected in the organic law." 1 Street, Foundations of Legal Liability, 1906, 460, 470.

48. Smith, Torts Without Particular Names, 1921, 69 U.Pa.L.Rev. 91; Winfield, The Foundation of Liability in Tort, 1927, 27 Col.L.Rev. 1.

49. As to negligent acts causing mental disturbance, see infra, § 54.

50. The classic article on the subject is Magruder, Mental and Emotional Disturbance in the Law of Torts, 1936, 49 Harv.L.Rev. 1033. See also Prosser, Insult and Outrage, 1956, 44 Cal.L.Rev. 40; Wade, Tort Liability for Abusive and Insulting Language, 1951, 4 Vand.L.Rev. 63; Prosser, Intentional Infliction of Mental Suffering: A New Tort, 1939, 37 Mich.L.Rev. 874; Vold, Tort Recovery for Intentional Infliction of Emotional Distress, 1939, 18 Neb.L.B. 222; Borda, One's Right to Enjoy Mental Peace and Tranquillity, 1939, 28 Geo.L.J. 55; Seitz, Insults, Practical Jokes, Threats of Future Harm, 1940, 28 Ky.L.J. 411; Smith, An Independent Tort Action for Mental Suffering and Emotional Distress, 1957, 7 Drake L.Rev. 53; Notes, 1952, 52 Col.L.Rev. 939; 1952, 25 So.Cal.L.Rev. 440; Restatement of Torts, §§ 46, 48.

51. Chamberlain v. Chandler, C.C.Mass.1823, 3 Mason 242, 5 Fed.Cas.No.2,575; Cole v. Atlanta & W. P. R. Co., 1897, 102 Ga. 474, 31 S.E. 107; Texas & Pac. R. Co. v. Jones, Tex.Civ.App.1897, 39 S.W. 124; Knoxville Traction Co. v. Lane, 1899, 103 Tenn. 376, 53 S.W. 557.

52. Chamberlain v. Chandler, C.C.Mass.1823, 3 Mason 242, 5 Fed.Cas.No.2,575; Knoxville Traction Co. v. Lane, 1899, 103 Tenn. 376, 53 S.W. 557; Bleecker v. Colorado & So. R. Co., 1911, 50 Colo. 140, 114 P. 481. Cf. Frewen v. Page, 1921, 238 Mass. 499, 131 N.E. 475 (innkeeper).

53. Texas & Pac. R. Co. v. Jones, Tex.Civ.App.1897, 39 S.W. 124. Accord: St. Louis-San Francisco R. Co. v. Clark, 1924, 104 Okl. 24, 229 P. 779; Jones v. Atlantic Coast Line R. Co., 1917, 108 S.C. 217, 94

decisions rest the liability upon the special obligation of the carrier to the public, and regard it as sounding in tort.[54] In this field the decisions have gone to considerable lengths, holding the carrier liable for language which is merely profane or indecent,[55] or grossly [56] insulting [57] to people of ordinary sensibility,[58] even though the mental disturb-

ance is not attended by any illness or other physical consequences.[59]

The same liability has been imposed upon innkeepers, whose position toward the public is analogous to that of carriers; and the hotel detective who bursts into a room crying that the occupants are unmarried and threatening jail makes his employer liable for the mental suffering which results.[60] It has also been extended in a few cases to telegraph companies; [61] and there appears to be little doubt that it would be applied to any other public utility grossly insulting its patrons.[62] Although there has been a little indication of a desire on the part of a few courts to extend this liability for mere insult to the owners of shops and other premises held open to the public,[63] the majority of the cases [64] thus far

---

S.E. 490 (in freight depot to pick up package); Moody v. Kenny, 1923, 153 La. 1007, 97 So. 21 (hotel guest not yet registered).

54. Cole v. Atlanta & W. P. R. Co., 1897, 102 Ga. 474, 31 S.E. 107; Goddard v. Grand Trunk R. Co., 1869, 57 Me. 202, 2 Am.Rep. 39; cf. Boyce v. Greeley Square Hotel Co., 1920, 228 N.Y. 106, 126 N.E. 647 (hotel).

55. Birmingham Ry. L. & P. Co. v. Glenn, 1912, 179 Ala. 263, 60 So. 111; Bleecker v. Colorado & Southern R. Co., 1911, 50 Colo. 140, 114 P. 481; Fort Worth & R. G. R. Co. v. Bryant, Tex.Civ.App.1918, 210 S. W. 556; St. Louis-San Francisco R. Co. v. Clark, 1924, 104 Okl. 24, 229 P. 779; Southeastern Greyhound Corp. v. Graham, 1943, 69 Ga.App. 621, 26 S.E. 2d 371.

56. Mere discourtesy, as distinguished from gross insult, apparently is not enough. Thus a mere rough tone of voice was held not to be actionable in New York, L. E. & W. R. Co. v. Bennett, 6 Cir. 1892, 50 F. 496; Crutcher v. Cleveland, C. C. & St. L. R. Co., 1908, 132 Mo.App. 311, 111 S.W. 891; Daniels v. Florida C. & P. R. Co., 1901, 62 S.C. 1, 39 S.E. 762; and cf. Campopiano v. Rhode Island Co., 1916, 39 R.I. 105, 97 A. 597.

The mildest insult found for which recovery was allowed was in Haile v. New Orleans Ry. & Light Co., 1914, 135 La. 229, 65 So. 225: "A big fat woman like you." Even this might be expected to be highly offensive to a big fat woman like her.

57. Gillespie v. Brooklyn Heights R. Co., 1904, 178 N.Y. 347, 70 N.E. 857 ("deadbeat" and "swindler"); Lipman v. Atlantic Coast Line R. Co., 1917, 108 S. C. 151, 93 S.E. 714 ("lunatic"); Knoxville Traction Co. v. Lane, 1899, 103 Tenn. 376, 53 S.W. 557 ("whore"); Barbknecht v. Great Northern R. Co., 1927, 55 N.D. 104, 212 N.W. 776 (opprobrious epithets and indecent proposal); Huffman v. Southern R. Co., 1913, 163 N.C. 171, 79 S.E. 307 ("cheap, common scalawag").

58. The liability was so limited in Georgia Ry. & Elec. Co. v. Baker, 1907, 1 Ga.App. 832, 58 S.E. 88; Birmingham Ry. L. & P. Co. v. Glenn, 1912, 179 Ala. 263, 60 So. 111.

The personality of the plaintiff is to be taken into account, and a lady or a child may recover where a man hardened to profane language might not. Fort

Worth & R. G. R. Co. v. Bryant, Tex.Civ.App.1918, 210 S.W. 556.

59. Lipman v. Atlantic Coast Line R. Co., 1917, 108 S.C. 151, 93 S.E. 714; Humphrey v. Michigan United R. Co., 1911, 166 Mich. 645, 132 N.W. 447; Gillespie v. Brooklyn Heights R. Co., 1904, 178 N.Y. 347, 70 N.E. 857; Texas & Pac. R. Co. v. Jones, Tex.Civ. App.1897, 39 S.W. 124.

60. Emmke v. De Silva, 8 Cir.1923, 293 F. 17; De Wolf v. Ford, 1908, 193 N.Y. 397, 86 N.E. 527; Dixon v. Hotel Tutwiler Operating Co., 1926, 214 Ala. 396, 108 So. 26; Frewen v. Page, 1921, 238 Mass. 499, 131 N.E. 475; Milner Hotels v. Dougherty, 1943, 195 Miss. 718, 15 So.2d 358.

61. Dunn v. Western Union Tel. Co., 1907, 2 Ga.App. 845, 59 S.E. 189 ("Go to hell with your God damn message"); Buchanan v. Western Union Tel. Co., 1920, 115 S.C. 433, 106 S.E. 159 (indecent proposal by messenger at home); Magouirk v. Western Union Tel. Co., 1902, 79 Miss. 632, 31 So. 206; cf. Western Union Tel. Co. v. Watson, 1902, 82 Miss. 101, 33 So. 76; Butler v. Western Union Tel. Co., 1901, 62 S.C. 222, 40 S.E. 162.

62. The plaintiff must qualify as a patron making use of the facilities of the carrier, innkeeper, or public utility, as such. Thus recovery was denied in Jenkins v. Kentucky Hotel, Inc., 1935, 261 Ky. 419, 87 S.W.2d 951, where plaintiff made use of defendant's hotel lobby to meet a friend; and cf. Wallace v. Shoreham Hotel Corp., Mun.App.D.C. 1946, 49 A.2d 81 (customer in cocktail lounge of hotel not hotel guest).

63. Davis v. Tacoma Ry. & Power Co., 1904, 35 Wash. 203, 77 P. 209 (amusement park; plaintiff ordered

64. See note 64 on page 54.

do not support the liability, and treat the owners of such premises upon the same footing as other defendants who are not under the special obligation of the public utility toward the public.[65]

There is virtually unanimous agreement that such ordinary defendants are not liable for mere insult, indignity, annoyance, or even threats, where the case is lacking in other circumstances of aggravation. The reasons are not far to seek. Our manners, and with them our law, have not yet progressed to the

point where we are able to afford a remedy in the form of tort damages for all intended mental disturbance. Liability of course cannot be extended to every trivial indignity. There is no occasion for the law to intervene with balm for wounded feelings in every case where a flood of billingsgate is loosed in an argument over a back fence. The plaintiff must necesssarily be expected and required to be hardened to a certain amount of rough language, and to acts that are definitely inconsiderate and unkind.[66] There is still, in this country at least, such a thing as liberty to express an unflattering opinion of another, however wounding it may be to his feelings; and in the interest not only of freedom of speech but also of avoidance of other more dangerous conduct, it is still very desirable that some safety valve be left through which irascible tempers may blow off relatively harmless steam.

There is the further, and still more significant, evident and serious danger of fictitious claims and vexatious suits in such cases. Petty insult or indignity lacks, from its very nature, any convincing assurance that the asserted mental distress is genuine, or that if genuine it is serious, and reasonable. When a citizen who has been called a son of a bitch testifies that the epithet has destroyed his slumber, ruined his digestion, wrecked his nervous system, and permanently impaired his health, other citizens who on occasion have been called the same thing without catastrophic harm may have legitimate doubts that he was really so upset, or that if he were his sufferings could possibly be so reasonable and justified under the circumstances as to be entitled to compensation.

Accordingly, it is generally held that there can be no recovery for mere profanity, obscenity, or abuse,[67] without circumstances of

out, with imputation of immoral conduct); Malczewski v. New Orleans Ry. & Light Co., 1924, 156 La. 830, 101 So. 213. In both cases the defendant was a carrier, but not acting as such. Other cases in which plaintiff was ejected from the premises are probably to be distinguished as involving a clear breach of contract. Weber-Stair Co. v. Fisher, Ky.1909, 119 S.W. 195 (theatre); Planchard v. Klaw & Erlanger New Orleans Theatres Co., 1928, 166 La. 235, 117 So. 132 (theatre); Aaron v. Ward, 1911, 203 N.Y. 351, 96 N.E. 736 (bathhouse); Smith v. Leo, 1895, 92 Hun. 242, 36 N.Y.S. 949 (dance hall).

64. Flowers v. Price, 1939, 190 S.C. 392, 3 S.E.2d 38 (tobacco warehouse; profanity and abuse); Wallace v. Shoreham Hotel Corp., Mun.App.D.C.1946, 49 A.2d 81 (cocktail lounge, insinuation of dishonesty); Republic Iron & Steel Co. v. Self, 1915, 192 Ala. 403, 68 So. 328 (shop; "liar," "dirty liar," and "no lady"); Miller v. Friedman's Jewelers, Inc., 1963, 107 Ga. App. 841, 131 S.E.2d 663 (shop; abuse, ordered out); Slocum v. Food Fair Stores of Florida, Fla.1958, 100 So.2d 396 ("You stink to me"); Stavnezer v. Sage-Allen & Co., 1959, 146 Conn. 460, 152 A.2d 312 (false accusation goods not paid for).

Cf. Nance v. Mayflower Tavern, 1944, 106 Utah 517, 150 P.2d 773 (restaurant refusing to serve plaintiff); Mann v. Roosevelt Shop, Fla.1949, 41 So.2d 894 (similar refusal by shop); Larson v. R. B. Wrigley Co., 1931, 183 Minn. 28, 235 N.W. 393 (restaurant refusing, plaintiff "too dirty.")

65. Thus the owner of premises, like anyone else, can be held liable for extreme outrage (see infra, pp. 55–58). Saenger Theatres Corp. v. Herndon, 1938, 180 Miss. 791, 178 So. 86 (picture theatre; schoolgirl bullied, accused of immoral conduct, threatened with arrest); Interstate Amusement Co. v. Martin, 1913, 8 Ala.App. 481, 62 So. 404 (plaintiff called up on stage of theatre and publicly humiliated); Boswell v. Barnum & Bailey, 1916, 135 Tenn. 35, 185 S.W. 692 (insult and abuse in argument over circus seats; "outrageous"); O'Connor v. Dallas Cotton Exchange, Tex.Civ.App.1941, 153 S.W.2d 266 (white woman ordered into elevator reserved for Negroes; an extreme outrage at the time in Texas?).

66. Magruder, Mental and Emotional Disturbance in the Law of Torts, 1936, 49 Harv.L.Rev. 1033, 1035.

67. Brooker v. Silverthorne, 1919, 111 S.C. 553, 99 S.E. 350; Ex parte Hammett, 1953, 259 Ala. 240, 66 So.2d 600; Halliday v. Cienkowski, 1939, 333 Pa.

aggravation, or for insults,[68] indignities or threats [69] which are considered to amount to nothing more than mere annoyances. The plaintiff cannot recover merely because he has had his feelings hurt.[70] Even the dire affront of inviting an unwilling woman to illicit intercourse has been held by most courts [71] to be no such outrage as to lead to liability—"the view being, apparently," in Judge Magruder's well-known words,[72] "that there is no harm in asking." It is only under the old statutes in Mississippi, Virginia, and West Virginia,[73] which had their origin as

part of an anti-dueling code, and which provide an action for "all words which from their usual construction and acceptation are considered as insults, and lead to violence and breach of the peace," that such an action will lie.

Extreme Outrage

There are, however, special situations of extreme misconduct in which recovery is allowed. The leading case which first broke through the shackles of the older law was Wilkinson v. Downton,[74] in which a practical joker amused himself by telling a woman that her husband had been smashed up in an accident and was lying at The Elms at Leytonstone with both legs broken, and that she was to go at once in a cab with two pillows to fetch him home. The shock to her nervous system produced serious and permanent physical consequences, which at one time threatened her reason, and entailed weeks of suffering and incapacity. The court obviously had no love for the defendant; and as in many another hard case, the enormity of the outrage overthrew the settled rule of law.

As other outrageous cases began to accumulate, the courts continued to struggle to find some familiar and traditional basis of liability; and when it was possible without too obvious pretense, the recovery was rested upon a technical assault,[75] battery,[76] false im-

---

123, 3 A.2d 372; Atkinson v. Bibb Mfg. Co., 1935, 50 Ga.App. 434, 178 S.E. 537; Johnson v. General Motors Acc. Corp., 5 Cir.1955, 228 F.2d 104.

68. Slocum v. Food Fair Stores of Florida, Fla.1958, 100 So.2d 396; Wallace v. Shoreham Hotel Corp., Mun.App.D.C.1946, 49 A.2d 81; Stavnezer v. Sage-Allen & Co., 1959, 146 Conn. 460, 152 A.2d 312; Republic Iron & Steel Co. v. Self, 1915, 192 Ala. 403, 68 So. 328; McPherson v. McCarrick, 1900, 22 Utah 232, 61 P. 1004.

69. Taft v. Taft, 1867, 40 Vt. 229; Stratton v. Posse Normal School of Gymnastics, 1928, 265 Mass. 223, 163 N.E. 905; State Nat. Bank of Iowa Park v. Rogers, Tex.Civ.App.1935, 89 S.W.2d 825; Gefter v. Rosenthal, 1956, 384 Pa. 123, 119 A.2d 250; McKinzie v. Huckaby, D.Okl.1953, 112 F.Supp. 642. Cf. Meek v. Harris, 1916, 110 Miss. 805, 71 So. 1; People's Finance & Thrift Co. v. Harwell, 1938, 183 Okl. 413, 82 P.2d 994; Perati v. Atkinson, 1963, 213 Cal. App.2d 472, 28 Cal.Rptr. 898.

70. Wallace v. Shoreham Hotel Corp., Mun.App.D.C. 1946, 49 A.2d 81.

71. Bennett v. McIntire, 1889, 121 Ind. 231, 23 N.E. 78; Reed v. Maley, 1903, 115 Ky. 816, 74 S.W. 1079; Prince v. Ridge, 1900, 32 Misc. 666, 66 N.Y.S. 454; Davis v. Richardson, 1905, 76 Ark. 348, 89 S.W. 318; Shepard v. Lamphier, 1914, 84 Misc. 498, 146 N.Y.S. 745. Cf. Clack v. Thomason, 1938, 57 Ga.App. 253, 195 S.E. 218 (making love to married woman and soliciting her to divorce her husband). In Erwin v. Milligan, 1934, 188 Ark. 658, 67 S.W.2d 592, recovery was allowed without mention of the technical battery apparent on the stated facts; and in Kurpgeweit v. Kirby, 1910, 88 Neb. 72, 129 N.W. 177, an "assault" was found where there was apparently no apprehension of force.

72. Magruder, Mental and Emotional Disturbance in the Law of Torts, 1936, 49 Harv.L.Rev. 1033, 1055.

73. Miss.Code Ann.1942, § 1059; Va.Code Ann.1950, § 8–630; W.Va.Code Ann.1955, § 5471. See Land-

rum v. Ellington, 1929, 152 Miss. 569, 120 So. 444; Michaelson v. Turk, 1916, 79 W.Va. 31, 90 S.E. 395; Huckabee v. Nash, 1938, 182 Miss. 754, 183 So. 500; Boyd v. Boyd, 1914, 116 Va. 326, 82 S.E. 110; Wade, Tort Liability for Abusive and Insulting Language, 1950, 4 Vand.L.Rev. 63, 82; Malone, Insult in Retaliation, 1939, 11 Miss.L.J. 333; Note, 1941, 27 Va.L.Rev. 405.

74. [1897] 2 Q.B.D. 57.

75. Atlanta Hub Co. v. Jones, 1933, 47 Ga.App. 778, 171 S.E. 470; Kurpgeweit v. Kirby, 1910, 88 Neb. 72, 129 N.W. 177; Leach v. Leach, 1895, 11 Tex. Civ.App. 699, 33 S.W. 703.

76. De May v. Roberts, 1881, 46 Mich. 160, 9 N.W. 146; Interstate Life & Accident Co. v. Brewer, 1937, 56 Ga.App. 599, 193 S.E. 458.

prisonment,[77] trespass to land,[78] nuisance,[79] or invasion of the right of privacy.[80] Gradually too many cases appeared in which no such traditional ground could be discovered; and somewhere around 1930 it began to be recognized that the intentional infliction of mental disturbance by extreme and outrageous conduct constituted a cause of action in itself.

So far as it is possible to generalize from the cases, the rule which seems to have emerged is that there is liability for conduct exceeding all bounds usually tolerated by decent society, of a nature which is especially calculated to cause, and does cause, mental distress of a very serious kind.[81] Such extreme outrage has been found, as in the leading Wilkinson case,[82] in decoying a woman

suspected of insanity to a hospital by a concocted tale of an injured husband and child;[83] in spreading the false rumor that the plaintiff's son had hanged himself;[84] in bringing a mob to the plaintiff's door at night with a threat to lynch him unless he left town;[85] and in wrapping up a very gory dead rat instead of a loaf of bread, for a sensitive soul to open.[86] The invitation to a woman to illicit intercourse, insufficient in itself,[87] becomes extreme outrage when it is prolonged or repeated to the point of hounding, and accompanied by advertising in the form of indecent pictures or exposure.[88]

The extreme and outrageous nature of the conduct may arise not so much from what is done as from abuse by the defendant of some relation or position which gives him actual or apparent power to damage the plaintiff's interests. The result is something very like extortion. Again the leading case is an English one, Janvier v. Sweeney,[89] where a private detective, representing himself to be a police officer, threatened to charge plaintiff with espionage unless she

77. Salisbury v. Poulson, 1918, 51 Utah 552, 172 P. 315.

78. Engle v. Simmons, 1906, 148 Ala. 92, 41 So. 1023; American Security Co. v. Cook, 1934, 49 Ga.App. 723, 176 S.E. 798; Continental Cas. Co. v. Garrett, 1935, 173 Miss. 676, 161 So. 753; Watson v. Dilts, 1902, 116 Iowa 249, 89 N.W. 1068; Bouillon v. Laclede Gas Light Co., 1910, 148 Mo.App. 462, 129 S.W. 401.

79. Shellabarger v. Morris, 1905, 115 Mo.App. 566, 91 S.W. 1005. Cf. Acadia, California, Ltd. v. Herbert, 1960, 54 Cal.2d 328, 5 Cal.Rptr. 686, 353 P.2d 294 (refusal to supply water to desert lands).

80. Brents v. Morgan, 1927, 221 Ky. 765, 299 S.W. 967.

81. Restatement of the Law, 1948 Supp., Torts, § 46, Comment *g*: "In short, the rule stated in this section imposes liability for intentionally causing severe emotional distress in those situations in which the actor's conduct has gone beyond all reasonable bounds of decency. The prohibited conduct is conduct which in the eyes of decent men and women in a civilized community is considered outrageous and intolerable. Generally, the case is one in which the recitation of the facts to an average member of the community would arouse his resentment against the actor and lead him to exclaim 'Outrageous!'"

Ohio has held back, in Bartow v. Smith, 1948, 149 Ohio St. 301, 78 N.E.2d 735, where defendant reviled a pregnant woman on the public street. The case is commented on, in 1949, 27 Mich.L.Rev. 436; 1949, 27 Tex.L.Rev. 730 ("distinctly and inexcusably retrogressive").

82. Supra, p. 74.

83. Savage v. Boies, 1954, 77 Ariz. 355, 272 P.2d 349.

84. Bielitski v. Obadiak, 1921, 61 Dom.L.Rep. 494.

85. Wilson v. Wilkins, 1930, 181 Ark. 137, 25 S.W.2d 428. Cf. Ruiz v. Bertolotti, 1962, 37 Misc.2d 1067, 236 N.Y.S.2d 854 (threat of harm to plaintiffs, Negroes, and their children, if they moved into neighborhood); Flamm v. Van Nierop, 1968, 56 Misc.2d 1059, 291 N.Y.S.2d 189 (hounding plaintiff on the streets).

86. Great A. & P. Tea Co. v. Roch, 1930, 160 Md. 189, 153 A. 22.

87. See supra, p. 40.

88. Samms v. Eccles, 1961, 11 Utah 2d 289, 358 P.2d 344; Mitran v. Williamson, 1960, 21 Misc.2d 106, 197 N.Y.S.2d 689. Cf. Webber v. Gray, 1957, 228 Ark. 289, 307 S.W.2d 80, where defendant, a former mistress of plaintiff, hounded him and his family, with incidents of aggravation, in an effort to renew the association. Also Halio v. Lurie, 1961, 15 App. Div.2d 62, 222 N.Y.S.2d 759, where a man who had jilted a woman wrote her jeering verses and taunting letters; and Tate v. Canonica, 1960, 180 Cal. App.2d 898, 5 Cal.Rptr. 28, where a man was driven to suicide by threats and accusations not set forth.

89. [1919] 2 K.B. 316.

surrendered private letters in her possession. Not far removed from this are the cases of bullying a school girl, with threats of prison and public disgrace, unless she signed a confession of immoral misconduct,[90] and the threats of an association of rubbish collectors to beat the plaintiff up, destroy his truck, and put him out of business, unless he paid over proceeds from a territory which they had allocated to one of their members.[91]

It is on this basis that the tort action has been used as a potent counter-weapon against the more outrageous high-pressure methods of collection agencies and other creditors. These are sufficiently well known,[92] ranging from violent cursing, abuse, and accusations of dishonesty,[93] through a series of letters in lurid envelopes bearing a picture of lightning about to strike, which repeatedly threaten arrest, ruination of credit, or a suit which is never brought,[94] or telephone calls around the clock,[95] or attempts to pile up the pressure by involving the plaintiff's employer, his relatives, his neighbors or the public in the controversy,[96] up to a call to a neighbor's telephone for an "emergency message" which will be a "great shock," [97] and a proposal to a woman to "take it out in trade." [98] It is seldom that any one such item of conduct is found alone in a case; and the liability usually has rested on a prolonged course of hounding by a variety of extreme methods.[99] Similar outrageous bullying tactics on the part of insurance adjusters seeking to force a settlement,[1] or evicting landlords seeking to

debtor's landlady with telephone calls. Her only remedy was held to be an action for the nuisance, since she was not the debtor.

90. Johnson v. Sampson, 1926, 167 Minn. 203, 208 N.W. 814.

91. State Rubbish Collectors Assn. v. Siliznoff, 1952, 38 Cal.2d 330, 240 P.2d 282.

92. See Birkhead, Collection Tactics of Illegal Lenders, 1941, 8 Law & Contemp.Prob. 78 ; Borda, One's Right to Enjoy Mental Peace and Tranquillity, 1939, 28 Geo.L.J. 55 ; Berger, The Bill Collector and the Law, 1968, 17 De Paul L.Rev. 327 ; Notes, 1939, 34 Ill.L.Rev. 505 ; 1957, 24 U.Chi.L.Rev. 572 ; 1957, 14 Wash. & Lee L.Rev. 167 ; 1957, 35 Chicago-Kent L.Rev. 145.

93. Kirby v. Jules Chain Stores Corp., 1936, 210 N.C. 808, 188 S.E. 625 ; American Security Co. v. Cook, 1934, 49 Ga.App. 723, 176 S.E. 798 ; American Finance & Loan Corp. v. Coots, 1962, 105 Ga.App. 849, 125 S.E.2d 689 (including pointing revolver).

94. Barnett v. Collection Service Co., 1932, 214 Iowa 1303, 242 N.W. 25 ; LaSalle Extension University v. Fogarty, 1934, 126 Neb. 457, 253 N.W. 424. Cf. Christensen v. Swedish Hospital, 1962, 59 Wash.2d 545, 368 P.2d 897 (threat of criminal prosecution); Abraham Used Car Co. v. Silva, Fla.App.1968, 208 So.2d 500 (same).

95. Moore v. Savage, Tex.Civ.App.1962, 359 S.W.2d 95, writ of error refused, N.R.E., 362 S.W.2d 298. Cf. Housh v. Peth, 1956, 165 Ohio St. 35, 133 N.E.2d 340 (held invasion of privacy). In Wiggins v. Moskins Credit Clothing Store, E.D.S.C.1956, 137 F. Supp. 764, there was continued harassing of the

96. Quina v. Roberts, La.App.1944, 16 So.2d 558 ; Barnett v. Collection Service Co., 1932, 214 Iowa 1303, 242 N.W. 25 ; LaSalle Extension University v. Fogarty, 1934, 126 Neb. 457, 253 N.W. 424 ; Moore v. Savage, Tex.Civ.App.1962, 359 S.W.2d 95, writ of error refused, n. r. e. 362 S.W.2d 298 ; Booty v. American Finance Corp. of Shreveport, La.App.1969, 224 So.2d 512, application denied 254 La. 782, 226 So.2d 771.
Cf. Tollefson v. Price, 1967, 247 Or. 398, 430 P.2d 990 (publication of name in list of undisputed delinquent accounts, where disputed).

97. Bowden v. Spiegel, Inc., 1950, 96 Cal.App.2d 793, 216 P.2d 571. Cf. Lyons v. Zale Jewelry Co., 1963, 246 Miss. 139, 150 So.2d 154 (swearing at woman over telephone).

98. Digsby v. Carroll Baking Co., 1948, 76 Ga.App. 656, 47 S.E.2d 203.

99. There was not much that the defendant overlooked in Duty v. General Finance Co., 1954, 154 Tex. 16, 273 S.W.2d 64. See also Advance Loan Service v. Mandik, Tex.Civ.App.1957, 306 S.W.2d 754 ; Salazar v. Bond Finance Co., Tex.Civ.App. 1966, 410 S.W.2d 839, refused n. r. e. ; Lyons v. Zale Jewelry Co., 1963, 246 Miss. 139, 150 So.2d 154 ; Warren v. Parrish, Mo.1969, 436 S.W.2d 670.
It goes without saying that reasonable attempts at collection are not actionable. Berrier v. Beneficial Finance, Inc., D.Ind.1964, 234 F.Supp. 204 ; Passman v. Commercial Credit Plan of Hammond, Inc., La. App.1969, 220 So.2d 758, application denied 254 La. 287, 223 So.2d 410 ; Whatley v. K-Mart Discount Stores, Tex.Civ.App.1970, 451 S.W.2d 568 (wrong person).

1. Continental Cas. Co. v. Garrett, 1935, 173 Miss. 676, 161 So. 753 ; Pacific Mut. Ins. Co. v. Tetirick, 1938, 185 Okl. 37, 89 P.2d 774 ; National Life & Acc. Ins. Co. v. Anderson, 1940, 187 Okl. 180, 102 P.2d

harass unwanted tenants,[2] have been subjected to the same liability.

Still another basis on which extreme outrage can be found is the defendant's knowledge [3] that the plaintiff is especially sensitive, susceptible and vulnerable to injury through mental distress at the particular conduct. This goes back to a Louisiana case [4] in which the defendants buried a "pot of gold" for an eccentric and mentally deficient old maid to find, and when she dug it up escorted her in triumph to the city hall, where she opened the pot under circumstances of public humiliation. In line with this case there are a number of decisions in which sick people [5] children,[6] and pregnant women [7]

have recovered, on the basis of the defendant's knowledge of their condition, for profanity and abuse, threatening letters, or other conduct which apparently would not otherwise have been sufficient to constitute a tort.

Finally, there are a great many cases involving the mishandling of dead bodies, whether by mutilation,[8] disinterment,[9] interference with proper burial,[10] or other forms of intentional [11] disturbance.[12] In most of

S.E. 458; Pacific Mut. Life Ins. Co. v. Tetirick, 1938, 185 Okl. 37, 89 P.2d 774; National Life & Acc. Ins. Co. v. Anderson, 1940, 187 Okl. 180, 102 P.2d 141. This is apparently the basis on which "nigger" to a black man has been held actionable. Alcorn v. Anbro Engineering Inc., 1970, 2 Cal.2d 568, 86 Cal. Rptr. 88, 468 P.2d 216.

6. Delta Finance Co. v. Ganakas, 1956, 93 Ga.App. 297, 91 S.E.2d 383 (intimidation); Korbin v. Berlin, Fla.App.1965, 177 So.2d 551 (vilifying mother).

7. Alabama Fuel & Iron Co. v. Baladoni, 1916, 15 Ala.App. 316, 73 So. 205; Richardson v. Pridmore, 1950, 97 Cal.App.2d 124, 217 P.2d 113; Vargas v. Ruggiero, 1961, 197 Cal.App.2d 709, 17 Cal.Rptr. 568. Cf. Turner v. ABC Jalousie Co. of N. C., 1968, 251 S.C. 92, 160 S.E.2d 528 (frightening lone woman).

8. Alderman v. Ford, 1937, 146 Kan. 698, 72 P.2d 981; Hill v. Travelers Ins. Co., 1927, 154 Tenn. 295, 294 S.W. 1097; Crenshaw v. O'Connell, 1941, 235 Mo.App. 1085, 150 S.W.2d 489; French v. Ochsner Clinic, La. App.1967, 200 So.2d 371, writ refused 251 La. 34, 202 So.2d 652; Jackson v. Rupp, Fla.App.1970, 228 So.2d 916.

9. Gostkowski v. Roman Catholic Church of Sacred Hearts of Jesus and Mary, 1933, 262 N.Y. 320, 186 N.E. 798; England v. Central Pocahontas Coal Co., 1920, 86 W.Va. 575, 104 S.E. 46; Spomer v. City of Grand Junction, 1960, 144 Colo. 207, 355 P.2d 960. Cf. Boyle v. Chandler, 1927, 3 W.W.Harr., Del., 323, 138 A. 273 (removal from casket).

10. Finley v. Atlantic Transport Co., 1917, 220 N.Y. 249, 115 N.E. 715 (burial at sea); Spiegel v. Evergreen Cemetery, 1936, 117 N.J.L. 90, 186 A. 585 (in absence of relatives); Kirksey v. Jernigan, Fla.1950, 45 So.2d 188 (holding unburied); Papieves v. Lawrence, 437 Pa. 373, 263 A.2d 118.

11. As to negligence, see infra, p. 329.

12. Sworski v. Simons, 1940, 208 Minn. 201, 293 N.W. 309 (unauthorized embalming); Wilson v. St. Louis & S. F. R. Co., 1912, 160 Mo.App. 649, 142 S.W. 775 (mishandling); Sanford v. Ware, 1950, 191 Va. 43, 60 S.E.2d 10 (misburial); Brownlee v. Pratt, 1946, 77 Ohio App. 533, 68 N.E.2d 798 (burial of intruder in lot). See Note, 1958, 19 Ohio St.L.J. 455.

141; Frishett v. State Farm Mut. Auto. Ins. Co., 1966, 3 Mich.App. 688, 143 N.W.2d 612. Cf. Fletcher v. Western Nat. Life Ins. Co., 1970, 10 Cal.App.3d 376, 89 Cal.Rptr. 78 (bad faith refusal to settle claim, to put pressure on insured).

But coming to plaintiff's home and cajoling her into a settlement is not actionable. Cluff v. Farmers Ins. Exchange, 1969, 10 Ariz.App. 560, 460 P.2d 666.

2. Emden v. Vitz, 1948, 88 Cal.App.2d 313, 198 P.2d 696; Duncan v. Donnell, Tex.Civ.App.1928, 12 S.W. 2d 811; Louisville & N. R. Co. v. Roberts, 1925, 207 Ky. 310, 269 S.W. 333; Scheman v. Schlein, 1962, 35 Misc.2d 581, 231 N.Y.S.2d 548; Kaufman v. Abramson, 4 Cir. 1966, 363 F.2d 865.

Compare, as unusual cases, Curnett v. Wolf, 1953, 244 Iowa 683, 57 N.W.2d 915 (threat to have plaintiff discharged unless he dismissed a suit); Guillory v. Godfrey, 1955, 134 Cal.App.2d 628, 286 P.2d 474 (intimidation of customers away from liquor store); Tate v. Canonica, 1960, 180 Cal.App.2d 898, 5 Cal.Rptr. 28 (driven to suicide by unspecified threats and blackmail).

3. If there is no such knowledge, conduct otherwise not sufficiently extreme leads to no liability, even though plaintiff may in fact suffer injury because of it. Braun v. Craven, 1898, 175 Ill. 401, 51 N.E. 657; Carrigan v. Henderson, 1943, 192 Okl. 254, 135 P.2d 330; Haas v. Metz, 1898, 78 Ill.App. 46; Kramer v. Ricksmeier, 1913, 159 Iowa 48, 139 N.W. 1091.

4. Nickerson v. Hodges, 1920, 146 La. 735, 84 So. 37. The pot of gold came to her heirs, in the form of $500 damages.

5. Clark v. Associated Retail Credit Men, 1939, 70 App.D.C. 183, 105 F.2d 62; Continental Cas. Co. v. Garrett, 1935, 173 Misc. 676, 161 So. 753; Interstate Life & Acc. Co. v. Brewer, 1937, 56 Ga.App. 599, 193

these cases the courts have talked of a somewhat dubious "property right" [13] to the body, usually in the next of kin,[14] which did not exist while the decedent was living, cannot be conveyed, can be used only for the one purpose of burial, and not only has no pecuniary value but is a source of liability for funeral expenses. It seems reasonably obvious that such "property" is something evolved out of thin air to meet the occasion, and that it is in reality the personal feelings of the survivors which are being protected, under a fiction likely to deceive no one but a lawyer.

There are two cases [15] which have avoided all of these difficulties by recognizing what is sufficiently obvious, that the tort is in reality merely the intentional infliction of mental distress.

The emotional distress must in fact exist, and it must be severe. If the plaintiff is not impressed by the defendant's threatening letter, and is only sufficiently concerned to make an effort to discover who wrote it, the minor annoyance and affront to his dignity are too trivial to support a tort action.[16] Furthermore, except in cases where the defendant has knowledge of the plaintiff's peculiar susceptibility and practices upon it, the distress must be such as a reasonable man "of ordinary sensibilities" would undergo under the circumstances.[17]

In the great majority of the cases allowing recovery the genuineness of the mental disturbance has been evidenced by resulting physical illness of a serious character, and both the mental and the physical elements have been compensated. Texas has said flatly that physical illness or some other non-mental damage is essential to the existence of the tort,[18] and there are other cases which look as if it were considered indispensable.[19] On the other hand, there are a substantial number of decisions which have found liability for mere mental disturbance without any evidence of physical consequences. The mere recital, for example, of the fact that a mob came to the plaintiff's house at night with a threat to lynch him unless he left town, leaves no doubt at all that the emotional upset to which the plaintiff testifies was real.[20]

---

13. See Note, 1934, 18 Minn.L.Rev. 204.

14. See Koerber v. Patek, 1920, 123 Wis. 453, 102 N. W. 40; Gostkowski v. Roman Catholic Church of Sacred Hearts of Jesus and Mary, 1933, 262 N.Y. 320, 186 N.E. 798; Boyle v. Chandler, 1927, 3 W.W. Harr., Del. 323, 138 A. 273; Stephens v. Waits, 1936, 53 Ga.App. 44, 184 S.E. 781. See, Generally, Green, Relational Interests, 1934, 29 Ill.L.Rev. 460, 489; Notes, 1934, 18 Minn.L.Rev. 204; 1926, 74 U.Pa.L. Rev. 404; 1933, 19 Corn.L.Q. 108.

15. Gadbury v. Bleitz, 1925, 133 Wash. 134, 233 P. 299; Stephens v. Waits, 1936, 53 Ga.App. 44, 184 S.E. 781.

16. Taft v. Taft, 1867, 40 Vt. 229.

17. March v. Cacioppo, 1962, 37 Ill.App.2d 235, 185 N.E.2d 397 (obtaining void judgment and garnishment of bank account, not enough); cf. Nelson v.

Crawford, 1899, 122 Mich. 466, 81 N.W. 335 (hysterical fright at man dressed in woman's clothing); Oehler v. L. Bamberger & Co., 1927, 103 N.J.L. 703, 137 A. 425, affirming 1926, 4 N.J.Misc. 1003, 135 A. 71 (stroke at repossession of vacuum cleaner).

18. Duty v. General Finance Co., 1954, 154 Tex. 16, 273 S.W.2d 64, distinguishing on this basis Harned v. E–Z Finance Co., 1953, 151 Tex. 641, 254 S.W.2d 81. But in Western Guaranty Loan Co. v. Dean, Tex.Civ. App.1958, 309 S.W.2d 857, refused n. r. e., where there was other damage in plaintiff's discharge from his employment, it was held that physical illness was not required.

19. Kirby v. Jules Chain Stores Corp., 1936, 210 N.C. 808, 188 S.E. 625; Carrigan v. Henderson, 1943, 192 Okl. 254, 135 P.2d 330; Clark v. Associated Retail Credit Men, 1939, 70 U.S.App.D.C. 183, 105 F.2d 62.

20. Wilson v. Wilkins, 1930, 181 Ark. 137, 25 S.W.2d 428. Cf. Savage v. Boies, 1954, 77 Ariz. 355, 272 P. 2d 349 (police decoying plaintiff to hospital by report her husband and child were injured); Barnett v. Collection Service Co., 1932, 214 Iowa 1303, 242 N.W. 25 (extreme collection letters); La Salle Extension University v. Fogarty, 1934, 126 Neb. 457, 253 N.W. 424 (same); Delta Finance Co. v. Ganakas, 1956, 93 Ga.App. 297, 91 S.E.2d 383 (frightening child); Samms v. Eccles, 1961, 11 Utah 2d 289, 358 P.2d 344 (invitation to illicit intercourse and indecent exposure); Mitran v. Williamson, 1960, 21 Misc.2d 106, 197 N.Y.S.2d 689 (same); Curnett v. Wolf, 1953, 244 Iowa 683, 57 N.W.2d 915 (threat to have plaintiff discharged unless he dismissed suit); State Rubbish Collectors Ass'n v. Siliznoff,

In 1948 a section of the Restatement of Torts [21] was amended to reject any absolute necessity for physical results. Probably the conclusion to be reached is that where physical harm is lacking the courts will properly tend to look for more in the way of extreme outrage as an assurance that the mental disturbance claimed is not fictitious; but that if the enormity of the outrage itself carries conviction that there has in fact been severe and serious mental distress, which is neither feigned nor trivial, bodily harm is not required.

In the great majority of the cases allowing recovery the mental distress has been inflicted intentionally, either in the sense that the defendant desired to cause it, or that he knew that it was substantially certain to follow from his conduct. There are, however, a few cases which indicate that liability for extreme outrage is broader than intent, and that it extends to situations in which there is no certainty, but merely a high degree of probability that the mental distress will follow, and the defendant goes ahead in conscious disregard of it. This is the type of conduct which commonly is given the name of wilful or wanton, or sometimes recklessness. The most striking case is one in Iowa [22] in which the defendant decided that it would be a good idea to commit suicide by cutting his throat in the plaintiff's kitchen, and she returned to be confronted with his corpse, with blood all over the premises. There are a few other decisions [23] of the same general nature, which appear to indicate very definitely that the category of extreme outrage is to be extended to include conduct not intended to cause mental disturbance, but wilful, wanton or reckless in its deliberate disregard of a known high degree of risk of it.

Acts Directed at a Third Person

Where the mental distress is caused by the defendant's conduct which is not directed at the plaintiff, but at a third person, other problems arise. The first possibility that comes to mind is that the doctrine of "transferred intent" [24] found in the battery cases might be applied to permit recovery. There seems to be little reason to apply it when the plaintiff suffers physical harm, and to reject it where there is mental damage. It is a strange distinction which allows damages when the plaintiff is struck by a bullet aimed at another, and denies them when it frightens her into serious illness,[25] or finds a cause of action in mental disturbance at the mistreatment of household furniture, and none in shock at the sight of the mutilated body of a murdered sister.[26] But, probably for the simple reason that emotional distress did not fall within the framework of the old action of trespass where "transferred intent" arose, there is only one

---

1952, 38 Cal.2d 330, 240 P.2d 282 (threats of violence in gangster atmosphere).

21. Restatement of the Law, 1948 Supp., Torts, § 46. This has been retained, and covered by Comment *k*, in the Second Restatement of Torts, § 46.

22. Blakeley v. Shortal's Estate, 1945, 236 Iowa 787, 20 N.W.2d 28. Compare the appalling story in Mahnke v. Moore, 1951, 197 Md. 61, 77 A.2d 923, where, however, the shock to the child was so certain that it clearly must be classified as intentional.

23. Bielitski v. Obadiak, 1921, 15 Sask. 153, 61 Dom. L.Rep. 494 (defendant spread rumor plaintiff's son had hanged himself, knowing that it was very likely

to reach her); Price v. Yellow Pine Paper Mill Co., Tex.Civ.App.1922, 240 S.W. 588 (injured husband brought home in shocking condition and delivered abruptly to his pregnant wife); Boyle v. Chandler, 1927, 33 Del. 323, 138 A. 273 (reckless handling of dead body); Lindh v. Great Northern R. Co., 1906, 99 Minn. 408, 109 N.W. 823 (same); Anderson v. Knox, 9 Cir. 1961, 297 F.2d 702, cert. denied 370 U.S. 915 (reckless bad advice as to insurance program). See, however, Alsteen v. Gehl, 1963, 21 Wis. 2d 349, 124 N.W.2d 312, rejecting recklessness as a basis for the tort.

24. See supra p. 32.

25. Compare Corn v. Sheppard, 1930, 179 Minn. 490, 229 N.W. 869, with Renner v. Canfield, 1886, 36 Minn. 90, 30 N.W. 435.

26. Compare Rose Co. v. Lowery, 1929, 33 Ohio App. 488, 169 N.E. 716 (and see the trespass cases, supra, note 78), with Koontz v. Keller, 1936, 52 Ohio App. 265, 3 N.E.2d 694.

West Virginia case [27] which has so much as mentioned it by analogy in allowing recovery for fright at a battery committed upon the plaintiff's father.

Other courts, rejecting "transferred intent," have rather regarded the plaintiff's mental distress as so substantially certain to follow, under the circumstances, that it must be treated as itself intended, and have allowed recovery on that basis.[28] In others stress is laid upon the foreseeability of the mental effect upon the plaintiff, and it seems to have been concluded that there was some kind of negligence toward her,[29] which justifies the recovery. On the facts of all of these cases, it would appear that there was a very high degree of probability that the mental disturbance would follow, and that the defendant proceeded in conscious and deliberate disregard of it, so that his conduct would properly be called wilful, wanton or reckless.

There are other cases in which recovery has been denied, usually on the ground that the mental disturbance was not a thing that could reasonably have been anticipated.[30]

The decisions indicate that recovery in such cases is limited to plaintiffs who are not only present at the time,[31] but are known by the defendant to be present,[32] so that the mental effect can reasonably be anticipated by the defendant. The distinction between the wife who sees her husband shot down before her eyes, and the one who hears about it five minutes later, may be a highly artificial one; but it is perhaps justified by the obvious necessity of drawing a line somewhere short of the widow who learns of the decease ten years afterward, when the genuineness and gravity of her distress may very reasonably be doubted.

There is the further question of whether the recovery should be limited to near relatives of the person attacked, or at least to close associates, where there is some additional guarantee that the mental disturbance is real and extreme. Nearly all of the cases allowing recovery have involved members of the immediate family; but there are two [33] which have not. It may be suggested that when a complete stranger is asked for a match on the street and the individual who asks for it is suddenly shot down before his eyes, the mental shock may be very genuine and severe, and that a pregnant bystander

27. Lambert v. Brewster, 1924, 97 W.Va. 124, 125 S.E. 244.

28. Jeppsen v. Jensen, 1916, 47 Utah 536, 155 P. 429 ("assault" upon the plaintiff); Rogers v. Williard, (1920) 144 Ark. 587, 223 S.W. 15 (quarrel in presence of pregnant woman); Purdy v. Woznesensky, Sask. [1937] 2 W.W.R. 116. A clear case of intent is Knierim v. Izzo, 1961, 22 Ill.2d 73, 174 N.E.2d 157, where defendant told plaintiff that he would murder her husband, and then did so. See Note, [1961] U.Ill.Law Forum 535.

29. Hill v. Kimball, 1890, 76 Tex. 210, 13 S.W. 59; Young v. Western & Atlantic R. Co., 1929, 39 Ga.App. 761, 148 S.E. 414; Duncan v. Donnell, Tex.Civ.App. 1929, 12 S.W.2d 811; Watson v. Dilts, 1902, 116 Iowa 249, 89 N.W. 1068. See Hallen, Hill v. Kimball—A Milepost in the Law, 1933, 12 Tex.L.Rev. 1.

30. Phillips v. Dickerson, 1877, 85 Ill. 11; Hutchinson v. Stern, 1906, 115 App.Div. 791, 101 N.Y.S. 145, dismissed 1908, 189 N.Y. 577, 82 N.E. 1128; Ellsworth v. Massacar, 1921, 215 Mich. 511, 184 N.W. 408; Reed v. Ford, 1908, 129 Ky. 471, 112 S.W. 600; Goddard v. Watters, 1914, 14 Ga.App. 722, 82 S.E. 304.

31. There is no case allowing recovery where the plaintiff was not present. Magruder, Mental and Emotional Disturbance in the Law of Torts, 1936, 49 Harv.L.Rev. 1033, 1044. Recovery was denied in Koontz v. Keller, 1936, 52 Ohio App. 265, 3 N.E.2d 694 (discovery of body of murdered sister); Ellsworth v. Massacar, 1921, 215 Mich. 511, 184 N.W. 408 (later discovery of attack on husband); Knox v. Allen, 1926, 4 La.App. 223 (same as to attack on child).

32. Phillips v. Dickerson, 1877, 85 Ill. 11 (plaintiff in another room); Hutchinson v. Stern, 1906, 115 App. Div. 791, 101 N.Y.S. 145 ("present and nearby" but not in sight); Reed v. Ford, 1908, 129 Ky. 471, 112 N.W. 600 (near, but not known to be there); Goddard v. Watters, 1914, 14 Ga.App. 722, 82 S.E. 304 (plaintiff ran out to see what was happening); Taylor v. Vallelunga, 1959, 171 Cal.App.2d 107, 339 P.2d 910 (plaintiff witnessed beating of her father; not pleaded defendant knew she was present). In Bunyan v. Jordan, Aust.1936, 57 Comm.L.Rep. 1, defendant pretended to commit suicide to frighten A, and B, who overheard but was not known to be present, was not allowed to recover.

33. Hill v. Kimball, 1890, 76 Tex. 210, 13 S.W. 59; Rogers v. Williard, 1920, 144 Ark. 587, 223 S.W. 15.

who witnesses a bloody beating may suffer a real injury entitled to compensation. The language of the cases themselves does not suggest any such arbitrary limitation, and it does not appear to be called for.

In short, the law appears to be moving in the direction of liability; but thus far recovery is clearly limited to the most extreme cases of violent attack, where there is some especial likelihood of fright or shock, usually on the part of a woman.[34]

34. Thus recovery was denied in Hunt v. Calacino, D.D.C.1953, 114 F.Supp. 254 (threat of jail sentence to son); Bucknam v. Great Northern R. Co., 1899, 76 Minn. 373, 79 N.W. 98 (violent language to husband); Sanderson v. Northern Pac. R. Co., 1902, 88 Minn. 162, 92 N.W. 542 (putting children off of train); Ellis v. Cleveland, 1883, 55 Vt. 358 (wrongful arrest of husband); Sperier v. Ott, 1906, 116 La. 1087, 41 So. 323 (wrongful arrest of son).

CHAPTER 3

INTENTIONAL INTERFERENCE WITH

PROPERTY

13. TRESPASS TO LAND

The law pertaining to trespass upon land has been described as "both exceptionally simple and exceptionally rigorous." [1] In the eyes of the common law, every unauthorized entry upon the soil of another was a trespass, [2] "for the law bounds every man's property and is his fence." [3] The strict and severe rules of the action of trespass, to which reference has previously been made, [4] have survived to a considerable extent until quite modern times, and the courts have been slow to modify them as in the case of injuries to the person. Some of them are only now passing out of the picture. This survival, which sometimes has resulted in distinctions between person and property that can only be described as highly artificial and unreasonable, probably was due primarily to the fact that upon the action of trespass was placed the burden of vindicating property rights, and claims to possession and ownership. Since in the usual case the important question was the disputed title, and any technical invasion would serve as the basis of litigation to settle it, the rules as to the character of the tort itself tended to become fixed, [5] and to remain so.

Strict Liability

The most important of the trespass rules to survive was that which imposed liability for invasions of property which were neither intended nor negligent. The defendant was not liable so long as he had done no voluntary act, as where he was carried onto the plaintiff's land by others against his will. [6] But if, without negligence, he felled a tree, [7] or dammed a stream, [8] or operated a street car [9]

---

1. 1 Street, Foundations of Legal Liability, 1906, 19.

2. 3 Bl.Comm. 209; Brame v. Clark, 1908, 148 N.C. 364, 62 S.E. 418.

3. Star v. Rookesby, 1711, 1 Salk. 336, 91 Eng.Rep. 295; 3 Bl.Comm. 209.

4. See supra, § 7.

5. "The law unquestionably does not prize property more than it does personal security, but at some points it has put forth more energetic efforts to protect property than it has to protect personal security. When it was once determined that a man could resort to a form of trespass to settle a matter of disputed title, the character of the trespass upon realty was fixed. Thenceforth the common law, in considering liability for intrusions upon realty, could not undertake to discriminate between the much and the little." 1 Street, Foundations of Legal Liability, 1906, 25. See also 8 Holdsworth, History of English Law, 1923, 467; Note, 1933, 5 Rocky Mt.L.Rev. 286.

6. Smith v. Stone, 1647, Style 65, 82 Eng.Rep. 533; Carter v. Thurston, 1877, 58 N.H. 104 (logs carried onto plaintiff's land by a stream). Thus one who slips and falls, or is otherwise carried onto the land by something beyond his control, is not a trespasser. Puchlopek v. Portsmouth Power Co., 1926, 82 N.H. 440, 136 A. 259; Durst v. Wareham, 1931, 132 Kan. 785, 297 P. 675; Edgarton v. H. P. Welch Co., 1947, 321 Mass. 603, 74 N.E.2d 674.

7. Newsom v. Anderson, 1841, 2 Ired., N.C., 42.

8. Lawson v. Price, 1876, 45 Md. 123; McKee v. Delaware & H. Canal Co., 1891, 125 N.Y. 353, 26 N.E. 305. This was apparently, and rather unaccountably, followed in Corrington v. Kalicak, Mo. App.1959, 319 S.W.2d 888.

9. Louisville R. Co. v. Sweeney, 1914, 157 Ky. 620, 163 S.W. 739. Cf. Happy Coal Co. v. Smith, 1929, 229 Ky. 716, 17 S.W.2d 1008; West Virginia Cent. & P. R. Co. v. Fuller, 1903, 96 Md. 652, 54 A. 669; Van Alstyne v. Rochester Tel. Corp., 1937, 163 Misc. 258, 296 N.Y.S. 726. These results are actually

upon his own property, and his act resulted in the tree, stream or car going directly upon the land of another, he was liable for the consequences. The same result was reached in a number of cases [10] in which the defendant, engaged in blasting operations, threw rocks or rubbish upon the plaintiff's land; and here it was perhaps justified by the highly dangerous and unusual character of the enterprise.[11]

There is no great triumph of reason in a rule which makes a street railway, whose car jumps the track, liable only for negligence to a pedestrian on the sidewalk, but absolutely liable to the owner of the plate-glass window behind him. The strict rule appears to have been repudiated in England,[12] where it was born, and it is safe to say that it is almost at its last gasp in the United States. In the famous Nitro-Glycerine Case,[13] the servants

of a carrier innocently opened with a hammer a box which was leaking nitro-glycerine, and the resulting explosion damaged the plaintiff's premises. The Supreme Court refused to hold the carrier liable for trespass, in the absence of intent or negligence. Other cases, in a variety of situations,[14] have agreed, and Kentucky, which was one of the strongholds of the old rule, has thrown it overboard in a case [15] where a rock was thrown up by the wheels of a truck, and onto the land of the plaintiff. The rule still survives in New York and Texas, which may be the only states; but the latest decisions in both jurisdictions [16] narrowly limit it to cases in which the defendant has done some affirmative volitional act which immediately causes the invasion of the land; and this appears to foreshadow ultimate abandonment. The present prevailing position is that of the Restatement of Torts,[17] which finds liability for tres-

---

defended in Clark, Trespass Quare Clausum Fregit, 1960, 12 Ala.L.Rev. 301.

10. Hay v. Cohoes County, 1849, 2 N.Y. 159; Mulchanock v. Whitehall Cement Mfg. Co., 1916, 253 Pa. 262, 98 A. 554; Adams & Sullivan v. Sengel, 1917, 177 Ky. 535, 197 S.W. 974; Asheville Const. Co. v. Southern R. Co., 4 Cir.1927, 19 F.2d 32; Hakkila v. Old Colony Broken Stone & Concrete Co., 1928, 264 Mass. 447, 162 N.E. 895. Cf. Wheeler v. Norton, 1904, 92 App.Div. 368, 86 N.Y.S. 1095 (blasting resulting in flooding); Rochester Gas & Elec. Co. v. Dunlop, 1933, 148 Misc. 849, 266 N.Y.S. 469 (airplane crash). See Smith, Liability for Substantial Physical Damage to Land by Blasting, 1920, 33 Harv.L. Rev. 442.

11. See infra, p. 513. Cf. United Electric Light Co. v. Deliso Const. Co., 1943, 315 Mass. 313, 52 N.E.2d 553, where the defendant constructed an underground tunnel, and forced liquid cement at high pressure against plaintiff's wires. The court found strict liability for "an improper and unreasonable use by the defendant of the space allotted to it."

12. It was rejected as to trespass to chattels, with implications as to any trespass, in National Coal Board v. J. C. Evans Co., [1951] 2 K.B. 861. The decision was at least foreshadowed in Gayler & Pope v. Davies & Son, [1924] 2 K.B. 75; and see Fowler v. Lanning, [1959] 1 Q.B. 426. See Winfield and Goodhart, Trespass and Negligence, 1933, 49 L.Q.Rev. 359.

13. Parrott v. Wells Fargo & Co., 1872, 15 Wall., U.S., 524.

14. Brown v. Collins, 1873, 53 N.H. 442 (runaway horse); Boyd v. White, 1954, 128 Cal.App.2d 641, 276 P.2d 92 (airplane crash); Wisconsin Power & Light Co. v. Columbia County, 1958, 3 Wis.2d 1, 87 N.W.2d 279 (tower caused to tilt by dirt dumped near it); Smith v. Pate, 1957, 246 N.C. 63, 97 S.E. 2d 457 (automobile crashed into building); Gallin v. Poulou, 1956, 140 Cal.App.2d 638, 295 P.2d 958 (damage to building from vibration); Hawke v. Maus, 1967, 141 Ind.App. 126, 226 N.E.2d 713 (entry due to collision).

15. Randall v. Shelton, Ky.1956, 293 S.W.2d 559. See Notes, 1957, 46 Ky.L.J. 187; 1957, 14 Wash. & Lee L.Rev. 319.

16. Phillips v. Sun Oil Co., 1954, 307 N.Y. 328, 121 N.E.2d 249 (leakage of oil from tank); Wood v. United Airlines, 1962, 32 Misc.2d 955, 223 N.Y.S.2d 692, affirmed 1962, 16 App.Div.2d 659, 226 N.Y.S.2d 1022, appeal dismissed 11 N.Y.2d 1053, 230 N.Y.S.2d 207, 184 N.E.2d 180 (crash of plane out of control); First City Nat. Bank of Houston v. Japhet, Tex. Civ.App.1965, 390 S.W.2d 70, error dismissed (motorist suffered heart attack, ran onto land).

17. "Except where the actor is engaged in an abnormally dangerous activity, an unintentional and non-negligent entry on land in the possession of another or causing a thing or third person to enter the land, does not subject the actor to liability to the possessor, even though the entry causes harm to the possessor or to a thing or third person in whose security the possessor has a legally protected interest." Second Restatement of Torts, § 166.

pass only in the case of intentional intrusion, or negligence,[18] or some "abnormally dangerous activity" [19] on the part of the defendant.

The problem arises in connection with damage to land caused by the forced landing [20] of airplanes, or by objects falling from them.[21]

In cases arising in New York [22] strict liability has been imposed on the basis of trespass; but most of the other decisions have turned upon the dispute as to whether aviation is to be treated as an abnormal and excessively hazardous activity, which is to be considered in a later chapter.[23]

Direct and Indirect Invasions

A second survival is that of the old distinction between direct and indirect invasions of the property, found in the actions of trespass and case.[24] If the defendant threw water on his neighbor's land, it was a trespass; [25] but if he merely constructed a spout,[26] or obstructed or diverted a stream so that as a result the water ultimately flowed onto the premises of the plaintiff,[27] the action was on the case. The chief importance of the distinction lay in the fact that case required proof of negligence or intent, as well as substantial damage, while trespass did not.

In a series of blasting cases,[28] a number of courts have held that injuries due to vibration or concussion, as distinguished from the actual arrival of a rock in the plaintiff's parlor, were indirect and so not actionable without proof of negligence. This distinction is now rejected by most courts,[29] and would appear to be slowly on its way to oblivion. The Restatement of Torts [30] has abandoned any distinction between direct and indirect invasions where there is an actual entry of a person or thing upon the plaintiff's land, and classes both as trespass. Injuries due to concussion are left to fall into the category of nuisance,[31] or strict liability based on the dangerous character of the enterprise.[32] But

18. Thus Zimmer v. Stephenson, 1965, 66 Wash.2d 477, 403 P.2d 343.

19. Thus Loe v. Lenhardt, 1961, 227 Or. 242, 362 P.2d 312; Young v. Darter, Okl.1961, 363 P.2d 829 (crop dusting).

20. Wood v. United Airlines, 1962, 32 Misc.2d 955, 223 N.Y.S.2d 692, affirmed 1962, 16 App.Div.2d 659, 226 N.Y.S.2d 1022, draws a distinction, suggested by some writers, between a forced but intentional landing, and a plane entirely out of control. In the latter case it was held that the invasion was not due to any volitional act of the defendant, as where his horse runs away with him. Cf. Gibbons v. Pepper, 1695, 1 Ld.Raym. 38, 91 Eng.Rep. 922. In the former, the invasion might be privileged to a limited extent, but the defendant might be required to pay for any damage which resulted. See infra, § 24; Notes, 1933, 33 Col.L.Rev. 1459; 1933, 47 Harv.L.Rev. 345.

21. See Bohlen, Aviation Under the Common Law, 1934, 45 Harv.L.Rev. 216; Vold and Wolf, Aircraft Operator's Liability for Ground Damage and Passenger Injury, 1935, 13 Neb.L.B. 373; Sweeney, Adjusting the Conflicting Interests of Landowner and Aviator in Anglo-American Law, 1932, 3 J.Air Law 329, 531.

22. Rochester Gas & Elec. Corp. v. Dunlop, 1933, 148 Misc. 849, 266 N.Y.S. 469; Margosian v. United States Airlines, E.D.N.Y.1955, 127 F.Supp. 464; Hahn v. United States Airlines, E.D.N.Y.1954, 127 F.Supp. 950.

23. See infra, p. 514.

24. See supra, § 7.

25. Prewitt v. Clayton, 1827, 5 T.B.Mon., Ky., 4; Wheeler v. Norton, 1904, 92 App.Div. 368, 86 N.Y.S. 1095 (breaking water pipe). Cf. Van Alstyne v. Rochester Tel. Corp., 1937, 163 Misc. 258, 296 N.Y.S. 726.

26. Reynolds v. Clarke, 1725, 1 Strange 634, 2 Ld. Raym. 1399, 93 Eng.Rep. 747. Or if water is discharged onto A's property, and then flows onto that of B, B's action is on the case. Nicholls v. Ely Beet Sugar Factory, [1931] 2 Ch. 84.

27. Suter v. Wenatchee Water Power Co., 1904, 35 Wash. 1, 76 P. 298; Butala v. Union Elec. Co., 1924, 70 Mont. 580, 226 P. 899; Norwood v. Eastern Oregon Land Co., 1931, 139 Or. 25, 5 P.2d 1057, modified 1932, 139 Or. 25, 7 P.2d 996; Scheurich v. Empire Dist. Elec. Co., Mo.1916, 188 S.W. 114; Walter v. Wagner, 1928, 225 Ky. 255, 8 S.W.2d 421.

28. See infra, p. 513.

29. See infra, p. 543.

30. Second Restatement of Torts, § 158, Comment i.

31. See infra, ch. 15.

32. See infra, § 13.

if strict liability for trespass is likewise to be limited to such "abnormally dangerous activities," the classification seems to become a matter of purely academic interest. The same historical background accounts for the insistence of some courts [33] upon the entry of something tangible, with appreciable mass, and visible to the naked eye, before trespass can be found—so that industrial dust [34] or noxious fumes [35] will not be enough. This may very possibly have been due to the refusal of the ancient courts to pay any attention to what they could not see—a point of view no longer valid in the light of modern scientific tests.[36] The end of the old forms of action under the codes, however, has had its effect in relaxing the tight requirements; and there are now decisions finding a trespass in the entry of invisible gases and microscopic particles, where they do harm.[37] One of these same courts has refused to go so far as to include light rays falling upon the

land, [38] but a later decision throws real doubt upon even this conclusion.[39]

Necessity of Damage

The common law action of trespass could be maintained without proof of any actual damage. From every direct entry upon the soil of another, "the law infers some damage; if nothing more, the treading down grass or herbage." [40] The plaintiff recovered nominal damages where no substantial damage was shown,[41] or even where the trespass was a benefit to him.[42] The action was directed at the vindication of the legal right, without which the defendant's conduct, if repeated, might in time ripen into prescription; and there was no room for the application of the maxim that the law does not concern itself with trifles.[43]

On the other hand, the action on the case required proof of actual damage, and could not be maintained without it.[44] Here again the distinction between direct and indirect invasions is quite illogical. It seems more reasonable to limit the recovery without proof of damage to cases of intentional invasion, where the trespass action may serve an important purpose in determining and vindicat-

---

33. The cases are reviewed in excellent Notes in 1960, 60 Col.L.Rev. 877; 1966, 19 Okl.L.Rev. 117.

34. Thackery v. Union Portland Cement Co., 1924, 64 Utah 437, 231 P. 813; Riblet v. Spokane-Portland Cement Co., 1952, 41 Wash.2d 249, 248 P.2d 380.

35. Arvidson v. Reynolds Metals Co., W.D.Wash. 1954, 125 F.Supp. 481, affirmed 1954, 236 F.2d 224, cert. denied 352 U.S. 968; Ryan v. City of Emmetsburg, 1942, 232 Iowa 600, 4 N.W.2d 435; Waschak v. Moffatt, 1954, 379 Pa. 441, 109 A.2d 310; Bartlett v. Grasselli Chem. Co., 1922, 92 W.Va. 445, 115 S.E. 451; Davis v. Georgia-Pacific Corp., 1968, 251 Or. 239, 445 P.2d 481.

36. See Fairview Farms, Inc. v. Reynolds Metals Co., D.Or.1959, 176 F.Supp. 178.

37. Gregg v. Delhi-Taylor Oil Corp., 1961, 162 Tex. 26, 344 S.W.2d 411 (gas); Martin v. Reynolds Metals Co., 1959, 221 Or. 86, 342 P.2d 790, cert. denied 362 U.S. 918 (gas and microscopic deposit); Reynolds Metals Co. v. Martin, 9 Cir. 1964, 337 F.2d 780 (same); Hall v. De Weld Mica Corp., 1956, 244 N.C. 182, 93 S.E.2d 56 (dust); Zimmer v. Stephenson, 1965, 66 Wash.2d 477, 403 P.2d 343 (spark); Martin v. Union Pac. R. Co., Or.1970, 474 P.2d 739 (fire).

Compare, as to vibration, Gallin v. Poulou, 1956, 140 Cal.App.2d 638, 295 P.2d 958; and see the blasting concussion cases cited infra, p. 513.

38. Amphitheatres, Inc. v. Portland Meadows, 1948, 184 Or. 336, 198 P.2d 847.

39. Martin v. Reynolds Metals Co., 1959, 221 Or. 86, 342 P.2d 790.

40. Dougherty v. Stepp, 1835, 18 N.C. 371.

41. Dixon v. Clow, 1840, 24 Wend., N.Y., 188; Pfeiffer v. Grossman, 1853, 15 Ill. 492; Giddings v. Rogalewski, 1916, 192 Mich. 319, 158 N.W. 951; Fletcher v. Howard, 1928, 226 Ky. 258, 10 S.W.2d 825; Forest City Cotton Co. v. Miller, 1940, 218 N.C. 294, 10 S.E.2d 806.

42. Harmony Ditch Co. v. Sweeney, 1924, 31 Wyo. 1, 222 P. 577; Longenecker v. Zimmerman, 1954, 175 Kan. 719, 267 P.2d 543.

43. Norvell v. Thompson, 1834, 2 Hill L., S.C., 470; Bragg v. Laraway, 1893, 65 Vt. 673, 27 A. 492; Foust v. Kinney, 1918, 202 Ala. 392, 80 So. 474; Reeves v. Jackson, 1944, 207 Ark. 1089, 184 S.W.2d 256.

44. Thompson v. Crocker, 1829, 9 Pick., Mass., 59; Cooper v. Hall, 1832, 5 Ohio 320, 321; Garrett v. McKie, 1843, 1 Rich.L., S.C., 444.

ing the right to exclusive possession of the property.[45] No such necessity is apparent in the case of invasions due to mere negligence or dangerous activities.[46]

Furthermore, once it is determined that a trespass has been committed, the trespasser's responsibility has been carried to an extreme length as to the consequences for which he is liable. While it cannot be said that he is liable for everything that follows as a result of his trespass,[47] he is held responsible, under a rule apparently derived originally from the principle of "transferred intent," [48] for any visible and tangible damage inflicted upon the land itself, although such damage is not the result of any negligent or wrongful act beyond the mere trespass, and could not reasonably have been anticipated at the time of the unlawful entry. Thus if the trespasser lights a fire in the stove, using all possible care, and the fire burns down the house, he is liable for the consequences; [49] and the

same is true as to any other such damage.[50] The same liability has been extended to the person of the possessor,[51] and to his chattels on the land,[52] and even to the members of his family.[53] Since the question is one of an accomplished trespass to the land, and liability for its consequences, the ancient trespass requirement of direct and immediate injury has not been insisted upon,[54] and recovery

45. Second Restatement of Torts, § 163.

46. Second Restatement of Torts, § 165. One important consequence would be the effect upon the statute of limitations. In cases of intentional trespass, the cause of action is now held to accrue when the invasion occurs. Kansas Pac. R. Co. v. Mihlman, 1876, 17 Kan. 224; Williams v. Pomeroy Coal Co., 1882, 37 Ohio St. 583; National Copper Co. v. Minnesota Min. Co., 1885, 57 Mich. 83, 23 N.W. 781. In the case of nuisance, or other indirect invasion, it usually is held to accrue only when damage results. Hempstead v. Cargill, 1891, 46 Minn. 118, 48 N.W. 558; Hooker v. Farmers' Irr. Dist., 8 Cir.1921, 272 F. 600; Heckaman v. Northern Pac. R. Co., 1933, 93 Mont. 363, 20 P.2d 258. See Note, 1937, 21 Minn.L.Rev. 334. If the view of the Restatement is adopted, the distinction would of course be between intentional and non-intentional invasions.

47. See cases cited infra, note 54.

48. See Prosser, Transferred Intent, 1967, 45 Tex.L. Rev. 650; supra, p. 82.

49. Wyant v. Crouse, 1901, 127 Mich. 158, 86 N.W. 527; Southern Counties Ice Co. v. RKO Radio Pictures, S.D.Cal.1941, 39 F.Supp. 157; Lee v. Stewart, 1940, 218 N.C. 287, 10 S.E.2d 804; Newsom v. Meyer, 1925, 102 Conn. 93, 128 A. 699; Wetzel v. Satterwhite, 1910, 59 Tex.Civ.App.1910, 125 S.W. 93.

50. Cleveland Park Club v. Perry, Mun.App.D.C.1960, 165 A.2d 485 (drain plugged with tennis ball, swimming pool damaged); Curtis v. Fruin-Colnon Contracting Co., 1952, 363 Mo. 676, 253 S.W.2d 158 (foundation cracked, building settled); Garland v. White, Tex.Civ.App.1963, 368 S.W.2d 12 (shot at dog, damaged house); Whitehead v. Zeiller, Tex.Civ. App.1954, 265 S.W.2d 689 (soil removed, erosion damage to trees); Garrett v. Sewell, 1895, 108 Ala. 521, 18 So. 737 (fence removed, cattle entered).

51. Rogers v. Kent Board of County Road Comm'rs, 1948, 319 Mich. 661, 30 N.W.2d 358; Brackett v. Bellows Falls Hydro-Elec. Corp., 1934, 87 N.H. 173, 175 A. 822; Kopka v. Bell Tel. Co., 1952, 371 Pa. 444, 91 A.2d 232; Ham v. Maine-New Hampshire Interstate Bridge Authority, 1943, 92 N.H. 268, 30 A.2d 1; Mitchell v. Mitchell, 1893, 54 Minn. 301, 55 N.W. 1134.

52. Van Alstyne v. Rochester Tel. Corp., 1937, 163 Misc. 258, 296 N.Y.S. 726 (dogs swallowed dropped lead); Renaire Corp. v. Vaughn, Mun.App.D.C.1958, 142 A.2d 148 (window broken, tools stolen); Eten v. Luyster, 1875, 60 N.Y. 252 (box of money lost); Damron v. Roach, 1843, 4 Humph. 134, 23 Tenn. 134 (fence removed, cattle strayed).

53. Wardrop v. City of Manhattan Beach, 1958, 160 Cal.App.2d 779, 326 P.2d 15 (child contracting polio); St. Petersburg Coca-Cola Bottling Co. v. Cuccinello, Fla.1950, 44 So.2d 670 (child run down); Brabazon v. Joannes Bros. Co., 1939, 231 Wis. 426, 286 N.W. 21 (wife); Keesecker v. G. M. McKelvey Co., 1940, 64 Ohio App. 29, 27 N.E.2d 787, reversed on other grounds, 1941, 68 Ohio App. 505, 42 N.E.2d 223, second appeal, 1943, 141 Ohio St. 162, 47 N.E.2d 211 (child).

54. Except in Alabama and Nebraska. Jackson v. Bohlin, 1917, 16 Ala.App. 105, 75 So. 697; Connolly v. Omaha Pub. Power Dist., 1970, 185 Neb. 501, 177 N.W.2d 492. Recovery was denied, however, for consequential injury in Leonard v. Nat Harrison Associates, Fla.App.1960, 122 So.2d 432 (fall nine days after damage to steps); Clifford v. Metropolitan Life Ins. Co., 1923, 197 Ky. 828, 248 S.W. 180 (injury sustained in pursuing the intruder); Mawson v. Vess Beverage Co., Mo.App.1943, 173 S. W.2d 606 (injury in attempting to remove a sign); Clark v. Gay, 1901, 112 Ga. 777, 38 S.E. 81 (loss

quite frequently has been allowed for harm brought about in a very indirect manner.[55] Even the requirement of physical harm has been relaxed to permit recovery of damages for mental distress at the trespass, not only on the part of the possessor of the land,[56] but even of the members of his family.[57] This rather curious survival, and extension, of an early notion of strict liability is an excellent illustration of the great importance which the courts have attached to the right to exclusive possession of land.

Necessity of Possession

The action for trespass is designed to protect the interest in exclusive possession of the land in its intact physical condition. Therefore any person in the actual and exclusive possession [58] of the property may main-

tain the action, although he has no legal title, and is himself in wrongful occupation,[59] as for example under a void lease,[60] or in mere adverse possession.[61] As against the fact of possession in the plaintiff, no defendant in a trespass action may set up the right of a third person, unless he is able to connect himself with that right.[62] "Any possession is a legal possession against a wrongdoer." [63] The reason usually is stated to be that it is more conducive to the maintenance of order to protect existing, although wrongful, possession against the depredations of other wrongdoers, than to lay any one with a defective title open to such depredations without redress. But the land may of course be held through a servant; [64] and the American courts have developed the fiction that where the land is vacant and occupied by no one, the owner is deemed to be the man in posses-

of sale value of house because of murder committed in it).

55. Kopka v. Bell Tel. Co., 1952, 371 Pa. 444, 91 A. 2d 232 (fall into hole); Rogers v. Kent Board of County Road Comm'rs, 1948, 319 Mich. 661, 30 N.W. 2d 358 (fall from mowing machine); Brackett v. Bellows Falls Hydro-Elec. Corp., 1934, 87 N.H. 173, 175 A. 822 (same); Van Alstyne v. Rochester Tel. Corp., 1937, 163 Misc. 258, 296 N.Y.S. 726 (dogs eating dropped lead); Keesecker v. G. M. McKelvey Co., 1940, 64 Ohio App. 29, 27 N.E.2d 787 reversed on other grounds, 1941, 68 Ohio App. 505, 42 N.E.2d 223, second appeal, 1943, 141 Ohio St. 162, 47 N.E.2d 211.

56. Walker v. Ingram, 1948, 251 Ala. 395, 37 So.2d 685; Kornoff v. Kingsburg Cotton Oil Co., 1955, 45 Cal.2d 265, 288 P.2d 507; Barrow v. Georgia Lightweight Aggregate Co., 1961, 103 Ga.App. 704, 120 S.E. 2d 636; J. B. McCrary Co. v. Phillips, 1930, 222 Ala. 117, 130 So. 805; Sager v. Sisters of Mercy, 1927, 81 Colo. 498, 256 P. 8.

57. Engle v. Simmons, 1906, 148 Ala. 92, 41 So. 1023; American Security Co. v. Cook, 1934, 49 Ga.App. 723, 176 S.E. 798; Watson v. Dilts, 1902, 116 Iowa 249, 89 N.W. 1068; Lesch v. Great Northern R. Co., 1906, 97 Minn. 503, 106 N.W. 955; Bouillon v. Laclede Gaslight Co., 1910, 148 Mo.App. 462, 129 S.W. 401; Second Restatement of Torts, § 162.

58. If both parties can be considered in any sense as in possession, such mixed possession inures to the benefit of the one having the legal title. Leach v. Woods, 1833, 31 Mass., 14 Pick., 461; Abbott v. Abbott, 1863, 51 Me. 575; cf. Kentucky Land & Immigration Co. v. Crabtree, 1902, 113 Ky. 922, 70 S.W. 31.

A mere licensee, having no interest in the premises, can bring no action for trespass, or damage to the realty. Powers v. Clarkson, 1876, 17 Kan. 218; Sabine & E. T. R. Co. v. Johnson, 1886, 65 Tex. 389; Bakersfield Religious Cong. Soc. v. Baker, 1843, 15 Vt. 119. The same is true of the holder of an easement. State ex rel. Green v. Gibson Circuit Court, 1965, 246 Ind. 446, 206 N.E.2d 135; Morgan v. Boyes, 1876, 65 Me. 124; Chloupek v. Perotka, 1895, 89 Wis. 551, 62 N.W. 537. See Note, 1925, 11 Va.L.Rev. 476.

59. Barstow v. Sprague, 1859, 40 N.H. 27; Nickerson v. Thacher, 1888, 146 Mass. 609, 16 N.E. 581; Langdon v. Templeton, 1894, 66 Vt. 173, 28 A. 866; Frisbee v. Town of Marshall, 1898, 122 N.C. 760, 30 S.E. 21; Southern R. Co. v. Horine, 1904, 121 Ga. 386, 49 S.E. 285.

60. Graham v. Peat, 1801, 1 East 244, 102 Eng.Rep. 95; Brenner v. Haley, 1960, 185 Cal.App.2d 183, 8 Cal.Rptr. 224 (illegal lease in violation of zoning ordinance).

61. Catteris v. Cowper, 1812, 4 Taunt. 546, 128 Eng. Rep. 444; Evertson v. Sutton, 1830, 5 Wend., N.Y., 281; Langdon v. Templeton, 1893, 66 Vt. 173, 28 A. 866.

62. As in Danforth v. Briggs, 1896, 89 Me. 316, 36 A. 452; Kirk v. Cassady, 1926, 217 Ky. 87, 288 S.W. 1045.

63. Graham v. Peat, 1801, 1 East 244, 102 Eng.Rep. 95, per Lord Kenyon, C. J.

64. Bertie v. Beaumont, 1812, 16 East 33, 104 Eng. Rep. 1001.

sion.[65] The same policy of favoring possession operates to protect the defendant, once he is in occupancy of the land for some appreciable period of time under a colorable claim of ownership. He is then no longer subject to an action of trespass on the part of the true owner, whose proper remedy is in the form of an action of ejectment.[66]

On the other hand, an owner who is out of possession cannot maintain trespass.[67] Thus a landlord cannot sue for a mere trespass to land in the occupation of his tenant.[68] He is not without legal remedy, in the form of an action on the case for the injury to the reversion;[69] but in order to maintain it, he must show more than the trespass—namely, actual permanent harm to the property of such sort as to affect the value of his interest.[70] The tenant may recover damages for the injury to his interest up to the end of his term, but any permanent damage beyond this is recoverable by the landlord.[71] It is the common law rule that an owner forcibly dispossessed of the property may bring trespass for the ouster, but not for damage done afterward;[72] his remedy is by way of an action for ejectment, and for mesne profits.[73]

Vertical Extent of Possession

Any physical entry upon the surface of the land is a trespass, whether it be by walking upon it,[74] flooding it with water,[75] casting objects upon it,[76] or otherwise. One may commit a trespass upon the vertical surface of another's premises, as well as the horizontal —as where he piles dirt[77] or attaches wires[78] against a boundary wall. But the interest in exclusive possession is not limited to the surfaces; it extends above and below. There is

65. Church v. Meeker, 1867, 34 Conn. 421; Miller v. Miller, 1874, 41 Md. 623; Randall v. Sanders, 1882, 87 N.Y. 578; Falejczyk v. Meo, 1961, 31 Ill.App.2d 372, 176 N.E.2d 10; Dodson v. Culp, 1963, 108 Ga. App. 408, 133 S.E.2d 631. But this fiction of "constructive possession" has no application when another is in actual possession.

66. LaRue v. Russell, 1866, 26 Ind. 386; Mosseller v. Deaver, 1890, 106 N.C. 494, 11 S.E. 529.

67. Kelman v. Wilen, 1954, 283 App.Div. 113, 131 N. Y.S.2d 679; Bacon v. Sheppard, 1830, 11 N.J.L. 197; Hawkins v. Roby, 1882, 77 Mo. 140; Ruggles v. Sands, 1879, 40 Mich. 559; Kay v. Adams, 1931, 223 Ala. 33, 134 So. 628.
This has always been subject to the exception that one who has the right to immediate possession at the time of the tort can, after entry, maintain an action for trespass. Ocean Accident Co. v. Ilford Gas Co., [1905] 2 K.B. 493.

68. Daisey v. Hudson, 1855, 5 Harr., Del., 320; Bascom v. Dempsey, 1887, 143 Mass. 409, 9 N.E. 744; Walden v. Conn, 1886, 84 Ky. 312, 1 S.W. 537.
Some courts have held that where the tenant in possession is merely a tenant at will, the landlord may bring trespass, as having "constructive" possession. Starr v. Jackson, 1814, 11 Mass. 519; Davis v. Nash, 1851, 32 Me. 411. Others hold that the right to immediate possession is not the equivalent of possession. Campbell v. Arnold, 1806, 1 Johns., N.Y., 511; Gunsolus v. Lormer, 1882, 54 Wis. 630, 12 N.W. 62.
The holder of a contract to purchase, which gives no right to possession before payment, cannot bring trespass. Greve v. Wood-Harmon Co., 1899, 173 Mass. 45, 52 N.E. 1070; Des Jardins v. Thunder Bay River Boom Co., 1893, 95 Mich. 140, 54 N.E. 718.

69. Bucki v. Cone, 1889, 25 Fla. 1, 6 So. 160; Devlin v. Snellenburg, 1890, 132 Pa. 186, 18 A. 1119; Hersey

v. Chapin, 1894, 162 Mass. 176, 38 N.E. 442; Cherry v. Lake Drummond Canal & Water Co., 1906, 140 N.C. 422, 53 S.E. 138; Croasdale v. Butell, 1955, 177 Kan. 487, 280 P.2d 593.

70. Bascom v. Dempsey, 1887, 143 Mass. 409, 9 N.E. 744.

71. Gilbert v. Kennedy, 1870, 22 Mich. 5; O. W. Zimmerman Mfg. Co. v. Daffin, 1906, 149 Ala. 380, 42 So. 858.

72. Smith v. Wunderlich, 1873, 70 Ill. 426.

73. Anderson v. Radcliffe, 1860, 29 L.J.Q.B. 128.

74. Dougherty v. Stepp, 1835, 18 N.C. 371.

75. Herro v. Board of County Road Comm'rs, 1962, 368 Mich. 263, 118 N.W.2d 271; Union Pac. R. Co. v. Vale Irr. Dist., D.Or.1966, 253 F.Supp. 251; Conner v. Woodfill, 1890, 126 Ind. 85, 25 N.E. 876.

76. Prewitt v. Clayton, 1827, 5 T.B.Mon., Ky., 4 (breaking in door with stones and clubs); Clark v. Wiles, 1884, 54 Mich. 323, 20 N.W. 63 (throwing dirt).

77. Miller v. McClelland, Iowa, 1919, 173 N.W. 910; Hutchinson v. Schimmelfeder, 1861, 40 Pa. 396.

78. Boomer v. Southern Cal. Edison Co., 1928, 91 Cal. App. 382, 267 P. 181; Wells Amusement Co. v. Eros, 1920, 204 Ala. 239, 85 So. 692; cf. Mawson v. Vess Beverage Co., Mo.App.1943, 173 S.W.2d 606 (tacking sign).

a property right in the air space above land, which may be invaded by overhanging structures,[79] or telephone wires,[80] by thrusting an arm across the boundary line,[81] or by shooting across the land,[82] even though the bullets do not fall upon it.[83]

The upward extent of this property right has been a subject of much discussion in recent years,[84] since it has been brought into sharp relief by the progress of aviation. Lord Coke once gave utterance [85] to the statement that *"cujus est solum ejus est usque ad coelum"*—which, taken literally, means that he who has the soil owns upward unto heaven, and by analogy, downward to perdition. This dictum was repeated in many cases [86]

where there was no question of anything more than the immediate space above the soil, and it remains to trouble the law of the air. No one now advocates that it be applied literally; if it were, and no way were found to evade it, it is obvious that no airplane would ever leave the ground. But the exact extent of the landowner's rights in the air column is still in process of determination.

At least four distinct theories have been advanced in the state courts to adjust the conflicting interests of the surface owner and the aviator.[87] One is the "zone" theory, which divides the airspace into two strata, with the landowner owning that contained in the lower zone, but not that in the upper. The line is drawn at the limit of the owner's "effective possession," or in other words, at so much of the space above him as is essential to the complete use and enjoyment of his land. This was the rule applied in the early case of Smith v. New England Aircraft Co.,[88] where flights at the level of one hundred feet were held to be trespasses, since the land was used for the cultivation of trees which reached that height. A few other cases have adopted the same view.[89] The height of the zone of ownership must vary according to

---

79. Smith v. Smith, 1872, 110 Mass. 302 (eaves); Puorto v. Chieppa, 1905, 78 Conn. 401, 62 A. 664 (projection of one inch held trespass for which at least nominal damages recoverable); Cumberland Tel. & Tel. Co. v. Barnes, 1907, 30 Ky.L.Rev. 1290, 101 S.W. 301 (cross-arm of telegraph pole); Kelsen v. Imperial Tobacco Co., [1957] 2 Q.B. 334 (advertising sign). Cf. Harris v. Central Power Co., 1922, 109 Neb. 500, 191 N.W. 711.

80. Butler v. Frontier Tel. Co., 1906, 186 N.Y. 486, 79 N.E. 716; McKenzie v. Pacific Gas & Elec. Co., 1962, 200 Cal.App.2d 731, 19 Cal.Rptr. 628.

81. Hannabalson v. Sessions, 1902, 116 Iowa 457, 90 N.W. 93. Cf. Ellis v. Loftus Iron Co., 1874, L.R. 10 C.P. 19 (horse kicking through fence).

82. Whittaker v. Stangvick, 1907, 100 Minn. 386, 111 N.W. 295; Munro v. Williams, 1920, 94 Conn. 377, 109 A. 129; Herrin v. Sutherland, 1925, 74 Mont. 587, 241 P. 328; Hall v. Browning, 1943, 195 Ga. 423, 24 S.E.2d 392.

83. Davies v. Bennison, 1927, 22 Tas.L.Rev. 52. This is the famous "Tasmanian cat case," in which defendant shot the cat on the roof of plaintiff's house, and the bullet remained in the cat. It was held that A could recover for trespass to his land.

84. See Hackley, Trespassers in the Sky, 1937, 21 Minn.L.Rev. 773; Hunter, The Conflicting Interests of Airport Owners and Nearby Property Owners, 1945, 11 Law & Con.Prob. 539; Mace, Ownership of Airspace, 1948, 17 U.Cin.L.Rev. 343; Calkins, Landowner and Aircraft, 1958, 25 J.Air Law 373; Anderson, Airspace Trespass, 1960, 27 J.Air Law 341; Note, 1967, 9 W. & M.L.Rev. 460.

85. Coke, Littleton, 4a. See Klein, Cujus Est Solum Ejus Est—Quousque Tandem? 1959, 26 J.Air Law & Comm. 237.

86. See for example Hannabalson v. Sessions, 1902, 116 Iowa 457, 458, 90 N.W. 93, 95: " * * * the

title of the owner of the soil extends not only downward to the centre of the earth, but upward usque ad coelum, although it is, perhaps, doubtful whether owners as quarrelsome as the parties in this case will ever enjoy the usufruct of their property in the latter direction. * * * "

87. Hackley, Trespassers in the Sky, 1937, 21 Minn.L. Rev. 773; Hunter, The Conflicting Interests of Airport Owners and Nearby Property Owners, 1945, 11 Law & Con.Prob. 539; Mace, Ownership of Airspace, 1948, 17 U.Cin.L.Rev. 343; Notes, 1957, 19 U.Pitt. L.Rev. 154; 1961, 74 Harv.L.Rev. 1581. Much the best discussion is in Harvey, Landowners' Rights in the Air Age: The Airport Dilemma, 1958, 56 Mich. L.Rev. 1313.

88. 1930, 270 Mass. 511, 170 N.E. 385.

89. Burnham v. Beverly Airways, 1942, 311 Mass. 628, 42 N.E.2d 575; Delta Air Corp. v. Kersey, 1942, 193 Ga. 862, 20 S.E.2d 245; Thrasher v. City of Atlanta, 1934, 178 Ga. 514, 173 S.E. 817; Swetland v. Curtiss Airports Corp., 6 Cir.1931, 55 F.2d 201.

the facts of each case,[90] and the objections to this solution are that the extent of the right is left in doubt until adjudication, and that there apparently is to be a cause of action, with nominal damages and the possibility of an injunction, for flights which do no present harm to anyone.

A second view was adopted in a decision of the Ninth Circuit,[91] where the court refused to find a trespass in flights even within five feet of the surface of unoccupied waste land. It denies any ownership of the unused airspace, and limits the owner's rights to his actual use of it, with the rule that there is no tort unless there is interference with the present enjoyment of the property. Quite a different approach is that of the Restatement of Torts,[92] which was taken over by the Uniform State Law for Aeronautics[93] and enacted in one form or another in some twenty-two states.[94] This recognizes unlimited ownership of upward space, subject to a privilege of flight similar to the public right to make use of a navigable stream.[95] With flights now ranging into the verge of outer space, and carried on by rockets and many objects other than airplanes, this notion of private ownership of a segment of space reaching to the moon, and limited only by a privilege of flight, is now pretty well discredited. The Uniform Act was withdrawn by the Commissioners on Uniform State Laws in 1943; and while it remains on the books in a good many states, its approach is not likely to be applied so long as others are available.

Finally there is the "nuisance" theory, which is finding increasing support. It ignores arguments about ownership of the air, and gives a remedy in the form of an action for nuisance, or possibly negligence, when the flight results in actual interference with the use of the land,[96] but denies it unless there is such interference.[97]

All of these theories represent obvious attempts to strike a balance between the property interests of the landowner and the demands of a growing industry highly important to the public. Thus far it cannot be said that any one of them has predominated, largely because the courts have been so exceedingly cautious about committing them-

---

90. See Swetland v. Curtiss Airports Corp., D.Ohio 1930, 41 F.2d 929, [1930] U.S.Av.Rep. 21; Cory v. Physical Culture Hotel, D.C.N.Y.1936, 14 F.Supp. 977, 982, affirmed 2 Cir. 1937, 88 F.2d 411 [1936] U.S.Av.Rep. 16.

91. Hinman v. Pacific Air Transport, 9 Cir. 1936, 84 F.2d 755, cert. denied 300 U.S. 654, discussed in Green, Trespass by Airplane, 1937, 31 Ill.L.Rev. 499. Accord, applying a Georgia statute, Wall v. Trogdon, 1959, 249 N.C. 747, 107 S.E.2d 757.

92. Restatement of Torts, § 194.

93. See Keuhnl, Uniform State Aviation Liability Legislation, [1948] Wis.L.Rev. 356.

94. Hunter, The Conflicting Interests of Airport Owner and Nearby Property Owner, 1945, 11 Law & Con. Prob. 539, 547, gives the following list: Arizona, Arkansas, California, Colorado, Delaware, Georgia, Idaho, Indiana, Maryland, Michigan, Minnesota, Missouri, Nevada, New Jersey, North Carolina, North Dakota, Pennsylvania, South Carolina, South Dakota, Tennessee, Vermont, Wisconsin, Wyoming.

See, applying such legislation, Capitol Airways v. Indianapolis Power & Light Co., 1939, 215 Ind. 462, 18 N.E.2d 776; Guith v. Consumers Power Co., E.D. Mich.1940, 36 F.2d 21; Vanderslice v. Shawn, 1942, 26 Del.Ch. 225, 27 A.2d 87. In Strother v. Pacific Gas & Elec. Co., 1949, 94 Cal.App.2d 525, 211 P.2d 624, the same conclusion was reached without a statute.

95. At lower levels, and except in the case of unreasonable activities such as "stunt" flying, the practical result would seem to be much the same as under the "zone" theory. See Eubank, Doctrine of the Airspace Zone of Effective Possession, 1932, 12 Bos. U.L.Rev. 414. One possible difference is that under the "zone" theory the landowner has the burden of proof that his zone of effective possession has been invaded; under the theory recognizing a public privilege of flight, the burden would be upon the aviator to show that his flight was privileged. See Thurston, Trespass to Airspace, Harvard Legal Essays, 1934, 521.

96. Delta Air Corp. v. Kersey, 1942, 193 Ga. 862, 20 S.E.2d 245; Warren Township School Dist. No. 7 v. City of Detroit, 1944, 308 Mich. 460, 14 N.W.2d 134; Brandes v. Mitterling, 1948, 67 Ariz. 349, 196 P.2d 464; Hyde v. Somerset Air Service, 1948, 1 N.J.Super. 346, 61 A.2d 645; Anderson v. Souza, 1952, 38 Cal.2d 825, 243 P.2d 497.

97. See Swetland v. Curtiss Airports Corp., 6 Cir. 1931, 55 F.2d 201; Delta Air Corp. v. Kersey, 1942, 193 Ga. 862, 20 S.E.2d 245.

selves; and most of the decisions do not identify and distinguish them very clearly. But the emphasis placed by the great majority of the decisions upon unreasonable interference with actual use of the land, even when trespass is relied upon,[98] tends to indicate that it is the nuisance theory which will ultimately prevail. It is obviously a highly artificial distinction which allows recovery to one plaintiff over whose land an airplane passes, and denies it to another whose boundary is fifty feet away, when any interference with the ground is the same as to both. A late Oregon decision,[99] which completely jettisons trespass, and relies upon nuisance as the sole basis of liability, is so well reasoned in pointing out that unreasonable interference with the surface is the only reliable criterion for liability, that it appears likely to be followed.

In 1946 the Supreme Court of the United States took a hand in the matter with United States v. Causby,[1] holding that continued low-altitude flights by military aircraft, which ruined the plaintiff's poultry business, constituted a wrongful "taking" of private property, for which the Fifth Amendment required compensation. The Court began by declaring that the federal statutes, together with the regulations of the Civil Aeronautics Board, had the effect of making the airspace above the prescribed minimum altitudes a public, and a federal, domain and highway, so that it must follow that there can be no

trespass in flight at such levels.[2] Apparently this has the effect of invalidating all state law to the contrary.[3] The case has left several unanswered questions. One of them is as to the extent to which Congress has occupied the field, so that state law may be precluded from allowing recovery even for flights below the minimum.[4] Another is whether there can be a "taking," or, inferentially, a trespass, in flights over the land below the prescribed minimum altitude, but above the "immediate reaches" of the land, which do not interfere with the use of the land. Here the only federal decisions[5] since the Causby Case have said that there cannot. There is the further question of liability for flights above the minimum which do so interfere; and here the Supreme Court itself has found a "taking" in a subsequent case,[6]

---

98. See for example Cheskov v. Port of Seattle, 1960, 55 Wash.2d 416, 348 P.2d 673; Antonik v. Chamberlain, 1947, 81 Ohio App. 465, 78 N.E.2d 752.

99. Atkinson v. Bernard, Inc., 1960, 223 Or. 624, 355 P.2d 229.

1. 1946, 328 U.S. 256. In accord is Gardner v. Allegheny County, 1955, 382 Pa. 88, 114 A.2d 491. Both decisions came before the amendment of Civil Aeronautics regulations to set minimum altitudes for glide paths in landing and taking off. See also Ackerman v. Port of Seattle, 1960, 55 Wash.2d 400, 348 P.2d 664; Wildwood Mink Ranch v. United States, D.Minn.1963, 218 F.Supp. 67.

2. This was not a new idea. In Maitland v. Twin City Aviation Corp., 1949, 254 Wis. 541, 37 N.W.2d 74, the court applied the Civil Aeronautics minimum altitude of 500 feet as a "zone" limit. This possibility was rejected in Thrasher v. City of Atlanta, 1934, 178 Ga. 514, 173 S.E. 817, as too simple a solution, since liability must depend upon the use to which the surface is put, and a single rule for all cases was regarded as too arbitrary.

3. Antonik v. Chamberlain, 1947, 81 Ohio App. 465, 78 N.E.2d 752; Cheskov v. Port of Seattle, 1960, 55 Wash.2d 416, 348 P.2d 673; Allegheny Airlines v. Village of Cedarhurst, E.D.N.Y.1955, 132 F.Supp. 871, affirmed 2 Cir.1956, 238 F.2d 812.

4. See Note, 1961, 74 Harv.L.Rev. 1581. The Causby decision apparently has been taken to mean that Congress has occupied the field, and that any state law inconsistent with federal rules is invalidated. Antonik v. Chamberlain, 1947, 81 Ohio App. 465, 78 N.E.2d 752; Cheskov v. Port of Seattle, 1960, 55 Wash.2d 416, 348 P.2d 673; Allegheny Airlines v. Village of Cedarhurst, E.D.N.Y.1955, 132 F.Supp. 871, affirmed 2 Cir.1956, 238 F.2d 812.

5. City of Newark v. Eastern Airlines, D.N.J.1958, 159 F.Supp. 750; Freeman v. United States, W.D. Okl.1958, 167 F.Supp. 541; Palisades Citizens Ass'n, Inc. v. Civil Aeronautics Board, D.C.Cir.1969, 420 F.2d 188.

6. Griggs v. County of Allegheny, 1962, 369 U.S. 84, rehearing denied 369 U.S. 857, noted in 1962, 57 Nw.U.L.Rev. 346. Accord: Matson v. United States, 1959, 145 Ct.Cl. 225, 171 F.Supp. 283; Thornburg v. Port of Portland, 1962, 233 Or. 178, 376 P.2d 100. See Hill, Liability for Aircraft Noise—The After-

although apparently not upon any basis of trespass.

The interest in the possession of land extends also below the surface, and may present similar problems there.[7] It is a trespass to mine under another's land,[8] or to construct a tunnel and force water through it,[9] or to invade it by a projecting foundation,[10] or by driving earth under the soil.[11] But the limits of this downward right have received little consideration. In a Kentucky case,[12] notwithstanding a forceful dissenting opinion,[13] the court permitted the surface owner to recover for trespass in a cave extending laterally beneath his property three hundred and sixty feet below. Since it is quite apparent that he had no slightest practical possibility of access to the cave, either now or in the future, the decision is dog-in-the-manger law, and can only be characterized as a very bad one. Much to be preferred is the conclusion

of a New York court [14] that a sewer one hundred fifty feet below the surface is not an invasion of the owner's rights. It is only where some damage to the surface results, or there is some interference with a use that can be made of the property, present or prospective, that a trespass action should be permitted in such a case.

Character of Defendant's Act

The trespass may be committed not only by entry upon the land, or by casting objects upon it, but also by causing a third person to enter. The defendant may carry him on the land by force,[15] pursue him so that he enters through fear,[16] or lead him to enter by false representations,[17] or by a grant of the land,[18] or other inducement.[19]

In an old New York case,[20] a balloonist came down in the plaintiff's garden, and was held liable for the damage done by the crowd which rushed in, upon the ground that he had caused their intrusion.

The trespass may also be committed by remaining on the land after a right of entry

---

math of Causby and Griggs, 1964, 19 U.Miami L. Rev. 1.

7. Ball, The Vertical Extent of Ownership in Land, 1928, 76 U.Pa.L.Rev. 631, 684–689.

8. Maye v. Yappen, 1863, 23 Cal. 306; North Jellico Coal Co. v. Helton, 1920, 187 Ky. 394, 219 S.W. 185; Chartiers Block Coal Co. v. Mellon, 1893, 152 Pa. 286, 25 A. 597. In many western states, however, the miner is permitted to follow the lode, as in Bowen v. Chemi-Cote Perlite Co., 1967, 5 Ariz.App. 28, 423 P.2d 104, vacated on other grounds 102 Ariz. 423, 432 P.2d 435. As to slant drilling of oil wells, see Note, 1939, 27 Cal.L.Rev. 192.

9. City of Chicago v. Troy Laundry Machinery Co., 7 Cir. 1908, 162 F. 678.

10. Wachstein v. Christopher, 1907, 128 Ga. 229, 57 S.E. 511; Harrington v. City of Huron, 1891, 86 Mich. 46, 48 N.W. 641.

11. Costigan v. Pennsylvania R. Co., 1892, 54 N.J.L. 233, 23 A. 810. Cf. United Elec. Light Co. v. Deliso Const. Co., 1943, 315 Mass. 313, 52 N.E.2d 553.

12. Edwards v. Lee, 1929, 230 Ky. 375, 19 S.W.2d 992; Edwards v. Sims, 1929, 232 Ky. 791, 24 S.W.2d 619; Edwards v. Lee, 1933, 250 Ky. 166, 61 S.W.2d 1049; Edwards v. Lee's Adm'r, 1936, 265 Ky. 418, 96 S.W. 2d 1028. The case is discussed in 1937, 31 Ill.L.Rev. 680; 1937, 37 Col.L.Rev. 503. Accord: Marengo Cave Co. v. Ross, 1937, 212 Ind. 624, 10 N.E.2d 917.

13. Logan, J., in Edwards v. Sims, 1929, 232 Ky. 791, 24 S.W.2d 619, 622.

14. Boehringer v. Montalto, 1931, 142 Misc. 560, 254 N.Y.S. 276.

15. Smith v. Stone, 1647, Style 65, 82 Eng.Rep. 533.

16. Vandenburgh v. Truax, 1847, 4 Denio, N.Y., 464.

17. Kirby Lumber Co. v. Karpel, 5 Cir. 1956, 233 F.2d 373 (inaccurate information about boundary lines).

18. Sanburn v. Sturtevant, 1882, 17 Minn. 200; Donovan v. Consolidated Coal Co., 1900, 187 Ill. 28, 58 N.E. 290; Hendrix v. Black, 1918, 132 Ark. 473, 201 S.W. 283; Murrell v. Goodwill, 1925, 159 La. 1057, 106 So. 564; Darden v. McMillan, 1956, 93 Ga.App. 892, 93 S.E.2d 169. See, however, McDermott v. Sway, 1951, 78 N.D. 521, 50 N.W.2d 235, holding that the negligent but bona fide granting of an easement does not make the grantor liable for the trespass.

19. Castleberry v. Mack, 1943, 205 Ark. XIX, 167 S.W.2d 489. Cf. State v. Lasiter, Tex.Civ.App. 1961, 352 S.W.2d 915, where the state authorized and directed a city to trespass on the land by laying a sewer line across it.

20. Guille v. Swan, 1822, 19 Johns., N.Y., 381. The case is the subject of a poem by Irving Browne, The Balloon and the Garden-Sauce, in 1889, 1 Green Bag 281.

has terminated.[21] Thus it is a trespass to refuse to leave after a license to remain has been revoked,[22] or to fail to remove property at the end of an agreed period.[23] At common law the action must be on the case,[24] since there was no forcible invasion; but since the forms of action have been discarded, it is commonly held that there is an actionable trespass.[25]

The defendant is liable for an intentional entry although he has acted in good faith, under the mistaken belief, however reasonable, that he is committing no wrong.[26] Thus he is a trespasser although he believes that the land is his own,[27] or that he has the consent of the owner,[28] or the legal privilege of entry;[29] or although he is a child too young to understand that what he is doing is wrong.[30] The interest of the landowner is protected at the expense of those who make innocent mistakes. But if the mistake is induced by the conduct of the owner himself, there will be no liability for the intrusion; the only possibility of recovery lies in quasi-contract, to the extent of any unjust enrichment.[31]

Continuing Trespass

The ordinary trespass is complete when it is committed; the cause of action accrues, and the statute of limitations begins to run at that time, although the consequence may be a permanent injury to the land.[32] But in

21. Second Restatement of Torts, § 158; Wood v. Leadbitter, 1848, 13 M. & W. 838, 153 Eng.Rep. 351; People v. Weinberg, 1967, 6 Mich.App. 345, 149 N.W.2d 248; Rager v. McCloskey, 1953, 305 N.Y. 75, 111 N.E.2d 214; Hubbard v. Commonwealth, 1967, 207 Va. 673, 152 S.E.2d 250; Johnson v. State, 1965, 277 Ala. 655, 173 So.2d 824.

22. Mitchell v. Mitchell, 1893, 54 Minn. 301, 55 N.W. 1134; Davis v. Stone, 1876, 120 Mass. 228. Cf. McKenzie v. Minis, 1909, 132 Ga. 323, 63 S.E. 900 (discharged servant); Emry v. Roanoke Nav. & Water Power Co., 1892, 111 N.C. 94, 16 S.E. 18 (lessee).

This is subject to the qualification that the Federal Civil Rights Act of 1964, requiring all places of public accommodation whose business affects interstate commerce to serve customers "without discrimination or segregation on the ground of race, color, religion, or national origin," is held to entitle the customer not only to enter and demand service, but to remain and insist upon it after he is ordered to leave. Hamm v. City of Rock Hill, 1964, 379 U.S. 306, rehearing denied 379 U.S. 995; Dilworth v. Riner, 5 Cir. 1965, 343 F.2d 226.

23. Rogers v. Kent Board of County Road Comm'rs, 1948, 319 Mich. 661, 30 N.W.2d 358; Ross v. Williams Mfg. Co., 1928, 38 Ga.App. 178, 143 S.E. 448; Benjamin v. American Tel. & Tel. Co., 1907, 196 Mass. 454, 82 N.E. 681 (failure to remove telephone pole on demand).

24. Winterbourne v. Morgan, 1809, 11 East 395, 103 Eng.Rep. 1056; Boults v. Mitchell, 1850, 15 Pa. 371; Stone v. Knapp, 1857, 29 Vt. 501.

25. Mitchell v. Mitchell, 1893, 54 Minn. 301, 55 N.W. 1134; Snedecor v. Pope, 1904, 143 Ala. 275, 39 So. 318; cf. Beers v. McGinnis, 1906, 191 Mass. 279, 77 N.E. 768.

26. Second Restatement of Torts, § 164; State v. Cobb, 1964, 262 N.C. 262, 136 S.E.2d 674.

27. Maye v. Yappan, 1863, 23 Cal. 306; Isle Royale Min. Co. v. Hertin, 1877, 37 Mich. 332; Ball & Bro. Lumber Co. v. Simms Lumber Co., 1908, 121 La. 627, 46 So. 674; Alabama Great Southern R. Co. v. Broach, 1960, 238 Miss. 618, 119 So.2d 923; Bihm v. Hirsch, La.App.1967, 193 So.2d 865.

28. Anderson v. United States, E.D.Pa.1966, 259 F. Supp. 148; Jackson v. Pettigrew, 1908, 133 Mo.App. 508, 113 S.W. 672; Jernigan v. Clark, 1901, 134 Ala. 313, 32 So. 686; Southern Counties Ice Co. v. RKO Radio Pictures, S.D.Cal.1941, 39 F.Supp. 157; Serota v. M. & M. Utilities, Inc., 1967, 55 Misc.2d 286, 285 N.Y.S.2d 121.

29. Connor v. Greenberg, 1916, 198 Ill.App. 129; Blatt v. McBarron, 1894, 161 Mass. 21, 36 N.E. 468; Concanan v. Boynton, 1889, 76 Iowa 543, 41 N.W. 213.

30. Cleveland Park Club v. Perry, Mun.App.D.C.1960, 165 A.2d 485; Brown v. Dellinger, Tex.Civ.App. 1962, 355 S.W.2d 742.

31. See Gunn v. Parsons, 1925, 213 Ala. 217, 104 So. 390; Merriweather v. Bell, 1900, 139 Ky. 402, 58 S.W. 987; Leach v. Fosburgh Lumber Co., 1912, 159 N.C. 532, 75 S.E. 716; Restatement of Restitution, § 129.

Contra: Holmes v. Wilson, 1839, 10 Ad. & El. 503, 113 Eng.Rep. 190; Russell v. Brown, 1874, 63 Me. 203; McGann v. Hamilton, 1890, 58 Conn. 69, 19 A. 376; Stowers v. Gilbert, 1898, 156 N.Y. 600, 51 N.E. 282. See also Fergerson v. Utilities Elkhorn Coal Co., Ky.1958, 313 S.W.2d 395, looking to the ease of removal of the condition, as in the cases in the next succeeding note.

32. Williams v. Pomeroy Coal Co., 1882, 37 Ohio St. 583; National Copper Co. v. Minnesota Min. Co.,

many cases, as where the defendant erects a structure or dumps rubbish upon the land of the plaintiff, the invasion is continued by a failure to remove it. In such a case, there is a continuing wrong so long as the offending object remains.[33] A purchaser of the land may recover for the continuing trespass,[34] and a transferee of the defendant's interest in the chattel or structure may be liable.[35]

A question of considerable difficulty arises as to whether the plaintiff may maintain successive actions for such a continuing trespass, or must recover in a single action for all damages, past and prospective. The first alternative may be inconvenient to the plaintiff, and compel him to harass the defendant with repeated suits over a matter which could better be disposed of in one. The second means that the statute of limitations will run from the initial trespass, and that the damages claimed may be largely speculative, or that the trespass may terminate after the judgment.

The courts are not in accord in dealing with this question. In the case of actual encroachments, as by building a structure upon the plaintiff's land, the prevailing view is that there must be a single recovery of all damages, upon the ground that the defendant is not privileged to commit a second trespass to remove it.[36] Where the trespass results from a condition on the defendant's own land, as in the case of a dam which floods the plaintiff's premises, most courts have made the solution turn upon the permanent nature of the condition, in the light of its physical durability and the likelihood that the defendant will terminate it rather than pay the plaintiff's claim.[37] In view of the uncertain and illogical nature of these distinctions, it has been suggested [38] that in all cases the plaintiff be given the option of a single recovery for all damages, or successive actions, upon the condition that he is in no way responsible for the continuance of the trespass.[39]

1885, 57 Mich. 83, 23 N.W. 781; Houston Water Works Co. v. Kennedy, 1888, 70 Tex. 233, 8 S.W. 36.

33. Second Restatement of Torts, § 161; 509 Sixth Ave. Corp. v. New York City Transit Authority, 1964, 15 N.Y.2d 48, 255 N.Y.S.2d 89, 203 N.E.2d 486.

34. Konskier v. Goodman, [1928] 1 K.B. 421; Peck v. Smith, 1814, 1 Conn. 103; Milton v. Puffer, 1911, 207 Mass. 416, 93 N.E. 634.

35. Lyons v. Fairmont Real Estate Co., 1913, 71 W. Va. 754, 77 S.E. 525; Rahn v. Milwaukee Electric Railway & Light Co., 1899, 103 Wis. 467, 79 N.W. 747; cf. Zenith Bathing Pavilion v. Fair Oaks S. S. Corporation, 1925, 240 N.Y. 307, 148 N.E. 532.

36. Finley v. Hershey, 1875, 41 Iowa 389; Ziebarth v. Nye, 1890, 42 Minn. 541, 44 N.W. 1027; Cherry

v. Lake Drummond Canal & Water Co., 1906, 140 N.C. 422, 53 S.E. 138; Blankenship v. Kansas Explorations, 1930, 325 Mo. 998, 30 S.W.2d 471.

37. Stodghill v. Chicago, B. & Q. R. Co., 1880, 53 Iowa 341, 5 N.W. 495; Louisville, H. & St. L. R. Co. v. Roberts, 1911, 144 Ky. 820, 139 S.W. 1073; Smith v. Dallas Utility Co., 1921, 27 Ga.App. 22, 107 S.E. 381; Southern R. Co. v. White, 1920, 128 Va. 551, 104 S.E. 865; Razzano v. Kent, 1947, 78 Cal.App.2d 254, 177 P.2d 612.

If the defendant's structure is not subject to abatement or injunction, because authorized by eminent domain statutes, many courts regard it as a "permanent nuisance," and permit a single recovery for prospective damages. Jacksonville, T. & K. W. R. Co. v. Lockwood, 1894, 33 Fla. 573, 15 So. 327; Phillips v. Postal Tel. Cable Co., 1902, 130 N.C. 513, 41 S.E. 1022; cf. Pappenheim v. Metropolitan Elev. R. Co., 1891, 128 N.Y. 436, 28 N.E. 518.

38. McCormick, Damages, 1935, 511–515; McCormick, Damages for Anticipated Injury to Land, 1924, 37 Harv.L.Rev. 574, 593–601; Goodrich, Permanent Structure and Continuing Injuries—The Iowa Rule, 1918, 4 Iowa L.B. 65. A good case to this effect is Kornoff v. Kingsburg Cotton Oil Co., 1955, 45 Cal.2d 265, 288 P.2d 507. See also Strange v. Cleveland, C., C. & St. L. R. Co., 1910, 245 Ill. 246, 91 N.E. 1036; City of Ottumwa v. Nicholson, 1913, 161 Iowa 473, 143 N.W. 439; Thompson v. Illinois Central R. Co., 1920, 191 Iowa 35, 179 N.W. 191.

39. Thus if the plaintiff refuses to permit the defendant to enter the land and remove the thing, there is no liability for the continuation of the trespass. Restatement of Torts, § 161, Comment d. If the plaintiff elects to retain the structure as a part of his land, the defendant will be liable for a second trespass if he enters to remove it. Druse v. Wheeler, 1872, 26 Mich. 189.

14. TRESPASS TO CHATTELS

The earliest cases in which the action of trespass was applied to chattels involved asportation, or carrying off, and a special form of the writ, known as trespass de bonis asportatis, was devised to deal with such situations.[40] Later the action was extended to include cases where the goods were damaged but not taken—as where animals were killed[41] or beaten.[42] Later decisions extended the tort to include any direct and immediate intentional interference with a chattel in the possession of another. Thus it is a trespass to damage goods or destroy them,[43] to make an unpermitted use of them,[44] or to move them from one place to another.[45] Under the common law forms, the interference must be direct and forcible, otherwise the action must be on the case;[46] but as in the case of trespass to land, the tendency has long been to ignore any such artificial distinction.[47]

The later development of the common law action of trover, and the tort of conversion[48] provided a substitute for trespass which usually was the more convenient action. As a result trespass tended to fall more or less into disuse in the case of chattels. Some occasional confusion followed as to which was the appropriate remedy in a given case.[49] The disappearance of the forms of action has made the distinction immaterial, and the name of the tort of little consequence, in most cases of intentional interference with chattels. Its chief importance now is that there may be recovery where trespass would lie at common law, for interferences with the possession of chattels which are not sufficiently important to be classed as conversion, and so to compel the defendant to pay the full value of the thing with which he has interfered.[50] Trespass to chattels survives

---

40. 1 Street, Foundations of Legal Liability, 1906, 15; Ames, History of Trover, 1898, 11 Harv.L.Rev. 277, 285–286.

41. Wright v. Ramscot, 1668, 1 Wms.Saund. 108, 85 Eng.Rep. 93; Sheldrick v. Abery, 1793, 1 Esp. 55, 170 Eng.Rep. 278.

42. Dand v. Sexton, 1789, 3 Term.Rep. 37, 100 Eng. Rep. 442; Marlow v. Weekes, 1744, Barnes' Notes 452; Slater v. Swann, 1730, 2 Stra. 872, 93 Eng.Rep. 906.

43. Parker v. Mise, 1855, 27 Ala. 480 (shooting dog); Brittain v. McKay, 1840, 23 N.C. 265 (cutting crop); Cole v. Fisher, 1814, 11 Mass. 137 (frightening horse into runaway and damaging chaise); Cole v. Schweer, 1910, 159 Ill.App. 278 (releasing fish); Post v. Munn, 1818, 4 N.J.L. 61 (damaging fishing net). Cf. Bankston v. Dumont, 1949, 205 Misc. 272, 38 So.2d 721 (opening and searching purse, removing money).

44. Penfolds Wines, Ltd. v. Elliott, Aust.1946, 74 Comm.L.Rep. 204.

45. Kirk v. Gregory, 1876, 1 Ex.Div. 55; G. W. K., Ltd. v. Dunlop Rubber Co., K.B. (1926) 42 T.L.R. 376 (taking tire from automobile and replacing it two days later); Bruch v. Carter, 1867, 32 N.J.L. 554; Zaslow v. Kroenert, 1946, 29 Cal.2d 541, 176 P.2d 1. A fortiori if the defendant takes the goods away. Peeples v. Brown, 1894, 42 S.C. 81, 20 S.E. 24; Guttner v. Pacific Steam Whaling Co., D.Cal. 1899, 96 F. 617; Danley-Evers Furniture Co. v. Cauley, 1929, 220 Ala. 542, 126 So. 844; Vaughn v. Glenn, 1932, 44 Ga.App. 426, 161 S.E. 672.

46. See Covell v. Laming, 1808, 1 Camp. 497, 170 Eng. Rep. 1034; Hopper v. Reeve, 1817, 7 Taunt. 698, 129 Eng.Rep. 278.

47. See Cole v. Fisher, 1814, 11 Mass. 137; Loubz v. Hafner, 1827, 12 N.C. 185; Waterman v. Hall, 1844, 17 Vt. 128; cf. Tennessee Coal, Iron & R. Co. v. Kimball, 1923, 209 Ala. 466, 96 So. 329.

48. See Ames, The History of Trover, 1898, 11 Harv. L.Rev. 374.

49. Thus it was held that trespass would lie, as well as trover, where an officer levied upon goods and took them under his legal control, although there was no physical interference with the property itself. Wintringham v. Lafoy, 1827, 7 Cow., N.Y., 735; Miller v. Baker, 1840, 1 Metc., Mass., 27.

Cf. Van Dresor v. King, 34 Pa.St. 201 (sale on execution); C. I. T. Corp. v. Brewer, 1941, 146 Fla. 247, 200 So. 910 (repossessing car).

One distinction of some importance was that trespass would not lie for a mere detention of goods rightfully acquired, without any taking or damage to them. Hartley v. Moxham, 1842, 3 Q.B. 701, 114 Eng. Rep. 675; Furlong v. Bartlett, 1838, 21 Pick., Mass., 401; Bradley v. Davis, 1836, 14 Me. 44. See infra, 89.

50. See infra, p. 80.

today, in other words, largely as a little brother of conversion.

In common with other progeny of the old action of trespass, such as assault and battery,[51] trespass to chattels has become, in modern usage, exclusively a wrong of intentional interference.[52] The strict liability which persisted in the case of trespass to land[53] did not survive as to chattels, and today there is no trespass on that basis.[54] While there may be liability for negligence which results in harm to the chattel, as in the case of a damaged car in an automobile collision, the remedy has been absorbed into the broader field of negligence actions,[55] leaving trespass for the intentional wrong.[56] But, as in the case of other torts derived from the old writ of trespass, the "intent" requires no wrongful motive; and it is no defense that the defendant believed the goods to be his own, so long as he voluntarily interfered with them by the act which constituted the trespass.[57] As in the case of trespass to land and conversion, the property right is protected at the expense of an innocent mistake.

Another departure from the original rule of the old writ of trespass concerns the necessity of some actual damage to the chattel before the action can be maintained. Where the defendant merely interferes without doing any harm—as where, for example, he merely lays hands upon the plaintiff's horse, or sits in his car—there has been a division of opinion among the writers, and a surprising dearth of authority. By analogy to trespass to land there might be a technical tort in such a case; and it has been contended that there is a real necessity for nominal damages to protect property from intermeddlers.[58] Such scanty authority as there is, however, has considered that the dignitary interest in the inviolability of chattels, unlike that as to land, is not sufficiently important to require any greater defense than the privilege of using reasonable force when necessary to protect them. Accordingly it has been held that nominal damages will not be awarded, and that in the absence of any actual damage the action will not lie.[59] This must be qualified, however, to the extent that any loss of possession by the plaintiff is regarded as necessarily a loss of something of value, even if only for a brief interval—so that wherever there is found to be dispossession, as in the case of seizure of goods on

51. See supra, p. 30.

52. Second Restatement of Torts, §§ 217, 222.

53. Supra, p. 63.

54. National Coal Board v. Evans, [1951] 2 K.B. 861; Socony-Vacuum Oil Co. v. Bailey, 1952, 202 Misc. 364, 109 N.Y.S.2d 799; Mountain States Tel. & Tel. Co. v. Horn Tower Const. Co., 1961, 147 Colo. 166, 363 P.2d 175; Texas-New Mexico Pipe Co. v. Allstate Construction, Inc., 1962, 70 N.M. 15, 369 P.2d 401.

55. Gayler & Pope, Ltd. v. Davies & Son, Ltd., [1924] 2 K.B. 75; see Winfield and Goodhart, Trespass and Negligence, 1933, 49 L.Q.Rev. 359. As in the case of battery, there is occasional reference in the cases to a negligent "trespass," as in Percival v. Hickey, 1820, 18 Johns., N.Y. 257, 259; but this is obviously pure carelessness.

56. With the resulting distinction that, while mere possession of the chattel will support an action for trespass (see infra, note 63), one for negligence cannot be maintained unless the plaintiff has title, or some special property interest in the chattel, which has suffered damage. Engelman v. Bird, D.Alaska, 1955, 16 Alaska 61, 136 F.Supp. 501; Veltri v. City of Cleveland, 1957, 167 Ohio St. 90, 146 N.E.2d 442; Northern Pacific R. Co. v. Lewis, 1895, 162 U.S. 366; Murphy v. Sioux City & Pac. R. Co., 1881, 55 Iowa 473, 8 N.W. 320; Lockhart v. Western & A. R. Co., 1884, 73 Ga. 472.

57. Brooks v. Olmstead, 1851, 17 Pa. 24; Dexter v. Cole, 1858, 6 Wis. 319; Hobart v. Hagget, 1835, 12 Me. 67; Shell Petroleum Corp. v. Liberty Gravel & Sand Co., Tex.Civ.App.1939, 128 S.W.2d 471. Cf. Medairy v. McAllister, 1903, 97 Md. 488, 55 A. 461 (advice of counsel as to legal right to take goods).

58. Pollock, Law of Torts, 13th ed. 1929, 264; Salmond, Law of Torts, 8th ed. 1934, 353; see Leitch & Co. v. Leydon, [1931] A.C. 106.

59. De Marentille v. Oliver, 1808, 2 N.J.L. 379; Paul v. Slason, 1850, 22 Vt. 231; Graves v. Severens, 1868, 40 Vt. 636; Glidden v. Szybiak, 1949, 95 N.H. 318, 63 A.2d 233; Koller v. Duggan, 1963, 346 Mass. 270, 191 N.E.2d 475; J. & C. Ornamental Iron Co. v. Watkins, 1966, 114 Ga.App. 688, 152 S.E.2d 613; Second Restatement of Torts, § 218, Comment e.

execution,[60] the requirement of actual damage is satisfied.[61]

The property interest protected by the old action of trespass was that of possession; and this has continued to affect the character of the action. It follows that anyone in possession of the chattel, under some colorable claim of right to it,[62] at the time of the defendant's interference, can maintain a trespass action.[63] The defendant is not permitted to set up as a defense to the plaintiff's claim the "jus tertii," which is to say the right of some third person to the chattel, superior to that of the plaintiff,[64] unless he can connect himself in his own right with that third person's claim.[65] The reason has been said to be that any other rule would be "an invitation to all the world to scramble for * * * possession;" [66] or in other words, that the main-

tenance of decent order requires that peaceable possession be protected against wrongdoers with no rights at all.

The original common law rule required that the plaintiff be in possession of the chattel at the time of the trespass, or the action could not be maintained.[67] This was relaxed slightly, at a later date, to allow trespass to be maintained by one who is entitled to possession immediately, or upon demand, as in the case of a bailor at will, or a mortgagee after default.[68] Furthermore, even one out of possession but entitled to it at some future time, as in the case of a bailor for a term, was not without all remedy; and while he could not bring trespass, he might recover in an action on the case for any harm to his interest in the chattel.[69] With the abolition of the forms of trespass and case under modern procedure, it would seem that the only distinction of any consequence is that the man entitled only to future possession recovers only to the extent of any damage to his interest.[70] Complications must arise when the claims of the present possessor and of the reversioner are both asserted; but since these develop most frequently in cases of conver-

60. Wintringham v. Lafoy, 1827, 7 Cow., N.Y., 735; Jaquith v. Stanger, 1957, 79 Idaho 49, 310 P.2d 805; Ohio Finance Co. v. Berry, 1941, 219 Ind. 94, 37 N.E.2d 2; Beede v. Nides Finance Corp., 1941, 209 Minn. 354, 296 N.W. 413.

61. Bankston v. Dumont, 1949, 205 Miss. 272, 38 So.2d 721 ($10 bill taken from purse, returned shortly thereafter on request); Lowery v. McTier, 1959, 99 Ga.App. 423, 108 S.E.2d 771; Stallworth v. Doss, 1967, 280 Ala. 409, 194 So.2d 566.

62. As in the case of conversion (infra, p. 94), it appears probable that a thief without colorable claim would not be allowed to recover. But trespass cases are lacking.

63. "The finder of an article may maintain trespass against any person but the real owner; and a person having an illegal possession may support this action against any person other than the true owner." Hoyt v. Gelston & Schenck, 1816, 13 Johns., N.Y., 141 affirmed 13 Johns. 561, affirmed 3 Wheat. 246; Sewell v. Harrington, 1839, 11 Vt. 141; Browning v. Skillman, 1854, 24 N.J.L. 351; Cole v. Schweer, 1910, 159 Ill.App. 278; W. K. Syson Timber Co. v. Dickens, 1906, 146 Ala. 471, 40 So. 753; cf. Priester v. Milleman, 1947, 161 Pa.Super. 507, 55 A.2d 540; Stone v. C. I. T. Corp., 1936, 122 Pa.Super. 71, 184 A. 674.

64. Woadson v. Nawton, 1727, 2 Stra. 777, 93 Eng.Rep. 842.

65. Blades v. Higgs, 1865, 20 C.B.,N.S., 214, 144 Eng. Rep. 1087.

66. Kenyon, C. J., in Webb v. Fox, 1797, 7 Term Rep. 391, 397, 101 Eng.Rep. 1037.

67. Ward v. Macauley, 1791, 4 Term Rep. 489, 100 Eng.Rep. 1135; Putnam v. Wyley, 1811, 8 Johns., N.Y., 432; Winship v. Neale, 1858, 10 Gray, Mass., 382; Holman v. Ketchum, 1907, 153 Ala. 360, 45 So. 206.

68. Lotan v. Cross, 1810, 2 Camp. 464, 170 Eng.Rep. 1219; Staples v. Smith, 1861, 48 Me. 470; Strong v. Adams, 1858, 30 Vt. 221. Cf. Edwards v. Edwards, 1839, 11 Vt. 587 (buyer); Roberts v. Messinger, 1890, 134 Pa. 298, 19 A. 625 (beneficiary of unadministered estate); Ker v. Bryan, 4 Cir. 1908, 163 F. 233, reversed on other grounds 222 U.S. 107 (owner of land in possession of trespasser); Manning v. Wells, 1894, 104 Ala. 383, 16 So. 23 (conditional seller after default).

69. Hall v. Pickard, 1812, 3 Camp. 186, 170 Eng.Rep. 1348; Mears v. London & S. W. R. Co., 1862, 11 C.B., N.S., 850, 142 Eng.Rep. 1029; Devlin v. Snellenburg, 1890, 132 Pa.St. 186, 18 A. 1119; Perry v. Bailey, 1900, 94 Me. 50, 46 A. 789; Second Restatement of Torts, § 219.

70. Juniata Acceptance Corp. v. Hoffman, 1940, 139 Pa.Super. 87, 11 A.2d 494.

sion,[71] the rules are identical, and there are almost no trespass cases, they are best dealt with at a later point.

15. CONVERSION

Conversion is a fascinating tort, although it has largely eluded the attention of legal writers.[72] Highly technical in its rules and complications, perhaps more so than any other except defamation, it almost defies definition.[73] The chief reason is that the hand of history, with its old common law forms of action,[74] lies heavy upon this particular field.

Although the term had made some earlier appearances,[75] conversion had its real genesis in the old common law action of trover. Trover emerged late in the fifteenth century, as a branch of the action on the case. We probably do not have the earliest examples of its use, but they were almost certainly cases in which the finder of lost goods did not return them, but used them himself, or disposed of them to someone else. The new writ was invented to fill the gap left by the action of trespass, which lay for the wrongful taking of a chattel, and detinue, which lay for its wrongful detention.[76] By 1554 the allegations of the complaint had become more or less standardized: [77] that the plaintiff was possessed of certain goods, that he casually lost them, that the defendant found them, and that the defendant did not return them, but instead "converted them to his own use." From that phrase in the pleading came the name of the tort.

Trover, as it developed, had certain definite procedural advantages over the older forms of action, not the least of which was that it avoided wager of law, a form of licensed perjury which made detinue singularly unattractive to an honest plaintiff suing a dishonest defendant. Almost from the beginning, therefore, the effort was made to expand trover into the fields occupied by the other actions. The device by which this was accomplished was that of treating, first the allega-

71. See infra, p. 96.

72. The scanty literature on the subject includes Ames, History of Trover, 1898, 11 Harv.L.Rev. 277, 374; Salmond, Observations on Trover and Conversion, 1905, 21 L.Q.Rev. 43; Clark, The Test of Conversion, 1908, 21 Harv.L.Rev. 408; Warren, Qualifying as Plaintiff in an Action for a Conversion, 1936, 49 Harv.L.Rev. 1084; Rubin, Conversion of Choses in Action, 1941, 10 Ford.L.Rev. 415; Prosser, The Nature of Conversion, 1957, 42 Corn.L.Q. 168; Faust, Distinction Between Conversion and Trespass to Chattel, 1958, 37 Or.L.Rev. 256; Note, 1935, 21 Corn. L.Q. 112. See also Professor Warren's small book, Trover and Conversion, 1936.

73. The few attempts have been either so general and vague as to be quite meaningless, or so broad as to include conduct which is clearly not a conversion, or so narrow as to exclude some conduct which clearly is. See for example: "an act of wilful interference with a chattel, done without lawful justification, by which any person entitled thereto is deprived of use and possession." Salmond, Law of Torts, 10th Ed. 1945, 286. "Conversion is the unlawful and wrongful exercise of dominion, ownership or control over the property of another to the exclusion of the exercise of the same rights by the owner, either permanently or for an indefinite time." Pugh v. Hassell, 1952, 206 Okl. 290, 291, 242 P.2d 701, 702.

74. "Forms of action are dead, but their ghosts still haunt the precincts of the law. In their life they were powers of evil, and even in death they have not wholly ceased from troubling. * * * In no branch of the law is this more obvious than in that which relates to the different classes of wrongs which may be committed with respect to chattels. In particular the law of trover and conversion is a region still darkened with the mists of legal formalism, through which no man will find his way by the light of nature or with any other guide save the old learning of writs and forms of action and the mysteries of pleading." Salmond, Observations on Trover and Conversion, 1905, 21 L.Q.Rev. 43.

75. Simpson, The Introduction of the Action on the Case for Conversion, 1959, 75 L.Q.Rev. 364, traces it back to 1479, Y.B. 18 Edw. IV, f. 23, pl. 5, where there is reference to an earlier action on the case, in which the defendant "converted" the goods by changing their character, making clothes out of cloth of gold.

76. See Fifoot, History and Sources of the Common Law, 1949, 102–25; Ames, History of Trover, 1898, 11 Harv.L.Rev. 277, 374; Salmond, Observations on Trover and Conversion, 1905, 21 L.Q.Rev. 43.

77. Lord Mounteagle v. Countess of Worcester, 1554, 2 Dyer 121a, 73 Eng.Rep. 265.

tion of losing the goods, and then that of finding them, as a fiction.[78]

The defendant was not permitted to deny the losing and finding, so that the only issues to be litigated were those of the plaintiff's right to possession and the conversion itself. With losing and finding no longer essential, trover became the standard remedy for any form of interference with a chattel. It entirely replaced detinue, which fell into complete disuse; and it so far replaced trespass to chattels that that action appeared only very infrequently. For some two centuries it was said that "whenever trespass for taking goods will lie, that is, where they are taken wrongfully, trover will lie."[79] The two actions, in other words, were regarded as alternative remedies for the same wrong.

There were, however, significant differences between them, which for these two centuries passed almost entirely unremarked. One was that trover would lie for a wrongful detention of goods which had not been wrongfully taken, while trespass would not.[80] More important, however, was a basic difference in theory. The theory of trespass was that the plaintiff remained the owner of the chattel, with his possession only interrupted or interfered with, so that when it was tendered back to him he must accept it. His recovery was limited to the damages he had sustained through loss of possession, or harm to the chattel, which were usually considerably less than its value. The theory of trover was that the defendant had appropriated the plaintiff's chattel, for which he must pay. The plaintiff was therefore not required to

accept it when it was tendered back to him; and he recovered as damages the full value of the chattel at the time and place of conversion. When the defendant satisfied the judgment in trover, the title to the chattel passed to him, and the plaintiff had nothing more to do with it.[81] The effect was that the defendant was compelled, because of his wrongful appropriation, to buy the chattel at a forced sale, of which the action of trover was the judicial instrument.[82]

The modern law of conversion began when this basic difference between the theories of trespass and trover was brought into sharp focus in Fouldes v. Willoughby[83] in England in 1841. The defendant wrongfully refused to carry plaintiff's horses on a ferry-boat, and put them off. The plaintiff remained on the boat, and as a result lost his horses. It was held that this was a trespass, but not a conversion, since there was no interference with the plaintiff's "general right of dominion" over the horses. At about the same time, in an American case,[84] a young lawyer named Abraham Lincoln succeeded in convincing the court that there was no conversion when a horse left with the defendant to be agisted and fed was ridden, on one occasion, for a distance of fifteen miles, since it was not a sufficiently serious invasion of the owner's rights.

Following such decisions, the tort of conversion has been confined to those major interferences with the chattel, or with the plaintiff's rights in it, which are so serious, and so important, as to justify the forced ju-

---

78. Gumbleton v. Grafton, 1600, Cro.Eliz. 781, 78 Eng. Rep. 1011; Kinaston v. Moore, 1626, Cro.Car. 89, 79 Eng.Rep. 678; Ratcliff v. Davies, 1611, Cro.Jac. 244, 79 Eng.Rep. 210; Isaack v. Clark, 1614, 2 Bulst. 306, 80 Eng.Rep. 1143.

79. Lord Mansfield, in Cooper v. Chitty, 1756, 1 Burr. 20, 31, 97 Eng.Rep. 166, 172; Serjeant Williams, Note to Saunders' Reports, Wilbraham v. Snow, 1670, 2 Wms.Saund. 47aa, 85 Eng.Rep. 624.

80. Put and Hardy v. Rawsterne, 1682, T.Raym. 472, 83 Eng.Rep. 246. See supra, p. 76.

81. Adams v. Broughton, 1737, Andrews 18, 95 Eng. Rep. 278; Gunther v. Morey Larue Laundry Co., 1943, 129 N.J.L. 345, 29 A.2d 713 affirmed, 1943, 130 N.J.L. 557, 33 A.2d 893. The mere entry of judgment, without satisfaction, did not affect the title. Hepburn v. Sewell, 1821, 5 Har. & J., Md., 211; Miller v. Hyde, 1894, 161 Mass. 472, 37 N.E. 760.

82. See Hale, Bailments, 1896, 188; May v. Georger, 1897, 21 Misc. 622, 47 N.Y.S. 1057.

83. 1841, 8 M. & W. 540, 151 Eng.Rep. 1153.

84. Johnson v. Weedman, 1843, 5 Ill. 495.

dicial sale to the defendant which is the distinguishing feature of the action. Trespass remains as an occasional remedy for minor interferences, resulting in some damage, but not sufficiently serious or sufficiently important to amount to the greater tort.[85] In determining the seriousness of the interference, and the justice of requiring the defendant to pay the full value, all of the relevant factors in the case are to be considered. These include the extent and duration of the defendant's exercise of control over the chattel; his intent to assert a right which is in fact inconsistent with the plaintiff's right of control; the defendant's good faith or bad intentions; the extent and duration of the resulting interference with the plaintiff's right of control; the harm done to the chattel; and the expense and inconvenience caused to the plaintiff.[86] It follows that in cases of similar conduct, and similar interference, the question becomes one of degree, as to which no definite rules can be laid down —although similar cases are amazingly consistent with one another.

What May Be Converted

What property may be the subject of an action for conversion was at first determined on the basis of the fiction of losing and find-ing.[87] Any tangible chattel could be lost and found, and so could be converted.[88] Land, on the other hand, was obviously incapable of getting lost, and therefore trover would not lie for the dispossession or withholding of real property. The same was true of sand and gravel, timber, crops and fixtures, so long as they were regarded as a part of the land, so that no action of trover would lie for their severance. Once there was severance, however, such goods became personal property, and trover could be maintained for their removal from the land.[89]

Intangible rights of all kinds could not be lost or found, and the original rule was that there could be no conversion of such property. But this hoary limitation has been discarded to some extent by all of the courts.[90] The first relaxation of the rule was with respect to the conversion of a document in which intangible rights were merged, so that the one became the symbol of the other —as in the case of a promissory note,[91] a

---

85. See for example Bankston v. Dumont, 1949, 205 Miss. 272, 38 So.2d 721 (opening and searching purse, removing money); Bruch v. Carter, 1867, 32 N.J.L. 554 (moving chattel); Post v. Munn, 1818, 4 N.J.L. 61 (damaging fishing net); Brittain v. McKay, 1840, 23 N.C. 265 (cutting crop). "Where the conduct complained of does not amount to a substantial interference with possession or the right thereto, but consists of intermeddling with or use of or damage to the personal property, the owner has a cause of action for trespass or case, and may recover only the actual damages suffered by reason of the impairment of the property or the loss of its use." Zaslow v. Kroenert, 1946, 29 Cal.2d 541, 551, 176 P.2d 1, 7.

86. Second Restatement of Torts, § 222A, accepted in Mustola v. Toddy, 1969, — Or. —, 456 P.2d 1004; Pearson v. Dodd, D.C.Cir.1969, 410 F.2d 701. Cases are collected in Prosser, The Nature of Conversion, 1957, 42 Corn.L.Q. 168.

87. See Ayers v. French, 1874, 41 Conn. 142.

88. Graham v. Smith, 1897, 100 Ga. 434, 28 S.E. 225 (dog); State v. Omaha Nat. Bank, 1899, 59 Neb. 483, 81 N.W. 319 (money); Vaughn v. Wright, 1913, 139 Ga. 736, 78 S.E. 123 (tax receipts).

89. Cage Bros. v. Whiteman, 1942, 139 Tex. 522, 163 S.W.2d 638; Palumbo v. Harry M. Quinn, Inc., 1944, 323 Ill.App. 404, 55 N.E.2d 825; Luhmann v. Schaefer, Mo.App.1940, 142 S.W.2d 1088; Pettigrew v. W & H Development Co., Fla.App.1960, 122 So.2d 813; Giuliano Const. Co. v. Simmons, 1960, 147 Conn. 441, 162 A.2d 511. As to the appreciated value of cut timber, see Smith v. Shiflett, 1965, 66 Wash.2d 462, 403 P.2d 364.

90. See Rubin, Conversion of Choses in Action, 1941, 10 Fordham L.Rev. 415.

91. Citizens' Bank of Madison v. Shaw, 1909, 132 Ga. 771, 65 S.E. 81; Capps v. Vasey Bros., 1909, 23 Okl. 554, 101 P. 1043; Hoyt v. Stuart, 1915, 90 Conn. 41, 96 A. 166; Security Bank of Minnesota v. Fogg, 1889, 148 Mass. 273, 19 N.E. 378; Griggs v. Day, 1892, 136 N.Y. 152, 32 N.E. 612, rehearing denied 137 N.Y. 542, 32 N.E. 1001. In the absence of evidence, the measure of damages for conversion of a negotiable instrument usually is taken to be its face value. Allied Building Credits v. Grogan Builders Supply Co., Tex.Civ.App.1963, 365 S.W.2d 692, refused n. r. e.

check,[92] a bond,[93] a bill of lading,[94] or a stock certificate.[95] This was then extended to include intangible rights to which a tangible object, converted by the defendant, was highly important—as in the case of a savings bank book,[96] an insurance policy,[97] a tax receipt,[98] account books,[99] or a receipted account.[1] In all of these cases the conversion

of the tangible thing was held to include conversion of the intangible rights, and to carry damages for it. The final step was to find conversion of the rights themselves where there was no accompanying conversion of anything tangible—as, for example, where a corporation refuses to register a transfer of the rights of a shareholder on its books.[2]

The process of expansion has stopped with the kind of intangible rights which are customarily merged in, or identified with some document. There is perhaps no very valid and essential reason why there might not be conversion of an ordinary debt,[3] the good will of a business,[4] or even an idea,[5] or "any species of personal property which is the subject of private ownership;"[6] but thus far

92. First Nat. Bank of Montgomery v. Montgomery Cotton Mfg. Co., 1924, 211 Ala. 551, 101 So. 186; Bentley, Murray & Co. v. La Salle St. Trust & Sav. Bank, 1916, 197 Ill.App. 322; Craven v. Wright, 1925, 114 Or. 692, 236 P. 1043; Lovell v. Hammond Co., 1895, 66 Conn. 500, 34 A. 511; Graton & Knight Mfg. Co. v. Redelsheimer, 1902, 28 Wash. 370, 68 P. 879. Cf. Hooten v. State to Use of Cross County, 1915, 119 Ark. 334, 178 S.W. 310 (draft).

93. Knight v. Seney, 1919, 290 Ill. 11, 124 N.E. 813; Varney v. Curtis, 1913, 213 Mass. 309, 100 N.E. 650; Simon v. Reilly, 1926, 321 Ill. 431, 151 N.E. 884; Thompson v. Metropolitan Bldg. Co., 1917, 95 Wash. 546, 164 P. 222; Chew v. Louchheim, 3 Cir., 1897, 80 F. 500.

94. Alderson v. Gulf, C. & S. F. R. Co., Tex.Civ.App. 1893, 23 S.W. 617, error refused; Market State Bank v. Farmers' Sav. Bank of Meservey, 1921, 190 Iowa 1112, 181 S.W. 486. Accord, as to warehouse receipts: Canadian Bank of Commerce v. McCrea, 1882, 106 Ill. 281; Latimer v. Stubbs, 1935, 173 Miss. 436, 159 So. 857, 161 So. 869; cf. R. L. Rothstein Corp. v. Kerr S. S. Co., 1964, 21 App.Div.2d 463, 251 N.Y.S.2d 81 (mate's receipt).

95. Pierpoint v. Hoyt, 1932, 260 N.Y. 26, 182 N.E. 235; United States Cities Corp. v. Sautbine, 1927, 126 Okl. 172, 259 P. 253; Pardee v. Nelson, 1922, 59 Utah 497, 205 P. 332; Reading Finance & Sec. Co. v. Harley, 3 Cir. 1911, 186 F. 673.

96. Stebbins v. North Adams Trust Co., 1922, 243 Mass. 69, 136 N.E. 880; Iavazzo v. Rhode Island Hospital Trust Co., 1931, 51 R.I. 459, 155 A. 407.

97. Commercial Credit Co. v. Eisenhour, 1925, 28 Ariz. 112, 236 P. 126; Hayes v. Massachusetts Mut. Life Ins. Co., 1888, 125 Ill. 626, 18 N.E. 322; Mutual Life Ins. Co. v. Allen, 1904, 212 Ill. 134, 72 N.E. 200; Handley v. Home Ins. Co. of New York, 1933, 112 Fla. 225, 150 So. 902.

98. Vaughn v. Wright, 1913, 139 Ga. 736, 78 S.E. 123.

99. Plunkett-Jarrell Grocery Co. v. Terry, 1954, 222 Ark. 784, 263 S.W.2d 229. See Note, 1954, 9 Ark.L. Rev. 72.

1. Moody v. Drown, 1876, 58 N.H. 45. Cf. Pickford Corp. v. De Luxe Laboratories, S.D.Cal.1958, 161 F.Supp. 367, supplemented, 1959, 169 F.Supp. 118, finding conversion of literary property when defendant duplicated motion picture negatives delivered to it, and turned the prints over to a television company for exhibition.

2. Herrick v. Humphrey Hardware Co., 1905, 73 Neb. 809, 103 N.W. 685; Humphreys v. Minnesota Clay Co., 1905, 94 Minn. 469, 103 N.W. 338; Mears v. Crocker First Nat. Bank, 1948, 84 Cal.App.2d 637, 191 P.2d 501; Mastellone v. Argo Oil Corp., 1951, Del., 7 Terry, 102, 82 A.2d 379; Ballenger v. Liberty Nat. Life Ins. Co., 1957, 266 Ala. 407, 96 So.2d 728.

3. In Englehart v. Sage, 1925, 73 Mont. 139, 235 P. 767, and McAllister v. Bailey, 1891, 127 N.Y. 583, 28 N.E. 591, conversion was found in the wrongful attachment of an ordinary debt. To the contrary are Rothchild v. Schwarz, 1899, 28 Misc. 521, 59 N.Y.S. 527; Wright v. School District, 1912, 36 Okl. 294, 128 P. 241; Knox v. Moskins Stores, 1951, 341 Ala. 346, 2 So.2d 449; and Petroleum Marketing Corp. v. Metropolitan Petroleum Corp., 1959, 396 Pa. 48, 151 A.2d 616.

4. No conversion: Powers v. Fisher, 1937, 279 Mich. 442, 272 N.W. 737 (names of customers); Olschewski v. Hudson, 1927, 87 Cal.App. 282, 262 P. 43 (same); Illinois Minerals Co. v. McCarty, 1943, 318 Ill.App. 423, 48 N.E.2d 424 (same); Stern v. Kaufman's Bakery, Inc., Sup.Ct.1959, 191 N.Y.S.2d 734 (bakery route); Whiteley v. Foremost Dairies, W.D.Ark. 1957, 151 F.Supp. 914, affirmed, 1958, 254 F.2d 36 (milk route); Meier v. Wilkens, 1897, 15 App.Div. 97, 44 N.Y.S. 274 (right to occupy a market stall).

5. No conversion: Mackay v. Benjamin Franklin Realty & Holding Co., 1927, 288 Pa. 207, 135 A. 613; Thompson v. Mobil Producing Co., D.Mont.1958, 163 F.Supp. 402 (confidential information).

6. Vaughn v. Wright, 1913, 139 Ga. 736, 78 S.E. 123.

other remedies apparently have been adequate, and there has been no particular need or demand for any extension of the rather drastic relief of conversion beyond rights customarily represented by documents.

Character of Defendant's Act

A conversion can result only from conduct intended to affect the chattel. For merely negligent interference with it, such as failure to protect it against loss, damage or theft, the remedy is an action for negligence; but there is no conversion, and trover would not lie.[7] It usually is said that mere nonfeasance is not a conversion;[8] but it seems clear that there are situations in which a wilful omission which deprives the plaintiff of his property can serve as a foundation for the action.[9]

The intent required is not necessarily a matter of conscious wrongdoing. It is rather an intent to exercise a dominion or control over the goods which is in fact inconsistent with the plaintiff's rights.[10] A purchaser of

stolen goods[11] or an auctioneer who sells them[12] in the utmost good faith becomes a converter, since his acts are an interference with the control of the property. A mistake of law or fact is no defense. "Persons deal with the property in chattels or exercise acts of ownership over them at their peril,"[13] and must take the risk that there is no lawful justification for their acts. The essential problem is whether the interference is of so serious a character as to require the defendant to buy the goods.

Given the intent to affect the chattel, conversion may be committed in a number of different ways, as follows:

Acquiring Possession

The defendant may, first of all, wrongfully acquire possession of the plaintiff's chattel.

---

7. Heald v. Carey, 1852, 11 C.B. 977, 138 Eng.Rep. 762; Dearbourn v. Union Nat. Bank, 1870, 58 Me. 273; Wamsley v. Atlas S. S. Co., 1901, 168 N.Y. 533, 61 N.E. 896; Emmert v. United Bank & Trust Co., 1936, 14 Cal.App.2d 1, 57 P.2d 963; Armored Car Service v. First Nat. Bank of Miami, Fla.App.1959, 114 So.2d 431.

8. Farrar v. Rollins, 1864, 37 Vt. 295; Forehand v. Jones, 1889, 84 Ga. 508, 10 S.E. 1090; Evans v. Mason, 1886, 64 N.H. 98, 5 A. 766; Bolling v. Kirby, 1889, 90 Ala. 215, 7 So. 914; Dearbourn v. Union Nat. Bank, 1870, 58 Me. 273; Second Restatement of Torts, § 224.

9. See Donnell v. Canadian Pac. R. Co., 1912, 109 Me. 500, 84 A. 1002. "Where B is in possession of the property, or where he has such control over it that he can readily get possession (as where he has stored it with a bailee), and A demands it, and B fails to deliver it, no modern court is going to save B from being a converter on the ground that there was only a nonfeasance." Warren, Trover and Conversion, 1936, 36.

10. See Fouldes v. Willoughby, 1841, 8 M. & W. 540, 151 Eng.Rep. 1153; Hiort v. Bott, 1874, L.R. 9 Ex. 86; Hollins v. Fowler, 1875, L.R. 7 H.L. 757; Allred v. Hinkley, 1958, 8 Utah, 2d 73, 328 P.2d 726.

In Poggi v. Scott, 1914, 167 Cal. 372, 139 P. 815, defendant, on moving into a building, found in the cellar plaintiff's barrels of wine, left there for sto-

rage. Assuming that they were abandoned, he sold them for junk. He was held liable for conversion.

In Salt Springs Nat. Bank v. Wheeler, 1872, 48 N.Y. 492, plaintiff sent three bills of exchange to defendant for acceptance. Defendant allowed them to get mixed up with other papers, which he threw into the waste basket, and the bills were burned. He was held not liable for conversion.

The difference between the two cases is that in the first defendant intended to affect the chattels, by disposing of them, although under a mistake of fact as to what they were. In the second there was no intent to dispose of the chattels at all, although there was no doubt negligence.

11. See infra, p. 84.

12. See infra, p. 88. Cf. Judkins v. Sadler-MacNeil, 1962, 61 Wash.2d 1, 376 P.2d 837 (good faith refusal to surrender goods).

13. Cleasby, B., in Hollins v. Fowler, 1874, L.R. 7 Q.B. 639. "The foundation for the action of conversion rests neither in the knowledge nor the intent of the defendant. It rests upon the unwarranted interference by defendant with the dominion over the property of the plaintiff from which injury to the latter results. Therefore neither good nor bad faith, neither care nor negligence, neither knowledge nor ignorance, are of the gist of the action." Poggi v. Scott, 1914, 167 Cal. 372, 139 P. 815. Cf. Wilson Freight Forwarding Co. v. Cleveland, C. & C. Highway, 1944, 74 Ohio App. 54, 57 N.E.2d 796 (wrong carrier shipped goods by mistake); McGlynn v. Schultz, 1966, 90 N.J.Super. 505, 218 A.2d 408, affirmed 95 N.J.Super. 412, 231 A.2d 386 (good faith and advice of counsel no defense); Newhart v. Pierce, 1967, 254 Cal.App.2d 783, 62 Cal.Rptr. 553.

He may, without legal justification, take it out of the plaintiff's possession, or that of a third person. Thus conversion will lie against a trespasser,[14] or a thief.[15] It will also lie for an unjustified levy or attachment under legal process, even though possession is not otherwise disturbed, since the interference is equally serious.[16] In all such cases the taking itself is wrongful, and the tort is complete without any demand for the return of the goods.[17] The same rule has been extended to the acquisition of possession of the chattel by fraud,[18] even though title may have passed to the defendant,[19] by means of a rather fine-spun and anomalous theory which permits the plaintiff to exercise of his own motion the equitable remedy of rescission of the transaction, and thereafter to recover for the wrongful taking as if his consent to it had never been given.

Upon the same basis, a bona fide purchaser of goods from one who has stolen them, or who merely has no power to transfer them, becomes a converter when he takes possession to complete the transaction.[20] The courts of New York, and those of two or three other states, have held that such possession is not in itself a sufficiently serious interference with the owner's rights to amount to conversion, so that the purchaser is liable only when he refuses to return the goods on demand.[21] But the great weight of authority regards the mere acquisition of the goods under such circumstances as in itself an assertion of an adverse claim, so detrimental to the dominion of the owner that it completes the tort, and no demand is required.[22] An exception is

14. Plaintiff may waive the trespass and sue for the conversion. Hunt v. City of Boston, 1903, 183 Mass. 303, 67 N.E. 244. As to the local or transitory character of the action, see American Union Tel. Co. v. Middleton, 1880, 80 N.Y. 408; Ellenwood v. Marietta Chair Co., 1895, 158 U.S. 105; Stone v. United States, 1897, 167 U.S. 178.

15. Hutchinson v. Merchants' & Mechanics' Bank of Wheeling, 1861, 41 Pa. 42.

16. Tinkler v. Poole, 1770, 5 Burr. 2657, 98 Eng.Rep. 396; Morse v. Hurd, 1845, 17 N.H. 246; Kloos v. Gatz, 1906, 97 Minn. 167, 105 N.W. 639; Zion v. De Jonge, 1902, 39 Misc. 839, 81 N.Y.S. 491; Johnson v. Farr, 1880, 60 N.H. 426. It is not necessary that the defendant apply the property to his own use. McPheters v. Page, 1891, 83 Me. 234, 22 A. 101. See Note, 1939, 23 Minn.L.Rev. 799.

17. Bruen v. Roe, 1665, 1 Sid. 264, 82 Eng.Rep. 1095; Porell v. Cavanaugh, 1898, 69 N.H. 364, 41 A. 860; New York Cent. R. Co. v. Freedman, 1921, 240 Mass. 200, 133 N.E. 101; Atlantic Finance Corp. v. Graham, 1942, 311 Mass. 49, 39 N.E.2d 951 (attachment of goods of wrong party).

18. Roehrich v. Holt Motor Co., 1938, 201 Minn. 586, 277 N.W. 274; McCrillis v. Allen, 1884, 57 Vt. 505; Douglas Motor Sales v. Cy Owens, Inc., 1959, 99 Ga.App. 890, 109 S.E.2d 874 (payment stopped on check); Gottesfeld v. Mechanics & Traders Ins. Co., 1961, 196 Pa.Super. 109, 173 A.2d 763. Contra, Christensen v. Pugh, 1934, 84 Utah 440, 36 P.2d 100.

19. Holland v. Bishop, 1895, 60 Minn. 23, 61 N.W. 681; Hagar v. Norton, 1905, 188 Mass. 47, 73 N.E. 1073. Since the theory of the recovery is a wrongful taking rather than wrongful detention, a demand is not essential to the cause of action. Thurston v. Blanchard, 1839, 22 Pick., Mass., 18; Yeager v. Wallace, 1868, 57 Pa. 365; Luckey v. Roberts, 1857, 25 Conn. 486; Baird v. Howard, 1894, 51 Ohio St. 57, 36 N.E. 732; Second Restatement of Torts, § 252A.

Cf. Bolton v. Stewart, Tex.Civ.App.1945, 191 S.W.2d 798 (purchase of goods from lunatic incapable of contract).

20. Second Restatement of Torts, § 229. See Newmark, Conversion by Purchase, 1881, 15 Am.L.Rev. 363.

21. Gillet v. Roberts, 1874, 57 N.Y. 28. Accord: Parker v. Middlebrook, 1855, 24 Conn. 207; see Burckhalter v. Mitchell, 1887, 27 S.C. 240, 3 S.E. 225. But demand is held to be unnecessary where it would obviously be futile, as where the defendant after knowledge of the plaintiff's rights claims to be the owner. Employers' Fire Ins. Co. v. Cotten, 1927, 245 N.Y. 102, 156 N.E. 629.

22. Hyde v. Noble, 1843, 13 N.H. 494; Hovland v. Farmers Union Elevator Co., 1936, 67 N.D. 71, 269 N.W. 842; Culp v. Signal Van & Storage Co., 1956, 142 Cal.App.2d 859, 298 P.2d 162; Lovinger v. Hix Green Buick Co., 1964, 110 Ga.App. 698, 140 S.E.2d 83; McRae v. Bandy, 1959, 270 Ala. 12, 115 So.2d 479; Second Restatement of Torts, § 229; Note, 1933, 32 Yale L.J. 292.

The purchaser is also a converter when he resells the chattel without notice that it is stolen. Rogers v. Citizens Bank, 1955, 92 Ga.App. 399, 88 S.E.2d 548; Culp v. Signal Van & Storage Co., 1956, 142 Cal.App.2d 859, 298 P.2d 162.

A fortiori if the defendant either buys or resells with notice. Fowler v. Kragel, 1956, 93 Ga.App. 403, 91

recognized in the case of negotiable instruments, whose character protects those who rely upon them.[23] Similar rules are applied to those who in good faith take stolen goods in rental or pledge.[24]

Complications arise where there is a bona fide purchase of goods which the true owner was originally induced to sell by fraud.[25] In such a case title has passed on the sale, and there is only a right to rescind the transaction and recover back the goods. This right, although it is enforced at law, originated in equity, and is essentially equitable in character. Since it is fundamental that a bona fide purchase always cuts off equitable rights, such a purchaser is not liable to the original owner for conversion.[26] On the other hand, a purchaser with notice of the fraud obtains no better rights than the one from whom he buys, and so is liable.[27]

It is not, however, every unauthorized taking of goods from the possession of another which is sufficiently serious to amount to conversion. Intention may be good, the duration brief, the event harmless; and if so, the severe remedy of the forced sale to the defendant will not be applied. If A takes B's hat from the rack in a restaurant, immediately discovers his mistake, and returns the hat, it is clearly no conversion.[28] If he takes the hat intending to steal it,[29] or if he keeps it six months, or if a sudden gust of wind blows it off of his head into an open manhole and it is lost, the interference with the rights of the owner becomes sufficiently serious to amount to conversion.[30]

It is generally agreed that a bailee who merely receives possession of the chattel for storage, safekeeping or transportation, in ignorance of the fact that it is lost or stolen, does not thereby become liable to the owner for conversion.[31] Sometimes this is explained

S.E.2d 794; Burns v. Commonwealth Trailer Sales, 1956, 163 Neb. 308, 79 N.W.2d 563.

23. Spooner v. Holmes, 1869, 102 Mass. 503; Pratt v. Higginson, 1918, 230 Mass. 256, 119 N.E. 661; Security-First Nat. Bank of Los Angeles v. Lutz, 9 Cir. 1961, 297 F.2d 159. The purchaser must take in due course or he is not protected. United States F. & G. Co. v. Leon, 1937, 165 Misc. 549, 300 N.Y.S. 331.

24. Warner v. Martin, 1850, 49 U.S. (11 How.) 209; Bott v. McCoy & Johnson, 1852, 20 Ala. 578; O'Connell v. Chicago Park District, 1941, 376 Ill. 550, 34 N.E.2d 836; McCreary & Barlow v. Gaines, 1881, 55 Tex. 485; Thrall v. Lathrop, 1858, 30 Vt. 307. A few courts, however, represented by Varney v. Curtis, 1913, 213 Mass. 309, 100 N.E. 650, have held that the mere taking in pledge is not sufficient for conversion, and that the pledgee is not liable until demand is made upon him.

25. See supra, note 18.

26. McCullen v. Hereford State Bank, 5 Cir. 1954, 214 F.2d 185; Parr v. Helfrich, 1922, 108 Neb. 801, 189 N.W. 281; Martin v. Green, 1918, 117 Me. 138, 102 A. 977; Porell v. Cavanaugh, 1898, 69 N.H. 364, 41 A. 860; Hoffman v. Alpern, 1948, 193 Misc. 695, 85 N.Y.S.2d 561.

Where the transferee has obtained only possession by his fraud, and not title, he can convey no title, and the bona fide purchaser becomes a converter. Alexander v. Swackhamer, 1886, 105 Ind. 81, 4 N. E. 433, 5 N.E. 908; Moody v. Blake, 1874, 117 Mass. 23; Hamet v. Letcher, 1881, 37 Ohio St. 356; Ashton v. Allen, 1903, 70 N.J.L. 117, 56 A. 165; Barker v. Dinsmore, 1872, 72 Pa. 427.

27. Luckey v. Roberts, 1857, 25 Conn. 486; Traywick v. Keeble, 1890, 93 Ala. 498, 8 So. 573; Shaw v. North Pennsylvania R. Co., 1879, 101 U.S. 557; Yeomans v. Jones, 1936, 54 Ga.App. 330, 188 S.E. 62; Charles Kreisler, Inc. v. Matusow, Sup.Ct.1955, 144 N.Y.S.2d 568.

28. Cf. Blackinton v. Pillsbury, 1927, 260 Mass. 123, 156 N.E. 895 (removal of property from locker by mistake); Hushaw v. Dunn, 1916, 62 Colo. 109, 160 P. 1037 (money taken from person of prisoner before he was locked up); Frome v. Dennis, 1883, 45 N.J.L. 515 (brief and innocent borrowing of a plow from one with no right to lend it); MacBryde v. Burnett, D.Mo.1942, 44 F.Supp. 833, affirmed, 1943, 132 F.2d 898 (trustee by mistake transferred shares of stock into his own name).

29. Cf. Lawyers' Mortgage Inv. Co. v. Paramount Laundries, 1934, 287 Mass. 357, 191 N.E. 398; Hutchinson v. Merchants' & Mechanics' Bank, 1861, 41 Pa. 42.

30. Cf. Donahue v. Shippee, 1887, 15 R.I. 453, 8 A. 541 (cutting grass, which was appropriated by third persons); and see Blackinton v. Pillsbury, 1927, 260 Mass 123, 156 N.E. 895 (dictum, if the property were lost or destroyed there would be conversion).

31. Gurley v. Armstead, 1889, 148 Mass. 267, 19 N.E. 389; Shellnut v. Central of Georgia R. Co., 1908,

upon the basis that the interference with the owner's rights is not a sufficiently serious one;[32] but the rule appears in reality to be one of commercial convenience, which protects those who are needed in our society to receive such goods, against the necessity of inquiry as to the title to what is delivered to them, and so protects their patrons against the delay attending such inquiry. It may thus be regarded as in the nature of a privilege, which does not exist if the bailee receives the goods with knowledge, or reason to know, that the bailor has no right to deliver them.[33]

The liability of a servant or agent who receives possession from another on behalf of his principal or master has presented more difficulty. The prevailing view is that if the agent himself has negotiated the transaction for his principal, in which he takes possession of the goods, he thereby asserts such an adverse claim, of so serious a character, that he is liable to the true owner of the goods for conversion, notwithstanding his innocence and good faith.[34] But if he innocently receives or transports the goods and has no other part in the transaction, he is not responsible for the conversion by his principal.[35]

Removing the Chattel

The unauthorized change of the location of the chattel, without other interference with it, may or may not amount to a conversion. If there is no intent to assume any other control over it, or to deprive the owner of it, and the interference is brief in duration and otherwise harmless, it is not so serious a matter as to call for a forced sale to the defendant. Thus the defendant who finds in a newly purchased house the plaintiff's furniture, which the plaintiff refuses to remove, does not become a converter, although there may perhaps be trespass,[36] when he sends the furniture to a storage warehouse, and informs the plaintiff where it is.[37] But if he removes the furniture to a great distance,[38] or fails to notify the plaintiff or to follow his instructions,[39] and so puts him to unnecessary inconvenience and expense, or if he removes the furniture intending to keep it for him-

---

131 Ga. 404, 62 S.E. 294; Thoms v. D. C. Andrews & Co., 2 Cir. 1931, 54 F.2d 250; Williams v. Roberts, 1939, 59 Ga.App. 473, 1 S.E.2d 587; Manny v. Wilson, 1910, 137 App.Div. 140, 122 N.Y.S. 16, affirmed 1912, 203 N.Y. 535, 96 N.E. 1121.

32. "The carrier and the packing agent are generally held not to have converted because by their acts they merely purport to change the position of the goods and not the property." Barker v. Furlong, [1891] 2 Ch.Div. 172, 182.

33. Warder-Bushnell & Glessner Co. v. Harris, 1890, 81 Iowa 153, 46 N.W. 859; Beckwith v. Independent Transfer & Storage Co., 1928, 105 W.Va. 26, 141 S.E. 443; McAnelly v. Chapman, 1856, 18 Tex. 198; Thorp v. Burling, 1814, 11 Johns., N.Y., 285; Dodson v. Economy Equipment Co., 1936, 188 Wash. 340, 62 P.2d 708.

34. Hollins v. Fowler, 1875, L.R. 7 H.L. 757; Flannery v. Harley, 1903, 117 Ga. 483, 43 S.E. 765; Richtmyer v. Mutual Livestock Commission Co., 1932, 122 Neb. 317, 240 N.W. 315; First Nat. Bank of Pipestone v. Siman, 1937, 65 S.D. 514, 275 N.W. 347; Nahm v. J. R. Fleming & Co., Tex.Civ.App. 1938, 116 S.W.2d 1174.

35. Cases as to liability for mere receipt are few. In Burditt v. Hunt, 1885, 25 Me. 419, and Silver v. Martin, 1880, 59 N.H. 580, the agent was held not to be a converter. To the contrary are Stephens v. Elwall, 1815, 4 M. & S. 259, 105 Eng.Rep. 830, and Miller v. Wilson, 1896, 98 Ga. 567, 25 S.E. 578. See however, the cases of delivery by an agent, infra, note 60, all of which necessarily involved his receipt. If the agent receives possession with notice of the owner's rights, he is a converter. Warder-Bushnell & Glessner Co. v. Harris, 1890, 81 Iowa 153, 46 N.W. 859.

36. See Zaslow v. Kroenert, 1946, 29 Cal.2d 541, 176 P.2d 1; Burgess v. Graffam, C.C.Mass.1883, 18 F. 251; Bruch v. Carter, 1867, 32 N.J.L. 554.

37. Zaslow v. Kroenert, 1946, 29 Cal.2d 541, 176 P.2d 1; Lucas v. Durrence, (1920) 25 Ga.App. 264, 103 S.E. 36; Geisler v. David Stevenson Brewing Co., 1908, 126 App.Div. 715, 111 N.Y.S. 56; Lee Tung v. Burkhart, 1911, 59 Or. 194, 116 P. 1066; Oge v. Resolute Ins. Co., La.App.1969, 217 So.2d 738.

38. Cf. Forsdick v. Collins, 1816, 1 Stark. 173, 171 Eng.Rep. 437; Electric Power Co. v. Mayor of New York, 1899, 36 App.Div. 383, 55 N.Y.S. 460.

39. McGonigle v. Victor H. Belleisle Co., 1904, 186 Mass. 310, 71 N.E. 569; Borg & Powers Furniture Co. v. Reiling, 1943, 213 Minn. 539, 7 N.W.2d 310.

self,[40] or it is destroyed by fire while it is in the warehouse, there is conversion.[41]

Thus the liability of one who moves another's car upon the street will depend upon whether he intends to steal it, or merely wants parking space for himself; and in the latter case, whether he moves it only a few feet or locks it up in an unknown garage without informing the owner.[42] As in the case of receiving possession,[43] carriers and other bailees are protected in their transportation of stolen goods if they move them in good faith, but not if they have notice of the adverse claim.

Transferring Possession

Perhaps the most common way in which conversion is committed is by an unauthorized transfer or disposal of possession of the goods to one who is not entitled to them. Normally this is a sufficiently serious interference with the true owner's right of control, although cases are possible in which the consequences of an innocent mistake are so unimportant that conversion will not be found.[44]

Ordinarily the defendant has "set the goods afloat upon a sea of strangers," and it follows that, in Professor Warren's well-known phrase, he has "bought something." Thus a sale and delivery of the plaintiff's goods to another,[45] a lease,[46] a pledge,[47] a mortgage,[48] or even a gift,[49] or a mere erroneous delivery to the wrong person,[50] will constitute a conversion. It is no answer that the defendant acted in good faith, in the honest belief that the delivery was lawful, proper, or authorized. Thus an auctioneer who sells and delivers stolen or mortgaged goods under instructions from his principal becomes liable as a converter notwithstanding his innocence,[51] and so does a carrier or other bailee who, by an innocent mistake, misdelivers the goods to the wrong party.[52] This liability has even

---

40. Hicks Rubber Distributors v. Stacy, Tex.Civ.App. 1939, 133 S.W.2d 249.

41. McCurdy v. Wallblom Furniture & Carpet Co., 1905, 94 Minn. 326, 102 N.W. 873. Cf. Ryan v. Chown, 1910, 160 Mich. 204, 125 N.W. 46; Tobin v. Deal, 1884, 60 Wis. 87, 18 N.W. 634. In Egge v. West Dependable Stores, 1932, 171 Wash. 64, 17 P.2d 609, distance, intent to appropriate, and destruction by fire were all involved. Conversion was found.

42. Cf. Howard v. Deschambeault, 1959, 154 Me. 383, 148 A.2d 706; Fouldes v. Willoughby, 1841, 8 M. & W. 540, 151 Eng.Rep. 1153; Wilson v. McLaughlin, 1871, 107 Mass. 587; Mattice v. Brinkman, 1889, 74 Mich. 705, 42 N.W. 172; O. J. Gude Co. v. Farley, 1898, 25 Misc. 502, 54 N.Y.S. 998.

43. See supra, notes 31, 35.

44. For example, Gulf, C. & S. F. R. Co. v. Wortham, Tex.Civ.App.1913, 154 S.W. 1071, where a carrier by mistake delivered plaintiff's goods to a stranger, immediately discovered the mistake, and within twenty-four hours retrieved the goods and delivered them to plaintiff. Also Brandenburg v. Northwestern Jobbers Credit Bureau, 1915, 128 Minn. 411, 151 N.W. 134, where plaintiff's furniture was delivered to a stranger with a house, and there was delay in notifying plaintiff to come and get it.

45. Poggi v. Scott, 1914, 167 Cal. 372, 139 P. 815; Miller v. Long, 1956, 126 Ind.App. 482, 131 N.E.2d 348, rehearing denied 126 Ind.App. 482, 132 N.E.2d 272; Royal-Liverpool Ins. Group v. Macarthy, 1956, 229 S.C. 72, 91 S.E.2d 881; Presley v. Cooper, 1955, 155 Tex. 168, 284 S.W.2d 138; Kenney v. Ranney, 1893, 96 Mich. 617, 55 N.W. 982.

46. Crocker v. Gullifer, 1858, 44 Me. 491.

47. Parker v. Godin, 1728, 2 Stra. 813, 93 Eng.Rep. 866; Singer Mfg. Co. v. Clark, 1879, 5 Ex.Div. 37.

48. Stevens v. Eames, 1851, 22 N.H. 568.

49. Block v. Talge, 1943, 221 Ind.App. 658, 51 N.E.2d 81 (to junk man). See, however, Row v. Home Sav. Bank, 1940, 306 Mass. 522, 29 N.E.2d 552, finding no conversion where the defendant gave away goods apparently abandoned.

50. Hiort v. Bott, 1874, L.R. 9 Ex. 86; Hall v. Bost. & W. R. Corp., 1867, 14 Allen, Mass., 439; Knapp v. Guyer, 1909, 75 N.H. 397, 74 A. 873; Suzuki v. Small, 1925, 214 App.Div. 541, 212 N.Y.S. 589.

51. Morin v. Hood, 1951, 96 N.H. 485, 79 A.2d 4; United States v. Matthews, 9 Cir. 1957, 244 F.2d 626; Kearney v. Clutton, 1894, 101 Mich. 106, 59 N.W. 419; Kelly v. Lang, N.D., 1954, 62 N.W.2d 770; Sig Ellingson & Co. v. De Vries, 8 Cir. 1952, 199 F.2d 677, cert. denied 73 S.Ct. 505, 344 U.S. 934. Cf. Swim v. Wilson, 1891, 90 Cal. 126, 27 P.2d 33 (market agent). See Notes, 1962, 41 Neb.L.Rev. 617; 1957, 45 Cal.L.Rev. 776.

52. Youl v. Harbottle, 1791, Peake 49, 170 Eng.Rep. 74; Baer v. Slater, 1927, 261 Mass. 153, 158 N.E. 328; Potomac Ins. Co. v. Nickson, 1924, 64 Utah 395, 231 P. 445; Sullivan & O'Brien v. Kennedy, 1940, 107 Ind.App. 457, 25 N.E.2d 267; Marshall & Michel

been extended to a so-called "involuntary bailee," such as a finder,[53] or one who comes into possession of the chattel by accident or mistake,[54] and then misdelivers it to one not the owner. This has not gone without criticism,[55] and the severity and hardship of such a result can be justified only by the policy of protecting the property right, and placing the burden of tracing and retrieving goods misdelivered by mistake upon the man who made the mistake, rather than upon the equally innocent owner.

But again, as in the case of receipt of possession,[56] commercial convenience and common sense have led to some relaxation of the responsibility of bailees, agents and servants. Such a person will not be liable to his bailor, principal or master if he delivers the goods,

contrary to instructions, to one who is legally entitled to possession,[57] or to an officer armed with legal process.[58] Beyond this, if he has received such possession from a thief he does not become a converter as against the true owner when, as directed and in good faith, he returns it to the thief,[59] or turns the goods over to a third party.[60] The line is drawn where the agent himself negotiates the transaction by which the goods are transferred to a third party, and then makes the delivery. In such a case, unless what is transferred is negotiable paper,[61] there is general agreement that there is such a major interference with the rights of the true owner that there must be liability for conversion.[62]

Grain Co. v. Kansas City & Ft. Scott R. Co., 1903, 176 Mo. 480, 75 S.W. 638. See Note, 1957, 45 Cal.L. Rev. 776.

53. See Dolitsky v. Dollar Bank, 1952, 203 Misc. 262, 118 N.Y.S.2d 65; and compare Ryan v. Chown, 1910, 160 Mich. 204, 125 N.W. 46; Poggi v. Scott, 1914, 167 Cal. 372, 139 P. 815.

54. Cowen v. Pressprich, 1922, 117 Misc. 663, 192 N.Y.S. 242, reversed on other grounds in 1924, 202 App.Div. 796, 194 N.Y.S. 926; Knapp v. Guyer, 1909, 75 N.H. 397, 74 A. 873; Suzuki v. Small, 1925, 214 App.Div. 541, 212 N.Y.S. 589, affirmed 1927, 243 N.Y. 590, 154 N.E. 618. Compare Hiort v. Bott, 1874, L.R. 9 Ex. 86; Helson v. McKenzies, [1950] N.Z.L. Rep. 878; McCurdy v. Wallblom Furniture & Carpet Co., 1905, 94 Minn. 326, 102 N.W. 873; McGonigle v. Victor H. Belleisle Co., 1904, 186 Mass. 310, 71 N.E. 569. See Note, 1922, 6 Minn.L.Rev. 579.

In New York, where a bona fide purchaser is not liable until demand and refusal, he is nevertheless liable if he has sold the goods. Pease v. Smith, 1875, 61 N.Y. 477.

55. Burnett, Conversion by Involuntary Bailee, 1960, 76 L.Q.Rev. 364; Fleming, Law of Torts, 3d ed. 1965, 58–9; 1 Harper & James, Law of Torts, 1956, 177– 178. This position was taken by Elvin & Powell, Ltd. v. Plummer Roddie, Ltd., 1934, 50 T.L.R. 158, and Morris v. Third Ave. R. Co., 1862, 1 Daly, N.Y., 202. Cohen v. Koster, 1909, 133 App.Div. 570, 118 N.Y.S. 142, looks like a case of doing nothing, where defendant never had come into possession. The Second Restatement of Torts, § 235, reverses the position of the First Restatement, § 236(2), and supports the text.

56. Supra, p. 86.

57. Herring v. Creech, 1954, 241 N.C. 233, 84 S.E.2d 886; Farmers Union Warehouse Co. v. Barnett, 1925, 214 Ala. 202, 107 So. 46; Davis v. Donohoe-Kelly Banking Co., 1907, 152 Cal. 282, 92 P. 639; Eisiminger v. Dinwiddie, 1935, 170 Okl. 396, 40 P.2d 1029; Schrowang v. Von Hoffman Press, Mo.App. 1934, 75 S.W.2d 649, affirmed 1935, 337 Mo. 522, 85 S.W.2d 417.

58. Clegg v. Boston Storage Warehouse Co., 1889, 149 Mass. 454, 21 N.E. 877; American Express Co. v. Mullins, 1909, 212 U.S. 311; Cornell v. Mahoney, 1906, 190 Mass. 265, 76 N.E. 664; Branch v. Bekins Van & Storage Co., 1930, 106 Cal.App. 623, 290 P. 146.

59. Thoms v. D. C. Andrews & Co., 2 Cir. 1931, 54 F.2d 250; Steele v. Marcicano, 1894, 102 Cal. 666, 36 P. 920; Coleman v. Francis, 1925, 102 Conn. 612, 129 A. 718; Shellnut v. Central of Georgia R. Co., 1908, 131 Ga. 404, 62 S.E. 294; Nanson v. Jacob, 1887, 93 Mo. 331, 6 S.W. 246.

60. Ashcraft v. Tucker, 1923, 73 Colo. 363, 215 P. 877; Hodgson v. St. Paul Plow Co., 1899, 78 Minn. 172, 80 N.W. 956; Leuthold v. Fairchild, 1886, 35 Minn. 99, 27 N.W. 503, 28 N.W. 218; Walker v. First Nat. Bank of Athena, 1903, 43 Or. 102, 72 P. 635; In re Samuel Kernan, [1945] Ch. 408.

61. Even here, where the property sold is negotiable paper, it has been held that the agent is protected by the character of the instrument, on which he is entitled to rely. Spooner v. Holmes, 1869, 102 Mass. 503; Pratt v. Higginson, 1918, 230 Mass. 256, 119 N.E. 661; First Nat. Bank v. Goldberg, 1941, 340 Pa. 337, 17 A.2d 377; Gruntal v. United States F. & G. Co., 1930, 254 N.Y. 468, 173 N.E. 682; Second Restatement of Torts, § 233.

62. Swim v. Wilson, 1891, 90 Cal. 126, 27 P. 33; Flannery v. Harley, 1903, 117 Ga. 483, 43 S.E. 765; Richtmyer v. Mutual Live Stock Commission Co.,

Once the bailee, agent or servant has received notice of the true owner's claim, the situation is changed. There is no longer the same reason to protect him, and he is required, at his peril, to avoid a wrongful delivery to a third person.[63] Even after such notice, however, the common law developed a curious rule which permitted him to redeliver the goods to his bailor without liability, so long as no demand or other claim had been made upon him by the true owner.[64] The origin of this is obscure, but it apparently rested upon the idea of a special obligation undertaken by the bailee to the bailor. Its only practical justification has been one of commercial expediency for the protection of the bailee himself. It usually has been explained upon the basis of an "estoppel" to dispute the title of the bailor; but this explanation fails when demand or other claim has been made by the true owner. The bailee then re-delivers at his peril, and is liable for conversion if he turns out to be wrong.[65] His proper course in such a case is interpleader, or deposit in court.[66]

Withholding Possession

Another very common way in which conversion may occur is by way of a refusal to surrender possession of the chattel to one who is entitled to it. Normally this is a sufficiently serious interference with the plaintiff's right of control. Here, however as elsewhere throughout this chapter, there will obviously be occasional cases where the detention is a relatively unimportant matter, so that conversion will not be found. If a garage, even quite intentionally, delays for half an hour the return of the plaintiff's parked car, it is no conversion.[67] But if the detention is for a month, or the intent is to appropriate the car,[68] or if it is destroyed by fire during the delay,[69] then there is clearly conversion.[70]

Where there has been no wrongful taking or disposal of the goods, and the defendant has merely come rightfully into possession and then refused to surrender them, demand and refusal are necessary to the existence of the tort.[71] When demand is made, an abso-

---

1932, 122 Neb. 317, 240 N.W. 315; Kelly v. Lang, N.D.1954, 62 N.W.2d 770; First Nat. Bank of Pipestone v. Siman, 1937, 65 S.D. 514, 275 N.W. 347. See Notes, 1947, 14 U.Chi.L.Rev. 713; 1962, 41 Neb.L.Rev. 617; 1957, 45 Cal.L.Rev. 776.

63. Edwards v. Max Thieme Chevrolet Co., La.App. 1939, 191 So. 569; Thorp v. Burling, 1814, 11 Johns., N.Y., 285; Beckwith v. Independent Transfer & Storage Co., 1928, 105 W.Va. 26, 141 S.E. 443; Hudmon v. Du Bose, 1888, 85 Ala. 446, 5 So. 162; Dodson v. Economy Equipment Co., 1936, 188 Wash. 340, 62 P.2d 708.

64. Hill v. Hayes, 1871, 38 Conn. 532; Succession of Macon, 1922, 150 La. 1026, 91 So. 441; Rembaugh v. Phipps, 1882, 75 Mo. 422; Paccos v. Rosenthal, 1926, 137 Wash. 423, 242 P. 651. See Second Restatement of Agency, § 417.

65. Hattiesburg Auto Sales Co. v. Mossiron, 1924, 136 Miss. 632, 101 So. 690; Maser v. Farmers' & Merchants' Bank, 1931, 90 Mont. 33, 300 P. 207; Bonner v. McDonald, App.Term 1916, 162 N.Y.S. 324; Roberts v. Yarboro, 1874, 41 Tex. 449; cf. Smith v. Bell & Stephens, 1846, 9 Mo. 873.

66. Winter v. Bancks, 1901, 84 L.T. 504; Cass v. Higenbotam, 1885, 100 N.Y. 248, 3 N.E. 189.

67. Mattice v. Brinkman, 1889, 74 Mich. 705, 42 N.W. 172; Peck v. Patterson, 1956, 119 Vt. 280, 125 A.2d 813 (brief detention of cars); Daggett v. Davis, 1884, 53 Mich. 35, 18 N.W. 548 (stock certificate). In accord are the cases in which defendant, to keep out intruders, has locked up plaintiff's goods in a building, and so delayed him in obtaining possession. Poor v. Oakman, 1870, 117 Mass. 309; Edinburg v. Allen Squire Co., 1938, 299 Mass. 206, 12 N.E.2d 718; Zaslow v. Kroenert, 1946, 29 Cal.2d 451, 176 P.2d 1.

68. Thomas v. Westbrook, 1944, 206 Ark. 841, 177 S.W.2d 931; Kirby v. Porter, 1923, 144 Md. 261, 125 A. 41; Jones v. Stone, 1917, 78 N.H. 504, 102 A. 377; Henderson v. Beggs, Tex.Civ.App.1918, 207 S.W. 565.

69. Donnell v. Canadian Pacific R. Co., 1912, 109 Me. 500, 84 A. 1002.

70. "The very denial of goods to him that has a right to demand them is an actual conversion, and not only evidence of it." Baldwin v. Cole, 1704, 6 Mod.Rep. 212, 87 Eng.Rep. 964; Bristol v. Burt, 1810, 7 Johns., N.Y., 254; Vilas v. Mason, 1870, 25 Wis. 310; Smith v. Durham, 1900, 127 N.C. 417, 37 S.E. 473.

71. Spackman v. Foster, 1883, 11 Q.B.Div. 99. Hence the cause of action does not accrue until demand.

lute, unqualified refusal to surrender, which puts the plaintiff to the necessity of force or a lawsuit to recover his own property, is of course a conversion.[72] Denial of possession,[73] equivocation,[74] or a lying promise to return,[75] or even continued silence and inaction for several days,[76] may amount to the same thing. Ordinarily the defendant is not required to do more than permit the plaintiff to come and get the goods,[77] but if some positive act, easily done, is called for, such as disclosure of their location or turning over a key, a failure to perform it may be a conversion.[78]

Not every failure to deliver upon demand, however, will constitute a conversion. The defendant does not become a converter when the goods are no longer in his possession or control, so that he is unable to comply with the demand,[79] even though they may have been lost or destroyed through his own fault.[80] The remedy in such a case is an action for negligence. The defendant is not required to comply with a demand made at an unreasonable time or place, or in an unreasonable manner,[81] or upon an employee who has no authority to take any action.[82] And even when he has possession, a qualified refusal, for a reasonable purpose and for a reasonable length of time,[83] is not a conversion. The defendant may detain the goods for a reasonable time to identify the plaintiff,[84] to determine his right to possession,[85] to

In the case of gratuitous bailments without a time limit, however, it has been held that the demand must be made within a reasonable time, which, in the absence of other determining factors, will be taken to be that of the statute of limitations. Lowney v. Knott, 1956, 83 R.I. 505, 120 A.2d 552; Schupp v. Taendler, 1946, 81 App.D.C. 59, 154 F.2d 849; Southward v. Foy, 1948, 65 Nev. 694, 201 P.2d 302; cf. Norwood Trust Co. v. Twenty-Four Federal St. Corp., 1936, 295 Mass. 234, 3 N.E.2d 826.

72. Singer Mfg. Co. v. King, 1884, 14 R.I. 511; Vilas v. Mason, 1870, 25 Wis. 310; Smith v. Durham, 1900, 127 N.C. 417, 37 S.E. 473; Preble v. Hanna, 1926, 117 Or. 306, 244 P. 75 (fastening door securely, denying access); Molski v. Bendza, 1933, 116 Conn. 710, 164 A. 387 (refusal to allow plaintiff to enter premises). Even though the defendant refuses in the good faith belief that he has the right to detain the goods. Judkins v. Sadler-MacNeil, 1962, 61 Wash.2d 1, 376 P.2d 837.

73. Dunlap v. Hunting, 1846, 2 Denio, N.Y., 643; Wright v. Frank A. Andrews Co., 1912, 212 Mass. 186, 98 N.E. 798; Russell-Vaughn Ford, Inc. v. Rouse, 1968, 281 Ala. 567, 206 So.2d 371.

74. Gray v. Frazier, 1930, 158 Md. 189, 148 A. 457 (stalling plaintiff off).

75. Lopard v. Symons, Sup.Ct.1904, 85 N.Y.S. 1025. Compare, however, Severin v. Kepple, 1803, 4 Esp. 156, 170 Eng.Rep. 674, where continued promises and excuses, apparently in good faith, were held not sufficient.

76. Willis v. Midland Finance Co., 1958, 97 Ga.App. 443, 103 S.E.2d 185.

77. Farrar v. Rollins, 1864, 37 Vt. 295; Forehand v. Jones, 1889, 84 Ga. 508, 10 S.E. 1090.

78. Donnell v. Canadian Pac. R. Co., 1912, 109 Me. 500, 84 A. 1002; Bank of America v. McNeil, 1873, 73 Ky., 10 Bush. 54.

79. Rushworth v. Taylor, 1842, 3 Q.B. 669, 114 Eng. Rep. 674; Dozier v. Pillot, 1891, 79 Tex. 224, 14 S.W. 1027; Nelen v. Colwell, 1924, 45 R.I. 465, 123 A. 897, 124 A. 257; State ex rel. Sporleder v. Staed, 1896, 65 Mo.App. 487; Magnin v. Dinsmore, 1877, 70 N.Y. 410.

80. Hawkins v. Hoffman, 1844, 6 Hill, N.Y., 586; Dearbourn v. Union Nat. Bank, 1870, 58 Me. 273; Wamsley v. Atlas S. S. Co., 1901, 168 N.Y. 533, 61 N.E. 896; Salt Springs Nat. Bank v. Wheeler, 1872, 48 N.Y. 492.

81. Fifield v. Maine Central R. Co., 1873, 62 Me. 77; Durgin v. Gage, 1860, 40 N.H. 302; Phelps v. Gilchrist, 1854, 28 N.H. 266 (place); cf. Pantz v. Nelson, 1939, 234 Mo.App. 1043, 135 S.W.2d 397 (place); St. Louis Fixture & Show Case Co. v. F. W. Woolworth Co., 1935, 232 Mo.App. 10, 88 S.W.2d 254 (demand not specifying the chattels).

82. Mueller v. Technical Devices Corp., 1951, 8 N.J. 201, 84 A.2d 620; Fletcher v. Pump Creek Gas & Oil Syndicate, 1928, 38 Wyo. 329, 266 P. 1062.

83. Felcher v. McMillan, 1895, 103 Mich. 494, 61 N.W. 791 (24 hours); Buffington v. Clarke, 1887, 15 R.I. 437, 8 A. 247 (12 days); St. Louis Fixture & Show Case Co. v. F. W. Woolworth Co., 1935, 232 Mo.App. 10, 88 S.W.2d 254 (22 days); Farming Corp. v. Bridgeport Bank, 1925, 113 Neb. 323, 202 N.W. 911 (30 days). An offer of indemnity may cut down the time, and require the defendant to surrender the goods or interplead promptly. Ball v. Liney, 1871, 48 N.Y. 6.

84. McEntee v. New Jersey Steamboat Co., 1871, 45 N.Y. 34; Flood v. Moore, [1933] 4 Dom.L.Rep. 392.

85. Bradley v. Roe, 1940, 282 N.Y. 525, 27 N.E.2d 35, certified questions answered 257 App.Div. 1074, 14

ascertain whether charges against the goods are correct,[86] or if he is an agent, to consult the principal from whom he received them.[87] All such detentions must, however, be made in good faith,[88] with the reason stated. An unqualified refusal to surrender, stating no reason,[89] or one stating the wrong reason,[90] is still a conversion, even where there are unstated justifications. And if the defendant insists upon charges,[91] or other conditions of delivery,[92] which he has no right to impose, there is conversion. After the lapse of a reasonable time for investigation, the defendant is required to make up his mind, and he becomes liable as a converter if he refuses delivery to the rightful claimant.[93] Again his way out of the difficulty is by interpleader, or deposit in court.[94]

Destruction or Alteration

If the defendant, intending to do so, completely destroys the plaintiff's chattel, as by burning a paper, there is obviously a complete interference with the plaintiff's rights, and an obvious conversion;[95] and the same must be true if he so radically damages or alters it that its character is substantially changed, as by adulterating rum,[96] cutting down a fur coat so that it becomes too small for the plaintiff to wear,[97] disassembling a complicated piece of machinery into many

N.Y.S.2d 996; Buffington v. Clarke, 1887, 15 R.I. 437, 8 A. 247; Hansen v. Village of Ralston, 1945, 145 Neb. 838, 18 N.W.2d 213; Banque de France v. Equitable Trust Co., S.D.N.Y. 1929, 33 F.2d 202; Wolfe v. Lewisburg Trust & Safe Deposit Co., 1931, 305 Pa. 583, 158 A. 567. Cf. Wood v. Pierson, 1881, 45 Mich. 313, 7 N.W. 888 (finder); Giacomelos v. Bank of America Nat. Trust & Sav. Ass'n, 1965, 237 Cal.App.2d 99, 46 Cal.Rptr. 612 (trustee).

86. Beasley v. Baltimore & Potomac R. Co., 1906, 27 App.D.C. 595; Stahl v. Boston & Maine R. Co., 1901, 71 N.H. 57, 51 A. 176; Hett v. Boston & Maine R. Co., 1897, 69 N.H. 139, 44 A. 910; Bolling v. Kirby, 1889, 90 Ala. 215, 7 So. 914; Felcher v. McMillan, 1895, 103 Mich. 494, 61 N.W. 791.

87. Alexander v. Southey, 1821, 5 B. & Ad. 247, 106 Eng.Rep. 1183. Cf. Beasley v. Baltimore & Potomac R. Co., 1906, 27 U.S.App.D.C. 595.

88. Flannery v. Brewer, 1887, 66 Mich. 509, 33 N.W. 522; Holbrook v. Wight, 1840, 24 Wend., N.Y., 169.

89. Boardman v. Sill, 1809, 1 Camp. 410, 170 Eng.Rep. 1003; Hanna v. Phelps, 1855, 7 Ind. 21; Clark v. Rideout, 1859, 39 N.H. 238; Williams v. Smith, 1893, 153 Pa. 462, 25 A. 1122; Rapid Sewing Center v. Sanders, 1961, 79 S.D. 373, 112 N.W.2d 233.

90. Ingalls v. Bulkley, 1853, 15 Ill. 224; Pantz v. Nelson, 1940, 234 Mo.App. 1043, 135 S.W.2d 397.

91. Jones v. Tarleton, 1842, 9 M. & W. 675, 152 Eng. Rep. 285; Semple v. Morganstern, 1922, 97 Conn. 402, 116 A. 906; Long-Lewis Hardware Co. v. Abston, 1938, 235 Ala. 599, 180 So. 261.

92. Pennsylvania Fire Ins. Co. v. Levy, 1929, 85 Colo. 565, 277 P. 779 (settlement); Herbertson v. Cohen, 1955, 132 Colo. 231, 287 P.2d 47 (complete release); Charles F. Curry Co. v. Hedrick, Mo.1964, 378 S.W.2d 522 (waiver of all claims); Boiseau v. Morrisette, Mun.App.D.C.1951, 78 A.2d 777 (dismissal of other suit); Citizens Ind. Bank of Austin v. Oppenheim, Tex.Civ.App.1936, 92 S.W.2d 312, error dismissed (holding as security for other loans).

93. Beasley v. Baltimore & Potomac R. Co., 1906, 27 App.D.C. 595; Buffington v. Clarke, 1887, 15 R.I. 437, 8 A. 247.

As in the case of conversion by misdelivery, supra, p. 89, there are cases holding that a bailee is "estopped" to dispute the title of his bailor, and cannot justify refusal to surrender the chattel to him because of the claim of a third person, unless the third person has asserted the claim against the bailee. See Thorne v. Tilbury, 1858, 3 H. & N. 534, 157 Eng.Rep. 581; Biddle v. Bond, 1865, 6 Best & S. 225, 122 Eng.Rep. 1179; Ball v. Liney, 1871, 48 N.Y. 6; Powell v. Robinson, 1884, 76 Ala. 423; Flannery v. Brewer, 1887, 66 Mich. 509, 33 N.W. 522. The question may be raised, how long this antique rule for the restoration of stolen property into the hands of thieves is entitled to survive.

94. Wilson v. Anderton, 1830, 1 B. & Ad. 450, 109 Eng. Rep. 855.

95. Keyworth v. Hill, 1820, 3 B. & Ald. 684, 106 Eng. Rep. 811; Simmons v. Sikes, 1841, 24 N.C., 2 Ired. 98. Cf. Aschermann v. Philip Best Brewing Co., 1878, 45 Wis. 262 (melting ice). As to damages for loss of use where there is complete destruction, see Note, 1960, 33 So.Cal.L.Rev. 451.

96. Dench v. Walker, 1780, 14 Mass. 500. Cf. Richardson v. Atkinson, 1723, 1 Stra. 576, 93 Eng.Rep. 710 (drawing out part of wine and substituting water); Penfolds Wines, Ltd. v. Elliott, Aust. 1946, 74 Comm.L.Rep. 204, 229 (cutting seals from a deed); Colby v. Porter, 1925, 124 Me. 446, 129 A. 298 (changes in sleds).

97. Douglass v. Hart, 1925, 103 Conn. 685, 131 A. 401; May v. Georger, 1897, 21 Misc. 622, 47 N.Y.S. 1057.

parts,[98] grinding wheat into flour,[99] or commingling the plaintiff's goods with others so that identification becomes impossible.[1] On the other hand, mere damage, falling short of destruction or material alteration, usually may be compensated without the forced purchase which is the distinguishing feature of the remedy, and so is not treated as conversion.[2] Questions of degree will of course arise. One of these may concern the destruction or removal of a part of a chattel, such as the tire of an automobile: is it conversion only of the part, or of the whole? Probably the answer is that if replacement is quick and easy, only the tire is converted; but if it is slow and difficult, with the car in the midst of a distant desert, there is conversion of the car.[3]

Using the Chattel

If the defendant has only made use of the chattel without harming it, one would expect to find much the same distinctions made. A casual and harmless use, involving no defiance of the owner's right of dominion, as where a car left to be sold is driven, on one occasion, for ten miles,[4] will not be treated as a conversion, although the defendant will of course be liable in damages for the use of the car. But if it is driven 2,000 miles,[5] or driven even the ten with the intention to steal it,[6] or if it is used for the illegal transportation of narcotics and confiscated by the government,[7] there is a conversion.

The more serious questions arise where an agent or bailee is authorized to make some use of the chattel, but exceeds or departs from what is permitted. In general, any major and serious departure will be held to be a conversion,[8] while minor ones which

98. Symphony Player Co. v. Hackstadt, 1918, 182 Ky. 546, 206 S.W. 803 (pin-cylinder organ). Cf. Jackson v. Innes, 1919, 231 Mass. 558, 121 N.E. 489.

99. Mayer v. Springer, 1901, 192 Ill. 270, 61 N.E. 348. Cf. McPheters v. Page, 1891, 83 Me. 234, 22 A. 101 (cutting up carcass of deer); Wilson Cypress Co. v. Logan, 1935, 120 Fla. 124, 162 So. 489 (sawing logs).

1. Peltola v. Western Workmen's Pub. Soc., 1920, 113 Wash. 283, 193 P. 691; Crane Lumber Co. v. Bellows, 1898, 116 Mich. 304, 74 N.W. 481; Martin v. Mason, 1886, 78 Me. 452, 7 A. 11; Royce v. Oakes, 1897, 20 R.I. 252, 38 A. 371; Wells v. Batts, 1893, 112 N.C. 283, 17 S.E. 417.

2. Simmons v. Lillystone, 1853, 8 Ex. 431, 155 Eng. Rep. 1417. Cf. Philpott v. Kelley, 1835, 3 Ad. & El. 106, 111 Eng.Rep. 353 (bottling wine to preserve it). Cf. Donovan v. Barkhausen Oil Co., 1929, 200 Wis. 194, 227 N.W. 940.

3. In G. W. K., Ltd. v. Dunlop Rubber Co., K.B. 1926, 42 T.L.R. 376, where a set of tires was removed from a car on exhibition in a showroom, it was held that there was no conversion of the car. Otherwise in Nielsen v. Warner, 1938, 66 S.D. 214, 281 N.W. 110, where the motor was removed. In Klam v. Koppel, 1941, 63 Idaho 171, 118 P.2d 729, some parts of a tractor were removed, others smashed with a sledge-hammer, and it was held that there was conversion of the tractor.

4. Jeffries v. Pankow, 1924, 112 Or. 439, 229 P. 903. Cf. Buice v. Campbell, 1959, 99 Ga.App. 334, 108 S.E.2d 339 (left to be repaired, driven to dealer to match parts); Johnson v. Weedman, 1843, 5 Ill. 495 (agister to feed horse rode him once for fifteen miles); Frome v. Dennis, 1883, 45 N.J.L. 515 (unauthorized borrowing of plow, used for three days); McNeill v. Brooks, 1882, 9 Tenn. 73 (horse rented for riding used once to carry goods); Donovan v. Barkhausen Oil Co., 1929, 200 Wis. 194, 227 N.W. 940 (minor repairs on automobile against orders).

5. Miller v. Uhl, 1929, 37 Ohio App. 276, 174 N.E. 591. Cf. E. J. Caron Enterprises v. State Operating Co., 1935, 87 N.H. 371, 179 A. 665 (theatre fixtures used in wrong theatre); West Jersey R. Co. v. Trenton Car Works Co., 1866, 32 N.J.L. 517 (car defendant was under duty to forward used in its own service); Schulte v. Florian, Mo.App.1963, 370 S.W.2d 623 (using plaster mixer, removing to another job, leaving it dirty).

6. Cf. Cheshire R. Co. v. Foster, 1871, 51 N.H. 490; Forster v. Juniata Bridge Co., 1851, 16 Pa. 393; Oakley v. Lyster, [1931] 1 K.B. 148. Cf. Lord Petre v. Heneage, 1699, 12 Mod.Rep. 519, 88 Eng.Rep. 1490; Bryant v. Wardell, 1848, 2 Exch. 479, 154 Eng.Rep. 580; Hillhouse v. Wolf, 1958, 166 Cal.App.2d Supp. 833, 333 P.2d 454; Peterson v. Wolff, 1938, 68 N.D. 354, 280 N.W. 187.

7. Vermont Acceptance Corp. v. Wiltshire, 1931, 103 Vt. 219, 153 A. 199; Moorgate Merc. Co. v. Finch, [1962] 1 Q.B. 701. Cf. Collins v. Bennett, 1871, 46 N.Y. 490 (horse used and foundered).

8. McMorris v. Simpson, 1839, 21 Wend., N.Y., 610 (sending goods to unauthorized market); Laverty v. Snethen, 1877, 68 N.Y. 522 (surrendering note without payment); Juzeler v. Buchli, 1933, 63 N.D. 657, 249 N.W. 790 (surrendering check on compromise of col-

do no harm will not.[9] A series of old cases concerned with the driving of rented horses beyond the agreed destination,[10] worked out the rule that if the departure is a minor one and no harm ensues, there is no conversion;[11] but that if substantial damage occurs to the chattel in the course of the deviation, even without the fault of the bailee, he is an insurer against it, and is liable as a converter.[12] This, of course, is consistent with the position taken throughout, that the severe and drastic remedy of a forced sale to the defendant is properly limited to cases where there has been an intent to deny the rights of ownership, or major interference with a substantial part of them.

Asserting Ownership

The gist of conversion is the interference with control of the property. It follows that a mere assertion of ownership, without any disturbance of possession, or any other interference with the right to it, is not sufficiently

serious to be classed as conversion.[13] A sale,[14] an advertisement for sale,[15] or a purchase [16] of the chattel by one who has no right to it, while the owner's possession remains undisturbed, does not make the defendant a converter. But obviously very little more is required. A claim of title by one who is in possession, which reasonably implies that the owner will not be permitted to obtain the goods, will be enough;[17] and so of course will any legal proceeding, such as an injunction [18] which restricts the actual control.

Plaintiff's Interest

In order to maintain the common law action of trover, the plaintiff must establish

---

lection); Maynard v. James, 1929, 109 Conn. 365, 146 A. 614 (driving car left to be washed); Regas v. Helios, 1922, 176 Wis. 56, 186 N.W. 165 (making different investment of money).

9. See cases cited supra, note 4.

10. One of the minor mysteries of the law is why there are no automobile cases. This remains horse-and-buggy law, but none the less sound.

11. Wentworth v. McDuffie, 1869, 48 N.H. 402; Farkas v. Powell, 1891, 86 Ga. 800, 13 S.E. 200; Doolittle v. Shaw, 1894, 92 Iowa 348, 60 N.W. 621; Carney v. Rease, 1906, 60 W.Va. 676, 55 S.E. 729; Daugherty v. Reveal, 1915, 54 Ind.App. 71, 102 N.E. 381.

12. Palmer v. Mayo, 1907, 80 Conn. 353, 68 A. 369; Perham v. Coney, 1875, 117 Mass. 102; Baxter v. Woodward, 1916, 191 Mich. 379, 158 N.W. 137; Woodman v. Hubbard, 1862, 25 N.H. 67; Disbrow v. Tenbroeck, 1855, 4 E.D. Smith, N.Y., 397.

Cf. Ledbetter v. Thomas, 1901, 130 Ala. 299, 30 So. 342; Cartlidge v. Sloan, 1899, 124 Ala. 596, 26 So. 918; Fryer v. Cooper, 1928, 53 S.D. 286, 220 N.W. 486; De Voin v. Michigan Lumber Co., 1885, 64 Wis. 616, 25 N.W. 552. In Spooner v. Manchester, 1882, 133 Mass. 270, where the driver unintentionally deviated from the route, and the horse was injured while he was trying to get back to it, it was held that there was no conversion.

13. Hein v. Marcante, 1941, 57 Wyo. 81, 113 P.2d 940; Irish v. Cloyes, 1836, 8 Vt. 30; Jenkins v. Holly, 1920, 204 Ala. 519, 86 So. 390; Knowles v. Knowles, 1903, 25 R.I. 464, 56 A. 775; Dietzman v. Ralston Purina Co., 1967, 246 Or. 367, 425 P.2d 163 (refusal to release invalid chattel mortgage). See, 1931, 47 L.Q.Rev. 168.

Cf. Martin v. Sikes, 1951, 38 Wash.2d 274, 229 P.2d 546 (plaintiff served with criminal complaint asserting ownership, told to leave goods in status quo); Richstein v. Roesch, 1946, 71 S.D. 451, 25 N.W.2d 558 (filing and assignment of mechanic's lien).

14. Traylor v. Horrall, 1837, 4 Blackf., Ind., 317. But cf. Ramsby v. Beezley, 1883, 11 Or. 49, 8 P. 288, where the plaintiff apparently lost possession as a result of the sale.

15. Brandenburg v. Northwestern Jobbers' Credit Bureau, 1915, 128 Minn. 411, 151 N.W. 134; Carroll v. M. & J. Finance Corp., 1958, 233 S.C. 200, 104 S.E.2d 171.

16. Andrews v. Shattuck, 1860, 32 Barb., N.Y., 396; Hall v. Merchants' State Bank, 1925, 199 Iowa 483, 202 N.W. 256; Matteawan Co. v. Bentley, 1852, 13 Barb., N.Y., 641 (taking mortgage).

17. Baker v. Beers, 1936, 64 N.H. 102, 6 A. 35; Adams v. Mizell, 1852, 11 Ga. 106; Oakley v. Lyster, [1931] 1 K.B. 148; Laverriere v. Casco Bank & Trust Co., 1959, 155 Me. 97, 151 A.2d 276; Gowin v. Heider, 1964, 237 Or. 266, 391 P.2d 630 (obtaining power of attorney by fraud to register car in own name).

18. Interstate Nat. Bank v. McCormick, 1920, 67 Mont. 80, 214 P. 949. In General Finance Corp. of Jacksonville v. Sexton, Fla.App.1963, 155 So.2d 159, obtaining a transfer of title from the Motor Vehicle Commission was regarded as sufficient, apparently because of the serious disadvantages to which the plaintiff would be put.

that he was in possession of the goods, or entitled to possession, at the time of the conversion.[19] The early law, which was preoccupied with tangible objects and the repression of physical violence, attached an undue importance to possession, as distinguished from ownership,[20] and permitted the man in possession to recover the full value of the chattel, although he did not own it, and might be responsible over to some one else who did. Thus a finder of goods [21] might recover, or a sheriff who had seized them,[22] or a bailee,[23] or a mortgagor in default.[24] The rule

has even been applied to permit recovery by one whose possession is wrongful, and in defiance of the owner,[25] although in all such cases the plaintiff has been in possession under some colorable claim of right. A few courts have said that the plaintiff cannot recover unless his possession is under such colorable claim.[26] No court ever has allowed an admitted, or even a clearly proved, thief without claim of right to recover, and it seems improbable that one ever will. Not only is all policy against giving him the money to make away with, but the case law is clear that the courts will not lend their aid by an action for conversion of property possessed for an illegal purpose.[27]

The procedural method by which all this has been accomplished has been a refusal to permit the defendant in a conversion action to set up as a defense the "jus tertii," which is the claim of a third person to the chattel,

19. 1 Street, Foundations of Legal Liability, 1906, 250.

20. Ames, Disseisin of Chattels, 1890, 3 Harv.L. Rev. 23, 313, 337; Holmes, The Common Law, 1881, 163–166; Pollock and Wright, Possession in the Common Law, 1888, 91.

21. Armory v. Delamirie, 1722, 1 Stra. 505, 93 Eng. Rep. 664; Clark v. Maloney, 1839, 3 Harr., Del., 68; McLaughlin v. Waite, 1827, 9 Cow., N.Y., 670, affirmed, 1830, 5 Wend. 404; Weeks v. Hackett, 1908, 104 Me. 264, 71 A. 858. See Reisman, Possession and the Law of Finders, 1939, 52 Harv.L.Rev. 1105; Aigler, Rights of Finders, 1923, 21 Mich.L.Rev. 664, 57 Am.L.Rev. 511; Moreland, Rights of Finders of Lost Property, 1927, 16 Ky.L.J. 1; Note, 1937, 21 Minn.L.Rev. 191.

22. Wilbraham v. Snow, 1670, 2 Wms.Saund. 47, 85 Eng.Rep. 624; Barker v. Miller, 1810, 6 Johns., N. Y., 195; Witherspoon v. Clegg, 1880, 42 Mich. 484, 4 N.W. 209. ·

23. Nicolls v. Bastard, 1835, 2 Cr.M. & R. 659, 150 Eng.Rep. 279; Vining v. Baker, 1866, 53 Me. 544; Chamberlain v. West, 1887, 37 Minn. 54, 33 N.W. 114; Baker v. Troy Compress Co., 1896, 114 Ala. 415, 21 So. 496.

There was, however, a very odd little rule that a servant entrusted with the chattel by his master had only "custody" of it, with possession "constructively" in the master, so that the servant could not maintain trover, although he could be liable in such an action. The origin of this is obscure; it may have been a survival from the time when servants were slaves, or merely a device to get around some of the larceny rules of the criminal law. See Holmes, The Common Law, 1881, 227–228; Pollock and Wright, Possession, 1888, 58–59; Becher v. Great Eastern R. Co., 1870, L.R. 5 Q.B. 241; Ludden v. Leavitt, 1812, 9 Mass. 104; Richard v. Nowlan, 1959, 19 Dom.L.Rev. 239.

It may seriously be doubted that this antique bit of lore survives in the United States. In Moore v. Robinson, 1831, 2 B. & Ad. 817, 109 Eng.Rep. 1346,

the captain of a ship was held to be in such possession that he could maintain trover; and in Poole v. Symonds, 1818, 1 N.H. 289, and Thayer v. Hutchinson, 1841, 13 Vt. 504, custodians were allowed to recover because they were "responsible" for the goods and "accountable" to the owner. But is this not always true of servants? Cf. Mitchell v. Georgia & A. R. Co., 1900, 111 Ga. 760, 36 S.E. 971; Gunzburger v. Rosenthal, 1910, 226 Pa. 300, 75 A. 418 (manager of business and salesman).

24. Ellis v. Snell, 1955, 44 Tenn.App. 294, 313 S.W. 2d 558.

25. Jeffries v. Great Western R. Co., 1856, 5 El. & Bl. 802, 119 Eng.Rep. 680; Cook v. Patterson, 1859, 35 Ala. 102; Shaw v. Kaler, 1871, 106 Mass. 448; Wheeler v. Lawson, 1886, 103 N.Y. 40, 8 N.E. 360; Anderson v. Gouldberg, 1892, 51 Minn. 294, 53 N.W. 636.

26. Turley v. Tucker, 1840, 6 Mo. 583; Barwick v. Barwick, 1850, 11 Ired., 33 N.C. 80; Stephenson v. Little, 1862, 10 Mich. 433; Rexroth v. Coon, 1885, 15 R.I. 35, 23 A. 37.

27. Miller v. Chicago & N. W. R. Co., 1913, 153 Wis. 431, 141 N.W. 263 (slot machine); Du Bost v. Beresford, 1810, 2 Camp. 511, 170 Eng.Rep. 1235 (libelous portrait); Suttori v. Peckham, 1920, 48 Cal.App. 88, 191 P. 960 (fish taken in violation of law); Hofferman v. Simmons, 1943, 290 N.Y. 449, 49 N.E.2d 523 (gaming money); Carr v. Hoy, 1957, 2 N.Y.2d 185, 158 N.Y.S.2d 572, 139 N.E.2d 531 (money collected for photographing nude women).

superior to that of the plaintiff, unless the defendant can connect himself with that claim. The result is that the man in possession recovers the full value of the chattel, although he may not be the full owner, or any owner at all. The original justification for this lay in the convenience of treating the possessor as the owner, and the encouragement to peace and security expected to result from the protection of any possession against a wrongdoer with no rights at all. Modern law has discovered new reasons of business convenience for permitting the possessor to maintain the action, and recover the full value of the chattel. It is said that the possession is a sufficient title against the wrongdoer, because the man in possession is, of the two, the proper party to account to the true owner for the amount recovered, and to adjust with him any question as to their respective rights.[28] But, since a full recovery by one in possession will bar any subsequent action by the true owner,[29] the disadvantages are obvious. Such a rule may result in considerable hardship where the possessor mishandles the suit,[30] or is not to be trusted with the proceeds. For these reasons it has been suggested [31] that the possessor's right to recover more than the value of his own interest in the chattel should be limited to cases where

he has the express or implied consent of the owner to bring the action, or the owner cannot be found; and that the proper procedure when the question of the jus tertii arises is for the court, of its own motion, to stay proceedings until the owner can be notified, and permitted to decide whether he wishes to intervene in the action, or take other measures of his own.

The common law rule was extended to permit recovery by one who had the immediate right to possession, as in the case of a bailor entitled to possession on demand,[32] or a chattel mortgagee or conditional seller after default.[33] But an owner who had neither possession nor the immediate right to it at the time of the conversion could not maintain trover.[34] His remedy was an action on the case for the damage to his interest in the goods.[35] Although the distinction persists to-

28. The Winkfield, [1902] P. 42; Warren, Qualifying as Plaintiff in an Action for a Conversion, 1936, 49 Harv.L.Rev. 1084, 1095; Warren, Trover and Conversion, 1936, 12; Note, 1938, 22 Minn.L.Rev. 863.

29. Knight v. Davis Carriage Co., 5 Cir. 1896, 71 F. 662; Lord, Stone & Co. v. Buchanan, 1897, 69 Vt. 320, 37 A. 1048.

30. As, for example, by a settlement which does not protect the owner's interests. See First Nat. Bank v. Union R. Co., 1926, 153 Tenn. 386, 284 S.W. 363; Ellis Motor Co. v. Hancock, 1928, 38 Ga.App. 788, 145 S.E. 518; Harris v. Seaboard Air Line R. Co., 1925, 190 N.C. 480, 130 S.E. 319; Juniata Acceptance Corp. v. Hoffman, 1940, 139 Pa.Super. 87, 11 A.2d 494. See, 1937, 21 Minn.L.Rev. 449.

31. Warren, Qualifying as Plaintiff in an Action for a Conversion, 1936, 49 Harv.L.Rev. 1084, 1098; Warren, Trover and Conversion, 1936, 15–17; Note, 1928, 22 Minn.L.Rev. 863. The only case found which has so held is Panama Canal Co. v. Stockard & Co., 1958, 391 Pa. 374, 137 A.2d 793.

32. Manders v. Williams, 1849, 4 Ex. 339, 154 Eng. Rep. 1242; Drake v. Reddington, 1838, 9 N.H. 243; Robinson v. Bird, 1893, 158 Mass. 357, 33 N.E. 391. The wrongful act of the bailee may of course terminate the bailment and give the bailor the right to immediate possession. Sanborn v. Colman, 1832, 6 N.H. 14; Swift v. Moseley, 1838, 10 Vt. 208.

33. Nichols & Shepard Co. v. Minnesota Threshing Mfg. Co., 1897, 70 Minn. 528, 73 N.W. 415; Worthington v. A. G. Rhodes & Son Co., 1905, 145 Ala. 656, 39 So. 614; Howard v. Burns, 1890, 44 Kan. 543, 24 P. 981; Reynolds v. Fitzpatrick, 1899, 23 Mont. 52, 57 P. 452; First Nat. Bank of Bay Shore v. Stamper, 1966, 93 N.J.Super. 150, 225 A.2d 162 (assignee of conditional seller).

34. Gordon v. Harper, 1796, 7 Term Rep. 9, 101 Eng. Rep. 828 (landlord); Citizens' Bank of St. Louis v. Tiger Tail Mill & Land Co., 1890, 152 Mo. 145, 53 S.W. 902 (owner not in possession); Raymond Syndicate v. Guttentag, 1901, 177 Mass. 562, 59 N.E. 446 (bailor for a term); Newhall v. Kingsbury, 1881, 131 Mass. 445 (conditional seller before default); Adams & Frederick Co. v. South Omaha Nat. Bank, 8 Cir. 1903, 123 F. 641. See Note, 1944, 19 Ohio St.L.J. 758.

35. Mears v. London & S. W. R. Co., 1862, 11 C.B., N.S., 850, 142 Eng.Rep. 1029; Ayer v. Bartlett, 1829, 9 Pick., 26 Mass., 156; New York, L. E. & W. R. Co. v. New Jersey Elec. R. Co., 1897, 60 N.J.L. 338, 38 A. 828, affirmed, 1897, 61 N.J.L. 287, 41 A. 1116; Adams & Frederick Co. v. South Omaha Nat. Bank, 8 Cir. 1903, 123 F. 641. Compare, as to a negligence action, Bell Finance Co. v. Gefter, 1958, 337 Mass. 69, 147 N.E.2d 815; Cashman v. Soulia, 1957, 120 Vt.

day in a good many courts,[36] it is an antique procedural survival, with nothing to recommend it. The important fact is that the man entitled only to future possession can recover, in whatever form of action, the full value of his interest in the goods which has been appropriated by the defendant, and no more. If this is not to be called conversion, it is at least the same thing by another name.[37] There are a substantial number of courts which have discarded the procedural distinction, and have called the action one of conversion.[38]

Complications arise when the converter is sued both by the bailee and by the bailor. They are not peculiar to conversion, and arise also in cases of negligent destruction of the chattel, or damage to it. The bailee, using the term in the general sense of one in possession when rights to possession are outstanding, is entitled to recover the full value of the chattel,[39] being accountable to the bailor for any excess over the value of his own interest.[40] The bailor may recover the full

value if he was entitled to immediate possession at the time of the conversion,[41] but if he was then entitled only to future possession, he recovers only the damages he can prove to his own interest in the chattel.[42]

The converter may be subjected to two of these actions, or conceivably to all three; and the mere reduction of any one of them to judgment does not bar a subsequent judgment in another. The defendant is, however, required to pay only once. The satisfaction of a judgment against him by one who was in possession, or was entitled to immediate possession, and so was entitled to recover the full damages, has the effect of extinguishing all claims against the defendant, and is a complete bar to any further recovery, or any further enforcement of other judgments.[43] A settlement or release covering the full value, from the person entitled to it, has the same effect. The one whose claim is thus settled remains accountable to the other claimant to the extent of the latter's interest in the chattel, but the converter is no longer liable to anyone.[44] On the other hand, the satisfac-

171, 136 A.2d 355. See Notes, 1912, 25 Harv.L.Rev. 655; 1944, 19 Ohio St.L.J. 758.

36. See for example Breault v. Merrill & Ring Lumber Co., 1898, 72 Minn. 143, 75 N.W. 122; Goebel v. Clark, 1934, 242 App.Div. 408, 275 N.Y.S. 43.

37. Salmond, Observations on Trover and Conversion, 1905, 21 L.Q.Rev. 43, 54. See also Warren, Qualifying as Plaintiff in an Action for a Conversion, 1936, 49 Harv.L.Rev. 1084, 1100–1109; Warren, Trover and Conversion, 1936, 19–28.

38. Morin v. Hood, 1951, 96 N.H. 485, 79 A.2d 4 (chattel mortgage); Wall v. Colvard, Inc., 1966, 268 N.C., 43, 149 S.E.2d 559; Redd Chemical & Nitrate Co. v. W. T. Clay Merc. Co., 1929, 219 Ala. 478, 122 So. 652 (equitable lien); Moore v. Carey Bros. Oil Co., Tex.Com.App.1925, 269 S.W. 75, 272 S.W. 440 (materialmen's lien); and see Nash v. Lang, 1929, 268 Mass. 407, 414, 167 N.E. 762, 765.

39. The Winkfield, [1902] P. 42; Hopkins v. Colonial Stores, 1944, 224 N.C. 137, 29 S.E.2d 455; Hudson Transit Corp. v. Antonucci, 1948, 137 N.J.L. 704, 61 A.2d 180; Chamberlain v. West, 1887, 37 Minn. 54, 33 N.W. 114; Herries v. Bell, 1915, 220 Mass. 243, 107 N.E. 944.

40. The Winkfield, [1902] P. 42; Walsh v. United States Tent Co., 1910, 153 Ill.App. 229; Baggett v. McCormack, 1896, 73 Miss. 552, 19 So. 89; Smyth v.

Fidelity & Deposit Co. of Md., 1937, 125 Pa.Super. 597, 190 A. 398; Fletcher v. Perry, 1932, 104 Vt. 279, 158 A. 679.

41. Clark v. Rideout, 1859, 39 N.H. 238; Knox v. Binkoski, 1923, 99 Conn. 582, 122 A. 400; Hussey v. Flanagan, 1923, 237 N.Y. 227, 142 N.E. 594; Reynolds v. Fitzpatrick, 1899, 23 Mont. 52, 57 P. 452.

42. Mears v. London & S. W. R. Co., 1862, 11 C.B., N.S., 850, 142 Eng.Rep. 1029; Gordon v. Harper, 1796, 7 Term Rep. 9, 101 Eng.Rep. 828; White v. Griffin, 1856, 4 Jones, 49 N.C. 139.

43. Juniata Acceptance Corp. v. Hoffman, 1940, 139 Pa.Super. 87, 11 A.2d 494; Railway Express Agency v. Goodman's N. Y. & C. E. Corp., 1942, 129 Conn. 386, 28 A.2d 869; The W. C. Block, 2 Cir. 1934, 71 F.2d 682, cert. denied Cornell Steamboat Co. v. Scholl, 293 U.S. 579; Eaton v. Schild, 1930, 8 N.J. Misc. 245, 149 A. 637; Industrial Inv. Co. v. King, 1931, 159 Mass. 491, 132 So. 333.

44. Associates Discount Corp. v. Gillineau, 1948, 322 Mass. 490, 78 N.E.2d 192; Motor Finance Co. v. Noyes, 1942, 139 Me. 159, 28 A.2d 235; Jolly v. Thornton, 1940, 40 Cal.App.2d Supp. 819, 102 P.2d 467; Lowery v. Louisville & N. R. Co., 1934, 228 Ala. 137, 153 So. 467; Gas City Transfer Co. v. Miller, 1939, 107 Ind.App. 210, 21 N.E.2d 428.

tion of a judgment, or a settlement and release, from one who was entitled only to future possession, and so not entitled to the full value of the chattel, covers only the damages for the harm to his own interest, and so does not extinguish the defendant's liability, but only reduces it pro tanto when the man in possession seeks to recover against him.[45]

Return of the Chattel

The conversion is complete when the defendant takes, detains or disposes of the chattel. At that point, it is the traditional view that the plaintiff acquires the right to enforce a sale, and recover the full value of the property. The defendant cannot undo his wrong by forcing the goods back upon their owner, either as a bar to the action,[46] or in mitigation of damages.[47]

Such a rule is unduly severe upon comparatively innocent defendants who have converted in good faith or by mistake, and are entirely willing to restore the goods when they discover the facts. The English courts

have moderated it by giving the trial judge discretion to allow the return of the goods in mitigation of damages, provided that they are uninjured, and no special damage has resulted from the detention.[48] A few American courts have recognized a similar discretion,[49] where the conversion was not intentionally wrongful,[50] and there has been no deterioration in the value of the chattel,[51] or other special damage to the plaintiff.[52] This limitation of the forced sale involved in the action of trover seems necessary to prevent occasional over-drastic remedy for relatively inoffensive legal fault.[53] In any case, return of the chattel, whether consented to by the plaintiff or compelled by the court, does not bar the action, but goes merely to reduce the damages.[54]

In Belli v. Forsyth, 1938, 301 Mass. 203, 16 N.E.2d 656, where the settlement purported to satisfy only the bailee's own damages, it was held that further action by the bailor was not barred.

45. Gaines v. Briggs, 1848, 9 Ark. 46; Missouri, K. & T. R. Co. v. Hunter, Tex.Civ.App.1919, 216 S.W. 1107; see Hudson Transit Corp. v. Antonucci, 1948, 137 N.J.L. 704, 61 A.2d 180.

46. Olivant v. Baring, 1743, 1 Wils. 23, 95 Eng.Rep. 471; De Celles v. Casey, 1914, 48 Mont. 568, 139 P. 586; Hofschulte v. Panhandle Hardware Co., Tex. Civ.App. 1899, 50 S.W. 608; Wall v. Colvard, Inc., 1966, 268 N.C. 43, 149 S.E.2d 559. The same as to repossession by the plaintiff. Schulte v. Florian, Mo.App.1963, 370 S.W.2d 623.

47. Baltimore & O. R. Co. v. O'Donnell, 1892, 49 Ohio St. 489, 32 N.E. 476; Sloan v. Butler, 1921, 148 Ark. 117, 228 S.W. 1046; West Tulsa Belt R. Co. v. Bell, 1915, 54 Okl. 175, 153 P. 622; Ketchum v. Amsterdam Apartments Co., 1920, 94 N.J.L. 7, 110 A. 590; Gorham v. Massillon Iron & Steel Co., 1918, 284 Ill. 594, 120 N.E. 467.

48. Fisher v. Prince, 1782, 3 Burr. 1363, 97 Eng.Rep. 876; Tucker v. Wright, 1826, 3 Bing. 601, 130 Eng. Rep. 645.

49. The relief is within the discretion of the court, and there is no absolute right to it. Rutland & W. R. Co. v. Bank of Middlebury, 1860, 32 Vt. 639.

50. It is not permitted where the conversion was not an innocent one. Baltimore & Ohio R. Co. v. O'Donnell, 1892, 49 Ohio St. 489, 32 N.E. 476; Ketchum v. Amsterdam Apartments Co., 1920, 94 N.J.L. 7, 110 A. 590; Gorham v. Massillon Iron & Steel Co., 1918, 284 Ill. 594, 120 N.E. 467.

51. It will not be granted where the goods have been damaged, or partly sold or destroyed. Magic City Steel & Metal Corp. v. Mitchell, Okl.1954, 265 P. 2d 473; Hart v. Skinner, 1844, 16 Vt. 138.

52. Farr v. State Bank of Phillips, 1894, 87 Wis. 223, 58 N.W. 377; Moody v. Sindlinger, 1915, 27 Colo.App. 290, 149 P. 263; Whittler v. Sharp, 1913, 43 Utah 419, 135 P. 112; Gilbert & Miller v. Peck, 1891, 43 Mo. App. 577; Carpenter v. American Bldg. & Loan Ass'n, 1893, 54 Minn. 403, 56 N.W. 95.

53. Notes, 1925, 9 Minn.L.Rev. 392; 1942, 40 Mich.L. Rev. 437.

54. Cernahan v. Chrisler, 1900, 107 Wis. 645, 83 N.W. 778; Plummer v. Reeves, 1907, 83 Ark. 10, 102 S.W. 376; Jackson v. Innes, 1919, 231 Mass. 558, 121 N.E. 489; Truth Seeker Co. v. Durning, 2 Cir. 1945, 147 F.2d 54; Schulte v. Florian, Mo.App.1963, 370 S.W.2d 623 (repossession).

CHAPTER 4

DEFENSES TO INTENTIONAL INTERFERENCE
WITH PERSON OR PROPERTY

16. PRIVILEGE

Even though the defendant has intentionally invaded the interests of the plaintiff, so that under ordinary circumstances liability would result, he may not be liable because his conduct is privileged. The early common law classified defenses to intentional torts as "justification" or "excuse," and developed technical rules distinguishing between the two, which no longer have any great importance.[1] "Privilege" is the modern term applied to those considerations which avoid liability where it might otherwise follow.[2] In its broader sense, it is applied to any immunity which prevents the existence of a tort; but in its more common usage, it signifies that the defendant has acted to further an interest of such social importance that it is entitled to protection, even at the expense of damage to the plaintiff. He is allowed freedom of action because his own interests, or those of the public require it, and social policy will best be served by permitting it. The boundaries of the privilege are marked out by current ideas of what will most effectively promote the general welfare.

The question of "privilege" arises almost exclusively in connection with intentional torts. Much the same considerations have weight in negligence cases, in determining whether the defendant's conduct is reasonable under the circumstances.[3] Negligence, however, is a matter of risk and probability of harm; and where the likelihood of injury to the plaintiff is relatively slight, the defendant will necessarily be allowed greater latitude than where the harm is intended, or substantially certain to follow.[4]

---

1. See Beale, Justification for Injury, 1928, 41 Harv. L.Rev. 553.

   "There is no justification for a tort. The so-called justification is an exceptional fact which shows that no tort was committed." Stevenson, V. C., in Booth & Bro. v. Burgess, 1906, 72 N.J.Eq. 181, 188, 65 A. 226.

2. Second Restatement of Torts, § 10.

3. See infra, § 31.

4. "Even assuming that the defendant's interest is of slightly less value than that of the plaintiff, he may be permitted to do without liability an act which is certain to advance it even though it contains five chances out of a hundred of injuring a more important interest of the plaintiff, but he is not privileged to do it if the chances for and against injury reach or approach equality. Where the defendant intends to inflict the very invasion which his act causes, there is no room for such considerations. It is the bare value of the respective interests involved and the extent of the harm from which the act is intended to protect the one as compared with that which it is intended to cause to the other which determines the existence or nonexistence of

As the defendant's interest gains weight in the scale of social values, his privilege becomes greater. It may be absolute, in the sense that there is immunity from all liability, regardless of the motive or purpose for which he acts. The acts of judicial officers, done under authority of law, for example, are absolutely privileged, even though malicious or corrupt.[5] It may be conditioned upon a proper motive and reasonable behavior, as in the case of the privilege of self-defense.[6] It may be limited, in the sense that the defendant may not be restrained in advance from acting, and is not liable for any mere technical tort, but is still liable for any substantial damage that he may cause.[7] The sliding scale by which the law balances the interests of the parties to accomplish a social purpose is nowhere better illustrated than in the field of privilege.

17. MISTAKE

The question of mistake frequently arises in connection with privilege. There is an essential distinction between mistake and accident, which is to be considered in a later chapter.[8] The plea of unavoidable accident is that the result complained of as a wrong was not intended by the defendant, and could not have been foreseen and avoided by the exercise of reasonable care. The plea of unavoidable mistake, on the other hand, is that, although the act was voluntary, and the result was intended, the defendant acted under an erroneous belief, formed upon reasonable grounds, that circumstances existed which would justify his conduct. It is an accident if the defendant's horse runs away with him and carries him upon the land of another, a mistake if he intentionally enters upon it in the belief that it is his own.[9]

While unavoidable accident is commonly recognized as a defense against liability, unavoidable mistake is in itself generally held to be no defense at all. However valid the excuse may be under the criminal law,[10] in a civil action one who intentionally interferes with the person or property of another does so at his peril, and must assume the risk that he is wrong. The line which is drawn between accident and mistake has been condemned as anomalous and unreasonable;[11] it can be justified only upon the basis of a policy which makes the defendant responsible for the physical result which he intended, and, as between two parties equally free from moral blame, places the loss upon the one who made the mistake.

Thus it is no defense to an action for battery[12] or false imprisonment[13] that the defendant mistook the plaintiff for another person on whom he might properly lay hands. A trespasser upon land, who honestly believes that he is the owner,[14] or that he has authority from the owner,[15] or who has merely mis-

the privilege." Bohlen, Incomplete Privilege to Inflict Intentional Invasions of Interests of Property and Personality, 1926, 39 Harv.L.Rev. 307, 309 note.

5. See infra, § 132.

6. See infra, § 19.

7. Bohlen, Incomplete Privilege to Inflict Intentional Invasions of Interests of Property and Personality, 1926, 39 Harv.L.Rev. 307. See infra, § 24.

8. See infra, § 29.

9. Salmond, Law of Torts, 8th Ed. 1934, 27; Whittier, Mistake in the Law of Torts, 1902, 15 Harv.L.Rev. 325.

10. See Keedy, Ignorance and Mistake in the Criminal Law, 1908, 22 Harv.L.Rev. 75; Perkins, Ignorance and Mistake in Criminal Law, 1939, 88 U.Pa.L. Rev. 35.

11. Whittier, Mistake in the Law of Torts, 1902, 15 Harv.L.Rev. 335. But see Holmes, The Common Law, 1881, 96–100.

12. Seigel v. Long, 1910, 169 Ala. 79, 53 So. 753; Gill v. Selling, 1928, 125 Or. 587, 267 P. 812, affirmed 126 Or. 584, 270 P. 411; Samuelson v. Taylor, 1931, 160 Wash. 369, 295 P. 113; Moos v. United States, 8 Cir. 1955, 225 F.2d 705 (operation on wrong leg). See supra, p. 36.

13. Cooter v. Bronson, 1875, 67 Barb., N.Y., 444; Formwalt v. Hylton, 1886, 66 Tex. 288, 1 S.W. 376; Holmes v. Blyler, 1890, 80 Iowa 365, 45 N.W. 756; National Food Stores v. Utley, 8 Cir. 1962, 303 F.2d 284. See supra, p. 48.

14. Perry v. Jefferies, 1901, 61 S.C. 292, 39 S.E. 515; Isle Royale Min. Co. v. Hertin, 1877, 37 Mich. 332.

15. Higginson v. York, 1809, 5 Mass. 341; Hazelton v. Week, 1880, 49 Wis. 661, 6 N.W. 309; Lowenburg v. Rosenthal, 1889, 18 Or. 178, 22 P. 601.

taken the boundary,[16] is nevertheless a trespasser. One who sells a chattel,[17] or takes
possession of it, even by bona fide purchase,[18]
becomes a converter, although he does not
know that it is stolen property. In all of
these cases, the defendant may be free from
moral blame, but the rights of others are protected at his expense against the physical
effect which he intends to accomplish.

But such a rule must of necessity have its
limitations. Although mistake as to the existence of a privilege, or a mistake of fact in
itself, will not excuse the defendant, still his
mistake of fact may be important in determining whether the privilege exists. One
who reasonably believes that he is being attacked is privileged to defend himself by injuring another, although it turns out that he
was wrong.[19] An officer armed with a warrant apparently valid on its face is privileged
to make an arrest, although the warrant is
in fact invalid because improperly issued; [20]
or, if he mistakenly thinks that a felony has
been committed, and arrests one whom he
reasonably supposes to be the culprit, he is
likewise privileged.[21] In such cases the in-

terest to be protected is of such outstanding
importance that the defendant is permitted
greater freedom of action. The burden of the
mistake is placed upon the innocent plaintiff
because it is socially necessary that men be
free to defend themselves against apparent
attack, and that officers have leeway to make
arrests.

It is not possible to state a general rule
which will determine when a mistake is privileged.[22] The boundaries of the privilege will
be marked out in each situation upon the
basis of the special reasons of policy and expediency bearing upon the facts.[23] In general, without attempting to state a rule, it
may be said that a mistake is privileged in
cases where it appears necessary for the defendant to act quickly to protect a right as to
the existence of which he is not mistaken, or
where he is under a duty to act for the protection of a public interest. A private citizen, for example, unlike an officer, is privileged to arrest only when a crime has in fact
been committed, and must take the risk that
it has not.[24] The reason is that he has no
public responsibility; there is less necessity
for such arrests, and more occasion to deter
private citizens from taking the law into
their own hands.

If the mistake has been induced by the
plaintiff's own conduct, it is generally held
that the defendant will be absolved from any
liability in tort,[25] so long as he has not acted
unreasonably.[26] The plaintiff will not be
heard to complain of a mistake for which he

---

16. Maye v. Yappan, 1863, 23 Cal. 306; Jeffries v.
     Hargis, 1887, 50 Ark. 65, 6 S.W. 328. See supra,
     p. 74.

Compare, as to trespass to chattels, Ranson v. Kitner,
     1888, 31 Ill.App. 241, where defendant shot plaintiff's
     dog believing it to be a wolf; and see supra, p. 79.

17. Hoffman v. Carow, 1839, 22 Wend., N.Y., 285;
     Kearney v. Clutton, 1894, 101 Mich. 106, 59 N.W. 419.

18. Galvin v. Bacon, 1833, 11 Me. 28; Hyde v. Noble,
     1843, 13 N.H. 494; Eldred v. Oconto Co., 1873, 33
     Wis. 133. See supra, p. 84. Cf. Dexter v. Cole,
     1858, 6 Wis. 319 (trespass).

19. Keep v. Quallman, 1887, 68 Wis. 451, 32 N.W. 233;
     Courvoisier v. Raymond, 1896, 23 Colo. 113, 47 P.
     284; Crabtree v. Dawson, 1904, 119 Ky. 148, 83 S.W.
     557. See infra, p. 109.

20. Rush v. Buckley, 1905, 100 Me. 322, 61 A. 774;
     McIntosh v. Bullard, Earnheart & Magness, 1910, 95
     Ark. 227, 129 S.W. 85; Johnson v. Scott, 1909, 134
     Ky. 736, 121 S.W. 695. See infra, § 25.

21. Beckwith v. Philby, 1827, 6 B. & C. 635, 108 Eng.
     Rep. 585; Grau v. Forge, 1919, 183 Ky. 521, 209
     S.W. 369; White v. McQueen, 1893, 96 Mich. 249,
     55 N.W. 843. See infra, § 26.

22. Whittier, Mistake in the Law of Torts, 1902, 15
     Harv.L.Rev. 335.

23. Smith, Tort and Absolute Liability, 1917, 30 Harv.
     L.Rev. 319, 326.

24. Holley v. Mix, 1829, 3 Wend., N.Y., 350; Reuck
     v. McGregor, 1866, 32 N.J.L. 70; Morley v. Chase,
     1887, 143 Mass. 396, 9 N.E. 767. See infra, § 26.

25. Hills v. Snell, 1870, 104 Mass. 173; Tousley v.
     Board of Education, 1888, 39 Minn. 419, 40 N.W. 509;
     Parker v. Walrod, 1836, 16 Wend., N.Y., 514; Cf.
     Row v. Home Savings Bank, 1940, 306 Mass. 522,
     29 N.E.2d 552.

26. Moore v. Bowman, 1867, 47 N.H. 494.

is himself responsible. If the defendant is unjustly enriched by his act, however, he may be accountable in a quasi-contract action.[27]

18. CONSENT

The consent of the person damaged will ordinarily avoid liability for intentional interference with person or property. It is not, strictly speaking, a privilege, or even a defense,[28] but goes to negative the existence of any tort in the first instance.[29] It is a fundamental principle of the common law that *volenti non fit injuria*—to one who is willing, no wrong is done. The attitude of the courts has not, in general, been one of paternalism. Where no public interest is contravened, they have left the individual to work out his own destiny, and are not concerned with protecting him from his own folly in permitting others to do him harm.[30] In the field of negligence, this policy has been given effect by the doctrine of assumption of risk, which relieves the defendant of the obligation to exercise care.[31] As to intentional invasions of the plaintiff's interests, his consent negatives the wrongful element of the defendant's act, and prevents the existence of a tort. "The absence of lawful consent," said Mr. Justice Holmes, "is part of the definition of an assault."[32] The same is true of false imprisonment,[33] conversion,[34] and trespass.[35]

"Implied" Consent

Consent to an act is simply willingness that it shall occur. Actual willingness, established by competent evidence, will prevent liability; and, if it can ever be proved, will no doubt do so even though the plaintiff has done nothing to manifest it to the defendant.[36] But the converse is also true, that a manifestation of consent, upon which the defendant may reasonably rely, will be equally effective even though there is no willingness in fact. In our society we must perforce rely upon the overt words and acts of others, rather than upon their undisclosed minds. Consent may therefore be manifested by words, or by the kind of actions which often speak louder than words. The defendant is entitled to rely upon what any reasonable man would understand from the plaintiff's conduct. If the plaintiff expressly says, "It's all right with me," he will of course not be permitted to deny that he did consent. By the same taken, if he holds up his arm without objection to be vaccinated, he will not be heard to deny that he has consented after the defendant has relied upon his action.[37]

---

27. Pearson v. Inlow, 1855, 20 Mo. 322.

28. Except in the case of trespass to land, where by the weight of authority the burden of proving a license is upon the defendant. Sims v. Alford, 1908, 218 Ala. 216, 118 So. 395; Milton v. Puffer, 1911, 207 Mass. 416, 419, 93 N.E. 634, 635; Schiffmann v. Hickey, 1921, 101 Or. 596, 604, 200 P. 1035.

29. Lord Denman, in Christopherson v. Bare, 1848, 11 Q.B. 473, 116 Eng.Rep. 554, 556: "to say that the defendant assaulted the plaintiff by his permission * * * is a manifest contradiction in terms." It was therefore held that as a matter of pleading the consent must be shown under a general denial, and that if the defendant admitted the assault he could not defend on the ground that he did it by consent.

30. Bohlen, Contributory Negligence, 1908, 21 Harv.L. Rev. 233; Bohlen, Consent as Affecting Civil Liability for Breaches of the Peace, 1924, 24 Col.L.Rev. 819.

31. Bohlen, Voluntary Assumption of Risk, 1906, 20 Harv.L.Rev. 14, 17; see infra, § 68.

32. Ford v. Ford, 1887, 143 Mass. 577, 578, 10 N.E. 474, 475. Accord: Wright v. Starr, 1919, 42 Nev. 441, 179 P. 877; Cadwell v. Farrell, 1862, 28 Ill. 438 (action must be on the case for negligence, rather than in trespass).

33. Ellis v. Cleveland, 1882, 54 Vt. 437; Kirby v. Harker, 1909, 143 Iowa 478, 121 N.W. 1071; Kirk v. Garrett, 1896, 84 Md. 383, 35 A. 1089.

34. Tousley v. Board of Education, 1888, 39 Minn. 319, 40 N.W. 509.

35. Bennett v. McIntire, 1889, 121 Ind. 231, 23 N.E. 78. But see supra, note 28.

36. What if plaintiff writes in his secret diary, later produced in evidence, that he would be glad to have the defendant come upon his land and use his tennis court? There are no cases.

37. O'Brien v. Cunard S. S. Co., 1891, 154 Mass. 272, 28 N.E. 266. Accord: Dicenzo v. Berg, 1940, 340 Pa. 305, 16 A.2d 15; Barfield v. South Highland In-

Silence and inaction may manifest consent where a reasonable person would speak if he objected. The girl who makes no protest at a proposal to kiss her in the moonlight may have mental reservations that it is without her consent, but the man who does it is none the less privileged.[38] On the other hand, of course, silence does not operate as consent where no reasonable man would so interpret it, as where one defiantly stands his ground under the threat of a blow.

The defendant is sometimes at liberty to infer consent as a matter of usage or custom, and to proceed upon the assumption that it is given. Thus the general habit of the community to permit strangers to enter at will upon wild land may justify a trespass;[39] consent may be assumed to the ordinary contacts of daily life,[40] and a continued course of practical joking between the parties may permit the inference that there is leave to continue it further.[41] One who enters into a sport, game or contest may be taken to consent to physical contacts consistent with the understood rules of the game.[42] It is only

when notice is given that all such conduct will no longer be tolerated [43] that the defendant is no longer free to assume consent.

If the plaintiff is known to be incapable of giving consent because of infancy,[44] intoxication,[45] or mental incompetence,[46] his failure to object, or even his active manifestation of consent will not protect the defendant. The question arises often enough in connection with surgeons and unconscious, delirious, or otherwise irresponsible patients. While the interest of the state in the preservation of human life and health may justify a court order for compulsory treatment even over objection,[47] it does not protect the surgeon when he goes ahead without such an order, and without the consent of the patient,[48] or at least that of a near relative.[49] In the case

---

firmary, 1915, 191 Ala. 553, 68 So. 30; Knowles v. Blue, 1923, 209 Ala. 27, 95 So. 481.

38. Restatement of Torts, § 50. Cf. Wright v. Starr, 1919, 42 Nev. 441, 179 P. 877; Thibault v. Lalumiere, 1945, 318 Mass. 72, 60 N.E.2d 349. Otherwise where the plaintiff does not fully understand what is going on. Shulman v. Lerner, 1966, 2 Mich.App. 705, 141 N.W.2d 348 (preparation for injection).

39. McKee v. Gratz, 1922, 260 U.S. 127; Marsh v. Colby, 1878, 39 Mich. 626.

40. Wiffin v. Kincard, 1807, 2 Bos. & P. 471, 126 Eng. Rep. 1391; Coward v. Baddeley, 1859, 4 H. & N. 478, 157 Eng.Rep. 927.

41. Wartman v. Swindell, 1892, 54 N.J.L. 589, 25 A. 356.

42. McAdams v. Windham, 1922, 208 Ala. 492, 94 So. 742 (boxing match); Vendrell v. School Dist. No. 26C, 1962, 233 Or. 1, 376 P.2d 406 (football); Gibeline v. Smith, 1904, 106 Mo.App. 545, 80 S.W. 961 (friendly scuffle); Tavernier v. Maes, 1966, 242 Cal.App.2d 532, 51 Cal.Rptr. 575 (baseball); Ogden v. Rabinowitz, 1957, 294 R.I. 86, 134 A.2d 416 (college fracas); Note, 1929, 26 Mich.L.Rev. 322. Cf. Second Restatement of Torts, § 50, Comment b, to the effect that there is no liability for a violation of rules not intended for the protection of the players, but merely

to further better playing of the game, such as the offside rule in football. No cases have been found.

43. Richmond v. Fiske, 1893, 160 Mass. 34, 35 N.E. 103. Cf. Breitenbach v. Trowbridge, 1887, 64 Mich. 393, 31 N.W. 402 (revocation of license to enter place of business).

44. Robalina v. Armstrong, 1852, 15 Barb., N.Y., 247; Commonwealth v. Nickerson, 1862, 5 Allen, Mass., 518.

45. McCue v. Klein, 1883, 60 Tex. 168; Ibach v. Jackson, 1934, 148 Or. 92, 35 P.2d 672; Hollerud v. Malamis, 1970, 20 Mich.App. 748, 174 N.W.2d 626; Note, 1935, 14 Or.L.Rev. 281.

46. Pratt v. Davis, 1906, 224 Ill. 300, 79 N.E. 562; Bolton v. Stewart, Tex.Civ.App.1945, 191 S.W.2d 798.

47. Application of President & Directors of Georgetown College, D.C. Cir. 1964, 331 F.2d 1000, 1010, cert. denied 377 U.S. 978; In re Brooks' Estate, 1965, 32 Ill.2d 361, 205 N.E.2d 435; Raleigh Fitkin-Paul Morgan Mem. Hosp. v. Anderson, 1964, 42 N.J. 421, 201 A.2d 537, cert. denied 377 U.S. 985. See Notes, 1964, 51 Minn.L.Rev. 293; 1964, 77 Harv.L. Rev. 1539.

48. Mulloy v. Hop Sang, [1935] 1 W.W.R. 714; Schloendorff v. Society of New York Hospital, 1914, 211 N.Y. 125, 105 N.E. 92; Mohr v. Williams, 1905, 95 Minn. 261, 263, 104 N.W. 12, 13; Hively v. Higgs, 1927, 120 Or. 588, 253 P. 363; Rolater v. Strain, 1913, 39 Okl. 572, 137 P. 96.

49. In Pratt v. Davis, 1906, 224 Ill. 300, 79 N.E. 562, the consent of the husband was held to be required for an operation on an insane wife. But where the patient is competent to consent, and does so, consent of the spouse is not required. State to Use of Jan-

of operations on young children, the consent of the parent has been held to be required,[50] although minors approaching maturity have been held to be capable of giving their own consent.[51] But in an emergency which threatens death or serious bodily harm, as where the patient is bleeding to death and it is necessary to amputate his foot to save his life, it is generally recognized that these requirements must be waived, and the surgeon must be free to operate without delaying to obtain consent.[52] It is said in these cases that the consent is "implied" under the cir-

cumstances. This is obviously a fiction, since consent does not exist, and there is no act which indicates it.[53] It is probably more accurate here, and perhaps likewise in many other cases of so-called "implied" consent, to say that the defendant is privileged because he is reasonably entitled to assume that, if the patient were competent and understood the situation, he would consent, and therefore to act as if it has been given.

Exceeding Consent

The consent is to the plaintiff's conduct, rather than to its consequences. If the plaintiff willingly engages in a boxing match, he does not of course consent to be killed, but he does consent to the defendant's striking at him, and hitting him if he can; and if death unexpectedly results, his consent to the act will defeat any action for the resulting invasion of his interests.[54] He does not, on the other hand, consent to being hit with brass knuckles, which is the same invasion by an act of a different character.

The defendant's privilege is limited to the conduct to which the plaintiff consents, or at least to acts of a substantially similar nature. A consent to a fight with fists is not a consent to an act of a different nature, such as biting off a finger,[55] or stabbing with a

ney v. Housekeeper, 1889, 70 Md. 162, 16 A. 382; Burroughs v. Crichton, 1919, 48 App.D.C. 596; Mc-Clallen v. Adams, 1837, 19 Pick., Mass., 333. It is also ineffective when given. Gravis v. Physicians & Surgeons Hospital of Alice, 1968, — Tex. —, 427 S.W.2d 310.

50. Zoski v. Gaines, 1939, 271 Mich. 1, 260 N.W. 99 (9½ years); Moss v. Rishworth, Tex.Com.App., 1920, 222 S.W. 225 (11 years); Bonner v. Moran, 1941, 75 U.S.App.D.C. 156, 126 F.2d 121 (15 years); Rogers v. Sells, 1936, 178 Okl. 103, 61 P.2d 1018 (14 years).

Where the parent unreasonably refuses consent a court may, as in other cases where it is necessary to act for the welfare of the child, remove him from the custody of the parent, and appoint a custodian, who may then consent to the operation. Matter of Brooklyn Hospital v. Torres, 1965, 45 Misc.2d 914, 258 N.Y.S.2d 621; Notes, 1955, 12 Wash. & Lee L. Rev. 239; 1953, 41 Geo.L.J. 226.

51. At least to minor operations. Bakker v. Welsh, 1906, 144 Mich. 632, 108 N.W. 94 (17 years); Gulf & S. I. R. Co. v. Sullivan, 1928, 155 Miss. 1, 119 So. 501 (same); Bishop v. Shurly, 1926, 237 Mich. 76, 211 N.W. 75 (19 years); Lacey v. Laird, 1956, 166 Ohio St. 12, 139 N.E.2d 25 (18 years). The reasoning is that the minor is competent to consent, which would apply also to major operations; but there are as yet no cases so holding. See Notes, 1957, 10 Vand.L.Rev. 619; 1957, 9 West.Res.L.Rev. 101.

52. Even in the case of a minor, where the parents cannot be reached quickly. Luka v. Lowrie, 1912, 171 Mich. 122, 136 N.W. 1106; Wells v. McGehee, La. App.1949, 39 So.2d 196; Jackovach v. Yocom, 1931, 212 Iowa 914, 237 N.W. 444. Cf. King v. Carney, 1922, 85 Okl. 62, 204 Pa. 270; McGuire v. Rix, 1929, 118 Neb. 434, 225 N.W. 120; Delahunt v. Finton, 1928, 244 Mich. 226, 221 N.W. 168; Preston v. Hubbell, 1948, 87 Cal.App.2d 53, 196 P.2d 113; Barnett v. Bachrach, Mun.App.D.C.1943, 34 A.2d 626. See also Sullivan v. Montgomery, 1935, 155 Misc. 448, 279 N.Y.S. 575 (necessary to relieve pain).

53. Second Restatement of Torts, § 62. Cf. Ollet v. Pittsburg, C. C. & St. L. R. Co., 1902, 201 Pa. 361, 50 A. 1011, holding that emergency measures were privileged although the patient objected.

54. McAdams v. Windham, 1922, 208 Ala. 492, 94 So. 742; cf. Nicholls v. Colwell, 1903, 113 Ill.App. 219. See Puttkammer, Consent in Criminal Assault, 1925, 19 Ill.L.Rev. 617.

It seems clear that the consent must be to the act rather than the resulting invasion of the plaintiff's interests. A consents to a boxing match with B, and unknown to A, B uses a set of brass knuckles. B punches A in the nose, inflicting exactly the same damage as if he had hit him with his fist. The consent is ineffective. On the other hand, A permits B to punch him in the chest as hard as he can. Unknown to either A or B, A has a defective heart, and drops dead. The consent is effective.

55. Milam v. Milam, 1907, 46 Wash. 468, 90 P. 595. Cf. Fitzgerald v. Cavin, 1872, 110 Mass. 153 (foul

knife.[56] Permission to dump "a few stones" upon property is not a permission to cover it with boulders.[57] If the defendant goes beyond the consent given, and does a substantially different act, he is liable.[58]

The rule frequently is applied to surgical operations.[59] Consent to operate on the right ear is not necessarily consent to operate on the left,[60] and a patient who agrees to a blood test [61] or a minor operation on his nose [62]

does not thereby consent to a spinal puncture, or the removal of his tonsils. With the patient unconscious under an anaesthetic, and unable to be consulted, the mere desirability of the operation does not protect the surgeon, who becomes liable for battery—which, in addition to making him liable for at least nominal and perhaps punitive damages, renders quite immaterial any question of whether he has complied with good professional practice.[63] It is of course possible that the situation may be one of unforeseen emergency, critical in its nature, which will justify the surgeon in proceeding [64] on the assumption that the patient would consent if he were conscious and understood the situation.[65] It is also possible that the consent given will be sufficiently general in its terms to cover the particular operation, or that the surgeon may be authorized with complete freedom to do whatever he thinks best to remedy whatever he finds,[66] particularly where the patient has signed one of the written forms in common use in hospitals.[67] Such questions are matters of fact, which normally are to be determined by the jury. The general approach of the law has certainly changed from quite a rigorous one at the beginning of the century [68] to much greater liberality

hold in wrestling match); Nicholls v. Colwell, 1903, 113 Ill.App. 219 (excessive force in scuffle).

56. Teolis v. Moscatelli, 1923, 44 R.I. 494, 119 A. 161.

57. Wheelock v. Noonan, 1888, 108 N.Y. 179, 15 N.E. 67.

58. Francis v. Sun Oil Co., 1959, 135 Mont. 307, 340 P.2d 824 (seismographic operations on plaintiff's land, too close to a spring); Shiffer v. Broadhead, 1889, 126 Pa. 260, 17 A. 592 (cutting trees below customary limit in size); Cartan v. Cruz Const. Co., 1965, 89 N.J.Super. 414, 215 A.2d 356.

This is true in particular where the consent is effectively withdrawn before or during the act. Mims v. Boland, 1964, 110 Ga.App. 477, 138 S.E.2d 902; Regina v. Miller, [1954] 2 Q.B. 282 (wife's withdrawal of consent to intercourse).

But consent to the entry of the defendants to remove heavy goods may reasonably imply consent to the entry of his servants to assist. Sterling v. Warden, 1871, 51 N.H. 217.

59. An exceptionally good discussion of the problems involved is McCoid, A Reappraisal of Liability for Unauthorized Medical Treatment, 1957, 41 Minn.L.Rev. 381. See also Straub, Antecedent Grounds of Liability in the Practice of Surgery, 1942, 14 Rocky Mt.L.Rev. 233; Smith, The Surgeon and the Unconscious Patient, 1929, 33 Law Notes 29; Kelly, The Physician, the Patient, and the Consent, 1960, 8 Kan.L.Rev. 405; Notes, 1940, 14 U.Cin.L.Rev. 161; 1946, 19 Tenn.L.Rev. 374; 1953, 42 Ky.L.J. 98; 1957, 6 Duke Bar J. 41. Cases are collected in Morris, Medical Malpractice—A Changing Picture, [1956] Ins.L.J. 318.

60. Mohr v. Williams, 1905, 95 Minn. 261, 104 N.W. 12. Cf. Moos v. United States, 8 Cir. 1955, 225 F.2d 705 (wrong leg); Hershey v. Peake, 1924, 115 Kan. 562, 223 P. 1113 (wrong tooth); Paulsen v. Gundersen, 1935, 218 Wis. 578, 260 N.W. 448; Franklyn v. Peabody, 1930, 249 Mich. 363, 228 N.W. 681.

61. Gill v. Selling, 1928, 125 Or. 587, 267 P. 812. Cf. Throne v. Wandell, 1922, 176 Wis. 97, 186 N.W. 146 (consent to examination; extraction of all teeth).

62. Hively v. Higgs, 1927, 120 Or. 588, 253 P. 363; Rolater v. Strain, 1913, 39 Okl. 572, 137 P. 96; Tabor v. Scobee, Ky.1952, 254 S.W.2d 474; Markart v.

Zeimer, 1924, 67 Cal.App. 363, 227 P. 683; Wells v. Van Nort, 1919, 100 Ohio St. 101, 125 N.E. 910.

63. Perry v. Hodgson, 1929, 168 Ga. 678, 148 S.E. 659; Tabor v. Scobee, Ky.1952, 254 S.W.2d 474; Franklyn v. Peabody, 1930, 249 Mich. 363, 228 N.W. 681.

64. Delahunt v. Finton, 1928, 244 Mich. 226, 221 N.W. 168; Preston v. Hubbell, 1948, 87 Cal.App.2d 53, 196 P.2d 113; Barnett v. Bachrach, Mun.App.D.C.1943, 34 A.2d 626.

65. See supra, p. 104.

66. Bennan v. Parsonnet, 1912, 83 N.J.L. 20, 83 A. 948; Crippen v. Pulliam, 1963, 61 Wash.2d 725, 380 P.2d 475; King v. Carney, 1922, 85 Okl. 62, 204 P. 270; Rothe v. Hull, 1944, 352 Mo. 926, 180 S.W.2d 7; Dicenzo v. Berg, 1940, 340 Pa. 305, 16 A.2d 15.

67. Danielson v. Roche, 1952, 109 Cal.App.2d 832, 241 P.2d 1028 (surgeon to "perform all treatments deemed advisable by him" during appendectomy. Held to cover removal of parts of Fallopian tubes).

68. Mohr v. Williams, 1905, 95 Minn. 261, 104 N.W. 12, is the classic case. See also Pratt v. Davis, 1906, 224 Ill. 300, 79 N.E. 562.

toward the surgeon, in the light of the conditions under which operations are now performed.[69] But it is still at least true that where an operation is found to have been prohibited,[70] the surgeon is not saved from liability by his good intentions in proceeding with it.

Mistake, Fraud and Duress

If the plaintiff manifests consent to the defendant's act under a mistake as to its nature or character, the consent will still be effective, unless the defendant is aware of the mistake and takes advantage of it, as where he has misrepresented the matter to the plaintiff.[71] If he gives the plaintiff a box of candy, in ignorance of the fact that it contains poison, the consent to eat it will prevent any liability for battery. But if the defendant knows that the candy is poisoned, and that the plaintiff is unaware of the fact, he is not privileged to rely on the consent.[72] The "fraud" usually said to be involved in such a case may be simply the advantage taken of the plaintiff's ignorance to injure him. Thus a woman who consents to intercourse may still recover when she is infected with venereal disease, although nothing was said about it,[73] or equally when she finds that she is the victim of a mock marriage;[74] and a physician may be liable for inducing an innocent girl to submit to indecent liberties, when he knows that she is ignorant of the fact that they are unnecessary for medical treatment.[75] Apparently, however, the mistake must extend to the essential character of the act itself, which is to say that which makes it harmful or offensive,[76] rather than to some collateral matter which merely operates as an inducement. Thus consent to intercourse is still consent, although it is in return for counterfeit money, and the woman has no action for battery when she subsequently decides that she has been raped.[77] The remedy, if any, for such collateral fraud, is an action for deceit, or upon the contract for the consideration promised.

The question sometimes has arisen in cases involving medical or surgical treatment, where the defendant is aware that the patient does not understand the nature of the operation, or the risk of undesirable consequences involved in it.[78] Where there is active misrepresentation, this has been held to invali-

69. See for example Kennedy v. Parrott, 1956, 243 N.C. 355, 90 S.E.2d 754; Barnett v. Bachrach, Mun. App.D.C.1943, 34 A.2d 626; Rothe v. Hull, 1944, 352 Mo. 926, 180 S.W.2d 7; Russell v. Jackson, 1950, 37 Wash.2d 66, 221 P.2d 516.

70. Schloendorff v. Society of New York Hospital, 1914, 211 N.Y. 125, 105 N.E. 92; Chambers v. Nottebaum, Fla.App.1957, 96 So.2d 716; Corn v. French, 1955, 71 Nev. 280, 289 P.2d 173; Woodson v. Huey, Okl.1954, 261 P.2d 199. Cf. Mulloy v. Hop Sang, [1935] 1 W.W.R. 714 (amputation expressly forbidden, although necessary to save life).

71. Second Restatement of Torts, § 55.

72. Cf. Commonwealth v. Stratton, 1873, 114 Mass. 303; State v. Monroe, 1897, 121 N.C. 677, 28 S.E. 547; People v. Steinberg, 1947, 190 Misc. 413, 73 N.Y.S. 475 (pretended smallpox vaccination, with water). See Note, 1935, 14 Or.L.Rev. 281.

73. Crowell v. Crowell, 1920, 180 N.C. 516, 105 S.E. 206, rehearing denied, 1921, 181 N.C. 66, 106 S.E. 149; De Vall v. Strunk, Tex.Civ.App.1936, 96 S.W.2d 245; State v. Lankford, 1917, 29 Del. 594, 102 A. 63.

74. Blossom v. Barrett, 1868, 37 N.Y. 434.

75. Bartell v. State, 1900, 106 Wis. 342, 82 N.W. 142; Commonwealth v. Gregory, 1938, 132 Pa.Super. 507, 1 A.2d 501; Bowman v. Home Life Ins. Co., 3 Cir. 1957, 243 F.2d 331. Cf. Hobbs v. Kizer, 8 Cir. 1916, 236 F. 681 (abortion represented to be other operation); People v. Steinberg, 1947, 190 Misc. 413, 73 N.Y.S.2d 475 (pretended vaccination, with water).

76. Second Restatement of Torts, §§ 55, 57.

77. Restatement of Torts, § 57. Cf. Oberlin v. Upson, 1911, 84 Ohio St. 111, 95 N.E. 511 (seduction under promise of marriage); Martin v. Carbide & Carbon Chemicals Corp., 1946, 184 Tenn. 166, 197 S.W.2d 798 (treatment by unlicensed physician). Compare the cases of conversion by a sale induced by fraud, supra, p. 84.

78. See McCoid, The Care Required of Medical Practitioners, 1959, 12 Vand.L.Rev. 549, 586–597; Plant, An Analysis of "Informed Consent," 1968, 36 Ford.L.Rev. 639; Karchmer, Informed Consent: A Plaintiff's Malpractice "Wonder Drug," 1966, 31 Mo. L.Rev. 29; Notes, 1960, 60 Col.L.Rev. 1193; 1961, 34 So.Cal.L.Rev. 209, 1962, 75 Harv.L.Rev. 1445; 1966, 44 Tex.L.Rev. 799; 1967, 52 Iowa L.Rev. 786; 1967, 20 Okl.L.Rev. 214; 1967, 21 Sw.L.Rev. 843.

date the consent, so that there is battery; [79] and the same has been held where there has been mere nondisclosure of consequences which the surgeon knew to be certain to follow.[80] Beyond this, there have been a few decisions finding battery where there was failure to disclose only a known risk of the treatment.[81]

The greater number of decisions now regard the failure to disclose a mere risk of treatment as involving a collateral matter, and negligence rather than intent, and so have treated the question as one of negligent malpractice only, which brings into question professional standards of conduct. The matter is therefore more fully considered in connection with negligence.[82]

Relatively few cases have dealt with the problem of consent given under duress. Duress is an important defense in the criminal law,[83] and will justify recission of a contract or other transaction, with restitution,[84] but there has been no discussion of its place in the law of torts. There are odd cases [85] which have held that duress is a tort in itself; but much more commonly it is held merely to invalidate the consent given, and so permit any other tort action which would

arise if there were no consent. As to false imprisonment or battery, it is clear that yielding to a threat of force,[86] or the assertion of legal authority,[87] must be treated as no consent at all, but submission against the plaintiff's will; and the same is undoubtedly true as to trespass or conversion.[88] The same is probably true where the threat is directed against a member of the plaintiff's immediate family,[89] or his valuable property.[90] But if the threat is less direct, being merely one of future arrest,[91] or of "economic" duress such as loss of employment,[92] the courts have refused to say that the consent given, however reluctant it may be, is ineffective, so as to establish another tort. The distinction is of course one of degree. The growing tendency to recognize and extend the intentional inflic-

79. Paulsen v. Gundersen, 1935, 218 Wis. 578, 260 N.W. 448; Wall v. Brim, 5 Cir. 1943, 138 F.2d 478.

80. Bang v. Charles T. Miller Hospital, 1958, 251 Minn. 427, 88 N.W.2d 186 (sterilization).

81. Bang v. Charles T. Miller Hospital, 1958, 251 Minn. 427, 88 N.W.2d 186; Gray v. Grunnagle, 1966, 423 Pa. 144, 223 A.2d 663; Belcher v. Carter, 1967, 13 Ohio App.2d 113, 234 N.E.2d 311; Shulman v. Lerner, 1966, 2 Mich.App. 705, 141 N.W.2d 348.

82. See infra, p. 165.

83. Newman and Weitzer, Duress, Free Will and the Criminal Law, 1957, 30 So.Cal.L.Rev. 313.

84. See Notes, 1941, 6 Mo.L.Rev. 73; 1968, 53 Iowa L. Rev. 892.

85. Neibuhr v. Gage, 1906, 99 Minn. 149, 108 N.W. 884, affirmed, 1906, 99 Minn. 149, 109 N.W. 1 (duress a "form of fraud"); Smith v. Blakesburg Sav. Bank, 1917, 182 Iowa 1190, 164 N.W. 762 (following case last cited); Woodham v. Allen, 1900, 130 Cal. 194, 62 P. 398 (relying upon apparently irrelevant Code provision).

86. Meints v. Huntington, 8 Cir. 1921, 276 F. 245; W. T. Grant Co. v. Owens, 1928, 149 Va. 906, 141 S.E. 860; Cordell v. Standard Oil Co., 1930, 131 Kan. 221, 289 P. 472 (false imprisonment); Miller v. Balthasser, 1875, 78 Ill. 302 (battery). But where consent to sexual intercourse is concerned, an overwhelming personality is no sufficient substitute for force. Rouse v. Creech, 1932, 203 N.C. 378, 166 S.E. 174.

87. Whitman v. Atchison, T. & S. F. R. Co., 1911, 85 Kan. 150, 116 P. 234; Hebrew v. Pulis, 1906, 73 N.J.L. 621, 64 A. 121; Johnson v. Norfolk & W. R. Co., 1918, 82 W.Va. 692, 97 S.E. 189.

88. Grainger v. Hill, 1838, 4 Bing.N.C. 212, 132 Eng. Rep. 769 (arrest and imprisonment); Murphy v. Hobbs, 1884, 8 Colo. 17, 5 P. 637 (threats of force); General Motors Acceptance Corp. v. Davis, 1931, 151 Okl. 255, 7 P.2d 157 (issue of warrant and threat of prosecution); see Millsap v. National Funding Corp., 1943, 57 Cal.App.2d 772, 135 P.2d 407; Saunders v. Mullinix, 1950, 195 Md. 235, 72 A.2d 720.

89. Second Restatement of Torts, § 58. See Note, 1928, 12 Minn.L.Rev. 409.

90. See supra, p. 45.

91. Payson v. Macomber, 1861, 3 Allen, Mass., 69; Knowlton v. Ross, 1915, 114 Me. 18, 95 A. 281; Sweeney v. F. W. Woolworth Co., 1924, 247 Mass. 277, 142 N.E. 50; Blumenfeld v. Harris, 1957, 3 App. Div.2d 219, 159 N.Y.S.2d 561; Priddy v. Bunton, Tex. Civ.App.1943, 177 S.W.2d 805, error refused; see Powell v. Champion Fiber Co., 1908, 150 N.C. 12, 63 S.E. 159.

92. Latter v. Braddell, 1880, 50 L.J.Q.B. 166; Weiler v. Herzfeld-Phillipson Co., 1926, 189 Wis. 554, 208 N.W. 599.

tion of mental suffering as an independent cause of action [93] may perhaps afford a remedy for some of the more extreme cases. In the field of contracts, duress is more generally recognized as a ground for relief,[94] and it may in time receive more acceptance in the field of torts.

Consent to a Criminal Act

If the defendant's act is a crime, affecting the interest of the public, the criminal law in many cases refuses to recognize the consent of the injured party as a defense.[95] This is true, for example, of a fight by mutual consent, which is a breach of the peace. The considerable majority of the courts have attempted, in cases of mutual combat [96] and similar batteries [97] to vindicate a conception of public policy by holding that the consent given will likewise not protect the defendant against a civil action for the damage inflicted. This rule has been traced [98] to a dictum in an early English case,[99] at a time when the action of trespass still had a criminal character, and the state was directly concerned in it. Its survival is due to a combination of the two notions that the interests of the state require protection by allowing a civil action, and that the parties will be deterred from fighting by the fear of liability. But the cases have been roundly criticized [1] on the grounds that no one should be rewarded with damages for his own voluntary participation in a wrong, particularly where, as is usually the case, he himself commits a crime; that the state is fully able to protect itself by a criminal prosecution; and that the parties, if they give any thought to the law at all, which is quite improbable, are quite as likely to be encouraged by the hope that if they get hurt they can still win in court. A minority of some eight states,[2] with the support of the Restatement,[3] have held that the consent will defeat the civil action, except where the force used exceeds the consent.

There are, however, certain criminal statutes, such as those fixing the age of consent to sexual intercourse, which obviously are intended to protect a limited class of persons against their own lack of judgment, and so against their own consent. In such a case, the direction of public policy has been con-

---

93. See supra, § 12.

94. Notes, 1925, 39 Harv.L.Rev. 108; Note 1938, 22 Minn.L.Rev. 891. As in the case of fraud (supra, note 85), any duress which will avoid a contract of sale may permit the seller to rescind and sue for conversion. General Motors Acceptance Corp. v. Davis, 1931, 151 Okl. 255, 7 P.2d 157; Borderland Hardware Co. v. Saenz, Tex.Civ.App.1928, 9 S.W.2d 1049.

95. Beale, Consent in the Criminal Law, 1895, 8 Harv.L.Rev. 317; Miller, Criminal Law, 1934, 171.

96. McNeil v. Mullin, 1905, 70 Kan. 634, 79 P. 168; Schwaller v. McFarland, 1940, 228 Iowa 405, 291 N.W. 852; Lewis v. Fountain, 1915, 168 N.C. 277, 84 S.E. 278; Condict v. Hewitt, 1962, — Wyo. —, 369 P.2d 278; Strawn v. Ingram, 1937, 118 W.Va. 603, 191 S.E. 401 (in mitigation of punitive damages only). See Notes, 1931, 17 Va.L.Rev. 374; 1949, 2 Okl.L.Rev. 108; 1949, 2 Vand.L.Rev. 301.

97. Teeters v. Frost, 1930, 145 Okl. 273, 292 P. 356 (prize fight); Gilmore v. Fuller, 1902, 198 Ill. 130, 65 N.E. 84 (unlawful charivari); Logan v. Austin, 1828, 1 Stew., Ala., 476; cf. Evans v. Waite, 1892, 83 Wis. 286, 53 N.W. 445.

98. Bohlen, Consent as Affecting Civil Liability for Breaches of the Peace, 1924, 24 Col.L.Rev. 819.

99. In Matthews v. Ollerton, 1693, Comb. 218, 90 Eng. Rep. 438.

1. Bohlen, Consent as Affecting Civil Liability for Breaches of the Peace, 1924, 24 Col.L.Rev. 819; Notes, 1924, 73 U.Pa.L.Rev. 74; 1931, 17 Va.L.Rev. 374; 1931, 3 Rocky Mt.L.Rev. 285; 1938, 22 Minn. L.Rev. 546.

2. Galbraith v. Fleming, 1886, 60 Mich. 408, 27 N.W. 583; Lykins v. Hamrick, 1911, 144 Ky. 80, 137 S.W. 852; Wright v. Starr, 1919, 42 Nev. 441, 179 P. 877; Hart v. Geysel, 1930, 159 Wash. 632, 294 P. 570; Dixon v. Samartino, Tex.Civ.App.1942, 163 S.W.2d 739, error refused. See also the abortion cases cited infra, note 6.

Even in such jurisdictions, the conclusion may be affected by the language of particular criminal statutes. Thus in Hudson v. Craft, 1949, 33 Cal.2d 654, 204 P.2d 1, a statute prohibiting unlicensed boxing matches was found to be filled with so many provisions for the protection of the boxers as to indicate an intention to protect them even though they consented.

3. Second Restatement of Torts, § 60.

sidered to be clearly indicated, and it is generally agreed, except for one or two cases,[4] that the consent will not bar the action.[5] There is a good deal of dispute over the category into which to put the statutes making abortion a crime. A scant majority of the jurisdictions,[6] with almost an equal number to the contrary,[7] have considered that the abortion statutes are intended for the protection of the unborn child and the public interest rather than the woman,[8] and have held that her consent bars her recovery. Here perhaps the argument that the public interest demands that the plaintiff be allowed a civil action as an incentive to disclose a crime peculiarly likely to remain secret, has strengthened the opinions of the minority. It would appear that in any case recovery should be allowed for negligence in performing the operation, to which there has been no consent;[9] but there are courts which have

denied even this, in order to avoid giving any aid to the voluntary wrongdoer.[10]

19.   SELF–DEFENSE

The privilege of self-defense rests upon the necessity of permitting a man who is attacked to take reasonable steps to prevent harm to himself, where there is no time to resort to the law. The early English law, with its views of strict liability, did not recognize such a privilege; concerning such cases, it was said that "the man who commits homicide by misadventure or in self-defense deserves but needs a pardon." [11] But since about 1400 the privilege has been recognized,[12] and it is now undisputed, in the law of torts as well as in the criminal law. The privilege extends to the use of all reasonable force to prevent any threatened harmful or offensive bodily contact, or any confinement, whether intended or negligent.[13] Since it originated as a

4.   Barton v. Bee Line, 1933, 238 App.Div. 501, 265 N.Y.S. 284, vigorously attacked the idea of allowing the girl to recover. See also Note, 1938, 7 Ford.L. Rev. 274, pointing out the opportunities for extortion. In Braun v. Heidrich, 1932, 62 N.D. 85, 241 N.W. 599, recovery was denied where the statute, apparently unique, expressly made the girl a criminal.

5.   Bishop v. Liston, 1924, 112 Neb. 559, 199 N.W. 825; Priboth v. Haveron, 1914, 41 Okl. 692, 139 P. 973; Hough v. Iderhoff, 1914, 69 Or. 568, 139 P. 931; Glover v. Callahan, 1937, 299 Mass. 55, 12 N.E.2d 194; Gaither v. Meacham, 1926, 214 Ala. 343, 108 So. 2; Koch v. Stone, Ky.1960, 332 S.W.2d 529 (indecent liberties); Restatement of Torts, § 61.

6.   Miller v. Bennett, 1949, 190 Va. 162, 56 S.E.2d 217; Sayadoff v. Warda, 1954, 125 Cal.App.2d 626, 271 P. 2d 140; Szadiwicz v. Cantor, 1926, 257 Mass. 518, 154 N.E. 251; Bowlan v. Lunsford, 1936, 176 Okl. 115, 54 P.2d 666; Martin v. Morris, 1931, 163 Tenn. 186, 42 S.W.2d 207.

7.   Joy v. Brown, 1953, 173 Kan. 833, 252 P.2d 889; Milliken v. Heddesheimer, 1924, 110 Ohio St. 381, 144 N.E. 264; Martin v. Hardesty, 1928, 91 Ind.App. 239, 163 N.E. 610; Androws v. Coulter, 1931, 163 Wash. 429, 1 P.2d 320. See Notes, 1951, 45 Ill.L.Rev. 395; 1953, 26 So.Cal.L.Rev. 472; Wolcott v. Gaines, 1969, 225 Ga. 373, 169 S.E.2d 165 (not in pari delictur).

8.   See Herman v. Turner, 1925, 117 Kan. 733, 232 P. 864.

9.   Courts which do not bar the action for the abortion itself of course allow recovery for the dam-

ages resulting from negligence. Kimberly v. Ledbetter, 1958, 183 Kan. 644, 331 P.2d 307. But some courts which treat consent as a bar to a battery action have allowed recovery for negligence. Androws v. Coulter, 1931, 163 Wash. 429, 1 P.2d 320; True v. Older, 1948, 227 Minn. 154, 34 N.W.2d 700; Henrie v. Griffith, Okl.1964, 395 P.2d 809; Gaines v. Wolcott, 1969, 119 Ga.App. 313, 167 S.E.2d 366, affirmed 225 Ga. 373, 169 S.E.2d 165.

10.   Hunter v. Wheate, 1923, 53 App.D.C. 206, 289 F. 604; Nash v. Meyer, 1934, 54 Idaho 283, 31 P.2d 273; Castronovo v. Murawsky, 1954, 3 Ill.App.2d 168, 120 N.E.2d 871.

11.   2 Pollock and Maitland, History of English Law, 2d Ed.1898, 479. See Ames, Law and Morals, 1908, 22 Harv.L.Rev. 97; Wigmore, Responsibility for Tortious Acts: Its History, 1894, 7 Harv.L.Rev. 315.

12.   Chapleyn of Greye's Inn v. ———, 1400, Y.B. 2 Hen. IV 8, pl. 40.

There are relatively few tort cases. The tort rules are apparently completely identical with those of the criminal law. An excellent review of the latter is Perkins, Self-Defense Re-examined, 1954, 1 U.C. L.A.L.Rev. 133.

13.   Second Restatement of Torts, §§ 64, 66, 68: Haeussler v. De Loretto, 1952, 109 Cal.App.2d 363, 240 P.2d 654.

defense, the burden is upon the defendant to establish the facts creating the privilege.[14]

Apparent Necessity

The privilege to act in self-defense arises, not only where there is real danger, but also where there is a reasonable belief that it exists. The defendant is not liable where he acts under a reasonable, but mistaken, apprehension that the man advancing toward him intends to attack him,[15] or that the hand which goes to a pocket is reaching for a gun.[16] He is not required to wait until a blow is struck, for, as was quaintly observed in the earliest case, "perhaps it will come too late afterwards." [17] Undoubtedly the criminal law, with its concern with moral guilt, has had its influence in casting the loss due to an innocent mistake upon the party who is hurt; but the interest in self-protection, "the first law of nature," is perhaps sufficiently important in the mind of the public to justify the result.

The belief must, however, be one which a reasonable man would have entertained under the circumstances. The defendant is not required to behave with unusual courage,[18] but neither is he free to behave with abnormal timidity, or to be a complete fool; [19] and it is not enough that he really believes that he is about to be attacked, unless he has some reasonable ground for the belief.[20] Evidence as to his state of mind and nerves, and the threats, past conduct, and reputation of his assailant which may have induced it, is important and admissible on the issue of what was reasonable,[21] which is frequently one for the jury,[22] but the standard to be applied is the external one of reasonable conduct.

Reasonable Force

The privilege is limited to the use of force which is, or reasonably appears to be,[23] necessary for protection against the threatened injury.[24] The defendant is not privileged to inflict a beating which goes beyond the real or apparent necessities of his own defense.[25] If he does, he is committing a tort as to the

14. Wells v. Englehart, 1905, 118 Ill.App. 217; Marriott v. Williams, 1908, 152 Cal. 705, 93 P. 875; see Note, 1928, 6 Tex.L.Rev. 553.

15. Paxton v. Boyer, 1873, 67 Ill. 132; Courvoisier v. Raymond, 1896, 23 Colo. 113, 47 P. 284; Crabtree v. Dawson, 1904, 119 Ky. 148, 83 S.W. 557; Pearson v. Taylor, La.App.1959, 116 So.2d 833; Laffin v. Apalucci, 1943, 130 Conn. 153, 32 A.2d 648. As to the effect of a threat, see Hughes v. State, 1937, 212 Ind. 577, 10 N.E.2d 629.

16. Keep v. Quallman, 1887, 68 Wis. 451, 32 N.W. 233; Godwin v. Collins, 1914, 67 Fla. 197, 64 So. 752; Landry v. Hill, La.App.1957, 94 So.2d 308. The supposed assailant may be privileged in turn to defend himself, and in the resulting fracas it is entirely possible that neither party may be liable. Jamison v. Moseley, 1892, 69 Miss. 478, 10 So. 582.

17. Chapleyn of Greye's Inn v. ——, 1400, Y.B. 2 Hen. IV 8, pl. 40.

18. Petterson v. Standley, 1900, 91 Ill.App. 671.

19. Courvoisier v. Raymond, 1896, 23 Colo. 113, 47 P. 284; Beck v. Minneapolis Union R. Co., 1905, 95
Minn. 73, 103 N.W. 746; McQuiggan v. Ladd, 1906, 79 Vt. 90, 64 A. 503; Daggs v. St. Louis-S. F. R. Co., 1930, 326 Mo. 555, 31 S.W.2d 769.

20. State v. Bryson, 1864, 60 N.C. 476, 2 Winst.L. 86; Higgins v. Minaghan, 1891, 78 Wis. 602, 47 N.W. 941; Fixico v. State, 1928, 39 Okl.Cr.App. 95, 263 P. 171.

21. Cain v. Skillin, 1929, 219 Ala. 228, 121 So. 521; Woodson v. State, 1926, 30 Ariz. 448, 247 P. 1103; State v. Mark Len, 1932, 108 N.J.L. 439, 158 A. 749; State v. Padula, 1927, 106 Conn. 454, 138 A. 456; Simms v. D'Avillier, La.App.1965, 179 So.2d 707; Notes, 1932, 18 Va.L.Rev. 794; 1940, 24 Minn.L.Rev. 426.

22. Zell v. Dunaway, 1911, 115 Md. 1, 80 A. 215.

23. Enright v. People, 1895, 155 Ill. 32, 39 N.E. 561; Shorter v. People, 1849, 2 Comst., N.Y., 193; Beck v. Minneapolis Union R. Co., 1905, 95 Minn. 73, 103 N.W. 746. The relative size and strength of the parties is to be considered in determining what is reasonable. Thomason v. Gray, 1886, 82 Ala. 291, 3 So. 38; Davis v. State, 1898, 152 Ind. 34, 51 N.E. 928. The same is of course true as to the number of the assailants. Thornton v. Taylor, 1899, 21 Ky.L. Rep. 1082, 54 S.W. 16; Higgins v. Minaghan, 1891, 78 Wis. 602, 47 N.W. 941.

24. It is generally agreed that the defendant need not be threatened with death, or with "great" or "serious" bodily injury to justify an ordinary battery. Boston v. Muncy, 1951, 204 Okl. 603, 233 P.2d 300; State v. Woodward, 1937, 58 Idaho 385, 74 P.2d 92; Shires v. Boggess, 1913, 72 W.Va. 109, 77 S.E. 542.

25. Ogden v. Claycomb, 1859, 52 Ill. 365; Nichols v. Brabazon, 1896, 94 Wis. 549, 69 N.W. 342; Beavers v. Bowen, 1906, 26 Ky.L.Rep. 291, 80 S.W. 1165.

excessive force, and it is entirely possible that each party may have an action against the other.[26]

There is no privilege to use violence after the assailant is disarmed or helpless, or all danger is clearly past.[27] Revenge is not defense, and for compensation the defendant must look to the law. Threats and insults may give color to an act of aggression;[28] but in themselves they do not ordinarily justify an apprehension of immediate harm,[29] and the defendant is not privileged to vindicate his outraged personal feelings at the expense of the physical safety of another.[30] Such provocation is to be considered only in mitigation of the damages; and the prevailing view, with some little authority to the contrary,[31] is that it operates only to reduce or avoid punitive, as distinguished from compensatory, damages.[32] Even though the plaintiff was the aggressor in the first instance, if he withdraws from the encounter, and clearly brings his withdrawal home to the mind of his opponent,[33] there is no privilege to renew the conflict and attack him.[34]

Ordinarily the question of what is reasonable force is to be determined by the jury. Certain boundaries have, however, been marked out by the law. It is unreasonable to use force which is calculated to inflict death or serious bodily harm, such as a deadly weapon, unless one has reason to believe that he is in similar serious danger, and that there is no other safe means of defense.[35] Where

26. Elliott v. Brown, 1829, 2 Wend., N.Y., 497; Dole v. Erskine, 1857, 35 N.H. 503; Gutzman v. Clancy, 1902, 114 Wis. 589, 90 N.W. 1081; McCulloch v. Goodrich, 1919, 105 Kan. 1, 181 P. 556.

27. Germolus v. Sausser, 1901, 83 Minn. 141, 85 N.W. 946; Monize v. Begaso, 1906, 190 Mass. 87, 76 N.E. 460; Custer v. Kroeger, 1922, 209 Mo.App. 450, 240 S.W. 241; Drabek v. Sabley, 1966, 31 Wis.2d 184, 142 N.W.2d 798; McCombs v. Hegarty, 1954, 205 Misc. 937, 130 N.Y.S.2d 547 (kicking man when he is down).

28. Keep v. Quallman, 1887, 68 Wis. 451, 32 N.W. 233; see Hulse v. Tollman, 1853, 49 Ill.App. 490.

29. Rippy v. State, 1858, 2 Head, Tenn., 217.

30. Eisentraut v. Madden, 1915, 97 Neb. 466, 150 N.W. 627 ("Hello, Professor" does not justify battery with a shovel); Rackett v. Rackett, 1940, 5 Wash.2d 262, 105 P.2d 22; Gargotto v. Isenberg, 1932, 244 Ky. 493, 51 S.W.2d 443; Cunningham v. Reagan, Mo. 1954, 273 S.W.2d 174; Prell Hotel Corp. v. Antonacci, Nev.1970, 469 P.2d 399. Cf. Johnson v. Johnson, 1917, 201 Ala. 41, 77 So. 335 (the exasperating wife).

Louisiana is unique in holding that provocative words may be a complete justification for battery, if the words were such that under the circumstances they should reasonably be expected to produce physical retaliation. Davis v. Maddox, La.App.1958, 100 So. 2d 905; Walsh v. Shriner, La.App.1936, 168 So. 345; Jumonville v. Frey's, Inc., La.App.1937, 173 So. 227. Other words go merely to mitigate damages. Wells v. Perkins, La.App.1958, 101 So.2d 740. See Note, 1944, 5 La.L.Rev. 617.

In Mississippi a statute has been interpreted to the same effect. Thomas v. Carter, 1927, 148 Miss. 637, 114 So. 736. See Malone, Insult in Retaliation, 1939, 11 Miss.L.J. 333.

31. Jackson v. Old Colony St. R. Co., 1910, 206 Mass. 477, 92 N.E. 725; Bascom v. Hoffman, 1925, 199 Iowa 941, 203 N.W. 273; Mohler v. Owens, Tex. Civ.App.1962, 352 S.W.2d 855; Arnold v. Wiley, 1955, 39 Tenn.App. 391, 284 S.W.2d 296.

32. Heil v. Zink, 1949, 120 Colo. 481, 210 P.2d 610; Gissendanner v. Temples, 1936, 232 Ala. 608, 169 So. 231; Royer v. Belcher, 1926, 100 W.Va. 694, 131 S.E. 556; Barth v. Stewart, 1929, 229 Ky. 840, 18 S.W.2d 275; Patterson v. Henry, 1953, 72 Ohio L. Abs. 403, 136 N.E.2d 764. See Note, 1945, 14 Ford. L.Rev. 95.

In Ulrich v. Schwarz, 1929, 199 Wis. 24, 225 N.W. 195 it was held that evidence of provocation was admissible as bearing on the extent of plaintiff's mental suffering.

33. People v. Button, 1895, 106 Cal. 628, 39 P. 1073 (insanity preventing). Cf. Eisentraut v. Madden, 1915, 97 Neb. 466, 150 N.W. 627.

34. Rowe v. United States, 1898, 164 U.S. 546; Stoffer v. State, 1864, 15 Ohio St. 47; Allen v. State, 1859, 28 Ga. 395; McNatt v. McRae, 1903, 117 Ga. 898, 45 S.E. 248.

35. Coats v. State, 1911, 101 Ark. 51, 141 S.W. 197; State v. Meyers, 1910, 57 Or. 50, 110 P. 407; State v. Clark, 1909, 64 W.Va. 625, 63 S.E. 402; Roberson v. State, 1901, 43 Fla. 156, 157, 29 So. 535; Second Restatement of Torts, § 65. See Note, 1967, 69 W.Va. L.Rev. 361.

Thus there is no privilege to kill in resisting unlawful arrest, except where it involves such serious personal danger. Creighton v. Commonwealth, 1886, 84 Ky. 103; Baxter v. State, 1955, 225 Ark. 239, 281 S.W.2d 931.

On the other hand, self-defense with fists is not limited to cases where the defendant reasonably believes

a reasonably safe way of escape is open, the courts have not agreed as to the rule to be applied. It is clear that the defendant may stand his ground and use force short of that likely to cause serious physical injury.[36] A considerable majority of the American courts, centering largely in the south and west, have had a high regard for the dignity and sense of honor of the individual, and have held that he may stand his ground and use deadly force against an attack which calls for it, even to the extent of killing his assailant.[37] A minority of some fifteen jurisdictions have adopted the view, which seems much to be preferred in a civilized community,[38] that personal honor does not justify the killing or wounding of a human being, and that the defendant must retreat if it appears that he can do so with safety.[39] The obligation to retreat is ended when it is no longer apparent that it is safe to do so. "Detached reflection cannot be demanded in the presence of an uplifted knife,"[40] and if there is any reason-

able doubt, he need not run.[41] With firearms what they are today, and the possibility of safe retreat accordingly curtailed, the whole controversy has lost most of its importance; and the intelligent rule would appear to be that it is merely one element to be considered in judging reasonable conduct.[42]

The courts have continued the ancient rule that there is no obligation to retreat when the defendant is attacked in his own dwelling house, "his castle,"[43] apparently because of "an instinctive feeling that a home is sacred, and that it is improper to require a man to submit to pursuit from room to room in his own house."[44] There are courts which have extended this to include the yard around the dwelling,[45] the defendant's place of busi-

---

that he is in danger of great bodily harm. Boston v. Muncy, 1951, 204 Okl. 603, 233 P.2d 300.

36. State v. Abbott, 1961, 36 N.J. 63, 174 A.2d 881; Beyer v. Birmingham R. L. & P. Co., 1914, 186 Ala. 56, 64 So. 609; State v. Gough, 1919, 187 Iowa 363, 174 N.W. 279; People v. Katz, 1942, 263 App. Div. 883, 32 N.Y.S.2d 157; State v. Sherman, 1889, 16 R.I. 631, 18 A. 1040; Second Restatement of Torts, § 63.

37. Brown v. United States, 1921, 256 U.S. 335; People v. Bush, 1953, 414 Ill. 441, 111 N.E.2d 326; State v. Ellerbe, 1944, 223 N.C. 770, 28 S.E.2d 519; State v. Hiatt, 1936, 187 Wash. 226, 60 P.2d 71; People v. Ligouri, 1940, 284 N.Y. 309, 31 N.E.2d 37.

38. Beale, Retreat from Murderous Assault, 1903, 16 Harv.L.Rev. 567; Beale, Homicide in Self-Defense, 1903, 3 Col.L.Rev. 526; Restatement of Torts, § 65. Contra, Perkins, Self-Defense Re-examined, 1954, 1 U.C.L.A.L.Rev. 133.

39. King v. State, 1936, 233 Ala. 198, 171 So. 254; Ford v. State, 1953, 222 Ark. 16, 257 S.W.2d 30; State v. Cox, 1941, 138 Me. 151, 23 A.2d 634; State v. Stevenson, 1936, 8 W.W.Harr., Del., 105, 188 A. 750; Scholl v. State, 1927, 94 Fla. 1138, 115 So. 43.

40. Holmes, J., in Brown v. United States, 1921, 256 U.S. 335.

41. Cf. State v. Bartlett, 1902, 170 Mo. 658, 71 S.W. 148 (retreat impossible); People v. Macard, 1888, 73 Mich. 15, 40 N.W. 784; State v. Roberts, 1891, 63 Vt. 139, 21 A. 424; State v. Gardner, 1909, 96 Minn. 318, 104 N.W. 971. See Inbau, Firearms and Legal Doctrine, 1933, 7 Tul.L.Rev. 529, 531.

42. See Regina v. Howe, 1058, 100 Comm.L.Rep. (Aust.) 448; Fontin v. Katapodis, 1962, 108 Comm. L.Rep. (Aust.) 117; Fleming, Law of Torts, 3d ed. 1965, 86.

43. State v. Johnson, 1964, 261 N.C. 727, 136 S.E.2d 84; Crawford v. State, 1963, 231 Md. 354, 190 A.2d 538; Dunn v. State, 1957, 237 Ind. 398, 146 N.E.2d 529; State v. Preece, 1935, 116 W.Va. 176, 179 S.E. 524; Bowen v. State, 1928, 217 Ala. 574, 117 So. 204.

44. First Restatement of Torts, Tent. Draft, Commentary to § 84. Where the attack is made in the dwelling of both parties, authority is divided. See, holding that the defendant must retreat if he can safely do so: State v. Grierson, 1949, 96 N.H. 36, 69 A.2d 851; Baker v. Commonwealth, 1947, 305 Ky. 88, 202 S.W.2d 1010; Watts v. State, 1912, 177 Ala. 24, 59 So. 270; State v. Dyer, 1910, 147 Iowa 217, 124 N.W. 629. This is the position taken by the Second Restatement of Torts, § 65.

Contra: Bryant v. State, 1949, 252 Ala. 153, 39 So. 2d 657; State v. Phillips, 1936, 38 Del. 24, 187 A. 721; People v. Tomlins, 1914, 213 N.Y. 240, 107 N.E. 496; State v. Gordon, 1924, 128 S.C. 422, 122 S.E. 501; People v. McGrandy, 1967, 9 Mich.App. 187, 156 N.W.2d 48.

45. State v. Frizelle, 1955, 243 N.C. 49, 89 S.E.2d 725; cf. State v. Davis, 1948, 214 S.C. 34, 51 S.E. 2d 86 (anywhere on his own premises). Contra, Brown v. Oestman, 1961, 362 Mich. 614, 107 N.W. 2d 837.

ness,[46] or his club,[47] or even his automobile; [48] but such extensions have an obvious artificial air, and are scarcely to be recommended.

The privilege to resist unlawful arrest is subject, in general, to the same rules of reasonable conduct as that of defense against assault and battery.[49]

Injury to Third Person

If, in defending himself, the defendant accidentally shoots a stranger, there is no liability in the absence of some negligence,[50] and on the issue of negligence, the necessity of defending against the assailant must be considered in determining whether he has acted reasonably.[51] The same policy which gives the defendant the privilege of acting under a reasonable mistake protects him in such a case.

But if the injury is inflicted intentionally, as where the defendant deliberately rides another down in order to escape from a pursuer, there is a closer approach to moral blame. It may be that there is no liability in such a case for the mere technical tort, but, by analogy to a similar rule as to the invasion of property in case of "necessity," [52] it seems reasonable to say that the privilege is qualified, and that he should be required to pay for it by making compensation for any actual damage.[53] Thus the defendant who, with a pistol held at his head, kills a third person to save his own life, is guilty at least of manslaughter,[54] as well as liable in tort for the death.

20. DEFENSE OF OTHERS

The early common law recognized a feudal privilege in the master of the household to defend the members of his family and his servants against attack.[55] Later this was extended to permit any members of the same family to defend one another,[56] and servants to defend their employers.[57] No reason is apparent today for any such artificial limitation; and the privilege should exist whenever defense of another is called for, or sanctioned,

---

46. Askew v. State, 1891, 94 Ala. 4, 10 So. 657; State v. Baratta, 1951, 242 Iowa 1308, 49 N.W.2d 866; State v. Griggs, 1950, 218 S.C. 86, 61 S.E.2d 653; State v. Turner, 1938, 95 Utah 129, 79 P.2d 46.

47. State v. Marlowe, 1922, 120 S.C. 205, 112 S.E. 921.

48. State v. Borwick, 1922, 193 Iowa 639, 187 N.W. 460. Contra, State v. McGee, 1937, 185 S.C. 184, 193 S.E. 303. As to such extensions generally, see State v. Sipes, 1926, 202 Iowa 173, 209 N.W. 458; People v. Tomlins, 1914, 213 N.Y. 240, 107 N.E. 496; Madry v. State, 1918, 201 Ala. 512, 78 So. 866; State v. Bowers, 1923, 122 S.C. 275, 115 S.E. 303; Beale, Retreat from Murderous Assault, 1903, 16 Harv.L.Rev. 567; Note, 1922, 7 Minn.L.Rev. 59.

49. Coats v. State, 1911, 101 Ark. 51, 141 S.W. 197; Creighton v. Commonwealth, 1886, 84 Ky. 103; Baxter v. State, 1955, 225 Ark. 239, 281 S.W.2d 931; Second Restatement of Torts, § 68.

50. Morris v. Platt, 1864, 32 Conn. 75; Shaw v. Lord, 1914, 41 Okl. 347, 137 P. 885; Paxton v. Boyer, 1873, 67 Ill. 132; State v. Fielder, 1932, 330 Mo. 747, 50 S.W.2d 1031; Mayweather v. State, 1926, 29 Ariz. 460, 242 P. 864. This operates as a limitation upon the principle of "transferred intent," supra, p. 32.
Negligence was found in Bartosh v. Banning, 1967, 251 Cal.App.2d 378, 59 Cal.Rptr. 382.

51. Shaw v. Lord, 1914, 41 Okl. 347, 137 P. 885; United States v. Jasper, 4 Cir.1955, 222 F.2d 632.

52. See infra, § 24.

53. Cf. Regina v. Dudley, 1884, 14 Q.B.D. 273, 15 Cox C.C. 624; United States v. Holmes, 1842, Fed. Cas.No.15,383, 1 Wall.Jr. 1; and see Bohlen, Incomplete Privilege to Inflict Intentional Invasions of Interests of Property and Personality, 1926, 39 Harv.L.Rev. 307.

54. Arp v. State, 1893, 97 Ala. 5, 12 So. 301; People v. Repke, 1895, 103 Mich. 459, 61 N.W. 861; State v. Capaci, 1934, 179 La. 462, 154 So. 419; State v. Fisher, 1900, 23 Mont. 540, 59 P. 919; Brewer v. State, 1904, 72 Ark. 145, 78 S.W. 773.

55. Seaman v. Cuppledick, c. 1610, Owen 150, 74 Eng.Rep. 966.

56. Martin v. Costa, 1934, 140 Cal.App. 494, 35 P.2d 362 (husband); Sheward v. Magit, 1951, 106 Cal. App.2d 163, 234 P.2d 708 (son); State v. Browers, 1947, 356 Mo. 1195, 205 S.W.2d 721 (brother); Tubbs v. Commonwealth, 1900, 22 Ky.L.Rep. 481, 57 S.W. 623 (uncle); Frew v. Teagarden, 1922, 111 Kan. 107, 205 P. 1023 (brother-in-law).

57. Barfoot v. Reynolds, 1734, 2 Strange 953, 93 Eng.Rep. 963; Malley v. Lane, 1921, 97 Conn. 133, 115 A. 674.

by recognized social usage, or commonly accepted standards of decent conduct.[58] Thus the driver of an automobile is permitted to defend his guest,[59] and it would seem, since there are a few decisions so holding,[60] that one complete stranger is privileged to defend another whenever it is reasonable for him to do so.

The privilege extends to the use of all force reasonably necessary for such defense, although there will be liability if unnecessary force is used.[61] It is said that the defender may do whatever the person attacked might do to protect himself.[62] As in the case of self-defense, the necessity must be immediate, and attacks made in the past, or threats for the future, will not justify such action.[63]

As to the effect of a mistaken but reasonable belief that intervention is necessary, or that the force used is called for, the courts have not agreed. The majority of them have said that the intermeddler takes the risk that the man he is defending would not be privileged to defend himself in the same manner.[64] But if an honest mistake is to relieve the defendant of liability when he thinks that he must defend himself, his meritorious defense of another should receive the same consideration. The minority view to this effect[65] seems greatly to be preferred.

21. DEFENSE OF PROPERTY

The privilege to defend the possession of property rests upon the same considerations of policy as that of self-defense.[66] The interest in peaceful possession and enjoyment justifies protection by self-help, in situations where there is usually no time to resort to the law. The limitations upon the privilege are much the same as in the case of self-defense: the force must be, or reasonably appear to be, necessary, and not excessive in view of the interest involved.

The interest to be protected is that of possession. The privilege may be exercised by anyone in possession of property who has, as against the invader, the better right to it.[67] It is the privilege to resist a trespass,

---

58. Second Restatement of Torts, § 78. The idea that the privilege is limited to the defense of relatives, servants, or at least close associates, apparently was derived from some loose language in Leward v. Baseley, 1695, 1 Ld. Raym. 62, 91 Eng.Rep. 937.

59. State v. Borwick, 1922, 193 Iowa 639, 187 N.W. 460.

60. State v. Totman, 1899, 80 Mo.App. 125; Brouster v. Fox, 1906, 117 Mo.App. 711, 93 S.W. 318; Fink v. Thomas, 1909, 66 W.Va. 487, 66 S.E. 650; Williams v. State, 1943, 70 Ga.App. 10, 27 S.E.2d 109; Beavers v. Calloway, 1946, 270 App.Div. 873, 61 N.Y.S.2d 804. "Every man has the right of defending any man by reasonable force against unlawful force." Salmond, Law of Torts, 8th Ed. 1934, 44.
There are a good many other cases in which some relation has existed, but the court has made no point of it. See for example Thompson v. State, 1954, 195 Ala. 65, 70 So.2d 282 (friend); People v. Roe, 1922, 189 Cal. 548, 209 P. 560 (friend); Johnson v. Commonwealth, 1949, 311 Ky. 182, 223 S.W.2d 741 (brother); Reeves v. State, 1949, 153 Tex.Cr. 32, 217 S.W.2d 19 (fellow officer).

61. Lopez v. Surchia, 1952, 112 Cal.App.2d 314, 246 P.2d 111.

62. People v. Forte, 1915, 269 Ill. 505, 110 N.E. 47; Roberson v. Stokes, 1921, 181 N.C. 59, 106 S.E. 151; Downs v. Jackson, Ky.1910, 128 S.W. 339.

63. People v. Cook, 1878, 39 Mich. 236; State v. Young, 1908, 52 Or. 227, 96 P. 1067; Sexton v. Commonwealth, 1922, 193 Ky. 495, 236 S.W. 956; Webb v. Snow, 1942, 102 Utah 435, 132 P.2d 114.

64. People v. Young, 1962, 11 N.Y.2d 274, 229 N.Y.S.2d 1, 183 N.E.2d 319; Commonwealth v. Hounchell, 1939, 280 Ky. 217, 132 S.W.2d 921; Robinson v. City of Decatur, 1947, 32 Ala.App. 654, 29 So.2d 429; State v. Melton, 1891, 102 Mo. 683, 15 S.W. 139; State v. Cook, 1907, 78 S.C. 253, 59 S.E. 862.

65. Sloan v. Pierce, 1906, 74 Kan. 65, 85 P. 812; State v. Harper, 1899, 149 Mo. 514, 51 S.W. 89; Warnack v. State, 1908, 3 Ga.App. 590, 60 S.E. 288; Mayhew v. State, 1912, 65 Tex.Cr. 290, 144 S.W. 229; Patterson v. Kuntz, La.App. 1946, 28 So.2d 278; Second Restatement of Torts, § 76; Note, 1924, 8 Minn. L.Rev. 340.

66. See also the cases as to abatement of a nuisance, infra, p. 605.

67. Cole v. Rowen, 1891, 88 Mich. 219, 50 N.W. 138 (servant); Brendlin v. Beers, 1911, 144 App.Div. 403, 129 N.Y.S. 222 (janitor); Chew v. Gilliland, 1965, — Tex. —, 398 S.W.2d 98 (custodian); Moore v. Camden & T. R. Co., 1907, 74 N.J.L. 498, 65 A. 1021 (wife of owner); Hoagland v. Forest Park High-

by force which would otherwise amount to assault, battery or false imprisonment. It extends not only to the prevention of wrongful interference with the possession of chattels, and entry upon land, but also to the expulsion of those who have entered by right or permission, whose right to remain has terminated.[68]

Apparent Necessity

As in the case of self-defense, the existence of the privilege does not depend upon the real necessities of the situation, but rather upon the appearance it would present to a reasonable man in the defendant's position.[69] Here again, the loss due to an innocent mistake is cast upon the injured party, because the importance of the property interest is considered to justify reasonable means to defend it. But if the mistake is as to some matter of fact or law which confers upon the intruder a privilege of his own to enter, there is no privilege to defend the property at his expense,[70] unless he is himself responsible for the misunderstanding, as by an unreasonable failure to disclose the facts.[71] It is only a mistake as to the immediate and urgent necessity for action which will excuse the defendant.

The use of force is not privileged when it is apparent that no immediate interference with the property is threatened,[72] or that all danger is past.[73] Ordinarily the use of any force at all will be unreasonable unless a request has first been made to the intruder to desist. Blows are not justified where it is not clear that words alone would not be enough.[74] But a futile request is not required where the conduct of the intruder has indicated clearly that it would be disregarded,[75] or where he is proceeding with such violence that it is clear that it could not be made in time, or with safety.[76]

Reasonable Force

The reasonableness of the force used is usually a question of fact for the jury.[77] But as in the case of self-defense, the law has marked out certain limitations. The force used must be of a kind appropriate to the defense of the property.[78] A push in the right direction may be proper where a slap

lands Amusement Co., 1902, 170 Mo. 335, 70 S.W. 878 (finder).

68. Austin v. Metropolitan Life Ins. Co., 1919, 106 Wash. 371, 180 P. 134 (insurance office); Brookside-Pratt Min. Co. v. Booth, 1924, 211 Ala. 268, 100 So. 240 (merchant); Ramirez v. Chavez, 1951, 71 Ariz. 239, 226 P.2d 143 (bar); Yoder v. Yoder, 1913, 239 Pa. 12, 86 A. 523 (hotel).

69. Bunten v. Davis, 1926, 82 N.H. 304, 133 A. 16; Foster v. Shepherd, 1913, 258 Ill. 164, 101 N.E. 411; People v. Flanagan, 1881, 60 Cal. 2; Smith v. Delery, 1959, 238 La. 180, 114 So.2d 857.

70. Stuyvesant v. Wilcox, 1882, 92 Mich. 233, 52 N. W. 465; Arlowski v. Foglio, 1926, 105 Conn. 342, 135 A. 397; Second Restatement of Torts, § 77.

71. Leach v. Francis, 1868, 41 Vt. 670.

72. State v. Sorrentino, 1924, 31 Wyo. 129, 224 P. 420; Shea v. Cassidy, 1930, 257 Ill.App. 557; McAuley v. State, 1852, 3 G. Greene, Iowa, 435.

73. Hamilton v. Howard, 1930, 234 Ky. 321, 28 S. W.2d 7; Territory v. Drennan, 1868, 1 Mont. 41.

74. Tullay v. Reed, 1823, 1 C. & P. 6, 171 Eng.Rep. 1078; Chapell v. Schmidt, 1894, 104 Cal. 511, 38 P. 892; Emmons v. Quade, 1903, 176 Mo. 22, 75 S.W. 103; Miller v. McGuire, 1918, 202 Ala. 351, 80 So. 433; State v. Woodward, 1871, 50 N.H. 527.

75. Higgins v. Minaghan, 1891, 78 Wis. 602, 47 N.W. 941; State v. Steele, 1890, 106 N.C. 766, 11 S.E. 478.

76. State v. Cessna, 1915, 170 Iowa 726, 153 N.W. 194; Scribner v. Beach, 1847, 4 Denio, N.Y., 448; Polkinghorn v. Wright, 1845, 8 Q.B. 197, 115 Eng. Rep. 849.

77. Hughes v. Babcock, 1944, 349 Pa. 475, 37 A.2d 551; Olesen v. Fader, 1915, 160 Wis. 473, 152 N.W. 290; Bunten v. Davis, 1926, 82 N.H. 304, 133 A. 16.

78. Collins v. Renison, 1754, Sayer 138, 96 Eng.Rep. 830 (inappropriate to overturn a ladder on which plaintiff was standing); Rowe v. Hawkins, 1858, 1 F. & F. 91, 175 Eng.Rep. 640 (force necessary to make plaintiff let go of bridle); Cunningham v. Reagan, Mo.1954, 273 S.W.2d 174 (battery not privileged where only in retaliation for insulting words).

in the face is not,[79] and assault by a threat of force or violence may be proper where the battery itself would be excessive.[80] And, since the law has always placed a higher value upon human safety than upon mere rights in property, it is the accepted rule that there is no privilege to use any force calculated to cause death or serious bodily injury to repel the threat to land or chattels,[81] unless there is also such a threat to the defendant's personal safety as to justify self-defense.[82] Where the intruder is not proceeding with violence, the defendant may normally, in the first instance, use only the mildest of force, for which the old form of pleading had a phrase—"molliter manus imposuit;" he gently laid hands upon him.[83] But if the plaintiff resists, the defendant may use the force reasonably necessary to overcome his resistance and expel him,[84] and if in the process his

own safety is threatened, he may defend himself, and even kill if necessary;[85] but in the first instance a mere trespass does not justify such an act. Even the tradition that a man's house is his castle, and that one may kill in defense of his dwelling, has given way in most jurisdictions [86] to the view that such force is not justified [87] unless the intrusion threatens the personal safety of the occupants, or the commission of a felony.[88]

In certain situations, there may be no privilege to use any force at all to expel an intruder. Just as the defendant may not kill a trespasser to eject him, he will not be privileged to put him out when he will be exposed to serious danger of physical harm.

---

79. Symalla v. Dusenka, 1939, 206 Minn. 280, 288 N.W. 385; Newman v. Southern Kraft Corp., La. App.1940, 197 So. 197; Maddran v. Mullendore, 1955, 206 Md. 291, 111 A.2d 608.

80. State v. Yancey, 1876, 74 N.C. 244; Silas v. Bowen (D.S.C.1967) 277 F.Supp. 314 (shooting at the ground); cf. Daluiso v. Boone, 1968, 71 A.Cal.2d 503, 78 Cal.Rptr. 707, 455 P.2d 811.

81. McIlvoy v. Cockran, 1820, 9 Ky. (2 A.K. Marsh.) 271; Anderson v. Jenkins, 1954, 220 Miss. 145, 70 So.2d 535; Scheufele v. Newman, 1949, 187 Or. 263, 210 P.2d 573; Haworth v. Elliott, 1944, 67 Cal.App. 2d 77, 153 P.2d 804; Commonwealth v. Emmons, 1945, 157 Pa.Super. 495, 43 A.2d 568.

Even assault with a deadly weapon, without battery, has been held to be excessive. People v. Doud, 1923, 223 Mich. 120, 193 N.W. 884; State v. Paxton, 1916, 6 Boyce, Del., 249, 99 A. 46; Brown v. Martinez, 1961, 68 N.M. 271, 361 P.2d 152; Ross v. Michael, 1923, 246 Mass. 126, 140 N.E. 292.

The defendant, even when exercising reasonable force, is required to do so with reasonable care, and will be liable for any negligence which injures the plaintiff. Phillips v. Wilpers, 1869, 2 Lans., N.Y., 389.

82. Eldred v. Burns, 1947, 182 Or. 394, 182 P.2d 397, rehearing denied 182 Or. 394, 188 P.2d 154; Wade v. Gennaro, La.App.1942, 8 So.2d 561.

83. Weaver v. Bush, 1798, 8 Term Rep. 78, 101 Eng. Rep. 1276.

84. Coleman v. New York & N. H. R. Co., 1870, 106 Mass. 160; State v. Benson, 1959, 155 Me. 115, 151

A.2d 266; Penn v. Henderson, 1944, 174 Or. 1, 146 P.2d 760; Holley v. Kelley, Fla.1957, 91 So.2d 862.

Considerable force may sometimes be used, as in Kent v. Southern R. Co., 1936, 52 Ga.App. 731, 184 S.E. 638 (tear gas against strikers); State v. Goode, 1902, 130 N.C. 651, 41 S.E. 3 (indignant colored lady and the baseball bat). But the defendant will still be liable for the use of any force which does not reasonably appear to be necessary to overcome the resistance. Gosselin v. Silver, 1938, 301 Mass. 481, 17 N.E.2d 706.

85. Tipsword v. Potter, 1918, 31 Idaho 509, 174 P. 133; Eldred v. Burns, 1947, 182 Or. 394, 182 P.2d 397, 188 P.2d 154; McMurrey Corp. v. Yawn, Tex. Civ.App.1940, 143 S.W.2d 664.

86. But see In re J. J. Hussey, Eng.1924, 18 Crim. App.Rep. 160.

87. Hamilton v. Howard, 1930, 234 Ky. 321, 28 S.W. 2d 7; Hudgens v. State, 1933, 166 Tenn. 231, 60 S.W.2d 153; State v. Sorrentino, 1924, 31 Wyo. 129, 224 P. 420; Bradshaw v. Commonwealth, 1939, 174 Va. 391, 4 S.E.2d 752; Anderson v. Jenkins, 1954, 220 Miss. 145, 70 So.2d 535.

88. State v. Miller, 1966, 267 N.C. 409, 148 S.E.2d 279, appeal after remand 272 N.C. 243, 158 S.E.2d 47; Morrison v. State, 1963, 212 Tenn. 633, 371 S.W.2d 441; Nakashima v. Takase, 1935, 8 Cal.App. 2d 35, 46 P.2d 1020; People v. Wilcox, 1927, 245 N.Y. 404, 157 N.E. 509; State v. Taylor, 1898, 143 Mo. 150, 44 S.W. 785.

Quite often this will be the case; but it is another matter entirely to say that, with a speedy remedy at law available in all jurisdictions, the occupant is justified in shooting an evicting landlord. See Notes, 1926, 25 Mich.L.Rev. 57; 1936, 9 So.Cal.L. Rev. 375.

A tramp on a railway train may not be thrown off at forty miles an hour,[89] nor may a trespasser who is ill and unable to look out for himself be thrust out on a winter night,[90] unless his illness is of a contagious character which threatens the inmates of the house.[91] The necessities of the situation create a privilege to remain, which prevails over the vindication of the property right.[92]

The defendant may not do indirectly what he could not do directly. The privilege to protect property by dangerous mechanical devices is no greater than that of defense by a personal act.[93] Barbed wire and spiked railings, which are not intended to cause serious injury, and carry their own warning by day or might reasonably be anticipated and guarded against by night, will ordinarily be privileged,[94] in the absence of some neg-

ligence in their location or construction.[95] But spring guns and other man-killing devices are not justifiable against a mere trespasser, or even a petty thief.[96] They are privileged only against those upon whom the landowner, if he were present in person, would be free to inflict injury of the same kind. There is thus considerable authority[97] that such devices may be used without liability for protection against a burglar, where the owner's inability to be present in person makes the use of such force reasonable for the prevention of the felony. He must take the risk that he may injure the wrong man. Even where notice of the device is given, it will no more justify shooting the plaintiff than if the defendant were there acting in person.[98]

Although few cases have considered the question, and it is somewhat complicated by statutes, as well as by the common law rule of strict liability for keeping dangerous animals,[99] it would seem that a vicious watchdog is to be classed with a spring gun, and

---

89. Chesapeake & O. R. Co. v. Ryan, 1919, 183 Ky. 428, 209 S.W. 538; Kobbe v. Chicago & N. W. R. Co., 1928, 173 Minn. 79, 216 N.W. 543; Ansteth v. Buffalo R. Co., 1896, 145 N.Y. 210, 39 N.E. 708; Kansas City, Ft. S. & G. R. Co. v. Kelly, 1887, 36 Kan. 655, 14 P. 172; cf. Iaconio v. D'Angelo, 1928, 104 N.J.L. 506, 142 A. 46 (boy on automobile). But a verbal order to get off has been held to impose no liability where it was not accompanied by a show of force. Bjornquist v. Boston & A. R. Co., 1904, 185 Mass. 130, 70 N.E. 53; Osalek v. Baltimore & O. R. Co., 1929, 295 Pa. 553, 145 A. 582; cf. Lo Castro v. Long Island R. Co., 1959, 6 N.Y.2d 470, 190 N.Y.S.2d 366, 160 N.E.2d 846.

90. Depue v. Flatau, 1907, 100 Minn. 299, 111 N.W. 1; Bradshaw v. Frazier, 1901, 113 Iowa 579, 85 N.W. 752; Waldrop v. Nashville, C. & St. L. R. Co., 1913, 183 Ala. 226, 62 So. 769; Adams v. Chicago G. W. R. Co., 1912, 156 Iowa 31, 135 N.W. 21. Cf. Feiges v. Racine Dry Goods Co., 1939, 231 Wis. 270, 285 N.W. 799. Also Dierkes v. Hauxhurst Land Co., 1911, 80 N.J.L. 369, 79 A. 361 (frightening trespasser over cliff with dogs); but cf. Miller v. Oscar Schmidt, Inc., 1924, 100 N.J.L. 324, 126 A. 309.

91. Tucker v. Burt, 1908, 152 Mich. 68, 115 N.W. 722.

92. See infra, § 24.

93. Bohlen and Burns, The Privilege to Protect Property by Dangerous Barriers and Mechanical Devices, 1926, 35 Yale L.J. 527; Hart, Injuries to Trespassers, 1931, 47 L.Q.Rev. 92, 101–105.

94. Quigley v. Clough, 1899, 173 Mass. 429, 53 N.E. 884; Kelly v. Bennett, 1890, 132 Pa. 218, 19 A. 69; Skaling v. Sheedy, 1924, 101 Conn. 545, 126 A. 721; Worthington v. Wade, 1891, 82 Tex. 26, 17 S.W. 520.

95. Hurd v. Lacy, 1890, 93 Ala. 427, 9 So. 378; Sisk v. Crump, 1887, 112 Ind. 504, 14 N.E. 381; cf. Kelly v. Bennett, 1890, 132 Pa. 218, 19 A. 69.

96. Bird v. Holbrook, 1828, 4 Bing. 628, 130 Eng. Rep. 911; State v. Childers, 1938, 133 Ohio St. 508, 14 N.E.2d 767; Starkey v. Dameron, 1933, 92 Colo. 420, 21 P.2d 1112, 22 P.2d 640; State v. Plumlee, 1933, 177 La. 687, 149 So. 425; State v. Beckham, 1924, 306 Mo. 566, 267 S.W. 817; Second Restatement of Torts, § 85. See Note, 1934, 18 Minn.L.Rev. 77.

97. Gray v. Combs, 1832, 7 J.J. Marsh., Ky., 478; Scheuermann v. Scharfenberg, 1909, 163 Ala. 337, 50 So. 335; Marquis v. Benfer, Tex.Civ.App.1957, 298 S.W.2d 601, ref. n. r. e.; Pierce v. Commonwealth, 1923, 135 Va. 635, 115 S.E. 686; Second Restatement of Torts, § 85. In Allison v. Fiscus, 1951, 156 Ohio St. 120, 100 N.E.2d 237, it was held that the unreasonableness of setting a dynamite trap merely to frighten one breaking and entering on industrial premises was for the jury. As to shooting a burglar when the landowner is present in person, see infra, p. 134.

98. Johnson v. Patterson, 1840, 14 Conn. 1; State v. Childers, 1938, 133 Ohio St. 508, 14 N.E.2d 767; Bruister v. Haney, 1958, 233 Miss. 527, 102 So.2d 806; Second Restatement of Torts, § 85.

99. See infra, § 76.

that the owner will be liable if he leaves him at large[1] to attack trespassers,[2] at least where he would not be privileged to call the dog to his assistance if he were present himself.[3]

The privilege to destroy property,[4] such as a trespassing dog, in order to save property, is governed by much the same rules. Although the dog need not be in the very act of killing the defendant's hens,[5] it is not reasonable to shoot him if there is any other reasonably available means of defense.[6] And even where there is none, the killing may not be privileged where it is obvious at the time that the value of the dog, considered with other circumstances,[7] is far in excess of the damage threatened.[8]

22. RECAPTURE OF CHATTELS

The privilege of an owner dispossessed of his chattel to recapture it by force differs from that of defending his possession in the first instance,[9] in that the owner is no longer maintaining the status quo and defending an existing peaceable state of affairs, but is himself an aggressor, seeking to disturb the possession of another. Nevertheless, to a limited extent, the privilege has been recognized. It had its origin in cases where there was a "momentary interruption of possession," so that it was not difficult to regard the owner as still defending his original possession against one who had not got clean away.[10] Its survival, and extension to interference with the established possession of another, has been due to the recognized necessity of a speedy remedy where legal process is slow and cumbersome, and likely to be ineffective because it cannot operate in time, or cannot compel the specific return of the chattel.[11] One consequence, however, of the fact that

1. Otherwise if the dog is properly chained, and kept only for warning. Woodbridge v. Marks, 1897, 17 App.Div. 139, 45 N.Y.S. 156.

2. Loomis v. Terry, 1837, 17 Wend., N.Y., 496; Conway v. Grant, 1891, 88 Ga. 40, 13 S.E. 803; Brewer v. Furtwangler, 1933, 171 Wash. 617, 18 P.2d 837; Gerulis v. Lunecki, 1936, 284 Ill.App. 44, 1 N.E.2d 440.

3. See Woolf v. Chalker, 1862, 31 Conn. 121. Cf. Ryan v. Marren, 1914, 216 Mass. 556, 104 N.E. 353.

4. As to property other than trespassing animals, see Louisville & N. R. Co. v. Joullian, 1917, 116 Miss. 40, 76 So. 769; McKeesport Sawmill Co. v. Pennsylvania Co., C.C.Pa.1903, 122 F. 184; Berry v. Carle, 1825, 3 Green, Me., 269; Note, 1918, 27 Yale L.J. 569.

5. Hull v. Scruggs, 1941, 191 Miss. 66, 2 So.2d 543; McChesney v. Wilson, 1903, 132 Mich. 252, 93 N.W. 627; Aldrich v. Wright, 1873, 53 N.H. 398; Fisher v. Badger, 1902, 95 Mo.App. 289, 69 N.W. 26; Helsel v. Fletcher, 1924, 98 Okl. 285, 225 P. 514; cf. Brill v. Flagler, 1840, 23 Wend., N.Y., 354. The privilege is of course all the clearer if the dog is caught in the act. Granier v. Chagnon, 1949, 122 Mont. 327, 203 P.2d 982.

6. Leonard v. Wilkins, 1812, 9 Johns., N.Y. 233; Livermore v. Batchelder, 1886, 141 Mass. 179, 5 N.E. 275; Johnson v. Patterson, 1840, 14 Conn. 1; State v. Dickens, 1939, 215 N.C. 303, 1 S.E.2d 837. Thus past depredations do not justify killing the animal. Clark v. Keliher, 1870, 107 Mass. 406 (see the poem on this case by Austin A. Martin in 1889, 1 Green Bag 292); Wells v. Head, 1831, 4 C. & P. 568, 172 Eng.Rep. 828; Brent v. Kimbell, 1871, 60 Ill. 211.

7. " * * * the value of the animal doing the mischief, the disturbance and mischief likely to be wrought; the probability of less severe measures being successful and the necessity for immediate action, are all elements to be considered in reaching a conclusion." Lipe v. Blackwelder, 1886, 25 Ill. App. 119; Kershaw v. McKown, 1916, 196 Ala. 123, 72 So. 47; see Nesbett v. Wilbur, 1900, 177 Mass. 200, 58 N.E. 586; O'Leary v. Wangensteen, 1928, 175 Minn. 368, 221 N.W. 430; Skog v. King, 1934, 214 Wis. 591, 254 N.W. 354.

8. Anderson v. Smith, 1880, 7 Ill.App. 354; Ex parte Minor, 1919, 203 Ala. 481, 83 So. 475; Johnston v. Wilson, 1924, 32 Ga.App. 348, 123 S.E. 222.

9. See supra, § 21.

10. Commonwealth v. Donahue, 1889, 148 Mass. 529, 20 N.E. 171; Winter v. Atkinson, 1900, 92 Ill.App. 162; Hamilton v. Arnold, 1898, 116 Mich. 684, 75 N.W. 133; Wright v. Southern Exp. Co., C.C.Tenn. 1897, 80 F. 55; Donnell v. Great A. & P. Tea Co., 1934, 229 Ala. 320, 156 So. 844.

11. Branston, The Forcible Recaption of Chattels, 1918, 28 L.Q.Rev. 262; Notes, 1935, 19 Minn.L.Rev. 602; 1945, 34 Ky.L.J. 65.

the defendant is here the aggressor, is that he is required to take his chances on being right as to the facts which he believes to give him the privilege; and the loss due to any mistake, however reasonable, must fall upon the one who makes it.[12]

For obvious reasons, in the interest of the preservation of order, the privilege has been restricted to those extreme cases where the emergency justifies the risk of a breach of the peace. It is properly exercised when there has been a wrongful dispossession of the property by force or fraud, and prompt action to retake it. The "momentary interruption" was extended later to situations where the wrongdoer had made his escape with the chattel, but the owner was in "fresh pursuit."[13] The meaning of "fresh pursuit" apparently never has been defined by any court; but it seems fairly clear that it is limited to prompt discovery of the dispossession, and prompt and persistent efforts to recover the chattel thereafter.[14] Any undue lapse of time during which it may be said that the pursuit has come to a halt will mean that the owner no longer is privileged to fight himself back into possession, but must resort to

the law.[15] It seems quite likely that the advent of the automobile and the airplane must affect rules which developed in the days when the fastest possible pursuit was on a horse; but there are no modern cases which have considered the question.

There is the further limitation that the force used must be reasonable under the circumstances, and there will be liability for any excess. As in the case of one defending his possession, it is not reasonable to use any force calculated to inflict serious bodily harm to protect the property interest.[16] But there is no privilege on the part of the wrongdoer to resist, and if he does, the owner may use any force required to defend his own person.[17] Ordinarily, of course, a resort to any force at all will not be justified until a demand has been made for the return of the property.[18]

The privilege does not exist unless possession is taken wrongfully from the defend-

12. Dixon v. Harrison Naval Stores, 1926, 143 Miss. 638, 109 So. 605; Dunlevy v. Wolferman, 1904, 106 Mo.App. 46, 79 S.W. 1165; S. H. Kress & Co. v. Musgrove, 1929, 153 Va. 348, 149 S.E. 453; Binder v. General Motors Acc. Corp., 1943, 222 N.C. 512, 23 S.E.2d 894; see Estes v. Brewster Cigar Co., 1930, 156 Wash. 465, 287 P. 36; Second Restatement of Torts, § 100, Comment *d* (adding "unless the mistake was induced by the other.")

In this respect the privilege differs from that of defending possession, supra, p. 114.

13. State v. Elliot, 1841, 11 N.H. 540 (100 rods); Hodgeden v. Hubbard, 1846, 18 Vt. 504 (several miles); State v. Dooley, 1894, 121 Mo. 591, 26 S.W. 558; Spelina v. Sporry, 1935, 279 Ill.App. 376; McLean v. Colf, 1918, 179 Cal. 237, 176 P. 169.

14. Second Restatement of Torts, § 103. See also the definition in § 5 of the Uniform Act on the Fresh Pursuit of Criminals, drafted by the Interstate Commission on Crime, and passed to date in rather more than half of the states: "Fresh pursuit as used herein shall not necessarily imply instant pursuit, but pursuit without unreasonable delay."

15. Bobb v. Bosworth, 1808, 16 Ky. 81; Barr v. Post, 1898, 56 Neb. 698, 77 N.W. 123. Whether, even then, the owner may not act to prevent destruction of the chattel, or its removal from the jurisdiction, has not been determined. See Second Restatement of Torts, § 100, Caveat.

Some reasonable leeway is certainly permitted. Cf. People v. Pool, 1865, 27 Cal. 572 (pursuit of felons three or four hours after felony committed); White v. State, 1892, 70 Miss. 253, 11 So. 632 (felony at night, pursuit on discovery next morning).

16. Spelina v. Sporry, 1935, 279 Ill.App. 376; Carter v. Sutherland, 1884, 52 Mich. 597, 18 N.W. 375; Wingate v. Bunton, 1916, 193 Mo.App. 470, 186 S.W. 32; McLean v. Colf, 1918, 179 Cal. 237, 176 P. 169; Second Restatement of Torts, § 106. Use of a deadly weapon in a non-deadly manner may, however, be reasonable. State v. Metcalfe, 1927, 203 Iowa 155, 212 N.W. 382.

17. Gyre v. Culver, 1867, 47 Barb., N.Y. 592; Hodgeden v. Hubbard, 1846, 18 Vt. 504; Hamilton v. Barker, 1898, 116 Mich. 684, 75 N.W. 133; Curlee v. Scales, 1931, 200 N.C. 612, 158 S.E. 89.

18. Dyk v. De Young, 1889, 35 Ill.App. 138, affirmed 133 Ill. 82, 24 N.E. 520. But demand should not be required where it reasonably appears that it will be dangerous. Second Restatement of Torts, § 104.

ant.[19] Any wrongful and forcible taking, even under claim of right,[20] will be sufficient. But the courts have extended the privilege beyond this, and have recognized it where the goods were obtained by fraud.[21] The owner is permitted to rescind his consent, by much the same anomalous theory which is found in actions for conversion,[22] and recover the property by his own act. The same rule is applied where the owner is induced by fraud to give temporary custody of the chattel for some particular purpose, and the wrongdoer is proceeding to make off with it.[23] It would seem that force may be used against any third person who receives the goods with notice of the circumstances under which they were taken, but not against an innocent party.[24]

If the plaintiff has come rightfully into possession in the first instance, no force may be used against him.[25] A defendant who has consented, without fraud, to part with his possession, must look to his legal remedy to recover it.[26] The question frequently arises in connection with the conditional sale of chattels. It is generally agreed that when the buyer defaults, the seller may retake possession, provided that he can do so peaceably, and without violence,[27] but not otherwise, so that if he is obstructed by the buyer he is not privileged to commit assault and battery,[28] or to resort to fraud.[29] The majority of the courts have even held that any clause in the contract which gives the seller the right to use such force against the person as may be necessary, is void as inviting a breach of the peace, and so contrary to the policy of the state.[30]

Entry upon Land to Remove Chattels

The courts have experienced some difficulty with the problems which arise where

19. Watson v. Rinderknecht, 1901, 82 Minn. 235, 84 N.W. 798; Monson v. Lewis, 1905, 123 Wis. 583, 101 N.W. 1094; Ryerson v. Carter, 1919, 92 N.J.L. 363, 105 A. 723.

20. See Heminway v. Heminway, 1890, 58 Conn. 443, 19 A. 766; Cox v. Klein, 1907, 149 Mich. 162, 112 N.W. 729.

21. Hodgeden v. Hubbard, 1846, 18 Vt. 504; Anderson v. State, 1872, 6 Baxt., Tenn., 608; Commonwealth v. Donahue, 1889, 148 Mass. 529, 20 N.E. 171.

22. See supra, p. 84.

23. Baldwin v. Hayden, 1827, 6 Conn. 453; Commonwealth v. Donahue, 1889, 148 Mass. 529, 20 N.E. 171; see Commonwealth v. Lynn, 1877, 123 Mass. 218.

24. See Branston, The Forcible Recaption of Chattels, 1912, 28 L.Q.Rev. 262, 266; Pollock, Law of Torts, 15th Ed. 1951, 293; Second Restatement of Torts, § 101(2) (b).

25. Bowman v. Brown, 1882, 55 Vt. 184; Shellabarger v. Morris, 1905, 115 Mo.App. 566, 91 S.W. 1005; Sabre v. Mott, C.C.Vt.1898, 88 F. 780; Rohr v. Riedel, 1922, 112 Kan. 130, 210 P. 644.

26. Rogers v. Kabakoff, 1947, 81 Cal.App.2d 487, 184 P.2d 312; Kirby v. Foster, 1891, 17 R.I. 437, 22 A. 1111; Watson v. Rinderknecht, 1901, 82 Minn. 235,

84 N.W. 798; Ryerson v. Carter, 1919, 92 N.J.L. 363, 105 A. 723, affirmed 1920, 93 N.J.L. 477, 108 A. 927; Monson v. Lewis, 1905, 123 Wis. 583, 101 N.W. 1094.

27. Blackford v. Neaves, 1922, 23 Ariz. 501, 205 P. 587; Westerman v. Oregon Automobile Credit Corp., 1942, 168 Or. 216, 122 P.2d 435; First Nat. Bank & Trust Co. of Muskogee v. Winter, 1936, 176 Okl. 400, 55 P.2d 1029; Commonwealth v. Larson, 1932, 242 Ky. 317, 46 S.W.2d 82. If the seller obtains possession peaceably, he may then defend it with reasonable force against the buyer's efforts to retake it. Biggs v. Seufferlein, 1914, 164 Iowa 241, 145 N.W. 507.

28. Kensinger Acceptance Corp. v. Davis, 1954, 223 Ark. 942, 269 S.W.2d 792; Roberts v. Speck, 1932, 169 Wash. 613, 14 P.2d 33; Deevy v. Tassi, 1942, 21 Cal.2d 109, 130 P.2d 389; Lamb v. Woodry, 1936, 154 Or. 30, 58 P.2d 1257; Stowers Furniture Co. v. Brake, 1908, 158 Ala. 639, 48 So. 89.

29. Stallworth v. Doss, 1967, 280 Ala. 409, 194 So.2d 566; Barham v. Standridge, 1941, 201 Ark. 1143, 148 S.W.2d 648.

30. Fredericksen v. Singer Mfg. Co., 1888, 38 Minn. 356, 37 N.W. 453; Abel v. M. H. Pickering Co., 1914, 58 Pa.Super. 439; Singer Sewing Machine Co. v. Phipps, 1911, 49 Ind.App. 116, 94 N.E. 793; Geissler v. Geissler, 1917, 96 Wash. 150, 164 P.2d 746, remittitur modified 96 Wash.2d 150, 166 P.2d 1119; Girard v. Anderson, 1934, 219 Iowa 142, 257 N.W. 400.

Contra: Lambert v. Robinson, 1894, 162 Mass. 34, 37 N.E. 753; W. T. Walker Furniture Co. v. Dyson, 1908, 32 App.D.C. 90. See Notes, 1935, 19 Minn.L. Rev. 602; 1933, 31 Mich.L.Rev. 987.

an entry upon the land of another is necessary in order to take property as to which the defendant is entitled to immediate possession. It is not disputed that if the goods have come upon the land through the wrongful conduct of the landowner, there is a privilege to enter to recover them.[31] The same would probably be true in the case of a wrongful taking by a third person, of which the landowner has knowledge.[32] The entry must of course be made at a reasonable time, and in a reasonable manner, and ordinarily there must first be a demand for the surrender of the chattel.[33] It has been held that "fresh pursuit" is not necessary to justify the trespass.[34] Reasonable force may be used, even to the extent of breaking down a fence or a door,[35] but any violence against the person of the landowner will not be justified,[36] unless the pursuit is fresh, or his resistance threatens the personal safety of the defendant.[37] The privilege is a complete one, and, so long as only reasonable force is used, the

defendant is not liable for any damage he may do.[38]

Where the goods have come upon the land through some force of nature, such as a flood, the privilege of entry is recognized;[39] and it would seem that it should exist also where they have been placed there by a third person, either without the consent of the landowner, or with his consent but without any knowledge that they are stolen goods.[40] But in such cases, the privilege resembles that of necessity,[41] and since the plaintiff is not a wrongdoer, it seems fair to require the defendant to make good any actual damage he may do in the course of entry, if he chooses to resort to self-help instead of the law.[42]

If the chattel has come upon the land through the fault of the defendant, or with his consent, he has no privilege to enter.[43]

---

31. Blades v. Higgs, 1861, 10 C.B.,N.S., 713, 142 Eng. Rep. 634; Patrick v. Colerick, 1838, 3 M. & W. 483, 150 Eng.Rep. 1235; Richardson v. Anthony, 1840, 12 Vt. 273; Arlowski v. Foglio, 1926, 105 Conn. 342, 135 A. 397; Wheelden v. Lowell, 1862, 50 Me. 499 (fraud).

32. See McLeod v. Jones, 1870, 105 Mass. 403; Richardson v. Anthony, 1840, 12 Vt. 273.

33. See Chambers v. Bedell, 1841, 2 Watts & S., Pa., 225; Richardson v. Anthony, 1840, 12 Vt. 273; Second Restatement of Torts, § 198, Comment d. Contra, Salisbury v. Green, 1892, 17 R.I. 758, 24 A. 787.

34. Cunningham v. Yeomans, 1868, 7 N.S.W. 149. But see Salisbury v. Green, 1892, 17 R.I. 758, 24 A. 787.

35. Wheelden v. Lowell, 1862, 50 Me. 499; Hamilton v. Calder, 1883, 23 N.B. 373. A felonious taking will justify even breaking into a dwelling house. Madden v. Brown, 1896, 8 App.Div. 454, 40 N.Y.S. 714.

36. Barnes v. Martin, 1862, 15 Wis. 240; Huppert v. Morrison, 1870, 27 Wis. 365; cf. Churchill v. Hulbert, 1872, 110 Mass. 42.

37. Cf. Arlowski v. Foglio, 1926, 105 Conn. 342, 135 A. 397; Madden v. Brown, 1896, 8 App.Div. 454, 40 N.Y.S. 714.

38. Patrick v. Colerick, 1838, 3 M. & W. 483, 150 Eng.Rep. 1235; Wheelden v. Lowell, 1862, 50 Me. 499; Robson v. Jones, 1830, 2 Bailey, S.C., 4.

39. Carter v. Thurston, 1877, 58 N.H. 104; Polebitzke v. John Week Lbr. Co., 1921, 173 Wis. 509, 181 N.W. 730; Pierce v. Finerty, 1910, 76 N.H. 38, 76 A. 194; Stuyvesant v. Wilcox, 1892, 92 Mich. 233, 52 N.W. 465. Cf. Shehyn v. United States, D.C.App.1969, 256 A.2d 404 (retrieving stray cat).

40. Hamilton v. Calder, 1883, 23 N.B. 373; Chapman v. Thumblethorpe, 1595, 1 Cro.Eliz. 329, 78 Eng.Rep. 579; Cunningham v. Yeomans, 1868, 7 N.S.W. 149; Salisbury v. Green, 1892, 17 R.I. 758, 24 A. 787; Richardson v. Anthony, 1840, 12 Vt. 273; Second Restatement of Torts, § 198, Comment a. Contra: Chess v. Kelly, 1834, 3 Blackf., Ind., 438; Roach v. Damron, 1841, 2 Humph., Tenn., 425.

41. Infra, § 24.

42. Sheldon v. Sherman, 1870, 42 N.Y. 484. See also Anthony v. Haney, 1832, 8 Bing. 186, 131 Eng.Rep. 372; Carter v. Thurston, 1877, 58 N.H. 104; Maulsby v. Cook, 1925, 134 Wash. 133, 235 P. 23; Polebitzke v. John Week Lumber Co., 1921, 173 Wis. 509, 181 N.W. 730; Second Restatement of Torts, § 198, Comment k. See Bohlen, Incomplete Privilege to Inflict Intentional Invasions of Interests of Property and Personality, 1925, 39 Harv.L.Rev. 307.

43. Newkirk v. Sabler, 1850, 9 Barb., N.Y., 652; Roach v. Damron, 1841, 2 Humph., Tenn., 425; Crocker v. Carson, 1851, 33 Me. 436; Ryerson v. Carter, 1919, 92 N.J.L. 363, 105 A. 723, affirmed, 1920, 93 N.J.L. 477, 108 A. 927; see Pierce v. Finerty, 1911, 76 N.H.

Having put the goods where they are, he has no remedy to recover them except legal process. A conditional seller of goods may acquire, by a clause in the contract, an irrevocable license to enter the buyer's premises upon his default, and remove the property,[44] but even such a provision gives him no right to do more than enter peaceably, at a reasonable time and in a reasonable manner,[45] and he will be liable if he uses any force to break in.[46] Even a clause in the contract authorizing him to do so has been held void as contrary to public policy.[47]

Temporary Detention for Investigation

If property is taken wrongfully, and the pursuit is fresh, the owner may use reasonable force to recover it which otherwise would amount to false imprisonment. At the same time, a private citizen has no legal authority to arrest upon the mere suspicion of a crime, and will be justified only if the crime has in fact been committed.[48] Still less has he any authority to imprison another for a debt,[49] or a civil claim for damages.[50] It follows that a shopkeeper, who has good reason to believe that he has caught a customer in the act of stealing, of defrauding him of goods, or of sneaking out without paying for goods or services, is placed in a difficult position. He must either permit the suspected wrongdoer to walk out, and very probably say goodbye to both goods and payment, or run the risk that he will be liable for heavy damages for any detention. Many courts have held him liable for false imprisonment under an honest mistake in such a case.[51] The problem is a major one, with theft losses ranging into many millions every year.[52]

38, 76 A. 194, 79 A. 23; McGill v. Holman, 1922, 208 Ala. 9, 93 So. 848.

44. White Sewing Mach. Co. v. Conner, 1901, 111 Ky. 827, 64 S.W. 841; North v. Williams, 1888, 120 Pa. 109, 13 A. 723. Such a license has been implied merely from the reservation of the right to repossess. Heath v. Randall, 1849, 4 Cush., Mass., 195; Proctor v. Tilton, 1889, 65 N.H. 3, 17 A. 638; Blackford v. Neaves, 1922, 23 Ariz. 501, 205 P. 587; C. I. T. Corp. v. Reeves, 1933, 112 Fla. 424, 150 So. 638. Cf. Plate v. Southern Bell Tel. & Tel. Co., E.D.S.C.1951, 98 F.Supp. 355 (removing telephone); C. I. T. Corp. v. Short, 1938, 273 Ky. 190, 115 S.W.2d 899 (towing car out of garage). Contra: Kirkwood v. Hickman, 1955, 223 Miss. 372, 78 So.2d 351; Reed v. Shreveport Furn. Co., 1927, 7 La.Ann. 134.

45. Flaherty v. Ginsberg, 1907, 135 Iowa 743, 110 N.W. 1050; Drury v. Hervey, 1879, 126 Mass. 519.

46. Evers-Jordan Furniture Co. v. Hartzog, 1939, 237 Ala. 407, 187 So. 491; General Motors Acc. Corp. v. Hicks, 1934, 189 Ark. 62, 70 S.W.2d 509; Dominick v. Rea, 1924, 226 Mich. 594, 198 N.W. 184; Wilson Motor Co. v. Dunn, 1928, 129 Okl. 211, 264 P. 194; Soulios v. Mills Novelty Co., 1941, 198 S.C. 355, 17 S.E.2d 869. See Note, 1952, 30 N.C.L.Rev. 149.

Comparatively slight force has been held to be tortious. Driver v. Commonwealth, Ky.1957, 299 S.W.2d 260 (breaking glass of car); Renaire Corp. v. Vaughn, Mun.App.D.C.1958, 142 A.2d 148 (breaking in); Lyda v. Cooper, 1933, 169 S.C. 451, 169 S.E. 236 (entering through unbroken window); M. J. Rose Co. v. Lowery, 1929, 33 Ohio App. 488, 169 N.E. 716 (opening lock with key); Commercial Credit Co. v. Spence, 1938, 185 Miss. 293, 184 So. 439 (breaking into car).

47. Girard v. Anderson, 1934, 219 Iowa 42, 257 N.W. 400; Stewart v. F. A. North Co., 1916, 65 Pa.Super. 195; Sturman v. Polito, 1936, 161 Misc. 536, 291 N.Y.S. 621.

48. See infra, § 26.

49. Gadsden General Hospital v. Hamilton, 1925, 212 Ala. 531, 105 So. 553 (hospital bill); Salisbury v. Poulson, 1918, 51 Utah 552, 172 P. 315 (dentist's bill); Vail v. Pennsylvania R. Co., 1927, 103 N.J.L. 213, 136 A. 425 (railway fare); Estes v. Brewster Cigar Co., 1930, 156 Wash. 465, 287 P. 36 (gambling debt); C. N. Robinson & Co. v. Greene, 1906, 148 Ala. 434, 43 So. 797.

50. Kearley v. Cowan, 1928, 217 Ala. 295, 116 So. 145 (automobile collision).

51. Zayre of Virginia, Inc. v. Gowdy, 1966, 207 Va. 47, 147 S.E.2d 710; Schantz v. Sears, Roebuck & Co., 1934, 12 N.J.Misc. 689, 174 A. 162, affirmed, 1935, 115 N.J.L. 174, 178 A. 768; Fitscher v. Rollman & Sons Co., 1939, 31 Ohio App. 340, 343, 167 N.E. 469; Mannaugh v. J. C. Penney Co., 1933, 61 S.D. 550, 250 N.W. 38; Great Atlantic & P. Tea Co. v. Smith, 1939, 281 Ky. 583, 136 S.W.2d 759.

52. It is discussed in Notes in 1953, 62 Yale L.J. 788; 1952, 46 Ill.L.Rev. 887, 47 Nw.U.L.Rev. 82; 1966, 17 S.C.L.Rev. 729.

Starting with a California case [53] in 1936, there have been a number of decisions which have permitted a business man who reasonably [54] suspects a customer of theft,[55] or of failure to pay,[56] to detain the suspected individual for a short time in order to investigate. This seems entirely reasonable, and justified by all ordinary usage among decent people: an honest man might be expected to remain voluntarily to assist in clearing the matter up. The privilege is, however, a very restricted one, confined to what is reasonably necessary for its limited purpose, of enabling the defendant to do what is possible on the spot to discover the facts. There will be liability if the detention is for a length of time beyond that which is reasonably necessary for such a short investigation,[57] or if the plaintiff is assaulted, insulted or bullied,[58] or public accusation is made against him,[59] or the privilege is exercised in an unreasonable manner; [60] and certainly if the defendant purports to make a definite arrest and take the plaintiff into legal custody,[61] or to use the detention to coerce payment,[62] or the signing of a confession.[63] In most of the decisions, the privilege apparently has been limited to detention on the defendant's premises, and does not extend to one who has left them.[64]

---

53. Collyer v. S. H. Kress & Co., 1936, 5 Cal.2d 175, 54 P.2d 20, followed in Bettolo v. Safeway Stores, Inc., 1936, 11 Cal.App.2d 430, 54 P.2d 24. The California decisions are noted with approval in 1936, 25 Cal.L.Rev. 119; 1936, 10 So.Cal.L.Rev. 103; 1936, 21 Minn.L.Rev. 107; 1936, 84 U.Pa.L.Rev. 912.

54. Otherwise where there is no reasonable ground for suspicion, even though a statute authorizes detention if there is. J. C. Penney Co. v. Cox, 1963, 246 Miss. 1, 148 So.2d 679; Isaian v. Great A. & P. Tea Co., 1959, 111 Ohio App. 537, 174 N.E.2d 128.

55. Teel v. May Department Stores Co., 1941, 348 Mo. 696, 155 S.W.2d 74; Montgomery Ward & Co. v. Freeman, 4 Cir. 1952, 199 F.2d 720; Little Stores v. Isenberg, 1943, 26 Tenn.App. 357, 172 S.W. 13; Cohen v. Lit Bros., 1950, 166 Pa.Super. 206, 70 A.2d 419; Kroger Grocery & Baking Co. v. Waller, 1945, 208 Ark. 1063, 189 S.W.2d 361.

Statutes in several states now have confirmed and regulated the privilege. See Isaian v. Great A. & P. Tea Co., 1959, 111 Ohio App. 537, 174 N.E.2d 128; Burnaman v. J. C. Penney Co., S.D.Tex.1960, 181 F. Supp. 633; Notes, 1958, 11 Okl.L.Rev. 102; 1965, 25 La.L.Rev. 956.

The only recent cases found which have denied the existence of the privilege are Zayre of Virginia, Inc. v. Gowdy, 1966, 207 Va. 47, 147 S.E.2d 710;

56. Standish v. Narragansett S. S. Co., 1873, 111 Mass. 512; Lynch v. Metropolitan Elev. R. Co., 1882, 90 N.Y. 77; Jacques v. Childs Dining Hall, 1923, 244 Mass. 438, 138 N.E. 843. Cf. Cox v. Rhodes Ave. Hospital, 1916, 198 Ill.App. 82.

57. Jacques v. Childs Dining Hall, 1923, 244 Mass. 438, 138 N.E. 843 (half an hour); Herbrick v. Sam-

ardick & Co., 1960, 169 Neb. 833, 101 N.W.2d 488 (hour and a half); J. J. Newberry Co. v. Judd, 1935, 259 Ky. 309, 82 S.W.2d 359 (four or five hours); Little Stores v. Isenberg, 1943, 26 Tenn.App. 357, 172 S.W.2d 13 (after cashier stated plaintiff had paid).

58. W. T. Grant Co. v. Owens, 1928, 149 Va. 906, 141 S.E. 860; S. H. Kress & Co. v. Musgrove, 1929, 153 Va. 348, 149 S.E. 453; A. Harris & Co. v. Caldwell, Tex.Civ.App.1925, 276 S.W. 298, error dismissed; Moffatt v. Buffum's, Inc., 1937, 21 Cal.App.2d 371, 69 P.2d 424.

59. Chretien v. F. W. Woolworth Co., La.App.1964, 160 So.2d 854, writ refused 246 La. 75, 163 So.2d 356; Southwest Drug Stores of Miss. v. Garner, Miss.1967, 195 So.2d 837 (both under statute).

60. Lukas v. J. C. Penney Co., 1963, 233 Or. 345, 378 P.2d 717.

61. McLoughlin v. New York Edison Co., 1929, 252 N.Y. 202, 169 N.E. 277; Lindquist v. Friedman's, Inc., 1937, 366 Ill. 232, 8 N.E.2d 625; S. H. Kress & Co. v. Bradshaw, 1940, 186 Okl. 588, 99 P.2d 508; Moseley v. J. G. McCrory Co., 1926, 101 W.Va. 480, 133 S.E. 73; Martin v. Castner-Knott Dry Goods Co., 1944, 27 Tenn.App. 421, 181 S.W.2d 638.

62. Standish v. Narragansett S. S. Co., 1873, 111 Mass. 512; Lynch v. Metropolitan Elev. R. Co., 1882, 90 N.Y. 77; Cox v. Rhodes Ave. Hospital, 1916, 198 Ill.App. 82; Sweeten v. Friedman, 1928, 9 La.App. 44, 118 So. 787.

63. Moffatt v. Buffums, Inc., 1937, 21 Cal.App.2d 371, 69 P.2d 424; Teel v. May Department Stores Co., 1941, 348 Mo. 696, 155 S.W.2d 74; W. T. Grant Co. v. Owens, 1928, 149 Va. 906, 141 S.E. 860. But a mere request to sign a statement is within the privilege. Collyer v. S. H. Kress & Co., 1936, 5 Cal. 2d 175, 54 P.2d 20.

64. In McCrory Stores Corp. v. Satchell, 1925, 148 Md. 279, 129 A. 348, and Moseley v. J. G. McCrory Co., 1926, 101 W.Va. 480, 133 S.E. 73, detention on the street was held not to be privileged. In Simmons v. J. C. Penney Co., La.App.1966, 186 So.2d 358, the sidewalk in front of the store was held to

But a Michigan decision [65] has recently allowed pursuit and detention where the plaintiff had left the store, but was in the immediate vicinity.

23. FORCIBLE ENTRY ON LAND

The privilege of one entitled to the possession of land to enter and recover it by force has been a source of long standing confusion in the courts. In 1381, under Richard the Second, a statute [66] made such forcible entry a criminal offense. The English courts refused to treat this statute as a basis for any civil action for trespass to the land, on the ground that the plaintiff, having no right to the possession, could sustain no injury when he was deprived of it.[67] But in Newton v. Harland,[68] it was held that the privilege of entry did not extend to the use of force upon the person of the occupant, and that an action for assault and battery would lie in such a case. This decision was overruled in England in 1920,[69] but in the meantime it had received a great deal of acceptance in the United States.

The criminal statute of Richard II has been accepted as part of the common law, or re-enacted, by nearly all of the American states. In addition, many states also provide a specific, and speedy, civil remedy for such forcible entry.[70] The interpretation placed upon

such statutes necessarily controls the rule to be adopted, and discussion of them obviously is beyond the scope of this treatise.[71] With due regard to the varying effect of such legislation, it may be said in general that the majority of the states have followed Newton v. Harland, and hold that the occupant may recover for assault and battery,[72] or for trespass to his goods,[73] if any such force is used in the course of the forcible entry. A smaller group adopt the present English rule, that the privilege extends to the use of reasonable force to expel the occupant and his property.[74]

The majority rule seems clearly the desirable one. In virtually all jurisdictions, a summary procedure exists by which the owner may recover possession by legal process, with only a brief delay. Few things are more likely to lead to a brawl than an evicting landlord, throwing out his tenant by main force. Land cannot be sequestered or removed, and the public interest in preserving the peace would seem to justify the temporary inconvenience to the owner.

The same arguments might be advanced, with somewhat less force, against the mere privilege of entry itself. Most states, however, deny any common law remedy for trespass,[75] and permit recovery, if at all, only

---

be part of the premises. Cf. Montgomery Ward & Co. v. Freeman, 4 Cir. 1952, 199 F.2d 720; J. C. Penney Co. v. O'Daniell, 10 Cir. 1959, 263 F.2d 849.

65. Bonkowski v. Arlan's Dept. Store, 1968, 12 Mich. App. 88, 162 N.W.2d 347, affirmed 1970, 383 Mich. 90, 174 N.W.2d 765.

66. Statute of Forcible Entry, 5 Rich. II, c. 2.

67. Turner v. Maymott, 1823, 1 Bing. 158, 130 Eng. Rep. 64; Pollen v. Brewer, 1859, 7 C.B.,N.S., 371, 141 Eng.Rep. 860.

68. 1840, 1 Man. & G. 644, 133 Eng.Rep. 490. Accord, Beddall v. Maitland, 1881, 17 Ch.Div. 174.

69. Hemmings v. Stoke Poges Golf Club, [1920] 1 K. B. 720. See Note, 1920, 36 L.Q.Rev. 205.

70. As to the New York legislation, which is more or less typical, see Wood v. Phillips, 1870, 43 N.Y. 152, 153; Fults v. Munro, 1911, 202 N.Y. 34, 95 N.E. 23.

71. See cases collected in 121 Am.St.Rep. 369; 45 A.L.R. 313; 141 A.L.R. 250. Also Sharpe, Forcible Trespass to Real Property, 1961, 39 N.C.L.Rev. 121.

72. Daluiso v. Boone, 1969, 71 Cal.2d 484, 78 Cal. Rptr. 707, 455 P.2d 811; Lobdell v. Keene, 1901, 85 Minn. 90, 88 N.W. 426; Weatherly v. Manatt, 1919, 72 Okl. 138, 179 P. 470; Ray v. Dyer, Tex.Civ.App. 1929, 20 S.W.2d 328, error dismissed; Mosseller v. Deaver, 1890, 106 N.C. 494, 11 S.E. 529; Second Restatement of Torts, § 185.

73. Whitney v. Brown, 1907, 75 Kan. 678, 90 P. 277; Sinclair v. Stanley, 1888, 69 Tex. 718, 7 S.W. 511.

74. Low v. Elwell, 1876, 121 Mass. 309; Allen v. Kelly, 1892, 17 R.I. 731, 24 A. 776; Shorter v. Shelton, 1945, 183 Va. 819, 33 S.E.2d 643; Gower v. Waters, 1926, 125 Me. 223, 132 A. 550; Vaughn v. Mesch, 1939, 107 Mont. 498, 87 P.2d 177.

75. Sampson v. Henry, 1832, 13 Pick., Mass., 36; Weeks v. Sly, 1881, 61 N.H. 89; Levy v. McClintock,

in the form of an action provided by statute for forcible entry.[76] Even here, a provision in the lease may give the landlord the privilege of entry by force, notwithstanding the statute.[77] In all cases, however, he is liable for the use of any force beyond that reasonably necessary.[78]

The statutes of forcible entry protect only a plaintiff who is himself in peaceable possession of the property. A mere "scrambling" possession is not enough. A trespasser who ousts the owner acquires no such possession as will entitle him to protection against an immediate forcible reentry, even though it may involve assault and battery.[79] What is required is "something like acquiescence in the physical fact of his occupation on the part of the rightful owner."[80] Mere delay in taking effective action, even for a period of months, will not make the entry tortious, where the owner has not discovered his dispossession,[81] or has made persistent efforts

to enter;[82] but acquiescence or toleration of the wrongful possession, even for a day,[83] may bring him within the statute.[84]

It is quite generally conceded that the owner may await his opportunity, and if he can regain possession peaceably, may then maintain it, and lawfully resist an attempt to oust him.[85] But what constitutes such "peaceable" entry is very largely a question of the terms of the particular statute; and in some jurisdictions unlocking a door,[86] or breaking it down,[87] is regarded as peaceable, while in others deception,[88] or a mere entry without the consent of the possessor,[89] remains wrongful.

24. NECESSITY

A defendant who acts to prevent a threatened injury from some force of nature, or some other independent cause not connected with the plaintiff, is said to be acting under necessity. The term is unfortunate, since it is broad enough to apply to any situation

1910, 141 Mo.App. 593, 125 S.W. 546; Gower v. Waters, 1926, 125 Me. 223, 132 A. 550; Southern R. Co. v. Hayes, 1913, 183 Ala. 465, 63 So. 874.

Contra: Dustin v. Cowdry, 1851, 23 Vt. 631; Mosseller v. Deaver, 1890, 106 N.C. 494, 11 S.E. 529; Raniak v. Krukowski, 1924, 226 Mich. 695, 198 N.W. 190.

76. Moyer v. Gordon, 1887, 113 Ind. 282, 14 N.E. 476; Walker v. Chanslor, 1908, 153 Cal. 118, 94 P. 606; Wilson v. Campbell, 1907, 75 Kan. 159, 88 P. 548; Greeley v. Spratt, 1883, 19 Fla. 644.

77. Princess Amusement Co. v. Smith, 1911, 174 Ala. 342, 56 So. 979; Goshen v. People, 1896, 22 Colo. 270, 44 P. 503, 504; Backus v. West, 1922, 104 Or. 129, 205 P. 533; cf. Clark v. Service Auto Co., 1926, 143 Miss. 602, 108 So. 704.

78. Gilbert v. Peck, 1912, 162 Cal. 54, 121 P. 315; Saros v. Avenue Theatre Co., 1912, 172 Mich. 238, 137 N.W. 559; Whitney v. Swett, 1850, 22 N.H. 10. Cf. Allison v. Hodo, 1951, 84 Ga.App. 790, 67 S.E.2d 606 (exposing furniture).

79. Cox v. Cunningham, 1875, 77 Ill. 545; Taylor v. Adams, 1885, 58 Mich. 187, 24 N.W. 864; Hodgkins v. Price, 1882, 132 Mass. 196; O'Donohue v. Holmes, 1895, 107 Ala. 489, 18 So. 263. See cases collected in 121 Am.St.Rep. 384.

80. Pollock, Law of Torts, 13th Ed. 1929, 403.

81. Anderson v. Mills, 1882, 40 Ark. 192; Wray v. Taylor, 1876, 56 Ala. 188; Jones v. Czaza, 1935, 19

Tenn.App. 327, 86 S.W.2d 1096; Hoag v. Pierce, 1865, 28 Cal. 187; Benevides v. Lucio, Tex.Com. App.1929, 13 S.W.2d 71.

82. Bowers v. Cherokee Bob, 1873, 45 Cal. 495; Voll v. Butler, 1874, 49 Cal. 74 (nearly four years).

83. Browne v. Dawson, 1840, 12 Ad. & El. 624, 113 Eng.Rep. 950.

84. Schwinn v. Perkins, 1910, 79 N.J.L. 515, 78 A. 19.

85. Winn v. State, 1892, 55 Ark. 360, 18 S.W. 375; Clarke v. Mylkes, 1921, 95 Vt. 460, 115 A. 492; Goldstein v. Webster, 1908, 7 Cal.App. 705, 95 P. 677; Mershon v. Williams, 1899, 62 N.J.L. 779, 42 A. 778; Richter v. Cordes, 1894, 100 Mich. 278, 58 N.W. 1110.

86. Smith v. Detroit Loan & Bldg. Ass'n, 1897, 115 Mich. 340, 73 N.W. 395.

87. Mussey v. Scott, 1859, 32 Vt. 82.

88. Pelavin v. Misner, 1928, 241 Mich. 209, 217 N.W. 36.

89. Casey v. Kitchens, 1917, 66 Okl. 169, 168 P. 812. Of course a violent entry is not peaceable. Thus where defendant, breathing curses and threats, "kicked down the door, entered the house, and fell over something, by which his leg was unfortunately broken, instead of his neck." State v. Jacobs, 1886, 94 N.C. 950.

where it obviously is desirable to do something to avoid unpleasant consequences, including for example the cases of self-defense. The privilege considered here is in fact closely related to that of self-defense. But there is the important difference that the plaintiff is not an aggressor, or even apparently a wrongdoer, and that the defendant, instead of protecting himself against a danger created by the plaintiff, is injuring an innocent man in order to avoid a danger from another source. It follows that the plaintiff's interest has correspondingly greater weight in the scale, and the defendant's privilege may be limited accordingly.[90]

The privilege of necessity, whose basis has been said to be "a mixture of charity, the maintenance of the public good and self-protection," [91] has been recognized in a comparatively small number of cases which have dealt with the problem. It appeared very early in a decision permitting the Crown to enter private land and dig for saltpeter to make gunpowder,[92] and one allowing goods to be jettisoned from a boat during a storm in order to save the passengers.[93] Later cases permitted a traveler on a public highway to turn out to avoid a temporary obstruction, and pass over the adjoining land.[94] But the privilege was not recognized where the way was a private one, and the interest in having it open did not extend to the public.[95]

Out of these early decisions, two lines of cases have developed, involving so-called "public" and "private" necessity. Where the danger affects the entire community, or so many people that the public interest is involved,[96] that interest serves as a complete justification to the defendant who acts to avert the peril to all. Thus one who dynamites a house to stop the spread of a conflagration that threatens a town,[97] or shoots a mad dog in the street,[98] or burns clothing infected with smallpox germs,[1] or, in time of war, destroys property which should not be allowed to fall into the hands of the enemy,[2] is not liable to the owner, so long as

---

90. Bohlen, Incomplete Privilege to Inflict Intentional Invasions of Interests of Property and Personality, 1926, 39 Harv.L.Rev. 307; Williams, The Defence of Necessity, [1953] Curr.Leg.Prob. 216.

91. Winfield, Law of Torts, 1937, 62.

92. King's Prerogative in Saltpetre, 1607, 12 Co. Rep. 12, 77 Eng.Rep. 1294. Even earlier is Maleverer v. Spinke, 1538, 1 Dyer 35b, 73 Eng.Rep. 79.

93. Mouse's Case, 1609, 12 Co.Rep. 63, 77 Eng.Rep. 1341.

94. Taylor v. Whitehead, 1781, 2 Dougl. 745, 99 Eng. Rep. 475; Campbell v. Race, 1851, 7 Cush., Mass., 408; Morey v. Fitzgerald, 1884, 56 Vt. 487; Shriver v. Marion County Court, 1910, 66 W.Va. 685, 66 S.E. 1062. Cf. Chicago & A. R. Co. v. Mayer, 1904, 112 Ill.App. 149 (defendant blocking highway); Dodwell v. Missouri Pac. R. Co., Mo.1964, 384 S.W.2d 643 (same).

95. Williams v. Safford, 1849, 7 Barb., N.Y., 309; Bullard v. Harrison, 1815, 4 M. & S. 387, 105 Eng. Rep. 877. But cf. Haley v. Colcord, 1879, 59 N.H. 7; Kent v. Judkins, 1865, 53 Me. 160.

96. The act must be for the purpose of protecting the public. A private benefit to the actor is not sufficient. Newcomb v. Tisdale, 1881, 62 Cal. 575; Whalley v. Lancashire R. Co., 1884, 13 Q.B.D. 131; Grant v. Allen, 1874, 41 Conn. 156.

97. Surocco v. Geary, 1853, 3 Cal. 69; Conwell v. Emrie, 1850, 2 Ind. 35; Russell v. Mayor of New York, 1845, 2 Denio, N.Y., 461; American Print Works v. Lawrence, 1837, 23 N.J.L. 9, 590; Stocking v. Johnson Flying Service, 1963, 143 Mont. 61, 387 P.2d 312 (fighting forest fire).

98. Putnam v. Payne, 1816, 13 Johns., N.Y., 312.

1. Seavey v. Preble, 1874, 64 Me. 120; State v. Mayor of Knoxville, 1883, 80 Tenn. (12 Lea) 146. Cf. McGuire v. Amyx, 1927, 317 Mo. 1061, 297 S.W. 968 (committing suspected smallpox patient to pesthouse).

2. Harrison v. Wisdom, 1872, 7 Heisk., 54 Tenn., 99 (liquor); United States v. Caltex, Inc., 1952, 344 U.S. 149, rehearing denied, 344 U.S. 919 (stored petroleum and refinery). Cf. Juragua Iron Co. v. United States, 1909, 212 U.S. 297.

To the contrary is Burmah Oil Co. v. Lord Advocate, [1962] Scot.L.T. 347, holding that when the crown does an act of confiscation which would not be open to the ordinary citizen, and justifies it under the prerogative for reasons of state, it does not have the privilege of public necessity, and must pay compensation.

See Abend, Federal Liability for Takings and Torts: An Anomalous Relationship, 1963, 31 Ford.L.Rev. 481; Note, 1964, 39 Tul.L.Rev. 133.

the emergency is great enough, and he has acted reasonably under the circumstances.[3] The "champion of the public" is not required to pay out of his own pocket for the general salvation. The number of persons who must be endangered in order to create a public necessity has not been determined by the courts. It would seem that the moral obligation upon the group affected to make compensation in such a case should be recognized by the law,[4] but recovery usually has been denied.[5]

Where no public interest is involved, and the defendant acts merely to protect a private one, usually his own, the privilege is properly more limited. If the emergency is sufficiently great,[6] he may trespass upon the property of another to save himself[7] or his own property,[8] or even a third person[9] or his property[10] from harm. The privilege to deviate from a blocked public highway[11] falls into this category, as the protection of the individual's private interest in going where he wants to go. In all such cases there is no liability for the technical tort, and no privilege in the landowner to resist or expel the intruder.[12] But in the leading case of Vincent v. Lake Erie Transportation Co.,[13] which has been accepted by a few other decisions,[14] and by the Restatement of Torts,[15] it was held that the privilege does not extend to the infliction of actual damage, and that a shipowner who kept his vessel moored to a dock

3. Beach v. Trudgain, 1845, 2 Grat., 43 Va., 219 (fire); Allen v. Camp, 1915, 14 Ala.App. 341, 70 So. 290 (mad dog). One who destroys property under claim of public necessity has the burden of showing an emergency which will justify the action, as distinguished from mere convenience. Hicks v. Dorn, 1870, 42 N.Y. 47.

4. Hall and Wigmore, Compensation for Property Destroyed to Stop the Spread of a Conflagration, 1907, 1 Ill.L.Rev. 501; Bishop v. Mayor, etc., of Macon, 1849, 7 Ga. 200; cf. Jarvis v. Pinckney, 1836, 3 Hill, S.C., 123. Many jurisdictions provide compensation by statute. See **Mayor of New York v. Lord**, 1837, 17 Wend., N.Y. 285; Taylor v. Inhabitants of Plymouth, 1844, 8 Metc., Mass., 462.

5. Field v. City of Des Moines, 1874, 39 Iowa 575; McDonald v. City of Red Wing, 1868, 13 Minn. 38; Bowditch v. Boston, 1879, 101 U.S. 16.

6. Mere convenience or advantage is not sufficient, in the absence of real emergency. Allen v. Camp, 1915, 14 Ala.App. 341, 70 So. 290 (entering to kill dog suspected of rabies); Uhlein v. Cromack, 1872, 109 Mass. 273 (same as to dog accustomed to bite); Gulf Production Co. v. Gibson, Tex.Civ.App.1921, 234 S.W. 906 (deviating from blocked highway, with other route available); Mitchell v. Oklahoma Cotton Growers' Ass'n, 1925, 108 Okl. 200, 235 P. 597 (entering to claim reward); Currie v. Silvernale, 1919, 142 Minn. 254, 171 N.W. 782 (continued entries after emergency past).

7. Depue v. Flatau, 1907, 100 Minn. 299, 111 N.W. 1; Bradshaw v. Frazier, 1901, 113 Iowa 579, 85 N.W. 752; Rossi v. Del Duca, 1962, 344 Mass. 66, 181 N.E.2d 591 (child frightened by dog).

8. Ploof v. Putnam, 1908, 81 Vt. 471, 71 A. 188; Carter v. Thurston, 1877, 58 N.H. 104; Boutwell v. Champlain Realty Co., 1915, 89 Vt. 80, 94 A. 108. Cf. Hetfield v. Baum, 1852, 35 N.C. 394 (hauling purchased wreck over plaintiff's land).

9. People v. Roberts, 1956, 47 Cal.2d 374, 303 P.2d 721; State v. Lukus, 1967, 149 Mont. 45, 423 P.2d 49; People v. Gallmon, 1967, 19 N.Y.2d 389, 280 N.Y.S.2d 356, 227 N.E.2d 284, cert. denied 390 U.S. 911.

10. Proctor v. Adams, 1873, 113 Mass. 376. Cf. Northern Assur. Co. v. New York Central R. Co., 1935, 271 Mich. 569, 260 N.W. 763; Metallic Compression Casting Co. v. Fitchburg R. Co., 1873, 109 Mass. 277.

11. Supra, note 94.

12. Ploof v. Putnam, 1908, 81 Vt. 471, 71 A. 188; Irwin v. Yeagar, 1888, 74 Iowa 174, 37 N.W. 136; Rossi v. Del Duca, 1962, 344 Mass. 66, 181 N.E.2d 591.

13. 1910, 100 Minn. 456, 124 N.W. 221.

14. Currie v. Silvernale, 1919, 142 Minn. 254, 171 N.W. 782; Swan-Finch Oil Corp. v. Warner-Quinlan Co., 1933, 11 N.J. Misc. 469, 167 A. 211, affirmed, 1934, 112 N.J.Law 519, 171 A. 800; Latta v. New Orleans & N. W. R. Co., 1912, 131 La. 272, 59 So. 250. Cf. Whalley v. Lancashire & York R. Co., 1884, 13 Q.B. D. 131; Whitecross Wire & Iron Co. v. Savill, 1882, 8 Q.B.D. 653 (application of general average); Cope v. Sharpe, [1912] 1 K.B. 496.

The only case found to the contrary is Commercial Union Assur. Co. v. Pacific Gas & Elec. Co., 1934, 220 Cal. 515, 31 P.2d 793, which, however, turned upon the pleading claiming negligence.

15. Second Restatement of Torts, § 263. See also Bohlen, Incomplete Privilege to Inflict Intentional Invasions of Interests of Property and Personality, 1926, 39 Harv.L.Rev. 307.

during a storm must pay for the salvation of his boat by making compensation for the injury to the dock. There is, in other words, an incomplete and partial privilege, which does not extend to the infliction of any substantial harm.[16]

So far as the decisions indicate, the privilege of necessity resembles those of self-defense and defense of property,[17] in that, assuming the reasonable appearance of necessity, an honest mistake as to its existence will not destroy the privilege.[18]

Although the privilege to inflict personal injury under necessity has received little consideration,[19] it would seem that it should be dealt with upon the same basis.

25. LEGAL PROCESS

The privilege to interfere with person or property under legal process is merely one phase of the broader problem of the liability of public officers for their official acts [20] but because of its close relation to intentional interference with person and property, it is convenient to consider it here. A public officer, of course, cannot be held liable for doing in a proper manner an act which is commanded or authorized by a valid law.[21] The immunity of such officers, in its broader aspects, remains to be considered in a later chapter.[22] As a defense to intentional torts against the person or property, it frequently arises in connection with the execution of legal process—for example, the arrest of an individual under a warrant, or the seizure of property under a writ of attachment or execution. This privilege may be considered briefly here.

Arrest under a warrant, or the levy of civil process, is considered a "ministerial act," [23] for which the officer will not be liable if he acts duly and properly,[24] but will be liable if he steps outside of his authority. If the court which issues the process is entirely without jurisdiction to do so, it is commonly held that the invalid process will afford the officer no protection.[25] It may nevertheless be questioned whether there is any desirable policy in requiring sheriffs and constables to know, at their peril, the limitations of the power of the court whose orders they obey, particularly where those limits are likely to depend upon questions of law utterly beyond their comprehension.[26] The rigors of the

16. Compare Taylor v. Chesapeake & Ohio R. Co., 1919, 84 W.Va. 442, 100 S.E. 218; Higgins v. New York, L. E. & W. R. Co., 1894, 78 Hun 567, 29 N.Y.S. 563; Noyes v. Shepherd, 1849, 30 Me. 173; Newcomb v. Tisdale, 1881, 62 Cal. 575, in all of which a defendant who saved his own land by casting flood waters on the plaintiff's land was held liable for the damage done.

17. Supra, pp. 109, 114.

18. Cope v. Sharpe, [1912] 1 K.B. 496; Conwell v. Emrie, 1850, 2 Ind. 35; Surocco v. Geary, 1853, 3 Cal. 69; Seavey v. Preble, 1874, 64 Me. 120, all so indicate. A striking illustration of the unwisdom of confining this privilege within too narrow limits is given in Respublica v. Sparhawk, 1788, 1 Dall., Pa., 357, 1 L.Ed. 174, attributing the destruction of London by the Great Fire to the timidity of the Lord Mayor about destroying houses in its path.

19. Cf. Regina v. Dudley, 1884, 14 Q.D.B. 273, 15 Cox C.C. 273; United States v. Holmes, 1842, Fed. Cas.No.15,383, 1 Wall.Jr. 1; Phillips v. Pickwick Stages, 1927, 85 Cal.App. 571, 259 P. 968 (goes off on negligence). See also the criminal cases cited supra, p. 114.

20. See infra, § 132.

21. Burton v. Fulton, 1865, 49 Pa. 151; Highway Commissioners v. Ely, 1884, 54 Mich. 173, 19 N.W. 940; Thibodaux v. Town of Thibodeaux, 1894, 46 La.Ann. 1528, 16 So. 450. See Gray, Private Wrongs of Public Servants, 1959, 47 Cal.L.Rev. 303.

22. See infra, § 132.

23. See infra, p. 989.

24. Mathews v. Murray, 1960, 101 Ga.App. 216, 113 S.E.2d 232; James v. Southwestern Ins. Co., Okl. 1960, 354 P.2d 408; Bradford v. Harding, E.D.N.Y. 1959, 180 F.Supp. 855, affirmed, 2 Cir. 1959, 284 F.2d 307.

25. Warren v. Kelley, 1888, 80 Me. 512, 15 A. 49; Heller v. Clarke, 1904, 121 Wis. 71, 98 N.W. 952; Strozzi v. Wines, 1899, 24 Nev. 389, 55 P. 828, 57 P. 832; Smith v. Hilton, 1906, 147 Ala. 642, 41 So. 747; Grove v. Van Duyn, 1882, 44 N.J.L. 654.

26. See State v. McNally, 1852, 34 Me. 210; Brooks v. Mangan, 1891, 86 Mich. 576, 49 N.W. 633; Rapacz, Protection of Officers Who Act Under Unconstitutional Statutes, 1927, 11 Minn.L.Rev. 585.

rule have been relaxed to some extent by holding that if the court has general jurisdiction to issue similar process, the officer will be protected, provided that the warrant or the writ is "fair on its face." [27] Any errors or irregularities in the proceedings, even though they may affect jurisdiction in the particular case, will not make him liable.[28]

The more modern and better reasoned cases,[29] with many still to the contrary,[30] have extended this even to the protection of officers who act under statutes subsequently declared to be unconstitutional, reasoning that the mentality of the average policeman, whose life is traditionally not a happy one, should not be charged with the decisions of questions which baffle the best lawyers in the land.

Process is not "fair on its face" if the kind of examination which the reasonable officer can fairly be expected to make would show that it is not valid. The officer is required to know at least the superficial characteristics of a valid warrant; and he will be liable

if it is too general in its terms,[31] fails properly to name the party wanted,[32] or is returnable at the wrong time,[33] or does not charge a crime.[34] But so long as it is valid upon its face, the weight of authority probably is that the officer is privileged to execute it even though he has personal knowledge of facts which should prevent the arrest, and may safely leave all responsibility to the court.[35]

The officer is of course charged with the valid and lawful execution of the process placed in his hands, and will be liable if he departs from the proper procedure, no matter how excellent his intentions.[36] He will be liable if he mistakenly arrests another than the person named,[37] or seizes property not

27. Robinette v. Price, 1943, 214 Minn. 521, 8 N.W. 2d 800; Williams v. Franzoni, 2 Cir. 1954, 217 F.2d 533; Peterson v. Lutz, 1942, 212 Minn. 307, 3 N.W. 2d 489; Hansen v. Lowe, 1940, 61 Idaho 138, 100 P.2d 51; Morrill v. Hamel, 1958, 337 Mass. 83, 148 N.E.2d 283.

28. Wilbur v. Stokes, 1903, 117 Ga. 545, 43 S.E. 856 (void judgment); Bohri v. Barnett, 7 Cir. 1906, 144 F. 389 (invalid ordinance); Rush v. Buckley, 1905, 100 Me. 322, 61 A. 774 (invalid statute); Vittorio v. St. Regis Paper Co., 1924, 239 N.Y. 148, 145 N.E. 913; David v. Larochelle, 1936, 296 Mass. 302, 5 N.E.2d 571.

29. Yekhtikian v. Blessing, 1960, 90 R.I. 287, 157 A.2d 669; McCray v. City of Lake Louisville, Ky.1960, 332 S.W.2d 837; Manson v. Wabash R. Co., Mo.1960, 338 S.W.2d 54; Brooks v. Mangan, 1891, 86 Mich. 576, 49 N.W. 633; Henke v. McCord, 1880, 55 Iowa 378, 7 N.W. 623. See Rapacz, Protection of Officers Who Act Under Unconstitutional Statutes, 1927, 11 Minn.L.Rev. 585; Field, The Effect of an Unconstitutional Statute in the Law of Public Officers, 1928, 77 U.Pa.L.Rev. 155; Note, 1936, 22 Va.L.Rev. 316.

30. Smith v. Costello, 1955, 77 Idaho 205, 290 P.2d 742; Sumner v. Beeler, 1875, 50 Ind. 341; Campbell v. Sherman, 1874, 35 Wis. 103; Kelly v. Bemis, 1855, 4 Gray, Mass., 83; Dennison Mfg. Co. v. Wright, 1923, 156 Ga. 789, 120 S.E. 120.

31. Commonwealth v. Crotty, 1865, 10 Allen, Mass., 403; Grumon v. Raymond, 1814, 1 Conn. 40; Lynchard v. State, 1938, 183 Miss. 691, 184 So. 805; Reichman v. Harris, 6 Cir. 1918, 252 F. 371.

32. Goldberg v. Markowitz, 1904, 94 App.Div. 237, 87 N.Y.S. 1045, affirmed, 1905, 182 N.Y. 540, 75 N.E. 1129 ("John"); Harwood v. Siphers, 1880, 70 Me. 464 (no party named).

33. Toof v. Bently, 1830, 5 Wend., N.Y., 276; Hussey v. Davis, 1878, 58 N.H. 317 (no return specified). Cf. Hazen v. Creller, 1910, 83 Vt. 460, 76 A. 145 (unsigned complaint).

34. Frazier v. Turner, 1890, 76 Wis. 562, 45 N.W. 411; Lueck v. Heisler, 1894, 87 Wis. 644, 58 N.W. 1101; Minor v. Selega, 1958, 168 Ohio St. 1, 150 N.E.2d 852. The officer is not held to the standard of a trained legal mind, but merely to that of an ordinary intelligent and informed layman. Ætna Ins. Co. v. Blumenthal, 1943, 129 Conn. 545, 29 A.2d 751.

35. People v. Warren, 1843, 5 Hill, N.Y., 440; Watson v. Watson, 1832, 9 Conn. 140; O'Shaughnessy v. Baxter, 1876, 121 Mass. 515; Heath v. Halfhill, 1898, 106 Iowa 131, 76 N.W. 522; Rice v. Miller, 1888, 70 Tex. 613, 8 S.W. 317; Second Restatement of Torts, § 124, Comment b. Contra: Tellefsen v. Fee, 1897, 168 Mass. 188, 46 N.E. 562; Leachman v. Dougherty, 1872, 81 Ill. 324.

36. See, generally, Perkins, The Law of Arrest, 1940, 25 Iowa L.Rev. 201, 212–228.

37. Holmes v. Blyler, 1890, 80 Iowa 365, 45 N.W. 756; Walton v. Will, 1944, 66 Cal.App.2d 509, 152 P.2d 639; Jordan v. C. I. T. Corp., 1939, 302 Mass. 281, 19 N.E.2d 5; Hays v. Creary, 1883, 60 Tex. 445; Johnson v. Weiner, 1944, 155 Fla. 169, 19 So.2d 699. The officer is liable if he arrests the person intended, under a warrant bearing the wrong name. Gris-

covered by the writ.[38] He is protected only if he acts with the process in his possession; it is not enough that it has been issued and is in the hands of another person.[39] He must ordinarily make known his authority, his intention to arrest, and the nature of the charge.[40] He must act at a reasonable time,[41] and use only reasonable force.[42] The execution of civil process, by long tradition, does not authorize breaking into a dwelling house without a separate court order, and such

wold v. Sedgwick, 1826, 6 Cow., N.Y., 456; West v. Cabell, 1894, 153 U.S. 78; Scheer v. Keown, 1872, 29 Wis. 586; Harris v. McReynolds, 1898, 10 Colo. App. 532, 51 P. 1016. But it has been held that an arrest in good faith of the wrong person bearing the same name is privileged. Schneider v. Kessler, 3 Cir. 1938, 97 F.2d 542; Blocker v. Clark, 1906, 126 Ga. 484, 54 S.E. 1022; Clark v. Winn, 1898, 19 Tex.Civ.App. 223, 46 S.W. 915; King v. Robertson, 1933, 227 Ala. 378, 150 So. 154.

There is no liability where the mistake is knowingly induced by the plaintiff. Dunston v. Paterson, 1857, 2 C.B.,N.S., 495, 140 Eng.Rep. 509.

38. Symonds v. Hull, 1853, 37 Me. 354; Buck v. Colbath, 1865, 70 U.S., 3 Wall., 334 (goods of wrong party); Kane v. Hutchinson, 1892, 93 Mich. 488, 53 N.W. 624 (goods other than those specifically named).

39. Galliard v. Laxton, 1862, 2 B. & S. 363, 121 Eng. Rep. 1109; Adams v. State, 1904, 121 Ga. 163, 48 S.E. 910; People v. McLean, 1888, 68 Mich. 480, 36 N.W. 231; Webb v. State, 1889, 51 N.J.L. 189, 17 A. 113; Second Restatement of Torts, § 126. See Bohlen and Shulman, Arrest With and Without a Warrant, 1927, 75 U.Pa.L.Rev. 485, 492.

40. Hodge v. Piedmont & N. R. Co., 1917, 109 S.C. 62, 95 S.E. 138; State v. Phinney, 1856, 42 Me. 384; State v. Freeman, 1859, 8 Iowa 428; cf. Crosswhite v. Barnes, 1924, 139 Va. 471, 124 S.E. 242 (reading warrant). See Second Restatement of Torts, § 128; Note, 1965, 25 Md.L.Rev. 48. But such manifestation is not required where the one arrested knows the officer's authority and the charge. Wolf v. State, 1869, 19 Ohio St. 248; State v. Byrd, 1905, 72 S.C. 104, 51 S.E. 542.

41. Keith v. Tuttle, 1848, 28 Me. 326 (Sunday); Malcolmson v. Scott, 1885, 56 Mich. 459, 23 N.W. 166 (Sunday); Bryan v. Comstock, 1920, 143 Ark. 394, 220 S.W. 475, (Saturday night). An arrest for a serious offense, however, may be justified at an inconvenient time.

42. As to what is reasonable force in effecting an arrest, with or without a warrant, see infra, p. 134.

forcible entry may be resisted.[43] But there is no privilege to resist the mere seizure of goods, even under a void writ, since the property interest involved does not justify force against the person of the officer asserting legal authority, and other remedies are available.[44]

Trespass Ab Initio

One who enters upon land, seizes property, or makes an arrest by virtue of legal authority, is of course liable for any subsequent tortious conduct. But by a curious and unique fiction, the common law courts held that his abuse of authority related back to his original act, and that he was liable as a trespasser from the beginning, however innocent of wrong he might have been up to the moment of misconduct. The fiction had its origin in the ancient law of distress of property,[45] and received its first full statement in the Six Carpenters Case,[46] in 1610. It was a procedural device, "due to the misplaced ingenuity of some medieval pleader," [47] which was designed to circumvent the rule that the action of trespass would not lie where the original entry was not wrongful.[48] It originated at a time when punitive damages were still in the far distant future, and no doubt it accomplished, in at least some outrageous cases of abuse of legal authority, much the same deterrent purpose.

Equally curious limitations were placed about the fiction. It was held that it had

43. Semayne's Case, 1604, 5 Co.Rep. 91a, 77 Eng. Rep. 194; Ilsley v. Nichols, 1831, 12 Pick., Mass., 270; Kelley v. Schuyler, 1898, 20 R.I. 432, 39 A. 893; Frothingham v. Maxim, 1928, 127 Me. 58, 141 A. 99.

44. State v. Downer, 1836, 8 Vt. 424; Faris v. State, 1854, 3 Ohio St. 159; State v. Selengut, 1915, 38 R.I. 302, 95 A. 503. Contra, Commonwealth v. Kennard, 1829, 8 Pick., Mass., 133.

45. Ames, History of Trover, 1898, 11 Harv.L.Rev. 277, 287; 7 Holdsworth, History of English Law, 1925, 499; Williams, A Strange Offspring of Trespass Ab Initio, 1936, 52 L.Q.Rev. 106.

46. 1610, 8 Co.Rep. 146a, 77 Eng.Rep. 695.

47. Salmond, Law of Torts, 8th Ed. 1934, 222.

48. 1 Street, Foundations of Legal Liability, 1906, 47.

no application to those who entered, not by authority of law, but by a private license, upon the theory that in such a case the landowner might choose his own licensee, and should take the risk that the license might be abused.[49] It was also held that the subsequent act must be one which in itself would amount to a trespass,[50] and that a mere omission, such as a failure to pay for drinks after entering an inn,[51] was not sufficient.[52] This was perhaps due to some respect for the formal requirements of the trespass action.

Notwithstanding vigorous and unanimous denunciation on the part of all writers who have discussed it,[53] the fiction has survived. Since the development of punitive damages, its effect has been to pile Ossa upon Pelion by adding damages for an innocent and rightful act on top of fair compensation for the wrong plus punishment. Its commonest application has been in the case of damage done after an entry of land under authority of law,[54] or the misuse or wrongful disposition of goods seized under process,[55] where its chief importance has lain in the fact that the defendant may be required to pay greater damages such as the entire value of the chattel.[56]

The reasons given by the courts for the continuance of the doctrine do not carry conviction. It is said that the abuse of the privilege creates a conclusive presumption that the actor intended from the outset to use the public authority as a cloak under which to enter for a wrongful purpose. While it may be important evidence to that effect, it scarcely justifies a rule of law.[57] The best argument in favor of the doctrine is that it affords a valuable correction for abuses by public officers; but the existence of adequate remedies for the subsequent misconduct should be sufficient.[58]

Since the turn of the century, there has been very little use of trespass ab initio in any field except that of arrest, where there has been much dispute as to its application.[59] A failure to make a return of process, even though it is only an omission, has been regarded as so identified with the arrest itself

49. Page v. Town of Newbury, 1943, 113 Vt. 336, 34 A.2d 218; Carton v. Cruz Const. Co., 1965, 89 N.J. Super. 414, 215 A.2d 356; Katsonas v. W. M. Sutherland Bldg. & Const. Co., 1926, 104 Conn. 54, 132 A. 553; Nichols v. Sonia, 1913, 113 Me. 529, 95 A. 209; Mertz v. J. M. Covington Corp., Alaska 1970, 470 P.2d 532.

Apparently it is only ignorance of the history which has made occasional courts hold the contrary, as in Francis v. Sun Oil Co., 1959, 135 Mont. 307, 340 P.2d 824; Ercanbrack v. Clark, 1932, 79 Utah 233, 8 P.2d 1093.

50. Adams v. Rivers, 1851, 11 Barb., N.Y., 390; Fullam v. Stearns, 1857, 30 Vt. 443; Ordway v. Ferrin, 1824, 3 N.H. 69; Hale v. Clark, 1838, 19 Wend., N.Y., 498; Louisville & N. R. Co. v. Bartee, 1920, 204 Ala. 539, 86 So. 394 (mere words not sufficient).

51. Six Carpenters Case, 1610, 8 Co.Rep. 146a, 77 Eng.Rep. 695.

52. Waterbury v. Lockwood, 1810, 4 Day, Conn., 257; Gardner v. Campbell, 1818, 15 Johns, N.Y., 401; Fullam v. Stearns, 1857, 30 Vt. 443.

53. "It is revolting to have no better reason for a rule of law than that so it was laid down in the time of Henry IV. It is still more revolting if the grounds upon which it was laid down have vanished long since, and the rule simply persists from blind imitation of the past." Holmes, The Path of the Law, 1897, 10 Harv.L.Rev. 457, 469.

See also the denunciation in McGuire v. United States, 1927, 273 U.S. 95; also Smith, Surviving Fictions, 1918, 27 Yale L.J. 147, 164; Bohlen and Shulman, Effect of Subsequent Misconduct Upon a Lawful Arrest, 1928, 28 Col.L.Rev. 841; Salmond, Law of Torts, 6th Ed. 1924, 232; Pollock, Law of Torts, 12th Ed. 1923, 402.

54. Cole v. Drew, 1871, 44 Vt. 49; McClannan v. Chaplain, 1923, 136 Va. 1, 116 S.E. 495; Second Restatement of Torts, § 214.

55. Malcom v. Spoor, 1847, 12 Metc., Mass., 279; Barrett v. White, 1825, 3 N.H. 210; Walsh v. Brown, 1907, 194 Mass. 317, 80 N.E. 465.

56. Cf. Mussey v. Cahoon, 1852, 34 Me. 74; Smith v. Gates, 1838, 21 Pick., Mass., 55; Bear v. Harris, 1896, 118 N.C. 476, 24 S.E. 364.

57. Smith, Surviving Fictions, 1918, 27 Yale L.J. 147, 164.

58. Bohlen and Shulman, Effect of Subsequent Misconduct Upon a Lawful Arrest, 1928, 28 Col.L.Rev. 841.

59. Bohlen and Shulman, Effect of Subsequent Misconduct Upon a Lawful Arrest, 1928, 28 Col.L.Rev. 841; Notes, 1940, 28 Cal.L.Rev. 646; 1945, 6 Mont. L.Rev. 61.

as to render it invalid, and make the defendant liable from the beginning.[60] Failure to use due diligence to bring the prisoner promptly before a magistrate has been given the same effect by many courts,[61] although there has been authority to the contrary.[62] A release of the prisoner without any presentment before a court, over his objection, has been regarded as a trespass ab initio by some courts,[63] and not by others.[64] As to any mistreatment of the prisoner,[65] or efforts to coerce him into compliance with orders,[66] there are surprisingly few cases.

Since around 1930 there have been decisions in some dozen jurisdictions, most of them overruling earlier cases, which have rejected the whole doctrine of trespass ab initio as applied to arrest, and have refused to hold

that there is any liability for the original privileged act, unless it was intended only as a cover for the subsequent misconduct.[67] This position has received the support of the Restatement of Torts, which has rejected the doctrine of trespass ab initio in all situations.[68] For these reasons, there is good reason to expect that the entire doctrine is on its way to oblivion.

26. ARREST WITHOUT A WARRANT

The details of the complex rules which have grown up around arrest without a warrant might better be considered in a treatise on criminal law.[69] A distinction necessarily has been made between the authority of officers of the law,[70] charged with the official duty of enforcing it, and that of private citizens.[71] The power to arrest has been limited according to the gravity of the crime with

60. Tubbs v. Tukey, 1893, 3 Cush., Mass., 438; Gibson v. Holmes, 1905, 78 Vt. 110, 62 A. 11; see Boston & Me. R. Co. v. Small, 1893, 85 Me. 462, 27 A. 349.

61. Nelson v. Eastern Air Lines, 1942, 128 N.J.L. 46, 24 A.2d 371; Bass v. State, 1949, 196 Misc. 177, 92 N.Y.S.2d 42; Peckham v. Warner Bros. Pictures, 1939, 36 Cal.App.2d 214, 97 P.2d 472; Leger v. Warren, 1900, 62 Ohio St. 500, 57 N.E. 506; Piedmont Hotel Co. v. Henderson, 1911, 9 Ga.App. 672, 72 S.E. 51.

62. Atchison, T. & S. F. R. Co. v. Hinsdell, 1907, 76 Kan. 74, 90 P. 800; Oxford v. Berry, 1913, 204 Mich. 197, 170 N.W. 83; Mulberry v. Fuellhart, 1902, 203 Pa. 573, 53 A. 504.

63. Keefe v. Hart, 1913, 213 Mass. 476, 100 N.E. 558; Stewart v. Feeley, 1902, 118 Iowa 524, 92 N.W. 670; Newhall v. Egan, 1908, 28 R.I. 584, 68 A. 471.

64. Atchison, T. & S. F. R. Co. v. Hinsdell, 1907, 76 Kan. 74, 90 P. 800; Harness v. Steele, 1902, 159 Ind. 286, 64 N.E. 875; Mulberry v. Fuellhart, 1902, 203 Pa. 573, 53 A. 504; Second Restatement of Torts, § 136.

65. Dumas v. Erie R. Co., 1935, 243 App.Div. 792, 278 N.Y.S. 197 (trespass ab initio); Grau v. Forge, 1919, 183 Ky. 521, 209 S.W. 369 (liability only for subsequent misconduct).

66. See Holley v. Mix, 1829, 3 Wend., N.Y., 350; Clark v. Tilton, 1907, 74 N.H. 330, 68 A. 335; Robbins v. Swift, 1894, 86 Me. 197, 29 A. 981 (all holding trespass ab initio).

The officer's subsequent misconduct does not impose liability upon one who assisted in a valid arrest. Dehm v. Hinman, 1887, 56 Conn. 320, 15 A. 741.

67. Dragna v. White, 1955, 45 Cal.2d 469, 289 P.2d 428; Anderson v. Foster, 1953, 73 Idaho 340, 252 P.2d 199; Shaw v. Courtney, 1943, 317 Ill.App. 422, 46 N.E.2d 170, affirmed 1943, 385 Ill. 559, 53 N.E.2d 432; Cline v. Tait, 1942, 113 Mont. 475, 129 P.2d 89; Brown v. Meier & Frank Co., 1939, 160 Or. 608, 86 P.2d 79.

68. See Second Restatement of Torts, §§ 214(2), 136, 278.

69. See Perkins, The Law of Arrest, 1940, 25 Iowa L.Rev. 201; Stone, Arrest Without Warrant, [1939] Wis.L.Rev. 385; Hall, The Law of Arrest in Relation to Contemporary Social Problems, 1936, 3 U. Chi.L.Rev. 345; Waite, The Law of Arrest, 1946, 24 Tex.L.Rev. 270; Potts, The Law of Arrest, 1949, 1 Baylor L.Rev. 397; Machen, Arrest Without Warrant in Misdemeanor Cases, 1954, 33 N.C.L.Rev. 17; Notes, 1953, 41 Ky.L.J. 455; 1969, 64 Nw.U.L. Rev. 229.

Also, as to particular jurisdictions, Perkins, The Tennessee Law of Arrest, 1949, 2 Vand.L.Rev. 509; Kauffman, The Law of Arrest in Maryland, 1941, 5 Md.L.Rev. 125; Miller, Arrest Without a Warrant by a Peace Officer in New York, 1946, 21 N.Y.U. L.Q.Rev. 61; Lugar, Arrest Without a Warrant in West Virginia, 1948, 48 W.Va.L.Q. 207; Note, 1956, 24 Tenn.L.Rev. 258.

70. As to the historical development of the law, as affected by the development of a professional police, see Hall, Legal and Social Aspects of Arrest Without a Warrant, 1936, 49 Harv.L.Rev. 566.

71. See Note, 1965, 65 Col.L.Rev. 502.

which the wrongdoer is to be charged. Highly technical distinctions have been drawn between felonies, which in general are major crimes; breaches of the peace, which are public offenses done by violence, or likely to create public disturbance; [72] and the greater number of minor criminal violations which are mere misdemeanors. The classification of a particular offense is very largely a matter of statute, and will vary in each jurisdiction. The unfortunate officer or citizen is required to know these distinctions, or to act at his peril. [73]

Broadly speaking, either an officer or a private citizen may arrest without a warrant to prevent a felony or a breach of the peace [74] which is being committed, or reasonably appears about to be committed, [75] in his presence. [76] Once the crime has been committed,

the jealous safeguards which the law always has thrown about the personal liberty of the individual have led to a restriction of the privilege. The officer, representing the state, may still arrest without legal process if he has information which affords a reasonable ground for suspicion that a felony has been committed, and that he has the right criminal. [77] The burden rests upon him to show that he has reasonable grounds, [78] and mere suspicion, unsupported by information, is not enough. [79] The private person may arrest if a felony has in fact been committed, and he has reasonable grounds to suspect the man whom he arrests, [80] but his authority depends upon the fact of the crime, and he must take the full risk that none has been committed. [81] A reasonable mistake as to the

---

72. Second Restatement of Torts, § 116.

73. "The rules adopted in the American Restatement of the Law of Torts are nearly as complicated as those in our [English] law. Both systems did right in grading crimes according to their gravity so far as the criminal is concerned. Both made a cardinal blunder in making this gradation a determinant not merely of the extent of liability of the criminal, but also of the liability of an innocent third person in a collateral matter like the arrest of the offender." Winfield, Law of Tort, 1st Ed. 1937, 236.

74. People v. Rounds, 1887, 67 Mich. 482, 35 N.W. 77 (officer); State v. Mancini, 1917, 91 Vt. 507, 101 A. 581 (officer); Commonwealth v. Gorman, 1934, 288 Mass. 294, 192 N.E. 618 (officer); Baltimore & O. R. Co. v. Cain, 1895, 81 Md. 87, 31 A. 801 (private person); Marcuchi v. Norfolk & W. R. Co., 1918, 81 W.Va. 548, 94 S.E. 979 (private person).

75. Handcock v. Baker, 1800, 2 Bos. & P. 260, 120 Eng.Rep. 1270 (murder about to be committed); State v. Hughlett, 1923, 124 Wash. 366, 214 P. 841 (reasonable belief felony being committed); Malley v. Lane, 1921, 97 Conn. 133, 115 A. 674 (felony committed); State v. Hum Quock, 1931, 89 Mont. 503, 300 P. 220 (felony committed); Byrd v. Commonwealth, 1932, 158 Va. 897, 164 S.E. 400 (felony and breach of the peace).

76. "In his presence" requires that the officer shall be aware of the offense by some perception before the arrest. Snyder v. United States, 4 Cir.1922, 285 F. 1; Black v. State, 1937, 63 Okl.Cr. 317, 74 P.2d 1172. But it is sufficient if the crime is per-

ceived by sight, Robertson v. Commonwealth, 1923, 198 Ky. 699, 249 S.W. 1010; People v. Martin, 1955, 45 Cal.App.2d 755, 290 P.2d 855; People v. Esposito, 1922, 118 Misc. 867, 194 N.Y.S. 326; hearing, State v. Blackwelder, 1921, 182 N.C. 899, 109 S.E. 644; Davis v. Commonwealth, Ky.1955, 280 S.W.2d 714; smell, United States v. Fischer, D.Pa. 1930, 38 F.2d 830; People v. Bock Leung Chew, 1956, 142 Cal.App.2d 400, 298 P.2d 118; mechanical devices, United States v. Harnish, D.Me.1934, 7 F. Supp. 305, or even a confession. State v. Gulczynski, 1922, 2 W.W.Harr., Del., 120, 120 A. 88.

77. Beckwith v. Philby, 1827, 6 B. & C. 635, 108 Eng. Rep. 585; State v. Smith, 1960, 56 Wash.2d 368, 353 P.2d 155; Stephens v. United States, 1959, 106 U.S.App.D.C. 249, 271 F.2d 832; Chesapeake & O. R. Co. v. Welch, 1937, 268 Ky. 93, 103 S.W.2d 698; Kirk v. Garrett, 1896, 84 Md. 383, 35 A. 1089. See Note, 1936, 24 Ky.L.J. 229.

78. Jackson v. Knowlton, 1899, 173 Mass. 94, 52 N.E. 134.

79. Laster v. Chaney, 1937, 180 Miss. 110, 177 So. 524; People v. Caruso, 1930, 339 Ill. 258, 171 N.E. 128; United States v. Gowen, 2 Cir. 1930, 40 F.2d 593; Kilkanes v. Willestoft, 1942, 13 Wash.2d 127, 124 P.2d 219.

80. Burns v. Erben, 1869, 40 N.Y. 463; Reuck v. McGregor, 1866, 32 N.J.L. 70; Davis v. United States, 1900, 16 U.S.App.D.C. 442; American Ry. Express Co. v. Summers, 1922, 208 Ala. 531, 94 So. 737.

81. Carr v. State, 1884, 43 Ark. 99; Garnier v. Squires, 1900, 62 Kan. 321, 62 P. 1005; Martin v. Houck, 1906, 141 N.C. 317, 54 S.E. 291; Enright v. Gibson, 1906, 219 Ill. 550, 76 N.E. 689. A fortiori

individual will protect him, but a mistake as to the felony will not. It has even been held that the felony which has occurred must be the very one for which he purports to make the arrest.[82]

For a past breach of the peace which is not a felony, neither the officer nor the citizen may arrest without a warrant,[83] unless the offense was committed in his presence, and he is in fresh pursuit.[84] For mere misdemeanors, the accepted common law rule is that neither the officer [85] nor the citizen [86] may arrest without a warrant, although some few jurisdictions have extended the power to an officer where the misdemeanor is committed in his presence.[87]

The person arrested must be informed of the charges against him,[88] and an arrest made upon an improper ground cannot later be justified because there was a proper one available.[89] An officer may call upon private persons to assist him in making any arrest, and those who do so will be privileged, even though the officer himself is without authority,[90] so long as he is known to be a peace cfficer.[91] But one who assists another private person must take the risk that there is authority for the arrest.[92]

These rules have been subjected to vigorous criticism, particularly as they allow obviously guilty criminals time to escape in a very mobile civilization, and invalidate arrests or prevent the admission of evidence, where guilt might clearly be proved.[93] They have been altered by statute in many states, and are likely to undergo further modification in the future.

The arrest and confinement of supposed lunatics, without a court order directing it, is at the risk of the person making the arrest, to the extent that the only possible jus-

where there is no reasonable ground to suspect the plaintiff. Maliniemi v. Gronlund, 1892, 92 Mich. 222, 52 N.W. 627; Morley v. Chase, 1887, 143 Mass. 396, 9 N.E. 767.

Even where there is a felony, there may be liability for failure to take proper precautions to see that the right person is arrested. Wallner v. Fidelity & Deposit Co., 1948, 253 Wis. 66, 33 N.W.2d 215. As to the privilege of temporary detention to investigate, see supra, p. 121.

82. Walters v. Smith & Sons, [1914] 1 K.B. 595.

83. State v. Lewis, 1893, 50 Ohio St. 179, 33 N.E. 405; Wahl v. Walton, 1883, 30 Minn. 506, 16 N.W. 397; John Bad Elk v. United States, 1900, 177 U.S. 529 (officers); Baynes v. Brewster, 1841, 2 Q.B. 375 (private person).

84. Curry v. Commonwealth, 1923, 199 Ky. 90, 250 S.W. 793; Wiegand v. Meade, 1932, 108 N.J.L. 471, 158 A. 825. Cf. Yates v. State, 1907, 127 Ga. 813, 56 S.E. 1017 (delay of several months).

85. State v. Mobley, 1954, 240 N.C. 476, 83 S.E.2d 100; People v. McLean, 1888, 68 Mich. 480, 36 N.W. 231; Caffini v. Hermann, 1914, 112 Me. 282, 91 A. 1009; Davids v. State, 1955, 208 Md. 377, 118 A.2d 636; McCrary v. State, 1936, 131 Tex.Cr.R. 233, 97 S.W. 2d 236 (sexual intercourse in presence of officer).

86. Fox v. Gaunt, 1832, 3 B. & Ad. 798, 110 Eng.Rep. 293; Palmer v. Maine Cent. R. Co., 1899, 92 Me. 399, 42 A. 800; Union Depot & R. Co. v. Smith, 1891, 16 Colo. 361, 37 P. 329. Cf. Jennings v. Riddle, 1935, 20 Tenn.App. 89, 95 S.W.2d 946.

87. Coverstone v. Davies, 1952, 38 Cal.2d 315, 239 P. 2d 876, cert. denied Mock v. Davies, 344 U.S. 840; St. Clair v. Smith, Okl.1956, 293 P.2d 597; State v. Deitz, 1925, 136 Wash. 228, 239 P. 386; State ex rel. Verdis v. Fidelity & Cas. Co., 1938, 120 W.Va. 593, 199 S.E. 884; see Carroll v. United States, 1925, 267

U.S. 132. See Bohlen and Shulman, Arrest With and Without a Warrant, 1927, 75 U.Pa.L.Rev. 485; Note, 1925, 25 So.Cal.L.Rev. 449.

88. Squadrito v. Griebsch, 1955, 1 App.Div.2d 760, 147 N.Y.S.2d 553, reversed, 1956, 1 N.Y.2d 471, 154 N.Y.S. 2d 37, 136 N.E.2d 504.

89. Noe v. Meadows, 1929, 229 Ky. 53, 16 S.W.2d 505 (adding that if the arrest is made on more than one ground, and justification is found for one only, the arrest is justified).

90. Watson v. State, 1887, 83 Ala. 60, 3 So. 441; Firestone v. Rice, 1888, 71 Mich. 377, 38 N.W. 885; Peterson v. Robison, 1954, 43 Cal.2d 690, 277 P.2d 19. In any case the citizen is privileged to the same extent as the officer. Byrd v. Commonwealth, 1932, 158 Va. 897, 164 S.E. 400. See Note, 1958, 13 Wyo. L.J. 72.

91. Dietrichs v. Schaw, 1873, 43 Ind. 175; Cincinnati, N. O. & T. P. R. Co. v. Cundiff, 1915, 166 Ky. 594, 179 S.W. 615.

92. Salisbury v. Commonwealth, 1908, 79 Ky. 425; Ryan v. Donnelly, 1873, 71 Ill. 100.

93. Waite, Some Inadequacies in the Law of Arrest, 1931, 29 Mich.L.Rev. 448; Waite, Public Policy and the Arrest of Felons, 1933, 31 Mich.L.Rev. 749.

tification is the apparent necessity of protecting others, or the insane person himself. It is not enough that the person arrested is believed to be insane,[94] but there must be good reason to believe that he will do serious harm to himself or another,[95] before the privilege exists.

Reasonable Force

Since very few arrests are with the consent of the criminal, the authority to make the arrest, whether it be with or without a warrant, must necessarily carry with it the privilege of using all reasonable force to effect it. Whether the force used is reasonable is a question of fact, to be determined in the light of the circumstances of each particular case.[96] In any case the defendant can never use more force than reasonably appears to be necessary, or subject the person arrested to unnecessary risk of harm. The use of deadly force, likely to cause serious injury is a matter upon which the courts have not always agreed.[97] There is no dispute that such force may be used to prevent the commission of a felony which threatens the life or safety of a human being,[98] including the burglary of a dwelling house, which from its nature is so regarded.[99] As to felonies which involve no such danger, the tendency in the modern cases is to say that the use of deadly force is unreasonable in proportion to the offense.[1]

Once the crime has been committed, the interest chiefly concerned is that of the state in apprehending the criminal. It is reasonable that much the same distinction should be made, although the courts have not agreed upon it: deadly force may certainly be used to enforce the arrest of the dangerous criminal whose offense has threatened human life or safety,[2] but not one guilty of such felonies as theft,[3] for which the state never punishes by death, and seldom by a major penalty. There are, however, a considerable number of decisions which have held that any felony

---

94. Fletcher v. Fletcher, 1859, 28 L.J.Q.B. 134; Witte v. Haben, 1915, 131 Minn. 71, 154 N.W. 662; Crawford v. Brown, 1926, 321 Ill. 305, 151 N.E. 911; Maxwell v. Maxwell, 1920, 189 Iowa 7, 177 N.W. 541; Porter v. Ritch, 1898, 70 Conn. 235, 39 A. 169; see Note, 1950, 35 Corn.L.Q. 904. But mental irresponsibility will be sufficient, and technical insanity need not be proved. Forsythe v. Ivey, 1932, 162 Miss. 471, 139 So. 615.

95. Look v. Dean, 1871, 108 Mass. 116; Keleher v. Putnam, 1880, 60 N.H. 30; Crawford v. Brown, 1926, 321 Ill. 305, 151 N.E. 911; cf. Christiansen v. Weston, 1930, 36 Ariz. 200, 284 P. 149. But a reasonable appearance of necessity usually has been held to be enough. Babb v. Carson, 1924, 116 Kan. 690, 229 P. 76; Dyer v. Dyer, 1941, 178 Tenn. 234, 156 S.W.2d 445; Forsythe v. Ivey, 1932, 162 Miss. 471, 139 So. 615; Springer v. Steiner, 1919, 91 Or. 100, 178 P. 592; Bisgaard v. Duvall, 1915, 169 Iowa 711, 151 N.W. 1051. Even here, however, it has been held that the defendant must follow the procedure prescribed by statute, if he can. Jillson v. Caprio, 1950, 86 U.S.App.D.C. 168, 181 F.2d 523.

96. Coles v. McNamara, 1924, 131 Wash. 377, 230 P. 430; State v. Montgomery, 1910, 230 Mo. 660, 132 S.W. 232; State v. Pugh, 1888, 101 N.C. 737, 7 S.E. 757. See, generally, Perkins, The Law of Arrest, 1940, 25 Iowa L.Rev. 201, 265–289.

97. See Pearson, The Right to Kill in Making Arrests, 1930, 28 Mich.L.Rev. 957; Bohlen and Shulman, Arrest With and Without a Warrant, 1927, 75 U.Pa.L.Rev. 485, 494; Note, 1938, 24 Iowa L.Rev. 154.

98. Dill v. State, 1854, 25 Ala. 15; In re Neagle, 1890, 135 U.S. 1.

99. Cf. State v. Patterson, 1873, 45 Vt. 308; People v. Kuehn, 1892, 93 Mich. 619, 53 N.W. 721; Wright v. Commonwealth, 1887, 85 Ky. 123, 2 S.W. 904.

1. Storey v. State, 1862, 71 Ala. 329; Demato v. People, 1910, 49 Colo. 147, 111 P. 703. Cf. State v. Plumlee, 1933, 177 La. 687, 149 So. 425; State v. Beckham, 1924, 306 Mo. 566, 267 S.W. 817.

2. State v. Smith, 1905, 127 Iowa 534, 103 N.W. 944; Harvey v. City of Bonner Springs, 1917, 102 Kan. 9, 169 P. 563; Crawford v. Commonwealth, 1931, 241 Ky. 391, 44 S.W.2d 286. See the discussion in the Notes, 1950, 38 Ky.L.Rev. 609, 618.

3. State v. Bryant, 1871, 65 N.C. 327; Storey v. State, 1882, 71 Ala. 329, 339; Thomas v. Kinkead, 1891, 55 Ark. 502, 18 S.W. 854; Donehy v. Commonwealth, 1916, 170 Ky. 474, 186 S.W. 161. See Pearson, The Right to Kill in Making Arrests, 1930, 28 Mich.L.Rev. 957, 974; Note, 1938, 24 Iowa L.Rev. 154.

justifies killing to enforce an arrest.[4] Arrest for a misdemeanor, it is everywhere agreed, does not justify the use of such deadly force, even though the criminal is in flight, and there is no other possible way to apprehend him.[5] If there is resistance, the arresting party may of course defend himself, and kill if it is necessary for his own protection,[6] and he is not required to retreat if a way is open, but may assert his legal authority and stand his ground.[7] But if the resistance does not threaten his safety, the better view, notwithstanding decisions in some states to the contrary,[8] is that the public interest in an arrest for a misdemeanor does not justify the use of deadly force.[9] By the same token, it is regarded as reasonable force to break in the door of a dwelling house to prevent a serious crime,[10] or to arrest after it has occurred,[11] but not to arrest for a misdemeanor,[12] unless the arrest is under a warrant.[13]

If the arrest is unlawful, the traditional rule has been that it may be resisted by reasonable force.[14] But here again, the harm which is likely to be inflicted by unlawful arrest is not sufficiently important to justify the infliction of serious injury, and the use of deadly force is not reasonable, where the personal safety of the one resisting is not in danger.[15] The whole modern trend has been in the direction of requiring submission to asserted legal authority, in the interest of keeping the peace; and the Uniform Arrest Act,[16] as well as the Model Penal Code,[17] has closely limited the privilege of resistance.

It must be repeated once more that these rules, which represent a wavering attempt to strike some balance between the public interest in the prevention of crime and the speedy apprehension of criminals, and the interest

4. Jackson v. State, 1898, 66 Miss. 89, 5 So. 690; Stinnett v. Commonwealth, 4 Cir.1932, 55 F.2d 644; Ex parte Warner, D.Okl.1927, 21 F.2d 542; Thompson v. Norfolk & W. R. Co., 1935, 116 W.Va. 705, 182 S.E. 880; Johnson v. Chesapeake & O. R. Co., 1935, 259 Ky. 789, 83 S.W.2d 521. Cf. Davis v. Hellwig, 1956, 21 N.J. 412, 122 A.2d 497.

5. Moore v. Foster, 1938, 182 Miss. 15, 180 So. 73; Evans v. Walker, 1939, 237 Ala. 385, 187 So. 189; Padilla v. Chavez, 1957, 62 N.M. 170, 306 P.2d 1094; State ex rel. Harbin v. Dunn, 1943, 39 Tenn.App. 190, 282 S.W.2d 203; Stevens v. Adams, 1930, 181 Ark. 816, 27 S.W.2d 999; Notes, 1938, 24 Iowa L.Rev. 154; 1940, 5 Mo.L.Rev. 93.

6. Donehy v. Commonwealth, 1916, 170 Ky. 474, 186 S.W. 161; State v. Smith, 1905, 127 Iowa 534, 103 N.W. 944; People v. Hardwick, Cal.App.1928, 260 P. 946, subsequent opinion 204 Cal. 582, 269 P. 427; Gordy v. State, 1956, 93 Ga.App. 743, 92 S.E.2d 737. A fortiori where the force used is not calculated to cause death or serious injury. State v. Phillips, 1903, 119 Iowa 652, 94 N.W. 229.

7. Durham v. State, 1927, 199 Ind. 567, 159 N.E. 145; State v. Dunning, 1919, 177 N.C. 559, 98 S.E. 530; State v. Vargas, 1937, 42 N.M. 1, 74 P.2d 62.

8. State v. Dierberger, 1888, 96 Mo. 666, 10 S.W. 168; Commonwealth v. Marcum, 1909, 135 Ky. 1, 122 S.W. 215; Krueger v. State, 1920, 171 Wis. 566, 177 N.W. 917.

9. Thomas v. Kinkead, 1892, 55 Ark. 502, 18 S.W. 854; People v. Klein, 1922, 305 Ill. 141, 137 N.E. 145; Meldrum v. State, 1914, 23 Wyo. 12, 146 P. 596; People v. Newsome, 1921, 51 Cal.App. 42, 195 P. 938.

10. Handcock v. Baker, 1800, 2 Bos. & P. 260, 120 Eng.Rep. 1270; State v. Stouderman, 1851, 6 La. Ann. 286.

11. Shanley v. Wells, 1873, 71 Ill. 78; Commonwealth v. Phelps, 1911, 209 Mass. 396, 95 N.E. 868; Read v. Case, 1822, 4 Conn. 166.

12. Adair v. Williams, 1922, 24 Ariz. 422, 210 P. 853; McLennon v. Richardson, 1860, 15 Gray, Mass., 74; Hughes v. State, 1922, 145 Tenn. 544, 238 S.W. 588.

13. Hawkins v. Commonwealth, 1854, 14 B.Mon., Ky., 395; Commonwealth v. Reynolds, 1876, 120 Mass. 190.

14. Finch v. State, 1960, 101 Ga.App. 73, 112 S.E.2d 824; Jenkins v. State, 1963, 232 Md. 529, 194 A.2d 618; People v. Cherry, 1954, 307 N.Y. 308, 121 N.E. 2d 238; State v. Morrissey, 1962, 257 N.C. 679, 127 S.E.2d 283; State v. Rousseau, 1952, 40 Wash.2d 92, 241 P.2d 447.

15. State v. Perrigo, 1895, 67 Vt. 406, 31 A. 844; State v. Gum, 1910, 68 W.Va. 105, 69 S.E. 463.

16. Uniform Arrest Act, §§ 5, 6. See Warner, The Uniform Arrest Act, 1942, 28 Va.L.Rev. 315.

17. Model Penal Code, § 3.04(2). In State v. Koonce, 1965, 89 N.J.Super. 169, 214 A.2d 428, the court accomplished the same result without a statute. See Notes, 1966, 27 U.Pitt.L.Rev. 716; 1966, 12 Wayne L.Rev. 883.

of the individual in freedom from interference at the hands of the law, have been modified extensively by statutes in many jurisdictions. Reference must be made to the legislation and decisions of each state, as to the validity of any particular rule.

27. DISCIPLINE

In certain situations, the necessity of some degree of orderly discipline vests in persons in control of others the authority to use summary force and restraint, and they will be protected in the exercise of it, if they act in good faith, and in a reasonable manner.

A husband or father, as the head of the household, was recognized by the early law as having authority to discipline the members of his family. He might administer to his wife "moderate correction," and "restrain" her by "domestic chastisement," [18] although there is probably no truth whatever in the legend that he was permitted to beat her with a stick no thicker than his thumb.[19] The altered position and independent legal status of married women in modern society has done away with any such discipline. Physical chastisement [20] or imprisonment [21] of a wife is everywhere a crime. As a tort, it is limited by the rule which still prevails in many jurisdictions, that one spouse may not maintain an action against the other for a personal tort.[22] Where this rule has been abandoned, the wife may recover.[23] The

early privilege to chastise domestic servants also is no longer recognized, and the employer's only remedy is discharge, or an action for damage done.[24]

As to children, the privilege remains, despite any modern theories that to spare the rod is not to spoil the child. A parent, or one who stands in the place of a parent,[25] may use reasonable force, including corporal punishment, for discipline and control. A school teacher has the same authority.[26] It is sometimes said that the parent, by sending the child to school, has delegated his discipline to the teacher; [27] but since many children go to public schools under compulsion of law, and the child may well be punished over the objection of the parent, a sounder reason is the necessity for maintaining order in and about the school.[28] The teacher's authority extends to all offenses which directly and immediately affect the decorum and morale of the school,[29] including acts done away from

---

18. 1 Bl.Comm., 1765, 444; Stedman, Right of Husband to Chastise Wife, 1917, 3 Va.L.Reg., N.S., 241.

19. See State v. Rhodes, 1868, 61 N.C. 453. But cf. Lord Leigh's Case, 1675, 3 Keble, 433, 84 Eng.Rep. 807, saying that "the salva moderata castigatione in the register is not meant of beating, but only admonition and confinement to the house, in case of extravagance. The Court agreed, she being not as an apprentice."

20. Fulgham v. State, 1871, 46 Ala. 143; Commonwealth v. McAfee, 1871, 108 Mass. 458.

21. Regina v. Jackson, [1891] 1 Q.B. 671.

22. See infra, § 122.

23. Brown v. Brown, 1914, 88 Conn. 42, 89 A. 889; Johnson v. Johnson, 1917, 201 Ala. 41, 77 So. 335; Fiedler v. Fiedler, 1914, 42 Okl. 124, 140 P. 1022.

24. Tinkle v. Dunivant, 1886, 16 Lea, Tenn., 503.

25. Steber v. Norris, 1925, 188 Wis. 366, 206 N.W. 173; Clasen v. Pruhs, 1903, 69 Neb. 278, 95 N.W. 640; Fortinberry v. Holmes, 1907, 89 Miss. 373, 42 So. 799 (one caring for child); Gorman v. State, 1875, 42 Tex. 221 (stepfather); State v. Alford, 1873, 68 N.C. 322 (paramour of mother).

26. See Proehl, Tort Liability of Teachers, 1959, 12 Vand.L.Rev. 723; Notes, 1926, 11 Corn.L.Q. 266; 1964, 15 Hast.L.J. 567.

27. State v. Pendergrass, 1837, 19 N.C. 365; Cleary v. Booth, [1893] 1 Q.B. 465; Quinn v. Nolan, 1878, 7 Ohio Dec.Repr. 585.

28. Stevens v. Fassett, 1847, 27 Me. 266; Lander v. Seaver, 1859, 32 Vt. 114; McLeod v. Grant County School District, 1953, 42 Wash.2d 316, 255 P.2d 360. See Sumption, The Control of Pupil Conduct by the School, 1955, 20 Law & Con.Prob. 80; Proehl, Tort Liability of Teachers, 1959, 12 Vand.L.Rev. 723, 726–7; Note, 1932, 26 Ill.L.Rev. 815.

29. Fertich v. Michener, 1887, 111 Ind. 472, 11 N.E. 605, 14 N.E. 68; Heritage v. Dodge, 1886, 64 N.H. 297, 9 A. 722; Sheehan v. Sturges, 1885, 53 Conn. 481, 2 A. 841; Wilson v. Abilene Independent School District, Tex.Civ.App.1945, 190 S.W.2d 406. Various kinds of rules and regulations which have been unheld are discussed in Sumption, The Control of Pupil Conduct by the School, 1955, 20 Law & Con. Prob. 80, 82–87.

the school premises,[30] but not to outside misconduct by which the school is only remotely affected.[31]

The privilege of either parent or teacher [32] extends to the infliction of any corporal punishment which is reasonable under the circumstances; but neither is privileged to use any force which goes beyond that reasonably necessary for the purpose to be accomplished.[33] All of the circumstances are to be taken into consideration, including the nature of the offense, the age, sex and strength of the child, his past behavior, the kind of punishment, and the extent of the harm inflicted.[34]

There are some courts, particularly in the older cases, which have said that the judgment of the parent or teacher must control as to the reasonableness of the force used, so long as he acts without malice, and inflicts no serious injury,[35] but the later cases have decided, it would seem more properly for the protection of the helpless at the mercy of the merciless, that the defendant is held to an external standard of what is reasonable under the circumstances.[36]

In most jurisdictions, the old rule that a child may not maintain an action against a parent for a personal tort still prevents any civil remedy for excessive force.[37] Where the action can be brought, the child may recover.[38] The rule, of course, affords no immunity to a teacher.

For obvious reasons, military and naval officers have a power of discipline over their subordinates, which is governed by military law.[39] The necessities of the sea have established a time-honored authority in the master of a ship, not only over the crew, but also over passengers. But here again, the

---

30. Cleary v. Booth, [1893] 1 Q.B. 465; Lander v. Seaver, 1859, 32 Vt. 114 (insulting teacher); O'Rourke v. Walker, 1925, 102 Conn. 130, 128 A. 25 (abusing other pupils); Hutton v. State, 1887, 23 Tex.App. 386, 5 S.W. 122 (fighting); Morrison v. Lawrence, 1904, 186 Mass. 456, 72 N.E. 91 (insulting teacher); Jones v. Cody, 1902, 132 Mich. 13, 92 N.W. 495 (failure to go home from school). See Note, 1926, 11 Corn.L.Q. 266.

31. Murphy v. Board of Directors, 1870, 30 Iowa 429 (article ridiculing school board); State ex rel. Clark v. Osborne, 1887, 24 Mo.App. 309; 1888, 32 Mo.App. 536 (attending social gathering). The privilege does not extend to forcible treatment of injury or disease. Guerrieri v. Tyson, 1942, 147 Pa.Super. 239, 24 A.2d 468.

32. Suits v. Glover, 1954, 260 Ala. 449, 71 So.2d 49; Drake v. Thomas, 1941, 310 Ill.App. 57, 33 N.E.2d 889; State v. Pendergrass, 1837, 19 N.C. 365; People v. Curtiss, 1931, 116 Cal.App.Supp. 771, 300 P. 801.

33. People v. Green, 1909, 155 Mich. 524, 119 N.W. 1087; Clasen v. Pruhs, 1903, 69 Neb. 278, 95 N.W. 640; State v. Vanderbilt, 1888, 116 Ind. 11, 18 N.E. 266; Calway v. Williamson, 1944, 130 Conn. 575, 36 A.2d 377 (kneeling on stomach); Frank v. Orleans Parish School Board, La.App. 1967, 195 So.2d 451, writ refused 250 La. 635, 197 So.2d 653 (lifting, shaking and dropping boy).

34. Fabian v. State, 1964, 235 Md. 306, 201 A.2d 511; Tinkham v. Kole, 1961, 252 Iowa 1303, 110 N.W.2d 258; Marlar v. Bill, 1944, 181 Tenn. 100, 178 S.W.2d 634 ("slight punishment with a ruler" reasonable); Fertich v. Michener, 1887, 111 Ind. 472, 11 N.E. 605, rehearing denied 14 N.E. 68 (detention after school); Patterson v. Nutter, 1886, 78 Me. 509, 7 A. 273. See Miller, Resort to Corporal Punishment in Enforcing School Discipline, 1950, 1 Syr.L.Rev. 247; Note, 1926, 11 Corn.L.Q. 266.

Considerable force may be justified in the case of an insolent or incorrigible pupil. Drake v. Thomas,

---

1941, 310 Ill.App. 57, 33 N.E.2d 889; Andreozzi v. Rubano, 1958, 145 Conn. 280, 141 A.2d 639.

35. State v. Pendergrass, 1837, 19 N.C. 365; Boyd v. State, 1889, 88 Ala. 169, 7 So. 268; Heritage v. Dodge, 1886, 64 N.H. 297, 9 A. 722; Dean v. State, 1890, 89 Ala. 46, 8 So. 38; People v. Green, 1909, 155 Mich. 524, 119 N.W. 1087. In other words, only good faith is required. This position is defended in Cooperrider, Child v. Parent in Tort: A Case for the Jury? 1958, 43 Minn.L.Rev. 73.

36. Patterson v. Nutter, 1886, 78 Me. 509, 7 A. 273; Steber v. Norris, 1925, 188 Wis. 366, 206 N.W. 173; People v. Curtiss, 1931, 116 Cal.App.Supp. 771, 300 P. 801; Clasen v. Pruhs, 1903, 69 Neb. 278, 95 N.W. 640; State v. Fischer, 1953, 245 Iowa 170, 60 N.W.2d 105; cf. Drum v. Miller, 1904, 135 N.C. 204, 47 S.E. 421. See Note, 1932, 26 Ill.L.Rev. 815.

37. See infra, § 122.

38. Treschman v. Treschman, 1901, 28 Ind.App. 206, 61 N.E. 961. Criminal liability for battery never was affected by the immunity. Cf. State v. Black, 1950, 360 Mo. 261, 227 S.W.2d 1006.

39. See for example Keppleman v. Upston, N.D.Cal. 1949, 84 F.Supp. 478 (false imprisonment); Wright v. White, 1941, 166 Or. 136, 110 P.2d 948 (malicious prosecution).

authority is limited, and the use of unreasonable force becomes a tort. The captain will be liable if he attacks a steward with a belaying pin for disobedience,[40] or puts a passenger in irons for calling him the landlord of a floating hotel.[41]

In many cases, the order of a superior officer has been held to protect a soldier or inferior officer from liability, where it was apparently lawful, and any want of authority was unknown to the inferior.[42] By analogy to the case of a civil officer executing a warrant "fair on its face,"[43] this seems the desirable rule, notwithstanding occasional cases to the contrary.[44]

---

40. Padmore v. Piltz, D.Wash.1890, 44 F. 104; Brown v. Howard, 1817, 14 Johns., N.Y., 119 (brutal punishment). The flogging of sailors, upheld in Michaelson v. Denison, C.C.Conn.1808, Fed.Cas.No.9,523, 3 Day 294, would quite certainly not be permitted today.

41. King v. Franklin, 1858, 1 F. & F. 360, 175 Eng.Rep. 764. In all cases which will admit of the delay, due inquiry should precede the act of punishment, and the party charged should be heard in his own defense. The Agincourt, 1824, 1 Hagg. 271, 166 Eng. Rep. 96.

42. Herlihy v. Donohue, 1916, 52 Mont. 601, 161 P. 164; Franks v. Smith, 1911, 142 Ky. 232, 134 S.W. 484; Trammell v. Bassett, 1866, 24 Ark. 299; cf. United States v. Clark, C.C.Mich. 1887, 31 F. 710; Neu v. McCarthy, 1941, 309 Mass. 17, 33 N.E.2d 570. See Second Restatement of Torts, § 146.

43. See supra, p. 128.

44. Bates v. Clark, 1877, 95 U.S. 204.

CHAPTER 5

NEGLIGENCE: STANDARD OF CONDUCT

28. HISTORY

Negligence was scarcely recognized as a separate tort before the earlier part of the nineteenth century.[1] Prior to that time the word had been used in a very general sense to describe the breach of any legal obligation, or to designate a mental element, usually one of inadvertence or indifference, entering into the commission of other torts.[2] Some writers, in fact, once maintained that negligence was merely one way of committing any other tort, and itself had no particular legal significance,[3] just as some courts, for example, still speak occasionally of a negligent "battery." [4] But for more than a century, it has received more or less general recognition as an independent basis of liability, with distinct features of its own, differing on the one hand from the intentional torts, and on the other from those in which strict liability is imposed.

One of the earliest appearances of what we now know as negligence was in the liability of those who professed to be competent in certain "public" callings. A carrier, an innkeeper, a blacksmith, or a surgeon, was regarded as holding himself out to the public as one in whom confidence might be reposed, and hence as assuming an obligation to give proper service, for the breach of which, by any negligent conduct, he might be liable.[5] But in the field of trespass and nuisance, the notion also developed, thinly disguised, that there might be liability for negligence; and in later years, the action on the case produced a large, undigested group of situations in which negligence was the essence of the tort.[6] Since the early law found its hands full in dealing with the more outrageous forms of misbehavior, it was natural that the early cases should be concerned almost exclusively with positive acts, rather than with omissions to act, or with "misfeasance" rather than "nonfeasance." There was a slow development of the idea that certain relations between the parties might impose an obligation to take affirmative action, so that there might be liability for nonfeasance.[7]

---

1. Winfield, The History of Negligence in the Law of Torts, 1926, 42 L.Q.Rev. 184; Miles, On Treatment of Negligence, Digest English Civil Law, 1910, 545; Gregory, Trespass to Negligence to Absolute Liability, 1951, 37 Va.L.Rev. 359.

2. Wigmore, Responsibility for Tortious Acts: Its History, 1894, 7 Harv.L.Rev. 315, 441, 453.

3. Salmond, Law of Torts, 6th Ed. 1924, 21–26; Jenks, History of English Law, 1934, 319, 320.

4. See supra, p. 30.

5. Winfield, The History of Negligence in the Law of Torts, 1926, 42 L.Q.Rev. 184; Ames, History of Assumpsit, 1888, 2 Harv.L.Rev. 1; Arterburn, The Origin and First Test of Public Callings, 1927, 75 U. Pa.L.Rev. 411.

6. Winfield, The History of Negligence in the Law of Torts, 1926, 42 L.Q.Rev. 184.

7. Bohlen, The Basis of Affirmative Obligations in the Law of Torts, 1905, 53 Am.L.Reg., N.S., 209, 293.

Any such obligation remains to this day very largely a matter of some specific relation, by reason of which the defendant may be regarded as having undertaken a duty to act.[8]

About the year 1825, negligence began to be recognized as a separate and independent basis of tort liability. Its rise coincided in a marked degree with the Industrial Revolution; and it very probably was stimulated by the rapid increase in the number of accidents caused by industrial machinery, and in particular by the invention of railways.[9] It undoubtedly was greatly encouraged by the disintegration of the old forms of action, and the disappearance of the distinction between direct and indirect injuries, found in trespass and case.[10] The cause of action which at last emerged from this process of reshuffling took on, in general, the aspects of the action on the case, largely because the facts upon which the initial decisions were based fitted that action. Intentional injuries, whether direct or indirect, began to be grouped as a distinct field of liability, and negligence remained as the main basis for unintended torts. Today it is not at all disputed that separate problems and principles, as well as distinct questions of policy, arise in negligence cases.

29. UNAVOIDABLE ACCIDENT

An unavoidable accident is an occurrence which was not intended, and which, under all the circumstances, could not have been foreseen or prevented by the exercise of reason-

8. See infra, § 56.

9. "Perhaps one of the chief agencies in the growth of the idea is industrial machinery. Early railway trains, in particular, were notable neither for speed nor for safety. They killed any object from a Minister of State to a wandering cow, and this naturally reacted on the law." Winfield, The History of Negligence in the Law of Torts, 1926, 42 L.Q.Rev. 184, 195.

10. See supra, § 7.

able precautions.[11] No accident, of course, is entirely inevitable, so long as it results from any voluntary act. If the defendant rides a horse, which runs away with him and injures the plaintiff, the accident is not strictly inevitable, since the defendant intentionally rode the horse, and might have prevented all harm by keeping him in the barn. But the runaway is called "unavoidable" if it did not result from any lack of proper care in the management of the horse, because both wrongful intent and negligence are lacking. There is no liability in such a case.[12] Upon exactly the same basis, the driver of an automobile who suddenly loses control of his car because he is seized with a heart attack,[13] a stroke,[14] a fainting spell,[15] or an epileptic

11. Uncapher v. Baltimore & O. R. Co., 1933, 127 Ohio St. 351, 188 N.E. 553; Morris v. Platt, 1864, 32 Conn. 75; Larrow v. Martell, 1918, 92 Vt. 435, 104 A. 826. As to the distinction between accident and mistake, see supra, § 17.

12. Gibbons v. Pepper, 1695, 1 Ld.Raym. 38, 91 Eng. Rep. 922; Steudle v. Rentchler, 1872, 64 Ill. 161.

As to the "unavoidable accident" instruction to the jury, see Rees, Unavoidable Accident—A Misunderstood Concept, 1964, 5 Ariz.L.Rev. 225. Also Note, 1966, 19 Okl.L.Rev. 308.

13. Ford v. Carew & English, 1948, 89 Cal.App.2d 199, 200 P.2d 828; Kreis v. Owens, 1955, 38 N.J. Super. 148, 118 A.2d 420; Weldon Tool Co. v. Kelley, 1947, 81 Ohio App. 427, 76 N.E.2d 629; McGovern v. Tinglof, 1962, 344 Mass. 114, 181 N.E.2d 573; First City Nat. Bank of Houston v. Japhet, Tex.Civ.App. 1965, 390 S.W.2d 70, error dismissed.

See Kraig, Heart Attack as a Defense in Negligence Actions, 1963, 12 Clev.Marsh.L.Rev. 59; Kerchner, Sudden Illness as a Defense in Auto Accidents, 1967, 16 Clev.Marsh.L.Rev. 523.

14. Baker v. Hausman, Fla.1953, 68 So.2d 572; Keller v. Wonn, 1955, 140 W.Va. 860, 87 S.E.2d 453. Cf. Haddox v. Indiana Lumbermen's Mut. Ins. Co., La. App.1963, 147 So.2d 732 (dog fight in front seat of car).

15. Armstrong v. Cook, 1930, 250 Mich. 180, 229 N.W. 433; Cohen v. Petty, 1933, 62 U.S.App.D.C. 187, 65 F.2d 820; Lehman v. Haynam, 1956, 164 Ohio St. 595, 133 N.E.2d 97. Cf. Kaiser v. Suburban Transp. System, 1965, 65 Wash.2d 461, 398 P.2d 14, amended 65 Wash.2d 461, 401 P.2d 350 (effect of drug taken on prescription); Porter v. Price, 1960, 11 Utah 2d 80, 355 P.2d 666 (insulin reaction).

fit,[16] or is merely overcome by slumber,[17] is not liable unless he knew that he was likely to become ill [18] or go to sleep,[19] in which case he is to be found negligent in driving the car at all. The same conclusions are reached when the defendant's car is struck by another vehicle and thrown out of control,[20] or a child unforeseeably dashes out in front of the car.[21]

Such rules are adopted because the line must be drawn somewhere, and if the defendant is to be held liable merely because he has ridden the horse or driven the car, it would be quite as logical, at least in the eyes of the law, to hold him liable for owning it, or even for drawing his breath or being born. To hold that he does every voluntary act at his peril, and must insure others against all of the consequences that may occur, would be an entirely unreasonable and quite intolerable burden upon all human activity.[22]

Nevertheless, as to injuries to person or property which followed as the more direct and immediate consequences of a voluntary act, and for which an action of trespass would lie, the early common law imposed a very strict responsibility.[23] The defendant who fired a gun, and accidentally wounded the plaintiff, was held liable unless he could establish that the accident was inevitable— "judged utterly without his fault; as if a man by force take my hand and strike you—" [24] and the burden was upon him to prove that such was the case.[25] As has been stated above,[26] the progress of the law [27] has been away from this position. There were jurisdictions in which the rule survived well into

16. Wishone v. Yellow Cab Co., 1936, 20 Tenn.App. 229, 97 S.W.2d 452; Shirks Motor Express v. Oxenham, 1954, 204 Md. 626, 106 A.2d 46, cert. denied 350 U.S. 966; Moore v. Capitol Transit Co., D.C.Cir. 1955, 96 U.S.App.D.C. 335, 226 F.2d 57, cert. denied 1956, 350 U.S. 966; Malcolm v. Patrick, Fla.App. 1962, 147 So.2d 188. Cf. Reeg v. Hodgson, 1964, 1 Ohio App.2d 272, 202 N.E.2d 310 (sudden cramp in foot); Haddox v. Indiana Lumbermen's Mut. Ins. Co., La.1963, 147 So.2d 732 (dog fight in car).

17. Bushnell v. Bushnell, 1925, 103 Conn. 583, 131 A. 432. Cf. Lobert v. Pack, 1939, 337 Pa. 103, 9 A.2d 365; Ballew v. Aiello, Mo.App.1967, 422 S.W.2d 396; Stokes v. Carlson, Mo.1951, 240 S.W.2d 132; Diamond State Tel. Co. v. Hunter, 1941, 2 Terry, Del., 336, 21 A.2d 286. But in Theisen v. Milwaukee Auto Mut. Ins. Co., 1962, 18 Wis.2d 91, 118 N.W.2d 140, rehearing denied, 1962, 18 Wis.2d 91, 119 N.W.2d 393, going to sleep while driving was held to be negligence as a matter of law, apparently on the basis that prior conduct must have been negligent. It was said that no facts can exist which will justify, excuse or exculpate falling asleep, except in cases of illness.

18. Eleason v. Western Cas. & Surety Co., 1948, 254 Wis. 134, 35 N.W.2d 301; Goodis v. Finkelstein, Fla. App.1965, 174 So.2d 600; Jackson v. Co-op. Cab Co., 1960, 102 Ga.App. 688, 117 S.E.2d 627; Goldman v. New York Ry. Co., 1919, 185 App.Div. 739, 173 N.Y.S. 737; see Kreis v. Owens, 1955, 38 N.J.Super. 148, 118 A.2d 420. Cf. Kohler v. Sheffert, 1959, 250 Iowa 899, 96 N.W.2d 911 (loss of consciousness from fright does not excuse prior negligence which caused it).

19. Bushnell v. Bushnell, 1925, 103 Conn. 583, 131 A. 432; Keller v. De Long, 1967, 108 N.H. 212, 231 A.2d 633; White v. King, 1966, 244 Md. 348, 223 A.2d 763, appeal after remand, 1968, 250 Md. 192, 242 A.2d 494; Shine v. Wujick, 1959, 89 R.I. 22, 150 A.2d 1; Wisconsin Nat. Gas Co. v. Employers' Mut. Liability Ins. Co., 1953, 263 Wis. 633, 58 N.W.2d 424.

See Kaufman and Kantrowitz, The Case of the Sleeping Motorist, 1950, 25 N.Y.U.L.Q.Rev. 362; Notes, [1950] Wis.L.Rev. 334; 1944, 18 St.Johns.L.Rev. 95.

20. Radcliffe v. Kostanden, Ohio Com.Pl.1959, 154 N.E.2d 671.

21. Geren v. Lowthian, 1957, 152 Cal.App.2d 230, 313 P.2d 12; Howell v. Roueche, 1955, 263 Ala. 83, 81

So.2d 297; Underwood v. Fultz, Okl.1958, 331 P.2d 375. Cf. Stephenson v. Wallis, 1957, 181 Kan. 254, 311 P.2d 355 (foot slipping from brake pedal found to be pure accident).

22. Holmes, The Common Law, 1881, 93–96.

23. 3 Holdsworth, History of English Law, 1931, 375 ff.; 1 Street, Foundations of Legal Liability, 1906, 73–85; Wigmore, Responsibility for Tortious Acts: Its History, 1884, 7 Harv.L.Rev. 315, 383, 441; Bohlen, Liability in Tort of Infants and Insane Persons, 1924, 23 Mich.L.Rev. 9. But compare Winfield, Law of Torts, 5th Ed. 1950, 43–44.

24. Weaver v. Ward, 1616, Hob. 134, 80 Eng.Rep. 284.

25. Weaver v. Ward, 1616, Hob. 134, 80 Eng.Rep. 284; Dickenson v. Watson, 1682, T. Jones 205, 84 Eng.Rep. 148; Leame v. Bray, 1803, 3 East 593, 102 Eng.Rep. 724.

26. Supra, § 7.

27. See 1 Street, Foundations of Legal Liability, 1906, 73–85; Wigmore, Responsibility for Tortious Acts: Its History, 1884, 7 Harv.L.Rev. 315, 383, 441.

the nineteenth century, that if the defendant voluntarily discharged the gun, he was liable for the injury.[28] But in Brown v. Kendall,[29] where the defendant, interfering in a dog fight, raised his stick and accidentally struck a man behind him, the Massachusetts court held that there was no liability in the absence of some wrongful intent or negligence. This case is now uniformly followed. The man who fires a gun,[30] the automobile driver whose tire blows out,[31] the boy on a bicycle who frightens a horse,[32] the man who instinctively and reasonable seizes another to save himself from falling,[33] are responsible for the damage done only if they have been at fault; and by the great weight of authority, the burden of proof of such fault is upon the plaintiff.[34]

There have been some vestiges of the older rule which have died hard. Strict liability for unavoidable accident still appears in one or two states, as a more or less antiquated survival, in trespass to land, where the trespasser is held liable not only for any accidental damage he may do in the course of his trespass, but for an accidental trespass itself.[35] It appears also in the case of the keeping of dangerous animals and other abnormally dangerous activities, where considerations of policy have been found to support it.[36] In a few states, it has been said in gunshot cases that the burden is upon the defendant to show that he was free from negligence; [37] but it is not clear that these cases mean to say more than that there is sufficient evidence of negligence in the occurrence of the accident itself to make out a prima facie case.

In England, the rule survived [38] until 1959, when it was finally laid to rest,[39] that where the injury to the plaintiff was direct and immediate, so that the ancient action of trespass would have lain, the defendant had the burden of proving that he was not negligent.

One form in which the older rule sometimes still appears is the statement found occasionally, that if the act itself was "unlawful," the actor is liable for all accidental consequences. Upon this basis, a defendant hunting on Sunday in violation of a statute was once held liable for shooting a companion by pure accident,[40] and one beating a horse was held for

28. Vincent v. Stinchour, 1835, 7 Vt. 62; Wright v. Clark, 1877, 50 Vt. 130; cf. Jennings v. Fundeburg, 1827, 4 McCord, S.C., 161; Morgan v. Cox, 1856, 22 Mo. 373.

29. 1850, 6 Cush. 292, 60 Mass. 292.

30. Fortier v. Stone, 1919, 79 N.H. 235, 107 A. 342; Tally v. Ayres, 1856, 3 Sneed, Tenn., 677; Annear v. Swartz, 1915, 46 Okl. 98, 148 P. 706; Davison v. Flowers, 1930, 123 Ohio St. 89, 174 N.E. 137; see Judd v. Ballard, 1894, 66 Vt. 668, 30 A. 96; cf. Taylor v. Franklin, 1925, 208 Ky. 43, 270 S.W. 462.

31. Kelly v. Gagnon, 1931, 121 Neb. 113, 236 N.W. 160; Hester v. Hall, 1919, 17 Ala.App. 25, 81 So. 361 (hogs darting in front of car); Rainwater v. Boatright, La.App.1952, 61 So.2d 212 (child darting in front of car); Larrow v. Martell, 1918, 92 Vt. 435, 104 A. 826 (moving car without knowledge of plaintiff's presence).

32. Holland v. Bartch, 1889, 120 Ind. 46, 22 N.E. 83. Cf. Stevens v. Gallagher, 1922, 224 Ill.App. 195 (golf ball flying off at right angle).

33. Filippone v. Reisenburger, 1909, 135 App.Div. 707, 119 N.Y.S. 632. Cf. Missouri Pac. R. Co. v. Richardson, 1932, 185 Ark. 472, 47 S.W.2d 794 (broken knee due to loose gravel on defendant's right of way); Leutine v. McAvoy, 1927, 105 Conn. 528, 136 A. 76.

34. Brown v. Kendall, 1850, 6 Cush., Mass., 292; Salerno v. Sheern, 1939, 62 R.I. 121, 2 A.2d 657; Fortier v. Stone, 1919, 79 N.H. 235, 107 A. 342; Cottrell v. Platt, 1897, 101 Iowa 231, 70 N.W. 177; Russo v. Porga, 1954, 141 Conn. 706, 109 A.2d 585. Thus inevitable accident may be shown under a general denial of an allegation of negligence, on which the plaintiff has the burden of proof. Jolley v. Clemens, 1938, 28 Cal.App.2d 55, 82 P.2d 51.

35. See supra, p. 64.

36. See infra, ch. 13.

37. Hawksley v. Peace, 1916, 38 R.I. 544, 96 A. 856; Atchison v. Dullam, 1884, 16 Ill.App. 42; Morgan v. Mulhall, 1908, 214 Mo. 451, 114 S.W. 4. Cf. In re Reichert Towing Line, 2 Cir. 1918, 251 F. 214, cert. denied, 248 U.S. 565.

38. Stanley v. Powell, [1891] 1 Q.B. 86, was taken as so holding. See Fleming, Law of Torts, 2d Ed. 1961, 22–23.

39. In Fowler v. Lanning, [1959] 1 Q.B. 426. See also Beals v. Hayward, [1960] N.Z.L.Rep. 131; Walmsley v. Humenick, [1954] 2 Dom.L.Rep. 232.

40. White v. Levarn, 1917, 93 Vt. 218, 108 A. 564.

an injury to a man.[41]   Under modern law, such a principle is certainly far too broad, except as it may perhaps have reference to the doctrine of "transferred intent,"[42] or perhaps to certain situations involving negligence.[43]   The conception of absolute fault, extending to all unavoidable consequences, is not workable in modern society; "with the increasing catalogue of unlawful acts, it can not be followed through."[44]   If the "unlawfulness" of the act consists merely in the violation of a statute designed to protect the interests of the state, or the public at large, against an entirely different kind of harm— as in the case of the Sunday statute—[45] there is no liability for results which could not have been avoided by reasonable care in the act itself.[46]

30. ELEMENTS OF CAUSE OF ACTION

Negligence, as we shall see,[47] is simply one kind of conduct.   But a cause of action founded upon negligence, from which liability will follow, requires more than conduct. The traditional formula for the elements nec-essary to such a cause of action may be stated briefly as follows: [48]

1. A duty, or obligation, recognized by the law, requiring the actor to conform to a certain standard of conduct, for the protection of others against unreasonable risks.[49]

2. A failure on his part to conform to the standard required.   These two elements go to make up what the courts usually have called negligence; but the term quite frequently is applied to the second alone.   Thus it may be said that the defendant was negligent, but is not liable because he was under no duty to the plaintiff not to be.

3. A reasonable close causal connection between the conduct and the resulting injury. This is what is commonly known as "legal cause," or "proximate cause." [50]

4. Actual loss or damage resulting to the interests of another.   Since the action for negligence developed chiefly out of the old form of action on the case, it retained the rule of that action, that proof of damage was an essential part of the plaintiff's case. Nominal damages, to vindicate a technical right, cannot be recovered in a negligence action, where no actual loss has occurred.[51]   The threat of future harm, not yet realized, is not enough.[52]   Negligent conduct in itself is not

---

41. Osborne v. Van Dyke, 1901, 113 Iowa 557, 85 N.W. 784.

42. Supra, p. 32.

43. See infra, p. 260.

44. Green, Judge and Jury, 1930, 318; Note 1918, 18 Col.L.Rev. 603.

45. Tingle v. Chicago, B. & Q. R. Co., 1882, 60 Iowa 333, 14 N.W. 320; Sutton v. Town of Wauwatosa, 1871, 29 Wis. 21; White v. Lang, 1880, 128 Mass. 598; Platz v. City of Cohoes, 1882, 89 N.Y. 219.

46. Bourne v. Whitman, 1911, 209 Mass. 155, 95 N.E. 404 (driving automobile without license); Cobb v. Cumberland County Power & Light Co., 1918, 117 Me. 455, 104 A. 844 (driving unregistered automobile); Muller v. West Jersey & S. R. Co., 1923, 99 N.J.L. 186, 122 A. 693 (same); Brown v. Shyne, 1926, 242 N.Y. 176, 151 N.E. 197 (practice of medicine without a license).   See infra, § 36.

Cf. Potter v. State, 1904, 162 Ind. 213, 70 N.E. 129 (carrying concealed weapon).

47. See infra, p. 145.

48. See Second Restatement of Torts, § 281; and for example, Mudrich v. Standard Oil Co., 1949, 87 Ohio App. 8, 86 N.E.2d 324, affirmed, 1950, 153 Ohio St. 31, 90 N.E.2d 859; Lee Street Auto Sales v. Warren, 1960, 102 Ga.App. 345, 116 S.E.2d 243.

49. See infra, § 53.

50. See infra, ch. 7.

51. Hall v. Cornett, 1952, 193 Or. 634, 240 P.2d 231; Kirby v. Carlisle, 1955, 178 Pa.Super. 389, 116 A. 2d 220; Elfer v. Hibernia Nat. Bank, La.App. 1937, 174 So. 287; Sullivan v. Old Colony St. R. Co., 1908, 200 Mass. 303, 86 N.E. 511; Northern Pac. R. Co. v. Lewis, 1896, 162 U.S. 366.   Contra, and clearly out of line, is Edwards v. Ely, 1943, 317 Ill.App. 599, 47 N.E.2d 344.

52. Johnson v. Rouchleau-Ray Iron Land Co., 1918, 140 Minn. 289, 168 N.W. 1.   It should be noted, however, that the danger of future harm may in itself cause present damage, as in nuisance cases,

such an interference with the interests of the world at large that there is any right to complain of it, or to be free from it, except in the case of some individual whose interests have suffered.

Such a statement must, however, be qualified to the extent that, as in the case of other torts, where irreparable injury is threatened, a court of equity may act by injunction to prevent the harm before it occurs. Even here the damage, even though only potential, is the basis for granting relief.

It follows that the statute of limitations does not begin to run against a negligence action until some damage has occurred.[53] This has led to real difficulties where, as is frequently the case in actions for medical malpractice,[54] the statute has run before the plaintiff discovers that he has suffered any injury at all. The older approach to such cases was a literal application of the statute to bar the action, regarding it as intended to protect the defendant not only against fictitious claims, but also against the difficulty of obtaining evidence after lapse of time even when he is confronted with a genuine one; and considering the hardship upon the plaintiff as merely part of the price to be paid for such protection.[55] The obvious and flagrant injustice of such cases has led to the adoption of a series of transparent devices to get around the rule. Thus the negligent treatment, or at least the defendant's duty, is held to continue until the relation of physician and patient has ended;[56] or the court finds fraudulent concealment of the damage, which tolls the running of the statute;[57] or it finds "constructive" fraud in silence with probable knowledge;[58] or the failure to discover and remove the sponge or other foreign object left in the plaintiff's body is held to be "continuing" negligence.[59] Quite recently there have been a wave of decisions meeting the issue head-on, and holding that the statute will no longer be construed as intended to run until the plaintiff has in fact discovered that he has suffered injury, or by the exercise of reasonable diligence should have discovered it.[60] While there will un-

215 N.E.2d 319; Stacey v. Pantano, 1964, 177 Neb. 694, 131 N.W.2d 163; Pickett v. Aglinsky, 4 Cir. 1940, 110 F.2d 628.

56. Hotelling v. Walther, 1952, 169 Or. 559, 130 P.2d 944; Williams v. Elias, 1941, 140 Neb. 656, 1 N.W. 2d 121; Samuelson v. Freeman, 1969, 75 Wash.2d 894, 454 P.2d 406; Huysman v. Kirsch, 1936, 6 Cal. 2d 302, 57 P.2d 908; Borgia v. City of New York, 1962, 12 N.Y.2d 151, 237 N.Y.S.2d 319, 187 N.E.2d 777. In Siegel v. Kranis, 1968, 29 App.Div.2d 477, 288 N.Y.S.2d 831, the "continued course of treatment" rule was applied to the malpractice of an attorney.

57. Lakeman v. La France, 1959, 102 N.H. 300, 156 A. 2d 123; Baker v. Hendrix, 1943, 126 W.Va. 37, 27 S.E.2d 275; Hinkle v. Hargens, 1957, 76 S.D. 520, 81 N.W.2d 888; Hall v. De Saussure, 1956, 41 Tenn. App. 572, 297 S.W.2d 90, cert. denied, 1956, 201 Tenn. 164, 297 S.W.2d 90; Murphy v. Dyer, D.Colo. 1966, 260 F.Supp. 822.

58. Burton v. Tribble, 1934, 189 Ark. 58, 70 S.W.2d 503; Morrison v. Acton, 1948, 68 Ariz. 27, 198 P.2d 590; Perrin v. Rodriquez, La.1934, 153 So. 555.

59. Gillette v. Tucker, 1902, 67 Ohio St. 106, 65 N.E. 865; Hotelling v. Walther, 1952, 169 Or. 559, 130 P.2d 944; Sly v. Van Lengen, 1923, 120 Misc. 420, 198 N.Y.S. 608; Frazor v. Osborne, 1966, 57 Tenn. App. 10, 414 S.W.2d 118, appeal after remand, 1968, 425 S.W.2d 768.

60. Flanagan v. Mount Eden General Hospital, 1969, 24 N.Y.2d 427, 301 N.Y.S.2d 23, 248 N.E.2d 871; Frohs v. Greene, 1969, — Or. —, 452 P.2d 564; Acker v. Sorenson, 1969, 183 Neb. 866, 165 N.W.2d

where it interferes with the enjoyment of land. See infra, p. 592.

53. See for example White v. Schnoebelen, 1941, 91 N.H. 273, 18 A.2d 185; Kitchener v. Williams, 1951, 171 Kan. 540, 236 P.2d 64; Theurer v. Condon, 1949, 34 Wash.2d 448, 209 P.2d 311; Essex Wire Corp. v. M. H. Hilt Co., 7 Cir. 1959, 263 F.2d 599; Rosenau v. City of New Brunswick, 1966, 93 N.J.Super. 49, 224 A.2d 689, modified, 1968, 51 N.J. 130, 238 A.2d 169.

54. See Anderson, The Application of Statutes of Limitation to Actions Against Physicians and Surgeons, 1958, 29 Ins.Couns.J. 237; Lilich, The Malpractice Statute of Limitations in New York and Other Jurisdictions, 1962, 47 Corn.L.Q. 339; Notes, 1956, 42 Iowa L.Rev. 97; 1957, 32 Ind.L.J. 528; 1957, 12 Wyo.L.J. 30. The statutes are surveyed in Note, 1969, 3 Suff.L.Rev. 597.

55. Hawks v. De Hart, 1966, 206 Va. 810, 146 S.E.2d 187; Vaughn v. Langmack, 1964, 236 Or. 542, 390 P.2d 142; Pasquale v. Chandler, 1966, 350 Mass. 450,

doubtedly be cases in which this will result in shifting the hardship which must be borne by some one to the defendant, it has been said [61] that "If, as is to be hoped, the resulting jeopardy to defendants produces a greater measure of care in connection with surgical operations, so much the better."

There are already a sprinkling of cases in which this "discovery" rule has been applied to other professional negligence, such as that of an accountant [62] or architect,[63] or even to damage to an adjoining landowner.[64]

31. UNREASONABLE RISK

Negligence is a matter of risk—that is to say, of recognizable danger of injury. It has been defined as "conduct which involves an unreasonably great risk of causing damage," [65] or, more fully, conduct "which falls below the standard established by law for the protection of others against unreasonably great risk of harm." [66] "Negligence is conduct, and not a state of mind." [67] In most instances, it is caused by heedlessness or carelessness, which makes the negligent party unaware of the results which may follow from his act. But it may also exist where he

has considered the possible consequences carefully, and has exercised his own best judgment.[68] The standard imposed by society is an external one, which is not necessarily based upon any moral fault of the individual; and a failure to conform to it is negligence, even though it may be due to stupidity,[69] forgetfulness,[70] an excitable temperament,[71] or even sheer ignorance.[72] The almost universal use of the phrase "due care" to describe conduct which is not negligent, should not be permitted to obscure the fact that the real basis of negligence is not carelessness, but behavior which should be recognized as involving unreasonable danger to others.[73]

Previous reference has been made [74] to the distinction between negligence and intent. In negligence, the actor does not desire to bring about the consequences which follow, nor does he know that they are substantially certain to occur, or believe that they will. There is merely a risk of such consequences, sufficiently great to lead a reasonable man in his position to anticipate them, and to guard against them.[75] If an automobile driver runs down a man in the street before him, with the desire to hit him, or with the belief that he is certain to do so, it is an intentional battery; but if he has no such desire or belief, but merely acts unreasonably in failing to guard against a risk which he should appreciate, it is negligence. As the probability of injury to another, apparent from the facts

---

74; Wilkinson v. Harrington, 1968, —— R.I. ——, 243 A.2d 745; Iverson v. Lancaster, N.D.1968, 158 N.W. 2d 507. In Ruth v. Dight, 1969, 75 Wash.2d 660, 453 P.2d 631, this was carried to the remarkable length of applying it to a sponge left in plaintiff's body for 23 years.

See Sacks, Statutes of Limitations and Undiscovered Malpractice, 1967, 16 Clev.Marsh.L.Rev. 65; Note, 1969, 30 Ohio St.L.J. 425.

61. Fernandi v. Strully, 1961, 35 N.J. 434, 173 A.2d 277, 286.

62. Moonie v. Lynch, 1967, 256 Cal.App.2d 361, 64 Cal.Rptr. 55. Cf. Downing v. Vaine, Fla.App.1969, 228 So.2d 622 (attorney).

63. Chrischilles v. Griswold, 1967, 260 Iowa 453, 150 N.W.2d 94.

64. Basque v. Yuk Lin Liau, 1969, 50 Haw. 397, 441 P.2d 636.

65. Terry, Negligence, 1915, 29 Harv.L.Rev. 40.

66. Restatement of Torts, § 282.

67. Terry, Negligence, 1915, 29 Harv.L.Rev. 40.

68. Vaughan v. Menlove, 1837, 3 Bing., N.C., 467, 132 Eng.Rep. 490; The Germanic, 1905, 196 U.S. 589; Edgerton, Negligence, Inadvertence and Indifference, 1926, 39 Harv.L.Rev. 849.

69. See infra, p. 152.

70. See infra, p. 158.

71. Bessemer Land & Imp. Co. v. Campbell, 1898, 121 Ala. 50, 25 So. 793; Taylor v. Richmond & D. R. Co., 1891, 109 N.C. 233, 13 S.E. 736.

72. See infra, p. 157.

73. Edgerton, Negligence, Inadvertence and Indifference, 1926, 39 Harv.L.Rev. 849, 860.

74. Supra, p. 32.

75. Seavey, Negligence—Subjective or Objective, 1927, 41 Harv.L.Rev. 1, 17.

within his knowledge, becomes greater, his conduct takes on more of the attributes of intent, until it reaches that substantial certainty of harm which juries, and sometimes courts,[76] may find inseparable from intent itself. Such intermediate mental states, based upon a recognizable great probability of harm, may still properly be classed as "negligence," [77] but are commonly called "reckless," "wanton," or even "wilful." They are dealt with, in many respects, as if the harm were intended, so that they become in effect a hybrid between intent and negligence, occupying a sort of penumbra between the two. They will be dealt with in a later section.[78]

Negligence already has been defined as conduct which falls below a standard established by the law for the protection of others against unreasonable risk of harm.[79] The idea of risk necessarily involves a recognizable danger, based upon some knowledge of the existing facts, and some reasonable belief that harm may follow.[80] A risk is a danger which is apparent, or should be apparent, to one in the position of the actor. The culpability of the actor's conduct must be judged in the light of the possibilities apparent to him at the time, and not by looking backward "with the wisdom born of the event." [81] The standard must be one of conduct, rather than of consequences. It is not enough that everyone can see now that the risk was great, if it was not apparent when the conduct occurred.[82] The court must put itself in the actor's place. At the same time, the standard imposed must be an external one, based upon what society demands of the individual, rather than upon his own notions of what is proper. An honest blunder, or a mistaken belief that no damage will result, may absolve him from moral blame, but the harm to others is still as great, and the actor's individual standards must give way to those of the public.[83] In other words, society may require of him not to be a fool.

In the light of the recognizable risk, the conduct, to be negligent, must be unreasonable. Nearly all human acts, of course, carry some recognizable but remote possibility of harm to another. No man so much as rides a horse without some chance of a runaway, or drives a car without the risk of a broken steering gear or a heart attack. But these are not unreasonable risks. Those against which the actor is required to take precautions are those which society, in general, considers sufficiently great to demand them. No man can be expected to guard against harm from events which are not reasonably to be anticipated at all, or are so unlikely to occur that the risk, although recognizable, would commonly be disregarded. An unprecedented frost [84] or flood,[85] an automo-

76. See Lambrecht v. Schreyer, 1915, 129 Minn. 271, 152 N.W. 645; Mercer v. Corbin, 1889, 117 Ind. 450, 20 N.E. 132.

77. Terry, Negligence, 1915, 29 Harv.L.Rev. 40, 41. But see Elliott, Degrees of Negligence, 1933, 6 So. Cal.L.Rev. 91.

78. See infra, § 34.

79. See supra, p. 145.

80. Seavey, Negligence—Subjective or Objective, 1927, 41 Harv.L.Rev. 1, 5–7.

81. Cardozo, C. J., in Greene v. Sibley, Lindsay & Curr Co., 1931, 257 N.Y. 190, 177 N.E. 416. Accord: Ismert-Hincke Milling Co. v. Union Pac. R. Co., 10 Cir. 1956, 238 F.2d 14; Hunter Packing Co. v. Baltimore & O. R. Co., 7 Cir. 1954, 210 F.2d 448; Gerber v. McCall, 1953, 175 Kan. 433, 264 P.2d 490.

82. Austin v. Eastern Mass. St. R. Co., 1929, 269 Mass. 420, 169 N.E. 484; Libby v. Maine Cent. R. Co., 1892, 85 Me. 34, 44, 26 A. 943; Baran v. Reading Iron Co., 1902, 202 Pa. 274, 51 A. 979 (evidence of precautions taken after accident to prevent repetition, not admissible). "Nothing is so easy as to be wise after the event." Bramwell, B., in Cornman v. Eastern Counties R. Co., 1859, 4 H. & N. 781, 786, 157 Eng. Rep. 1050.

83. Vaughan v. Menlove, 1837, 3 Bing.N.C. 468, 132 Eng.Rep. 490; The Germanic, 1904, 196 U.S. 589; Teepen v. Taylor, 1910, 141 Mo.App. 282, 124 S.W. 1062.

84. Blyth v. Birmingham Waterworks Co., 1856, 11 Exch. 781, 156 Eng.Rep. 1047; cf. Sutphen v. Hedden, 1902, 67 N.J.L. 324, 51 A. 721 (wind); King v. Queen Anne Food Products, 1958, 5 App.Div.2d 596, 173 N.Y.S.2d 975 (hurricane); Missouri Pac. R. Co. v. Columbia, 1902, 65 Kan. 390, 69 P. 338.

85. McCauley v. Logan, 1893, 152 Pa. 202, 25 A. 499; Power v. Village of Hibbing, 182 Minn. 66, 223 N.W.

bile thrown unexpectedly against a pillar on the corner,[86] a child picking up a plank with a nail in it and dropping it on his foot,[87] a pedestrian slipping on a small bit of gravel in the highway,[88] the ricochet of a bullet at an almost impossible angle [89]—all of these things have happened, and will occur again; but they are not so likely to do so on any particular occasion as to make it necessary to burden the freedom of human action with precau-

tions against them.[90] Such events are regarded as "unavoidable accidents,"[91] for which there is no liability.

On the other hand, if the risk is an appreciable one, and the possible consequences are serious, the question is not one of mathematical probability alone. The odds may be a thousand to one that no train will arrive at the very moment that an automobile is crossing a railway track, but the risk of death is nevertheless sufficiently serious to require the driver to look for the train.[92] It may be highly improbable that lightning will strike at any given place or time; but the possibility is there, and it requires precautions for the protection of inflammables.[93] As the gravity of the possible harm increases, the apparent likelihood of its occurrence need be correspondingly less.[94]

597; Louisville & N. R. Co. v. Finlay, 1939, 237 Ala. 116, 185 So. 904; Pleasure Beach Park Co. v. Bridgeport Dredge & Dock Co., 1933, 116 Conn. 496, 165 A. 691. See also the cases cited supra, note 84. Contrast Mayor of New York v. Bailey, 1845, 2 Denio, N.Y., 433 (higher flood 20 years before, one "nearly as great" 2 years before).

86. Leachman v. City of Louisville, 1937, 270 Ky. 260, 109 S.W.2d 614. Cf. Martin v. Hodsdon, 1943, 93 N.H. 66, 35 A.2d 402 (car swerving on wrong side of road); Rogers v. Cambridge Taxi Co., 1945, 317 Mass. 578, 59 N.E.2d 89 (passenger in taxicab impaled on ashtray); Wire v. Williams, 1965, 270 Minn. 390, 133 N.W.2d 840 (jump rope jerked out of hand); Reaves v. Wiggs, Miss.1966, 192 So.2d 401 (explosion of cleaning solution); Feldman v. Whipkey's Drug Shop, 1970, —— Ga.App. ——, 174 S.E.2d 474 (automobile jumping curb).

87. Spiering v. City of Hutchinson, 1921, 150 Minn. 305, 185 N.W. 375. Cf. Geary v. H. P. Hood & Sons, Inc., 1957, 336 Mass. 369, 145 N.E.2d 716 (ice on top of case of milk); Lubitz v. Wells, 1955, 19 Conn. Sup. 322, 113 A.2d 147 (boy picking up golf club, hitting other child with it); Chipokas v. Peterson, 1935, 219 Iowa 1072, 260 N.W. 37 (child darting into path of vehicle); Lance v. Senior, 1967, 36 Ill.2d 516, 224 N.E.2d 231 (child with hemophilia swallowing needle); Johnson v. Wichita Valley R. Co., Tex. Civ.App.1937, 104 S.W.2d 128 (chip struck out by adz flew into eye).

88. Missouri Pac. R. Co. v. Richardson, 1932, 185 Ark. 472, 47 S.W.2d 794. Cf. Gagnon v. Divittorio, 1941, 310 Mass. 475, 38 N.E.2d 629 (cuff on coat sleeve caught on truck); Lydon v. Warehouse 13, Inc., 1957, 335 Mass. 729, 142 N.E.2d 325 (machinery breaking); Scurfield v. Federal Laboratories, 1939, 335 Pa. 145, 6 A.2d 559 (accident with tear gas gun); Hauser v. Chicago, R.I. & P. R. Co., 1928, 205 Iowa, 940, 219 N.W. 60 (injury from inaccessible steampipe); cf. Republic of France v. United States, 5 Cir. 1961, 290 F.2d 395, cert. denied, 1962, 369 U.S. 804 (unprecedented explosion of chemical).

89. Cleghorn v. Thompson, 1901, 62 Kan. 727, 64 P.2d 605; Jensen v. Minard, 1955, 44 Cal.2d 325, 282 P.2d 7. Cf. Rose v. Morris, 1958, 97 Ga.App. 764, 104 S.E.2d 485 (golf ball hooked onto wrong fairway).

90. The particular circumstances are, however, always to be taken into account. Compare, as to an automobile tire throwing an object to a considerable distance, Miller v. Gonzalez, 1956, 4 Misc.2d 223, 156 N.Y.S.2d 775, reversed and held for jury, 9 Misc.2d 190, 163 N.Y.S.2d 687, and Randall v. Shelton, Ky. 1956, 293 S.W.2d 559 (no negligence) with Ridley v. Grifall Trucking Co., 1955, 136 Cal.App.2d 682, 289 P.2d 31 (negligence).

91. See supra, § 29.

92. Gallagher v. Montpelier & Wells River R. Co., 1927, 100 Vt. 299, 137 A. 207. And the fact that the train is off schedule does not absolve the driver. Truelove v. Durham & S. R. Co., 1943, 222 N.C. 704, 24 S.E.2d 537. Cf. Barker v. East Side Bldg. Corp., Mo.App.1961, 344 S.W.2d 299 (child crawling under merry-go-round); Smith-Kasson Co. v. Dirr, 1931, 41 Ohio App. 385, 180 N.E. 197 (crutch went through very small opening in sidewalk); La Plant v. E. I. Du Pont de Nemours & Co., Mo.App.1961, 346 S.W. 2d 231 (cattle poisoned by chemical deposited in willow leaves).

93. Jackson v. Wisconsin Tel. Co., 1894, 88 Wis. 243, 60 N.W. 430; Clark's Adm'r v. Kentucky Utilities Co., 1942, 289 Ky. 225, 158 S.W.2d 134; Texas Jersey Oil Corp. v. Beck, Tex.Civ.App.1956, 292 S.W.2d 803, affirmed in part, reversed in part, 1957, 157 Tex. 541, 305 S.W.2d 162.

94. Tullgren v. Amoskeag Mfg. Co., 1926, 82 N.H. 268, 133 A. 4; Gulf Refining Co. v. Williams, 1938, 183 Miss. 723, 185 So. 234; Pease v. Sinclair Refining Co., 2 Cir. 1939, 104 F.2d 183; Ridley v. Grifall Trucking Co., 1955, 136 Cal.App.2d 682, 289 P.2d 31.

Against this probability, and gravity, of the risk, must be balanced in every case the utility of the type of conduct in question. The problem is whether "the game is worth the candle." [95] Many risks may reasonably be run, with the full approval of the community. Chief among the factors which must be considered is the social value of the interest which the actor is seeking to advance. A man may be justified in dashing into the path of a train to save the life of a child, where it would be arrant folly to save his hat.[96] A railway will be permitted, or even required, to blow a whistle to warn travelers at a crossing, although it is likely to frighten horses on the highway; [97] it may be negligence to blow the same whistle without the same occasion for warning.[98] The public interest will justify the use of dangerous machinery, so long as the benefits outweigh the risk,[99] and a railroad may reasonably be constructed near a highway, even at the expense of some danger to those who use it.[1]

The same balance between the threatened harm and the utility of the actor's conduct appears, of course, in the various privileges, such as that of self-defense, which are recognized as defenses to intentional torts. The difference lies in the fact that, for historical reasons derived from the old action of trespass, such intentional invasions of the interests of another are regarded as prima facie wrongful, and the privilege is a matter of excuse or defense; while in negligence, which is to be traced primarily to the action on the case, it is considered that no wrong at all has occurred unless the defendant's conduct has been unreasonable in the light of the risk, and the burden is upon the plaintiff from the outset to establish the fact.

Consideration must also be given to any alternative course open to the actor. Whether it is reasonable to travel a dangerous road may depend upon the disadvantages of another route; [2] and while mere inconvenience [3] or cost [4] may not in themselves be sufficient to justify proceeding in the face of great danger, they may justify taking other risks which are not too extreme.[5] A county will not be

---

95. Second Restatement of Torts, § 291, Comment *a*. See Osborne v. Montgomery, 1931, 203 Wis. 223, 234 N.W. 372.

96. Eckert v. Long Island R. Co., 1871, 43 N.Y. 502; Louisville & N. R. Co. v. Orr, 1898, 121 Ala. 489, 26 So. 35; Dixon v. New York, N. H. & H. R. Co., 1910, 207 Mass. 126, 92 N.E. 1030; Note, 1933, 67 U.S.L. Rev. 54. Otherwise where the apparent danger of the person rescued is slight. Eversole v. Wabash R. Co., 1913, 249 Mo. 523, 155 S.W. 419. See the excellent statement in Wolfinger v. Shaw, 1940, 138 Neb. 229, 292 N.W. 731.

97. Mitchell v. Central Vermont R. Co., 1927, 261 Mass. 29, 158 N.E. 336.

98. Dugan v. St. Paul & Duluth R. Co., 1890, 43 Minn. 414, 45 N.W. 851.

99. Chicago, B. & Q. R. Co. v. Krayenbuhl, 1902, 65 Neb. 889, 91 N.W. 880. Cf. Ott v. Washington Gas Light Co., D.D.C.1962, 205 F.Supp. 815, affirmed, 1963, 115 U.S.App.D.C. 74, 317 F.2d 138 (open flare pot in street, night and day); Winsor v. Smart's Auto Freight Co., 1941, 25 Wash.2d 383, 171 P.2d 251 (backing truck to make coupling); Vezina v. City of Hartford, 1927, 106 Conn. 378, 138 A. 145 (obstructing sidewalk with fire hose).

1. Beatty v. Central Iowa R. Co., 1882, 58 Iowa 242, 12 N.W. 332. Cf. Bennett v. Illinois Power & Light Corp., 1934, 355 Ill. 564, 189 N.E. 899 (spool of wire by roadside frightening horse); Rosston v. Sullivan,

1931, 278 Mass. 31, 179 N.E. 173 (darkness in motion picture theater).

2. Musselman v. Borough of Hatfield, 1902, 202 Pa. 489, 52 A. 15; Pomeroy v. Inhabitants of Westfield, 1891, 154 Mass. 462, 28 N.E. 899.

3. "The mere fact that the safe course is disagreeable is not sufficient to justify conduct which is manifestly perilous to life and limb." Williams v. East Bay Motor Coach Lines, 1936, 16 Cal.App.2d 169, 60 P.2d 320. Accord, Saetz v. Braun, N.D.1962, 116 N.W.2d 628 (safe route difficult to drive, other with unsafe bridge). But the use of the most direct route is not necessarily negligent because the alternative would have been safer. Hopton v. Donora Borough, 1964, 415 Pa. 173, 202 A.2d 814.

4. Silver Falls Timber Co. v. Eastern & Western Lumber Co., 1935, 149 Or. 126, 40 P.2d 703 (failure to shut down operation emitting sparks during dry season); Haverstick v. Southern Pac. Co., 1934, 1 Cal.App.2d 605, 37 P.2d 146 (looking after train instead of extinguishing conflagration); Greenlee v. Southern R. Co., 1898, 122 N.C. 977, 30 S.E. 115 (failure to provide safety coupling devices).

5. Farrell v. Hidish, 1933, 132 Me. 57, 165 A. 903 (tenement child allowed to play in street); Grace

required, at ruinous expense, to build a bridge which will be safe against any accident that might be anticipated;[6] but the converse is also true, and where it can cheaply and easily post a warning, it may be required to do so.[7] A railroad need not do without a turntable because there is some chance that children will play on it and be hurt; but it is quite another matter to keep it locked.[8]

The alternative dangers to the actor himself [9] and to others [10] must be thrown into

the scale, and a balance struck in which all of these elements are weighed.

It is fundamental that the standard of conduct which is the basis of the law of negligence is determined by balancing the risk, in the light of the social value of the interest threatened, and the probability and extent of the harm, against the value of the interest which the actor is seeking to protect, and the expedience of the course pursued.[11] For this reason, it is seldom possible to reduce negligence to any definite rules; it is "relative to the need and the occasion," [12] and conduct which would be proper under some circumstances becomes negligence under others.

32. THE REASONABLE MAN

The whole theory of negligence presupposes some uniform standard of behavior.

& Co. v. City of Los Angeles, S.D.Cal.1958, 168 F. Supp. 344, affirmed, 9 Cir.1960, 278 F.2d 771 (failure to inspect water pipe); Kimbar v. Estis, 1956, 1 N. Y.2d 399, 153 N.Y.S.2d 197, 135 N.E.2d 708 (summer camp not required to floodlight woods).

Where both alternatives appear to involve equivalent risk, the actor may reasonably choose on the basis of convenience. McManamon v. Hanover Township, 1911, 232 Pa. 439, 81 A. 440.

6. Davison v. Snohomish County, 1928, 149 Wash. 109, 270 P. 422; Gavin v. City of Chicago, 1880, 97 Ill. 66; Vellante v. Town of Watertown, 1938, 300 Mass. 207, 14 N.E.2d 955 (perfection not required in sidewalks). Cf. Adams v. Bullock, 1919, 227 N.Y. 208, 125 N.E. 93 (not practicable to insulate trolley wires); Cooley v. Public Service Co., 1940, 90 N.H. 460, 10 A.2d 673 (or to install mesh basket device under them).

7. Stephani v. City of Manitowoc, 1895, 89 Wis. 467, 62 N.W. 176. Even a slight risk may be unreasonable, where it can be avoided with relatively slight effort, cost and inconvenience. Pease v. Sinclair Refining Co., 2 Cir. 1939, 104 F.2d 183 (water labeled "kerosene"); Yoffee v. Pennsylvania Power & Light Co., 1956, 385 Pa. 520, 123 A.2d 636 (improving visibility of transmission lines).

8. Chicago, B. & Q. R. Co. v. Krayenbuhl, 1902, 65 Neb. 889, 91 N.W. 880, Cf. Ott v. Washington Gas Lights Co., D.D.C.1962, 205 F.Supp. 815, affirmed 4 Cir.1963, 317 F.2d 138 (not negligence to have open flare pot in street, but negligence in not turning off before 10 A. M.); Logan v. Hennepin Ave. M. E. Church, 1941, 210 Minn. 96, 297 N.W. 333 (method of stacking folding chairs). See Bauer, The Degree of Danger and the Degree of Difficulty of Removal in "Attractive Nuisance" Cases, 1934, 18 Minn.L. Rev. 523.

9. Thurmond v. Pepper, Tex.Civ.App.1938, 119 S.W. 2d 900 (failure to stop truck because of danger of being crushed by pipes). But cf. Central R. Co. v. Crosby, 1885, 74 Ga. 737 (failure of engineer to jump).

10. Cooley v. Public Service Co., 1940, 90 N.H. 460, 10 A.2d 673 (power line devices); Hoosac Tunnel &

W. R. Co. v. New England Power Co., 1942, 311 Mass. 667, 42 N.E.2d 832 (opening sluice gates of dam in time of flood).

When either course involves danger to others, a choice either way may be reasonable, depending of course upon apparent probabilities. Compare Lucchese v. San Francisco-Sacramento R. Co., 1930, 106 Cal.App. 242, 289 P. 188, and Wheat v. New Orleans & N. E. R. Co., 1964, 245 La. 1099, 163 So.2d 65 (failure to stop car suddenly), with cases where such a stop was made. Cleveland City R. Co. v. Osborn, 1902, 66 Ohio St. 45, 63 N.E. 604; Bowers v. New York, N. H. & H. R. Co., 1959, 146 Conn. 437, 151 A.2d 704; Kopp v. Louisville Taxicab & Transfer Co., Ky.1953, 257 S.W.2d 891.

11. Terry, Negligence, 1915, 29 Harv.L.Rev. 40, 42; Restatement of Torts, §§ 291–293.

"Since there are occasions when every vessel will break away from her moorings, and, since, if she does, she becomes a menace to those about her, the owner's duty, as in other similar situations, to provide against resulting injuries is a function of three variables: (1) The probability that she will break away; (2) the gravity of the resulting injury, if she does; (3) the burden of adequate precautions. Possibly it serves to bring this notion into relief to state it in algebraic terms: if the probability be called P; the injury L; and the burden B; liability depends upon whether B is less than L multiplied by P; i. e., whether B is less than PL." Learned Hand, C. J., in United States v. Carroll Towing Co., 2 Cir., 1947, 159 F.2d 169.

12. Cardozo, C. J., in Babington v. Yellow Taxi Corp., 1928, 250 N.Y. 14, 164 N.E. 726.

Yet the infinite variety of situations which may arise makes it impossible to fix definite rules in advance for all conceivable human conduct. The utmost that can be done is to devise something in the nature of a formula, the application of which in each particular case must be left to the jury, or to the court.[13] The standard of conduct which the community demands must be an external and objective one,[14] rather than the individual judgment, good or bad, of the particular actor;[15] and it must be, so far as possible, the same for all persons, since the law can have no favorites. At the same time, it must make proper allowance for the risk apparent to the actor, for his capacity to meet it, and for the circumstances under which he must act.

The courts have dealt with this very difficult problem by creating a fictitious person, who never has existed on land or sea: the "reasonable man of ordinary prudence."[16]

Sometimes he is described as a reasonable man,[17] or a prudent man,[18] or a man of average prudence,[19] or a man of ordinary sense using ordinary care and skill.[20] It is evident that all such phrases are intended to mean very much the same thing. The actor is required to do what such an ideal individual would be supposed to do in his place. A model of all proper qualities, with only those human shortcomings and weaknesses which the community will tolerate on the occasion, "this excellent but odious character stands like a monument in our Courts of Justice, vainly appealing to his fellow-citizens to order their lives after his own example."[21]

13. Green, The Negligence Issue, 1928, 37 Yale L.J. 1029, reprinted in Green, Judge and Jury, 1930, 153, 154.

14. "Instead, therefore, of saying that the liability for negligence should be coextensive with the judgment of each individual, which would be as variable as the length of the foot of each individual, we ought rather to adhere to the rule, which requires in all cases a regard to caution such as a man of ordinary prudence would observe." Tindal, C. J., in Vaughan v. Menlove, 1837, 3 Bing.N.C. 468, 132 Eng.Rep. 490.

"To the extent that the solution of these problems involves standardized elements, or phrasing it differently, to the extent that the actor's conduct is determined with reference to the community valuations, we may say that an objective test applies." Seavey, Negligence—Subjective or Objective, 1927, 41 Harv.L.Rev. 1, 8.

15. Thus it is error to instruct the jury that the actor was not negligent if he used his own best judgment. The Germanic, 1904, 196 U.S. 589; Mertz v. Connecticut Co., 1916, 217 N.Y. 475, 112 N.E. 166; Maguire v. Barrett, 1918, 223 N.Y. 49, 119 N.E. 79; Beahan v. St. Louis Public Service Co., 1951, 361 Mo. 807, 237 S.W.2d 105, affirming Mo.App.1950, 230 S.W.2d 173. The actor's belief that he is using reasonable care is immaterial. Hankins v. Harvey, 1964, 248 Miss. 639, 160 So.2d 63; Hover v. Barkhoof, 1870, 44 N.Y. 113.

16. First mentioned in Vaughan v. Menlove, 1738, 3 Bing.N.C. 468, 132 Eng.Rep. 490.

17. "Negligence is the omission to do something which a reasonable man, guided upon those considerations which ordinarily regulate the conduct of human affairs, would do, or doing something which a prudent and reasonable man would not do." Alderson, B., in Blyth v. Birmingham Waterworks Co., 1856, 11 Ex. 781, 784, 156 Eng.Rep. 1047. Cf. Restatement of Torts, § 283.

18. Drown v. New England Telephone & Telegraph Co. & Consolidated Lighting Co., 1908, 81 Vt. 358, 70 A. 599.

19. Davis v. Concord & Montreal R. Co., 1895, 68 N. H. 247, 44 A. 388; Osborne v. Montgomery, 1931, 203 Wis. 223, 234 N.W. 372 ("ordinarily prudent man"); Warrington v. New York Power & Light Corp., 1937, 252 App.Div. 364, 300 N.Y.S. 154 ("typical prudent man"); Charbonneau v. MacRury, 1931, 84 N.H. 501, 153 A. 457 ("average person of ordinary prudence").

20. Brett, M. R., in Heaven v. Pender, 1883, 11 Q.B.D. 503, 507. He is "not necessarily a supercautious individual devoid of human frailties and constantly preoccupied with the idea that danger may be lurking in every direction about him at any time." Whitman v. W. T. Grant Co., 1964, 16 Utah 2d 81, 395 P.2d 918, 920; Public Service Co. of New Hampshire v. Elliott, 1 Cir. 1941, 123 F.2d 2, 7.

21. A. P. Herbert, Misleading Cases in the Common Law, 1930, 12–16: "He is an ideal, a standard, the embodiment of all those qualities which we demand of the good citizen. * * * He is one who invariably looks where he is going, and is careful to examine the immediate foreground before he executes a leap or a bound; who neither star-gazes nor is lost in meditation when approaching trapdoors or the margin of a dock; * * * who never mounts a moving omnibus and does not alight from any car while the train is in motion * * * and will inform himself of the history and habits of a dog before administering a caress; * * * who never

The courts have gone to unusual pains to emphasize the abstract and hypothetical character of this mythical person. He is not to be identified with any ordinary individual, who might occasionally do unreasonable things; he is a prudent and careful man, who is always up to standard.[22] Nor is it proper to identify him even with any member of the very jury who are to apply the standard; he is rather a personification of a community ideal of reasonable behavior, determined by the jury's social judgment.[23] It is sometimes difficult to escape the conviction that the refinements which have been developed in instructing the jury, in the effort to avoid any personal standard which one of them might be tempted to apply, are artificial and unreal, and quite beyond the comprehension of the average man in the box. Their only possible justification lies in a basis of experience justifying considerable uneasiness about what any jury may conceivably do, which has led to an excess of precaution in the effort to give them proper guidance.

drives his ball until those in front of him have definitely vacated the putting-green which is his own objective; who never from one year's end to another makes an excessive demand upon his wife, his neighbors, his servants, his ox, or his ass; * * * who never swears, gambles or loses his temper; who uses nothing except in moderation, and even while he flogs his child is mediating only on the golden mean. * * * In all that mass of authorities which bears upon this branch of the law there is no single mention of a reasonable woman."

22. Reynolds v. City of Burlington, 1880, 52 Vt. 300, 308; Austin & N. W. R. Co. v. Beatty, 1889, 73 Tex. 592, 593, 11 S.W. 858; Hennessey v. Chicago & N. W. R. Co., 1898, 99 Wis. 109, 74 N.W. 554; St. Louis, A. & T. R. Co. v. Finley, 1890, 79 Tex. 85, 15 S.W. 266.

23. Louisville & N. R. Co. v. Gower, 1887, 85 Tenn. 465, 3 S.W. 824; Freeman v. Adams, 1923, 63 Cal.App. 225, 218 P. 600; Warrington v. New York Power & Light Corp., 1937, 252 App.Div. 364, 300 N.Y.S. 154; Terry v. Fredette, 1970, —— N.H. ——, 261 A.2d 431; cf. Green v. United States, 5 Cir. 1962, 332 F.2d 788, cert. denied, 1965, 379 U.S. 949. See Allen, Learned and Unlearned Reason, 1924, 36 Jurid.Rev. 254; Bohlen, Mixed Questions of Law and Fact, 1924, 72 U.Pa.L.Rev. 111, 113.

Physical Attributes

The conduct of the reasonable man will vary with the situation with which he is confronted. The jury must therefore be instructed to take the circumstances into account; negligence is a failure to do what the reasonable man would do "under the same or similar circumstances." [24] Under the latitude of this phrase, the courts have made allowance not only for the external facts, but for many of the characteristics of the actor himself, and have applied, in many respects, a more or less subjective standard. "It would appear that there is no standardized man; that there is only in part an objective test; that there is no such thing as reasonable or unreasonable conduct except as viewed with reference to certain qualities of the actor— his physical attributes, his intellectual powers, probably, if superior, his knowledge and the knowledge he would have acquired had he exercised standard moral and at least average mental qualities at the time of action or at some connected time." [25]

As to his physical characteristics, the reasonable man may be said to be identical with the actor.[26] The man who is blind [27] or

24. "The rule has been repeatedly laid down that no definition is complete or correct which does not embody that element." Yerkes v. Northern Pac. R. Co., 1901, 112 Wis. 184, 193, 88 N.W. 33, 36; Garland v. Boston & Me. R. Co., 1913, 76 N.H. 556, 86 A. 141.

25. Seavey, Negligence—Subjective or Objective, 1927, 41 Harv.L.Rev. 1, 27; Green, The Negligence Issue, 1928, 37 Yale L.J. 1029, reprinted in Green, Judge and Jury, 1930, 153, 166; James, The Qualities of the Reasonable Man in Negligence Cases, 1951, 16 Mo.L. Rev. 1. A good workout on all this is Parsons, Negligence, Contributory Negligence, and the Man Who Does Not Ride the Bus to Clapham, 1958, 1 Melb.U.L.Rev. 163.

26. ten Broek, The Right to Live in the World: The Disabled and the Law of Torts, 1966, 54 Cal.L. Rev. 841.

27. Balcom v. City of Independence, 1916, 178 Iowa 685, 160 N.W. 305; Argo v. Goodstein, 1970, 438 Pa. 468, 265 A.2d 783; Cook v. City of Winston-Salem, 1954, 241 N.C. 422, 85 S.E.2d 696; Hefferon v. Reeves, 1918, 140 Minn. 505, 167 N.W. 423; Apper-

deaf,[28] or lame, or is otherwise physically disabled,[29] is entitled to live in the world and to have allowance made by others for his disability,[30] and he cannot be required to do the impossible by conforming to physical standards which he cannot met. Similar allowance has been made for the weaknesses of age [31] and sex.[32] At the same time, the conduct of the handicapped individual must be reasonable in the light of his knowledge of his infirmity, which is treated merely as one of the circumstances under which he acts. A blind man may be negligent in going into a place of known danger, just as one who knows that

he is subject to epileptic fits,[33] or is about to fall asleep,[34] may be negligent in driving a car. It is sometimes said that a blind man must use a greater degree of care than one who can see; [35] but it is now generally agreed that as a fixed rule this is inaccurate, and that the correct statement is merely that he must take the precautions, be they more or less, which the ordinary reasonable man would take if he were blind.[36] In theory the standard remains the same, but it is sufficiently flexible to take his physical defects into account.

Mental Capacity

As to the mental attributes of the actor, the standard remains of necessity an external one. "The law," says Mr. Justice Holmes in a much quoted passage, "takes no account of the infinite varieties of temperament, intellect, and education which make the internal character of a given act so different in different men. It does not attempt to see men as God sees them, for more than one sufficient reason." [37] The fact that the individual is a congenital fool, cursed with inbuilt

son v. Lazro, 1909, 44 Ind.App. 186, 87 N.E. 97, rehearing denied 88 N.E. 99.

Compare, as to impaired vision, Masters v. Alexander, 1967, 424 Pa. 65, 225 A.2d 905; Bernard v. Russell, 1960, 103 N.H. 76, 164 A.2d 577; Pennington v. Southern Pac. Co., 1956, 146 Cal.App.2d 605, 304 P.2d 22.

28. McCann v. Sadowski, 1926, 287 Pa. 294, 135 A. 207; Jakubiec v. Hasty, 1953, 337 Mich. 205, 59 N.W. 385; Rhimer v. Davis, 1923, 126 Wash. 470, 218 P. 193; Kerr v. Connecticut Co., 1928, 107 Conn. 304, 140 A. 751; Otterbeck v. Lamb, 1969, 85 Nev. 456, 456 P.2d 855.

29. Texas & N. O. R. Co. v. Bean, 1909, 55 Tex.Civ. App. 341, 119 S.W. 328, error refused (club foot); Bianchetti v. Luce, 1928, 222 Mo.App. 282, 2 S.W.2d 129 (lame); Goodman v. Norwalk Jewish Center, Inc., 1958, 145 Conn. 146, 139 A.2d 812 (crippled, lacking coordination, on crutches); Wray v. Fairfield Amusement Co., 1940, 126 Conn. 221, 10 A.2d 600 (bone condition); City and County of Denver v. Willson, 1927, 81 Colo. 134, 254 P. 153. Accord, as to short stature, Mahan v. State of New York, to Use of Carr, 1937, 172 Md. 373, 191 A. 575; Singletary v. Atlantic Coast Line R. Co., 1950, 217 S.C. 212, 60 S.E.2d 305. See, generally, Note, 1955, 34 N.C.L.Rev. 142.

30. Thus a city must govern its excavations on sidewalks by the expectation that the blind will use them. Fletcher v. City of Aberdeen, 1959, 54 Wash. 174, 338 P.2d 743. Cf. Garbutt v. Schechter, 1959, 167 Cal.App.2d 396, 334 P.2d 225 (200 pound woman); Robinson v. Pioche, Bayerque & Co., 1885, 5 Cal. 460 (drunk).

31. Johnson v. St. Paul City R. Co., 1897, 67 Minn. 260, 69 N.W. 900; Rosenthal v. Chicago & A. R. Co., 1912, 255 Ill. 552, 99 N.E. 672; Kitsap County Transp. Co. v. Harvey, 9 Cir. 1927, 15 F.2d 166.

32. Hassenyer v. Michigan Cent. R. Co., 1882, 48 Mich. 205, 12 N.W. 155.

33. Eleason v. New York R. Co., 1948, 254 Wis. 134, 35 N.W.2d 301; Goldman v. New York Rys. Co., 1919, 185 App.Div. 739, 173 N.Y.S. 737.

34. Bushnell v. Bushnell, 1925, 103 Conn. 583, 131 A. 432; Baird v. Baird, 1943, 223 N.C. 730, 28 S.E.2d 225; Manser v. Eder, 1933, 263 Mich. 107, 248 N.W. 563. Cf. Felton v. Horner, 1896, 97 Tenn. 579, 37 S.W. 696 (aged and infirm person risking jolt of train).

35. Winn v. City of Lowell, 1861, 1 Allen, Mass., 177; Karl v. Juniata County, 1903, 206 Pa. 633, 56 A. 78. See also Armstrong v. Warner Bros. Theatres, 1947, 161 Pa.Super. 285, 54 A.2d 831 (age).

36. Florida Central & P. R. Co. v. Williams, 1896, 37 Fla. 406, 20 So. 558; Keith v. Worcester & B. V. St. R. Co., 1907, 196 Mass. 478, 82 N.E. 680; Hill v. City of Glenwood, 1904, 124 Iowa 479, 100 N.W. 522; Jones v. Bayley, 1943, 49 Cal.App.2d 647, 122 P.2d 293; Weinstein v. Wheeler, 1932, 141 Or. 246, 15 P.2d 383. Cf. Fenneman v. Holden, 1891, 75 Md. 1, 22 A. 1049 (deafness).

37. Holmes, The Common Law, 1881, 108.

bad judgment,[38] or that in the particular instance he "did not stop to think," [39] or that he is merely a stupid ox, or of an excitable temperament which causes him to lose his head and get "rattled," obviously cannot be allowed to protect him from liability. Apart from the very obvious difficulties of proof as to what went on in his head, it may be no bad policy to hold a fool according to his folly. The harm to his neighbors is quite as great, and may be greater, than if he had a modicum of brains; [40] and if he is to live in the community, he must learn to conform to its standards or pay for what he breaks. As to all such mental deficiency, no allowance is made; [41] the standard of reasonable conduct is applied, and "it is not enough that the defendant did the best he knew how." [42]

Obviously, however, an extreme is reached at which the mental deficiency has prevented the individual from comprehending the danger, or from taking action to avoid it; and the question then becomes, how can we find the tort of negligence at all? Can a complete imbecile, for example, be negligent? It is a rather mysterious fact that no case can be found involving such a condition on the part of a defendant. There are, however, quite a few cases dealing with contributory negligence of plaintiffs; and in all of them except one,[43] it has been held that the jury could find that there was no negligence.[44] There are even one or two cases making allowance for inability to exercise the judgment of a reasonable man; [45] but in the light of the difficulty of distinguishing, for example, excitable temperament causing the man to lose his head,[46] this appears unworkable as a practical matter.

In cases in which the mental aberration has reached the point of actual insanity, the tendency has been to carry over the standard of the reasonable man, and to apply it even to the negligence of those who are definitely insane.[47] This has not gone without criticism,

38. Fritscher v. Billiot, La.App.1959, 112 So.2d 755; Vaughan v. Menlove, 1837, 3 Bing.N.C. 467, 132 Eng. Rep. 490.

39. Cronin v. Columbian Mfg. Co., 1909, 75 N.H. 319, 74 A. 180; Masters v. Public Service Co. of N. H., 1942, 92 N.H. 85, 25 A.2d 499.

40. "If, for instance, a man is born hasty and awkward, is always hurting himself or his neighbors, no doubt his congenital defects will be allowed for in the courts of Heaven, but his slips are no less troublesome to his neighbors than if they sprang from guilty neglect. His neighbors accordingly require him, at his peril, to come up to their standard, and the courts which they establish decline to take his personal equation into account." Holmes, The Common Law, 1881, 108.

41. Worthington v. Mencer, 1892, 96 Ala. 310, 11 So. 72; Feldman v. Howard, 1966, 5 Ohio App.2d 65, 214 N.E.2d 235, reversed on other grounds 1967, 10 Ohio St.2d 189, 226 N.E.2d 564; Johnson v. Texas & Pac. R. Co., 1931, 16 La.App. 464, 133 So. 517, rehearing denied 135 So. 114; Riesbeck Drug Co. v. Wray, 1942, 111 Ind.App. 467, 39 N.E.2d 776; Deisenreiter v. Kraus-Merkel Malting Co., 1897, 97 Wis. 279, 72 N.W. 735.

42. Vaughan v. Menlove, 1837, 3 Bing. N.C. 468, 471, 132 Eng.Rep. 490.

43. Wright v. Tate, 1967, 208 Va. 291, 156 S.E.2d 562.

44. Lynch v. Rosenthal, Mo.App.1965, 396 S.W.2d 272; De Martini v. Alexander Sanitarium, Inc., 1961, 192 Cal.App.2d 442, 13 Cal.Rptr. 564; Feldman v. Howard, 1966, 5 Ohio App.2d 65, 214 N.E.2d 235, reversed on other grounds 1967, 10 Ohio St.2d 189, 226 N.E.2d 564; Johnson v. Texas & Pac. R. Co., 1931, 16 La.App. 464, 133 So. 517, rehearing denied 135 So. 114; Riesbeck Drug Co. v. Wray, 1942, 111 Ind.App. 467, 39 N.E.2d 776. In Snider v. Callahan, W.D.Mo.1966, 250 F.Supp. 1022, a distinction was suggested between negligence and contributory negligence, with allowance made only for the latter.

45. Seattle Elec. Co. v. Hoveden, 9 Cir. 1911, 190 F. 7; Dassinger v. Kuhn, N.D.1958, 87 N.W.2d 720.

See Note, 1968, 9 W. & M. L.Rev. 896.

46. No allowance was made for this in Bessemer Land & Imp. Co. v. Campbell, 1898, 121 Ala. 50, 25 So. 793.

47. Williams v. Hays, 1894, 143 N.Y. 442, 38 N.E.2d 449, qualified in 1899, 157 N.Y. 541, 52 N.E. 589; Kuhn v. Zabotsky, 1967, 9 Ohio St.2d 129, 224 N.E. 2d 137; Johnson v. Lambotte, 1961, 147 Colo. 203, 363 P.2d 165; Sforza v. Green Bus Lines, 1934, 150 Misc. 180, 268 N.Y.S.2d 446; Shapiro v. Thernowitz, 1956, 3 Misc.2d 617, 155 N.Y.S.2d 1011; Ellis v. Fixico, 1935, 174 Okl. 116, 50 P.2d 162 (statute).

The Restatement of Torts at first left the question open, but was amended to adopt the rule of liability.

and there has been much argument that an exception should be made when mental deficiency reaches such an extreme.[48] There are a handful of contributory negligence cases in which the mental state has prevented the individual from comprehending or avoiding the danger, and the jury has been permitted to find that there is no negligence.[49] There are two decisions in Wisconsin and Ontario [50] which have come to the same conclusion as to insane defendants. It seems rather probable that the cases as to lunatics will follow the line of mental deficiency in general.

On the other hand a transitory unconsciousness,[51] or delirium due to illness, commonly is regarded as a "circumstance" depriving the actor of control over his conduct, which will relieve him of liability.

Whether intoxication is to be regarded as a physical or a mental disability is probably of no importance at all to anyone. On either basis, it is common enough; and it is uniformly held that voluntary [52] or negligent intoxication cannot serve as excuse or absolution for acts done in that condition which would otherwise be negligent.[53] One good reason is that such an excuse would be far too common and too easy to assert; another is that drunkenness is so anti-social that one who indulges in it ought to be held to the consequences. It is sometimes said [54] that such intoxication is negligence in itself; but this is scarcely correct, since a drunken man may still behave in a perfectly reasonable manner. The proper statement would seem to be that one who intentionally or negligently becomes intoxicated is held thereafter to the same standard of conduct as if he were sober.[55]

Children

As to one very important group of individuals, it has been necessary, as a practical matter, to depart to a considerable extent from the objective standard of capacity. Children, although they are liable for their

---

See 1948 Supp. § 283; Second Restatement of Torts, § 283B.

As to the tort liability of insane persons generally, see infra, § 135.

48. See Hornblower, Insanity and the Law of Negligence, 1905, 5 Col.L.Rev. 278; Bohlen, Liability in Tort of Infants and Insane Persons, 1924, 23 Mich. L.Rev. 9; Cook, Mental Deficiency in Relation to Tort, 1921, 21 Col.L.Rev. 333; Ague, The Liability of Insane Persons in Torts Actions, 1956, 60 Dick.L. Rev. 211; Wilkinson, Mental Deficiency as a Defense to Tort Liability, 1944, 17 Rocky Mt.L.Rev. 38; Green, Public Policy Underlying the Law of Mental Incompetency, 1940, 38 Mich.L.Rev. 1189; Curran, Tort Liability of the Mentally Ill and Mentally Deficient, 1960, 21 Ohio St.L.J. 52.

49. Emory University v. Lee, 1958, 97 Ga.App. 680, 104 S.E.2d 234; De Martini v. Alexander Sanitarium, 1961, 192 Cal.App.2d 442, 13 Cal.Rptr. 564; Johnson v. Texas & Pac. R. Co., 1931, 16 La.App. 464, 133 So. 517, rehearing denied 135 So. 114.

50. Breunig v. American Family Ins. Co., 1970, 45 Wis.2d 536, 173 N.W.2d 619; Buckley & Toronto Transp. Comm'n v. Smith Transport, Ltd., [1946] Ont.L.Rep. 798, [1946] 4 Dom.L.Rep. 721.

51. See supra, p. 140.

52. The cases all say that involuntary, non-negligent intoxication, as where the old lady who never has tasted whiskey is given a cup of "tea," is to be treated like illness or physical disability. As to the interesting problem of the chronic alcoholic, who escapes criminal liability, see Driver v. Hinnant, 4 Cir. 1966, 356 F.2d 761; Easter v. District of Columbia, D.C.Cir.1966, 361 F.2d 50; Note, 1967, 52 Corn.L.Q. 470.

53. Louisville & N. R. Co. v. Howser, 1923, 201 Ky. 548, 257 S.W. 1010; Bageard v. Consolidated Traction Co., 1900, 64 N.J.L. 316, 45 A. 620; Denman v. St. Paul & Duluth R. Co., 1880, 26 Minn. 357, 4 N.W. 605; Besserman v. Hines, 1920, 219 Ill.App. 606. Cf. Mikula v. Balogh, 1965, 9 Ohio App.2d 250, 224 N.E.2d 148 (voluntary influence of drugs).

A good discussion of this, with various other problems arising from intoxication, is McCoid, Intoxication and Its Effect Upon Civil Responsibility, 1956, 42 Iowa L.Rev. 38.

54. Woods v. Board of County Commissioners of Tipton County, 1890, 128 Ind. 289, 27 N.E. 611.

55. Wise v. Cleveland, C. C. & St. L. R. Co., 1915, 183 Ind. 484, 108 N.E. 369; McMichael v. Pennsylvania R. Co., 1938, 331 Pa. 584, 1 A.2d 242; State ex rel. Miser v. Hay, Mo.1959, 328 S.W.2d 672; Scott v. Gardner, 1941, 137 Tex. 628, 156 S.W.2d 513; Lynch v. Clark, 1948, 183 Or. 431, 194 P.2d 416. See Mc-

torts,[56] obviously cannot be held to the same standard as adults, because they cannot in fact meet it.[57] It is possible to apply a special standard to them, because "their normal condition is one of incapacity and the state of their progress toward maturity is reasonably capable of determination,"[58] and because there is a sufficient basis of community experience, on the part of those who have been children or dealt with them, to permit the jury to apply a special standard.

Conceding this, it is nevertheless true that the capacities of children vary greatly, not only with age, but also with individuals of the same age; and it follows that no very definite statement can be made as to just what standard is to be applied to them. To a great extent it must necessarily be a subjective one. The formula which has been worked out, and which is customarily given to the jury, is that of "what it is reasonable to expect of children of like age, intelligence and experience."[59] There is something of an individual standard: the capacity of the particular child to appreciate the risk and form

a reasonable judgment must be taken into account. This means that more will be required of a child of superior intelligence for his age,[60] and less of one who is mentally backward,[61] which is precisely what the same courts have refused to do in the case of an adult.[62] But the standard is still not entirely subjective,[63] and if the conclusion is that the conduct of the child was unreasonable in view of his estimated capacity, he may still be found negligent, even as a matter of law.[64]

Some courts have attempted to fix a minimum age, below which the child is held to be incapable of all negligence.[65] Although other limits have been set,[66] those most commonly accepted are taken over from the arbitrary rules of the criminal law, as to the age at which children are capable of crime. Below

Coid, Intoxication and Its Effect Upon Civil Responsibility, 1956, 42 Iowa L.Rev. 38, discussing a number of related problems.

56. See infra, § 134.

57. See, generally, Shulman, The Standard of Care Required of Children, 1927, 37 Yale L.J. 618; Bohlen, Liability in Tort of Infants and Insane Persons, 1924, 23 Mich.L.Rev. 9; Wilderman, Contributory Negligence of Infants, 1935, 10 Ind.L.J. 427; Notes, 1921, 21 Col.L.Rev. 697; 1925, 74 U.Pa.L.Rev. 79; 1937, 36 Mich.L.Rev. 328; 1959, 34 Ind.L.J. 511.

58. Snow, J., in Charbonneau v. MacRury, 1931, 84 N.H. 501, 153 A. 457, 463.

59. Dodwell v. Missouri Pac. R. Co., Mo.1964, 384 S.W. 2d 643; Ackerman v. Advance Petroleum Transport, 1942, 304 Mich. 96, 7 N.W.2d 235; Maker v. Wellin, 1958, 214 Or. 332, 327 P.2d 793, rehearing denied 329 P.2d 1114; Government Employees Ins. Co. v. Davis, 5 Cir. 1959, 266 F.2d 760; McCain v. Bankers Life & Cas. Co., Fla.App.1959, 110 So.2d 718; Second Restatement of Torts, § 283A.

"Age is only one of the elements to be considered, along with experience and judgment, the latter, involving discretion and power of self-control, being predominant." Marfyak v. New England Transp. Co., 1935, 120 Conn. 46, 179 A. 9.

60. Western & A. R. Co. v. Young, 1888, 81 Ga. 397, 7 S.E. 912; Thomas v. Oregon Short Line R. Co., 1916, 47 Utah 394, 154 P. 777; Grealish v. Brooklyn, Q. C. & S. R. Co., 1909, 130 App.Div. 238, 114 N.Y.S. 582, affirmed, 1910, 197 N.Y. 540, 91 N.E. 1114.

61. Harris v. Indiana General Service Co., 1934, 206 Ind. 351, 189 N.E. 410 (18 year old deaf mute with mental age of 6); Vitale v. Smith Auto Sales Co., 1929, 101 Vt. 477, 144 A. 380; Zajaczkowski v. State, 1947, 189 Misc.2d 299, 71 N.Y.S.2d 261 (7 year old with mental age of 2½); Garrison v. St. Louis, I. M. & S. R. Co., 1909, 92 Ark. 437, 123 S.W. 657; Linthicum v. Truitt, 1911, 2 Boyce, Del., 338, 80 A. 245.

62. See supra, p. 152.

63. Shulman, The Standard of Care Required of Children, 1927, 37 Yale L.J. 618.

64. Studer v. Southern Pac. Co., 1898, 121 Cal. 400, 53 P. 942; Colomb v. Portland & Brunswick St. R. Co., 1905, 100 Me. 418, 61 A. 898; Ackerman v. Advance Petroleum Transport, 1942, 304 Mich. 96, 7 N.W.2d 235; Lobsenz v. Rubinstein, 1939, 258 App. Div. 164, 15 N.Y.S.2d 848, affirmed, 1940, 283 N.Y. 600, 28 N.E.2d 22.

As to the effect of a child's violation of statute, see infra, p. 199.

65. See Note, 1966, 18 S.C.L.Rev. 648.

66. Thomas v. Tesch, 1954, 268 Wis. 338, 67 N.W.2d 367, rehearing denied, 1955, 268 Wis. 338, 68 N.W. 2d 457 (five and one-half); Conner v. Houtman, Okl.1960, 350 P.2d 311 (five); Christian v. Goodwin, 1961, 188 Cal.App.2d 650, 10 Cal.Rptr. 507 (five); Verni v. Johnson, 1946, 295 N.Y. 436, 68 N.E.2d 431 (four).

the age of seven, the child is arbitrarily held to be incapable of any negligence; [67] between seven and fourteen he is presumed to be incapable, but may be shown to be capable; [68] from fourteen to twenty-one he is presumed to be capable, but the contrary may be shown.[69] These multiples of seven are derived originally from the Bible, which is a poor reason for such arbitrary limits; and the analogy of the criminal law is certainly of dubious value where neither crime nor intent is in question.[70] The great majority of the courts have rejected any such fixed and arbitrary rules of delimitation, and have held that children well under the age of seven can be capable of some negligent conduct.[71] Undoubtedly there is an irreducible minimum, probably somewhere in the neighborhood of four years of age,[72] but it ought not to be fixed by rules laid down in advance without regard to the particular case. As the age decreases, there are simply fewer possibilities of negligence, until finally, at some indeterminate point, there are none at all. There is even more reason to say that there is no arbitrary maximum age, beyond which a minor is to be held to the same standard as an adult.[73]

The great bulk of the decisions in which all these questions have been considered have involved the contributory negligence of child plaintiffs. It has been contended [74] that where the child is a defendant no allowance should be made for his age, and he should in all cases be treated like an adult, for the reason that in practice children do not pay judgments against them for injuries inflicted, and such payment comes, if at all, from an adult, or from insurance paid for by an adult. Whether this is universally true may perhaps be questioned; but however that may be, the existing case law does not at all sustain this point of view.[75] Instead the courts have developed the rule, which is now quite generally accepted, that whenever a child, wheth-

---

67. Baker v. Alt, 1965, 374 Mich. 492, 132 N.W.2d 614; Dixon v. Stringer, 1939, 277 Ky. 347, 126 S.W.2d 448; Dodd v. Spartansburg, Ry. Gas & Elec. Co., 1913, 95 S.C. 9, 78 S.E. 525; Burns v. Eminger, 1927, 81 Mont. 79, 261 P. 613; Walston v. Greene, 1958, 247 N.C. 693, 102 S.E.2d 124. Cf. Bush v. New Jersey & N. Y. Transit Co., 1959, 30 N.J. 345, 153 A.2d 28 (presumption).

68. Kuhns v. Brugger, 1957, 390 Pa. 331, 135 A.2d 395; Virginian Ry. Co. v. Rose, 4 Cir. 1959, 267 F.2d 312, cert. denied 361 U.S. 837; Read v. Daniel, 1956, 197 Va. 853, 91 S.E.2d 400. This part of it, at least, was abandoned in Williamson v. Garland, Ky.1966, 402 S.W.2d 80.

69. Nagle v. Allegheny Valley R. Co., 1879, 88 Pa. 35; Atlanta Gas Light Co. v. Brown, 1956, 94 Ga.App. 351, 94 S.E.2d 612.

70. See Johnson's Adm'r v. Rutland R. Co., 1919, 93 Vt. 132, 106 A. 682.

71. Eckhardt v. Hanson, 1936, 196 Minn. 270, 264 N.W. 776; State for Use of Taylor v. Barlly, 1958, 216 Md. 94, 140 A.2d 173; Mann v. Fairbourn, 1961, 12 Utah 2d 342, 366 P.2d 603; Witt v. Houston, 1952, 207 Okl. 25, 246 P.2d 753; De Groot v. Van Akkeren, 1937, 225 Wis. 105, 273 N.W. 725.

72. Cf. Watts v. Erickson, 1955, 244 Minn. 264, 69 N.W.2d 626 (at four years, nine months, negligence not submitted to the jury unless there is some evidence as to experience, intelligence, maturity, training and capacity of the child).

See also Wilderman, Contributory Negligence of Infants, 1935, 10 Ind.L.J. 427.

73. Atlanta Gas Light Co. v. Brown, 1956, 94 Ga.App. 351, 94 S.E.2d 612 (20 years, presumed like adult); Smith v. Bailey, 1941, 91 N.H. 507, 23 A.2d 363 (19, treated as adult); Barga v. Longfellow, 1959, 111 Ohio App., 357, 172 N.E.2d 624 (17, standard of age and experience); Charbonneau v. MacRury, 1931, 84 N.H. 501, 153 A. 457 (17, same); Bridges v. Arkansas-Missouri Power Co., Mo.App.1966, 410 S.W. 2d 106 (16, same); Parzych v. Town of Branford, 1957, 20 Conn.Sup. 378, 136 A.2d 223 (15, treated like adult on particular facts).

74. James, Accident Liability Reconsidered: The Impact of Liability Insurance, 1948, 57 Yale L.J. 549, 554–6; Note, 1967, 46 Neb.L.Rev. 699.

75. Charbonneau v. MacRury, 1931, 84 N.H. 501, 153 A. 457; Faith v. Massengill, 1961, 104 Ga.App. 348, 121 S.E.2d 657; Chernotik v. Schrank, 1956, 76 S.D. 374, 79 N.W.2d 4; Hoyt v. Rosenberg, 1947, 80 Cal. App.2d 500, 182 P.2d 234; Kuhns v. Brugger, 1957, 390 Pa. 331, 135 A.2d 395; see Note, 1959, 38 Or.L. Rev. 268.

Neal v. Gillett, 1855, 23 Conn. 437, which has been cited as supporting the double standard, appears to hold only that the children were too old to have their age considered.

er as plaintiff [76] or as defendant, engages in an activity which is normally one for adults only,[77] such as driving an automobile [78] or flying an airplane, the public interest and the public safety require that any consequences due to his own incapacity shall fall upon him rather than the innocent victim, and that he must be held to the adult standard, without any allowance for his age. This position has been rapidly gaining ground in recent years.

There are a few occasional cases [79] indicating that a similar allowance is to be made at the other end of the scale, for persons at the extreme of life whose mental faculties have been impaired by age; but there is really not a great deal on it.

Knowledge

One of the most difficult questions in connection with negligence is that of what the actor may be required to know. Knowledge has been defined [80] as belief in the existence of a fact, which coincides with the truth. It rests upon perception of the actor's surroundings, memory of what has gone before, and a power to correlate the two with previous experience.[81] So far as perception is concerned, it seems clear that, unless his attention is legitimately distracted,[82] the actor must give to his surroundings the attention which a standard reasonable man would consider necessary under the circumstances, and that he must use such senses as he has to discover what is readily apparent. He may be negligent in failing to look,[83] or in failing to observe what is visible when he does look.[84]

76. Daniels v. Evans, 1966, 107 N.H. 407, 224 A.2d 63; Prichard v. Veterans Cab Co., 1965, 63 Cal.2d 727, 47 Cal.Rptr. 904, 408 P.2d 360; Harrelson v. Whitehead, 1963, 236 Ark. 325, 365 S.W.2d 868; Adams v. Lopez, 1965, 75 N.M. 503, 407 P.2d 50; Garatoni v. Teegarden, 1958, 129 Ind.App. 500, 154 N.E.2d 379. See Note, 1966, 9 Ariz.L.Rev. 134.

77. The leading case is probably Dellwo v. Pearson, 1961, 259 Minn. 452, 107 N.W.2d 859, which involved the operation of a motorboat. The rule has been applied to motorcycles. Harrelson v. Whitehead, 1963, 236 Ark. 325, 365 S.W.2d 868; Daniels v. Evans, 1966, 107 N.H. 407, 224 A.2d 63; Powell v. Hartford Acc. & Ind. Co., 1966, 217 Tenn. 503, 398 S.W.2d 727 (motor scooter); Medina v. McAllister, Fla.1967, 202 So.2d 755 (same); Adams v. Lopez, 1965, 75 N.M. 503, 407 P.2d 50. But not to bicycles. Williams v. Gilbert, 1965, 239 Ark. 935, 395 S.W.2d 333; Conway v. Tamborini, 1966, 68 Ill.App.2d 190, 215 N.E.2d 303; Bixenman v. Hall, 1968, — Ind. —, 242 N.E.2d 837; Ransom v. Melegi, 1969, 18 Mich.App. 476, 171 N.W.2d 482; Davis v. Bushnell, 1970, — Idaho —, 465 P.2d 652.

Perhaps the extreme case is Neumann v. Shlansky, App.Term 1970, 312 N.Y.S.2d 951, applying the adult standard to a teenager playing golf.

78. Baxter v. Fugett, Okl.1967, 425 P.2d 462; Allen v. Ellis, 1963, 191 Kan. 311, 380 P.2d 408; Prichard v. Veterans Cab Co., 1965, 63 Cal.2d 727, 47 Cal. Rptr. 904, 408 P.2d 360; Nielsen v. Brown, 1962, 232 Or. 426, 374 P.2d 896; Dawson v. Hoffmann, 1963, 43 Ill.App.2d 17, 192 N.E.2d 695. See Notes, 1966, 33 Tenn.L.Rev. 533; 1966, 9 Ariz.L.Rev. 134; 1969, 20 Syr.L.Rev. 823.

In Karr v. McNeil, 1952, 92 Ohio App. 458, 110 N.E.2d 714; Wilson v. Shumate, Mo.1956, 296 S.W.2d 72; Betzold v. Erickson, 1962, 35 Ill.App.2d 203, 182 N.E. 2d 342; and Harrelson v. Whitehead, 1963, 236 Ark. 325, 365 S.W.2d 868, statutes making no specific exception as to minors driving cars were held to require an adult standard.

79. "All that the law requires of an infant is a degree of care commensurate with its age and discretion. We think the same rule should apply to old people, whose senses are blunted, and mental faculties impaired by age." Johnson v. St. Paul City Ry. Co., 1897, 67 Minn. 260, 69 N.W. 900. Accord: Kitsap County Transp. Co. v. Harvey, 9 Cir. 1927, 15 F.2d 166; Daly v. Liverpool Corp., [1939] 2 All Eng. Rep. 142; see La Cava v. City of New Orleans, La. App.1964, 159 So.2d 362.

80. Seavey, Negligence—Subjective or Objective, 1927, 41 Harv.L.Rev. 1, 17; Second Restatement of Torts, § 289.

81. Second Restatement of Torts, § 289.

82. Marietta v. Springer, 1964, 193 Kan. 266, 392 P.2d 858; Conner v. Farmers & Merchants Bank, 1963, 243 S.C. 132, 132 S.E.2d 385; Ramsey v. Mellon Nat. Bank & Trust Co., W.D.Pa.1964, 231 F.Supp. 1.

83. Jackson v. Cockill, 1964, 149 W.Va. 78, 138 S.E. 2d 710; Belcher v. City & County of San Francisco, 1945, 69 Cal.App.2d 457, 158 P.2d 996; Syck v. Duluth St. R. Co., 1920, 146 Minn. 118, 177 N.W. 944; Waitkus v. Chicago & N. W. R. Co., 1931, 204 Wis. 566, 236 N.W. 531, 237 N.W. 259; Pennsylvania R. Co. v. Moses, 1932, 125 Ohio St. 621, 184 N.E. 8.

84. Payne v. Kingsley, 1965, 59 Ill.App.2d 245, 207 N.E.2d 177; Southern Md. Elec. Co-op., Inc. v. Blanchard, 1965, 239 Md. 481, 212 A.2d 301; Roux v. Pettus, Mo.App.1956, 293 S.W.2d 144; Southern Cal.

As to memory, he is required to fix in his mind those matters which would make such an impression upon the standard man,[85] and, unless he is startled,[86] or his attention is distracted for some sufficient reason,[87] to bear them in mind,[88] at least for a reasonable length of time.[89]

The real difficulty lies with the question of experience. The late Henry T. Terry [90] came to the conclusion that "there are no facts whatever which every person in the community is absolutely bound at his peril to know." It seems clear, however, that there are certain things which every adult [91] with a minimum of intelligence must necessarily have learned: [92] the law of gravity,[93] the fact that fire burns and water will drown,[94] that inflammable objects will catch fire,[95] that a loose board will tip when it is trod on,[96] the ordinary features of the weather to which he is accustomed,[97] and similar phenomena of

---

Freight Lines v. San Diego Elec. R. Co., 1944, 66 Cal. App.2d 672, 152 P.2d 470; Shelton v. Jones, W.D. Va.1967, 272 F.Supp. 139.

It is sometimes said that the actor's testimony that he looked and did not see will not be credited. Glaria v. Washington Southern R. Co., 1908, 30 App. D.C. 559; Danks v. Pittsburgh Rys. Co., 1937, 328 Pa. 356, 195 A. 16. But he is required to see only where a reasonable man would do so. Clewell v. Plummer, 1956, 384 Pa. 515, 121 A.2d 459.

85. Second Restatement of Torts, § 289, Comment *f*; City of Charlottesville v. Jones, 1918, 123 Va. 682, 97 S.E. 316, 324. Cf. Bassett v. Fish (1878) 75 N.Y. 303 (no reason to believe condition would cause injury); Deacy v. McDonnell, 1944, 131 Conn. 101, 38 A.2d 181 (not unreasonable as matter of law to forget step seen four times); Clewell v. Plummer, 1956, 384 Pa. 515, 121 A.2d 459 (otherwise occupied).

86. Williams v. Ballard Lumber Co., 1906, 41 Wash. 338, 83 P. 323.

87. Kingsul Theatres v. Quillen, 1946, 29 Tenn.App. 248, 196 S.W.2d 316; Crites v. City of New Richmond, 1897, 98 Wis. 55, 73 N.W. 322; West Kentucky Tel. Co. v. Pharis, 1904, 78 S.W. 917, 25 Ky. Law Rep. 1838; Houston v. Town of Waverly, 1932, 225 Ala. 98, 142 So. 80; Dennis v. City of Albemarle, 1955, 242 N.C. 263, 87 S.E.2d 561, on rehearing 243 N.C. 221, 90 S.E.2d 532. See Note, 1950, 2 Ala.L. Rev. 373. What is reasonable under particular circumstances is frequently a question for the jury. Powell v. Vracin, 1957, 150 Cal.App.2d 454, 310 P.2d 27.

Cf. Gilman v. Inhabitants of Deerfield, 1860, 15 Gray, Mass., 577 (preoccupation not enough); Buckley v. Westchester Lighting Co., 1905, 93 App.Div. 436, 87 N.Y.S. 763, affirmed 1906, 183 N.Y. 506, 76 N.E. 1090 (same); Davis v. California St. Cable R. Co., 1894, 105 Cal. 131, 38 P. 647 (curiosity as to fire). Cf. Ferrie v. D'Arc, 1959, 31 N.J. 92, 155 A.2d 257 (concentration on another matter).

88. Mickel v. Haines Enterprises, Inc., 1965, 240 Or. 369, 400 P.2d 518; Tomlinson v. Wilson & Toomer Fertilizer Co., Fla.App.1964, 165 So.2d 801; Lazzarotto v. Atchison, T. & S. F. R. Co., 1958, 157 Cal. App.2d 455, 321 P.2d 29; Ramos v. Service Bros., 1931, 118 Cal.App. 432, 5 P.2d 623, 624; Anderson v. Northern Pac. R. Co., 1898, 19 Wash. 340, 53 P. 345.

89. Failure of memory was excused in Bassett v. Fish, 1878, 75 N.Y. 303 (three weeks); West Kentucky

Tel. Co. v. Pharis, 1904, 78 S.W. 917, 25 Ky.Law Rep. 1838 (four days, with attention distracted). Cf. Wood v. Richmond & D. R. Co., 1893, 100 Ala. 660, 13 So. 552 (forgetting pile of timber in one day not excused).

90. Terry, Leading Principles of Anglo-American Law, 1884, § 200.

91. Here again a special standard based on age and capacity obviously is necessary for children. Second Restatement of Torts, § 283A.

92. See the exhaustive collection of cases in the Note, 1939, 23 Minn.L.Rev. 68. In Lange v. Hoyt, 1932, 114 Conn. 590, 159 A. 575, it was held that beliefs and theories held by a large number of reasonable and intelligent people, as for example, Christian Science, cannot be disregarded, even though the court itself might consider them unfounded.

93. Blomberg v. Trupukka, 1941, 210 Minn. 523, 299 N.W. 11; Seaboard Air Line R. Co. v. Hackney, 1928, 217 Ala. 382, 115 So. 869; Sidwell v. Economy Coal Co., 1912, 154 Iowa 475, 135 N.W. 59; Lyttle v. Harlan Town Coal Co., 1915, 167 Ky. 345, 180 S.W. 519.

94. Gates v. Boston & Me. R. Co., 1926, 255 Mass. 297, 151 N.E. 320; Peters v. Bowman, 1896, 115 Cal. 345, 350, 47 P. 113, 114, rehearing denied, 1897, 115 Cal. 345, 47 P. 598; City of Evansville v. Blue, 1937, 212 Ind. 130, 8 N.E.2d 224. See Lexington & E. R. Co. v. White, 1918, 182 Ky. 267, 279, 206 S.W. 467, 472, 473 (smoke).

95. Lillibridge v. McCann, 1898, 117 Mich. 84, 75 N.W. 288; Gates v. Boston & Maine R. Co., 1926, 255 Mass. 297, 151 N.E. 320; Mensik v. Cascade Timber Co., 1927, 144 Wash. 528, 258 P. 323.

96. City of Huntingburgh v. First, 1896, 15 Ind.App. 552, 43 N.E. 17; cf. Stobba v. Fitzsimmons & Connell Co., 1895, 58 Ill.App. 427.

97. Mayor of Baltimore v. Thompson, 1937, 171 Md. 460, 189 A. 822 (fog); Staples v. City of Spencer,

nature. He must know in addition a few elementary facts about himself: the amount of space he occupies,[98] the principles of balance and leverage as applied to his own body,[99] and, to the extent that it is reasonable to demand it of him, the limits of his own strength,[1] as well as some elementary rules of health.[2]

But beyond this, it seems clear that any individual who has led a normal existence will have learned much more: the traits of common animals,[3] the normal habits, capacities and reactions of other human beings,[4] including their propensities toward negligence and crime,[5] the danger involved in ex-

plosives,[6] inflammable liquids,[7] electricity,[8] moving machinery,[9] slippery surfaces [10] and firearms,[11] the fact that an automobile is not easy to control in deep sand,[12] that worn tires will blow out,[13] and many other things.[14] Such an individual will not be credited or excused when he denies knowledge of the risk; and to this extent, at least, there is a mini-

---

1937, 222 Iowa 1241, 271 N.W. 200 (ice); Olson v. McMullen, 1885, 34 Minn. 94, 24 N.W. 318 (effect of thaw); King v. Interstate Consol. St. R. Co., 1902, 23 R.I. 583, 51 A. 301.

98. See Jennings v. Tacoma Railway & Motor Co., 1893, 7 Wash. 275, 34 P. 937; Mellott v. Louisville & N. R. Co., 1897, 101 Ky. 212, 40 S.W. 696.

99. Sharp v. Higbee Co., 1936, 56 Ohio App. 278, 282, 10 N.E.2d 932, 934; Hesse v. National Casket Co., 1902, 66 N.J.L. 652, 52 A. 384.

1. Sweeney v. Winebaum, 1930, 84 N.H. 217, 149 A. 77; Worlds v. Georgia R. Co., 1896, 99 Ga. 283, 25 S.E. 646; Nashville, C. & St. L. R. Co. v. Cleaver, 1938, 274 Ky. 410, 118 S.W.2d 748; Missouri Pac. R. Co. v. Vinson, 1938, 196 Ark. 500, 118 S.W.2d 672.

2. Jurovich v. Interstate Iron Co., 1930, 181 Minn. 588, 233 N.W. 465 (working in ice water); Hicks v. Southern R. Co., 1919, 23 Ga.App. 594, 99 S.E. 218, affirmed, 1920, 149 Ga. 713, 101 S.E. 798 (exposure in a cold room); Kroger Grocery & Baking Co. v. Woods, 1943, 205 Ark. 131, 162 S.W.2d 869 (eating moldy food). Cf. Osborn v. Leuffgen, 1943, 381 Ill. 295, 45 N.E.2d 622 (alcoholic beverages are intoxicating).

3. Lloyd v. Alton R. Co., 1941, 348 Mo. 1222, 159 S.W. 2d 267 (dog); Linnehan v. Sampson, 1879, 126 Mass. 506 (bull); Haack v. Rodenbour, 1944, 234 Iowa 368, 12 N.W.2d 861 (bull); Hammond v. Melton, 1891, 42 Ill.App. 186 (stallion); Tolin v. Terrell, 1909, 133 Ky. 210, 117 S.W. 290 (mule).

4. Second Restatement of Torts, § 290. Cf. Easler v. Downie Amusement Co., 1926, 125 Me. 334, 133 A. 905. Compare, as to children, Davoren v. Kansas City, 1925, 308 Mo. 513, 273 S.W. 401; Louisville & N. R. Co. v. Vaughn, 1943, 292 Ky. 120, 166 S.W.2d 43; Femling v. Star Pub. Co., 1938, 195 Wash. 395, 81 P.2d 293.

5. Second Restatement of Torts, § 290. See infra, pp. 172–176.

6. City of Waco v. Dool, Tex.Civ.App.1923, 254 S.W. 353, 354, error dismissed; Comanche Duke Oil Co. v. Texas Pac. Coal & Oil Co., Tex.Com.App.1927, 298 S.W. 554. Cf. Schultz v. Kinabrew, La.App. 1937, 177 So. 450 (lye).

7. Burnett v. Amalgamated Phosphate Co., 5 Cir. 1938, 96 F.2d 974, cert. denied 305 U.S. 647 (gasoline); Parton v. Phillips Petroleum Co., 1937, 231 Mo.App. 585, 107 S.W.2d 167 (kerosene); Simkins v. R. L. Morrison & Sons, 5 Cir. 1939, 107 F.2d 121 (gasoline fumes). Cf. Lanigan v. New York Gaslight Co., 1877, 71 N.Y. 29 (gas).

8. Peterson v. Minnesota Power & Light Co., 1939, 206 Minn. 268, 288 N.W. 588; Roland v. Griffith, 1942, 291 Ky. 248, 163 S.W.2d 496; Aller v. Iowa Elec. L. & P. Co., 1939, 227 Iowa 185, 288 N.W. 66; LeVonas v. Acme Paper Board Co., 1944, 184 Md. 16, 40 A.2d 43.

9. Gossens v. Mattoon Mfg. Co., 1899, 104 Wis. 406, 80 N.W. 589; American Malting Co. v. Lelivelt, 1902, 101 Ill.App. 320; Dillenberger v. Weingartner, 1900, 64 N.J.L. 292, 45 A. 638.

10. McCann v. Gordon, 1934, 315 Pa. 367, 172 A. 644; Raymond v. Sauk County, 1918, 167 Wis. 125, 166 N.W. 29; McDonald v. State Highway Department, 1932, 166 S.C. 415, 164 S.E. 920; Wolfe v. State for Use of Brown, 1937, 173 Md. 103, 117, 194 A. 832, 838, 839.

11. See McMillen v. Steele, 1923, 275 Pa. 584, 119 A. 721.

12. Michigan City v. Rudolph, 1938, 104 Ind.App. 643, 12 N.E.2d 970.

13. Delair v. McAdoo, 1936, 324 Pa. 392, 188 A. 181. Cf. Crupe v. Spicuzza, Mo.App.1935, 86 S.W.2d 347 (blowouts occur at excessive speed); Grant v. Matson, 1942, 68 S.D. 402, 3 N.W.2d 118 (same); McIntyre v. Pope, 1937, 326 Pa. 172, 191 A. 607 (dangers of overcrowding driver's seat).

14. See Note, 1939, 23 Minn.L.Rev. 628. The First Restatement of Torts, § 289, Comment m, Illustration 15, may perhaps have gone too far in requiring the individual to know the possibility of spontaneous combustion. Cf. Gobrecht v. Beckwith, 1926, 82 N.H. 415, 135 A. 20; Baumgartner v. Pennsylvania R. Co., 1928, 292 Pa. 106, 140 A. 622 (dangers of carbon monoxide not a matter of common knowledge).

mum standard of knowledge, based upon what is common to the community.

The few cases [15] which have considered the question have held that when an abnormal individual who lacks the experience common to the particular community comes into it, as in the case of the old lady from the city who comes to the farm without ever having learned that a bull is a dangerous beast, the standard of knowledge will still be applied, and it is the individual who must conform to the community, rather than vice versa.

Above this minimum, once it is determined, the individual will not be held to knowledge of risks which are not known or apparent to him.[16] He may, however, know enough to be conscious of his own ignorance, and of possible danger into which it may lead him; and if that is the case, as where a layman attempts to give medical treatment,[17] or one enters a strange dark passage,[18] or an automobile driver proceeds with a mysterious wobble in his front wheels,[19] or traverses a strange town without an attempt to discover the meaning of unfamiliar purple traffic lights which suddenly confront him,[20] he will be found negligent in proceeding in the face of known ignorance. He may, furthermore, be engaged in an activity, or stand in a relation to others, which imposes upon him an obligation to investigate and find out,[21] so that he becomes liable not so much for being ignorant as for remaining ignorant; and this obligation may require him to know at least enough to conduct an intelligent inquiry as to what he does not know. The occupier of premises who invites business visitors to enter,[22] the landlord who installs a gas heater in a bathroom used by his tenants,[23] the telephone company which erects wires in the street,[24] the manufacturer of goods to be sold to the public,[25] the carrier who undertakes to transport passengers,[26] all are charged with

---

15. Linnehan v. Sampson, 1879, 126 Mass. 506 (bull); Haack v. Rodenbour, 1944, 234 Iowa 368, 12 N.W. 2d 861 (bull); Tolin v. Terrell, 1909, 133 Ky. 210, 117 S.W. 290 (mule); Borden v. Falk Co., 1903, 97 Mo.App. 566, 71 S.W. 478 (mule); Michigan City v. Rudolph, 1938, 104 Ind.App. 643, 12 N.E.2d 670 (deep sand on country road); Weirs v. Jones County, 1892, 86 Iowa 625, 53 N.W. 321 (inability to read English). See, however, Seavey, Negligence—Subjective or Objective, 1927, 41 Harv.L.Rev. 1, 19, arguing that a hermit or a savage dropped suddenly into the streets of New York should be judged only by the knowledge he has had the opportunity to acquire.

16. Stedman v. O'Neil, 1909, 82 Conn. 199, 72 A. 923; The Nitroglycerine Case, 1872, 15 Wall., U.S., 524; Wickert v. Wisconsin Central R. Co., 1910, 142 Wis. 375, 125 N.W. 943; Orr v. Bradley, 1907, 126 Mo. App. 146, 103 S.W. 1149.

17. Conner v. Winton, 1856, 8 Ind. 315. Cf. Commonwealth v. Pierce, 1884, 138 Mass. 165.

18. Benton v. Watson, 1919, 231 Mass. 582, 121 N.E. 399. Cf. Plahn v. Masonic Hall Bldg. Ass'n, 1939, 206 Minn. 232, 288 N.W. 575.

19. Prokey v. Hamm, 1941, 91 N.H. 513, 23 A.2d 327.

20. Second Restatement of Torts, § 289, Comment j.

21. "Where a duty to use care is imposed and where knowledge is necessary to careful conduct, voluntary ignorance is equivalent to negligence." Gobrecht v. Beckwith, 1926, 82 N.H. 415, 420, 135 A. 20, 22. See Note, 1939, 23 Minn.L.Rev. 628, 654.

22. Ness Creameries v. Barthes, 1934, 170 Miss. 865, 155 So. 222 (crystallization of metal); Haefeli v. Woodrich Eng. Co., 1931, 255 N.Y. 442, 175 N.E. 123 (strength of cement). Cf. Washington Market Co. v. Clagett, 1901, 19 App.D.C. 12; Easler v. Downie Amusement Co., 1926, 125 Me. 334, 133 A. 905; Falkenberry v. Shaw, 1931, 183 Ark. 1019, 39 S.W.2d 708.

23. Gobrecht v. Beckwith, 1926, 82 N.H. 415, 135 A. 20. Cf. Fireman's Mut. Ins. Co. v. High Point Sprinkler Co., 1966, 266 N.C. 134, 146 S.E.2d 53 (business of installing sprinkler systems). But only reasonable care is required. In Doherty v. Arcade Hotel, 1943, 170 Or. 374, 134 P.2d 118, an innkeeper was held not bound as a matter of law to know the dangers of porcelain faucets within 3½ years after the plumbing trade had abandoned them.

24. Western Union Tel. Co. v. Engler, 9 Cir. 1896, 75 F. 102; Thompson v. Reed, 1912, 29 S.D. 85, 135 N.W. 679.

25. Hopkins v. E. I. DuPont de Nemours & Co., 3 Cir. 1952, 199 F.2d 930; Maize v. Atlantic Refining Co., 1945, 352 Pa. 51, 41 A.2d 850; Carter v. Yardley & Co., 1946, 319 Mass. 92, 64 N.E.2d 693; Marsh Wood Products Co. v. Babcock & Wilcox Co., 1932, 207 Wis. 209, 218, 240 N.W. 392; Goullon v. Ford Motor Co., 6 Cir. 1930, 44 F.2d 310.

26. Central of Ga. R. Co. v. Robertson, 1919, 203 Ala. 358, 360, 83 So. 102, 104.

the duty of the affirmative action which would be taken by a reasonable man in their position, to discover dangers of which they may not be informed. As scientific knowledge advances, and more and more effective tests become available, what was excusable ignorance yesterday becomes negligent ignorance today.[27]

Superior Knowledge, Skill and Intelligence

Thus far the question has been one of a minimum standard, below which the individual will not be permitted to fall. But if he has in fact knowledge, skill, or even intelligence [28] superior to that of the ordinary man, the law will demand of him conduct consistent with it. The vendor of fur coats who has learned from experience that some few persons are especially susceptible to dermatitis caused by a particular dye must take precautions which might not be required if he had remained in ignorance.[29] Upon the same basis, a physician who is possessed of unusual skill or knowledge must use care which is reasonable in the light of his special ability and information, and may be negligent where an ordinary doctor would not.[30]

Cf. Mattson v. Central Elec. & Gas Co., 8 Cir. 1949, 174 F.2d 215 (gas company laying pipes in street); Cornbrooks v. Terminal Barber Shops, 1940, 282 N.Y. 217, 26 N.E.2d 25 (barber using vibrator); Zesch v. Abrasives Co. of Philadelphia, 1944, 353 Mo. 558, 183 S.W.2d 140 (defect in grinding wheel).

27. Marsh Wood Products Co. v. Babcock & Wilcox Co., 1932, 207 Wis. 209, 240 N.W. 392; Zesch v. Abrasives Co. of Philadelphia, 1944, 353 Mo. 558, 183 S.W.2d 140.

28. Seavey, Negligence—Subjective or Objective, 1927, 41 Harv.L.Rev. 1, 13; Second Restatement of Torts, § 289, Comment m.

29. Gerkin v. Brown & Sehler Co., 1913, 177 Mich. 45, 143 N.W. 48. Cf. Muller v. A. B. Kirschbaum Co., 1930, 298 Pa. 560, 148 A. 851 (knowledge that bottom of coffee urn had blown out on previous occasions).

30. Harris v. Fall, 7 Cir. 1910, 177 F. 79 ("his own best ability, skill and care," over and above the minimum standard). But the care required is still only the ordinary care of a reasonable man, assuming that he has such special knowledge. See Beach v. Chollet, 1928, 31 Ohio App. 8, 166 N.E. 145. And it has been said that this does not mean that

Professional men in general, and those who undertake any work calling for special skill, are required not only to exercise reasonable care in what they do,[31] but also to possess a standard minimum of special knowledge and ability. Most of the decided cases have dealt with physicians and surgeons,[32] but the same is undoubtedly true of dentists,[33] pharmacists,[34] psychiatrists,[35] attorneys,[36] archi-

a man must be always at his best. Dorris v. Warford, 1907, 124 Ky. 768, 100 S.W. 312; Loudon v. Scott, 1920, 58 Mont. 645, 194 P. 488.

31. As to the distinction between care and skill, see Akridge v. Noble, 1902, 114 Ga. 949, 41 S.E. 78; Kline v. Nicholson, 1911, 151 Iowa 710, 130 N.W. 722; Sullivan v. McGraw, 1898, 118 Mich. 39, 76 N.W. 149; Gillette v. Tucker, 1902, 67 Ohio St. 106, 65 N.E. 865; Newport v. Hyde, 1962, 244 Miss. 870, 147 So.2d 113.

32. A very good article is McCoid, The Care Required of Medical Practitioners, 1959, 12 Vand.L. Rev. 549. Older ones are Posten, The Law of Medical Malpractice in West Virginia, 1934, 41 W.Va. L.Q. 35; Swan, The California Law of Malpractice of Physicians, Surgeons, and Dentists, 1945, 33 Cal.L.Rev. 248; Notes, 1951, 35 Minn.L.Rev. 186; 1951, 36 Iowa L.Rev. 681; 1940, 26 Va.L.Rev. 919; 1929, 29 Col.L.Rev. 985; 1929, 78 U.Pa.L.Rev. 91; Symposium, 1967, 44 Chi.Kent.L.Rev. 106 ff.

As to osteopaths, naturopaths, chiropractors, and the like, See Note, 1965, 9 Utah L.Rev. 705.

33. United Dentists v. Bryan, 1932, 158 Va. 880, 164 S.E. 554; Lane v. Calvert, 1958, 215 Md. 457, 138 A.2d 902; Hurley v. Johnston, 1956, 143 Conn. 364, 122 A.2d 732; Wintersteen v. Semler, 1952, 197 Or. 601, 250 P.2d 420, rehearing denied 1953, 197 Or. 601, 255 P.2d 138.

34. Tremblay v. Kimball, 1910, 107 Me. 53, 77 A. 405; Allan v. State S. S. Co., 1892, 132 N.Y. 91, 30 N.E. 482; see King, Liability for Negligence of Pharmacists, 1959, 12 Vand.L.Rev. 695.

35. Hammer v. Rosen, 1960, 7 N.Y.2d 376, 198 N.Y.S.2d 65, 165 N.E.2d 756. See Dawidoff, The Malpractice of Psychiatrists, [1966] Duke L.J. 696; Morse, The Tort Liability of the Psychiatrist, 1967, 16 Buff.L.Rev. 649.

36. Ward v. Arnold, 1958, 52 Wash.2d 581, 328 P.2d 164; Hodges v. Carter, 1954, 239 N.C. 517, 80 S.E. 2d 144; Lucas v. Hamm, 1961, 56 Cal.2d 583, 15 Cal.Rptr. 821, 364 P.2d 685, cert. denied, 1962, 368 U.S. 987; Humboldt Bldg. Ass'n v. Ducker's Ex'x, 1901, 111 Ky. 759, 64 S.W. 671; Citizens' Loan Fund & Sav. Ass'n v. Friedley, 1890, 123 Ind. 143, 23 N.E. 1075.

See Wade, The Attorney's Liability for Negligence, 1959, 12 Vand.L.Rev. 755; Blaustein, Liability of

tects and engineers,[37] accountants,[38] abstracters of title,[39] and many other professions [40] and even skilled trades.[41] Since, allowing for the inevitable differences in the work done, the principles applied to all of these appear to be quite identical, and since the medical cases are by far the most numerous, it will be convenient to talk only of physicians and surgeons.

A physician may, although he seldom does, contract to cure his patient, or to accomplish a particular result, in which case he may be liable for breach of contract when he does not succeed.[42] In the absence of such an express agreement, he does not warrant or insure the outcome of his treatment,[43] and he will not be liable for an honest mistake of judgment, where the proper course is open to reasonable doubt.[44] But by undertaking to render medical services, even though gratuitously,[45] he will ordinarily be understood to hold himself out as having standard professional skill and knowledge. The formula under which this usually is put to the jury is that he must have the skill and learning commonly possessed by members of the profession in good standing; and he will be liable if harm results because he does not have them.[46]

Attorney to Client in New York for Negligence, 1953, 19 Brook.L.Rev. 233; Isaacs, Liability of the Lawyer for Bad Advice, 1935, 24 Cal.L.Rev. 39; DesChamps, Lawyers' and Accountants' Professional Liability, 1955, 22 Ins.Couns.J. 279; Notes, 1951, 37 Va.L.Rev. 429; 1959, 26 Tenn.L.Rev. 525; 1963, 63 Col.L.Rev. 1292; 1967, 8 Ariz.L.Rev. 343.

37. Cowles v. City of Minneapolis, 1915, 128 Minn. 452, 151 N.W. 184; Hubert v. Aitken, N.Y.C.P. 1888, 19 St.R. 914, 2 N.Y.S. 711, affirmed, 1889, 5 N.Y.S. 839, affirmed, 1891, 123 N.Y. 655, 25 N.E. 954; Surf Realty Corp. v. Standing, 1953, 195 Va. 431, 78 S.E.2d 901; Miller v. DeWitt, 1965, 59 Ill. App.2d 38, 208 N.E.2d 249. See Bell, Professional Negligence of Architects and Engineers.

38. L. B. Laboratories v. Mitchell, 1952, 39 Cal.2d 56, 244 P.2d 385; City of East Grand Forks v. Steele, 1913, 121 Minn. 296, 141 N.W. 181. See Hawkins, Professional Negligence Liability of Public Accountants, 1959, 12 Vand.L.Rev. 797; Witherspoon, When is an Architect Liable? [1954] Ins. Counsel J. 468, 1954, 59 Commercial L.J. 237, 1954, 31 N.D.L.J. 54; DesChamps, Lawyers' and Accountants' Professional Liability, 1955, 22 Ins.Counsel J. 279.

39. Adams v. Greer, W.D.Ark.1953, 114 F.Supp. 770; Savings Bank v. Ward, 1879, 100 U.S. 195, 25 L.Ed. 621. See Roady, Professional Liability of Abstractors, 1959, 12 Vand.L.Rev. 783.

40. Stern v. Lanng, 1901, 106 La. 738, 31 So. 303 (oculist); Kahn v. Shaw, 1941, 65 Ga.App. 563, 16 S.E.2d 99 (optometrist); Ballance v. Dunnington, 1928, 241 Mich. 383, 217 N.W. 329 (X-ray operator); The Tom Lysle, D.Pa.1892, 48 F. 690 (pilot).

The symposium on professional negligence in 1959, 12 Vand.L.Rev. 535–850 is particularly valuable. It has been republished in Roady and Anderson, Professional Negligence, 1960. See also Strobel, Malpractice by Veterinarians, 1966, 15 Cleve.-Marsh.L. Rev. 276; North, Valuers: A Study in Professional Liability, 1965, 29 Convey. 186.

41. Jackson v. Central Torpedo Co., 1926, 117 Okl. 245, 246 P. 426 (shooting oil well); Van Nortwick v. Holbine, 1901, 62 Neb. 147, 86 N.W. 1057 (thresher); Louis Pizitz Dry Goods Co. v. Waldrop, 1939, 237 Ala. 208, 186 So. 151 (restaurant); Milliken v. Woodward, 1900, 64 N.J.L. 444, 45 A. 796 (insurance agent); Weissman v. Prashker, 1961, 405 Pa. 226, 175 A.2d 63 (airplane pilot). See Moore, Liability of Artisans and Tradesmen for Negligence, in Roady and Anderson, Professional Negligence, 1960, 309.

42. Frankel v. Wolper, 1918, 181 App.Div. 485, 169 N.Y.S. 15, affirmed, 1920, 228 N.Y. 582, 127 N.E. 913; McQuaid v. Michou, 1932, 85 N.H. 299, 157 A. 881; Noel v. Proud, 1961, 189 Kan. 6, 367 P.2d 61; Brooks v. Herd, 1927, 144 Wash. 173, 257 P. 238; Crawford v. Duncan, 1923, 61 Cal.App. 647, 215 P. 573. See Miller, The Contractual Liability of Physicians and Surgeons, [1953] Wash.U.L.Q. 413. Such promises are construed wherever possible as agreements merely to use proper skill and care to accomplish the result. Kuhn v. Brownfield, 1890, 34 W.Va. 252, 12 S.E. 519; Reynolds v. Graves, 1854, 3 Wis. 416.

43. Thornburg v. Long, 1919, 178 N.C. 589, 101 S.E. 99; Bonnet v. Foote, 1910, 47 Colo. 282, 107 P. 252; Coombs v. King, 1910, 107 Me. 376, 78 A. 468; Champion v. Kieth, 1906, 17 Okl. 204, 87 P. 845.

44. Loudon v. Scott, 1920, 58 Mont. 645, 194 P. 488; Staloch v. Holm, 1907, 100 Minn. 276, 111 N.W. 264; Maxwell v. Howell, 1934, 114 W.Va. 771, 174 S.E. 553; Coon v. Shields, 1934, 88 Utah 76, 39 P.2d 348.

45. McNevins v. Lowe, 1866, 40 Ill. 209; Du Bois v. Decker, 1891, 130 N.Y. 325, 29 N.E. 313; Napier v. Greenzweig, 2 Cir. 1919, 256 F. 196.

46. Harris v. Graham, 1926, 124 Okl. 196, 255 P. 710; Ayers v. Parry, 3 Cir. 1951, 192 F.2d 181, cert. denied 343 U.S. 980, rehearing denied 344 U.S. 849, 344 U.S. 916, and 345 U.S. 961; Adkins v. Ropp, 1938, 105 Ind.App. 331, 14 N.E.2d 727; Kelly v. Carroll, 1950, 36 Wash.2d 482, 219 P.2d 79, cert.

Sometimes this is called the skill of the "average" member of the profession; but this is clearly misleading, since only those in good professional standing are to be considered; and of these it is not the middle but the minimum common skill which is to be looked to.[47] If the defendant represents himself as having greater skill than this, as for example where he holds himself out as a specialist,[48] or as having less,[49] and the patient accepts treatment with that understanding, the standard is modified accordingly.

The courts have been compelled to recognize that there are areas in which even experts will disagree. Where there are different schools of medical thought, it is held that the dispute cannot be settled by the law, and the doctor is entitled to be judged according to the tenets of the school he professes to follow.[50] This does not mean, however, that any quack, charlatan or crackpot can set himself up as a "school," and so apply his individual ideas without liability. A "school" must be a recognized one with definite principles, and it must be the line of thought of at least a respectable minority of the profession.[51] In addition, there are minimum requirements of skill and knowledge as to both diagnosis and treatment,[52] particularly in the light of modern licensing statutes,[53] which anyone who holds himself out as competent to treat human ailments is required to have, regardless of his personal views on medical subjects. Furthermore the physician is required to exercise reasonable care in ascertaining the operational facts upon which his diagnosis is based, and will be liable if he fails to do so.[54]

denied 340 U.S. 892; Johnson v. Colp, 1941, 211 Minn. 245, 300 N.W. 791.

47. Holtzman v. Hoy, 1886, 118 Ill. 534, 8 N.E. 832; Sim v. Weeks, 1935, 7 Cal.App.2d 28, 45 P.2d 350.

48. Rann v. Twitchell, 1909, 82 Vt. 79, 71 A. 1045; Atkins v. Clein, 1940, 3 Wash.2d 168, 100 P.2d 1, opinion adhered to 104 P.2d 489; Worster v. Caylor, 1953, 231 Ind. 625, 110 N.E.2d 337; Rule v. Cheeseman, 1957, 181 Kan. 957, 317 P.2d 472; Carbone v. Warburton, 1953, 11 N.J. 418, 94 A.2d 680. See Rosenbaum, The Degree of Skill and Care Required of a Specialist, 1932, 49 Med.-Leg.J. 85.

49. Higgins v. McCabe, 1878, 126 Mass. 13 (midwife); Spead v. Tomlinson, 1904, 73 N.H. 46, 59 A. 376 (Christian Science healer); Cummins v. Donley, 1952, 173 Kan. 463, 249 P.2d 695 (osteopath); Josselyn v. Dearborn, 1948, 143 Me. 328, 62 A.2d 174 (same).

50. "Who shall decide when doctors disagree?" Pope, Moral Essays, 1732, Epistle III, Line 1; Force v. Gregory, 1893, 63 Conn. 167, 27 A. 1116 (homeopath); Nelson v. Dahl, 1928, 174 Minn. 574, 219 N.W. 941 (chiropractor); Atkinson v. American School of Osteopathy, 1912, 240 Mo. 338, 144 S.W. 816 (osteopath).

Where there is legislative recognition of a method of treatment, the courts have no choice but to accept it as a recognized school. Cummins v. Donley, 1952, 173 Kan. 463, 249 P.2d 695 (osteopath); Hardy v. Dahl, 1936, 210 N.C. 530, 187 S.E. 788 (naturopath); Forrest v. Eason, 1953, 123 Utah 610, 261 P.2d 178 (same); Willett v. Rowekamp, 1938, 134 Ohio St.

285, 16 N.E.2d 457 (chiropractor). See Note, 1956, 10 Wyo.L.J. 124.

51. Thus one who belongs to no recognized school is held to the minimum standards of the profession in general. Nelson v. Harrington, 1888, 72 Wis. 591, 40 N.W. 228 ("spiritualist or clairvoyant physician"); Hansen v. Pock, 1920, 57 Mont. 51, 187 P. 282 (Chinese herb doctor); Longan v. Weltmer, 1904, 180 Mo. 322, 79 S.W. 655 ("magnetic healer").

52. Kelly v. Carroll, 1950, 36 Wash.2d 482, 219 P.2d 79, cert. denied, 1950, 340 U.S. 892; Treptau v. Behrens Spa, 1945, 247 Wis. 438, 20 N.W.2d 108; Hardy v. Dahl, 1936, 210 N.C. 530, 187 S.E. 788; Spead v. Tomlinson, 1904, 73 N.H. 46, 59 A. 376 (Christian Science healer). Regardless of any question of "school," however, the doctor will not be held liable for error, where he is not lacking in skill, and there is genuine difference of opinion among physicians. Blankenship v. Baptist Memorial Hospital, 1942, 26 Tenn.App. 131, 168 S.W. 401; Rakowski v. Raybestos-Manhattan, Inc., 1949, 5 N.J. Super. 203, 68 A.2d 641.

53. Whipple v. Grandchamp, 1927, 261 Mass. 40, 158 N.E. 270; Monahan v. Devinny, 1928, 223 App.Div. 547, 229 N.Y.S. 60; see Harris v. Graham, 1926, 124 Okl. 196, 255 P. 710; Brown v. Shyne, 1926, 242 N.Y. 176, 151 N.E. 197. The last named case held that mere absence of a license was in itself no evidence of lack of skill or care. Accord: Hardy v. Dahl, 1936, 210 N.C. 530, 187 S.E. 788; Janssen v. Mulder, 1925, 232 Mich. 183, 205 N.W. 159; Willett v. Rowekamp, 1938, 134 Ohio St. 285, 16 N.E.2d 457. See Notes, 1937, 22 Corn.L.Q. 276; 1928, 6 Tex.L. Rev. 398; 1937, 21 Minn.L.Rev. 463.

54. Clark v. United States, 4 Cir. 1968, 402 F.2d 950; Hicks v. United States, 4 Cir. 1966, 368 F.2d 626;

Formerly it was generally held that allowance must be made for the type of community in which the physician carries on his practice, and for the fact, for example, that a country doctor could not be expected to have the equipment, facilities, libraries, contacts, opportunities for learning, or experience afforded by large cities. Since the standard of the "same locality" [55] was obviously too narrow, this was commonly stated as that of "similar localities," thus including other towns of the same general type.[56] Improved facilities of communication, available medical literature, consultation and the like, led gradually to the abandonment of any fixed rule, and to treating the community as merely one factor to be taken into account in applying the general professional standard.[57] In a few jurisdictions the "locality rule" has been entirely discarded, and the general standard applied in all cases.[58]

Since juries composed of laymen are normally incompetent to pass judgment on questions of medical science or technique, it has been held in the great majority of malpractice cases that there can be no finding of

negligence in the absence of expert testimony to support it.[59] The well known reluctance of doctors to testify against one another, which has been mentioned now and then in the decisions,[60] may make this difficult or impossible to obtain, and so deprive the plaintiff of any remedy for a real and grievous wrong. In several cities, medical and bar associations are now cooperating to meet the problem by setting up panels of competent and unbiased experts, who will examine the plaintiff, and agree to testify for him if they find there has been negligence. Where the matter is regarded as within the common knowledge of laymen, as where the surgeon saws off the wrong leg, or there is injury to a part of the body not within the operative field,[61] it has

Steeves v. United States, D.S.C.1968, 294 F.Supp. 446; Alden v. Providence Hospital, D.C.Cir.1967, 382 F.2d 163; Betenbaugh v. Princeton Hospital, 1967, 50 N.J. 390, 235 A.2d 889.

55. Small v. Howard, 1880, 128 Mass. 131; Burk v. Foster, 1902, 114 Ky. 20, 69 S.W. 1096; Mason v. Geddes, 1926, 258 Mass. 40, 154 N.E. 519.

56. Michael v. Roberts, 1941, 91 N.H. 499, 23 A.2d 361; Weintraub v. Rosen, 7 Cir. 1937, 93 F.2d 544; Hoover v. Goss, 1940, 2 Wash.2d 237, 97 P.2d 689; Nation v. Gueffroy, 1943, 172 Or. 673, 142 P.2d 688; Wiggins v. Piver, 1969, 276 N.C. 134, 171 S.E.2d 393.

57. Sinz v. Owens, 1949, 33 Cal.2d 749, 205 P.2d 3; Tvedt v. Haugen, 1940, 70 N.D. 338, 294 N.W. 183; Hundley v. Martinez, 1967, 151 W.Va. 977, 158 S.E. 2d 159; McGulpin v. Bessmer, 1950, 241 Iowa 1119, 43 N.W.2d 121; Carbone v. Warburton, 1953, 11 N.J. 418, 94 A.2d 680. See Notes, 1962, 14 Stan.L.Rev. 884; 1951, 36 Iowa L.Rev. 681; 1951, 35 Minn. L.Rev. 186.

58. Brune v. Belinkoff, 1968, 354 Mass. 102, 235 N.E. 2d 793; Pederson v. Dumouchel, 1967, 72 Wash.2d 73, 431 P.2d 973. See Notes, 1969, 8 Washb.L.Rev. 339; 1970, 23 Vand.L.Rev. 729.

59. Shea v. Phillips, 1957, 213 Ga. 269, 98 S.E.2d 552, conformed to, 1957, 95 Ga.App. 800, 99 S.E.2d 168; Beane v. Perley, 1954, 99 N.H. 309, 109 A.2d 848; Boyce v. Brown, 1938, 51 Ariz. 416, 77 P.2d 455; Bierstein v. Whitman, 1949, 360 Pa. 537, 62 A.2d 843; Winters v. Rance, 1933, 125 Neb. 577, 251 N.W. 167. See, generally, Morris, The Role of Expert Testimony in the Trial of Negligence Issues, 1947, 26 Tex.L.Rev. 1, Notes, 1957, 30 Temple L.Q. 448; [1956] Ins.L.J. 329, 1966, 60 Nw.U.L.Rev. 834. This may, however, be supplied by admissions of the defendant. Sheffield v. Runner, 1958, 163 Cal.App. 2d 48, 328 P.2d 828.

60. See Morgan v. Rosenberg, Mo.1963, 370 S.W.2d 685; Halldin v. Peterson, 1968, 39 Wis.2d 668, 159 N.W.2d 738; Coleman v. McCarthy, 1933, 53 R.I. 266, 165 A. 900; Simon v. Friedrich, 1937, 163 Misc. 112, 296 N.Y.S. 367; Reynolds v. Struble, 1933, 128 Cal.App. 716, 18 P.2d 690; Seidelson, Medical Malpractice Cases and the Reluctant Expert, 1966, 16 Cath.U.L.Rev. 187; Markus, Conspiracy of Silence. 1965, 14 Cleve.Marsh.L.Rev. 520.

This is discussed infra, p. 227.

61. Evans v. Roberts, 1915, 172 Iowa 653, 154 N.W. 923 (tongue cut off in removing adenoids); Steinke v. Bell, 1954, 32 N.J.Super. 67, 107 A.2d 825 (dentist pulling wrong tooth); Caldwell v. Knight, 1955, 92 Ga.App. 747, 89 S.E.2d 900 (manhandled by chiropractor); Daly v. Lininger, 1930, 87 Colo. 401, 288 P. 633 (dentist severing nerve); Ybarra v. Spangard, 1944, 25 Cal.2d 486, 154 P.2d 687 (traumatic injury to shoulder during appendectomy); Whetstine v. Moravec, 1940, 228 Iowa 352, 291 N.W. 425 (fragment of tooth lodged in lung). Cf. Corn v. French, 1955, 71 Nev. 280, 289 P.2d 173 (cancer operation without preliminary biopsy).

been held that the jury may infer negligence without the aid of any expert.[62]

The cumulative effect of all of these rules has meant that the standard of conduct becomes one of "good medical practice," which is to say, what is customary and usual in the profession.[63]

It has been pointed out often enough [64] that this gives the medical profession, and also the others, the privilege, which is usually emphatically denied to other groups,[65] of setting their own legal standards of conduct, merely by adopting their own practices. It is sometimes said that this is because the physician has impliedly represented that he will follow customary methods, and so has undertaken to do so. Another explanation,[66] perhaps more valid, is the healthy respect which the courts have had for the learning of a fellow profession, and their reluctance to overburden it with liability based on uneducated judgment. It seems clear, in any case, that the result is closely tied in with the layman's ignorance of medical matters and the necessity of expert testimony, since, when the jury are considered competent to do so, they are permitted to find that a practice generally followed by the medical profession is negligent. This has frequently been done in the cases of sponges left in the patient's abdomen after an operation, where the task of keeping track of them has been delegated by the surgeon to a nurse. Although this was, and perhaps still is, universal practice, it has still been found to be negligent.[67]

A considerable number of late cases have involved the doctrine of "informed consent," which concerns the duty of the physician or surgeon to inform the patient of the risk which may be involved in treatment or surgery. The earliest cases treated this as a matter of vitiating the consent, so that there was liability for battery.[68] Beginning with a decision in Kansas [69] in 1960, it began to be recognized that this was really a matter of the standard of professional conduct, since there will be some patients to whom disclosure may be undesirable or even dangerous for success of the treatment or the patient's own welfare; [70] and that what should be done is a matter for professional judgment in the light of the applicable medical standards. Accordingly, the prevailing view now is that the action, regardless of its form, is in reality one for negligence in failing to conform to the proper standard, to be determined on the basis of expert testimony as to what disclosure should be made.[71] The factors to be con-

62. Such cases usually involve the doctrine of res ipsa loquitur. See infra, p. 226.

63. Regan, Doctor and Patient and the Law, 3d Ed. 1956, 30. This means that in the absence of expert testimony, the jury may not be permitted to find that what is customarily done is negligent. Trindle v. Wheeler, Cal.App.1943, 133 P.2d 425, reversed on other grounds in 1943, 23 Cal.2d 330, 143 P.2d 932; Gray v. McDermott, 1933, 188 Ark. 1, 64 S.W. 2d 94; Ferrell v. Ellis, 1906, 129 Iowa 614, 105 N.W. 993; Mason v. Geddes, 1926, 258 Mass. 40, 154 N.E. 519.

64. See for example Morris, Custom and Negligence, 1942, 42 Col.L.Rev. 1147; James, Particularizing the Standards of Conduct in Negligence Trials, 1952, 5 Vand.L.Rev. 697, 710.

65. See infra, p. 167.

66. See McCoid, The Care Required of Medical Practitioners, 1959, 12 Vand.L.Rev. 549, 608.

67. Ault v. Hall, 1928, 119 Ohio St. 422, 164 N.E. 518; Ales v. Ryan, 1936, 8 Cal.2d 82, 64 P.2d 409; Johnson v. Ely, 1947, 30 Tenn.App. 294, 205 S.W.2d 759; Leonard v. Watsonville Community Hospital, 1957, 47 Cal.2d 509, 305 P.2d 36; Rule v. Cheeseman, 1957, 181 Kan. 957, 317 P.2d 472. See Bohlen, Some Recent Decisions on Tort Liability, 1930, 4 Tul.L.Rev. 370, 379.

68. See supra, p. 105.

69. Natanson v. Kline, 1960, 186 Kan. 393, 350 P.2d 1093, on rehearing 187 Kan. 186, 354 P.2d 670.

70. See Lund, The Doctor, the Patient, and the Truth, 1946, 19 Tenn.L.Rev. 344; Smith, Therapeutic Privilege to Withhold Specific Diagnosis from Patient Sick with Serious or Fatal Illness, 1946, 19 Tenn. L.Rev. 349.

Cf. Ferrara v. Galluchio, 1958, 5 N.Y.2d 16, 176 N.Y.S. 2d 996, 152 N.E.2d 249; Furness v. Fitchett, [1958] N.Z.L.Rep. 398.

71. Wilson v. Scott, Tex.1967, 412 S.W.2d 299; Kaplan v. Haines, 1969, 96 N.J.Super. 242, 232 A.2d 840, affirmed, 1968, 51 N.J. 404, 241 A.2d 235 (good

sidered by the physician or surgeon include the likelihood and seriousness of the bad result, the feasibility of alternative methods, the interest of the patient, knowledge of his past history, his emotional stability, the necessity of treatment, and the existence of an emergency.[72]

33. APPLICATION OF THE STANDARD

The application of this standard of reasonable conduct is as wide as all human behavior. There is scarcely any act which, under some conceivable circumstances, may not involve an unreasonable risk of harm. Even going to sleep becomes negligence when it is done on a railway track, or at the wheel of an automobile. In so broad a field, there is space to select for consideration only a few problems, whose frequent appearance indicates that they are of sufficient importance to call for special notice.

Custom

Since the standard is a community standard, evidence of the usual and customary conduct of others under similar circumstances is normally relevant and admissible,[74] as an in-

dication of what the community regards as proper, and a composite judgment as to the risks of the situation and the precautions required to meet them.[75] If the actor does only what everyone else has done, there is at least an inference that he is conforming to the community's idea of reasonable behavior.[76] Custom also bears upon what others will expect the actor to do, and what, therefore, reasonable care may require him to do; upon the feasibility of taking precautions, the difficulty of change, and the actor's opportunity to learn the risks and what is called for to meet them.[77]

In a particular case, where there is nothing in the evidence or in common experience to lead to the contrary conclusion,[78] this inference may be so strong that it calls for a directed verdict on the issue of negligence.[79] Thus, in the absence of some special circumstances, where an automobile is driven along a private road, with no applicable highway statute, it seems quite impossible to conclude that it is negligence to drive it on the right

---

review of the cases); Di Filippo v. Preston, 1961, 53 Del. 539, 173 A.2d 333; Bowers v. Talmage, Fla.App.1963, 159 So.2d 888; Aiken v. Clary, Mo. 1965, 396 S.W.2d 668.

72. See Note, 1967, 20 Okl.L.Rev. 214.

There are good discussions of all this in Plant, An Analysis of "Informed Consent," 1968, 36 Ford. L.Rev. 639; McCoid, A Reappraisal of Liability for Unauthorized Medical Treatment, 1957, 41 Minn. L.Rev. 381; McCoid, The Care Required of Medical Practitioners, 1969, 12 Vand.L.Rev. 549; Waltz and Scheuneman, Informed Consent to Therapy, 1969, 64 Nw.U.L.Rev. 628; Note, 1967, 21 Sw.L.Rev. 843.

74. Cadillac Motor Car Co. v. Johnson, 2 Cir. 1915, 221 F. 801; Denning Warehouse Co. v. Widener, 10 Cir. 1949, 172 F.2d 910; Hellweg v. Chesapeake & Potomac Tel. Co., D.C.Cir. 1940, 71 U.S.App.D.C. 346, 110 F.2d 546; Murphy v. American Barge Line, W.D.Pa.1948, 76 F.Supp. 276; Levine v. Russell Blaine Co., 1937, 273 N.Y. 386, 7 N.E.2d 673.

To be admissible, the custom must be general, and not, for example, that of a particular block in a

town. Weisbart v. Flohr, 1968, 260 Cal.App.2d 281, 67 Cal.Rptr. 114.

75. 2 Wigmore, Evidence, 3d Ed.1940, § 461.

76. Weireter v. Great Northern R. Co., 1920, 146 Minn. 350, 353, 178 N.W. 887–889; Hellweg v. Chesapeake & Potomac Tel. Co., D.C.Cir. 1940, 71 App.D.C. 346, 110 F.2d 546; Honea v. Coca Cola Bottling Co., 1944, 143 Tex. 272, 183 S.W.2d 968.

77. See Morris, Custom and Negligence, 1942, 42 Col. L.Rev. 1147; James, Particularizing Standards of Conduct in Negligence Trials, 1952, 5 Vand.L.Rev. 697, 709–714; Note, 1944, 18 Tul.L.Rev. 646.

78. See Grammer v. Mid-Continent Petroleum Corp., 10 Cir. 1934, 71 F.2d 38; Higgins v. Fanning, 1900, 195 Pa. 599, 46 A. 102; Houston & T. C. R. Co. v. Alexander, 1910, 103 Tex. 594, 132 S.W. 119.

79. Corthell v. Great A. & P. Tea Co., 1935, 291 Mass. 242, 196 N.E. 850; Ketterer v. Armour & Co., 2 Cir. 1917, 247 F. 921; Dibble v. New York, N. H. & H. R. Co., 1923, 100 Conn. 130, 123 A. 124; Cleary v. R. E. Dietz Co., 1917, 222 N.Y. 126, 118 N.E. 509.

Some courts have said that customary conduct is prima facie due care, in the absence of evidence from which the jury might find the contrary. Weireter v. Great Northern R. Co., 1920, 146 Minn. 350, 178 N.W. 887; Sanford-Day Iron Works v. Moore, 1915, 132 Tenn. 709, 179 S.W. 373.

side of the road, or that it is not negligence to drive it on the left. It should be obvious, however, that this is a matter of the custom itself, of its general acceptance by the community and the general reliance upon it, and of all of the circumstances of the case. Some few courts formerly made the effort to treat all customs in this manner, and to enlarge the normal inference into an "unbending test" of negligence, under which the ordinary usages of a business or industry became the sole criterion as to what the actor should, as a reasonable man, have done.[80]

Such an arbitrary rule proved in the long run impossible to justify. First of all, customs which are entirely reasonable under the ordinary circumstances which give rise to them in the first instance, may become entirely unreasonable in the light of a single fact altering the situation in the particular case. It may become highly dangerous to follow the usual practice of bumping railroad cars together, on a day when brakemen must stand on top of cars which are covered with ice;[81] or to clean a floor with a compound which is in general use for the purpose, but quite unsuited to the particular floor.[82] But beyond this, customs and usages themselves are many and various;[83] some are the result of careful thought and decision, while others arise from the kind of inadvertence, carelessness, indifference, cost-paring and corner-cutting that normally is associated with negligence. There can certainly be such a thing as customary negligence, as the unchecked habit of jaywalking in some communities will suggest.

Even an entire industry, by adopting such careless methods to save time, effort or money, cannot be permitted to set its own uncontrolled standard.[84] The fact that all other beverage bottlers use the same slipshod methods cannot serve as absolution for the bottler who is being sued.[85] And if the only test is to be what has been done before, no industry or group will ever have any great incentive to make progress in the direction of safety. Cases will no doubt be infrequent in which any defendant will be held liable for failing to do what no one in his position has ever done before;[86] but there appears to be no doubt that they can arise.[87] Much the better view, therefore, is that of the great majority of the cases, that every custom is

80. Wommack v. Orr, 1943, 352 Mo. 113, 176 S.W.2d 477; Ellis v. Louisville & N. R. Co., Ky.1952, 251 S.W.2d 577; Titus v. Bradford, B. & K. R. Co., 1890, 136 Pa. 618, 20 A. 517; Shadford v. Ann Arbor St. R. Co., 1897, 111 Mich. 390, 69 N.W. 661; Kilbride v. Carbon Dioxide & Magnesia Co., 1902, 201 Pa. 552, 51 A. 347.

81. Texas & Pac. R. Co. v. Behymer, 1903, 189 U. S. 468. A good opinion from the very early days of railroads is Bradley v. Boston & Maine R. Co., 1848, 2 Cush., Mass., 539. See Miller, The So-Called Unbending Test of Negligence, 1916, 3 Va.L.Rev. 537.

82. S. H. Kress & Co. v. Telford, 5 Cir. 1957, 240 F.2d 70.

83. See William Laurie Co. v. McCullough, 1910, 174 Ind. 477, 90 N.E. 1014, 92 N.E. 337, rehearing denied, 1910, 174 Ind. 477, 92 N.E. 337; annotation, 1930, 68 A.L.R. 1400, 1401. Thus in Mennis v. Cheffings, 1962, 233 Or. 215, 376 P.2d 672, a custom on a private road, by which the loaded truck was to take the inside lane, was held to be merely evidence for the jury on the issue of negligence.

84. Shafer v. H. B. Thomas Co., 1958, 53 N.J.Super. 19, 146 A.2d 483 (unchecked swinging doors); Tite v. Omaha Coliseum Corp., 1943, 144 Neb. 22, 12 N.W. 2d 90; Maize v. Atlantic Ref. Co., 1945, 352 Pa. 51, 41 A.2d 850; Pan American Petroleum Corp. v. Like, Wyo.1963, 381 P.2d 70; Marietta v. Cliffs Ridge, Inc., 1970, 20 Mich.App. 449, 174 N.W.2d 164.

85. Grant v. Graham Chero-Cola Bottling Co., 1918, 176 N.C. 256, 97 S.E. 27; Morrison v. Kansas City Coca Cola Bottling Co., 1953, 175 Kan. 212, 263 P.2d 217.

86. Cf. Broad St. Bank v. National Bank, 1922, 183 N.C. 463, 112 S.E. 11 (failure of banks to use protective devices on checks); Northwest Airlines v. Glenn L. Martin Co., 6 Cir. 1955, 224 F.2d 120, cert. denied, 1956, 350 U.S. 937, rehearing denied 229 F.2d 434, 350 U.S. 976 (plane without radar, where not yet commercially available).

See, as to failure to carry radar at the present day, Note, 1966, 41 Ind.L.J. 522.

87. Marsh Wood Products Co. v. Babcock & Wilcox Co., 1932, 207 Wis. 209, 240 N.W. 392 (microscopic tests of steel for boiler tubes); The T. J. Hooper, 2 Cir. 1932, 60 F.2d 737, cert. denied 287 U.S. 662 (radio sets for ocean going tugs). This was suggested as long ago as 3 Labatt, Master and Servant, 1913, § 947.

not conclusive merely because it is a custom, and that it must meet the challenge of "learned reason," [88] and be given only the evidentiary weight which the situation deserves.[89] It follows that where common knowledge and ordinary judgment will recognize unreasonable danger, what everyone does may be found to be negligent; [90] and that there will be extreme cases where it is so clearly negligent in itself that it may even be excluded from evidence.[91]

Upon the same basis, the omission of a customary precaution may, in a particular case, be negligence in itself, especially where it is known that others may rely on it.[92] But as a general rule, the fact that a thing is done in an unusual manner is merely evidence to be considered in determining negligence, and is not in itself conclusive.[93]　A custom to be

relevant, must be reasonably brought home to the actor's locality,[94] and must be so general, or so well known, that the actor may be charged with knowledge of it or with negligent ignorance.[95]　The actor's own record of past conduct, which is commonly called "habit" rather than custom, is no evidence of any standard of reasonable care,[96] but when he has departed from it, it may be used against him as indicating his knowledge of the risk and the precautions necessary to meet it.[97]　The same, in general, is true of rules made by the defendant to govern the conduct of his employees,[98] and of the safety or accident record bearing upon the particular practice.[99]

Emergency

The courts have been compelled to recognize that an actor who is confronted with an

---

88.　Allen, Learned and Unlearned Reason, 1924, 36 Jurid.Rev. 254.

89.　"What usually is done may be evidence of what ought to be done, but what ought to be done is fixed by a standard of reasonable prudence, whether it usually is complied with or not." Texas & Pac. R. Co. v. Behymer, 1903, 189 U.S. 468, per Holmes, J. Accord: Wabash R. Co. v. McDaniels, 1882, 107 U.S. 454; Dempsey v. Addison Crane Co., D.D.C.1965, 247 F.Supp. 584; Atchison, T. & S. F. Ry. Co. v. Paar, 1964, 96 Ariz. 13, 391 P.2d 575; Maynard v. Buck, 1868, 100 Mass. 40; Cameron Compress Co. v. Whitington, Tex.Com.App.1926, 280 S.W. 527.

90.　MacDougall v. Pennsylvania Power & Light Co., 1932, 311 Pa. 387, 166 A. 589; Simonds v. City of Baraboo, 1896, 93 Wis. 40, 67 N.W. 40.

One apparent exception arises in the case of professional customs, such as those of physicians and surgeons. See supra, p. 165.

91.　Mayhew v. Sullivan Min. Co., 1884, 76 Me. 100 (unguarded shafts in coal mines); A. & N. R. Co. v. Bailey, 1881, 11 Neb. 332, 9 N.W. 50 (leaving turntable unsecured when accessible to children); Sanchez v. J. Barron Rice, Inc., 1967, 77 N.M. 717, 427 P.2d 240 (customary violation of safety ordinance).

92.　St. Louis & S. F. R. Co. v. Jeffries, 8 Cir. 1921, 276 F. 73; Greenlee v. Southern Ry. Co., 1898, 122 N.C. 977, 30 S.E. 115; Jensen v. Hudson Sawmill Co., 1897, 98 Wis. 73, 73 N.W. 434; Joliet Steel Co. v. Shields, 1893, 146 Ill. 603, 34 N.E. 1108; Roberts v. Indiana Gas & Water Co., 1966, 140 Ind.App. 409, 218 N.E.2d 556.

93.　Turner v. Chicago Housing Authority, 1956, 11 Ill. App.2d 160, 136 N.E.2d 543; Silver Falls Timber

Co. v. Eastern & Western Lumber Co., 1935, 149 Or. 126, 40 P.2d 703; Levine v. Russell Blaine Co., 1937, 273 N.Y. 386, 7 N.E.2d 673; Chicago Great Western R. Co. v. McDonough, 8 Cir. 1908, 161 F. 657; Dilburn v. Louisville & N. R. Co., 1908, 156 Ala. 228, 47 So. 210.

94.　Sprecher v. Roberts, 1933, 272 Wis. 69, 248 N.W. 795.

95.　Rhine v. Duluth, M. & I. R. Co., 1941, 210 Minn. 281, 297 N.W. 852; Garthe v. Ruppert, 1934, 264 N. Y. 290, 190 N.E. 643.

96.　Bimberg v. Northern Pac. R. Co., 1944, 217 Minn. 187, 14 N.W.2d 410, cert. denied 323 U.S. 752; Schiro v. Oriental Realty Co., 1959, 7 Wis.2d 556, 97 N.W.2d 385.

97.　Strong v. Chronicle Pub. Co., 1939, 34 Cal.App.2d 335, 93 P.2d 649; Zinnel v. United States Shipping Board E. F. Corp., 2 Cir. 1925, 10 F.2d 47; James, Particularizing Standards of Conduct in Negligence Cases, 1952, 5 Vand.L.Rev. 697, 712–713.

98.　Phillips v. Montgomery Ward & Co., 5 Cir. 1942, 125 F.2d 248; Montgomery v. Baltimore & O. R. Co., 6 Cir. 1927, 22 F.2d 359; Bryan v. Southern Pac. Co., 1955, 79 Ariz. 253, 286 P.2d 761; Dunham v. Des Moines R. Co., 1949, 240 Iowa 421, 35 N. W.2d 578; Hurley v. Connecticut Co., 1934, 118 Conn. 276, 172 A. 86. See Winters, The Evidentiary Value of Defendant's Safety Rules in a Negligence Action, 1959, 38 Neb.L.Rev. 906.

99.　A somewhat more complicated question, as to which see Morris, Proof of Safety History in Negligence Cases, 1948, 61 Harv.L.Rev. 205.

emergency is not to be held to the standard of conduct normally applied to one who is in no such situation.[1] An emergency has been defined as a sudden or unexpected event or combination of circumstances which calls for immediate action;[2] and although there are courts[3] which have laid stress upon the "instinctive action" which usually accompanies such a situation, it seems clear that the basis of the special rule is merely that the actor is left no time for thought, or is reasonably so disturbed or excited, that he cannot weigh alternative courses of action, and must make a speedy decision, based very largely upon impulse or guess.[4] Under such conditions, the actor cannot reasonably be held to the same conduct as one who has had full opportunity to reflect, even though it later appears that he made the wrong decision, which no reasonable man could possibly have made after due deliberation.[5] His choice "may be mistaken and yet prudent."[6]

There are, however, a number of limitations which have hedged the "emergency" rule. It does not mean that any different standard is to be applied in the emergency. The conduct required is still that of a reasonable man under the circumstances,[7] as they would appear to one who was using proper care,[8] and the emergency is only one of the circumstances. An objective standard must still be applied, and the actor's own judgment or impulse is still not the sole criterion.[9] He may still be found to be negligent if, notwithstanding the emergency, his acts are found to be unreasonable.[10] The "emergency doctrine" is applied only where the situation which arises is sudden and unexpected, and such as to deprive the actor of reasonable opportunity for deliberation and considered de-

---

1. See Evans, The Standard of Care in Emergencies, 1943, 21 Ky.L.J. 207; Notes, 1965, 36 Miss.L.J. 392; 1969, 21 U.Fla.L.Rev. 667. "The law takes account of the impulses of humanity when placed in dangerous positions, and does not expect thoughtful care from the persons whose lives are thus endangered." Elmore v. Des Moines City R. Co., 1929, 207 Iowa 862, 224 N.W. 28; Pennington's Adm'r v. Pure Milk Co., 1939, 279 Ky. 235, 130 S.W.2d 24.

2. Trinity Universal Ins. Co. v. Farmers Coop. Exchange, 1951, 171 Kan. 501, 233 P.2d 468; Colfax County v. Butler County, 1909, 83 Neb. 803, 120 N.W. 444. The Texas courts have distinguished between "imminent peril" and "emergency," with a large measure of resulting confusion. See Thode, Imminent Peril and Emergency in Texas, 1962, 40 Tex.L.Rev. 441.

3. Whicher v. Phinney, 1 Cir. 1942, 124 F.2d 929; Collette v. Boston & Me. R. Co., 1927, 83 N.H. 210, 140 A. 176; Cook v. Thomas, 1964, 25 Wis.2d 467, 131 N.W.2d 299.

4. Thus the rule has been applied where the actor testified that he was perfectly calm, and not at all excited. Triestram v. Way, 1938, 286 Mich. 13, 281 N.W. 420. See also Napier v. Du Bose, 1932, 45 Ga. App. 661, 165 S.E. 773; Graham v. Hines, Tex.Civ. App.1922, 240 S.W. 1015, error refused, indicating that shortage of time for decision, together with circumstances which would perturb or upset the judgment of the ordinary reasonable man, is the gist of emergency.

5. Kelley v. Safeway Stores, Inc., 1959, 105 U.S.App. D.C. 406, 267 F.2d 683; Heermen v. Burke, 8 Cir. 1959, 266 F.2d 935; St. Johnsbury Trucking Co. v. Rollins, 1950, 145 Me. 217, 74 A.2d 465; McClard v. Reid, 1950, 190 Tenn. 337, 229 S.W.2d 505; Majure v. Herrington, 1962, 243 Miss. 692, 139 So.2d 635; Second Restatement of Torts, § 296.

6. Holmes, C. J., in Kane v. Worcester Consol. St. R. Co., 1902, 182 Mass. 201, 65 N.E. 54.

7. Seele v. Purcell, 1941, 45 N.M. 176, 113 P.2d 320; Triestram v. Way, 1938, 286 Mich. 13, 281 N.W. 420; Dahlstrom v. Hurtig, 1940, 209 Minn. 72, 295 N.W. 508; Alabama Great Southern R. Co. v. Hunt, 1920, 204 Ala. 504, 86 So. 100; Barkshadt v. Gresham, 1922, 120 S.C. 219, 112 S.E. 923. The emergency is merely one of the factors to be considered by the triers of fact. Jones v. Boston & Me. R. Co., 1927, 83 N.H. 73, 139 A. 214; Luper Transp. Co. v. Barnes, 5 Cir. 1948, 170 F.2d 880.

8. Lederer v. Connecticut Co., 1920, 95 Conn. 520, 111 A. 785; Lunzer v. Pittsburgh & L. E. R. Co., 1929, 296 Pa. 393, 145 A. 907.

9. Gravel v. Roberge, 1926, 125 Me. 399, 134 A. 375.

10. Cook v. Thomas, 1964, 25 Wis.2d 467, 131 N.W. 2d 299; Raolaslovic v. New York Cent. R. Co., 1927, 245 N.Y. 91, 156 N.E. 625; Phillips v. Delta Motor Lines, Inc., 1959, 235 Miss. 1, 108 So.2d 409; Warnke v. Essex, 1958, 217 Md. 183, 141 A.2d 728; Leonard v. United States, D.Wyo.1955, 131 F.Supp. 694, affirmed, 1956, 235 F.2d 330, case remanded 352 U.S. 996.

cision.[11] Furthermore, it obviously cannot serve to excuse the actor when the emergency has been created through his own negligence, since he cannot be permitted to shield himself behind a situation resulting from his own fault.[12] It is, however, not the conduct after the emergency has arisen which is not excused, but the prior negligence; [13] and where the question is one of the last clear chance,[14] the defendant may still not be liable.[15]

A further qualification which must be made is that some "emergencies" must be anticipated, and the actor must be prepared to meet them when he engages in an activity in which they are likely to arise. Thus under present day traffic conditions, any driver of an automobile must be prepared for the sudden appearance of obstacles in the highway, or of other vehicles at intersections,[16] just as one who sees a child on the curb may be required to anticipate its sudden dash into

the street,[17] and his failure to act properly when they appear may be found to amount to negligence.

Anticipating Conduct of Others

There are many situations in which the hypothetical reasonable man would be expected to anticipate and guard against the conduct of others. Anyone with normal experience is required to have knowledge of the traits and habits of common animals, and of other human beings,[18] and to govern himself accordingly. He may expect that horses left unattended in the road may become frightened and run away,[19] that a bull or a stallion will attack a man,[20] that stampeded cattle or sheep will get upon a railway track,[21] or be killed by bears in the vicinity.[22] Upon much the same basis, he may be required to anticipate that persons who are ill or intoxicated may wander into places of danger,[23]

---

11. Hercules Powder Co. v. Crawford, 8 Cir. 1947, 163 F.2d 968; Kaestner v. Milwaukee Automobile Ins. Co., 1948, 254 Wis. 12, 35 N.W.2d 190; Horton Motor Lines v. Currie, 4 Cir. 1937, 92 F.2d 164; Henderson v. Land, 1931, 42 Wyo. 369, 295 P. 271. The actor must be aware of the sudden peril or the necessity for immediate action. Feck's Adm'r v. Bell Line, 1940, 284 Ky. 288, 144 S.W.2d 483. But a short time interval, of three or four seconds, will not as a matter of law prevent the application of the emergency rule. Kardasinski v. Koford, 1937, 88 N.H. 444, 109 A. 702.

12. Bellere v. Madsen, Fla.1959, 114 So.2d 619; Daugherty v. May Bros. Co., 1963, 265 Minn. 310, 121 N.W.2d 594; Lindberg v. Goode, 1959, 200 Va. 784, 108 S.E.2d 364; Tucker v. Blankenmeier, Mo. 1958, 315 S.W.2d 724; Mitchell v. Mitchell, Ky. 1968, 428 S.W.2d 222.

13. Windsor v. McKee, Mo.App.1929, 22 S.W.2d 65.

14. See infra, § 66.

15. Norwood Transp. Co. v. Bickell, 1922, 207 Ala. 232, 92 So. 464; Spoeneman v. Uhri, 1933, 332 Mo. 821, 60 S.W.2d 9. He will, however, be liable for any negligence after the emergency is over. Shank v. Baker, 4 Cir. 1964, 333 F.2d 301.

16. Ritter v. Johnson, 1931, 163 Wash. 153, 300 P. 518 (approaching traffic); Jones v. Boston & Me. R. Co., 1927, 83 N.H. 73, 139 A. 214 (car crossing railroad); May v. Pace, Miss.1967, 197 So.2d 220 (sudden stop of car ahead).

17. Potts v. Krey, Ky.1962, 362 S.W.2d 726; Ennis v. Dupree, 1962, 258 N.C. 141, 128 S.E.2d 231; Kachman v. Blosberg, 1958, 251 Minn. 224, 87 N.W.2d 687; Bermudez v. Jenkins, Fla.App.1962, 144 So.2d 859; Conery v. Tackmeier, 1967, 34 Wis.2d 511, 149 N.W. 2d 575 (failure to look out for children).

The actor may be required to provide the necessary mechanical equipment for dealing with such emergencies. Pappaceno v. Picknelly, 1949, 135 Conn. 660, 68 A.2d 117; Strahl v. Miller, 1915, 97 Neb. 820, 151 N.W. 952, affirmed, 1916, 239 U.S. 426. And to hire or train suitable personnel. Collins v. Riverside Amusement Park Co., 1944, 61 Ariz. 135, 145 P.2d 853; Pickett v. City of Jacksonville, 1945, 155 Fla. 439, 20 So.2d 484.

18. Second Restatement of Torts, §§ 290, 302. See supra, p. 160.

19. Griggs v. Fleckenstein, 1869, 14 Minn. 81, 14 Gil. 62.

20. Linnehan v. Sampson, 1879, 126 Mass. 506; Hammond v. Melton, 1891, 42 Ill.App. 186.

21. Sneesby v. Lancashire & York R. Co., 1874, L.R. 9 Q.B. 263.

22. Gilman v. Noyes, 1876, 57 N.H. 627.

23. Atchison, T. & S. F. R. Co. v. Parry, 1903, 67 Kan. 515, 73 P. 105; Black v. New York, N. H. & H. R. Co., 1907, 193 Mass. 448, 79 N.E. 797; cf. Southern R. Co. v. Webb, 1902, 116 Ga. 152, 42 S.E. 395. "A drunken man is as much entitled to a safe street, as a sober one, and much more in need of it."

and that human beings who are placed in a position of peril will endeavor, more or less instinctively, to escape, and may do harm to themselves or others in the attempt.[24] Thus he may be held liable if he causes an automobile to turn from its course,[25] or a passenger to leap from a car,[26] to avoid a collision.

But beyond this, he is required to realize that there will be a certain amount of negligence in the world. In general, where the risk is relatively slight, he is free to proceed upon the assumption that other people will exercise proper care. It would not be easy to move traffic if motorists could not assume that other cars will keep to the right, and drive accordingly;[27] or that those who use the highway will be reasonably intelligent, competent and careful, and will look out for

themselves.[28] But when the risk becomes a serious one, either because the threatened harm is great, or because there is an especial likelihood that it will occur, reasonable care may demand precautions against "that occasional negligence which is one of the ordinary incidents of human life and therefore to be anticipated."[29] "It is not due care to depend upon the exercise of care by another when such reliance is accompanied by obvious danger."[30] Thus an automobile driver may not proceed blindly across a railway track, upon the assumption that any approaching train will sound bell and whistle,[31] or into an intersection in the confidence that other vehicles will yield the right of way.[32] One who leaves another helpless in the highway,[33] or forces a pedestrian to walk in the

Robinson v. Pioche, Bayerque & Co., 1855, 5 Cal. 460, 461.

24. Ricker v. Freeman, 1870, 50 N.H. 420; Tuttle v. Atlantic City R. Co., 1901, 66 N.J.L. 327, 49 A. 450; Lowery v. Manhattan R. Co., 1885, 99 N.Y. 158, 1 N.E. 608. In Atlantic Coast Line R. Co. v. Daniels, 1910, 8 Ga.App. 775, 70 S.E. 203, where a badly excited plaintiff, having escaped being struck by a train, was injured while cranking his automobile with the maximum power turned on, it was held to be a "natural" and "normal" result of the defendant's negligence.

25. Gedeon v. East Ohio Gas Co., 1934, 128 Ohio St. 335, 190 N.E. 924; Fraser v. Flanders, 1924, 248 Mass. 62, 142 N.E. 836; Smith v. Yellow Cab Co., 1926, 285 Pa. 229, 132 A. 124; Rohrman v. Denzinger, 1925, 208 Ky. 832, 272 S.W. 16.

26. Jones v. Boyce, 1816, 1 Stark. 493, 171 Eng.Rep. 540; Twomley v. Central Park, N. & E. R. Co., 1877, 69 N.Y. 158; Jackson v. Galveston, H. & S. A. R. Co., 1897, 90 Tex. 372, 38 S.W. 745.

27. O'Mally v. Eagan, 1931, 43 Wyo. 233, 2 P.2d 1063, rehearing denied 43 Wyo. 350, 5 P.2d 276; Trout Auto Livery Co. v. People's Gas Light & Coke Co., 1912, 168 Ill.App. 56. Cf. Abeyta v. Carroll, 1963, 153 Colo. 575, 388 P.2d 756 (motorist running red light); Bennett v. Sears, Roebuck & Co., La.App.1966, 183 So.2d 737 (man in crowd stepping on plaintiff's foot); Sonnenburg v. Monumental Motor Tours, 1951, 198 Md. 227, 81 A.2d 617 (boulevard stop); Murphy v. Hawthorne, 1926, 117 Or. 319, 244 P. 79 (negligent parking); Jackson v. Geiger, 1924, 100 N.J.L. 330, 126 A. 438 (signal).

28. Cf. Lorenzo v. Wirth, 1897, 170 Mass. 596, 49 N.E. 1010 (one seeing pile of coal on sidewalk may be expected to know there is a coal hole). Also Warnken v. Moody, 5 Cir. 1927, 22 F.2d 960 (guest in motorboat may assume host knows what he is doing when he asks guest to pour gasoline into carburetor).

29. Second Restatement of Torts, § 302A; Gibson, J., in Murphy v. Great Northern R. Co., [1897] 2 Ir. Rep. 301. See, generally, Eldredge, Culpable Intervention as Superseding Cause, 1937, 86 U.Pa.L.Rev. 121.

30. Dragotis v. Kennedy, 1933, 190 Minn. 128, 250 N.W. 804; Tollisen v. Lehigh Valley Transp. Co., 3 Cir. 1956, 234 F.2d 121 (may not rely solely on traffic signal in crossing street).

31. Lehigh Valley R. Co. v. Kilmer, 2 Cir. 1916, 231 F. 628. Accord: Lanier v. Minneapolis, St. P. & S. S. M. R. Co., 1920, 209 Mich. 302, 176 N.W. 410; Buelow v. Chicago, R. I. & P. R. Co., 1925, 164 Minn. 52, 204 N.W. 571; Gunby v. Colorado & S. R. Co., 1925, 77 Colo. 225, 235 P. 566.

32. Nichols v. City of Phoenix, 1949, 68 Ariz. 124, 202 P.2d 201 (arterial intersection); Chiles v. Rohl, 1924, 47 S.D. 580, 201 N.W. 154; Pederson v. O'Rourke, 1926, 54 N.D. 428, 209 N.W. 798; Thrapp v. Meyers, 1926, 114 Neb. 689, 209 N.W. 238.

33. Morrison v. Medaglia, 1934, 287 Mass. 46, 191 N.E. 133; Thornton v. Eneroth, 1934, 177 Wash. 1, 30 P.2d 951; Adams v. Parrish, 1920, 189 Ky. 628, 225 S.W. 467. As to obstacles in the highway and negligently driven vehicles, cf. Wedel v. Johnson, 1936, 196 Minn. 170, 264 N.W. 689; City of Louisville v. Hart's Adm'r, 1911, 143 Ky.

street,[34] creates the risk [35] that he will be struck by a negligently driven car. If the defendant floods the premises with gasoline, he may be negligent because of the danger that someone will cause a spark or light a match.[36]

The duty to take precautions against the negligence of others thus becomes merely a matter of the customary process [37] of multiplying the probability that such negligence will occur by the magnitude of the harm likely to result if it does, and weighing the result against the burden upon the defendant of exercising such care. The duty arises, in other words, only where a reasonable man would recognize the existence of an unreasonable risk of harm to others through the intervention of such negligence.[38] It becomes

most obvious when the actor has reason to know that he is dealing with persons whose characteristics make it especially likely that they will do unreasonable things. He may be required to guard an insane patient to prevent him from jumping from the hospital window, [39] or to refrain from putting an intoxicated person off of a train into a railroad yard,[40] or letting him have an automobile,[41] or more liquor.[42]

And when children are in the vicinity, much is necessarily to be expected of them which would not be looked for on the part of an adult. It may be anticipated that a child will dash into the street in the path

171, 136 S.W. 212; Wagner v. Village of Waterbury, 1938, 109 Vt. 368, 196 A. 745 (ice).

34. McKenna v. Stephens, [1923] Ir.Rep. 2 K.B.D. 112; O'Malley v. Laurel Line Bus Co., 1933, 311 Pa. 251, 166 A. 868; Donovan v. Bender, 1961, 9 N.Y.2d 854, 175 N.E.2d 463; McDonald v. Central School District, 1941, 179 Misc. 333, 39 N.Y.S.2d 103, affirmed, 1942, 264 App.Div. 943, 36 N.Y.S.2d 438, affirmed, 1943, 289 N.Y. 800, 47 N.E.2d 50.

35. This, however, is a matter of unreasonable risk. In a quiet residential thoroughfare with one-way traffic, there may be, as a matter of law, no negligence. De Luca v. Manchester Laundry & Dry Cleaning Co., 1955, 380 Pa. 484, 112 A.2d 372. Cf. Smith v. Mabrey, 1941, 348 Mo. 644, 154 S.W.2d 770 (not the "proximate cause").

36. Watson v. Kentucky & Indiana Bridge & R. Co., 1910, 137 Ky. 619, 126 S.W. 146, 129 S.W. 341; Teasdale v. Beacon Oil Co., 1929, 266 Mass. 25, 164 N.E. 612; State Highway Comm. v. Empire Oil & Ref. Co., 1935, 141 Kan. 161, 40 P.2d 355; Robert R. Walker, Inc. v. Burgdorf, 1951, 150 Tex. 603, 244 S.W.2d 506 ("You know that gasoline and water will not burn.")

37. See supra, p. ——.

38. Nunan v. Bennett, 1919, 184 Ky. 591, 212 S.W. 570 (tenant leaving faucets turned on); Koppalan v. Martin Hotel Co., 1941, 230 Iowa 739, 298 N.W. 901 (hotel guest knocking out window screen); McDonald v. Fryberger, 1951, 233 Minn. 156, 46 N. W.2d 260 (employee standing on drawer of cabinet); Hendricks v. Pyramid Motor Freight Corp., 1937, 328 Pa. 570, 195 A. 907 (negligently starting truck on ferry); Rosenberg v. Hartman, 1943, 313 Mass. 54, 46 N.E.2d 406 (walking into glass door).

Sometimes different views are taken as to foreseeability. Compare, as to going too fast through a revolving door, Wiedanz v. May Department Stores Co., Mo.App.1941, 156 S.W.2d 44, with Hansen v. Henrici's, 1943, 319 Ill.App. 458, 49 N.E.2d 737.

39. Mulliner v. Evangelischer Diakonniessenverein, 1920, 144 Minn. 392, 175 N.W. 699; Misfeldt v. Hospital Authority of City of Marietta, 1960, 101 Ga.App. 579, 115 S.E.2d 244; Durfee v. Dorr, 1916, 123 Ark. 542, 186 S.W. 62; Paulen v. Shinnick, 1939, 291 Mich. 288, 289 N.W. 162; Collins v. State, 1965, 23 App.Div.2d 898, 258 N.Y.S.2d 938, affirmed, 1966, 17 N.Y.2d 542, 268 N.Y.S.2d 314, 215 N.E.2d 500.

But even on the part of an insane person, there are some acts so unlikely that reasonable care does not call for guarding against them. Mesedahl v. St. Luke's Hospital Ass'n of Duluth, 1935, 194 Minn. 198, 259 N.W. 819 (climbing out top of barred window); Prudential Society v. Ray, 1924, 207 App.Div. 496, 202 N.Y.S. 614, affirmed, 1925, 239 N.Y. 600, 147 N.E. 212 (pawning ring); Fisher v. Mutimer, 1938, 293 Ill.App. 201, 12 N.E.2d 315 (murder). Cf. Fetzer v. Aberdeen Clinic, 1925, 48 S.D. 308, 204 N.W. 364 (patient jumping from window).

40. Atchison, T. & S. F. R. Co. v. Parry, 1903, 67 Kan. 515, 73 P. 105; Fagan v. Atlantic Coast Line R. Co., 1917, 220 N.Y. 301, 115 N.E. 704. Cf. Black v. New York, N. H. & H. R. Co., 1907, 193 Mass. 448, 79 N.E. 797.

41. Owensboro Undertaking Ass'n v. Henderson, 1938, 273 Ky. 112, 115 S.W.2d 563; Mitchell v. Churches, 1922, 119 Wash. 547, 206 P. 6; Tolbert v. Jackson, 5 Cir. 1938, 99 F.2d 513; Rounds v. Phillips, 1934, 166 Md. 151, 170 A. 532 (notoriously reckless driver).

42. Rappaport v. Nichols, 1959, 31 N.J. 188, 156 A.2d 1; Waynick v. Chicago's Last Dept. Store, 7 Cir. 1959, 269 F.2d 322, cert. denied 362 U.S. 903.

of a car,[43] or meddle with a turntable.[44] It may be clear negligence to entrust him with a gun,[45] or to allow him to drive an automobile,[46] or to throw candy where a crowd of boys will scramble for it.[47] There have been a number of "pied piper" cases, in which street vendors of ice cream, and the like, which attract children into the street, have been held liable for failure to protect them against traffic.[48] It may be quite as negligent to leave the gun, or to leave dynamite caps, where children are likely to come, and and can easily find them.[49] In all such cases,

the question comes down essentially to one of whether the risk outweighs the utility of the actor's conduct.[50] He may be required to guard a power line pole located in a public park, but not one in the open country;[51] and whether he must take steps to prevent children from interfering with such an object as a stationary vehicle is entirely a matter of the circumstances of the particular case.[52]

There is normally much less reason to anticipate acts on the part of others which are malicious and intentionally damaging than those which are merely negligent; and this is all the more true where, as is usually the case, such acts are criminal.[53] Under all or-

---

43. Skeens v. Gemmell, 6 Cir. 1965, 353 F.2d 38 (near school); Vought v. Jones, 1965, 205 Va. 719, 139 S.E.2d 810; Bean v. Butler, 1959, 155 Me. 106, 151 A.2d 271; Washington v. Davis, 1958, 249 N.C. 65, 105 S.E.2d 202; Paschka v. Carsten, 1942, 231 Iowa 1185, 3 N.W.2d 542. Compare, as to starting a car, Butler v. Temples, 1955, 227 S.C. 496, 88 S.E.2d 586; Conrad v. Taylor, 1955, 197 Va. 188, 89 S.E.2d 40.

44. See the "attractive nuisance" cases, infra, pp. ——, ——.

45. Dixon v. Bell, 5 M. & S. 198, 105 Eng.Rep. 1023; Binford v. Johnston, 1882, 82 Ind. 426; Meers v. McDowell, 1901, 110 Ky. 926, 62 S.W. 1013; cf. Carter v. Towne, 1868, 98 Mass. 567.

Otherwise as to a 15 year old boy. Hartnett v. Boston Store, 1914, 265 Ill. 331, 106 N.E. 837; Poland v. Earhart, 1886, 70 Iowa 285, 30 N.W. 637. It has been held, in the absence of statute, that it is not negligence to entrust an air gun to a child. Chaddock v. Plummer, 1891, 88 Mich. 225, 50 N.W. 135; Harris v. Cameron, 1892, 81 Wis. 239, 51 N.W. 437.

46. Anderson v. Daniel, 1924, 136 Miss. 456, 101 So. 498; Hopkins v. Droppers, 1924, 184 Wis. 400, 198 N.W. 738.

47. Shafer v. Keeley Ice Cream Co., 1925, 65 Utah 46, 234 P. 300.

48. Jacobs v. Draper, 1966, 274 Minn. 110, 142 N.W.2d 628; Mackey v. Spradlin, Ky.1965, 397 S.W.2d 33; Ellis v. Trowen Frozen Products, Inc., 1968, 264 Cal. App.2d 499, 70 Cal.Rptr. 487; Thomas v. Goodies Ice Cream Co., 1968, 13 Ohio App.2d 67, 233 N.E.2d 876; Reid v. Swindler, 1967, 249 S.C. 483, 154 S.E.2d 910.

49. Vills v. City of Cloquet, 1912, 119 Minn. 277, 138 N.W. 33; Luhman v. Hoover, 6 Cir. 1938, 100 F.2d 127; Fehrs v. City of McKeesport, 1935, 318 Pa. 279, 178 A. 380; City of Tulsa v. McIntosh, 1923, 90 Okl. 50, 215 P. 624.

Otherwise where the caps are left where children are not likely to interfere with them. Perry v. Rochester Lime Co., 1916, 219 N.Y. 60, 113 N.E.

529; Vining v. Amos D. Bridges Sons Co., 1928, 127 Me. 544, 142 A. 773; cf. Dahl v. Valley Dredging Co., 1914, 125 Minn. 90, 145 N.W. 796; Beickert v. G. M. Laboratories, 1926, 242 N.Y. 168, 151 N.E. 195. But even then past experience of meddling may call for precautions. Katz v. Helbing, 1932, 215 Cal. 449, 10 P.2d 1001.

50. See Bauer, The Degree of Danger and the Degree of Difficulty of Removal in "Attractive Nuisance" Cases, 1934, 18 Minn.L.Rev. 523.

51. Compare Znidersich v. Minnesota Utilities Co., 1923, 155 Minn. 293, 193 N.W. 449, with Keep v. Otter Tail Power Co., 1937, 201 Minn. 475, 277 N.W. 213.

52. No negligence: Marengo v. Roy, 1945, 318 Mass. 719, 63 N.E.2d 893; Union Carbide & Carbon Corp. v. Peters, 4 Cir. 1953, 206 F.2d 366; Dennis v. Odend'Hal-Monks Corp., 1943, 182 Va. 77, 28 S.E.2d 4; Touris v. Brewster & Co., 1923, 235 N.Y. 226, 139 N.E. 249, reargument denied, 1924, 236 N.Y. 510, 142 N.E. 263; Bergman v. Williams, 1927, 173 Minn. 250, 217 N.W. 127.

Negligence: Lane v. Atlantic Works, 1872, 111 Mass. 136; Tierney v. New York Dugan Bros., 1942, 288 N.Y. 16, 41 N.E.2d 161; Vaughan v. Industrial Silica Corp., 1942, 140 Ohio St. 17, 42 N.E.2d 156; Johnson v. John Deere Plow Co., 1959, 214 Ga. 645, 106 S.E.2d 901 (tractor); Arnett v. Yeago, 1957, 247 N.C. 356, 100 S.E.2d 855 (car parked on hill).

See Glassey v. Worcester Consol. St. R. Co., 1904, 185 Mass. 315, 70 N.E. 199, and Second Restatement of Torts, § 302B, Illustration 14, to the effect that such acts may be anticipated on Halloween.

53. See Watson v. Kentucky & Ind. Bridge & R. Co., 1910, 137 Ky. 619, 126 S.W. 146, 129 S.W. 341; Crandall v. Consolidated Telephone, Telegraph & Electric Co., 1912, 14 Ariz. 322, 127 P. 994; Eldredge, Culpable Intervention as Superseding Cause, 1937, 86 U.Pa.L.Rev. 121.

dinary and normal circumstances, in the absence of any reason to expect the contrary, the actor may reasonably proceed upon the assumption that others will obey the criminal law. Under such ordinary circumstances, it is not reasonably to be expected that anyone will intentionally tamper with a railway track,[54] blow up a powder magazine,[55] forge a check,[56] push another man into an excavation,[57] assault a railway passenger,[58] or hold up a bowling alley and shoot a patron.[59] Although such things do occur, as must be known to anyone who reads the daily papers, they are still so unlikely in any particular instance that the burden of taking continual precautions against them exceeds the apparent risk.

There are, however, other situations, in which either a special responsibility resting upon the defendant for the protection of the plaintiff, or an especial temptation and opportunity for criminal misconduct, brought about by the defendant, will call upon him to take precautions against it.[60] The responsibility for protection may arise out of a contract, by which the defendant has agreed to provide it;[61] or it may be founded upon some relation existing between the parties, such as carrier and passenger, innkeeper and guest,[62] invitor and business visitor,[63] school district and pupil,[64] employer and employee,[65] landlord and tenant,[66] and no doubt others.[67] The

---

54. Deyo v. New York Central R. Co., 1865, 34 N.Y. 9; Bowers v. Southern R. Co., 1912, 10 Ga.App. 367, 73 S.E. 677 (switch); cf. Mars v. Delaware & H. Canal Co., 1889, 54 Hun 625, 8 N.Y.S. 107 (engine); Schmidt v. United States, 10 Cir. 1950, 179 F.2d 724, cert. denied 339 U.S. 986 (bazooka shell).

55. Kleebauer v. Western Fuse & Explosives Co., 1903, 138 Cal. 497, 71 P. 617. Cf. Bellows v. Worcester Storage Co., 1937, 297 Mass. 188, 7 N.E.2d 588 (setting fire to warehouse); Galanis v. Mercury Int. Ins. Underwriters, 1967, 247 Cal.App.2d 690, 55 Cal.Rptr. 890 (suicide-murder in plane for insurance).

56. Benenson v. National Surety Co., 1932, 260 N.Y. 299, 183 N.E. 505; Glasscock v. First Nat. Bank, 1924, 114 Tex. 207, 266 S.W. 393; Walsh v. Hunt, 1898, 120 Cal. 46, 52 P. 115. But the circumstances may make it foreseeable. Foutch v. Alexandria Bank & Trust Co., 1941, 177 Tenn. 348, 149 S.W.2d 76, where a check drawn in pencil was raised, contains a good review of the cases.

57. Alexander v. Town of New Castle, 1888, 115 Ind. 51, 17 N.E. 200; Milostan v. City of Chicago, 1909, 148 Ill.App. 540; Miller v. Bahmmuller, 1908, 124 App.Div. 558, 108 N.Y.S. 924. Cf. Village of Carterville v. Cook, 1889, 129 Ill. 152, 22 N.E. 14, as to anticipating negligent acts.

58. Hoff v. Public Service R. Co., 1918, 91 N.J.L. 641, 103 A. 209. Cf. Chancey v. Norfolk & W. R. Co., 1917, 174 N.C. 351, 93 S.E. 834 (theft); Ellinger v. Philadelphia W. & B. R. Co., 1893, 153 Pa. 213, 25 A. 1132 (jostling).

59. Genovay v. Fox, 1958, 50 N.J.Super. 538, 143 A.2d 229, reversed on the particular facts, 1959, 29 N.J. 436, 149 A.2d 212.

60. Second Restatement of Torts, § 302B, Comments e and f; Eldredge, Culpable Intervention as Superseding Cause, 1937, 86 U.Pa.L.Rev. 121; Feezer, Intervening Crime and Liability for Negligence, 1940, 24 Minn.L.Rev. 635; Notes, 1940, 24 Minn.L.Rev. 666; 1931, 29 Mich.L.Rev. 846; 1932, 30 Mich.L.Rev. 806.

61. Silverblatt v. Brooklyn Telegraph & Messenger Co., 1911, 73 Misc. 38, 132 N.Y.S. 253, reversed, 1912, 150 App.Div. 268, 134 N.Y.S. 765.

62. McFadden v. Bancroft Hotel Corp., 1943, 313 Mass. 56, 46 N.E.2d 573; Dickson v. Waldron, 1893, 135 Ind. 507, 34 N.E. 506, rehearing denied, 1893, 135 Ind. 507, 35 N.E. 1.

63. Peck v. Gerber, 1936, 154 Or. 126, 59 P.2d 675; Sinn v. Farmers Deposit Savings Bank, 1930, 300 Pa. 85, 150 A. 163; Stotzheim v. Djos, 1959, 256 Minn. 316, 98 N.W.2d 129; Wallace v. Der-Ohanian, 1962, 199 Cal.App.2d 141, 18 Cal.Rptr. 892; Grasso v. Blue Bell Waffle Shop, Mun.App.D.C.1960, 164 A.2d 475. See Note, 1955, 9 Vand.L.Rev. 106.

64. McLeod v. Grant County School District No. 128, 1953, 42 Wash.2d 316, 255 P.2d 360.

65. David v. Missouri Pac. R. Co., 1931, 328 Mo. 437, 41 S.W.2d 179, reversed on other grounds, 1932, 284 U.S. 460.

66. Ramsay v. Morrisette, D.C.App.1969, 252 A.2d 509; Kendall v. Gore Properties, 1956, 98 U.S.App. D.C., 236 F.2d 673; Mozer v. Semenza, Fla.App. 1965, 177 So.2d 880. See Note, 1965, 18 U.Fla.L.Rev. 538.

67. Two cases indicate the possible wide range. In Schuster v. City of New York, 1958, 5 N.Y.2d 75, 180 N.Y.S.2d 265, 154 N.E.2d 534, the city was held liable for failure to provide proper police protection for an informer, who was murdered. In Liberty Nat. Life Ins. Co. v. Weldon, 1958, 267 Ala. 171, 100 So.2d 696, a company which issued a

carrier, for example, may be required to protect its passengers from third persons who have threatened them with violence,[68] or are drunk or quarrelsome,[69] or to guard them against external attack [70] or look after its switches [71] in a neighborhood which is known to be frequented by criminal characters. Another possibility is that the defendant's special responsibility may arise because he is in a position to control the criminal himself and so is held to be under an obligation to do so, extending to anyone who may be injured by his failure to exercise reasonable care.[72]

There are other situations in which the defendant will be held liable because his affirmative conduct has greatly increased the risk of harm to the plaintiff through the criminal acts of others. The defendant may bring the plaintiff into contact with individuals of known criminal tendencies, as for example, by hiring them, under conditions in which opportunity for crime is afforded.[73] He may, by his acts, defeat a protection which the plaintiff himself has set up about his own person or property, against criminal interference. Thus if valuable property is left unguarded and exposed to the public view, it may be anticipated that it will be stolen,[74] and if the key is left in the lock of a jewelry store over a holiday, it is not at all unlikely that there will be a burglary.[75]

Other situations could no doubt be suggested. In all of them, however, there is liabili-

policy insuring the life of a child to one with no insurable interest was held liable when the beneficiary murdered the child. The case relied upon a statute. See Duesenberg, Insurer's Tort Liability for Issuing Policy Without Insurance Interest, 1959, 47 Cal.L.Rev. 64; Note, 1958, 58 Col.L.Rev. 1087.

68. Quigley v. Wilson Line of Massachusetts, 1958, 338 Mass. 125, 154 N.E.2d 77; Bullock v. Tamiami Trail Tours, Inc., 5 Cir.1959, 266 F.2d 326; Jones v. Yellow Cab & Baggage Co., 1954, 176 Kan. 558, 271 P.2d 249; Kinsey v. Hudson & Manhattan R. Co., 1943, 130 N.J.L. 285, 32 A.2d 497, affirmed, 1944, 130 N.J.L. 161, 35 A.2d 888; Smith v. Camel City Cab Co., 1947, 227 N.C. 572, 42 S.E.2d 657.

69. Liljegren v. United Rys. Co., Mo.App.1921, 227 S.W. 925; Hillman v. Georgia R. R. & Banking Co., 1906, 126 Ga. 814, 56 S.E. 68; Thompson v. St. Louis Public Service Co., Mo.1951, 242 S.W.2d 299. Cf. McFadden v. Bancroft Hotel Corp., 1943, 313 Mass. 56, 46 N.E.2d 573 (innkeeper); Peck v. Gerber, 1936, 154 Or. 126, 59 P.2d 675 (restaurant).

70. Neering v. Illinois Central R. Co., 1943, 383 Ill. 366, 50 N.E.2d 497, conformed to, 1944, 321 Ill.App. 625, 53 N.E.2d 271 (rape); Hines v. Garrett, 1921, 131 Va. 125, 108 S.E. 690 (same); Harpell v. Public Service Coordinated Transport, 1956, 20 N.J. 309, 120 A.2d 43 (rock thrown through train window). Cf. McLeod v. Grant County School District No. 128, 1953, 42 Wash.2d 316, 255 P.2d 360 (rape of school-girl).

71. International & G. N. R. Co. v. Johnson, 1900, 23 Tex.Civ.App. 160, 203, 55 S.W. 772, 796–797, reversed and dismissed by agreement; St. Louis S. F. R. Co. v. Mills, 5 Cir. 1925, 3 F.2d 882, cert. granted 267 U.S. 589; Green v. Atlanta & C. A. L. R. Co., 1924, 131 S.C. 124, 126 S.E. 441; Second Restatement of Torts, § 302B, Illustration 15.

72. Austin W. Jones Co. v. State, 1923, 122 Me. 214, 119 A. 577 (dangerous pyromaniac in asylum); St.

George v. State, 1953, 203 Misc. 340, 118 N.Y.S.2d 596, reversed on other grounds, 1953, 283 App.Div. 245, 127 N.Y.S.2d 147, settled, 1954, 128 N.Y.S.2d 583, motion denied, 1954, 307 N.Y. 689, 120 N.E. 2d 860, affirmed, 1955, 308 N.Y. 681, 124 N.E.2d 320. Finkel v. State, 1962, 37 Misc.2d 757, 237 N.Y.S.2d 66. Cf. Missouri, K. & T. R. Co. v. Wood, 1902, 95 Tex. 223, 66 S.W. 449 (smallpox patient); University of Louisville v. Hammock, 1907, 127 Ky. 564, 106 S.W. 219 (delirium tremens).

73. Hall v. Smathers, 1925, 240 N.Y. 486, 148 N.E. 654 (record of violence, hired as janitor); Kendall v. Gore Properties, 1956, 98 U.S.App.D.C. 378, 236 F.2d 673 (lunatic hired to do work in tenant's apartment); Hipp v. Hospital Authority of City of Marietta, 1961, 104 Ga.App. 174, 121 S.E.2d 273 (sex record, employed in hospital); Georgia Bowling Enterprises v. Robbins, 1961, 103 Ga.App. 286, 119 S.E.2d 52 (record of violence, hired in bowling alley); De la Bere v. Pearson, Ltd., [1908] 1 K.B. 280 (dishonest broker recommended).

74. Brower v. New York Central & H. R. R. Co., 1918, 91 N.J.L. 190, 103 A. 166; Whitehead v. Stringer, 1919, 106 Wash. 501, 180 P. 486; Filson v. Pacific Exp. Co., 1911, 84 Kan. 614, 114 P. 863; Morse v. Homer's, Inc., 1936, 295 Mass. 606, 4 N.E.2d 625; National Ben Franklin Ins. Co. v. Careccta, 1959, 21 Misc.2d 279, 193 N.Y.S.2d 904.

75. Garceau v. Engel, 1926, 169 Minn. 62, 210 N.W. 68. Cf. Southwestern Bell Tel. Co. v. Adams, 1939, 199 Ark. 254, 133 S.W.2d 867; Jesse French Piano & Organ Co. v. Phelps, 1907, 47 Tex.Civ.App. 385, 105 S.W. 225; Marshall v. Caledonian Ry., [1899] 1 Sess. Cas. (5th Ser.) 1060.

ty only if the defendant is negligent in not guarding against the possible crime—which is to say, if the foreseeable risk is an unreasonable one, in the light of the burden of taking precautions. A state prison may be under no obligation to use care in guarding a forger, with no record of any violence, for the protection of the plaintiff; [76] a mere unfastened window may create no undue risk of burglary; [77] a carrier may be required to take no precautions in a neighborhood apparently safe.[78] Leaving the key in the ignition lock of a car parked on the street may be found not to involve any unreasonable risk of harm to those in the vicinity, notwithstanding the obvious foreseeability of theft; [79] but if the vehicle is a twenty-six-ton bulldozer, poised on a plateau, and curious individuals have shown a disposition to meddle with it, the risk becomes entirely unreasonable.[80]

Shifting Responsibility

A large number of negligence cases have turned on the problem of what might be called shifting responsibility—that is to say, that the defendant may not be required to take any precautions for the plaintiff's safety, because he is free to assume that someone else will do it or will be fully responsible in case he does not. Whether it be said that the defendant is under no duty to act in such a case, or that he has exercised reasonable care in relying upon another, the result is the same.

Thus a common laborer, hired to dig a ditch in the street, may ordinarily leave it to his superiors to set out a red lantern to warn traffic,[81] and one who deposits cotton in a warehouse is not required to keep anyone from coming near the pile of bales.[82] A surgeon may leave routine duties following an operation to competent hospital attendants,[83] and an automobile driver may of course have his car overhauled by a reliable garage, rather than do it himself.[84] A landlord who leases premises without a covenant to keep them in repair is not responsible for injuries due to defects unknown to him at the time,[85] and one who sells another a chattel in safe condition may rely upon the buyer's agreement to inspect it for defects that may develop later.[86] In the ordinary case, one who employs an independent contractor to do work on his premises may leave all responsibility to him, and is not liable for his negligence.[87]

---

76. Williams v. State, 1955, 308 N.Y. 548, 127 N.E.2d 545.

77. Strong v. Granite Furniture Co., 1930, 77 Utah 292, 294 P. 303. Cf. Jenkins v. Louisville Home Tel. Co., Ky.1909, 120 S.W. 276 (burglar entered via telephone pole).

78. Sira v. Wabash R. Co., 1893, 115 Mo. 127, 21 S.W. 905.

79. Richards v. Stanley, 1954, 43 Cal.2d 60, 271 P.2d 23. See, as to the dispute over this, infra, p. ——.

80. Richardson v. Ham, 1955, 44 Cal.2d 772, 285 P.2d 269. Cf. Zuber v. Clarkson Const. Co., 1952, 363 Mo. 352, 251 S.W.2d 52; Hergenrether v. East, 1964, 61 Cal.2d 440, 39 Cal.Rptr. 4, 393 P.2d 164; Anderson v. Bushong Pontiac Co., 1961, 404 Pa. 382, 171 A.2d 771. See Note, 1965, 38 So.Cal.L.Rev. 125.

81. Jessup v. Sloneker, 1891, 142 Pa. 527, 21 A. 988; Carter v. Franklin, 1937, 234 Ala. 116, 173 So. 861; Schaefer v. Iron City Sand Co., 1906, 31 Pa.Super. 476.

82. Murphey v. Caralli, 1864, 3 H. & C. 461, 159 Eng. Rep. 611.

83. Harris v. Fall, 7 Cir. 1910, 177 F. 79; Stewart v. Manasses, 1914, 244 Pa. 221, 90 A. 574; Malkowski v. Graham, 1919, 169 Wis. 398, 172 N.W. 785.

84. Phillips v. Britannia Hygienic Laundry Co., [1923] 1 K.B. 539, affirmed [1923] 2 K.B. 832.

85. Harpel v. Fall, 1896, 63 Minn. 520, 65 N.W. 913; McKenzie v. Cheetham, 1891, 83 Me. 543, 22 A. 469; Campbell v. Elsie S. Holding Co., 1929, 251 N.Y. 446, 167 N.E. 582. See infra, p. ——.

86. Goar v. Village of Stephen, 1923, 157 Minn. 228, 196 N.W. 171. Compare, as to warning of the defect, Ford Motor Co. v. Wagoner, 1946, 183 Tenn. 392, 192 S.W.2d 840; Foster v. Ford Motor Co., 1926, 139 Wash. 341, 246 P. 945; J. C. Penny Co. v. Morris, 1935, 173 Miss. 710, 163 So. 124.

87. Engel v. Eureka Club, 1893, 137 N.Y. 100, 32 N.E. 1052; Pickett v. Waldorf System, 1922, 241 Mass. 569, 136 N.E. 64; Atlanta & F. R. Co. v. Kimberly, 1891, 87 Ga. 161, 13 S.E. 277. See infra, p. 468.

Yet in many situations, where the risk is unduly great, it is not reasonable care to rely upon the responsibility of others. The operating surgeon may be required to keep an eye on the count of sponges himself, rather than leave it to the nurse.[88] If premises are leased in such condition that they are unreasonably dangerous to those outside of them,[89] or to the general public who are known to be about to be admitted to them,[90] the landlord is not free to rely upon the tenant, and even the tenant's agreement to repair will not relieve him, if injury is to be anticipated before the repairs will be made.[91] A carrier who turns over a defective car may not leave it to the shipper or connecting carrier to inspect it for the benefit of employees who may be hurt.[92] The seller of a chattel which will be dangerous unless carefully made may not assume that the buyer will inspect it and discover the defects before resale,[93] and if the danger is very great, even actual discovery by the buyer, or a warning to him, may not be sufficient.[94] Quite apart from any question of vicarious liability, the employer of an independent contractor may be required to take precautions against his negligence if the work to be done is such that unreasonably dangerous conditions are likely to arise.[95] In all of these cases the defendant is not relieved, by his reliance upon another, of responsibility for a risk he has created.

It is not easy to state any general principle to govern these cases. Many factors must be taken into account: the competence and reliability of the person upon whom reliance is placed,[96] his understanding of the situation, the seriousness of the danger and the number of persons likely to be affected, the length of time elapsed,[97] and above all the likelihood that proper care will not be used, and the ease with which the actor himself may take precautions.[98] If an attempt must be made to generalize, it may be said that when the defendant is under a duty to act reasonably for the protection of the plaintiff, and may anticipate that a third person may fail to use proper care if the responsibility is transferred to him, and that serious harm will follow if he does not, it is not reasonable care to place reliance upon him.

Misrepresentation and Nondisclosure

In a relatively large number of negligence cases, liability has rested upon some form of misrepresentation on the part of the defendant, by which the plaintiff, or some third person, has been misled to the plaintiff's damage. The remedy of an action for deceit, which is considered elsewhere,[99] has tended to be confined to cases in which the interest

---

88. Ault v. Hall, 1928, 119 Ohio St. 422, 164 N.E. 518; Ales v. Ryan, 1936, 8 Cal.2d 82, 64 P.2d 409; Walker v. Holbrook, 1915, 130 Minn. 106, 153 N.W. 305; Davis v. Kerr, 1913, 239 Pa. 351, 86 A. 1007.

89. See infra, p. 402.

90. See infra, p. 403.

91. Swords v. Edgar, 1894, 59 N.Y. 28; Isham v. Broderick, 1905, 89 Minn. 397, 95 N.W. 224; Folkman v. Lauer, 1914, 244 Pa. 605, 91 A. 218. Otherwise where the lessor exacts an agreement that the premises will be put in safe condition before the public is admitted. Nickelsen v. Minneapolis, N. & S. R. Co., 1926, 168 Minn. 118, 209 N.W. 646; Beaman v. Grooms, 1917, 138 Tenn. 320, 197 S.W. 1090. See Second Restatement of Torts, § 359, Comment *i*.

92. See infra, p. 676.

93. See infra, p. 667.

94. Kentucky Independent Oil Co. v. Schnitzler, 1925, 208 Ky. 507, 271 S.W. 570; Clement v. Crosby & Co., 1907, 148 Mich. 293, 295, 111 N.W. 745; cf. Trusty v. Patterson, 1930, 299 Pa. 469, 149 A. 717; Ferraro v. Taylor, 1936, 197 Minn. 5, 265 N.W. 829; Bryson v. Hines, 4 Cir. 1920, 268 F. 290. See Second Restatement of Torts, § 389, Comment *f*.

95. See infra, p. 472.

96. Thus the defendant may be liable if he turns over his automobile to one who is intoxicated (infra, p. 482), or employs an independent contractor who is incompetent. Mueller v. Winston Bros. Co., 1931, 165 Wash. 130, 4 P.2d 854; Wabash County v. Pearson, 1889, 120 Ind. 426, 22 N.E. 134.

97. Cf. Goar v. Village of Stephen, 1923, 157 Minn. 228, 196 N.W. 171.

98. Cf. Malkowski v. Graham, 1919, 169 Wis. 398, 172 N.W. 785; Skogland v. St. Paul Gaslight Co., 1903, 89 Minn. 1, 93 N.W. 668.

99. See infra, ch. 18.

affected is a pecuniary one, such as sales and credit transactions. In those areas, the action for negligence makes its appearance, but has been kept within somewhat more narrow limits than where the harm is to person or property.[1] Deceit has served as an occasional remedy where there is such harm to tangible interests,[2] but for the most part cases of misrepresentation resulting in such harm have been dealt with in an action for negligence.

If the defendant consciously misstates the facts in such a way as to lead the plaintiff to place himself or his property in danger of harm which the defendant still does not intend, he may nevertheless not be exercising proper care for the plaintiff's safety, and so be liable for his negligent use of language.[3] But even where the defendant is not consciously misstating the facts, he may still be liable for negligence in speaking where he has not exercised proper care to ascertain the truth, or to communicate it. An assurance that a bridge is safe,[4] or that there is no danger from blasting operations[5] may result in liability for negligence when the plaintiff relies upon the assurance and suffers injury. The same is true when a physician informs those in contact with his patient that the illness is not contagious, when with proper skill and care he should have known better.[6]

Sellers of dangerous chattels who assure the buyer that there is no danger frequently have been held liable for negligent failure to ascertain the truth.[7] The misrepresentation may be by conduct rather than by words. A truck driver who waves a following motorist on to pass,[8] a railroad which opens its crossing gates,[9] or a seller who paints over a stepladder to conceal its defects,[10] may become liable for negligent misrepresentation when someone is hurt as a result.

Such liability is not necessarily confined to the person to whom the false statement is made. It extends to others who may reasonably be expected to be endangered by it. Thus in many cases the seller of a dangerous article who misrepresents its character,[11] or assures the buyer that it is safe,[12] has been

1. See infra, p. 704.

2. Langridge v. Levy, 1836, 2 M. & W. 519, 150 Eng.Rep. 863; Kuelling v. Roderick Lean Mfg. Co., 1905, 183 N.Y. 78, 75 N.E. 1098; see infra, p. 684. See Smith, Liability for Negligent Language, 1901, 14 Harv.L.Rev. 184.

3. Span v. Ely, 1876, 8 Hun, N.Y., 255 (assurance from physician smallpox was not contagious).

4. Washington & Berkeley Bridge Co. v. Pennsylvania Steel Co., 4 Cir.1915, 226 F. 169.

5. Valz v. Goodykoontz, 1911, 112 Va. 853, 72 S.E. 730. Cf. Virginia Dare Stores v. Schuman, 1938, 175 Md. 287, 1 A.2d 897 (assurance to workman place safe to stand); Robb v. Gylock Corp., 1956, 384 Pa. 209, 120 A.2d 174 (same, acid carboys empty); Benoit v. Perkins, 1918, 79 N.H. 11, 104 A. 254 (insane person safe to work for).

6. Jones v. Stanko, 1928, 118 Ohio St. 147, 160 N.E. 456; Skillings v. Allen, 1919, 143 Minn. 323, 173

N.W. 663; Edwards v. Lamb, 1899, 69 N.H. 599, 45 A. 480.

7. Cunningham v. C. R. Pease House Furnishing Co., 1908, 74 N.H. 435, 69 A. 120 (inflammable stove blacking; "the warmer the stove the better it works"); Flies v. Fox Bros. Buick Co., 1928, 196 Wis. 196, 218 N.W. 855; Segal v. Carroll Furniture Co., 1935, 51 Ga.App. 164, 179 S.E. 775; Ebbert v. Philadelphia Elec. Co., 1937, 126 Pa.Super. 351, 191 A. 384, affirmed, 1938, 330 Pa. 257, 198 A. 323.

8. Shirley Cloak & Dress Co. v. Arnold, 1956, 92 Ga.App. 885, 90 S.E.2d 622; Thelen v. Spillman, 1957, 251 Minn. 89, 86 N.W.2d 700; Haralson v. Jones Truck Lines, 1954, 223 Ark. 813, 270 S.W.2d 892; Petroleum Carrier Corp. v. Carter, 5 Cir.1956, 233 F.2d 402; Armstead v. Holbert, 1961, 146 W. Va. 582, 122 S.E.2d 43. Cf. Sweet v. Ringwelski, 1961, 362 Mich. 138, 106 N.W.2d 742 (motioning child to cross); Miller v. Watkins, Mo.1962, 355 S.W.2d 1 (waving truck driver on to pass bus).

9. Johnson v. Director General of Railroads, 1924, 278 Pa. 491, 123 A. 484; Philadelphia & R. R. Co. v. Le Barr, 3 Cir. 1920, 265 F. 129 (flagman's signal); Cunningham Hardware Co. v. Louisville & N. R. Co., 1923, 209 Ala. 327, 96 So. 358 (same).

10. Schubert v. J. R. Clark Co., 1892, 49 Minn. 331, 51 N.W. 1103.

11. Waters-Pierce Oil Co. v. Deselms, 1909, 212 U.S. 159 (gasoline sold as kerosene); Wright v. Howe, 1915, 46 Utah 588, 150 P. 956; Andreottala v. Gaeta, 1927, 260 Mass. 105, 156 N.E. 731; Fort Wayne Drug Co. v. Flemion, 1931, 93 Ind.App. 40, 175 N.E. 670.

12. West Disinfecting Co. v. Plummer, 1916, 44 App. D.C. 345; Lewis v. Terry, 1896, 111 Cal. 39, 43 P.

held liable to an ultimate purchaser, or to others in the vicinity of its expected use; and on the same basis a boiler inspector who certifies that a boiler is safe without proper inspection becomes liable to a third person who is injured when the boiler explodes.[13] In such cases the basis of liability is the fact that the misrepresentation has led the person to whom it is made to forego precautions which he might otherwise have taken for the protection of the plaintiff. The liability of a landlord who negligently repairs the premises and assures his tenant that the repairs are safe may be rested upon this basis.[14]

In all cases of negligent misrepresentation, however, the circumstances must be such that the defendant is under a duty to the plaintiff to exercise reasonable care in giving the information, and that reliance upon what he says, with resulting danger is reasonably to be expected.[15] An assurance from a cas-

ual bystander, asked for his opinion, that he thinks the situation is safe, involves no such duty or expectation, and has been held not to be sufficient for negligence liability.[16]

In many situations, a failure to disclose the existence of a known danger may be the equivalent of misrepresentation, where it is to be expected that another will rely upon the appearance of safety. The surgeon who remains silent when he discovers that he has left his tools in the patient's anatomy,[17] the landlord who leases defective premises,[18] the landowner who permits a licensee to enter without warning of hidden perils,[19] the seller or supplier[20] of a chattel who fails to disclose its dangerous nature[21] or its concealed

398; Jones v. Raney Chevrolet Co., 1938, 213 N.C. 775, 197 S.E. 757.

13. Van Winkle v. American Steam-Boiler Ins. Co., 1890, 52 N.J.L. 240, 19 A. 472.

14. Cf. Good v. Von Hemert, 1911, 114 Minn. 393, 131 N.W. 466; Finer v. Nichols, 1913, 175 Mo.App. 525, 157 S.W. 1023; see Harkrider, Tort Liability of a Landlord, 1928, 26 Mich.L.Rev. 260, 407. "The question, then, is whether or not we have a case of misrepresentation by conduct and reliance thereupon." Kirshenbaum v. General Outdoor Advertising Co., 1932, 258 N.Y. 489, 180 N.E. 245.

15. "There must be knowledge, or its equivalent, that the information is desired for a serious purpose; that he to whom it is given intends to rely and act upon it; that, if false or erroneous, he will because of it be injured in person or property. Finally, the relationship of the parties, arising out of contract or otherwise, must be such that in morals and good conscience the one has the right to rely upon the other for information, and the other giving the information owes a duty to give it with care." International Products Co. v. Erie R. Co., 1927, 244 N.Y. 331, 155 N.E. 662.

The Second Restatement of Torts, § 311, discards the limitation of the First Restatement to cases where the information is given in a business or professional capacity. Cf. Buttersworth v. Swint, 1936, 53 Ga.App. 602, 186 S.E. 770 (advice of physician to one not a patient); Fish v. Kelly, 1864, 17 C.B., N.S., 194, 144 Eng.Rep. 78 (of attorney to one not a client).

16. Avery v. Palmer, 1918, 175 N.C. 378, 95 S.E. 553 (weight of tombstone); Holt v. Kolker, 1948, 189 Md. 636, 57 A.2d 287 (safety of porch); Webb v. Cerasoli, 1949, 275 App.Div. 45, 87 N.Y.S.2d 884, affirmed, 1949, 300 N.Y. 603, 90 N.E.2d 64 (owner assuring contractor in presence of workman).

17. Benson v. Dean, 1921, 232 N.Y. 52, 133 N.E. 125; Slimak v. Foster, 1927, 106 Conn. 366, 138 A. 153; Ernen v. Crofwell, 1930, 272 Mass. 172, 172 N.E. 73; Shutan v. Bloomenthal, 1939, 371 Ill. 244, 20 N.E.2d 570. Cf. Tvedt v. Haugen, 1940, 70 N.D. 338, 294 N.W. 183 (duty of physician to disclose existence of better method of treatment).

18. Cowen v. Sunderland, 1887, 145 Mass. 363, 14 N.E. 117 (injury to tenant); Coke v. Gutkese, 1883, 80 Ky. 598 (members of tenant's family); Maywood v. Logan, 1889, 78 Mich. 135, 43 N.W. 1052 (same); Rushton v. Winters, 1938, 331 Pa. 78, 200 A. 60 (licensee of tenant).

19. Campbell v. Boyd, 1883, 88 N.C. 129; Phipps v. Oregon R. & Nav. Co., C.C.Wash.1908, 161 F. 376; Hamblet v. Buffalo Library Garage Co., 1929, 222 App.Div. 335, 225 N.Y.S. 716; cf. Waters v. Markham, 1931, 204 Wis. 332, 235 N.W. 797 (guest in automobile).

20. Griffin v. Payne, 1921, 95 N.J.L. 490, 113 A. 247 (carrier turning over car; injury to employee).

21. Weiser v. Holzman, 1903, 33 Wash. 87, 73 P. 797 (injury to employee of buyer); Guinan v. Famous Players-Lasky Corp., 1929, 267 Mass. 501, 167 N.E. 235 (bystander); Genesee County Patrons Fire Relief Ass'n v. L. Sonneborn Sons, 1934, 263 N.Y. 463, 189 N.E. 551 (property of third party); Farley v. Edward E. Tower & Co., 1930, 271 Mass. 230, 171 N.E. 639 (customer of buyer).

defects,[22] each may be liable to the person with whom he deals, or to others to whom harm is to be expected through that person's reliance.[23] The "something like fraud on the part of the giver," [24] which the courts have found so frequently in these cases, consists in permitting another to rely upon a tacit assurance of safety, when it is known that there is danger.

34. DEGREES OF NEGLIGENCE— AGGRAVATED NEGLIGENCE

The amount of care demanded by the standard of reasonable conduct must be in proportion to the apparent risk. As the danger becomes greater, the actor is required to exercise caution commensurate with it.[25] Those who deal with instrumentalities that are known to be dangerous, such as high tension electricity,[26] gas,[27] explosives,[28] or elevators,[29] must exercise a great amount of care

because the risk is great. They may be required to take every reasonable precaution suggested by experience or prudence.[30] Likewise those who accept an unusual responsibility are required to act in accordance with it. Common carriers, who enter into an undertaking toward the public for the benefit of all those who wish to make use of their services, must use great caution to protect passengers entrusted to their care; and this has been described as "the utmost caution characteristic of very careful prudent men," [31] or "the highest possible care consistent with the nature of the undertaking." [32] Where the carrier receives goods for transportation, his responsibility is even higher, and the common law made him an insurer of their safety, against all hazards except the act of God and the public enemy.[33] A private or contract carrier, or any other bailee receiving goods for hire or for his own benefit, although not an insurer of the goods,[34] is still recognized as assuming great responsibility, and must use great care,[35] whereas one who accepts the same goods gratuitously, for the sole benefit of the bail-

22. Huset v. J. I. Case Threshing Mach. Co., 8 Cir. 1903, 120 F. 865 (customer of buyer).

23. See cases cited supra, notes 11–14.

24. Willes, J., in Gautret v. Egerton, 1867, L.R. 2 C.P. 371.

25. Meredith v. Reed, 1866, 26 Ind. 334 (only ordinary care required in keeping a stallion, but that is more care than in keeping a mare); Tom v. Days of '47, Inc., 1965, 16 Utah 2d 386, 401 P.2d 946 (Brahma bull at rodeo); Foy v. Friedman, 1960, 108 U.S.App. D.C. 176, 280 F.2d 724 (greater the hazard, greater the care required). See Note, 1942, 30 Ky.L.J. 321.

26. Brillhart v. Edison Light & Power Co., 1951, 368 Pa. 307, 82 A.2d 44; Toney v. Interstate Power Co., 1917, 180 Iowa 1362, 163 N.W. 394; Lynn v. Pinehurst Silk Mills, 1935, 208 N.C. 7, 179 S.E. 11; Smith v. Appalachian Elec. Power Co., 4 Cir. 1935, 74 F.2d 647. See Feezer, Tort Liability of Suppliers of Electricity, 1937, 22 Wash.U.L.Q. 357; Note, 1956, 24 Tenn.L.Rev. 362.

27. Koelsch v. Philadelphia Co., 1893, 152 Pa. 355, 25 A. 522; Applegate v. Portland Gas & Coke Co., 1933, 142 Or. 66, 18 P.2d 211. See Note, 1933, 17 Minn.L. Rev. 518; Webb v. Wisconsin Southern Gas Co., 1965, 27 Wis.2d 343, 134 N.W.2d 407. See Note, 1933, 17 Minn.L.Rev. 518.

28. Rafferty v. Davis, 1918, 260 Pa. 563, 103 A. 951; Briglio v. Holt & Jeffery, 1916, 91 Wash. 644, 158 P. 347.

29. Goodsell v. Taylor, 1889, 41 Minn. 207, 42 N.W. 873; Mitchell v. Marker, 6 Cir. 1894, 62 F. 139;

Strobel v. Park, 1927, 292 Pa. 200, 140 A. 877; Shielee v. Hill, 1955, 47 Wash.2d 362, 287 P.2d 479. Cf. Galveston City R. Co. v. Hewitt, 1887, 67 Tex. 473, 3 S.W. 705. See Note, 1955, 34 N.C.L.Rev. 145.

30. Koelsch v. Philadelphia Co., 1893, 152 Pa. 355, 363, 25 A. 522, 524.

31. Pennsylvania Co. v. Roy, 1880, 102 U.S. 451, 456. Accord: Marshall v. Wabash R. Co., 1915, 184 Mich. 593, 151 N.W. 696; Gulf, C. & S. F. R. Co. v. Conley, 1924, 113 Tex. 472, 260 S.W. 561.

32. Carson v. Boston Elev. R. Co., 1941, 309 Mass. 32, 33 N.E.2d 701; Francis v. Fitzpatrick, D.C.Cir. 1937, 89 F.2d 813; Grigsby v. Smith, 1940, 258 Ky. 48, 146 S.W.2d 719. See Notes, 1937, 17 N.C.L.Rev. 453; 1938, 25 Va.L.Rev. 250.

33. See Note, 1959, 10 West.Res.L.Rev. 276, as to the present status of this rule in a state such as Ohio.

34. Erwin Mills, Inc. v. Williams, 1960, 238 Miss. 335, 118 So.2d 339. As to the distinction between common and private carriers, see Home Ins. Co. v. Riddell, 5 Cir. 1958, 252 F.2d 1; Jackson v. Stancil, 1960, 253 N.C. 291, 116 S.E.2d 817.

35. Howard v. Babcock, 1859, 21 Ill. 259; Cameron v. Bissonette, 1930, 103 Vt. 93, 152 A. 87; Mitchell v. Violette, Mo.App.1918, 203 S.W. 218.

or, is required to exercise much less caution.[36]

Although the language used by the courts sometimes seems to indicate that a special standard is being applied, it would appear that none of these cases should logically call for any departure from the usual formula. What is required is merely the conduct of the reasonable man of ordinary prudence under the circumstances, and the greater danger,[37] or the greater responsibility,[38] is merely one of the circumstances, demanding only an increased amount of care.

A substantial number of courts, however, have dealt with some such cases by instructing the jury in terms of a higher, or the highest, "degree" of care, as for example in the case of the common carrier.[39] They thus purport to recognize a higher or lower basic standard of conduct for different defendants, or different situations. There is seldom reason to think that they mean to say anything more than that greater or less care will be required under the circumstances. Technically the "high degree" instruction is incorrect, as a matter of principle; but it is not

likely ever really to mislead the jury, and almost never can be called prejudicial.

A different, and older, approach has recognized distinct "degrees" of negligence itself, which is to say degrees of legal fault, corresponding to required "degrees" of care. This idea was borrowed from the Roman law[40] in 1704 by Chief Justice Holt in a bailment case,[41] and given support by learned writers on the law of bailments.[42] It recognizes, in general, three "degrees" of negligence: slight negligence, which is failure to use great care; ordinary negligence, which is failure to use ordinary care; and gross negligence, which is failure to use even slight care.[43] The doctrine has received considerable acceptance, and is still the prevailing law, in the field of bailments,[44] and has been said to be so thoroughly rooted there that it is not likely to be eradicated.[45] A few courts have extended it

36. Smith v. Poor Hand Maids of Jesus Christ, 1927, 193 Wis. 63, 213 N.W. 667; Lincoln Reserve Life Ins. Co. v. Armes, 1928, 217 Ala. 464, 117 So. 46; Hargis v. Spencer, 1934, 254 Ky. 297, 71 S.W.2d 666.

37. Denver Consol. Elec. Co. v. Simpson, 1895, 21 Colo. 371, 41 P. 499 (electricity); Hanna v. Central States Elec. Co., 1930, 210 Iowa 864, 232 N.W. 421 (same); Senske v. Washington Gas & Elec. Co., 1931, 165 Wash. 1, 4 P.2d 523 (gas); Ambrose v. Cyphers, 1959, 29 N.J. 138, 148 A.2d 465 (U-turn); Archuleta v. Jacobs, 1939, 43 N.M. 425, 94 P.2d 706 (dealing with children).

38. Union Traction Co. of Indiana v. Berry, 1919, 188 Ind. 514, 121 N.E. 655, rehearing denied 124 N.E. 737 (carrier); Thomas v. Central Greyhound Lines, 1958, 6 App.Div.2d 649, 180 N.Y.S.2d 461 (carrier); Frederick v. City of Detroit, 1963, 370 Mich. 425, 121 N.W.2d 918 (carrier); Scoles v. Weaver, 1923, 157 Ark. 167, 247 S.W. 773 (bailee); Mason v. St. Louis Union Stock Yards Co., 1894, 60 Mo.App. 93 (bailee).

39. See for example Peck v. Fanion, 1938, 124 Conn. 549, 1 A.2d 143; Pennsylvania Co. v. Roy, 1880, 102 U.S. 451.

40. See Green, The Three Degrees of Negligence, 1874, 8 Am.L.Rev. 649; Elliott, Degrees of Negligence, 1932, 6 So.Cal.L.Rev. 91.

41. Coggs v. Bernard, 1704, 2 Ld.Raym. 909, 92 Eng. Rep. 107.

42. Jones, Essay on the Law of Bailments, 3d Ed. 1828, 5–36; Story, Commentaries on the Law of Bailments, 1832, 12.

43. New York Central R. Co. v. Lockwood, 1873, 17 Wall., U.S., 357. See Green, High Care and Gross Negligence, 1928, 23 Ill.L.Rev. 4, 62 Am.L.Rev. 545; Note, 1939, 24 Ky.L.J. 334.

44. Altman v. Aronson, 1913, 231 Mass. 588, 121 N.E. 505; Cadwell v. Peninsular State Bank, 1917, 195 Mich. 407, 162 N.W. 89; Smith v. Burks, 1954, 89 Ga. App. 278, 79 S.E.2d 52; E. P. Dutton & Co. v. Isaac Goldmann Co., 1950, 277 App.Div. 556, 101 N.Y.S.2d 379; Ryan v. Schwab, Tex.Civ.App.1953, 261 S.W.2d 605. Sometimes, however, the doctrine has been stated, and then defined away. See for example Preston v. Prather, 1891, 137 U.S. 604, where "gross" negligence of a bailee was said to be merely failure to exercise such ordinary care as the bailor would use for his own goods. See Note, 1935, 24 Ky.L.J. 334.

45. 1 Street, Foundations of Legal Liability, 1906, 100; Hanes v. Shapiro & Smith, 1915, 168 N.C. 24, 84 S.E. 33. But the doctrine has been repudiated as to bailments, in England, where it originated. Grill v. General Iron Screw Collier Co., 1866, L.R. 1 C.P. 600. And it has been rejected by a substantial minority of the American courts. Sherwood

to other situations, particularly in holding that an automobile driver is not liable to a gratuitous guest except for gross negligence.[46] Late in the nineteenth century there were experiments in Illinois [47] and Kansas,[48] which extended the doctrine to all negligence cases. These courts found themselves deluged with appeals and struggling in impossible confusion,[49] and finally repudiated and overruled the whole theory.[50]

Although the idea of "degrees of negligence" has not been without its advocates,[51] it has been condemned by most writers,[52] and, except in bailment cases, rejected at common law by nearly all courts,[53] as a dis-

tinction "vague and impracticable in its nature, unfounded in principle,"[54] which adds only difficulty and confusion to the already nebulous and uncertain standards which must be given to the jury. The prevailing view is that there are no "degrees" of care or negligence, as a matter of law; there are only different amounts of care as a matter of fact;[55] and "gross" negligence is merely the same thing as ordinary negligence, "with the addition," as Baron Rolfe once put it, "of a vituperative epithet." [56] This much-quoted phrase may be a bit unfair, since it is not difficult to understand that there are such things as major or minor departures from reasonable conduct; but the extreme difficulty of classification, because of the almost complete impossibility of drawing any satisfactory lines of demarcation, together with the unhappy history, fully justifies the rejection.

Nevertheless, the idea of degrees of negligence, or at least of some kind of aggravated negligence which will result in liability where ordinary negligence will not, has been adopted in a number of statutes,[57] which have forced the courts, however reluctantly,[58] to attempt to do again what they have declared that they could not do, and to make such efforts as are possible to supply a definition for the undefinable. Some of these statutes have attempted to codify the entire doc-

v. Home Sav. Bank, 1906, 131 Iowa 528, 109 N.W. 9; Maddock v. Riggs, 1920, 106 Kan. 808, 190 P. 12; Leonard v. Bartle, 1927, 48 R.I. 101, 135 A. 853.

46. Massaletti v. Fitzroy, 1917, 228 Mass. 487, 118 N.E. 168; Boggs v. Plybon, 1931, 157 Va. 30, 160 S.E. 77.

47. Galena & Chicago Union R. Co. v. Jacobs, 1858, 20 Ill. 478; Illinois Cent. R. Co. v. Hammer, 1874, 72 Ill. 347; Wabash R. Co. v. Henks, 1879, 91 Ill. 406.

48. Sawyer v. Sauer, 1872, 10 Kan. 466; Union Pac. R. Co. v. Henry, 1883, 36 Kan. 565, 14 P. 1; Wichita & W. R. Co. v. Davis, 1887, 37 Kan. 743, 16 P. 78.

49. Described in Chicago, B. & Q. R. Co. v. Johnson, 1882, 103 Ill. 512; Chicago, R. I. & P. R. Co. v. Hamler, 1905, 215 Ill. 525, 74 N.E. 705. See Green, Illinois Negligence Law, 1944, 39 Ill.L.Rev. 39, 51; Malone, The Formative Era of Contributory Negligence, 1946, 41 Ill.L.Rev. 151.

50. Lake Shore & M. S. R. Co. v. Hessions, 1894, 150 Ill. 546, 37 N.E. 905; City of Lanark v. Dougherty, 1894, 153 Ill. 163, 38 N.E. 892; Atchison, T. & S. F. R. Co. v. Morgan, 1883, 31 Kan. 77, 1 P. 298; Atchison, T. & S. F. R. Co. v. Henry, 1896, 57 Kan. 156, 45 P. 576.

51. See Green, High Care and Gross Negligence, 1928, 23 Ill.L.Rev. 4, 62 Am.L.Rev. 545.

52. Salmond, Law of Torts, 10th Ed. 1945, 439; 1 Beven, Negligence, 4th Ed. 1928, 15; Harper, Law of Torts, 1933, 176; 1 Street, Foundations of Legal Liability, 1906, 99; Elliott, Degrees of Negligence, 1932, 6 So.Cal.L.Rev. 91.

53. Dickerson v. Connecticut Co., 1922, 98 Conn. 87, 118 A. 518; Denny v. Chicago, R. I. & P. R. Co., 1911, 150 Iowa 460, 130 N.W. 363; Raymond v. Portland R. Co., 1905, 100 Me. 529, 62 A. 602; Thompson v. Ashba, 1951, 122 Ind.App. 58, 102 N.E.2d 519; Nadeau v. Fogg, 1950, 145 Me. 10, 70 A.2d 730.

54. Salmond, Law of Torts, 10th Ed. 1945, 440 note.

55. Smith, Liability for Substantial Physical Damage to Land by Blasting, 1920, 33 Harv.L.Rev. 542, 553.

56. Wilson v. Brett, 1843, 11 M. & W. 113, 116, 152 Eng.Rep. 737. Cf. McAdoo v. Richmond & D. R. Co., 1890, 105 N.C. 140, 150, 11 S.E. 316 ("a mere expletive").

57. See Elliott, Degrees of Negligence, 1932, 6 So. Cal.L.Rev. 91, 127.

58. One of the most vigorous protests is that of Stephenson, J., in Universal Concrete Pipe Co. v. Bassett, 1936, 130 Ohio St. 567, 200 N.E. 843. Cf. John v. Northern Pac. R. Co., 1910, 42 Mont. 18, 111 P. 632.

trine,[59] or apply it to particular situations such as bailments,[60] criminal negligence,[61] or contributory negligence cases.[62] Most of them, however, are automobile guest statutes.[63]

To the extent that "degrees of negligence" survive, the distinctions most commonly made are as follows:

Slight Negligence. This has been defined as "an absence of that degree of care and vigilance which persons of extraordinary prudence and foresight are accustomed to use," or in other words, a failure to exercise great care.[64] It is said, therefore, not to be the same thing as a slight want of ordinary care, which is merely ordinary negligence.[65] It finds its chief application in cases, such as those of bailments for hire or of carriers injuring passengers, where there is an obligation to use great care, and it results in liability where lack of ordinary care would not.[66] But the term also has been used in a very general comparative sense, as contrasted with gross negligence, where the comparative negligence rule is applied.[67]

Gross Negligence. As it originally appeared, this was very great negligence, or the want of even scant care.[68] It has been described as a failure to exercise even that care which a careless person would use.[69] Several courts, however, dissatisfied with a term so nebulous, and struggling to assign some more or less definite point of reference to it, have construed gross negligence as requiring wilful misconduct,[70] or recklessness,[71] or such utter lack of all care as will be evidence of either—sometimes on the ground that this must necessarily have been the intent of the legislature.[72] But it is still true that most courts consider that "gross negligence" falls short of a reckless disregard of consequences, and differs from ordinary negligence only in degree, and not in kind.[73] There is, in

---

59. Cf. NDCC 1–01–16, 1–01–17; 25 Okl.St.Ann. §§ 3–6.

60. Cf. Cal.Civ.Code 1931, §§ 1846, 1928; S.D.Comp. Laws 1929, §§ 991, 1019.

61. Cf. Wis.Stats. § 340.26. See Riesenfeld, Negligent Homicide—A Study in Statutory Interpretation, 1936, 25 Cal.L.Rev. 1; Robinson, Manslaughter by Motorists, 1938, 22 Minn.L.Rev. 755.

62. See infra, § 65.

63. See infra, p. 382.

64. Astin v. Chicago, M. & St. P. R. Co., 1910, 143 Wis. 477, 128 N.W. 265. See Note, 1929, 5 Wis. L.Rev. 184.

65. Van Dunk v. Chicago & N. W. R. Co., 1926, 188 Wis. 476, 206 N.W. 852.

66. Putney v. Keith, 1900, 98 Ill.App. 285.

67. Morrison v. Scotts Bluff County, 1920, 104 Neb. 254, 177 N.W. 158; Roby v. Auker, 1949, 151 Neb. 421, 37 N.W.2d 799. The Nebraska court has refused to define the term under its statute, saying that "any one of common sense knows that slight negligence actually means small or little negligence, and gross negligence mans just what it indicates, gross or great negligence." Monasmith v. Cosden Oil Co.,

1933, 124 Neb. 327, 246 N.W. 623. Cf. Friese v. Gulbrandson, 1943, 69 S.D. 179, 8 N.W.2d 438 ("ordinary negligence, small in quantum").

68. Altman v. Aronson, 1919, 231 Mass. 588, 591, 121 N.E. 505; Dawson v. Fusco's Auto Service, 1941, 178 Va. 350, 17 S.E.2d 364; Field v. Serpico, 1946, 24 N.J.Misc. 289, 49 A.2d 21. See Note, 1956, 42 Va.L. Rev. 97; Swengil v. Martin, 1933, 125 Neb. 745, 252 N.W. 207.

69. Louisville & N. R. Co. v. McCoy, 1883, 81 Ky. 403, 5 Ky.L.Rep. 397; Peavy v. Peavy, 1926, 36 Ga.App. 202, 204, 136 S.E. 96, 97; Crowley v. Barto, 1962, 59 Wash.2d 280, 367 P.2d 828.

70. De Wald v. Quarnstrom, Fla.1952, 60 So.2d 919; Rideout v. Winnebago Traction Co., 1904, 123 Wis. 297, 101 N.W. 672; Farmers Merc. Co. v. Northern Pac. R. Co., 1914, 27 N.D. 302, 310, 146 N.W. 550; Murner v. Thorpe, 1938, 284 Mich. 331, 279 N.W. 849.

71. Williamson v. McKenna, 1960, 223 Or. 366, 354 P. 2d 56 (very complete); La Plante v. Rousseau, 1940, 91 N.H. 330, 18 A.2d 777 (Georgia law; good review of the whole question); Millard v. Cohen, 1948, 187 Va. 44, 46 S.E.2d 2; In re Wright's Estate, 1951, 170 Kan. 600, 228 P.2d 911; Rokusek v. Bertsch, 1951, 78 N.D. 420, 50 N.W.2d 657. There seems at least to be no doubt that reckless conduct will satisfy a requirement of gross negligence. Desrosiers v. Cloutier, 1942, 92 N.H. 100, 25 A.2d 123.

72. Craig v. Stagner, 1929, 159 Tenn. 511, 19 S.W.2d 234; Melby v. Anderson, 1936, 64 S.D. 249, 266 N.W. 135. See, again, Williamson v. McKenna, 1960, 223 Or. 366, 354 P.2d 56, for complete discussion.

73. Altman v. Aronson, 1919, 231 Mass. 588, 121 N.E. 505; Sorrell v. White, 103 Vt. 277, 153 A. 359; Kastel v. Steiber, 1932, 215 Cal. 37, 8 P.2d 474. Cf.

short, no generally accepted meaning; but the probability is, when the phrase is used, that it signifies more than ordinary inadvertence or inattention,[74] but less than conscious indifference to consequences;[75] and that it is, in other words, merely an extreme departure from the ordinary standard of care.[76]

Wilful, Wanton and Reckless. A different approach, at least in theory, looks to the actor's real or supposed state of mind. Lying between intent to do harm, which, as we have seen,[77] includes proceeding with knowledge that the harm is substantially certain to occur, and the mere unreasonable risk of harm to another involved in ordinary negligence, there is a penumbra of what has been called "quasi intent."[78] To this area the words "wilful," "wanton," or "reckless," are customarily applied; and sometimes, in a single sentence, all three. Although efforts have

been made to distinguish them,[79] in practice all such distinctions have consistently been ignored, and the three terms have been treated as meaning the same thing, or at least as coming out at the same legal exit. They have been grouped together as an aggravated form of negligence, differing in quality rather than in degree from ordinary lack of care.[80] These terms are in common use in the automobile guest statutes,[81] but even before the statutes, they represented an idea which had a legitimate place in the common law. They apply to conduct which is still merely negligent, rather than actually intended to do harm, but which is so far from a proper state of mind that it is treated in many respects as if it were so intended. Thus it is held to justify an award of punitive damages,[82] and may justify a broader duty,[83] and more extended liability for consequences;[84] and it will avoid the defense of ordinary con-

---

Dinardi v. Herook, 1952, 328 Mass. 572, 105 N.E. 2d 197 (40 seconds inattention enough).

74. Driscoll v. Pagano, 1943, 313 Mass. 464, 48 N.E.2d 11; Ottersberg v. Holz, 1954, 159 Neb. 239, 66 N.W. 2d 571; Nehring v. Smith, 1952, 243 Iowa 225, 49 N.W.2d 831; Keefer v. Givens, 1951, 191 Or. 611, 232 P.2d 808; Nist v. Tudor, 1965, 67 Wash.2d 322, 407 P.2d 798 (negligence "appreciably greater than ordinary negligence.")

75. Alspaugh v. Diggs, 1953, 195 Va. 1, 77 S.E.2d 362; Hamblen v. Steckley, 1947, 148 Neb. 283, 27 N.W.2d 178; Crowley v. Barto, 1962, 59 Wash.2d 280, 367 P. 2d 828; Wyseski v. Collette, N.D.1965, 126 N.W.2d 896; Hodge v. Borden, 1966, 91 Idaho 125, 417 P.2d 75. See Spikes, Gross Negligence Under the Guest Statute, 1943, 22 Neb.L.Rev. 264; Note, 1963, 38 Wash.L.Rev. 357.

76. Weld v. Postal Telegraph-Cable Co., 1913, 210 N. Y. 59, 72, 103 N.E. 957 (negligence of "an aggravated character"); Learned v. Hawthorne, 1930, 269 Mass. 554, 169 N.E. 557 (something between ordinary negligence and reckless conduct).

77. See supra, § 8.

78. Elliott, Degrees of Negligence, 1932, 6 So.Cal.L. Rev. 91, 143. In Amaro v. Moss, 1959, 65 N.M. 373, 337 P.2d 948, it was said that this does not differ from the kind of negligence necessary to a conviction of involuntary manslaughter, citing State v. Clarkson, 1954, 58 N.M. 56, 265 P.2d 670.

79. "Negligence and wilfulness are as unmixable as oil and water. 'Wilful negligence' is as self-contradictory as 'guilty innocence.' " Kelly v. Malott, 7 Cir. 1905, 135 F. 74; Neary v. Northern Pac. R. Co., 1910, 41 Mont. 480, 490, 110 P. 226; Michels v. Boruta, Tex.Civ.App.1938, 122 S.W.2d 216.

80. Sorrell v. White, 1931, 103 Vt. 277, 153 A. 359; Ressmeyer v. Jones, 1941, 210 Minn. 423, 298 N.W. 709; Bedwell v. De Bolt, 1943, 221 Ind. 600, 50 N. E.2d 875; Wilhite v. Webb, 1950, 253 Ala. 606, 46 So.2d 414; Titus v. Lonergan, 1941, 322 Mich. 112, 33 N.W.2d 685. See Appleman, Wilful and Wanton Conduct in Automobile Guest Cases, 1937, 13 Ind. L.J. 131; Weber, Guest Statutes, 1937, 11 U.Cin.L. Rev. 24, 51.

81. See infra, p. 382.

82. Buford v. Hopewell, 1912, 140 Ky. 666, 131 S.W. 502; Hintz v. Roberts, 1923, 98 N.J.L. 768, 121 A. 711. See McCormick, Damages, 1935, 251; Morris, Punitive Damages in Tort Cases, 1931, 44 Harv.L. Rev. 1173; supra, p. 9.

83. See for example, as to trespassers, infra, p. 362.

84. See Derosier v. New England Telephone & Telegraph Co., 1925, 81 N.H. 451, 130 A. 145; Bremer v. Lake Erie & W. R. Co., 1925, 318 Ill. 11, 148 N.E. 862; Bauer, The Degree of Moral Fault as Affecting Defendant's Liability, 1933, 81 U.Pa. L.Rev. 586; Bauer, The Degree of Defendant's Fault as Affecting the Administration of the Law of Excessive Compensatory Damages, 1934, 82 U.Pa.L.Rev. 583.

tributory negligence on the part of the plaintiff.[85]

The usual meaning assigned to "wilful," "wanton" or "reckless," according to taste as to the word used, is that the actor has intentionally done an act of an unreasonable character [86] in disregard of a risk known to him or so obvious that he must be taken to have been aware of it, and so great as to make it highly probable that harm would follow.[87] It usually is accompanied by a conscious indifference to the consequences,[88] amounting almost to willingness that they shall follow; and it has been said that this is indispensable.[89] Since, however, it is almost never admitted, and can be proved only by the conduct and the circumstances, an objective standard must of necessity in practice be applied. This requirement therefore breaks down, and receives at best lip service, in any case where it is clear from the facts that the defendant, whatever his state of mind, has proceeded in disregard of a high degree of danger, either known to him or apparent to a reasonable man in his position.[90]

The result is that "wilful," "wanton" or "reckless" conduct tends to take on the aspect of highly unreasonable conduct, or an extreme departure from ordinary care, in a situation where a high degree of danger is apparent. As a result there is often no clear distinction at all between such conduct and "gross" negligence, and the two have tended to merge and take on the same meaning, of an aggravated form of negligence, differing in quality rather than in degree from ordinary lack of care.[91] It is at least clear, however, that such aggravated negligence must be more than any mere mistake resulting from inexperience, excitement, or confusion,[92] and more than mere thoughtlessness or inadvertence,[93] or simple inattention,[94]

---

85. See infra, p. 426.

86. Thus it has been held not to be wilful or wanton negligence for a motorist to go through a red light while taking a seriously injured man to the hospital. Banks v. Banks, 1938, 283 Mich. 506, 278 N.W. 665. But in La Marra v. Adam, 1949, 164 Pa.Super. 268, 63 A.2d 497, the jury were permitted to find recklessness in similar conduct on a similar occasion. There may in other words, be recklessness even in an emergency; and it becomes a question of fact.

87. Second Restatement of Torts, § 500; Ellis v. Ferguson, 1965, 238 Ark. 776, 385 S.W.2d 154; Cope v. Davison, 1947, 30 Cal.2d 193, 180 P.2d 873; Sullivan v. Hartford Acc. & Indem. Co., La.App.1963, 155 So.2d 432, writ refused 245 La. 64, 156 So.2d 604; Thomas v. Margoni, 1938, 285 Mich. 547, 281 N.W. 321; Mathes v. Robinson, 1970, 205 Kan. 402, 469 P.2d 259.

88. Helleren v. Dixon, 1949, 152 Ohio St. 40, 86 N.E. 2d 777; Whiting v. Stephas, 1956, 247 Iowa 473, 74 N.W.2d 228; Elliott v. Peters, 1947, 163 Kan. 631, 185 P.2d 139; McHugh v. Brown, 1956, 11 Terry, Del., 154, 125 A.2d 583; Kasanovich v. George, 1943, 348 Pa. 199, 34 A.2d 523.

89. See for example Tyndall v. Rippon, 1948, 5 Terry, Del., 458, 61 A.2d 422; Wolters v. Venhaus, 1953, 350 Ill.App. 322, 112 N.E.2d 747; Clarke v. Storchak, 1944, 384 Ill. 564, 52 N.E.2d 229, appeal dismissed 322 U.S. 713; Tighe v. Diamond, 1948, 149 Ohio St. 520, 80 N.E.2d 122.

90. Second Restatement of Torts, § 500, Comment c; Taylor v. Lawrence, 1961, 229 Or. 259, 366 P.2d 735; Muhn v. Schell, 1966, 196 Kan. 713, 413 P.2d 997; Britton v. Doehring, Ala.1970, 242 So.2d 666; Cramer v. Dye, 1950, 328 Mich. 370, 43 N.W.2d 892; Turner v. McCready, 1950, 190 Or. 28, 222 P.2d 1010.

91. See Mescher v. Brogan, 1937, 223 Iowa 573, 272 N.W. 645; Williamson v. McKenna, 1960, 223 Or. 366, 354 P.2d 56; Note, 1937, 35 Mich.L.Rev. 804. Compare Ascher v. H. E. Friedman, Inc., 1929, 110 Conn. 1, 147 A. 263, and Berman v. Berman, 1928, 110 Conn. 169, 147 A. 568 ("reckless") with Burke v. Cook, 1923, 246 Mass. 518, 141 N.E. 585, and Manning v. Simpson, 1928, 261 Mass. 494, 159 N.E. 440 ("gross negligence").

92. Seisseger v. Puth, 1931, 213 Iowa 164, 239 N.W. 46; Willett v. Smith, 1932, 260 Mich. 101, 244 N.W. 246; Rauch v. Stecklein, 1933, 142 Or. 286, 20 P. 2d 387; Anderson v. Olson, 1934, 106 Vt. 70, 169 A. 781; Krueger v. Taylor, U.S.App.D.C.1942, 132 F.2d 736.

93. Shoop v. Hubbard, 1966, 259 Iowa 1362, 147 N.W. 2d 51; Donnelly v. Southern Pac. Co., 1941, 18 Cal. 2d 863, 118 P.2d 465; Silver v. Silver, 1928, 108 Conn. 371, 143 A. 240, affirmed, 1929, 280 U.S. 117; Sayre v. Malcolm, 1934, 139 Kan. 378, 31 P.2d 8; Craig v. McAtee, 1931, 160 Wash. 337, 295 P. 146.

94. Boward v. Leftwich, 1955, 197 Va. 227, 89 S.E. 2d 32; Hawkins v. Sydner, 1938, 170 Va. 267, 196 S.E. 619; Porter v. Hofman, 1938, 12 Cal.2d 445, 85 P.2d 447; Mooney v. Wabrek, 1942, 129 Conn.

even to the extent of falling asleep at the wheel of an automobile,[95] or even of an intentional omission to perform a statutory duty,[96] except in those cases where a reasonable man in the actor's place would have been aware of great danger, and proceeding in the face of it is so entirely unreasonable as to amount to aggravated negligence.[97]

A few peculiar jurisdictions have added no little to the confusion which surrounds "wilful and wanton negligence" by defining it, under the automobile guest acts or in contributory negligence cases, as a mere failure to exercise ordinary care after discovery of ordinary danger—or in other words, ordinary negligence in the case of a known ordinary risk.[98] Such negligence may consist

of an unintentional failure to act promptly, or even an honest mistake in judgment.[99] This definition has rightly been condemned as unsound in principle, and as leading the jury either to deny recovery where it should be allowed, or to give punitive damages in the belief that the defendant's conduct was more than ordinary negligence; [1] and at least one such court has been compelled, in cases arising in other states, to recognize the anomaly of its definition.[2]

Automobile Guest Statutes

The automobile guest statutes, which have been mentioned in passing, have been adopted in rather more than half of the states.[3] They provide that the driver of an automobile is liable to one who is riding as a gratuitous guest in his car only for some form of aggravated misconduct. These statutes,

302, 27 A.2d 631; Bashor v. Bashor, 1938, 103 Colo. 232, 85 P.2d 732.

95. Kaplan v. Kaplan, 1931, 213 Iowa 646, 239 N.W. 682; Perkins v. Roberts, 1935, 272 Mich. 545, 262 N. W. 305; De Shetler v. Kordt, 1931, 43 Ohio App. 236, 183 N.E. 85.

But in Lankford v. Mong, 1968, 283 Ala. 24, 214 So.2d 301, going to sleep while driving was held to permit a finding of wanton conduct, on the basis that the driver must have known that he was getting sleepy.

96. Memphis & Charleston R. Co. v. Martin, 1897, 117 Ala. 367, 23 So. 231; Olson v. Jones, 1959, 172 Cal. App.2d 539, 342 P.2d 440; Kennedy v. Carter, 1967, 249 S.C. 168, 153 S.E.2d 312 (speed limit).

97. Lewis v. Zell, 1965, 279 Ala. 33, 181 So.2d 101; (running a red light); White v. King, 1966, 244 Md. 348, 223 A.2d 763, appeal after remand, 1968, 250 Md. 192, 242 A.2d 494 (driving in danger of sleep); Manser v. Eder, 1933, 263 Mich. 107, 248 N.W. 563 (knowledge of fatigue); Davis v. McCree, 6 Cir. 1924, 299 F. 142, error dismissed 266 U.S. 582 (same); Jones v. Pasco, 1942, 179 Va. 7, 18 S.E.2d 258. Compare, as to inattention in the face of known great danger, Cole v. Metropolitan St. R. Co., 1906, 121 Mo.App. 605, 97 S.W. 555. See Note, 1934, 18 Minn.L.Rev. 218.

98. Sloniker v. Great Northern R. Co., 1899, 76 Minn. 306, 79 N.W. 168; Cowan v. Minneapolis, St. P. & S. S. M. R. Co., 1919, 42 N.D. 170, 172 N.W. 322; cf. Wilson v. Southern Traction Co., 1921, 111 Tex. 361, 234 S.W. 663; Gibbard v. Cursan, 1923, 225 Mich. 311, 196 N.W. 398 ("gross negligence"). See Notes, 1924, 8 Minn.L.Rev. 239; 1939, 24 Minn.L.Rev. 81.

The Minnesota rule may be traced to a misinterpretation of the rule as to discovered trespassers.

Studley v. St. Paul & Duluth R. Co., 1892, 48 Minn. 249, 51 N.W. 115; Fonda v. St. Paul City R. Co., 1898, 71 Minn. 438, 74 N.W. 166.

99. Rawitzer v. St. Paul City R. Co., 1906, 98 Minn. 294, 108 N.W. 271; Langdon v. Minneapolis St. Ry. Co., 1912, 120 Minn. 6, 138 N.W. 790; Gill v. Minneapolis, St. P., R. & D. Electric Traction Co., 1915, 129 Minn. 142, 151 N.W. 896.

1. See Burrell, A New Approach to the Problem of Wilful and Wanton Misconduct, [1949] Ins.L.J. 716; Jaggard, J., dissenting in Anderson v. Minneapolis, St. P. & S. S. M. R. Co., 1908, 103 Minn. 224, 114 N.W. 1123; Note, 1939, 24 Minn.L.Rev. 81.

2. Pickering v. Northern Pac. R. Co., 1916, 132 Minn. 205, 156 N.W. 3.

3. See Weber, Guest Statutes, 1937, 11 U.Cin.L.Rev. 24; Corish, The Automobile Guest, 1934, 14 Bos.U. L.Rev. 728; Hodges, The Automobile Guest Statutes, 1934, 12 Tex.L.Rev. 303; White, The Liability of an Automobile Driver to a Non-Paying Passenger, 1934, 20 Va.L.Rev. 326; Richards, The Washington Guest Statute, 1940, 15 Wash.L.Rev. 87; Richards, Another Decade Under the Guest Statute, 1949, 24 Wash.L.Rev. 101; Notes, 1932, 17 Iowa L.Rev. 268; 1933, 18 Corn.L.Q. 621; 1937, 35 Mich.L.Rev. 804; 1935, 8 So.Cal.L.Rev. 140; 1959, 54 Nw.U.L.Rev. 263; 1965, 17 Hast.L.J. 337. The statutes are collected and classified in Notes, 1947, 1 Wyo.L.J. 182; 1949, 3 Wyo.L.J. 225.

As to similar statutes applicable to airplane guests, see Note, 1963, 15 Syr.L.Rev. 1.

which have been held constitutional,[4] vary considerably in their language from state to state, according to the fancy of the legislature or compromises in drawing the particular act. The required form of aggravation is specified as "gross negligence," "intentional," "wilful," "wanton," or "reckless" misconduct, acting "in disregard of the safety of others," "intoxication," or some combination of two or more. There is so much individual variation in the statutes, and in their interpretation,[5] that it may safely be said that there are as many different guest laws as there are acts.

Such statutes have been the result of persistent and effective lobbying on the part of liability insurance companies.[6] The chief argument advanced in support of them has been that in guest cases the insurer, who is required to pay the damages, is peculiarly exposed to collusion between the injured guest and a host anxious to see compensation paid, so long as he does not have to pay it—so that the truth does not come out in court, and there is a resulting increase in insurance rates.[7] Essentially, however, the theory of the acts is that one who receives a gratuitous favor in the form of a free ride has no right to demand that his host shall exercise ordinary care not to injure him. The typical guest act case[8] is that of the driver who offers his friend a lift to the office or invites him out to dinner, negligently drives him into a collision, and fractures his skull—after which the driver and his insurance company take refuge in the statute, step out of the picture, and leave the guest to bear his own loss. If this is good social policy, it at least appears under a novel front.

There is perhaps no other group of statutes which have filled the courts with appeals on so many knotty little problems involving petty and otherwise entirely inconsequential points of law. There is first of all the question of who is a "guest." What is the effect of sharing expenses, or of the guest buying a tank of gasoline? Of an indirect, prospective, or merely remotely potential, benefit to the host in the form of some business interest or hope in having the guest take the ride? Of an employer's order prohibiting the driver from taking free riders; of the fact that the guest is not invited, but allowed to stay after he trespasses; of the fact that the plaintiff is a child too young to know that he is a guest? Of the fact that the guest was out of the car for a moment when he was run down; of his demand to be let out of the car; of his assent even to the aggravated misconduct? Can the owner of the car be a guest in it when someone else is driving? And finally, what is the meaning, and application, of "gross," "wilful," "wanton," "reckless," or whatever other terms the statute may adopt?

No short text can hope to deal with the infinite variety of answers to these questions, under the different statutes, in so many states. The reader can only be referred to the law of the jurisdiction in which he may be interested.

---

4. Silver v. Silver, 1929, 280 U.S. 117. See Note, 1930, 18 Cal.L.Rev. 184; Westover v. Schaffer, 1970, 205 Kan. 62, 468 P.2d 251.

5. See the articles cited supra, note 78. Also Appleman, Wilful and Wanton Conduct in Automobile Guest Cases, 1937, 13 Ind.L.J. 131; Notes, 1944, 19 Ind.L.J. 145; 1946, 31 Iowa L.Rev. 428; 1945, 30 Iowa L.Rev. 283; 1951, 4 U.Fla.L.Rev. 79.

As to the effect of a comparative negligence statute upon an automobile guest act, see Spikes, Gross Negligence Under the Guest Statute, 1943, 22 Neb. L.Rev. 264; Gradwohl, Comparative Negligence of an Automobile Guest, 1953, 33 Neb.L.Rev. 54.

6. See, attacking the statutes on this basis, Allen, Why Do Courts Coddle Insurance Companies, 1927, 61 Am.L.Rev. 77; White, The Liability of an Automobile Driver to a Non-Paying Passenger, 1934, 20 Va.L.Rev. 326; Weinstein, Should We Kill the Guest Passenger Act, 1965, 33 U.Det.L.Rev. 185; Note, 1966, 7 W. & M.L.Rev. 321. See also Talbot Smith, J., in Stevens v. Stevens, 1959, 355 Mich. 363, 94 N.W.2d 858.

7. See Naudzius v. Lahr, 1931, 253 Mich. 216, 234 N.W. 581.

8. In legislative hearings there is frequent mention of the hitch-hiker, who gets little sympathy. The writer once found a hitch-hiker case, but has mislaid it. He has been unable to find another.

35. RULES OF LAW

The entire system of common law jurisprudence has been built upon the principle of stare decisis, that a decision of an appellate court establishes a precedent, to be followed in that jurisdiction when similar fact situations shall arise again. The principle has value in so far as it makes it possible to predict in advance the course which the administration of justice will take, and secures against bad motives or errors in judgment on the part of individual judges, or serves to prevent the sacrifice of ultimate social interests to the immediate demands of a particular case.[9] But it is not, and never has been, an ironclad and absolute principle, and such precedents may be departed from when the court subsequently concludes that they are unreasonable, or out of line with altered social conditions.[10] Nor do they control when the facts which arise are essentially different; and many writers have devoted thought to the sometimes highly artificial technique by which the facts of earlier cases are "distinguished."[11]

A decision of an appellate court that under certain circumstances a particular type of conduct is clearly negligent, or that it clearly is not negligent, or that the issue is for the jury as one on which reasonable men may differ, establishes a precedent for other cases where the facts are identical, or substantially the same. To that extent it may define the standard of reasonable conduct which the community requires.[12] Unfortunately the inevitable tendency to crystallize the law into mechanical rules [13] has led the courts in many cases to treat such precedents as fixing definite rules of universal application. Almost invariably the rule has broken down in the face of the obvious necessity of basing the standard upon the particular circumstances, the apparent risk and the actor's opportunity to deal with it.

Especially noteworthy in this respect is the attempt of Mr. Justice Holmes, in Baltimore & Ohio Railway v. Goodman,[14] to "lay down a standard once for all," which would require an automobile driver approaching a railroad crossing with an obstructed view to stop, look and listen, and if he cannot be sure otherwise that no train is coming, to get out of the car. The basic idea behind this is sound enough: it is by no means proper care to cross a railroad track without taking reasonable precautions against a train, and normally such precautions will require looking, hearing, and a stop, or at least slow speed, where the view is obstructed.[15] But the attempt to specify conduct for all cases virtually made it certain that there could never be a recovery for a crossing accident. A long series of cases in which gates were left open,[16] or the driver

<hr/>

9. Pound, Justice According to Law, 1913, 13 Col.L. Rev. 696, 709.

10. Cardozo, The Nature of the Judicial Process, 1921, 149; Von Moschzisker, Stare Decisis in Courts of Last Resort, 1924, 37 Harv.Lev.Rev. 409; MacMurray, Changing Conceptions of Law, 1915, 4 Cal.L.Rev. 411; Aumann, Judicial Law Making and Stare Decisis, 1933, 21 Ky.L.J. 156.

11. Allen, Law in the Making, 1927, 164; Green, Judge and Jury, 1930, 274.

12. Second Restatement of Torts, § 285, Comments e, h.

13. Pound, Mechanical Jurisprudence, 1908, 8 Col. L.Rev. 605. An interesting attempt to fix the standard of care by a rule which would very probably have strangled the automobile, if it had succeeded, is Berry, Rights and Duties of Automobile Drivers When Meeting and Passing Horse-Drawn Vehicles, 1916, 82 Cent.L.J. 315.

14. 1927, 275 U.S. 66. See Notes, 1930, 43 Harv.L.Rev. 926; 1933, 17 Minn.L.Rev. 771; 1928, 16 Cal.L.Rev. 238; 1928, 14 Va.L.Rev. 379; 1928, 4 Wis.L.Rev. 467.

15. This has been applied quite consistently in Pennsylvania. Cf. Benner v. Philadelphia & R. R. Co., 1918, 262 Pa. 307, 105 A. 283; and see Note, 1951, 13 U.Pitt.L.Rev. 117. Accord: Hanson v. Duluth, M. & N. Ry. Co., 1963, 267 Minn. 24, 124 N.W.2d 486; Atchison, T. & S. F. Ry. Co. v. Herbold, 10 Cir. 1948, 169 F.2d 12; McNealy v. Portland Traction Co., 1958, 213 Or. 659, 327 P.2d 410; McCune v. Thompson, 1938, 147 Kan. 57, 75 P.2d 294.

16. Wabash R. Co. v. Glass, 6 Cir. 1929, 32 F.2d 697; Canadian Pac. R. Co. v. Slayton, 2 Cir. 1928, 29 F.2d 687; Lindekugel v. Spokane, P. & S. R. Co., 1935, 149 Or. 634, 42 P.2d 907. Cf. Wabash R. Co. v. Walczak, 6 Cir. 1931, 49 F.2d 763 (flasher signal

relied upon the absence of a flagman,[17] or it was clear that the conduct specified would have added nothing to the driver's safety,[18] made it quite apparent that no such inflexible rule could be applied. Finally, in the subsequent case of Pokora v. Wabash Ry.,[19] where the only effective stop must be made upon the railway tracks themselves, in a position of obvious danger, the court discarded any such uniform rule, rejecting the "get out of the car" requirement as "an uncommon precaution, likely to be futile and sometimes even dangerous," and saying that the driver need not always stop. "Illustrations such as these," said Mr. Justice Cardozo, "bear witness to the need for caution in framing standards of behavior that amount to rules of law. * * * Extraordinary situations may not wisely or fairly be subjected to tests or regulations that are fitting for the commonplace or normal."

A similar fate is overtaking the rule which many courts have stated,[20] that it is always

negligence to drive at such a speed that it is impossible to stop within the range of vision. Again the principle is sound enough; but universal application becomes quite impossible. The rule has proved to be much too stringent when the visibility is obscured by fog or rain,[21] when the driver is suddenly blinded by the lights of an approaching car,[22] or when unanticipated defects or obstacles suddenly appear on an apparently safe highway.[23] The reaction from the rule has been so marked that some courts have gone to the

---

23 Cal.L.Rev. 498; 1948, 27 N.C.L.Rev. 153; 1956, 25 Ford.L.Rev. 371; 1958, 12 Wyo.L.J. 116; 1969, 30 La.L.Rev. 129; Schmeling, The Range of Vision Rule in Nebraska, 1969, 49 Neb.L.Rev. 7.

The application of the rule often leaves the driver in the familiar dilemma, that he must have driven at such a speed as to be unable to stop or have failed to keep a proper lookout, or else have disregarded obvious danger. Lee v. Atlantic Coast Line R. Co., 1937, 212 N.C. 340, 193 S.E. 395; Peckinpaugh v. Engelke, 1933, 215 Iowa 1248, 247 N.W. 822; Dalley v. Mid-Western Dairy Products Co., 1932, 80 Utah 331, 15 P.2d 309; Bagan v. Bitterman, 1935, 65 N.D. 23, 259 N.W. 266.

21. Langill v. First Nat. Stores, 1937, 298 Mass. 559, 11 N.E.2d 593; Rabenold v. Hutt, 1939, 226 Iowa 321, 283 N.W. 865; Devoto v. United Auto Transp. Co., 1924, 128 Wash. 604, 223 P. 1050, affirmed, 1924, 130 Wash. 707, 226 P. 1118; Morehouse v. City of Everett, 1926, 141 Wash. 399, 252 P. 157. Cf. Murphy v. Hawthorne, 1926, 117 Or. 319, 244 P. 79 (dust).

22. Watson v. Southern Bus Lines, 6 Cir. 1951, 186 F. 2d 981; Emerson v. Bailey, 1959, 102 N.H. 360, 156 A.2d 762; Nesbit v. Everette, 5 Cir. 1955, 227 F.2d 157; Winfough v. Tri-State Ins. Co., 1956, 179 Kan. 525, 297 P.2d 159; Ryan v. Cameron, 1955, 270 Wis. 325, 71 N.W.2d 408. But it may still be negligent as a matter of law not to slow down. Wolfe v. Beatty Motor Express, Inc., 1957, 143 W.Va. 238, 101 S.E.2d 81.

23. Tidwell v. Lewis, 6 Cir. 1949, 174 F.2d 173; Western Production Co. v. Yarbrough, 5 Cir. 1956, 234 F. 2d 889; Parsons v. Noel Bros., Mo.1954, 271 S.W.2d 543; Gruenhagen v. Brelje, 1958, 252 Minn. 203, 89 N.W.2d 738; Halfacre v. Hart, 1951, 192 Tenn. 342, 241 S.W.2d 421. Cf. Cerny v. Domer, 1968, 13 Ohio St.2d 117, 235 N.E.2d 132 (car ahead backing up). In Iowa and Ohio, where the rule has been adopted by statute, the courts have found it necessary to introduce similar modifications. See Note, 1938, 24 Iowa L.Rev. 128; Rogers v. Anchor Motor Freight, 1953, 95 Ohio App. 62, 117 N.E.2d 451.

---

not working); Shewmaker v. Louisville & N. R. Co., Ky.1966, 403 S.W.2d 283 (same).

17. Leuthold v. Pennsylvania R. Co., 6 Cir. 1929, 33 F.2d 758; cf. Weinstein v. Powell, 5 Cir. 1932, 61 F.2d 411; Malone v. St. Louis-S. F. R. Co., 1926, 270 Mo.App. 9, 285 S.W. 123 (fog).

18. Torgeson v. Missouri-Kansas-Texas R. Co., 1928, 124 Kan. 798, 262 P. 564; Swift & Co. v. St. Louis Transfer R. Co., Mo.App.1929, 15 S.W.2d 387; Williams v. Minneapolis, St. P. & S. S. M. R. Co., 1928, 57 N.D. 279, 221 N.W. 42; Norfolk & W. R. Co. v. Holbrook, C.C.A.Ky.1928, 27 F.2d 326 (heavy fog); Hoffman v. Southern Pac. Co., 1929, 101 Cal.App. 218, 281 P. 681 (same).

19. 1934, 292 U.S. 98. Accord: Doyel v. Thompson, 1948, 357 Mo. 963, 211 S.W.2d 704; Gleaton v. Southern Ry. Co., 1940, 208 S.C. 507, 38 S.E.2d 710; Union Pac. R. Co. v. Lumbert, 10 Cir. 1968, 401 F.2d 699 (Wyoming law); and cf. Macartney v. Westbrook, 1930, 132 Or. 488, 286 P. 525 (entering main highway from private road, with obstructed view).

20. The leading case is Lauson v. Town of Fond du Lac, 1909, 141 Wis. 57, 123 N.W. 629. Accord: Fridley v. Brush, 1955, 161 Neb. 318, 73 N.W.2d 376; Metro v. Long Transp. Co., 1956, 387 Pa. 354, 127 A.2d 716; Harris v. Hendrixson, 1941, 25 Tenn. App. 221, 155 S.W.2d 876; Haines v. Carroll, 1928, 126 Kan. 408, 267 P. 986; Russell v. Szczawinski, 1934, 268 Mich. 112, 255 N.W. 731. See Notes, 1935,

other extreme, of saying that such speed is never more than evidence of negligence for the jury.[24] Similar difficulties have arisen as to the ordinary traffic "rules of the road,"[25] and the rule that a pedestrian must look when crossing a street,[26] that a driver must constantly watch the road ahead,[27] or that it is negligence to board or leave a train while it is in motion.[28]

Such rules may be useful to fix a standard for the usual, normal case, but they are a hindrance to any just decision in the large number of unusual situations presenting new factors which may affect the standard. A standard which requires only conduct proportionate to the circumstances and the risk seldom, if ever, can be made a matter of absolute rule.[29]

24. Kendall v. City of Des Moines, 1918, 183 Iowa 866, 167 N.W. 684; Tresise v. Ashdown, 1928, 118 Ohio St. 307, 160 N.E. 898. North Carolina has a statute making it only evidence of negligence. See Burchette v. Davis Distributing Co., 1955, 243 N.C. 120, 90 S.E.2d 232.

25. Primock v. Goldenberg, 1924, 161 Minn. 160, 200 N.W. 920; George Ast Candy Co. v. Kling, 1929, 121 Ohio St. 362, 169 N.E. 292; Kimball v. Bauckman, 1932, 131 Me. 14, 158 A. 694; Richards v. Warner Co., 1933, 311 Pa. 50, 166 A. 496; Carlin v. Haas, 1938, 124 Conn. 259, 199 A. 430.

26. Knapp v. Barrett, 1915, 216 N.Y. 226, 110 N.E. 428. Cf. Lundberg v. Zimmer, 1924, 159 Minn. 179, 198 N.W. 407; Baker v. Close, 1912, 204 N.Y. 92, 97 N.E. 501; Hempel v. Hall, 1920, 136 Md. 174, 110 A. 210. See Note, 1929, 77 U.Pa.L.Rev. 427.

27. Duby v. Columbia County, 1927, 194 Wis. 172, 215 N.W. 819; Kendall v. City of Des Moines, 1918, 183 Iowa 866, 167 N.W. 684; Baldwin v. City of Norwalk, 1921, 95 Conn. 1, 112 A. 660.

28. Gavett v. Manchester & Lawrence R. Co., 1860, 16 Gray, Mass., 501. Cf. Eppendorf v. Brooklyn City & N. R. Co., 1877, 69 N.Y. 195; Guidry v. Morgan's Louisiana & T. R. & S. Co., 1917, 140 La. 1007, 74 So. 534; Gunn v. United Rys. Co. of St. Louis, 1917, 270 Mo. 517, 193 S.W. 814.

29. See Nixon, Changing Rules of Liability in Automobile Accident Litigation, 1936, 3 Law & Contemp. Prob. 478.

There is good discussion of all this in McKinney v. Yelavich, 1958, 352 Mich. 687, 90 N.W.2d 883.

36. VIOLATION OF STATUTE

The standard of conduct required of a reasonable man may be prescribed by legislative enactment.[30] When a statute provides that under certain circumstances particular acts shall or shall not be done, it may be interpreted as fixing a standard for all members of the community, from which it is negligence to deviate.[31] Within the limits of municipal authority, the same may be true of ordinances.[32] The fact that such legislation is usually penal in character, and carries with it a criminal penalty, will not prevent its use in imposing civil liability,[33] except in the

30. Second Restatement of Torts, §§ 285, 286. See, generally, Morris, The Relation of Criminal Statutes to Tort Liability, 1933, 46 Harv.L.Rev. 453; Morris, The Role of Criminal Statutes in Negligence Actions, 1949, 49 Col.L.Rev. 21; James, Statutory Standards and Negligence in Accident Cases, 1951, 11 La.L.Rev. 95; Williams, The Effect of Penal Legislation in the Law of Tort, 1960, 23 Mod.L.Rev. 232; Fricke, The Juridical Nature of the Action Upon the Statute, 1960, 76 L.Q.Rev. 240; Notes, 1932, 32 Col.L.Rev. 712; 1935, 19 Minn.L.Rev. 666; 1940, 27 Va.L.Rev. 240; 1950, 15 Brook L.Rev. 246; 1966, 39 U.Colo.L.Rev. 164.

31. "Negligence is the breach of legal duty. It is immaterial whether the duty is one imposed by the rule of common law requiring the exercise of ordinary care not to injure another, or is imposed by a statute designed for the protection of others. * * * The only difference is that in the one case the measure of legal duty is to be determined upon common law principles, while in the other the statute fixes it, so that the violation of the statute constitutes conclusive evidence of negligence, or, in other words, negligence per se. * * * All that the statute does is to establish a fixed standard by which the fact of negligence may be determined." Mitchell, J., in Osborne v. McMasters, 1889, 40 Minn. 103, 105, 41 N.W. 543, 544.

32. McLeod v. Tri-State Milling Co., 1946, 71 S.D. 362, 24 N.W.2d 485; Greyhound Terminal v. Thomas, 1947, 307 Ky. 44, 209 S.W.2d 478; Tralle v. Hartman Furniture Co., 1928, 116 Neb. 418, 217 N.W. 952; Schell v. Du Bois, 1916, 94 Ohio St. 93, 113 N.E. 664. See Kepner, Violation of a Municipal Ordinance as Negligence Per Se in Kentucky, 1949, 37 Ky.L.J. 358; Note, 1928, 14 Va.L.Rev. 591.

33. Parker v. Barnard, 1883, 135 Mass. 116; Stehle v. Jaeger Automatic Mach. Co., 1908, 220 Pa. 617, 69 A. 1116; Kavanagh v. New York, O. & W. R. Co., 1921, 196 App.Div. 384, 187 N.Y.S. 859, affirmed, 1922, 233 N.Y. 597, 135 N.E. 933.

comparatively rare case where the penalty is made payable to the person injured, and clearly is intended to be in lieu of all other compensation.[34]

Much ingenuity has been expended in the effort to explain why criminal legislation should result in a rule for civil liability. If there is a specific provision in the statute to that effect, there is of course no difficulty, since it is clear that that is the intent of the legislature.[35] The only questions open are whether the legislation is constitutional, whether it is applicable to the particular case, and whether it has in fact been violated. But where the statute merely declares that conduct is a crime, and makes no mention of any civil remedy, justification becomes more difficult, since the court is then obviously under no compulsion to apply the statute. Many courts have, however, purported to "find" in the statute a supposed "implied," "constructive," or "presumed" intent to provide for tort liability. In the ordinary case this is pure fiction, concocted for the purpose. The obvious conclusion can only be that when the legislators said nothing about it, they either did not have the civil suit in mind at all, or deliberately omitted to provide for it.[36] Again, it is said that the reasonable man would obey the criminal law, and that one who does not is not acting as a reasonable man, and therefore must be negligent.[37]

While this may serve to explain a decision that a breach of the statute is evidence of negligence, it is not clear that it justifies the prevailing rule under which the court must refuse to leave the issue to the jury,[38] nor does it account for the numerous violations which are held not to give rise to any civil action at all,[39] or for the cases in which, on the basis of analogy or association, the liability has been rested upon some other tort, such as trespass, deceit, nuisance, or even strict liability.[40]

Perhaps the most satisfactory explanation is that the courts are seeking, by something in the nature of judicial legislation, to further the ultimate policy for the protection of individuals which they find underlying the statute, and which they believe the legislature must have had in mind.[41] The statutory

34. Mack v. Wright, 1897, 180 Pa. 472, 36 A. 913; Town of Brattleboro v. Wait, 1872, 44 Vt. 459. In determining this, the amount of the penalty is important as an indication of legislative intent. Cf. Groves v. Wimborne, [1898] 2 Q.B. 402.

35. See for example Daggett v. Keshner, 1954, 284 App.Div. 733, 134 N.Y.S.2d 524, noted in 1955, 40 Corn.L.Q. 810. This case held that the express provision for the tort action justified holding the defendant liable for consequences which would otherwise not be "proximate."

36. Lowndes, Civil Liability Created by Criminal Legislation, 1932, 16 Minn.L.Rev. 361, 363; Thayer, Public Wrong and Private Action, 1913, 27 Harv. L.Rev. 317, 320.

37. Thayer, Public Wrong and Private Action, 1914, 27 Harv.L.Rev. 317, 322. Cf. Cardozo, J., in Martin

v. Herzog, 1920, 228 N.Y. 164, 126 N.E. 814: "By the very terms of the hypothesis, to omit, willfully or heedlessly, the safeguards prescribed by law for the benefit of another that he may be preserved in life or limb, is to fall short of the standard of diligence to which those who live in organized society are under a duty to conform."

38. Lowndes, Civil Liability Created by Criminal Legislation, 1932, 16 Minn.L.Rev. 361, 367. But see Morris, The Relation of Criminal Statutes to Tort Liability, 1933, 46 Harv.L.Rev. 453, 465, to the effect that it is a question of leeway for judicial discrimination.

39. See infra, pp. 192–193. As to Professor Thayer's argument that the jury should not be permitted to say that a reasonable man would disobey the law, see Stevens v. Luther, 1920, 105 Neb. 184, 190, 180 N.W. 87; Walker v. Lee, 1921, 115 S.C. 495, 106 S.E. 682.

40. " * * * when a statute is passed the courts generally tend to associate it with the type of common-law liability most closely related to the statute. For example, a statute prohibiting going on property and cutting timber is thought of in the classification of a trespass statute; one prohibiting the receiving of bank deposits after insolvency as a fraud statute; one prohibiting the blocking of public highways as a public nuisance statute; and one laying down rules of safety for the protection of the public or any class or group of individuals, as a negligence statute." Dart v. Pure Oil Co., 1947, 223 Minn. 526, 27 N.W.2d 555.

41. Well stated in Phoenix Refining Co. v. Powell, Tex.Civ.App.1952, 251 S.W.2d 892.

standard of conduct is simply adopted voluntarily, out of deference and respect for the legislature.[42] This is borne out by a considerable number of cases in which the terms of a criminal statute have been applied in a civil action, notwithstanding the fact that the statute was for some reason totally ineffective as a basis for criminal conviction—as where it had not been properly enacted,[43] or did not exactly cover the situation,[44] or the defendant was incapable of crime, and could not be prosecuted;[45] and by one or two others in which there has been flat refusal to accept a standard regarded as unreasonable.[46]

The question thus becomes one of when the court will look to a criminal statute for its negligence standard of the conduct of a reasonable man.

Class of Persons Protected

It is not every provision of a criminal statute or ordinance which will be adopted by the court in a civil action for negligence, as the standard of conduct of a reasonable man. Otherwise stated, there are statutes which are considered to create no duty of conduct toward the plaintiff, and to afford no basis for the creation of such a duty by the court.[47] The courts have been careful not to exceed the purpose which they attribute to the legislature. This judicial self-restraint has served as an argument for those who contend that an action cannot be founded upon a duty to another;[48] but there is of course a special reason, in the theory of the separation of powers, for such reluctance to go beyond the legislative policy.

There are many statutes, such as those directed against various activities on Sunday, which obviously are intended only to protect such interests of the state, or the community at large, as public peace, morality and quiet, rather than those of any particular class of individuals.[49] It follows that if a railroad

---

42. "We adopt the statutory test rather than that of the ordinarily prudent man as the more accurate one to determine negligence because the Legislature, by reason of its organization and investigating processes, is generally in a better position to establish such tests than are the judicial tribunals." Rudes v. Gottschalk, 1959, 159 Tex. 552, 324 S.W.2d 201.

43. Clinkscales v. Carver, 1943, 22 Cal.2d 72, 136 P. 2d 777 (faulty publication); Comfort v. Penner, 1932, 166 Wash. 177, 6 P.2d 604 (municipal action contrary to statute); Sellman v. Haddock, 1959, 66 N.M. 206, 345 P.2d 416 (same); Geisking v. Sheimo, 1960, 252 Iowa 37, 105 N.W.2d 599 (same); Alviar v. Garza, Tex.Civ.App.1965, 387 S.W.2d 905, reversed on other grounds, 395 S.W.2d 821 (ordinance not complying with city charter).

Accord: Ponca City v. Reed, 1925, 115 Okl. 166, 242 P. 164 (unlawful penalty); West Texas Coaches v. Madi, Tex.Comm.App.1930, 26 S.W.2d 199 (vagueness and uncertainty).

44. Black v. Stith, 1940, 164 Or. 117, 100 P.2d 485; Kern v. Autman, Del.Super.1961, 177 A.2d 525. Cf. Willy v. Mulledy, 1879, 78 N.Y. 310 (no notice to defendant).

45. Hopkins v. Droppers, 1924, 184 Wis. 400, 198 N.W. 738; Pelzer v. Lange, 1958, 254 Minn. 46, 93 N.W.2d 666.

46. Stafford v. Chippewa Valley Elec. R. Co., 1901, 110 Wis. 331, 85 N.W. 1036; Sardo v. Herlihy, 1932, 143 Misc. 397, 256 N.Y.S. 690. See also Stevens v. Luther, 1920, 105 Neb. 184, 190, 180 N.W. 87, 89; Morris, The Relation of Criminal Statutes to Tort Liability, 1933, 46 Harv.L.Rev. 453, 460. The former Kentucky rule that violation of an ordinance is not even evidence of negligence may be traced to the speed limit of six miles an hour for trains in Louisville & N. R. Co. v. Dalton, 1897, 102 Ky. 290, 43 S.W. 431. See, generally, Note, 1947, 25 Tex.L.Rev. 286.

47. "Even if a defendant owes a duty to some one else, but does not owe it to the person injured, no action will lie. The duty must be due to the person injured. These principles are elementary, and are equally applicable, whether the duty is imposed by positive statute or is founded on general common-law principles." Mitchell, J., in Akers v. Chicago, St. P., M. & O. Ry. Co., 1894, 58 Minn. 540, 544, 60 N.W. 669, 670.

48. See infra, p. 254.

49. Second Restatement of Torts, § 288, Illustration 2. Compare Fitzgerald v. Pan Am. World Airways, 2 Cir. 1956, 229 F.2d 499, reversing, S.D.N.Y.1955, 132 F.Supp. 798, as to a civil rights statute; and see Colley, Civil Actions for Damages Arising Out of Violations of Civil Rights, 1965, 17 Hast.L.J. 189; Notes, 1967, 45 Tex.L.Rev. 1015; 1956, 104 U.Pa.L. Rev. 864.

A decision at least open to question is Strauel v. Peterson, 1952, 155 Neb. 448, 52 N.W.2d 307, holding that

violates such a statute, by running a train on Sunday, a private individual, as for example the owner of a cow killed on the track, cannot found an action upon that violation alone,[50] without other evidence of negligence. Likewise ordinances which require householders to keep sidewalks in repair, or to remove snow and ice from them, are considered to be intended only for the benefit of the municipality, and not for any individual who may suffer a fall.[51] The same is true, in general, as to the statutory duties of public officers.[52] The great weight of authority, outside of Massachusetts,[53] has held that automobile registration statutes are for revenue purposes only and create only a public duty, and do not make the driver of an unlicensed car liable to those with whom he collides if

he is otherwise exercising proper care.[54] A similar conclusion was reached by the Minnesota court in a case [55] involving a war-time speed limit intended to conserve gasoline.

The explanation quite often given in these cases is that the violation of the statute is not the proximate cause of the injury to the plaintiff.[56] In such a statement there is an obvious fallacy. In all such cases the act of the defendant has clearly caused the damage. If a train run on Sunday hits a cow, it cannot be said that the act of running the train did not have a real causal connection, and a very direct and important one, with the death of the cow; and Sunday, when the cow was there, is quite as relevant as would be, for example, the month of July or a given year. On the other hand the violation of the statute, as such, never kills a cow, since the same result would certainly follow if no statute existed.[57] When a car is driven without a license, the act of driving the car certainly causes a collision; the absence of the license, or the existence of the statute, of course does not. What the statute does, or does not do, is to condition the legality of the act, and to qualify or characterize it as negligent. Upon cause and effect it has no bearing at all. It is, of course, quite possible that the act or omission itself may have no sufficient causal connection with the result—a

the Bang's Disease Act was intended to protect no one except the interests of the public.

50. Tingle v. Chicago, B. & Q. R. Co., 1882, 60 Iowa 333, 14 N.W. 320. Cf. Platz v. City of Cohoes, 1882, 89 N.Y. 219; Hoadley v. International Paper Co., 1899, 72 Vt. 79, 47 A. 169.

51. Brown v. Kelly, 1964, 42 N.J. 362, 200 A.2d 781; Vissman v. Koby, Ky.1958, 309 S.W.2d 345; Grooms v. Union Guardian Trust Co., 1944, 309 Mich. 437, 15 N.W.2d 698; McEvoy v. City of New York, 1943, 266 App.Div. 445, 42 N.Y.S.2d 746, affirmed, 1944, 292 N.Y. 654, 55 N.E.2d 517; Second Restatement of Torts, § 288, Comment b.

52. Routh v. Quinn, 1942, 20 Cal.2d 488, 127 P.2d 1; Strong v. Campbell, 1851, 11 Barb., N.Y., 125; Stevens v. North States Motor, 1925, 161 Minn. 345, 201 N.W. 435. But where a ministerial duty obviously is imposed for the benefit of a particular class of persons, one within that class may found an action on the statute. Howley v. Scott, 1913, 123 Minn. 159, 143 N.W. 257.

53. This state formerly had a unique rule that the driver of an unregistered car was a "trespasser on the highway," who was liable for all injuries he caused, regardless of other fault, and could not recover himself except for injuries caused intentionally or recklessly. After the Massachusetts court, in Comeau v. Harrington, 1955, 333 Mass. 768, 130 N.E. 2d 554, had expressed disapproval of the rule, the legislature changed it in Mass.Laws 1959, c. 250, by an amendment to the licensing section. It is now provided that violation shall not be a defense in an action by the violator, but shall be evidence of negligence in any action against him.

54. Dervin v. Frenier, 1917, 91 Vt. 398, 100 A. 760; Armstrong v. Sellers, 1913, 182 Ala. 582, 62 So. 28; Opple v. Ray, 1935, 208 Ind. 450, 195 N.E. 81; Black v. Moree, 1916, 135 Tenn. 73, 185 S.W. 682.

55. Cooper v. Hoeglund, 1946, 221 Minn. 446, 22 N.W. 2d 450.

56. See Falk v. Finkelman, 1929, 268 Mass. 524, 168 N.E. 89; Falvey v. Hamelburg, 1964, 347 Mass. 430, 198 N.E.2d 400; Jacobs v. Marquette Cas. Co., La. App.1964, 164 So.2d 612; Marland Refining Co. v. Duffy, 1923, 94 Okl. 16, 220 P. 846; and cf. Roos v. Loeser, 1919, 41 Cal.App. 782, 183 P. 204 (the case of the pampered, pedigreed, patrician Pomeranian pup).

57. Lowndes, Civil Liability Created by Criminal Legislation, 1932, 16 Minn.L.Rev. 361, 370; Green, Are There Dependable Rules of Causation, 1929, 77 U. Pa.L.Rev. 601, 618.

railway whistle means nothing to a cow.[58] But where such a connection is found, the only question concerning the statute is whether it is to be construed to afford protection against the conduct of the defendant, and so give the character of negligence to his act.

In many cases the evident policy of the legislature is to protect only a limited class of individuals. If so, the plaintiff must bring himself within that class in order to maintain an action based on the statute. Thus a factory act providing that dangerous machinery, or elevators, must be guarded, may be clearly intended only for the benefit of employees, and so afford no protection to others who enter the building.[59] Statutes requiring railroad trains to whistle for crossings are to protect those who are about to cross, and not parallel traffic,[60] and the ordinary rules of the highway are not for the benefit of those on the sidewalk.[61] It is generally agreed that

regulations governing the condition of land or buildings are to protect only those who are rightfully upon the premises, and not trespassers.[62]

The class of persons to be protected may of course be a very broad one, extending to all those likely to be injured by the violation. Thus a statute requiring druggists to label poisons,[63] a pure food act,[64] a law prohibiting the sale of firearms to minors,[65] or an ordinance against leaving horses unattended in the street,[66] must clearly be intended for the benefit of any member of the public who may be injured by the act or thing prohibited. Sometimes the courts have disagreed over a broad and a narrow construction of similar statutes, as where a provision requiring that parked cars shall be locked has been held to be intended,[67] and not to be intended,[68] for

58. Holman v. Chicago, R. I. & P. R. Co., 1876, 62 Mo. 562; Hayes Freight Lines v. Wilson, 1948, 226 Ind. 1, 77 N.E.2d 580 (causal connection must be proved). Cf. Weeks v. McNulty, 1898, 101 Tenn. 495, 48 N.W. 809; Hinton v. Southern R. Co., 1916, 172 N.C. 587, 90 S.E. 756; Powers v. Standard Oil Co., 1923, 98 N.J.L. 730, 119 A. 273, affirmed, 1923, 98 N.J.L. 893, 121 A. 926; Sullivan v. Boone, 1939, 205 Minn. 437, 286 N.W. 350.

59. Kelly v. Henry Muhs Co., 1904, 71 N.J.L. 358, 59 A. 23; Alsaker v. De Graff Lumber Co., 1951, 234 Minn. 280, 48 N.W.2d 431; Gibson v. Leonard, 1892, 143 Ill. 182, 32 N.E. 182. Cf. Davy v. Greenlaw, 1957, 101 N.H. 134, 135 A.2d 900; Aldworth v. F. W. Woolworth Co., 1936, 295 Mass. 344, 3 N.E.2d 1008.

60. Everett v. Great Northern R. Co., 1907, 100 Minn. 309, 111 N.W. 281; Hutto v. Southern R. Co., 1915, 100 S.C. 181, 84 S.E. 719. Accord: Williams' Adm'r v. Chesapeake & O. R. Co., 1918, 181 Ky. 313, 204 S. W. 292 (employee); Cooper v. Louisville & N. R. Co., Ky.1959, 321 S.W.2d 53 (trespasser); Hill v. Chicago, I. & L. R. Co., 1919, 188 Ind. 130, 122 N.E. 321 (invitee in yards); Central of Ga. R. Co. v. Griffin, 1926, 35 Ga.App. 161, 132 S.E. 255 (required stop where railways cross not for benefit of automobiles); Yazoo & M. V. R. Co. v. Green, 1933, 167 Miss. 137, 147 So. 333 (warning not for benefit of those fully warned).

61. Westlund v. Iverson, 1922, 154 Minn. 52, 191 N. W. 253 (keep to right); Boronkay v. Robinson & Carpenter, 1928, 247 N.Y. 365, 160 N.E. 400 (parking);

Erickson v. Kongsli, 1952, 40 Wash.2d 79, 240 P.2d 1209 (building owner).

62. Flanagan v. Sanders, 1904, 138 Mich. 253, 101 N.W. 581; Bennett v. Odell Mfg. Co., 1911, 76 N.H. 180, 80 A. 642; Akers v. Chicago, St. P., M. & O. R. Co., 1894, 58 Minn. 540, 60 N.W. 669. Cf. Garrett v. E. I. DuPont de Nemours & Co., 3 Cir. 1958, 257 F.2d 687 (I.C.C. regulations as to packing of sulphuric acid for transit not intended to protect employee of consignee).

63. Osborne v. McMasters, 1889, 40 Minn. 103, 41 N.W. 543.

64. Meshbesher v. Channellene Oil & Mfg. Co., 1909, 107 Minn. 104, 119 N.W. 428.

65. Anderson v. Settergren, 1907, 100 Minn. 294, 111 N.W. 279; Henningsen v. Markowitz, 1928, 132 Misc. 547, 230 N.Y.S. 313; Tamiami Gun Shop v. Klein, Fla.1959, 116 So.2d 421. See Note, 1960, 20 La.L.Rev. 797.

66. Bott v. Pratt, 1885, 33 Minn. 323, 23 N.W. 237.

67. Ross v. Hartman, 1943, 78 App.D.C. 217, 139 F.2d 14, cert. denied, 321 U.S. 790; Ney v. Yellow Cab Co., 1954, 2 Ill.2d 74, 117 N.E.2d 74; Garbo v. Walker, 1955, 129 N.E.2d 537, 57 Ohio Op. 363. In Justus v. Wood, 1961, 209 Tenn. 55, 348 S.W.2d 332, cert. denied, 209 Tenn. 55, 349 S.W.2d 793, it was held that the statute was intended to protect against injury during police pursuit of the thief, but not after he got away.
Cf. Boyer v. Atchison, T. & S. F. R. Co., 1962, 34 Ill. App.2d 330, 181 N.E.2d 372 (Federal Safety Appliance Act for protection of passengers as well as employees).

68. Galbraith v. Levin, 1948, 323 Mass. 255, 81 N.E.2d 560; Anderson v. Theisen, 1950, 231 Minn. 369, 43

the protection of a person run down by a thief escaping with a stolen car.

The purpose of the legislation is of course a matter of interpretation of its terms, in the light of the evil to be remedied. The title,[69] the provisions made and the language used,[70] may indicate the object to be accomplished, and so no doubt may the records of the legislature itself. The infinite variety of the statutes accounts for the lack of any general agreement as to their effect—for example, as to whether railway fencing statutes are for the protection of children as well as cattle,[71] or the class of persons to be protected by building regulations.[72]

Type of Risk Covered

The same limitation of the effect of the statute to accomplish only the supposed policy of the legislature is found in the requirement that the harm suffered must be of the kind which the statute was intended, in general, to prevent.[73] In the leading English case of Gorris v. Scott,[74] the defendant violated a statute, obviously intended merely as a sanitation measure, which required carriers by water to provide separate pens for animals transported. As a result of this violation, the plaintiff's sheep were washed overboard during a storm at sea. It was held that, while there might have been recovery if the overcrowding had resulted in disease, no action for loss during the storm could be maintained, because "the damage is of such a nature as was not contemplated at all by the statute, and as to which it was not intended to confer any benefit on the plaintiffs."

The same principle runs through a great many cases. Statutes which limit the time during which railway trains may obstruct crossings usually are held to be intended to prevent delays of traffic, and so may give rise to an action for damages resulting from such delay,[75] but afford no protection against personal injuries caused by the position of the train.[76] Nor are railway fencing statutes de-

---

N.W.2d 272; Frank v. Ralston, W.D.Ky.1956, 145 F.Supp. 294, affirmed, 1957, 248 F.2d 541; Kiste v. Red Cab, Inc., 1952, 122 Ind.App. 587, 106 N.E.2d 395; Corinti v. Wittkopp, 1959, 355 Mich. 170, 93 N.W.2d 906. See, assuming that the ordinance is a safety measure, but finding no proximate cause: Permenter v. Milner Chevrolet Co., 1956, 229 Miss. 385, 91 So.2d 243; Hersh v. Miller, 1959, 169 Neb. 517, 99 N.W.2d 878. See Notes, [1951] Wis.L.Rev. 740; 1958, 37 N.C.L.Rev. 104.

69. Compare the factory acts in Kelly v. Henry Muhs Co., 1904, 71 N.J.L. 358, 59 A. 23, and Hamilton v. Minneapolis Desk Mfg. Co., 1899, 78 Minn. 3, 80 N.W. 693, with the general building codes, which are construed to protect anyone rightfully entering the premises. Maloney v. Hearst Hotels Corp., 1937, 274 N.Y. 106, 8 N.E.2d 296; Sheyer v. Lowell, 1904, 134 Cal. 357, 66 P. 307.

70. See Gibson v. Leonard, 1892, 143 Ill. 182, 32 N.E. 182.

71. Protecting children: Hayes v. Michigan Cent. R. Co., 1884, 111 U.S. 228; Rosse v. St. Paul & Duluth R. Co., 1897, 68 Minn. 216, 71 N.W. 20; Heiting v. Chicago, R. I. & P. R. Co., 1911, 252 Ill. 466, 96 N.E. 842; Chicago, B. & Q. R. Co. v. Grablin, 1893, 38 Neb. 90, 56 N.W. 796, 57 N.W. 522.

Contra: Bischof v. Illinois Southern R. Co., 1908, 232 Ill. 446, 83 N.E. 948; Kapernaros v. Boston & Maine R. Co., 1916, 115 Me. 467, 99 A. 441; Menut v. Boston & Maine R. Co., 1910, 207 Mass. 12, 92 N.E. 1032; Di Caprio v. New York Central R. Co., 1921, 231 N.Y. 94, 131 N.E. 746.

72. See supra, note 69.

73. Thayer, Public Wrong and Private Action, 1914, 27 Harv.L.Rev. 317, 335; Morris, The Relation of Criminal Statutes to Tort Liability, 1933, 46 Harv.L. Rev. 453, 473; Lowndes, Civil Liability Created by Criminal Legislation, 1932, 16 Minn.L.Rev. 361, 372; Second Restatement of Torts, § 286, Comment *i*.

74. 1874, L.R. 9 Ex. 125. The rule has been adopted by the Second Restatement of Torts, §§ 286, 288. The only case found which is definitely to the contrary is Grey's Ex'r v. Mobile Trade Co., 1876, 55 Ala. 387.

75. Patterson v. Detroit, L. & N. R. Co., 1885, 56 Mich. 172, 22 N.W. 260; Terry v. New Orleans Great Northern R. Co., 1912, 103 Miss. 679, 60 So. 729. Cf. Kalkopf v. Donald Sales & Mfg. Co., 1967, 33 Wis.2d 247, 147 N.W.2d 277 (anti-littering statute not for safety).

76. Simpson v. Pere Marquette R. Co., 1936, 276 Mich. 653, 268 N.W. 769; Hendley v. Chicago & N. W. R. Co., 1929, 198 Wis. 569, 225 N.W. 205; Jones v. Atchison, T. & S. F. R. Co., 1929, 129 Kan. 314, 282 P. 593; Megan v. Stevens, 8 Cir. 1937, 91 F.2d 419, cert. denied 302 U.S. 746; Fox v. Illinois Cent. R.

signed to prevent a cow from eating herself to death,[77] or regulations requiring landlords to heat premises intended to protect children from burns from an electric heater.[78]

Ordinances regulating the place where vehicles may stop [79] or park [80] usually are not intended to prevent collisions or personal injuries to bus passengers, or to keep automobiles from running down pedestrians.[81] Most licensing statutes, such as those applicable

to automobile drivers [82] or physicians,[83] have been construed as intended only for the protection of the public against injury at the hands of incompetents, and to create no liability where the actor is in fact competent but unlicensed. Particular statutes may, however, be construed as establishing a specific standard of competence, so that those who do not meet them are treated as negligent in acting at all.[84]

In determining whether the plaintiff's injury is within the "purpose" of the statute, three lines of approach can be discovered in the cases. Sometimes there is an exceedingly narrow and even, apparently, quite unreasonable interpretation, as in the Missouri case [85] where a requirement that emery

Co., 1941, 308 Ill.App. 367, 31 N.E.2d 805. Contra: Budkiewicz v. Elgin, J. & E. R. Co., 1958, 238 Ind. 535, 150 N.E.2d 897; Paul v. Atlantic Coast Line R. Co., 1915, 170 N.C. 230, 87 S.E. 66.

77. Kansas, O. & G. R. Co. v. Keirsey, Okl.1954, 266 P.2d 617; Ingalsbe v. St. Louis-San Francisco R. Co., 1922, 295 Mo. 177, 243 S.W. 323. Cf. Brei v. Chicago, B. & Q. R. Co., 1936, 130 Neb. 496, 265 N.W. 539 (poison); Victory Sparkler & Specialty Co. v. Price, 1927, 146 Miss. 192, 111 So. 437 (sale of fireworks, eaten by child); Larrimore v. American Nat. Ins. Co., 1939, 184 Okl. 614, 89 P.2d 340 (laying out rat poison, which exploded); Sinclair Prairie Oil Co. v. Stell, 1942, 190 Okl. 344, 124 P.2d 255 (decedent drowned in salt water from oil well); Louisville & N. R. Co. v. Sloan, 1941, 246 Ky. 328, 155 S.W.2d 23 (cinder in eye from locomotive without spark arrester).

78. Cook v. Seidenverg, 1950, 36 Wash.2d 256, 217 P.2d 799. Cf. Nunneley v. Edgar Hotel, 1951, 36 Cal.2d 403, 225 P.2d 497 (sitting on low parapet of vent shaft on roof and falling over); Brown Hotel v. Levitt, 1948, 306 Ky. 804, 209 S.W.2d 70 (no handrail on steps; plaintiff knocked down by falling man); Belk v. Boyce, 1964, 263 N.C. 24, 138 S.E.2d 789 (cruelty to animals statute, man injured); Pelkey v. Brennan, 1961, 12 App.Div.2d 215, 209 N.Y.S.2d 691 (unaccompanied minor in skating rink).

79. Smith v. Portland Transaction Co., 1961, 226 Or. 221, 359 P.2d 899 (bus to discharge passengers at curb); Reque v. Milwaukee & Suburban Transp. Corp., 1959, 7 Wis.2d 111, 97 N.W.2d 182 (same); Mahone v. Birmingham Elec. Co., 1954, 261 Ala. 132, 73 So.2d 378 (same); Smith v. Virginia Transit Co., 1966, 206 Va. 951, 147 S.E.2d 110 (designated stopping point).

80. Ennis v. Atkin, 1946, 354 Pa. 165, 47 A.2d 217; Falk v. Finkelman, 1929, 268 Mass. 524, 168 N.E. 89; Denson v. McDonald Bros., 1919, 144 Minn. 252, 175 N.W. 108.

81. Shelden v. Wichita R. & L. Co., 1928, 125 Kan. 476, 264 P. 732; cf. Flynn v. Gordon, 1933, 86 N.H. 198, 165 A. 715 (obstruction of sidewalk).

82. Hertz Driv-Ur-Self System v. Hendrickson, 1942, 109 Colo. 1, 121 P.2d 483; Schuster v. Gillispie, 1933, 217 Iowa 386, 251 N.W. 735; Wilson v. Rogers, 1935, 140 Kan. 647, 38 P.2d 124; Halsan v. Johnson, 1937, 155 Or. 583, 65 P.2d 661; Seaboard Coast Line R. Co. v. Ziegler, 1969, 120 Ga.App. 276, 170 S.E.2d 60. Here again the decisions frequently and erroneously go off on "proximate cause." See for example Cirosky v. Smathers, 1924, 128 S.C. 358, 122 S.E. 864; Flanigan v. Carswell, 1959, 159 Tex. 598, 324 S.W.2d 835. See Gregory, Breach of Criminal Licensing Statutes in Civil Litigation, 1951, 36 Corn. L.Q. 622.

Contra, Johnson v. Boston & Me. R. Co., 1928, 83 N.H. 350, 143 A. 516. Massachusetts refused to hold that the unlicensed driver, as distinguished from the unlicensed car, was a "trespasser on the highway," and treated such a violation merely as evidence of negligence. Bourne v. Whitman, 1911, 209 Mass. 155, 95 N.E. 404.

83. Brown v. Shyne, 1926, 242 N.Y. 176, 151 N.E. 197; Hardy v. Dahl, 1936, 210 N.C. 530, 187 S.E. 788; Janssen v. Mulder, 1925, 232 Mich. 183, 205 N.W. 159.

84. Andreen v. Escondido Citrus Union, 1928, 93 Cal. App. 182, 269 P. 556 (fumigation); Cragg v. Los Angeles Trust Co., 1908, 154 Cal. 663, 98 P. 1063 (elevator operator); Whipple v. Grandchamp, 1927, 261 Mass. 40, 158 N.E. 270, (medical); Monahan v. Devinny, 1928, 223 App.Div. 547, 229 N.Y.S. 60 (medical).

85. Mansfield v. Wagner Elec. Mfg. Co., 1922, 294 Mo. 235, 242 S.W. 400. Cf. Moore v. Dering Coal Co., 1909, 242 Ill. 84, 89 N.E. 674 (requirement of flanges on drum for sinking mine shaft held to have no application where mine under construction, not yet in operation); Hatch v. Ford Motor Co., 1958,

wheels be hooded was held to be intended to guard only against the dust hazard, and not to prevent injuries to workmen's eyes. This sort of thing has become quite unfashionable in recent years. A much more reasonable attitude is that of the New York court in a decision [86] holding that an act requiring elevator shafts to be guarded covered the risk of objects falling down the shaft, to the effect that the accident need only be included within the same general risk, or class of risks, at which the statute is directed. Thus in the absence of any other guide, a statute may well be assumed to include all risks that may reasonably be anticipated as likely to follow from its violation.[87] There are, however, occasional cases which have gone to an extreme, and apparently have included all risks which would occur to anyone as possible, following the violation.[88] A broad purpose of maximum protection, found as the basis of the statute, will of course encourage such an interpretation.[89]

Excused Violations

It is entirely possible that a statute may impose an absolute duty, for whose violation there is no recognized excuse.

163 Cal.App.2d 393, 329 P.2d 605 (prohibition of radiator ornaments on automobiles held not to protect child coming in contact with parked vehicle).

86. De Haen v. Rockwood Sprinkler Co., 1932, 258 N.Y. 350, 179 N.E. 764. Accord: Middaugh v. Waseca Canning Co., 1938, 203 Minn. 456, 281 N.W. 818 (length of vehicle); Wildwood Mink Ranch v. United States, D.Minn.1963, 218 F.Supp. 67 (low flight frightening mink); Huckleberry v. Missouri Pac. R. Co., 1930, 324 Mo. 1025, 26 S.W.2d 980. See Note, 1933, 27 Ill.L.Rev. 318.

87. See Note, 1935, 19 Minn.L.Rev. 666, 674.

88. See for example Ross v. Hartman, 1943, 78 App. D.C. 217, 139 F.2d 14; Ney v. Yellow Cab Co., 1954, 2 Ill.2d 74, 117 N.E.2d 74. Compare, as to wrongful death following violation of a Civil Rights Act, Brazier v. Cherry, M.D.Ga.1960, 188 F.Supp. 817; and see Note, 1956, 104 U.Pa.L.Rev. 864.

89. Cf. Kernan v. American Dredging Co., 1958, 355 U.S. 426, construing the Jones Act and the Federal Employers' Liability Act to include even injuries found not to be within the type of harm the statute

The legislature, within its constitutional powers, may see fit to place the burden of injuries "upon those who can measurably control their causes, instead of upon those who are in the main helpless in that regard."[90] In such a case the defendant may become liable on the mere basis of his violation of the statute. No excuse is recognized, and neither reasonable ignorance nor all proper care will avoid liability. Such a statute falls properly under the head of strict liability, rather than any basis of negligence —although the courts not infrequently continue, out of habit, to speak of the violation as "negligence per se."

Thus the Federal Safety Appliance Act, regulating the equipment of trains moving in interstate commerce, has been construed to impose such an absolute duty,[91] as have nearly all of the statutes prohibiting the employment of child labor,[92] many of the factory or scaffolding acts making specific requirements for the safety of employees,[93] various types

was intended to prevent. See Note, 1958, 46 Cal.L. Rev. 847.

90. St. Louis, I. M. & S. R. Co. v. Taylor, 1907, 210 U.S. 281. This may be done even for criminal purposes. See Remington, Liability Without Fault Criminal Statutes, [1956] Wis.L.Rev. 625.

91. O'Donnell v. Elgin, J. & E. Ry. Co., 1949, 338 U.S. 384, rehearing denied, 338 U.S. 945; Trout v. Pennsylvania R. Co., 3 Cir. 1961, 300 F.2d 826. Accord, as to the Boiler Inspection Act, St. Louis S. W. Ry. Co. v. Williams, 5 Cir. 1968, 397 F.2d 147.

92. Beauchamp v. Sturges & Burns Mfg. Co., 1911, 250 Ill. 303, 95 N.E. 204, affirmed, 1914, 231 U.S. 320; Krutlies v. Bulls Head Coal Co., 1915, 249 Pa. 162, 94 A. 459; Blanton v. Kellioka Coal Co., 1921, 192 Ky. 220, 232 S.W. 614; Second Restatement of Torts, § 288A, Comment c; Note, 1930, 39 Yale L.J. 908.

93. Koenig v. Patrick Const. Corp., 1948, 298 N.Y. 313, 83 N.E.2d 133; Schmidt v. Merchants Despatch Transp. Co., 1936, 270 N.Y. 287, 200 N.E. 824, reargument denied, 1936, 271 N.Y. 531, 2 N.E.2d 680; Pankey v. Hiram Walker & Sons, S.D.Ill.1958, 167 F.Supp. 609; Continental Can Co. v. Horton, 8 Cir. 1957, 250 F.2d 637.

In Major v. Waverly & Ogden, Inc., 1960, 7 N.Y.2d 332, 197 N.Y.S.2d 165, 165 N.E.2d 181, it was held that such effect cannot be given to an administrative regulation, as distinguished from a statute.

of building regulations,[94] and many of the pure food [95] or animal food [96] cases in which the question has been decided, as well as two or three statutes [97] requiring effective brakes on vehicles operating on the public highway.

These statutes are, however, the exception; and in the aggregate they make up only a very small percentage of the total safety legislation. Normally no such interpretation will be placed upon a statute, and no such conclusion reached, unless the court finds that it was clearly the purpose of the legislature.[98] In the ordinary case, all that is re-

quired is reasonable diligence to obey the statute,[99] and it frequently has been recognized that a violation of the law is reasonable, and may be excused. Although such cases often speak of a supposed intent and an "implied exception" which makes the statute inapplicable to the case even for criminal purposes,[1] they seem rather to indicate that, in the absence of a clear declaration by the legislature, the courts reserve the final authority to determine whether the civil standard of reasonable conduct will always require obedience to the criminal law.[2]

Thus it has been held not to be negligence to violate the letter of a statute because of physical circumstances beyond the driver's control, as where his lights suddenly go out on the highway at night,[3] or without prior

94. Monsour v. Excelsior Tobacco Co., Mo.App.1938, 115 S.W.2d 219. Occasionally other statutes have received a very strict construction which in effect eliminates most possible excuses. Cf. Andrew v. White Bus Lines Corp., 1932, 115 Conn. 464, 161 A. 799; McDowell v. Federal Tea Co., 1942, 129 Conn. 455, 23 A.2d 512.

95. Meshbesher v. Channellene Oil & Mfg. Co., 1909, 107 Minn. 104, 119 N.W. 428; Culbertson v. Coca Cola Bottling Co., 1930, 157 S.C. 352, 154 S.E. 424; Donaldson v. Great A. & P. Tea Co., 1938, 186 Ga. 870, 199 S.E. 213, answers conformed to, 1939, 59 Ga.App. 79, 200 S.E. 498; Bolitho v. Safeway Stores, 1939, 109 Mont. 213, 95 P.2d 443; Yochem v. Gloria, Inc., 1938, 134 Ohio St. 427, 17 N.E.2d 731. See Note, 1939, 26 Va.L.Rev. 100.

Contra: Howson v. Foster Beef Co., 1935, 87 N.H. 200, 177 A. 656; Cheli v. Cudahy Bros. Co., 1934, 267 Mich. 690, 255 N.W. 414; Gearing v. Berkson, 1916, 223 Mass. 257, 111 N.E. 785.

96. Valdosta Milling Co. v. Garretson, 5 Cir. 1954, 217 F.2d 625; Metz v. Medford Fur Foods, Inc., 1958, 4 Wis.2d 96, 90 N.W.2d 106.

97. Albers v. Ottenbacher, 1962, 79 S.D. 637, 116 N.W. 2d 529; Bird v. Hart, 1965, 2 Ohio St.2d 9, 205 N.E. 2d 887; Hamill v. Smith, 1964, 25 Conn.Sup. 183, 199 A.2d 343. Oregon held this in Nettleton v. James, 1958, 212 Or. 375, 319 P.2d 879, but retreated from the position in McConnell v. Herron, 1965, 240 Or. 486, 402 P.2d 726.

Cf. Smulczeski v. City Center of Music & Drama, Inc., 1957, 3 N.Y.2d 498, 169 N.Y.S.2d 1, 146 N.E.2d 769 (no notice lights had gone out). Also Van Gaasbeck v. Webatuck Central School Dist. No. 1, 1967, 21 N.Y.2d 239, 287 N.Y.S.2d 77, 234 N.E.2d 243 (driver of school bus required to direct children).

98. Hammond v. Vestry of St. Pancras, 1874, L.R. 9 C.P. 319; Phillips v. Britannia Hygienic Laundry Co., [1923] 1 K.B. 539; Baldwin v. Washington Motor Coach Co., 1938, 196 Wash. 117, 82 P.2d 131;

Musgrave v. Southern Pac. Co., 1937, 49 Ariz. 512, 68 P.2d 202; Jenkins v. City of Fort Wayne, 1965, 139 Ind.App. 1, 210 N.E.2d 390, rehearing denied, 1966, 212 N.E.2d 916.

99. Iudica v. De Nezzo, 1932, 115 Conn. 233, 161 A. 81; Romansky v. Cestaro, 1929, 109 Conn. 654, 145 A. 156; Nashville & C. R. Co. v. Peacock, 1854, 25 Ala. 229; Chicago & N. W. R. Co. v. Barrie, 1870, 55 Ill. 226.

1. Second Restatement of Torts, § 288A; Note, 1935, 19 Minn.L.Rev. 666, 675; see Traynor, J., concurring in Satterlee v. Orange Glenn School District, 1947, 29 Cal.2d 581, 177 P.2d 279.

"Where a statutory general rule of conduct fixes no definite standard of care which would under all circumstances tend to protect life, limb or property, but merely codifies or supplements a common-law rule, which always has been subject to limitations or exceptions; or where the statutory rule of conduct regulates conflicting rights and obligations in manner calculated to promote public convenience and safety, then the statute, in the absence of clear language, should not be construed as intended to wipe out the limitations and exceptions which judicial decisions have attached to the common law duty." Tedla v. Ellman, 1939, 280 N.Y. 124, 19 N.E. 2d 987, 990.

2. Morris, The Relation of Criminal Statutes to Civil Liability, 1933, 46 Harv.L.Rev. 453. Well stated in Phoenix Refining Co. v. Powell, Tex.Civ. App.1952, 251 S.W.2d 892, ref. n. r. e.

3. Brotherton v. Day & Night Fuel Co., 1937, 192 Wash. 362, 73 P.2d 788; Taber v. Smith, Tex.Civ. App.1930, 26 S.W.2d 722.

negligence, his brakes fail [4] or his car crosses the center line of the highway.[5] The same is true where his violation is due to innocent ignorance of the operative facts which make the statute applicable, as where he reasonably does not know that he is approaching an intersection or a railroad track.[6] Another valid excuse is that of emergency, as where one drives on the left because the right is blocked,[7] or a child dashes into the street,[8]

or there is any other real necessity.[9] Undoubtedly there are even situations, such as that of the child, where it would be negligence as a matter of law to obey the literal terms of the statute at all.[10] There is respectable authority to the effect that at least a violation will be excused whenever it would be more dangerous to comply with the statute.[11] Although there are cases to the contrary,[12] the great majority of the cases have held that the immaturity of an infant can excuse him from

4. Alarid v. Vanier, 1958, 50 Cal.2d 617, 327 P.2d 897; Pollack v. Olson, 1963, 20 Wis.2d 394, 122 N.W.2d 426; Peters v. Rieck, 1964, 257 Iowa 12, 131 N.W.2d 529; Dayton v. Palmer, 1965, 1 Ariz.App. 184, 400 P.2d 855; Hills v. McGillvrey, 1965, 240 Or. 476, 402 P.2d 722. See Note, 1966, 45 Or.L.Rev. 156.

Cf. Moore v. Capitol Transit Co., D.C.Cir. 1955, 96 U.S.App.D.C. 335, 226 F.2d 57, cert. denied 350 U.S. 966 (motorman with "convulsive seisure" went through red light); Martin v. Atchison, T. & S. F. R. Co., 1914, 92 Kan. 595, 141 P. 599 (snow on railway fences); Krebs v. Rubsam, 1918, 91 N.J.L. 426, 104 A. 83.

5. Herman v. Sladofsky, 1938, 301 Mass. 534, 17 N.E. 2d 879 (skid); Dohm v. R. N. Cardozo & Bro., 1925, 165 Minn. 193, 206 N.W. 377; Wilson v. Wright, 1958, 52 Wash.2d 805, 329 P.2d 461 (hit chuck hole). Cf. Martinson v. Scherbel, 1964, 268 Minn. 509, 129 N.W.2d 802 (passing on right when car ahead stopped suddenly).

6. Hullander v. McIntyre, 1960, 78 S.D. 453, 104 N.W. 2d 40 (intersection); McEachen v. Richmond, 1957, 150 Cal.App.2d 546, 310 P.2d 122 (same); Johnson v. Chicago & N. W. Ry. Co., 1946, 71 S.D. 132, 22 N.W.2d 725 (grade crossing); Mitchell v. Emblade, 1956, 80 Ariz. 398, 298 P.2d 1034, adhered to 81 Ariz. 121, 301 P.2d 1032 (misleading speed signs); Wood v. Chicago, M. St. P. & P. R. Co., 1954, 45 Wash.2d 601, 277 P.2d 345, adhered to, 1955, 283 P.2d 688 (speed, approaching town). Cf. Baldwin v. Washington Motor Coach Co., 1938, 196 Wash. 117, 82 P.2d 131 (ignorance he had hit traffic signal).

7. Conder v. Griffith, 1916, 61 Ind.App. 218, 111 N.E. 816; Dugan v. Fry, 3 Cir. 1929, 34 F.2d 723; Hammer v. Connecticut Co., 1919, 94 Conn. 127, 108 A. 534. Cf. Sathrum v. Lee, 1930, 180 Minn. 163, 230 N.W. 580 (approaching vehicle); Discargar v. City of Seattle, 1946, 25 Wash.2d 306, 171 P.2d 205 (entering car on left side); Walker v. Missouri Pac. R. Co., 1915, 95 Kan. 702, 149 P. 677 (disabled train on crossing).

8. Chase v. Tingdale Bros., 1914, 127 Minn. 401, 149 N.W. 654; R. & L. Transfer Co. v. State for Use of Schmidt, 1931, 160 Md. 222, 153 A. 87; Burlie v.

Stephens, 1920, 113 Wash. 182, 193 P. 684. Cf. Riceland Petroleum Co. v. Moore, 1928, 178 Ark. 599, 12 S.W.2d 415; Lawson v. Dye, 1928, 106 W.Va. 494, 145 S.E. 817; Kosrofian v. Donnelly, R.I.1922, 117 A. 421.

9. Giancarlo v. Karabanowski, 1938, 124 Conn. 223, 198 A. 752 (useless steering gear); Seligmann v. Hammond, 1931, 205 Wis. 199, 236 N.W. 115 (blowout); Martin v. Nelson, 1947, 82 Cal.App.2d 733, 187 P.2d 78 (result of collision). Cf. Sidle v. Baker, 1936, 52 Ohio App. 89, 3 N.E.2d 537; Swoboda v. Brown, 1935, 129 Ohio St. 512, 196 N.E. 274. See Note, [1942] Wis.L.Rev. 422.

The emergency must of course be such that there is no reasonable opportunity to obey the statute. Toothaker v. Hines, 1922, 112 Kan. 304, 210 P. 1110 (snow on fences for three weeks); Hand v. Greathouse, 1938, 294 Ill.App. 383, 13 N.E.2d 1010 (parking car on highway after broken chain removed); Fairchild v. Dean, 1939, 198 Wash. 1, 86 P.2d 271 (passing truck without clear view ahead).

10. Walker v. Lee, 1921, 115 S.C. 495, 106 S.E. 682; Sims v. Eleazar, 1921, 116 S.C. 41, 106 S.E. 854; Phillips v. Davis, 3 Cir. 1925, 3 F.2d 798; Mora v. Favilla, 1921, 186 Cal. 199, 199 P. 17.

11. Hopson v. Goolsby, 1955, 196 Va. 832, 86 S.E.2d 149 (crossing street at point other than intersection); Tedla v. Ellman, 1939, 280 N.Y. 124, 19 N.E.2d 987 (walking on right side of highway where all heavy traffic on left); Cameron v. Stewart, 1957, 153 Me. 47, 134 A.2d 474 (walking on wrong side where sidewalk defective).

There is also authority that the violation will be excused where compliance with the statute would be simply foolish. Ridenhour v. Oklahoma Contracting Co., Mo.1932, 45 S.W.2d 108 (no lights in daylight); Sheehan v. Nims, 2 Cir. 1935, 75 F.2d 293 (same); Simpson v. Miller, 1934, 97 Mont. 328, 34 P.2d 528 (no lights under street lamp).

12. D'Ambrosio v. City of Philadelphia, 1946, 354 Pa. 403, 47 A.2d 256; Patrician v. Garvey, 1934, 287 Mass. 62, 190 N.E. 9; Sagor v. Joseph Burnett Co., 1937, 122 Conn. 447, 190 A. 258.

a violation which would be negligence on the part of an adult.[13]

A troublesome problem is presented by the deplorable array of trivial, obsolete, or entirely unreasonable legislation, such as speed limits of six miles an hour, which persists in our statute books. Since no officer has the power to authorize a violation of the law, the fact that such a provision is not and never has been enforced,[14] or that it is customary to violate it,[15] cannot affect its validity; nor, of course, may the court declare that it is not the law. In several cases the courts have struggled hard to construe such a provision to require only reasonable conduct,[16] or have found that its unreasonableness makes it unconstitutional or otherwise invalid;[17] but in others they have considered that they had no alternative but to treat the violation as negligence.[18] But there is after all no compulsion by which a purely criminal statute must lead to any civil liability, and it is the court's own decision which brings about such a result; and where such legislation clearly is utterly foolish, there seems to be no reason to ignore the fact that the community standard in fact permits a reasonable man to disobey it.[19]

Negligence Per Se and Evidence of Negligence

Once the statute is determined to be applicable—which is to say, once it is interpreted as designed to protect the class of persons in which the plaintiff is included, against the risk of the type of harm which has in fact occurred as a result of its violation—the great majority of the courts hold that an unexcused violation is conclusive on the issue of negligence, and that the court must so direct the jury.[20] The standard of conduct is taken over by the court from that fixed by the legislature, and "jurors have no dispensing power by which to relax it,"[21] except in so far as the court may recognize the possibility of a valid excuse for disobedience of the law. This usually is expressed by saying that the unexcused violation is negligence "per se," or in itself. The effect of such a rule is to stamp the defendant's conduct as ngligence, with all of the effects of common law negligence, but with no greater effect. There will still re-

13. Simmons v. Holm, 1961, 229 Or. 373, 367 P.2d 368; Daun v. Truax, 1961, 56 Cal.2d 647, 16 Cal.Rptr. 351, 365 P.2d 407; Rudes v. Gottschalk, 1959, 159 Tex. 552, 324 S.W.2d 201; Baldwin v. Hosley, Ky.1959, 328 S.W.2d 426; Gough v. Shaner, 1955, 197 Va. 572, 90 S.E.2d 171. See Mertz, The Infant and Negligence Per Se in Pennsylvania, 1947, 51 Dick.L.Rev. 79; Notes, 1960, 48 Ky.L.J. 601; 1953, 26 So.Cal.L. Rev. 335; 1958, 37 Tex.L.Rev. 255; 1949, 3 Vand.L. Rev. 145.

14. Riser v. Smith, 1917, 136 Minn. 417, 162 N.W. 520; Day v. Pauly, 1925, 186 Wis. 189, 202 N.W. 363; Pitcher v. Lennon, 1896, 12 App.Div. 356, 42 N.Y.S. 156; Cleveland R. Co. v. Harrington, 1892, 131 Ind. 426, 30 N.E. 37.

15. Stultz v. Thomas, 1921, 182 N.C. 470, 109 S.E. 361; Stogdon v. Charleston Transit Co., 1944, 127 W.Va. 286, 32 S.E.2d 276; Casey v. Boyer, 1921, 270 Pa. 492, 113 A. 364; Sanchez v. J. Barron Rice, Inc., 1967, 77 N.M. 717, 427 P.2d 240.

16. Lone Star Gas Co. v. Kelly, 1942, 140 Tex. 15, 165 S.W.2d 446, answer conformed to Tex.Civ.App., 166 S.W.2d 191; Nashville, C. & St. L. R. Co. v. White, 1929, 278 U.S. 456; Malloy v. New York Real Estate Ass'n, 1898, 156 N.Y. 205, 50 N.E. 853; Gallagher v. New York & N. E. R. Co., 1889, 57 Conn. 442, 18 A. 786.

17. Meyers v. Chicago, R. I. & P. R. Co., 1881, 57 Iowa 555, 10 N.W. 896; Evison v. Chicago, St. P., M. & O. R. Co., 1891, 45 Minn. 370, 48 N.W. 6; Zumault v. Kansas City & I. Air Line, 1897, 71 Mo.App. 670. See Note, 1947, 25 Tex.L.Rev. 286; Morris, The Role of Criminal Statutes in Negligence Actions, 1949, 49 Col.L.Rev. 21, 39–42.

18. Kansas City Suburban Belt R. Co. v. Herman, 1902, 64 Kan. 546, 68 P. 46, affirmed, 1902, 187 U.S. 63; Conrad v. Springfield Consol. R. Co., 1909, 240 Ill. 12, 88 N.E. 180; Cleveland, C. C. & I. R. Co. v. Harrington, 1892, 131 Ind. 426, 30 N.E. 37; Riser v. Smith, 1917, 136 Minn. 417, 162 N.W. 520.

19. See supra, p. 193.

20. Martin v. Herzog, 1920, 228 N.Y. 164, 126 N.E. 814; Hardaway v. Consolidated Paper Co., 1962, 366 Mich. 190, 114 N.W.2d 236; White v. Gore, 1959, 201 Va. 239, 110 S.E.2d 228; Larkins v. Kohlmeyer, 1951, 229 Ind. 391, 98 N.E.2d 896; Second Restatement of Torts, § 288B. See Notes, 1932, 32 Cal.L.Rev. 712; 1941, 29 Ky.L.J. 489.

21. Cardozo, J., in Martin v. Herzog, 1920, 228 N.Y. 164, 126 N.E. 814.

main open such questions as the causal relation between the violation and the harm to the plaintiff,[22] and, in the ordinary case, the defenses of contributory negligence,[23] and assumption of the risk.[24] There are, however, statutes, such as the child labor laws,[25] so clearly intended to protect a particular class of persons against their own inability to protect themselves, that the policy of the legislature is interpreted to mean even that such defenses are not available.

California has arrived at what appears to be precisely the same result by holding that the violation creates a presumption of negligence,[26] which may be rebutted by a showing of an adequate excuse but calls for a binding instruction in the absence of such evidence. A considerable minority have held that a violation is only evidence of negligence, which the jury may accept or reject as it sees fit.[27] Some of the courts which follow the majority rule as to statutes have held that the breach of ordinances,[28] or traffic laws,[29] or the regulations of administrative bodies,[30] even though the latter are authorized by statute, is only evidence for the jury. Such cases seem to indicate a considerable distrust of the arbitrary character of the provision, and a desire to leave some leeway for cases where its violation may not be necessarily unreasonable.[31] Even in such jurisdictions, however, it is recognized that there are cases [32] in which, merely as a matter of evidence, reasonable men could not fail to agree that the violation is negligence.

If the statute is not construed to cover the plaintiff, or the particular type of harm, many courts have held that its violation is not even evidence of negligence, and can have no effect on liability at all.[33] Obviously such a result is called for in the case of such statutes as the Sunday blue laws, which

22. Richardson v. Gregory, 1960, 108 U.S.App.D.C. 263, 281 F.2d 626; Somerville v. Keeler, 1933, 165 Miss. 244, 145 So. 721; White v. Peters, 1958, 52 Wash.2d 824, 329 P.2d 471.

23. See infra, § 65.

24. See infra, § 68. Cf. Greiving La Plante, 1942, 156 Kan. 196, 131 P.2d 898.

25. See infra, pp. 425, 453.

26. Satterlee v. Orange Glenn School District, 1947, 29 Cal.2d 581, 177 P.2d 279. Vermont held this in Landry v. Hubert, 1928, 101 Vt. 111, 141 A. 593, but it was said in Shulins v. New England Ins. Co., 2 Cir. 1966, 360 F.2d 781, that the violation makes a prima facie case for the jury.

27. New Amsterdam Cas. Co. v. Novick Transfer Co., 4 Cir. 1960, 274 F.2d 916 (Maryland law); Guinan v. Famous Players-Lasky Corp., 1929, 267 Mass. 501, 167 N.E. 235; Chiapparine v. Public Service R. Co., 1918, 91 N.J.L. 581, 103 A. 180; Gill v. Whiteside-Hemby Drug Co., 1939, 197 Ark. 425, 122 S.W.2d 597.

28. Carlock v. Westchester Lighting Co., 1935, 268 N.Y. 345, 197 N.E. 306; Rotter v. Detroit United R. Co., 1919, 205 Mich. 212, 171 N.W. 514. The prevailing view is that an ordinance is not to be distinguished from a statute. See supra, p. 190.

29. Silvia v. Pennock, 1962, 253 Iowa 779, 113 N.W. 2d 749; Attleson v. Boomgarden, N.D.1955, 73 N.W. 2d 448.

30. Claypool v. Mohawk Motors, 1951, 155 Ohio St. 8, 97 N.E.2d 32; Schumer v. Caplin, 1925, 241 N.Y. 346, 150 N.E. 139; Town of Kirklin v. Everman, 1940, 217 Ind. 683, 29 N.E.2d 206; Douglas v. Edgewater Park Co., 1963, 369 Mich. 320, 119 N.W.2d 567. Somewhat less frequently the violation has been held to be negligence as a matter of law. Rinehart v. Woodford Flying Service, 1940, 122 W.Va. 392, 9 S.E.2d 521; Hyde v. Connecticut Co., 1936, 122 Conn. 236, 188 A. 266; Phoenix Amusement Co. v. White, 1948, 306 Ky. 361, 208 S.W.2d 64; Weeks v. Prostrollo Sons, Inc., 1969, — S.D. —, 169 N.W. 2d 725.

Possibly the answer depends upon the importance and standing of an administrative agency. Violation of a regulation of the Interstate Commerce Commission may be negligence per se, as in Kane v. Branch Motor Express Co., 2 Cir.1961, 290 F.2d 503, where violation of one of a city fire marshal would not. See Morris, The Role of Administrative Safety Measures in Negligence Actions, 1949, 28 Tex.L.Rev. 143.

31. See Morris, The Relation of Criminal Statutes to Civil Liability, 1933, 46 Harv.L.Rev. 453; James, Statutory Standards and Negligence in Accident Cases, 1950, 11 La.L.Rev. 95.

32. Cantwell v. Cermins, 1941, 347 Mo.App. 836, 149 S.W.2d 343; Wojtowicz v. Belden, 1942, 211 Minn. 461, 1 N.W.2d 409.

33. Di Caprio v. New York Cent. R. Co., 1921, 231 N. Y. 94, 131 N.E. 746; Exner v. Sherman Power Const. Co., 2 Cir.1931, 54 F.2d 510; Mansfield v. Wagner Electric Mfg. Co., 1922, 294 Mo. 235, 242 S.W. 400; Robertson v. Yazoo & M. V. R. Co., 1929, 154 Miss. 182, 122 So. 371; Carter v. Redmond, 1920, 142 Tenn. 258, 218 S.W. 217.

do not purport to protect anyone, or to set any standard of care. But the existence of a statute does not prevent an action for common law negligence; and where the statute does set up standard precautions, although only for the protection of a different class of persons, or the prevention of a distinct risk, this may be a relevant fact, having proper bearing upon the conduct of a reasonable man under the circumstances, which the jury should be permitted to consider. There is, in other words, a statutory custom, which is entitled to admission as evidence. Thus a statute requiring hogs to be fenced in with a fence of specified build and strength, in order to prevent misbreeding, is some indication of the kind of fence required to keep the hogs out of the way of automobiles. Some courts have reached such a conclusion.[34] The arbitrary classification of all breaches of statute as negligence per se or no negligence at all leaves too little flexibility for the standard of reasonable care.[35]

Violation by Plaintiff

Where it is the plaintiff who violates the statute, a slightly different problem is presented. In early cases a few courts, influenced by the idea that no man should be permitted to base a cause of action upon his own illegal conduct,[36] held that a plaintiff who was violating the criminal law, as by driving on Sunday, could not recover for any injury that he might sustain while so engaged.[37] The anomalous Massachusetts rule, only lately abandoned,[38] that the driver of an unregistered automobile was a trespasser on the highway who had no right of action, may be traced to such an early Sunday law decision.[39] But with few exceptions, the courts have long since discarded the doctrine that any violator of a statute is an outlaw with no rights against anyone, and have recognized that, except in so far as he must resort to an illegal contract,[40] or an illegal status[41] as the basis of the defendant's duty to him, one who violates a criminal statute is not deprived of all protection against the torts of others. Thus the Sunday driver[42] or the unlicensed operator[43] of an unlicensed car,[44]

---

34. Hansen v. Kemmish, 1926, 201 Iowa 1008, 208 N. W. 277; cf. Union Pac. R. Co. v. McDonald, 1894, 152 U.S. 262; Slick Oil Co. v. Coffey, 1919, 72 Okl. 32, 177 P. 915; Dohm v. R. N. Cardozo & Bro., 1925, 165 Minn. 193, 206 N.W. 377. Compare, as to subsequent statutes, not retroactive, Geisking v. Sheimo, 1960, 252 Iowa 37, 105 N.W.2d 599; Gann v. Keith, 1952, 151 Tex. 626, 253 S.W.2d 413; Mitchell v. Emblade, 1956, 80 Ariz. 398, 298 P.2d 1034, adhered to 81 Ariz. 121, 301 P.2d 1032. See Note, 1966, 51 Iowa L.Rev. 1148.

35. See Morris, The Relation of Criminal Statutes to Civil Liability, 1933, 46 Harv.L.Rev. 453.

36. See Davis, The Plaintiff's Illegal Act as a Defense in Actions of Tort, 1905, 18 Harv.L.Rev. 505; Thayer, Public Wrong and Private Action, 1914, 27 Harv.L.Rev. 317, 338; Note, 1926, 39 Harv.L.Rev. 1088. Compare the earlier cases holding one who violates a statute liable for accidental consequences, supra, p. 142.

37. Bosworth v. Inhabitants of Swansey, 1845, 10 Metc., Mass., 363; Johnson v. Irasburgh, 1874, 47 Vt. 28; Hinckley v. Penobscot, 1856, 42 Me. 89.

38. See supra, p. 193.

39. See Note, 1933, 46 Harv.L.Rev. 319; Altshuler, Use and Operation of Automobiles in Violation of Statute, 1930, 10 Boston U.L.Rev. 211.

40. Cf. McNeill v. Durham & Charlotte R. Co., 1903, 132 N.C. 510, 44 S.E. 34, reversed on rehearing, 1904, 135 N.C. 682, 47 S.E. 765. See Note, 1933, 13 Bos. U.L.Rev. 365.

41. Cf. Illinois Cent. R. Co. v. Messina, 1916, 240 U.S. 395; Wickenburg v. Minneapolis, St. P. & S. S. M. R. Co., 1905, 94 Minn. 276, 102 N.W. 713; Texas-Louisiana Power Co. v. Daniels, 1936, 127 Tex. 126, 91 S. W.2d 302.

42. Sutton v. Town of Wauwatosa, 1871, 29 Wis. 21; Platz v. City of Cohoes, 1882, 89 N.Y. 219; Hoadley v. International Paper Co., 1899, 72 Vt. 79, 47 A. 169; cf. Welch v. Wesson, 1856, 6 Gray, Mass., 505. See also Bagre v. Daggett Chocolate Co., 1940, 126 Conn. 659, 13 A.2d 757 (winning candy box in bingo game does not bar recovery for negligence in manufacture).

43. Moore v. Hart, 1916, 171 Ky. 725, 188 S.W. 861; Kurtz v. Morse Oil Co., 1932, 114 Conn. 336, 158 A. 906; Speight v. Simonsen, 1925, 115 Or. 618, 239 P. 542. But cf. Johnson v. Boston & Me. R. R., 1928, 83 N.H. 350, 143 A. 516, interpreting the statute as fixing a standard of competence.

44. Armstead v. Lounsberry, 1915, 129 Minn. 34, 151 N.W. 542; Muller v. West Jersey & S. R. Co., 1923, 99 N.J.L. 186, 122 A. 693; Cobb v. Cumberland County Power & Light Co., 1918, 117 Me. 455, 104 A. 844.

although he is a criminal, can recover for his injuries if in other respects he is exercising proper care.

The accepted rule now is that a breach of statute by the plaintiff is to stand on the same footing as a violation by the defendant.[45] A few courts have held that the plaintiff's breach does not constitute contributory negligence as a matter of law, upon the ground that the statutes were enacted for the protection of others, and not of the actor himself.[46] But it seems clear that safety statutes, such as speed laws and traffic rules,[47] usually are designed for the broad purpose of preventing accidents or dangerous situations,[48] in which the plaintiff is quite as likely to be hurt as the defendant; and it is not difficult to discover a purpose to protect him by setting up a standard of his own conduct, the unexcused violation of which is negligence in itself.[49] If, as is infrequently the case, the statute is found to be intended solely for the protection of other persons,[50] or the prevention of a different type of risk,[51] the

breach will be irrelevant, or at best evidence of negligence for the jury.[52] The often repeated statement that in such cases the breach of statute is not the proximate cause of the harm has no more validity here than in the case of a violation on the part of the defendant.[53]

Compliance with Statute

Where the violation of a criminal statute is negligence, it does not follow that compliance with it is always due care. The statutory standard is no more than a minimum, and it does not necessarily preclude a finding that the actor was negligent in failing to take additional precautions. Thus the requirement of a hand signal on a left turn does not mean that the legislature has conferred immunity upon a driver who is otherwise negligent in making the turn, and that he is absolved from all obligation to slow down, keep a proper lookout, and proceed with reasonable care.[54] The same is of course true of administrative regulations.[55] Where there is a normal situation, clearly identical with that contemplated by the statute or regulation, and no special circumstances or danger are involved, it may be found, and can be ruled

45. Second Restatement of Torts, § 469; Notes, 1926, 39 Harv.L.Rev. 1088; 1935, 19 Minn.L.Rev. 666, 693; see Mechler v. McMahon, 1931, 184 Minn. 476, 239 N.W. 605, overruling a line of cases to the contrary.

46. See Dohm v. R. N. Cardozo & Bro., 1925, 165 Minn. 193, 206 N.W. 377; Watts v. Montgomery Traction Co., 1912, 175 Ala. 102, 106, 57 So. 471.

47. Henthorne v. Hopwood, 1959, 218 Or. 336, 338 P. 2d 373, rehearing denied, 1959, 218 Or. 336, 345 P.2d 249; Leap v. Royce, 1955, 203 Or. 566, 279 P.2d 887; Cardarelli v. Simon, 1942, 149 Pa.Super. 364, 27 A.2d 250; Le Tourneau v. Johnson, 1931, 185 Minn. 46, 239 N.W. 768; Lloyd v. Pugh, 1914, 158 Wis. 441, 149 N.W. 150. Contra, Kline v. Pennsylvania R. Co., 6 Cir.1925, 9 F.2d 290.

48. Second Restatement of Torts, § 469; Notes, 1935, 19 Minn.L.Rev. 666, 696; 1926, 39 Harv.L.Rev. 1088.

49. Dimick v. Linnell, 1965, 240 Or. 509, 402 P.2d 734; Fay v. Boston & Me. R. Co., 1959, 338 Mass. 531, 156 N.E.2d 24; Brown v. Jennings-Lawrence Co., 1958, 107 Ohio App. 409, 154 N.E.2d 154; Leap v. Royce, 1955, 203 Or. 566, 279 P.2d 887; and see cases cited supra, note 47.

50. Kline v. Pennsylvania R. Co., 6 Cir.1925, 9 F.2d 290; Dohm v. R. N. Cardozo & Bro., 1925, 165 Minn. 193, 206 N.W. 377.

51. Salvitti v. Throppe, 1942, 343 Pa. 642, 23 A.2d 445; Chattanooga R. & L. Co. v. Bettis, 1918, 139 Tenn. 332, 202 S.W. 70; Berry v. Sugar Notch Borough, 1899, 191 Pa. 345, 43 A. 240.

52. Corbett v. Scott, 1926, 243 N.Y. 66, 152 N.E. 467; Dohm v. R. N. Cardozo & Bro., 1925, 165 Minn. 193, 206 N.W. 377.

53. Green, Contributory Negligence and Proximate Cause, 1927, 6 N.C.L.Rev. 3, 13.

54. Curtis v. Perry, 1933, 171 Wash. 542, 18 P.2d 840. Cf. Mitchell v. Hotel Berry Co., 1929, 34 Ohio App. 259, 171 N.E. 39 (requirements as to hotel exits in case of fire); Caviote v. Shea, 1933, 116 Conn. 569, 165 A. 788 (parking car on highway in fog with tail light on); Peterson v. Salt River Project Agr. Imp. & Power District, 1964, 96 Ariz. 1, 391 P.2d 567 (red flag on end of towed long pole).

55. Hubbard-Hall Chemical Co. v. Silverman, 1 Cir. 1965, 340 F.2d 402; McGettigan v. New York Cent. R. Co., 1935, 268 N.Y. 66, 196 N.E. 745; Paolinelli v. Dainty Foods Mfrs., 1944, 322 Ill.App. 586, 54 N.E. 2d 759; Mississippi Power & Light Co. v. Whitescarver, 5 Cir.1934, 68 F.2d 628; Hayes v. New England Tel. & Tel. Co., 1934, 86 N.H. 486, 174 A. 49.

as matter of law, that the actor has done his full duty by complying with the statute, and nothing more is required. Thus a railroad may not be required to protect a country crossing, with an unobstructed view, which is little used, by anything more than the statutory warning sign.[56] But if there are unusual circumstances, or increased danger beyond the minimum which the statute was designed to meet, it may be found that there is negligence in not doing more.[57]

---

56. Leisy v. Northern Pac. R. Co., 1950, 230 Minn. 61, 40 N.W. 626; Gigliotti v. New York, C. & St. L. R. Co., 1958, 107 Ohio App. 174, 157 N.E.2d 447 (ordinary crossing with ordinary hazard). Cf. Turner v. Bennett, 1913, 161 Iowa 379, 142 N.W. 999 (turning on lights an hour after sunset); Shramek v. Huff, 1938, 135 Neb. 178, 280 N.W. 450 (stairway railing).

57. Grand Trunk R. Co. v. Ives, 1892, 144 U.S. 408; Pratt, Read & Co. v. New York, N. H. & H. R. Co., 1925, 102 Conn. 735, 130 A. 102, reargument denied 103 Conn. 508, 131 A. 395; Licha v. Northern Pac. R. Co., 1937, 201 Minn. 427, 276 N.W. 813; New York Cent. R. Co. v. Chernew, 8 Cir.1960, 285 F.2d 189; Southern Pac. R. Co. v. Mitchell, 1956, 80 Ariz. 50, 292 P.2d 827. See Morris, The Role of Criminal Statutes in Negligence Actions, 1949, 49 Col.L.Rev. 21, 42; Notes, 1938, 22 Minn.L.Rev. 901; 1938, 37 Mich.L.Rev. 150.

CHAPTER 6

NEGLIGENCE: PROOF

37. FUNCTIONS OF COURT AND JURY

The existence of negligence in a particular case often is said to be a mixed question of law and fact. By this it is meant, not only that both the court and the jury have an important part to play in the determination of the issue, and that separate functions are assigned to each, but further, that these functions to some extent overlap, and that it is not easy to fix any definite line of demarcation.[1] It is said also that the court must decide questions of law, and the jury questions of fact. But this means little or nothing until some method of classification is provided, by which "law" may be distinguished from "fact;" and the division of functions between court and jury is a matter rather of historical origins and present policy than of any such definitions.[2]

The issue of negligence presents at least five more or less distinct questions, as to which the court and the jury have separate parts to play in reaching a decision. These are as follows:

1. The sufficiency of the evidence to permit a finding of the facts. Before any duty, or any standard of conduct may be set, there must first be proof of facts which give rise to it; and once the standard is fixed, there must be proof that the actor has departed from it. If it be assumed that the driver of an automobile approaching a visible intersection will be required to moderate his speed, there is still the question whether the intersection was visible, and whether he did in fact slow down. These are purely questions of fact, and within the recognized province of the jury as the triers of fact. But over such questions of fact the courts always have reserved a preliminary power of decision, as to whether the issue shall be submitted to the jury at all.[3] If the evidence is such that no reasonably intelligent man would accept it as sufficient to establish the existence of a fact essential to negligence, it becomes the duty of the court to remove the issue from the jury, and to nonsuit the plaintiff, or direct a verdict for the defendant, or even to set aside a verdict once rendered.[4] Less frequently, the evidence may be so overwhelm-

---

1. Bohlen, Mixed Questions of Law and Fact, 1924, 72 U.Pa.L.Rev. 111, 112; James, Functions of Judge and Jury in Negligence Cases, 1949, 58 Yale L.J. 667. There are particularly good discussions of detail in Weiner, The Civil Jury Trial and the Law-Fact Distinction, 1966, 54 Cal.L.Rev. 1867; Baer, The Relative Roles of Legal Rules and Non-Legal Factors in Accident Litigation, 1952, 31 N.C.L.Rev. 46.

2. See the excellent and exhaustive discussion in James, Functions of Judge and Jury in Negligence Cases, 1949, 58 Yale L.J. 667. Also Thayer, Law and Fact in Jury Trials, 1890, 4 Harv.L.Rev. 147; Smith, Judges and Justice—The Judge's Role in Personal Injury Cases, [1962] U.Ill.L.Forum 172; Green, Juries and Justice—The Jury's Role in Personal Injury Cases, [1962] U.Ill.L.Forum 152.

3. Thayer, Preliminary Treatise on Evidence, 1898, 185, 202; Wigmore, Evidence, 3d ed.1940, § 2494; James, Functions of Judge and Jury in Negligence Cases, 1949, 58 Yale L.J. 667, 672–675.

4. Metropolitan R. Co. v. Jackson, [1877] 3 A.C. 193; Scott v. Hansen, 1940, 228 Iowa 37, 289 N.W. 710; Louisville & N. R. Co. v. Chambers, 1915, 165 Ky. 703, 178 S.W. 1041; Morgan v. Citizens' Bank, 1925, 190 N.C. 209, 129 S.E. 585; O'Connor v. Omaha & C. B. St. R. Co., 1920, 104 Neb. 534, 177 N.W. 838.

ing that no reasonable man could fail to accept the fact as proved; and the court must then direct the jury accordingly.[5] This is, of course, merely a part of the general law of evidence, and in this respect negligence cases do not differ from any other cases where essential facts must be proved.

2. The weight of the evidence as establishing the facts. Once it is determined that reasonable men may differ as to whether a fact has been proved, the probative value of the evidence, and the conclusion to be drawn from it, lies in the hands of the jury. They must not only decide as to the credibility of the testimony, but draw or refuse to draw any inferences from the testimony as to which there may be reasonable difference of opinion.[6] In this respect again, negligence cases do not differ from any others.

3. The existence of a duty. In other words, whether, upon the facts in evidence, such a relation exists between the parties that the community will impose a legal obligation upon one for the benefit of the other —or, more simply, whether the interest of the plaintiff which has suffered invasion was entitled to legal protection at the hands of the defendant. This is entirely a question of law, to be determined by reference to the body of statutes, rules, principles and precedents which make up the law; and it must

be determined only by the court.[7] It is no part of the province of a jury to decide whether a manufacturer of goods is under any obligation for the safety of the ultimate consumer, or whether the Long Island Railroad is required to protect Mrs. Palsgraf from fireworks explosions.[8] A decision by the court that, upon any version of the facts, there is no duty, must necessarily result in judgment for the defendant. A decision that, if certain facts are found to be true, a duty exists, leaves open the other questions now under consideration.

4. The general standard of conduct. As will be seen hereafter,[9] this is the necessary complement of duty. In negligence cases, once a duty is found, the duty, in theory at least, always requires the same standard of conduct, that of a reasonable man under the same or similar circumstances [10]—except perhaps in those jurisdictions where statutory or common law modifications have recognized "degrees" of care, and a higher or lower standard in particular cases.[11] Since the standard is a legal rule, from which the jury are not free to deviate, it is a matter of law, and is to be applied by the court. Almost invariably this application takes the form of an instruction to the jury declaring, briefly or more fully,[12] a formula such as that

---

5. This is true, for example, where the "incontrovertible physical facts" contradict the actor's testimony as to his use of care—as where he is placed in the familiar dilemma that he either must not have looked, must have failed to observe what was plainly visible, or must have disregarded what he saw. Heindel v. Transcontinental Ins. Co., La.App.1955, 82 So.2d 491; Miller v. North Carolina R. Co., 1942, 220 N.C. 562, 18 S.E.2d 232; Krause v. Baltimore & O. R. Co., 1944, 183 Md. 664, 39 A.2d 795; Danks v. Pittsburgh R. Co., 1937, 328 Pa. 356, 195 A. 16; Chandler v. Buchanan, 1927, 173 Minn. 31, 216 N.W. 254. See Note, 1932, 37 Dick.L.Rev. 58.

6. Loveland v. Nelson, 1926, 235 Mich. 623, 209 N.W. 835; Sweeney v. Erving, 1912, 228 U.S. 233; Kleinman v. Banner Laundry Co., 1921, 150 Minn. 515, 186 N.W. 123; Hughes v. Atlantic City & S. R. Co., 1914, 85 N.J.L. 212, 89 A. 769.

7. "Hence it becomes imperative before legal liability for conceded damages can be imposed upon a defendant, for the court in the first instance to inquire and determine the character of the duty which the law under the facts imposed upon the defendant as the basis of liability; for manifestly it cannot be conceded that the jury from their inner consciousness may evolve in every variety of tort-feasance a legal duty as the standard of liability." Minturn, J., in Morril v. Morril, 1928, 104 N.J.L. 557, 142 A. 337, 339. See Georgia Ry. & Electric Co. v. Cole, 1907, 1 Ga.App. 33, 57 S.E. 1026; Green, Judge and Jury, 1930, 55.

8. See infra, p. 254.

9. Infra, § 53.

10. See supra, p. 150.

11. See supra, p. 181.

12. Perhaps the most scholarly attempt at an elaborate instruction is that of Rosenberry, C. J., in

of the reasonable man of ordinary prudence. There is room for considerable skepticism as to how far such instructions are understood by the average jury, or have any weight with them,[13] but they represent the attempt, so far as is reasonably possible, to enlighten the layman's ignorance of the law, and to impose a social, rather than an individual standard.[14]

5. The particular standard of conduct. Since it is impossible to prescribe definite rules in advance for every combination of circumstances which may arise, the details of the standard must be filled in in each particular case. The question then is what the reasonable man would have done under the circumstances. Under our system of procedure, this question is to be determined in all doubtful cases by the jury, because the public insists that its conduct be judged in part by the man in the street rather than by lawyers, and the jury serves as a shock-absorber to cushion the impact of the law.[15]

The question usually is said to be one of fact, but it should be apparent that the function of the jury in fixing the standard differs from that of the judge only in that it cannot be reduced to anything approaching a definite rule.[16]

In many cases, however, the court may be required to remove the issue of the particular standard from the jury. It is possible to say, in many cases, that the conduct of the individual clearly has or has not conformed to what the community requires, and that no reasonable judgment could reach a contrary conclusion. The court must then direct a verdict for the plaintiff or for the defendant, or even set aside a verdict once rendered;[17] or, if the evidence as to the facts is in conflict, instruct the jury as to the conclusion it must draw from a particular version of the facts. Thus the court may rule that it is necessarily negligence to drive across a railway track without stopping to look and listen,[18] to cross the street without looking,[19] or to walk into the side of a passing automobile,[20] to drive at such a speed that it is impossible to stop within the range of vision,[21] or to ride with a driv-

Osborne v. Montgomery, 1931, 203 Wis. 223, 234 N.W. 372, inspired by the Restatement of Torts:

"Every person is negligent when, without intending to do any wrong, he does such an act or omits to take such precaution that under the circumstances he, as an ordinarily prudent person, ought reasonably to foresee that he will thereby expose the interests of another to an unreasonable risk of harm. In determining whether his conduct will subject the interests of another to an unreasonable risk of harm, a person is required to take into account such of the surrounding circumstances as would be taken into account by a reasonably prudent person and possess such knowledge as is possessed by an ordinarily reasonable person and to use such judgment and discretion as is exercised by persons of reasonable intelligence under the same or similar circumstances."

13. See Farley, Instructions to Juries—Their Role in the Judicial Process, 1932, 42 Yale L.J. 194.

14. See Green, The Negligence Issue, 1928, 37 Yale L.J. 1029, reprinted in Green, Judge and Jury, 1930, 153–185; James, Functions of Judge and Jury in Negligence Cases, 1949, 58 Yale L.J. 667, 680–685.

15. Bohlen, Mixed Questions of Law and Fact, 1924, 72 U.Pa.L.Rev. 111, 116. Cf. Prickett v. Sulzberger & Sons Co., 1916, 57 Okl. 567, 594, 157 P. 356; and see Heimer v. Salisbury, 1928, 108 Conn. 180, 142 A. 749.

16. See Bohlen, Mixed Questions of Law and Fact, 1924, 72 U.Pa.L.Rev. 111, 115, describing the function as "administrative." Also Weiner, The Civil Nonjury Trial and the Law-Fact Distinction, 1967, 55 Cal.L.Rev. 1021.

17. See Smith, The Power of a Judge to Direct a Verdict, 1924, 24 Col.L.Rev. 111.

18. Baltimore & O. R. Co. v. Goodman, 1927, 275 U.S. 66; Baltimore & O. R. Co. v. Bruchy, 1931, 161 Md. 175, 155 A. 346; Murray v. Southern Pac. Co., 1917, 177 Cal. 1, 169 P. 675; Fitzpatrick v. Kansas City Southern R. Co., 1940, 347 Mo. 57, 146 S.W.2d 560. See Note, 1933, 17 Minn.L.Rev. 771.

19. Boaze v. Windridge & Handy, 1939, 70 U.S.App. D.C. 24, 102 F.2d 628; Boyd v. Maruski, 1948, 321 Mich. 71, 32 N.W.2d 53; Standard Oil Co. v. Noakes, 6 Cir. 1932, 59 F.2d 897; Turnquist v. Rosaia Bros., 1938, 196 Wash. 434, 83 P.2d 353.

20. Provinsal v. Peterson, 1918, 141 Minn. 122, 169 N.W. 481; Mayer v. Anderson, 1918, 36 Cal.App. 740, 173 P. 174; Wood v. Woodlawn Improv. Ass'n Transp. Corp., 1926, 215 App.Div. 628, 214 N.Y.S. 398.

21. Bielecki v. United Trucking Service, 1929, 247 Mich. 661, 226 N.W. 675; Kelly v. Knabb, D.Fla.

er who is known to be drunk;[22] or that it is not negligence to fail to take precautions which no reasonable man would consider necessary under the circumstances.[23] Particularly where the standard of conduct is taken from a statute, the court must ordinarily rule that a departure from it is negligence in itself.[24] An uneasy distrust of the jury, and of the layman's known propensity to be charitable with other people's money and to compensate any injury which has occurred, especially at the expense of corporations, has played no small part in this process by which "learned reason"[25] and the greater experience of the judge[26] are substituted for the opinion of twelve more or less good men and true.[27]

While the function of the court, then, is primarily to determine the law, it must also decide some questions of fact, as to whether the evidence makes an issue sufficient for the jury; and the function of the jury in fixing the standard of reasonable conduct is so closely related to law that it amounts to a mere filling in of the details of the legal standard.

Courts seldom divide the issue of negligence into such separate questions. The most common statement is that if men of reasonable intelligence may differ as to the conclusion to be drawn, the issue must be left to the jury; otherwise it is for the court.[28]

38. BURDEN OF PROOF AND PRESUMPTIONS

Under our adversary system of litigation, which requires that all evidence be produced by the parties themselves, some method must be found to dispose of those cases in which the evidence is so inadequate, or so conflicting, that neither party can satisfy the triers of fact as to the truth of his version of the case. Some one must lose. This "risk of non-persuasion"[29] is called the burden of proof. It is of practical importance in relatively few cases, since few cases ever are so evenly balanced as to require decision on any such basis; but it often appears in instructions to the jury, based upon the possibility that such may be the case.

In civil suits, unlike criminal prosecutions, the burden of proof does not require that the jury be convinced beyond all reasonable doubt, but only that they be persuaded that a preponderance of the evidence is in favor of the party sustaining the burden.[30] This is true as to the issue of negligence, even though the act to be proved may also be a crime.[31] The burden of proof of the defendant's negligence is quite uniformly upon the

---

1924, 300 F. 256; Serfas v. Lehigh & N. E. R. Co., 1921, 270 Pa. 306, 113 A. 370.

22. Schwartz v. Johnson, 1926, 152 Tenn. 586, 280 S.W. 32; Wayson v. Rainier Taxi Co., 1925, 136 Wash. 274, 239 P. 559.

23. Noll v. Marian, 1943, 347 Pa. 213, 32 A.2d 18; Pennsylvania R. Co. v. Cook, 1942, 180 Md. 633, 26 A.2d 384; Carlstrom v. North Star Concrete Co., 1917, 138 Minn. 151, 164 N.W. 661; Troutman's Adm'x v. Louisville & N. R. Co., 1918, 179 Ky. 145, 200 S.W. 488.

24. See supra, p. 200.

25. Allen, Learned and Unlearned Reason, 1924, 36 Jurid.Rev. 254, 262.

26. Holmes, The Common Law, 1881, 124.

27. Bohlen, Mixed Questions of Law and Fact, 1924, 72 U.Pa.L.Rev. 111, 118.

28. Grand Trunk R. Co. v. Ives, 1892, 144 U.S. 408; Faucett v. Bergmann, 1927, 57 U.S.App.D.C. 290, 22 F.2d 718, 720; Downing v. Merchants' Nat. Bank, 1921, 192 Iowa 1250, 1254, 184 N.W. 722, 725; Cleveland, C. C. & St. L. R. Co. v. Stewart, 1903, 161 Ind. 242, 63 N.E. 170.

29. Wigmore, Evidence, 3d Ed. 1940, § 2485.

30. Botta v. Brunner, 1958, 26 N.J. 82, 138 A.2d 713 (error to charge that plaintiff must prove his case by "clear and convincing evidence" and with "reasonable certainty"). See Wigmore, Evidence, 3d ed. 1940, § 2498; Groom, Proof of Crime in a Civil Proceeding, 1929, 13 Minn.L.Rev. 556. Also the discussion of techniques of proof in Morris, Proof of Negligence, 1953, 47 Northw.U.L.Rev. 817.

31. Galloway v. United Railroads of San Francisco, 1921, 51 Cal.App. 575, 197 P. 663; Grella v. Lewis Wharf Co., 1912, 211 Mass. 54, 97 N.E. 745.

plaintiff,[32] since he is asking the court for relief, and must lose if his case does not outweigh that of his adversary. Notwithstanding a great deal of confused and careless language in the opinions, this appears to be true, except in Louisiana,[33] both as to the action of a bailor against his bailee for loss or damage to the goods,[34] and that of a passenger injured on a common carrier,[35] although in each case the plaintiff may be aided by a presumption.[36] It is generally agreed, however, that a carrier of goods, who is an insurer against everything but a few exceptional perils, has the burden of proving that the loss or damage to the goods falls within one of the exceptions,[37] after which it is the prevailing

view that the burden is upon the plaintiff to show any negligence of the carrier responsible for the harm under such circumstances.[38]

In some types of cases, such as those of medical malpractice,[39] where laymen on the jury are not competent to judge whether the actor's conduct meets the proper standard, expert testimony may be essential, and the burden of proof cannot be sustained without it;[40] and even where it is not indispensable, it may be a valuable aid to the plaintiff.[41]

Presumptions

The party having the burden of proof may be aided by the procedural devices known as presumptions. A presumption has been defined as "an assumption of the existence of one fact which the law requires the trier of fact to make on account of the existence of another fact or group of facts, standing alone."[42] It is, in other words, a rule of law for the determination of a question of fact, in the absence of sufficient evidence to prove the fact itself. The classic illustration of a presumption is the rule which calls for the conclusion that a man is dead when it is shown that he has disappeared for seven

32. Clark v. Lang, 1919, 124 Va. 544, 98 S.E. 673; Lane v. Cardwell, Ky.1957, 306 S.W.2d 290; Memphis St. R. Co. v. Cavell, 1916, 135 Tenn. 462, 187 S.W. 179; Mulligan v. Atlantic Coast Line R. Co., 1916, 104 S.C. 173, 88 S.E. 445, affirmed, 1917, 242 U.S. 620; Klein v. Beeten, 1919, 169 Wis. 385, 172 N.W. 736. As to contributory negligence of the plaintiff, see infra, p. 416.

33. A civil law jurisdiction, which puts this burden on the defendant. Jeter v. Lachle, La.App.1958, 106 So.2d 808 (bailee); Johnson v. Continental Southern Lines, Inc., La.App.1959, 113 So.2d 114 (carrier of passengers); Coleman v. Continental Southern Lines, Inc., La.App.1958, 107 So.2d 69 (same).

34. Commercial Molasses Corp. v. New York Tank Barge Corp., 1941, 314 U.S. 104; Edward Hines Lumber Co. v. Purvine Logging Co., 1965, 240 Or. 60, 399 P.2d 893; Revenue Aero Club v. Alexandria Airport, 1951, 192 Va. 231, 64 S.E.2d 671; Banachowski v. Saunders, Mun.App.D.C.1963, 187 A.2d 891; Deloach v. Automatic Transmission & Brake Shop, 1962, 106 Ga.App. 797, 128 S.E.2d 512. See Sweet, Burden of Proof of Bailee's Negligence in Connection With His Failure to Redeliver, 1957, 8 Hast. L.J. 89; Brodkey, Practical Aspects of Bailment Proof, 1962, 45 Marq.L.Rev. 531.

35. Old South Lines v. McCuistan, 5 Cir. 1937, 92 F.2d 441; Jones v. Baltimore Transit Co., 1956, 211 Md. 423, 127 A.2d 649; Oppenheim v. Pitcairn, 1940, 293 Mich. 475, 292 N.W. 374; Ginsberg v. Metropolitan Transit Authority, 1956, 333 Mass. 514, 131 N.E.2d 919; Byron v. Public Service Coordinated Transport, 1939, 122 N.J.L. 451, 5 A.2d 483; see Note, 1966, 42 Wash.L.Rev. 273.

36. See infra, p. 210.

37. Atlantic Coast Line R. Co. v. J. W. Maddox & Co., 1923, 210 Ala. 444, 98 So. 276; Goodman v. New York, N. H. & H. R. Co., 1936, 295 Mass. 330, 3 N.E.

2d 777; Blair v. Pennsylvania Greyhound Lines, 1936, 275 Mich. 636, 267 N.W. 578; Barnet v. New York Cent. & H. R. R. Co., 1918, 222 N.Y. 195, 118 N.E. 625; Port Terminal R. R. Ass'n v. Rohm & Haas Co., Tex.Civ.App.1963, 371 S.W.2d 403.

38. Dobie, Bailments and Carriers, 1914, 348–9; Oakland Meat Co. v. Railway Express Agency, 1964, 46 Ill.App.2d 176, 196 N.E.2d 361.

39. See supra, p. 164.

40. Cf. Kelly v. McKay, 1950, 149 Tex. 343, 233 S.W.2d 121 (quantity of explosive); Air Reduction Co. v. Philadelphia Storage Battery Co., 3 Cir., 1926, 14 F.2d 734 (handling oxygen); Jones v. Chicago, B. & Q. R. Co., 1939, 343 Mo. 1104, 125 S.W.2d 5 (drainage capacity of a waterway).

41. Cf. Muller v. Kirschbaum Co., 1930, 298 Pa. 560, 148 A. 851; Higgins v. Town of Carroll, 1933, 86 N.H. 312, 167 A. 271; Heinmiller v. Winston Bros., 1906, 131 Iowa 32, 107 N.W. 1102. See Morris, The Role of Expert Testimony in the Trial of Negligence Issues, 1947, 26 Tex.L.Rev. 1.

42. Morgan, Some Observations Concerning Presumptions, 1931, 44 Harv.L.Rev. 906.

years without explanation. The nature and effect of presumptions is a matter of vigorous controversy, which lies beyond the scope of this text. Courts and writers have not agreed as to the precise meaning of the term in all respects, or as to the procedural effect which is to follow when a presumption is found.[43]

There is, however, general agreement that presumptions are rules of law, and their application is for the court. Probably the greater number of presumptions are created merely for the purpose of giving effect, as a settled rule, to the normal inference or conclusion which most people would draw, if permitted, from a given set of facts, in the absence of satisfactory definite evidence as to the conclusion itself. Most of the presumptions associated with negligence are of this kind: for example, the presumptions, often stated, that a person is in possession of normal faculties and reason,[44] and that the instinct of self-preservation has made him exercise proper care for his own safety.[45] Such

presumptions require that in the absence of evidence to the contrary, the court must decide the issue and direct the jury. They place upon the adverse party the "burden" of going forward and offering further evidence, in the sense that a verdict will be directed against him if he does not; but they do not affect the ultimate burden of proof, as to the preponderance of the total evidence required, once all the evidence is in. When persuasive evidence to the contrary is introduced, the occasion for the presumptions, as rules of law, is gone, and they simply cease to exist, "like bats of law flitting in the twilight, but disappearing in the sunshine of actual facts."[46] All that remains is whatever inference from ordinary experience is to be drawn from the facts, which has whatever probative value the facts may justify.[47]

There are, however, other presumptions which obviously are imposed in part as a matter of policy, to compel persons in a position of special responsibility to disclose evidence within their control, under penalty of a procedural disadvantage in the case if they do not. They are, in other words, "smoking out" presumptions, designed to bring about a result rather than to give effect to probabilities.[48] Such, for example, are the presumptions that when goods are delivered to a bailee in good condition, and are either not returned or returned in bad condition, the loss or damage is due to the negligence of the bailee;[49] that when a passenger is injured

43. See Thayer, Preliminary Treatise on Evidence, 1898, 313–352; Wigmore, Evidence, 3d Ed. 1940, § 2490; Bohlen, The Effect of Rebuttable Presumptions of Law Upon the Burden of Proof, 1920, 68 U.Pa.L.Rev. 307; McCormick, Charges on Presumptions and Burden of Proof, 1927, 5 N.C.L.Rev. 291; Morgan, Some Observations Concerning Presumptions, 1931, 44 Harv.L.Rev. 906; Morgan, Instructing the Jury Upon Presumptions and Burden of Proof, 1933, 47 Harv.L.Rev. 59; McBaine, Presumptions: Are They Evidence, 1938, 26 Cal.L.Rev. 519; Reaugh, Presumptions and the Burden of Proof, 1942, 36 Ill.L.Rev. 703, 819; Gausewitz, Presumptions in a One-Rule World, 1952, 5 Vand.L.Rev. 324.

44. Artman v. Kansas Cent. R. Co., 1879, 22 Kan. 296; Brown v. Union Pac. R. Co., 1910, 81 Kan. 701, 106 P. 1001; Kramm v. Stockton Elec. Co., 1909, 10 Cal.App. 271, 101 P. 914.

45. Baltimore & Potomac R. Co. v. Landrigan, 1903, 191 U.S. 461; Korab v. Chicago, R. I. & P. R. Co., 1910, 149 Iowa 711, 128 N.W. 529; Wilkins v. Bradford, 1929, 247 Mich. 157, 225 N.W. 609; Odgers v. Clark, 1941, 2 Terry, Del., 232, 19 A.2d 724.

This presumption would seem to be of importance only in jurisdictions which place the burden of proof of the issue of contributory negligence upon the plaintiff. Wabash R. Co. v. De Tar, 8 Cir., 1905, 141 F. 932. Otherwise it amounts merely to an application of the rule as to the burden of proof,

or a permissible inference from ordinary experience. See Note, 1931, 15 Minn.L.Rev. 473.

46. Lamm, J., in Mockowik v. Kansas City St. J. & C. B. R. Co., 1906, 196 Mo. 550, 571, 94 S.W. 256.

47. Wigmore, Evidence, 3d Ed. 1940, § 2491.

48. The basic idea is set forth at length in Jaffe, Res Ipsa Loquitur Vindicated, 1951, 1 Buff.L.Rev. 1.

49. Girard Trust Corn Exchange Bank v. Brinks, Inc., 1966, 422 Pa. 48, 220 A.2d 827; McKenzie v. Hanson, N.D.1966, 143 N.W.2d 697; Milwaukee Automobile Mut. Ins. Co. v. Hansord Pontiac Co., 1965, 271 Minn. 567, 136 N.W.2d 381; Banachowski v. Saunders, Mun.App.D.C.1963, 187 A.2d 891; Falls Church Airpark Co. v. Mooney Aircraft, Inc., 5 Cir. 1958, 254 F.2d 920.

by a cause within the carrier's control the carrier has been negligent;[50] and that when goods are damaged in transit over a series of carriers, the last carrier has caused the damage.[51] Quite frequently careless use of language, or genuine confusion, has led to a statement of such presumptions in terms of a "burden of proof" upon the defendant, rather than the mere "burden" of going forward with the production of evidence under penalty of a direction on the issue.[52] Some writers have contended that the policy underlying such presumptions can only be carried out by allowing them to persist in the face of contrary evidence, or by shifting the burden of proof to the adverse party and requiring a preponderance of the evidence to overthrow the presumption.[53] Others consider that the policy may be sufficiently served by instructing the jury that they must apply the presumption unless they believe the contrary evidence.[54] The writers, if not all of the courts, seem to have agreed that in any case a presumption, as a rule of law applied in the absence of evidence, is not itself evidence, and can no more be balanced against evidence than two and a half pounds of sugar can

be weighed against half-past two in the afternoon.

39. CIRCUMSTANTIAL EVIDENCE— RES IPSA LOQUITUR

It is often said that negligence must be proved, and never will be presumed.[55] The mere fact that an accident or an injury has occurred, with nothing more, is not evidence of negligence on the part of anyone. The fact that a man is found dead upon a railway track after a train has passed is no proof that the train was run without proper care.[56] There is of course, as a matter of speculation, sufficiently interesting in itself, always the possibility that the man may have been killed by reason of negligent operation of the train; but for a decision imposing liability to respond in damages, this is not enough. What is required is evidence, which means some form of proof; and it must be evidence from which reasonable men may conclude that, upon the whole, it is more likely that the event was caused by negligence than that it was not. As long as the conclusion is a matter of mere speculation or conjecture,[57] or where the probabilities are at best evenly balanced between negligence and its absence,[58] it becomes the duty of the court to direct the

---

50. Southern Pac. Co. v. Cavin, 9 Cir., 1906, 144 F. 348; Steele v. Southern R. Co., 1899, 55 S.C. 389, 33 S.E. 509; Williams v. Spokane Falls & N. R. Co., 1905, 39 Wash. 77, 80 P. 1100.

51. Dunlap v. Great Northern R. Co., 1914, 34 S.D. 320, 148 N.W. 529; St. Louis, I. M. & S. R. Co. v. Coolidge, 1904, 73 Ark. 112, 83 S.W. 333. The presumption is not affected by the Carmack Amendment to the Interstate Commerce Act, 49 U.S.C.A. § 20 (11, 12), making the initial carrier liable for the damage. Chicago & N. W. R. Co. v. C. C. Whitnack Produce Co., 1922, 258 U.S. 369.

52. Cf. Holmes v. Harden, 1957, 96 Ga.App. 365, 100 S.E.2d 101; Central Mut. Ins. Co. v. Whetstone, 1957, 249 Minn. 334, 81 N.W.2d 849.

53. Morgan, Some Observations Concerning Presumptions, 1931, 44 Harv.L.Rev. 906; Bohlen, The Effect of Rebuttable Presumptions of Law Upon the Burden of Proof, 1920, 68 U.Pa.L.Rev. 307.

54. McBaine, Presumptions: Are They Evidence, 1938, 26 Cal.L.Rev. 519. Cf. McCormick, Charges on Presumptions and Burden of Proof, 1927, 5 N.C.L.Rev. 291.

55. Kemp v. McNeil Cooperage Co., 1918, 7 Boyce, Del., 146, 104 A. 639; McCombe v. Public Service R. Co., 1920, 95 N.J.L. 187, 112 A. 255.

56. Johnson v. Mobile & O. R. Co., 1917, 178 Ky. 108, 198 S.W. 538. Accord: Tower v. Humboldt Transit Co., 1917, 176 Cal. 602, 169 P. 227; Mardo v. Valley Smokeless Coal Co., 1924, 279 Pa. 209, 123 A. 779; New v. Bradshaw, 1922, 89 Okl. 205, 214 P. 557.

57. Benedick v. Potts, 1898, 88 Md. 52, 40 A. 1067; Southwestern Greyhound Lines v. Smith, Okl.1954, 277 P.2d 157; Wardwell v. George H. Taylor Co., 1955, 333 Mass. 302, 130 N.E.2d 586; Digelormo v. Weil, 1932, 260 N.Y. 192, 183 N.E. 360, reargument denied, 1933, 261 N.Y. 536, 185 N.E. 728; West v. United States, 3 Cir.1957, 246 F.2d 443.

58. Tower v. Humboldt Transit Co., 1917, 176 Cal. 602, 169 P. 227; Johnson v. Mobile & O. R. Co., 1917, 178 Ky. 108, 198 S.W. 538; Lawson v. Anderson & Kerr Drilling Co., 1938, 184 Okl. 107, 84 P.2d 1104; Mardo v. Valley Smokeless Coal Co., 1924, 279 Pa. 209, 123 A. 779.

jury that the burden of proof has not been sustained.

This does not mean, however, that there must be in every case eye-witnesses of the defendant's conduct. Negligence, like any other fact, may be proved by circumstantial evidence.[59] This is evidence of one fact, or of a set of facts, from which the existence of the fact to be determined may reasonably be inferred.[60] It involves, in addition to the assertion of witnesses as to what they have observed, a process of reasoning, or inference, by which a conclusion is drawn. Thus it may be reasonable to infer, from skid marks or other traces of an accident, that an automobile was driven at excessive speed;[61] from the usual operation of lights that they were turned out by those who had done so before;[62] or from the fact that soon after the passage of a train a fire started up beside the track, that it was caused by negligence in controlling sparks from the train.[63]

Defense counsel in criminal cases have long made us familiar with the weaknesses of some kinds of circumstantial evidence; but there is still no man who would not accept dog tracks in the mud against the sworn testimony of a hundred eye-witnesses that no dog has passed by. Like all other evidence, it may be strong or weak; it may be so unconvincing as to be quite worthless, or it may be irresistible and overwhelming. The gist of it, and the key to it, is the inference, or process of reasoning by which the conclusion is reached. This must be based upon the evidence given, together with a sufficient background of human experience to justify the conclusion. It is not enough that plaintiff's counsel can suggest a possibility of negligence. The evidence must sustain the burden of proof by making it appear more likely than not. The inference must cover all of the necessary elements of negligence,[64] and must point to a breach of the defendant's duty. The mere fact of the presence of a banana peel on a floor may not be sufficient to show that it has been there long enough for reasonable care to require the defendant to discover and remove it;[65] but if it is "black, flattened out and gritty,"[66] the conclusion

59. Wigmore, Evidence, 3d Ed. 1940, § 25; Miller, Some Problems of Proof in Negligence Actions, 1950, 2 Syr.L.Rev. 8.

60. Dixon v. Gaso P. & Burner Mfg. Co., 1937, 183 Okl. 249, 80 P.2d 678; Mathews v. Alabama Great Southern R. Co., 1917, 200 Ala. 251, 76 So. 17; Loveland v. Nelson, 1926, 235 Mich. 623, 209 N.W. 835; Mulligan v. Atlantic Coast Line R. Co., 1915, 104 S.C. 173, 88 S.E. 445.

61. Yates v. Chappell, 1965, 263 N.C. 461, 139 S.E.2d 728 (position of cars, violence of impact, extent of damage); McAlexander v. Lewis' Estate, 1958, 167 Neb. 524, 93 N.W.2d 632 (position of cars); Burkett v. Johnston, 1955, 39 Tenn.App. 276, 282 S.W.2d 647 (multiple facts); Gutierrez v. Public Service Int. Transp. Co., 2 Cir.1948, 168 F.2d 678 (fender of bus bent, plaintiff in gutter with torn trousers and smear of grease). Cf. Neff v. Firth, 1946, 354 Pa. 308, 47 A.2d 193 (failure to look); Kuntz v. Stelmachuk, N.D.1965, 136 N.W.2d 810 (same).

62. Korel v. United States, 4 Cir.1957, 246 F.2d 424. Cf. Drahmann's Adm'x v. Brink's Adm'x, Ky.1956, 290 S.W.2d 449 (plane piloted by one who usually did so); Frankel v. Johns-Manville Corp., E.D.Pa. 1955, 134 F.Supp. 108 (from what point did workman fall?); Brady v. Great A. & P. Tea Co., 1957, 336 Mass. 386, 145 N.E.2d 828 (reasons for fall of baby from shopping carriage).

63. Viera v. Atchison, T. & S. F. R. Co., 1909, 10 Cal.App. 267, 101 P. 690. Cf. Maus v. Broderick,

1899, 51 La.App. 1153, 25 So. 977 (runaway horse in the street); Breidenbach v. McCormick Co., 1913, 21 Cal.App. 709, 132 P. 771 (same).

64. Wigmore, Evidence, 3d Ed. 1940, § 2487.

65. Goddard v. Boston & Me. R. Co., 1901, 179 Mass. 52, 60 N.E. 486; Jones v. Sanitary Market, 1958, 185 Pa.Super. 163, 137 A.2d 859; Koer v. Mayfair Markets, 1967, 19 Utah 2d 339, 431 P.2d 566 (grape). Cf. Great A. & P. Tea Co. v. Bennett, 1958, 267 Ala. 538, 103 So.2d 177 (vegetable leaf); Food Fair Stores of Fla. v. Patty, Fla.1959, 109 So.2d 5, conformed to 109 So.2d 399 (green beans); Bell v. F. W. Woolworth Co., 1957, 44 Tenn.App. 587, 316 S.W.2d 34 (ice cream wrapper); White v. Sears, Roebuck & Co., 4 Cir.1957, 242 F.2d 821 (slippery substance).

Other circumstances may, however, supply the inference. Bozza v. Vornado, Inc., 1964, 42 N.J. 355, 200 A.2d 777 (litter on floor of cafeteria near counter); cf. Mahoney v. J. C. Penney Co., 1962, 71 N.M. 244, 377 P.2d 663; Wollerman v. Grand Union Stores, Inc., 1966, 47 N.J. 426, 221 A.2d 513.

66. Anjou v. Boston Elev. R. Co., 1911, 208 Mass. 273, 94 N.E. 386; Williamson v. F. W. Woolworth Co.,

may reasonably be drawn. It is for the court to determine, in the first instance, whether reasonable men on the jury may draw it.[67]

One type of circumstantial evidence, concerning which there has been much difference of opinion, is that which is given the name of res ipsa loquitur.[68] The Latin phrase, which means nothing more than "the thing speaks for itself," is the offspring of a casual word of Baron Pollock during argument with counsel in a case [69] in 1863 in which a barrel of flour rolled out of a warehouse window and fell upon a passing pedestrian. In its inception the principle was nothing more than a reasonable conclusion, from the circumstances of an unusual accident, that it was probably the defendant's fault. It soon became involved, however, in cases of injuries to passengers at the hands of carriers, with the aftermath of an older decision [70] which had held that the carrier had the burden of proving that it had not been negligent. The two principles, one concerned with the suffi-

ciency of circumstantial evidence, the other of the burden of proof, gradually became confused and intermingled; [71] and from this fusion there developed an uncertain "doctrine" of res ipsa loquitur, which has been the source of so much trouble to the courts that the use of the phrase itself has become a definite obstacle to any clear thought, and it might better be discarded entirely.[72] It is nevertheless accepted and applied by all of our courts, including those of South Carolina, which purport to reject it by name,[73] Michigan, which formerly did so,[74] and Pennsylvania, which purports to limit its application to cases in which the defendant has voluntarily undertaken some responsibility.[75]

The statement of this doctrine most often quoted is that of Chief Justice Erle in 1865: [76]

1960, 237 Miss. 141, 112 So.2d 529; Vaughn v. National Tea Co., 7 Cir.1964, 328 F.2d 128. Cf. Jacobs v. Great A. & P. Tea Co., 2 Cir.1963, 324 F.2d 50 (baby food); Kaplan v. Grand Department Stores, 1934, 118 Conn. 714, 174 A. 76 (worn rubber mat); Morton v. Manhattan Lunch Co., 1940, 41 Cal.App.2d 70, 106 P.2d 212 (worn linoleum).

67. See James, Proof of the Breach in Negligence Cases, 1951, 37 Va.L.Rev. 179.

68. See Carpenter, The Doctrine of Res Ipsa Loquitur, 1934, 1 U.Chi.L.Rev. 519; Carpenter, The Doctrine of Res Ipsa Loquitur in California, 1937, 10 So.Cal. L.Rev. 166; Malone, Res Ipsa Loquitur and Proof by Inference, 1941, 4 La.L.Rev. 70; Morris, Res Ipsa Loquitur in Texas, 1948, 26 Tex.L.Rev. 257, 761; Prosser, Res Ipsa Loquitur in California, 1949, 37 Cal.L.Rev. 183, reprinted in Prosser, Selected Topics on the Law of Torts, 1954, 302; James, Proof of the Breach in Negligence Cases, 1951, 37 Va.L.Rev. 179; Ghiardi, Res Ipsa Loquitur in Wisconsin, 1956, 39 Marq.L.Rev. 361; Notes, 1935, 3 U.Chi.L.Rev. 126; 1936, 85 U.Pa.L.Rev. 212; 1950, 35 Iowa L.Rev. 393; 1956, 5 U.Kan.L.Rev. 88; 1957, 33 Ind.L.J. 45.

69. Byrne v. Boadle, 1863, 2 H. & C. 722, 159 Eng. Rep. 299. Repeated, on substantially identical facts, in Hake v. George Wiedemann Brewing Co., 1970, —— Ohio St.2d ——, 262 N.E.2d 702.

70. Christie v. Griggs, 1809, 2 Camp. 79, 170 Eng.Rep. 1088.

71. See, illustrating the process: Southern Pac. Co. v. Cavin, 9 Cir.1906, 144 F. 348; George v. St. Louis, I. M. & S. R. Co., 1879, 34 Ark. 613; Central R. R. Co. v. Freeman, 1885, 75 Ga. 331; Cleveland, C. C. & I. R. Co. v. Newell, 1885, 104 Ind. 264, 3 N.E. 836; Baltimore & O. R. Co. v. State, to Use of Mahone, 1884, 63 Md. 135. See Note, 1957, 33 Ind.L.J. 45.

72. "It adds nothing to the law, has no meaning which is not more clearly expressed for us in English, and brings confusion to our legal discussions. It does not represent a doctrine, is not a legal maxim, and is not a rule." Bond, C. J., dissenting in Potomac Edison Co. v. Johnson, 1930, 160 Md. 33, 152 A. 633. See Bond, The Use of the Phrase Res Ipsa Loquitur, 1908, 66 Cent.L.J. 386; Prosser, The Procedural Effect of Res Ipsa Loquitur, 1936, 20 Minn.L.Rev. 241, 271.

"If that phrase had not been in Latin, nobody would have called it a principle." Lord Shaw, in Ballard v. North British R. Co., [1923] Sess.Cas., H.L., 43.

73. Shepherd v. U. S. Fidelity & Guaranty Co., 1958, 233 S.C. 536, 106 S.E.2d 381; Boyd v. Marion Coca Cola Bottling Co., 1962, 240 S.C. 383, 126 S.E.2d 178.

74. Michigan applies res ipsa loquitur "much as a disdainful lady might proclaim her profound aversion to strong drink just as she is tossing off a bumper of patent medicine harboring enough alcohol to floor a stevedore." Mitcham v. City of Detroit, 1959, 355 Mich. 182, 94 N.W.2d 388, 391.

75. See Skeen v. Stanley Co. of America, 1949, 362 Pa. 174, 66 A.2d 774; Fitzpatrick v. Penfield, 1920, 267 Pa.St. 564, 109 A. 653; Note, 1921, 70 U.Pa.L. Rev. 105.

76. In Scott v. London & St. Katherine Docks Co., 1865, 3 H. & C. 596, 159 Eng.Rep. 665.

"There must be reasonable evidence of negligence; but where the thing is shown to be under the management of the defendant or his servants, and the accident is such as in the ordinary course of things does not happen if those who have the management use proper care, it affords reasonable evidence, in the absence of explanation by the defendants, that the accident arose from want of care."

The conditions usually stated in America as necessary for the application of the principle of res ipsa loquitur were derived originally from the first edition of Wigmore on Evidence,[77] which appeared in 1905. They are as follows: (1) the event must be of a kind which ordinarily does not occur in the absence of someone's negligence; (2) it must be caused by an agency or instrumentality within the exclusive control of the defendant; (3) it must not have been due to any voluntary action or contribution on the part of the plaintiff. Some courts have at least suggested a fourth condition, that evidence as to the true explanation of the event must be more readily accessible to the defendant than to the plaintiff. As will be seen, this traditional formula is neither complete nor accurate so far as it goes. The various elements of the problem remain to be considered.

Inference that Someone was Negligent

The requirement that the occurrence be one which ordinarily does not happen without negligence is of course only another way of stating an obvious principle of circumstantial evidence: that the event must be such that in the light of ordinary experience it gives rise to an inference that some one must have been negligent. On this basis res ipsa loquitur has been applied to a wide variety of situations, and its range is as broad as the possible events which reasonably justify such a conclusion. It finds common application, for example, in the case of objects such as

bricks or window panes falling from the defendant's premises,[78] falling elevators,[79] the collapse of structures,[80] live stock loose on the highway,[81] the escape of gas or water from mains,[82] or of electricity from wires or appliances,[83] the explosion of boilers or other objects under the defendant's control,[84] or the escape of dust or noxious gases from his premises,[85] the sudden starting of machin-

77. 4 Wigmore, Evidence, 1st Ed. 1905, § 2509.

78. Kearney v. London, B. & S. C. R. Co., 1870, L.R. 5 Q.B. 411; Lipsitz v. Schechter, 1966, 377 Mich. 685, 142 N.W.2d 1; Both v. Harband, 1958, 164 Cal.App. 2d 743, 331 P.2d 140; Kelly v. Laclede Real Estate & Inv. Co., (1941) 348 Mo. 407, 155 S.W.2d 90; Levit's Jewelers, Inc. v. Friedman, Tex.Civ.App.1967, 410 S. W.2d 947.

79. Griffen v. Manice, 1901, 166 N.Y. 188, 59 N.E. 925; Littlefield v. Laughlin, Mo.1959, 327 S.W.2d 863; O'Connor v. Mennie, 1915, 169 Cal. 217, 146 P. 674; Cleary v. Cavanaugh, 1914, 219 Mass. 281, 106 N.E. 998; Kunzie v. Leeds, 1941, 66 Ohio App. 469, 34 N.E.2d 448.

80. Suko v. Northwestern Ice & Cold Storage Co., 1941, 166 Or. 557, 113 P.2d 209; Katz v. Goldring, 1933, 237 App.Div. 824, 260 N.Y.S. 796; Boyer v. Iowa High School Athletic Ass'n, 1967, 260 Iowa 1061, 152 N.W.2d 293.

81. O'Connor v. Black, 1958, 80 Idaho 96, 326 P.2d 376; Bender v. Welsh, 1942, 344 Pa. 392, 25 A.2d 182; Mercer v. Byrons, 1 Cir.1952, 200 F.2d 284.

82. George Foltis, Inc. v. City of New York, 1941, 287 N.Y. 108, 38 N.E.2d 455; Quigley v. Village of Hibbing, 1964, 268 Minn. 541, 129 N.W.2d 765; Skaggs Drug Centers, Inc. v. City of Idaho Falls, 1965, 90 Idaho 1, 407 P.2d 695; Adam Hat Stores, Inc. v. Kansas City, Mo.1958, 316 S.W.2d 594; Carmody v. Boston Gaslight Co., 1895, 162 Mass. 539, 39 N.E. 184.

83. Humphrey v. Twin State Gas & Elec. Co., 1927, 100 Vt. 414, 139 A. 440; Arkansas Light & Power Co. v. Jackson, 1925, 166 Ark. 633, 267 S.W. 359; Cain v. Southern Massachusetts Tel. Co., 1914, 219 Mass. 504, 107 N.E. 380; Mares v. New Mexico Public Service Co., 1938, 42 N.M. 473, 82 P.2d 257.

84. Kleinman v. Banner Laundry Co., 1921, 150 Minn. 515, 186 N.W. 123; Souden v. Fore River Shipbuilding Co., 1916, 223 Mass. 509, 112 N.E. 82. Cf. Metz v. Central Ill. Elec. & Gas Co., 1965, 32 Ill.2d 446, 207 N.E.2d 305 (gas line); Zurich Ins. Co. v. Missouri Edison Co., Mo.1964, 384 S.W.2d 623 (same); Baker v. Thompson-Hayward Chem. Co., Mo.App. 1958, 316 S.W.2d 652 (chlorine plant).

85. Reynolds Metals Co. v. Yturbide, 1958, 258 F.2d 321, cert. denied 358 U.S. 840; Martin v. Reynolds Metals Co., D.Or.1952, 135 F.Supp. 379, affirmed 258 F.2d 321, cert. denied 358 U.S. 840; McKenna v. Al-

ery,[86] injuries to passengers from causes within the control of the carrier, such as derailment,[87] the sudden stop of a bus,[88] or its defective equipment;[89] some kinds of automobile accidents, such as a car suddenly leaving the highway and going into the ditch[90] or colliding with a stationary object,[91] or starting down hill not long after it has been parked at the curb;[92] defective food in sealed containers,[93] and many other similar occurrences. There is an element of drama,[94] and of the freakish and improbable in a good many of these cases, which has led the courts on occasion to say that the event must be an "unusual" one;[95] but this is not at all indispensable, and very commonplace events, such as an ordinary movement of a street car at the wrong time, will be quite enough.[96]

On the other hand there are many accidents which, as a matter of common knowledge, occur frequently enough without anyone's fault. A tumble downstairs,[97] a fall in alighting from a standing street car,[98] a tire

---

lied Chem. & Dye Corp., 1959, 8 A.D.2d 463, 188 N. Y.S.2d 919. An interesting assembly of what is now known as to a vitally important problem of the future is Hutton, Res Ipsa Loquitur and Actionable Radiation Injury, 1958, 25 Tenn.L.Rev. 327.

86. Ross v. Double Shoals Cotton Mills, 1905, 140 N.C. 115, 52 S.E. 121; Chiuccariello v. Campbell, 1912, 210 Mass. 532, 96 N.E. 1101.

87. Hunt v. Atlantic Coast Line R. Co., E.D.S.C.1956, 144 F.Supp. 877; Edgerton v. New York & H. R. Co., 1868, 39 N.Y. 227; Chicago Union Traction Co. v. Giese, 1907, 229 Ill. 260, 82 N.E. 232; Washington-Virginia R. Co. v. Bouknight, 1912, 113 Va. 696, 75 S.E. 1032.

88. Shaw v. Pacific Greyhound Lines, 1958, 50 Cal. App.2d 153, 323 P.2d 391; Mitcham v. City of Detroit, 1959, 355 Mich. 182, 94 N.W.2d 388.

89. Bressler v. New York Rapid Transit Corp., 1938, 277 N.Y. 200, 13 N.E.2d 772; Chicago Union Traction Co. v. Newmiller, 1906, 215 Ill. 383, 74 N.E. 410; Hughes v. Atlantic City & S. R. Co., 1914, 85 N.J.L. 212, 89 A. 769; Adam v. Los Angeles Transit Lines, 1957, 154 Cal.App.2d 535, 317 P.2d 642.

90. Johnson v. Foster, Miss.1967, 202 So.2d 520; Bagby v. Commonwealth, Ky.1968, 424 S.W.2d 119; Badela v. Karpowich, 1965, 152 Conn. 360, 206 A.2d 838; Novakofski v. State Farm Mut. Auto Ins. Co., 1967, 34 Wis.2d 154, 148 N.W.2d 714; Merriman v. Kraft, 1969, —— Ind. ——, 249 N.E.2d 485.

91. Corson v. Wilson, 1940, 56 Wyo. 218, 108 P.2d 260; Wisconsin Tel. Co. v. Matson, 1950, 256 Wis. 304, 41 N.W.2d 268; Grigsby v. Smith, 1940, 285 Ky. 48, 146 S.W.2d 719; Bryne v. Great A. & P. Tea Co., 1929, 269 Mass. 130, 168 N.E. 540; Whitwell v. Wolf, 1914, 127 Minn. 529, 149 N.W. 299.

92. Colla v. Mandella, 1955, 271 Wis. 145, 72 N.W.2d 755; Kroger Co. v. Perpall, 1962, 105 Ga.App. 682, 125 S.E.2d 511; Lewis v. Wolk, 1950, 312 Ky. 536, 228 S.W.2d 432; Pelland v. D'Alessandro, 1947, 321 Mass. 387, 73 N.E.2d 590; Knippenberg v. Windemuth, 1968, 249 Md. 159, 238 A.2d 915; cf. Grant v. Malkerson Sales, Inc., 1961, 259 Minn. 419, 108 N.W. 2d 347 (standing car suddenly took off). See Lloyd, The Parking of Automobiles, 1928, 77 U.Pa.L.Rev. 336; Note, 1951, 39 Ky.L.J. 328.

93. Richenbacher v. California Packing Corp., 1924, 250 Mass. 198, 145 N.E. 281; Dryden v. Continental Baking Co., 1938, 11 Cal.2d 33, 77 P.2d 833; Coca Cola Bottling Co. v. Creech, 1932, 245 Ky. 414, 53 S. W.2d 745; Cassini v. Curtis Candy Co., 1934, 113 N.J.L. 91, 172 A. 519; Gross v. Loft, 1936, 121 Conn. 394, 185 A. 80. See Jeanblanc, Manufacturers' Liability to Persons Other than Their Immediate Vendees, 1937, 24 Va.L.Rev. 134; Notes, 1935, 21 Va.L. Rev. 306; 1935, 23 Ky.L.J. 534; 1935, 15 Boston U.L. Rev. 851.

94. Thus Marshall v. Suburban Dairy Co., 1921, 96 N. J.L. 81, 114 A. 750 (horse leaped over hood of motor truck and arrived in cab); Guthrie v. Powell, 1955, 178 Kan. 587, 290 P.2d 834 (800 pound steer came through ceiling); Armstrong v. New Orleans Public Service, La.App.1939, 188 So. 189 (uninvited street car entering restaurant); Harlow v. Standard Imp. Co., 1904, 145 Cal. 477, 78 P. 1045 (vagrant steam roller crossed lawn and crashed into house); Pilars v. R. J. Reynolds Tobacco Co., 1918, 117 Miss. 490, 78 So. 365 (human toe in chewing tobacco); Fowler v. Seaton, 1964, 61 Cal.2d 681, 39 Cal.Rptr. 881, 394 P.2d 697 (child sent to nursery school, returned with bruised head, crossed eyes and concussion); Wolfe v. Feldman, 1936, 158 Misc. 656, 286 N.Y.S. 118 (the extraordinary case of the unfortunate dentist).

95. See for example Rystinki v. Central Cal. Traction Co., 1917, 175 Cal. 336, 165 P. 952.

96. Mudrick v. Market St. R. Co., 1938, 11 Cal.2d 724, 81 P.2d 950.

97. Hutsell v. Edens, 1961, 172 Neb. 592, 111 N.W.2d 388; Hiner v. Hubbard, 1966, 240 Cal.App.2d 63, 49 Cal.Rptr. 157. Cf. Haynes v. Horton, 1964, 261 N.C. 615, 135 S.E.2d 582 (slip and fall on defendant's floor).

98. Wyatt v. Pacific Elec. R. Co., 1909, 156 Cal. 170, 103 P. 892; Greeley v. Baltimore Transit Co., 1941, 180 Md. 10, 22 A.2d 460.

of an ordinary automobile which blows out,[99] a skidding car,[1] the explosion of a stick of dynamite,[2] a broken milk bottle,[3] a fire of unknown origin,[4] will not in themselves[5]

99. Klein v. Beeten, 1919, 169 Wis. 385, 172 N.W. 736; Cox v. Wilson, Ky.1954, 267 S.W.2d 83; Pawlowski v. Eskofski, 1932, 209 Wis. 189, 244 N.W. 611. But in Simpson v. Gray Line Co., 1961, 226 Or. 71, 358 P. 2d 516, and Greyhound Corp. v. Brown, 1959, 269 Ala. 520, 113 So.2d 916, where the tire of a bus blew out, res ipsa loquitur was applied, on the basis of the carrier's extraordinary duty of care. And where the defect in the tire is such as could be discovered by proper inspection, res ipsa loquitur will be applied. Merriman v. Kraft, 1969, — Ind. —, 249 N.E.2d 485.

1. This is the prevailing view, in the usual case. Rickert v. Geppert, 1964, 64 Wash.2d 350, 391 P.2d 964; Wray v. King, Mo.App.1965, 385 S.W.2d 831; Shepherd v. Ball, 1959, 47 Tenn.App. 189, 337 S.W. 2d 243; Kaufman v. Bieker, 1959, 110 Ohio App. 496, 165 N.E.2d 453; Lithgow v. Lithgow, 1939, 334 Pa. 262, 5 A.2d 573.

But cases have begun to appear in which, under particular circumstances, the inference has been permitted. Evans v. S. J. Groves & Sons Co., 2 Cir. 1963, 315 F.2d 335; Vespe v. Di Marco, 1964, 43 N.J. 430, 204 A.2d 874; Campbell v. Fiorot, 1963, 411 Pa. 157, 191 A.2d 657; Schaubhut v. Liberty Mut. Ins. Co., La.App.1963, 157 So.2d 346; Calvetti v. Seipp, 1967, 37 Ill.2d 596, 227 N.E.2d 758. See Note, 1967, 16 Buff.L.Rev. 456.

2. Matievitch v. Hercules Powder Co., 1955, 3 Utah 2d 283, 282 P.2d 1044. Cf. Caplinger v. Werner, Ky. 1958, 311 S.W.2d 201 (motorboat).

3. Honea v. City Dairy, 1943, 22 Cal.2d 614, 140 P.2d 369.

4. Tedrow v. Des Moines Housing Corp., 1958, 249 Iowa 766, 87 N.W.2d 463; Arledge v. Scherer Freight Lines, 1955, 269 Wis. 142, 68 N.W.2d 821; Watenpaugh v. L. L. Coryell & Son, 1939, 135 Neb. 607, 283 N.W. 204; The President Wilson, D.Cal.1933, 5 F.Supp. 684; Foerster v. Fischback-Moore, Inc., N.D.1970, 178 N.W.2d 258. Cf. Randall v. Shelton, Ky.1956, 293 S.W.2d 559 (stone thrown up by truck); Cunningham v. Neil House Hotel Co., Ohio App.1941, 33 N.E.2d 859 (insect bite).

5. Additional facts may still justify the inference. Cf. Ruerat v. Stevens, 1931, 113 Conn. 333, 155 A. 219, where defendant was the only person to smoke on a davenport all evening; Seeley v. Combs, 1966, 65 Cal.2d 127, 52 Cal.Rptr. 578, 416 P.2d 810 (started in vicinity of defendant's hot sparks and gases); John Rooff & Sons, Inc. v. Winterbottom, 1957, 249 Iowa 122, 86 N.W.2d 131 (same as to sparks); McManus v. Pennsylvania Elec. Co., 1957, 389 Pa. 168, 132 A.2d 242 (same as to excessive current in wires).

justify the conclusion that negligence is the most likely explanation; and to such events res ipsa loquitur does not apply The earlier cases dealing with aviation took the position that there was not yet such common knowledge and experience of its hazards as to permit such a conclusion from the unexplained crash of a plane.[6] With rapid technological improvement, the position began to change; and all of the later cases now agree that the safety record justifies the application of res ipsa loquitur to such a crash,[7] or even to the complete disappearance of a plane.[8] There are, however, other kinds of aviation mishaps, such as the lurch or bump of a plane when unexpected air currents are suddenly encountered,[9] which still lead to no such conclusion.

6. Wilson v. Colonial Air Transports, 1932, 278 Mass. 420, 180 N.E. 212; Herndon v. Gregory, 1935, 190 Ark. 702, 81 S.W.2d 849; Morrison v. Le Tourneau, 5 Cir. 1943, 138 F.2d 339; Smith v. Whitley, 1943, 223 N.C. 534, 27 S.E.2d 442; Towle v. Phillips, 1943, 180 Tenn. 121, 172 S.W.2d 806.

7. United States v. Kesinger, 10 Cir. 1951, 190 F.2d 529; Rogow v. United States, S.D.N.Y.1959, 173 F. Supp. 547; Lobel v. American Airlines, 2 Cir. 1951, 192 F.2d 217, cert. denied 342 U.S. 945; Capital Airlines v. Barger, 1960, 47 Tenn.App. 636, 341 S.W.2d 579; Newberger v. Pokrass, 1967, 33 Wis.2d 569, 148 N.W.2d 80. See McLarty, Res Ipsa Loquitur in Airline Passenger Litigation, 1951, 37 Va.L.Rev. 55; Goldin, The Doctrine of Res Ipsa Loquitur in Aviation Law, 1944, 18 So.Cal.L.Rev. 15, 124; Notes, 1949, 16 U.Chi.L.Rev. 365; 1952, 37 Corn.L.Q. 543; 1955, 33 N.C.L.Rev. 670; 1963, 15 Syr.L.Rev. 1.

8. Cox v. Northwest Airlines, Inc., 7 Cir. 1967, 379 F. 2d 893, cert. denied 389 U.S. 1044; Haasman v. Pacific Alaska Air Express, 1951, 13 Alaska 439, 100 F.Supp. 1, affirmed, De Marais v. Beckman, 1952, 13 Alaska 745, 198 F.2d 550, cert. denied 344 U.S. 922. Cf. O'Connor v. United States, 2 Cir. 1958, 251 F.2d 939, cert. denied 344 U.S. 922 (collision between defendant's planes); Goodwin v. United States, E.D.N.C.1956, 141 F.Supp. 445 (practice bomb falling from plane).

The aviation picture has changed rapidly. In the early days of jet aircraft, it was held in Williams v. United States, 5 Cir. 1955, 218 F.2d 473, that the explosion of a jet in midair was no matter for res ipsa loquitur. It appears inconceivable that such a decision would be reached today.

9. Cudney v. Midcontinent Airlines, 1953, 363 Mo.App. 922, 254 S.W.2d 662; Cudney v. Braniff Airways,

There has been much the same history in the law of exploding beverage bottles, where it was at one time held that the explosion of a single bottle, which apparently then was not at all an uncommon occurrence, was no sufficient indication of negligence.[10] Both bottles and bottling methods have improved greatly since; and there is now general agreement that even a single bottle is enough to permit a finding of negligence.[11] Whether the inference may be drawn is often a matter of the details of the evidence. If minute particles of glass are found in a can of spinach, it may be that negligence cannot reasonably be inferred, since ordinary inspection might not discover them; if the particles are somewhat larger, res ipsa loquitur applies.[12]

In the usual case the basis of past experience from which the conclusion may be drawn that such events usually do not occur without negligence, is one common to the whole community, upon which the jury are simply permitted to rely. Even where such a basis of common knowledge is lacking, however, expert testimony may provide a sufficient foundation;[13] and by the same token it may destroy an inference which would otherwise arise.[14] In many cases the inference to be drawn is a double one, that the accident was caused in a particular manner, and that the defendant's conduct with reference to that cause was negligent.[15] But the inference of negligence may also arise where a definite cause is known,[16] or where the accident is more or less a mystery, with no particular cause indicated. When a gasoline filling station mysteriously explodes, many possible explanations can be suggested, but the most likely one may be negligence on

Mo.1957, 300 S.W.2d 412; Gafford v. Trans-Texas Airways, 6 Cir. 1962, 299 F.2d 60; Lazarus v. Eastern Air Lines, 1961, 110 U.S.App.D.C. 255, 292 F.2d 748; see Ness v. West Coast Airlines, 1965, 90 Idaho 111, 410 P.2d 965. Cf. Herman v. United Air Lines, D.C.Colo.1957, 157 F.Supp. 65 (murderer blew up plane); Capps v. American Airlines, 1956, 81 Ariz. 232, 303 P.2d 717 (passenger tripped while boarding plane).

10. Dail v. Taylor, 1909, 151 N.C. 284, 66 S.E. 135; Loebig's Guardian v. Coca Cola Bottling Co., 1935, 259 Ky. 124, 81 S.W.2d 910; Wheeler v. Laurel Bottling Works, 1916, 111 Miss. 442, 71 So. 743. Even then, however, the inference could be drawn if several bottles exploded. Coca Cola Bottling Works v. Shelton, 1926, 214 Ky. 118, 282 S.W. 778; Boyd v. Marion Coca Cola Bottling Co., 1962, 240 S.C. 383, 126 S.E.2d 178; cf. Ashkenazi v. Nehi Bottling Co., 1940, 217 N.C. 552, 8 S.E.2d 818.

11. Zentz v. Coca Cola Bottling Co., 1952, 39 Cal.2d 436, 247 P.2d 344; Johnson v. Coca-Cola Bottling Co., 1960, 239 Miss. 759, 125 So.2d 537; Evangelio v. Metropolitan Bottling Co., 1959, 339 Mass. 177, 158 N.E.2d 342; Ferrell v. Royal Crown Bottling Co., 1959, 144 W.Va. 465, 109 S.E.2d 489; Bornstein v. Metropolitan Bottling Co., 1957, 45 N.J.Super. 365, 132 A.2d 825, affirmed, 1958, 26 N.J. 263, 139 A.2d 404. See Notes, [1951] Wash.U.L.Q. 216; 1957, 24 Tenn.L.Rev. 1219.

12. Compare O'Brien v. Louis K. Liggett Co., 1926, 255 Mass. 553, 152 N.E. 57 with Richenbacher v. California Pack. Corp., 1924, 250 Mass. 198, 145 N.E. 291.

13. Baker v. B. F. Goodrich Co., 1953, 115 Cal.App.2d 221, 252 P.2d 24 (tire exploded while being mounted); Gordon v. Aztec Brewing Co., 1949, 33 Cal. 2d 514, 203 P.2d 522 (beer bottle exploded); Buffum's v. City of Long Beach, 1931, 111 Cal.App. 327, 295 P. 540 (broken water main); Hanaman v. New York Tel. Co., 1951, 278 App.Div. 875, 104 N.Y.S.2d 315, reargument and appeal denied, 1951, 278 A.D. 986, 105 N.Y.S.2d 1007 (escape of current from telephone); McCray v. Galveston, H. & S. A. R. Co., 1896, 89 Tex. 168, 34 S.W. 95 (steel rails falling off); and see the cases of medical malpractice cited infra, p. 227, note 1. See Fricke, The Use of Expert Evidence in Res Ipsa Loquitur Cases, 1959, 5 Vill.L. Rev. 59; Note, 1958, 106 U.Pa.L.Rev. 731.

14. Ray v. United States, 5 Cir. 1956, 228 F.2d 574, cert. denied 351 U.S. 968 (failure in electric cable splice). Cf. Deojay v. Lyford, 1942, 139 Me. 234, 29 A.2d 111; Lehner v. McLennan, 1921, 54 Cal.App. 491, 202 P. 41; Texas & N. O. R. Co. v. Schreiber, Tex.Civ.App.1937, 104 S.W.2d 929.

15. See O'Dea v. Amodeo, 1934, 118 Conn. 58, 170 A. 486; Frenkil v. Johnson, to Use of National Retailers Mut. Ins. Co., 1939, 175 Md. 592, 3 A.2d 479; Peterson v. Minnesota Power & Light Co., 1940, 207 Minn. 387, 291 N.W. 705.

16. Khanoyan v. All American Sports Enterprises, 1964, 229 Cal.App.2d 785, 40 Cal.Rptr. 596; Barney v. Hudson & M. R. Co., 1929, 105 N.J.L. 274, 145 A. 5, affirmed 106 N.J.Law 230, 231, 148 A. 917; Russ v. Eastman Car Co., 1923, 122 Me. 380, 120 A. 176; cf. Texas-La. Power Co. v. Daniels, Tex.Civ.App. 1933, 61 S.W.2d 179, affirmed, 1936, 127 Tex. 126, 91 S.W.2d 302.

the part of those in charge.[17] The plaintiff is not required to eliminate with certainty all other possible causes or inferences,[18] which would mean that he must prove a civil case beyond a reasonable doubt. All that is needed is evidence from which reasonable men can say that on the whole it is more likely that there was negligence associated with the cause of the event than that there was not.[19] It is enough that the court cannot say that the jury could not reasonably come to that conclusion.[20] Where no such balance of probabilities in favor of negligence can reasonably be found, res ipsa loquitur does not apply.[21]

Inference the Negligence was Defendant's

It is never enough for the plaintiff to prove merely that he has been injured by the negligence of someone unidentified. Even though there is beyond all possible doubt negligence in the air, it is still necessary to bring it home to the defendant. On this too the plaintiff has the burden of proof by a preponderance of the evidence; and in any case where it is clear that it is at least equally probable that the negligence was that of another, the court must direct the jury that the plaintiff has not proved his case.[22] The injury must either be traced to a specific instrumentality or cause for which the defendant was responsible,[23] or it must be shown that he was responsible for all reasonably probable causes to which the accident could be attributed.[24] Accordingly res ipsa loquitur is held not to apply where a chair is thrown from an unidentified window in the defendant's hotel,[25] or where the presence of such an object as a bolt on a railway platform might easily have been due to the act of a third party,[26]

---

17. Nelson v. Zamboni, 1925, 164 Minn. 314, 204 N.W. 943; Hiell v. Golco Oil Co., 1940, 137 Ohio St. 180, 28 N.E.2d 561; Keck v. Bairs, Inc., 1968, 150 Mont. 562, 437 P.2d 380. Cf. Judson v. Giant Powder Co., 1895, 107 Cal. 549, 40 P. 1020 (nitroglycerine factory); Glaser v. Schroeder, 1929, 269 Mass. 337, 168 N.E. 809 (stationary automobile starting into motion); Nicol v. Geitler, 1933, 188 Minn. 69, 247 N.W. 8 (automobile leaving the highway); Cox v. Northwest Airlines, Inc., 7 Cir. 1967, 379 F.2d 893, cert. denied 389 U.S. 1044 (disappearance of airplane).

18. Adam Hat Stores v. Kansas City, Mo.1958, 316 S.W.2d 594; Rocona v. Guy F. Atkinson Co., 9 Cir. 1949, 173 F.2d 661; Burlington-Rock Island R. Co. v. Ellison, 1943, 140 Tex. 353, 167 S.W.2d 723.

19. Graham v. Badger, 1895, 164 Mass. 42, 41 N.E. 61; Kleinman v. Banner Laundry Co., 1921, 150 Minn. 515, 186 N.W. 123; Mintzer v. Wilson, 1937, 21 Cal.App.2d 85, 68 P.2d 370; Pack v. Nazareth Literary & Ben. Institute, 1962, 50 Tenn.App. 540, 362 S.W.2d 816; Shahinian v. McCormick, 1963, 59 Cal.2d 554, 30 Cal.Rptr. 521, 381 P.2d 377.

20. Dunn v. Vogel Chevrolet Co., 1959, 168 Cal.App. 2d 117, 335 P.2d 492; Gordon v. Aztec Brewing Co., 1949, 33 Cal.2d 514, 203 P.2d 522; Seneris v. Haas, 1955, 45 Cal.2d 811, 291 P.2d 915.

21. Carson v. Boston Elev. R. Co., 1941, 309 Mass. 32, 33 N.E.2d 701; Owen v. Beauchamp, 1944, 66 Cal. App.2d 750, 152 P.2d 756; Benedick v. Potts, 1898, 88 Md. 52, 40 A. 1067.

22. Emmons v. Texas & Pac. R. Co., Tex.Civ.App.1941, 149 S.W.2d 167, error dismissed; Olson v. Whitthorne & Swan, 1928, 203 Cal. 206, 263 P. 518; Joffre v. Canada Dry Ginger Ale, Inc., 1960, 222 Md. 1, 158 A.2d 631; Ginsberg v. Metropolitan Transit Authority, 1956, 333 Mass. 514, 131 N.E.2d 919; Lea v. Carolina Power & Light Co., 1957, 246 N.C. 287, 98 S.E.2d 9.

23. Manley v. New York Tel. Co., 1951, 303 N.Y. 18, 100 N.E.2d 113 (severe nervous shock while using telephone); Nahigian v. Belcher & Loomis Hardware Co., 1941, 66 R.I. 194, 18 A.2d 388 (injury from electric ironer not shown to be due to repairs); Monaghan v. Equitable Life Ins. Co., 1918, 184 Iowa 352, 168 N.W. 892 (plaintiff fell over and died in defendant's elevator).

24. As in Judson v. Giant Powder Co., 1895, 107 Cal. 549, 40 P. 1020.

25. Larson v. St. Francis Hotel, 1948, 83 Cal.App.2d 210, 188 P.2d 513. Cf. Sipe v. Helgerson, 1944, 159 Kan. 290, 153 P.2d 934 (bottle thrown from baseball grandstand); Davidson's, Inc. v. Scott, 1965, 149 W.Va. 470, 140 S.E.2d 807 (fire in room to which several people had keys); Quinn v. Southard, 1967, 269 N.C. 385, 152 S.E.2d 538 (fire while delivering gasoline).

26. O'Mara v. Pennsylvania R. Co., 6 Cir. 1938, 95 F.2d 762. Cf. German v. Kienow's Food Stores, 1967, 246 Or. 334, 425 P.2d 523 (grape on floor of store); McGillivray v. Great Northern R. Co., 1917, 138 Minn. 278, 164 N.W. 922 (pile of sand on track); Owen v. Beauchamp, 1944, 66 Cal.App.2d 750, 152 P.2d 756 (slippery substance on floor of dentist's office); Biaggi v. Giant Food Shopping Center, 1957, 100 U.S.App.D.C. 338, 244 F.2d 786 (dis-

or where gas or water or electricity escape from fixtures controlled in part by another.[27]

Where such other causes are in the first instance equally probable, there must be evidence which will permit the jury to eliminate them. This means, for example, that a plaintiff injured by the explosion of a beer bottle purchased from a retailer will be required to make some sufficient showing that the bottle was not cracked by mishandling after it left the defendant's plant.[28] Again, however, the evidence need not be conclusive, and only enough is required to permit a finding as to the greater probability.[29] The plaintiff is not required to do the impossible by accounting for every moment of the bottle's existence

since it left the defendant's plant;[30] and it is enough if he produces sufficient evidence of careful handling in general, and of the absence of unusual incidents, to permit reasonable men to conclude that, more likely than not, the event was due to the defendant's negligence.[31] As to dead mice, and the like, in capped bottles, the possibility of deliberate tampering by a stranger has been ruled out as too unlikely, in the absence of some evidence to indicate it.[32] The same kind of question arises when the defendant's car, parked on the side of a hill, is found in motion shortly afterward.[33] Various explanations suggest themselves, including the same tampering stranger; but it can still be found that the most probable one is negligence in parking the car.[34]

This element usually is stated as meaning that the defendant must be in "exclusive control" of the instrumentality which has caused

arranged boxes in room where others had been working).

Otherwise where it is shown that the condition has existed so long that reasonable care would have discovered it. Kaplan v. Grand Department Stores, 1934, 118 Conn. 714, 174 A. 76; Hudson v. F. W. Woolworth Co., 1931, 275 Mass. 469, 176 N.E. 188.

27. Barker v. Withers, 1956, 141 W.Va. 713, 92 S.E.2d 705; Okmulgee Gas Co. v. Kelly, 1924, 105 Okl. 189, 232 P. 428; Bell v. Huntington Development & Gas Co., 1928, 106 W.Va. 155, 145 S.E. 165; Hernandez v. Southern Cal. Gas Co., 1931, 213 Cal. 384, 2 P.2d 360; Arkansas Power & Light Co. v. Butterworth, 1953, 222 Ark. 67, 258 S.W.2d 36. Cf. In re Hayden's Estate, 1953, 174 Kan. 140, 254 P.2d 813 (plane crash, three pilots and dual controls).

28. Keffer v. Logan Coca-Cola Bottling Works, Inc., 1956, 141 W.Va. 839, 93 S.E.2d 225; Miami Coca-Cola Bottling Co. v. Reisinger, Fla.1953, 68 So.2d 589; Trust v. Arden Farms Co., 1958, 50 Cal.2d 217, 324 P.2d 583; Joffre v. Canada Dry Ginger Ale, Inc., 1960, 222 Md. 1, 158 A.2d 631; Johnson v. Coca Cola Bottling Co., 1952, 235 Minn. 471, 51 N.W.2d 573. Cf. Huggins v. John Morrell & Co., 1964, 176 Ohio St. 171, 198 N.E.2d 448 (pickled pigs' feet).

The manufacturer's duty may, however, extend to protection during all normal intermediate handling. Ryan v. Zweck-Wollenberg Co., 1954, 266 Wis. 630, 64 N.W.2d 226.

29. Weggeman v. Seven-Up Bottling Co., 1958, 5 Wis. 2d 503, 93 N.W.2d 467, rehearing denied, amended 94 N.W.2d 645; Gordon v. Aztec Brewing Co., 1949, 33 Cal.2d 514, 203 P.2d 522; Honea v. Coca Cola Bottling Co., 1944, 143 Tex. 272, 183 S.W.2d 968. Cf. Dennis v. Carolina Pines Bowling Center, 1967, 248 Cal.App.2d 369, 56 Cal.Rptr. 453; Leidenfrost v. Atlantic Masonry, Inc., 1964, 235 Md. 244, 201 A.2d 336.

30. Zarling v. La Salle Coca Cola Bottling Co., 1958, 2 Wis.2d 596, 87 N.W.2d 263; Macon Coca-Cola Bottling Co. v. Chancey, 1960, 101 Ga.App. 166, 112 S.E.2d 811, affirmed, 1960, 216 Ga. 61, 114 S.E.2d 517.

31. Gordon v. Aztec Brewing Co., 1949, 33 Cal.2d 514, 203 P.2d 522; Groves v. Florida Coca-Cola Bottling Co., Fla.1949, 40 So.2d 128; Ryan v. Adam Scheidt Brewing Co., 3 Cir. 1952, 197 F.2d 614; Coca Cola Bottling Works, Inc. v. Crow, 1956, 200 Tenn. 161, 291 S.W.2d 589; Lanza v. De Ridder Coca Cola Bottling Co., La.App.1941, 3 So.2d 217. Cf. Maybach v. Falstaff Brewing Corp., 1949, 359 Mo. 446, 222 S.W.2d 87.

32. Wichita Coca-Cola Bottling Co. v. Tyler, Tex. Civ.App.1956, 288 S.W.2d 903, ref. n. r. e., Zarling v. La Salle Coca Cola Bottling Co., 1958, 2 Wis.2d 596, 87 S.W.2d 263; Coast Coca Cola Bottling Co. v. Bryant, 1959, 236 Miss. 880, 112 So.2d 538.

33. In Hughes v. Jolliffe, 1957, 50 Wash.2d 554, 313 P.2d 678, the lapse of several hours was held to defeat the inference of any negligence in parking. But in Gresser v. Taylor, 1967, 276 Minn. 440, 150 N.W.2d 869, and Roberts v. Ray, 1959, 45 Tenn.App. 280, 322 S.W.2d 435, res ipsa loquitur was applied notwithstanding an interval of three hours.

34. McCloud v. City of La Follette, 1954, 38 Tenn. App. 553, 276 S.W.2d 763; Colla v. Mandella, 1955, 271 Wis. 145, 72 N.W.2d 755; Kroger Co. v. Perpall, 1962, 105 Ga.App. 682, 125 S.E.2d 511; Lewis v. Wolk, 1950, 312 Ky. 536, 228 S.W.2d 432; Pelland v. D'Allesandro, 1947, 321 Mass. 387, 73 N.E.2d 590.

the accident.[35] Such control of course does serve effectively to focus any negligence upon the defendant; but the strict and literal application of the formula has led some courts to ridiculous conclusions, requiring that the defendant be in possession at the time of the plaintiff's injury—as in the Rhode Island case [36] denying recovery where a customer in a store sat down in a chair, which collapsed. Of course this is wrong: it loses sight of the real purpose of the reasoning process in an attempt to reduce it to a fixed, mechanical and rigid rule. "Control," if it is not to be pernicious and misleading, must be a very flexible term. It must be enough that the defendant has the right or power of control, and the opportunity to exercise it, as in the case of an owner who is present while another is driving his car,[37] or a landowner who permits visitors to come on his premises.[38] It is enough that he is under a duty which he cannot delegate to another, as in the case of a surgeon who allows a nurse to count the sponges.[39] It is enough that he shares the duty and the responsibility, as in the case of

the landlord of a building from which an electric sign falls into the street.[40]

There are other cases, however, in which it is clear that "control" is simply the wrong word. The plaintiff who is riding a horse is in exclusive control of it, but when the saddle slips off the inference is still that it is the fault of the defendant who put it on.[41] There is now quite general agreement that the fact that the plaintiff is sitting on the defendant's stool when it collapses,[42] or has possession of an exploding bottle,[43] or a loaf of bread with glass baked inside of it,[44] or is using an appliance,[45] which the defendant has manufac-

---

35. The statement is derived from the formula stated by Wigmore, Evidence, 3d Ed.1940, § 2509: "Both inspection and user must have been at the time of the injury in the control of the party charged."

36. Kilgore v. Shepard Co., 1932, 52 R.I. 151, 158 A. 720. Cf. Stanolind Oil & Gas Co. v. Bunce, 1936, 51 Wyo. 1, 62 P.2d 1297; Terrell v. First Nat. Bank, 1950, 204 Okl. 24, 226 P.2d 431; Wheeler v. Laurel Bottling Works, 1916, 111 Miss. 442, 71 So. 743. See Note, 1952, 5 Okl.L.Rev. 99.

37. Mein v. Reed, 1938, 224 Iowa 1274, 278 N.W. 307; Price v. McDonald, 1935, 7 Cal.App.2d 77, 45 P.2d 425.

38. Pandjiris v. Oliver Cadillac Co., 1936, 339 Mo. 711, 98 S.W.2d 969. Cf. International-Great Northern R. Co. v. Lucas, Tex.Com.App.1936, 128 Tex. 480, 99 S.W.2d 297; Van Horn v. Pacific Refining & Roofing Co., 1915, 27 Cal.App. 105, 148 P. 951. Miles v. St. Regis Paper Co., 1970, — Wash.2d —, 467 P.2d 307.

39. Ales v. Ryan, 1936, 8 Cal.2d 82, 64 P.2d 409; Voss v. Bridwell, 1961, 188 Kan. 643, 364 P.2d 955. Cf. Poulsen v. Charlton, 1964, 224 Cal.App.2d 262, 36 Cal.Rptr. 347 (independent contractor); Knell v. Morris, 1952, 39 Cal.2d 450, 247 P.2d 352 (same).

40. Smith v. Claude Neon Lights, 1933, 110 N.J.L. 326, 164 A. 423; Barb v. Farmers Ins. Exchange, Mo.1955, 281 S.W.2d 297; Both v. Harband, 1958, 164 Cal.App.2d 743, 331 P.2d 140. Cf. Corcoran v. Banner Super Market, 1967, 19 N.Y.2d 425, 280 N.Y.S.2d 385, 227 N.E.2d 304, remittitur amended 21 N.Y.2d 793, 288 N.Y.S.2d 484, 235 N.E.2d 455; Decatur & Macon Hospital Ass'n v. Erie City Iron Works, 1966, 75 Ill.2d 144, 220 N.E.2d 590; Bond v. Otis Elevator Co., Tex.App.1965, 388 S.W.2d 681, on remand 391 S.W.2d 519.

41. Rafter v. Dubrock's Riding Academy, 1946, 75 Cal.App.2d 621, 171 P.2d 459. Cf. Kronmer v. Dahl, 1965, 145 Mont. 491, 402 P.2d 979 (owner last person to exercise control over car); van der Hout v. Johnson, 1968, 251 Or. 435, 446 P.2d 99 (grating gave way when plaintiff stepped on it).

42. Sweet v. Swangel, 1969, — Iowa —, 166 N.W.2d 776; Gow v. Multnomah Hotel, 1950, 191 Or. 45, 224 P.2d 552, motion granted 228 P.2d 791; Couris v. Casco Amusement Corp., 1956, 333 Mass. 740, 133 N.E.2d 250; Keena v. Scales, 1964, 61 Cal.2d 779, 40 Cal.Rptr. 65, 394 P.2d 809; Benedict v. Eppley Hotel Co., 1954, 159 Neb. 23, 65 N.W.2d 224.

43. Goldman & Freiman Bottling Co. v. Sindell, 1922, 140 Md. 488, 117 A. 886; Zentz v. Coca Cola Bottling Co., 1952, 39 Cal.2d 436, 247 P.2d 344. Cf. Ryan v. Zweck-Wollenberg Co., 1954, 266 Wis. 630, 64 N.W.2d 226; Killian v. Logan, 1932, 115 Conn. 437, 162 A. 30.

44. Dryden v. Continental Baking Co., 1938, 11 Cal. 2d 33, 77 P.2d 333; cf. Coca Cola Bottling Works v. Williams, 1941, 111 Ind.App. 502, 37 N.E.2d 702.

45. Peterson v. Minnesota Power & Light Co., 1940, 207 Minn. 387, 291 N.W. 705; Bustamante v. Carborundum Co., 7 Cir. 1967, 375 F.2d 688; Ozark v. Wichita Manor, Inc., 5 Cir. 1958, 252 F.2d 671, rehearing denied 258 F.2d 805; Black v. Partridge, 1953, 115 Cal.App.2d 639, 252 P.2d 760; **May v.**

tured, will not prevent the application of res ipsa loquitur when the evidence reasonably eliminates other explanations than the defendant's negligence.   Some courts have said [46] that it is enough that the defendant was in exclusive control at the time of the indicated negligence.   It would be far better, and much confusion would be avoided, if the idea of "control" were discarded altogether, and we were to say merely that the apparent cause of the accident must be such that the defendant would be responsible for any negligence connected with it.

Multiple Defendants

Some quite intricate questions arise where the plaintiff proceeds against two or more defendants.[47]   Unless there is vicarious liability or shared control,[48] the logical rule usually is applied, that the plaintiff does not make out a preponderant case against either of two defendants by showing merely that he has been injured by the negligence of one or the other.[49]   Occasional statutes permitting the plaintiff to join the two as defendants, and to proceed against them with pleading in the alternative, have been held to be intended to avoid a nonsuit,[50] but not to affect the ultimate burden of proof by a preponderance of the evidence against someone.[51]   The questions which arise are amply illustrated by the cases of colliding vehicles.

All courts are agreed that the mere fact of a collision of two automobiles gives rise to no inference of negligence against either driver in an action brought by the other.[52]   The great majority of the decisions reach the same conclusion where the action is brought by a third party, such as a bystander, injured by the collision,[53] on the ground that neither driver is in exclusive control of the situation.   It is only where one vehicle is stationary,[54] or its driver's fault is eliminated

Columbian Rope Co., 1963, 40 Ill.App.2d 264, 189 N.E.2d 394 (rope).

Otherwise when the intervening history might reasonably account for the accident. Tayer v. York Ice Mach. Corp., 1938, 342 Mo. 912, 119 S.W.2d 240; Brooks v. Hill-Shaw Co., 7 Cir. 1941, 117 F. 2d 682, cert. denied 314 U.S. 610; Weston v. Gold & Co., 1959, 167 Neb. 692, 94 N.W.2d 380; Ford Motor Co. v. McDavid, 4 Cir. 1958, 259 F.2d 261, cert. denied 358 U.S. 908; Johnson v. Latimer, 1957, 180 Kan. 720, 308 P.2d 65.

46. See for example Escola v. Coca Cola Bottling Co., 1944, 24 Cal.2d 453, 150 P.2d 436; Gadde v. Michigan Consol. Gas Co., 1966, 377 Mich. 117, 139 N.W. 2d 722.

47. See McCoid, Negligence Actions Against Multiple Defendants, 1955, 7 Stan.L.Rev. 480; Nagy, Res Ipsa Loquitur in Joint Tortfeasor Cases, 1967, 16 Cleve.Marsh.L.Rev. 550; Note, 1969, 34 Alb.L.J. 106.

48. See supra, p. 220.

49. Turner v. North American Van Lines, Mo.App. 1956, 287 S.W.2d 384; Casey Pure Milk Co. v. Booth Fisheries Co., 1913, 124 Minn. 117, 144 N.W. 450; Oglesby's Sureties v. State, 1889, 73 Tex. 658, 11 S.W. 873; Louisville Gas & Elec. Co. v. Nall, 1917, 178 Ky. 33, 198 S.W. 745; Hartzell v. Bank of Murray, 1925, 211 Ky. 263, 277 S.W. 270.

Where, however, there is a res ipsa loquitur case against one defendant, it is not necessarily de-

stroyed by specific evidence of negligence on the part of another. McCarty v. Hosang, W.D.Mo. 1957, 154 F.Supp. 852.

50. Hummerstone v. Leary, [1921] K.B. 664; S. & C. Clothing Co. v. United States Trucking Corp., 1926, 216 App.Div. 482, 215 N.Y.S. 349; Thermoid Rubber Co. v. Baird Rubber & Trading Co., 1925, 124 Misc. 774, 249 N.Y.S. 277.

51. Julius Klugman's Sons v. Oceanic Steam Nav. Co., S.D.N.Y.1930, 42 F.2d 461.

52. Schofield v. King, 1957, 388 Pa. 132, 130 A.2d 93; Busch v. Los Angeles R. Co., 1918, 178 Cal. 536, 174 P. 665; McCarthy v. Kenosha Auto Transport Corp., 1966, 2 Ariz.App. 620, 411 P.2d 58; Sandler v. Boston Elev. R. Co., 1921, 238 Mass. 148, 130 N.E. 104. Even a rear-end collision, between moving vehicles. Mickelson v. Forney, 1966, 259 Iowa 91, 143 N.W.2d 390; Brehm v. Lorenz, 1955, 206 Md. 500, 112 A.2d 475.

53. Diamond v. Weyerhaeuser, 1918, 178 Cal. 540, 174 P. 38; Tibbetts v. Nyberg, 1967, 276 Minn. 431, 150 N.W.2d 687; Hot Springs St. R. Co. v. Hildreth, 1904, 72 Ark. 572, 82 S.W. 245; Union Traction Co. v. Alstadt, 1924, 195 Ind. 389, 143 N.E. 879; Stangy v. Boston Elev. R. Co., 1915, 220 Mass. 414, 107 N.E. 933. Cf. Denman v. Denman, 1961, 242 Miss. 59, 134 So.2d 457, and Denman v. Spain, 1961, 242 Miss. 431, 135 So.2d 195, where the two drivers were sued separately.

54. Bondar v. Ar Jay Paint Co., 1959, 20 Misc.2d 643, 191 N.Y.S.2d 767; Ponce v. Black, 1964, 224 Cal. App.2d 159, 36 Cal.Rptr. 419; Bryne v. Great A. & P. Tea Co., 1929, 269 Mass. 130, 168 N.E. 540; Hardman v. Younkers, 1942, 15 Wash.2d 483, 131 P.2d 177; Bellere v. Madsen, Fla.1959, 114 So.2d 619.

by some other specific evidence,[55] that res ipsa loquitur can apply against the other. In about half of the jurisdictions which have considered the question, this is true even though in the particular case one of the vehicles is a common carrier, and the plaintiff is its passenger.[56] But in such a case other courts have proceeded to apply res ipsa loquitur in favor of the passenger in his action against his carrier,[57] but not against the other driver,[58] and not in favor of one who is not a passenger of the defendant.[59] The reason sometimes given for this apparently freakish rule is that the carrier's duty of the highest care toward its passenger makes it more likely that the accident was due to its negligence

than to that of the other driver.[60] Ingenious as this is, a better explanation would appear to be that these courts are in fact continuing the older rule which formerly [61] imposed special responsibility upon the carrier by setting up a procedural disadvantage requiring it to exonerate itself from fault or pay,[62] and that this policy has little relation to any inference of negligence, or to the principle of res ipsa loquitur as it is commonly applied.[63]

The question may legitimately be raised, however, whether all this is the reasonable and logical approach. When moving vehicles collide on the highway, whether or not one of them is a carrier, is there not a reasonable inference, based merely upon the known probabilities, that not one but *both* drivers have been negligent? Certainly there is an inference that due care has not been used by some one,[64] as is demonstrated by the cases where one defendant has operated both vehicles.[65]

---

55. Chicago City R. Co. v. Barker, 1904, 209 Ill. 321, 70 N.E. 624 (defendant's car out of control); Hendler v. Coffey, 1932, 278 Mass. 339, 179 N.E. 801 (rear-end collision); Linberg v. Stanto, 1931, 211 Cal. 771, 297 P. 9 (automobile on sidewalk).

56. Reardon v. Boston Elevated R. Co., 1923, 247 Mass. 124, 141 N.E. 857; Blew v. Philadelphia Rapid Transit Co., 1910, 227 Pa. 319, 76 A. 17; Yellow Cab Co. v. Hodgson, 1932, 91 Colo. 365, 14 P.2d 1081; Riggsby v. Tritton, 1925, 143 Va. 903, 129 S.E. 493, 133 S.E. 580. Cases are collected in Prosser, Res Ipsa Loquitur: Collisions of Carriers with Other Vehicles, 1936, 30 Ill.L.Rev. 980.

57. St. Clair v. McAllister, 1932, 216 Cal. 95, 13 P.2d 924; Zichler v. St. Louis Public Service Co., 1933, 332 Mo. 902, 59 S.W.2d 654; Crozier v. Hawkeye Stages, 1929, 209 Iowa 313, 228 N.W. 320; Pickwick Stages Corp. v. Messinger, 1934, 44 Ariz. 174, 36 P.2d 168; Capital Transit Co. v. Jackson, D.C. Cir. 1945, 149 F.2d 839.

California, overlooking its automobile guest statute, once applied the same rule to a guest in a private automobile; but the case is now discredited. Contra, State ex rel. Brancato v. Trimble, 1929, 322 Mo. 318, 18 S.W.2d 4.

58. The distinction is clearly made in Capital Transit Co. v. Jackson, D.C.Cir.1945, 149 F.2d 839; Preston v. Des Moines R. Co., 1932, 214 Iowa 156, 241 N.W. 648; Loudoun v. Eighth Ave. R. Co., 1900, 162 N.Y. 380, 56 N.E. 988; Kilgore v. Brown, 1928, 90 Cal. App. 555, 266 P. 297.

59. Little Rock & M. R. Co. v. Harrell, 1894, 58 Ark. 454, 25 S.W. 117; St. Clair v. McAllister, 1932, 216 Cal. 95, 13 P.2d 924; Loudoun v. Eighth Ave. R. Co., 1900, 162 N.Y. 380, 56 N.E. 988; Zichler v. Missouri Pac. R. Co., 1933, 332 Mo. 902, 59 S.W.2d 654.

60. See for example Housel v. Pacific Elec. R. Co., 1914, 167 Cal. 245, 139 P. 73; Plumb v. Richmond Light & R. Co., 1922, 233 N.Y. 285, 135 N.E. 504; Central Passenger R. Co. v. Kuhn, 1888, 86 Ky. 578, 6 S.W. 441; James, Proof of the Breach in Negligence Cases, 1951, 37 Va.L.Rev. 179. Cf. Simpson v. Gray Line Co., 1961, 226 Or. 71, 358 P.2d 516, applying the same reasoning to the blowout of a bus tire.

61. In Christie v. Griggs, 1809, 2 Camp. 79, 170 Eng. Rep. 1088.

62. Cf. Greyhound Corp. v. Brown, 1959, 269 Ala. 520, 113 So.2d 916, which not only applies res ipsa loquitur to a blowout of a bus tire, but puts the burden of proof upon the carrier. See also Slife, The Iowa Doctrine of Res Ipsa Loquitur, 1950, 35 Iowa L.Rev. 393, 400 ff.

63. See Prosser, Res Ipsa Loquitur: Collisions of Carriers with Other Vehicles, 1936, 30 Ill.L.Rev. 980.

64. Hence it has been held error to give an "unavoidable accident" instruction. Cobb v. Chubeck, 1960, 399 Pa. 201, 160 A.2d 207; McClarren v. Buck, 1955, 343 Mich. 300, 72 N.W.2d 31. And in Sheehan v. Allred, Fla.App.1962, 146 So.2d 760, it was held that a verdict should have been directed for the plaintiff, leaving it to the jury to decide which driver was liable.

65. Birdsall v. Duluth-Superior Transit Co., 1936, 197 Minn. 411, 267 N.W. 363; Campbell v. Con-

It is not a question of assigning this fault to one or the other, but of recognizing that, more probably than not, careful drivers do not have collisions even with careless ones. If the driver collides with a stationary object, an inference of negligence arises; why any other conclusion when he collides with a moving object which proper care requires him to look out for and avoid? There is a little authority to this effect; [66] but it cannot be pretended that the argument has made much headway since it was first advanced.[67]

An even more striking departure from the idea of exclusive control is found in Ybarra v. Spangard,[68] where an unconscious patient undergoing an operation for appendicitis suffered a traumatic injury to his shoulder, and res ipsa loquitur was applied against all of the doctors and hospital employees connected with the operation, although it seemed quite clear that not all of them could have been responsible. The basis of the decision appears quite definitely to have been the special responsibility for the plaintiff's safety undertaken by everyone concerned.[69] Again there is obviously a deliberate policy, similar to that found in the carrier cases, which requires the defendants to explain or pay, and goes beyond any reasonable inference from the facts; and one may surmise that this is not unconnected with the refusal of the medical profession to testify against one another.

Beyond this there are a handful of sporadic decisions which have applied res ipsa loquitur against multiple defendants. Pennsylvania and Kansas [70] have done so where the bottler and the distributor of a beverage were sued together, without any such element of assumed special responsibility. There are in

solidated Traction Co., 1902, 201 Pa. 167, 50 A. 829; Greinke v. Chicago City R. Co., 1908, 234 Ill. 564, 85 N.E. 327; Niebalski v. Pennsylvania R. Co., 1915, 249 Pa. 530, 94 A. 1097. Cf. O'Connor v. United States, 2 Cir. 1958, 251 F.2d 939 (collision of planes).

66. La Rocco v. Fernandez, 1954, 130 Colo. 523, 277 P.2d 232; Krump v. Highlander Ice Cream Co., 1961, 30 Ill.App.2d 103, 173 N.E.2d 822; Pearlman v. W. O. King Lumber Co., 1939, 302 Ill.App. 190, 23 N.E.2d 826; Weddle v. Phelan, La.App.1937, 177 So. 407; Overstreet v. Ober, 1930, 14 La.App. 633, 130 So. 648. Contra, Dunaway v. Marroun, La. App.1937, 178 So. 710.

67. It was accepted in a vacated opinion, Phillips v. Noble, Cal.App.1957, 313 P.2d 22. The supreme court rejected it because the automobile guest statute applicable to one driver would have led to an unfair distinction between the two. Phillips v. Noble, 1958, 50 Cal.2d 163, 323 P.2d 385.

68. 1944, 25 Cal.2d 486, 154 P.2d 687, 162 A.L.R. 1258. The outcome was judgment against all of the defendants because they were unable, or unwilling, to explain. Ybarra v. Spangard, 1949, 93 Cal.App.2d 43, 208 P.2d 445.

The case was followed, upon parallel facts, in Oldis v. La Société Française De Bienfaisance Mutuelle, 1955, 130 Cal.App.2d 461, 279 P.2d 184; Frost v. Des Moines Still College of Osteopathy & Surgery, 1956, 248 Iowa 294, 79 N.W.2d 306; Meyer v. St. Paul-Mercury Ind. Co., La.App.1952, 61 So.2d 901, affirmed 225 La. 618, 73 So.2d 781; Horner v. Northern Pacific Ben. Ass'n Hospitals, 1963, 62 Wash.2d 351, 382 P.2d 518; Beaudoin v. Watertown Memorial Hospital, 1966, 32 Wis.2d 132, 145 N.W.2d 166. It was rejected in Rhodes v. De Haan, 1959, 184 Kan. 473, 337 P.2d 1043; Talbot v. Dr. W. H. Groves' Latter-Day Saints Hospital, Inc., 1968, 21 Utah 2d 73, 440 P.2d 872. See Thode, Unconscious Patient: Who Should Bear the Risk of Unexplained Injuries to a Healthy Part of His Body, [1969] Utah L.Rev. 1.

The case was criticized in no very friendly vein in Seavey, Res Ipsa Loquitur: Tabula in Naufragio, 1950, 63 Harv.L.Rev. 643; Adamson, Medical Malpractice: Misuse of Res Ipsa Loquitur, 1962, 46 Minn.L.Rev. 1043.

69. The case was explained on this basis in Gobin v. Avenue Food Mart, 1960, 178 Cal.App.2d 345, 2 Cal.Rptr. 822, which refused to apply res ipsa loquitur against the retailer and wholesaler of a toy gun in a sealed container.

In Sanchez v. Rodriguez, 1964, 226 Cal.App.2d 439, 38 Cal.Rptr. 110, the court was careful to limit the rule to cases which laymen know do not usually occur without medical negligence.

70. Loch v. Confair, 1953, 372 Pa. 212, 93 A.2d 451; Nichols v. Nold, 1953, 174 Kan. 613, 258 P.2d 317. Cf. Lafleur v. Coca-Cola Bottling Co., La.App.1967, 195 So.2d 419, writ refused 250 La. 488, 196 So.2d 802. It should be noted that at the time all three states imposed strict liability upon sellers of food to the ultimate consumer. (See infra, § 97). The extension is thus not an extreme one. See Cowan and Malinak, Res Ipsa Loquitur—The Application of the Doctrine to Products Liability Cases, 1964, 31 Ins.Couns.J. 71.

addition odd cases [71] in which the principle has been applied against all of those who have contributed component parts to an integrated whole, apparently on the basis that they were so closely tied together that they must be treated in effect as one defendant. With these infrequent exceptions, res ipsa loquitur still has not been held to apply against multiple defendants, where it is inferable only that one has been negligent.[72]

Eliminating the Plaintiff

Allied to the condition of exclusive control in the defendant is that of absence of any action on the part of the plaintiff contributing to the accident. Its purpose, of course, is to eliminate the possibility that it was the plaintiff who was responsible. If the boiler of a locomotive explodes while the plaintiff engineer is operating it, the inference of his own negligence is at least as great as that of the defendant, and res ipsa loquitur will not apply until he has accounted for his own conduct.[73] But the requirement may easily be misunderstood. The plaintiff is seldom entirely static, and it is not necessary that he be completely inactive, but merely that there be evidence removing the inference of his own responsibility.[74]

This possibility of contribution by the plaintiff, together with the possible inference of negligence on the part of a fellow servant, originally played an important part in leading many courts to say that res ipsa loquitur could not apply in an action by an employee against his employer.[75] But no such arbitrary rule can be justified, and employment cases do not differ in principle from any others.[76] If the evidence is sufficient to eliminate the plaintiff's contribution, and the negligence of fellow servants is out of the case,[77] as it usually is today, it is now

---

71. Dement v. Olin-Mathieson Chem. Corp., 5 Cir. 1960, 282 F.2d 76 (manufacturers of dynamite and cap); Becker v. American Airlines, S.D.N.Y.1961, 200 F.Supp. 839 (maker of plane, maker of altimeter, and air line). Cf. Schroeder v. City & County Sav. Bank of Albany, 1944, 293 N.Y. 370, 57 N.E.2d 57, motion denied, 1944, 293 N.Y. 764, 57 N.E.2d 842, where "control" of a barricade in front of a building passed back and forth among three parties.

72. A red flag must be hung out as to three opinions of the intermediate courts of California, which frequently have been cited as changing the whole rule in that state: Knell v. Morris, Cal.App.1951, 234 P.2d 1025; Burr v. Sherwin Williams Co., Cal. App.1953, 258 P.2d 58; and Litzmann v. Humboldt County, Cal.App.1954, 273 P.2d 82. Actually there are no such opinions.

In all three a hearing was granted by the supreme court. The first two were disposed of on other grounds in 1952, 39 Cal.2d 450, 247 P.2d 352, and 1954, 42 Cal.2d 682, 268 P.2d 1041; the third was settled. Under the peculiar California procedure, a hearing by the supreme court is on appeal de novo from the trial court. The opinion of the District Court of Appeal is vacated and stricken from the record. It is never officially published, and becomes as if never written. In California it is considered a breach of etiquette for counsel to cite such an opinion.

73. Mathews v. Chicago & N. W. R. Co., 1925, 162 Minn. 313, 202 N.W. 896. Accord: Dorman v. T. Smith & Son, 1953, 223 La. 29, 64 So.2d 833; Simmons v. F. W. Woolworth Co., 1958, 163 Cal.App.2d 709, 329 P.2d 999; Orr v. Southern Pac. Co., 9 Cir. 1955, 226 F.2d 841; Phillips v. Klepfer, 1940, 217 Ind. 237, 27 N.E.2d 340.

In Wisconsin, under a comparative negligence statute, it has been held that the plaintiff need not be eliminated as a possible cause, since his contributory negligence would not be an absolute bar. Turk v. H. C. Prange Co., 1963, 18 Wis.2d 547, 119 N.W.2d 365.

74. Shahinian v. McCormick, 1963, 59 Cal.2d 554, 30 Cal.Rptr. 521, 381 P.2d 377. This is true particularly where the plaintiff has done nothing abnormal, and has only used a thing for the purpose for which it was intended. Baker v. B. F. Goodrich Co., 1953, 115 Cal.App.2d 221, 252 P.2d 24. Compare the obvious cases, supra, notes 63–65, where the plaintiff eats defective food prepared by the defendant, and the like.

75. Patton v. Texas & Pac. R. Co., 1901, 179 U.S. 658; Spees v. Boggs, 1901, 198 Pa. 112, 47 A. 875; City of Greeley v. Foster, 1904, 32 Colo. 292, 75 P. 351.

76. Berry, The Application of Res Ipsa Loquitur in Master and Servant Cases, 1917, 84 Cent.L.J. 67, 53 Can.L.J. 104; Note, 1944, 9 Mo.L.Rev. 283.

77. The fellow servant rule is eliminated, for example, by the Federal Employers' Liability Act, 45 U.S.C.A. § 51 et seq. Central Railroad of N. J. v. Peluso, 2 Cir., 1923, 286 F. 661; Pitcairn v. Perry, 8 Cir., 1941, 122 F.2d 881; Terminal R. Ass'n v. Staengel, 8 Cir., 1941, 122 F.2d 271.

quite uniformly agreed that res ipsa loquitur may apply to actions by employees.[78] Even where the plaintiff's own contribution is left in doubt by reason of conflicting evidence, or is shared control of the situation, it is still possible to apply the principle under proper instructions to the jury.[79]

Evidence More Accessible to Defendant

Courts frequently have said, and on rare occasions have held [80] that res ipsa loquitur cannot be applied unless evidence of the true explanation of the accident is more accessible to the defendant than to the plaintiff. Usually this has been said when the inference of negligence did not arise anyway,[81] or the evidence of the plaintiff provided a complete explanation.[82]

It is difficult to believe that this factor ever can be controlling, or more than at best a makeweight. If the circumstances are such as to create a reasonable inference of the defendant's negligence, it cannot be supposed that the inference would ever be defeated by a showing that the defendant knew nothing about what had happened; [83] and if the facts give rise to no such inference, a plaintiff who has the burden of proof in the first instance could scarcely make out a case merely by proving that he knew less about the matter than his adversary.[84]

Res ipsa loquitur has been applied where the defendant or his agent in charge is dead or vanished,[85] or it is otherwise clear from the facts in evidence that the defendant has no more information than the plaintiff.[86] It has been applied where the plaintiff himself has introduced definite evidence of negligence,[87] or has pleaded specific allegations,[88]

78. Marceau v. Rutland R. Co., 1914, 211 N.Y. 203, 105 N.E. 206; Rose v. Minneapolis, St. P. & S. S. M. R. Co., 1913, 121 Minn. 363, 141 N.W. 487; O'Connor v. Mennie, 1915, 169 Cal. 217, 146 P. 674; Wyldes v. Patterson, 1915, 31 N.D. 282, 153 N.W. 630; F. W. Martin & Co. v. Cobb, 8 Cir. 1940, 110 F.2d 159 (Arkansas law).

79. Jesionowski v. Boston & Me. R. Co., 1947, 329 U.S. 452; Johnson v. United States, 1947, 333 U.S. 46, 865; Keller v. Morrison-Knudsen Co., 1957, 149 Cal. App.2d 205, 308 P.2d 370; Lamb v. Hartford Acc. & Ind. Co., 1956, 180 Kan. 157, 300 P.2d 387; Seffert v. Los Angeles Transit Lines, 1958, 56 Cal.2d 498, 15 Cal.Rptr. 161, 364 P.2d 337.

80. Hughes v. Jolliffe, 1957, 50 Wash.2d 554, 313 P.2d 678; Appalachian Ins. Co. v. Knutson, 8 Cir. 1966, 358 F.2d 679; Ellis v. Henderson, W.Va.1956, 95 S.E.2d 801, withdrawn on rehearing, 1957, 142 W. Va. 824, 98 S.E.2d 719; Wilson v. East St. Louis & Interurban Water Co., 1938, 295 Ill.App. 603, 15 N.E.2d 599; Levendusky v. Empire Rubber Mfg. Co., 1913, 84 N.J.L. 698, 87 A. 338.

Cf. Johnson v. Jackson, 1967, 245 Md. 589, 226 A.2d 883, where plaintiff introduced into evidence only a part of the facts available to him.

81. Shinofield v. Curtis, 1954, 245 Iowa 1352, 66 N.W. 2d 465; Cox v. Wilson, Ky.1954, 267 S.W.2d 83; Guthrie v. Carter, 1950, 190 Va. 354, 57 S.E.2d 45.

82. Johnson v. Ostrom, 1932, 128 Cal.App. 38, 16 P. 2d 794; Collis v. Ashe, 1956, 212 Ga. 746, 95 S.E. 2d 654; Hebert v. General Accident F. & L. Ass. Corp., La.App.1950, 48 So.2d 107; Johnson v. Bosch, 1929, 178 Minn. 363, 227 N.W. 181; McKinney v. Frodsham, 1960, 57 Wash.2d 126, 356 P.2d 100, amended 360 P.2d 576.

83. "And that the defendant does not know the cause is no explanation." Williams v. Field Transp. Co., Cal.App.1946, 166 P.2d 884. Accord, Ireland v. Marsden, 1930, 108 Cal.App. 632, 291 P. 912.

84. See Galbraith v. Busch, 1935, 267 N.Y. 230, 196 N.E. 36; Monkhouse v. Johns, La.App.1932, 142 So. 347.

85. Weller v. Worstall, 1934, 50 Ohio App. 11, 197 N.E. 410, affirmed, 1935, 129 Ohio St. 596, 196 N.E. 637; Burkett v. Johnston, 1955, 39 Tenn.App. 276, 282 S.W.2d 647; Nicol v. Geitler, 1933, 188 Minn. 69, 247 N.W. 8; cf. Lane v. Dorney, 1960, 252 N.C. 90, 113 S.E.2d 33. See, however, Larkin v. State Farm Mut. Auto. Ins. Co., 1957, 233 La. 544, 97 So.2d 389, refusing to draw the inference on the facts.

86. Judson v. Giant Powder Co., 1885, 107 Cal. 549, 40 P. 1020 (explosion "scattered all the witnesses to the four winds"); Haasman v. Pacific Alaska Air Express, D.Alaska 1951, 13 Alaska 439, 100 F.Supp. 1, affirmed, De Marais v. Beckman, 9 Cir. 1952, 13 Alaska 745, 198 F.2d 550, cert. denied 344 U.S. 922 (airplane disappeared in flight); Cox v. Northwest Airlines, Inc., 7 Cir. 1967, 379 F.2d 893 (same), cert. denied 389 U.S. 1044; cf. Seffert v. Los Angeles Transit Lines, 1961, 56 Cal.2d 498, 15 Cal.Rptr. 161, 364 P.2d 337.

87. See infra, p. 231.

88. See infra, p. 232. Cf. Klatt v. Hoboken Bank for Savings, 1941, 126 N.J.L. 96, 18 A.2d 602, where plaintiff, himself an expert, "may have had some opinion as to how or why the accident happened."

and so has indicated that prima facie at least he is at no disadvantage. And in a large number of cases in which there has been no consideration of the point it is apparent from the facts that the accident was a mysterious occurrence, as to which the defendant was as much in the dark as the plaintiff.[89]

The plaintiff's comparative ignorance of the facts in the type of cases under consideration no doubt provides some argument for the validity of the principle of res ipsa loquitur, and undoubtedly it has had some persuasive effect in making courts more willing to apply the doctrine.[90] It is sometimes advanced as a reason by those who seek to give the principle a greater procedural effect than that of a mere inference from circumstantial evidence.[91] But it cannot be regarded as an indispensable requirement, and there are few cases in which it can be said to have had any real importance.

Breach of Defendant's Duty

Res ipsa loquitur leads only to the conclusion that the defendant has not exercised reasonable care, and is not in itself any proof that he was under a duty to do so. Thus a trespasser or a licensee injured by the condition of premises may still have no right to recover even though the facts speak for themselves.[92] In many cases the problem becomes one of whether the apparent cause of the accident lies within the scope of the defendant's obligation. Where an automobile unaccountably leaves the road and injures a guest, and under a guest statute the host is liable only for wilful or wanton misconduct, or for gross negligence, res ipsa loquitur furnishes no proof of it.[93] And something slippery on a floor affords no res ipsa case against the owner of the premises, unless it is shown to have been there long enough so that he should have discovered and removed it.[94]

This question of duty arises frequently in cases of medical malpractice.[95] Since a physician or surgeon normally undertakes only to exercise the skill and care common to the profession,[96] there usually is not enough in a

---

89. For example Nelson v. Zamboni, 1925, 164 Minn. 314, 204 N.W. 943; Hiell v. Golco Oil Co., 1940, 137 Ohio St. 180, 28 N.E.2d 561; Smith v. Southern Counties Gas Co., 1928, 89 Cal.App. 81, 264 P. 532.

90. See for example Oakdale Bldg. Corp. v. Smithereen Co., 1944, 322 Ill.App. 222, 54 N.E.2d 231; Ybarra v. Spangard, 1944, 25 Cal.2d 486, 154 P.2d 687.

91. See infra, p. 230. Also Jaffe, Res Ipsa Loquitur Vindicated, 1951, 1 Buffalo L.Rev. 1.

92. Brust v. C. J. Kubach Co., 1933, 130 Cal.App. 152, 19 P.2d 845; Pennebaker v. San Joaquin Light & Power Co., 1910, 158 Cal. 579, 112 P. 459; Heaton v. Kagley, 1955, 198 Tenn. 530, 281 S.W.2d 385.

Cf. Stocking v. Johnson Flying Service, 1963, 143 Mont. 61, 387 P.2d 312 (privilege of public necessity).

93. Nehring v. Smith, 1951, 243 Iowa 225, 49 N.W. 2d 831; Fiske v. Willkie, 1945, 67 Cal.App.2d 440, 154 P.2d 725; Minkovitz v. Fine, 1942, 67 Ga.App. 176, 19 S.E.2d 561; Garland v. Greenspan, 1958, 74 Nev. 88, 323 P.2d 27; Burghardt v. Olson, 1960, 223 Or. 155, 354 P.2d 871. See Note, 1955, 7 S.C.L.Rev. 480.

A discredited case is Galbraith v. Busch, 1935, 267 N.Y. 230, 196 N.E. 36, reversed on other grounds, 242 App. Div. 793, 275 N.Y.S. 655, holding that even in the absence of such a statute res ipsa loquitur will not apply in favor of the guest, since it is equally likely that the accident may have been due to a latent defect in the car as to which the driver owed him no duty. Cases in other jurisdictions have not agreed. See supra, p. 215. The decision apparently was overruled in Pfaffenbach v. White Plains Express Corp., 1966, 17 N.Y.2d 132, 269 N.Y.S.2d 115, 216 N.E.2d 324.

94. F. W. Woolworth Co. v. Jones, 1955, 126 Ind. App. 118, 130 N.E.2d 672; Deptula v. New Britain Trust Co., 1955, 19 Conn.Sup. 434, 116 A.2d 773; Owen v. Beauchamp, 1944, 66 Cal.App.2d 650, 152 P.2d 756.

95. See Louisell and Williams, Res Ipsa Loquitur—Its Future in Medical Malpractice, 1960, 48 Cal.L. Rev. 252; Rubsamen, Res Ipsa Loquitur in California Medical Malpractice Law, 1962, 14 Stan.L.Rev. 251; Morris, "Res Ipsa Loquitur"—Liability Without Fault, 1957, 12 J.Am.Med.Ass'n 1055, 1958, 25 Ins.Couns.J. 97; Johnson, Medical Malpractice—Doctrine of Res Ipsa Loquitur and Informed Consent, 1965, 37 U.Colo.L.Rev. 182; Notes, 1957, 9 Stan.L.Rev. 731; 1956, 30 So.Cal.L.Rev. 80; 1940, 26 Va.L.Rev. 919; 1940, 40 Col.L.Rev. 161; 1940, 9 Brook.L.Rev. 335; 1941, 19 N.C.L.Rev. 617; 1966, 60 Nw.U.L.Rev. 852.

96. See supra, p. 162.

mistaken diagnosis alone,[97] or the unfortunate choice of the wrong method of treatment,[98] or the kind of accident or undesirable result which happens in spite of all reasonable precautions,[99] to show the necessary lack of skill or care. What this means is that ordinarily laymen are not qualified to say that a good doctor would not go wrong, and that expert testimony [1] is indispensable before any negligence can be found.[2] Such decisions, together with the notorious unwillingness of members of the medical profession to testify against one another,[3] may impose

an insuperable handicap upon a plaintiff who cannot obtain the proof.

There are, however, some medical and surgical errors on which any layman is competent to pass judgment and conclude from common experience that such things do not happen if there has been proper skill and care. When an operation leaves a sponge in the patient's interior,[4] or removes or injures an inappropriate part of his anatomy,[5] or when a tooth is dropped down his windpipe,[6]

---

97. Carraway v. Graham, 1928, 218 Ala. 453, 118 So. 807; Boyce v. Brown, 1938, 51 Ariz. 416, 77 P.2d 455; Meador v. Arnold, 1936, 264 Ky. 378, 94 S.W. 2d 626; Patterson v. Marcus, 1928, 203 Cal. 550, 265 P. 222.

98. Gephart v. Rike-Kumler Co., 1956, 145 N.E.2d 197, 76 Ohio Law Abs. 9; Loudon v. Scott, 1920, 58 Mont. 645, 194 P. 488; Farber v. Olkon, 1953, 40 Cal.2d 503, 254 P.2d 520; Ewing v. Goode, S.D.Ohio 1897, 78 F. 442; Goode v. Lothrop, 1929, 266 Mass. 518, 165 N.E. 688.

99. Hoffman v. Naslund, 1966, 274 Minn. 521, 144 N.W.2d 580; Hasemeier v. Smith, Mo.1962, 361 S.W.2d 697; Shurpit v. Brah, 1966, 30 Wis.2d 388, 141 N.W.2d 266; Mogensen v. Hicks, 1961, 253 Iowa 139, 110 N.W.2d 563; Johnston v. Rodis, 1958, 102 U.S.App.D.C. 209, 251 F.2d 917.

1. Such testimony that such events do not usually occur if due care is used may lay a sufficient foundation for res ipsa loquitur. Fehrman v. Smirl, 1963, 20 Wis.2d 1, 121 N.W.2d 255; Seneris v. Haas, 1955, 45 Cal.2d 811, 291 P.2d 915; Mayor v. Dowsett, 1965, 240 Or. 196, 400 P.2d 234; Raza v. Sullivan, D.C.Cir.1970, 432 F.2d 617; Tomei v. Henning, 1967, 67 Cal.2d 319, 62 Cal.Rptr. 9, 431 P.2d 633. See Notes, 1964, 77 Harv.L.Rev. 333; 1967, 18 Hast.L.J. 691.

2. Dees v. Pace, 1953, 118 Cal.App.2d 284, 257 P.2d 756; Toy v. Rickert, 1958, 53 N.J.Super. 27, 146 A.2d 510; Callahan v. Hahnemann Hospital, 1934, 1 Cal.2d 447, 35 P.2d 536; April v. Peront, 1936, 88 N.H. 309, 188 A. 457; Nelson v. Murphy, 1953, 42 Wash.2d 737, 258 P.2d 472.

3. This has been mentioned from time to time in the decisions. See Morgan v. Rosenberg, Mo.1963, 370 S.W.2d 685; Coleman v. McCarthy, 1933, 53 R.I. 266, 165 A. 900; Simon v. Freidrich, 1937, 163 Misc. 112, 296 N.Y.S. 367; Reynolds v. Struble, 1933, 128 Cal.App. 716, 18 P.2d 690; Halldin v. Peterson, 1968, 39 Wis.2d 668, 159 N.W.2d 738; Seidelson, Medical Malpractice Cases and the Reluctant Expert, 1966, 16 Cath.U.L.Rev. 187; Markus, Con-

spiracy of Silence, 1965, 14 Cleve.Marsh.L.Rev. 530; Note, 1961, 45 Minn.L.Rev. 1019.

A survey made by the Boston University Law-Medicine Research Institute, and reported in Medical Economics, Aug. 28, 1961, found that out of 214 doctors, only 31% of the specialists and 27% of the general practitioners said that they would be willing to appear for the plaintiff if a surgeon, operating on a diseased kidney, removed the wrong one. In Agnew v. Parks, 1959, 172 Cal.App.2d 756, 343 P.2d 118, a suit was actually brought against a group of doctors for "conspiracy to obstruct the ends of justice" by refusal to testify. In L'Orange v. Medical Protective Co., 6 Cir. 1968, 394 F.2d 57, one was brought against a malpractice insurer for cancelling the insurance of a dentist because he testified. See also Douglas v. Bussabarger, 1968, 73 Wash.2d 476, 438 P.2d 829.

But in Gould v. Winokur, 1968, 98 N.J.Super. 554, 237 A.2d 916, affirmed 104 N.J.Super. 329, 250 A.2d 38, plaintiff's inability to obtain expert testimony was held not to justify the application of res ipsa loquitur where it was not otherwise applicable.

4. French v. Fischer, 1962, 50 Tenn.App. 587, 362 S.W. 2d 926; Young v. Fishback, 1958, 104 U.S.App.D.C. 372, 262 F.2d 469; Dietze v. King, E.D.Va.1960, 184 F.Supp. 944; Mitchell v. Saunders, 1941, 219 N.C. 178, 13 S.E.2d 242; Easterling v. Walton, 1967, 208 Va. 214, 156 S.E.2d 787. See Note, 1963, 30 Tenn. L.Rev. 666.

5. Evans v. Roberts, 1915, 172 Iowa 653, 154 N.W. 923; Vergeldt v. Hartzell, 8 Cir. 1924, 1 F.2d 633; Brown v. Shortlidge, 1929, 98 Cal.App. 352, 277 P. 134; Horner v. Northern Pac. Ben. Ass'n Hospitals, 1963, 62 Wash.2d 351, 382 P.2d 518. See also Dee v. Beck, La.App.1962, 141 So.2d 920 (dentist).

6. Nelson v. Parker, 1930, 104 Cal.App. 770, 286 P. 1078; cf. Higdon v. Carlebach, 1957, 348 Mich. 363, 83 N.W.2d 296 (cutting tongue); Butts v. Watts, Ky. 1956, 290 S.W.2d 777 (portion of extracted tooth left in jaw). Compare, as to fractures so badly set or treated as to be apparent to any layman: Olson v. Weitz, 1950, 37 Wash.2d 70, 221 P.2d 537; Atkins v. Humes, Fla.1959, 110 So.2d 663; Shirey v. Schlemmer, 1967, 140 Ind.App. 606, 223 N.E.2d 759,

or he suffers a serious burn from a hot water bottle,[7] or when instruments are not sterilized,[8] the thing speaks for itself without the aid of any expert's advice.[9]

One of the difficult questions arising in malpractice cases is that of the calculated risk, where the defendant, for perfectly sound and valid medical reasons, adopts a method of treatment which, as he knows from experience, will produce damaging results in a small percentage of cases in spite of all possible professional skill and care. Courts occasionally have fallen into the error of saying that because in the ordinary case no injury occurs, the jury may be permitted to conclude that there must have been negligence in the particular instance. This is clearly wrong; and the same courts have almost invariably been compelled to retreat from it.[10]

40. RES IPSA LOQUITUR—PROCEDURAL EFFECT

There is more agreement as to the type of case to which res ipsa loquitur is applicable than as to its procedural effect when it is applied. The confusion is due in no small part to the original merger of two basic ideas in the development of the doctrine,[11] and to the continued cross-purposes under which courts have sought at the same time merely to permit a conclusion to be drawn from evidence which is purely circumstantial in character, and to make use of the principle as an instrument of policy to impose a procedural disadvantage upon certain defendants.[12]

In the ordinary case, absent special circumstances or some special relation between the parties, the great majority of the American courts regard res ipsa loquitur as nothing more than one form of circumstantial evidence.[13] "When the facts and circumstances

---

rev'd 249 Ind. 1, 230 N.E.2d 534. See Note, 1963, 47 Marq.L.Rev. 239. Cf. Berry v. American Cyanamid Co., 6 Cir. 1965, 341 F.2d 14 (basis of common knowledge as to oral polio vaccine).

7. Timbrell v. Suburban Hospital, 1935, 4 Cal.2d 68, 47 P.2d 737; Vonault v. O'Rourke, 1934, 97 Mont. 92, 33 P.2d 535; cf. Jensen v. Linner, 1961, 260 Minn. 22, 108 N.W.2d 705; Becker v. Eisenstodt, 1960, 60 N.J.Super. 240, 158 A.2d 706; Terhune v. Margaret Hague Maternity Hospital, 1960, 63 N.J. Super. 106, 164 A.2d 75; McDonald v. Foster Memorial Hospital, 1959, 170 Cal.App.2d 85, 338 P.2d 607.

Earlier cases treated an X-ray burn as indicative of negligence. Shockley v. Tucker, 1905, 127 Iowa 456, 103 N.W. 360; Jones v. Tri-State Tel. & Tel. Co., 1912, 118 Minn. 217, 136 N.W. 741; Lewis v. Casenburg, 1928, 157 Tenn. 187, 7 S.W.2d 808. Later decisions have tended to recognize that some X-ray injuries are unavoidable, or due to personal idiosyncrasy of the patient. Christie v. Callahan, 1941, 75 U.S.App.D.C. 133, 124 F.2d 825; Costa v. Regents of University of California, Cal.App.1952, 247 P.2d 21, on rehearing, 1953, 116 Cal.App.2d 445, 254 P.2d 85; Nixon v. Pfahler, 1924, 279 Pa. 377, 124 A. 130. See Note, 1946, 19 Tenn.L.Rev. 372.

8. Barham v. Widing, 1930, 210 Cal. 206, 291 P. 173.

See also Pederson v. Dumouchel, 1967, 72 Wash.2d 73, 431 P.2d 973 (plaintiff did not awake from general anaesthetic for almost a month, and then with brain damage).

9. As to the possibility of placing the burden of proof on the defendant, see infra, p. 230.

10. See Siverson v. Weber, 1962, 57 Cal.2d 834, 22 Cal.Rptr. 337, 372 P.2d 97, overruling Valentine

v. Kaiser Foundation Hospitals, 1961, 194 Cal.App. 2d 282, 15 Cal.Rptr. 26, McDonald v. Foster Memorial Hospital, 1959, 170 Cal.App.2d 85, 338 P.2d 607, and Wolfsmith v. Marsh, 1959, 51 Cal.2d 832, 337 P. 2d 70. See also Fehrman v. Smirl, 1963, 20 Wis.2d 1, 121 N.W.2d 255, rehearing denied, 1963, 20 Wis. 2d 1, 122 N.W.2d 439; Cavero v. Franklin General Ben. Soc., 1950, 36 Cal.2d 301, 223 P.2d 471; Note, 1956, 10 So.Cal.L.Rev. 80.

11. See supra, p. 213.

12. See, generally, Heckel and Harper, Effect of the Doctrine of Res Ipsa Loquitur, 1928, 22 Ill.L.Rev. 724; Carpenter, The Doctrine of Res Ipsa Loquitur, 1934, 1 U.Chi.L.Rev. 519; Prosser, The Procedural Effect of Res Ipsa Loquitur, 1936, 20 Minn.L.Rev. 241; Rosenthal, The Procedural Effect of Res Ipsa Loquitur in New York, 1936, 22 Corn.L.Q. 39; Prosser, Res Ipsa Loquitur in California, 1949, 37 Cal.L.Rev. 183, reprinted in Prosser, Selected Topics on the Law of Torts, 1954, 302.

13. Palmer Brick Co. v. Chenall, 1904, 119 Ga. 837, 47 S.E. 329; Kleinman v. Banner Laundry Co., 1921, 150 Minn. 515, 186 N.W. 123; Glowacki v. North Western Ohio R. & P. Co., 1927, 116 Ohio St. 451, 157 N.E. 21; Levine v. Union & New Haven Trust Co., 1941, 127 Conn. 435, 17 A.2d 500; Merriman v. Kraft, 1968, —— Ind.App. ——, 242 N.E.2d 526. Cases are collected, and the jurisdictions classified, in Prosser, The Procedural Effect of Res Ipsa Loquitur, 1936, 20 Minn.L.Rev. 241; but there have been many shifts of position since that date.

from which the jury is asked to infer negligence are those immediately attendant upon the occurrence, we speak of it as a case of 'res ipsa loquitur;' when not immediately connected with the occurrence, then it is an ordinary case of circumstantial evidence." [14] This means that the inference of negligence to be drawn from the circumstances is left to the jury. They are permitted, but not compelled to find it.[15] The plaintiff escapes a nonsuit, or a dismissal of his case, since there is sufficient evidence to go to the jury; but the burden of proof is not shifted to the defendant's shoulders,[16] nor is any "burden" of introducing evidence cast upon him, except in the very limited sense that if he fails to do so, he runs the risk that the jury may, and very likely will, find against him.[17]

The reason for this is that in the ordinary case, such as that of an automobile unaccountably leaving the highway, or a stationary car starting into motion, reasonable men may differ as to the conclusion to be drawn, both as to the probable cause of the event and as to the likelihood that negligence was associated with it. Other possibilities than negligence are in the case, which counsel should be entitled to argue to the jury; and the facts are not so definitely proved that the court can rule on them as a matter of law. In other words, many inferences are possible, and none of them is so clear that the court can say that it is compulsory.

In all such jurisdictions, however, there may be occasional cases, such as those of the human toe in the plug of chewing tobacco,[18] the collision of railway trains trying to run on the same track,[19] rear end collisions with a stationary vehicle,[20] and the like,[21] where

---

"What is a res ipsa loquitur case anyhow? Reduced to simple terms, does it not merely mean that negligence can be proved by circumstantial evidence and that certain circumstances, as to the character of an accident, are sufficient to take the case to the jury?" Harke v. Haase, 1934, 335 Mo. 1104, 75 S.W.2d 1001.

14. Cullen, J., in Griffen v. Manice, 1901, 166 N.Y. 188, 59 N.E. 925. See Seavey, Res Ipsa Loquitur: Tabula in Naufragio, 1950, 63 Harv.L.Rev. 643.

15. George Foltis, Inc. v. City of New York, 1941, 287 N.Y. 108, 38 N.E.2d 455; Gardner v. Coca Cola Bottling Co., 1964, 267 Minn. 505, 127 N.W.2d 557; Bell & Koch, Inc. v. Stanley, Ky.1964, 375 S.W.2d 696; Sullivan v. Crabtree, 1953, 36 Tenn.App. 469, 258 S.W.2d 782; Weggeman v. Seven-Up Bottling Co., 1958, 5 Wis.2d 503, 93 N.W.2d 467, rehearing denied, amended, 94 N.W.2d 645.

16. Munzert v. American Stores Co., 1963, 232 Md. 97, 192 A.2d 59; Ziino v. Milwaukee Elec. R. & T. Co., 1956, 272 Wis. 21, 74 N.W.2d 791; Tuso v. Markey, 1956, 61 N.M. 77, 294 P.2d 1102; Calhoun v. Northeast Airlines, Inc., S.D.N.Y.1959, 180 F.Supp. 532; Rutherford v. Huntington Coca-Cola Bottling Co., 1957, 142 Va. 681, 97 S.E.2d 803.

17. "Res ipsa loquitur means that the facts of the occurrence warrant the inference of negligence, not that they compel such an inference; that they furnish circumstantial evidence of negligence where direct evidence of it may be lacking, but it is evidence to be weighed, not necessarily to be accepted as sufficient. * * *" Sweeney v. Erving, 1913, 228 U.S. 233.

18. "We can imagine no reason why, with ordinary care, human toes could not be left out of chewing tobacco, and if toes are found in chewing tobacco, it seems to us that somebody has been very careless." Cook, P. J., in Pillars v. R. J. Reynolds Tobacco Co., 1918, 117 Miss. 490, 500, 78 So. 365, 366.

19. "The time will probably never come when a collision resulting from an attempt to have two trains going at full speed, in opposite directions, pass each other, on the same track, will not be held to be negligence, in law." Rouse v. Hornsby, 8 Cir. 1895, 67 F. 219, 221, error dismissed 161 U.S. 558. Accord, where one train went through a red light, Moore v. Atchison, T. & S. F. R. Co., 1961, 28 Ill. App.2d 340, 171 N.E.2d 393. The same conclusion is of course implicit in the old anecdote: "What a hell of a way to run a railroad."

20. Gagosian v. Burdick's Television & Appliances, 1967, 254 Cal.App.2d 316, 62 Cal.Rptr. 70.

21. Whitley v. Hix, 1961, 207 Tenn. 683, 343 S.W.2d 851 (driver lost control of car at curve); Koehler v. Thiensville State Bank, 1944, 245 Wis. 281, 14 N.W. 2d 15 (eruption of tear gas system in bank); Alabama & V. R. Co. v. Groome, 1910, 97 Miss. 201, 52 So. 703 (unsafe place to work). See Angerman Co. v. Edgemon, 1930, 76 Utah 394, 290 P. 169; Weggeman v. Seven-Up Bottling Co., 1958, 5 Wis.2d 503, 93 N.W.2d 467, 94 N.W.2d 645.

California resorted to an eccentric, and apparently indefensible, procedural quirk under which for the sake of convenience of trial judges in giving juries a uniform instruction, they must be told that they must infer negligence, although they are not in fact required to do so, and a verdict for the defendant will not be set aside. Burr v. Sherwin Williams

the inference of negligence is so clear that no reasonable man could fail to accept it; and in such cases, if the defendant offers no explanation, a verdict should be directed for the plaintiff. In other words, the procedural effect of a res ipsa case is a matter of the strength of the inference to be drawn, which will vary with the circumstances of the case.

A small minority of the courts, however, uniformly give res ipsa loquitur a greater effect than that of a mere permissible inference from the evidence. They have held that it creates a presumption, which always requires a directed verdict for the plaintiff unless the defendant offers sufficient evidence to meet it.[22] Colorado, Louisiana, and perhaps Mississippi, have gone further, and have held that it shifts to the defendant the ultimate burden of proof, requiring him to introduce evidence of greater weight than that of the plaintiff.[23] Such courts frequently have been compelled to retreat from this position, either by occasional decisions to the contrary, or by recognizing, under other names, the type of res ipsa case which creates only a permissible inference of negligence.

The source of these decisions is usually to be traced to early cases involving injuries to passengers at the hands of carriers, in which it was held that the carrier had the burden of proof on the issue of negligence.[24] The sur-

vival of such an early attitude, however, may have been due to a more or less conscious policy of requiring the defendant to produce evidence explaining the accident or pay. Since in some cases at least he will be unable to explain, this results in imposing upon him the losses due to such unexplainable events, and so may amount to the imposition of strict liability without fault.[25]

In an able defense of this position,[26] one of the leading writers has contended that the policy is justified by a combination of three factors: the balance of probabilities in favor of the plaintiff, the defendant's exclusive control of the causes, and his superior information or opportunity to obtain evidence. There is, in other words, a deliberate policy of "smoking out" evidence which the defendant has or can get. But this is to give to circumstantial evidence, even though the jury might regard it as unconvincing, a greater effect than direct evidence could have. The balance of probabilities usually is a matter upon which reasonable men may differ, and therefore for the jury; and the defendant's exclusive control, although not at all necessary to a res ipsa case, is important only in fixing the inference of negligence upon the defendant rather than another. It is the normal thing in all kinds of negligence cases for the defendant to have greater knowledge of his own conduct than the plaintiff, and the plaintiff's comparative ignorance is not held to relieve him of the burden of establishing his case by evidence which the jury will accept.

Co., 1954, 42 Cal.2d 682, 268 P.2d 1041. As applied by the intermediate appellate courts, however, this instruction is given only when all of the elements of res ipsa loquitur are beyond dispute. See Exploration Drilling Co. v. Heavy Transport, Inc., Cal. App.1963, 33 Cal.Rptr. 747.

22. Ten Ten Chestnut St. Corp. v. Quaker State Bottling Co., 1958, 186 Pa.Super. 585, 142 A.2d 306 (Pennsylvania doctrine of "exclusive control"); Coca Cola Bottling Co. of Helena v. Mattice, 1951, 219 Ark. 428, 243 S.W.2d 15; Florence Coca Cola Bottling Co. v. Sullivan, 1953, 259 Ala. 56, 65 So.2d 169.

23. Weiss v. Axler, 1958, 137 Colo. 544, 328 P.2d 88; Jones v. Shell Petroleum Corp., 1936, 185 La. 1067, 171 So. 447; Johnson v. Coca Cola Bottling Co., 1960, 239 Miss. 759, 125 So.2d 537.

24. See for example Sullivan v. Philadelphia & R. R. Co., 1858, 30 Pa. 234; Grignoli v. Chicago & G. E. R. Co., 1871, 4 Daly, N.Y., 182; Patton v. Pickles,

1898, 50 La.Ann. 857, 24 So. 290. The origin is recognized in Klingman v. Loew's, Inc., 1941, 209 Minn. 449, 296 N.W. 528. See supra, p. 213.

25. See Note, 1935, 3 U.Chi.L.Rev. 126; Bohlen, The Effect of Rebuttable Presumptions of Law Upon the Burden of Proof, 1920, 68 U.Pa.L.Rev. 307, 316.

26. Carpenter, The Doctrine of Res Ipsa Loquitur in California, 1937, 10 So.Cal.L.Rev. 166. See the ensuing discussion in Prosser, Res Ipsa Loquitur, 1937, 10 So.Cal.L.Rev. 459; Carpenter, Res Ipsa Loquitur, 1937, 10 So.Cal.L.Rev. 467. See also, repeating essentially the same arguments, Jaffe, Res Ipsa Loquitur Vindicated, 1951, 1 Buffalo L. Rev. 1.

Such a policy seems called for and desirable only in cases, such as those of carrier and passenger, where some special responsibility assumed by the defendant toward the plaintiff justifies placing upon him the burden of proof, requiring him to exonerate himself by a preponderance of the evidence or make good the loss. In such a case, the same burden should rest upon him even when the plaintiff offers the direct testimony of eyewitnesses; and such a policy does not seem properly to be connected with res ipsa loquitur at all.

Actually this enlarged procedural effect of res ipsa loquitur is fast disappearing from the courts, as recent decisions in many jurisdictions [27] have swung over to the view that there is as a general rule no more than a permissible inference which merely gets the plaintiff to the jury. There was at one time considerable support for the position that where the action is by a passenger against his carrier, res ipsa loquitur is given increased procedural effect, in the form of a presumption, or even a shifted burden of proof; [28] but except in Alabama and Oklahoma [29] there appears to have been a retreat from this distinction.[30] There may perhaps

be other such relations, such as that of physician and patient,[31] where special conclusions are called for. Apart from such instances, however, remarkably few jurisdictions now treat res ipsa loquitur as anything more than a simple matter of circumstantial evidence.

It has been suggested [32] that the whole procedural argument is only a tempest in a teapot, for the reason that res ipsa loquitur at least gets the plaintiff to the jury, and the jury in practice finds in his favor. Academically speaking, this may be true; but the rule to be adopted still has its importance for the trial lawyer. Not only do occasional juries find for the defendant, even though he offers no explanation,[33] but "inference," "presumption," and "burden of proof" have been involved in literally thousands of instructions, each of them replete with possibilities of reversible error.

Specific Evidence Introduced by Plaintiff

Where the plaintiff introduces specific evidence of the defendant's negligence, the question arises whether he may still rely upon the inference provided by a res ipsa loquitur case. It is sometimes said that where the facts are disclosed by evidence there is no room for inference, or that by attempting specific proof the plaintiff has "waived" the benefit of the doctrine.[34]

---

27. See, overruling or clarifying previous decisions: George Foltis, Inc. v. City of New York, 1941, 287 N.Y. 108, 38 N.E.2d 455; Bell & Koch, Inc. v. Stanley, Ky.1964, 375 S.W.2d 696; Ritchie v. Thomas, 1950, 190 Or. 95, 224 P.2d 543; Wildauer v. Rudnevitz, 1938, 119 N.J.L. 471, 197 A. 252; Roscigno v. Colonial Beacon Oil Co., 1936, 294 Mass. 234, 200 N.E. 883.

28. See Bond v. St. Louis-San Francisco R. Co., 1926, 315 Mo. 987, 288 S.W. 777; Hartnett v. May Department Stores, 1935, 231 Mo.App. 1116, 85 S.W.2d 644; Ritchie v. Thomas, 1950, 190 Or. 95, 224 P.2d 543; Weber v. Chicago, R. I. & P. R. Co., 1916, 175 Iowa 358, 151 N.W. 852; Montgomery & E. R. Co. v. Mallette, 1890, 92 Ala. 209, 9 So. 363. Cf. Hardin v. San Jose City Lines, 1953, 41 Cal.2d 432, 260 P.2d 63.

29. Greyhound Corp. v. Brown, 1959, 269 Ala. 520, 113 So.2d 916; Transcontinental Bus System, Inc. v. Simons, Okl., 1961, 367 P.2d 160.

30. Simpson v. Gray Line Co., 1961, 226 Or. 71, 358 P.2d 516; Duncker v. St. Louis Public Service Co., Mo.App.1951, 241 S.W.2d 64.

31. Cf. Ybarra v. Spangard, 1944, 25 Cal.2d 486, 154 P.2d 687.

32. 2 Harper and James, Law of Torts, 1956, 1104.

33. See for example Sullivan v. Crabtree, 1953, 36 Tenn.App. 469, 258 S.W.2d 782; Weggeman v. Seven-Up Bottling Co., 1958, 5 Wis.2d 503, 93 N.W.2d 467, rehearing denied, amended, 1959, 94 N.W.2d 645; Tuengel v. Stobbs, 1962, 59 Wash.2d 477, 367 P.2d 1008 (decision by trial court); Simpson v. Gray Line Co., 1961, 226 Or. 71, 358 P.2d 516.

34. Jackson v. 919 Corp., 1951, 344 Ill.App. 519, 101 N.E.2d 594; Heffter v. Northern States Power Co., 1927, 173 Minn. 215, 217 N.W. 102; Anderson v. Northern Pac. R. Co., 1915, 88 Wash. 139, 152 P. 1001; Baldwin v. Smitherman, 1916, 171 N.C. 772, 88 S.E. 854; cf. Langeland v. 78th & Park Ave. Corp., Sup.1954, 129 N.Y.S.2d 719.

Plaintiff is of course bound by his own evidence; but proof of some specific facts does not necessarily exclude inferences of others. When the plaintiff shows that the railway car in which he was a passenger was derailed, there is an inference that the defendant has somehow been negligent. When he goes further and shows that the derailment was caused by an open switch, he destroys any inference of other causes; but the inference that the defendant has not used proper care in looking after its switches is not destroyed, but considerably strengthened.[35] If he goes further still and shows that the switch was left open by a drunken switchman on duty, there is nothing left to infer; and if he shows that the switch was thrown by an escaped convict with a grudge against the railroad, he has proved himself out of court.[36] It is only in this sense that when the facts are known there is no inference, and res ipsa loquitur simply vanishes from the case.[37] On the basis of such reasoning as this, it is quite generally agreed that the introduction of some evidence which tends to show specific acts of negligence on the part of the defendant, but which does not purport to furnish a full and complete explanation of the occurrence does not destroy the inferences which are consistent with the evidence, and so does not deprive the plaintiff of the benefit of res ipsa loquitur.[38]

Pleading Specific Negligence

A similar problem arises where the plaintiff has alleged specific negligence in his pleadings, and seeks to take advantage of res ipsa loquitur at the trial.[39] No less than four positions have been taken by the courts: that the plaintiff by his specific allegations has waived or lost his right to rely on the doctrine;[40] that he may take advantage of it if the inference of negligence to be drawn supports the specific allegations;[41] that it may be applied only if the specific pleading is accompanied by a general allegation of negligence;[42] and that it is available without regard to the form of the pleading.[43]

35. Bolander v. Northern Pac. R. Co., 1964, 63 Wash. 2d 659, 388 P.2d 729. Cf. Citrola v. Eastern Air Lines, 2 Cir. 1959, 264 F.2d 815; Vogreg v. Shepard Ambulance Co., 1955, 47 Wash.2d 659, 289 P.2d 350; New York C. & St. L. R. Co. v. Henderson, 1957, 237 Ind. 456, 146 N.E.2d 531, rehearing denied 147 N.E. 2d 237.

36. Cf. Rea v. St. Louis-San Francisco R. Co., Mo. 1967, 411 S.W.2d 96; Augspurger v. Western Auto Supply Co., 1963, 257 Iowa 777, 134 N.W.2d 913; Hill v. Hill, Mo.1966, 401 S.W.2d 438; Hall v. National Supply Co., 5 Cir. 1959, 270 F.2d 379; Tillery v. Ellison, Okl.1959, 345 P.2d 434.

37. Cf. Strasburger v. Vogel, 1906, 103 Md. 85, 62 A. 202; Binns v. Standen, 1931, 118 Cal.App. 625, 5 P.2d 637; Taylor v. Prudential Ins. Co., Mo.App. 1939, 131 S.W.2d 226; Southwestern Gas & Elec. Co. v. Deshazo, 1940, 199 Ark. 1078, 138 S.W.2d 397; Snethen v. Gomez, 1967, 6 Ariz.App. 366, 432 P.2d 914.

38. Hugo v. Manning, 1968, 201 Kan. 391, 441 P.2d 145; Fehrman v. Smirl, 1964, 25 Wis.2d 645, 131 N.W.2d 314; Throop v. F. E. Young Co., 1963, 94 Ariz. 146, 382 P.2d 560; Weigand v. Pennsylvania R. Co., 3 Cir. 1959, 267 F.2d 281; Citrola v. Eastern Air Lines, Inc., 2 Cir. 1959, 264 F.2d 815. See Note, 1968, 42 St. Johns L.Rev. 410.

39. See Niles, Pleading Res Ipsa Loquitur, 1930, 7 N.Y.U.L.Rev. 415; Notes, 1958, 27 Ford.L.Rev. 411; 1964, 29 Mo.L.Rev. 382.

40. Sankey v. Williamsen, 1966, 180 Neb. 714, 144 N.W.2d 429; Kerby v. Chicago Motor Coach Co., 1960, 28 Ill.App.2d 259, 171 N.E.2d 412; Highland Ave. & B. R. Co. v. South, 1896, 112 Ala. 642, 20 So. 1003; Langeland v. 78th & Park Ave. Corp., Sup.Ct.1954, 129 N.Y.S.2d 719.

41. Pickwick Stages Corp. v. Messinger, 1934, 44 Ariz. 174, 36 P.2d 168; Wallace v. Norris, 1940, 310 Ky. 424, 220 S.W.2d 867; Short v. D. R. B. Logging Co., 1951, 192 Or. 383, 235 P.2d 340; Atkinson v. United Railroads of San Francisco, 1925, 71 Cal.App. 82, 234 P. 863; Terre Haute & I. R. Co. v. Sheeks, 1900, 155 Ind. 74, 56 N.E. 434.

42. Whitby v. One-O-One Trailer Rental Co., 1963, 191 Kan. 653, 383 P.2d 560; Erckman v. Northern Ill. Gas Co., 1965, 61 Ill.App.2d 137, 210 N.E.2d 42; Williams v. St. Louis Public Service Co., 1952, 363 Mo. 625, 253 S.W.2d 97; Sherman v. Hartman, 1955, 137 Cal.App.2d 589, 290 P.2d 894; Rauch v. Des Moines Elec. Co., 1928, 206 Iowa 309, 218 N.W. 340.

43. Johnson v. Greenfield, 1946, 210 Ark. 985, 198 S.W.2d 403; Nashville Interurban Ry. Co. v. Gregory, 1917, 137 Tenn. 422, 193 S.W. 1053; Briganti v. Connecticut Co., 1934, 119 Conn. 316, 175 A. 679; Loos v. Mountain Fuel Supply Co., 1940, 99 Utah 496, 108 P.2d 254.

If the plaintiff pleads only the specific negligence, without general allegations, the general inference of res ipsa loquitur may not support the specific pleadings. A derailment alone is no proof of an open switch. The policy underlying the rule that specific pleadings limit proof is that a defendant who comes into court with notice only of a specific claim should not be required to litigate other issues, or to meet inferences based on a theory advanced for the first time at the trial. But any inferences which will support the specific pleading should not be excluded.[44] And if the specific allegations are accompanied by a claim of negligence in general terms, the defendant has at least received notice that the plaintiff is not relying exclusively upon the specific allegations, and can scarcely claim to have been surprised or misled. Where both general and specific negligence are pleaded, the rule which permits the plaintiff to rely upon res ipsa loquitur if he does not succeed with his specific proof seems less artificial, and more likely to lead to a fair result on the merits.[45]

Effect of Rebutting Evidence

When the defendant in turn offers evidence to show that the event was not due to his negligence, there is the further question of the extent to which the principle of res ipsa loquitur will survive in the face of such proof. It is generally agreed, except in two or three jurisdictions,[46] that the burden of proof is not

upon the defendant, and that he is required to do no more than to introduce evidence which, if believed will permit the jury to say that it is as probable that he was not negligent as that he was.[47] Against this evidence must be balanced the inference of negligence to be drawn from the circumstances of the case, which has weight so long as reasonable men may still draw it from the facts in evidence.[48] Probably no more than this is meant by most of the cases which have said that the "presumption" of res ipsa loquitur is itself evidence, to be weighed against that of defendant.[49]

If the defendant seeks a directed verdict in his favor, he must produce evidence which will destroy any reasonable inference of negligence, or so completely contradict it that reasonable men could no longer accept it. The evidence necessary to do this will vary with the strength of the inference. It takes more of an explanation to justify a falling elephant than a falling brick, more to account for a hundred defective bottles than for one. If the defendant proves definitely by uncontradicted evidence that the occurrence was caused by some outside agency over which he had no control,[50] that it was of a kind

---

44. See cases cited supra, note 41.

45. If specific pleading is required in the first instance, or if the defendant succeeds in a motion to make the pleading more definite, the plaintiff obviously should not be denied the benefit of res ipsa loquitur. Rapp v. Butler-Newark Bus Lines, 1927, 103 N.J.L. 512, 138 A. 377, affirmed, 1928, 104 N.J.L. 444, 140 A. 921; Sutcliffe v. Fort Dodge Gas & Electric Co., 1934, 218 Iowa 1386, 257 N.W. 406. The possibility that res ipsa loquitur will be relied on furnishes an excellent reason for denying such a motion. See Harvey v. Borg, 1934, 218 Iowa 1228, 257 N.W. 190.

46. See supra, note 230.

47. Nopson v. Wockner, 1952, 40 Wash.2d 645, 245 P. 2d 1022; Micek v. Weaver-Jackson Co., 1936, 12 Cal.App.2d 19, 54 P.2d 768; Vonault v. O'Rourke, 1934, 97 Mont. 92, 33 P.2d 535; White v. Hines, 1921, 182 N.C. 275, 109 S.E. 31.

48. Motiejaitis v. Johnson, 1933, 117 Conn. 631, 169 A. 606; Humphrey v. Twin State Gas & Elec. Co., 1927, 100 Vt. 414, 139 A. 440; Lipsky v. C. Reiss Coal Co., 1908, 136 Wis. 307, 117 N.W. 803; Note, 1967, 43 N.D.L.Rev. 556.

49. Bush v. Barnett, 1892, 96 Cal. 202, 31 P. 2; Kay v. Metropolitan St. Ry. Co., 1900, 163 N.Y. 447, 57 N.E. 751. See McBaine, Presumptions: Are They Evidence, 1938, 26 Cal.L.Rev. 519.

50. Lopes v. Narragansett Elec. Co., 1967, 102 R.I. 128, 229 A.2d 55; Scarpelli v. Washington Water Power Co., 1911, 63 Wash. 18, 114 P. 870; Gray v. Baltimore & O. R. Co., 7 Cir. 1928, 24 F.2d 671; Tyreco Ref. Co. v. Cook, Tex.Civ.App.1937, 110 S.W. 2d 219, error dismissed; cf. Lea v. Carolina Power & Light Co., 1957, 246 N.C. 287, 98 S.E.2d 9.

which commonly occurs without negligence on the part of anyone,[51] or that it could not have been avoided by the exercise of all reasonable care,[52] the inference of negligence is no longer permissible, and the verdict is directed for the defendant. The res ipsa case has been overthrown by showing that it is not a res ipsa case.

But if the defendant merely offers evidence of his own acts and precautions amounting to reasonable care, it is seldom that a verdict can be directed in his favor.[53] The inference

from the circumstances remains in the case to contradict his evidence. If he testifies that he used proper care to insulate his wires,[54] to inspect his chandelier,[55] to drive his bus,[56] or to keep defunct mice and wandering insect life out of his bottled beverage,[57] the fact that electricity escaped from the wires, that the chandelier fell, that the bus went into the ditch and the bug was in the bottle, with the background of common experience that such things do not usually happen if proper care is used, may permit reasonable men to find that his witnesses are not to be believed, that the precautions described were not sufficient to conform to the standard required [58] or were not faithfully

But the mere introduction of contradicted or otherwise inconclusive evidence suggesting another cause will not entitle the defendant to a directed verdict. Glowacki v. North Western Ohio R. & P. Co., 1927, 116 Ohio St. 451, 157 N.E. 21; Wood v. Indemnity Ins. Co. of North America, 1956, 273 Wis. 93, 76 N.W.2d 610; Furr v. McGrath, Okl.1959, 340 P.2d 243; Manuel v. Pacific Gas & Elec. Co., 1933, 134 Cal.App. 512, 25 P.2d 509.

The evidence may of course be such that the jury is not compelled to accept it. Cf. Bressler v. New York Rapid Transit Corp., 1938, 277 N.Y. 200, 13 N.E.2d 772.

51. Bollenbach v. Bloomenthal, 1930, 341 Ill. 539, 173 N.E. 670; Tavani v. Swift & Co., 1918, 262 Pa. 184, 105 A. 55; Engelking v. Carlson, 1939, 13 Cal.2d 216, 88 P.2d 695; Chesapeake & Ohio R. Co. v. Baker, 1927, 149 Va. 549, 140 S.E. 648, 141 S.E. 753, addendum opinion, 1928, 150 Va. 647, 143 S.E. 299. Cf. Keefer v. Public Service Co., 1939, 185 Okl. 94, 90 P.2d 409.

52. Oliver v. Union Transfer Co., 1934, 17 Tenn.App. 694, 71 S.W.2d 478; Richards v. Oregon Short Line R. Co., 1912, 41 Utah 99, 123 P. 933; Ryder v. Kinsey, 1895, 62 Minn. 85, 64 N.W. 94.

53. Directed verdicts for defendant were upheld in Swenson v. Purity Baking Co., 1931, 183 Minn. 289, 236 N.W. 310; Dunning v. Kentucky Utilities Co., 1937, 270 Ky. 44, 109 S.W.2d 6; Nichols v. Continental Baking Co., 3 Cir., 1929, 34 F.2d 141. The correctness of these decisions seems open to question. As the defendant's evidence approaches definite proof that the defect could not be present, it is all the more clearly rebutted by the fact that the defect is there. See Prosser, The Procedural Effect of Res Ipsa Loquitur, 1936, 20 Minn.L.Rev. 241, 268; James, Proof of the Breach in Negligence Cases, 1951, 37 Va.L.Rev. 179, 227.

It is, however, possible that the evidence of due care may be found conclusively to refute the contention that the injury was traceable to the defendant, and to point to another possible cause. Cf. Rowe v.

Oscar Ewing Dist. Co., Ky.1962, 357 S.W.2d 882; Rogers v. Coca Cola Bottling Co., Tex.Civ.App.1941, 156 S.W.2d 325, error refused.

54. Humphrey v. Twin State Gas & Elec. Co., 1927, 100 Vt. 414, 139 A. 440. Cf. Ryan v. Zweck-Wollenberg Co., 1954, 266 Wis. 630, 64 N.W.2d 226; Reynolds Metals Co. v. Yturbide, 9 Cir. 1958, 258 F.2d 321, cert. denied 358 U.S. 840; Langlinais v. Geophysical Service, Inc., 1959, 237 La. 585, 111 So.2d 781.

55. Goldstein v. Levy, 1911, 74 Misc. 463, 132 N.Y.S. 373. Cf. Kemalyan v. Henderson, 1954, 45 Wash.2d 693, 277 P.2d 372 (administering anaesthetic).

56. Francisco v. Circle Tours Sightseeing Co., 1928, 125 Or. 80, 265 P. 801. Cf. Lewis v. Wolk, 1950, 312 Ky. 536, 228 S.W.2d 432; Terminal R. Ass'n v. Staengel, 8 Cir. 1941, 122 F.2d 271, cert. denied 314 U.S. 680; Union Pac. R. Co. v. Stanger, 9 Cir. 1943, 132 F.2d 982; Knippenberg v. Windemuth, 1968, 249 Md. 159, 238 A.2d 915; Tarter v. Souderton Motor Co., E.D.Pa.1966, 257 F.Supp. 598.

57. Crystal Coca Cola Bottling Co. v. Cathey, 1957, 83 Ariz. 163, 317 P.2d 1094; Coca-Cola Bottling Co. v. Davidson, 1937, 193 Ark. 825, 102 S.W.2d 833; Bagre v. Daggett Chocolate Co., 1940, 126 Conn. 659, 13 A.2d 757 (tooth filling in candy); Gustafson v. Gate City Co-op. Creamery, 1964, 80 S.D. 430, 126 N.W.2d 121 (glass in butter); Atlanta Coca-Cola Bottling Co. v. Burke, 1964, 109 Ga.App. 53, 134 S.E. 2d 909 (exploding bottle).

58. Crigger v. Coca Cola Bottling Co., 1915, 132 Tenn. 545, 179 S.W. 155; Collins Baking Co. v. Savage, 1933, 227 Ala. 408, 150 So. 336; Minutilla v. Providence Ice Cream Co., 1929, 50 R.I. 43, 144 A. 884; Webb v. Brown & Williamson Tobacco Co., 1939, 121 W.Va. 115, 2 S.E.2d 898.

carried out,[59] and that the whole truth has not been told. It is of course not impossible that proof of proper care may be so over-whelming as to call for a directed verdict, but in the ordinary case it will not be sufficient to destroy the inference from res ipsa loquitur.[60]

59. Richenbacher v. California Packing Corp., 1924, 250 Mass. 198, 145 N.E. 281; Try-Me Beverage Co. v. Harris, 1928, 217 Ala. 302, 116 So. 147; cf. Rozumailski v. Philadelphia Coca Cola Bottling Co., 1929, 296 Pa. 114, 145 A. 700. See Notes, 1935, 21 Va.L.Rev. 306; 1935, 23 Ky.L.J. 534.

60. Evans v. Missouri Pac. R. Co., 1937, 342 Mo. 420, 116 S.W.2d 8; J. C. Penny Co. v. Forrest, 1938, 183 Okl. 106, 80 P.2d 640; Landerman v. Hamilton, 1964, 230 Cal.App.2d 782, 41 Cal.Rptr. 335. See Note, 1963, 51 Ky.L.J. 771.

CHAPTER 7

PROXIMATE CAUSE

41. CAUSATION IN FACT

An essential element of the plaintiff's cause of action for negligence, or for that matter for any other tort, is that there be some reasonable connection between the act or omission of the defendant and the damage which the plaintiff has suffered. This connection usually is dealt with by the courts in terms of what is called "proximate cause," or "legal cause." There is perhaps nothing in the entire field of law which has called forth more disagreement, or upon which the opinions are in such a welter of confusion. Nor, despite the manifold attempts which have been made to clarify the subject,[1] is there yet any general agreement as to the proper approach. Much of this confusion is due to the fact that no one problem is involved, but a number of different problems, which are not distinguished clearly, and that language appropriate to a discussion of one is carried over to cast a shadow upon the others.[2]

"Proximate cause"—in itself an unfortunate term—is merely the limitation which the courts have placed upon the actor's responsibility for the consequences of his conduct. In a philosophical sense, the consequences of an act go forward to eternity, and the causes of an event go back to the discovery of America and beyond. "The fatal trespass done by Eve was cause of all our woe." But any attempt to impose responsibility upon such a basis would result in infinite liability for all wrongful acts, and would "set society on edge and fill the courts with endless litigation."[3] As a practical

1. Green, Rationale of Proximate Cause, 1927; Bohlen, The Probable or the Natural Consequence as the Test of Liability in Negligence, 1901, 49 Am.L. Reg. 79, 148; Bingham, Some Suggestions Concerning "Legal Cause" at Common Law, 1909, 9 Col. L.Rev. 16, 136; Smith, Legal Cause in Actions of Tort, 1911, 25 Harv.L.Rev. 102, 233; Beale, The Proximate Consequences of an Act, 1920, 33 Harv.L. Rev. 633; Green, Are Negligence and "Proximate" Cause Determined by the Same Test, 1923, 1 Tex.L. Rev. 224, 423; Edgerton, Legal Cause, 1924, 72 U.Pa. L.Rev. 211, 343; McLaughlin, Proximate Cause, 1925, 39 Harv.L.Rev. 149; Green, Are There Dependable Rules of Causation, 1929, 77 U.Pa.L.Rev. 601; Carpenter, Workable Rules for Determining Proximate Cause, 1932, 20 Cal.L.Rev. 229, 396, 471; Prosser, The Minnesota Court on Proximate Cause, 1936, 21 Minn.L.Rev. 19; Campbell, Duty, Fault and Legal Cause, [1938] Wis.L.Rev. 402; Gregory, Proximate Cause in Negligence—A Retreat from Rationalization, 1938, 6 U.Chi.L.Rev. 36; Carpenter, Proximate Cause, 1940–43, 14 So.Cal.L.Rev. 1, 115, 416, 15 So. Cal.L.Rev. 187, 304, 427, 16 So.Cal.L.Rev. 1, 61, 275; Morris, Proximate Cause in Minnesota, 1950, 34 Minn.L.Rev. 185; Green, Proximate Cause in Texas Negligence Law, 1950, 28 Tex.L.Rev. 71, 621, 755; Prosser, Proximate Cause in California, 1950, 38 Cal.L.Rev. 369; James and Perry, Legal Cause, 1951, 60 Yale L.J. 761; Myers, Causation and Common Sense, 1951, 5 U.Miami L.Q. 238; Morris, Duty, Negligence and Causation, 1952, 101 U.Pa.L. Rev. 189; Pound, Causation, 1957, 67 Yale L.J. 1. Williams, Causation in the Law, [1961] Camb.L.J. 62; Green, The Causal Relation Issue in Negligence Law, 1962, 60 Mich.L.Rev. 543.

2. See Prosser, Proximate Cause in California, 1950, 38 Cal.L.Rev. 369.

3. Mitchell, J., in North v. Johnson, 1894, 58 Minn. 242, 59 N.W. 1012. The same problems arise in the criminal law, where the limits of criminal responsibility are in question; and they are dealt with, broadly speaking, in the same manner. See Note, 1962, 56 Northw.U.L.Rev. 791. As to the comparative law, see Ryu, Causation in Criminal Law, 1958, 106 U.Pa.L.Rev. 773.

matter, legal responsibility must be limited to those causes which are so closely connected with the result and of such significance that the law is justified in imposing liability. Some boundary must be set to liability for the consequences of any act, upon the basis of some social idea of justice or policy.

This limitation is sometimes, although rather infrequently, one of the fact of causation. More often it is purely one of policy, of our more or less inadequately expressed ideas of what justice demands, or of administrative possibility and convenience, none of which have any connection with questions of causation at all. If the defendant excavates a hole by the side of the road, and the plaintiff's runaway horse runs into it,[4] it scarcely can be pretended that the hole was not a cause of the harm, and a very important one. If the defendant escapes responsibility, it is because the policy of the law does not require him to safeguard the plaintiff against such a risk. On the same basis, if the defendant drives through the state of New Jersey at an excessive speed, and arrives in Philadelphia in time to be struck by lightning,[5] his speed is a not unimportant cause of the accident, since without it he would not have been there in time; and if he is not liable to his passenger, it is because in the eyes of the law his negligence did not extend to such a risk. The attempt to deal with such cases in the language of causation can lead only to confusion.[6]

Although it is not without its complications, the simplest and most obvious problem connected with "proximate cause" is that of causation in fact.[7] Of all of the questions involved, it is easiest to dispose of that which has been regarded, traditionally, as the most difficult: has the conduct of the defendant caused the plaintiff's harm? This is a question of fact. It is, furthermore, a fact upon which all the learning, literature and lore of the law are largely lost. It is a matter upon which any layman is quite as competent to sit in judgment as the most experienced court. For that reason, in the ordinary case, it is peculiarly a question for the jury.

Causation is a fact. It is a matter of what has in fact occurred. A cause is a necessary antecedent: in a very real and practical sense, the term embraces all things which have so far contributed to the result that without them it would not have occurred.[8] It covers not only positive acts and active physical forces, but also pre-existing passive conditions which have played a material part in bringing about the event.[9] In particular, it covers the defendant's omissions as well as his acts. The failure to extinguish a fire may

---

child? Cf. Dombeck v. Chicago, St. P. M. & P. R. Co., 1964, 24 Wis.2d 420, 129 N.W.2d 185.

Suppose that he knew in advance the precise moment when the child would dash into the highway, and purposely operated his car at a carefully calculated speed, to arrive precisely at that instant, in order to kill the child. Would the speed be a cause of the death? So far as causation is concerned, can there be any difference between intent and negligence?

4. Cf. La Londe v. Peake, 1901, 82 Minn. 124, 84 N.W. 726; Alexander v. Town of New Castle, 1888, 115 Ind. 51, 17 N.E. 200; Milostan v. City of Chicago, 1909, 148 Ill.App. 540.

5. Cf. Berry v. Sugar Notch Borough, 1899, 191 Pa. 345, 43 A. 240; Balfe v. Kramer, 1936, 249 App. Div. 746, 291 N.Y.S. 842; Doss v. Town of Big Stone Gap, 1926, 145 Va. 520, 134 S.E. 563; Lewis v. Flint & P. M. R. Co., 1884, 54 Mich. 55, 19 N.W. 744.

6. Defendant operates his automobile over five miles of highway at a speed in excess of what is proper, and so arrives at a point in the street just at the moment that a child unexpectedly darts out from the curb. Is his speed a cause of the death of the

7. See, generally, Hart and Honoré, Causation in the Law, 1959; Becht and Miller, The Test of Factual Causation, 1961; Malone, Ruminations on Cause-in-Fact, 1956, 9 Stan.L.Rev. 60; Green, The Causal Relation Issue in Negligence Law, 1962, 60 Mich.L.Rev. 543.

8. "In a comprehensive sense, all the circumstances (powers, occasions, actions and conditions) necessary to an event and necessarily followed by it; in general, whatever in reality stands in relations analogous to those between a necessitated conclusion and its antecedent grounds." Funk & Wagnalls, New Standard Dictionary, 1923.

9. See infra, p. 247.

be quite as important in causing the destruction of a building as setting it in the first place.[10] The failure to fence a railway track may be a cause, and an important one, that a child is struck by a train.[11] It is familiar law that if such omissions are culpable they will result in liability.

On the other hand, an act or an omission is not regarded as a cause of an event if the particular event would have occurred without it. A failure to fence a hole in the ice plays no part in causing the death of runaway horses which could not have been halted if the fence had been there.[12] A failure to have a lifeboat ready is not a cause of the death of a man who sinks without trace immediately upon falling into the ocean.[13] The failure to install a proper fire escape on a hotel is no cause of the death of a man suf-

focated in his bed by smoke.[14] The omission of a traffic signal to an automobile driver who could not have seen it if it had been given is not a cause of the ensuing collision.[15] The omission of crossing signals by an approaching train is of no significance when an automobile driver runs into the sixty-eighth car.[16] The presence of a railroad embankment may be no cause of the inundation of the plaintiff's land by a cloudburst which would have flooded it in any case.[17]

From such cases [18] many courts have derived a rule, commonly known as the "but

---

10. McNally v. Colwell, 1892, 91 Mich. 527, 52 N.W. 70; Cobb v. Twitchell, 1926, 91 Fla. 539, 108 So. 186; Musgrove v. Pandelis, [1919] 2 K.B. 43.

11. Hayes v. Michigan Cent. R. Co., 1884, 111 U.S. 228; Heiting v. Chicago, R. I. & P. R. Co., 1911, 252 Ill. 466, 96 N.E. 842.

12. Stacy v. Knickerbocker Ice Co., 1893, 84 Wis. 614, 54 N.W. 1091; Sowles v. Moore, 1893, 65 Vt. 322, 26 A. 629. Cf. Ellis v. H. S. Finke, Inc., 6 Cir. 1960, 278 F.2d 54 (fall would not have been prevented by safety device on a hoist); Southern Bell Tel. & Tel. Co. v. Spears, 1956, 212 Ga. 537, 93 S.E.2d 659, conformed to 94 Ga.App. 329, 94 S.E.2d 514 (location of pole too close to highway; would have been hit if at proper distance); People's Service Drug Stores v. Somerville, 1931, 161 Md. 662, 158 A. 12 (poison label on prescription medicine would not have prevented too heavy a dose).

13. Ford v. Trident Fisheries Co., 1919, 232 Mass. 400, 122 N.E. 399; New York Cent. R. Co. v. Grimstad, 2 Cir. 1920, 264 F. 334; Russell v. Merchants & Miners Transp. Co., E.D.Va.1937, 19 F.Supp. 349. But cf. Kirincich v. Standard Dredging Co., 3 Cir. 1940, 112 F.2d 163, and Zinnel v. United States Shipping Board E. F. Corp., 2 Cir. 1925, 10 F.2d 47, where there was evidence that the drowning man might have been saved.

Cf. Berryhill v. Nichols, 1935, 171 Miss. 769, 158 So. 470, and Lippold v. Kidd, 1928, 126 Or. 160, 269 P. 210, where the evidence was that the best possible medical treatment would not have averted the injury.

14. Weeks v. McNulty, 1898, 101 Tenn. 495, 48 S.W. 809; Lee v. Carwile, La.App.1964, 168 So.2d 469; Smith v. The Texan, Inc., Tex.Civ.App.1944, 180 S.W.2d 1010, error refused (no showing guest made any effort to use it); Tibbits v. Crowell, Tex.1968, 434 S.W.2d 919 (no showing could have used it); Rosser v. Atlantic Trust & Security Co., 1937, 168 Va. 389, 191 S.E. 651 (at least two available exits).

15. Rouleau v. Blotner, 1931, 84 N.H. 539, 152 A. 916; Harvey v. Chesapeake & Potomac Tel. Co., 1956, 198 Va. 213, 93 S.E.2d 309. Accord: Gunnels v. Roach, 1963, 243 S.C. 248, 133 S.E.2d 757 (motorist inattentive, boy running into side of car); Peterson v. Nielsen, 1959, 9 Utah 2d 302, 343 P.2d 731 (slower speed would not have avoided collision); Sun Cab Co. v. Faulkner, 1932, 163 Md. 477, 163 A. 194 (same); Waugh v. Suburban Club Ginger Ale Co., 1948, 83 U.S.App.D.C. 226, 167 F.2d 758 (no lookout, but would not have seen).

16. Sullivan v. Boone, 1939, 205 Minn. 437, 286 N.W. 350; Wink v. Western Md. R. Co., 1935, 116 Pa. Super. 374, 176 A. 760. Accord: Holman v. Chicago, R. I. & P. R. Co., 1876, 62 Mo. 562 (a whistle means nothing to a cow); New Orleans & N. E. R. Co. v. Burge, 1941, 191 Miss. 303, 2 So.2d 825 (would not have been heard); Haire v. Brooks, 1938, 42 N.M. 634, 83 P.2d 980 (good brakes would not have stopped in time).

17. Baltimore & O. R. Co. v. Sulphur Spring Ind. School Dist., 1880, 96 Pa. 65; City of Piqua v. Morris, 1918, 98 Ohio St. 42, 120 N.E. 300; Illinois Cent. R. Co. v. Wright, 1924, 135 Miss. 435, 100 So. 1; Cole v. Shell Petroleum Corp., 1939, 149 Kan. 25, 86 P.2d 470.

18. Accord: Laidlaw v. Sage, 1899, 158 N.Y. 73, 52 N.E. 679; Powers v. Standard Oil Co., 1923, 98 N.J.L. 730, 119 A. 273, affirmed 98 N.J.Law 893, 121 A. 926; Boronkay v. Robinson & Carpenter, 1928, 247 N.Y. 365, 160 N.E. 400; Ham v. Greensboro Ice & Fuel Co., 1933, 204 N.C. 614, 169 S.E. 180; Schoonmaker v. Kaltenbach, 1940, 236 Wis. 138, 294 N.W. 794; Second Restatement of Torts, § 432(1).

for" or "sine qua non" rule, which may be stated as follows: The defendant's conduct is not a cause of the event, if the event would have occurred without it.[19] At most this must be a rule of exclusion: if the event would not have occurred "but for" the defendant's negligence, it still does not follow that there is liability, since considerations other than causation, which remain to be discussed, may prevent it.[20] It should be quite obvious that, once events are set in motion, there is, in terms of causation alone, no place to stop. The event without millions of causes is simply inconceivable; and causation alone can provide no clue of any kind to singling out those which are to be held legally responsible. It is for this reason that instructions to the jury that they must find the defendant's conduct to be "the sole cause," or "the dominant cause," or "the proximate cause" of the injury are rightly condemned as misleading error.[21]

Restricted to the question of causation alone, and regarded merely as a rule of exclusion, the "but for" rule serves to explain the greater number of cases; but there is one type of situation in which it fails. If two causes concur to bring about an event, and either one of them, operating alone, would have been sufficient to cause the identical result, some other test is needed. Two motorcycles simultaneously pass the plaintiff's horse, which is frightened and runs away; either one alone would have caused the fright.[22] A stabs C with a knife, and B fractures C's skull with a rock; either wound would be fatal, and C dies from the effects of both.[23] The defendant sets a fire, which merges with a fire from some other source; the combined fires burn the plaintiff's property, but either one would have done it alone.[24] In such cases it is quite clear that each cause has in fact played so important a part in producing the result that responsibility should be imposed upon it; and it is equally clear that neither can be absolved from that responsibility upon the ground that the identical harm would have occurred without it, or there would be no liability at all.[25]

    T. S. A. v. Newtown Creek T. Co., 2 Cir. 1938, 98 F.2d 694.

23. Wilson v. State, Tex.Cr.1893, 24 S.W. 409. Accord: Glick v. Ballentine Produce, Inc., Mo.1965, 396 S.W.2d 609, appeal dismissed 385 U.S. 5; Thompson v. Louisville & N. R. Co., 1890, 91 Ala. 496, 8 So. 406; People v. Lewis, 1899, 124 Cal. 551, 57 P. 470. A further situation might be suggested, where no one of the acts would alone have caused the result, and no one act was essential to it—as where five men independently beat a sixth, and he dies from the effect of all of the beatings, and would have died from any three.

Cf. McAllister v. Workmen's Compensation Appeals Board, 1968, 69 Cal.2d 408, 71 Cal.Rptr. 697, 445 P.2d 313 (lung cancer from smoke inhaled in fighting fires, and from smoking cigarettes); Basko v. Sterling Drug Co., 2d Cir. 1969, 416 F.2d 417 (blindness resulting from use of two drugs).

24. Anderson v. Minneapolis, St. P. & S. S. M. R. Co., 1920, 146 Minn. 430, 179 N.W. 45; Seckerson v. Sinclair, 1913, 24 N.D. 625, 140 N.W. 239. Cf. Appalachian Power Co. v. Wilson, 1925, 142 Va. 468, 129 S.E. 277.

In Cook v. Minneapolis, St. P. & S. S. M. R. Co., 1898, 98 Wis. 624, 74 N.W. 561, the court drew a fine distinction between the case of two fires, both of responsible origin, and the case where one fire has no responsible source, holding that in the latter case there is no liability upon the responsible defendant. Later, in Kingston v. Chicago & N. W. R. Co., 1927, 191 Wis. 610, 211 N.W. 913, the court more or less nullified the effect of the rule by holding that the burden was upon the defendant to prove the natural origin of the other fire. The distinction has been rejected elsewhere. See Carpenter, Concurrent Causation, 1935, 83 U.Pa.L.Rev. 941.

25. An interesting negative application of the same problem, where the negligence of each of two parties prevents the other from being a cause, is suggested by Saunders System Birmingham Co. v.

---

19. See Smith, Legal Cause in Actions of Tort, 1911, 25 Harv.L.Rev. 103, 106, 109; McLaughlin, Proximate Cause, 1925, 39 Harv.L.Rev. 149, 155.

20. See Gilman v. Noyes, 1876, 57 N.H. 627, 631.

21. Barringer v. Arnold, 1960, 358 Mich. 594, 101 N. W.2d 365; Strobel v. Chicago, R. I. & P. R. Co., 1959, 255 Minn. 201, 96 N.W.2d 195; Henthorne v. Hopwood, 1959, 218 Or. 336, 345 P.2d 249; Pigg v. Brockman, 1963, Idaho 492, 381 P.2d 286; Gantt v. Sissell, 1954, 222 Ark. 902, 263 S.W.2d 916.

22. Corey v. Havener, 1902, 182 Mass. 250, 65 N.E. 69. Cf. Oulighan v. Butler, 1905, 189 Mass. 287, 75 N.E. 726; Orton v. Virginia Carolina Chemical Co., 1918, 142 La. 790, 77 So. 632; Navigazione Libera

It was in a case of this type [26] that the Minnesota court applied a broader rule, which has found general acceptance: [27] The defendant's conduct is a cause of the event if it was a material element and a substantial factor in bringing it about. Whether it was such a substantial factor is for the jury to determine, unless the issue is so clear that reasonable men could not differ. It has been considered [28] that "substantial factor" is a phrase sufficiently intelligible to the layman to furnish an adequate guide in instructions to the jury, and that it is neither possible nor desirable to reduce it to any lower terms. As applied to the fact of causation alone, no better test has been devised.[29]

> Adams, 1928, 217 Ala. 621, 117 So. 72, and Rouleau v. Blotner, 1931, 84 N.H. 539, 152 A. 916, neither of which considered the point. A supplies B with a car with no brakes; B makes no attempt to apply the brakes, and C is hit. Or A fails to signal for a left turn; B is not looking, but would see no signal if he did; there is a collision, and C is injured. It may be said with some confidence that if any such case is considered, both parties will be held liable; but the theory of liability is not so clear. Perhaps the best guess is that each, by his negligence, has deprived the plaintiff of a cause of action against the other, and so should be liable.

26. Anderson v. Minneapolis, St. P. & S. S. M. R. Co., 1920, 146 Minn. 430, 179 N.W. 45. The court no doubt was influenced by the suggestion of the test in Smith, Legal Cause of Actions of Tort, 1911, 25 Harv.L.Rev. 103, 223, 229.

27. Carney v. Goodman, 1954, 38 Tenn.App. 55, 270 S.W.2d 572; Walton v. Blauert, 1949, 256 Wis. 125, 40 N.W.2d 545; New Orleans & N. E. R. Co. v. Burge, 1941, 191 Miss. 303, 2 So.2d 825; Dunham v. Village of Canisteo, 1952, 303 N.Y. 498, 104 N.E.2d 872; Edgecomb v. Great A. & P. Tea Co., 1941, 127 Conn. 488, 18 A.2d 364; Second Restatement of Torts, §§ 431, 433. See Note, 1964, 15 West.Res.L.Rev. 807.

28. Green, Rationale of Proximate Cause, 1927, 132–141; Green, The Causal Relation Issue, 1962, 60 Mich.L.Rev. 543, 554. Hart and Honoré, Causation in the Law, 1959, 216–218, 263–266, object strongly to the phrase as undefinable. So, Green suggests, is "reasonable;" but that does not prevent its use to pose an issue for the jury.

29. The test is one of significance, rather than of largeness or smallness, or quantum. McDowell v. Davis, 1969, 104 Ariz. 69, 448 P.2d 869.

Such a formula, for it can scarcely be called a test, is clearly an improvement over the "but for" rule. It disposes of the cases mentioned above, and likewise of the difficulties presented by two other types of situations which have proved troublesome. One is that where a similar, but not identical result would have followed without the defendant's act; [30] the other where one defendant has made a clearly proved but quite insignificant contribution to the result, as where he throws a lighted match into a forest fire.[31] But in the great majority of cases, it amounts to the same thing. Except as indicated, no case has been found where the defendant's act could be called a substantial factor when the event would have occurred without it; [32] nor will cases very often arise where it would not be such a factor when it was so indispensable a cause that without it the result would not have followed.[33]

If the defendant's conduct was a substantial factor in causing the plaintiff's injury, it follows that he will not be absolved from liability merely because other causes have contributed to the result, since such causes, innumerable, are always present. In particu-

As to the use of "substantial factor" in a broader sense, to include elements of "proximate" cause, see infra, p. 248.

30. Thus the case put by Carpenter, Workable Rules for Determining Proximate Cause, 1932, 20 Cal.L. Rev. 229, 396, where A and B each sell a rope to C, who is bent on hanging himself, and C hangs himself with A's rope. A's act is a substantial factor in causing C's death, while B's is not. Whether A is liable is not a question of causation, but of the effect of the intervening act of C. See infra, § 51.

31. See Golden v. Lerch Bros., 1938, 203 Minn. 211, 281 N.W. 249; Connellan v. Coffey, 1936, 122 Conn. 136, 187 A. 901; Huey v. Milligan, 1961, 242 Ind. 93, 175 N.E.2d 698.

32. Well stated in Texas & Pac. T. Co. v. McCleery, Tex.1967, 418 S.W.2d 494.

33. See, indicating the identity of the two rules, Schultz v. Brogan, 1947, 251 Wis. 390, 29 N.W.2d 719; New Orleans & N. E. R. Co. v. Burge, 1941, 191 Miss. 303, 2 So.2d 825; West Texas Utilities v. Harris, Tex.Civ.App.1950, 231 S.W.2d 558.

lar, however, a defendant is not necessarily relieved of liability because the negligence of another person is also a contributing cause, and that person, too, is to be held liable.[34] Thus where two vehicles collide and injure a bystander, or a passenger in one of them, each driver may be liable for the harm inflicted.[35] The law of joint tortfeasors rests very largely upon recognition of the fact that each of two or more causes may be charged with a single result.[36]

It cannot be repeated too often that, while causation is essential to liability, it does not determine it. Other considerations, which remain to be considered, may prevent liability for results clearly caused.

Proof

On the issue of the fact of causation, as on other issues essential to his cause of action for negligence, the plaintiff, in general,[37] has the burden of proof. He must introduce evidence which affords a reasonable basis for the conclusion that it is more likely than not that the conduct of the defendant was a substantial factor in bringing about the result. A mere possibility of such causation is not enough;[38] and when the matter remains one

of pure speculation or conjecture,[39] or the probabilities are at best evenly balanced,[40] it becomes the duty of the court to direct a verdict for the defendant. Where the conclusion is not one within the common knowledge of laymen, expert testimony may provide a sufficient basis for it,[41] but in the absence of such testimony it may not be drawn.[42] But on medical matters on which laymen are compe-

34. Washington & G. R. Co. v. Hickey, 1897, 166 U.S. 521; Nees v. Minneapolis St. R. Co., 1944, 218 Minn. 532, 16 N.W.2d 758; Erie County United Bank v. Berk, 1943, 73 Ohio St. 314, 56 N.E.2d 285, motion overruled; Hill v. Edmonds, 1966, 26 App.Div.2d 554, 270 N.Y.S.2d 1020.

35. Chiles v. Rohl, 1924, 47 S.D. 580, 201 N.W. 154; Kinley v. Hines, 1927, 106 Conn. 82, 137 A. 9; Peters v. Johnson, 1928, 124 Or. 237, 264 P. 459; Glazener v. Safety Transit Lines, 1929, 196 N.C. 504, 146 S.E. 134; McDonald v. Robinson, 1929, 207 Iowa 1293, 224 N.W. 820.

36. See infra, § 47.

37. As to the special situation of alternative tort feasors, see infra, p. 243.

38. Kramer Service v. Wilkins, 1939, 184 Miss. 483, 186 So. 625; Gipson v. Memphis St. R. Co., 1962, 51 Tenn.App. 31, 364 S.W.2d 110; Rutherford v. Modern Bakery, Ky.1958, 310 S.W.2d 274; Florig v. Sears, Roebuck & Co., 1957, 388 Pa. 419, 130 A.2d 445; Tombigbee Elec. Power Co. v. Gandy, 1953, 216 Miss. 444, 62 So.2d 567.

39. Wintersteen v. Semler, 1953, 197 Or. 601, 255 P.2d 138; Sears v. Mid-City Motors, Inc., 1965, 178 Neb. 175, 132 N.W.2d 361, withdrawn 179 Neb. 100, 136 N.W.2d 428; Atchison, T. & S. F. R. Co. v. Hamilton Bros., 8 Cir. 1951, 192 F.2d 817; Alling v. Northwestern Bell Tel. Co., 1923, 156 Minn. 60, 194 N.W. 313; Gipson v. Memphis St. R. Co., 1962, 51 Tenn. App. 31, 364 S.W.2d 110.

40. Farmers Home Mut. Ins. Co. v. Grand Forks Imp. Co., 1952, 79 N.D. 177, 55 N.W.2d 315; Lane v. Hampton, 1955, 197 Va. 46, 87 S.E.2d 803; Eckley v. Seese, 1955, 382 Pa. 425, 115 A.2d 227; Altrichter v. Shell Oil Co., D.Minn.1958, 161 F.Supp. 46; Phillips Petroleum Co. v. West, Tex.Civ.App.1955, 284 S.W.2d 196, ref. n. r. e. But where the choice is between two causes, with negligence of the defendant shown as to each, the plaintiff's case is made out. Brumm v. Goodall, 1958, 16 Ill.App.2d 212, 147 N.E.2d 699.

41. Dunham v. Village of Canisteo, 1952, 303 N.Y. 498, 104 N.E.2d 872; Pritchard v. Liggett & Myers Tobacco Co., 3 Cir. 1961, 295 F.2d 292; Lee v. Blessing, 1945, 131 Conn. 569, 41 A.2d 337; Oklahoma Nat. Gas Co. v. Gray, 1951, 204 Okl. 362, 230 P.2d 256; Foley v. Pittsburgh-Des Moines Co., 1949, 363 Pa. 1, 68 A.2d 517. See Small, Gaffing at a Thing Called Cause, 1953, 31 Tex.L.Rev. 630.

As to the medical problem of cancer following traumatic injury, see Dyke, Traumatic Cancer? 1966, 15 Cleve.Marsh.L.Rev. 472; Parsons, Sufficiency of Proof in Traumatic Cancer Cases, 1961, 45 Corn. L.Q. 581; Elliott, Traumatic Cancer and "An Old Misunderstanding Between Doctors and Lawyers," 1964, 13 Kan.L.Rev. 79; Note, 1961, 46 Corn.L.Q. 581.

As to the meaning of "causation" to a doctor, see Powers, After All, Doctors Are Human, 1963, 15 U.Fla.L.Rev. 463.

42. Kramer Service v. Wilkins, 1939, 184 Miss. 483, 186 So. 625; Christensen v. Northern States Power Co., 1946, 222 Minn. 474, 25 N.W.2d 659; Blizzard v. Fitzsimmons, 1942, 193 Miss. 484, 10 So.2d 343; Blarjeske v. Thompson's Restaurant Co., 1945, 325 Ill.App. 189, 59 N.E.2d 320; Goodwin v. Misticos, 1949, 207 Miss. 361, 42 So.2d 397.

tent to judge, no expert testimony is required to permit a conclusion as to causation.[43]

The plaintiff is not, however, required to prove his case beyond a reasonable doubt. He need not negative entirely the possibility that the defendant's conduct was not a cause,[44] and it is enough that he introduces evidence from which reasonable men may conclude that it is more probable that the event was caused by the defendant than that it was not.[45] The fact of causation is incapable of mathematical proof, since no man can say with absolute certainty what would have occurred if the defendant had acted otherwise. Proof of what we call the relation of cause and effect, that of necessary antecedent and inevitable consequence, can be nothing more than "the projection of our habit of expecting certain consequents to follow certain antecedents merely because we had observed these sequences on previous occasions."[46] If as a matter of ordinary experience a particular act or omission might be expected, under the circumstances, to produce a particular result, and that result in fact has followed, the conclusion may be permissible that the causal relation exists.

Circumstantial evidence,[47] expert testimony,[48] or common knowledge may provide a basis from which the causal sequence may be inferred. Thus it is every day experience that unlighted stairs create a danger that someone will fall. Such a condition "greatly multiplies the chances of accident, and is of a character naturally leading to its occurrence."[49] When a fat woman tumbles down the steps, it is a reasonable conclusion that it is more likely than not that the bad lighting has played a substantial part in the fall. When a child is drowned in a swimming pool, no one can say with certainty that a lifeguard would have saved him; but the experience of the community permits the conclusion that the absence of the guard played a significant part in the drowning.[50] Such questions are peculiarly for the jury; and whether proper construction of a building would have withstood an earthquake,[51] or whether reasonable police precautions would have prevented a boy from shooting the plaintiff in the eye with an airgun,[52] are questions on which a court can

43. See for example Mitchell v. Coca Cola Bottling Co., 1960, 11 App.Div.2d 579, 200 N.Y.S.2d 478, where a child drank a beverage containing an insect, immediately vomited, and was subsequently made ill.

44. Ominsky v. Charles Weinhagen & Co., 1911, 113 Minn. 422, 129 N.W. 845; Gates v. Boston & Me. R. Co., 1926, 255 Mass. 297, 151 N.E. 320; Cornbrooks v. Terminal Barber Shops, 1940, 282 N.Y. 217, 26 N.E.2d 25.

45. State of Maryland for Use of Pumphrey v. Manor Real Estate & Trust Co., 4 Cir. 1949, 176 F.2d 414; Saad v. Pappageorge, 1926, 82 N.H. 294, 133 A. 24; MacIntosh v. Great Northern R. Co., 1922, 151 Minn. 527, 188 N.W. 551; Harmon v. Richardson, 1936, 88 N.H. 312, 188 A. 468 ("a little more probable than otherwise"); Simpson v. Logan Motor Co., Mun. App.D.C.1963, 192 A.2d 122.

46. See Wolf, Causality, 5 Encyclopedia Britannica, 14th Ed. 1929, 61, 62; Pearson, The Grammar of Science, 1911, 113 ff.

47. Emery v. Tilo Roofing Co., 1937, 89 N.H. 165, 195 A. 409; Paine v. Gamble Stores, 1938, 202 Minn. 462, 279 N.W. 257; Messing v. Judge & Dolph Drug Co., 1929, 322 Mo. 901, 18 S.W.2d 408; Mulligan v. Atlantic Coast Line R. Co., 1916, 104 S.C. 173, 88 S.E. 445, affirmed 1917, 242 U.S. 620; Casey v. Phillips Pipeline Co., 1967, 199 Kan. 538, 431 P.2d 518.

48. See supra, note 241.

49. Reynolds v. Texas & Pac. R. Co., 1885, 37 La. Ann. 694. Cf. Sullivan v. Hamacher, 1959, 339 Mass. 190, 158 N.E.2d 301; Ingersoll v. Liberty Bank, 1938, 278 N.Y. 1, 14 N.E.2d 828; Parkinson v. California Co., 10 Cir. 1956, 233 F.2d 432; Kirincich v. Standard Dredging Co., 3 Cir. 1940, 112 F.2d 163; Texas Sling Co. v. Emanuel. Tex.Civ.App.1967, 418 S.W.2d 565, affirmed in part, reversed in part 431 S.W.2d 538.

50. Rovegno v. San Jose Knights of Columbus Hall, 1930, 108 Cal.App. 591, 291 P. 848. Otherwise when there is evidence indicating the man could not have been saved. Blacka v. James, 1964, 205 Va. 646, 139 S.E.2d 47.

51. Finch v. McKee, 1936, 18 Cal.App.2d 90, 62 P.2d 1380.

52. Stockwell v. Board of Trustees of Leland Stanford Jr. University, 1944, 64 Cal.App.2d 197, 148 P.

seldom rule as a matter of law. And whether the defendant's negligence consists of the violation of some statutory safety regulation, or the breach of a plain common law duty of care, the court can scarcely overlook the fact that the injury which has in fact occurred is precisely the sort of thing that proper care on the part of the defendant would be intended to prevent, and accordingly allow a certain liberality to the jury in drawing its conclusion.[53]

There is one special type of situation in which the usual rule that the burden of proof as to causation is on the plaintiff has been relaxed. It may be called that of clearly established double fault and alternative liability. Where, for example, two defendants negligently shoot across a public highway at the same time, and the plaintiff is struck by one shot, which might have been fired from either gun, it is clear that both marksmen were at fault, and that one of them, and only one, has caused the injury. Instead of dismissing the action against both for lack of a

preponderance of proof against either, the courts have displayed some eagerness to find concert of action, and so permit recovery against both.[54]

In this situation the California supreme court has solved the problem by placing the burden of proof on the issue of causation upon the two defendants.[55] There is support for this in three Canadian decisions,[56] and in American automobile cases of "chain collisions," in which the plaintiff is injured by one of two or more negligently driven cars, but cannot prove which.[57] It seems a very desirable solution where negligence on the part of both defendants is clear, and it is only the issue of causation which is in doubt, so that the choice must be made between letting the loss due to failure of proof fall upon the innocent plaintiff or the culpable defendants. But where there is no evidence even as to where culpability lies, the hardship may be equally great upon an innocent

2d 405. Cf. Chavira v. Carnahan, 1967, 77 N.M. 467, 423 P.2d 988; Tullgren v. Amoskeag Mfg. Co., 1926, 82 N.H. 268, 133 A. 4; Gates v. Boston & M. R. Co., 1926, 255 Mass. 297, 151 N.E. 320; Houren v. Chicago, M. & St. P. R. Co., 1908, 236 Ill. 620, 86 N.E. 611.

53. See for example Louisville Trust Co. v. Morgan, 1918, 180 Ky. 609, 203 S.W. 555; Kohn v. Clark, 1912, 236 Pa. 18, 84 A. 692. This is well discussed in Malone, Ruminations on Cause-in-Fact, 1956, 9 Stan.L.Rev. 60.

Two striking exceptional cases, both based on statutory policy, appear to have carried this to an extreme length. One is Pierce v. Albanese, 1957, 144 Conn. 241, 129 A.2d 606, appeal dismissed 355 U.S. 15, holding that where the Dramshop Act is violated, the defendant will not be heard to say that there is no causation of intoxication. As a constitutional exercise of the police power, there is a complete departure from "the common law precepts of proximate cause." The other is Wilson v. Hanley, 1960, 224 Or. 570, 356 P.2d 556, where apparently much the same effect is given to a regulation of the State Industrial Commission. See also Virginian R. Co. v. Calhoun, 1959, 200 Va. 908, 108 S.E.2d 239, holding that under the Federal Employers' Liability Act it is enough that the employer's negligence has made any contribution whatever to the result, however slight.

54. Oliver v. Miles, 1927, 144 Miss. 852, 110 So. 666; Benson v. Ross, 1906, 143 Mich. 452, 106 N.W. 1120; Kuhn v. Bader, 1951, 89 Ohio App. 203, 101 N.E.2d 322; cf. Regina v. Salmon, 1880, 6 Q.B.D. 79; State v. Newberg, 1929, 129 Or. 564, 278 P. 568.

55. Summers v. Tice, 1948, 33 Cal.2d 80, 199 P.2d 1. The court merely extended the rule as to the burden of proof on the issue of apportionment of damages. See infra, p. 319.

56. Cook v. Lewis, [1952] 1 Dom.L.Rep. 1, [1951] S.C. Rep. 830 (similar facts); Woodward v. Begbie, 1961, 31 Dom.L.Rep.2d 22; Saint-Pierre v. McCarthy, [1957] Que.Rep. 421 (merchants selling cartridges to boys). The first of these cases is attacked in Hogan, Cook v. Lewis Re-examined, 1961, 24 Mod.L.Rev. 331.

57. Murphy v. Taxicabs of Louisville, Inc., Ky.1959, 330 S.W.2d 395; Cummings v. Kendall, 1940, 41 Cal.App.2d 549, 107 P.2d 282; Eramdjian v. Interstate Bakery Corp., 1957, 153 Cal.App.2d 590, 315 P. 2d 19; Copley v. Putter, 1949, 93 Cal.App.2d 453, 207 P.2d 876. Cf. Micelli v. Hirsch, Ohio App.1948, 83 N.E.2d 240 (result accomplished by presumption of continuing life). See also, as to apportionment of damages, infra, p. 319.

A badly confused case is Clark v. Gibbons, 1967, 66 Cal. 2d 399, 58 Cal.Rptr. 125, 426 P.2d 525, where this principle apparently was applied, under the misnomer of res ipsa loquitur, to the negligence of two physicians, which might possibly have been causal.

defendant; and except in very special cases [58] the courts have refused to shift the burden of proof.[59]

42. PROXIMATE CAUSE: SCOPE OF THE PROBLEM

Once it is established that the defendant's conduct has in fact been one of the causes of the plaintiff's injury,[60] there remains the question whether the defendant should be legally responsible for what he has caused. Unlike the fact of causation, with which it is often hopelessly confused, this is essentially a problem of law.[61] It is sometimes said to be a question of whether the conduct has been so significant and important a cause that the defendant should be legally responsible. But both significance and importance turn upon conclusions in terms of legal policy, so that this becomes essentially a question of whether the policy of the law will extend the responsibility for the conduct to the consequences which have in fact occurred. Quite often this has been stated, and properly so, as an issue of whether the defendant is under any duty to the plaintiff, or whether his duty includes protection against such consequences. This is not a question of causation, or even a question of fact, but quite far removed from both; and the attempt to deal with it in such terms has led and can lead only to utter confusion.[62]

The term "proximate cause" is applied by the courts to those more or less undefined considerations which limit liability even where the fact of causation is clearly established. The word "proximate" is a legacy of Lord Chancellor Bacon,[63] who in his time committed other sins. The word means nothing more than near or immediate; and when it was first taken up by the courts it had connotations of proximity in time and space which have long since disappeared. It is an unfortunate word, which places an entirely wrong emphasis upon the factor of physical or mechanical closeness. For this reason "legal cause" [64] or perhaps even "responsible cause" would be a more appropriate term. There is, however, no present prospect that long ingrained practice will ever be altered by the substitution of either.

Relation to Duty

It is quite possible, and often helpful, to state every question which arises in connection with "proximate cause" in the form of a single question: was the defendant under a duty to protect the plaintiff against the event which did in fact occur?[65] Such a form of statement does not, of course, provide any answer to the question, or solve anything whatever; [66] but it does serve to direct attention to the policy issues which determine the extent of the original obligation and of its continuance, rather than to the mechanical sequence of events which goes to make up causation in fact. The question becomes par-

---

58. See supra, p. 231.

59. See supra, p. 223.

60. See supra, § 41.

61. Well stated in Green, Proximate Cause in Texas Negligence Law, 1950, 28 Tex.L.Rev. 471, 621, 755.

62. See the odd museum collection of utterances on the subject, some of them quite profound and others quite leather-headed, in Lewis, Proximate Cause in Law, 1933, 7 U.Fla.Bar Ass'n J. 109, 138, 158.

63. "In jure non remota causa, sed proxima, spectatur. [In law the near cause is looked to, not the remote one.] It were infinite for the law to judge the cause of causes, and their impulsion of one another; therefore it contenteth itself with the immediate cause, and judgeth of acts by that, without looking to any further degree." Bacon, Maxims of the Law, Reg. I.

64. See Edgerton, Legal Cause, 1924, 72 U.Pa.L.Rev. 211; Morris, On the Teaching of Legal Cause, 1939, 39 Col.L.Rev. 1087; Second Restatement of Torts, § 431.

65. Green, Rationale of Proximate Cause, 1927, 11–43; Campbell, Duty, Fault and Legal Cause, [1938] Wis. L.Rev. 402. See O'Connell, J., concurring, in Dewey v. A. F. Klaveness & Co., 1963, 233 Or. 515, 379 P.2d 560.

66. Prosser, Palsgraf Revisited, 1953, 52 Mich.L.Rev. 1, reprinted in Prosser, Selected Topics on the Law of Torts, 1954, 191.

ticularly helpful in cases where the only issue is in reality one of whether the defendant is under any duty to the plaintiff at all— which is to say, whether he stands in any such relation to the plaintiff as to create any legally recognized obligation of conduct for his benefit. Or, reverting again to the starting point, whether the interests of the plaintiff are entitled to legal protection at the defendant's hands against the invasion which has in fact occurred. Or, again reverting, whether the conduct is the "proximate cause" of the result. The circumlocution is unavoidable, since all of these questions are, in reality, one and the same.

This has been common enough in cases where the plaintiff was outside of the zone of any obvious danger from the defendant's conduct, and so no harm to him was to have been anticipated,[67] as where a fire set by the defendant spreads to an unusual distance,[68] or a train strikes an object on the track and throws it against a person in a position of apparent safety;[69] and likewise where harm results from a violation of a statute, such as a Sunday law, which was not designed to afford the plaintiff any protection.[70] It appears also in cases, such as those involving mental disturbance,[71] where the court is in reality

saying that the particular interest invaded is not entitled to legal redress. In all such cases the causal connection between the act and the harm is usually clear and direct, and the attempt to subdivide the indivisible by way of "proximate" only offers obstacles to the determination of the real issue.

The ordinary usage of the courts has been to confine the word "duty" to questions of the existence of some relation between the defendant and the plaintiff which gives rise to the obligation of conduct in the first instance, and to deal with the connection between that obligation, once it has arisen, and the consequences which have followed in the language of "proximate cause." The usage is no doubt well enough, so long as it is not allowed to obscure the fact that identical questions are often still involved, and buried under the two terms, sometimes so deeply that a good deal of digging is called for to uncover them.

Confusion with Standard of Conduct

In other cases the standard of reasonable conduct does not require the defendant to recognize the risk, or to take precautions against it. The owner of an automobile who leaves it unattended in the street ordinarily is not required to anticipate that other persons will move it;[72] a city need not provide all its bridges with railings sufficient to keep any car from going over the edge;[73] the owner of premises need not foresee that the wind will swing a door against a boy and put out his eye;[74] and no one is required to anticipate a storm of unprecedented violence,[75] or foresee that a cow will knock a

67. See infra, p. 254.

68. Cf. Ryan v. New York Cent. R. Co., 1866, 35 N.Y. 210, 91 Am.Dec. 49; Hoag & Alger v. Lake Shore & M. S. R. Co., 1877, 85 Pa. 293; Smith v. London & S. W. R. Co., 1870, L.R. 6 C.P. 14; Kuhn v. Jewett, 1880, 32 N.J.Eq. 647.

69. See infra, p. 263.

70. Cf. Tingle v. Chicago, B. & Q. R. Co., 1882, 60 Iowa 333, 14 N.W. 320; Dervin v. Frenier, 1917, 91 Vt. 398, 100 A. 760; Armstead v. Lounsberry, 1915, 129 Minn. 34, 151 N.W. 542; Falk v. Finkelman, 1929, 268 Mass. 524, 168 N.E. 89.

Compare also the cases of Howard v. Redden, 1919, 93 Conn. 604, 107 A. 509 (liability of building contractor where owner failed to inspect); Missouri, K. & T. R. Co. v. Merrill, 1902, 65 Kan. 436, 70 P. 358 (carrier delivering defective car to connecting line), where the decision must be supported, if at all, upon the ground that there was no duty to the plaintiff.

71. See infra, § 54.

72. Cf. Slater v. T. C. Baker Co., 1927, 261 Mass. 424, 158 N.E. 778; Squires v. Brooks, 1916, 44 App.D.C. 320; Kennedy v. Hedberg, 1924, 159 Minn. 76, 198 N.W. 302.

73. Cf. Tracey v. City of Minneapolis, 1932, 185 Minn. 380, 241 N.W. 390. Compare Jones v. City of Fort Dodge, 1919, 185 Iowa 600, 171 N.W. 16.

74. Cf. Morril v. Morril, 1928, 104 N.J.L. 557, 142 A. 337, 60 A.L.R. 102.

75. Cf. Strobeck v. Bren, 1904, 93 Minn. 428, 101 N. W. 795.

man under a train.[76] In these cases the defendant is simply not negligent. When the courts say that his conduct is not the "proximate cause" of the harm, they not only obscure the real issue, but suggest artificial distinctions of causation which have no sound basis, and can only arise to plague them in the future.

Confusion with Defenses to Negligence Action

In many cases where the negligence of the defendant is clearly established the plaintiff is barred from recovery by his contributory negligence.[77] It is said sometimes that this is because the defendant's negligence is not the proximate cause of the harm, since the plaintiff's act has intervened.[78] But certainly in the ordinary contributory negligence case, as where two automobiles collide, the causal connection is quite clear, and there is no doubt that both parties have played an important part in bringing about the result. A rule which has its foundations in the common law's individualistic notions of policy is rationalized by distorting the facts to create imaginary distinctions between causes.[79] Similar fictitious reasoning is found as to the doctrine of the "last clear chance," [80] the

defense of assumption of risk,[81] and the rule as to avoidable consequences,[82] which bars the plaintiff from recovery for damages which he might himself have avoided with reasonable care. "Proximate cause," in short, has been all things to all men. "Having no integrated meaning of its own, its chameleon quality permits it to be substituted for any one of the elements of a negligence case when decision on that element becomes difficult. * * * No other formula * * * so nearly does the work of Aladdin's lamp." [83]

Proposed Formulae

The search for some test or formula which will serve as a universal solvent for all of the problems of "proximate cause" has occupied many writers. Among the dozens of touchstones and panaceas which have been proposed, the following deserve special mention: [84]

The nearest cause. The word "proximate," in itself, means nothing more than near, or possibly nearest. Bacon's maxim,[85] taken literally, would mean that only the antecedent which is nearest in time or space is to be regarded as the legal cause, and none other will be held responsible. Whether Bacon really meant anything of the sort is at least doubtful.[86] If he did, the courts have long since ceased to pay attention to him. It is of course obvious that if a defendant sets a

---

76. Cf. Schreiner v. Great Northern R. Co., 1902, 86 Minn. 245, 90 N.W. 400.

77. See infra, § 65.

78. Cf. Nieboer v. Detroit Elec. R. Co., 1901, 128 Mich. 486, 489, 87 N.W. 626, 627; Henry v. St. Louis, K. C. & N. R. Co., 1882, 76 Mo. 288; Studer v. Southern Pac. Co., 1898, 121 Cal. 400, 53 P. 942; Curwen v. Appleton Mfg. Co., 1916, 133 Minn. 28, 157 N.W. 899. Compare the reduction of the whole matter to a complete absurdity in Hinkle v. Minneapolis, A. & C. R. Co., 1926, 162 Minn. 112, 202 N.W. 340.

79. See Green, Contributory Negligence and Proximate Cause, 1927, 6 North Car.L.Rev. 3; Bohlen, Contributory Negligence, 1908, 21 Harv.L.Rev. 233, 234–242; Lowndes, Contributory Negligence, 1934, 22 Georgetown L.J. 674, 675 ff.

80. Cf. Girdner v. Union Oil Co., 1932, 216 Cal. 197, 13 P.2d 915; Nehring v. Connecticut Co., 1912, 86 Conn. 109, 84 A. 301, 524; Drown v. Northern Ohio Traction Co., 1907, 76 Ohio St. 234, 81 N.E. 326. See infra, p. 427.

81. Cf. Hagglund v. St. Hilaire Lumber Co., 1906, 97 Minn. 94, 106 N.W. 91; The San Onofre, [1922] P. 243. See Note, 1923, 36 Harv.L.Rev. 486.

82. Loker v. Damon, 1835, 17 Pick., Mass., 284; 1 Sedgwick, Damages, 9th Ed. 1920, § 202.

83. Green, Proximate Cause in Texas Negligence Law, 1950, 28 Tex.L.Rev. 471.

84. See Smith, Legal Cause in Actions of Tort, 1911, 25 Harv.L.Rev. 103, 106–128; Carpenter, Workable Rules for Determining Proximate Cause, 1932, 20 Cal.L.Rev. 229, 235–246; James and Perry, Legal Cause, 1951, 60 Yale L.J. 761, 801–811.

85. See supra, p. 246.

86. See Beale, Recovery for Consequences of an Act, 1895, 9 Harv.L.Rev. 80, 81, offering the interpretation that the defendant must be *responsible* for the immediate or final cause.

fire which burns the plaintiff's house, no court in the world will relieve him of liability upon the ground that the fire, rather than his act, was the nearest, or next cause of the destruction of the house. It is everywhere recognized that there must be some degree of progression into the causal sequence. There may have been considerable confusion about this in the distant past, but the question is certainly no longer open.

The last human wrongdoer. A similar formula, which has been stated and followed by some courts,[87] would place the legal responsibility upon the last culpable human actor in point of time, and exempt all those antecedent to him. This rule may have been due, at least in part, to the idea, which once had some currency,[88] that the law fulfilled its function if it provided *one* legally responsible defendant, and that it was superfluous, uneconomical, and confusing to the issue to offer more. Such a rule is unworkable in two respects. The last human wrongdoer is not always responsible; he may be relieved because his negligence did not extend to the particular risk, or by reason of unforeseen intervening forces over which he had no control.[89] And the earlier actor may be held responsible if he was under an obligation to protect the plaintiff against the later wrongful conduct, as in the numerous cases where the defendant is required to anticipate and safeguard the plaintiff against the negligent, or even the criminal acts of others.[90] Although British law still has some trouble with

it,[91] the rule is now of purely historical interest in the United States, except for odd bits and pieces of peculiar law which survive here and there,[92] and for the influence which it has had in the development of the doctrine of the last clear chance.[93]

Cause and condition. Many courts have sought to distinguish between the active "cause" of the harm and the existing "conditions" upon which that cause operated. If the defendant has created only a passive, static condition which made the damage possible, he is said not to be liable.[94] But so far as the fact of causation is concerned, in the sense of necessary antecedents which have played an important part in producing the result, it is quite impossible to distinguish between active forces and passive situations, particularly since, as is invariably the case, the latter are the result of other active forces which have gone before.[95] If the defendant spills gasoline about the premises, he creates a "condition;" but his act may be culpable because of the danger of fire. When a spark ignites the gasoline, the condition has done quite as much to bring about the fire as the

---

90.　See supra, pp. 274–275.

91.　Fleming, Law of Torts, 3d Ed. 1965, 205–210.

92.　See for example the exoneration of a municipality for a highway defect if the wrongful act of a third person contributed to plaintiff's injury. Hayes v. Hyde Park, 1891, 153 Mass. 514, 27 N.E. 522; Stone v. City of Philadelphia, 1930, 302 Pa. 340, 153 A. 550. See Eldredge, Culpable Intervention as Superseding Cause, 1937, 86 U.Pa.L.Rev. 121, reprinted in Eldredge, Modern Tort Problems, 1941, 205. Also such cases as Medved v. Doolittle, 1945, 220 Minn. 352, 19 N.W.2d 788; Kline v. Moyer, 1937, 325 Pa. 357, 191 A. 43; Hubbard v. Murray, 1939, 173 Va. 448, 3 S.E.2d 397, where one who negligently parks a car is held not liable because another driver has run into it.

93.　See infra, § 66.

94.　Gilman v. Central Vermont R. Co., 1919, 93 Vt. 340, 107 A. 122; White v. Lang, 1880, 128 Mass. 598; Kryger v. Panaszy, 1937, 123 Conn. 353, 196 A. 795. See Green, Proximate Cause in Connecticut Negligence Law, 1950, 24 Conn.B.J. 24, 33.

95.　Smith, Legal Cause in Actions of Tort, 1914, 25 Harv.L.Rev. 103, 110; Levitt, Cause, Legal Cause and Proximate Cause, 1922, 21 Mich.L.Rev. 34, 160.

87.　See Wharton, Negligence, 1st Ed. 1874, § 134; Vicars v. Wilcocks, 1806, 8 East 1; Singleton Abbey v. Paludina, [1927] 1 A.C. 16; Stone v. City of Philadelphia, 1931, 302 Pa. 340, 153 A. 550; Medved v. Doolittle, 1945, 220 Minn. 352, 19 N.W.2d 788; Hubbard v. Murray, 1939, 173 Va. 448, 3 S.E.2d 397. See Eldredge, Culpable Intervention as Superseding Cause, 1937, 86 U.Pa.L.Rev. 121, reprinted in Eldredge, Modern Tort Problems, 1941, 205; Note, 1928, 76 U.Pa.L.Rev. 720.

88.　Bohlen, Contributory Negligence, 1908, 21 Harv. L.Rev. 232, 238; Wharton, Negligence, 1st Ed. 1874, § 139.

89.　See infra, § 44.

spark; and since that is the very risk which the defendant has created, he will not escape responsibility.[96] Even the lapse of a considerable time during which the "condition" remains static will not necessarily affect liability; one who digs a trench in the highway may still be liable to another who falls into it a month afterward.[97] "Cause" and "condition" still find occasional mention in the decisions;[98] but the distinction is now almost entirely discredited. So far as it has any validity at all, it must refer to the type of case where the forces set in operation by the defendant have come to rest in a position of apparent safety, and some new force intervenes.[99] But even in such cases, it is not the distinction between "cause" and "condition" which is important, but the nature of the risk and the character of the intervening cause.

The substantial factor test. The late Jeremiah Smith once proposed[1] as a test of proximate cause, that "the defendant's tort must have been a substantial factor in producing the damage complained of." This was picked up by the supreme court of Minnesota in a case[2] of merging fires presenting an issue of causation in fact, and was used by the court as a substitute for the obviously inapplicable "but for" rule of causation.[3] This case in turn was taken over by the Restatement of Torts, which, in its original form,[4] adopted "substantial factor" as a test not only of causation, but also of the "proximate." A number of courts have followed this, apparently accepting the phrase as the answer to all prayers and some sort of universal solvent.[5] As applied to the fact of causation alone, the test is of considerable assistance, and perhaps no better guide can be found.[6] But when the "substantial factor" is made to include all of the ill-defined considerations of policy which go to limit liability once causation in fact is found, it has no more definite meaning than "proximate cause," and it becomes a hindrance rather than a help. It is particularly unfortunate in so far as it suggests that the questions involved are only questions of causation, obscuring all other issues, and as it tends to leave to the jury matters which should be decided by the court.[7] Some courts which have once proclaimed adherence to it as such a general catch-all formula have been compelled to reject it later,[8] and the 1948 revision of the Restatement has limited its application very definitely to the fact of causation alone.[9]

---

96. Teasdale v. Beacon Oil Co., 1929, 266 Mass. 25, 164 N.E. 612; Watson v. Kentucky & Ind. Bridge & R. Co., 1910, 137 Ky. 619, 126 S.W. 146, 129 S.W. 341; Johnson v. Kosmos Portland Cement Co., 6 Cir. 1933, 64 F.2d 193; Riley v. Standard Oil Co. of Indiana, 1934, 214 Wis. 15, 252 N.W. 183.

97. Pyke v. City of Jamestown, 1906, 15 N.D. 157, 107 N.W. 359; Page v. Town of Bucksport, 1874, 64 Me. 51 (defective bridge); Quaker Oats Co. v. Grice, 2 Cir. 1912, 195 F. 441 (mill permitted to become filled with dust, which exploded).

98. Briske v. Burnham, 1942, 379 Ill. 193, 39 N.E.2d 976, 979; Stewart v. Kroger Grocery, 1945, 198 Miss. 371, 21 So.2d 914; Oklahoma Gas & Elec. Co. v. Butler, 1942, 190 Okl. 393, 124 P.2d 397, 399; Atchison v. Texas & P. R. Co., 1945, 143 Tex. 466, 186 S.W.2d 228, 232.

99. See infra, § 44.

1. Smith, Legal Cause in Actions of Tort, 1911, 25 Harv.L.Rev. 103, 223, 229.

2. Anderson v. Minneapolis, St. P. & S. S. M. R. Co., 1920, 146 Minn. 430, 179 N.W. 45.

3. See supra, p. 240.

4. First Restatement of Torts, §§ 431, 433, 435.

5. Mahoney v. Beatman, 1929, 110 Conn. 184, 147 A. 762; Hayes Freight Lines v. Wilson, 1948, 226 Ind. 1, 77 N.E.2d 580; Simon v. Hudson Coal Co., 1944, 350 Pa. 82, 38 A.2d 259; Hatch v. Smail, 1946, 249 Wis. 183, 23 N.W.2d 460; Weaver v. McClintock-Trunkey Co., 1941, 8 Wash.2d 154, 111 P.2d 570, 114 P.2d 1004.

6. See supra, p. 240. See for example Schultz v. Brogan, 1947, 251 Wis. 390, 29 N.W.2d 719; Goudy v. State, 1948, 203 Miss. 366, 35 So.2d 308.

7. See Green, The Torts Restatement, 1935, 29 Ill. L.Rev. 582, 602; Prosser, The Minnesota Court on Proximate Cause, 1936, 21 Minn.L.Rev. 19.

8. See for example Seward v. Minneapolis St. R. Co., 1946, 222 Minn. 454, 25 N.W.2d 221, retreating from Peterson v. Fulton, 1934, 192 Minn. 360, 256 N.W. 901.

9. Restatement of Torts, 1948 Supp. § 433; Second Restatement of Torts, § 433.

Justly attachable cause. Professor, later Judge, Edgerton once maintained [10] that the essential question is whether the harm which has been suffered is "justly attachable" to the defendant's conduct. While this perhaps comes closer to stating the problem than anything else that has been said, it offers no solution. Justice, as every law student soon discovers, is an abstract, undefinable thing, about which men disagree. The necessity of being able to predict, to some reasonable extent at least, what the court is likely to do with any particular case, is so great that no one can be satisfied with anything so vague. Something more closely approaching a definite guide is possible, and essential.[11] The gist of the proposal, so far as there was anything concrete about it, was that the jury should be permitted to consider the imposition of liability upon "justly attachable" causes, on grounds of fairness and social advantage. Other writers, and the courts, have not, however, considered the jury to be a fit body to make such decisions.

Systems of rules. At the opposite extreme are the various attempts, the most noted of which is identified with the name of Professor Carpenter,[12] to establish a fixed system of rules to cover all cases. Thus it has been said, for example, in summary, that the defendant is liable if he has created a force which "remained active itself or created another force that remained active until it directly caused the result; or created a new active risk of being acted upon by the active force that caused the result." [13] Apart from the mechanical terminology used, which is more appropriate to physics than to law, such ironclad systems ignore the interplay of the various problems of policy which may arise in particular situations, and break down under the numerous obviously correct decisions which cannot be fitted into the structure erected.[14] "Proximate cause" cannot be reduced to absolute rules. No better statement ever has been made concerning the problem than that of Street: "It is always to be determined on the facts of each case upon mixed considerations of logic, common sense, justice, policy and precedent. * * * The best use that can be made of the authorities on proximate cause is merely to furnish illustrations of situations which judicious men upon careful consideration have adjudged to be on one side of the line or the other." [15]

Problems Involved

Abandoning the fruitless quest for a universal formula, it is possible to approach "proximate cause" as a series of distinct problems, more or less unrelated, to be determined upon different considerations.[16] The list, which is not necessarily exclusive, would include at least the following problems:

1. The problem of causation in fact: what part has the defendant's conduct played in bringing about the result? This has been considered above.[17]

2. The problem of apportionment of damages among causes. This will be considered below.[18]

10. Edgerton, Legal Cause, 1924, 72 U.Pa.L.Rev. 211, 343.

11. McLaughlin, Proximate Cause, 1925, 39 Harv.L. Rev. 149, 187; James and Perry, Legal Cause, 1951, 60 Yale L.J. 761, 802–803.

12. Carpenter, Workable Rules for Determining Proximate Cause, 1932, 20 Cal.L.Rev. 229, 396, 471; Carpenter, Proximate Cause, 1940–1943, 14 So.Cal.L. Rev. 1, 115, 416, 15 So.Cal.L.Rev. 187, 304, 427, 16 So.Cal.L.Rev. 1, 61, 275.

13. Beale, The Proximate Consequences of an Act, 1920, 33 Harv.L.Rev. 633.

14. See Edgerton, Legal Cause, 1924, 72 U.Pa.L.Rev. 211, 343.

15. 1 Street, Foundations of Legal Liability, 1906, 110.

16. See Green, Rationale of Proximate Cause, 1929, 77–121; Prosser, Proximate Cause in California, 1950, 38 Cal.L.Rev. 369.

17. See supra, § 41.

18. See post, § 52.

3. The problem of liability for unforeseeable consequences: to what extent should the defendant be liable for results which he could not reasonably have been expected to foresee?

4. The problem of intervening causes: should the defendant be relieved of liability by some new cause of external origin coming into operation at a time subsequent to his conduct and superseding his responsibility?

5. The problem of shifting responsibility: is there another person to whom the defendant was free to leave the duty of protecting the plaintiff? This has been mentioned before,[19] but it becomes a factor of importance in many cases of proximate cause.

Only the first of these problems has anything whatever to do with the factual relation of cause and effect. The attempt to deal with the others in terms of causation is at the bottom of much of the existing confusion.

43. UNFORESEEABLE CONSEQUENCES

Negligence, it must be repeated, is conduct which falls below the standard established by law for the protection of others against unreasonable risk. It necessarily involves a foreseeable risk, a threatened danger of injury, and conduct unreasonable in proportion to the danger. If the defendant could not reasonably foresee any injury as the result of his act, or if his conduct was reasonable in the light of what he could anticipate, there is no negligence, and no liability.[20] But what if he does unreasonably fail to guard against harm which he should foresee, and consequences which he could in no way have anticipated in fact follow? Suppose, for example, that a defect in his railway platform offers at most the foreseeable possibility of a

sprained ankle; but as a result of it a passenger dies of inflammation of the heart?[21] Or his negligent driving threatens the plaintiff with something like a broken leg, but instead causes him to be shot?[22]

There is perhaps no other one issue in the law of torts over which so much controversy has raged, and concerning which there has been so great a deluge of legal writing.[23] At the risk of becoming wearisome, it must be repeated that the question is in no way one of causation, and never arises until causation has been established. It is rather one of the fundamental policy of the law, as to whether the defendant's responsibility should extend to such results. In so far as he is held liable for consequences which do not lie within the original risk which he has created, a strict liability without fault is superimposed upon the liability that is logically to be attributed to his negligence itself. It is simpler, and no doubt more accurate, to state the problem in terms of "duty:" is the defendant under a legal obligation to protect the plaintiff against such unforeseeable consequences of his own negligent acts?[24] But to

19. See supra, p. 176.

20. Stephens v. Mutual Lumber Co., 1918, 103 Wash. 1, 173 P. 1031; Mendelson v. Davis, 8 Cir., 1922, 281 F. 18; Nunan v. Bennett, 1919, 184 Ky. 591, 212 S.W. 570; Sears v. Texas & N. O. R. Co., Tex.Civ. App.1923, 247 S.W. 602; Gaupin v. Murphy, 1928, 295 Pa. 214, 145 A. 123.

21. Keegan v. Minneapolis & St. Louis R. Co., 1899, 76 Minn. 90, 78 N.W. 965 (liable).

22. Lynch v. Fisher, La.App.1947, 34 So.2d 513 (liable). Cf. Walmsley v. Rural Tel. Ass'n, 1917, 102 Kan. 139, 169 P. 197 (liable); Gouna v. O'Neill, Tex. Civ.App.1941, 149 S.W.2d 138 (not liable).

23. See the articles cited supra, p. 236, note 1. Also Dias, The Duty Problem in Negligence, 1955, 13 Camb.L.J. 198; Dias, The Breach Problem and the Duty of Care, 1956, 30 Tulane L.Rev. 377; Fleming, The Passing of Polemis, 1961, 39 Can.Bar Rev. 489; Goodhart, The Imaginary Necktie and the Rule in Re Polemis, 1952, 68 L.Q.Rev. 514; Goodhart, Liability and Compensation, 1960, 76 L.Q.Rev. 567; Green, Foreseeability in Negligence Law, 1961, 61 Col.L.Rev. 1401; Payne, The "Direct" Consequences of a Negligent Act, 1952, 5 Curr.Leg.Prob. 189; Payne, Foreseeability and Remoteness of Damage in Negligence, 1962, 25 Mod.L.Rev. 1; Williams, The Risk Principle, 1961, 77 L.Q.Rev. 179; Wilson and Slade, A Re-examination of Remoteness, 1952, 15 Mod.L.Rev. 458; Wright, Re Polemis, 1951, 14 Mod.L.Rev. 393.

24. Green, Rationale of Proximate Cause, 1927, 11–43; Campbell, Duty, Fault and Legal Cause, [1938] Wis. L.Rev. 402.

state the question in this manner is merely to make use of other words to ask it, and can of course provide no answer. Whether there is to be such an obligation is a matter of policy, of the end to be accomplished; and when we say that the defendant is or is not under a "duty" to protect the plaintiff against such consequences, "duty" is only a word, and no more, with which we state our conclusion. But at least to deal with the problem in terms of causation, or to talk of the "proximate," is merely to obscure the issue. As to this problem, there are two basic, fundamental, opposing and irreconcilable views, which have been in conflict for more than a century; and each has developed complications of its own. First one may be considered, then the other, and finally, the possibility of compromise between the two.

Limitation of Liability to Risk

The first of these positions begins in 1850 with Baron Pollock,[25] who expressed the view that the same criterion of foreseeability and risk of harm which determined whether the defendant was negligent in the first instance should determine the extent of his liability for that negligence; and that no defendant should ever be held liable for consequences which no reasonable man would expect to follow from his conduct. The limitation, in other words, is to foreseeable consequences, and liability is restricted to the scope of the original risk created, with the test of responsibility for the result identical with the test for negligence.[26] In 1876, the same posi-

tion was taken by Mr. Justice Strong in Milwaukee & St. Paul Railway Co. v. Kellogg,[27] which became the leading American case. It has had a great deal of support in a long line of cases,[28] although it is nowhere carried to its logical extreme of eliminating *all* damages which could not reasonably have occurred to the defendant's mind,[29] and in nearly every jurisdiction there are occasional odd cases which appear impossible to reconcile with it. It represents the rule which is quite uniformly adopted where the defendant's negligence consists of the violation of an applicable statute;[30] and here the explanation has been offered that the written rule, and the policy of strict construction which seeks not to go beyond legislative purpose or intent, justify the result. It is also the rule generally applied in cases of what are called intervening causes,[31] where it may be necessitated by the absence of any other place to stop, if nothing more. There are, however, so many possible factors which may interplay in any given situation, that some caution must be exercised in classifying decisions as examples of the application of the rule.

This position has been justified as more rational, since the factors which define negligence should also limit liability for negligence; as easier to administer, since it fixes the nearest thing to a definite boundary of liability which is possible; and as more just,

---

not within the circle—in all of which time, place and circumstance play their respective and important parts." Griffith, J., in Mauney v. Gulf Refining Co., 1942, 193 Miss. 421, 9 So.2d 780.

27. 1876, 94 U.S. 469.

28. Engle v. Director General of Railroads, 1921, 78 Ind.App. 547, 133 N.E. 138; Cone v. Inter County Tel. & Tel. Co., Fla.1949, 40 So.2d 148; Dixon v. Kentucky Utilities Co., 1943, 295 Ky. 32, 174 S.W.2d 19; Shideler v. Habiger, 1952, 172 Kan. 718, 243 P.2d 211; Republic of France v. United States, 5 Cir. 1961, 290 F.2d 395 (Texas law).

29. See infra, p. 261. As to the various tests adopted in such a state as Oklahoma, and the resulting problem of the federal court, see Hardware Mut. Ins. Co. v. Lukken, 10 Cir. 1967, 372 F.2d 8.

30. See supra, pp. 192–195.

31. See infra, § 44.

---

25. In Greenland v. Chaplin, 1850, 5 Ex. 243, 155 Eng.Rep. 104, and Rigby v. Hewitt, 1850, 5 Ex. 240, 155 Eng.Rep. 103.

26. "The area within which liability is imposed is that which is within the circle of reasonable foreseeability, using the original point at which the negligent act was committed or became operative, and thence looking in every direction as the semi-diameters of the circle; and those injuries which from this point could or should have been reasonably foreseen, as something likely to happen, are within the field of liability, while those which, although foreseeable, were foreseeable only as remote possibilities, those only slightly probable, are beyond and

since negligence may consist of only a slight deviation from the community standard of conduct, and even be free from all moral blame, while its consequences may be catastrophic, and out of all proportion to the fault.[32] It is, however, by no means free from difficulties, which have led, in nearly all jurisdictions, to some modification of the rule in its pristine purity.[33]

Natural and probable consequences. To some extent there are difficulties of language. Many courts have said that the defendant is liable only if the harm suffered is the "natural and probable" consequence of his act.[34] These words frequently appear to have been given no more definite meaning than "proximate" itself. Strictly speaking, all consequences are "natural" which occur through the operation of forces of nature, without human intervention. But the word, as used, obviously appears not to be intended to mean this at all, but to refer to consequences which are normal, not extraordinary, not surprising in the light of ordinary experience. "Probable," if it is to add anything to this, must refer to consequences which were to be anticipated at the time of the defendant's conduct.[35] The phrase therefore appears to come

out as the equivalent of the test of foreseeability, of consequences within the scope of the original risk, so that the likelihood of their occurrence was a factor in making the defendant negligent in the first instance.

Time and space. The New York courts have attempted to set an arbitrary rule, in terms of what is foreseeable, by requiring that the consequences be not too far removed in time or space from the defendant's conduct. This revival of the original meaning of "proximate" originated in a case [36] in which, apparently because of the possibility of subrogation claims on the part of fire insurance companies, the court was unwilling to extend liability for a fire negligently set, beyond the first adjoining building. In later fire cases New York has retained the arbitrary rule.[37]

All other jurisdictions have rejected any such attempt to fix a rule.[38] Remoteness in

---

32. Pollock, Liability for Consequences, 1922, 38 L.Q. Rev. 165; Goodhart, The Unforeseeable Consequences of a Negligent Act, 1930, 39 Yale L.J. 449; Seavey, Mr. Justice Cardozo and the Law of Torts, 1939, 52 Harv.L.Rev. 372, 48 Yale L.J. 390, 39 Col.L. Rev. 20; Foster, Grant and Green, The Risk Theory and Proximate Cause, 1952, 32 Neb.L.Rev. 72; Wilson, Some Thoughts About Negligence, 1949, 2 Okl. L.Rev. 275; Keeton, Legal Cause in the Law of Torts, 1963.

See, however, condemning the whole approach, Smith, Legal Cause in Actions of Tort, 1911, 25 Harv.L.Rev. 103, 114–128; and the attack upon policy grounds in Green, Rationale of Proximate Cause, 1927, 177–185.

33. See infra, p. 261.

34. In the United States, this apparently originated in Milwaukee & St. Paul R. Co. v. Kellogg, 1876, 94 U.S. 469; and the phrase was repeated from that case, and from one decision to another.

35. Bohlen, The Probable or the Natural Consequences as the Test of Liability in Negligence, 1901, 49 Am.L.Reg. 79, 85.

36. Ryan v. New York Central R. Co., 1866, 35 N.Y. 210.

37. See Bird v. St. Paul Fire & Marine Ins. Co., 1918, 224 N.Y. 47, 120 N.E. 86; Notes, 1932, 32 Col.L.Rev. 911; 1933, 2 Brook.L.Rev. 113. In O'Neill v. New York, O. & W. R. Co., 1889, 115 N.Y. 579, 22 N.E. 217, it was suggested, but not decided, that the rule did not apply to forest fires in the country (where, incidentally, there would probably be no insurance). But in Hoffman v. King, 1899, 160 N.Y. 618, 55 N.E. 401, the suggestion was repudiated, and liability for forest fires restricted to the first owner affected. The legislature then by statute changed the rule to extend liability to other lands "however distant". See Nicoll v. Long Island R. Co., 1931, 232 App.Div. 435, 250 N.Y.S. 366. The court has refused to apply this statute to property other than "forest land." Rose v. Pennsylvania R. Co., 1923, 236 N.Y. 568, 142 N.E. 287.

The court has, however, shown some tendency to be liberal in its application of the rule. Thus recovery has been allowed to a next adjoining landowner, although his was not the first building to catch fire. Webb v. Rome, W. & O. R. Co., 1872, 49 N.Y. 420. Also to the first building to which the fire jumps, although it is not adjoining. Homac Corp. v. Sun Oil Co., 1932, 258 N.Y. 462, 180 N.E. 172, affirmed 1931, 233 App.Div. 890, 251 N.Y.S. 877, affirmed 137 Misc. 551, 244 N.Y.S. 51. See also Davies v. Delaware, L. & W. R. Co., 1915, 215 N.Y. 181, 109 N.E. 95.

38. Smith v. London & S. W. R. Co., 1870, L.R. 6 C.P. 14; Kuhn v. Jewett, 1880, 32 N.J.Eq. 647; Silver

time or space undoubtedly has its importance in determining whether the defendant has been a substantial factor in causing the harm at all, and may well lead to the conclusion that he has not; or it may give rise to the likelihood that other intervening causes have taken over the responsibility.[39] But when causation is found, and other factors are eliminated, it is not easy to discover any merit whatever in the contention that such physical remoteness should of itself bar recovery. The defendant who sets a bomb which explodes ten years later,[40] or mails a box of poisoned chocolates from California to Delaware,[41] has caused the result, and should obviously bear the consequences.

The "same hazard." Sometimes the foreseeability limitation is stated in a form which,

on its face, would seem to narrow the scope of liability. It is said that the defendant's responsibility must be limited to harm which results from the realization of the particular risk or hazard which he has created.[42] Just what this means is a problem, although there are decisions which have purported to apply it,[43] just as there are others which have purported to reject it.[44] The difficulty lies in the meaning to be assigned to "hazard." Does it signify the harm which is to result, and if so, does it refer to the particular harm or merely to a general class or type of damage? Does it mean the manner in which that harm is to be brought about, and if so, a broad general class of possible events, the particular details, or something undefined in between? Or does it mean merely the absence of anything very unexpected? The illustration most often given[45] is that of the child who is given a gun, and instead of shooting himself, suffers injury by dropping it on his toe; and the best discussion[46] gives only similar examples of unpredictable intervening causes.[47] If, as this might indicate, the significance of the

Falls Timber Co. v. Eastern & W. Lbr. Co., 1935, 149 Or. 126, 40 P.2d 703; Phillips v. Durham & C. R. Co., 1905, 138 N.C. 12, 50 S.E. 462; Osborn v. City of Whittier, 1951, 103 Cal.App.2d 609, 230 P.2d 132 and cases cited infra, p. 262. The New York rule was followed in Pennsylvania R. Co. v. Kerr, 1870, 62 Pa. 353, but was repudiated in Pennsylvania R. Co. v. Hope, 1876, 80 Pa. 373.

39. Thus in Firman v. Sacia, 1958, 11 Misc.2d 243, 173 N.Y.S.2d 440, affirmed, 1959, 7 App.Div.2d 579, 184 N.Y.S.2d 945, where injuries inflicted by defendant drove A insane, and seven years later he was "unable to resist the impulse" to shoot B, the court refused to permit a finding that this was proximate. It said that lapse of time will not defeat recovery in itself, but it "militates against foreseeability and proximate cause of the injury. * * * The intervention of other causes is very likely to occur where the time lapse is considerable in length."

40. Cf. Western Union Tel. Co. v. Preston, 3 Cir. 1918, 254 F. 229, cert. denied 248 U.S. 585 (death ten years after negligence); Bishop v. St. Paul City R. Co., 1892, 48 Minn. 26, 50 N.W. 927 (seven months); Parks v. Starks, 1955, 342 Mich. 443, 70 N.W.2d 805 (nine hours). It should, however, be noted that when the plaintiff suffers actual injury, the statute of limitations and the rule against splitting a cause of action may bar his recovery for long delayed damages.

41. People v. Botkin, 1901, 132 Cal. 231, 64 P. 286. Cf. Mize v. Rocky Mountain Bell Tel. Co., 1909, 38 Mont. 521, 100 P. 971 (nine or ten miles); Chase v. Washington Water Power Co., 1941, 62 Idaho 298, 111 P.2d 872 (over a mile); Kroeger v. Safranek, 1955, 161 Neb. 182, 72 N.W.2d 831; Thornton v. Weaber, 1955, 380 Pa. 590, 112 A.2d 344.

42. Second Restatement of Torts, § 281, Comment *e.* Followed in Duncan v. Lumbermen's Mut. Cas. Co., 1941, 91 N.H. 349, 23 A.2d 325. Cf. New York Eskimo Pie Co. v. Rataj, 3 Cir. 1934, 73 F.2d 184 ("substantially the manner in which it was brought about"); Harper, The Foreseeability Factor in the Law of Torts, 1932, 7 Notre Dame Lawyer 468, 470.

43. See for example Verkamp Corp. of Ky. v. Hubbard, Ky.1956, 296 S.W.2d 740 (safety valves on gas cylinder intended to prevent explosion, not ignition of gas after release).

44. See for example Norfolk & W. R. Co. v. Whitehurst, 1919, 125 Va. 260, 99 S.E. 568 (railroad switchman falling over unlighted switch target in the dark).

45. From Second Restatement of Torts, § 281, Illustration 3.

46. Eldredge, Modern Tort Problems, 17–24.

47. In addition to the boy and the gun, the following: Gorris v. Scott, 1874, L.R. 9 Ex. 125; Falk v. Finkelman, 1929, 268 Mass. 524, 168 N.E. 89; Hudson v. Lehigh Valley R. Co., 1913, 54 Pa.Super. 107; Bruggeman v. York, 1917, 259 Pa. 94, 102 A. 415; Hassett v. Palmer, 1940, 126 Conn. 468, 12 A.2d 646; New York, L. E. & W. R. Co. v. Ball, 1891, 53 N.J.L. 283, 21 A. 1052.

"same hazard" is merely to eliminate the results of such causes, it would appear to be subject to the rule that where the result is foreseeable but the intervention is not, there is liability.[48] With such uncertainties surrounding it, the "same hazard" approach is in all probability no real aid of any kind, and merely a means of covering up or disguising somewhat complicated problems.

Unforeseeable Plaintiffs

In 1928 something of a bombshell burst upon this field, when the New York Court of Appeals, forsaking "proximate cause," stated the issue of foreseeability in terms of duty. The case was Palsgraf v. Long Island Railroad Co.,[49] which has become the most discussed and debated of all torts cases,[50] and over which the argument still goes on. It involved what may be called, instead of unforeseeable consequences, the unforeseeable plaintiff. If the defendant's conduct threatens harm, which a reasonable man would foresee, to A, and A is in fact injured, we start with negligence toward A, and the problem is purely one of the extent of liability for consequences. But what if harm results instead to B, who was in no way threatened, stood outside of the zone of all apparent danger, and to whom no harm could reasonably be foreseen? Is the defendant's duty of care limited to A, toward whom he has created a foreseeable risk, or does it extend also to the plaintiff whom he has in fact injured, but could not reasonably foresee? We have seen the doctrine of "transferred intent," by which one who shoots at A, and instead unexpectedly hits B, becomes liable to B.[51] Is there such a thing as "transferred negligence," which will accomplish the same result?

Actually the problem was not a new one in 1928. It had arisen before, and courts had already considered it in terms of duty,[52] as well as "proximate cause," [53] and arrived at conflicting conclusions upon either basis. What the Palsgraf case actually did was to submit to the nation's then most excellent state court a law professor's dream of an examination question. A passenger was running to catch one of the defendant's trains. The defendant's servants, trying to assist him to board it, dislodged a package from his arms, and it fell upon the rails. The package contained fireworks, which exploded with some violence. The concussion overturned

48. See infra, p. 286.

49. Palsgraf v. Long Island R. Co., 1928, 248 N.Y. 339, 162 N.E. 99.

50. Green, The Palsgraf Case, 1930, 30 Col.L.Rev. 789, reprinted in Green, Judge and Jury, 1930, c. 8; Goodhart, The Unforeseeable Consequences of a Negligent Act, 1930, 39 Yale L.J. 449; Campbell, Duty, Fault and Legal Cause, [1938] Wis.L.Rev. 402; Cowan, The Riddle of the Palsgraf Case, 1938, 23 Minn.L.Rev. 46; Gregory, Proximate Cause in Negligence—A Retreat from Rationalization, 1938, 6 U.Chi.L.Rev. 36; Seavey, Mr. Justice Cardozo and the Law of Torts, 1939, 52 Harv.L.Rev. 372, 48 Yale L.J. 390, 39 Col.L.Rev. 20; Ehrenzweig, Loss-Shifting and Quasi-Negligence, 1941, 8 U.Chi.L.Rev. 729; Eldredge, The Role of Foreseeable Consequences in Negligence Law, 1952, 23 Pa. B.A.Q. 158; Morris, Duty, Negligence and Causation, 1952, 101 U.Pa.L. Rev. 189; James, Scope of Duty in Negligence Cases, 1953, 47 Nev.U.L.Rev. 778; Prosser, Palsgraf Revisited, 1953, 52 Mich.L.Rev. 1, reprinted in Prosser, Selected Topics on the Law of Torts, 1954, 191; Note, 1954, 29 Ind.L.Rev. 622.

51. See supra, p. 32.

52. Duty: Stevens v. Dudley, 1883, 56 Vt. 158; Wilson v. Northern Pac. R. Co., 1915, 30 N.D. 456, 153 N.W. 429; Hollidge v. Duncan, 1908, 199 Mass. 121, 85 N.E. 186; Mize v. Rocky Mountain Bell Tel. Co., 1909, 38 Mont. 521, 100 P. 971; and see Poffenbarger, J., in Bond v. Baltimore & Ohio R. Co., 1918, 82 W. Va. 557, 96 S.E. 932.

No duty: Boyd v. City of Duluth, 1914, 126 Minn. 33, 147 N.W. 710; Goodlander Mill Co. v. Standard Oil Co., 7 Cir. 1894, 63 F. 400; Trinity & B. V. R. Co. v. Blackshear, 1915, 106 Tex. 515, 172 S.W. 544.

53. Proximate: Wolfe v. Checker Taxi Co., 1938, 299 Mass. 225, 12 N.E.2d 849; Robinson v. Standard Oil Co., 1929, 89 Ind.App. 167, 166 N.E. 160; Kommerstad v. Great Northern R. Co., 1913, 120 Minn. 376, 139 N.W. 713, second appeal, 1915, 128 Minn. 505, 151 N.W. 177; Ramsey v. Carolina-Tenn. Power Co., 1928, 195 N.C. 788, 143 S.E. 861; Walmsley v. Rural Tel. Co., 1917, 102 Kan. 139, 169 P. 197. See also the cases of fires spreading to unforeseeable distances, infra, p. 262.

Not proximate: Wood v. Pennsylvania R. Co., 1896, 177 Pa. 306, 35 A. 699; Ryan v. New York Central R. Co., 1866, 35 N.Y. 210.

some scales,[54] many feet away on the platform, and they fell upon the plaintiff and injured her. The defendant's servants, who were found by the jury to have been negligent in what they did, could have foreseen harm from their clumsiness to the package, or at most to the passenger boarding the train; but no harm to the plaintiff could possibly have been anticipated.

In this situation Judge Cardozo, speaking for a majority of four, held that there was no liability, because there was no negligence toward the plaintiff. Negligence, he said, was a matter of relation between the parties, which must be founded upon the foreseeability of harm to the person in fact injured. The defendant's conduct was not a wrong toward her merely because it was negligence toward someone else. She must "sue in her own right for a wrong personal to her, and not as the vicarious beneficiary of a breach of duty to another."

Three judges dissented in the Palsgraf Case. Judge Andrews stated their contention that "Due care is a duty imposed upon each one of us to protect society from unnecessary danger, not to protect A, B or C alone. * * * Every one owes to the world at large the duty of refraining from those acts which unreasonably threaten the safety of others. * * * Not only is he wronged to whom harm might reasonably be expected to result, but he also who is in fact injured, even if he be outside what would generally be thought the danger zone."

The Restatement of Torts [55] almost immediately afterward accepted the view of the Palsgraf Case, that there is no duty, and hence no negligence, and so never any liability, to the unforeseeable plaintiff. Subsequent decisions, however, cannot be said as yet definitely to have settled the question so far as American law is concerned.[56] It has become fashionable to cite the case in connection with almost every kind of negligence problem, and most of the extensive list of references to it have no significance whatever, unless it is recognition that the decision has acquired a reputation. In particular, it has been cited in a long list of cases in which no injury to anyone was to be anticipated, and therefore there was simply no negligence at all.[57]

Even where a negligent defendant and an unforeseeable plaintiff have in fact been involved, the Palsgraf rule has become rather hopelessly entangled with other rules, and other bases of policy. Thus it has been cited [58] in support of the familiar rule [59] that a statute intended to protect only a particular class of persons or to guard only against a particular risk or type of harm, creates no duty to any other class or risk; but the written law and the policy of strict construction which refuses to extend its effect beyond the legislative purpose seem definitely to set this apart from any court-made rule. It has been

---

54. The Record of the case is set forth in Scott and Simpson, Cases on Civil Procedure, 1950, at pp. 891–940. A study of it indicates that the event could not possibly have happened in the manner described, and that the scale must have been knocked over by a stampede of frightened passengers. See Prosser, Palsgraf Revisited, 1953, 52 Mich.L.Rev. 1, 3, reprinted in Prosser, Selected Topics on the Law of Torts, 1953, 191, 194. This would of course make no difference in the result.

55. § 281, Comment c. For the background of Cardozo's position as an Adviser in drafting the Re-

statement, see Prosser, Palsgraf Revisited, 1953, 52 Mich.L.Rev. 1, 4–8, reprinted in Prosser, Selected Topics on the Law of Torts, 1954, 191.

56. See Prosser, Palsgraf Revisited, 1953, 52 Mich.L. Rev. 1, 8–12, reprinted in Prosser, Selected Topics on the Law of Torts, 1954, 191.

57. See for example Hetrick v. Marion-Reserve Power Co., 1943, 141 Ohio St. 347, 48 N.E.2d 103; Birckhead v. Mayor and City Council of Baltimore, 1938, 174 Md. 32, 197 A. 615; Andreu v. Wellman, 1949, 144 Me. 36, 63 A.2d 926; Foreman v. Texas & New Orleans R. Co., 5 Cir. 1953, 205 F.2d 79; Union Carbide & Carbon Corp. v. Peters, 4 Cir. 1953, 206 F.2d 366.

58. Flynn v. Gordon, 1933, 86 N.H. 198, 165 A. 715; Chicago, B. & Q. R. Co. v. Murray, 1929, 40 Wyo. 324, 277 P. 703; Coray v. Southern Pac. Co., 1947, 112 Utah 166, 185 P.2d 963.

59. See supra, pp. 192, 195.

cited [60] in holding that a railroad's duty toward drivers at crossings does not extend to its employees; but here, as in the case of the trespasser,[61] there is an element of assumption of risk which limits the duty. It has been relied on in holding that a contract obligation does not extend to third parties,[62] and that a contract interest is not protected against negligence toward one of the parties to the contract; [63] but here again the kind of obligation or interest involved seems to be an adequate explanation. Finally the case has been relied on [64] in holding that a plaintiff who is himself in a position of safety cannot recover for mental shock and injury brought about by the sight of harm or peril to another person within the danger zone. The reluctance of the courts to enter this field even where the mental injury is clearly foreseeable, and the frequent mention of the difficulties of proof, the facility of fraud, and the problem of finding a place to stop and draw the line,[65] suggest that here it is the nature of the interest invaded and the type of damage which is the real obstacle.

It is difficult to conclude that such cases represent any general and established principle of non-liability. For each of them there are others to be found which come to the same conclusion on similar facts, but on other

and better grounds. They suggest rather that the duty problem [66] is a very involved and complex one, and that the opinion of Cardozo has perhaps greatly over-simplified the whole matter. The cases which have dealt with the Palsgraf question, and which cannot be so distinguished, are few, and divided. The majority of the small number of them have accepted and followed the case.[67] There has been, however, an undercurrent of disagreement,[68] which suggests that there is something more here than meets the casual eye; and this is borne out by the conflict in the earlier decisions,[69] most of which went off on "proximate cause." It would be easy to dismiss these last opinions on the ground that they never saw the point of "duty;" but there is in them so much explicit consideration of the bearing of foreseeability that they seem in reality to have decided it under another name.[70]

60. Karr v. Chicago, R. I. & P. R. Co., 1937, 341 Mo. 536, 108 S.W.2d 44.

61. Cf. Garland v. Boston & Me. R. Co., 1913, 76 N.H. 556, 86 A. 141; Wickenburg v. Minneapolis, St. P. & S. S. M. R. Co., 1905, 94 Minn. 276, 102 N.W. 713; Peterson v. South & W. R. Co., 1906, 143 N.C. 260, 55 S.E. 618.

62. Harris v. Lewistown Trust Co., 1937, 326 Pa. 145, 191 A. 34 (landlord's covenant to repair). See infra, p. 408.

63. Sinram v. Pennsylvania R. Co., 2 Cir., 1932, 61 F.2d 767. As to negligent interference with contract, see infra, p. 938.

64. Waube v. Warrington, 1935, 216 Wis. 603, 258 N.W. 497; Curry v. Journal Pub. Co., 1937, 41 N.M. 318, 68 P.2d 168; Blanchard v. Reliable Transfer Co., 1944, 71 Ga.App. 843, 32 S.E.2d 420; Cote v. Litawa, 1950, 96 N.H. 174, 71 A.2d 792; Resavage v. Davies, 1952, 199 Md. 479, 86 A.2d 879.

65. See infra, § 54.

66. See infra, § 53.

67. Dahlstrom v. Shrum, 1951, 368 Pa. 423, 84 A.2d 289 (A struck by bus, thrown off at an angle against B, in position of apparent safety); Radigan v. W. J. Halloran Co., 1963, 97 R.I. 122, 196 A.2d 160 (crane brought in contact with power line, resulting in gas explosion on third floor); West v. Cruz, 1952, 75 Ariz. 13, 251 P.2d 311 (motorist failed to pull to curb when siren sounded, caused collision between two other vehicles); Tucker v. Collar, 1955, 79 Ariz. 141, 285 P.2d 178 (defective machinery threatened premises of tenant, injured those of landlord); Diamond State Tel. Co. v. Atlantic Ref. Co., 3 Cir. 1953, 205 F.2d 402 (barge threatened, cable injured); Geo. D. Barnard Co. v. Lane, Tex.Civ.App. 1965, 392 S.W.2d 769 (collision at intersection damaging air conditioning unit in distant building).

68. Jackson v. B. Lowenstein & Bros., 1940, 175 Tenn. 535, 136 S.W.2d 495; Pfeifer v. Standard Gateway Theater, 1952, 262 Wis. 229, 55 N.W.2d 29; Longberg v. H. L. Green Co., 1962, 15 Wis.2d 505, 113 N. W.2d 129, 114 N.W.2d 435.

69. See supra, p. 254.

70. Compare, upon essentially similar facts, Wood v. Pennsylvania R. Co., 1896, 177 Pa. 306, 35 A. 699 (proximate cause, no liability); Mellon v. Lehigh Valley R. Co., 1925, 282 Pa. 39, 127 A. 444 (proximate cause, liability); and Dahlstrom v. Shrum, 1951, 368 Pa. 423, 84 A.2d 289 (duty, no liability). Is there any difference in the analysis in the three cases, except one of terminology?

The present state of the law is, then, still one of troubled waters, in which any one may fish. The holding that duty in a negligence action extends only to those within a definite area of danger has obvious merits. In support of it, it has been argued [71] that it simplifies the problem and facilitates administration by restricting the defendant's responsibility within some reasonable bounds— which may, however, be somewhat illusory because of the difficulties of a fragmentary analysis of the risk.[72] It has been contended that such a limitation is desirable because the negligence may consist of a momentary inadvertence, or an honest error of judgment, while the harm that results may be out of all proportion to the nature or extent of the departure from ordinary standards of conduct. The rule has been defended as more consistent with the basic theory of negligence, that of the creation of an unreasonable risk; but a cause of action for negligence requires compensable damage as well as fault, and the conclusion that the plaintiff's damages are not to be included can only beg the question.

There is, however, something to be said for the idea of an absolute wrong adopted by the dissent. As between an entirely innocent plaintiff and a defendant who admittedly has departed from the social standard of conduct, if only toward one individual, who should bear the loss? If the result is out of all proportion to the defendant's fault, it can be no less out of proportion to the plaintiff's entire innocence. If it is unjust to the defendant to make him bear a loss which he could not have foreseen, it is no less unjust to the plaintiff to make him bear a loss which he too could not have foreseen, and which is not even due to his own negligence. The defendant is required to be reasonably careful, for the protection of those to whom harm can be foreseen. If we extend this liability to others, we impose upon the defendant no new obligation of conduct, and reasonable care will still protect him from liability. The issue is whether the plaintiff's interests are to be afforded protection against the defendant's negligence where the consequences exceed the fault; there is nothing sacred about "duty," which is nothing more than a word, and a very indefinite one, with which we state our conclusion.

Such an approach, of course, does nothing to solve the problem of a place to stop short of infinite liability, and throws the question of any limitation back into the morass of "proximate cause," and the search for some reasonably close connection between the defendant's conduct and the injury.[73]

The real problem, and the one to which attention should be directed, would seem to be one of social policy: whether the defendants in such cases should bear the heavy negligence losses of a complex civilization, rather than the individual plaintiff.[74] Because these defendants are in large measure public utilities, governmental bodies, industries, automobile drivers, and others who by rates, prices, taxes or insurance are better able to distribute the loss to the general public, many courts may reasonably consider that the burden should rest upon them, and experience no great difficulty in finding a "duty" of protection. So far as policy is concerned, different answers might well be given in different communities, according to the view that is taken as to where the loss should fall; [75] but the issue is not to be determined

---

71. See for example Seavey, Mr. Justice Cardozo and the Law of Torts, 1939, 52 Harv.L.Rev. 372, 48 Yale L.J. 390, 39 Col.L.Rev. 20.

72. See infra, p. 268.

73. See supra, § 42.

74. See Green, The Duty Problem in Negligence Cases, 1928, 28 Col.L.Rev. 1014, 1929, 29 Col.L.Rev. 255, reprinted in Green, Judge and Jury, 1930, ch. 3–4; Note, 1929, 29 Col.L.Rev. 53.

75. New York limits liability for the spread of fire to the first adjoining building. Ryan v. New York Cent. R. Co., 1866, 35 N.Y. 210, 91 Am.Dec. 49. Kansas, carrying direct causation to an extreme, holds that it extends for at least four miles. Atchison, T. & S. F. R. Co. v. Stanford, 1874, 12 Kan. 354, 15 Am. Rep. 362. New York's prosperity depends upon railroads and heavy industry; its courts have had in

by any talk of "duty," or an assumption of the conclusion. There is room for argument that the foreseeability of harm to the plaintiff should be but one factor in determining the existence of a duty, and not always conclusive,[76] and that situations will more or less inevitably arise which do not fit within any fixed and inflexible rule.[77] Also that in a field of freak accidents, which do not recur without significant differences, there should be no absolute rule as a prediction for the unpredictable; that there might well be different results not only in different jurisdictions but in different types of cases; [78] and that where there is so much dispute among lawyers the court should be rather slow to take the case from the jury.[79]

Thus, while the trend is definitely in favor of acceptance of the Palsgraf rule, it cannot be said that the issue is finally determined for all cases in the United States.

One group of cases especially difficult to fit into the "duty" formula have been those in which a defendant has endangered one man, and has been held liable to another who is in-

jured in an attempt to rescue him.[80] The duty to the rescuer is clearly an independent one; and it has been held that the contributory negligence of the person rescued will not bar the rescuer's recovery,[81] and even that the latter may still recover where the former is owed no duty because he is a trespasser.[82] Since anticipation of rescue, and all the more so of harm to the rescuer, unduly strains the limitation of the "foreseeable risk," these cases were formerly regarded as an exception to the rule, or at least a considerable extension of it.[83] When Cardozo himself was confronted with the question, he rationalized the apparent anomaly by declaring, as a more or less arbitrary rule, that rescuers, as a class, are always foreseeable when the defendant's negligence endangers anyone.[84] A series of later decisions in which the defendant's negligence endangered only himself,[85]

mind urban communities in which nearly all property of any value carries fire insurance, and the possibility of a windfall for the insurers in the form of subrogation claims. Kansas has miles of uninsured wheat, and its community attitude toward railroads is by no means the same. Who is to say that each decision is not defensible for the jurisdiction; and what reason is there that both must come to the same conclusion?

76. Green, Judge and Jury, 1930, 71.

77. Green, Foreseeability in Negligence Law, 1961, 61 Col.L.Rev. 1401; Note, 1961, 36 N.Y.U.L.Rev. 1043. Compare the cases in which statutes have been held to call for a relaxation of rules of "proximate cause." Daggett v. Keshner, 1954, 284 App.Div. 733, 134 N.Y. S.2d 524, noted in 1955, 40 Corn.L.Q. 810; Pierce v. Albanese, 1957, 144 Conn. 241, 129 A.2d 606, appeal dismissed 355 U.S. 15; Kernan v. American Dredging Co., 1958, 355 U.S. 426.

78. See Prosser, Palsgraf Revisited, 1953, 52 Mich.L. Rev. 1, 28–32, reprinted in Prosser, Selected Topics on the Law of Torts, 1954, 191.

79. See Jackson v. B. Lowenstein & Bros., 1940, 175 Tenn. 535, 538, 136 S.W.2d 495; Pfeifer v. Standard Gateway Theater, 1952, 262 Wis. 229, 55 N.W.2d 29.

80. Eckert v. Long Island R. Co., 1871, 43 N.Y. 502; Perpich v. Leetonia Min. Co., 1912, 118 Minn. 508, 137 N.W. 12; Bond v. Baltimore & O. R. Co., 1918, 82 W.Va. 557, 96 S.E. 932; Sarratt v. Holston Quarry Co., 1934, 174 S.C. 262, 177 S.E. 135; Hatch v. Globe Laundry Co., 1934, 132 Me. 379, 171 A. 387. See Tilley, The Rescue Principle, 1967, 30 Mod.L.Rev. 25; Gordon, Moral Challenge to the Legal Doctrine of Rescue, 1965, 14 Cleve.Marsh.L.Rev. 334.

81. Pittsburgh, C. C. & St. L. R. Co. v. Lynch, 1903, 69 Ohio St. 123, 68 N.E. 703; Highland v. Wilsonian Inv. Co., 1932, 171 Wash. 34, 17 P.2d 631.

82. Videan v. British Transport Commission, [1963] 2 Q.B. 650. Contra: Brady v. Chicago & N. W. R. Co., 1954, 265 Wis. 618, 62 N.W.2d 415; Rose v. Peters, Fla.1955, 82 So.2d 585.

83. See Bohlen, Review of Harper, Law of Torts, 1934, 47 Harv.L.Rev. 556, 557.

84. "Danger invites rescue. The cry of distress is the summons to relief. The law does not ignore these reactions of the mind in tracing conduct to its consequences. It recognizes them as normal. It places their effects within the range of the natural and probable. The wrong that imperils life is a wrong to the imperiled victim; it is a wrong also to his rescuer." Cardozo, C. J., in Wagner v. International R. Co., 1921, 232 N.Y. 176, 133 N.E. 437.

85. Carney v. Buyea, 1946, 271 App.Div. 338, 65 N.Y.S. 2d 902, appeal denied 1947, 271 App.Div. 949, 68 N.Y.S.2d 446; Brugh v. Bigelow, 1944, 310 Mich. 74, 16 N.W.2d 668; Longacre v. Reddick, Tex.Civ. App.1948, 215 S.W.2d 404, mandamus overruled;

or his own property,[86] have confirmed the rationalization, since if the defendant is under a duty to anyone, and is negligent because he can foresee harm to anyone, it must be to the rescuer. One may perhaps swallow this, with a grain of salt; but when the same arbitrary rule is extended further, to hold that a rescuer of the rescuer is to be held to be foreseeable,[87] its artificial and fanciful character becomes more apparent.

Particular interest. In a dictum in the Palsgraf Case [88] Cardozo suggested a further refinement, with a distinction to be made between interests of the plaintiff as to which the defendant owes him a duty, and those as to which he does not. For example, that if only harm to his property is to be foreseen, there can be no recovery for injuries to his person which may in fact result, and vice versa. The First Restatement of Torts [89]

formerly approved this dictum also. While it may follow logically enough from what has gone before, there is almost no authority in support of such a proposition,[90] and quite a bit to the contrary, in cases where property was threatened, and injury to the person [91] or to other property [92] has in fact been caused. Although there are writers who have approved this idea,[93] it has terrified others [94]

Dodson v. Maddox, 1949, 359 Mo. 742, 223 S.W.2d 434; Usry v. Small, 1961, 103 Ga.App. 144, 118 S.E. 2d 719. Cf. Talbert v. Talbert, 1960, 22 Misc.2d 782, 199 N.Y.S.2d 212, where the defendant attempted suicide, and his son was injured while trying to save him.

86. Rushton v. Howle, 1949, 79 Ga.App. 360, 53 S.E. 2d 768; Henjum v. Bok, 1961, 261 Minn. 74, 110 N. W.2d 461; Green v. Britton, 1960, 22 Conn.Super. 71, 160 A.2d 497; George A. Fuller Const. Co. v. Elliott, 1955, 92 Ga.App. 309, 88 S.E.2d 413.

87. Richards v. Kansas Elec. Power Co., 1928, 126 Kan. 521, 268 P. 847; Brown v. Ross, 1956, 345 Mich. 54, 75 N.W.2d 68; Richardson v. United States, E.D. Okl.1965, 248 F.Supp. 99.

88. Palsgraf v. Long Island R. Co., 1928, 248 N.Y. 339, 346–347, 162 N.E. 89, 101: "There is room for argument that a distinction is to be drawn according to the diversity of interests invaded by the act, as where conduct negligent in that it threatens an insignificant invasion of an interest in property results in an unforeseeable invasion of an interest of another order, as, e. g., one of bodily security."

89. § 281, Comment *g.* In Comment *c* under the same Section, the First Restatement approved the rule of the "same hazard," supra, p. 253.

90. One such case is Texas & Pacific R. Co. v. Bigham, 1896, 90 Tex. 223, 38 S.W. 162, discussed in Green, Are Negligence and Proximate Cause Determined by the Same Test, 1923, 1 Tex.L.Rev. 399, where defendant's negligence threatened harm only to plaintiff's cattle, and he was injured personally when they stampeded.

See also Seale v. Gulf, Colorado & S. F. R. Co., 1886, 65 Tex. 274, where a railroad negligently starting a fire was held liable for loss of adjoining property, but not for death of the owner's daughter fighting the fire. This looks wrong, at least under present-day law.

The contention of the Restatement was advanced by the dissenting opinion of Jaggard, J., in Lesch v. Great Northern R. Co., 1906, 97 Minn. 503, 106 N.W. 955, where the plaintiff recovered for mental anguish following the invasion of her property, but it was rejected by the majority of the court.

91. Rasmussen v. Benson, 1938, 135 Neb. 232, 280 N.W. 890 (poisoning of cattle led to death of owner); Isham v. Dow's Estate, 1898, 70 Vt. 588, 41 A. 585 (harm to plaintiff's dog, resulting in personal injury); Mitchell v. Friedman, 1951, 11 N.J.Super. 344, 78 A.2d 417 (negligent failure to repair toilet, resulting in personal injury from carrying water); Chicago & N. W. R. Co. v. Hunerberg, 1885, 16 Ill.App. 387, (threatened harm to land, resulting personal injury); Brackett v. Bellows Falls Hydro-Electric Corp., 1934, 87 N.H. 173, 175 A. 822 (threatened harm to land, resulting personal injury); Barker v. City of Philadelphia, E.D.Pa.1955, 134 F.Supp. 231 (threatened harm to chattel, death of child) In re Guardian Casualty Co., 1938, 253 App.Div. 360, 2 N.Y.S.2d 232, aff'd 1938, 278 N.Y. 674, 16 N.E.2d 397 (damage to building, personal injury). Cf. Law v. Visser, [1961] Queensland Rep. 46, where a motorist ran over an object on the highway at night, with no reason to expect it to be a man.

92. John C. Kupferle Foundry Co. v. St. Louis Merchants' Bridge Term R. Co., 1918, 275 Mo. 451, 205 S.W. 57 (threatened harm to tank in street, resulting harm to factory behind it); and cf. Atherton v. Goodwin, 1947, 163 Kan. 22, 180 P.2d 296 (threatened harm to scales, resulting pecuniary loss); The Glendola, 2 Cir. 1931, 47 F.2d 206, cert. denied 283 U.S. 857.

93. Tilley, The English Rule as to Liability for Unintended Consequences, 1935, 33 Mich.L.Rev. 829, 848–851; Machin, Negligence and Interest, 1954, 17 Mod.L.Rev. 405.

94. "If the courts once adopt such a distinction, then we are faced with the terrifying prospect of a whole new series of cases in which it will be necessary

with the prospect of either a whole series of hair-splitting distinctions, or else broad categories unreasonable in themselves. There is something of an analogy to the rule which does not permit the plaintiff to split his cause of action between personal injury and property damage,[95] or even between two pieces of property.[96] There is a very obvious artificiality about the whole thing. If A drops B's clock upon B's floor, it may be that A should foresee the risk of harm to the clock, and not to the floor. It may be that B's interest in his floor is not the same as his interest in his clock, or for that matter his toe; and that the risk of disarranging the internal workings of the clock is distinct from the possibility of marring the varnish of the floor, or breaking the toe. These things might be; but if the floor is in fact damaged, or the toe broken, none of this is of any real aid in determining who should bear the loss—the innocent owner, or the clumsy lout who carelessly let go the clock.[97] For such reasons the Second Restatement, in the absence of case support for its proposition, has reversed it.[98]

The analogy of the cases holding that liability for the violation of a statute is limited to the particular risk covered is scarcely to be relied on, since they clearly involve the

effect given to a legislative policy narrow in its scope. There are of course interests which, as a matter of policy, should not be protected against certain types of wrongful conduct,[1] but it does not follow from this that protection should always be limited to the interest which is threatened in advance.

Liability Beyond the Risk

There remains the opposing view, which has been urged from time to time by a good many writers,[2] that a defendant who is negligent must take existing circumstances as he finds them, and may be liable for consequences brought about by his acts, even though they were not reasonably to be anticipated. Or, as it is sometimes put, that what he could foresee is important in determining whether he was negligent in the first instance, but not at all decisive in determining the extent of the consequences for which, once negligent, he will be liable.[3] This posi-

---

to consider whether or not a person has the same interest in his foot and his eye, in his two adjoining houses, in his ship and the cargo which it carries. Obviously a single distinction between bodily security on the one hand and property security on the other, would be too broad." Goodhart, The Unforeseeable Consequences of a Negligent Act, 1930, 39 Yale L.J. 449, 467. See also Porter, The Measure of Damages in Contract and Tort, 1934, 5 Camb.L.J. 178, 183; Payne, Negligence and Interest, 1955, 18 Mod.L.Rev. 43.

95. See for example King v. Chicago, M. & St. P. R. Co., 1900, 80 Minn. 83, 82 N.W. 1113; and cases collected in the annotation, 1958, 62 A.L.R.2d 977.

96. Knowlton v. New York & N. E. R. Co., 1888, 147 Mass. 606, 18 N.E. 580; Jeffrey v. Copeland Flour Mills, [1923] 4 Dom.L.Rep. 1140.

97. See Porter, The Measure of Damages in Contract and Tort, 1934, 5 Camb.L.J. 178, 183.

98. Second Restatement of Torts, § 281, Comment j.

1. For example, the financial interests which are refused protection in Carsten v. Northern Pac. R. Co., 1890, 44 Minn. 454, 47 N.W. 49; Northern States Contracting Co. v. Oakes, 1934, 191 Minn. 88, 253 N.W. 371. Liesbosch Dredger v. S. S. Edison, [1933] A.C. 449. See, infra, as to negligent misrepresentation, p. 708, and interference with contract, p. 938.

2. Bohlen, The Probable or the Natural Consequences as the Test of Liability in Negligence, 1901, 49 Am.L.Reg. 79, 148; Smith, Legal Cause in Actions of Tort, 1911, 25 Harv.L.Rev. 103, 223; Carpenter, Workable Rules for Determining Proximate Cause, 1932, 20 Cal.L.Rev. 229, 396; Myers, Causation and Common Sense, 1951, 5 Miami L.Q. 238; Hart and Honore, Causation in the Law, 1959, 151 ff.

3. "If a person had no reasonable ground to anticipate that a particular act would or might result in any injury to anybody, then, of course, the act would not be negligent at all; but if the act itself is negligent, then the person guilty of it is equally liable for all its natural and proximate consequences, whether he could have foreseen them or not. Otherwise expressed, the law is that if the act is one which the party ought, in the exercise of ordinary care, to have anticipated was liable to result in injury to others, then he is liable for any injury proximately resulting from it, although he could not have anticipated the particular injury which did happen. Consequences which follow in unbroken sequence, without an intervening efficient cause, from the original negligent act, are natural and proximate, and for such consequences the original wrongdoer is responsible, even though he could not

tion appears to have originated in 1870 in England, in the case of Smith v. London & Southwestern Ry. Co.,[4] where it was considered unforeseeable that a fire set by the defendant on its right of way would reach the plaintiff's house. Although the present trend is definitely against it, this view still displays a great deal of vitality, and will not entirely down. Its continued prevalence has been due in no small part to the more or less instinctive feeling that, as between an entirely innocent plaintiff and a defendant who has been negligent as to results lying within the risk, the burden of the loss due to consequences beyond the risk should fall, within some quite undefined ultimate limits, upon the wrongdoer.

There are some areas in which even the courts which have been most vocal in favor of the "foreseeable risk" limitation upon liability have been forced to discard it. There is almost universal agreement upon liability beyond the risk, for quite unforeseeable consequences, when they follow an impact upon the person of the plaintiff.[5]

It is as if a magic circle were drawn about the person, and one who breaks it, even by so much as a cut on the finger, becomes liable for all resulting harm to the person, although it may be death.[6] The defendant is held li-

able when his negligence operates upon a concealed physical condition, such as pregnancy,[7] or a latent disease,[8] or susceptibility to disease,[9] to produce consequences which he could not reasonably anticipate. He is held liable for unusual results of personal injuries which are regarded as unforeseeable, such as tuberculosis,[10] paralysis,[11] pneumonia,[12] heart or kidney disease,[13] blood poisoning,[14] cancer,[15] or the loss of hair from

---

have foreseen the particular result which did follow." Mitchell, J., in Christianson v. Chicago, St. P. M. & O. R. Co., 1896, 67 Minn. 94, 69 N.W. 640. Accord: Dodge v. McArthur, 1966, 126 Vt. 81, 223 A.2d 453; Osborne v. Montgomery, 1931, 203 Wis. 223, 234 N.W. 372; Dellwo v. Pearson, 1961, 259 Minn. 452, 107 N.W.2d 859; Lynch v. Fisher, La. App.1949, 34 So.2d 513.

4. 1870, L.R. 6 C.P. 14.

5. Compare the suggestion of Burke, Rules of Legal Cause in Negligence Cases, 1926, 15 Cal.L.Rev. 1, 14, that a distinction is to be made between unforeseeable consequences following "after the first impingement of the defendant's wrong," and cases in which the "impingement" itself is of an unforeseeable character. But why the distinction, the author does not succeed in making so clear.

6. Koehler v. Waukesha Milk Co., 1926, 190 Wis. 52, 208 N.W. 901. See Notes, 1960, 43 Marq.L.Rev. 511; 1959, 34 Notre Dame Lawyer 224; 1966, 16 Drake L.Rev. 49.

7. Mann Boudoir Car Co. v. Dupre, 5 Cir. 1893, 54 F. 646; Brown v. Chicago, M. & St. P. R. Co., 1882, 54 Wis. 342, 11 N.W. 356, rehearing denied 1882, 54 Wis. 342, 11 N.W. 911; Malone v. Monongahela Valley Traction Co., 1927, 104 Va. 417, 140 S.E. 340. Cf. Thompson v. Lupone, 1948, 135 Conn. 236, 62 A.2d 861 (obesity).

8. Owen v. Dix, 1946, 210 Ark. 562, 196 S.W.2d 913; Sentilles v. Inter-Caribbean Shipping Corp., 1959, 361 U.S. 107; Heppner v. Atchison, T. & S. F. R. Co., Mo.1956, 297 S.W.2d 497; City of Port Arthur v. Wallace, 1943, 141 Tex. 201, 171 S.W.2d 480; Flood v. Smith, 1940, 126 Conn. 644, 13 A.2d 677.

9. Steinhauser v. Hertz Corp., 2 Cir. 1970, 421 F.2d 1169 (psychotic tendencies); Alexander v. Knight, 1962, 197 Pa.Super. 79, 177 A.2d 142 (neurotic predisposition); Lockwood v. McCaskill, 1964, 262 N.C. 663, 138 S.E.2d 541 (predisposition to amnesia); Trascher v. Eagle Ind. Co., La.App.1950, 48 So.2d 695 (ruptured disc); McCahill v. New York Transp. Co., 1911, 201 N.Y. 221, 94 N.E. 616 (delirium tremens).

10. Champlin Refining Co. v. Thomas, 10 Cir. 1937, 93 F.2d 133; Larson v. Boston Elevated R. Co., 1912, 212 Mass. 262, 98 N.E. 1048; Healy v. Hoy, 1911, 115 Minn. 321, 132 N.W. 208.

11. Bishop v. St. Paul City R. Co., 1892, 48 Minn. 26, 50 N.W. 927; Homans v. Boston Elev. R. Co., 1902, 180 Mass. 456, 62 N.E. 737.

12. Louisville & N. R. Co. v. Jones, 1887, 83 Ala. 376, 3 So. 902; cf. Beauchamp v. Saginaw Mining Co., 1893, 50 Mich. 163, 15 N.W. 65.

13. Keegan v. Minneapolis & St. L. R. Co., 1899, 76 Minn. 90, 78 N.W. 965 (endocarditis); Turner v. Minneapolis St. R. Co., 1918, 140 Minn. 248, 167 N.W. 1041 (nephritis); Sullivan v. Boston Elevated R. Co., 1904, 185 Mass. 602, 71 N.E. 90 (appendicitis).

14. Armstrong v. Montgomery St. Ry. Co., 1899, 123 Ala. 233, 26 So. 349; Carr v. Minneapolis, St. P. & S. S. M. R. Co., 1919, 140 Minn. 91, 167 N.W. 299; Koehler v. Waukesha Milk Co., 1926, 190 Wis. 52, 208 N.W. 901; Wolfe v. Checker Taxi Co., 1938, 299 Mass. 225, 12 N.E.2d 849.

15. Baltimore City Pass. R. Co. v. Kemp, 1884, 61 Md. 74; Heppner v. Atchison, T. & S. F. R. Co., Mo. 1956, 297 S.W.2d 497.

fright.[16] The defendant of course is liable only for the extent to which his conduct has resulted in an aggravation of the pre-existing condition, and not for the condition as it was;[17] but as to the aggravation, foreseeability is not a factor. One of the illustrations which runs through the English cases is that of the man with the "eggshell skull," who suffers death where a normal man would have had only a bump on the head;[18] and an obviously related rule is that one who kills a man must take his chances, as to damages for the death, that the man has a large income, although he had no reason to expect it.[19]

Perhaps all this might be dismissed as a more or less arbitrary rule of policy, that one who negligently inflicts any personal injury upon another is to be held liable for all the injury to him which follows, and that the courts will refuse to attempt any division in terms of the unforeseeable. But the problem is broader than this. There have been a substantial number of decisions, at one time certainly amounting to a majority rule in the United States, but now undoubtedly on the decline, which have held the defendant liable where the initial impact or harm to the plaintiff itself was unforeseeable. Thus where an object struck by a train is hurled through the air at an angle or to a distance which could not reasonably have been anticipated, and strikes a man,[20] or a fire spreads to an

unanticipated distance,[21] the greater number of American decisions, never expressly overruled, hold that there is liability, although the event was to be regarded as utterly beyond foresight. There have been, in addition, a considerable number of more or less unclassifiable cases of what can only be described as freak accidents of a preposterous character, in which the fact that the defendant could not possibly have foreseen the harm to the plaintiff has been held to be no bar to his recovery.[22]

Typical of these is the North Carolina case[23] in which a railroad over-enthusiastically shunted a freight car into a cornfield, and succeeded in killing a workman some miles away. On their facts many of these

N.E. 160; Wolfe v. Checker Taxi Co., 1938, 299 Mass. 225, 12 N.E.2d 849; Solomon v. Branfman, Sup.Ct.1919, 175 N.Y.S. 835.

21. Hoyt v. Jeffers, 1874, 30 Mich. 181; Atchison, T. & S. F. R. Co. v. Stanford, 1874, 12 Kan. 354; Poeppers v. Missouri, K. & T. R. Co., 1878, 67 Mo. 715; Kuhn v. Jewett, 1880, 32 N.J.Eq. 647; E. T. & H. K. Ide v. Boston & Maine R. Co., 1909, 83 Vt. 66, 74 A. 401. Contra, Hoag v. Lake Shore & M. S. R. Co., 1877, 85 Pa. 293.

It may of course be anticipated that fire will spread to a considerable distance. Cf. Gudfelder v. Pittsburgh, C. C. & St. L. R. Co., 1904, 207 Pa. 629, 57 A. 70; Osborn v. City of Whittier, 1951, 103 Cal.App. 2d 609, 230 P.2d 132. But in the foregoing cases it is assumed that the particular distance was beyond all foreseeable limits.

22. Walmsley v. Rural Tel. Ass'n, 1917, 102 Kan. 139, 169 P. 197 (plaintiff shot because of low hanging wires); Lynch v. Fisher, La.App.1947, 34 So.2d 513 (plaintiff shot by deranged motorist because of collision); Chavers v. A. R. Blossman, Inc., La.App. 1950, 45 So.2d 398 (plaintiff struck by wire severed by fire resulting from collision); Dellwo v. Pearson, 1961, 259 Minn. 452, 107 N.W.2d 859 (motorboat entangled fishline, caught and broke plaintiff's glasses, damaged her eye); Perkins v. Vermont Hydro-Electric Corp., 1934, 106 Vt. 367, 177 A. 631 (defective water diversion system and unprecedented flood); Cameron v. Bissonette, 1930, 103 Vt. 93, 152 A. 87 (mare left out in rain, drowned in brook). See also Bunting v. Hogsett, 1890, 139 Pa. 363, 21 A. 31; Osborne v. Montgomery, 1931, 203 Wis. 223, 234 N.W. 372; Pfeifer v. Standard Gateway Theater, 1952, 262 Wis. 229, 55 N.W.2d 29.

23. Ramsey v. Carolina-Tennessee Power Co., 1928, 195 N.C. 788, 143 S.E. 861.

16. Ominsky v. Charles Weinhagen & Co., 1911, 113 Minn. 422, 129 N.W. 845.

17. Schwingschlegl v. City of Monroe, 1897, 113 Mich. 683, 72 N.W. 7; Watson v. Rinderknecht, 1901, 82 Minn. 235, 84 N.W. 798; Gates v. Fleischer, 1886, 67 Wis. 504, 30 N.W. 674.

18. This originated in Dulieu v. White, [1901] 2 K.B. 669, 679. See Williams, The Risk Principle, 1961, 77 L.Q.Rev. 179, 193–197.

19. First suggested by Blackburn, J., in Smith v. London & S. W. R. Co., 1870, L.R. 6 C.P. 14, 22–23.

20. Kommerstad v. Great Northern R. Co., 1913, 120 Minn. 376, 139 N.W. 713, id., 1915, 128 Minn. 505, 151 N.W. 177; Alabama Great Southern R. Co. v. Chapman, 1886, 80 Ala. 615, 2 So. 738; Robinson v. Standard Oil Co. of Ind., 1929, 89 Ind.App. 167, 166

cases have involved the Palsgraf problem,[24] but it has been either ignored or taken in stride. The courts which have been most consistent in this rejection of foreseeability as a test of the "proximate" have been Louisiana, Minnesota, Vermont, and Wisconsin.

One area in which it may be especially likely that the "foreseeability" limitation will be cast aside is that of intentional torts, as to which it has been said often enough [25] that there is more extended liability. This appears to be, however, more of a general attitude and an unexpressed tendency than anything like a concrete rule.[26]

The objection frequently has been made that such decisions may impose a ruinous liability which no private fortune could meet,[27]

and which is out of all proportion to the defendant's fault. To this it has been answered that if a great loss is to be suffered, it is better that it should fall upon the wrongdoer than upon one innocent victim, or a hundred. "The simple question is, whether a loss, that must be borne somewhere, is to be visited on the head of the innocent or guilty." [28] But the difficulty lies not so much in any injustice to the defendant as in the delimitation of such liability beyond the risk.[29] It is still inconceivable that any defendant should be held liable to infinity for all of the consequences which flow from his act, and some boundary must be set. If nothing more than "common sense" or a "rough sense of justice" is to be relied on,[30] the law becomes to that extent unpredictable, and at the mercy of whatever the court, or even the jury, may decide to do with it.

"Direct Causation"

The alternative to the limitation of the foreseeable risk proposed by a good many courts and writers [31] is that of "direct causation." A distinction is made, which is easier of comprehension than of any exact definition, between consequences which may be regarded as caused "directly" by the defendant's act, and those which result from the intervention of other causes at a later time. "Direct" consequences [32] are those which fol-

---

24. See supra, p. 254.

25. "In determining how far the law will trace causation and afford a remedy, the facts as to the defendant's intent, his imputable knowledge, or his justifiable ignorance are often taken into account. The moral element is here the factor that has turned these cases one way or the other. For an intended injury the law is astute to discover even very remote causation. For one which the defendant merely ought to have anticipated it has often stopped at an earlier stage of the investigation of causal connection. And as to those where there was neither knowledge nor duty to foresee, it has usually limited accountability to direct and immediate results." Derosier v. New England Tel. & Tel. Co., 1925, 81 N.H. 451, 130 A. 145. See also, Seidel v. Greenberg, 1969, 108 N.J.Super. 248, 260 A.2d 863; Bauer, The Degree of Moral Fault as Affecting Defendant's Liability, 1933, 81 U.Pa.L.Rev. 586, 592–596; Note, 1962, 14 Stan.L.Rev. 362.

26. Two cases which clearly illustrate it are Tate v. Canonica, 1960, 180 Cal.App.2d 898, 5 Cal.Rptr. 28, and Cauverian v. De Metz, 1959, 20 Misc.2d 144, 188 N.Y.S.2d 627, both cases of voluntary suicide because of an intentional and outrageous tort of the defendant. Recovery was allowed, where it would not have been for mere negligence. See infra, p. 280. See also criminal cases such as Regina v. Saunders, 1573, 2 Plowd. 473, 75 Eng.Rep. 706; Regina v. Mitchell, 1840, 2 Moody 120, 169 Eng.Rep. 48, where poison intended for the plaintiff was given to A, but unforeseeably administered to B. See also the cases of "transferred intent," supra, p. 32, and of liability for the consequences of trespass to land, supra, p. 67.

27. See Ryan v. New York Cent. R. Co., 1866, 35 N.Y. 210; Pennsylvania R. Co. v. Kerr, 1869, 62 Pa. 353.

28. Fent v. Toledo, P. & W. R. Co., 1871, 59 Ill. 349.

29. Seavey, Mr. Justice Cardozo and the Law of Torts, 1939, 52 Harv.L.Rev. 372, 48 Yale L.J. 390, 39 Col.L.Rev. 20.

30. Cf. Andrews, J., dissenting in Palsgraf v. Long Island R. Co., 1928, 248 N.Y. 339, 162 N.E. 99.

31. Beale, The Proximate Consequences of an Act, 1920, 33 Harv.L.Rev. 633; McLaughlin, Proximate Cause, 1925, 39 Harv.L.Rev. 149; Carpenter, Proximate Cause, 1940, 14 So.Cal.L.Rev. 1, 115 ff; Myers, Causation and Common Sense, 1951, 5 Miami L.Q. 238.

32. It should be noted that "direct" sometimes is used in other senses—referring, for example, to the immediate physical consequences, as distinguished from later ones. See Bauer, Confusion of the Terms "Proximate" and "Direct," 1919, 86 Cent.L.J. 226;

low in sequence from the effect of the defendant's act upon conditions existing and forces already in operation at the time, without the intervention of any external forces which come into active operation later. Thus if the defendant stabs the plaintiff with a knife, the bacteria which enter the wound upon the blade of the knife may cause infection, which may cause septicemia, which may cause death.[33] No new external factor of significance intervenes. There is an analogy to knocking over the first of a row of blocks, after which all of the rest fall down without the assistance of any other force. Upon the same basis, if the defendant sets a fire with a strong wind blowing at the time, there is "direct" causation of any damage which the fire may do when the same wind blows it to any distance,[34] so long as new forces do not intervene.

It seems very likely that the ultimate origins of this distinction between the direct and the indirect sequence are to be sought in the old actions of trespass and case. Applying it, it has frequently been said that direct consequences are always proximate. The defendant is liable for all such consequences of his negligence, although they were unforeseeable, and lie entirely beyond the scope of the

risk created;[35] but his liability for the intervention of new causes is limited to the risk involved in his conduct.[36]

This approach is obviously an arbitrary one, and of course not a matter of causal connection at all, but only of convenience in limiting liability. If there is any justification for it, it must rest in the fact that when a defendant acts upon a set stage, the boundaries of the direct consequences are always limited, not by foreseeability, but by the way the stage is set.[37] The defendant may be expected to take existing circumstances as he finds them, and be responsible for the effect of his act upon them. But the possibilities of intervening causes which may enlarge the consequences at some later time are virtually infinite, and the necessity for some restriction obviously is more imperative. It is another thing to extend the defendant's liability to cover the unlimited number of independent factors which may enter at some later moment to change the situation he has created.

Artificial as it is, "direct" causation has been seized in quite a few cases as affording some way of steering a course between the alternatives of limiting all liability to the risk on the one hand, and unlimited liability on the other. But the limitation is scarcely a logical one, and it is not always easy of application. Apart from the fact that it offers a mechanical solution of a problem which is primarily and essentially one of policy,[38]

Bauer, Confusion of the Terms "Proximate" and "Direct," 1936, 11 Notre Dame Lawyer 395; cf. Berkovitz v. American River Gravel Co., 1923, 191 Cal. 195, 215 P. 675. It is also used vaguely as a general synonym for "proximate," as in Coates v. Dewoskin, Mo.App.1964, 379 S.W.2d 146; Mailton v. Vare, 1931, 184 Minn. 580, 239 N.W. 659. An unsatisfactory term, but it is used by the courts, and no better is at hand.

33. Cf. State v. James, 1913, 123 Minn. 487, 144 N.W. 216; McGarrahan v. New York, N. H. & H. R. Co., 1898, 171 Mass. 211, 50 N.E. 610; Koehler v. Waukesha Milk Co., 1926, 190 Wis. 52, 208 N.W. 901.

34. Burlington & M. R. Co. v. Westover, 1876, 4 Neb. 268; cf. Kuhn v. Jewett, 1880, 32 N.J.Eq. 647. Compare, as cases of direct causation, Rich v. Finley, 1949, 325 Mass. 99, 89 N.E.2d 213 (aviation student freezing at controls); Loftus v. McCramie, Fla.1950, 47 So.2d 298 (escaped steers wandering about and doing damage); Brown v. Travelers' Indemnity Co., 1947, 251 Wis. 188, 28 N.W.2d 306 (stunned cow revived and injured plaintiff).

35. See for example Chicago, R. I. & P. R. Co. v. Goodson, 5 Cir. 1957, 242 F.2d 203 (Texas law); Dixon v. Kentucky Utilities Co., 1943, 295 Ky. 32, 37, 174 S.W.2d 19, 22; Williams v. Brennan, 1912, 213 Mass. 28, 99 N.E. 516. See also the cases cited supra, notes 6 to 22, all of which are examples of direct causation.

36. See infra, § 44. The distinction is well stated in Nunan v. Bennett, 1919, 184 Ky. 591, 212 S.W. 570.

37. Cf. the suggestion in Winfield, Law of Torts, 1937, 80, that cases will be relatively infrequent in which direct consequences will not be foreseeable. See also, justifying the distinction, Carpenter, Proximate Cause, 1940, 14 So.Cal.L.Rev. 1, 115.

38. The attitude is well illustrated in Collier v. Citizens Coach Co., 1959, 231 Ark. 489, 330 S.W.2d

it is not always easy to say whether new forces have intervened—as where for example, a wind changes its direction—[39] and in nearly all cases of "direct" causation it is necessary to ignore as unimportant a number of external factors which have intervened before the result.[40] More important, however, is the objection that no really successful and satisfactory limitation is provided which will eliminate the consequences which most of us feel, more or less instinctively, to be going too far. Although direct consequences are not unlimited, they may still be fantastic; and it is not likely that any court would ever carry the direct liability to all of the extreme lengths to which it might lead.

The spectacular case applying the theory of direct causation is the English one of In re Polemis,[41] in which a plank dropped by defendant's workman into the hold of a ship struck out a spark, which exploded petrol vapor, and destroyed the ship and its cargo. Although the arbitrators had specifically found that this was not a foreseeable result of the negligence, recovery was allowed because it was all "direct." The case remained

something of a storm center in England for forty years, with much outpouring of attack [42] and support.[43] In 1961 the decision was flatly overruled by the Privy Council in the first of two cases which have been nicknamed The Wagon Mound,[44] after the oil tanker involved. Her bunker crew negligently allowed furnace oil to overflow into Sydney harbor, where it was carried to the plaintiff's dock, some 600 feet away. It might have been expected that the oil would do minor damage to the plaintiff's slipways, which it did; but it was found that because of the high flash point of the oil it could not reasonably be foreseen that it would become ignited when spread upon the water. Molten metal falling from the dock ignited cotton waste floating on the oil, which acted as a wick, and the dock was burned. The court repudiated the "direct causation" rule, adopting a straight limitation of the liability to the foreseeable risk, and so denied recovery for the loss of the dock. The decision is the logical aftermath of Cardozo's position in the Palsgraf case,[45] since there is an obvious ab-

74, 76, where it is actually said that "proximate cause is a rule of physics and not a criterion of negligence!"

39. Compare Stephens v. Mutual Lumber Co., 1918, 103 Wash. 1, 173 P. 1031 (considered a new intervening force) with E. T. & H. K. Ide v. Boston & Me. R. Co., 1909, 83 Vt. 66, 74 A. 401 (considered direct).

40. "The entire assumption that the physiological disturbances which follow from a wound are part of the defendant's direct force rests upon a refusal to analyze the physiological processes. It is necessary only to note here that obvious intervening forces, such as a man's eating, may often be neglected for practical purposes in analyzing a case. Eating bacteria is so foreseeable that it would not be an isolating force, and so the question of classification as direct causation or some other type may be ignored. It must be obvious, however, that the limits of direct causation are not sharply defined." McLaughlin, Proximate Cause, 1925, 39 Harv.L.Rev. 149, 165.

41. In re Polemis and Furness, Withy & Co., [1921] 3 K.B. 560.

42. Goodhart, The Unforeseeable Consequences of a Negligent Act, 1930, 39 Yale L.J. 449; Goodhart, The Imaginary Necktie and the Rule of Re Polemis, 1952, 68 L.Q.Rev. 514; Goodhart, Liability and Compensation, 1960, 76 L.Q.Rev. 567; Goodhart, The Brief Life Story of the Direct Consequence Rule in English Tort Law, 1967, 53 Va.L.Rev. 857.

(Among the great one-man crusades of history, that of Sir Arthur Goodhart against the Polemis rule must certainly be numbered; and there can be little doubt that its ultimate overthrow was due in large part to him).

See also Seavey, Mr. Justice Cardozo and the Law of Torts, 1939, 52 Harv.L.Rev. 372, 48 Yale L.J. 390, 39 Col.L.Rev. 20; Payne, The "Direct" Consequences of a Negligent Act, 1952, 5 Curr.Leg.Prob. 189.

43. Porter, The Measure of Damages in Contract and Tort, 1934, 5 Camb.L.J. 176; Wright, Re Polemis, 1951, 14 Mod.L.Rev. 393; Hart and Honoré, Causation in the Law, 1959, 151 ff; Wilson and Slade, A Re-examination of Remoteness, 1952, 15 Mod.L.Rev. 458.

44. Overseas Tankship (U.K.) Ltd. v. Morts Dock & Engineering Co., Ltd., [1961] A.C. 388.

45. Supra, p. 254.

surdity in holding that one who can foresee some harm to A is liable for consequences to A which he cannot foresee, but is not liable for similar consequences to B.

The decision appeared to have settled the issue for the British Commonwealth,[46] although it left a legacy of vexatious unsettled questions,[47] and the prediction was made [48] that any such flat and final rule could not possibly hold good for all situations. This was borne out by decisions holding that foreseeability was not required as to consequences following an injury to the person,[49] as in the case of the man with the "egg-shell skull," and that if the consequences themselves were foreseeable, it was not necessary to foresee the manner in which they were brought about.[50]

Six years later the Privy Council retreated somewhat from its position in Wagon Mound No. 2,[51] where the action was for damage to

ships docked at the same wharf. This time there was evidence justifying the conclusion that the defendants were, or should have been, aware that there was some slight risk that the oil on the water would be ignited, although it was very unlikely. It was held that since the conduct of the defendants had no justification or social value, they were not justified in neglecting even that slight risk, and they were therefore liable. The decision would appear to have adopted the American formula of balancing magnitude of risk and gravity of harm against utility of conduct,[52] and to have applied it to foreseeability in relation to "proximate cause." The effect would appear to be to let the Polemis Case in again by the back door, since cases will obviously be quite infrequent in which there is not some recognizable slight risk of this character.

It is still a matter of speculation, what effect the Wagon Mound decisions may have in the United States.[53] Although in the beginning the American courts were much influenced by English cases,[54] in later years they have been preoccupied with the somewhat over-ample supply of American decisions, and the English ones have tended to pass unremarked. The Polemis Case itself has been a subject of discussion very largely in the law schools, and its passing may very possibly have no great effect on this side of the water.

Two important decisions bearing upon the Palsgraf Case are involved in Petition of Kinsman Transit Co. In the first of these,[55]

---

46. There was for a time some doubt as to whether the decision of the Privy Council would be followed as to Great Britain itself. This was finally set at rest by Doughty v. Turner Mfg. Co., Ltd., [1964] 1 Q.B. 518.

47. Two excellent articles in which the situation following Wagon Mound No. 1 is reviewed are Fleming, The Passing of Polemis, 1961, 39 Can.Bar Rev. 489, and Williams, The Risk Principle, 1961, 77 L.Q.Rev. 179. See also Morison, The Victory of Reasonable Foresight, 1961, 34 Aust.L.J. 317; Payne, Foresight and Remoteness of Damage in Negligence, 1962, 25 Mod.L.Rev. 1; Dias, Remoteness of Liability and Legal Policy, [1962] Camb.L.J. 178; see also Smith, The Limits of Tort Liability in Canada, included in Linden, Studies in Canadian Tort Law (1968).

48. Green, Foreseeability in Negligence Law, 1961, 61 Col.L.Rev. 1401.

49. Smith v. Leech Brain & Co., Ltd., [1962] 2 Q.B. 405; Oman v. McIntyre, [1962] Scot.L.T. 168.

50. Hughes v. Lord Advocate, [1963] A.C. 837.

51. Overseas Tankship (U.K.) Ltd. v. Miller Steamship Co., [1967] 1 A.C. 617. The whole story of the Wagon Mound cases is narrated in Goodhart, The Brief Life Story of the Direct Consequence Law in English Tort Law, 1967, 53 Va.L.Rev. 857; Smith, The Limits of Tort Liability in Canada, included in Linden, Studies in Canadian Tort Law (1968); Green, The Wagon Mound No. 2—Foreseeability Revisited, [1967] Utah L.Rev. 197; Dias, Trouble on

Oiled Waters: Problems of the Wagon Mound (No. 2), [1967] Camb.L.J. 62.

52. See Learned Hand, in United States v. Carroll Towing Co., 2 Cir. 1947, 159 F.2d 169.

53. The only reference to either decision found to date is in Petition of Kinsman Transit Co., 2 Cir. 1964, 338 F.2d 708, where Wagon Mound No. 1 was rejected, so far as the limitation to foreseeable consequences was concerned.

54. Particularly Smith v. London & Southwestern Ry. Co., 1870, L.R. 6 C.P. 14.

55. Petition of Kinsman Transit Co., 2 Cir. 1964, 338 F.2d 308.

a ship negligently moored in the Buffalo River was set adrift by floating ice, collided with a bridge and overthrew it, creating an ice jam in the river, which backed up water to damage factories on the bank below the point of mooring. The court, bound by New York law, proceeded to limit the Palsgraf rule by holding that if any harm to the plaintiff was foreseeable, the defendant was liable for unforeseeable consequences to him. In the second,[56] the action was for pecuniary loss due to the necessity of transporting ship cargoes around the jam. The court was unwilling to hold that there could be no liability for pecuniary loss caused by negligence,[57] and held instead that the connection between the negligence and these damages was too "tenuous and remote" to permit recovery. Just what this may mean would appear to be anybody's guess.

Anatomy of Foresight

From what has gone before in this chapter, the conclusion may well be drawn that, while there are still rearguard actions, and cases that do not fit, the "scope of the foreseeable risk" is on its way to ultimate victory as the criterion of what is "proximate," if it has not already achieved it. One very possible explanation for the triumph of the concept is that it so completely lacks all clarity and precision that it amounts to nothing more than a convenient formula for disposing of the case—usually by leaving it to the jury under instructions calling for "foreseeable," or "natural and probable" consequences. What, then, does foresight mean?[58]

In one sense, almost nothing is entirely unforeseeable, since there is a very slight math-

ematical chance, recognizable in advance, that even the most freakish accident which is possible will occur, particularly if it has ever happened in history before.[59] In another, no event whatever is entirely foreseeable, since the exact details of a sequence never can be predicted with complete omniscience and accuracy. What is meant must lie somewhere between the two extremes; but where? The usual answer has been that "foreseeability" means, in "proximate cause," the same thing as in negligence; and that the same considerations which determine the original culpability are to be used again to determine liability for consequences. This has a comforting sound of predictable certainty and facility of administration. But, with deference, it is submitted that both are quite illusory.

Foreseeability of consequences, or, as it is sometimes called, the risk of harm, is only one of the factors which are important in determining negligence. Into the scale with it there must also be thrown the gravity of the harm if it is to occur, and against both must be balanced the utility of the challenged conduct.[60] But even the risk of harm itself, when

---

56. Petition of Kinsman Transit Co., 2 Cir. 1968, 388 F.2d 821.

57. See infra, p. 938.

58. Well considered in Fleming, The Passing of Polemis, 1961, 39 Can.Bar Rev. 489, 508–529; Linden, Down with Foreseeability! Of Thin Skulls and Rescuers, 1969, 47 Can.Bar Rev. 545.

59. Compare the argument of Edgerton, Legal Cause, 1924, 72 U.Pa.L.Rev. 211, 238, that there may be a sight chance of the particular result (as of a fire spreading several miles), which a reasonable man would recognize in advance, but which would not in itself influence his conduct. When there is negligence because of other risks, recovery, says Edgerton, should be allowed for such consequences. Cf. Morey v. Lake Superior Terminal & Transfer Co., 1905, 125 Wis. 148, 103 N.W. 271; Pittsburgh Fore & Iron Co. v. Dravo Contracting Co., 1922, 272 Pa. 118, 116 A. 147.

Compare also Green, Foreseeability in Negligence Law, 1961, 61 Col.L.Rev. 1401, explaining In re Polemis, [1921] 3 K.B. 560, on the ground that blowing up the ship was just what was to be expected—despite the fact that the arbitrator specifically found, and the whole court assumed throughout, that it was quite "unforeseeable."

60. See supra, p. 148.

the defendant is found to be negligent, is usually an aggregate risk of many possibilities.

If a train is operated without a proper lookout, it is relatively easy to say that the total risk, made up of everything that can happen, be it probable or fantastic, is so great that the reasonable man of ordinary prudence would not do this, and therefore there is negligence. But how easy is it, by a process of fragmentation of that risk, to sort it out into particular consequences, and to say that they are, or are not, such substantial parts of the original total foreseeable risk that liability is to be attached to them? There is some likelihood that the train will collide with an automobile or a cow, or be derailed and injure its passengers; less that it will endanger a child on the track and injure its rescuer; still less that the cow will be thrown against a man a hundred feet from the track and break his leg, that the train wreck will start a forest fire and burn a distant village, or twist a power line pole and electrocute a man ten miles away; and what of the likelihood that the injured man's watch will be stolen, that he will contract pneumonia and die of it, or that he will receive negligent medical treatment and be further injured? [61]

All of these things have happened, and all of them have been held "proximate" by some court. But which of them are to be called "foreseeable," in the sense that any reasonable man would really have had them in mind at the time of his operation of the train?

Recognizing these difficulties, there are courts which have thrown over the language of foreseeability, and have said outright that this becomes a matter of hindsight, which is to say of relating the consequences back into the picture of the original negligence after they have in fact occurred. [62]

The Restatement of Torts [63] has offered much the same approach by saying that the defendant is not to be liable for consequences which, looking backward after the event with full knowledge of all that has occurred, would appear to be "highly extraordinary." The language may be unfortunate; to one gifted with omniscience as to all existing circumstances, no result could appear remarkable, or indeed anything but inevitable, as a matter of hindsight. Certainly no element of mystery is necessary, or of ignorance as to what has happened. Perhaps the Restatement has come close to expressing the underlying idea of a limitation of liability short of the remarkable, the preposterous, the highly unlikely, in the language of the street the cock-eyed and far-fetched, even when we look at the event, as we must, after it has occurred.

The problem is in no way simplified by the quite universal agreement that what is required to be foreseeable is only the "general character" or "general type" of the event or the harm, [64] and not its "precise" nature, de-

---

61. See Gregory, Proximate Cause in Negligence—A Retreat from Rationalization, 1938, 6 U.Chi.L.Rev. 36, 50; Prosser, Proximate Cause in California, 1950, 38 Cal.L.Rev. 369, 396.

62. Leposki v. Railway Express Agency, 3 Cir. 1962, 297 F.2d 849 is an excellent example. Defendant allowed gasoline to drip from its truck into the gutter; boys ignited it, and it burned the plaintiff's home. It was held improper to charge that defendant was not liable unless this act was foreseeable; the Pennsylvania test is whether the intervening act was extraordinary, looking back. See also Dellwo v. Pearson, 1961, 259 Minn. 452, 107 N.W.2d 859 ("Negligence is tested by foresight, but proximate cause is determined by hindsight").

63. Second Restatement of Torts, § 435(2). Cf. Wabash R. Co. v. Coker, 1898, 81 Ill.App. 660; Wallin v. Eastern R. Co., 1901, 83 Minn. 149, 158, 86 N.W. 76, 79; Butts v. Anthis, 1937, 181 Okl. 276, 73 P.2d 843 (" * * * all the consequences which a prudent and experienced person, fully acquainted with the circumstances which in fact existed * * * would at the time of the negligent act have thought reasonably possible if they had occurred to his mind.")

64. Danner v. Arnsberg, 1961, 227 Or. 420, 362 P.2d 758 ("the same general character"); Tropea v. Shell Oil Co., 2 Cir. 1962, 307 F.2d 757 ("in a general

tails, or above all manner of occurrence.[65] This goes back to two early cases in which a workman who might have been expected to be knocked down by the collision of a tug with a bridge was pinched between piles instead when the collision knocked out a brace,[66] and an engine involved in a collision was thrown out of control, traveled in a circle, and collided again with the same train.[67] Some "margin of leeway" has to be left for the unusual and the unexpected.[68] But this has opened a very wide door; and the courts have taken so much advantage of the leeway that it can scarcely be doubted that a great deal of what the ordinary man would regard as freakish, bizarre, and unpredictable has crept within the bounds of liability by the simple device of permitting the jury to foresee at least its very broad, and vague, general outlines.[69] This becomes, in

the courtroom, a matter for the skill of the advocate who can lay stress upon broad, general, and very simple things, and stay away from all complications of detail.[70]

With such a background, one would expect confusion as to what is or is not foreseeable; and confusion there is. On the one hand there are limitations which appear to be amazingly short-sighted. The New York court has solemnly held that it is unforeseeable that a fire will spread beyond the first adjoining house.[71] Learned Hand, a great judge, has assured us that it is not sufficiently to be anticipated that a barge with which the defendant collides will later sink, and will be carrying insurance.[72] Pennsylvania has twice held that no reasonable man can foresee that when a speeding vehicle strikes a man his body will fly off at an angle, and hit a person not directly in the path.[73] Wisconsin has considered that when a child is run down in the street there is no sufficient recognizable risk that its mother will be somewhere in the vicinity, and will suffer severe nervous shock.[74] Opinions may differ;

way"); Byrnes v. Stephens, Tex.Civ.App.1961, 349 S.W.2d 611 ("such general character as might have been anticipated"); Smith v. Prater, 1966, 206 Va. 693, 146 S.E.2d 179; Nobles v. Unruh, Miss.1967, 198 So.2d 245; Thornton v. Weaber, 1955, 380 Pa. 590, 112 A.2d 344 ("some injury of the same general character"); Carey v. Pure Dist. Corp., 1939, 133 Tex. 31, 124 S.W.2d 847. Perhaps the best statement of all this is that of Magruder, J., in Marshall v. Nugent, 1 Cir. 1955, 222 F.2d 604, 58 A.L.R.2d 251.

65. Biggers v. Continental Bus System, 1957, 157 Tex. 351, 303 S.W.2d 359; Bondurant v. Holland, Mastin & Sales Co., 1960, 252 N.C. 190, 113 S.E.2d 292; Chase v. Washington Water Power Co., 1941, 62 Idaho 298, 111 P.2d 872; Foss v. Chicago, B. & Q. R. Co., 1922, 151 Minn. 506, 187 N.W. 609; Pulaski Gas Light Co. v. McClintock, 1911, 97 Ark. 576, 134 S.W. 1189.

66. Hill v. Winsor, 1875, 118 Mass. 251.

67. Bunting v. Hogsett, 1890, 139 Pa. 363, 21 A. 31.

68. In Lady Nelson v. Creole Petroleum Co., 2 Cir. 1955, 224 F.2d 591, cert. denied 350 U.S. 935, this was applied even in a Palsgraf type of situation. In accord is the striking case of Petition of Kinsman Transit Co., 2 Cir. 1964, 338 F.2d 708, where a negligently moored ship, drifting down a winding river amid floating ice, might have been expected to do some kind of damage to shore installations, and actually resulting in flooding several factories. See Note, 1965, 49 Minn.L.Rev. 1052.

69. See Coatney v. Southwest Tenn. Elec. Membership Corp., 1956, 40 Tenn.App. 541, 292 S.W.2d 420: "some such harm of a like general character * * *

almost any harm from electricity which could humanly have been avoided would render the company liable in damages."

70. Well stated in Morris, Proximate Cause in Minnesota, 1950, 34 Minn.L.Rev. 185, who attributes the decision in Hines v. Morrow, Tex.Civ.App.1922, 236 S.W. 183, error refused, to the summary of the facts in plaintiff's brief, as follows: "The case stated in its briefest form, is simply this: Appellee was on the highway using it in a lawful manner, and slipped into this hole, created by appellant's negligence, and was injured in attempting to extricate himself."

71. Ryan v. New York Central R. Co., 1866, 35 N.Y. 210.

72. Sinram v. Pennsylvania R. Co., 2 Cir. 1932, 61 F.2d 767.

73. Wood v. Pennsylvania R. Co., 1896, 177 Pa. 306, 35 A. 699; Dahlstrom v. Shrum, 1951, 368 Pa. 423, 84 A.2d 289. But cf. Mellon v. Lehigh Valley R. Co., 1925, 282 Pa. 39, 127 A. 444, which appears to contradict both.

74. Waube v. Warrington, 1935, 216 Wis. 603, 258 N.W. 497. Cf. Davis v. Shiappacossee, Fla.App.1962, 145 So.2d 758, holding that it is not really foreseeable that when intoxicating liquor is sold to minors they will be injured in an automobile crash.

but surely it is permissible to say that to agree with these things requires the faith that moveth mountains.

On the other hand, there are quite remarkable events which have been taken in stride by various courts as within the boundaries of the jury's permission to find foreseeability. The defendant negligently drives his car so that it leaves the roadway and collides with a power line pole; this shuts off power from a traffic control box, traffic signals cease to function, and two other cars collide at an intersection.[75] A power line pole breaks, falls upon a telephone wire and charges it; the plaintiff's power shovel, elevated above the ground, comes in contact with the wire.[76] A negligently driven car collides with a taxicab, which is rammed against the stone stoop of a building, where it becomes wedged among stones knocked down. While a wrecking car is attempting to remove the taxicab, a stone which has been dislodged is loosened, and falls upon a bystander.[77] Defendant parks his car and leaves it without setting the brake. Five hours later a drunken driver rams the car, shoving it into the plaintiff.[78] A mudhole is negligently left in a highway; a car gets stuck in it, and a man with a wooden leg attempts to pull the car out with a tow rope. His wooden leg becomes stuck in the mud and a loop in the tow rope lassos his good leg and breaks it.[79] It is all found to be foreseeable. Illustrations might be multiplied, but surely enough has been said to indicate

the essential conflict in the cases, all of which are making use of the same words, to mean whatever they are desired to mean. With so much leeway and flexibility in "foreseeability," it is not surprising that "unforeseeable consequences" and "direct causation" are falling into disrepute.

It seems evident that in all of these proposed rules and formulae the courts and the writers have been groping for something that is difficult, if not impossible, to put into words: some method of limiting liability to those consequences which have some reasonably close connection with the defendant's conduct and the harm which it originally threatened, and are in themselves not so remarkable and unusual as to lead one to stop short of them. It may be questioned whether anyone has yet succeeded in accomplishing more than the courts themselves have been able to achieve with the idea of such a reasonably close connection contained in the despised word "proximate," which may have more in the way of merit than is usually credited to it.

44. INTERVENING CAUSES

In dealing with a large group of cases, it is convenient to adopt the language frequently used by the courts, and to speak of intervening causes, or intervening forces. On its face, the problem is one of whether the defendant is to be held liable for an injury to which he has in fact made a substantial contribution, when it is brought about by a later cause of independent origin, for which he is not responsible. In its essence, however, it becomes again a question of the extent of the defendant's original obligation; and once more the problem is not one of causation at all, since it does not arise until causation is established. It is rather one of the policy as to imposing legal responsibility. The older cases tend to ask the question, why should the defendant be held liable for harm brought about by something for which he is not re-

75. Ferroggiaro v. Bowline, 1957, 153 Cal.App.2d 759, 315 P.2d 446. Reference to the Record discloses that it was not even the same intersection, but one at a considerable distance.

76. Jackson v. Utica Light & Power Co., 1944, 64 Cal. App.2d 885, 149 P.2d 748.

77. In re Guardian Casualty Co., 1938, 253 App.Div. 360, 2 N.Y.S.2d 232, affirmed, 1938, 278 N.Y. 674, 16 N.E.2d 397.

78. Byrnes v. Stephens, Tex.Civ.App.1961, 349 S.W.2d 611.

79. Hines v. Morrow, Tex.Civ.App.1922, 236 S.W. 183, error refused.

sponsible? The later ones tended to ask instead, why should he be relieved of liability for something that he has caused, along with other causes? It is for this reason that the Restatement [80] has stated the problem in terms of whether there is a "superseding cause."

"Intervening cause," like "direct causation," is a term easier of general comprehension than of any exact definition. An intervening cause is one which comes into active operation in producing the result *after* the negligence of the defendant.[81] "Intervening" is used in a time sense; it refers to later events. If the defendant sets a fire with a strong wind blowing at the time, which carries the fire to the plaintiff's property, the wind does not intervene, since it was already in operation; but if the fire is set first, and the wind springs up later, it is then an intervening cause.[82] Neither are forces caused or set in motion by the operation of the defendant's conduct upon the existing situation—as where his spark ignites gasoline vapor already present—to be considered as intervening, since their origin is not external

and independent, and they are to be attributed to the defendant himself.[83]

It must be conceded that "intervening cause" is a highly unsatisfactory term, since we are dealing with problems of responsibility, and not physics.[84] It is used in default of a better, because it is useful in dealing with the type of case where a new and independent cause acts upon a situation once created by the defendant. It should be understood in the very general sense of concurring [85] causes of either natural or human

---

80. Second Restatement of Torts, § 440: "A superseding cause is an act of a third person or other force which by its intervention prevents the actor from being liable for harm to another which his antecedent negligence is a substantial factor in bringing about."

81. Second Restatement of Torts, § 441: "An intervening force is one which actively operates in producing harm to another after the actor's negligent act or omission has been committed."
"An intervening force is a force which is neither operating in the defendant's presence, nor at the place where the defendant's act takes effect at the time of the defendant's act, but comes into effective operation at or before the time of the damage." McLaughlin, Proximate Cause, 1925, 39 Harv.L.Rev. 149, 159.

82. Cf. Burlington & M. R. Co. v. Westover, 1876, 4 Neb. 268, and Kuhn v. Jewett, 1880, 32 N.J.Eq. 647 (direct), with Haverly v. State Line & S. R. Co., 1890, 135 Pa. 50, 19 A. 1013 (intervening). Some confusion has arisen from an occasional use of "intervening" to include forces operating at the time and place of the defendant's act, as in Hoag & Alger v. Lake Shore & M. S. R. Co., 1877, 85 Pa. 293.

83. In re Polemis and Furness, Withy & Co., [1921] 3 K.B. 560. Cf. Larson v. Boston Elev. R. Co., 1912, 212 Mass. 262, 98 N.E. 1048 (latent tuberculosis). "The new, independent intervening cause must be one not produced by the wrongful act or omission, but independent of it, and adequate to bring about the injurious result." Purcell v. St. Paul City R. Co., 1892, 48 Minn. 134, 50 N.W. 1034.

84. "Force obviously must be a word of practical application, rather than a scientific term. Thus a spreading fire, for practical purposes, may be regarded as a continuous force, rather than a series of chemical reactions from one blade of grass to another, resulting from the interplay of many forces." Atchison, T. & S. F. R. Co. v. Stanford, 1874, 12 Kan. 354, 375. There will of course be occasional difficulty in determining whether a "force" is to be regarded as a new one—as where the wind shifts from east to north. Compare Stephens v. Mutual Lumber Co., 1918, 103 Wash. 1, 173 P. 1031 (new force) with E. T. & H. K. Ide v. Boston & Me. R. Co., 1909, 83 Vt. 66, 74 A. 401 (same force). But so long as the emphasis is placed upon the risk, such questions are seldom important.

85. There is some confusion as to the meaning of "concurring causes" and "intervening causes." All causes, whether intervening or otherwise, which materially contribute to the result, may properly be called "concurring" in a causal sense, while only those which come into active operation later in point of time are "intervening." See Notes, 1934, 12 Tex.L.Rev. 518; 1936, 26 Georgetown L.J. 167. It is entirely possible that each of two concurring causes may be an intervening force as to the other. For example, suppose that each of two defendants leaves an automobile at the top of a hill without setting the brakes. The two cars run down hill and collide at the bottom, and one of them is deflected so that it injures the plaintiff. Each car has intervened after the original negligence connected with the other; both are concurring causes. Many courts confuse the terms, and use them interchangeably. See Johnson v. Plymouth Gypsum Plaster Co., 1916, 174 Iowa 498, 156 N.W. 721.

origin, which come into active operation at a later time to change a situation resulting from the defendant's conduct.

The number and variety of causes which may intervene after the negligence of the defendant is an accomplished fact, are obviously without any limit whatever. In the effort to hold the defendant's liability within some reasonable bounds, the courts have been compelled, out of sheer necessity and in default of anything better, to fall back upon the scope of the original foreseeable risk which he has created. The question is always one of whether he is to be relieved of responsibility, and his liability superseded, by the subsequent event. In general, this has been determined by asking whether the intervention of the later cause is a significant part of the risk involved in the defendant's conduct, or is so reasonably connected with it that the responsibility should not be terminated. It is therefore said that the defendant is to be held liable if, but only if, the intervening cause is "foreseeable." [86]

But here, as before,[87] this overworked and undefined word covers a multitude of sins. It is at least clear that in many cases recovery has been allowed where the intervening cause was not one which any reasonable actor could be expected to anticipate or have in mind, but it is regarded as "normal" to the situation which he has created.[88] In other words, although the theory of the cases is one of foreseeability, the practical application has always involved a considerable element of hindsight.

Foreseeable Intervening Causes

If the intervening cause is one which in ordinary human experience is reasonably to be anticipated, or one which the defendant has reason to anticipate under the particular circumstances,[89] he may be negligent, among other reasons, because he has failed to guard against it; or he may be negligent only for that reason. Thus one who sets a fire may be required to foresee that an ordinary, usual and customary wind arising later will spread it beyond his own property, and therefore to take precautions to prevent that event.[90] The man who leaves combustible or explosive material exposed in a public place may foresee the risk of fire from some independent source.[91] One who leaves uninsulated electric wires where people may come in contact with them may anticipate that they will do so as a result of their own acts.[92] A

---

86. See for example Payne v. City of New York, 1938, 277 N.Y. 393, 14 N.E.2d 449 (stone in street thrown by wheel of passing car through windshield); Silver Falls Timber Co. v. Eastern & Western Lumber Co., 1935, 149 Or. 126, 40 P.2d 703 (fire carried by wind); Pease v. Sinclair Refining Co., 2 Cir. 1939, 104 F.2d 183 (mislabeled water mixed with sodium caused explosion); Royal Indemnity Co. v. Midland Counties Public Service Corp., 1919, 42 Cal.App. 628, 183 P. 960 (horse entangled in improperly insulated guy wire); Mize v. Rocky Mountain Bell Tel. Co., 1909, 38 Mont. 521, 100 P. 971 (telephone wire electrified, current carried ten miles).

87. See supra, § 43.

88. Second Restatement of Torts, § 435, Comment *d*.

89. Cf. Bell Lumber Co. v. Bayfield Transfer R. Co., 1919, 169 Wis. 357, 172 N.W. 955 (notice of forest fires); Chesapeake & O. R. Co. v. J. Wix & Sons, 4 Cir., 1937, 87 F.2d 257 (weather forecast of storm of great intensity); Toledo & O. C. R. Co. v. S. J. Kibler & Bros. Co., 1918, 97 Ohio St. 262, 119 N.E. 733 (notice of flood); Ithaca Roller Mills v. Ann Arbor R. Co., 1922, 217 Mich. 348, 186 N.W. 516 (same).

90. Haverly v. State Line & S. R. Co., 1890, 135 Pa. 50, 19 A. 1013; Olson v. Riddle, 1911, 22 N.D. 144, 132 N.W. 655; Silver Falls Timber Co. v. Eastern & Western Lumber Co., 1935, 149 Or. 126, 40 P.2d 703.

91. Watson v. Kentucky & Indiana Bridge & R. Co., 1910, 137 Ky. 619, 126 S.W. 146, 129 S.W. 341 modified, 1911, 129 S.W. 341; Teasdale v. Beacon Oil Co., 1929, 266 Mass. 25, 164 N.E. 612; Trapp v. Standard Oil Co., 1954, 176 Kan. 39, 269 P.2d 469. Cf. Williams v. American Mut. Liability Ins. Co., La.App.1960, 121 So.2d 545; McClure v. Hoopeston Gas & Elec. Co., 1922, 303 Ill. 89, 135 N.E. 43. Contrast the older attitude toward such cases, in Stone v. Boston & Albany R. Co., 1898, 171 Mass. 536, 51 N.E. 1.

92. Asher v. City of Independence, 1913, 177 Mo.App. 1, 163 S.W. 574; Davidson v. Otter Tail Power Co., 1921, 150 Minn. 446, 185 N.W. 644.

defendant who has a hole in his sidewalk may expect that some person walking by will slip or catch his foot in it.[93] An unguarded elevator shaft involves the risk that someone will fall into it;[94] unprotected dangerous machinery means that someone may get himself caught.[95] If a gun is entrusted to a child, it suggests at once to anyone with any imagination at all that someone, the child or another, is likely to be shot.[96] In all of these cases there is an intervening cause combining with the defendant's conduct to produce the result, and in each case the defendant's negligence consists in failure to protect the plaintiff against that very risk.

Obviously the defendant cannot be relieved from liability by the fact that the risk, or a substantial and important part of the risk, to which he has subjected the plaintiff has indeed come to pass. Foreseeable intervening forces are within the scope of the original risk, and hence of the defendant's negligence. The courts are quite generally agreed that intervening causes which fall fairly in this category will not supersede the defendant's responsibility.[97]

Thus it has been held that a defendant will be required to anticipate the usual weather of the vicinity, including all ordinary forces of nature such as usual wind or rain,[98] or snow[99] or frost[1] or fog[2] or even lightning;[3] that one who leaves an obstruction on the road[4] or a railroad track[5] should foresee that a vehicle or a train will run into it; that if defective goods are sold to a dealer he may be expected to resell them,[6] and they may be passed on into the hands of those who will be injured by them;[7] that workmen who are furnished with a defective appliance may be

93. Magay v. Claflin-Sumner Coal Co., 1926, 257 Mass. 244, 153 N.E. 534. Cf. Rodgers v. Yellow Cab Co., 1959, 395 Pa. 412, 147 A.2d 611; Hastings v. F. W. Woolworth Co., 1933, 189 Minn. 523, 250 N.W. 362; Duteny v. Pennichuck Water Co., 1929, 84 N.H. 65, 146 A. 161.

94. Landy v. Olson & Serley Sash & Door Co., 1927, 171 Minn. 440, 214 N.W. 659. Cf. Mawson v. Eagle Harbor Transp. Co., 1928, 148 Wash. 258, 268 P. 595; Eggen v. Hickman, 1938, 274 Ky. 550, 119 S.W.2d 633.

95. Nelson v. William H. Ziegler Co., 1933, 190 Minn. 313, 251 N.W. 534.

96. Dixon v. Bell, 1816, 5 M. & S. 198, 105 Eng.Rep. 1023; Mautino v. Piercedale Supply Co., 1940, 338 Pa. 435, 13 A.2d 51; Milton Bradley Co. v. Cooper, 1949, 79 Ga.App. 302, 53 S.E.2d 761; Anderson v. Settergren, 1907, 100 Minn. 294, 111 N.W. 279. Accord: Pudla v. Dubiel, 1930, 273 Mass. 172, 173 N.E. 536 (shot for air rifle); Allen v. Gornto, 1959, 100 Ga.App. 744, 112 S.E.2d 368 (fireworks); Rappaport v. Nichols, 1959, 31 N.J. 188, 156 A.2d 1 (liquor).

97. Two early decisions to this effect which have been cited frequently are Lane v. Atlantic Works,

1872, 111 Mass. 136, and Gilman v. Noyes, 1876, 57 N.H. 627.

98. Holter Hardware Co. v. Western Mortgage & W. T. Co., 1915, 51 Mont. 94, 149 P. 489; Kimble v. Mackintosh Hemphill Co., 1948, 359 Pa. 461, 59 A.2d 68; Fairbrother v. Wiley's, Inc., 1958, 183 Kan. 579, 331 P.2d 330; Cachick v. United States, S.D.Ill.1958, 161 F.Supp. 15; The Mariner, 5 Cir. 1927, 17 F.2d 253.

99. Bowman v. Columbia Tel. Co., 1962, 406 Pa. 455, 179 A.2d 197; Klein v. United States, 2 Cir. 1964, 339 F.2d 512.

1. Fox v. Boston & Maine R. Co., 1889, 148 Mass. 220, 19 N.E. 222; Benedict Pineapple Co. v. Atlantic Coast Line R. Co., 1908, 55 Fla. 514, 46 So. 732. But not a frost beyond all prior experience. Blyth v. Birmingham Waterworks Co., 1856, 11 Ex. 781, 156 Eng.Rep. 1047.

2. White v. Dickerson, 1958, 248 N.C. 723, 105 S.E. 2d 51.

3. Clark's Adm'r v. Kentucky Utilities Co., 1942, 289 Ky. 225, 158 S.W.2d 134; Jackson v. Wisconsin Tel. Co., 1894, 88 Wis. 243, 60 N.W. 430.

4. Hyatt v. Murray, 1907, 101 Minn. 507, 112 N.W. 881; cf. Stemmler v. City of Pittsburgh, 1926, 287 Pa. 365, 135 A. 100.

5. Martin v. North Star Iron Works, 1884, 31 Minn. 407, 18 N.W. 109; cf. American Express Co. v. Risley, 1899, 179 Ill. 295, 53 N.E. 558.

6. Meshbesher v. Channellene Oil & Mfg. Co., 1909, 107 Minn. 104, 119 N.W. 428; Farley v. Edward E. Tower & Co., 1930, 271 Mass. 230, 171 N.E. 639. Cf. Skinn v. Reutter, 1903, 135 Mich. 57, 97 N.W. 152.

7. Mossrud v. Lee, 1916, 163 Wis. 229, 157 N.W. 758; Burk v. Creamery Package Mfg. Co., 1905, 126 Iowa 730, 102 N.W. 793; cf. Moehlenbrock v. Parke Davis & Co., 1918, 141 Minn. 154, 169 N.W. 541 (doctors administering impure ether).

expected to try to make it work;[8] that it may be foreseen that animals which are loose will wander into danger[9] or take fright and run away if they are left unguarded,[10] or that mosquitoes will breed in a swamp.[11]

The risk created by the defendant may include the intervention of the foreseeable negligence of others. As we have seen above,[12] the standard of reasonable conduct may require the defendant to protect the plaintiff against "that occasional negligence which is one of the ordinary incidents of human life, and therefore to be anticipated."[13] Thus a defendant who blocks the sidewalk and forces the plaintiff to walk in a street where he will be exposed to the risks of heavy traffic becomes liable when he is run down by a car,[14]

even though the car is negligently driven;[15] and one who parks his automobile on the highway without lights at night is not relieved of responsibility when another negligently drives into it.[16] By the same token, one who spills gasoline can expect it to be negligently set afire,[17] and when a drunken passenger is ejected from a bus into the midst of traffic it may be anticipated that he will be negligently run down.[18] The circumstances of the particular case may of course indicate the danger of some quite unusual negligence, as when children are in the vicinity, and conduct is to be expected of them which would not be foreseen on the part of an adult.[19] The question is essentially one of the defendant's original obligation, and far removed from causation.

8. Arko v. Shenango Furnace Co., 1909, 107 Minn. 220, 119 N.W. 789; Liberty Mut. Ins. Co. v. Great Northern R. Co., 1928, 174 Minn. 466, 219 N.W. 755; Anderson v. Baltimore & Ohio R. Co., 2 Cir. 1937, 89 F.2d 629; Frederick v. Goff, 1960, 251 Iowa 290, 100 N.W.2d 624 (citing numerous cases in accord).

9. Sneesby v. Lancashire & Y. R. Co., 1874, L.R. 8 Q.B. 263; Wilder v. Stanley, 1893, 65 Vt. 145, 26 A. 189. Cf. Gilman v. Noyes, 1876, 57 N.H. 627.

10. McDonald v. Snelling, 1867, 14 Allen, Mass., 290; Collins v. West Jersey Exp. Co., 1905, 72 N.J.L. 231, 62 A. 675; cf. Murchison v. Powell, 1967, 269 N.C. 656, 153 S.E.2d 352. But it is not foreseeable that a horse will take fright at a keg by the side of the road. Rozell v. Northern Pac. R. Co., 1918, 39 N.D. 475, 167 N.W. 489.

11. Towaliga Falls Power Co. v. Sims, 1909, 6 Ga.App. 749, 65 S.E. 844.

12. Supra, p. 171.

13. Murphy v. Great Northern R. Co., [1897] 2 Ir.Rep. 301; Second Restatement of Torts, § 302A. Cf. McEvoy v. American Pool Corp., 1948, 32 Cal.2d 295, 195 P.2d 783; Nance v. Parks, 1966, 266 N.C. 206, 146 S.E.2d 24. See Eldredge, Culpable Intervention as Superseding Cause, 1937, 86 U.Pa.L.Rev. 121.

14. The case is of course all the clearer where there is no showing of any negligence on the part of the driver. O'Neill v. City of Port Jervis, 1930, 253 N.Y. 423, 171 N.E. 694. Cf. Brechtel v. Lopez, La. App.1962, 140 So.2d 189, where a speeding driver, pursued by the police, was held liable when the police car struck a utility pole.

15. Johnson v. City of Rockford, 1962, 35 Ill.App.2d 107, 182 N.E.2d 240; Shafir v. Sieben, Mo.1921, 233 S.W. 419; O'Malley v. Laurel Line Bus Co., 1933, 311 Pa. 251, 166 A. 868. Cf. Boese v. Love, Mo.1957, 300 S.W.2d 453, where an improperly parked truck blocked the view of an automobile driver, and a boy crossing the street was run down. But cf. City of Okmulgee v. Hemphill, 1938, 183 Okl. 450, 83 P.2d 189, where, on the particular facts, the negligent driving was held to relieve the defendant.

16. Kline v. Moyer, 1937, 325 Pa. 357, 191 A. 43; Butts v. Ward, 1938, 227 Wis. 387, 279 N.W. 6; Leveillee v. Wright, 1938, 300 Mass. 382, 15 N.E.2d 247; Berry v. Visser, 1958, 354 Mich. 38, 92 N.W.2d 1; Washington v. Kemp, 1959, 99 Ga.App. 635, 109 S.E.2d 294.

17. Watson v. Kentucky & Indiana Bridge & R. Co., 1910, 137 Ky. 619, 126 S.W. 146, 129 S.W. 341; Teasdale v. Beacon Oil Co., 1929, 266 Mass. 25, 164 N.E. 612; Miles v. Southeastern Motor Truck Lines, 1943, 295 Ky. 156, 173 S.W.2d 990; Robert R. Walker, Inc. v. Burgdorf, 1951, 150 Tex. 603, 244 S.W.2d 506.

18. Houston v. Strickland, 1946, 184 Va. 994, 37 S.E. 2d 64.

19. Such as tampering with dangerous articles left exposed to them. Vaughan v. Industrial Silica Corp., 1942, 140 Ohio St. 17, 42 N.E.2d 156; Kingsland v. Erie County Agr. Soc., 1949, 298 N.Y. 409, 84 N.E.2d 38; New York Eskimo Pie Co. v. Rataj, 3 Cir., 1934, 73 F.2d 184; Butrick v. Snyder, 1926, 236 Mich. 300, 310 N.W. 311. Cf. Shafer v. Keeley Ice Cream Co., 1925, 65 Utah 46, 234 P. 300 (scrambling for candy).

The same is true as to those intervening intentional or criminal acts which the defendant might reasonably anticipate, and against which he would be required to take precautions.[20] It must be remembered that the mere fact that misconduct on the part of another might be foreseen is not of itself sufficient to place the responsibility upon the defendant. As we have seen,[21] there are situations in which he may reasonably say that it is not his concern. But once it is determined that the defendant's duty requires him to anticipate the intervening misconduct, and guard against it, it follows that it cannot supersede his liability.

Even though the intervening cause may be regarded as foreseeable, the defendant is not liable unless his conduct has created or increased an unreasonable risk of harm through its intervention. A wind might be expected to blow at any time, and it might damage the plaintiff in a hundred different ways, but the defendant is not responsible for it unless he has set a fire or done some other act which increases the foreseeable danger that the wind will do harm.[22] There may be an appreciable danger that the plaintiff will be struck by lightning,[23] or by an automobile in the street,[24] or a mail sack thrown from a train,[25] or that a kerosene lamp will explode in his face,[26] but there is no liability unless what the defendant has done has increased the risk. Railway trainmen are subject to a constant risk of falling from trains and bridges, but the railway company is not liable for such an accident unless its negligence has increased the danger.[27] And although the defendant's excessive speed in driving his car may be in fact a cause of his killing a child which suddenly darts out from behind a tree on a lonely road —since without it he would not have been there in time for the event to occur—there is no liability if the speed is found not to have increased the risk.[28]

20. Wallinga v. Johnson, 1964, 269 Minn. 436, 131 N.W.2d 216; J. H. Welch & Son Contracting Co. v. Gardner, 1964, 96 Ariz. 94, 392 P.2d 567; McLeod v. Grant County School Dist., 1953, 42 Wash. 316, 255 P.2d 360; Hines v. Garrett, 1921, 131 Va. 125, 108 S.E. 690; Morse v. Homer's, Inc., 1936, 295 Mass. 606, 4 N.E.2d 625.

The liability is of course all the clearer where the foreseeable act of the third person, although intended to affect the plaintiff adversely, is not of itself wrongful. Thus where a bank dishonors a check, and plaintiff is arrested under a bad check law. Weaver v. Bank of America Nat. Trust & Sav. Ass'n, 1962, 59 Cal.2d 428, 30 Cal.Rptr. 4, 380 P.2d 644; Collins v. City Nat. Bank & Trust Co., 1944, 131 Conn. 167, 38 A.2d 582; cf. Segal v. Horwitz, 1929, 32 Ohio App. 1, 167 N.E. 406 (selling plaintiff stolen goods); Wilson v. Capital Automobile Co., 1939, 59 Ga.App. 834, 2 S.E.2d 147 (failing to change registration of car in name of criminal).

21. Supra, p. 176.

22. Cf. Rex v. Gill, 1719, 1 Stra. 190, 93 Eng.Rep. 465; San Antonio & A. P. R. Co. v. Behne, Tex.Comm. App.1921, 231 S.W. 354; Strong v. Granite Furn. Co., 1930, 77 Utah 292, 294 P. 303.

23. Shell Oil Co. v. Mahler, Tex.Civ.App.1965, 385 S.W.2d 684; Bennett v. Southern R. Co., 1957, 245 N.C. 261, 96 S.E.2d 31, cert. denied 353 U.S. 958; Alling v. Northwestern Bell Tel. Co., 1923, 156 Minn. 60, 194 N.W. 313 (no increased risk). Compare, where the risk was held to be increased; Jackson v. Wisconsin Tel. Co., 1894, 88 Wis. 243, 60 N.W. 430; Johnson v. Kosmos Portland Cement Co., 6 Cir. 1933, 64 F.2d 193, cert. denied 290 U.S. 641.

24. Balfe v. Kramer, 1936, 249 App.Div. 746, 291 N. Y.S. 842; cf. Fulton v. Kalbach, Sup.Ct.1920, 179 N.Y.S. 604 (collision after plaintiff carried past stop on street car). Compare, where the risk was increased, O'Malley v. Laurel Line Bus Co., 1933, 311 Pa. 251, 166 A. 868, and O'Neill v. City of Port Jervis, 1930, 253 N.Y. 423, 171 N.E. 694.

25. Louisville & N. R. Co. v. Daniels, 1924, 135 Miss. 33, 99 So. 434. Cf. Berry v. Sugar Notch Borough, 1899, 191 Pa. 345, 43 A. 240.

26. Central of Georgia R. Co. v. Price, 1898, 106 Ga. 176, 32 S.E. 77.

27. Goneau v. Minneapolis, St. P. & S. S. M. R. Co., 1922, 154 Minn. 1, 191 N.W. 279; Bohm v. Chicago, M. & St. P. R. Co., 1924, 161 Minn. 74, 200 N.W. 804.

28. Howk v. Anderson, 1934, 218 Iowa 358, 253 N.W. 32; Burlie v. Stephens, 1920, 113 Wash. 182, 193 P. 684; see Wallace v. Suburban R. Co., 1894, 26 Or. 174, 177, 37 P. 477, 478. Cf. Berry v. Sugar Notch Borough, 1899, 191 Pa. 345, 43 A. 240 (struck by falling tree); Doss v. Town of Big Stone Gap, 1926, 145 Va. 520, 134 S.E. 563 (driver forced to detour, injured by crashing airplane).

Normal Intervening Causes

There are other intervening causes which could scarcely have been contemplated by any reasonable man in the place of the defendant at the time of his conduct, but which are nevertheless to be regarded as normal incidents of the risks he has created. Here "foreseeability" has undergone the same process of dilution and attenuation which we have encountered before,[29] but the results are even more striking. When the defendant negligently drives an automobile, he may reasonably foresee that he may run down a man, or collide with another car. It would be straining anticipation to the breaking point to say that, while he is driving, he should have in mind the possibility that the man might be left unconscious in the highway, and run over there by another car,[30] or that the automobile might be left across the highway and cause a second collision.[31] He might have even less reason to contemplate the possibility that if he endangered a child, a rescuer dashing out from the sidewalk might be injured.[32] But such events are certainly not abnormal incidents of the situation in fact created—the unconscious

man, the blocked highway, or the danger to the child.

It is perhaps a pointless quibble over the meaning of a term to debate whether such normal intervening causes are to be called "foreseeable."[33] They are at least not unforeseeable, in the sense that any event which is not abnormal may reasonably be expected to occur now and then, and would be recognized as not highly unlikely if it did suggest itself to the actor's mind. They are closely and reasonably associated with the immediate consequences of the defendant's act, and form a normal part of its aftermath; and to that extent they are not foreign to the scope of the risk created by the original negligence. For the most part they have been called foreseeable by the courts; but that word obviously has traveled a long way from its original meaning in connection with the risk created by negligence.

In a large number of cases these normal intervening causes have been held not to supersede the defendant's liability. Thus defensive acts, such as the reasonable attempt of an individual threatened with harm to escape it, as by leaping from a vehicle[34] or swerving aside[35] will not relieve the original wrongdoer of liability, whether the act be in-

29. See supra, p. 267.

30. Bunda v. Hardwick, 1965, 376 Mich. 640, 138 N.W. 2d 305; Morrison v. Medaglia, 1934, 287 Mass. 46, 191 N.E. 133; Thornton v. Eneroth, 1934, 177 Wash. 1, 30 P.2d 951; Adams v. Parrish, 1920, 189 Ky. 628, 225 S.W. 467; Hill v. Peres, 1934, 136 Cal.App. 132, 28 P.2d 946. Compare the even more remarkable case of Matthews v. Porter, 1962, 239 S.C. 620, 124 S.E.2d 321.

31. Sworden v. Gross, 1966, 243 Or. 83, 409 P.2d 897; Evans v. Farmer, 1963, 148 W.Va. 142, 133 S.E.2d 710; Anderson v. Jones, 1966, 66 Ill.App.2d 407, 213 N.E.2d 627; Garbe v. Halloran, 1948, 150 Ohio St. 476, 83 N.E.2d 217; Caylor v. B. C. Motor Transp., 1937, 191 Wash. 365, 71 P.2d 162. Cf. Wedel v. Johnson, 1936, 196 Minn. 170, 264 N.W. 689 (horse); and see Note, 1949, 9 La.L.Rev. 421. See, however, Millirons v. Blue, 1934, 48 Ga.App. 483, 173 S.E. 443, where it was held unforeseeable that anyone would have collided with a car left across the road at a 45 degree angle, with all lights on and the horn continually sounding.

32. See supra, p. 267.

33. See Restatement of Torts, 1948 Supp., § 435; Bohlen, Review of Harper, Law of Torts, 1934, 47 Harv.L.Rev. 556, 557; Goodhart, Rescue and Voluntary Assumption of Risk, 1934, 5 Camb.L.J. 192, 197.

34. Jones v. Boyce, 1816, 1 Stark. 493, 171 Eng.Rep. 540. Accord: Tuttle v. Atlantic City R. Co., 1901, 66 N.J.L. 327, 49 A. 450; Danner v. Arnsberg, 1961, 227 Or. 420, 362 P.2d 758; Hill v. Associated Transport, Inc., 1962, 345 Mass. 55, 185 N.E.2d 642; Quigley v. Delaware & Hudson Canal Co., 1891, 142 Pa. 388, 21 A. 827.

35. Ryan v. Cameron, 1955, 270 Wis. 325, 71 N.W.2d 408; Wilson v. Goscinske, 6 Cir. 1956, 233 F.2d 759. Cf. Hall v. Macco Corp., 1961, 198 Cal.App.2d 415, 18 Cal.Rptr. 273 (crowd stampeding from fire and explosion); Sayers v. Harlow U.D.C., [1958] 2 All Eng.Rep. 342 (climbing out of lavatory to avoid inconvenience when locked in).

stinctive [36] or after time for reflection,[37] and whether the resulting injury is to the person so seeking to escape, or to another.[38] The same is true of attempts to defend the actor's property,[39] or his rights or privileges.[40]

Upon the same basis, under the "rescue doctrine," efforts to protect the personal safety of another have been held not to supersede the liability for the original negligence which has endangered it.[41] Whether or not the res-

cuer is to be regarded as "foreseeable," [42] it has been recognized since the early case of the crowd rushing to assist the descending balloonist [43] that he is nothing abnormal. "The risk of rescue, if only it be not wanton, is born of the occasion. The emergency begets the man." [44] There is thus an independent duty of care owed to the rescuer himself,[45] which arises even when the defendant endangers no one's safety but his own.[46] The rule is not limited to spontaneous or instinctive action, but applies even when there is time for thought.[47] And whether the rescuer succeeds in injuring himself,[48] or the person rescued,[49] or a stranger,[50] the original wrongdoer is still liable.

36. Scott v. Shepherd, 1773, 3 Wils. 403, 95 Eng.Rep. 1124; Ricker v. Freeman, 1870, 50 N.H. 420; Hill v. Associated Transport, 1962, 345 Mass. 55, 185 N.E.2d 642 (frightened when truck crashed through door of house in middle of night; leaped out of bed and fell on scatter rug). Cf. Russo v. Dinerstein, 1951, 138 Conn. 220, 83 A.2d 222 (letting child fall out of door).

37. Schumaker v. St. Paul & Duluth R. Co., 1891, 46 Minn. 39, 48 N.W. 559; Yazoo & M. V. R. Co. v. Aden, 1900, 77 Miss. 382, 27 So. 385; Reimard v. Bloomsburg & S. R. Co., 1910, 228 Pa. 384, 77 A. 560.

But not, of course, where the plaintiff's defensive efforts are foolhardy and unreasonable. Fowlks v. Southern Ry. Co., 1899, 96 Va. 742, 32 S.E. 464; Weeks v. Great Northern R. Co., 1919, 43 N.D. 426, 175 N.W. 726; Brady v. Oregon Lbr. Co., 1926, 117 Or. 188, 243 P. 96.

38. Jackson v. Galveston, H. & S. A. Ry. Co., 1897, 90 Tex. 372, 38 S.W. 745; Griffin v. Hustis, 1919, 234 Mass. 95, 125 N.E. 387; Gedeon v. East Ohio Gas Co., 1934, 128 Ohio St. 335, 190 N.E. 924; Crow v. Colson, 1927, 123 Kan. 702, 256 P. 971; Smith v. Carlson, 1941, 209 Minn. 268, 296 N.W. 132.

39. Illinois Cent. R. Co. v. Siler, 1907, 229 Ill. 390, 82 N.E. 362; Glanz v. Chicago, M. & St. P. R. Co., 1903, 119 Iowa 611, 93 N.W. 575; Cooper v. Richland County, 1907, 76 S.C. 202, 56 S.E. 958; Esposito v. Christopher, 1968, 166 Colo. 361, 443 P.2d 731; Lowden v. Shoffner Merc. Co., 8 Cir. 1940, 109 F.2d 956. See Second Restatement of Torts, § 445.

A few cases to the contrary have proceeded on the ground that it is unreasonable and so contributory negligence for the plaintiff to risk serious personal injury to save his property. See Cook v. Johnston, 1885, 58 Mich. 437, 25 N.W. 388; Morris v. Lake Shore & M. S. R. Co., 1896, 148 N.Y. 182, 42 N.E. 579; Taylor v. Home Tel. Co., 1910, 163 Mich. 458, 128 N.W. 728; see Note, 1935, 8 So.Cal.L.Rev. 159.

40. See Clark v. Chambers, 1878, 3 Q.B.D. 327; Cieplinski v. Severn, 1929, 269 Mass. 261, 168 N.E. 722; O'Neill v. City of Port Jervis, 1930, 253 N.Y. 423, 171 N.E. 694; Second Restatement of Torts, § 446.

41. Bond v. Baltimore & O. R. Co., 1918, 82 W.Va. 557, 96 S.E. 932; Brock v. Peabody Coop. Equity

Exchange, 1960, 186 Kan. 657, 352 P.2d 37; Mitchell v. Pettigrew, 1958, 65 N.M. 137, 333 P.2d 879; Silbernagel v. Voss, 7 Cir. 1959, 265 F.2d 390; Hatch v. Globe Laundry Co., 1934, 132 Me. 379, 171 A. 387. See Note, 1950, 3 Okl.L.Rev. 476.

42. See supra, p. 267.

43. Guille v. Swan, 1822, 19 Johns., N.Y., 381.

44. Cardozo, J., in Wagner v. International R. Co., 1921, 232 N.Y. 176, 133 N.E. 437.

45. See supra, p. 258. Thus actual danger to the rescued is not essential, and it is enough that the rescuer reasonably believes that his act is necessary. Ellmaker v. Goodyear Tire & Rubber Co., Mo.App.1963, 372 S.W.2d 650.

46. Ruth v. Ruth, 1963, 213 Tenn. 82, 372 S.W.2d 285; Dodson v. Maddox, 1949, 359 Mo. 742, 223 S.W.2d 434; Provenzo v. Sam, 1968, 23 N.Y.2d 256, 296 N.Y.S.2d 322, 244 N.E.2d 26. Brugh v. Bigelow, 1944, 310 Mich. 74, 16 N.W.2d 668; Usry v. Small, 1961, 103 Ga.App. 144, 118 S.E.2d 719. Cf. Talbert v. Talbert, 1960, 22 Misc.2d 782, 199 N.Y.S.2d 212 (rescuing one attempting suicide).

47. Wagner v. International R. Co., 1921, 232 N.Y. 176, 133 N.E. 437; Luce v. Hartman, 1959, 6 N.Y.2d 786, 159 N.E.2d 677, reversing, 1957, 5 App.Div.2d 19, 168 N.Y.S.2d 501; Da Rin v. Casualty Co. of America, 1910, 41 Mont. 175, 108 P. 649. In Parks v. Starks, 1955, 342 Mich. 443, 70 N.W.2d 805, the lapse of nine hours after the original negligence was held not to prevent liability to the rescuer.

48. Including stress and strain. Williams v. Chick, 8 Cir. 1967, 373 F.2d 330 (death from stress); Britt v. Mangum, 1964, 261 N.C. 250, 134 S.E.2d 235 (strained back).

49. Second Restatement of Torts, § 445.

50. Guille v. Swan, 1822, 10 Johns., N.Y., 381; Woodcock's Adm'r v. Hallock, 1925, 98 Vt. 284, 127 A.

Although there has been some disagreement,[51] the great majority of the courts now apply the same rule to one who tries to rescue the property of another,[52] even when he is under no duty to do so,[53] and even though the property involved is that of the defendant.[54] Even a rescuer of a rescuer of property has been allowed to recover;[55] and the same type of rule has been applied where the plaintiff seeks only to remedy a dangerous situation, such as a blocked highway, which threatens harm to person or property of those in the vicinity.[56] If any such defensive act is itself unreasonable, or done in an unreasonable manner, it may amount to contributory negligence which will bar any recovery by the actor himself,[57] but it will not necessarily prevent the defendant's liability to a third person who is injured.[58] The scope of the risk created may still extend to the possibility that such defensive efforts may be negligent, and so may endanger others. It is only when they are so utterly foolhardy and extraordinary that they cannot be regarded as any normal part of the original risk, that they will be considered a superseding cause.[59]

A similar group of cases hold the defendant liable for the results of medical treat-

---

380; Thomas v. Casey, 1956, 49 Wash.2d 14, 297 P.2d 614.

51. Sometimes on the basis that the rescuer is a "volunteer," as in Glines v. Maine Central R. Co., 1947, 94 N.H. 299, 52 A.2d 298; Johnson v. Terminal Ry. Ass'n, 1928, 320 Mo. 884, 8 S.W.2d 891, cert. denied 278 U.S. 644. Sometimes on the basis that the "rescue doctrine" applies only to volunteers, and so not to a fireman whose duty it is to rescue. Nastasio v. Cinnamon, Mo.1956, 295 S.W.2d 117.

52. Foster v. LaPlante, Me.1968, 244 A.2d 803; George A. Fuller Const. Co. v. Elliott, 1955, 92 Ga.App. 309, 88 S.E.2d 413; Keystone-Fleming Transport v. City of Tahoka, Tex.Civ.App.1958, 315 S.W.2d 656, ref. n. r. e. (city fire equipment damaged); Henshaw v. Belyea, 1934, 220 Cal. 458, 31 P.2d 348; Stewart v. Jefferson Plywood Co., 1970, — Or. —, 469 P.2d 783. See Notes, 1929, 77 U. Pa.L.Rev. 393; 1934, 23 Cal.L.Rev. 110.

53. Liming v. Illinois Cent. R. Co., 1890, 81 Iowa 246, 47 N.W. 66; Superior Oil Co. v. Richmond, 1935, 172 Miss. 407, 159 So. 850; Burnett v. Conner, 1938, 299 Mass. 604, 13 N.E.2d 417; Pike v. Grand Trunk R. Co., 1 Cir. 1889, 39 F. 255.

54. Rushton v. Howle, 1949, 79 Ga.App. 360, 53 S.E.2d 768; Henjum v. Bok, 1961, 261 Minn. 74, 110 N.W. 2d 461; Green v. Britton, 1960, 22 Conn.Super. 71, 160 A.2d 497; Schmartz v. Harger, 1961, 22 Conn. Super. 308, 171 A.2d 89.

55. Richards v. Kansas Elec. Power Co., 1928, 126 Kan. 521, 268 P. 847; Brown v. Ross, 1956, 345 Mich. 54, 75 N.W.2d 68; Richardson v. United States, E.D.Okl.1965, 248 F.Supp. 99.

56. Marshall v. Nugent, 1 Cir. 1955, 222 F.2d 604, 58 A.L.R.2d 251 (warning traffic); Scott v. Texaco, Inc., 1966, 239 Cal.App.2d 431, 48 Cal.Rptr. 785 (same); Bilyeu v. Standard Freight Lines, 1960, 182 Cal.App.2d 536, 6 Cal.Rptr. 65 (police clearing wreckage); Rovinski v. Brown, 6 Cir. 1942, 131 F.2d 687 (trying to move disabled truck); Hatch v. Smail, 1946, 249 Wis. 183, 23 N.W.2d 460 (trying to right overturned car).

57. Taylor v. Home Tel. Co., 1910, 163 Mich. 458, 128 N.W. 728; Hogan v. Bragg, 1918, 41 N.D. 203, 170 N.W. 324; Berg v. Great Northern R. Co., 1897, 70 Minn. 272, 73 N.W. 648; Illinois Cent. R. Co. v. Oswald, 1930, 338 Ill. 270, 170 N.E. 247; Barnett v. Des Moines Elec. Co., 8 Cir. 1925, 10 F.2d 111. See the excellent statement in Wolfinger v. Shaw, 1940, 138 Neb. 229, 292 N.W. 731.

58. Turner v. Page, 1904, 186 Mass. 600, 72 N.E. 329; Williams v. Koehler, 1899, 41 App.Div. 426, 58 N.Y.S. 863; Henry v. Dennis, 1883, 93 Ind. 452; Woodcock's Adm'r v. Hallock, 1925, 98 Vt. 284, 127 A. 380.

59. Atchison, T. & S. F. R. Co. v. Calhoun, 1909, 213 U.S. 1 (injuring child in hopeless effort to catch train); Robinson v. Butler, 1948, 226 Minn. 491, 33 N.W.2d 821 (excited passenger seizing wheel); Weller v. Chicago & N. W. R. Co., 1952, 244 Iowa 149, 55 N.W.2d 720 (excited mother unreasonably seizing child). Compare the cases of foolhardy exposure to danger in Cone v. Inter County Tel. & Tel. Co., Fla. 1949, 40 So.2d 148; Central Wis. Trust Co. v. Chicago & N. W. R. Co., 1939, 232 Wis. 536, 287 N.W. 699.

It has been held that the rescuer may not recover where his injury is an abnormal one, not reasonably to be expected as a result of the situation. Whitman v. Mobile & O. R. Co., 1927, 217 Ala. 70, 114 So. 912 (wrenching side carrying water to extinguish fire). But compare the unusual events for which recovery was allowed in Lynch v. Fisher, La.App. 1949, 41 So.2d 692; Hines v. Morrow, Tex.Civ.App. 1921, 236 S.W. 183; St. Louis-San Francisco R. Co. v. Ginn, Okl.1954, 264 P.2d 351.

If the rescuer himself is partly responsible for creating the danger, he cannot recover. Tarnowski v. Fite, 1952, 335 Mich. 267, 55 N.W.2d 824; Atlanta & A. A. L. R. Co. v. Leach, 1893, 91 Ga. 419, 17 S.E. 619.

ment of the injured victim.[60] Even where such treatment is itself negligent, because of lack of proper skill or care, recovery for its consequences is permitted.[61] It would be an undue compliment to the medical profession to say that bad surgery is no part of the risk of a broken leg.[62] So long as the plaintiff himself has exercised reasonable care in his selection of a physician,[63] the defendant

will be liable for all ordinary forms of professional negligence. There undoubtedly is a line to be drawn, short of the highly unusual varieties of medical misconduct, such as, for example, the infliction of an intentional injury,[64] or the misperformance of an entirely independent and unrelated operation,[65] which cannot fairly be regarded as normal incidents of the risk; but the few cases which have approached the problem have been far from affording any very reliable guide to the location of the line.[66]

Where the injured plaintiff subsequently contracts a disease, similar principles are applied. If the injury renders him peculiarly susceptible to the disease, as where an open

60. This is not limited to cases where the medical treatment is negligent. Thus in Simmons v. Lollar, 10 Cir. 1962, 304 F.2d 774, recovery was allowed for death on the operating table, without negligence. In accord is Adams v. Dantin, La.App.1958, 107 So.2d 809. Also Lane v. Southern R. Co., 1926, 192 N.C. 287, 134 S.E. 855, where recovery was allowed for pain and suffering due to treatment which was proper, although not beneficial.

The familiar rule that plaintiff may recover expenses of reasonably necessary medical care rests upon the same basis. Alt v. Konkle, 1927, 237 Mich. 264, 211 N.W. 661; Dreyfus & Co. v. Wooters, 1918, 123 Va. 42, 96 S.E. 235.

61. Thompson v. Fox, 1937, 326 Pa. 209, 192 A. 107; Harris v. Brian, 10 Cir. 1958, 255 F.2d 176; Jess Edwards, Inc. v. Goergen, 10 Cir. 1958, 256 F.2d 542; Kansas City Southern R. Co. v. Justis, 5 Cir. 1956, 232 F.2d 267, cert. denied 352 U.S. 833; City of Covington v. Keal, 1939, 280 Ky. 237, 133 S.W.2d 49.

This is not limited to the negligence of physicians, but extends to that of members of plaintiff's family who are looking after him. Ewing v. Duncan, 1935, 209 Ind. 33, 197 N.E. 901; Lange v. Hoyt, 1932, 114 Conn. 590, 159 A. 575; H. T. Whitson Lumber Co. v. Upchurch, 1923, 198 Ky. 127, 248 S.W. 243.

But in Exner Sand & Gravel Corp. v. Petterson Lighterage & Towage Corp., 2 Cir. 1958, 258 F.2d 1, the court, in a 2–1 decision, refused to extend it to the negligence of the repair crew after damage to a barge.

62. Pullman Palace Car Co. v. Bluhm, 1884, 109 Ill. 20 ("The liability to mistakes in curing is incident to a broken arm"); Thompson v. Fox, 1937, 326 Pa. 209, 192 A. 107.

63. Cf. Flint v. Connecticut Hassam Pav. Co., 1918, 92 Conn. 576, 103 A. 840.

Some courts have held that there is no such liability where the negligent physician has been selected with reasonable care by the defendant himself on the ground that the physician is then an independent contractor. Nall v. Alabama Utilities Co., 1931, 224 Ala. 33, 138 So. 411; Andrews v. Davis, 1930, 128 Me. 464, 148 A. 684. This is no less true where the doctor is chosen by the plaintiff,

and the distinction appears quite indefensible. It was rejected in Martin v. Cunningham, 1916, 93 Wash. 517, 161 P. 355; Edmondson v. Hancock, 1929, 40 Ga.App. 652, 151 S.E. 114.

64. Second Restatement of Torts, § 457, Comment e. Cf. Brown v. New York State Training School for Girls, 1941, 285 N.Y. 37, 32 N.E.2d 783, where, to alleviate pain, the injured man took a bichloride of mercury tablet instead of the sedative prescribed by the physician.

65. Cf. Hoyt v. Independent Asphalt Pav. Co., 1909, 52 Wash. 672, 101 P. 367 (operation rendered necessary not by injury but by childbirth); Upham's Case, 1923, 245 Mass. 31, 139 N.E. 433 (appendicitis).

66. In Purchase v. Seelye, 1918, 231 Mass. 434, 121 N.E. 413, a clerical error in a hospital, as a result of which a surgeon operated on the wrong patient, was held to be a superseding cause. This looks wrong; surely such a routine mistake is a normal part of the risk of going to a hospital. The same appears to be true of Corbett v. Clarke, 1948, 187 Va. 222, 46 S.E.2d 327, where a second dentist, trying to repair the ravages of a first, left a foreign substance in the cavity; and of Bush v. Commonwealth, 1880, 78 Ky. 268, where plaintiff caught scarlet fever from the physician. Contrary to this last case is Schafer & Olson v. Varney, 1926, 191 Wis. 186, 210 N.W. 359, a workmen's compensation case, where plaintiff contracted smallpox in the hospital. See Second Restatement of Torts, § 457.

On the other hand, in Lucas v. City of Juneau, D. Alaska 1955, 127 F.Supp. 730, and State ex rel. Smith v. Weinstein, Mo.App.1965, 398 S.W.2d 41, one who injured the plaintiff was held liable when he was further injured while being transported in an ambulance.

wound becomes infected,[67] there is little difficulty in holding the defendant for the consequences of the disease and its treatment. Likewise where his weakened condition creates an especial susceptibility to such an ailment as pneumonia or tuberculosis,[68] it is not difficult to regard it as a normal intervention. Even where the disease is one such as smallpox, which appears equally likely to attack a person in good health, recovery will probably be allowed if it is found that the effects of the disease have been more serious because of the lowered vitality.[69] So also, if the plaintiff's weakened condition or physical disability subjects him, while he is exercising proper care,[70] to the risk of a fall or some similar mishap, he may recover if the accident was one normally to be expected in view of his condition,[71] even though the second accident injures some entirely different part of the body.[72] On the other hand, if the second accident is such an abnormal consequence as drowning, because of a cast on the arm, when the plaintiff falls out of a boat, it has been held to operate as a superseding cause.[73]

Some difficulty has arisen in cases where the injured person becomes insane and commits suicide. Although there are cases to the contrary,[74] it is the prevailing view that when his insanity prevents him from realizing the nature of his act or controlling his conduct, the suicide is to be regarded as a direct result, and no intervening force at all, or else as a normal incident of the consequences inflicted, for which the defendant will be liable.[75] The situation is the same as if he should hurt himself during unconsciousness or delirium brought on by the injury.[76] But if the man is sane, or if the suicide is during a lucid interval, when he is in full command of his faculties, but his life has become unendurable to him by reason of his

67. Dickson v. Hollister, 1888, 123 Pa. 421, 16 A. 484; cf. Day v. Great Eastern Cas. Co., 1919, 104 Wash. 575, 177 P. 650.

68. Hazelwood v. Hodge, Ky.1961, 357 S.W.2d 711 (tuberculosis); Beauchamp v. Saginaw Mining Co., 1883, 50 Mich. 163, 15 N.W. 65 (pneumonia); Anderson v. Anderson, 1933, 188 Minn. 602, 248 N.W. 35 (same); Terre Haute & I. R. Co. v. Buck, 1884, 96 Ind. 346 (malarial fever); Wallace v. Ludwig, 1935, 292 Mass. 251, 198 N.E. 159 (streptococcus infection); see Second Restatement of Torts, § 458.

69. There are few cases. This is the conclusion in St. Louis, I. M. & S. R. Co. v. Steel, 1915, 119 Ark. 349, 178 S.W. 320, second appeal, 1917, 129 Ark. 520, 197 S.W. 288, and in Schafer & Olson v. Varney, 1926, 191 Wis. 186, 210 N.W. 359. To the contrary is Upham's Case, 1923, 245 Mass. 31, 139 N.E. 433 (appendicitis).

70. The limitation is necessary, both from the point of view of contributory negligence, and that of proximate cause. Cf. Svorna v. Kalina, 1931, 184 Minn. 89, 237 N.W. 841; Ault v. Kuiper, 1937, 279 Mich. 1, 271 N.W. 530; S. S. Kresge Co. v. Kenney, 1936, 66 App.D.C. 274, 86 F.2d 651.

71. Wagner v. Mittendorf, 1922, 232 N.Y. 481, 134 N. E. 539; Squires v. Reynolds, 1939, 125 Conn. 366, 5 A.2d 877; Mitchell v. Logarsky, 1948, 95 N.H. 214, 60 A.2d 136; Green v. Orion Shipping & Trading Co., D.Md.1956, 139 F.Supp. 431; Wilder v. General Motorcycle Sales Co., 1919, 232 Mass. 305, 122 N.E. 319. See Second Restatement of Torts, § 460; Vance, Liability for Subsequent Injuries, 1963, 42 Tex.L.Rev. 86; Note, 1937, 22 Wash.U.L.Q. 139.

72. Bowyer v. Te-Co., Mo.1958, 310 S.W.2d 892; Eichstadt v. Underwood, Ky.1960, 337 S.W.2d 684; Eli Witt Cigar & Tobacco Co. v. Matatics, Fla.1951, 55 So.2d 549.

73. Linder v. City of Payette, 1943, 64 Idaho 656, 135 P.2d 440. Cf. Armstrong v. Bergeron, 1962, 104 N. H. 85, 178 A.2d 293 (aggravation of whiplash injury due to second rear-end collision); Koch v. Zimmermann, 1903, 85 App.Div. 370, 83 N.Y.S. 339; Ault v. Kuiper, 1937, 279 Mich. 1, 271 N.W. 530.

74. Scheffer v. Washington City, V. M. & G. S. R. Co., 1881, 105 U.S. 249; Salsedo v. Palmer, 2 Cir. 1921, 278 F. 92.

75. Orcutt v. Spokane County, 1961, 58 Wash.2d 846, 364 P.2d 1102; State ex rel. Richardson v. Edgeworth, Miss.1968, 214 So.2d 579. Appling v. Jones, 1967, 115 Ga.App. 301, 154 S.E.2d 406. See Daniels v. New York, N. H. & H. R. Co., 1903, 183 Mass. 393, 67 N.E. 424; Long v. Omaha & C. B. St. R. Co., 1922, 108 Neb. 342, 187 N.W. 930.

This is of course all the clearer when the defendant knows of the mental condition, and should take precautions against the suicide. Trapani v. State, 1965, 23 A.D.2d 709, 257 N.Y.S.2d 224; Muhlmichl v. State, 1964, 20 A.D.2d 837, 247 N.Y.S.2d 770.

76. Cf. Koch v. Fox, 1902, 71 App.Div. 288, 75 N.Y.S. 913; Hall v. Coble Dairies, 1951, 234 N.C. 206, 67 S.E.2d 63; Millman v. United States Mortgage & T. G. Co., 1938, 121 N.J.L. 28, 1 A.2d 265.

injury, it is agreed in negligence cases [77] that his voluntary choice is an abnormal thing, which supersedes the defendant's liability.[78] A recent English decision, recognizing that the neurosis and depression brought about by the original injury may still be the producing cause, has allowed recovery even in the latter case.[79]

Unforeseeable Results of Unforeseeable Causes

If the defendant can foresee neither any danger of direct injury, nor any risk from an intervening cause, he is simply not negligent. Negligence cannot be predicated solely upon a failure to anticipate that extraordinary and unprecedented rainfall will flood the streets,[80] that a pedestrian will slip and fall upon an apparently safe highway,[81] that the wind will blow a door latch against the eye of a boy,[82] or that a ribbon held across a street to stop a wedding procession will cause one carriage to run into another.[83] But once the defendant's negligence is established, because injury of some kind was to be anticipated, intervening causes which could not reasonably be foreseen, and which are no normal part of the risk created, may bring about results of an entirely different kind.

It is here at least that the line must of necessity be drawn to terminate the defendant's responsibility. The courts have exhibited a more or less instinctive feeling that it would be unfair to hold him liable. The virtually unanimous agreement that the liability must be limited to cover only those intervening causes which lie within the scope of the foreseeable risk, or have at least some reasonable connection with it, is based upon a recognition of the fact that the independent causes which may intervene to change the situation created by the defendant are infinite, and that as a practical matter responsibility simply cannot be carried to such lengths.

Accordingly, it has been held that the defendant is not liable for the results of unforeseeable, abnormal forces of nature, such

77. Where the tort is intentional, recovery has been allowed. Tate v. Canonica, 1960, 180 Cal.App.2d 898, 5 Cal.Rptr. 28 (intentional infliction of mental disturbance by unspecified threats, apparently blackmail); Stephenson v. State, 1932, 205 Ind. 141, 179 N.E. 633, petition dismissed, 1933, 205 Ind. 141, 186 N.E. 293 (rape and torture; in its day a very famous case). See also Cauverien v. De Metz, 1959, 20 Misc.2d 144, 188 N.Y.S.2d 627, where "irresistible impulse" was alleged. See Note, 1960, 20 La.L.Rev. 791.

78. Arsnow v. Red Top Cab Co., 1930, 159 Wash. 137, 292 P. 436; Tucson Rapid Transit Co. v. Tocci, 1966, 3 Ariz.App. 330, 414 P.2d 179; Lancaster v. Montesi, 1965, 216 Tenn. 50, 390 S.W.2d 217; Stasiof v. Chicago Hoist & Body Co., 1964, 50 Ill.App. 2d 115, 200 N.E.2d 88; Wallace v. Bounds, Mo.1963, 369 S.W.2d 138. See Second Restatement of Torts, § 455; Notes, 1949, 2 Vand.L.Rev. 330; 1966, 33 Tenn.L.Rev. 540.

79. Pigney v. Pointers Transport Service, [1957] 2 All Eng.Rep. 121. Contra, however, are Murdoch v. British Israel Fed., [1942] N.Z.L.Rep. 600; Cowan v. National Coal Board, [1958] Scot.L.T. (Notes) 19.

There are occasional workmen's compensation cases that have held that suicide is compensable even though it is an act of conscious volition. Harper v. Industrial Commission, 1962, 24 Ill.2d 103, 180 N.E. 2d 480; Burnlight v. Industrial Accident Commission, 1960, 181 Cal.App.2d 816, 5 Cal.Rptr. 786; Graver Tank & Mfg. Co. v. Arizona Industrial Commission, 1965, 97 Ariz. 256, 399 P.2d 664.

80. Power v. Village of Hibbing, 1930, 182 Minn. 66, 233 N.W. 597; McCauley v. Logan, 1893, 152 Pa. 202, 25 A. 499; Fairmont Creamery Co. v. Thomp-son, 1941, 139 Neb. 677, 298 N.W. 551; Blyth v. Birmingham Waterworks Co., 1856, 11 Ex. 781, 156 Eng.Rep. 1047 (frost); Sutphen v. Hedden, 1902, 67 N.J.L. 324, 51 A. 721 (wind).

81. Missouri Pac. R. Co. v. Richardson, 1932, 185 Ark. 472, 47 S.W.2d 794. Cf. Spiering v. City of Hutchinson, 1921, 150 Minn. 305, 185 N.W. 375 (child picked up plank with nail in it and dropped it on his foot); Smith v. Lampe, 6 Cir. 1933, 64 F. 2d 201 (sounding automobile horn which caused steamboat collision in fog); Gaupin v. Murphy, 1928, 295 Pa. 214, 145 A. 123 (defendant's automobile wheel picked up rope dropped by one child, and dragged another child into the street).

82. Morril v. Morril, 1928, 104 N.J.L. 557, 142 A. 337.

83. Simek v. Korbel, 1911, 114 Minn. 533, 131 N.W. 1134. Cf. Briglia v. City of St. Paul, 1916, 134 Minn. 97, 158 N.W. 794 (automobile going off of apparently safe highway); Tracey v. City of Minneapolis, 1932, 185 Minn. 380, 241 N.W. 390 (same).

as unpredictable storms or floods; [84] the unlikely acts of animals, such as a cow knocking a man under a train; [85] the fall of an airplane upon the plaintiff when the defendant has caused him to make a detour; [86] and the more unpredictable behavior of irresponsible persons [87] or children [88] who get themselves into trouble or injure others. The more unusual, extraordinary forms of negligent conduct of adults, against which the defendant was under no obligation to take precautions, have been held to be superseding causes: the reckless or unusual driving of vehicles, [89]

tampering with dangerous articles, [90] with stationary vehicles, [91] or other articles left unguarded, [92] the violation of express orders by workmen, [93] the unreasonable stampede of a crowd of frightened men, [94] abnormal mistakes in medical treatment, [95] unlikely, foolhardy efforts to avert a threatened danger. [96]

The same is true of those intentional or criminal acts against which no reasonable standard of care would require the defendant to be on his guard: unforeseeable personal attacks upon the plaintiff, [97] destructive med-

---

84. Gerber v. McCall, 1953, 175 Kan. 433, 264 P.2d 490; Strobeck v. Bren, 1904, 93 Minn. 428, 101 N.W. 795; Seaboard Air Line R. Co. v. Mullin, 1915, 70 Fla. 450, 70 So. 467; see Kimble v. Mackintosh Hemphill Co., 1948, 359 Pa. 461, 59 A.2d 68. Apparently contra is Bushnell v. Telluride Power Co., 10 Cir. 1944, 145 F.2d 950.

85. Schreiner v. Great Northern R. Co., 1902, 86 Minn. 245, 90 N.W. 400. Cf. Loiseau v. Arp, 1908, 21 S.D. 566, 114 N.W. 701; Eberhardt v. Glasco Mut. Tel. Ass'n, 1914, 91 Kan. 763, 139 P. 416; La Londe v. Peake, 1901, 82 Minn. 124, 84 N.W. 726.

86. Doss v. Town of Big Stone Gap, 1926, 145 Va. 520, 134 S.E. 563. Cf. Dunnivant v. Nafe, 1960, 206 Tenn. 458, 334 S.W.2d 717 (brake failure after car stopped on hill by obstructed highway). See Note, 1960, 27 Tenn.L.Rev. 634.

87. Fisher v. Mutimer, 1938, 293 Ill.App. 201, 12 N.E.2d 315 (murder by discharged lunatic); Mesedahl v. St. Luke's Hospital Ass'n, 1935, 194 Minn. 198, 259 S.W. 819 (climbing out of top of barred window); Bellows v. Worcester Storage Co., 1937, 297 Mass. 188, 7 N.E.2d 588 (insane person set fire to warehouse).

88. Leoni v. Reinhard, 1937, 327 Pa. 391, 194 A. 490 (child injuring self with lime found on highway); Dahl v. Valley Dredging Co., 1914, 125 Minn. 90, 145 N.W. 796 (heating naphtha on stove); Glassey v. Worcester Consol. St. R. Co., 1904, 185 Mass. 315, 70 N.E. 199 (rolling reel of wire down hill); Perry v. Rochester Lime Co., 1916, 219 N.Y. 60, 113 N.E. 529 (finding dynamite concealed in apparent safety); Paquin v. Wisconsin Cent. R. Co., 1906, 99 Minn. 170, 108 N.W. 882 (starting railway cars down grade). See, as to "attractive nuisance," infra, § 59.

89. Hendricks v. Pyramid Motor Freight Corp., 1938, 328 Pa. 570, 195 A. 907; Mayette v. Canadian Pac. R. Co., 1939, 110 Vt. 345, 6 A.2d 33; Butner v. Spease, 1940, 217 N.C. 82, 6 S.E.2d 808; Mull v.

Ford Motor Co., 2 Cir. 1966, 368 F.2d 713; Batts v. Faggart, 1963, 260 N.C. 641, 133 S.E.2d 504. Cf. Salt River Valley Water Users' Ass'n v. Cornum, 1937, 49 Ariz. 1, 63 P.2d 639; Frerichs v. Eastern Neb. Pub. Power Dist., 1951, 154 Neb. 777, 49 N.W.2d 619; Merlo v. Public Service Co., 1942, 381 Ill. 300, 45 N.E.2d 665.

90. Larson v. Duluth, M. & N. R. Co., 1919, 142 Minn. 366, 172 N.W. 762. Cf. Spence v. American Oil Co., 1938, 171 Va. 62, 197 S.E. 468 (defendant sold watered gasoline to A; A's servant drained it into the gutter, where B threw a match into it to see whether it would burn).

91. Kinsley v. Von Atzingen, 1952, 20 N.J.Super. 378, 90 A.2d 37; Reti v. Vaniska, 1951, 14 N.J.Super. 94, 81 A.2d 377; Mars v. Delaware & Hudson Canal Co., 1889, 54 Hun. 625, 8 N.Y.S. 107.

92. Quill v. Empire State Telephone & Telegraph Co., 1899, 159 N.Y. 1, 53 N.E. 679 (telephone insulator); Schwartz v. California Gas & Electric Corporation, 1912, 163 Cal. 398, 125 P. 1044 (same); Bentley v. Fisher Lumber & Mfg. Co., 1899, 51 La.Ann. 451, 25 So. 262 (levee); cf. Bellino v. Columbus Const. Co., 1905, 188 Mass. 430, 74 N.E. 684 (workmen putting gasoline in stove).

93. Schendel v. Chicago, M. & St. P. R. Co., 1924, 158 Minn. 378, 197 N.W. 744.

94. Southern Transp. Co. v. Harper, 1903, 118 Ga. 672, 45 S.E. 458.

95. See supra, p. 279.

96. See supra, p. 278.

As to the obligation to guard against the negligence of others in general, see supra, p. 274.

97. Hoff v. Public Service R. Co., 1918, 91 N.J.L. 641, 103 A. 209; Sira v. Wabash R. Co., 1893, 115 Mo. 127, 21 S.W. 905; Toone v. Adams, 1964, 262 N.C. 403, 137 S.E.2d 132 (baseball umpire); United States v. Shively, 5 Cir. 1965, 345 F.2d 294.

dling with property,[98] and the forgery of a check.[99]

Almost invariably these cases present no issue of causation, since there is no doubt whatever that the defendant has created the situation acted upon by another force to bring about the result; and to deal with them in terms of "cause" or "proximate cause" is only to avoid the real issue. The question is one of negligence and the extent of the obligation: whether the defendant's responsibility extends to such interventions, which are foreign to the risk he has created. It is best stated as a problem of duty to protect the plaintiff against such an intervening cause.[1] A decision that the defendant's conduct is not the "proximate cause" of the result means only that he has not been negligent at all, or that his negligence, if any, does not cover such a risk. The element of shifting responsibility[2] frequently enters. In general, when a third person becomes aware of the danger, and is in a position to deal with it, the defendant will be free to assume that he would act reasonably.[3] It is only where such misconduct was to be anticipated, and the risk of it was unreasonable, that liability will be imposed for such intervening acts.

One recurring type of case in which the problem is nicely illustrated[4] is that in which the defendant parks his car, leaving the key in the ignition lock, and the plaintiff is run down and injured by a thief who has stolen the car and is making his getaway. Here two courts have found liability at common law,[5] and three have construed legislation to create a duty to the plaintiff and impose liability.[6]

The great majority have refused to hold the defendant liable, either with[7] or without[8] a car-locking ordinance. The opinions have run the gamut of all possible grounds, ranging from no duty through no lack of reasonable care to no proximate causation. Actually the problem appears to be a very simple one. Leaving a car unlocked certainly creates a foreseeable likelihood that it will be stolen, which endangers the interests of

98. Deyo v. New York Cent. R. Co., 1865, 34 N.Y. 9; Aune v. Oregon Truck R. R., 1935, 151 Or. 622, 51 P.2d 663; Bellows v. Worcester Storage Co., 1937, 297 Mass. 188, 7 N.E.2d 588; Stasulat v. Pacific Gas & Elec. Co., 1937, 8 Cal.2d 631, 67 P.2d 678.

99. Glasscock v. First Nat. Bank, 1924, 114 Tex. 207, 266 S.W. 393; Saugerties Bank v. Delaware & Hudson R. Co., 1923, 236 N.Y. 425, 141 N.E. 904; Walsh v. Hunt, 1898, 120 Cal. 46, 52 P. 115.

As to the obligation to guard against criminal acts in general, see supra, p. 275.

1. See Campbell, Duty, Fault and Legal Cause, [1938] Wis.L.Rev. 402.

2. See supra, p. 176.

3. Cf. Rulane Gas Co. v. Montgomery Ward & Co., 1949, 231 N.C. 270, 56 S.E.2d 689; Venorick v. Revetta, 1943, 152 Pa.Super. 455, 33 A.2d 655; Ford Motor Co. v. Wagoner, 1946, 183 Tenn. 392, 192 S. W.2d 840; Dooley v. Borough of Charleroi, 1937, 328 Pa. 57, 195 A. 6.

4. See Notes, [1951] Wis.L.Rev. 740; 1955, 43 Cal.L. Rev. 140; 1956, 21 Mo.L.Rev. 197; 1956, 24 Tenn. L.Rev. 395; 1958, 37 N.C.L.Rev. 104; 1949, 34 Iowa L.Rev. 376; 1964, 29 Mo.L.Rev. 379; 1965, 38 So. Cal.L.Rev. 125.

5. Mellish v. Cooney, 1962, 23 Conn.Sup. 350, 183 A. 2d 753; Schaff v. R. W. Claxton, Inc., 1944, 79 U. S.App.D.C. 207, 144 F.2d 532, overruling Brooks v. Squires, 1916, 44 App.D.C. 320. The District of Columbia now has a statute. See the following note.

6. Ross v. Hartman, 1943, 78 App.D.C. 217, 139 F.2d 14, cert. denied 321 U.S. 790; Ney v. Yellow Cab Co., 1954, 2 Ill.2d 74, 117 N.E.2d 74; Garbo v. Walker, Ohio C.P.1955, 129 N.E.2d 537 (ordinance). See supra, p. 107.

7. Meihost v. Meihost, 1966, 29 Wis.2d 537, 139 N.W. 2d 116; Galbraith v. Levin, 1948, 323 Mass. 255, 81 N.E.2d 560; Corinti v. Wittkopp, 1959, 355 Mich. 170, 93 N.W.2d 906; Hersh v. Miller, 1959, 169 Neb. 517, 99 N.W.2d 878; Anderson v. Theisen, 1950, 231 Minn. 369, 43 N.W.2d 272. Some car-locking statutes specifically provide that they shall have no effect upon civil liability. Richards v. Stanley, 1954, 43 Cal.2d 60, 271 P.2d 23; Gower v. Lamb, Mo.App. 1955, 282 S.W.2d 867.

8. Richards v. Stanley, 1954, 43 Cal.2d 60, 271 P.2d 23; Liney v. Chestnut Motors, Inc., 1966, 421 Pa. 26, 218 A.2d 336; Rass v. Nutt, 1964, 177 Ohio St. 113, 203 N.E.2d 118; Williams v. Mickens, 1957, 247 N.C. 262, 100 S.E.2d 511; Kalberg v. Anderson Bros. Motor Co., 1958, 251 Minn. 458, 88 N.W.2d 197.

the owner; but is it so likely that the thief, getting away, will drive negligently, that there is any unreasonable risk of harm to anyone else? [9] When the plaintiff is run down five days after the theft, the decisions agree [10] that there is no liability, since there is nothing more than the ordinary risk of being run down by any car. Is there so much more danger while the thief is escaping that the owner is required to take precautions for the protection of those down the highway? The bulk of the decisions have said no.[11] But when the danger is increased, as where the car is parked with the engine running and children about,[12] or there has been past experience of meddling with an enormous bulldozer left unlocked on a plateau at the top of a canyon,[13] liability is found. The

same kind of distinction may be made between public authorities who have a dangerous pyromaniac in prison,[14] and those who have one merely convicted of forgery.[15]

In only one considerable group of cases [16] has the defendant been held liable where unforeseeable intervening causes have brought about unforeseeable results. It is quite often said in the cases that when the negligence of a defendant "concurs" with an act of God, which is to say an unforeseeable force of nature, he is to be held liable.[17] Sometimes it is a problem what this is supposed to mean. In most of the cases the result brought about by the act of God is the same as that threatened by the defendant's negligence, so that

v. George W. Bowers Co., 1965, 63 Ill.App.2d 27, 211 N.E.2d 563.

9. It has been contended that a thief making his getaway is likely to be the most careful of all drivers, to avoid attracting attention. See, however, Peck, An Exercise Based upon Empirical Data: Liability for Harm Caused by Stolen Automobiles, [1969] Wis.L.Rev. 909, demonstrating rather clearly that the accident rate is much higher among drivers of stolen cars.

There has been recent statistical research verifying this conclusion, which may very well lead to a change in the attitude of the courts. See Davis v. Thornton, 1970, — Mich. —, 180 N.W.2d 11; Gaither v. Meyers, D.C.Cir.1968, 404 F.2d 216.

10. Wannebo v. Gates, 1948, 227 Minn. 194, 34 N.W. 2d 695; Dersookian v. Helmick, 1970, 256 Md. 627, 261 A.2d 472; see Justus v. Wood, 1961, 209 Tenn. 55, 348 S.W.2d 332, 349 S.W.2d 793.

11. There is especially good discussion, with a dissent, in Richards v. Stanley, 1954, 43 Cal.2d 60, 271 P.2d 23.

12. Hatch v. Globe Laundry Co., 1934, 132 Me. 379, 171 A. 387; Lomano v. Ideal Towel Supply Co., 1947, 25 N.J.Misc. 162, 51 A.2d 888. Cf. Anderson v. Bushong Pontiac Co., 1961, 404 Pa. 382, 171 A.2d 771 (car keys stolen); Murray v. Wright, 1958, 166 Cal.App.2d 589, 333 P.2d 111 (many unlocked cars in open car lot); Pfaehler v. Ten Cent Taxi Co., 1942, 198 S.C. 476, 18 S.E.2d 331 (taxi left with ignition key in lock and drunken passenger on front seat).

13. Richardson v. Ham, 1955, 44 Cal.2d 772, 285 P.2d 269. Cf. Hergenrether v. East, 1964, 61 Cal.2d 440, 39 Cal.Rptr. 4, 393 P.2d 164 (character of neighborhood); Anderson v. Bushong Pontiac Co., 1961, 404 Pa. 382, 171 A.2d 771; Mezyk v. National Repossessions, Inc., 1965, 241 Or. 333, 405 P.2d 840; Kacona

14. Austin W. Jones Co. v. State, 1923, 122 Me. 214, 119 A. 577; St. George v. State, 1953, 203 Misc. 340, 118 N.Y.S.2d 596, reversed on other grounds, 1953, 283 App.Div. 245, 127 N.Y.S.2d 147, settled, 1954, 128 N.Y.S.2d 583, motion denied, 1954, 307 N.Y. 689, 120 N.E.2d 860, affirmed, 1955, 308 N.Y. 681, 124 N. E.2d 320; University of Louisville v. Hammock, 1907, 127 Ky. 564, 106 S.W. 219 (delirium tremens). Cf. Missouri, K. & T. R. Co. v. Wood, 1902, 95 Tex. 223, 66 S.W. 449 (smallpox patient); Webb v. State, La.App.1956, 91 So.2d 156 (dangerous criminal).

15. Williams v. State, 1955, 308 N.Y. 548, 127 N.E.2d 545. Accord, Green v. State through Department of Institutions, La.App.1956, 91 So.2d 153 (negligent driving by escaped inmates of state institution for youths).

16. Mention should be made, however, of Daggett v. Keshner, 1954, 284 App.Div. 733, 134 N.Y.S.2d 524, affirmed, App.Div.1950, 149 N.Y.S.2d 422, again, 304 N.Y. 968, 110 N.E.2d 892, again, 305 N.Y. 553, 111 N.E.2d 246. A statute penalizing the sale of gasoline compounds unless there was a permit or delivery into a fuel tank of a vehicle, provided a tort action for any person injured as a result of violation. This was held to make the seller liable when the gasoline was used for arson, and detectives trying to apprehend the criminals were injured. The case is noted in 1955, 40 Corn.L.Q. 810. Contrast, however, Gonzalez v. Derrington, 1961, 56 Cal.2d 130, 14 Cal.Rptr. 1, 363 P.2d 1, where violation of a statute prohibiting sale of gasoline in open cans, without provision for any tort action, was held not to make defendant liable for arson.

17. See for example Manila School Dist. No. 15 v. Sanders, 1956, 226 Ark. 270, 289 S.W.2d 529.

he is held liable for the foreseeable result.[18] Where a totally different result is brought about, most cases agree that there is no liability, even though there is concurrence in causation.[19] The exceptional cases are those in which a carrier delays goods in transit, and during such delay the goods are destroyed by an unforeseeable flood or other force of nature. Here a number of courts have held the carrier liable.[20]

Here again the talk of "proximate cause" has obscured the real problem. The common law always has held a common carrier so far an insurer of the goods entrusted to its care that it is liable for all damage to them, whether caused by its negligence or entirely accidental, except that resulting from the acts of the public enemy or the act of God.[21] But when the carrier is itself guilty of misconduct, there are cases in which it forfeits even this exemption. If the carrier deviates from the prescribed route it is liable when the goods are lost by the act of God in the course of the deviation.[22] If it fails to make delivery of goods on hand to deliver, it is liable for their subsequent destruction through natural causes.[23] It is quite arguable that this strict liability, which is of course based upon the special responsibility assumed by the carrier, should be extended to cases where the delay has exposed the goods to a loss which could not have been anticipated.

Another group of courts, representing the view which has been preferred by most writers, have rejected any such extension, and have held that a carrier is not responsible for the results of a force of nature which is no part of the risk created by the delay.[24] If a flood is unforeseeable, it would of course be equally likely to occur at any time or place.[25] Upon any ordinary principles of negligence, there is no more reason to hold the carrier when it occurs during a delayed transit than if the flood should destroy the goods, with the delay still operating to keep them behind schedule, in the hands of a connecting carrier, or even after delivery to the

---

18. See infra, p. 286.

19. See cases cited supra, p. 281, note 84.

20. Bibb Broom Corn Co. v. Atchison, T. & S. F. R. Co., 1905, 94 Minn. 269, 102 N.W. 709; Green-Wheeler Shoe Co. v. Chicago, R. I. & P. R. Co., 1906, 130 Iowa 123, 106 N.W. 498; Alabama G. S. R. Co. v. Quarles, 1906, 145 Ala. 436, 40 So. 120; Sunderland Bros. Co. v. Chicago, B. & Q. R. Co., 1911, 89 Neb. 660, 131 N.W. 1047; Michaels v. New York Cent. R. Co., 1864, 30 N.Y. 564.

21. To these exceptions "native justice and the genius of our jurisprudence" have added losses due to the act of the shipper, the public authority, and the inherent nature of the goods. Dobie, Bailments and Carriers, 1914, 325. See generally, Holmes, Common Carriers and the Common Law, 1879, 13 Am. L.Rev. 609; Beale, The Carrier's Liability: Its History, 1898, 11 Harv.L.Rev. 158.

But see the strict interpretation of "act of God" in Forward v. Pittard, 1785, 1 Term Rep. 27, 99 Eng. Rep. 953 (fire of possible human origin); Schaff v. Roach, 1925, 116 Okl. 205, 243 P. 976 (sale); Leister v. Kelley, 1939, 279 Ky. 767, 132 S.W.2d 67 (confiscation of whiskey during flood); Lysaght, Ltd. v. Lehigh Valley R. Co., D.N.Y.1918, 254 F. 351 (Black Tom explosion).

22. Davis v. Garrett, 1830, 6 Bing. 716, 130 Eng.Rep. 1456; Seavey Co. v. Union Transit Co., 1900, 106

Wis. 394, 82 N.W. 285; Louisville & C. Packet Co. v. Rogers, 1898, 20 Ind.App. 594, 49 N.E. 970.

23. Richmond & D. R. Co. v. Benson, 1890, 86 Ga. 203, 12 S.E. 357; East Tennessee, V. & G. R. Co. v. Kelly, 1892, 91 Tenn. 699, 20 S.W. 312.

24. Rodgers v. Missouri Pac. R. Co., 1907, 75 Kan. 222, 88 P. 885; Morrison v. Davis & Co., 1852, 20 Pa. 171; Seaboard Air Line R. Co. v. Mullin, 1915, 70 Fla. 450, 70 So. 467; Yazoo & M. V. R. Co. v. Millsaps, 1899, 76 Miss. 855, 25 So. 672; Little Rock Packing Co. v. Chicago, B. & Q. R. Co., W.D. Mo.1953, 116 F.Supp. 213; Second Restatement of Torts, § 451.

25. It has been suggested that there is a slight risk of the flood, which the carrier has increased by the delay. See Green, Rationale of Proximate Cause, 1927, 29; Bauer, Common Carrier's Negligent Delay Plus Act of God, 1933, 8 Notre Dame Lawyer 394. Such a suggestion overlooks the fact that the courts imposing liability have been willing to assume that the intervening force was beyond all human foresight, and in no way a normal part of the risk created by the delay, and still hold the carrier. Cf. the Bibb Broom Corn Case, supra, note 20 where it was conceded "that it was unprecedented, and beyond the reasonable anticipation of the most prudent residents of the vicinity where it occurred."

consignee.[26] The problem is purely one of the extent of the responsibility which the policy of the law is to impose upon the carrier. The federal courts have held that the carrier is not liable for such unforeseeable forces of nature.[27] The federal rule controls as to all shipments in interstate commerce,[28] and for this reason alone it should be adopted by the state courts, since it is obviously indefensible that recovery should depend upon the fortuitous circumstances that the goods did not cross a state line.[29]

Foreseeable Results of Unforeseeable Causes

Suppose that the defendant is negligent because his conduct threatens a result of a particular kind which will injure the plaintiff, and an intervening cause which could not be anticipated changes the situation, but ultimately produces the same result?[30] The problem is well illustrated by a well-known federal case.[31] The defendant failed to clean the residue out of an oil barge, tied to a dock, leaving it full of explosive gas. This was of course negligence, since fire or explosion, resulting in harm to any person in the vicinity, was to be anticipated from any one of several possible sources. A bolt of lightning struck the barge, exploded the gas, and injured workmen on the premises. The defendant was held liable. If it be assumed that the lightning was an unforeseeable intervening cause, still the result itself was to be anticipated, and the risk of it imposed upon the defendant the original duty to use proper care.

In such a case, the result is within the scope of the defendant's negligence. His obligation to the plaintiff was to protect him against the risk of such an accident. It is only a slight extension of his responsibility to hold him liable when the danger he has created is realized through external factors which could not be anticipated. An instinctive feeling of justice leads to the conclusion that the defendant is morally responsible in such a case, and that the loss should fall upon him rather than upon the innocent plaintiff.

Many cases have held the defendant liable where the result which was to be foreseen was brought about by causes that were unforeseeable: a ladder left standing in the street blown down by an unforeseeable wind;[32] an obstruction in the highway with which a runaway horse collides;[33] delay up-

---

26. Cf. Denny v. New York Cent. R. Co., 1859, 13 Gray, Mass., 481, where the goods had arrived at destination but had not yet been delivered. Compare also Berry v. Borough of Sugar Notch, 1899, 191 Pa. 345, 43 A. 240, where the speed of the car brought it under a tree in time to be struck when it fell. Is there any real distinction?

27. Memphis & C. R. Co. v. Reeves, 1870, 10 Wall., U.S., 176.

28. Northwestern Consol. Milling Co. v. Chicago, B. & Q. R. Co., 1917, 135 Minn. 363, 160 N.W. 1028, cert. denied 245 U.S. 644; Toledo & Ohio Cent. R. Co. v. S. J. Kibler & Bros. Co., 1918, 97 Ohio St. 262, 119 N.E. 733, cert. denied 248 U.S. 569; Barnet v. New York Cent. & H. R. R. Co., 1918, 222 N.Y. 195, 118 N.E. 625; Continental Paper Bag Co. v. Maine Cent. R. Co., 1916, 115 Me. 449, 99 A. 259.

29. Second Restatement of Torts, § 451, Comment *a*.

30. Suppose the defendant, in dry weather, runs its train without proper spark arresters. A spark from the engine sets fire to a field of hay on the south side of the track; a cyclone blows the fire in a circle of a hundred miles, and a wheat field adjoining the right of way on the north side at the same point is burned. Is the defendant liable? See Note, 1966, 18 U.Fla.L.Rev. 538.

31. Johnson v. Kosmos Portland Cement Co., 6 Cir. 1933, 64 F.2d 193.

32. Moore v. Townsend, 1899, 76 Minn. 64, 78 N.W. 880. Accord: O'Connor v. Chicago, M. & St. P. R. Co., 1916, 163 Wis. 653, 158 N.W. 343, affirmed, 1918, 248 U.S. 536 (tree and storm); Mars v. Meadville Tel. Co., 1942, 344 Pa. 29, 23 A.2d 856 (pole and cow); Mummaw v. Southwestern Tel. & Tel. Co., Mo.App.1918, 208 S.W. 476 (pole and fire); Blanks v. Saenger Theaters, 1932, 19 La.App. 305, 138 So. 883 (fire escape ladder tipped by child trespasser). See Second Restatement of Torts, § 442B.

It should be noted that in some cases it is possible to apportion the damages. See infra, § 52.

33. McDowell v. Village of Preston, 1908, 104 Minn. 263, 116 N.W. 470; Baldwin v. Greenwoods Turnpike Co., 1873, 40 Conn. 238.

Cf. McDermott v. McClain, Fla.App.1969, 220 So.2d 394 (car parked at forbidden place, plaintiff helping to pour gasoline into it struck by drunken driver).

on a railway track because of the unexpected lowering of the crossing gates; [34] an insecure gas pipe bursting because it was struck by an automobile; [35] a loose pile of lumber knocked over by a stranger; [36] a termite-riddled telephone pole thrown down by an automobile which comes up on the sidewalk,[37] cattle driven from a farmyard wandering back onto a railway onto which they had escaped in the first instance because of improper fencing.[38] In all such cases the courts have taken refuge in the rule, stated to be well settled, that if the result is foreseeable, the manner in which it is brought about need not be, and is immaterial.[39]

Yet there are other cases [40] in which it seems equally clear that the defendant should not be liable. What if A knocks B down and leaves him lying unconscious in the street, where he may be run over by negligently driven automobiles, and C, a personal enemy of B, discovers him there and intentionally runs him down? When the defendant excavates a hole in the sidewalk into which someone might fall, he may be liable if the plaintiff is negligently pushed into it by a stranger,[41] but what if he is pushed deliberately? [42] Nor should the defendant be liable where a chair seat is left on a balcony railing, and it is purposely thrown down,[43] or a policeman aware of the danger of a live wire knocks it with his club against the plaintiff,[44] or a stranger impersonating an elevator operator deliberately invites the plaintiff to step into an open shaft.[45]

The difference between the two groups of cases is a matter of intangible factors not easy to express. It apparently lies in the conclusion of the courts that in the latter type of case the responsibility is shifted to the second actor. Where there is a malicious or criminal act,[46] the original actor might be free to say, even if he had anticipated the misconduct, that it was not his concern, whereas he might still be responsible for

---

34. Washington & G. R. Co. v. Hickey, 1897, 166 U.S. 521. Cf. Munsey v. Webb, 1913, 231 U.S. 150 (passenger in unsafe elevator falling down); Teasdale v. Beacon Oil Co., 1929, 266 Mass. 25, 164 N.E. 612 (spark from unexpected source igniting gasoline); Robert R. Walker, Inc. v. Burgdorf, 1951, 150 Tex. 603, 244 S.W.2d 506 (gasoline negligently ignited).

35. Carroll v. Central Counties Gas Co., 1925, 74 Cal.App. 303, 240 P. 53. Accord: Van Cleef v. City of Chicago, 1909, 240 Ill. 318, 88 N.E. 815; Dalton v. Great A. & P. Tea Co., 1922, 241 Mass. 400, 135 N.E. 318; Hughes v. Lord Advocate, [1963] A.C. 837.

36. Pastene v. Adams, 1874, 49 Cal. 87. Accord: Chacey v. City of Fargo, 1895, 5 N.D. 173, 64 N.W. 932.

37. Gibson v. Garcia, 1950, 96 Cal.App.2d 681, 216 P. 2d 119; Friendship Tel. Co. v. Russom, 1957, 43 Tenn.App. 441, 309 S.W.2d 416; cf. Blunt v. Spears, 1956, 93 Ga.App. 623, 92 S.E.2d 573, reversed on other grounds in 1956, 212 Ga. 537, 93 S.E.2d 659. Contra, Indiana Service Corp. v. Johnston, 1941, 109 Ind.App. 204, 34 N.E.2d 157.

38. Turner v. Chicago, R. I. & P. R. Co., 1917, 136 Minn. 383, 162 N.W. 469. Cf. Riley v. Standard Oil Co., 1934, 214 Wis. 15, 252 N.W. 183 (fire communicated in unexpected manner); Chase v. Washington Water Power Co., 1941, 62 Idaho 298, 111 P.2d 872 (high tension electric arc caused by fighting chicken-hawks); Billups Petroleum Co. v. Entrekin, 1950, 209 Miss. 302, 46 So.2d 781; Steele v. Rapp, 1958, 183 Kan. 371, 327 P.2d 1053. A quite extraordinary case is United Novelty Co. v. Daniels, Miss.1949, 42 So.2d 395, where fire was carried by a rat.

39. See supra, p. 286.

40. See Carpenter, Workable Rules for Determining Proximate Cause, 1932, 20 Cal.L.Rev. 229, 471, 515–

520, contending that "probable consequences" of unforeseeable intervening forces are never "proximate."

41. Village of Carterville v. Cook, 1889, 129 Ill. 152, 22 N.E. 14.

42. Milostan v. City of Chicago, 1909, 148 Ill.App. 540; Alexander v. Town of New Castle, 1888, 115 Ind. 51, 17 N.E. 200; Miller v. Bahmmuller, 1908, 124 App.Div. 558, 108 N.Y.S. 924; Loftus v. Dehail, 1901, 133 Cal. 214, 65 P. 379.

43. Klaman v. Hitchcock, 1930, 181 Minn. 109, 231 N.W. 716.

44. Seith v. Commonwealth Elec. Co., 1909, 241 Ill. 252, 89 N.E. 425. Accord: Polloni v. Ryland, 1915, 28 Cal.App. 51, 151 P. 296; and cf. Watson v. Kentucky & Ind. Bridge & R. Co., 1910, 137 Ky. 619, 126 S.W. 146, modified, 1910, 129 S.W. 341 (setting fire to spilled gasoline).

45. Cole v. German Sav. & Loan Society, 8 Cir. 1903, 124 F. 113. But see contra, Mozer v. Semenza, Fla.App.1965, 177 So.2d 880 (arson).

46. See cases cited supra, notes 41, 45.

inadvertence or ignorant blunders.[47] Where he would be relieved of responsibility even if the act were to be anticipated, he should be no less relieved when it is unforeseeable, even though the result is part of the risk he has created.

Such a suggestion may resolve the apparent confusion surrounding two types of cases. One is that in which the defendant permits dynamite caps, or something similarly dangerous, to get into the hands of a child, and the parents of the child, after taking the caps away from him, fail to prevent him from obtaining possession of them again, to his subsequent injury. The injury, of course, is what was to be expected in the first place; and ordinarily a defendant is not free to rely upon others to avert the danger which he creates. If he sets a fire, the failure of a third person to extinguish it, however unreasonable, will not relieve him from liability.[48] If the parents do not discover the nature of the dynamite, their failure to take it from the child, or to keep it from him, although it may be negligent, does not end the defendant's responsibility when the risk he has created is realized.[49] But once the parent be-

comes aware of the danger and interferes, it is at least possible to conclude that from that point forward the responsibility is his rather than the defendant's.[50] Whether, in such a case, the danger is not so extreme that the defendant could not reasonably rely upon even the parent to protect the child, is a question which is open to debate.[51]

The other group of cases involve the situation in which a third person fully discovers the danger, and then proceeds, in deliberate disregard of it, to resell, pass on to his employees, or continue to make use of a defective chattel which the defendant has sold him,[52] or otherwise to inflict upon the plaintiff the danger which he has discovered.[53] Again the explanation appears to be that the responsibility is shifted, as it would be if the third party were notified of the danger in advance, and then elected to proceed. Again, however, there will be situations of extreme

---

47. See for example The Lusitania, D.C.N.Y.1918, 251 F. 715 (published threat of German government to sink passenger liner in violation of international law); Graves v. Johnson, 1901, 179 Mass. 53, 60 N. E. 383 (liquor sold to one known to intend to make illegal resale); Beatty v. Gilbanks, 1882, 15 Cox.C. C. 138 (riot started by group known to oppose Salvation Army).

48. Wiley v. West Jersey R. Co., 1882, 44 N.J.L. 247. Accord: Nicholson v. Buffalo, R. & P. R. Co., 1930, 302 Pa. 41, 153 A. 128; Diehl v. Fidelity Philadelphia Trust Co., 1946, 159 Pa.Super. 513, 49 A.2d 190; Bixby v. Thurber, 1922, 80 N.H. 411, 118 A. 99; Harber v. Gledhill, 1922, 60 Utah 391, 208 P. 1111.

Nor is the defendant relieved when a third person attempts to halt the consequences, but fails. Haverly v. State Line & S. R. Co., 1890, 135 Pa. 50, 19 A. 1013; Mathis v. Granger Brick & Tile Co., 1915, 85 Wash. 634, 149 P. 3; Clark v. E. I. Du Pont de Nemours Powder Co., 1915, 94 Kan. 268, 146 P. 320.

49. Mathis v. Granger Brick & Tile Co., 1915, 85 Wash. 634, 149 P. 3; Diehl v. A. P. Green Fire Brick Co., 1923, 299 Mo. 641, 253 S.W. 984.

50. Carter v. Towne, 1870, 103 Mass. 507; Peterson v. Martin, 1917, 138 Minn. 195, 164 N.W. 813; Pittsburg Reduction Co. v. Horton, 1908, 87 Ark. 576, 113 S.W. 647; Kingsland v. Erie County Agr. Soc., 1949, 298 N.Y. 409, 84 N.E.2d 28. Cf. Pollard v. Oklahoma City R. Co., 1912, 36 Okl. 96, 128 P. 300.

51. See Henningsen v. Markowitz, 1928, 132 Misc. 547, 230 N.Y.. 313; Clark v. E. I. Du Pont de Nemours Powder Co., 1915, 94 Kan. 268, 146 P. 320. In McGettigan v. National Bank of Washington, D. C. Cir. 1963, 320 F.2d 703, and Caskins v. Albi, 1967, 163 Colo. 370, 431 P.2d 17, the court refused to say as a matter of law that the negligence of the parent was a superseding cause.

52. Ford Motor Co. v. Wagoner, 1946, 183 Tenn. 392, 192 S.W.2d 840; Foster v. Ford Motor Co., 1926, 139 Wash. 341, 246 P. 945; Ford Motor Co. v. Atcher, Ky.1957, 310 S.W.2d 510; Stultz v. Benson Lumber Co., 1936, 6 Cal.2d 688, 59 P.2d 100; J. C. Penny Co. v. Morris, 1935, 173 Miss. 710, 163 So. 124. See Note, 1959, 48 Ky. L.J. 177.

53. Cf. Drazen v. Otis Elevator Co., 1963, 96 R.I. 114, 189 A.2d 693; Dooley v. Borough of Charleroi, 1937, 328 Pa. 57, 195 A. 6; Rulane Gas Co. v. Montgomery Ward & Co., 1949, 231 N.C. 270, 56 S.E.2d 689; Goede v. Rondorf, 1950, 231 Minn. 322, 43 N. W.2d 770; McMurdie v. Underwood, 1959, 9 Utah 2d 400, 346 P.2d 711. Otherwise where, after knowledge of the danger, the third person forgets it, instead of proceeding deliberately. Comstock v. General Motors Corp., 1959, 358 Mich. 163, 99 N.W.2d 627.

danger, or special relations, in which, as a matter of policy, the defendant will not be allowed to shift the responsibility, and intervening discovery of the danger will not relieve him.[54]

Still more difficult to explain are the occasional cases in which mere lapse of time has been held to shift the responsibility to another—as where, for example, an electric company which installed a defective transformer pole was held to be relieved by the failure of the village, for more than a year and a half, to perform its agreement to inspect and maintain the pole.[55] Such decisions are perhaps to be explained merely on the ground that there must be a terminus somewhere, short of eternity, at which the second party becomes responsible in lieu of the first.

45. FUNCTIONS OF COURT AND JURY

The confusion which has surrounded the whole subject of "proximate cause" has extended to the respective functions of the court and the jury. There is a decided tendency to leave every question to the bewildered jury,[56] under some vague instruction which provides no effective guide.[57] At the other extreme, it has been contended [58] that the only question of "proximate cause" which is properly left to the jury at all is that of causation in fact, and that the limitations to be imposed upon liability are always a matter for the court.

It must be remembered that the primary function of the jury is the determination of questions of fact upon which reasonable men might differ. The administration of rules of law, and the determination of facts upon which there could be no reasonable difference of opinion is in the hands of the court.[59] If the foregoing analysis is correct, it follows that the duties of the court in any case in which "proximate cause" is involved are as follows:

1. The determination of any question of duty—that is, whether the defendant stands in such a relation to the plaintiff that the law will impose upon him any obligation of reasonable conduct for the benefit of the plaintiff.[60] This issue is one of law, and is never for the jury.

2. The determination of causation in fact, in any case where reasonable men could not differ as to whether the defendant's conduct was, or was not, a substantial factor in producing the result.[61] In cases where reasonable men might differ—which will include all but a few of the cases in which the issue is in dispute at all—the question is one for the jury.[62]

---

54. Clement v. Crosby & Co., 1907, 148 Mich. 293, 111 N.W. 745 (inflammable stove polish); Farley v. Edward E. Tower & Co., 1930, 271 Mass. 230, 171 N.E. 639, 86 A.L.R. 941 (inflammable beauty shop combs); Kentucky Independent Oil Co. v. Schnitzler, 1925, 208 Ky. 507, 271 S.W. 570 (gasoline in kerosene); Ferraro v. Taylor, 1936, 197 Minn. 5, 265 N.W. 829 (highly dangerous rented automobile); Trusty v. Patterson, 1930, 299 Pa. 469, 149 A. 717 (same).

55. Goar v. Village of Stephen, 1923, 157 Minn. 228, 196 N.W. 171. A very similar case is Greenwood v. Lyles & Buckner, Inc. Okl., 1958, 329 P.2d 1063.

Compare, as to putting an ill or intoxicated person off a train in a place of danger, Atchison, T & S. F. R. Co., v. Parry, 1903, 67 Kan. 515, 73 P. 105, with Lammers v. Pacific Elec. R. Co., 1921, 186 Cal. 379, 199 P. 523.

56. See Green, Rationale of Proximate Cause, 1927, 122–127.

57. See Prosser, Proximate Cause in California, 1950, 38 Cal.L.Rev. 369, 419–425. Also Ray's Adm'r v. Standard Oil Co., 1933, 250 Ky. 111, 61 S.W.2d 1067,

to the effect that the jury should not be given any definition of "proximate cause" because the term has no definite meaning. If the courts are unable to attach a meaning to the term, what can be expected of the jury?

58. Green, Rationale of Proximate Cause, 1927, 122.

59. See supra, § 37.

60. See Morril v. Morril, 1922, 104 N.J.L. 557, 142 A. 337; Palsgraf v. Long Island R. Co., 1928, 248 N.Y. 339, 162 N.E. 99.

61. Stacy v. Knickerbocker Ice Co., 1893, 84 Wis. 614, 54 N.W. 1091; Illinois Cent. R. Co. v. Wright, 1924, 135 Miss. 435, 100 So. 1.

62. Reynolds v. Texas & Pac. R. Co., 1885, 37 La. Ann. 694; Tullgren v. Amoskeag Mfg. Co., 1926, 82

3. The determination of the question whether the damages are of such a character that they may be apportioned and assigned in part to several causes.[63] It would seem that the only function of the jury as to such an issue is to make such apportionment as it can, once the apportionment is permitted.

4. The determination of the standard of conduct, and of the extent of the defendant's obligation, in all cases where reasonable men could not differ, or any limitation is imposed by the law. This would include, of course, any limitation of liability as to consequences directly caused,[64] or any case in which the defendant's responsibility is superseded by abnormal intervening forces.[65]

In any case where there might be reasonable difference of opinion as to the foreseeability of a particular risk, the reasonableness of the defendant's conduct with respect to it, or the normal character of an intervening cause, the question is for the jury,[66] subject of course to suitable instructions from the court as to the legal conclusion to be drawn as the issue is determined either way. By far the greater number of the cases which have arisen have been of this description; and to this extent it may properly be said that "proximate cause is ordinarily a question of fact for the jury, to be solved by the exercise of good common sense in the consideration of the evidence of each particular case."[67]

N.H. 268, 133 A. 4; Pfeifer v. Standard Gateway Theatre, 1952, 262 Wis. 229, 55 N.W.2d 29.

63. Rix. v. Town of Alamogordo, 1938, 42 N.M. 325, 77 P.2d 765; Jenkins v. Pennsylvania R. Co., 1902, 67 N.J.L. 331, 51 A. 704; McAllister v. Pennsylvania R. Co., 1936, 324 Pa. 65, 187 A. 415.

64. Cf. Ryan v. New York Cent. R. Co., 1866, 35 N.Y. 210; Wood v. Pennsylvania R. Co., 1896, 177 Pa. 306, 35 A. 699. See supra, § 50.

65. Schreiner v. Great Northern R. Co., 1902, 86 Minn. 245, 90 N.W. 400; Perry v. Rochester Lime

Co., 1916, 219 N.Y. 60, 113 N.E. 529; Toney v. Interstate Power Co., 1917, 180 Iowa 1362, 163 N.W. 394.

66. See Gilman v. Noyes, 1876, 57 N.H. 627; Holter Hardware Co. v. Western Mortgage & Warranty Title Co., 1915, 51 Mont. 94, 149 P. 489; Henry v. City of Philadelphia, 1919, 264 Pa. 33, 107 A. 315.

67. Healy v. Hoy, 1911, 115 Minn. 321, 132 N.W. 208. There is a very good discussion of all this in Pfeifer v. Standard Gateway Theatre, 1952, 262 Wis. 229, 55 N.W.2d 29.

CHAPTER 8

JOINT TORTFEASORS

46. CONCERTED ACTION

The terms "joint tort" and "joint tort-feasors" have been surrounded by no little uncertainty and confusion.[1] There have been various attempts to define them, and to propose tests [2] of one kind or another as to when this may be found to exist. An examination of the multitude of cases in which they are to be found leads to the conclusion that they have meant very different things to different courts, and often to the same court, and that much of the existing confusion is due to a failure to distinguish the different senses in which the terms are used, which often has had an unfortunate effect upon the substance of the law. Since a "joint tort" can have significance only in so far as it may involve some definite legal result, it is possible to approach the problem by distinguishing the various consequences which follow from it, and to indicate how far they are related, or unrelated, to one another.

Concerted Action

The original meaning of a "joint tort" was that of vicarious liability for concerted action. All persons who acted in concert to commit a trespass, in pursuance of a common design, were held liable for the entire result. In such a case there was a common purpose, with mutual aid in carrying it out; in short, there was a joint enterprise, so that "all coming to do an unlawful act, and of one party, the act of one is the act of all of the same party being present." [3] Each was therefore liable for the entire damage done, although one might have battered the plaintiff, while another imprisoned him, and a third stole his silver buttons.[4] All might be joined as defendants in the same action at law, and since each was liable for all, the jury would not be permitted to apportion the damages.[5] The

1. See Prosser, Joint Torts and Several Liability, 1937, 25 Cal.L.Rev. 413; Jackson, Joint Torts and Several Liability, 1939, 17 Tex.L.Rev. 399.

2. Thus, the identity of a cause of action against each of two or more defendants; the existence of a common, or like, duty; whether the same evidence will support an action against each; the single, indivisible nature of the injury to the plaintiffs; identity of the facts as to time, place or result; whether the injury is direct and immediate, rather than consequential; responsibility of the defendants for the same *injuria*, as distinguished from the same *damnum*. See 1 Cooley, Torts, 4th Ed. 1932, 276–278; Clerk and Lindsell, Torts, 8th Ed. 1929, 58; Brunsden v. Humphrey, 1884, 14 Q.B.D. 141, 147; Petcoff v. St. Paul City R. Co., 1913, 124 Minn. 531, 144 N.W. 474; Farley v. Crystal Coal & Coke Co., 1920, 85 W.Va. 595, 102 S.E. 265; The Koursk, [1924] P. 140.

3. Sir John Heydon's Case, 1613, 11 Co.Rep. 5, 77 Eng.Rep. 1150.

4. Smithson v. Garth, 1601, 3 Lev. 324, 83 Eng.Rep. 711. Cf. Clark v. Newsam, 1847, 1 Exch. 131, 154 Eng.Rep. 55; Sir Charles Stanley's Case, 1663, Kel. 86, 84 Eng.Rep. 1094.

5. Austen v. Willward, 1601, Cro.Eliz. 860, 78 Eng. Rep. 1086; Crane and Hill v. Hummerstone, 1606, Cro.Jac. 118, 79 Eng.Rep. 102; Sir John Heydon's Case, 1613, 11 Co.Rep. 5, 77 Eng.Rep. 1150; Matthews v. Coal, 1615, Cro.Jac. 384, 79 Eng.Rep. 329. Cf. Hill v. Goodchild, 1771, 5 Burr. 2790, 98 Eng. Rep. 465. A late decision to the same effect is Miller v. Singer, 1955, 131 Colo. 112, 279 P.2d 846.

rule goes back to the early days when the action of trespass was primarily a criminal action; and it has survived also in the criminal law.[6] This principle, somewhat extended beyond its original scope, is still law.[7] All those who, in pursuance of a common plan or design to commit a tortious act, actively take part in it, or further it by cooperation or request,[8] or who lend aid or encouragement to the wrongdoer,[9] or ratify and adopt his acts done for their benefit,[10] are equally liable with him.

Express agreement is not necessary, and all that is required is that there be a tacit understanding,[11] as where two automobile drivers suddenly and without consultation decide to race their cars on the public highway.[12] There are even occasional statements that mere knowledge by each party of what the other is doing is sufficient "concert" to make each liable for the acts of the other;[13] but this seems clearly wrong. Such knowledge may very well be important evidence that a tacit understanding exists; but since there is ordinarily no duty to take affirmatice steps to interfere,[14] the mere presence of the particular defendant at the commission of the wrong, or his failure to object to it, is not enough to charge him with responsibility.[15] It is, furthermore, essential that each particular defendant who is to be charged with responsibility shall be proceeding tortiously, which is to say with intent to commit a tort, or with negligence. One who innocently, and carefully, does an act which furthers the tortious purpose of another is not acting in concert with him.[16]

---

6. Sir Charles Stanley's Case, 1663, Kel. 86, 84 Eng. Rep. 1094; State v. Newberg, 1929, 129 Or. 564, 278 P. 568.

7. Garrett v. Garrett, 1948, 228 N.C. 530, 46 S.E.2d 302; Moore v. Foster, 1938, 182 Miss. 15, 180 So. 73; Drake v. Keeling, 1941, 230 Iowa 1038, 299 N.W. 919; Wrabek v. Suchomel, 1920, 145 Minn. 468, 177 N.W. 764; Olive v. Miles, 1926, 144 Minn. 852, 110 So. 666. And see the amusing opinion of Minturn, J., in Tricoli v. Centalanza, 1924, 100 N.J.L. 231, 126 A. 214.

It makes no difference that the damage inflicted by one tortfeasor exceeds what the others might reasonably have foreseen. Thompson v. Johnson, 5 Cir., 1950, 180 F.2d 431.

8. Sourbier v. Brown, 1919, 188 Ind. 554, 123 N.E. 802; Kirby Lumber Co. v. Karpel, 5 Cir. 1956, 233 F.2d 373; Thompson v. Fehlig Bros. Box & Lbr. Co., Mo.App.1941, 155 S.W.2d 279; Johnson v. Sartain, 1962, 46 Haw. 112, 375 P.2d 229, rehearing denied 46 Haw. 134, 375 P.2d 856; Jaffray v. Hill, 1963, 41 Ill.App.2d 470, 191 N.E.2d 399.

9. Daingerfield v. Thompson, 1880, 33 Grat., Va., 136; Hilmes v. Stroebel, 1883, 59 Wis. 74, 17 N.W. 539; Thompson v. Johnson, 5 Cir. 1950, 180 F.2d 431; Knott v. Litton, La.App.1955, 81 So.2d 124; Thomas v. Doorley, 1959, 175 Cal.App.2d 545, 346 P. 2d 491. As to what is meant by encouragement, see Bird v. Lynn, 1850, 10 B.Mon., Ky., 422; Brown v. Perkins, 1861, 1 Allen, Mass., 89.

10. Stull v. Porter, 1921, 100 Or. 514, 196 P. 1116; Weinberg Co. v. Bixby, 1921, 185 Cal. 87, 196 P. 25; see Myers v. Shipley, 1922, 140 Md. 380, 116 A. 645.

11. Patnode v. Westenhaver, 1902, 114 Wis. 460, 90 N.W. 467; Stapler v. Parler, 1925, 212 Ala. 644, 103 So. 573; Troop v. Dew, 1921, 150 Ark. 560, 234 S. W. 992; Daggy v. Miller, 1917, 180 Iowa 1146, 162 N.W. 854; Larimer & Weld Irr. Co. v. Walker, 1918, 65 Colo. 320, 176 P. 282.

12. Bierczynski v. Rogers, 1968, — Del. —, 239 A. 2d 218; Nelson v. Nason, 1961, 343 Mass. 220, 177 N.E.2d 887; Lemons v. Kelly, 1964, 239 Or. 354, 397 P.2d 784; Skipper v. Hartley, 1963, 242 S.C. 221, 130 S.E.2d 486; Anderson v. Esposito, 1966, 90 N.J.Super. 170, 216 A.2d 607. Compare, as to physicians acting in concert in negligent medical treatment, Sprinkle v. Lemley, 1966, 243 Or. 521, 414 P. 2d 797.

13. Moses v. Town of Morgantown, 1926, 192 N.C. 102, 133 S.E. 421; see Sloggy v. Dilworth, 1888, 38 Minn. 179, 36 N.W. 451; Bowman v. Humphrey, 1904, 124 Iowa 744, 100 N.W. 854. Knowledge of what another is doing may of course be important in determining the tortious character of the defendant's own conduct. See Folsom v. Apple River Log-Driving Co., 1877, 41 Wis. 602; McKay v. Southern Bell Tel. & Tel. Co., 1896, 111 Ala. 337, 19 So. 695.

14. See infra, § 56.

15. Duke v. Feldman, 1967, 245 Md. 454, 226 A.2d 345; Ramirez v. Chavez, 1951, 71 Ariz. 239, 226 P. 2d 143; Bukowski v. Juranek, 1948, 227 Minn. 313, 35 N.W.2d 427; Heisler v. Heisler, 1911, 151 Iowa 503, 131 N.W. 676; Rhinehart v. Whitehead, 1885, 64 Wis. 42, 24 N.W. 401.

16. Day v. Walton, 1955, 199 Tenn. 10, 281 S.W.2d 685; Knight v. Western Auto Supply Co., 1946, 239 Mo.App. 643, 193 S.W.2d 771.

It is in connection with such vicarious liability that the word conspiracy is often used. The original writ of conspiracy was employed only in the case of combinations of two or more persons to abuse legal procedure, and was the forerunner of the action for malicious prosecution.[17] This was replaced at a later date by an action on the case in the nature of conspiracy, and the word gradually came to be used to extend liability in tort, as well as crime, beyond the active wrongdoer to those who have merely planned, assisted or encouraged his acts. There has been a good deal of discussion as to whether conspiracy is to be regarded as a separate tort in itself.[18] On the one hand, it is clear that the mere agreement to do a wrongful act can never alone amount to a tort, whether or not it may be a crime; and that some act must be committed by one of the parties in pursuance of the agreement, which is itself a tort.[19] "The gist of the action is not the conspiracy charged, but the tort working damage to the plaintiff." [20] It is only where means are employed,[21] or purposes are accomplished,[22] which are themselves tortious, that the conspirators who have not acted but have promoted the act

will be held liable. On the other hand, it now seems generally agreed, although there has been authority to the contrary, that there are certain types of conduct, such as boycotts,[23] in which the element of combination adds such a power of coercion, undue influence or restraint of trade, that it makes unlawful acts which one man alone might legitimately do. It is perhaps pointless to debate whether in such a case the combination or conspiracy becomes itself the tort, or whether it merely gives a tortious character to the acts done in furtherance of it. On either basis, it is the determining factor in liability.

47. JOINDER OF DEFENDANTS

A second meaning of a joint tort is that two or more persons may be joined as defendants in the same action at law. The common law rules as to joinder were extremely strict. It was limited to cases of concerted action, where a mutual agency might be found. Given such joint responsibility, the identity of the cause of action against each defendant was clear.[24] The joinder was merely permitted, and was not compulsory, and the defendants might each be sued severally for the entire damages; but the plaintiff could recover only one judgment, because it was considered that he had but one cause of action against the several parties.[25] Where the defendants did not act

17. Winfield, History of Conspiracy, 1921, ch. II.

18. See Charlesworth, Conspiracy as a Ground of Liability in Tort, 1920, 36 L.Q.Rev. 38; Burdick, Conspiracy as a Crime and as a Tort, 1907, 7 Col. L.Rev. 229; Burdick, The Tort of Conspiracy, 1908, 8 Col.L.Rev. 117.

19. Beechley v. Mulville, 1897, 102 Iowa 602, 70 N.W. 107, 71 N.W. 428; Delz v. Winfree, 1891, 80 Tex. 400, 16 S.W. 111; Robertson v. Parks, 1892, 76 Md. 118, 24 A. 411; City of Boston v. Simmons, 1890, 150 Mass. 461, 23 N.E. 210; Van Horn v. Van Horn, 1894, 56 N.J.L. 318, 28 A. 669.

20. James v. Evans, 3 Cir. 1906, 149 F. 136, 140.

21. Wickersham v. Johnson, 1873, 51 Mo. 313; Van Horn v. Van Horn, 1890, 52 N.J.L. 284, 20 A. 485; see Fleming v. Dane, 1939, 304 Mass. 46, 22 N.E.2d 609.

22. White v. White, 1907, 132 Wis. 121, 111 N.W. 1116; Hutton v. Watters, 1915, 132 Tenn. 527, 179 S.W. 134; Hudgens v. Chamberlain, 1911, 161 Cal. 710, 120 P. 422; Newton Co. v. Erickson, 1911, 70 Misc. 291, 126 N.Y.S. 949.

23. See infra, p. 961. Cf. Gregory v. Duke of Brunswick, 1844, 6 M. & G. 205, 1 C. & K. 24, 134 Eng. Rep. 866; Collins v. Cronin, 1887, 117 Pa. 35, 11 A. 869; Morris Run Coal Co. v. Barclay Coal Co., 1871, 68 Pa. 173; Place v. Minster, 1875, 65 N.Y. 89.

24. Crane and Hill v. Hummerstone, 1606, Cro.Jac. 118, 79 Eng.Rep. 102; Sir John Heydon's Case, 1613, 11 Co.Rep. 5, 77 Eng.Rep. 1150; Austen v. Willward, 1601 Cro.Eliz. 860, 78 Eng.Rep. 1086; Matthews v. Coal, 1615, Cro.Jac. 384, 79 Eng.Rep. 329.

25. Brown v. Wootton, 1600, Cro.Jac. 73, 79 Eng.Rep. 62; Barlye v. Martin, 1647, Sty. 20, 82 Eng.Rep. 498; Mitchell v. Tarbutt, 1794, 5 Term Rep. 649, 101 Eng.Rep. 362; Sutton v. Clarke, 1815, 6 Taunt.

in concert, the English courts consistently [26] refused to allow them to be joined, even though they had done acts identical in character, which had combined in their effect to cause a single, more or less indivisible injury to the plaintiff. Thus two persons who had independently uttered the same slanderous words could not be joined,[27] nor could successive converters of the same goods,[28] nor those who separately blocked the highway with their vans and prevented access to the plaintiff's property.[29]

The early American cases adopted the same position, although they showed some tendency to liberalize it.[30] Joinder was permitted where the defendants had acted in concert,[31] but not where the acts were independent.[32] A different rule developed in equity suits, where the purpose was the prevention of a wrong, and it was not necessary for such prevention to ascertain what particular share of damage each defendant had inflicted or threatened to inflict.[33] The attitude of the American courts toward joinder of parties was materially altered, however, by the passage of the Field Code of Procedure in New York in 1848, and similar codes in a majority of the other states. The codes contained a provision, intentionally framed to permit, at law as in equity, the complete settlement of all questions connected with a transaction in a single suit,[34] to the effect that "Any person may be made a defendant who has or claims an interest in the controversy adverse to the plaintiff or who is a necessary party to the complete determination or settlement of the questions involved therein."

This provision received, at the outset, most uncharitable treatment at the hands of the courts, which tended to follow the earlier precedents,[35] and to preserve the rule as to

---

29, 128 Eng.Rep. 943; Brinsmead v. Harrison, 1872, L.R. 7 C.P. 547.

26. A servant and the master vicariously liable for his acts could be joined, but of course it is obvious that each is held responsible for the same act. Cf. Wilson v. Tumman, 1843, 6 M. & G. 236, 134 Eng. Rep. 879. In Arneil v. Peterson, [1931] A.C. 560, the principle was extended to two defendants whose dogs together killed sheep; but the court was at some pains to lay stress on the fact that the dogs, if not the defendants, were acting in concert.

27. Chamberlain v. White and Goodwin, 1617, Cro. Jac. 647, 79 Eng.Rep. 558.

28. Nicoll v. Glennie, 1817, 1 M. & S. 588, 105 Eng. Rep. 220. Cf. Morris v. Robinson, 1824, 3 B. & C. 196, 107 Eng.Rep. 706.

29. Sadler v. Great Western R. Co., [1896] A.C. 450. Accord: Thompson v. London County Council, [1899] 1 Q.B. 840 (one defendant negligently excavated, another left its water main insufficiently stopped, and plaintiff's property was undermined); The Koursk, [1924] P. 140 (collision between two vessels, injuring a third. The court notes the occasional use of the term "joint tortfeasor" to signify nothing more than concurrent liability for the same loss).

30. Thus Wright v. Cooper, 1802, 1 Tyler, Vt., 425 (two dams flooding plaintiff's land); Ellis v. Howard, 1845, 17 Vt. 330; Stone v. Dickinson, 1862, 5 Allen, Mass., 29 (officers executing process on behalf of different parties).

31. Halsey v. Woodruff, 1830, 9 Pick., Mass., 555; Williams v. Sheldon, 1833, 10 Wend., N.Y., 654; Fuller v. Chamberlain, 1846, 11 Metc., Mass., 503.

32. Russell v. Tomlinson, 1817, 2 Conn. 206; Adams v. Hall, 1829, 2 Vt. 9; Hopkins v. Hersey, 1841, 20 Me. 449; Webb v. Cecil, 1848, 9 B.Mon., Ky., 198; Bard v. Yohn, 1856, 26 Pa. 482.

This antique procedural rule survived as late as 1939 in Desforge v. American-Bristol Home Bldg. Ass'n, 1939, 63 R.I. 305, 7 A.2d 788, where the court refused to allow joinder of a lessor and a lessee through whose breach of separate duties as to the condition of the premises the plaintiff was injured.

33. Woodruff v. North Bloomfield Gravel Min. Co., C.C.Cal.1883, 8 Sawy. 628, 16 F. 25; Miller v. Highland Ditch Co., 1891, 87 Cal. 430, 25 P. 550; Kelley v. Boettcher, 8 Cir.1898, 85 F. 55.

34. See First Report of New York Commissioners on Pleading and Practice, 1848, 124; Clark, Code Pleading, 2d Ed.1947, §§ 60, 61; Note, 1924, 33 Yale L.J. 817; Yankwich, Joinder of Parties, 1929, 2 So. Cal.L.Rev. 315; Harris, Joinder of Parties and Causes, 1930, 36 W.Va.L.Q. 192.

35. See for example Cogswell v. Murphy, 1877, 46 Iowa 44 (trespassing cattle); Blaisdell v. Stephens, 1879, 14 Nev. 17 (flooding land); Farley v. Crystal Coal & Coke Co., 1920, 85 W.Va. 595, 102 S.E. 265 (pollution of stream); Johnson v. City of Fairmont, 1933, 188 Minn. 451, 247 N.W. 572 (same); Key v. Armour Fertilizer Works, 1916, 18 Ga.App. 472, 89 S.E. 593 (smoke nuisance).

concerted action as the test of permissive joinder. The chief reason for this failure to accomplish the manifest intention of the code was the retention of the common law notion that the same "cause of action" must affect all of the joined defendants.[36] Nevertheless with the passage of time the code provision has had its effect, and joinder has been permitted in a number of situations where the acts of two defendants have combined to produce a single, indivisible result. Thus in the common case where the vehicles of two defendants collide and injure the plaintiff, it is held in most jurisdictions that there may be joinder under the codes.[37] The same liberality has been extended to other similar situations, where the negligence of both defendants has been necessary to produce a single injury which from its nature obviously cannot be apportioned.[38]

Joinder usually is permitted where it can be found that the defendants were under a common duty, as in the case of the fall of a party wall,[39] or the failure of two defendants to keep property in repair.[40] There has been much rather pointless argument as to whether, in a given case, the duties are sufficiently identical to permit joinder; and some cases, for example, refuse to allow a city and a property owner responsible for the condition of a sidewalk to be sued together.[41] If joinder is merely a matter of procedural convenience, no reason is apparent for refusing to permit it in such a case, and the weight of authority allows it.[42] There has been similar disagreement as to the joinder of a servant and the master vicariously liable for his tort in one action, with a small and dwindling minority of the courts still refusing to allow it unless the act

---

36. Clark, Code Pleading, 2d Ed.1947, § 61. Thus in Ader v. Blau, 1924, 241 N.Y. 7, 148 N.E. 771, it was held that an original tortfeasor and a surgeon who negligently treated the injured man could not be joined, since there was a distinct "cause of action" against each defendant. Accord: Bost v. Metcalfe, 1941, 219 N.C. 607, 14 S.E.2d 648; cf. Rose v. Sprague, 1933, 248 Ky. 635, 59 S.W.2d 554 (successive physicians); Kniess v. Armour & Co., 1938, 134 Ohio St. 432, 17 N.E.2d 734, (meat packer and dealer); Dorsey v. Material Service Corp., 1956, 9 Ill. App.2d 428, 133 N.E.2d 730 (damage from three different blasters). See criticisms in Notes, 1925, 35 Yale L.J. 85; 1925, 25 Col.L.Rev. 975; 1925, 11 Corn. L.Q. 113.

37. See cases cited supra, p. 241. Also Tillman v. Bellamy, 1955, 242 N.C. 211, 87 S.E.2d 253; Way v. Waterloo, C. F. & N. R. Co., 1947, 239 Iowa 244, 29 N.W.2d 867; Meyer v. Cincinnati St. R. Co., 1952, 157 Ohio St. 38, 104 N.E.2d 173; Sutterfield v. District Court, 1968, 165 Colo. 225, 438 P.2d 236 (chain collision). Peters v. Johnson, 1928, 124 Or. 237, 264 P. 459. Cf. Kirby Lumber Corp. v. Walters, Tex. Civ.App.1955, 277 S.W.2d 796 (several defendants putting mud on highway, plaintiff lost control); De Bardelaben v. Stallings, 4 Cir.1955, 226 F.2d 951 (truck left on highway, motorist swerved to avoid it); Carpini v. Pittsburgh & Weirton Bus. Co., 3 Cir.1954, 216 F.2d 404 (manufacturer and operator of bus); Tracy v. Rublein, 1955, 342 Mich. 623, 70 N.W.2d 819 (truck stalled on highway, other driver).

38. Carstesen v. Town of Stratford, 1896, 67 Conn. 428, 35 A. 276 (horse fell successively into two excavations); Fleming v. Arkansas Fuel Co., 1957, 231

S.C. 42, 97 S.E.2d 76 (three successive sellers of liquid which exploded); Cassity v. Brady, 1958, 182 Kan. 381, 321 P.2d 171 (successive physicians); Robertson v. Chicago, B. & Q. R. Co., 1922, 108 Neb. 569, 188 N.W. 190 (two defendants delaying shipment); Smith v. McDowell Furniture Co., 1941, 220 N.C. 155, 16 S.E.2d 685 (motorist blinded by steam).

39. Johnson v. Chapman, 1897, 43 W.Va. 639, 28 S.E. 744; Klauder v. McGrath, 1860, 35 Pa. 128; Simmons v. Everson, 1891, 124 N.Y. 319, 26 N.E. 911.

40. Lindsay v. Acme Cement Plaster Co., 1922, 220 Mich. 367, 190 N.W. 275. Cf. Schaffer v. Pennsylvania R. Co., 7 Cir.1939, 101 F.2d 369; Wisconsin Cent. R. Co. v. Ross, 1892, 142 Ill. 9, 31 N.E. 412; Doeg v. Cook, 1899, 126 Cal. 213, 58 P. 707; Walton, Witten & Graham Co. v. Miller's Adm'x, 1909, 109 Va. 210, 63 S.E. 458; Nelson v. Illinois Cent. R. Co., 1910, 98 Miss. 295, 53 So. 619.

41. Bennett v. Fifield, 1880, 13 R.I. 139, 43 Am.Rep. 17; Morris v. Woodburn, 1897, 57 Ohio St. 330, 48 N.E. 1097; Wiest v. City of Philadelphia, 1901, 200 Pa. 148, 49 A. 891. Cf. Cole v. Lippitt, 1900, 22 R.I. 31, 46 A. 43. The reason often given is the possibility that one defendant may be entitled to indemnity from the other. But if joinder is a matter of procedural convenience, it should not bar adjustment of the rights of the defendants, among themselves. Schneider v. City Council of Augusta, 1903, 118 Ga. 610, 45 S.E. 459.

42. City of Peoria v. Simpson, 1884, 110 Ill. 294; Fortmeyer v. National Biscuit Co., 1911, 116 Minn. 158, 133 N.W. 461; Scearce v. Mayor of Gainesville, 1925, 33 Ga.App. 411, 126 S.E. 883; Rowe v. Richards, 1913, 32 S.D. 66, 142 N.W. 664.

was positively authorized or commanded,[43] while the rest permit it in any case.[44]

In the remaining common law states, the passage of statutes similar to the code provisions, or precedents from the code jurisdictions, have led to a similar limited relaxation of the earlier rule.[45] Cases are extremely rare, however, in which even the code states have allowed joinder in situations where the defendants clearly have committed separate, independent wrongs, resulting in distinct injuries, but the difficulty of determining questions of fact, such as the apportionment of damages, has made joinder "necessary;" [46] and there has been a general refusal to do so.[47] It is highly unfortunate that the common law concept of the identity of a "cause of action" is carried over to defeat the obvious intent of the statutes. The advantages of joinder are obvious; [48] and the rules

against misjoinder are rules of convenience and expediency, and should be construed in the light of the broader policy against multiplicity of suits.[49] It is still more unfortunate that the uncertainty of procedural rules should have affected the substantive liability of the defendants.

When joinder is permitted, it is not compelled, and each tortfeasor may be sued severally, and held responsible for the damage he is found to have caused, although other wrongdoers have contributed to it. He cannot compel the plaintiff to make the others parties to the action,[50] or complain because they have not been joined,[51] or because the action against one is dismissed out of court; [52] nor is it a defense to him

---

43. Hobbs v. Hurley, 1918, 117 Me. 449, 104 A. 815; Shaver v. Shirks Motor Express Corp., 1955, 163 Ohio St. 484, 127 N.E.2d 355.

44. Daniels v. Parker, 1956, 119 Vt. 348, 126 A.2d 85; Feger v. Concrete Materials & Const. Co., 1951, 172 Kan. 75, 238 P.2d 708; Skala v. Lehon, 1931, 343 Ill. 602, 175 N.E. 832; Putnam Memorial Hospital v. Allen, 2 Cir.1929, 34 F.2d 927; Allen v. Trester, 1924, 112 Neb. 515, 199 N.W. 841. See Notes, 1942, 26 Minn.L.Rev. 730; 1959, 44 Iowa L.Rev. 542.

45. See for example Arnst v. Estes, 1939, 136 Me. 272, 8 A.2d 201; Carlton v. Boudar, 1916, 118 Va. 521, 88 S.E. 174; Matthews v. Delaware, L. & W. R. Co., 1893, 56 N.J.L. 34, 27 A. 919; Feneff v. Boston & M. R. R. Co., 1907, 196 Mass. 575, 82 N.E. 705; Smith v. Yellow Cab Co., 1926, 285 Pa. 229, 132 A. 124.

46. For example, Gunder v. Tibbitts, 1899, 153 Ind. 591, 55 N.E. 762; Sherlock v. Manwaren, 1924, 208 App.Div. 538, 203 N.Y.S. 709. But the former case arrives at the extraordinary conclusion that the doctor who performs an abortion is liable for the original seduction!

47. McGannon v. Chicago & N. W. R. Co., 1924, 160 Minn. 143, 199 N.W. 894; Miller v. Highland Ditch Co., 1891, 87 Cal. 430, 25 P. 550; Albrecht v. St. Hedwig's Roman Cath. Benev. Soc., 1919, 205 Mich. 395, 171 N.W. 461; Ader v. Blau, 1925, 241 N.Y. 7, 148 N.E. 771; White v. Arizona Eastern R. Co., 1924, 26 Ariz. 590, 229 P. 101.

48. The result of the refusal to permit joinder is that: (1) in the separate suits it is open to each de-

fendant to prove that the other was solely responsible, or responsible for the greater part of the damage, and so defeat or minimize recovery; (2) it is equally open to the plaintiff to prove that each defendant was solely responsible, or responsible for the greater part of the damage, and so recover excessive compensation; (3) the two verdicts will seldom have any relation to one another; (4) different witnesses may be called in the two suits, or the same witness may tell different stories, so that the full truth is told in neither; (5) neither defendant may cross-examine the other, or his witnesses, and plaintiff may not cross-examine both in one action; (6) time and expense are doubled.

In some jurisdictions, these difficulties may be obviated by consolidation of the actions, usually at the discretion of the court. But if this is possible, why not permit joinder in the first instance, and treat it as the equivalent of consolidation? See Snow v. Rudolph, 1910, 62 Tex.Civ.App. 235, 131 S. W. 249; Note, 1920, 18 Mich.L.Rev. 708.

49. See Great Southern Life Ins. Co. v. Dolan, Tex. Civ.App.1922, 239 S.W. 236, reversed on other grounds in, Tex.Com.App.1924, 262 S.W. 475.

50. Hoosier Stone Co. v. McCain, 1892, 133 Ind. 231, 31 N.E. 956; Melichar v. Frank, 1959, 78 S.D. 58, 98 N.W.2d 345; Sox v. Hertz Corp., D.S.C.1967, 262 F.Supp. 531. Cf. Johns v. Castles, 1956, 229 S.C. 51, 91 S.E.2d 721 (when plaintiff sues only one, he may not be heard to demand joinder of the others).

51. Berkson v. Kansas City Cable Ry. Co., 1898, 144 Mo. 211, 45 S.W. 1119; Coleman v. Bennett, 1902, 111 Tenn. 705, 69 S.W. 734; Farmers' State Bank v. Jeske, 1924, 50 N.D. 813, 197 N.W. 854; Tower v. Camp, 1925, 103 Conn. 41, 130 A. 86.

52. Arnst v. Estes, 1939, 136 Me. 272, 8 A.2d 201; Yellow Cab Co. of Nashville v. Pewitt, 1958, 44

that his own participation was slight in comparison with that of others not joined.[53] Since each is severally liable, a verdict in favor of one will not discharge the others,[54] either in the same or in separate suits,[55] unless, as in the case of vicarious liability, it is clear that one cannot be discharged without also discharging the other.[56] In such a case

it is common practice to accept the verdict for the defendant, and deny the plaintiff any recovery; but since the inconsistency calls into question the validity of one verdict as much as the other, much the preferable procedure is to refuse to accept the entire verdict from the jury, or if it be too late for that, to order a complete new trial.[57]

Entire Liability

Quite apart from any question of vicarious liability or joinder of defendants, the common law developed a separate principle, that a tortfeasor might be liable for the entire loss sustained by the plaintiff, even though his act concurred or combined with that of another wrongdoer to produce the result— or, as the courts have put it, that the defendant is liable for all consequences proximately caused by his wrongful act. The rule was first applied in actions against a single defendant, where there was no concert of action, and therefore no joinder would have been possible, and there was no suggestion of a "joint tort." [58] The extent to which such entire liability has been imposed has been considered above.[59]

In England, such concurrent but independent wrongdoers were not confused with joint tortfeasors because there could be no

Tenn.App. 572, 316 S.W.2d 17; May v. Bradford, Mo.1963, 369 S.W.2d 225; Farmers' State Bank v. Jeske, 1924, 50 N.D. 813, 197 N.W. 854; Eyak River Packing Co. v. Huglen, 1927, 143 Wash. 229, 255 P. 123, judgment affirmed on rehearing 257 P. 638.

Likewise vacation or reversal of a judgment against one joint tortfeasor does not affect the judgments with respect to the others. Chmielewski v. Marich, 1954, 2 Ill.2d 568, 119 N.E.2d 247; Regent Coop. Equity Exchange v. Johnston's Fuel Liners, Inc., N.D. 1964, 130 N.W.2d 165 (new trial). One alone may appeal. Wright v. Royse, 1963, 43 Ill.App.2d 267, 193 N.E.2d 340; see Note, 1966, 31 Mo.L.Rev. 141.

53. Wrabek v. Suchomel, 1920, 145 Minn. 468, 177 N. W. 764; Wisecarver & Stone v. Chicago, R. I. & P. R. Co., 1909, 141 Iowa 121, 119 N.W. 532; Riverside Cotton Mills v. Lanier, 1903, 102 Va. 148, 45 S.E. 875; City of Atlanta v. Chattanooga Foundry & Pipeworks, 6 Cir. 1903, 127 F. 23.

54. Doran v. Chicago, St. P., M. & O. R. Co., 1915, 128 Minn. 193, 150 N.W. 800; Garrison v. Everett, 1924, 112 Neb. 230, 199 N.W. 30; Miller v. Alaska S. S. Co., 1926, 139 Wash. 207, 246 P. 296; Wood v. Rolfe, 1924, 128 Wash. 55, 221 P. 982; San Antonio Gas Co. v. Singleton, 1900, 24 Tex.Civ.App. 341, 59 S.W. 920.

55. Nelson v. Illinois Cent. R. Co., 1910, 98 Miss. 295, 53 So. 619; City of Tulsa v. Wells, 1920, 79 Okl. 39, 191 P. 186.

56. Pangburn v. Buick Motor Co., 1914, 211 N.Y. 228, 105 N.E. 423; Walker v. St. Louis-San Francisco R. Co., 1926, 214 Ala. 492, 108 So. 388; Chesapeake & Ohio R. Co. v. Williams' Adm'x, 1945, 300 Ky. 850, 190 S.W.2d 549; Eckleberry v. Kaiser Foundation Northern Hospital, 1961, 226 Or. 616, 359 P.2d 1090; Jentick v. Pacific Gas & Elec. Co., 1941, 18 Cal.2d 117, 114 P.2d 343. The same principle prevents verdicts differing in amount in the same action. Goines v. Pennsylvania R. Co., 1957, 3 A.D.2d 307, 160 N.Y.S.2d 39, reargument denied 4 A.D.2d 831, 166 N.Y.S.2d 303; Biel, Inc. v. Kirsch, 1958, 130 Ind.App. 46, 153 N.E.2d 140; cf. Miller v. Singer, 1955, 131 Colo. 112, 279 P.2d 846 (concerted action). See Note, 1964, 17 Okl.L.Rev. 432.

Mississippi, however, has a unique rule permitting inconsistent verdicts as to master and servant, on the ground that either could have been sued and held liable separately. Gulf Refining Co. v. Myrick,

1954, 220 Miss. 429, 71 So.2d 217. See Note, 1955, 26 Miss.L.J. 265.

57. Monumental Motor Tours v. Eaton, 1945, 184 Va. 311, 35 S.E.2d 105; Berger v. Podolsky Bros., 1950, 360 Mo. 239, 227 S.W.2d 695; Begin v. Liederbach Bus Co., 1926, 167 Minn. 84, 208 N.W. 546; Tolley v. Engert, 1925, 71 Cal.App. 439, 235 P. 651.

58. Dixon v. Bell, 1816, 5 M. & S. 198, 105 Eng.Rep. 1023 (defendant gave loaded gun to young servant, who negligently shot plaintiff); Illidge v. Goodwin, 1831, 5 C. & P. 190, 172 Eng.Rep. 934 (defendant left horse unguarded in street, passing stranger whipped it); Lynch v. Nurdin, 1841, 1 Q.B. 29, 113 Eng.Rep. 1041 (defendant left horse and cart in street, and boy made it move); cf. Hume v. Oldacre, 1816, 1 Stark. 351, 171 Eng.Rep. 494; King v. Moore, 1832, 3 B. & Ad. 184, 110 Eng.Rep. 68; Guille v. Swan, 822, 19 Johns., N.Y., 381.

59. See supra, § 41.

joinder in the absence of concerted action.[60] They must be sued separately, and although each might be liable for the entire loss, the juries were under no compulsion to return verdicts for the same amount. Under the more liberal American rules as to joinder, defendants whose negligence has concurred to produce a single result have been joined in one action, and by careless usage have been called joint tortfeasors.[61]

One immediate result has been to confuse joinder of parties with liability for entire damages, and to crystallize the prejudice of the courts against joinder of defendants liable for separate results. Another has been the rigid enforcement of the common law rule that a verdict for one sum must be returned against all those who are found liable in the joint action.[62] This rule, which developed in cases of concerted action, was of course reasonable where the act of one was considered the act of all, and no basis could be found to permit the jury to apportion the damages.[63] It has unfortunate results where

joinder is permitted only as a matter of convenience, and it is clear that not all of those who are "necessary parties to the complete determination of the questions involved" are liable for the same damages. Thus an earlier tortfeasor may be liable for the damages inflicted by a later one, while the later wrongdoer is not liable for the earlier damage;[64] and yet there are obvious reasons of convenience for the joinder of both defendants in a single action.[65] The rule against separate verdicts has meant either that the courts insist upon separate suits,[66] or what is even worse, that joinder is permitted and each defendant is held liable for the entire damage.[67] No reason can be found for refusing to allow joinder without making the parties "joint" for any other purpose than the convenient trial of the case.

Where the jury improperly returns verdicts for separate amounts against two or more defendants, various rules have been adopted.[68] The plaintiff is permitted by some courts to take judgment against all for the higher damages,[69] and by others to enter

60. Sadler v. Great Western R. Co., [1896] A.C. 450; Thompson v. London County Council, [1899] 1 Q.B. 840; The Koursk, [1924] P. 140.

61. Carolina, C. & O. R. Co. v. Hill, 1916, 119 Va. 416, 89 S.E. 902; Riley v. Industrial Finance Service Co., 1957, 157 Tex. 306, 302 S.W.2d 652; Tracy v. Rublein, 1955, 342 Mich. 623, 70 N.W.2d 819; De Bardelaben v. Stallings, 4 Cir. 1955, 226 F.2d 951; Carpini v. Pittsburgh & Weirton Bus Co., 3 Cir. 1954, 216 F.2d 404.

62. See Note, 1928, 14 Va.L.Rev. 677; Marriott v. Williams, 1908, 152 Cal. 705, 93 P. 875; Jordan v. Koerth, 1933, 212 Wis. 109, 248 N.W. 918; Ross v. Pennsylvania R. Co., 1927, 5 N.J.Misc. 811, 138 A. 383; Lake Erie & W. R. Co. v. Halleck, 1922, 78 Ind.App. 495, 136 N.E. 39; Hall v. McClure, 1923, 112 Kan. 752, 212 P. 875.

The length to which the rule is carried is illustrated by Fort Worth & N. O. Ry. Co. v. Enos, 1897, 15 Tex.Civ.App. 673, 39 S.W. 1095, where the power of the jury to assess damages severally was denied, even though the acts and defenses of the defendants were so distinct that each was held entitled to a separate continuance.

63. Austen v. Willward, 1601, Cro.Eliz. 860, 78 Eng. Rep. 1086; Crane and Hill v. Hummerstone, 1606, Cro.Jac. 118, 79 Eng.Rep. 102; Sir John Heydon's Case, 1613, 11 Co.Rep. 5, 77 Eng.Rep. 1150; Mat-

thews v. Coal, 1615, Cro.Jac. 384, 79 Eng.Rep. 329; Hill v. Goodchild, 1771, 5 Burr. 2790, 98 Eng.Rep. 465.

64. See infra, p. 320.

65. Compare the procedure in La Bella v. Brown, 1926, 103 N.J.L. 491, 133 A. 82, affirmed, 1927, 103 N.J.L. 491, 135 A. 918, where the actions were consolidated by agreement and separate verdicts were returned. Also Young v. Dille, 1923, 127 Wash. 398, 220 P. 782; and see Sherlock v. Manwaren, 1924, 208 App.Div. 538, 203 N.Y.S. 709.

66. Cf. Albrecht v. St. Hedwig's Roman Catholic Benev. Soc., 1919, 205 Mich. 395, 171 N.W. 461; McGannon v. Chicago & N. W. R. Co., 1924, 160 Minn. 143, 199 N.W. 894; Schafer v. Ostmann, 1910, 148 Mo.App. 644, 129 S.W. 63; Barton v. Barton, 1906, 119 Mo.App. 507, 94 S.W. 574; Ader v. Blau, 1925, 241 N.Y. 7, 148 N.E. 771.

67. Sawdey v. R. W. Rasmussen Co., 1930, 107 Cal. App. 467, 290 P. 684; Owens v. Cerullo, 1931, 9 N. J.Misc. 776, 155 A. 759. Cf. Gunder v. Tibbitts, 1899, 153 Ind. 591, 55 N.E. 762.

68. See Notes, 1928, 14 Va.L.Rev. 677; 1938, 22 Minn.L.Rev. 569.

69. Halsey v. Woodruff, 1830, 9 Pick., Mass., 555; Kinsey v. William Spencer & Son Corp., 1937, 165

judgment against one defendant and dismiss his action against the others.[70] A few courts have adopted the most reasonable solution, which is to return the case to the jury with instructions to render a single verdict.[71] A defendant, however, usually is not permitted to complain at all, as he might have been sued severally, and the smaller verdict against another defendant does not relieve him of his own liability, as determined by the jury.[72]

48. JUDGMENT AND SATISFACTION

The English rule, until it was altered by statute[73] in 1935, was that the plaintiff could obtain but one judgment on a joint tort. Since the act of each tortfeasor was the act of all, it was considered that there was only one cause of action, which was "reduced to certainty" or merged in the judgment, and judgment against one alone, even though unsatisfied, barred any later action against another.[74] But if the defendants had not acted in concert, the tort was not joint, there were two or more causes of action, and an unsatisfied judgment against one did not prevent a later action against the others.[75] At the same time there developed a quite distinct principle, that the plaintiff was entitled to but one compensation for his loss, and that satisfaction of his claim, even by a stranger to the action,[76] would prevent its further enforcement.[77] It is obvious that this rule is equitable in its nature,[78] and that its purpose is to prevent unjust enrichment. It is equally obvious that it applies not only to concerted wrongdoers, but also to concurrent tortfeasors not acting in concert, or even to payments made by parties who have no connection with the tort at all.[79]

American courts have shown a tendency to confuse these two rules. The first has generally been repudiated in the United States,[80] and it is now held everywhere that

Misc. 143, 300 N.Y.S. 391; Rochester v. Anderson, 1809, 1 Bibb., Ky., 439.

70. Koltz v. Jahaaske, 1942, 312 Ill.App. 623, 38 N.E. 2d 973; Whitney v. Tuttle, 1936, 178 Okl. 170, 62 P.2d 508; Warren v. Westrup, 1890, 44 Minn. 237, 46 N.W. 347; Crawford v. Morris, 1848, 5 Grat., Va., 90.

71. City of Tuscaloosa v. Fair, 1936, 232 Ala. 129, 167 So. 276; Forslund v. Swenson, 1923, 110 Neb. 188, 192 N.W. 649; Chrudinsky v. Evans, 1917, 85 Or. 548, 167 P. 562; Cullen v. City of Minneapolis, 1937, 201 Minn. 102, 275 N.W. 414.

72. Kelly v. Schneller, 1927, 148 Va. 573, 139 S.E. 275; Ohio Valley Bank v. Greenbaum Sons Bank & Trust Co., 4 Cir. 1926, 11 F.2d 87; Crawford v. Morris, 1848, 5 Grat., Va., 90; Nashville Ry. & Light Co. v. Trawick, 1907, 118 Tenn. 273, 99 S.W. 695.

73. 25 & 26 Geo. V, ch. 30, § 6(1).

74. Brown v. Wootton, 1600, Cro.Jac. 73, 79 Eng.Rep. 62; King v. Hoare, 1844, 13 M. & W. 494, 153 Eng. Rep. 206; Day v. Porter, 1838, 2 Moody & R. 151, 174 Eng.Rep. 245; Brinsmead v. Harrison, 1872, L. R. 7 C.P. 547.

75. Morris v. Robinson, 1824, 3 B. & C. 196, 107 Eng. Rep. 706; Ellis v. Stenning, [1932] 2 Ch. 81; The Koursk, [1924] P. 140.

76. Welby v. Drake, 1825, 1 C. & P. 557, 171 Eng. Rep. 1315; Belshaw v. Bush, 1851, 11 C.B. 191, 138 Eng.Rep. 444; Freshwater v. Bulmer Rayon Co., [1933] Ch. 162. See Gold, Accord and Satisfaction by a Stranger, 1941, 19 Can.Bar Rev. 165.

77. Morris v. Robinson, 1824, 3 B. & C. 196, 107 Eng. Rep. 706; Cooper v. Shepherd, 1846, 3 C.B. 266, 136 Eng.Rep. 107; Ellis v. Stenning, [1932] 2 Ch. 81.

78. See the statement in Morris v. Robinson, 1824, 3 B. & C. 196, 107 Eng.Rep. 706, that equity will prevent double satisfaction.

79. See Miller v. Beck, 1899, 108 N.W. 575, 79 N.W. 344. And cf. Schoenly v. Nashville Speedways, Inc., 1961, 208 Tenn. 107, 344 S.W.2d 349, where an award of a Board of Claims, based on the negligence of a state highway patrolman, was held to be in satisfaction, and so to bar action against other tortfeasors.

80. See Note, 1955, 68 Harv.L.Rev. 700. Virginia adopted the English rule in Petticolas v. City of Richmond, 1897, 95 Va. 456, 28 S.E. 566, but it was later changed by statute. Fitzgerald v. Campbell, 1921, 131 Va. 486, 109 S.E. 308. An early Rhode Island case, Hunt v. Bates, 1862, 7 R.I. 217, was later limited strictly to its own facts. Parmenter v. Barstow, 1899, 21 R.I. 410, 43 A. 1035. Earlier cases holding that suing out an unsatisfied execution against one bars action against another were overruled in Cleveland v. City of Bangor, 1895, 87 Me. 259, 32 A. 892; Ketelson v. Stilz, 1916, 184 Ind. 702, 111 N.E. 423; Verhoeks v. Gillivan, 1928, 244 Mich. 367, 221 N.W. 287.

an unsatisfied judgment against one tort-feasor does not bar an action against another. The plaintiff may bring separate suits, pursue each to judgment, and elect to enforce either or both.[81] It has even been held [82] that he may refuse tender of payment of the first judgment, and still proceed to speculate upon the possibility of a larger recovery by means of a second. And even a partial satisfaction of one judgment will not prevent obtaining or enforcing another, although it is everywhere agreed that the amount received must be credited pro tanto against the amount to be collected.[83] It has been held, however, that full satisfaction of a lesser judgment will extinguish a greater one, apparently on the ground that it has been adjudicated in court that the amount paid is the complete equivalent of the plaintiff's damage.[84]

The second rule, as to satisfaction itself, has become involved in the confused concept of "joint torts." [85] When payment of the judgment in full is made by the judgment debtor, there is no doubt that the plaintiff is barred from a further action against another who is liable for the same damages,[86] or from enforcement of another judgment against him.[87] But where the plaintiff's claim, whether reduced to judgment or not, is paid in full by a stranger who is not connected with the tort at all, there are a good many cases [88] which have held that it does not discharge the plaintiff's claim against the real tortfeasor even though it has been agreed that it shall do so. Such decisions thus in effect permit double compensation. The weight of authority is now definitely to the contrary.[89] It is supported by deci-

---

81. Lovejoy v. Murrah, 1866, 3 Wall., U.S. 1; Black v. Bringhurst, 1935, 7 Cal.App.2d 711, 46 P.2d 993; Irwin v. Jetter Brewing Co., 1917, 101 Neb. 409, 163 N.W. 470; Squire v. Ordemann, 1909, 194 N.Y. 394, 87 N.E. 435; Moss v. Jones, 1966, 93 N.J.Super. 179, 225 A.2d 369.

As to the related problem of the privity between defendants which will make a judgment in favor of one bar action against the other, see Restatement of Judgments, 1942, §§ 96(1) (a), 99; 1 Freeman, Judgments, 5th Ed. 1925, § 451; Note, 1952, 65 Harv.L.Rev. 818, 862. The problem is beyond the scope of this text.

82. Bradford v. Carson, 1931, 223 Ala. 594, 137 So. 426; Skelly Oil Co. v. Jordan, 1939, 186 Okl. 130, 96 P.2d 524; Fitzgerald v. Campbell, 1921, 131 Va. 486, 109 S.E. 308; Restatement of Torts, 1939, § 886, Comment c.

83. Laurenzi v. Vranizan, 1945, 25 Cal.2d 806, 155 P. 2d 633; Meixell v. Kirkpatrick, 1883, 29 Kan. 679; McVey v. Marratt, 1890, 80 Iowa 132, 45 N.W. 548; Stusser v. Mutual Union Ins. Co., 1923, 127 Wash. 449, 221 P. 331; Boyles v. Knight, 1899, 123 Ala. 289, 26 So. 939.

84. Thomas' Adm'r v. Maysville St. R. & Transfer Co., 1910, 136 Ky. 446, 124 S.W. 398; Cox v. Smith, 1882, 10 Or. 418; Larson v. Anderson, 1919, 108 Wash. 157, 182 P. 957; cf. Simpson v. Plyler, 1963, 258 N.C. 390, 128 S.E.2d 843; Battle v. Morris, 1957, 265 Ala. 581, 93 So.2d 428. By statute in England, the plaintiff is limited to satisfaction of the *first* judgment. See Williams, Joint Torts and Contributory Negligence, 1951, 1–194; Note, 1955, 68 Harv.L.Rev. 697, 701.

85. See for example Price-Bass Co. v. Owen, 1940, 24 Tenn.App. 474, 146 S.W.2d 149.

86. City of Wetumka v. Crowell-Franklin Oil Co., 1935, 171 Okl. 565, 43 P.2d 434; Laver v. Kingston, 1956, 11 Ill.App.2d 323, 137 N.E.2d 113; Viehweg v. Mountain States Tel. & Tel. Co., D.Idaho 1956, 141 F.Supp. 848; Theobald v. Kenney's Suburban House, Inc., 1966, 48 N.J. 203, 225 A.2d 10; Bundt v. Embro, 1965, 48 Misc.2d 802, 265 N.Y.S.2d 872.

But satisfaction of a judgment against an original tortfeasor may not bar a subsequent malpractice action against a physician aggravating the injury, where it is found that there was not satisfaction of such damages. Selby v. Kuhns, 1963, 345 Mass. 600, 188 N.E.2d 861; Knutsen v. Brown, 1966, 93 N.J.Super. 522, 226 A.2d 460, affirmed, 1967, 96 N. J.Super. 229, 232 A.2d 833. And vice versa. Mathis v. Virgin, Fla.App.1964, 167 So.2d 897.

87. Thomas' Adm'r v. Maysville St. R. & Transfer Co., 1910, 136 Ky. 446, 124 S.W. 398. In Hilbert v. Roth, 1959, 395 Pa. 270, 149 A.2d 648, this was carried to the length of refusing to permit collection of punitive damages, awarded in the second judgment but not the first.

88. Papenfus v. Shell Oil Co., 1949, 254 Wis. 233, 35 N.W.2d 920; Deatley's Adm'r v. Phillips, Ky.1951, 243 S.W.2d 918; Brimer v. Scheibel, 1926, 154 Tenn. 253, 290 S.W. 5; Carroll v. Kerrigen, 1938, 173 Md. 627, 197 A. 127; Phillips Sheet & Tin Plate Co. v. Griffith, 1918, 98 Ohio St. 73, 120 N.E. 207.

89. Latham v. Des Moines Elec. Co., 1942, 232 Iowa 1038, 6 N.W.2d 853; Harris v. City of Roanoke, 1942, 179 Va. 1, 18 S.E.2d 303; Husky Ref. Co. v. Barnes, 8 Cir. 1941, 119 F.2d 715; Jacobsen v.

sions [90] as to accord and satisfaction of contracts, and appears definitely to represent the preferable view, at least where the intent of the parties is clear that the claim shall be satisfied. The problem has been further complicated, however, by the matter of releases, which remains to be considered.

49. RELEASE

There is a genuine distinction between a satisfaction and a release. A satisfaction is an acceptance of full compensation for the injury; a release is a surrender of the cause of action, which may be gratuitous, or given for inadequate consideration.[91] Releases at common law were under seal,[92] which disposed of any possible dispute as to the adequacy of consideration. Such a release to one of two tortfeasors who had acted in concert necessarily released the other, since there was in the eyes of the law but one cause of action against the two, liable for the same acts, which was surrendered.[93] But as to independent wrongdoers, not acting in concert, who were liable for the same loss, there seems to be no reason to conclude that

a release of one would release the others, except in so far as it was based upon actual satisfaction of the claim.[94]

The American courts, possibly because of the diminished effect given to the seal,[95] have rather hopelessly confused release with satisfaction. When, in turn, concurrent wrongdoers who have caused the same loss become "joint tort-feasors," for the sole reason that they can be joined, the result is still more confusion. Until quite recent years, most of the courts have continued to hold that a release to one of two concurrent tortfeasors is a complete surrender of any cause of action against the other, and a bar to any suit against him,[96] without regard to the sufficiency of the compensation actually received.[97] This has been held to be true even though the release is accompanied by an oral agreement that it shall have no such effect,[98] or the agreement is inserted in the

Woerner, 1939, 149 Kan. 598, 89 P.2d 24; Bacich v. Northland Transp. Co., 1932, 185 Minn. 544, 242 N. W. 379. See Notes, 1944, 22 N.C.L.Rev. 167; 1950, 15 Mo.L.Rev. 115; 1955, 8 Vand.L.Rev. 509.

90. Abrahamson v. Brown, 1948, 149 Neb. 267, 30 N. W.2d 675; Somers & Sons v. Le Clerc, 1939, 110 Vt. 408, 8 A.2d 663; Welsh v. Loomis, 1940, 5 Wash.2d 377, 105 P.2d 500; Restatement of Contracts, § 421. See King, Accord and Satisfaction by a Third Person, 1950, 15 Mo.L.Rev. 115; Gold, Accord and Satisfaction by a Stranger, 1941, 19 Can.Bar Rev. 165.

91. See Miller v. Beck, 1899, 108 Iowa 575, 79 N.W. 344; Ellis v. Essau, 1880, 50 Wis. 138, 6 N.W. 518; Cleveland, C. C. & St. L. R. Co. v. Hilligoss, 1908, 171 Ind. 417, 86 N.E. 485. See, generally, Havighurst, The Effect of a Settlement with One Co-obligor upon the Obligations of the Others, 1959, 45 Corn.L.Q. 1.

92. 2 Williston, Contracts, Rev.Ed. 1936, § 333A.

93. Cocke v. Jenner, 1614, Hob. 66, 80 Eng.Rep. 214; Duck v. Mayeu, [1892] 2 Q.B. 511. See Winfield, Province of the Law of Tort, 1931, 40, suggesting that the rule was influenced by the fact that until 1695 the court would not interfere with an award of excessive damages.

94. Amazingly enough, the point seems never to have been presented directly to an English court; but the conclusion would seem to follow from the fact that an unsatisfied judgment was not a bar in such a case, because the causes of action were separate. See Salmond, Law of Torts, 8th Ed. 1934, 82, note; and cf. Freshwater v. Bulmer Rayon Co., [1933] Ch. 162; The Koursk, [1924] P. 140.

95. 2 Williston, Contracts, Rev.Ed. 1936, § 333A. So long as the seal remained conclusive as to adequate consideration, the release necessarily imported full satisfaction. Gunther v. Lee, 1876, 45 Md. 60; Carpenter v. W. H. McElwain Co., 1916, 78 N.H. 118, 97 A. 560.

96. Price v. Baker, 1959, 143 Colo. 264, 352 P.2d 90; McFarland v. News & Observer Pub. Co., 1963, 260 N.C. 397, 132 S.E.2d 752; Lucio v. Curran, 1956, 2 N.Y.2d 157, 157 N.Y.S.2d 948, 139 N.E.2d 133; Jackman v. Jones, 1953, 198 Or. 564, 258 P.2d 133; Atlantic Coast Line R. Co. v. Boone, Fla.1956, 85 So. 2d 834.

97. The release is said to be "conclusive evidence" of full satisfaction. Greene v. Waters, 1951, 260 Wis. 40, 49 N.W.2d 919; J. E. Pinkham Lumber Co. v. Woodland State Bank, 1930, 156 Wash. 117, 286 P. 95; Hawber v. Raley, 1928, 92 Cal.App. 701, 268 P. 943.

98. Martin v. Setter, 1931, 184 Minn. 457, 239 N.W. 219; Muse v. De Vito, 1923, 243 Mass. 384, 137 N.E. 730; Colby v. Walker, 1934, 86 N.H. 568, 171 A. 774; Williams v. Le Bar, 1891, 141 Pa. 149, 21 A. 525. As to the parol evidence rule, see infra, p. 304.

release itself.[99] No better reason has been offered than that such terms are necessarily repugnant to the legal operation and effect of the instrument itself, and hence are void,[1] or that the cause of action is by its nature indivisible in the eyes of the law.[2]

This result has been justly condemned[3] because it compels the plaintiff either to forego any opportunity of obtaining what he can get from one defendant without suit, or to give up his entire claim against the other without full compensation. Historically, and logically, it has no justification, since causes of action against mere concurrent tortfeasors not acting in concert have always been separate,[4] and their separate character should not be affected by the possibility of joinder for procedural convenience. A surrender of one therefore should not on any logical or reasonable basis discharge the other, except to the extent that there has been full compensation. Even as applied to cases of concerted action,[5] the rule seems at best an antiquated survival of an arbitrary common law procedural concept, arising out of long forgotten semi-criminal forms of action; and it has no reasonable application at all to cases of mere concurrent negligence. The fear of double recovery[6] is meaningless, since the amount paid under the release must be credited to the second tortfeasor in any case;[7] and the argument[8] that the plaintiff should not be permitted to make piecemeal collections from different defendants is quite pointless when he is allowed to do precisely that after judgment.[9]

Such was the original state of the American law; but the last fifty years have seen wholesale changes in it. Actually the only states which continue to cling to the old rule, and make it impossible to settle with one tortfeasor without releasing another, are

---

99. Friday v. United States, 9 Cir. 1957, 239 F.2d 701; Shortt v. Hudson Supply & Equip. Co., 1950, 191 Va. 306, 60 S.E.2d 900; Morris v. Diers, 1956, 134 Colo. 39, 298 P.2d 957; Roper v. Florida Public Utilities Co., 1938, 131 Fla. 709, 179 So. 904; Bryan v. Creaves, 7 Cir. 1943, 138 F.2d 377, cert. denied 321 U.S. 778 (Illinois law).

1. McBride v. Scott, 1903, 132 Mich. 176, 93 N.W. 243; Abb v. Northern Pac. R. Co., 1902, 28 Wash. 428, 68 P. 954; Price v. Baker, 1959, 143 Colo. 264, 352 P.2d 90. This reached a peak of absurdity when one who was never liable at all to the plaintiff was released, and this was held to release the real wrongdoer, upon the basis that the plaintiff was "estopped" or "precluded" from denying that they were joint tortfeasors. See for example Bittner v. Little, 3 Cir. 1959, 270 F.2d 286 (Virginia law); Connelly v. United States Steel Co., 1954, 161 Ohio St. 448, 119 N.E.2d 843; Note, 1955, 8 Vand.L.Rev. 509.

See, however, Hamm v. Thompson, 1960, 143 Colo. 298, 353 P.2d 73, holding that a release to a master does not release a servant, since the master would be entitled to indemnity over against him.

2. McBride v. Scott, 1903, 132 Mich. 176, 93 N.W. 243; Muse v. De Vito, 1923, 243 Mass. 384, 137 N.E. 730; Sunset Copper v. Zickrick, 1924, 125 Wash. 565, 217 P. 5; Kirkland v. Ensign-Bickford Co., D. Conn.1920, 267 F. 472.

3. Havighurst, The Effect of a Settlement with One Co-obligor upon the Obligations of the Others, 1959, 45 Corn.L.Q. 1; Notes, 1959, 12 Vand.L.Rev. 1414; 1961, 40 N.C.L.Rev. 88; 1951, 24 So.Cal.L.Rev. 466; 1943, 28 Iowa L.Rev. 515; 1941, 3 Wash. & Lee L. Rev. 151; 1938, 22 Minn.L.Rev. 692.

4. Milwaukee Ins. Co. v. Gas Service Co., 1959, 185 Kan. 604, 347 P.2d 394. Suppose that the damages inflicted by an original wrongdoer are aggravated by the negligent treatment of a physician. If a release is given to the original wrongdoer before the malpractice occurs, does it discharge the physician before the cause of action against him even accrues? The answer invariably has been no. Western Express Co. v. Smeltzer, 6 Cir. 1937, 88 F. 2d 94, cert. denied 302 U.S. 678; Smith v. Golden State Hospital, 1931, 111 Cal.App. 667, 296 P. 127; De Nike v. Mowery, 1966, 69 Wash.2d 357, 418 P.2d 1010, amended 422 P.2d 328 (discovered later). Cf. Dakin v. Allis, 1964, 25 Wis.2d 49, 130 N.W.2d 191; Lackey v. Brooks, 1963, 204 Va. 428, 132 S.E.2d 461. See Note, 1933, 18 Corn.L.Q. 257.

5. The American cases rely in general upon two early decisions of this type: Ruble v. Turner, 1808, 2 Hen. & M., Va., 38; Gunther v. Lee, 1876, 45 Md. 60.

6. See McBride v. Scott, 1903, 132 Mich. 176, 182, 93 N.W. 243, 245; J. E. Pinkham Lumber Co. v. Woodland State Bank, 1930, 156 Wash. 117, 286 P. 95.

7. See infra, p. 305.

8. Advanced in Price v. Baker, 1959, 143 Colo. 264, 352 P.2d 90.

9. See supra, p. 300.

Washington [10] and Virginia.[11] The rest of the courts have retreated, in one way or another, from the common law rule. The device commonly accepted is that of a covenant not to sue,[13] by which the plaintiff does not surrender his cause of action, but merely agrees that he will not enforce it, and so becomes liable for an equivalent amount of damages if he breaks the agreement and sues.[14] Such a covenant is held not to release other tortfeasors,[15] even in the absence of any reservation of rights against them,[16] unless it is found that there has in fact been full satisfaction of the claim.[17] Under this technical evasion, which is the most obvious of subterfuges for circumventing an inconvenient common law rule, the form of the instrument becomes highly important in some jurisdictions; and the draftsman who uses the language of covenant may succeed where any mention of the word release would be fatal.[18] It has been said often enough that intent governs rather than form, and that the court will look to the four corners of the instrument to determine it.[19]

There still remain, however, some instruments which by any fair construction are not covenants, but releases. Even as to these the common law rule has been changed by statute in some nineteen states.[20] Without a statute, another thirteen jurisdictions have held that the release does not discharge the second tortfeasor if it provides in terms that it shall not do so.[21] Some of them even have recognized an accompanying oral agreement to that effect,[22] and have met the objection

10. Rust v. Schaitzer, 1933, 175 Wash. 331, 27 P.2d 571; Haney v. Cheatham, 1941, 8 Wash.2d 310, 111 P.2d 1003. Although Richardson v. Pacific Power & Light Co., 1941, 11 Wash.2d 288, 118 P.2d 985, suggested a change in the Washington law, it does not appear to have taken place.

11. Bland v. Warwickshire Corp., 1933, 160 Va. 131, 168 S.E. 443; Goldstein v. Gilbert, 1942, 125 W.Va. 250, 23 S.E.2d 606 (Virginia law).

Colorado had held likewise in Price v. Baker, 1959, 143 Colo. 264, 352 P.2d 90; but the case was overruled in Cox v. Pearl Inv. Co., 1969, — Colo. —, 450 P.2d 60.

12. Omitted.

13. Or not to proceed further, as in Hicklin v. Anders, 1953, 201 Or. 128, 253 P.2d 897; or not to enforce judgment, as in Pellett v. Sonotone Corp., 1945, 26 Cal.2d 705, 160 P.2d 783; Whittlesea v. Farmer, 1970, — Nev. —, 469 P.2d 57. A mere dismissal of the action against some defendants may have the same practical effect, although it is not satisfactory protection for the one released. Adolph Gottscho, Inc. v. American Market Corp., 1955, 18 N.J. 467, 114 A.2d 438, cert. denied 350 U.S. 834.

14. The effect of the covenant between the parties is well stated in Pellett v. Sonotone Corp., 1945, 26 Cal.2d 705, 160 P.2d 783.

15. Johnson v. Harnisch, 1966, 259 Iowa 1090, 147 N.W.2d 11; Lyons v. Durocher, 1960, 341 Mass. 382, 169 N.E.2d 911; Burke v. Burnham, 1952, 97 N.H. 203, 84 A.2d 918; Southern Pac. Co. v. Raish, 9 Cir. 1953, 205 F.2d 389 (Oregon law); Boucher v. Thomsen, 1950, 328 Mich. 312, 43 N.W.2d 866.

16. Joyce v. Massachusetts Real Estate Co., 1928, 173 Minn. 310, 217 N.W. 337. The intent not to release other tortfeasors is a question of fact, and open to inquiry. Fagerburg v. Phoenix Flour Mills Co., 1937, 50 Ariz. 227, 71 P.2d 1022; Richardson v. Pacific Power & Light Co., 1941, 11 Wash.2d 288, 118 P.2d 985.

17. Daniels v. Celeste, 1939, 303 Mass. 358, 21 N.E. 2d 1; Haase v. Employers Mut. Liability Ins. Co., 1947, 250 Wis. 422, 27 N.W.2d 468; Shortt v. Hudson Supply & Equipment Co., 1950, 191 Va. 306, 60 S.E.2d 900.

18. Compare Oliver v. Williams, 1935, 19 Tenn.App. 54, 83 S.W.2d 271, with Byrd v. Crowder, 1933, 166 Tenn. 215, 60 S.W.2d 171. See Note, 1964, 7 South Tex.L.Rev. 134.

19. See for example Atlantic Coast Line R. Co. v. Boone, Fla.1956, 85 So.2d 834; Albert's Shoes, Inc. v. Crabtree Const. Co., Fla.1956, 89 So.2d 491.

20. See Note, 1959, 12 Vand.L.Rev. 1414, listing statutes in Alabama, Arkansas, Delaware, Hawaii, Louisiana, Maryland, Michigan, Missouri, Montana, Nevada, New Mexico, New York, North Dakota, Pennsylvania, Rhode Island, South Dakota, Utah, West Virginia, and Wisconsin. To these must be added California.

21. McKenna v. Austin, 1943, 77 U.S.App.D.C. 228, 134 F.2d 659; Gronquist v. Olson, 1954, 242 Minn. 119, 64 N.W.2d 159; Jukes v. North American Van Lines, 1957, 181 Kan. 12, 309 P.2d 692; Riley v. Industrial Finance Service Co., 1957, 157 Tex. 306, 302 S.W.2d 652; Standard Sanitary Mfg. Co. v. Brian's Adm'r, 1928, 224 Ky. 419, 6 S.W.2d 491.

22. Couillard v. Charles T. Miller Hospital, 1958, 253 Minn. 418, 92 N.W.2d 96; Safety Cab Co. v. Fair,

of the parol evidence rule [23] with the argument that the second tortfeasor is not a party to the instrument.[24] Still others have accomplished the same result by the short and simple method of calling a release with reservation of rights against others a covenant not to sue.[25]

The only desirable rule would seem to be that a plaintiff should never be compelled to surrender his cause of action against any wrongdoer unless he has intentionally done so, or unless he has received such full compensation that he is no longer entitled to maintain it.[26] If the statutes are taken into account, this is now the rule actually applied in some two-thirds of the American jurisdictions. Where there has been such full satisfaction,[27] or where it is agreed that the amount paid under the release is so received,[28] no claim should remain as to any other tortfeasor; but these are questions of fact, and normally to be determined by the jury, where the amount of the claim is unliquidated.[29] The release, however, may very well be taken as a prima facie acknowledgment of satisfaction, and the burden placed upon the plaintiff to prove that it is not.[30] The requirement that an express reservation of rights against other tortfeasors be inserted in the release itself [31] seems unfortunate, when releases frequently are signed by plaintiffs ignorant of the law and without legal advice. If it is clear that the satisfaction received was understood to be only partial, it should not discharge the claim against the second tortfeasor.[32] All courts are agreed,

1937, 181 Okl. 264, 74 P.2d 607; Standard Sanitary Mfg. Co. v. Brian's Adm'r, 1928, 224 Ky. 419, 6 S. W.2d 491; Fitzgerald v. Union Stock Yards Co., 1911, 89 Neb. 393, 131 N.W. 612; Weldon v. Lehmann, 1956, 226 Miss. 600, 84 So.2d 796. See also Breen v. Peck, 1958, 28 N.J. 351, 146 A.2d 665; Daily v. Somberg, 1959, 28 N.J. 372, 146 A.2d 676.

23. See Goss v. Ellison, 1884, 136 Mass. 503; Martin v. Setter, 1931, 184 Minn. 457, 239 N.W. 219; Cannon v. Pearson, Tex.1964, 383 S.W.2d 565.

24. See for example Fitzgerald v. Union Stock Yards Co., 1911, 89 Neb. 393, 131 N.W. 612.

25. Carey v. Bilby, 8 Cir. 1930, 129 F. 203; Bolton v. Ziegler, N.D.Iowa 1953, 111 F.Supp. 516; Natrona Power Co. v. Clark, 1924, 31 Wyo. 284, 225 P. 586; Cox v. Pearl Inv. Co., 1969, — Colo. —, 450 P.2d 60.

26. See the excellent opinion of Rutledge, J., in McKenna v. Austin, 1943, 77 U.S.App.D.C. 228, 134 F. 2d 659, which seems to leave nothing more to be said. Also Black v. Martin, 1930, 88 Mont. 256, 292 P. 577; Aldrich v. Charles Beauregard & Sons, Inc., 1964, 105 N.H. 330, 200 A.2d 14; Gronquist v. Olson, 1954, 242 Minn. 119, 64 N.W.2d 159.

See also, holding that a release to an original tortfeasor does not necessarily release a negligent physician who aggravates the injury: Derby v. Prewitt, 1962, 12 N.Y.2d 100, 236 N.Y.S.2d 953, 187 N.E. 2d 556; Smith v. Conn, 1969, — Iowa —, 163 N.W.2d 407; Hansen v. Collett, 1963, 79 Nev. 159, 380 P.2d 301; Couillard v. Charles T. Miller Hospital, 1958, 253 Minn. 418, 92 N.W.2d 96; Galloway v. Lawrence, 1965, 263 N.C. 433, 139 S.E.2d 761.

27. Berry v. Pullman Co., 5 Cir. 1918, 249 F. 816; Cleveland, C. C. & St. L. R. Co. v. Hilligoss, 1908, 171 Ind. 417, 86 N.E. 485; Urton v. Price, 1881, 57 Cal. 270; Bowman v. Davis, 1889, 13 Colo. 297, 22 P. 507; State ex rel. Cox v. Maryland Elec. R. Co., 1915, 126 Md. 300, 95 A. 43.

28. Beedle v. Carolan, 1944, 115 Mont. 587, 148 P.2d 559; Greenhalch v. Shell Oil Co., 10 Cir. 1935, 78 F. 2d 942; Fitzgerald v. Union Stock Yards Co., 1911, 89 Neb. 393, 131 N.W. 612; Hartigan v. Dickson, 1900, 81 Minn. 284, 83 N.W. 1901.

29. Ellis v. Essau, 1880, 50 Wis. 138, 6 N.W. 518; Fitzgerald v. Union Stock Yards Co., 1911, 89 Neb. 393, 131 N.W. 612; Berry v. Pullman Co., 5 Cir. 1918, 249 F. 816; O'Neil v. National Oil Co., 1918, 231 Mass. 20, 120 N.E. 107; Arnett v. Missouri Pac. R. Co., 1895, 64 Mo.App. 368.

30. See Dwy v. Connecticut Co., 1915, 89 Conn. 74, 92 A. 883; Smith v. Mann, 1931, 184 Minn. 485, 239 N.W. 223; Moss v. Cherdak, 1935, 114 N.J.L. 332, 176 A. 333; Tanana Trading Co. v. North American Trading & Transp. Co., 9 Cir. 1915, 220 F. 783; Snyder v. Mutual Tel. Co., 1907, 135 Iowa 215, 112 N.W. 776. Contra, Booker v. Kansas City Gas Co., 1936, 231 Mo.App. 214, 96 S.W.2d 919.

31. See supra, p. 303; Restatement of Torts, § 885.

In Young v. State, Alaska 1969, 455 P.2d 889, the court took the converse position, that a release without full compensation does not release other tortfeasors unless they are specifically named in the release.

32. Adams Express Co. v. Beckwith, 1919, 100 Ohio St. 348, 126 N.E. 300; Louisville & E. Mail Co. v. Barnes' Adm'r, 1904, 117 Ky. 860, 79 S.W. 261; Kropidlowski v. Pfister & Vogel Leather Co., 1912, 149 Wis. 421, 135 N.W. 839; Robertson v. Trammell, 1904, 37 Tex.Civ.App. 53, 83 S.W. 258, error refused 98 Tex. 364, 83 S.W. 1098.

however, that it must be credited pro tanto to diminish the amount of damages recoverable against him,[33] irrespective of an agreement that it shall not,[34] and regardless of whether it is received under a release or a covenant not to sue.[35] The prevailing view, with some authority to the contrary,[36] is that it must be so credited even where the person released was not in fact a joint tortfeasor, or was not liable to the plaintiff at all.[37]

33. McKenna v. Austin, 1943, 77 U.S.App.D.C. 228, 134 F.2d 659; McNair v. Goodwin, 1964, 262 N.C. 1, 136 S.E.2d 218; Hutchinson v. Rubel Baking Co., 1939, 34 Ohio Abs. 15, 34 N.E.2d 472, motion overruled; Natrona Power Co. v. Clark, 1924, 31 Wyo. 284, 225 P. 586; Dwy v. Connecticut Co., 1915, 89 Conn. 74, 92 A. 883. Normally the deduction is to be made by the jury; but it may be made after judgment, by credit against the judgment. Price v. Wabash R. Co., 1961, 30 Ill.App.2d 115, 174 N.E.2d 5; Hardin v. New York Cent. R. Co., 1960, 145 W.Va. 676, 116 S.E.2d 697. Many statutes now require this. See Daugherty v. Hershberger, 1956, 386 Pa. 367, 126 A.2d 730; Note, 1957, 106 U.Pa.L.Rev. 311.

A few courts, under statute or at common law, have held that there must be a pro rata reduction in the amount to be recovered, rather than a lump sum. Theobald v. Angelos, 1965, 44 N.J. 228, 208 A.2d 129; Palestine Contractors, Inc. v. Perkins, Tex.1964, 386 S.W.2d 764; Martello v. Hawley, 1962, 112 U.S.App.D.C. 129, 300 F.2d 721; Harvey v. Travelers Ins. Co., La.App.1964, 163 So.2d 915. See Notes, 1966, 18 Stan.L.Rev. 486; 1966, 14 Kan.L. Rev. 541; 1964, 43 Tex.L.Rev. 118.

34. Home Tel. Co. v. Fields, 1907, 150 Ala. 306, 43 So. 711.

35. Ramsey v. Camp, 1961, 254 N.C. 443, 119 S.E.2d 209; Price v. Wabash R. Co., 1961, 30 Ill.App.2d 115, 174 N.E.2d 5; Burke v. Burnham, 1952, 97 N. H. 203, 84 A.2d 918; Bolton v. Ziegler, N.D.Iowa 1953, 111 F.Supp. 516; Harmon v. Givens, 1953, 88 Ga.App. 629, 77 S.E.2d 223. Contra, Mink v. Majors, 1954, 39 Tenn.App. 50, 279 S.W. 714, criticized in Note, 1956, 24 Tenn.L.Rev. 390.

36. Harlee v. City of Gulfport, 5 Cir. 1941, 120 F.2d 41; Herberger v. Anderson Motor Service Co., 1933, 268 Ill.App. 403; Brandstein v. Ironbound Transp. Co., 1934, 112 N.J.L. 585, 172 A. 580; Carroll v. Kerrigen, 1938, 173 Md. 627, 197 A. 127; Scoggins v. Village of Hartford, 1967, 86 Ill.App.2d 233, 229 N.E.2d 550, appeal after remand, 1969, 104 Ill.App. 2d 403, 244 N.E.2d 433.

37. Holland v. Southern Pac. Utilities Co., 1935, 208 N.C. 289, 180 S.E. 592; Jacobsen v. Woerner, 1939, 149 Kan. 598, 89 P.2d 24; Husky Ref. Co. v. Barnes, 8 Cir. 1941, 119 F.2d 715; Steger v. Egyud,

50. CONTRIBUTION

Still another significance attached to a "joint tort" is the common law rule that there can be no contribution between those who are regarded as "joint tortfeasors," when one has discharged the claim of the injured plaintiff.[38] The rule had its origin in 1799 in the case of Merryweather v. Nixan.[39] There is a very meagre report of the case, but it seems clear that there had been an action for conversion and a joint judgment against two defendants, and that they had acted in concert, since they were joined at a time when joinder was not possible on any other basis. One of the two, who had been levied on for the whole judgment, sought "contribution of a moiety" from the other, on the theory of an implied promise, "as for so much money paid to his use." Lord Kenyon said that there could be no doubt that he should be nonsuit; and that he had never heard of such an action where the former judgment was for a tort. The ground of the decision would appear to have been simply the fact that the parties had acted intentionally and in concert, and the plaintiff's claim for contribution rested upon what was, in the eyes of the law, entirely his own deliberate wrong.[40]

1959, 219 Md. 331, 149 A.2d 762; Caplan v. Caplan, 1940, 62 Ga.App. 577, 9 S.E.2d 96.

38. See, generally, Leflar, Contribution and Indemnity Between Tortfeasors, 1932, 81 U.Pa.L.Rev. 130; Bohlen, Contribution and Indemnity Between Tortfeasors, 1936, 21 Corn.L.Q. 552, 1937, 22 Corn.L.Q. 469; Hodges, Contribution and Indemnity Among Tortfeasors, 1947, 26 Tex.L.Rev. 150; Notes, 1931, 45 Harv.L.Rev. 349; 1947, 35 Geo.L.J. 382; 1953, 37 Minn.L.Rev. 470; 1958, 37 Neb.L.Rev. 820; 1959, 68 Yale L.J. 964; 1970, 31 Mont.L.Rev. 69.

Contribution and indemnity are generally allowed in the continental law. See Cohn, Responsibility of Joint Wrongdoers in Continental Law, 1935, 51 L. Q.Rev. 46.

39. 1799, 8 Term.Rep. 186, 101 Eng.Rep. 1337. See Reath, Contribution Between Persons Jointly Charged with Negligence—Merryweather v. Nixan, 1799, 12 Harv.L.Rev. 176; Hatcher, Battersey's Case, 1941, 47 W.Va.L.Q. 123.

40. Compare the celebrated Highwayman's Case, Everet v. Williams, Ex. 1725, reported in 1893, 9 L.Q.

Lord Kenyon expressly stated that the decision "would not affect cases of indemnity, where one man employed another to do acts, not unlawful in themselves." Later cases seized upon this limitation, and held that the rule against contribution did not apply unless the plaintiff was a wilful and conscious wrongdoer.[41] It was not until 1894 that the question was even raised in England in a case of concurrent negligence,[42] and the better English view, even before their statute,[43] appears clearly to have been that contribution is not denied in cases of mere vicarious liability, negligence, accident, mistake, or other unintentional breaches of the law.[44]

The early American cases applied the rule against contribution to cases of wilful misconduct,[45] but refused to recognize it where the tort committed by the claimant was a matter of negligence or mistake.[46] But once the door was thrown open to joinder in one action of those who had merely caused the same damage, the origin of the rule and the reason for it were lost to sight. The great majority of our courts proceeded to apply it generally, and refused to permit contribution even where independent, although concurrent, negligence had contributed to a single result.[47] Over a period of more than a century, only nine American jurisdictions have come to the contrary conclusion, allowing contribution without legislation: the District of Columbia,[48] Iowa,[49] Louisiana,[50] Maine,[51]

Rev. 197, and Costigan's Cases on Legal Ethics, 1917, 399. This was a suit by one highwayman against another for an accounting of their plunder. The bill was dismissed with costs to be paid by the defendant; the plaintiff's solicitors were attached and fined fifty pounds each for contempt. Both plaintiff and defendant were subsequently hanged. In short, contribution was not allowed.

41. Adamson v. Jarvis, 1827, 4 Bing. 66, 130 Eng.Rep. 693 (indemnity to an auctioneer innocently selling goods). See also Betts v. Gibbins, 1834, 2 Ad. & El. 57, 111 Eng.Rep. 22 (exception "where the act is not clearly illegal in itself"); Pearson v. Skelton, 1836, 1 M. & W. 504, 150 Eng.Rep. 533 (same).

42. Palmer v. Wick & Pultneytown Steam Shipping Co., [1894] A.C. 318, a case arising in Scotland, where a workman was killed when one defendant furnished defective tackle and the other negligently used it. Lord Herschell allowed contribution, saying that the rule did not apply to mere negligence, and in any case should not extend to Scots law. Even prior to this, in Wooley v. Batte, 1826, 2 C. & P. 417, 172 Eng.Rep. 188, contribution had been allowed between two joint proprietors of a stage-coach, not personally at fault, but held liable because of the negligence of the coachman.

43. Contribution is now provided by statute in England. See Williams, Joint Torts and Contributory Negligence, 1951, §§ 25–54.

44. Salmond, Law of Torts, 8th Ed. 1934, 86, relying on the cases cited, as well as Burrows v. Rhodes, [1890] 1 Q.B. 816; Hillen v. I. C. I., [1934] 1 K.B. 455. Contra, The Englishman and The Australia, [1895] P. 212.

45. Peck v. Ellis, 1816, 2 Johns.Ch., N.Y., 131; Miller v. Fenton, 1844, 11 Paige, N.Y., 18; Hunt v. Lane, 1857, 9 Ind. 248; Rhea v. White, 1859, 3 Head, Tenn., 121; Atkins v. Johnson, 1870, 43 Vt. 78, 5 Am.Rep. 260; cf. Spalding v. Oakes' Adm'r, 1869, 42 Vt. 343 (keeping ram known to be vicious).

46. Thweatt's Adm'r v. Jones, 1825, 1 Rand., Va., 328; Horbach's Adm'rs v. Elder, 1851, 6 Harris, Pa., 33; Acheson v. Miller, 1853, 2 Ohio St. 203; Bailey v. Bussing, 1859, 28 Conn. 455; Armstrong County v. Clarion County, 1870, 66 Pa. 218; Nickerson v. Wheeler, 1875, 118 Mass. 295. See Reath, Contribution Between Persons Jointly Charged for Negligence, 1899, 12 Harv.L.Rev. 176, 180–182; Hatcher, Battersey's Case, 1941, 47 W.Va.L.Q. 123.

47. Union Stock Yards Co. v. Chicago, B. & Q. R. Co., 1905, 196 U.S. 217; National Trailer Convoy, Inc. v. Oklahoma Turnpike Authority, Okl.1967, 434 P.2d 238; Denneler v. Aubel Ditching Service, 1969, 203 Kan. 117, 453 P.2d 88; Riexinger v. Ashton Co., 1969, 9 Ariz.App. 406, 453 P.2d 235; Fidelity & Cas. Co. of New York v. Chapman, 1941, 167 Or. 661, 120 P.2d 223. The rule could not be evaded by the assignment of a judgment from the plaintiff to one tortfeasor. Adams v. White Bus Line, 1921, 184 Cal. 710, 195 P. 389.

48. Knell v. Feltman, 1949, 85 App.D.C. 22, 174 F.2d 662.

49. Best v. Yerkes, 1956, 247 Iowa 800, 77 N.W.2d 23; Hawkeye-Security Ins. Co. v. Lowe Const. Co., 1959, 251 Iowa 27, 99 N.W.2d 421.

50. Quatray v. Wicker, 1933, 178 La. 289, 151 So. 208; Linkenburger v. Owens, 5 Cir. 1950, 181 F.2d 97. Louisiana now has a statute, permitting contribution only between joint judgment defendants.

51. Bedell v. Reagan, 1963, 159 Me. 292, 192 A.2d 24.

Minnesota,[52] Nevada,[53] Pennsylvania,[54] Tennessee,[55] and Wisconsin.[56]

There is obvious lack of sense and justice in a rule which permits the entire burden of a loss, for which two defendants were equally, unintentionally responsible, to be shouldered onto one alone, according to the accident of a successful levy of execution, the existence of liability insurance, the plaintiff's whim or spite, or his collusion with the other wrongdoer,[57] while the latter goes scot free. The only kind words said by any writer over the last century for the rule denying contribution[58] have been addressed to the proposition that contribution will be used chiefly to permit liability insurance companies to shift a part of the loss which they have been paid to bear to the shoulders of uninsured defendants. In reply it has been suggested[59] that if this is true it is at least

odd that the insurance companies are among the most vigorous opponents of the change, and that it is by no means yet true that there will be insurance in every case.

However this may be, half a century of vigorous attack upon the original rule has had its effect in the passage of statutes in some twenty-three states, which to a greater or less extent permit contribution among tortfeasors.[60] Some of these acts are limited to contribution between defendants against whom a joint judgment has been rendered.[61] Others are quite broad and general in scope, declaring the principle of contribution and leaving its administration to the courts.[62] Still others provide methods by which the tortfeasor from whom contribution is sought may be joined as a defendant, and his liability determined in the original action.[63] The

52. Ankeny v. Moffett, 1887, 37 Minn. 109, 33 N.W. 320; Underwriters at Lloyds of Minneapolis v. Smith, 1926, 166 Minn. 388, 208 N.W. 13; Skaja v. Andrews Hotel Co., 1968, 281 Minn. 417, 161 N.W.2d 657. See Note, 1953, 37 Minn. L.Rev. 470.

53. Probably, concludes the federal court in Wiener v. United Airlines, S.D.Cal.1962, 216 F.Supp. 701.

54. Goldman v. Mitchell-Fletcher Co., 1928, 292 Pa. 354, 141 A. 231. Pennsylvania subsequently adopted a statute providing for contribution.

55. Davis v. Broad St. Garage, 1950, 191 Tenn. 320, 232 S.W.2d 355; Huggins v. Graves, E.D.Tenn. 1962, 210 F.Supp. 98. There is, however, apparently some confusion of the ideas of contribution and indemnity. See American Cas. Co. v. Billingsley, 1953, 195 Tenn. 448, 260 S.W.2d 173.

56. Ellis v. Chicago & N. W. R. Co., 1918, 167 Wis. 392, 167 N.W. 1048; Mitchell v. Raymond, 1923, 181 Wis. 591, 195 N.W. 855. Wisconsin subsequently adopted a statute providing for contribution.

57. As examples of such collusion, see Pennsylvania Co. v. West Penn Rys., 1924, 110 Ohio St. 516, 144 N.E. 51; Norfolk So. R. Co. v. Beskin, 1924, 140 Va. 744, 125 S.E. 678.

58. James, Contribution Among Joint Tortfeasors: A Pragmatic Criticism, 1941, 54 Harv.L.Rev. 1156; Jones, Contribution Among Tortfeasors, 1958, 11 U. Fla.L.Rev. 175.

59. The James article led to the ensuing debate: Gregory, Contribution Among Joint Tortfeasors: A Defense; James, Replication; Gregory, Rejoinder, all in 1941, 54 Harv.L.Rev. 1170 ff.

60. The jurisdictions are collected and classified in the Note, 1959, 68 Yale L.J. 964, 981–984. See, for former discussions, Gregory, Legislative Loss Distribution in Negligence Actions, 1936; Gregory, Contribution Among Tortfeasors: A Uniform Practice, [1938] Wis.L.Rev. 365; Notes, 1932, 32 Col.L. Rev. 94; 1931, 45 Harv.L.Rev. 349.

61. See for example Kahn v. Urania Lbr. Co., La. App.1958, 103 So.2d 476; Powell v. Barker, 1957, 96 Ga.App. 592, 101 S.E.2d 113; State ex rel. McClure v. Dinwiddie, 1948, 358 Mo. 15, 213 S.W.2d 127; Buckner v. Foster, E.D.Mich. 1952, 105 F.Supp. 279; Distefano v. Lamborn, 1951, 7 Terry (Del.) 195, 83 A.2d 300. See Gregory, Tort Contribution Practice in New York, 1935, 20 Corn.L.Q. 269; Note, 1950, 24 St. Johns L.Rev. 276.

62. See for example Consolidated Coach Corp. v. Burge, 1932, 245 Ky. 631, 54 S.W.2d 16; Callihan Interests, Inc. v. Duffield, Tex.Civ.App.1965, 385 S. W.2d 586, error refused.

63. See for example Brotman v. McNamara, 1942, 181 Md. 224, 29 A.2d 264. See Gregory, Procedural Aspects of Securing Contribution in the Injured Plaintiff's Action, 1933, 47 Harv.L.Rev. 209.

The original Uniform Contribution Among Tortfeasors Act, proposed by the Commissioners on Uniform State Laws in 1939, contained elaborate provisions for such joinder. It was adopted in nine jurisdictions, but was so extensively amended everywhere that there was no real uniformity. The Act was withdrawn by the Commissioners, and a new Uniform Contribution Among Tortfeasors Act proposed in 1955. This Act avoids any attempt to deal with procedural questions such as joinder.

drafting has not been free from difficulty.[64] Where there is so much variation in the terms of the statutes, and even in the decisions apart from them, little more can be done here than to indicate some of the more important questions, and how they have been dealt with.

1. It is necessary first of all to distinguish between contribution and indemnity.[65] In any case where there is a right to indemnity, contribution statutes and rules do not apply.[66]

2. Under the statutes or apart from them, the tendency has been to continue the original rule that there is no contribution in favor of those who commit intentional torts,[67] and even to extend it to include aggravated negligence;[68] but some statutes

have been construed to allow contribution even in such cases.[69]

3. Notwithstanding arguments as to policy,[70] there appears to be general agreement, except as to the construction of the North Carolina statute,[71] that the contribution suit will lie in favor of a liability insurer who has paid the plaintiff's judgment and become subrogated to the claim.[72]

4. A more difficult question is whether a tortfeasor who has settled with the original plaintiff shall be entitled to contribution. The argument against it is that the other defendant may take no part in the settlement, violently oppose it, and regard it as outrageous, and still be held liable for his share. It is for this reason that the statutes of several jurisdictions limit contribution to those against whom judgments have been rendered, which fix both liability and amount. Where there is no such provision, it is almost invariably held that one who settles without judgment can recover contribution.[73] It is usually held, however, that in the

---

64. See Stevens, A Proposal for Contribution Among Joint Tortfeasors in Ohio, 1951, 3 West.Res.L.Rev. 50; Jones, Contribution Among Tortfeasors, 1958, 11 U.Fla.L.Rev. 175; Note, 1936, 24 Cal.L.Rev. 546; Reports of New York Law Revision Commission, 1936, 699; 1937, 67; 1938, 65; 1939, 27; 1941, 17; 1952. An unhappy lawyer's estimate of the New Jersey statute is Orlando, The Operation of the "Joint Tortfeasors Contribution Law" in New Jersey, 1955, 22 Ins.Counsel J. 480.

65. See infra, § 309.

66. See for example Melichar v. Frank, 1959, 78 S.D. 58, 98 N.W.2d 345 (master and servant); Weis v. A. T. Hipke & Sons, 1955, 271 Wis. 140, 72 N.W.2d 715.

67. Turner v. Kirkwood, 10 Cir. 1931, 49 F.2d 590, cert. denied 284 U.S. 635; Jacobs v. General Acc., F. & L. Assur. Corp., 1961, 14 Wis.2d 1, 109 N.W.2d 462; Best v. Yerkes, 1956, 247 Iowa 800, 77 N.W.2d 23 ("intentional wrong, concerted action, or moral turpitude"). The statutes of Kentucky and Virginia so provide. Ky.Rev.Stat.1953, § 412.030; Va.Code Ann. 1950, § 8–627. So does § 1(c) of the current Uniform Act, 9 U.L.A., 1961 Pocket Part 68, after the earlier Act had been silent on the matter.

68. Hardware Mut. Cas. Co. v. Danberry, 1951, 234 Minn. 391, 48 N.W.2d 567 (wilful negligence); Cage v. New York Cent. R. Co., W.D.Pa.1967, 276 F.Supp. 778, affirmed 3d Cir. 1968, 386 F.2d 998. The 1955 Uniform Act brackets this as optional in § 1(c).

Minnesota carried this too far in Fidelity & Cas. Co. v. Christenson, 1931, 183 Minn. 182, 236 N.W. 618, denying contribution because there had been intentional violation of a statute. This was modified in Skaja v. Andrews Hotel Co., 1968, 281 Minn. 417,

161 N.W.2d 657, to limit it to cases of conscious wrongdoing.

69. Judson v. Peoples Bank & Trust Co. of Westfield, 1954, 17 N.J. 67, 110 A.2d 24, second appeal, 1957, 25 N.J. 17, 134 A.2d 761; Brenneis v. Marley, 1955, 5 Pa.D. & C.2d 24; cf. Maryland Lumber Co. v. White, 1954, 205 Md. 180, 107 A.2d 73.

70. See supra, p. 307.

71. Lumbermen's Mut. Cas. Co. v. United States Fid. & Guar. Co., 1936, 211 N.C. 13, 188 S.E. 634. See Notes, 1963, 41 N.C.L.Rev. 890; 1965, 44 N.C.L.Rev. 142.

72. Coble v. Lacey, 1960, 257 Minn. 352, 101 N.W.2d 594; Hudgins v. Jones, 1964, 205 Va. 495, 138 S.E. 2d 16; Zeglen v. Minkiewicz, 1963, 12 N.Y.2d 497, 240 N.Y.S.2d 965, 191 N.E.2d 450; Hawkeye-Security Ins. Co. v. Lowe Const. Co., 1959, 251 Iowa 27, 99 N.W.2d 421; State Farm Mut. Auto Ins. Co. v. Continental Cas. Co., 1953, 264 Wis. 493, 59 N.W.2d 425. See Note, 1936, 45 Yale L.J. 151.

73. Harger v. Caputo, 1966, 420 Pa. 528, 218 A.2d 108; Morris v. Kospelich, 1969, 253 La. 413, 218 So.2d 316; Huggins v. Graves, 6 Cir. 1964, 337 F.2d 486 (Tennessee law); Zontelli Bros. v. Northern Pac. Ry. Co., 8 Cir. 1959, 263 F.2d 194; Hawkeye-Security Ins. Co. v. Lowe Const. Co., 1959, 251 Iowa 27, 99 N.W.2d 421.

contribution suit such a compromiser must sustain the burden of proof, not only as to his own liability to the original plaintiff, but also as to the amount of the damages and the reasonableness of the settlement.[74]

5. The contribution defendant must be a tortfeasor, and originally liable to the plaintiff. If there was never any such liability, as where he has the defense of family immunity,[75] assumption of risk,[76] or the application of an automobile guest statute,[77] or the substitution of workmen's compensation for common law liability,[78] then he is not liable for contribution.

6. Once liability has existed, however, there is more difficulty as to subsequent events discharging it. It is generally agreed that the fact that the statute of limitations has run against the original plaintiff's action does not bar a suit for contribution,[79] since that cause of action does not arise until payment.[80]

7. The effect of a settlement with the plaintiff by the contribution defendant, in which he received a release or a covenant not to sue, has perhaps given more difficulty than any other problem. The usual holding has been that the defendant so relieved of liability is not released from contribution.[81] There has been much dissatisfaction with this because it becomes impossible for a defendant to settle the case, take a release, and close the file, since the potential liability for contribution is still open. On the other hand, the proposed solution of a pro rata reduction of the amount remaining due [82] discourages

74. Farmers Mut. Auto Ins. Co. v. Milwaukee Auto. Ins. Co., 1959, 8 Wis.2d 512, 99 N.W.2d 746. Accord: Allied Mut. Cas. Co. v. Long, 1961, 252 Iowa 829, 107 N.W.2d 682 ("The whole matter may be summed up in the statement that before there can be contribution among tortfeasors, there must be tortfeasors"); Clemmons v. King, 1965, 265 N.C. 199, 143 S.E.2d 83; Consolidated Coach Corp. v. Burge, 1932, 245 Ky. 631, 54 S.W.2d 16; McKenna v. Austin, 1943, 77 U.S.App.D.C. 228, 134 F.2d 659; Duluth, M. & N. R. Co. v. McCarthy, 1931, 183 Minn. 414, 236 N.W. 766.

75. Yellow Cab Co. of D. C. v. Dreslin, 1950, 86 U.S. App.D.C. 327, 181 F.2d 626; Chamberlain v. McCleary, E.D.Tenn.1963, 217 F.Supp. 591; Blunt v. Brown, S.D.Iowa 1963, 225 F.Supp. 326; Rodgers v. Galindo, 1961, 68 N.M. 215, 360 P.2d 400; Zaccari v. United States, D.Md.1955, 130 F.Supp. 50.

There is something of a movement on foot to change this rule and allow the contribution, on the ground that the immunity does not go to tort liability, but merely to suit. Bedell v. Reagan, 1963, 159 Me. 292, 192 A.2d 24; Zarrella v. Miller, 1966, 100 R.I. 545, 217 A.2d 673; Restifo v. McDonald, 1967, 426 Pa. 5, 230 A.2d 199; Weinberg v. Underwood, 1968, 101 N.J.Co. 448, 244 A.2d 538.

76. Shonka v. Campbell, 1967, 260 Iowa 1178, 152 N. W.2d 242; Troutman v. Modlin, 8 Cir. 1965, 353 F. 2d 382; Burmeister v. Youngstrom, 1965, 81 S.D. 578, 139 N.W.2d 226; Shrofe v. Rural Mut. Cas. Ins. Co., 1950, 258 Wis. 128, 45 N.W.2d 76.

77. Troutman v. Modlin, 8 Cir. 1965, 353 F.2d 382; Blunt v. Brown, S.D.Iowa 1963, 225 F.Supp. 326; Patterson v. Tomlinson, Tex.Civ.App.1938, 118 S.W. 2d 645, error refused; Hill Hardware Corp. v. Hesson, 1956, 198 Va. 425, 94 S.E.2d 256; Downing v. Dillard, 1951, 55 N.M. 267, 232 P.2d 140.

78. Hunsucker v. High Point Bending & Chair Co., 1953, 237 N.C. 559, 75 S.E.2d 768; Bertone v. Turco Products, Inc., 3 Cir. 1958, 252 F.2d 726 (New Jer-

sey law); Auld v. Globe Ind. Co., W.D.La.1963, 220 F.Supp. 96; Mahone v. McGraw-Edison Co., E.D. Va.1968, 281 F.Supp. 582; Iowa Power & Light Co. v. Abild Const. Co., 1966, 259 Iowa 314, 144 N.W.2d 303.

79. Keleket X-Ray Corp. v. United States, D.C.Cir. 1960, 275 F.2d 167; Cooper v. Philadelphia Dairy Products Co., 1955, 34 N.J.Sup. 301, 112 A.2d 308; Godfrey v. Tidewater Power Co., 1943, 223 N.C. 647, 27 S.E.2d 736; Ainsworth v. Berg, 1948, 253 Wis. 438, 34 N.W.2d 790, 35 N.W.2d 911.

80. The problem of long deferred payment has been dealt with in several of the statutes, by short limitation provisions applicable to the contribution suit itself. See for example, § 3(c) and (d) of the later Uniform Act, 9 U.L.A., 1961 Pocket Part 71.

81. State Farm Mut. Auto Ins. Co. v. Continental Cas. Co., 1953, 264 Wis. 493, 59 N.W.2d 425; Employers Mut. Cas. Co. v. Chicago, St. P., M. & O. R. Co., 1951, 235 Minn. 304, 50 N.W.2d 689; Blauvelt v. Village of Nyack, 1931, 141 Misc. 730, 252 N.Y.S. 746; Blanchard v. Wilt, 1963, 410 Pa. 356, 188 A.2d 722; Buckley v. Basford, D.Me.1960, 184 F.Supp. 870. This was the position taken by § 4 of the first Uniform Act, 9 U.L.A. 242.

82. See Larson, A Problem in Contribution: The Tortfeasor with an Individual Defense Against the Injured Party, [1940] Wis.L.Rev. 467. This was actually applied under the New Jersey statute in Judson v. Peoples Bank & Trust Co. of Westfield, 1954,

plaintiffs from accepting smaller settlements from one defendant. In either case both parties complain. For these reasons the current Uniform Act [83] has gone the whole length of holding that the release discharges the one to whom it is given from all liability for contribution.

8. Normally the apportionment of liability effected by contribution is on the basis that "equality is equity," which means that each tortfeasor is required ultimately to pay his pro rata share,[84] arrived at by dividing the damages by the number of tortfeasors. In some instances, as where the owner and the driver of a car are joined as defendants, equity may require treating the two together as liable for a single share,[85] or that the share of a tortfeasor who is insolvent or absent from the jurisdiction be borne by the others.[86]

In some jurisdictions, however, either by express provision of statute or by interpretation of it, the distribution of the liability is in proportion to the comparative fault of the defendants.[87]

51. INDEMNITY

There is an important distinction between contribution, which distributes the loss among the tortfeasors by requiring each to pay his proportionate share, and indemnity, which shifts the entire loss from one tortfeasor who has been compelled to pay it to the shoulders of another who should bear it instead.[88] The two are often confused, and there are many decisions in which indemnity has been allowed under the name of "contribution." [89] One of the common, and simple, bases for indemnity is a contract which provides for it.[90] The right to indemnity may, however, arise without agreement, and by operation of law to prevent a result which is regarded as unjust or unsatisfactory. Al-

17 N.J. 67, 110 A.2d 24, but was doubted on a second appeal in 1957, 25 N.J. 17, 134 A.2d 761. It remains, however, the New Jersey law. Theobald v. Angelos, 1965, 44 N.J. 228, 208 A.2d 129; see Note, 1966, 21 Rut.L.Rev. 130. See also the cases cited supra, p. 305, note 33.

83. Uniform Contribution Among Tortfeasors Act, 1955, § 4, 9 U.L.A.1961 Pocket Part 72. See also Levi v. Montgomery, N.D.1960, 120 N.W.2d 383; Pilosky v. Dougherty, E.D.Pa.1959, 179 F.Supp. 148; Augustin v. General Acc., Fire & Life Assur. Corp., 7 Cir. 1960, 283 F.2d 82; and cf. Tino v. Stout, 1967, 49 N.J. 289, 229 A.2d 793.

84. Early Settlers Ins. Co. v. Schweid, D.C.App.1966, 221 A.2d 920; Russell v. United States, D.Pa.1953, 113 F.Supp. 353; Hutcherson v. Slate, 1928, 105 W. Va. 184, 142 S.E. 444; Mulderig v. St. Louis, K. C. & C. R. Co., 1906, 116 Mo.App. 655, 94 S.W. 801. This is provided by the current Uniform Act, § 1(b), 9 U. L.A. 1961 Pocket Part, 68.

85. See for example Larsen v. Minneapolis Gas Co., 1968, 282 Minn. 135, 163 N.W.2d 755 (independent contractor); Ramirez v. Redevelopment Agency of City & County of San Francisco, 1970, 4 Cal.App. 3d 397, 84 Cal.Rptr. 356 (same); Bundy v. City of New York, 1965, 23 App.Div.2d 392, 261 N.Y.S.2d 221; Zeglen v. Minkiewicz, 1963, 12 N.Y.2d 497, 240 N.Y.S.2d 965, 191 N.E.2d 450 (master and servant); and cf. Wold v. Grozalsky, 1938, 277 N.Y. 364, 14 N.E.2d 437 (joint owners of building).

86. See Moody v. Kirkpatrick, M.D. Tenn. 1964, 234 F.Supp. 537; Judson v. Peoples Bank & Trust Co. of Westfield, 1957, 25 N.J. 17, 134 A.2d 761. See

Notes, 1958, 12 Rut.L.Rev. 533; 1934, 47 Harv.L. Rev. 209.

87. Bielski v. Schulze, 1962, 16 Wis.2d 1, 114 N.W.2d 105; Mitchell v. Branch, 1961, 45 Hawaii 128, 363 P.2d 969; Little v. Miles, 1948, 213 Ark. 725, 212 S. W.2d 935.

88. Well stated in McFall v. Compagnie Maritime Belge, 1952, 304 N.Y. 314, 107 N.E.2d 463.

89. See for example Horrabin v. City of Des Moines, 1924, 198 Iowa 549, 199 N.W. 988; Seaboard Air Line R. Co. v. American Dist. Elec. Protective Co., 1932, 106 Fla. 330, 143 So. 16; Preferred Acc. Ins. Co. v. Musante, Berman & Steinberg, 1947, 133 Conn. 536, 52 A.2d 862; Skala v. Lehon, 1931, 343 Ill. 602, 175 N.E. 832.

90. A contract agreeing to indemnify a party against the consequences of his own negligence is not against public policy. Southern Pac. Co. v. Morrison-Knudsen Co., 1959, 216 Or. 398, 338 P.2d 665; Indemnity Ins. Co. v. Koontz-Wagner Elec. Co., 7 Cir. 1956, 233 F.2d 380. But such a construction will not be put upon a contract unless it is very clearly intended. Barrus v. Wilkinson, 1965, 16 Utah 2d 204, 398 P.2d 207. An agreement of indemnity against intentional trespass has been held to be ineffective as against public policy. Pruet v. Dugger-Holmes & Associates, 1964, 276 Ala. 403, 162 So.2d 613.

though the ancient specious argument that the courts will not aid one tortfeasor against another because no one should be permitted to found a cause of action on his own wrong, would appear to apply quite as fully to indemnity as to contribution, the courts have been much more disposed to reject it where indemnity is involved.[91]

Thus it is generally agreed that there may be indemnity in favor of one who is held responsible solely by imputation of law because of his relation to the actual wrongdoer, as where an employer is vicariously liable for the tort of a servant [92] or an independent contractor; [93] or an innocent partner [94] or carrier [95] is held liable for the acts of another, or the owner of an automobile for the conduct of the driver.[96] Likewise where one is directed or employed by another [97] to do an act not manifestly wrong,[98] or is induced to act by the misrepresentations of the other,[99] he is uniformly entitled to indemnity when a third party recovers against him.

The principle is not, however, limited to those who are personally free from fault. A similar rule has been applied to indemnity against a supplier of goods when a retail-

---

91. See Davis, Indemnity Between Negligent Tortfeasors: A Proposed Rationale, 1952, 37 Iowa L. Rev. 517; Meriam and Thornton, Indemnity Between Tort-Feasors, 1950, 25 N.Y.U.L.Rev. 845; Leflar, Contribution and Indemnity Between Tortfeasors, 1932, 81 U.Pa.L.Rev. 130; Cohlen, Contribution and Indemnity Between Tortfeasors, 1936, 21 Corn.L.Q. 552, 1937, 22 Corn.L.Q. 469; Shark, Common Law Indemnity Among Joint Tortfeasors, 1965, 7 Ariz.L.Rev. 59; Note, 1966, 33 Tenn.L.Rev. 184.

92. Canadian Indem. Co. v. United States Fid. & Guar. Co., 9 Cir. 1954, 213 F.2d 658; Thomas v. Malco Refineries, 10 Cir. 1954, 214 F.2d 884; American Southern Ins. Co. v. Dime Taxi Service, 1963, 275 Ala. 51, 151 So.2d 783; McLaughlin v. Siegel, 1936, 166 Va. 374, 185 S.E. 873; Skala v. Lehon, 1931, 343 Ill. 602, 175 N.E. 832; Restatement of Restitution, § 96. See Jolowicz, The Right to Indemnity Between Master and Servant, [1956] Camb.L.J. 100.

This has been vigorously attacked as subverting the policy behind respondeat superior. Steffen, The Employer's "Indemnity" Action, 1958, 25 U.Chi.L. Rev. 465; Williams, Vicarious Liability and the Master's Indemnity, 1957, 20 Mod.L.Rev. 220; James, Contribution, Indemnity and Subrogation, and the Efficient Distribution of Accident Losses, 1958, 21 NACCA L.J. 360, 369; Note, 1954, 63 Yale L.J. 570. In United States v. Gilman, 1953, 347 U. S. 507, it was held that the United States, held liable under the Federal Tort Claims Act, had no right to indemnity. See, however, McCrary v. United States, D.Tenn.1964, 235 F.Supp. 33; Gahagan v. State Farm Mut. Auto Ins. Co., D.La.1964, 233 F.Supp. 171.

93. Tipaldi v. Riverside Memorial Chapel, 1948, 273 App.Div. 414, 78 N.Y.S.2d 12, motion denied 297 N. Y.S.2d 1029, 80 N.E.2d 544, affirmed, 298 N.Y. 686, 82 N.E.2d 585; Waylander-Peterson Co. v. Great Northern Ry. Co., 8 Cir. 1953, 201 F.2d 408; George

A. Fuller Co. v. Otis Elevator Co., 1918, 245 U.S. 489; Standard Oil Co. v. Robins Dry Dock & Repair Co., 2 Cir. 1929, 32 F.2d 182; Griffiths & Son Co. v. National Fireproofing Co., 1923, 310 Ill. 331, 141 N.E. 739.

94. Farney v. Hauser, 1921, 109 Kan. 75, 198 P. 178; In re Ryan's Estate, 1914, 157 Wis. 576, 147 N.W. 993; Smith v. Ayrault, 1888, 71 Mich. 475, 39 N.W. 724.

95. Joest v. Clarendon & Rosedale Packet Co., 1916, 122 Ark. 353, 183 S.W. 759; Produce Trading Co. v. Norfolk Southern R. Co., 1919, 178 N.C. 175, 100 S. E. 316; Orlove v. Philippine Air Lines, 2 Cir.1958, 257 F.2d 384; Merchant Shippers Ass'n v. Kellogg Express & Draying Co., 1946, 28 Cal.2d 594, 170 P. 2d 923.

96. Fontainebleau Hotel Corp. v. Postol, Fla.App. 1962, 142 So.2d 299; Lunderberg v. Bierman, 1954, 241 Minn. 349, 63 N.W.2d 355; Traub v. Dinzler, 1955, 309 N.Y. 395, 131 N.E.2d 564. Compare, as to an original tortfeasor held liable for the negligence of a physician treating the victim, Herrero v. Atkinson, 1964, 227 Cal.App.2d 69, 38 Cal.Rptr. 490; Musco v. Conte, 1964, 22 App.Div.2d 121, 254 N.Y.S. 2d 589.

97. Horrabin v. City of Des Moines, 1924, 198 Iowa 549, 199 N.W. 988; Oats v. Dublin Nat. Bank, 1936, 127 Tex. 2, 90 S.W.2d 824; Culmer v. Wilson, 1896, 13 Utah 129, 44 P. 833; Aberdeen Const. Co. v. City of Aberdeen, 1915, 84 Wash. 429, 147 P. 2; Higgins v. Russo, 1899, 72 Conn. 238, 43 A. 1050.

98. Plasikowski v. Arbus, 1919, 92 Conn. 556, 103 A. 642; Cox v. Cameron Lumber Co., 1905, 39 Wash. 562, 82 P. 116. Cf. Russell v. Walker, 1890, 150 Mass. 531, 23 N.E. 383 (sheriff attaching wrong goods).

99. Kennedy v. Colt, 1959, 216 Or. 647, 339 P.2d 450; Philadelphia, B. & W. R. Co. v. Roberts, 1919, 134 Md. 308, 106 A. 615; Henderson v. Sevey, 1822, 2 Greenl., Me., 139. Otherwise where he was not entitled to rely on the representation. Trimble v. Exchange Bank, 1901, 23 Ky.L.Rep. 367, 62 S.W. 1027.

er [1] or user [2] of the goods incurs liability by reason of negligent reliance upon his proper care. The same is true where the owner of a building negligently relies upon a contractor who makes improvements or repairs.[3] Again, it is quite generally agreed that there may be indemnity in favor of one who was under only a secondary duty where another was primarily responsible, as where a municipal corporation, held liable for failure to keep its streets in safe condition, seeks recovery from the person who has created the condition, or a property owner who has permitted it; [4] or an owner of land held liable for injury received upon it sues the wrongdoer who created the hazard.[5]

There is in addition considerable language in the cases to the effect that one whose negligence has consisted of mere passive neglect may have indemnity from an active wrongdoer.[6] Where this has validity, it appears to be in situations where one tortfeasor, by his active conduct, has created a danger to the plaintiff, and the other has merely failed to discover or to remedy it. Certainly there is no general principle that one who has failed to turn on the lights on a parked automobile is entitled to indemnity against a driver who runs into it and injures his passenger.

Carrying this to a possible logical conclusion, it has been suggested [7] that one who is liable merely for ordinary negligence should have indemnity from another who has been guilty of intentionally wrongful or reckless conduct. There is, however, no visible support for such a proposition, other than the obvious fact that there can be no indemnity in favor of the intentional or reckless tortfeasor himself; [8] and it has been firmly re-

---

1. Tromza v. Tecumseh Products Co., 3 Cir. 1967, 378 F.2d 601; Frank R. Jelleff, Inc. v. Pollak Bros., N. D.Ind. 1959, 171 F.Supp. 467; Popkin Bros. v. Volk's Tire Co., 1941, 20 N.J.Misc. 1, 23 A.2d 162; Busch & Latta Paint Co. v. Woermann Const. Co., 1925, 310 Mo. 419, 276 S.W. 614; Farr v. Armstrong Rubber Co., 1970, —— Minn. ——, 179 N.W.2d 64. See Degnan and Barton, Vouching to Quality Warranty: Case Law and Commercial Code, 1963, 51 Cal.L.Rev. 471.

2. Allied Mut. Cas. Corp. v. General Motors Corp., 10 Cir. 1960, 279 F.2d 455; Blair v. Cleveland Twist Drill Co., 7 Cir. 1952, 197 F.2d 842; Crouse v. Wilbur-Ellis Co., 1954, 77 Ariz. 359, 272 P.2d 352; McFall v. Compagnie Maritime Belge, 1952, 304 N.Y. 314, 107 N.E.2d 463; Peters v. Lyons, 1969, —— Iowa ——, 168 N.W.2d 759.

3. Bethlehem Shipbuilding Corp. v. Joseph Gutradt Co., 9 Cir. 1926, 10 F.2d 769; Pennsylvania Steel Co. v. Washington & Berkeley Bridge Co., D.W.Va. 1912, 194 F. 1011; Georgia Power Co. v. Banning Cotton Mills Co., 1931, 42 Ga.App. 671, 157 S.E. 525; Barb v. Farmers Ins. Exchange, Mo. 1955, 281 S.W.2d 297; Bond v. Otis Elevator Co., Tex. 1965, 388 S.W.2d 681, on remand Tex.Civ.App., 391 S.W. 2d 519.

4. City & County of San Francisco v. Ho Sing, Cal. App. 1958, 323 P.2d 1054, replaced by, 1958, 51 Cal. 2d 127, 330 P.2d 802 (long list of cases); Washington Gaslight Co. v. District of Columbia, 1895, 161 U.S. 316; City of Des Moines v. Barnes, 1947, 238 Iowa 1192, 30 N.W.2d 170; City of Fort Scott v. Pen Lucric-Oil Co., 1927, 122 Kan. 369, 252 P. 268; Township of Hart v. Noret, 1916, 191 Mich. 427, 158 N.W. 17.

5. Preferred Acc. Ins. Co. v. Musante, Berman & Steinberg, 1947, 133 Conn. 536, 52 A.2d 862; Middlesboro Home Tel. Co. v. Louisville & N. R. Co., 1926, 214 Ky. 822, 284 S.W. 104; Eureka Coal Co.

v. Louisville & N. R. Co., 1929, 219 Ala. 286, 122 So. 169; cf. United States v. Chicago, R. I. & P. R. Co., 10 Cir. 1949, 171 F.2d 377.

6. Chicago G. W. Ry. Co. v. Casura, 8 Cir. 1956, 234 F.2d 441; Western Cas. & Surety Co. v. Shell Oil Co., Mo.App. 1967, 413 S.W.2d 550; Jackson v. Associated Dry Goods Corp., 1963, 13 N.Y.2d 112, 242 N.Y.S.2d 210, 192 N.E.2d 167; Daly v. Bergstedt, 1964, 267 Minn. 244, 126 N.W.2d 242; D'Amico v. Moriarty Meat Co., 1964, 47 Ill.App.2d 63, 197 N.E. 2d 445. See Notes, 1960, 28 Ford.L.Rev. 782; 1966, 30 Mo.L.Rev. 624.

Otherwise where there is more than mere failure to discover. Kenyon v. F. M. C. Corp., 1970, 286 Minn. 283, 176 N.W.2d 69.

The converse is sometimes stated: no indemnity when plaintiff's active negligence contributed to the injury. Spivack v. Hara, 1966, 69 Ill.App.2d 22, 216 N. E.2d 173; Campbell v. Preston, Mo.1964, 379 S.W. 2d 557; Miller v. Pennsylvania R. Co., 2 Cir. 1956, 236 F.2d 295; Public Service Elec. & Gas Co. v. Waldroup, 1955, 38 N.J.Super. 419, 119 A.2d 172. See, however, Seiden v. Savings & Loan Ass'n, 1958, 10 Misc.2d 720, 172 N.Y.S.2d 403, still allowing recovery on the basis of a difference in degree.

7. Keeton, Contribution and Indemnity Among Tortfeasors, 1960, 27 Ins.Counsel J. 630, 631.

8. Cf. Padgett v. Boswell, Tex.Civ.App.1952, 250 S. W.2d 234.

jected when the question has arisen.[9] Finally, it has even been held that the doctrine of the last clear chance [10] is to be applied to permit indemnity for the earlier liability against the later.[11] It is difficult to see any logical reason why the mere difference in time which is the basis of the last clear chance rule should lead to any such conclusion as to liability between the tortfeasors themselves.

Out of all this, it is extremely difficult to state any general rule or principle as to when indemnity will be allowed and when it will not.[12] It has been said that it is permitted only where the indemnitor has owed a duty of his own to the indemnitee; [13] that it is based on a "great difference" in the gravity of the fault of the two tortfeasors; [14] or that

it rests upon a disproportion or difference in character of the duties owed by the two to the injured plaintiff.[15] Probably none of these is the complete answer, and, as is so often the case in the law of torts, no one explanation can be found which will cover all of the cases. Indemnity is a shifting of responsibility from the shoulders of one person to another; and the duty to indemnify will be recognized in cases where community opinion would consider that in justice the responsibility should rest upon one rather than the other. This may be because of the relation of the parties to one another, and the consequent duty owed; or it may be because of a significant difference in the kind or quality of their conduct.

52. APPORTIONMENT OF DAMAGES

Once it is determined that the defendant's conduct has been a cause of some damage suffered by the plaintiff, a further question may arise as to the portion of the total damage sustained which may properly be assigned to the defendant, as distinguished from other causes. The question is primarily not one of the fact of causation, but of the feasibility and practical convenience of splitting up the total harm into separate parts which may be attributed to each of two or more causes.[16] Where a logical basis can be found for some rough practical apportionment, which limits a defendant's liability to that part of the harm which he has in fact caused, it may be expected that the division

9. Jacobs v. General Acc., Fire & Life Assur. Corp., 1961, 14 Wis.2d 1, 109 N.W.2d 462; Panasuk v. Seaton, D.Mont.1968, 277 F.Supp. 979. Cf. Warner v. Capital Transit Co., D.D.C.1958, 162 F.Supp. 253 (contribution, but not indemnity, when one of the defendants violated carrier's higher duty of care). Contrary to this last case is United Airlines, Inc. v. Wiener, 9 Cir. 1964, 335 F.2d 379, cert. dismissed, 1965, 379 U.S. 951.

10. See infra, § 66.

11. Nashua Iron & Steel Co. v. Worcester & N. R. Co., 1882, 62 N.H. 159; Colorado & S. R. Co. v. Western Light & Power Co., 1923, 73 Colo. 107, 214 P. 30; Knippenberg v. Lord & Taylor, 1920, 193 App.Div. 753, 184 N.Y.S. 785; Eastern Texas Electric Co. v. Joiner, Tex.Civ.App.1930, 27 S.W.2d 917. Cf. Parchefsky v. Kroll Bros., 1935, 267 N.Y. 410, 196 N.E. 308.

12. Two careful attempts at analysis of indemnity are Hendrickson v. Minnesota Power & Light Co., 1960, 258 Minn. 368, 104 N.W.2d 843, and Jacobs v. General Accident, Fire & Life Assur. Corp., 1961, 14 Wis.2d 1, 109 N.W.2d 462. Both arrived at a brief list, similar to the foregoing.

As in the case of contribution, indemnity is not allowed against one who has a defense, such as family immunity, against the original plaintiff. Chamberlain v. McCleary, E.D.Tenn.1963, 217 F.Supp. 591.

13. Humble Oil & Ref. Co. v. Martin, 1949, 148 Tex. 175, 222 S.W.2d 995.

14. See United Air Lines v. Wiener, 9 Cir. 1964, 335 F.2d 379, cert. dismissed, 1965, 379 U.S. 951; Slattery v. Marra Bros., 2 Cir. 1951, 186 F.2d 134, cert. denied 341 U.S. 915; Atchison, T. & S. F. R. Co. v. Lan Franco, 1968, 267 Cal.App.2d 881, 73 Cal.Rptr. 660.

15. Davis, Indemnity Between Negligent Tortfeasors: A Proposed Rationale, 1952, 37 Iowa L.Rev. 517.

16. See Prosser, Joint Torts and Several Liability, 1937, 25 Cal.L.Rev. 413; Jackson, Joint Torts and Several Liability, 1939, 17 Tex.L.Rev. 399; Conant, Recent Developments in Joint and Several Tort Liability, 1962, 14 Baylor L.Rev. 421. An analogy may be suggested to the problem of splitting a cause of action against a single defendant, in the pleading cases. See Clark, Code Pleading, 1928, 84; McCaskill, The Elusive Cause of Action, 1937, 4 U. Chi.L.Rev. 281; Gavit, The Code Cause of Action, 1930, 30 Col.L.Rev. 802; Harris, What is a Cause of Action, 1928, 16 Cal.L.Rev. 459.

will be made. Where no such basis can be found, and any division must be purely arbitrary, there is no practical course except to hold the defendant for the entire loss, notwithstanding the fact that other causes have contributed to it.

The distinction is one between injuries which are reasonably capable of being divided, and injuries which are not. If two defendants, struggling for a single gun, succeed in shooting the plaintiff, there is no logical or reasonable basis for dividing the injury between them, and each will be liable for all of it. If they shoot him independently, with separate guns, and he dies from the effect of both wounds, there can still be no division, for death cannot be divided or apportioned except by an arbitrary rule devised for that purpose.[17] If they merely inflict separate wounds, and he survives, a basis for division exists, because it is possible to regard the two wounds as separate injuries;[18] and the same is of course true as to wounds negligently inflicted.[19] There will be obvious difficulties of proof as to the apportionment of certain elements of damages, such as physical and mental suffering and medical expenses, but such difficulties are not insuperable, and it is better to attempt some rough divi-

sion than to hold one defendant for the wound inflicted by the other. Upon the same basis, if two defendants each pollute a stream with oil, it is possible to say that each has interfered to a separate extent with the plaintiff's rights in the water, and to make some division of the damages.[20] It is not possible if the oil is ignited, and burns the plaintiff's barn.[21]

In general, it may be said that entire liability will be imposed only where there is no reasonable alternative. Each case must turn upon its own particular facts; but it is possible to make a classification of the more common types of situations.[22]

Concerted Action

Where two or more persons act in concert, it is well settled both in criminal[23] and in civil cases that each will be liable for the entire result.[24] Such concerted wrongdoers were

---

17. Cf. Wilson v. State, Tex.Cr.1893, 24 S.W. 409; People v. Lewis, 1899, 124 Cal. 551, 57 P. 470; Thompson v. Louisville & N. R. Co., 1890, 91 Ala. 496, 8 So. 406; Hawkes v. Goll, 1939, 256 App.Div. 940, 9 N.Y.S.2d 924, appeal granted, 1939, 256 App. Div. 1002, 11 N.Y.S.2d 556, affirmed, 1940, 281 N.Y. 808, 24 N.E.2d 484. Upon the same basis. it has been held that insanity cannot be apportioned among several causes. Rooney v. New York, N. H. & H. R. Co., 1899, 173 Mass. 222, 53 N.E. 435.

18. Le Laurin v. Murray, 1905, 75 Ark. 232, 87 S.W. 131; Schafer v. Ostmann, 1910, 148 Mo.App. 644, 129 S.W. 63; Albrecht v. St. Hedwig's Roman Catholic Ben. Soc., 1919, 205 Mich. 395, 171 N.W. 461.

19. McAllister v. Pennsylvania R. Co., 1936, 324 Pa. 65, 187 A. 415; Meier v. Holt, 1956, 347 Mich. 430, 80 N.W.2d 207; Hughes v. Great Am. Indem. Co., 5 Cir. 1956, 236 F.2d 71, cert. denied 352 U.S. 989; Corbett v. Clarke, 1948, 187 Va. 222, 46 S.E.2d 327; De Witt v. Gerard, 1936, 274 Mich. 299, 264 N.W. 379.

20. Watson v. Pyramid Oil Co., 1923, 198 Ky. 135, 248 S.W. 227; Snavely v. City of Goldendale, 1941, 10 Wash.2d 453, 117 P.2d 221; Farley v. Crystal Coal & Coke Co., 1920, 85 W.Va. 595, 102 S.E. 265; Johnson v. City of Fairmont, 1933, 188 Minn. 451, 247 N.W. 572.

21. Northup v. Eakes, 1918, 72 Okl. 66, 178 P. 266; Phillips Petroleum Co. v. Vandergriff, 1942, 190 Okl. 280, 122 P.2d 1020. Accord, as to poisoning livestock, Tidal Oil Co. v. Pease, 1931, 153 Okl. 137, 5 P.2d 389; as to damage to crops, Phillips Petroleum Co. v. Hardee, 5 Cir. 1951, 189 F.2d 205; Robillard v. Selah-Moxee Irr. Dist., 1959, 54 Wash.2d 582, 343 P.2d 565. Cf. Neville v. Mitchell, 1902, 28 Tex.Civ.App. 89, 66 S.W. 579 (illness resulting from nuisance). On this basis Griffith v. Kerrigan, 1952, 109 Cal.App.2d 637, 241 P.2d 296, where water damaged fruit trees, appears wrongly decided.

22. See Prosser, Joint Torts and Several Liability. 1937, 25 Cal.L.Rev. 413; Notes, 1924, 24 Col.L.Rev. 891; 1931, 19 Cal.L.Rev. 630; 1937, 21 Minn.L.Rev. 616.

23. Sir Charles Stanley's Case, 1663, Kel. 86, 84 Eng.Rep. 1094; State v. Newberg, 1929, 129 Or. 564, 278 P. 568.

24. Garrett v. Garrett, 1948, 228 N.C. 530, 46 S.E.2d 302; Wrabek v. Suchomel, 1920, 145 Minn. 468, 177 N.W. 764; Bunker Hill & Sullivan Min. & Con. Co. v. Polak, 9 Cir. 1925, 7 F.2d 583, cert. denied 269 U.S. 581; Oliver v. Miles. 1926, 144 Miss. 852, 110 So. 666; Bobich v. Dackow, 1929, 229 Ky. 830, 18 S.W.2d 280. See also the amusing opinion of Min-

considered "joint tort feasors" by the early common law.[25] In legal contemplation, there is a joint enterprise, and a mutual agency, so that the act of one is the act of all,[26] and liability for all that is done must be visited upon each. It follows that there is no logical basis upon which the jury may be permitted to apportion the damages.[27]

Vicarious Liability

The liability of a master for the acts of his servant,[28] or that of a principal for those of his agent,[29] within the scope of the employment or agency, stands upon much the same footing. Under the doctrine of respondeat superior,[30] the master becomes responsible for the same act for which the servant is liable, and for the same consequences. Again there is no logical basis for any division of damages between the two.[31]

Common Duty

Two defendants may be under a similar duty to exercise care to prevent a particular occurrence. The most obvious illustration is the case of the fall of a party wall, which each of two adjoining landowners was re-

quired to maintain.[32] So likewise two or more defendants may each be under an obligation to keep the same railway track[33] or highway[34] in repair. When both defendants fail to perform their obligation, and harm results, each will be liable for the event; and here likewise there is no reasonable basis for any division of damages.

Single Indivisible Result

Certain results, by their very nature, are obviously incapable of any logical, reasonable, or practical division. Death is such a result,[35] and so is a broken leg or any single wound, the destruction of a house by fire, or the sinking of a barge.[36] No ingenuity can suggest anything more than a purely arbitrary apportionment of such harm. Where two or more causes combine to produce such a single result, incapable of any logical division, each may be a substantial factor in bringing about the loss, and if so, each must

turn, J., in Tricoli v. Centalanza, 1924, 100 N.J.L. 231, 126 A. 214, affirmed, 1925, 101 N.J.L. 570, 129 A. 923.

25. As to joinder of defendants in one action, and the meaning of "concert", see supra, § 46.

26. "* * * all coming to do an unlawful act, and of one party, the act of one is the act of all of the same party being present." Sir John Heydon's Case, 1613, 11 Co.Rep. 5, 77 Eng.Rep. 1150.

27. See Note, 1928, 14 Va.L.Rev. 677.

28. Schumpert v. Southern R. Co., 1903, 65 S.C. 332, 43 S.E. 813; Mayberry v. Northern Pac. R. Co., 1907, 100 Minn. 79, 110 N.W. 356; Verlinda v. Stone & Webster Eng. Corp., 1911, 44 Mont. 223, 119 P. 573; Allen v. Trester, 1924, 112 Neb. 515, 199 N. W. 841.

29. Bradford v. Brock, 1934, 140 Cal.App. 47, 34 P.2d 1048 (statutory agency); Tucker v. Cole, 1882, 54 Wis. 539, 11 N.W. 703 (partnership).

30. See infra, § 70.

31. As to joinder of defendants and contradictory verdicts, see supra, § 47.

32. Johnson v. Chapman. 1897, 43 W.Va. 639, 28 S.E. 744; Klauder v. McGrath, 1860, 35 Pa. 128; Simmons v. Everson, 1891, 124 N.Y. 319, 26 N.E. 911.

33. Lindsay v. Acme Cement Plaster Co., 1922, 220 Mich. 367, 190 N.W. 275; Wisconsin Cent. R. Co. v. Ross, 1892, 142 Ill. 9, 31 N.E. 412; Schaffer v. Pennsylvania R. Co., 7 Cir. 1939, 101 F.2d 369; cf. Galveston, H. & S. A. R. Co. v. Nass, 1900, 94 Tex. 255, 59 S.W. 870; Hoye v. Great Northern R. Co., C.C.Mont.1903, 120 F. 712.

34. Doeg v. Cook, 1899, 126 Cal. 213, 58 P. 707. Cf. Walton, Witten & Graham Co. v. Miller's Adm'x, 1909, 109 Va. 210, 63 S.E. 458 (employer and contractor both under duty to warn of blasting); Nelson v. Illinois Cent. R. Co., 1910, 98 Miss. 295, 53 So. 619 (railroad and Pullman company liable for loss of baggage); Woods v. Kansas City, K. V. & W. R. Co., 1932, 134 Kan. 755, 8 P.2d 404; Economy Light & Power Co. v. Hiller, 1903, 203 Ill. 518, 68 N.E. 72.

35. Blanton v. Sisters of Charity, 1948, 82 Ohio App. 20, 79 N.E.2d 688; Bolick v. Gallagher, 1955, 268 Wis. 421, 67 N.W.2d 860; Hackworth v. Davis, 1964, 87 Idaho 98, 390 P.2d 422.

36. Cf. Brown v. Murdy, 1960, 78 S.D. 367, 102 N.W. 2d 664 (loss of foot through negligence of two physicians); Watts v. Smith, 1965, 375 Mich. 120, 134 N.W.2d 194 (morning and afternoon accidents causing indivisible injury). But see, as to the possibility of a division on the basis of potential damage from the earlier cause, infra, p. 321.

be charged with all of it. Here again the typical case is that of two vehicles which collide and injure a third person.[37] The duties which are owed to the plaintiff by the defendants are separate, and may not be identical in character or scope,[38] but entire liability rests upon the obvious fact that each has contributed to the single result, and that no rational division can be made.[39]

Such entire liability is imposed both where some of the causes are innocent, as where a fire set by the defendant is carried by a wind,[40] and where two or more of the causes are culpable. It is imposed where either cause would have been sufficient in itself to bring about the result, as in the case of merg-

ing fires which burn a building,[41] and also where both were essential to the injury, as in the vehicle collision suggested above.[42] It is not necessary that the misconduct of two defendants be simultaneous. One defendant may create a situation upon which the other may act later to cause the damage. One may leave combustible material, and the other set it afire;[43] one may leave a hole in the street, and the other drive into it.[44] Liability in such a case is not a matter of causation, but of the effect of the intervening agency upon culpability.[45] If a defend-

---

37. See Arnst v. Estes, 1939, 136 Me. 272, 8 A.2d 201 (stating clearly that entire liability rests upon the absence of any logical basis for apportionment). Also Schools v. Walker, 1948, 187 Va. 619, 47 S.E.2d 418; Way v. Waterloo, C. F. & N. R. Co., 1947, 239 Iowa 244, 29 N.W.2d 867; Nees v. Minneapolis St. R. Co., 1944, 218 Minn. 532, 16 N.W.2d 755. Cf. Crowe v. Domestic Loans, Inc., 1963, 242 S.C. 310, 130 S.E.2d 845 (procuring discharge of employee).

38. In Matthews v. Delaware, L. & W. R. Co., 1893, 56 N.J.L. 34, 27 A. 919, and Carlton v. Boudar, 1916, 118 Va. 521, 88 S.E. 174, the court specifically held this to be immaterial.

39. Except in Kentucky, where an unusual statute permits but does not require the jury to apportion the damages arbitrarily. Elpers v. Kimbel, Ky. 1963, 366 S.W.2d 157; Note, 1960, 48 Ky.L.J. 606. This has been carried to the length of permitting apportionment of damages between two defendants held liable for deceit. Evola Realty Co. v. Westerfield, Ky.1952, 251 S.W.2d 298.

In Rourk v. Selvey, 1968, 252 S.C. 25, 164 S.E.2d 909, The court overruled a line of South Carolina cases which had permitted the jury to do the same thing.

40. Haverly v. State Line & S. R. Co., 1890, 135 Pa. 50, 19 A. 1013. Cf. Holter Hardware Co. v. Western Mortgage & Warranty Title Co., 1915, 51 Mont. 94, 149 P. 489; Long v. Crystal Refrigerator Co., 1938, 134 Neb. 44, 277 N.W. 830; Jackson v. Wisconsin Tel. Co., 1894, 88 Wis. 243, 60 N.W. 430 (lightning); Fox v. Boston & Me. R. Co., 1889, 148 Mass. 220, 19 N.E. 222 (frost).

Obviously only culpable causes will be held responsible. Thus where a negligent automobile driver collides with an innocent one and injures a third person, only the negligent driver is liable.

41. Anderson v. Minneapolis, St. P. & S. S. M. R. Co., 1920, 146 Minn. 430, 179 N.W. 45; Seckerson v. Sinclair, 1913, 24 N.D. 625, 140 N.W. 239; Miller v. Northern Pac. R. Co., 1913, 24 Idaho 567, 135 P. 845. Cf. Oulighan v. Butler, 1905, 189 Mass. 287, 75 N.E. 726; Orton v. Virginia Carolina Chemical Co., 1918, 142 La. 790, 77 So. 632; Luengene v. Consumers' Light, Heat & Power Co., 1912, 86 Kan. 866, 122 P. 1032.

42. Washington & Georgetown R. Co. v. Hickey, 1897, 166 U.S. 521 (horse car driven onto railway tracks with negligent operation of crossing gates); Folsom v. Apple River Log-Driving Co., 1877, 41 Wis. 602 (dam and bridge causing flood); Drown v. New England Telephone & Telegraph Co., 1907, 80 Vt. 1, 66 A. 801 (light wires and telephone wires crossed); Ramsey v. Carolina-Tennessee Power Co., 1928, 195 N.C. 788, 143 S.E. 861 (railway shunting cars which struck negligently maintained power line pole); Barnes v. Masterson, 1899, 38 App.Div. 612, 56 N.Y.S. 939 (defendants successively deposited sand against plaintiff's wall, which collapsed).

43. Johnson v. Chicago, M. & St. P. R. Co., 1883, 31 Minn. 57, 16 N.W. 488. Cf. Watson v. Kentucky & Ind. Bridge & R. Co., 1910, 137 Ky. 619, 126 S.W. 146, 129 S.W. 341 (defendant flooded vicinity with gasoline, another person struck a match); Oviatt v. Garretson, 1943, 205 Ark. 792, 171 S.W.2d 287 (one defendant burned leaves, another drove into smoke pall).

44. Tobin v. City of Seattle, 1923, 127 Wash. 644, 221 P. 583. Cf. Ethridge v. Nicholson, 1950, 80 Ga.App. 693, 57 S.E.2d 231 (dog chasing boy on bicycle into obstruction in street); Stemmler v. City of Pittsburgh, 1926, 287 Pa. 365, 135 A. 100 (defective street and cyclist splashing mud); Butts v. Ward, 1938, 227 Wis. 387, 279 N.W. 6 (truck parked without lights and negligently driven car); Hill v. Edmonds, 1966, 26 A.D.2d 554, 270 N.Y.S.2d 1020 (same).

45. See supra, § 45.

ant is liable at all, he will be liable for all the damage caused.[46]

Damage of Same Kind Capable of Apportionment

Certain other results, by their nature, are more capable of apportionment. If two defendants independently shoot the plaintiff at the same time, and one wounds him in the arm and the other in the leg, the ultimate result may be a badly damaged plaintiff in the hospital, but it is still possible, as a practical matter, to regard the two wounds as separate wrongs.[47] Mere coincidence in time does not make the two one tort, nor does similarity of design or conduct, without concert.[48] Evidence may be entirely lacking upon which to apportion some elements of the damages, such as medical expenses, or permanent disability, or the plaintiff's pain and suffering; but this never has been regarded as sufficient reason to hold one defendant liable for the damage inflicted by the other.[49]

There have appeared in the decisions a number of similar situations, in some of which the extent of the harm inflicted by the separate torts has been almost incapable of any definite and satisfactory proof, and has been left merely to the jury's estimate. Thus the owners of trespassing cattle,[50] or of dogs

which together kill sheep,[51] are held liable only for the separate damage done by their own animals, unless there has been some concerted action, such as keeping the animals in a common herd.[52] Nuisance cases, in particular, have tended to result in apportionment of the damages, largely because the interference with the plaintiff's use of his land has tended to be severable in terms of quantity, percentage, or degree. Thus defendants who independently pollute the same stream,[53] or who flood the plaintiff's land from separate sources,[54] are liable only severally for the damages individually caused, and the same is

1904, 45 Or. 103, 76 P. 1079; Wood v. Snider, 1907, 187 N.Y. 28, 79 N.E. 858; Hill v. Chappel Bros. of Montana, 1933, 93 Mont. 92, 18 P.2d 1106. Cf. King v. Ruth, 1924, 136 Miss. 377, 101 So. 500.

51. Anderson v. Halverson, 1904, 126 Iowa 125, 101 N.W. 781; Nohre v. Wright, 1906, 98 Minn. 477, 108 N.W. 865; Stine v. McShane, 1927, 55 N.D. 745, 214 N.W. 906; Miller v. Prough, 1920, 203 Mo.App. 413, 221 S.W. 159.

In a number of states owners of dogs which kill sheep are made liable for the entire damage by statute. See Worcester County v. Ashworth, 1893, 160 Mass. 186, 35 N.E. 773; McAdams v. Sutton, 1873, 24 Ohio St. 333; Dole v. Hardinger, 1917, 204 Ill.App. 640.

52. Ushirohira v. Stuckey, 1921, 52 Cal.App. 526, 199 P. 339; Wilson v. White, 1906, 77 Neb. 351, 109 N.W. 367; cf. Stephens v. Schadler, 1919, 182 Ky. 833, 207 S.W. 704.

53. Chipman v. Palmer, 1879, 77 N.Y. 51; Johnson v. City of Fairmont, 1933, 188 Minn. 451, 247 N.W. 572; Farley v. Crystal Coal & Coke Co., 1920, 85 W.Va. 595, 102 S.E.2d 265; Somerset Villa, Inc. v. City of Lee's Summit, Mo.1969, 436 S.W.2d 658; Snavely v. City of Goldendale. 1941, 10 Wash.2d 453, 117 P.2d 221. See Note, 1953, 31 N.C.L.Rev. 237. As to indivisible consequences, see supra, p. 315.

54. Miller v. Highland Ditch Co., 1891, 87 Cal. 430, 23 P. 550; William Tackaberry Co. v. Sioux City Service Co., 1911, 154 Iowa 358, 132 N.W. 945, rehearing denied, 1912, 134 N.W. 1064; Verheyen v. Dewey, 1915, 27 Idaho 1, 146 P. 1116; Boulger v. Northern Pac. Ry. Co., 1918, 41 N.D. 316, 171 N.W. 632; Ryan Gulch Reservoir Co. v. Swartz, 1925, 77 Colo. 60, 234 P. 1059. Cf. Connor v. Grosso, 1953, 41 Cal.2d 229, 259 P.2d 435 (trespass by dumping earth), Wm. G. Roe & Co. v. Armour & Co., 5 Cir. 1969, 414 F.2d 862 (damages to citrus crop from two sources).

46. As to joinder of defendants and the possibility of contribution from one to the other, see infra, §§ 47, 50.

47. Le Laurin v. Murray, 1905, 75 Ark. 232, 87 S.W. 131; Albrecht v. St. Hedwig's Roman Catholic Ben. Soc., 1919, 205 Mich. 395, 171 N.W. 461; McAllister v. Pennsylvania R. Co., 1936, 324 Pa. 65, 187 A. 415; Corbett v. Clarke, 1948, 187 Va. 222, 46 S.E.2d 327; Phillips v. Gulf & South American S. S. Co., Tex.Civ.App.1959, 323 S.W.2d 631, error refused.

48. Dickson v. Yates, 1922, 194 Iowa 910, 188 N.W. 948 (battery and trespass at same time by different persons); Millard v. Miller, 1907, 39 Colo. 103, 88 P. 845 (independent appropriations of different parts of pasture).

49. As to joining defendants in one action, see supra, § 47.

50. Dooley v. Seventeen Thousand Five Hundred Head of Sheep, 1894, 4 Cal.Unrep. 479, 101 Cal. xvii, 35 P. 1011; Pacific Live Stock Co. v. Murray,

true as to nuisances due to noise,[55] or pollution of the air.[56] Perhaps the most extreme example is the case of separate repetitions of the same defamatory statement,[57] or separate acts which result in alienation of affections.[58] One may speculate that the effort to apportion the damages whenever some rational and possible basis could be found has been due in no small measure in the past to the lack of any rule of contribution if one tortfeasor should be compelled to pay the entire damages.

The same kind of apportionment is, however, entirely possible where some part of the damage may logically and conveniently be assigned to an innocent cause. Thus a defendant's dam or embankment might reasonably be expected to flood the plaintiff's property in the event of any ordinary rainfall, but a quite unprecedented and unforeseeable cloudburst may cause a flood similar in kind but far greater in extent. In such cases the weight of authority[59] holds that the defend-

ant is liable only for such portion of the total damage as may properly be attributed to his negligence—or in other words, the flood which would have resulted from his obstruction with an ordinary rain. A similar distinction has been made between damages which would have followed in any case from the defendant's reasonable conduct, and those in excess which may be attributed to his negligence,[60] and likewise between those damages caused by the defendant and those by the plaintiff himself.[61]

The difficulty of any complete and exact proof in assessing such separate damages has received frequent mention in all these cases, but it has not been regarded as sufficient justification for entire liability. The emphasis is placed upon the logical possibility of apportionment, and the distinct and separate invasion of the plaintiff's interests which may be attributed to each cause. The difficulty

55. Sherman Gas & Elec. Co. v. Belden, 1909, 103 Tex. 59, 123 S.W. 119; Neville v. Mitchell, 1902, 28 Tex.Civ.App. 89, 66 S.W. 579.

56. Swain v. Tennessee Copper Co., 1903, 111 Tenn. 430, 78 S.W. 93; Key v. Armour Fertilizer Works, 1916, 18 Ga.App. 472, 89 S.E. 593; O'Neal v. Southern Carbon Co., 1949, 216 La. 96, 43 So.2d 230.

57. Harriott v. Plimpton, 1896, 166 Mass. 585, 44 N. E. 992; Yocum v. Husted, 1918, 185 Iowa 119, 167 N.W. 663; Howe v. Bradstreet Co., 1911, 135 Ga. 564, 69 S.E. 1082; Hall v. Frankel, 1924, 183 Wis. 247, 197 N.W. 820.

58. Barton v. Barton, 1906, 119 Mo.App. 507, 94 S.W. 574; Heisler v. Heisler, 1911, 151 Iowa 503, 131 N. W. 676.

59. Radburn v. Fir Tree Lumber Co., 1915, 83 Wash. 643, 145 P. 632; McAdams v. Chicago, R. I. & P. R. Co., 1925, 200 Iowa 732, 205 N.W. 310; Rix v. Town of Alamogordo, 1938, 42 N.M. 325, 77 P.2d 765; Wilson v. Hagins, 1927, 116 Tex. 538, 295 S.W. 922; Brown v. Chicago, B. & Q. R. Co., D.Neb.1912, 195 F. 1007. See Notes, 1938, 23 Minn.L.Rev. 91; 1950, 15 Mo.L.Rev. 93.

§ 450 of the First Restatement of Torts, to the contrary, has been reversed by the Second Restatement, §§ 433A and 450. It was based on Elder v. Lykens Valley Coal Co., 1893, 157 Pa. 490, 27 A. 545.

60. Jenkins v. Pennsylvania R. Co., 1902, 67 N.J.L. 331, 51 A. 704 (smoke nuisance); Middleton v. Melbourne Tramway Co., 1913, 16 Comm.L.Rep. (Aust.) 572 (motorist hitting pedestrian).

61. Philadelphia & R. R. Co. v. Smith, 3 Cir. 1894, 64 F. 679; Bowman v. Humphrey, 1906, 132 Iowa 234, 109 N.W. 714; Randolf v. Town of Bloomfield, 1889, 77 Iowa 50, 41 N.W. 562; Walters v. Prairie Oil & Gas Co., 1922, 85 Okl. 77, 204 P. 906.

Compare also the cases where a separate part of the plaintiff's suffering or disability may be found to result from a pre-existing condition not caused by the defendant. Nelson v. Twin City Motor Bus Co., 1953, 239 Minn. 276, 58 N.W.2d 561; Gates v. Fleischer, 1886, 67 Wis. 504, 30 N.W. 674; Dallas Ry. & T. Co. v. Ector, Com.App.1938, 131 Tex. 505, 116 S.W.2d 683; Texas Coca Cola Bottling Co. v. Lovejoy, Tex.Civ.App.1940, 138 S.W.2d 254; Pittsburgh S. S. Co. v. Palo, 6 Cir. 1933, 64 F.2d 198; O'Keefe v. Kansas City Western R. Co., 1912, 87 Kan. 322, 124 P. 416. Cf. Gould v. McKenna, 1878, 86 Pa. 297 (part of flooding due to condition of wall).

Compare also the "last clear chance" cases, in which the plaintiff is struck by a vehicle because of his own negligence, but after he is helpless the defendant inflicts further injuries by negligent failure to stop the vehicle. Cleveland, C., C. & St. L. Ry. Co. v. Klee, 1900, 154 Ind. 430, 56 N.E. 234; Teakle v. San Pedro, L. A. & S. L. R. Co., 1907, 32 Utah 276, 90 P. 402; Weitzman v. Nassau Electric R. Co., 1898, 33 App.Div. 585, 53 N.Y.S. 905.

of proof may have been overstated. The courts necessarily have been very liberal in permitting the jury to award damages where the uncertainty as to their extent arises from the nature of the wrong itself, for which the defendant, and not the plaintiff, is responsible.[62] The requirements of proof usually have been somewhat relaxed in such cases, and it has been said that no very exact evidence will be required, and that general evidence as to the proportion in which the causes contributed to the result will be sufficient to support a verdict.[63] Cases are few in which recovery has actually been denied for lack of such proof.[64] As a last resort, in the absence of anything to the contrary, it has been presumed that certain causes are equally responsible, and the damages have been divided equally between them.[65] The difficulty is certainly no greater than in cases where part of the damage is to be attributed to the unreasonable conduct of the plaintiff himself, and the rule of avoidable consequences is applied to limit his recovery.[66]

There has remained, however, enough in the way of real difficulty experienced, and possible injustice feared, to lead several writers [67] to urge that in any case where two or more defendants are shown to have been negligent, and to have caused each some damage, and only the extent as to each is in question, the burden of proof should be shifted to the defendants, and each should be held liable to the extent that he cannot produce evidence to limit his liability. The justification for this rests upon the fact that a choice must be made, as to where the loss due to failure of proof shall fall, between an entirely innocent plaintiff and defendants who are clearly proved to have been at fault, and to have done him harm. A few courts have accepted this position, and have placed the burden of proof as to apportionment upon the defendants in such cases,[68] as for example where there are chain automobile collisions, and there is doubt as to the injuries inflicted by each driver.[69] Texas decisions [70] refusing to permit

---

62. Little Schuylkill Nav. R. & Coal Co. v. Richards' Adm'r, 1858, 57 Pa. 142; Jenkins v. Pennsylvania R. Co., 1902, 67 N.J.L. 331, 51 A. 704; Inland Power & Light Co. v. Grieger, 9 Cir. 1937, 91 F.2d 811; De Witt v. Gerard, 1936, 274 Mich. 299, 264 N.W. 379; Hughes v. Great Amer. Ind. Co., 5 Cir. 1956, 236 F.2d 71, cert. denied 352 U.S. 989.

63. Eckman v. Lehigh & Wilkes-Barre Coal Co., 1912, 50 Pa.Super. 427; William Tackaberry Co. v. Sioux City Service Co., 1911, 154 Iowa 358, 132 N.W. 945, 134 N.W. 1064; Miller v. Prough, 1920, 203 Mo.App. 413, 221 S.W. 159; Hill v. Chappel Bros. of Montana, 1933, 93 Mont. 92, 18 P.2d 1106; Sellick v. Hall, 1879, 47 Conn. 260.

64. The only cases found are Deutsch v. Connecticut Co., 1923, 98 Conn. 482, 119 A. 891; Maas v. Perkins, 1953, 42 Wash.2d 38, 253 P.2d 427; Slater v. Pacific American Oil Co., 1931, 212 Cal. 648, 300 P. 31; Tucker Oil Co. v. Matthews, Tex.Civ.App.1938, 119 S.W.2d 606. All of these cases are believed no longer to be law.

65. Wood v. Snider, 1907, 187 N.Y. 28, 79 N.E. 858; Anderson v. Halverson, 1904, 126 Iowa 125, 101 N.W. 781; Miller v. Prough, 1920, 203 Mo.App. 413, 221 S.W. 159; Powers v. Kindt, 1874, 13 Kan. 74.

66. Cf. Bowman v. Humphrey, 1906, 132 Iowa 234, 109 N.W. 714; Randolf v. Town of Bloomfield, 1889, 77 Iowa 50, 41 N.W. 562; Philadelphia &

R. Co. v. Smith, 3 Cir. 1894, 64 F. 679; Walters v. Prairie Oil & Gas Co., 1922, 85 Okl. 77, 204 P. 906.

67. Wigmore, Joint Tortfeasors and Severance of Damages, 1923, 17 Ill.L.Rev. 458; Carpenter, Workable Rules for Determining Proximate Cause, 1932, 20 Cal.L.Rev. 306, 406; Jackson, Joint Torts and Several Liability, 1939, 17 Tex.L.Rev. 399.

68. Phillips Petroleum Co. v. Hardee, 5 Cir. 1951, 189 F.2d 205 (pollution of irrigation waters); Finnegan v. Royal Realty Co., 1950, 35 Cal.2d 409, 218 P.2d 17 (aggravation of injuries from fire because of failure to provide exit doors); De Corsey v. Purex Corp., 1949, 92 Cal.App.2d 669, 207 P.2d 616 (aggravation of injuries from exploding bottle due to deterioration of compound); cf. Colonial Ins. Co. v. Industrial Acc. Comm'n, 1946, 29 Cal.2d 79, 172 P.2d 884 (workmen's compensation, with multiple insurance carriers).

69. Maddux v. Donaldson, 1961, 362 Mich. 425, 108 N.W.2d 33; Maroulis v. Elliot, 1966, 247 Va. 503, 151 S.E.2d 339; Holtz v. Holder, 1966, 101 Ariz. 247, 418 P.2d 584; Mathews v. Mills, 1970, —— Minn. ——, 178 N.W.2d 841; Ruud v. Grimm, 1961, 252 Iowa 1266, 110 N.W.2d 321. See Doyle, Multiple Causes and Apportionment of Damages, 1966, 43 Denv.L.Rev. 490; Notes, 1966, 44 N.C.L.Rev. 249; 1967, 9 Ariz.L.Rev. 129; 1967, 18 Syr.L.Rev. 898.

That there may be limitations on this is indicated by Loui v. Oakley, 1968, 50 Haw. 260, 272, 438 P.2d

apportionment because the injury is regarded as "indivisible" appear in reality to mean no more than that the defendants have the burden of proving any basis for division. There are even courts [71] which have placed upon the defendant the burden of apportionment where part of the damages have been due to an innocent cause. There are, however, some comparatively recent cases [72] which have rejected all idea of shifting the burden of proof to the defendant.

Successive Injuries

The damages may be conveniently severable in point of time. If two defendants, independently operating the same plant, pollute a stream over successive periods, it is clear that each has caused separate damage, limited in time, and that neither has any responsibility for the loss caused by the other.[73]

The same may be true where a workman's health is impaired by the negligence of successive employers,[74] and of course where successive batteries or other personal injuries are inflicted upon the plaintiff.[75]

It is important to note that there are situations in which the earlier wrongdoer will be liable for the entire damage, while the later one will not. If an automobile negligently driven by defendant A strikes the plaintiff, fractures his skull, and leaves him helpless on the highway, where shortly afterward a second automobile, negligently driven by defendant B, runs over him and breaks his leg, A will be liable for both injuries, for when the plaintiff was left in the highway, it was reasonably to be anticipated that a second car would run him down.[76] But defendant B should be liable only for the broken leg, since he had no part in causing the fractured skull, and could not foresee or avoid it.[77] On the

393, where plaintiff was injured in four different accidents, widely spaced over months, and it was considered unfair to hold one defendant liable for the consequences of all four.

As to the burden on defendants, when it is a question of all or nothing as to each, see supra, p. 243.

70. Landers v. East Texas Salt Water Disposal Co., 1952, 151 Tex. 251, 248 S.W.2d 731 (pollution); Burns v. Lamb, Tex.Civ.App.1958, 312 S.W.2d 730, ref. n. r. e. (same); Western Guaranty Loan Co. v. Dean, Tex.Civ.App.1958, 309 S.W.2d 857, ref. n. r. e. (mental distress at collection methods); Riley v. Industrial Finance Service Co., 1957, 157 Tex. 306, 302 S.W.2d 652 (same). See, as to this interpretation of these cases, Phillips v. Gulf & South American S. S. Co., Tex.Civ.App.1959, 323 S.W.2d 631, error refused.

71. City of Oakland v. Pacific Gas & Elec. Co., 1941, 47 Cal.App.2d 444, 118 P.2d 328 (increased damage to books from delay in shutting off steam); Newbury v. Vogel, 1962, 151 Colo. 520, 379 P.2d 811 (pre-existing diseased condition); Kawamoto v. Yasutake, 1966, 49 Haw. 42, 410 P.2d 976 (same); Wise v. Carter, Fla.App.1960, 119 So.2d 40 (prior injury). See Note, 1964, 43 N.C.L.Rev. 1011.

72. Panther Coal Co. v. Looney, 1946, 185 Va. 758, 40 S.E.2d 298; Grzybowski v. Connecticut Co., 1933, 116 Conn. 292, 164 A. 632; Maas v. Perkins, 1953, 42 Wash.2d 38, 253 P.2d 427; Sweet Milk Co. v. Stanfield, 9 Cir. 1965, 353 F.2d 811.

73. Midland Empire Packing Co. v. Yale Oil Corp., 1946, 119 Mont. 36, 169 P.2d 732; Coleman Vitrified

Brick Co. v. Smith, Tex.Civ.App.1915, 175 S.W. 860; Southern Iron & Steel Co. v. Acton, 1913, 8 Ala. App. 502, 62 So. 402; Freshwater v. Bulmer Rayon Co., [1933] Ch. 162.

74. McGannon v. Chicago & N. W. R. Co., 1924, 160 Minn. 143, 199 N.W. 894; cf. Pieczonka v. Pullman Co., 2 Cir. 1937, 89 F.2d 353. Contrast the interesting case of silicosis developed three years after the latter of two successive employments, in Golden v. Lerch Bros., 1938, 203 Minn. 211, 281 N.W. 249. The original opinion, holding each employer liable for the full damage on the ground that the injury could not be apportioned, was withdrawn on rehearing as not supported by sufficient evidence that one employer contributed substantially to the result, and remains unpublished. It is discussed in Note, 1937, 21 Minn.L.Rev. 616.

75. See cases cited supra, pp. 313–314.

76. Adams v. Parrish, 1920, 189 Ky. 628, 225 S.W. 467; Morrison v. Medaglia, 1934, 287 Mass. 46, 191 N.E. 133; Thornton v. Eneroth, 1934, 177 Wash. 1, 30 P.2d 951; Hill v. Peres, 1934, 136 Cal.App. 132, 28 P.2d 946.

77. Bowles v. Lindley, Tex.Civ.App.1967, 411 S.W.2d 751, refused n. r. e.; Grzybowski v. Connecticut Co., 1933, 116 Conn. 292, 164 A. 632; Frye v. City of Detroit, 1932, 256 Mich. 466, 239 N.W. 886; Ristan v. Frantzen, 1953, 26 N.J.Super. 225, 97 A.2d 726, affirmed, 1954, 14 N.J. 455, 102 A.2d 614;

same basis, an original wrongdoer may be liable for the additional damages inflicted by the negligent treatment of his victim by a physician,[78] while the physician will not be liable for the original injury.[79]

Potential Damage

Chief Justice Peaslee of New Hampshire, in an extremely interesting article,[80] pointed out that there are situations in which an apparently indivisible injury may be apportioned upon the basis of potential damage from one cause, which reduces the value of the loss inflicted by another. In the case which prompted the article,[81] a boy standing on the high beam of a bridge trestle lost his balance and started to fall to substantially certain death or serious injury far below. He came in contact with defendant's wires, and was electrocuted. The incipient fall was an accomplished fact before the defendant's negligence caused any harm at all. The court allowed damages only for such a sum as his prospects for life and health were worth when the defendant killed him.

Hughes v. Great American Ind. Co., 5 Cir. 1956, 236 F.2d 71, cert. denied 352 U.S. 989.

Compare, however, Gibson v. Bodley, 1943, 156 Kan. 338, 133 P.2d 112, where the events were treated as substantially simultaneous, and entire liability was found.

78. Thompson v. Fox, 1937, 326 Pa. 209, 192 A. 107; Aubuschon v. Witt, Mo.1967, 412 S.W.2d 136; Herrero v. Atkinson, 1964, 227 Cal.App.2d 69, 38 Cal. Rptr. 490; Sauter v. New York Cent. & H. R. R. Co., 1876, 66 N.Y. 50; Selleck v. City of Janesville, 1898, 100 Wis. 157, 75 N.W. 975.

79. See Viou v. Brooks-Scanlon Lumber Co., 1906, 99 Minn. 97, 108 N.W. 891; Pederson v. Eppard, 1930, 181 Minn. 47, 231 N.W. 393; Staehlin v. Hochdoerfer, Mo.1921, 235 S.W. 1060; Pedigo & Pedigo v. Croom, Tex.Civ.App.1931, 37 S.W.2d 1074; Notes, 1929, 29 Col.L.Rev. 630; 1933, 18 Corn.L.Q. 257.

80. Peaslee, Multiple Causation and Damage, 1934, 47 Harv.L.Rev. 1127. See also, adopting opposing views, Carpenter, Concurrent Causation, 1935, 83 U.Pa.L.Rev. 941.

81. Dillon v. Twin State Gas & Elec. Co., 1932, 85 N.H. 449, 163 A. 111.

Prosser Torts 4th Ed. HB—21

In the same manner, it has been held that an existing disease[82] or a prior accident[83] which reduces the plaintiff's life expectancy will limit accordingly the value of his life in an action for wrongful death. Then what is the value of a burning house which the defendant prevents a fire engine from extinguishing,[84] or one in the path of a conflagration which he destroys?[85] What damage has the plaintiff suffered when the defendant blocks the passage of his barge into a canal in which passage was already blocked by a landslide?[86]

Value is an estimate of worth at the time and place of the wrong. It is obvious that if such factors as these are to be considered as reducing value, they must be in operation when the defendant causes harm, and so imminent that reasonable men would take them into account.[87] There is a clear distinction

82. Pieczonka v. Pullman Co., 2 Cir. 1937, 89 F.2d 353. Cf. Evans v. S. J. Groves & Sons Co., 2 Cir. 1963, 315 F.2d 335; Henderson v. United States, 5 Cir. 1964, 328 F.2d 502; Denman v. Johnston, 1891, 85 Mich. 387, 48 N.W. 565; Fortner v. Koch, 1935, 272 Mich. 273, 261 N.W. 762 ($25,000 reduced to $7,000).

83. Slaven v. Germain, 1892, 64 Hun 506, 19 N.Y.S. 492. Cf. Pittsburgh S. S. Co. v. Palo, 6 Cir. 1933, 64 F.2d 198.

84. Felter v. Delaware & Hudson R. Corporation, D. Pa.1937, 19 F.Supp. 852, affirmed 3 Cir. 1938, 98 F. 2d 868 (damages for only portion of total value), discussed in, 1937, 12 Temple L.Q. 132.

85. Peaslee, Multiple Causation and Damage, 1934, 47 Harv.L.Rev. 1127, approves on this basis the decision in Cook v. Minneapolis, St. P. & S. S. M. R. Co., 1898, 98 Wis. 624, 74 N.W. 561, where a fire set by the defendant merged with a fire of innocent origin to burn the plaintiff's property. It may be suggested that this is unsound, since any decrease in value of the property before destruction must be attributed equally to the threat of each fire.

86. Douglas Burt & Buchanan Co. v. Texas & Pac. R. Co., 1922, 150 La. 1038, 91 So. 503 (none).

87. In Morris v. St. Paul City R. Co., 1908, 105 Minn. 276, 117 N.W. 500, where defendant caused a miscarriage, the court refused to permit the jury to balance against the pain suffered the pain to be expected from the normal birth of the child, saying that it was "too remote, speculative and uncertain to be taken as a basis for estimating damages."

between a man who is standing in the path of an avalanche when the defendant shoots him, and one who is about to embark on a steamship doomed later to strike an iceberg and sink.[88] The life of the latter has value at the time, as any insurance company would agree, while that of the former has none. So a forest fire a mile away may affect the market value of a building, while one a hundred miles away will not, although it may afterwards destroy it.

So far as the feasibility of such apportionment is concerned, it is equally possible where both causes are culpable.[89] If A shoots B and kills him instantly, two minutes after C has administered to him a slow poison for which there is no known antidote, it can still be said that his life had little value when A killed him. But in such a case A has deprived the plaintiff, not only of the life, but of a possible redress against C. Because A has killed B, C has not caused his death, and so has not become liable, as he was otherwise certain to do. There was not only potential damage, but a potential cause of action in compensation for it, which A has destroyed. It is therefore proper to hold A liable for the full value of B's life, in contrast to the case where B has poisoned himself by mistake. Such questions, however, apparently have not been considered by any court.

Reference to the record in the case discloses that plaintiff was pregnant only two months. But in a case where the miscarriage occurred three weeks before birth was due, the deduction was made. Hawkins v. Front St. Cable R. Co., 1898, 3 Wash. 592, 28 P. 1021. See 1 Joyce, Damages, 1903, § 185.

88. Peaslee, Multiple Causation and Damage, 1934, 47 Harv.L.Rev. 1127, 1139.

89. To vary slightly a case suggested by McLaughlin, Proximate Cause, 1925, 39 Harv.L.Rev. 149, 155: Suppose A is entering a desert. B secretly empties A's water keg, leaving only three days' supply. A takes the keg into the desert, where C steals it. both A and C believing that it is full. A dies of thirst. Should C be liable for the loss of more than three days of A's life?

Acts Harmless in Themselves Which Together Cause Damage

A very troublesome question arises where the acts of each of two or more parties, standing alone, would not be wrongful, but together they cause harm to the plaintiff. If several defendants independently pollute a stream, the impurities traceable to each may be negligible and harmless, but all together may render the water entirely unfit for use. The difficulty lies in the fact that each defendant alone would have committed no tort. There would have been no negligence, and no nuisance, since the individual use of the stream would have been a reasonable use, and no harm would have resulted.

Obviously the plaintiff's interests have been invaded, and if each defendant is to escape on the ground that his contribution was harmless in itself, there will be no redress.[90] A number of courts have held that acts which individually would be innocent may be tortious if they thus combine to cause damage, in cases of pollution,[91] flooding of land,[92] diversion of water,[93] obstruction of a highway,[94] or even a noise nuisance.[95] The explanation of the paradox is that the standard of reasonable conduct applicable to each defendant is governed by the surrounding cir-

90. Hill v. Smith, 1867, 32 Cal. 166; James, L. J., in Thorpe v. Brumfitt, 1873, L.R. 8 Ch.App. 650.

91. Duke of Buccleuch v. Cowan, 1866, 5 Sess.Cas. (Macph.) 214; Woodyear v. Schaefer, 1881, 57 Md. 1, 40 Am.Rep. 419; Warren v. Parkhurst, 1904, 45 Misc. 466, 92 N.Y.S. 725; Northup v. Eakes, 1918, 72 Okl. 66, 178 P. 266. Compare the case suggested in Blair v. Deakin, 1887, 57 L.T., N.S., 522, of two defendants each discharging a chemical harmless in itself, which combined with the other renders the water unusable.

92. Sloggy v. Dilworth, 1888, 38 Minn. 179, 36 N.W. 451; Wright v. Cooper, 1802, 1 Tyler, Vt., 425; Town of Sharon v. Anahama Realty Corp., 1924, 97 Vt. 336, 123 A. 192; Woodland v. Portneuf Marsh Valley Irr. Co., 1915, 26 Idaho 789, 146 P. 1106.

93. Hillman v. Newington, 1880, 57 Cal. 56.

94. Thorpe v. Brumfitt, 1873, L.R. 8 Ch.App. 650; Sadler v. Great Western R. Co., [1895] L.R. 2 Q.B. 688.

95. Lambton v. Mellish, [1894] 3 Ch. 163.

cumstances, including the activities of the other defendants. Pollution of a stream to even a slight extent becomes unreasonable when similar pollution by others makes the condition of the stream approach the danger point. The single act itself becomes wrongful because of what others are doing.[96]

Where, as in the usual case, such liability must be based on negligence or intent rather than any ultra-hazardous activity, it would seem that there can be no tortious conduct unless the individual knows, or is at least negligent in failing to discover, that his conduct may concur with that of others to cause damage.[97] And liability need not necessarily be entire, for there is no reason why damages may not be apportioned here, to the same extent as in any other case.[98]

96. "The acts of the other company must be taken into account because it may be that the one company ought not to be doing what it was when the other company was doing what it did." Sadler v. Great Western R. Co., [1895] 2 Q.B. 688. Accord; Woodyear v. Schaefer, 1881, 57 Md. 1; Hillman v. Newington, 1880, 57 Cal. 56; United States v. Luce, C.C.Del.1905, 141 F. 385, 411; Lawton v. Herrick, 1910, 83 Conn. 417, 428, 76 A. 986, 990; cf. Weidman Silk Dyeing Co. v. East Jersey Water Co., N. J.Sup.1914, 91 A. 338.

It has been said. however, that to be liable the defendant must have "contributed substantially" rather than infinitesimally—a clear application of the substantial factor test of causation. See Duke of Buccleuch v. Cowan, 1866, 5 Sess.Cas., Macph., 214.

97. See the stress placed upon knowledge of the situation by each defendant in Warren v. Parkhurst, 1904, 45 Misc. 466, 92 N.Y.S. 725; Lambton v. Mellish, [1894] 3 Ch. 163; also the instruction approved in Folsom v. Apple River Log-Driving Co., 1877, 41 Wis. 602; cf. McKay v. Southern Bell Tel. & Tel. Co., 1896, 111 Ala. 337, 19 So. 695.

98. Sloggy v. Dilworth. 1888, 38 Minn. 179, 36 N.W. 451; Woodland v. Portneuf Marsh Valley Irr. Co., 1915, 26 Idaho 789, 146 P. 1106.

CHAPTER 9

LIMITED DUTY

53. DUTY

"Duty" we have already encountered, in connection with the problem of the unforeseeable plaintiff.[1] It is quite possible, and not at all uncommon, to deal with most of the questions which arise in a negligence case in terms of "duty." Thus the standard of conduct required of the individual may be expressed by saying that the driver of an automobile approaching an intersection is under a duty to moderate his speed, to keep a proper lookout, or to blow his horn, but that he is not under a duty to take precautions against an unexpected explosion of a manhole cover in the street. But the problems of "duty" are sufficiently complex without subdividing it in this manner to cover an endless series of details of conduct. It is better to reserve "duty" for the problem of the relation between individuals which imposes upon one a legal obligation for the benefit of the other, and to deal with particular conduct in terms of a legal standard of what is required to meet the obligation. In other words, "duty" is a question of whether the defendant is under any obligation for the benefit of the particular plaintiff; and in negligence cases, the duty is always the same, to conform to the legal standard of reasonable conduct in the light of the apparent risk. What the defendant must do, or must not do, is a question of the standard of conduct required to satisfy the duty. The distinction is one of convenience only, and it must be remembered that the two are

correlative, and one cannot exist without the other.

A duty, in negligence cases, may be defined as an obligation, to which the law will give recognition and effect, to conform to a particular standard of conduct toward another. In the early English law, there was virtually no consideration of duty. Liability was imposed with no great regard even for the fault of the defendant.[2] The requirements as to conduct were absolute, and once the act was found to be wrongful, the actor was liable for the damage that might result. Such few limitations upon his responsibility as are found in the earlier cases are stated, not in any terms of duty, but of remoteness of the damage, or what we now call "proximate cause."[3] Certainly there is little trace of any notion of a relation between the parties, or an obligation to any one individual, as essential to the tort.[4] The defendant's obligation to behave properly apparently was owed to all the world, and he was liable to any person whom he might injure by his misconduct.

The conception of an absolute wrong remains in the criminal law,[5] and in the field

1. See supra, p. 254.

2. See supra, p. 17.

3. 2 Holdsworth, History of English Law, 1931, 50–54; 3 Holdsworth, History of English Law, 1931, 375–382.

4. Winfield, Duty in Tortious Negligence, 1934, 34 Col.L.Rev. 41.

5. State v. Renfrow, 1892, 111 Mo. 589, 20 S.W. 299; State v. Levelle, 1891, 34 S.C. 120, 13 S.E. 319; Commonwealth v. Mink, 1877, 123 Mass. 422; State v. Dalton, 1919, 178 N.C. 779, 101 S.E. 548.

of intentional torts, where the doctrine of "transferred intent" makes any one who attempts to injure another liable to any stranger whom he may injure instead.[6] But when negligence began to take form as a separate basis of tort liability, the courts developed the idea of duty, as a matter of some specific relation between the plaintiff and the defendant, without which there could be no liability.[7] We owe this to three English cases,[8] decided between 1837 and 1842. The rule which developed out of them was that no action could be founded upon the breach of a duty owed only to some person other than the plaintiff. He must bring himself within the scope of a definite legal obligation, so that it might be regarded as personal to him.[9] "Negligence in the air, so to speak, will not do." [10] The first cases [11] in which this idea was stated held only that the obligation of a contract could give no right of action to one who was not a contracting party; but it was soon extended to the whole field of negligence. The period during which it developed was that of the industrial revolution, and there is good reason to believe that it was a means by which the courts sought, perhaps more or less unconsciously, to limit the responsibilities of growing industry within some reasonable bounds.

This concept of a relative duty is not regarded as essential by the continental law, and it has been assailed as serving no useful purpose, and producing only confusion in ours.[12] Its artificial character is readily apparent; in the ordinary case, if the court should desire to find liability, it would be quite as easy to find the necessary "relation" in the position of the parties toward one another, and hence to extend the defendant's duty to the plaintiff.[13] The statement that there is or is not a duty begs the essential question—whether the plaintiff's interests are entitled to legal protection against the defendant's conduct.[14] It is therefore not surprising to find that the problem of duty is as broad as the whole law of negligence, and that no universal test for it ever has been formulated. It is a shorthand statement of a conclusion, rather than an aid to analysis in itself. It is embedded far too firmly in our law to be discarded,[15] and no satisfactory substitute for it, by which the defendant's responsibility may be limited, has been devised.[16] But it should be recognized that "duty" is not sacrosanct in itself, but only an expression of the sum total of those considerations of policy which lead the law to

---

6. See supra, p. 32.

7. Winfield, Duty in Tortious Negligence, 1934, 34 Col.L.Rev. 41.

8. Vaughan v. Menlove, 1837, 3 Bing.N.C. 468, 132 Eng.Rep. 490; Langridge v. Levy, 1837, 2 M. & W. 519, 150 Eng.Rep. 863; Winterbottom v. Wright, 1842, 10 M. & W. 109, 152 Eng.Rep. 402.

9. "The question of liability for negligence cannot arise at all until it is established that the man who has been negligent owed some duty to the person who seeks to make him liable for his negligence. * * * A man is entitled to be as negligent as he pleases toward the whole world if he owes no duty to them." Lord Esher, in Le Lievre v. Gould, [1893] 1 Q.B. 491, 497.

10. Pollock, Law of Torts, 13th Ed. 1929, 468.

11. See supra, note 8.

12. Winfield, Duty in Tortious Negligence, 1934, 34 Col.L.Rev. 41; Buckland, The Duty to Take Care, 1935, 51 L.Q.Rev. 637.

13. Compare the opinions of Cardozo, C. J., in MacPherson v. Buick Motor Co., 1916, 217 N.Y. 382, 111 N.E. 1050, where a duty was found, and H. R. Moch Co. v. Rensselaer Water Co., 1928, 247 N.Y. 160, 159 N.E. 896, where it was not.

14. See Green, The Duty Problem in Negligence Cases, 1928, 28 Col.L.Rev. 1014, 1929, 29 Col.L.Rev. 255; Green, Judge and Jury, 1930, ch. 3; Prosser, Palsgraf Revisited, 1953, 52 Mich.L.Rev. 1, reprinted in Prosser, Selected Topics on the Law of Torts, 1954, 191; 1 Street, Foundations of Legal Liability, 1906, 93; Morison, A Re-examination of the Duty of Care, 1948, 11 Mod.L.Rev. 9; Heuston, Donoghue v. Stevenson in Retrospect, 1957, 20 Mod.L.Rev. 1.

15. Cf. Restatement of Torts, § 4.

16. As to the deficiencies of "remoteness of damage," or "proximate cause" as a limitation, see Green, Rationale of Proximate Cause, 1927; Edgerton, Legal Cause, 1924, 72 U.Pa.L.Rev. 211, 343; Prosser, The Minnesota Court on Proximate Cause, 1936, 21 Minn.L.Rev. 19.

say that the particular plaintiff is entitled to protection.

There is little analysis of the problem of duty in the courts. Frequently it is dealt with in terms of what is called "proximate cause," usually with resulting confusion. In such cases, the question of what is "proximate" and that of duty are fundamentally the same: whether the interests of the plaintiff are to be protected against the particular invasion by the defendant's conduct.

Scope of Duty

In Heaven v. Pender,[17] Brett, M.R., afterwards Lord Esher, made the first attempt to state a formula of duty. "Whenever one person," he said, "is by circumstances placed in such a position with regard to another that every one of ordinary sense who did think would at once recognize that if he did not use ordinary care and skill in his own conduct with regard to those circumstances he would cause danger of injury to the person or property of the other, a duty arises to use ordinary care and skill to avoid such danger." But this formula, which afterwards was rejected by Lord Esher himself,[18] was soon recognized as far too broad. As a general proposition to be applied in the ordinary negligence case, where the defendant has taken some affirmative action such as driving an automobile, it holds good. That is to say, that whenever the automobile driver should, as a reasonable man, foresee that his conduct will involve an unreasonable risk of harm to other drivers or to pedestrians, he is then under a duty to them to exercise the care of a reasonable man as to what he does or does not do. There are, however, a good many defendants, and a good many situations, as to which there is no such duty. In other words, the defendant is under no legal obligation toward the particular plaintiff to act with the

care of a reasonable man, and he is not liable even though his conduct falls far short of that standard, and the other is injured as a result.

A later attempt at a formula for duty was that of Lord Atkin in Donoghue v. Stevenson: [19]

"The rule that you are to love your neighbor becomes in law, you must not injure your neighbor; and the lawyer's question, Who is my neighbor? receives a restricted reply. You must take reasonable care to avoid acts or omissions which you can reasonably foresee would be likely to injure your neighbor. Who, then, in law is my neighbor? The answer seems to be—persons who are so closely and directly affected by my act that I ought reasonably to have them in contemplation as being so affected when I am directing my mind to the acts or omissions which are called in question."

As a formula this is so vague as to have little meaning, and as a guide to decision it has had no value at all. Within some such undefined general limits, it may be said that the courts have merely "reacted to the situation in the way in which the great mass of mankind customarily react," [20] and that as our ideas of human relations change the law as to duties has changed with them.[21] Various factors undoubtedly have been given conscious or unconscious weight,[22] including con-

---

17. 1883, 11 Q.B.D. 503. The other members of the court stated definitely that they did not concur in this formula.

18. In Le Lievre v. Gould, [1893] 1 Q.B. 491.

19. [1932] A.C. 579. See Pollock, The Snail in the Bottle, and Thereafter, 1933, 49 L.Q.Rev. 22.

20. Bohlen, Review of Green, Judge and Jury, 1932, 80 U.Pa.L.Rev. 781, 785. The New York cases as to duty are considered in Steuer, The Conception of Duty in Personal Injury Cases in New York, 1932, 18 Corn.L.Q. 51.

21. Prosser Palsgraf Revisited, 1953, 52 Mich.L.Rev. 1, 12–15, reprinted in Prosser, Selected Topics on the Law of Torts, 1954, 191.

22. Green, The Duty Problem in Negligence Cases, 1928, 28 Col.L.Rev. 1014, 1929, 29 Col.L.Rev. 255, reprinted in Green, Judge and Jury, 1930, ch. 3–4. See supra, § 4.

There are particularly good statements as to the factors affecting duty in Amaya v. Home Ice, Fuel &

venience of administration, capacity of the parties to bear the loss, a policy of preventing future injuries, the moral blame attached to the wrongdoer, and many others. Changing social conditions lead constantly to the recognition of new duties. No better general statement can be made, than that the courts will find a duty where, in general, reasonable men would recognize it and agree that it exists.

54. MENTAL DISTURBANCE

Certain types of interests, because of the various difficulties which they present, have been afforded relatively little protection at the hands of the law against negligent invasions. Thus interests of a pecuniary nature, such as the right to have a contract performed,[23] the expectation of financial advantage,[24] or the integrity of the pocketbook which may be damaged by reliance upon a representation,[25] all present special problems, which are considered elsewhere in this text. In general, however, it may be said that the law gives protection against negligent acts to the interest in security of the person, and all interests in tangible property. In other words, negligence may result in liability for personal injury or property damage. One interest which is still a subject of controversy is that in freedom from mental disturbance. No general agreement has yet been reached as to the liability for negligence resulting in fright, shock, or other "mental suffering," or its physical consequences.

Previous reference has been made [26] to the reluctance with which the courts have recog-

nized the interest in peace of mind, even where the interference with it is intentional. This reluctance has of course been more pronounced where the defendant's conduct is merely negligent. The same objections against allowing recovery have been advanced: it is said that mental disturbance cannot be measured in terms of money, and so cannot serve in itself as a basis for the action; [27] that its physical consequences are too remote, and so not "proximately caused;" [28] that there is a lack of precedent,[29] and that a vast increase in litigation would follow.[30] All these objections have been demolished many times,[31] and it is threshing old straw to deal with them. Mental suffering is no more difficult to estimate

---

Supply Co., 1963, 59 Cal.2d 295, 29 Cal.Rptr. 33, 379 P.2d 513; Raymond v. Paradise Unified School Dist., 1963, 218 Cal.App.2d 1, 31 Cal.Rptr. 847; Wright v. Arcade School Dist., 1964, 230 Cal.App.2d 272, 40 Cal.Rptr. 812.

23. See infra, p. 938.

24. See infra, p. 952.

25. See infra, § 704.

26. Supra, p. 49.

27. See Lynch v. Knight, 1861, 9 H.L.C. 577, 598, 11 Eng.Rep. 854; Mitchell v. Rochester R. Co., 1896, 151 N.Y. 107, 45 N.E. 354; Cleveland, C. C. & St. L. R. Co. v. Stewart, 1899, 24 Ind.App. 374, 56 N.E. 917; Perry v. Capital Traction Co., 1929, 59 App. D.C. 42, 32 F.2d 938.

28. Victorian Rys. Comm'rs v. Coultas, 1888, 13 A.C. 222; Mitchell v. Rochester R. Co., 1897, 151 N.Y. 107, 45 N.E. 354; Chittick v. Philadelphia Rapid Transit Co., 1909, 224 Pa. 13, 73 A. 4.

29. Lehman v. Brooklyn City R. Co., 1888, 47 Hun, N.Y., 355; Victorian Rys. Commrs. v. Coultas, 1888, 13 A.C. 222.

30. Mitchell v. Rochester R. Co., 1897, 151 N.Y. 107, 45 N.E. 354; Spade v. Lynn & Boston R. Co., 1896, 168 Mass. 285, 47 N.E. 88; Ward v. West Jersey & S. R. Co., 1900, 65 N.J.L. 383, 47 A. 561.

31. Bohlen, The Right to Recover for Injury Resulting from Negligence Without Impact, 1902, 41 Am.L.Reg.,N.S., 141; Goodrich, Emotional Disturbance as Legal Damage, 1922, 20 Mich.L.Rev. 497; Magruder, Mental and Emotional Disturbance in the Law of Torts, 1936, 49 Harv.L.Rev. 1033; Harper and McNeely, A Re-examination of the Basis for Liability for Emotional Distress, [1938] Wis.L. Rev. 426; Smith, Relation of Emotions to Injury and Disease, 1944, 30 Va.L.Rev. 193; Campbell, Injury Without Impact, [1951] Ins.L.J. 654; Rendall, Nervous Shock and Tortious Liability, 1962, 2 Osg. Hall L.J. 291; Anderson, The Interest in Mental Tranquillity, 1964, 13 Buff.L.Rev. 339; Notes, 1964, 16 U.Fla.L.Rev. 540; 1969, 54 Iowa L.Rev. 737. See also the excellent, although outdated, review of the entire problem in the Report of the New York Law Revision Commission, Study Relating to Injuries Resulting from Fright or Shock, 1936, Leg.Doc. No. 65(E).

in financial terms, and no less a real injury than "physical" pain; [32] it is not an independent intervening cause, but a thing brought about by the defendant's negligence itself, and its consequences follow in unbroken sequence from that negligence; [33] and while it may be true that its consequences are seldom very serious unless there is some predisposing physical condition, [34] the law is not for the protection of the physically sound alone. [35] It is the business of the courts to make precedent where a wrong calls for redress, even if lawsuits must be multiplied, [36] and by this time there is precedent enough, and no such increase in litigation is to be observed. [37]

It is now more or less generally conceded [38] that the only valid objection against recovery for mental injury is the danger of vexatious suits and fictitious claims, which has loomed very large in the opinions as an obstacle. [39] The danger is a real one, and must be met. Mental disturbance is easily simulated, and courts which are plagued with fraudulent personal injury claims may well

be unwilling to open the door to an even more dubious field. But the difficulty is not insuperable. Not only fright and shock, but other kinds of mental injury are marked by definite physical symptoms, which are capable of clear medical proof. [40] It is entirely possible to allow recovery only upon satisfactory evidence and deny it when there is nothing to corroborate the claim, [41] or to look for some guarantee of genuineness in the circumstances of the case. [42] The problem is one of adequate proof, and it is not necessary to deny a remedy in all cases because some claims may be false. The very clear tendency of the recent cases is to refuse to admit incompetence to deal with such a problem, and to find some basis for redress in a proper case.

Mental Disturbance Alone

Where the defendant's negligence causes only mental disturbance, without accompanying physical injury or physical consequences, or any other independent basis for tort liability, there is still general agreement that in the ordinary case there can be no re-

---

32. Goodrich, Emotional Disturbance as Legal Damage, 1922, 20 Mich.L.Rev. 497; Hargis v. Knoxville Power Co., 1917, 175 N.C. 31, 94 S.E. 702; Nashville, C. & St. L. R. Co. v. Miller, 1904, 120 Ga. 453, 47 S.E. 959.

33. Purcell v. St. Paul City R. Co., 1892, 48 Minn. 134, 50 N.W. 1034; Simone v. Rhode Island Co., 1907, 28 R.I. 186, 66 A. 202; Hanford v. Omaha & C. B. St. R. Co., 1925, 113 Neb. 423, 203 N.W. 643.

34. Havard, Reasonable Foresight of Nervous Shock, 1956, 19 Mod.L.Rev. 478; Note, 1947, 15 U.Chi.L. Rev. 188. The latter is particularly misleading in ignoring the possibility of predisposition.

35. See supra, p. 261.

36. Chiuchiolo v. New England Wholesale Tailors, 1930, 84 N.H. 329, 150 A. 540; Alabama Fuel & Iron Co. v. Baladoni, 1916, 15 Ala.App. 316, 73 So. 205.

37. Gulf, C. & S. F. R. Co. v. Hayter, 1900, 93 Tex. 239, 54 S.W. 944.

38. "Whatever justification there may be rests in the courts' fear that unscrupulous lawyers with the aid of equally unscrupulous doctors may obtain from sympathetic juries verdicts upon purely fabricated evidence." Bohlen, Fifty Years of Torts, 1937, 50 Harv.L.Rev. 725, 733.

39. Spade v. Lynn & Boston R. Co., 1897, 168 Mass. 285, 47 N.E. 88; Miller v. Baltimore & O. S. W. R. Co., 1908, 78 Ohio St. 309, 85 N.E. 499; Huston v. Freemansburg Borough, 1905, 212 Pa. 548, 61 A. 1022.

40. Crile, The Origin and Nature of the Emotions, 1915; Goodrich, Emotional Disturbance as Legal Damage, 1922, 20 Mich.L.Rev. 497; Earengey, The Legal Consequences of Shock, 1934, 2 Medico-Leg. & Crim.Rec. 14; Smith and Solomon, Traumatic Neuroses in Court, 1943, 30 Va.L.Rev. 87; Smith, Relation of Emotions to Injury and Disease, 1944, 30 Va.L.Rev. 193.

41. Compare the cases refusing to sustain verdicts based on subjective testimony as to physical pain or injury. Johnson v. Great Northern R. Co., 1909, 107 Minn. 285, 119 N.W. 1061; Sprogis v. Butler, 1919, 40 Cal.App. 647, 181 P. 246; Paderas v. Stauffer, 1929, 10 La.App. 50, 119 So. 757, 120 So. 886; City of Pawhuska v. Crutchfield, 1932, 155 Okl. 222, 8 P.2d 685. See, as to mental injury, Johnson v. Sampson, 1926, 167 Minn. 203, 208 N.W. 814.

42. Cf. Nelson v. Crawford, 1899, 122 Mich. 466, 81 N.W. 335; Prude v. Sebastian, 1902, 107 La. 64, 31 So. 764; Meek v. Harris, 1916, 110 Miss. 805, 71 So. 1.

covery. The temporary emotion of fright,[43] so far from serious that it does no physical harm, is so evanescent a thing, so easily counterfeited, and usually so trivial, that the courts have been quite unwilling to protect the plaintiff against mere negligence, where the elements of extreme outrage and moral blame which have had such weight in the case of the intentional tort [44] are lacking. Other unpleasant emotions, such as the distress of a mother at being given the wrong baby by a hospital, have been dealt with on the same basis.[45] It makes no difference that there has been a harmless but emotionally disturbing contact with the plaintiff's person, as where he gets a mouthful of broken glass without actually being cut.[46]

In only two groups of special cases has there been any tendency to break away from the settled rule, and to allow recovery for mental disturbance alone. In one of them a respectable minority [47] of the courts allow recovery against a telegraph company for the negligent transmission of a message, such as one announcing death, which indicates upon its face that there is an especial likelihood that such mental distress will result. The federal rule, which controls as to interstate messages,[48] and the greater number of state decisions [49] are to the contrary. The other group of cases has involved the negligent mishandling of corpses. Here the older rule denied recovery for mere negligence, without circumstances of aggravation.[50] There are by now, however, quite a series of cases allowing recovery for negligent embalming,[51] negligent shipment,[52] or

---

43. Memphis St. R. Co. v. Bernstein, 1917, 137 Tenn. 637, 194 S.W. 902; Pullman Co. v. Strang, 1926, 35 Ga.App. 59, 132 S.E. 399; Gulf & S. I. R. Co. v. Beard, 1922, 129 Miss. 827, 93 So. 357; Weissman v. Wells, 1924, 306 Mo. 82, 267 S.W. 400; Logan v. St. Luke's General Hospital, 1965, 65 Wash.2d 914, 400 P.2d 296.

To be distinguished is shock to the nervous system, which commonly is regarded as injury to the body rather than to the mind, and hence satisfies the requirement of physical injury. See for example Vanoni v. Western Airlines, 1967, 247 Cal.App.2d 793, 56 Cal.Rptr. 115.

44. See supra, § 11.

45. Espionosa v. Beverly Hospital, 1952, 114 Cal. App.2d 232, 249 P.2d 843. Cf. Seidenbach's, Inc. v. Williams, Okl.1961, 361 P.2d 185 (failure to deliver wedding gown in time for wedding); Manie v. Matson Oldsmobile-Cadillac Co., 1967, 378 Mich. 650, 148 N.W.2d 779 (mental distress when stopped by police); The Black Gull, 2 Cir. 1936, 82 F.2d 758, cert. denied American Diamond Lines v. Peterson, 298 U.S. 684 (anxiety); Verhagen v. Gibbons, 1970, 47 Wis.2d 220, 177 N.W.2d 83. A strongly slanted brief for the plaintiff in such cases is Brody, Negligently Inflicted Psychic Injuries: A Return to Reason, 1962, 7 Vill.L.Rev. 232.

46. Tuttle v. Meyer Dairy Products Co., 1956, 100 Ohio App. 133, 138 N.E.2d 429. Cf. Sullivan v. H. P. Hood & Sons, 1960, 341 Mass. 216, 168 N.E.2d 80 (dead mouse in milk); Cushing Coca-Cola Bottling Co. v. Francis, 1952, 206 Okl. 553, 245 P.2d 84 (same in Coca Cola); Monteleone v. Cooperative Transit Co., 1945, 128 W.Va. 340, 36 S.E.2d 475 (cut the size of a pimple).

47. So Relle v. Western Union Tel. Co., 1881, 55 Tex. 308; Mentzer v. Western Union Tel. Co., 1895, 93 Iowa 752, 62 N.W. 1; Russ v. Western Union Tel. Co., 1943, 222 N.C. 504, 23 S.E.2d 681; Western Union Tel. Co. v. Redding, 1930, 100 Fla. 495, 129 So. 743; Western Union Tel. Co. v. Crumpton, 1903, 138 Ala. 632, 36 So. 517.

48. Western Union Tel. Co. v. Speight, 1920, 254 U.S. 17; Western Union Tel. Co. v. Junker, Tex.Civ. App.1941, 153 S.W.2d 210, error refused. See Notes, 1942, 20 Tex.L.Rev. 210; 1956, 34 Tex.L.Rev. 487. The federal rule does, however, allow recovery where the mental disturbance results in physical illness. Kaufman v. Western Union Tel. Co., 5 Cir. 1955, 224 F.2d 723, cert. denied 350 U.S. 947.

49. Western Union Tel. Co. v. Choteau, 1911, 28 Okl. 664, 115 P. 879; Morton v. Western Union Tel. Co., 1895, 53 Ohio St. 431, 41 N.E. 689; Corcoran v. Postal Tel. Cable Co., 1917, 80 Wash. 570, 142 P. 29; Seifert v. Western Union Tel. Co., 1907, 129 Ga. 181, 58 S.E. 699; Connelly v. Western Union Tel. Co., 1900, 100 Va. 51, 40 S.E. 618.

50. Dunahoo v. Bess, 1941, 146 Fla. 182, 200 So. 541; Beaulieu v. Great Northern R. Co., 1907, 103 Minn. 47, 114 N.W. 353; Nail v. McCullough & Lee, 1923, 88 Okl. 243, 212 P. 981; Nichols v. Central Vermont R. Co., 1919, 94 Vt. 14, 109 A. 905; Kneass v. Cremation Society of Washington, 1918, 103 Wash. 521, 175 P. 172.

51. Brown Funeral Homes & Ins. Co. v. Baughn, 1933, 226 Ala. 661, 148 So. 154; Chelini v. Nieri, 1948, 32 Cal.2d 480, 196 P.2d 915; Carey v. Lima, Salmon & Tully Mortuary, 1959, 168 Cal.App.2d 42, 335 P.2d 181; cf. Lamm v. Shingleton, 1949, 231 N. C. 10, 55 S.E.2d 810 (leaky casket).

52. Louisville & N. R. Co. v. Wilson, 1905, 123 Ga. 62, 51 S.E. 24; Clemm v. Atchison, T. & S. F. R.

running over the body,[53] and the like,[54] without such circumstances of aggravation, which now are in the majority. What all of these cases appear to have in common is an especial likelihood of genuine and serious mental distress, arising from the special circumstances, which serves as a guarantee that the claim is not spurious. There may perhaps be other such cases. Where the guarantee can be found, and the mental distress is undoubtedly real and serious, there is no essential reason to deny recovery.[55] But cases will obviously be rare in which "mental anguish," not so severe as to cause physical harm, will be so clearly a serious wrong worthy of redress, or sufficiently attested by the circumstances of the case.[56]

Mental Disturbance with Physical Injury

Where the defendant's negligence inflicts an immediate physical injury, such as a broken leg, none of the foregoing objections has prevented the courts from allowing compensation for purely mental elements of damage accompanying it, such as fright at the time of the injury,[57] apprehension as to its effects,[58] nervousness,[59] or humiliation at disfigurement.[60] With a cause of action established by the physical harm, "parasitic" damages are awarded, and it is considered that there is sufficient assurance that the mental injury is not feigned.[61]

If the physical harm is not immediate, but follows subsequently as a result of the plaintiff's fright or shock—as in the case of the miscarriage which appears so frequently in these cases that it has come to typify them—[62] there is still dispute. After England had led off by denying liability,[63] a large

Trade School Contracting Co., 1916, 173 Cal. 199, 159 P. 567; Louisville & N. R. Co. v. Brown, 1908, 127 Ky. 732, 106 S.W. 795.

58. Ferrara v. Galluchio, 1958, 5 N.Y.2d 16, 176 N.Y. S.2d 996, 152 N.E.2d 249 (fear of cancer); Murray v. Lawson, Ky.1969, 441 S.W.2d 136 ("phobic reaction" anxiety neurosis); Hamilan Corp. v. O'Neill, 1959, 106 U.S.App.D.C. 354, 273 F.2d 89 (worry over drinking beverage containing glass); Domenico v. Kaherl, 1964, 160 Me. 182, 200 A.2d 844 (worry over unborn child); Fehely v. Senders, 1943, 170 Or. 457, 135 P.2d 283 (same). See Note, 1926, 24 Mich.L. Rev. 306.

Cf. Rome Ry. & Light Co. v. Duke, 1920, 26 Ga.App. 52, 105 S.E. 386 (mental suffering at diminished capacity for work); Templin v. Erkekedis, 1949, 119 Ind.App. 171, 84 N.E.2d 728 (virgin whose hymen was ruptured); Dulaney Inv. Co. v. Wood, Tex.Civ. App.1940, 142 S.W.2d 379 (fear of paralysis).

59. Redick v. Peterson, 1918, 99 Wash. 368, 169 P. 804.

60. Patterson v. Blatti, 1916, 133 Minn. 23, 157 N.W. 717; Erie R. Co. v. Collins, 1920, 253 U.S. 77; Main v. Grand Rapids, G. H. & M. R. Co., 1919, 207 Mich. 473, 174 N.W. 157. Contra: Diamond Rubber Co. v. Harryman, 1907, 41 Colo. 415, 92 P. 922; Camenzind v. Freeland Furniture Co., 1918, 89 Or. 158, 174 P. 139.

61. 1 Street, Foundations of Legal Liability, 1906, 470.

62. "With few exceptions, recoveries have been restricted to women, and for the most part, pregnant women." Green, "Fright" Cases, 1933, 27 Ill.L.Rev. 761. Actually, this has now become something of an overstatement. Although miscarriages are still plentiful, there is also a good supply of cases of heart attacks, and the like, occurring to mere males.

63. In Victorian Railways Commissioners v. Coultas, P.C.1888, 13 App.Cas. 222. This was subsequently rejected in Dulieu v. White, [1901] 2 K.B. 669. But

Co., 1928, 126 Kan. 181, 268 P. 103; Louisville & N. R. Co. v. Hull, 1902, 113 Ky. 561, 68 S.W. 433; Missouri, K. & T. R. Co. v. Hawkins, 1908, 50 Tex.Civ. App. 128, 109 S.W. 221; Hale v. Bonner, 1891, 82 Tex. 33, 17 S.W. 605.

53. St. Louis S. W. R. Co. v. White, 1936, 192 Ark. 350, 91 S.W.2d 277; Pollard v. Phelps, 1937, 56 Ga. App. 408, 193 S.E. 102; Morrow v. Southern R. Co., 1938, 213 N.C. 127, 195 S.E. 383; cf. Owens v. Liverpool Corp., [1939] 1 K.B. 394.

54. Renihan v. Wright, 1890, 125 Ind. 536, 25 N.E. 822 (misdelivery); Torres v. State, 1962, 34 Misc.2d 488, 228 N.Y.S.2d 1005 (autopsy and unauthorized burial); Lott v. State, 1962, 32 Misc.2d 296, 225 N. Y.S.2d 434 (confusion of bodies); Weingast v. State, 1964, 44 Misc.2d 824, 254 N.Y.S.2d 952 (same); Blanchard v. Brawley, La.App.1954, 75 So. 2d 891 (burning body trying to cut it out of wreck). See Note, [1960] Duke L.J. 135.

55. See Note, 1936, 21 Corn.L.Q. 166.

56. Cf. St. Louis, I. M. & S. R. Co. v. Bragg, 1901, 69 Ark. 402, 64 S.W. 226 (not a "natural" consequence).

57. Canning v. Inhabitants of Williamstown, 1848, 1 Cush., 55 Mass., 451; Baltimore & O. R. Co. v. Mc-Bride, 6 Cir. 1930, 36 F.2d 841; Easton v. United

number of the American courts, including those of all of the leading industrial states of the country,[64] refused to permit recovery for such consequences unless there had been some "impact" upon the person of the plaintiff. Apart from some quite untenable notions of causal connection,[65] the theory seems to be that the "impact" affords the desired guarantee that the mental disturbance is genuine. But the same courts have found "impact" in minor contacts with the person which play no part in causing the real harm,[66] and in themselves can have no importance whatever. "Impact" has meant a slight blow,[67] a trifling burn[68] or electric shock,[69] a trivial jolt or jar,[70] a forcible seat-

ing on the floor,[71] dust in the eye,[72] or the inhalation of smoke.[73] The requirement has even been satisfied by a fall brought about by a faint after a collision,[74] or the plaintiff's own wrenching of her shoulder[75] in reaction to the fright. "The magic formula 'impact' is pronounced; the door opens to the full joy of a complete recovery."[76] A Georgia circus case[77] has reduced the whole matter to a complete absurdity by finding "impact" where the defendant's horse "evacuated his bowels" into the plaintiff's lap.

If there is any value at all in such a distinction, it must lie in the opportunity which is afforded to the defendant to testify that there was no impact. He may be able to swear that within the period of the statute of limitations he has struck no one with his automobile, where he cannot be sure whom he may have frightened.[78] But so far as sub-

since the decisions of the Privy Council are controlling for other portions of the British Commonwealth, they still have some difficulty getting around the Victorian Case. See Toms v. Toronto W. R. Co., 1911, 44 Can.S.C. 268, 20 Ann.Cas. 985; Chester v. Waverley Corp., 1939, 62 Comm.L.Rep., Aust., 1, 46–47; Stevenson v. Basham, [1922] N.Z. L.Rep. 225, 232. See Fleming, Law of Torts, 3d Ed. 1965, 156.

64. Bosley v. Andrews, 1958, 393 Pa. 161, 142 A.2d 263; Brisboise v. Kansas City Pub. Serv. Co., Mo. 1957, 303 S.W.2d 619; Spade v. Lynn & Boston R. Co., 1897, 168 Mass. 285, 47 N.E. 88; Miller v. Baltimore & Ohio S. W. R. Co., 1908, 78 Ohio St. 309, 85 N.E. 499; West Chicago St. R. Co. v. Liebig, 1898, 79 Ill.App. 567. See Notes, 1959, 13 U.Miami L.Q. 370; 1966, 39 Temple L.Q. 229.

At this writing, the following jurisdictions so hold: Arkansas, Illinois, Indiana, Kentucky, Maine, Massachusetts, Michigan, Missouri, Ohio, Virginia (doubtful), Washington. Florida allows recovery without impact where the defendant's conduct is wanton or malicious, but not otherwise. Crane v. Loftin, Fla.1954, 70 So.2d 574.

65. See Mitchell v. Rochester R. Co., 1896, 151 N.Y. 107, 45 N.E. 354.

66. Cf. Homans v. Boston Elev. R. Co., 1902, 180 Mass. 456, 62 N.E. 737; Kentucky Traction & Term. Co. v. Roman's Guardian, 1929, 232 Ky. 285, 23 S.W.2d 272.

67. Homans v. Boston Elev. R. Co., 1902, 180 Mass. 456, 62 N.E. 737; Spade v. Lynn & Boston R. Co., 1898, 172 Mass. 488, 52 N.E. 747.

68. Kentucky Traction & Term. Co. v. Roman's Guardian, 1929, 232 Ky. 285, 23 S.W.2d 272.

69. Hess v. Philadelphia Transp. Co., 1948, 358 Pa. 144, 56 A.2d 89; Clark v. Choctawhatchee Elec. Cooperative, Fla.1958, 107 So.2d 609.

70. Zelinsky v. Chimics, 1961, 196 Pa.Super. 312, 175 A.2d 351 ("any degree of physical impact, however slight"); Johnson Freight Lines, Inc. v. Tallent, 1964, 53 Tenn.App. 464, 384 S.W.2d 46; Boston v. Chesapeake & Ohio R. Co., 1945, 223 Ind. 425, 61 N. E.2d 326; McCardle v. George B. Peck Dry Goods Co., 1915, 191 Mo.App. 263, 177 S.W. 1095; Kasey v. Suburban Gas Heat of Kennewick, Inc., 1962, 60 Wash.2d 468, 374 P.2d 549 (shock wave from explosion).

71. Driscoll v. Gaffey, 1910, 207 Mass. 102, 92 N.E. 1010. Cf. Block v. Pascucci, 1930, 111 Conn. 58, 149 A. 210.

72. Porter v. Delaware, L. & W. R. Co., 1906, 73 N. J.L. 405, 63 A. 860.

73. Morton v. Stack, 1930, 122 Ohio St. 115, 170 N.E. 869.

74. Comstock v. Wilson, 1931, 257 N.Y. 231, 177 N.E. 431.

75. Freedman v. Eastern Mass. St. R. Co., 1938, 299 Mass. 246, 12 N.E.2d 739.

76. Goodrich, Emotional Disturbance as Legal Damage, 1922, 20 Mich.L.Rev. 497, 504.

77. Christy Bros. Circus v. Turnage, 1928, 38 Ga. App. 581, 144 S.E. 680.

78. The fear of accident "fakers" is reflected by the fact that the list of jurisdictions which, at one time or another, have insisted upon the "impact" requirement, is very largely the list of the states with our largest cities. Conspicuous exceptions are California and Texas, both of which had adopted

stantial justice is concerned, it would seem that it is possible to have equal assurance that the mental disturbance is genuine when the plaintiff escapes "impact" by a yard. Beginning with an Irish decision[79] in 1890, a considerable and rather rapidly increasing[80] majority of the courts have repudiated the requirement of "impact," and have regarded the physical consequences themselves, or the circumstances of the accident, as sufficient guarantee.[81] The same tendency is apparent in cases arising under the workmen's compensation acts.[82]

The impact requirement received something of a body blow in 1961, when New York, which had been one of its chief supporters, threw it overboard, and overruled one of the leading cases.[83] When Pennsyl-

vania followed suit in 1970,[84] overruling one of the most unappetizing of the earlier decisions,[85] which had provoked a blistering, disgusted, and highly literary dissent from Justice Musmanno, which may well be one of the classics of the law, it became apparent that the impact rule is destined for rapid extinction, and might perhaps even never be applied again.

Undoubtedly the change in the law has led to recovery by the plaintiff in some cases in which it has not been medically justifiable,[86] although these are almost certainly outweighed by the far greater number in which it is. It would seem that there must necessarily be, in lieu of impact, some requirement of satisfactory proof,[87] and at least in the absence of knowledge of the plaintiff's unusual susceptibility,[88] there should be no recovery for hypersensitive mental disturbance where a normal individual would not be affected

---

the contrary rule before any city reached major size.

79. Bell v. Great Northern Ry., 1890, L.R. 26 Ir.Rep. 428. The parent American case was Hill v. Kimball, 1890, 76 Tex. 210, 13 S.W. 59.

80. At this writing twenty-seven states so hold, and all but four of them have taken the position since 1900.

81. Purcell v. St. Paul City R. Co., 1892, 48 Minn. 134, 50 N.W. 1034; Orlo v. Connecticut Co., 1941, 128 Conn. 231, 21 A.2d 402; Colla v. Mandella, 1957, 1 Wis.2d 594, 85 N.W.2d 345; Houston Elec. Co. v. Dorsett, 1946, 145 Tex. 95, 194 S.W.2d 546; Simone v. Rhode Island Co., 1907, 28 R.I. 186, 66 A. 202.

The Second Restatement of Torts, § 313, adopts this view, with a Caveat in § 436 as to possible unreliability of testimony.

82. Compensation is allowed even by jurisdictions which deny recovery at common law, on the ground that the statute is to be construed liberally. Klein v. Len H. Darling Co., 1922, 217 Mich. 485, 187 N. W. 400; Hall v. Doremus, 1934, 12 N.J.Misc. 319, 171 A. 781; Pickerell v. Schumacher, 1925, 215 App.Div. 745, 212 N.Y.S. 899, affirmed, 1926, 242 N. Y. 577, 152 N.E. 434. The absence of a jury may have had some influence on these decisions.

83. Battalla v. State, 1961, 10 N.Y.2d 237, 219 N.Y.S. 2d 34, 176 N.E.2d 729, overruling Mitchell v. Rochester R. Co., 1896, 151 N.Y. 107, 45 N.E. 354. This was followed, quite promptly, by Falzone v. Busch, 1965, 45 N.J. 559, 214 A.2d 12; Robb v. Pennsylvania R. Co., 1965, — Del. —, 210 A.2d 709; aud Savard v. Cody Chevrolet, Inc., 1967, 126 Vt. 405, 234 A.2d 656, all overruling previous cases.

84. Niederman v. Brodsky, 1970, 436 Pa. 401, 261 A. 2d 84. In subsequent accord are Wallace v. Coca-Cola Bottling Plants, Inc., 1970, — Me. —, 269 A.2d 117, and Daley v. La Croix, 1970, — Mich. —, 179 N.W.2d 390.

85. Bosley v. Andrews, 1958, 393 Pa. 161, 142 A.2d 263.

86. See the opinion of a qualified medical writer, doubting the extent to which recovery has really been justified in all such cases, in Smith, Relation of Emotions to Injury and Disease: Legal Liability for Psychic Stimuli, 1944, 30 Va.L.Rev. 193. Also Notes, 1947, 15 U.Chi.L.Rev. 188; 1956, 19 Mod.L. Rev. 478, as to the "customary miscarriage."

87. "It may be that a distinction might properly be drawn between those effects of fright or shock which the common experience of the ordinary man recognizes as likely to result therefrom, such as a miscarriage after a severe fright, and those obscure nervous disorders as to which even medical experts may and do not agree. If trial courts could and would exercise an intelligent control over jury trials such a differentiation might be possible." Bohlen and Polikoff, Liability in New York for the Physical Consequences of Emotional Disturbance, 1932, 32 Col.L.Rev. 409, 417.

88. Cf. Price v. Yellow Pine Paper Mill Co., Tex. Civ.App.1922, 240 S.W. 588; Chiuchiolo v. New England Wholesale Tailors, 1930, 84 N.H. 329, 150 A. 540; Mitnick v. Whalen Bros., 1932, 115 Conn. 650, 163 A. 414.

under the circumstances.[89] But in general, it seems clear that the courts which deny all remedy in such cases are fighting a rearguard action.

Peril or Harm to Another

Where the mental disturbance and its consequences are not caused by any fear for the plaintiff's own safety, but by distress at some peril or harm to another person—as in the case of a mother witnessing the death of her child—additional problems arise. The courts which require an "impact" upon the person of course deny recovery,[90] although if there is impact some of them have been willing to allow damages due in part to fear for another.[91] But even in the courts which do not insist upon "impact," there have been a long array of cases [92] denying all recovery.

The reason usually assigned, as in a Wisconsin case [93] which is commonly regarded as the leading decision, is that the defendant could not reasonably anticipate any harm to the plaintiff, and therefore owes her no duty of care. She stands, in other words, in the position of Mrs. Palsgraf.[94] Accordingly, if the plaintiff herself is threatened with physical injury by the defendant's negligence, as where she is standing in the path of his vehicle, and suffers physical harm instead through fright at the peril to her child, it was held in the English case of Hambrook v. Stokes Brothers [95] that, with an initial breach of duty to her established, it becomes merely a matter of the unexpected manner in which the forseeable harm has occurred, and recovery was allowed. There have been a few American decisions which have accepted this conclusion in similar situations.[96]

---

89. Williamson v. Bennett, 1960, 251 N.C. 498, 112 S. E.2d 48 (fear for safety of child plaintiff imagined that she had struck); Legac v. Vietmayer Bros., 1929, 7 N.J.Misc. 685, 147 A. 110 (made ill by sight of a bug in a loaf of bread); Koplin v. Louis K. Liggett Co., 1936, 322 Pa. 333, 185 A. 744 (same as to centipede in soup); Davis v. Cleveland R. Co., 1939, 135 Ohio St. 401, 21 N.E.2d 169 (major hysteria and paralysis at being caught in bus door); Caputzal v. Lindsay Co., 1966, 48 N.J. 69, 222 A.2d 513 (heart attack at sight of brownish water from faucet). Cf. Kaufman v. Miller, Tex.1967, 414 S.W.2d 164 (must be foreseeable). See Note, 1961, 39 N.C. L.Rev. 303.

Even the normal individual, however, may suffer a good deal of hysteria, with serious consequences. See for example Sundquist v. Madison Rys. Co., 1928, 197 Wis. 83, 221 N.W. 392.

90. Knaub v. Gotwalt, 1966, 422 Pa. 267, 220 A.2d 646 (since overruled); Ellsworth v. Massacar, 1921, 215 Mich. 511, 184 N.W. 408.

91. Chesapeake & Ohio R. Co. v. Robinett, 1913, 151 Ky. 778, 152 S.W. 976; Greenberg v. Stanley, 1958, 51 N.J.Super. 90, 143 A.2d 588.

92. Burroughs v. Jordan, 1970, —— Tenn. ——, 456 S. W.2d 652; Barber v. Pollock, 1963, 104 N.H. 379, 187 A.2d 788; McMahon v. Bergeson, 1960, 9 Wis.2d 256, 101 N.W.2d 63; Lula v. Sivaco Wire & Nail Co., S.D.N.Y.1967, 265 F.Supp. 222; Rogers v. Hexol, Inc., D.Or.1962, 218 F.Supp. 453. Much the best discussion of the arguments on both sides of the question is in the two opinions in Amaya v. Home Ice, Fuel & Supply Co., 1963, 59 Cal.2d 295, 29 Cal. Rptr. 33, 379 P.2d 513.

See Goodhart, The Shock Cases and the Area of Risk, 1953, 16 Mod.L.Rev. 4; Havard, Reasonable Foresight of Nervous Shock, 1956, 19 Mod.L.Rev. 478; Tymann, Bystander's Recovery for Psychic Injury in New York, 1968, 32 Alb.L.Rev. 489; Notes, 1969, 37 Ford.L.Rev. 429; [1969] Utah L.Rev. 396; (1969) 44 Ind.L.J. 478; (1969) 43 Temp.L.Q. 59; (1965) 14 Buff.L.Rev. 499.

93. Waube v. Warrington, 1935, 216 Wis. 603, 258 N. W. 497. Accord: Cote v. Litawa, 1950, 96 N.H. 174, 71 A.2d 792; Resavage v. Davies, 1952, 199 Md. 479, 86 A.2d 879; Curry v. Journal Pub. Co., 1937, 41 N.M. 318, 68 P.2d 168; Bourhill v. Young, [1943] A. C. 92. See Goodhart, Shock Cases and the Area of Risk, 1953, 16 Mod.L.Rev. 14; Goodhart, Emotional Distress and the Unimaginative Taxicab Driver, 1953, 69 L.Q.Rev. 347; Notes, 1953, 31 N.C.L.Rev. 233; 1953, 10 Wash. & Lee L.Rev. 267.

94. See supra, p. 254.

95. [1925] 1 K.B. 141.

96. Bowman v. Williams, 1933, 164 Md. 397, 165 A. 182; Cosgrove v. Beymer, D.Del.1965, 244 F.Supp. 824; H. E. Butt Grocery Co. v. Perez, Tex.Civ.App. 1966, 408 S.W.2d 576; Frazee v. Western Dairy Products Co., 1935, 182 Wash. 578, 47 P.2d 1037; see Hopper v. United States, D.Colo.1965, 244 F. Supp. 314. In Holland v. St. Paul Mercury Ins Co., La.App.1961, 135 So.2d 145, it was held to be sufficient that there was breach of an independent duty to the parent, to inform him of the nature of the poison taken by his child; and that this was enough for liability, although the parent himself was never in any danger.

Other courts, however, have rejected this, and have denied recovery even though the plaintiff herself has been in the path of danger,[97] which suggests that it is not the unforeseeable plaintiff but the nature of the injury which is the real obstacle.

Until 1968 the only cases allowing recovery for mental disturbance at the peril of another were old ones in intermediate courts,[98] which were ambiguous, and probably to be explained on the basis of threatened physical injury to the plaintiff herself. In that year California kicked over the traces, and held [99] that a mother who saw her child run down and killed could recover, although she was herself in a position of complete safety. The decision has not yet been followed elsewhere, and has been rejected by name in both New Hampshire [1] and Vermont.[2]

It seems sufficiently obvious that the shock of a mother at danger or harm to her child may be both a real and a serious injury. All ordinary human feelings are in favor of her action against the negligent defendant. If a duty to her requires that she herself be in some recognizable danger, then it has properly been said that when a child is endangered, it is not beyond contemplation that its mother will be somewhere in the vicinity, and will suffer serious shock.[3] There is surely no great triumph of logic in a rule which permits recovery for anxiety about an unborn child,[4] and denies it once the child is born, or compensates for distress at the discovery of ransacked furniture but not the body of a murdered sister.[5] Yet it is equally obvious that if recovery is to be permitted, there must be some limitation. It would be an entirely unreasonable burden on all human activity if the defendant who has endangered one man were to be compelled to pay for the lacerated feelings of every other person disturbed by reason of it, including every bystander shocked at an accident, and every distant relative of the person injured, as well as his friends. And obviously the danger of fictitious claims, and the necessity of some guarantee of genuineness, are even greater here than before. It is no doubt such considerations that have made the law extremely cautious.

Some limitations might, however, be suggested. It is clear that the injury threatened or inflicted upon the third person must be a

---

97. Strazza v. McKittrick, 1959, 146 Conn. 714, 156 A.2d 149; Lessard v. Tarca, 1957, 20 Conn.Super. 295, 133 A.2d 625.

98. Spearman v. McCrary, 1912, 4 Ala.App. 473, 58 So. 927, cert. denied 177 Ala. 672, 58 So. 1038; Gulf, C. & S. F. R. Co. v. Coopwood, Tex.Civ.App. 1906, 96 S.W. 102; Cohn v. Ansonia Realty Co., 1914, 162 App.Div. 791, 148 N.Y.S. 39; Id., 1914, 162 App.Div. 794, 148 N.Y.S. 41. Compare also the cases, supra, p. 61, in which intentional attacks on third persons are regarded as negligence toward the plaintiff.

In Rasmussen v. Benson, 1937, 133 Neb. 449, 275 N.W. 674; Id., 1938, 135 Neb. 232, 280 N.W. 890, plaintiff's cattle were poisoned, and plaintiff died of heart trouble brought on by shock at their loss and fear that he had poisoned his milk customers. See Note, 1939, 27 Cal.L.Rev. 201. Contra, as to property loss, Buchanan v. Stout, 1908, 123 App.Div. 648, 108 N.Y.S. 38 (loss of pet cat mangled by defendant's dog).

99. Dillon v. Legg, 1968, 68 Cal.2d 728, 69 Cal.Rptr. 72, 441 P.2d 912. In Hopper v. United States, D. Colo.1965, 244 F.Supp. 314, the court wanted to allow recovery, but could not find support for it in the law of Colorado.

1. Jelley v. La Flame, 1968, 108 N.H. 471, 238 A.2d 728.

2. Guilmette v. Alexander, 1969, — Vt. —, 259 A. 2d 12. In accord, since the text was written, is Tobin v. Grossman, 1969, 24 N.Y.2d 609, 301 N.Y.S. 2d 554, 249 N.E.2d 419.

3. Hallen, Damages for Physical Injuries Resulting from Fright or Shock, 1933, 19 Va.L.Rev. 253, 270. Compare the rescue cases, infra, where the mental reactions of a bystander are regarded as normal p. 277). See, however, Magruder, Mental and Emotional Disturbance in the Law of Torts, 1936, 49 Harv.L.Rev. 1033, 1042, to the effect that the chance of injuring the third person may be relatively slight, and that of causing shock to an onlooker even more so.

4. See cases cited supra, p. 330.

5. Compare M. J. Rose Co. v. Lowery, 1929, 33 Ohio App. 488, 169 N.E. 716; Koontz v. Keller, 1936, 52 Ohio App. 265, 3 N.E.2d 694.

serious one, of a nature to cause severe mental disturbance to the plaintiff,[6] and that the shock must result in actual physical harm.[7] The action might, at least initially, well be confined to members of the immediate family of the one endangered, or perhaps to husband, wife, parent, or child,[8] to the exclusion of mere bystanders,[9] and remote relatives. As an additional safeguard, it might be required that the plaintiff be present at the time of the accident or peril, or at least that the shock be fairly contemporaneous with it,[10] rather than follow when the plaintiff is informed of the whole matter at a later date.[11] Admittedly such restrictions are quite arbitrary, have no reason in themselves, and would be imposed only in order to draw a line somewhere short of undue liability; but they may be necessary in order not to "leave the liability of a negligent defendant open to undue extension by the verdict of sympathetic juries, who under our system must define and apply any general rule to the facts of the case before them."[12]

55. PRENATAL INJURIES

One area in which the limitation imposed by the concept of "duty" has played a predominant part is that of prenatal injuries. When a pregnant woman is injured, and as a result the child subsequently born suffers deformity or some other injury, nearly all of the decisions [13] prior to 1946 denied recovery to the child.[14] Two reasons usually were given: First, that the defendant could owe no duty of conduct to a person who was not in existence at the time of his action; and second, that the difficulty of proving any causal connection between negligence and damage was too great, and there was too much danger of fictitious claims.

---

6.   Sperier v. Ott, 1906, 116 La. 1087, 41 So. 323; Bucknam v. Great Northern R. Co., 1899, 76 Minn. 373, 79 N.W. 98; Ellis v. Cleveland, 1883, 55 Vt. 358; Sanderson v. Northern Pacific R. Co., 1902, 88 Minn. 162, 92 N.W. 542.

7.   Keyes v. Minneapolis & St. L. R. Co., 1886, 36 Minn. 290, 30 N.W. 888; Wyman v. Leavitt, 1880, 71 Me. 227.

8.   Cf. Gardner v. Cumberland Tel. Co., 1925, 207 Ky. 249, 268 S.W. 1108; Western Union Tel. Co. v. Taulbee, Tex.Civ.App.1929, 20 S.W.2d 232 (negligent transmission of telegram).

In Dillon v. Legg, 1968, 68 Cal.2d 728, 69 Cal.Rptr. 72, 441 P.2d 912, a sister was allowed to recover; but she was herself physically endangered.

9.   Bourhill v. Young, [1943] A.C. 92; cf. Blanchard v. Reliable Transfer Co., 1944, 71 Ga.App. 843, 32 S.E.2d 420; Van Hoy v. Oklahoma Coca-Cola Bottling Co., 1951, 205 Okl. 135, 235 P.2d 948.

10.   Cf. Hambrook v. Stokes Bros., [1925] 1 K.B. 141, 152; Robertson v. Aetna Cas. & Surety Co., La. App.1970, 232 So.2d 829.

In Archibald v. Braverman, 1969, 275 Cal.App.2d 290, 79 Cal.Rptr. 723, recovery was allowed to a mother who did not actually see her child injured, but appeared on the scene moments afterward and saw his condition. In accord is Boardman v. Sanderson, [1964] 1 W.L.R. 1317, where a father, known to defendant to be on the premises, heard the screams and came running to the scene.

11.   Koontz v. Keller, 1936, 52 Ohio App. 265, 3 N.E. 2d 694; Kelly v. Fretz, 1937, 19 Cal.App.2d 356, 65 P.2d 914; Kalleg v. Fassio, 1932, 125 Cal.App. 96, 13 P.2d 763; Herrick v. Evening Express Pub. Co., 1921, 120 Me. 138, 113 A. 16; Finbow v. Domino, 1957, 23 W.W.R. 97.

12.   Bohlen, Fifty Years of Torts, 1937, 50 Harv.L. Rev. 725, 735. Compare the liberal rule in workmen's compensation cases, where there is no jury. Yates v. South Kirkby Collieries, [1910] 2 K.B. 538. But see, opposing all liability, Note, 1937, 26 Geo.L. J. 144.

13.   Recovery was allowed in Cooper v. Blanck, La. App.1923, 39 So.2d 352, and in Scott v. McPheeters, 1939, 33 Cal.App.2d 629, 92 P.2d 678, rehearing denied 33 Cal.App.2d 629, 93 P.2d 562, both relying on statutory language. Kine v. Zuckerman, 1924, 4 Pa.D. & C. 227, allowed recovery, but was overruled by Berlin v. J. C. Penney Co., 1940, 339 Pa. 547, 16 A.2d 28. Finally, Montreal Tramways v. Leveille, [1933] S.C.Rep. 456, 4 Dom.L.Rep. 337, was influenced by the civil law.

14.   Walker v. Great Northern R. Co., [1891] L.R. 28 Ir. 69; Allaire v. St. Luke's Hospital, 1900, 184 Ill. 359, 56 N.E. 638; Lipps v. Milwaukee Elec. R. & L. Co., 1916, 164 Wis. 272, 159 N.W. 916; Drobner v. Peters, 1921, 232 N.Y. 220, 133 N.E. 567.

A fortiori, that there could be no action for wrongful death of the child after its birth. Dietrich v. Inhabitants of Northampton, 1884, 138 Mass. 14; Gorman v. Budlong, 1901, 23 R.I. 169, 49 A. 704; Buel v. United Railways Co., 1913, 248 Mo. 126, 154 S.W. 71; Magnolia Coca Cola Bottling Co. v. Jordan, 1935, 124 Tex. 347, 78 S.W.2d 944; Newman v. City of Detroit, 1937, 281 Mich. 60, 274 N.W. 710.

So far as duty is concerned, if existence at the time is necessary,[15] medical authority has recognized long since that the child is in existence from the moment of conception,[16] and for many purposes its existence is recognized by the law.[17] The criminal law regards it as a separate entity,[18] and the law of property considers it in being for all purposes which are to its benefit, such as taking by will or descent.[19] After its birth, it has been held that it may maintain a statutory action for the wrongful death of the parent.[20] So far as causation is concerned, there will certainly be cases in which there are difficulties of proof, but they are no more frequent, and the difficulties, are no greater,

than as to many other medical problems.[21] All writers who have discussed the problem have joined in condemning the old rule, in maintaining that the unborn child in the path of an automobile is as much a person in the street as the mother, and in urging that recovery should be allowed upon proper proof.[22]

A good many years of this rather devastating criticism finally had its effect. Beginning with a decision [23] in the District of Columbia in 1946, a rapid series of cases, many of them expressly overruling prior holdings, have brought about what was up till that time the most spectacular abrupt reversal of a well settled rule in the whole history of the law of torts. The child, if he is born alive,[24] is permitted to maintain an action for the consequences of prenatal injuries,[25] and if

---

15. Cf. Kine v. Zuckerman, 1924, 4 Pa.D. & C. 227, saying the case is the same as if the defendant had installed a dangerous apparatus in the home of the unborn child, and shortly after birth the child had been injured by it. Cf. Piper v. Hoard, 1887, 107 N.Y. 73, 13 N.E. 626, where equitable relief was given to a child not even conceived at the time of an intentional fraud.

16. See Herzog, Medical Jurisprudence, 1931, §§ 860–975; Malloy, Legal Anatomy and Surgery, 1930, 669–687.

17. "Let us see what this non-entity can do. He may be vouched in a recovery, though it is for the purpose of making him answer over in value. He may be an executor. He may take under the Statute of Distributions. He may take by devise. He may be entitled under a charge for raising portions. He may have an injunction, and he may have a guardian." Butler, J., in Thellusson v. Woodford, 1798, 4 Ves. 227, 322, 31 Eng.Rep. 117.

18. Cf. State v. Walters, 1929, 199 Wis. 68, 225 N. W. 167; Morgan v. State, 1923, 148 Tenn. 417, 256 S.W. 433; Clarke v. State, 1898, 117 Ala. 1, 23 So. 671 (child born alive died as a result of unlawful beating of mother; held to be murder).

19. Deal v. Sexton, 1907, 144 N.C. 157, 56 S.E. 691; Biggs v. McCarty, 1882, 86 Ind. 352; cf. Hall v. Hancock, 1834, 15 Pick., Mass., 255; Campbell v. Everhart, 1905, 139 N.C. 503, 52 S.E. 201; Texas & Pac. R. Co. v. Robertson, 1891, 82 Tex. 657, 17 S.W. 1041.

20. The George and Richard, 1871, 3 Ad. & El. 466, 111 Eng.Rep. 491; Herndon v. St. Louis & S. F. R. Co., 1912, 37 Okl. 256, 128 P. 727; Nelson v. Galveston, H. & S. A. R. Co., 1890, 78 Tex. 621, 14 S.W. 1021.

21. Herzog, Medical Jurisprudence, 1931, §§ 860–975; 1 Gray, Attorney's Handbook of Medicine, 3d Ed. 1949, 611; Malloy, Legal Anatomy and Surgery, 1930, 669–687. "The questions of causation, reasonable certainty, etc., which will arise in these cases are no different, in kind, from the ones which have arisen in thousands of other negligence cases decided in this State, in the past." Woods v. Lancet, 1951, 303 N.Y. 349, 102 N.E.2d 691.

22. Winfield, The Unborn Child, 1942, 4 U.Toronto L.J. 278; Muse and Spinella, Right of Infant to Recover for Prenatal Injury, 1950, 36 Va.L.Rev. 611; Del Tufo, Recovery for Prenatal Torts: Actions for Wrongful Death, 1950, 15 Rut.L.Rev. 61; Gordon, The Unborn Plaintiff, 1965, 12 J.For.Med. 111; Notes, 1949, 63 Harv.L.Rev. 173; 1950, 3 Vand.L.Rev. 283; 1950, 48 Mich.L.Rev. 550; 1950, 35 Corn.L.Q. 648; 1951, 12 Md.L.Rev. 223; [1951] Wash.U.L.Q. 408, [1951] Wis.L.Rev. 518; 1959, 26 Tenn.L.Rev. 494; 1963, 38 Wash.L.Rev. 390; 1965, 37 U.Colo.L.Rev. 271.

23. Bonbrest v. Kotz, D.D.C.1946, 65 F.Supp. 138.

The real start of the movement was the dissenting opinion of Boggs, J., in Allaire v. St. Luke's Hospital, 1900, 184 Ill. 359, 56 N.E. 638.

24. As to stillborn infants, see infra, p. 338.

25. Williams v. Marion Rapid Transit Co., 1949, 152 Ohio St. 114, 87 N.E.2d 334; Woods v. Lancet, 1951, 303 N.Y. 349, 102 N.E.2d 691; Damasiewicz v. Gorsuch, 1951, 197 Md. 417, 79 A.2d 550; Rodriquez v. Patti, 1953, 415 Ill. 496, 114 N.E.2d 271; Mallison v. Pomeroy, 1955, 205 Or. 690, 291 P.2d 225. There is a complete collection and classification of cases to date in the Note in 1963, 38 Wash.L.Rev. 390.

he dies of such injuries after birth an action will lie for his wrongful death.[26] So rapid has been the overturn that after the lapse of a scant twenty-three years from the beginning, it is now apparently literally true that there is no authority left still supporting the older rule. The last jurisdiction to overrule it was Texas,[27] in 1967.

There are, however, two problems on which there is as yet no complete agreement. One concerns the stage of development of the unborn child at the time of the original injury. Most of the cases allowing recovery have involved a foetus which was then viable, meaning capable of independent life, if only in an incubator.[28] Many of them have said, by way of dictum, that recovery must be limited to such cases,[29] and two or three have said that the child, if not viable, must at least be "quick." [30] But when actually faced with the issue for decision, almost all of the jurisdictions have allowed recovery even though the injury occurred during the early weeks of pregnancy, when the child was neither viable nor quick.[31]

There is something to be said on both sides of this. Viability of course does not affect the question of the legal existence of the foetus, and therefore of the defendant's duty; and it is a most unsatisfactory criterion, since it is a relative matter, depending on the health of mother and child and many other matters in addition to the stage of development.[32] Certainly the infant may be no less injured; and all logic is in favor of ignoring the stage at which it occurs. But with our knowledge of embryology what it is, as we approach the beginning of pregnancy medical knowledge, and therefore medical testimony and medical proof of causes, becomes increasingly unreliable and unsatisfactory, so that there is good reason for caution.[33] This,

26. Amann v. Faidy, 1953, 415 Ill. 422, 114 N.E.2d 412; Peterson v. Nationwide Mut. Ins. Co., 1964, 175 Ohio St. 551, 197 N.E.2d 194; Steggall v. Morris, 1953, 363 Mo. 1224, 258 S.W.2d 577; Keyes v. Construction Service, Inc., 1960, 340 Mass. 633, 165 N.E.2d 912; Shousha v. Matthews Drivurself Service, 1962, 210 Tenn. 384, 358 S.W.2d 471. In Torigian v. Watertown News Co., 1967, 352 Mass. 446, 225 N.E.2d 926, recovery was allowed where the child, although it lived two or three hours, was not even viable at the time of the injury.

27. Leal v. C. C. Pitts Sand & Gravel Co., Tex.1967, 419 S.W.2d 820, overruling Magnolia Coca Cola Bottling Co. v. Jordan, 1935, 124 Tex. 347, 78 S.W.2d 944.

28. "Viable: Capable of living, especially capable of living outside the uterus; said of a fetus that has reached such a stage of development that it can live outside the uterus." Dorland, American Illustrated Medical Dictionary, 21st Ed. 1948, 1616.

29. New Hampshire so held in Poliquin v. Macdonald, 1957, 101 N.H. 104, 135 A.2d 249, but this was apparently overruled in Bennett v. Hymers, 1958, 101 N.H. 483, 147 A.2d 108.

30. Kelly v. Gregory, 1953, 282 App.Div. 542, 125 N.Y.S.2d 696, appeal granted, 1954, 283 App.Div. 914, 129 N.Y.S.2d 914; Damasiewicz v. Gorsuch, 1951, 197 Md. 417, 79 A.2d 550. Porter v. Lassiter, 1955, 91 Ga.App. 712, 87 S.E.2d 100 so held, but the supreme court has gone beyond it.

31. Sylvia v. Gobeille, 1966, 101 R.I. 76, 220 A.2d 222; Hornbuckle v. Plantation Pipe Line Co., 1956, 212 Ga. 504, 93 S.E.2d 727, conformed to 94 S.E.2d 328, 94 S.E.2d 523; Bennett v. Hymers, 1958, 101 N.H. 483, 147 A.2d 108; Sinkler v. Kneale, 1960, 401 Pa. 267, 164 A.2d 93; Smith v. Brennan, 1960, 31 N.J. 353, 157 A.2d 497. See Note, 1968, 21 Okl. L.Rev. 114.

California and Louisiana have construed their statutory language to reach this result. Scott v. McPheeters, 1939, 33 Cal.App.2d 629, 92 P.2d 678, rehearing denied 33 Cal.App.2d 629, 93 P.2d 562; Cooper v. Blanck, La.App.1923, 39 So.2d 352.

32. Greenhill, Principles and Practice of Obstetrics, 10th Ed. 1951, 391, 794. Infants have been born as early as the twenty-sixth week and survived; others have been unable to sustain life when born even at term. De Lee, Principles and Practice of Obstetrics, 7th Ed. 1938, 58. See Notes, 1950, 38 Corn.L.Q. 648; 1953, 14 U.Pitt.L.Rev. 344.

33. The problem is nicely illustrated by Sinkler v. Kneale, 1960, 401 Pa. 267, 164 A.2d 93, and Puhl v. Milwaukee Auto. Ins. Co., 1959, 8 Wis.2d 343, 99 N. W.2d 163. In each case there was traumatic injury to the mother in the early stages of pregnancy, and the child was born a Mongolian idiot. Pennsylvania, on the pleadings, held that a cause of action was stated. Wisconsin, after trial, held that the burden of proof of causation had not been sustained.

The writer cannot venture any medical opinion; but if, as may very possibly be the case, the causation is really a matter of pure scientific speculation, or even of sheer medical nonsense, the dangers are in-

however, goes to proof rather than principle; and if, as is undoubtedly the case [34] there are injuries as to which reliable medical proof is possible, it makes no sense to deny recovery on any such arbitrary basis.

The other problem is whether the child must be born alive, or whether an action can be maintained for its wrongful death if it is stillborn as a result of the injury. This may turn on the construction of a wrongful death statute, as to whether such an infant is the kind of "person" intended by the legislature; but there are also obvious difficulties of proof of causation and damages, and some possibility of double recovery, since the mother has an action for her own miscarriage.[35] For such reasons several courts have refused to permit the action.[36] Others, by now in a slight majority, have been more concerned with compensation for a distressing wrong in the loss of a child, and have allowed it.[37]

Some mention should also be made here of the curious problem presented by two cases [38] in which recovery was denied for the alleged tort of causing the plaintiff to be born in a state of illegitimacy. Although these gave rise to quite a bit of law review discussion,[39] there is no decision whch has yet allowed any such action.

56. ACTS AND OMISSIONS

In the determination of the existence of a duty, there runs through much of the law a distinction between action and inaction.[40] In the early common law one who injured another by a positive, affirmative act, was held liable without any great regard even for his fault.[41] But the courts were far too much occupied with the more flagrant forms of misbehavior to be greatly concerned with one who merely did nothing, even though another might suffer harm because of his omission to act. Hence there arose very early a difference, still deeply rooted in the law of negligence, between "misfeasance" and "nonfeasance"—that is to say, between active misconduct working positive injury to others and passive inaction or a failure to take

dicated. See the excellent discussion in the Notes, [1962] Wis.L.Rev. 554; 1962, 110 U.Pa.L.Rev. 554. Also Culiner, Trauma to the Unborn Child, 5 Trauma, No. 1, June 1963, 5–126.

34. The large number of injuries resulting in Europe from the use of the tranquillizer thalidomide during early weeks of pregnancy appear to offer an excellent example. Consider also the well-known effect of rubella (German measles) in the early stages of pregnancy.

35. The mother's action does not, however, include damages for the loss of the child. Occhipinti v. Rheem Mfg. Co., 1965, 252 Miss. 172, 172 So.2d 186.

36. Drabbels v. Skelly Oil Co., 1951, 155 Neb. 17, 50 N.W.2d 229; Graf v. Taggert, 1964, 43 N.J. 303, 204 A.2d 140; Padillow v. Elrod, Okl.1967, 424 P.2d 16; Durrett v. Owens, 1963, 212 Tenn. 614, 371 S.W.2d 433; Carroll v. Skloff, 1964, 415 Pa. 47, 202 A.2d 9. See Del Tufo, Recovery for Prenatal Torts: Actions for Wrongful Death, 1960, 15 Rut.L.Rev. 61; Notes, 1965, 18 Vand.L.Rev. 847; 1964, 29 Mo.L. Rev. 174; 1964, 26 U.Pitt.L.Rev. 134; 1969, 21 Syr. L.Rev. 186; 1966, 18 Me.L.Rev. 105; 1965, 22 Wash. & Lee L.Rev. 146.

37. Kwaterski v. State Farm Mut. Auto Ins. Co., 1967, 34 Wis.2d 14, 148 N.W.2d 107; State to Use of Odham v. Sherman, 1964, 234 Md. 179, 198 A.2d 71; Fowler v. Woodward, 1964, 244 S.C. 608, 138 S. E.2d 42; White v. Yup, 1969, 85 Nev. 527, 458 P.2d 617; Rice v. Rizk, Ky.1970, 453 S.W.2d 901. See Notes, 1969, 71 W.Va.L.Rev. 389; 1970, 7 Houst.L. Rev. 449.

38. Zepeda v. Zepeda, 1963, 41 Ill.App.2d 240, 190 N. E.2d 849, cert. denied 379 U.S. 945; Williams v. State, 1966, 18 N.Y.2d 481, 276 N.Y.S.2d 885, 223 N. E.2d 343.

39. Ploscowe, An Action for "Wrongful Life," 1963, 38 N.Y.U.L.Rev. 1078; Notes, 1966, 66 Col.L.Rev. 127; 1966, 18 Stan.L.Rev. 530; [1963] U.Ill.L.F. 733; 1966, 35 U.Cin.L.Rev. 120; 1966, 11 S.Dak.L. Rev. 180.

40. See Bohlen, The Basis of Affirmative Obligations in the Law of Tort, 1905, 44 Am.L.Reg.,N.S., 209, 273, 337; Bohlen, The Moral Duty to Aid Others as a Basis of Tort Liability, 1908, 56 U.Pa.L.Rev. 217; McNiece and Thornton, Affirmative Duties in Tort, 1949, 58 Yale L.J. 1272; Gregory, Gratuitous Undertakings and the Duty of Care, 1951, 1 De Paul L. Rev. 30; Seavey, Reliance on Gratuitous Promises or Other Conduct, 1951, 64 Harv.L.Rev. 913; Wright, Negligent "Acts or Omissions," 1941, 19 Can.Bar Rev. 465.

41. See supra, p. 7.

steps to protect them from harm.[42] The reason for the distinction may be said to lie in the fact that by "misfeasance" the defendant has created a new risk of harm to the plaintiff, while by "nonfeasance" he has at least made his situation no worse, and has merely failed to benefit him by interfering in his affairs.[43] The highly individualistic philosophy of the older common law had no great difficulty in working out restraints upon the commission of affirmative acts of harm, but shrank from converting the courts into an agency for forcing men to help one another.[44]

Liability for nonfeasance was therefore slow to receive recognition in the law. It first appears in the case of those engaged in "public" callings, who, by holding themselves out to the public, were regarded as having undertaken a duty to give service, for the breach of which they were liable.[45] This idea still survives in the obligation of common carriers, innkeepers, public warehousemen, and public utilities to serve all comers.[46] With the development of the action of assumpsit, this principle was extended to anyone who, for a consideration, has undertaken to perform a promise—[47] or what we now call a contract. During the last century, liability for "nonfeasance" has been extended still further to a limited group of relations, in which custom, public sentiment and views of social policy have led the courts to find a duty of affirmative action. It is not likely that this process of extension has ended. For the most part such a duty has been imposed where the relation is of some actual or potential economic advantage to the defendant, and the expected benefit justifies the requirement of special obligations.[48] The largest single group upon whom the duty of affirmative conduct has been imposed are the owners and occupiers of land, who are to be considered later.[49]

Liability for "misfeasance," then, may extend to any person to whom harm may reasonably be anticipated as a result of the defendant's conduct, or perhaps even beyond;[50] while for "nonfeasance" it is necessary to find some definite relation between the parties, of such a character that social policy justifies the imposition of a duty to act.

In theory the difference between the two is simple and obvious; but in practice it is not always easy to draw the line and say whether conduct is active or passive.[51] It is clear that

---

42. Bohlen, The Moral Duty to Aid Others as a Basis of Tort Liability, 1908, 56 U.Pa.L.Rev. 217, 219.

43. Bohlen, The Moral Duty to Aid Others as a Basis of Tort Liability, 1908, 56 U.Pa.L.Rev. 217, 221.

44. Green, Judge and Jury, 1930, 62.

45. Arterburn, The Origin and First Test of Public Callings, 1927, 75 U.Pa.L.Rev. 411.

46. See for example Williams v. Carolina & N. W. R. Co., 1907, 144 N.C. 498, 57 S.E. 216; Zabron v. Cunard S. S. Co., 1911, 151 Iowa 345, 131 N.W. 18; Jackson v. Virginia Hot Springs Co., 1914, 130 C.C. A. 375, 213 F. 969; Oklahoma Natural Gas Co. v. Pack, 1939, 186 Okl. 330, 97 P.2d 768; Capital Elec. Power Ass'n v. Hinson, 1957, 230 Miss. 211, 92 So. 2d 867.

It survives also under the civil rights statutes, requiring places of public accommodation to serve the public without discrimination on the basis of race or color. See for example Lambert v. Mandel's of California, 1957, 156 Cal.App.2d 855, 319 P.2d 469; Amos v. Prom, Inc., N.D.Iowa 1953, 115 F.Supp. 127. See Niles, Civil Actions for Damages Under the Federal Civil Rights Statutes, 1967, 45 Tex.L. Rev. 1015; Colley, Civil Actions for Damages Aris-

ing Out of Violations of Civil Rights, (1965) 17 Hast.L.J. 189; Note, 1966, 18 West.Res.L.Rev. 278.

47. Ames, History of Assumpsit, 1888, 2 Harv.L.Rev. 1, 53; Jenks, On Negligence and Deceit in the Law of Torts, 1910, 26 L.Q.Rev. 159.

As to the interrelation of tort and contract, see infra, § 92.

48. Bohlen, The Basis of Affirmative Obligations in the Law of Tort, 1905, 44 Am.L.Reg.,N.S., 209, 273, 337; McNiece and Thornton, Affirmative Duties in Tort, 1949, 58 Yale L.J. 1272.

49. See infra, ch. 10.

50. See supra, pp. 260–267.

51. "So, while to use an article known to be defective is palpably misfeasance, and while a mere failure to provide protection for those who by one's bare permission use one's premises is plainly passive nonfeasance, the use of a chattel for a particular purpose without having first ascertained whether it is fit for such purpose is a compound of both.

it is not always a matter of action or inaction as to the particular act or omission which has caused the plaintiff's damage. Failure to blow a whistle or to shut off steam,[52] although in itself inaction, is readily treated as negligent operation of a train, which is affirmative misconduct; an omission to repair a gas pipe is regarded as negligent distribution of gas;[53] and failure to supply heat for a building can easily become mismanagement of a boiler.[54] On the other hand the discharge of an employee, which is certainly an affirmative act, is uniformly considered to be no more than non-performance of an agreement to continue employment,[55] and a similar conclusion has been reached as to the revocation of a theater ticket and expulsion of a patron.[56] But a physician who starts in to treat a patient and then neglects or abandons him is held liable in tort for breach of a duty undertaken.[57] The question appears to

be essentially one of whether the defendant has gone so far in what he has actually done, and has got himself into such a relation with the plaintiff, that he has begun to affect the interests of the plaintiff adversely, as distinguished from merely failing to confer a benefit upon him.[58]

Duty to Aid One in Peril

Because of this reluctance to countenance "nonfeasance" as a basis of liability, the law has persistently refused to recognize the moral obligation of common decency and common humanity, to come to the aid of another human being who is in danger, even though the outcome is to cost him his life.[59] Some of the decisions have been shocking in the extreme. The expert swimmer, with a boat and a rope at hand, who sees another drowning before his eyes, is not required to do anything at all about it, but may sit on the dock, smoke his cigarette, and watch the man drown.[60] A physician is under no duty to an-

There is both action, i. e., the use of the chattel, and nonfeasance, the failure to perform the positive duty of inspecting it to ascertain if it be defective. * * * Still, the final cause of whatever injury is sustained being the use of the chattel, the tendency is to consider that the whole constitutes an act of misfeasance." Bohlen, The Moral Duty to Aid Others as a Basis of Tort Liability, 1908, 56 U.Pa.L.Rev. 217, 220.

52. Southern R. Co. v. Grizzle, 1906, 124 Ga. 735, 53 S.E. 244. Cf. Kelly v. Metropolitan R. Co., [1895] 1 Q.B. 944.

53. Consolidated Gas Co. v. Connor, 1911, 114 Md. 140, 78 A. 725. Cf. Osborne v. Morgan, 1881, 130 Mass. 102; Horner v. Lawrence, 1874, 37 N.J.L. 46; Lottman v. Barnett, 1876, 62 Mo. 159.

54. Pittsfield Cottonwear Mfg. Co. v. Pittsfield Shoe Co., 1902, 71 N.H. 522, 53 A. 807.

55. Addis v. Gramophone Co., Ltd., [1909] A.C. 488; Elmore v. Atlantic Coast Line R. Co., 1926, 191 N.C. 182, 131 S.E. 633; Manley v. Exposition Cotton Mills, 1933, 47 Ga.App. 496, 170 S.E. 711; W. B. Davis & Son v. Ruple, 1930, 222 Ala. 52, 130 So. 772.

56. Horney v. Nixon, 1905, 213 Pa. 20, 61 A. 1088; Marrone v. Washington Jockey Club, 1913, 227 U.S. 633; Boswell v. Barnum & Bailey, 1916, 135 Tenn. 35, 185 S.W. 692; Shubert v. Nixon Amusement Co., 1912, 83 N.J.L. 101, 83 A. 369.

57. Braun v. Riel, Mo.1931, 40 S.W.2d 621, 80 A.L.R. 875; Thaggard v. Vafes, 1928, 218 Ala. 609, 119 So.

647; Cochran v. Laton, 1918, 78 N.H. 562, 103 A. 658; Mehigan v. Sheehan, 1947, 94 N.H. 274, 51 A. 2d 632.

58. There is a much quoted, but quite lengthy, passage to this effect in the opinion of Cardozo in H. R. Moch Co. v. Rensselaer Water Co., 1928, 247 N. Y. 160, 159 N.E. 896, 898.

59. In several other countries statutes, for the most part of a criminal character, have imposed a duty, under some limited conditions, to rescue another in peril. See Feldbrugge, Good and Bad Samaritans: A Comparative Survey, 1967, 14 Am.J.Comp.Law, 630. An earlier Note more concerned with tort liability is in 1952, 52 Col.L.Rev. 631. A good Canadian study is Linden, Tort Liability for Criminal Nonfeasance, 1966, 44 Can.Bar Rev. 25.

60. Osterlind v. Hill, 1928, 263 Mass. 73, 160 N.E. 301. Here the defendant had even rented a canoe to the intoxicated plaintiff, who upset it. Still worse is Yania v. Bigan, 1959, 397 Pa. 316, 155 A.2d 343, where plaintiff was not a stranger, but a business visitor, and defendant incited him to jump into the water and let him drown. There is also Handiboe v. McCarthy, 1966, 114 Ga.App. 541, 151 S.E.2d 905, where it was held that there was no duty whatever to rescue a child licensee drowning in a swimming pool. It would be hard to find a more unappetizing trio of decisions. See Seavey, I Am Not My Guest's Keeper, 1960, 13 Vand.L.Rev. 699.

swer the call of one who is dying and might be saved,[61] nor is anyone required to play the part of Florence Nightingale and bind up the wounds of a stranger who is bleeding to death,[62] or to prevent a neighbor's child from hammering on a dangerous explosive,[63] or to remove a stone from the highway where it is a menace to traffic,[64] or a train from a place where it blocks a fire engine on its way to save a house,[65] or even to cry a warning to one who is walking into the jaws of a dangerous machine.[66] The remedy in such cases is left to the "higher law" and the "voice of conscience," [67] which, in a wicked world, would seem to be singularly ineffective either to prevent the harm or to compensate the victim.

Such decisions are revolting to any moral sense. They have been denounced with vigor by legal writers.[68] Thus far the difficul-

ties of setting any standards of unselfish service to fellow men, and of making any workable rule to cover possible situations where fifty people might fail to rescue one,[69] has limited any tendency to depart from the rule to cases where some special relation between the parties has afforded a justification for the creation of a duty, without any question of setting up a rule of universal application. Thus a carrier has been required to take reasonable affirmative steps to aid a passenger in peril,[70] and an innkeeper to aid his guest.[71] Maritime law has long recognized the duty of a ship to save its seaman who has fallen overboard; [72] and there is now quite a general tendency to extend the

---

61. Hurley v. Eddingfield, 1901, 156 Ind. 416, 59 N.E. 1058; see Randolph's Adm'r v. Snyder, 1910, 139 Ky. 159, 129 S.W. 562. As to hospitals, see Note, 1966, 18 U.Fla.L.Rev. 475.

62. Allen v. Hixson, 1900, 111 Ga. 460, 36 S.E. 810; Riley v. Gulf, C. & S. F. R. Co., Tex.Civ.App.1913, 160 S.W. 595; cf. People v. Beardsley, 1907, 150 Mich. 206, 113 N.W. 1128.

63. Sidwell v. McVay, Okl.1955, 282 P.2d 756.

64. O'Keefe v. W. J. Barry Co., 1942, 311 Mass. 517, 42 N.E.2d 267.

65. Louisville & Nashville R. Co. v. Scruggs & Echols, 1909, 161 Ala. 97, 49 So. 399.

66. See Gautret v. Egerton, 1887, L.R. 2 C.P. 381; Buch v. Amory Mfg. Co., 1897, 69 N.H. 257, 44 A. 809; Toadvine v. Cincinnati, N. O. & T. P. R. Co., D.Ky.1937, 20 F.Supp. 226. Compare Schichowski v. Hoffmann, 1933, 261 N.Y. 389, 185 N.E. 676 (no duty to aid another to avoid imprisonment).

67. Union Pac. R. Co. v. Cappier, 1903, 66 Kan. 649, 72 P. 281.

68. Ames, Law and Morals, 1908, 22 Harv.L.Rev. 97, 112; Bohlen, The Moral Duty to Aid Others as a Basis of Tort Liability, 1908, 56 U.Pa.L.Rev. 217, 316; Bruce, Humanity and the Law, 1911, 73 Cent. L.J. 335; Warner, Duty of a Railroad to Care for a Person Rendered Helpless, 1919, 7 Cal.L.Rev. 312; Cardozo, The Paradoxes of Legal Science, 1928, 25; Seavey, I Am Not My Guest's Keeper, 1960, 13 Vand.L.Rev. 699; Rudolph, The Duty to Act: A Proposed Rule, 1965, 44 Neb.L.J. 499; Note, 1966, 28 U.Pitt.L.Rev. 61.

69. The difficulties are considered in the Report of the Commissioners on the Indian Penal Code (1838), Note M. 103–6. Compare the provision of the Dutch Penal Code, Art. 450: "One who, witnessing the danger of death with which another is suddenly threatened, neglects to give or furnish him such assistance as he can give or procure without reasonable fear of danger to himself, is to be punished, if the death of the person in distress follows, by a detention of three months at most and an amende of three hundred florins at most."

70. Yu v. New York, N. H. & H. R. Co., 1958, 145 Conn. 451, 144 A.2d 56; Middleton v. Whitridge, 1915, 213 N.Y. 499, 108 N.E. 192; Kambour v. Boston & Me. R. Co., 1913, 77 N.H. 33, 86 A. 624; Layne v. Chicago & Alton R. Co., 1913, 175 Mo.App. 34, 157 S.W. 850; Yazoo & M. V. R. Co. v. Byrd, 1906, 89 Miss. 308, 42 So. 286. Even where the passenger has been injured through his own negligence. Continental Southern Lines v. Robertson, 1961, 241 Miss. 796, 133 So.2d 543; Southern R. Co. v. Sewell, 1916, 18 Ga.App. 544, 90 S.E. 94.

71. At least in case of fire. Dove v. Lowden, W.D. Mo.1942, 47 F.Supp. 546; West v. Spratling, 1920, 204 Ala. 478, 86 So. 32; Stewart v. Weiner, 1922, 108 Neb. 49, 187 N.W. 121; Texas Hotel Co. of Longview v. Cosby, Tex.Civ.App.1939, 131 S.W.2d 261. Cf. Hercules Powder Co. v. Crawford, 8 Cir. 1947, 163 F.2d 968. See also, as to protection of the guest against attacks of third persons, infra, p. 395.

72. Harris v. Pennsylvania R. Co., 4 Cir. 1931, 50 F. 2d 866; Di Nicola v. Pennsylvania R. Co., 2 Cir. 1946, 158 F.2d 856; Pacific-Atlantic S. S. Co. v. Hutchison, 9 Cir. 1957, 242 F.2d 691; Kirincich v. Standard Dredging Co., 3 Cir. 1940, 112 F.2d 163. Cf. Cortes v. Baltimore Insular Lines, 1932, 287 U. S. 367 (sick); Scarff v. Metcalf, 1887, 107 N.Y. 211, 13 N.E. 796 (same). See Note, 1932, 17 Corn.L.Q. 505.

same duty to any employer when his employee is injured or endangered in the course of his employment.[73] There is now respectable authority imposing the same duty upon a shopkeeper to his business visitor,[74] upon a host to his social guest,[75] upon a jailer to his prisoner,[76] and upon a school to its pupil.[77] There are undoubtedly other rela-

tions calling for the same conclusion. Two that appear likely to receive early recognition are those of husband and wife, and parent and child, where the duty to aid has been established in the criminal law,[78] and with the rapidly growing tendency to abrogate family immunities to suit [79] may be expected to be taken over into tort cases.

It also is recognized that if the defendant's own negligence has been responsible for the plaintiff's situation, a relation has arisen which imposes a duty to make a reasonable effort to give assistance, and avoid any further harm.[80] Where the original danger is created by innocent conduct, involving no fault on the part of the defendant, it was formerly the rule [81] that no such duty arose; but this appears to have given way, in recent decisions, to a recognition of the duty to take action, both where the prior innocent conduct has created an unreasonable risk of harm to the plaintiff,[82] and where it

73. Anderson v. Atchison, T. & S. F. R. Co., 1948, 333 U.S. 821; Rival v. Atchison, T. & S. F. R. Co., 1957, 62 N.M. 159, 306 P.2d 648; Szabo v. Pennsylvania R. Co., 1945, 132 N.J.L. 331, 40 A.2d 562; Hunicke v. Meramec Quarry Co., 1914, 262 Mo. 560, 172 S.W. 43; Carey v. Davis, 1921, 190 Iowa 720, 180 N.W. 889.

It has been held that there is no duty to an employee outside of the course of his employment. Allen v. Hixson, 1900, 111 Ga. 460, 36 S.E. 810; Matthews v. Carolina & N. W. R. Co., 1918, 175 N.C. 35, 94 S. E. 714. And of course none in the absence of reason to believe that he needs aid. Wilke v. Chicago Great Western R. Co., 1933, 190 Minn. 89, 251 N.W. 11; Gypsy Oil Co. v. McNair, 1937, 179 Okl. 182, 64 P.2d 885.

Accord, as to cities: Whitacre v. City of Charlotte, 1940, 216 N.C. 687, 6 S.E.2d 558; Knight v. Sheffield Corp., [1942] 2 All Eng.Rep. 411.

Cf. O'Leary v. Erie R. Co., 1900, 169 N.Y. 289, 62 N.E. 346; but cf. Hieber v. Central Ky. Traction Co., 1911, 145 Ky. 108, 140 S.W. 54.

74. L. S. Ayres & Co. v. Hicks, 1942, 220 Ind. 86, 40 N.E.2d 334, 41 N.E.2d 356; Connelly v. Kaufmann & Baer Co., 1944, 349 Pa. 261, 37 A.2d 125; Larkin v. Saltair Beach Co., 1905, 30 Utah 86, 83 P. 686; see Harold's Club v. Sanchez, 1954, 70 Nev. 518, 275 P.2d 384; Blizzard v. Fitzsimmons, 1942, 193 Miss. 484, 10 So.2d 343. That this is "premises liability" seems to be made clear by Gilbert v. Gwin-McCollum Funeral Home, 1958, 268 Ala. 372, 106 So.2d 646, holding that a funeral director had no duty to protect a mourner, riding in the car of another mourner in a funeral procession.

75. Hutchinson v. Dickie, 6 Cir. 1947, 162 F.2d 103, cert. denied, 332 U.S. 830 (on yacht); Tubbs v. Argus, 1967, 140 Ind.App. 695, 225 N.E.2d 841; Matthews v. MacLaren, [1969] 2 Ont.L.Rep. 137.

76. Farmer v. State, 1955, 224 Miss. 96, 79 So.2d 528; Dunham v. Village of Canisteo, 1952, 303 N.Y. 498, 104 N.E.2d 872; Thomas v. Williams, 1962, 105 Ga. App. 321, 124 S.E.2d 409; Smith v. Miller, 1950, 241 Iowa 625, 40 N.W.2d 597; O'Dell v. Goodsell, 1948, 149 Neb. 261, 30 N.W.2d 906.

77. See Pirkle v. Oakdale Union Grammar School Dist., 1953, 40 Cal.2d 207, 253 P.2d 1. Cf. Barbarisi v. Caruso, 1957, 47 N.J.Super. 125, 135 A.2d 539 (grandmother volunteering to look after child).

78. Rex v. Russell, [1933] Vict.L.Rep. 59; Rex v. Smith, 1826, 2 C. & P. 449, 172 Eng.Rep. 203; State v. Rivers, 1958, 133 Mont. 129, 320 P.2d 1004; State v. Zobel, 1965, 81 S.D. 260, 134 N.W.2d 101, cert. denied 382 U.S. 833. See Linden, Tort Liability for Criminal Nonfeasance, 1966, 44 Am.Bar Rev. 25.

79. See infra, § 122.

80. Parrish v. Atlantic Coast Line R. Co., 1942, 221 N.C. 292, 20 S.E.2d 299. Trombley v. Kolts, 1938, 29 Cal.App.2d 699, 85 P.2d 541. Both Whitesides v. Southern R. Co., 1901, 128 N.C. 229, 38 S.E. 878, and Ward v. Morehead City Sea Food Co., 1916, 171 N. C. 33, 87 S.E. 958, are probably to be explained on this basis, although the decisions are far from clear.

81. Griswold v. Boston & Maine R. Co., 1903, 183 Mass. 434, 67 N.E. 354; Union Pac. R. Co. v. Cappier, 1903, 66 Kan. 649, 72 P. 281; Turbeville v. Mobile Light & R. Co., 1930, 221 Ala. 91, 127 So. 519. Cf. Rose v. Buchanan, Tex.Civ.App.1940, 140 S.W.2d 203, affirmed, 1942, 138 Tex. 390, 159 S.W. 2d 109.

82. Hollinbeck v. Downey, 1962, 261 Minn. 481, 113 N.W.2d 9 (hooked golf ball, duty to cry warning); Montgomery v. National Convoy & Trucking Co., 1938, 186 S.C. 167, 195 S.E. 247 (blocked highway); Hardy v. Brooks, 1961, 103 Ga.App. 124, 118 S.E.2d 492 (same); Chandler v. Forsyth Royal Crown Bottling Co., 1962, 257 N.C. 245, 125 S.E.2d 584 (glass on road); Zylka v. Leikvoll, 1966, 274 Minn. 435,

has already injured him.[83] In a few states "hit and run driver" statutes have been construed to result in civil liability for failure to stop and aid a person injured in an automobile accident, even without the fault of the driver.[84] This process of extension has been slow, and marked with extreme caution; but there is reason to think that it may continue until it approaches a general holding that the mere knowledge of serious peril, threatening death or great bodily harm to another, which an identified defendant might avoid with little inconvenience, creates a sufficient relation, recognized by every moral and social standard, to impose a duty of action.[85]

Where the duty is recognized, it is agreed that it calls for nothing more than reasonable care under the circumstances. The defendant is not liable when he neither knows nor should know of the unreasonable risk, or of the illness or injury. He is not required to give aid to one whom he has no reason to know to be ill. He will seldom be required to do more than give such first aid as he reasonably can, and take reasonable steps to turn the sick man over to a physician, or to those who will look after him until one can be brought.[86]

Affirmative Conduct

If there is no duty to come to the assistance of a person in difficulty or peril, there is at least a duty to avoid any affirmative acts which make his situation worse. When we cross the line into the field of "misfeasance," liability is far easier to find. A truck driver may be under no obligation whatever to signal to a car behind him that it may safely pass; but if he does signal, he will be liable if he fails to exercise proper care and injury results.[87] There may be no duty to take care of a man who is ill or intoxicated, and unable to look out for himself; but it is another thing entirely to eject him into the danger of a railroad yard; and if he is injured there will be liability.[88] But further, if the defendant does attempt to aid him, and takes charge and control of the situation, he is regarded as entering voluntarily into a relation which is attended with responsibility. The same is true, of course, of a physician who accepts a charity patient.[89] Such a defendant will then be liable

---

144 N.W.2d 358. See Second Restatement of Torts, § 321; Note, 1966, 51 Minn.L.Rev. 362.

83. L. S. Ayres & Co. v. Hicks, 1942, 220 Ind. 86, 40 N.E.2d 334, 41 N.E.2d 336; Whitesides v. Southern R. Co., 1901, 128 N.C. 229, 38 S.E. 878; Holland v. St. Paul Mercury Ins. Co., La.App.1961, 135 So.2d 145; cf. Connelly v. Kaufmann & Baer Co., 1944, 349 Pa. 261, 37 A.2d 125; Ward v. Morehead City Sea Food Co., 1916, 171 N.C. 33, 87 S.E. 958.

Cf. Rains v. Heldenfels Bros., Tex.Civ.App.1969, 443 S.W.2d 280, refused n. r. e. (plaintiff barred by contributory negligence from recovery for original injury, but may still recover for failure to give aid after it).

84. Summers v. Dominguez, 1938, 29 Cal.App.2d 308, 84 P.2d 237; Brumfield v. Wofford, 1958, 143 W. Va. 332, 102 S.E.2d 103; Hallman v. Cushman, 1941, 196 S.C. 402, 13 S.E.2d 498; Battle v. Kilcrease, 1936, 54 Ga.App. 808, 189 S.E. 573; Brooks v. E. J. Willig Truck Transp. Co., 1953, 40 Cal.2d 669, 255 P.2d 802. See Note, 1931, 6 Notre Dame Lawyer 379.

85. Cf. Warshauer v. Lloyd Sabaudo S. A., 2 Cir., 1934, 71 F.2d 146 (duty to rescue ship at sea; relying on general maritime law).

86. Owl Drug Co. v. Crandall, 1938, 52 Ariz. 322, 80 P.2d 952; Ohio & Mississippi R. Co. v. Early, 1894, 141 Ind. 73, 40 N.E. 257; Baltimore & Ohio R. Co. v. State to Use of Woodward, 1874, 41 Md. 268; Shaw v. Chicago, M. & St. P. R. Co., 1907, 103 Minn. 8, 114 N.W. 85; Fitzgerald v. Chesapeake & Ohio R. Co., 1935, 116 W.Va. 239, 180 S.E. 766.

87. Shirley Cloak & Dress Co. v. Arnold, 1955, 92 Ga. App. 885, 90 S.E.2d 622; Thelen v. Spilman, 1957, 251 Minn. 89, 86 N.W.2d 700; Haralson v. Jones Truck Lines, 1954, 223 Ark. 813, 270 S.W.2d 892; Petroleum Carrier Corp. v. Carter, 5 Cir. 1956, 233 F.2d 402. Cf. Sweet v. Ringwelski, 1961, 362 Mich. 138, 106 N.W.2d 742; Wulf v. Rebbun, 1964, 25 Wis.2d 499, 131 N.W.2d 303.

88. Fagg's Adm'r v. Louisville & N. R. Co., 1901, 111 Ky. 30, 31, 63 S.W. 580; Cincinnati, N. O. & T. P. R. Co. v. Marrs' Adm'x, 1905, 119 Ky. 954, 85 S.W. 188; Weymire v. Wolfe, 1879, 52 Iowa 533, 3 N.W. 541. Cf. Depue v. Flatau, 1907, 100 Minn. 299, 111 N.W. 1; Raasch v. Elite Laundry Co., 1906, 98 Minn. 357, 108 N.W. 477.

89. Christie v. Callahan, 1941, 75 U.S.App.D.C. 133, 124 F.2d 825; Le Juene Road Hospital, Inc. v. Watson, Fla.App.1965, 171 So.2d 102; Du Bois v.

for a failure to use reasonable care for the protection of the plaintiff's interests.[90] And on the same basis one who, without any legal obligation to do so, attempts to remove ice from the sidewalk, may find himself liable when he makes the situation worse.[91] The result of all this is that the good Samaritan who tries to help may find himself mulcted in damages, while the priest and the Levite who pass by on the other side go on their cheerful way rejoicing. It has been pointed out often enough that this in fact operates as a real, and serious, deterrent to the giving of needed aid. Physicians, who are so frequently called upon for needed help, have been much concerned about potential liability.[92] This

has led to active lobbying by medical associations, which has resulted in the adoption, in a good many states, of statutes absolving a doctor who renders aid in an emergency from all liability for negligence. These statutes have not escaped criticism, as special legislation not really called for by any necessity.[93]

This idea of voluntary assumption of a duty by affirmative conduct runs through a variety of cases. Just when the duty is undertaken, when it ends and what conduct is required, are nowhere clearly defined, and perhaps cannot be. Following an old leading decision in New York,[94] never overruled, a large body of case law has been built up, which holds that a mere gratuitous promise [95] to render service or assistance, with nothing more, imposes no tort obligation upon the promisor, even though the plaintiff may rely on the promise and suffer damage because of that reliance. Most of the decisions have involved only pecuniary loss, as where the promise is to obtain insurance upon a building, and the uninsured building is destroyed by fire.[96] There are, however, a good many

---

Decker, 1891, 130 N.Y. 325, 29 N.E. 313; Napier v. Greenzweig, 1919, 167 C.C.A. 412, 256 F. 196. See Notes, 1964, 31 Tenn.L.Rev. 525; 1965, 19 U.Miami L.Rev. 652; 1966, 18 U.Fla.L.Rev. 475. An extreme case of this is O'Neill v. Montefiore Hospital, 1960, 11 App.Div.2d 132, 202 N.Y.S.2d 436, where a physician and a nurse attempted to give free advice over the telephone. Cf. Le Juene Road Hosp., Inc. v. Watson, Fla.App.1965, 171 So.2d 202.

90. Slater v. Illinois Cent. R. Co., M.D.Tenn.1911, 209 F. 480; Devlin v. Safeway Stores, S.D.N.Y.1964, 235 F.Supp. 882; Gates v. Chesapeake & O. R. Co., 1919, 185 Ky. 24, 213 S.W. 564; Yazoo & M. V. R. Co. v. Leflar, 1933, 168 Miss. 255, 150 So. 220; Bascho v. Pennsylvania R. Co., 1949, 3 N.J.Super. 86, 65 A.2d 613.

91. Nelson v. Schultz, 1939, 170 Misc. 681, 11 N.Y.S. 2d 184; Foley v. Ulrich, 1967, 94 N.J.Sup. 410, 228 A.2d 702, reversed on other grounds 50 N.J. 426, 236 A.2d 137. Cf. Mistretta v. Alessi, 1957, 45 N.J.Super. 176, 131 A.2d 891; Jediny v. City of New York, 2 Cir. 1966, 368 F.2d 523; Ellsworth Bros. v. Crook, Wyo.1965, 406 P.2d 520. See also Cox v. Wagner, Ala.App.1964, 162 So.2d 527 (attempt to steady step-ladder); Briere v. Mathrop Co., 1970, 22 Ohio St.2d 166, 258 N.E.2d 597 (volunteer help in moving scaffold).

Cf. Kurzweg v. Hotel St. Regis Corp., 2 Cir. 1962, 309 F.2d 746 (hotel provided doorman who did not protect plaintiff from traffic); Roberts v. Indiana Gas & Water Co., 1966, 140 Ind.App. 409, 221 N.E.2d 693 (gas company odorized gas, discontinued the practice without warning); Shannon v. City of Anchorage, Alaska 1967, 429 P.2d 17 (city provided access to dock from vessels, failed to provide safe one).

92. One poll of 1209 doctors, reported in Medical Tribune, Aug. 28, 1961, p. 23, resulted in only about half of them saying that they would stop to give medical aid at the scene of an emergency. An-

other poll of 214 led to 16% saying they would refuse to come forward for an emergency in a theater. See Notes, 1962, 75 Harv.L.Rev. 641; 1963, 51 Cal.L.Rev. 816.

93. See the discussion of these "Good Samaritan Acts" in Notes, 1964, 64 Col.L.Rev. 1301; 1964, 10 Vill.L.Rev. 130; [1964] Wis.L.Rev. 494; 1964, 13 De Paul L.Rev. 297; 1964, 42 Or.L.Rev. 328; 1965, 17 U.Fla.L.Rev. 586; 1966, 44 N.C.L.Rev. 508.

In Dahl v. Turner, 1969, 80 N.M. 564, 458 P.2d 816, cert. denied 80 N.M. 608, 458 P.2d 860, such a statute was held to have no application to injury to the victim while transporting him to the hospital.

94. Thorne v. Deas, 1809, 4 Johns., N.Y., 84.

95. Where there is consideration for the promise, there may of course be liability for breach of contract; but the same rule, in general, is applied to bar recovery in tort. This is more conveniently dealt with in connection with the interrelation of tort and contract. See infra, § 92.

96. Brawn v. Lyford, 1907, 103 Me. 362, 69 A. 544; Northern Commercial Co. v. United Airmotive, Inc., 1951, 13 Alaska 503, 101 F.Supp. 169; Comfort v. McCorkle, 1933, 149 Misc. 826, 268 N.Y.S. 192 (proof of fire loss). Cf. Miller v. Bennett, 1943, 237 Mo.

in which reliance upon the promise has led to injury to the person,[97] or to damage to tangible property.[98] The rule frequently has been applied in cases where the defendant has agreed to accept employment whose duties would require him to act for the protection of others such as the plaintiff. If he never appears on the job at all, he is not liable; but if he enters upon performance of his duties and then fails to act, he is.[99]

Actually, however, the old rule has served chiefly as a point of departure; and very little extra is required for the assumption of the duty. If the defendant receives the plaintiff's property or papers, and undertakes, without consideration, to obtain insurance on them,[1] to record a deed,[2] to collect a

note,[3] or otherwise to act as agent,[4] he assumes the duty to use proper care in the performance of the task. The duty is of course all the more clear when he has actually entered upon performance of the promise. But such initiation of the "undertaking" is commonly found in minor acts, of no significance in themselves and without any effect of their own upon the plaintiff's interests, such as

Rather less than half of the courts which have considered the question have held that an insurance company whose agent is entrusted with an application for insurance is liable in tort for undue delay in acting on the application. While there have been a variety of theories, the prevalent explanation is that the agent has assumed a duty of care in dealing with the application. Boyer v. State Farms' Mut. Hail Ins. Co., 1912, 86 Kan. 442, 121 P. 329, rehearing denied, 1912, 87 Kan. 293, 123 P. 742; United States Fire Ins. Co. v. Cannon, 8 Cir. 1965, 349 F.2d 941; Dyer v. Missouri State Life Ins. Co., 1925, 132 Wash. 378, 232 P. 346, affirmed 135 Wash. 693, 236 P. 807; Security Ins. Co. v. Cameron, 1922, 85 Okl. 171, 205 P. 151; Travelers Ins. Co. v. Anderson, W.D.S.C.1962, 210 F.Supp. 735.

Contra: Patten v. Continental Cas. Co., 1954, 162 Ohio St. 18, 120 N.E.2d 441; Swentusky v. Prudential Ins. Co. of America, 1933, 116 Conn. 526, 165 A. 686; Schliep v. Commercial Cas. Ins. Co., 1934, 191 Minn. 479, 254 N.W. 618; Thornton v. National Council, 1930, 110 W.Va. 412, 158 S.E. 507; Zaye v. John Hancock Mut. Life Ins. Co., 1940, 338 Pa. 426, 13 A.2d 34. See Funk, The Duty of an Insurer to Act Promptly on Applications, 1927, 75 U.Pa.L.Rev. 207; Prosser, Delay in Acting on an Application for Insurance, 1935, 3 U.Chi.L.Rev. 39; Notes, 1955, 16 Ohio St.L.J. 111; 1963, 36 Temple L.Q. 84; 1967, 18 S.C.L.Rev. 863.

App. 1285, 172 S.W.2d 960 (conversion of bonds into stock); Newton v. Brook, 1902, 134 Ala. 269, 32 So. 722 (preparation of corpse for shipment by certain train); Louisville & Nashville R. Co. v. Spinks, 1898, 104 Ga. 692, 30 S.E. 968 (transportation home if plaintiff not employed); Farabee-Treadwell Co. v. Union & Planters Bank & Trust Co., 1916, 135 Tenn. 208, 186 S.W. 92 (lending money for purchase of corn).

97. Long v. Patterson, 1945, 198 Miss. 554, 22 So.2d 490 (warn of approaching traffic); Willey v. Alaska Packers Ass'n., N.D.Cal.1926, 9 F.2d 937, affirmed 1937, C.C.A., 18 F.2d 8; Galveston, H. & S. A. R. Co. v. Hennigan, 1903, 33 Tex.Civ.App. 314, 76 S.W. 452 (provide medical treatment); Stone v. Johnson, 1938, 89 N.H. 329, 197 A. 713 (promise to light stair; treated as case of pure nonfeasance). See Randolph's Adm'r v. Snyder, 1910, 139 Ky. 159, 129 S.W. 562 (physician's promise to attend).

98. Tomko v. Sharp, 1915, 87 N.J.L. 385, 94 A. 793 (take car to garage for repairs and bring it back; treated as case of pure nonfeasance); Houston Milling Co. v. Carlock, Tex.Civ.App.1944, 183 S.W.2d 1013 (notify when hay stored in building); see Brown v. T. W. Phillips Gas & Oil Co., 3 Cir. 1952, 195 F.2d 643 (repair gas regulator).

99. Waters v. Anthony, 1949, 252 Ala. 244, 40 So.2d 316; Franklin v. May Department Stores, E.D. Miss.1938, 25 F.Supp. 735; Landreth v. Phillips Petroleum Co., W.D.Mo.1947, 74 F.Supp. 801.

1. Siegel v. Spear & Co., 1925, 234 N.Y. 479, 138 N.E. 414; Schroeder v. Mauzy, 1911, 16 Cal.App. 443, 118 P. 459; cf. Maddock v. Riggs, 1920, 106 Kan. 808, 190 P. 12. See Arterburn, Liability for Breach of Gratuitous Promises, 1927, 22 Ill.L.Rev. 161; Shattuck, Gratuitous Promises—A New Writ, 1937, 35 Mich.L.Rev. 908.

2. Hyde v. Moffat, 1844, 16 Vt. 271; cf. Carr v. Maine Cent. R. Co., 1917, 78 N.H. 502, 102 A. 532 (filing claim for rebate); Melbourne & Troy v. Louisville & N. R. Co., 1889, 88 Ala. 443, 6 So. 762 (failure to notify second carrier of goods).

3. Herzig v. Herzig, 1910, 67 Misc. 250, 122 N.Y.S. 440.

4. Stockmen's Nat. Bank v. Richardson, 1933, 45 Wyo. 306, 18 P.2d 635.

Cf. McGuigan v. Southern Pac. Co., 1952, 112 Cal. App.2d 704, 247 P.2d 415 (employer undertook to decide whether employee was physically fit for his duties).

There is no visible reason for the limitation of the principle to bodily harm found in Restatement of Torts, §§ 325, 497.

writing a letter [5] or attending a meeting,[6] or merely accepting a general agency.[7] These decisions have so much of an air of courts seeking some kind of excuse to impose tort liability for the breach of the promise itself, that it has been urged by one or two writers [8] that the excuse should be thrown overboard, and liability imposed outright for breach of the promise alone, when it is relied on to the plaintiff's detriment.

Actually there are three [9] late decisions in which this has been done. The leader is the fascinating Louisiana cat case,[10] in which the defendant broke a promise to confine a cat which had bitten the plaintiff during a rabies scare, and in consequence she was compelled to undergo the Pasteur treatment. Two others, in New Jersey, involved a gratuitous promise to call medical help,[11] and one to put salt on icy steps.[12] In all three personal injury resulted from reliance on the promise.[13] These decisions may possibly represent the beginning of the overthrow of the traditional rule.

Where performance clearly has been begun, there is no doubt that there is a duty of care.[14] Thus a landlord who makes repairs on leased premises, although he is under no obligation to do so, assumes a duty to his tenant and to those entering in the right of the tenant, to exercise proper care to see that the repairs are safe, or at least that the tenant is not left in ignorance of his danger.[15] The same principle frequently has been applied in the very common case where a railway company has made a practice of maintaining a flagman or giving warning signals at a crossing, and when it fails to do so on a particular occasion, is held liable to a traveler who has relied on the absence of warning.[16] This has recently been extended

---

5. Condon v. Exton-Hall Brokerage & Vessel Agency, 1913, 80 Misc. 369, 142 N.Y.S. 548, reversed on other grounds in 1913, 83 Misc. 130, 144 N.Y.S. 760; Evan L. Reed Mfg. Co. v. Wurts, 1914, 187 Ill.App. 378. Cf. Warrener v. Federal Land Bank, 1936, 266 Ky. 668, 99 S.W.2d 817 (calling for and receiving insurance premium); Sunflower Compress Co. v. Clark, 1933, 165 Miss. 219, 145 So. 617 (tax collector took taxpayer's check).

6. Kirby v. Brown, Wheelock, Harris, Vought & Co., 1930, 229 App.Div. 155, 241 N.Y.S. 255, reversed on other grounds, 1931, 255 N.Y. 274, 174 N.E. 652, reargument denied, 1931, 255 N.Y. 632, 175 N.E. 346. Cf. O'Neill v. Montefiore Hospital, 1960, 11 App. Div.2d 132, 202 N.Y.S.2d 436 (physician telling patient to come back and see another doctor that evening).

7. Phoenix Ins. Co. v. Thomas, 1927, 103 W.Va. 574, 138 S.E. 381.

8. Seavey, Reliance Upon Gratuitous Promises or Other Conduct, 1951, 64 Harv.L.Rev. 913; Gregory, Gratuitous Undertakings and the Duty of Care, 1951, 1 De Paul L.Rev. 30.

9. Three others, which have been cited as cases of tort liability for breach of the promise alone, appear merely to be cases in which the promise was given in connection with a sale, and the sale was performed. Brunelle v. Nashua Bldg. & Loan Ass'n, 1949, 95 N.H. 391, 64 A.2d 315; Valdez v. Taylor Automobile Co., 1954, 129 Cal.App.2d 810, 278 P.2d 91; Lester v. Marshall, 1960, 143 Colo. 189, 352 P. 2d 786.

10. Marsalis v. La Salle, La.App.1957, 94 So.2d 120. See Note, 1958, 18 La.L.Rev. 585. It should be noted, however, that the case began with defendant's cat biting the plaintiff, who was an invitee, so that a duty to take care might have been imposed on either ground. See supra, p. 342.

11. Dudley v. Victor Lynn Lines, 1958, 48 N.J.Super. 457, 138 A.2d 53, reversed on other grounds, 1960, 32 N.J. 479, 161 A.2d 479.

12. Johnson v. Souza, 1961, 71 N.J.Super. 240, 176 A. 2d 797. See also Jobidon v. Lussier, 1964, 124 Vt. 242, 204 A.2d 88; Fabricius v. Montgomery Elev. Co., 1963, 254 Iowa 1319, 121 N.W.2d 361; Morgan v. County of Yuba, 1964, 230 Cal.App.2d 938, 41 Cal.Rptr. 508; Fair v. United States, 5 Cir.1956, 234 F.2d 288.

13. All three were encouraged by the ambiguity in § 325 of the First Restatement of Torts, which stated that one who gratuitously "undertakes" to give aid to another is subject to liability, without defining "undertaking." This is replaced, but of course not clarified, by the Caveat under § 323 of the Second Restatement, expressing no opinion as to whether a bare promise can be a sufficient undertaking.

14. See for example Abresch v. Northwestern Bell Tel. Co., 1956, 246 Minn. 408, 75 N.W.2d 206 (telephone company attempting to call fire department for plaintiff); Thompson v. Southwestern Bell Tel. Co., Mo.1970, 451 S.W.2d 147 (same).

15. See infra, p. 410.

16. Burns v. North Chicago Rolling Mill Co., 1886, 65 Wis. 312, 27 N.W. 43; Langston v. Chicago & N. W.

to the maintenance of a lighthouse by the United States government,[17] and to an emergency ward maintained by a private hospital.[18] There are a number of cases in which a liability insurer, making a voluntary inspection of premises to determine their safety for the purpose of workmen's compensation insurance, has been held liable to an injured workman, for its negligence in doing so.[19]

In most of the cases finding liability the defendant has made the situation worse, either by increasing the danger,[20] or by misleading the plaintiff into the belief that it has been removed,[21] or depriving him of the possibility of help from other sources,[22] as where he is induced voluntarily to forego it. In a few decisions [23] it has been said that some such element is necessary, and that there can be no liability where the conduct in no way aggravates the situation or misleads the plaintiff, and he is left no worse off than he was before. There are, however, a considerable group of cases [24] involving gratuitous repairs by landlords, in which any such requirement has been rejected, and the defendant has been held to the obligation of reasonable care in his undertaking, although

R. Co., 1947, 398 Ill. 248, 75 N.E.2d 363; Westaway v. Chicago, St. P., M. & O. R. Co., 1893, 56 Minn. 28, 57 N.W. 222; Will v. Southern Pac. Co., 1941, 18 Cal.2d 468, 116 P.2d 44; cf. Teall v. City of Cudahy, 1963, 60 Cal.2d 431, 34 Cal.Rptr. 869, 386 P.2d 493 (city traffic signal).

17. Indian Towing Co. v. United States, 1955, 350 U. S. 61. Cf. Ingham v. Eastern Air Lines, Inc., 2 Cir.1967, 373 F.2d 227, cert. denied 389 U.S. 931 (weather service to aircraft). Also Armiger v. United States, 1964, 168 Ct.Cl. 379, 339 F.2d 625 (obtaining flight insurance for Navy band).

18. Wilmington General Hospital v. Manlove, 1961, 4 Storey 15, 174 A.2d 135; Harris v. State, 1969, 119 Ga.App. 684, 168 S.E.2d 337; New Biloxi Hospital v. Frazier, 1962, 245 Miss. 185, 146 So.2d 882; Stanturf v. Sipes, Mo.1969, 447 S.W.2d 558; Methodist Hospital v. Ball, 1963, 50 Tenn.App. 460, 362 S.W.2d 475. See Notes, 1962, 40 Tex.L.Rev. 732; 1966, 18 U.Fla.L.Rev. 475.

19. Nelson v. Union Wire Rope Corp., 1964, 31 Ill.2d 69, 199 N.E.2d 769; Ray v. Transamerica Ins. Co., 1968, 10 Mich.App. 55, 158 N.W.2d 786; Fabricius v. Montgomery Elevator Co., 1963, 254 Iowa 1319, 121 N.W.2d 361; Mays v. Liberty Mut. Ins. Co., 3 Cir.1963, 323 F.2d 174; Smith v. American Employers' Ins. Co., 1960, 102 N.H. 530, 163 A.2d 564.

The greater number have held to the contrary. Gerace v. Liberty Mut. Ins. Co., D.D.C.1966, 264 F. Supp. 95; De Jesus v. Liberty Mut. Ins. Co., Pa. 1966, 223 A.2d 849; Williams v. United States Fid. & Guar. Co., 4 Cir.1966, 358 F.2d 799; Kerner v. Employers Mut. Liab. Ins. Co. of Wis., 1967, 35 Wis.2d 391, 151 N.W.2d 72; Matthews v. Liberty Mut. Ins. Co., 1968, 354 Mass. 470, 238 N.E.2d 348.

See Boynton and Evans, What Price Liability for Insurance Carriers Who Undertake Voluntary Safety Inspections, 1967, 43 Notre Dame L. 193; McCoid, The Third Person in the Compensation Picture, 1959, 37 Tex.L.Rev. 389; Hammond and Poust, Safety Inspection by Workmen's Compensation Insurer, 1969, 10 For the Defense No. 9, Nov. 1969; Note, 1968, 21 Vand.L.Rev. 395.

20. See for example United States v. Lawter, 5 Cir. 1955, 219 F.2d 559 (Coast Guard rescue; clumsy work with a helicopter).

21. Cf. Case v. Northern Pac. Terminal Co., 1945, 176 Or. 643, 160 P.2d 313.

22. See the stress laid on this element in United States v. Gavagan, 5 Cir.1960, 280 F.2d 319, cert. denied 364 U.S. 933 (Coast Guard rescue); Zelenko v. Gimbel Bros., 1935, 158 Misc. 904, 287 N.Y.S. 134, affirmed, 1936, 247 App.Div. 867, 287 N.Y.S. 136; Owl Drug Co. v. Crandall, 1938, 52 Ariz. 322, 80 P. 2d 952; O'Leary v. Erie R. Co., 1900, 169 N.Y. 289, 62 N.E. 346; Finer v. Nichols, 1913, 175 Mo.App. 525, 157 S.W. 1023. See Seavey, Reliance Upon Gratuitous Promises or Other Conduct, 1951, 64 Harv.L.Rev. 913.

23. Lacey v. United States, D.Mass.1951, 98 F.Supp. 219 (Coast Guard rescue); United States v. De Vane, 5 Cir.1962, 306 F.2d 182; Kuchynski v. Ukryn, 1938, 89 N.H. 400, 200 A. 416; Kirshenbaum v. General Outdoor Adv. Co., 1932, 258 N.Y. 489, 180 N.E. 245, motion denied, 1929, 259 N.Y. 525, 182 N. E. 165; Kearns v. Smith, 1942, 55 Cal.App.2d 532, 131 P.2d 36.

24. Bartlett v. Taylor, 1943, 351 Mo. 1060, 174 S.W.2d 844; Janofsky v. Garland, 1941, 42 Cal.App.2d 655, 109 P.2d 750; Olsen v. Mading, 1935, 45 Ariz. 423, 45 P.2d 23; Bauer v. 141–149 Cedar Lane Holding Co., 1957, 24 N.J. 139, 130 A.2d 833; Conner v. Farmers & Merchants Bank, 1963, 243 S.C. 132, 132 S.E.2d 385.

See also Westaway v. Chicago, St. P., M. & O. R. Co., 1893, 56 Minn. 28, 57 N.W. 222; Bluhm v. Byram, 1927, 193 Wis. 346, 214 N.W. 364; Stewart v. Standard Pub. Co., 1936, 102 Mont. 43, 55 P.2d 694; Cummings v. Henninger, 1925, 28 Ariz. 207, 236 P. 701; Edwards v. Stein, 1938, 121 N.J.L. 233, 2 A.2d 44.

the plaintiff has not been more endangered, misled, or deprived of other help.

It is quite possible that this obligation of reasonable care under all the circumstances provides all the limitation that is really necessary. The defendant is never required to do more than is reasonable;[25] and he may terminate his responsibility by turning an injured man over to a doctor[26] or to his friends,[27] or where it is reasonable to do so he may discontinue his performance and step out of the picture upon notice of his intention[28] and disclosure of what remains undone.[29] It seems very unlikely that any court will ever hold that one who has begun to pull a drowning man out of the river after he has caught hold of the rope is free, without good reason, to abandon the attempt, walk away and let him drown, merely because he was already in extremis before the effort was begun. It may therefore be suggested that whether or not the situation has been made worse is only one fact to be considered, as bearing upon what the reasonable man would do under the circumstances.

Preventing Aid by Others

Even though the defendant may be under no obligation to render assistance himself, he is at least required to take reasonable care that he does not prevent others from giving it. A railway company is liable if it runs over a fire hose which is in use to put out a fire,[30] or obstructs a crossing so that the fire engines cannot arrive in time.[31] The principle has been carried even to the length of holding that there is liability for interfering with the possibility of such aid, before it is actually being given.[32] Such acts are of course "misfeasance," but the real basis of liability would appear to be the interference with the plaintiff's opportunity of obtaining assistance, and the principle might perhaps be applied to other situations.[33]

Controlling Conduct of Others

The general duty which arises in many relations to take reasonable precautions for the safety of others may include the obligation to exercise control over the conduct of third persons.[34] Thus the duty of a carrier toward

---

25. Shaw v. Chicago, M. & St. P. R. Co., 1907, 103 Minn. 8, 114 N.W. 85; Owl Drug Co. v. Crandall, 1938, 52 Ariz. 322, 80 P.2d 952.

26. Baltimore & O. R. Co. v. State to Use of Woodward, 1874, 41 Md. 268; Ohio & Miss. R. Co. v. Early, 1894, 141 Ind. 73, 40 N.E. 257. Cf. Lindgren v. Shepard S.S. Co., 2 Cir., 1940, 108 F.2d 806 (ship's duty to seaman ends when he is as completely cured as possible).

27. Fitzgerald v. Chesapeake & O. R. Co., 1935, 116 W.Va. 239, 180 S.E. 766.

28. Backus v. Ames, 1900, 79 Minn. 145, 81 N.W. 766; Pennsylvania R. Co. v. Yingling, 1925, 148 Md. 169, 129 A. 36.

29. Kirshenbaum v. General Outdoor Advertising Co., 1932, 258 N.Y. 489, 180 N.E. 245.

30. Metallic Compression Casting Co. v. Fitchburg R. Co., 1872, 109 Mass. 277; Erickson v. Great Northern R. Co., 1912, 117 Minn. 348, 135 N.W. 1129; Phenix Ins. Co. of Brooklyn v. New York Cent. & H. R. R. Co., 1909, 196 N.Y. 554, 90 N.E. 1164; Eclipse Lumber Co. v. Davis, 1923, 196 Iowa 1349, 195 N.W. 337.

31. Luedeke v. Chicago & N. W. R. Co., 1930, 120 Neb. 124, 231 N.W. 695; Globe Malleable Iron & Steel Co. v. New York Cent. & H. R. R. Co., 1919, 227 N.Y. 58, 124 N.E. 109, 5 A.L.R. 1648; Hanlon Drydock & Shipbuilding Co. v. Southern Pac. Co., 1928, 92 Cal.App. 230, 268 P. 385; Felter v. Delaware & H. R. Corporation, D.Pa.1937, 19 F.Supp. 852, affirmed, 3 Cir., 1938, 98 F.2d 868. See, 1938, 23 Corn.L.Q. 349.

32. Concordia Fire Ins. Co. v. Simmons Co., 1918, 167 Wis. 541, 168 N.W. 199. Cf. Gilbert v. New Mexico Const. Co., 1935, 39 N.M. 216, 44 P.2d 489.

33. See infra, p. 952. Cf. International Products Co. v. Erie R. Co., 1927, 244 N.Y. 331, 155 N.E. 662 (misinformation depriving plaintiff of opportunity to obtain insurance). The minority group of cases which have held an insurance company liable for failure to act promptly on an application for insurance might rest upon this principle. See Budge, C. J., in Wallace v. Hartford Fire Ins. Co., 1918, 31 Idaho 481, 174 P. 1009; Funk, The Duty of an Insurer to Act Promptly on Applications, 1927, 75 U. Pa.L.Rev. 207; Note, 1930, 40 Yale L.J. 121; but see Prosser, Delay in Acting in an Application for Insurance, 1935, 3 U.Chi.L.Rev. 39.

34. Harper and Kime, The Duty to Control the Conduct of Another, 1934, 43 Yale L.J. 886, 898; Note, 1958, 19 La.L.Rev. 228; Second Restatement of Torts, § 315.

its passengers may require it to maintain order in its trains and stations, and to use reasonable care to prevent not only conduct which is merely negligent,[35] but also personal attacks [36] or thefts of property [37] on the part of other passengers or strangers.[38] A similar obligation rests upon innkeepers toward their guests,[39] upon employers toward their employees,[40] a jailor toward his prisoner,[41] a hospital toward its patients,[42] a school toward its pupils,[43] and in a large number of cases it has been extended to owners of premises who hold them open to business visitors.[44] The list appears to include all those who are under an affirmative duty to render aid,[45] and may possibly include other relations.[46]

But even in the absence of such a special relation toward the person injured, the defendant may stand in such a relation toward the third person himself as to give him a definite control over his actions, and carry with it a duty to exercise that control to protect the plaintiff.[47] Thus the owner of an automobile is in such a position to control the conduct of one who is driving it in his presence that he is required to act reasonably to prevent negligent driving.[48] An employer must prevent his employees from throwing

35. La Sota v. Philadelphia Transp. Co., 1966, 421 Pa. 386, 219 A.2d 296 (controlling unruly mob of passengers); Kuhlen v. Boston & N. St. R. Co., 1907, 193 Mass. 341, 79 N.E. 815; Exton v. Central R. Co. of New Jersey, 1899, 62 N.J.L. 7, 42 A. 486, affirmed, 1900, 63 N.J.L. 356, 46 A. 1099.

36. McPherson v. Tamiami Trail Tours, Inc., 5 Cir. 1967, 383 F.2d 527; Bullock v. Tamiami Trail Tours, Inc., 5 Cir. 1959, 266 F.2d 326; Kinsey v. Hudson & Manhattan R. Co., 1943, 130 N.J.L. 285, 32 A.2d 497, aff'd 1944, 131 N.J.L. 161, 35 A.2d 888; Birmingham Elec. R. Co. v. Driver, 1936, 232 Ala. 36, 166 So. 701; Nute v. Boston & Me. R. Co., 1913, 214 Mass. 184, 100 N.E. 1099.

37. Robinson v. Southern R. Co., 1913, 40 U.S.App.D. C. 549; Pullman Palace-Car Co. v. Adams, 1898, 120 Ala. 581, 24 So. 921.

38. St. Louis, 1. M. & S. R. Co. v. Hatch, 1906, 116 Tenn. 580, 94 S.W. 671; Harpell v. Public Service Coordinated Transport, 1955, 20 N.J. 309, 120 A.2d 43; Melicharek v. Hill Bus Co., 1961, 70 N.J.Super. 150, 175 A.2d 238. A difference in the care required has been suggested, apparently on the theory that the carrier has more control over the passenger. Tate v. Illinois Cent. R. Co., 1904, 26 Ky.L. Rep. 309, 341, 81 S.W. 256.

39. Knott Corp. v. Furman, 4 Cir. 1947, 163 F.2d 199, cert. denied 332 U.S. 809, rehearing denied 332 U.S. 826; Fortney v. Hotel Bancroft, 1955, 5 Ill.App.2d 327, 125 N.E.2d 544; McFadden v. Bancroft Hotel Corp., 1943, 313 Mass. 56, 46 N.E.2d 573; Miller v. Derusa, La.App.1955, 77 So.2d 748; Gurren v. Casperson, 1928, 147 Wash. 257, 265 P. 472.

40. David v. Missouri Pac. R. Co., 1931, 328 Mo. 437, 41 S.W.2d 179; St. Louis-San Francisco R. Co. v. Mills, 5 Cir., 1934, 3 F.2d 882.

41. Taylor v. Slaughter, 1935, 171 Okl. 152, 42 P.2d 235; Cohen v. United States, N.D.Ga.1966, 252 F. Supp. 679; Kusah v. McCorkle, 1918, 100 Wash. 318, 170 P. 1023; St. Julian v. State, La.App.1955, 82 So.2d 85.

42. Sylvester v. Northwestern Hospital of Minneapolis, 1952, 236 Minn. 384, 53 N.W.2d 17.

43. Cashen v. Riney, 1931, 239 Ky. 779, 40 S.W.2d 339; McLeod v. Grant County School Dist., 1953, 42 Wash.2d 316, 255 P.2d 360; Morris v. Ortiz, 1966, 3 Ariz.App. 399, 415 P.2d 114, vacated on other grounds, 103 Ariz. 119, 437 P.2d 652. Cf. Wallace v. Der-Ohanian, 1962, 199 Cal.App.2d 141, 18 Cal.Rptr. 892 (children's camp). See Note, 1967, 19 Me.L.Rev. 111.

44. Peck v. Gerber, 1936, 154 Or. 126, 59 P.2d 675; Sparks v. Ober, Fla.App.1966, 192 So.2d 81; Winn v. Holmes, 1956, 143 Cal.App.2d 501, 299 P.2d 994; Sinn v. Farmers Deposit Sav. Bank, 1930, 300 Pa. 85, 150 A. 163; Hughes v. Coniglio, 1946, 147 Neb. 829, 25 N.W.2d 405. Cf. Ellis v. D'Angelo, 1953, 116 Cal.App.2d 310, 253 P.2d 675 (duty to warn baby-sitter at private home).

45. See supra, pp. 341–342.

46. In Schuster v. City of New York, 1958, 5 N.Y.2d 75, 180 N.Y.S.2d 265, 154 N.E.2d 534, the city was held to be obligated to guard a key witness in a criminal case, who was shot after receiving a threatening letter. See Note, 1959, 59 Col.L.Rev. 488.

47. Second Restatement of Torts, § 315; Harper and Kime, The Duty to Control the Conduct of Another, 1934, 43 Yale L.J. 886; Note, 1938, 36 Mich.L.Rev. 505. Cf. Brooke v. Bool, [1928] 2 K.B. 578, 585.

48. Wheeler v. Darmochwat, 1932, 280 Mass. 553, 183 N.E. 55; Beaudoin v. W. F. Mahaney, Inc., 1932, 131 Me. 118, 159 A. 567; Parks v. Pere Marquette R. Co., 1946, 315 Mich. 38, 23 N.W.2d 196; Bell v. Jacobs, 1918, 261 Pa. 204, 104 A. 587; Second Restatement of Torts, § 318.

objects from his factory windows,[49] and this has been extended quite generally to include an obligation on the part of any occupier of premises to exercise reasonable care to control the conduct of any one upon them, for the protection of those outside.[50] The physician in charge of an operation may be liable for failure to prevent the negligence of his assistants.[51] In a New York case, a hospital was held liable for permitting a quack doctor to treat a patient on its premises.[52] The same rule has been applied to those who have taken charge of dangerous lunatics,[53] and logically should apply, in cases where there is recognizable great danger,[54] to those who have charge of criminals.[55] In all such cases, the duty is not an absolute one to insure safety, but requires only reasonable care,[56] and there is no liability when such care has been used,[57] or where the defendant neither knows nor has any reason to know that it is called for.[58]

A common application of the principle is found in the liability of parents for failure to exercise proper control over their children, which remains to be considered in the chapter on domestic relations.[59]

49. Hogle v. H. H. Franklin Mfg. Co., 1910, 199 N.Y. 388, 92 N.E. 794. Accord, Fletcher v. Baltimore & P. R. Co., 1897, 168 U.S. 135; Palmer v. Keene Forestry Ass'n, 1921, 80 N.H. 68, 112 A. 798; Second Restatement of Torts, § 317.

50. De Ryss v. New York Cent. R. Co., 1937, 275 N.Y. 85, 9 N.E.2d 788 (trespassers shooting on land); Connolly v. Nicollet Hotel, 1959, 254 Minn. 373, 95 N.W.2d 657 (rowdy conduct in hotel convention); Kapphahn v. Martin, 1941, 230 Iowa 739, 298 N.W. 901; Holly v. Meyers Hotel & Tavern, 1952, 9 N.J. 493, 89 A.2d 6; Brogan v. City of Philadelphia, 1943, 346 Pa. 208, 29 A.2d 671.

51. Davis v. Potter, 1931, 51 Idaho 81, 2 P.2d 318; Morey v. Thybo, 7 Cir. 1912, 199 F. 760; Beck v. German Klinik, 1889, 78 Iowa 696, 43 N.W. 617.

52. Hendrickson v. Hodkin, 1937, 276 N.Y. 252, 11 N.E.2d 899. See Note, 1938, 48 Yale L.J. 81.

53. Austin W. Jones Co. v. State, 1923, 122 Me. 214, 119 A. 577; University of Louisville v. Hammock, 1907, 127 Ky. 564, 106 S.W. 219; St. George v. State, 1953, 203 Misc. 340, 118 N.Y.S.2d 596, reversed on other grounds, 1953, 283 App.Div. 245, 127 N.Y.S.2d 147, settled, 1954, 128 N.Y.S.2d 583, motion denied, 1954, 307 N.Y. 689, 120 N.E.2d 860, affirmed, 1955, 308 N.Y. 681, 124 N.E.2d 320. Cf. Missouri, K. & T. R. Co. v. Wood, 1902, 95 Tex. 223, 66 S.W. 449 (smallpox patient); Second Restatement of Torts, § 319.

54. It has been held that the possible escape of a forger, or of inmates of a youth correction institution, is not sufficiently dangerous to require precautions for the protection of the public. Williams v. State, 1955, 308 N.Y. 548, 127 N.E.2d 545; Green v. State through Department of Institutions, La. App.1956, 91 So.2d 153.

55. Webb v. State, La.App.1956, 91 So.2d 153. See Note, 1957, 17 La.L.Rev. 857. Contra are Henderson v. Dade Coal Co., 1897, 100 Ga. 568, 28 S.E. 251; Hullinger v. Worrell, 1876, 83 Ill. 220. Cf. Ballinger v. Rader, 1910, 153 N.C. 488, 69 S.E. 497 (held unforeseeable); Fisher v. Mutimer, 1938, 293 Ill.App. 201, 12 N.E.2d 315 (same).

56. Chicago, R. I. & P. R. Co. v. Brown, 1914, 111 Ark. 288, 163 S.W. 525; Hoff v. Public Service Co., 1915, 91 N.J.L. 641, 103 A. 209; City of Dallas v. Jackson, 1970, —— Tex. ——, 450 S.W.2d 62.

57. Landry v. News-Star-World Pub. Co., La.App. 1950, 46 So.2d 140; Harrington v. Border City Mfg. Co., 1921, 240 Mass. 170, 132 N.E. 721; Holly v. Meyers Hotel & Tavern, 1952, 9 N.J. 493, 89 A.2d 6.

58. Gold v. Heath, Mo.1965, 392 S.W.2d 298; Kapphahn v. Martin, 1941, 230 Iowa 739, 298 N.W. 901; Bruner v. Seelbach Hotel, 1909, 133 Ky. 41, 117 S.W. 373; Brogan v. City of Philadelphia, 1943, 346 Pa. 208, 29 A.2d 671; Ford v. Grand Union, 1935, 268 N.Y. 243, 197 N.E. 266, reargument denied, 1935, 268 N.Y. 664, 198 N.E. 546.

59. See infra, p. 872.

CHAPTER 10

OWNERS AND OCCUPIERS OF LAND

57. OUTSIDE OF THE PREMISES

The largest single area in which the concept of "duty" has operated as a limitation upon liability has concerned owners and occupiers of land. Largely for historical reasons, the rights and liabilities arising out of the condition of land, and activities conducted upon it, have been concerned chiefly with the possession of the land,[1] and this has continued into the present day, for the obvious reason that the man in possession is in a position of control, and normally best able to prevent any harm to others. He has a privilege to make use of the land for his own benefit, and according to his own desires, which is an integral part of our whole system of private property; but it has been said many times by the courts that this privilege is qualified by a due regard for the interests of others who may be affected by it. The possessor is under the obligation to make only a reasonable use of his property, which causes no unreasonable harm to others in the vicinity.[2]

His liability for a breach of this obligation may fall into any of the three categories into which tort liability has been divided. It may

rest upon intent, as where he fills the air with poisonous fumes knowing that they are certain to damage the plaintiff's adjoining land.[3] It may be based upon negligence in the creation of an unreasonable risk, as when he runs a gasoline engine that frightens horses in the street,[4] or allows a building to fall into such disrepair that it is a menace to passers-by.[5] It may be strict liability, for the keeping of animals [6] or for abnormal activities which, as a matter of social policy, are required to pay their way by making good the harm they do.[7] When any of the three results in an unreasonable interference with the use and enjoyment of the land of another, it has been treated by the courts as a question of private nuisance;[8] and when the interference is with a public right, as in the case of a danger to the highway or a disturbance of the public morals or the peace, it has been

---

1. The obligation arises from possession and control, even without legal ownership. Jacobs v. Mutual Mortgage & Inv. Co., 1966, 6 Ohio St.2d 92, 216 N.E.2d 49; Trainor v. Frank Mercede & Sons, Inc., 1965, 152 Conn. 364, 207 A.2d 54. As to ownership without possession, see infra, § 80.

2. Smith, Reasonable Use as a Justification for Damage to a Neighbor, 1917, 17 Col.L.Rev. 383.

3. Vaughn v. Missouri Power & Light Co., Mo.App. 1935, 89 S.W.2d 699; Smith v. Staso Milling Co., 2 Cir.1927, 18 F.2d 736.

4. Wolf v. Des Moines Elevator Co., 1905, 126 Iowa 659, 98 N.W. 301, affirmed 102 N.W. 517; Fort Wayne Cooperage Co. v. Page, 1908, 170 Ind. 585, 84 N.E. 145.

5. Mitchell v. Brady, 1907, 124 Ky. 411, 99 S.W. 266; McCarthy v. Thompson Square Theatre Co., 1926, 254 Mass. 373, 150 N.E. 170; cf. Frenkil v. Johnson, 1939, 175 Md. 592, 3 A.2d 479.

6. See infra, § 76.

7. See infra, § 78.

8. See infra, § 89.

dealt with as a public nuisance.[9] In the great majority of other cases, such as those of personal injury outside of the premises or upon them, the problem has been treated as one of simple negligence. The only distinguishing feature involved is the weight which must be given to the interest in the free use of the property, which must be thrown into the scale in determining both the duty to exercise any care at all, and the reasonableness of the defendant's conduct.

The possessor of land is first of all required to exercise reasonable care with regard to any activities which he carries on, for the protection of those outside of his premises. He may be liable if he blows a whistle where it will frighten horses in the street,[10] or operates a barrel hoist which is dangerous to adjoining property,[11] or runs a factory so that it gives out unnecessary noise or smoke.[12] Likewise, he must use similar care as to the erection of structures on his land,[13] or the digging of excavations,[14] to see that

they are not unreasonably dangerous to persons or property in the vicinity. In addition, he is under the affirmative duty to take reasonable steps [15] to inspect his premises and keep them in repair, and he may be liable if through his negligence a ruined house,[16] a fire escape [17] or a loose sign [18] falls and injures the plaintiff.

Danger to Highway

A large proportion of the cases have involved danger to an adjacent public highway. The public right of passage carries with it, once the highway has been established,[19] an

---

793; Buesching v. St. Louis Gaslight Co., 1880, 73 Mo. 219; Downes v. Silva, 1937, 57 R.I. 343, 190 A. 42.

9. See infra, § 88. In cases of personal injury to those on the highway, the courts have talked indiscriminately of public nuisance or negligence. Compare Buesching v. St. Louis Gaslight Co., 1880, 73 Mo. 219; City of Lincoln v. First Nat. Bank, 1903, 67 Neb. 401, 93 N.W. 698 (nuisance), with McCarthy v. Thompson Square Theatre Co., 1926, 254 Mass. 373, 150 N.E. 170; Mitchell v. Brady, 1907, 124 Ky. 411, 99 S.W. 266; Wolf v. Des Moines Elevator Co., 1905, 126 Iowa 659, 98 N.W. 301, affirmed 102 N.W. 517 (negligence).

10. Dugan v. St. Paul & D. R. R. Co., 1890, 43 Minn. 414, 45 N.W. 851.

11. Weitzmann v. A. L. Barber Asphalt Co., 1908, 190 N.Y. 452, 83 N.E. 477. Accord: Howser v. Cumberland & Pa. R. Co., 1894, 80 Md. 146, 30 A. 906 (improperly loaded train); Cessna v. Coffeyville Racing Ass'n, 1956, 179 Kan. 766, 298 P.2d 265 (automobile race track, insufficiently fenced).

12. See infra, p. 596.

13. Smethurst v. Proprietors of Barton Square Church, 1889, 148 Mass. 261, 19 N.E. 387 (roof shedding snow); Ferris v. Board of Education, 1899, 122 Mich. 315, 81 N.W. 98 (same). Cf. Davis v. Niagara Falls Tower Co., 1902, 171 N.Y. 336, 64 N.E. 4.

14. Barnes v. Ward, 1850, 9 C.B. 392, 137 Eng.Rep. 945; Mayhew v. Burns, 1885, 103 Ind. 328, 2 N.E.

15. The defendant is not an insurer of safe condition, and is not liable where he has exercised reasonable care. Schell v. Second Nat. Bank, 1869, 14 Minn. 43, 14 Gil. 34.

16. Domina Regina v. Watts, 1703, 1 Salk. 357, Ld. Raym. 856, 91 Eng.Rep. 311; Mullen v. St. John, 1874, 57 N.Y. 567; Pope v. Reading Co., 1931, 304 Pa. 326, 156 A. 106.

17. McCarthy v. Thompson Square Theatre Co., 1926, 254 Mass. 373, 150 N.E. 170. Accord: Restaino v. Griggs Motor Sales, 1937, 118 N.J.L. 442, 193 A. 543 (show window); Pearson v. Ehrich, 1912, 148 App. Div. 680, 133 N.Y.S. 273 (same); Mitchell v. Brady, 1907, 124 Ky. 411, 99 S.W. 266 (downspout); Crow v. Colson, 1927, 123 Kan. 702, 256 P. 971 (screen).

18. Smith v. Claude Neon Lights, 1933, 110 N.J.L. 326, 164 A. 423. Accord: Houston v. Brush, 1894, 66 Vt. 331, 29 A. 380 (iron plate falling from railway).

19. The weight of authority is strongly with the Second Restatement of Torts, § 368, Comment c, to the effect that the responsibility for remedying a condition, such as an excavation, which exists when the highway is constructed, is upon those charged with the duty of maintaining the highway, and the adjoining landowner is not liable. Fisher v. Prowise, 1852, 2 B. & S. 770, 121 Eng.Rep. 1258; City of Fort Worth v. Lee, 1945, 143 Tex. 551, 186 S.W.2d 954; Harvell v. City of Wilmington, 1939, 214 N.C. 608, 200 S.E. 367; Galiano v. Pacific Gas & Elec. Co., 1937, 20 Cal.App.2d 534, 67 P.2d 388; State v. Society for Establishing Useful Manufactures, 1892, 44 N.J.L. 502. This is consistent with the fact that eminent domain proceedings do not compensate for any imposition of liability. Contra: White v. Suncook Mills, 1940, 91 N.H. 92, 13 A.2d 729; City of Holyoke v. Hadley Water-Power Co., 1899, 174 Mass. 424, 54 N.E. 889.

obligation upon the occupiers of abutting land to use reasonable care to see that the passage is safe.[20] They are not required to maintain or repair the highway itself,[21] but they will be liable for any unreasonable risk to those who are on it, such as an open coal hole in the sidewalk, or overhanging objects ready to fall.[22] The obligation extends also to any conditions, such as an excavation next to the street,[23] which are dangerous to those who use it.

The status of a user of the highway has been extended to those who stray a few feet from it inadvertently.[24] It has been extended also to those who deviate intentionally for some purpose reasonably connected with the travel itself, such as detouring an obstruction,[25] or stepping out to avoid others on the sidewalk,[26] or even stopping in a doorway to tie a shoelace.[27] On the other hand, one who intentionally leaves the highway for some purpose of his own not reasonably connected with travel is not regarded as a user of the highway, and becomes a trespasser, or at most a licensee.[28] And one who wanders into a pit a considerable distance from the road after traversing the adjoining land, even though he does so inadvertently, is denied such protection, and treated as a trespasser.[29] The distance would appear not to be so important in itself, but merely to bear upon the existence of a recognizable danger to the normal users of the highway.[30] On

20. Pindell v. Rubenstein, 1921, 139 Md. 567, 115 A. 859; Davis v. Pennsylvania R. Co., 1907, 218 Pa. 463, 67 A. 777; De Ark v. Nashville Stone Setting Corp., 1955, 38 Tenn.App. 678, 279 S.W.2d 518.

21. Second Restatement of Torts, § 349, adding (§ 350), unless the dangerous condition is "created in the highway by him for his sole benefit subsequent to dedication." See Gabrielson v. City of Seattle, 1928, 150 Wash. 157, 272 P. 723, aff'd 152 Wash. 700, 278 P. 1071; Washington Gaslight Co. v. District of Columbia, 1895, 161 U.S. 316; Callaway v. Newman Merc. Co., 1928, 321 Mo. 766, 12 S.W.2d 491; Korricks Dry Goods Co. v. Kendall, 1928, 33 Ariz. 325, 264 P. 692.

22. Magay v. Claflin-Sumner Coal Co., 1926, 257 Mass. 244, 153 N.E. 534; Hass v. Booth, 1914, 182 Mich. 173, 148 N.W. 337; Crow v. Colson, 1927, 123 Kan. 702, 256 P. 971; Thompson v. Commercial Nat. Bank, 1924, 156 La. 479, 100 So. 688; Feeney v. New York Waist House, 1927, 105 Conn. 647, 136 A. 554. Cf. Thompson v. White, 1963, 274 Ala. 413, 149 So.2d 797 (performing clowns on highway).

23. Downes v. Silva, 1937, 57 R.I. 343, 190 A. 42; Bennett v. Citizens' State Bank, 1917, 100 Kan. 90, 163 P. 625; Sinclair Texas Pipe Line Co. v. Ross, 1936, 175 Okl. 435, 54 P.2d 204; Fenton v. Ackerman, 1939, 66 S.D. 465, 285 N.W. 516; White v. Suncook Mills, 1940, 91 N.H. 92, 13 A.2d 729.

24. Puchlopek v. Portsmouth Power Co., 1926, 82 N. H. 440, 136 A. 259 (slip); Durst v. Wareham, 1931, 132 Kan. 785, 297 P. 675 (motorcycle out of control); Edgarton v. H. P. Welch Co., 1947, 321 Mass. 603, 74 N.E.2d 674 (truck out of control); Louisville & N. R. Co. v. Anderson, 5 Cir. 1930, 39 F.2d 403 (automobile missing turn); Gaylord Container Corp. v. Miley, 5 Cir. 1956, 230 F.2d 177 (drunk). Massachusetts is contra, but apparently alone. Lioni v. Marr, 1946, 320 Mass. 17, 67 N.E.2d 766.

25. Vale v. Bliss, 1869, 50 Barb., N.Y., 358; Sawicki v. Connecticut Ry. & Light Co., 1943, 129 Conn. 626, 30 A.2d 556.

26. Weidman v. Consolidated Gas, E. L. & P. Co., 1930, 158 Md. 39, 148 A. 270; Gibson v. Johnson, 1941, 69 Ohio App. 19, 42 N.E. 689. Cf. Larkin v. Andrews, 1921, 27 Ga.App. 685, 109 S.E. 518 (dodging car).

27. Murray v. McShane, 1879, 52 Md. 217. Accord Healy v. Vorndrin, 1901, 65 App.Div. 353, 72 N.Y.S. 877 (stepping out to rescue child); Ruocco v. United Advertising Corp., 1922, 98 Conn. 241, 119 A. 48 (boy touching electrically charged chain); Goodwin v. Columbia Tel. Co., 1911, 157 Mo.App. 596, 138 S. W. 940 (reaching into overhead tree). Cf. Hynes v. New York Cent. R. Co., 1921, 231 N.Y. 229, 131 N.E. 898 (using springboard to dive into navigable stream). See Note, 1938, 36 Mich.L.Rev. 159.

28. Collins v. Decker, 1907, 120 App.Div. 645, 105 N. Y.S. 657 (short cut); Foley v. H. F. Farnham Co., 1936, 135 Me. 29, 188 A. 708 (conversation with a friend); Racine v. Morris, 1910, 136 App.Div. 467, 121 N.Y.S. 146, affirmed, 1911, 201 N.Y. 240, 94 N.E. 864 (policeman on official duty); Anderson v. Speer, 1926, 36 Ga.App. 29, 134 S.E. 811 (viewing show window); Chickering v. Thompson, 1912, 76 N.H. 311, 82 A. 829 (on way to back of lot).

29. Hardcastle v. South Yorkshire R. & R. D. Co., 1859, 4 H. & N. 67, 157 Eng.Rep. 761; Flint v. Bowman, 1906, 42 Tex.Civ.App. 354, 93 S.W. 479; Daneck v. Pennsylvania R. Co., 1896, 59 N.J.L. 415, 37 A. 59; Knapp v. Doll, 1913, 180 Ind. 526, 103 N.E. 385; cf. Winegardner v. City of St. Louis, Mo.1961, 346 S.W.2d 219; Selve v. Pilosi, 1916, 253 Pa. 571, 98 A. 723.

30. See City of Norwich v. Breed, 1852, 30 Conn. 535. Cf. Hildebrand v. Hines, 1921, 270 Pa. 86, 112 A.

the same basis the occupier of abutting land is required to guard against the tendency of children to stray from the road, where there is a condition close to it which will be unreasonably dangerous to them if they do.[31] Likewise, if he so maintains a part of his land that it appears to be a highway, as where he paves a strip next to the street,[32] or gives a private way the appearance of a public one,[33] he must use reasonable care to see that there is no danger to those who are misled into using it. It is often said in such cases that there is an implied "invitation" to enter, but the true basis of liability seems to be the misrepresentation as to the character of the property.[34]

Natural Conditions

The one important limitation upon the responsibility of the possessor of land to those outside of his premises has been the traditional rule of both the English and the American courts, that he is under no affirmative duty to remedy conditions of purely natural origin upon his land, although they may be highly dangerous or inconvenient to his neighbors.[35] The origin of this, in both countries, lay in an early day when much land, in fact most, was unsettled or uncultivated, and the burden of inspecting it and putting it in safe condition would have been not only unduly onerous, but out of all proportion to any harm likely to result. Thus it has been held that the landowner is not liable for the existence of a foul swamp,[36] for falling rocks,[37] for the spread of weeds or thistles growing on his land,[38] for harm done by indigenous animals,[39] or for the normal, natural flow of surface water.[40] Closely allied to this is the generally accepted holding that an abutting owner is under no duty to remove ice and snow which has fallen upon his own land or upon the highway.[41]

35. Second Restatement of Torts, § 363. See Noel, Nuisances from Land in its Natural Condition, 1943, 56 Harv.L.Rev. 772; Goodhart, Liability for Things Naturally on the Land, 1930, 4 Camb.L.J. 13.

36. Roberts v. Harrison, 1897, 101 Ga. 773, 28 S.E. 995.

37. Pontardawe R. D. C. v. Moore-Gwynn, [1929] 1 Ch. 656.

38. Giles v. Walker, 1890, 24 Q.B.D. 656 (thistles); Salmon v. Delaware, L. & W. R. Co., 1875, 38 N.J.L. 5 (leaves); Harndon v. Stultz, 1904, 124 Iowa 734, 100 N.W. 851 (weeds); Langer v. Goode, 1911, 21 N.D. 462, 131 N.W. 258 (wild mustard); Boarts v. Imperial Irr. Dist., 1947, 80 Cal.App.2d 574, 182 P. 2d 246 (weeds). The fact that in some such cases cultivation of the land has contributed to the growth of the weeds has been largely ignored. Statutes in several states require railroads and others to destroy weeds. See for example Chicago, T. H. & S. E. R. Co. v. Anderson, 1916, 242 U.S. 283.

39. Brady v. Warren, [1909] 2 Ir.Rep. 632; Stearn v. Prentice Bros., [1919] 1 K.B. 394; Seaboard Air Line R. Co. v. Richmond-Petersburg Turnpike Authority, 1961, 202 Va. 1029, 121 S.E.2d 499 (pigeons); Merriam v. McConnell, 1961, 31 Ill.App.2d 241, 175 N.E.2d 293 (box elder bugs).

40. Mohr v. Gault, 1860, 10 Wis. 513; Livezey v. Schmidt, 1895, 96 Ky. 441, 29 S.W. 25. Cf. Middlesex Co. v. McCue, 1889, 149 Mass. 103, 21 N.E. 230.

41. Ainey v. Rialto Amusement Co., 1925, 135 Wash. 56, 236 P. 801; Bailey v. Blacker, 1929, 267 Mass. 73, 165 N.E. 699; Moore v. Gadsden, 1881, 87 N.Y.

875; Boutelje v. Tarzian, 1940, 142 Pa.Super. 275, 16 A.2d 146; Mineral City v. Gilbow, 1909, 81 Ohio St. 263, 90 N.E. 800; Hydraulic Works v. Orr, 1877, 83 Pa. 332.

31. Duffy v. Sable Iron Works, 1904, 210 Pa. 326, 59 A. 1100 (vat three feet from sidewalk); Wells v. Henry W. Kuhs Realty Co., Mo.1954, 269 S.W.2d 761 (broken glass near sidewalk); Haywood v. South Hill Mfg. Co., 1925, 142 Va. 761, 128 S.E. 362 (uninsulated wires); Sedita v. Steinberg, 1926, 105 Conn. 1, 134 A. 243 (open pipe from gasoline tank); Rasmus v. Pennsylvania R. Co., 1949, 164 Pa.Super. 635, 67 A.2d 660 (excavation). Cf. Cumberland River Oil Co. v. Dicken, 1939, 279 Ky. 700, 131 S.W.2d 927; and see infra, § 59.

32. Holmes v. Drew, 1890, 151 Mass. 578, 25 N.E. 22; Crogan v. Schiele, 1885, 53 Conn. 186, 1 A. 899, 5 A. 673; Beckwith v. Somerset Theatres, 1942, 139 Me. 65, 27 A.2d 596; Williamson v. Southern R. Co., 1930, 42 Ga.App. 9, 155 S.E. 113; Mercier v. Naugatuck Fuel Co., 1953, 139 Conn. 521, 95 A.2d 263.

33. Allen v. Yazoo & M. V. R. Co., 1916, 111 Miss. 267, 71 So. 386; Baltimore & O. S. W. R. Co. v. Slaughter, 1906, 167 Ind. 330, 79 N.E. 186; Reddington v. Getchell, 1919, 40 R.I. 463, 101 A. 123; Southern v. Cowan Stone Co., 1949, 188 Tenn. 576, 221 S.W.2d 809.

34. See infra, p. 389.

On the other hand, if the occupier has himself altered the condition of the premises, as by erecting a structure which discharges water upon the sidewalk,[42] setting up a parking lot upon which water will collect,[43] weakening rocks by the construction of a highway,[44] damming a stream so that it forms a malarial pond,[45] planting a row of trees next to the highway,[46] or piling sand where the wind may blow it,[47] the condition is no longer to be regarded as a natural one, and he will be held liable for the damage resulting from any negligence.

The rule of non-liability for natural conditions was obviously a practical necessity in the early days, when land was very largely in a primitive state. It remains to a considerable extent a necessity in rural communities, where the burden of inspecting and improving the land is likely to be entirely disproportionate not only to any threatened harm but even to the value of the land itself. Almost without exception the cases applying it have arisen in the country. But it is scarcely suited to cities, to say that a landowner may escape all liability for serious damage to his neighbors, merely by allowing nature to take its course. There are indications that a different rule is developing as to urban centers.

This is well illustrated by the cases of dangerous trees. It is still the prevailing rule that the owner of rural land is not required to inspect it to make sure that every tree is safe, and will not fall over into the public highway and kill a man,[48] although there is already some little dissent even as to this,[49] and at least if the defendant knows that the tree is dangerous he will be required to take affirmative steps.[50] But when the tree is in an urban area, and falls into a city street, there is no dispute as to the landowner's duty of reasonable care, including inspection to make sure that the tree is safe.[51] The cases of trees

---

84; Norville v. Hub Furniture Co., 1929, 59 App.D. C. 29, 32 F.2d 430. Ordinances requiring the property owner to remove snow and ice usually are construed to impose no duty to any private individual. Hanley v. Fireproof Bldg. Co., 1922, 107 Neb. 544, 186 N.W. 534; Smith v. Meier & Frank Inv. Co., 1918, 87 Or. 683, 171 P. 555; Griswold v. Camp, 1912, 149 Wis. 399, 135 N.W. 754. See Note, 1937, 21 Minn.L.Rev. 703, 711; DeGraff, Snow and Ice, 1936, 21 Corn.L.Q. 436.

42. Leahan v. Cochran, 1901, 178 Mass. 566, 60 N.E. 382; Adlington v. City of Viroqua, 1914, 155 Wis. 472, 144 N.W. 1130; Tremblay v. Harmony Mills, 1902, 171 N.Y. 598, 64 N.E. 501; Updegraff v. City of Ottumwa, 1929, 210 Iowa 382, 226 N.W. 928. See Note, 1937, 21 Minn.L.Rev. 703, 713.

43. Moore v. Standard Paint & Glass Co. of Pueblo, 1960, 145 Colo. 151, 358 P.2d 33.

44. McCarthy v. Ference, 1948, 358 Pa. 485, 58 A.2d 49.

45. Mills v. Hall, 1832, 9 Wend., N.Y. 315; Towaliga Falls Power Co. v. Sims, 1909, 6 Ga.App. 749, 65 S. E. 844. Cf. Proprietors of Margate Pier v. Town Council of Margate, 1869, 20 L.T. 564 (pier causing accumulation of seaweed); Andrews v. Andrews, 1955, 242 N.C. 382, 88 S.E.2d 88 (artificial pond collecting wild geese, which destroyed plaintiff's crops).

46. Coates v. Chinn, 1958, 51 Cal.2d 304, 332 P.2d 289. Accord, Wisher v. Fowler, 1970, 7 Cal.App.3d 225, 86 Cal.Rptr. 582 (maintaining hedge). Cf. Crowhurst v. Amersham Burial Board, 1878, 4 Exch.Div. 5, 48 L.J.Ex. 109 (planting poisonous trees near boundary line).

47. Ettl v. Land & Loan Co., 1939, 122 N.J.L. 401, 5 A.2d 689. Accord: Bishop v. Readsboro Chair Mfg. Co., 1911, 85 Vt. 141, 81 A. 454; Long v. Crystal Refrigerator Co., 1938, 134 Neb. 44, 277 N.W. 830; Holter Hardware Co. v. Western Mortgage & Warranty Title Co., 1915, 51 Mont. 94, 149 P. 489.

48. Chambers v. Whelen, 4 Cir. 1930, 44 F.2d 340; Zacharias v. Nesbitt, 1921, 150 Minn. 369, 185 N.W. 295; O'Brien v. United States, 9 Cir. 1960, 275 F.2d 696; Lemon v. Edwards, Ky.1961, 344 S.W.2d 822; see Hay v. Norwalk Lodge, 1952, 92 Ohio App. 14, 109 N.E.2d 481.

49. Brandywine Hundred Realty Co. v. Cotillo, 3 Cir. 1931, 55 F.2d 231; Medeiros v. Honomu Sugar Co., 1912, 21 Hawaii 155. England, thickly settled, requires reasonable care as to all trees. Davey v. Harrow Corp., [1958] 1 Q.B. 60.

50. Hay v. Norwalk Lodge, 1951, 92 Ohio App. 14, 109 N.E.2d 481. Cf. Plesko v. City of Milwaukee, 1963, 19 Wis.2d 210, 120 N.W.2d 130 (urban).

51. Kurtigian v. City of Worcester, 1965, 348 Mass. 284, 203 N.E.2d 692; Mizell v. Cauthen, 1964, 251 Miss. 418, 169 So.2d 814; Plesko v. Allied Inv. Co., 1961, 12 Wis.2d 168, 107 N.W.2d 201; Turner v.

therefore suggest that the ordinary rules as to negligence should apply in the case of natural conditions, and that it becomes a question of the nature of the locality, the seriousness of the danger, and the ease with which it may be prevented.[52]

Statutes in a number of states, which have been held constitutional,[53] require the owner of land to alter its natural condition.

Conduct of Others

The defendant will of course be liable for any acts of his servants within the scope of their employment which create an unreasonable risk of harm to those outside of his premises. In addition, his possession and control of his land gives him a power of control over the conduct of those whom he allows to enter it, which he is required to exercise for the protection of those outside. Thus he will be liable if he stands idly by and permits others on his land to throw junk upon adjoining property,[54] or to play golf [55] or baseball [56] or turn a hotel convention into

a minor riot,[57] where it will be dangerous to persons on the highway.

A large number of the cases involving liability for the torts of an independent contractor, which are to be considered later,[58] have concerned work done on the premises of the employer. The possessor of land is not free to delegate his responsibility for its condition, or for activities carried on upon it, where the work to be done is regarded as "inherently dangerous" to those outside of the land, and he remains liable for the negligence of the contractor in such a case.[59] On the other hand he is not liable for "collateral" or "casual" negligence in the operative details of the work, which he could not reasonably contemplate as likely to occur.[60]

There have been surprisingly few cases dealing with liability for the conduct of trespassers and others acting without the possessor's knowledge or consent. It seems clear, however, that he is not liable for such conduct, or for conditions resulting from it, until he knows or should know of the dan-

---

Ridley, Mun.App.D.C.1958, 144 A.2d 269; Edgett v. State, 1959, 7 A.D.2d 570, 184 N.Y.S.2d 952. See McCleary, The Possessor's Responsibility as to Trees, 1964, 29 Mo.L.Rev. 159.

52. This is borne out by Carver v. Salt River Valley Water Users' Ass'n, 1968, 8 Ariz.App. 386, 446 P.2d 492, vacated on other grounds, 104 Ariz. 513, 456 P.2d 371, finding a duty to inspect rural trees adjacent to a well-traveled highway, and rejecting the arbitrary distinction. See Noel, Nuisances from Land in its Natural Condition, 1943, 56 Harv.L.Rev. 772; Goodhart, Liability for Things Naturally on the Land, 1930, 4 Camb.L.J. 13, 30.

53. Missouri, K. & T. R. Co. v. May, 1904, 194 U.S. 267 (Johnson grass); Wurts v. Hoagland, 1885, 114 U.S. 606 (drainage).

54. Hogle v. H. H. Franklin Mfg. Co., 1910, 199 N.Y. 388, 92 N.E. 794; Fletcher v. Baltimore & P. R. Co., 1897, 168 U.S. 135; cf. Brogan v. City of Philadelphia, 1943, 346 Pa. 208, 29 A.2d 671; De Ryss v. New York Cent. R. Co., 1937, 275 N.Y. 85, 9 N.E.2d 788.

55. Castle v. St. Augustine's Links, 1922, 38 T.L.R. 615; Gleason v. Hillcrest Golf Course, 1933, 148 Misc. 246, 265 N.Y.S. 886. See Note, 1933, 13 Boston U.L.Rev. 772.

56. Harrington v. Border City Mfg. Co., 1921, 240 Mass. 170, 132 N.E. 721; cf. Young v. New York, N.

H. & H. R. Co., 1910, 136 App.Div. 730, 121 N.Y.S. 517. Also Thompson v. White, 1963, 274 Ala. 413, 149 So.2d 797 (performing clowns distracting attention of driver on highway).

57. Connolly v. Nicollet Hotel, 1959, 254 Minn. 373, 95 N.W.2d 657. Cf. Stevens v. City of Pittsburgh, 1938, 329 Pa. 496, 198 A. 655 (shooting in park); De Rosa v. Fordham University, 1963, 18 App.Div. 2d 1056, 238 N.Y.S.2d 778 (using sledge hammer on rock).

58. See infra, § 71.

59. Rohlfs v. Weil, 1936, 271 N.Y. 444, 3 N.E.2d 588 (fall of painter from scaffold); Richman Bros. v. Miller, 1936, 131 Ohio St. 424, 3 N.E.2d 360 (work on building); Hudgins v. Hann, 5 Cir. 1917, 240 F. 387 (repair of wall after fire); Covington & C. Bridge Co. v. Steinbrock & Patrick, 1899, 61 Ohio St. 215, 55 N.E. 618 (wrecking); St. Louis & S. F. R. Co. v. Madden, 1908, 77 Kan. 80, 93 P. 586 (clearing land by fire).

60. Hyman v. Barrett, 1918, 224 N.Y. 436, 121 N.E. 271 (dropping plank); Pickett v. Waldorf System, 1922, 241 Mass. 569, 136 N.E. 64 (water flowing on sidewalk); Drennan Co. v. Jordan, 1913, 181 Ala. 570, 61 So. 938 (whitewash bucket through window).

ger,[61] but that once he has had a reasonable opportunity to discover the situation he is under a duty to exercise proper care to prevent harm to others.[62]

58. TRESPASSING ADULTS

Where the injury occurs on the premises of the defendant, rather than outside of them, additional factors enter the case. The result has been a set of limitations of liability in terms of duty, quite complicated in their detailed variations, and tending to be quite rigidly distinguished and enforced.[63] Those who enter upon land are divided into three fixed categories: trespassers, licensees, and invitees, and there are subdivided duties as to each. They make out, as a general pattern, a rough sliding scale, by which, as the legal status of the visitor improves, the possessor of the land owes him more of an obligation of protection. This system has long made legal writers, and some of the courts, quite unhappy because of its arbitrary and sometimes unreasonable character; and there are present indications [64] that it may have started

on its way to the discard. But since it represents the existing law in the overwhelming majority of the jurisdictions, the categories must first be considered one by one.

Lowest in the legal scale is the trespasser, defined as "a person who enters or remains upon land in the possession of another without a privilege to do so, created by the possessor's consent or otherwise." [65] The possessor of land [66] has a legally protected interest in the exclusiveness of his possession. In general, no one has any right to enter without his consent, and he is free to fix the terms on which that consent will be given. Intruders who come without his permission have no right to demand that he provide them with a safe place to trespass, or that he protect them in their wrongful use of his property. When they enter where they have no right or privilege, the responsibility is theirs, and they must assume the risk of what they may encounter,[67] and are expected to look out for themselves. Such has always been the point of view of the common law, with its traditional regard for the rights of private ownership of property. Accordingly, it is the general rule, subject to a number of qualifications which remain to be considered, that the possessor is not liable for injury to

---

61. Barker v. Herbert, [1911] 2 K.B. 633; Spiker v. Eikenberry, 1907, 135 Iowa 79, 110 N.W. 457.

62. De Ryss v. New York Central R. Co., 1937, 275 N.Y. 85, 9 N.E.2d 788; Brogan v. City of Philadelphia, 1943, 346 Pa. 208, 29 A.2d 671; Katz v. Helbing, 1932, 215 Cal. 449, 10 P.2d 1001; City of Bowie v. Hill, Tex.Civ.App.1923, 258 S.W. 568; Sedleigh-Denfield v. O'Callaghan, [1940] A.C. 880; Attorney-General v. Heatley, [1897] 1 Ch. 500; Barker v. Herbert, [1911] 2 K.B. 633. See Note, 1944, 18 Temple L.Q. 526.

In Rayonier, Inc. v. United States, 9 Cir. 1955, 225 F. 2d 642, vacated, 1957, 352 U.S. 315, it was held that the government had no duty to fight a fire which originated on the land of a third party, spread to the government's land, and thence to the land of the plaintiff.

63. "What I particularly wish to emphasize is that there are the three different classes—invitees, licensees, trespassers * * * Now the line that separates each of these three classes is an absolutely rigid line. There is no half-way house, no no-man's land between adjacent territories." Lord Dunedin, in Robert Addie & Sons v. Dumbreck, [1929] A.C. 358, 371. See Note, 1964, 31 Tenn.L.Rev. 485.

64. See infra, § 62.

65. Second Restatement of Torts, § 329. See Eldredge, Tort Liability to Trespassers, 1937, 12 Temple L.Q. 32, reprinted in Eldredge, Modern Tort Problems, 1941, 163, 167–173.

66. Most of the cases have involved trespassers on land; but the same rules are applied to trespassers on personal property, such as automobiles. Jefferson v. King, 1929, 12 La.App. 249, 124 So. 589 (automobile); Kuharski v. Somers Motor Lines, 1945, 132 Conn. 269, 43 A.2d 777 (truck); Rolfe v. Hewitt, 1920, 227 N.Y. 486, 125 N.E. 804; Lavallee v. Pratt, 1960, 122 Vt. 90, 166 A.2d 195 (truck). See the discussion in Falardeau v. Malden & Melrose Gas Co., 1931, 275 Mass. 196, 175 N.E. 471.

67. McPheters v. Loomis, 1939, 125 Conn. 526, 7 A.2d 437; Lary v. Cleveland, C., C. & I. R. Co., 1881, 78 Ind. 323; Sheehan v. St. Paul & Duluth R. Co., 7 Cir. 1896, 76 F. 201; Augusta R. Co. v. Andrews, 1892, 89 Ga. 653, 16 S.E. 203. Cf. Petrak v. Cooke Contracting Co., 1951, 329 Mich. 564, 46 N.W.2d 574 (the principle of assumption of risk will be "conservatively applied" in trespasser cases).

trespassers caused by his failure to exercise reasonable care to put his land in a safe condition for them, or to carry on his activities in a manner which does not endanger them.[68] He is under no obligation to guard a concealed pitfall [69] or a dangerous electric wire,[70] or to repair a defective building [71] for their benefit, or to keep a lookout for them as he operates his machinery,[72] or runs his train.[73] Even involuntary trespassers, such as those

who wander too far from the highway in the dark,[74] have no right to such protection.

Sometimes reasons have been given for this immunity which are difficult to support. It has been said that the presence of a trespasser is not to be anticipated, and hence that a reasonable man would not take steps to protect him. In many cases this is no doubt true; [75] but it is common knowledge that people do trespass upon the land of others, especially upon railway property,[76] and yet, in most jurisdictions, the foreseeability of such general trespassing is said to impose no obligation.[77] It has been said that the trespasser is contributorily negligent, or that he is a wrongdoer, who may not recover for the consequences of his own wrong. But in the usual case the trespass is complete, and the trespasser is helpless to protect himself, before the defendant's conduct occurs, and yet even the courts which accept the doctrine of the "unconscious last clear chance" [78] refuse to find any duty to him.[79]

68. Restatement of Torts, § 333. See Eldredge, Tort Liability to Trespassers, 1937, 12 Temple L.Q. 32, reprinted in Eldredge, Modern Tort Problems, 1941, 163; James, Tort Liability of Occupiers of Land: Duties Owed to Trespassers, 1953, 63 Yale L.J. 144; Green, Landowner v. Intruder; Intruder v. Landowner: Basis of Responsibility in Tort, 1923, 21 Mich.L.Rev. 495; Hughes, Duties to Trespassers: A Comparative Survey and Revaluation, 1959, 68 Yale L.J. 633; Notes, 1955, 38 Marq.L.Rev. 194; 1958, 12 Rutgers L.Rev. 599; 1947, 22 St. Johns L. Rev. 118.

69. Blyth v. Topham, 1607, Cro.Jac. 158, 79 Eng.Rep. 139 ("for he shows not any right why his mare should be in the said common, and the digging of the pit is lawful as against him"). Accord: Sutton v. West Jersey & S. R. Co., 1900, 78 N.J.L. 17, 73 A. 256 (third rail); Hooker v. Routt Realty Co., 1938, 102 Colo. 8, 76 P.2d 431; Previte v. Wanskuck Co., 1952, 80 R.I. 1, 90 A.2d 769; Blavatt v. Union Elec. L. & P. Co., 1934, 335 Mo. 151, 71 S.W.2d 736.

70. Gramlich v. Wurst, 1878, 86 Pa. 74; Klix v. Nieman, 1887, 68 Wis. 271, 32 N.W. 223; Susquehanna Power Co. v. Jeffress, 1930, 159 Md. 465, 150 A. 788; Farmer v. Modern Motors Co., 1930, 235 Ky. 483, 31 S.W.2d 716.

71. Lary v. Cleveland, C., C. & I. R. Co., 1881, 78 Ind. 323; Pittsburgh, Ft. W. & C. Ry. Co. v. Bingham, 1876, 29 Ohio St. 364. Cf. Chattanooga So. R. Co. v. Wheeler, 1905, 123 Ga. 41, 50 S.E. 987.

72. Wilson v. City of Long Beach, 1945, 71 Cal.App. 2d 235, 163 P.2d 501; Woodward Iron Co. v. Goolsby, 1942, 242 Ala. 329, 6 So.2d 11; Mergenthaler v. Kirby, 1894, 79 Md. 182, 28 A. 1065; cf. Rome Furnace Co. v. Patterson, 1904, 120 Ga. 521, 48 S.E. 166 (handling dynamite).

73. Hill v. Baltimore & Ohio R. Co., 7 Cir. 1946, 153 F.2d 91, cert. denied 328 U.S. 849; Sawler v. Boston & Albany R. Co., 1959, 339 Mass. 34, 157 N.E.2d 615; Reasoner v. Chicago, R. I. & P. R. Co., 1960, 251 Iowa 506, 101 N.W.2d 739; Miller v. Delaware, L. & W. R. Co., 2 Cir. 1957, 241 F.2d 116, cert. denied 354 U.S. 923; Davies v. Delaware, L. & W. R. Co., 1952, 370 Pa. 181, 87 A.2d 183.

74. See supra, p. 353.

75. See for example Hume v. Hart, 1952, 109 Cal. App.2d 614, 241 P.2d 25; Preston v. Austin, 1919, 206 Mich. 194, 172 N.W. 377; McCaffrey v. Concord Elec. Co., 1921, 80 N.H. 45, 114 A. 395; Keep v. Otter Tail Power Co., 1937, 201 Minn. 475, 277 N.W. 213. Compare also the startling accident which befell the uninvited stranger in Cleveland Elec. Illum. Co. v. Van Benshoten, 1929, 120 Ohio St. 438, 166 N.E. 374.

76. At least in the United States. It still appears to be quite uncommon in England. The explanation may be found in Kipling's short story, "An Error in the Fourth Dimension." As to the English rule, see Commissioners for Railways v. Quinlan, [1964] 1 All Eng.Rep. 897; Goodhart, An Adult Trespasser on the Railway Lines, 1964, 80 L.Q.Rev. 559.

77. Rowland v. Byrd, 1938, 57 Ga.App. 390, 195 S.E. 458; Eastern Ky. R. Co. v. Powell, 1895, 17 Ky.L. Rep. 1051, 33 S.W. 629; Hanks v. Great Northern R. Co., 1915, 131 Minn. 281, 154 N.W. 1088. "A landowner may in fact reasonably anticipate an invasion of his property, but in law he is entitled to assume that he will not be interfered with." Guinn v. Delaware & A. Tel. Co., 1905, 72 N.J.L. 276, 278, 62 A. 412.

78. See infra, p. 430.

79. Newman v. Louisville & N. R. Co., 1925, 212 Ala. 580, 103 So. 856; Dyrcz v. Missouri Pac. R. Co.,

And so far as contributory negligence is concerned, recovery has been denied to children too young to be negligent.[80] And while it is often said that the trespasser assumes the risk of injury, this is rather a way of describing the rule and its effect than of accounting for it, since he is quite usually unaware of any risk at all.[81] The true explanation seems to be merely that, in a civilization based on private ownership, it is considered a socially desirable policy to allow a man to use his own land in his own way, without the burden of watching for and protecting those who come there without permission or right.[82]

This is indicated very definitely by the prevailing view [83] which refuses to extend the immunity to other defendants who are not in possession of the land. It is shared, of course, by members of the possessor's household,[84] by his servants in the course of their employment, and by contractors who are

doing work for him on the land.[85] But other trespassers,[86] adjoining landowners,[87] and even the possessor himself when he carries his activities outside of his premises,[88] are held liable for a failure to exercise reasonable care, notwithstanding the fact that the plaintiff is a trespasser. Although there is considerable authority to the contrary, the greater number of courts have placed a similar responsibility upon gratuitous licensees,[89] invitees,[90] and the holders of easements, such

---

1911, 238 Mo. 33, 141 S.W. 861; Castile v. O'Keefe, 1916, 138 La. 479, 70 So. 481. See Peaslee, Duty to Seen Trespassers, 1914, 27 Harv.L.Rev. 403, 406–408.

80. Thomas v. Chicago, M. & St. P. R. Co., 1895, 93 Iowa 248, 61 N.W. 967; Ling v. Great Northern R. Co., C.C.Mont.1908, 165 F. 813; Conn v. Pennsylvania R. Co., 1927, 288 Pa. 494, 136 A. 779; Santora v. New York, N. H. & H. R. Co., 1912, 211 Mass. 464, 98 N.E. 90 (child of 27 months); Moore v. Pennsylvania R. Co., 1882, 99 Pa. 301, 305.

81. See infra, p. 447.

82. McPheters v. Loomis, 1939, 125 Conn. 526, 7 A.2d 437; Bagby v. Kansas City, 1936, 338 Mo. 771, 92 S.W.2d 142; Bottum's Adm'r v. Hawks, 1911, 84 Vt. 370, 79 A. 858. See Goodrich, Landowner's Duty to Strangers on His Premises, 1927, 7 Iowa L.B. 65, 71.

83. See Notes, 1929, 77 U.Pa.L.Rev. 506; 1934, 19 Corn.L.Q. 125; 1928, 12 Minn.L.Rev. 420; 1937, 21 Minn.L.Rev. 333; 1933, 12 Tex.L.Rev. 98. In Ellis v. Orkin Exterminating Co., 1939, 24 Tenn.App. 279, 143 S.W.2d 108, an exterminating company to which a building was turned over for twenty-four hours was held to be in possession, so that a child of the occupant was a trespasser against it.

84. Sohn v. Katz, 1934, 112 N.J.L. 106, 169 A. 838; Second Restatement of Torts, § 382.

85. Hamakawa v. Crescent Wharf & Warehouse Co., 1935, 4 Cal.2d 499, 50 P.2d 803; Mikaelian v. Palaza, 1938, 300 Mass. 354, 15 N.E.2d 480; Ireland v. Complete Machinery & Equipment Co., 1940, 174 Misc. 91, 21 N.Y.S.2d 430; Hollett v. Dundee, Inc., D.Del.1967, 272 F.Supp. 1; cf. Toomey v. Wichison Industrial Gas Co., 1936, 144 Kan. 534, 61 P.2d 891 (licensee); Waller v. Smith, 1921, 116 Wash. 645, 200 P. 95 (same).

86. Cf. Reichvalder v. Borough of Taylor, 1936, 322 Pa. 72, 185 A. 270; Wittleder v. Citizens Elec. Ill. Co., 1900, 47 App.Div. 410, 62 N.Y.S. 297, affirmed, 1900, 50 App.Div. 478, 64 N.Y.S. 114; Guinn v. Delaware & Atlantic Tel. Co., 1905, 72 N.J.L. 276, 62 A. 412.

87. Fitzpatrick v. Penfield, 1920, 267 Pa. 564, 109 A. 653; Wilson v. American Bridge Co., 1902, 74 App. Div. 596, 77 N.Y.S. 820; Prairie Pipe Line Co. v. Dalton, Tex.Civ.App.1922, 243 S.W. 619. Cf. Schiermeier v. Hoefken, 1941, 309 Ill.App. 250, 33 N.E.2d 147 (truck driver in street).

88. Ehret v. Village of Scarsdale, 1935, 269 N.Y. 198, 199 N.E. 56 (pipes laid in street). See Notes, 1936, 84 U.Pa.L.Rev. 795; 1936, 49 Harv.L.Rev. 1010.

89. Edwards v. Kansas City, 1919, 104 Kan. 684, 180 P. 271; Law v. Railway Express Agency, 1 Cir. 1940, 111 F.2d 427; Benton v. North Carolina Pub. Serv. Co., 1914, 165 N.C. 354, 81 S.E. 448; Lynchburg Tel. Co. v. Bokker, 1905, 103 Va. 594, 50 S.E. 148; Temple v. McComb Elec. L. & P. Co., 1906, 89 Miss. 1, 42 So. 874. See Hart, Injuries to Trespassers, 1931, 47 L.Q.Rev. 92.

Contra: Parshall v. Lapeer Gas-Electric Co., 1924, 228 Mich. 80, 199 N.W. 599; Stansfield v. Chesapeake & Potomac Tel. Co., 1914, 123 Md. 120, 91 A. 149; Brown v. Panola Light & Power Co., 1911, 137 Ga. 352, 73 S.E. 580.

90. Lewis v. I. M. Shapiro Co., 1945, 132 Conn. 342, 44 A.2d 124; Kribs v. Jefferson City L. H. & P. Co., Mo.App.1917, 199 S.W. 261; O'Gara v. Philadelphia Elec. Co., 1914, 244 Pa. 156, 90 A. 529; Ellis v. Ashton & S. A. Power Co., 1925, 41 Idaho 106, 238 P. 517.

as power companies stringing wires over the land.[91] The Restatement of Torts [92] has taken the position, which will explain much of the apparent conflict, that persons on the premises who are working for or acting on behalf of the possessor are subject to the same liability and entitled to the same immunity, while other third persons are not.

Frequent Trespass on Limited Area

Once the foregoing general rule of nonliability has been stated, the rest of the law of trespassers is a list of exceptions to it. These have developed because of an increasing feeling that human safety is of more importance than the defendant's interest in unrestricted freedom to make use of his land as he sees fit, which usually has meant no more than his desire to be free from all burden of trouble and expense in taking precautions. If that burden is diminished until it is not unreasonable, and if the risk of harm to trespassers is correspondingly increased, there may be good reason to hold the defendant liable. This has been true first of all in the case of frequent trespass upon a limited area.

Where, to the knowledge of the occupier of the land, trespassers in substantial number [93]

are in the habit of entering it at a particular point, or of traversing an area of small size, the burden of looking out for them is reduced and the risk of harm increased, so that most of the courts [94] have held that there is a duty of reasonable care to discover and protect them in the course of any activities which the defendant carries on. The typical case is that of frequent use of a particular part of a railroad track, as by a path across it, which is held to impose a duty of reasonable care as to the operation of trains.[95] While there are fewer cases, the same duty has been found as to dangerous passive conditions known to the possessor, such as concealed high tension wires,[96] or a bull in a pasture near a path.[97] In a number of cases the court has attempted to explain the liability by saying that the

cautious about applying the rule. It has held that fewer than 150 persons a day, at a point on a railroad track, is not enough. Louisville & N. R. Co. v. Jones, 1944, 297 Ky. 528, 180 S.W.2d 555; Dietz v. Cincinnati, N. O. & T. P. R. Co., 1943, 296 Ky. 279, 176 S.W.2d 699 (75 a day). Where larger numbers were involved, recovery was allowed, in Louisville & N. R. Co. v. Spoonamore, 1939, 278 Ky. 673, 129 S.W.2d 175. In Wise v. Chicago, R. I. & P. R. Co., 1934, 335 Mo. 1168, 76 S.W.2d 118, the presence of a path across the track was held sufficient evidence of frequent use.

94. There have been occasional cases in some jurisdictions to the contrary, such as Jackson v. Pennsylvania R. Co., 1939, 176 Md. 1, 3 A.2d 719.

95. Southern R. Co. v. Campbell, 5 Cir.1962, 309 F.2d 569; Cheslock v. Pittsburgh R. Co., 1949, 363 Pa. 157, 69 A.2d 108; Carter v. Seaboard Air Line R. Co., 1950, 114 S.C. 517, 104 S.E. 186; Thomas v. Southern R. Co., 5 Cir.1937, 92 F.2d 445; Smith v. Boston & Me. R. Co., 1935, 87 N.H. 246, 177 A. 729; Second Restatement of Torts, § 334. Cf. Lyshak v. City of Detroit, 1958, 351 Mich. 230, 88 N.W.2d 596 (struck by golf ball).

96. Clark v. Longview Public Service Co., 1927, 143 Wash. 319, 255 P. 380. Accord: Imre v. Riegel Paper Corp., 1957, 24 N.J. 438, 132 A.2d 505; Franc v. Pennsylvania R. Co., 1967, 424 Pa. 99, 225 A.2d 528; Hanson v. Bailey, 1957, 249 Minn. 495, 83 N.W.2d 252; Mix v. City of Minneapolis, 1945, 219 Minn. 389, 18 N.W.2d 130; Cornucopia Gold Mines v. Locken, 9 Cir.1945, 150 F.2d 75, cert. denied 326 U. S. 763; Second Restatement of Torts, § 335.

97. Lowery v. Walker, [1911] A.C. 10; Glidden v. Moore, 1883, 14 Neb. 84, 15 N.W. 326.

Contra: Louisville Trust Co. v. Horn, 1925, 209 Ky. 827, 273 S.W. 549; Kirkpatrick v. Damianakes, 1936, 15 Cal.App.2d 446, 59 P.2d 556; Key West Elec. Co. v. Roberts, 1921, 81 Fla. 743, 89 So. 122; Robbins v. Minute Tapioca Co., 1920, 236 Mass. 387, 128 N.E. 417. See Note, 1937, 21 Minn.L.Rev. 338.

91. Humphrey v. Twin State Gas & Elec. Co., 1927, 100 Vt. 414, 139 A. 440; Earl W. Baker Utilities Co. v. Haney, 1950, 203 Okl. 91, 218 P.2d 621; Texas-Louisiana Power Co. v. Webster, 1936, 127 Tex. 126, 91 S.W.2d 302; Langazo v. San Joaquin L. & P. Corp., 1939, 32 Cal.App.2d 678, 90 P.2d 825; Blackwell v. Alabama Power Co., 1963, 275 Ala. 123, 152 So.2d 670.

Contra, on the ground that the easement holder had the right to exclude the trespasser from his easement: Kesterson v. California-Oregon Power Co., 1924, 114 Or. 22, 228 P. 1092; Roe v. Narragansett Elec. Co., 1933, 53 R.I. 342, 166 A. 695.

92. §§ 383–385.

93. The only court which has attempted to be more specific is that of Kentucky, which has been very

defendant's continued toleration of the trespass amounts to permission to make use of the land, so that the plaintiff is not a trespasser but a licensee.[98] While it is undoubtedly true that a failure to object may amount to tacit permission,[99] it seems clear that the mere fact that a railroad company does not take burdensome and expensive precautions, which are likely to be futile, to keep trespassers out, does not in itself indicate that it is willing to have them enter.[1] The real basis of liability to such "tolerated intruders" would seem to be only the ordinary duty to protect another, where the harm to be anticipated from a risk for which the defendant is responsible outweighs the inconvenience of guarding against it.[2]

Dangerous Activities

A second exception which a few courts have developed, almost entirely in railroad cases, requires the defendant to exercise reasonable care for the safety of trespassers on any part of his land where their presence is to be anticipated, and the activity carried on involves a high degree of danger to them.[3]

The argument in favor of such a rule proceeds upon the ground that the trespass is to be foreseen, and the defendant's active and dangerous conduct places upon him the special obligation to use care for the safety of other human beings.[4] The great majority of the courts, however, have felt that it is too great a burden to require a railroad company to watch every mile of its tracks for the protection of those who have no right to be there, and have found no such duty.[5] As to activities and conditions so abnormally dangerous that strict liability to those outside of the premises would follow, reference must be made to a later chapter.[6]

Discovered Trespassers

The most important exception as to the adult trespasser is the now generally accepted requirement that the occupier must exercise reasonable care for his safety once his presence is known. This is lineally descended from the older rule, that the possessor of land was not free to inflict unreasonable intentional injury upon his unwelcome visitor. A trespasser, while he may be a wrongdoer, is not an outlaw, and an intentional, unprivileged battery upon him was too much to be tolerated even by the great veneration of the English courts for rights in land. The defendant was not permitted to set traps for the

---

98. Davis v. Chicago & N. W. R. Co., 1883, 58 Wis. 646, 17 N.W. 406; St. Louis Southwestern R. Co. v. Douthit, Tex.Civ.App.1919, 208 S.W. 201; Smith v. Philadelphia & R. R. Co., 1922, 274 Pa. 97, 117 A. 786.

99. See for example Meitzner v. Baltimore & O. R. Co., 1909, 224 Pa. 352, 73 A. 434; Lodge v. Pittsburgh & L. E. R. Co., 1914, 243 Pa. 10, 89 A. 790.

1. See Bohlen, The Duty of a Landowner Toward Those Entering His Premises of Their Own Right, 1921, 69 U.Pa.L.Rev. 142, 237; Eldredge, Tort Liability to Trespassers, 1937, 12 Temple L.Q. 32, 34–38, reprinted in Eldredge, Modern Tort Problems, 1941, 163.

2. Green, Landowner v. Intruder; Intruder v. Landowner, 1923, 21 Mich.L.Rev. 495, 57 Am.L.Rev. 321.

3. Pickett v. Wilmington & W. R. Co., 1895, 117 N.C. 616, 23 S.E. 264; Gulf, C. & S. F. R. Co. v. Russell, 1935, 125 Tex. 443, 82 S.W.2d 948; Tillman v. Public Belt R. Comm'n, La.App.1949, 42 So.2d 888. West Virginia requires the railroad to look out for child trespassers on the track, but not for adults. Virginian R. Co. v. Rose, 4 Cir.1959, 267 F.2d 312, cert. denied 361 U.S. 837. In Arkansas and Tennessee the rule as to railroads is enacted by statute.

See Thompson v. Carley, 8 Cir.1944, 140 F.2d 656 (Arkansas); Gordon v. Tennessee Cent. R. Co., 1934, 167 Tenn. 302, 69 S.W.2d 611.

In Stevens v. Missouri Pac. R. Co., Mo.1962, 355 S.W. 2d 122, the same rule was applied to a defendant handling explosives.

4. Green, Landowner v. Intruder; Intruder v. Landowner, 1923, 21 Mich.L.Rev. 495, 57 Am.L.Rev. 321.

5. Hanks v. Great Northern R. Co., 1915, 131 Minn. 281, 154 N.W. 1088; State for Use of Anderson v. Baltimore & O. R. Co., 1924, 144 Md. 571, 125 A. 393; Eastern Ky. R. Co. v. Powell, 1895, 17 Ky.L. Rep. 1051, 33 S.W. 629; McIntyre v. Northern Pac. R. Co., 1920, 58 Mont. 256, 191 P. 1065; Capitula v. New York Cent. R. Co., 1925, 213 App.Div. 526, 210 N.Y.S. 651. See Note, 1947, 22 St. John's L.Rev. 118.

6. See infra, p. 520.

trespasser,[7] or to use unreasonable force to expel him from the premises.[8] Nor, in later cases, was he allowed to injure him negligently by an act specifically directed toward him,[9] or recklessly by conduct in conscious disregard of his peril.[10] The usual phrase which summarized the exception was that there was liability for any "wilful or wanton" injury to a trespasser.[11]

In a few states the courts, so far as their express language goes, have stopped at this point, and have refused to find any liability to the trespasser, even after his presence is known, unless there is "wilful or wanton" conduct.[12] Some of these courts have in fact retreated from this position by the expedient, also adopted in other types of cases,[13] of misdefining "wilful or wanton" to include any failure to use ordinary care after it is discovered that the trespasser is there.[14] The

great majority have discarded "wilful or wanton" entirely as a limitation, and have said outright that once the presence of the trespasser is discovered, there is a duty to use ordinary care to avoid injuring him, as in the case of any other human being. The defendant is then required to govern his active conduct, such as running a train,[15] conducting a circus,[16] or operating an elevator,[17] with the caution of a reasonable man for the trespasser's safety.

The trespasser's presence is discovered when he is perceived in a situation of possible danger,[18] even though the defendant is unaware that he is a trespasser, as where, for example, a boy has crawled under a circus tent and become one of the crowd.[19] But it

---

7. See supra, § 21.

8. See supra, § 21.

9. Palmer v. Gordon, 1899, 173 Mass. 410, 53 N.E. 909; Magar v. Hammond, 1906, 183 N.Y. 387, 76 N. E. 474.

10. Aiken v. Holyoke St. R. Co., 1903, 184 Mass. 269, 68 N.E. 238; McVoy v. Oakes, 1895, 91 Wis. 214, 64 N.W. 748; Trico Coffee Co. v. Clemens, 1933, 168 Miss. 748, 151 So. 175. Cf. Bremer v. Lake Erie & W. R. Co., 1925, 318 Ill. 11, 148 N.E. 862 (reckless conduct, trespasser undiscovered).

11. The "wilful or wanton" element does not necessarily require active conduct, but may be found in an omission to remedy a highly dangerous condition, or to give warning of it. Blaylock v. Malernee, 1939, 185 Okl. 381, 92 P.2d 357; McLaughlin v. Bardsen, 1915, 50 Mont. 177, 145 P. 954; Romana v. Boston Elev. R. Co., 1917, 226 Mass. 532, 116 N.E. 218; City of Shawnee v. Cheek, 1913, 41 Okl. 227, 137 P. 724. Cf. Wunderlich v. Franklin, 5 Cir.1939, 100 F.2d 164, cert. denied 307 U.S. 631.

12. Duff v. United States, 4 Cir. 1949, 171 F.2d 846 (Maryland law); Westmoreland v. Mississippi Power & Light Co., 5 Cir. 1949, 172 F.2d 643 (Mississippi law); Nalepinski v. Durner, 1951, 259 Wis. 583, 49 N.W.2d 601; Columbus Min. Co. v. Napier's Adm'r, 1931, 239 Ky. 642, 40 S.W.2d 285; McIntyre v. Converse, 19–1, 238 Mass. 592, 131 N.E. 198.

13. See supra, p. 186.

14. Frederick v. Philadelphia Rapid Transit Co., 1940, 337 Pa. 136, 10 A.2d 576; Sloniker v. Great

Northern R. Co., 1899, 76 Minn. 306, 79 N.W. 168; Western & A. R. Co. v. Bailey, 1898, 105 Ga. 100, 31 S.E. 547; Tempfer v. Joplin & P. R. Co., 1913, 89 Kan. 374, 131 P. 592. See Note, 1924, 8 Minn.L.Rev. 329.

15. Omaha & R. V. R. Co. v. Cook, 1894, 42 Neb. 477, 60 N.W. 899; Baltimore & O. R. Co. v. State to Use of Welch, 1911, 114 Md. 536, 80 A. 170; Gulf & S. I. R. Co. v. Williamson, 1932, 162 Miss. 726, 139 So. 601; Wimsatt's Adm'x v. Louisville & N. R. Co., 1930, 235 Ky. 405, 31 S.W.2d 729; Denver & Rio Grande Western R. Co. v. Clint, 10 Cir. 1956, 235 F.2d 445. Cf. McManus v. Rogers, 1959, 106 U.S. App.D.C. 369, 273 F.2d 104 (automobile); Nielsen v. Henry H. Stevens, Inc., 1960, 359 Mich. 130, 101 N. W.2d 284 (truck).

16. Herrick v. Wixom, 1899, 121 Mich. 384, 80 N.W. 117, 81 N.W. 333. Cf. Fernandez v. Consolidated Fisheries, 1950, 98 Cal.App.2d 91, 219 P.2d 73 (delivering fish); Lyshak v. City of Detroit, 1958, 351 Mich. 230, 88 N.W.2d 596 (driving golf ball).

17. Davis' Adm'r v. Ohio Valley Banking & Trust Co., 1908, 127 Ky. 800, 106 S.W. 843. Accord: Moore v. Kurn, 10 Cir. 1939, 108 F.2d 906; Averch v. Johnston, 1932, 90 Colo. 321, 9 P.2d 291; St. Louis-San Francisco R. Co. v. Fletcher, 1923, 159 Ark. 344, 253 S.W. 12 (spraying poison near trespassing cattle).

18. A "position of peril" means only that the trespasser may be injured if the defendant is negligent. Kakluskas v. Somers Motor Lines, 1947, 134 Conn. 35, 54 A.2d 592.

19. Herrick v. Wixom, 1899, 121 Mich. 384, 80 N.W. 117; Cleveland-Cliffs Iron Co. v. Metzner, 6 Cir. 1945, 150 F.2d 206; cf. Carney v. Concord St. R. Co., 1903, 72 N.H. 364, 57 A. 218.

is not essential that he be perceived. It is enough that the defendant is notified, by information which would lead a reasonable man to conclude that a man is there, or to proceed upon that assumption.[20] There is, however, some authority that the defendant must at least have reason to think that an object which he has discovered may be a human being, or valuable property,[21] so that something unidentified ahead on a railroad track which looks like a discarded bundle of waste paper will not necessarily call for slowing down,[22] unless there is something about the situation, as for example its locality, to suggest a risk that the thing is a man.[23]

Whether the duty to the discovered trespasser extends to warning or otherwise protecting him against a purely passive condition of the premises was for a long time uncertain. A well-known old New Hampshire case[24] held that there was no more obliga-

tion to rescue the trespasser from peril than to rescue any other stranger. But the Restatement of Torts[25] has disagreed, taking the position that possession of the land carries with it the duty to see that it does not become an instrument of harm to others, and the discovery makes the warning reasonable. There are now a few decisions in support of this;[26] and the whole trend of the law has been such that they are likely to be followed. It is agreed that there is at least a duty to control operating forces, such as machinery in motion,[27] or to give warning of them.

The obligation is of course only to exercise reasonable care under the circumstances. Thus the engineer of a train who discovers a trespasser ahead on the track may ordinarily assume that he is in possession of his faculties, and that after proper warning he will remove himself to safety.[28] It is only when it becomes apparent that he is insensible[29] or otherwise helpless,[30] or that the

20. Frederick v. Philadelphia Rapid Transit Co., 1940, 337 Pa. 136, 10 A.2d 576 (tripping device, and warning of man under train); Cleveland-Cliffs Iron Co. v. Metzner, 6 Cir. 1945, 150 F.2d 206 (from facts known to defendant, he should have known); Lavallee v. Pratt, 1960, 122 Vt. 90, 166 A.2d 195 (on information available defendant required to "know or apprehend"). Cf. Kumkumian v. City of New York, 1953, 305 N.Y. 167, 111 N.E.2d 865; Chadwick v. City of New York, 1950, 301 N.Y. 176, 93 N.E.2d 625.

21. Haskins v. Grybko, 1938, 301 Mass. 322, 17 N.E. 2d 146 (shooting at object believed to be a wild animal).

22. Missouri Pac. R. Co. v. Gordon, 1939, 186 Okl. 424, 98 P.2d 39; Cochran v. Thompson, 1941, 347 Mo. 649, 148 S.W.2d 532; Sorey v. Yazoo & M. V. R. Co., 1931, 17 La.App. 538, 136 So. 155; Joy v. Chicago, B. & Q. R. Co., 1914, 263 Ill. 465, 105 N.E. 330; Southern R. Co. v. Wahl, 1925, 196 Ind. 581, 149 N.E. 72.

23. See for example Jones v. Chicago, R. I. & P. R. Co., 1946, 4 La.App. 457 (locality); Central of Ga. R. Co. v. Pelfry, 1912, 11 Ga.App. 119, 74 S.E. 854 (failure to watch); Hyde v. Union Pac. R. Co., 1891, 7 Utah 356, 26 P. 979 (place frequented by children); Owen v. Delano, Mo.App.1917, 194 S.W. 756 (locality); Norfolk & Western R. Co. v. Henderson, 1922, 132 Va. 297, 111 S.E. 277 (locality).

24. Buch v. Amory Mfg. Co., 1897, 69 N.H. 257, 44 A. 809. See also, Carroll v. Spencer, 1954, 204 Md. 387,

104 A.2d 628 (no duty, at least where the peril is not imminent).

25. Second Restatement of Torts, § 337 (with a caveat, however, as to natural conditions).

26. Martin v. Jones, 1953, 122 Utah 597, 253 P.2d 359, 261 P.2d 174; Oklahoma Biltmore v. Williams, 1938, 182 Okl. 574, 577, 79 P.2d 202; Gaylord Container Corp. v. Miley, 5 Cir. 1956, 230 F.2d 177; Appling v. Stuck, 1969, —— Iowa ——, 164 N.W.2d 810. Cf. Hobbs v. George W. Blanchard & Sons Co., 1908, 74 N.H. 116, 65 A. 382.

27. Castonguay v. Acme Knitting Mach. & Needle Co., 1927, 83 N.H. 1, 136 A. 702; Walsh v. Pittsburg R. Co., 1908, 221 Pa. 463, 70 A. 826; Second Restatement of Torts, § 338.

28. Campbell v. Kansas City, Ft. S. & M. R. Co., 1895, 55 Kan. 536, 40 P. 997; Lawrence v. Bamberger R. Co., 1955, 3 Utah 2d 247, 282 P.2d 335; Brimeyer v. Chicago, M. & St. P. R. Co., 1931, 213 Iowa 1289, 241 N.W. 409; Northern Alabama R. Co. v. Elliott, 1929, 219 Ala. 423, 122 So. 402; Young v. Louisville & N. R. Co., 1931, 228 Ky. 771, 15 S. W.2d 1001.

29. Tyson v. Eastern Carolina R. Co., 1914, 167 N.C. 215, 83 S.E. 318 (drunk); Bragg v. Central New England R. Co., 1920, 228 N.Y. 54, 126 N.E. 253 (asleep).

30. Chicago Terminal Transfer R. Co. v. Kotoski, 1902, 199 Ill. 383, 65 N.E. 350 (on trestle); Pollard v. Nicholls, 5 Cir. 1938, 99 F.2d 955 (on a horse).

warning has not been heard,[31] that something more than the whistle is required.

59. TRESPASSING CHILDREN

When the trespasser is a child, one important reason for the general rule of non-liability may be lacking. Because of his immaturity and want of judgment, the child may be incapable of understanding and appreciating all of the possible dangers which he may encounter in trespassing, or of making his own intelligent decisions as to the chances he will take. While it is true that his parents or guardians are charged with the duty of looking out for him, it is obviously neither customary nor practicable for them to follow him around with a keeper, or chain him to the bedpost. If he is to be protected at all, the person who can do it with the least inconvenience is the one upon whose land he strays. Added to this is the traditional social interest in the safety and welfare of children, and, it must be admitted frankly, some of the same sentimental considerations which affect a jury when an injured child comes into the courtroom. On the other hand, the burden of making the premises safe against harm to the child is certainly no less than in the case of an adult, and is very likely to be a great deal heavier. The interest in unrestricted freedom to make use of the land may be required, within reasonable limits, to give way to the greater social interest in the safety of the child; but this cannot reasonably be unlimited. The struggle in the courts has been to arrive at some reasonable compromise between the conflicting interests.[32]

Although it was foreshadowed in England,[33] the special rule as to trespassing children first appeared in 1873 in the Supreme Court of the United States,[34] where recovery was allowed, virtually without discussion, when a child trespassed on railroad land and was injured while playing with a turntable. The situation was repeated, and the rule first clearly stated, two years later in Minnesota.[35] In this second opinion the court displayed a great deal of ingenuity in inventing the theory that the child had been allured or enticed upon the land by the turntable "as a bait attracts a fish or a piece of stinking meat draws a dog," [36] so that the defendant was himself

1923, 21 Mich.L.Rev. 495, 57 Am.L.Rev. 321; Hudson, The Turntable Doctrine in the Federal Courts, 1923, 26 Harv.L.Rev. 826; Wilson, Limitations on the Attractive Nuisance Doctrine, 1923, 1 N.C.L. Rev. 162; Eldredge, Tort Liability to Trespassers, 1937, 12 Temple L.Q. 32, reprinted in Eldredge, Modern Tort Problems, 1941, 163; Green, Landowners' Responsibility to Children, 1948, 27 Tex.L.Rev. 1; James, Tort Liability of Occupiers of Land: Duties Owed to Trespassers, 1953, 63 Yale L.J. 144; Prosser, Trespassing Children, 1959, 47 Cal.L.Rev. 427; Note, 1966, 20 Vand.L.Rev. 139.

As to the law of particular jurisdictions, see Noel, The Attractive Nuisance in Tennessee, 1951, 21 Tenn.L.Rev. 658; Fulford, The Tort Liability of Possessors of Property to Trespassing Children in Alabama, 1958, 11 Ala.L.Rev. 1; Prewitt, Attractive Nuisance Doctrine in Missouri, 1964, 29 Mo.L.Rev. 24; Notes 1953, 41 Cal.L.Rev. 138; 1950, 15 Mo.L. Rev. 97; 1950, 10 La.L.Rev. 469; 1954, 8 Rut.L. Rev. 578; 1952, 40 Ky.L.J. 204; 1948, 26 Tex.L. Rev. 821; 1953, 10 Wash. & Lee L.Rev. 20; 1958, 42 Marq.L.Rev. 64.

33. In Lynch v. Nurdin, 1841, 1 Q.B. 29, 113 Eng. Rep. 1041, where a child was hurt as the result of tampering with a negligently loaded cart on the highway. English courts, however, for reasons that remain difficult to determine, never have evolved any special rule as to children, although they have shown a great deal of liberality in finding some "implied" license or invitation which will make the child no trespasser. See Fleming, Torts, 3d Ed. 1965, 443–445.

34. Sioux City & Pac. R. Co. v. Stout, 1873, 17 Wall., U.S., 657.

35. Keffe v. Milwaukee & St. Paul R. Co., 1875, 21 Minn. 207.

36. 1 Thompson, Negligence, 1st Ed. 1886, 305. There is an obvious effort to find an analogy to

31. Yazoo & M. V. R. Co. v. Lee, 1927, 148 Miss. 809, 114 So. 866; Russo v. Texas & Pac. R. Co., 1938, 189 La. 1042, 181 So. 485; cf. Hines v. Angle, 5 Cir. 1920, 264 F. 497. See, generally, Carlton, Mississippi Rules on the Liability of Railroads to Trespassers, 1938, 10 Miss.L.J. 305.

32. Smith, Liability of Landowners to Children Entering Without Permission, 1898, 11 Harv.L.Rev. 349, 434; Green, Landowner v. Intruder; Intruder v. Landowner: Basis of Responsibility in Tort,

responsible for the trespass, and therefore could not be allowed to set it up against the child. From these decisions, and others like them, the rule became known as the "turntable doctrine;" and from the second one it was sadly miscalled by the name of "attractive nuisance." [37]

Almost from the beginning the new rule met with vigorous opposition on the part of some of the courts, who denounced it, sometimes in quite unrestrained language,[38] as a barefaced fiction and a piece of sentimental humanitarianism, founded on sympathy rather than law or logic, which imposed an undue burden upon landowners and industry by giving the jury a free hand to express its feelings for the injured child out of the defendant's pocketbook. The number of such jurisdictions has diminished in recent years as earlier decisions have been overruled;[39] and today there are only seven courts,[40]

which still purport to reject the special rule without qualification. Even most of these proceed to apply it when the child is injured while climbing on a chattel in the street,[41] usually upon the rather naive ground that he is then "where he has a right to be." Since he has no more right to be upon the truck, the power line pole, or the lumber pile than upon the land, this appears in reality to represent a half-hearted acceptance of the principle, which might be expected, in time, to lead to full recognition.

As a logical consequence of the "attraction" theory, the Supreme Court, in a much criticized opinion of Mr. Justice Holmes,[42] held that a child could not recover when he was not induced to trespass by the presence of the pool of poisoned water that killed him, but discovered it after he had come upon the land. Thirteen years later the decision ap-

such cases as Townsend v. Wathen, 1808, 9 East 277, 103 Eng.Rep. 579, where baited traps were set for plaintiff's dogs. Cf. Buckeye Cotton Oil Co. v. Horton, 1915, 117 Ark. 1, 173 S.W. 423; Williams Estate Co. v. Nevada Wonder Mining Co., 1921, 45 Nev. 25, 196 P. 844.

37. "Nuisance" because of a supposed analogy to conditions dangerous to children in the highway or otherwise outside of the premises; "attractive" because it was thought essential that the child be allured onto the premises. See infra, p. 366.

38. The classic denunciation is in Ryan v. Towar, 1901, 128 Mich. 463, 87 N.W. 644. See also Bottum's Adm'r v. Hawks, 1911, 84 Vt. 370, 79 A. 858; Frost v. Eastern R. Co., 1886, 64 N.H. 220, 9 A. 790.

39. Thompson v. Reading Co., 1942, 343 Pa. 585, 23 A.2d 729; Strang v. South Jersey Broadcasting Co., 1952, 9 N.J. 38, 86 A.2d 777; McGill v. United States, 3 Cir. 1953, 200 F.2d 873; Angelier v. Red Star Yeast & Products Co., 1934, 215 Wis. 47, 254 N.W. 351. Michigan, formerly one of the most vigorous opponents of the doctrine, now applies it "conservatively." Patrak v. Corke Contracting Co., 1951, 329 Mich. 564, 46 N.W.2d 151.

40. Cogswell v. Warren Bros. Road Co., Me.1967, 229 A.2d 215; Hicks v. Hitaffer, 1970, 256 Md. 659, 261 A.2d 769; Prudhomme v. Calvine Mills, Inc., 1967, 352 Mass. 767, 225 N.E.2d 592; Devost v. Twin State Gas & Elec Co., 1920, 79 N.H. 411, 109 A. 839; Ware v. City of Cincinnati, 1952, 93 Ohio App. 431, 111 N.E.2d 401; Houle v. Carr-Consolidated Biscuit

Co., 1956, 85 R.I. 1, 125 A.2d 143; Trudo v. Lazarus, 1950, 116 Vt. 221, 73 A.2d 306. Even New Hampshire may be doubtful, in view of Labore v. Davison Constr. Co., 1957, 101 N.H. 123, 135 A.2d 591.

New York for many years purported to reject the doctrine, but developed so many exceptions that it became apparent that it was in reality accepted. This was finally recognized by the court in Patterson v. Proctor Paint & Varnish Co., 1968, 21 N.Y.2d 447, 288 N.Y.S.2d 622, 235 N.E.2d 765.

Virginia and West Virginia also purport to reject, but have substituted their own doctrine of "dangerous instrumentalities," which apparently covers most of the situations in which other courts allow recovery. See for example Washabaugh v. Northern Va. Const. Co., 1948, 187 Va. 767, 48 S.E.2d 276; Hatten v. Mason Realty Co., 1964, 148 W.Va. 380, 135 S.E. 2d 236. In Sutton v. Monongahela Power Co., 1967, 151 W.Va. 961, 158 S.E.2d 98, this was treated as the equivalent of the "attractive nuisance" doctrine.

41. Pindell v. Rubinstein, 1921, 139 Md. 567, 115 A. 859; Lane v. Atlantic Works, 1871, 107 Mass. 104, 111 Mass. 136; De Groodt v. Skrbina, 1924, 111 Ohio St. 108, 144 N.E. 601; Rine v. Norris, 1925, 99 W.Va. 52, 127 S.E. 908.

42. United Zinc & Chemical Co. v. Britt, 1921, 258 U.S. 268. It is worthy of note that the Massachusetts court, of which Holmes had been a member, had rejected the doctrine entirely. Daniels v. New York & N. E. R. Co., 1891, 154 Mass. 349, 28 N.E. 283.

parently was overruled;[43] but in the meantime it had been accepted and followed by a number of other courts. It has been discredited by degrees, until at the present time there are only six jurisdictions [44] which still adhere to it. Early in the twenties a different theory began to gain ground [45] as a justification for the liability to the child, which discarded the necessity of allurement, enticement or attraction onto the land, and considered that this was important only in so far as it meant that the trespass was to be anticipated.[46] The basis of the liability was held to be nothing more than the foreseeability of harm to the child, and the considerations of common humanity and social policy which, in other negligence cases, operate to bring about a balancing of the conflicting interests, and to curtail to some reasonable extent the defendant's privilege to act as he sees fit without taking care for the protection of others. In other words, child trespasser law is merely ordinary negligence

law, and the fact that the child is a trespasser merely one fact to be taken into account, with others, in determining the defendant's duty, and the care required of him. The result has been a compromise between the conflicting claims, which gives the child a limited degree of protection.[47]

Foreseeable Trespass

In 1934 the Restatement of Torts, in what has been perhaps its most effective single section,[48] threw its support behind the special rule. It discarded the idea of allurement to trespass, and treated the rule as one of ordinary negligence liability. The Section has been cited so frequently, and has received such general acceptance on the part of the great majority of the courts, as the best available statement of the law, that it must be taken as a new point of departure. It has now been somewhat modified, in minor particulars, by the Second Restatement,[49] and since it may reasonably be assumed that this is likely to meet with the same reception, it may be reviewed in some detail.

The Restatement rule is stated in terms of liability to trespassing children; but it is quite clear that the principle is not limited to them. In any case where the child could recover if he were a trespasser, he can recover at least as well when he is a licensee [50]

43. In Best v. District of Columbia, 1934, 291 U.S. 411. The Britt Case was cited with apparent approval, but the decision is quite inconsistent with it, and later cases have said it is overruled. Eastburn v. Levin, 1940, 72 U.S.App.D.C. 190, 113 F.2d 176; McGettigan v. National Bank of Washington, 1963, 115 U.S.App.D.C. 384, 320 F.2d 703.

44. Esquibel v. City and County of Denver, 1944, 112 Colo. 546, 151 P.2d 757; Indianapolis Motor Speedway Co. v. Shoup, 1929, 88 Ind.App. 572, 165 N.E. 246; Saxton v. Plum Orchards, 1949, 215 La. 378, 40 So.2d 791; Shemper v. Cleveland, 1951, 212 Miss. 113, 54 So.2d 215; Miller v. Perry, D.S.C.1970, 308 F.Supp. 863; Gouger v. Tennessee Valley Authority, 1949, 188 Tenn. 96, 216 S.W.2d 739.

45. Largely under the impetus of two noted law review articles: Green, Landowner v. Intruder; Intruder v. Landowner: Basis of Responsibility in Tort, 1923, 21 Mich.L.Rev. 495, 57 Am.L.Rev. 321; Hudson, The Turntable Doctrine in the Federal Courts, 1923, 36 Harv.L.Rev. 826.

46. See Banker v. McLaughlin, 1948, 146 Tex. 434, 208 S.W.2d 843; Weber v. St. Anthony Falls Water Power Co., 1942, 214 Minn. 1, 7 N.W.2d 339; Lone Star Gas Co. v. Parsons, 1932, 159 Okl. 52, 14 P.2d 369; Verrichia v. Society di M. S. del Lazio, 1951, 366 Pa. 629, 79 A.2d 237; Nichols v. Consolidated Dairies of Lake County, 1952, 125 Mont. 460, 239 P.2d 740.

47. "The decisions show an effort to hammer out a compromise between the interest of society in preserving the safety of its children and the legitimate interest of landowners to use their land for their own purposes with reasonable freedom, and so are naturally in a state of flux and motion." Bohlen, The Duty of a Landowner Towards Those Entering His Premises of Their Own Right, 1921, 69 U.Pa.L. Rev. 142, 237, 340, 348.

48. Restatement of Torts, § 339. See Gladstone, The Supreme Court of Pennsylvania and Section 339 of the Restatement of Torts, 1965, 113 U.Pa.L.Rev. 563.

49. Discussed, in its earlier drafting stages, in Prosser, Trespassing Children, 1959, 47 Cal.L.Rev. 427.

50. Gross v. Bloom, Ky.1967, 411 S.W.2d 326; Kemline v. Simonds, 1965, 231 Cal.App.2d 165, 41 Cal. Rptr. 653; Petree v. Davison-Paxon-Stokes Co.,

or an invitee [51] on the premises. This means, in particular, that account must be taken of his propensity to meddle with interesting objects, and his inability to understand and appreciate their danger; and in this respect his status upon the land makes no significant difference.[52] There are also occasional cases in which the plaintiff is a third person, not upon the land at all, who is injured when the child finds something like a dynamite cap and carries it away. Here there is no question involved of any immunity toward the plaintiff as a trespasser; but the decisions have proceeded upon the same basis,[53] which indicates again that this is only a phase of a broader negligence rule.

The Restatement limits its rule to "a structure or other artificial condition which he maintains upon the land." There are a few decisions involving natural waters [54] and rocks,[55] in which recovery has been denied, and a good many more in which artificial ponds [56] and other conditions [57] have duplicated nature, and that fact has been given as one reason among others for denying liability. In all such cases, however, the condition was one which the child might be expected to understand and appreciate,[58] so that, whether natural or artificial, there could be no recovery. The case of the natural condition which the child would not appreciate apparently has not yet arisen.[59] It is difficult to see why the origin of the condition should in itself make all the difference, if the possessor could easily remove it or protect against it, and fails to do so. It is at least not necessary that he create the condition himself, or "maintain" it in any active sense; and he has been held liable for conditions created by adjoining landowners,[60] trespassers,[61] a prior occu-

1923, 30 Ga.App. 490, 118 S.E. 697; Peterson v. Richfield Plaza, 1958, 252 Minn. 215, 89 N.W.2d 712; Ramage Min. Co. v. Thomas, 1935, 172 Okl. 24, 44 P.2d 19.

51. Thacker v. J. C. Penney Co., 5 Cir. 1958, 254 F. 2d 672, cert. denied 358 U.S. 820; Crane v. Smith, 1943, 23 Cal.2d 288, 144 P.2d 356; Weinberg v. Hartman, 1949, 6 Terry (45 Del.) 9, 65 A.2d 805; Zazkowski v. Choyce, 1945, 324 Ill.App. 582, 59 N. E.2d 324; Nesmith v. Starr, 1967, 115 Ga.App. 472, 155 S.E.2d 24. Contra, and apparently wrong, Williams v. Primary School Dist. No. 3, 1966, 3 Mich. App. 468, 142 N.W.2d 894.

52. Meagher v. Hirt, 1951, 232 Minn. 336, 45 N.W.2d 563.

53. Katz v. Helbing, 1928, 205 Cal. 629, 271 P. 1062 (boys throwing mortar); Kahn v. James Burton Co., 1955, 5 Ill.2d 614, 126 N.E.2d 836 (upsetting lumber into street); Commercial Union Fire Ins. Co. v. Blocker, La.App.1956, 86 So.2d 760 (starting tractor, running it into house); Lone Star Gas Co. v. Parsons, 1932, 159 Okl. 52, 14 P.2d 369 (dynamite caps); McGettigan v. National Bank of Washington, D.C.Cir.1963, 320 F.2d 703, cert. denied 375 U. S. 943 (explosive flare).

54. Fitch v. Selwyn Village, 1951, 234 N.C. 632, 68 S.E.2d 255; Gandy v. Copeland, 1920, 204 Ala. 366, 86 So. 3; Anneker v. Quinn-Robbins Co., 1958, 80 Idaho 1, 323 P.2d 1073; Adams v. Brookwood Country Club, 1958, 16 Ill.App.2d 263, 148 N.E.2d 39; Woolf v. City of Dallas, Tex., Civ.App.1958, 311 S. W.2d 78.

55. Bagby v. Kansas City, 1936, 338 Mo. 771, 92 S. W.2d 142; McComb City v. Hayman, 1920, 124 Miss. 525, 87 So. 11. Cf. Ostroski v. Mount Prospect Shop-Rite, Inc., 1967, 94 N.J.Super. 374, 228 A. 2d 545 (coasting on icy slope).

56. Plotzki v. Standard Oil Co., 1950, 228 Ind. 518, 92 N.E.2d 632; Raeside v. City of Sioux City, 1930, 209 Iowa 975, 229 N.W. 216; Harper v. City of Topeka, 1914, 92 Kan. 11, 139 P. 1018; Baker v. Prayer & Sons, Mo.1962, 361 S.W.2d 667; Atchison, T. & S. F. R. Co. v. Powers, 1952, 206 Okl. 322, 243 P.2d 688.

57. Anderson v. Reith-Riley Const. Co., 1942, 112 Ind.App. 170, 44 N.E.2d 184 (sand bank caving in); Zagar v. Union Pac. R. Co., 1923, 113 Kan. 240, 214 P. 107.

58. See infra, p. 371.

59. See, however, Corporation of City of Glasgow v. Taylor, [1922] 1 A.C. 44, to the effect that there is no distinction between a natural poisonous bush and a planted one; the question is whether the child can be expected to appreciate either danger. Also Norton v. Black, 1970, —— Ariz.App. ——, 469 P.2d 101. Notes, 1949, 2 Okl.L.Rev. 537; 1951, 26 Ind.L.J. 266.

60. Smith v. Otto Hendrickson Post 212, American Legion, 1954, 241 Minn. 46, 62 N.W.2d 354; Halloran v. Belt Ry. of Chicago, 1960, 25 Ill.App.2d 114, 166 N.E.2d 98 (condition actually on adjoining land); Chapman v. Parking, Inc., Tex.Civ.App.1959, 329 S.W.2d 439 (same).

61. Roman v. City of Leavenworth, 1913, 90 Kan. 379, 133 P. 551; Simmel v. New Jersey Coop. Co.,

pant,[62] or an independent contractor.[63] Again the origin of the condition appears to be of no consequence, so long as the possessor knows of its existence, can easily take precautions against it, and can reasonably anticipate that it will injure children.

Given such conditions, the Restatement sets up four conditions for liability:

1.   The place where the condition is found must be one upon which the possessor knows or has reason to know that children are likely to trespass.[64] The occupier, in other words, must have reason to anticipate the presence of the child at the place of danger. He is not required to take precautions when he has no reason to expect that the children will come upon his land.[65] If a power line pole is located in the open country, at a distance from any highway or habitation,[66] or can be

1957, 47 N.J.Super. 509, 136 A.2d 301, reversed on other grounds, 1958, 28 N.J. 1, 143 A.2d 521; Johnson v. Clement F. Sculley Const. Co., 1959, 255 Minn. 41, 95 N.W.2d 409; Lorusso v. De Carlo, 1957, 48 N.J.Super. 112, 136 A.2d 900; Pickens v. Southern R. Co., E.D.Tenn.1959, 177 F.Supp. 553; cf. McGettigan v. National Bank of Washington, D.C., Cir. 1963, 320 F.2d 703 (person unknown).

62.   Coeur d'Alene Lumber Co. v. Thompson, 9 Cir. 1914, 215 F. 8.   Contra, Calore v. Domnitch, 1957, 5 Misc.2d 895, 162 N.Y.S.2d 173.

63.   Foster v. Lusk, 1917, 129 Ark. 1, 194 S.W. 855.   Cf. Dehn v. S. Brand Coal & Oil Co., 1954, 241 Minn. 237, 63 N.W.2d 6 (lessee); Menneti v. Evans Const. Co., 3 Cir. 1958, 259 F.2d 367 ("maintains" includes leaving the condition unchanged after it is known); and see Cooper v. City of Reading, 1958, 392 Pa. 452, 140 A.2d 792 (passive neglect enough).

64.   The chief application is to trespassers on land; but the same rules will obviously apply to those on chattels.   Browning v. Eichelman, 1968, 12 Mich. App. 408, 162 N.W.2d 898; Schmit v. Village of Cold Spring, 1944, 216 Minn. 465, 13 N.W.2d 382; Wytupeck v. City of Camden, 1957, 25 N.J. 450, 136 A.2d 887; O'Donnell v. City of Chicago, 1937, 289 Ill.App. 41, 6 N.E.2d 449.

65.   Shell Petroleum Co. v. Beers, 1939, 185 Okl. 331, 91 P.2d 777; Walker v. Sprinkle, 1966, 267 N.C. 626, 148 S.E.2d 631; Klaus v. Eden, 1962, 70 N.M. 371, 374 P.2d 129; Long v. Sutherland-Backer Co., 1967, 48 N.J. 134, 224 A.2d 321; Ewing v. George Benz & Sons, 1947, 224 Minn. 508, 28 N.W.2d 733.

66.   Keep v. Otter Tail Power Co., 1937, 201 Minn. 475, 277 N.W. 213; James v. Wisconsin Power &

climbed only with great difficulty and ingenuity,[67] there may be no duty to guard it; but if it is in or near a street,[68] or a park or playground,[69] and is easily climbed,[70] the duty may arise.   It is here that the element of attractiveness to children outside of the premises plays its legitimate part.[71]   But, except in a very few states,[72] as a requirement it is on its way to limbo.   Without it the presence of the children may still be foresee-

Light Co., 1954, 266 Wis. 290, 63 N.W.2d 116; Shell Petroleum Co. v. Beers, 1939, 185 Okl. 331, 91 P.2d 777; Jennings v. Glen Alden Coal Co., 1952, 369 Pa. 532, 87 A.2d 206; Puckett v. City of Louisville, 1938, 273 Ky. 349, 116 S.W.2d 627.

67.   Empire Dist. Elec. Co. v. Harris, 8 Cir. 1936, 82 F.2d 48; Cole v. Mississippi Power & Light Co., 5 Cir. 1938, 100 F.2d 351; Fredericks' Adm'r v. Kentucky Utilities Co., 1938, 276 Ky. 13, 122 S.W.2d 1000; Ross v. Sequatchie Valley Elec. Co-op., 1955, 198 Tenn. 638, 281 S.W.2d 646; Tampa Elec. Co. v. Larisey, Fla.App.1964, 166 So.2d 227.   Cf.   Slinker v. Wallner, 1960, 258 Minn. 243, 103 N.W.2d 377; Callahan v. Dearborn Developments, 1959, 57 N.J. Super. 437, 154 A.2d 865, affirmed 1960, 32 N.J. 27, 158 A.2d 830.

68.   Clark v. Pacific Gas & Elec. Co., 1931, 118 Cal. App. 344, 5 P.2d 58, 6 P.2d 297; Koch v. City of Chicago, 1938, 297 Ill.App. 103, 17 N.E.2d 411; Kentucky Utilities Co. v. Garland, 1950, 314 Ky. 252, 234 S.W.2d 753; Ekdahl v. Minnesota Utilities Co., 1938, 203 Minn. 374, 281 N.W. 517.   Cf.   Cumberland River Oil Co. v. Dicken, 1939, 279 Ky. 700, 131 S.W.2d 927.

69.   Wolczek v. Public Service Co., 1931, 342 Ill. 482, 174 N.E. 577; McKiddy v. Des Moines Elec. Co., 1926, 202 Iowa 225, 206 N.W. 815; Znidersich v. Minnesota Utilities Co., 1923, 155 Minn. 293, 193 N. W. 449; Wytupeck v. City of Camden, 1957, 25 N.J. 450, 136 A.2d 887.

70.   Bartleson v. Glen Alden Coal Co., 1949, 361 Pa. 519, 64 A.2d 846; O'Donnell v. City of Chicago, 1937, 289 Ill.App. 41, 6 N.E.2d 449; Henry v. Mississippi Power & Light Co., 1933, 166 Miss. 827, 146 So. 857; Afton Elec. Co. v. Harrison, 1936, 49 Wyo. 367, 54 P.2d 540; Clark v. Pacific Gas & Elec. Co., 1931, 118 Cal.App. 344, 5 P.2d 58, 6 P.2d 297.

71.   Holbrook Light & Power Co. v. Gordon, 1944, 61 Ariz. 256, 148 P.2d 360; Simkins v. Dowis, 1937, 100 Colo. 355, 67 P.2d 627; Koch v. City of Chicago, 1938, 297 Ill.App. 103, 17 N.E.2d 411; Commercial Union Fire Ins. Co. v. Blocker, La.App.1956, 86 So.2d 760; Pickens v. Southern Ry. Co., E.D.Tenn. 1959, 177 F.Supp. 553.

72.   See supra, p. 366.

able on the basis of past trespasses,[73] proximity to places where children are likely to be,[74] accessibility of the dangerous condition,[75] or any other evidence which would lead a reasonable man to anticipate the trespass.[76] The circumstances which make the trespass foreseeable must be known to the possessor, and he is not required in the first instance to police his premises, or to make any inquiry, to discover whether there is any likelihood that children will enter.[77]

Foreseeable Risk of Injury

2. The condition must be one which the occupier should recognize as involving an unreasonable risk of harm to such children. Again he must know of the condition, or have

reason to know of it;[78] and no case[79] has ever held that, in the absence of any notice that something may be wrong, he is required to inspect his land, or otherwise investigate, to discover whether there is any condition on it which might harm trespassing children.[80] But even though the condition is known, if it is not one from which any unreasonable danger to children is reasonably to be anticipated, there is no negligence in failing to protect them against it, and no liability.[81]

The stress here is upon "unreasonable." There is virtually no condition upon any land with which a child may not possibly get himself into trouble. He may choke to death upon a green apple, pick up a stick and poke it into his eye, or have his skull fractured by a rock found and thrown by his companion. Unless the possessor is to shoulder the im-

---

73. Mann v. Kentucky & Ind. R. Co., Ky.1955, 290 S. W.2d 820, second appeal 1958, 312 S.W.2d 451; Wagner v. Kepler, 1951, 411 Ill. 368, 104 N.E.2d 231; Chase v. Luce, 1953, 239 Minn. 364, 58 N.W.2d 565; Patterson v. Palley Mfg. Co., 1948, 360 Pa. 259, 61 A.2d 861; Strang v. South Jersey Broadcasting Co., 1952, 9 N.J. 38, 86 A.2d 777.

Isolated instances of trespass, in a remote place, may not be enough to require anticipation that they will be repeated. Jennings v. Glen Alden Coal Co., 1952, 369 Pa. 532, 87 A.2d 206. In Clover Fork Coal Co. v. Daniels, Ky.1960, 340 S.W.2d 210, it was held that the children need not be shown to have been present at the exact point of danger.

74. Wolczek v. Public Service Co., 1931, 342 Ill. 482, 174 N.E. 577; Long v. Standard Oil Co., 1949, 92 Cal.App.2d 455, 207 P.2d 837; Commercial Union Fire Ins. Co. v. Blocker, La.App.1956, 86 So.2d 760.

75. Swanson v. City of Marquette, 1959, 357 Mich. 424, 98 N.W.2d 574; Healing v. Security Steel Equip. Corp., 1958, 51 N.J.Super. 123, 143 A.2d 844; United States v. Stoppelmann, 8 Cir. 1959, 266 F.2d 13; Burns v. City of Chicago, 1929, 338 Ill. 89, 169 N.E. 811; Thompson v. Reading Co., 1942, 343 Pa. 585, 23 A.2d 729.

76. See for example Smith v. Otto Hendrickson Post 212, American Legion, 1954, 241 Minn. 46, 62 N.W. 2d 354 (condition extending onto adjoining land); Wolfe v. Rehbein, 1931, 123 Conn. 110, 193 A. 608 (same).

77. Hickey v. Nulty, 1960, 182 Cal.App.2d 237, 5 Cal. Rptr. 914; Jones v. Louisville & N. R. Co., 1944, 297 Ky. 197, 179 S.W.2d 874; Empire Dist. Elec. Co. v. Harris, 8 Cir. 1936, 82 F.2d 48; Hedgepath v. City of Durham, 1944, 223 N.C. 822, 28 S.E.2d 503; Rahe v. Fidelity-Philadelphia Trust Co., 1935, 318 Pa. 376, 178 A. 467.

78. Contra, 2 Harper & James, Torts, 1956, 1458–1459.

79. Menneti v. Evans Const. Co., 3 Cir. 1958, 259 F.2d 367, where defendant knew that it was raining heavily, seems to be a case where he knew enough to put him on inquiry, and so had notice, or "reason to know." So do Dezendorf Marble Co. v. Gartman, Tex.Civ.App.1960, 333 S.W.2d 404, affirmed, 1961, 161 Tex. 535, 343 S.W.2d 441, where defendant knew that dynamite caps were not accounted for; Dehn v. S. Brand Coal & Oil Co., 1954, 241 Minn. 237, 63 N.W.2d 6, and Johnson v. Clement F. Sculley Const. Co., 1959, 255 Minn. 41, 95 N.W.2d 409. This is where the court came out on rehearing in McGettigan v. National Bank of Washington, 1963, 115 U.S.App.D.C. 384, 320 F.2d 703.

80. Recovery was denied where the defendant had no knowledge at all in Rush v. Plains Township, 1952, 371 Pa. 117, 89 A.2d 200; Pocholec v. Giustina, 1960, 224 Or. 245, 355 P.2d 1104; Pier v. Schultz, 1962, 243 Ind. 200, 182 N.E.2d 255; Simmel v. New Jersey Co-op. Co., 1958, 28 N.J. 1, 143 A.2d 521; Lynch v. Kentucky Utilities Co., Ky.1959, 328 S. W.2d 520.

81. Martin v. Latex Const. Co., W.D.La.1943, 50 F. Supp. 424 (pipe and burner); Lee v. Salt River Valley Water Users' Ass'n, 1951, 73 Ariz. 122, 238 P.2d 945 (pump house and power line pole); Giddings v. Superior Oil Co., 1951, 106 Cal.App.2d 607, 235 P.2d 843 (oil well pump); Deffland v. Spokane Portland Cement Co., 1947, 26 Wash.2d 891, 176 P.2d 311 (charged wire and pigeons in cupola); J. C. Penney Co. v. Clark, Okl.1961, 366 P.2d 637 (stool in shoe store).

possible burden of making his land complete-ly "child-proof," which might mean razing it to the bare earth, something more is called for than the general possibility of somehow coming to some harm which follows the child everywhere throughout his daily existence. Accordingly, there is a long line of cases involving normally harmless objects, such as a sharp-pointed pole,[82] railroad spikes,[83] a wooden horse,[84] a piece of shingle on a roof,[85] a red lantern,[86] or even stationary vehicles,[87] which have been held to be so innocuous that as a matter of law there was no liability,

unless the possessor had some special reason to anticipate injury.[88]

Struggling to characterize these cases, the courts sometimes have said that the condition must be an unusual one,[89] or that the doctrine has no application to common objects,[90] or to conditions arising from the ordinary conduct of a business,[91] or that it is limited to special and unusual conditions of modern industry;[92] but all such statements appear to be made with reference to the particular case, and to be directed at nothing more than the existence of a recognizable and unreasonable risk of harm to the child. A recognizable and unreasonable risk of harm may arise from a very ordinary condition; and where there has been past meddling, a concealed danger, a special attraction to children, or any other special reason to expect harm, even so commonplace a thing as a mailbox may be found to be enough for liability.[93]

82. Mail v. M. R. Smith Lumber & Shingle Co., 1955, 47 Wash.2d 447, 287 P.2d 877. Cf. Southern Bell Tel. & Tel. Co. v. Brackin, 1959, 215 Ga. 225, 109 S. E.2d 782 (piece of wire).

83. Genovese v. New Orleans Pub. Service Co., La. App.1950, 45 So.2d 642. Cf. Bruce v. Housing Authority of City of Pittsburgh, 1950, 365 Pa. 571, 76 A.2d 400 (broken glass on floor, child on roller skates); Johnson v. Williams, Fla.App.1966, 192 So.2d 339 (low wire cable between trees). On the other hand, in Brittain v. Cubbon, 1963, 190 Kan. 641, 378 P.2d 141, rusty nails protruding from a plank in a razed building were held to be sufficient, as unlikely to be discovered by trespassing children.

84. Ray v. Hutchinson, 1933, 17 Tenn.App. 477, 68 S. W.2d 948, Cf. State ex rel. W. E. Callahan Const. Co. v. Hughes, 1941, 348 Mo. 1209, 159 S.W.2d 251 (bucket).

85. Massino v. Smaglick, 1958, 3 Wis.2d 607, 89 N.W. 2d 223. Cf. Landman v. M. Susan & Associates, 1965, 63 Ill.App.2d 292, 211 N.E.2d 407 (pile of sand on beach); Krakowiak v. Sampson, 1967, 85 Ill. App.2d 71, 229 N.E.2d 578 (mounds of earth, tree stumps, overhanging branches).

86. Brown v. City of Minneapolis, 1917, 136 Minn. 177, 161 N.W. 503. Cf. Camp v. Peel, 1939, 33 Cal. App.2d 612, 92 P.2d 428 (lime putty); St. Louis, I. M. & S. R. Co. v. Waggoner, 1914, 112 Ark. 593, 166 S.W. 948 (empty alcohol barrel); Esquibel v. City and County of Denver, 1944, 112 Colo. 546, 151 P.2d 757 (old auto bodies and parts); Bonhomie & H. S. R. Co. v. Hinton, 1929, 155 Miss. 173, 124 So. 271 (sliding door).

87. Anderson v. B. F. Goodrich Co., 1961, 103 Ga. App. 453, 119 S.E.2d 603 (truck with hanging chain and hook); Harris v. Winston-Salem Southbound R. Co., 1942, 220 N.C. 698, 18 S.E.2d 204 (railroad car); Sydenstricker v. Chicago & N. W. R. Co., 1969, 107 Ill.App.2d 427, 247 N.E.2d 15 (tank car); Gear v. General Cas. Ins. Co., 1953, 263 Wis. 261, 57 N. W.2d 340 (automobile); Harris v. Roberson, 1943, 78 U.S.App.D.C. 246, 139 F.2d 529 (trailer).

88. Britten v. City of Eau Claire, 1952, 260 Wis. 382, 51 N.W.2d 30 (past meddling); Gimmestad v. Rose Bros. Co., 1935, 194 Minn. 531, 261 N.W. 194 (way lumber was piled).

89. See for example Hunsche v. Southern Pac. Co., N.D.Cal.1945, 62 F.Supp. 634; Denver Tramway Co. v. Garcia, 1964, 154 Colo. 417, 390 P.2d 952; Vincent v. Barnhill, 1948, 203 Miss. 740, 34 So.2d 363.

90. Hayko v. Colorado & Utah Coal Co., 1925, 77 Colo. 143, 235 P. 373; Goss v. Shawnee Post No. 3204, V.F.W., Ky.1954, 265 S.W.2d 799; Brown v. Salt Lake City, 1908, 33 Utah 222, 93 P. 570; Heva v. Seattle School Dist. No. 1, 1920, 110 Wash. 668, 188 P. 776.

91. Brown v. Rockwell City Canning Co., 1906, 132 Iowa 631, 110 N.W. 12; Holt v. Fuller Cotton Oil Co., Tex.Civ.App.1943, 175 S.W.2d 272; Stamford Oil Mill Co. v. Barnes, 1910, 103 Tex. 409, 128 S.W. 375.

92. Giannini v. Campodonico, 1917, 176 Cal. 548, 169 P. 80; San Antonio & A. P. R. Co. v. Morgan, 1898, 92 Tex. 98, 46 S.W. 28. See Green, Judge and Jury, 1930, 128–133.

93. United States v. Bernhardt, 5 Cir. 1957, 244 F.2d 154. Cf. Garcia v. Soogian, 1959, 52 Cal.2d 107, 338 P.2d 433 (stacked building materials); Hoff v. Natural Ref. Products Co., 1955, 38 N.J.Super. 222, 118 A.2d 714 (refuse mound); Crutchfield v. Adams, Fla.App.1963, 152 So.2d 808 (unguarded fan belt); Eastburn v. Levin, D.C.Cir.1940, 72 U.S.App.D.C. 190, 113 F.2d 176 (junk yard).

While it is evident that there must be some aggravated danger to the child, greater than the ordinary risks which attend his daily life, it is equally clear that this cannot be reduced to a definite formula, and that it must be the product of all the factors bearing on the case.[94] A high degree of probability of relatively slight harm, as in the case of concealed barbed wire,[95] may be sufficient, and so may a relatively slighter probability of death, as in the case of high tension electric wires.[96]

One very important factor is that of whether any trespassing child may reasonably be expected to comprehend the situation. Sometimes this is expressed by saying that the danger must be latent,[97] meaning apparently nothing more than that the child can be expected not to understand and appreciate the peril, or protect himself against it.[98] The question here is not whether he does in fact understand, although that too has its importance;[99] it is rather what the possessor may reasonably expect of him. Here the courts have displayed a tendency to set up

certain more or less arbitrary categories of conditions which trespassing children, as a matter of law, can be expected to understand. This means that the possessor is free to rely upon the assumption that any child of sufficient age to be allowed at large by his parents, and so to be at all likely to trespass, will appreciate the danger and avoid it, or at least make his own intelligent and responsible choice. The danger to which such a fixed rule most often has been applied is that of drowning in water;[1] but there are numerous cases showing a similar rigidity as to the perils of fire,[2] falling from a height[3] or into an excavation,[4] moving vehicles,[5] ordinary visible machinery in motion,[6] sliding or

94. Well stated in Lone Star Gas Co. v. Parsons, 1932, 159 Okl. 52, 14 P.2d 369.

95. Cincinnati & Hammond Spring Co. v. Brown, 1903, 32 Ind.App. 58, 69 N.E. 197. Cf. Penso v. McCormick, 1890, 125 Ind. 116, 25 N.E. 156; Borinstein v. Hansbrough, 1948, 119 Ind.App. 134, 82 N. E.2d 266; City of Indianapolis v. Williams, 1915, 58 Ind.App. 447, 108 N.E. 387.

96. Harris v. Indiana General Service Co., 1933, 206 Ind. 351, 189 N.E. 410; Fort Wayne & N.I.T. Co. v. Stark, 1920, 74 Ind.App. 669, 127 N.E. 460. Cf. Carradine v. City of New York, 1962, 16 App.Div.2d 928, 229 N.Y.S.2d 328, reversed on other grounds, 1964, 13 N.Y.2d 291, 246 N.Y.S.2d 620, 196 N.E.2d 259 (explosives); Medlin v. United States, W.D.S.C. 1965, 244 F.Supp. 403 (same).

97. Republic Steel Corp. v. Tillery, 1954, 261 Ala. 34, 72 So.2d 719; Bass v. Quinn-Robbins Co., 1950, 70 Idaho 308, 216 P.2d 944; Fourseam Coal Corp. v. Greer, Ky.1955, 282 S.W.2d 129; McHugh v. Reading Co., 1943, 346 Pa. 266, 30 A.2d 122; Schroeder v. Texas & Pac. R. Co., Tex.Civ.App.1951, 243 S.W. 2d 261.

98. Montgomery Ward & Co. v. Ramirez, Tex.Civ. App.1939, 127 S.W.2d 1034.

99. See infra, p. 373.

1. Gordon v. C. H. C. Corp., Miss.1970, 236 So.2d 733; Roberson v. City of Kinston, 1964, 261 N.C. 135, 134 S.E.2d 193; Alabama Great Southern R. Co. v. Green, 1964, 276 Ala. 120, 159 So.2d 823; Jones v. Comer, 1964, 237 Ark. 500, 374 S.W.2d 465; Plotzki v. Standard Oil Co., 1950, 228 Ind. 518, 92 N.E.2d 632. See Note, 1963, 48 Iowa L.Rev. 939.

2. Rhodes v. City of Kansas City, 1949, 167 Kan. 719, 208 P.2d 275; Goss v. Shawnee Post No. 3204, V.F. W., Ky.1954, 265 S.W.2d 799; Lentz v. Schuerman Bldg. & Realty Co., 1949, 359 Mo. 103, 220 S.W.2d 58; Botticelli v. Winters, 1939, 125 Conn. 537, 7 A. 2d 443; Hancock v. Aiken Mills, 1935, 180 S.C. 93, 185 S.E. 188.

3. Fourseam Coal Co. v. Greer, Ky.1955, 282 S.W.2d 129; Kravetz v. B. Perini & Sons, 3 Cir. 1958, 252 F.2d 905; Crawford v. Cox Planing Mill & Lumber Co., 1964, 238 Ark. 588, 383 S.W.2d 291; Mikkelson v. Risovi, N.D.1966, 141 N.W.2d 150; Malloy v. Pennsylvania R. Co., 1956, 387 Pa. 408, 128 A.2d 40.

4. Fain v. Standard Oil Co., 1940, 284 Ky. 561, 145 S.W.2d 39; Savannah, F. & W. R. Co. v. Beavers, 1901, 113 Ga. 398, 39 S.E. 82.

5. Harris v. Roberson, 1943, 78 App.D.C. 246, 139 F. 2d 529 (trailer); Walker v. Pacific Elec. R. Co., 1944, 66 Cal.App.2d 290, 152 P.2d 226 (electric car); Louisville & N. R. Co. v. Spence's Adm'r, Ky.1955, 282 S.W.2d 826 (train); Smith v. Illinois Cent. R. Co., 1952, 214 Miss. 293, 58 So.2d 812 (train); Courtright v. Southern Compress & Warehouse Co., Tex.Civ.App.1957, 299 S.W.2d 169 (trailer).

6. Giddings v. Superior Oil Co., 1951, 106 Cal.App.2d 607, 235 P.2d 843 (oil well pump); Teagarden v. Russell's Adm'x, 1947, 306 Ky. 328, 207 S.W.2d 18 (conveyor belt); Erickson v. Minneapolis, St. P. & S. S. M. R. Co., 1925, 165 Minn. 106, 205 N.W. 889, 45 A.L.R. 973 (drive belt); Ford v. Planters' Chem.

caving soil,[7] and piles of lumber, crossties, and other building material.[8]

These fixed rules have broken down in two groups of cases. One of these arises where the possessor of the land knows or has reason to know [9] that the children who are likely to trespass are so extremely young that they cannot appreciate the danger. When an infant of three or four is known to be in the vicinity of fire [10] water, [11] or these other conditions,[12] it is "pure fantasy, straight from

outer space" [13] to say that he will be fully able to protect himself against them. The other group have involved some reason to say that there is an enhanced risk, greater than the ordinary one normally attending such a condition, as where some part of the danger is concealed or masked,[14] or there is some special attraction, such as a diving board,[15] or special reason to anticipate trespasses, such as past experience [16] or proximity to a place where children congregate.[17] There are so many of these exceptional cases that the present tendency is to reject any such fixed and arbitrary rules, and to say that

& Oil Co., 1930, 220 Ala. 669, 126 So. 866 (spiral conveyor).

7. Anderson v. Reith-Riley Const. Co., 1942, 112 Ind. App. 170, 44 N.E.2d 184; Knight v. Kaiser Co., 1957, 48 Cal.2d 778, 312 P.2d 1089; Zagar v. Union Pac. R. Co., 1923, 113 Kan. 240, 214 P. 107; Powell v. Ligon, 1939, 334 Pa. 250, 5 A.2d 373.

8. Lovell v. Southern Ry. Co., 1952, 257 Ala. 561, 59 So.2d 807 (steel girders); Branan v. Wimsatt, 1924, 54 U.S.App.D.C. 374, 298 F. 833, cert. denied 265 U. S. 591 (lumber); Morris v. Lewis Mfg. Co., 1951, 331 Mich. 252, 49 N.W.2d 164 (lumber); Emery v. Thompson, 1941, 347 Mo. 494, 148 S.W.2d 479 (ties); Boyette v. Atlantic Coast Line R. Co., 1947, 227 N. C. 406, 32 S.E.2d 462 (ties and timbers).

9. Where the defendant has no reason to anticipate such very young children, recovery is denied. Davis v. Goodrich, 1959, 171 Cal.App.2d 92, 340 P.2d 48; Meyer v. General Elec. Co., 1955, 46 Wash.2d 251, 280 P.2d 257; Holifield v. Wigdor, 1951, 361 Mo. 636, 235 S.W.2d 564; Nichols v. Atlantic Coast Line R. Co., 1947, 228 N.C. 222, 44 S.E.2d 879; Cox v. Ince, Tex.Civ.App.1954, 274 S.W.2d 865.

10. Louisville Trust Co. v. Nutting, Ky.1968, 437 S. W.2d 484 (3 years); Wozniczka v. McKean, 1969, — Ind.App. —, 247 N.E.2d 215 (5 years); Missouri Pac. R. Co. v. Lester, 1951, 219 Ark. 413, 242 S.W. 714; Courtell v. McEachen, 1959, 51 Cal.2d 448, 334 P.2d 870 (5 years); Ford v. Blythe Bros. Co., 1955, 242 N.C. 347, 87 S.E.2d 879 (3 years).

11. Everett v. White, 1965, 245 S.C. 331, 140 S.E.2d 582 (5 years); Davies v. Land O'Lakes Racing Ass'n, 1955, 244 Minn. 248, 69 N.W.2d 642 (5 years); Barlow v. Gurney, 1944, 224 N.C. 223, 29 S.E.2d 681 (4 years); Banker v. McLaughlin, 1948, 146 Tex. 434, 208 S.W.2d 843 (5 years); Altenbach v. Lehigh Valley R. Co., 1944, 349 Pa. 272, 37 A.2d 429 (3 years).

12. Cockerham v. R. E. Vaughan, Inc., Fla.1955, 82 So.2d 890 (2½ years, excavation); Kentucky & Ind. Terminal R. Co. v. Mann, Ky.1958, 312 S.W.2d 451, affirming Ky.1955, 290 S.W.2d 820 (2½ years, moving train); Peterson v. Richfield Plaza, 1958, 252 Minn. 215, 89 N.W.2d 712 (2 years, fall from balco-

ny); Gould v. De Beve, 1964, 117 U.S.App.D.C., 330 F.2d 826, 829 (2½ years, fall from window); Eaton v. R. B. George Investments, 1953, 152 Tex. 523, 260 S.W. 587 (3 years, cattle dipping vat).

13. Smith, J., in Elbert v. City of Saginaw, 1961, 363 Mich. 463, 109 N.W.2d 879.

14. Cooper v. City of Reading, 1958, 392 Pa. 452, 140 A.2d 792 (ice-covered pool with concealed step-off); Lehmkuhl v. Junction City, 1956, 179 Kan. 389, 295 P.2d 621 (deceptive surface); Ansin v. Thurston, Fla.App.1957, 98 So.2d 87, cert. denied 101 So.2d 808 (concealed drop-off); Skaggs v. Junis, 1960, 27 Ill. App.2d 251, 169 N.E.2d 684 (concealed stump in pond); Hoff v. Natural Ref. Products Co., 1955, 38 N.J.Super. 222, 118 A.2d 714 (pile of refuse caved in).

15. Smith v. Evans, 1955, 178 Kan. 259, 284 P.2d 1065. Cf. Allen v. William P. McDonald Corp., Fla. 1949, 42 So.2d 706 (pond with white sand bank); Galleher v. City of Wichita, 1956, 179 Kan. 513, 296 P.2d 1062 (deceptive water with sand beach); Cargill, Inc. v. Zimmer, 8 Cir.1967, 374 F.2d 924 (72 foot ladder with pigeons at top); Salanski v. Enright, Mo.1970, 452 S.W.2d 143 (tree house).

16. Dickeson v. Baltimore & O. C. T. R. Co., 1965, 73 Ill.App.2d 5, 220 N.E.2d 43, affirmed, 1969, 42 Ill.2d 103, 245 N.E.2d 762 (moving trains); Weber v. St. Anthony Falls Water Power Co., 1942, 214 Minn. 1, 7 N.W.2d 339 (pile of lumber); Barlow v. Gurney, 1944, 224 N.C. 223, 29 S.E.2d 681 (pond); Talbott v. Farmers Union Co-op. Elevator Co., 1953, 174 Kan. 435, 256 P.2d 856 (well); Nechodomu v. Lindstrom, 1956, 273 Wis. 313, 77 N.W.2d 707, rehearing denied 78 N.W.2d 417 (mud mixer machine).

17. Saxton v. Plum Orchards, 1949, 215 La. 378, 40 So.2d 791; Kahn v. James Burton Co., 1955, 5 Ill.2d 614, 126 N.E.2d 836; Heitman v. City of Lake City, 1947, 225 Minn. 117, 30 N.W.2d 18; Gimmestad v. Rose Bros. Co., 1935, 194 Minn. 531, 261 N.W. 194; Hull v. Gillioz, 1939, 344 Mo. 1227, 130 S.W.2d 623.

each case must be considered in the light of all of its particular facts.[18]

Child's Ignorance of Danger

3. The child, because of his immaturity, either does not discover the condition or does not in fact appreciate the danger involved. Since the one basic reason for a rule distinguishing trespassing children from trespassing adults is the inability of the child to protect himself, the courts have been quite firm in their insistence that if the child is fully aware of the condition, understands and appreciates the risk which it carries, and is quite able to avoid it, he stands in no better position than any adult with similar knowledge and understanding.[19]

This is not merely a matter of contributory negligence,[20] but of lack of duty to the child. Thus the fact that he has been warned of the danger may be enough to defeat his re-

covery, where it is found to have been effective in making him fully aware of the situation.[21] But it is appreciation of the danger which is required to bar recovery, rather than mere knowledge of the existence of the condition itself;[22] and where the child is too young to understand,[23] or not sufficiently impressed to forego the attractive hazard,[24] the warning may be found not to relieve the defendant of liability, if he could reasonably be expected to do more.

The age of the child is obviously an important factor throughout. The original turntable cases involved children of the ages of six and seven; and prior to 1925 it was very rarely that a child over twelve was allowed to recover.[25] Even today the great majority of the recoveries have been on the part of children of twelve or under; and there is a long list of decisions refusing to permit the jury to find for a plaintiff of thirteen,[26] four-

---

18. King v. Lennen, 1959, 53 Cal.2d 340, 1 Cal.Rptr. 665, 348 P.2d 98 (swimming pool, overruling a long line of cases); Pocholec v. Giustina, 1960, 224 Or. 245, 355 P.2d 1104 (pond); Elbert v. City of Saginaw, 1961, 363 Mich. 463, 109 N.W.2d 879; Kahn v. James Burton Co., 1955, 5 Ill.2d 614, 126 N.E.2d 836; Garcia v. Soogian, 1959, 52 Cal.2d 107, 338 P. 2d 433.

See, as to swimming pools, Note, 1967, 9 Ariz.L.Rev. 339.

19. Nolley v. Chicago, M., St. P. & P. R. Co., 8 Cir. 1950, 183 F.2d 566, cert. denied 340 U.S. 913; Idzi v. Hobbs, Fla.App.1965, 176 So.2d 606, quashed, 1966, 186 So.2d 20; Ostroski v. Mount Prospect Shop-Rite, Inc., 1967, 94 N.J.Super. 374, 228 A.2d 545; Brady v. Chicago & N. W. R. Co., 1954, 265 Wis. 618, 62 N.W.2d 415; Luttrell v. Carolina Mineral Co., 1942, 220 N.C. 782, 18 S.E.2d 412.

Missouri Pac. R. Co. v. Hance, Tex.Civ.App.1958, 310 S.W.2d 374, and Nicolosi v. Clark, 1915, 169 Cal. 746, 147 P. 971, appear to be alone in denying recovery because of the boy's "moral turpitude" in stealing explosives. In both cases he was aware of the danger.

20. Pocholec v. Giustina, 1960, 224 Or. 245, 355 P.2d 1104; Nechodomu v. Lindstrom, 1956, 273 Wis. 313, 77 N.W.2d 707, 78 N.W.2d 417; Nashville Lumber Co. v. Busbee, 1911, 100 Ark. 76, 139 S.W. 301; Courtell v. McEachen, 1959, 51 Cal.2d 448, 334 P.2d 870; Van Alst v. Kansas City, 1949, 239 Mo. App. 346, 186 S.W.2d 762. Contra, Larnel Builders v. Martin, Fla.1959, 110 So.2d 649.

21. Phipps v. Mitze, 1947, 116 Colo. 288, 180 P.2d 233; Nolley v. Chicago, M., St. P. & P. R. Co., 8 Cir. 1950, 183 F.2d 566, cert. denied 340 U.S. 913; McCulley v. Cherokee Amusement Co., 1944, 182 Tenn. 68, 184 S.W.2d 170; Harriman v. Incorporated Town of Afton, 1938, 225 Iowa 659, 281 N.W. 183; Vincent v. Barnhill, 1948, 203 Miss. 740, 34 So.2d 363.

22. Novicki v. Blaw-Knox Co., 3 Cir. 1962, 304 F.2d 931; Helguera v. Cirone, 1960, 178 Cal.App.2d 232, 3 Cal.Rptr. 64; Buckeye Irr. Co. v. Askren, 1935, 45 Ariz. 566, 46 P.2d 1068.

23. Missouri Pac. R. Co. v. Lester, 1951, 219 Ark. 413, 242 S.W.2d 714; Tucker Bros. v. Menard, Fla. 1956, 90 So.2d 908; Ramsay v. Tuthill Bldg. Materials Co., 1920, 295 Ill. 395, 129 N.E. 127; Cumberland River Oil Co. v. Dicken, 1939, 279 Ky. 700, 131 S.W.2d 927; Ziehm v. Vale, 1918, 98 Ohio St. 306, 120 N.E. 702.

24. Selby v. Tolbert, 1952, 56 N.M. 718, 249 P.2d 498; Roman v. City of Leavenworth, 1913, 90 Kan. 379, 133 P. 551.

25. See Schulte v. Willow River Power Co., 1940, 234 Wis. 188, 290 N.W. 629, 631.

26. Harriman v. Incorporated Town of Afton, 1938, 225 Iowa 659, 281 N.W. 183; Deffland v. Spokane Portland Cement Co., 1947, 26 Wash.2d 891, 176 P. 2d 311; Edwards v. City of Kansas City, 1919, 104 Kan. 684, 180 P. 271; Marquette v. Cangelosi, La. App.1933, 148 So. 88.

teen,[27] fifteen,[28] sixteen,[29] and above.[30] It is commonly said that the special rule applied only to "young" children, or those of "tender years;" and the original rule of the Restatement of Torts was so limited.

A small number of courts have declared a fixed age limit of fourteen,[31] which is taken over from their rule as to the presumed incapacity of children under that age for contributory negligence. All this authority is not, however, quite as impressive as it may appear, since the cases have involved, for the most part, conditions which would have been understood and appreciated by even younger children.

On the other hand, with the increasing development of conditions, such as high tension wires, which a boy of high school age may reasonably be expected not to appreciate,

there are now a considerable number of cases in which such children have been allowed to recover, at the age of thirteen[32] and fourteen,[33] with a few instances of even older children.[34] No definite line is drawn, but as the age goes up the possible conditions diminish, until at some uncertain point they vanish.[35] For these reasons, the Second Restatement of Torts[36] has eliminated the limitation to "young" children originally stated. There is even a little authority[37] that the infant's mental development is to be taken into account, as in cases of contributory negligence;

27. Empire Dist. Elec. Co. v. Harris, 8 Cir. 1936, 82 F.2d 48; Giddings v. Superior Oil Co., 1951, 106 Cal.App.2d 607, 235 P.2d 843; Gouger v. Tennessee Valley Authority, 1949, 188 Tenn. 96, 216 S.W.2d 739; Massie v. Copeland, 1950, 149 Tex. 319, 233 S.W.2d 449.

28. Hanson v. Freigang, 1959, 55 Wash.2d 70, 345 P.2d 1109; Roach v. Dozier, 1958, 97 Ga.App. 568, 103 S.E.2d 691; James v. Wisconsin Power & Light Co., 1954, 266 Wis. 290, 63 N.W.2d 116; Scheffer v. Braverman, 1965, 89 N.J.Super. 452, 215 A.2d 378; O'Keefe v. South End. Rowing Club, 1966, 64 Cal. 2d 729, 51 Cal.Rptr. 534, 414 P.2d 830.

29. Republic Steel Co. v. Tillery, 1954, 261 Ala. 34, 72 So.2d 719; Moseley v. City of Kansas City, 1951, 170 Kan. 585, 228 P.2d 699; Peters v. Town of Ruston, La.App.1936, 167 So. 491; Schulte v. Willow River Power Co., 1940, 234 Wis. 188, 290 N.W. 629.

30. E. I. Du Pont de Nemours & Co. v. Edgerton, 8 Cir.1956, 231 F.2d 430 (seventeen); Garrett v. Arkansas Power & Light Co., 1951, 218 Ark. 575, 237 S.W.2d 895 (same); Midkiff v. Watkins, La.App. 1951, 52 So.2d 573 (same); Texas Power & Light Co. v. Burt, Tex.Civ.App.1937, 104 S.W.2d 941 (eighteen); Soles v. Ohio Edison Co., 1945, 144 Ohio St. 373, 59 N.E.2d 138 (nineteen).

31. Central of Georgia R. Co. v. Robins, 1923, 209 Ala. 6, 95 So. 367; Moseley v. City of Kansas City, 1951, 170 Kan. 585, 228 P.2d 699; Bentley v. South-East Coal Co., Ky.1960, 334 S.W.2d 349; Briscoe v. Henderson L. & P. Co., 1908, 148 N.C. 396, 62 S.E. 600; Keck v. Woodring, 1948, 201 Okl. 665, 208 P.2d 1133. See Note, 1961, 50 Ky.L.Rev. 100.

32. Buckeye Irr. Co. v. Askren, 1935, 45 Ariz. 566, 46 P.2d 1068; Gillespie v. Sanitary District, 1942, 315 Ill.App. 405, 43 N.E.2d 141; Smith v. Evans, 1955, 178 Kan. 259, 284 P.2d 1065; Johnson v. Clement F. Sculley Const. Co., 1959, 255 Minn. 41, 95 N.W.2d 409; Hoff v. Natural Ref. Products Co., 1955, 38 N.J.Super. 222, 118 A.2d 714.

33. Kleren v. Bowman, 1957, 15 Ill.App.2d 148, 145 N.E.2d 810; Dezendorf Marble Co. v. Gartman, Tex. Civ.App.1960, 333 S.W.2d 404, affirmed, 1961, 161 Tex. 535, 343 S.W.2d 441; Patterson v. Palley Mfg. Co., 1948, 360 Pa. 259, 61 A.2d 861; McKiddy v. Des Moines Elec. Co., 1926, 202 Iowa 225, 206 N.W. 815; McCoy v. Texas Power & Light Co., Tex. Comm.App.1922, 239 S.W. 1105.

34. Ekdahl v. Minnesota Utilities Co., 1938, 203 Minn. 374, 281 N.W. 517 (fifteen, cable attached to power line pole); Johns v. Fort Worth L. & P. Co., Tex.Civ.App.1930, 30 S.W.2d 549 (fifteen, power line tower); Skaggs v. Junis, 1960, 27 Ill.App.2d 251, 169 N.E.2d 684 (sixteen, diving into pool with concealed stump); Schorr v. Minnesota Utilities Co., 1938, 203 Minn. 384, 281 N.W. 523 (sixteen, cable attached to power line pole); Klingensmith v. Scioto Valley Traction Co., 1924, 18 Ohio App. 290 (sixteen, power line pole); Boyer v. Guidicy Marble Terrazzo & Tile Co., Mo.1952, 246 S.W.2d 742 (seventeen, dynamite cap); cf. Fouraker v. Mullis, Fla.App.1960, 120 So.2d 808 (seventeen, throwing wet plaster).

35. There is a very good discussion of this in Hoff v. Natural Ref. Products Co., 1955, 38 N.J.Super. 222, 118 A.2d 714. See also Notes, 1939, 23 Minn.L.Rev. 241; 1937, 25 Ky.L.J. 277.

36. Second Restatement of Torts, § 339.

37. Stephens v. Blackwood Lumber Co., 1926, 191 N. C. 23, 131 S.E. 314; Giacona v. Tapley, 1967, 5 Ariz.App. 494, 428 P.2d 439; Lynch v. Motel Enterprises, Inc., 1966, 248 S.C. 490, 151 S.E.2d 435; see Moseley v. City of Kansas City, 1951, 170 Kan. 585, 228 P.2d 699; Grube v. Mayor of Baltimore, 1918, 132 Md. 355, 103 A. 948.

and on this basis, the extreme case allowing recovery has been one in Indiana [38] of an eighteen-year old deaf mute with the mind of a child of six.

4. The utility to the possessor of maintaining the condition must be slight as compared with the risk to children involved.[39] Here, as elsewhere,[40] negligence is to be determined by weighing the probability and the gravity of the possible harm against the utility of the defendant's conduct.[41] The public interest in the free use of land is such that, in general, he will not be required to take precautions which are so burdensome or expensive as to be unreasonable in the light of the risk,[42] or to make his premises "child-proof." [43] Such things as standing freight cars [44] and moving vehicles [45] are undeniably

attractive to children, but are socially useful and very difficult to safeguard, and so may call for very little in the way of care. On the other hand dynamite caps,[46] or uninsulated wires,[47] which can easily be removed or guarded, may properly serve as a basis of liability. A railroad company may not be negligent in having a turntable where children frequently play, but may be negligent in failing to keep it locked when it is not in use.[48] At one stage of its construction an unfinished house may be practically impossible to safeguard so that children cannot get into it; [49] while at a later stage it becomes possible, and reasonable, to barricade or lock the door.[50] The defendant is to be held liable only for negligence, which means that he is required to exercise only reasonable care, and to take only those precautions which would be taken by a reasonable man under

---

38. Harris v. Indiana General Service Co., 1934, 206 Ind. 351, 189 N.E. 410.

39. See Bauer, The Degree of Danger and the Degree of Difficulty of Removal of the Danger as Factors in Attractive Nuisance Cases, 1934, 18 Minn.L.Rev. 523.

40. See supra, § 31.

41. Chicago, B. & Q. R. Co. v. Krayenbuhl, 1902, 65 Neb. 889, 91 N.W. 880; Scibelli v. Pennsylvania R. Co., 1954, 379 Pa. 282, 108 A.2d 348; Hunsche v. Southern Pac. Co., N.D.Cal.1945, 62 F.Supp. 634; Courtright v. Southern Compress & Warehouse Co., Tex.Civ.App.1957, 299 S.W.2d 169; Coughlin v. United States Tool Co., 1958, 52 N.J.Super. 341, 145 A.2d 482.

42. Jesko v. Turk, 1966, 421 Pa. 434, 219 A.2d 591; Powell v. Ligon, 1939, 334 Pa. 250, 5 A.2d 373; Hickey v. Nulty, 1960, 182 Cal.App.2d 237, 5 Cal.Rptr. 914; McGaughey v. Haines, 1962, 189 Kan. 453, 370 P.2d 120; Brown v. Salt Lake City, 1908, 33 Utah 222, 93 P. 570.

43. McLendon v. Hampton Cotton Mills Co., 1917, 109 S.C. 238, 95 S.E. 781; Taylor v. Minneapolis & St. L. R. Co., 1917, 180 Iowa 702, 163 N.W. 405; Colligen v. Philadelphia Electric Co., 1930, 301 Pa. 87, 151 A. 699.

44. Dugan v. Pennsylvania R. Co., 1956, 387 Pa. 25, 127 A.2d 343, cert. denied 353 U.S. 946; Barnhill's Adm'r v. Mt. Morgan Coal Co., D.Ky.1910, 215 F. 608; Buddy v. Union Terminal R. Co., 1918, 276 Mo. 276, 207 S.W. 821; Kressine v. Janesville Traction Co., 1921, 175 Wis. 192, 184 N.W. 777.

45. Allred v. Pioneer Truck Co., 1918, 179 Cal. 315, 176 P. 455; Courtright v. Southern Compress &

Warehouse Co., Tex.Civ.App.1957, 299 S.W.2d 169; Routt v. Look, 1923, 180 Wis. 1, 191 N.W. 557; Zigman v. Beebe & Runyan Furniture Co., 1915, 97 Neb. 689, 151 N.W. 166.

46. Mattson v. Minnesota & N. W. R. Co., 1905, 95 Minn. 477, 104 N.W. 443; Nelson v. McLellan, 1903, 31 Wash. 208, 71 P. 747; Sandeen v. Tschider, 8 Cir.1913, 205 F. 252.

47. Hayes v. Southern Power Co., 1913, 95 S.C. 230, 78 S.E. 956; Fort Wayne & Northern Indiana Traction Co. v. Stark, 1920, 74 Ind.App. 669, 127 N.E. 460; Meyer v. Menominee & Marinette Light & Traction Co., 1912, 151 Wis. 279, 138 N.W. 1008.

48. Chicago, B. & Q. R. Co. v. Krayenbuhl, 1902, 65 Neb. 889, 91 N.W. 880; Louisville & N. R. Co. v. Vaughn, 1942, 292 Ky. 120, 166 S.W.2d 43; Accord: Chase v. Luce, 1953, 239 Minn. 364, 58 N.W.2d 565 (closing door of unfinished house); Nichols v. Consolidated Dairies, 1952, 125 Mont. 460, 239 P.2d 740, (safety catch on elevator out of repair).

49. Puchta v. Rothman, 1950, 99 Cal.App.2d 285, 221 P.2d 744; Neal v. Home Builders, 1953, 232 Ind. 160, 111 N.E.2d 280; Callahan v. Dearborn Developments, 1959, 57 N.J.Super. 437, 154 A.2d 865. Cf. Camp v. Peel, 1939, 33 Cal.App.2d 612, 92 P.2d 428.

50. Chase v. Luce, 1953, 239 Minn. 364, 58 N.W.2d 565; Woods v. City and County of San Francisco, 1957, 148 Cal.App.2d 958, 307 P.2d 698; Wilinski v. Belmont Builders, 1957, 14 Ill.App.2d 100, 143 N.E. 2d 69; Greene v. De Fazio, 1961, 148 Conn. 419, 171 A.2d 411. Cf. Goben v. Sidney Winer Co., Ky.1960, 342 S.W.2d 706.

the circumstances.[51] A warning to the child may be all that is required,[52] particularly where other precautions are difficult or impossible.[53]

60. LICENSEES

In its broadest sense, the term "licensee" includes anyone who has a license, which is to say a privilege,[54] to enter upon land.[55] It has sometimes been employed [56] to designate any person who comes upon the land with a privilege arising from the consent of the possessor, including all invitees. But as the word is most commonly used by the courts, it is limited to those who enter with that consent and nothing more.

Such a person is not a trespasser, since he is permitted to enter; but he comes for his own purposes rather than for any purpose or interest of the possessor of the land. He has only the consent to distinguish him from a trespasser; and for this reason he is sometimes unflatteringly referred to as a "bare"

or a "naked" licensee. He receives the use of the premises as a gift, and comes well within the old saying that one may not look a gift horse in the mouth. He has no right to demand that the land be made safe for his reception, and he must, in general, assume the risk of whatever he may encounter, and look out for himself.[57] The permission to enter carries with it no obligation to inspect the premises to discover dangers which are unknown to the possessor,[58] nor, a fortiori, to give warning or protection against conditions which are known or should be obvious to the licensee.[59] Here again, as in the case of trespassers,[60] the immunity is limited to persons in possession or those acting on their behalf,[61] and it is generally held that it does not

51. Morton v. Rome, La.App.1959, 110 So.2d 192; Slinker v. Wallner, 1960, 258 Minn. 243, 103 N.W.2d 377; Matheny v. Stonecutter Mills Corp., 1959, 249 N.C. 575, 107 S.E.2d 143; Betts v. City and County of San Francisco, 1952, 108 Cal.App.2d 701, 239 P.2d 456; Kressine v. Janesville Traction Co., 1921, 175 Wis. 192, 184 N.W. 777.

52. Colligen v. Philadelphia Elec. R. Co., 1930, 301 Pa. 87, 151 A. 699; McCulley v. Cherokee Amusement Co., 1944, 182 Tenn. 68, 184 S.W.2d 170; Olson v. Ottertail Power Co., 8 Cir. 1933, 65 F.2d 893; Niernberg v. Gavin, 1950, 123 Colo. 1, 224 P.2d 215.

53. Hernandez v. Santiago Orange Growers Ass'n, 1930, 110 Cal.App. 229, 293 P. 875; Jarvis v. Howard, 1949, 310 Ky. 38, 219 S.W.2d 958; Shock v. Ringling Bros. & B. B. Combined Shows, 1940, 5 Wash.2d 599, 105 P.2d 838; Lucas v. Hammond, 1928, 150 Miss. 369, 116 So. 536; Galbraith-Foxworth Lumber Co. v. Gerneth, Tex.Civ.App.1933, 66 S.W.2d 471.

54. This has served as justification for holding that public officers entering the performance of their duties are licensees. See infra, p. 395.

55. As to licensees on personal property, and automobile guests, see infra, p. 382.

56. Particularly by the First Restatement of Torts, §§ 330–332.

57. See James, Tort Liability of Occupiers of Land: Duties Owed to Licensees and Invitees, 1954, 63 Yale L.J. 605; Marsh, The History and Comparative Law of Invitees, Licensees and Trespassers, 1953, 69 L.Q.Rev. 182, 359; Bohlen, The Duty of a Landowner Towards Those Entering His Premises of Their Own Right, 1921, 69 U.Pa.L.Rev. 142, 237, 340.

58. Brauner v. Leutz, 1943, 293 Ky. 406, 169 S.W.2d 4; Myszkiewicz v. Lord Baltimore Filling Stations, 1935, 168 Md. 642, 178 A. 856; Steinmeyer v. McPherson, 1951, 171 Kan. 275, 232 P.2d 236; Ford v. United States, 10 Cir. 1952, 200 F.2d 272; Rosenberger v. Consolidated Coal Co., 1943, 318 Ill.App. 8, 47 N.E.2d 491.

59. Reardon v. Thompson, 1889, 149 Mass. 267, 21 N.E. 369; Branan v. Wimsatt, 1924, 54 U.S.App.D.C. 374, 298 F. 833, cert. denied 265 U.S. 591; Mazey v. Loveland, 1916, 133 Minn. 210, 158 N.W. 44; Mississippi Power & Light Co. v. Griffin, 5 Cir.1936, 81 F.2d 292; Standard Oil Co. of Ind. v. Meissner, 1936, 102 Ind.App. 552, 200 N.E. 445.

The special rules as to trespassing children apply also, however, to child licensees. See supra, p. ——.

60. See supra, p. 359.

61. Ireland v. Complete Machinery & Equipment Co., 1940, 174 Misc. 91, 21 N.Y.S.2d 430 (contractor); Dishington v. A. W. Kuettel & Sons, 1959, 255 Minn. 325, 96 N.W.2d 684 (subcontractor); State Compensation Fund v. Allen, 1930, 104 Cal.App. 400, 285 P. 1053 (general building contractor); Toomey v. Wichison Industrial Gas Co., 1936, 144 Kan. 534, 61 P.2d 891 (removing gas connections); Harris v. Mentes-Williams Co., 1952, 23 N.J.Super. 9, 92 A.2d 498, reversed on other grounds in 1953, 11 N.J. 559, 95 A.2d 388 (bulldozing contractor).

extend to trespassing third parties,[62] to other licensees,[63] or even to invitees who have paid for the privilege of entry.[64]

Persons Included

Among the more common classes of persons who enter with nothing more than consent are those taking short cuts across the property [65] or making merely permissive use of crossings and ways [66] or other parts of the premises; [67] loafers, loiterers, and people who come in only to get out of the weather; [68] those in search of their children, servants or

other third persons; [69] spectators and sight-seers not in any way invited to come; [70] those who enter for social visits [71] or personal business dealings with employees of the possessor of the land; [72] tourists visiting a plant at their own request; [73] those who come to borrow tools [74] or to pick up and remove refuse for their own benefit; [75] salesmen canvassing at the door of private homes,[76] and those

62. Davoust v. City of Alameda, 1906, 149 Cal. 69, 84 P. 760; Boutlier v. City of Malden, 1917, 226 Mass. 479, 116 N.E. 251; Williams v. Springfield Gas & Elec. Co., 1918, 274 Mo. 1, 202 S.W. 1.

63. Constantino v. Watson Contracting Co., 1916, 219 N.Y. 443, 114 N.E. 802; Duel v. Mansfield Plumbing Co., 1914, 86 N.J.L. 582, 92 A. 367; Mullen v. Wilkes-Barre Gas & Elec. Co., 1910, 229 Pa. 54, 77 A. 1108; Thompson v. Tilton Elec. L. & P. Co., 1913, 77 N.H. 92, 88 A. 216.

Contra: Hafey v. Dwight Mfg. Co., 1921, 240 Mass. 155, 133 N.E. 107; New Omaha T. H. Elec. L. Co. v. Anderson, 1905, 73 Neb. 84, 102 N.W. 89.

64. Barnett v. Atlantic City Elec. Co., 1915, 87 N.J.L. 29, 93 A. 108; Oil Belt Power Co. v. Touchstone, Tex.Civ.App.1924, 266 S.W. 432. See, generally, Note, 1929, 77 U.Pa.L.Rev. 506.

65. Draper v. Switous, 1963, 370 Mich. 468, 122 N.W. 2d 698; Bruno v. Seigel, Fla.1954, 73 So.2d 674; Baird v. Goldberg, 1940, 283 Ky. 558, 142 S.W.2d 120; Myszkiewicz v. Lord Baltimore Filling Stations, 1935, 168 Md. 642, 178 A. 856; Cook v. 177 Granite St., 1949, 95 N.H. 397, 64 A.2d 327.

66. Barry v. New York Cent. & H. R. R. Co., 1883, 92 N.Y. 289; Phipps v. Oregon R. & Nav. Co., C.C. Wash.1908, 161 F. 376; Reardon v. Thompson, 1889, 149 Mass. 267, 21 N.E. 369; Matthews v. Seaboard Air Line R. Co., 1903, 67 S.C. 499, 46 S.E. 335; Carskaddon v. Mills, 1892, 5 Ind.App. 22, 31 N.E. 559.

67. Babcock & Wilcox Co. v. Nolton, 1937, 58 Nev. 133, 71 P.2d 1051; Standard Oil Co. of Indiana v. Meissner, 1936, 102 Ind.App. 552, 200 N.E. 445; Brinkmeyer v. United Iron & Metal Co., 1935, 168 Md. 149, 177 A. 171.

68. Dye v. Rule, 1934, 138 Kan. 808, 28 P.2d 758; Murry Chevrolet Co. v. Cotten, 1934, 169 Miss. 521, 152 So. 657; Kneiser v. Belasco-Blackwood Co., 1913, 22 Cal.App. 205, 133 P. 989; Texas Co. v. Haggard, 1939, 23 Tenn.App. 475, 134 S.W.2d 880;

Cumberland Tel. & Tel. Co. v. Martin's Adm'r, 1903, 116 Ky. 554, 76 S.W. 394, 77 S.W. 718.

69. Plummer v. Dill, 1892, 156 Mass. 426, 31 N.E. 128; Flatley v. Acme Garage, 1923, 196 Iowa 82, 194 N.W. 180; Faris v. Hoberg, 1892, 134 Ind. 269, 33 N.E. 1028.

70. Gillis v. Pennsylvania R. Co., 1868, 59 Pa.St. 129; Midland Valley R. Co. v. Littlejohn, 1914, 44 Okl. 8, 143 P. 1; Polio v. Ohio River R. Co., 1893, 38 W.Va. 645, 18 S.E. 782.

71. Snyder v. I. Jay Realty Co., 1959, 30 N.J. 303, 153 A.2d 1; Gunnarson v. Robert Jacob, Inc., 2 Cir. 1938, 94 F.2d 170, cert. denied 303 U.S. 660, rehearing denied 304 U.S. 588; Gotch v. K. & B. Packing & Provision Co., 1933, 93 Colo. 276, 25 P.2d 719; Yazoo & M. V. R. Co. v. Mansfield, 1931, 160 Miss. 672, 134 So. 577; Lange v. St. Johns Lumber Co., 1925, 115 Or. 337, 237 P. 696.

72. Roadman v. C. E. Johnson Motor Sales Co., 1941, 210 Minn. 59, 297 N.W. 166; Hamakawa v. Crescent Wharf & Warehouse Co., 1935, 4 Cal.2d 499, 50 P.2d 803; Roth v. Schaefer, 1939, 300 Ill.App. 464, 21 N.E.2d 328; Pries v. Atlanta Enterprises, 1941, 66 Ga.App. 464, 17 S.E.2d 902. Cf. Eisen v. Sportogs, Inc., Fla.1956, 87 So.2d 44 (wife returning work to shop as accommodation to husband employee).

73. Benson v. Baltimore Traction Co., 1893, 77 Md. 535, 26 A. 973; Roe v. St. Louis Independent Packing Co., 1920, 203 Mo.App. 11, 217 S.W. 335.

74. Laporta v. New York Central R. Co., 1916, 224 Mass. 100, 112 N.E. 643; Aguilar v. Riverdale Coop. Creamery Ass'n, 1930, 104 Cal.App. 263, 285 P. 889; Forbrick v. General Elec. Co., 1904, 45 Misc. 452, 92 N.Y.S. 36.

75. Lavoie v. Nashua Gummed & Coated Paper Co., 1918, 79 N.H. 97, 105 A. 4; Cowart v. Meeks, 1938, 131 Tex. 36, 111 S.W.2d 1105; Pelon v. Easthampton Gas Co., 1924, 248 Mass. 57, 142 N.E. 640.

76. Prior v. White, 1938, 132 Fla. 1, 180 So. 347; Malatesta v. Lowry, La.App.1961, 130 So.2d 785; De Berry v. City of La Grange, 1940, 62 Ga.App. 74, 8 S.E.2d 146; Phillips v. Bush, 1961, 50 Tenn. App. 639, 363 S.W.2d 401; City of Osceola v. Blair, 1942, 231 Iowa 770, 2 N.W.2d 83.

soliciting money for charity;[77] a stranger entering an office building to post a letter in a mail-box provided for the use of tenants only.[78] The permission may of course be tacit, and may be manifested by the defendant's conduct, or by the condition of the land itself.[79] It is often a question for the jury. But notwithstanding occasional great liberality on the part of some courts,[80] it is generally agreed that the mere toleration of continued intrusion where objection or interference would be burdensome or likely to be futile, as in the case of habitual trespasses on railroad tracks, is not in itself and without more a manifestation of consent.[81]

Early decisions, seeking to find some justification for liability to licensees, sometimes struggled hard to find some element of invitation or allurement in the permission given.[82] While there is occasional language to this effect today, it is now very generally recognized that permission is not necessarily

invitation,[83] and that even where there is encouragement to enter or the occupier takes the initiative, it adds nothing to the permission unless the circumstances are such as to imply an assurance that the premises have been prepared and made safe for the particular visit.

Thus nearly all of the decisions are agreed that a social guest, however cordially he may have been invited and urged to come, is not in law an invitee—a distinction which has puzzled generations of law students, and even some lawyers. The guest is legally nothing more than a licensee, to whom the possessor owes no duty of inspection and affirmative care to make the premises safe for his visit.[84] The fact that in the course of his visit he gratuitously performs incidental services for his host, such as picking fruit, washing the dishes, or feeding the dog, does not improve his legal position.[85] The reason usually given is

---

77. Jones v. Asa G. Candler, Inc., 1918, 22 Ga.App. 717, 97 S.E. 112; Ockerman v. Faulkner's Garage, Ky.1953, 261 S.W.2d 296.

78. Brosnan v. Kaufman, 1936, 194 Mass. 495, 2 N.E. 2d 441.

79. Meitzner v. Baltimore & O. R. Co., 1909, 224 Pa. 352, 73 A. 434; Rooney v. Woolworth, 1905, 78 Conn. 167, 61 A. 366; Ellsworth v. Metheney, 6 Cir.1900, 104 F. 119.

80. As for example in Brinilson v. Chicago & N. W. R. Co., 1911, 144 Wis. 614, 129 N.W. 664; Kremposky v. Mt. Jessup Coal Co., 1920, 266 Pa. 568, 109 A. 766; Lowery v. Walker, [1911] A.C. 10.

81. Arkansas Short Line v. Bellars, 1928, 176 Ark. 53, 2 S.W.2d 683; Bailey v. Lehigh Valley R. Co., 1908, 220 Pa. 516, 69 A. 998; Indiana Harbor Belt R. Co. v. Jones, 1942, 220 Ind. 139, 41 N.E.2d 361. See Bohlen, The Duty of a Landowner Toward Those Entering His Premises of Their Own Right, 1921, 69 U.Pa.L.Rev. 142, 237; Eldredge, Tort Liability to Trespassers, 1937, 12 Temple L.Q. 32, 34–38, reprinted in Eldredge, Modern Tort Problems, 1941, 163; Second Restatement of Torts, § 330, Comment c.

82. Sweeny v. Old Colony & N. R. Co., 1865, 10 Allen, Mass., 368, 87 Am.Dec. 644; Holmes v. Drew, 1890, 151 Mass. 578, 25 N.E. 22. See further, as to the distinction between licensees and invitees, infra, pp. 389, 390.

83. Plummer v. Dill, 1892, 156 Mass. 426, 31 N.E. 128; Branan v. Wimsatt, 1924, 54 U.S.App.D.C. 374, 298 F. 833, cert. denied 265 U.S. 591; Larmore v. Crown Point Iron Co., 1886, 101 N.Y. 391, 4 N.E. 752.

84. Laube v. Stevenson, 1951, 137 Conn. 469, 78 A.2d 693; Walker v. Williams, 1964, 215 Tenn. 195, 384 S.W.2d 447; Krause v. Alper, 1958, 4 N.Y.2d 518, 176 N.Y.S.2d 349, 151 N.E.2d 895; Lomberg v. Renner, 1960, 121 Vt. 311, 157 A.2d 222; Cordula v. Dietrich, 1960, 9 Wis.2d 211, 101 N.W.2d 126.

85. Ciaglo v. Ciaglo, 1959, 20 Ill.App.2d 360, 156 N. E.2d 376. Accord: Pearlstein v. Leeds, 1958, 52 N. J.Super. 450, 145 A.2d 650 (aiding in preparations for party); Murrell v. Handley, 1957, 245 N.C. 559, 96 S.E.2d 717 (fetching scissors); Cochran v. Abercrombie, Fla.App.1958, 118 So.2d 636 (looking over motor); Dotson v. Haddock, 1955, 46 Wash.2d 52, 278 P.2d 338 (baby sitter).

A guest who brings a gift does not become an invitee. Blackman v. Crowe, 1967, 149 Mont. 253, 425 P.2d 323; Kapka v. Urbaszewski, 1964, 47 Ill.App.2d 321, 198 N.E.2d 569.

Otherwise when the guest comes in response to a request to render gratuitous services, such as nursing —in which case he is an invitee. Murdock v. Petersen, 1958, 74 Nev. 363, 332 P.2d 649; see Maxwell v. Maxwell, 1962, 140 Mont. 59, 367 P.2d 308; Brant v. Matlin, Fla.App.1965, 172 So.2d 902. Cf. Weyburn v. California Kamloops, Inc., 1962, 200

that the guest understands when he comes that he is to be placed on the same footing as one of the family, and must take the premises as the occupier himself uses them, without any inspection or preparation for his safety; and that he also understands that he must take his chances as to any defective conditions unknown to the occupier, and is entitled at most to a warning of dangers that are known.[86] There has, however, been quite a vigorous undercurrent of dissent, as to whether this is really in accord with present social customs, under which it is contended that the guest, invited and even urged to come, rightfully expects more than mere inactivity for his safety;[87] and some writers[88] have urged that the social guest be treated as an invitee. The prevalence of liability insurance covering injuries due to defective premises has been advanced as a reason for the change.[89] Thus far, however, the only courts which have accepted these arguments are those of Louisiana[90] and Michigan,[91] which have held that the guest is an invitee.

Cal.App.2d 239, 19 Cal.Rptr. 357 (corporation inviting business man to camp and fish).

86. Well stated in Pagliaro v. Pezza, 1961, 92 R.I. 110, 167 A.2d 139; Wolfson v. Chelist, Mo.1955, 284 S.W.2d 447.

87. See particularly Laube v. Stevenson, 1951, 137 Conn. 469, 78 A.2d 693, and Scheibel v. Lipton, 1951, 156 Ohio St. 308, 102 N.E.2d 453. The arguments are considered at length in Wolfson v. Chelist, Mo. 1955, 284 S.W.2d 447.

88. See Laube v. Stevenson, A Discussion, 1951, 25 Conn.Bar J. 123; McCleary, The Liability of a Possessor of Land in Missouri to Persons Injured While on the Land, 1936, 1 Mo.L.Rev. 45, 58; Notes, 1959, 19 La.L.Rev. 906; 1957, 22 Mo.L.Rev. 186; 1958, 12 Rutgers L.Rev. 599; 1966, 7 Wm. & M.L.Rev. 313.

89. 2 Harper and James, Torts, 1956, 1476–1478.

90. Alexander v. General Accident Fire & Life Ins. Co., La.App.1957, 98 So.2d 730; Daire v. Southern Farm Bureau Cas. Ins. Co., La.App.1962, 143 So.2d 389.

91. Preston v. Sleziak, 1969, 16 Mich.App. 18, 167 N. W.2d 477; Genesee Merchants Bank & Trust Co. v. Payne, 1967, 6 Mich.App. 204, 148 N.W.2d 503, affirmed, 1968, 381 Mich. 234, 161 N.W.2d 17.

Activities Dangerous to Licensees

As in the case of trespassers,[92] the earlier decisions frequently said that there was no duty to a licensee except to refrain from injuring him intentionally, or by wilful, wanton or reckless conduct.[93] The statement is still sometimes repeated,[94] usually in cases holding that there is no duty to inspect the premises to discover unknown conditions. Again, as in the case of trespassers, there is something of a tendency to find "wanton" or "reckless" conduct in what clearly appears to be nothing more than ordinary negligence.[95] As in the case of trespassers, however, an increasing regard for human safety has led to a gradual modification of this position, and the greater number of courts now expressly reject it.[96] It is now generally held that as to any active operations which the occupier carries on, there is an obligation to exercise reasonable care for the protection of a licensee.[97] He must run his train,[98] operate his

92. See supra, p. 362.

93. See for example O'Brien v. Union Freight R. Co., 1911, 209 Mass. 449, 95 N.E. 861; Cleveland, C. C. & St. L. R. Co. v. Potter, 1925, 113 Ohio St. 591, 150 N.E. 44; Kahn v. Graper, 1966, 114 Ga.App. 572, 152 S.E.2d 10. Recklessness is enough for liability in all jurisdictions. See for example Blackburn v. Colvin, 1963, 191 Kan. 239, 380 P.2d 432.

94. Tennessee Valley Authority v. Stratton, 1948, 306 Ky. 753, 209 S.W.2d 318; Carbone v. Mackchil Realty Co., 1947, 296 N.Y. 154, 71 N.E.2d 447; McGillivray v. First Nat. Stores, 1951, 326 Mass. 678, 96 N.E.2d 159; Willnes v. Ludwig, 1947, 136 N.J.L. 208, 55 A.2d 48; Cavezzi v. Cooper, Fla.1950, 47 So.2d 860.

95. See for example Petree v. Davison-Paxon-Stokes Co., 1923, 30 Ga.App. 490, 118 S.E. 697; Holcombe v. Buckland, 4 Cir.1942, 130 F.2d 544; King v. Patrylow, 1951, 15 N.J.Super. 429, 83 A.2d 639.

96. Oettinger v. Stewart, 1944, 24 Cal.2d 133, 148 P. 2d 19; Kentucky & W. Va. Power Co. v. Stacy, 1942, 291 Ky. 325, 164 S.W.2d 537; Davis v. Tredwell, 1943, 347 Pa. 341, 32 A.2d 411; Lordi v. Spiotta, 1946, 133 N.J.L. 581, 45 A.2d 491; Weighmunk v. Harrington, 1936, 274 Mich. 409, 264 N.W. 845.

97. Second Restatement of Torts, § 341. Active negligence, to create liability to a licensee, must be more than prior creation of a condition. Kaslo v. Hahn, 1967, 36 Wis.2d 87, 153 N.W.2d 33.

98. Louisville & Nashville R. Co. v. Blevins, Ky.1956, 293 S.W.2d 246; Seaboard Air Line R. Co. v. Bran-

machinery,[99] or back his truck[1] with due regard for the possibility that the permission given may have been accepted and the licensee may be present. The obligation is higher than that owed to a trespasser, because the possessor may be required to look out for licensees before their presence is discovered; but reasonable care will of course be affected by the probability that the licensee will come, whether he may be expected to follow a particular path,[2] the time of day,[3] and the nature of the danger. No more than reasonable care is required,[4] and ordinarily

a proper warning will be sufficient.[5] The licensee has no right to demand that the occupier change his method of conducting activities for his safety, and in the usual case, if he is fully informed as to what is going on or it is obvious to him, he has all that he is entitled to expect, and assumes the risk thereafter.[6]

Dangerous Conditions Known to the Occupier

As to passive conditions on the land, it is still the settled rule that the possessor is under no obligation to the licensee with respect to anything that the possessor does not know.[7] He is not required to inspect his land for unknown dangers, nor, of course, to disclose their existence or take precautions against them.[8] But another special rule which developed in England[9] was that the occupier was not permitted to "set a trap" for the licensee. This phrase originally was used in

ham, Fla.App.1958, 99 So.2d 621, certiorari discharged, 1958, 104 So.2d 356; Barry v. New York Cent. & H. R. R. Co., 1883, 92 N.Y. 289; Pomponio v. New York, N. H. & H. R. Co., 1895, 66 Conn. 528, 34 A. 491; Smithwick v. Pacific Elec. R. Co., 1920, 206 Cal. 291, 274 P. 980.

Contra, Jackson v. Pennsylvania R. Co., 1939, 176 Md. 1, 3 A.2d 719.

99. Boardman v. McNeff, 1964, 177 Neb. 534, 129 N. W.2d 457 (harrow and truck); Standard Steel Car Co. v. McGuire, 1908, 88 C.C.A. 469, 161 F. 527 (crane); De Haven v. Hennessey Bros. & Evans Co., 1905, 69 C.C.A. 620, 137 F. 472 (elevator). Cf. Cropanese v. Martinez, 1955, 35 N.J.Super. 118, 113 A.2d 433 (joining pipe); Draper v. Switous, 1963, 370 Mich. 468, 122 N.W.2d 698 (washing rack); Szafranski v. Radetzky, 1966, 31 Wis.2d 119, 141 N.W.2d 902 (handling gun powder); Perry v. St. Jean, 1966, 100 R.I. 622, 218 A.2d 484 (providing horse to be ridden).

1. Brigman v. Fiske-Carter Const. Co., 1927, 192 N.C. 791, 136 S.E. 125; Cullmann v. Mumper, 1967, 83 Ill.App.2d 395, 228 N.E.2d 276; Potter Title & Trust Co. v. Young, 1951, 367 Pa. 239, 80 A.2d 76; Babcock & Wilcox Co. v. Nolton, 1937, 58 Nev. 133, 71 P.2d 1051; Gay v. Cadwallader Gibson Co., 1939, 34 Cal.App.2d 566, 93 P.2d 1051.

Cf. Lordi v. Spiotta, 1946, 133 N.J.L. 581, 45 A.2d 491 (shutting off gas); Potts v. Amis, 1963, 62 Wash.2d 777, 384 P.2d 825 (swinging golf club); Blystone v. Kiesel, 1967, 247 Or. 528, 431 P.2d 262 (running to front door); Bradshaw v. Minter, 1965, 206 Va. 450, 143 S.E.2d 827 (giving guest horse).

2. Cf. Olderman v. Bridgeport-City Trust Co., 1939, 125 Conn. 177, 4 A.2d 646; Morrison v. Carpenter, 1914, 179 Mich. 207, 146 N.W. 106.

3. Cf. Sherman v. Maine Cent. R. Co., 1913, 110 Me. 228, 85 A. 755.

4. Musto v. Lehigh Valley R. R., 1937, 327 Pa. 35, 192 A. 888 (train properly inspected); cf. Texas & P. R. Co. v. Endsley, 1910, 103 Tex. 434, 129 S.W.

342; Missouri-Kansas-Texas R. Co. v. Sowards, 1933, 165 Okl. 219, 25 P.2d 641.

5. Second Restatement of Torts, § 341. Thus in Peitruszka v. Bethlehem Mines Corp., W.D.Pa.1957, 156 F.Supp. 523, it was held there was no liability where the plaintiff was warned and disregarded it. But more than warning may be required where it is obvious that the warning is not heard or the danger is not realized. Ahnefeld v. Wabash R. Co., 1908, 212 Mo. 280, 111 S.W. 95.

6. Downes v. Elmira Bridge Co., 1904, 179 N.Y. 136, 71 N.E. 743; Fox v. Warner-Quinlan Asphalt Co., 1912, 204 N.Y. 240, 97 N.E. 497; Roe v. St. Louis Independent Packing Co., 1920, 203 Mo.App. 11, 217 S.W. 335; Shafer v. Tacoma Eastern R. Co., 1916, 91 Wash. 164, 157 P. 485.

7. See supra, p. 376.

8. Fleck v. Nickerson, 1965, 239 Or. 641, 399 P.2d 353; Brauner v. Leutz, 1943, 293 Ky. 406, 169 S.W. 2d 4; Steinmeyer v. McPherson, 1951, 171 Kan. 275, 232 P.2d 236; Ford v. United States, 10 Cir. 1952, 200 F.2d 272; Gabbert v. Wood, 1954, 127 Cal.App. 2d 188, 273 P.2d 319.

Statutes in a number of jurisdictions, however, impose the duty of reasonable care. See, as to the Wisconsin "Safe Place" statute, Note, [1953] Wis.L. Rev. 311.

9. Corby v. Hill, 1858, 4 C.B.,N.S., 556, 140 Eng.Rep. 1209; Bolch v. Smith, 1862, 7 H. & N. 736, 158 Eng.Rep. 666.

the sense of presenting an appearance of safety where it did not exist;[10] but the significance which gradually became attached to it was not one of intent to injure, or even of any active misconduct, but was merely that the possessor of the land was under an obligation to disclose to the licensee any concealed dangerous conditions of the premises of which he had knowledge.[11] The theory usually advanced in support of this duty is that by extending permission to enter the land he represents that it is as safe as it appears to be, and when he knows that it is not there is "something like fraud"[12] in his failure to give warning.[13] The licensee may be required to accept the premises as the occupier uses them, but he is entitled to at least equal knowledge of the danger, and should not be expected to assume the risk of a defective bridge,[14] an uninsulated wire,[15] an unusually slippery floor,[16] or a dangerous step,[17] in the face of a misleading silence.

While there are still occasional cases[18] which deny the existence of any such obligation of disclosure, it is accepted by the overwhelming weight of authority.

The duty arises only when the occupier has actual knowledge of the risk,[19] although this may be shown by circumstantial evidence, and he is held to the standard of a reasonable man in realizing the significance of what he has discovered.[20] It includes disclosure of natural[21] as well as artificial conditions, and it extends also to any activities of third persons on the premises which may create a danger to the licensee.[22] The duty is not to maintain the land in safe condition, but to exercise reasonable care to see that the licensee is aware of the danger;[23] and if it is known[24] or must be obvious[25] to him he

10. Griffith, Licensors and "Traps," 1925, 41 L.Q. Rev. 255.

11. Second Restatement of Torts, § 342.

12. Willes, J., in Gautret v. Eberton, 1867, L.R. 2 C. P. 271, 36 L.J.C.P. 191. See Eldredge, Landlord's Tort Liability for Disrepair, 1936, 84 U.Pa.L.Rev. 467, 468–470, reprinted in Eldredge, Modern Tort Problems, 1941, 113.

13. See supra, p. 179, as to nondisclosure as negligence.

14. Campbell v. Boyd, 1883, 88 N.C. 129; Lawson v. Shreveport Waterworks Co., 1903, 111 La. 73, 35 So. 390.

15. Smith v. Southwest Missouri R. Co., 1933, 333 Mo. 314, 62 S.W.2d 761. Cf. Snow v. Judy, 1968, 96 Ill.App.2d 420, 239 N.E.2d 327 (barbed wire).

16. The Blue Moon III, D.N.Y.1932, 60 F.2d 653; Choate v. Carter, 1958, 98 Ga.App. 375, 105 S.E.2d 909; Newman v. Fox West Coast Theatres, 1948, 86 Cal.App.2d 428, 194 P.2d 706; Hennessey v. Hennessey, 1958, 145 Conn. 211, 140 A.2d 473.

17. Berger v. Shapiro, 1959, 30 N.J. 89, 152 A.2d 20; Haffey v. Lemieux, 1966, 154 Conn. 185, 224 A.2d 551. Accord: Miniken v. Carr, 1967, 71 Wash.2d 325, 428 P.2d 716 (two doors); Rushton v. Winters, 1938, 331 Pa. 78, 200 A. 60 (porch railing); Smith v. Benson's Wild Animal Farm, 1954, 99 N.H. 243, 109 A.2d 39 (loose pony); Maxfield v. Maxfield, 1959, 102 N.H. 101, 151 A.2d 226 (oily rags).

18. See for example Fisher v. General Petroleum Corp., 1954, 123 Cal.App.2d 770, 267 P.2d 841, criticized in Note, 1954, 7 Stan.L.Rev. 130.

19. Sandstrom v. AAD Temple Bldg. Ass'n, 1964, 267 Minn. 407, 127 N.W.2d 173; cf. Paquin v. Mc-Ginnis, 1967, 246 Md. 569, 229 A.2d 86.

20. Hennessey v. Hennessey, 1958, 145 Conn. 211, 140 A.2d 473. He is not, however, required to know more than the standard reasonable man about the dangers of a situation; and if he knows of the existence of a condition, but is reasonably ignorant of its dangers, he is not liable. Schlaks v. Schlaks, 1962, 17 App.Div.2d 153, 232 N.Y.S.2d 814.

21. Windsor Reservoir & Canal Co. v. Smith, 1933, 92 Colo. 464, 21 P.2d 1116; Kittle v. State, 1935, 245 App.Div. 401, 284 N.Y.S. 657, affirmed, 1936, 272 N.Y. 420, 3 N.E.2d 850.

22. Murry Chevrolet Co. v. Cotten, 1934, 169 Miss. 521, 152 So. 657. Cf. Oliver v. Oakwood Country Club, Mo.1951, 245 S.W.2d 37.

23. Second Restatement of Torts, § 342, Comment e.

24. Kopp v. R. S. Noonan, Inc., 1956, 385 Pa. 460, 123 A.2d 429; Maxfield v. Maxfield, 1959, 102 N.H. 101, 151 A.2d 226; Mississippi Power & Light Co. v. Griffin, 5 Cir. 1936, 81 F.2d 292; Cutler v. Peck Lumber Mfg. Co., 1944, 350 Pa. 8, 37 A.2d 739.

25. Dishington v. A. W. Kuettel & Sons, 1959, 255 Minn. 325, 96 N.W.2d 684; Fentress v. Co-op. Refinery Ass'n, 1948, 149 Neb. 355, 31 N.W.2d 225; Cook v. 177 Granite St., 1949, 95 N.H. 397, 64 A.2d 327; Standard Oil Co. of Ind. v. Meissner, 1936, 102 Ind.App. 552, 200 N.E. 445; Griffin v. State, 1937, 250 App.Div. 244, 295 N.Y.S. 304. See Keeton, Personal Injuries Resulting from Open and Obvious

must look out for himself, and there is no further obligation. If, however, the possessor knows of a physical infirmity of the visitor, such as bad eyesight, which will make discovery difficult, there may be a duty to disclose even the otherwise obvious.[26] The perils of darkness usually are held to be assumed by one who voluntarily proceeds into it,[27] but if the occupier has any special reason to believe that the licensee will encounter a particular danger there, of which he is unaware, there may still be a duty to give warning.[28] In short, the duty of disclosure arises only where a reasonable man in the position of the occupier would conclude that it is called for.[29] Account must, however, be taken of the curiosity and meddling propensities of children and their inability to protect themselves; and the doctrine of "attractive nuisance" applies to licensees as fully as to trespassers.[30]

Liability frequently is imposed where the occupier, knowing that licensees are in the habit of entering or are likely to come, alters the condition of his premises so as to create a new danger without giving notice of the change or taking other precautions to prevent injury. Thus he may be liable if he places an obstruction in a private way or path,[31] or digs a hole,[32] installs a dangerous electric wire,[33] or sets a vicious horse [34] where licensees customarily pass, or establishes or permits some similar new danger [35] where it may reasonably be expected that they will not discover it. The liability is based, not so much on the "setting of a trap" or the active conduct of the occupier, as on the duty to give warning of a known danger.

Automobile Guests

The law as to the duty owed by the driver of an automobile to a guest in his car is in a tangle of confusion, concerning which only very general statements can be made, and reference must be made to the cases in each jurisdiction for further enlightenment.[36] In the absence of statute, the problem has been one primarily of the analogy to be applied.

Conditions, 1952, 100 U.Pa.L.Rev. 629; Malone, Contributory Negligence and the Landowner Cases, 1945, 29 Minn.L.Rev. 61.

26. Berger v. Shapiro, 1959, 30 N.J. 89, 152 A.2d 20; Choate v. Carter, 1958, 98 Ga.App. 375, 105 S.E.2d 909.

27. Tempest v. Richardson, 1956, 5 Utah 2d 174, 299 P.2d 124; Reardon v. Thompson, 1889, 149 Mass. 267, 21 N.E. 369; Rodefer v. Turner, 1942, 232 Iowa 691, 6 N.W.2d 17; Porchey v. Kelling, 1945, 353 Mo. 1034, 185 S.W.2d 820; Sherman v. Maine Cent. R. Co., 1913, 110 Me. 228, 85 A. 755.

28. Malmquist v. Leeds, 1955, 245 Minn. 130, 71 N.W.2d 863; Deacy v. McDonnell, 1944, 131 Conn. 101, 38 A.2d 181; Morrison v. Carpenter, 1914, 179 Mich. 207, 146 N.W. 106; John v. Reick-McJunkin Dairy Co., 1924, 281 Pa. 543, 127 A. 143.

29. Birdsong v. City of Chattanooga, 1958, 204 Tenn. 264, 319 S.W.2d 233 (no duty to warn one using well defined path of dangers off path); Sokoloski v. Pugliese, 1962, 149 Conn. 299, 179 A.2d 603 (must have reason to believe plaintiff would not discover and realize risk); Mathias v. Denver Union Terminal R. Co., 1958, 137 Colo. 224, 323 P.2d 624 (when aware licensee has embarked on dangerous course, duty to warn him).

30. See supra, p. 366.

31. Corby v. Hill, 1858, 4 C.B.,N.S., 556, 140 Eng.Rep. 1209; Carskaddon v. Mills, 1892, 5 Ind.App. 22, 31 N.E. 559; Nashville, C. & St. L. R. Co. v. Blackwell, 1918, 201 Ala. 657, 79 So. 129; Batts v. Home Tel. & Tel. Co., 1923, 186 N.C. 120, 118 S.E. 893.

32. Phipps v. Oregon R. & Nav. Co., C.C.Wash.1908, 161 F. 376; Morrison v. Carpenter, 1914, 179 Mich. 207, 146 N.W. 106; Oliver v. City of Worcester, 1869, 102 Mass. 489; Burton v. Western & A. R. Co., 1896, 98 Ga. 783, 25 S.E. 736.

33. Ellsworth v. Metheney, 6 Cir. 1900, 104 F. 119.

34. Lowery v. Walker, [1911] A.C. 10.

35. Newman v. Fox West Coast Theatres, 1948, 86 Cal.App.2d 428, 194 P.2d 706; Olderman v. Bridgeport-City Trust Co., 1939, 125 Conn. 177, 4 A.2d 646; Jones v. Southern R. Co., 1930, 199 N.C. 1, 153 S.E. 637; John v. Reick-McJunkin Dairy Co., 1924, 281 Pa. 543, 127 A. 143; Burns v. Union Carbide Co., 1933, 265 Mich. 584, 251 N.W. 925.

36. See Corish, The Automobile Guest, 1934, 14 Boston U.L.Rev. 728; Gammon, The Automobile Guest, 1943, 17 Tenn.L.Rev. 452; Campbell, Host-Guest Rules in Wisconsin, [1943] Wis.L.Rev. 180; Georgetta, The Major Issues in a Guest Case, [1954] Ins.L.J. 583; White, The Liability of an Automobile Driver to a Non-Paying Passenger, 1934, 20 Va.L.Rev. 326.

A small number of courts have applied their rules as to gratuitous bailments, holding that there is liability to the guest only for "gross" negligence or other aggravated misconduct.[37] By far the greater number have treated the guest as a licensee on personal property,[38] in essentially the same position as one entering by permission upon the land of another. The application of the analogy has led to decisions in several states holding that, while the driver is under a duty to exercise reasonable care for the protection of the guest in his active operation of the car,[39] and is required to disclose to him any defects in the vehicle of which he has knowledge,[40] he is not required to inspect the automobile to make sure that it is safe, and is not liable for defects of which he does not know.[41] It has sometimes been said that the guest "assumes the risk" of such unknown defects.[42]

The soundness of the analogy to passive conditions on land may be doubted, since one who is driving a car with bad brakes is certainly engaged in a dangerous active operation, even though he does not know that they are bad; and there are other courts which have not agreed.[43] Wisconsin, which originated the rule,[44] has lately overthrown it, rejecting the analogy of the licensee on land as inappropriate to a moving, and highly dangerous instrumentality, as to which liability insurance is widely prevalent, and requiring that the driver exercise reasonable care for the protection of his guest in all respects, including inspection of the car.[45] The decision has the appearance of being right, and no doubt may be expected to be followed. In some twenty-eight states,[46] however, the matter has been taken out of the hands of the courts by automobile guest statutes, which have been considered in a prior chapter.[47] Under these acts some form of aggravated misconduct is always required, so that there is no liability to the guest for ordinary derelictions of duty, such as simple inadvertence or inattention, failure to look for defects, and the like.

Under either the common law or the guest acts, the peculiar mobility and mutiple uses of the automobile raise numerous problems as to who is a "guest," which seldom if ever arise in connection with the licensee on land. Where the ride is a purely gratuitous one, which confers no benefit upon the host except the pleasure of hospitality and an agreeable social relation, everyone agrees that

---

37. Lippman v. Ostrum, 1956, 22 N.J. 14, 123 A.2d 230 (gross); Passler v. Mowbray, 1945, 318 Mass. 231, 61 N.E.2d 120 (gross); Slaton v. Hall, 1931, 172 Ga. 675, 158 S.E. 747 (gross).

38. Cf. Baines v. Collins, 1942, 310 Mass. 523, 38 N. E.2d 626 (bicyclist holding on to truck).

39. Spivey v. Newman, 1950, 232 N.C. 281, 59 S.E.2d 844; Alexander v. Corey, 1951, 13 Alaska 382, 98 F.Supp. 1013; Dashiell v. Moore, 1940, 177 Md. 657, 11 A.2d 640; Rudolph v. Ketter, 1940, 233 Wis. 329, 289 N.W. 674; Lorance v. Smith, 1932, 173 La. 883, 138 So. 871.

40. Waters v. Markham, 1931, 204 Wis. 332, 235 N.W. 797; In re O'Byrne's Estate, 1938, 133 Neb. 750, 277 N.W. 74; cf. Eastman v. Silva, 1930, 156 Wash. 613, 287 P. 656.

41. Higgins v. Mason, 1930, 255 N.Y. 104, 174 N.E. 77; Marple v. Haddad, 1927, 103 W.Va. 508, 138 S. E. 113; Olson v. Buskey, 1945, 220 Minn. 155, 19 N.W.2d 57; Howe v. Little, 1931, 182 Ark. 1083, 34 S.W.2d 218; Clark v. Parker, 1933, 161 Va. 480, 171 S.E. 600.

42. As to the extent to which the absence of duty is often stated in terms of assumption of risk, see Rice, The Automobile Guest and the Rationale of Assumption of Risk, 1943, 27 Minn.L.Rev. 323; Kluwin, The Problems of Host-Guest Cases as They Relate to Contributory Negligence and Assumption of Risk, 1953, 37 Marq.L.Rev. 35.

43. Dostie v. Lewiston Crushed Stone Co., 1939, 136 Me. 284, 8 A.2d 393; Woodward v. Tillman, La.App. 1955, 82 So.2d 121.

44. In O'Shea v. Lavoy, 1921, 175 Wis. 456, 185 N.W. 525, which has been the leading case.

45. McConville v. State Farm Mut. Auto. Ins. Co., 1962, 15 Wis.2d 374, 113 N.W.2d 14. See also Pfaffenbach v. White Plains Express Corp., 1966, 17 N. Y.2d 132, 269 N.Y.S.2d 115, 216 N.E.2d 324.

46. Listed in Georgetta, The Major Issues in a Guest Case, [1954] Ins.L.J. 583, 584.

47. See supra, p. 187.

the occupant is a guest.[48] On the other hand, if he pays for his ride, or in return for it confers any consideration of pecuniary value upon his host, he is not a guest, but a paying passenger, to whom there is a full obligation of reasonable care.[49] The difficult cases have arisen where there is some more or less indirect benefit to the host from the ride. If it is intended to further his business advantage, as where the guest is a prospective customer to whom he hopes to make a sale,[50] or the two are going together to further mutual business interests,[51] the usual conclusion has been that there is indirect compensation, and the man is not a guest. On the other hand, if there is only mutual convenience in making a pleasure trip together,[52] or in traveling together to transact separate

business,[53] or to conduct a political campaign,[54] any benefit has been held to be more of a social accommodation, so that he remains a guest.

The sharing of expenses has offered considerable difficulty. Where it is done without prearrangement, as where the courtesy of the ride is reciprocated by insistence upon buying a tank full of gasoline, there is general agreement that this is not compensation, and the occupant is a guest.[55] Where there is agreement beforehand for sharing expenses or pooling cars, it is probably the prevailing view that this is enough to take the rider out of the guest category and make him a passenger.[56] Some courts have insisted, in addition, that the prearrangement be one that is legally binding;[57] but the trend is

48. Chaplowe v. Powsner, 1934, 119 Conn. 188, 175 A. 470; Boyd v. Mueller, 1943, 320 Ill.App. 303, 50 N. E.2d 847; see Whitechat v. Guyette, 1942, 19 Cal.2d 428, 122 P.2d 47, 49.

49. Ward v. Dwyer, 1954, 177 Kan. 212, 277 P.2d 644; Parrish v. Ash, 1949, 32 Wash.2d 637, 203 P.2d 330; O'Connell v. Scott Paper Co., 1969, — Wash. 2d —, 460 P.2d 282 (advice); Trujillo v. Chavez, 1966, 76 N.M. 703, 417 P.2d 893 (promise to pay). Cf. Taylor v. Goldstein, 1952, 329 Mass. 161, 107 N. E.2d 14; Vest v. Kramer, 1952, 158 Ohio St. 78, 107 N.E.2d 105; Whitechat v. Guyette, 1941, 19 Cal.2d 428, 122 P.2d 47. See Notes, 1938, 26 Cal.L.Rev. 251; 1938, 51 Harv.L.Rev. 545; 1941, 27 Va.L. Rev. 559; 1948, 34 Va.L.Rev. 954.

50. Sullivan v. Richardson, 1931, 119 Cal.App. 367, 6 P.2d 567; Robb v. Ramey Associates, 1940, 1 Terry, Del., 520, 14 A.2d 394; Bookhart v. Greenlease-Lied Motor Co., 1932, 215 Iowa 8, 244 N.W. 721.

51. Gage v. Chapin Motors, 1932, 115 Conn. 546, 162 A. 17; Tucker v. Landucci, 1962, 57 Cal.2d 762, 22 Cal.Rptr. 10, 371 P.2d 754; Markham v. Giannani, 1964, 74 N.M. 543, 395 P.2d 677; Greene v. Morse, Mo.App.1964, 375 S.W.2d 411. See also, as to co-employees on business of the employer: Carman v. Harrison, 8 Cir.1966, 362 F.2d 694; Spring v. Liles, 1963, 236 Or. 140, 387 P.2d 578.

Cf. Zwick v. Burdin, 1965, 239 Or. 629, 399 P.2d 362 (mother-in-law being driven for baby-sitting).

52. Chaplowe v. Powsner, 1934, 119 Conn. 188, 175 A. 470; Johnson v. Fischer, 1940, 292 Mich. 78, 290 N. W. 334; McCann v. Hoffman, 1937, 9 Cal.2d 279, 70 P.2d 909; Ernest v. Bellville, 1936, 53 Ohio App. 110, 4 N.E.2d 286.

53. Eubanks v. Kielsmeier, 1933, 171 Wash. 484, 18 P.2d 48; Hasbrook v. Wingate, 1949, 152 Ohio St. 50, 87 N.E.2d 87.

54. Delk v. Young, Ohio App.1941, 35 N.E.2d 969; Boyson v. Porter, 1935, 10 Cal.App.2d 431, 52 P.2d 582. Cf. Thuente v. Hart Motors, 1944, 234 Iowa 1294, 15 N.W.2d 622 (wartime scrap drive); Forsling v. Mickelson, 1938, 66 S.D. 366, 283 N.W. 169 (community Corn Carnival). In Druzanich v. Criley, 1941, 19 Cal.2d 439, 122 P.2d 53, plaintiff was a delegate to a labor conference, given a ride on condition that he assist in the driving. This was held to be a specific benefit to the driver, which made him a passenger.

55. Urban v. Chars, 1957, 1 Wis.2d 582, 85 N.W.2d 386; Burt v. Richardson, 1958, 251 Minn. 335, 87 N.W.2d 833; Kuser v. Barengo, 1953, 70 Nev. 66, 254 P.2d 447; Brody v. Harris, 1944, 308 Mich. 234, 13 N.W.2d 273; Scholz v. Leuer, 1941, 7 Wash.2d 76, 109 P.2d 294.

56. Sylvia v. Helfer, 1965, 241 Or. 98, 404 P.2d 238; Gilliland v. Singleton, 1963, 204 Va. 115, 129 S.E.2d 641; Baynes v. McElrath, 1962, 106 Ga.App. 805, 128 S.E.2d 348; Huebotter v. Follett, 1946, 27 Cal. 2d 765, 167 P.2d 193; Pence v. Berry, 1942, 13 Wash.2d 564, 125 P.2d 645; Autry v. Spiering, Tex. Civ.App.1966, 407 S.W.2d 826, refused n.r.e. (reciprocal driving arrangement). See Note, 1967, 4 Houst. L.Rev. 690 (car pools).

57. Kerstetter v. Elfman, 1937, 327 Pa. 17, 192 A. 663; Hasbrook v. Wingate, 1949, 152 Ohio St. 50, 87 N.E. 2d 87; Hale v. Hale, 1941, 219 N.C. 191, 13 S.E.2d 221. See Notes, 1945, 31 Iowa L.Rev. 143; 1951, 29 Tex.L.Rev. 384.

clearly against this requirement. There are, however, so many other factors which may affect the situation [58] that the proper statement probably is that the sharing of expenses is merely one factor, albeit an important one, to be considered in determining whether there is a guest relation.

Other problems that have arisen with some frequency have involved the protesting guest who demands to be let out of the car, which is refused—there is general agreement that he ceases to be a guest, and becomes rather a prisoner.[59] Also there is the question of the owner of the car himself, when he surrenders the driving to another; and here the prevailing view is that the basic relation is not changed, and he does not become a guest in his own car.[60] Also the question of children, too young to understand the situation and to enter voluntarily into the position of a guest, with its assumption of any risks. Here there is some authority [61] that the child is

none the less a guest, on the theory that the ride had been accepted for the child by the parent; but other courts, more realistically, have discarded this fiction, and held the child incapable of becoming a guest.[62]

61. INVITEES

The leading English case of Indermaur v. Dames [63] laid down the rule that as to those who enter premises upon business which concerns the occupier, and upon his invitation express or implied, the latter is under an affirmative duty to protect them, not only against dangers of which he knows, but also against those which with reasonable care he might discover. The case has been accepted in all common law jurisdictions, and the invitee, or as he is sometimes called the business visitor,[64] is placed upon a higher footing than a licensee. The typical example, of course, is the customer in a store.[65] Patrons of restaurants,[66] banks,[67] theatres,[68] bathing

58. As, for example, the fact that the parties are members of the same family. See Hasbrook v. Wingate, 1949, 152 Ohio St. 50, 87 N.E.2d 87; Bradley v. Clarke, 1934, 118 Conn. 641, 174 A. 72; Hale v. Hale, 1941, 219 N.C. 191, 13 S.E.2d 221.

59. Andrews v. Kirk, Fla.App.1958, 106 So.2d 110; Anderson v. Williams, 1957, 95 Ga.App. 684, 98 S.E. 2d 579; cf. Redis v. Lynch, 1959, 169 Ohio St. 305, 159 N.E.2d 597. The host becomes liable for false imprisonment. Cieplinski v. Severn, 1929, 269 Mass. 261, 168 N.E. 722. This makes it at least difficult to regard the guest relation as continuing. Cf. Coffman v. Godsoe, 1960, 142 Colo. 575, 351 P.2d 808, where misrepresentation by the host that he had a driver's license and ability to drive was held to vitiate the relation.

60. Naphtali v. Lafazan, 1959, 8 App.Div.2d 22, 186 N.Y.S.2d 1010, affirmed, 1960, 8 N.Y.2d 1097, 209 N.Y.S.2d 317, 171 N.E.2d 462; Peterson v. Winn, 1962, 84 Idaho 523, 373 P.2d 925; Henline v. Wilson, 1960, 111 Ohio App. 515, 174 N.E.2d 122; Wilson v. Workman, D.Del.1961, 192 F.Supp. 852; Lorch v. Eglin, 1952, 369 Pa. 314, 85 A. 841. But see Patton v. La Bree, 1963, 60 Cal.2d 606, 35 Cal.Rptr. 622, 387 P.2d 398 (statute). See Note, 1966, 38 U.Colo. L.Rev. 346.

61. Welker v. Sorenson, 1957, 209 Or. 402, 306 P.2d 737; Horst v. Holtzen, 1958, 249 Iowa 958, 90 N.W. 2d 41; In re Wright's Estate, 1951, 170 Kan. 600, 228 P.2d 911.

62. Burhans v. Witbeck, 1965, 375 Mich. 253, 134 N.W.2d 225; Wood v. Morris, 1964, 109 Ga.App. 148, 135 S.E.2d 484; Green v. Jones, 1957, 136 Colo. 512, 319 P.2d 1083; Kudrna v. Adamski, 1950, 188 Or. 396, 216 P.2d 262; Hart v. Hogan, 1933, 173 Wash. 598, 24 P.2d 99. See Notes, 1958, 30 Rocky Mt.L. Rev. 372; 1958, 11 U.Fla.L.Rev. 124.

63. 1866, L.R. 1 C.P. 274, 35 L.J.C.P. 184, affirmed L.R. 2 C.P. 311, 36 L.J.C.P. 181.

64. Second Restatement of Torts, § 332.

65. Royer v. Najarian, 1938, 60 R.I. 368, 198 A. 562; Glowacki v. A. J. Bayless Markets, 1953, 76 Ariz. 295, 263 P.2d 799; Huber v. American Drug Stores, 1932, 19 La.App. 430, 140 So. 120; F. W. Woolworth Co. v. Williams, 1930, 59 App.D.C. 147, 41 F. 2d 970; Greeley v. Miller's, 1930, 111 Conn. 584, 150 A. 500.

66. Holmes v. Ginter Restaurant Co., 1 Cir. 1932, 54 F.2d 876; Coston v. Skyland Hotel, 1950, 231 N.C. 546, 57 S.E.2d 793. Cf. Braun v. Vallade, 1917, 33 Cal.App. 279, 164 P. 904 (saloon).

67. Sinn v. Farmers' Deposit Sav. Bank, 1930, 300 Pa. 85, 150 A. 163; Downing v. Merchants' Nat. Bank, 1921, 192 Iowa 1250, 184 N.W. 722; Howlett v. Dorchester Trust Co., 1926, 256 Mass. 544, 152 N.E. 895.

68. Dickson v. Waldron, 1893, 135 Ind. 507, 34 N.E. 506, 35 N.E. 1; Durning v. Hyman, 1926, 286 Pa.

beaches,[69] fairs [70] and other places of amusement,[71] and other businesses open to the public [72] are included, as are drivers calling for or delivering goods purchased or sold,[73] independent contractors doing work on the premises [74] and the workmen employed by such contractors,[75] as well as a large and miscel-

laneous group of similar persons who are present in the interest of the occupier as well as of their own.

There is, however, an important conflict of opinion as to the definition of an invitee, as well as to whether certain visitors are to be included in this category.[76] The argument turns on the fundamental theory as to the basis of the special obligation which is placed upon the occupier of the land. One theory, which has received approval from a number of legal writers,[77] and was adopted by the First Restatement of Torts,[78] is that the duty of affirmative care to make the premises safe is imposed upon the man in possession as the price he must pay for the economic benefit he derives, or expects to derive, from the presence of the visitor; and that when no such benefit is to be found, he is under no such duty. On this basis the "business" on

---

376, 133 A. 568; Knapp v. Connecticut Theatrical Corp., 1937, 122 Conn. 413, 190 A. 291.

69. Beverly Beach Club v. Marron, 1937, 172 Md. 471, 192 A. 278; Maehlman v. Reuben Realty Co., 1928, 32 Ohio App. 54, 166 N.E. 920; Knight v. Moore, 1942, 179 Va. 139, 18 S.E.2d 266.

70. Dunn v. Brown County Agricultural Society, 1888, 46 Ohio St. 93, 18 N.E. 496; Smith v. Cumberland County Agricultural Society, 1913, 163 N.C. 346, 79 S.E. 632.

71. Scott v. University of Michigan Athletic Ass'n, 1908, 152 Mich. 684, 116 N.W. 624 (football); Crane v. Kansas City Baseball & Exhibition Co., 1913, 168 Mo.App. 301, 153 S.W. 1076 (baseball); Brown v. Rhoades, 1927, 126 Me. 186, 137 A. 58 (amusement park); Mastad v. Swedish Brethren, 1901, 83 Minn. 40, 85 N.W. 913 (Swedish picnic); Nicholas v. Tri-State Fair & Sales Ass'n, 1967, 82 S.D. 450, 148 N.W.2d 183 (rodeo).

72. Jay v. Walla Walla College, 1959, 53 Wash.2d 590, 335 P.2d 458 (college); Ilgenfritz v. Missouri Power & Light Co., 1933, 340 Mo. 648, 101 S.W.2d 723 (light company); Chatkin v. Talarski, 1937, 123 Conn. 157, 193 A. 611 (undertaker); Elkton Auto Sales Corp. v. State to Use of Ferry, 4 Cir. 1931, 53 F.2d 8 (garage); Smith v. Mottman, 1938, 194 Wash. 100, 77 P.2d 376 (seamstress).

73. Harvill v. Swift & Co., 1960, 102 Ga.App. 543, 117 S.E.2d 202; Atlantic Greyhound Corp. v. Newton, 4 Cir. 1942, 131 F.2d 845; Riggs v. Pan-American Wall Paper & Paint Co., 1939, 225 Iowa 1051, 283 N.W. 250; Kulka v. Nemirovsky, 1934, 314 Pa. 134, 170 A. 261; Strong v. Chronicle Pub. Co., 1939, 34 Cal.App.2d 335, 93 P.2d 649. Cf. Albers v. Gehlert, Mo. 1966, 409 S.W.2d 682 (demonstrator).

74. Haefeli v. Woodrich Eng. Co., 1931, 255 N.Y. 442, 175 N.E. 123; Happertz v. The Jerseyman, 1923, 98 N.J.L. 836, 121 A. 718; Arizona Binghampton Copper Co. v. Dickson, 1921, 22 Ariz. 163, 195 P. 538. See Stein v. Battenfeld Oil & Grease Co., 1931, 327 Mo. 804, 39 S.W.2d 345.

75. Sullivan v. Shell Oil Co., 9 Cir. 1956, 234 F.2d 733, cert. denied 352 U.S. 925; Crane Co. v. Simpson, 6 Cir. 1957, 242 F.2d 734; Dobbie v. Pacific Gas & Elec. Co., 1928, 95 Cal.App. 781, 273 P. 630; Davis Bakery Co. v. Dozier, 1924, 139 Va. 628, 124 S.E. 411; McCready v. Southern Pac. Co., 9 Cir. 1928, 26 F.2d 569.

76. See Prosser, Business Visitors and Invitees, 1942, 26 Minn.L.Rev. 573, 20 Can.Bar Rev. 446, reprinted in Prosser, Selected Topics on the Law of Torts, 1954, 243; James, Tort Liability of Occupiers of Land: Duties Owed to Licensees and Invitees, 1954, 63 Yale L.J. 605; Notes, 1958, 44 Va.L.Rev. 804; 1958, 46 Ky.L.J. 501; 1966, 42 Wash.L.Rev. 299.

77. Salmond, Law of Torts, 11th Ed. 1953, § 162; Harper, Law of Torts, 1933, § 98; Charlesworth, Law of Negligence, 2d Ed. 1947, § 181 ff.

In the United States this theory appears to have originated with the writer of a forgotten treatise on the law of negligence, Robert Campbell, who derived it from the rather ambiguous use of the word "business" in some of the early English cases. Campbell, Law of Negligence, 2d Ed. 1878, 63–64. The theory received support in Bennett v. Louisville & N. R. Co., 1880, 102 U.S. 577, and Plummer v. Dill, 1892, 156 Mass. 426, 31 N.E. 128. It was first fully developed in Bohlen, The Basis of Affirmative Obligations in the Law of Tort, 1905, 53 U.Pa.L.Rev. 209, 237, 337, reprinted in Bohlen, Studies in the Law of Torts, 1926, 33, and Bohlen, The Duty of a Landowner Towards Those Entering His Premises of Their Own Right, 1920, 69 U.Pa.L.Rev. 142, 340.

78. §§ 332, 343, Comment a. It should be noted that the Reporter for this part of the First Restatement was Professor Bohlen, the leading advocate of the economic benefit theory. Late cases still adopting it are Richey v. Kemper, Mo.1965, 392 S.W.2d 266; Vogel v. Fetter Livestock Co., 1964, 144 Mont. 127, 394 P.2d 766.

which the visitor comes must be one of at least potential pecuniary profit to the possessor.

The application of the economic benefit theory has led to a good deal of what looks like legal ingenuity. Potential gain is not difficult to find in the case of one who enters a store to make a purchase,[79] or forms such an intention after entering,[80] or one who is shopping in the hope of finding something that he wants,[81] or even one with the "vague purpose of buying something if she saw anything she took a fancy to"[82]—although obviously any such test is at the mercy of the plaintiff's own testimony as to his reasons.[83] And no doubt the customer who returns to pay a bill, or to retrieve a purse left at the store is still to be treated as on the original business.[84] But many courts which have proceeded on this basis have endeavored to find in other cases some even more tenuous economic advantage, in the form of advertising or good will, encouragement of customers to come, possible advice or assistance which might be given to another about to buy,[85] or

even the chance that the plaintiff might see something he likes,[86] which would appear to be true of any person whatever on the premises, and to exclude virtually no one, even a policeman coming to confer "benefit" upon the landowner by arresting him.

Thus children[87] and friends[88] who accompany customers with no intention of buying anything themselves, or go to visit patients in hospitals,[89] or to railway stations to see people off,[90] guests in automobiles who go

H. & H. R. Co., 1934, 286 Mass. 7, 189 N.E. 574 (railway station); St. Louis, I. M. & S. R. Co. v. Grimsley, 1909, 90 Ark. 64, 117 S.W. 1064 (same).

Or that the parent might be unable to come if she must leave her child at home. Grogan v. O'Keefe's, Inc., 1929, 267 Mass. 189, 166 N.E. 721; Anderson v. Cooper, 1958, 214 Ga. 164, 104 S.E.2d 90.

86. Campbell v. Weathers, 1941, 153 Kan. 316, 111 P.2d 72; Kennedy v. Phillips, 1928, 319 Mo. 573, 5 S.W.2d 33.

87. Murphy v. Kelly, 1954, 15 N.J. 608, 105 A.2d 841; Hostick v. Hall, Okl.1963, 386 P.2d 758; Valunas v. J. J. Newberry Co., 1957, 336 Mass. 305, 145 N.E.2d 685; Jackson v. Pike, Fla.1956, 87 So.2d 410; Carlisle v. J. Weingarten, Inc., 1941, 137 Tex. 220, 152 S.W.2d 1073 (specifically rejecting pecuniary benefit).

Accord, Radle v. Hennepin Ave. Theatre & Realty Co., 1941, 209 Minn. 415, 296 N.W. 510 (mother accompanying child entered in "talent contest"); Goyette v. Sousa, 1959, 90 R.I. 8, 153 A.2d 509, reargument denied 154 A.2d 697 (wife accompanying fisherman).

In Burchell v. Hickisson, 1880, 50 L.J.C.P. 101, and Dunleavy v. Constant, 1964, 106 N.H. 64, 204 A.2d 236, children accompanying those on business at a private residence were held to be only licensees.

88. Kennedy v. Phillips, 1928, 319 Mo. 573, 5 S.W.2d 33; Smigielski v. Nowak, 1940, 124 N.J.L. 235, 11 A.2d 251; Farrier v. Levin, 1959, 176 Cal.App.2d 791, 1 Cal.Rptr. 742; Briggs v. John Yeon Co., 1942, 168 Or. 239, 122 P.2d 444.

89. Viosca v. Touro Infirmary, La.App.1964, 170 So. 2d 222, application denied 1965, 247 La. 416, 171 So.2d 668; North Broward Hospital Dist. v. Adams, Fla.App.1961, 143 So.2d 355; Alabama Baptist Hospital Board v. Carter, 1932, 226 Ala. 109, 145 So. 443; McLeod v. St. Thomas Hospital, 1936, 170 Tenn. 423, 95 S.W.2d 917. Accord, Goldstein v. Healy, 1921, 187 Cal. 206, 201 P. 462 (visiting guest in hotel).

90. McCann v. Anchor Line, 2 Cir. 1933, 79 F.2d 338; Powell v. Great Lakes Transit Corp., 1922, 152 Minn. 90, 188 N.W. 61; Hutchins v. Penobscot Bay

79. Kroger Co. v. Thomas, 6 Cir. 1960, 277 F.2d 854; Holmes v. Ginter Restaurant Co., 1 Cir. 1932, 54 F. 2d 876; Coston v. Skyland Hotel, 1950, 231 N.C. 546, 57 S.E.2d 793; Smith v. Sears, Roebuck & Co., Mo.App.1935, 84 S.W.2d 414; Durham v. Hubert W. White, Inc., 1938, 203 Minn. 82, 279 N.W. 839.

80. Braun v. Vallade, 1917, 33 Cal.App. 279, 164 P. 904.

81. J. G. Christopher Co. v. Russell, 1912, 63 Fla. 191, 58 So. 45; Finnegan v. The Goerke Co., 1929, 106 N.J.L. 59, 147 A. 442; Dickey v. Hochschild, Kohn & Co., 1929, 157 Md. 448, 146 A. 282; Nelson v. F. W. Woolworth Co., 1930, 211 Iowa 592, 231 N. W. 665.

82. MacDonough v. F. W. Woolworth Co., 1918, 91 N.J.L. 677, 103 A. 74.

83. See Shulman and James, Cases and Materials on the Law of Torts, 2d ed. 1952, 631.

84. Andrews v. Goetz, Fla.App.1958, 104 So.2d 653; H. L. Green Co. v. Bobbitt, 4 Cir. 1938, 99 F.2d 281; Sulhoff v. Everett, 1944, 235 Iowa 396, 16 N.W.2d 737.

85. Sears, Roebuck & Co. v. Donovan, Mun.App.D.C. 1958, 137 A.2d 716; Kennedy v. Phillips, 1928, 319 Mo. 573, 5 S.W.2d 33; cf. Fournier v. New York, N.

with drivers to garages,[91] filling stations [92] or parking lots,[93] tourists who visit factories at the invitation of the owner,[94] those who bring employees their lunch with the encouragement of the management,[95] and even possible purchasers who look at displays in shop windows,[96] or who desire on the particular occasion only to use a toilet [97] or a telephone [98]

open to the public, or even the man who goes into a bank to change a five dollar bill,[99] or into a building to read a notice required by law to be posted there,[1] all have been held to be invitees. While it has been said often enough that the "mutuality of interest" may be indirect and remote from the object of the particular visit,[2] there is at least ground for suspecting that in some of these cases, at least, it has been dredged up for the occasion.

The alternative theory, which appears to have been the earlier one,[3] is that the basis of liability is not any economic benefit to the occupier, but a representation to be implied when he encourages others to enter to further a purpose of his own, that reasonable care has been exercised to make the place safe for those who come for that purpose.

& River Steamboat Co., 1913, 110 Me. 369, 86 A. 250; Atchison, T. & S. F. R. Co. v. Cogswell, 1909, 23 Okl. 181, 90 P. 923. Cf. Mathias v. Denver Union Term. R. Co., 1958, 137 Colo. 224, 323 P.2d 624 (photographer in railroad station to photograph visiting celebrity).

91. De Soto Auto Hotel v. McDonough, 6 Cir. 1955, 219 F.2d 253; Pope v. Willow Garages, 1930, 274 Mass. 440, 174 N.E. 727; Gordon v. Freeman, 1934, 193 Minn. 97, 258 N.W. 19; Warner v. Lucey, 1923, 207 App.Div. 241, 201 N.Y.S. 658, affirmed, 1924, 238 N.Y. 638, 144 N.E. 924.

92. Nave v. Hixenbaugh, 1956, 180 Kan. 370, 304 P. 2d 482; Wingrove v. Home Land Co., 1938, 120 W. Va. 100, 196 S.E. 563. Contra, Morse v. Sinclair Automobile Service Co., 5 Cir. 1936, 86 F.2d 298.

93. Goldsmith v. Cody, 1958, 351 Mich. 380, 88 N.W. 2d 268; Nary v. Parking Authority of Town of Dover, 1959, 58 N.J.Super. 222, 156 A.2d 42; Kelley v. Goldberg, 1938, 288 Mass. 79, 192 N.E. 513; Gray v. Watson, 1936, 54 Ga.App. 885, 189 S.E. 616; Parking, Inc. v. Dalrymple, Tex.Civ.App.1964, 375 S.W.2d 758.

94. Gilliland v. Bondurant, Mo.App.1932, 51 S.W.2d 559, affirmed, 1933, 332 Mo. 881, 59 S.W.2d 679; Deach v. Woolner Distilling Co., 1914, 187 Ill.App. 524 ("mutuality of interest" specifically rejected).

95. Illinois Cent. R. Co. v. Hopkins, 1902, 200 Ill. 122, 65 N.E. 656; Bustillos v. Southwestern Portland Cement Co., Tex.Com.App.1919, 211 S.W. 929; Taylor v. McCowat-Mercer Printing Co., D.Tenn. 1939, 27 F.Supp. 880, affirmed, 6 Cir. 1940, 115 F.2d 868; Coburn v. Village of Swanton, 1921, 94 Vt. 320, 115 A. 153. In Handleman v. Cox, 1963, 39 N. J. 95, 187 A.2d 708, the court rejected the necessity of any pecuniary benefit in finding that a salesman collecting from the employee, encouraged to come by the employer, was an invitee.

96. Leighton v. Dean, 1917, 117 Me. 40, 102 A. 565 ("All are invited that some may be persuaded").

97. Campbell v. Weathers, 1941, 153 Kan. 316, 111 P.2d 72; Dym v. Merit Oil Corp., 1944, 130 Conn. 585, 36 A.2d 276.

98. Ward v. Avery, 1931, 113 Conn. 394, 155 A. 502; Dowling v. MacLean Drug Co., 1928, 248 Ill.App. 270; Haley v. Deer, 1938, 135 Neb. 459, 282 N.W. 389; Coston v. Skyland Hotel, 1950, 231 N.C. 546,

57 S.E.2d 793; Randolph v. Great A. & P. Tea Co., W.D.Pa.1932, 2 F.Supp. 462, affirmed, 3 Cir. 1933, 64 F.2d 247. Contra, Argus v. Michler, Mo.App. 1963, 349 S.W.2d 389. In Hartman v. Di Lello, 1959, 109 Ohio App. 387, 157 N.E.2d 127, the defendant apparently received payment for the use of the telephone, since the plaintiff is called a business visitor.

99. First Nat. Bank of Birmingham v. Lowery, 1955, 263 Ala. 36, 81 So.2d 284; American Nat. Bank v. Wolfe, 1938, 22 Tenn.App. 642, 125 S.W.2d 193. Contrast, where the place was not open for such a purpose, and the visitor was held only a licensee: Stewart v. Texas Co., Fla.1953, 67 So.2d 653 (changing bill in filling station); Cobb v. First Nat. Bank of Atlanta, 1938, 58 Ga.App. 160, 198 S.E. 111 (entering bank to obtain blank form for promissory note).

1. Walker v. County of Randolph, 1960, 251 N.C. 805, 112 S.E.2d 551 (courthouse); St. Louis, I. M. & S. R. Co. v. Fairbairn, 1886, 48 Ark. 491, 4 S.W. 50 (railroad station). Cf. Bell v. Houston & S. R. Co., 1913, 132 La. 88, 60 So. 1029 (mailing letter on train); Hale v. Grand Trunk R. Co., 1888, 60 Vt. 605, 15 A. 300 (same).

2. See for example Knudsen v. Duffee-Freeman, Inc., 1959, 99 Ga.App. 520, 109 S.E.2d 339.

3. The early history is traced in Prosser, Business Visitors and Invitees, 1942, 26 Minn.L.Rev. 573, 1943, 20 Can.Bar Rev. 446, reprinted in Prosser, Selected Topics on the Law of Torts, 1954, 243; Marsh, The History and Comparative Law of Invitees, Licensees and Trespassers, 1953, 69 L.Q.Rev. 182, 359.

This idea of course underlies the stress laid upon "invitation" in so many of the cases; but, as in the case of the social guest,[4] invitation is not enough without the circumstances which convey the implied assurance. When premises are thrown open to the public, the assurance is ordinarily given; and this explains, more satisfactorily than any indirect hope of pecuniary gain, the foregoing cases. It accounts also for decisions holding that when a strip of land abutting upon the highway is so paved that it is indistinguishable from the sidewalk,[5] or a private way is given the appearance of a public thoroughfare,[6] those who use it are to be treated as invitees. It is the implied representation made to the public, by holding the land open to them, that it has been prepared for their reception, which is the basis of the liability. There is thus a distinction between a landowner who tacitly permits the boys of the neighborhood to play ball on his vacant lot, in which case they are only licensees,[7] and the man who installs playground equipment and throws the lot open gratuitously to the children of the town as offered and provided for the purpose, in which case there is a public invitation.[8]

It is this second theory which is now accepted by the great majority of the courts; and many visitors from whose presence no shadow of pecuniary benefit is to be found are held to be invitees. The list has included persons attending free public lectures,[9] church services and meetings,[10] and college reunions; [11] free spectators invited to public

---

4. See supra, p. 378.

5. Latzoni v. City of Garfield, 1956, 22 N.J. 84, 123 A.2d 531; Daisey v. Colonial Parking, Inc., 1963, 118 U.S.App.D.C. 31, 331 F.2d 277; Concho Const. Co. v. Oklahoma Nat. Gas Co., 10 Cir. 1953, 201 F. 2d 673; Weidman v. Consolidated Gas, Elec. Light & Power Co., 1929, 158 Md. 39, 148 A. 270; Olsen v. Macy, 1959, 86 Ariz. 72, 340 P.2d 985.

Otherwise if the boundary line is clearly marked out so that the private land does not appear to be intended for public use. Kelley v. City of Columbia, 1884, 41 Ohio St. 263. Or if the defendant did not create the appearance or know of it. Conroy v. Allison Storage Whse. Co., 1935, 292 Mass. 133, 197 N.E. 454.

6. Black v. Central R. Co., 1913, 85 N.J.L. 197, 89 A. 24; Diotiollavi v. United Pocahontas Coal Co., 1924, 95 W.Va. 692, 122 S.E. 161; Aluminum Co. of America v. Walden, 1959, 230 Ark. 337, 322 S.W.2d 696; Southern v. Cowan Stone Co., 1949, 188 Tenn. 576, 221 S.W.2d 809; Chronopoulos v. Gil Wyner Co., 1956, 334 Mass. 593, 137 N.E.2d 667.

Compare, as to permissive use: Renfro Drug Co. v. Lewis, 1950, 149 Tex. 507, 235 S.W.2d 609 (short cut through drug store); Sandford v. Firestone Tire & Rubber Co., Fla.App.1962, 139 So.2d 916 (filling station next to sidewalk).

Otherwise if a notice is posted that the way is not open to the public. Bowler v. Pacific Mills, 1909, 200 Mass. 364, 86 N.E. 767; Mitchell v. Ozan-Graysonia Lbr. Co., 1921, 151 Ark. 6, 235 S.W. 44.

7. Cf. Adams v. American Enka Corp., 1932, 202 N.C. 767, 164 S.E. 367; Dalton v. Philadelphia & Reading R. Co., 1926, 285 Pa. 209, 131 A. 724; Indiana Harbor Belt R. Co. v. Jones, 1942, 220 Ind. 139, 41 N.E.2d 361; O'Keefe v. South End Rowing Club, 1966, 64 Cal.2d 729, 51 Cal.Rptr. 534, 414 P.2d 830.

8. Cf. Dorsey v. Chautauqua Institution, 1922, 203 App.Div. 251, 196 N.Y.S. 798; Maehlman v. Reuben Realty Co., 1928, 32 Ohio App. 54, 166 N.E. 920; Millum v. Lehigh & Wilkes-Barre Coal Co., 1909, 225 Pa. 214, 73 A. 1106; Hutzler Bros. v. Taylor, 1967, 247 Md. 228, 230 A.2d 663 (parking lot). Cf. McKinnon v. Washington Federal Savings & Loan Ass'n, 1966, 68 Wash.2d 644, 414 P.2d 773.

9. Bunnell v. Waterbury Hospital, 1925, 103 Conn. 520, 131 A. 501; Howe v. Ohmart, 1893, 7 Ind.App. 32, 33 N.E. 466.

10. Davis v. Central Congregational Society, 1880, 129 Mass. 367; Weigel v. Reintjes, Mo.App.1941, 154 S.W.2d 412; Geiger v. Simpson M. E. Church, 1928, 174 Minn. 389, 219 N.W. 463; Price v. Central Assembly of God, 1960, 144 Colo. 297, 356 P.2d 240; cf. Napier v. First Congregational Church, 1937, 157 Or. 110, 70 P.2d 43 (coming to see minister for advice). Cf. Dowd v. Portsmouth Hospital, N.H.1963, 193 A.2d 788 (charitable hospital). Contra, McNulty v. Hurley, Fla.1957, 97 So.2d 185. There was pecuniary benefit in De Mello v. St. Thomas the Apostle Church Corp., R.I.1960, 165 A.2d 500.

11. Guilford v. Yale University, 1942, 128 Conn. 449, 23 A.2d 917. Cf. American Legion, Dept. of Georgia, v. Simonton, 1956, 94 Ga.App. 184, 94 S.E.2d 66 (meeting of American Legion Auxiliary, at state headquarters); Rovegno v. San Jose Knights of Columbus Hall Ass'n, 1930, 108 Cal.App. 591, 291 P. 848 (600 members regularly using swimming pool).

places of amusement;[12] those who enter in the reasonable expectation of buying something not sold on the premises,[13] or come in response to advertisements of something to be given away;[14] and a long array of members of the public making use of municipal parks and playgrounds,[15] swimming pools,[16] libraries,[17] comfort stations,[18] wharves,[19] golf courses,[20] community centers,[21] and state[22] and federal[23] land.

Without this element of "invitation," and the assurance that it carries, the potentiality of benefit to the occupier is not enough to make the visitor an invitee. Thus salesmen,[24] workmen seeking employment,[25] or prospective purchasers[26] or tenants[27] of

---

12. Demarest v. Palisades Realty & Amusement Co., 1925, 101 N.J.L. 66, 127 A. 536, 38 A.L.R. 352; Recreation Centre Corp. v. Zimmerman, 1937, 172 Md. 309, 191 A. 233; Blakeley v. White Star Line, 1908, 154 Mich. 635, 118 N.W. 482; Richmond & Manchester R. Co. v. Moore's Adm'r, 1897, 94 Va. 493, 27 S. E. 70. Cf. Watford by Johnston v. Evening Star Newspaper Co., 1954, 93 U.S.App.D.C. 260, 211 F.2d 31 (soap box derby on public property).

13. Vanderdoes v. Rumore, La.App.1941, 2 So.2d 284 (sold out); Talcott v. National Exhibition Co., 1911, 144 App.Div. 337, 128 N.Y.S. 1059 (same); Schmidt v. George H. Hurd Realty Co., 1927, 170 Minn. 322, 212 N.W. 903 (not yet open); Lewis-Kures v. Edwards R. Walsh & Co., 2 Cir. 1939, 102 F.2d 42, cert. denied 308 U.S. 596 (out of business); Rasmussen v. National Tea Co., 1940, 304 Ill.App. 353, 26 N.E. 2d 523 (rummage sale, not yet open).

Otherwise where the plaintiff has no reason to think the article is sold there. Fraters v. Keeling, 1937, 20 Cal.App.2d 490, 67 P.2d 118.

14. Roper v. Commercial Fibre Co., 1928, 105 N.J.L. 10, 143 A. 741 ("Ashes and boxes given away"); Edwards v. Gulf Oil Corp., 1943, 69 Ga.App. 140, 24 S.E.2d 843 (free comic books at filling station).

15. Caldwell v. Village of Island Park, 1952, 304 N.Y. 268, 107 N.E.2d 441; City of Anadarko v. Swain, 1914, 42 Okl. 741, 142 P. 1104; Warden v. City of Grafton, 1925, 99 W.Va. 249, 128 S.E. 375; Ramirez v. City of Cheyenne, 1925, 34 Wyo. 67, 241 P. 710; Paraska v. City of Scranton, 1933, 313 Pa.St. 227, 169 A. 434.

16. City of Longmont v. Swearingen, 1927, 81 Colo. 246, 254 P. 1000; Ashworth v. City of Clarksburg, 1937, 118 W.Va. 476, 190 S.E. 763; City of Columbia v. Wilks, Miss.1936, 166 So. 925; Taylor v. Kansas City, Mo.App.1961, 353 S.W.2d 814, transferred to 361 S.W.2d 797.

17. Abbott v. New York Public Library, 1942, 263 App.Div. 314, 32 N.Y.S.2d 963; Nickell v. Windsor, [1927] 1 Dom.L.Rev. 379, 59 Ont.L.Rep. 618.

18. Pitman v. City of New York, 1910, 141 App.Div. 670, 125 N.Y.S. 941.

19. Hise v. City of North Bend, 1931, 138 Or. 150, 6 P.2d 30.

20. Lowe v. City of Gastonia, 1937, 211 N.C. 564, 191 S.E. 7.

21. Kelly v. Board of Education, 1920, 191 App.Div. 251, 180 N.Y.S. 796.

22. Le Roux v. State, 1954, 307 N.Y. 397, 121 N.E.2d 386 (public hunting ground); Hall v. State, 1940, 173 Misc. 903, 19 N.Y.S.2d 20, affirmed, 1943, 265 App.Div. 1037, 41 N.Y.S.2d 183 (canal lock); Surmanek v. State, 1960, 24 Misc.2d 102, 202 N.Y.S.2d 756 (beach).

23. Claypool v. United States, S.D.Cal.1951, 98 F. Supp. 702 (misunderstanding with a bear in national park); Ashley v. United States, D.Neb.1963, 215 F.Supp. 39, affirmed 8 Cir. 1964, 326 F.2d 499 (same); Adams v. United States, E.D.Okl.1965, 239 F.Supp. 503 (national park); Smith v. United States, N.D.Cal.1953, 117 F.Supp. 525 (campground); Phillips v. United States, E.D.Tenn.1952, 102 F.Supp. 943 (visitor seeking pass at Oak Ridge). See Note, 1967, 2 L. & W.Rev. 447.

24. Hartman v. Miller, 1941, 143 Pa.Super. 143, 17 A.2d 652; C. R. Anthony Co. v. Williams, 1939, 185 Okl. 564, 94 P.2d 836; Austin v. Beuttner, 1956, 211 Md. 61, 124 A.2d 793; see Liveright v. Max Lifsits Furniture Co., 1936, 117 N.J.L. 243, 187 A. 583; Alberts v. Brockelman Bros., 1942, 312 Mass. 486, 45 N.E.2d 392.

25. Steiskal v. Marshall Field & Co., 1909, 238 Ill. 92, 87 N.E. 117; St. Louis, I. M. & S. R. Co. v. Wirbel, 1912, 104 Ark. 236, 149 S.W. 92 (well stated); Ziegler v. Oil Country Specialties Mfg. Co., 1921, 108 Kan. 589, 196 P. 603; Brigman v. Fiske-Carter Const. Co., 1926, 192 N.C. 791, 136 S.E. 125; Mideastern Contracting Co. v. O'Toole, 2 Cir. 1932, 55 F.2d 909.

26. Harry Poretsky & Sons v. Hurwitz, 4 Cir. 1956, 235 F.2d 295; Singleton v. Kubiak & Schmitt, 1960, 9 Wis.2d 472, 101 N.W.2d 619; Smith v. Jackson, 1903, 70 N.J.L. 183, 56 A. 118; Bonello v. Powell, Mo.App.1920, 223 S.W. 1075; Petluck v. McGoldrick Realty Co., 1934, 240 App.Div. 61, 268 N.Y.S. 782.

27. Ware v. Cattaneo, 1962, 69 N.M. 394, 367 P.2d 705; Tutwiler v. I. Beverally Nalle, Inc., 1943, 152 Fla. 479, 12 So.2d 163; Eggen v. Hickman, 1938, 274 Ky. 550, 119 S.W.2d 633; Oettinger v. Stewart, 1943, 24 Cal.2d 133, 148 P.2d 19; Lord v. Lowell Institution for Savings, 1939, 304 Mass. 212, 23 N.E.2d 101.

land are considered invitees when they come to a place which they have good reason to believe to be open for possible dealings with them, but not when they enter without such encouragement.[28] On the other hand an unsuccessful canvasser calling at a private home is at most a licensee, because the place is not held open to him for the purpose,[29] although the potentialities of benefit to the occupier would appear to be no less. The Second Restatement of Torts [30] has bowed to this spate of authority, and has reversed the position of its predecessor.

It is in connection with invitations to enter private land, not held open to the public, that possible pecuniary benefit has its importance; but only as justifying an expectation that the place has been prepared and made safe for the visit. Anyone invited to transact business [31] or do work [32] on private premises

not open to the public normally has the assurance that the place is prepared for him; but one who comes to volunteer assistance, although he confers benefit, is treated as a licensee,[33] unless the circumstances indicate that he has reason to expect protection in return.[34]

Area of Invitation

The special obligation toward invitees exists only while the visitor is upon the part of the premises which the occupier has thrown open to him for the purpose which makes him an invitee. This "area of invitation" [35] will of course vary with the circumstances of the case. It extends to the entrance to the property,[36] and to a safe exit after the purpose is concluded; [37] and it extends to all parts of the

---

28. Larmore v. Crown Point Iron Co., 1886, 101 N.Y. 391, 4 N.E. 752; American Ry. Express Co. v. Gilbreath, 6 Cir. 1931, 48 F.2d 809; Cohen v. Great A. & P. Tea Co., 1933, 11 N.J.Misc. 817, 168 A. 792; Mills v. Heidingsfield, La.App.1939, 192 So. 786; Mortgage Comm'n Service Corp. v. Brock, 1939, 60 Ga.App. 695, 4 S.E.2d 669. But if business is in fact transacted, the salesman becomes an invitee, regardless of whether the office was originally held open for the purpose. Lavitch v. Smith, 1960, 224 Or. 498, 356 P.2d 531.

29. Prior v. White, 1938, 132 Fla. 1, 180 So. 347; Malatesta v. Lowry, La.App.1961, 130 So.2d 785; De Berry v. City of La Grange, 1940, 62 Ga.App. 74, 8 S.E.2d 146; City of Osceola v. Blair, 1942, 231 Iowa 770, 2 N.W.2d 83; Reuter v. Kenmore Bldg. Co., 1934, 153 Misc. 646, 276 N.Y.S. 545.

30. § 332.

31. Finch v. W. R. Roach Co., 1941, 299 Mich. 703, 1 N.W.2d 46 (picking cherries purchased); Fishang v. Eyerman Contracting Co., 1933, 333 Mo. 874, 63 S.W.2d 30 (paying for privilege of dumping refuse); Sills v. Forbes, 1939, 33 Cal.App.2d 219, 91 P.2d 246 (paying for use of road by maintaining it).

32. Schlicht v. Thesing, 1964, 25 Wis. 436, 130 N.W.2d 763 (baby-sitter); Cozine v. Shuff, Ky.1964, 378 S.W.2d 635 (helping invalid); Speece v. Browne, 1964, 229 Cal.App.2d 487, 40 Cal.Rptr. 384 (cooking Sunday dinner). See supra, notes 74 and 75. If the circumstances do not justify such an expectation, the visitor is not an invitee, notwithstanding any pecuniary benefit. Fuchs v. Mapes, 1958, 74 Nev. 366, 332 P.2d 1002.

Those entering in response to a request for gratuitous services are commonly held to be invitees. Drews v. Mason, 1961, 29 Ill.App.2d 269, 172 N.E.2d 383; Murdock v. Petersen, 1958, 74 Nev. 363, 332 P.2d 649; Brant v. Matlin, Fla.App.1965, 172 So.2d 902.

33. Davis v. Silverwood, 1953, 116 Cal.App.2d 39, 253 P.2d 83; Krantz v. Nichols, 1956, 11 Ill.App.2d 37, 135 N.E.2d 816; Wurm v. Allen Cadillac Co., 1938, 301 Mass. 413, 17 N.E.2d 305; Mallory v. Day Carpet & Furniture Co., 1927, 245 Ill.App. 465 (good statement); Smedley v. Mashek Chemical & Iron Co., 1915, 189 Mich. 64, 155 N.W. 537. See other cases of social guests performing services, supra, p. 378.

34. As where he is asked to come for the sole purpose of doing the gratuitous work. Drews v. Mason, 1961, 29 Ill.App.2d 269, 172 N.E.2d 383; Cain v. Friend, 1959, 171 Cal.App.2d 806, 341 P.2d 753; Murdock v. Petersen, 1958, 74 Nev. 363, 332 P.2d 649; see Maxwell v. Maxwell, 1962, 140 Mont. 59, 367 P.2d 308. Cf. Henry W. Cross Co. v. Burns, 8 Cir. 1936, 81 F.2d 856 (advice on how to run plant); Nevada Transfer & Warehouse Co. v. Peterson, 1940, 60 Nev. 87, 99 P.2d 633; Supornick v. Supornick, 1928, 175 Minn. 579, 222 N.W. 275; Tucker v. Buffalo Cotton Mills, 1907, 76 S.C. 539, 57 S.E. 626.

35. Second Restatement of Torts, § 332, Comment *l*.

36. Downing v. Merchants' Nat. Bank, 1921, 192 Iowa 1250, 184 N.W. 722; Hochschild v. Cecil, 1917, 131 Md. 70, 101 A. 700; Norton v. Chandler & Co., 1915, 221 Mass. 99, 108 N.E. 897; Morris v. Atlantic & Pacific Tea Co., 1956, 384 Pa. 464, 121 A.2d 135 (parking lot).

37. Gray v. First Nat. Bank of Crosby, 1957, 250 Minn. 539, 85 N.W.2d 668; Seng v. American Stores

premises to which the purpose may reasonably be expected to take him,[38] and to those which are so arranged as to lead him reasonably to think that they are open to him.[39] If a toilet or a telephone is provided and maintained for the use of customers, as is usual in theatres and department stores, the customer is an invitee while he makes use of it;[40] but if it is kept for the private use of the occupier and his employees, as is often the case in the corner drug store and the butcher shop, he is at most a licensee.[41] Again it should be noted that any expectation of pecuniary benefit, which can only come through a pleased visitor, is the same in either case.

If the customer is invited or encouraged to go to an unusual part of the premises, such as behind a counter or into a storeroom, for the purpose which has brought him, he remains an invitee;[42] but if he goes without such encouragement and solely on his own initiative, he is only a licensee if there is consent, or a trespasser if there is not.[43] Since the potentiality of benefit through a possible purchase or a satisfied customer is the same in all of these cases, they offer an additional argument against the theory of pecuniary advantage as the basis of liability.[44] There are similar limitations of time; and if the invitee remains on the land beyond the time reasonably necessary to accomplish the purpose for which he came, and to withdraw from the premises, he becomes at most a licensee thereafter.[45]

Care Required

The occupier is not an insurer of the safety of invitees, and his duty is only to exercise reasonable care for their protection.[46]   But

Co., 1956, 384 Pa. 338, 121 A.2d 123; Royer v. Najarian, 1938, 60 R.I. 368, 198 A. 562; Carr v. W. T. Grant Co., 1933, 188 Minn. 216, 246 N.W. 743; Cooley v. Makse, 1964, 46 Ill.App.2d 25, 196 N.E.2d 396.

38. Pauckner v. Wakem, 1907, 231 Ill. 276, 83 N.E. 202; Williams v. Morristown Memorial Hospital, 1960, 59 N.J.Super. 384, 157 A.2d 840 (short cut across grass).

39. Crown Cork & Seal Co. v. Kane, 1957, 213 Md. 153, 131 A.2d 470 (smoking room); Montgomery Ward & Co. v. Steele, 8 Cir. 1965, 352 F.2d 822 (warehouse aisle); Morris v. Granato, 1946, 133 Conn. 295, 50 A.2d 416 (basement door looked like toilet); McAdams v. Raymond S. Roberts, Inc., 1952, 117 Vt. 309, 91 A.2d 706 (open door and call); Plewes v. City of Lancaster, 1952, 171 Pa. Super. 312, 90 A.2d 279 (obstructed portion of airport).

40. Dickau v. Rafala, 1954, 141 Conn. 121, 104 A.2d 214; Bass v. Hunt, 1940, 151 Kan. 740, 100 P.2d 696; McClusky v. Duncan, 1927, 216 Ala. 388, 113 So. 250; Main v. Lehman, 1922, 294 Mo. 579, 243 S.W. 91; Randolph v. Great A. & P. Tea Co., D.Pa. 1932, 2 F.Supp. 462, affirmed, 3 Cir. 1933, 64 F.2d 247.

41. Hashim v. Chimiklis, 1941, 91 N.H. 456, 21 A.2d 166; Westbrock v. Colby, 1942, 315 Ill.App. 494, 43 N.E.2d 405; McNamara v. MacLean, 1939, 302 Mass. 428, 19 N.E.2d 544; McMullen v. M. & M. Hotel Co., 1940, 227 Iowa 1061, 290 N.W. 3; Liveright v. Max Lifsitz Furniture Co., 1936, 117 N.J.L. 243, 187 A. 583.

42. Bullock v. Safeway Stores, 8 Cir. 1956, 236 F.2d 29 (back room); Blackburn v. Consolidated Rock Products, 1956, 140 Cal.App.2d 858, 295 P.2d 929 (truck driver motioned to area normally outside invitation); Hupfer v. National Distilling Co., 1902, 114 Wis. 279, 99 N.W. 191 (top of tank); Duffy v. Stratton, 1926, 169 Minn. 136, 210 N.W. 866 (behind counter); Foley v. Hornung, 1917, 35 Cal.App. 304, 169 P. 705. In Stein v. Powell, 1962, 203 Va. 423, 124 S.E.2d 889, where a child got into a storeroom-dressing room, it was said that there was no apparent limitation as to what parts of the store the invitation extended to.

43. Whelan v. Van Natta, Ky.1964, 382 S.W.2d 205; Langford v. Mercurio, 1966, 254 Miss. 788, 183 So.2d 150; Sabo v. Reading Co., 3 Cir. 1957, 244 F.2d 692, cert. denied 355 U.S. 847; Campbell v. Hoffman, 1963, 51 Tenn.App. 672, 371 S.W.2d 174; Gayer v. J. C. Penney Co., Mo.App. 1959, 326 S.W.2d 413 (stock room).

44. See also the cases involving the liability of lessors for common passageways and premises leased for admission of the public, infra, pp. 403, 405.

45. Hansen v. Cohen, 1954, 203 Or. 157, 276 P.2d 391, rehearing denied, 1955, 203 Or. 157, 278 P.2d 898; Robillard v. Tillotson, 1954, 118 Vt. 294, 108 A.2d 524.

46. S. S. Kresge Co. v. Fader, 1927, 116 Ohio St. 718, 158 N.E. 174; F. W. Woolworth Co. v. Williams, 1930, 59 App.D.C. 347, 41 F.2d 970; Engdal v. Owl Drug Co., 1935, 183 Wash. 100, 48 P.2d 232.

the obligation of reasonable care is a full one, applicable in all respects, and extending to everything that threatens the invitee with an unreasonable risk of harm. The occupier must not only use care not to injure the visitor by negligent activities,[47] and warn him of latent dangers of which the occupier knows,[48] but he must also inspect the premises to discover possible dangerous conditions of which he does not know,[49] and take reasonable precautions to protect the invitee from dangers which are foreseeable from the arrangement [50] or use.[51] The obligation extends to the original construction of the premises, where it results in a dangerous condition.[52] The fact that the premises are open to the public must be taken into account, and will call for greater care than in the case of a visitor at a private home.[53] If the presence of children is to be expected, their meddling propensities must be anticipated; and the principle of "attractive nuisance" applies to child invitees no less than to trespassers.[54]

On the other hand there is no liability for harm resulting from conditions from which no unreasonable risk was to be anticipated,[55] or those which the occupier did not know and could not have discovered with reasonable care.[56] The mere existence of a defect or danger is not enough to establish liability, unless it is shown to be of such a character or of such duration that the jury may reasonably conclude that due care would have discovered it.[57]

He may, for example, await the end of a storm before removing ice and snow from church steps. Hadglin v. Church of St. Paul of Sauk Center, 1968, 280 Minn. 119, 158 N.W.2d 269.

47.　Clark v. Glosser Bros. Dept. Stores, 1944, 156 Pa.Super. 193, 39 A.2d 733; Potter Title & Trust Co. v. Young, 1951, 367 Pa. 239, 80 A.2d 76; Gay v. Cadwallader-Gibson Co., 1939, 34 Cal.App.2d 566, 93 P.2d 1051; Second Restatement of Torts, § 341A.

48.　Johnston v. De La Guerra Properties, 1946, 28 Cal.2d 394, 170 P.2d 5; Straight v. B. F. Goodrich Co., 1946, 354 Pa. 391, 47 A.2d 605; Jurgens v. American Legion, 1969, 1 Wash.2d 39, 459 P.2d 79; see Puleo v. H. E. Moss & Co., 2 Cir. 1947, 159 F. 2d 842, 845, cert. denied 331 U.S. 847.

49.　Durning v. Hyman, 1926, 286 Pa. 376, 133 A. 568; Kallum v. Wheeler, 1937, 129 Tex. 74, 101 S. W.2d 225; Dickey v. Hochschild, Kohn & Co., 1929, 157 Md. 448, 146 A. 282; Stark v. Great A. & P. Tea Co., 1926, 102 N.J.L. 694, 133 A. 172; Forcier v. Grand Union Stores, Inc., Vt.1970, 264 A.2d 796; Second Restatement of Torts, § 343.

50.　Dean v. Safeway Stores, Mo.1957, 300 S.W.2d 431 (lighting parking lot); Johnston v. De La Guerra Properties, 1946, 28 Cal.2d 394, 170 P.2d 5; Kmiotek v. Anast, 1944, 350 Pa. 593, 39 A.2d 923; Donahoo v. Kress House Moving Corp., 1944, 25 Cal.2d 237, 153 P.2d 349; Peaster v. William Sikes Post No. 4825 V.F.W., 1966, 113 Ga.App. 211, 147 S.E.2d 686 (safe chairs).

51.　Schwartzmann v. Lloyd, 1936, 65 U.S.App.D.C. 216, 82 F.2d 822 (crowd at advertised sale); Greeley v. Miller's, Inc., 1930, 111 Conn. 584, 150 A. 500 (same); Lee v. National League Baseball Club of Milwaukee, 1958, 4 Wis.2d 168, 89 N.W.2d 811 (scramble by baseball spectators for foul ball); Rowell v. City of Wichita, 1947, 162 Kan. 294, 176 P.2d 590 (thrown bottle at baseball park); Philpot v. Brooklyn Baseball Club, 1951, 303 N.Y. 116, 100 N.E.2d 164 (same).

52.　De Weese v. J. C. Penney Co., 1956, 5 Utah 2d 116, 297 P.2d 898 (terrazzo floor likely to become slippery when wet); Rose v. Melody Lane of Wilshire, 1952, 39 Cal.2d 481, 247 P.2d 335 (defective stool at counter); Magnolia Petroleum Co. v. Barnes, 1947, 198 Okl. 406, 179 P.2d 132. Cf. Gallagher v. St. Raymond's Roman Catholic Church, 1968, 21 N.Y.2d 554, 289 N.Y.S.2d 401, 236 N.E.2d 632 (duty of church to provide exterior lighting).

53.　Criterion Theatre Corp. v. Starns, 1944, 194 Okl. 624, 154 P.2d 92.

54.　See supra, p. 367.

55.　Greenfield v. Freedman, 1952, 328 Mass. 272, 103 N.E.2d 242 (leaves on sidewalk); Home Public Market v. Newrock, 1943, 111 Colo. 428, 142 P.2d 272 (swinging doors); Sheridan v. Great A. & P. Tea Co., 1945, 353 Pa. 11, 44 A.2d 280 (double entrance doors); Chew v. Paramount-Richards Theatres, La. App.1943, 14 So.2d 853 (gentle slope).

56.　Brown v. Dorney Park Coaster Co., 3 Cir. 1948, 167 F.2d 433; Schnatterer v. Bamberger, 1911, 81 N.J.L. 558, 79 A. 324; Downing v. Jordan Marsh Co., 1919, 234 Mass. 159, 125 N.E. 207; Penny v. Sears, Roebuck & Co., 1934, 193 Minn. 65, 258 N.W. 522; Dudley v. Abraham, 1906, 122 App.Div. 480, 107 N.Y.S. 97.

57.　Jones v. Jarvis, Ky.1969, 437 S.W.2d 189; Smith v. Mr. D's Inc., 1966, 197 Kan. 83, 415 P.2d 251; J. C. Penney Co. v. Norris, 5 Cir. 1958, 250 F.2d 385; McVeigh v. McCullough, 1963, 96 R.I. 412, 192 A.2d 437; Frank v. J. C. Penney Co., 1955, 133 Cal.App. 2d 123, 283 P.2d 291.

Likewise, in the usual case, there is no obligation to protect the invitee against dangers which are known to him,[58] or which are so obvious and apparent to him that he may reasonably be expected to discover them.[59] Against such conditions it may normally be expected that the visitor will protect himself. It is for this reason that it is so frequently held that reasonable care requires nothing more than a warning of the danger.[60] But this is certainly not a fixed rule, and all of the circumstances must be taken into account. In any case where the occupier, as a reasonable man, should anticipate an unreasonable risk of harm to the invitee notwithstanding his knowledge, warning, or the obvious nature of the condition, something more in the way of precautions may be required. This is true, for example, where there is reason to expect that the invitee's attention will be distracted, as by goods on display,[61] or that after lapse of time he may forget the existence of the condition, even though he has discovered it or been warned;[62] or where the condition is one which would not reasonably be expected, and for some reason, such as an arm full of bundles, it may be anticipated that the visitor will not be looking for it.[63] It is true also where the condition is one such as icy steps, which cannot be negotiated with reasonable safety even though the invitee is fully aware of it, and, because the premises are held open to him for his use, it is to be expected that he will nevertheless proceed to

Circumstantial evidence may, however, indicate that the defendant should have discovered the condition. Bozza v. Vornado, Inc., 1964, 42 N.J. 355, 200 A.2d 777; Mahoney v. J. C. Penney Co., 1962, 71 N.M. 244, 377 P.2d 663; Strack v. Great A. & P. Tea Co., 1967, 35 Wis.2d 51, 150 N.W.2d 361; Wollerman v. Grand Union Stores, Inc., 1966, 47 N.J. 426, 221 A. 2d 513. See Notes, 1966, 35 Ford.L.Rev. 375; 1967, 12 Vill.L.Rev. 396.

58.   Atherton v. Hoenig's Grocery, 1957, 249 Iowa 50, 86 N.W.2d 252; Schild v. Schild, 1964, 176 Neb. 282, 125 N.W.2d 900.

59.   Harrison v. Williams, 1963, 260 N.C. 392, 132 S. E.2d 869; Dukek v. Farwell Ozmun Kirk & Co., 1956, 248 Minn. 374, 80 N.W.2d 53; Waters v. Banning, 1959, 339 Mass. 777, 162 N.E.2d 41; Ludloff v. Hanson, 1959, 220 Md. 218, 151 A.2d 753; Gottlieb v. Andrus, 1958, 200 Va. 114, 104 S.E.2d 743. See Keeton, Personal Injuries Resulting from Open and Obvious Conditions, 1952, 100 U.Pa.L.Rev. 629.

60.   Burk v. Walsh, 1902, 118 Iowa 397, 92 N.W. 65; Hordes v. Kessner, App.Term 1916, 159 N.Y.S. 891; Paubel v. Hitz, 1936, 339 Mo. 274, 96 S.W.2d 369.

The Restatement of Torts, § 347, has taken the position that in the case of a public utility, which has no right to exclude the public, the duty is not merely to give warning, but always to provide reasonably safe premises. This is no doubt true where the plaintiff has no reasonable alternative except to forego the use of the premises, as in Hayes v. Illinois Cent. R. Co., La.App.1955, 83 So.2d 160; Letang v. Ottawa Elec. R. Co., [1926] A.C. 725; Burnison v. Sauders, 1931, 225 Mo.App. 1159, 35 S.W.2d 619. But where the patron can easily avoid known or obvious danger and still make use of the facilities, it has been held often enough that the utility is not liable. Pennsylvania R. Co. v. O'Neil, 2 Cir. 1913, 204 F. 584; McNaughton v. Illinois Cent. R. Co., 1907, 136 Iowa 177, 113 N.W. 844; Lookner v. New York, N. H. & H. R. Co., 1956, 333 Mass. 555, 132 N.E.2d 160; Illinois Cent. R. Co. v. Nichols, 1938, 173 Tenn. 602, 118 S.W.2d 213.

61.   Jaudon v. F. W. Woolworth Co., 4 Cir. 1962, 303 F.2d 61; J. J. Newberry Co. v. Lancaster, Okl.1964, 391 P.2d 224; Grall v. Meyer, 1969, —— Iowa ——, 173 N.W.2d 61; Yuma Furniture Co. v. Rehwinkle, 1968, 8 Ariz.App. 576, 448 P.2d 420; Gowdy v. United States, W.D.Mich.1967, 271 F.Supp. 733, reversed on other grounds, C.A.6th 1969, 412 F.2d 525, cert. denied 396 U.S. 960, rehearing denied 396 U.S. 1063.

62.   Walgreen-Texas Co. v. Shivers, 1941, 137 Tex. 493, 154 S.W.2d 625; Hechler v. McDonnell, 1941, 42 Cal.App.2d 515, 109 P.2d 426; Simpson v. Doe, 1952, 39 Wash.2d 934, 239 P.2d 1051; Powell v. Vracin, 1957, 150 Cal.App.2d 454, 310 P.2d 27.

63.   Seng v. American Stores Co., 1956, 384 Pa. 338, 121 A.2d 123; Hanson v. Town & Country Shopping Center, Inc., 1966, 259 Iowa 542, 144 N.W.2d 870; Stofer v. Montgomery Ward & Co., 8 Cir. 1957, 249 F.2d 285; Ackerberg v. Muskegon Osteopathic Hospital, 1962, 366 Mich. 596, 115 N.W.2d 290 (hospital visitor dizzy from odors); Valdes v. Karoll's Inc., 7 Cir. 1960, 277 F.2d 637 (stairwell just inside revolving door).

The visitor is entitled to assume that proper care has been exercised to make the premises safe, and is not required to be on the alert for unusual conditions. Holmes v. Ginter Restaurant Co., 1 Cir. 1932, 54 F.2d 876; Glenn v. W. T. Grant Co., 1935, 129 Neb. 173, 269 N.W. 811; Smith v. S. S. Kresge Co., 1933, 116 Conn. 706, 164 A. 206.

encounter it.[64] In all such cases the jury may be permitted to find that obviousness, warning or even knowledge is not enough. It is generally agreed that the obligation as to the condition of the premises is of such importance that it cannot be delegated, and that the occupier will be liable for the negligence of an independent contractor to whom he entrusts maintenance and repair.[65]

In particular, the possessor must exercise the power of control or expulsion which his occupation of the premises gives him over the conduct of a third person who may be present, to prevent injury to the visitor at his hands. He must act as a reasonable man to avoid harm from the negligence of contractors and concessionaires as to activities on the land,[66] as well as that of other persons who have entered it,[67] or even from intentional attacks on the part of such third persons.[68] But he is required to take action only when he has reason to believe, from what he has observed or from past experience, that the conduct of the other will be dangerous to the invitee.[69] Again, in the usual case, a warning will be a sufficient precaution,[70] unless it is apparent that, either because of lack of time or by reason of the character of the conduct to be expected on the part of the third person, it will not be effective to give protection.[71]

Public Employees

The courts have encountered considerable difficulty in dealing with those who come upon the land in the exercise of a privilege not conferred by the consent of the occupier.[72] Apart from patrons of public utilities, who are quite obviously to be regarded as invitees,[73] these have consisted for the most part of public officers and employees, who enter in the performance of their public

---

64. Peterson v. W. T. Rawleigh Co., 1966, 274 Minn. 495, 144 N.W.2d 555; Csizmadia v. P. Ballantine & Sons, 2 Cir. 1961, 287 F.2d 423 (slippery floor); Adams v. R. S. Bacon Veneer Co., 1968, — Iowa —, 162 N.W.2d 470; Dawson v. Payless for Drugs, 1967, 248 Or. 334, 433 P.2d 1019; King Soopers, Inc. v. Mitchell, 1959, 140 Colo. 119, 342 P.2d 1006.

65. Besner v. Central Trust Co. of New York, 1921, 230 N.Y. 357, 130 N.E. 577; Corrigan v. Elsinger, 1900, 81 Minn. 42, 83 N.W. 492; Lineaweaver v. Wanamaker Co., 1930, 299 Pa. 45, 149 A. 91; Curtis v. Kiley, 1891, 153 Mass. 125, 26 N.E. 421; see Note, 1921, 31 Yale L.J. 99.

66. McCordic v. Crawford, 1943, 23 Cal.2d 1, 142 P.2d 7; Thornton v. Maine State Ag. Soc., 1903, 97 Me. 108, 53 A. 979; Smith v. Cumberland County Ag. Soc., 1913, 163 N.C. 346, 79 S.E. 632; Stickel v. Riverview Sharpshooters' Park Co., 1911, 250 Ill. 452, 95 N.E. 445.

67. Moran v. Valley Forge Drive-in Theatres, Inc., 1968, 431 Pa. 432, 246 A.2d 875; Adamson v. Hand, 1955, 93 Ga.App. 5, 90 S.E.2d 669; Fleming v. Allied Supermarkets, Inc., W.D.Okl.1964, 236 F.Supp. 306; Easler v. Downie Amusement Co., 1926, 125 Me. 334, 133 A. 905; Hill v. Merrick, 1934, 147 Or. 244, 31 P.2d 663. See Notes, 1958, 12 Vand.L. Rev. 299; 1959, 6 U.C.L.A.L.Rev. 494; 1959, 19 La. L.Rev. 890; 1957, 56 Mich.L.Rev. 137.

68. Sinn v. Farmers' Deposit Sav. Bank, 1930, 300 Pa. 85, 150 A. 163; Peck v. Gerber, 1936, 154 Or. 126, 59 P.2d 675; Glen Park Democratic Club, Inc. v. Kylsa, 1966, 139 Ind.App. 393, 213 N.E.2d 812;

Taylor v. Centennial Bowl, Inc., 1966, 65 Cal.2d 114, 52 Cal.Rptr. 561, 416 P.2d 793; Kimple v. Foster, Kan.1970, 469 F.2d 281. See Harper and Kime, The Duty to Control the Conduct of Another, 1934, 43 Yale L.J. 886; Note, 1937, 35 Mich.L.Rev. 843.

69. Napper v. Kenwood Drive-In Theatre Co., Ky. 1958, 310 S.W.2d 270; Weihert v. Piccione, 1956, 273 Wis. 448, 78 N.W.2d 757; Richter v. Adobe Creek Lodge, 1956, 143 Cal.App.2d 514, 299 P.2d 941; Barnes v. J. C. Penney Co., 1937, 190 Wash. 633, 70 P.2d 311; Leonard v. Standard Lumber Co., 1938, 196 Ark. 800, 120 S.W.2d 5. Actual knowledge of threats is not required, if the defendant should have heard them. Coca v. Arceo, 1962, 71 N.M. 186, 376 P.2d 970.

70. Western Auto Supply Co. v. Campbell, Tex.1963, 373 S.W.2d 735.

71. Taylor v. Centennial Bowl, Inc., 1966, 65 Cal.2d 114, 52 Cal.Rptr. 561, 416 P.2d 793; Chicago, T. H. & S. E. R. Co. v. Fisher, 1915, 61 Ind.App. 10, 110 N. E. 240; Terre Haute, I. & E. T. Co. v. Scott, 1930, 91 Ind.App. 690, 170 N.E. 341, rehearing denied, 1961, 172 N.E.2d 659; Second Restatement of Torts, § 344. But see § 343A(2), suggesting that in the case of a public utility, where the customer cannot be required to forego its use, more in the way of protection may be required than in the case of an occupier of private land.

72. See Notes, 1966, 19 Vand.L.Rev. 407; 1961, 47 Corn.L.Q. 119.

73. See supra, p. 385.

duties. Such individuals do not fit very well into any of the arbitrary categories which the law has established for the classification of visitors. They are not trespassers, since they are privileged to come. The privilege is independent of any permission, consent or license of the occupier, and they would be privileged to enter, and would insist upon doing so, even if he made active objection. They normally do not come for any of the purposes for which the premises are held open to the public, and frequently, upon private premises, they do not enter for any benefit of the occupier, or under circumstances which justify any expectation that the place has been prepared to receive them. For these reasons some writers,[74] particularly in England, have advocated an additional and separate category for them. Thus far, however, the American courts always have proceeded to cram them, with some straining at the seams, into the sack of either licensees or invitees.

Where it can be found that the public employee comes for a purpose which has some connection with business transacted on the premises by the occupier, he is almost invariably treated as an invitee. Quite often, however, this has a very artificial look. It is no doubt possible to spell out pecuniary benefit to the occupier in the case of a garbage collector,[75] a city water meter reader,[76] or even a postman,[77] but it becomes quite fanciful, to say the least, in the case of sanitary[78] or building[79] inspectors, and especially so as to a tax[80] or a customs[81] collector. The courts are reduced to saying that the occupier cannot legally do business without such visits.

While this is true, pecuniary benefit on such a basis appears to be quite unrealistic. The visitor is an unsought and often resented condition of doing business at all. The freedom of choice to admit or exclude him, which is so essential to ordinary invitation, is entirely lacking, and he is a burden thrust upon the occupier as the fruit of compulsion.[82] This is not to say, however, that the duty owed to him is not properly the same as that owed to an invitee. At least he knows that the occupier is required by law to receive him, and to prepare for his reception, and so he has some reason to believe that his coming is not unanticipated, and that the premises are ready for him. On this basis there is justification for holding that there is an affirmative duty of reasonable care to make the premises safe.

---

74. Bohlen, The Duty of a Landowner Towards Those Entering His Premises of Their Own Right, 1921, 69 U.Pa.L.Rev. 142, 237, 340; Paton, The Responsibility of an Occupier to Those Who Enter as of Right, 1941, 19 Can.Bar Rev. 1; Wallis-Jones, Liability of Public Authorities as Occupiers of Dangerous Premises, 1949, 65 L.Q.Rev. 367.

Australian courts have shown some preference for this. Aiken v. Municipality of Kingborough, 1939, 62 Comm.L.Rep. 179, 190–1, 209; Currum Corp. v. Richardson, 1939, 62 Comm.L.Rep. 214, 228–30; Vale v. Whiddon, 1949, 50 S.R., N.S.W., 90, 112.

75. Toomey v. Sanborn, 1888, 146 Mass. 28, 14 N.E. 921.

76. Finnegan v. Fall River Gas Works, 1893, 159 Mass. 311, 34 N.E. 523; Kennedy v. Heisen, 1913, 182 Ill.App. 200; Sheffield Co. v. Phillips, 1943, 69 Ga.App. 41, 24 S.E.2d 834.

77. Paubel v. Hitz, 1936, 339 Mo. 274, 96 S.W.2d 369; Sutton v. Penn, 1925, 238 Ill.App. 182; Gordon v. Cummings, 1890, 152 Mass. 513, 25 N.E. 978. See Notes, 1926, 26 Col.L.Rev. 116; 1937, 2 Mo.L.Rev. 110.

78. Jennings v. Industrial Paper Stock Co., Mo.App. 1952, 248 S.W.2d 43; Swift & Co. v. Schuster, 10 Cir.1951, 192 F.2d 615; Cudahy Packing Co. v. McBride, 8 Cir.1937, 92 F.2d 737, cert. denied, 303 U.S. 639; Mitchell v. Barton & Co., 1923, 126 Wash. 232, 217 P. 993; Boneau v. Swift & Co., Mo.App. 1934, 66 S.W.2d 172. See Note, 1938, 22 Minn.L. Rev. 898.

79. Fred Howland, Inc. v. Morris, 1940, 143 Fla. 189, 196 So. 472; Robey v. Keller, 4 Cir.1940, 114 F.2d 790; Miller v. Pacific Constructors, 1945, 68 Cal. App.2d 529, 157 P.2d 57; McCormack v. Windsort, 1931, 9 N.J.Misc. 543, 154 A. 765.

80. Anderson & Nelson Distilling Co. v. Hair, 1898, 103 Ky. 196, 44 S.W. 658.

81. Low v. Grand Trunk Ry. Co., 1881, 72 Me. 313; Wilson v. Union Iron Works Dry Dock Co., 1914, 167 Cal. 539, 140 P. 250.

82. 2 Harper and James, Torts, 1956, 1500.

On the other hand firemen [83] and policemen [84] traditionally have been held to be only mere licensees, entering under a privilege conferred by legal authority, toward whom there is no such duty. The occupier is still required to exercise reasonable care for their protection in carrying on his activities,[85] and to give warning of dangers of which he knows [86] as in the case of other licensees; but there is no obligation to inspect and prepare the premises for them. And the fact that the occupier himself has been negligent in starting the fire for which the fireman is called makes no difference.[87]

There always has been something of an aspect of absurdity about these decisions. It is of course quite foolish to say that a fireman who comes to extinguish a blaze or a policeman who enters to prevent a burglary confers no pecuniary benefit upon the occupier; and if invitation is called for, it is at least clearly present when he comes in response to a desperate call for help.[88] The argument, occasionally offered,[89] that tort liability might deter landowners from uttering such cries of distress is surely preposterous rubbish. It is quite true, as has been pointed out,[90] that injuries to firemen and policemen are covered by compensation and pension funds; but this is no less true of the other public employees mentioned above, or even of many private employees who are held to be invitees.

The one really valid basis for the distinction must lie in the fact that firemen and policemen are likely to enter at unforeseeable times, upon unusual parts of the premises, and under circumstances of emergency, where care in looking after the premises, and in preparation for the visit, cannot reasonably be looked for.[91] A man who climbs

83. Krauth v. Geller, 1960, 31 N.J. 270, 157 A.2d 129; Baxley v. Williams Const. Co., 1958, 98 Ga. App. 662, 106 S.E.2d 799; Roberts v. Rosenblatt, 1959, 146 Conn. 110, 148 A.2d 142; Anderson v. Cinnamon, 1955, 365 Mo. 304, 282 S.W.2d 445; Aldworth v. F. W. Woolworth Co., 1936, 295 Mass. 344, 3 N.E.2d 1008. See Notes, 1965, 30 Mo.L.Rev. 395; 1966, 25 Md.L.Rev. 348; 1959, 48 Geo.L.J. 187.

In Mulcrone v. Wagner, 1942, 212 Minn. 478, 4 N.W.2d 97, this was carried to the length of holding that a fire inspector on a back stair was a licensee only. In Texas Cities Gas Co. v. Dickens, 1943, 140 Tex. 433, 168 S.W.2d 208, where the defendant occupied only part of a building, it was held that a fireman injured in another part was not a mere licensee as to him.

84. Scheurer v. Trustees of Open Bible Church, 1963, 175 Ohio St. 163, 192 N.E.2d 38; Casey v. Adams, 1908, 234 Ill. 350, 84 N.E. 933; Burroughs Adding Machine Co. v. Fryar, 1915, 132 Tenn. 612, 179 S.W. 127; Brennan v. Keene, 1921, 237 Mass. 556, 130 N. E. 82; Pincock v. McCoy, 1929, 48 Idaho 227, 281 P. 371. See Note, 1943, 28 Corn.L.Q. 232.

85. Houston Belt & Terminal R. Co. v. O'Leary, Tex. Civ.App.1911, 136 S.W. 601; Cameron v. Kenyon-Connell Commercial Co., 1899, 22 Mont. 312, 56 P. 358.

86. Shypulski v. Waldorf Paper Products Co., 1951, 232 Minn. 394, 45 N.W.2d 549; Rogers v. Cato Oil & Grease Co., Okl.1964, 396 P.2d 1000; Bartels v. Continental Oil Co., Mo.1964, 384 S.W.2d 667; Scottish Rite Supreme Council v. Jacobs, 1959, 105 U.S. App.D.C. 271, 266 F.2d 675; Schwab v. Rubel Corp., 1941, 286 N.Y. 525, 37 N.E.2d 234. There is, however, no duty to warn a fireman of dangers in a place where there is no reason to expect him to go. Anderson v. Cinnamon, 1955, 365 Mo. 304, 282 S.W. 2d 445.

87. Giorgi v. Pacific Gas & Elec. Co., 1968, 266 Cal. App.2d 355, 72 Cal.Rptr. 119; Buren v. Midwest In-

dustries, Inc., Ky.1964, 380 S.W.2d 96; Eckert v. Refiners' Oil Co., 1923, 17 Ohio App. 221; Cities Service Oil Co. v. Dixon, 1932, 14 Ohio L.Abs. 203; Suttie v. Sun Oil Co., 1931, 15 Pa.D. & C. 3.

88. A fireman who is employed by private persons, or who responds to such a call as a volunteer, has been allowed to recover, as an invitee or a rescuer. Clinkscales v. Mundkoski, 1938, 183 Okl. 12, 79 P.2d 562; Buckeye Cotton Oil Co. v. Campagna, 1922, 146 Tenn. 389, 242 S.W. 646; Walker Hauling Co. v. Johnson, 1964, 110 Ga.App. 620, 139 S.E.2d 496. Compare, as to policemen, St. Louis-San Francisco R. Co. v. Williams, 1936, 176 Okl. 465, 56 P.2d 815; San Angelo Water, Light & Power Co. v. Anderson, Tex.Civ.App.1922, 244 S.W. 571, error dismissed.

89. See Shypulski v. Waldorf Paper Products Co., 1951, 232 Minn. 394, 397, 398, 45 N.W.2d 549, 551; Suttie v. Sun Oil Co., 1931, 15 Pa.D. & C. 3, 5, 6.

90. Lunt v. Post Printing & Pub. Co., 1910, 48 Colo. 316, 110 P. 203.

91. See Boneau v. Swift & Co., Mo.App.1934, 66 S.W. 2d 172, 173; Shypulski v. Waldorf Paper Products Co., 1951, 232 Minn. 394, 397, 45 N.W.2d 549, 551;

in through a basement window in search of a fire or a thief cannot expect any assurance that he will not find a bulldog in the cellar. But this appears to bear upon the issue of negligent conduct itself, as a matter of foreseeable harm and reasonable care, rather than affording an arbitrary basis for denying recovery in all cases. There is an easy solution, requiring the occupier to take precautions only where it is reasonable to expect him to do so. On this basis, there is obvious merit in the position taken by a small number of courts,[92] that such visitors are entitled to the status of invitees and to the full duty of reasonable care when they come, under the same circumstances as other members of the public, to a part of the premises at that time held open to the public. This means that a policeman calling to make an inquiry at a business office is an invitee; and that the occupier must exercise ordinary care to see that the usual means of access to his premises are safe for a visiting fireman. The additional obligation in fact requires no more care than is already required for other invitees.

In 1960 the supreme court of Illinois [93] carried this to its logical conclusion by throwing over the arbitrary rules as to firemen, and by inference also as to policemen, holding that they are to be treated in all respects, as in-

vitees, and that any unforeseeability of harm to them goes only to the issue of reasonable care. Although this appears oviously reasonable, the Illinois decision met with no immediate enthusiasm on the part of other courts.[94] Vermont, however, has recently adopted the same position; [95] and it may still possibly prevail.

62. ABOLITION OF CATEGORIES

The system of rigid categories of trespasser, licensee or invitee, into one of which the plaintiff must be forced to fit, has long made legal writers unhappy,[96] and has disturbed some judges,[97] particularly since there are cases which are difficult to dispose of under any of the three specifications.[98] This dis-

---

Notes, 1926, 26 Col.L.Rev. 116; 1938, 22 Minn.L. Rev. 898.

92. Meiers v. Fred Koch Brewery, 1920, 229 N.Y. 10, 127 N.E. 491 (fireman on driveway); Learoyd v. Godfrey, 1885, 138 Mass. 315 (policeman on walk); see Beedenbender v. Midtown Properties, 1957, 4 App.Div.2d 276, 164 N.Y.S.2d 276; Jenkins v. 313–321 W. 37th St. Corp., 1939, 257 App.Div. 228, 12 N.Y.S.2d 739, motion denied, 1940, 282 N.Y. 595, 25 N. E.2d 148, modified, 1941, 284 N.Y. 397, 31 N.E.2d 503, reargument denied, 1941, 285 N.Y. 614, 33 N.E. 2d 547, and cf. Ryan v. Chicago & N. W. R. Co., 1942, 314 Ill.App. 65, 42 N.E.2d 128 ("more than a licensee"). See Note, 1943, 28 Corn.L.Q. 232.

93. In Dini v. Naiditch, 1960, 20 Ill.2d 406, 170 N.E. 2d 881. The case was somewhat weakened as authority by the fact that the violation of statutes was given as an alternative ground. See Notes, 1961, 47 Corn.L.Q. 119; 1961, 14 Vand.L.Rev. 1541; 38 Chi.Kent L.Rev. 75.

94. The Dini case was emphatically rejected in Aravanis v. Eisenberg, 1965, 237 Md. 242, 206 A.2d 148; Scheurer v. Trustees of Open Bible Church, 1963, 175 Ohio St. 163, 192 N.E.2d 38; Rogers v. Cato Oil & Grease Co., Okl.1964, 396 P.2d 1000.

95. Cameron v. Abatiell, 1968, 127 Vt. 111, 241 A.2d 310.

96. See for example 2 Harper and James, Law of Torts, 1956, 1430–1505; Notes, 1957, 22 Mo.L.Rev. 186; 1958, 12 Rutgers L.Rev. 599. See the lengthy discussion in Wolfson v. Chelist, Mo.1955, 284 S.W. 2d 447.

97. Thus Lord Denning, in Dunster v. Abbott, [1953] 2 All Eng.Rep. 1572: "A canvasser who comes on your premises without your consent is a trespasser. Once he has your consent he is a licensee. Not until you do business with him is he an invitee. Even when you have done business with him, it seems rather strange that your duty towards him should be different when he comes up to your door from what it is when he goes away. Does he change his colour in the middle of the conversation? What is the position when you discuss business with him and it comes to nothing? No confident answer can be given to these questions. Such is the morass into which the law has floundered in trying to distinguish between licensees and invitees."

98. See in particular the cases of public officers entering in performance of their duties, supra, p. 395. Also Hynes v. New York Cent. R. Co., 1921, 231 N. Y. 229, 131 N.E. 898, where a boy was injured while on a diving board, which was anchored on defendant's land, but extended out over a navigable stream.

satisfaction finally led to the adoption in England, in 1957, of a statute [99] which abrogated the distinction between licensees and invitees, and declared that the occupier owes the same "common duty of care" to both, with reasonable care modified according to the circumstances of the entry. The law as to trespassers has, however, not been affected. The fact that the jury has virtually disappeared from negligence actions may have played some part in encouraging the passage of the act. There has as yet been no similar legislation in the United States.

There are, however, courts which have abolished the categories at common law. This began with admiralty cases,[1] in which the distinctions were held to have no application to maritime law. In 1968 this was followed in California, in Rowland v. Christian,[2] which held that whether plaintiff was a trespasser, a licensee or an invitee made no difference as to the duty of reasonable care owed to him, but was to be considered only on the issue of what was reasonable care. In 1969 Hawaii followed suit.[3] These decisions are still too recent to permit any guess whether they will be followed elsewhere, although it certainly is not unlikely; or as to the extent to which the former rules of law may survive in the form of decisions that as a matter of law there was no lack of reasonable care.[4]

63. LESSOR AND LESSEE

When land is leased to a tenant, the law of property regards the lease as equivalent to a sale of the premises for the term.[5] The lessee acquires an estate in the land, and becomes for the time being the owner and occupier, subject to all of the responsibilities of one in possession, both to those who enter upon the land and to those outside of its boundaries. But, as in the case of a vendee,[6] it is generally held that he is free to assume when he rents that no private nuisance exists upon the property without the consent of those in the neighborhood, and he is not liable for such a nuisance until he has at least discovered or been notified of the condition, and had a reasonable opportunity to remedy it.[7]

---

4. One may question, for example, whether the rules as to trespassing children (supra, § 59, which were worked out over so many years with so much blood, sweat, toil and tears, will be jettisoned completely in favor of a free hand for the jury.

See, however, Beard v. Atchison, T. & S. F. R. Co., 1970, 4 Cal.App.3d 129, 84 Cal.Rptr. 449 (child hopping moving freight train), where the effect of the Rowland decision was held to be to shift to the defendant the burden of proving the child's knowledge of the risk.

5. See, generally, Harkrider, Tort Liability of a Landlord, 1928, 26 Mich.L.Rev. 260, 383; Eldredge, Landlord's Tort Liability for Disrepair, 1936, 84 U. Pa.L.Rev. 467, reprinted in Eldredge, Modern Tort Problems, 1941, 113; Eldredge, Tort Liability of a Connecticut Landlord, 1950, 24 Conn.Bar J. 49; Jacobs, Tort Liability of a Connecticut Landlord, 1941, 15 Conn.Bar J. 315; James, Tort Risks of Land Ownership: How Affected by Lease or Sale, 1954, 28 Conn.Bar J. 127; Notes, 1949, 62 Harv.L. Rev. 669; 1941, 29 Geo.L.J. 1046.

6. See infra, p. 414.

7. McDonough v. Gilman, 1861, 3 Allen, Mass., 264 (request to abate required); Philadelphia & R. R. Co. v. Smith, 3 Cir. 1894, 64 F. 679 (same); Martin v. Chicago, R. I. & P. R. Co., 1909, 81 Kan. 344, 105 P. 451 (knowledge sufficient); Dickson v. Chicago, R. I. & P. R. Co., 1880, 71 Mo. 575 (same). Otherwise in the case of a public nuisance. Irvine v. Wood, 1872, 51 N.Y. 224; see infra, p. 415.

---

99. Occupiers' Liability Act, 5 & 6 Eliz. II, c. 31. Discussed in Odgers, Occupiers' Liability: A Further Comment, [1957] Camb.L.J. 39; Payne, The Occupiers' Liability Act, 1958, 21 Mod.L.Rev. 359.

1. Kermarec v. Compagnie Generale Transatlantique, 1959, 358 U.S. 625. See also Judy v. Belk, Fla.App. 1966, 181 So.2d 694.

2. 1968, 69 Cal.2d 108, 70 Cal.Rptr. 97, 443 P.2d 561. This was followed in Carlson v. Ross, 1969, 271 Cal. App.2d 29, 76 Cal.Rptr. 209; Beauchamp v. Los Gatos Golf Course, 1969, 275 Cal.App.2d 25, 77 Cal. Rptr. 914; and Fitch v. LeBeau, 1969, 1 Cal.App.3d 320, 81 Cal.Rptr. 722. See Notes, 1969, 44 N.Y.U.L. Rev. 426; 1969, 14 S.D.L.Rev. 332; 1969, 23 Ark.L. Rev. 153.

3. Pickard v. City of Honolulu, 1969, 51 Haw. 134, 452 P.2d 445, followed in Gibo v. City & County of Honolulu, 1969, 51 Haw. 299, 459 P.2d 198.

In the absence of agreement to the contrary, the lessor surrenders both possession and control of the land to the lessee, retaining only a reversionary interest; and he has no right even to enter without the permission of the lessee. Consequently, it is the general rule that he is under no obligation to anyone to look after the premises or keep them in repair, and is not responsible, either to persons injured on the land [8] or to those outside of it,[9] for conditions which develop or are created by the tenant after possession has been transferred. Neither is he responsible, in general, for the activities which the tenant carries on upon the land after such transfer,[10] even when they create a nuisance.[11] Furthermore, the doctrine of *caveat emptor* applies to the lessee quite as much as to a vendee,

and a tenant who does not exact an express warranty must inspect the land for himself and take it as he finds it, for better or for worse. There is therefore, as a general rule, no liability upon the landlord, either to the tenant [12] or to others entering the land,[13] for defective conditions existing at the time of the lease.

Modern ideas of social policy have given rise to a number of exceptions to these general rules of non-liability of the lessor, which remain to be considered below. There is increasing recognition of the fact that the tenant who leases defective premises is likely to be impecunious and unable to make the necessary repairs, and that the financial burden is best placed upon the landlord, who receives a benefit from the transaction in the form of rent. This policy is expressed by statutes in a number of states, which require the landlord to put and keep certain types of premises, such as tenement houses, in good condition and repair, and have been held to impose liability in tort upon him for his failure to do so.[14]

8. Corcione v. Ruggieri, 1958, 87 R.I. 182, 139 A.2d 388; Avron v. Plummer, N.D.1964, 132 N.W.2d 198; Anderson v. Valley Feed Yards, 1963, 175 Neb. 719, 123 N.W.2d 839; Schafer v. Mascola, 1958, 163 Cal. App.2d 53, 328 P.2d 865; Kauffman v. First Central Trust Co., 1949, 151 Ohio St. 298, 85 N.E.2d 796.

Massachusetts has held that one who leases a furnished house for a short term impliedly agrees that it is fit for the purpose. Hacker v. Nitschke, 1942, 310 Mass. 754, 39 N.E.2d 644. See Note, 1949, 23 St.Johns L.Rev. 357.

9. Jackson v. 919 Corp., 1951, 344 Ill.App. 519, 101 N.E.2d 594; Hester v. Hubbuch, 1942, 26 Tenn.App. 246, 170 S.W.2d 922; Nash v. Goritson, 1944, 174 Or. 368, 149 P.2d 325; Spinelli v. Golda, 1950, 6 N. J. 68, 77 A.2d 233; Blanchard v. Stone's, 1939, 304 Mass. 634, 24 N.E.2d 688; Poley v. Browne, 1947, 199 Okl. 416, 186 P.2d 812.

10. Sherwood Bros. v. Eckard, 1954, 204 Md. 485, 105 A.2d 207; Wells v. Whitaker, 1966, 207 Va. 616, 151 S.E.2d 422; Howell Gas Co. of Athens, Inc. v. Coile, 1965, 112 Ga.App. 732, 146 S.E.2d 145; Manning v. Leavitt, 1939, 90 N.H. 167, 5 A.2d 667; Brittain v. Atlantic Refining Co., 1941, 126 N.J.L. 528, 19 A.2d 793. See Second Restatement of Torts, § 379A; Note, 1964, 50 Iowa L.Rev. 648.

11. Midland Oil Co. v. Thigpen, 8 Cir.1924, 4 F.2d 85, error dismissed 273 U.S. 658; Pinnell v. Woods, 1938, 275 Ky. 290, 121 S.W.2d 679; Meloy v. City of Santa Monica, 1932, 124 Cal.App. 622, 12 P.2d 1072; Lufkin v. Zane, 1892, 157 Mass. 117, 31 N.E. 757. As to consent to the activity at the time of the lease, see infra, p. 402.

12. Taylor v. Stimson, 1958, 52 Wash.2d 278, 324 P.2d 1070; Newman v. Sears, Roebuck & Co., 1950, 77 N.D. 466, 43 N.W.2d 411; Bowe v. Hunking, 1883, 135 Mass. 380; Valin v. Jewell, 1914, 88 Conn. 151, 90 A. 36. Cf. Finney v. Steele, 1906, 148 Ala. 197, 41 So. 976 (child of tenant); Clark v. Sharpe, 1912, 76 N.H. 446, 83 A. 1090 (same).

13. Bowles v. Mahoney, 1952, 91 U.S.App.D.C. 155, 202 F.2d 320, cert. denied 344 U.S. 935 (invitee); O'Malley v. Twenty-Five Associates, 1901, 178 Mass. 555, 60 N.E. 387 (invitee); Hanson v. Beckwith, 1897, 20 R.I. 165, 37 A. 702 (same); McKenzie v. Cheetham, 1891, 83 Me. 543, 22 A. 469 (guest); Roche v. Sawyer, 1900, 176 Mass. 71, 57 N.E. 216 (guest). See Note, 1964, 39 Wash.L.Rev. 345.

14. See Morningstar v. Strich, 1950, 326 Mich. 541, 40 N.W.2d 719 (Housing Law); Daniels v. Brunton, 1951, 7 N.J. 102, 80 A.2d 547 (Tenement House Act); Pharm v. Lituchy, 1940, 283 N.Y. 130, 27 N. E.2d 811 (Multiple Dwelling Law); McLain v. Haley, 1949, 53 N.M. 327, 207 P.2d 1013 (city ordinance held to apply even to patent defect). See Feuerstein and Shestack, The Statutory Duty to Repair, 1951, 45 Ill.L.Rev. 205; Note, 1922, 7 Corn.L.Q. 386.

Concealed Dangerous Conditions Known to Lessor

One exception developed by the common law is that the lessor, like a vendor,[15] is under the obligation to disclose to the lessee concealed dangerous conditions existing when possession is transferred, of which he has knowledge. There is "something like fraud" in a failure to give warning of a known hidden danger to one who enters upon the assumption that it does not exist; and the lessor will be liable to the lessee[16] or to members of his family[17] for his non-disclosure. The liability extends likewise to guests and others who enter in the right of the tenant,[18] since they have been deprived of an opportunity for protection at the hands of the tenant by the landlord's silence.

It is not necessary that the lessor shall believe the condition to be unsafe,[19] or even that he have definite knowledge of its existence, before he is under any duty in regard to it. It is enough that he is informed of facts from which a reasonable man would conclude that there is danger; and the decisions run the gamut of "reasonable notice,"[20] "reason to know,"[21] or "should have known."[22] If he has such information, and it would lead a reasonable man to suspect the existence of an unreasonable risk of harm, it is his duty to communicate at least that suspicion.[23] Tennessee[24] has gone even further, and has imposed upon the lessor an affirmative duty to use reasonable care to inspect the premises before transfer; but the decision has not been followed in other jurisdictions, where it is generally agreed that there is no obligation to inspect or investigate in the absence of some reason to believe that there is a danger.[25]

There is of course no duty to disclose conditions which are known to the tenant,[26] or

15. See infra, p. 413.

16. Smith v. Green, 1970, —— Mass. ——, 260 N.E.2d 656; Wright v. Peterson, 1966, 259 Iowa 1239, 146 N.W.2d 617 (condition of water heater); Anderson v. Shuman, 1967, 257 Cal.App.2d 272, 64 Cal.Rptr. 662; Earle v. Kuklo, 1953, 26 N.J.Super. 471, 98 A. 2d 107 (tuberculosis infection); Miner v. McNamara, 1909, 81 Conn. 690, 72 A. 138. See Eldredge, Landlord's Tort Liability for Disrepair, 1936, 84 U.Pa.L.Rev. 467, reprinted in Eldredge, Modern Tort Problems, 1941, 113; Note, 1951, 49 Mich.L. Rev. 1082.

17. Faber v. Creswick, 1959, 31 N.J. 234, 156 A.2d 252; Knox v. Sands, Mo.1967, 421 S.W.2d 497; Rahn v. Beurskens, 1966, 66 Ill.App.2d 423, 213 N. E.2d 301; Keegan v. G. Heilman Brewing Co., 1915, 129 Minn. 496, 152 N.W. 877; Moore v. Parker, 1901, 63 Kan. 52, 64 P. 975.

18. Ames v. Brandvold, 1912, 119 Minn. 521, 138 N. W. 786; Kaylor v. Magill, 6 Cir. 1950, 181 F.2d 179; Anderson v. Hayes, 1899, 101 Wis. 538, 77 N.W. 891; Second Restatement of Torts, § 358.

19. Murphy v. Barlow Realty Co., 1943, 214 Minn. 64, 7 N.W.2d 684; Cutter v. Hamlen, 1888, 147 Mass. 471, 18 N.E. 397.

20. Cohen Bros. v. Krumbein, 1922, 28 Ga.App. 788, 113 S.E. 58; Cesar v. Karutz, 1875, 60 N.Y. 229; Cohen v. Cotheal, 1913, 156 App.Div. 784, 142 N.Y.S. 90, affirmed, 1915, 215 N.Y. 659, 109 N.E. 1070 ("constructive notice").

But notice of a leaking faucet is not notice of the danger of scalding. Campbell v. Hagen-Burger, 1951, 327 Mass. 159, 97 N.E.2d 409.

21. Meade v. Montrose, 1913, 173 Mo.App. 722, 160 S. W. 11 ("adequate reason to suspect"); Jaffe v. Harteau, 1874, 56 N.Y. 398 (same); Cummings v. Prater, Ariz.1963, 386 P.2d 27 (same).

22. Cutter v. Hamlen, 1888, 147 Mass. 471, 18 N.E. 397; Rhoades v. Seidel, 1905, 139 Mich. 608, 102 N. W. 1025 ("ought to have known"); Reckert v. Roco Petroleum Corp., Mo.1966, 411 S.W.2d 199 (same); Taylor v. First Nat. Bank, 1912, 119 Minn. 525, 138 N.W. 783; Idel v. Mitchell, 1899, 158 N.Y. 134, 52 N.E. 740. See Harkrider, Tort Liability of a Landlord, 1928, 26 Mich.L.Rev. 260, 268; Note, 1926, 11 Corn.L.Q. 253.

23. Johnson v. O'Brien, 1960, 258 Minn. 502, 105 N. W.2d 244.

24. Willcox v. Hines, 1898, 100 Tenn. 538, 46 S.W. 297; Kaylor v. Magill, 6 Cir.1950, 181 F.2d 179. See Noel, Landlord's Tort Liability in Tennessee, 1963, 30 Tenn.L.Rev. 368; Note, 1954, 23 Tenn.L. Rev. 219.

25. State for Use of Bohon v. Feldstein, 1955, 207 Md. 20, 113 A.2d 100; Newman v. Golden, 1929, 108 Conn. 676, 144 A. 467; Pyburn v. Fourseam Coal Co., 1946, 303 Ky. 443, 197 S.W.2d 921; Harrill v. Sinclair Refining Co., 1945, 225 N.C. 421, 35 S.E.2d 240; Kurtz v. Pauly, 1914, 158 Wis. 534, 149 N.W. 143.

26. Marston v. Andler, 1923, 80 N.H. 564, 122 A. 329; Godfrey v. Barton, 1939, 184 Okl. 237, 86 P.2d

which are so open and obvious that he cannot reasonably be expected to fail to discover them when he takes possession,[27] or are of a kind, such as a flight of steps, or poison ivy on a campsite,[28] which anyone might expect to encounter upon similar premises, and therefore to look out for himself.

Conditions Dangerous to Those Outside of the Premises

A second exception is that, as in the case of a vendor,[29] the responsibility to which the lessor would have been subject as occupier continues for at least a considerable time when he transfers possession of land in such condition that it involves an unreasonable risk of harm to others outside of it. Most of the cases have involved either private nuisances [30] or dangers to the highway, such as awnings likely to fall into the street,[31] or

holes in the sidewalk.[32] The liability extends not only to dangerous conditions and disrepair existing at the time of the transfer, but also to conditions which are then potentially dangerous, and likely to become so in the course of the use of the land for the purpose for which it is leased.[33] The lessor's responsibility to adjoining landowners and to the public is such that he is not permitted to shift it to another, and even a covenant on the part of the lessee to repair the defect will not relieve him of liability.[34]

In a few cases the responsibility of the lessor has been carried even beyond that of a vendor,[35] and he has been held liable for a nuisance created by the activities of the tenant to which he consented at the time of the lease, and which he should have known would necessarily involve such a result. If he leases his land for a stone quarry, he cannot escape responsibility for the blasting and rock crushing carried on by the lessee.[36] But

---

621; Manes v. Hines & McNair Hotels, 1946, 184 Tenn. 210, 197 S.W.2d 889; Carusi v. Schulmerick, 1938, 69 U.S.App.D.C. 76, 98 F.2d 605.

Cf. Bupy v. Fidelity-Philadelphia Trust Co., 1940, 338 Pa. 5, 12 A.2d 7 (agreement to take premises "as is").

27. Branstetter v. Robbins, 1955, 178 Kan. 8, 283 P. 2d 455; Hyde v. Bryant, 1966, 114 Ga.App. 535, 151 S.E.2d 925; Stover v. Fechtman, 1966, 140 Ind.App. 62, 222 N.E.2d 281; Shegda v. Hartford-Connecticut Trust Co., 1944, 131 Conn. 186, 38 A.2d 668; Kearns v. Smith, 1943, 55 Cal.App.2d 532, 131 P.2d 36.

28. Hersch v. Anderson Acres, Ohio C.P.1957, 146 N. E.2d 648.

29. See infra, p. 413.

30. Wofford v. Rudick, 1957, 63 N.M. 307, 318 P.2d 605; Boyle v. Pennsylvania R. Co., 1943, 346 Pa. 602, 31 A.2d 89 (explosion danger); Mylander v. Beimschla, 1906, 102 Md. 689, 62 A. 1038. Cf. Whiffen v. De Tweede N. W. & P. H. Bank, 1932, 52 Idaho 165, 12 P.2d 271 (private nuisance created by another; lessor liable only for negligence). See Note, 1949, 37 Ky.L.J. 322.

31. Both v. Harband, 1958, 164 Cal.App.2d 743, 331 P.2d 140 (piece of building material); City of Knoxville v. Hargis, 1946, 184 Tenn. 262, 198 S.W. 2d 555; Whalen v. Shivek, 1950, 326 Mass. 142, 93 N.E.2d 393 (parapet); Kelly v. Laclede Real Estate & Inv. Co., 1941, 348 Mo. 407, 155 S.W.2d 90 (portion of building wall); Barrett v. Stoneburg, 1947, 238 Iowa 1068, 29 N.W.2d 420 (ruined building).

32. Wells v. Ballou, 1909, 201 Mass. 244, 87 N.E. 576; McLaughlin v. Kelly, 1911, 230 Pa. 251, 79 A. 552 (rotten grating); Mitchell v. Foran, 1936, 143 Kan. 191, 53 P.2d 490 (hook); Isham v. Broderick, 1903, 89 Minn. 397, 95 N.W. 224 (pipe discharging water); Granucci v. Claasen, 1928, 204 Cal. 509, 264 P. 437 (driveway).

33. Larson v. Calder's Park Co., 1919, 54 Utah 325, 180 P. 599 (unguarded shooting gallery); Rose v. Gunn Fruit Co., 1919, 201 Mo.App. 262, 211 S.W. 85 (potentially dangerous hole in sidewalk); Knauss v. Brua, 1884, 107 Pa. 85 (obstructed sewer pipe).

34. Whalen v. Shivek, 1950, 326 Mass. 142, 93 N.E.2d 393; Updegraff v. City of Ottumwa, 1929, 210 Iowa 382, 226 N.W. 928; Isham v. Broderick, 1903, 89 Minn. 397, 95 N.W. 244; Mitchell v. Brady, 1907, 124 Ky. 411, 99 S.W. 266; Wells v. Ballou, 1909, 201 Mass. 244, 87 N.E. 576.

35. A possible reason for the distinction is the policy against restraints in the case of a vendor, and the greater ease with which the activities of the tenant may be restricted by a clause in the lease.

36. Benton v. Kernan, 1940, 127 N.J.Eq. 434, 13 A.2d 825, modified in 1941, 130 N.J.Eq. 193, 21 A.2d 755; Harris v. James, 1876, 45 L.J.Q.B. 545; Fagan v. Silver, 1920, 57 Mont. 427, 188 P. 900; Laurenzi v. Vranizan, 1945, 25 Cal.2d 806, 155 P.2d 633; City of San Angelo v. Sitas, 1944, 143 Tex. 154, 183 S.W.2d 417.

he is not responsible for activities to which he did not consent and which he had no reason to contemplate or expect,[37] or for dangers created by the tenant which he has not authorized;[38] and if the nuisance is not a necessary consequence of the expected activity, and it could be conducted without such interference with the interests of others, the tenant alone is liable.[39]

Premises Leased for Admission of the Public

A third exception arises where the land is leased for a purpose which involves the admission of the public. There is then quite general agreement,[40] that the lessor is under an affirmative duty to exercise reasonable care [41] to inspect and repair the premises before possession is transferred, to prevent any unreasonable risk of harm to the public who may enter. The earliest decisions involved wharves and piers,[42] and the principle has been applied to amusement parks,[43] theatres [44] and other halls of entertainment,[45] beaches,[46] hotels,[47] and baseball grandstands.[48] Various reasons for the landlord's liability have been advanced. It has been regarded as an extension of his obligation to the public outside of the land, and the defective condition has been called, quite unjustifiably, a nuisance. Some courts have said that the lessor has "invited" the public to enter, or that he has represented, or has authorized the lessee to represent, that the premises are safe for public admission. Perhaps the best explanation is merely the arbitrary one that his responsibility to the public is so great that he will not be permitted to

Compare, as to criminal liability for a public nuisance, Montgomery v. Commonwealth, 1947, 306 Ky. 275, 207 S.W.2d 27; and cf. Tedescki v. Berger, 1907, 150 Ala. 649, 48 So. 960 (injunction).

37. Edgar v. Walker, 1899, 106 Ga. 454, 32 S.E. 582; Lufkin v. Zane, 1892, 157 Mass. 117, 31 N.E. 757; Fleischner v. Citizens' Real Estate & Inv. Co., 1893, 25 Or. 119, 35 P. 174.

38. Brazinskos v. A. S. Fawcett, Inc., 1945, 318 Mass. 263, 61 N.E.2d 105; Britton v. Donwin Realty Corp., 1940, 123 N.J.L. 540, 10 A.2d 262; Olin v. Houstead, 1939, 60 Idaho 211, 91 P.2d 380.

39. Meloy v. City of Santa Monica, 1932, 124 Cal. App. 622, 12 P.2d 1072; Maas v. Perkins, 1953, 42 Wash.2d 38, 253 P.2d 427; Poley v. Browne, 1947, 199 Okl. 416, 186 P.2d 812; Wasilewski v. McGuire Art Shop, 1936, 117 N.J.L. 264, 187 A. 530; Anderson v. Kopelman, 1932, 279 Mass. 140, 181 N.E. 239.

40. Massachusetts appears to be quite alone to the contrary. Mallard v. Waldman, 1960, 340 Mass. 288, 163 N.E.2d 658. See, however, Oxford v. Leathe, 1896, 165 Mass. 254, 43 N.E. 92, giving limited recognition to the principle.

41. The lessor is not an insurer, and is liable only for negligence. O'Toole v. Thousand Island Park Assn., 1923, 206 App.Div. 31, 200 N.Y.S. 502. There is no obligation as to conditions which are obvious, and which the entering public may be expected to avoid. Lyman v. Herrmann, 1938, 203 Minn. 225, 280 N.W. 862. But liability is not limited to known defects, and there is an obligation to inspect. Colorado Mortgage & Inv. Co. v. Giacomini, 1913, 55 Colo. 540, 136 P. 1039; Junkermann v. Tilyou Realty Co., 1915, 213 N.Y. 404, 108 N.E. 190.

42. Swords v. Edgar, 1874, 59 N.Y. 28; Campbell v. Portland Sugar Co., 1873, 62 Me. 552; Albert v. State, 1887, 66 Md. 325, 7 A. 697; Joyce v. Martin, 1887, 15 R.I. 558, 10 A. 620. Cf. Nugent v. Boston, C. & M. R. Co., 1880, 80 Me. 62, 12 A. 797 (railway station).

43. Junkermann v. Tilyou Realty Co., 1915, 213 N.Y. 404, 108 N.E. 190; Larson v. Calder's Park Co., 1919, 54 Utah 325, 180 P. 599.

44. Lang v. Stadium Purchasing Corp., 1926, 216 App.Div. 558, 215 N.Y.S. 502.

45. Oxford v. Leathe, 1896, 165 Mass. 254, 43 N.E. 92 (horse training exhibition); Camp v. Wood, 1879, 76 N.Y. 92 (dance); Johnson v. Zemel, 1932, 109 N.J.L. 197, 160 A. 356 (boxing); Brown v. Reorganization Inv. Co., 1942, 350 Mo. 407, 166 S.W.2d 476 (wrestling); Friedman v. Richman, 1914, 85 Misc. 376, 147 N.Y.S. 461 (auditorium leased to religious society).

46. Barrett v. Lake Ontario Beach Imp. Co., 1903, 174 N.Y. 310, 66 N.E. 968; Martin v. City of Asbury Park, 1933, 111 N.J.L. 364, 168 A. 612.

47. Colorado Mortgage & Inv. Co. v. Giacomini, 1913, 55 Colo. 540, 136 P. 1039; Copley v. Balle, 1900, 9 Kan.App. 465, 60 P. 656; see Goodman v. Harris, 1953, 40 Cal.2d 254, 253 P.2d 447.

48. Tulsa Entertainment Co. v. Greenlees, 1922, 85 Okl. 113, 205 P. 179; Folkman v. Lauer, 1914, 244 Pa. 605, 91 A. 218; Lusk v. Peck, 1909, 132 App. Div. 426, 116 N.Y.S. 1051, affirmed, 1910, 199 N.Y. 546, 93 N.E. 377.

Accord, as to race tracks, Fox v. Buffalo Park, 1900, 163 N.Y. 559, 57 N.E. 1109, affirming, 1897, 21 App. Div. 321, 47 N.Y.S. 488; Gibson v. Shelby County Fair Ass'n, 1950, 241 Iowa 1349, 44 N.W.2d 362.

shift it to the tenant, and he may not allow his land to be used in a manner which involves a public, rather than a private, danger.[49] This is borne out by the decisions holding that the mere agreement of the tenant to repair or remedy the condition will not of itself relieve the landlord of liability,[50] but if the agreement is that the land is not to be open to the public until the repairs have been made, the lessor may rely on the lessee, and his responsibility is terminated.[51]

The First Restatement of Torts[52] rather unaccountably took the position that the "public use" exception applied only to places leased for the purpose of admitting the public in large numbers; and there have been a few cases[53] that have accepted the limitation. It appears quite impossible to find

any justification for it, if the landlord's responsibility is a public one; and it is now rejected by the overwhelming majority of the courts. The liability has been found in the case of small stores[54] and shops,[55] a restaurant,[56] taverns,[57] a garage,[58] gasoline filling stations,[59] a parking lot,[60] a voting precinct,[61] small meetings,[62] a doctor's office,[63] a boarding house,[64] a motel,[65] and even premises across which there is a passageway used by the public.[66] On the other hand it is not

49. "We may say more simply, and perhaps more wisely, rejecting the fiction of invitation, that the nature of the use itself creates the duty, and that an owner is just as much bound to repair a structure that endangers travelers on a walk in an amusement park as he is to repair a structure that endangers travelers on a highway." Cardozo, J., in Junkermann v. Tilyou Realty Co., 1915, 213 N.Y. 404, 408, 409, 108 N.E. 190, 191. Accord, Fitchett v. Buchanan, 1970, 2 Wash.App. 965, 472 P.2d 623.

50. Folkman v. Lauer, 1914, 244 Pa. 605, 91 A. 218; Warner v. Lucey, 1923, 207 App.Div. 241, 201 N.Y.S. 658, affirmed, 1924, 238 N.Y. 638, 144 N.E. 924.

51. Beaman v. Grooms, 1917, 138 Tenn. 320, 197 S.W. 1090; Nickelsen v. Minneapolis, N. & S. R. Co., 1926, 168 Minn. 118, 209 N.W. 646.

In Maglin v. People's City Bank, 1940, 141 Pa.Super. 329, 14 A.2d 827, the lessee's covenant to repair was held to give the lessor adequate reason to believe that the public would not be admitted until repairs were made.

52. § 359. This was relied on in Zinn v. Hill Lumber & Inv. Co., 1954, 176 Kan. 669, 272 P.2d 1106.

53. Hayden v. Second Nat. Bank of Allentown, 1938, 331 Pa. 29, 199 A. 218 (garage); Warner v. Fry, 1950, 360 Mo. 496, 228 S.W.2d 729 (tavern); Marx v. Standard Oil Co., 1949, 6 N.J.Super. 39, 69 A.2d 748 (gasoline filling station).

Still less accountable is the limitation to places of amusement, as distinguished from commercial premises, found in Gentry v. Taylor, 1945, 182 Tenn. 223, 185 S.W.2d 521 (restaurant); Clark v. Chase Hotel Co., 1934, 230 Mo.App. 739, 74 S.W.2d 498 (Turkish bath); Bender v. Weber, 1913, 250 Mo. 51, 157 S.W. 570 (grocery store).

54. Schlender v. Andy Jansen Co., Okl. 1962, 380 P.2d 523; Turner v. Kent, 1932, 134 Kan. 574, 7 P.2d 513; Senner v. Danewolf, 1932, 139 Or. 93, 6 P.2d 240; Corrigan v. Antupit, 1944, 131 Conn. 71, 37 A. 2d 697; see Lyman v. Herrmann, 1938, 203 Minn. 225, 280 N.W. 862.

55. Webel v. Yale University, 1939, 125 Conn. 515, 7 A.2d 215 (beauty shop); Wood v. Prudential Ins. Co., 1942, 212 Minn. 551, 4 N.W.2d 617 (same).

56. Hilleary v. Earle Restaurant, D.D.C.1952, 109 F. Supp. 829.

57. Nelson v. Hokuf, 1941, 140 Neb. 290, 299 N.W. 472; Austin v. Beuttner, 1956, 211 Md. 61, 124 A.2d 793; Spain v. Kelland, 1963, 93 Ariz. 172, 379 P.2d 149.

58. Warner v. Lucey, 1923, 207 App.Div. 241, 201 N. Y.S. 658, affirmed, 1924, 238 N.Y. 638, 144 N.E. 924.

59. Hayes v. Richfield Oil Corp., 1952, 38 Cal.2d 375, 240 P.2d 580; Bluemer v. Saginaw Central Oil & Gas Service, 1959, 356 Mich. 399, 97 N.W.2d 90.

60. Burroughs v. Ben's Auto Park, 1945, 27 Cal.2d 449, 164 P.2d 897.

61. Boothby v. Town of Yreka City, 1931, 117 Cal. App. 643, 4 P.2d 589.

62. Howe v. Jameson, 1940, 91 N.H. 55, 13 A.2d 471 (domestic science lectures); King v. New Masonic Temple Ass'n, 1942, 51 Cal.App.2d 512, 125 P.2d 559 (woman's club and guests); Bunnell v. Waterbury Hospital, 1925, 103 Conn. 520, 131 A. 501 (Salvation Army); Rau v. Redwood City Woman's Club, 1952, 111 Cal.App.2d 546, 245 P.2d 12 (piano recital).

63. Gilligan v. Blakesley, 1933, 92 Colo. 370, 26 P.2d 808; McCarthy v. Maxon, 1947, 134 Conn. 170, 55 A.2d 912 (veterinarian).

64. Stenberg v. Wilcox, 1896, 96 Tenn. 163, 33 S.W. 917.

65. Goodman v. Harris, 1953, 40 Cal.2d 254, 253 P.2d 447.

66. Standard Oil Co. v. Decell, 1936, 175 Miss. 251, 166 So. 379.

found in the case of private dwellings,[67] a warehouse leased for private storage,[68] or a private pier.[69]

It is not necessary that the members of the public enter, or be expected to enter, as paying customers, or that they come on any business purpose of either the lessor or the lessee; and the lessor's duty arises when the land is leased for a free public lecture, piano recital, or social gathering.[70] It has been held that it is not even necessary that the lessor be paid rent, and that a gratuitous lease for the admission of the public is enough.[71] The lessor's liability extends only to those parts of the premises which are in fact thrown open to the public,[72] and to those invitees who enter for the purpose for which

the place was leased.[73] Since he has no control over the land after the tenant has taken possession, he is not liable for the negligence of the tenant in maintaining the premises, once they are turned over in good condition;[74] and for the same reason he is not liable if the land is used for a public purpose not contemplated by the lease.[75] Since the basis of liability is the likelihood that the public will be permitted to enter before the dangerous condition is changed, it is logical that it should be limited to the time within which there is reason to believe that it will remain unaltered.[76]

Parts of Premises Retained in Control of Lessor

When different parts of a building, such as an office building or an apartment house, are leased to several tenants, the approaches and common passageways normally do not pass to the tenant, but remain in the possession and control of the landlord.[77] The tenants are permitted to make use of them but do not occupy them, and the responsibility for their condition remains upon the lessor. His position is closely analogous to

---

67. Areal v. Home Owners Loan Corp., Sup.Ct.1943, 43 N.Y.S.2d 538; Patton v. Texas Co., 1951, 13 N.J. Super. 42, 80 A.2d 231. Cf. La Freda v. Woodward, 1940, 125 N.J.L. 489, 15 A.2d 798 (doctor's office in private dwelling); De Motte v. Arkell, 1926, 77 Cal.App. 610, 247 P. 254 (private lodge meeting).

68. Campbell v. Elsie S. Holding Co., 1929, 251 N.Y. 446, 167 N.E. 582; O'Brien v. Fong Wan, 1960, 185 Cal.App.2d 112, 8 Cal.Rptr. 124. Cf. Brittain v. Atlantic Refining Co., 1941, 126 N.J.L. 528, 19 A.2d 793 (workroom of gasoline filling station).

69. Lafredo v. Bush Terminal Co., 1933, 261 N.Y. 323, 185 N.E. 398.

70. Bunnell v. Waterbury Hospital, 1925, 103 Conn. 521, 131 A. 501; Howe v. Jameson, 1940, 91 N.H. 55, 13 A.2d 471; Rau v. Redwood City Woman's Club, 1952, 111 Cal.App.2d 546, 245 P.2d 12; King v. New Masonic Temple Ass'n, 1942, 51 Cal.App.2d 512, 125 P.2d 559; Eckman v. Atlantic Lodge, 1902, 68 N.J.L. 10, 52 A. 293. Cf. Standard Oil Co. v. Decell, 1936, 175 Miss. 251, 166 So. 379.

71. In Tulsa Entertainment Co. v. Greenlees, 1922, 85 Okl. 113, 205 P. 179, the owner was held liable where he donated the premises for the admission of the public. Accord, Second Restatement of Torts, § 359, comment g. Contra: Davis v. Schmitt Bros., 1922, 199 App.Div. 683, 192 N.Y.S. 15; Karlowski v. Kissock, 1931, 275 Mass. 180, 175 N.E. 500.

72. Wilson v. Dowtin, 1939, 215 N.C. 547, 2 S.E.2d 576; Van Avery v. Platte Valley Land & Inv. Co., 1937, 133 Neb. 314, 275 N.W. 288; Kelly v. McGreevy, 1918, 182 App.Div. 584, 169 N.Y.S. 923; Morong v. Spofford, 1914, 218 Mass. 50, 105 N.E. 454.

73. Kneiser v. Belasco-Blackwood Co., 1913, 22 Cal. App. 205, 133 P. 989; Second Restatement of Torts, § 359, Comment e.

74. Goodman v. Harris, 1953, 40 Cal.2d 254, 253 P.2d 447; Bonfield v. Blackmore, 1917, 90 N.J.L. 252, 100 A. 161; Dawson v. Kitch, 1910, 156 Ill.App. 185; Cunningham v. Rogers, 1909, 225 Pa. 132, 73 A. 1094.

75. Edwards v. New York & H. R. Co., 1885, 98 N.Y. 245.

76. Second Restatement of Torts, § 359, Comment i. No cases definitely supporting this position have been found. See, however, Volz v. Williams, 1944, 112 Colo. 592, 152 P.2d 996; Corrigan v. Antupit, 1944, 131 Conn. 71, 37 A.2d 697; Maglin v. People's City Bank, 1940, 141 Pa.Super. 329, 14 A.2d 827.

77. Sawyer v. McGillicuddy, 1889, 81 Me. 318, 17 A. 124; Inglehardt v. Mueller, 1914, 156 Wis. 609, 146 N.W. 808; Looney v. McLean, 1880, 129 Mass. 33. Cf. Nunan v. Dudley Properties, 1950, 325 Mass. 551, 91 N.E.2d 840 (retained control of part of single building); Coleman v. Steinberg, 1969, 54 N.J. 58, 253 A.2d 167 (single control heating unit in two-family apartment).

that of a possessor who permits visitors to enter for a purpose of his own; and those who come in the course of the expected use may be considered his invitees, as a good many courts have said.[78] He is therefore under an affirmative obligation to exercise reasonable care to inspect and repair such parts of the premises for the protection of the lessee;[79] and the duty extends also to members of the tenant's family,[80] his employees,[81] his invitees,[82] his guests,[83] and oth-

ers on the land in the right of the tenant,[84] since their presence is a part of the normal use of the premises for which the lessor holds them open. It extends also to those outside of the premises who may be injured as a result of their condition.[85] It is entirely possible that as to any of these plaintiffs the landlord may be liable where the tenant is not.[86] The duty does not extend to intruders who come for a purpose for which the building is not open and provided,[87] and such individuals are at best licensees.

The obligation is one of reasonable care only,[88] and the lessor is not liable where no injury to anyone was reasonably to be antici-

78. Wool v. Larner, 1942, 112 Vt. 431, 26 A.2d 89; Sockett v. Gottlieb, 1960, 187 Cal.App.2d 760, 9 Cal. Rptr. 831; Temple v. Congress Square Garage, 1950, 145 Me. 274, 75 A.2d 459; Snyder v. I. Jay Realty Co., 1959, 30 H.J. 303, 153 A.2d 1; City of Richmond v. Grizzard, 1964, 205 Va. 298, 136 S.E. 2d 827.

79. Arnold v. Walters, 1950, 203 Okl. 503, 224 P.2d 261; Ross v. Belzer, 1952, 199 Md. 187, 85 A.2d 799; Braimaster v. Wolf, 1947, 320 Mass. 620, 70 N.E.2d 697; Franklin Drug Stores v. Gur-Sil Corp., 1967, 269 N.C. 169, 152 S.E.2d 77 (property of tenant damaged); Levine v. Katz, 1968, 132 U.S.App. D.C. 173, 407 F.2d 303 (mat on polished floor of hallway).

80. Primus v. Bellevue Apartments, 1950, 241 Iowa 1055, 44 N.W.2d 347, 25 A.L.R.2d 565; Inglehardt v. Mueller, 1914, 156 Wis. 609, 146 N.W. 808; McGinley v. Alliance Trust Co., 1901, 168 Mo. 257, 66 S.W. 153; Harper v. Vallejo Housing Authority, 1951, 104 Cal.App.2d 621, 232 P.2d 262; Conroy v. 10 Brewster Ave. Corp., 1967, 97 N.J.App. 75, 234 A.2d 415.

81. White v. Ellison Realty Corp., 1950, 5 N.J. 228, 74 A.2d 401; Lunde v. Citizens Nat. Bank of Mankato, 1942, 213 Minn. 278, 6 N.W.2d 809; Rowe v. Ayer & Williams, 1933, 86 N.H. 127, 164 A. 761.

82. Chalfen v. Kraft, 1949, 324 Mass. 1, 84 N.E.2d 454; Siegel v. Detroit City Ice & Fuel Co., 1949, 324 Mich. 205, 36 N.W.2d 719; Swenson v. Slawik, 1952, 236 Minn. 403, 53 N.W.2d 107; Johnston v. De La Guerra Properties, 1946, 28 Cal.2d 394, 170 P.2d 5. Also as to the property of invitees. Whellkin Coat Co. v. Long Branch Trust Co., 1938, 121 N.J.L. 106, 1 A.2d 394.

83. Temple v. Congress Square Garage, 1950, 145 Me. 274, 75 A.2d 459; Wool v. Larner, 1942, 112 Vt. 431, 26 A.2d 89; Sockett v. Gottlieb, 1960, 187 Cal.App. 2d 760, 9 Cal.Rptr. 831; Snyder v. I. Jay Realty Co., 1959, 30 N.J. 303, 153 A.2d 1; Bowers v. City Bank Farmers Trust Co., 1940, 282 N.Y. 442, 26 N. E.2d 970.

84. Menard v. Cashman, 1947, 94 N.H. 428, 55 A.2d 156 (licensee); Urseleo v. Rosengard, 1924, 248 Mass. 542, 143 N.E. 497 (lodger).

See Second Restatement of Torts, §§ 360, 361; Note, 1946, 40 Ill.L.Rev. 142.

85. Washington Loan & Trust Co. v. Hickey, 1943, 78 U.S.App.D.C. 59, 137 F.2d 677; Laskowski v. Manning, 1950, 325 Mass. 393, 91 N.E.2d 231; Gilland v. Maynes, 1914, 216 Mass. 581, 104 N.E. 555; O'Connor v. Andrews, 1891, 81 Tex. 28, 16 S.W. 628.

86. Goodman v. Corn Exchange Nat. Bank & Trust Co., 1938, 331 Pa. 587, 200 A. 642; Sockett v. Gottlieb, 1960, 187 Cal.App.2d 760, 9 Cal.Rptr. 831; Snyder v. I. Jay Realty Co., 1959, 30 N.J. 303, 153 A.2d 1; Temple v. Congress Square Garage, 1950, 145 Me. 274, 75 A.2d 459.

The point is strikingly illustrated in Taneian v. Meghrigian, 1954, 15 N.J. 567, 104 A.2d 689, where a lessor who lived in one unit of a multi-family house was held liable to his own social guest as a landlord, where he would not be liable as an occupier.

87. Stacy v. Shapiro, 1925, 212 App.Div. 723, 209 N. Y.S. 305 (canvasser); Reuter v. Kenmore Bldg. Co., 1934, 153 Misc. 646, 276 N.Y.S. 545 (canvasser); Jolles v. 3720 Corp., 1937, 163 Misc. 51, 296 N.Y.S. 354 (peddler); Hart v. Cole, 1892, 156 Mass. 475, 31 N.E. 644 (uninvited interloper coming to see a wake); Medcraft v. Merchants Exchange, 1931, 211 Cal. 404, 295 P. 822 (using toilet in office building).

88. Tair v. Rock Inv. Co., 1942, 139 Ohio St. 629, 41 N.E.2d 867. Massachusetts has a unique rule that the lessor is only required to maintain the common passageways in the same condition as when the premises were first leased. Mallard v. Waldman, 1960, 340 Mass. 288, 163 N.E.2d 658.

By analogy to the rule as to trespassing children, supra, § 59, due care may require the lessor to protect children against dangerous objects attractive to them. Nesmith v. Starr, 1967, 115 Ga.App. 472, 155 S.E.2d 24. Or against the acts of other children.

pated,[89] or the condition was not discoverable by reasonable inspection,[90] or it was created by the tenant or another,[91] unless it is shown to have been of such duration as to permit the conclusion that due care would have discovered it.[92] The landlord is not necessarily required to light passageways,[93] unless there is some unusual danger in the darkness.[94] The prevailing view, by a scant margin, is that the duty extends to conditions of purely natural origin, such as ice and snow on the steps;[95] and there seems to be little reason

in the distinction as to such conditions made by some of the courts.[96]

The lessor's obligation extends to hallways,[97] stairs,[98] elevators,[99] approaches and entrances,[1] yards,[2] basements,[3] bathrooms,[4]

Mayer v. Housing Authority of Jersey City, 1964, 84 N.J.Super. 411, 202 A.2d 439, affirmed, 1965, 44 N.J. 567, 210 A.2d 617.

89. American Fire & Cas. Co. v. Jackson, 5 Cir. 1951, 187 F.2d 379; Security Bldg. Co. v. Lewis, 1953, 127 Colo. 139, 255 P.2d 405; Anderson v. Reeder, 1953, 42 Wash.2d 45, 253 P.2d 423.

90. Fernandes v. Medeiros, 1950, 325 Mass. 293, 90 N.E.2d 9; C. W. Simpson Co. v. Langley, 1942, 76 U.S.App.D.C. 365, 131 F.2d 869; Revell v. Deegan, 1951, 192 Va. 428, 65 S.E.2d 543.

91. Aldrich v. Laul, 1908, 126 App.Div. 427, 110 N.Y. S. 897; Hunter v. Goldstein, 1929, 267 Mass. 183, 166 N.E. 577; White v. E & F Const. Co., 1963, 151 Conn. 110, 193 A.2d 716.

92. Barb v. Farmers Insurance Exchange, Mo.1955, 281 S.W.2d 297; Brunsilius v. Farmers & Merchants State Bank, 1936, 143 Kan. 148, 53 P.2d 476; Morris v. King Cole Stores, 1946, 132 Conn. 489, 45 A.2d 710; Henry v. First Nat. Bank of Kansas City, 1938, 232 Mo.App.1071, 115 S.W.2d 121 (fires frequently set by tenants); Rosenberg v. Rosenberg, 1936, 247 App.Div. 765, 285 N.Y.S. 859 (habit of leaving door in aisle).

93. Denny v. Burbeck, 1955, 333 Mass. 310, 130 N.E. 2d 542; Agosta v. Granite City Real Estate Co., 1951, 116 Vt. 526, 80 A.2d 534; Westerbeke v. Reynolds, 1944, 155 Fla. 2, 19 So.2d 413; Knight v. Fourth Buckingham Community, 1942, 179 Va. 13, 18 S.E.2d 264; Rietzel v. Cary, 1941, 66 R.I. 418, 19 A.2d 760, affirmed, 1941, 67 R.I. 101, 21 A.2d 5.

94. May v. Hexter, Mo.App.1950, 226 S.W.2d 383; Given v. Tobias, 1933, 137 Kan. 58, 19 P.2d 472; Gibson v. Hoppman, 1928, 108 Conn. 401, 143 A. 635; Marwedel v. Cook, 1891, 154 Mass. 235, 28 N. E. 140. But in Sullivan v. Hamacher, 1959, 339 Mass. 190, 158 N.E.2d 301, failure to replace a light bulb in a hallway for three months was held enough to go to the jury.

95. Bostian v. Jewell, 1963, 254 Iowa 1289, 121 N.W. 2d 141; Langhorne Road Apartments, Inc. v. Bisson, 1966, 207 Va. 474, 150 S.E.2d 540; Klein v. United States, 2 Cir. 1964, 339 F.2d 512; Langley Park Apartments v. Lund, 1964, 234 Md. 402, 199

A.2d 620; Skupienski v. Maly, 1958, 27 N.J. 240, 142 A.2d 220. See Notes, 1967, 2 L. & W. Rev. 492; 1967, 16 De Paul L.Rev. 510; 1965, 25 Md.L.Rev. 81; 1953, 31 Chicago-Kent L.Rev. 271; 1941, 41 Col.L.Rev. 349; 1937, 21 Minn.L.Rev. 703.

Reasonable care may, however, permit the landlord to wait until the end of a storm. Reuter v. Iowa Trust & Savings Bank, 1953, 244 Iowa 939, 57 N.W. 2d 225; Young v. Saroukos, 1962, 55 Del. 149, 185 A.2d 274, judgment affirmed, 1963, 189 A.2d 437.

96. Carey v. Malley, 1951, 327 Mass. 189, 97 N.E.2d 645; Pomfret v. Fletcher, 1965, 99 R.I. 452, 208 A. 2d 743; Cronin v. Brownlee, 1952, 348 Ill.App. 448, 109 N.E.2d 352; Burke v. O'Neil, 1934, 192 Minn. 492, 257 N.W. 81; Turoff v. Richman, 1944, 76 Ohio App. 83, 61 N.E.2d 486.

97. Temple v. Congress Square Garage, 1950, 145 Me. 274, 75 A.2d 459.

98. Chalfen v. Kraft, 1949, 324 Mass. 1, 84 N.E.2d 454; Geesing v. Pendergrass, Okl.1966, 417 P.2d 322; Ross v. Belzer, 1952, 199 Md. 187, 85 A.2d 799; Menard v. Cashman, 1947, 94 N.H. 428, 55 A. 2d 156; West v. Hanley, 1950, 73 S.D. 540, 45 N.W. 2d 455. Cf. Sonne v. Booker, Ky.1958, 310 S.W.2d 526 (fire escape).

99. Lee v. Jerome Realty, Inc., 1958, 338 Mass. 150, 154 N.E.2d 126; Swenson v. Slawik, 1952, 236 Minn. 403, 53 N.W.2d 107; Bosze v. Metropolitan Life Ins. Co., 1948, 1 N.J. 5, 61 A.2d 499; Carter v. United Novelty & Premium Co., 1957, 389 Pa. 198, 132 A.2d 202; Story v. Lyon Realty Corp., 1941, 308 Mass. 66, 30 N.E.2d 845.

1. Trimble v. Spears, 1958, 182 Kan. 406, 320 P.2d 1029; Johnston v. De La Guerra Properties, 1946, 28 Cal.2d 394, 170 P.2d 5; Arnold v. Walters, 1950, 203 Okl. 503, 224 P.2d 261; Siegel v. Detroit City Ice & Fuel Co., 1949, 324 Mich. 205, 36 N.W.2d 719; Lunde v. Citizens Nat. Bank of Mankato, 1942, 213 Minn. 278, 6 N.W.2d 809. Cf. Ruby v. Casello, 1964, 204 Pa.Super. 9, 201 A.2d 219 (alleyway); Cooper v. City of Philadelphia, 1955, 178 Pa.Super. 205, 115 A.2d 849 (sidewalk in front of premises).

2. Reek v. Lutz, 1960, 90 R.I. 340, 158 A.2d 145; Lake v. Emigh, 1948, 121 Mont. 87, 190 P.2d 550; Hussey v. Long Dock R. Co., 1924, 100 N.J.L. 380, 126 A. 314; Rosmo v. Amherst Holding Co., 1951, 235 Minn. 320, 50 N.W.2d 698 (alleyway).

3. McNab v. Wallin, 1916, 133 Minn. 370, 158 N.W. 623; Wright & Taylor v. Smith, Ky.1958, 315 S.W. 2d 624.

4. Lennox v. White, 1949, 133 W.Va. 1, 54 S.E.2d 8; Iverson v. Quam, 1948, 226 Minn. 290, 32 N.W.2d 596 (toilet).

common rooms,[5] porches,[6] the roof of the building,[7] and any other parts of the premises maintained for the benefit of the tenants within the purposes of the lease.[8] It extends also to any appliances, such as a heating plant or a water system,[9] or a washing machine,[10] over which the lessor retains control, and which he furnishes for common use by the tenants. It does not extend to parts of the premises to which the tenant or his visitors may not reasonably be expected to go,[11]

or to their use for an unintended purpose.[12] If the lessee discovers the dangerous condition he may, but does not necessarily,[13] assume the risk or become contributorily negligent in dealing with it; but his knowledge will not prevent recovery by a third party who is himself ignorant of the danger.[14]

Lessor's Agreement to Repair

The effect of an agreement on the part of the lessor to keep the premises in repair is a subject of considerable dispute.[15] In the past, the considerable majority of the courts have held that when a landlord's contract to repair is broken, the only remedy of the tenant is an action in contract for the breach.[16] In many of them this has been carried to the very dubious length of holding that the damages which may be recovered are limited to the cost of repair of the loss of rental value of the property,[17] on the ground that injury to the

5. Primus v. Bellevue Apartments, 1950, 241 Iowa 1055, 44 N.W.2d 347 (laundry room).

6. Hinthorn v. Benfer, 1913, 90 Kan. 731, 136 P. 247; Klahr v. Kostopoulos, 1952, 138 Conn. 653, 88 A.2d 332. Cf. Lipsitz v. Schechter, 1966, 377 Mich. 685, 142 N.W.2d 1 (window screen).

7. Whellkin Coat Co. v. Long Branch Trust Co., 1938, 121 N.J.L. 106, 1 A.2d 394; 2310 Madison Avenue, Inc. v. Allied Bedding Mfg. Co., 1956, 209 Md. 399, 121 A.2d 203; Hunkins v. Amoskeag Mfg. Co., 1933, 86 N.H. 356, 169 A. 3; Graeber v. Anderson, 1952, 237 Minn. 20, 53 N.W.2d 642 (knob on door to roof); see Rogers v. Dudley Realty Corp., 1938, 301 Mass. 104, 16 N.E.2d 244 (eaves and gutters).

8. Baldwin v. McEldowney, 1936, 324 Pa. 399, 188 A. 154 (fire escape); Rowe v. Ayer & Williams, 1933, 86 N.H. 127, 164 A. 761 (same); Sizzin v. Stark, 1946, 187 Md. 241, 49 A.2d 742 (air shaft); Stupka v. Scheidel, 1953, 244 Iowa 442, 56 N.W.2d 874 (window washer's screw eye).

9. Allen v. William H. Hall Free Library, 1942, 68 R.I. 80, 26 A.2d 751; Conroy v. 10 Brewster Ave. Corp., 1967, 97 N.J.Super. 75, 234 A.2d 415 (water-heater); Paratino v. Gildenhorn, 1925, 55 U.S.App. D.C. 271, 4 F.2d 938; Gladden v. Walker & Dunlop, 1948, 83 U.S.App.D.C. 224, 168 F.2d 321 (electrical wiring system); Wardman v. Hanlon, 1922, 52 U.S. App.D.C. 14, 280 F. 988 (toilet tank).

10. Shaefer v. Investors' Co. of Oregon, 1935, 150 Or. 16, 41 P.2d 440; Marsh v. Riley, 1936, 118 W.Va. 52, 188 S.E. 748 (gas heater); Lake v. Emigh, 1948, 121 Mont. 87, 190 P.2d 550 (clothesline).

11. Matthews v. Spiegel, 1956, 385 Pa. 203, 122 A.2d 696 (tenant with no right under lease to use cellar); Cohen v. Davies, 1940, 305 Mass. 152, 25 N.E.2d 223 (walking across lawn); Roessler v. O'Brien, 1949, 119 Colo. 222, 201 P.2d 901 (use of fire escape not contemplated); Morong v. Spofford, 1914, 218 Mass. 50, 105 N.E. 454; Seavy v. I. X. L. Laundry Co., 1941, 60 Nev. 324, 108 P.2d 853 (toilet).

12. Seaman v. Henriques, 1953, 139 Conn. 561, 95 A.2d 701.

13. Looney v. McLean, 1880, 129 Mass. 33; Dollard v. Roberts, 1891, 130 N.Y. 269, 29 N.E. 104; Roman v. King, 1921, 289 Mo. 641, 233 S.W. 161.

14. Gibson v. Hoppman, 1928, 108 Conn. 401, 143 A. 635; Loucks v. Dolan, 1914, 211 N.Y. 237, 105 N.E. 411; Foley v. Everett, 1908, 142 Ill.App. 250; Hunn v. Windsor Hotel Co., 1937, 119 W.Va. 215, 193 S.E. 57.

15. See Bohlen, Landlord and Tenant, 1922, 35 Harv.L.Rev. 633; Harkrider, Tort Liability of a Landlord, 1928, 26 Mich.L.Rev. 260, 383, 392–400; Eldredge, Landlord's Tort Liability for Disrepair, 1936, 84 U.Pa.L.Rev. 467, reprinted in Eldredge, Modern Tort Problems, 1941, 113; Notes, 1950, 48 Mich.L.Rev. 689; 1951, 49 Mich.L.Rev. 1080; 1951, 30 Tex.L.Rev. 131.

16. Goff v. United States, D.Me. 1958, 159 F.Supp. 415; Tuttle v. George H. Gilbert Mfg. Co., 1887, 145 Mass. 169, 13 N.E. 465; Caudill v. Gibson Fuel Co., 1946, 185 Va. 233, 38 S.E.2d 465; Berkowitz v. Winston, 1934, 128 Ohio St. 611, 193 N.E. 343; Young v. Beattie, 1935, 172 Okl. 250, 45 P.2d 470.

17. Cooper v. Roose, 1949, 151 Ohio St. 316, 85 N.E. 2d 545; Leavitt v. Twin County Rental Co., 1942, 222 N.C. 81, 21 S.E.2d 14; Spinks v. Asp, 1921, 192 Ky. 550, 234 S.W. 14; Murrell v. Crawford, 1917, 102 Kan. 118, 169 P. 561; Hanson v. Cruse, 1900, 155 Ind. 176, 57 N.E. 904.

person or property of the tenant was not contemplated by the parties at the time of the agreement. It follows that no action can be maintained by any third person, such as a member of the tenant's family or a guest, who was not a party to the contract.[18] The lessor's liability for his nonperformance is no greater than that of a carpenter or any other person contracting to make repairs.[19]

A slowly increasing number of the courts, which by now has reached a slight majority,[20] have worked out a liability in tort for such injuries to person or property, finding a duty arising out of the contract relation. This duty extends not only to the tenant,[21] but also to the members of his family,[22] his employees,[23] guests [24] and invitees,[25] and to others on the land in his right,[26] or even those outside of it who are endangered.[27]

A variety of ingenious theories have been advanced in support of this liability. The most popular one is that under the agreement to repair the lessor retains the privilege to enter and supervise the condition of the property, and so is in "control" of it, and therefore subject to the same duties as an occupier.[28] On this basis a few courts have held him liable to persons outside of the premises where he merely reserves the right to enter and repair, without obligating himself to do so; [29] but as to persons on the land most of the courts have refused to go so far.[30]

About as many jurisdictions now allow recovery for personal injuries in the contract action. Maday v. New Jersey Title Guarantee & Trust Co., 1941, 127 N.J.L. 426, 23 A.2d 178, modified, 1942, 129 N.J.L. 53, 28 A.2d 104; Busick v. Home Owners Loan Corp., 1941, 91 N.H. 257, 18 A.2d 190; Hodges v. Hilton, 1935, 173 Miss. 343, 161 So. 686; Hart v. Coleman, 1917, 201 Ala. 345, 78 So. 201; Ross v. Haner, Tex.Com.App.1924, 258 S.W. 1036.

18. Huey v. Barton, 1950, 328 Mich. 584, 44 N.W.2d 132; Chelefou v. Springfield Institute for Savings, 1937, 297 Mass. 236, 8 N.E.2d 769; Timmons v. Williams Wood Products Corp., 1932, 164 S.C. 361, 162 S.E. 329; Harris v. Lewistown Trust Co., 1937, 236 Pa. 145, 191 A. 34; Soulia v. Noyes, 1940, 111 Vt. 323, 16 A.2d 173.

19. Jacobson v. Leventhal, 1930, 128 Me. 424, 148 A. 281.

20. With the overruling of earlier decisions in Reitmeyer v. Sprecher, 1968, 431 Pa. 284, 243 A.2d 395; Rampone v. Wanskuck Bldgs., Inc., 1967, 102 R.I. 30, 227 A.2d 586; Williams v. Davis, 1961, 188 Kan. 385, 362 P.2d 641; Zuroski v. Estate of Strickland, 1964, 176 Neb. 633, 126 N.W.2d 888.

21. Michaels v. Brookchester, Inc., 1958, 26 N.J. 379, 140 A.2d 199; 2310 Madison Avenue, Inc. v. Allied Bedding Mfg. Co., 1956, 209 Md. 399, 121 A.2d 203; Scibek v. O'Connell, 1945, 131 Conn. 557, 41 A.2d 251; Ashmun v. Nichols, 1919, 92 Or. 223, 178 P. 234, affirmed, 1919, 92 Or. 223, 180 P. 510.

22. Faber v. Creswick, 1959, 31 N.J. 234, 156 A.2d 252; Williams v. Davis, 1961, 188 Kan. 385, 362 P. 2d 641; Wallace v. Schrier, Fla.App.1958, 107 So.2d 754; Saturnini v. Rosenblum, 1944, 217 Minn. 155, 14 N.W.2d 108; Ross v. Haner, Tex.Com.App.1924, 258 S.W. 1036.

23. Merchants' Cotton Press & Storage Co. v. Miller, 1916, 135 Tenn. 187, 186 S.W. 87; Alaimo v. Du Pont, 1954, 4 Ill.App.2d 85, 123 N.E.2d 583.

24. Flood v. Pabst Brewing Co., 1914, 158 Wis. 626, 149 N.W. 489; Mesher v. Osborne, 1913, 75 Wash. 439, 134 P. 1092.

25. Collison v. Curtner, 1919, 141 Ark. 122, 216 S.W. 1059; Scholey v. Steele, 1943, 59 Cal.App.2d 402, 138 P.2d 733; Krieger v. Ownership Corp., 3 Cir. 1959, 270 F.2d 265 (New Jersey law).

26. Barron v. Liedloff, 1905, 95 Minn. 474, 104 N.W. 289 (sublessee); Hodges v. Hilton, 1935, 173 Miss. 343, 161 So. 686 (same).

27. Lommori v. Milner Hotels, 1957, 63 N.M. 342, 319 P.2d 949; Johnson v. Prange-Geussenhainer Co., 1942, 240 Wis. 363, 2 N.W.2d 723; Marzotta v. Gay Garment Co., 1951, 11 N.J.Super. 368, 78 A.2d 394.

28. See Barron v. Liedloff, 1905, 95 Minn. 474, 104 N.W. 289; Flood v. Pabst Brewing Co., 1914, 158 Wis. 626, 149 N.W. 489. Also Bohlen, Landlord and Tenant, 1922, 35 Harv.L.Rev. 633, 640, to the effect that the lessor's duty is "suspended" by the ordinary lease, but not if there is a covenant to repair.

It is of course quite possible for the lessor to reserve and exercise a genuine control over the premises. See for example Brown v. Cleveland Baseball Co., 1952, 158 Ohio St. 1, 106 N.E.2d 632.

29. Appel v. Muller, 1933, 262 N.Y. 278, 186 N.E. 785; City of Dalton v. Anderson, 1945, 72 Ga.App. 109, 33 S.E.2d 115; Fjellman v. Weller, 1942, 213 Minn. 457, 7 N.W.2d 521; Johnson v. Prange-Geussenhainer Co., 1942, 240 Wis. 363, 2 N.W.2d 723; Wilchick v. Marks and Silverstone, [1934] 2 K.B. 56.

30. Keegan v. G. Heilman Brewing Co., 1915, 129 Minn. 496, 152 N.W. 877; Senk v. City Bank Farmers Trust Co., 2 Cir. 1940, 108 F.2d 630; Flynn v.

It seems obvious that the lessor's "control," even under a covenant, is a fiction devised to meet the case, since he has no power to exclude any one, or to direct the use of the land, and it is difficult to see how his privilege to enter differs in any significant respect from that of any carpenter hired to do the work.[31] The fiction becomes quite threadbare when the tort liability is extended, as some courts have extended it, to the breach of an agreement to heat the premises.[32]

A second theory is that the landlord by his promise has induced the tenant to forego repairs of his own, and by his misleading undertaking has made himself responsible for the consequences, and that he is distinguished from other contractors by the peculiar probability that the tenant will rely on him.[33] Recovery quite uniformly has been denied, however, where such a promise is made after the lease and without consideration,[34] in

which case it would appear that the tenant is no less misled. It seems clear that it is the contract itself which gives rise to the tort liability, and that it is distinguished from other contracts to enter and repair by reason of the peculiar relation existing between the parties, which gives the lessee a special reason and right to rely upon the promise. This, together with an undeclared policy which places the responsibility for harm caused by disrepair upon the party best able to bear it, and most likely to prevent the injuries, at least where he has expressed willingness to assume responsibility, is perhaps the best explanation of the result.[35] The minority position has received the support of the Restatement of Torts,[36] and has been slowly gaining ground.

The jurisdictions which find a tort duty usually construe the lessor's covenant, in the absence of an express provision to the contrary, to mean merely that he must repair only within a reasonable time after he has been notified of the dangerous condition, or has otherwise discovered it.[37]

Negligence in Making Repairs

When the lessor does in fact attempt to make repairs, whether he is bound by a covenant to do so or not,[38] and fails to exercise

---

Pan American Hotel Co., 1944, 143 Tex. 219, 183 S. W.2d 446; Ripple v. Mahoning Nat. Bank, 1944, 143 Ohio St. 614, 56 N.E.2d 289.

New York, which rejected tort liability founded on the covenant to repair in Cullings v. Goetz, 1931, 256 N.Y. 287, 176 N.E. 397, has permitted the jury to find "control" on the basis of the mere right to repair, in Noble v. Marx, 1948, 298 N.Y. 106, 81 N. E.2d 40; Antonsen v. Bay Ridge Sav. Bank, 1944, 292 N.Y. 143, 54 N.E.2d 338, plus maintenance of a repair force in De Clara v. Barber S. S. Lines, 1956, 309 N.Y. 620, 132 N.E.2d 871. This may foreshadow a complete change of position. See Murphy and Bundy, The Erosion of Cullings v. Goetz, 1956, 8 Syr.L.Rev. 50; Note, 1950, 48 Mich.L.Rev. 689.

31. See Cavalier v. Pope, [1906] A.C. 428; Harkrider, Tort Liability of a Landlord, 1928, 26 Mich.L. Rev. 260, 383, 394–398. In Strand Enterprises v. Turner, 1955, 223 Miss. 588, 78 So.2d 769, a landlord entering premises to inspect them was held to have the status of an invitee of the tenant.

32. Glidden v. Goodfellow, 1913, 124 Minn. 101, 144 N. W. 428; O'Donnell v. Rosenthal, 1903, 110 Ill.App. 225; Pabst v. Schwarzstein, 1925, 101 N.J.L. 431, 128 A. 279.

33. See Merchants' Cotton Press & Storage Co. v. Miller, 1916, 135 Tenn. 187, 186 S.W. 87; Note, 1931, 45 Harv.L.Rev. 166; 1935, 83 U.Pa.L.Rev. 1035.

34. Metcalf v. Chiprin, 1963, 217 Cal.App.2d 305, 31 Cal.Rptr. 571; Redden v. James T. McCreery Co.,

1941, 123 W.Va. 367, 15 S.E.2d 150; Papallo v. Meriden Sav. Bank, 1942, 128 Conn. 563, 24 A.2d 472; Rosenberg v. Krinick, 1936, 116 N.J.L. 597, 186 A. 446; Margolen v. deHaan, 1922, 226 Ill.App. 110.

35. The opinion of Maltbie, J., in Dean v. Hershowitz, 1935, 119 Conn. 398, 177 A. 262, recognizes this, and contains the best discussion. It is not necessary to establish, however, that the covenant was made for the purpose of preventing personal injury. Harvey v. Seale, Tex.1962, 362 S.W.2d 310.

36. Second Restatement of Torts, §§ 357, 378.

37. Cooper v. Roose, 1949, 151 Ohio St. 316, 85 N.E.2d 545; Sieber v. Blanc, 1888, 76 Cal. 173, 18 P. 260; Staples v. Casey, 1915, 43 U.S.App.D.C. 477; Second Restatement of Torts, § 357, Comment d.

The obligation is one of reasonable care only. Asheim v. Fahey, 1943, 170 Or. 330, 133 P.2d 246.

38. Massachusetts has a unique rule, that as to gratuitous repairs there is liability only to the tenant, and only for gross negligence. Bergeron v. Forest,

reasonable care, there is general agreement that he is liable for resulting injuries to the tenant [39] or to members of his family [40] or others on the premises in his right.[41] It has been said that the lessor's liability does not rest upon his standing in the relation of landlord, but rather on his course of affirmative conduct [42] endangering the plaintiff. The landlord's duty is not necessarily to complete the repairs,[43] but merely to exercise due care for the safety of those on the premises, which may require no more than a warning. In most of the cases the attempt to repair has either made the situation worse by increasing the danger,[44] or has given the tenant a deceptive assurance of safety; [45] and there

are cases,[46] approved by the Restatement of Torts,[47] which have held that there is no liability when it does neither. There are, however, several decisions [48] which have rejected any such requirement, and have said that the mere failure of the lessor to exercise reasonable care under the circumstances is enough for liability. This position appears preferable, since there will be situations in which the tenant is unable to leave the premises and is therefore endangered, even though the situation has been made no worse than it was.

When the lessor entrusts the repairs to an independent contractor, the general weight of authority is that his duty of care in making them cannot be delegated, and he will be liable for the contractor's negligence.[49] Nearly all courts are agreed on this where the work is done on a part of the premises over which the lessor has retained control,[50]

1919, 233 Mass. 392, 124 N.E. 74; Barrett v. Wood Realty Co., 1956, 334 Mass. 370, 135 N.E.2d 660. This has not been followed elsewhere. See Bohlen, Landlord and Tenant, 1922, 35 Harv.L.Rev. 633.

39. Barham v. Baca, 1969, 80 N.M. 502, 458 P.2d 228; Marks v. Nambil Realty Co., 1927, 245 N.Y. 256, 157 N.E. 129; Finer v. Nichols, 1913, 175 Mo.App. 525, 157 S.W. 1023; Meecke v. Morguies, 1929, 128 Kan. 423, 278 P. 45; Mahan-Jellico Coal Co. v. Dulling, 1940, 282 Ky. 698, 139 S.W.2d 749. Cf. Tarnogurski v. Rzepski, 1916, 252 Pa. 507, 97 A. 697 (tenant's goods).

40. Gill v. Middleton, 1870, 105 Mass. 477; Shaw v. Butterworth, 1931, 327 Mo. 622, 38 S.W.2d 57; Good v. Von Hemert, 1911, 114 Minn. 393, 131 N.W. 466.

41. Ginsberg v. Wineman, 1946, 314 Mich. 1, 22 N.W.2d 49 (employee); Olsen v. Mading, 1935, 45 Ariz. 423, 45 P.2d 23 (invitee); Larson v. Dauphin Realty Co., E.D.Pa.1964, 224 F.Supp. 989, affirmed in part, reversed in part on other grounds, 3rd Cir. 1965, 340 F.2d 180 (same); Bloecher v. Duerbeck, 1933, 333 Mo. 359, 62 S.W.2d 553 (guest); Broame v. New Jersey Conference, 1912, 83 N.J.L. 621, 83 A. 901 (employee of sublessee).

42. Holmes, J., in Riley v. Lissner, 1894, 160 Mass. 330, 35 N.E. 1130; see supra, § 56.

43. Kirshenbaum v. General Outdoor Advertising Co., 1932, 258 N.Y. 489, 180 N.E. 245, motion denied, 1932, 259 N.Y. 525, 182 N.E. 165; Bauer v. 141–149 Cedar Lane Holding Co., 1957, 24 N.J. 139, 130 A.2d 833.

44. See for example Buck v. Miller, 1947, 198 Okl. 617, 181 P.2d 264.

45. See for example Smith v. Kravitz, 1953, 173 Pa. Super. 11, 93 A.2d 889; Verplanck v. Morgan, Ohio App.1948, 90 N.E.2d 872; Dunnigan v. Kirkorian, 1942, 67 R.I. 472, 25 A.2d 221.

46. Kuchynski v. Ukryn, 1938, 89 N.H. 400, 200 A. 416; Kirshenbaum v. General Outdoor Advertising Co., 1932, 258 N.Y. 489, 180 N.E. 245, motion denied, 1932, 259 N.Y. 525, 182 N.E. 165; Kearns v. Smith, 1943, 55 Cal.App.2d 532, 131 P.2d 36; Hill v. Day, 1911, 108 Me. 467, 81 A. 581; Rhoades v. Seidel, 1905, 139 Mich. 608, 102 N.W. 1025; Dapolito v. Morrison, 1938, 166 Misc. 849, 2 N.Y.S.2d 765. See supra, p. 347.

47. § 362.

48. Bartlett v. Taylor, 1943, 351 Mo. 1060, 174 S.W. 2d 844, transferred 168 S.W.2d 168; Janofsky v. Garland, 1941, 42 Cal.2d 655, 109 P.2d 750; Olsen v. Mading, 1935, 45 Ariz. 423, 45 P.2d 23; Bauer v. 141–149 Cedar Lane Holding Co., 1957, 24 N.J. 139, 130 A.2d 833; Conner v. Farmers & Merchants Bank, 1963, 243 S.C. 132, 132 S.E.2d 385.

49. See Notes, 1939, 87 U.Pa.L.Rev. 728; 1938, 18 Boston U.L.Rev. 458. There is, however, no liability for "casual" or "collateral" negligence of the contractor. Hyman v. Barrett, 1918, 224 N.Y. 436, 121 N.E. 271; Zarrillo v. Satz, 1937, 118 N.J.L. 576, 194 A. 241; Jackson v. Butler, 1913, 249 Mo. 342, 155 S.W. 1071.

50. Brown v. George Pepperdine Foundation, 1943, 23 Cal.2d 256, 143 P.2d 929; Hussey v. Long Dock R. Co., 1924, 100 N.J.L. 380, 126 A. 314; Koskoff v. Goldman, 1912, 86 Conn. 415, 85 A. 588; Cramblitt v. Percival-Porter Co., 1916, 176 Iowa 733, 158 N.W. 541; Lebright v. Gentzlinger, 1931, 232 App.Div. 274, 249 N.Y.S. 501.

or where it is pursuant to his contract with the tenant,[51] but there is a division of opinion where no control is retained and the repairs to the leased premises are gratuitous.[52] Even here the better view seems to be that the tenant's right to rely on the landlord is such that the responsibility cannot be shifted;[53] and the more recent cases have tended to take this position.[54]

64. VENDOR AND VENDEE

The vendor of real property who parts with title, possession and control of it ceases to be either an owner or an occupier. Ordinarily, therefore, he is permitted to step out of the picture and shift all responsibility for the condition of the land to the purchaser. As to sales of land the ancient doctrine of *caveat emptor* lingered on, and is still very largely in force; and it is only in recent years, and then to a very limited extent [55] that the implied warranties which have grown up around the sale of chattels [56] have been parallelled as to land. This was perhaps for the

reason that great importance is attached to the deed of conveyance, which is taken to represent the full agreement of the parties, and to exclude all other terms; [57] the lack of any standard marketable quality, or even standard use, of land; [58] and the fact that the vendee normally inspects the property before purchase, and so is assumed to have accepted it as it is.[59] Thus in the absence of express agreement or misrepresentation [60] the purchaser is expected to make his own examination and draw his own conclusions as to the condition of the land; and the vendor is, in general, not liable for any harm resulting to him from any defects existing at the time of transfer.[61] Still less is he liable to other persons who may come upon the land.[62]

With the passage of time, an increased regard for human safety, and a sadly needed improvement in bargaining business ethics, have led to the development of two exceptions to this once universal rule.[63] One of them, which finds support in the cases of lessors,[64] and in the Restatement of Torts,[65]

---

51. Peerless Mfg. Co. v. Bagley, 1901, 126 Mich. 225, 85 N.W. 568; Vitale v. Duerbeck, 1933, 332 Mo. 1184, 62 S.W.2d 559; Wertheimer v. Saunders, 1897, 95 Wis. 573, 70 N.W. 824; Blumenthal v. Prescott, 1902, 70 App.Div. 560, 75 N.Y.S. 710.

52. Liability: Ryce v. Whitley, 1901, 115 Iowa 784, 87 N.W. 694; Bancroft v. Godwin, 1905, 41 Wash. 253, 83 P. 189; O'Rourke v. Feist, 1899, 42 App.Div. 136, 59 N.Y.S. 157; Dalkowitz v. Schreiner, Tex. Civ.App.1908, 110 S.W. 564.

No liability: Jefferson v. Jameson & Morse Co., 1896, 165 Ill. 138, 46 N.E. 272; Bains v. Dank, 1917, 199 Ala. 250, 74 So. 341; Eblin v. Miller's Ex'rs, 1880, 78 Ky. 371; Schatzky v. Harber, Sup.Ct.1917, 164 N.Y.S. 610.

53. Second Restatement of Torts, § 420.

54. Bailey v. Zlotnick, 1945, 80 App.D.C. 117, 149 F. 2d 505; Rubin v. Girard Trust Co., 1944, 154 Pa.Super. 257, 35 A.2d 601; Arlington Realty Co. v. Lawson, 1934, 228 Ala. 214, 153 So. 425; Livingston v. Essex Inv. Co., 1941, 219 N.C. 416, 14 S.E.2d 489.

55. See infra, p. 680.

56. See infra, § 95. The leading case holding that there are no implied warranties on the sale of land is Hart v. Windsor, 1843, 12 M. & W. 68, 152 Eng. Rep. 1114.

57. See Williston, Contracts, Rev.Ed.1936, § 426.

58. Dunham, Vendor's Obligation as to Fitness of Land for a Particular Purpose, 1953, 37 Minn.L. Rev. 110.

59. See Notes, 1959, 44 Minn.L.Rev. 144; 1956, 5 De Paul L.Rev. 263.

60. See infra, ch. 18.

61. Levy v. C. Young Const. Co., 1957, 46 N.J.Super. 293, 134 A.2d 717, affirmed, 1958, 26 N.J. 330, 139 A.2d 738; Stone v. Heyman Bros., 1932, 124 Cal. App. 46, 12 P.2d 126; Combow v. Kansas City Ground Inv. Co., 1949, 358 Mo. 934, 218 S.W.2d 539; Ramsey v. Mading, 1950, 36 Wash.2d 303, 217 P.2d 1041; Kordig v. Grovedale Oleander Homes, Inc., 1958, 18 Ill.App.2d 48, 151 N.E.2d 470.

62. Copfer v. Golden, 1955, 135 Cal.App.2d 623, 288 P.2d 90; Kilmer v. White, 1930, 254 N.Y. 64, 171 N.E. 908; cf. Slavitz v. Morris Park Estates, 1917, 98 Misc. 314, 162 N.Y.S. 888; Upp v. Darner, 1911, 150 Iowa 403, 130 N.W. 409; see Note, 1930, 16 Corn.L.Q. 130.

63. See Notes, 1965, 53 Cal.L.Rev. 1062; 1966, 51 Corn.L.Q. 389.

64. See supra, p. 401.

65. Second Restatement of Torts, § 353, adding that the liability extends to others upon the land in the right of the vendee.

is that the vendor is at least under a duty to disclose to the vendee any concealed conditions known to him which involve an unreasonable danger to the health or safety of those upon the premises, and which he may anticipate that the vendee will not discover.[66] If he fails to make such disclosure, he becomes liable for injury resulting from such conditions to the vendee, or to members of his family, or others upon the land in the right of the vendee.[67] The older view was to the contrary,[68] and there are still courts whose latest decisions deny even this obligation;[69] but the duty should certainly exist, if only because of the analogy to the "something like fraud" in permitting even a licensee[70] to enter in the face of a concealed and undisclosed hazard, and because the risk to the vendee is clearly great in proportion to the relatively slight burden of disclosure cast upon the vendor.

The recognition of this duty of disclosure has thus far ended the progress of any neg-

ligence liability of the vendor. There have been, however, important developments along the lines of strict liability, which have superseded the ground of negligence, and which remain to be considered in a later chapter.[71]

The other exception to the general rule of nonliability of the vendor is found in a number of cases where the land, when it is transferred, is in such condition that it involves an unreasonable risk of harm to those outside of the premises. In nearly all of the decided cases, this has amounted to either a public or a private nuisance, but this is clearly not essential. In such a case the vendor remains subject, at least for a reasonable time, to any liability which he would have incurred if he had remained in possession, for injuries to persons or property outside of the land, caused by such a condition.[72] The reason usually given is the obviously fictitious one that by selling the land in such condition he has "authorized the continuance of the nuisance." A more reasonable explanation would appear to be merely that the vendor's responsibility to those outside of his land is regarded as of such social importance that he is not permitted to shift it, even by an outright sale. A Pennsylvania case,[73] approved by the Restatement of Torts,[74] once limited this liability to structures or artificial conditions created by the vendor himself, as distinguished from mere disrepair or inactivity; and it has been urged in support of this position that liability for the act of creation would continue even if the actor were a

---

66. There is no duty to seek out and discover such defects, in the absence of any such knowledge. Whiten v. Orr Const. Co., 1964, 109 Ga.App. 267, 136 S.E.2d 136.

67. Belote v. Memphis Development Co., 1961, 208 Tenn. 434, 346 S.W.2d 441; Bray v. Cross, 1958, 98 Ga.App. 612, 106 S.E.2d 315; Caporaletti v. A–F Corp., D.D.C.1956, reversed on other grounds, 1957, 99 U.S.App.D.C. 367, 240 F.2d 53; Derby v. Public Service Co., 1955, 100 N.H. 53, 119 A.2d 335; Southern v. Floyd, 1954, 89 Ga.App. 602, 80 S.E.2d 490; Herzog v. Capital Co., 1945, 27 Cal.2d 349, 164 P.2d 8.

As to the parallel development of liability for pecuniary loss resulting from nondisclosure, see infra, § 106.

68. One of the leading American cases has been Smith v. Tucker, 1925, 151 Tenn. 347, 270 S.W. 66, which apparently is now of questionable authority.

69. Bottomley v. Bannister, [1932] 1 K.B. 458; Swinton v. Whitinsville Sav. Bank, 1942, 311 Mass. 677, 42 N.E.2d 808; Day v. Frederickson, 1922, 153 Minn. 380, 190 N.W. 788; Riley v. White, Mo.App. 1950, 231 S.W.2d 291.

70. See supra, p. 380. Compare, as to lessors, Eldredge, Landlord's Tort Liability for Disrepair, 1936, 84 U.Pa.L.Rev. 467, 468–470, reprinted in Eldredge, Modern Tort Problems, 1941, 113.

71. See infra, p. 639.

72. Plumer v. Harper, 1824, 3 N.H. 88; Keeley v. Manor Park Apartments, Del.Ch.1953, 99 A.2d 248; Walter v. Wagner, 1928, 225 Ky. 255, 8 S.W.2d 421; Wilks v. New York Tel. Co., 1926, 243 N.Y. 351, 153 N.E. 444; Derby v. Public Service Co., 1955, 100 N. H. 53, 119 A.2d 335; Second Restatement of Torts, § 373.

73. Palmore v. Morris, Tasker & Co., 1897, 182 Pa. 82, 37 A. 995. Cf. Wilks v. New York Tel. Co., 1926, 243 N.Y. 351, 153 N.E. 444 (no liability for maintaining nuisance later taken over by government).

74. § 374.

trespasser on the land, while the duty to maintain safe conditions is based on possession, and should terminate with it.[75] It is difficult, however, to find any real basis for distinguishing the contrary view taken in the cases of lessors,[76] and it appears unlikely that the case will be followed.

As to both of these exceptions under which the vendor is held liable for injuries occurring after possession is transferred, it seems obvious that there must be some time limit upon the duration of the potential liability. A corporation, still in existence, can scarcely be required to pay for damages which occur a century after the grant. There are, however, very few cases which have considered the question. The indications are that the vendor is no longer liable once the vendee has had a reasonable time to discover and remedy the condition,[77] unless the vendor has actively concealed it, in which case, as in other instances of fraud, his liability will continue until actual discovery, and a reasonable time thereafter to take action.[78]

Vendees

The vendee to whom possession is transferred becomes himself an occupier, and subject to all of the obligations of a possessor. The most important problem which has arisen in connection with such vendees is that of liability for injuries to persons outside of the premises resulting from conditions of which the vendee has no knowledge, or which he has not yet had an opportunity to remedy after entering into possession. Most of the cases have involved a private nuisance existing on the land at the time of transfer. The First Restatement of Torts,[79] supported by almost nothing in the way of authority,[80] took the position that the vendee is required at his peril to make full inspection before he buys, and that as to all artificial conditions which are not latent he assumes responsibility from the moment he takes possession, regardless of knowledge of the danger or of any opportunity whatever to guard against it.

The weight of authority is heavily against this proposition. A long line of nuisance cases have held that the vendee becomes liable only after he is given notice of the existence of the condition, and requested to abate it.[81] He is entitled to a reasonable time after such notice, to take action.[82] This is said to be because the vendee is entitled to

---

75. Salmond, Law of Torts, 8th Ed. 1934, 251.

76. See supra, p. 402. Both lessor and vendor surrender possession and control, and the vendor receives a price for the sale which is no less economic benefit than the lessor's rent. Why should the retention of legal title make the difference, when it gives no effective power of action after the transfer?

77. Walter v. Wagner, 1928, 225 Ky. 255, 8 S.W.2d 421 ("until the liability of the purchaser becomes fixed"); Farragher v. City of New York, 1966, 26 App.Div.2d 494, 275 N.Y.S.2d 542, motion denied, 1967, 19 N.Y.2d 1014, 281 N.Y.S.2d 1010, 228 N.E.2d 904, affirmed, 1968, 21 N.Y.2d 756, 288 N.Y.S.2d 232, 235 N.E.2d 218 (to same effect); Brown v. St. Louis & S. F. R. Co., Mo.App.1925, 268 S.W. 678. Compare, as to lessors under the New York Multiple Dwelling Law: Pharm v. Lituchy, 1940, 283 N.Y. 130, 27 N.E.2d 811 ("a reasonable time to discover"); Tri-Boro Bowling Center v. Roosevelt Eighty-Fifth St. Estates, Sup.Ct.1947, 77 N.Y.S.2d 74 (4 years too long).

78. Pavelchak v. Finn, Sup.Ct.1956, 153 N.Y.S.2d 795, affirmed, 1958, 6 App.Div.2d 841, 176 N.Y.S.2d 933. Narsh v. Zirbser Bros., Inc., 1970, 111 N.J.Super. 203, 268 A.2d 46.

79. § 366. See Note, 1930, 79 U.Pa.L.Rev. 236. But cf. the Note, 1930, 16 Corn.L.Q. 130, misinterpreting the case of Kilmer v. White, 1930, 254 N.Y. 64, 171 N.E. 908.

80. The only support found is some very dubious dictum in Harvey v. Machtig, 1925, 73 Cal.App. 667, 239 P. 78, and Palmore v. Morris, Tasker & Co., 1897, 182 Pa. 82, 37 A. 995.

81. Penruddock's Case, 1598, 5 Co.Rep. 101b, 77 Eng. Rep. 210; Union Pac. R. Co. v. Campbell, 1916, 150 C.C.A. 40, 236 F. 708; Edwards v. Atchison, T. & S. F. R. Co., 9 Cir. 1926, 15 F.2d 37; Roberts v. Georgia Ry. & Power Co., 1921, 151 Ga. 241, 106 S.E. 258; Glenn v. Crescent Coal Co., 1911, 145 Ky. 137, 140 S.W. 43.

82. Rychlicki v. City of St. Louis, 1893, 115 Mo. 662, 22 S.W. 908; Beauchamp v. Excelsior Brick Co., 1911, 143 App.Div. 48, 127 N.Y.S. 686.

assume, when he takes possession, that any existing private nuisance has the consent of the adjoining landowners, and that if compensation for it is required, it has been paid. No particular form of notice or request is necessary, so long as the vendee is informed of the condition and the plaintiff's unwillingness to have it continued.[83] A good many other cases [84] have held that express notice or request is not required, and that it is sufficient that the vendee knows of the condition or has information which should put him on inquiry, and has had a reasonable opportunity to remedy it. It may be that these two lines of authority are not inconsistent, since in many of the cases where knowledge alone is held sufficient the condition has been such that consent to its existence could not reasonably be assumed. In either case there is no strict liability, and the vendee is held responsible only for his own unreasonable conduct.[85]

This is borne out by the fact that where the condition of the premises creates a public nuisance, it is generally agreed that there is liability as soon as the vendee knows of the condition and fails to remedy it, without any notice or request.[86] This is because a public nuisance, being criminal in character and an invasion of the rights of the public, cannot reasonably be assumed by anyone to exist with public consent. The possessor is therefore required to know the condition of his land, and to take all reasonable steps to insure that it does not interfere with the public right.

83. Weimer v. Cauble, 1959, 214 Ga. 634, 106 S.E.2d 781; Bishop v. Readsboro Chair Mfg. Co., 1911, 85 Vt. 141, 81 A. 454. Neither notice nor request is required where it is clear that it would be useless. Clarke v. Boysen, 10 Cir. 1930, 39 F.2d 800, cert. denied 282 U.S. 869.

84. Conhocton Stone Road Co. v. Buffalo, N.Y. & E. R. Co., 1873, 51 N.Y. 573; Willitts v. Chicago, B. & K. C. R. Co., 1893, 88 Iowa 281, 55 N.W. 313; City of Turlock v. Bristow, 1930, 103 Cal.App. 750, 284 P. 962; Lamb v. Roberts, 1916, 196 Ala. 679, 72 So. 309.

85. Restatement of Torts, § 839 (obviously contrary to § 366). This is in accord with the general holding that a possessor is not liable for nuisance in the absence of negligence, intent or abnormally dangerous activity. See infra, § 87. The vendee will of course be liable if he continues or, increases the nuisance by his own active conduct. Philadelphia & R. R. Co. v. Smith, 3 Cir. 1894, 64 F. 679; Daniels v. St. Louis & S. F. R. Co., 1912, 36 Okl. 421, 128 P. 1089.

86. Leahan v. Cochran, 1901, 178 Mass. 566, 60 N.E. 382; Turner v. Ridley, Mun.App.D.C.1958, 144 A.2d 269; Corby v. Ramsdell, 2 Cir. 1931, 48 F.2d 701; Bixby v. Thurber, 1922, 80 N.H. 411, 118 A. 99; Matthews v. Missouri Pac. R. Co., 1887, 26 Mo.App. 75.

CHAPTER 11
NEGLIGENCE: DEFENSES

65. CONTRIBUTORY NEGLIGENCE

The two most common defenses in a negligence action are contributory negligence and assumption of risk. Since both developed at a comparatively late date in the law of negligence,[1] and since both clearly operate to the advantage of the defendant, they are commonly regarded as defenses to a tort which would otherwise be established. The great majority of the courts hold that the burden of pleading and proof of the contributory negligence of the plaintiff is on the defendant.[2] Some few jurisdictions, because of various theories as to the basis of the rule, have held that freedom from such negligence is an essential part of the plaintiff's cause of action, as to which he has the burden of proof.[3] This obviously means that where

there is no evidence on the issue the plaintiff must lose; and the hardship of this is so apparent in many cases that such jurisdictions have tended to relax the rule, either by aiding the plaintiff by a presumption of his own due care, supposedly based upon the instinct of self-preservation,[4] or by allowing proof, not ordinarily admissible, of the plaintiff's habit of being careful,[5] or even by holding that it is enough that the plaintiff, in proving the defendant's negligence, discloses nothing but prudent conduct of his own.[6] In a good many states the rule has been changed by statute, particularly in death cases, where the plaintiff is especially likely to be unable to produce any satisfactory evidence.[7]

Contributory negligence is conduct on the part of the plaintiff, contributing as a legal

---

1. Assumption of risk first appears in a negligence case in Cruden v. Fentham, 1799, 2 Esp. 685, 170 Eng.Rep. 496, although it was not unknown previously in trespass actions. See Ilott v. Wilkes, 1820, 3 B. & Ald. 304, 106 Eng.Rep. 674; Warren, Volenti Non Fit Injuria in Actions of Negligence, 1895, 8 Harv.L.Rev. 457, 462. The earliest contributory negligence case is Butterfield v. Forrester, 1809, 11 East 60, 103 Eng.Rep. 926. The first American case appears to have been Smith v. Smith, 1824, 2 Pick., Mass., 621.

2. Washington & Georgetown R. Co. v. Gladmon, 1872, 82 U.S. 401; Bullard v. Boston Elev. R. Co., 1917, 226 Mass. 262, 115 N.E. 294; Hopper, McGaw & Co. v. Kelly, 1924, 145 Md. 161, 125 A. 779; Vanceburg Tel. Co. v. Bevis, 1912, 148 Ky. 285, 146 S.W. 420.

3. West Chicago St. R. Co. v. Liderman, 1900, 187 Ill. 463, 58 N.E. 367; Kotler v. Lalley, 1930, 112 Conn. 86, 151 A. 433; Dreier v. McDermott, 1913, 157 Iowa 726, 141 N.W. 315. See Green, Illinois Negligence Law II, 1944, 39 Ill.L.Rev. 116, 125–130. It has been held that this is matter of substance

rather than procedure, so that federal and foreign courts must apply the law of the state where the tort occurs. Palmer v. Hoffman, 1943, 318 U.S. 109, rehearing denied 318 U.S. 800; Redick v. M. B. Thomas Auto Sales, Inc., 1954, 364 Mo. 1174, 273 S. W.2d 228.

4. Way v. Illinois Cent. R. Co., 1875, 40 Iowa 341; Breker v. Rosema, 1942, 301 Mich. 685, 4 N.W.2d 57; Savage v. Rhode Island Co., 1907, 28 R.I. 391, 67 A. 633. See Note, 1920, 6 Iowa L.J. 55.

5. Chicago, R. I. & P. R. Co. v. Clark, 1883, 108 Ill. 113; Wallis v. Southern Pac. Co., 1921, 184 Cal. 662, 195 P. 408. See Notes, 1922, 16 Ill.L.Rev. 628; 1932, 20 Cal.L.Rev. 208.

6. Duggan v. Heaphy, 1912, 85 Vt. 515, 83 A. 726; Wood v. City of Danbury, 1899, 72 Conn. 69, 43 A. 554; Murphy v. Chicago, R. I. & P. R. Co., 1877, 45 Iowa 661.

7. See for example Me.Rev.Stat.1954, c. 113, § 50; N.Y. Decedent Estate Law § 131; Cooperstein v. Eden Brick & Supply Co., 1924, 238 N.Y. 200, 144 N.E. 501.

cause to the harm he has suffered, which falls below the standard to which he is required to conform for his own protection.[8] Unlike assumption of risk, the defense does not rest upon the idea that the defendant is relieved of any duty toward the plaintiff. Rather, although the defendant has violated his duty, has been negligent, and would otherwise be liable, the plaintiff is denied recovery because his own conduct disentitles him to maintain the action. In the eyes of the law both parties are at fault; and the defense is one of the plaintiff's disability, rather than the defendant's innocence.

Many theories have been advanced to explain the defense of contributory negligence. It has been said that it has a penal basis, and that the plaintiff is denied recovery to punish him for his own misconduct.[9] But, while this may perhaps once have been an explanation, it is certainly so no longer, in the light of the many cases in which a plaintiff who is grievously, and even criminally, at fault is still permitted to recover.[10] The same objection may be made to the theory, sometimes advanced,[11] that the plaintiff is required to come into court with "clean hands." The defense has been said to rest upon voluntary assumption of risk; but this is clearly error, since it may exist in the absence of knowledge of the risk, or any consent, other than an obviously fictitious one, to encounter it.[12]

The greater number of courts have explained it in terms of "proximate cause," saying that the plaintiff's negligence is an intervening, or insulating, cause between the defendant's negligence and the result.[13] But this cannot be supported unless a meaning is assigned to "proximate cause" which goes beyond anything applied elsewhere.[14] If two automobiles collide and injure a bystander, the negligence of one driver is not held to be an "insulating cause" which relieves the other of liability. So far as causation is concerned, it can hardly have any different effect when the action is by one driver against the other.[15] It has been said also that the rule is intended to discourage accidents, by denying recovery to those who fail to use proper care for their own safety.[16] But the assumption that the speeding motorist is, or should be, meditating on the possible failure of a lawsuit for his possible injuries, lacks all genuine reality or basis in human experience; and it would be quite as reasonable to say that the rule promotes accidents by en-

8 Harv.L.Rev. 457, 458–461; James, Assumption of Risk, 1952, 61 Yale L.J. 141.

8. Second Restatement of Torts, § 463. See, generally, Malone, The Formative Era of Contributory Negligence, 1946, 41 Ill.L.Rev. 151; James, Contributory Negligence, 1953, 62 Yale L.J. 691; Bohlen, Contributory Negligence, 1908, 21 Harv.L.Rev. 233; Lowndes, Contributory Negligence, 1934, 22 Geo.L.J. 674.

9. See Lord Halsbury, L. C., in Wakelin v. London & S. W. R. Co., 1886, 12 A.C. 41, 45.

10. See infra, p. 421.

11. Owen, C.J., in Davis v. Guarnieri, 1887, 45 Ohio St. 470, 15 N.E. 350.

12. See Bohlen, Contributory Negligence, 1908, 21 Harv.L.Rev. 233; Lowndes, Contributory Negligence, 1934, 22 Geo.L.J. 674, 679–681; Warren, Volenti Non Fit Injuria in Actions of Negligence, 1895,

13. Bowen, L.J., in Thomas v. Quartermaine, 1897, 18 Q.B.D. 685, 697; Gilman v. Central Vermont R. Co., 1919, 93 Vt. 340, 107 A. 122; Ware v. Saufley, 1922, 194 Ky. 53, 237 S.W. 1060; Exum v. Atlantic Coast Line R. Co., 1911, 154 N.C. 408, 70 S.E. 845; Chesapeake & O. R. Co. v. Wills, 1910, 111 Va. 32, 68 S.E. 395. English writers have tended to accept this explanation. Pollock, Law of Torts, 13th Ed. 1929, 474; Winfield, Law of Torts, 4th Ed. 1948, 414.

14. Green, Contributory Negligence and Proximate Cause, 1927, 6 North Car.L.Rev. 3; Lowndes, Contributory Negligence, 1934, 22 Georgetown L.J. 674; Bohlen, Contributory Negligence, 1908, 21 Harv.L. Rev. 233.

15. Austin Elec. R. Co. v. Faust, 1910, 63 Tex.Civ. App. 91, 133 S.W. 449, error refused in part and error dismissed in part; Albritton v. Hill, 1925, 190 N.C. 429, 130 S.E. 5; Etheridge v. Norfolk Southern R. Co., 1925, 143 Va. 789, 129 S.E. 680; McDonald v. Robinson, 1929, 207 Iowa 1293, 224 N.W. 820; Fraser v. Flanders, 1924, 248 Mass. 62, 142 N.E. 836.

16. Schofield, Davies v. Mann: Theory of Contributory Negligence, 1890, 3 Harv.L.Rev. 263, 270.

couraging the negligent defendant to hope that the person he injures will be negligent too.

Perhaps no one theory can ever explain the doctrine of contributory negligence. In its essence, it is an expression of the highly individualistic attitude of the common law, and its policy of making the personal interests of each party depend upon his own care and prudence.[17] Its development was at least encouraged, if not entirely explained, by three factors.[18] Chief among these was the uneasy distrust of the plaintiff-minded jury which grew upon the courts in the earlier part of the nineteenth century, and a desire to keep the liabilities of growing industry within some bounds. Another was the tendency of the courts of the day to look for some single, principal, dominant, "proximate" cause of every injury.[19] The third was the inability of the courts, apart from admiralty cases where there was no jury, to conceive of a satisfactory method by which the damages for a single, indivisible injury could be apportioned between the parties, so that, although both were at fault, the loss must fall entirely upon the negligent plaintiff or upon the negligent defendant.[20]

All this, however, is the antique heritage of an older day. Criticism of the denial of all recovery was not slow in coming, and it has been with us for more than a century.[21]

The history of the doctrine has been that of a chronic invalid who will not die. With the gradual change in social viewpoint, stressing the humanitarian desire to see injuries compensated, the defense of contributory negligence has gradually come to be looked upon with increasing disfavor by the courts,[22] and its rigors have been quite extensively modified, as will be seen below.

Compared with Negligence

It is perhaps unfortunate that contributory negligence is called negligence at all. "Contributory fault" would be a more descriptive term. Negligence as it is commonly understood is conduct which creates an undue risk of harm to others. Contributory negligence is conduct which involves an undue risk of harm to the actor himself.[23] Negligence requires a duty, an obligation of conduct to another person. Contributory negligence involves no duty, unless we are to be so ingenious as to say that the plaintiff is under an obligation to protect the defendant against liability for the consequences of his own negligence.[24]

Nevertheless, and largely because of the long-continued process of setting one over against the other, contributory negligence, in general, is determined and governed by the same tests and rules as the negligence of

---

17. Schofield, Davies v. Mann: Theory of Contributory Negligence, 1890, 3 Harv.L.Rev. 270; Owen, C. J., in Davis v. Guarnieri, 1887, 45 Ohio St. 470, 15 N.E. 350.

18. Malone, The Formative Era of Contributory Negligence, 1947, 41 Ill.L.Rev. 151.

19. Wright, Contributory Negligence, 1950, 13 Mod.L. Rev. 2, 5.

20. See Lowndes, Contributory Negligence, 1934, 22 Geo.L.J. 674, 683–685; Beach, Contributory Negligence, 3d Ed. 1899, § 12.

21. One of the best statements of the attack on contributory negligence is found in Green, Illinois Negligence Law, 1944, 39 Ill.L.Rev. 36, 116, 197. See also Lowndes, Contributory Negligence, 1934, 22 Geo.L.J. 674; James, Last Clear Chance: A Transitional Doctrine, 1938, 47 Yale L.J. 704.

22. See Leflar, The Declining Defense of Contributory Negligence, 1946, 1 Ark.L.Rev. 1; James, Contributory Negligence, 1953, 62 Yale L.J. 691.

In Layton v. Rocha, 1962, 90 Ariz. 369, 368 P.2d 444, relying upon a constitutional provision, it was held that when contributory negligence is found, the jury "may," not "must," find for the defendant.

23. Second Restatement of Torts, § 463, Comment b; Pappas v. Evans, 1951, 242 Iowa 804, 48 N.W.2d 298.

24. See Atkin, L.J., in Ellerman Lines v. Grayson, [1919] 2 K.B. 535; Lord Parmoor, in Grayson v. Ellerman Lines, [1920] A.C. 477. See also Dean Green's attempt to deal with contributory negligence in terms of "duty," in Green, Mahoney v. Beatman: A Study in Proximate Cause, 1930, 39 Yale L.J. 532, reprinted in Green, Judge and Jury, 1930, ch. 7, and the criticism of Bohlen in his Review, 1932, 80 U.Pa.L.Rev. 781, 784.

the defendant. The plaintiff is required to conform to the same broad standard of conduct, that of the reasonable man of ordinary prudence under like circumstances.[25] The unreasonableness of the risks which he incurs is judged by the same process of weighing the importance of the interest he is seeking to advance against the probability, and probable gravity, of the anticipated harm to himself. Thus it may not be contributory negligence to dash into the path of a train to save a child,[26] or to try to put out a fire which threatens valuable property,[27] or to stand in the street to warn travelers of an obstruction to traffic.[28]

The same intelligence, attention, knowledge[29] and judgment are required of the actor for the protection of his own interests as for the protection of others, and the same allowance is made for his physical inferiorities,[30] and for the immaturity of children,[31]

diverted attention,[32] and the burden of taking precautions.[33]

The similarity of negligence and contributory negligence does not, however, necessarily mean that identical conduct is to be demanded of the plaintiff and the defendant in any given situation. Too many varying factors may affect what the standard of the reasonable man requires, to permit any such rigid rule. The defendant may have more information than the plaintiff as to the risk,[34] or by reason of the enterprise in which he is engaged may be required to obtain it;[35] or the risk of harm to others may be more apparent, or apparently more serious, than the risk to the actor himself; or he may have reasonable confidence in his own awareness of the risk, and his ability to avoid it, where he cannot reasonably have such confidence in the awareness or ability of others. He may have undertaken a responsibility toward others, which will require him to exercise an amount of care for their protection which he would not be required to exercise for his own safety.[36] It is not necessarily contributory negligence as a matter of law for one riding in an automobile to fail to use a seat belt,[37] although it is negligence for the

25.   Second Restatement of Torts, § 464.

26.   Brock v. Peabody Co-op. Equity Exchange, 1960, 186 Kan. 657, 352 P.2d 37; Brown v. Ross, 1956, 345 Mich. 54, 75 N.W.2d 68; Bond v. Baltimore & Ohio N. R. Co., 1918, 82 W. Va. 557, 96 S.E. 932; Williams v. City of Baton Rouge, La.App.1967, 200 So.2d 420, affirmed and amended, 1968, 252 La. 770, 214 So.2d 138.

27.   Liming v. Illinois Cent. R. Co., 1890, 81 Iowa 246, 47 N.W. 66; Henshaw v. Belyea, 1934, 220 Cal. 458, 31 P.2d 348.

28.   Hammonds v. Haven, Mo.1955, 280 S.W.2d 814; Marshall v. Nugent, 1 Cir. 1955, 222 F.2d 604; cf. Rovinski v. Rowe, 6 Cir. 1942, 131 F.2d 687; Wolfinger v. Shaw, 1940, 138 Neb. 229, 292 N.W. 731.

29.   Public Service Co. of N. H. v. Elliott, 1 Cir. 1941, 123 F.2d 2; Peterson v. Minnesota Power & Light Co., 1939, 206 Minn. 268, 288 N.W. 588.

30.   Second Restatement of Torts, § 464, Comments a, b. See supra, p. 151.

31.   Shulman, The Standard of Care Required of Children, 1927, 37 Yale L.J. 618; Bohlen, Liability in Tort of Infants and Insane Persons, 1924, 23 Mich.L.Rev. 9; Wilderman, Contributory Negligence of Infants, 1935, 10 Ind.L.J. 427; Notes, 1921, 21 Col.L.Rev. 697; 1925, 74 U.Pa.L.Rev. 79; 1937, 36 Mich.L.Rev. 328. As to possible different rules for plaintiffs and defendants, see supra, p. 156.

32.   Johnson v. Rulon, 1950, 363 Pa. 585, 70 A.2d 325; Dennis v. City of Albemarle, 1955, 242 N.C. 263, 87 S.E.2d 561, rehearing dismissed, 1956, 243 N.C. 221, 90 S.E.2d 532; Public Service Co. of N. H. v. Elliott, 1 Cir. 1941, 123 F.2d 2; Houston v. Town of Waverly, 1932, 225 Ala. 98, 142 So. 80; Kingsul Theatres v. Quillen, 1946, 29 Tenn.App. 248, 196 S. W.2d 316.

33.   Starr v. Philadelphia Transp. Co., 1960, 191 Pa. Super. 559, 159 A.2d 10.

34.   Haverly v. State Line & S. R. Co., 1890, 135 Pa. 50, 19 A. 1013. Cf. Oil City Gas Co. v. Robinson, 1881, 99 Pa. 1.

35.   See supra, p. 160.

36.   Gobrecht v. Beckwith, 1926, 82 N.H. 415, 135 A. 20. Cf. Sollinger v. Himchak, 1961, 402 Pa. 232, 166 A.2d 531 (driver of car may be found negligent toward his own passengers, but not contributorily negligent in his action against driver of car with which he collided).

37.   Woods v. Smith, N.D.Fla.1969, 296 F.Supp. 1128; Romankewiz v. Black, 1969, 16 Mich.App. 119, 167

manufacturer of the car to fail to supply one.[38] Or the plaintiff may be justified in relying upon the defendant to protect him; or, even without such factors, the jury may find that in the particular situation a reasonable man would have been more careful for others than for himself.

Thus the greater number of courts have recognized that a passenger in an automobile is entitled to rely upon the driver, and may take and keep his eyes off of the road,[39] and may even go to sleep,[40] where it is quite clear that the driver cannot reasonably do either. There has been so much of this differentiation in the decisions that eminent writers [41] have advocated outright recognition of the double standard. Whether this is at all necessary, or even desirable, may seriously be questioned, in the light of the flexibility which has developed in the decided cases under the present single formula for both.

The result of all this is that, while the theory is the same, and the formula put to the jury is the same, the practical application of both is not the same for negligence and for contributory negligence. As to the latter, in part because of these differentiating factors, and in part, perhaps, because of the healthy dislike and distaste which nearly all courts have developed for this defense, the marked tendency has been to let the issue go to the jury whenever it is at all possible. It is still not entirely impossible for the defendant to get a directed verdict, where the negligence of the plaintiff is beyond all dispute—as where, for example, he runs without excuse into the side of a train, and collides with a car ten feet high, painted red with bright yellow letters on the side.[42] But in the ordinary case, where enough uncertainty can be conjured up to make an issue as to what the reasonable man would have done, that issue goes to the jury.[43]

N.W.2d 606; Cierpisz v. Singleton, 1967, 247 Md. 215, 230 A.2d 629; Brown v. Kendrick, Fla.App. 1966, 192 So.2d 49; Bertsch v. Spears, 1969, 20 Ohio App.2d 137, 252 N.E.2d 194. Cf. Rogers v. Frush, 1970, 257 Md. 233, 262 A.2d 549 (motorcycle helmet). See Kleist, The Seat Belt Defense, 1967, 18 Hast.L. J. 613; Notes, 1967, 12 S.D.L.Rev. 130; 1967, 16 De Paul L.Rev. 521; 1967, 9 Ariz.L.Rev. 118; [1967] Wis.L.Rev. 288; 1969, 38 Ford.L.Rev. 94.

38. Mortenson v. Southern Pacific Co., 1966, 245 Cal.App.2d 241, 53 Cal.Rptr. 851.

39. O'Toole v. Pittsburgh & L. E. R. Co., 1893, 158 Pa. 99, 27 A. 737; Love v. Cardwell, 8 Cir. 1966, 368 F.2d 289; Leclair v. Boudreau, 1928, 101 Vt. 270, 143 A. 401; Bradford v. Carson, 1931, 223 Ala. 594, 137 So. 426; Scales v. Boynton Cab Co., 1929, 198 Wis. 293, 223 N.W. 836. Cf. Stubbs v. Pancake Corner of Salem, Inc., 1969, — Or. —, 458 P.2d 676. See Mechem, The Contributory Negligence of Automobile Passengers, 1930, 78 U.Pa.L.Rev. 736; Notes, 1932, 8 Wis.L.Rev. 69; 1940, 38 Mich.L.Rev. 556.

40. The distinction is clearly made in Shine v. Wujick, 1959, 89 R.I. 22, 150 A.2d 1, where both driver and passenger went to sleep. Accord: Newell v. Riggins, 1955, 197 Va. 490, 90 S.E.2d 150; Nelson v. Nygren, 1932, 259 N.Y. 71, 181 N.E. 52; Taylor v. Birks, Okl.1958, 325 P.2d 737 (intoxicated plaintiff); Jesse v. Dunn, 1932, 244 Ky. 613, 51 S.W.2d 918; White v. Stanley, 1932, 169 Wash. 342, 13 P.2d 457. See Notes, 1933, 17 Minn.L.Rev. 222; 1959, 44 Iowa L.Rev. 622.

41. 2 Harper and James, Law of Torts, 1956, 1227–1234.

42. Union Pac. R. Co. v. Cogburn, 1957, 136 Colo. 184, 315 P.2d 209; Jenkins v. Atlantic Coast Line R. Co., 1962, 258 N.C. 58, 127 S.E.2d 778 (side of engine). Cf. Sargent v. Williams, 1953, 152 Tex. 413, 258 S.W.2d 787 (riding with driver with reputation for recklessness, who traveled 110 miles per hour); Badders v. Lassiter, 1954, 240 N.C. 413, 82 S.E.2d 357 (crossing highway after seeing approaching car, without looking again); Haeg v. Sprague, Warner & Co., 1938, 202 Minn. 425, 281 N.W. 261 (same).

43. "It is not disputed by appellant, that we must view the evidence in the light most favorable to plaintiff; that it is only the exceptional case in which the issue of freedom from contributory negligence should not be submitted to the jury—only where such negligence is so palpable, flagrant and manifest that reasonable minds may fairly reach no other conclusion; that if there is any evidence tending to establish plaintiff's freedom from contributory negligence, the question is one of fact for the jury, and doubts should be resolved in favor of such submission." Goman v. Benedik, 1962, 253 Iowa 719, 113 N.W.2d 738. Cf. Gills v. New York, C. & St. L. R. Co., 1930, 342 Ill. 455, 174 N.E. 523; Williams v. Henderson, 1949, 230 N.C. 707, 55 S.E. 2d 462. See Notes, 1955, 34 N.C.L.Rev. 137; [1953] U.Ill.L.Forum 52; 1966, 55 Ky.L.J. 192.

There is one rather curious but not infrequent aberration which makes an apparent distinction between negligence and contributory negligence. It is said by a number of courts [44] that the plaintiff is barred from recovery if his own negligence has contributed to his injury "in any degree, however slight." On the face of it this means that any insignificant contribution, such as the addition of a lighted match to a forest fire, would bar the action. In all probability this is nothing more than a confusion of words, which fails to distinguish slight negligence from slight contribution; and what is really meant is that the plaintiff's negligence can be a defense, no matter how slight his departure from ordinary standards of conduct.[45] The intent, in other words, is to reject any idea of comparative negligence. If so, it is a mistake peculiarly likely to mislead the jury when an instruction is given in such terms. Most courts, when the distinction has been pointed out to them, have held that the rules as to causation [46] are the same for contributory negligence as for negligence,[47] and that the plaintiff is not barred unless his negligence, of whatever degree, has been a substantial factor in causing his injury.[48]

Particular Risk

One respect in which there is general agreement that there is a difference between negligence and contributory negligence, is that the latter bars recovery only when the injury results from a hazard, or risk, which made the plaintiff's conduct negligent.[49] The "clean hands" theory of contributory negligence, which induced a few early courts to deny recovery to a plaintiff whose conduct was unlawful in any way whatever, as in the case of one driving quite carefully in violation of a Sunday law,[50] was soon found to be neither just nor workable. It has long since been discarded, even in the case of criminal acts; [51] and there is now no doubt, for example, that one who goes upon land for the purpose of engaging in fornication [52] or gaming [53] is not an outlaw, and is not for that reason barred from recovery when he is injured on the premises; nor is an alien unlawfully in the United States, when he is run down by a car.[54] From this it has been an

---

The Arizona constitution requires that the issue of contributory negligence always be left to the jury. See Heimke v. Munoz, Ariz.1970, 470 P.2d 107.

44. Crane v. Neal, 1957, 389 Pa. 329, 132 A.2d 675; Ferris v. Patch, 1956, 119 Vt. 274, 126 A.2d 114; Aitchison v. Reter, 1954, 245 Iowa 1005, 64 N.W.2d 923; Silva v. Waldie, 1938, 42 N.M. 514, 82 P.2d 282; Keck v. Pozorski, 1963, 135 Ind.App. 192, 191 N.E.2d 325.

45. Made clear in Bahm v. Pittsburgh & Lake Erie R. Co., 1966, 6 Ohio St.2d 192, 217 N.E.2d 217; Daigle v. Twin City Ready Mix Concrete Co., 1964, 268 Minn. 136, 128 N.W.2d 148; Bazydlo v. Placid Marcy Co., 2 Cir. 1970, 422 F.2d 842; Juaire v. Narden, 2 Cir. 1968, 395 F.2d 373, cert. denied 393 U.S. 938, 380n.

46. See supra, § 41.

47. Second Restatement of Torts, § 465. See Malone, Ruminations on Dixie Drive It Yourself v. American Beverage Co., 1970, 30 La.L.Rev. 363.

48. Mack v. Precast Industries, Inc., 1963, 369 Mich. 439, 120 N.W.2d 225; Bahm v. Pittsburgh & Lake-

Erie R. Co., 1966, 6 Ohio St.2d 192, 217 N.E.2d 217; Huey v. Milligan, 1961, 242 Ind. 93, 175 N.E.2d 698; Busch v. Lilly, 1960, 257 Minn. 343, 101 N.W.2d 199; McManus v. Getter Trucking Co., Wyo.1963, 384 P.2d 974.

49. As to negligence, see supra, p. 253.

50. Bosworth v. Inhabitants of Swansey, 1845, 10 Metc., Mass., 363; Johnson v. Irasburgh, 1874, 47 Vt. 28; Hinckley v. Penobscot, 1856, 42 Me. 89. See Davis, The Plaintiff's Illegal Act as a Defense in Actions of Tort, 1905, 18 Harv.L.Rev. 505; Thayer, Public Wrong and Private Action, 1914, 27 Harv.L.Rev. 317, 338.

51. See supra, p. 143.

52. Rapee v. Beacon Hotel Corp., 1944, 293 N.Y. 196, 56 N.E.2d 548; Cramer v. Tarr, D.Me.1958, 165 F. Supp. 130; Holcomb v. Meeds, 1952, 173 Kan. 321, 246 P.2d 239; Meador v. Hotel Grover, 1942, 193 Miss. 392, 9 So.2d 782. See Notes, 1945, 31 Corn.L. Q. 89; 1938, 4 U.Pitt.L.Rev. 223.

53. Manning v. Noa, 1956, 345 Mich. 130, 76 N.W.2d 75; Shiroma v. Itano, 1956, 10 Ill.App.2d 428, 135 N.E.2d 123. Cf. Bagre v. Daggett Chocolate Co., 1940, 126 Conn. 659, 13 A.2d 757 (bingo game prize); Johnson v. Thompson, 1965, 111 Ga.App. 654, 143 S. E.2d 51 (same).

54. Janusis v. Long, 1933, 284 Mass. 403, 188 N.E. 228; Mulhall v. Fallon, 1900, 176 Mass. 266, 57 N.E.

easy step, for courts unhappy with the defense, to the conclusion that the plaintiff is not barred when his failure to exercise reasonable care for his own safety exposes him to a foreseeable risk of injury through one event, and he is in fact injured through another which he could not foresee.[55]

In a leading Connecticut case [56] in which a workman violated instructions not to work on the unguarded end of a slippery platform, and was injured by the fall of a brick wall, it was held that he might recover, since his negligence did not extend to such a risk. Upon the same basis, it has been held that a passenger riding upon the platform of a street car is not negligent with respect to a collision,[57] nor is an automobile driver who parks near a fire hydrant negligent as to any vehicle which may drive into him, except a fire engine,[58] nor is one who drives at excessive speed negligent as to a tree which falls on him.[59] In one or two instances this

has been carried to extreme and hair-splitting lengths, as by holding that negligence as to being hit by an eastbound train does not bar recovery when it is a westbound train on a second track,[60] or that the risk of falling is not the risk of falling upon a hook.[61]

Such cases frequently say that the plaintiff's negligence is not the "proximate cause" of his own damage.[62] It is, of course, quite possible that his conduct may not have been a substantial contributing factor at all, where the harm would have occurred even if he had exercised proper care.[63] But in the usual case the causal connection is clear and beyond dispute, and no problem of causation is involved.[64] What is meant is that the plaintiff's conduct has not exposed him to any foreseeable risk of the particular injury through the defendant's negligence, and therefore is not available as a defense.[65]

Distinguished from Avoidable Consequences

Closely allied to the doctrine of contributory negligence is the rule of "avoidable con-

---

386. As to unlicensed vehicles or drivers, see supra, p. 196.

55. Second Restatement of Torts, § 468. See Green, Contributory Negligence and Proximate Cause, 1927, 6 N.C.L.Rev. 3.

56. Smithwick v. Hall & Upson Co., 1890, 59 Conn. 261, 21 A. 924. Accord, Gray & Bell v. Scott, 1870, 66 Pa. 345.

57. Dewire v. Boston & Maine R. Co., 1889, 148 Mass. 343, 19 N.E. 523; Montambault v. Waterbury & Milldale Tramway Co., 1923, 98 Conn. 584, 120 A. 145; Webster v. Rome, W. & O. R. Co., 1889, 115 N.Y. 112, 21 N.E. 725; New York, L. E. & W. R. Co. v. Ball, 1891, 53 N.J.L. 283, 21 A. 1052. Cf. Cosgrove v. Shusterman, 1942, 129 Conn. 1, 26 A.2d 471 (riding on running board); Guile v. Greenberg, 1934, 192 Minn. 548, 257 N.W. 649 (on fender). But cf. Pennsylvania R. Co. v. Langdon, 1879, 92 Pa. 21, where the court considered that the risk of injury through collision was increased by riding in the baggage car.

58. Denson v. McDonald Bros., 1919, 144 Minn. 252, 175 N.W. 108.

59. Nesta v. Meyer, 1968, 100 N.J.Super. 434, 242 A. 2d 386; Berry v. Sugar Notch Borough, 1899, 191 Pa. 345, 43 A. 240. Cf. Hyde v. Avalon Air Transport, Inc., 1966, 243 Cal.App.2d 88, 52 Cal.Rptr. 309 (spear fishing in city limits, struck by airplane); Graft v. Crooker, D.Mont.1967, 263 F.Supp. 941

(plane taking off in bad weather, obstruction at end of field).

60. Kinderavich v. Palmer, 1940, 127 Conn. 85, 15 A. 2d 83. Cf. Brazel v. McMurray, 1961, 404 Pa. 188, 171 A.2d 151 (plaintiff struck by one car, left helpless in the highway, run over by a second); Sherman v. Millard, 1932, 144 Misc. 748, 259 N.Y.S. 415, reversed on other grounds Sherman v. Leicht, 1933, 238 App.Div. 271, 264 N.Y.S. 492 (similar).

61. Furukawa v. Yoshio Ogawa, 9 Cir. 1956, 236 F.2d 272. The case is criticized, and the difficulties of defining the "particular hazard" pointed out, in Note, [1958] Wash.U.L.Q. 111.

62. See for example Garland v. Nelson, 1944, 219 Minn. 1, 17 N.W.2d 28. See Notes, 1938, 22 Minn. L.Rev. 410; 1953, 41 Ky.L.J. 317.

63. Boulfrois v. United Traction Co., 1904, 210 Pa. 263, 59 A. 1007; Hawthorne v. Gunn, 1932, 123 Cal.App. 452, 11 P.2d 411; Tennessee Cent. R. Co. v. Page, 1926, 153 Tenn. 84, 282 S.W. 376; Stobie v. Sullivan, 1919, 118 Me. 483, 105 A. 714; Travis v. Hay, Ky.1961, 352 S.W.2d 209.

64. Payne v. Chicago & Alton R. Co., 1895, 129 Mo. 405, 31 S.W. 885; Green, Contributory Negligence and Proximate Cause, 1927, 6 North Car.L.Rev. 3, 11; Note, 1938, 22 Minn.L.Rev. 410, 414.

65. Compare the "intervening cause" cases, as to the negligence of the defendant. See supra, § 44.

sequences," which denies recovery for any damages which could have been avoided by reasonable conduct on the part of the plaintiff. Both rest upon the same fundamental policy of making recovery depend upon the plaintiff's proper care for the protection of his own interests, and both require of him only the standard of the reasonable man under the circumstances.[66] The statement commonly made as to the distinction between the two is that contributory negligence is negligence of the plaintiff before any damage, or any invasion of his rights, has occurred, which bars all recovery. The rule of avoidable consequences comes into play after a legal wrong has occurred, but while some damages may still be averted, and bars recovery only for such damages.[67] Thus, if the plaintiff is injured in an automobile collision, his contributorily negligent driving before the collision will prevent any recovery at all, but his failure to obtain proper medical care for his broken leg will bar only his damages for the subsequent aggravated condition of the leg.[68]

It may be suggested that the underlying basis for the distinction is merely the practical feasibility of assigning a part of the damages to the defendant's negligence alone in the latter case. Here as elsewhere [69] the courts have been willing to apportion damages to separate causes when a logical basis

may be found. In the "avoidable consequence" cases, the initial damage can not logically be charged to the plaintiff's own negligence as a cause, while the later damages may be. If no such division can be made, the plaintiff's negligence will bar all recovery, notwithstanding that it is subsequent in point of time to that of the defendant.[70]

In a limited number of situations, the plaintiff's unreasonable conduct, although it is prior or contemporaneous, may be found to have caused only a separable part of the damage. In such a case, even though it is called contributory negligence, the apportionment will be made. This is true, for example, where plaintiff, and defendant both pollute the same stream,[71] or flood the plaintiff's property,[72] or cause other damage similar in kind but capable of logical division. A more difficult problem is presented when the plaintiff's prior conduct is found to have played no part in bringing about an impact or accident, but to have aggravated the ensuing damages. In such a case,[73] upon a

66. See McCormick, Damages, 1935, §§ 33, 35; American Ry. Express Co. v. Judd, 1925, 213 Ala. 242, 104 So. 418; James B. Berry's Sons Co. v. Presnall, 1931, 183 Ark. 125, 35 S.W.2d 83; Stewart Dry Goods Co. v. Boone, 1918, 180 Ky. 199, 202 S.W. 489.

67. See McCormick, Damages, 1935, § 33; Dippold v. Cathlamet Timber Co., 1924, 111 Or. 199, 225 P. 202; Armfield v. Nash, 1856, 31 Miss. 361; Bailey v. J. L. Roebuck Co., 1929, 135 Okl. 216, 275 P. 329.

68. Wingrove v. Home Land Co., 1938, 120 W.Va. 100, 196 S.E. 563; City of Duncan v. Nicholson, 1926, 118 Okl. 275, 247 P. 979; Hendler Creamery Co. v. Miller, 1927, 153 Md. 264, 138 A. 1; Potts v. Guthrie, 1925, 282 Pa. 200, 127 A. 605. Cf. Socony Vacuum Oil Co. v. Marvin, 1946, 313 Mich. 528, 21 N.W.2d 841 (preventing fire after accident).

69. See supra, § 52.

70. See the interesting case of continuing negligence of both plaintiff and defendant, with progressive damage to the plaintiff's cattle, in Atchison, T. & S. F. R. Co. v. Merchants' Live Stock Co., 8 Cir. 1923, 293 F. 987, where recovery was denied "because it is impossible to determine the amount of damage respectively caused by the negligence of each."
It has been held that a plaintiff seeking apportionment of damages caused by his contributory negligence and damages that would have occurred anyway has the burden of proof on the issue. Dziedzic v. St. John's Cleaners & Shirt Launderers, Inc., 1968, 99 N.J.Super. 565, 240 A.2d 697, reversed on other grounds, 53 N.J. 157, 249 A.2d 382.

71. Randolf v. Town of Bloomfield, 1889, 77 Iowa 50, 41 N.W. 562; Bowman v. Humphrey, 1906, 132 Iowa 234, 109 N.W. 714. Cf. Walters v. Prairie Oil & Gas Co., 1922, 85 Okl. 77, 204 P. 906.

72. Philadelphia & R. R. Co. v. Smith, 3 Cir. 1894, 64 F. 679; Thomas v. Kenyon, 1861, 1 Daly, N.Y., 132; Gould v. McKenna, 1878, 86 Pa. 297.

73. Mahoney v. Beatman, 1929, 110 Conn. 184, 147 A. 762. Accord: Guile v. Greenberg, 1934, 192 Minn. 548, 257 N.W. 649; Hamilton v. Boyd, 1934, 218 Iowa 885, 256 N.W. 290. See Green, Mahoney v. Beatman: A Study in Proximate Cause, 1930, 39

finding that the plaintiff's excessive speed in driving was not responsible for a collision, but greatly increased the damages resulting from it, the Connecticut court refused to make any division, and held that the plaintiff could recover the entire amount. On the other hand the courts of Iowa [74] and Kansas,[75] in analogous situations, have apportioned the damages, holding that the plaintiff's recovery will be reduced to the extent that they have been aggravated by his own antecedent negligence. This would seem to be the better view, unless we are to place an entirely artificial emphasis upon the moment of impact, and the pure mechanics of causation. Cases will be infrequent, however, in which the extent of aggravation can be determined with any reasonable degree of certainty, and the court may properly refuse to divide the damages upon the basis of mere speculation.[76]

Yale L.J. 532, reprinted in Green, Judge and Jury, 1930, ch. 7; Gregory, Justice Maltbie's Dissent in Mahoney v. Beatman, 1950, 24 Conn.Bar J. 78.

74. Wright v. Illinois & Miss. Tel. Co., 1866, 20 Iowa 195. Plaintiff's damages from a runaway enhanced by his negligent failure to have more than one helper.

75. O'Keefe v. Kansas City Western R. Co., 1912, 87 Kan. 322, 124 P. 416 (plaintiff's injuries from a fall increased by his prior intoxication, which did not contribute to the fall). See Note, 1938, 22 Minn.L. Rev. 410; also the dictum in Smithwick v. Hall & Upson Co., 1890, 59 Conn. 261, 21 A. 924: "An act or omission that merely increases or adds to the extent of the loss or injury will not have that effect [to bar the action], though of course it may affect the amount of damages recovered in a given case." Also Gould v. McKenna, 1878, 86 Pa. 297, one possible interpretation of which is in accord, and the dissenting opinion of Maltbie, J., in Mahoney v. Beatman, supra, note 73.

This has been applied where plaintiff's failure to use a seat belt has not caused the collision, but has contributed to the damages from it. Barry v. Coca Cola Co., 1968, 99 N.J.Super. 270, 239 A.2d 273; see Sonnier v. Ramsey, Tex.Civ.App.1968, 424 S.W.2d 684, refused n. r. e.; Lawrence v. Westchester Fire Ins. Co., La.App.1968, 213 So.2d 784, application denied 252 La. 969, 215 So.2d 131; Walker and Beck, Seat Belts and the Second Accident, 1967, 34 Ins. Couns.J. 352.

76. Thane v. Scranton Traction Co., 1899, 191 Pa. 249, 43 A. 136 (increased damage because of plain-

It is suggested, therefore, that the doctrines of contributory negligence and avoidable consequences are in reality the same, and that the distinction which exists is rather one between damages which are capable of assignment to separate causes, and damages which are not.

Negligence Toward Known Danger

Contributory negligence may consist not only in a failure to discover or appreciate a risk which would be apparent to a reasonable man, or an inadvertent mistake in dealing with it, but also in an intentional exposure to a danger of which the plaintiff is aware.[77] Thus it may be negligence, even as a matter of law, to continue to ride with a drunken automobile driver at high speed, after there is an opportunity to leave the car,[78] or to walk through a dark passage with which the plaintiff is unfamiliar without taking appropriate precautions.[79] In such cases the plaintiff's conduct may be such as to indicate his consent or willingness to encounter the danger and relieve the defendant of responsibility, and hence the controversial defense of assumption of risk may also be available as a defense, overlapping contributory negligence.[80] So far as contributory negligence

tiff's position on car too speculative); Schomaker v. Havey, 1927, 291 Pa. 30, 139 A. 495 (same).

77. Second Restatement of Torts, § 466; Cleveland-Cliffs Iron Co. v. Metzner, 6 Cir. 1945, 150 F.2d 206; Chisenall v. Thompson, 1952, 363 Mo. 538, 252 S.W.2d 335; Dezelan v. Duquesne Light Co., 1939, 334 Pa. 246, 5 A.2d 552; Wayson v. Rainier Taxi Co., 1925, 136 Wash. 274, 239 P. 559; Pennsylvania R. Co. v. Townsend, 1936, 130 Ohio St. 554, 200 N.E. 772.

Otherwise when it is not voluntary. Cole v. United States, N.D.Ga.1965, 249 F.Supp. 7 (convict laborer).

78. See for example Hutchinson v. Mitchell, 1957, 143 W.Va. 280, 101 S.E.2d 73.

79. Wolfe v. Green Mears Const. Co., 1955, 134 Cal. App.2d 654, 286 P.2d 433; Bridges v. Hillman, 1957, 249 Minn. 451, 82 N.W.2d 615; Brant v. Van Zandt, Fla.1955, 77 So.2d 858; cf. Fogle v. Shaffer, 1958, 167 Ohio St. 353, 148 N.E.2d 687; Lundy v. City of Ames, 1926, 202 Iowa 100, 209 N.W. 427.

80. See infra, § 68.

itself is concerned, however, the reasonableness of the plaintiff's conduct is to be determined by balancing the risk against the value which the law attaches to the advantages which he is seeking.

In particular, the plaintiff may not be required to surrender a valuable right or privilege merely because the defendant's conduct threatens him with what would otherwise be an unreasonable risk. Because the defendant builds a powder mill [81] or runs a railroad [82] near his property, he need not abandon it, or take special precautions against fire. He is not to be deprived of the free, ordinary and proper use of his land because his neighbor is negligent, and he may leave the responsibility to the defendant. At least this is true where the danger is still relatively slight, and the alternative means of protection expensive or burdensome. And due regard must be given to the importance of the plaintiff's interest in asserting the legal right itself. But on the other hand, there are situations where insistence upon a right, such as the use of a highway,[83] or the right of way,[84] or the boarding of an overcrowded street car,[85] may clearly involve a risk out of all proportion to its value, and the plaintiff may then be negligent.

Scope of the Defense

Within the limits above indicated, and in the absence of modifying legislation,[86] the contributory negligence of the plaintiff is a complete bar to his action for any common law negligence of the defendant. Whether it is a bar to the liability of a defendant who has violated a statutory duty is a matter of the legislative purpose which the court finds in the statute. If it is found to be intended merely to establish a standard of ordinary care for the protection of the plaintiff against a risk, his contributory negligence with respect to that risk will bar his action, as in the case of common law negligence.[87] But there are certain unusual types of statutes, such as child labor acts,[88] those prohibiting the sale of dangerous articles such as firearms to minors,[89] the Federal Safety Appliance and

take precautions against defendant's threat of fire: Pribonic v. Fulton, 1922, 178 Wis. 393, 190 N.W. 190; Nashville, C. & St. L. R. Co. v. Nants, 1933, 167 Tenn. 1, 65 S.W.2d 189; Morgan & Bros. v. Missouri, K. & T. R. Co. of Texas, 1917, 108 Tex. 331, 193 S.W. 134.

86. See infra, § 67.

87. Dart v. Pure Oil Co., 1947, 223 Minn. 526, 27 N. W.2d 555; Wertz v. Lincoln Liberty Life Ins. Co., 1950, 152 Neb. 451, 41 N.W.2d 740; Payne v. Vance, 1921, 103 Ohio St. 59, 133 N.E. 85; Richardson v. Fountain, Fla.App.1963, 154 So.2d 709; Browne v. Siegel, Cooper & Co., 1901, 191 Ill. 226, 60 N.E. 815.

88. Karpeles v. Heine, 1919, 227 N.Y. 74, 124 N.E. 101; Pinoza v. Northern Chair Co., 1913, 152 Wis. 473, 140 N.W. 84; Dusha v. Virginia & Rainy Lake Co., 1920, 145 Minn. 171, 176 N.W. 482; Terry Dairy Co. v. Nalley, 1920, 146 Ark. 448, 225 S.W. 887; Boyles v. Hamilton, 1965, 235 Cal.App.2d 492, 45 Cal.Rptr. 399.

89. Tamiami Gun Shop v. Klein, Fla.1959, 116 So.2d 421; McMillen v. Steele, 1923, 275 Pa. 584, 119 A. 721. Compare, as to protection of intoxicated persons: Hauth v. Sambo, 1916, 100 Neb. 160, 158 N. W. 1036; Soronen v. Olde Milford Inn, 1964, 84 N. J.Super. 372, 202 A.2d 208; Schelin v. Goldberg, 1958, 188 Pa.Super. 341, 146 A.2d 648. Also Van Gaasbeck v. Webatuck Cent. School Dist. No. 1, 1968, 21 N.Y.2d 239, 287 N.Y.S.2d 77, 234 N.E.2d 243 (instructing children on school bus how to cross

81. Judson v. Giant Powder Co., 1895, 107 Cal. 549, 40 P. 1020. Cf. North Bend Lumber Co. v. City of Seattle, 1921, 116 Wash. 500, 199 P. 988 (dam); Spencer v. Gedney, 1927, 45 Idaho 64, 260 P. 699 (fire).

82. Leroy Fibre Co. v. Chicago, M. & St. P. R. Co., 1914, 232 U.S. 340; Louisville & N. R. Co. v. Malone, 1897, 116 Ala. 600, 22 So. 897; Martin v. Western Union R. Co., 1868, 23 Wis. 437; Donovan v. Hannibal & St. J. R. Co., 1886, 89 Mo. 147, 1 S. W. 232; Kellogg v. Chicago & N. W. R. Co., 1870, 26 Wis. 223.

83. Wright v. City of St. Cloud, 1893, 54 Minn. 94, 55 N.W. 819; Harris v. Clinton, 1887, 64 Mich. 447, 31 N.W. 425. Cf. Clayards v. Dethick, 1848, 12 Q.B. 439; Holle v. Lake, 1965, 194 Kan. 200, 398 P.2d 300; Provenzo v. Sam, 1967, 27 App.Div.2d 442, 280 N.Y.S.2d 308, reversed on other grounds, 1968, 23 N. Y.2d 256, 296 N.Y.S.2d 322, 244 N.E.2d 26.

84. Rosenau v. Peterson, 1920, 147 Minn. 95, 179 N. W. 647.

85. Harding v. Philadelphia Rapid Transit Co., 1907, 217 Pa. 69, 66 A. 151. Compare, as to failure to

Boiler Inspection Acts,[90] factory acts for the protection of workmen,[91] or railway fencing[92] or fire[93] statutes which have been construed as intended to place the entire responsibility upon the defendant, and to protect the particular class of plaintiffs against their own negligence. In such a case, as in the case of the statutes involving the age of consent,[94] the object of the statute itself would be defeated if the plaintiff's fault were a defense, and the courts refuse to recognize it.

The ordinary contributory negligence of the plaintiff is to be set over against the ordinary negligence of the defendant, to bar the action. But where the defendant's conduct is actually intended to inflict harm upon the plaintiff, there is a difference, not merely in degree but in the kind of fault; and the defense never has been extended to such intentional torts. Thus it is no defense to assault and battery.[95] The same is true of that

aggravated form of negligence, approaching intent, which has been characterized variously as "wilful," "wanton," or "reckless,"[96] as to which all courts have held that ordinary negligence on the part of the plaintiff will not bar recovery.[97] Such conduct differs from negligence not only in degree but in kind, and in the social condemnation attached to it. Many courts have said that in such cases the defendant's conduct is not the "proximate cause" of the harm; but this is clearly unsound, for the causal connection is the same as in any ordinary contributory negligence case. It is in reality a rule of comparative fault which is being applied, and the court is refusing to set up the lesser fault against the greater. Thus if the defendant's negligence is merely "gross," an extreme departure from ordinary standards, but still without elements of "wilfulness" or "wantonness," it is generally held that the plaintiff's ordinary negligence is a defense.[98] And if the plaintiff's own conduct is "wilful," "wanton," or "reckless," it will be balanced against similar conduct on the part of the defendant, and recognized as a bar to his action.[99]

street); McCallie v. New York Cent. R. Co., 1969, 23 Ohio App.2d 152, 261 N.E.2d 179 (warning sign at grade crossing).

90. Bass v. Seaboard Airline R. Co., 1949, 205 Ga. 458, 53 S.E.2d 895; Gowins v. Pennsylvania R. Co., 6 Cir. 1962, 299 F.2d 431, cert. denied, 371 U.S. 824.

91. Osborne v. Salvation Army, 2 Cir. 1939, 107 F.2d 929; Koenig v. Patrick Const. Corp., 1948, 298 N.Y. 313, 83 N.E.2d 133; Carterville Coal Co. v. Abbott, 1899, 181 Ill. 495, 55 N.E. 131; Caspar v. Lewin, 1910, 82 Kan. 604, 109 P. 657; Alber v. Owens, 1967, 66 Cal.2d 790, 59 Cal.Rptr. 117, 427 P.2d 781.

92. Flint & Pere Marquette R. Co. v. Lull, 1874, 28 Mich. 510; Congdon v. Central Vermont R. Co., 1883, 56 Vt. 390; Welty v. Indianapolis & V. R. Co., 1885, 105 Ind. 55, 4 N.E. 410; Atchison, T. & S. F. R. Co. v. Paxton, 1907, 75 Kan. 197, 88 P. 1082.

93. Matthews v. Missouri Pac. R. Co., 1897, 142 Mo. 645, 44 S.W. 802; Peter v. Chicago & N. W. R. Co., 1899, 121 Mich. 324, 80 N.W. 295; Bowen v. Boston & A. R. Co., 1901, 179 Mass. 524, 61 N.E. 141.

94. See supra, p. 107.

95. Jenkins v. North Carolina Dept. of Motor Vehicles, 1956, 244 N.C. 560, 94 S.E.2d 577; Steinmetz v. Kelly, 1880, 72 Ind. 442; Birmingham Ry., Light & Power Co. v. Jones, 1906, 146 Ala. 277, 41 So. 146; Brendle v. Spencer, 1899, 125 N.C. 474, 34 S.E. 634; cf. City of Garland v. White, Tex.Civ.App.1963, 368 S.W.2d 12, refused n. r. e. (killing dog); Hawks v.

Slusher, 1912, 55 Or. 1, 104 P. 883 (frightening horse). But if the plaintiff voluntarily places himself in the way of attack, his conduct may amount to consent and bar recovery. See Moore v. Atchison, T. & S. F. R. Co., 1910, 26 Okl. 682, 695, 110 P. 1059, 1064.

Also, the rule as to avoidable consequences may apply to intentional torts, once some damage has been committed. Power Mfg. Co. v. Lindley, Tex.Civ. App.1927, 296 S.W. 653 (wrongful attachment).

96. See supra, p. 185.

97. Kellerman v. J. S. Durig Co., 1964, 176 Ohio St. 320, 199 N.E.2d 562; Tabor v. O'Grady, 1960, 61 N.J.Super. 446, 161 A.2d 267; Kasanovich v. George, 1943, 348 Pa. 199, 34 A.2d 523; Newman v. Piazza, 1967, 6 Ariz.App. 396, 433 P.2d 47; Liebhart v. Calahan, 1967, 72 Wash.2d 620, 434 P.2d 605.

98. Banks v. Braman, 1905, 188 Mass. 367, 74 N.E. 594; Taylor v. Volfi, 1927, 86 Cal.App. 244, 260 P. 927.

99. Zank v. Chicago, R. I. & P. R. Co., 1959, 17 Ill.2d 473, 161 N.E.2d 848, on remand 1960, 26 Ill.App.2d 389, 168 N.E.2d 472; Ardis v. Griffin, 1962, 239 S.C. 529, 123 S.E.2d 876; Tabor v. O'Grady, 1960, 61 N.

In cases involving strict liability, not based upon wrongful intent or negligence, certain types of contributory negligence may also serve as a defense. The problem is more appropriately considered in connection with the basis of the defendant's liability.[1]

66. LAST CLEAR CHANCE

The most commonly accepted modification of the strict rule of contributory negligence is the doctrine of the last clear chance. This doctrine, as to the basis or extent of which there has been little agreement and endless discussion,[2] had its origin in 1842 in the English case of Davies v. Mann,[3] in which the plaintiff left his ass fettered in the highway, and the defendant drove into it. It was held that the plaintiff might recover, notwithstanding any negligence of his own, if the defendant might, by proper care, have avoided injuring the animal.

No very satisfactory reason for the rule ever has been suggested. The first explanation given,[4] and the one which still is most often stated,[5] is that if the defendant has the last clear opportunity to avoid the harm, the plaintiff's negligence is not a "proximate cause" of the result. While this coincides rather well with the attempt made in an older day to fix liability upon the "last human wrongdoer,"[6] it is quite out of line with modern ideas of proximate cause.[7] In such a case the negligence of the plaintiff undoubtedly has been a cause, and a substantial and important one, of his own damage, and it cannot be said that injury through the defendant's negligence was not fully within the risk which the plaintiff has created. If the injury should be to a third person, such as a passenger in the defendant's vehicle, the plaintiff's negligence would clearly be recognized as a responsible cause,[8] and it is an

---

J.Super. 446, 161 A.2d 267; Kniffen v. Hercules Powder Co., 1948, 164 Kan. 196, 188 P.2d 980; Elliott v. Philadelphia Transp. Co., 1947, 356 Pa. 643, 53 A.2d 81.

1. See infra, p. 522.

2. Schofield, Davies v. Mann: Theory of Contributory Negligence, 1890, 3 Harv.L.Rev. 263; Bohlen, Contributory Negligence, 1908, 21 Harv.L.Rev. 233; Smith, Last Clear Chance, 1916, 82 Cent.L.J. 425, 55 Am.L.Rev. 897; Lowndes, Contributory Negligence, 1934, 22 Geo.L.J. 674; James, Last Clear Chance: A Transitional Doctrine, 1938, 47 Yale L.J. 704; MacIntyre, The Rationale of Last Clear Chance, 1940, 53 Harv.L.Rev. 1225.

See also, as to the law of particular jurisdictions: DeMuth, Derogation of the Common Law Rule of Contributory Negligence, 1935, 7 Rocky Mt.L.Rev. 161; Slife, The Iowa Doctrine of Last Clear Chance, 1949, 34 Iowa L.Rev. 480; Donley, Observations on the Last Clear Chance in West Virginia, 1931, 37 W.Va.L.Q. 362; Donley, Last Clear Chance—Some Further Observations, 1942, 49 W. Va.L.Q. 51; Rozas, The Last Clear Chance Doctrine in Louisiana, 1967, 27 La.L.Rev. 269; Van Dyck, Last Clear Chance in Virginia, 1954, 40 Va. L.Rev. 637; Notes, 1954, 40 Va.L.Rev. 666; 1958, 36 N.C.L.Rev. 545.

3. 1842, 10 M. & W. 546, 152 Eng.Rep. 588. Hence the nickname of the "jackass doctrine," with whatever implications it may carry.

4. Dowell v. General Steam Nav. Co., 1855, 5 El. & Bl. 195, 119 Eng.Rep. 454; Tuff v. Warman, 1857, 2 C.B.,N.S., 740, 140 Eng.Rep. 607, 5 C.B.,N.S., 573, 141 Eng.Rep. 231.

5. Dunn Bus Service v. McKinley, 1937, 130 Fla. 778, 178 So. 865; Girdner v. Union Oil Co., 1932, 216 Cal. 197, 13 P.2d 915; Wall v. King, 1932, 280 Mass. 577, 182 N.E. 855; Nehring v. Connecticut Co., 1912, 86 Conn. 109, 84 A. 301; Bragg v. Central New England R. Co., 1920, 228 N.Y. 54, 126 N.E. 253.

6. Bohlen, Contributory Negligence, 1908, 21 Harv.L. Rev. 233. See supra, p. 247.

7. Green, Contributory Negligence and Proximate Cause, 1927, 6 North Car.L.Rev. 3, 21. The proximate cause explanation is reduced to a complete absurdity in Hinkle v. Minneapolis, A. & C. R. R. Co., 1925, 162 Minn. 112, 202 N.W. 340, where it is said that "wilful and wanton" negligence (discovered peril) on the part of the defendant alone will be the proximate cause of the injury, but that where there is such negligence on the part of both, *neither* is the proximate cause.

It is of course possible that the plaintiff's negligence may have played such an insignificant part that it is not to be regarded as a substantial factor in causing the result. This is the theory relied on in Jaggers v. Southeastern Greyhound Lines, D.Tenn. 1940, 34 F.Supp. 667, and Kinderavich v. Palmer, 1940, 127 Conn. 85, 15 A.2d 83, 89, although the facts of the cases do not appear to justify it.

8. Lincoln City Lines, Inc. v. Schmidt, 8 Cir. 1957, 245 F.2d 600; Petition of Kinsman Transit Co., 2

utterly artificial distinction which applies any other rule when the plaintiff himself is injured.

Other courts have said that the later negligence of the defendant involves a higher degree of fault, and that it is a rule of comparative negligence which is being applied.[9] This may be true in many cases where the defendant has discovered the plaintiff's helpless situation, or his conduct approaches reckless or intentional disregard of the danger; but it can scarcely explain many others in which the defendant's fault consists merely in a failure to discover the danger at all,[10] or in slowness, clumsiness, inadvertence or an error in judgment in dealing with it.[11]

The real explanation would seem to be a dislike for the defense of contributory negligence which has made the courts rebel at its application in many situations,[12] and ac-

cept without reasoning the conclusion that the last wrongdoer is necessarily the worst wrongdoer, or at least the decisive one, and should pay. The doctrine has been called a transitional one, a way station on the road to apportionment of damages;[13] but its effect has been to freeze the transition rather than to speed it. As an ultimate just solution, it is obviously inadequate, since, except in a few cases where a part of the plaintiff's damages have occurred before the "last clear chance,"[14] it merely transfers from the plaintiff to the defendant an entire loss due to the fault of both.

The application of the doctrine has been attended with much confusion. Virtually every possible rule has been adopted, often in a single jurisdiction,[15] including a repudiation of the last clear chance rule by name[16] on the part of courts which nevertheless proceed to apply it under the guise of "wantonness" or "proximate cause."[17] It is quite

---

Cir. 1964, 338 F.2d 708, cert. denied 1965, 380 U.S. 944; Evans v. Phoenix Ins. Co., La.App.1965, 175 So.2d 425; Atlantic Coast Line R. Co. v. Coxwell, 1955, 93 Ga.App. 159, 91 S.E.2d 135; Fontaine v. Charas, 1935, 87 N.H. 424, 181 A. 417.

It has been held, however, that the defendant who has the last clear chance may be required to indemnify the other defendant. Nashua Iron & Steel Co. v. Worcester & N. R. Co., 1882, 62 N.H. 159; Colorado & Southern R. Co. v. Western Light & Power Co., 1923, 73 Colo. 107, 214 P. 30; see Knippenberg v. Lord & Taylor, 1920, 193 App.Div. 753, 184 N.Y.S. 785; Leflar, Contribution and Indemnity Between Tortfeasors, 1932, 81 U.Pa.L.Rev. 130, 152. There are dicta to the contrary in Shield v. F. Johnson & Son Co., 1913, 132 La. 773, 61 So. 787; Pacific Tel. & Tel. Co. v. Parmenter, 9 Cir. 1909, 170 F. 140; Bradley v. Becker, 1928, 321 Mo. 405, 11 S.W.2d 8.

9.   Wilson v. Southern Traction Co., 1921, 111 Tex. 361, 234 S.W. 663; Rawitzer v. St. Paul City R. Co., 1904, 93 Minn. 84, 100 N.W. 664; Moreno v. Los Angeles Transfer Co., 1920, 44 Cal.App. 551, 186 P. 800; Dildine v. Flynn, 1924, 116 Kan. 563, 227 P. 340; Notes, 1924, 8 Minn.L.Rev. 329; 1939, 24 Minn.L.Rev. 81. See infra, § 67. Cf. Walldren Express & Van Co. v. Krug, 1920, 291 Ill. 472, 126 N.E. 97.

10.   See infra, p. 430.

11.   See infra, p. 430.

12.   "It may be that neither explanation is strictly logical, and that the real foundation for the rule is merely its fundamental justice and reasonableness.

The justice of the rule * * * may be a sufficient foundation for it." Cavanaugh v. Boston & Me. R. R., 1911, 76 N.H. 68, 79 A. 694.

13.   James, Last Clear Chance: A Transitional Doctrine, 1938, 47 Yale L.J. 704; MacIntyre, The Rationale of Last Clear Chance, 1940, 53 Harv.L.Rev. 1225.

14.   In such cases the courts have been willing to regard the damages as divisible and apportion them. Cleveland, C., C. & St. L. Ry. Co. v. Klee, 1900, 154 Ind. 430, 56 N.E. 234; Weitzman v. Nassau Electric R. Co., 1898, 33 App.Div. 585, 53 N.Y.S. 905; Teakle v. San Pedro, L. A. & S. L. R. Co., 1907, 32 Utah 276, 90 P. 402.

15.   See De Muth, Derogation of the Common Law Rule of Contributory Negligence, 1935, 7 Rocky Mt. L.Rev. 161.

16.   Brennan v. Public Service R. Co., 1930, 106 N.J. L. 464, 148 A. 775; Carson, Pirie Scott & Co. v. Chicago Rys. Co., 1923, 309 Ill. 346, 141 N.E. 172; Switzer v. Detroit Inv. Co., 1925, 188 Wis. 330, 206 N.W. 407; Spillers v. Griffin, 1917, 109 S.C. 78, 95 S.E. 133.

17.   Walldren Express & Van Co. v. Krug, 1920, 291 Ill. 472, 126 N.E. 97; Clyde v. Southern Public Utilities Co., 1918, 109 S.C. 290, 96 N.E. 116; Bryant v. Northern Pac. R. Co., 1946, 221 Minn. 577, 23 N.W. 2d 174; Sutton v. Public Service I. T. Co., 2 Cir. 1946, 157 F.2d 947 (New Jersey law).

literally true that there are as many variant forms and applications of this doctrine as there are jurisdictions which apply it. A few courts, with something resembling billiard-parlor reverse English, have even purported to recognize a "last clear chance" doctrine in favor of the defendant, to bar the plaintiff's recovery; [18] but since this comes out at exactly the same place as the defense of contributory negligence without the doctrine at all, and is calculated only to bewilder the jury with incomprehensible instructions, most courts have rejected any such idea. [19] In such a general area of confusion and disagreement, only very general statements can be offered, and reference must of necessity be made to the law of each particular state. The situations which have arisen may be classified as follows: [20]

Plaintiff Helpless

Where the plaintiff's prior negligence has placed him in a position from which he is powerless to extricate himself by the exercise of any ordinary care, [21] and the defendant discovers his danger while there is still time to avoid it, and then fails to do so, all of the courts, including those which purport to reject the whole doctrine by name, have held

that the plaintiff can recover. [22] This "conscious last clear chance," sometimes distinguished as the "doctrine of discovered peril," occasionally has been explained on the basis that negligence after the danger is known to the defendant necessarily involves a greater degree of fault, and amounts to "wilful" or "wanton" misconduct, to which the ordinary negligence of the plaintiff is no defense. [23] Such an explanation does not meet a number of cases where the defendant's conduct consists of nothing more than confusion, inadvertence, or a mistake in judgment, [24] and the greater number of courts treat the issue as one of negligence only, and apply the rule of the last clear chance. [25]

There must be proof that the defendant discovered the situation, [26] that he then had

18. Umberger v. Koop, 1952, 194 Va. 123, 72 S.E.2d 370; Miami Beach R. Co. v. Doheme, 1938, 131 Fla. 171, 179 So. 166; Island Express v. Frederick, 1934, 5 W.W.Harr., Del., 569, 171 A. 181; Louisville & N. R. Co. v. Patterson, 1948, 77 Ga.App. 406, 49 S.E.2d 218. See Note, 1934, 14 Boston U.L.Rev. 850.

19. Rein v. Jarvis, 1955, 131 Colo. 377, 281 P.2d 1019; Rollman v. Morgan, 1952, 73 Ariz. 305, 240 P.2d 1196; Durant v. Stuckey, 1952, 221 S.C. 342, 70 S.E.2d 473; Barr v. Curry, 1952, 137 W.Va. 364, 71 S.E.2d 313; Rondinelli v. City of Pittsburgh, 1962, 407 Pa. 89, 180 A.2d 74.

20. Cases are classified in Bradford and Carlson, Last Clear Chance in Automobile Negligence Cases, 1962, 11 Defense L.J. 61.

21. Including cases where the plaintiff's only effective means of escape would not be expected of a reasonable man, as in Schaaf v. Coen, 1936, 131 Ohio St. 279, 2 N.E.2d 605; Bence v. Teddy's Taxi, 1931, 112 Cal.App. 636, 297 P. 128.

22. Southern R. Co. v. Williams, 1942, 243 Ala. 429, 10 So.2d 273; Barry v. Southern Pac. R. Co., 1946, 64 Ariz. 116, 166 P.2d 825; New York Cent. R. Co. v. Thompson, 1939, 215 Ind. 652, 21 N.E.2d 625; Collins v. Maine Cent. R. Co., 1939, 136 Me. 149, 4 A.2d 100; Sutton v. Public Service Interstate Transp., 2 Cir. 1946, 157 F.2d 947, cert. denied 330 U.S. 828 (New Jersey law).

23. Esrey v. Southern Pac. Co., 1894, 103 Cal. 541, 37 P. 500; Tempfer v. Joplin & P. R. Co., 1913, 89 Kan. 374, 131 P. 592; Labarge v. Pere Marquette R. Co., 1903, 134 Mich. 139, 95 N.W. 1073; cf. Bryant v. Northern Pac. R. Co., 1946, 221 Minn. 577, 23 N.W.2d 174.

24. As, for example, in Smith v. Connecticut Ry. & Lighting Co., 1907, 80 Conn. 268, 67 A. 888; Clark v. Wilmington & W. R. Co., 1891, 109 N.C. 430, 14 S.E. 43.

25. Bragg v. Central New England R. Co., 1920, 228 N.Y. 54, 126 N.E. 253; Chappell v. San Diego & A. R. Co., 1927, 201 Cal. 560, 258 P. 73; Hutchinson Purity Ice Cream Co. v. Des Moines City R. Co., 1915, 172 Iowa 527, 154 N.W. 890; Muskogee Electric Traction Co. v. Tanner, 1923, 93 Okl. 284, 220 P. 655; Louisville & N. R. Co. v. Harrod's Adm'r, 1913, 155 Ky. 155, 159 S.W. 685.

26. Srogi v. New York Cent. R. Co., 1936, 247 App. Div. 95, 286 N.Y.S. 215; Curt v. Zinan, 1940, 140 Pa.Super. 25, 12 A.2d 802; Erenkrantz v. Palmer, 1944, 69 R.I. 478, 35 A.2d 224.

It is enough that the defendant has discovered that someone is in peril. Bolus v. Martin L. Adams & Son, Ky.1969, 438 S.W.2d 79; Chadwick v. City of New York, 1950, 301 N.Y. 176, 93 N.E.2d 625. Or that he may be. Kumkumian v. City of New York, 1953, 305 N.Y. 167, 111 N.E.2d 865.

the time to take action which would have saved the plaintiff,[27] and that he failed to do something which a reasonable man would have done.[28] In the absence of any one of these elements, these courts deny recovery.

Where the plaintiff has become helpless, and the defendant does not discover his danger in time to avoid the injury, but is under a duty to discover it,[29] and with proper vigilance could do so in time to avoid the result, there is a division in the courts. In such an "unconscious last clear chance" situation, a substantial number of the courts still follow their original rule and deny recovery.[30] A considerable majority by now have swung over to the position that it is to be allowed.[31]

There is an astonishing lack of reasoning in the decisions to support either conclusion. Much emphasis is placed upon the time sequence of events, and the interval during which the defendant is still able to prevent the harm while the plaintiff is not, as if this in itself were a sufficient explanation not only for the absolution given the plaintiff, but for the requirement or nonrequirement of discovery of the situation. The usual reason given is merely that the defendant's later negligence is, or is not, the "proximate cause" of the injury, rather than that of the plaintiff.

Plaintiff Inattentive

In another group of cases, the plaintiff's situation is not one of helplessness and he is still in a position to escape, but his negligence consists of failure to pay attention to his surroundings and discover his own peril. If the defendant discovers his danger and his inattentiveness, and is then negligent, most courts hold, with an occasional contrary view,[32] that the plaintiff may recover.[33] It is sometimes said that the defendant has a "conscious" and the plaintiff an "unconscious" chance, although obviously neither is "last" nor "clear." There is much the same vague talk of "wanton" conduct and comparative fault, or of proximate cause; but here all of the usual explanations and excuses for the doctrine would appear to fall particularly flat. There is the same tendency to avoid any explanation at all, and to lay stress upon the time interval during which the defendant might have done something, as if

---

27. Louisville & N. R. Co. v. Griffin, 1940, 240 Ala. 213, 198 So. 345; Kurn v. McCoy, 1940, 187 Okl. 210, 102 P.2d 177; Doran v. City & County of San Francisco, 1955, 44 Cal.2d 477, 283 P.2d 1; Couture v. Lewis, 1963, 105 N.H. 224, 196 A.2d 60.

28. Stokes v. Johnstone, 1955, 47 Wash.2d 323, 287 P.2d 472; Johnson v. J. E. Morris' Adm'x, Ky.1955, 282 S.W.2d 835; Elliott v. New York Rapid Transit Co., 1944, 293 N.Y. 145, 56 N.E.2d 86; McClain v. Missouri Pac. R. Co., La.App.1941, 200 So. 57.

29. Without such a duty, the doctrine does not apply. Thus in the case of trespassers, to whom the defendant owes no duty of viligance to discover their presence, actual discovery may be necessary before the defendant can be found negligent at all. Southern R. Co. v. Drake, 1910, 166 Ala. 540, 51 So. 996; Dyrcz v. Missouri Pac. R. Co., 1911, 238 Mo. 33, 141 S.W. 861; Castile v. O'Keefe, 1916, 138 La. 479, 70 So. 481; Atchison, T. & S. F. R. Co. v. Howard, 1939, 186 Okl. 446, 98 P.2d 914.

30. Hayman v. Pennsylvania R. Co., 1945, 77 Ohio App. 135, 62 N.E.2d 724; Storr v. New York Cent. R. Co., 1933, 261 N.Y. 348, 185 N.E. 407; Kurn v. Casey, 1943, 193 Okl. 192, 141 P.2d 1001; New England Pretzel Co. v. Palmer, 1949, 75 R.I. 387, 67 A. 2d 39; Griffith Freight Lines v. Benson, 1937, 234 Ala. 613, 176 So. 370.

In many cases the court has made the broad statement that the defendant must actually discover the danger, but the plaintiff has not been helpless but merely inattentive. Thus in Iowa Cent. R. Co. v. Walker, 8 Cir. 1913, 203 F. 685; Woloszynowski v. New York Cent. R. Co., 1930, 254 N.Y. 206, 172 N.E. 471; Morser v. Southern Pac. Co., 1924, 110 Or. 9, 222 P. 736. As to this situation, see infra, p. 430.

31. Exum v. Boyles, 1968, 272 N.C. 567, 158 S.E.2d 845; French v. Mozzali, Ky.1968, 433 S.W.2d 122; Minton v. Southern Ry. Co., 6 Cir. 1966, 368 F.2d

719; Letcher v. Derricott, 1963, 191 Kan. 596, 383 P.2d 533; Spenser v. Fondry, 1960, 122 Vt. 149, 167 A.2d 372; Second Restatement of Torts, § 479.

32. Middletown Trust Co. v. Armour & Co., 1937, 122 Conn. 615, 191 A. 532; Butler v. Rockland T. & C. St. R. Co., 1904, 99 Me. 149, 58 A. 775; Hanson v. New Hampshire Pre-Mix Concrete, Inc., N.H.1970, 268 A.2d 841.

33. Burnham v. Yellow Checker Cab, Inc., 1964, 74 N.M. 125, 391 P.2d 413; Greear v. Noland Co., 1955, 197 Va. 233, 89 S.E.2d 49; McCormick v. Gilbertson, 1952, 41 Wash.2d 495, 250 P.2d 546; Leon v.

that were a reason in itself.[34] As to what it is necessary for the defendant to discover, there is further disagreement among courts adhering to the prevailing view. Some of them apparently hold that he must in fact realize the plaintiff's danger and his inattention;[35] the greater number apply a more objective standard, and require only that he discover the situation, and that the danger and lack of attention be apparent to a reasonable man.[36] But the discovery may be proved by circumstantial evidence,[37] and there is in the decisions so much hair-splitting as to whether "ought to have seen" is equivalent to "saw" that the result of any particular case is likely to be unpredictable in a given jurisdiction. There is the further necessary qualification that the defendant may often reasonably assume until the last moment that the plaintiff will look out for himself, and has no reason to act until he has some notice to the contrary.[38]

If the defendant does not discover the plaintiff's situation, but merely might do so by proper vigilance, it is obvious that neither party can be said to have a "last clear" chance. The plaintiff is still in a position to escape, and his lack of attention continues up to the point of the accident, without the interval of superior opportunity of the defendant,[39] which has been considered so important. The plaintiff may not reasonably demand of the defendant greater care for his own protection than that which he exercises himself. Accordingly, nearly all of the courts have held that there can be no recovery.[40] The great exception is Missouri,[41]

Penn Central Co., 7 Cir. 1970, 428 F.2d 528; Connolly v. Steakley, Fla.App.1964, 165 So.2d 784, cert. discharged Fla.1967, 197 So.2d 524.

34. In the absence of sufficient time to act, the doctrine does not apply. De Vore v. Faris, 1948, 88 Cal.App.2d 576, 199 P.2d 391. But in Wylie v. Vellis, 1955, 132 Cal.App.2d 854, 283 P.2d 327, the court refused to rule as matter of law that four seconds was insufficient for the last clear chance in an intersection collision.

35. See Woloszynowski v. New York Cent. R. Co., 1930, 254 N.Y. 206, 172 N.E. 471; St. Louis & S. F. R. Co. v. Summers, 8 Cir. 1909, 173 F. 358. But such knowledge may be proved by circumstantial evidence over the defendant's denial. Arnold v. Owens, 4 Cir. 1935, 78 F.2d 495; Groves v. Webster City, 1936, 222 Iowa 849, 270 N.W. 329.

36. Menke v. Peterschmidt, 1955, 246 Iowa 722, 69 N.W.2d 65; Meyn v. Dulaney-Miller Auto Co., 1937, 118 W.Va. 545, 191 S.E. 558; Standard Oil Co. v. McDaniel, 1922, 52 U.S.App.D.C. 19, 280 F. 993; Tyrrell v. Boston & Me. R. Co., 1914, 77 N.H. 320, 91 A. 179; Yazoo & M. V. R. Co. v. Lee, 1927, 148 Miss. 809, 114 So. 866. Cf. Kumkumian v. City of New York, 1953, 305 N.Y. 167, 111 N.E.2d 865 (discovery of man on subway track by automatic tripper device).

37. See for example the complete alteration of the California rule, starting with Selinsky v. Olsen, 1951, 38 Cal.2d 102, 237 P.2d 645, through Peterson v. Burkhalter, 1951, 38 Cal.2d 107, 237 P.2d 977, to Gulley v. Warren, 1959, 174 Cal.App.2d 470, 345 P. 2d 17. See Garon, Recent Developments in California's Last Clear Chance Doctrine, 1952, 40 Cal.L. Rev. 404. This finally led to Brandelius v. City and County of San Francisco, 1957, 47 Cal.2d 729, 306 P.2d 432, holding that the time for action starts when defendant "should have known" from facts apparent to him that plaintiff was in peril. All this in a "discovered peril" jurisdiction.

38. Ralph v. Union Pacific R. Co., 1960, 82 Idaho 240, 351 P.2d 464; Marks v. Southern Pacific Co., 1957, 211 Or. 539, 316 P.2d 523; Lawrence v. Bamberger R. Co., 1955, 3 Utah 2d 247, 282 P.2d 335; Harvey v. Burr, 1954, 224 Ark. 62, 271 S.W.2d 777; Lee v. Atlantic Coast Line R. Co., 1953, 237 N.C. 357, 75 S.E.2d 143.

39. It usually is said that the defendant's chance must be later by the amount of time it would take a normal human being to react to the situation. Milby v. Diggs, 1937, 118 W.Va. 56, 189 S.E. 107; Morrison v. Boston & Me. R. R., 1933, 86 N.H. 176, 180, 164 A. 553, 556; Hutcheson v. Misenheimer, 1938, 169 Va. 511, 194 S.E. 665; Swadling v. Cooper, [1931] A.C. 1.

40. Donohue v. Rolando, 1965, 16 Utah 2d 294, 400 P.2d 12; Hester v. Watson, 1968, 74 Wash.2d 924, 448 P.2d 320; J. D. Ball Ford, Inc. v. Roitman, Fla.App.1968, 206 So.2d 661; Gessel v. Smith, Okl. 1967, 435 P.2d 587; Underwood v. Gardner, Ky. 1952, 249 S.W.2d 950.

41. Both Virginia and North Carolina have had decisions which have allowed recovery. See Notes, 1954, 40 Va.L.Rev. 666; 1958, 36 N.C.L.Rev. 545. The latest decisions in both states apparently deny it. See Anderson v. Payne, 1949, 189 Va. 712, 54 S. E.2d 82; Craighead v. Sellers, 1953, 194 Va. 920, 76 S.E.2d 212; Cagle v. Norfolk Southern R. Co., M. D.N.C.1956, 144 F.Supp. 710, reversed on other grounds, 1957, 242 F.2d 405.

which has evolved a rather marvelous so-called "humanitarian doctrine," [42] fearful and wonderful in its ramifications, which allows recovery. It appears to have begun as a distinction between a defendant operating a dangerous machine, such as a railroad train or an automobile, and a plaintiff who was not, and to have become transformed instead into a doctrine favoring the plaintiff where both parties were equally, and similarly, at fault.[43] Unquestionably it represents an attempt to stress the greater importance of human safety over the convenience and financial interests of defendants; but its application has been marked by such great confusion, and so many appeals, that no other court has been tempted to follow the Missouri cases.

Defendant's Antecedent Negligence

A further problem arises where the defendant, after discovery of the danger, does what he can to avoid the injury, but his prior negligence prevents his efforts from being effective—as, for example, where he tries to stop his car, but cannot do so because of defective brakes. No reason is evident in such a case for distinguishing between the antecedent negligence of the defendant and that of the plaintiff who has got himself into danger; [44] and most courts deny recovery.[45] It was allowed in an English case,[46] upon the ground that "a last opportunity which the defendant would have had but for his own negligence is equivalent in law to one he actually had"—a line of reasoning which the court refuses to apply to the plaintiff. A small number of American cases [47] have reached such a result. The Restatement of Torts [48] has not approved it, even in the limited situation once advocated by one distinguished legal writer,[49] where the defendant's lack of equipment, such as headlights, has prevented him from discovering the danger at all, and the argument has been that his duty "would not be discharged by vigilant effort in the absence of means to make the lookout effectual." It is not easy to find any distinction between the duty to see and the duty to avoid what is seen, or to justify an obvious fiction which says that negligent inability to have the last clear chance is the same thing as negligence on the part of one who actually has it.

42. Womack v. Missouri Pac. R. Co., 1935, 337 Mo. 1160, 88 S.W.2d 368; McCall v. Thompson, 1941, 348 Mo. 795, 155 S.W.2d 161; Barrie v. St. Louis Transit Co., 1903, 102 Mo.App. 87, 76 S.W. 706; Murphy v. Wabash R. Co., 1910, 228 Mo. 56, 128 S. W. 481; Maginnis v. Missouri Pac. R. Co., 1916, 268 Mo. 667, 187 S.W. 1165. See Otis, The Humanitarian Doctrine, 1912, 46 Am.L.Rev. 381; Gaines, The Humanitarian Doctrine in Missouri, 1935, 20 St. Louis L.Rev. 113; Stryker, A Comparison—Last Clear Chance Doctrine of Kansas and Humanitarian Doctrine of Missouri, 1950, 18 Kan.Bar A.J. 334.

43. The ultimate length was reached in Miller v. St. Louis Pub. Serv. Co., Mo.App.1964, 375 S.W.2d 641, when the "humanitarian doctrine" was applied to allow recovery for damage to the plaintiff's property, notwithstanding his contributory negligence. See Note, 1964, 9 St.Louis L.Rev. 285.

44. Suppose that A is lying drunk and unconscious in the street, and B, driving a car, sees him and endeavors to stop, but cannot do so because of defective brakes. Are we to say that B's antecedent negligence makes him liable for A's injuries, but that A's antecedent negligence does not make him responsible for B's—or his own?

45. Andersen v. Bingham & Garfield R. Co., 1950, 117 Utah 197, 214 P.2d 607; Johnson v. Director-General of Railroads, 1924, 81 N.H. 289, 125 A. 147; Chesapeake & O. R. Co. v. Conley's Adm'x, 1935, 261 Ky. 669, 88 S.W.2d 683; Illinois Cent. R. Co. v. Nelson, 8 Cir. 1909, 173 F. 915; Noe v. Chicago Great Western R. Co., 1969, — Ill.App.2d —, 263 N.E.2d 889 (Iowa law).

Compare, as to excessive speed, Brager v. Milwaukee Elec. R. & L. Co., 1936, 220 Wis. 65, 264 N.W. 733; State ex rel. Fleming v. Bland, 1929, 322 Mo. 565, 15 S.W.2d 798.

46. British Columbia Elec. R. Co. v. Loach, [1916] 1 A.C. 719. See Bohlen, The Rule in British Columbia R. R. Co. v. Loach, 1917, 66 U.Pa.L.Rev. 73.

47. Fairport, P. & E. R. Co. v. Meredith, 1933, 46 Ohio App. 457, 189 N.E. 10; Little Rock Traction & Elec. Co. v. Morrison, 1901, 69 Ark. 289, 62 S.W. 1045; Dent v. Bellows Falls & S. R. St. R. Co., 1922, 95 Vt. 523, 116 A. 83; Neary v. Northern Pac. R. Co., 1910, 41 Mont. 480, 110 P. 226.

48. Second Restatement of Torts, §§ 479, 480.

49. Harper, Law of Torts, 1933, § 139, notes 79, 81.

Criticism

This variety of irreconcilable rules, all purporting to be the same, and the lack of any rational fundamental theory to support them, suggest that the "last clear chance" doctrine is more a matter of dissatisfaction with the defense of contributory negligence than anything else. In its application, it is not infrequent that the greater the defendant's negligence, the less his liability will be. The driver who looks carefully and discovers the danger, and is then slow in applying his brakes, may be liable, while the one who does not look at all, or who has no effective brakes to apply, may not. Recognition of the absurdity of such distinctions has played a considerable part in the extension of the doctrine to new situations. Nor is it easy to defend a rule which absolves the plaintiff entirely from his own negligence, and places the loss upon the defendant, whose fault may be the lesser of the two. It is probable that the future development of the law of contributory negligence will lie along the lines of statutory or common law apportionment of the damages, rather than the last clear chance.[50]

67. COMPARATIVE NEGLIGENCE

The hardship of the doctrine of contributory negligence upon the plaintiff is readily apparent. It places upon one party the entire burden of a loss for which two are, by hypothesis, responsible. The negligence of the defendant has played no less a part in causing the damage; the plaintiff's deviation from the community standard of conduct may even be relatively slight, and the defendant's more extreme; the injured man is in all probability, for the very reason of his injury, the less able of the two to bear the financial burden of his loss; and the answer of the law to all this is that the defendant goes scot free of all liability, and the plaintiff bears it all. Nor is it any answer to say that the contributory negligence rule promotes caution by making the plaintiff responsible for his own safety. It is quite as reasonable to say that it encourages negligence, by giving the defendant reason to hope that he will escape the consequences.[51] Actually any such idea of deterrence is quite unrealistic. In the usual case, the negligence on both sides will consist of mere inadvertence or inattention, or an error in judgment, and it is quite unlikely that forethought of any legal liability will in fact be in the mind of either party. No one supposes that an automobile driver, as he approaches an intersection, is in fact meditating upon the golden mean of the reasonable man of ordinary prudence, and the possibility of tort damages, whether for himself or for another.

There has been for many years an increasing dissatisfaction with the absolute defense of contributory negligence.[52] Courts are becoming more reluctant to rule that the plaintiff's conduct is negligent as a matter of law,[53] and juries are notoriously inclined to find that there has been no such negligence, or to make some more or less haphazard reduction of the plaintiff's damages in proportion to his fault. This dissatisfaction has led to a number of attempts to find

---

50. See, however, the seemingly unjustifiable application of the last clear chance doctrine under statutes providing for apportionment, infra, p. 438.

51. Lowndes, Contributory Negligence, 1934, 22 Georgetown L.J. 674, 681–682.

52. "No one can appreciate more than we the hardship of depriving plaintiff of his verdict and of all right to collect damages from defendant; but the rule of contributory negligence, through no fault of ours, remains in our law and gives us no alternative other than to hold that defendant is entitled to judgment notwithstanding the verdict. It would be hard to imagine a case more illustrative of the truth that in operation the rule of comparative negligence would serve justice more faithfully than that of contributory negligence. * * * But as long as the legislature refuses to substitute the rule of comparative for that of contributory negligence, we have no option but to enforce the law in a proper case." Holt, J., in Haeg v. Sprague, Warner & Co., 1938, 202 Minn. 425, 281 N.W. 261.

53. Nixon, Changing Rules of Liability in Automobile Accident Litigation, 1936, 3 Law & Con.Prob. 476.

some substitute method of dealing with cases where there is negligence on the part of both parties.[54]

The makeshift doctrine of the last clear chance [55] has been adopted to some extent in nearly all jurisdictions. Apart from this, both Illinois and Kansas [56] at one time endeavored to modify the rigors of contributory negligence by classifying negligence into "degrees," and saying that if the plaintiff's negligence was "ordinary," while that of the defendant was "gross," the plaintiff might recover. Such a result was still unsatisfactory, since it merely shifted the entire loss from the plaintiff to the defendant, when both parties were still at fault. Furthermore, it proved extremely difficult to assign any definite meaning to "gross" negligence, or to furnish the jury with any satisfactory guide as to the distinction; and the result was to fill the courts with appeals in which they were invited to struggle with the creature to which they had given birth.[57] Both states finally abandoned the experiment,[58] and this

form of "comparative negligence" is now entirely discarded at common law.[59]

Apportionment of Damages

An entirely different approach to the whole problem would be to divide the damages between the two parties. The common law courts always have been entirely unwilling to make or permit any such division. Their reasons seldom have been given; but, in addition to judicial inertia and the survival of tradition, they appear to include the indivisibility of any single injury and the lack of any definite basis for apportionment,[60] and a marked distrust of the bias and general unreliability of the jury which would be expected to make any division. There never has been any essential reason why the change could not be made without a statute by the courts which made the contributory negligence rule in the first place; [61] but it is so sweeping an alteration of the law, affecting so many thousands of cases, that there has been understandable reluctance on the part of the courts to take such a step. In 1967 it looked for a time as if Illinois were about to do so, when the Supreme Court asked the Appellate Court for an opinion as to whether it was desirable; but after receiving an affirmative answer [62]

54. See Mole and Wilson, A Study of Comparative Negligence, 1932, 17 Corn.L.Q. 333, 604; Gregory, Loss Distribution by Comparative Negligence, 1936, 21 Minn.L.Rev. 1; Prosser, Comparative Negligence, 1953, 51 Mich.L.Rev. 465, reprinted in Prosser, Selected Topics on the Law of Torts, 1954, 1; Dobbs, Comparative Negligence, 1955, 9 Ark.L.Rev. 357; Leflar, Comparative Negligence—A Study for Arkansas Lawyers, 1956, 10 Ark.L.Rev. 54; Maloney, From Contributory to Comparative Negligence: A Needed Law Reform, 1958, 11 U.Fla.L. Rev. 135; Haugh, Comparative Negligence: A Reform Long Overdue, 1969, 49 Or.L.Rev. 38. In opposition to the whole idea, see Benson, Comparative Negligence—Boon or Bane, (1956) 23 Ins.Couns.J. 204.

55. See supra, § 66.

56. Galena & Chicago Union R. Co. v. Jacobs, 1858, 20 Ill. 478; Chicago, B. & Q. R. Co. v. Payne, 1871, 59 Ill. 534; Union Pac. R. Co. v. Henry, 1883, 36 Kan. 565, 14 P. 1; Wichita & W. R. Co. v. Davis, 1887, 37 Kan. 743, 16 P. 78. See Malone, The Formative Era of Contributory Negligence, 1946, 41 Ill.L.Rev. 151.

57. See supra, p. 182.

58. Lake Shore & M. S. R. Co. v. Hessions, 1894, 150 Ill. 546, 37 N.E. 905; City of Lanark v. Dougherty,

1894, 153 Ill. 163, 38 N.E. 892; Atchison, T. & S. F. R. Co. v. Morgan, 1883, 31 Kan. 77, 1 P. 298.

59. It has, however, been adopted in several statutes providing for apportionment of damages. See infra, § 67.

60. "The reason why, in cases of mutual concurring negligence, neither party can maintain an action against the other, is, not that the wrong of the one is set off against the wrong of the other; it is that the law cannot measure how much the damage suffered is attributable to the plaintiff's own fault. If he were allowed to recover, it might be that he would obtain from the other party compensation for his own misconduct." Heil v. Glanding, 1862, 42 Pa. 493, 499.

As to avoidable consequences, where such a basis may be found, see supra, p. 422.

61. See Keeton, Creative Continuity in the Law of Torts, 1962, 75 Harv.L.Rev. 463; Symposium, 1968, 21 Vand.L.Rev. 889–949.

62. Maki v. Frelk, 1967, 85 Ill.App.2d 439, 229 N.E.2d 284.

the higher court was still of the opinion that the matter should be left to the legislature.[63] There thus appears to be very little likelihood of any immediate relief from the courts, at least until legislation becomes much more common and unopposed than it is.

Civil law jurisdictions [64] on the other hand, quite uniformly apportion the damages, and seem to experience no particular difficulties in administration, perhaps because in negligence cases they have no jury. The law of admiralty, which is derived by descent from the civil law, follows it even in common law countries, again without a jury. The original English admiralty rule divided the damages equally between the negligent parties; but in 1911 England conformed to the Brussels Maritime Convention by adopting a statute providing for a division "in proportion to the degree in which each vessel was at fault." [65] The United States never has adhered to the Brussels Convention; and in collision cases the federal courts have continued to divide the damages equally. This always has been supposed to be required by early decisions of the Supreme Court; [66] and

it has been deplored on occasion by the lower federal courts [67] as an arbitrary and unjust rule. In cases of negligent injuries to maritime employees several of them, before legislation required it, broke away from the limitation, and apportioned the damages according to fault.[68]

All other leading maritime countries make the division in proportion to the relative fault of the parties. The objections commonly made to such apportionment, that it is not possible to make a fair estimate, that it places too heavy a reliance and a burden upon the triers of fact, that it will lead to too many appeals, and the like, all have been considered and rejected long since in admiralty law, and have not been borne out by subsequent experience.[69]

In the United States numerous statutes have been enacted providing for similar apportionment of damages according to fault. The Federal Employers' Liability Act,[70] the

---

L.Rev. 223. See the humorous application of the rule in The Niobe, D.Ga.1887, 31 F. 164.

67. Tank Barge Hygrade, Inc. v. The Gatco New Jersey, 3 Cir.1957, 250 F.2d 485; Luckenbach S.S. Co. v. United States, 2 Cir.1946, 157 F.2d 250, 252. See also The City of Chattanooga, 2 Cir.1935, 79 F.2d 23; The Margaret, 3 Cir.1929, 30 F.2d 923, 928. See Jackson, The Archaic Rule of Dividing Damages in Marine Collisions, 1967, 19 Ala.L.Rev. 263. In N. M. Paterson & Sons v. City of Chicago, N.D. Ill.1962, 209 F.Supp. 576, called the Supreme Court rule dictum, and proceeded to break away and apportion the damages according to fault. But this was reversed in 7 Cir.1963, 324 F.2d 254.

68. The Explorer, D.La.1884, 20 F. 135; Olson v. Flavel, D.Or.1888, 34 F. 477; The Mystic, D.N.Y. 1890, 44 F. 398; Cricket S. S. Co. v. Parry, 2 Cir. 1920, 263 F. 523. See Note, 1969, 64 Nw.U.L.Rev. 765.

69. See Franck, Collisions at Sea in Relation to International Maritime Law, 1896, 12 L.Q.Rev. 260; Scott, Collisions at Sea, 1897, 13 L.Q.Rev. 17; Huger, Proportional Damage Rule in Collisions at Sea, 1927, 13 Corn.L.Q. 531; Sprague, Divided Damages, 1929, 6 N.Y.U.L.Rev. 15; Mole and Wilson, A Study of Comparative Negligence, 1932, 17 Corn.L.Q. 333, 339–359.

70. 1910, 45 U.S.C.A. §§ 51–59. See Norfolk & W. R. Co. v. Earnest, 1913, 229 U.S. 114, 122.

---

63. Maki v. Frelk, 1968, 40 Ill.2d 193, 239 N.E.2d 445. This is discussed in the Symposium, 1968, 21 Vand. L.Rev. 889–949; Note [1969] Wis.L.Rev. 647.

In accord, that the remedy is for the legislature, are Bissen v. Fujii, 1970, 51 Haw. 636, 466 P.2d 429; Peterson v. Culp, 1970, — Or. —, 465 P.2d 876; and Vincent v. Pabst Brewing Co., 1970, 47 Wis.2d 120, 177 N.W.2d 513. There are, however, intimations in all three that if the legislature will not act, the court may have to.

64. Turk, Comparative Negligence on the March, 1950, 28 Chicago-Kent L.Rev. 189, 238–244; Montreal Tramways v. McAllister, 1916, 26 Quebec K.B. 174, 34 Dom.L.Rep. 556; Del Prado v. Maila Elec. Co., 1929, 52 Philippine Rep. 900; Ubeda y Salazar v. San Juan L. & T. Co., 1909, 4 Puerto Rico 553. The exception is Louisiana, which follows the common law and does not apportion damages. Mathes v. Schwing, 1929, 169 La. 272, 125 So. 121.

65. Maritime Conventions Act of 1911, 1 & 2 Geo. V, c. 57, § 1.

66. Particularly The Schooner Catharine, 1855, 17 How., U.S., 170. See also The Max Morris, 1890, 137 U.S. 1; Robinson, Legal Adjustments of Personal Injury in the Maritime Industry, 1930, 44 Harv.

Jones Act and the Merchant Marine Act,[71] and many of the state railway [72] and other [73] labor acts all provide that the contributory negligence of an injured workman shall not bar his recovery, but his damages shall be reduced in proportion to his negligence. Florida [74] and Iowa [75] have had similar provisions as to any injury inflicted by a railroad, and Virginia [76] as to railway crossing accidents arising out of failure to give the required signals—although it would appear that all three are unconstitutional as a denial of equal protection of the laws.[77] There are altogether some thirty special statutes on the books, applicable to particular classes of plaintiffs or defendants, or to particular situations.

The first state to adopt a general "comparative negligence" act was Mississippi, which in 1910 enacted a statute applicable to all actions for personal injuries, and expanded it in 1920 to include damages to property.[78] Georgia [79] accomplished the same result by a rather remarkable tour de force of construction by which a statute applicable only to damage inflicted by a railroad was expanded into a general act. Succeeding years saw the adoption of general apportionment statutes, applicable to all negligence actions, in Wisconsin and Nebraska in 1913, South Dakota in 1941, Arkansas in 1957, Maine in 1964, and in Hawaii, Massachusetts, Minnesota, New Hampshire and Vermont in 1969. The Canadian provinces [80] all divide the damages in all such cases, as do all the states of Australia except New South Wales.[81]

Under all these apportionment statutes, if the defendant's fault is found to be twice as great as that of the plaintiff, the latter will recover two-thirds of his damages, and himself bear the remainder of his loss.[82] To the objection that no jury can estimate so intangible a thing as relative fault in any precise terms, it may be replied that it is an open secret that juries do in fact adjust the damages according to fault, even where there is no apportionment statute and they are in-

71. See Lindgren v. United States, 4 Cir. 1930, 281 U.S. 38.

72. See for example Louisville & N. R. Co. v. Chapman's Adm'x, 1945, 300 Ky. 835, 190 S.W.2d 542; Great Northern R. Co. v. Wojtala, 9 Cir.1940, 112 F.2d 609; McLean v. Andrews Hardwood Co., 1931, 200 N.C. 312, 156 S.E. 528; Boyleston v. Southern R. Co., 1947, 211 S.C. 232, 44 S.E.2d 537.

73. See for example Benson v. Brady, 1960, 177 Cal. App.2d 280, 2 Cal.Rptr. 124; Tampa Elec. R. Co. v. Bryant, 1931, 101 Fla. 204, 133 So. 887; Price v. McNeill, 1946, 237 Iowa 1120, 24 N.W.2d 464; Dierks Lumber & Coal Co. v. Noles, 1941, 201 Ark. 1088, 148 S.W.2d 650; Fitzgerald v. Oregon-Wash. R. & N. Co., 1932, 141 Or. 1, 16 P.2d 27.

74. Fla.Stat.Ann.1944, § 768.06.

75. 2 Iowa Code, 1946, p. 1843, Civil Proc. Rule 97.

76. See Chesapeake & O. R. Co. v. Pulliam, 1947, 185 Va. 908, 41 S.E.2d 54; Southern R. Co. v. Whetzel, 1933, 159 Va. 796, 167 S.E. 427; Norfolk & W. R. Co. v. White, 1931, 158 Va. 243, 163 S.E. 530.

A Tennessee statute, by construction, has been given the same effect. Illinois Cent. R. Co. v. Sigler, 6 Cir.1941, 122 F.2d 279; Tennessee Cent. R. Co. v. Page, 1926, 153 Tenn. 84, 282 S.W. 376.

77. So held as to the Florida statute in Georgia So. & Fla. Ry. Co. v. Seven Up Bottling Co., Fla.1965, 175 So.2d 39; Turman v. Florida East Coast Ry. Co., Fla.App.1967, 195 So.2d 604. See Note, 1965, 28 U.Fla.L.Rev. 166.

78. Now Miss.Code Ann.1942, § 1454. See Shell and Bufkin, Comparative Negligence in Mississippi, 1956, 27 Miss.L.Rev. 105. A similar provision is found in Canal Zone Civil Code, 1934, § 977.

79. See Goodrich, Origin of the Georgia Rule of Comparative Negligence and Apportionment of Damages, [1940] Ga.Bar.A.J. 174; Wynne v. Southern Bell Tel. Co., 1925, 159 Ga. 623, 126 S.E. 388; Moore v. Sears, Roebuck & Co., 1934, 48 Ga.App. 185, 172 S.E. 680.

80. Alberta Rev.Stat.1942, c. 116; British Columbia Rev.Stat.1936, c. 52, amended by Rev.Stat.1948, c. 68; Manitoba R.S.M.1940, c. 215; New Brunswick Rev.Stat.1927, c. 143; Nova Scotia Stat.1926, c. 3; Ontario Rev.Stat.1937, c. 115; Prince Edward Island Stat.1938, c. 5; Saskatchewan Stat.1944, c. 23. Quebec, with its civil law heritage, divides the damages without a statute. Nichols Chemical Co. v. Lefebvre, 1909, 42 Can.S.C.Rep. 402.

81. See Fleming, Law of Torts, 2d Ed. 1961, 228.

82. See, correcting prior confusion as to this, Cameron v. Union Automobile Ins. Co., 1933, 210 Wis. 659, 246 N.W. 420, 247 N.W. 453.

structed not to do it,[83] and that any approximate division is at least better than a rule which throws one hundred per cent of the loss upon the plaintiff, and none upon the defendant—an arbitrary method of apportionment which is demonstrably wrong. There is more substance in the objection that juries frequently fail to follow the instruction to apportion the damages because of contributory negligence, and that it is often impossible to know whether they have done so. For this reason the special verdict procedure followed in Wisconsin appears to be a very desirable check upon the verdict.[84] It was originally provided in the Arkansas statute, but almost immediately removed by the next session of the legislature.[85] The Maine statute has accomplished much the same result by requiring the jury to report the damages found before and after any reduction.[86]

In Nebraska [87] and South Dakota [88] the general comparative negligence acts are lim-ited to situations in which the negligence of the plaintiff is "slight" while that of the defendant is "gross" in comparison; and this limitation is found in some of the special statutes.[89] Its effect has been to revive the old unhappy experience of headaches for the courts in Illinois and Kansas,[90] and seriously to curtail the effectiveness of the statutes by depriving them of application in any case where the negligence of the parties is anywhere near approximately equal. Wisconsin [91] and Georgia,[92] as well as some of the special statutes,[93] limit the recovery to cases where the plaintiff's negligence is "not as great" as that of the defendant; and this was added to the Arkansas act [94] originally adopted without it. It has subsequently been adopted in the statutes of Hawaii, Maine, Massachusetts, Minnesota, New Hampshire and Vermont.

All of these restrictions are obviously the result of compromise between conflicting interests in the legislatures, and smack of political expediency rather than of any reason or logic in the situation. They have led, under all of the statutes, to an excessive number of appeals, in which the court is asked to review the jury's finding as to the

---

83. "We but blind our eyes to obvious reality to the extent that we ignore the fact that in many cases juries apply it [apportionment] in spite of us." Holt, J., in Haeg v. Sprague, Warner & Co., 1938, 202 Minn. 425, 430, 281 N.W. 261. See also Ulman, A Judge Takes the Stand, 1933, 30–34.

84. See Prosser, Comparative Negligence, 1953, 51 Mich.L.Rev. 465, 475, 497–503, reprinted in Prosser, Selected Topics on the Law of Torts, 1954, 1.

85. See Note, 1958, 11 Ark.L.Rev. 391. The symposium in 1956, 10 Ark.L.Rev. 54–100 is one of the most valuable sources of information about comparative negligence.

86. See Note, 1966, 18 Me.L.Rev. 65.

87. See Johnson Comparative Negligence—The Nebraska View, 1957, 36 Neb.L.Rev. 240; Union Pac. R. Co. v. Denver-Chicago Trucking Co., 8 Cir.1953, 202 F.2d 31; Krepcik v. Interstate Transit Lines, 1949, 152 Neb. 39, 40 N.W.2d 252, affirmed in 1950, 153 Neb. 98, 43 N.W.2d 609; McDonald v. Wright, 1934, 125 Neb. 871, 252 N.W. 411; Roby v. Auker, 1949, 151 Neb. 421, 37 N.W.2d 799.

88. See Note, 1962, 7 S.D.L.Rev. 114. In 1964 the statute was amended to eliminate "gross" negligence, and to require only that the plaintiff's negligence be "slight" in comparison with that of defendant. See Crabb v. Wade, 1969, —— S.D. ——, 167 N.W.2d 546. The effect appears to be to adopt the Wisconsin position, infra, note 91.

89. See for example Baltimore & Ohio R. Co. v. McTeer, 1936, 55 Ohio App. 217, 9 N.E.2d 627; Lassen v. Southern Pac. Co., 1916, 173 Cal. 71, 159 P. 143.

90. See supra, p. 182.

91. See Campbell, Wisconsin's Comparative Negligence Law, 1932, 7 Wis.L.Rev. 224; Padway, Comparative Negligence, 1931, 16 Marq.L.Rev. 3; Whelan, Comparative Negligence, [1938] Wis.L.Rev. 465; Campbell, Ten Years of Comparative Negligence, [1941] Wis.L.Rev. 289; Heine v. Oswald Jaeger Baking Co., 1957, 275 Wis. 26, 80 N.W.2d 791.

92. Southern Stages, Inc. v. Clements, 1944, 71 Ga. App. 169, 30 S.E.2d 429; Whatley v. Henry, 1941, 65 Ga.App. 668, 16 S.E.2d 214; Southern R. Co. v. Parkman, 1939, 61 Ga.App. 62, 5 S.E.2d 685; Gahring v. Brown, 1963, 108 Ga.App. 530, 133 S.E.2d 389.

93. See for example St. Louis-San Francisco R. Co. v. Hovley, 1940, 199 Ark. 853, 137 S.W.2d 231; English v. Michigan Cent. R. Co., 1915, 188 Mich. 286, 154 N.W. 98.

94. See Note, 1958, 11 Ark.L.Rev. 391.

comparative fault. Since each case must turn upon all of the circumstances, there can be no definite rules, and cases which on their face appear to involve more or less identical conduct on each side quite frequently have come out with quite different results.[95]

The opposition to the apportionment legislation has come, naturally enough, from the habitual defendants and the liability insurance companies, with some occasional support from personal injury attorneys alarmed at the prospect of diminished verdicts and correspondingly lower fees. There has been much controversy over the prospective effect upon liability insurance rates, which, so far as appears, has been nothing very unsettling in the states where the statutes have been adopted.[96]

Such "comparative negligence"[97] statutes offer a fairly simple problem where only two parties are involved. Their administration is very much complicated when there are multiple plaintiffs or defendants.[98] If there is a triple collision of automobiles driven by A, B and C, or if two cars collide and injure a passenger or a bystander, there may be three distinct sets of damages, and three different proportions of fault. No adjudication in an action between A and B can do full justice unless C is made a party, and his liability and his claims are determined in the same

suit. The English statute[99] and some of those in Canada[1] provide for bringing C into court, for the hearing of all claims at one time, and for adding up the total damages and dividing them according to the respective fault of each party. Theoretically perfect as this procedure is, it may lead to almost incredible complexity in the resulting issues,[2] which may well be beyond the capacity of the ordinary American jury; and as yet no American state has been led to follow the foreign example.

One quite troublesome question which has arisen under the comparative negligence acts is whether the fact that the defendant has the last clear chance is to entitle him, as it did before the statute, to recover all of his damages notwithstanding his own negligence. The very questionable "proximate cause" explanation of the last clear chance doctrine[3] has led the greater number of the courts which have dealt with this to hold that the doctrine survives, and the plaintiff recovers all, on the theory that his own negligence has not contributed "proximately" to his injury at all. This has been true in state decisions under the Federal Employers' Liability Act,[4] under several of the state statutes,[5] and in

---

95. See Prosser, Comparative Negligence, 1953, 51 Mich.L.Rev. 465, 484–494, reprinted in Prosser, Selected Topics on the Law of Torts, 1954, 1; Winkler v. State Farm Mut. Auto. Ins. Co., 1960, 11 Wis.2d 170, 105 N.W.2d 302; Fronczek v. Sink, 1940, 235 Wis. 398, 291 N.W. 850, 293 N.W. 153.

96. See Rosenberg, Comparative Negligence in Arkansas: A "Before and After" Survey, 1959, 13 Ark.L.Rev. 89; Peck, Comparative Negligence and Automobile Liability Insurance, 1960, 58 Mich.L. Rev. 689.

97. More properly called "comparative damages" or "damage apportionment" statutes. See Note, 1926, 12 Corn.L.Q. 113.

98. See Gregory, Legislative Loss Distribution in Negligence Actions, 1936; Gregory, Loss Distribution by Comparative Negligence, 1936, 21 Minn.L. Rev. 1.

99. Law Reform (Married Women and Tortfeasors) Act, 1935, 25 & 26 Geo. 5, c. 30; Law Reform (Contributory Negligence) Act, 1945, 8 & 9 Geo. 6, c. 28. See Williams, Joint Torts and Contributory Negligence, 1951.

1. Ontario, Alberta, British Columbia, Manitoba, and Saskatchewan.

2. See Prosser, Comparative Negligence, 1953, 51 Mich.L.Rev. 465, 503–507, reprinted in Prosser, Selected Topics on the Law of Torts, 1954, 1; and cf. Haines v. Williams, 1933, 47 Brit.Col. 69.

3. See supra, p. 427.

4. Chicago, R. I. & P. R. Co. v. Adams, 1933, 187 Ark. 816, 62 S.W.2d 947; Hamilton v. Chicago, B. & Q. R. Co., 1931, 211 Iowa 924, 234 N.W. 810; Washington & O. D. R. Co. v. Weakley, 1924, 140 Va. 796, 125 S.E. 672; Soles v. Atlantic Coast Line R. Co., 1922, 184 N.C. 283, 114 S.E. 305; Barnes v. Red River & G. R. Co., 1930, 14 La.App. 188, 128 So. 724.

5. Southland Butane Gas Co. v. Blackwell, 1955, 211 Ga. 665, 88 S.E.2d 6, conformed to 92 Ga.App. 288, 88 S.E.2d 424; Wilfong v. Omaha & C. B. R. Co.,

most of the decisions under the Canadian apportionment acts.[6] In all probability this defeats the purpose of the legislation, since the system of apportionment breaks down in one important group of cases, where a loss from the fault of two parties is still visited on one; and while the statutes are silent on the last clear chance, the very probable reason is that the question simply never occurred to the legislature. The causation explanation appears to have been something which was itself invented as a justification; and any necessity for the last clear chance as a palliative of the hardships of contributory negligence obviously disappears when the loss can be apportioned.[7] The tendency in the latest decisions [8]

has been to hold that the apportionment statute takes effect, notwithstanding the fact that the defendant has the last clear chance.

68. ASSUMPTION OF RISK

Like contributory negligence, assumption of risk developed late in the law of negligence.[9]

It has been a subject of much controversy,[10] and has been surrounded by much confusion, because "assumption of risk" has been used by the courts in several different senses,[11] which have been lumped together under the one name, usually without realizing that any differences exist, and certainly with no effort to make them clear. There are even courts which have limited the use of the term "assumption of risk" to cases in which the parties stand in the relation of master and servant, or at least some other contractual relation; but they have been compelled to invent other names for other cases, such as

---

1935, 129 Neb. 600, 262 N.W. 537; Pecos & N. T. R. Co. v. Rosenbloom, 1915, 107 Tex. 291, 173 S.W. 215, 177 S.W. 952, reversed on other grounds 240 U.S. 439; Vaughn v. Alcoa, 1952, 194 Tenn. 449, 251 S. W.2d 304; Wilson's Adm'x v. Virginia Portland R. Co., 1917, 122 Va. 160, 94 S.E. 347. See Note, 1965, 1 Ga. State Bar J. 500.

6. Farber v. Toronto Transp. Co., [1925] 2 Dom.L. Rep. 729, 56 Ont.L.Rep. 537; Key v. British Columbia Elec. R. Co., 1930, 43 B.C.Rep. 288; McLaughlin v. Long, [1927] Can.S.C.Rep. 303, [1927] 2 Dom.L. Rep. 186; McDonald v. Thomas, 1933, 41 Man.Rep. 657.

7. See Weir, Davies v. Mann and Contributory Negligence Statutes, 1931, 9 Can.Bar Rev. 470; MacDonald, The Negligence Action and the Legislature, 1933, 13 Can.Bar Rev. 535; MacIntyre, The Rationale of the Last Clear Chance, 1940, 53 Harv.L. Rev. 1225; Williams, The Law Reform (Contributory Negligence) Act, 1946, 9 Mod.L.Rev. 105; MacIntyre, Last Clear Chance After Thirty Years, 1955, 33 Can.Bar Rev. 257; Wright, The Law of Torts, 1948, 26 Can.Bar Rev. 46, 70; Gregory, Legislative Loss Distribution in Negligence Actions, 1936, 126–133.

8. Cushman v. Perkins, Me.1968, 245 A.2d 846, noted in 1969, 2 Creighton L.Rev. 376; Atlantic Coast Line R. Co. v. Anderson, 5 Cir. 1959, 267 F.2d 329, cert. denied 361 U.S. 841, reh. denied 361 U.S. 904 (Federal Employers' Liability Act); Loftin v. Nolin, Fla.1956, 86 So.2d 161, noted in 1956, 10 U. Miami L.Q. 594. An older decision is Switzer v. Detroit Inv. Co., 1925, 188 Wis. 330, 206 N.W. 407. The Arkansas statute expressly applies to cases of the last clear chance. See also Davies v. Swan Motor Co., [1949] 2 K.B. 291; Winter v. Bennett, [1956] Vict. L.Rep. 612; Richie v. Dunedin City Corp., [1953] N.Z.L.Rep. 899; Bruce v. McIntyre [1954] Ont.L. Rep. 265, [1954] 2 Dom.L.Rep. 799. See Garner,

Comparative Negligence and Discovered Peril, 1956, 10 Ark.L.Rev. 72.

9. Cruden v. Fentham, 1799, 2 Esp. 685, 170 Eng.Rep. 496, is perhaps the first clearly distinguishable case. The defense received its greatest impetus from Priestley v. Fowler, 1837, 3 M. & W. 1, 150 Eng.Rep. 1030, a case of master and servant.

10. See Bohlen, Voluntary Assumption of Risk, 1906, 20 Harv.L.Rev. 14, 91; Rice, The Automobile Guest and the Rationale of Assumption of Risk, 1943, 27 Minn.L.Rev. 33; Keeton, Assumption of Risk and the Landowner, 1942, 20 Tex.L.Rev. 562; Gordon, Wrong Turns in the Volens Cases, 1945, 61 L.Q.Rev. 140; Keeton, Personal Injuries Resulting from Open and Obvious Conditions, 1952, 100 U.Pa.L.Rev. 629; James, Assumption of Risk, 1952, 61 Yale L.J. 141; Payne, Assumption of Risk and Negligence, 1957, 35 Can.Bar Rev. 350; Wade, The Place of Assumption of Risk in the Law of Negligence, 1961, 22 La.L.Rev. 5; Mansfield, Informed Choice in the Law of Torts, 1961, 22 La.L.Rev. 17; Green, Assumed Risk as a Defense, 1961, 22 La.L.Rev. 77; James, Assumption of Risk: Unhappy Reincarnation, 1968, 78 Yale L.J. 185.

11. See Keeton, Assumption of Risk in Products Liability Cases, 1961, 22 La.L.Rev. 122, classifying assumption of risk into six different categories: express, subjectively consensual, objectively consensual, by consent to conduct or condition, associational, and imposed.

"incurred risk," or "volenti non fit injuria." [12] This appears to be a distinction without a difference; and most courts have made general use of the one term. [13] It is possible to classify the cases in which assumption of risk has been recognized into three broad basic types of situations, as follows:

In its simplest and primary sense, assumption of risk means that the plaintiff, in advance, has given his consent to relieve the defendant of an obligation of conduct toward him, and to take his chances of injury from a known risk arising from what the defendant is to do or leave undone. [14] The situation is then the same as where the plaintiff consents to the infliction of what would otherwise be an intentional tort, [15] except that the consent is to run the risk of unintended injury, to take a chance, rather than a matter of the greater certainty of intended harm. The result is that the defendant is relieved of all legal duty to the plaintiff; and being under no duty, he cannot be charged with negligence.

A second, and closely related situation, is where the plaintiff voluntarily enters into some relation with the defendant, with knowledge that the defendant will not protect him against the risk. He may then be regarded as tacitly or impliedly consenting to the negligence, and agreeing to take his own chances. Thus he may accept employment, knowing that he is expected to work with a dangerous horse; or a ride in a car with knowledge that the brakes are defective and the driver in-

competent; or he may enter a baseball park, sit in an unscreened seat, and so consent that the players may proceed with the game without taking any precautions to protect him from being hit by the ball. [16] Again the legal result is that the defendant is simply relieved of the duty which would otherwise exist.

In the third type of situation the plaintiff, aware of a risk already created by the negligence of the defendant, proceeds voluntarily to encounter it—as where he has been supplied with a chattel which he knows to be unsafe, and proceeds to use it after he has discovered the danger. If this is a voluntary choice, it may be found that he has accepted the situation, and consented to relieve the defendant of his duty. [17]

In all three of these situations the plaintiff may be acting quite reasonably, and not be at all negligent in taking the chance, because the advantages of his conduct outweigh the risk. His decision may be the right one, and he may even act with unusual caution because he knows the danger he is to meet. [18] If that is the case, the defense operates only to deny the defendant's negligence by denying the duty of care which would give rise to it; and the plaintiff does not recover only because as to him the defendant's conduct is not a legal wrong. On the other hand, and particularly in the second and third situations, [19] the plaintiff's conduct in encountering a known risk may be in itself unreason-

---

12. See for example Walsh v. West Coast Mines, 1948, 31 Wash.2d 396, 197 P.2d 233; Conrad v. Springfield Consol. R. Co., 1909, 240 Ill. 12, 88 N.E. 180; Emhardt v. Perry Stadium, 1943, 113 Ind.App. 197, 46 N.E.2d 704; Fletcher v. Kemp, Mo.1959, 327 S.W.2d 178; Cummins v. Halliburton Oil Well Cementing Co., Tex.Civ.App.1958, 319 S.W.2d 379.

13. Bugh v. Webb, 1959, 231 Ark. 27, 328 S.W.2d 379; Cassady v. Billings, 1959, 135 Mont. 390, 340 P.2d 509; Wright v. Valan, 1947, 130 W.Va. 466, 43 S.E.2d 364; Evans v. Johns Hopkins University, 1961, 224 Md. 234, 167 A.2d 591.

14. See infra, p. 442.

15. See supra, § 18.

16. See infra, p. 446. Cf. La Fleur v. Vergilia, 1952, 280 App.Div. 1035, 117 N.Y.S.2d 244 (teaching learner to drive car); Corbett v. Curtis, 1967, — Me. —, 225 A.2d 402 (same).

17. See infra, p. 445.

18. Miner v. Connecticut River R. Co., 1891, 153 Mass. 398, 26 N.E. 994; Peirce v. Clavin, 7 Cir. 1897, 82 F. 550; Hunn v. Windsor Hotel Co., 1937, 119 W.Va. 215, 193 S.E. 57. The unusual care exercised may itself be evidence that the plaintiff knew the risk and assumed it. Hotchkin v. Erdrich, 1906, 214 Pa. 460, 63 A. 1035.

19. Also, no doubt, in the first; but here the express agreement always has been regarded as a sufficient basis in itself for the defense, without looking further.

able,[20] because the danger is out of all proportion to the advantage which he is seeking to obtain—as where, with other transportation available, he elects to ride with a drunken automobile driver in an unlighted car on a dark night,[21] or dashes into a burning building to save his hat. If that is the case, his conduct is a form of contributory negligence, in which the negligence consists in making the wrong choice and voluntarily encountering a known unreasonable risk.[22] In such cases it is clear that the defenses of assumption of risk and contributory negligence overlap, and are as intersecting circles, with a considerable area in common, where neither excludes the possibility of the other.

In this area of intersection, the traditional position of the courts has been that the defendant may at his election avail himself of either defense, or of both.[23] Since normally either will be sufficient to bar the action, it ordinarily makes no practical difference what the defense is called,[24] and it is not surprising

that the two have not been at all clearly distinguished, and are quite commonly confused.[25] Where they have been distinguished, the traditional basis has been that assumption of risk is a matter of knowledge of the danger and intelligent acquiescence in it, while contributory negligence is a matter of some fault or departure from the standard of conduct of the reasonable man, however unaware, unwilling, or even protesting the plaintiff may be.[26] Obviously the two may coexist when the plaintiff makes an unreasonable choice to incur the risk; but either may exist without the other. The significant difference, when there is one, is likely to be one between risks which were in fact known to the plaintiff,[27] and risks which he merely might have discovered by the exercise of ordinary care.[28]

---

20. Or, even after accepting an entirely reasonable risk, the plaintiff may fail to exercise proper care for his own protection against it. Hartwick v. Chicago & A. R. Co., 7 Cir. 1922, 286 F. 672; Miller v. White Bronze Monument Co., 1908, 141 Iowa 701, 118 N.W. 518; Choctaw, O. & G. R. Co. v. Jones, 1906, 77 Ark. 367, 92 S.W. 244. In such a case it is quite clear that two distinct defenses, assumption of risk and contributory negligence, are involved.

21. Sutherland v. Davis, 1941, 286 Ky. 743, 151 S.W. 2d 1021; Hutzler v. McDonnell, 1943, 242 Wis. 256, 7 N.W.2d 835; Powell v. Berry, 1916, 145 Ga. 696, 89 S.E. 753; Clise v. Prunty, 1929, 108 W.Va. 635, 152 S.E. 201. Cf. Adair v. Valley Flying Service, 1952, 196 Or. 479, 250 P.2d 104 (drunken pilot of plane).

22. See supra, p. 424.

23. See Bugh v. Webb, 1959, 231 Ark. 27, 328 S.W.2d 379; Schmidt v. Fontaine Ferry Enterprises, Ky. 1958, 319 S.W.2d 468; Evans v. Johns Hopkins University, 1961, 224 Md. 234, 167 A.2d 591; Centrello v. Basky, 1955, 164 Ohio St. 41, 128 N.E.2d 80; Krolikowski v. Allstate Ins. Co., 7 Cir. 1960, 283 F. 2d 889.

24. Compare the following cases. Assumption of risk: Cruden v. Fentham, 1799, 2 Esp. 685, 170 Eng.Rep. 496; Clayards v. Dethick, 1848, 12 Q.B. 439, 116 Eng.Rep. 932; Howey v. Fisher, 1899, 122

Mich. 43, 80 N.W. 1004; Pomeroy v. Westfield, 1891, 154 Mass. 462, 28 N.E. 899.

Contributory negligence: Wright v. City of St. Cloud, 1893, 54 Minn. 94, 55 N.W. 819; Mosheuvel v. District of Columbia, 1903, 191 U.S. 247; Houston, E. & W. T. R. Co. v. McHale, 1907, 47 Tex.Civ.App. 360, 105 S.W. 1149. Cf. Poole v. Lutz & Schmidt, 1938, 273 Ky. 586, 117 S.W.2d 575.

25. See James, Assumption of Risk, 1952, 61 Yale L. J. 141; Notes, 1952, 26 Temple L.Q. 206; 1966, 23 Wash. & Lee L.Rev. 91. Also Petrone v. Margolis, 1952, 20 N.J.Super. 180, 89 A.2d 476, saying that the two are now treated as "convertible terms."

26. Erie R. Co. v. Purucker, 1917, 244 U.S. 320; Kingwell v. Hart, 1954, 45 Wash.2d 401, 275 P.2d 431; Koshorek v. Pennsylvania R. Co., 3 Cir. 1963, 318 F.2d 364; Sullivan v. Shell Oil Co., 9 Cir. 1956, 234 F.2d 733, cert. denied 352 U.S. 925; Kleppe v. Prawl, 1957, 181 Kan. 590, 313 P.2d 227. See Notes, 1959, 26 Tenn.L.Rev. 565; [1960] Wis.L.Rev. 460.

See also Borchard v. Sicard, 1944, 113 Vt. 429, 35 A. 2d 439, to the effect that assumption of risk is a matter of preliminary conduct in getting into a dangerous situation, contributory negligence a matter of the act more immediately leading to the specific accident.

27. See Gila Valley, G. & N. R. Co. v. Hall, 1914, 232 U.S. 94, 102; Chesapeake & O. R. Co. v. De Atley, 1916, 241 U.S. 310; McAdoo v. Anzellotti, 2 Cir. 1921, 271 F. 268.

28. Hayes v. Richfield Oil Corp., 1952, 38 Cal.2d 375, 240 P.2d 580; Yazoo & M. V. R. Co. v. Wright, 1914, 235 U.S. 376; Erie R. Co. v. Purucker, 1917, 244 U.

Express Agreement

It is quite possible for the parties expressly [29] to agree in advance that the defendant is under no obligation of care for the benefit of the plaintiff, and shall not be liable for the consequences of conduct which would otherwise be negligent.[30] There is in the ordinary case no public policy which prevents the parties from contracting as they see fit, as to whether the plaintiff will undertake the responsibility of looking out for himself. Thus one who accepts a gratuitous pass on a railway train,[31] or enters into a lease,[32] or

rents a horse,[33] or employs an agent,[34] or enters into a variety of similar relations involving free and open bargaining between the parties,[35] may agree that there shall be no obligation to take precautions, and hence no liability for negligence.

The courts have refused to uphold such agreements, however, where one party is at such obvious disadvantage in bargaining power that the effect of the contract is to put him at the mercy of the other's negligence. Thus it is generally held that a contract exempting an employer from all liability for negligence toward his employees is void as against public policy.[36] The same is true as

---

S. 320; Westcott v. Chicago G. W. R. Co., 1923, 157 Minn. 325, 196 N.W. 272.

"It may well be said that the notice of danger which a prudent plaintiff should have taken, and the knowledge of that danger which the actual plaintiff must have had, are things which shade into each other and are different in degree, but not in kind. Indeed, the jury will have difficulty in distinguishing between that danger which was merely so apparent that every reasonably prudent man would observe it, and that danger which was so obvious that the plaintiff could not help but know it; yet the knowledge which the plaintiff should have had and the actual knowledge to be imputed to him are distinct—at least in theory—and the authoritative cases cited in the opinion must be accepted as establishing the distinction." Denison, C. J., concurring in Cincinnati, N. O. & T. P. R. Co. v. Thompson, 6 Cir. 1916, 236 F. 1, 16. See, criticizing the distinction, Note, 1932, 32 Col.L.Rev. 1384.

29. Or by fair implication from what has been agreed. As where, for example, the plaintiff is employed to correct a condition negligently created by the defendant. Broecker v. Armstrong Cork Co., 1942, 128 N.J.L. 3, 24 A.2d 194; Byars v. Moore-McCormack Lines, 2 Cir. 1946, 155 F.2d 587; Brucker v. Matsen, 1943, 18 Wash.2d 375, 139 P.2d 276.

30. See Arensberg, Limitation by Bailees and by Landlords of Liability for Negligent Acts, 1947, 51 Dick.L.Rev. 36; Notes, 1938, 86 U.Pa.L.Rev. 772; 1939, 4 Mo.L.Rev. 55; 1942, 40 Mich.L.Rev. 897; 1965, 17 Ala.L.Rev. 283; 1964, 52 Cal.L.Rev. 350.

31. Gonzales v. Baltimore & Ohio R. Co., 4 Cir. 1963, 318 F.2d 294; Quimby v. Boston & Me. R. Co., 1890, 150 Mass. 365, 23 N.E. 205; Atchison, T. & S. F. R. Co. v. Smith, 1913, 38 Okl. 157, 132 P. 494; Atlantic Greyhound Lines v. Skinner, 1939, 172 Va. 428, 2 S.E.2d 441; Louisville & N. R. Co. v. George, 1939, 279 Ky. 24, 129 S.W.2d 986. See Note, 1940, 38 Mich.L.Rev. 1310.

32. O'Callaghan v. Waller & Beckwith Realty Co., 1958, 15 Ill.2d 436, 155 N.E.2d 545; Hartford Fire

Ins. Co. v. Chicago, M. & St. P. R. Co., 1899, 175 U. S. 91; Weirick v. Hamm Realty Co., 1929, 179 Minn. 25, 228 N.W. 175; Griswold v. Illinois Cent. R. Co., 1894, 90 Iowa 265, 57 N.W. 843. See Note, 1959, 54 N.W.U.L.Rev. 61. Such decisions have led to statutes in some states invalidating exculpatory clauses in leases. See for example Billie Knitwear, Inc. v. New York Life Ins. Co., 1940, 174 Misc. 978, 22 N.Y.S.2d 324, affirmed, 1941, 262 App.Div. 714, 27 N.Y.S.2d 328, affirmed memo. 1942, 288 N.Y. 682, 43 N.E.2d 80.

Even without a statute there are some respects in which it has been held that the landlord cannot contract away his liability. Kuzmiak v. Brookchester, Inc., 1955, 33 N.J.Super. 575, 111 A.2d 425 (affirmative misconduct); Kessler v. The Ansonia, 1930, 253 N.Y. 453, 171 N.E. 704 (same); Hollander v. Wilson Estate Co., 1932, 214 Cal. 582, 7 P.2d 177 (common passageways); Myron W. McIntyre Ltd. v. Chandler Holding Corp., 1939, 172 Misc. 917, 16 N.Y.S.2d 642, affirmed 1940, 259 App.Div. 710, 19 N.Y.S.2d 149 (concealment of known defect).

33. Moss v. Fortune, 1960, 207 Tenn. 426, 340 S.W.2d 902. Cf. Hall v. Sinclair Refining Co., 1955, 242 N. C. 707, 89 S.E.2d 396 (defendant installed tank for plaintiff); Ciofalo v. Vic Tanney Gyms, Inc., 1961, 10 N.Y.2d 294, 220 N.Y.S.2d 962, 177 N.E.2d 925 (joining club with gymnasium and swimming pool).

34. Griffiths v. Henry Broderick, Inc., 1947, 27 Wash.2d 901, 182 P.2d 18.

35. Jefferson County Bank of Lakewood v. Armored Motors Service, 1961, 148 Colo. 343, 366 P.2d 134; Nichols v. Hitchcock Motor Co., 1937, 22 Cal.App.2d 151, 70 P.2d 654; Freeman v. United Fruit Co., 1916, 223 Mass. 300, 111 N.E. 789; Peterson v. Chicago & N. W. R. Co., 1903, 119 Wis. 197, 96 N.W. 532; Gaita v. Windsor Bank, 1929, 251 N.Y. 152, 167 N.E. 203.

36. Tarbell v. Rutland R. Co., 1901, 73 Vt. 347, 51 A. 6; Blanton v. Dodd, 1892, 109 Mo. 64, 18 S.W.

to the efforts of public utilities to escape liability for negligence in the performance of their duty of public service.[37] A carrier who transports goods [38] or passengers for hire,[39] or a telegraph company transmitting a message,[40] may not contract away its public responsibility, and this is true although the agreement takes the form of a limitation of recovery to an amount less than the probable damages.[41] It has been held, however, that the contract will be sustained where it represents an honest attempt to fix a value as liquidated damages in advance, and the carrier graduates its rates according to such value, so that full protection would be open to the plaintiff upon paying a higher rate.[42] The same rules apply to innkeepers [43] and public warehousemen.[44]

There has been a definite tendency to extend the same rule to other professional bailees who are under no public duty but deal with the public, such as garagemen and owners of parking lots,[45] and of parcel check-

1149; Johnston v. Fargo, 1906, 184 N.Y. 379, 77 N. E. 388; Pittsburgh, C. C. & St. L. R. Co. v. Kinney, 1916, 95 Ohio St. 64, 115 N.E. 505; Hughes v. Warman Steel Casting Co., 1917, 174 Cal. 556, 163 P. 885. Cf. Feigenbaum v. Brink, 1965, 66 Wash.2d 125, 401 P.2d 642 (landlord and tenant). Also McCarthy v. National Ass'n for Stock Car Auto Racing, 1966, 90 N.J.App. 574, 218 A.2d 871 (automobile racing).

37. Restatement of Contracts, § 575(1); Denver Consol. Elec. Co. v. Lawrence, 1903, 31 Colo. 301, 73 P. 39; Collins v. Virginia Power & Elec. Co., 1933, 204 N.C. 320, 168 S.E. 500; Oklahoma Natural Gas Co. v. Appel, Okl.1954, 266 P.2d 442; Reeder v. Western Gas & Power Co., 1953, 42 Wash.2d 542, 256 P. 2d 825; Bowman & Bull Co. v. Postal Telegraph-Cable Co., 1919, 290 Ill. 155, 124 N.E. 851, cert. denied 251 U.S. 562.

38. Boston & Me. R. Co. v. Piper, 1918, 246 U.S. 439; Franklin v. Southern Pac. Co., 1928, 203 Cal. 680, 265 P. 936; Oceanic Steam Nav. Co. v. Corcoran, 2 Cir. 1925, 9 F.2d 724; 4 Williston, Contracts, Rev.Ed. 1936, § 1109. See Goddard, The Liability of the Common Carrier as Determined by Recent Decisions of the United States Supreme Court, 1915, 15 Col.L.Rev. 399, 475.

39. York Co. v. Central R. Co., 1865, 70 U.S. (3 Wall.) 107; School District in Medfield v. Boston, H. & E. R. Co., 1869, 102 Mass. 552. Thus a caretaker travelling on a pass is regarded as a passenger for hire, and the agreement is void. New York Cent. R. Co. v. Lockwood, 1873, 84 U.S. (17 Wall.) 357; Buckley v. Bangor & Aroostook R. Co., 1915, 113 Me. 164, 93 A. 65; cf. Warner v. New York Cent. R. Co., 1964, 43 Misc.2d 848, 252 N.Y.S.2d 515, reversed on other grounds, 23 App.Div.2d 642, 256 N.Y.S.2d 969, appeal after remand 34 App.Div.2d 275, 311 N.Y.S.2d 351 (union representative); Rogow v. United States, S.D.N.Y.1959, 173 F.Supp. 547 (free lance writer travelling for government purpose).

40. Western Union Tel. Co. v. James, 1896, 162 U.S. 650; Vermilye v. Western Union Tel. Co., 1911, 207 Mass. 401, 93 N.E. 635; Dickerson v. Western Union Tel. Co., 1917, 114 Miss. 115, 74 So. 779. But as to interstate messages, the Interstate Commerce Act, 49 U.S.C.A. § 1 et seq., which permits a limitation of liability as to unrepeated messages, now controls. Postal Telegraph-Cable Co. v. Warren-Goodwin Lumber Co., 1919, 251 U.S. 27.

41. Union Pac. R. Co. v. Burke, 1921, 255 U.S. 317; Southern Exp. Co. v. Owens, 1906, 146 Ala. 412, 41 So. 752; Adams Express Co. v. Mellichamp, 1912, 138 Ga. 443, 75 S.E. 596. See Bikle, Agreed Valuation as Affecting the Liability of Common Carriers for Negligence, 1907, 21 Harv.L.Rev. 32.

42. Hart v. Pennsylvania R. Co., 1884, 112 U.S. 331; Alair v. Northern Pac. R. Co., 1893, 53 Minn. 160, 54 N.W. 1072; Greenwald v. Barrett, 1910, 199 N.Y. 170, 92 N.E. 218; Franklin v. Southern Pac. Co., 1928, 203 Cal. 680, 265 P. 936, cert. denied 278 U.S. 621; Zeidenberg v. Greyhound Lines, 1965, 3 Conn. Cir. 176, 209 A.2d 697. See Smith, Contractual Limitations of Damages in Commercial Transactions, 1960, 12 Hast.L.J. 122. That the value fixed is entirely inadequate is immaterial. Pierce Co. v. Wells Fargo Co., 1914, 236 U.S. 278.

43. Oklahoma City Hotel Co. v. Levine, 1941, 189 Okl. 331, 116 P.2d 997; Maxwell Operating Co. v. Harper, 1918, 138 Tenn. 640, 200 S.W. 515; see Gardner v. Jonathan Club, 1950, 35 Cal.2d 343, 217 P.2d 961; Hirsch, Limited Liability of Innkeepers Under Statutory Regulations, 1928, 76 U.Pa.L.Rev. 272.

44. 4 Williston, Contracts, Rev.Ed.1936, 2926; George v. Bekins Van & Storage Co., 1949, 33 Cal.2d 834, 205 P.2d 1037; England v. Lyon Fireproof Storage Co., 1928, 94 Cal.App. 562, 271 P. 532; Inland Compress Co. v. Simmons, 1916, 59 Okl. 287, 159 P. 262.

45. Miller's Mut. Fire Ins. Ass'n of Alton, Ill. v. Parker, 1951, 234 N.C. 20, 65 S.E.2d 341; Nagaki v. Stockfleth, 1942, 141 Neb. 676, 4 N.W.2d 766; Scott Auto & Supply Co. v. McQueen, 1924, 111 Okl. 107, 226 P. 372; Pilson v. Tip-Top Auto Co., 1913, 67 Or. 528, 136 P. 642.

rooms,[46] on the ground that the indispensable need for their services deprives the customer of all real equal bargaining power. As to other private bailees for hire, the courts are divided as to the validity of a contract against liability for negligence—some holding that such a general agreement is valid,[47] while others regard it as against public policy.[48] The decision is likely to turn upon the extent to which it is considered that the public interest is involved. Where it is not, it seems the better view that there is an unfair advantage to the bailee in permitting him to set the terms upon which he will receive the goods, so long as the bailor is free without any serious disadvantage to himself to reject them.[49] It is generally agreed that he may at least contract that he is not required to exercise care to protect the deposited goods against a specific limited risk.[50]

If an express agreement exempting the defendant from liability for his negligence is to be sustained, it must appear that its terms were brought home to the plaintiff;[51] and if he did not know of the provision in his contract and a reasonable person in his position would not have known of it, it is not binding upon him, and the agreement fails for want of mutual assent.[52] It is also necessary that the expressed terms of the agreement be applicable to the particular misconduct of the defendant.[53] In general, and on the basis either of common experience as to what is intended, or of public policy to discourage aggravated wrongs, such agreements are not construed to cover the more extreme forms of negligence which are described as wilful, wanton, reckless or gross,[54] or to any conduct

46. Denver Union Terminal R. Co. v. Cullinan, 1922, 72 Colo. 248, 210 P. 602; Hotels Statler Co. v. Safier, 1921, 103 Ohio St. 638, 134 N.E. 460. In Tunkl v. Regents of University of California, 1963, 32 Cal.Rptr. 33, 383 P.2d 441, the same rule was applied to a charitable hospital accepting patients from the public, upon the ground that the "public interest" was involved.

47. Fidelity Storage Co. v. Kingsbury, 1935, 65 U.S. App.D.C. 69, 79 F.2d 705; Marlow v. Conway Iron Works, 1924, 130 S.C. 256, 125 S.E. 569; Gashweiler v. Wabash, St. L. & P. R. Co., 1884, 83 Mo. 112.

48. Sporsem v. First Nat. Bank, 1925, 133 Wash. 199, 233 P. 641; Downs v. Sley System Garages, 1937, 129 Pa.Super. 68, 194 A. 772. Cf. Hunter v. American Rentals, Inc., 1962, 189 Kan. 615, 371 P.2d 131 (business of renting trailers).

49. See Note, 1938, 86 U.Pa.L.Rev. 772, concluding that such provisions should be upheld, but that there is a slight numerical majority against their validity.

50. Taussig v. Bode & Haslett, 1901, 134 Cal. 260, 66 P. 259 (no obligation to watch casks for leakage); Gesford v. Star Van & Storage Co., 1920, 104 Neb. 453, 177 N.W. 794 (freezing); Patterson v. Wenatchee Canning Co., 1910, 59 Wash. 556, 110 P. 379; see Note, 1922, 35 Harv.L.Rev. 478.

51. Lebkeucher v. Pennsylvania R. Co., 1922, 97 N.J. L. 112, 116 A. 323, affirmed, 1922, 98 N.J.L. 271, 118 A. 926; Van Noy Interstate Co. v. Tucker, 1921, 125 Miss. 260, 87 So. 643; Dodge v. Nashville, C. & St. L. R. Co., 1919, 142 Tenn. 20, 215 S.W. 274. But the plaintiff may be bound by a general custom to print such limitations in bills of lading, or by a tariff on file. Porteous v. Adams Express Co., 1911, 115 Minn. 281, 132 N.W. 296; Kansas City Southern R. Co. v. C. H. Albers Commission Co., 1911, 223 U.S. 573.

52. Agricultural Ins. Co. v. Constantine, 1944, 144 Ohio St. 275, 58 N.E.2d 658; Dodge v. Nashville, C. & St. L. R. Co., 1919, 142 Tenn. 20, 215 S.W. 274; cf. Raynale v. Yellow Cab Co., 1931, 115 Cal.App. 90, 300 P. 991; Restatement of Contracts, 1932, § 70. While it is true that one who accepts a contract is normally bound by its terms even though he does not read them, as in U Drive & Tour v. System Auto Parks, 1937, 28 Cal.App.2d Supp. 782, 71 P.2d 354, this does not apply where he reasonably believes that a ticket handed him is only a token of identification. Maynard v. James, 1929, 109 Conn. 365, 146 A. 614. Cf. The Majestic, 1897, 166 U.S. 375; Jones v. Great Northern R. Co., 1923, 68 Mont. 231, 217 P. 673.

53. Langford v. Nevin, 1927, 117 Tex. 130, 298 S. W. 536; Gulf Compress Co. v. Harrington, 1909, 90 Ark. 256, 119 S.W. 249; Willard Van Dyke Products, Inc. v. Eastman Kodak Co., 1963, 12 N.Y.2d 301, 239 N.Y.S.2d 337, 189 N.E.2d 693; Galligan v. Arovitch, 1966, 421 Pa. 301, 219 A.2d 463.

54. Friedman v. Lockheed Aircraft Corp., E.D.N.Y. 1956, 138 F.Supp. 530; Thomas v. Atlantic Coast Line R. Co., 5 Cir. 1953, 201 F.2d 167; Cooper v. Raleigh & G. R. Co., 1899, 110 Ga. 659, 36 S.E. 240; Wabash R. Co. v. Brown, 1894, 152 Ill. 484, 39 N.E. 273; Ringling Bros., Barnum & Bailey Combined Shows v. Olvera, 9 Cir. 1941, 119 F.2d 584. In Pratt v. Western Pac. R. Co., 1963, 213 Cal.App.2d

which constitutes an intentional tort.[55] It follows, for example, that when a warehouseman negligently misdelivers goods, a clause in the contract of storage limiting his liability, which would be effective if the action were for negligence, can be circumvented by suing for conversion.[56]

Implied Acceptance of Risk

In by far the greater number of cases, the consent to assume the risk has not been a matter of express agreement, but has been found to be implied from the conduct of the plaintiff under the circumstances. Although it was said in early decisions,[57] and is still repeated by some courts,[58] that assumption of risk will not be found apart from a contract relation between the parties, it is now generally recognized that the basis of the defense is not contract but consent, and that it is available in many cases where no agreement exists.[59] It has been said also, on occasion, that the plaintiff never assumes the risk of the defendant's negligence, once it exists;[60] but the case law is strongly to the effect that once the plaintiff is informed of such negligence, the risks arising from it can be assumed.[61]

It is here that there is the greatest misapprehension and confusion as to assumption of risk, and its most frequent misapplication. It is not true that in any case where the plaintiff voluntarily encounters a known danger he necessarily consents to negligence of the defendant which creates it. A pedestrian who walks across the street in the middle of a block, through a stream of traffic travelling at high speed, cannot by any stretch of the imagination be found to consent that the drivers shall not use care to avoid running him down. On the contrary, he is insisting that they shall. This is contributory negligence pure and simple; it is not assumption of risk. And if A leaves an automobile stopped at night on the travelled portion of the highway, and his passenger remains sitting in it, it can readily be found that there is consent to the negligence of A, but not to that of B, who runs into the car from the rear.[62] This is a distinction which has baffled a great many law students, some judges, and unhappily a few very learned legal writers.

Implied assumption of risk has been found in a variety of cases, in some of which the plaintiff's conduct has apparently been quite reasonable, while in others it has amounted to contributory negligence.[63] By entering freely and voluntarily into any relation or situation where the negligence of the defendant is obvious, the plaintiff may be found to

573, 29 Cal.Rptr. 108, it was held to be contrary to public policy to allow a carrier to exonerate itself for gross negligence.

55. Cf. Sands v. American Ry. Exp. Co., 1923, 154 Minn. 308, 193 N.W. 721, reversed, 1924, 159 Minn. 25, 198 N.W. 402.

56. Page v. Allison, 1935, 173 Okl. 205, 47 P.2d 134; Arizona Storage & Dist. Co. v. Rynning, 1930, 37 Ariz. 232, 293 P. 16; Glinsky v. Dunham & Reid, 1930, 230 App.Div. 470, 245 N.Y.S. 359; Menuez v. Julius Kindermann & Sons, S.D.N.Y.1937, 19 F. Supp. 7; see D'Aloisio v. Morton's, Inc., 1961, 342 Mass. 231, 172 N.E.2d 819. Contra, George v. Bekins Van & Storage Co., 1949, 33 Cal.2d 834, 205 P. 2d 1037.

57. See B. Shoninger Co. v. Mann, 1905, 219 Ill. 242, 76 N.E. 354; and cf. Papakalos v. Shaka, 1941, 91 N.H. 265, 18 A.2d 377. See Note, 1941, 40 Mich.L. Rev. 137.

58. See supra, p. 439.

59. Scanlon v. Wedger, 1898, 156 Mass. 462, 31 N.E. 642; Shafer v. Tacoma Eastern R. Co., 1916, 91 Wash. 164, 157 P. 485; Mountain v. Wheatley, 1951, 106 Cal.App.2d 333, 234 P.2d 1031; Bohnsack v. Driftmier, 1952, 243 Iowa 383, 52 N.W.2d 79; Miner v. Connecticut River R. Co., 1891, 153 Mass. 398, 26 N.E. 994. See Note, 1954, 32 N.C.L.Rev. 366.

60. See for example Jewell v. Kansas City Bolt & Nut Co., 1910, 231 Mo. 176, 132 S.W. 703. See supra, p. 453.

61. Choctaw, O. & G. R. Co. v. Jones, 1906, 77 Ark. 367, 92 S.W. 244; Chicago, B. & Q. R. Co. v. Shalstrom, 8 Cir. 1912, 195 F. 725; De Kallands v. Washtenaw Home Tel. Co., 1908, 153 Mich. 25, 116 N.W. 564; Kath v. East St. Louis & S. R. Co., 1908, 232 Ill. 126, 83 N.E. 533.

62. Suggested by Calahan v. Wood, 1970, 24 Utah 2d 8, 465 P.2d 169.

63. See supra, p. 440.

accept and consent to it, and to undertake to look out for himself and relieve the defendant of the duty. Thus those who participate [64] or sit as spectators at sports and amusements may be taken to assume all the known risks of being hurt by roller coasters,[65] flying baseballs,[66] golf balls,[67] or wrestlers,[68] or such things as fireworks explosions.[69] Cardozo once summarized all this quite neatly: "The timorous may stay at home." [70]

On the same basis, plaintiffs who enter business premises as invitees and discover dangerous conditions, such as slippery floors and unsafe stairways, may be found to assume the risks when they nevertheless proceed freely and voluntarily to encounter them.[71] The guest who accepts a ride with an automobile driver may assume the risk of his known incompetence,[72] or intoxication,[73] of his continued or threatened negligent driving,[74] or of known defects in the car.[75] Likewise the user of a product sup-

64. McLeod Store v. Vinson, 1926, 213 Ky. 667, 281 S.W. 799.

65. Lumsden v. L. A. Thompson Scenic R. Co., 1909, 130 App.Div. 209, 114 N.Y.S. 421; Sullivan v. Ridgeway Const. Co., 1920, 236 Mass. 75, 127 N.E. 543; Murphy v. Steeplechase Amusement Co., 1929, 250 N.Y. 479, 166 N.E. 173. See Note, 1929, 15 Corn.L.Q. 132.

66. Hudson v. Kansas City Baseball Club, 1942, 349 Mo. 1215, 164 S.W.2d 318; Hunt v. Portland Baseball Club, 1956, 207 Or. 337, 296 P.2d 495; Shaw v. Boston American League Baseball Co., 1930, 325 Mass. 419, 90 N.E.2d 840; Brisson v. Minneapolis Baseball & Athletic Ass'n, 1932, 185 Minn. 507, 240 N.W. 903; Williams v. Houston Baseball Ass'n, Tex.Civ.App.1941, 154 S.W.2d 874. See Notes, 1936, 10 So.Cal.L.Rev. 67; 1936, 24 Cal.L.Rev. 429; 1937, 17 Bos.U.L.Rev. 485; [1951] Wash.U.L.Q. 434; 1952, 26 Temple L.Q. 206.

67. Schlenger v. Weinberg, 1930, 107 N.J.L. 130, 150 A. 434; Everett v. Goodwin, 1931, 201 N.C. 734, 161 S.E. 316; Slotnick v. Cooley, 1933, 166 Tenn. 373, 61 S.W.2d 462; Alexander v. Wrenn, 1932, 158 Va. 486, 164 S.E. 715; Stober v. Embry, 1932, 243 Ky. 117, 47 S.W.2d 921. Cf. Douglas v. Converse, 1915, 248 Pa. 232, 93 A. 955 (polo); Ingerson v. Shattuck School, 1931, 185 Minn. 16, 239 N.W. 667 (football); Hammel v. Madison Square Garden Corp., 1935, 156 Misc. 311, 279 N.Y.S. 815 (hockey); Filler v. Stenvick, 1953, 79 N.D. 422, 56 N.W.2d 798 (skater, crack in ice).

68. Dusckiewicz v. Carter, 1947, 115 Vt. 122, 52 A.2d 419.

69. Scanlon v. Wedger, 1892, 156 Mass. 462, 31 N.E. 642. Cf. Morton v. California Sports Car Club, 1958, 163 Cal.App.2d 685, 329 P.2d 967 (wheel from car in automobile race); Johnson v. City of New York, 1906, 186 N.Y. 139, 78 N.E. 715 (automobile speed test); Shafer v. Tacoma Eastern R. Co., 1916, 91 Wash. 164, 157 P. 485 (raising derailed engine). See, Generally, Calapietro, The Promoters' Liability for Sports Spectator Injuries, 1960, 46 Corn.L.Q. 140.

70. In Murphy v. Steeplechase Amusement Co., 1929, 250 N.Y. 479, 166 N.E. 173. Cf. Rauch v. Pennsyl-

vania Sports & Enterprises, 1951, 367 Pa. 632, 81 A.2d 548 (voluntary return to rink where reckless skating going on).

71. Hunn v. Windsor Hotel Co., 1937, 119 W.Va. 215, 193 S.E. 57; Crone v. Jordan Marsh Co., 1929, 269 Mass. 289, 169 N.E. 136; Fillis v. Wahlig, 1943, 267 App.Div. 781, 45 N.Y.S.2d 609, affirmed memo. 1944, 293 N.Y. 710, 56 N.E.2d 729; Curtis v. Traders Nat. Bank, 1951, 314 Ky. 765, 237 S.W.2d 76; Cole v. L. D. Willcutt & Sons Co., 1914, 218 Mass. 71, 105 N.E. 461. See, with a critical approach to such cases, Keeton, Assumption of Risk and the Landowner, 1942, 20 Tex.L.Rev. 562; Keeton, Personal Injury Resulting from Open and Obvious Conditions, 1952, 100 U.Pa.L.Rev. 629; Keeton, Assumption of Risk and the Landowner, 1961, 22 La.L.Rev. 108.

72. Cleary v. Eckart, 1926, 191 Wis. 114, 210 N.W. 267; Powell v. Berry, 1916, 145 Ga. 696, 89 S.E. 753; Schubring v. Weggen, 1940, 234 Wis. 517, 291 N.W. 788. Cf. Wall v. Gill, 1950, 311 Ky. 796, 225 S.W.2d 670 (inexperienced student, permanent wave).

73. Ven Rooy v. Farmers Mut. Ins. Co., 1958, 5 Wis. 2d 374, 92 N.W.2d 771; Young v. Wheby, 1944, 126 W.Va. 741, 30 S.E.2d 6; Waltanen v. Wiitala, 1960, 361 Mich. 504, 105 N.W.2d 400; Borstad v. La Roque, N.D.1959, 98 N.W.2d 16; see Bohnsack v. Driftmier, 1952, 243 Iowa 383, 52 N.W.2d 79. Cf. Adair v. Valley Flying Service, 1952, 196 Or. 479, 250 P.2d 104 (drunken pilot of plane).

74. Bugh v. Webb, 1959, 231 Ark. 27, 328 S.W.2d 379 (drag racing); Sprague v. Hauck, 1958, 3 Wis.2d 616, 89 N.W.2d 226 (speed); Kelly v. Checker White Cab Co., 1948, 131 W.Va. 816, 50 S.E.2d 888 (snow and ice on road). See Note, 1942, 48 W.Va.L.Q. 80.

75. Clise v. Prunty, 1930, 108 W.Va. 635, 152 S.E. 201 (chains and brakes); Sloan v. Gulf Ref. Co. of La., La.App.1924, 139 So. 26 (lights); Mitchell v. Heaton, 1941, 231 Iowa 269, 1 N.W.2d 284 (defective wheel bolts). See Rice, The Automobile Guest and the Rationale of Assumption of Risk, 1943, 27 Minn.L.Rev. 323; Pedrick: Taken for a Ride: The Automobile Guest and Assumption of Risk, 1961, 22 La.L.Rev. 90.

plied to him may assume the risks of its known dangerous defects.[76] In all of these cases the plaintiff may be barred by his voluntary choice to go ahead with full knowledge of the risk. In all of them, however, other factors, which remain to be considered, may affect the "voluntary choice;" and the fact that the risk *may* be assumed is by no means conclusive as to whether it has been assumed.

Knowledge of Risk

The defense of assumption of risk is in fact quite narrowly confined and restricted by two requirements: first, that the plaintiff must know and understand the risk he is incurring, and second, that his choice to incur it must be entirely free and voluntary. Since in the ordinary case there is no conclusive evidence against the plaintiff on these issues, they normally go to the jury;[77] and since juries are notoriously unfavorable to the defense, the percentage of cases in which the plaintiff has actually been barred from recovery by his assumption of the risk is quite small.

"Knowledge of the risk is the watchword of assumption of risk."[78] Under ordinary circumstances the plaintiff will not be taken to assume any risk of either activities or conditions of which he is ignorant.[79] Furthermore, he must not only know of the facts which create the danger, but he must comprehend and appreciate the danger itself.[80] "A defect and the danger arising from it are not necessarily to be identified, and a person may know of one without appreciating the other."[81] The standard to be applied is, in theory at least, a subjective one, geared to the particular plaintiff and his situation, rather than that of the reasonable man of ordinary prudence who appears in contributory negligence. If because of age[82] or lack of information or experience,[83] he does not comprehend the risk involved in a known situation, he will not be taken to consent to

---

76. Gallegos v. Nash, 1955, 137 Cal.App.2d 14, 289 P. 2d 835; Runnels v. Dixie Drive-It-Yourself System Jackson Co., 1954, 220 Miss. 678, 71 So.2d 453; Saeter v. Harley-Davidson Motor Co., (1960) 186 Cal. App.2d 248, 8 Cal.Rptr. 747; Sanders v. Kalamazoo Tank & Silo Co., (1919) 205 Mich. 339, 171 N.W. 523.

See also Erickson v. Van Web Equipment Co., 1965, 270 Minn. 42, 132 N.W.2d 814; De Eugenio v. Allis-Chalmers Mfg. Co., 3 Cir. 1954, 210 F.2d 409; Baldridge v. Wright Gas Co., 1961, 154 Ohio St. 452, 96 N.E.2d 300. See Keeton, Assumption of Risk in Products Liability Cases, 1961, 22 La.L.Rev. 122.

77. Silvia v. Woodhouse, 1969, 356 Mass. 119, 248 N. E.2d 260; Cox v. Johnston, 1959, 139 Colo. 376, 339 P.2d 989; Reeves v. Winslow, 1959, 394 Pa. 291, 147 A.2d 357; Turner v. Johnson, Ky.1960, 333 S.W.2d 749; Quigley v. Roath, 1961, 227 Or. 336, 362 P.2d 328.

78. Cincinnati, N. O. & T. P. R. Co. v. Thompson, 6 Cir. 1916, 236 F. 1, 9.

79. Guerrero v. Westgate Lumber Co., 1958, 164 Cal. App.2d 612, 331 P.2d 107; Ricks v. Jackson, 1959, 169 Ohio St. 254, 159 N.E.2d 225; Wiltz v. Esso Standard Oil Co., La.App.1961, 126 So.2d 649; Evans v. Buchner, 1963, — Alaska —, 386 P.2d 836; Calanchini v. Bliss, 9 Cir. 1937, 88 F.2d 82.

80. Shufelberger v. Worden, 1962, 189 Kan. 379, 369 P.2d 382; Ellis v. Moore & Wardlaw, Tex.1966, 401 S.W.2d 789; Stotzheim v. Djos, 1959, 256 Minn. 316, 98 N.W.2d 129; Dean v. Martz, Ky.1959, 329 S.W.2d 371; Gilbert v. City of Los Angeles, 1967, 249 Cal.App.2d 1006, 58 Cal.Rptr. 56.

81. Errico v. Washburn Williams Co., C.C.Pa.1909, 170 F. 852, 853. Cf. Dean v. Martz, Ky.1959, 329 S. W.2d 371; Shufelberger v. Worden, 1962, 189 Kan. 379, 369 P.2d 382; Sparks v. Porcher, 1964, 109 Ga. App. 334, 136 S.E.2d 153 (knowledge that driver has been drinking not as matter of law knowledge he is too drunk to drive).

82. Aldes v. St. Paul Baseball Club, 1958, 251 Minn. 440, 88 N.W.2d 94; Moore v. City of Bloomington, 1912, 51 Ind.App. 145, 95 N.E. 374 and City of Bloomington v. Moore, 1915, 183 Ind. 283, 109 N.E. 42; Freedman v. Hurwitz, 1933, 116 Conn. 283, 164 A. 647; Everton Silica Sand Co. v. Hicks, 1939, 197 Ark. 980, 125 S.W.2d 793.

In Greene v. Watts, 1962, 21 Cal.App.2d 103, 26 Cal. Rptr. 334, it was held that a child aged 3½ was incapable of assumption of risk, as well as contributory negligence.

83. Dee v. Parish, 1959, 160 Tex. 171, 327 S.W.2d 449, on remand, 1960, 332 S.W.2d 764; Hanley v. California Bridge & Constr. Co., 1899, 127 Cal. 232, 59 P. 577; Perham v. Portland General Elec. Co., 1897, 33 Or. 451, 53 P. 14, rehearing denied, 1898, 53 P. 24; Gill v. Homrighausen, 1891, 79 Wis. 634, 48 N.W. 862; Dawson v. Lawrence Gaslight Co., 1905, 188 Mass. 481, 74 N.E. 912.

assume it. His failure to exercise ordinary care to discover the danger is not properly a matter of assumption of risk, but of the defense of contributory negligence.[84]

At the same time, it is evident that a purely subjective standard opens a very wide door for the plaintiff who is willing to testify that he did not know or understand the risk; and there have been a good many cases in which the courts have said in effect that he is not to be believed, so that in effect something of an objective element enters the case, and the standard applied in fact does not differ greatly from that of the reasonable man. The plaintiff will not be heard to say that he did not comprehend a risk which must have been quite clear and obvious to him.[85] There are some things, as for example the risk of injury if one is hit by a baseball driven on a line,[86] which are so far a matter of common knowledge in the community, that in the absence of some satisfactory explanation a de-

nial of such knowledge simply is not to be believed.[87]

As in the case of negligence itself,[88] there are certain risks which anyone of adult age must be taken to appreciate: the danger of slipping on ice,[89] of falling through unguarded openings,[90] of lifting heavy objects,[91] of being squeezed in a narrow space,[92] of inflammable liquids,[93] of driving an automobile whose brakes will not operate,[94] or of unguarded circular saws or similar dangerous machinery,[95] and doubtless many others. Furthermore, a plaintiff who has been for a substantial length of time in the immediate vicinity of a dangerous situation will be taken to have discovered and to understand the normal, ordinary risks involved in that situation, such as the danger of trains in motion in a railroad yard,[96] or of standardized ob-

---

84. Ward v. Knapp, 1955, 134 Cal.App.2d 538, 286 P. 2d 370; Halepeska v. Callihan Interests, Inc., Tex. 1963, 371 S.W.2d 368, on remand 376 S.W.2d 932; Fisher v. United States Steel Corp., 5 Cir. 1964, 334 F.2d 904; Dana v. Bursey, Fla.App.1964, 169 So.2d 845. See supra, p. 445.

85. 4 Labatt, Master and Servant, 2d Ed.1913, § 1313.

86. Crane v. Kansas City Baseball Co., 1913, 168 Mo.App. 301, 153 S.W. 1076; Brown v. San Francisco Ball Club, 1950, 99 Cal.App.2d 484, 222 P.2d 19. Compare, as to the obligation to discover the risk, Brisson v. Minneapolis Baseball Ass'n, 1932, 185 Minn. 507, 240 N.W. 903; Keys v. Alamo City Baseball Club, Tex.Civ.App.1941, 150 S.W.2d 368.

As to the effect of community knowledge of the risk of attending ice hockey games, compare Modec v. City of Eveleth, 1947, 224 Minn. 556, 29 N.W.2d 453, with Tite v. Omaha Coliseum Co., 1943, 144 Neb. 22, 12 N.W.2d 90; Morris v. Cleveland Hockey Club, 1952, 157 Ohio St. 225, 105 N.E.2d 419; Lemoine v. Springfield Hockey Ass'n, 1940, 307 Mass. 102, 29 N.E.2d 716; Thurman v. Ice Palace, 1939, 36 Cal. App.2d 364, 97 P.2d 999. See Notes, 1948, 31 Marq. L.Rev. 298; 1952, 26 Temple L.Q. 206; 1953, 22 U. Cin.L.Rev. 118.

Cf. Alden v. Norwood Arena, 1955, 332 Mass. 267, 124 N.E.2d 505 as to a wheel coming off of a car at an automobile race.

87. Even a minor may be taken to appreciate those risks with which one of his age, experience and intelligence must be familiar. Ciriack v. Merchants' Woolen Co., 1890, 151 Mass. 152, 23 N.E. 829.

88. See supra, p. 157.

89. Shea v. Kansas City, Ft. S. & M. R. Co., 1898, 76 Mo.App. 29. Cf. McIntire v. White, 1898, 171 Mass. 170, 50 N.E. 524.

90. Moulton v. Gage, 1885, 138 Mass. 390; Schwartz v. Cornell, 1891, 59 Hun 623, 13 N.Y.S. 355.

91. Brown v. Oregon Lumber Co., 1893, 24 Or. 315, 33 P. 557; Ferguson v. Phoenix Cotton Mills, 1901, 106 Tenn. 236, 61 S.W. 53. Cf. Gibson v. Beaver, 1967, 245 Md. 418, 226 A.2d 273; Duffy v. New York, N. H. & H. R. Co., 1906, 192 Mass. 28, 77 N.E. 1031.

92. Toledo, St. L. & W. R. Co. v. Allen, 1928, 276 U. S. 165; Mellott v. Louisville & N. R. Co., 1897, 101 Ky. 212, 40 S.W. 696.

93. Johnson v. Webster Mfg. Co., 1909, 139 Wis. 181, 120 N.W. 832.

94. Gallegos v. Nash, 1955, 137 Cal.App.2d 14, 289 P. 2d 835.

95. Hanson v. Ludlow Mfg Co., 1894, 162 Mass. 187, 38 N.E. 363; Findlay v. Russell Wheel & Foundry Co., 1896, 108 Mich. 286, 66 N.W. 50 (pulley); Ruchinsky v. French, 1897, 168 Mass. 68, 46 N.E. 417 (cogwheels); Dillenberger v. Weingartner, 1900, 64 N.J.L. 292, 45 A. 638 (fan).

96. Wolfe v. Atlantic Coast Line R. Co., 1930, 199 N. C. 613, 155 S.E. 459; Hines v. Pershin, 1923, 89 Okl. 297, 215 P. 599; Chesapeake & O. R. Co. v. Nixon, 1926, 271 U.S. 218.

structions near the track.[97] Once the plaintiff fully understands the risk, the fact that he has momentarily forgotten it will not protect him.[98] In the usual case, his knowledge and appreciation of the danger will be a question for the jury; but where it is clear that any person of normal intelligence [99] in his position must have understood the danger, the issue may be decided by the court.[1]

Even where there is knowledge and appreciation of a risk, the plaintiff may not be barred from recovery where the situation changes to introduce a new element, such as several balls in the air at one time in a baseball park.[2] The fact that the plaintiff is fully aware of one risk, as for example that of the speed at which a car is being driven, does not mean that he assumes another of which he is unaware, such as the failure of the driver to watch the road.[3] And his knowl-

edge of the negligence of one person does not mean that he assumes the risk of that of another, of which he does not know.[4]

Since the basis of assumption of the risk is not so much knowledge of the risk as consent to assume it, it is quite possible for the plaintiff to assume risks of whose specific existence he is not aware, provided that his intent to do so is made clear. He may, in other words, consent to take his chances as to unknown conditions. He may certainly do so expressly; and there are a few cases in which the assumption has been found by implication. Thus a guest who accepts a gratuitous ride in an automobile has been taken to assume the risk of defects in the car unknown to the driver,[5] just as the same has been said of a licensee who enters another's premises.[6] Workmen used to be said to assume risks of employment of which they had at least equal means or opportunities of knowledge or discovery with the employer, even though they were unaware of what they were.[7]

---

97. Southern Pac. Co. v. Berkshire, 1921, 254 U.S. 415; Reese v. Philadelphia & R. R. Co., 1915, 239 U.S. 463.

98. Jacobs v. Southern R. Co., 1916, 241 U.S. 229; New York, C. & St. L. R. Co. v. McDougall, 6 Cir. 1926, 15 F.2d 283.

99. Luebke v. Berlin Mach. Works, 1894, 88 Wis. 442, 60 N.W. 711; 4 Labatt, Master and Servant, 2d Ed. 1913, § 1313. It was said in Ingerman v. Moore, 1891, 90 Cal. 410, 27 P. 306, that the plaintiff's capacity to acquire knowledge must be taken into account. It would seem that where consent to incur the risk is in issue, as distinguished from the departure from external standards of conduct involved in contributory negligence, the lack of normal intelligence should be considered. Cf. Greene v. Watts, 1962, 21 Cal.App.2d 103, 26 Cal.Rptr. 334. In general, however, the distinction is seldom made.

1. 4 Labatt, Master and Servant, 2d Ed.1913, § 1309.

2. Cincinnati Baseball Club v. Eno, 1925, 112 Ohio St. 175, 147 N.E. 86.

3. Jewell v. Schmidt, 1957, 1 Wis.2d 241, 83 N.W.2d 487. Accord: Cassidy v. Quisenberry, Ky.1961, 346 S.W.2d 304 (speed of car and roller-coaster road, inexperience of driver); Haugen v. Wittkopf, 1943, 242 Wis. 276, 7 N.W.2d 886 (frosted windshield, inattention of driver); Fred Harvey Corp. v. Mateas, 9 Cir. 1948, 170 F.2d 612 (inexperienced and untrained mule at Grand Canyon); Lee v. National League Baseball Club of Milwaukee, 1958, 4 Wis.2d 168, 89 N.W.2d 811 (negligent supervision in scramble for foul ball); American Cooperage Co. v. Clem-

ons, Tex.Civ.App.1963, 364 S.W.2d 705 (electric lineman; failure of fellow servant to direct traffic). Vierra v. Fifth Ave. Rental Service, 1963, 60 Cal.2d 266, 32 Cal.Rptr. 193, 383 P.2d 777 (known danger of flying particles of concrete, unknown as to flying metal fragments broken off of tool).

4. Host driver and other colliding driver: Berkstresser v. Voight, 1958, 63 N.M. 470, 321 P.2d 1115; Giemza v. Allied American Mut. Fire Ins. Co., 1960, 10 Wis.2d 555, 103 N.W.2d 538; Kauth v. Landsverk, 1937, 224 Wis. 554, 271 N.W. 841; Smith v. Harris, 1952, 41 Wash.2d 291, 248 P.2d 551; Miller v. Treat, 1960, 57 Wash.2d 524, 358 P.2d 143; Contra, Baltimore County v. State to Use of Keenan, 1963, 232 Md. 350, 193 A.2d 30. Employer and third person: Wright v. Concrete Co., 1962, 107 Ga.App. 190, 129 S.E.2d 351. Cf. Farley v. Hampson, 1949, 323 Mass. 550, 83 N.E.2d 165; Harrop v. Beckman, 1963, 15 Utah 2d 78, 387 P.2d 554.

5. Higgins v. Mason, 1930, 255 N.Y. 104, 174 N.E. 77; Gagnon v. Dana, 1897, 69 N.H. 264, 39 A. 982. See supra, p. 383. A line of cases so holding, headed by O'Shea v. Lavoy, 1921, 175 Wis. 456, 185 N.W. 525, was overruled in McConville v. State Farm Mut. Auto. Ins. Co., 1962, 15 Wis.2d 374, 113 N.W.2d 14.

6. See supra, p. 376.

7. Miller v. Moran Bros. Co., 1905, 39 Wash. 631, 81 P. 1089; Peterson v. American Ice Co., 1912, 83 N.

All that such decisions mean, of course, is that the defendant is under no duty to protect the plaintiff because the plaintiff is in an equal position to protect himself. Rather than the defense of assumption of risk, they appear fairly to go to duty in the first instance. The law merely distributes the hazards in accordance with a more or less common understanding of the position in which the plaintiff consents to be placed, or the obligation which the defendant may reasonably be taken to assume.[8]

Voluntary Assumption

The second important limitation upon the defense of assumption of risk is that the plaintiff is not barred from recovery unless his choice is a free and voluntary one. There must first of all, of course, be some manifestation of consent to relieve the defendant of the obligation of reasonable conduct. It is not every deliberate encountering of a known danger which is reasonably to be interpreted as evidence of such consent. The jaywalker who dashes into the street in the middle of the block, in the path of a stream of cars driven in excess of the speed limit, certainly does not manifest consent that they shall use no care and run him down. On the contrary, he is insisting that they shall take immediate precautions for his safety; and while this is certainly contributory negligence, it is not assumption of risk.[9] This is undoubtedly the most frequent error of attorneys, and even of the courts, in dealing with the defense.

But even though his conduct may indicate consent, the risk will not be taken to be as-

sumed if it appears from his words, or from the facts of the situation, that he does not in fact consent to relieve the defendant of the obligation to protect him.[10] The difficulty in the administration of this principle arises from the fact that, notwithstanding vigorous protests, if the plaintiff proceeds to enter voluntarily into a situation which exposes him to the risk, it will normally indicate that he does not stand on his objection, and has consented, however reluctantly, to accept the risk and look out for himself.[11] If, however, he surrenders his better judgment upon an assurance that the situation is safe, or that it will be remedied, or a promise of protection, he does not assume the risk,[12] unless the danger is so obvious and so extreme that there can be no reasonable reliance upon the assurance.[13] The rule which was worked out in employment cases is that a workman does not assume the risk of defects or dangerous conditions which the employer has promised to remedy,[14] until so long a time has elapsed

J.L. 579, 83 A. 872; Dube v. Gay, 1899, 69 N.H. 670, 46 A. 1049. See 4 Labatt, Master and Servant, 2d Ed. 1913, §§ 1327, 1328.

8. "When, therefore, it is said, in this connection, that a servant assumes, by entering the service of his master, any given hazard, it is merely another form of saying that, under all the circumstances, the law imposes that hazard upon him." Chicago & N. W. R. Co. v. Moranda, 1879, 93 Ill. 302, 320.

9. See Second Restatement of Torts, § 496C, Comment *h*.

10. Smith v. Baker & Sons, [1891] A.C. 325; Krause v. Hall, 1928, 195 Wis. 565, 217 N.W. 290; Ridgway v. Yenny, 1944, 223 Ind. 16, 57 N.E.2d 581. In Boyce v. Black, 1941, 123 W.Va. 234, 15 S.E.2d 588, it was held that where one automobile guest protests against the negligence of the driver, others are not necessarily required to protest.

11. Atchison, T. & S. F. R. Co. v. Schroeder, 1891, 47 Kan. 315, 27 P. 965; Galveston, H. & S. A. R. Co. v. Drew, 1883, 59 Tex. 10; Talbot v. Sims, 1905, 213 Pa. 1, 62 A. 107; Loynes v. Loring B. Hall Co., 1907, 194 Mass. 221, 80 N.E. 472.

12. Oltmanns v. Driver, 1961, 252 Iowa 1066, 109 N. W.2d 446; Brown v. Lennane, 1908, 155 Mich. 686, 118 N.W. 581; McKee v. Tourtellotte, 1896, 167 Mass. 69, 44 N.E. 1071; Manks v. Moore, 1909, 108 Minn. 284, 122 N.W. 5. Even without express assurance, the plaintiff may reasonably believe that his protests, as against reckless driving of a car, have been effective. Renfro v. Keen, 1935, 19 Tenn.App. 345, 89 S.W.2d 170.

13. Burke v. Davis, 1906, 191 Mass. 20, 76 N.E. 1039; Milby & Dow Coal & Mining Co. v. Balla, 1907, 7 Ind.T. 629, 104 S.W. 860; Rohrabacher v. Woodard, 1900, 124 Mich. 125, 82 N.W. 797; Blume v. Ballis, 1940, 207 Minn. 393, 291 N.W. 906.

14. Clarke v. Holmes, 1862, 7 H. & N. 937, 158 Eng. Rep. 751; Deshazer v. Tompkins, 1965, 89 Idaho 347, 404 P.2d 604; Schumaker v. King, Fla.App.

without action that he can no longer continue work in reasonable reliance upon such a promise.[15]

Even where the plaintiff does not protest, the risk is not assumed where the conduct of the defendant has left him no reasonable alternative. Where the defendant puts him to a choice of evils, there is a species of duress, which destroys all idea of freedom of election. Thus a shipper does not assume the risk of a defective car supplied him by a carrier where the only alternative to shipment in it is to let his cabbages rot in the field;[16] and a tenant does not assume the risk of the landlord's negligence in maintaining a common passageway when it is the only exit to the street.[17] In general, the plaintiff is not required to surrender a valuable legal right, such as the use of his own property as he sees fit, merely because the defendant's conduct has threatened him with harm if the right is exercised. He is not, for example, required to forego pasturing his cattle in a field because the defendant has failed in its duty to fence its adjoining railway track.[18] By plac-

ing him in the dilemma, the defendant has deprived him of his freedom of choice, and so cannot be heard so say that he has voluntarily assumed the risk. Those who dash in to save their own property,[19] or the lives [20] or property [21] of others, from a peril created by the defendant's negligence, do not assume the risk where the alternative is to allow the threatened harm to occur. In all of these cases, of course, the danger may be so extreme as to be out of all proportion to the value of the interest to be protected, and the plaintiff may be charged with contributory negligence in his own unreasonable conduct.[22] And where there is a reasonably safe alternative open, the plaintiff's choice of the dangerous way is a free one, and may amount

But if the danger is more imminent, as where fire already set on the defendant's land is spreading to plaintiff's property, there may be negligence in failure to avoid the damage. Pribonic v. Fulton, 1922, 178 Wis. 393, 190 N.W. 190; Hall v. Meister, 1932, 42 Ohio App. 425, 182 N.E. 350. Cf. Spencer v. Gedney, 1927, 45 Idaho 64, 260 P. 699.

19. Illinois Cent. R. Co. v. Siler, 1907, 229 Ill. 390, 82 N.E. 362; Glanz v. Chicago, M. & St. P. R. Co., 1903, 119 Iowa 611, 93 N.W. 575; Owen v. Cook, 1899, 9 N.D. 134, 81 N.W. 285.

20. Eckert v. Long Island R. Co., 1871, 43 N.Y. 502; Bond v. Baltimore & O. R. Co., 1918, 82 W.Va. 557, 96 S.E. 932; Perpich v. Leetonia Mining Co., 1912, 118 Minn. 508, 137 N.W. 12; Cote v. Palmer, 1940, 127 Conn. 321, 16 A.2d 595. See Goodhart, Rescue and Voluntary Assumption of Risk, 1934, 5 Camb. L.J. 192.

21. Liming v. Illinois Cent. R. Co., 1890, 81 Iowa 246, 47 N.W. 66; Dixon v. New York, N. H. & H. R. Co., 1910, 207 Mass. 126, 92 N.E. 1030; Pegram v. Seaboard Air Line R. Co., 1905, 139 S.C. 303, 51 S. E. 975; Henshaw v. Belyea, 1934, 220 Cal. 458, 31 P.2d 348. "Undoubtedly more risks may be taken to protect life than to protect property without involving imputation of negligence, but the rule is that a reasonable effort may be made even in the latter case." Andrews, J., in Wardrop v. Santi Moving & Express Co., 1922, 233 N.Y. 227, 135 N.E. 272.

1962, 141 So.2d 807; Illinois Steel Co. v. Mann, 1902, 100 Ill.App. 367, affirmed, 1903, 197 Ill. 186, 64 N.E. 328; Hermanek v. Chicago & N. W. R. Co., 8 Cir. 1911, 186 F. 142. Cf. Ferraro v. Ford Motor Co., 1966, 423 Pa. 324, 223 A.2d 746.

15. Gunning System v. Lapointe, 1904, 212 Ill. 274, 72 N.E. 393; Heathcock v. Milwaukee Platteville Lead & Zinc Min. Co., 1906, 128 Wis. 46, 107 N.W. 463; Andrecsik v. New Jersey Tube Co., 1906, 73 N.J.L. 664, 63 A. 719.

16. Missouri, K. & T. R. Co. of Texas v. McLean, 1909, 55 Tex.Civ.App. 130, 118 S.W. 161.

17. Dollard v. Roberts, 1891, 130 N.Y. 269, 29 N.E. 104; Conroy v. Briley, Fla.App.1966, 191 So.2d 601; Brandt v. Thompson, Mo.1952, 252 S.W.2d 339; cf. Rush v. Commercial Realty Co., 1929, 7 N.J.Misc.R. 337, 145 A. 476; English v. Amidon, 1902, 72 N.H. 301, 56 A. 548.

18. Donovan v. Hannibal & St. Joseph R. Co., 1886, 89 Mo. 147, 1 S.W. 232; Judson v. Giant Powder Co., 1895, 107 Cal. 549, 40 P. 1020; Leroy Fibre Co. v. Chicago, M. & St. P. R. Co., 1914, 232 U.S. 340; Taulbee v. Campbell, 1931, 241 Ky. 410, 44 S.W.2d 275; North Bend Lumber Co. v. City of Seattle, 1921, 116 Wash. 500, 199 P. 988.

22. Harding v. Philadelphia Rapid Transit Co., 1907, 217 Pa. 69, 66 A. 151; Cook v. Johnston, 1885, 58 Mich. 437, 25 N.W. 388; Devine v. Pfaelzer, 1917, 277 Ill. 255, 115 N.E. 126; Berg v. Great Northern R. Co., 1897, 70 Minn. 272, 73 N.W. 648.

to both contributory negligence and assumption of risk.[23]

The economic pressure which rests upon workmen under threat of loss of employment received considerable recognition under the common law of England.[24] Notwithstanding violent denunciation at the hands of every writer who has dealt with the subject,[25] the American law was very slow to keep pace; and in the absence of a statute the greater number of courts for a long time held that a risk was assumed even when a workman acted under a direct command carrying an express or implied threat of discharge for disobedience.[26] Some vestiges of this old law no doubt still remain in fragments here and there; but it has been largely superseded by the workmen's compensation acts, [27] and even where these acts do not apply the defense of assumption of risk has been removed, in most instances, by statute,[28] or by decision in those areas where no statute applies.[29]

The defendant may be under a legal duty, which he is not free to refuse to perform, to exercise reasonable care for the plaintiff's safety, so that the plaintiff has a corresponding legal right to insist on that care. In such a case it is commonly said that the plaintiff does not assume the risk when he proceeds to make use of the defendant's services or facilities, notwithstanding his knowledge of the danger. This is undoubtedly true where the plaintiff acts reasonably, and the defendant has left him with no reasonable alternative, other than to forego the right entirely. Thus a common carrier,[30] or other public utility,[31] which has negligently provided a dangerously defective set of steps to its waiting room, cannot set up assumption of risk against a patron who makes use of the steps as the only convenient means of access. The same is true of a city maintaining a public highway or sidewalk,[32] or other public place which the plaintiff has a right to use,[33] and

---

23. King v. Woodward Iron Co., 1912, 177 Ala. 487, 59 So. 264; Donahue v. Chicago, M. & St. P. R. Co., 1930, 179 Minn. 138, 228 N.W. 556; Watson v. Mound City R. Co., 1895, 133 Mo. 246, 34 S.W. 573; Tharp v. Pennsylvania R. Co., 1938, 332 Pa. 233, 2 A.2d 695 (contributory negligence). Thus the decision oftens turns upon the existence of some reasonable alternative, as of leaving a negligently driven car at a point of reasonable convenience and safety. Compare Ridgway v. Yenny, 1944, 223 Ind. 16, 57 N.E.2d 581, with Kelly v. Checker White Cab, Inc., 1948, 131 W.Va. 816, 50 S.E.2d 888. Compare Hidden v. Malinoff, 1959, 174 Cal.App.2d 845, 345 P.2d 499, where a motorist, with car trouble at night, pulled over to the edge of the highway, and was struck and killed by an overtaking car.

24. Yarmouth v. France, 1887, 19 Q.B.D. 647; Smith v. Baker & Sons, [1891] A.C. 325; Thrussell v. Handyside & Co., 1888, 20 Q.B.D. 359.

25. See for example Labatt, Volenti Non Fit Injuria as a Defense to Actions by Injured Servants, 1898, 32 Am.L.Rev. 57, 66; 3 Labatt, Master and Servant, 2d Ed. 1913, §§ 960–964.

26. Dougherty v. West Superior Iron & Steel Co., 1894, 88 Wis. 343, 60 N.W. 274; Hallstein v. Pennsylvania R. Co., 6 Cir. 1929, 30 F.2d 594; Worlds v. Georgia R. Co., 1896, 99 Ga. 283, 25 S.E. 646; Nashville, C. & St. L. R. Co. v. Cleaver, 1938, 274 Ky. 410, 118 S.W.2d 748.

27. See Gow, The Defense of Volenti Non Fit Injuria, 1949, 61 Jurid.Rev. 37; 1 Schneider, Workmen's Compensation, Perm.Ed.1941, c. 1.

28. See infra, p. 533.

29. See for example Inouye v. Pacific Gas & Elec. Co., 1960, 53 Cal.2d 361, 1 Cal.Rptr. 848, 348 P.2d 208; Hedding v. Pearson, 1946, 76 Cal.App.2d 481, 173 P.2d 382.

30. Letang v. Ottawa Elec. R. Co., [1926] A.C. 725; Osborne v. London & N. W. R. Co., 1888, 21 Q.B.D. 220; Toroian v. Parkview Amusement Co., 1932, 331 Mo. 700, 56 S.W.2d 134; Dierks v. Alaska Air Transport, D.Alaska 1953, 109 F.Supp. 695. Even express assumption of risk would not be effective. See supra, p. 443.

31. Williamson v. Derry Elec. Co., 1938, 89 N.H. 216, 196 A. 265.

32. Ahern v. City of Des Moines, 1943, 234 Iowa 113, 12 N.W.2d 296; Campion v. City of Rochester, 1938, 202 Minn. 136, 277 N.W. 422; Dougherty v. Chas. H. Tompkins Co., 1957, 99 U.S.App.D.C. 348, 240 F. 2d 34; Patton v. City of Grafton, 1935, 116 W.Va. 311, 180 S.E. 267; Mosheuvel v. District of Columbia, 1903, 191 U.S. 247.

33. Orrison v. City of Rapid City, 1956, 76 S.D. 145, 74 N.W.2d 489 (municipal swimming pool); City of Madisonville v. Poole, Ky.1952, 249 S.W.2d 133 (city clubhouse). Compare, as to a safe means of access to the plaintiff's land, Clayards v. Dethick, 1848, 12 Q.B. 439, 116 Eng.Rep. 932; Hickey v. City of Waltham, 1893, 159 Mass. 460, 34 N.E. 681.

c̣ premises upon which the plaintiff has a contract right to enter.[34] But where a reasonable alternative is left open which will provide the service to which the plaintiff is entitled, such as another safe route involving no undue inconvenience, his unreasonable [35] insistence upon unnecessarily encountering danger becomes contributory negligence; and under one name or the other the choice of a dangerous highway,[36] or of an unsafe place to get off of a street car,[37] will bar his recovery. In this area it is reasonably clear that assumption of risk and contributory negligence always coincide, and that it is relatively unimportant which the defense is called.

Violation of Statute

Where the defendant's negligence consists of the violation of a statute, the traditional view has been that the plaintiff may still assume the risk. Thus a guest who accepts a night ride in an automobile without lights has been held to consent to relieve the defendant of the duty of conforming to the standard established by the statute for his protection, and cannot be heard to complain when he is injured as a result.[38] There have

34. Seelbach, Inc. v. Mellman, 1943, 293 Ky. 790, 170 S.W.2d 18 (employee of tenant in office building). In accord, as to the tenant himself, are Looney v. McLean, 1880, 129 Mass. 33; Rush v. Commercial Realty Co., 1929, 7 N.J.Misc. 337, 145 A. 476; Roman v. King, 1921, 289 Mo. 641, 233 S.W. 161.

35. The existence of a reasonable alternative does not necessarily make the plaintiff's choice unreasonable. It depends upon the apparent danger. Willetts v. Butler Township, 1940, 141 Pa.Super. 394, 15 A.2d 392.

36. Marlowe v. City of Los Angeles, 1957, 147 Cal. App.2d 680, 305 P.2d 604; Porter v. Toledo T. R. Co., 1950, 152 Ohio St. 463, 90 N.E.2d 142; Ahern v. City of Des Moines, 1943, 234 Iowa 113, 12 N.W.2d 296; Smith v. City of Pittsburgh, 1940, 338 Pa. 216, 12 A.2d 788; Neal v. Town of Marion, 1900, 126 N. C. 412, 35 S.E. 812.

37. Chesley v. Waterloo, C. F. & N. R. Co., 1920, 188 Iowa 1004, 176 N.W. 961. Cf. W. H. Blodget Co. v. New York Cent. R. Co., 1927, 261 Mass. 365, 159 N. E. 45 (shipper of goods in winter assumes risk of freezing).

38. White v. Cochrane, 1933, 189 Minn. 300, 249 N.W. 328; Le Doux v. Alert Transfer & Storage Co.,

been certain statutes, however, which clearly are intended to protect the plaintiff against his own inability to protect himself, including his own lack of judgment or inability to resist various pressures. Such, for example, are the child labor acts,[39] and various safety statutes for the benefit of employees,[40] as to which the courts have recognized the economic inequality in bargaining power which has induced the passage of the legislation. Since the fundamental purpose of such statutes would be defeated if the plaintiff were permitted to assume the risk, it is generally held that he cannot do so, either expressly or by implication.[41] Quite recently Connecticut [42] and California [43] have tak-

1927, 145 Wash. 115, 259 P. 24; Knipfer v. Shaw, 1933, 210 Wis. 617, 246 N.W. 328; Scory v. La Fave, 1934, 215 Wis. 21, 254 N.W. 643; Rittenberry v. Robert E. McKee, Inc., Tex.Civ.App.1960, 337 S. W.2d 197, ref. n. r. e.

39. Lenahan v. Pittston Coal Mining Co., 1907, 218 Pa. 311, 67 A. 642; Terry Dairy Co. v. Nalley, 1920, 146 Ark. 448, 225 S.W. 887; Dusha v. Virginia & Rainy Lake Co., 1920, 145 Minn. 171, 176 N.W. 482; Clark v. Arkansas Democrat Co., 1967, 242 Ark. 133, 497, 413 S.W.2d 629.

40. Suess v. Arrowhead Steel Products Co., 1930, 180 Minn. 21, 230 N.W. 125; Osborne v. Salvation Army, 2 Cir. 1939, 107 F.2d 929; Thomas v. Carroll Const. Co., 1957, 14 Ill.App.2d 205, 144 N.E.2d 461; Gould v. State, 1949, 196 Misc. 488, 92 N.Y.S.2d 251; Farmers Coop. El. Ass'n Non-Stock of Big Springs, Neb. v. Strand, 8 Cir. 1967, 382 F.2d 224, cert. denied 389 U.S. 1014, rehearing denied 390 U.S. 913.

41. See Narramore v. Cleveland, C. C. & St. L. R. Co., 6 Cir. 1899, 96 F. 298, cert. denied 175 U.S. 724; Davis Coal Co. v. Polland, 1901, 158 Ind. 607, 62 N.E. 492; Fitzwater v. Warren, 1912, 206 N.Y. 355, 99 N.E. 1042.

Other instances include the Safe Place statutes in Powless v. Milwaukee County, 1959, 6 Wis.2d 78, 94 N.W.2d 187; Justice v. Shelby Ice & Fuel Co., 1969, 18 Ohio App.2d 197, 248 N.E.2d 195, and the act as to the sale of animal food in Metz v. Medford Fur Foods, Inc., 1958, 4 Wis.2d 96, 90 N.W.2d 106.

42. Casey v. Atwater, 1960, 22 Conn.Super. 225, 167 A.2d 250; L'Heureux v. Hurley, 1933, 117 Conn. 347, 168 A. 8.

43. Finnegan v. Royal Realty Co., 1950, 35 Cal.2d 409, 218 P.2d 17; Maia v. Security Lumber & Concrete Co., 1958, 160 Cal.App.2d 16, 324 P.2d 657; Guerrero v. Westgate Lumber Co., 1958, 164 Cal. App.2d 612, 331 P.2d 107; Mulder v. Casho, 1964, 61

en the lead in holding that the risk cannot be assumed as to the violation of any safety statute enacted for the protection of the public, on the somewhat ingenious ground that the obligation and the right so created are public ones, which it is not within the power of any private individual to waive. This amounts to saying that the policy of the statutes overrides private agreements and understandings. Such decisions are quite likely to appear in other states in the near future.

Abolition of the Defense

Assumption of risk has been a defense cordially disliked by the friends of the plaintiff, because of its long history of barring recovery in cases of genuine hardship.[44] There has been a strong movement among one group of legal writers [45] to abrogate the defense as such in all but the cases of express agreement; to refuse to admit that in other cases it has any valid, or even factual separate existence; and to distribute it between the concepts of duty and contributory negligence. The argument is that assumption of risk serves no purpose which is not fully taken care of by the other doctrines; that it adds only duplication leading to confusion; and

that it results in some denial of recovery in cases where it should not be denied.

This attack has had its effect. In addition to the cases of violation of statute, to which reference has been made,[46] a few courts have been led to abolish the defense completely in certain specific area, such as the liability of an employer to his employee,[47] or that of an automobile driver to his guest.[48] In 1959 New Jersey took the lead in abolishing the defense of implied assumption of risk completely in all cases;[49] and this has now been followed by New Hampshire,[50] Kentucky,[51] and Michigan.[52] The arguments in favor of the abolition have been as follows:

Where the plaintiff acts reasonably in making his choice of conduct, it is insisted that the only effect of assumption of risk is to deny the defendant's duty of care, and hence his negligence. This is certainly true. But it is said further, that it follows that, just as there can be no duty when there is assumption of risk, there can be no assumption of risk when there is a duty owed to the plaintiff. This ignores entirely the procedure of a lawsuit, and in particular the burden of

---

Cal.2d 633, 39 Cal.Rptr. 705, 394 P.2d 545; Johnson v. Schilling, 1964, 224 Cal.App.2d 281, 36 Cal.Rptr. 735.

In Shahinian v. McCormick, 1963, 59 Cal.2d 554, 30 Cal.Rptr. 521, 381 P.2d 377, it was held that there was no assumption of risk as to defendant's violation of a statute by driving a boat at excessive speed, but that plaintiff assumed the risk of defendant's inexpertness, which was not statutory.

44. Particularly in cases of injury to employees. See infra, p. 527.

45. See 2 Harper and James, Law of Torts, 1956, 1162–1192; Fleming, Law of Torts, 2d Ed.1961, 249–258; Bohlen, Voluntary Assumption of Risk, 1906, 20 Harv.L.Rev. 14, 91; Rice, The Automobile Guest and the Rationale of Assumption of Risk, 1943, 27 Minn.L.Rev. 33; Payne, Assumption of Risk and Negligence, 1957, 35 Can.Bar Rev. 350; Wade, The Place of Assumption of Risk in the Law of Negligence, 1961, 22 La.L.Rev. 5; James, Assumption of Risk: Unhappy Reincarnation, 1968, 78 Yale L.J. 185.

46. Supra, p. 453.

47. Siragusa v. Swedish Hospital, 1962, 60 Wash.2d 310, 373 P.2d 767; Ritter v. Beals, 1961, 225 Or. 504, 358 P.2d 1080; Hines v. Continental Baking Co., Mo.App.1960, 334 S.W.2d 140.

48. McConville v. State Farm Mut. Auto. Ins. Co., 1962, 15 Wis.2d 374, 113 N.W.2d 14; Zumwalt v. Lindland, 1964, 239 Or. 26, 396 P.2d 205; Leavitt v. Gillaspie, 1968, —— Alaska ——, 443 P.2d 61. See Note, 1963, 38 Wash.L.Rev. 349.

49. In Meistrich v. Casino Arena Attractions Inc., 1959, 31 N.J. 44, 155 A.2d 90, the court urged the elimination of the term; and when this had no effect, McGrath v. American Cyanamid Co., 1963, 41 N.J. 272, 196 A.2d 238, declared that assumption of risk would no longer be recognized as a distinct doctrine.

50. Bolduc v. Crain, 1962, 104 N.H. 163, 181 A.2d 641.

51. Parker v. Redden, Ky.1967, 421 S.W.2d 586.

52. Except in cases of employment. Felgner v. Anderson, 1965, 375 Mich. 23, 133 N.W.2d 136.

See Notes, 1965, 50 Iowa L.Rev. 141; 1966, 35 U.Cin. L.Rev. 26; 1965, 41 Notre Dame L. Rev. 104.

pleading and proof. If the question is only one of duty, then the burden of proof of the duty and its breach must normally fall upon the plaintiff;[53] and in any case where the plaintiff is dead, or otherwise unable to produce evidence that he did not consent, or where the evidence is no more than evenly balanced, he must lose. On the other hand, assumption of risk is a defense, which the defendant is required to plead and prove;[54] and if he does not, the plaintiff will recover. If, for example, there is a crash of a private airplane in which everyone is killed, including a passenger, and it appears that the plane was defective and the pilot knew it, treating disclosure to the passenger and his consent as a matter of duty means that he will lose; but if it is a matter of assumption of risk he will recover.[55] The shift of ground to "duty" is thus a disservice to the plaintiff, imposing upon him a real procedural disadvantage, with no corresponding gain. Furthermore, duty is traditionally an issue for the court, whereas assumption of risk is a jury question in all but the clearest cases.[56]

This becomes most readily apparent in the cases where there has been a time sequence.

In the ordinary case the plaintiff makes out a prima facie case of a duty owed to him [57] by proving the existence of some relation, such as that of invitor and invitee,[58] which imposes the full obligation of reasonable care for his protection. This duty does not coincide with those risks which the plaintiff does not in fact assume; rather it is based upon what the defendant can reasonably expect of him. Thus the obligation of the owner of a baseball park is to provide screened seats only for the number of patrons who may reasonably be expected to want them.[59] If he fails to do so he has, on the face of it, failed in his duty toward anyone seeking a screened seat, and he is liable when such an individual is hit by a ball. But it is still possible for such a person, after entering the park, to change his mind and decide to sit in an unscreened seat, or, on discovering a hole in the screen in front of him, to refuse to move—in each case, without any negligence of his own.[60] What, in such a case, changes "duty"

53. Cf. Drible v. Village Improvement Co., 1937, 123 Conn. 20, 192 A. 308; Berger v. Shapiro, 1959, 30 N.J. 89, 152 A.2d 20; Hopkins v. E. I. Du Pont de Nemours & Co., 3 Cir. 1954, 212 F.2d 623, cert. denied 348 U.S. 872; Valles v. Peoples-Pittsburgh Trust Co., 1940, 339 Pa. 33, 13 A.2d 19; Hannon v. Hayes-Bickford Lunch System, 1957, 336 Mass. 268, 145 N.E.2d 191.

54. Smith v. Baker, 1891, A.C. 325; Catura v. Romanofsky, 1954, 268 Wis. 11, 66 N.W.2d 693; Frederick v. Goff, 1960, 251 Iowa 290, 100 N.W.2d 624; Goldberg v. Norton Co., 1957, 335 Mass. 605, 141 N.E.2d 377; Lyon v. Dr. Scholl's Foot Comfort Shops, Inc., 1958, 251 Minn. 285, 87 N.W.2d 651; Pall v. Pall, 1950, 137 Conn. 347, 77 A.2d 345.

As in the case of contributory negligence, when assumption of risk appears from the plaintiff's evidence, the defendant may take advantage of it, even though it is not pleaded. Centrello v. Basky, 1955, 164 Ohio St. 41, 128 N.E.2d 80.

55. Suggested by Bruce v. O'Neal Flying Service, 1949, 231 N.C. 181, 56 S.E.2d 560.

56. Pona v. Boulevard Arena, 1955, 35 N.J.Super. 148, 113 A.2d 529.

57. See Williams, Joint Torts and Contributory Negligence, 1951, 195; Winfield, Torts, 6th Ed. 1954, 28. It should be remembered that the duty of the defendant is not necessarily discharged by a warning of the danger. See supra, p. 394.

58. See supra, § 61. Where the plaintiff proves only that he is a licensee, there is only a limited duty to him—for example, to warn him against latent dangers of which he does not know. See supra, § 60. It is quite often said that he "assumes the risk" of other dangers. This has been a fertile source of confusion in the law review articles. Much of it apparently has been due to the different meanings assigned to "duty." See Keeton, Assumption of Risk in Products Liability Cases, 1961, 22 La.L.Rev. 122, 160–164.

59. Brown v. San Francisco Baseball Club, 1950, 99 Cal.App.2d 484, 222 P.2d 19; Brisson v. Minneapolis Baseball & Athletic Ass'n, 1932, 185 Minn. 508, 240 N.W. 903; Anderson v. Kansas City Baseball Club, Mo.1950, 231 S.W.2d 170; Keys v. Alamo City Baseball Co., Tex.Civ.App.1941, 150 S.W.2d 368; Ingersoll v. Onondaga Hockey Club, 1935, 245 App. Div. 137, 281 N.Y.S. 505 (ice hockey).

60. Kavafian v. Seattle Baseball Club Ass'n, 1919, 105 Wash. 215, 177 P. 776, reversed in 105 Wash. 215, 181 P. 679; Hudson v. Kansas City Baseball Club, 1942, 349 Mo. 1215, 164 S.W.2d 318; Hunt v. Portland Baseball Club, 1956, 207 Or. 337, 296 P. 2d 495; Shaw v. Boston American League Baseball

to "no duty;" and if it is not to be called assumption of risk, what better name can be found? And should not the burden be upon the defendant to establish the change in the situation?

It has been proposed [61] that, when the matter is dealt with in terms of duty, the burden of proof as to "no duty" be placed upon the defendant. It is difficult to see how this amounts to anything more than a change of terminology, or how it offers any advantage, other than the elimination of a phrase which is so cordially disliked by some writers and courts as to amount almost to a phobia. If the consent of the plaintiff to the defendant's negligence is to negative a duty which would clearly otherwise exist, and the burden of proof on the issue is upon the defendant, why not continue to call it assumption of risk, which is the term the courts have always used?

Where the plaintiff acts unreasonably in making his choice, it is said that there is merely one form of contributory negligence, which is certainly true; and from this it is argued that there is, or should be, no distinction between the two defenses, and that there is only useless and confusing duplication. But this is a distinctive kind of contributory negligence, in which the plaintiff knows the risk and voluntarily accepts it; and it has been held to differ from contributory negligence which merely fails to discover the danger in several minor respects. Thus assumption of risk is governed by the subjective standard of the plaintiff himself, whereas contributory negligence is measured by the objective standard of the reasonable man.[62]

Assumption of risk, whether or not it is called contributory negligence, will bar recovery in an action founded on strict liability, where the plaintiff's ordinary negligence may not.[63] The plaintiff may assume the risk where the conduct of the defendant is wilful, wanton or reckless,[64] and his ordinary negligence is not a defense; and while there will certainly be many cases in which the encountering of a known high degree of danger will itself be wilful, wanton and reckless, and so a bar under either theory,[65] there will be others where it is not. It seems clear that assumption of risk may also be a defense where the defendant has the last clear chance.[66]

The attack on the separate recognition of assumption of risk is largely an attack upon the validity of such distinctions; and as such it has a good deal of merit. The matter is brought to a head by statutes apportioning the damages between plaintiff and defendant, which have been held to affect one defense and not the other. The first answer given, under the Federal Employers' Liability Act, was that while contributory negligence went only to reduce the plaintiff's damages, assumption of risk remained as a complete defense, which barred the action entirely.[67] The same conclusion has been reached under some of the state apportionment statutes.[68]

Co., 1950, 325 Mass. 419, 90 N.E.2d 840; Chickasha Cotton Oil Co. v. Holloway, Tex.Civ.App.1964, 378 S.W.2d 695. See cases collected in Notes, [1951] Wash.U.L.Q. 434; 1960, 46 Corn.L.Q. 140.

61. James, Assumption of Risk: Unhappy Reincarnation, 1968, 78 Yale L.J. 185; Meistrich v. Casino Arena Attractions, 1959, 31 N.J. 44, 155 A.2d 90.

62. See Schrader v. Kriesel, 1950, 232 Minn. 238, 45 N.W.2d 395; Landrum v. Roddy, 1943, 143 Neb. 934, 12 N.W.2d 82; Eisenhower v. United States, E.D.

N.Y.1963, 216 F.Supp. 803. See Note, [1960] Wis.L. Rev. 460.

63. See infra, p. 522.

64. Waltanen v. Wiitala, 1960, 361 Mich. 504, 105 N. W.2d 400; Evans v. Holsinger, 1951, 242 Iowa 990, 48 N.W.2d 250; Pierce v. Clemens, 1943, 113 Ind. App. 65, 46 N.E.2d 836; Gill v. Arthur, 1941, 69 Ohio App. 386, 43 N.E.2d 894; Schubring v. Weggen, 1940, 234 Wis. 517, 291 N.W. 788.

65. See Brown v. Barber, 1943, 26 Tenn.App. 534, 174 S.W.2d 298; Second Restatement of Torts, § 503.

66. Boyles v. Hamilton, 1965, 235 Cal.App.2d 492, 45 Cal.Rptr. 399; cf. Gover v. Central Vermont R. Co., 1922, 96 Vt. 208, 118 A. 874.

67. Seaboard Air Line R. Co. v. Horton, 1914, 233 U. S. 492.

68. Scory v. La Fave, 1934, 215 Wis. 21, 254 N.W. 643; Saxton v. Rose, 1947, 201 Miss. 814, 29 So.2d

In all probability this defeats the basic intention of the statute, since it continues an absolute bar in the case of one important, and very common, type of negligent conduct on the part of the plaintiff. It can scarcely be supposed in reason that the legislature has intended to allow a partial recovery to the plaintiff who has been so negligent as not to discover his peril at all, and deny it to one who has at least exercised proper care in that respect, but has made a mistake of judgment in proceeding to encounter the danger after it is known.[69] In 1939 the Federal Employers' Liability Act was amended to eliminate the defense of assumption of risk,[70] and the Nebraska statute has been interpreted to mean that the damages are to be apportioned where there is negligent assumption of risk, as in other cases of negligence of the plaintiff.[71] Wisconsin, which has been one of the leading advocates of the contrary position, has now changed its rule to the same effect.[72]

All this goes to say, however, not that there is no such defense as assumption of risk, but that in many cases, at least, where it overlaps and coincides with contributory negligence, the rules of that defense should be applied to it. The term does serve to focus attention upon the element of voluntary acceptance of the defendant's negligence, which is sometimes, but not always, involved in contributory negligence. For that reason, the predication may be ventured that it is not likely to disappear from the court decisions, at least for some time to come, and that courts which have abolished it may be forced to recognize it, if only under another name. But it is by no means a favored defense, and it is likely to be at least limited and restricted in the future.

646; Bugh v. Webb, 1959, 231 Ark. 27, 328 S.W.2d 379. Cf. Vee Bar Airport v. De Vries, 1950, 73 S.D. 356, 43 N.W.2d 369; Seymour v. Maloney [1955] 1 Dom.L.Rep. 824. See Note, 1963, 41 Tex.L.Rev. 459.

69. See Campbell, Wisconsin's Comparative Negligence Law, 1932, 7 Wis.L.Rev. 222, 235; Baylor, Assumption of Risk and Contributory Negligence Under the Guest Statute, 1937, 15 Neb.L.B. 318, 326; Note, 1951, 30 Neb.L.Rev. 608.

70. 45 U.S.C.A. § 54. See Tiller v. Atlantic Coast Line R. Co., 1943, 318 U.S. 54; Blair v. Baltimore & O. R. Co., 1945, 323 U.S. 600.

71. Landrum v. Roddy, 1943, 143 Neb. 934, 12 N.W. 2d 82; Anthony v. City of Lincoln, 1950, 152 Neb. 320, 41 N.W.2d 147.

72. Meyer v. Val-Lo-Will Farms, Inc., 1961, 14 Wis. 2d 616, 111 N.W.2d 500; McConville v. State Farm Mut. Auto. Ins. Co., 1962, 15 Wis.2d 374, 113 N.W.2d 14; Colson v. Rule, 1962, 15 Wis.2d 387, 113 N.W.2d 21.

CHAPTER 12

IMPUTED NEGLIGENCE

69. VICARIOUS LIABILITY

A is negligent, B is not. "Imputed negligence" means that, by reason of some relation existing between A and B, the negligence of A is to be charged against B, although B has played no part in it, has done nothing whatever to aid or encourage it, or indeed has done all that he possibly can to prevent it. The result may be that B, in an action against C for his own injuries, is barred from recovery because of A's negligence, to the same extent as if he had been negligent himself. This is commonly called "imputed contributory negligence."[1] Or the result may be that B, in C's action against him, becomes liable as a defendant for C's injuries, on the basis of A's negligence. This is sometimes called imputed negligence. More often it is called vicarious liability, or the principle is given the Latin name of *respondeat superior.*

Since B himself has been free from all fault, when he is held liable to C it is in one sense a form of strict liability. In another it is not.[2] The foundation of the action is still negligence, or other fault, on the part of A; and all that the law has done is to broaden the liability for that fault by imposing it upon an additional, albeit innocent, defendant. It is still an action for negligence, and the ordinary rules of negligence liability are still applied to it.[3] The most familiar illustration, of course, is the liability of a master for the torts of his servant in the course of his employment.

The idea of vicarious liability was common enough in primitive law. Not only the torts of servants and slaves, or even wives, but those of inanimate objects, were charged against their owner. The movement of the early English law was away from such strict responsibility, until by the sixteenth century it was considered that the master should not be liable for his servant's torts unless he had commanded the particular act.[4] But soon after 1700 this rule was found to be far too narrow to fit the expanding complications

---

1. See infra, § 74.

2. See Williams, Vicarious Liability: Tort of the Master or of the Servant? 1956, 72 L.Q.Rev. 522; Note, 1957, 20 Mod.L.Rev. 655.

3. Thus the defenses of contributory negligence and assumption of risk are open to B as well as A; and a judgment for A in an action brought against him by C is res judicata as to B's vicarious liability to C. See McGinnis v. Chicago, R. I. & P. R. Co., 1906, 200 Mo. 347, 98 S.W. 590; Doremus v. Root, 1901, 23 Wash. 710, 63 P. 572; Bradley v. Rosenthal, 1908, 154 Cal. 420, 97 P. 875; Pangburn v. Buick Motor Co., 1914, 211 N.Y. 228, 105 N.E. 423. See Note, 1926, 12 Corn.L.Q. 92.

   One important distinction is that some courts refuse to hold B liable for punitive damages; but even here there are others to the contrary. See supra, p. 12. Another is that B does not necessarily have the benefit of immunity from suit, as where A is a husband and the plaintiff is his wife. See infra, p. 868; Hughes and Hudson, The Nature of a Master's Liability in the Law of Tort, 1953, 31 Can.Bar Rev. 18.

4. Wigmore, Responsibility for Tortious Acts: Its History, 1894, 7 Harv.L.Rev. 315, 383, 441; Holdsworth, History of English Law, 4th Ed. 1935, vol. 3, 382–387, vol. 8, 472–482; Baty, Vicarious Liability, 1916, ch. 1.

of commerce and industry, and the courts began to revert to something like the earlier rule, at first under the fiction of a command to the servant "implied" from the employment itself,[5] and at last, by slow degrees, by minimizing and finally abandoning the fiction of command.

A multitude of very ingenious reasons have been offered for the vicarious liability of a master:[6] he has a more or less fictitious "control" over the behavior of the servant; he has "set the whole thing in motion," and is therefore responsible for what has happened; he has selected the servant and trusted him, and so should suffer for his wrongs, rather than an innocent stranger who has had no opportunity to protect himself; it is a great concession that any man should be permitted to employ another at all, and there should be a corresponding responsibility as the price to be paid for it—or, more frankly and cynically, "In hard fact, the reason for the employers' liability is the damages are taken from a deep pocket."[7] None of these reasons is so self-sufficient as to carry conviction, although they are all in accord with the general common law notion that one who is in a position to exercise some general control over the situation must exercise it or bear the loss. All of them go beyond that notion in holding the defendant liable even though he has done his best. Most courts have made little or no effort to explain the result, and have taken refuge in rather empty phrases, such as "he who does a thing through another does it himself," or the endlessly repeated formula of "respondeat superior," which in itself means nothing more than "look to the man higher up."

What has emerged as the modern justification[8] for vicarious liability is a rule of policy, a deliberate allocation of a risk. The losses caused by the torts of employees, which as a practical matter are sure to occur in the conduct of the employer's enterprise, are placed upon that enterprise itself, as a required cost of doing business. They are placed upon the employer because, having engaged in an enterprise which will, on the basis of all past experience, involve harm to others through the torts of employees, and sought to profit by it, it is just that he, rather than the innocent injured plaintiff, should bear them; and because he is better able to absorb them, and to distribute them, through prices, rates or liability insurance, to the public, and so to shift them to society, to the community at large.[9] Added to this is the makeweight argument that an employer who is held strictly liable is under the greatest incentive to be careful in the selection, instruction and supervision of his servants, and to take every precaution to see that the enterprise is conducted safely. Notwithstanding the occasional condemnation of the entire doctrine which used to appear in the past,[10] the tendency is clearly to justify it on such grounds, and gradually to extend it.[11]

---

5. 1 Bl.Comm. 429; Hern v. Nichols, 1708, 1 Salk. 289, 91 Eng.Rep. 256; Brucker v. Fromont, 1796, 6 Term Rep. 659, 101 Eng.Rep. 758.

6. See Baty, Vicarious Liability, 1916, ch. 8; Baty, The Basis of Responsibility, 1920, 32 Jurid.Rev. 159; Smith, Frolic and Detour, 1923, 23 Col.L.Rev. 444, 454; James, Vicarious Liability, 1954, 28 Tulane L.Rev. 161.

7. Baty, Vicarious Liability, 1916, 154.

8. See Seavey, Speculations as to "Respondeat Superior," Harvard Legal Essays, 1934, 433; Laski, The Basis of Vicarious Liability, 1916, 26 Yale L.J. 105; Smith, Frolic and Detour, 1923, 23 Col.L.Rev. 444, 456; Douglas, Vicarious Liability and Administration of Risk, 1929, 38 Yale L.J. 584, 720; Miller, The Master-Servant Concept and Judge-Made Law, 1941, 1 Loyola L.Rev. 25; Neuner, Respondeat Superior in the Light of Comparative Law, 1941, 4 La.L.Rev. 1; Ferson, Bases for Master's Liability and for Principal's Liability to Third Persons, 1951, 4 Vand.L.Rev. 260.

9. As to proposals to extend this "enterprise liability" to other defendants, see infra, § 85.

10. See Holmes, Agency, 1891, 5 Harv.L.Rev. 14; Baty, Vicarious Liability, 1916, ch. 8; Baty, Basis of Responsibility, 1920, 32 Jurid.Rev. 159. Cf. the testimony of Bramwell before the parliamentary committee of 1876, 1887, Cd. 285, p. 46.

11. Seavey, Speculations as to "Respondeat Superior," Harvard Legal Essays, 1934, 433, 451.

70. SERVANTS

The traditional definition of a servant is that he is a person employed to perform services in the affairs of another, whose physical conduct in the performance of the service is controlled, or is subject to a right of control, by the other.[12]

This is, however, a great over-simplification of a complex matter. In determining the existence of "control" or the right to it, many factors are to be taken into account and balanced against one another—the extent to which, by agreement, the employer may determine the details of the work; the kind of occupation and the customs of the community as to whether the work usually is supervised by the employer; whether the one employed is engaged in a distinct business or occupation, and the skill required of him; who supplies the place and instrumentalities of the work; the length of time the employment is to last; the method of payment, and many others.[13] Consideration of

the extensive and detailed ramification of all this must be left to other texts; but it is probably no very inaccurate summary of the whole matter to say that the person employed is a servant when, in the eyes of the community, he would be regarded as a part of the employer's own working staff, and not otherwise.

Once it is determined that the man at work is a servant, the master becomes subject to vicarious liability for his torts. He may, of course, be liable on the basis of any negligence of his own in selecting or dealing with the servant, or for the latter's acts which he has authorized or ratified,[14] upon familiar principles of agency law. But his vicarious liability, for conduct which is in no way his own, extends to any and all tortious conduct of the servant which is within the "scope of the employment."[15] This highly indefinite phrase, which sometimes is varied with "in the course of the employment," is so devoid of meaning in itself that its very vagueness has been of value in permitting a desirable degree of flexibility in decisions. It is obviously no more than a bare formula to cover the unordered and unauthorized acts of the servant for which it is found to be expedient to charge the master with liability, as well as to exclude other acts for which it is not. It refers to those acts which are so closely connected with what the servant is employed to do, and so fairly and reasonably incidental to it, that they may be regarded as methods, even though quite improper ones,

12. Second Restatement of Agency, § 220(1); Newspapers, Inc. v. Love, Tex.1964, 380 S.W.2d 582; Chicago, R. I. & P. R. Co. v. Bennett, 1912, 36 Okl. 358, 128 P. 705; Nichols v. Harvey Hubbell, Inc., 1918, 92 Conn. 611, 103 A. 835; Stewart v. California Imp. Co., 1900, 131 Cal. 125, 63 P. 177; cf. Turner v. Lewis, Ky.1955, 282 S.W.2d 624; Globe Indemnity Co. v. Victill Corp., 1956, 208 Md. 573, 119 A.2d 423.

13. See Second Restatement of Agency, § 220(2); Stevens, The Test of the Employment Relation, 1939, 38 Mich.L.Rev. 188; Note, 1964, 6 Ariz.L.Rev. 150. As to the "borrowed servant," lent by one employer to another, see Smith, Scope of the Business: The Borrowed Servant Problem, 1940, 38 Mich.L.Rev. 1222; Notes, 1962, 29 Tenn.L.Rev. 448; 1967, 28 Ohio St.L.Rev. 550.

The problem is not limited to vicarious tort liability, and arises in workmen's compensation cases, as well as in connection with social security and other forms of social legislation. See Wolfe, Determination of Employer-Employee Relationships in Social Legislation, 1941, 41 Col.L.Rev. 1015; Jacobs, Are "Independent Contractors" Really Independent? 1953, 3 De Paul L.Rev. 23.

A signed agreement as to the status of the employee is evidence, but not necessarily conclusive. Texaco, Inc. v. Layton, Okl.1964, 395 P.2d 393; Gulf Refining Co. v. Brown, 4 Cir. 1938, 93 F.2d 870; Humble

Oil & Ref. Co. v. Martin, 1949, 148 Tex. 175, 222 S. W.2d 995; Scorpion v. American-Republican, 1944, 131 Conn. 42, 37 A.2d 802.

14. Second Restatement of Agency, §§ 212–218. As to ratification, see Dempsey v. Chambers, 1891, 154 Mass. 330, 28 N.E. 279; Crotty v. Horn, 1914, 186 Ill.App. 74; Kirk v. Montana Transfer Co., 1919, 56 Mont. 292, 184 P. 987; and cf. State ex rel. Kansas City Public Service Co. v. Shain, 1939, 345 Mo. 543, 134 S.W.2d 58.

15. See Smith, Scope of the Business: The Borrowed Servant Problem, 1940, 38 Mich.L.Rev. 1222; Notes, 1936, 21 Corn.L.Q. 294; 1957, 24 Tenn.L.Rev. 241.

of carrying out the objectives of the employment.

As in the case of the existence of the relation itself, many factors enter into the question: [16] the time, place and purpose of the act, and its similarity to what is authorized; whether it is one commonly done by such servants; the extent of departure from normal methods; the previous relations between the parties; whether the master had reason to expect that such an act would be done; and many other considerations, as to which the reader must be referred to texts dealing with the subject at length.[17] It has been said [18] that in general the servant's conduct is within the scope of his employment if it is of the kind which he is employed to perform, occurs substantially within the authorized limits of time and space, and is actuated, at least in part, by a purpose to serve the master.

The fact that the servant's act is expressly forbidden by the master, or is done in a manner which he has prohibited, is to be considered in determining what the servant has been hired to do,[19] but it is usually not conclusive, and does not in itself prevent the act from being within the scope of employment. A master cannot escape liability merely by ordering his servant to act carefully. If he could, no doubt few employers would ever be held liable. Thus instructions to a sales clerk never to load a gun while exhibiting it will not prevent liability when the clerk does so, in an effort to sell the gun.[20] If the other factors involved indicate that the forbidden conduct is merely the servant's own way of accomplishing an authorized purpose, the master cannot escape responsibility no matter how specific, detailed and emphatic his orders may have been to the contrary.[21] This has been clear since the leading English case [22] in which an omnibus company was held liable notwithstanding definite orders to its driver not to obstruct other vehicles. It is still the master's enterprise, and the policy which places the risk of the servant's misconduct upon him requires that he shall not be permitted to avoid it by such instructions.

Frolic and Detour

In 1834 Baron Parke [23] uttered the classic phrase, that a master is not liable for the torts of his servant who is not at all on his master's business, but is "going on a frolic of his own." If the servant steps outside of his employment to do some act for himself, not connected with the master's business, there is no more responsibility for what he does than for the acts of any stranger.[24] If he

16. Second Restatement of Agency, § 229; Great A. & P. Tea Co. v. Noppenberger, 1937, 171 Md. 378, 189 A. 434; De Parcq v. Liggett & Myers Tobacco Co., 8 Cir. 1936, 81 F.2d 777, cert. denied 298 U.S. 680; Loper v. Yazoo & M. V. R. Co., 1933, 166 Miss. 79, 145 So. 743; Poundstone v. Whitney, 1937, 189 Wash. 494, 65 P.2d 1261.

17. See 6 Labatt, Master and Servant, 1913, ch. 92–105; 2 Mechem Agency, 1914, ch. 5.

18. Second Restatement of Agency, § 228; White v. Pacific Tel. & Tel. Co., D.Or.1938, 24 F.Supp. 871; Hubbard v. Lock Joint Pipe Co., E.D.Mo.1947, 70 F.Supp. 589; Hall Grocery Co. v. Wall, 1930, 13 Tenn.App. 203.

19. Thus in Gurley v. Southern Power Co., 1916, 172 N.C. 690, 90 S.E. 943, a custodian of a private swimming pool was instructed not to admit unauthorized swimmers. He did so, and rented them suits. It was held that the orders were conclusive that this was beyond the scope of his employment.

20. Garretzen v. Duenckel, 1872, 50 Mo. 104. Accord: Mautino v. Piercedale Supply Co., 1940, 338 Pa. 435, 13 A.2d 51 (selling cartridges to minor); Central Truckaway System v. Moore, 1947, 304 Ky. 533, 201 S.W.2d 725 (intoxication on the job); Carroll v. Beard-Laney, Inc., 1945, 207 S.C. 339, 35 S.E.2d 425 (same).

21. Cosgrove v. Ogden, 1872, 49 N.Y. 255; Barrett v. Minneapolis, St. P. & S. S. M. R. Co., 1908, 106 Minn. 51, 117 N.W. 1047; Great A. & P. Tea Co. v. Noppenberger, 1937, 171 Md. 378, 189 A. 434; Rankin v. Western Union Tel. Co., 1946, 147 Neb. 411, 23 N.W.2d 676; Second Restatement of Agency, § 230.

22. Limpus v. London General Omnibus Co., 1862, 1 H. & C. 526, 158 Eng.Rep. 993.

23. In Joel v. Morrison, 1834, 6 C. & P. 501, 172 Eng.Rep. 1338.

24. Lemarier v. A. Towle Co., 1947, 94 N.H. 246, 51 A.2d 42; Vadyak v. Lehigh & N. E. R. Co., 1935,

has no intention, at least in part, to perform any service for the employer, but only to further a personal end, his act is not within the scope of the employment.[25] This is true, for example, where he borrows the owner's car to go for a ride for his own amusement,[26] or lends it to a friend for the same purpose.[27] But so long as there is an intent, even though it be a subordinate one, to serve the master's purpose, the master may be liable if what is done is otherwise within the service.[28]

Certain activities for the personal benefit of the employee, such as going to the toilet,[29] or lighting a fire to keep warm,[30] are quite generally recognized as so necessary, usual, and closely tied in with the work, that they are held not to constitute deviations from the employment. There has been an argument about smoking.[31] The prevailing view has been that it is solely for the amusement of the servant, so that it is in itself outside of the scope of employment,[32] although in conjunction with authorized acts, such as pouring gasoline, it may amount to an unauthorized way of doing something which is within it.[33]

A comparatively recent California decision [34] has taken the position that smoking on the part of employees is so usual and foreseeable that it is to be regarded as one of the normal risks of the enterprise, and so within the scope of vicarious liability.

Questions of fact of unusual difficulty arise in determining whether the servant's conduct is an entire departure from the master's business, or only a roundabout way of doing it—and likewise, the point at which the departure is terminated, and the servant may be said to have reentered the employment. This is particularly true in the "detour" cases,[35] where the servant deviates from his route on a personal errand, and later returns to it. Various tests have been proposed. One approach makes the question turn ex-

---

318 Pa. 580, 179 A. 435; Reilly v. Connable, 1915, 214 N.Y. 586, 108 N.E. 853; Adomaities v. Hopkins, 1920, 99 Conn. 239, 111 A. 178.

Cf. District Certified TV Service, Inc. v. Neary, 1965, 122 U.S.App.D.C. 21, 350 F.2d 998 (hit and run driver trying to excape).

25. Salomone v. Yellow Taxi Corp., 1926, 242 N.Y. 251, 151 N.E. 442, reargument denied 242 N.Y. 602, 152 N.E. 445; Herr v. Simplex Paper Box Corp., 1938, 330 Pa. 129, 198 A. 309; Kelly v. Louisiana Oil Ref. Co., 1934, 167 Tenn. 101, 66 S.W.2d 997; Lucas v. Friedman, 1928, 58 App.D.C. 5, 24 F.2d 271; Pratt v. Duck, 1945, 28 Tenn.App. 502, 191 S. W.2d 562; Second Restatment of Agency, § 235.

26. Fiske v. Enders, 1900, 73 Conn. 338, 47 A. 681.

27. Robinson v. McNeil, 1897, 18 Wash. 163, 51 P. 355. On the other hand, permitting a friend to drive while the employee remains in the vehicle on the employer's business, is not beyond the scope of employment. Meagher v. Garvin, 1964, 80 Nev. 211, 391 P.2d 507.

28. Nelson v. American-West African Line, 2 Cir. 1936, 86 F.2d 730, cert. denied 300 U.S. 665; Forsberg v. Tevis, 1937, 191 Wash. 355, 71 P.2d 358; Tuttle v. Dodge, 1922, 80 N.H. 304, 116 A. 627; Jones v. Lozier, 1922, 195 Iowa 365, 191 N.W. 103; McKinley v. Rawls, 4 Cir. 1964, 333 F.2d 198; Second Restatement of Agency, § 236.

Cf. Erwin v. United States, D.C.Okl.1969, 302 F.Supp. 693 (operating government car for purpose of catching airplane on vacation and leaving car in safe place of storage).

29. J. C. Penney Co. v. McLaughlin, 1939, 137 Fla. 594, 188 So. 785.

30. Brown v. Anzalone, 3 Cir. 1962, 300 F.2d 177.

31. See Note, 1950, 4 Ark.L.Rev. 217.

32. Williams v. Jones, 1865, 3 H. & C. 602, 159 Eng. Rep. 668; Kelly v. Louisiana Oil Ref. Co., 1934, 167 Tenn. 101, 66 S.W.2d 997; Shuck v. Carney, 1938, 22 Tenn.App. 125, 118 S.W.2d 896; Herr v. Simplex Paper Box Co., 1938, 330 Pa. 129, 198 A. 309; Tomlinson v. Sharpe, 1946, 226 N.C. 177, 37 S.E.2d 498.

33. Mack v. Hugger Bros. Const. Co., 1929, 10 Tenn.App. 402 (laying explosive floor mixture); Wood v. Saunders, 1930, 228 App.Div. 69, 238 N.Y.S. 571; Jefferson v. Derbyshire Farmers, Ltd., [1921] 2 K.B. 281; George v. Bekins Van & Storage Co., 1949, 33 Cal.2d 834, 205 P.2d 1037.

34. George v. Bekins Van & Storage Co., 1949, 33 Cal.2d 834, 205 P.2d 1037. Cf. Vincennes Steel Corp. v. Gibson, 1937, 194 Ark. 58, 106 S.W.2d 173.

35. See Smith, Frolic and Detour, 1923, 23 Col.L.Rev. 444, 716; Rouse, Deviation and Departure by Servant, 1929, 17 Ky.L.J. 123; Douglas, Vicarious Liability and Administration of Risk, 1929, 38 Yale L. J. 584; James, Vicarious Liability, 1954, 28 Tulane L.Rev. 161.

clusively on the servant's purpose in the deviation, holding to the strict rule that he is outside of his employment while he is off on his own concerns,[36] but that he is still within it while he intends in part to serve his master by or during the departure,[37] or as soon as he starts to return to his route.[38]

This very mechanical solution has been losing ground in recent years, and has given way to another approach, now more generally accepted, which looks to the foreseeability of such a deviation,[39] and holds the employer liable only for torts occurring in a "zone of risk" within which the servant might reasonably be expected to deviate, even for purposes entirely his own.[40] Under this view distance becomes controlling, and the servant

who intends to return to his master's business does not resume it at least until he is reasonably near the authorized route.[41] It seems to be more or less generally agreed that the master will be liable at least for those slight departures from the performance of the work which might reasonably be expected on the part of servants similarly employed, and that the foreseeability of such deviations is an important factor in determining the "scope of employment." [42] The tendency has been to recognize a number of factors as affecting the result, which vary with the circumstances.[43] Essentially the question is one of major and minor departures, having always in mind that the employer is to be held liable for those things which are fairly to be regarded as risks of his business.[44]

---

36. Skapura v. Cleveland Elec. Illuminating Co., 1950, 89 Ohio App. 403, 100 N.E.2d 700; Carter Truck Line v. Gibson, 1938, 195 Ark. 994, 115 S.W. 2d 270; McCauley v. Steward, 1945, 63 Ariz. 524, 164 P.2d 465; Lemarier v. A. Towle Co., 1947, 94 N.H. 246, 51 A.2d 42; Lucas v. Friedman, 1928, 58 U.S.App.D.C. 5, 24 F.2d 271; Note, 1952, 21 U.Cin. L. Rev. 156.

37. Edwards v. Earnest, 1922, 208 Ala. 539, 94 So. 598; Hayes v. Wilkins, 1907, 194 Mass. 223, 80 N.E. 449; Eckel v. Richter, 1926, 191 Wis. 409, 211 N.W. 158; Westberg v. Willde, 1939, 14 Cal.2d 360, 94 P. 2d 590; Clawson v. Pierce-Arrow Motor Co., 1921, 231 N.Y. 273, 131 N.E. 914, reargument denied, 1921, 231 N.Y. 640, 132 N.E. 921.

38. Sleath v. Wilson, 1839, 9 C. & P. 607, 173 Eng. Rep. 976; McKiernan v. Lehmaier, 1911, 85 Conn. 111, 81 A. 969; Duffy v. Hickey, 1922, 151 La. 274, 91 So. 733; Riley v. Standard Oil Co., 1921, 231 N. Y. 301, 132 N.E. 97; Note, 1952, 35 Marq.L.Rev. 383.

39. Smith, Frolic and Detour, 1923, 23 Col.L.Rev. 444, 716. Much the same idea may be expressed by the question: if the master should send out a search party to find the servant, within what area would they reasonably be expected to look?

40. Leuthold v. Goodman, 1945, 22 Wash.2d 583, 157 P.2d 326; Healey v. Cockrill, 1918, 133 Ark. 327, 202 S.W. 229; Kohlman v. Hyland, 1926, 54 N.D. 710, 210 N.W. 643; Edwards v. Benedict, 1946, 79 Ohio App. 134, 70 N.E.2d 471; Fleischmann Co. v. Howe, 1926, 213 Ky. 110, 280 S.W. 496. These cases indicate that the distance the servant may depart without getting outside of his employment is somewhat proportional to the length of the authorized journey. See Second Restatement of Agency, § 234.

41. Bell v. Martin, 1941, 241 Ala. 182, 1 So.2d 906; A. S. Abell Co. v. Sopher, 1941, 179 Md. 687, 22 A.2d 462; Riley v. Standard Oil Co. of New York, 1921, 231 N.Y. 301, 132 N.E. 97; Crady v. Greer, 1919, 183 Ky. 675, 210 S.W. 167; Tuttle v. Dodge, 1927, 80 N.H. 304, 116 A. 627; Second Restatement of Agency, § 237.

42. Compare: Not within scope, Jasper v. Wells, 1943, 173 Or. 114, 144 P.2d 505; Summerville v. Gillespie, 1947, 181 Or. 144, 179 P.2d 719; McCauley v. Steward, 1945, 63 Ariz. 524, 164 P.2d 465; Gordoy v. Flaherty, 1937, 9 Cal.2d 524, 164 P.2d 465. Within scope: Loper v. Morrison, 1944, 23 Cal.2d 600, 145 P.2d 1; George v. Bekins Van & Storage Co., 1949, 33 Cal.2d 834, 205 P.2d 1037; Leuthold v. Goodman, 1945, 22 Wash.2d 583, 157 P.2d 326; Edwards v. Benedict, 1946, 79 Ohio App. 134, 70 N.E. 2d 471.

43. See McConville v. United States, 2 Cir.1952, 197 F.2d 680, cert. denied 344 U.S. 877; Osipoff v. City of New York, 1941, 286 N.Y. 422, 36 N.E.2d 646; Kohlman v. Hyland, 1926, 54 N.D. 710, 210 N.W. 643; Glass v. Davison, 1964, 276 Ala. 328, 161 So.2d 811; Leuthold v. Goodman, 1945, 22 Wash.2d 583, 157 P.2d 326; Second Restatement of Agency, §§ 229–237.

44. See Ryan v. Western Pac. Ins. Co., 1965, 224 Or. 84, 408 P.2d 84; Luke v. St. Paul Mercury Indem. Co., 1941, 140 Nev. 557, 300 N.W. 577; Standard Tire & Battery Co. v. Sherrill, 1936, 170 Tenn. 418, 95 S.W.2d 915; McCarthy v. Timmins, 1901, 178 Mass. 378, 59 N.E. 1038. But quite extreme deviations have been held not to take the servant out of employment, where the automobile is involved. Cf. Carroll v. Beard-Laney, Inc., 1945, 207 S.C. 339, 35

It has been suggested [45] that such questions ought to be determined by the convenience with which the employer may obtain liability insurance to cover the risk; but as a matter of realistic actuarial practice it appears that this is largely pure theorizing.[46]

Intentional Torts

Early decisions,[47] adhering to the fiction of an "implied command" of the master, refused to hold him liable for intentional or "wilful" wrongdoing on the part of the servant, on the ground that it could not be implied that such conduct was ever authorized. Under modern theories of allocation of the risk of the servant's misbehavior, it has been recognized that even intentional torts may be so reasonably connected with the employment as to be within its "scope," and the present tendency is to extend the employer's responsibility for such conduct.[48] Here again space does not permit any extended discussion of the subject.[49] It may be said, in general, that the master is held liable for any intentional tort committed by the servant where its purpose, however misguided, is wholly or in part to further the master's business.

Thus he will be held liable where his bus driver crowds a competitor's bus into a ditch,[50] or assaults a trespasser to eject him from the bus,[51] or a salesman makes fraudulent statements about the products he is selling,[52] or defames a competitor [53] or disparages his product;[54] or where the servant resorts to false imprisonment,[55] or malicious prosecution [56] for a like purpose. Thus a

S.E.2d 425 (25 mile trip, 15 miles off route); M. K. Hall Co. v. Caballero, Tex.Civ.App.1962, 358 S.W.2d 179 (off route, drunk, picked up girl, stopped on highway to allow her to relieve herself, passed out on seat).

45. Douglas, Vicarious Liability and Administration of Risk, 1929, 38 Yale L.J. 584–594; Smith, Frolic and Detour, 1923, 23 Col.L.Rev. 444, 716.

46. Morris, Enterprise Liability and the Actuarial Process—The Insignificance of Foresight, 1961, 70 Yale L.J. 554.

47. McManus v. Crickett, 1800, 1 East 105, 102 Eng. Rep. 43; Wright v. Wilcox, 1838, 19 Wend., N.Y., 343; Poulton v. London & S. W. R. Co., 1867, L.R. 2 Q.B. 534; Maille v. Lord, 1868, 39 N.Y. 381.

48. Seavey, Speculations as to "Respondeat Superior," Harvard Legal Essays, 1934, 433, 453; Laski, Basis of Vicarious Liability, 1916, 26 Yale L.J. 105, 118; Notes, 1932, 45 Harv.L.Rev. 348; 1927, 21 Ill. L.Rev. 619. See Limpus v. London General Omnibus Co., 1862, 1 H. & C. 526, 158 Eng.Rep. 993; Cohen v. Dry Dock E. B. & B. R. Co., 1877, 69 N.Y. 170; Howe v. Newmarch, 1866, 12 Allen, Mass., 49; Osipoff v. City of New York, 1941, 286 N.Y. 422, 36 N.E.2d 646.

49. See 2 Mechem, Agency, 2d Ed. 1914, §§ 1916–1927; James, Vicarious Liability, 1954, 28 Tulane L.Rev. 161, 187; Seavey, Studies in Agency, 1949, 249 ff.; Second Restatement of Agency, § 245. Brill, The Liability of an Employer for the Wilful Torts of His Servants, 1968, 45 Chi.Kent L.Rev. 1.

50. Limpus v. London General Omnibus Co., 1862, 1 H. & C. 526, 158 Eng.Rep. 993.

51. Pelletier v. Bilbiles, 1967, 154 Conn. 544, 227 A.2d 251; Hyde v. Baggett Transp. Co., E.D.Tenn.1964, 236 F.Supp. 194; Tarman v. Southard, 1953, 92 U. S.App.D.C. 297, 205 F.2d 705; Joyce v. Southern Bus Lines, 5 Cir.1949, 172 F.2d 432. Cf. Florida East Coast R. Co. v. Morgan, Fla.App.1968, 213 So. 2d 632 (assault on picket). See Note, 1967, 9 Ariz. L.Rev. 110.

52. Moynes v. Applebaum, 1922, 218 Mich. 198, 187 N.W. 241; Rutherford v. Rideout Bank, 1938, 11 Cal.2d 479, 80 P.2d 978; Gleason v. Seaboard Air Line R. Co., 1929, 278 U.S. 349; McCord v. Western Union Tel. Co., 1888, 39 Minn. 181, 39 N.W. 315; Downey v. Finucane, 1912, 205 N.Y. 251, 98 N.E. 391. See Second Restatement of Agency, §§ 249, 257–264.

As to negligent misrepresentation, see Note, 1968, 41 Temp.L.Q. 185.

53. Hooper-Holmes Bureau v. Bunn, 5 Cir.1947, 161 F.2d 102; Baker v. Atlantic C. L. R. Co., 1939, 141 Fla. 184, 192 So. 606; Draper v. Hellman Commercial Trust & Sav. Bank, 1928, 203 Cal. 26, 263 P. 240; West v. F. W. Woolworth Co., 1939, 215 N.C. 211, 1 S.E.2d 546. See Note, 1936, 20 Minn.L.Rev. 805. Cf. Grist v. Upjohn Co., 1962, 368 Mich. 578, 118 N.W.2d 985.

54. Rosenberg v. J. C. Penney Co., 1939, 30 Cal.App. 2d 609, 623, 86 P.2d 696, 704; Second Restatement of Agency, §§ 247, 248.

55. Staples v. Schmid, 1893, 18 R.I. 224, 26 A. 193; Cobb v. Simon, 1903, 119 Wis. 597, 97 N.W. 276; Gearity v. Strasbourger, 1909, 133 App.Div. 701, 118 N.Y.S. 257; Nash v. Sears, Roebuck & Co., 1968, 12 Mich.App. 553, 163 N.W.2d 471.

56. Chicago, R. I. & P. R. Co. v. Gage, 1918, 136 Ark. 122, 206 S.W. 141; O'Donnell v. Chase Hotel, Inc.,

railway ticket agent who assaults, arrests or slanders a passenger, in the belief that he has been given a counterfeit bill for a ticket, is within the scope of his employment,[57] although the employer has not authorized such conduct, or has even expressly prohibited it. But if he acts from purely personal motives, because of a quarrel over his wife which is in no way connected with the employer's interests, he is considered in the ordinary case to have departed from his employment, and the master is not liable.[58] Where the conduct of the servant is unprovoked, highly unusual, and quite outrageous, there has been something of a tendency to find that this in itself is sufficient to indicate that the motive was a purely personal one;[59] but it seems clear that this cannot hold true in all cases.[60]

Even where the servant's ends are entirely personal, the master may be under such a duty to the plaintiff that responsibility for the servant's acts may not be delegated to him.[61] This is true in particular in those cases where the master, by contract or otherwise, has entered into some relation requiring him to be responsible for the protection of the plaintiff. The employees of a carrier, for example, would be under a duty to a passenger to exercise reasonable care to protect him against assaults on the part of third persons, even for personal motives;[62] and they are no less under a duty to protect him against their own assaults, which is the duty of the master as well.[63] It follows that the master will be liable even for such entirely personal torts as the rape of a passenger.[64] The same is true of innkeepers [65] and hospitals.[66]

The most difficult questions arise where the servant, for strictly personal reasons and not in furtherance of his employment, loses his temper and attacks the plaintiff in a quarrel which arises out of the employment—as

Mo.App.1965, 388 S.W.2d 489; Eastman v. Leiser Co., 1921, 148 Minn. 96, 181 N.W. 109; Ruth v. St. Louis Transit Co., 1903, 98 Mo.App. 1, 71 S.W. 1055.

57. Palmeri v. Manhattan R. Co., 1892, 133 N.Y. 261, 30 N.E. 1001. Accord: Bergman v. Hendrickson, 1900, 106 Wis. 434, 82 N.W. 304 (barkeeper attacking customer who refused to pay); Johnson v. Monson, 1920, 183 Cal. 149, 190 P. 635 (same as to drunken and noisy customer); Rice v. Marler, 1940, 107 Colo. 57, 108 P.2d 868 (taxicab driver assaulting passenger in argument over attempt to collect fare).

58. Cary v. Hotel Rueger, 1954, 195 Va. 980, 81 S.E. 2d 421; Brazier v. Betts, 1941, 8 Wash.2d 549, 113 P.2d 34; Park Transfer Co. v. Lumbermen's Cas. Co., App.D.C.1944, 142 F.2d 100; Georgia Power Co. v. Shipp, 1943, 195 Ga. 446, 24 S.E.2d 764; Sauter v. New York Tribune, 1953, 305 N.Y. 442, 113 N.E. 2d 790.

59. Ochsrider v. Reading Co., E.D.Pa.1959, 172 F. Supp. 830 (sudden and unprovoked assault, "strongly suggestive of personal motivation"); Averill v. Luttrell, 1958, 44 Tenn.App. 56, 311 S.W.2d 812 (fight between baseball players); Linden v. City Car Co., 1941, 239 Wis. 236, 300 N.W. 925 (taxi driver assaulting one who refused to ride in his cab); Craig's Adm'x v. Kentucky Utilities Co., 1919, 183 Ky. 274, 209 S.W. 33 (shooting a debtor). Cf. Western Ry. of Alabama v. Milligan, 1902, 135 Ala. 205, 33 So. 438 (tickling fellow employee).

60. Davis v. Merrill, 1922, 133 Va. 69, 112 S.E. 628 (railroad gateman shooting at car); Jackson v. American Tel. & Tel. Co., 1905, 139 N.C. 347, 51 S. E. 1015 (having plaintiff arrested so as to put poles on his land while he was in jail).

61. Second Restatement of Agency, § 214; Notes, 1932, 45 Harv.L.Rev. 342; 1927, 21 Ill.L.Rev. 619.

62. See supra, p. 395.

63. Korner v. Cosgrove, 1923, 108 Ohio St. 484, 141 N.E. 267; Garvik v. Burlington, C. R. & N. R. Co., 1906, 131 Iowa 415, 108 N.W. 327; Southern R. Co. v. Beaty, 1925, 212 Ala. 608, 103 So. 658; Pine Bluff & A. R. R. Co. v. Washington, 1915, 116 Ark. 179, 172 S.W. 872.

64. Co-op. Cab Co. v. Singleton, 1942, 66 Ga.App. 874, 19 S.E.2d 541; Berger v. Southern Pac. Co., 1956, 144 Cal.App.2d 1, 300 P.2d 170; cf. Jenkins v. General Cab Co. of Nashville, 1940, 175 Tenn. 409, 135 S.W.2d 448. The same is almost certainly true as to other public utilities. Munick v. City of Durham, 1921, 181 N.C. 188, 106 S.E. 665 (water company).

65. Danile v. Oak Park Arms Hotel, Inc., 1965, 55 Ill.App.2d 2, 203 N.E.2d 706; Clancy v. Barker, 1904, 71 Neb. 83, 98 N.W. 440, affirmed 103 N.W. 446; cf. Beilke v. Carroll, 1909, 51 Wash. 395, 98 P. 1119 (saloon). But cf. Smothers v. Welch & Co. House Furnishing Co., 1925, 310 Mo. 144, 274 S.W. 678 (storekeeper not liable for rape by salesman).

66. Vannah v. Hart Private Hospital, 1917, 228 Mass. 132, 117 N.E. 328.

where, for example, a truck driver collides with the plaintiff, and an altercation follows. Here, unless some non-delegable duty can be found, the older rule denied recovery, and this is still the holding of the majority of the decisions.[67] There has been a tendency in the later cases, however, to allow recovery on the ground that the employment has provided a peculiar opportunity and even incentive for such loss of temper;[68] and there have been California decisions [69] which have found something of an analogy to the workmen's compensation acts, and have considered that the intentional misconduct arises out of and in the course of the employment.

Dangerous Instrumentalities

In a small group of cases a master who has entrusted his servant with an instrumentality which is highly dangerous in itself, or is capable of being misused in some way involving a high degree of risk to others, has been held liable when the servant has misused it for a purpose entirely his own.[70] Thus the rule has been applied in the case of steam locomotives,[71] torpedoes,[72] and poisons.[73] The cases indicate that the master will be held liable only while the servant is engaged in his employment, and while so engaged has custody of the instrumentality.[74] The doctrine has been rejected by perhaps the greater number of courts.[75] It is not very difficult to find a justification for it in the case of things such as dynamite or vicious animals, which are

---

67. Thus in the collision situation stated: Johnson v. M. J. Uline Co., Mun.App.D.C.1949, 40 A.2d 260; Georgia Power Co. v. Shipp, 1943, 195 Ga. 446, 24 S.E.2d 764; Plotkin v. Northland Transp. Co., 1939, 204 Minn. 422, 283 N.W. 758; Sauter v. New York Tribune, 1953, 305 N.Y. 442, 113 N.E.2d 790; State ex rel. Gosselin v. Trimble, 1931, 328 Mo. 760, 41 S. W.2d 801. Cf. Dieas v. Associates Loan Co., Fla. 1957, 99 So.2d 279 (collecter entered residence and assaulted plaintiff).

68. Fields v. Sanders, 1947, 29 Cal.2d 834, 180 P.2d 684; United Brotherhood of Carpenters and Joiners of America, AFL–CIO v. Humphreys, 1962, 203 Va. 781, 127 S.E.2d 98, cert. denied 371 U.S. 954 (strike violence by union representatives); Dilli v. Johnson, 1939, 71 U.S.App.D.C. 139, 107 F.2d 669; Tri-State Coach Corp. v. Walsh, 1948, 188 Va. 299, 49 S.E.2d 363; and cf. Bowman v. Home Life Ins. Co., of America, 3 Cir.1957, 243 F.2d 331, where an insurance company's field underwriter represented himself to be a doctor, and made an indecent examination of an applicant for insurance. Also Andrews v. Norvell, 1941, 65 Ga.App. 241, 15 S.E.2d 808.

69. Fields v. Sanders, 1947, 29 Cal.2d 834, 180 P.2d 684; George v. Bekins Van & Storage Co., 1949, 33 Cal.2d 834, 205 P.2d 1037; Carr v. Wm. C. Crowell Co., 1946, 28 Cal.2d 652, 171 P.2d 5; Caldwell v. Farley, 1955, 134 Cal.App.2d 84, 285 P.2d 294. See Small, The Effect of Workmen's Compensation Trends on Agency-Tort Concepts of Scope of Employment, 1953, 11 NACCA L.J. 19, 12 NACCA L.J. 21.

Much the same result was accomplished in Ira S. Bushey & Sons, Inc. v. United States, 2 Cir.1968, 398 F.2d 167, where the court rejected the "motive" test and held that damage to a ship by a drunken sailor was one of the "characteristic" risks of his employment. See Note, 1969, 82 Harv.L.Rev. 1568.

70. See Horack, The Dangerous Instrument Doctrine, 1917, 26 Yale L.J. 224.

71. Alsever v. Minneapolis & St. L. R. Co., 1902, 115 Iowa 338, 88 N.W. 841; (blowing off steam to frighten child); Toledo, W. & W. R. Co. v. Harmon, 1868, 47 Ill. 298 (similar facts); Stewart v. Cary Lumber Co., 1907, 146 N.C. 47, 59 S.E. 545 (blowing whistle to "make the mule dance"). Cf. Danbeck v. New Jersey Traction Co., 1895, 57 N.J.L. 463, 31 A. 1038 (electric car).

In Southern Cotton Oil Co. v. Anderson, 1920, 80 Fla. 441, 86 So. 629, this rule was applied to an automobile; and this has continued to be the Florida doctrine. All other courts have rejected such an application. See for example Terrett v. Wray, 1937, 171 Tenn. 448, 105 S.W.2d 93.

72. Harriman v. Pittsburgh, C. & St. L. R. Co., 1887, 45 Ohio St. 11, 12 N.E. 451; Euting v. Chicago & N. W. R. Co., 1902, 116 Wis. 13, 92 N.W. 358.

73. Smith's Adm'x v. Middleton, 1902, 112 Ky. 588, 66 S.W. 388.

74. Obertoni v. Boston & M. R. Co., 1904, 186 Mass. 481, 71 N.E. 980; Johnson v. Chicago, R. I. & P. R. Co., 1913, 157 Iowa 738, 141 N.W. 430. See Horack, The Dangerous Instrument Doctrine, 1917, 26 Yale L.J. 224.

75. American Ry. Exp. Co. v. Davis, 1922, 152 Ark. 258, 238 S.W. 50, 1063 (pistol); Galveston, H. & S. A. R. Co. v. Currie, 1906, 100 Tex. 136, 96 S.W. 1073 (compressed air); Vadyak v. Lehigh & N. E. R. Co., 1935, 318 Pa. 580, 179 A. 435 (steam locomotive); Thomas-Kincannon-Elkin Drug Co. v. Hendrix, 1936, 175 Miss. 767, 168 So. 287 (powerful laxative); second Restatement of Agency, § 238, Comment *d*.

so extremely dangerous in themselves that strict liability may properly be imposed upon the enterprise which makes use of them, and the employer would be liable even if they were entrusted to an independent contractor.[76] The courts which have extended it beyond such instrumentalities are pursuing a policy of holding the enterprise responsible for the danger, which goes beyond the limitations usually imposed upon strict liability at the present time. The justification for it must lie in the especial opportunity and temptation afforded to the servant to misuse the instrumentality under the conditions likely to arise in the employment—or in other words, again, the foreseeability and indeed especial likelihood of the tort.

Agents Other Than Servants

Since an agent who is not a servant is not subject to any right of control by his employer over the details of his physical conduct, the responsibility ordinarily rests upon the agent alone, and the principal is not liable for the torts which he may commit.[77] There are, however, a number of situations in which such liability may exist. These include all cases in which a tort may be based upon the apparent authority of the agent to act for his principal,[78] or in which a tort such as deceit occurs in the course of a consensual transaction between the agent and the injured person.[79] Thus a client may be made liable for the improper institution of legal proceedings by his attorney,[80] and a seller of land or goods may, in most states, be subject to an action of deceit for the fraud of his agent committed in the course of the sale.[81] In such cases liability is based wholly upon the relation of principal and agent, but it is subject, in general, to the same limitations as those placed upon the liability of a master for the tort of a servant.[82] Thus it must appear either that the representations made were within the actual or apparent authority of the agent,[83] or of a kind reasonably to be expected by the employer in connection with the transaction,[84] or that the agent has been placed by the principal in a position which enables him to commit the fraud, while apparently acting within his authority.[85]

The field of vicarious liability is a very large one, and any full discussion of it must be left to texts on the law of master and servant, agency, partnership and the like. The space here available permits only the briefest review of some of the more common problems which have arisen in tort cases.

---

76. Cf. Baker v. Snell, [1908] 2 K.B. 352, 825, 77 L.J. K.B. 1090 (vicious animal); Stapleton v. Butensky, 1919, 188 App.Div. 237, 177 N.Y.S. 18 (same). As to the similarity of the rule as to independent contractors, see Montgomery v. Gulf Refining Co. of Louisiana, 1929, 168 La. 73, 121 So. 578.

77. Second Restatement of Agency, § 250; Great American Indemnity Co. v. Fleniken, 5 Cir., 1943, 134 F.2d 208; Hurla v. Capper Publications, 1939, 149 Kan. 369, 87 P.2d 552; Vert v. Metropolitan Life Ins. Co., 1938, 342 Mo. 629, 117 S.W.2d 252.

78. Rhone v. Try Me Cab. Co., 1933, 62 App.D.C. 201, 65 F.2d 834; Middleton v. Frances, 1934, 257 Ky. 42, 77 S.W.2d 425; Standard Oil Co. v. Gentry, 1941, 241 Ala. 62, 1 So.2d 29; Acherman v. Robertson, 1942, 240 Wis. 421, 3 N.W.2d 723. See Notes, 1931, 11 Boston U.L.Rev. 85; 1938, 22 Minn.L.Rev. 741.

79. Second Restatement of Agency, §§ 256–261. See Horack, Vicarious Liability for Fraud and Deceit in Iowa, 1931, 16 Iowa L.Rev. 361.

80. Otto v. Levy, 1935, 244 App.Div. 349, 279 N.Y.S. 462; Second Restatement of Agency, § 253.

81. Heidegger v. Burg, 1917, 137 Minn. 53, 162 N.W. 889; Howe v. Johnson, 1920, 236 Mass. 379, 128 N. E. 634; Moynes v. Applebaum, 1922, 218 Mich. 198, 187 N.W. 241; Gulf Electric Co. v. Fried, 1929, 218 Ala. 684, 119 So. 685.

82. Second Restatement of Agency, §§ 251–262.

83. Second Restatement of Agency, § 257.

84. Second Restatement of Agency, § 258.

85. Second Restatement of Agency, § 261. Cf. Wise v. Western Union Tel. Co., 1934, 6 W.W.Harr. 155, Del., 172 A. 757; Ripon Knitting Works v. Railway Express Agency, 1932, 207 Wis. 452, 240 N.W. 840.

71. INDEPENDENT CONTRACTORS

For the torts of an independent contractor, as distinguished from a servant,[86] it has long been said to be the general rule that there is no vicarious liability upon the employer.[87] This doctrine developed, both in English [88] and in American [89] law at a time when such liability for the torts of a servant was well established, and it seems to have been, in its inception, something of a retreat from the rigors of that rule. Various reasons have been advanced for it, but the one most commonly accepted [90] is that, since the employer

has no right of control over the manner in which the work is to be done, it is to be regarded as the contractor's own enterprise, and he, rather than the employer, is the proper party to be charged with the responsibility of preventing the risk, and administering and distributing it.

Against this argument, it has been contended [91] that the enterprise is still the employer's, since he remains the person primarily to be benefited by it; that he selects the contractor, and is free to insist upon one who is financially responsible, and to demand indemnity from him, and that the insurance necessary to distribute the risk is properly a cost of his business. Upon this basis, the prediction has been made [92] that ultimately the "general rule" will be that the employer is liable for the negligence of an independent contractor, and that he will be excused only in a limited group of cases where he is not in a position to select a responsible contractor, or the risk of any harm to others from the enterprise is obviously slight. The English courts have taken steps in this direction,[93] until the position of the ordinary independent contractor in England approaches that of a servant. The American courts, have not gone so far, and have continued to repeat the "general rule" of non-liability with exceptions, whose very number is sufficient to cast doubt upon the validity of the rule.[94]

---

86. See supra, § 70.

87. Globe Indemnity Co. v. Victill Corp., 1956, 208 Md. 573, 119 A.2d 423; Turner v. Lewis, Ky.1955, 282 S.W.2d 624; Pickett v. Waldorf System, 1922, 241 Mass. 569, 136 N.E. 64; Kruse v. Wiegand, 1931, 204 Wis. 195, 235 N.W. 426; Jourdenais v. Hayden, 1932, 104 Vt. 215, 158 A. 664. See McCleary, Liability of an Employer for the Negligence of an Independent Contractor in Missouri, 1933, 18 St. Louis L.Rev. 289; Notes, 1930, 39 Yale L.J. 871; 1956, 44 Cal.L.Rev. 762.

88. In Bush v. Steinman, 1799, 1 Bos. & P. 404, 121 Eng.Rep. 978, the employer was held liable, despite "great difficulty in stating with accuracy the grounds for liability." But in Laugher v. Pointer, 1826, 5 B. & C. 547, 108 Eng.Rep. 204, the employer was held not liable for the negligence of a hired driver, and this decision was followed in subsequent cases. Quarman v. Burnett, 1840, 6 M. & W. 499, 151 Eng.Rep. 509; Milligan v. Wedge, 1840, 12 Ad. & El. 737, 113 Eng.Rep. 993; Reedie v. London & N. W. R. Co., 1849, 4 Ex. 244, 154 Eng.Rep. 1201.

89. Early cases held the employer liable. Lowell v. Boston & L. R. Corp., 1839, 23 Pick., Mass., 24; Stone v. Cheshire R. Corp., 1839, 19 N.H. 427. Later decisions to the contrary apparently were influenced by the English cases. Blake v. Ferris, 1851, 5 N.Y. 48; Hilliard v. Richardson, 1855, 3 Gray, Mass., 349; Painter v. City of Pittsburgh, 1863, 46 Pa. 213. See Note, 1902, 2 Col.L.Rev. 112.

90. See Harper, The Basis of the Immunity of an Employer of an Independent Contractor, 1935, 10 Ind.L.J. 494; Morris, the Torts of an Independent Contractor, 1935, 29 Ill.L.Rev. 339; Douglas, Vicarious Liability and Administration of Risk, 1929, 38 Yale L.J. 584, 594; Steffen, Independent Contractor and the Good Life, 1935, 2 U.Chi.L.Rev. 501; Brown, Liability for the Torts of an Independent Contractor in West Virginia, 1953, 55 W.Va.L.Rev. 216; Ferson, Liability of Employers for Misrepresentations Made by Independent Contractors, 1949, 3 Vand.L.Rev. 1; James, Vicarious Liability, 1954,

28 Tulane L.Rev. 161. Also N.Y. Law Revision Comm'n Report, 1939, 411–688.

91. See the articles cited in the preceding note.

92. Morris, The Torts of an Independent Contractor, 1935, 29 Ill.L.Rev. 339. But see, to the contrary, Steffen, Independent Contractor and the Good Life, 1935, 2 U.Chi.L.Rev. 501, pointing out the difficulties involved.

93. See Chapman, Liability for the Negligence of Independent Contractors, 1934, 50 L.Q.Rev. 71; Williams, Liability for Independent Contractors, [1956] Camb.L.J. 180; Jolowicz, Liability for Independent Contractors in the English Common Law—A Suggestion, 1957, 9 Stan.L.Rev. 690; Charlesworth, Law of Negligence, 1938, 58–66.

94. See Note, 1930, 39 Yale L.J. 861. "Indeed it would be proper to say that the rule is now primar-

The Restatement of Torts [95] has devoted no less than twenty-four sections to the list.

These exceptions making the employer liable overlap and shade into one another; and cases are comparatively rare in which at least two of them do not appear. The method of decision then has been almost invariably to state and rely upon both or all, as alternative or cumulative grounds. The various types of situations can be roughly grouped together as follows:

Negligence of the Employer

In the first place, quite apart from any question of vicarious responsibility, the employer may be liable for any negligence of his own in connection with the work to be done. Where there is a foreseeable risk of harm to others unless precautions are taken, it is his duty to exercise reasonable care to select a competent,[96] experienced,[97] and careful [98] contractor with the proper equipment,[99] and to provide, in the contract or otherwise, for

such precautions as reasonably appear to be called for.[1] So far as he in fact gives directions for the work,[2] furnishes equipment for it,[3] or retains control over any part of it,[4] he is required to exercise reasonable care for the protection of others; and he must likewise interfere to put a stop to any unnecessarily dangerous practices of which he becomes informed,[5] and make a reasonable inspection of the work after it is completed,

---

ily important as a preamble to the catalog of its exceptions." Pacific Fire Ins. Co. v. Kenny Boiler & Mfg. Co., 1937, 201 Minn. 500, 503, 277 N.W. 226. It may be suggested that the chief reason why a "general rule" of liability never has been stated, is that the only way of stating exceptions to it would be to say that the exceptional cases are those which do not fit into the numerous categories now rated as exceptions.

95. Second Restatement of Torts, §§ 410–429.

96. Huntt v. McNamee, 4 Cir. 1905, 141 F. 293; Mooney v. Stainless, Inc., 6 Cir. 1964, 338 F.2d 127, cert. denied 381 U.S. 925; Norwalk Gaslight Co. v. Borough of Norwalk, 1893, 63 Conn. 495, 28 A. 32; Board of Comm'rs of Wabash County v. Pearson, 1889, 120 Ind. 426, 22 N.E. 134; Baker v. Scott County Milling Co., 1929, 323 Mo. 1089, 20 S.W.2d 494.

97. Ellis & Lewis v. Warner, 1929, 180 Ark. 53, 20 S. W.2d 320; Mullich v. Brocker, 1905, 119 Mo.App. 332, 97 S.W. 549.

98. Ozan Lumber Co. v. McNeely, 1949, 214 Ark. 657, 217 S.W.2d 341; Brannock v. Elmore, 1893, 114 Mo. 55, 21 S.W. 451; Richardson v. Carbon Hill Coal Co., 1893, 6 Wash. 52, 32 P. 1012.

99. Risley v. Lenwell, 1954, 129 Cal.App.2d 608, 277 P.2d 897; Kuhn v. P. J. Carlin Const. Co., 1935, 154 Misc. 892, 278 N.Y.S. 635; L. B. Foster & Co. v. Hurnblad, 9 Cir. 1969, 418 P.2d 727.

1. Mountain States Tel. & Tel. Co. v. Kelton, 1955, 79 Ariz. 126, 285 P.2d 168 (failure to warn against underground cable); A. M. Holter Hardware Co. v. Western Mortgage & W. T. Co., 1915, 51 Mont. 94, 149 P. 489; State Highway & Public Works Comm'n v. Diamond S.S. Transp. Corp., 1946, 226 N.C. 371, 38 S.E.2d 214; Fegles Const. Co. v. McLaughlin Const. Co., 9 Cir.1953, 205 F.2d 637; Whalen v. Shivek, 1950, 326 Mass. 142, 93 N.E.2d 393.

2. Ellis v. Sheffield Gas Co., 1853, 2 El. & Bl. 767, 118 Eng.Rep. 955; Posner v. Paul's Trucking Service, Inc., 1 Cir. 1967, 380 F.2d 757; Keldon v. Steiner, 1939, 138 Pa.Super. 66, 10 A.2d 19 (undue risk); Besner v. Central Trust Co. of New York, 1921, 230 N.Y. 357, 130 N.E. 577 (dangerous method); Humphries v. Kendall, 1937, 195 Ark. 45, 111 S.W.2d 492 (interference with the work).

3. Johnson v. J. I. Case Threshing Mach. Co., 1916, 193 Mo.App. 198, 182 S.W. 1089; Brady v. Jay, 1904, 111 La. 1071, 36 So. 132; Willis v. San Bernardino Lumber & Box Co., 1927, 82 Cal.App. 751, 256 P. 224.

4. Terry v. A. P. Green Fire Brick Co., E.D.Ark. 1958, 164 F.Supp. 184; Bergquist v. Penterman, 1957, 46 N.J.Super. 74, 134 A.2d 20; McGrath v. Pennsylvania Sugar Co., 1925, 282 Pa. 265, 127 A. 780; Willis v. San Bernardino Lumber & Box Co., 1927, 82 Cal.App. 751, 256 P. 224; Fluor Corp. v. Sykes, 1966, 3 Ariz.App. 211, 413 P.2d 270, rehearing denied 3 Ariz.App. 599, 416 P.2d 610. But this must be more than the mere general supervisory right to object to something unsatisfactory, which is retained by nearly every employer. McDonald v. Shell Oil Co., 1955, 44 Cal.2d 785, 285 P.2d 902.

Such cases of course shade into those in which such complete control is retained that the employee is regarded as a servant, and the distinction seldom is made clear.

5. United States v. Standard Oil Co. of New Jersey, D.Md.1919, 258 F. 697, affirmed 4 Cir., 1920, 264 F. 66; Bergen v. Morton Amusement Co., 1917, 178 App.Div. 400, 165 N.Y.S. 348; Lamb v. South Unit Jehovah's Witnesses, 1950, 232 Minn. 259, 45 N.W.2d 403.

to be sure that it is safe.[6] If the work is done on the employer's own land, he will be required to exercise reasonable care to prevent activities or conditions which are dangerous to those outside of it,[7] or to those who enter it as invitees.[8] In all of these cases, he is liable for his personal negligence, rather than that of the contractor.

Non-delegable Duty

A different approach, adopted in several of the exceptions to the general rule of non-liability, has been to hold that the employer's enterprise, and his relation to the plaintiff, are such as to impose upon him a duty which cannot be delegated to the contractor. It has been mentioned earlier[9] that there are numerous situations in which it may be negligence to rely upon another person, and the defendant is not relieved of the obligation of taking reasonable precautions himself. But the cases of "non-delegable duty" go further, and hold the employer liable for the negligence of the contractor, although he has himself done everything that could reason-

ably be required of him. They are thus cases of vicarious liability.

Such a duty may be imposed by statute,[10] by contract,[11] by franchise or charter,[12] or by the common law.[13] The catalogue is a long one: the duty of a carrier to transport its passengers in safety,[14] of a railroad to fence its tracks properly[15] or to maintain safe crossings,[16] and of a municipality to keep its streets in repair;[17] the duty to afford lateral

---

6. Hickman v. Toole, 1926, 35 Ga.App. 697, 134 S.E. 635; McGuire v. Hartford Buick Co., 1944, 131 Conn. 417, 40 A.2d 269; Bethlehem Steel Co. v. Variety Iron & Steel Co., 1921, 139 Md. 313, 115 A. 59; Pulaski Housing Authority v. Smith, 1955, 39 Tenn.App. 213, 282 S.W.2d 213; Rumetsch v. John Wanamaker, N. Y., Inc., 1915, 216 N.Y. 379, 110 N.E. 760. Cf. Sheridan v. Rosenthal, 1923, 206 App.Div. 279, 201 N.Y.S. 169 (holding that under the circumstances there was a duty to inspect the work as it proceeded).

7. Inhabitants of Rockport v. Rockport Granite Co., 1901, 177 Mass. 246, 58 N.E. 1017; Wright v. Tudor City Twelfth Unit, 1938, 276 N.Y. 303, 12 N.E.2d 307; United States v. Standard Oil Co., of New York, D.C.Md.1919, 258 F. 697, affirmed, 1919, 264 F. 66; Lamb v. South Unit Jehovah's Witnesses, 1950, 232 Minn. 259, 45 N.W.2d 403; Probst v. Hinesley, 1909, 133 Ky. 64, 117 S.W. 389.

8. Lineaweaver v. Wanamaker, 1930, 299 Pa. 45, 149 A. 91; Thornton v. Maine State Ag. Society, 1903, 97 Me. 108, 53 A. 979; Stickel v. Riverview Sharpshooters' Park Co., 1911, 250 Ill. 452, 95 N.E. 445; Smith v. Cumberland County Ag. Society, 1913, 163 N.C. 346, 79 S.E. 632; Hartman v. Tennessee State Fair Ass'n, 1915, 134 Tenn. 149, 183 S.W. 733.

9. See supra, p. 177.

10. Snyder v. Southern Cal. Edison Co., 1955, 44 Cal. 2d 793, 285 P.2d 912; Blount v. Tow Fong, 1927, 48 R.I. 453, 138 A. 52; Semanchuck v. Fifth Ave. & Thirty-Seventh St. Corp., 1943, 290 N.Y. 412, 49 N. E.2d 507; John Griffiths & Son Co. v. National Fire Proofing Co., 1923, 310 Ill. 331, 141 N.E. 739.

11. Colgrove v. Smith, 1894, 102 Cal. 220, 36 P. 411. Particularly where the contract calls for the employer to do the work himself. Radel v. Borches, 1912, 147 Ky. 506, 145 S.W. 155; Maryland Dredging & Contracting Co. v. Maryland, 4 Cir. 1919, 262 F. 11; Mahany v. Kansas City R. Co., Mo.1923, 254 S.W. 16; Sciolaro v. Asch, 1910, 198 N.Y. 77, 91 N. E. 263.

12. Dixie Stage Lines v. Anderson, 1931, 222 Ala. 673, 134 So. 23; Cotton v. Ship-By-Truck Co., 1935, 337 Mo. 270, 85 S.W.2d 80; City of Chicago v. Murdoch, 1904, 212 Ill. 9, 72 N.E. 46; Murray v. Lehigh Valley R. Co., 1895, 66 Conn. 512, 34 A. 506; Sanford v. Pawtucket St. R. Co., 1896, 19 R.I. 537, 35 A. 67. See Note, 1930, 79 U.Pa.L.Rev. 90. Cf. Louis v. Youngren, 1956, 12 Ill.App.2d 198, 138 N.E.2d 696.

13. Woodman v. Metropolitan R. Co., 1889, 149 Mass. 335, 21 N.E. 482; Corrigan v. Elsinger, 1900, 81 Minn. 42, 83 N.W. 492. See Note, 1965, 44 N.C.L. Rev. 242.

14. Dixie Stage Lines v. Anderson, 1931, 222 Ala. 673, 134 So. 23. Or freight. Eli v. Murphy, 1952, 39 Cal.2d 598, 248 P.2d 756.

15. Rockford, R. I. & St. L. R. Co. v Heflin, 1872, 65 Ill. 366; Chicago, K. & W. R. Co. v. Hutchinson, 1891, 45 Kan. 186, 25 P. 576. Compare, as to crossings, Boucher v. New York, N. H. & H. R. Co., 1907, 196 Mass. 355, 82 N.E. 15; Choctaw, O. & W. R. Co. v. Wilker, 1906, 16 Okl. 384, 84 P. 1086.

16. Boucher v. New York, N. H. & H. R. Co., 1907, 196 Mass. 355, 82 N.E. 15; Choctaw, O. & W. R. Co. v. Wilker, 1906, 16 Okl. 384, 84 P. 1086.

17. Storrs v. City of Utica, 1858, 17 N.Y. 104; Prowell v. City of Waterloo, 1909, 144 Iowa 689, 123 N. W. 346; City of Baltimore v. Leonard, 1917, 129 Md. 621, 99 A. 891; City of Glasgow v. Gillenwaters, 1902, 113 Ky. 140, 67 S.W. 381. See Hepburn, Liability of Municipal Corporations for Negligent

support to adjoining land,[18] to refrain from obstructing or endangering the public highway,[19] to keep premises reasonably safe for business visitors,[20] to provide employees with a safe place to work; [21] the duty of a landlord to maintain common passageways,[22] to make repairs according to covenant,[23] or to use proper care in making them,[24] and no doubt

several others.[25] The owner of land or a building who entrusts repairs or other work on it to a contractor remains liable for any negligence injuring those on or outside the land, while he retains possession during the progress of the work,[26] or resumes it after completion,[27] but not while he has vacated the premises during the work.[28]

It is difficult to suggest any criterion by which the non-delegable character of such duties may be determined, other than the conclusion of the courts that the responsibility is so important to the community that the employer should not be permitted to transfer it to another. So far as they may be willing to broaden the category in the future, the law may approach an ultimate rule that any duty which can be found to rest upon the em-

Acts of Independent Street Contractors, 1930, 6 Notre Dame Lawyer 55. The same rule has been applied to the state, where it can be sued. Saari v. State, 1953, 203 Misc. 859, 119 N.Y.S.2d 507, affirmed, 1953, 282 App.Div. 526, 125 N.Y.S.2d 507.

18. Wharam v. Investment Underwriters, 1943, 58 Cal.App.2d 346, 136 P.2d 363; Kolodkin v. Griffin, 1953, 87 Ga.App. 725, 75 S.E.2d 197; Levi v. Schwartz, 1953, 201 Md. 575, 95 A.2d 322; Law v. Phillips, 1952, 136 W.Va. 761, 68 S.E.2d 452; Davis v. Summerfield, 1903, 133 N.C. 325, 45 S.E. 654.

19. Globe Indemnity Co. v. Schmitt, 1944, 142 Ohio St. 595, 53 N.E.2d 790; Brown Hotel Co. v. Sizemore, 1946, 303 Ky. 431, 197 S.W.2d 911; May v. Hrinko, 1948, 137 N.J.L. 324, 59 A.2d 823; Campus v. McElligott, 1936, 122 Conn. 14, 187 A. 29; Magay v. Claflin-Sumner Coal Co., 1926, 257 Mass. 244, 153 N.E. 534.

20. Blancher v. Bank of California, 1955, 47 Wash.2d 1, 286 P.2d 92; Besner v. Central Trust Co. of New York, 1921, 230 N.Y. 357, 130 N.E. 577; Lineaweaver v. John Wanamaker, Inc., 1930, 299 Pa. 45, 149 A. 91; Daly v. Bergstedt, 1964, 267 Minn. 244, 126 N.W.2d 242; Modlin v. Washington Ave. Food Center, Fla.App.1965, 178 So.2d 596, cert. denied 201 So.2d 70, quashed, cause remanded 205 So.2d 295, conformed to 208 So.2d 862.

21. Myers v. Little Church by the Side of the Road, 1951, 37 Wash.2d 897, 227 P.2d 165; Webb v. Old Salem, Inc., 4 Cir. 1969, 416 F.2d 223. Cf. Van Arsdale v. Hollinger, 1968, 68 Cal.2d 245, 66 Cal.Rptr. 20, 437 P.2d 508 (marking lines on busy street).

22. Brown v. George Pepperdine Foundation, 1943, 23 Cal.2d 256, 143 P.2d 929; Koskoff v. Goldman, 1912, 86 Conn. 415, 85 A. 588; Cramblitt v. Percival-Porter Co., 1916, 176 Iowa 733, 158 N.W. 541; Hussey v. Long Dock R. Co., 1924, 100 N.J.L. 380, 126 A. 314.

23. Peerless Mfg. Co. v. Bagley, 1901, 126 Mich. 225, 85 N.W. 568; Vitale v. Duerbeck, 1933, 332 Mo. 1184, 62 S.W.2d 559; Paltey v. Egan, 1910, 200 N.Y. 83, 93 N.E. 267.

24. Arlington Realty Co. v. Lawson, 1934, 228 Ala. 214, 153 So. 425; Bailey v. Zlotnick, 1945, 80 U.S. App.D.C. 117, 149 F. 505; Covington Co. v. Masonic

Temple Co., 1917, 176 Ky. 729, 197 S.W. 420; Livingston v. Essex Inv. Co., 1941, 219 N.C. 416, 14 S. E.2d 489; Rubin v. Girard Trust Co., 1944, 154 Pa. Super. 257, 35 A.2d 601.

25. California has applied this to the statutory duty to have automobile brakes in good operating condition. Maloney v. Rath, 1968, 69 Cal.2d 442, 71 Cal. Rptr. 897, 445 P.2d 513; Dutcher v. Weber, 1969, 275 Cal.App.2d 1078, 80 Cal.Rptr. 378. See Note, 1969, 14 Vill.L.Rev. 560.

26. E. R. Harding Co. v. Paducah St. R. Co., 1926, 208 Ky. 728, 271 S.W. 1046; Lineaweaver v. John Wanamaker, Inc., 1930, 299 Pa. 45, 149 A. 91; S. H. Kress & Co. v. Reaves, 4 Cir. 1936, 85 F.2d 915, cert. denied 299 U.S. 616; De Palma v. Weinman, 1909, 15 N.M. 68, 103 P. 782; Walker v. Strosnider, 1910, 67 W.Va. 39, 67 S.E. 1087. The distinction between repair and original construction made by § 422 of the First Restatement of Torts is simply not borne out by the cases, and is abandoned by the Second Restatement, § 422, Comment b.

27. Connolly v. Des Moines Inv. Co., 1905, 130 Iowa 633, 105 N.W. 400; Cork v. Blossom, 1894, 162 Mass. 330, 38 N.E. 495; Wilkinson v. Detroit Steel & Spring Works, 1888, 73 Mich. 405, 41 N.W. 490; McCrorey v. Thomas, 1909, 109 Va. 373, 63 S.E. 1011; Walker v. Strosnider, 1910, 67 W.Va. 39, 67 S.E. 1087.

28. Prest-o-lite Co. v. Skeel, 1914, 182 Ind. 593, 106 N.E. 365; Burke v. Ireland, 1901, 166 N.Y. 305, 59 N.E. 914; Csaranko v. Robilt, Inc., 1967, 93 N.J.Super. 428, 226 A.2d 43; Boswell v. Laird, 1857, 8 Cal. 469.

ployer himself cannot be delegated to an independent contractor.[29]

"Inherently Dangerous" Activities

The leading English case of Bower v. Peate,[30] in which the foundation of the plaintiff's building was undermined by an excavation, adopted still another approach, saying that the employer would be liable for the negligence of the contractor if, in the course of the work, injurious consequences might be expected to result "unless means are taken to prevent them." This gave rise to an exceptional category of work likely to be peculiarly dangerous "unless special precautions are taken." [31] American courts on the whole have preferred to adopt the language of Judge Dillon [32] as to work which is "inherently dangerous." Neither phrase has ever yet been very well defined by anyone, and they are apparently intended to mean very much the same thing. They have been used more or less interchangeably by the courts, which usually state and rely upon both as the basis of an exceptional rule. If there is a distinction, it is that the "special precautions" exception is more commonly applied where the employer should anticipate the need for some one specific precaution, such as a railing around an excavation in the sidewalk while "inherent danger" is used where the work calls for a whole set of precautions, against a number of hazards, as in the case of painting carried on upon a scaffold above a highway.

Obviously included within either concept are activities, such as the construction of

reservoirs,[33] the use or keeping of vicious animals,[34] high tension electric wires,[35] blasting,[36] crop dusting,[37] and the exhibition of fireworks,[38] which will be dangerous in spite of all reasonable care, so that strict liability might be imposed upon the employer if he should carry them out himself.

But liability on either basis has been extended beyond this, to work which, in its nature, will create some peculiar risk of injury to others unless special precautions are taken —as, for example, excavations in or near a public highway,[39] or construction or repair work on buildings adjoining it [40] or likely to

---

29. Compare the English rule, which approaches this result. Chapman, Liability for the Negligence of Independent Contractors, 1934, 50 L.Q.Rev. 71.

30. 1876, 1 Q.B. 321.

31. Second Restatement of Torts, § 416.

32. Dillon, Municipal Corporations, 1st Ed. 1872, § 792. See Note, 1950, 38 Ky.L.J. 282; Second Restatement of Torts, § 427. "Inherent danger" converges not only with "special precautions," but also with "non-delegable duty." The courts not infrequently state all three. Cf. Besner v. Central Trust Co. of New York, 1921, 230 N.Y. 357, 130 N.E. 577.

33. Rylands v. Fletcher, 1868, L.R. 3 H.L. 330 was itself a case involving an independent contractor.

34. Stapleton v. Butensky, 1919, 188 App.Div. 237, 177 N.Y.S. 18; Austin v. Bridges, 1912, 3 Tenn.Civ. App. 151; Yazoo & M. V. R. Co. v. Gordon, 1939, 184 Miss. 885, 186 So. 631.

35. Person v. Cauldwell-Wingate Co., 4 Cir. 1949, 176 F.2d 237.

36. Garden of the Gods Village v. Hellman, 1956, 133 Colo. 286, 294 P.2d 597; Wilson v. Rancho Sespe, 1962, 207 Cal.App.2d 10, 24 Cal.Rptr. 296; J. C. Carland & Co. v. Burke, 1916, 197 Ala. 435, 73 So. 10; Freebury v. Chicago, M. & P. S. R. Co., 1914, 77 Wash. 464, 137 P. 1044; Giem v. Williams, 1949, 215 Ark. 705, 222 S.W.2d 800.

37. S. A. Gerrard Co. v. Fricker, 1933, 42 Ariz. 503, 27 P.2d 678; Alexander v. Seaboard Air Line R. Co., 1952, 221 S.C. 477, 71 S.E.2d 299; Pendergrass v. Lovelace, 1953, 57 N.M. 661, 262 P.2d 231; Miles v. A. Arena & Co., 1938, 23 Cal.App.2d 680, 73 P.2d 1260; Southwestern Bell Tel. Co. v. Smith, 1952, 220 Ark. 223, 247 S.W.2d 16.

38. Blue Grass Fair Ass'n v. Bunnell, 1924, 206 Ky. 462, 267 S.W. 237; see Note, 1927, 37 Yale L.J. 113. Cf. Trexler v. Tug Raven, D.C.Va.1968, 290 F.Supp. 429, reversed on other grounds 419 F.2d 536, cert. denied Crown Central Petroleum Corp. v. Texler, 398 U.S. 938 (loading and discharging combustible fuel).

39. Thomas v. Harrington, 1902, 72 N.H. 45, 54 A. 285; Campus v. McElligott, 1936, 122 Conn. 14, 187 A. 29; Evans v. Elliott, 1941, 220 N.C. 253, 17 S.E. 2d 125; McGinley v. Edison Elec. Ill. Co., 1924, 248 Mass. 583, 143 N.E. 537; Olah v. Katz, 1926, 234 Mich. 112, 207 N.W. 892.

40. Rohlfs v. Weil, 1936, 271 N.Y. 444, 3 N.E.2d 588; Richman Bros. Co. v. Miller, 1936, 131 Ohio St. 424, 3 N.E.2d 360 (both painting over sidewalk); Whalen v. Shivek, 1950, 326 Mass. 142, 93 N.E.2d 393;

obstruct it,[41] and similar activities,[42] such as the clearing of land by fire,[43] tearing down high walls or chimneys,[44] the construction of a dam,[45] and many other kinds of work.[46]

So far as the cases indicate the principle seems to be limited to work in which there is a high degree of risk in relation to the particular surroundings,[47] or some rather spe-

cific risk or set of risks to those in the vicinity, recognizable in advance as calling for definite precautions. The emphasis is upon the "peculiar" character of the risk, and the need for special, unusual care. One who hires a trucker to transport his goods must, as a reasonable man, always realize that if the truck is driven at an excessive speed, or with defective brakes, some collision or other harm to persons on the highway is likely to occur. But this is not "inherent danger," as the courts have used the term; and for such more or less usual negligence the employer will not be liable.[48] When the trucker is to transport over the highway giant logs which require special care to fasten them securely,[49] there is obviously a special danger, and the exception applies. On the other hand, it is certainly not at all essential that the risk be an unavoidable one, necessarily [50] involved in the work itself. It is enough that the usual or contemplated [51] methods of doing the

Stubblefield v. Federal Reserve Bank of St. Louis, 1947, 356 Mo. 1018, 204 S.W.2d 718; Warden v. Pennsylvania R. Co., 1931, 123 Ohio St. 304, 175 N. E. 207.

41. Girdzus v. Van Etten, 1918, 211 Ill.App. 524 (piled building materials); Boylhart v. Di Marco & Reimann, 1936, 270 N.Y. 217, 200 N.E. 793 (same); Wright v. Tudor City Twelfth Unit, 1938, 276 N.Y. 303, 12 N.E.2d 307, (washing mats on sidewalk).

42. Besner v. Central Trust Co. of New York, 1921, 230 N.Y. 357, 130 N.E. 577 (installing safety doors on elevator while in use); Watkins v. Gabriel Steel Co., 1932, 260 Mich. 692, 245 N.W. 801 (installing joists on steel building frame); Nashua Gummed & Coated Paper Co. v. Noyes Buick Co., 1945, 93 N.H. 348, 41 A.2d 920 (use of acetylene torch near inflammable materials); Fegles Const. Co. v. McLaughlin Const. Co., 9 Cir. 1953, 205 F.2d 637 (red hot rivets dropped into work below); Banaghan v. Dewey, 1959, 340 Mass. 73, 162 N.E.2d 807 (installing elevator).

43. St. Louis & S. F. R. Co. v. Madden, 1908, 77 Kan. 80, 93 P. 586; Cameron v. Oberlin, 1897, 19 Ind. App. 142, 48 N.E. 386; cf. Black v. Christchurch Fin. Co., [1894] A.C. 48.

44. Bonczkiewicz v. Merberg Wrecking Corp., 1961, 148 Conn. 573, 172 A.2d 917; Covington & C. Bridge Co. v. Steinbrock, 1899, 61 Ohio St. 215, 55 N.E. 618; Hanley v. Central Sav. Bank, 1938, 255 App. Div. 542, 8 N.Y.S.2d 371, affirmed 1939, 280 N.Y. 734, 21 N.E.2d 513; Hevel v. Stangier, 1964, 238 Or. 44, 395 P.2d 201.

45. Trump v. Bluefield Waterworks & Imp. Co., 1925, 99 W.Va. 425, 129 S.E. 309.

46. Medley v. Trenton Inv. Co., 1931, 205 Wis. 30, 236 N.W. 713 (exterminating bedbugs); Alabama Power Co. v. McIntosh, 1929, 219 Ala. 546, 122 So. 677 (cleaning floors with gasoline); Beauchamp v. B. & L. Motor Freight, Inc., 1958, 106 Ohio App. 530, 152 N.E.2d 334 (brakes on heavy tractor-trailer); T. E. Ritter Corp. v. Rose, 1959, 200 Va. 736, 107 S.E.2d 479 (crossing railroad with heavy equipment); Nechodomu v. Lindstrom, 1955, 269 Wis. 455, 69 N. W.2d 608 (mixer machine attracting child).

47. See Evans v. Elliott, 1941, 220 N.C. 253, 17 S.E.2d 125. Thus the employer has been held not liable

for blasting in an uninhabited area. Holt v. Texas-New Mexico Pipeline Co., 5 Cir. 1945, 145 F.2d 862.

48. Cf. Fitzgerald v. Conklin Limestone Co., D.R.I. 1955, 131 F.Supp. 532 (dust hazard); Jacob v. Mosler Safe Co., 1940, 127 Conn. 186, 14 A.2d 736 (same); Oklahoma City v. Caple, 1940, 187 Okl. 600, 105 P.2d 209 (excavating sewer ditch); Millstone Corp. v. Laurel Oil Co., 1945, 131 Conn. 636, 41 A.2d 711 (steaming out gasoline tank); Jennings v. Vincent's Adm'x, 1940, 284 Ky. 614, 145 S.W.2d 537 (insulating floor with plastic).

49. Risley v. Lenwell, 1954, 129 Cal.App.2d 608, 277 P.2d 897. Cf. Van Arsdale v. Hollinger, 1968, 68 Cal.2d 245, 66 Cal.Rptr. 20, 437 P.2d 508 (marking lines on busy street, special precautions to detour traffic).

50. In this the First Restatement of Torts, § 416, appears definitely to have been in error, and the position is reversed in the Second Restatement, § 416, Comment e.

51. Where the acts of the contractor were neither usual nor contemplated, it is held that the employer is not liable. Oklahoma City v. Caple, 1940, 187 Okl. 600, 105 P.2d 209 (failure to repair leak in other sewer line discovered in course of excavation); Swearsky v. Stanley Dry Goods Co., 1936, 122 Conn. 7, 186 A. 556 (washing windows, water allowed to flow onto sidewalk); Von Longerke v. City of New York, 1912, 150 App.Div. 98, 134 N.Y.S. 832, af-

work are likely to lead to such a special risk, as where, for example, a contractor laying pavement in the street may be expected to follow the usual practice of piling the gravel in the street, and so to create a special hazard for travelers.[52]

"Collateral" Negligence

Another distinction, as yet not very exactly defined, is the rule generally accepted, that the employer is liable only for risks inherent in the work itself, and not for "collateral" or "casual" negligence on the part of the contractor.[53] This doctrine, apparently originated in some dicta in an English case [54] where, in violation of statutory provisions, the construction of a bridge was permitted to delay traffic on a river for more than three days. It is very closely related to the exception as to "inherent danger," and seems in reality to represent nothing more than a negative statement of it, describing the type of situa-

tion in which the special danger is not necessarily involved in the work to be done, and not contemplated in connection with the way it is expected to be done.

There are many cases [55] in which the language of the court seems to regard "collateral" or "casual" negligence as referring to negligence in the operative details of the work, easily controlled by the contractor, and not ordinarily considered or contemplated by the employer, as distinguished from its general objective or plan, which must necessarily be so contemplated. This, however, appears to be an illusory distinction, not borne out by the decisions themselves. Thus it has been held to be "collateral" negligence for the servant of an independent contractor to splash mortar from a mortar box on the ground into the eye of a man passing on the sidewalk, but not to splash mortar from a wall in the course of construction over the plaintiff's windows, and the clothes hanging in her yard; [56] to drop a paint bucket out of a window while the workman is painting an inside storeroom, but not to drop a paint bucket while he is painting a sign over a sidewalk; [57] to dislodge a board from a windowsill while working on a building on private land, but not a stone from a bridge over

---

52. Pine Bluff Natural Gas Co. v. Senyard, 1913, 108 Ark. 229, 158 S.W. 1091. Accord: Philadelphia, B. & W. R. Co. v. Mitchell, 1908, 107 Md. 600, 69 A. 422 ("probable consequences" which "might have been anticipated" unless, etc.); Mallory v. Louisiana Pure Ice & Supply Co., 1928, 320 Mo. 95, 6 S. W.2d 617 ("would likely result in damage unless," etc.); Evans v. Elliott, 1941, 220 N.C. 253, 17 S.E. 2d 125 ("in the natural course of things injurious consequences must be expected to arise"); State v. Williams, 1941, 12 Wash.2d 1, 120 P.2d 496 (same); Richman Bros. Co. v. Miller, 1936, 131 Ohio St. 424, 3 N.E.2d 360 ("danger likely to attend the doing of certain work unless," etc).

firmed 211 N.Y. 558, 105 N.E. 1101 (contractor changed course of tunnel, broke a water main); Kunan v. De Matteo, 1941, 308 Mass. 427, 32 N.E.2d 613 (gasoline shovel used in resurfacing sidewalk broke meter box set in walk); Barrabee v. Crescenta Mut. Water Co., 1948, 88 Cal.App.2d 192, 198 P. 2d 558 (contractor drilling a well allowed water to flow into highway).

53. Second Restatement of Torts, § 426. See the excellent discussion in Talbot Smith, Collateral Negligence, 1941, 25 Minn.L.Rev. 399. The leading American case making the distinction is Robbins v. City of Chicago, Ill.1866, 4 Wall., 71 U.S. 657, 18 L.Ed. 427.

54. Hole v. Sittingbourne R. Co., 1861, 6 H. & N. 488, 158 Eng.Rep. 201.

55. See for example Hyman v. Barrett, 1918, 224 N. Y. 436, 121 N.E. 271 (dropping board while doing repair work); Long v. Moon, 1891, 107 Mo. 334, 17 S. W. 810 (plank allowed to remain against elevator); Wilton v. City of Spokane, 1913, 73 Wash. 619, 132 P. 404 (leaving stick of dynamite under improved street); Pickett v. Waldorf System, 1922, 241 Mass. 569, 136 N.E. 64 (allowing water to flow onto sidewalk in washing windows); O'Hara v. Laclede Gaslight Co., 1912, 244 Mo. 395, 148 S.W. 884 (pipes carelessly loaded).

56. Compare Strauss v. City of Louisville, 1900, 108 Ky. 155, 55 S.W. 1075, with Pye v. Faxon, 1892, 156 Mass. 471, 31 N.E. 640.

57. Compare Drennan Co. v. Jordan, 1913, 181 Ala. 570, 61 So. 938, with Richman Bros. Co. v. Miller, 1936, 131 Ohio St. 424, 3 N.E.2d 360; Rohlfs v. Weil, 1936, 271 N.Y. 444, 3 N.E.2d 588. And see Lockowitz v. Melnyk, 1956, 1 App.Div.2d 138, 148 N.Y.S.2d 232, where the precise distinction is made.

a public highway;[58] to blast negligently when the contract does not contemplate blasting, but not when it does;[59] to allow water to run onto the sidewalk when the employer has no reason to expect it, but not where he has reason.[60]

The test of "collateral" negligence, therefore, appears to be, not its character as a minor incident or operative detail of the work to be done, but rather its disassociation from any inherent or contemplated special risk which may be expected to be created by the work. The employer is not liable because the negligence is "collateral" to the risk created—which is to say, that the performance of the work contracted for in the normal manner contemplated by the contract would involve no expectation of such a risk of harm to the plaintiff, and it is the abnormal departure from usual or contemplated methods by the servants of the contractor which has created the danger. Where the peculiar risk is involved in the work to be done itself, as where a sign is to be painted over the sidewalk,[61] the fact that the risk which was to be expected materializes through the incidental negligence of the servant in dropping the bucket will not relieve the employer of liability. But where the employer reasonably expects that windows will be painted in place on the building, and the contractor decides to remove them and in the process drops one five floors,[62] the negligence is collateral to the risk.

72. JOINT ENTERPRISE

The doctrine of vicarious responsibility in connection with joint enterprises rests upon an analogy to the law of partnership. In a partnership, there is a more or less permanent business arrangement, creating a mutual agency between the partners for the purpose of carrying on some general business, so that the acts of one are to be charged against another. A "joint enterprise" is something like a partnership,[63] for a more limited period of time, and a more limited purpose. It is an undertaking to carry out a small number of acts or objectives, which is entered into by associates under such circumstances that all have an equal voice in directing the conduct of the enterprise. The law then considers that each is the agent or servant of the others, and that the act of any one within the scope of the enterprise is to be charged vicariously against the rest.[64] Whether such a relation exists between the parties is normally a question for the jury, under proper instructions from the court.[65]

---

58. Compare Hyman v. Barrett, 1918, 224 N.Y. 436, 121 N.E. 271, with Philadelphia B. & W. R. Co. v. Mitchell, 1908, 107 Md. 600, 69 A. 422.

59. Compare McNamee v. Huntt, 4 Cir. 1898, 87 F. 298, with Giem v. Williams, 1949, 215 Ark. 705, 222 S.W.2d 800.

60. Compare Pickett v. Waldorf System, 1922, 241 Mass. 569, 136 N.E. 64, with Wright v. Tudor City Twelfth Unit, 1938, 276 N.Y. 303, 12 N.E.2d 307.

61. Rohlfs v. Weil, 1936, 271 N.Y. 444, 3 N.E.2d 588. Cf. Olah v. Katz, 1926, 234 Mich. 112, 207 N.W. 892 (installing plumbing through street to building, hole in street left unguarded); Watkins v. Gabriel Steel Co., 1932, 260 Mich. 692, 245 N.W. 801 (erecting steel building, failure to secure joists); Hammond Ranch Corp. v. Dodson, 1940, 199 Ark. 846, 136 S.W.2d 484 (spraying field, failure to cut off spray over plaintiff's land); McCarrier v. Hollister, 1902, 15 S.D. 366, 89 N.W. 862 (sewer in street, hole unguarded); Thomas v. Harrington, 1902, 72 N.H. 45, 54 A. 285 (same as to water pipe).

62. Davis v. John L. Whiting & Son Co., 1909, 201 Mass. 91, 87 N.E. 199. Cf. Hoff v. Shockley, 1904, 122 Iowa 720, 98 N.W. 573 (piling sand in street); Yellow Poplar Lumber Co. v. Adkins, 1927, 221 Ky. 794, 299 S.W. 963; Callahan v. Salt Lake City, 1912, 41 Utah 300, 125 P. 863; May v. 11½ East 49th St. Co., 1945, 269 App.Div. 180, 54 N.Y.S.2d 860, affirmed 1946, 296 N.Y. 599, 68 N.E.2d 881.

63. "The rule is founded on the theory of partnership or a relation akin to partnership." Kokesh v. Price, 1917, 136 Minn. 304, 309, 161 N.W. 715, 717; see Connellee v. Nees, Tex.Comm.App.1924, 266 S.W. 502.

64. One of the best statements of this is in Howard v. Zimmerman, 1926, 120 Kan. 77, 242 P. 131, 132.

65. Hollister v. Hines, 1921, 150 Minn. 185, 184 N.W. 856; Farthing v. Hepinstall, 1928, 243 Mich. 380, 220 N.W. 708; Clark v. Missouri Pac. R. Co., 1924, 115 Kan. 823, 224 P. 920. It is a "mixed question

Nearly all courts have accepted the principle of vicarious tort responsibility in such a case, but there is no complete agreement upon any one criterion by which the relation is to be determined.

Where the enterprise is for some commercial or business purpose, and particularly where the parties have agreed to share profits and losses, it usually is called a joint adventure.[66] It is then governed, as to tort liability, by the law applicable to partnerships, which is beyond the limited scope of this text.[67] The extension of "joint enterprise" beyond such business ventures is almost entirely a creature of the American courts.[68]

Except in comparatively rare instances,[69] its application has been in the field of automobile law, where it has meant that the negligence of the driver of the vehicle is to be imputed to a passenger riding in it. In relatively few cases, the passenger has been charged with liability as a defendant to a third person who has been injured by the negligence.[70] It is not altogether clear why this has not occurred more frequently, unless it is that, with a financially responsible defendant available in the negligent driver, the plaintiff has not thought it desirable to complicate matters by joining one who is personally innocent. In by far the greater number of cases, the question has been one of contributory negligence, and the driver's misconduct has been imputed to the passenger to bar his own recovery.[71] "Joint enterprise" is thus of importance chiefly as a defendant's doctrine, imputing the negligence of another to the plaintiff; and as such, it has not been slow to draw the wrath of the plaintiff's partisans.

Considerable confusion still surrounds the doctrine,[72] which no one has succeeded in re-

---

of law and fact." Robison v. Oregon-Washington R. & Nav. Co., 1918, 90 Or. 490, 176 P. 594.

66. Houston v. Dexter & Carpenter, D.Va.1924, 300 F. 354. See Mechem, The Law of Joint Adventures, 1931, 15 Minn.L.Rev. 644. The terms "joint enterprise" and "joint adventure" have been used more or less interchangeably. See Masterson v. Leonard, 1921, 116 Wash. 551, 556, 200 P. 320, 322; Wagner v. Kloster, 1920, 188 Iowa 174, 175 N.W. 840, 841; Coleman v. Bent, 1924, 100 Conn. 527, 124 A. 224, 225.

67. Cases dealing with various types of "joint adventure" situations are collected in annotations in 1927, 48 A.L.R. 1077, and 1929, 63 A.L.R. 909.

68. Only one English case, Brooke v. Bool, [1928] 2 K.B. 578, contains any indication of recognition of the principle. It has been applied in a Canadian case, Grand Trunk R. Co. v. Dixon, [1920] 51 Dom. L.Rep. 576.

69. One such case is Cullinan v. Tetrault, 1923, 123 Me. 302, 122 A. 770, where the negligence of one boy purchasing liquor for a drinking party was imputed to his companion. See also O'Neil v. Sea Bee Club, 1954, 118 N.E.2d 175, 69 Ohio St. 442 (club members); Ruth v. Hutchinson Gas Co., 1941, 209 Minn. 248, 296 N.W. 136 (hunting party); Eagle Star Ins. Co. v. Bean, 9 Cir. 1943, 134 F.2d 755 (dismantling a sawmill); Shell Oil Co. v. Prestidge, 9 Cir. 1957, 249 F.2d 413 (prospecting for oil).
But compare the refusal to apply the doctrine to pedestrians walking together in Barnes v. Town of Marcus, 1896, 96 Iowa 675, 65 N.W. 984; Bailey v. City of Centerville, 1901, 115 Iowa 271, 88 N.W. 379. Also Brigham Young University v. Lillywhite, 10 Cir. 1941, 118 F.2d 836, cert. denied 314 U.S. 638 (chemistry students working in laboratory). With these few exceptions, all "joint enterprise" cases found have involved business ventures or vehicles.

70. Manley v. Horton, Mo.1967, 414 S.W.2d 254; Straffus v. Barclay, 1949, 147 Tex. 600, 219 S.W.2d 65; Jones v. Kasper, 1941, 109 Ind.App. 465, 33 N.E.2d 816; Ahlstedt v. Smith, 1936, 130 Neb. 372, 264 N.W. 889; Fox v. Lavender, 1936, 89 Utah 115, 56 P.2d 1049. See Note, 1949, 1 Baylor L.Rev. 492. In Willoughby v. Flem, D.Mont.1958, 158 F.Supp. 258, a judgment against the plaintiff in his action against one person engaged in a joint enterprise was held to bar his action against another.

71. However, in Pierson v. Edstrom, 1970, —— Minn. ——, 174 N.W.2d 712, the court prospectively abolished the imputation of contributory negligence in joint enterprise cases, leaving only the imputation of negligence to the defendant.

72. See, generally, Weintraub, The Joint Enterprise Doctrine in Automobile Law, 1931, 16 Corn.L.Q. 320; Rollison, The "Joint Enterprise" in the Law of Imputed Negligence, 1931, 6 Notre Dame Lawyer 172; Keeton, Imputed Contributory Negligence, 1935, 13 Tex.L.Rev. 161; James, Vicarious Liability 1954, 28 Tulane L.Rev. 161, 210; Notes, 1924, 12 Cal.L.Rev. 238; 1926, 12 Va.L.Rev. 341; 1929, 38 Yale L.J. 810; 1929, 77 U.Pa.L.Rev. 676; 1934, 12 N.C.L.Rev. 385; 1936, 20 Minn.L.Rev. 385; 1940, 14 Temple L.Q. 535; 1950, 48 Mich.L.Rev. 372; 1953, 33 Bos.U.L.Rev. 90.

ducing to any very exact formula or definition. A statement frequently quoted from an opinion of the supreme court of Washington [73] attempts the following:

"Briefly stated, a joint adventure arises out of, and must have its origin in, a contract, express or implied, in which the parties thereto agree to enter into an undertaking in the performance of which they have a community of interest, and further, a contract in which each of the parties has an equal right of control over the agencies used in the performance. Thus we note (1) a contract, (2) a common purpose, (3) a community of interest, (4) equal right to a voice, accompanied by an equal right of control."

Common Purpose

One group of cases, now definitely very much in the minority and almost passing out of the picture, have found a joint enterprise in the mere association of the driver and the passenger in the use of the vehicle for any purpose in which they have a common interest of any kind. Thus friends on a pleasure trip together,[74] members of the same family on the way to church,[75] a group proceeding together to witness a prize fight,[76] a prospective purchaser riding with a salesman,[77] and fellow servants riding together in the course of their employment,[78] have at various times been found to be engaged in a joint enterprise, by reason of that association alone, with the mutual right of control conjured up from the community of interest without more. Such decisions were condemned [79] as in effect a restoration of discarded fictions of imputed contributory negligence [80] in nearly all passenger cases, since it is seldom that some element of common purpose cannot be found when two persons are travelling together in a private vehicle. So many of the jurisdictions in which these decisions appear have repudiated them, or departed from them in later cases,[81] that they are now almost entirely discredited; and it is generally agreed that something more is required for a joint enterprise than the mere showing of a contract or agreement to travel together to a destination for a common purpose.[82] Some-

73. Carboneau v. Peterson, 1939, 1 Wash.2d 347, 95 P.2d 1043.

74. Washington & O. D. R. Co. v. Zell's Adm'x, 1916, 118 Va. 755, 88 S.E. 309; Wentworth v. Town of Waterbury, 1916, 90 Vt. 60, 96 A. 334. Contra: Schweidler v. Caruso, 1955, 269 Wis. 438, 69 N.W.2d 611; Elfers v. Bright, 1958, 108 Ohio App. 495, 162 N.E.2d 535; Meyers v. Southern Pac. Co., 1923, 63 Cal.App. 164, 218 P. 284; Koplitz v. City of St. Paul, 1902, 86 Minn. 373, 90 N.W. 794.

75. Hurley v. City of Spokane, 1923, 126 Wash. 213, 217 P. 1004; Delaware & Hudson Co. v. Boyden, 3 Cir. 1921, 269 F. 881 (fishing excursion); Caliando v. Huck, D.Fla.1949, 84 F.Supp. 598 (trip to Florida); Stam v. Cannon, Iowa 1970, 176 N.W.2d 794 (to different jobs). Contra: Hunter v. Brand, 1960, 186 Kan. 415, 350 P.2d 805 (wife with husband on his business trip); Virginia Transit Co. v. Simmons, 1956, 198 Va. 122, 92 S.E.2d 291. But a husband and wife, operating a supper club business together, and going together to pick up steaks for a banquet, are engaged in a joint enterprise. Vanderbloemen v. Suchosky, 1959, 7 Wis.2d 367, 97 N.W.2d 183.

76. Jensen v. Chicago, M. & St. P. R. Co., 1925, 133 Wash. 208, 233 P. 635.

77. Lawrence v. Denver & R. G. R. Co., 1918, 52 Utah 414, 174 P. 817.

78. Martin v. Puget Sound Elec. R. Co., 1926, 136 Wash. 663, 241 P. 360; Otis v. Kolsky, 1929, 94 Pa. Super. 548. Cf. Campagna v. Lyles, 1929, 298 Pa. 352, 148 A. 527 (servant riding with employer on employer's business). Contra: Parton v. Weilnau, 1959, 169 Ohio St. 145, 158 N.E.2d 719; Flynn v. Wallace, 1959, 173 Cal.App.2d 592, 343 P.2d 767.

79. Bryant v. Pacific Elec. R. Co., 1917, 174 Cal. 737, 164 P. 385; Pope v. Halpern, 1924, 193 Cal. 168, 223 P. 470; Coleman v. Bent, 1924, 100 Conn. 527, 124 A. 224. See Weintraub, The Joint Enterprise Doctrine in Automobile Law, 1931, 16 Corn.L.Q. 320, 332.

80. See infra, § 74.

81. See for example Director General of Railroads v. Pence's Adm'x, 1923, 135 Va. 329, 116 S.E. 351; Landry v. Hubert, 1927, 100 Vt. 268, 137 A. 97; Rosenstrom v. North Bend Stage Line, 1929, 154 Wash. 57, 280 P. 932; Kocher v. Creston Transfer Co., 3 Cir. 1948, 166 F.2d 680; Alperdt v. Paige, 1928, 292 Pa. 1, 140 A. 555.

82. Thompson v. Bell, 6 Cir. 1942, 129 F.2d 211; Powers v. State for Use of Reynolds, 1940, 178 Md. 23, 11 A.2d 909; Mosson v. Liberty Fast Freight Co., 2

thing in the nature of a common business, financial or pecuniary interest in the objective of the journey is said to be essential. In this form the requirement of a mutual interest persists as a minimum in all courts, to the exclusion of all cases in which the parties are casually together for pleasure [83] or for independent ends.[84]

Mutual Right of Control

The prevailing view is that a joint enterprise requires something, beyond the mere association of the parties for a common end, to show a mutual "right of control" over the operation of the vehicle—or in other words, an equal right in the passenger to be heard as to the manner in which it is driven.[85] It is not the fact that he does [86] or does not [87] give directions which is important in itself, but rather the understanding between the parties that he has the right to have his

wishes respected, to the same extent as the driver. In the absence of circumstances indicating such an understanding, it has been held that companions on a pleasure trip,[88] members of the same family,[89] parties engaged in a commercial transaction,[90] servants riding with the employer,[91] or fellow servants in the course of their employment,[92] although they may have a common purpose in the ride, are not engaged in a joint enterprise. Nor, of course, is the fact that the passenger has requested the driver to make the trip for his benefit sufficient to establish such a right of control.[93]

Cir. 1942, 124 F.2d 448; Horchler v. Van Zandt, 1938, 120 W.Va. 452, 199 S.E. 65.

83. Hall v. Blackham, 1966, 18 Utah 2d 164, 417 P.2d 664 (duck hunting); Young v. Bynum, Tex.Civ.App. 1953, 260 S.W.2d 696; Edlebeck v. Hooten, 1963, 20 Wis.2d 83, 121 N.W.2d 240 (deer hunting).

84. Kepler v. Chicago, St. P., M. & O. R. Co., 1923, 111 Neb. 273, 196 N.W. 161 (passenger driven as accommodation to mail letters); Hilton v. Blose, 1929, 297 Pa. 458, 147 A. 100 (on way to bowl on different teams in different games); Carlson v. Erie R. Co., 1931, 305 Pa. 431, 158 A. 163 (going to work for same employer on different jobs); Conner v. Southland Corp., Fla.App.1970, 240 So.2d 822 (car pool); Kuser v. Barengo, 1953, 70 Nev. 66, 254 P.2d 447 (delegates to convention).

85. Cunningham v. City of Thief River Falls, 1901, 84 Minn. 21, 86 N.W. 763; Pope v. Halpern, 1924, 193 Cal. 168, 223 P. 470; Churchill v. Briggs, 1938, 225 Iowa 1187, 282 N.W. 280; Carroll v. Hutchinson, 1939, 172 Va. 43, 200 S.E. 644.

86. Churchill v. Briggs, 1938, 225 Iowa 1187, 282 N.W. 280; Southern Pac. Co. v. Wright, 9 Cir. 1918, 248 F. 261; Bryant v. Pacific Elec. R. Co., 1917, 174 Cal. 737, 164 P. 385; Webb v. Huffman, Tex. Civ.App.1959, 320 S.W.2d 893, ref. n.r.e.

87. Crescent Motor Co. v. Stone, 1924, 211 Ala. 516, 101 So. 49; Carpenter v. Campbell Automobile Co., 1913, 159 Iowa 52, 140 N.W. 225; Howard v. Zimmerman, 1926, 120 Kan. 77, 242 P. 131.

88. Edlebeck v. Hotten, 1963, 20 Wis.2d 83, 121 N.W. 2d 240; Hall v. Blackham, 1966, 18 Utah 2d 164, 417 P.2d 664; Padgett v. Southern R. Co., 1951, 219 S.C. 353, 65 S.E.2d 297; MacGregor v. Bradshaw, 1952, 193 Va. 787, 71 S.E.2d 361; Carnes v. Day, 1949, 309 Ky. 163, 216 S.W.2d 901.

Compare, as to car pools driving to work: Allen v. Clark, 1947, 148 Neb. 627, 28 N.W.2d 439.

89. Rodgers v. Saxton, 1931, 305 Pa. 479, 158 A. 166; Edwards v. Freeman, 1949, 34 Cal.2d 589, 212 P.2d 883; Gardner v. Hobbs, 1949, 69 Idaho 288, 203 P. 2d 539, Greenwood v. Bridgeways, Inc., Mo.App. 1951, 243 S.W.2d 111; Square Deal Cartage Co. v. Smith's Adm'r, 1948, 307 Ky. 135, 210 S.W.2d 340.

90. Spradley v. Houser, 1966, 247 S.C. 208, 146 S.E.2d 621; Bloom v. Leech, 1929, 120 Ohio St. 239, 166 N.E. 137; Gilmore v. Grass, 10 Cir. 1933, 68 F.2d 150; Ryan v. Snyder, 1923, 29 Wyo. 146, 211 P. 482; Churchill v. Briggs, 1938, 225 Iowa 1187, 282 N.W. 280.

91. Sylvester v. St. Paul City R. Co., 1922, 153 Minn. 516, 191 N.W. 46; Robertson v. United Fuel & Supply Co., 1922, 218 Mich. 271, 187 N.W. 300; Johnson v. Turner, 1943, 319 Ill.App. 265, 49 N.E.2d 297; Neagle v. City of Tacoma, 1923, 127 Wash. 528, 221 P. 588; Flynn v. Wallace, 1959, 173 Cal.App.2d 592, 343 P.2d 767 (employee driving).

92. Slowik v. Union St. R. Co., 1933, 282 Mass. 249, 184 N.E. 469; Melville v. State of Maryland to Use of Morris, 4 Cir. 1946, 155 F.2d 440; Kocher v. Creston Transfer Co., 3 Cir. 1948, 166 F.2d 680; Dameron v. Yellowstone Trail Garage, 1934, 54 Idaho 646, 34 P.2d 417; Loomis v. Abelson, 1928, 101 Vt. 459, 144 A. 378.

Cf. Oklahoma R. Co. v. Thomas, 1917, 63 Okl. 219, 164 P. 120 (firemen); Denver Tramway Co. v. Orbach, 1918, 64 Colo. 511, 172 P. 1063 (policemen); Bartholomew v. Oregonian Pub. Co., 1950, 188 Or. 407, 216 P.2d 257 (policemen).

93. Southern Pac. Co. v. Wright, 9 Cir. 1918, 248 F. 261; Tronto v. Reo Motor Co., 1919, 92 N.J.L. 595,

If the purpose of the journey is a business or financial one, in which the parties have a common interest, the mutual right to direct the operation of the car is much more readily found.[94] There are courts[95] which have gone so far as to say that the mutual right of control does not exist, and so a joint enterprise does not exist, in the absence of such a common pecuniary interest in the use of the car for the trip. The justification for this position may be that such a financial venture involves a closer analogy to the law of partnership, and affords more reason for regarding the risk as properly to be charged against all those engaged in it. This is certainly the direction toward which the courts are tending to move; but there are still older cases which have rejected any such limitation.[96]

In the past the theoretical right to an equal voice in the operation of the car has quite often been found when the driver and the passenger have a common property interest in the vehicle—as where they own it in common,[97] or have joined in hiring[98] or borrow-

ing[99] it. This not infrequently has meant that an entirely innocent plaintiff is barred from all recovery by the negligence of one with whom he happens to be a joint owner; and since the right to an equal voice in the operation is sometimes, and particularly in the case of husband and wife,[1] more theoretical than real, there has been quite a pronounced reaction against such decisions. The present tendency is to hold that joint ownership, while it may be a fact to be considered, does not of itself necessarily establish the "right of control" required for a joint enterprise.[2]

Beyond this, there are other factors which tend to establish such a mutual right of control, but usually are not regarded as conclusive. An agreement to share the expenses of the trip is some evidence of such a right in the passenger,[3] as is the fact that he de-

106 A. 383; Parker v. Ullom, 1928, 84 Colo. 433, 271 P. 187; Gregory v. Jenkins, Mo.App.1932, 43 S.W.2d 877; Webb v. Huffman, Tex.Civ.App.1959, 320 S. W.2d 893, ref. n. r. e.

94. Eagle Star Ins. Co. v. Bean, 9 Cir. 1943, 134 F.2d 755; Judge v. Wallen, 1915, 98 Neb. 154, 152 N.W. 318; Van Horn v. Simpson, 1915, 35 S.D. 640, 153 N.W. 883; Derrick v. Salt Lake & O. R. Co., 1917, 50 Utah 573, 168 P. 335; Vanderbloemen v. Suchosky, 1959, 7 Wis.2d 367, 97 N.W.2d 183.

95. Robison v. Oregon-Washington R. & Nav. Co., 1918, 90 Or. 490, 176 P. 594; Fisher v. Johnson, 1925, 238 Ill.App. 25; Jessup v. Davis, 1926, 115 Neb. 1, 211 N.W. 190.

96. Smith v. Wells, 1930, 326 Mo. 525, 31 S.W.2d 1014; Archer v. Chicago, M., St. P. & P. R. Co., 1934, 215 Wis. 509, 255 N.W. 67; Hurley v. City of Spokane, 1923, 126 Wash. 213, 217 P. 1004; Howard v. Zimmerman, 1926, 120 Kan. 77, 242 P. 131.

97. Moore v. Skiles, 1954, 130 Colo. 191, 274 P.2d 311; Roddy v. Francis, Mo.App.1961, 349 S.W.2d 488; Shoe v. Hood, 1960, 251 N.C. 719, 112 S.E.2d 543; Caliando v. Huck, N.D.Fla.1949, 84 F.Supp. 598; Archer v. Chicago, M., St. P. & P. R. Co., 1934, 215 Wis. 509, 255 N.W. 67. Cf. Fox v. Lavender, 1936, 89 Utah 115, 56 P.2d 1049 (presumption).

98. Christopherson v. Minneapolis, St. P. & S. S. M. R. Co., 1914, 28 N.D. 128, 147 N.W. 791; Wosika v.

St. Paul City R. Co., 1900, 80 Minn. 364, 83 N.W. 386; Dixon v. Grand Trunk R. Co., 1920, 47 Ont.L. Rep. 115, 51 Dom.L.Rep. 576.

99. Curran v. Lehigh Valley R. Co., 1930, 299 Pa. 584, 149 A. 885; El Paso Elec. Co. v. Leeper, Tex. Com.App.1933, 60 S.W.2d 187; Union Bus Co. v. Smith, 1932, 104 Fla. 569, 140 So. 631; Hurley v. City of Spokane, 1923, 126 Wash. 213, 217 P. 1004. Cf. Jones v. Kasper, 1941, 109 Ind.App. 465, 33 N.E. 2d 816 (wrongful appropriation of car by party of four).

1. Clemens v. O'Brien, 1964, 85 N.J.Super. 404, 204 A.2d 895; Workman v. City of San Diego, 1968, 267 Cal.App.2d 36, 72 Cal.Rptr. 509.

2. Burdick v. Bongard, 1959, 256 Minn. 24, 96 N.W.2d 868; Sherman v. Korff, 1958, 353 Mich. 387, 91 N. W.2d 485; Mooneyham v. Kats, Wyo.1965, 405 P.2d 267; Clemens v. O'Brien, 1964, 85 N.J.Super. 404, 204 A.2d 895; Rushing v. Polk, 1962, 258 N.C. 256, 128 S.E.2d 675.

3. Pence v. Berry, 1942, 13 Wash.2d 564, 125 P.2d 645; Hopkins v. Golden, 1937, 281 Mich. 389, 275 N.W. 184; Derrick v. Salt Lake & O. R. Co., 1917, 50 Utah 573, 168 P. 335; Alexiou v. Nockas, 1933, 171 Wash. 369, 17 P.2d 911; Grubb v. Illinois Terminal Co., 1937, 366 Ill. 330, 8 N.E.2d 934. See Note, 1943, 41 Mich.L.Rev. 962.

But the jury may still find that the management of the car was left entirely to the driver. Zeigler v. Ryan, 1937, 65 S.D. 110, 271 N.W. 767; Coleman v. Bent, 1924, 100 Conn. 527, 124 A. 224; Noel v. La Pointe, 1933, 86 N.H. 162, 164 A. 769. Cf. Carboneau v. Peterson, 1939, 1 Wash.2d 347, 95 P.2d 1043.

termines the route to be taken,[4] or alternates in the driving,[5] but none of these is necessarily inconsistent with his status as a mere paying passenger, or a guest, who will not be responsible for the driver's misconduct. The essential question is whether the parties can be found by implication to have agreed to an equal voice in the management of the vehicle,[6] which in the normal and usual case is merely an issue of fact for the jury.

Passenger v. Driver

A few courts, entirely mistaking the nature of the vicarious liability in the joint enterprise cases, have held that the negligence of the driver is to be imputed to the passenger to bar recovery even when he brings his action against the negligent driver himself.[7]

And the absence of an agreement to share expenses of course does not preclude a joint enterprise. Duvall v. Pioneer Sand & Gravel Co., 1937, 191 Wash. 417, 71 P.2d 567.

There are cases which have held that the sharing of expenses does not even permit an inference of joint enterprise. Bonney v. San Antonio Transit Co., 1959, 160 Tex. 11, 325 S.W.2d 117; McCann v. Hoffman, 1937, 9 Cal.2d 279, 70 P.2d 909.

4. Anthony v. Kiefner, 1915, 96 Kan. 194, 150 P. 524; Cram v. City of Des Moines, 1919, 185 Iowa 1292, 172 N.W. 23; Johnston v. Kincheloe, 1935, 164 Va. 370, 180 S.E. 540; Webb v. Huffman, Tex.Civ.App. 1959, 320 S.W.2d 893. The "normal and usual courtesies, deferring to one another's wishes on the trip," do not show any mutual right of control. Virginia Transit Co. v. Simmons, 1956, 198 Va. 122, 92 S.E.2d 291.

5. Isaacson v. Boston, W. & N. Y. St. R. Co., 1932, 278 Mass. 378, 180 N.E. 118; Fisher v. Johnson, 1925, 238 Ill.App. 25; Carroll v. Hutchinson, 1938, 172 Va. 43, 200 S.E. 644; Webb v. Huffman, Tex. Civ.App.1959, 320 S.W.2d 893, ref. n. r. e.
The jury may still find that control was left entirely to the driver of the moment. Zeigler v. Ryan, 1937, 65 S.D. 110, 271 N.W. 767; MacGregor v. Bradshaw, 1952, 193 Va. 787, 71 S.E.2d 361; Hollister v. Hines, 1921, 150 Minn. 185, 184 N.W. 856.

6. See Sanderson v. Hartford Eastern R. Co., 1930, 159 Wash. 472, 294 P. 241; Rogers v. Goodrich, 1933, 131 Cal.App. 245, 21 P.2d 122; Krause v. Hall, 1928, 195 Wis. 565, 217 N.W. 290; Hasty v. Pittsburgh County R. Co., 1925, 112 Okl. 144, 240 P. 1056.

7. Frisorger v. Shepse, 1930, 251 Mich. 121, 230 N.W. 926; Barnett v. Levy, 1919, 213 Ill.App. 129; see

There seems to be no possible justification for such a result.[8] It is well settled that the vicarious liability which is designed for the protection of third persons against the risks of the enterprise does not extend to any action between the parties themselves, and that a negligent servant will be liable to his master,[9] or one member of a partnership to another.[10] Most of the courts which have considered the question have recognized this, and have held that the driver's negligence, which is itself the cause of action, will not bar the passenger's recovery.[11] It has been held, however, that as between two passengers in a joint enterprise, neither may recover from the other for the negligence of the driver,[12] upon analogy to the agency rule that where two principals employ the same agent to deal with their common interests, one cannot charge the other with the misconduct of their mutual agent, unless the other is personally at fault.[13]

Jacobs v. Jacobs, 1917, 141 La. 272, 286, 74 So. 992, 997.

8. See Notes, 1932, 20 Cal.L.Rev. 458; 1936, 20 Minn.L.Rev. 401, 410. It is suggested by Weintraub, The Joint Enterprise Doctrine in Automobile Law, 1934, 16 Corn.L.Q. 320, 324, that these courts have been influenced by the apparent unfairness of absolving a negligent third party and holding the driver for the same accident. But this, of course, occurs also in the case of a master's action against a negligent servant.

9. Mechem, Agency, 2d Ed. 1914, § 1275.

10. Rowley, Modern Law of Partnership, 1916, § 758.

11. Williams v. Knapp, 1968, 248 Md. 506, 237 A.2d 450; Dosher v. Hunt, 1955, 243 N.C. 247, 90 S.E.2d 374; Le Sage v. Pryor, 1941, 137 Tex. 455, 154 S. W.2d 446; Sackett v. Haeckel, 1957, 249 Minn. 290, 81 N.W.2d 833; Brown v. Sohn, Ky.1970, 449 S.W. 2d 920.

12. Murphy v. Keating, 1939, 204 Minn. 269, 283 N. W. 389; Hume v. Crane, Mo.1962, 352 S.W.2d 610; O'Neil v. Sea Bee Club, 1954, 118 N.E.2d 175, 69 O. L.A. 442; Stearns v. Lindow, 1934, 63 U.S.App.D.C. 134, 136, 70 F.2d 738, 740; Zeigler v. Ryan, 1937, 65 S.D. 110, 271 N.W. 767. See Note, 1939, 23 Minn.L. Rev. 666.

13. Cf. Brown & Co. v. St. John Trust Co., 1905, 71 Kan. 134, 80 P. 37; Martin v. Northern Pac. Ben. Ass'n, 1897, 68 Minn. 521, 71 N.W. 701; Roschmann

Criticism

If the question were now to be raised for the first time, arguments might be advanced against the vicarious responsibility, whether as plaintiff or as defendant, of the passenger who is engaged in a "joint enterprise" for the negligence of his driver.[14] The contractual agreement by which he is said to enter into such an arrangement is all too obviously a fiction in situations where the parties have merely got together for the ride; and upon this there is erected a second fiction, that the passenger shares a "right of control" of the operation of the vehicle; and on this is erected in turn a third fiction, that the driver is his agent or servant. This topheavy structure tends to fall of its own weight. In the usual case the passenger has no physical ability to control the operation of the car, and no opportunity to interfere with it; and any attempt on his part to do so in fact would be a dangerously distracting piece of backseat driving which might very well amount to negligence in itself.

Unless the limitation to business ventures of a character really approaching a partnership[15] is to be accepted, the doctrine will most often be applied to enterprises which are not commercial and are matters of friendly cooperation and accommodation, where there is not the same reason for placing all risks upon the enterprise itself. Normally it is the driver, and not the passenger, who might be expected to carry insurance. The apparent restriction of the doctrine to vehicle cases[16] suggests of course that its real basis is in some way connected with the peculiar hazards of traffic; but it is difficult to see why a point should be stretched to bar the innocent passenger. It has been said that the courts do not regard the doctrine with favor.[17] It has nevertheless a long history of application in American law; and while its rigors are in process of being ameliorated, if only by the greatly increased tendency to leave the question to the jury, it is perhaps too firmly established to permit any hope that it will soon disappear.

73. OTHER APPLICATIONS

As in the case of the doctrine of joint enterprise,[18] the advent of the automobile has been responsible for a number of other extensions of the principle of vicarious liability. The alarming increase in traffic accidents, together with the frequent financial irresponsibility of the individual driving the car,[19] has led to a search for some basis for imposing liability upon the owner of the vehicle, even though he is free from negligence himself. Bluntly put, it is felt that, since automobiles are expensive, the owner is more likely to be able to pay any damages than the driver, who may be entirely impecunious; and that the owner is the obvious person to carry the necessary insurance to cover the risk, and so to distribute any losses among motorists as a class. Beyond this, also, is the feeling that one who originates such a danger by setting the car upon the highway in the first instance should be held responsible for the negligence of the person to whom he entrusts it; and also the reasonable idea that the assumption of such responsibility is the price which the owner should be required to pay for the privilege of having the car operated, at the cost of the taxpayers, over the expensive highways of the state.

v. Sanborn, 1934, 315 Pa. 188, 172 A. 657; Koogler v. Koogler, 1933, 127 Ohio St. 57, 186 N.E. 725.

14. See Weintraub, The Joint Enterprise Doctrine in Automobile Law, 1931, 16 Corn.L.Q. 320, 334; James, Vicarious Liability, 1954, 28 Tulane L.Rev. 161, 214.

15. See supra, p. 477.

16. See supra, p. 476.

17. See Gilmore v. Grass, 10 Cir. 1933, 68 F.2d 150, 153; Berry, Automobiles, 4th Ed. 1924, 502; 4 Blashfield, Cyclopedia of Automobile Law, 1935, 176.

18. Supra, § 72.

19. See infra, ch. 14.

This quest for a financially responsible defendant has led, in the automobile cases, to a variety of measures. Where the owner of the car entrusts it to an unsuitable driver,[20] he is held liable for the negligence of the driver, upon the basis of his own negligence in not preventing it. But even where the owner has exercised all due care of his own, vicarious responsibility has been imposed. When the owner is present as a passenger in his own car, a number of courts have held that he retains such a "right of control" over the operation of the vehicle that the driver is to be regarded as his agent or servant. In many of these cases, it is not clear that anything more is meant than that the owner has failed, when he had the opportunity, to interfere with the negligent driving, and so has been negligent himself.[21] In others, special circumstances have indicated that the owner in fact retained the authority to give directions as to the operation of the car.[22] But some courts clearly have gone further, and have held that the right of control, sufficient to impose responsibility, is established by the mere presence of the owner in the car.[23]

Most jurisdictions have rejected such an arbitrary rule, and have held that the owner may surrender his right to give directions, and become a guest in his own car.[24] It is generally agreed that the plaintiff may be aided by a presumption that the driver is an agent or servant,[25] but the owner may prove the contrary.

If the owner is not present in the car, but has entrusted it to a driver who is not his servant, there is merely a bailment, and usually no basis can be found for even any fiction of a "right of control."[26] It is here that the owner's liability to the injured plaintiff breaks down at common law.[27] Only the

---

20. See infra, p. 678.

21. Cf. Wheeler v. Darmochwat, 1932, 280 Mass. 553, 183 N.E. 55; Fixico v. Ellis, 1935, 173 Okl. 5, 46 P. 2d 519; Powers v. State for Use of Reynolds, 1940, 178 Md. 23, 11 A.2d 909. See Harper and Kime, The Duty to Control the Conduct of Another, 1934, 43 Yale L.J. 886.

22. Archambault v. Holmes, 1939, 125 Conn. 167, 4 A.2d 420 (prospective purchaser); Doyon v. Massoline Motor Car Co., 1923, 98 N.J.L. 540, 120 A. 204 (same); Kelley v. Thibodeau, 1921, 120 Me. 402, 115 A. 162 (inexperienced driver); Chambers v. Hawkins, 1930, 233 Ky. 211, 25 S.W.2d 363 (driving at owner's request); Smith v. Spirek, 1923, 196 Iowa 1328, 195 N.W. 736 (driving under actual directions).

23. Sutton v. Inland Const. Co., 1944, 144 Neb. 721, 14 N.W.2d 387; Reetz v. Mansfield, 1935, 119 Conn. 563, 178 A. 53; Atchison, T. & S. F. R. Co. v. McNulty, 8 Cir. 1923, 285 F. 97; Wisconsin & Ark. Lumber Co. v. Brady, 1923, 157 Ark. 449, 248 S.W. 278. Cf. Baker v. Maseeh, 1919, 20 Ariz. 201, 179 P. 53 ("consent" of the owner).

Such "control" is frequently found where one spouse is driving the other's car. Malone Freight Lines v.

Tutton, 5 Cir. 1949, 177 F.2d 901; Lucey v. Allen, 1922, 44 R.I. 379, 117 A. 539; Gochee v. Wagner, 1931, 257 N.Y. 344, 178 N.E. 553; Fisch v. Waters, 1948, 136 N.J.L. 651, 57 A.2d 471. "If the law supposes that," said Mr. Bumble, "the law is a ass."

24. Davis v. Spindler, 1952, 156 Neb. 276, 56 N.W.2d 107; Sackett v. Haeckel, 1957, 249 Minn. 290, 81 N. W.2d 833; Reiter v. Grober, 1921, 173 Wis. 493, 181 N.W. 739; Rodgers v. Saxton, 1931, 305 Pa. 479, 158 A. 166; Virginia R. & P. Co. v. Gorsuch, 1917, 120 Va. 655, 91 S.E. 632. His presence is merely "an important element in showing agency or control by inference." Neese v. Toms, 1941, 196 S.C. 67, 12 S.E.2d 859.

25. Moore v. Watkins, 1956, 41 Tenn.App. 246, 293 S.W.2d 185; Ross v. Burgan, 1955, 163 Ohio St. 211, 126 N.E.2d 592; Potts v. Pardee, 1917, 220 N.Y. 431, 116 N.E. 78; Haigh v. Hill, 1924, 65 Cal.App. 517, 224 P. 474; Fox v. Kaminsky, 1942, 239 Wis. 559, 2 N.W.2d 199 (rebutted). See Note, [1941] Wis. L.Rev. 521.

26. Mimick v. Beatrice Foods Co., 1958, 167 Neb. 470, 93 N.W.2d 627 (milk dispenser); Florenzie v. Fey, 1960, 26 Misc.2d 295, 205 N.Y.S.2d 91 (motorboat); Burke v. Auto Mart, 1955, 37 N.J.Super. 451, 117 A. 2d 624 (license plates); see McChord, Liability of Bailor for Bailee's Negligence in Operating Motor Vehicle, 1927, 15 Geo.L.J. 402.

27. Field v. Evans, 1928, 262 Mass. 315, 159 N.E. 751; Cornish v. Kreuer, 1929, 179 Minn. 60, 228 N. W. 445; Eklof v. Waterston, 1930, 132 Or. 479, 285 P. 201; Brady v. B. & B. Ice Co., 1931, 242 Ky. 138, 45 S.W.2d 1051; Williams v. Younghusband, 5 Cir. 1932, 57 F.2d 139.

courts of Florida [28] have gone the length of saying that an automobile is a "dangerous instrumentality," for which the owner remains responsible when it is negligently driven by another. Other courts have refused to accept this simple but sweeping conclusion,[29] and have fallen back instead upon a mere presumption that the driver is the servant of the owner, which may be rebutted,[30] or have struggled hard to find some foundation for vicarious liability in the circumstances of the particular case.

Family Purpose Doctrine

One of the devices most commonly resorted to is the "family car," or "family purpose" doctrine,[31] which has been accepted by about half of the American courts. Under this doctrine, the owner of an automobile who permits members of his household to drive it for their own pleasure or convenience is regarded as making such a family purpose his "business," so that the driver is treated as his servant. Sometimes it is said that the owner would be liable for the negligence of a chauffeur whom he hires to drive his family, and therefore should be liable when he entrusts the same task to a member of his family instead.[32] There is obviously an element of unblushing fiction in this manufactured agency; and it has quite often been recognized, without apology, that the doctrine is an instrument of policy, a transparent device intended to place the liability upon the party most easily held responsible.[33]

To come within the application of the doctrine, the defendant must own the automo-

---

28. Southern Cotton Oil Co. v. Anderson, 1920, 80 Fla. 441, 86 So. 629; Lynch v. Walker, 1947, 159 Fla. 188, 31 So.2d 268; May v. Palm Beach Chemical Co., Fla.1955, 77 So.2d 468. See Notes, 1952, 5 U.Fla.L.Rev. 412; 1958, 11 U.Fla.L.Rev. 381; 1967, 21 U.Miami L.Rev. 491. This has been extended to make a bailee liable when he permitted another to drive, in Martin v. Lloyd Motor Co., Fla.App.1960, 119 So.2d 413, and to make a car rental company liable when the bailee broke his contract by permitting another to drive, in Susco Car Rental System of Florida v. Leonard, Fla.1959, 112 So.2d 832.

29. Hunter v. First State Bank of Morrilton, 1930, 181 Ark. 907, 28 S.W.2d 712; Leonard v. North Dakota Coop. W. M. Ass'n, 1942, 72 N.D. 310, 6 N.W.2d 576; Elliott v. Harding, 1923, 107 Ohio St. 501, 140 N.E. 338; Ford Motor Co. v. Livesay, 1916, 61 Okl. 231, 160 P. 901; Mullen & Haynes Co. v. Crisp, 1925, 207 Ky. 31, 268 S.W. 576. Cf. Boyd v. White, 1954, 128 Cal.App.2d 641, 276 P.2d 92 (airplane).

30. Enea v. Pfister, 1923, 180 Wis. 329, 192 N.W. 1018; Heavilin v. Wendell, 1932, 214 Iowa 844, 241 N.W. 654; Ferris v. Sterling, 1915, 214 N.Y. 249, 108 N.E. 406; Judson v. Bee Hive Auto Service Co., 1930, 136 Or. 1, 294 P. 588, 297 P. 1050.
Contra: White Oak Coal Co. v. Rivoux, 1913, 88 Ohio St. 18, 102 N.E. 302; Middletown Trust Co. v. Bregman, 1934, 118 Conn. 651, 174 A. 67.

31. King v. Smythe, 1918, 140 Tenn. 217, 204 S.W. 296; Dibble v. Wolff, 1949, 135 Conn. 428, 65 A.2d 479; Benton v. Regeser, 1919, 20 Ariz. 273, 179 P. 966; Hutchins v. Haffner, 1917, 63 Colo. 365, 167 P. 966; Allison v. Bartelt, 1922, 121 Wash. 418, 209

P. 863. The doctrine is at least as old as Lashbrook v. Patten, 1864, i Duv., 62 Ky. 316, where "the son must be regarded as in the father's employment, discharging a duty usually performed by a slave."
See, generally, Lattin, Vicarious Liability and the Family Automobile, 1928, 26 Mich.L.Rev. 846; Hope, The Doctrine of the Family Automobile, 1922, 8 A.B.A.J. 72; Notes, 1936, 14 Tex.L.Rev. 234; 1932, 12 Or.L.Rev. 72; 1938, 24 Va.L.Rev. 931; 1941, 16 Notre Dame L. 394; 1950, 38 Ky.L.J. 156; 1952, 22 Tenn.L.Rev. 535; 1966, 18 S.C.L.Rev. 638; 1967, 55 Ky.L.J. 502.

32. See Birch v. Abercrombie, 1913, 74 Wash. 486, 133 P. 1020, modified, 1913, 135 P. 821; Davis v. Littlefield, 1914, 97 S.C. 171, 81 S.E. 487; Griffin v. Russell, 1915, 144 Ga. 275, 87 S.E. 10.

33. "The Family Purpose Doctrine is a humanitarian one designed for the protection of the public generally, and resulted from recognition of the fact that in the vast majority of instances an infant has not sufficient property in his own right to indemnify one who may suffer from his negligent act." Turner v. Hall's Adm'x, Ky.1952, 252 S.W.2d 30, 32.
Compare the accomplishment of the same thing by statute, in Hawkins v. Ermatinger, 1920, 211 Mich. 578, 179 N.W. 249 (if car driven by a minor, conclusive presumption it is with owner's consent); Wilson v. Grace, 1930, 273 Mass. 146, 173 N.E. 524 (registration of car in name of defendant prima facie evidence it was being operated by his authorized agent); Arizona Code Ann.1939, §§ 66–242 and 66–254 (father or mother must sign application of minor under 18 for driver's license, and by doing so become liable for his negligence); Sizemore v. Bailey's Adm'r, Ky.1956, 293 S.W.2d 165 (same).

bile,[34] or be in control of its use,[35] or at least have some recognized property interest in it [36] or supply it; [37] and he must have made it available for family use, rather than for use in his business.[38] It usually is held that the car must be made available for general use, and not merely to take out on a particular occasion,[39] although whatever policy may underlie this odd business would appear to apply no less to the special permission. The owner need not, however, be the head of the family.[40] The driver must be a member of

the defendant's immediate household,[41] as distinguished from a more distant or collateral relative such as a brother-in-law.[42] The fact that the driver is an adult son usually is held, however, not to prevent the agency relation where he is still a member of the household.[43]

The car must be found to have been driven at the time with the permission or acquiescence of the defendant,[44] although his con-

---

34. McNamara v. Prather, 1939, 277 Ky. 754, 127 S. W.2d 160; Stevens v. Van Deusen, 1952, 56 N.M. 128, 241 P.2d 331.

35. Durso v. A. D. Cozzolino, Inc., 1941, 128 Conn. 24, 20 A.2d 392; Hexter v. Burgess, 1936, 52 Ga. App. 819, 184 S.E. 769; Gray v. Golden, 1946, 301 Ky. 477, 192 S.W.2d 371.

36. In Emanuelson v. Johnson, 1921, 148 Minn. 417, 182 N.W. 521, the doctrine was applied to a bailee of an automobile who permitted his daughter to use it. Cf. Mann v. Cook, Tex.Civ.App.1929, 23 S.W.2d 860 (servant-bailee). In Smith v. Doyle, 1938, 68 App.D.C. 60, 98 F.2d 341, nominal ownership of a car bought by members of the family for their own use was held not to be enough.

37. In Gray v. Golden, 1945, 301 Ky. 477, 192 S.W.2d 371, a defendant who bought a car for family use and put legal title in another member of the family was held to fall within the rule.

38. Hanford v. Goehry, 1946, 24 Wash.2d 859, 167 P. 2d 678; Lambert v. Polen, 1943, 346 Pa. 352, 30 A. 2d 115; Cook v. Hall, 1948, 308 Ky. 500, 214 S.W.2d 1017; Rubenstein v. Williams, 1932, 61 App.D.C. 266, 61 F.2d 575, second appeal, 1934, 63 App.D.C. 57, 69 F.2d 231; Hawes v. Haynes, 1941, 219 N.C. 535, 14 S.E.2d 503.

39. Costanzo v. Sturgill, 1958, 145 Conn. 92, 139 A.2d 51; Cronenberg v. United States, E.D.N.C.1954, 123 F.Supp. 693; Studdard v. Turner, 1954, 91 Ga.App. 318, 85 S.E.2d 537; Greenwood v. Kier, 1952, 125 Colo. 333, 243 P.2d 417; Cook v. Hall, 1948, 308 Ky. 500, 214 S.W.2d 1017.

40. Hill v. Smith, 1949, 32 Tenn.App. 172, 222 S.W.2d 207 (mother); Smith v. Overstreet's Adm'r, 1935, 258 Ky. 781, 81 S.W.2d 571 (same); Perfetto v. Wesson, 1952, 138 Conn. 506, 86 A.2d 565 (same); Turner v. Gackle, 1926, 168 Minn. 514, 209 N.W. 626 (child). See Note, 1950, 3 Vand.L.Rev. 644.

It has been held that a corporation cannot have a "family" or "household" within the doctrine. Keller v. Federal Bob Brannon Truck Co., 1924, 151 Tenn. 427, 269 S.W. 914. But in Durso v. A. D.

Cozzolino, Inc., 1941, 128 Conn. 24, 20 A.2d 392, it was applied to a family corporation where the car was used for family purposes.

41. In Smart v. Bissonette, 1927, 106 Conn. 447, 138 A. 365, the doctrine was applied to the use of a car by the housekeeper of a Catholic priest. But cf. Scott v. Greene, 1926, 242 Ill.App. 405, 413.

In Rutherford v. Smith, 1940, 284 Ky. 592, 145 S.W.2d 533, a grandson was held to be included.

42. Bryant v. Keen, 1931, 43 Ga.App. 251, 158 S.E. 445; Jones v. Golick, 1922, 46 Nev. 10, 206 P. 679; Scott v. Greene, 1926, 242 Ill.App. 405; McBroom v. Wolsleger, 1966, 180 Neb. 622, 144 N.W.2d 199 (brother); Johnston v. Hare, 1926, 30 Ariz. 253, 246 P. 546 (second cousin).

43. Burkhart v. Corn, 1955, 59 N.M. 343, 284 P.2d 226; Garska v. Harris, 1961, 172 Neb. 339, 109 N. W.2d 529 (need not be permanent member of household); Dillon v. Burnett, 1938, 197 Wash. 371, 85 P.2d 656; Cockerham v. Potts, 1933, 143 Or. 80, 20 P.2d 423; Hubert v. Harpe, 1935, 181 Ga. 168, 182 S.E. 167. Cf. Robinson v. Hartley, 1958, 98 Ga.App. 765, 106 S.E.2d 861 (nephew). Contra; Adkins v. Nanney, 1935, 169 Tenn. 67, 82 S.W.2d 867; Bradley v. Schmidt, 1928, 223 Ky. 784, 4 S.W.2d 703.

An adult son living apart is not included. Walker v. Farley, 1948, 308 Ky. 163, 213 S.W.2d 1016; McGinn v. Kimmel, 1950, 36 Wash.2d 786, 221 P.2d 467; Bryan v. Schatz, 1949, 77 N.D. 9, 39 N.W.2d 435, But see Dunn v. Caylor, 1962, 218 Ga. 256, 127 S.E.2d 367 (military service).

44. Todd v. Hargis, 1945, 299 Ky. 841, 187 S.W.2d 739 (negligently leaving car unlocked not enough); Sale v. Atkins, 1924, 206 Ky. 224, 267 S.W. 223; Jensen v. Fischer, 1916, 134 Minn. 366, 159 N.W. 827; Dow v. Legg, 1930, 120 Neb. 271, 231 N.W. 747.

It is not, however, required that the car be actually driven by the person to whom the permission was given, if that person is present in the car. Dibble v. Wolff, 1949, 135 Conn. 482, 65 A.2d 479; Golden v. Medford, 1940, 189 Ga. 614, 7 S.E.2d 236; Turner v. Hall's Adm'x, Ky.1952, 252 S.W.2d 30; Kayser v. Van Nest, 1914, 125 Minn. 277, 146 N.W. 1091.

sent may be inferred from a failure to protest at frequent violations of his orders not to use the car.[45] His liability does not extend to any use beyond the "family purpose,"[46] which, however, will include all normal family activities, including mere driving for the pleasure of an individual.[47] Questions of deviation from the precise scope of the consent given have been dealt with [48] much as in the case of a servant's deviation from the scope of his employment.[49] A few courts have held that there can be a family purpose only when two or more members of the family are in the car; [50] but most of those

which accept the doctrine have said that there is no such requirement.[51]

The question of the application of the family car doctrine to impute the contributory negligence of the driver to the owner when he is suing for damage to the car or to his own person seldom has arisen. Logically, if there is an agency, it should apply both ways; and it has been so held.[52] But since the whole purpose of the device has been to protect plaintiffs against financial irresponsibility, rather than to cut down their recoveries, there are a few courts [53] which of late have declared that the policy involved does not require the imputation of the contributory negligence.

The family car doctrine has been repudiated entirely by an equal number of courts,[54] as a fictitious agency without any basis in fact. It is of course entirely contrary to the accepted rule that the head of a household is not liable when, without negligence, he entrusts other chattels, such as shotguns or golf clubs, to members of his family for simi-

45. Watson v. Burley, 1928, 105 W.Va. 416, 143 S.E. 95. Cf. Grier v. Woodside, 1931, 200 N.C. 759, 158 S.E. 491 (habitual use).

46. Rowland v. Spalti, 1923, 196 Iowa 208, 194 N.W. 90; Rauckhorst v. Kraut, 1926, 216 Ky. 323, 287 S.W. 895; Hildock v. Grosso, 1939, 334 Pa. 222, 5 A. 2d 565; Johnson v. Brant, 1955, 93 Ga.App. 44, 90 S.E.2d 587 (lending car to a friend).

47. Harmon v. Haas, 1932, 61 N.D. 772, 241 N.W. 70; Hanson v. Eilers, 1931, 164 Wash. 185, 2 P.2d 719; McCullough v. Harshman, 1924, 99 Okl. 262, 226 P. 555.

48. See for example McDowell v. Hurner, 1933, 142 Or. 611, 20 P.2d 395; Evans v. Caldwell, 1937, 184 Ga. 203, 190 S.E. 582; King v. Cann, 1935, 184 Wash. 554, 52 P.2d 900; Vaughn v. Booker, 1940, 217 N.C. 479, 8 S.E.2d 603; Forman v. Shields, 1935, 183 Wash. 333, 48 P.2d 599.

49. See supra, p. 461. If the use is within the general scope of the consent given, liability is not defeated by the fact that the car is being used at a place or in a manner which the owner has forbidden. Evans v. Caldwell, 1937, 184 Ga. 203, 190 S.E. 582; Richardson v. True, Ky.1953, 259 S.W.2d 70; Turner v. Hall's Adm'x, Ky.1952, 252 S.W.2d 30; Jones v. Cook, 1924, 96 W.Va. 60, 123 S.E. 407. In Driver v. Smith, 1959, 47 Tenn.App. 505, 339 S.W.2d 135, a daughter turned the car over to her boy friend to drive, and was injured while enthusiastically kissing him, when he lost control of the car. The father was held liable for her negligent failure to supervise the driver.

50. See Doran v. Thomsen, 1908, 76 N.J.L. 754, 71 A. 296; Stumpf v. Montgomery, 1924, 101 Okl. 257, 226 P. 65. Compare Missell v. Hayes, 1914, 86 N.J.L. 348, 91 A. 322; McNeal v. McKain, 1912, 33 Okl. 449, 126 P. 742.

51. Landry v. Oversen, 1919, 187 Iowa 284, 174 N.W. 255; Miller v. Weck, 1920, 186 Ky. 552, 217 S.W. 904; Crittenden v. Murphy, 1918, 36 Cal.App. 803, 173 P. 595; Griffin v. Russell, 1915, 144 Ga. 275, 87 S.E. 10; Davis v. Littlefield, 1913, 97 S.C. 171, 81 S.E. 487.

An automobile guest act does not protect the owner of the car liable under the family car doctrine. Lopez v. Barreras, 1966, 77 N.M. 52, 419 P.2d 251.

52. Prendergast v. Allen, 1922, 44 R.I. 379, 117 A. 539; Pearson v. Northland Transp. Co., 1931, 184 Minn. 560, 239 N.W. 602.

53. Michaelsohn v. Smith, N.D.1962, 113 N.W.2d 571; Pinaglia v. Beaulieu, 1969, 28 Conn.Sup. 90, 250 A. 2d 522; White v. Yup, 1969, 85 Nev. 527, 458 P.2d 617.

54. Grimes v. Labreck, 1967, 108 N.H. 26, 226 A.2d 787; Trice v. Bridgewater, 1935, 125 Tex. 75, 81 S. W.2d 63; Sare v. Stetz, 1950, 67 Wyo. 55, 214 P.2d 486; Andersen v. Byrnes, 1931, 344 Ill. 240, 176 N. E. 374; Hackley v. Robey, 1938, 170 Va. 55, 195 S. E. 689 (overruling prior cases).

A finding of actual agency will still render the parent liable. Smith v. Jordan, 1912, 211 Mass. 269, 97 N. E. 761 (father instructed son to drive mother); Zeidler v. Goelzer, 1926, 191 Wis. 378, 211 N.W. 140 (implied request to operate car for father's benefit).

lar purposes.[55] It fails to distinguish between mere permissive use for the driver's own ends and a use subject to the control of the owner as master and connected with his affairs.[56] Its connection with the peculiar dangers and financial responsibilities of the automobile is clearly indicated by decisions in jurisdictions which adopt it, that it has no application to motorboats or motorcycles.[57] It clearly is to be regarded as an ingenious fiction, resorted to as a partial and inadequate step in the direction of an ultimate rule which will hold the owner of the car liable in all cases for the negligence of the driver to whom he entrusts it. When such a rule is adopted by statute, the doctrine will have served its purpose, and is to be discarded.[58]

Legislation

At this writing about a dozen states have accomplished this result outright by legislation.[59] The first such "automobile consent" statute was adopted in Michigan in 1909, and four years later was held constitutional.[60] Such statutes make the owner of the automobile liable for injuries to third persons caused by the negligence of any person, whether a member of the family or not, who is operating the car on the public highway with the owner's consent. In effect an arbitrary statutory agency is created, which results in vicarious liability.[61]

The term "owner" has been construed to exclude persons, such as conditional sellers, who have legal title without power to control the use of the vehicle.[62] The liability is limited to the scope of the consent given, and the owner is not liable where the car is being used at a time [63] or a place [64] or for a purpose [65] which is clearly beyond the scope of the permission. This limitation is, however, very similar to, although of course not

55. Chaddock v. Plummer, 1891, 88 Mich. 225, 50 N. W. 135; Harris v. Cameron, 1892, 81 Wis. 239, 51 N.W. 437; Fleming v. Kravitz, 1918, 260 Pa. 428, 103 A. 831. See Van Blaricom v. Dodgson, 1917, 220 N.Y. 111, 115 N.E. 443; Piquet v. Wazelle, 1927, 288 Pa. 463, 136 A. 787.

56. See Doran v. Thomsen, 1908, 76 N.J.L. 754, 71 A. 296; Lattin, Vicarious Liability and the Family Automobile, 1928, 26 Mich.L.Rev. 846, 860.

57. Felcyn v. Gamble, 1932, 185 Minn. 357, 241 N.W. 37; Meinhardt v. Vaughn, 1929, 159 Tenn. 272, 17 S.W.2d 5. Cf. Pflugmacher v. Thomas, 1949, 34 Wash.2d 687, 209 P.2d 443 (bicycle). See Note, 1932, 16 Minn.L.Rev. 970.

Contra, Stewart v. Stephens, 1969, 225 Ga. 185, 166 S. E.2d 890, conformed to 119 Ga.App. 629, 168 S.E.2d 325.

58. McMartin v. Saemisch, 1962, 254 Iowa 45, 116 N. W.2d 491.

59. See Chamberlain, Automobiles and Vicarious Liability, 1924, 10 A.B.A.J. 788; Brodsky, Motor Vehicle Owners' Statutory Vicarious Liability in Rhode Island, 1939, 19 Boston U.L.Rev. 448; Notes, 1937, 21 Minn.L.Rev. 823; 1933, 81 U.Pa.L.Rev. 513; 1943, 16 So.Cal.L.Rev. 242; 1951, 25 St.Johns L. Rev. 306.

60. In Daugherty v. Thomas, 1913, 174 Mich. 371, 140 N.W. 615. Accord: Young v. Masci, 1933, 289 U.S. 253; Holmes v. Lilygren Motor Co., 1937, 201 Minn. 44, 275 N.W. 416; Robinson v. Bruce Rent-A-Ford Co., 1927, 205 Iowa 261, 215 N.W. 724; Stapleton v. Independent Brewing Co., 1917, 198 Mich. 170, 164 N.W. 520.

61. See Secured Finance Co. v. Chicago, R.I. & P. R. Co., 1929, 207 Iowa 1105, 1108, 224 N.W. 88, 69; Psota v. Long Island R. Co., 1927, 246 N.Y. 388, 393, 159 N.E. 180; Wolf v. Sulik, 1919, 93 Conn. 431, 106 A. 443; Young v. Masci, 1933, 289 U.S. 253.

62. Smith v. Simpson, 1963, 260 N.C. 601, 133 S.E.2d 474 (father nominal owner of son's car); Federated Mut. Imp. & Hardware Ins. Co. v. Rouse, N.D.Iowa 1955, 133 F.Supp. 226; Lennon v. L.A.W. Acceptance Corp. of R.I., 1927, 48 R.I. 363, 138 A. 215; Swing v. Lingo, 1933, 129 Cal.App. 518, 19 P.2d 56; Mason v. Automobile Finance Co., 1941, 73 U.S. App.D.C. 284, 121 F.2d 32. Cf. O'Tier v. Sell, 1930, 252 N.Y. 400, 169 N.E. 624 (mechanic inspecting car not within statute).

63. Union Trust Co. v. American Commercial Car Co., 1922, 219 Mich. 557, 189 N.W. 23; Truman v. United Products Corp., 1944, 217 Minn. 155, 14 N. W.2d 120; De Rebaylio v. Herndon, 1935, 6 Cal. App.2d 567, 44 P.2d 581.

64. Henrietta v. Evans, 1938, 10 Cal.2d 526, 75 P.2d 1051; Chaika v. Vandenberg, 1929, 252 N.Y. 101, 169 N.E. 103; Robinson v. Shell Petroleum Corp., 1933, 217 Iowa 1252, 251 N.W. 613 (time and place).

65. Heavilin v. Wendell, 1932, 214 Iowa 844, 241 N. W. 654; Krausnick v. Haegg Roofing Co., 1945, 236 Iowa 985, 20 N.W. 432; Muma v. Brown, 1967, 378 Mich. 637, 148 N.W.2d 760.

identical with, the "scope of employment" where the driver is a servant; [66] and a minor deviation from the permitted use, [67] or a violation of specific instructions as to the manner in which the car is to be operated, [68] will not absolve the owner. This has led to decisions, for example, that if the person to whom the consent is given turns the car over to a stranger, without permission to do so, the owner's liability terminates; [69] but if the bailee himself remains in the car and rides while the stranger is driving, there is still a permitted use, and even the owner's express prohibition will not defeat his liability. [70]

As to the effect of the automobile consent statutes in imputing the contributory negligence of the driver to the owner who sues for damage to the car or to his own person, agreement has not been reached. Decision has been affected to some extent by the language of the particular act. A few courts have interpreted the statute to impute the

driver's negligence both ways, so that the owner's action is barred. [71] The greater number of courts have looked to the purpose of the statute, which is obviously to protect injured plaintiffs against the financial irresponsibility of drivers, and not to diminish any recovery which would otherwise be allowed; and accordingly they have held that the legislation does not have the effect of imputing contributory negligence. [72]

Apart from the law of automobiles, there are occasional instances of other statutes creating vicarious liability. [73] Owners of aircraft have been made strictly liable for damage to persons or property beneath, although the craft may be operated by another person. [74] Another quite interesting group of statutes are the "lynching" acts, making municipalities liable for damages within their corporate limits which result from mob violence. [75]

---

66. See Flaugh v. Egan Chevrolet, Inc., 1938, 202 Minn. 615, 279 N.W. 582; Chaika v. Vandenberg, 1929, 252 N.Y. 101, 106, 169 N.E. 103, 104; Guerin v. Mongeon, 1928, 49 R.I. 414, 143 A. 674; Kieszkowski v. Odlewany, 1937, 280 Mich. 388, 273 N.W. 741. See Notes, 1929, 24 Minn.L.Rev. 271; 1964, 31 U.Chi.L.Rev. 355. The differences are made clear in Moore v. Palmer, 1957, 350 Mich. 363, 86 N.W.2d 585, where the owner consented to an employee driving the car.

Proof that defendant owned a car which was operated on the highway by another in lawful possession of it makes out a prima facie of consent. Schultz v. Swift & Co., 1941, 210 Minn. 533, 299 N.W. 7; Houseman v. Walt Neal, Inc., 1962, 368 Mich. 631, 118 N.W.2d 964.

67. Kieszkowski v. Odlewany, 1937, 280 Mich. 388, 273 N.W. 741; Senator Cab Co. v. Rothberg, Mun. App.D.C.1945, 42 A.2d 245.

68. Sweeney v. Hartman, 1941, 296 Mich. 343, 296 N. W. 282; Herbert v. Casswelli, 1943, 61 Cal.App.2d 661, 143 P.2d 792; Grant v. Knopper, 1927, 245 N.Y. 158, 156 N.E. 650; cf. Arcara v. Moresse, 1932, 258 N.Y. 211, 179 N.E. 389.

69. Fischer v. McBride, 1941, 296 Mich. 671, 296 N. W. 834.

70. Souza v. Corti, 1937, 22 Cal.2d 454, 139 P.2d 645; Arcara v. Moresse, 1932, 258 N.Y. 211, 179 N.E. 389; Webb v. Moreno, 8 Cir. 1966, 363 F.2d 97.

71. McCants v. Chenault, 1954, 98 Ohio App. 529, 130 N.E.2d 382; National Trucking & Storage Co. v. Driscoll, Mun.App.D.C.1949, 64 A.2d 304; Birnbaum v. Blunt, 1957, 152 Cal.App.2d 371, 313 P.2d 86; Davis Pontiac, Inc. v. Sirois, 1954, 82 R.I. 32, 105 A.2d 792; cf. Di Leo v. Du Montier, La.App.1940, 195 So. 74.

72. Wick v. Widdell, 1967, 276 Minn. 51, 149 N.W.2d 20; Houlahan v. Brockmeier, 1966, 258 Iowa 1197, 141 N.W.2d 545 supplemented 141 N.W.2d 924; Bush v. Oliver, 1963, 86 Idaho 380, 386 P.2d 967; York v. Day's, Inc., 1958, 153 Me. 441, 140 A.2d 730; Mills v. Gabriel, 1940, 259 App.Div. 60, 18 N.Y.S.2d 78, affirmed, 1940, 284 N.Y. 755, 31 N.E.2d 512, appeal granted 259 App.Div. 818, 19 N.Y.S.2d 771. See Note, 1956, 31 Notre Dame L. 724. In Mason v. Russell, 1958, 158 Cal.App.2d 391, 322 P.2d 486, it was held that the statute was inapplicable to an action by the owner against the negligent driver.

73. See note, 1931, 45 Harv. L.Rev. 171.

74. Uniform State Law of Aeronautics, § 5.

75. One of the early ones was in Clark v. Inhabitants of the Hundred of Blything, 1823, 2 B. & C. 254, 107 Eng.Rep. 378, which involved a Riot Act making the hundred liable. See also Slaton v. City of Chicago, 1955, 8 Ill.App.2d 47, 130 N.E.2d 205; A. & B. Auto Stores of Jones St., Inc. v. City of Newark, 1968, 103 N.J.Super. 559, 248 A.2d 258; City of Iola v. Birnbaum, 1905, 71 Kan. 600, 81 P. 198; Butte Miners' Union v. City of Butte, 1920, 58 Mont. 391, 194 P. 149.

74. IMPUTED CONTRIBUTORY NEGLIGENCE

Ordinarily the plaintiff's action for his damages will not be barred by the negligence of any third person who may have contributed to them. He may treat the defendant and the stranger as joint tort feasors, so far as each is a legal cause of the harm, and recover from either.[76] But if the plaintiff and the third person stand in such a relation to one another—as for example that of master and servant [77]—that the plaintiff will be charged with that person's negligence as a defendant, it will ordinarily follow that he will likewise be charged with it as a plaintiff.[78] Normally the responsibility is applied "both ways." As we have seen, however,[79] there may be special reasons of policy in particular cases which will lead to the imputation of the negligence to a defendant, but not to a plaintiff.[80]

There are additional complications, which are now largely a matter of purely historical interest. "Imputed contributory negligence" has had a very bad name of its own, because of a group of quite unreasonable and rather senseless rules which were at one time applied to defeat the recovery of the injured plaintiff by imputing to him the negligence of another, even though he would not have been at all liable for that negligence as a defendant. This was done where the plaintiff and the third person stood within a limited group of special relations to one another, on the basis of which fictitious agencies were created to accomplish the result. There was much denunciation of these fictions and their consequences,[81] as a result of which they steadily lost ground. Except for vestigial remnants which are at most moribund historical survivals, "imputed contributory negligence" in its own right has now disappeared. The result at which the courts have arrived is that the plaintiff will never be barred from recovery by the negligence of a third person unless the relation between them is such that the plaintiff would be vicariously liable as a defendant to another who might be injured.[82]

The various relations in which contributory negligence was formerly imputed may be considered briefly, as follows:

Driver and Passenger

In 1849 an unfortunate English decision [83] imputed the negligence of the driver of an omnibus to his passenger, who was injured through the negligent operation of another vehicle. The reason given was that there was an agency relation, since the plaintiff must be taken to be in "control" of the driver, for the reason that he had selected the means of conveyance. This resulted in imputing the contributory negligence of every driver to his passenger. This nonsensical fiction was overruled in England [84]

76. See supra, § 47.

77. See Notes, 1967, 51 Minn.L.Rev. 377; 1966, 45 Tex.L.Rev. 364.

78. As to master and servant, see for example Louisville & N. R. Co. v. Tomlinson, Ky.1963, 373 S.W.2d 601.

79. See, as to the family car doctrine, supra, p. 483; as to automobile consent statutes, supra, p. 486.

80. In Weber v. Stokely-Van Camp, Inc., 1966, 274 Minn. 482, 144 N.W.2d 540, the court overthrew the "both ways" rule as to master and servant, and held that the contributory negligence of the servant would not be imputed. The case has not been followed, and was rejected in Wilson v. Great Northern R. Co., 1968, 83 S.D. 207, 157 N.W.2d 19.

81. See Gilmore, Imputed Negligence, 1921, 1 Wis.L. Rev. 193, 237; Keeton, Imputed Contributory Negligence, 1936, 13 Tex.L.Rev. 161; Gregory, Vicarious Responsibility and Contributory Negligence, 1932, 41 Yale L.J. 831; Lessler, Imputed Negligence, 1951, 25 Conn.Bar J. 30; Lessler, The Proposed Discard of the Doctrine of Imputed Contributory Negligence, 1951, 20 Ford L.Rev. 156; James, Imputed Contributory Negligence, 1954, 14 La.L.Rev. 340; Notes, 1924, 12 Cal.L.Rev. 238; 1928, 14 Va. L.Rev. 213; 1932, 80 U.Pa.L.Rev. 1123; 1953, 33 Bos.U.L.Rev. 90; 1959, 26 Tenn.L.Rev. 531.

82. Second Restatment of Torts, § 485.

83. Thorogood v. Bryan, 1849, 8 C.B. 115, 137 Eng. Rep. 452.

84. Mills v. Armstrong (The Bernina), 1888, L.R. 13 A.C. 1.

some forty years later, but in the meantime it had been taken up in the United States. The American cases which accepted it now have been overruled everywhere.[85] The last state to abandon the idea was Michigan,[86] in 1946. It is now held that the driver's negligence will not be imputed to the passenger, whether the transportation be in a common carrier,[87] a hired vehicle,[88] or a gratuitous conveyance,[89] unless the relation between them is such that the passenger would be vicariously liable as a defendant.[90]

Such vicariously imputed negligence must be distinguished from the contributory negligence of the passenger himself. He is required to exercise reasonable care for his own safety,[91] and will be barred from recovery if he voluntarily rides with a driver whom he knows to be intoxicated, reckless or incompetent,[92] or unreasonably fails to warn the driver of a danger which he discovers, or to make use of any ability to control the negligence which he may possess.[93] In the ordinary case the question of the reasonableness of the passenger's conduct is for the jury;[94] and it is now the prevailing view that he need not be on the alert or watch the road, and may trust himself to the driver[95] until he has reason to believe that there is danger.[96]

Domestic Relations

Another old rule imputed the contributory negligence of one spouse to another, by reason of the marital relation alone. The origin of this lay in the legal identity of the wife with her husband at common law,[97] which meant that each was to be charged with the negligence of the other, and any recovery by

85. Ashworth v. Baker, 1956, 197 Va. 582, 90 S.E.2d 860; Reiter v. Grober, 1921, 173 Wis. 493, 181 N.W. 739; Bessey v. Salemme, 1939, 302 Mass. 188, 19 N. E.2d 75; Koplitz v. City of St. Paul, 1902, 86 Minn. 373, 90 N.W. 794; Fechley v. Springfield Traction Co., 1906, 119 Mo.App. 358, 96 S.W. 421.

86. Bricker v. Green, 1946, 313 Mich. 218, 21 N.W.2d 105.

87. Bennett v. New Jersey R. & T. Co., 1873, 36 N.J. L. 225.

88. Little v. Hackett, 1886, 116 U.S. 366.

89. Rodgers v. Saxton, 1931, 305 Pa. 479, 158 A. 166; Schoenrock v. City of Sisseton, 1960, 78 S.D. 419, 103 N.W.2d 649; Olson v. Kennedy Trading Co., 1937, 199 Minn. 493, 272 N.W. 381.

90. See supra, §§ 70, 72. It is still possible that the negligence of the driver may be such an intervening cause as to relieve the third person from liability on the basis of "proximate cause." See for example Rusczck v. Chicago & N. W. R. Co., 1926, 191 Wis. 130, 210 N.W. 361.

91. Murphy v. Shibiya, 1933, 125 Neb. 487, 250 N.W. 746; Highton v. Pennsylvania R. Co., 1938, 132 Pa. Super. 559, 1 A.2d 568; Cotton v. Willmar & Sioux Falls R. Co., 1906, 99 Minn. 366, 109 N.W. 835; Darrington v. Campbell, 1939, 150 Kan. 407, 94 P.2d 305. See Mechem, Contributory Negligence of Automobile Passengers, 1930, 78 U.Pa.L.Rev. 736.

92. Schwartz v. Johnson, 1926, 152 Tenn. 586, 280 S. W. 32; Wayson v. Rainier Taxi Co., 1925, 136 Wash. 274, 239 P. 559; Winston's Adm'r v. Henderson, 1918, 179 Ky. 220, 200 S.W. 330; Hemington v. Hemington, 1922, 221 Mich. 206, 190 N.W. 683.

93. Garrow v. Seattle Taxicab Co., 1925, 135 Wash. 630, 238 P. 623; Whitman v. Fisher, 1904, 98 Me. 575, 57 A. 895; Bush v. Union Pac. R. Co., 1901, 62 Kan. 709, 64 P. 624; Thompson v. Pennsylvania R. Co., 1906, 215 Pa. 113, 64 A. 323. In some cases it has been held that failure to protest against improper driving is contributory negligence as a matter of law. Sharp v. Sproat, 1922, 111 Kan. 735, 208 P. 613. In others, that it is a question for the jury. Codner v. Stowe, 1926, 201 Iowa 800, 208 N. W. 330; Jones v. Schreiber, 1926, 166 Minn. 177, 207 N.W. 322.

It may depend upon whether the passenger has reason to believe his interference to be necessary. See Senft v. Western Maryland Ry. Co., 1914, 246 Pa. 446, 92 A. 553; Beach v. City of Seattle, 1915, 85 Wash. 379, 148 P. 39. But it is generally held that if his protest is disregarded, he is not necessarily negligent in failing to leave the vehicle, and the question is one for the jury. Mendler v. Town Taxi, 1936, 295 Mass. 90, 3 N.E.2d 15; Adams v. Hilton, 1937, 270 Ky. 818, 110 S.W.2d 1088.

94. Baltimore & O. R. Co. v. Faubion, 1930, 92 Ind. App. 592, 170 N.E. 94.

95. Longino v. Moore, 1936, 53 Ga.App. 674, 187 S.E. 203; Zank v. Chicago, R. I. & P. R. Co., 1959, 17 Ill.2d 473, 161 N.E.2d 848, on remand, 1960, 26 Ill. App.2d 389, 168 N.E.2d 472; Leclair v. Boudreau, 1928, 101 Vt. 270, 143 A. 401; Bradford v. Carson, 1931, 223 Ala. 594, 137 So. 426; Schmidt v. Leuthener, 1929, 199 Wis. 567, 227 N.W. 17.

96. Parker v. Helfert, 1931, 140 Misc. 905, 252 N.Y.S. 35; cf. Nelson v. Nygren, 1932, 259 N.Y. 71, 181 N. E. 52.

97. See infra, p. 859.

one inured to the benefit of the other. In all states the Married Women's Acts have long since terminated this legal identity, and permit the wife to maintain an action for a personal tort in her own name, without joining her husband.[98] As a result the wife is regarded as a separate individual, whose negligence is no more to be attributed to the husband, or his to her, than in the case of any other person; and imputed contributory negligence on the basis of the marriage alone has vanished from the law of most jurisdictions.[99] The only exception is found in the case of one or two jurisdictions which, under the influence of the civil law, treat the damages recoverable by either spouse as community property, and therefore continue to impute the negligence of one to the other in order to prevent the negligent party from profiting as community owner by his own wrong.[1]

Another old rule, of a particularly hideous character, imputed the contributory negligence of a parent to his child. Here there was never any legal identity; but in 1829, in one of those bleak decisions which have here and there marred the face of our law,

it was held in New York [2] that a child two years old who was injured by the negligence of the defendant in running him down with a sleigh was barred from recovery by the negligence of his father, who was supposed to be looking after him at the time. The mistake was repeated, but subsequently overruled, in England.[3] This barbarous rule, which denied to the innocent victim of the negligence of two parties any recovery against either, and visited the sins of the fathers upon the children,[4] was accepted in several American States until it was at one time very nearly the prevailing rule; but it is now abrogated, by statute [5] or by decision [6] everywhere except in Maine,[7] where it appears exceedingly unlikely that it will long survive. The "agency" of the parent to look after the child is of course the sheerest nonsense, and the fear that the parent may profit by his own negligence is now removed by the power of the court to put the proceeds in trust for the child.[8]

---

98. See infra, p. 861.

99. Ward v. Baskin, Fla.1957, 94 So.2d 859; Ditty v. Farley, 1959, 219 Or. 208, 347 P.2d 47; Painter v. Lingon, 1952, 193 Va. 840, 71 S.E.2d 355; Schoenrock v. City of Sisseton, 1960, 78 S.D. 419, 103 N. W.2d 649; Sherman v. Korff, 1958, 353 Mich. 387, 91 N.W.2d 485; Second Restatement of Torts, § 487.

1. Dallas Ry. & Term. Co. v. High, 1937, 129 Tex. 219, 103 S.W.2d 735; Tinker v. Hobbs, 1956, 80 Ariz. 166, 294 P.2d 659; Clark v. Foster, 1964, 87 Idaho 134, 391 P.2d 853. Contra, Cook v. Faria, 1958, 74 Nev. 262, 328 P.2d 568. As to the tangled California history, see Brunn, California Personal Injury Damage Awards to Married Persons, 1966, 13 UCLA L.Rev. 587. Effective January 1, 1970, the legislature restored the community property status of the action, but abolished the imputed negligence.

There are one or two states in which the negligence of one spouse is still imputed to the other to bar an action for wrongful death of a child. See for example Martinez v. Rodriquez, Fla.1969, 215 So.2d 305.

2. Hartfield v. Roper, 1829, 21 Wend., N.Y., 615. As this developed, it was limited to cases where both parent and child were negligent, and the parent's negligence consisted in failure properly to look after the child. See Cadman v. White, 1936, 296 Mass. 117, 5 N.E.2d 19; Kupchinsky v. Vacuum Oil Co., 1933, 263 N.Y. 128, 188 N.E. 278; Notes, 1934, 47 Harv.L.Rev. 874; 1934, 34 Col.L.Rev. 575.

3. Waite v. North Eastern R. Co., 1858, 1 El.Bl. & El. 719, 120 Eng.Rep. 679, overruled by Oliver v. Birmingham & Midland Omnibus Co., [1933] 1 K.B. 35.

4. See the denunciation in Neff v. City of Cameron, 1908, 213 Mo. 350, 111 S.W. 1139.

5. See Novak v. State, 1950, 199 Misc. 588, 99 N.Y.S. 2d 962; Gill v. Jakstas, 1950, 325 Mass. 309, 90 N. E.2d 527; Zaccari v. United States, D.Md.1956, 144 F.Supp. 860 (Maryland law).

6. Price v. Seaboard Air Line R. Co., 1968, 274 N.C. 32, 161 S.E.2d 590; Shelton v. Mullins, 1966, 207 Va. 17, 147 S.E.2d 754; McKeon v. Goldstein, 1960, 3 Storey, Del., 24, 164 A.2d 260; Lucas v. Ambridge Yellow Cab Co., 1958, 185 Pa.Super. 350, 137 A.2d 819; Botelho v. Curtis, 1970, 28 Conn.Sup. 493, 267 A.2d 675.

7. Gravel v. Le Blanc, 1932, 131 Me. 325, 162 A. 789; Wood v. Balzano, 1940, 137 Me. 87, 15 A.2d 188.

8. See Note, 1932, 80 U.Pa.L.Rev. 1123, 1131; Beach, Contributory Negligence, 3d Ed. 1899, § 127; Zarzana v. Neve Drug Co., 1919, 180 Cal. 32, 179 P.

Imputed negligence in domestic relations also appears in connection with actions for loss of services [9] and wrongful death,[10] which are more conveniently considered at a later point.

Bailments

Until the year 1897, nearly all courts imputed the contributory negligence of a bailee to his bailor, in an action by the latter for damage to the chattel inflicted by the defendant.[11] The basis for the rule was obscure; but it appears to have rested upon the fact that the bailor had selected the bailee, that either might sue the tortfeasor and recover, and therefore it was assumed that there was an identity of their interests, and so the rule in the two suits should be the same.[12] This is still the law in Texas; [13] but with modern acceptance of the interests of the bailor and the bailee as quite separate and distinct, the earlier decisions have been overruled everywhere else.[14] It is now held that in the ab-

sence of statute the bailment is not sufficient in itself to impute the contributory negligence of the bailee, and that the bailor will be charged with such negligence only where there are additional factors which would make him liable to a third person as a defendant.[15] The negligence of the bailee will bar his recovery for any damage to his own interest, but will not prevent a recovery by the bailor.[16] A similar result has been reached in the case of various analogous legal relations, such as conditional sales.[17] In some states, however, statutes making the owner of an automobile liable as a defendant for the negligence of one driving with his consent have been construed to impute also the contributory negligence of the driver,[18] although other courts have refused to give their statutes such an interpretation.

203. When the parent receives such funds, he is regarded as a trustee for the infant. Bedford v. Bedford, 1891, 136 Ill. 354, 26 N.E. 662.

9. See infra, § 125.

10. See infra, § 127.

11. Forks Township v. King, 1877, 84 Pa. 230; Texas & Pac. R. Co. v. Tanskersley, 1885, 63 Tex. 57; Illinois Cent. R. Co., v. Sims, 1899, 77 Miss. 325, 27 So. 527; Welty v. Indianapolis & V. R. Co., 1886, 105 Ind. 55, 4 N.E. 410.

12. Gregory, Vicarious Responsibility and Contributory Negligence, 1932, 41 Yale L.J. 831, 834; Reno, Imputed Contributory Negligence in Automobile Bailments, 1934, 82 U.Pa.L.Rev. 213; Notes, 1930, 78 U.Pa.L.Rev. 1009; 1930, 24 Ill.L.Rev. 603; 1930, 5 Temple L.Q. 129. It should be recalled that originally the bailor could not maintain the action at all, and all damages must be recovered by the bailee. See Holmes, The Common Law, 1881, 164 ff.; Bordwell, Property in Chattels, 1916, 29 Harv. L.Rev. 731.

13. Rose v. Baker, 1942, 138 Tex. 554, 160 S.W.2d 515; Socony Mobil Oil Co. v. Slater, Tex.Civ.App. 1967, 412 S.W. 349.

14. The leading case is New York, L. E. & W. R. Co. v. New Jersey Elec. R. Co., 1897, 60 N.J.L. 338, 38 A. 828, affirmed 61 N.J.Law 287, 41 A. 1116. Accord: Fisher v. Andrews & Pierce, 1950, 76 R.I. 464, 72 A.2d 172; White v. Saunders, 1942, 289 Ky. 268, 158 S.W.2d 393; Robinson v. Warren, 1930, 129 Me.

172, 151 A. 10; Nash v. Lang, 1929, 268 Mass. 407, 167 N.E. 762; Jones v. Taylor, Mo.App.1966, 401 S. W.2d 183; Second Restatement of Torts, § 489.

15. Howle v. McDaniel, 1957, 232 S.C. 125, 101 S.E.2d 255; Eggerding v. Bicknell, 1955, 20 N.J. 106, 118 A.2d 820; Seibly v. City of Sunnyside, 1934, 178 Wash. 632, 35 P.2d 56; English v. Stevens, 1952, 35 Tenn.App. 557, 249 S.W.2d 908; Asher v. Fox, E.D. Ky.1955, 134 F.Supp. 27.

16. In the bailor's action, the defendant and the bailee are merely co-tortfeasors, neither of whom can found a defense on the negligence of the other. Wellwood v. King, [1921] 2 Ir.Rep. 290; New York, L. E. & W. R. Co. v. New Jersey Electric Ry. Co., 1897, 60 N.J.L. 338, 38 A. 828. If the bailee sues first and recovers the entire damages, the bailor's action will be barred, as the defendant cannot be required to pay twice. Lord Stone & Co. v. Buchanan, 1897, 69 Vt. 320, 37 A. 1048; Knight v. Davis Carriage Co., 5 Cir. 1896, 71 F. 662. But a judgment for the defendant on the basis of the contributory negligence of the bailee is not binding upon the bailor. Peck v. Merchants' Transfer & Storage Co., of Topeka, 1911, 85 Kan. 126, 116 P. 365; Standard Foundry Co. v. Schloss, 1891, 43 Mo.App. 304.

17. Commercial Credit Corp. v. Satterthwaite, 1930, 107 N.J.L. 17, 150 A. 235, affirmed, 1931, 108 N.J.L. 188, 154 A. 769; Lacey v. Great Northern R. Co., 1924, 70 Mont. 346, 225 P. 808 (conditional sales); Contos v. Jamison, 1908, 81 S.C. 488, 62 S.E. 867 (tenant and landlord); Higgins v. Los Angeles Gas & Elec. Co., 1911, 159 Cal. 651, 115 P. 313 (real property mortgage).

18. See supra, p. 486.

CHAPTER 13

STRICT LIABILITY

75. BASIS OF LIABILITY

As we have seen,[1] the early law of torts was not concerned primarily with the moral responsibility, or "fault" of the wrongdoer. It occupied itself chiefly with keeping the peace between individuals, by providing a remedy which would be accepted in lieu of private vengeance.[2] While it is probable that even from the beginning the idea of moral guilt never was entirely absent from the minds of the judges,[3] it was not the most important consideration. Originally the man who hurt another by pure accident,[4] or in self-defense,[5] was required to make good the damage inflicted. "In all civil acts," it was said, "the law doth not so much regard the intent of the actor, as the loss and damage of the party suffering."[6] There was, in other words, a rule, undoubtedly supported by the general feeling in the community, that "he who breaks must pay."

Until about the close of the nineteenth century, the history of the law of torts was that of a slow, and somewhat unsteady,[7] progress toward the recognition of "fault" or moral responsibility as the basis of the remedy.[8] With a growing moral consciousness in the community, there was a general movement in the direction of identifying legal liability with conduct which would not be expected of a good citizen.[9] This tendency was so marked that efforts were made by noted writers to construct a consistent theory of tort law upon the basic principle that there should be no liability without fault.[10]

But "fault," in this sense never has become quite synonymous with moral blame. Not only is a great deal of morally reprehensible conduct vested with complete legal immunity—as where the expert swimmer who sees another drowning before his eyes is permitted to stand on the dock and watch

---

1. Supra, p. 17.

2. Holmes, The Common Law, 1881, 2, 3.

3. Winfield, The Myth of Absolute Liability, 1926, 42 L.Q.Rev. 37.

4. See supra, § 29.

5. 1319, Y.B. 12 Ed. II, 381.

6. Lambert v. Bessey, 1681, T.Ray. 421, 83 Eng.Rep. 220. As late as 1783, "Erskine said in his argument in the celebrated case of The Dean of St. Asaph [21 St.Tr. 1022] (and he said it by way of a familiar illustration of the difference between civil and criminal liability) that 'if a man rising in his sleep walks into a china shop and breaks everything about him, his being asleep is a complete answer to an *indictment* for trespass, but he must answer in an *action* for everything he has broken.'" Pollock, Law of Torts, 13th Ed.1929, 146.

7. Isaacs, Fault and Liability, 1918, 31 Harv.L.Rev. 954, 966, contends that the law has moved in cycles, alternating periods of strict liability with liability based on fault.

8. Wigmore, Responsibility for Tortious Acts: Its History, 1894, 7 Harv.L.Rev. 315, 383, 441.

9. Ames, Law and Morals, 1908, 22 Harv.L.Rev. 97.

10. Holmes, The Common Law, 1881, 144–163; Salmond, Law of Torts, 7th Ed.1924, 11–12; Smith, Tort and Absolute Liability, 1917, 30 Harv.L.Rev. 241, 319, 409.

him drown—[11] but at the same time the law finds "fault" in much that is morally innocent. "Fault" is a failure to live up to an ideal of conduct to which no one conforms always and which may be beyond the capacity of the individual. It may consist of sheer ignorance [12] lack of intelligence [13] or an honest mistake.[14] It may consist even in acts which are the normal and usual thing in the community.[15] Even the infant and the lunatic[16] who cannot help what they do are held liable for their torts.

So much can be collected in the way of cases imposing liability without any vestige of moral blame that a number of writers [17] have maintained that negligence is rapidly losing, if it has not entirely lost, its character as a branch of "fault" liability, so that those who are entirely innocent are now required to pay for the damage they do, and that negligence should therefore largely be jettisoned. This perhaps begs the question, by assigning to "fault" a criminal law connotation of moral blame which it seldom has been given in the law of torts. There is a broader sense in which "fault" means nothing more than a departure from a standard of conduct required of a man by society for the protection of his neighbors; [18] and if the departure is an innocent one, and the defendant cannot help it, it is none the less a departure, and a social wrong. The distinction still remains between the man who has deviated from the standard, and the man who has not. The defendant may not be to blame for being out of line with what society requires of him, but he is none the less out of line.

In this broader sense there is "fault" in much innocent conduct. Tort liability never has been inconsistent with the ignorance which is bliss, or the good intentions with which hell is said to be paved. A trespasser is not excused by the honest, reasonable belief that the land is his own; [19] a bona fide purchaser of stolen goods is held liable for conversion; [20] the publisher of a libel commits a tort, although he has no means of knowing the defamatory nature of his words.[21] There are many situations in which a careful person is held liable for an entirely reasonable mistake.[22] In all this there is nothing new. Socially, and legally, these defendants are at fault; whether they are individually so, in spite of the fact that they are blameless, appears to be entirely a mat-

11. Yania v. Bigan, 1959, 397 Pa. 316, 155 A.2d 343; Osterlind v. Hill, 1928, 263 Mass. 73, 160 N.E. 301. See supra, p. 340.

12. Michigan City v. Rudolph, 1938, 104 Ind.App. 643, 12 N.E.2d 970; Note, 1939, 23 Minn.L.Rev. 628. See supra, p. 157.

13. Worthington v. Mencer, 1892, 96 Ala. 310, 11 So. 72. See supra, p. 152.

14. The Germanic, 1905, 196 U.S. 589.

15. Ault v. Hall, 1928, 119 Ohio St. 422, 164 N.E. 518; Marsh Wood Products Co. v. Babcock & Wilcox Co., 1932, 207 Wis. 209, 240 N.W. 392; Grant v. Graham Chero-Cola Bottling Co., 1918, 176 N.C. 256, 97 S.E. 27.

16. See infra, §§ 134, 135.

17. Ehrenzweig, Negligence Without Fault, 1951; Leflar, Negligence in Name Only, 1952, 27 N.Y.U.L. Rev. 564; McNiece and Thornton, Is the Law of Negligence Obsolete, 1952, 26 St.Johns L.Rev. 255; James, Accident Proneness and Accident Law, 1950, 63 Harv.L.Rev. 769.

18. "In fact, legal fault upon which liability is based has little connection with personal morality or with justice to the individual; it is always tinctured with a supposed expediency in shifting the loss from one harmed to one who has caused the harm by acting below the standard imposed by the courts or legislators." Seavey, Speculations as to "Respondeat Superior," Harvard Legal Essays, 1934, 433, 442.

19. Loewenberg v. Rosenthal, 1899, 18 Or. 178, 22 P. 601; Hazelton v. Week, 1880, 49 Wis. 661, 6 N.W. 309; Perry v. Jefferies, 1901, 61 S.C. 292, 39 S.E. 515.

20. Stephens v. Elwall, 1815, 4 M. & S. 259, 105 Eng. Rep. 830; Hyde v. Noble, 1843, 13 N.H. 494. See supra, p. 84.

21. Hulton & Co. v. Jones, [1909] 2 K.B. 444, [1910] A.C. 20; Taylor v. Hearst, 1895, 107 Cal. 262, 40 P. 392; Washington Post Co. v. Kennedy, 1924, 55 App.D.C. 162, 3 F.2d 207.

22. Gill v. Selling, 1928, 125 Or. 587, 267 P. 812; Holmes v. Blyler, 1890, 80 Iowa 365, 45 N.W. 756. See supra, § 17.

ter of definition, rather than substance, and the argument leads only to a pointless dispute over the meaning of a word.[23]

Strict Liability

But even beyond all this, the last hundred years have witnessed the overthrow of the doctrine of "never any liability without fault," even in the legal sense of a departure from reasonable standards of conduct. It has seen a general acceptance of the principle that in some cases the defendant may be held liable, although he is not only charged with no moral wrongdoing, but has not even departed in any way from a reasonable standard of intent or care. In some instances, as where liability is imposed upon the keepers of animals,[24] new reasons of social policy have been found for the continuance of an older rule of strict liability. In others, involving abnormally dangerous conditions or activities,[25] the courts have in effect recognized a new doctrine, that the defendant's enterprise, while it will be tolerated by the

law, must pay its way.[26] There is "a strong and growing tendency, where there is blame on neither side, to ask, in view of the exigencies of social justice, who can best bear the loss and hence to shift the loss by creating liability where there has been no fault." [27] An entire field of legislation, illustrated by the workmen's compensation acts,[28] has been based upon the same principle.

This new policy frequently has found expression where the defendant's activity is unusual and abnormal in the community, and the danger which it threatens to others is unduly great—and particularly where the danger will be great even though the enterprise is conducted with every possible precaution. The basis of the liability is the defendant's intentional behavior in exposing those in his vicinity to such a risk. The conduct which is dealt with here occupies something of a middle ground. It is conduct which does not so far depart from social standards as to fall within the traditional boundaries of negligence—usually because the advantages which it offers to the defendant and to the community outweigh even the abnormal risk; but

---

23. "To be of any service as a test of liability, fault must be used in its actual, its subjective meaning of some conduct repugnant to accepted moral or ethical ideals or some act or omission falling below the standard of conduct required of society of its members. It is possible to state all liabilities in terms of fault, to say that one is legally, if not morally or socially, in fault, wherever the law holds him liable.

"Compare Jaco v. Baker, 1944, 174 Or. 191, 148 P.2d 938, where the intentional creation of the risk involved in keeping a vicious dog was held to be sufficient "malice" to prevent a discharge under the Bankruptcy Act. But this is reasoning in a vicious circle. It involves as the premise, the assumption of the very point in dispute, that legal liability cannot exist without fault. The reasoning is this, there can be no legal liability without fault, the defendant is liable, therefore he is at fault, if not actually at least legally. Not only is such reasoning vicious as reasoning, but, by confounding liability and fault, it destroys all value of fault as an element determinative of liability." Bohlen, The Rule in Rylands v. Fletcher, 1911, 59 U.Pa.L.Rev. 298, 313.

24. See infra, § 76.

25. See infra, § 78.

26. The theory is developed at length in Ehrenzweig, Negligence Without Fault, 1951.

27. See Pound, The End of Law as Developed in Legal Rules and Doctrines, 1914, 27 Harv.L.Rev. 195, 233; Bohlen, The Rule in Rylands v. Fletcher, 1911, 59 U.Pa.L.Rev. 298; Harris, Liability Without Fault, 1932, 6 Tulane L.Rev. 337; Carpenter, The Doctrine of Green v. General Petroleum Corporation, 1932, 5 So.Cal.L.Rev. 263; Stallybrass, Dangerous Things and the Non-Natural Use of Land, 1929, 3 Camb.L.J. 376; Feezer, Capacity to Bear Loss as a Factor in the Decision of Certain Types of Tort Cases, 1930, 78 U.Pa.L.Rev. 805, 1931, 79 U. Pa.L.Rev. 742; James, Some Reflections on the Bases of Strict Liability, 1958, 18 La.L.Rev. 293; Ognall, Some Facets of Strict Tortious Liability in the United States and Their Implications, 1958, 33 Notre Dame L. 239. As to similar developments on the continent, see Takayanagi, Liability Without Fault in the Modern Civil and Common Law, 1921–1923, 16 Ill.L.Rev. 163, 268; 17 Ill.L.Rev. 185, 416.

28. Smith, Sequel to Workmen's Compensation Acts, 1914, 27 Harv.L.Rev. 235; Bohlen, The Drafting of Workmen's Compensation Acts, 1912, 25 Harv.L. Rev. 544. See infra, § 80.

which is still so far socially unreasonable that the defendant is not allowed to carry it on without making good any actual harm which it does to his neighbors.

The courts have tended to lay stress upon the fact that the defendant is acting for his own purposes, and is seeking a benefit or a profit of his own from such activities, and that he is in a better position to administer the unusual risk by passing it on to the public than is the innocent victim. The problem is dealt with as one of allocating a more or less inevitable loss to be charged against a complex and dangerous civilization, and liability is imposed upon the party best able to shoulder it. The defendant is held liable merely because, as a matter of social adjustment, the conclusion is that the responsibility should be his. This modern attitude, which is largely a thing of the last four decades, is of course a far cry from the individualistic viewpoint of the common law courts.

While such strict liability often is said to be imposed "without fault," it can scarcely be said that there is less of a moral point of view involved in the rule that one who innocently causes harm should make it good. The traditional analysis regards such a result as something of an exception to more or less well established rules, and says that the defendant is not at "fault" because he has only done a reasonable thing in a reasonable way, and that he is liable notwithstanding.[29] But it may be questioned whether "fault," with its popular connotation of personal guilt and moral blame, and its more or less arbitrary legal meaning, which will vary with the requirements of social conduct imposed by the law,[30] is of any real assistance in dealing with such questions, except perhaps as a descriptive term. It might be quite as easy to say

that one who conducts blasting operations which may injure his neighbor is at "fault" in conducting them at all,[31] and is privileged to do so only in so far as he insures that no harm shall result, as to say that he is not at fault, but is liable nevertheless. If he is not "at fault" because the social desirability of the blasting justifies the risk,[32] his conduct is still so far socially questionable that it does not justify immunity. The basis of his liability in either case is the creation of an undue risk of harm to other members of the community.[33] It has been said [34] that there is "conditional fault," meaning that the defendant is not to be regarded as at fault unless or until his conduct causes some harm to others, but he is then at fault, and to be held responsible. If this analysis helps anyone, it is certainly as permissible as another.[35]

29. Smith, Tort and Absolute Liability, 1917, 30 Harv.L.Rev. 241, 319, 409; Harper, Law of Torts, 1933, §§ 155, 203.

30. Seavey, Speculations as to "Respondeat Superior," Harvard Legal Essays, 1934, 433, 435–442.

31. See Smith, Liability for Substantial Physical Damage to Land by Blasting, 1920, 33 Harv.L.Rev. 542, 549. Compare the view that liability for the keeping of vicious animals is based on negligence, 2 Cooley, Torts, 3d Ed.1906, ch. XI; also the view that Rylands v. Fletcher, 1868, L.R. 3 H.L. 330, could have been decided upon grounds of negligence. 1 Street, Foundations of Legal Liability, 1906, 62, 63; Smith, Tort and Absolute Liability, 1917, 30 Harv.L.Rev. 409, 414, n. 23; Bishop, Non-Contract Law, 1889, § 839; see Thayer, Liability Without Fault, 1916, 29 Harv.L.Rev. 801. See also the conclusion in Salmond, Law of Torts, 8th Ed.1934, 596–599, that there is no sufficient reason for any line of demarcation between strict liability and negligence; also the editorial comment in [1928] 4 Dom.L.Rep.No. 3, and the ensuing controversy between A. L. MacDonald and V. C. MacDonald in 1929, 7 Can.Bar Rev. 140, 208, 330.

32. Harper, Law of Torts, 1933, 203.

33. Harper, The Foreseeability Factor in the Law of Torts, 1932, 7 Notre Dame Lawyer 468.

34. Keeton, Conditional Fault in the Law of Torts, 1959, 72 Harv.L.Rev. 401.

35. It has often been said that strict liability arises from conduct which is so far legitimate that it will not be enjoined, but it will make the defendant liable when it causes damage. The writer has been unable to trace the origin of this notion; but since there appears to be nothing whatever to support it, it may have come from a law professor. Decisions are not lacking in which conduct has been enjoined on the ground that it would entail strict liability.

Once the legal concept of "fault" is divorced, as it has been, from the personal standard of moral wrongdoing, there is a sense in which liability with or without "fault" must beg its own conclusion. The term requires such extensive definition, that it seems better not to make use of it at all, and to refer instead to strict liability, apart from either wrongful intent or negligence.

76. ANIMALS

Primitive law tended to hold the owner of property strictly liable for the harm it did. The owner of a slave, an animal, or even an inanimate thing, was so far identified with his chattel that he was liable, without any fault of his own, for the damage it might inflict on his neighbors.[36] It is characteristic of certain stages of development in all legal systems of which we have knowledge, that he might escape liability by surrendering the harmful agent itself, either to the injured party or to the crown.[37] The present state of the common law may be said to begin with the disappearance of this "noxal surrender" and the rule of strict liability for harm done by harmless things. So far as the responsibility of keepers of animals is concerned, the survival of the primitive notion of strict liability has been due in part to modern views of policy. Certain kinds of animals involve an obvious danger to the community, even if they are carefully kept; everyone knows the propensity of cattle and horses to escape and roam and do mischief,[38] and a bear or an elephant [39] can never be regarded as safe. Those who keep such animals for their own purposes are required to protect the community, at their peril, against the risk involved. The strict liability is, in general, co-extensive with the obvious risk.

Trespassing Animals

It was said in an early case [40] that "where my beasts of their own wrong without my will and knowledge break another's close I shall be punished, for I am the trespasser with my beasts * * * for I am held by the law to keep my beasts without their doing wrong to anyone." The action was in trespass rather than case,[41] but the liability was similar to that of a defendant who had trespassed in person.[42] While this primitive idea of the identity of the owner with the animal has vanished, it remains the common law in most jurisdictions that the keeper of animals of a kind likely to roam and do damage is strictly liable for their trespasses.

See for example Attorney-General v. Cory Bros., [1921] 1 A.C. 521; Attorney-General v. Corke, [1933] Ch. 89; Gas Light & Coke Co. v. Vestry of St. Mary Abbott's, 1885, 15 Q.B.D. 1; Jones v. Llanrwst Urban District Council, [1911] 1 Ch. 393; Snow v. Whitehead, 1884, 27 Ch. Div. 588; Mallett v. Taylor, 1915, 78 Or. 208, 152 P. 873. And as to denying injunction even where there is clear fault, see McClintock, Discretion to Deny Injunction Against Trespass and Nuisance, 1928, 12 Minn.L. Rev. 565; Walsh, Equity, 1930, 284–298.

36. There is a controversy as to whether this was the earliest rule, or a somewhat later development. See Williams, Liability for Animals, 1939; Holmes, The Common Law, 1881, 15–24; Wigmore, Responsibility for Tortious Acts: Its History, 1894, 7 Harv.L.Rev. 315, 352 et seq.; 2 Pollock and Maitland, History of English Law, 2d Ed. 1911, 472 et seq.

37. 1 Street, Foundations of Legal Liability, 1906, 50; 2 Pollock and Maitland, History of English Law, 2d Ed. 1911, 473. As late as 1842, in Regina v. Eastern Counties R. Co., 10 M. & W. 58, 152 Eng.Rep. 380, a railway engine which had run over a man was forfeited as a deodand.

38. Page v. Hollingsworth, 1855, 7 Ind. 317; Gresham v. Taylor, 1874, 51 Ala. 505.

39. Crunk v. Glover, 1959, 167 Neb. 816, 95 N.W.2d 135; Filburn v. People's Palace & Aquarium Co., 1890, L.R. 25 Q.B.D. 258.

40. 12 Hen. VII, Keilwey 3b, 72 Eng.Rep. 156. This was repeated in substance in Wells v. Howell, 1822, 19 Johns, N.Y. 385. In Tonawanda R. Co. v. Munger, 1848, 5 Denio, N.Y., 255, affirmed, 1850, 4 N.Y. 349 it was added that there is absolute liability for the trespass of cattle even though the defendant has exercised all ordinary care and prudence in taking care of them.

41. See 27 Lib.Assis. pl. 56.

42. See supra, § 13.

This has been true in the case of cattle,[43] horses,[44] sheep,[45] hogs,[46] and such wandering fowls as turkeys, chickens and pigeons;[47] and also, no doubt, to any kept wild animals of a kind likely to escape, trespass and do damage.[48] On the other hand, in the case of such domestic favorites as dogs[49] and cats,[50] nearly all courts have refused to impose strict liability for the trespass, although such liability may be rested upon knowledge on the part of the owner of any mischievous propensity.[51]

This is perhaps to be traced to the old rule, long since discarded, that the owner could have no property right in such "base" animals;[52] but the justification now given is, together with the community custom to allow such animals to wander, that their trespasses are likely to be trivial and to do no serious harm, so that there is no necessity for protection against anything more than negligence.[53] This justification has been criticized[54] as unlikely to appeal to adjoining owners of flower beds and poultry; and statutes in many states have imposed strict liability for all damages done by dogs.[55]

In earlier days in the United States, many courts rejected entirely the rule of strict liability for animal trespasses, as contrary to established local custom, particularly in western country where cattle were allowed to graze at large on the range.[56] This view still prevails in some parts of our western states. But as the country has become more closely settled, the tendency has been to restore the common law rule, either by statute or by decision.[57] The matter is now very largely governed by statutory provisions. The first leg-

43. McKee v. Trisler, 1924, 311 Ill. 536, 143 N.E. 69; Page v. Hollingsworth, 1855, 7 Ind. 317; Angus v. Radin, 1820, 5 N.J.L. 815; Stackpole v. Healy, 1819, 16 Mass. 33.

44. Decker v. Gammon, 1857, 44 Me. 322; Morgan v. Hudnell, 1895, 52 Ohio St. 552, 40 N.E. 716; Ellis v. Loftus Iron Co., 1874, L.R. 10 C.P. 10.

45. Theyer v. Purnell, [1918] 2 K.B. 333; see Marsh v. Hand, 1890, 120 N.Y. 315, 24 N.E. 463.

46. Gresham v. Taylor, 1874, 51 Ala. 505. See, as to trespassing animals generally, Notes, 1919, 32 Harv.L.Rev. 420; 1949, 34 Iowa L.Rev. 318.

47. McPherson v. James, 1896, 69 Ill.App. 337; Lapp v. Stanton, 1911, 116 Md. 197, 81 A. 675; Adams Bros. v. Clark, 1920, 189 Ky. 279, 224 S.W. 1046; Taylor v. Granger, 1896, 19 R.I. 410, 34 A. 153, 37 A. 13; see Tate v. Ogg, 1938, 170 Va. 95, 195 S.E. 496. But see contra, repudiating the common law rule as not applicable to the customs of the state: Kimple v. Schafer, 1913, 161 Iowa 659, 143 N.W. 505; Evans v. McLalin, 1915, 189 Mo.App. 310, 175 S.W. 294. See Notes, 1924, 9 Va.L.Reg.,N.S., 481; 1921, 19 Mich.L.Rev. 422.

48. King v. Blue Mountain Forest Ass'n, 1956, 100 N.H. 212, 123 A.2d 151 (wild boar).

49. Sanders v. Teape & Swan, 1884, 51 L.T. 263; Van Etten v. Noyes, 1908, 128 App.Div. 406, 112 N.Y.S. 888; Blair v. Forehand, 1838, 100 Mass. 136; McDonald v. Castle, 1925, 116 Okl. 46, 243 P. 215; Olson v. Pederson, 1939, 206 Minn. 415, 288 N.W. 856. Otherwise where the owner is himself responsible for the trespass, as in the case of fox hunting. Pegg v. Gray, 1954, 240 N.C. 548, 82 S.E.2d 757; Baker v. Howard County Hunt, 1936, 171 Md. 159, 188 A. 223, (negligence). See Note, 1954, 33 N.C.L. Rev. 134.

50. Buckle v. Holmes, [1926] 2 K.B. 125; McDonald v. Jodry, 1890, 8 Pa.Co.Ct. 142; see Bischoff v. Cheney, 1914, 89 Conn. 1, 92 A. 660. See Alderman, Legal Status of the Cat, 1917, 20 Law Notes 204; Hibschman, The Cat and the Law, 1937, 12 Temple L.Q. 89; Note, 1928, 13 Corn.L.Q. 150.

51. See infra, p. 501.

52. Mason v. Keeling, 1691, 12 Mod. 332, 1 Ld.Raym. 606, 88 Eng.Rep. 1359.

53. Buckle v. Holmes, [1926] 2 K.B. 125; McDonald v. Castle, 1925, 116 Okl. 46, 243 P. 215.

54. See Note, 1928, 13 Corn.L.Q. 150.

55. See for example Granniss v. Weber, 1928, 107 Conn. 622, 141 A. 877. Three courts have reached the same result, as to trespassing dogs, at common law. Chunot v. Larson, 1868, 43 Wis. 536; Doyle v. Vance, 1880, 6 Vict.L.Rep. 87; McClain v. Lewiston Interstate Fair & Racing Ass'n, 1909, 17 Idaho 63, 104 P. 1015.

56. Delaney v. Errickson, 1880, 10 Neb. 492, 6 N.W. 300, reversed on other grounds, 1881, 11 Neb. 533, 10 N.W. 451; Wagner v. Bissell, 1856, 3 Iowa 396; Beinhorn v. Griswold, 1902, 27 Mont. 79, 69 P. 557; Overbey v. Poteat, 1960, 206 Tenn. 146, 332 S.W.2d 197.

57. Phillips v. Bynum, 1906, 145 Ala. 549, 39 So. 911; Bulpit v. Matthews, 1893, 145 Ill. 345, 34 N.E. 525; Puckett v. Young, 1901, 112 Ga. 578, 37 S.E. 880; Gumm v. Jones, 1906, 115 Mo.App. 597, 92 S.W. 169; Nelson v. Tanner, 1948, 113 Utah 293, 194 P.2d 468.

islation to be adopted consisted of "fencing out" statutes, which provided that if the plaintiff properly fenced his land there was strict liability when the animals broke through the fence, but otherwise there was liability only when the owner was at fault.[58] As the country became more settled, the conflict between the grazing and the agricultural interests resulted in many states in "fencing in" statutes, which required the owner of the animals to fence or otherwise restrain them, and made him strictly liable if he did not do so.[59] Sometimes the final step was taken, by legislation restoring the common law rule. In a good many states individual counties are permitted to choose the rule that they wish to apply, so that the law varies in different parts of the state. It is of course generally agreed that there is liability for any negligence leading to the animal trespass.[60]

One exception to the common law rule which the courts were compelled to recognize early[61] was the case of animals straying from a highway on which they were being driven lawfully.[62] While the owner would be liable for any negligence in failing to control them, or to pursue them promptly and bring

them back,[63] the privilege to make use of the highway to move them from one place to another[64] involves, as a more or less inevitable incident, immunity as to any casual trespass on adjoining lands by the way.[65] But the privilege extends only to property immediately abutting on the highway, and not to any lands removed from it, upon which the cattle may trespass once they have strayed from the road.[66] On the highway itself, even an escaped animal is not a trespasser, and there is no strict liability for any harm which it may do upon that basis.[67]

The foundation of the strict liability is commonly said to be possession and the power of control of the animals. Thus one whose lands are crossed, without his consent, by the cattle of another before they enter the plaintiff's land, is not liable for the trespass.[68] But

58. See for example Buford v. Houtz, 1890, 133 U.S. 320; Garcia v. Sumrall, 1942, 58 Ariz. 526, 121 P.2d 640; Osborne v. Osmer, 1927, 82 Colo. 80, 256 P. 1092; Johnston v. Mack Mfg. Co., 1909, 65 W.Va. 544, 64 S.E. 841. In Robinson v. Kerr, 1960, 144 Colo. 48, 355 P.2d 117, it was held that such a statute applied only to damage to land, and not to personal injuries inflicted by a trespassing horse.

58. See also, at common law, Johnson v. Robinson, 1968, 11 Mich.App. 707, 162 N.W.2d 161.

59. See for example Arizona Code Ann., 1949, § 50–606.

60. Howland v. Cressy, 1948, 95 N.H. 205, 60 A.2d 128; Lyons v. Merrick, 1870, 105 Mass. 71; Grimes v. Eddy, 1894, 126 Mo. 168, 28 S.W. 756.

61. Harvy v. Gulson, 1604, Noy 107, 74 Eng.Rep. 1072.

62. The rule has no application when cattle are at large unlawfully upon the highway. Stackpole v. Healy, 1819, 16 Mass. 33; Avery v. Maxwell, 1827, 4 N.H. 36; Harrison v. Brown, 1856, 5 Wis. 27.

63. Goodwyn v. Cheveley, 1859, 4 H. & N. 631, 157 Eng.Rep. 989; Erdman v. Gottshall, 1899, 9 Pa.Super. 295; Wood v. Snider, 1907, 187 N.Y. 28, 79 N. E. 858. Cf. Bender v. Welsh, 1942, 344 Pa. 392, 25 A.2d 182.

64. Including, at common law, the privilege to drive them through city streets. Tillett v. Ward, 1882, L.R. 10 Q.B. 17 (no liability to shop owner). It may be suggested that, even if not forbidden by ordinance, this might now be negligence in large cities.

65. Goodwyn v. Cheveley, 1859, 4 H. & N. 631, 157 Eng.Rep. 989; Rightmire v. Shepard, 1891, 36 St.R. 768, 59 Hun 620, 12 N.Y.S. 800; Cool v. Crommet, 1836, 13 Me. 250; Hartford v. Brady, 1874, 114 Mass. 466; Boutwell v. Champlain Realty Co., 1915, 89 Vt. 80, 94 A. 108.

66. Wood v. Snider, 1907, 187 N.Y. 28, 79 N.E. 858; McDonnell v. Pittsfield & N. A. R. Corp., 1874, 115 Mass. 564.

67. Gardner v. Black, 1940, 217 N.C. 573, 9 S.E.2d 10; Eddy v. Union R. Co., 1903, 25 R.I. 451, 56 A. 677; Bombard v. Newton, 1920, 94 Vt. 354, 111 A. 510. There may, however, be liability for negligence in looking after the animal. Deen v. Davies, [1935] 2 K.B. 282; Shaw v. Joyce, 1959, 249 N.C. 415, 106 S.E.2d 459; Traill v. Ostermeier, 1941, 140 Neb. 432, 300 N.W. 375. Or strict liability on the basis of scienter as to dangerous traits. See infra, p. 501.

68. Lawrence v. Combs, 1858, 37 N.H. 331; Hanson v. Northern Pac. R. Co., 1916, 90 Wash. 516, 156 P. 553; Little v. McGuire, 1876, 43 Iowa 447.

a bailee to whom they are delivered becomes strictly responsible for their escape.[69] Whether the owner is also liable in such a case is a matter on which the courts have not agreed. There is authority that his duty of keeping the animals safe is so absolute that he cannot delegate it to another.[70] Such a view may be appropriate to the ownership of such a dangerous beast as a tiger,[71] but it is scarcely called for in the case of animals so relatively harmless and so easily restrained as cattle. It seems the better conclusion that the owner is relieved of responsibility by the bailment.[72]

The consequences of the trespass for which the defendant will be held liable are more appropriately considered at a later point.[73]

Liability Apart from Trespass

Strict liability for damage done by dangerous animals, apart from any trespass on land, is of very ancient origin, but finds its first modern statement in 1846, in the English case of May v. Burdett,[74] where the plaintiff was bitten by the defendant's monkey. It has been thought [75] to rest on the basis of negligence in keeping the animal at all; but this does not coincide with the modern analysis of negligence as conduct which is unreasonable in view of the risk, since it may not be an unreasonable thing to keep even a tiger in a zoo. It is rather an instance of the strict responsibility placed upon those who, even with proper care, expose the community to the risk of a very dangerous thing. While two or three jurisdictions insist that there is no liability without some negligence in keeping the animal,[76] by far the greater number impose strict liability.

"Dangerous" animals requires definition. It means, in general, animals which are known in fact, or which must necessarily be known, by the one who keeps them to be likely to inflict serious damage. A distinction has been made between animals which, by reason of their species, are by nature ferocious, mischievous or intractable, and those of a species normally harmless. In the first category are lions and tigers,[77] bears,[78]

69. Moulton v. Moore, 1884, 56 Vt. 700; Tewksbury v. Bucklin, 1835, 7 N.H. 518; Van Slyck v. Snell, 1872, 6 Lans., N.Y., 299.

70. 1638, 2 Rolle Abr. 526(b) 1; Sheridan v. Bean, 1844, 8 Metc., Mass., 284; Blaisdell v. Stone, 1881, 60 N.H. 507; Weymmouth v. Gile, 1882, 72 Me. 446; see Marsh v. Hand, 1890, 120 N.Y. 315, 24 N. E. 463.

71. See infra, p. 500.

72. Rossell v. Cottom, 1858, 31 Pa. 525; Reddick v. Newburn, 1882, 76 Mo. 423; Ward v. Brown, 1872, 64 Ill. 307; Mott v. Scott, 1905, 35 Colo. 68, 83 P. 779; Restatement of Torts, § 504, Comment f. Cf. Reuter v. Swarthout, 1924, 182 Wis. 453, 196 N.W. 847.

73. See infra, p. 518.

74. 1846, 9 Q.B. 101, 115 Eng.Rep. 1213.

75. See Williams, Liability for Animals, 1939, 327; 3 Bl.Comm. 211; 2 Cooley, Torts, 3d Ed. 1906, ch. XI.

76. Vaughan v. Miller Bros. "101" Ranch Wild West Show, 1931, 109 W.Va. 170, 153 S.E. 289; Panorama Resort v. Nichols, 1935, 165 Va. 289, 182 S.E. 235; Hansen v. Brogan, 1965, 145 Mont. 224, 400 P.2d 265. See Note, 1931, 25 Ill.L.Rev. 962. In all of these cases the plaintiff was injured while on the defendant's premises, and the statements made as to the state of the authorities are misleading, to say the least. An attempt was made to add Louisiana in Briley v. Mitchell, La.App.1959, 110 So.2d 169, but this was overruled, and the strict liability reinstated, in Briley v. Mitchell, 1959, 238 La. 551, 115 So.2d 851, on remand, 1960, 119 So.2d 668.

See the excellent analysis in McNeely, A Footnote on Dangerous Animals, 1939, 37 Mich.L.Rev. 1181, concluding that the decisions might be harmonized on the basis of strict liability outside of the keeper's land, but liability only for negligence for harm occurring upon it, because of assumption of risk.

77. Stamp v. Eighty-Sixth St. Amusement Co., 1916, 95 Misc. 599, 159 N.Y.S. 683 (lion); see Opelt v. Al. G. Barnes Co., 1919, 41 Cal.App. 776, 183 P. 241 (leopard).

78. Crunk v. Glover, 1959, 167 Neb. 816, 95 N.W.2d 135; City of Tonkawa v. Danielson, 1933, 166 Okl. 241, 27 P.2d 348; Vredenburg v. Behan, 1881, 33 La.Ann. 627; City of Mangum v. Brownlee, 1938, 181 Okl. 515, 75 P.2d 174; see Bottcher v. Buck, 1928, 265 Mass. 4, 163 N.E. 182; Malloy v. Starin, 1908, 191 N.Y. 21, 83 N.E. 588.

elephants,[79] wolves,[80] and monkeys,[81] and other similar animals.[82] No individual of such a species, however domesticated, can ever be regarded as safe, and liability does not rest upon any experience with the particular animal.[83] In the second class are cattle, sheep, horses, dogs and cats, and other creatures regarded as usually harmless. As to these, it must be shown that the defendant knew, or had reason to know, of a dangerous propensity in the one animal in question.[84] Undoubtedly the customs of the community, and the social utility of keeping the animal in the particular locality, have entered into the classification to a considerable extent, since an elephant is regarded as a safe, domesticated animal in Burma,[85] but a Burmese elephant transported to England is not;[86] and such uncooperative creatures as stallions,[87] mules,[88] bulls[89] and bees,[90] in spite of the known characteristics of their kind, are called harmless, while deer[91] and raccoons[92] have been regarded as inherently dangerous. The emphasis is placed upon the abnormal character of the animal in the particular community, and

---

79. Filburn v. People's Palace & Aquarium Co., 1890, 25 Q.B.D. 258; Behrens v. Bertram Mills Circus, Ltd., [1957] 2 Q.B. 1; see Scribner v. Kelley, 1862, 38 Barb., N.Y. 14.

80. Hayes v. Miller, 1907, 150 Ala. 621, 43 So. 818; Collins v. Otto, 1962, 149 Colo. 489, 369 P.2d 564 (coyote); Temple v. Elvery, Sask., [1926] 3 W.W.R. 652 (cross between Great Dane and coyote).

81. May v. Burdett, 1846, 9 Q.B. 101, 115 Eng.Rep. 1213; Copley v. Wills, Tex.Civ.App.1913, 152 S.W. 830; Phillips v. Garner, 1914, 106 Miss. 828, 64 So. 735; Garelli v. Sterling-Alaska Fur & Game Farms, Inc., 1960, 25 Misc.2d 1032, 206 N.Y.S.2d 130; cf. Candler v. Smith, 1935, 50 Ga.App. 667, 179 S.E. 395 (baboon). But in Abrevaya v. Palace Theatre & Realty Co., 1960, 25 Misc.2d 600, 197 N.Y.S.2d 27, it was held that a domesticated rhesus monkey was not a matter for strict liability in the absence of scienter.

82. Marlor v. Ball, 1900, 16 T.L.R. 239 (zebras); Smith v. Jalbert, 1966, 351 Mass. 432, 221 N.E.2d 744 (same). A humorous extension of the idea is York, In re Wrestlers, 1941, 13 Rocky Mt. L.Rev. 171.

83. Filburn v. People's Palace & Aquarium Co., 1890, 25 Q.B.D. 258, 59 L.J.Q.B. 471; Hayes v. Miller, 1907, 150 Ala. 621, 43 So. 818; Copley v. Wills, Tex.Civ.App.1913, 152 S.W. 830.

84. Talley v. Travelers Ins. Co., La.App.1967, 197 So. 2d 92 (horse) writ refused 250 La. 913, 199 So.2d 920; Berry v. Kegans, 1966, 196 Kan. 388, 411 P.2d 707 (dog); Maxwell v. Fraze, Mo.App.1961, 344 S. W.2d 262 (dog); Mann v. Stanley, 1956, 141 Cal. App.2d 438, 296 P.2d 921 (bull); Pallman v. Great A. & P. Tea Co., 1933, 117 Conn. 667, 167 A. 733 (cat); May Co. v. Drury, 1931, 160 Md. 143, 153 A. 61 (parrot); Olson v. Pederson, 1939, 206 Minn. 415, 288 N.W. 856 (dog); Restatement of Torts, § 518.

85. Maung Kyan Dun v. Ma Kyian, 1900, 2 Upper Burma Rulings, Civ. 570.

86. Behrens v. Bertram Mills Circus, Ltd., [1957] 2 Q.B. 1. Similarly, the Indian buffalo is regarded as "cattle" in India. Madho v. Akaji, 1912, 17 Ind. Cas. 899. But not in Ceylon, where it is said not to be so domesticated as to be "harmless." Anonymous, 1851, Austin's Rep., Ceylon, 153.

Camels, which are now domesticated virtually everywhere they are found, were held not to be "wild" animals in McQuacker v. Goddard, [1940] 1 K.B. 687, and Nada Shah v. Sleeman, 1917, 19 West. Aust.L.Rep. 119; but the contrary was held in Gooding v. Chutes Co., 1909, 155 Cal. 620, 102 P. 819.

87. Hammond v. Melton, 1891, 42 Ill.App. 186.

88. Rector v. Southern Coal Co., 1926, 192 N.C. 804, 136 S.E. 113; Robidoux v. Busch, Mo.App. 1966, 400 S.W.2d 631. See the justly noted remarks of Lamm, J., on the Missouri mule in Lyman v. Dale, 1914, 262 Mo. 353, 360, 171 S.W. 352, 354.

89. Banks v. Maxwell, 1933, 205 N.C. 233, 171 S.E. 70; Mann v. Stanley, 1956, 141 Cal.App.2d 438, 296 P.2d 921. Cf. Yazoo & M. V. R. Co. v. Gordon, 1939, 184 Miss. 885, 186 So. 631 (steer); Young v. Blaum, La.App.1933, 146 So. 168 (male goat); Oakes v. Spaulding, 1867, 40 Vt. 347 (the battering ram). As to this last, see Browne, The Sign of the Ram, 1889, 1 Green Bag 328.

90. Earl v. Van Alstyne, 1850, 8 Barb., N.Y., 630; Parsons v. Manser, 1903, 119 Iowa 88, 93 N.W. 86; Ammons v. Kellogg, 1925, 137 Miss. 551, 102 So. 562.

Thus it has been said that the keeper of such animals is not liable for acts normal to the kind, in the absence of some notice of a special propensity in the individual, or some negligence. Clinton v. Lyons & Co., [1912] 3 K.B. 198; Manton v. Brocklebank, [1923] 2 K.B. 212; Buckle v. Holmes, [1926] 2 K.B. 125; Goodwin v. E. B. Nelson Groc. Co., 1921, 239 Mass. 232, 132 N.E. 51.

91. Congress & Empire Spring Co. v. Edgar, 1879, 99 U.S. 645; Marble v. Ross, 1878, 124 Mass. 44; Briley v. Mitchell, 1959, 238 La. 551, 115 So.2d 851, on remand, 1960, 119 So.2d 668.

92. Andrew v. Kilgour, 1910, 19 Man.L.Rep. 545.

hence the abnormal character of the risk to which the defendant exposes his neighbors, as the justification for creating the strict responsibility. The more offensive members of a species customarily kept, domesticated, and traditionally devoted to the service of mankind are considered as so far sanctioned by common usage that there is no liability merely for keeping such an animal.

The special notice of the character of the particular animal which is required in such a case is known technically as "scienter." It must extend to the trait or propensity which has caused the damage. Notice that a dog or a horse will attack other animals is not necessarily notice that it will attack human beings,[93] and the vicious character of a dog is no notice that it will collide with a man and knock him down.[94] A horse which is difficult to control is not necessarily likely to bite or kick.[95] The strict liability is limited to the particular risk known to the defendant.

But a known tendency to attack others, even in playfulness,[96] as in the case of the overly friendly large dog with a propensity for enthusiastically jumping up on visitors,[97] or to chase motor vehicles,[98] will be enough to make the defendant liable for any damage resulting from such an act.

While the owner may not be liable for a mere failure to discover the traits of his dog,[99] it is sufficient that he has notice of facts which would put a reasonable man on his guard, and he is charged with knowledge of the characteristics that are reasonably apparent to him.[1] Notice that a dog has once bitten a man is ordinarily sufficient to establish scienter that he may do it again,[2] but the often repeated statement that "every dog is entitled to one bite" is not and never has

---

93. Fowler v. Helck, 1939, 278 Ky. 361, 128 S.W.2d 564; Warrick v. Farley, 1914, 95 Neb. 565, 145 N. W. 1020; Keightlinger v. Egan, 1872, 65 Ill. 235; Glanville v. Sutton, [1928] 1 K.B. 571.

In Perkins v. Drury, 1953, 57 N.M. 269, 258 P.2d 379, this together with the fact that the owner kept the dog on a leash and frequently warned others to keep their children away from it was held to justify a finding of scienter. See Note, 1954, 11 Wash. & Lee L.Rev. 119.

94. Koetting v. Conroy, 1936, 223 Wis. 550, 270 N.W. 625, 271 N.W. 369. Cf. Melicker v. Sedlacek, 1920, 189 Iowa 946, 179 N.W. 197 (dog barking at car). The Massachusetts court seems to have carried this entirely too far in holding that notice that a horse will bite is not notice that he will kick. Greeley v. Jameson, 1928, 265 Mass. 465, 164 N.E. 385. See contra, Reynolds v. Hussey, 1886, 64 N.H. 64, 5 A. 458 (frontal attack by horse known to kick); cf. McCullar v. Williams, 1928, 217 Ala. 278, 116 So. 137 (dog attacking in street rather than on premises). Fright at a vicious dog is clearly within the risk. Netusil v. Novak, 1931, 120 Neb. 751, 235 N. W. 335; cf. Candler v. Smith, 1935, 50 Ga.App. 667, 179 S.E. 395. See Note, 1935, 13 Neb.L.B. 422.

95. Webber v. McDonnell, 1926, 254 Mass. 387, 150 N.E. 189; Cockerham v. Nixon, 1850, 11 Ired. 269, 33 N.C. 269. The dangerous trait must be pleaded and proved. F. Giovannozzi & Sons v. Luciani, 1941, 2 Terry, Del., 211, 18 A.2d 435.

96. Evans v. McDermott, 1886, 49 N.J.L. 163, 6 A. 653; Oakes v. Spaulding, 1867, 40 Vt. 347; Mercer v. Marston, 1925, 3 La.App. 97.

97. Crowley v. Groonell, 1901, 73 Vt. 45, 50 A. 546; Groner v. Hedrick, 1961, 403 Pa. 148, 169 A.2d 302; Dansker v. Gelb, Mo.1961, 352 S.W.2d 12. Cf. Russo v. Schieber, 1958, 11 Misc.2d 842, 175 N.Y.S.2d 188, affirmed memo., 1959, 8 App.Div.2d 986, 191 N.Y.S.2d 146, reargument denied and appeal denied, 1959, 9 App.Div.2d 629, 191 N.Y.S.2d 549 (dog lunging out of window); Owen v. Hampson, 1952, 258 Ala. 228, 62 So.2d 245 (running after motor vehicles).

98. Owen v. Hampson, 1952, 258 Ala. 228, 62 So.2d 245. See, generally, Note as to liability in non-bite cases, 1969, 23 U. Miami L.Rev. 848.

99. Domm v. Hollenbeck, 1913, 259 Ill. 382, 102 N.E. 782. But if such failure to discover is unreasonable, it may amount to negligence. Lloyd v. Bowen, 1915, 170 N.C. 216, 86 S.E. 797.

1. Knowles v. Mulder, 1889, 74 Mich. 202, 41 N.W. 896; Butts v. Houston, 1915, 76 W.Va. 604, 86 S.E. 473; Bachman v. Clark, 1916, 128 Md. 245, 97 A. 440; Mungo v. Bennett, 1961, 238 S.C. 79, 119 S.E. 2d 522.

2. Zarek v. Fredericks, 3 Cir. 1943, 138 F.2d 689; Grissom v. Hofius, 1905, 39 Wash. 51, 80 P. 1002; Tubbs v. Shears, 1916, 55 Okl. 610, 155 P. 549; Tamburello v. Jaeger, La.App.1965, 176 So.2d 707, affirmed 249 La. 25, 184 So.2d 544 (horse had kicked two others). But in Chandler v. Vaccaro, 1959, 167 Cal.App.2d 786, 334 P.2d 998, it was held that a bite five years before, with good behavior in the meantime, was not enough.

been the law.[3] It is enough that the dog has manifested a vicious disposition, and a desire to attack or annoy people or other animals.[4] Such knowledge may be inferred from the fact that the dog is kept confined,[5] or even from continued ownership of an animal whose tendencies are obvious,[6] or from its reputation in the neighborhood.[7] Under familiar agency principles, the owner is charged with the knowledge of a servant,[8] or a member of his family,[9] to whom he has entrusted its custody. In some jurisdictions statutes have been enacted imposing absolute liability for certain types of damage done by animals, such as dog bites—usually with an exception made in the case of injuries to trespassers or tortfeasors.[10] And scienter is of course not required where any negligence can be shown in the keeping or control of the animal.[11]

Since the gist of the tort is the keeping of a thing known to be dangerous, one who keeps or harbors an animal owned by another may be liable if he has such knowledge.[12]

3. Mailhot v. Crowe, 1918, 99 Wash. 623, 170 P. 131; Carrow v. Haney, 1920, 203 Mo.App. 485, 219 S.W. 710; Harris v. Williams, 1932, 160 Okl. 103, 15 P.2d 580; Andrews v. Smith, 1936, 324 Pa. 455, 188 A. 146. The statement may perhaps be traced to "the dog has the privilege of one worry," Burton v. Moorhead, 1881, 8 Sess.Cas., 4th Ser., 892.

4. Barger v. Jimerson, 1955, 130 Colo. 459, 276 P.2d 744; Perrotta v. Picciano, 1919, 186 App.Div. 781, 175 N.Y.S. 16; Perazzo v. Ortega, 1927, 32 Ariz. 154, 256 P. 503; Warwick v. Mulvey, 1964, 80 S.D. 511, 127 N.W.2d 433; Davis v. Bedell, 1963, 123 Vt. 441, 194 A.2d 67.

5. Radoff v. Hunter, 1958, 158 Cal.App.2d 770, 323 P.2d 202; Barger v. Jimerson, 1955, 130 Colo. 459, 276 P.2d 744; Shuffian v. Garfola, 1959, 9 App. Div.2d 910, 195 N.Y.S.2d 45. Cf. Perkins v. Drary, 1953, 57 N.M. 269, 258 P.2d 379 (warning children to keep away); Ford v. Steindon, 1962, 35 Misc.2d 339, 232 N.Y.S.2d 473 ("Beware of the Dog").

6. Thompson v. Wold, 1955, 47 Wash.2d 782, 289 P.2d 712; Dauber v. Boyajian, 2 Cir. 1933, 62 F.2d 1002; Stapleton v. Butensky, 1919, 188 App.Div. 237, 177 N.Y.S. 18; Radoff v. Hunter, 1958, 158 Cal.App.2d 770, 323 P.2d 202.

7. Fake v. Addicks, 1890, 45 Minn. 37, 47 N.W. 450; Stewart v. Gwinn, 1924, 136 Miss. 806, 101 So. 689; Hill v. Moseley, 1941, 220 N.C. 485, 17 S.E.2d 676.

See, generally, Note, 1968, 33 Mo.L.Rev. 99.

8. Herbert v. Ziegler, 1958, 216 Md. 212, 139 A.2d 699; Buck v. Brady, 1909, 110 Md. 568, 73 A. 277; Grissom v. Hofius, 1905, 39 Wash. 51, 80 P. 1002; Dauber v. Boyajian, 2 Cir. 1933, 62 F.2d 1002; Restatement of Agency, Second, § 283.

9. Perazzo v. Ortega, 1927, 32 Ariz. 154, 256 P. 503; Harris v. Williams, 1932, 160 Okl. 103, 15 P.2d 580.

10. See McEvoy v. Brown, 1958, 17 Ill.App.2d 470, 150 N.E.2d 652; Tanga v. Tanga, 1967, 94 N.J.Super. 5, 226 A.2d 723; Nelson v. Hansen, 1960, 10 Wis.2d 107, 102 N.W.2d 251; Schonwald v. Tapp, 1955, 142 Conn. 719, 118 A.2d 302; Dragonette v. Brandes, 1939, 135 Ohio St. 223, 20 N.E.2d 367 (leash law). See Hallen, Liability of Dog Owners, 1951, 12 Ohio St.L.J. 343; Notes, 1948, 1 Okl.L. Rev. 110; [1960] Duke L.J. 146.

It has been held that the statute does not abrogate the common law action based on scienter. Reeves v. Eckles, 1966, 77 Ill.App.2d 408, 222 N.E.2d 530. Or negligence. Warner v. Wolfe, 1964, 176 Ohio St. 389, 199 N.E.2d 860.

11. Weaver v. National Biscuit Co., 7 Cir. 1942, 125 F.2d 463; Drew v. Gross, 1925, 112 Ohio St. 485, 147 N.E. 757; Parsons v. Manser, 1903, 119 Iowa 88, 93 N.W. 86; Gardner v. Koenig, 1961, 188 Kan. 135, 360 P.2d 1107; McAbee v. Daniel, 1968, —— Tenn. ——, 445 S.W.2d 917.

12. Missio v. Williams, 1914, 129 Tenn. 504, 167 S.W. 473; Dauber v. Boyajian, 2 Cir. 1933, 62 F.2d 1002; Smith v. Royer, 1919, 181 Cal. 165, 183 P. 660; Harris v. Williams, 1932, 160 Okl. 103, 15 P.2d 580. A corporation may be liable for harboring an animal kept by its employee. Tidal Oil Co. v. Forcum, 1941, 189 Okl. 268, 116 P.2d 572. But not where it is outside of the scope of his employment, unauthorized, and unknown. Dickson v. Graham-Jones Paper Co., Fla.1956, 84 So.2d 309.

"Harboring" has been said to mean protecting. Wood v. Campbell, 1911, 28 S.D. 197, 132 N.W. 785. Probably more than this is required, since the United States has been held not to harbor wild bears in its national parks. Ashley v. United States, D.C.Neb. 1963, 215 F.Supp. 39, affirmed 326 F.2d 449; Claypool v. United States, D.C.Cal.1951, 98 F.Supp. 702. It seems to mean housing, keeping or caring for the animal as it usually is kept by an owner. Hancock v. Finch, 1939, 126 Conn. 121, 9 A.2d 811; Schulz v. Griffith, 1897, 103 Iowa 150, 72 N.W. 445. Feeding deer is not enough. Swain v. Tillett, 1967, 269 N.C. 46, 152 S.E.2d 297. One who has given away a dog and will not take him back is not harboring him when he keeps returning. Hunt v. Hazen, 1953, 197 Or. 637, 254 P.2d 210.

A bailee with scienter is of course liable.[13] What little authority there is tends to hold the owner strictly liable, as well as the bailee in such a case, either upon the basis of negligence in allowing the animal to be used,[14] or on the ground that the danger is such that the responsibility cannot be shifted.[15] While the latter view has been criticized,[16] there is perhaps a sufficient analogy to the entrusting of a dangerous activity to an independent contractor.[17]

The various questions which arise as to the extent of the liability for the keeping of abnormally dangerous animals can more conveniently be dealt with at a later point.[18]

77. FIRE

The dangerous potentialities of fire seem to have been recognized very early. Something approaching strict liability for fire apparently was imposed upon landholders by the early common law, although it is a matter of dispute just what its limitations may have been.[19] Certainly some excuses were

recognized, such as the intervention of an act of God, or the act of a stranger.[20] But whatever the early rule may have been, it was altered by a statute passed in 1707, and amended in 1774,[21] which provided that no action should be maintained against one in whose building or estate a fire accidentally began. Under this statute, the English courts have held that the landholder ordinarily is not liable,[22] unless the fire originates or spreads through his negligence,[23] or is intentionally set.[24] But where the fire has its origin in the course of an activity which is regarded as abnormally dangerous, even on the defendant's land, they have reverted to their present understanding of the earlier rule, and have held him to strict responsibility.[25] Thus the owner of a steam engine, driven along the highway, has been held liable without

13. Quilty v. Battie, 1892, 135 N.Y. 201, 32 N.E. 47; Frammell v. Little, 1861, 16 Ind. 251.

See Donaldson, Liability Arising from Owning or Harboring Animals, 1969, 26 Ins.Couns.J. 268.

14. White v. Steadman, [1913] 3 K.B. 340; Corliss v. Keown, 1910, 207 Mass. 149, 93 N.E. 143.

15. Stapleton v. Butensky, 1919, 188 App.Div. 237, 177 N.Y.S. 18. Cf. Austin v. Bridges, 1912, 3 Tenn.Civ. App. 151; Pinn v. Rew, 1916, 32 T.L.R. 451 (independent contractor authorized to take dangerous animals upon the highway); Yazoo & M. R. Co. v. Gordon, 1939, 184 Miss. 885, 186 So. 631 (independent contractor loading cattle); Luick v. Sondrol, 1925, 200 Iowa 728, 205 N.W. 331 (under statute).

16. See Note, 1920, 20 Col.L.Rev. 89; Harper, Law of Torts, 1933, § 175.

17. See supra, § 70. Cf. Black v. Christchurch Finance Co., [1894] A.C. 48. "Can the person who has acquired a tiger, so long as he remains its owner, relieve himself of responsibility by contracting with a third person for its custody?" Atkin, L. J., in Belvedere Fish Guano Co. v. Rainham Chemical Works, [1920] 2 K.B. 497, 504.

18. See infra, p. 518.

19. See Beaulieu v. Fingham, 1401, Y.B. 2 Hen. 4, 18, pl. 61; Tubervil v. Stamp, 1697, variously reported

in 1 Salk. 13, 1 Ld.Raym. 264, Carthew 425, 91 Eng.Rep. 1072. The allegation was for "negligently" keeping the fire; but it seems clear that this meant less than the modern significance of negligence, and the only uncertainty is as to how much less. See Wigmore, Responsibility for Tortious Acts: Its History, 1893, 7 Harv.L.Rev. 315, 448; Winfield, The Myth of Absolute Liability, 1926, 42 L.Q.Rev. 37, 46.

20. Tubervil v. Stamp, 1697, 1 Salk. 13, 1 Ld.Raym. 264, 91 Eng.Rep. 1072. Cf. Rayonier, Inc. v. United States, 9 Cir. 1955, 225 F.2d 642, vacated on other grounds 352 U.S. 315 (fire from other land sweeping across defendant's).

21. 6 Anne, c. 31, § 6, made permanent by 10 Anne, c. 14, § 1, later amended by 14 Geo. 3, c. 78, § 86.

22. Job Edwards, Ltd. v. Birmingham Navigations, [1924] 1 K.B. 341; Collingwood v. Home and Colonial Stores, [1936] 3 All Eng.Rep. 200.

23. Vaughan v. Menlove, 1837, 3 Bing. 468, 132 Eng. Rep. 490; Maclenan v. Segar, [1917] 2 K.B. 325; Sochacki v. Sas, [1947] 1 All.Eng.Rep. 344; Vaughan v. Taff Vale R. Co., 1860, 5 H. & N. 679, 157 Eng.Rep. 1357; Howard v. Furness Houlder Argentine Lines, [1936] 2 All Eng.Rep. 781, 41 Com.Cas. 290.

24. In Filliter v. Phippard, 1847, 11 Q.B. 347, 116 Eng.Rep. 506, the statute was held inapplicable to a fire intentionally kindled, as not of "accidental" origin.

25. See Bankes, L. J., in Musgrove v. Pandelis, [1919] 2 K.B. 43.

negligence for sparks setting fire to a hay-stack.[26]

The American courts, influenced by the English statutes as a part of the common law taken over in this country,[27] have consistently rejected the older rule, and have held, in the absence of legislation, that there is no liability for the escape of fire where the defendant was not negligent.[28] It is recognized, of course, that fire is a dangerous thing, and a great amount of care is required in dealing with it.[29] There may be liability for negligence in starting a fire,[30] or in failing to take precautions against its occurrence, as where combustible materials are left unprotected,[31] or in failing to control it

after it is started,[32] or neglecting to have the means to extinguish it at hand.[33] But its utility is so great, and it is so clearly sanctioned by universal use, that strict liability, even on the part of industrial enterprises, is not considered convenient or desirable.[34]

Statutes, however, in many states, have restored the rule of strict liability in certain very dangerous situations—as where a fire is set during a specified dry season,[35] or a prairie fire is started intentionally.[36] A very common type of statute makes railroad companies strictly liable, without negligence, for fires set by their locomotives,[37] or provides that the fire shall be "conclusive" as to negligence,[38] which of course amounts to the same thing. Such statutes have been held constitutional, as reasonable measures for the protection of property and the adjustment of an inevitable risk.[39] The only question in

26. Mansell v. Webb, 1919, 88 L.J.K.B. 323; Powell v. Fall, 1880, 3 Q.B.D. 597; cf. Musgrove v. Pandelis, [1919] 2 K.B. 43. The same rule was applied to railway locomotives, Jones v. Festiniog R. Co., 1868, L.R. 3 Q.B. 733, except where they were run under statutory privilege. Vaughan v. Taff Vale R. Co., 1860, 5 H. & N. 678, 157 Eng.Rep. 1351; Canadian Pac. R. Co. v. Roy, [1902] A.C. 220. The liability of railways is now governed by special statute. See Attorney General v. Great Western R. Co., [1924] 2 K.B. 1.

27. Lansing v. Stone, 1862, 37 Barb., N.Y., 15, 14 Abb.Prac. 199; Bachelder v. Heagan, 1840, 18 Me. 32.

28. B. W. King, Inc. v. Town of West New York, 1967, 49 N.J. 318, 230 A.2d 133; Clark v. Foot, 1811, 8 Johns., N.Y., 421; Fahn v. Reichert, 1859, 8 Wis. 255; Mitchell v. Reitchick, 1923, 123 Me. 30, 121 A. 91; Wallace v. New York, N. H. & H. R. Co., 1911, 208 Mass. 16, 94 N.E. 306.

29. Piraccini v. Director General of Railroads, 1920, 95 N.J.L. 114, 112 A. 311; Cobb v. Twitchell, 1926, 91 Fla. 539, 108 So. 186. In McNally v. Colwell, 1892, 91 Mich. 527, 52 N.W. 70, it is suggested that greater care is required as to an industrial fire than as to one in the home.

30. Burlington & M. R. Co. v. Westover, 1876, 4 Neb. 268; Brummit v. Furniss, 1891, 1 Ind.App. 401, 27 N.E. 656; Piraccini v. Director General of Railroads, 1920, 95 N.J.L. 114, 112 A. 311.

31. Eisenkramer v. Eck, 1924, 162 Ark. 501, 258 S.W. 368; Collins v. George, 1904, 102 Va. 509, 46 S.E. 684; Keyser Canning Co. v. Klots Throwing Co., 1923, 94 W.Va. 346, 118 S.E. 521; Phillips Petroleum Co. v. Berry, 1933, 188 Ark. 431, 65 S.W.2d 533; cf. Riley v. Standard Oil Co., 1934, 214 Wis. 15, 252 N.W. 183.

32. Cobb v. Twitchell, 1926, 91 Fla. 539, 108 So. 186; Farrell v. Minneapolis & R. R. R. Co., 1913, 121 Minn. 357, 141 N.W. 491; Sandberg v. Cavanaugh Timber Co., 1917, 95 Wash. 556, 164 P. 200.

33. McNally v. Colwell, 1892, 91 Mich. 527, 52 N.W. 70; Keyser Canning Co. v. Klots Throwing Co., 1923, 94 W.Va. 346, 118 S.E. 521.

34. O'Day v. Shouvlin, 1922, 104 Ohio St. 519, 136 N. E. 289.

35. See Seckerson v. Sinclair, 1913, 24 N.D. 625, 140 N.W. 239; Thoburn v. Campbell, 1890, 80 Iowa 338, 45 N.W. 769.

36. See Interstate Galloway Cattle Co. v. Kline, 1893, 51 Kan. 23, 32 P. 628; State v. Phillips, 1929, 176 Minn. 472, 233 N.W. 912.

37. Peck Iron & Metal Co. v. Seaboard Air Line R. Co., 1959, 200 Va. 698, 107 S.E.2d 421; Baltimore & O. R. Co. v. Kreager, 1899, 61 Ohio St. 312, 56 N.E. 203; Hooksett v. Concord R. Co., 1859, 38 N.H. 242; Fleming v. Southern R. Co., 1922, 120 S.C. 242, 113 S.E. 73; Carr v. Davis, 1924, 159 Minn. 485, 199 N.W. 237. A striking case is Dickelman Mfg. Co. v. Pennsylvania R. Co., N.D.Ohio 1929, 34 F.2d 70, where the railroad was held liable for a fire resulting from a train wreck, caused by an undiscoverable defect in a car which it was required by law to accept and transport.

38. See Schaff v. Coyle, 1926, 121 Okl. 228, 249 P. 947; and cf. Martin v. New York & N. E. R. Co., 1892, 62 Conn. 331, 25 A. 239 (presumption).

39. St. Louis & S. F. R. Co. v. Mathews, 1896, 165 U.S. 1; Union Pac. R. Co. v. De Busk, 1886, 12

such a case is one of whether the fire was in fact started by the locomotive, which is frequently one of circumstantial evidence.[40] Presumptions have been created in many jurisdictions to aid the plaintiff in his proof, based on the passage of an engine shortly before the fire begins, or proof of the emission of sparks, or similar facts.[41]

Again the question of the extent of the liability created by such statutes is more conveniently left to a later section.[42]

78. ABNORMALLY DANGEROUS THINGS AND ACTIVITIES

The doctrine of strict liability for abnormally dangerous conditions and activities [43] is a comparatively recent one in the law. The leading case from which it has developed is Rylands v. Fletcher,[44] decided in England in 1868. The defendants, mill owners in Lan-

cashire, constructed a reservoir upon their land. The water broke through into the disused and filled-up shaft of an abandoned coal mine, and flooded along connecting passages into the adjoining mine of the plaintiff. The actual work was done by independent contractors, who were probably negligent,[45] but the arbitrator who stated the case found that the defendants themselves were ignorant of the existence of the old coal workings, and free from all personal blame. No trespass could be found, since the flooding was not direct or immediate; nor any nuisance, as the term was then understood, since there was nothing offensive to the senses and the damage was not continuous or recurring. But it was held, upon the analogy of the strict liability for trespassing cattle, dangerous animals and "absolute" nuisance, which was extended to cover the facts in question, that the plaintiff might recover.

Justice Blackburn, in the Exchequer Chamber, used language which has been much quoted since, and is often erroneously said to be the "rule" of the case: "We think that the true rule of law is that the person who for his own purposes brings on his land and collects and keeps there anything likely to do mischief if it escapes, must keep it at his peril, and if he does not do so is prima facie answerable for all the damage which is the natural consequence of its escape." [46]

In the House of Lords this broad statement was sharply limited, and placed upon a different footing. Lord Cairns said that the principle applied only to a "non-natural" use of the defendant's land, as distinguished from "any purpose for which it might in the ordinary course of the enjoyment of land be used." [47] The emphasis was thus shifted to

Colo. 294, 20 P. 752; Grissell v. Housatonic R. Co., 1886, 54 Conn. 447, 9 A. 137.

40. See Harper and Harper, Establishing Railroad Liability for Fires, 1929, 77 U.Pa.L.Rev. 629; Note, 1937, 31 Ill.L.Rev. 549. The plaintiff has the burden of proof on the issue. State v. Pennsylvania R. Co., 1956, 101 Ohio App. 521, 136 N.E.2d 738.

41. Gibbons v. Wisconsin Valley R. Co., 1886, 66 Wis. 161, 28 N.W. 170; Nelson v. Chicago, B. & Q. R. Co., 1924, 47 S.D. 228, 197 N.W. 288; Missoula Trust & Sav. Bank v. Northern Pac. R. Co., 1926, 76 Mont. 201, 245 P. 949; Stockdale v. Midland Valley R. Co., 1923, 113 Kan. 635, 215 P. 1021.

42. See infra, § 79.

43. See, generally, Bohlen, The Rule in Rylands v. Fletcher, 1911, 59 U.Pa.L.Rev. 298; Pollock, Duties of Insuring Safety: The Rule in Rylands v. Fletcher, 1886, 2 L.Q.Rev. 52; Thayer, Liability Without Fault, 1916, 29 Harv.L.Rev. 801; Carpenter, The Doctrine of Green v. General Petroleum Corporation, 1932, 5 So.Cal.L.Rev. 263; Morris, Hazardous Enterprises and Risk Bearing Capacity, 1952, 61 Yale L.J. 1172; Stallybrass, Dangerous Things and the Non-Natural User of Land, 1929, 3 Camb.L.J. 376; Prosser, The Principle of Rylands v. Fletcher, in Prosser, Selected Topics in the Law of Torts, 1954, 134.

44. Fletcher v. Rylands, 1865, 3 H. & C. 774, 159 Eng.Rep. 737, reversed in Fletcher v. Rylands, 1866, L.R. 1 Ex. 265, affirmed in Rylands v. Fletcher, 1868, L.R. 3 H.L. 330.

45. The case arose eleven years before it was first held, in Bower v. Peate, 1876, 1 Q.B.D. 321, that an employer might be liable for the negligence of an independent contractor.

46. Fletcher v. Rylands, 1866, L.R. 1 Ex. 265, 279–80.

47. Rylands v. Fletcher, 1868, L.R. 3 H.L. 330, 338. The attempt of Newark, Non-Natural User and Rylands v. Fletcher, 1961, 24 Mod.L.Rev. 21, to explain

the abnormal and inappropriate character of the defendant's reservoir in coal mining country, rather than the mere tendency of all water to escape.

More than a hundred subsequent decisions in British jurisdictions have fully borne out this interpretation of the case. The strict liability has been said many times to be confined to things or activities which are "extraordinary," [48] or "exceptional," [49] or "abnormal," [50] and not to apply to the "usual and normal." [51] There must be "some special use bringing with it increased danger to others, and must not merely be the ordinary use of land or such a use as is proper for the general benefit of the community." [52]

In determining what is a "non-natural use" the English courts have looked not only to the character of the thing or activity in question, but also to the place and manner in which it is maintained and its relation to its surroundings.[53]   Water collected in large

quantity in hydraulic power mains,[54] a cellar,[55] or a plant for washing film,[56] all in dangerous proximity to the plaintiff's land, is a non-natural use" for which there is strict liability. But water in a cistern,[57] in household pipes,[58] or in a barnyard tank supplying cattle,[59] is a natural use for which the defendant will not be liable in the absence of negligence. Gas [60] or electricity [61] in household pipes or wires is a natural use; gas in quantity [62] or high-powered electricity [63] under the street is another matter entirely. Fire in a fireplace [64] or in an authorized railway engine [65] is a normal thing, and so is a

---

so it seems that there is scarcely anything which is in all circumstances safe." See also Fleming, Torts, 3d ed. 1965, 302–303.

54. Charing Cross Elec. Supply Co. v. Hydraulic Power Co., [1914] 3 K.B. 772.

55. Snow v. Whitehead, 1884, 27 Ch.Div. 588. Cf. Ballard v. Tomlinson, 1885, 29 Ch.Div. 115 (pollution of well by percolation).

56. Western Engraving Co. v. Film Laboratories, Ltd., [1936] 1 All Eng.Rep. 106.

57. Blake v. Land and House Property Corp., Q.B. 1887, 3 T.L.R. 667.

58. Rickards v. Lothian, [1913] A.C. 263; A. Prosser & Son, Ltd. v. Levy, [1955] 1 W.L.R. 1224; Tilley v. Stevenson, [1939] 4 All Eng.Rep. 207; Torette House v. Berkman, 1940, 62 Comm.L.Rep., Aust., 637. Cf. Ross v. Fedden, 1872, L.R. 7 Q.B. 661 (water closet); Peters v. Prince of Wales Theatre, [1943] K.B. 73 (sprinkler system).

59. Bartlett v. Tottenham, [1932] 1 Ch. 114.

60. Miller v. Robert Addie & Son's Collieries, [1934] S.C. 150.

61. Collingwood v. Home & Colonial Stores, [1936] 1 All Eng.Rep. 74; Spicer v. Smee, [1946] 1 All Eng. Rep. 489.

62. Northwestern Utilities v. London Guarantee & Accident Co., [1936] A.C. 108; Hanson v. Wearmouth Coal Co., [1939] 3 All Eng. Rep. 47; Batcheller v. Tunbridge Wells Gas Co., 1901, 84 T.L.R. 765.

63. National Tel. Co. v. Baker, [1893] 2 Ch. 186; Eastern & South African Tel. Co. v. Cape Town Tramways Co., [1902] A.C. 381; Midwood & Co. v. Manchester Corp. [1905] 2 K.B. 597.

64. Sochacki v. Sas, [1947] 1 All Eng.Rep. 344; Hazlewood v. Webber, 1934, 52 Comm.L.Rep., Aust., 268 (household cooking).

65. Vaughan v. Taff Vale R. Co., 1860, 5 H. & N. 679, 157 Eng.Rep. 1351.

"natural" as meaning arising in the course of nature, appears to run counter to the language of the opinion, the cases cited, and certainly all the subsequent English interpretation of the case.

48. Kekewich, J., in National Tel. Co. v. Baker, [1893] 2 Ch. 186; Farwell, L. J., in West v. Bristol Tramways, [1908] 2 K.B. 14; Wright, J., in Noble v. Harrison, [1926] 2 K.B. 332.

49. Lord Buckmaster, in Rainham Chemical Works v. Belvedere Fish Guano Co., [1921] 2 A.C. 465, 471.

50. Farwell, L. J., in Barker v. Herbert, [1911] 2 K. B. 633, 645.

51. Wright, J., in Noble v. Harrison, [1926] 2 K.B. 332, 342; Fletcher Moulton, L. J., in Barker v. Herbert, [1911] 2 K.B. 633. Cf. Sutton and Ash v. Card, [1886] W.N. 120 ("ordinary way of using a man's own property").

52. Lord Moulton, in Rickards v. Lothian, [1913] A.C. 263, 280; Lord Wright, in Sedleigh-Denfield v. O'Callaghan, [1940] A.C. 880, 888; Scott, L. J., in Read v. J. Lyons & Co., 1944, 61 T.L.R. 149, 153; Bramwell, B., in Nichols v. Marsland, 1875, L.R. 10 Ex. 255, 259; Wright, J., in Blake v. Woolf, [1898] 2 Q.B. 426, 427.

53. Stallybrass, Dangerous Things and the Non-Natural User of Land, (1929) 3 Camb. L.J. 376, 387, comes to the conclusion that it is all a matter of relativity, and that "just as there is nothing which is at all times and in all circumstances dangerous,

steam boiler on a ship; [66] but fire in an un-licensed locomotive [67] or in a steam engine travelling on the highway and shooting out sparks [68] is not normal, and is a proper matter for strict liability. The automobile, dangerous and fatal to thousands as it undoubtedly is, is today a usual, customary phenomenon on the street, for which there is no strict liability, [69] but a ten ton traction engine [70] or a steam roller [71] which crushes conduits under the street is definitely extraordinary. The storage in quantity of explosives [72] or inflammable liquids, [73] or blasting, [74] or the accumulation of sewage, [75] or the emission of creosote fumes, [76] or pile driving which sets up excessive vibration, [77] all have

the same element of the unusual, excessive and bizarre, and have been considered "non-natural" uses, leading to strict liability when they result in harm to another.

The place where all this occurs, the customs of the community, and the natural fitness or adaptation of the premises for the purpose, all are highly important in determining whether the rule applies. In Burma an elephant is nót a non-natural creature, but a domestic animal, no more a subject for strict liability than a horse; [78] but the same elephant, transported to England in a circus, becomes an abnormal danger to that community. [79] Just so coal mining, [80] gravel pits, [81] and the removal of shingle from the seashore, [82] are regarded as natural uses of the particular land, since that is what such land is for; and it is only when the methods adopted are unusual or abnormal, as in the case of letting in a river [83] or pumping water to a level from which it will flow onto the plaintiff's land, [84] that the strict liability is held to apply.

66. Howard v. Furness Houlder Argentine Lines, [1936] 2 All Eng.Rep. 781, 41 Com.Cas. 290. Accord, Wise Bros. Pty. v. Commissioner for Railways, 1947, 75 Comm.L.Rep., Aust., 59 (in flour mill for manufacturing).

67. Jones v. Festiniog R. Co., 1868, L.R. 3 Q.B. 733.

68. Powell v. Fall, 1880, 5 Q.B.D. 597; Mansel v. Webb, 1918.

69. Wing v. London General Omnibus Co., [1909] 2 K.B. 652; Phillips v. Britannia Hygienic Laundry Co., [1923] 1 K.B. 539.

70. Chichester Corp. v. Foster, [1906] 1 K.B. 167.

71. Gas Light & Coke Co. v. Vestry of St. Mary Abbott's, 1885, 15 Q.B.D. 1.

72. Rainham Chemical Works v. Belvedere Fish Guano Co., [1921] 2 A.C. 465; J. P. Porter v. Bell, [1955] 1 Dom.L.Rep. 62.

73. Mulholland & Tedd, Ltd. v. Baker, [1939] 3 All Eng.Rep. 253; Smith v. Great Western R. Co., 1926, 135 L.T. 112; Ekstrom v. Deagon & Montgomery, [1946] 1 Dom.L.Rep. 208.

74. Miles v. Forest Rock Granite Co., 1918, 34 T.L.R. 500.

75. Humphries v. Cousins, 1877, 2 C.P.Div. 239; Jones v. Llanrwst Urban District Council, [1911] 1 Ch. 393.

76. West v. Bristol Tramways, [1908] 2 K.B. 14. Accord, Halsey v. Esso Petroleum Co., [1961] 1 W.L.R. 683. See Note, [1961] Camb.L.J. 168.

77. Hoare & Co. v. McAlpine, [1923] 1 Ch. 167. Compare the following:

"Natural" uses: Wilkins v. Leighton, [1932] 2 Ch. 106 (ordinary building); Noble v. Harrison, [1926] 2 K.B. 332 (ordinary tree); Ilford Urban District Council v. Beal and Judd, [1925] 1 K.B. 671 (retaining

wall); Barker v. Herbert, [1911] 2 K.B. 633 (area protected by a railing); Haseldine v. C. A. Dow & Son, Ltd., [1941] 3 K.B. 343 (elevator in apartment building).

"Non-natural" uses: Attorney-General v. Cory Bros. & Co., [1921] 1 A.C. 521 (pile of sliding coal mine refuse); Hurdman v. North Eastern R. Co., 1878, 3 C.P.Div. 168 (artificial mound shedding water); Cheater v. Cater, [1918] 1 K.B. 247 (poisonous tree); Hale v. Jennings Bros., [1938] 1 All Eng.Rep. 579 (centrifugal amusement device whirling chairs at a giddy angle); Shiffman v. Order of St. John, [1936] 1 All Eng.Rep. 557 (unsafe flagpole in the wrong place).

78. Maung Hyan Dun v. Ma Kyian, 1900, 2 Upper Burma Rulings (Civ.) 570.

79. Behrens v. Bertam Mills Circus, [1957] 2 Q.B. 1.

80. Smith v. Kenrick, 1849, 7 C.B. 515, 137 Eng.Rep. 205; Wilson v. Waddell, 1876, 2 A.C. 95; Westhoughton Coal & Cannel Co. v. Wigan Coal Corp., [1939] Ch. 800.

81. Rouse v. Gravelworks, Ltd., [1940] 1 K.B. 489.

82. Attorney-General v. Tomline, 1879, 12 Ch.Div. 214.

83. Crompton v. Lea, 1874, 19 Eq. 115.

84. Baird v. Williamson, 1863, 15 C.B., N.S., 376, **143** Eng.Rep. 531; Westminster Brymbo Coal & Coke

In short, what emerges from the English decisions as the "rule" of Rylands v. Fletcher is that the defendant will be liable when he damages another by a thing or activity unduly dangerous and inappropriate to the place where it is maintained, in the light of the character of that place and its surroundings.[85]

In 1947 the House of Lords abruptly put a stop to the expansion of the doctrine of Rylands v. Fletcher, in a case[86] in which a government inspector was injured by an explosion in the defendant's munitions plant. On its face the case looks like one in which the plaintiff might have been held to have assumed the risk;[87] but the court elected instead to limit the principle of strict liability to cases in which there has been an "escape" of a dangerous substance from land under the control of the defendant. Two of the judges[88] thought that it was not applicable at all to cases of personal injury. The decision appears definitely out of line with other English cases;[89] and if it is to be followed,

which is not yet entirely certain as to either point,[90] it is at least a sudden, and rather unexplained, reversal of what had before appeared to be a definite trend in the English law.

American Cases

In the United States Rylands v. Fletcher was promptly accepted by the courts of Massachusetts and Minnesota.[91] Almost immediately afterward the whole doctrine was received with a triple bath of ice water, and entirely repudiated, by decisions in New Hampshire,[92] New York,[93] and New Jersey.[94] Two of these cases involved the explosion of ordinary steam boilers, and the third a runaway horse on the highway. They were obviously cases of customary, natural uses, to which the English courts would never have applied the rule.[95] In all three cases the attack was directed at Blackburn's broad statement in the intermediate court, and the final decision of the House of Lords was ignored. Rylands v. Fletcher was treated as holding that the defendant is absolutely liable in all cases whenever anything under his control escapes and does damage. In other words, the law of the case was misstated, and as

---

Co. v. Clayton, 1867, 36 L.J.Ch. 476; Hodgkinson v. Ennor, 1863, 4 B. & S. 229, 122 Eng.Rep. 446 (discharging pollution into stream); West Cumberland Iron & Steel Co. v. Kenyon, 1877 L.R. 6 Ch.Div. 773 ("any means not in the ordinary and proper course of working his mine").

85. Cf. Sutherland, J., in Village of Euclid v. Ambler Realty Co., 1926, 272 U.S. 365, 388, speaking of nuisance: " . . . merely the right thing in the wrong place—like a pig in the parlor instead of the barnyard." See Prosser, The Principle of Rylands v. Fletcher, in Prosser, Selected Topics on the Law of Torts, 1954, 134–149.

86. Read v. J. Lyons & Co., Ltd., [1947] A.C. 156.

87. Cf. E. I. Du Pont De Nemours & Co. v. Cudd, 10 Cir.1949, 176 F.2d 855, as to an employee.

88. Per Lord Macmillan, at p. 173, and Lord Uthwatt, at 186.

89. Cf. Hoare & Co. v. McAlpine, [1923] 1 Ch. 167 (vibration); Midwood v. Mayor of Manchester, [1905] 2 K.B. 597 (fusing of defendant's electric cable under the public highway); Powell v. Fall, 1880, 5 Q.B.D. 597 (engine emitting sparks on the highway); Mansel v. Webb, 1918, 88 L.J.K.B. 323 (same); Rainham Chemical Works v. Belvedere Fish Guano Co., [1921] 2 A.C. 465. As to personal injuries, see Miles v. Forest Rock Granite Co., 1918,

34 T.L.R. 500; Shiffman v. Order of St. John, [1936] 1 All Eng.Rep. 557; Hale v. Jennings Bros., [1938] 1 All Eng.Rep. 579; Schubert v. Sterling Trust Co., [1943] 4 Dom.L.Rep. 584.

90. As to "escape," the case was followed in Barrette v. Franki Compressed Pile Co., [1955] 2 Dom.L.Rep. 665, in holding that vibration is not a matter for strict liability. As to personal injuries, it was disregarded in Aldridge v. Van Patter, [1952] 4 Dom. L.Rep. 93, and in Perry v. Kendrick's Transp., [1956] 1 W.L.R. 85, 92.

91. Ball v. Nye, 1868, 99 Mass. 582 (percolation of filthy water); Cahill v. Eastman, 1871, 18 Minn. 324 (underground water tunnel broke through into plaintiff's property).

92. Brown v. Collins, 1873, 53 N.H. 442.

93. Losee v. Buchanan, 1873, 51 N.Y. 476.

94. Marshall v. Welwood, 1876, 38 N.J.L. 339.

95. Cf. Howard v. Furness Houlder Argentine Lines, [1936] 2 All Eng.Rep. 781, 41 Com.Cas. 290; Huff v. Austin, 1889, 46 Ohio St. 386, 21 N.E. 864.

misstated rejected, on facts to which it had no proper application in the first place.

On the heels of these decisions, the doctrine was condemned by legal writers [96] as an unjustifiable extension of liability to unavoidable accidents, in a field where the law of negligence, aided by the principle of res ipsa loquitur, would be adequate to cover the cases where recovery should be allowed. One important reason often given for the rejection of the strict liability was that it was not adapted to an expanding civilization. Dangerous enterprises, involving a high degree of risk to others, were clearly indispensable to the industrial and commercial development of a new country and it was considered that the interests of those in the vicinity of such enterprises must give way to them, and that too great a burden must not be placed upon them.[97] With the disappearance of the frontier, and the development of the country's resources, it was to be expected that the force of this objection would be weakened, and that it would be replaced in time by the view that the hazardous enterprise, even though it be socially valuable, must pay its way, and make good the damage inflicted. After a long period during which Rylands v. Fletcher was rejected by the large majority of the American courts which considered it,[98] the pendulum has swung to acceptance of the case and its doctrine in the United States.

At this writing, Rylands v. Fletcher still is rejected by name in seven American jurisdictions: Maine,[99] New Hampshire,[1] New York,[2] Oklahoma,[3] Rhode Island,[4] Texas,[5] and probably Wyoming.[6] It has been approved by name, or a statement of principle clearly derived from it has been accepted, in some thirty jurisdictions, with the number expanding at the rate of about one a year.[7]

The conditions and activities to which the rule has been applied have followed the English pattern. They include water collected in quantity in a dangerous place,[8] or allowed

---

96. Holmes, The Theory of Torts, 1873, 7 Am.L.Rev. 652; Thayer, Liability Without Fault, 1916, 29 Harv.L.Rev. 801; Smith, Tort and Absolute Liability, 1917, 30 Harv.L.Rev. 241, 319, 408. Cf. Pollock, Duties of Insuring Safety: The Rule in Rylands v. Fletcher, 1886, 2 L.Q.Rev. 52.

97. On this basis, it had been held, in earlier cases, that the owners of mill dams in the natural bed of streams were not liable, in the absence of negligence, for the escape of the water. Shrewsbury v. Smith, 1853, 12 Cush., Mass., 177; Livingston v. Adams, 1828, 8 Cow., N.Y., 175; Everett v. Hydraulic Flume Tunnel Co., 1863, 23 Cal. 225. Again, surely, a "natural use."

98. It is still commonly, and erroneously, said that Rylands v. Fletcher is rejected by the great majority of the American courts. The writer pleads guilty. Prosser, Torts, 1st Ed. 1941, 452.

99. Reynolds v. W. H. Hinman Co., 1950, 145 Me. 343, 75 A.2d 802.

1. Brown v. Collins, 1873, 53 N.H. 442; Garland v. Towne, 1874, 55 N.H. 55.

2. Losee v. Buchanan, 1873, 51 N.Y. 476; cf. Cosulich v. Standard Oil Co., 1890, 122 N.Y. 118, 25 N.E. 259.

3. Gulf Pipe Line Co. v. Sims, 1934, 168 Okl. 209, 32 P.2d 902; Sinclair Prairie Oil Co. v. Stell, 1942, 190 Okl. 344, 124 P.2d 255. See Foster and Keeton, Liability Without Fault in Oklahoma, 1950, 3 Okl. L. Rev. 1, 172.

4. Rose v. Socony-Vacuum Corp., 1934, 54 R.I. 411, 173 A. 627.

5. Gulf, C. & S. F. R. Co. v. Oakes, 1900, 94 Tex. 155, 58 S.W. 999; Turner v. Big Lake Oil Co., 1936, 128 Tex. 155, 96 S.W.2d 221. See Prosser, Nuisance Without Fault, 1942, 20 Tex.L.Rev. 399.

6. Jacoby v. Town of City of Gillette, 1947, 62 Wyo. 487, 174 P.2d 505.

7. See for example Healey v. Citizens Gas & Elec. Co., 1924, 199 Iowa 82, 201 N.W. 118; Central Exploration Co. v. Gray, 1954, 219 Miss. 757, 70 So.2d 33; Thigpen v. Skousen & Hise, 1958, 64 N.M. 290, 327 P.2d 802; Berg v. Reaction Motors Division, Thiokol Chemical Corp., 1962, 37 N.J. 396, 181 A.2d 487; Loe v. Lenhardt, 1961, 227 Or. 242, 362 P.2d 312; Enos Coal Min. Co. v. Schuchart, 1962, 243 Ind. 692, 188 N.E.2d 406; Wallace v. A. H. Guion & Co., 1960, 237 S.C. 349, 117 S.E.2d 359.

8. Wilson v. City of New Bedford, 1871, 108 Mass. 261; Defiance Water Co. v. Olinger, 1896, 54 Ohio St. 532, 44 N.E. 238; Bridgeman-Russell Co. v. City of Duluth, 1924, 158 Minn. 509, 197 N.W. 971; Weaver Merc. Co. v. Thurmond, 1911, 68 W.Va. 530, 70 S.E. 126; Smith v. Board of County Road Comm'rs of Chippewa County, 1966, 5 Mich.App. 370,

to percolate;[9] explosives[10] or inflammable liquids[11] stored in quantity in the midst of a city; blasting;[12] pile driving;[13] crop dusting;[14] the fumigation of part of a building with cyanide gas;[15] drilling oil wells or operating refineries in thickly settled communi-

ties;[16] an excavation letting in the sea;[17] factories emitting smoke, dust or noxious gases in the midst of a town;[18] roofs so constructed as to shed snow into a highway;[19] and a dangerous party wall.[20]

On the other hand the conditions and activities to which the American courts have refused to apply Rylands v. Fletcher, whether they purport to accept or to reject the case in principle, have been with few exceptions what the English courts would regard as a "natural" use of land, and not within the rule at all. They include water in household pipes,[21] the tank of a humidity system,[22] or authorized utility mains;[23] gas in a

146 N.W.2d 702. Cf. Kennecott Copper Corp. v. McDowell, 1966, 100 Ariz. 276, 413 P.2d 749 (water in stream diverted against bridge).

9. Ball v. Nye, 1868, 99 Mass. 582; Kall v. Carruthers, 1922, 59 Cal.App. 555, 211 P. 43; Healey v. Citizens Gas & Elec. Co., 1924, 199 Iowa 82, 201 N.W. 118; Norfolk & Western R. Co. v. Amicon, 4 Cir. 1920, 269 F. 559.

10. Exner v. Sherman Power Const. Co., 2 Cir.1931, 54 F.2d 510; Bradford Glycerine Co. v. St. Mary's Woolen Mfg. Co., 1899, 60 Ohio St. 560, 54 N.E. 528; French v. Center Creek Powder Mfg. Co., 1913, 173 Mo.App. 220, 158 S.W. 723; cf. Koster & Wythe v. Massey, 9 Cir.1961, 293 F.2d 922, cert. denied 368 U.S. 927 (incendiary bomb). See Notes, 1932, 17 Corn. L.Q. 703; 1966, 39 U.Colo.L.Rev. 161.

11. Brennan Const. Co. v. Cumberland, 1907, 29 U.S. App.D.C. 554; Berger v. Minneapolis Gaslight Co., 1895, 60 Minn. 296, 62 N.W. 336; Yommer v. McKenzie, 1969, 255 Md. 220, 257 A.2d 138. Cf. MacKenzie v. Fitchburg Paper Co., 1966, 351 Mass. 292, 218 N.E.2d 579 (dumping inflammable ink at city dump).

12. Colton v. Onderdonk, 1886, 69 Cal. 155, 10 P. 395; Britton v. Harrison Const. Co., S.D.W.Va.1948, 87 F.Supp. 405; Central Exploration Co. v. Gray, 1954, 219 Miss. 757, 70 So.2d 33; Brown v. L. S. Lunder Const. Co., 1942, 240 Wis. 122, 2 N.W.2d 859; Davis v. L. & W. Const. Co., Iowa 1970, 176 N.W.2d 223; see McNeal, Use of Explosives and Liability Questions Involved, 1956, 23 Ins.Counsel J. 125.

13. Caporale v. C. W. Blakeslee & Sons, Inc., 1961, 149 Conn. 79, 175 A.2d 561. Sachs v. Criat, 1968, 281 Minn. 540, 162 N.W.2d 243.

14. Young v. Darter, Okl.1961, 363 P.2d 829; Loe v. Lenhardt, 1961, 227 Or. 242, 362 P.2d 312; Gotreaux v. Gary, 1957, 232 La. 373, 94 So.2d 293, appeal transferred 80 So.2d 578.

Contra: S. A. Gerrard Co. v. Fricker, 1933, 42 Ariz. 503, 27 P.2d 678; Miles v. A. Arena & Co., 1937, 23 Cal.App.2d 680, 73 P.2d 1260; Lawler v. Skelton, 1961, 241 Miss. 274, 130 So.2d 565. See Notes, 1968, 19 Hast.L.J. 476; 1962, 40 Tex.L.Rev. 527; 1963, 49 Iowa L.Rev. 135.

15. Luthringer v. Moore, 1948, 31 Cal.2d 489, 190 P. 2d 1.

16. Green v. General Petroleum Corp., 1928, 205 Cal. 328, 270 P. 952; Niagara Oil Co. v Jackson, 1910, 48 Ind.App. 238, 91 N.E. 825; Helms v. Eastern Kansas Oil Co., 1917, 102 Kan. 164, 169 P. 208; Berry v. Shell Petroleum Co., 1934, 140 Kan. 94, 33 P.2d 953, rehearing denied, 1935, 141 Kan. 6, 40 P. 2d 359. Cf. State Highway Comm'n v. Empire Oil & Ref. Co., 1935, 141 Kan. 161, 40 P.2d 355. See Green, Hazardous Oil and Gas Operations: Tort Liability, 1955, 33 Tex.L.Rev. 574.

17. Mears v. Dole, 1883, 135 Mass. 508.

18. Susquehanna Fertilizer Co. v. Malone, 1890, 73 Md. 268, 20 A. 900; Frost v. Berkeley Phosphate Co., 1894, 42 S.C. 402, 20 S.E. 280; Holman v. Athens Empire Laundry Co., 1919, 149 Ga. 345, 100 S.E. 207.

19. Shipley v. Fifty Associates, 1869, 101 Mass. 251, affirmed in 1870, 106 Mass. 194; Hannem v. Pence, 1889, 40 Minn. 127, 41 N.W. 657.

20. Gorham v. Gross, 1878, 125 Mass. 232.

21. McCord Rubber Co. v. St. Joseph Water Co., 1904, 181 Mo. 678, 81 S.W. 189; Stevens-Salt Lake City, Inc. v. Wong, 1953, 123 Utah 309, 259 P.2d 586; Shanander v. Western Loan & Bldg. Co., 1951, 103 Cal.App.2d 507, 229 P.2d 864.

22. Fibre Leather Mfg. Corp. v. Ramsay Mills, 1952, 329 Mass. 575, 109 N.E.2d 910.

23. Midwest Oil Co. v. City of Aberdeen, 1943, 69 S.D. 343, 10 N.W.2d 701; Interstate Sash & Door Co. v. City of Cleveland, 1947, 148 Ohio St. 325, 74 N.E.2d 239; Grace & Co. v. City of Los Angeles, S.D. Cal. 1958, 168 F.Supp. 344, affirmed, 9 Cir.1960, 278 F.2d 771. But a city which deliberately adopted a policy of burying cast iron pipe six feet underground and leaving it there until leaks developed, was held to strict liability in Lubin v. Iowa City, 1964, 257 Iowa 383, 131 N.W.2d 765.

meter,[24] electric wiring in a machine shop,[25] and gasoline in a filling station;[26] a dam in the natural bed of a stream;[27] ordinary steam boilers;[28] an ordinary fire in a factory;[29] an automobile;[30] Bermuda grass on a railroad right of way;[31] a small quantity of dynamite kept for sale in a Texas hardware store;[32] barnyard spray in a farmhouse;[33] a division fence;[34] the wall of a house left standing after a fire;[35] coal mining operations regarded as usual and normal;[36] vibrations from ordinary building construction;[37] earth moving operations in grading a hillside;[38] the construction of a railroad tunnel;[39] and even a runaway horse.[40] There remain a few cases, including such things as water reservoirs or irrigation ditches in dry country,[41] or properly conducted[42] oil wells in Texas[43] or Oklahoma,[44] which are undoubtedly best explained upon the basis of a different community view which makes such things "natural" to the particular locality. The conclusion is, in short, that the American decisions, like the

24. Triple-State Natural Gas & Oil Co. v. Wellman, 1902, 114 Ky. 79, 70 S.W. 49. Cf. St. Mary's Gas Co. Brodbeck, 1926, 114 Ohio St. 423, 151 N.E. 323.

25. Mangan's Adm'r v. Louisville Elec. Light Co., 1906, 122 Ky. 476, 91 S.W. 703. Cf. McKenzie v. Pacific Gas & Elec. Co., 1962, 200 Cal.App.2d 731, 19 Cal.Rptr. 628 (power line).

26. Greene v. Spinning, Mo.App.1932, 48 S.W.2d 51. Cf. Collins v. Liquid Transporters, Inc., Ky.1953, 262 S.W.2d 382 (tank trucks on highway).

27. City Water Power Co. v. City of Fergus Falls, 1910, 113 Minn. 33, 128 N.W. 817; Barnum v. Handschiegel, 1919, 103 Neb. 594, 173 N.W. 593; McHenry v. Ford Motor Co., E.D.Mich.1956, 146 F. Supp. 897, affirmed, 6 Cir.1959, 261 F.2d 833, rehearing, 1959, 269 F.2d 18; New Brantner Extension Ditch Co. v. Ferguson, 1957, 134 Colo. 502, 307 P.2d 479. Cf. Esson v. Wattier, 1893, 25 Or. 7, 34 P. 756; Clark v. United States, D.Or.1952, 109 F. Supp. 213, affirmed, 9 Cir.1955, 218 F.2d 446.

28. Huff v. Austin, 1889, 46 Ohio St. 386, 21 N.E. 864; Losee v. Buchanan, 1873, 51 N.Y. 476; Marshall v. Welwood, 1876, 38 N.J.L. 339. Cf. Fritz v. E. I. Du Pont De Nemours & Co., 1950, 6 Terry, Del., 427, 75 A.2d 256 (chlorine gas in industrial plant where specific use not shown).

29. O'Day v. Shouvlin, 1922, 17 Ohio App. 62, affirmed 104 Ohio St. 519, 136 N.E. 289.

30. Steffen v. McNaughton, 1910, 142 Wis. 49, 124 N.W. 1016.

31. Gulf, C. & S. F. R. Co. v. Oakes, 1900, 94 Tex. 155, 58 S.W. 999.

32. Barnes v. Zettlemoyer, 1901, 25 Tex.Civ.App. 468, 62 S.W. 111. Cf. Henn v. Universal Atlas Cement Co., Ohio Com.Pl.1957, 144 N.E.2d 917 (blasting in a rural area, causing vibration).

33. Branstetter v. Robbins, 1955, 178 Kan. 8, 283 P. 2d 455.

34. Quinn v. Crimmings, 1898, 171 Mass. 255, 50 N.E. 624.

35. Ainsworth v. Lakin, 1902, 180 Mass. 397, 62 N.E. 746.

36. Pennsylvania Coal Co. v. Sanderson, 1886, 113 Pa. 126, 6 A. 453; Kentucky Block Fuel Co. v. Roberts, 1925, 207 Ky. 137, 268 S.W. 802; Venzel v. Valley Camp Coal Co., 1931, 304 Pa. 583, 156 A. 240; Jones v. Robertson, 1886, 116 Ill. 543, 6 N.E. 890.

37. Gallin v. Poulou, 1956, 140 Cal.App.2d 638, 295 P.2d 958.

38. Beck v. Bel Air Properties, 1955, 134 Cal.App.2d 834, 286 P.2d 503.

39. Marin Municipal Water District v. Northwestern Pac. R. Co., 1967, 253 Cal.App.2d 83, 61 Cal.Rptr. 520.

40. Brown v. Collins, 1873, 53 N.H. 442.

41. Turner v. Big Lake Oil Co., 1936, 128 Tex. 155, 96 S.W.2d 221; Anderson v. Rucker Bros., 1919, 107 Wash. 595, 183 P. 70, affirmed 186 P. 293; Clark v. Di Prima, 1966, 241 Cal.App.2d 823, 51 Cal.Rptr. 49; Jacoby v. Town of City of Gillette, 1947, 62 Wyo. 487, 174 P.2d 505, rehearing denied 177 P.2d 204. Contra, Union Pac. R. Co. v. Vale, Oregon Irr. Dist., D.Or.1966, 253 F.Supp. 251; see Note, 1967, 46 Or.L.Rev. 239.

42. Otherwise where the operation is abnormal. Teel v. Rio Bravo Oil Co., 1907, 47 Tex.Civ.App. 153, 104 S.W. 420.

43. Turner v. Big Lake Oil Co., 1936, 128 Tex. 155, 96 S.W.2d 221; Cosden Oil Co. v. Sides, Tex.Civ. App.1931, 35 S.W.2d 815; cf. East Texas Oil Refining Co. v. Mabee Consolidated Corp., Tex.Civ.App. 1937, 103 S.W.2d 795, appeal dismissed, 1939, 133 Tex. 300, 127 S.W.2d 445 (pipe line). See Green, Hazardous Oil and Gas Operations: Tort Liability, 1955, 33 Tex.L.Rev. 574.

44. Tidal Oil Co. v. Pease, 1931, 153 Okl. 137, 5 P.2d 389; Gulf Pipe Line Co. v. Alred, 1938, 182 Okl. 400, 77 P.2d 1155; Sinclair Prairie Oil Co. v. Stell, 1942, 190 Okl. 344, 124 P.2d 255. Cf. United Fuel Gas Co. v. Sawyers, Ky.1953, 259 S.W.2d 466. See Note, 1967, 20 Okl.L.Rev. 86.

English ones, have applied the principle of Rylands v. Fletcher only to the thing out of place, the abnormally dangerous condition or activity which is not a "natural" one where it is.[45]

The Restatement of Torts [46] has accepted the principle of Rylands v. Fletcher, but has limited it to an "ultrahazardous activity" of the defendant, defined as one which "necessarily involves a risk of serious harm to the person, land or chattels of others which cannot be eliminated by the exercise of the utmost care," and "is not a matter of common usage." This goes beyond the English rule in ignoring the relation of the activity to its surroundings, and falls short of it in the insistence on extreme danger and the impossibility of eliminating it with all possible care. The shift of emphasis is not at all reflected in the American cases, which have laid quite as much stress as the English ones upon the place where the thing is done.[47]

Actually even the jurisdictions which reject Rylands v. Fletcher by name have accepted and applied the principle of the case under the cloak of various other theories.[48] Most frequently, in all of the American courts, the same strict liability is imposed upon defendants under the name of nuisance.

The "absolute nuisances" [49] for which strict liability is found without intent to do harm or negligence fall into categories already familiar. They include water collected in quantity in the wrong place,[50] or allowed to percolate; [51] explosives [52] or inflammable liquids [53] stored in quantity in thickly settled communities or in dangerous proximity to valuable property; blasting; [54] fireworks set

---

45. See Prosser, The Principle of Rylands v. Fletcher, in Selected Topics on the Law of Torts, 1953, 135.

46. §§ 519, 520.

47. Tentative Draft No. 10 of the Second Restatement of Torts, § 520, tentatively approved by the American Law Institute, has eliminated "ultrahazardous" in favor of "abnormally dangerous," and has stated six factors to be considered, one of which is "whether the activity is inappropriate to the place where it is carried on." This was accepted and applied in Yommer v. McKenzie, 1969, 255 Md. 220, 257 A.2d 138, where gasoline was stored in a rural community, in dangerous proximity to the plaintiff's well. See also McLane v. Northwest Natural Gas Co., 1969, — Or. —, 467 P.2d 635.

48. See Prosser, The Principle of Rylands v. Fletcher, in Prosser, Selected Topics on the Law of Torts, 1954, 135, 159–177.

49. See infra, p. 575. In England there has been little confusion, because it is recognized that the application of Rylands v. Fletcher is one basis for finding a nuisance. See Miles v. Forest Rock Granite Co., 1918, 34 T.L.R. 500; Hoare & Co. v. McAlpine, [1923] 1 Ch. 167, 92 L.J.Ch. 81; National Tel. Co. v. Baker, [1893] 2 Ch. 186, 62 L.J.Ch. 699. See Winfield, Nuisance as a Tort, 1931, 4 Camb.L.J. 189. Also Newark, The Boundaries of Nuisance, 1949, 65 L.Q.Rev. 480, 488, contending that Rylands v. Fletcher is but a branch of a broader principle of nuisance, differing only in that it permits recovery for an isolated incident.

50. Filtrol Corp. v. Hughes, 1945, 199 Miss. 10, 23 So.2d 891; Pruitt v. Bethell, 1917, 174 N.C. 454, 93 S.E. 945; De Vaughn v. Minor, 1887, 77 Ga. 809, 1 S.E. 433; Alabama Western R. Co. v. Wilson, 1911, 1 Ala.App. 306, 55 So. 932; Smith v. Board of County Road Comm'rs, 1966, 5 Mich.App. 370, 146 N.W.2d 702.

51. Pixley v. Clark, 1866, 35 N.Y. 520; Goodyear Tire & Rubber Co. v. Gadsden Sand & Gravel Co., 1946, 248 Ala. 273, 27 So.2d 578; International & G. N. R. Co. v. Slusher, 1906, 42 Tex.Civ.App. 631, 95 S.W. 717; City of Barberton v. Miksch, 1934, 128 Ohio St. 169, 190 N.E. 387.

52. Heeg v. Licht, 1880, 80 N.Y. 579; McAndrews v. Collerd, 1880, 42 N.J.L. 189; Comminge v. Stevenson, 1890, 76 Tex. 642, 13 S.W. 556; Forster v. Rogers, 1915, 247 Pa. 54, 93 A. 26; Cumberland Torpedo Co. v. Gaines, 1923, 201 Ky. 88, 255 S.W. 1046; St. Joseph Lead Co. v. Prather, 8 Cir. 1956, 238 F.2d 301.

53. Whittemore v. Baxter Laundry Co., 1914, 181 Mich. 564, 148 N.W. 437; Great Northern Refining Co. v. Lutes, 1921, 190 Ky. 451, 227 S.W. 795; McGuffey v. Pierce-Fordyce Oil Ass'n, Tex.Civ.App. 1919, 211 S.W. 335; O'Hara v. Nelson, 1906, 71 N. J.Eq. 161, 63 A. 836.

54. Gossett v. Southern R. Co., 1905, 115 Tenn. 376, 89 S.W. 737; Blackford v. Heman Const. Co., 1908, 132 Mo.App. 157, 112 S.W. 287; Dixon v. New York Trap Rock Corp., 1944, 293 N.Y. 509, 58 N.E.2d 517, motion denied, 1945, 294 N.Y. 654, 60 N.E.2d 385; Fontenot v. Magnolia Petroleum Co., 1955, 227 La. 866, 80 So.2d 845; Opal v. Material Service Corp., 1956, 9 Ill.App.2d 433, 133 N.E.2d 733.

off in the public streets;[55] oil wells[56] or abnormal mining operations;[57] the accumulation of sewage;[58] concussion or vibration from a rock crusher;[59] and in addition such things as smoke, dust, bad odors, noxious gases and the like from industrial enterprises,[60] all obviously closely related to the cases following Rylands v. Fletcher. There has been general recognition in these nuisance cases that the relation of the activity to its surroundings is the controlling factor; and a magazine of explosives or a huge tank full of gasoline in the midst of a populous city may be an absolute nuisance, where the same explosive[61] or inflammable liquid[62] in the

wilderness or under less highly and obviously dangerous conditions is not. The "non-natural use" becomes an "unreasonable use."[63]

There is in fact probably no case applying Rylands v. Fletcher which is not duplicated in all essential respects by some American decision which proceeds on the theory of nuisance;[64] and it is quite evident that under that name the principle is in reality universally accepted.[65]

Blasting, which has been so commonly given as an illustration of an activity which falls clearly within Rylands v. Fletcher that it has come to typify all such activities, actually has run the gamut of all possible theories of liability.[66] The first cases to arise were those in which rocks were thrown upon the plaintiff's premises, and it was possible to impose strict liability upon the ground that there was a trespass to land.[67] The courts are still virtually unanimous in holding that there is

55. Landau v. City of New York, 1904, 180 N.Y. 48, 72 N.E. 631; Harris v. City of Findlay, 1938, 59 Ohio App. 375, 18 N.E.2d 413; Moore v. City of Bloomington, 1911, 51 Ind.App. 145, 95 N.E. 374.

56. Teel v. Rio Bravo Oil Co., 1907, 47 Tex.Civ.App. 153, 104 S.W.2d 420 (abnormal discharge of salt water); Niagara Oil Co. v. Ogle, 1912, 177 Ind. 292, 98 N.E. 60; McGregor v. Camden, 1899, 47 W.Va. 193, 34 S.E. 936. See Keeton and Jones, Tort Liability and the Oil and Gas Industry, 1956, 35 Tex.L. Rev. 1.

57. Jones v. Robertson, 1886, 116 Ill. 543, 6 N.E. 890; Beach v. Sterling Iron & Zinc Co., 1895, 54 N.J.Eq. 65, 33 A. 286; Pennsylvania R. Co. v. Sagamore Coal Co., 1924, 281 Pa. 233, 126 A. 386; H. B. Bowling Coal Co. v. Ruffner, 1907, 117 Tenn. 180, 100 S.W. 116.

58. Jutte v. Hughes, 1876, 67 N.Y. 267; In re Haugh's Appeal, 1883, 102 Pa. 42; Ryan v. City of Emmetsburg, 1942, 232 Iowa 600, 4 N.W.2d 435.

59. Gilbert v. Davidson Const. Co., 1922, 110 Kan. 298, 203 P. 1113; Dilucehio v. Shaw, 1922, 31 Del. 509, 115 A. 771.

60. See for example Dutton v. Rocky Mountain Phosphates, 1968, 151 Mont. 54, 438 P.2d 674; Bartel v. Ridgefield Lumber Co., 1924, 131 Wash. 183, 229 P. 306; Susquehanna Fertilizer Co. v. Malone, 1890, 73 Md. 268, 20 A. 900; King v. Columbian Carbon Co., 5 Cir. 1945, 152 F.2d 636; Columbian Carbon Co. v. Tholen, Tex.Civ.App.1947, 199 S.W.2d 825, error refused.

61. Tuckachinsky v. Lehigh & W. Coal Co., 1901, 199 Pa. 515, 49 A. 308; Kleebauer v. Western Fuse & Explosives Co., 1903, 138 Cal. 497, 71 P. 617; Henderson v. Sullivan, 6 Cir. 1908, 159 F. 46; Whaley v. Sloss-Sheffield Steel & Iron Co., 1909, 164 Ala. 216, 51 So. 419.

62. Thomas v. Jacobs, 1916, 254 Pa. 255, 98 A. 863; Adams Co. v. Buchanan, 1920, 42 S.D. 548, 176 N.W.

512; Shell Petroleum Co. v. Wilson, 1936, 178 Okl. 355, 65 P.2d 173; State ex rel. Stewart v. Cozad, 1923, 113 Kan. 200, 213 P. 654.

63. See infra, p. 596.

64. Even Attorney-General v. Corke, [1933] Ch. 89, where the defendant's harboring of disreputable gypsies was held to come within Rylands v. Fletcher, finds a close parallel in the tenement full of Mexican peons in Harty v. Guerra, Tex.Civ.App. 1925, 269 S.W. 1064, and the workhouse in District of Columbia v. Totten, App.D.C.1925, 5 F.2d 374. Compare also Shipley v. Fifty Associates, 1869, 101 Mass. 251 affirmed, 1870, 106 Mass. 194 (roof shedding snow), with Davis v. Niagara Falls Tower Co., 1902, 171 N.Y. 336, 64 N.E. 4 (tower shedding ice).

65. See Prosser, Nuisance Without Fault, 1942, 20 Tex.L.Rev. 399; Notes, 1934, 29 Ill.L.Rev. 372; 1947, 95 U.Pa.L.Rev. 781.

66. See McNeal, Use of Explosives and Liability Questions Involved, 1956, 23 Ins.Counsel J. 125; Smith, Liability for Substantial Physical Damage to Land by Blasting, 1920, 33 Harv.L.Rev. 542, 667; Gregory, Trespass to Negligence to Absolute Liability, 1951, 37 Va.L.Rev. 359; Notes, 1910, 10 Col.L. Rev. 465; 1935, 19 Minn.L.Rev. 322; 1937, 16 Tex. L.Rev. 426; 1962, 40 N.C.L.Rev. 640.

67. See supra, p. 64.

such liability when this occurs,[68] or where some flying object strikes a person.[69] Where the damage is the result merely of concussion or vibration, some five or six continue to adhere to the ancient distinction between trespass and case,[70] and regard the injury as an "indirect" one, for which there can be no recovery except on the basis of negligence.[71] This distinction, which has often been denounced[72] as a marriage of procedural technicality with scientific ignorance, is rejected by the great majority of the courts, which hold the defendant strictly liable for concussion damage.[73] Many of the later cases[74] have come to the conclusion, which might be drawn with fair success from the facts of the entire group of blasting cases,[75] that the strict liability is entirely a question of the relation of the activity to its surroundings; and that the use of explosives on an uninhabited mountainside is a matter of negligence only, while any one who blasts in the center of a large city does so at his peril, and must bear the responsibility for the damage he does, despite all proper care.

Ground damage from aviation has been a matter of controversy, not yet entirely determined.[76] Flying was of course regarded at first as a questionable and highly dangerous enterprise, the province exclusively of venturesome fools, and so properly subject to strict liability for any harm to persons and property beneath; and this was encouraged

---

68. Hay v. Cohoes County, 1849, 2 N.Y. 159; Mulchanock v. Whitehall Cement Mfg. Co., 1916, 252 Pa. 262, 98 A. 554; Adams & Sullivan v. Sengel, 1917, 177 Ky. 535, 197 S.W. 974; Central Iron & Coal Co. v. Vanderheurk, 1906, 147 Ala. 546, 41 So. 145; Asheville Const. Co. v. Southern R. Co., 4 Cir. 1927, 19 F.2d 32.

69. Sullivan v. Dunham, 1900, 161 N.Y. 290, 55 N.E. 923; Wells v. Knight, 1911, 32 R.I. 432, 80 A. 16; Louisville & N. R. Co. v. Smith's Adm'r, 1923, 203 Ky. 513, 263 S.W. 29.

70. See supra, § 7.

71. Coalite, Inc. v. Aldridge, 1969, —— Ala. ——, 229 So.2d 539; Wadleigh v. City of Manchester, 1956, 100 N.H. 277, 123 A.2d 831; Albison v. Robbins & White, 1955, 151 Me. 114, 116 A.2d 608.

Kentucky and Vermont have recently abandoned this position. Lynn Mining Co. v. Kelly, Ky.1965, 394 S.W.2d 755; Malloy v. Lane Const. Co., 1963, 123 Vt. 500, 194 A.2d 398. It has very probably received its death blow when New York joined them, in Spano v. Perini Corp., 1969, 25 N.Y.2d 11, 302 N. Y.S.2d 527, 250 N.E.2d 31, on remand 33 App.Div.2d 516, 304 N.Y.S.2d 15.

72. Smith, Liability for Substantial Physical Damage to Land by Blasting, 1920, 33 Harv.L.Rev. 542, 667; Salmond, Law of Torts, 7th Ed. 1928, 231; Notes, 1910, 10 Col.L.Rev. 465; 1935, 19 Minn.L.Rev. 322; 1937, 16 Tex.L.Rev. 426; 1967, 31 Alb.L.J. 370. It is, however, defended by Fleming, Torts, 3d Ed. 1965, 40 on the basis that a nuisance action allows for reasonable use and abnormal sensitivity, while trespass does not. This may be valid as to the form of action, but scarcely as to the substance of strict liability.

There is excellent discussion in Louden v. City of Cincinnati, 1914, 90 Ohio St. 144, 106 N.E. 970; and in Watson v. Mississippi River Power Co., 1916, 174 Iowa 23, 156 N.W. 188.

73. Western Geophysical Co. of America v. Mason, 1966, 240 Ark. 767, 402 S.W.2d 657; Enos Coal Min. Co. v. Schuchart, 1963, 243 Ind. 692, 188 N.E.2d 406; Wallace v. A. H. Guion & Co., 1960, 237 S.C. 349, 117 S.E.2d 359; Thigpen v. Skousen & Hise, 1958, 64 N.M. 290, 327 P.2d 802; Whitney v. Ralph Myers Contracting Corp., 1961, 146 W.Va. 130, 118 S.E.2d 622.

74. Robison v. Robison, 1964, 16 Utah 2d 2, 394 P. 2d 876; Boonville Collieries Corp. v. Reynolds, 1960, 130 Ind.App. 331, 163 N.E.2d 627; Alonso v. Hills, 1950, 95 Cal.App.2d 778, 214 P.2d 50; Cashin v. Northern Pac. R. Co., 1934, 96 Mont. 92, 28 P.2d 862; Carson v. Blodgett Const. Co., 1915, 189 Mo. App. 120, 174 S.W. 447.

75. Thus compare McKenna v. Pacific Elec. R. Co., 1930, 104 Cal.App. 538, 286 P. 445, with Houghton v. Loma Prieta Lumber Co., 1907, 152 Cal. 500, 93 P. 82; also Klepsch v. Donald, 1892, 4 Wash. 436, 30 P. 991, with Patrick v. Smith, 1913, 75 Wash. 407, 134 P. 1076; also Freebury v. Chicago, M. & P. S. R. Co., 1914, 77 Wash. 464, 137 P. 1044, with Kendall v. Johnson, 1909, 51 Wash. 477, 99 P. 310.

76. See Orr, Is Aviation Ultra-Hazardous? 1954, 21 Ins.Counsel J. 48; Vold, Strict Liability for Airplane Crashes, 1953, 5 Hastings L.J. 1; Eubank, Land Damage Liability in Aircraft Cases, 1953, 57 Dick.L.Rev. 155; Orr, Airplane Tort Law, 1952, 19 Ins.Counsel J. 67; Vold, Aircraft Operator's Liability for Ground Damage and Passenger Injury, 1935, 13 Neb.L.Rev. 373; Notes, 1955, 31 Ind.L.J. 63; 1957, 19 U.Pitt.L.Rev. 154; 1955, 43 Cal.L.Rev. 309.

by the fact that the first cases [77] arose in New York, where there was strict liability for any physical invasion of land.[78] Notwithstanding vigorous agitation on the part of the developing industry,[79] the Restatement of Torts [80] in 1939 took the position that aviation had not reached such a stage of safety as to justify treating it by analogy to the railroads, and classified it as an "ultrahazardous activity" upon which strict liability for ground damage was to be imposed. This position was also incorporated in Section 5 of the Uniform Aeronautics Act,[81] promulgated by the Commissioners on Uniform State Laws in 1922.

With the further development of the industry, and an improved safety record,[82] later years have witnessed a considerable amount of hesitancy over the strict liability, efforts to avoid passing upon it whenever possible, and at last a definite reversal of the trend. In 1943 the Uniform Act was withdrawn by the Commissioners for further study, and it has not been reissued.[83] Several of the states which have adopted it have eliminated, repealed or modified the section providing for strict liability for ground damage.[84]

In spite of all the discussion, cases dealing with the liability at common law have been astonishingly few. The cases arising in New York first adhered to the rule of that state as to strict liability for any land trespass,[85] but they are now apparently in process of being overruled,[86] in common with other accidental trespass cases. There have been two or three decisions from other jurisdictions which, without a statute, have imposed strict

---

77. Guille v. Swan, 1822, 19 Johns., N.Y., 381; Rochester Gas & Elec. Corp. v. Dunlop, 1933, 148 Misc. 849, 266 N.Y.S. 469. See Baldwin, Liability for Accidents in Aerial Navigation, 1910, 9 Mich.L.Rev. 20.

78. See supra, p. 63.

79. See, criticizing strict liability as putting its advocates in the "ranks of those passed on, but not forgotten, solons who required a man with a red lantern to precede a railroad train," 1931, 2 J.Air Law 549; Cooper, Aircraft Liability to Persons and Property on Ground, 1931, 17 A.B.A.J. 435; Ewing, The Ground Rule of Torts by Aircraft at the American Law Institute, 1934, 5 Air L.Rev. 323; Report of American Bar Ass'n Standing Committee on Aeronautical Law, 1931.

80. § 520, Comment b. See, upholding this position, Vold, Strict Liability for Aircraft Crashes and Forced Landings, 1953, 5 Hastings L.J. 1; Bohlen Aviation Under the Common Law, 1934, 45 Harv.L. Rev. 216.

81. See 9 Uniform Laws Ann. 17; Note, [1948] Wis. L.Rev. 356. The Act was applied in United States v. Praylou, 4 Cir. 1953, 208 F.2d 291, cert. denied 347 U.S. 934. (South Carolina law); United States v. Pendergrast, 4 Cir. 1957, 241 F.2d 687 (same); Prentiss v. National Airlines, D.N.J.1953, 112 F. Supp. 306 (New Jersey; held constitutional); Adler's Quality Bakery, Inc. v. Gaseteria, Inc., 1960, 32 N.J. 55, 159 A.2d 97.

Cf. D'Anna v. United States, 4 Cir. 1950, 181 F.2d 335 (presumption of negligence under Maryland statute).

82. See Orr, Is Aviation Ultra-Hazardous, 1954, 21 Ins.Counsel J. 48; Sweeney, Is Special Aviation Liability Legislation Essential, 1952, 19 J.Air Law

166, 311. Report of Civil Aeronautics Board, Bureau of Safety, Feb. 25, 1965.

83. See 9 Uniform Laws Ann. xvi.

84. The statutes are summarized up to 1953, in Eubank, Land Damage Liability in Aircraft Cases, 1953, 57 Dick.L.Rev. 188, 193. As of the end of 1967, the state of the statutory law was as follows:

Nine jurisdictions had strict liability provisions: Delaware, Hawaii, Minnesota, Montana, New Jersey, North Dakota, South Carolina, Tennessee, Wyoming; Five provided for a presumption of negligence, rebuttable by proof of due care: Georgia, Maryland, Nevada, Rhode Island, Wisconsin; Eight had provisions apparently rejecting strict liability, and stating that the "ordinary rules of law" shall govern: Arizona, Arkansas, California, Idaho, Missouri, Pennsylvania, South Dakota, Vermont; Five had repealed strict liability provisions, and were without legislation: Connecticut, Indiana, Michigan, North Carolina, Utah. The rest never have had any legislation.

85. Rochester Gas & Elec. Corp. v. Dunlop, 1933, 148 Misc. 849, 266 N.Y.S. 469; Margosian v. United States Airlines, E.D.N.Y.1955, 127 F.Supp. 464; Hahn v. U. S. Airlines, E.D.N.Y.1954, 127 F.Supp. 950.

86. Wood v. United Air Lines, Inc., 1961, 32 Misc.2d 955, 223 N.Y.S.2d 692, affirmed memo. 16 App.Div. 2d 659, 226 N.Y.S.2d 1022, appeal dismissed 11 N.Y. 2d 1053, 230 N.Y.S.2d 207, 184 N.E.2d 180; Crist v. Civil Air Patrol, 1967, 53 Misc.2d 289, 278 N.Y.S.2d 430.

liability for ground damage,[87] in line with the Uniform Act. About as many others [88] have rejected such a rule, and have insisted that the liability must rest upon proof of negligence. Most of the decisions have gone off upon proof of specific negligence,[89] or have resorted to res ipsa loquitur,[90] which by inference, at least, would indicate a rejection of

strict liability. The question cannot be said to be finally determined; and since nearly half of the jurisdictions now have statutes bearing on the matter, its ultimate solution appears very likely to be in the form of legislation.

One possible suggestion as to the ultimate outcome is that strict liability might be retained as to what may be called "abnormal" aviation, including all such things as stunt flying,[91] crop dusting,[92] experimental aircraft and military planes not designed primarily for safety,[93] and "sonic booms," [94] while "normal" aviation, including all common commercial flights, might require proof of negligence. Rapid technological changes would, however, make such a classification extremely difficult to maintain.

Although rockets already have made their appearance [95] in the field of strict liability, the first case raising the question as to the use of nuclear energy has yet to reach the courts.[96] When it does, it may be predicted with a good deal of confidence that this is an area in which no court will, at last, refuse to recognize and apply the principle of strict liability found in the cases which follow Rylands v. Fletcher.[97]

87. Parcell v. United States, S.D.W.Va.1951, 104 F. Supp. 110 F.Supp. 110 (collision of two military planes); Gaidys v. United States, D.Colo., [1951] U. S.Av.Rep. 352 (military aircraft crashed while flying low after take-off); D'Anna v. United States, 4 Cir. 1950, 181 F.2d 335 (fall of auxiliary gas tank from military plane); cf. Long v. United States, W.D.S.C.1965, 241 F.Supp. 286 (under South Carolina statute). See Notes, 1951, 4 Vand.L.Rev. 867; 1953, 38 Corn.L.Q. 570; 1963, 15 Syr.L.Rev. 1.

88. Johnson v. Dew, 1964, 204 Pa.Super. 526, 205 A. 2d 880; Southern Cal. Edison Co. v. Coleman, 1957, 150 Cal.App.2d Supp. 829, 310 P.2d 504; In re Kinsey's Estate, 1949, 152 Neb. 95, 40 N.W.2d 526, 531; State to Use of Birckhead v. Sammon, 1936, 171 Md. 178, 189 A. 265.

See also the following, where the action was against the owner of the plane, and the court rejected the contention that he was liable because the activity was "ultrahazardous," "inherently dangerous," and the like: Fosbroke-Hobbes v. Airwork, Ltd., [1936] 1 All Eng.Rep. 108; D'Aquilla v. Pryor, S.D.N.Y. 1954, 122 F.Supp. 346; Johnson v. Central Aviation Corp., 1951, 103 Cal.App.2d 102, 229 P.2d 114; Spartan Aircraft Co. v. Jamison, 1938, 181 Okl. 645, 75 P.2d 1096; Herrick & Olson v. Curtiss, Sup.Ct. Nassau County, N.Y., [1932] U.S.Av.Rep. 110.

89. San Diego Gas & Elec. Co. v. United States, 9 Cir. 1949, 173 F.2d 92 (low flying); Bright v. United States, E.D.Ill.1956, 149 F.Supp. 620 (flying into storm); Evans v. United States, W.D.La.1951, 100 F.Supp. 5 (inexperienced pilot); Leisy v. United States, D.Minn.1954, 102 F.Supp. 789 (low flying); Maitland v. Twin City Aviation Corp., 1949, 254 Wis. 541, 37 N.W.2d 74 (same); Murphy v. Neely, 1935, 319 Pa. 437, 179 A. 439 (bad operation).

90. United States v. Kesinger, 10 Cir. 1951, 190 F.2d 529; Northwestern Nat. Ins. Co. v. United States, N.D.Ill.1949, [1949] U.S.Av.Rep. 316; Kadylak v. O'Brien, W.D.Pa.1941, 32 F.Supp. 281; Goodwin v. United States, E.D.N.C.1956, 141 F.Supp. 445; Sollak v. State, N.Y.Ct.Cl.1927, [1929] U.S.Av.Rep. 42. See also the following, which refused to apply res ipsa loquitur, and denied recovery: Williams v. United States, 5 Cir. 1955, 218 F.2d 473 (jet bomber exploded, flaming fuel fell on plaintiff's house—a horrible case); Deojay v. Lyford, 1942, 139 Me. 234, 29 A.2d 111 (bad landing); Prokop v. Becker, 1942, 345 Pa. 607, 29 A.2d 23 (same).

91. Johnson v. Curtiss Northwest Airplane Co., D. Ramsey County, Minn.1923, [1928] U.S.Av.Rep. 42 (enjoined at any altitude).

92. See supra, p. 513.

93. Cf. Canney v. Rochester Agricultural & Mechanical Ass'n, 1911, 76 N.H. 60, 79 A. 517 (balloon).

94. See Note, 1958, 31 So.Cal.L.Rev. 259.

95. Berg v. Reaction Motors Division, Thiokol Chemical Corp., 1962, 37 N.J. 396, 181 A.2d 487; Smith v. Lockheed Propulsion Co., 1967, 247 Cal.App.2d 774, 56 Cal.Rptr. 128.

96. Both Bartholomae Corp. v. United States, S.D. Cal.1955, 135 F.Supp. 651, and Bulloch v. United States, D.Utah 1955, 133 F.Supp. 885, never reached the issue, but were disposed of on the basis of the exception, in the Federal Tort Claims Act, as to the "discretionary functions" of government officers. See infra, p. 973.

97. See Seavey, Torts and Atoms, 1958, 46 Cal.L.Rev. 3; Frampton, Radiation Exposure—The Need for a National Policy, 1957, 10 Stan.L.Rev. 7; Stason, Estep and Pierce, Atoms and the Law, 1959.

79. EXTENT OF LIABILITY

In dealing with the extent of strict liability, and the limitations upon it, it is convenient to group together all of the areas in which it is applied, since, with some occasional exceptions, reasonably consistent rules have developed which are common to all of them. It is clear, first of all, that unless a statute requires it, strict liability will never be found unless the defendant is aware of the abnormally dangerous condition or activity, and has voluntarily engaged in or permitted it.[98] Mere negligent failure to discover or prevent it is not enough, although it may, of course, be an independent basis of liability.

Once the responsibility is established, it frequently is stated, in cases of strict liability, that the defendant acts "at his peril," [99] and is an insurer against the consequences of his conduct. What is meant is usually that he is liable although he has taken every possible precaution to prevent the harm, and is not at "fault" in any moral or social sense. But there are not lacking indications that the liability itself is thought to be an extensive one. Baron Bramwell [1] once carried this to the length of saying that if a man kept a tiger and lightning broke his chain, he might be liable for all the mischief the tiger might do.

But such extended responsibility may undoubtedly impose too heavy a burden upon the defendant. It is one thing to say that a dangerous enterprise must pay its way within reasonable limits, and quite another to say that it must bear responsibility for every extreme of harm that it may cause.

The same practical necessity for the restriction of liability within some reasonable bounds, which arises in connection with problems of "proximate cause" in negligence cases,[2] demands here that some limit be set. It might be expected that this limit would be a narrower one where no initial departure from a social standard is to be found. In general, this has been true. Just as liability for negligence has tended to be restricted within narrower boundaries than when intentional misconduct is involved,[3] there is a visible tendency to restrict it still further when there is not even negligence. The intentional wrongdoer is commonly held liable for consequences extending beyond the scope of the foreseeable risk he creates,[4] and many courts have carried negligence liability beyond the risk to some extent.[5] But where there is neither intentional harm nor negligence, the line is generally drawn at the limits of the risk,[6] or even within it. This limitation has been expressed by saying that the defendant's duty to insure safety extends only to certain consequences.[7] More commonly, it is said that the defendant's conduct is not the "proximate cause" of the damage.[8] But ordinarily in such cases no question of causation is involved, and the limitation is one of the policy underlying liability.

Type of Harm Threatened

The type of damage threatened by the conduct which entails strict liability usually is

---

98. Zampos v. U. S. Smelting, Ref. & Min. Co., 10 Cir. 1953, 206 F.2d 171; The Nitroglycerine Case (Parrott v. Wells, Fargo & Co.), 1872, 15 Wall., U. S., 524; Hunt v. Hazen, 1953, 197 Or. 637, 254 P.2d 210; Dickson v. Graham-Jones Paper Co., Fla.1956, 84 So.2d 309.

99. Rylands v. Fletcher, 1868, L.R. 3 H.L. 330, 37 L. J.Ex. 161; Exner v. Sherman Power Const. Co., 2 Cir. 1931, 54 F.2d 510.

1. In Nichols v. Marsland, 1875, L.R. 10 Ex. 255.

2. See supra, § 42; Carpenter, Proximate Cause, 1942, 15 So.Cal.L.Rev. 188, 195–198.

3. See supra, p. 263.

4. Cf. Wyant v. Crouse, 1901, 127 Mich. 158, 86 N.W. 527; Isham v. Dow's Estate, 1898, 70 Vt. 588, 41 A. 585; Derosier v. New England Tel. & Tel. Co., 1925, 81 N.H. 451, 130 A. 145.

5. See supra, § 43.

6. See Harper, Liability Without Fault and Proximate Cause, 1932, 30 Mich.L.Rev. 1001.

7. See Pollock, Duties of Insuring Safety: The Rule in Rylands v. Fletcher, 1886, 2 L.Q.Rev. 52.

8. See Harper, Liability Without Fault and Proximate Cause, 1932, 30 Mich.L.Rev. 1001.

well defined. The keeping of vicious animals involves the risk that human beings or other animals will be attacked; the risk of abnormally dangerous things and activities, such as high tension electricity or blasting, is sufficiently obvious. In general, strict liability has been confined to consequences which lie within the extraordinary risk whose existence calls for such special responsibility.

Thus the owner of trespassing animals has been held strictly liable for consequences of the trespass which were reasonably to be expected from an invasion by animals of the particular kind—including, of course, damage to crops, attacks upon other animals,[9] infecting them with disease,[10] or the misalliance of a scrub bull with a pedigreed heifer.[11] The same has been true of personal injuries suffered by the owner in an attempt to put the animal out, which has been regarded as foreseeable, reasonably likely to occur, and to provoke resistance.[12] On the other hand, there are several cases [13] denying recovery for in-

juries from quite unprovoked attacks, on the ground that they could not reasonably be expected to follow from the trespass; and it has also been denied for more indirect and unlikely results, as where a trespassing cow breaks through a rotten floor, and the plaintiff, in the dark, later falls into the hole.[14] In general, the cases support the view that the defendant will be liable only for normal consequences of the trespass, lying within the risk,[15] which will vary with the type of animal involved,[16] and may often be a jury question.

If no trespass can be established, the question becomes one of strict liability for keeping the animal at all.[17] Here again the same conclusion is to be drawn. Thus the keeper of a wild animal, such as a bear or an elephant, has been held not liable for the fright of a horse at the mere sight of the animal on the highway, on the ground that the foreseeable risk of keeping the animal did not extend to

---

9. Dolph v. Ferris, 1844, 7 Watts & S., Pa., 367 (bull); McKee v. Trisler, 1924, 311 Ill. 536, 143 N.E. 69 (bull); Morgan v. Hudnell, 1893, 52 Ohio St. 552, 40 N.E. 716 (horse); Ellis v. Loftus Iron Co., 1874, L.R. 10 C.P. 10 (horse); Hilton v. Overly, 1918, 69 Pa.Super. 348 (boar hog). Cf. Houska v. Hrabe, 1915, 35 S.D. 269, 151 N.W. 1021 (playful horse).

10. Anderton v. Buckton, 1718, 11 Mod. 304, 88 Eng. Rep. 1054; Theyer v. Purnell, [1918] 2 K.B. 333; Lee v. Burk, 1884, 15 Ill.App. 651.

11. Crawford v. Williams, 1878, 48 Iowa 247; McLean v. Brett, 1919, 15 Alta.L.Rep. 43, 49 Dom.L. Rep. 162; Cousins v. Greaves, 1920, 13 Sask.L.Rep. 443, 54 Dom.L.Rep. 630. See, among the classics of legal humor on this subject, Kopplin v. Quade, 1911, 145 Wis. 454, 130 N.W. 511.

12. Troth v. Wills, 1897, 8 Pa.Super. 1; Nixon v. Harris, 1968, 15 Ohio St.2d 105, 238 N.E.2d 785; Walker v. Nickerson, 1935, 291 Mass. 522, 197 N.E. 451; Robinson v. Kerr, 1960, 144 Colo. 48, 355 P.2d 117; Harris Park Lakeshore, Inc. v. Church, 1963, 152 Colo. 278, 381 P.2d 459.

13. Leipske v. Guenther, 1959, 7 Wis.2d 86, 95 N.W. 2d 774, rehearing denied, 1959, 7 Wis.2d 86, 96 N. W.2d 821 (horse reached over high fence and bit schoolgirl in the ear); Harvey v. Buchanan, 1904, 121 Ga. 384, 49 S.E. 281 (mule killing kid); Klenberg v. Russell, 1890, 125 Ind. 531, 25 N.E. 596 (unprovoked attack on plaintiff by cow); Street v.

Craig, 1920, 48 Ont.L.Rep. 324, 56 Dom.L.Rep. 105 (same); Bradley v. Wallace's, Ltd., [1913] 3 K.B. 629 (horse killed a man).

14. Hollenbeck v. Johnson, 1894, 79 Hun 449, 29 N. Y.S. 945. Cf. Durrham v. Goodwin, 1870, 54 Ill. 469, where defendant's horses broke down a fence, and let in the horses of a third party, which did the damage.

15. See Troth v. Wills, 1898, 8 Pa.Super. 1; Theyer v. Purnell, [1918] 2 K.B. 333; Street v. Craig, 1920, 48 Ont.L.Rep. 324, 56 Dom.L.Rep. 105; Note, 1919, 32 Harv.L.Rev. 420; and compare Fox v. Koehnig, 1926, 190 Wis. 528, 209 N.W. 708. This seems to amount to saying that knowledge of the propensity of the animal to inflict such injuries is necessary, but that in certain cases the owner will not be heard to deny it.

16. See the dissenting opinion in Troth v. Wills, 1898, 8 Pa.Super. 1, putting the case of injury to a child by a trespassing pet lamb or hen.

17. Manton v. Brocklebank, [1923] 2 K.B. 212; Dufer v. Cully, 1871, 3 Or. 377; Van Leuven v. Lyke, 1848, 1 N.Y. 515. Thus in Peterson v. Conlan, 1909, 18 N.D. 205, 119 N.W. 367, a mere licensee on the land was not allowed to recover on the basis of trespass. See, however, Troth v. Wills, 1898, 8 Pa. Super. 1, allowing recovery by a member of the household of the landholder. The Restatement of Torts, § 504, seems clearly to go too far in permitting recovery for *any* harm done while upon the land to its possessor or a member of his household.

such an event;[18] but strict liability has been imposed for the fright of a person whom such an animal attempts to attack.[19] Recovery has been denied where a dog known to attack other animals but never human beings unexpectedly attacked a man;[20] where animals which escape onto the highway attack people[21] or interfere with vehicles,[22] or while trespassing cause unexpected personal injuries of a kind not to be anticipated from such an animal.[23] The statutory strict liability for the escape of fire has been held not to extend to cattle frightened into a stampede,[24] on the ground that this was not the risk at which the statute was directed. The doctrine of Rylands v. Fletcher has been held not to apply where dangerous electric current caused electrical interference with telegraph communications,[25] or the heat from the defendant's mill damaged a very delicate type of paper which the plaintiff was keeping for sale on his premises.[26]

Class of Persons Protected

In much the same manner, the class of persons who are threatened by the abnormal danger, and the kind of damage they may be expected to incur, usually are well marked out. Strict liability probably is limited to such plaintiffs and such damages. Thus, it has been held that where the defendant's blasting hurls a rock to such a distance that no experience would have recognized the danger,[27] or causes frightened mink to kill their young,[28] the plaintiff cannot recover without a finding of negligence.

Injuries occurring on the premises of the defendant involve primarily questions of duty. Although there are one or two cases[29]

---

18. Scribner v. Kelley, 1862, 38 Barb., N.Y., 14; Bostock-Ferari Amusement Co. v. Brocksmith, 1895, 34 Ind.App. 566, 73 N.E. 281.

19. Candler v. Smith, 1935, 50 Ga.App. 667, 179 S.E. 395 (baboon); cf. Netusil v. Novak, 1931, 120 Neb. 751, 235 N.W. 335.

20. Keightlinger v. Egan, 1872, 65 Ill. 235; Ewing v. Prince, Ky.1968, 425 S.W.2d 732 (mare); Glanville v. Sutton, [1928] 1 K.B. 571. Accord, Koetting v. Conroy, 1936, 223 Wis. 550, 270 N.W. 625, 271 N.W. 369 (vicious dog, instead of attacking plaintiff, accidentally ran into him).

21. Cox v. Burbidge, 1863, 13 C.B.,N.S., 430, 143 Eng.Rep. 171; Klenberg v. Russell, 1890, 125 Ind. 531, 25 N.E. 596; Brady v. Straub, 1917, 177 Ky. 468, 197 S.W. 938. But compare the view that a kick from a horse is not beyond the risk involved in allowing the horse to be free on the street. Healey v. P. Ballentine & Sons, 1901, 66 N.J.L. 339, 49 A. 511. Liability may of course be based on negligence in allowing the animal to be at large. Cf. Dickson v. McCoy, 1868, 39 N.Y. 400; Netusil v. Novak, 1931, 120 Neb. 751, 235 N.W. 335.

22. Hadwell v. Righton, [1907] 2 K.B. 345 (fowl flying into wheel of bicycle); Marsh v. Koons, 1908, 78 Ohio St. 68, 84 N.E. 599 (cow frightening horse); Zumstein v. Shrumm, [1895] 22 Ont.App. 262 (turkey frightening horse); Fox v. Koehnig, 1926, 190 Wis. 528, 209 N.W. 708 (automobile colliding with horse); Dyer v. Mudgett, 1919, 118 Me. 267, 107 A. 831 (same). Liability may, however, be predicated on negligence in allowing the animal to be at large. Drew v. Gross, 1925, 112 Ohio St. 485, 147 N.E. 757; Wedel v. Johnson, 1936, 196 Minn. 170, 264 N.W. 689; Roberts v. Griffith, 1929, 100 Cal.App. 456, 280 P. 199.

23. See supra, § 76.

24. Chicago, B. & Q. R. Co. v. Gelvin, 8 Cir. 1916, 238 F. 14.

25. Eastern & South African Tel. Co. v. Cape Town Tramways Co., [1902] A.C. 381, 71 L.J.P.C. 122; Lake Shore & M. S. R. Co. v. Chicago, L. S. & S. B. R. Co., 1911, 48 Ind.App. 584, 92 N.E. 989; Postal Telegraph-Cable Co. v. Pacific Gas & Elec. Co., 1927, 202 Cal. 382, 260 P. 1101; Amphitheatres, Inc. v. Portland Meadows, 1948, 184 Or. 336, 198 P.2d 847. See, 1928, 12 Minn.L.Rev. 414; 1928, 16 Cal. L.Rev. 331.

26. Robinson v. Kilvert, 1889, 41 Ch.Div. 88.

27. Klepsch v. Donald, 1892, 4 Wash. 436, 30 P. 991; cf. Houghton v. Loma Prieta Lumber Co., 1907, 152 Cal. 500, 93 P. 82.

28. Madsen v. East Jordan Irr. Co., 1942, 101 Utah 552, 125 P.2d 794; Foster v. Preston Mill Co., 1954, 44 Wash.2d 440, 268 P.2d 645; Gronn v. Rogers Construction, Inc., 1960, 221 Or. 226, 350 P.2d 1086. But there may be liability for negligence if the defendant, knowing the risk, is found to act unreasonably. Summit View, Inc. v. W. W. Clyde & Co., 1965, 17 Utah 2d 26, 403 P.2d 919; MacGibbon v. Robinson, [1952] 4 Dom.L.Rep. 142.

29. McGehee v. Norfolk & Southern R. Co., 1908, 147 N.C. 142, 60 S.E. 912 (stored dynamite, trespasser shot at the building). Similar, and in accord, is St. Joseph Lead Co. v. Prather, 8 Cir. 1956, 238 F.2d 301, where, however, recovery was allowed on other grounds.

in which, apparently on the ground of unforeseeability, trespassers were denied recovery for abnormally dangerous conditions, most of the cases have involved vicious dogs. It seems clear that the owner may not intentionally keep such a dog for the purpose of attacking mere trespassers,[30] where he would not be privileged to inflict serious injury if he were present in person.[31] But even where there is no such intent, the danger has been considered so extreme, and the situation so unreasonable, that even a trespasser is entitled to protection against it, and can recover when he establishes the necessary scienter.[32] In all of these cases, however, harm to the trespasser was considered foreseeable, and within the risk. It has been contended that unanticipated trespassers are not within the class of persons entitled to protection, and that liability to trespassers, as well as to others entering the owner's premises, should rest upon ordinary principles of negligence.[33]

Licensees and invitees are apparently denied recovery under the doctrine of Rylands v. Fletcher, by the last English decision.[34]

The American rule appears to be definitely to the contrary,[35] particularly as to abnormally dangerous animals. It has been held often enough that the strict liability, both as to vicious dogs [36] and as to wild animals,[37] applies in favor of both licensees and invitees upon the premises. While there are a few other decisions [38] that have held there is no liability in the absence of negligence, they are in a small minority and largely discredited.

Manner of Occurrence

Apparently there is some further limitation as to the manner in which the harm occurs. In the field of negligence, the defendant frequently is held liable when the risk he has created is realized through un-

30. Loomis v. Terry, 1837, 17 Wend., N.Y., 496; Brewer v. Furtwangler, 1933, 171 Wash. 617, 18 P. 2d 837; Conway v. Grant, 1891, 88 Ga. 40, 13 S.E. 803. Otherwise if the dog is safely confined, and kept only for warning. Woodbridge v. Marks, 1897, 17 App.Div. 139, 45 N.Y.S. 156.

31. Thus keeping the dog may be privileged against a felonious intruder, or where the owner would be privileged to set him on in person. See Woolf v. Chalker, 1862, 31 Conn. 121; cf. Ryan v. Marren, 1914, 216 Mass. 556, 104 N.E. 353.

32. Marble v. Ross, 1878, 124 Mass. 44; Eberling v. Mutillod, 1917, 90 N.J.L. 478, 101 A. 519; Woolf v. Chalker, 1862, 31 Conn. 121; Brewer v. Furtwangler, 1933, 171 Wash. 617, 18 P.2d 837; Darby v. Clare Food & Relish Co., 1934, 111 Pa.Super. 537, 170 A. 387; Radoff v. Hunter, 1958, 158 Cal.App.2d 770, 323 P.2d 202. Cf. Glidden v. Moore, 1883, 14 Neb. 84, 15 N.W. 326 (vicious bull).

33. McNeely, A Footnote on Dangerous Animals, 1939, 37 Mich.L.Rev. 1181; Williams, Liability for Animals, 1939, 349–352; Winfield, Torts, 5th Ed. 1950, 541. Thus the Restatement of Torts, §§ 511, 512, takes the position that there is liability to trespassers only where the land is subject to constant intrusion and the owner fails to give such warning. See Broke v. Copeland, 1794, 1 Esp. 202, 170 Eng.Rep. 328; Sarch v. Blackburn, 1830, 4 C. & P. 297, 172 Eng.Rep. 712. Compare, as to anticipated trespassers, Meibus v. Dodge, 1875, 38 Wis. 300.

34. Read v. J. Lyons & Co., [1947] A.C. 156. In E. I. Du Pont de Nemours & Co. v. Cudd, 10 Cir. 1949, 176 F.2d 855, a similar case, recovery was denied on the basis of assumption of risk.

35. McLane v. Northwest Natural Gas Co., 1969, —— Or. ——, 467 P.2d 635, specifically rejecting the English case.

36. Invitees: Zarek v. Fredericks, 3 Cir. 1943, 138 F.2d 689; Frederickson v. Kepner, 1947, 82 Cal. App.2d 905, 187 P.2d 800; Burke v. Fischer, 1944, 298 Ky. 157, 182 S.W.2d 638; Flynn v. Lindenfield, 1967, 6 Ariz.App. 459, 433 P.2d 639; Gerulis v. Lunecki, 1936, 284 Ill.App. 44, 1 N.E.2d 440.

Licensees: Thompson v. Wold, 1955, 47 Wash.2d 782, 289 P.2d 712; Carrow v. Haney, 1920, 203 Mo.App. 485, 219 S.W. 710.

37. Opelt v. Al. G. Barnes Co., 1919, 41 Cal.App. 776, 183 P. 241; Copley v. Wills, Tex.Civ.App.1913, 152 S.W. 830; Crunk v. Glover, 1959, 167 Neb. 816, 95 N.W.2d 135; City of Tonkawa v. Danielson, 1933, 166 Okl. 241, 27 P.2d 348; Bottcher v. Buck, 1928, 265 Mass. 4, 163 N.E. 182. See, however, McNeely, A Footnote on Dangerous Animals, 1939, 37 Mich. L.Rev. 1181, 1192, pointing out that in nearly all such cases liability might have been rested on negligence.

38. Panorama Resort v. Nichols, 1935, 165 Va. 289, 182 N.E. 235; Vaughan v. Miller Bros. "101" Ranch Wild West Show, 1930, 109 W.Va. 170, 153 S.E. 289; Hansen v. Brogan, 1965, 145 Mont. 224, 400 P.2d 265; Parker v. Cushman, 8 Cir. 1912, 195 F. 715; Marquet v. La Duke, 1893, 96 Mich. 596, 55 N. W. 1006.

foreseeable intervening causes.[39] But where strict liability is in question, the strong current of authority, notwithstanding the Restatement of Torts [40] to the contrary, relieves the defendant of liability in such a case.[41] Thus in the leading case of Rylands v. Fletcher,[42] where the defendant's reservoir broke through into the plaintiff's mine, it was suggested that the defendant might excuse himself by showing that the event was caused by an act of God—meaning, obviously, an unforeseeable intervening force of nature. In a later case,[43] where the defendant's dam was carried away by an unprecedented cloudburst, the "act of God" exception was applied, and the defendant was excused from liability. Subsequent decisions have applied the same rule to extraordinary rainfall,[44] a rat gnawing a hole in a receptacle for the storage of water,[45] and even the operation of frost in causing leakage from a pond.[46]

In the same manner, the defendant has been relieved from liability by the independent act of a third person, which he could not have foreseen or prevented. In still another reservoir case,[47] where the escape of the water was caused by a discharge from a reservoir upstream, it was held that the defendant's responsibility did not extend to the wrongful act of a stranger. The decision has been followed in cases involving the escape of water from the upper floor of a building,[48] and oil from a truck,[49] through the meddling of a stranger; and a very similar rule has been applied where the escape of fire from a locomotive was caused by the release of gasoline vapor by the plaintiff's employees.[50] On the same basis, where the defendant's cattle strayed onto the highway and were driven onto the plaintiff's land by an intermeddling stranger, it was held that the defendant was not responsible.[51] On the other hand, in two cases where the attack of an abnormally dangerous animal was brought

---

39. See supra, p. 286.

40. §§ 510, 522. The Tentative Draft, No. 12, p. 142, cites no authority for these sections, except Vredenburg v. Behan, 1881, 33 La.Ann. 627, and Baker v. Snell, [1908] 2 K.B. 825, both of which would appear to be distinguishable, and the dictum of Baron Bramwell, supra, note 1.

41. Harper, Liability Without Fault and Proximate Cause, 1932, 30 Mich.L.Rev. 1001, 1009.

42. 1868, L.R. 3 H.L. 330. Compare the dictum in Tubervil v. Stamp, 1601, 1 Salk. 13, 1 Ld.Raym. 264, Carthew 425, 91 Eng.Rep. 13, that liability for the escape of fire might be avoided "if a sudden storm had arisen, which he could not stop."

43. Nichols v. Marsland, 1876, L.R. 2 Ex.Div. 1.

44. Bratton v. Rudnick, 1933, 283 Mass. 556, 186 N.E. 669; Golden v. Amory, 1952, 329 Mass. 484, 109 N. E.2d 131; Barnum v. Handschiegel, 1919, 103 Neb. 594, 173 N.W. 593; Smith v. Board of County Road Comm'rs, 1966, 5 Mich.App. 370, 146 N.W.2d 702; McDougall v. Snider, [1913] 15 Dom.L.Rev. 111.

See also Jacoby v. Town of Gillette, 1947, 62 Wyo. 487, 174 P.2d 505; Sutliff v. Sweetwater Water Co., 1920, 182 Cal. 34, 186 P. 766; Charlesworth, Law of Negligence, 1938, 220–233; MacDonald, The Rule of Rylands v. Fletcher and Its Limitations, 1923, 1 Can.Bar Rev. 140, 145.

45. Carstairs v. Taylor, 1871, L.R. 6 Ex. 217.

46. Murphy v. Gillum, 1898, 73 Mo.App. 487. Cf. Tuckachinsky v. Lehigh & W. Coal Co., 1901, 199

Pa. 515, 49 A. 308 (magazine of explosives destroyed by lightning).

47. Box v. Jubb, 1879, L.R. 4 Ex.Div. 76. A fortiori where the escape is caused by the act of the plaintiff himself. Rosewski v. Simpson, 1937, 9 Cal.2d 515, 71 P.2d 72.

48. Rickards v. Lothian, [1913] A.C. 263, 82 L.J.P.C. 42.

49. Smith v. Great Western R. Co., 1926, 42 T.L.R. 391. Accord: Perry v. Kendricks Transport, Ltd., [1956] 1 W.L.R. 85; Kaufman v. Boston Dye House, 1932, 280 Mass. 161, 182 N.E. 297; Langabaugh v. Anderson, 1903, 68 Ohio St. 131, 67 N.E. 286; Cohen v. Brockton Sav. Bank, 1947, 320 Mass. 690, 71 N.E.2d 109. Compare, as to the result, Kleebauer v. Western Fuse & Explosives Co., 1903, 138 Cal. 497, 71 P. 617; McGehee v. Norfolk & Southern R. Co., 1908, 147 N.C. 142, 60 S.E. 912.

50. Davis v. Atlas Assur. Co., 1925, 112 Ohio St. 543, 147 N.E. 913. But cf. Spokane International R. Co. v. United States, 10 Cir. 1934, 72 F.2d 440, giving the statute a broader interpretation.

51. Hartford v. Brady, 1874, 114 Mass. 466. Accord, M'Gibbon v. M'Curry, 1909, 43 Ir.L.T. 132 (stranger left gate open). But apparently contra is Noyes v. Colby, 1855, 30 N.H. 143, where the defendant's cow was released from confinement by the act of a third party.

about by the deliberate interference of a third person,[52] it was held that the defendant was strictly liable, without any question of negligence on his part. These decisions appear to be out of line. If they are to be justified, it may be upon the ground that the extraordinary risk of keeping such abnormal animals includes the likelihood that strangers will interfere with them, since it is so easily done; and hence that the defendant's strict responsibility extends to the prevention of such an occurrence.[53]

Plaintiff's Conduct

It frequently is said that the contributory negligence of the plaintiff is not a defense in cases of strict liability.[54] This involves the seemingly illogical position that the fault of the plaintiff will relieve the defendant of liability when he is negligent, but not when he is innocent. The explanation must lie in part in the element of wilful creation of an unreasonable risk to others by abnormal conduct which is inherent in most of the strict liability cases; and in part in the policy which places the absolute responsibility for preventing the harm upon the defendant, whether his conduct is regarded as fundamentally anti-social, or he is considered merely to be in a better position to transfer the loss to the community.[55] The statutory policy of the workmen's compensation acts,[56] which places all risk upon the defendant, finds a parallel in strict liability at common law.

Thus a plaintiff who is injured by the defendant's dangerous animal is not barred from recovery by his own lack of ordinary care in failing to discover its presence,[57] or

---

52. In Vredenburg v. Behan, 1881, 33 La.Ann. 627, a bear chained to the corner of defendant's clubhouse was teased by a boy setting a dog on him, escaped his collar, and injured the plaintiff. It would seem that the defendant was negligent in keeping the bear without a cage; but in any case, in view of the public place, such interference would appear to be clearly within the risk. The same is true of the very similar case of Kinmouth v. McDougall, 1892, 64 Hun 636, 19 N.Y.S. 771, affirmed, 1893, 139 N.Y. 612, 35 N.E. 204.

In Baker v. Snell, [1908] 2 K.B. 352, 825, a vicious dog was entrusted to a servant to be taken for a run. The servant released the dog, and incited it to attack the plaintiff. The actual decision of the case ordered a new trial on the issue of whether the servant was acting in the course of his employment; but two of the three final judges, in quite unclear opinions, apparently thought that the owner should be liable even if he were not. In any case, since the servant was entrusted with the dog, the decision is scarcely authority as to the acts of complete strangers. It was followed, under compulsion, in Behrens v. Bertram Mills Circus, [1957] 2 Q.B. 1, where the negligence of a third party allowed a dog to frighten an elephant. Contra is the Scottish case of Fleeming v. Orr, 1857, 2 Macq. 14; also, apparently, Strubing v. Mahar, 1899, 46 App. Div. 409, 61 N.Y.S. 799.

English writers have, on the whole, disagreed with Baker v. Snell. See Pollock, The Dog and the Potman, or "Go It, Bob," 1909, 25 L.Q.Rev. 317; Beven, The Responsibility at Common Law for the Keeping of Animals, 1909, 22 Harv.L.Rev. 317; Williams, Liability for Animals, 1939, 334–335; Salmond, Law of Torts, 13th Ed.1961, 616–617; Winfield, Law of Tort, 6th Ed.1954, 647. Defending it are Goodhart, The Third Man, 1951, 4 Curr.Leg. Prob. 184–187; Fleming, Law of Torts, 2d Ed.1961, 317.

53. Compare City of Mangum v. Brownlee, 1938, 181 Okl. 515, 75 P.2d 174, where the act of a stranger in leading an escaped bear back to the zoo was held to be clearly within the risk. Also Andrew v. Kilgour,

[1910] 19 Man.L.Rep. 545, as to the act of a third person in fighting off an attack from a raccoon, and dumping it out in the yard. Cf. Clinkenbeard v. Reinert, 1921, 284 Mo. 569, 225 S.W. 667, discussed in Note, 1921, 34 Harv.L.Rev. 771, holding that it is within the risk that a vicious dog will go mad.

54. "As negligence, in the ordinary sense, is not the ground of liability, so contributory negligence, in its ordinary meaning, is not a defense." Muller v. McKesson, 1878, 73 N.Y. 195.

Cf. Osinger v. Christian, 1963, 43 Ill.App.2d 480, 193 N.E.2d 872 (not a defense in action under Dramshop Act); and see Note, 1942, 37 Ill.L.Rev. 57.

55. Lowndes, Contributory Negligence, 1934, 22 Georgetown L.J. 674, 689–697.

56. See infra, p. 530.

57. Muller v. McKesson, 1878, 73 N.Y. 195; Sandy v. Bushey, 1925, 124 Me. 320, 128 A. 513; Burke v. Fischer, 1944, 298 Ky. 157, 182 S.W.2d 638. Accord, under dog statutes: Wojewoda v. Rybarczyk, 1929, 246 Mich. 641, 225 N.W. 555; Siegfried v. Everhart, 1936, 55 Ohio App. 351, 9 N.E.2d 891.

Compare the cases of nuisance, infra, p. 610.

in inadvertently coming in contact with it.[58] Likewise the plaintiff's negligent failure to maintain fences on his own land will not prevent strict liability for the trespass of the defendant's horse.[59] Nor is contributory negligence in failing to take precautions a defense to the statutory liability for the escape of fire.[60] And in cases where the defendant is carrying on an abnormally dangerous activity, such as blasting, contributory negligence which merely fails to discover the peril and avoid it will not prevent the plaintiff's action.[61]

At the same time, the defense which consists of voluntarily and unreasonably encountering a known danger, and in negligence cases passes more or less indiscriminately under the names of contributory negligence and assumption of risk, will, in general, relieve the defendant of strict liability. Here, as elsewhere, the plaintiff will not be heard to complain of a risk which he has encountered voluntarily, or brought upon himself with full knowledge and appreciation of the danger. Thus if he agrees to work with dangerous animals, he assumes the risk, and cannot recover when they injure him.[62] If he consents to the

accumulation of a pile of debris on the defendant's adjoining property, he has no cause of action based on the mere escape of the material onto his own land, in the absence of some negligence to which he did not consent.[63] And where the defendant's activity is carried on in part for the plaintiff's benefit, as where water [64] or gas [65] pipes are maintained for his use, consent to the risk is found by implication from his acceptance of the situation.

Upon this basis, the kind of contributory negligence which consists of voluntary exposure to a known danger, and so amounts to assumption of risk, is ordinarily a defense. A plaintiff who voluntarily brings himself within reach of an animal which he knows to be dangerous,[66] or intentionally irritates or provokes it,[67] has no cause of action when it attacks him. The same is true when he rashly rushes into the path of the defendant's fire.[68] And where the defendant's ac-

---

58.   Fake v. Addicks, 1890, 45 Minn. 37, 47 N.W. 450 (stepping on dog); Wojewoda v. Rybarczyk, 1929, 246 Mich. 641, 225 N.W. 555 (same); Klatz v. Pfeffer, 1928, 333 Ill. 90, 164 N.E. 224; Tubbs v. Shears, 1916, 55 Okl. 610, 155 P. 549; Johnston v. Ohls, 1969, —— Wash.2d ——, 457 P.2d 194.

59.   Holgate v. Bleazard, [1917] 1 K.B. 443; Stackpole v. Healy, 1819, 16 Mass. 33; cf. Mozingo v. Cooley, 1930, 157 Miss. 636, 128 So. 771.

60.   Evins v. St. Louis & S. F. R. Co., 1912, 104 Ark. 79, 147 S.W. 452; Matthews v. Missouri Pac. R. Co., 1897, 142 Mo. 645, 44 S.W. 802; Fraser-Patterson Lumber Co. v. Southern R. Co., W.D.S.C.1948, 79 F.Supp. 424.

61.   See, as to "absolute" nuisances, Bowman v. Humphrey, 1906, 132 Iowa 234, 109 N.W. 714; Niagara Oil Co. v. Ogle, 1912, 177 Ind. 292, 98 N.E. 60; Wilks v. New York Tel. Co., 1924, 208 App.Div. 542, 203 N.Y.S. 665; Hoffman v. City of Bristol, 1931, 113 Conn. 386, 393, 155 A. 499. See Note, 1934, 29 Ill.L.Rev. 372.

62.   Cooper v. Robert Portner Brewing Co., 1900, 112 Ga. 894, 38 S.E. 91, rehearing and motion to modified judgment denied 113 Ga. 1, 38 S.E. 347; Ar-

mington v. Providence Ice Co., 1912, 33 R.I. 484, 82 A. 263; Bowles v. Indiana R. Co., 1901, 27 Ind.App. 672, 62 N.E. 94; Gomes v. Byrne, 1959, 51 Cal.2d 418, 333 P.2d 754; Brown v. Barber, 1943, 26 Tenn. App. 534, 174 S.W.2d 298.

63.   Attorney General v. Cory Bros. & Co., [1921] A.C. 521, 539.

64.   Carstairs v. Taylor, 1871, L.R. 6 Ex. 217; Rickards v. Lothian, [1913] A.C. 263; Blake v. Woolf, [1898] 2 Q.B. 426.

65.   Cf. Hess v. Greenway, Ont.1919, 48 Dom.L.Rep. 630; E. I. Du Pont de Nemours & Co. v. Cudd, 10 Cir. 1949, 176 F.2d 855 (plaintiff participating in activity).

66.   Opelt v. Al. G. Barnes Co., 1918, 41 Cal.App. 776, 183 P. 241 (crawling under rope near leopard's cage); Hosmer v. Carney, 1920, 228 N.Y. 73, 126 N.E. 650 (going behind vicious horse); Swerdfeger v. Krueger, 1960, 145 Colo. 180, 358 P.2d 479 (going within reach of vicious dog); Hughey v. Fergus County, 1934, 98 Mont. 98, 37 P.2d 1035 (entering field with bull); Heidemann v. Wheaton, 1948, 72 S.D. 375, 34 N.W.2d 492 (going within reach of bear).

67.   Lehnhard v. Robertson's Adm'x, 1917, 176 Ky. 322, 195 S.W. 441 (prodding bear); Wolff v. Lamann, 1900, 108 Ky. 343, 56 S.W. 408 (teasing dog); Donahue v. Frank E. Scott Transfer Co., 1908, 141 Ill.App. 174 (irritating jackass). Cf. Dorman v. Carlson, 1927, 106 Conn. 200, 137 A. 749 (under dog statute).

68.   Bowen v. Boston & A. R. Co., 1901, 179 Mass. 524, 61 N.E. 141. But an adjoining landowner does

tivity is a dangerous one imposing strict liability, such as blasting, a plaintiff who has discovered the danger will be barred from recovery by his own "wanton, wilful or reckless misconduct which materially increases the probabilities of injury," [69] or what amounts to "invitation to injury, or at least indifference to consequences." [70] This does not mean, however, that the defendant, by setting up a known dangerous condition, such as a magazine of explosives, may deprive the plaintiff of the ordinary uses of his property, or compel him to take precautions to protect himself. As in other cases of assumption of risk, [71] the imposition of an unreasonable alternative prevents his acceptance of the risk from being regarded as voluntary, even where he "comes to the nuisance" by buying property adjoining it. [72] Again, there are many cases in which the plaintiff may proceed on the assumption that the defendant will protect him against any danger, as in the case of a member of the public who attends a circus. [73] The plaintiff's appreciation of the risk, and his voluntary consent to encounter it, will often be a jury question, and juries frequently are reluctant to find that a true consent has been given. [74]

Privilege

There are certain conditions under which conduct which would otherwise result in strict liability may be privileged. The most obvious one is that of a sanction given by statutory authority, or by well defined local law. [75] Within the limitations of the constitution, [76] the legislature may authorize acts which involve a high degree of risk to others, and such authority amounts at least to a declaration that the acts are not anti-social, but desirable for the benefit of the community. In the absence of a provision expressly preserving the defendant's liability for any resulting damage, [77] the courts have on occasion interpreted the statute as condoning the consequences in advance, and have refused to hold the defendant liable for doing what he was authorized to do. Thus where gas, [78] wa-

---

not assume the risk of fire by failing to take precautions against it, where the defendant forces an unreasonable alternative upon him. Leroy Fibre Co. v. Chicago, M. & St. P. R. Co., 1914, 232 U.S. 340.

69. Worth v. Dunn, 1922, 98 Conn. 51, 62, 118 A. 467, 471; Wells v. Knight, 1911, 32 R.I. 432, 80 A. 16; Robison v. Robison, 1964, 16 Utah 2d 2, 394 P.2d 876.

70. See McFarlane v. City of Niagara Falls, 1928, 247 N.Y. 340, 160 N.E. 391; Muller v. McKesson, 1878, 73 N.Y. 195.

71. See supra, § 68.

72. Judson v. Giant Powder Co., 1895, 107 Cal. 549, 40 P. 1020. Accord: Campbell v. Seaman, 1876, 63 N.Y. 568; Bliss v. Hall, 1838, 4 Bing.N.C. 183, 132 Eng.Rep. 758; Risher v. Acken Coal Co., 1910, 147 Iowa 459, 124 N.W. 764; Laflin & Rand Powder Co. v. Tearney, 1890, 131 Ill. 322, 23 N.E. 389.

73. Parker v. Cushman, 8 Cir. 1912, 195 F. 715. Accord: Copley v. Wills, Tex.Civ.App.1913, 152 S.W. 830 (boy feeding peanuts to monkey at large in museum); Bottcher v. Buck, 1928, 265 Mass. 4, 163 N. E. 183 (child feeding candy to bear); Lynch v. McNally, 1878, 73 N.Y. 347 (offering candy to dog not known to be vicious).

74. Cf. Whitby v. Brock, 1888, 4 T.L.R. 241; McKee v. Malcolmson, [1925] N.Ir.Rep. 120.

Compare, as to the emergency created by the defendant's conduct, Terpstra v. Schinkel, 1944, 235 Iowa 547, 17 N.W.2d 106.

75. See Linden, Strict Liability—Nuisance and Legislative Authorization, 1966, 4 Osgoode Hall L.Rev. 196. Also Madras R. Co. v. Zemindar of Carvatenagarum, 1874, L.R. 1 Ind.App. 364, 30 L.T. 770; Notes, 1960, 12 Stan.L.Rev. 691; 1938, 13 Notre Dame L. 229.

76. See generally Bacon v. City of Boston, 1891, 154 Mass. 100, 28 N.E. 9; Cohen v. Mayor of New York, 1889, 113 N.Y. 532, 21 N.E. 700; Rose v. State, 1942, 19 Cal.2d 713, 123 P.2d 505; Chick Springs Water, Inc. v. State Highway Dept., 1931, 159 S.C. 481, 157 S.E. 842.

77. In such a case there is liability without negligence. Midwood & Co. v. Mayor of Manchester, [1905] 2 K.B. 597; Charing Cross Elec. Supply Co. v. Hydraulic Power Co., [1914] 3 K.B. 772.

78. Gould v. Winona Gas Co., 1907, 100 Minn. 258, 261, 111 N.W. 254, 255; Schmeer v. Gas Light Co., 1895, 147 N.Y. 529, 42 N.E. 202, 205; Price v. South Metropolitan Gas Co., 1895, 65 L.J.Q.B. 126.

ter,[79] or electric [80] conduits are laid in the street under legislative sanction, it has been held that there is no liability for the damage they may do, in the absence of some negligence.[81] Likewise a contractor, doing work involving blasting for the state, has been held not subject to strict liability.[82] The tendency in the later cases has been to avoid such a conclusion, by strict construction of the authorizing statute,[83] or by finding an implied condition that there shall be liability,[84] or that the manner of doing the work, or the resulting damage itself, are not authorized or necessary consequences of the sanctioned work.[85]

Upon much the same basis, those who are charged with a public duty are not liable unless they have been negligent in its performance. The custodians of a public zoological garden are not subject to strict liability for harm done by the animals kept,[86] and a carrier which is required to accept dangerous animals [87] or explosives [88] for transportation is liable only for negligence in dealing with them.

80. EMPLOYERS' LIABILITY

The outstanding statutory application of the principle of strict liability is in the workmen's compensation acts, which have very largely preëmpted the whole field of the liability of employers for injuries to their employees. Basically they do not rest upon any theory of tort liability, but upon one of social insurance.

The background of these statutes lay in the very limited tort liability of the master to his servant at common law. The extent of the employer's responsibility, although it was said to rest upon the understanding of the parties, undoubtedly was fixed by the courts upon the basis of old industrial condi-

79. Green v. Chelsea Waterworks Co., 1894, 70 L.T. 547.

80. National Tel. Co. v. Baker, [1893] 2 Ch. 186; Dumphy v. Montreal Light Co., [1907] A.C. 455. Compare the rule that a railway run under statutory authority is not liable for the escape of fire. Vaughan v. Taff Vale R. Co., 1860, 5 H. & N. 678, 157 Eng.Rep. 1351; Canadian Pac. R. Co. v. Roy, [1902] A.C. 220.

81. The statute does not relieve the defendant from liability for negligence. Northwestern Utilities v. London Guar. & Acc. Co., [1936] A.C. 105.

82. Pumphrey v. J. A. Jones Const. Co., 1959, 250 Iowa 559, 94 N.W.2d 737; Nelson v. McKenzie-Hague Co., 1934, 192 Minn. 180, 256 N.W. 96; V. N. Green & Co. v. Thomas, 1965, 205 Va. 903, 140 S.E. 2d 635. Accord: Benner v. Atlantic Dredging Co., 1892, 134 N.Y. 156, 31 N.E. 328; Fitzgibbon v. Western Dredging Co., 1908, 141 Iowa 328, 117 N.W. 878. See Notes, 1934, 19 Minn.L.Rev. 129; 1966, 23 Wash. & Lee L.Rev. 118.

83. Cogswell v. New York, N. H. & H. R. Co., 1886, 103 N.Y. 10, 8 N.E. 537; Messer v. City of Dickinson, 1942, 71 N.D. 568, 3 N.W.2d 241, 245. Cf. McLane v. Northwest Natural Gas Co., 1969, —— Or. ——, 467 P.2d 635.

84. Smith v. Aldridge, Mo.App.1962, 356 S.W.2d 532; Ferriter v. Herlihy, 1934, 287 Mass. 138, 191 N.E. 352, 354.

85. Whitney v. Ralph Myers Contracting Co., 1961, 146 W.Va. 130, 118 S.E.2d 622; Webster Co. v. Steelman, 1939, 172 Va. 342, 1 S.E.2d 305; Hakkila v. Old Colony Broken Stone Co., 1928, 264 Mass. 447, 162 N.E. 895. Cf. Monroe v. Razor Const. Co., 1961, 252 Iowa 1249, 110 N.W.2d 250 (negligence).

86. Jackson v. Baker, 1904, 24 App.D.C. 100; Guzzi v. New York Zoological Soc., 1920, 192 App.Div. 263, 182 N.Y.S. 257, affirmed, 1922, 233 N.Y. 511, 135 N.E. 897.

The city itself is not liable where it has legislative authority. McKinney v. City and County of San Francisco, 1952, 109 Cal.App.2d 844, 241 P.2d 1060; Hibbard v. City of Wichita, 1916, 98 Kan. 498, 159 P.2d 399. It is, however, strictly liable where it has no authority. City of Mangum v. Brownlee, 1938, 181 Okl. 515, 75 P.2d 174; Collentine v. City of New York, 1938, 279 N.Y. 119, 124, 17 N.E.2d 792, 795; Hyde v. City of Utica, 1940, 259 App.Div. 477, 20 N.Y.S.2d 335.

87. Malloy v. Starin, 1908, 191 N.Y. 21, 83 N.E. 588. The Restatement of Torts, § 517, takes the position that if the carrier is not required to accept the shipment it may be strictly liable. But see, to the effect that it is sufficient that it is authorized to accept it as a carrier, Stamp v. Eighty-Sixth St. Amusement Co., 1916, 95 Misc. 599, 159 N.Y.S. 683; cf. Pope v. Edward M. Rude Carrier Corp., 1953, 138 W.Va. 218, 75 S.E.2d 584 (dynamite).

88. Actiesselskabet Ingrid v. Central R. Co. of N. J., 2 Cir. 1914, 216 F. 72; Pope v. Edward M. Rude Carrier Corp., 1953, 138 W.Va. 218, 75 S.E.2d 584.

tions, and a social philosophy and an attitude toward labor, which are long since outmoded. The cornerstone of the common law edifice was the economic theory that there was complete mobility of labor, that the supply of work was unlimited, and that the workman was an entirely free agent, under no compulsion to enter into the employment. He was expected therefore to accept and take upon himself all of the usual risks of his trade, together with any unusual risks of which he had knowledge, and to relieve his employer of any duty to protect him. The economic compulsion which left him no choice except starvation, or equally dangerous employment elsewhere, was entirely disregarded. The employer's responsibility was limited to certain rather specific minimum obligations, which it was felt that any workman had the right to demand. Even as to these obligations, the employer was not an insurer of safety, and was liable only for a failure to exercise reasonable care;[89] and in addition, he was not responsible for the negligence of fellow-servants of the injured workman, as distinguished from the employer's own misconduct.[90] The result was that for the great majority of industrial accidents there was no recovery, either because no lack of proper care could be charged against the employer, or because the workman was taken to have assumed the risk.

The specific common law duties of the master for the protection of his servants were commonly classified as follows:

1. The duty to provide a safe place to work.[91]

2. The duty to provide safe appliances, tools and equipment for the work.[92]

3. The duty to give warning of dangers of which the employee might reasonably be expected to remain in ignorance.[93]

4. The duty to provide a sufficient number of suitable fellow servants.[94]

5. The duty to promulgate and enforce rules for the conduct of employees which would make the work safe.[95]

The possibility of the injured workman's recovery, which was limited at the outset to cases where the employer had failed to exercise proper care in the foregoing specific respects, was restricted further by the "unholy

---

The duty was not only to protect against dangers of which the employer knew, but also to exercise reasonable care to make inspections to discover conditions of which he did not. White v. Consolidated Freight Lines, 1937, 192 Wash. 146, 73 P.2d 358; Chicago & E. I. R. Co. v. Kneirim, 1894, 152 Ill. 458, 39 N.E. 324; Simone v. Kirk, 1902, 173 N.Y. 7, 65 N.E. 739; Smith v. Erie R. Co., 1902, 67 N.J.L. 636, 52 A. 634.

92. Petrol Corp. v. Curtis, 1948, 190 Md. 652, 59 A.2d 329; Toy v. United States Cartridge Co., 1893, 159 Mass. 313, 34 N.E. 461; Chicago Union Traction Co. v. Sawusch, 1905, 218 Ill. 130, 75 N.E. 797; Byrne v. Eastmans Co., 1900, 163 N.Y. 461, 57 N.E. 738; Daniels v. Luechtefeld, Mo.App.1941, 155 S.W. 2d 307.

93. Engelking v. City of Spokane, 1910, 59 Wash. 446, 110 P. 25; Baumgartner v. Pennsylvania R. Co., 1928, 292 Pa. 106, 140 A. 622; Brennan v. Gordon, 1890, 118 N.Y. 489, 23 N.E. 810; Moore v. Morse & Malloy Shoe Co., 1938, 89 N.H. 332, 197 A. 707; Bassett v. New York, C. & St. L. R. Co., 3 Cir. 1956, 235 F.2d 900 (obstructions in area where employee was to travel by motor car).

94. Flike v. Boston & A. R. Co., 1873, 53 N.Y. 549; Johnson v. Ashland Water Co., 1888, 71 Wis. 553, 37 N.W. 823; Peterson v. American Grass Twine Co., 1903, 90 Minn. 343, 96 N.W. 913; Di Bari v. J. W. Bishop Co., 1908, 199 Mass. 254, 85 N.E. 89; Wyman v. Lehigh Valley R. Co., 2 Cir. 1908, 158 F. 957.

95. Tremblay v. J. Rudnick & Sons, 1940, 91 N.H. 24, 13 A.2d 153; Lake Shore & M. S. R. Co. v. Lavalley, 1880, 36 Ohio St. 221; Cooper v. Central R. R. of Iowa, 1876, 44 Iowa 134; Doing v. New York, O. & W. R. Co., 1897, 151 N.Y. 579, 45 N.E. 1028; Southern Package Corp. v. Mitchell, 5 Cir. 1940, 109 F.2d 609.

89. Cf. Armour v. Hahn, 1884, 111 U.S. 313; Wonder v. Baltimore & O. R. Co., 1870, 32 Md. 411; Curley v. Hoff, 1899, 62 N.J.L. 758, 42 A. 731.

90. See infra, p. 528.

91. Armour v. Golkowska, 1903, 202 Ill. 144, 66 N.E. 1037; Burns v. Delaware & A. Tel. & Tel. Co., 1904, 70 N.J.L. 745, 59 A. 220, 592; McGuire v. Bell Tel. Co. of Buffalo, 1901, 167 N.Y. 208, 60 N.E. 433; Butterman v. McClintic-Marshall Const. Co., 1903, 206 Pa. 82, 55 A. 839.

trinity" of common law defenses—contributory negligence, assumption of risk, and the fellow servant rule. The effect of these defenses was to relieve the employer of responsibility even though he, or his other servants, had failed in respect of the specific obligations for the protection of the servant listed above. The second and third in particular offered formidable obstacles to any recovery for the usual industrial accident.

The workman was required to exercise reasonable care for his own safety, and his recovery was barred by his contributory negligence.[96] The defense was of course subject to all of the rules usually applicable to it, and the servant might recover if it could be found that the master had the last clear chance,[97] or that his conduct was wilful or wanton.[98] But it frequently meant that a momentary lapse of caution on the part of the workman was penalized by casting the entire burden of his injury upon him, in the face of continued and greater negligence of the employer.

The risks which did not lie within the scope of the specific obligations of the master were considered to be accepted by the servant as an incident of his employment, and the employer was under no duty to protect him against them. He was said to have bargained away his right to hold the employer responsible,[99] or to have assumed the

risk of hazards normally incident to his employment.[1] But even where the master had clearly violated his duty in the first instance, as to appliances,[2] the place to work,[3] or his rules and methods,[4] the workman might be denied recovery on the ground that he had assumed the risk, and consented[5] to relieve the employer of his obligation. If he re-

P. R. Co., 1918, 182 Iowa 1339, 1342, 166 N.W. 735, 736.

1. Cooper v. Mayes, 1959, 234 S.C. 491, 495, 109 S.E. 2d 12, 13; Jones v. Adams, 1952, 56 N.M. 510, 245 P.2d 843; Walsh v. West Coast Mines, Inc., 1948, 31 Wash.2d 396, 406, 197 P.2d 233, 238; Conboy v. Crofoot, 1964, 194 Kan. 46, 397 P.2d 326.

2. Errico v. Washburn Williams Co., M.D.Pa.1909, 170 F. 852; Crown v. Orr, 1893, 140 N.Y. 450, 35 N.E. 648; Painter v. Nichols, 1954, 118 Vt. 306, 108 A.2d 384; Abercrombie v. Ivey, 1938, 59 Ga.App. 296, 200 S.E. 551; see Bartlett v. Gregg, 1958, 77 S.D. 406, 92 N.W.2d 654.

3. Eiban v. Widsteen, 1948, 31 Wash.2d 655, 198 P. 2d 667; Kline v. Abraham, 1904, 178 N.Y. 377, 70 N.E. 923; Gutierrez v. Valley Irr. & Livestock Co., 1960, 68 N.M. 6, 357 P.2d 664, 666; Richter v. Razore, 1960, 56 Wash.2d 580, 354 P.2d 706; Morris & Co. v. Alvis, 1921, 130 Va. 434 107 S.E. 664.

4. Abbot v. McCadden, 1892, 81 Wis. 563, 51 N.W. 1079; Schultz v. Chicago & N. W. R. Co., 1887, 67 Wis. 616, 31 N.W. 321.

The usual form of statement was that the employee "assumes (1) such dangers as are ordinarily and normally incident to the work, and a workman of mature years is presumed to know them whether he does or not; (2) such extraordinary and abnormal risks as he (a) knows and appreciates and faces without complaint or (b) are obvious and apparent." Boatman v. Miles, 1921, 27 Wyo. 481, 487, 199 P. 933, 935.

5. See Note, 1961, 47 Va.L.Rev. 1444. Assumption of risk was sometimes said to be a matter of the contract of employment, as in Conway v. Furst, 1895, 57 N.J.L. 645, 32 A. 380; B. Shoninger Co. v. Mann, 1905, 219 Ill. 242, 76 N.E. 354. It is generally recognized, however, that it rests merely on consent, and that the risk may be assumed after the workman has been employed. O'Maley v. South Boston Gas Light Co., 1893, 158 Mass. 135, 32 N.E. 1119; Rase v. Minneapolis, St. P. & S. S. M. R. Co., 1909, 107 Minn. 260, 120 N.W. 360; Knisley v. Pratt, 1896, 148 N.Y. 372, 42 N.E. 986, reargument denied, 1896, 149 N.Y. 582, 43 N.E. 988.

As to the distinction between assumption of risk and contributory negligence, see supra, § 68.

96. Schlemmer v. Buffalo, R. & P. R. Co., 1911, 220 U.S. 590; Meunier v. Chemical Paper Co., 1901, 180 Mass. 109, 61 N.E. 810; Limberg v. Glenwood Lumber Co., 1900, 127 Cal. 598, 60 P. 176; Narramore v. Cleveland, C. C. & St. L. R. Co., 6 Cir. 1899, 96 F.2d 298, cert. denied 175 U.S. 724.

97. Small v. Boston & Me. R. Co., 1934, 87 N.H. 25, 173 A. 381; Raines v. Southern R. Co., 1915, 169 N.C. 189, 85 S.E. 294; see Louisville & N. R. Co. v. Young, 1910, 168 Ala. 551, 53 So. 213.

98. Louisville & N. R. Co. v. York, 1901, 128 Ala. 305, 30 So. 676; see Arkley v. Niblack, 1916, 272 Ill. 356, 112 N.E. 67.

99. Lang v. United States Reduction Co., 7 Cir. 1940, 110 F.2d 441, 442; Ehrenberger v. Chicago, R. I. &

mained at work voluntarily [6] after he knew [7] and appreciated [8] the danger, he was found to accept the situation, and to undertake to look out for himself, notwithstanding the employer's breach of his obligation. Even though he continued his work under protest,[9] or under a direct order carrying a threat of discharge,[10] he still was found to have consented, however reluctantly, to assume the risk. The fact that the alternative was the loss of his means of subsistence and that it was "his poverty and not his will which consented," [11] although it was recognized to some extent in England,[12] was almost entirely ignored by the American courts. It was only

where the peril was not imminent,[13] and the master gave an assurance of safety [14] or a promise to remedy the defect,[15] that the workman was held not to assume the risk by remaining in his employment, and then only until such time as it became apparent that the assurance was not to be relied on.[16]

The rule that the employer was not liable for injuries caused solely by the negligence of a fellow servant first appeared in England in 1837,[17] and almost immediately afterward in the United States,[18] where it was stated elaborately in a well known opinion of Chief Justice Shaw of Massachusetts in Farwell v. Boston & Worcester Railway.[19] Although it has been assailed as a direct departure from the established rule of vicarious liability for the torts of servants within the scope of their employment, it probably should be regarded as an inherent limitation upon that rule itself, which seems to have been conceived as

---

6. Thus the defense does not apply to one who is not free to leave the employment. Chattahoochee Brick Co. v. Braswell, 1893, 92 Ga. 631, 18 S.E. 1015; Sloss-Sheffield Steel & Iron Co. v. Long, 1910, 169 Ala. 337, 53 So. 910 (convicts); Lafourche Packet Co. v. Henderson, 5 Cir. 1899, 94 F. 871 (seaman). Cf. Olney v. Boston & Me. R. R., 1902, 71 N.H. 427, 52 A. 1097 (engineer would endanger others by leaving engine).

7. See supra, p. 447; Uhlrig v. Shortt, 1964, 194 Kan. 68, 397 P.2d 321.

8. Heinlen v. Martin Miller Orchards, 1952, 40 Wash.2d 356, 242 P.2d 1054; McDaniel v. Chicago, R. I. & P. R. Co., 1936, 338 Mo. 481, 92 S.W.2d 118; Choctaw, O. & G. R. Co. v. Jones, 1906, 77 Ark. 367, 92 S.W. 244; Davidson v. Cornell, 1892, 132 N.Y. 228, 30 N.E. 573.

9. Atchison, T. & S. F. Ry. Co. v. Schroeder, 1891, 47 Kan. 315, 27 P. 965; Galveston, H. & S. A. R. Co. v. Drew, 1883, 59 Tex. 10; Talbot v. Sims, 1905, 213 Pa. 1, 62 A. 107; Loynes v. Loring B. Hall Co., 1907, 194 Mass. 221, 80 N.E. 472.

10. Burke v. Davis, 1906, 191 Mass. 20, 76 N.E. 1039; Hallstein v. Pennsylvania R. Co., 6 Cir. 1929, 30 F.2d 594; Clairmont v. Cilley, 1931, 85 N.H. 1, 153 A. 465; Nashville, C. & St. L. R. Co. v. Cleaver, 1938, 274 Ky. 410, 118 S.W.2d 748. Contra: New York, N. H. & H. R. Co. v. Vizvari, 2 Cir. 1913, 210 F. 118; Goss v. Kurn, 1940, 187 Miss. 679, 193 So. 783.

11. Hawkins, J., in Thrussell v. Handyside & Co., 1888, 20 Q.B.D. 359.

12. Yarmouth v. France, 1887, 19 Q.B.D. 647; Smith v. Baker & Sons, [1891] A.C. 325; Bowalter v. Rowley Regis Corp., [1944] 1 K.B. 476. Accord, Groner v. Hedrick, 1961, 403 Pa. 148, 169 A.2d 302. See Gow, The Defense of Volenti Non Fit Injuria, 1949, 61 Jurid.Rev. 37.

13. Greene v. Minneapolis & St. L. R. Co., 1883, 31 Minn. 248, 17 N.W. 378; Dowd v. Erie R. Co., 1904, 70 N.J.L. 451, 57 A. 248; Curran v. A. H. Stange Co., 1898, 98 Wis. 598, 74 N.W. 377. Cf. Burke v. Davis, 1906, 191 Mass. 20, 76 N.E. 1039; Rohrabacher v. Woodward, 1900, 124 Mich. 125, 82 N.W. 797 (imminent danger).

14. Brown v. Lennane, 1908, 155 Mich. 686, 118 N.W. 581; McKee v. Tourtellotte, 1896, 167 Mass. 69, 44 N.E. 1071; Manks v. Moore, 1909, 108 Minn. 284, 122 N.W. 5.

15. Hough v. Texas & Pac. R. Co., 1879, 100 U.S. 213, 25 L.Ed. 612; Rice v. Eureka Paper Co., 1903, 174 N.Y. 385, 66 N.E. 979; Dowd v. Erie R. Co., 1904, 70 N.J.L. 451, 57 A. 248; Cheek v. Eyth, 1939, 149 Kan. 586, 89 P.2d 11. But a promise by an unauthorized agent, or other third person is not sufficient. Liptak v. Karsner, 1940, 208 Minn. 168, 293 N.W. 612.

16. Faulkner v. Big Rock Stone & Material Co., 1940, 201 Ark. 124, 143 S.W.2d 883; Gunning System v. Lapointe, 1904, 212 Ill. 274, 73 N.E. 393; Andrecsik v. New Jersey Tube Co., 1906, 73 N.J.L. 664, 63 A. 719; Heathcock v. Milwaukee Platteville Lead & Zinc Min. Co., 1906, 128 Wis. 46, 107 N.W. 463.

17. Priestley v. Fowler, 1837, 3 M. & W. 1, 150 Eng. Rep. 1030.

18. Murray v. South Carolina R. Co., 1938, 1 McMul. L., S.C., 385.

19. 1849, 4 Metc., Mass. 49.

an obligation of the head of the household to those who were not his servants.[20] The reasons usually assigned [21] for it, however, were that the plaintiff upon entering the employment assumed the risk of negligence on the part of his fellow servants,[22] and the master did not undertake to protect him against it; that he was as likely to know of their deficiencies and to be in a position to guard against them as his employer; and that it would promote the safety of the public and of all servants to make each one watchful of the conduct of others for his own protection. While these reasons might perhaps have been appropriate to small enterprises and shops, where the workmen had close contact and acquaintance with one another, they had little validity in the case of large industries, where the plaintiff might be injured by the negligence of a fellow servant whom he had never seen. The explanation of the rule probably lay in the highly individualistic viewpoint of the common law courts, and their desire to encourage industrial undertakings by making the burden upon them as light as possible.[23]

The general rule thus declared was later restricted in a number of respects, as its hardship upon labor became apparent.

The most important restriction was that generally accepted in the United States,[24] that the fellow servant rule did not apply to the negligence of a "vice-principal." By this was meant a servant who represented the employer in his responsibility to the plaintiff. In some decisions, it was held that a vice-principal must be a superior servant, such as a foreman, in a position of direct authority over the plaintiff.[25] Most courts rejected this requirement, and defined a vice-principal to include any servant, of whatever rank, who was charged by the master with the performance of his common law duties toward the plaintiff, such as the maintenance of a safe place to work [26] or safe appliances,[27] the employment of competent workmen,[28] or the giving of warning or instruction.[29] These duties were said to be non-delegable, in the sense that the employer could not escape responsibility for them by entrusting them to another, whether he be a servant or an in-

20. Holmes, Agency, 1891, 4 Harv.L.Rev. 345.

21. 2 Labatt, Master and Servant, 1904, §§ 472, 473; Powell, Some Phases of the Law of Master and Servant, 1910, 10 Col.L.Rev. 1, 30; Mechem, Employer's Liability, 1910, 44 Am.L.Rev. 221; Burdick, Is Law the Expression of Class Selfishness, 1912, 25 Harv.L.Rev. 349, 357–381; Farwell v. Boston & Worcester R. Co., 1849, 4 Metc., Mass., 49; Coon v. Syracuse & Utica R. Co., 1849, 6 Barb., N.Y., 231, affirmed, 1851, 5 N.Y. 492; Ryan v. Cumberland Valley R. Co., 1854, 23 Pa. 384.

22. Thus it was held that a convict entering employment under compulsion and a minor too inexperienced to appreciate the danger, were not subject to the fellow servant rule. Buckalew v. Tennessee Coal I. & R. Co., 1895, 112 Ala. 146, 20 So. 606; Kendrick v. Ideal Holding Co., 1939, 137 Fla. 600, 188 So. 778.

23. Dodd, Administration of Workmen's Compensation, 1936, 7.

24. Rejected in England, in Wilson v. Merry, 1868, L.R. 1 H.L.Sc.App.Cas. 326.

25. Berea Stone Co. v. Kraft, 1877, 31 Ohio St. 287; Lamb v. Littman, 1903, 132 N.C. 978, 44 S.E. 646; Chap-Tan Drilling Co. v. Myers, 1950, 203 Okl. 642, 225 P.2d 373; cf. May v. Sharp, 1936, 191 Ark. 1142, 89 S.W.2d 735; McDonald v. Louisville & N. R. Co., 1930, 232 Ky. 734, 24 S.W.2d 585.

26. Smith v. Erie R. Co., 1902, 38 Vroom. 636, 67 N. J.L. 636, 52 A. 634; Nuckolls v. Great A. & P. Tea Co., 1939, 192 S.C. 156, 5 S.E.2d 862; Boettger v. Moran, 1940, 64 R.I. 340, 12 A.2d 285; Cadden v. American Steel Barge Co., 1894, 88 Wis. 409, 60 N. W. 800.

27. Union Pac. R. Co. v. Daniels, 1894, 152 U.S. 684; Green River Light & Water Co. v. Beeler, 1923, 197 Ky. 818, 248 S.W. 201; Nuckolls v. Great A. & P. Tea Co., 1939, 192 S.C. 156, 5 S.E.2d 862; Herdler v. Bucks Stove Co., 1896, 136 Mo. 3, 37 S.W. 115; cf. Plemmons v. Antles, 1958, 52 Wash.2d 269, 324 P.2d 823 (truck driver with exclusive control).

28. Flike v. Boston & A. R. Co., 1873, 53 N.Y. 549; Gilman v. Eastern R. Co., 1866, 13 Allen, Mass., 433.

29. Tedford v. Los Angeles Elec. Co., 1901, 134 Cal. 76, 66 P. 76; Brennan v. Gordon, 1890, 118 N.Y. 489, 23 N.E. 810; Moore v. Morse & Malloy Shoe Co., 1938, 89 N.H. 332, 197 A. 707; Carey Reed Co. v. McDavid, 5 Cir. 1941, 120 F.2d 843.

dependent contractor.[30] Consequently he remained liable for the negligence of a fellow servant who represented him in that capacity. The vice-principal rule was, however, subject to the qualification that it did not apply to incidental dangers arising in the operative details of the fellow servant's work,[31] against which the master had no duty to take precautions, as distinct from a specific responsibility for the performance of a duty placed upon the servant.

Some slow progress toward the imposition of liability upon the employer may be traced through the common law cases, but the tendency in this direction was in large part superseded by the passage of the workmen's compensation acts.

Statutory Changes

Under the common law system, by far the greater proportion [32] of industrial accidents remained uncompensated, and the burden fell upon the workman, who was least able to support it. Furthermore, the litigation which usually was necessary to any recovery meant delay, pressure upon the injured man to settle his claim in order to live, and heavy attorneys' fees and other expenses which frequently left him only a small part of the money finally paid.[33] Coupled with this were

working conditions of an extreme inhumanity in many industries, which the employer was under no particular incentive to improve. Early legislative attempts to regulate these conditions sometimes were nullified by decisions holding that the workman assumed the risk of the employer's violation of the statute.[34] The reluctance of the courts to face the problem and modify the common law rules made it clear that any change must come through some general legislation, and led to a movement for the passage of workmen's compensation acts, modeled upon the statute already in existence in Germany.[35] Increasing agitation at last brought about the first statutes, in England in 1897, and in the United States, for government employees, in 1908. This was followed by the first state statute in New York in 1910. By 1921 all but a few of the American states had enacted such legislation. It is now in effect in all of the states, with Hawaii the last to fall into line in 1963. It has been said that no subject of labor legislation ever has made such progress or received such general acceptance of its principles in so brief a period.[36]

The theory underlying the workmen's compensation acts never has been stated better than in the old campaign slogan,[37] "the cost of the product should bear the blood of the workman." [38] The human accident losses of

---

30. Pullman's Palace Car Co. v. Laack, 1892, 143 Ill. 242, 32 N.E. 285; Moran v. Corliss Steam Engine Co., 1899, 21 R.I. 386, 43 A. 874.

31. Armour v. Hahn, 1884, 111 U.S. 313; James Stewart & Co. v. Newby, 4 Cir. 1920, 266 F. 287; Citrone v. O'Rourke Eng. Const. Co., 1907, 188 N.Y. 339, 80 N.E. 1092; Curley v. Hoff, 1899, 62 N.J.L. 758, 42 A. 731; Manning v. Genesee River & L. O. Steamboat Co., 1901, 66 App.Div. 314, 72 N.Y.S. 677.

32. Variously estimated as follows: 70 per cent, 1 Schneider, Workmen's Compensation, 2d Ed. 1932, 1; 80 per cent, Lumbermen's Reciprocal Ass'n v. Behnken, Tex.Civ.App.1920, 226 S.W. 154; 83 per cent, Downey, History of Work Accident Indemnity in Iowa, 1912, 71; 87 per cent, First Report of New York Employers' Liability Comm., 1910, vol. 1, p. 25; 94 per cent, Report of Ohio Employers' Liability Comm., 1911, part 1, xxxv-xliv.

33. First Report of New York Employers' Liability Comm., 1910, vol. 1, p. 31; Report of Michigan Em-

ployers' Liability Comm., 1911, p. 16; Wisconsin Bureau of Labor Statistics, 13th Bien.Rep., 1907–1908, 13.

34. St. Louis Cordage Co. v. Miller, 8 Cir. 1903, 126 F. 495; Knisley v. Pratt, 1896, 148 N.Y. 372, 42 N. E. 986; Cleveland & Eastern R. Co. v. Somers, 1902, 14 Ohio Cir.Ct.Rep. 67, reversed on other grounds, 1906, 74 Ohio St. 477, 78 N.E. 1122.

35. Passed in 1884, amended from time to time, and finally codified in an act of July 6th, 1911.

36. U. S. Bureau of Labor Statistics, Bull. No. 126, 1913, p. 9.

37. The writer has heard this attributed to Lloyd George, but has been unable to trace its origin.

38. Bohlen, A Problem in the Drafting of Workmen's Compensation Acts, 1912, 25 Harv.L.Rev. 328, 401, 517; Wambaugh, Workmen's Compensation Acts, 1911, 25 Harv.L.Rev. 129; Walton, Workmen's

modern industry are to be treated as a cost of production, like the breakage of tools or machinery. The financial burden is lifted from the shoulders of the employee, and placed upon the employer, who is expected to add it to his costs, and so transfer it to the consumer. In this he is aided and controlled by a system of compulsory liability insurance, which equalizes the burden over the entire industry. Through such insurance both the master and the servant are protected at the expense of the ultimate consumer.

Workmen's compensation is thus a form of strict liability. The employer is charged with the injuries arising out of his business, without regard to any question of his negligence, or that of the injured employee. He is liable for injuries caused by pure unavoidable accident, or by the negligence of the workman himself. The three wicked sisters of the common law—contributory negligence, assumption of risk and the fellow servant rule—are abolished as defenses.[39] The only questions remaining to be litigated are, first, were the workman and his injury within the act, and second, what shall be the compensation paid.[40] Since in most cases the compensation is fixed by the statute itself,[41] "the re-

sult has been most satisfactory in that injured employees receive immediate relief, a fruitful source of friction between employer and employee has been eliminated, * * * a tremendous amount of burden and expensive litigation has been eliminated, and a more harmonious relation between the employers and employees exists than was possible under the old system." [42]

The law of workmen's compensation lies outside of the scope of this text.[43] When an injury to a servant is found to be covered by a workmen's compensation act, it is uniformly held that the statutory compensation is the sole remedy, and that any recovery at common law is barred.[44] It is recognized that this remedy is in the nature of a compromise, by which the workman is to accept a limited compensation, usually less than the estimate which a jury might place upon his damages, in return for an extended liability of the employer, and an assurance that he will be paid. Accordingly, even though his damages are partly of a nature not compensated under the

Compensation and the Theory of Professional Risk, 1911, 11 Col.L.Rev. 36; Stertz v. Industrial Ins. Commission of Washington, 1916, 91 Wash. 588, 158 P. 256; In re Petrie, 1915, 215 N.Y. 335, 109 N.E. 549; Wangler Boiler & Sheet Metal Works v. Industrial Comm., 1919, 287 N.Y. 118, 122 N.E. 366; Bundy v. State of Vermont Highway Department, 1929, 102 Vt. 84, 146 A. 68.

39. Borgnis v. Falk Co., 1911, 147 Wis. 327, 133 N.W. 209; Imperial Brass Mfg. Co. v. Industrial Commission, 1922, 306 Ill. 11, 137 N.E. 411; American Ice Co. v. Fitzhugh, 1916, 128 Md. 382, 97 A. 999; see Grand Trunk R. Co. of Canada v. Knapp, 6 Cir. 1916, 233 F. 950.

40. First Report of New York Employers' Liability Comm., 1910, vol. 1, p. 56.

41. The statutes contain elaborate and detailed schedules of compensation for particular injuries. Thus: "For the loss of a thumb, sixty-six and two-thirds per centum of the daily wage at the time of injury during sixty-five weeks." Minn.Stat.Ann., § 176.101.

42. 1 Schneider, Workmen's Compensation, 2d Ed., 1932, 6.

43. See Schneider, Workmen's Compensation, 3d Ed. 16 vols., 1939–53; Larson, Workmen's Compensation Law, 2 vols. 1952; Somers and Somers, Workmen's Compensation, 1954; Kossoris et al., Workmen's Compensation in the United States, 1953, 76 Monthly Lab.Rev. 359, 480, 602, 709, 826, 1063, 1179, 1289; Bureau of Labor Statistics Bull. No. 1149, 1954; Riesenfeld, Study of the Workmen's Compensation Law in Hawaii, 1963, Hawaii Leg.Ref.Bureau Rep. No. 1; Dittmar, State Workmen's Compensation Laws, 1959; Cheit, Injury and Recovery in the Course of Employment, 1961; Larson, The Nature and Origins of Workmen's Compensation, 1952, 37 Corn.L.Q. 206; Riesenfeld, Forty Years of American Workmen's Compensation, 1951, 35 Minn.L.Rev. 525; Riesenfeld, Basic Problems in the Administration of Workmen's Compensation, 1952, 36 Minn.L.Rev. 119; Somers et al., Current Status of Workmen's Compensation, 1953, 7 Industrial & Lab.Rel.Rev. 31.

An excellent brief review of the comparatively recent state of the law is Riesenfeld, Contemporary Trends in Compensation for Industrial Accidents Here and Abroad, 1954, 42 Cal.L.Rev. 531.

44. See Note, 1936, 14 North Car.L.Rev. 199.

act, he has no cause of action based on the negligence of his employer.[45]

There are, however, many injuries to servants which still are not covered by the workmen's compensation acts. There are important groups, such as farm laborers,[46] domestic servants,[47] railway workmen,[48] corporate officers and working partners,[49] and those employed by enterprises having less than a minimum number of employees,[50] who are excluded from most of the statutes. In most instances such exclusions have been the result of political compromise at the time of the adoption of the act. One important group, of "casual" employees, or those "not in the usual course of trade or business of the employer," has been excluded largely because

of the difficulty of obtaining insurance coverage for such occasional work.[51]

In addition, many of the acts, because of early doubts as to constitutionality, were made elective and remain so, so that the servant may be deprived of coverage, either by his own choice or that of the employer.[52] Some of the statutes do not cover all industries, but apply only to "hazardous" employments.[53] Nearly all of the acts are limited to injuries arising "by accident;" and while there has been considerable expansion of the definition,[54] it may still in some states exclude damage caused gradually over a period of time,[55] or resulting merely from the usual work under the usual conditions.[56] The acts

45. Hyett v. Northwestern Hospital for Women and Children, 1920, 147 Minn. 413, 180 N.W. 552; Gregutis v. Waclark Wire Works, 1914, 86 N.J.L. 610, 38 N.J.L.J. 11, 92 A. 354; Smith v. Baker, 1932, 157 Okl. 155, 11 P.2d 132; Freese v. John Morrell & Co., 1931, 58 S.D. 634, 237 N.W. 886; Shanahan v. Monarch Eng. Co., 1916, 219 N.Y. 469, 114 N.E. 795. See Page, The Exclusivity of the Workmen's Compensation Remedy, 1963, 4 B.C.Ind. & Com.L.Rev. 555.

46. See for example Anderson v. Last Chance Ranch Co., 1924, 63 Utah 551, 228 P. 184; Greischar v. St. Mary's College, 1928, 176 Minn. 100, 222 N.W. 525; In re Roby, 1939, 54 Wyo. 439, 93 P.2d 940; Taylor v. Hostetler, 1960, 186 Kan. 788, 352 P.2d 1042; Pestlin v. Haxton Canning Co., 1949, 299 N.Y. 477, 87 N.E.2d 522.

47. See for example Anderson v. Ueland, 1936, 197 Minn. 518, 267 N.W. 517; cf. Congressional Country Club v. Baltimore & O. R. Co., 1950, 194 Md. 533, 71 A.2d 696; Barres v. Watterson Hotel Co., 1922, 196 Ky. 100, 244 S.W. 308. See Note, 1937, 21 Minn.L. Rev. 227.

48. See infra, p. 534.

49. See Grossman v. Industrial Commission, 1941, 376 Ill. 198, 33 N.E.2d 444; Carville v. A. F. Bornot & Co., 1927, 288 Pa. 104, 135 A. 652; Benson v. Hygienic Artificial Ice Co., 1936, 198 Minn. 250, 269 N.W. 460; Rasmussen v. Trico Feed Mills, 1947, 148 Neb. 855, 29 N.W.2d 641; Pederson v. Pederson, 1949, 229 Minn. 460, 39 N.W.2d 893.

50. Ranging from two in Nevada and Oklahoma to fifteen in South Carolina. See Bureau of Labor Standards, Bulletin No. 125, 1950.

51. See Bohlen, Casual Employment and Employment Outside of Business, 1923, 11 Cal.L.Rev. 221; Note, 1926, 10 Minn.L.Rev. 626; Billmayer v. Sanford, 1929, 177 Minn. 465, 225 N.W. 426; Moore v. Clark, 1936, 171 Md. 39, 187 A. 887; Cochrane v. William Penn Hotel, 1940, 339 Pa. 549, 16 A.2d 43; Ludwig v. Kirby, 1951, 13 N.J.Super. 116, 80 A.2d 239.

52. See Bureau of Labor Standards, Bulletin No. 125, 1950.

53. Cf. Illinois Pub. & Print. Co. v. Industrial Commission, 1921, 299 Ill. 189, 132 N.E. 511; Morris v. Department of Labor and Industries, 1934, 179 Wash. 523, 38 P.2d 395; Mattes v. City of Baltimore, 1942, 180 Md. 579, 26 A.2d 390.

54. See for example Caddy v. R. Maturi & Co., 1944, 217 Minn. 207, 14 N.W.2d 393; Winkelman v. Boeing Airplane Co., 1949, 166 Kan. 503, 203 P.2d 171; Atlas Coal Corp. v. Scales, 1947, 198 Okl. 658, 185 P.2d 177; Benjamin F. Shaw Co. v. Musgrave, 1949, 189 Tenn. 1, 222 S.W.2d 22; Hardin's Bakeries v. Ranager, 1953, 217 Miss. 463, 65 So.2d 461. See Riesenfeld, Forty Years of American Workmen's Compensation, 1951, 35 Minn.L.Rev. 524.

55. See for example Aistrop v. Blue Diamond Coal Co., 1943, 181 Va. 287, 24 S.E.2d 546; Kress & Co. v. Burkes, 1944, 153 Fla. 868, 16 So.2d 106; Di Maria v. Curtiss-Wright Corp., 1947, 135 N.J.L. 470, 52 A.2d 698; Wilson & Co. v. McGee, 1933, 163 Okl. 99, 21 P.2d 25; Industrial Commission v. Lambert, 1933, 126 Ohio St. 501, 186 N.E. 89.

56. See for example Hartford Acc. & Ind. Co. v. Industrial Commission, 1947, 66 Ariz. 259, 186 P.2d 959; Muff v. Brainard, 1949, 150 Neb. 650, 35 N.W. 2d 597; Rathmell v. Wesleyville Borough, 1944, 351 Pa. 14, 40 A.2d 28; Schlange v. Briggs Mfg. Co., 1950, 326 Mich. 552, 40 N.W.2d 454; Masse v.

of Mississippi and Wyoming still do not cover occupational diseases, while those of twenty-two other states cover only certain specified diseases.[57] Most of the statutes are limited to injuries "arising out of and in the course of employment," and it may still be found that damage caused by the negligence of the employer lies outside of the scope of this restriction.[58] In all such cases, the statute is held to have no application, and the workman is left to his remedy at common law.[59] There is thus a substantial, and still important, area of labor litigation in which the older law still has significance and vitality. The whole trend is toward cutting it down, making further inroads upon it by bringing as much as possible within the compensation acts; and its ultimate extinction appears to be only a question of time—which, however, may not mean anything immediate.

As in the past, the common law action is founded on a theory of negligence, and must be based upon proof of a violation of some specific duty of care resting upon the employer. In the absence of legislation it is still subject to the old trio of defenses,[60] assumption of risk,[61] contributory negligence,[62] and the fellow servant rule.[63] This last has been said to have "practically disappeared with workmen's compensation,"[64] and not to be at all popular with the courts, which will apply it only where it is unavoidable;[65] and

James H. Robinson Co., 1950, 301 N.Y. 34, 92 N.E.2d 56. See Sears and Groves, Worker Protection Under Occupational Disease Disability Statutes, 1959, 31 Rocky Mt.L.Rev. 462.

57. See Bureau of Labor Standards Bull. No. 125, 1950.

58. Thus the workman may be injured by negligence of his employer not connected with the employment, or while he is out of the course of his employment. National Biscuit Co. v. Litzky, 6 Cir. 1927, 22 F.2d 939; Collins v. Troy Laundry Co., 1931, 135 Or. 580, 297 P. 334; Conrad v. Youghiogheny & Ohio Coal Co., 1923, 107 Ohio St. 387, 140 N.E. 482; Norwood v. Tellico River Lumber Co., 1922, 146 Tenn. 682, 244 S.W. 490. See Note, 1936, 14 North Car.L. Rev. 199.

See Malone, The Compensable Risk, 1959, 31 Rocky Mt.L.Rev. 397; Larson, The Legal Aspects of Causation in Workmen's Compensation, 1954, 8 Rutgers L.Rev. 423.

59. See for example Billo v. Allegheny Steel Co., 1937, 328 Pa. 97, 195 A. 110; Triff v. National Bronze & Aluminum Foundry Co., 1939, 135 Ohio St. 191, 20 N.E.2d 232; Echord v. Rush, 1927, 124 Kan. 521, 261 P. 820; Jellico Coal Co. v. Adkins, 1923, 197 Ky. 684, 247 S.W. 972; Jones v. Rinehart & Dennis Co., 1933, 113 W.Va. 414, 168 S.E. 482.

Contra, as to a schedule of occupational diseases: Thomas v. Parker Rust Proof Co., 1938, 284 Mich. 260, 279 N.W. 504; Murphy v. American Enka Corp., 1938, 213 N.C. 218, 195 S.E. 538.

60. All of which may be involved in a single case. See Rawlins v. Nelson, 1951, 38 Wash.2d 570, 231 P.2d 281; McDonald v. Louisville & N. R. Co., 1930, 232 Ky. 734, 24 S.W.2d 585.

61. Jones v. Adams, 1952, 56 N.M. 510, 245 P.2d 843; Taylor v. Hostetler, 1960, 186 Kan. 788, 352 P.2d 1042; Syverson v. Nelson, 1955, 245 Minn. 63, 70 N.W.2d 880; Heinlen v. Martin Miller Orchards, 1952, 40 Wash.2d 356, 242 P.2d 1054; Painter v. Nichols, 1954, 118 Vt. 306, 108 A.2d 384. See Note, 1961, 47 Va.L.Rev. 1444.

62. Frei v. Frei, 1953, 263 Wis. 430, 57 N.W.2d 731; Price v. New Castle Refractories Co., 1939, 332 Pa. 537, 3 A.2d 418; Steiner v. Spencer, 1940, 24 Tenn. App. 389, 145 S.W.2d 547; Kolenko v. Certain-Teed Products Corp., W.D.N.Y.1937, 20 F.Supp. 920.

63. May v. Sharp, 1936, 191 Ark. 1142, 89 S.W.2d 735; Parker v. Nelson Grain & Milling Co., 1932, 330 Mo. 95, 48 S.W.2d 906; Richardson v. American Cotton Mills, 1925, 189 N.C. 653, 127 S.E. 834; Mariani v. Nanni, 1962, 95 R.I. 153, 185 A.2d 119, Cf. Taylor v. Hostetler, 1960, 186 Kan. 788, 352 P.2d 1042 (on basis of assumption of risk). See Note, 1948, 13 Mo.L.Rev. 327.

64. Reboni v. Case Bros., 1951, 137 Conn. 501, 78 A. 2d 887.

A number of states have deprived the employer of all three defenses where the tort liability survives because of the employer's election of non-coverage by workmen's compensation. See for example Fitch v. Mayer, Ky.1953, 258 S.W.2d 923; Kansas City Stockyards Co. v. Anderson, 8 Cir., 1952, 199 F.2d 91 (Missouri); Muldrow v. Weinstein, 1951, 234 N. C. 587, 68 S.E.2d 249; Baldassare v. West Oregon Lumber Co., 1952, 193 Or. 556, 239 P.2d 839.

Nearly all of the acts contain such a provision in the event of failure to obtain insurance. See for example Haralson v. Rhea, 1953, 76 Ariz. 74, 259 P.2d 246; McCoy v. Cornish, 1954, 220 Miss. 577, 71 So. 2d 304; Evans v. Phipps, 1953, 152 Tex. 487, 259 S. W.2d 723.

65. Buss v. Wachmuth, 1937, 190 Wash. 673, 70 P.2d 417.

the courts of Florida, Oregon and Washington have declared [66] that it will not be recognized in the future; but elsewhere it remains at least theoretically alive.

Legislation has not, however, stopped with the workmen's compensation acts. There are a good many scattered statutes regulating working conditions, which have been construed to place full responsibility upon the employer, so that he is under strict liability when an injury results from their violation, even though he has exercised all possible care.[67] There are other statutes which have abrogated the fellow servant rule,[68] and the defenses of assumption of risk [69] or contributory negligence; [70] and the last named defense frequently is limited to a reduction of the plaintiff's damages on a comparative neg-

ligence basis.[71]   Such legislation usually has been limited in its scope to particular industries or particular hazards; and while it has done a great deal to palliate the rigors of the common law, and the courts have been eager to seize almost any excuse to do the same, the uncompensated industrial injury remains one of the chief reproaches to the law, and a field in which further remedies are still badly needed.

Carrier Employees

The most important single group of employees not covered by the workmen's compensation acts are those of railroads. Legislation with respect to railway employees antedated workmen's compensation in the United States. In 1906 Congress enacted a Federal Employers' Liability Act, covering all employees of common carriers by rail when the carrier was engaged in interstate or foreign commerce. This act was held unconstitutional as exceeding the power of Congress, in that it applied to employees who were themselves engaged in intrastate commerce at the time of injury.[72] A second Act,[73] passed in 1908, and limited to employees who were themselves in interstate or foreign commerce, was held constitutional,[74] and is now in effect. Since the application of the statute thus depended upon the type of commerce in which the workman was engaged when he was hurt, the courts were

---

66. Crenshaw Bros. Produce Co. v. Harper, 1940, 142 Fla. 27, 194 So. 353; Ritter v. Beals, 1961, 225 Or. 504, 358 P.2d 1080; Siragusa v. Swedish Hospital, 1962, 60 Wash.2d 310, 373 P.2d 767.

67. Koenig v. Patrick Const. Corp., 1948, 298 N.Y. 313, 3 N.E.2d 133; Lu May v. Van Drisse Motors, 1929, 199 Wis. 310, 226 N.W. 301; Johnson v. Weborg, 1942, 142 Neb. 516, 7 N.W.2d 65; Grasty v. Sabin, 1927, 32 Ariz. 463, 259 P. 1049; O'Donnell v. Elgin, J. & E. R. Co., 1949, 338 U.S. 384 (Federal Safety Appliance Act).

68. See Ferguson v. Ringsby Truck Line, 10 Cir. 1949, 174 F.2d 744 (Colorado Employers' Liability Act); Pitzer v. M. D. Tomkies & Sons, 1951, 136 W.Va. 268, 67 S.E.2d 437 (child labor); Phillips Petroleum Co. v. Jenkins, 1936, 297 U.S. 629, second appeal, 298 U.S. 691, rehearing denied 298 U.S. 691 (employees of corporations in Arkansas); Union Oil Co. of Calif. v. Hunt, 9 Cir. 1940, 111 F.2d 269 (hazardous industries in Oregon).

69. Osborne v. Salvation Army, 2 Cir. 1939, 107 F.2d 929; Union Oil Co. of Calif. v. Hunt, 9 Cir. 1940, 111 F.2d 269 (Oregon law); Brown v. Hames, 1944, 207 Ark. 196, 179 S.W.2d 689; N. O. Nelson Mfg. Corp. v. Dickson, 1944, 114 Ind.App. 668, 53 N.E.2d 640; Price v. New Castle Refractories Co., 1939, 332 Pa. 507, 3 A.2d 418. The same result has been achieved by judicial decision. See supra, note 66.

70. Osborne v. Salvation Army, 2 Cir. 1939, 107 F.2d 929; Koenig v. Patrick Const. Corp., 1948, 298 N.Y. 313, 83 N.E.2d 133; Brown v. Hames, 1944, 207 Ark. 196, 179 S.W.2d 689; N. O. Nelson Mfg. Corp. v. Dickson, 1944, 114 Ind.App. 668, 53 N.E.2d 640; Maurizi v. Western Coal & Min. Co., 1928, 321 Mo. 378, 11 S.W.2d 268.

71. See for example Price v. McNeill, 1946, 237 Iowa 1120, 24 N.W.2d 464; Edwards v. Hollywood Canteen, 1945, 27 Cal.2d 802, 167 P.2d 729; McKee v. New Idea, Inc., Ohio App.1942, 44 N.E.2d 697; Tampa Elec. Co. v. Bryant, 1931, 101 Fla. 204, 133 So. 887.

72. Employers' Liability Cases, 1908, 207 U.S. 463.

73. Federal Employers' Liability Act, 45 U.S.C.A. § 51 et seq. See Symposium, 1953, 18 Law & Contemp. Prob. 110–431; Richter and Forer, Federal Employers' Liability Act, 1952, 12 F.R.D. 13; Richter and Forer, Federal Employers' Liability Act —A Real Compensatory Law for Railroad Workers, 1951, 36 Corn.L.Q. 203.

74. Second Employers' Liability Cases, 1912, 223 U.S. 1.

faced with the difficult problem of separating out the duties of employees or interstate railways into categories, and classifying them as interstate or intrastate, with some rather refined splitting of hairs in the process. This difficulty was removed to a considerable extent by an amendment to the Act in 1939, which broadened its terms to include all activities which further interstate commerce, or which directly or closely and substantially affect it.[75] Thus if the task performed by the workman at the time of his injury is to be regarded as a part of interstate commerce, or as directly, or closely and substantially, affecting it, the Federal Act applies, and since Congress has occupied the field, it operates to the exclusion of all state remedies.[76] On the other hand, as to injuries during activities which are strictly intrastate,[77] or as to employees of carriers other than by rail,[78] the states are not deprived of the power to legislate. Many of them have enacted special railway labor acts, modeled upon the federal statute.[79]

The Federal Employers' Liability Act, and the state acts patterned after it, included the modifications of the common law which had won popular favor up to the year 1908, and were regarded as important steps forward when they were enacted. Liability must still be based on negligence, the breach of some duty found to rest upon the employer,[80] and to this extent the statutes do no more than to preserve the common law remedy. The fellow servant rule, however, is abolished.[81] Assumption of risk was left untouched by the original Federal Act, except as to the employer's violation of statutes enacted for the safety of employees.[82] The amendments of 1939 specifically changed the Act to provide that the employee shall not be held to have assumed the risks of his employment in any case where injury results in whole or in part from the negligence of the carrier or its servants.[83] Contributory negligence is not allowed to bar recovery, but goes only to reduce it by an apportionment of damages according to fault. For a long time this provision was to some extent defeated by a rather unaccountable series of decisions of the Supreme Court beginning in 1916,[84] which

75. See Reed v. Pennsylvania R. Co., 1956, 351 U.S. 502; Southern Pac. R. Co. v. Gileo, 1956, 351 U.S. 493; Lillie v. Thompson, 1947, 332 U.S. 459; Bailey v. Central Vt. R. Co., 1943, 319 U.S. 350.

76. New York Cent. R. Co. v. Winfield, 1917, 244 U. S. 147.

As to coverage of employees, see Miller, F.E.L.A. Revisited, 1956, 6 Catholic U.L.Rev. 158.

77. Boston & Me. R. Co. v. Armburg, 1932, 285 U.S. 234.

78. State ex rel. Washington Motor Coach Co. v. Kelly, 1937, 192 Wash. 394, 74 P.2d 16; Hall v. Industrial Commission of Ohio, 1936, 131 Ohio St. 416, 3 N.E.2d 367; Ben Wolf Truck Lines v. Bailey, 1936, 102 Ind.App. 208, 1 N.E.2d 660. In these cases employees of motor carriers were engaged in interstate commerce.

79. See for example Louisville & N. R. Co. v. Chapman's Adm'x, 1945, 300 Ky. 835, 190 S.W.2d 452; Boyleston v. Southern R. Co., 1947, 211 S.C. 232, 44 S.E.2d 537.

80. Herdman v. Pennsylvania R. Co., 1957, 352 U.S. 518. See, generally, Smith, The Federal Employers' Liability Act. 1926, 12 A.B.A.J. 486; Funkhouser, What is a Safe Place to Work Under the F.E.L.A., 1956, 17 Ohio St.L.J. 367.

The negligence may, however, be proved by circumstantial evidence, including res ipsa loquitur. Jesionowski v. Boston & Me. R. Co., 1947, 329 U.S. 452. Or negligence per se may be found where a statute permitting no excuse is violated. Myers v. Reading Co., 1947, 331 U.S. 477 (Safety Appliance Act).

81. The Act makes the carrier liable for the negligence of its officers, agents and employees. In Sinkler v. Missouri Pac. R. Co., 1958, 356 U.S. 326, this was held to include an independent contractor "engaged in furthering the operational activities" of the railroad by conducting switching operations.

See Metzenbaum and Schwartz, Defenses Under the F.E.L.A., 1956, 17 Ohio St.L.J. 416.

82. Seaboard Airline R. Co. v. Horton, 1914, 233 U.S. 492.

83. 45 U.S.C.A. § 54; Tiller v. Atlantic Coast Line R. Co., 1943, 318 U.S. 54; Blair v. Baltimore & O. R. Co., 1945, 323 U.S. 600. See Metzenbaum and Schwartz, Defenses Under the F.E.L.A., 1956, 17 Ohio St.L.J. 416.

84. Great Northern R. Co. v. Wiles, 1916, 240 U.S. 444.

drew a distinction between the mere negligence of the plaintiff contributing to his injury, and his violation of a "primary duty," which was the "sole proximate cause" of his injury. In 1943 the Court quite as unexpectedly declared [85] that the "primary duty" rule had been in reality a form of assumption of risk, and that it had been eliminated by the amendments of 1939.

The history of the Federal Employers' Liability Act since that year has been one of gradual but persistent liberalization [86] in the direction of allowing the plaintiff to recover whenever he is injured in the course of his employment, as under a compensation act. Following a series of decisions in which the question of the railroad's negligence went to the jury although the evidence bearing upon it was circumstantial, sketchy, or the omission or departure from ordinary care was very slight,[87] the Supreme Court finally declared [88] that "Under this statute the text of a jury case is simply whether the proofs justify with reason the conclusion that employer negligence played *any part, even the slight-*

est,[89] in producing the injury or death for which damages are sought." This has been said to reduce the extent of the negligence required, as well as the quantum of proof necessary to establish it, to the "vanishing point." [90] While it is still undoubtedly true that there must be some shreds of proof both of negligence and of causation,[91] and that "speculation, conjecture and possibilities" will not be enough,[92] there appears to be little doubt that under the statute jury verdicts for the plaintiff can be sustained upon evidence which would not be sufficient in the ordinary negligence action.[93]

The Federal Employers' Liability Act has been, and is still a subject of much controversy. It undoubtedly has resulted in considerable extension of liability to the employee.[94] But it probably has resulted, on the

---

89. Italics supplied.

90. Atlantic Coast Line R. Co. v. Barrett, Fla.1958, 101 So.2d 37; see Corso, How FELA Became Liability Without Fault, 1966, 15 Cleve.Marsh.L.Rev. 344.

91. New York, N. H. & H. R. Co. v. Henagan, 1960, 364 U.S. 441; Herdman v. Pennsylvania R. Co., 1957, 352 U.S. 518; Dessi v. Pennsylvania R. Co., 3 Cir. 1958, 251 F.2d 149, 151, cert. denied 356 U.S. 967; Callihan v. Great Northern R. Co., 1960, 137 Mont. 93, 350 P.2d 369; Inman v. Baltimore & Ohio R. Co., 1959, 361 U.S. 138. As to causation, see Notes, 1966, 18 Stan.L.Rev. 829; 1966, 35 U.Cin.L. Rev. 140.

92. Memorandum of Mr. Justice Frankfurter, denying certiorari in Elgin, J. & E. R. Co. v. Gibson, 1957, 355 U.S. 897.

93. Cf. Gibson v. Thompson, 1957, 355 U.S. 18, rehearing denied 335 U.S. 900 (engineer on way from roundhouse to engine slipped and fell on loose gravel); Stinson v. Atlantic Coast Line R. Co., 1957, 355 U.S. 62, rehearing denied 355 U.S. 910, mandate conformed to, 1958, 267 Ala. 537, 103 So.2d 183 (nude body of engineer found on track under mysterious circumstances); Ringhiser v. Chesapeake & Ohio R. Co., 1957, 354 U.S. 901 (worker injured while answering call of nature in a gondola car). See McCoid, The Federal Railroad Safety Acts and the F.E.L.A.: A Comparison, 1956, 17 Ohio St.L.J. 494.

94. See Delisi, Federal Employers' Liability Act— Scope and Recent Developments, 1947, 18 Miss.L.J. 206; Richter and Forer, The Federal Employers' Liability Act, 1952, 12 F.R.D. 13; De Parcq, The

---

85. In Tiller v. Atlantic Coast Line R. Co., 1943, 318 U.S. 54, 63–64. See Keith v. Wheeling & L. E. R. Co., 6 Cir. 1947, 160 F.2d 654, cert. denied 332 U.S. 763; Rogers v. Missouri Pac. R. Co., 1957, 352 U.S. 500.

86. The initial stages of this are reviewed, without enthusiasm, in Alderman, The New Supreme Court and the Old Law of Negligence, 1953, 18 Law & Con.Prob. 111. A different view is taken in Griffith, The Vindication of a National Public Policy Under the Federal Employers' Liability Act, 1953, 18 Law & Con.Prob. 160.

87. Tennant v. Peoria & Pekin Union R. Co., 1944, 321 U.S. 29, rehearing denied 321 U.S. 802; Bailey v. Central of Vt. R. Co., 1943, 319 U.S. 350; Hayes v. Wabash R. Co., 1950, 360 Mo. 1223, 233 S.W.2d 12; Williams v. New York Central R. Co., 1949, 402 Ill. 494, 84 N.E.2d 399; Sadowski v. Long Island R. Co., 1944, 292 N.Y. 448, 55 N.E.2d 497. The last of these is Gallick v. Baltimore & Ohio R. Co., 1963, 372 U.S. 108, appeal dismissed, 1963, 172 Ohio St. 488, 178 N.E.2d 597, where there were inconsistent special findings.

88. In Rogers v. Missouri Pac. R. Co., 1957, 352 U.S. 500, rehearing denied 353 U.S. 943, and 352 U.S. 521.

whole, in increasing rather than diminishing litigation; and whether it has brought a sufficient advantage to the railway worker is a matter of dispute.[95] It has been said that "a law inspired by laudable motives at a time when remedial state legislation was in its infancy has outlived its usefulness and has become an obstacle to the fulfillment of its own purposes."[96] For more than forty years there has been discussion of some system similar to the workmen's compensation acts to cover injuries in the course of railway labor.[97] The same kind of agitation led to the passage in 1927 of a federal compensation act for longshoremen and harbor workers.[98] In the case of seamen, however, the Jones Act of 1915 and the Merchant Marine Act of 1920 have placed them on the same basis as railway employees under the Federal Employers' Liability Act.[99] On the whole the railway and maritime unions have been satisfied with the present statutes, and it is their opposition which has operated chiefly to prevent any change.[1]

81. OTHER APPLICATIONS

Writing in 1914, Jeremiah Smith[2] foresaw with trepidation the extension of the principle of strict liability into many new fields, either by statute or by modification of the common law, until the ultimate result would be the extinction of the requirement of legal fault for all tort liability. On the continent of Europe there has been considerable realization of this prediction, as to automobile accidents.[3] In this country, however, the expansion of strict liability, although it has occurred, still falls far short of this sweeping prediction.

A policy somewhat similar to that of the workmen's compensation acts is found in such

Ten Most Important Cases Under the Federal Employers' Liability Act, 1967, 44 N.D.L.Rev. 7.

95. Dodd, Administration of Workmen's Compensation, 1936, 773–780. Not the least of the reasons for this, as in the case of other federal acts, is the uncertainty as to which of the various industrial accident statutes is to apply. See Edises, Multiplicity of Remedies in the Field of Industrial Accident Law, 1933, 21 Cal.L.Rev. 430.

96. Schoene and Watson, Workmen's Compensation on Interstate Railways, 1934, 47 Harv.L.Rev. 389, 424. See also Miller, The Quest for a Federal Workmen's Compensation Law for Railroad Employees, 1953, 18 Law & Con.Prob. 188; Parker, Federal Employers' Liability Act or Uniform Compensation for All Workers, 1953, 18 Law & Con. Prob. 208.

97. See Schoene and Watson, Workmen's Compensation on Interstate Railways, 1934, 47 Harv.L.Rev. 389; Gellhorn, Federal Workmen's Compensation for Transportation Employees, 1934, 43 Yale L.J. 906; Miller, Workmen's Compensation for Railroad Employees, 1944, 2 Loyola L.Rev. 138; Miller, The Quest for a Federal Workmen's Compensation Law for Railroad Employees, 1953, 18 Law & Contemp. Prob. 188; Parker, FELA or Uniform Compensation for All Workers, 1953, 18 Law & Contemp. Prob. 208; Pollack, The Crisis in Work Injury Compensation On and Off the Railroads, 1953, 18 Law & Contemp.Prob. 296.

98. See Alaska Packers' Ass'n v. Industrial Accident Comm. of California, 1928, 276 U.S. 467; Athearn, The Longshoremen's Act and the Courts, 1935, 23 Cal.L.Rev. 129; Stumberg, Harbor Workers and Workmen's Compensation, 1929, 7 Tex.L.Rev. 197.

99. See Panama R. Co. v. Johnson, 1924, 264 U.S. 375; Stumberg, The Jones Act: Remedies of Seamen, 1956, 17 Ohio St.L.J. 416; Gardner, Remedies for Personal Injuries to Seamen, Railroadmen and Longshoremen, 1938, 71 Harv.L.Rev. 438.

1. See Richter and Forer, Federal Employers' Liability Act—A Real Compensatory Law for Railroad Workers, 1951, 36 Corn.L.Q. 203; Kossoris and Zisman, Workmen's Compensation for Seamen, 1946, 62 Monthly Lab.Rev. 851. See, however, suggesting improvements from the plaintiff's point of view, Richter and Forer, Proposed Changes in the Laws Governing Injuries in Interstate Transportation, 1954, 67 Harv.L.Rev. 1003.

2. Smith, Sequel to Workmen's Compensation Acts, 1914, 27 Harv.L.Rev. 235, 344. This has been referred to as a latter-day "Lamentations of Jeremiah." Malone, Damage Suits and the Contagious Principle of Workmen's Compensation, 1952, 12 La. L.Rev. 231.

3. See Malone, Damage Suits and the Contagious Principle of Workmen's Compensation, 1952, 12 La. L.Rev. 231; Esmein, Liability in French Law for Damages Caused by Motor Vehicle Accidents, 1953, 2 J.Am.Comp.Law 156; Ussing, the Scandinavian Law of Torts, 1952, 1 J.Am.Comp.Law 359; Deák, Automobile Accidents: A Comparative Study of the Laws of Liability in Europe, 1931, 79 U.Pa.L.Rev. 271.

statutes as the Federal Safety Appliance Act,[4] which requires railroads engaged in interstate commerce to equip their trains with certain safety devices, and makes them responsible without negligence for any deficiency which injures employees,[5] or others likely to suffer harm.[6] Child labor statutes,[7] by reason of the obvious social policy underlying them, generally have been construed to provide strict liability for injuries to the child, although the employer has exercised proper care and did not know his age. The same has been true of a number of factory acts, scaffold acts, and the like intended for the protection of employees.[8] The sale of goods involving a considerable risk to the public has been dealt with in much the same manner. Many of the pure food acts [9] make the seller of defective food liable to the injured consumer, even though he has used all reasonable care. "Dram Shop" or Civil Liability Acts [10] in some fourteen states impose

strict liability, without negligence, upon the seller of intoxicating liquors, when the sale results [11] in harm to the interests of a third person because of the intoxication of the buyer. These statutes, which have been held constitutional,[12] and are liberally construed,[13] protect the third party not only against injuries resulting directly from affirmative acts of the intoxicated man, such as assault and battery,[14] but also against the loss of family support due to injuries to the man himself,[15] including those inflicted upon him in self-defense by those whom he has attacked.[16] There are numerous other strict liability statutes applicable to particular situations, such as ground damage from airplane crashes,[17]

History and Appraisal of the Illinois Dram Shop Act, [1958] U.Ill.Law Forum 175; Note, 1959, 4 Villanova L.Rev. 575.

11. Pierce v. Albanese, 1957, 144 Conn. 241, 129 A.2d 606, appeal dismissed 355 U.S. 15; Galvin v. Jennings, 3 Cir. 1961, 289 F.2d 15; Kvanli v. Village of Watson, 1965, 272 Minn. 481, 139 N.W.2d 275.

12. Pierce v. Albanese, 1957, 144 Conn. 241, 129 A.2d 606, appeal dismissed 355 U.S. 15; Huckaba v. Cox, 1958, 14 Ill.2d 126, 150 N.E.2d 832.

13. Iszler v. Jorda, N.D.1957, 80 N.W.2d 665; Pierce v. Albanese, 1957, 144 Conn. 241, 129 A.2d 606, appeal dismissed, 355 U.S. 15; Hahn v. City of Ortonville, 1953, 238 Minn. 428, 57 N.W.2d 254; Danhof v. Osborne, 1956, 10 Ill.App.2d 529, 135 N.E.2d 492.

14. Fernandez v. Chamberlain, Fla.App.1967, 201 So. 2d 781; Geocaris v. Bangs, 1968, 91 Ill.App.2d 81, 234 N.E.2d 17 (battery); Wendelin v. Russell, 1966, 259 Iowa 1152, 147 N.W.2d 188 (drunken driving); St. Clair v. Douvas, 1959, 21 Ill.App.2d 444, 158 N. E.2d 642 (wife recovered for loss of support due to killing son); Manning v. Yokas, 1957, 389 Pa. 136, 132 A.2d 198 (negligent driving).

15. Bistline v. Ney Bros., 1907, 134 Iowa 172, 111 N. W. 422 (shooting himself); Bejnarowicz v. Bakos, 1947, 332 Ill.App. 151, 74 N.E.2d 614 (collision due to reckless driving); Sworski v. Coleman, 1940, 208 Minn. 43, 293 N.W. 297 (death from drinking). Cf. Iszler v. Jorda, N.D.1957, 80 N.W.2d 665 (funeral expenses). The intoxicated person himself usually is held not to be covered. Nolan v. Morelli, 1967, 154 Conn. 432, 226 A.2d 383.

16. Kiriluk v. Cohn, 1958, 16 Ill.App.2d 385, 148 N.E. 2d 607; Currier v. McKee, 1904, 99 Me. 364, 59 A. 442.

17. See supra, p. 516.

4. 45 U.S.C.A. § 1 et seq.

5. O'Donnell v. Elgin, J. & E. R. Co., 1949, 338 U.S. 384, rehearing denied 338 U.S. 945.

6. Fairport, P. & E. R. Co. v. Meredith, 1934, 292 U. S. 589 (highway traveler). See Note, 1938, 23 Minn.L.Rev. 103.

7. Beauchamp v. Sturges & Burn Mfg. Co., 1911, 250 Ill. 303, 95 N.E. 204, affirmed, 1914, 231 U.S. 320; Krutlies v. Bulls Head Coal Co., 1915, 249 Pa. 162, 94 A. 459; Blanton v. Kellioka Coal Co., 1921, 192 Ky. 220, 232 S.W. 614; Second Restatement of Torts, § 286, Comment f; Note, 1930, 39 Yale L.J. 908.

8. See supra, p. 107.

9. Meshbesher v. Channellene Oil & Mfg. Co., 1909, 107 Minn. 104, 119 N.W. 428; Culbertson v. Coca-Cola Bottling Co., 1930, 157 S.C. 352, 154 S.E. 424; Donaldson v. Great Atlantic & Pacific Tea Co., 1938, 186 Ga. 870, 199 S.E. 213; Great Atlantic & Pacific Tea Co. v. Hughes, 1936, 131 Ohio St. 501, 3 N.E.2d 415. Cf. Pine Grove Poultry Farm v. Newtown By-Products Mfg. Co., 1928, 248 N.Y. 293, 162 N.E. 84 (animal food); McAleavy v. Lowe, 1951, 259 Wis. 463, 49 N.W.2d 487 (same). Contra: Howson v. Foster Beef Co., 1935, 87 N.H. 200, 177 A. 656; Cheli v. Cudahy Bros. Co., 1934, 267 Mich. 690, 255 N.W. 414. See Melick, The Sale of Food and Drink, 1936, 284; Note, 1939, 26 Va.L.Rev. 100.

10. See Appleman, Civil Liability Under the Illinois Dramshop Act, 1939, 34 Ill.L.Rev. 30; Ogilvie,

or, for example, the Pennsylvania act making pipe lines strictly liable when oil escapes and pollutes a well.[18]

While the common law has not altogether kept pace with these statutory developments, it has shown in recent years a very marked tendency to extend strict liability into new fields. Sellers of goods have generally been held liable for defects which cause harm to the purchaser, under the guise of an "implied warranty" which becomes a term of the contract, and permits recovery without any proof of negligence.[19] First in food cases, and later as to all other products, the considerable majority of the American jurisdictions have extended the strict liability to the ultimate consumer even in the absence of privity of contract, either upon the theory of an implied warranty to the consumer by implication of law, or, more lately, on the basis of outright strict liability in tort.[20] In particular the tort liability has been found at the common law in the "Dramshop" situation, where the defendant sells liquor to an intoxicated person, and a third person suffers injury.[21] Strict liability has also been extended into the field of misrepresentation, to cover innocent statements made without negligence, for which some courts permit recovery in an action of deceit,[22] and, in the case of harm to third persons without privity of contract, recovery has been based upon an express "warranty" of truth.[23]

There are some survivals of older rules, as to which the fundamental policy of the law as to the administration of the risk involved is now advanced as a justification. The liability of a carrier [24] or an innkeeper [25] for goods entrusted to his care is one such instance. Defamatory statements [26] are subject to a similar strict rule, which is perhaps primarily an historical anomaly, but has been supported as an instrument of policy. Vicarious liability [27] is now quite generally recognized as a form of strict liability, designed to administer the risk. Still another instance is the common law rule, now often modified by statute, which makes a defendant strictly liable, despite all due care, if he removes naturally necessary lateral or subjacent support for the plaintiff's land.[28] On the other hand, there are other such rules that are now losing favor, particularly that as to trespass to land,[29] as it is realized that there is no longer any social necessity or justification for them.

Frequently, when the courts have been unwilling to say outright that the defendant is liable without negligence, something approaching this result has been accomplished by the creation of presumptions. Thus it has been held that upon proof of an injury at the hands of a carrier, a passenger is entitled to a presumption of the carrier's negligence, which the carrier must meet by producing affirmative evidence, or suffer a di-

riers, 1914, 324, 325; Hutchinson, Law of Carriers, 3d Ed.1906, § 4.

25. Hulett v. Swift, 1865, 33 N.Y. 571; Fisher v. Bonneville Hotel Co., 1920, 55 Utah 588, 188 P. 856, 12 A.L.R. 255; Featherstone v. Dessert, 1933, 173 Wash. 264, 22 P.2d 1050. The common law rule has been altered by statutes in many states and rejected by decisions in others. See Brown, Personal Property, 1936, § 102; Notes, 1929, 13 Minn.L.Rev. 615; 1942, 22 Or.L.Rev. 95.

26. See infra, p. 772.

27. See supra, § 69.

28. See 5 Powell, Real Property, 1961, ch. 63; Note, 1941, 50 Yale L.J. 1125; Obert v. Dunn, 1897, 140 Mo. 476, 41 S.W. 901; Schaefer v. Hoffman, 1929, 198 Wis. 233, 223 N.W. 847; Hemsworth v. Cushing, 1897, 115 Mich. 92, 72 N.W. 1108; Walker v. Strosnider, 1910, 67 W.Va. 39, 67 S.E. 1087; Chesapeake & Ohio R. Co. v. May, 1914, 157 Ky. 708, 163 S.W. 1112.

29. See supra, pp. 63–64.

18. Jackson v. United States Pipe Line, 1937, 325 Pa. 436, 191 A. 165.

19. See infra, § 95.

20. See infra, §§ 97, 98.

21. See infra, p. 678.

22. See infra, p. 710.

23. See infra, p. 651.

24. Thomas v. Boston & Prov. R. Corp., 1845, 10 Metc., Mass. 472; see Dobie, Bailments and Car-

rected verdict for the plaintiff.[30] In some cases, at whose number one may only guess, where there has in fact been no negligence but the defendant is unable to prove it, this will arrive at the same result as strict liability.[31] The difference between the two, however, lies in the fact that the door is not closed to whatever proof of proper care the defendant may be able to offer; and since he can often offer such proof, it is a difference of importance. A similar presumption of negligence has been created where goods are lost or damaged in the hands of a bailee.[32]

Subject to constitutional limitations, such presumptions have been created by some statutes.[33] The courts which give the doctrine of res ipsa loquitur [34] more than its normal procedural effect as circumstantial evidence regard it as an instrument of policy, requiring the defendant to prove that he was not negligent or pay.

The last few years have witnessed the renewed and more vigorous advocacy of strict liability on an even broader scale, in which liability insurance is to play the key and dominating role. Discussion of these proposals is best deferred to a later chapter.[35]

---

30. Southern Pac. Co. v. Cavin, 9 Cir. 1906, 144 F. 348; Steele v. Southern R. Co., 1899, 55 S.C. 389, 33 S.E. 509; Williams v. Spokane Falls & N. R. Co., 1905, 39 Wash. 77, 80 P. 1100. See Prosser, Res Ipsa Loquitur: Collisions of Carriers with Other Vehicles, 1936, 30 Ill.L.Rev. 980.

31. As to the policy underlying such presumptions, see Bohlen, The Effect of Rebuttable Presumptions of Law Upon the Burden of Proof, 1920, 68 U.Pa.L. Rev. 307; Morgan, Some Observations Concerning Presumptions, 1931, 44 Harv.L.Rev. 906.

32. Rustad v. Great Northern R. Co., 1913, 122 Minn. 453, 142 N.W. 727; Schaefer v. Washington Safety

Deposit Co., 1917, 281 Ill. 43, 117 N.E. 781. See Brown, Personal Property, 1936, § 87.

33. See Brosman, The Statutory Presumption 1930, 5 Tulane L.Rev. 17; Morgan, Federal Constitutional Limitations Upon Presumptions Created by State Legislation, Harvard Legal Essays, 1934, 323.

34. See supra, p. 230.

35. See infra, ch. 14.

CHAPTER 14

LIABILITY INSURANCE

82. WHAT LIABILITY INSURANCE IS

The last twenty-five years have brought forth a deluge of legal writing concerning the relation between liability insurance and the law of torts. There are now upwards of a hundred law review articles on the subject, as well as half a dozen books.[1] In the aggregate, this literature has constructed a magnificent new edifice of proposed tort law, built upon the theory that it is, or should be, a branch of the law of insurance. All personal injuries, and perhaps other damages, or at least all those in some particular fields, such as traffic accidents, are to become a matter of strict liability. The tortfeasor is to be required by statute to carry insurance against that liability, and the insurance is to be paid by way of compensation to the injured victim.

At the outset it must be said that thus far all this literature has made much more of an impression upon the writers than upon the courts. The authors cite one another in profusion, until there is a superficial impression of an abundance of authority, and great movement in the law; but up to the present time, at least, they have received little or no mention in judicial opinions, and the legislatures, for the most part, have remained unimpressed. But they are not for that reason to be disregarded, or lightly brushed aside. There are far too many instances in American law in which the theories of professors, received initially with a smile of disdain as radical innovations evolved in the disordered minds of those lacking in all practical experience, have come with the passage of time to be accepted, and have passed into our law as the prevailing rules. This book is full of them. Some legislatures are beginning to consider the proposals, and to order studies made; more bills are introduced into each new session; grants are being made by foundations for other studies. The agitation, if that is the proper name for it, is on the increase year by year. Anyone about to enter the practice of law may expect to live with these problems for a good many years to come.

Liability insurance is a form of indemnity.[2] The insurer, almost invariably a com-

---

[1]. Mention may be made of a few landmarks: Ehrenzweig, Negligence Without Fault, 1951; Green, Traffic Victims: Tort Law and Insurance, 1958; James, Accident Liability Reconsidered: The Impact of Liability Insurance, 1948, 57 Yale L.J. 549; James and Thornton, The Impact of Insurance on the Law of Torts, 1950, 15 Law & Con.Prob. 431; Friedmann, Social Insurance and the Principles of Tort Liability, 1950, 63 Harv.L.Rev. 241; Grad, Recent Developments in Automobile Accident Compensation, 1950, 50 Col.L.Rev. 300; McNiece and Thornton, Is the Law of Negligence Obsolete? 1952 26 St. Johns L.Rev. 255; Morris, Hazardous Enterprises and Risk-Bearing Capacity, 1952, 61 Yale L.J. 1172; McNiece and Thornton, Automobile Accident Prevention and Compensation, 1952, 27 N.Y.U.L. Rev. 585; Green, The Individual's Protection Under Negligence Law: Risk Sharing, 1953, 47 Northwestern U.L.Rev. 751; James, The Columbia Study of Compensation Law for Automobile Accidents: An Unanswered Challenge, 1959, 59 Col.L.Rev. 408. As to the European law, see Ehrenzweig, Assurance Oblige—A Comparative Study, 1950, 15 Law & Con. Prob. 445; O'Connell, Taming the Automobile, 1963, 58 Nw.U.L.Rev. 299.

[2]. Technically, only where the insured is required to pay the claim of the third person before he can have any action against the insurer, as in Teters v.

pany engaged in the business, undertakes to indemnify the insured against loss which he may sustain through payments made by reason of his becoming legally liable to a third person, or against such liability itself before payment. This is a matter of a contract, the insurance policy, between the insurer and the insured, to which in the first instance the third person is not a party, and with which, in the absence of statute so providing, he is not directly concerned. Liability insurance is thus to be distinguished from accident insurance, in which payment is to be made directly to the injured person. Unless there is statutory regulation, as there frequently may be, the insurer's undertaking is entirely a matter of the terms of the particular policy, in which there may be, and in fact is, a good deal of variation.[3]

Provisions indemnifying against liability were not unknown in early insurance policies, as for example those of marine insurance, by which the insurer undertook, among other risks, that of liability for damages inflicted on other ships through collision.[4] In its modern form, the separate liability policy began to appear in England not long after 1880, and developed first as a means of protecting employers against the increased litigation and liability resulting from employ-

ers' liability and workmen's compensation acts. As the experience with this proved satisfactory, new demands were made for protection against other risks, and the protection was expanded into other fields in a rather unplanned and haphazard manner.[5] In addition to the employer's liability, common subjects of insurance today are the risks resulting from the use of premises, whether open to the public or privately used; from faulty products which injure consumers; from the use of vehicles in all forms of transportation; and those arising out of the practice of professions, such as surgery, medicine, law, accounting, and trusteeship. There are even policies available for protection against relatively unusual risks, such as that of liability of a publisher for defamation. By far the greatest amount of liability insurance today, however, covers the risks arising from automobile accidents. This has become a business of enormous proportions. In 1959 the net premiums written for automobile personal injury liability in the United States totaled over ten billion dollars and the amount paid on claims over six billion.[6]

Almost from the beginning, the liability insurer began to undertake more than the indemnification for the loss or liability itself. One of the primary purposes of the policy always has been to protect the insured against the expense and inconvenience of litigation. The investigation of the third person's claim, negotiation with the claimant, the posting of a bond when it is required, or even providing bail where there is an arrest, the defense of the action brought against the insured, the payment of attorney's fees and all other expenses which it may involve, and frequently, today, the payment of first-aid medical ex-

Gass, 1927, 156 Tenn. 127, 299 S.W. 788; Frye v. Bath Gas & Elec. Co., 1903, 97 Me. 241, 54 A. 395; Luger v. Windell, 1921, 116 Wash. 375, 199 P. 760. Where the policy protects against incurring liability, before such payment, it usually is classified as a distinct form of insurance, differing from indemnity insurance. See for example Landaker v. Anderson, 1927, 145 Wash. 660, 261 P. 388.

3. There is a good short summary of this in Mowbray and Blanchard, Insurance, 5th Ed. 1961, ch. 13. See also Mehr and Cammack, Principles of Insurance, 1953, ch. 14.

4. See Delanoy v. Robson, 1814, 5 Taunt. 605, 606, 128 Eng.Rep. 827, mentioning "societies of persons, who insured each other's vessels not only against sea risks, but against all sums which the owner might be obliged to pay for damages done by their vessels." The marine insurance policy, which has not been changed substantially since it was first put into use in 1613, is set out in Patterson, Cases on Insurance, 3d Ed. 1955, 746.

5. "Like a New England Farmhouse, with unplanned additions stuck on as occasion demanded." McNeely, Illegality as a Factor in Liability Insurance, 1941, 41 Col.L.Rev. 26, 28. See, as a full description of one type, Arnold, Products Liability Insurance, [1957] Wis.L.Rev. 429.

6. 1969 Statistical Abstract of the United States, 547–52; National Safety Council, Accident Facts (1969 ed.) 5.40.

penses of the injured person even though there is no liability and no claim is made—all these have become recognized as the responsibility of the insurer.

For a time in the beginning, there was considerable uncertainty as to whether any contract by which an insured was to be protected against the consequences of his own negligence or other fault was not void as contrary to public policy. Liability insurance was attacked as a form of maintenance, by which professional litigants were provided to replace the true defendants, and as an encouragement to antisocial conduct and a relaxation of vigilance toward the rights of others, by relieving the actual wrongdoer of liability for his acts.[7] That the latter objection was not altogether without substance is illustrated by one case in which, a moment before the crash, the defendant replied to the plaintiff's protest against his reckless driving, "Don't worry, I carry insurance." [8] With the passage of time, when it became apparent that no dire consequences in fact resulted,[9] these objections passed out of the picture, and the validity of a liability insurance contract as such is no longer questioned.

Following two leading cases in which the insurance contract was sustained where an employer had hired the injured employee in violation of a statute setting an age limit,[10]

and the insured's car was being operated, against the law, by a person under age,[11] it is now generally agreed that even minor violations of criminal statutes, such as driving without a license,[12] speeding,[13] and the like,[14] will not invalidate the insurance, or deprive the violator of its protection. There will almost certainly be cases in which the misconduct is so flagrant and extreme that it will be considered entirely against public policy to indemnify against it; [15] but it seems equally clear that it is only in the plainest and most outrageous cases that this will be true.[16] Some vestiges of the old doubts and objections still appear, in the form of policy provisions excluding liability for some kinds of illegal conduct, such as assault and battery or other intentional infliction of harm, or cer-

7. See Coffman v. Louisville & N. R. Co., 1913, 184 Ala. 474, 63 So. 527; Employers' Liability Assur. Corp. Ltd. v. Kelly-Atkinson Const. Co., 1913, 182 Ill.App. 372; Aetna Life Ins. Co. v. Weck, 1915, 163 Ky. 37, 173 S.W. 317; Standard Life & Acc. Ins. Co. v. Bambrick Bros. Const. Co., 1912, 163 Mo.App. 504, 143 S.W. 845; In re Aldrich, 1913, 86 Vt. 531, 86 A. 801.

8. Herschensohn v. Weisman, 1923, 80 N.H. 557, 119 A. 705.

9. See the references to empirical data indicating that the number of accidents has not increased with the growth of liability insurance, in Merchants' Mut. Automobile Liability Ins. Co. v. Smart, 1925, 267 U.S. 126; In re Opinion of the Justices, 1925, 251 Mass. 569, 147 N.E. 681.

10. Edward Stern & Co. v. Liberty Mutual Ins. Co., 1921, 269 Pa. 559, 112 A. 865.

11. Messersmith v. American Fidelity Co., 1921, 232 N.Y. 161, 133 N.E. 432. Accord, Davis v. Highway Motor Underwriters, 1931, 120 Neb. 734, 235 N.W. 325.

12. McMahon v. Pearlman, 1922, 242 Mass. 367, 136 N.E. 154; Odden v. Union Indemnity Co., 1930, 156 Wash. 10, 286 P. 59; Neat v. Miller, 1932, 170 Wash. 625, 17 P.2d 32; Sills v. Schneider, 1939, 197 Wash. 659, 86 P.2d 203 (taxicab).

13. Miller v. U. S. Fidelity & Cas. Co., 1935, 291 Mass. 445, 197 N.E. 75; Firemen's Fund Ins. Co. v. Haley, 1922, 129 Miss. 525, 92 So. 635; Rothman v. Metropolitan Cas. Ins. Co., 1938, 134 Ohio St. 241, 16 N.E.2d 417 (plus improper driving).

14. Security Underwriters v. Rousch Motor Co., 1928, 88 Ind.App. 112, 161 N.E. 569 (cable across highway); Lopez v. Townsend, 1933, 37 N.M. 574, 25 P. 2d 809 (carrier violating operating rules); Bowman v. Preferred Risk Mut. Ins. Co., 1957, 348 Mich. 531, 83 N.W.2d 434 (moving another's car illegally); Wolff v. General Cas. Co. of America, 1963, 68 N.M. 292, 361 P.2d 330 (assault and battery). See Note, 1967, 12 S.D.L.Rev. 373.

15. See for example Acme Finance Co. v. National Ins. Co., 1948, 118 Colo. 445, 195 P.2d 728, refusing to enforce a liability policy because the accident occurred while the insured was engaged in robbery and murder.

16. See, allowing recovery where there was drunken driving, Neat v. Miller, 1932, 170 Wash. 625, 17 P.2d 32; Tinline v. White Cross Ins. Ass'n, [1921] 3 K.B. 327; James v. British Gen. Ins. Co., [1927] 2 K.B. 311. Contra, where the car was being operated at very high speed, O'Hearn v. Yorkshire Ins. Co., 1921, 67 Ont.L.Rep. 735.

tain specified criminal acts, including in particular the operation of a car by an unlicensed minor, or by a drunken driver.[17]

Since, in its inception, liability insurance was intended solely for the benefit and protection of the insured, which is to say the tortfeasor, it followed that the injured plaintiff, who was not a party to the contract, had at common law no direct remedy against the insurance company.[18] In order to make this quite certain, and so far as possible to delay or avoid the liability which they had been paid to assume, insurance companies inserted in the policy "no action" clauses, which required payment of a judgment by the insured before they became obligated to him.[19] This meant that insolvency of the insured, his settlement and release of the insurer, his death or his removal from the jurisdiction, or merely the fact that he was judgment-proof, would defeat all recovery in favor of anyone.[20] Unscrupulous companies were even known to put the insured through bankruptcy, as a cheap way of paying off the policy.[21] Vari-

ous theories which were resorted to in order to obtain a direct action against the insurer, such as subrogation,[22] garnishment,[23] and the like,[24] were singularly unsuccessful. The two which succeeded to some limited extent were the device by which a cooperative insured paid off the judgment with a note,[25] and an estoppel precluding the insurer from setting up the clause where it had assumed control of the lawsuit and defended it.[26]

All of this is now extensively modified by legislation.[27]   Statutes, variously worded,

---

17. These are considered at length, as to different types of liability insurance, in McNeely, Illegality as a Factor in Liability Insurance, 1941, 41 Col.L. Rev. 26.

18. Bain v. Atkins, 1902, 181 Mass. 240, 63 N.E. 414; Kinnan v. Fidelity & Cas. Co., 1903, 107 Ill.App. 406; Smith Stage Co. v. Eckert, 1919, 21 Ariz. 28, 184 P. 1001; Fidelity & Cas. Co. v. Martin, 1915, 163 Ky. 12, 173 S.W. 307. A noted diatribe in condemnation of this is Laube, The Social Vice of Accident Indemnity, 1931, 80 U.Pa.L.Rev. 189.

19. "No action shall lie against the company to recover for any loss or expense under this policy, unless it shall be brought by the assured for loss or expense actually sustained and paid in money by him after trial of the issue." Quoted in Patterson v. Adan, 1912, 119 Minn. 308, 309–311, 138 N.W. 281, 282. See also Goodman v. Georgia Life Ins. Co., 1914, 189 Ala. 130, 66 So. 649; Ohio Cas. Ins. Co. v. Beckwith, 5 Cir. 1934, 74 F.2d 75.

20. Hollings v. Brown, 1922, 202 Ala. 504, 80 So. 792; Shea v. U. S. Fidelity & Cas. Co., 1923, 98 Conn. 447, 120 A. 286; Cushman v. Carbondale Fuel Co., 1904, 122 Iowa 656, 98 N.W. 509; Transylvania Cas. Ins. Co. v. Williams, 1925, 209 Ky. 626, 273 S.W. 536.

21. See Roth v. National Automobile Mut. Cas. Co., 1922, 202 App.Div. 667, 669, 195 N.Y.S. 865, 867, dismissed, 1923, 235 N.Y. 605, 139 N.E. 752.

22. Pfeiler v. Penn Allen Portland Cement Co., 1913, 240 Pa. 468, 87 A. 623; Allen v. Aetna Life Ins. Co., 3 Cir. 1906, 145 F. 881.

23. Shea v. U. S. Fidelity & Cas. Co., 1923, 98 Conn. 453, 120 A. 286; Combs v. Hunt, 1924, 140 Va. 627, 125 S.E. 661; Hollings v. Brown, 1919, 202 Ala. 504, 80 So. 792; Fidelity & Cas. Co. v. Martin, 1915, 163 Ky. 12, 173 S.W. 307; Ford v. Aetna Life Ins. Co., 1912, 70 Wash. 29, 126 P. 69.

Where the policy is construed to insure against liability, before payment, the injured party, after judgment against the insured establishes the liability, may garnish the insurer. Fentress v. Rutledge, 1924, 140 Va. 685, 125 S.E. 668; Wehrhahn v. Fort Dearborn Cas. Underwriters, 1928, 221 Mo.App. 230, 1 S.W.2d 242.

24. Luger v. Windell, 1921, 116 Wash. 375, 199 P. 760 (assignment of the policy); Connolly v. Bolster, 1905, 187 Mass. 266, 72 N.E. 981 (resort to equity).

25. Herbo-Phosa Co. v. Philadelphia Cas. Co., 1912, 34 R.I. 567, 84 A. 1093; Taxicab Motor Co. v. Pacific Coast Cas. Co., 1913, 73 Wash. 631, 132 P. 393; Standard Printing Co. v. Fidelity & Deposit Co., 1917, 138 Minn. 304, 164 N.W. 1022; Hoagland Wagon Co. v. London Guarantee & Acc. Co., 1919, 201 Mo.App. 490, 212 S.W. 393. Even this failed in Wisconsin as a "mere subterfuge." Stenbohm v. Brown-Corliss Engine Co., 1909, 137 Wis. 564, 119 N.W. 308.

26. Patterson v. Adan, 1912, 119 Minn. 308, 138 N.W. 281; American Indemnity Co. v. Felbaum, 1924, 114 Tex. 127, 263 S.W. 908; Sanders v. Frankfort Marine, Accident & Plate Glass Ins. Co., 1904, 72 N.H. 485, 57 A. 655; Elliott v. Aetna Life Ins. Co., 1917, 100 Neb. 833, 161 N.W. 579; Elliott v. Belt Auto. Ass'n, 1924, 87 Fla. 545, 100 So. 797; Maryland Cas. Co. v. Peppard, 1915, 53 Okl. 515, 157 P. 106. Apart from statute, however, this was definitely a minority position. See Vance, Insurance, 3d Ed. 1951, 803.

27. See Dodge, An Injured Party's Rights Under an Automobile Liability Policy, 1952, 38 Iowa L.Rev. 116; Lassiter, Direct Actions Against the Insurer,

have prevented the insurer from conditioning his duty to pay upon prior payment by the insured, and provide that the injured person holding an unsatisfied judgment against the insured may proceed against the insurer,[28] or that the insolvency or bankruptcy of the insured shall not release the company.[29] The National Standard Automobile Liability policy now in general use provides specifically that bankruptcy or insolvency of the insured or of his estate shall not relieve the company of any of its obligations under the policy. Wisconsin and Louisiana [30] have gone farthest of all, and have provided a direct action in every case against the liability insurer; and Florida has accomplished the same result by judicial decision.[31]

Clauses in the policy almost invariably limit the liability of the insurer at a great deal less than that which the insured may possibly incur. Most obvious and important, of course, is the limitation in amount, which is graduated according to the premium paid. In addition, various plaintiffs, such as members of the insured's own family, are quite commonly excluded. The automobile guest statutes, to which reference has been made above,[32] and which are largely the work of insurance companies in the legislatures, have tended to cut down on liability to guests;

and where there are no such statutes, a clause in the policy may do so. Another important type of limitation is the "omnibus clause," found in the usual automobile liability policy, which specifies the persons driving the car for whose negligence the owner shall be insured. These may be limited to the owner himself or his immediate family; but the National Standard Policy now extends the liability to any person driving the car with the insured's permission. This has led to a large number of cases dealing with detailed questions,[33] which are beyond the scope of this text. It has been said [34] that in the application of these clauses three tendencies are to be observed: a strict rule, which denies coverage if the driver departs from the intended purposes of the owner; a minor deviation rule, holding that the policy covers if the deviation is slight; and the so-called liberal rule, which holds that the policy covers the driver although he completely deviates from the owner's intention, once he has obtained possession with the permission of the owner.

As in the case of other contracts of insurance, that of liability insurance may be defeated by misrepresentation of material facts on the part of the insured at the time of his application for the policy. Thus a misstatement as to ownership of an automobile,[35]

[1949] Ins.L.J. 411; Leigh, Direct Actions Against Liability Insurer, [1949] Ins.L.J. 633; Rudser, Direct Actions Against Insurance Companies, 1969, 45 N.D.L.Rev. 483; Notes, 1933, 46 Harv.L.Rev. 1325; 1952, 27 N.Y.U.L.Rev. 817; 1970, 23 Vand.L.Rev. 631.

28. See Guerin v. Indemnity Ins. Co., 1928, 107 Conn. 649, 142 A. 268; Stacey v. Fidelity & Cas. Co., 1926, 114 Ohio St. 633, 151 N.E. 718; Riding v. Travelers Ins. Co., 1927, 48 R.I. 433, 138 A. 186.

29. Merchants' Mut. Auto. Liability Ins. Co. v. Smart, 1925, 267 U.S. 126; Coleman v. New Amsterdam Cas. Co., 1927, 247 N.Y. 271, 160 N.E. 367; Indemnity Ins. Co. of North America v. Davis' Adm'r, 1928, 150 Va. 778, 143 S.E. 328.

30. See Notes, [1953] Wis.L.Rev. 688; 1937, 11 Tulane L.Rev. 443.

31. Shingleton v. Bussey, Fla.1969, 223 So.2d 713.

32. See supra, p. 187.

33. See Sawyer, Automobile Liability Insurance: An Analysis of the National Standard Policy Provisions, 1936, 84 ff.; Gosnell, Omnibus Clauses in Automobile Insurance Policies, [1950] Ins.L.J. 237, 38 Ill.Bar J. 468; Austin, Permissive User Under the Omnibus Clause of the Automobile Liability Policy, [1962] Ins. Counsel J. 49; Note, 1953, 10 Wash. & Lee L.Rev. 241.

34. In Branch v. U. S. Fidelity & Guar. Co., 6 Cir. 1952, 198 F.2d 1007, 1009. A late example of the "liberal" attitude is Hays v. Country Mut. Ins. Co., 1962, 38 Ill.App.2d 1, 186 N.E.2d 153.

35. Didlake v. Standard Ins. Co., 10 Cir. 1952, 195 F. 2d 247; Employers Liability Assur. Corp. v. Maguire, 1948, 65 Pa.D. & C. 231; Maryland Cas. Co. v. Powers, W.D.Va.1953, 113 F.Supp. 126; Ambrose v. Indemnity Ins. Co., 124 N.J.L. 438, 12 A.2d 693.

its place or purpose of use,[36] or the past history of the applicant,[37] all may afford the company an effective defense. In addition, practically all policies provide that the insured must give the insurer immediate notice, or notice as soon as practicable, of any accident which may result in a claim. This is construed to mean notice within a reasonable time;[38] and if at the time the accident appears trivial, with no apparent injury to anyone, so that the insured has no reason to contemplate any suit or claim, the requirement will be satisfied if notice is given within a reasonable time after he learns that a claim will probably result.[39] It may be given

by anyone, including the injured person,[40] and to any authorized agent of the company.[41] Legislation requiring insurance, or giving the injured person direct rights against the insurer, has been held, except in Louisiana and Maryland,[42] not to do away with this requirement of notice.[43] There has, however, been a tendency in some of the cases to hold that the insurer is not relieved of liability where he is not prejudiced by the delay,[44] although there are still courts which adhere to the older rule to the contrary.[45]

Another standard provision of liability insurance policies requires the insured to "co-

---

36. Farm Bureau Mut. Auto. Ins. Co. v. Georgiana, 1951, 14 N.J.Super. 459, 82 A.2d 217; Phoenix Indemnity Co. v. Anderson, 1938, 170 Va. 406, 196 S.E. 629. Cf. Government Employees Ins. Co. v. Powell, 2 Cir. 1947, 160 F.2d 89 (extent of permission to drive). But cf. Sutton v. Hawkeye Cas. Co., 6 Cir. 1943, 138 F.2d 781.

37. Allstate Ins. Co. v. Moldenhauer, 7 Cir. 1952, 193 F.2d 663 (prior cancellation); Allstate Ins. Co. v. Orloff, E.D.Mich.1952, 106 F.Supp. 114 (driving record); Allstate Ins. Co. v. Miller, 1950, 96 Cal. App.2d 778, 216 P.2d 565 (driving record). Cf. State Farm Mut. Auto. Ins. Co. v. Mossey, 7 Cir. 1952, 195 F.2d 56, cert. denied Du Bois v. Mossey, 344 U. S. 869 (age).

As to misstatements later withdrawn or corrected, see cases collected in the annotation, 1954, 34 A.L.R.2d 264.

38. Kravat v. Indemnity Ins. Co., 6 Cir. 1945, 152 F. 2d 336; Minnesota Elec. Distr. Co. v. United States F. & G. Co., 1927, 173 Minn. 114, 216 N.W. 784; Unverzagt v. Prestern, 1940, 339 Pa. 141, 13 A.2d 46; American Lumbermen's Mut. Cas. Co. of Ill. v. Klein, D.N.Y.1945, 63 F.Supp. 701; Young v. Travelers Ins. Co., 5 Cir. 1941, 119 F.2d 877.

39. Phoenix Indemnity Co. v. Anderson's Groves, 5 Cir. 1949, 176 F.2d 246; Baker v. Metropolitan Cas. Ins. Co., 1934, 118 Conn. 147, 171 A. 7; Maryland Cas. Co. v. Sammons, 4 Cir. 1938, 99 F.2d 323; Jackson v. State Farm Mut. Auto. Ins. Co., 1946, 211 La. 19, 29 So.2d 177; Burbank v. National Cas. Co., 1941, 43 Cal.App.2d 773, 111 P.2d 740.

Likewise where the insured is not aware that he has been involved in an accident. Vande Leest v. Basten, 1942, 241 Wis. 509, 6 N.W.2d 667; Chinn v. Butchers' Mut. Cas. Co., 1947, 190 Misc. 117, 71 N. Y.S.2d 70.

40. Superior Lloyds of America v. Boesch Loan Co., Tex.Civ.App.1939, 130 S.W.2d 1036; Pallasch v. U. S. Fidelity & Guar. Co., 1946, 329 Ill.App. 257, 67 N.E.2d 883; Deaven v. Baumgardner, 1947, 62 Pa. D. & C. 183.

41. Hankins v. Public Service Mut. Ins. Co., 1949, 192 Md. 68, 63 A.2d 606; Fleming v. Travelers Ins. Co., 1949, 206 Miss. 284, 39 So.2d 885; Stewart v. Commerce Ins. Co. of Glen Falls, N. Y., 1948, 114 Utah 278, 198 P.2d 467; Pickard v. Rice, 1946, 329 Ill.App. 185, 67 N.E.2d 425.

42. Edwards v. Fidelity & Cas. Co. of N. Y., 1929, 11 La.App. 176, 123 So. 162; West v. Monroe Bakery, 1950, 217 La. 189, 46 So.2d 122; National Indemnity Co. v. Simmons, 1962, 230 Md. 234, 186 A.2d 595. See also National Indemnity Co. v. Simmons, 1962, 230 Md. 234, 186 A.2d 595 (failure of insured to cooperate).

43. Lorando v. Gethro, 1917, 228 Mass. 181, 117 N.E. 185; Hynding v. Home Acc. Ins. Co., 1932, 214 Cal. 743, 7 P.2d 999; Coleman v. New Amsterdam Cas. Co., 1928, 247 N.Y. 271, 160 N.E. 367; Stacey v. Fidelity & Cas. Co., 1926, 114 Ohio St. 633, 151 N.E. 718.

44. Gibson v. Colonial Ins. Co., 1949, 92 Cal.App.2d 33, 206 P.2d 387; Kennedy v. Dashner, 1947, 319 Mich. 491, 30 N.W.2d 46; Massachusetts Bonding & Ins. Co. v. Arizona Concrete Co., 1936, 47 Ariz. 420, 56 P.2d 188; Brookville Elec. Co. v. Utilities Ins. Co., Mo.App.1940, 142 S.W.2d 803; Frank v. Nash, 1950, 166 Pa.Super. 470, 71 A.2d 835. See Note, 1952, 51 Mich.L.Rev. 275.

45. Standard Accident Ins. Co. v. Turgeon, 1 Cir. 1944, 140 F.2d 94; State Farm Mut. Auto. Ins. Co. v. Cassinelli, 1950, 67 Nev. 227, 216 P.2d 606, 18 A. L.R.2d 431; Preferred Acc. Ins. Co. of N. Y. v. Castellano, 2 Cir. 1945, 148 F.2d 761; State Farm Mut. Auto. Ins. Co. v. Arghyris, 1949, 189 Va. 913, 55

operate with" and assist the insurer in the defense of any action covered by the policy. This means first of all that he must give the company full and accurate information as to the facts of the accident.[46]

It requires also that he attend the trial, and take part in it,[47] and that he do nothing to aid the injured person against the insurer, as for example by giving him a statement admitting liability.[48] On the other hand, mere expressions of sympathy, or of a desire that the injured person recover, normally are held not to amount to a violation of the cooperation clause;[49] and most courts have held that the insurer is not released in any case unless it has been in some way prejudiced by the failure to cooperate.[50]

83. "IMPACT" UPON THE LAW OF TORTS

Dedicated advocates of sweeping change, in which liability insurance is to play a predominant part, have sought to buttress their arguments by the contention that such insurance already has revolutionized the law of torts; that it has rendered obsolete the rules of negligence, which have become a mere set of formulae to which the courts still afford lip service, while in fact looking to the insurance; that the change is half made, and therefore should be completed.[51]

While liability insurance undoubtedly has had its effect, it is difficult to escape the impression that all this has been very much overstated. A dispassionate observer, if such a one is to be found in this area, might quite as readily conclude that the "impact" of insurance upon the law of torts has been amazingly slight; that most of the changes that have been pointed out are due to other causes; and that it is in truth astonishing that a system by which the defendants can and do obtain relief from all liability upon payment of a relatively small premium has received so little mention and visible recognition in the tort decisions.

The difference between the two points of view will turn upon the extent to which one is willing to assume, without proof, that the

S.E.2d 16; New Amsterdam Cas. Co. v. Hamblen, 1945, 144 Tex. 306, 190 S.W.2d 56.

46. Coleman v. New Amsterdam Cas. Co., 1927, 247 N.Y. 271, 160 N.E. 367; Ohio Cas. Co. of Hamilton, Ohio v. Swan, 8 Cir. 1937, 89 F.2d 219; Hilliard v. United Pacific Cas. Co., 1938, 195 Wash. 478, 81 P. 2d 513; Standard Acc. Ins. Co. of Detroit, Mich. v. Winget, 9 Cir. 1952, 197 F.2d 97.

47. Maryland Cas. Co. v. Hallatt, 5 Cir. 1961, 295 F. 2d 64, cert. denied; Indemnity Ins. Co. of North America v. Smith, 1951, 197 Md. 160, 78 A.2d 461; Roberts v. Commercial Standard Ins. Co., D.Ark. 1956, 138 F.Supp. 363; Curran v. Connecticut Indem. Co., 1941, 127 Conn. 692, 20 A.2d 87; Hynding v. Home Acc. Ins. Co., 1932, 214 Cal. 743, 7 P.2d 999.

48. Kindervater v. Motorists Cas. Ins. Co., 1938, 120 N.J.L. 373, 199 A. 606. Compare, as to other instances of "collusion," Bassi v. Bassi, 1925, 165 Minn. 100, 205 N.W. 947; Collins' Ex'rs v. Standard Acc. Ins. Co., 1916, 170 Ky. 27, 185 S.W. 112; Conroy v. Commercial Cas. Co., 1928, 292 Pa. 219, 140 A. 905; State Farm Mut. Auto. Ins. Co. v. Bonacci, 8 Cir. 1940, 111 F.2d 412.

49. Maryland Cas. Co. v. Lamarre, 1928, 83 N.H. 206, 140 A. 174; Johnson v. Johnson, 1939, 228 Minn. 282, 37 N.W.2d 1.

50. State Farm Mut. Auto. Ins. Co. v. Koval, 10 Cir. 1944, 146 F.2d 118; MacClure v. Accident & Cas. Ins. Co., 1948, 229 N.C. 305, 49 S.E.2d 742; MFA Mut. Ins. Co. v. Sailors, 1966, 180 Neb. 201, 141 N. W.2d 846; Marcum v. State Auto. Mut. Ins. Co., 1950, 134 W.Va. 144, 59 S.E.2d 433; Billington v. Interinsurance Exch. of So. Cal., 1969, 71 Cal.2d 757, 79 Cal.Rptr. 326, 456 P.2d 982.

51. The pioneer piece of writing of this kind was Feezer, Capacity to Bear Loss as a Factor in the Decision of Certain Types of Tort Cases, 1930, 78 U.Pa.L.Rev. 805. Next, and fuller was James, Accident Liability Reconsidered: The Impact of Liability Insurance, 1948, 57 Yale L.J. 549. This was followed by the booklet by Ehrenzweig, Negligence Without Fault, 1951, which is the outstanding work along these lines. See also James and Thornton, The Impact of Insurance on the Law of Torts, 1950, 15 Law & Con.Prob. 431; Friedmann, Social Insurance and the Principles of Tort Liability, 1950, 63 Harv.L.Rev. 241; Leflar, Negligence in Name Only, 1952, 27 N.Y.U.L.Rev. 564; McNiece and Thornton, Is the Law of Negligence Obsolete? 1952, 26 St. Johns L.Rev. 255; Atkins, The Impact of the Growth of Enterprise Liability on the Theory of Damages in Accident Cases, 1959, 20 La.L. Rev. 50.

continued shift toward the red end of the spectrum which has been going on for the past half century, and which has resulted in increased protection for the plaintiff in nearly all areas, is due to this one factor rather than a number of others. One illustration will suffice. In 1915 it was held in Nebraska,[52] as a matter of law, that the failure of a surgeon dealing with a bone fracture to take X-ray photographs was not negligence, or evidence from which the jury could find negligence. In 1947, in California,[53] the court took judicial notice of the fact that good surgical practice always requires that such photographs be taken, and held that the failure to do so was in itself enough to support a finding of negligence. In the meantime, insurance against liability for medical malpractice, which was available but not prevalent in 1915, had expanded into an enormous business. It would be easy to attribute the change in the law to this alone, and no doubt some of the writers would do so. But this is to ignore the greatly advanced standards of medicine and surgery, the superior medical education, the increased familiarity of all medical men with X-rays, the improvement in the equipment, its lower cost, and its availability in nearly all communities; and above all the demands which the public now makes, and reasonably makes, upon the profession. It would be quite as logical to say that the spread of the malpractice insurance itself is a consequence of the expanded liability, which is rather the result of a multitude of such other factors.[54]

"Invisible" Effects

Two of the effects upon the law claimed for liability insurance have been so-called "invisible" ones, which are not reflected by or in any way apparent from the opinions of appellate courts. One of these is the settlement of cases. The insurance companies, engaged in the business for profit, and manned by unsentimental individuals interested only in financial results, customarily settle a substantial portion of their claims without regard to the existence of any liability. In other words, many claims are paid in which it is clear that the defendant was not at fault, or that the plaintiff was; and the result is compensation not based on fault at all, but on the existence of insurance. This is good business, since it retains the good will of both the plaintiff and the defendant, who may buy more insurance, and it helps the reputation of the company as a liberal payer of claims. It is also the cheapest way out in any case in which the "nuisance value" of the suit, which means the probable cost of investigation, preparation and trial, together with the off chance that the plaintiff might after all be able to prove his case, exceeds the amount paid. For obvious reasons, the claims so settled are almost invariably the smaller ones.

All this is certainly true; but its relevance is not so apparent. Contract claims are customarily settled on the same basis; the return of goods to a store by an unsatisfied cus-

---

52. In Van Boskirk v. Pinto, 1915, 99 Neb. 164, 155 N.W. 889.

53. In Agnew v. City of Los Angeles, 1947, 82 Cal. App.2d 616, 186 P.2d 450.

54. "It is often argued that 'liberal' legal policies in respect of tort liability, i. e., those which seem to broaden the base of what is compensable and raise the price of the penalty of carelessness, are moving in this direction [of compensation of every casualty without regard to predictability or fault]. The fact is that a century or more ago, the failure to guard against dangers that ought to be foreseen was treated in the same spirit as now; what has

changed in the accelerated pace and the enhanced mechanism utilized by society is merely the range and scope of the danger to be guarded against. The law of tort is more 'liberal' precisely because experience shows more predictable casualties. Compare the failure to tie up the horse which ran away and injured the plaintiff, considered by the Court of Common Pleas in 1854 (McCahill v. Kipp, 2 E.D. Smith 413) with the failure of a responsible third party to warn a workman engaged to thaw out a line by electricity of the presence of methane gas, an explosive which injured him, considered in 1949 in Appier v. Million, 299 N.Y. 715, 87 N.E.2d 125." Bergan, J., in McPartland v. State, 1950, 277 App. Div. 103, 98 N.Y.S.2d 665, 668, reargument and appeal denied In re Sage's Estate, 1951, 277 App.Div. 1063, 100 N.Y.S.2d 958.

tomer is a familiar example. Yet no one considers that this has had any particular effect upon the law of contracts. Such settlements are simply extra-legal. Habitual defendants, such as railroad companies, always have settled claims on this basis, and so does the ordinary individual if he has any sense. What insurance has done is to put the settlement of a great many such claims into the hands of professional adjusters who know what they are doing, and so are more disposed to settle. Where the amount of the claim exceeds the nuisance value, settlement may still be made; but it is always made on the basis of the prospects of establishing liability under the existing law, which remains unaffected.

The other "invisible" effect is upon the verdict of the jury. It is more or less notorious among lawyers [55] that juries, in general, tend to return verdicts, or larger verdicts, against defendants who have liability insurance, for the simple reason that they are aware that the defendant will not have to pay the judgment, and that the company has been paid a premium for undertaking the liability. In most jurisdictions the jury are not supposed to be told in so many words that there is insurance in the case,[56] unless the evidence is somehow relevant as bearing upon some other issue.[57] Plaintiff's attorneys have, however, become very adroit in managing to convey the information. The most common device is to ask the jurymen, upon voir dire, about their possible interest in or employment by a liability insurance company.[58] By way of emphasis of the idea, a question asked of a witness may produce an "unexpected" and unresponsive mention of insurance,[59] which, whether it is uttered in good faith or not, is virtually impossible to prevent or control. Even where no such information can be conveyed, jurymen are quite likely to assume that any defendant who owns an automobile and is worth suing is probably insured, and treat him accordingly—which in no way operates to the benefit of a defendant who in fact has no insurance. With financial responsibility laws in many states making insurance practically compulsory for every driver, the whole question of disclosure of insurance is no longer the burning issue that it formerly was; and courts in increasing numbers are asserting that the jurors assume anyway that the defendant is insured.[60]

The result of all this is said, and no doubt quite correctly, to be a substantial increase in the proportion of recoveries in some types

---

55. The tendency may not be so great as is commonly supposed, now that most jurymen drive cars and have liability insurance of their own. See Kalven, The Jury, the Law, and the Personal Injury Damage Award, 1958, 19 Ohio St.L.J. 158, 170–171, reporting on the University of Chicago jury study.

56. See McCormick, Evidence, 1954, 355–358; James Stewart Co. v. Newby, 4 Cir. 1920, 266 F. 287; Fielding v. Publix Cars, Inc., 1936, 130 Neb. 576, 265 N.W. 726, 105 A.L.R. 1306; Watson v. Adams, 1914, 187 Ala. 490, 65 So. 528; Roche v. Llewellyn Ironworks Co., 1903, 140 Cal. 563, 74 P. 147. See Note, 1966, 51 Iowa L.Rev. 726.

57. See Rapoport, Proper Disclosure During Trial that Defendant is Insured, 1940, 26 Corn.L.Q. 137; Aquilera v. Reynolds Well Service, Inc., Tex.Civ. App.1950, 234 S.W.2d 282.

58. See Kiernan v. Van Schaik, 3 Cir. 1965, 347 F.2d 775; Mathena v. Burchett, 1962, 189 Kan. 350, 369 P.2d 487; White v. Teague, 1944, 353 Mo. 247, 182 S.W.2d 288; Santee v. Haggart Const. Co., 1938, 202 Minn. 361, 278 N.W. 520; Wheeler v. Rudek, 1947, 397 Ill. 438, 74 N.E.2d 601. See Notes, 1948, 43 Ill.L.Rev. 650; 1966, 51 Iowa L.Rev. 726.

In Texas this is not permitted. See Green, Blindfolding the Jury, 1954, 33 Tex.L.Rev. 137; Gay, "Blindfolding" the Jury: Another View, 1956, 34 Tex.L. Rev. 368; Green, A Rebuttal 1956, 34 Tex.L.Rev. 382.

59. See for example Pillsbury Flour Mills v. Miller, 8 Cir. 1941, 121 F.2d 297; Williams v. Consumers' Co., 1933, 352 Ill. 51, 185 N.E. 217; Cain v. Kohlman, 1941, 344 Pa. 63, 22 A.2d 667; Sheldon v. River Lines, 1949, 91 Cal.App.2d 478, 205 P.2d 37.

60. "He [the juror] doesn't require a brick house to fall on him to give him an idea." Bliss, C. J., in Connelly v. Nolte, 1946, 237 Iowa 114, 21 N.W.2d 311, 320. Accord: Brown v. Walter, 2 Cir. 1933, 62 F.2d 798; Takoma Park Bank v. Abbott, 1941, 179 Md. 249, 19 A.2d 169, cert. denied, 314 U.S. 672; Odegard v. Connolly, 1941, 211 Minn. 342, 1 N.W.2d 137. Cf. Waid v. Bergschneider, 1963, 94 Ariz. 21, 381 P.2d 568 (mention not prejudicial).

of cases, as well as larger recoveries, by plaintiffs as a class. This in turn, of course, has had its effect upon liability insurance rates, which undoubtedly have increased at a pace not entirely to be accounted for by the increase in the accident rate itself.

Assuming that all this is true, it adds nothing that is new to the law. For many years railroad companies, public utilities, municipalities, industrial enterprises, and large corporations in general, who among them have made up the majority of all negligence defendants, have been subjected to this treatment at the hands of juries, and against them the recoveries always have run, and still run, quite as high as against insurance companies. All that the insurance has done is to provide, in lieu of many private individuals such as automobile drivers, a large new source of payment in the form of an additional group against whom the jury may give rein to their natural human desire to see compensation made to an injured human being, at the expense of another who, they feel, should be able to pay it without comparable hardship. From the social point of view this development of course has considerable significance; but it has taken place entirely within the framework of the existing law.

"Visible" Effects

When we come to the "visible" effects, reflected in the opinions of the courts, we find that some of them are not so visible. There is a tendency, already noted, to attribute virtually every change in the law which has favored the plaintiff to liability insurance. The increased responsibility of occupiers of land, of landlords, of professional men, of manufacturers and vendors of products, of all industry, of virtually every class of defendants, which is to be observed throughout the law of torts, is ascribed to the fact that the court is aware that the defendants have insurance, or that they and others like them can get it.

Concerning this all that can be said is that it could be true; that there is reason to doubt it; that assertion is easy, denial quite as easy, and proof impossible where the opinions themselves say nothing about it. If one is willing to ignore the improved standards of an advancing civilization, the higher scale of living, the new dangers which have accompanied it, the great improvement in facilities for safety, the change in public opinion, with an increased social consciousness as to the sick and injured even when no one else has caused the harm, and concentrate on the one thing that the courts have not mentioned, the conclusion can be drawn. Whether it is to be drawn the reader must decide for himself. Again it would be at least possible for one so disposed to say that the insurance is the effect, and not the cause.

Jury Issues

Over the last half century there has been a great decrease in the proportion of directed verdicts. Issues are now commonly left to the jury which fifty years ago would have been decided for the defendant by the court. Since juries are well known to favor the injured plaintiff when they are permitted to do so, this works to his advantage. This too has been ascribed to the presence, or availability, of insurance, either as the sole explanation or as the controlling and decisive factor.

Again there is nothing in the opinions to indicate it. Since the judge usually is aware of insurance when it is in the case, if only because he knows who the lawyers' clients are, and since he also cannot fail to be aware that the mere fact that the defendant has been sued is an indication that he has some means of payment, those who are inclined to think that courts always act for unexpressed reasons which they are unwilling to admit can readily assert that this is the only explanation. It is an assertion impossible to prove or to disprove. There are, however, other factors to be accounted for.

The tendency of the courts to abdicate control and decision in favor of the jury has not been confined to cases in which there is insurance, or any likelihood of it. It has not been confined to tort cases, but has been general across the law. It appears to have begun in the days of Theodore Roosevelt, when the "judicial oligarchy" was under violent attack, and the courts were subjected to severe criticism for what was called their arrogant assumption of power and authority. The tendency certainly has not been discouraged by the election of judges, who become reluctant to make unpopular decisions, and by the active resentment of the bar against interference from the court. The same judicial retreat has been apparent in the issuance of injunctions, in punishments for contempt, and in the refusal of the judge, in most American jurisdictions, to comment on the evidence even when he is permitted to do so.

The most likely explanation may be simply the same general shift in popular opinion, and in judicial response to it in favor of the plaintiff, which has been going on in all tort law, and which leads the judge quite reasonably to refuse to deprive the injured man of his chance in any case in which a doubtful question can fairly be conjured up. The tendency has been most marked as to the defenses of contributory negligence and assumption of risk, as to both of which directed verdicts have largely disappeared from the scene. Both defenses have been under attack for many years; [61] and the same reasons which have induced the courts to say that they are disfavored, and to develop such halfway measures as the last clear chance, and which have led to the adoption of comparative negligence acts, are in themselves quite adequate explanation. It can scarcely be supposed that insurance has not been something of a factor, if only as a makeweight; but there is no satisfactory indication that it is the whole story.

Shift of Emphasis in Negligence

Some writers have made a great deal of a supposed change in the character of negligence itself. Beginning, along with the criminal law, with a purpose only of "admonition" of the defendant and deterrence of others like him, and hence with an insistence upon moral blame as essential to liability, it is said to have altered in the direction of a primary concern with compensation of the victim, and so to have become negligence "without fault," or "in name only." Thus the man who is only stupid, ignorant, excitable or congenitally clumsy, or otherwise lacking in the capacity to behave as a normal individual, is held liable for negligence [62] even though he is in no way to blame for it. The psychologists have come up with the classification of the "accident prone," [63] who are predisposed to catastrophe and unable to protect themselves or others against it; and whether this is, as might be suspected, merely a matter of innate stupidity, slow reaction time, poor training and bad habits, or, as some of the psychologists would have it, of a "guilt complex" and a "death wish" subconsciously seeking punishment for past misdeeds,[64] it is undoubtedly true that there are such individuals who have a history of repetition, and that, whether they can help it or not, they are held liable. Professor Ehrenzweig [65] has even provided us with a "psychoanalysis of negligence," to explain

61. See supra, ch. 11.

62. See supra, p. 152.

63. See James and Dickinson, Accident Proneness and Accident Law, 1950, 63 Harv.L.Rev. 869; Maloney and Risk, The Accident-Prone Driver: The Automotive Age's Biggest Unsolved Problem, 1962, 14 U.Fla.L.Rev. 364.

64. See McLean, Accident Proneness—A Clinical Approach to Injury-Liability, 1955, 24 Indus.Med. & Surg. 121; Jenkins, The Accident-Prone Personality, Personnel, July, 1956, 29; Tillman & Hobbs, Accident-Prone Automobile Drivers: Study of Psychiatric and Social Background, 1949, 106 Am.J. Psychiatry 321.

65. Ehrenzweig, A Psychoanalysis of Negligence, 1953, 47 Northwestern U.L.Rev. 855.

our social attitude toward those who cannot help committing torts.

It may be suggested that much of this, at least, is setting up a straw man to knock him down. The dual purpose of tort law goes back to very ancient times, and moral blame never has been a requisite of legal liability. As long ago as 1616, it was said [66] that a lunatic is liable for his torts, although not for his crimes. At least since tort law finally split away from crime, it has been primarily concerned with compensation. The very first case in which the objective standard of the reasonable man first emerged was Vaughan v. Menlove [67] in 1837, one of a stupid mistake of an ignorant man who honestly used his own bad judgment. These are developments of earlier centuries, and not of the present day. Nor is liability without moral blame the same thing as liability without fault. There is still legal fault, which is a departure from a standard of conduct required by the community. The defendant may not be to blame for being out of line with it, but he is none the less out of line, and it is on that basis that he is held liable.

Mention has been made above [68] of how the principle of res ipsa loquitur has been used to permit recovery in cases where there is no direct proof of negligence or of its absence, and it may very possibly not have existed in fact. This also has been hailed as a part of the advancing front of strict liability,[69] and, inevitably, attributed to the existence of insurance, although the decisions never mention it.

This, at least, has almost certainly been overstated. In the ordinary case, res ipsa loquitur amounts to nothing more than recognition of a reasonable inference that there has been negligence, which the jury are entitled to draw on the basis of probabilities. The door is open to the defendant to refute it by proof; and so long as this is true, there is no liability without fault. One might as well say that conviction of an innocent man of crime upon circumstantial evidence amounts to a law of guilt without crime. In the relatively few situations [70] in which procedural disadvantages have been imposed upon defendants against whom no such inference was to be drawn, there has invariably been a special relation between the plaintiff and the defendants, or between two or more defendants, which justifies the special responsibility imposed.

Vicarious Liability

Mention has been made [71] of the manner in which the principle of respondeat superior, originating in cases of master and servant, has been extended to impose vicarious liability in other situations. One who is himself free from all moral blame or legal fault is held liable for the tort of another, so that so far as he is concerned there is a form of liability without fault. Some of these developments have been statutory; but others, as in the case of the family car doctrine and the employers of independent contractors,[72] have been a matter of common law.

The changes are undoubtedly there, although to attribute them to insurance may require some stretch of the imagination, where no court has said anything about it. They represent an obvious effort to find a financially responsible defendant who can be charged with the liability of another who, in general, cannot be relied on to pay a judgment. Two limitations are, however, to be pointed out. The basis of liability is still the negligence or other fault of the one actually at fault; and without such fault no one is lia-

---

66. In Weaver v. Ward, 1616, Hob. 134, 80 Eng.Rep. 284.

67. 1837, 3 Bing.N.C. 467, 132 Eng.Rep. 490.

68. Supra, p. 230.

69. This goes back to Thayer, Liability Without Fault, 1916, 29 Harv.L.Rev. 801.

70. See supra, p. 231.

71. Supra, § 73.

72. See supra, §§ 71, 73.

ble at all. And the defendant who is to be charged always stands in such a relation to the one at fault that he may properly be held responsible for his conduct; and in the absence of such a relation there is again no liability. What has been done, in other words, is not to institute a system of liability without fault, but to broaden the fault liability to include those who may properly be held responsible.

Nevertheless, this is so far a matter of judge-made policy, deliberately adopted to the end of insuring compensation of the injured, that it may serve as an analogy for holding other "enterprises" liable for the more or less inevitable harm which they inflict upon others.[73]

Specific Mention of Insurance

As has been indicated, there is really, in the opinions in tort cases, astonishingly little mention of insurance as a reason for holding the defendant liable. This is all the more remarkable when one considers the number of cases in which the court has been scrabbling hard for any reason or argument to support a change in the law. The failure even to mention insurance under such conditions suggests rather a determination *not* to take it into account than an important and influential, but unstated, reason. On the other hand, it has been said often enough that liability insurance does not create liability, but only provides a means of indemnity against it once it has arisen; and that it is not to be considered in determining whether anyone is liable in the first instance.

There are, however, a few cases, out of many thousand, in which insurance has received specific mention as a factor. As long ago as Ryan v. New York Central Railroad Co.,[74] in 1866, the prevalence of fire insurance among urban property owners was mentioned as one reason for applying a narrower

rule of "proximate cause" in fire cases; and this finds a parallel in some of the decisions denying recovery for private fire losses against a water company which has contracted to supply water to a city.[75]

There is a striking recent Wisconsin decision [76] in which the prevalence of liability insurance is given as one reason for a change in the rule that a host is not liable to his automobile guest for defects in the car of which he does not know. There is also a passage from a concurring opinion of Mr. Justice Traynor of California [77] which has been much

75. See Reimann v. Monmouth Consolidated Water Co., 1952, 9 N.J. 134, 87 A.2d 325; Wm. Burford & Co. v Glasgow Water Co., 1928, 223 Ky. 54, 2 S.W. 2d 1027; Ancrum v. Camden Water Co., 1908, 82 S. C. 284, 64 S.E. 151.

76. "Liability insurance is widely prevalent today. In few cases will the new rule shift the burden of loss from the injured guest to the negligent host personally. In the great majority of cases it will shift part or all the burden of loss from the injured individual to the motoring public. The policy concept that it is unfair to shift the burden from the injured person to his host where the injured person knowingly and voluntarily exposed himself to dangers created by the host is no longer applicable." McConville v. State Farm Mut. Auto. Ins. Co., 1962, 15 Wis.2d 374, 113 N.W.2d 14, 19.

Cf. Siragusa v. Swedish Hospital, 1962, 60 Wash.2d 310, 373 P.2d 767, mentioning the prevalence of "social insurance" covering employees as a reason for abrogating the defense of assumption of risk in cases of injury to them.

77. "Traynor, J. I concur in the judgment, but I believe the manufacturer's negligence should no longer be singled out as the basis of a plaintiff's right to recover in cases like the present one. In my opinion it should now be recognized that a manufacturer incurs an absolute liability when an article that he has placed on the market, knowing that it is to be used without inspection, proves to have a defect that causes injury to human beings.   *   *

"Even if there is no negligence, however public policy demands that responsibility be fixed wherever it will most effectively reduce the hazards to life and health inherent in defective products that reach the market. It is evident that the manufacturer can anticipate some hazards and guard against the recurrence of others, as the public cannot. Those who suffer injury from defective products are unprepared to meet its consequences. The cost of an injury and the loss of time or health may be an overwhelming misfortune to the person injured, and a

73. As to the proposals made, see infra § 85.

74. 1866, 35 N.Y. 210.

quoted, in which the possibility that the manufacturer of a product can insure against liability, and so distribute the risk, is mentioned as one reason, among others, for holding him to strict liability to the injured consumer. The liability for defective products is a field which has been undergoing rapid and spectacular change,[78] with many courts writing long opinions mustering all available reasons for holding manufacturers and sellers liable without negligence; and dissenting opinions, as well as challenges from other sources, have put them upon their mettle and under considerable pressure to ignore no possible justification. In view of this, it appears quite astonishing that, out of a few thousand opinions dealing with products liability, this was for a long time the *only* one in which there was any mention whatever of insurance. On any conceivable basis, it is not easy to account for the fact; but it is at least some indication that the changes in this area of the law have not been due primarily to this one factor.

The chief visible effect of insurance, however, has been in connection with the abrogation of various immunities from liability. All of these have been under attack for many years,[79] as outmoded vestiges of antique law arising out of historical origins that long since have passed away and been forgotten, and as without logical or moral justification. The presence, or availability, of liability insurance has provided an additional argument, since it means that, although the defendant will have to pay an insurance premium, he will not have to pay the judgment against him. In a few instances this has been enough to tip the scale. Thus there were four decisions [80] eliminating the "family" immunity of a parent toward his child, where the child is injured in the course of a business activity of the parent, which is covered by liability insurance. There were, however, two others in which the business activity alone, without the insurance, was held to be sufficient; [81] and a great many more in which the "family" immunity between husband and wife was abrogated,[82] or numerous other exceptions developed to that between parent and child,[83] in which insurance was not a visible factor at all. Where the question arose, the overwhelming majority of the decisions for a long time declared that liability insurance does not create liability, but only provides indemnity against it when it has arisen; that it is not in itself a sufficient reason for any change in the rule, and any such change must be for the legislature; and that the presence of insurance in the particular case makes no difference.[84] There were even several decisions

---

needless one, *for the risk of injury can be insured by the manufacturer and distributed among the public as a cost of doing business.* [Italics supplied]. It is to the public interest to discourage the marketing of products having defects that are a menace to the public. If such products nevertheless find their way into the market it is to the public interest to place the responsibility for whatever injury they may cause upon the manufacturer, who even if he is not negligent in the manufacture of the product, is responsible for its reaching the market. However, intermittently such injuries may occur and however haphazardly they may strike, the risk of their occurrence is a constant risk and a general one. Against such a risk there should be general and constant protection, and the manufacturer is best situated to afford such protection." Escola v. Coca Cola Bottling Co., 1944, 24 Cal.2d 453, 461–462, 150 P.2d 436, 440–441.

78. See infra, ch. 17.

79. See infra, §§ 122, 131–133.

80. Dunlap v. Dunlap, 1930, 84 N.H. 352, 150 A. 905; Lusk v. Lusk, 1932, 113 W.Va. 17, 166 S.E. 538; Worrell v. Worrell, 1939, 174 Va. 11, 4 S.E.2d 343 (under compulsory insurance statute); Edwards v. Royal Indemnity Co., 1935, 182 La. 171, 161 So. 191 (under statute providing for direct action of injured person against insurer).

81. Signs v. Signs, 1952, 156 Ohio St. 566, 103 N.E.2d 743; Borst v. Borst, 1952, 41 Wash.2d 642, 251 P.2d 149.

82. See infra, p. 864.

83. See infra, p. 866.

84. Levesque v. Levesque, 1954, 99 N.H. 147, 106 A.2d 563; Harralson v. Thomas, Ky.1954, 269 S.W.2d 276; Parker v. Parker, 1956, 230 S.C. 28, 94 S.E.2d 12; Prince v. Prince, 1959, 205 Tenn. 451, 326 S.W.

which gave the insurance as a reason for *not* abrogating the immunity, because of the opportunity for fraud and collusion against the insurance company.[85]

Finally, however, when the modern wave of decisions [86] began to engulf the family immunities, the existence or the possibility of liability insurance began to be stated in nearly all of the overruling cases, as one of the primary reasons for the change.[87]

The immunity of charities has had much the same history. Since 1942 it has been in full retreat, and it appears only a question of time before it is to disappear from American law.[88] The visible part which insurance has played in the change has been quite meagre. In some half dozen states, by statute or decision, the immunity is not recognized when the charity in fact has the insurance, on the ground that liability will not deplete trust funds or discourage donors.[89]

There have been two or three opinions [90] in which insurance has received mention as one

reason, among others, for the termination of the immunity; but most of the courts which have abrogated it entirely have made no mention of any such reason. And on the other hand, there are a very large number of cases in which it has been declared specifically that the presence or availability of insurance is not a factor to be considered at all in deciding whether any change shall be made in the law.[91] Governmental immunity, which is also under heavy fire,[92] has undergone little specific change that can be traced to insurance.[93] There are a few decisions [94] holding that statutory authorization to take out the insurance constitutes a "waiver" of the immunity, which makes the government liable; but the large majority of the cases have held that such authorization is not a waiver, and the immunity is not affected by the insurance.[95]

Avellone v. St. Johns Hospital, 1956, 165 Ohio St. 467, 135 N.E.2d 410.

2d 908; Fehr v. General Accident, F. & L. Assur. Corp., 1944, 246 Wis. 228, 16 N.W.2d 787.

85. Hastings v. Hastings, 1960, 33 N.J. 247, 163 A.2d 147; Villaret v. Villaret, 1948, 83 App.D.C. 311, 169 F.2d 677; Luster v. Luster, 1938, 299 Mass. 480, 13 N.E.2d 438; Parks v. Parks, 1957, 390 Pa. 287, 135 A.2d 65; Turner v. Carter, 1935, 169 Tenn. 553, 89 S.W.2d 751.

86. See infra, § 122.

87. See for example Gelbman v. Gelbman, 1969, 23 N.Y.2d 434, 297 N.Y.S.2d 529, 245 N.E.2d 192; Balts v. Balts, 1966, 273 Minn. 419, 142 N.W.2d 66; Tamashiro v. DeGama, 1969, 51 Haw. 74, 450 P.2d 998; Immer v. Risko, 1970, 56 N.J. 482, 267 A.2d 481; France v. A.P.A. Transport Corp., 1970, 56 N.J. 500, 267 A.2d 490.

88. See infra, § 133.

89. Michael v. St. Paul Mercury Indemnity Co., W.D. Ark.1950, 92 F.Supp. 140 (Arkansas statute); Michard v. Myron Stratton Home, 1960, 144 Colo. 251, 355 P.2d 1078 (no immunity, but judgment can be satisfied only out of funds not held in trust); Cox v. De Jarnette, 1961, 104 Ga.App. 664, 123 S.E.2d 16; Howard v. South Baltimore Hospital, 1948, 191 Md. 617, 62 A.2d 574 (statute); O'Quin v. Baptist Memorial Hospital, 1947, 184 Tenn. 570, 201 S.W.2d 694.

90. President and Directors of Georgetown University v. Hughes, D.C.Cir.1942, 130 F.2d 810, 823–824;

91. Cristini v. Griffin Hospital, 1948, 134 Conn. 282, 57 A.2d 262; Haynes v. Presbyterian Hospital, 1950, 241 Iowa 1269, 45 N.W.2d 151; Kreuger v. Schmiechen, 1954, 364 Mo. 568, 264 S.W.2d 311; Muller v. Nebraska Methodist Hospital, 1955, 160 Neb. 279, 70 N.W.2d 86; Pierce v. Yakima Valley Memorial Hospital Ass'n, 1953, 43 Wash.2d 162, 260 P.2d 765.

92. See infra, § 131.

93. Molitor v. Kaneland Community Unit Dist. Co. 302, 1959, 18 Ill.2d 11, 163 N.E.2d 89, cert. denied 362 U.S. 968, declared that insurance was immaterial. The other decisions (see infra, p. ——) abrogating governmental immunity have not mentioned it at all.

94. Bailey v. City of Knoxville, 6 Cir. 1954, 222 F.2d 520; Lynwood v. Decatur Park District, 1960, 26 Ill.App.2d 431, 168 N.E.2d 185; Rogers v. Butler, 1936, 170 Tenn. 125, 92 S.W.2d 414; Taylor v. Knox County Board of Education, 1942, 292 Ky. 767, 167 S.W.2d 700. Cf. Christie v. Board of Regents of University of Michigan, 1961, 364 Mich. 202, 111 N.W.2d 30.

95. Maffei v. Incorporated Town of Kemmerer, 1959, 80 Wyo. 33, 338 P.2d 808, rehearing denied 1959, 80 Wyo. 33, 340 P.2d 759; Hummer v. School City of Hartford City, 1953, 124 Ind.App. 30, 112 N.E.2d 891; Rittmiller v. School District No. 84, D.Minn. 1952, 104 F.Supp. 187; Jones v. Scofield Bros., D.

The list is far from being an impressive testimonial to the supreme importance of liability insurance in the law of torts up to the present day. The conclusion which seems to emerge is that it has served as a makeweight, as an additional reason, valid enough, for the overthrow in a few situations of obsolete rules long under attack because of their own inherent weakness and lack of logic or policy; but that it never has been sufficient in itself, and the courts have been strangely silent about it where important changes have been going on in the law.

84. PRESENT DEFICIENCIES

The deficiencies of our present system for compensating personal injuries are manifold, and have been pointed out many times. Because the problem is most acute in relation to automobile accidents, nearly all of the discussion has centered about them. The original study, and still the only comprehensive one ever made, is a rather remarkable Report of a Committee to Study Compensation for Automobile Accidents, for the Columbia University Council for Research in the Social Sciences,[96] which was published in 1932, and is in most law libraries. This called forth a real deluge of discussion, which has continued and even increased until the present day.[97]

No one needs to be told of the number of automobile accidents, and the gravity of the problem they present. In December, 1951, the millionth man was killed by an automobile in the United States. In 1968 there were 55,700 deaths, an annual number which had considerably more than tripled since 1921. In that same year there were 14 million automobile accidents in the United States, and over 2 million personal injuries. Somewhere in this country there was an automobile death every thirteen minutes, and an automobile injury every twenty-three seconds. The losses totaled at least eleven billion dollars, which is a good round sum.[98] The intervening years undoubtedly have carried these figures to new high levels.

Thus far liability insurance has been quite inadequate to provide and assure compensation to those who suffer such injuries. It had its inception solely as a device for the protection and benefit of the insured who paid for it, and not as any part of a scheme for social betterment; and it has largely retained that original character. The present evils may be reviewed briefly, as follows:

Uncompensated Plaintiffs

Unless the defendant is required by statute to carry insurance, he is under no incentive to do so, except for whatever fear of his own liability may trouble him. Even in fields where liability insurance is most prevalent, there are still a large number of defendants who do not have it. The last available estimate was that in 1960, out of some 73,000,000 automobiles registered in the Unit-

---

Md.1947, 73 F.Supp. 395. See Gibbons, Liability Insurance and the Tort Immunity of State and Local Governments, [1959] Duke L.J. 588; Notes, 1956, 54 Mich.L.Rev. 404; 1949, 33 Minn.L.Rev. 634.

96. Discussed, and to some extent summarized, in Smith, Lilly and Dowling, Compensation for Automobile Accidents: A Symposium, 1932, 32 Col.L.Rev. 785.

97. Kline and Pearson, The Problem of the Uninsured Motorist, 1951; Marx, Compulsory Compensation Insurance, 1925, 25 Col.L.Rev. 164; Corstvet, The Uncompensated Accident and Its Consequences, 1936, 3 Law & Con.Prob. 467; Lewis, The Merits of the Automobile Accident Compensation Plan, 1936,

3 Law & Con.Prob. 583; Marx, Compensation Insurance for Automobile Accident Victims: The Case for Compulsory Automobile Insurance, 1954, 15 Ohio St.L.J. 134; Netherton, Highway Safety Under Differing Types of Liability Legislation, 1954, 15 Ohio St.L.J. 110; James, The Columbia Study of Compensation Law for Automobile Accidents: An Unanswered Challenge, 1959, 59 Col.L.Rev. 408. A good summary in a nutshell appears in Ehrenzweig, "Full Aid" Insurance for the Traffic Victim, 1954, 1–8.

98. National Safety Council, Accident Facts, 1969, 5.40; Statistical Abstract of the United States, 1969, 547–52.

ed States, something like 11,000,000 carried no insurance at all.[99]

Even these figures cannot be fully appreciated unless account is taken of the fact that the uninsured are, as a group, those who are least responsible financially, and so unlikely to be able to pay a judgment. The Columbia Report estimated, in 1932, that *some* payment was made in over 85 per cent of all cases in which the defendant was insured, but that against an uninsured driver the injured plaintiff had only about once chance in four of collecting anything at all.[1] It is also undoubtedly true that uninsured drivers on the highway are those who tend on the whole to be driving unsafe vehicles, to be the most slipshod, law-violating and reckless, and to cause a disproportionately large percentage of the accidents. It is, in short, those who are unable to pay for the harm they do, who do most of the harm.[2]

Inadequate Coverage

Even where there is insurance, it is very often inadequate in amount. Coverage varies according to the premium paid, and poverty, economy and optimism tend to keep it down. A substantial percentage of the automobile liability policies are still written for five-and-ten, which is to say with a limit of $10,000 upon liability to any one person, and of $20,000 for the total liability arising out of any one accident. The bulk of them are written for not more than ten-and-twenty, which doubles these figures. With present-day verdicts for really serious personal injuries running well in excess of $50,000, and in a few cases over $300,000 or even $400,000, it is obvious that such insurance does not meet the risk. The injured plaintiff may still collect what he can,

in excess of the policy, on his judgment against the tortfeasor. To the extent that he can do so, the policy fails to protect the insured. To the extent that he cannot, it fails to meet the problem of compensating him for the tort.

Assuming that the amount is adequate, the coverage may still fail because the plaintiff is excepted from the terms of the policy, because an automobile guest act prevents his recovery, or because an excluded person is driving the car.[3] Misrepresentation or concealment on the part of the insured, his failure to give notice of the accident, or his failure to "cooperate" with the insurance company, may still defeat the recovery;[4] and in any jurisdiction where there is no direct remedy against the insurer, the insolvency of the insured, or anything which will prevent suit against him, will do the same.[5]

Liability Only for Fault

By its terms liability insurance does not purport to provide compensation for injuries, but only to protect the insured against legal ability. In the present state of our law, except in the case of abnormally dangerous animals, conditions or activities, and a few other instances, such liability is incurred only when the defendant has been at fault, which in the usual case means that he has been negligent. There are many types of enterprises and activities, of which the automobile is the common example, which are not classified as abnormally dangerous, and yet produce their inevitable quota of accidents and injuries, a substantial part of which occur without any negligence or other fault on the part of anyone.

Even where there is fault in fact, it must be proved before liability is established; and there are many cases in which the injured person, struck and knocked unconscious by

---

99. Best's Insurance Report, Fire and Casualty Volume, 1961, p. x.

1. Committee to Study Compensation for Automobile Accidents, Report to the Columbia University Council for Research in the Social Sciences, 1932, 75, 77, 86, 87, 203–04, 261–66, 269–73.

2. Kline and Pearson, The Problem of the Uninsured Motorist, 1951.

3. See supra, p. 545.

4. See supra, p. 546.

5. See supra, p. 544.

something that he never saw, is quite unable to offer such proof. To some extent he is aided by the doctrine of res ipsa loquitur;[6] but there are still many cases, such as those of collisions of moving vehicles, to which it does not apply. And even when the plaintiff succeeds in offering proof of the defendant's negligence, it can still be denied and refuted; and even when it is beyond dispute, the defenses of contributory negligence and assumption of risk can still be interposed to defeat the recovery.

The result is a substantial number of cases, known to exist by all trial lawyers, but impossible to number with any accuracy, in which legal fault either does not exist, or if it exists cannot be proved, or if proved can still be defeated. In all such cases the insurance, even if carried with full coverage, affords no protection to the victim.

Litigation

The process by which the question of legal fault, and hence of liability, is determined in our courts is a cumbersome, time-consuming, expensive, and almost ridiculously inaccurate one. The evidence given in personal injury cases usually consists of highly contradictory statements from the two sides, estimating such factors as time, speed, distance and visibility, offered months after the event by witnesses who were never very sure just what happened when they saw it, and whose faulty memories are undermined by lapse of time, by bias, by conversations with others, and by the subtle influence of counsel. Upon such evidence, a jury of twelve inexperienced citizens, called away from their other business if they have any, are invited to retire and make the best guess they can as to whether the defendant, the plaintiff, or both were "negligent," which is itself a wobbly and uncertain standard based upon the supposed mental processes of a hypothetical and non-existent reasonable man. European lawyers view the whole thing with utter

amazement; and the extent to which it has damaged the courts and the legal profession by bringing the law and its administration into public disrepute can only be guessed.

Delay

The process inundates our courts with tort cases, and particularly those involving automobile accidents. In many areas calendars are congested and fall months—they have been known to fall as much as three or four years—behind,[7] which means that the injured man must wait that long before his case can even be heard, to say nothing of the further delay that may result from various motions and an appeal. Since in the meantime he has to live, is unable to work if he is seriously injured, and has hospital bills and other expenses to meet, he is under the most extreme economic pressure to settle his claim on any terms he can get.[8] Since a hungry man cannot afford to litigate, it is still true, as it always has been, that in any personal injury case delay always works for the defendant; and in the poker game of negotiation for settlement, he always has that ace up his sleeve.

Attorneys and Fees

To combat all this, lawyers who specialize in personal injury cases abound. By and large they are reasonably reputable men, but there are those who definitely are not, and fake claim rackets are a major problem.[9]

---

6. See supra, § 39.

7. See Rosenberg and Sovern, Delay and the Dynamics of Personal Injury Litigation, 1959, 59 Col. L.Rev. 1116; Burger, The Courts on Trial: A Call for Action Against Delay, 1958, 44 A.B.A.J. 738; James and Law, Compensation for Auto Accident Victims: A Story of Too Little and Too Late, 1952, 26 Conn. Bar J. 70; Steinbrink and Lockwood, Facts, Figures and Recommendations re Trial Calendars of the Supreme Court, Kings County, 1932 to 1952, 1952; 1952, 19 Rep.N.Y.Judicial Council 32; Note, 1951, 51 Col.L.Rev. 1037.

8. Corstvet, The Uncompensated Accident and Its Consequences, 1936, 3 Law & Con.Prob. 466; Hogan and Stubbs, The Sociological and Legal Problem of the Uncompensated Motor Victim, 1938, 11 Rocky Mt.L.Rev. 12.

9. See Monaghan, The Liability Claim Racket, 1936, 3 Law & Con.Prob. 491.

The attorneys follow the accidents, interview the injured, investigate the facts, produce witnesses, prepare the case, settle it if they can, and end by trying it if they cannot. Since personal injury victims are not steady or recurring clients, their practice has to be built up by reliance upon such sources as labor unions or hospital staffs who will steer plaintiffs to them, or by solicitation of claims ("ambulance chasing") in defiance of the ethics of their profession; and in the interest of attracting customers some of them indulge in a degree of blatant self-advertising which decent lawyers find odious. As a group they have developed to an extreme the fine art of showmanship in the courtroom, and of extracting the last possible dime from sympathetic and impressionable juries; and some of the verdicts they have obtained run to staggering figures. While the case is pending they not infrequently advance money to support the injured man and his family, and to meet his medical bills and other expenses, which gives them a financial investment in his case that is scarcely consistent with a fair and scrupulously honest approach.

For these services they charge fees upon a contingent basis, which means that they are paid only if they win the case or succeed in obtaining a settlement. Since the successes must pay for the failures, these fees are high. Normally, they run to a third of the amount recovered; but in difficult cases, or those of protracted litigation, they may be as much as a half. Thus the plaintiff who finally recovers a verdict and judgment of $90,000 for the loss of his leg may find that $30,000 of it goes for his lawyer's fee, and an additional $10,000 for repayment of money advanced to him for expenses and subsistence in the meantime.

Summary

The whole picture is one of a fumbling and uncertain process of awarding a judgment upon the basis of unreliable evidence, fraught with ruinous delay, which fails entirely when proof of fault fails, leaves the entire remedy worthless against many defendants who are not financially responsible, and diverts a large share of the money to the plaintiff's attorney even when it can be collected. The Columbia Report found in 1932 that in ten states in which studies were made, 47% of the temporary injuries, 56% of the permanent injuries, and 55% of those that were fatal, resulted in actual receipt of less than the medical and other expenses of the accident, without any compensation for other damage such as disability and loss of earnings. Since 1932 the increased prevalence of insurance, and financial responsibility laws in most of the states, have brought about some uncertain improvement in these figures, whose extent can only be a matter of guess; but in its essence, it is reasonably certain that the situation is not a vast deal better at the present day. Later fragmentary studies have indicated that the fundamental picture is unchanged.[10]

85. REMEDIES

As the slaughter on the highways has mounted, and the problem of the uncompensated victim has become more and more acute, there has been a flood of proposals seeking to remedy an increasingly desperate

10. See Brown, Automobile Accident Litigation in Wisconsin: A Factual Study, 1935, 10 Wis.L.Rev. 170; Survey Analysis of Studied Cases of Victims: Report of the Joint Legislative Committee to Investigate Automobile Insurance, 1938, N.Y.Leg.Doc. No. 91; Temple University Bureau of Economic and Business Research, Economic-Financial Consequences of Personal Injuries Sustained in 1953 Philadelphia Auto Accidents, 1955, 7 J.Econ. & Bus., Bull. No. 3; James Compensation for Auto Accident Victims: A Study of Too Little and Too Late, 1952, 26 Conn.Bar J. 70; Marx, "Motorism," Not "Pedestrianism": Compensation for Automobile Victims, 1956, 42 Am.Bar Assn.J. 421; Morris and Paul, The Financial Impact of Automobile Accidents, 1962, 110 U.Pa.L.Rev. 913; Calabresi, The Cost of Accidents (1970); Conard et al., Automobile Accident Costs and Payments: Studies in the Economics of Injury Reparation (1964); Conard, The Economic Treatment of Automobile Injuries, 1964, 63 Mich.L.Rev. 279.

situation which clearly cries aloud for a remedy.[11]

In two minor respects[12] the insurance companies themselves have endeavored to meet the situation with extended policy provisions. One of these agrees to pay, without regard to any question of fault, first medical expenses of the injured person, or, for a higher premium, all such expenses incurred within a year after the accident.[13] The other provides, along with coverage of any liability of the insured, casualty protection against his inability to collect a valid claim or judgment against an uninsured motorist.[14] Both of these are of course voluntary schemes, and their weakness is that they must rely upon the common sense, good will or liberality of the insured. All of the other proposals have been for legislation.

Nearly all of them go back to the analogy of the workmen's compensation acts,[15] which, while they are admittedly far from perfect, are generally conceded to constitute a great advance upon the common law system of litigation based on fault which preceded them. The system of workmen's compensation involves five basic elements:

(1) strict liability of employers for injuries to workmen arising out of and in the course of employment;

(2) compulsory insurance against the liability, with resulting distribution of the losses over an entire industry through the premiums paid;

(3) a schedule of compensation limiting the workman's recovery considerably short of the damages recoverable in a tort action for negligence;

(4) a commission or other administrative body to hear claims and award compensation without a jury, in lieu of the courts;

(5) limitation of attorney's fees.

Nearly all of the proposals made for legislation dealing with automobile accidents have involved the first two of these elements. Most of them have involved all five.

Financial Responsibility Laws

Among the earliest proposals affecting automobiles, and the first steps actually taken were "financial responsibility" laws.[16] The

---

11. Literature on all this is legion; but mention may be made of Grad, Recent Developments in Automobile Accident Compensation, 1950, 50 Col.L. Rev. 300; Green, The Individual's Protection Under Negligence Law: Risk Sharing, 1953, 47 Northwestern U.L.Rev. 751; Marx, Compensation for Automobile Accident Victims, 1954, 15 Ohio St.L.J. 150; Plummer, The Uncompensated Automobile Accident Victim, [1956] Ins.L.J. 459; James, The Columbia Study of Compensation for Automobile Accidents: An Unanswered Challenge, 1959, 59 Col.L.Rev. 408; Berger, Compensation Plans for Personal Injuries, [1962] U.Ill.L.Forum 217.

Also the books of Ehrenzweig, Negligence Without Fault, 1951, and "Full Aid" Insurance for the Traffic Victim, 1954, and Green, Traffic Victims—Tort Law and Insurance, 1958.

12. See also, as to a new policy with an "absolute liability" option to the injured party, to take payment according to scheduled benefits without regard to whether the insured was at fault, Note, [1958] Ins.L.J. 32–33.

13. See Liability Revisions, 1947, 48 Best's Ins.Rep. No. 2, p. 45; Sawyer, Frontiers of Liability Insurance, 1938, 39 Best's 439, 440; Melendes and Craig, Medical Payments Provisions of the Automobile Insurance Policy, 1969, 52 Marq.L.Rev. 445.

14. See Widiss, A Guide to Uninsured Motorist Coverage (1969); Caverly, New Provisions for Protection from Injuries Inflicted by an Uninsured Automobile, [1956] Ins.L.J. 19; Morgenbesser, Some Legal Aspects of the New York Uninsured Motorists' Coverage, [1956] Ins.L.J. 241; Graham, The Uninsured Motorist Endorsement: Its Terms and Developing Case Law, 1968, 19 Fed.Ins.Couns. I. 85; Panel Discussion, Uninsured Motorist Coverage, 1970, 20 Fed.Ins.Couns. I. 56; Note, 1964, 15 West. Res.L.Rev. 386.

15. See supra, p. 531.

16. See Braun, The Financial Responsibility Law, 1936, 3 Law & Con.Prob. 505; Feinsinger, Operation of Financial Responsibility Laws, 1936, 3 Law & Con.Prob. 519; Feinsinger, Financial Responsibility Laws and Compulsory Insurance—The Problem in Wisconsin, 1935, 10 Wis.L.Rev. 192; Aberg, Effects of and Problems Arising from Financial Responsibility Laws, 1943–44 A.B.A.Proc. 45; Stoeckel, Administrative Problems of Financial Responsibility Laws, 1936, 3 Law & Con.Prob. 531; Burtis, Operation of the Kansas Financial Responsibility

first of these was enacted in Connecticut in 1925.[17] In their original form they required any motorist who had failed to satisfy a judgment against him for an accident to furnish proof that he was capable of satisfying future judgments up to a specified amount. This was under penalty of revocation of his license to drive, or of the registration of his automobile. The easy form of proof of such financial responsibility is obviously a certificate that the driver has taken out liability insurance; and the practical effect of the legislation is to require it of those who default on judgments. Such statutes have now been adopted in all of the states except Alaska. Their weaknesses are obvious. They leave the first person injured with no assurance of collecting his judgment, and no aid in doing so except the threat that a report to the authorities will compel insurance for the future, which is by no means a dire threat. In this respect they have been described as "locking the barn door after the horse is stolen," and as examples of a philosophy analogous to the old myth that "every dog is entitled to one bite." [18] Even as to future injuries, they fail to have any effect upon even the negligent driver who, because he is known to be judgment proof, is not worth suing, and so escapes a judgment; and even when there is an unpaid judgment, the administration of the acts has been at the mercy of some method of following it up. There are, in addition, many such drivers who fail to surrender registration or license cards, or who continue to drive without them.

For such reasons the original statutes have been replaced, in about half of the states,

by "security-responsibility laws," [19] the first of which [20] was adopted in New Hampshire in 1937. These have been held constitutional,[21] except in Colorado.[22] They require any driver involved in an accident, under the same penalties, to furnish proof that he is capable of paying a judgment for that accident, or to deposit security for such payment, up to the specified amounts. This clearly is better; but the amounts specified are usually grossly inadequate. The system may still fail to affect the driver who is willing to settle, is not sued, and so does not come before the court, or the obstinate individual who would rather forego the privilege of driving himself, and let his wife do it, rather than provide such proof or security. The American Automobile Association has a model bill of this type.

There appears to be very little doubt that such "security" legislation has greatly encouraged voluntary liability insurance.[23]

19. See Johnson, The Modern Trend in Financial Responsibility Legislation, 1944 A.B.A.Proc. 67, 69; Wagner, Safety Responsibility Laws—A Review of Recent Developments, 1946, 9 Ga.Bar J. 160; Braun, The Need for Revision of Financial Responsibility Legislation, 1945, 40 Ill.L.Rev. 237; Netherton, Highway Safety Under Different Types of Liability Legislation, 1954, 15 Ohio St.L.J. 110; Vorys, A Short Survey of Laws Designed to Exclude the Financially Irresponsible Driver from the Highway, 1954, 15 Ohio St.L.J. 101; Johnson, The Modern Trend in Financial Responsibility Legislation, 1944 A.B.A. Ins. Section 67.

20. N.H.Rev.Laws, 1942, c. 122.

21. Hadden v. Aitken, 1952, 156 Neb. 215, 55 N.W.2d 620; Escobedo v. State Dept. of Motor Vehicles, 1950, 35 Cal.2d 870, 222 P.2d 1; Doyle v. Kahl, 1951, 242 Iowa 153, 46 N.W.2d 52; Ballow v. Reeves, Ky.1951, 238 S.W.2d 141; Gillaspie v. Department of Public Safety, 1953, 152 Tex. 459, 259 S.W.2d 177, cert. denied 347 U.S. 933; State v. Stehlek, 1953, 262 Wis. 642, 56 N.W.2d 514.

22. People v. Nothaus, 1962, 147 Colo. 210, 363 P.2d 180.

23. See Wagner, Safety Responsibility Laws—A Review of Recent Developments, 1946, 9 Ga.Bar J. 160, 166, stating the following increases in the percentages of insured cars: New Hampshire, 36% before enactment of security law, about 85% after enactment; New York, 30% before, about 75% after;

Law, 1941, 9 Kan. Bar A.J. 367; Wagner, Safety Responsibility Laws—A Review of Recent Developments, 1946, 9 Ga.Bar J. 160; Notes, 1943, 20 N.C. L.Rev. 198; 1938, 16 N.Y.U.L.Q.Rev. 126; 1936, 24 Ky.L.J. 495; 1941, 41 Col.L.Rev. 1461; 1949, 1 Stan.L.Rev. 263.

17. Conn.Pub.Acts, 1925, c. 183. An early analysis of such statutes was Heyting, Automobiles and Compulsory Liability Insurance, 1930, 16 A.B.A.J. 362.

18. See supra, p. 501.

Compulsory Insurance

As to common carriers, and many commercial vehicles, virtually all states have gone beyond the financial responsibility laws, and have required the owner of the vehicle, as a condition of obtaining permission in the first instance to operate it on the public highway, to carry liability insurance.[24]

In 1927, following an affirmative advisory opinion as to constitutionality,[25] Massachusetts enacted a statute requiring all automobile drivers to carry insurance against liability up to specified amounts.[26] In part, at least, because of the opposition of the insurance companies themselves,[27] no other state followed this lead until New York, in 1956, adopted a statute requiring advance proof of financial responsibility on the part of all drivers of motor vehicles, and North Carolina followed suit the next year.[28] Compulsory insurance is common enough on the continent of Europe,[29] and similar bills have been intro-

duced without success into a number of American legislatures.[30] As in the case of some of the financial responsibility laws [31] the problem of the motorist who is so bad a risk that no insurance company wants him, is dealt with by "assigned risk" provisions, under which state authorities allocate the coverage of such individuals among the companies doing business in the state; and this, as much as any other single element, has aroused the opposition of the insurers. There has been a long experience under the Massachusetts act; [32] and while every other attempt to duplicate it has been defeated under heavy fire,[33] there appears to be little real

---

Indiana, 33% before, about 74% after; Maine, 36% before, 60% after. In Minnesota about 80% of the cars were insured eight months after a security law was enacted.

24. See Brownfield, Compulsory Liability Insurance for Commercial Motor Vehicles, 1936, 3 Law & Con.Prob. 571.

25. Opinion of the Justices, 1925, 251 Mass. 569, 147 N.E. 681. After the statute was adopted, its constitutionality was carried to the Supreme Court of the United States, which, in a brief per curiam opinion, affirmed a dismissal for lack of a federal question.

26. Mass.Ann.Laws 1932, c. 175, §§ 113A—113D. Now considerably modified, as of January 1, 1971, by the Massachusetts Personal Injury Protection Act, Mass.Laws 1970, ch. 670, 744. See infra, p. 567.

27. See McVay, The Case Against Compulsory Automobile Insurance, 1954, 15 Ohio St.L.J. 150; Virginia Assn. of Insurance Agents, The Uninsured Motorist, 1957; Kline and Pearson, The Problem of the Uninsured Motorist (State of New York Insurance Dept. 1951); Casualty Insurance Companies Serving Massachusetts, The First Thirty Years: A Commentary on the Operation of the Massachusetts Compulsory Liability Insurance Act, 1957.

28. N.Y.Vehicle & Traffic Laws, Art. 6, §§ 310–321.

29. See Ehrenzweig, Assurance Oblige—A Comparative Study, 1950, 15 Law & Con.Prob. 445; Deák,

Liability and Compensation for Automobile Accidents, 1937, 21 Minn.L.Rev. 123; Deák, Automobile Accidents: A Comparative Study of the Law of Liability in Europe, 1931, 79 U.Pa.L.Rev. 271; Bolgár, Motor Vehicle Accident Compensation: Types and Trends, 1953, 2 Am.J.Comp.Law 515.

30. See California Legislature, Assembly Interim Committee on Finance and Insurance, Semifinal Report, Sec. 3, 1953; Missouri State Chamber of Commerce, Motor Vehicle Financial Responsibility, [1952] Ins.L.J. 722; New Jersey Legislature, Report of Joint Committee on Improvements of the Motor Vehicle Financial Responsibility Law, 1952; North Dakota Legislature, Report on Automobile Liability Insurance, 1950; Wisconsin Report of Legislative Council Committee on Motor Vehicle Accidents, 1953; Kline and Pearson, The Problem of the Uninsured Motorist, State of New York Insurance Dept., 1951; Marx, The Case for Compulsory Automobile Compensation Insurance, 1954, 15 Ohio St. L.J. 134; McVay, The Case Against Compulsory Automobile Insurance, 1954, 15 Ohio St.L.J. 150.

31. See for example California State Auto. Assn. Inter-Insurance Bureau v. Maloney, 1951, 341 U.S. 105.

32. See Report of Mass. Senate Special Commission to Study Compulsory Motor Vehicle Liability Insurance and Related Matters, 1930, 15 Mass.L.Q. 8–288; Blanchard, Compulsory Motor Vehicle Liability Insurance in Massachusetts, 1936, 3 Law & Con. Prob. 537; Carpenter, Compulsory Motor Vehicle Insurance and Court Congestion in Massachusetts, 1936, 3 Law & Con.Prob. 554.

33. Wilkie, The Recurring Question of Compulsory Automobile Insurance, 1940, 30 Rep.Wis.Bar Assn. 77.

doubt that "For a law which has been loudly denounced as 'unworkable,' the Massachusetts law has for the last twenty-three years worked better than any other in the United States to protect the victim." [34]

Compulsory insurance obviously affords protection to more plaintiffs than the financial responsibility acts; but it has two definite inadequacies. One is that the amounts of insurance coverage required by the statutes are necessarily low, since they must be geared to fit the purse of the impecunious driver; and since the specified limits tend to set a standard, and such legislation apparently generates some hostility on the part of the motoring public, Massachusetts has the lowest percentage of policies above such limits of any state in the nation.[35] The other is that even the compulsory insurance covers only liability upon the basis of fault. It fails when proof of fault fails, or is defeated; and it does relatively little to meet the unsatisfactory situation of the delays in litigation and the attorney's fee.

Unsatisfied Judgment Funds

Three or four states,[36] as well as all of the Canadian provinces except Quebec and Sas-

katchewan, have attempted to meet the problem by setting up state funds for the purpose of paying unsatisfied automobile liability judgments up to specified limits. These are financed by additional taxation, either upon all motorists, upon those who do not have insurance, or upon liability insurance companies doing business in the jurisdiction. These measures, too, undoubtedly have been of some aid in relieving the situation.

The criticism of all of these steps is that they take only one bite at the cherry. They do not affect liability beyond the particular limits specified, which are low. These usually are set at not more than $10,000 for any one plaintiff, and $20,000 for any one accident. They do not affect any accident in which there is no fault, or in which it cannot be proved, or in which contributory negligence and assumption of risk will defeat recovery. Nor do they, obviously, affect materially the delay of litigation, with its inevitable pressure for cheap settlement, or the share mulcted for attorney's fees. It is for this reason that the other proposals all have gone back to the analogy of the workmen's compensation acts.

The Columbia Plan

Even before 1932 there had been several writers [37] who had advocated the extension of the workmen's compensation principle to automobile accidents. In that year there

34. Grad, Recent Developments in Automobile Accident Compensation, 1950, 50 Col.L.Rev. 300, 315–316.

35. See Netherton, Highway Safety Under Differing Types of Liability Legislation, 1954, 15 Ohio St.L. J. 110, 125. See also Virginia Assn. of Insurance Agents, The Uninsured Motorist, 1957, 3, reporting that only 38% of Massachusetts motorists carry insurance in excess of the $5,000/$10,000 statutory requirement, while 75 to 90% of those in Wisconsin, for example, buy higher limits. Also only 38% of Massachusetts drivers buy medical payments protection while the national average outside of Massachusetts is 61%.

36. New Jersey Laws 1952, ch. 174. See New Jersey's Uninsured Motorist Law, J.Am.Ins., March 1959, p. 8. Bambrick, A Look at the New Jersey Unsatisfied Claim and Judgment Fund, [1956] Ins. L.J. 825; Note, 1966, 65 Mich.L.Rev. 180. The act was applied in Dietz v. Meyer, 1963, 79 N.J.Super. 194, 191 A.2d 182. See also Bergeson, The North Dakota Unsatisfied Judgment Plan, 1953, 3 Fed. of Ins. Counsel Q. 35; Denny, Uninsured Motorist Coverage in Virginia, 1961, 47 Va.L.Rev. 145; Court,

Virginia's Experience with the "Uninsured Motorist" Act, 1962, 3 Wm. & Mary L.Rev. 237. As to South Carolina, see Note, 1963, 15 S.C.L.Rev. 739.

37. See Chamberlin, Make the Automobile Liable for the Injury, National Underwriter, May 2, 1898, summarized in Bowers, Compulsory Automobile Compensation, 1929, at 282; Rollins, A Proposal to Extend the Compensation Principle to Accidents in the Streets, 1919, 4 Mass.L.Q. 392; Carman, Is a Motor Vehicle Accident Compensation Act Advisable? 1919, 4 Minn.L.Rev. 1; Marx, Compulsory Compensation Insurance, 1925, 25 Col.L.Rev. 164; Elsbree and Roberts, Compulsory Insurance Against Motor Vehicle Accidents, 1928, 76 U.Pa.L. Rev. 690.

appeared the Columbia Report,[38] which was the work of a distinguished committee made up of Arthur A. Ballantine as chairman, Shippen Lewis, Dean Charles E. Clark, Walter F. Dodd, William Draper Lewis, Robert S. Marx, Horace Stern, and Ogden L. Mills. It proposed to take over the workmen's compensation system for all automobile accidents. Strict liability was to be imposed upon the owner of the vehicle, and he was to be required to carry liability insurance to cover it. A schedule of compensation was to be set up, substantially identical with that of the workmen's compensation law at the time. Claims were to be heard and awards to be made by a special board following workmen's compensation procedure, which was to have power to limit attorney's fees.

This plan never yet has been adopted anywhere, although it has received serious consideration in the legislatures of New York, Connecticut, Virginia, North Dakota, and Wisconsin, among others. But the proposal set off a torrent of discussion,[39] which has continued till the present day; and the Columbia Report has been the basis, or at least the point of departure, for a large number of suggestions, proposals, and even bills in the legislatures since, which never have got beyond committees.

The Saskatchewan Plan

Until 1970, the one English-speaking jurisdiction which had adopted a compensation plan for automobile accidents was the Canadian province of Saskatchewan. Conditions there are perhaps as favorable for the success of such a plan as can be found anywhere. Geographically the province is roughly comparable to the state of North Dakota. It has wide distances, no large cities and relatively few small ones, flat country, long winters in which traffic is at a minimum, and in comparison with any American state, few automobiles; and its accident rate is therefore low.

The Saskatchewan Automobile Accident Insurance Act was adopted in 1946, and has been amended from time to time since.[40] It sets up a state insurance fund for the compensation of all victims of automobile accidents, without regard to fault. Such accidents include every injury to the person as a result of driving in, riding in, colliding with, or being run down by a motor vehicle in Saskatchewan, whether or not another vehicle is involved. The fund is financed by annual assessment of all drivers and car owners, at the time of their registration. Essentially the plan is one of accident insurance. The terms of the insurance are contained in the statute, and the only "policy" issued is the registration certificate or the driver's license. The coverage expires with it, but the person injured by an unlicensed driver is still compensated, and the state is subrogated to his rights against the driver. The payment of claims is administered by the Government Insurance Office, and the claimant ordinarily has no need of an attorney. A schedule of compensation is set up, which is somewhat lower than the benefits under the New York workmen's compensation law.[41]

38. Report of Committee to Study Compensation for Automobile Accidents, for Columbia University Council for Research in the Social Sciences, 1932.

39. This is well reviewed in James, The Columbia Study of Compensation for Automobile Accidents: An Unanswered Challenge, 1959, 59 Col.L.Rev. 408. See also Ballantine, Compensation for Automobile Accidents, 1932, 18 A.B.A.J. 221; Smith, Lilly and Dowling, Compensation for Automobile Accidents, 1932, 32 Col.L.Rev. 785; Lewis, The Merits of the Automobile Compensation Plan, 1936, 3 Law & Con.Prob. 513; Malone, Damage Suits and the Contagious Principle of Workmen's Compensation, 1952, 12 La.L.Rev. 231.

40. It was re-enacted in its entirety in 1952. Sask. Rev.Stats. c. 409 (1965).

41. For a fuller summary, and discussion of many of the details of the plan, see Green, The Automobile Accident Insurance Act of Saskatchewan, 1949, 31 J.Comp.Leg. & Int.Law 39. See also Green, the Automobile Accident Insurance Act of Saskatchewan, 1952, 2 Chitty's L.J. 38; Fines, The Saskatchewan Plan, 1953, 3 Fed. of Ins.Counsel Q. 51; Shumiatcher, State Compulsory Insurance Act—An Ap-

The unique feature of the Saskatchewan plan is that it does not supersede tort liability, and leaves the plaintiff the possibility of an action in the courts to recover additional compensation on the basis of fault if he can prove it. In that event the defendant is covered by state liability insurance, in the amounts of $10,000 and $20,000. As to this insurance, the Government Insurance Office plays much the same part in litigation and settlement as private insurance companies elsewhere. Obviously the plaintiff is likely to resort to court only when he thinks that he has a good chance of establishing the defendant's fault, and that his damages exceed the state compensation by an amount sufficient to justify the litigation and his attorney's fees. Remarkably enough, the experience has been that few such suits are filed. In 1948–9 there were 1731 claims made for compensation under the plan, and only 103 claims under the additional liability insurance provided by the Act.

The reports from Saskatchewan, with some occasional dissent, are that the plan is working as well as workmen's compensation, which is to say, that while it may leave a good deal to be desired as an ultimate solution of the problem, it is regarded there as a considerable advance over what has gone before.[42] It has served as a point of departure for several proposals in American legislatures, and for a book by Dean Leon Green,[43] who advocates what is essentially the Saskatchewan plan, with the elimination of the schedule of compensation, and the substitution of common law damages other than pain and suffering. It also led to a report of a Committee of the Ontario Parliament in

1963,[44] and to a similar committee proposal in California[45] in 1965.

Academic Suggestions

Professor Ehrenzweig, in a booklet[46] has proposed an alternative of his own. It involves an extension of the "first aid" clauses which are now commonly written into liability insurance policies, by which the insurer obligates itself to compensate for the first medical expenses of the accident—or, for an additional premium, for all such expenses within a year—without regard to fault or legal liability of the insured. The proposal is that such clauses be expanded to include benefits, of the kind now found in accident insurance policies, which would be sufficient to afford a minimum of compensation to anyone injured in an automobile accident by the insured, without any question of fault or liability. Any owner or operator of an automobile who carries such "full aid" insurance in statutory minimum amounts, would be relieved of his common law liability for ordinary negligence, as distinguished from aggravated negligence such as drunken driving. In addition, anyone injured by a car not so insured, other than a member of the driver's family, would be entitled to recover the same "full aid" benefits from an uncompensated-injury fund, financed either by "tort fines" collected from those who are criminally negligent, or from tax sources deemed to correspond to the savings in relief payments, and to the taxpayer's fair share of automobile losses as a non-motorized user of the highways.

This plan has attracted considerable attention among the insurance companies, and has

praisal, 1961, 39 Can.Bar Rev. 107; Grad, Recent Developments in Automobile Accident Compensation, 1950, 50 Col.L.Rev. 300.

42. See articles cited in the preceding note, particularly Grad, Recent Developments in Automobile Accident Compensation, 1950, 50 Col.L.Rev. 300, 320–325.

43. Green, Traffic Victims—Tort Law and Insurance, 1958.

44. Ontario Select Committee on Automobile Insurance, Final Report (1963); Linden, The Report of the Osgoode Hall Study on Compensation for Victims of Automobile Accidents (1965); Linden, Automobile Accident Compensation in Ontario, 1967, 15 Am.J.Comp.L. 301.

45. Cal.State Bar., Report of Committee on Personal Injury Claims, 1965, 40 J.St.B.Cal. 148, 216.

46. Ehrenzweig, "Full Aid" Insurance for the Traffic Victim, 1954. Also covered in 1955, 43 Cal.L.Rev. 1.

received some support. It is still too novel to permit any estimate as yet as to its chances of adoption.

It is not to be supposed that the supply of plans has ended here. Proposals have proliferated, without much agreement. Among others may be mentioned the rather elaborate "social insurance" plan, with vocational rehabilitation of the victims and provision for their subsistence, offered by Professor Conard and his associates; [47] the general proposal of Professor Franklin [48] for compensation for all accidents, without limitation to automobiles; and the social welfare approach of Professors Blume and Kalven, [49] contending that the way out is not to impose the burden upon the automobile driver, but to broaden the scope of social security and put the burden on the state. There have been various other proposals emanating from the insurance companies, [50] and others, [51] which for the

most part have broadened the basis of recovery beyond fault, while limiting the amount of the damages.

The Keeton-O'Connell Plan

The most thorough and carefully prepared study in the area of automobile compensation is the one offered under the title of "Basic Protection" by Professors Robert E. Keeton and Jeffrey O'Connell, in a book of 600 pages [52] published in 1965. It was accompanied by a proposed statute which has been introduced before many state legislatures and given serious consideration, but thus far has failed of adoption in any state. It has nevertheless been the subject of a great deal of discussion and debate. [53]

Rather than traditional liability insurance with its three-party claims procedure, Basic Protection relies primarily on loss insurance, analogous to medical payments coverage, under which the victim ordinarily claims directly against the insurance company covering his own car, or, if a guest, his host's car, or, if a pedestrian, the car striking him. The coverage applies regardless of fault.

The plan calls for compulsory insurance providing "basic protection" for bodily injuries up to $10,000 for reasonable expenses incurred and loss of income from work, less a

47. Conard et al., Automobile Accident Costs and Payments: Studies in the Economics of Insuring Reparation (1964); Conard, The Economic Treatment of Automobile Injuries, 1964, 63 Mich.L.Rev. 279; Conard and Jacobs, New Hope for Consensus in Automobile Injury Impasse, 1966, 52 A.B.A.J. 533.

48. Franklin, Replacing the Negligence Lottery: Compensation and Selective Reimbursement, 1967, 53 Va.L.Rev. 774.

49. Blum and Kalven, Public Law Perspectives on a Private Law Problem, 1965, 83–85; Blum and Kalven, A Stopgap Plan for Compensating Auto Accident Victims, [1968] Ins.L.J. 661; Blum and Kalven, Public Law Perspectives on a Private Law Problem, 1964, 31 U.Chi.L.Rev. 641. This led to a lively exchange of polite brickbats in Calabresi, Fault, Accidents, and the Wonderful World of Blum and Kalven, 1966, 75 Yale L.J. 216; Blum and Kalven, The Empty Cabinet of Dr. Calabresi, 1967, 34 U.Chi.L.Rev. 239. See also Calabresi, Some Thoughts on Risk Distribution and the Law of Torts, 1961, 70 Yale L.J. 499; Note, 1949, 63 Harv. L.Rev. 330.

50. Collected in King, The Insurance Industry and Compensation Plans, 1968, 43 N.Y.U.L.Rev. 1137; Davies, The Minnesota No-Fault Auto Insurance, 1970, 54 Minn.L.Rev. 921; Logan, Insure the Driver, [1968] Ins. L.J. 682.

51. New York Insurance Dept., Automobile Insurance. . . . For Whose Benefit? (1970); Ghiardi & Kircher, Automobile Insurance: The Rockefeller-Stewart Plan, 1970, 37 Ins. Couns. J. 324; Conn.

Ins. Dept., A Program for Automobile Insurance and Accident Benefit Reform (1969).

52. Keeton and O'Connell, Basic Protection for the Traffic Victim: A Blueprint for Reforming Automobile Insurance (1965).

See O'Connell, Taming the Automobile, 1964, 58 Minn. L.Rev. 299; Keeton and O'Connell, Basic Protection—A Proposal for Improving Automobile Claims Systems, 1965, 78 Harv.L.Rev. 329; O'Connell, Basic Protection—Relief for the Ills of Automobile Insurance Cases, 1967, 27 La.L.Rev. 647.

53. Inst.Cont.Leg.Ed., Protection for the Traffic Victim: The Keeton-O'Connell Plan and Its Critics (1967); Am.Ins. Assn., Report of Special Committee to Study and Evaluate the Keeton-O'Connell Basic Protection Plan (1968); Marryott, The Tort System and Automobile Claims, 1966, 52 A.B.A.J. 639; Symposia, 1967, 3 Trial 10–54; [1967] U.Ill.L.F. 361–633; (1968), 1 Conn.L.Rev. 1; Keeton and O'Connell, Basic Protection: A Rebuttal to Its Critics, 1967, 53 A.B.A.J. 633.

small deductible amount, and less any losses covered by benefits from other sources. Unless damages for pain and suffering exceed $5,000, or other personal damages exceed $10,000, the basic protection coverage replaces any tort action for damages. If the damages do exceed these figures, the negligence action is preserved but recovery is reduced by these amounts.

A compulsory "property damage dual option" insurance coverage applies to all property damage which a policy holder negligently causes to others. For damages to his own car, he may elect a "liability option," entitling him to payment only if he can prove a valid tort claim against another person, or he may elect an "added protection option," entitling him to be paid for this damage regardless of fault. There are in addition numerous detailed provisions dealing with the mechanics of administration.

The First American Statutes

The first American statute actually adopted was in the Commonwealth of Puerto Rico in 1968, to take effect the following year.[54] It establishes an Automobile Accident Compensation Administration which will provide medical and rehabilitation services for traffic victims, pay death and disability benefits according to a schedule like workmen's compensation, and pay weekly compensation for 50% of wage loss for two years with a weekly maximum of $50 for the first year and $25 for the second year. Benefits from collateral sources are deducted. The Administration is financed by an initial appropriation of $1,000,000, and a tax on the registration of automobiles. A tort action remains open to the victim, subject to deductions. The whole program bears a great many similarities to that of Saskatchewan.[55]

The first, and to the date of publication the only, state to adopt an automobile accident reparations statute was Massachusetts in 1970, to become effective January 1, 1971. The Massachusetts Compulsory Personal Injuries Protection Act took many of its features from the Keeton-O'Connell Plan,[56] which had passed one house of the legislature a few years before; but it is obviously an independent piece of legislation.[57]

The statute is based on the existing compulsory bodily injury liability insurance provisions, as to $5,000 per person and $10,000 per accident, which are retained. Strict liability is required as a part of the liability insurance policy, in favor of the named insured, the members of his household, any authorized operator or passenger of his vehicle, or any pedestrian it strikes. There is also coverage for the insured and the members of his household if they are hit by an uninsured motorist.

The benefits run up to $2000. Within a period of two years after the accident they cover reasonable medical and hospital expenses; net loss of wages, or for unemployed persons, net loss of earning power, up to 75%; costs of substitute services, such as hiring individuals for family services which would have been rendered by the injured person. Some collateral benefits are not deducted, but others are, such as wages paid under a wage continuation program.

These benefits are in lieu of tort damages; and any person covered by the compulsory

---

56. See supra, p. 566.

57. There were successive statutes. The first, Mass. Laws 1970, ch. 670 contained provisions as to a 15% reduction in premiums, and forbidding cancellation or refusal to renew a policy. This was very unpalatable to the insurance companies, some of which threatened to withdraw from the state. A second Act, Mass. Laws 1970, ch. 744, authorized a refusal to renew under restricted conditions.

The two acts amend provisions found in various chapters of the Massachusetts General Laws, and are hence distributed. See Mass. Am. Laws, Cum. Supp. 1970, ch. 90, §§ 34A, 34D, 34M, 34N; ch. 231, § 6D; ch. 175, §§ 22E, 22F, 22G, 22H, 113B, 113C.

---

54. P. R. Laws Ann. (Supp.1968) tit. 9, §§ 2051–65. See Apoute and Denenberg, The Automobile Problem in Puerto Rico: Dimensions and Proposed Solution [1968] Ins.L.J. 884.

55. See supra, p. 564.

insurance is exempted from liability to the extent of the coverage. An injured person can recover in tort for pain and suffering only if reasonable medical expenses exceed $500, or the injury results in death, loss of a body member or sight or hearing, a fracture, or "permanent and serious disfigurement." Property damage is not covered, and is left to the common law. The policy may provide for exclusion of benefits to a person injured while driving under the influence of alcohol or drugs, committing a felony, or intending to cause injury to himself or others.

The Arguments

About all this verbal battle has been waged now for a good many years.[58] The chief arguments in favor of the adoption of some form of automobile accident compensation plan have been those decrying the evils of the present situation.[59] In addition, it has been contended that, as in the case of the law of respondeat superior applied to employers,[60] "enterprises" in which anyone chooses to engage should bear the losses which they must inevitably entail, and distribute them among those so engaged by insurance premiums; and that the man who is given the privilege of driving a high-powered automobile to the peril of the public, upon expensive highways provided by the state, should reasonably be required to assume the burden of compensating anyone whom he may injure, even without his fault.[61]

The automobile is singled out for such responsibility because of the social necessity arising from the enormous number of injuries it inflicts, and the peculiar difficulties in the way of obtaining satisfactory evidence of fault which attend litigation in which so much will turn upon split seconds. The theory of workmen's compensation, which is one of insurance at the cost of the enterprise for the benefit of individuals unable to protect themselves, is drawn upon and applied by analogy. Stress is also laid upon the expected saving in time and expense of litigation through prompt payment and settlement, the relief of the injured man during the time pending compensation, the discouragement of "ambulance chasing" and excessive fees, and the remedy afforded for the congestion of court calendars.

Opponents of the plans [62] have cried "socialism," and have been greatly alarmed at

58. See Smith, Lilly and Dowling, Compensation for Automobile Accidents: A Symposium, 1932, 32 Col. L.Rev. 785, 803, 813; Landis, Book Review 1932, 45 Harv.L.Rev. 1428; Thurston, Book Review, 1933, 43 Yale L.J. 160; Brown, Automobile Accident Litigation in Wisconsin: A Factual Study, 1934, 10 Wis. L.Rev. 170; Lewis, The Merits of the Automobile Accident Compensation Plan, 1936, 3 Law & Con. Prob. 583; Sherman, Grounds for Opposing the Automobile Accident Compensation Plan, 1936, 3 Law & Con.Prob. 598; Grad, Recent Developments in Automobile Accident Compensation, 1950, 50 Col. L.Rev. 300; Kline and Pearson, The Problem of the Uninsured Motorist (New York State Insurance Dept.), 1951; McNiece and Thornton, Automobile Accident Prevention and Compensation, 1952, 27 N. Y.U.L.Rev. 585; Green, The Individual's Protection Under Negligence Law: Risk Sharing, 1953, 47 Northwestern U.L.Rev. 751; James, The Columbia Study of Compensation Law for Automobile Accidents: An Unanswered Challenge, 1959, 59 Col.L. Rev. 408; James and Low, Compensation for Auto Accident Victims: A Story of Too Little and Too Late, 1952, 26 Conn.Bar J. 70; Morris, Torts, 1953, 353 ff.; Marx, The Case for Compulsory Automobile Compensation Insurance, 1954, 15 Ohio St.L.J. 134; McVay, The Case Against Compulsory Automobile Compensation Insurance, 1954, 15 Ohio St. L.J. 150; Ehrenzweig, "Full Aid" Insurance, 1954; Ryan and Greene, The Strange Philosophy of "Pedestrianism," 1956, 42 A.B.A.J. 117; Green, Traffic Victims—Tort Law and Insurance, 1958.

59. See supra, § 84.

60. See supra, § 70.

61. The leading proponent of this argument is still Ehrenzweig, Negligence Without Fault, 1951. There is a good discussion of it in Malone, This Brave New World—A Review of "Negligence Without Fault," 1951, 25 So.Cal.L.Rev. 14.

62. See Lilly, Criticism of the Proposed Solution, 1932, 32 Col.L.Rev. 803; Sherman, Grounds for Opposing the Automobile Accident Compensation Plan, 1936, 3 Law & Con.Prob. 598; McVay, The Case Against Compulsory Liability Insurance, 1954, 15 Ohio St.L.J. 150; Ryan and Greene, Pedestrianism: A Strange Philosophy, 1956, 42 A.B.A.J. 117, 183; Greene, Must We Discard Our Law of Negligence

an initial step in the direction of the "welfare state." They have insisted that no innocent man, or his insurer, should be required to pay for injuries which are in no way his fault. Workmen's compensation has been distinguished, upon the basis of the pre-existing relation between employer and workman, which does not exist between driver and victim, and the much greater simplicity of actuarial calculations of prospective losses in terms of the time the workman will lose from his employment, where he is necessarily employed— which is not true of the automobile victim. That ancient bugaboo of tort law, the danger of false claims, has arisen again, and is said to be much greater in automobile cases than in industrial accidents, where investigation of the facts is normally quite simple and easy; and so likewise has the invitation to carelessness on the highway on the part of an insured driver who knows that the result will be no worse from his own point of view than if he were careful.

Cost

The main dispute, however, has raged around the cost of the compulsory insurance necessary to any compensation plan. It is of course extremely easy to say, in theory, that an insured defendant is not required to pay the compensation himself, and that his liability is conveniently distributed among a large group by insurance premiums. But in saying this, we must not lose sight of the fact that the group as a group still have to pay. If the entire group are to be saddled with a new and extensive liability, and if the premiums are prohibitive, the objection that the cost of the plan is too high is by no means answered. With the annual increase in the accident rate, liability insurance premiums, even under the present system, have risen steadily to higher figures, until they are now a real and serious

obstacle to adequate coverage, or even any coverage at all, even on the part of those who really want it. There is many a man who now pays more every year for liability insurance than he paid for the first second-hand car that he ever bought. What will a compensation plan do to premium rates that are already too high?

This has been a matter of violent dispute, in the legislatures and elsewhere. In 1932 the Columbia Report estimated that its compensation plan could be put into operation in New York with only a relatively slight increase in the rates. This was promptly challenged by Lilly [63] as hopelessly optimistic. In 1950 a report of a committee of the North Dakota legislature [64] estimated that the Saskatchewan Plan, if adopted in that state, would cost almost twice as much as in Saskatchewan with state insurance, and from two to three times as much with private insurance carriers. In 1954 a former member of the Columbia Committee thought that the same plan could be put into effect in Ohio with an increase of only $19 per automobile.[65] This was vigorously disputed by the president of a group of insurance companies,[66] who contended that with seven times the population of Saskatchewan living in one-sixth the area, with more than twenty times as many automobiles, with several large cities, and with hilly driving conditions instead of the plains, the existing Ohio rates would have to be multiplied by at least two or three, and possibly as much as five or six. He also pointed out that, as of April 1, 1953, the Saskatchewan state fund had a taxpayers' deficit of $1,600,000. These dif-

in Personal Injury Cases, 1958, 19 Ohio St.L.J. 290; Kilroe, Necessity for Preservation of the Judicial Process in the Interests of Persons Injured in Automobile Accidents, 1953, 25 N.Y.State Bar Bull. 315, 324.

63. Lilly, Criticism of the Proposed Solution, 1932, 32 Col.L.Rev. 803.

64. North Dakota Legislature, Report on Automobile Liability Insurance, 1950.

65. Marx, Compensation Insurance for Automobile Accident Victims, 1954, 15 Ohio St.L.J. 134, 142–144.

66. McVay, Reply to "The Case for Compulsory Automobile Compensation Insurance," 1954, 15 Ohio St. L.J. 161.

ferent guesses at least indicate the range of the dispute. The one thing upon which there appears to be general, if tacit, agreement is that strict liability for all accidents upon the basis of our present rules of damages, with compulsory insurance, but without a compensation schedule limiting the recovery, would result in quite prohibitive rates.

The plain truth of the matter appears to be that no one knows what the cost would be. It is very likely that the insurance companies have made their own estimates, but if so they have not released them to the public. As has been well pointed out,[67] their actuarial processes are not very well set up for the calculation of new risks beyond the limits of their policies; and it may be that even they can only guess. There may be no way to find out except to try it, as was done in Saskatchewan. This remains the major obstacle to the adoption of any automobile compensation plan.

It must be said in all candor, that there are few states in which the adoption of an automobile accident compensation plan appears to be very imminent. Meanwhile the acci-

dent rate continues to mount every year, the victims remain uncompensated, and the social cost of caring for them becomes greater. There is much objection to the increased cost to the motorist of the higher insurance premium; little is expressed to the cost to taxpayers and others who have in no way contributed to the injury, of caring for the injured when the motorist does not. The cost is there, in either case; the question is simply one of who shall bear it. The agitation for a remedy has steadily increased; more books and articles are being written; more groups and organizations are becoming first interested and then convinced; legislative and foundation studies are being made again; more lawyers and legislators swing over every year in support; the pressure increases slowly but steadily in terms of ounces to the square inch. It is no mere speculation that sooner or later something will have to crack. Sooner or later, perhaps in a year of political overturn, a number of radically minded legislatures will come to the conclusion that, whatever the cost of automobile accident compensation may be, it is one that will have to be borne by the driver, because the cost of the present system in ruined human lives exceeds it.

67. In Morris, Enterprise Liability and the Actuarial Process—The Insignificance of Foresight, 1961, 70 Yale L.J. 550.

CHAPTER 15

NUISANCE

86. MEANING OF NUISANCE

There is perhaps no more impenetrable jungle in the entire law than that which surrounds the word "nuisance." It has meant all things to all men,[1] and has been applied indiscriminately to everything from an alarming advertisement[2] to a cockroach baked in a pie.[3] There is general agreement that it is incapable of any exact or comprehensive definition.[4] Few terms have afforded so excellent an illustration of the familiar tendency of the courts to seize upon a catchword as a substitute for any analysis of a problem; the defendant's interference with the plaintiff's interests is characterized as a "nuisance," and there is nothing more to be said. With this reluctance of the opinions to assign any particular meaning to the word, or to get to the bottom of it, there has been a rather astonishing lack of any full consideration of "nuisance" on the part of legal writers.[5] It was not until the publication of the Restatement of Torts[6] in 1939 that there was any really significant attempt to determine some definite limits to the types of tort liability which are associated with the name.

History

Most of this vagueness, uncertainty and confusion has been due to the fact that the word "nuisance," which in itself means no more than hurt, annoyance or inconvenience,[7] has come by a series of historical ac-

1. "*   *   * many wrongs are indifferently termed nuisance or something else, at the convenience or whim of the writer. Thus, injuries to ways, to private lands, various injuries through negligence, wrongs harmful to the physical health, disturbances of the peace, and numberless other things are often or commonly spoken of as nuisances while equally they are called by the other name, and the other name may include other things also which are not nuisances." Bishop, Non-Contract Law, 1889, § 411, note 1. See Smith, Torts Without Particular Names, 1921, 69 U.Pa.L.Rev. 91, 110–112.

   As to the difficulties which the English courts and writers have had with the term, see Newark, The Boundaries of Nuisance, 1949, 65 L.Q.Rev. 480; Winfield, Nuisance as a Tort, 1931, 4 Camb.L.J. 189; Paton, Liability for Nuisance, 1942, 37 Ill.L. Rev. 1.

2. Commonwealth v. Cassidy, 1865, 6 Phila, Pa., 82.

3. Carroll v. New York Pie Baking Co., 1926, 215 App.Div. 240, 213 N.Y.S. 553.

4. "It is indeed impossible, having regard to the wide range of subject-matter embraced under the term nuisance, to frame any general definition. *   *   *" Garrett and Garrett, Law of Nuisances, 3d Ed. 1908, 4; Winfield, Law of Tort, 1937, 462; Cooley, Torts, 2d Ed. 1888, 672; Terry, Leading Principles of Anglo-American Law, 1884, § 434.

5. Both Wood, Law of Nuisances, 3d Ed. 1893, and Garrett and Garrett, Law of Nuisances, 3d Ed. 1908, are of dubious value. Of the scanty literature on the subject, the following are helpful as general discussion: Winfield, Nuisance as a Tort, 1931, 4 Camb.L.J. 189; Winfield, Law of Tort, 5th Ed. 1950, ch. 18; Smith, Reasonable Use as Justification for Damage to Neighbor, 1917, 17 Col.L.Rev. 383; Paton, Liability for Nuisance, 1942, 37 Ill.L. Rev. 1.

   See also, as to the law of particular states, Kenworthy, The Private Nuisance Concept in Pennsylvania, 1949, 54 Dick.L.Rev. 109; Leesman, Private Nuisances, in Illinois, 1930, 24 Ill.L.Rev. 876; Notes, 1934, 29 Ill.L.Rev. 372; 1947, 95 U.Pa.L.Rev. 781; 1941, 13 Miss.L.Rev. 224.

6. Restatement of Torts, §§ 822–840.

7. The word is distantly derived from the Latin *nocumentum*, by way of the French *nuisance*. Thus

cidents to cover the invasion of different kinds of interests, and of necessity to refer to various kinds of conduct on the part of the defendant. The word first emerges in English law to describe interferences with servitudes or other rights to the free use of land. It became fixed in the law as early as the thirteenth century with the development of the assize of nuisance, which was a criminal writ affording incidental civil relief, designed to cover invasions of the plaintiff's land due to conduct wholly on the land of the defendant. This was superseded in time by the more convenient action on the case for nuisance, which became the sole common law action.[8] The remedy was limited strictly to interference with the use or enjoyment of land,[9] and thus was the parent of the law of private nuisance as it stands today.

Parallel with this civil remedy protecting rights in land, there developed an entirely separate principle, that an infringement of the rights of the crown, or of the general public, was a crime. The earliest cases appear to have involved purprestures, which were encroachments upon the royal domain or the public highway, and might be redressed by a suit by the crown.[10] There was enough of a superficial resemblance between the blocking of a private right of way and the blocking of a public highway to keep men contented with calling the latter a nuisance

as well; and "thus was born the public nuisance, that wide term which came to include obstructed highways, lotteries, unlicensed stage-plays, common scolds, and a host of other rag ends of the law." [11] By the time of Edward III the principle had been extended to such things as interference with a market, smoke from a lime-pit, and diversion of water from a mill, and by analogy the word "nuisance," which still had acquired no very definite meaning, was carried over and applied rather loosely to these matters too.[12] By degrees the class of offenses recognized as "common nuisances" was greatly enlarged, until it came to include any "act not warranted by law, or omission to discharge a legal duty, which inconveniences the public in the exercise of rights common to all Her Majesty's subjects." [13] The remedy remained exclusively a criminal one until the sixteenth century, when it was recognized that a private individual who had suffered special damage might have a civil action in tort for the invasion of the public right.[14]

Public and Private Nuisance

These two lines of development, the one narrowly restricted to the invasion of interests in the use or enjoyment of land, and the other extending to virtually any form of annoyance or inconvenience interfering with common public rights, have led to the prevailing uncertainty as to what a nuisance is. A private nuisance is a civil wrong, based on a disturbance of rights in land.[15] The rem-

---

in the Statute of Bridges, 22 Hen. VIII, ch. 5, the word used is "annoyance."

8. The history is traced in Winfield, Nuisance as a Tort, 1931, 4 Camb.L.J. 189; Winfield, Law of Tort, 5th Ed. 1950, ch. 18; 1 Street, The Foundations of Legal Liability, 1906, 213; Newark, The Boundaries of Nuisance, 1949, 65 L.Q.Rev. 480; McRae, Development of Nuisance in the Early Common Law, 1948, 1 U.Fla.L.Rev. 27.

9. Thus the action on the case for nuisance was always local in character. Warren v. Webb, 1808, 1 Taunt. 379, 127 Eng.Rep. 880.

10. Garrett and Garrett, Law of Nuisances, 3d Ed. 1908, 1. Modern examples of purprestures are Adams v. Commissioners of Town of Trappe, 1954, 204 Md. 165, 102 A.2d 830; Long v. New York Central R. Co., 1929, 248 Mich. 437, 227 N.W. 739; Sloan v. City of Greenville, 1959, 235 S.C. 277, 111 S.E.2d 573.

11. Newark, The Boundaries of Nuisance, 1949, 65 L.Q.Rev. 480, 482.

12. Garrett and Garrett, Law of Nuisances, 3d Ed. 1908, 2; Jeudwine, Tort, Crime, and Police in Mediaeval Britain, 1917, 218.

13. Stephen, General View of the Criminal Law of England, 1890, 105.

14. 8 Holdsworth, History of English Law, 2d Ed. 1937, 424–425; 1535, Y.B. 27 Hen. VIII, Mich., pl. 10; Williams's Case, 1595, 5 Co.Rep. 73a, 77 Eng. Rep. 164; Fineux v. Hovenden, 1598, Cro.Eliz. 664, 78 Eng.Rep. 902; Fowler v. Sanders, Cro.Jac. 446, 79 Eng.Rep. 382.

15. See infra, § 89.

edy for it lies in the hands of the individual whose rights have been disturbed. A public or common nuisance, on the other hand, is a species of catch-all criminal offense, consisting of an interference with the rights of the community at large,[16] which may include anything from the obstruction of a highway to a public gaming-house or indecent exposure.[17] As in the case of other crimes, the normal remedy is in the hands of the state. The two have almost nothing in common, except that each causes inconvenience to someone,[18] and it would have been for-

tunate if they had been called from the beginning by different names. Add to this the fact that a public nuisance may also be a private one, when it interferes with the enjoyment of land,[19] and that even apart from this there are circumstances in which a private individual may have a tort action for the public offense itself,[20] and it is not difficult to explain the existing confusion.

If "nuisance" is to have any meaning at all, it is necessary to dismiss a considerable number of cases [21] which have applied the term to matters not connected either with land or with any public right, as mere aberration, adding to the vagueness of an already uncertain word. Unless the facts can be brought within one of the two categories mentioned there is not, with any accurate use of the term, a nuisance.[22]

87. BASIS OF LIABILITY

Another fertile source of confusion is the fact that nuisance is a field of tort liability, rather than a type of tortious conduct. It has reference to the interests invaded, to the damage or harm inflicted, and not to any particular kind of act or omission which has led to the invasion.[23] The attempt frequently made to distinguish between nuisance and negligence,[24] for example, is based upon an entirely mistaken emphasis upon what the defendant has done rather than the result

---

16. Salmond, Law of Torts, 8th Ed. 1934, 233. "Public nuisances may be considered as offenses against the public by either doing a thing which tends to the annoyance of all the King's subjects, or by neglecting to do a thing which the common good requires." Russell, Crimes and Misdemeanors, 8th Ed. 1923, 1691.

17. A very good case on the distinction between the two is Mandell v. Pivnick, 1956, 20 Conn.Sup. 99, 125 A.2d 175, which found neither. Plaintiff was injured by a defectively installed awning on defendant's building. It was held that no private nuisance was pleaded, because there was no allegation of any interference with rights in land; and no public nuisance, because there was no allegation that the awning interfered with the public highway, or with plaintiff's rights as a member of the general public.

In accord is Radigan v. W. J. Halloran Co., 1963, 97 R.I. 122, 196 A.2d 160 (personal injury from negligent operation of a crane).

18. "Public and private nuisances are not in reality two species of the same genus at all. There is no generic concept which includes the crime of keeping a common gaming-house and the tort of allowing one's trees to overhang the land of a neighbor." Salmond, Law of Torts, 8th Ed. 1934, 233.

"What generic conception, it has been asked, connects public nuisances like the woman who is a common scold, or the boy who fires a squib, with private nuisances like blocking up the ancient lights of a building or excessive playing on the piano? The only link which we can suggest is inconvenience, and loose as this term is, it is probably the best that can be offered. At any rate, be the ground of the distinction what it may, the distinction itself cannot be cast aside without departing from settled legal terminology, and ignoring not only the fact that a public nuisance may become a private one but also the very practical consequence of the distinction which is that a public nuisance is a crime while a private nuisance is a tort." Winfield, Law of Tort, 1937, 466.

19. See infra, p. 589.

20. See infra, p. 586.

21. For example, Carroll v. New York Pie Baking Co., 1926, 215 App.Div. 240, 213 N.Y.S. 553.

22. Mandell v. Pivnick, 1956, 20 Conn.Sup. 99, 125 A. 2d 175; Dahlstrom v. Roosevelt Mills, Inc., 1967, 27 Conn.Sup. 355, 238 A.2d 431.

23. Restatement of Torts, Scope and Introductory Note to chapter 40, preceding § 822; Peterson v. King County, 1954, 45 Wash.2d 860, 278 P.2d 774.

24. See Hogle v. H. H. Franklin Mfg. Co., 1910, 199 N.Y. 388, 92 N.E. 794; Bell v. Gray-Robinson Const. Co., 1954, 265 Wis. 652, 62 N.W.2d 390; Winfield, Law of Tort, 5th Ed. 1950, § 138; Lowndes, Contributory Negligence, 1934, 22 Geo.L.J. 674, 697; Note, 1915, 1 Corn.L.Q. 55.

which has followed, and forgets completely the well established fact that negligence is merely one type of conduct which may give rise to a nuisance.[25] The same is true as to the attempted distinction between nuisance and strict liability for abnormal activities, which has plagued the English [26] as well as the American courts.

Again the confusion is largely historical. Early cases of private nuisance seem to have assumed that the defendant was strictly liable, and to have made no inquiry as to the nature of his conduct. As late as 1705, in a case where sewage from the defendant's privy percolated into the cellar of the plaintiff's adjoining house, Chief Justice Holt considered it sufficient that it was the defendant's wall and the defendant's filth, because "he was bound of common right to keep his wall so his filth would not damnify his neighbor." [27] Over a period of years the general modifications of the theory of tort liability to which reference has been made above [28] have included private nuisance. Today liability for nuisance may rest upon an intentional invasion of the plaintiff's interests, or a negligent one, or conduct which is abnormal and out of place in its surroundings, and so falls fairly within the principle of strict liability. With very rare exceptions, there is no liability unless the case can be fitted into one of these familiar categories.[29]

Any of the three types of conduct may result in liability for a private nuisance.[30] By far the greater number of such nuisances are intentional. Occasionally they proceed from a malicious desire to do harm for its own sake; [31] but more often they are intentional merely in the sense that the defendant has created or continued the condition causing the nuisance with full knowledge that the harm to the plaintiff's interests is substantially certain to follow.[32] Thus a defendant who continues to spray chemicals into the air after he is notified that they are blown onto the plaintiff's land is to be regarded as intending that result,[33] and the same is true when he knows that he is contaminating the plaintiff's water supply with his slag refuse,[34] or that blown sand from the land he is improving is ruining the paint on the plaintiff's house.[35] If there is no reasonable justifica-

---

25. See infra, notes 37–44.

26. See Winfield, Law of Tort, 5th Ed.1950, § 143; Newark, The Boundaries of Nuisance, 1949, 65 L.Q. Rev. 480.

27. Tenant v. Goldwin, 1705, 1 Salk. 360, 91 Eng.Rep. 314, adding, "and that it was a trespass [the action was on the case] on his neighbor, as if his beasts should escape, or one should make a great heap upon his ground, and it should tumble and fall down upon his neighbor's." See also Sutton v. Clarke, 1815, 6 Taunt. 29, 44, 128 Eng.Rep. 943; Humphries v. Cousins, 1877, 2 C.P.D. 239, 46 L.J.C. P. 438.

28. Supra, p. 17. See 8 Holdsworth, History of English Law, 2d Ed. 1937, 446–459.

29. Wright v. Masonite Corp., M.D. N.C.1965, 237 F. Supp. 129 affirmed 368 F.2d 661, cert. denied 386 U.S. 934; Power v. Village of Hibbing, 1930, 182

Minn. 66, 233 N.W. 597; Schindler v. Standard Oil Co. of Ind., 1921, 207 Mo.App. 190, 232 S.W. 735; Rose v. Socony Vacuum Corp., 1934, 54 R.I. 411, 173 A. 627; Ettl v. Land & Loan Co., 1939, 122 N.J.L. 401, 5 A.2d 689.

30. See the excellent discussion in Taylor v. City of Cincinnati, 1944, 143 Ohio St. 426, 55 N.E.2d 724. Also Rose v. Standard Oil Co. of N. Y., 1936, 56 R. I. 272, 185 A. 251, reargument denied, 1936, 56 R.I. 472, 188 A. 71.

31. See for example the spite fence cases, infra, p. 598. Also Medford v. Levy, 1888, 31 W.Va. 649, 8 S.E. 302; Smith v. Morse, 1889, 148 Mass. 407, 19 N.E. 393; Christie v. Davey, [1893] 1 Ch. 316; Hollywood Silver Fox Farm v. Emmett, [1936] 2 K.B. 468; Collier v. Ernst, 1941, 31 Del.Co., Pa., 49. See Friedmann, Motive in the English Law of Nuisance, 1954, 40 Va.L.Rev. 583.

32. See supra, § 8.

33. Vaughn v. Missouri Power & Light Co., Mo.App. 1935, 89 S.W.2d 699; Smith v. Staso Milling Co., 2 Cir. 1927, 18 F.2d 736; Jost v. Dairyland Power Cooperative, 1969, 45 Wis.2d 164 172 N.W.2d 647. Cf. Morgan v. High Penn Oil Co., 1953, 238 N.C. 185, 77 S.E.2d 682; E. Rauh & Sons Fertilizer Co. v. Shreffler, 6 Cir. 1943, 139 F.2d 38. See Note, 1955, 8 Vand.L.Rev. 921.

34. Burr v. Adam Eidemiller, Inc., 1956, 386 Pa. 416, 126 A.2d 403.

35. Waters v. McNearney, 1959, 8 App.Div.2d 13, 185 N.Y.S.2d 29, affirmed, 1960, 8 N.Y.2d 808, 202 N.Y. S.2d 24, 168 N.E.2d 255.

tion for such conduct,[36] it is tortious and subjects him to liability.

But a nuisance may also result from conduct which is merely negligent, where there is no intent to interfere in any way with the plaintiff, but merely a failure to take precautions against a risk apparent to a reasonable man. The defendant may, for example, carry on some entirely proper activity, such as burying dead animals,[37] firing his furnace,[38] or constructing a water main in the street,[39] without reasonable care against the stench or smoke or flow of water which may follow.[40] In particular, negligence is the usual basis of liability where the defendant is doing something authorized by the legislature,[41] or, without knowledge that anything is wrong, he has merely failed to inspect and repair his premises,[42] or he has

only failed to discover [43] or to repair or abate [44] a condition which he has not created, but which is under his control.

Finally, a nuisance may arise where the defendant carries on in an inappropriate place an abnormally dangerous activity such as blasting,[45] or the storage of explosives; [46] or where an enterprise such as a plant manufacturing carbon black,[47] or a stockyards and slaughterhouse,[48] or a workhouse from which

---

(percolation of petroleum products). Cf. Coates v. Chinn, 1958, 51 Cal.2d 304, 332 P.2d 289 (trees dropping limbs onto public highway).

43. City of Phoenix v. Harlan, 1953, 75 Ariz. 290, 255 P.2d 609; Terrell v. Alabama Water Service Co., 1943, 245 Ala. 68, 15 So.2d 727; Tennessee Coal, Iron & R. Co. v. Hartline, 1943, 244 Ala. 116, 11 So.2d 833; Maynard v. Carey Const. Co., 1939, 302 Mass. 530, 19 N.E.2d 304; Monzolino v. Grossman, 1933, 111 N.J.L. 325, 168 A. 673.

44. Cf. Lamb v. Roberts, 1916, 196 Ala. 679, 72 So. 309; Peterson v. King County, 1954, 45 Wash.2d 860, 278 P.2d 774; Griffith v. Lewis, 1885, 17 Mo. App. 605; Schindler v. Standard Oil Co., 1921, 207 Mo.App. 190, 232 S.W. 735; see Huntsman v. Smith, 1957, 62 N.M. 457, 312 P.2d 103; Friedmann, Incidence of Liability for Nuisance, 1940, 4 Mod.L. Rev. 139.

As to the relation of nuisance to negligence, see Friedmann, Nuisance, Negligence and the Overlapping of Torts, 1940, 3 Mod.L.Rev. 305; Note, 1935, 23 Cal.L.Rev. 427.

45. Patrick v. Smith, 1913, 75 Wash. 407, 134 P. 1076; Beecher v. Dull, 1928, 294 Pa. 17, 143 A. 498; Longtin v. Persell, 1904, 30 Mont. 306, 76 P. 699; Gossett v. Southern R. Co., 1905, 115 Tenn. 376, 89 S.W. 737; Opal v. Material Service Corp., 1956, 9 Ill.App.2d 433, 133 N.E.2d 733.

46. Liber v. Flor, 1966, 160 Colo. 7, 415 P.2d 332; Cumberland Torpedo Co. v. Gaines, 1923, 201 Ky. 88, 255 S.W. 1046; Bradford Glycerine Co. v. St. Mary's Woolen Mfg. Co., 1899, 60 Ohio St. 560, 54 N.E. 528; Laflin & Rand Powder Co. v. Tearney, 1890, 131 Ill. 322, 23 N.E. 389. Cf. Whittemore v. Baxter Laundry Co., 1914, 181 Mich. 564, 148 N.W. 437 (gasoline); Rider v. Clarkson, 1910, 77 N.J.Eq. 469, 78 A. 676 (vicious dog).

47. King v. Columbian Carbon Co., 5 Cir. 1946, 152 F.2d 636. Cf. Green v. General Petroleum Corp., 1928, 205 Cal. 328, 270 P. 952 (drilling oil well in city); Hauck v. Tidewater Pipe Line Co., 1893, 153 Pa. 366, 26 A. 644.

48. Sarraillon v. Stevenson, 1950, 153 Neb. 182, 43 N.W.2d 509.

---

36. See infra, p. 580.

37. Long v. Louisville & N. R. Co., 1908, 128 Ky. 26, 107 S.W. 203; Cumberland R. Co. v. Bays, 1913, 153 Ky. 159, 154 S.W. 929. Cf. Illinois Cent. R. Co. v. Grabill, 1869, 50 Ill. 241.

38. Cf. Dunsbach v. Hollister, 1888, 49 Hun 352, 2 N.Y.S. 94, affirmed, 1892, 132 N.Y. 602, 130 N.E. 1152. Also Miles v. A. Arena & Co., 1937, 23 Cal. App.2d 680, 73 P.2d 1260 (crop dusting; defendant "should have known" the chemical might drift); Bernard v. Whitefield Tanning Co., 1917, 78 N.H. 418, 101 A. 439; Schindler v. Standard Oil Co., 1921, 207 Mo.App. 190, 232 S.W. 735; Rose v. Standard Oil Co., 1936, 56 R.I. 272, 185 A. 251.

39. Interstate Sash & Door Co. v. City of Cleveland, 1947, 148 Ohio St. 325, 74 N.E.2d 239. Cf. Milstrey v. City of Hackensack, 1951, 6 N.J. 400, 79 A.2d 37; Reinhart v. Lancaster Area Refuse Authority, 1963, 201 Pa.Super. 614, 193 A.2d 670.

40. Cf. Bernard v. Whitefield Tanning Co., 1917, 78 N.H. 418, 101 A. 439 (failure to prevent discharge of anthrax bacteria into stream); Schindler v. Standard Oil Co., 1921, 207 Mo.App. 190, 232 S.W. 735 (pollution); Rose v. Standard Oil Co. of N. Y., 1936, 56 R.I. 272, 185 A. 251, reargument denied, 1936, 56 R.I. 472, 188 A. 71 (percolation of petroleum).

41. Jeffers v. Montana Power Co., 1923, 68 Mont. 114, 217 P. 652.

42. Schindler v. Standard Oil Co., 1921, 207 Mo.App. 190, 232 S.W. 735 (leaking water pipe); Rose v. Standard Oil Co. of N. Y., 1936, 56 R.I. 272, 185 A. 251, reargument denied, 1936, 56 R.I. 472, 188 A. 71

prisoners may easily escape [49] necessarily involves so great a risk to its surroundings that its location may be considered unreasonable, and a strict liability may be imposed. Attention has been called earlier [50] to the extent to which American courts have recognized such strict liability under the general vagueness of "nuisance."

There are relatively few situations in which it makes very much difference which basis of liability is to be relied on.[51] For this reason, and because the action on the case for nuisance was adequate to cover any of the three, the courts seldom have made the distinction, and have been content to say merely that a nuisance exists. Another reason for this has been the fact that the great majority of nuisance suits have been in equity, and concerned primarily with the prevention of future damage. Under such circumstances the original nature of the defendant's conduct frequently loses its importance, since his persistence, over the plaintiff's protest, in continuing conduct which may have been merely negligent or abnormal in its inception, is sufficient to establish its character as an intentional wrong.[52] In the usual

case, therefore, the problem is not discussed, but intent is the apparent basis of liability.[53]

In the field of public nuisance, the matter is somewhat complicated by the fact that many such nuisances are marked out by statute, and it is not necessary for the court to look further than the legislative declaration that the conduct is a criminal offense. Apart from such specific statutes, however, the same division exists.[54] Most public nuisances, such as the keeping of a disorderly house, or the odors from a fertilizer factory over half a town, are obviously intentional invasions of the rights of the public, and the same is of course true of the deliberate obstruction of the public highway,[55] or an encroachment upon it.[56] But a public nuisance may also arise through conduct which is merely negligent, such as failure to inspect and repair a sidewalk,[57] to guard against damage to the highway from heavy equipment,[58] to remove a

the creation of the risk may be called intentional, negligent, or abnormally dangerous activity, according to taste.

49. District of Columbia v. Totten, 1925, 55 U.S.App. D.C. 312, 5 F.2d 374, cert. denied 269 U.S. 562. Cf. Andrews v. Andrews, 1955, 242 N.C. 382, 88 S.E.2d 88, where defendant baited an artificial pond to attract wild geese, which destroyed plaintiff's crops.

50. Supra, p. 512. See, however, refusing to accept this as having any validity, Keeton, Trespass, Nuisance and Strict Liability, 1959, 59 Col.L.Rev. 457. Also the Note on absolute nuisance in Pennsylvania, 1947, 95 U.Pa.L.Rev. 781.

51. One is the situation where the defendant has not created the nuisance himself, supra, notes 43 and 44. Another involves the contributory negligence of the plaintiff. See infra, § 91.

52. An additional reason is the fact that in cases of private nuisance the risk of future damage may itself amount to a present interference with the enjoyment of land. Cumberland Torpedo Co. v. Gaines, 1923, 201 Ky. 88, 255 S.W. 1046 (fear of explosion); Fields v. Stokley, 1882, 99 Pa. 306 (fire hazard); cf. Everett v. Paschall, 1910, 61 Wash. 47, 111 P. 879 (fear of disease from hospital). In such cases the grounds of liability tend to merge, and

53. See for example the following, where the basis of liability is not stated, but the facts clearly indicate that the invasion was intentional in this sense: Phelps v. Winch, 1923, 309 Ill. 158, 140 N.E. 847; Stevens v. Rockport Granite Co., 1914, 216 Mass. 486, 104 N.E. 371; Stuhl v. Great Northern R. Co., 1917, 136 Minn. 158, 161 N.W. 501; Kennedy v. Frechette, 1924, 45 R.I. 399, 123 A. 146.

54. Taylor v. City of Cincinnati, 1944, 143 Ohio St. 426, 55 N.E.2d 724.

55. Hanson v. Hall, 1938, 202 Minn. 381, 279 N.W. 227; Flaherty v. Great Northern R. Co., 1944, 218 Minn. 488, 16 N.W.2d 553.

56. Curtis v. Kastner, 1934, 220 Cal. 185, 30 P.2d 26; Adams v. Commissioners of Town of Trappe, 1954, 204 Md. 165, 102 A.2d 830.

57. McFarlane v. City of Niagara Falls, 1928, 247 N. Y. 340, 160 N.E. 391; Reedy v. City of Pittsburgh, 1949, 363 Pa. 365, 69 A.2d 93. Cf. Khoury v. Saratoga County, 1935, 267 N.Y. 384, 196 N.E. 299 (dangerous highway); Downes v. Silva, 1937, 57 R.I. 343, 190 A. 42 (unguarded opening); City of Lincoln v. First Nat. Bank (1903) 67 Neb. 401, 93 N.W. 698 (defective coal hole).

58. Denny v. Garavaglia, 1952, 333 Mich. 317, 52 N. W.2d 521.

condition created by another,[59] or permitting a bridge to fall into a navigable stream.[60] When a private individual brings suit in such a case, the courts have spoken more or less indiscriminately of nuisance or negligence, with little reference to the relation between the two.[61] Finally, a public nuisance, like a private one, may be created by carrying on abnormal and inappropriate activities, such as the storage of explosives,[62] keeping vicious animals,[63] or shooting off fireworks in the streets,[64] which are properly a matter of strict liability.

Nuisance, in short, is not a separate tort in itself, subject to rules of its own. Nuisances are types of damage—the invasion of two quite unrelated kinds of interests, by conduct which is tortious because it falls into the usual categories of tort liability.[65]

Substantial Interference

Both public and private nuisances require some substantial interference with the interest involved.[66] Since nuisance is a common subject of equity jurisdiction,[67] the damage against which an injunction is asked is often merely threatened or potential; but even in such cases, there must be at least a threat of a substantial invasion of the plaintiff's interests.[68] The law does not concern itself with trifles, or seek to remedy all of the petty annoyances and disturbances of every day life in a civilized community. Thus it has been held that there is no nuisance arising from the mere unsightliness of the defendant's premises,[69] from roots and branches of a tree extending beyond a boundary line which do no harm,[70] from the temporary

---

59. Terrell v. Alabama Water Service Co., 1943, 245 Ala. 68, 15 So.2d 727; Hayes v. Brooklyn Heights R. Co., 1910, 200 N.Y. 183, 93 N.E. 469.

60. Piscataqua Nav. Co. v. New York, N. H. & H. R. Co., D.Mass.1898, 89 F. 362. Cf. Bush v. City of Norwalk, 1937, 122 Conn. 426, 189 A. 608 (slippery beam in school gymnasium).

61. See Hayes v. Brooklyn Heights R. Co., 1910, 200 N.Y. 183, 93 N.E. 469, making the distinction that the creation of an obstruction in the street is nuisance, but failure to remove it is negligence. There is nothing in the distinction; the nuisance is the same in either case, and the difference is merely between an intentional and a negligent invasion of the same public right.

62. McAndrews v. Collerd, 1880, 42 N.J.L. 189 (stored explosives); Schnitzer v. Excelsior Powder Mfg. Co., Mo.App.1912, 160 S.W. 282 (same).

63. King v. Kline, 1847, 6 Pa. 318; Browning v. Belue, 1928, 22 Ala.App. 437, 116 So. 509; Patterson v. Rosenwald, 1928, 222 Mo.App. 973, 6 S.W.2d 664.

64. Landau v. City of New York, 1904, 180 N.Y. 48, 72 N.E. 631; Jenne v. Sutton, 1881, 43 N.J.L. 257. Cf. Heller v. Smith, Iowa 1922, 188 N.W. 878, affirmed on rehearing, 1923, 196 Iowa 104, 194 N.W. 271.

65. Restatement of Torts, Scope and Introductory Note to Chapter 40, preceding § 822; Rose v. Standard Oil Co., 1936, 56 R.I. 272, 185 A. 251.

66. Thus even the legislature may not constitutionally declare a thing a nuisance when it does not interfere substantially with public or private interests. Yates v. City of Milwaukee, 1870, 10 Wall., U.S., 497, 19 L.Ed. 984; Boyd v. Board of Councilmen of Frankfort, 1903, 117 Ky. 199, 77 S.W. 669; Prior v. White, 1938, 132 Fla. 1, 180 So. 347; City of San Antonio v. Salvation Army, Tex.Civ.App. 1910, 127 S.W. 860, error refused.

67. See infra, p. 603.

68. Theil v. Cernin, 1955, 224 Ark. 854, 276 S.W.2d 677; McCann v. Chasm Power Co., 1914, 211 N.Y. 301, 105 N.E. 416; City of Richmond v. House, 1917, 177 Ky. 814, 198 S.W. 218; Cook v. City of Fall River, 1921, 239 Mass. 90, 131 N.E. 346; Gainey v. Folkman, D.Ariz.1954, 114 F.Supp. 231.

69. State Road Comm'n v. Oakes, 1966, 150 W.Va. 709, 149 S.E.2d 293; Livingston v. Davis, 1951, 243 Iowa 21, 50 N.W.2d 592; Feldstein v. Kammauf, 1956, 209 Md. 479, 121 A.2d 716; Crabtree v. City Auto Salvage Co., 1960, 47 Tenn.App. 616, 340 S.W. 2d 940; Vermont Salvage Corp. v. Village of St. Johnsbury, 1943, 113 Vt. 341, 34 A.2d 188.

In Mathewson v. Primeau, 1964, 64 Wash.2d 929, 395 P.2d 183, it was said that there was a trend toward the protection of aesthetic values, but it was by legislation and not by injunction.

Aesthetic considerations may, however, play an important part in determining reasonable use. See Parkersburg Builders Material Co. v. Barrack, 1937, 118 W.Va. 608, 191 S.E. 368, 192 S.E. 291; Noel, Unaesthetic Sights as Nuisance, 1939, 25 Corn.L.Q. 1; Note, 1937, 44 W.Va.L.Q. 58.

70. Grandona v. Lovdal, 1889, 70 Cal. 161, 11 P. 623; Smith v. Holt, 1939, 174 Va. 213, 5 S.E.2d 492;

muddying of a well,[71] or from an occasional unpleasant odor [72] or whiff of smoke.[73]

Where the invasion affects the physical condition of the plaintiff's land,[74] the substantial character of the interference is seldom in doubt. But where it involves mere personal discomfort or annoyance, some other standard must obviously be adopted than the personal tastes, susceptibilities and idiosyncracies of the particular plaintiff. The standard must necessarily be that of definite offensiveness, inconvenience or annoyance to the normal person in the community—[75] the nuisance must affect "the ordinary comfort of human existence as understood by the American people in their present state of enlightenment." [76] It is not a nuisance to ring a church bell, merely because it throws a hypersensitive individual into convulsions,[77]

to blow a whistle [78] or play croquet [79] or even baseball [80] where the noise affects the health of a nervous invalid, or to run a factory where the smoke aggravates the plaintiff's bronchitis,[81] or the vibration shakes down a rickety house.[82] Neither is a keg of spikes by the side of the road a public nuisance because it frightens an unduly skittish horse; [83]

Harndon v. Stultz, 1904, 124 Iowa 440, 100 N.W. 329.

71. Taylor v. Bennett, 1836, 7 C. & P. 329, 173 Eng. Rep. 146.

72. Jones v. Adler, 1913, 183 Ala. 435, 62 So. 777; Francisco v. Department of Institutions and Agencies, 1935, 13 N.J.Misc. 663, 180 A. 843; Thiel v. Cernin, 1955, 224 Ark. 854, 276 S.W.2d 677; cf. Wade v. Miller, 1905, 188 Mass. 6, 73 N.E. 849.

73. Holman v. Athens Empire Laundry Co., 1919, 149 Ga. 345, 100 S.E. 207. This may have been carried too far in Reynolds v. Community Fuel Co., 1949, 309 Ky. 716, 218 S.W.2d 950, where there appears to have been substantial noise and dust disturbing plaintiff's dwelling, but recovery was denied because most of the witnesses said that they would not have objected to it.

74. See infra, p. 591.

75. Restatement of Torts, § 822, Comment g. Compare the cases as to liability for negligent conduct causing abnormal mental disturbance, supra, p. 332.

76. Joyce, Nuisances, 1906, § 20; Everett v. Paschall, 1910, 61 Wash. 47, 111 P. 879. The customs of the community are to be taken into account. In a small Massachusetts town in 1905, poultry odors and noises were held not to be offensive to the ordinary citizen. Wade v. Miller, 1905, 188 Mass. 6, 73 N.E. 849.

77. Rogers v. Elliott, 1888, 146 Mass. 349, 15 N.E. 768. Accord: Dorsett v. Nunis, 1941, 191 Ga. 559, 13 S.E.2d 371 (church); Lord v. Dewitt, C.C.N.Y. 1902, 116 F. 713 (blasting; plaintiff had a weak heart); Gunther v. E. I. Du Pont de Nemours &

Co., N.D.W.Va.1957, 157 F.Supp. 25, appeal dismissed, 1958, 255 F.2d 710 (blasting; nervous woman frightened by noise); Myer v. Minard, La.App. 1945, 21 So.2d 72 (crowing rooster).

"Exceptionally nervous persons, or those whose refinement exceeds the standards of the 'American people in their present state of enlightenment,' as the Washington court put it, must seek refuge in sound proof rooms, if they can afford them, or take their chances of the padded cell." Lloyd, Noise as a Nuisance, 1934, 82 U.Pa.L.Rev. 567, 582.

78. Meeks v. Wood, 1918, 66 Ind.App. 594, 118 N.E. 591. The disturbing effect of a continued noise which is not unduly loud may, however, be enough to make it a nuisance. Kentucky & W. Va. Power Co. v. Anderson, 1941, 288 Ky. 501, 156 S.W.2d 857; Stodder v. Rosen Talking Mach. Co., 1922, 241 Mass. 245, 135 N.E. 251.

79. Akers v. Marsh, 1901, 19 App.D.C. 28. Accord: Wade v. Miller, 1905, 188 Mass. 6, 73 N.E. 849 (odor and noise from henhouse); Columbus Gaslight & Coke Co. v. Freeland, 1861, 12 Ohio St. 392 (factory odors); Meyer v. Kemper Ice Co., 1935, 180 La. 1037, 158 So. 378 (factory noise).

80. Warren Co. v. Dickson, 1938, 185 Ga. 481, 195 S. E. 568; Beckman v. Marshall, Fla.1956, 85 So.2d 552; Lieberman v. Township of Saddle River, 1955, 37 N.J.Super. 62, 116 A.2d 809.

81. Ladd v. Granite State Brick Co., 1894, 68 N.H. 185, 37 A. 1041. Accord: Aldridge v. Saxey, 1965, 242 Or. 238, 409 P.2d 184 (German shepherd dogs not a nuisance because plaintiff suffered from emphysema and was home all day); Erickson v. Hudson, 1952, 70 Wyo. 317, 249 P.2d 523 (allergy to creosote). Cf. Salvin v. North Brancepeth Coal Co., 1874 L.R. 9 Ch. 705 ("the damage must be such as can be shewn by a plain witness to a plain common juryman").

82. Cremidas v. Fenton, 1916, 223 Mass. 249, 111 N. E. 855. Accord: Henn v. Universal Atlas Cement Co., Ohio C.P. 1957, 144 N.E.2d 917 (blasting in farm area, causing non-damaging earth tremors). Cf. Hoare & Co. v. McAlpin & Sons, [1923] 1 Ch. 167, 92 L.J.Ch. 81.

83. Rozell v Northern Pac. R. Co., 1918, 39 N.D. 475, 167 N.W. 489. Cf. McMillan v. Kuehnle, 1909, 76 N.J.Eq. 256, 73 A. 1054, reversed on other grounds, 1911, 78 N.J.Eq. 251, 78 A. 185 (Sunday baseball

nor a door which occasionally opens onto the highway; [84] nor an occasional fall of ice and snow from a television tower,[85] nor a single call at people's houses by Jehovah's Witnesses.[86] The plaintiff cannot, by devoting his own land to an unusually sensitive use, such as a drive-in motion picture theatre easily affected by light,[87] make a nuisance out of conduct of the adjoining defendant which would otherwise be harmless. By the same token, the fact that there are people who are hardened to the discomfort will not prevent the existence of a nuisance affecting a normal person.[88] Fears and feelings common to

most of the community are to be considered; and the dread of contagion from a pesthouse, common to ordinary citizens, may make it a nuisance, although there is no foundation in scientific fact.[89]

It is sometimes said by courts [90] and writers [91] that a nuisance must involve the idea of continuance or recurrence over a considerable period of time. What is meant by this is not altogether clear. In many cases, of course, continuance or recurrence of the interference is necessary to cause any substantial harm.[92] In others, it is necessary as a

---

game); Phillips v. State, 1874, 7 Baxt., Tenn., 151 (slaughterhouse); King v. Tindall, 1837, 6 Ad. & El. 143, 112 Eng.Rep. 55 (obstruction of navigation); Jarvis v. Pinckney, 1836, 3 Hill, S.C., 123 (ship infected with cholera).

84. Rief v. Mountain States Tel. & Tel. Co., 1942, 63 Idaho 418, 120 P.2d 823.

85. State v. WOR–TV Tower, 1956, 39 N.J.Super. 583, 121 A.2d 764.

86. People v. Northum, 1940, 41 Cal.2d 284, 106 P.2d 433. Cf. Excelsior Baking Co. v. City of Northfield, 1956, 247 Minn. 387, 77 N.W.2d 188 (single calls by canvassers seeking to line up a delivery route for bakery goods).

87. Amphitheatres, Inc. v. Portland Meadows, 1948, 184 Or. 336, 198 P.2d 847; Sheridan Drive-In Theatre v. State, 1963, —— Wyo. ——, 384 P.2d 597; Belmar Drive-In Theatre Co. v. Illinois State Toll Highway Comm'n, 1966, 34 Ill.2d 544, 216 N.E.2d 788.

Accord, as to electrical interference: Eastern & South African Tel. Co. v. Cape Town Tramways Co., [1902] A.C. 381; Lake Shore & M. S. R. Co. v. Chicago, L. S. & S. B. R. Co., 1911, 48 Ind.App. 584, 92 N.E. 989, rehearing denied 48 Ind.App. 584, 95 N.E. 596; Postal Telegraph-Cable Co. v. Pacific Gas & Elec. Co., 1927, 202 Cal. 382, 260 P. 1101. Cf. Robinson v. Kilvert, 1889, 41 Ch.Div. 88 (sensitive photographic equipment).

The possibility should be noted, however, that if the defendant is aware of plaintiff's extra-sensitive use he may be liable for negligence, although not for nuisance. Bell v. Gray-Robinson Const. Co., 1954, 265 Wis. 652, 62 N.W.2d 390 (mink frightened by noisy machinery); Lahar v. Barnes, 1958, 353 Mich. 408, 91 N.W.2d 261 (same).

88. Powell v. Bentley & Gerwig Furn. Co., 1891, 34 W.Va. 804, 12 S.E. 1085; Cunningham v. Miller, 1922, 178 Wis. 220, 189 N.W. 531; Cumberland Corp. v. Metropoulos, 1922, 241 Mass. 491, 135 N.E.

693; Wheat Culvert Co. v. Jenkins, 1932, 246 Ky. 319, 55 S.W.2d 4; Board of Health of Lyndhurst Township v. United Cork Cos., 1934, 116 N.J.Eq. 4, 172 A. 347, affirmed, 1935, 117 N.J.Eq. 437, 176 A. 142.

89. Everett v. Paschall, 1910, 61 Wash. 47, 111 P. 879; City of Baltimore v. Fairfield Imp. Co., 1898, 87 Md. 352, 39 A. 1081; Cherry v. Williams, 1908, 147 N.C. 452, 61 S.E. 267; Stotler v. Rochelle, 1910, 83 Kan. 86, 109 P. 788; cf. Benton v. Pittard, 1944, 197 Ga. 843, 31 S.E.2d 6 (venereal disease clinic). See, however, Nicholson v. Connecticut Half-way House, Inc., 1966, 153 Conn. 507, 218 A.2d 383 (mere unfounded apprehension not enough in itself).

A tuberculosis hospital located in a proper place, instead of in the midst of a residential area, is not a nuisance. Board of Health v. North American Home, 1910, 77 N.J.Eq. 464, 78 A. 677; Jardine v. City of Pasadena, 1926, 199 Cal. 64, 248 P. 225.

90. See Cunard & Wife v. Antifyre, [1933] 1 K.B. 551, 557; McCalla v. Louisville & N. R. Co., 1909, 163 Ala. 107, 50 So. 971; United States v. Cohen, D.Mo.1920, 268 F. 420; Rogers v. Bond Bros., 1939, 279 Ky. 239, 130 S.W.2d 22. The statement was made in holding that a single instance of interference is not enough in Reese v. Wells, Mun.App.D.C. 1950, 73 A.2d 899; Ford v. Grand Union Co., 1934, 240 App.Div. 294, 270 N.Y.S. 162; Smillie v. Continental Oil Co., D.Colo.1954, 127 F.Supp. 508; Grover v. City of Manhattan, 1967, 198 Kan. 307, 424 P. 2d 256.

91. 1 Wood, Law of Nuisances, 3d ed. 1893, 33; Harper, Law of Torts, 1933, § 180; Bohlen, Studies in the Law of Torts, 1926, 413.

92. Taylor v. Bennett, 1836, 7 C. & P. 329, 173 Eng. Rep. 146; Jones v. Adler, 1913, 183 Ala. 435, 62 So. 777; Reese v. Wells, Mun.App.D.C.1950, 73 A.2d 899. Cf. Harnik v. Levine, 1953, 281 App.Div. 878, 120 N.Y.S.2d 62 (double parking), reversing, 1952, 202 Misc. 648, 115 N.Y.S.2d 25, which affirmed, 1951, 106 N.Y.S.2d 460.

ground for relief by injunction.[93] If the harm was not foreseeable in the first instance, some continuance of the defendant's conduct may be required to establish his intent and his liability; and the duration or frequency of the invasion may certainly bear upon the reasonableness of what he has done.[94] But in cases where the harm to the plaintiff has been instantaneous, although substantial, as where a powder magazine explodes,[95] it has been held that the plaintiff may maintain an action for damages for a nuisance; and likewise where the defendant has acted only briefly, as by setting off a single blast,[96] burying a dead cow,[97] or spraying his field with insecticide for twenty-five minutes.[98] A public nuisance may consist in a single prizefight[99] or indecent exposure.[1] The proper statement would therefore appear to be that the duration or recurrence of the interference is merely one—and not necessarily a conclusive—factor in determining whether the damage is so substantial as to amount to a nuisance.[2]

Reasonableness of Defendant's Conduct

The interference with the protected interest must not only be substantial, but it must also be unreasonable. "Life in organized society, and especially in populous communities, involves an unavoidable clash of individual interests. Practically all human activities, unless carried on in a wilderness, interfere to some extent with others or involve some risk of interference, and these interferences range from mere trifling annoyances to serious harms. It is an obvious truth that each individual in a community must put up with a certain amount of annoyance, inconvenience and interference, and must take a certain amount of risk in order that all may get on together. The very existence of organized society depends upon the principle of 'give and take, live and let live,' and therefore the law of torts does not attempt to impose liability or shift the loss in every case where one person's conduct has some detrimental effect on another. Liability is imposed only in those cases where the harm or risk to one is greater than he ought to be required to bear under the circumstances, at least without compensation."[3]

Where the basis of the nuisance is negligence, the reasonableness of the defendant's

---

93. Attorney-General v. Cambridge Consumers Gas. Co., 1868, L.R. 4 Ch. 71; Nelson v. Milligan, 1894, 151 Ill. 462, 38 N.E. 239.

94. See Garvey v. Long Island R. Co., 1899, 159 N.Y. 323, 54 N.E. 57; Herrlich v. New York Cent. & H. R. R. Co., 1910, 70 Misc. 115, 126 N.Y.S. 311; Harrison v. Southwark & Vauxhall Water Co., [1891] 2 Ch. 409, 413–414.

95. Heeg v. Licht, 1880, 80 N.Y. 579; Laflin & Rand Powder Co. v. Tearney, 1890, 131 Ill. 322, 23 N.E. 389; Fisher v. Western Fuse & Explosives Co., 1910, 12 Cal.App. 739, 108 P. 659. Cf. Midwood & Co. v. Mayor of Manchester, [1905] 2 K.B. 597 (electric main fused, causing gas explosion and fire).

96. Patrick v. Smith, 1913, 75 Wash. 407, 134 P. 1076. Accord, E. Rauh & Sons Fertilizer Co. v. Shreffler, 6 Cir. 1943, 139 F.2d 38 (single failure of defendant's apparatus); Ambrosini v. Alisal Sanitary District, 1957, 154 Cal.App.2d 720, 317 P.2d 33 (single overflow of sewer outfall line).

97. Long v. Louisville & N. R. Co., 1908, 128 Ky. 26, 107 S.W. 203. Cf. Yates v. Missouri Pac. R. Co., 1925, 168 Ark. 170, 269 S.W. 353 (burning carcasses for three days).

98. S. A. Gerrard Co. v. Fricker, 1933, 42 Ariz. 503, 27 P.2d 678.

99. Commonwealth v. McGovern, 1903, 116 Ky. 212, 75 S.W. 261.

1. Truet v. State, 1912, 3 Ala.App. 114, 57 So. 512, Cf. Cincinnati R. Co. v. Commonwealth, 1882, 80 Ky. 137 (obstruction of highway for one day); Hanson v. Hall, 1938, 202 Minn. 381, 279 N.W. 227 (stopping vehicle on highway).

2. Restatement of Torts, § 827, Comment b. "Thus, when it is said that the injury must be 'of a substantial character, not fleeting or evanescent,' apparently what is signified is that the temporary nature of the injury may be evidence, but certainly not conclusive evidence, that it is too trivial to be reckoned as a nuisance." Winfield, Law of Tort, 1st Ed. 1937, 473. See also Helms v. Eastern Kansas Oil Co., 1917, 102 Kan. 164, 168, 169 P. 208, 209; McCarty v. Natural Carbonic Gas Co., 1907, 189 N.Y. 40, 46–47, 81 N.E. 549, 550; and the dissenting (but not on this point) opinion of Pollock, C. B., in Bamford v. Turnley, 1862, 3 B. & S. 66, 122 Eng. Rep. 27.

3. Restatement of Torts, § 822, Comment j.

conduct is obviously in issue, and is determined by the familiar process of weighing the gravity and probability of the risk against the utility of his course.[4] But the same balance of interests is called into play when the interference is an intentional one. Each defendant is privileged, within reasonable limits, to make use of his own property or to conduct his own affairs at the expense of some harm to his neighbors. He may operate a factory whose noise and smoke cause some discomfort to others, so long as he keeps within reasonable bounds. It is only when his conduct is unreasonable, in the light of its utility and the harm which results, that it becomes a nuisance.[5] This privilege,[6] which is broader, more indefinite and more comprehensive than the specific privileges to interfere with the bodily security of another.[7] usually is expressed by saying that there is no liability for nuisance unless the defendant's conduct is unreasonable under the circumstances.

Most of the litigation in the field of nuisance has dealt with this ultimate question [8] of "reasonable use." The problem arises most frequently as to private nuisances, where the conflicting interests of landowners are involved;[9] but it also appears in cases of public nuisance. The obstruction of a highway caused by moving a house,[10] the smoke from an electric power plant,[11] and similar public inconveniences [12] are not nuisances where the harm is slight and the conduct reasonable. As it was said in an ancient case [13] in regard to candle-making in a town,

---

4. See supra, p. 148.

5. See McCarty v. Natural Carbonic Gas Co., 1907, 189 N.Y. 40, 46, 47, 81 N.E. 549, 550; Gulf, C. & S. F. R. Co. v. Oakes, 1900, 94 Tex. 155, 159–160, 58 S.W. 999, 1000; Meyer v. Kemper Ice Co., 1935, 180 La. 1037, 158 So. 378; Holman v. Athens Empire Laundry Co., 1919, 149 Ga. 345, 100 S.E. 207; Ebur v. Alloy Metal Wire Co., 1931, 304 Pa. 177, 155 A. 280.

6. Very few cases have considered the question whether reasonable use is matter of defense. It was held in Pawlowicz v. American Locomotive Co., 1915, 90 Misc. 450, 154 N.Y.S. 768; Canfield v. Quayle, 1939, 170 Misc. 621, 10 N.Y.S.2d 781; and Vestal v. Gulf Oil Corp., 1951, 149 Tex. 487, 235 S. W.2d 440, that the burden of pleading and proof of unreasonableness, as an essential element of nuisance, is on the plaintiff. Other cases have held the interference to be a prima facie nuisance, and the burden of proof of reasonable conduct to be on the defendant. Sexton v. Youngkau, 1924, 202 Ky. 256, 259 S.W. 335; Ohio Oil Co. v. Westfall, 1909, 43 Ind.App. 661, 88 N.E. 354; Pruner & Hubles v. Pendleton, 1881, 75 Va. 516. Cf. Holman v. Mineral Point Zinc Co., 1908, 135 Wis. 132, 115 N.W. 327.

It may be suggested that where the claim rests on negligence, unreasonable conduct should be proved by the plaintiff as in other negligence cases; but that where, as in the usual case, the interference is intentional, the burden should be on the defendant to justify the invasion.

7. See supra, ch. 4.

8. Well stated in Antonik v. Chamberlain, 1947, 81 Ohio App. 465, 78 N.E.2d 752; Louisville & Jefferson County Air Board v. Porter, Ky.1965, 397 S.W. 2d 146; see also Hannum v. Gruber, 1943, 346 Pa. 417, 31 A.2d 99; Roberts v. C. F. Adams & Son, 1947, 199 Okl. 369, 184 P.2d 634; Young v. Brown, 1948, 212 S.C. 156, 46 S.E.2d 673; Soukoup v. Republic Steel Corp., 1946, 78 Ohio App. 87, 66 N.E.2d 334.

"It is in the field of unreasonable use that the law of nuisance is operative. The ultimate question in each cause is whether the challenged use is reasonable in view of all the surrounding circumstances." Johnson v. Drysdale, 1939, 66 S.D. 436, 285 N.W. 301.

9. See infra, p. 596.

10. Graves v. Shattuck, 1857, 35 N.H. 257. Cf. Jones v. Hayden, 1941, 310 Mass. 90, 37 N.E.2d 243 (obstruction of sidewalk by bales of hay).

11. People v. Transit Development Co., 1909, 131 App.Div. 174, 115 N.Y.S. 297; Commonwealth v. Miller, 1890, 139 Pa. 77, 21 A. 138 (petroleum refinery; nuisance is a matter of locality); Commonwealth v. Upton, 1856, 6 Gray, Mass., 473 (changing surroundings).

12. King v. Tindall, 1827, 6 Ad. & El. 143, 112 Eng. Rep. 55 (obstruction of navigation); People v. Horton, 1876, 64 N.Y. 610 (same); Phillips v. State, 1874, 7 Baxt., Tenn., 151 (slaughterhouse near highway); City of Erie v. Gulf Oil Corp., 1959, 395 Pa. 383, 150 A.2d 351 (storage of petroleum products in quantity in commercial or industrial area); Excelsior Baking Co. v. City of Northfield, 1956, 247 Minn. 387, 77 N.W.2d 188 (initial calls of canvassers to line up delivery route for bakery products).

13. Mentioned in Stephen, General View of the Criminal Law of England, 1890, 106.

"Le utility del chose excusera le noisomeness del stink."

"Absolute" Nuisance

The emphasis which has been laid upon the invasion of the plaintiff's interests, rather than the defendant's conduct, has resulted in a half-developed notion that nuisance is a separate and peculiar variety of tort, and that some nuisances are "absolute," so that the defendant will be liable although he has acted reasonably in all respects. Sometimes this is expressed by saying that the condition or activity is a nuisance "per se," without regard to the care with which it is conducted or the circumstances under which it exists.[14]

In some types of cases, the conclusion that the nuisance is "absolute" rests upon the view of some courts that certain property rights and privileges, such as that of a riparian owner to the use of a stream in its "natural" condition,[15] of that of a landowner to make use of percolating or subterranean waters,[16] or particularly that of disposing of surface water,[17] are fixed and invariable, rather than relative. When the interests of landowners come into conflict, these courts seek some arbitrary rule which will give one complete protection at the expense of the other, as by holding that the lower riparian owner is entitled to the "natural flow" of the stream, and that any diversion which sub-

stantially interferes with it is a nuisance.[18] But the hardship and injustice to other owners becomes so apparent in such cases that these same courts, while ostensibly adhering to the rule laid down, often are compelled to retreat from such a position, and to recognize limitations upon rights and privileges in terms of reasonable use.[19] Except in the case of surface waters,[20] the prevailing view is that such property rights and privileges are not absolute, but relative, that there is no nuisance if the defendant has made a reasonable use of his property, and that any use which is unreasonable under the circumstances may be a nuisance.[21]

Usually the statement that a nuisance is "absolute" or "per se" means only that it does not arise out of negligent conduct. So far as the idea has any validity, it apparently

---

14. Evans v. Reading Chem. & Fert. Co., 1894, 160 Pa. 209, 28 A. 702 (fertilizer plant); Bartel v. Ridgefield Lumber Co., 1924, 131 Wash. 183, 229 P. 306 (sawmill); People v. Detroit White Lead Works, 1890, 82 Mich. 471, 46 N.W. 735 (lead works); Davis v. Niagara Falls Tower Co., 1902, 171 N.Y. 336, 64 N.E. 4 (tower shedding ice); Ducktown Sulphur, C. & I. Co. v. Barnes, Tenn.1900, 60 S.W. 593 (copper smelter).

15. See Kinyon, What Can a Riparian Proprietor Do, 1937, 21 Minn.L.Rev. 512.

16. See Clayberg, The Law of Percolating Waters, 1915, 14 Mich.L.Rev. 119; Huffcut, Percolating Waters: The Rule of Reasonable User, 1904, 13 Yale L.J. 222; MacArtor v. Graylyn Crest III Swim Club, Del.Ch.1963, 187 A.2d 417.

17. See Kinyon and McClure, Surface Waters, 1940, 24 Minn.L.Rev. 891; Note, 1962, 50 Ky.L.J. 254.

18. See for example Robertson v. Arnold, 1936, 182 Ga. 664, 186 S.E. 806; Roberts v. Martin, 1913, 72 W.Va. 92, 77 S.E. 535; Clark v. Pennsylvania R. Co., 1891, 145 Pa. 438, 22 A. 989; Exton v. Glen Gardner Water Co., 1925, 3 N.J.Misc. 613, 129 A. 255; Harvey Realty Co. v. Borough of Wallingford, 1930, 111 Conn. 352, 150 A. 60. See Kinyon, What Can a Riparian Proprietor Do, 1937, 21 Minn.L.Rev. 512, 517–522. There is a good review of all this in Harris v. Brooks, 1955, 225 Ark. 436, 283 S.W.2d 129.

19. See for example Southern Cal. Inv. Co. v. Wilshire, 1904, 144 Cal. 68, 77 P. 767; Nesalhous v. Walker, 1907, 45 Wash. 621, 88 P. 1032; Pennsylvania R. Co. v. Miller, 1886, 112 Pa. 34, 3 A. 780; Watkins Land Co. v. Clements, 1905, 98 Tex. 578, 86 S.W. 733; Helfrich v. Catonsville Water Co., 1891, 74 Md. 269, 22 A. 72.

20. As to surface waters, most of the states still adhere to either the civil law rule that the natural flow of surface water may not be interfered with (see Nininger v. Norwood, 1882, 72 Ala. 277), or the common law or "common enemy" rule, that a landowner may deal with surface water as he sees fit, regardless of the effect upon adjoining land (see Bowlsby v. Speer, 1865, 31 N.J.L. 351. An increasing minority of the jurisdictions have adopted the "reasonable use" doctrine expressly (see infra, p. 596), while others have accepted it in effect. See for example Keys v. Romley, 1966, 64 Cal.2d 396, 50 Cal.Rptr. 273, 412 P.2d 529. See Kinyon and McClure, Surface Waters, 1940, 24 Minn.L.Rev. 891; Note, 1962, 50 Ky.L.J. 254.

21. See infra, p. 596.

is restricted to three types of cases.[22] Certain public nuisances are designated specifically by statute. Within constitutional limitations, the declaration of the legislature is conclusive, and will preclude any inquiry into their unreasonable character.[23] In other cases the defendant is intentionally interfering for his own purposes with the plaintiff's interests, by maintaining something such as a fertilizer plant, a sawmill or a cesspool, which is clearly an unreasonable thing in view of its surroundings.[24] When the nature of the enterprise, its locality and the method of conducting it are reasonable in proportion to the resulting interference, the same courts have found that the same activity is not a nuisance at all.[25] Finally, nuisances which result from abnormal and unduly hazardous activities, such as the storage of explosives,[26] are said to be "absolute" in the sense that they do not require any intent to do harm, or any negligence. Even in such cases, however, the abnormal character of the enterprise itself will depend upon the place and the manner in which it is carried on, the harm which is inflicted or threatened, and the general utility of the defendant's conduct; and to this extent the question of reasonable use still is involved.[27]

When a court carries "absolute" nuisance beyond these limits,[28] it is saying in effect that certain property rights will be protected under any and all circumstances, and sooner or later may find itself compelled to retreat from such a generalization.

88. PUBLIC NUISANCE

No better definition of a public nuisance has been suggested than that of an act or omission "which obstructs or causes inconvenience or damage to the public in the exercise of rights common to all Her Majesty's subjects." [29] The term comprehends a miscellaneous and diversified group of minor criminal offenses, based on some interference with the interests of the community, or the comfort or convenience of the general public. It includes interferences with the public health, as in the case of a hogpen,[30] the keep-

---

22. Well stated in Taylor v. City of Cincinnati, 1944, 143 Ohio St. 426, 55 N.E.2d 724.

23. Harmison v. City of Lewiston, 1894, 153 Ill. 313, 38 N.E. 628 (slaughterhouse); City of Chicago v. Shaynin, 1913, 258 Ill. 69, 101 N.E. 224 (medical museum); Pompano Horse Club v. State, 1927, 93 Fla. 415, 111 So. 801 (horse racing); State v. Chicago, M. & St. P. R. Co., 1911, 114 Minn. 122, 130 N. W. 545 (burning soft coal). See Noel, Retroactive Zoning and Nuisances, 1941, 41 Col.L.Rev. 457.

24. See cases cited supra, p. 574.

25. Cf. Ebur v. Alloy Metal Wire Co., 1931, 304 Pa. 177, 155 A. 280; Gilbert v. Showerman, 1871, 23 Mich. 448; McCarty v. Natural Carbonic Gas Co., 1907, 189 N.Y. 40, 81 N.E. 549.

26. McAndrews v. Collerd, 1880, 42 N.J.L. 189; Schnitzer v. Excelsior Powder Mfg. Co., Mo.App. 1912, 160 S.W. 282; Cumberland Torpedo Co. v. Gaines, 1923, 201 Ky. 88, 255 S.W. 1046.

27. Cf. Heeg v. Licht, 1880, 80 N.Y. 579; In re Dilworth's Appeal, 1872, 91 Pa. 247; Tuckachinsky v.

Lehigh & W. Coal Co., 1901, 199 Pa. 515, 49 A. 308; Laflin & Rand Powder Co. v. Tearney, 1890, 131 Ill. 322, 23 N.E. 389; Burns v. Lamb, Tex.Civ.App.1958, 312 S.W.2d 730, ref. n. r. e.

28. A very slanted attempt at this is James, The Element of Fault in Private Nuisance, filed as a brief in (1970) Second Restatement of Torts, Tentative Draft No. 16, 132–157. All of the cases cited are clearly cases of intentional interference with the plaintiff's interests (see supra, p. 574), and the only question to be determined in any of them was whether such intentional interference was unreasonable—in other words, whether it was a nuisance at all. The writer, at least, has great difficulty in seeing what, if anything, this has to do with strict liability.

29. Stephen, General View of the Criminal Law of England, 1890, 105; Salmond, Law of Torts, 8th Ed. 1934, 233; Mayor and Council of Alpine v. Brewster, 1951, 7 N.J. 42, 80 A.2d 297.

"A common or public nuisance is the doing of or the failure to do something that injuriously affects the safety, health or morals of the public, or works some substantial annoyance, inconvenience or injury to the public." Commonwealth v. South Covington & C. St. R. Co., 1918, 181 Ky. 459, 463, 205 S.W. 581, 583, 6 A.L.R. 118; cf. City of Selma v. Jones, 1918, 202 Ala. 82, 83, 79 So. 476, 477.

30. Seigle v. Bromley, 1912, 22 Colo.App. 189, 124 P. 191; Gay v. State, 1891, 90 Tenn. 645, 18 S.W. 260.

ing of diseased animals,[31] or a malarial pond;[32] with the public safety, as in the case of the storage of explosives,[33] the shooting of fireworks in the streets,[34] harboring a vicious dog,[35] or the practice of medicine by one not qualified;[36] with public morals, as in the case of houses of prostitution,[37] illegal liquor establishments,[38] gambling houses,[39] indecent exhibitions,[40] bullfights,[41] unlicensed prize fights,[42] or public profanity;[43] with the public peace, as by loud and disturbing noises,[44] or an opera performance which threatens to cause a riot;[45] with the public comfort, as in the case of bad odors, smoke, dust and vibration;[46] with public convenience, as by obstructing a highway[47] or a navigable stream,[48] or creating a condition which makes

31. Durand v. Dyson, 1915, 271 Ill. 382, 111 N.E. 143; Fevold v. Board of Sup'rs of Webster County, 1926, 202 Iowa 1019, 210 N.W. 139. Cf. Rex v. Vantandillo, 1815, 4 M. & S. 73, 105 Eng.Rep. 762 (carrying child with smallpox along the highway).

32. Mills v. Hall & Richards, 1832, 9 Wend., N.Y., 315. Cf. Ajamian v. Township of North Bergen, 1968, 103 N.J.Super. 61, 246 A.2d 521, affirmed 107 N.J.Super. 175, 257 A.2d 726 (unsanitary conditions in tenement house).

33. State v. Excelsior Powder Mfg. Co., 1914, 259 Mo. 254, 169 S.W. 267; McAndrews v. Collerd, 1880, 42 N.J.L. 189.

34. Jenne v. Sutton, 1881, 43 N.J.L. 257; Landau v. City of New York, 1904, 180 N.Y. 48, 72 N.E. 631. Accord, Parker v. City of Fort Worth, Tex.Civ.App. 1955, 281 S.W.2d 721 (keeping and selling).

35. King v. Kline, 1847, 6 Pa. 318; Browning v. Belue, 1928, 22 Ala.App. 437, 116 So. 509; Patterson v. Rosenwald, 1928, 222 Mo.App. 973, 6 S.W.2d 664.

36. State v. Scopel, Mo.1958, 316 S.W.2d 515; State ex rel. Marron v. Compere, 1940, 44 N.M. 414, 103 P.2d 273.

37. Black v. Circuit Court of Eighth Judicial District, 1960, 78 S.D. 302, 101 N.W.2d 520; State v. Navy, 1941, 123 W.Va. 722, 17 S.E.2d 626; Tedescki v. Berger, 1907, 150 Ala. 649, 43 So. 960; People ex rel. Dyer v. Clark, 1915, 268 Ill. 156, 108 N.E. 994; State ex rel. Wilcox v. Ryder, 1914, 126 Minn. 95, 147 N.W. 953.

38. Brown v. Perkins, 1858, 12 Gray, Mass., 89; State v. Bertheol, 1843, 6 Blackf., Ind., 474.

39. State ex rel. Williams v. Karston, 1945, 208 Ark. 703, 187 S.W.2d 327; State ex rel. Johnson v. Hash, 1944, 144 Neb. 495, 13 N.W.2d 716; State ex rel. Leahy v. O'Rourke, 1944, 115 Mont. 502, 146 P.2d 168; State ex rel. Trampe v. Multerer, 1940, 234 Wis. 50, 289 N.W. 600. Compare, as to lotteries, State ex rel. Regez v. Blumer, 1940, 236 Wis. 129, 294 N.W. 491; State ex rel. Cowie v. La Crosse Theaters Co., 1939, 232 Wis. 153, 286 N.W. 707; Engle v. State, 1939, 53 Ariz. 458, 90 P.2d 988.

40. Weis v. Superior Court of San Diego County, 1916, 30 Cal.App. 730, 159 P. 464; Truet v. State, 1912, 3 Ala.App. 114, 57 So. 512. Cf. City of Chica-

go v. Shaynin, 1913, 258 Ill. 69, 101 N.E. 224; Adams v. Commonwealth, 1915, 162 Ky. 76, 171 S.W. 1006.

41. State v. Canty, 1907, 207 Mo. 439, 105 S.W. 1078.

42. Commonwealth v. McGovern, 1903, 116 Ky. 212, 75 S.W. 261.

43. State v. Chrisp, 1881, 85 N.C. 528; Wilson v. Parent, 1961, 228 Or. 354, 365 P.2d 72.

44. Rex v. Smith, 1725, 2 Stra. 704, 93 Eng.Rep. 795; People v. Rubenfeld, 1930, 254 N.Y. 245, 172 N.E. 485; Town of Davis v. Davis, 1895, 40 W.Va. 464, 21 S.E. 906. Cf. State v. Turner, 1942, 198 S.C. 487, 18 S.E.2d 372; McMillan v. Kuehnle, 1909, 76 N.J. Eq. 256, 73 A. 1054, reversed on other grounds, 1911, 78 N.J.Eq. 251, 78 A. 185 (Sunday baseball); Town of Preble v. Song Mountain, Inc., 1970, 62 Misc.2d 353, 308 N.Y.S.2d 1001 ("rock festival").

See Lloyd, Noise as a Nuisance, 1933, 82 U.Pa.L.Rev. 567.

45. Star Opera Co. v. Hylan, 1919, 109 Misc. 132, 178 N.Y.S. 179.

46. Transcontinental Gas Pipe Line Corp. v. Gault, 4 Cir. 1952, 198 F.2d 196; State v. Primeau, 1966, 70 Wash.2d 109, 422 P.2d 302; Potashnick Truck Service v. City of Sikeston, 1943, 351 Mo. 505, 173 S.W. 2d 96, transferred 157 S.W.2d 808; Soap Corp. of America v. Reynolds, 5 Cir. 1950, 178 F.2d 503; Bd. of Health of Lyndhurst Tp. v. United Cork Cos., 1934, 116 N.J.Eq. 4, 172 A. 347.

47. James v. Hayward, 1631, Cro.Car. 184, 79 Eng. Rep. 761; Harrower v. Ritson, 1861, 37 Barb., N.Y., 301; Pilgrim Plywood Corp. v. Melendy, 1938, 110 Vt. 12, 1 A.2d 700. Cf. Adams v. Commissioners of Town of Trappe, 1954, 204 Md. 165, 102 A.2d 830 (encroachment); Sloan v. City of Greenville, 1959, 235 S.C. 277, 111 S.E.2d 573 (enclosure by construction of an overhanging building); Salsbury v. United Parcel Service, 1953, 203 Misc. 1008, 120 N.Y.S.2d 33 (double parking).

48. Willard v. City of Cambridge, 1862, 3 Allen, Mass., 574; Piscataqua Nav. Co. v. New York, N. H. & H. R. Co., D.Mass.1898, 89 F. 362; Carver v. San Pedro, L. A. & S. L. R. Co., C.C.Cal.1906, 151 F. 334; Swain & Son v. Chicago, B. & Q. R. Co., 1912, 252 Ill. 622, 97 N.E. 247. See Waite, Public Rights to Use and Have Access to Navigable Waters, [1958] Wis.L.Rev. 335.

travel unsafe [49] or highly disagreeable,[50] or the collection of an inconvenient crowd; [51] and in addition, such unclassified offenses as eavesdropping on a jury,[52] or being a common scold.[53]

To be considered public, the nuisance must affect an interest common to the general public, rather than peculiar to one individu-

al,[54] or several.[55] Thus the pollution of a stream which merely inconveniences a number of riparian owners is a private nuisance only,[56] but it may become a public one if it kills the fish.[57] It is not necessary, however, that the entire community be affected, so long as the nuisance will interfere with those who come in contact with it in the exercise of a public right.[58] The most obvious illustration, of course, is the obstruction of a public highway, which inconveniences only those who are travelling upon it. It is, furthermore, rather obvious that any condition or activity which substantially interferes with the private interests of any considerable number of individuals in a community is very likely to interfere also with some public right, such as the comfortable use of the highway; [59] and for this reason the question

49. Lamereaux v. Tula, 1942, 312 Mass. 359, 44 N.E. 2d 789 (ice on sidewalk); State ex rel. Detienne v. City of Vandalia, 1906, 119 Mo.App. 406, 94 S.W. 1009 (noise frightening horse); Town of Newcastle v. Grubbs, 1908, 171 Ind. 482, 86 N.E. 757 (excavation); McFarlane v. City of Niagara Falls, 1928, 247 N.Y. 340, 160 N.E. 391 (defective sidewalk). It must, however, be travel on the public highway. Mandell v. Pivnick, 1956, 20 Conn.Sup. 99, 125 A.2d 175.

50. Town of Mount Pleasant v. Van Tassell, 1957, 7 Misc.2d 643, 166 N.Y.S.2d 458, affirmed, 1958, 6 App.Div.2d 880, 177 N.Y.S.2d 1010 (bad odors, rats and flies from piggery).

51. Lyons Sons & Co. v. Gulliver, [1914] 1 Ch. 631, Ann.Cas.1916B, 959; Shamhart v. Morrison Cafeteria, 1947, 159 Fla. 629, 32 So.2d 727, 2 A.L.R.2d 429; Tushbant v. Greenfield's, 1944, 308 Mich. 626, 14 N.W.2d 520; Shaw's Jewelry Shop v. New York Herald Co., 1915, 170 App.Div. 504, 156 N.Y.S. 651, affirmed, 1919, 224 N.Y. 731, 121 N.E. 890. See Notes, 1948, 26 Chicago-Kent L.Rev. 355; 1948, 1 Ala.L.Rev. 67.

In Rex v. Carlisle, 1834, 6 C. & P. 636, 172 Eng.Rep. 1397, there is reference in a note to the daughter of a Mr. Very, a confectioner in Regent Street, who was so wondrous fair that her presence in the shop caused three or four hundred people to assemble every day in the street before the window to look at her, so that her father was forced to send her out of town. Counsel was led to inquire whether she might not have been indicted as a public nuisance.

52. State v. Pennington, 1859, 3 Head, Tenn., 299.

53. Commonwealth v. Mohn, 1866, 52 Pa. 243. Cf. State ex rel. Goff v. O'Neil, 1939, 205 Minn. 366, 286 N.W. 316 (loan shark); State v. Hooker, N.D. 1957, 87 N.W.2d 337 (same). See Note, 1939, 38 Mich.L.Rev. 273.

54. City of Phoenix v. Johnson, 1938, 51 Ariz. 115, 75 P.2d 30; Pennsylvania Coal Co. v. Mahon, 1922, 260 U.S. 393. Cf. Attorney-General ex rel. Muskegon Co. v. Evart Booming Co., 1876, 34 Mich. 462. Thus in Miller v. Morse, 1959, 9 App.Div.2d 188, 192 N.Y. S.2d 571, appeal denied, 1959, 10 App.Div.2d 598, 195 N.Y.S.2d 398, followed, 1959, 194 N.Y.S.2d 462, it was held that a defect in the floor of a two-family house, not intended for public use, did not make it a public nuisance.

55. Rex v. Lloyd, 1802, 4 Esp. 200, 170 Eng.Rep. 691; Higgins v. Connecticut Light & Power Co, 1943, 129 Conn. 606, 30 A.2d 388; People v. Brooklyn & Queens Transit Corp., 1939, 258 App.Div. 753, 15 N. Y.S.2d 295, affirmed, 1940, 283 N.Y. 484, 28 N.E.2d 925.

There are, however, statutes in two or three states which define a public nuisance to include interference with any "considerable number of persons;" and under these no public right, as such, need be involved. See Boudinot v. State, Okl.1959, 340 P.2d 268; People v. Rubenfeld, 1930, 254 N.Y. 245, 172 N.E. 485; Ballenger v. City of Grand Saline, Tex. Civ.App.1955, 276 S.W.2d 874.

56. Smith v. City of Sedalia, 1899, 152 Mo. 283, 53 S. W. 907. Accord: Hartung v. County of Milwaukee, 1958, 2 Wis.2d 269, 86 N.W.2d 475, 87 N.W.2d 799 (quarry); Biggs v. Griffith, Mo.App.1950, 231 S.W. 2d 875 (outdoor public address system); Soap Corp. of America v. Reynolds, 5 Cir. 1950, 178 F.2d 503; District of Columbia v. Totten, 1925, 55 U.S.App.D. C. 312, 5 F.2d 374, cert. denied 269 U.S. 562; State v. Wright Hepburn Webster Gallory Ltd., Sup.Ct. 1970, 314 N.Y.S.2d 661.

57. State ex rel. Wear v. Springfield Gas & Elec. Co., Mo.App.1918, 204 S.W. 942.

58. State v. Hooker, N.D.1957, 87 N.W.2d 337; State v. Turner, 1942, 198 S.C. 487, 18 S.E.2d 372; Parker v. City of Fort Worth, Tex.Civ.App.1955, 281 S.W. 2d 721; Dean v. State, 1921, 151 Ga. 371, 106 S.E. 792; Finkelstein v. City of Sapulpa, 1925, 106 Okl. 297, 234 P. 187.

59. See for example Town of Mount Pleasant v. Van Tassell, 1957, 7 Misc.2d 643, 166 N.Y.S.2d 458, af-

of the number of persons affected has seldom arisen.

At common law, a public nuisance was always a crime, and punishable as such.[60] In the United States, all jurisdictions have enacted broad criminal statutes covering such nuisances without attempting to define them, or with at most a very general and rather meaningless definition. Such statutes commonly are construed to include anything which would have been a public nuisance at common law.[61] In addition there are in every state a multitude of specific provisions declaring that certain things, such as bawdy houses, black currant plants, buildings where narcotics are sold, mosquito breeding waters, or unhealthy multiple dwellings,[62] are public nuisances. Apparently the question has not arisen whether, in a state which has no common law crimes, there may be liability in tort for a common law public nuisance which is not covered by any general or specific statute. But since tort liability has been imposed upon municipal corporations, which are not criminally responsible but may be held liable for the creation or maintenance

of a nuisance,[63] one might hazard the guess that if the question should arise common law principles would be held to control in such a case.

Particular Damage

Tort liability for public nuisance originated in an anonymous case [64] in 1536, which is one of the two instances since the days of the old action of trespass in which a crime has become per se a tort.[65] In that case it was first held that the action would lie if the plaintiff could show that he had suffered damage particular to him, and not shared in common by the rest of the public. This qualification has persisted, and it is uniformly held that a private individual has no action for the invasion of the purely public right, unless his damage is in some way to be distinguished from that sustained by other members of the general public.[66] It is not enough that he suffers the same inconvenience or is exposed to the same threatened injury as everyone else.[67] Redress

firmed, 1958, 6 App.Div.2d 880, 177 N.Y.S.2d 1010 (odors, rats and flies from piggery).

60. 2 Russell, Crimes, 8th Ed. 1923, 1692; Mayor and Council of Alpine v. Brewster, 1951, 7 N.J. 42, 80 A.2d 297.

No case has been found of tort liability for a public nuisance which was not a crime. Cases of the liability of municipal corporations, infra, p. 982, are of course not in point—one might as well say that murder is not a crime because a lunatic or an infant cannot be convicted of it.

61. People v. Lim, 1943, 18 Cal.2d 872, 118 P.2d 472; Engle v. State, 1939, 53 Ariz. 458, 90 P.2d 988; People v. Clark, 1915, 268 Ill. 156, 108 N.E. 994; First Ave. Coal & Lumber Co. v. Johnson, 1911, 171 Ala. 470, 54 So. 598.

62. See New York Consol.Laws, Cahill 1930, ch. 46, §§ 343a, 409a, 434; ch. 10, § 57a; New York Sess. Laws 1937, ch. 353, § 2. As to the constitutionality of statutes declaring nuisances, see Noel, Retroactive Zoning and Nuisances, 1941, 41 Col.L.Rev. 457. See also Smith v. Costello, 1955, 77 Idaho 205, 290 P.2d 742, holding unconstitutional a statute as to dogs running at large in territory inhabited by deer.

63. Dubois v. City of Kingston, 1888, 102 N.Y. 219, 6 N.E. 273; Cohen v. Mayor of New York, 1889, 113 N.Y. 532, 21 N.E. 700; White, Negligence of Municipal Corporations, 1920, ch. VII; Note, 1923, 23 Col.L.Rev. 56.

64. Y.B. 27 Hen. VIII, Mich., pl. 10. See Holdsworth, History of English Law, 2d Ed. 1937, 424.

65. The other instance, of course, is libel. See infra, p. 751.

66. Alexander v. Wilkes-Barre Anthracite Coal Co., 1916, 254 Pa. 1, 98 A. 794 (coal mining); Dozier v. Troy Drive-In Theatres, Inc., 1956, 265 Ala. 93, 89 So.2d 537 (gaming); Taylor v. Barnes, 1946, 303 Ky. 562, 198 S.W.2d 297 (obstruction of highway); Painter v. Gunderson, 1913, 123 Minn. 323, 143 N.W. 910 (access to lake cut off); Bouquet v. Hackensack Water Co., 1916, 90 N.J.L. 203, 101 A. 379 (pollution of public waters); Missouri Veterinary Medical Ass'n v. Glisan, Mo.App.1950, 230 S.W.2d 169 (unlicensed professional activity).

But the rule does not preclude an ordinary negligence action for the particular damage, not founded in the invasion of the public right. Kneece v. City of Columbia, 1924, 128 S.C. 375, 123 S.E. 100.

67. Schroder v. City of Lincoln, 1952, 155 Neb. 599, 52 N.W.2d 808; Schlirf v. Loosen, 1951, 204 Okl. 651, 232 P.2d 928; Christy v. Chicago, B. & Q. R.

of the wrong to the community must be left to its appointed representatives. The best reason that has been given for the rule is that it relieves the defendant of the multiplicity of actions which might follow if everyone were free to sue for the common harm.[68]

Once this rule is accepted, however, the courts have not always found it at all easy to determine what is sufficient "particular damage" to support the private action, and some rather fine lines have been drawn in the

decisions.[69] There is general agreement on the requirement that the plaintiff's damage be different in kind, rather than in degree, from that shared by the general public;[70] and that, for example, the fact that the plaintiff has occasion to use a highway[71] or a navigable stream[72] five times as often as anyone else gives him no private right of action when it is obstructed. One good reason for such a conclusion is the extreme difficulty of fixing any lines of demarcation in terms of "degree" of public damage, since anyone who uses the highway or the stream at all will obviously suffer greater inconvenience than one who does not use it.

There have been writers[73] who have contended that, while the plaintiff should of course have no cause of action for the infringement of a purely theoretical right common to the public, he should not be denied

---

Co., 1948, 240 Mo.App. 632, 212 S.W.2d 476; Poulos v. Dover Boiler & Plate Fabricators, 1950, 5 N.J. 580, 76 A.2d 808.

68. 4 Bl.Comm. 166; Winfield, Law of Tort, 1st Ed. 1937, 466; 5 Pomeroy, Equity Jurisprudence, 2d Ed. 1919, § 1892. See, however, Smith, Private Action for Obstruction to Public Right of Passage, 1915, 15 Col.L.Rev. 1, 2–9, contending that actual, substantial damage is necessary, and that those who suffer it will be few, so that no undue burden will result from allowing them to recover.

Recent ferment in the field of environmental law has led to some agitation for abolition of the rule. See for example Davis, the Liberalized Law of Standing, 1970, 37 U.Chi.L.Rev. 450; Hanks and Hanks, an Environmental Bill of Rights: The Citizen Suit and the National Environmental Policy Act of 1969, 1970, 24 Rut.L.Rev. 230; Jaffe, Standing to Sue in Conservation Suits, in Law and Environment, 1970, 123.

Reliance has been placed by these writers on decisions under such statutes as the Federal Power Act and the Rivers and Harbors Act, which give a person "aggrieved" by the action of a Federal administrative agency the right to maintain a proceeding challenging the action of the agency. In such cases as Scenic Hudson Preservation Conference v. Federal Power Commission, 2 Cir. 1965, 354 F.2d 608, and Citizens Committee for the Hudson Valley v. Volpe, 2 Cir. 1970, 425 F.2d 97, this was held to authorized suits by groups interested in the protection of scenic values.

There are also statutes in a few states that provide for suit by individual citizens in the public interest to abate a public nuisance. For example Fla.Stat.1969, 60.05; Mich.Pub.Acts 1970, No. 127, Mich.Stat.Ann. 14.528; Wis.Stat.1958, 280.02. See Note, 1970, 16 Wayne L.Rev. 1085, 1127.

In the absence of such statutory authorization, no case has been found in which a private individual has been held to have standing to sue for a public nuisance in the absence of particular damage to him. The remedy was denied to a wildlife society in National Audubon Society v. Johnson, S.D.Tex.1970, 317 F.Supp. 1330.

69. See Smith, Private Action for Obstruction to Public Right of Passage, 1915, 15 Col.L.Rev. 1, 149; Prosser, Private Action for Public Nuisance, 1966, 52 Va.L.Rev. 997; Note, 1918, 2 Minn.L.Rev. 210.

Interesting questions of "proximate cause" were raised in the second Wagon Mound decision, Overseas Tankship (U.K.) Ltd. v. Morts Dock & Eng. Co., Ltd., [1961] A.C. 388. See Dias, Trouble on Oiled Waters: Problems of The Wagon Mound (No. 2), [1967] Camb.L.J. 62; Green, The Wagon Mound No. 2—Foreseeability Revisited, [1967] Utah L.Rev. 197.

70. Page v. Niagara Chemical Division of Food Machinery & Chemical Corp., Fla.1953, 68 So.2d 383; Smedberg v. Moxie Dam Co., 1952, 148 Me. 302, 92 A.2d 606; Willard v. City of Cambridge, 1862, 3 Allen (85 Mass.) 574; Bouquet v. Hackensack Water Co., 1916, 90 N.J.L. 203, 101 A. 379; Livingston v. Cunningham, 1920, 188 Iowa 254, 175 N.W. 980.

71. Poulos v. Dover Boiler & Plate Fabricators, 1950, 5 N.J. 580, 76 A.2d 808; Borton v. Mangus, 1915, 93 Kan. 719, 145 P. 835; Painter v. Gunderson, 1913, 123 Minn. 342, 143 N.W. 911; Christy v. Chicago, B. & Q. R. Co., 1948, 240 Mo.App. 632, 212 S.W.2d 476; Zettel v. City of West Bend, 1891, 79 Wis. 316, 48 N.W. 379.

72. Whitmore v. Brown, 1906, 102 Me. 47, 65 A. 516; Swanson v. Mississippi & Rum River Boom Co., 1890, 42 Minn. 532, 44 N.W. 986.

73. Smith, Private Action for Obstruction of Public Right of Passage, 1915, 15 Col.L.Rev. 1, 15–23; Fleming, Torts, 3d Ed. 1965, 367–369.

relief in any case where that infringement causes him substantial harm, even though he shares it with others. This has not been borne out at all by the decisions; and when a whole community has been commercially affected by the closing of a drawbridge or a river,[74] or the destruction of fish in a lake,[75] a plaintiff who has suffered greater pecuniary loss than anyone else has not been allowed to recover for it.

Degree cannot, however, be left entirely out of account in determining difference in kind. Normally there may be no difference in the kind of interference with one who travels a road once a week and with one who travels it once a day. But if he traverses it a dozen times a day,[76] he always has some special reason to do so, which will almost invariably be based upon some special interest of his own not common to the community. Substantial interference with that interest must be particular damage. Deprivation of immediate access to land, which is quite clearly a special kind of damage, shades off by imperceptible stages into the remote obstruction of a highway, which is just as clearly not.[77] It follows that the degree can never be ignored when it bears legitimately upon the issue of kind.[78]

Where the plaintiff suffers personal injury,[79] or harm to his health,[80] or even mental distress,[81] there is no difficulty in finding a different kind of damage. The same is true as to physical harm to his chattels,[82] or interference with the physical condition of land, as by flooding it; [83] or silting up irrigation ditches.[84] It is likewise true where there is any substantial interference with the plaintiff's use and enjoyment of his own land,[85]

---

74. Willard v. City of Cambridge, 1862, 3 Allen, (85 Mass.) 574; Swanson v. Mississippi & Rum River Boom Co., 1890, 42 Minn. 532, 44 N.W. 986. Cf. Hohmann v. City of Chicago, 1892, 140 Ill. 226, 29 N.E. 671; Prosser v. City of Ottumwa, 1876, 42 Iowa 509; Walls v. Smith & Co., 1910, 167 Ala. 138, 52 So. 320.

75. Smedberg v. Moxie Dam Co., 1952, 148 Me. 302, 92 A.2d 606. Cf. Anthony Wilkinson Live Stock Co. v. McIlquam, 1905, 14 Wyo. 209, 83 P. 364 (interference with grazing rights); Livingston v. Cunningham, 1920, 188 Iowa 254, 175 N.W. 980.

76. Wiggins v. Boddington, 1828, 3 Car. & P. 544, 172 Eng.Rep. 539 (hauling carts full of sand).

77. See infra, notes 95–98.

78. "Where to draw the line between cases where the injury is more general or more equally distributed, and cases where it is not, where, by reason of local situation, the damage is comparatively much greater to the special few, is often a difficult task. In spite of all the refinements and distinctions which have been made, it is often a mere matter of degree, and the courts have to draw the line between the more immediate obstruction or peculiar interference, which is ground for special damage, and the more remote obstruction or interference, which is not." Kaje v. Chicago, St. P., M. & O. R. Co., 1894, 57 Minn. 422, 424, 59 N.W. 493.

79. Downes v. Silva, 1937, 57 R.I. 343, 190 A. 42; Flaherty v. Great Northern R. Co., 1944, 218 Minn. 488, 16 N.W.2d 553; White v. Suncook Mills, 1940, 91 N.H. 92, 13 A.2d 729; Delaney v. Philhern Realty Holding Corp., 1939, 280 N.Y. 461, 21 N.E.2d 507; Beckwith v. Town of Stratford, 1942, 129 Conn. 506, 29 A.2d 775.

80. Sullivan v. American Mfg. Co. of Mass., 4 Cir. 1929, 33 F.2d 690; Hunnicutt v. Eaton, 1937, 184 Ga. 485, 191 S.E. 919; Savannah, F. & W. R. Co. v. Parish, 1903, 117 Ga. 893, 45 S.E. 280; De Vaughn v. Minor, 1887, 77 Ga. 809, 1 S.E. 433; Code v. Jones, 1923, 54 Ont.L.Rep. 425.

81. Wilson v. Parent, 1961, 228 Or. 354, 365 P.2d 72 (public profanity addressed to plaintiff).

82. Lynn v. Hooper, 1899, 93 Me. 46, 44 A. 127; Larson v. New England Tel. & Tel. Co., 1945, 141 Me. 326, 44 A.2d 1; Dygert v. Schenck, 1840, 23 Wend., N.Y., 446. Even where this is consequential, as where corn is spoiled when it cannot be moved over a blocked highway. Maynell v. Saltmarsh, 1665, 1 Keb. 847, 83 Eng.Rep. 1278; Cottman v. Lochner, 1929, 40 Wyo. 378, 278 P. 71.

83. Weinstein v. Lake Pearl Park, Inc., 1964, 347 Mass. 91, 196 N.E.2d 638. Cf. Lind v. City of San Luis Obispo, 1895, 109 Cal. 340, 42 P. 437 (depositing sewage); Hark v. Mountain Fork Lumber Co., 1945, 127 W.Va. 586, 34 S.E.2d 348 (laying tramway tracks).

84. Ravndal v. Northfork Placers, 1939, 60 Idaho 305, 91 P.2d 368.

85. Karpisek v. Cather & Sons Const., Inc., 1962, 174 Neb. 234, 117 N.W.2d 322 (dust from asphalt plant); Buckmaster v. Bourbon County Fair Ass'n, 1953, 174 Kan. 515, 256 P.2d 878 (noise and disturbance from automobile races); Weinstein v. Lake Pearl Park, Inc., 1964, 347 Mass. 91, 196 N.E.2d 638 (riparian land made wetter); Morris v. Borough of

as where a bawdy house, which disturbs the public morals, also makes life disagreeable in the house next door.[86] This makes the nuisance a private as well as a public one; and since the plaintiff does not lose his rights as a landowner merely because others suffer damage of the same kind, or even of the same degree, there is general agreement that he may proceed upon either theory, or upon both.[87] Where this is the case, the action founded on the public nuisance may sometimes be preferable, because it is well settled that prescriptive rights, laches and the statute of limitations do not run against it.[88]

There is more difficulty where the obstruction of a highway interferes with the landowner's access to his property, which is itself a property right. Where immediate ingress and egress are completely cut off, there is no doubt that there is particular damage, for which the private action will lie.[89] But there

need not be complete deprivation; and it is enough that one entrance is closed, although there is another available,[90] or that the obstruction makes use of the passage unreasonably burdensome or inconvenient,[91] or unsafe.[92] It is only when the obstruction is so minor or partial that it is not regarded as a substantial interference with access[93] that the remedy is denied.

More distant obstructions of the highway, preventing entry by a particular route, offer more of a problem. Where access is completely cut off by blocking the only road in, and the plaintiff is "marooned far up on the mountain side,"[94] there is no doubt that there is particular damage. But where other routes are open, and it is only one that is blocked, the line must somehow be drawn

---

Haledon, 1952, 24 N.J.Super. 171, 93 A.2d 781 (noises and smoke); Morse v. Liquor Control Comm'n, 1947, 319 Mich. 52, 29 N.W.2d 316 (illegal sale of liquor interfering with church).

86. Crawford v. Tyrrell, 1891, 128 N.Y. 341, 28 N.E. 514; Tedescki v. Berger, 1907, 150 Ala. 649, 43 So. 960.

87. Adams v. City of Toledo, 1939, 163 Or. 185, 96 P. 2d 1078; Tedescki v. Berger, 1907, 150 Ala. 649, 43 So. 960; Bishop Processing Co. v. Davis, 1957, 213 Md. 465, 132 A.2d 445; District of Columbia v. Totten, 1925, 55 U.S.App.D.C. 312, 5 F.2d 374, cert. denied 269 U.S. 562; McManus v. Southern R. Co., 1909, 150 N.C. 655, 64 S.E. 766.

88. Wade v. Campbell, 1962, 200 Cal.App.2d 54, 19 Cal.Rptr. 173; Elves v. King County, 1956, 49 Wash.2d 201, 299 P.2d 206; City of Meridian v. Tingle, 1956, 226 Miss. 317, 84 So.2d 388; Hazen v. Perkins, 1918, 92 Vt. 414, 105 A. 249; Long v. New York Cent. R. Co., 1929, 248 Mich. 437, 227 N.W. 739. The contention that this is true only when the private damages are of the same nature as the public invasion was effectively refuted in Weeks-Thorn Paper Co. v. Glenside Woolen Mills, 1909, 64 Misc. 205, 118 N.Y.S. 1027, affirmed 140 App.Div. 878, 124 N.Y.S. 2, affirmed 204 N.Y. 563, 97 N.E. 1118, reargument denied 204 N.Y. 639, 98 N.E. 1136.

89. Cushing-Wetmore Co. v. Gray, 1907, 152 Cal. 118, 92 P. 70; Owens v. Elliott, 1962, 257 N.C. 250, 125 S.E.2d 589; Lindauer v. Hill, Okl.1953, 262 P.2d 697; Stephens v. Hubbard, 1930, 234 Ky. 115, 27 S.

W.2d 665; Mayo v. Schumer, Mo.App.1923, 256 S. W. 549.

90. Brown v. Hendricks, 1947, 211 S.C. 395, 45 S.E.2d 603; Fassion v. Landrey, 1890, 123 Ind. 136, 24 N. E. 96; Hindi v. Smith, 1963, 73 N.M. 335, 388 P.2d 60; Purvis v. Busey, 1954, 260 Ala. 373, 71 So.2d 18; White Mountain Freezer Co. v. Levesque, 1954, 99 N.H. 15, 104 A.2d 525.

91. Graceland Corp. v. Consolidated Laundries Corp., 1958, 7 App.Div.2d 89, 180 N.Y.S.2d 644, affirmed 1959, 6 N.Y.2d 900, 190 N.Y.S.2d 708, 160 N.E.2d 926; Michelsen v. Dwyer, 1954, 158 Neb. 427, 63 N. W.2d 513; Fugate v. Carter, 1928, 151 Va. 108, 144 S.E. 483; Regester v. Lincoln Oil Ref. Co., 1933, 95 Ind.App. 425, 183 N.E. 693.

92. Baldocchi v. Four Fifty Sutter Corp., 1933, 129 Cal.App. 383, 18 P.2d 682.

93. Wynn v. Hale, 1957, 227 Ark. 765, 301 S.W.2d 466 (forced to open and close gates); Holland v. Grant County, 1956, 208 Or. 50, 298 P.2d 832 (minor detour); Ayers v. Stidham, 1954, 260 Ala. 390, 71 So. 2d 95 (seldom used route); Schroder v. City of Lincoln, 1952, 155 Neb. 599, 52 N.W.2d 808 (bank teller window at curb); Magee v. Omansky, 1948, 187 Va. 422, 46 S.E.2d 443 (encroachment of eighteen inches); Richard v. Gulf Theatres, 1945, 155 Fla. 626, 21 So.2d 715 (15 feet of street obstructed, leaving 60 feet clear).

94. Colvin v. Tallassee Power Co., 1930, 199 N.C. 353, 360, 154 S.E. 678, 682; Pilgrim Plywood Corp. v. Melendy, 1938, 110 Vt. 112, 1 A.2d 700; Smart v. Aroostook Lumber Co., 1907, 103 Me. 37, 68 A. 527; Miller v. Schenck, 1889, 78 Iowa 372, 43 N.W. 225; Stricker v. Hillis, 1909, 15 Idaho 709, 99 P. 831.

between deprivation of access to land, which is a property right, and mere deprivation of the public right of passage, which is not.[95] This is essentially a matter of degree. In general,[96] when the obstruction is close to the land, as for example two hundred feet away in the same block,[97] so that the plaintiff must detour to travel in one direction, it has been treated as interference with access, while more remote obstructions, permitting the plaintiff to make a substantial start on his journey before he is forced to detour, have been regarded as nothing more than interference with the public right of travel.[98]

Pecuniary loss to the plaintiff has been regarded as different in kind when the defendant's obstruction has prevented the plaintiff from performing a particular contract, as for example to transport goods over the highway in question,[99] or when it has put him to additional expense, or expensive delay, in performing it.[1] It has also been considered sufficient where the plaintiff has an established business[2] making a commercial use of the public right with which the defendant interferes, as where a river is blocked and plaintiff operates a steamboat line[3] or rafts logs,[4] or collects tolls for passage.[5] There are several cases in which commercial fisheries making a localized use of public waters have been allowed to recover for pollution,[6] where the ordinary citizen deprived of his occasional

95. See State ex rel. Anderson v. Preston, 1963, 2 Ohio App.2d 244, 207 N.E.2d 664, saying that otherwise "a bridge in Louisiana would logically subject that state to claims by all owners on the Mississippi and its many tributaries."

96. Missouri has adopted an arbitrary rule that unless access is completely cut off there must be an interference with entry to land at the point of the obstruction, and no detour is enough. Arcadia Realty Co. v. City of St. Louis, 1930, 326 Mo. 273, 30 S.W.2d 995; Christy v. Chicago, B. & Q. R. Co., 1948, 240 Mo.App. 632, 212 S.W.2d 476.

97. O'Brien v. Central Iron & Steel Co., 1902, 158 Ind. 218, 63 N.E. 302. Accord: Young v. Rothrock, 1903, 121 Iowa 588, 96 N.W. 1105; Purvis v. Busey, 1954, 260 Ala. 373, 71 So.2d 18; Bennett v. Nations, 1945, 49 N.M. 389, 164 P.2d 1019; Yates v. Tiffany, 1927, 126 Me. 128, 136 A. 668. The greatest distance found is two blocks, in Sloss-Sheffield Steel & Iron Co. v. Johnson, 1906, 147 Ala. 384, 41 So. 907.

98. Ayers v. Stidham, 1954, 260 Ala. 390, 71 So.2d 95; Magee v. Omansky, 1948, 187 Va. 422, 46 S.E.2d 443; McKay v. Enid, 1910, 26 Okl. 275, 109 P. 520; Guttery v. Glenn, 1903, 201 Ill. 275, 66 N.E. 305; Zettel v. City of West Bend, 1891, 79 Wis. 316, 48 N.W. 379.

99. Gulf States Steel Co. v. Beveridge, 1923, 209 Ala. 473, 96 So. 587 (taxi unable to deliver passenger); Brewer v. Missouri Pac. R. Co., 1923, 161 Ark. 525, 257 S.W. 53 (contract to do work on flooded road).

1. Tuell v. Marion, 1913, 110 Me. 460, 86 A. 980; Commissioners of Anne Arundel County v. Watts, 1910, 112 Md. 353, 76 A. 82; Sholin v. Skamania Boom Co., 1909, 56 Wash. 303, 105 P. 632; Knowles v. Pennsylvania R. Co., 1896, 175 Pa. 623, 34 A. 974; cf. Campbell v. Mayor of Paddington, [1911] 1 K.B. 869.

The mere delay and inconvenience of a detour around a highway obstruction, common to all who pass that way, is not enough in the way of particular damage, in the absence of some showing of special pecuniary loss. Winterbottom v. Lord Derby, 1867, L.R. 2 Ex. 316; Ayers v. Stidham, 1954, 260 Ala. 390, 71 So.2d 95; Magee v. Omansky, 1948, 187 Va. 422, 46 S.E.2d 443; McKay v. Enid, 1910, 26 Okl. 275, 109 P. 520; Guttery v. Glenn, 1903, 201 Ill. 275, 66 N.E. 305.

2. It is not enough that the plaintiff contemplates commercial transactions, since anyone might do so. Clark v. Chicago & N. W. R. Co., 1888, 70 Wis. 593, 36 N.W. 326; President & Fellows of Harvard College v. Stearns, 15 Gray. (81 Mass.) 1.

3. Carver v. San Pedro, L. A. & S. L. R. Co., S.D. Cal.1906, 151 F. 334; Piscataqua Nav. Co. v. New York, N. H. & H. R. Co., D.Mass.1898, 89 F. 362; Viebahn v. Board of Crow Wing Comm'rs, 1906, 96 Minn. 276, 104 N.W. 1089; City of Philadelphia v. Gilmartin, 1872, 71 Pa. 140.

4. Wakeman v. Wilbur, 1895, 147 N.Y. 657, 42 N.E. 341; Page v. Mille Lacs Lumber Co., 1893, 53 Minn. 492, 55 N.W. 608, vacated on other grounds, 55 N.W. 1119; Gates v. Northern Pac. R. Co., 1885, 64 Wis. 64, 24 N.W. 494, error dismissed Northern Pac. R. Co. v. Gates, 131 U.S. 442.

5. Wisconsin River Improvement Co. v. Lyons, 1872, 30 Wis. 61.

6. Hampton v. North Carolina Pulp Co., 1943, 223 N.C. 535, 27 S.E.2d 538; Columbia River Fishermen's Protective Union v. City of St. Helens, 1939, 160 Or. 654, 87 P.2d 195; Strandholm v. Barbey, 1933, 145 Or. 427, 26 P.2d 46; Morris v. Graham, 1897, 16 Wash. 343, 47 P. 752; Carson v. Hercules Powder Co., 1966, 240 Ark. 887, 402 S.W.2d 640. See Note, 1967, 20 Ark.L.Rev. 407.

piscatorial Sunday pleasure could not do so. Even where the business is not itself founded on the exercise of the public right, there may still be recovery for loss of customers,[7] or interference with transportation which prevents it from obtaining materials or labor,[8] or from shipping its goods to market.[9] Where, however, the pecuniary loss is common to the whole community, or a large part of it, as where a whole area of a town is cut off by a viaduct,[10] or the draining of a good fishing lake affects all the fishing camps in the vicinity,[11] it has been regarded as no different in kind from the common misfortune, and the private action cannot be maintained.

89. PRIVATE NUISANCE

The essence of a private nuisance is an interference with the use and enjoyment of land.[12] The ownership or rightful possession of land necessarily involves the right not only to the unimpaired condition of the property itself, but also to some reasonable comfort and convenience in its occupation. Thus many interferences with personal comfort, such as a dog next door which makes night hideous with his howls,[13] which at first glance would appear to be wrongs purely personal to the landholder, are treated as nuisances because they interfere with that right to the undisturbed enjoyment of the premises which is inseparable from ownership of the property.[14]

The different ways and combinations of ways in which the interest in the use or enjoyment of land may be invaded are infinitely variable. A private nuisance may consist of an interference with the physical condition of the land itself, as by vibration[15] or blasting[16] which damages a house, the de-

7. East Cairo Ferry Co. v. Brown, 1930, 233 Ky. 299, 25 S.W.2d 730; Johnson v. Town of Oakland, 1925, 148 Md. 432, 129 A. 648; Duy v. Alabama W. Ry., 1912, 175 Ala. 162, 57 So. 724; Aldrich v. City of Minneapolis, 1893, 52 Minn. 164, 53 N.W. 1072; Flynn v. Taylor, 1891, 127 N.Y. 596, 28 N.E. 418.

8. Farmers' Co-op. Mfg. Co. v. Albemarle & R. R. Co., 1895, 117 N.C. 579, 23 S.E. 43; Williams v. Tripp, 1878, 11 R.I. 447. A good case is Pedrick v. Raleigh & P. S. R. Co., 1906, 143 N.C. 485, 55 S.E. 877, in which the owner of a sawmill on the river was permitted to maintain the action, while citizens keeping sailboats on the water for pleasure were not.

9. E. A. Chatfield Co. v. City of New Haven, D. Conn.1901, 110 F. 788; Carl v. West Aberdeen Land & Imp. Co., 1896, 13 Wash. 616, 43 P. 890; Mehrhof Bros. Brick Mfg. Co. v. Delaware, L. & W. R. Co., 1888, 51 N.J.L. 56, 16 A. 12; Little Rock, M. R. & T. R. Co. v. Brooks, 1882, 39 Ark. 403.

10. Hohman v. City of Chicago, 1892, 140 Ill. 226, 29 N.E. 671 (construction of viaduct); Willard v. City of Cambridge, 1862, 85 Mass. (3 Allen) 574 (closing drawbridge); Swanson v. Mississippi & Rum River Boom Co., 1890, 42 Minn. 532, 44 N.W. 986 (blocking river); Prosser v. City of Ottumwa, 1876, 42 Iowa 509 (business of ferry).

11. Smedberg v. Moxie Dam Co., 1952, 148 Me. 302, 92 A.2d 606. Cf. Anthony Wilkinson Live Stock Co. v. McIlquam, 1905, 14 Wyo. 209, 83 P. 364 (public grazing rights).

12. And without it, the fact of personal injury, or of interference with some purely personal right, is not enough for such a nuisance. Cox v. Ray M. Lee Co., 1959, 100 Ga.App. 333, 111 S.E.2d 246; Stanley v. City of Macon, 1957, 95 Ga.App. 108, 97 S.E.2d 330; Lederman v. Cunningham, Tex.Civ.App.1955, 283 S.W.2d 108; Mandell v. Pivnick, 1956, 20 Conn. Sup. 99, 125 A.2d 175.

13. Brill v. Flagler, 1840, 23 Wend., N.Y., 354; Hubbard v. Preston, 1892, 90 Mich. 221, 51 N.W. 209; Adams v. Hamilton Carhartt Overall Co., 1943, 293 Ky. 443, 169 S.W.2d 294.

14. 1 Street, Foundations of Legal Liability, 1906, 211, 212; Restatement of Torts, § 822, Comment c. It is not necessary that the condition endanger the health of the occupant, if it is offensive to the senses and renders enjoyment of life and property uncomfortable. Miller v. Coleman, 1957, 213 Ga. 125, 97 S.E.2d 313 (dog kennel).

15. Hoare & Co. v. McAlpin & Sons, [1928] 1 Ch. 167, 92 L.J.Ch. 81; Sam Warren & Son Stone Co. v. Gruesser, 1948, 397 Ky. 98, 209 S.W.2d 817; Transcontinental Gas Pipe Line Co. v. Gault, 4 Cir. 1952, 198 F.2d 196.

16. Beecher v. Dull, 1928, 294 Pa. 17, 143 A. 498. Cf. Heeg v. Licht, 1880, 80 N.Y. 579; Laflin & Rand Powder Co. v. Tearney, 1890, 131 Ill. 322, 23 N.E. 389; Davis v. Niagara Falls Tower Co., 1902, 171 N.Y. 336, 64 N.E. 4 (ice falling on roof). See Notes, 1929, 77 U.Pa.L.Rev. 550; 1930, 19 Cal.L.Rev. 94.

struction of crops,[17] flooding,[18] raising the water table,[19] or the pollution of a stream [20] or of an underground water supply.[21] It may consist of a disturbance of the comfort or convenience of the occupant, as by unpleasant odors,[22] smoke or dust or gas,[23] loud noises,[24] excessive light or high temperatures,[25] or

even repeated telephone calls; [26] or of his health, as by a pond full of malarial mosquitoes.[27] Likewise, it may disturb merely his peace of mind, as in the case of a bawdy house,[28] the depressing effect of an undertaking establishment,[29] or the unfounded fear of contagion from a tuberculosis hospital.[30] A threat of future injury may be a present menace and interference with enjoyment, as in the case of stored explosives,[31] inflammable

17. United Verde Extension Min. Co. v. Ralston, 1931, 37 Ariz. 554, 296 P. 262; Andrews v. Andrews, 1955, 242 N.C. 382, 88 S.E.2d 88; Campbell v. Seaman, 1876, 63 N.Y. 568 (trees and plants); Stevens v. Moon, 1921, 54 Cal.App. 737, 202 P. 961 (trees).

18. Mueller v. Fruen, 1886, 36 Minn. 273, 30 N.W. 886; Rindge v. Sargent, 1886, 64 N.H. 294, 9 A. 723; William Tackaberry Co. v. Sioux City Service Co., 1911, 154 Iowa 358, 132 N.W. 945, 134 N.W. 1064. Cf. Spaulding v. Cameron, 1952, 38 Cal.2d 265, 239 P.2d 625 (mud).

19. Cason v. Florida Power Co., 1917, 74 Fla. 1, 76 So. 535; Shields v. Wondries, 1957, 154 Cal.App.2d 249, 316 P.2d 9.

20. Beach v. Sterling Iron & Zinc Co., 1895, 54 N.J. Eq. 65, 33 A. 286; Johnson v. City of Fairmont, 1933, 188 Minn. 451, 247 N.W. 572; Farley v. Crystal Coal & Coke Co., 1920, 85 W.Va. 595, 102 S.E. 265; Rose v. Standard Oil Co. of New York, 1936, 56 R.I. 272, 185 A. 251.

21. Cities Service Co. v. Merritt, Okl.1958, 332 P.2d 677; Burr v. Adam Eidemiller, Inc., 1956, 386 Pa. 416, 126 A.2d 403.

22. Aldred's Case, 1611, 9 Co.Rep. 57, 77 Eng.Rep. 816; Sarraillon v. Stevenson, 1950, 153 Neb. 182, 43 N.W.2d 509; Hedrick v. Tubbs, 1950, 120 Ind.App. 326, 92 N.E.2d 561; Johnson v. Drysdale, 1939, 66 S.D. 436, 285 N.W. 301; Higgins v. Decorah Produce Co., 1932, 214 Iowa 276, 242 N.W. 109.

23. Alster v. Allen, 1935, 141 Kan. 661, 42 P.2d 969; Riblet v. Spokane-Portland Cement Co., 1952, 41 Wash.2d 249, 248 P.2d 380; Dill v. Dance Freight Lines, 1966, 247 S.C. 159, 146 S.E.2d 574; Menolascino v. Superior Felt & Bedding Co., 1942, 313 Ill. App. 557, 40 N.E.2d 813; cf. Waters v. McNearney, 1959, 8 App.Div.2d 13, 185 N.Y.S.2d 29, affirmed, 1960, 8 N.Y.2d 808, 202 N.Y.S.2d 24, 168 N.E.2d 255 (blown sand).

24. Guarnia v. Bogart, 1962, 407 Pa. 307, 180 A.2d 557; Hooks v. International Speedways, Inc., 1965, 263 N.C. 686, 140 S.E.2d 387; Gorman v. Sabo, 1956, 210 Md. 155, 122 A.2d 475; Borsvold v. United Dairies, 1957, 347 Mich. 672, 81 N.W.2d 378; Jenner v. Collins, 1951, 211 Miss. 770, 52 So.2d 638; cf. Herbert v. Smyth, 1967, 155 Conn. 78, 230 A.2d 235 (barking dogs). See Lloyd, Noise as a Nuisance, 1933, 82 U.Pa.L.Rev. 567; Spater, Noise and the Law, 1965, 63 Mich.L.Rev. 1373.

25. Light: The Shelburne, Inc. v. Crossan Corp., 1923, 95 N.J.Eq. 188, 122 A. 749; Hansen v. Independent School District, 1940, 61 Idaho 109, 98 P. 2d 959. See Notes, 1949, 2 Okl.L.Rev. 259; 1948, 1 Ala.L.Rev. 67.

Temperature: Sanders-Clark v. Grosvenor Mansions Co., [1900] 2 Ch. 373; Grady v. Wolsner, 1871, 46 Ala. 381.

26. Brillhardt v. Ben Tipp, Inc., 1956, 48 Wash.2d 722, 297 P.2d 232; Wiggins v. Moskins Credit Clothing Store, E.D.S.C.1956, 137 F.Supp. 764; see Roland v. Slesinger, 1959, 16 Misc.2d 1087, 185 N.Y. S.2d 303. See Note, 1956, 55 Mich.L.Rev. 310.

27. Yaffe v. City of Fort Smith, 1928, 178 Ark. 406, 10 S.W.2d 886; Mills v. Hall, 1832, 9 Wend., N.Y., 315; Towaliga Falls Power Co. v. Sims, 1909, 6 Ga.App. 649, 65 S.E. 844.

28. Crawford v. Tyrrell, 1891, 128 N.Y. 341, 28 N.E. 514; Tedescki v. Berger, 1907, 150 Ala. 649, 43 So. 960; cf. Reid v. Brodsky, 1959, 397 Pa. 463, 156 A. 2d 334 (taproom frequented by disorderly characters).

29. Howard v. Etchieson, 1958, 228 Ark. 809, 310 S. W.2d 473; Tureman v. Ketterlin, 1924, 304 Mo. 221, 263 S.W. 202; Williams v. Montgomery, 1939, 184 Miss. 547, 186 So. 302; Kundinger v. Bagnasco, 1941, 298 Mich. 15, 298 N.W. 386. Cf. Lowe v. Prospect Hill Cemetery Ass'n, 1898, 58 Neb. 94, 78 N.W. 488 (cemetery); Jones v. Trawick, Fla.1954, 75 So.2d 785 (same); see Notes, 1938, 16 Tex.L.Rev. 278; 1934, 18 Minn.L.Rev. 482.

30. Everett v. Paschall, 1910, 61 Wash. 47, 111 P. 879; City of Baltimore v. Fairfield Imp. Co., 1898, 87 Md. 352, 39 A. 1081; Cherry v. Williams, 1908, 147 N.C. 452, 61 S.E. 267; Stotler v. Rochelle, 1910, 83 Kan. 86, 109 P. 788.

31. Cumberland Torpedo Co. v. Gaines, 1923, 201 Ky. 88, 255 S.W. 1046; Whittemore v. Baxter Laundry Co., 1914, 181 Mich. 564, 148 N.W. 437. Cf. Hogle v. H. H. Franklin Mfg. Co., 1910, 199 N.Y. 388, 92 N.E. 794 (throwing junk from windows).

buildings or materials,[32] or a vicious dog;[33] and even though no use is being made of the plaintiff's land at the time, the depreciation in the use value of the property because of such conditions or activities is sufficient present damage upon which an action may be based.[34] Many nuisances involve an assortment of interferences: a factory may cause vibration, smoke and dust, loud noises, pollution of a stream, and a fire hazard.[35] So long as the interference is substantial and unreasonable,[36] and such as would be offensive or inconvenient to the normal person,[37] virtually any disturbance of the enjoyment of the property may amount to a nuisance.

Property Rights Protected

The original character of private nuisance as an invasion of interests in land has been preserved. Apparently any interest sufficient to be dignified as a property right will support the action. Thus it will lie in favor of a tenant for a term,[38] or from week to week,[39] or a mortgagor in possession after foreclosure,[40] or even one in adverse possession without title.[41] Likewise it may be maintained by the holder of an easement, such as a right of way[42] or a right to passage, light and air.[43] But in each case the protection is limited to the interest of the plaintiff. Thus a tenant may recover damages for the depreciation in market value of his term,[44] but not for that of the reversion, in which he has no interest;[45] and a reversioner may recover for permanent harm to the property or loss of its rental value,[46] but not for harm which goes merely to the present enjoyment of the man in possession.[47]

32. Richardson v. Murphy, 1953, 198 Or. 640, 259 P. 2d 116; Griswold & Day v. Brega & Roster, 1895, 57 Ill.App. 554; Fields v. Stokley, 1882, 99 Pa. 306.

33. Rider v. Clarkson, 1910, 77 N.J.Eq. 469, 78 A. 676.

34. Wilson v. Townend, 1860, 1 Drew & Sm. 324, 62 Eng.Reg. 403; Busch v. New York, L. & W. R. Co., 1890, 34 N.Y.St.Rep. 7, 12 N.Y.S. 85; Bowden v. Edison Elec. Ill. Co., 1899, 29 Misc. 171, 60 N.Y.S. 835; Romano v. Birmingham Ry., L. & P. Co., 1913, 182 Ala. 335, 62 So. 677.

35. See for example McClung v. Louisville & N. R. Co., 1951, 255 Ala. 302, 51 So.2d 371; Kosich v. Poultrymen's Service Corp., 1945, 136 N.J.Eq. 571, 43 A.2d 15; Gus Blass Dry Goods Co. v. Reinman & Wolfort, 1912, 102 Ark. 287, 143 S.W. 1087; Vowinckel v. N. Clark & Sons, 1932, 216 Cal. 156, 13 P. 2d 733; Hoadley v. M. Seward & Son Co., 1899, 71 Conn. 649, 42 A. 997.

36. See supra, pp. 577, 580.

37. See supra, p. 577.

38. McClosky v. Martin, Fla.1951, 56 So.2d 916; Bly v. Edison Elec. Ill. Co., 1902, 172 N.Y. 1, 64 N.E. 745; Green v. T. A. Shoemaker & Co., 1909, 111 Md. 69, 73 A. 688; American Electronics, Inc. v. Christe Poules & Co., 1964, 43 Misc.2d 302, 250 N.Y. S.2d 738 (one tenant liable to another). A fortiori a life tenant. Price v. Grose, 1921, 78 Ind.App. 62, 133 N.E. 30.

39. See Jones v. Chappell, 1875, L.R. 20 Eq. 539; Bowden v. Edison Electric Illuminating Co., 1899, 29 Misc. 171, 60 N.Y.S. 835 (tenant from month to month); Towaliga Falls Power Co. v. Sims, 1909, 6 Ga.App. 749, 65 S.E. 844 (tenant at will).

40. Lurssen v. Lloyd, 1892, 76 Md. 360, 25 A. 294.

41. Brink v. Moeschl Edwards Corrugating Co., 1911, 142 Ky. 88, 133 S.W. 1147; cf. Denner v. Chicago, M. & St. P. R. Co., 1883, 57 Wis. 218, 15 N.W. 158.

42. Lane v. Capsey, [1891] 3 Ch. 411; Herman v. Roberts, 1890, 119 N.Y. 37, 23 N.E. 442.

43. Webber v. Wright, 1924, 124 Me. 190, 126 A. 737.

44. Bowden v. Edison Elec. Ill. Co., 1899, 29 Misc. 171, 60 N.Y.S. 835; Klassen v. Central Kansas Coop. Creamery Ass'n, 1946, 160 Kan. 697, 165 P.2d 601. He may maintain the action even against the landlord for interference with his present use. Jubb v. Maslanka, 1961, 22 Conn.Sup. 373, 173 A.2d 604.

45. Klassen v. Central Kansas Coop. Creamery Ass'n, 1946, 160 Kan. 697, 165 P.2d 601. Cf. National Glue Co. v. Thrash, 1921, 76 Ind.App. 381, 132 N. E. 311; Yoos v. City of Rochester, 1895, 92 Hun 481, 36 N.Y.S. 1072.

46. Jeffer v. Gifford, 1767, 4 Burr. 2141, 98 Eng.Rep. 116; Kidgill v. Moor, 1850, 9 C.B. 364, 137 Eng.Rep. 934. Cf. Smith v. Morse, 1889, 148 Mass. 407, 19 N.E. 393.

47. Gotwals v. City of Wessington Springs, 1932, 60 S.D. 428, 244 N.W. 649; Miller v. Edison Elec. Illuminating Co., 1906, 184 N.Y. 17, 76 N.E. 734; McDonnell v. Cambridge R. Co., 1890, 151 Mass. 159, 23 N.E. 841.

The interests of vendor and vendee are similarly divided before the conveyance. Missouri Pac. R. Co. v. Davis, 1932, 186 Ark. 401, 53 S.W.2d 851; Irvine v. City of Oelwein, 1915, 170 Iowa 653, 150 N.W. 674.

Once the invasion of the property interest is established, however, consequential damages to the possessor which result from it, such as injuries to his own health,[48] or loss of services of his family,[49] may be recovered.

On the other hand, it is generally agreed that anyone who has no interest in the property affected, such as a licensee;[50] an employee[51] or a lodger[52] on the premises, cannot maintain an action based on a private nuisance. But although there is authority to the contrary,[53] the greater number of cases have regarded member's of the family of the possessor as sharing the possession with him, and hence as entitled to recover damages which they have sustained, on the basis of nuisance.[54] The existence of a nuisance to

the land does not of course preclude an independent tort action for ordinary negligence resulting in interference with the bodily security of the individual.[55]

Distinguished from Trespass

The distinction between trespass and nuisance was originally that between the old action of trespass and the action on the case.[56] If there was a direct physical invasion of the plaintiff's land, as by casting water on it, it was a trespass; if the invasion was indirect, as where the defendant constructed a spout from which the water ultimately flowed upon the land, it was a nuisance.[57] Coupled with this was the fact that the old strict liability, which persisted as to trespass to land, was modified relatively early in nuisance cases—hence the anomalous rule, still followed in one or two jurisdictions,[58] that the defendant was strictly liable if his blasting operations cast rocks upon the plaintiff's premises, but not if they shook down his house.

With the abandonment of the old procedural forms, direct and indirect invasions have lost their significance, and the line between trespass and nuisance has become wavering and uncertain. The distinction

---

48. Vann v. Bowie Sewerage Co., 1936, 127 Tex. 97, 90 S.W.2d 561; O'Connor v. Aluminum Ore Co., 1922, 224 Ill.App. 613; Millett v. Minnesota Crushed Stone Co., 1920, 145 Minn. 475, 177 N.W. 641, reargument denied, 1920, 145 Minn. 475, 179 N. W. 682; Dixon v. New York Trap Rock Corp., 1944, 293 N.Y. 509, 58 N.E.2d 517, motion denied, 1945, 294 N.Y. 654, 60 N.E.2d 385. City of Evansville v. Rinehart, 1968, — Ind.App. —, 233 N.E.2d 495.

49. United States Smelting Co. v. Sisam, 8 Cir. 1911, 191 F. 293; Towaliga Falls Power Co. v. Sims, 1909, 6 Ga.App. 749, 65 S.E. 844; Millett v. Minnesota Crushed Stone Co., 1920, 145 Minn. 475, 177 N. W. 641.

50. Malone v. Laskey, [1907] 2 K.B. 141; Elliott v. Mason, 1911, 76 N.H. 229, 81 A. 701; Owen v. Henman, 1841, 1 Watts & S. (Pa.) 548.

51. Page v. Niagara Chemical Division, Fla.1953, 68 So.2d 383; Broderick v. City of Waterbury, 1944, 130 Conn. 601, 36 A.2d 585; Kilts v. Supervisors of Kent County, 1910, 162 Mich. 646, 127 N.W. 821; Daurizio v. Merchants' Despatch Transp. Co., 1934, 152 Misc. 716, 274 N.Y.S. 174.

52. Reber v. Illinois Cent. R. Co., 1932, 161 Miss. 885, 138 So. 574. Cf. Miller v. Edison Elec. Ill. Co., 1906, 184 N.Y. 17, 76 N.E. 734.

53. Cunard and Wife v. Antifyre, Ltd., [1933] 1 K.B. 551; Ellis v. Kansas City, St. J. & C. B. R. Co., 1876, 63 Mo. 131, 21 Am.Rep. 436; Hughes v. City of Auburn, 1899, 161 N.Y. 96, 55 N.E. 389; Millett v. Minnesota Crushed Stone Co., 1920, 145 Minn. 475, 177 N.W. 641, reargument denied 145 Minn. 475, 179 N.W. 682; Kavanagh v. Barber, 1892, 131 N.Y. 211, 30 N.E. 235.

54. Fort Worth & R. G. Ry. Co. v. Glenn, 1904, 97 Tex. 586, 80 S.W. 992; Hosmer v. Republic Iron

& Steel Co., 1913, 179 Ala. 415, 60 So. 801; Hodges v. Town of Drew, 1935, 172 Miss. 668, 159 So. 298; Pere Marquette R. Co. v. Chadwick, 1917, 65 Ind. App. 95, 115 N.E. 678.

55. See Kilts v. Supervisor of Kent County, 1910, 162 Mich. 646, 127 N.W. 821; Daurizio v. Merchants' Despatch Transp. Co., 1934, 158 Misc. 716, 274 N.Y. S. 174; Malone v. Laskey, [1907] 2 K.B. 141; Cunard and Wife v. Antifyre, [1933] 1 K.B. 551.

56. See supra, § 7.

57. Reynolds v. Clarke, 1725, 1 Strange 634, 93 Eng. Rep. 747. This distinction is repeated in such modern cases as Pan American Petroleum Co. v. Byars, 1934, 228 Ala. 372, 153 So. 616; Wright v. Syracuse, B. & N. Y. R. Co., 1888, 49 Hun 445, 3 N.Y.S. 480, affirmed, 1891, 124 N.Y. 668, 27 N.E. 854; Central of Georgia R. Co. v. Americas Const. Co., 1909, 133 Ga. 392, 65 S.E. 855.

58. See supra, p. 513.

which is now accepted [59] is that trespass is an invasion of the plaintiff's interest in the exclusive possession of his land, while nuisance is an interference with his use and enjoyment of it. The difference is that between walking across his lawn and establishing a bawdy house next door; between felling a tree across his boundary line and keeping him awake at night with the noise of a rolling mill. It is obvious, however, that there are many types of conduct which will interfere with both of these interests. The blasting nuisance which makes the plaintiff's home insufferable may be a trespass when it throws stones into his garden,[60] and the flooding of his land, which is a trespass, may deprive him of all use and enjoyment.[61] The same is true of covering the land with dirt, sand and mud,[62] or encroaching on the space above it.[63] In such cases there is both trespass and nuisance, and the plaintiff is free to pursue his remedy for either. It was formerly sometimes said that a nuisance may be caused only by conduct outside of the land affected; [64] but this is scarcely correct, since a dog which howls under the plaintiff's window,[65] cattle which wander over his fields,[66] or any other entry so long continued or repeated as to cause a substantial interference with his use or enjoyment [67] may amount to a nuisance.

The distinction between the two theories of liability becomes important chiefly in connection with the statute of limitations. A cause of action in trespass, for disturbance of the possession, becomes complete when the land is entered, although no actual damage has been done,[68] while liability in damages for a nuisance begins only when the interference causes substantial harm.[69] However, a

65. Brill v. Flagler, 1840, 23 Wend., N.Y., 354.

66. Barnes v. Hagar, Sup.Ct.1913, 148 N.Y.S. 395, affirmed 166 App.Div. 952, 151 N.Y.S. 1103.

67. Coulson v. White, 1743, 3 Atk. 21, 26 Eng.Rep. 816. Accord: Codman v. Evans, 1863, 7 Allen, Mass., 431 (building projecting over plaintiff's land); Graham v. Lowden, 1940, 137 Me. 48, 15 A. 2d 69 (building erected on plaintiff's land); Milton v. Puffer, 1911, 207 Mass. 416, 93 N.E. 634 (same).

68. Kansas Pac. R. Co. v. Mihlman, 1876, 17 Kan. 224; Williams v. Pomeroy Coal Co., 1882, 37 Ohio St. 583; National Copper Co. v. Minnesota Min. Co., 1885, 57 Mich. 83, 23 N.W. 781. See, however, the view of the Second Restatement of Torts, § 162, that liability without proof of actual damage should be limited to intentional invasions.

69. Barakis v. American Cyanamid Co., N.D.Tex. 1958, 161 F.Supp. 25; Yolande Coal & Coke Co. v. Pierce, 1915, 12 Ala.App. 431, 68 So. 563, cert. denied 193 Ala. 687, 69 So. 1021; Hooker v. Farmers Irr. Dist., 8 Cir. 1921, 272 F. 600; Hempstead v. Cargill, 1891, 46 Minn. 118, 48 N.W. 558; Heckaman v. Northern Pac. R. Co., 1933, 93 Mont. 363, 20 P.2d 258.

It should be noted that the threat of future harm may amount to present damage, by interfering with enjoyment. Cumberland Torpedo Co. v. Gaines, 1923, 201 Ky. 88, 255 S.W. 1046; Baldwin v. Simpson, 1935, 191 Ark. 448, 86 S.W.2d 420. Also that a threatened nuisance may be restrained in equity without proof of actual damage, because of the possibility of irreparable injury in the future; and the fact that the act of the defendant, if permitted to continue, would ripen into an easement, is sometimes considered enough to make the injury irreparable. Lindsay-Strathmore Irr. Dist. v. Superior Court of Tulare County, 1920, 182 Cal. 315, 187 P. 1056; Amsterdam Knitting Co. v. Dean, 1900, 162 N.Y. 278, 56 N.E. 757; Murphy v. Lincoln, 1891, 63 Vt. 278, 22 A. 418.

59. Restatement of Torts, Scope and Introductory Note to ch. 40, preceding § 822. See Ryan v. City of Emmetsburg, 1942, 232 Iowa 600, 4 N.W.2d 435.

60. Compare Beecher v. Dull, 1928, 294 Pa. 17, 143 A. 498; Green v. T. A. Shoemaker & Co., 1909, 111 Md. 69, 73 A. 688 (nuisance), with Asheville Const. Co. v. Southern R. Co., 4 Cir. 1927, 19 F.2d 32; Mulchanock v. Whitehall Cement Mfg. Co., 1916, 253 Pa. 262, 98 A. 554 (trespass); Hakkila v. Old Colony Broken Stone Co., 1928, 264 Mass. 447, 162 N.E. 895 (both).

61. Compare Lawson v. Price, 1876, 45 Md. 123; Groover v. Hightower, 1939, 59 Ga.App. 491, 1 S.E. 2d 446 (trespass), with Rindge v. Sargent, 1886, 64 N.H. 294, 9 A. 723 (nuisance); Mueller v. Fruen, 1886, 36 Minn. 273, 30 N.W. 886 (both); Irvine v. City of Oelwein, 1915, 170 Iowa 653, 150 N.W. 674 (both).

62. Burk v. High Point Homes, 1960, 22 Misc.2d 492, 197 N.Y.S.2d 969, appeal dismissed, 1960, 11 App. Div.2d 701, 205 N.Y.S.2d 862.

63. Pahl v. Ribero, 1961, 193 Cal.App.2d 154, 14 Cal. Rptr. 174.

64. 1 Wood, Law of Nuisances, 3d Ed. 1893, 33.

continuing trespass, such as the erection of a structure on the plaintiff's land, affords a continuing cause of action,[70] which can hardly be distinguished from nuisance, and has been dealt with indiscriminately as either.[71] Whether the plaintiff may bring a single action for past and prospective damages, or successive actions for the continuing tort, has been made to turn in the case of nuisance, as well as trespass,[72] upon the permanent nature of the condition created, and the likelihood that the defendant will terminate it rather than pay a subsequent claim.[73]

Reasonable Use

Most of the litigation as to private nuisance has dealt with the conflicting interests of landowners, and the question of the reasonableness of the defendant's conduct. The defendant's privilege of making a reasonable use of his own property for his own benefit and conducting his affairs in his own way is no less important than the plaintiff's right to use and enjoy his premises. The two are correlative and interdependent, and neither is entitled to prevail entirely, at the expense of the other. Some balance must be struck between the two. The plaintiff must be expected to endure some inconvenience rather than curtail the defendant's freedom of action, and the defendant must so use his own property that he causes no unreasonable harm to the plaintiff.[74] The law of private nuisance is very largely a series of adjustments to limit the reciprocal rights and privileges of both.[75] In every case the court must make a comparative evaluation of the conflicting interests according to objective legal standards, and the gravity of the harm to the plaintiff must be weighed against the utility of the defendant's conduct.[76]

Many factors must be considered in this evaluating process, any one of which is sel-

70. See supra, p. 75.

71. See Codman v. Evans, 1863, 89 (7 Allen) Mass. 431 (encroachment); Mueller v. Fruen, 1886, 36 Minn. 273, 30 N.W. 886 (flooding); Irvine v. City of Oelwein, 1915, 170 Iowa 653, 150 N.W. 674.

72. See supra, p. 75.

73. City of Springdale v. Weathers, 1967, 241 Ark. 772, 410 S.W.2d 754; Hawkins v. Wallace, Ky.1964, 384 S.W.2d 507; Robertson v. Cincinnati, N. O. & T. P. R. Co., 1960, 207 Tenn. 272, 339 S.W.2d 6; Reynolds Metals Co. v. Wand, 9 Cir. 1962, 308 F.2d 504; Spaulding v. Cameron, 1952, 38 Cal.2d 265, 239 P.2d 625.

The expense or inconvenience of abatement is an important factor to be considered, and may be decisive. Bainbridge Power Co. v. Ivey, 1930, 41 Ga. App. 193, 152 S.E. 306; Chesapeake & O. R. Co. v. Coleman, 1919, 184 Ky. 9, 210 S.W. 947; Wilmoth v. Limestone Products Co., Tex.Civ.App.1953, 255 S. W.2d 532, ref. n. r. e.

See McCormick, Damages, 1935, 511–515; McCormick, Damages for Anticipated Injury to Land, 1924, 37 Harv.L.Rev. 574, 593–601; Goodrich, Permanent Structure and Continuing Injuries—The Iowa Rule, 1918, 4 Iowa L.B. 65; Notes, 1927, 21 Ill.L.Rev. 629; 1933, 27 Ill.L.Rev. 953; 1937, 21 Minn.L.Rev. 334, 339; 1961, 28 Tenn.L.Rev. 433.

74. The often repeated phrase "sic utere tuo ut alienum non laedas" (use thine own so that thou dost no harm to another) apparently means no more than this. See Smith, Reasonable Use as Justification for Damage to a Neighbor, 1917, 17 Col.L.Rev. 383, 388–390.

75. "The law of nuisance plys [sic] between two antithetical extremes: The principle that every person is entitled to use his property for any purpose that he sees fit, and the opposing principle that everyone is bound to use his property in such a manner as not to injure the property or rights of his neighbor. For generations courts, in their task of judging, have ruled on these extremes according to the wisdom of the day, and many have recognized that the contemporary view of public policy shifts from generation to generation." Antonik v. Chamberlain, 1947, 81 Ohio App. 465, 78 N.E.2d 752. The case contains an excellent statement of the whole matter. See also Soukoup v. Republic Steel Corp., 1946, 78 Ohio App. 87, 66 N.E.2d 334; Roberts v. C. F. Adams & Son, 1947, 199 Okl. 369, 184 P.2d 634; Johnson v. Drysdale, 1939, 66 S.D. 436, 285 N.W. 301; Louisville Refining Co. v. Mudd, Ky.1960, 339 S.W.2d 181. See Note, 1961, 50 Ky.L.J. 104.

76. Restatement of Torts, §§ 826–831. See Smith, Reasonable Use as Justification for Damage to a Neighbor, 1917, 17 Col.L.Rev. 383; Johnson v. Drysdale, 1939, 66 S.D. 436, 285 N.W. 301; McCarty v. Natural Carbonic Gas Co., 1907, 189 N.Y. 40, 46, 81 N.E. 549, 550; Gulf, C. & S. F. R. Co. v. Oakes, 1900, 94 Tex. 155, 159, 58 S.W. 999, 1000; Holman v. Athens Empire Laundry Co., 1919, 149 Ga. 345, 100 S.E. 207; Ebur v. Alloy Metal Wire Co., 1931, 304 Pa. 177, 155 A. 280.

dom conclusive.[77] The gravity of the harm will of course depend upon the extent and duration of the interference. The plaintiff may be required to submit to a minor annoyance, such as an unsightly spectacle near his house,[78] a slight amount of noise and smoke,[79] or a disturbance which is merely temporary [80] or occurs only at long intervals,[81] where a greater one would be considered a nuisance.[82] The character of the harm is also important; if there is physical damage to property,[83] the courts have been more inclined to grant relief than where there is only personal discomfort. The social value of the use which the plaintiff makes of his land is always a material factor and may protect a residence against a stone crusher.[84] In addition, the extent to which the plaintiff may be able, without undue burden or hardship, to avoid the harm by taking precautions against it, as by closing his windows against occasional smoke, may have some bearing upon the seriousness of the invasion of his rights.[85]

So far as the defendant is concerned, the utility of his conduct is always affected by the social value which the law attaches to its ultimate purpose. The world must have factories,[86] smelters,[87] oil refineries,[88] noisy

77. Thus the character of the neighborhood, Jedneak v. Minneapolis General Elec. Co., 1942, 212 Minn. 226, 230, 4 N.W.2d 326, 327, 328; the nature of the thing complained of, Hofstetter v. Myers, Inc., 1951, 170 Kan. 564, 228 P.2d 522; its proximity to those complaining, Hasslinger v. Village of Hartland, 1940, 234 Wis. 201, 290 N.W. 647; the frequency and continuity of its operation, Hofstetter v. Myers, supra; the nature and extent of the harm done, Schott v. Appleton Brewery Co., Mo.App.1947, 205 S.W.2d 917; whether or not there are any means of preventing it, Godard v. Babson-Dow Mfg. Co., 1943, 313 Mass. 280, 47 N.E.2d 303; whether or not the operation is conducted in the only feasible locality, Robinson v. Westman, 1947, 224 Minn. 105, 29 N.W.2d 1; the importance of the defendant's business to the community, Soukoup v. Republic Steel Corp., 1946, 78 Ohio App. 87, 66 N. E.2d 334; the amount of defendant's investment, City of San Antonio v. Camp Warnecke, Tex.Civ. App.1954, 267 S.W.2d 468; the length of time his business has existed. Waschak v. Moffat, 1953, 173 Pa.Super. 209, 96 A.2d 163, reversed on other grounds, 1953, 379 Pa. 441, 109 A.2d 310.

78. State Road Comm'n v. Oakes, 1966, 150 W.Va. 709, 149 S.E.2d 293; Livingston v. Davis, 1951, 243 Iowa 21, 50 N.W.2d 592; Feldstein v. Kammauf, 1956, 209 Md. 479, 121 A.2d 716; Crabtree v. City Auto Salvage Co., 1960, 47 Tenn.App. 616, 340 S.W. 2d 940; Vermont Salvage Corp. v. Village of St. Johnsbury, 1943, 113 Vt. 341, 34 A.2d 188. But aesthetic considerations may be important in determining reasonable use. Noel, Unaesthetic Sights as Nuisances, 1939, 25 Corn.L.Q. 1; Note, 1937, 44 W. Va.L.Q. 58.

79. Holman v. Athens Empire Laundry Co., 1919, 149 Ga. 645, 100 S.E. 207; Hannum v. Gruber, 1943, 346 Pa. 417, 31 A.2d 99; Pawlowicz v. American Locomotive Co., 1915, 90 Misc. 450, 154 N.Y.S. 768. See Lloyd, Noise as a Nuisance, 1933, 82 U.Pa.L.Rev. 567.

Or even a considerable amount. Woschak v. Moffat, 1954, 379 Pa. 441, 109 A.2d 310.

80. Garvey v. Long Island R. Co., 1889, 159 N.Y. 323, 54 N.E. 57; Harrison v. Southwark & Vauxhall Water Co., [1891] 2 Ch. 409, 413, 414.

81. Molony v. Pounds, 1949, 361 Pa. 498, 64 A.2d 802 (occasional noise from restaurant); Heffenstall Co. v. Berkshire Chemical Co., 1944, 130 Conn. 485, 35

A.2d 845 (occasional injury to health of employees); Jones v. Adler, 1913, 183 Ala. 435, 62 So. 777.

82. Cf. Helms v. Eastern Kansas Oil Co., 1917, 102 Kan. 164, 169 P. 208; McCarty v. Natural Carbonic Gas Co., 1907, 189 N.Y. 40, 81 N.E. 549.

83. Cf. Rindge v. Sargent, 1886, 64 N.H. 294, 9 A. 723; Stevens v. Moon, 1921, 54 Cal.App. 737, 202 P. 961; Parsons v. Luhr, 1928, 205 Cal. 193, 270 P. 443; Hoadley v. M. Seward & Son Co., 1899, 71 Conn. 640, 42 A. 997; Beecher v. Dull, 1928, 294 Pa. 17, 143 A. 498.

84. Brede v. Minnesota Crushed Stone Co., 1919, 143 Minn. 374, 173 N.W. 805.

85. See Keeney & Wood Mfg. Co. v. Union Mfg. Co., 1873, 39 Conn. 576; Snow v. Parsons, 1856, 28 Vt. 459; Hazard Powder Co. v. Somersville Mfg. Co., 1905, 78 Conn. 171, 61 A. 519. Most courts have treated the question as one of the plaintiff's obligation to avoid the consequences of the defendant's tort. See Carroll Springs Distilling Co. v. Schnepfe, 1909, 111 Md. 420, 431, 74 A. 828; Sherman v. Fall River Iron Works Co., 1861, 2 Allen, Mass., 524, 526; Atchison, T. & S. F. R. Co. v. Jones, 1903, 110 Ill.App. 626; Southern R. Co. v. Poetker, 1910, 46 Ind.App. 295, 91 N.E. 610.

86. Monroe Carp Pond Co. v. River Raisin Paper Co., 1927, 240 Mich. 279, 215 N.W. 325; Daughtry v. Warren, 1881, 85 N.C. 136.

87. Clifton Iron Co. v. Dye, 1888, 87 Ala. 468, 6 So. 192; Madison v. Ducktown Sulphur, Copper & Iron Co., 1904, 113 Tenn. 331, 83 S.W. 658.

88. Rose v. Socony-Vacuum Corp., 1934, 54 R.I. 411, 173 A. 627; Helms v. Eastern Kansas Oil Co., 1917,

machinery,[89] and blasting,[90] as well as airports,[91] even at the expense of some inconvenience to those in the vicinity, and the plaintiff may be required to accept and tolerate some not unreasonable discomfort for the general good. It is only when the harm is excessive that he will be heard to complain.[92] On the other hand a foul pond,[93] or a vicious or noisy dog,[94] will have little if any social value, and relatively slight annoyance from it may justify relief. Conduct which is indecent, such as breeding animals before the plaintiff's windows,[95] or destructive of the general welfare, as in the case of a house of prostitution,[96] is nearly always a private nuisance when it interferes with the enjoyment of the plaintiff's property. Likewise, the motive of the defendant may

be important. In all but a few jurisdictions,[97] it is now settled that where the defendant acts out of pure malice or spite, as by erecting a fence for the sole purpose [98] of shutting off the plaintiff's view,[99] or drilling a well to cut off the plaintiff's underground water,[1] or leaving his kitchen door open in order to give the plaintiff the benefit of the aroma of cooking cabbage and onions,[2] or harassing him with repeated objectionable telephone calls,[3] or playing loud musical instruments to

---

102 Kan. 164, 169 P. 208; Louisville Refining Co. v. Mudd, Ky.1960, 339 S.W.2d 181.

89. Gilbert v. Showerman, 1871, 23 Mich. 448.

90. Booth v. Rome, W. & O. T. R. Co., 1893, 140 N.Y 267, 35 N.E. 592.

91. Antonik v. Chamberlain, 1947, 81 Ohio App. 465, 78 N.E.2d 752; Atkinson v. Bernard, Inc., 1960, 223 Or. 624, 355 P.2d 229. See Note, 1961, 74 Harv.L. Rev. 97.

92. Ross v. Butler, 1868, 19 N.J.Eq. 294; Helms v. Eastern Kansas Oil Co., 1917, 102 Kan. 164, 169 P. 208; McCarty v. Natural Carbonic Gas Co., 1907, 189 N.Y. 40, 81 N.E. 549; Hoadley v. M. Seward & Son Co., 1899, 71 Conn. 640, 42 A. 997.

93. Mills v. Hall & Richards, 1832, 9 Wend., N.Y., 315; Hosmer v. Republic Iron & Steel Co., 1913, 179 Ala. 415, 60 So. 801; cf. Fort Worth & R. G. R. Co. v. Glenn, 1904, 97 Tex. 586, 80 S.W. 992 (well full of decayed animal life).

94. Hubbard v. Preston, 1892, 90 Mich. 221, 51 N.W. 209; Rider v. Clarkson, 1919, 77 N.J.Eq. 469, 78 A. 676.

95. Hayden v. Tucker, 1866, 37 Mo. 214; Farrell v. Cook, 1884, 16 Neb. 483, 20 N.W. 720; cf. Magel v. Gruetli Benevolent Society, 1920, 203 Mo.App. 335, 218 S.W. 704 (obscene language and indecent exposure).

96. Crawford v. Tyrrell, 1891, 128 N.Y. 341, 28 N.E. 514; Tedescki v. Berger, 1907, 150 Ala. 649, 43 So. 960. Cf. Fox v. Corbitt, 1916, 137 Tenn. 466, 194 S. W. 88 (saloon); Paramount-Richards Theatres v. City of Hattiesburg, 1950, 210 Miss. 271, 49 So.2d 574 (Sunday night motion pictures).

97. The early common law rule was that a spite fence was not a nuisance. Mahan v. Brown, 1835, 13 Wend., N.Y., 261; Letts v. Kessler, 1896, 54 Ohio St. 73, 42 N.E. 765; Metzger v. Hochrein, 1900, 107 Wis. 267, 83 N.W. 308; Koblegard v. Hale, 1906, 60 W.Va. 37, 53 S.E. 793. In most such jurisdictions the rule has been altered by statute. See Rideout v. Knox, 1888, 148 Mass. 368, 19 N.E. 390; Horan v. Byrnes, 1903, 72 N.H. 93, 54 A. 945; Vojdich v. Jedelski, 1918, 140 Minn. 520, 168 N.W. 95.

The only two recent cases to take such a position are Cohen v. Perrino, 1947, 355 Pa. 455, 50 A.2d 348; Musumeci v. Leonardo, 1950, 71 R.I. 255, 75 A.2d 175.

98. It is generally agreed that if the structure serves a useful purpose, the addition of a spite motive does not make it a nuisance. Kuzniak v. Kozminski, 1895, 107 Mich. 444, 65 N.W. 275; White v. Bernhart, 1925, 41 Idaho 665, 241 P. 367; Campbell v. Hammock, 1955, 212 Ga. 90, 90 S.E.2d 415; D'Inzillo v. Basile, 1943, 180 Misc. 237, 40 N.Y.S.2d 293, affirmed, 1943, 266 App.Div. 875, 43 N.Y.S.2d 638.

99. Larkin v. Tsavaris, Fla.1956, 85 So.2d 731; Welsh v. Todd, 1963, 260 N.C. 527, 133 S.E.2d 171; Erickson v. Hudson, 1952, 70 Wyo. 317, 249 P.2d 523; Hornsby v. Smith, 1941, 191 Ga. 491, 13 S.E.2d 20; Hibbard v. Halliday, 1916, 58 Pkl. 244, 158 P. 1158.

1. Chesley v. King, 1882, 74 Me. 164; Gagnon v. French Lick Springs Hotel Co., 1904, 163 Ind. 687, 72 N.E. 849; Barclay v. Abraham, 1903, 121 Iowa 619, 96 N.W. 1080; Katz v. Walkinshaw, 1903, 141 Cal. 116, 70 P. 663, 74 P. 766; Stillwater Water Co. v. Farmer, 1903, 89 Minn. 58, 93 N.W. 907.

2. Medford v. Levy, 1888, 31 W.Va. 649, 8 S.E. 302. Cf. Burnett v. Rushton, Fla.1951, 52 So.2d 645 (spiteful noise, light, barking dog, obscene gestures); Hollywood Silver Fox Farm v. Emmett, [1936] 2 K.B. 468 (firing gun to interfere with fox breeding).

3. Wiggins v. Moskins Credit Clothing Store, E.D.S. C.1956, 137 F.Supp. 764.

annoy him,[4] such conduct is indefensible from a social point of view, and there is liability for the nuisance.

Finally, a very material factor in all cases is the practical possibility of preventing or avoiding the harm. If the defendant, by taking reasonable steps,[5] without too great hardship or expense, could reduce or eliminate the inconvenience to the plaintiff, and still carry on his enterprise effectively, his failure to do so may render him liable. Thus a factory, which is not a nuisance in itself, may become one when it is so operated that it gives out unnecessary noise or smoke.[6] It is in these cases of practically avoidable harm that a nuisance is most frequently found to rest on negligence.[7]

The interest of the community, or the public at large, must also be thrown into the scale, along with those of the contending parties; and a cement plant upon which the prosperity of a city depends,[8] or a sewage disposal system essential to its existence,[9] may not be enjoined or subjected to a heavy burden of damages, even though it is an unquestioned inconvenience to those in the vicinity.

The decisive consideration in many cases is the nature of the locality, and the suitability of the use made of the land by both the plaintiff and the defendant.[10] The courts have been compelled to recognize that certain areas, by reason of their physical character [11] or the accident of community growth, are devoted to certain types of activities, and that some uses of land are more or less segregated in certain localities, in order to avoid unnecessary conflict between those which are necessarily incompatible. Thus some districts are used primarily for residential purposes, others for industry, and others for agriculture. Sound public policy demands that the land in each locality be used for purposes suited to the character of that locality, and that anyone desiring to

---

4. Christie v. Davey, [1893] 1 Ch. 316; Collier v. Ernst, 1941, 31 Del.Co., Pa., 49.

See Ames, Tort Because of Wrongful Motive, 1905, 18 Harv.L.Rev. 411; Clayberg, The Law of Percolating Waters, 1915, 14 Mich.L.Rev. 119; Drukker, Spite Fences and Spite Wells, 1938, 26 Cal.L.Rev. 691; Friedmann, Motive in the English Law of Nuisance, 1954, 40 Va.L.Rev. 583; Notes, 1925, 11 Va.L.Rev. 122; 1954, 9 Wyo.L.J. 74.

5. A manufacturer may not be required to employ means of unknown or doubtful efficacy. Grzelka v. Chevrolet Motor Car Co., 1938, 286 Mich. 141, 281 N.W. 568.

But even the impossibility of purchasing the necessary equipment in war time will not necessarily prevent the nuisance from being enjoined in the meantime. Anderson v. Guerrein Sky-Way Amusement Co., 1943, 349 Pa. 80, 29 A.2d 682.

6. De Blois v. Bowers, D.Mass.1930, 44 F.2d 621; Sprague v. Sampson, 1921, 120 Me. 353, 114 A. 305; Illinois Central R. Co. v. Grabill, 1869, 50 Ill. 241; Dargan v. Waddill, 1848, 31 N.C. 244; Dauberman v. Grant, 1926, 198 Cal. 586, 246 P. 319; Higgins v. Decorah Produce Co., 1932, 214 Iowa 276, 242 N.W. 109. Cf. Sans v. Ramsey Golf & Country Club, 1959, 29 N.J. 438, 149 A.2d 599 (relocation of third tee of golf club); Kuhn v. Wood, Ohio App.1941, 36 N.E.2d 1006 (hogpen kept in unreasonable manner); Barrett v. Lopez, 1953, 57 N.M. 697, 262 P.2d 981 (uncontrolled dance hall).

It may be possible to apportion the damages, and hold the defendant liable only for the excess caused beyond his reasonable use. Jenkins v. Pennsylvania R. Co., 1902, 67 N.J.L. 331, 51 A. 704.

7. See supra, p. 575.

8. Compare Powell v. Superior Portland Cement, 1942, 15 Wash.2d 14, 129 P.2d 536, with Riblet v. Spokane Portland Cement Co., 1952, 41 Wash.2d 249, 248 P.2d 380. Cf. Hannum v. Gruber, 1943, 346 Pa. 417, 31 A.2d 99.

"Without smoke, Pittsburgh would have remained a very pretty *village.*" Musmanno, J., in Versailles Borough v. McKeesport Coal & Coke Co., 1935, 83 Pitts.Leg.J. 379, 385.

9. East St. Johns Shingle Co. v. City of Portland, 1952, 195 Or. 505, 246 P.2d 554.

10. Well stated in Soukoup v. Republic Steel Corp., 1946, 78 Ohio App. 87, 66 N.E.2d 334. See also Obrecht v. National Gypsum Co., 1960, 361 Mich. 399, 105 N.W.2d 143. Also Beuscher and Morrison, Judicial Zoning Through Recent Nuisance Cases, [1955] Wis.L.Rev. 440.

11. See Pennsylvania Coal Co. v. Sanderson, 1886, 113 Pa. 126, 6 A. 453; Robb v. Carnegie Bros. & Co., 1891, 145 Pa. 324, 22 A. 649; Turner v. Big Lake Oil Co., 1936, 128 Tex. 155, 96 S.W.2d 221; Gulf Pipe Line Co. v. Sims, 1934, 168 Okl. 209, 32 P.2d 902.

make a particular use of land should do it in a suitable place.[12]　Thus a plaintiff who makes his home in a manufacturing [13] or a business [14] district cannot be heard to complain of any noise, smoke, vibration or other inconvenience which is normal to such a locality, unless it is practically avoidable or is carried to an unreasonable extreme.[15]　On the other hand a factory,[16] a gas works,[17] a sawmill [18] or a livery stable [19] located in a residential district may become a nuisance when it causes the same interference with homes in the vicinity.　A funeral parlor [20] or

a gasoline filling station [21] which creates no nuisance in a business center may cause one in a locality given over to residences, and a powder mill in a city [22] may be a nuisance when one in the country is not.[23]

In this process of judicial zoning the courts frequently are called on to determine the paramount use to which a locality is devoted.[24]　The presence of some factories in a neighborhood which still is used chiefly for residences will not give it an industrial character such as to justify a new establishment which interferes with the plaintiff's use of his land.[25]　Furthermore the character of a

---

12. Restatement of Torts, § 827, Comment *f*.

13. Wagner v. Yale & Towne Mfg. Co., 1944, 348 Pa. 595, 36 A.2d 321; Grzelka v. Chevrolet Motor Car Co., 1938, 286 Mich. 141, 281 N.W. 568; Tortorella v. H. Traiser & Co., 1933, 284 Mass. 497, 188 N.E. 254; Dahl v. Utah Oil Refining Co., 1927, 71 Utah 1, 262 P. 269.

14. Irby v. Panama Ice Co., 1936, 184 La. 1082, 168 So. 306; Kasper v. H. P. Hood & Sons, 1935, 291 Mass. 24, 196 N.E. 149. Cf. Burke v. Hollinger, 1929, 296 Pa. 510, 146 A. 115; and see Beckman v. Marshall, Fla.1956, 85 So.2d 553 (day nursery in neighborhood with traffic lights, filling stations, four-lane highway with truck traffic, and railroad).

15. Cf. Kosich v. Poultrymen's Service Corp., 1945, 136 N.J.Eq. 571, 43 A.2d 15; Vowinckel v. N. Clark & Sons, 1932, 216 Cal. 156, 13 P.2d 733; Asmann v. Masters, 1940, 151 Kan. 281, 98 P.2d 419; Helms v. Eastern Kansas Oil Co., 1917, 102 Kan. 164, 169 P. 208.

16. Riblet v. Spokane Portland Cement Co., 1952, 41 Wash.2d 249, 248 P.2d 380; Kennedy v. Frechette, 1924, 45 R.I. 399, 123 A. 146; Stevens v. Rockport Granite Co., 1914, 216 Mass. 486, 104 N.E. 371.

17. Cleveland v. Citizens' Gaslight Co., 1869, 20 N.J. Eq. 201.

18. Krocker v. Westmoreland Planing Mill Co., 1922, 274 Pa. 143, 117 A. 669. Cf. Sarraillon v. Stevenson, 1950, 153 Neb. 182, 43 N.W.2d 509 (slaughterhouse); Obrecht v. National Gypsum Co., 1960, 361 Mich. 399, 105 N.W.2d 143 (loading dock for gypsum rock).

19. Johnson v. Drysdale, 1939, 66 S.D. 436, 285 N.W. 301; cf. Hansen v. Independent School Dist. No. 1 in Nez Perce County, 1939, 61 Idaho 109, 98 P.2d 959; City of Fredericktown v. Osborn, Mo.App.1968, 429 S.W.2d 17 (dog kennel).

20. Rutledge v. National Funeral Home of New Albany, Miss.1967, 203 So.2d 318; Jack v. Torrant, 1950, 136 Conn. 414, 71 A.2d 705; Mutual Service Funeral Homes v. Fehler, 1952, 257 Ala. 354, 58 So.

2d 770; Blair v. Yancy, 1958, 229 Ark. 745, 318 S. W.2d 589; Dawson v. Laufersweiler, 1950, 241 Iowa 850, 43 N.W.2d 726. See Lynch, Restricting Location of Undertaking Establishments, 1926, 24 Geo.L.J. 352. Cf. Overby v. Piet, Fla.App.1964, 163 So.2d 532 (cemetery).

There are cases contra, such as Mast v. Oakley-Metcalf Funeral Home, Tex.Civ.App.1937, 101 S.W.2d 819. See Notes, 1934, 18 Minn.L.Rev. 482; 1938, 16 Tex.L.Rev. 278.

21. Residential: Bortz v. Troth, 1948, 359 Pa. 326, 59 A.2d 93; McPherson v. First Presbyterian Church of Woodward, 1926, 120 Okl. 40, 248 P. 561; Huddleston v. Burnett, 1926, 172 Ark. 216, 287 S.W. 1013; Cities Service Oil Co. v. Roberts, 10 Cir. 1933, 62 F.2d 579.

Cf. Robinson v. Westman, 1947, 224 Minn. 105, 29 N. W.2d 1 (riding academy); Phelps v. Winch, 1923, 309 Ill. 158, 140 N.E. 847 (dance hall); Smith v. Nickoloff, 1938, 283 Mich. 188, 277 N.W. 880 (restaurant); Martin v. Williams, 1956, 141 W.Va. 595, 93 S.E.2d 835 (used car lot); Dale v. Bryant, Ohio C.P.1957, 141 N.E.2d 504 (burning automobile for salvage).

Business: Julian v. Golden Rule Oil Co., 1923, 112 Kan. 671, 212 P. 884; Coley v. Campbell, 1926, 120 Misc. 869, 215 N.Y.S. 679; Daniel v. Kosh, 1939, 173 Va. 352, 4 S.E.2d 381.

See Notes, 1928, 12 Minn.L.Rev. 669; 1940, 26 Va.L. Rev. 392.

22. Heeg v. Licht, 1880, 80 N.Y. 579; Cumberland Torpedo Co. v. Gaines, 1923, 201 Ky. 88, 255 S.W. 1046.

23. In re Dilworth's Appeal, 1879, 91 Pa. 247. Blasting in a farming area may not be a nuisance, even though it shakes the earth. Henn v. Universal Atlas Cement Co., Ohio C.P. 1957, 144 N.E.2d 917.

24. See Burke v. Hollinger, 1929, 296 Pa. 510, 146 A. 115.

25. Cleveland v. Citizens' Gaslight Co., 1869, 20 N.J. Eq. 201; Krocker v. Westmoreland Planing Mill

district may change with the passage of time, and an industry set up in the open country may become a nuisance, or be required to modify its activities, when residences spring up around it.[26] It will acquire no prescriptive right,[27] unless during the necessary period it was causing an unreasonable interference for which an action might have been maintained.[28] Zoning ordinances now affect the whole problem in all of the larger cities, and within constitutional limitations may be decisive as to the permissible uses to which particular areas may be put.[29] In an action for damages, the relative hardship upon the plaintiff and the defendant is not material, once the nuisance is found to exist.

In still other types of cases, it becomes necessary for the court to determine the extent to which either party is free to insist upon a property right or privilege to which each has a claim. Thus it is the prevailing view that the privilege of an upper riparian owner to abstract or divert water from a stream is limited to a reasonable use of the water which does no unreasonable harm to the interests of lower owners.[30] Any use is

privileged which does no harm,[31] or whose utility outweighs the gravity of the inconvenience which results;[32] but there will be liability for any diversion which unreasonably interferes with the use of the stream below.[33] The right of each to make use of the water is qualified by that of the other,[34] and the court must strike a balance between the two, having in view the same considerations as in the case of any other nuisance.[35] The same is true, in general, of the pollution of the stream,[36] and of the use of percolating or subterranean waters,[37] and it seems the

Co., 1922, 274 Pa. 143, 117 A. 669; Stevens v. Rockport Granite Co., 1914, 216 Mass. 486, 104 N.E. 371; cf. Graham & Wager v. Ridge, 1931, 41 Ohio App. 288, 179 N.E. 693.

26. City of Fort Smith v. Western Hide & Fur Co., 1922, 153 Ark. 99, 239 S.W. 724; Green v. Gilbert, 1880, 60 N.H. 144; City of Baltimore v. Fairfield Imp. Co., 1898, 87 Md. 352, 39 A. 1081; Campbell v. Seaman, 1876, 63 N.Y. 568. See Levitin, Change of Neighborhood in Nuisance Cases, 1964, 13 Coeve.-Marsh.L.Rev. 340.

27. Sturges v. Bridgman, 1879, 11 Ch.Div. 852; Ireland v. Bowman & Cockrell, 1908, 130 Ky. 153, 113 S.W. 56; Holsman v. Boiling Spring Bleaching Co., 1862, 14 N.J.Eq. 335.

28. As in Hudson v. Dailey, 1909, 156 Cal. 617, 105 P. 748; Charnley v. Shawano Water Power & River Imp. Co., 1901, 109 Wis. 563, 85 N.W. 507; Perley v. Hilton, 1875, 55 N.H. 444.

29. See Notes, 1956, 54 Mich.L.Rev. 267; 1965, 16 Syr.L.Rev. 860. Also Fuchs v. Curran Carbonizing & Eng. Co., Mo.App.1955, 279 S.W.2d 211.

30. See Kinyon, What Can a Riparian Proprietor Do, 1937, 21 Minn.L.Rev. 512, 523–528; Trelease, The Concept of Reasonable Beneficial Use in the Source of Surface Streams, 1957, 12 Wyo.L.J. 1; Restatement of Torts, § 832; Note, 1965, 19 Ark.L. Rev. 193. Also Harris v. Brooks, 1955, 225 Ark. 436, 283 S.W.2d 129.

31. Meyers v. Lafayette Club, 1936, 197 Minn. 241, 266 N.W. 861; Dyer v. Cranston Print Works Co., 1901, 22 R.I. 506, 48 A. 791; Baldwin v. Ohio Township, 1904, 70 Kan. 102, 78 P. 424; Stratton v. Mt. Hermon Boys' School, 1913, 216 Mass. 83, 103 N.E. 87; Brown v. Chase, 1923, 125 Wash. 542, 217 P. 23.

32. Hazard Powder Co. v. Somersville Mfg. Co., 1905, 78 Conn. 171, 61 A. 519; Davis v. Town of Harrisonburg, 1914, 116 Va. 864, 83 S.E. 401; Jones v. Conn, 1901, 39 Or. 30, 64 P. 855, 65 P. 1068; Joerger v. Mt. Shasta Power Corp., 1932, 214 Cal. 630, 7 P.2d 706.

33. Timm v. Bear, 1871, 29 Wis. 254; Woodin v. Wentworth, 1885, 57 Mich. 278, 23 N.W. 813; Red River Roller Mills v. Wright, 1883, 30 Minn. 249, 15 N.W. 167; Weare v. Chase, 1899, 93 Me. 264, 44 A. 900; Sturtevant v. Ford, 1932, 280 Mass. 303, 182 N.E. 560.

34. Cooley, J., in Dumont v. Kellogg, 1874, 29 Mich. 420.

35. Red River Roller Mills v. Wright, 1883, 30 Minn. 249, 15 N.W. 167; Snow v. Parsons, 1856, 28 Vt. 459; Jones v. Conn, 1901, 39 Or. 30, 64 P. 855, 65 P. 1068; Gehlen v. Knorr, 1897, 101 Iowa 700, 70 N.W. 757; Half Moon Bay Land Co. v. Cowell, 1916, 173 Cal. 543, 160 P. 675.

36. Borough of Westville v. Whitney Home Builders, 1956, 40 N.J.Super. 62, 122 A.2d 233; Monroe Carp Pond Co. v. River Raisin Paper Co., 1927, 240 Mich. 279, 215 N.W. 325; Stamford Extract Mfg. Co. v. Stamford Rolling Mills Co., 1924, 101 Conn. 310, 125 A. 623; McDonough v. Russell Miller Milling Co., 1917, 38 N.D. 465, 165 N.W. 504; Rose v. Socony-Vacuum Corp., 1934, 54 R.I. 411, 173 A. 627.

37. Meeker v. City of East Orange, 1909, 77 N.J.L. 623, 74 A. 379; Katz v. Walkinshaw, 1902, 141 Cal.

better view, notwithstanding a large body of cases to the contrary,[38] that interferences with the flow of surface waters should be governed by the same principles.[39] As has been said above,[40] in some cases the law has been complicated by the tendency of some courts to regard such property rights and privileges as "absolute," and to search for some rule by which one may prevail entirely at the expense of the other.

All of these factors must be thrown into the scale, and the decision must be made on the basis of what is reasonable under the circumstances. It is very seldom that the mat-

ter can be made one of definite rule,[41] and the cases are often of little value except as a general guide to the principles involved.

90. REMEDIES

Once the existence of a nuisance is established, the plaintiff normally has three possible remedies: an action for the damages which he has suffered, equitable relief by injunction, and abatement by self-help.

Damages

As in the case of any other tort, the plaintiff may recover his damages in an action at law. In such an action the principal elements of damages are the value attached to the use or enjoyment of which he has been deprived,[42] or—which often amounts to a measure of the same thing—the loss of the rental or use value of the property for the duration of a temporary nuisance,[43] or the permanent diminution in value from a permanent nuisance,[44] or specific losses such as

---

116, 70 P. 663, 74 P. 766; Stillwater Water Co. v. Farmer, 1903, 89 Minn. 58, 93 N.W. 907; Cason v. Florida Power Co., 1917, 74 Fla. 1, 76 So. 535. See Clayberg, The Law of Percolating Waters, 1915, 14 Mich.L.Rev. 119.

38. Most courts attempt to adopt one or the other of two definite rules. One is the "civil law" rule, that no one may interfere with the natural drainage of surface water. Heier v. Krull, 1911, 160 Cal. 441, 117 P. 530; Farkas v. Towns, 1897, 103 Ga. 150, 29 S.E. 700; Garland v. Aurin, 1899, 103 Tenn. 555, 53 S.W. 940. The other is the common law or "common enemy" rule, that a possessor of land has an unrestricted right to deal with surface water as he pleases, regardless of harm to others. Gannon v. Hargadon, 1865, 10 Allen, Mass., 106; Barkley v. Wilcox, 1881, 86 N.Y. 140; Baltzeger v. Carolina Midland Ry. Co., 1899, 54 S.C. 242, 32 S.E. 358. However, most courts have found it necessary to modify either rule, and many seem in effect to have come out at the "reasonable use" doctrine. See Kinyon and McClure, Surface Waters, 1940, 24 Minn.L.Rev. 891; Note, 1962, 50 Ky.L.J. 254.

39. Hopler v. Morris Hills Regional Dist., 1957, 45 N.J.Super. 409, 133 A.2d 336; Whitman v. Forney, 1943, 181 Md. 652, 31 A.2d 630; Swett v. Cutts, 1870, 50 N.H. 439; Bush v. City of Rochester, 1934, 191 Minn. 591, 255 N.W. 256. See Kinyon and McClure, Surface Waters, 1940, 24 Minn.L.Rev. 891; Note, 1962, 50 Ky.L.J. 254.

40. Supra, p. 581. The "absolute right" position may undoubtedly have some validity, particularly where constitutional rights are in question. See for example Stratton v. Conway, 1957, 201 Tenn. 582, 301 S.W.2d 332, where residential property in an exclusively white neighborhood was sold to a Negro. This was held to be a reasonable use of the land, notwithstanding resulting damage to the value of surrounding property.

41. Occasionally in particular jurisdictions certain cases may be said to have crystallized into more or less definite rules. Thus the attempt to classify different types of residence districts in Burke v. Hollinger, 1929, 296 Pa. 510, 146 A. 15; and cf. Nesbit v. Riesenman, 1930, 298 Pa. 475, 148 A. 695. Definite rules may of course be established by legislation, such as zoning ordinances.

42. Baltimore & Potomac R. Co. v. Fifth Baptist Church, 1883, 108 U.S. 317; Judson v. Los Angeles Suburban Gas Co., 1910, 157 Cal. 168, 106 P. 581; Oklahoma City v. Eylar, 1936, 177 Okl. 616, 61 P.2d 649; Millett v. Minnesota Crushed Stone Co., 1920, 145 Minn. 475, 177 N.W. 641, reargument denied 179 N.W. 682. See Notes, 1937, 21 Minn.L.Rev. 611; 1964, 50 Iowa L.Rev. 141 (stream pollution).

43. Love Petroleum Co. v. Jones, Miss.1967, 205 So. 2d 274; Kellerhals v. Kallenberger, 1960, 251 Iowa 974, 103 N.W.2d 691; Nitram Chemicals, Inc. v. Parker, Fla.App.1967, 200 So.2d 220; Adams Const. Co. v. Bentley, Ky.1960, 335 S.W.2d 912; Signal Mountain Portland Cement Co. v. Brown, 6 Cir. 1944, 141 F.2d 471.

44. Akers v. Ashland Oil & Refining Co., 1954, 139 W.Va. 682, 80 S.E.2d 884; Spaulding v. Cameron, 1952, 38 Cal.2d 265, 239 P.2d 625 (good discussion); Brown v. Virginia-Carolina Chemical Co., 1913, 162 N.C. 83, 77 S.E. 1102; City of Amarillo v. Ware, 1931, 120 Tex. 456, 40 S.W.2d 57.

crops,[45] or the income from an established business;[46] and in addition the value of any personal discomfort or inconvenience which the plaintiff has suffered,[47] or of any injury to health or other personal injury sustained by the plaintiff, or by members of his family so far as they affect his own enjoyment of the premises,[48] as well as any reasonable expenses which he has incurred on account of the nuisance.[49] Where the action is one for damages, the comparative hardship upon the parties is immaterial once the existence of the nuisance itself has been established.[50]

Equitable Relief

The power of a court of equity, in a proper case, to enjoin a nuisance is of long standing, and apparently never has been questioned since the earlier part of the eighteenth century.[51] As in other cases of equity jurisdiction, it must appear that the recovery of damages at law will not be an adequate remedy;[52] but since equity regards every tract of land as unique, it considers that damages are not adequate where its usefulness is seriously impaired.[53] The possibility that the defendant's act, if continued, may ripen into prescription has been regarded by some courts as enough to make the injury irreparable, and justify relief by injunction.[54]

One distinguishing feature of equitable relief is that it may be granted upon the threat of harm which has not yet occurred. The defendant may be restrained from entering upon an activity where it is highly probable[55] that it will lead to a nuisance, although if the possibility is merely uncertain or contingent he may be left to his remedy after the nuisance has occurred.[56] Furthermore, even where there is an existing nuisance and pres-

---

45. United Verde Copper Co. v. Ralston, 9 Cir. 1931, 46 F.2d 1; California Orange Co. v. Riverside Portland Cement Co., 1920, 50 Cal.App. 522, 195 P. 694; Vautier v. Atlantic Refining Co., 1911, 231 Pa. 8, 79 A. 814.

46. See Central Georgia Power Co. v. Pope, 1913, 141 Ga. 186, 80 S.E. 642.

47. Kornoff v. Kingsburg Cotton Oil Co., 1955, 45 Cal.2d 265, 288 P.2d 507; Phillips Petroleum Co. v. Ruble, 1942, 191 Okl. 37, 126 P.2d 526; Nailor v. C. W. Blakeslee & Sons, 1933, 117 Conn. 241, 167 A. 548; Kentucky West Virginia Gas Co. v. Lafferty, 6 Cir. 1949, 174 F.2d 848; Town of Braggs v. Slape, 1952, 207 Okl. 420, 250 P.2d 214.

48. Van v. Bowie Sewerage Co., 1936, 127 Tex. 97, 90 S.W.2d 561; Dodd v. Glen Rose Gasoline Co., 1940, 194 La. 1, 193 So. 349; Millett v. Minnesota Crushed Stone Co., 1920, 145 Minn. 475, 177 N.W. 641, 179 N.W. 682; United States Smelting Co. v. Sisam, 8 Cir. 1911, 191 F. 293. See supra, p. 594.

This has been held to include mental suffering and its physical consequences. Alonso v. Hills, 1950, 95 Cal.App.2d 778, 214 P.2d 50; Dixon v. New York Trap Rock Corp., 1944, 293 N.Y. 509, 58 N.E.2d 517, 60 N.E.2d 385.

49. Loughran v. City of Des Moines, 1887, 72 Iowa 382, 34 N.W. 172 (medical expenses); City of San Antonio v. Mackey's Estate, 1899, 22 Tex.Civ.App. 145, 54 S.W. 33 (expenses of avoiding nuisance).

50. North American Cement Corp. v. Price, 1933, 164 Md. 234, 164 A. 545.

51. See Baines v. Baker, 1752, Amb.158, 27 Eng.Rep. 105; Crowder v. Tinkler, 1816, 19 Ves. 617, 34 Eng.

Rep. 645; 3 Bl.Comm.Ch. 11; Wilmont Homes, Inc. v. Weiler, 1964, 42 Del.Ch. 8, 202 A.2d 576; De Funiak, Equitable Relief Against Nuisances, 1950, 38 Ky.L.J. 223; Walsh, Equitable Relief Against Nuisance, 1930, 7 N.Y.U.L.Rev. 352; Note, 1965, 78 Harv.L.Rev. 997 ff.

52. Swaine v. Great Northern R. Co., 1864, 4 De G.J. & S. 211, 46 Eng.Rep. 899; Rhodes v. Dunbar, 1868, 57 Pa. 274; Purcell v. Davis, 1935, 100 Mont. 480, 50 P.2d 255.

53. Shipley v. Ritter, 1855, 7 Md. 408; Wilson v. City of Mineral Point, 1875, 39 Wis. 160; McIntosh v. Brimmer, 1924, 68 Cal.App. 770, 230 P. 203; Krocker v. Westmoreland Planing Mill Co., 1922, 274 Pa. 143, 117 A. 669. See McClintock, Equity, 1936, § 132.

54. Lindsay-Strathmore Irr. Dist. v. Superior Court of Tulare County, 1920, 182 Cal. 315, 187 P. 1056; Amsterdam Knitting Co. v. Dean, 1900, 162 N.Y. 278, 56 N.E. 757; Murphy v. Lincoln, 1891, 63 Vt. 278, 22 A. 418.

55. Hamilton Corp. v. Julian, 1917, 130 Md. 597, 101 A. 558; De Give v. Seltzer, 1879, 64 Ga. 423; Edmunds v. Duff, 1924, 280 Pa. 355, 124 A. 489; Mullins v. Morgan, 1940, 176 Va. 201, 10 S.E.2d 593. Absolute certainty is not required. Nelson v. Swedish Evangelical Lutheran Cemetery Ass'n, 1910, 111 Minn. 149, 126 N.W. 723, 127 N.W. 626.

56. Hannum v. Oak Lane Shopping Center, 1956, 383 Pa. 618, 119 A.2d 213; Wilcher v. Sharpe, 1952, 236 N.C. 308, 72 S.E.2d 662; Kimmons v. Benson, 1952, 220 Ark. 299, 247 S.W.2d 468; Foster v. County of Genesee, 1951, 329 Mich. 665, 46 N.W.2d 426; Turn-

ent harm, the equity court may in its discretion deny the injunction where the balance of the equities involved is in favor of the defendant. It may take into consideration the relative economic hardship which will result to the parties from the granting or denial of the injunction,[57] the good faith or intentional misconduct of each,[58] and the interest of the general public in the continuation of the defendant's enterprise.[59] Where liability for damages is concerned, the defendant's conduct may be found to be so unreasonable that he should pay for the harm that his factory is causing, but where an injunction is in question, it may be found to be still so far reasonable that he should be allowed to continue it if payment is made.[60] For these reasons de-

nial of relief by way of injunction is not always a precedent for denial of relief by way of damages, and this fact has added no little to the confusion surrounding the law of nuisance.

As to public nuisance, the remedy by injunction may exist in favor of the state.[61] Its use is somewhat complicated by the traditional rule that equity will not enjoin a crime as such, where the effect will be to deprive the defendant of his constitutional safeguards;[62] but this will not prevent the injunction where the criminal penalty is inadequate to prevent the damage threatened by the continuation of the nuisance,[63] and it has been held that there is no double jeopardy in such a remedy.[64] A private individual may obtain an injunction against a public nuisance[65] only if he can show special damage, or the threat of special damage, to himself, distinct from the invasion of the public interest.[66]

er v. City of Spokane, 1951, 39 Wash.2d 332, 235 P. 2d 300.

57. City of Harrisonville v. W. S. Dickey Clay Mfg. Co., 1933, 289 U.S. 334; Canfield v. Quayle, 1939, 170 Misc. 621, 10 N.Y.S.2d 781; Dundalk Holding Co. v. Easter, 1958, 215 Md. 549, 137 A.2d 667, cert. denied 358 U.S. 821, rehearing denied 358 U.S. 901; Koseris v. J. R. Simplot Co., 1960, 82 Idaho 263, 352 P.2d 235; Akers v. Mathieson Alkali Works, 1928, 151 Va. 1, 144 S.E. 492. But the factor of disproportionate expense is not always controlling in itself. Metropoulos v. Macpherson, 1922, 241 Mass. 491, 135 N.E. 693.

58. Jack v. Torrant, 1950, 136 Conn. 414, 71 A.2d 705.

59. Haack v. Lindsay Light & Chemical Co., 1946, 393 Ill. 367, 66 N.E.2d 391 (essential war work); Storey v. Central Hide & Rendering Co., 1950, 148 Tex. 509, 226 S.W.2d 615 (only plant in county); Antonik v. Chamberlain, 1947, 81 Ohio App. 465, 78 N.E.2d 752 ("life and death of a legitimate and necessary business"); Koseris v. J. R. Simplot Co., 1960, 82 Idaho 263, 352 P.2d 235 (over 1,000 employees).

As to the balancing of several factors, see Elliott Nursery Co. v. Du Quesne Light Co., 1924, 281 Pa. 166, 126 A. 345; Edwards v. Allouez Min. Co., 1878, 38 Mich. 46; Bliss v. Washoe Copper Co., 9 Cir. 1911, 186 F. 789; McCarthy v. Bunker Hill & Sullivan Mining & Coal Co., 9 Cir. 1908, 164 F. 927.

See McClintock, Equity, 1936, §§ 140, 141; McClintock, Discretion to Deny Injunction Against Trespass and Nuisance, 1926, 12 Minn.L.Rev. 565; Morris and Keeton, Notes on "Balancing the Equities," 1940, 18 Tex.L.Rev. 412; Notes, 1927, 37 Yale L.J. 96; 1922, 36 Harv.L.Rev. 211; 1933, 40 W.Va. L.Q. 59.

60. Restatement of Torts, Scope and Introductory Note to chapter 40, preceding § 822.

61. Black v. Circuit Court of Eighth Judicial District, 1960, 78 S.D. 302, 101 N.W.2d 520; State v. Sportsmen's Club, 1943, 214 Minn. 151, 7 N.W.2d 495; Commonwealth v. McGovern, 1903, 116 Ky. 212, 75 S.W. 261; City of Fayetteville v. Spur Distributing Co., 1939, 216 N.C. 596, 5 S.E.2d 838; Attorney General v. Smith, 1901, 109 Wis. 532, 85 N. W. 512.

62. State v. Vaughan, 1906, 81 Ark. 117, 98 S.W. 685; State v. Ehrlick, 1909, 65 W.Va. 700, 64 S.E. 935. See McClintock, Equity, 1936, § 159; Schofield, Equity Jurisdiction to Enjoin Illegal Saloons as Public Nuisances, 1913, 8 Ill.L.Rev. 19.

63. Engle v. Scott, 1941, 57 Ariz. 383, 114 P.2d 236; State v. Karsten, 1945, 208 Ark. 703, 187 S.W.2d 327; Goose v. Commonwealth ex rel. Dimmit, 1947, 305 Ky. 644, 205 S.W.2d 326; Portage Township v. Full Salvation Union, 1947, 318 Mich. 693, 29 N.W. 2d 297.

64. State v. Boren, 1953, 42 Wash.2d 155, 253 P.2d 939.

65. Callanan v. Gilman, 1887, 107 N.Y. 360, 14 N.E. 264; First Nat. Bank of Montgomery v. Tyson, 1905, 144 Ala. 457, 39 So. 560; Edmunds v. Duff, 1924, 280 Pa. 355, 124 A. 489.

66. Alexander v. Wilkes-Barre Anthracite Coal Co., 1916, 254 Pa. 1, 98 A. 794; Cope v. District Fair Ass'n of Flora, 1881, 99 Ill. 489. As to what is such particular damage, see supra, p. 586.

Abatement

The privilege of abatement of a nuisance by self-help is of ancient origin, and existed at a time when early common law actions afforded a legal means of compelling the nuisance to be discontinued.[67] It is closely related to the privilege of using reasonable force to protect the exclusive possession of land against trespass,[68] and may be justified on the same basis, that injuries, "which obstruct or annoy such things as are of daily convenience and use, require an immediate remedy, and cannot wait for the slow process of the ordinary forms of justice."[69] Consequently the privilege must be exercised within a reasonable time after knowledge of the nuisance is acquired or should have been acquired by the person entitled to abate; if there has been sufficient delay to allow a resort to legal process, the reason for the privilege fails, and the privilege with it.[70]

Summary abatement of a private nuisance by self-help is open only to those whose interests in the enjoyment of land are interfered with, or in other words, to those to whom it is a nuisance.[71] It is often said that the privilege is available only to one who might have an action for damages,[72] but such a statement is perhaps too broad, since there must be situations of imminent dan-

ger which will justify action before any harm has occurred.[73] Likewise, a public nuisance may be abated by a private individual only when it causes or threatens special damage to himself apart from that to the general public,[74] and then only to the extent necessary to protect his own interests. Thus a traveller on a highway may remove only so much of an obstruction as is required to permit him to proceed on his journey.[75] Again, because nuisances so often involve debatable questions of reasonable conduct, the privilege of abating conditions outside of the land affected differs from that of defending possession from a trespass,[76] in that it depends upon the actual existence of a nuisance. The actor who adopts such a summary remedy rather than resort to the law must take his chances that he is justified, and an honest belief that he is right will not protect him from criminal prosecution[77] or civil liability.[78]

67. See, 1322, Y.B. 14 Edw. II, f. 422, pl. 3; 1469, Y.B. 8 Edw. IV, f. 5, pl. 14.

68. See supra, § 21.

69. 3 Bl.Com. 6.

70. Moffett v. Brewer, 1848, 1 G.Greene, Iowa, 348; Hentz v. Long Island R. Co., 1852, 13 Barb., N.Y., 646.

71. Lincoln v. Chadbourne, 1868, 56 Me. 197; Gates v. Blincoe, 1833, 2 Dana, Ky., 158; see Hummel v. State, 1940, 69 Okl.Cr. 38, 99 P.2d 913.

72. Adams v. Barney, 1853, 25 Vt. 225, 231; 2 Wood, Law of Nuisances, 3d Ed.1893, § 825. Cf. Priewe v. Fitzsimons & Connell Co., 1903, 117 Wis. 497, 94 N.W. 317; Toledo, St. L. & K. C. R. Co. v. Loop, 1894, 139 Ind. 542, 39 N.E. 306.

73. See Lipnik v. Ehalt, 1921, 76 Ind.App. 390, 132 N.E. 410; and cf. Restatement of Torts, § 203, Comment b.

74. Brown v. Perkins, 1858, 12 Gray, Mass, 89, 101; Corthell v. Holmes, 1896, 87 Me. 24, 32 A. 715; Harrower v. Ritson, 1861, 37 Barb., N.Y., 301; Nation v. District of Columbia, 1910, 34 App.D.C. 453. Earlier cases were to the contrary. Burnham v. Hotchkiss, 1841, 14 Conn. 311, 318; Day v. Day, 1853, 4 Md. 262, 270.

A private individual may, however, be privileged to act under public necessity to avert a public disaster. See supra, § 24. Cf. Seavey v. Preble, 1874, 64 Me. 120; Meeker v. Van Rensselaer, 1836, 15 Wend., N.Y., 397 (abating nuisance to prevent spread of disease).

75. Harrower v. Ritson, 1861, 37 Barb., N.Y., 301; James v. Hayward, 1631, Cro.Car. 184, 79 Eng.Rep. 761; Johnson v. Maxwell, 1891, 2 Wash. 482, 27 P. 1071.

76. Supra, § 21.

77. State v. Moffett, 1848, 1 G.Greene, Iowa, 247.

78. Graves v. Shattuck, 1847, 35 N.H. 257; Grant v. Allen, 1874, 41 Conn. 156; Humphreys Oil Co. v. Liles, Tex.Civ.App.1924, 262 S.W. 1058, affirmed, Tex.Com.App.1925, 277 S.W. 100; Tissot v. Great Southern Telephone & Telegraph Co., 1887, 39 La. App. 996, 3 So. 261 (public nuisance).

The privilege of abatement extends to entry upon the land of another,[79] and to the use of all reasonable force in a reasonable manner which is necessary to terminate the nuisance, even to the destruction of valuable property,[80] where the damage done is not greatly disproportionate to the threatened harm. But it does not extend to unnecessary or unreasonable damage, and there will be liability for any excess.[81] It may not be justifiable, for instance, to destroy a house merely because it is used for prostitution.[82] What is reasonable is of course to be determined in the light of all the circumstances of the case, including the gravity of the nuisance and the necessity for prompt action, and the existence of any reasonable alternative method.[83] It is quite generally agreed, however, that the abatement of a nuisance does not justify the infliction of personal injury,[84] or

conduct which amounts to a breach of the peace.[85] Most courts have held that before one is privileged to abate a nuisance he must notify the wrongdoer of its existence and demand its removal;[86] but obviously this will not be required in an emergency where there is no time for it,[87] or where it is apparent that he is already aware of the nuisance and that such a demand would be futile.[88]

91. DEFENSES

In an action founded on a claim of nuisance, the defendant may set up certain defenses, now to be considered.

Legislative Authority

Just as the legislature, within its constitutional limitations,[89] may declare particular conduct or a particular use of property to be a nuisance,[90] it may authorize that which would otherwise be a nuisance.[91] Zoning or-

---

79.   Jones v. Williams, 1843, 11 M. & W. 176, 152 Eng.Rep. 764.

80.   Amoskeag Mfg. Co. v. Goodale, 1865, 46 N.H. 53 (dam); Maryland Telephone & Telegraph Co. v. Ruth, 1907, 106 Md. 644, 68 A. 358 (telephone pole); McKeesport Sawmill Co. v. Pennsylvania Co., C.C. Pa.1903, 122 F. 184 (barge); Hubbard v. Preston, 1892, 90 Mich. 221, 51 N.W. 209 (dog).

81.   Gates v. Blincoe, 1833, 2 Dana, Ky., 158; Finley v. Hershey, 1875, 41 Iowa 389; Ely v. Niagara County Sup'rs, 1867, 36 N.Y. 297. Thus the defendant may be privileged to cut off branches of overhanging trees, but not to enter his neighbor's land and cut down the trees. Fick v. Nilson, 1950, 98 Cal.App.2d 683, 220 P.2d 752. Or to move a car from a place where it is illegally parked, but not negligently to release the brakes and let it roll down hill to destruction. Russell v. Aragon, 1961, 146 Colo. 332, 361 P.2d 346.

82.   Moody v. Board of Supervisors of Niagara County, 1866, 46 Barb., N.Y., 659. Accord: Ohio Valley Electric R. Co. v. Scott, 1916, 172 Ky. 183, 189 S.W. 7; Morrison v. Marquardt, 1867, 24 Iowa 35; Brightman v. Bristol, 1876, 65 Me. 426.

83.   Great Falls Co. v. Worster, 1844, 15 N.H. 412; Maryland Telephone & Telegraph Co. v. Ruth, 1907, 106 Md. 644, 68 A. 358; McKeesport Sawmill Co. v. Pennsylvania Co., C.C.Pa.1903, 122 F. 184; Ohio Valley Electric R. Co. v. Scott, 1916, 172 Ky. 183, 189 S.W. 7.

84.   See Rex v. Rosewell, 1699, 2 Salk. 459, 91 Eng. Rep. 396; Stiles & Davis v. Laird, 1855, 5 Cal. 120; Walker v. Davis, 1917, 139 Tenn. 475, 202 S.W. 78.

85.   Day v. Day, 1853, 4 Md. 262; Earp v. Lee, 1873, 71 Ill. 193; People v. Severance, 1901, 125 Mich. 556, 84 N.W. 1089.

86.   State v. Brown, 1926, 191 N.C. 419, 132 S.E. 5; Martin v. Martin, Tex.Civ.App.1952, 246 S.W.2d 718; Hickey v. Michigan Cent. R. Co., 1893, 96 Mich. 498, 55 N.W. 989; Maryland Telephone & Telegraph Co. v. Ruth, 1907, 106 Md. 644, 68 A. 358.

87.   Childers v. New York Power & Light Corp., 1949, 275 App.Div. 133, 89 N.Y.S.2d 11. See Jones v. Williams, 1843, 11 M. & W. 176, 152 Eng.Rep. 764; Buck v. McIntosh, 1908, 140 Ill.App. 9.

88.   See Jones v. Williams, 1843, 11 M. & W. 176, 152 Eng.Rep. 764; Hickey v. Michigan Cent. R. Co., 1893, 96 Mich. 498, 55 N.W. 989.

89.   See Yates v. City of Milwaukee, 1870, 10 Wall., U.S. 497; City of Evansville v. Miller, 1897, 146 Ind. 613, 45 N.E. 1054; Boyd v. Board of Councilmen of Frankfort, 1903, 117 Ky. 199, 77 S.W. 669; Prior v. White, 1938, 132 Fla. 1, 180 So. 347.

90.   City of Chicago v. Shaynin, 1913, 258 Ill. 69, 101 N.E. 224; Pompano Horse Club v. State, 1927, 93 Fla. 415, 111 So. 801; State v. Chicago, M. & St. P. R. Co., 1911, 114 Minn. 122, 130 N.W. 545; Laurel Hill Cemetery v. City and County of San Francisco, 1907, 152 Cal. 464, 93 P. 70; City of Rochester v. Gutberlett, 1914, 211 N.Y. 309, 105 N.E. 548.

91.   Delaware, L. & W. R. Co. v. Chiara, 3 Cir. 1938, 95 F.2d 663; People v. Brooklyn & Queens Transit

dinances, for example, may give legislative sanction to conditions or activities in particular localities where there might otherwise be liability.[92] In England, where parliamentary authority is not limited, such action is final, and it is a complete defense that nothing has been done except what the law of the land expressly permits.[93] In America the power of the legislature is of course subject to constitutional restrictions, discussion of which is beyond the scope of this text. In general, it may be said that there is power to authorize minor interferences with the convenience of property owners, but not major ones,[94] unless the land is condemned and compensation given under the law of eminent domain. Wherever possible the authority given will be construed to permit only reasonable conduct of the enterprise in a reasonable manner, with proper care and due regard for the interests of others, so that a permission to carry on blasting operations will not prevent liability for throwing stones on the plaintiff's land.[95]

Conduct of Others

The extent to which others in the vicinity are causing a similar interference with the plaintiff's convenience is a factor to be considered in determining whether the defendant's conduct is reasonable. If a locality is given over predominantly to manufacturing, the plaintiff will have less right to complain of factory noise or smoke than if it is of a residential character.[96] What is a nuisance in Palm Springs is not necessarily one in Pittsburgh. But where such other activities fall short of devoting the locality to a particular use,[97] or where the defendant's conduct is found to be unreasonable even in such a place,[98] the fact that others are polluting a stream,[99] diverting water from it,[1] flooding the plaintiff's land,[2] or filling the air with noise[3] or smells and smoke,[4] will not be a defense to an action based on the defendant's

---

Corp., 1940, 283 N.Y. 484, 28 N.E.2d 925; Strachan v. Beacon Oil Co., 1925, 251 Mass. 479, 146 N.E. 792; Dudding v. Automatic Gas Co., 1946, 145 Tex. 1, 193 S.W.2d 517. See Note, 1952, 52 Col.L.Rev. 781.

92. See Note, 1956, 34 Tex.L.Rev. 482.

93. Hammersmith R. Co. v. Brand, 1869, L.R. 4 H.L. 171; Quebec R. Co. v. Vandry, [1920] A.C. 662, 89 L.J.P.C. 99; Salmond, Law of Torts, 8th Ed.1934, 47.

94. See Richards v. Washington Terminal Co., 1914, 233 U.S. 546; Sawyer v. Davis, 1884, 136 Mass. 239; Bacon v. City of Boston, 1891, 154 Mass. 100, 28 N.E. 9; Sadlier v. City of New York, 1903, 40 Misc. 78, 81 N.Y.S. 308, reversed on other grounds, 1905, 104 App.Div. 28, 93 N.Y.S. 579, affirmed, 1906, 185 N.Y. 408, 78 N.E. 272.

95. Hakkila v. Old Colony Broken Stone & Concrete Co., 1928, 264 Mass. 447, 162 N.E. 895. Accord: Messer v. City of Dickinson, 1942, 71 N.D. 568, 3 N.W.2d 241; Louisville & N. Terminal Co. v. Lellyett, 1905, 114 Tenn. 368, 85 S.W. 881; Squaw Island Freight Terminal Co. v. City of Buffalo, 1937, 273 N.Y. 119, 7 N.E.2d 10; Bright v. East Side Mosquito Abatement Dist., 1959, 168 Cal.App.2d 7, 335 P.2d 527.

96. Thus activities of others which are in themselves no defense are to be considered in determining the nature of the locality. Hobson v. Walker, La.App. 1949, 41 So.2d 789; Waier v. Peerless Oil Co., 1933, 265 Mich. 398, 251 N.W. 552. See supra, p. 599.

97. Cleveland v. Citizens' Gaslight Co., 1869, 20 N.J. Eq. 201.

98. Waier v. Peerless Oil Co., 1933, 265 Mich. 398, 251 N.W. 552; Ross v. Butler, 1868, 19 N.J.Eq. 294.

99. Beach v. Sterling Iron & Zinc Co., 1895, 54 N.J. Eq. 65, 33 A. 286; Parker v. American Woolen Co., 1913, 215 Mass. 176, 102 N.E. 360; Weston Paper Co. v. Pope, 1900, 155 Ind. 394, 57 N.E. 719; Thomas v. Ohio Coal Co., 1916, 199 Ill.App. 50.

1. Gould v. Stafford, 1888, 77 Cal. 66, 18 P. 879; Elkhart Paper Co. v. Fulkerson, 1905, 36 Ind.App. 219, 75 N.E. 283.

2. Coleman v. Bennett, 1902, 111 Tenn. 705, 69 S.W. 734; Verheyen v. Dewey, 1915, 27 Idaho 1, 146 P. 1116; Birch v. Boston & Me. R. R., 1927, 259 Mass. 528, 156 N.E. 859.

3. Fox v. Ewers, 1949, 195 Md. 650, 75 A.2d 357; Robinson v. Baugh, 1875, 31 Mich. 290.

4. Bollinger v. American Asphalt Roof Co., 1929, 224 Mo.App. 98, 19 S.W.2d 544; Richards v. Daugherty, 1902, 133 Ala. 569, 31 So. 934; Waier v. Peerless Oil Co., 1933, 265 Mich. 398, 251 N.W. 552; Jordan v. United Verde Copper Co., D.Ariz.1925, 9 F.2d 144.

Custom is not necessarily a defense. Iverson v. Vint, 1952, 243 Iowa 949, 54 N.W.2d 494.

nuisance. A dozen nuisances do not each obtain immunity because they all interfere with the plaintiff's use of his land. Where the damage done is incapable of any practical division, as where a river polluted with oil burns a barn,[5] or poisons cattle,[6] each will be liable for the entire loss. But in the usual case the interference with the plaintiff's enjoyment, by noise, smoke, odors, pollution or flooding, is regarded by the courts as capable of some rough apportionment according to the extent to which each defendant has contributed, and it is held that each will be liable only for his proportionate share of the harm.[7]

There are occasional cases in which the conduct of each of two or more defendants, taken alone, would cause no unreasonable interference, but all together amount to a nuisance. One may pollute a stream to some extent without any harm, but if several do the same thing the plaintiff's use of the stream may be destroyed. It has been held consistently in these cases that each defendant is liable.[8] The explanation given is that mentioned earlier,[9] that the conduct of each,

however reasonable it would be in itself, becomes unreasonable in view of what the others are doing. It may not be a nuisance to obstruct a small part of a highway and leave room for passage, but it becomes one when some one else obstructs the rest of the street.[10]

Conduct of Plaintiff

It is very often said [11] that contributory negligence cannot be a defense to an action based on a nuisance. There is just enough truth in this to be misleading. It is true that in the ordinary, typical nuisance case, where the defendant has deliberately established a slaughterhouse or a powder mill, or an oil well pumping salt water,[12] with knowledge that it is certain to interfere with the plaintiff's use of his land, there is such an element of intent, or at least of wilful or reckless misconduct, that the mere failure of the plaintiff to anticipate harm, or to take precautions against it, should no more avoid liability than in the case of any other wilful or wanton tort.[13] The same is perhaps true of some public nuisances, where there is a deliberate infringement of the rights of the plaintiff, as by intentionally obstructing the highway for the purpose of preventing his passage.[14] So many qualifications must be attached to the statement, however, that it has no validity as

---

5. Northup v. Eakes, 1918, 72 Okl. 66, 178 P. 266; Phillips Petroleum Co. v. Vandergriff, 1942, 190 Okl. 280, 122 P.2d 1020. Cf. Slater v. Mersereau, 1878, 64 N.Y. 138; Folsom v. Apple River Log-Driving Co., 1877, 41 Wis. 602. See supra, p. 315.

6. Tidal Oil Co. v. Pease, 1931, 153 Okl. 137, 5 P.2d 389; see Orton v. Virginia Carolina Chemical Co., 1918, 142 La. 790, 77 So. 632.

7. See supra, p. 317. As to the burden of proof on the issue of apportionment, see supra, p. 319.

The distinction made in West Muncie Strawboard Co. v. Slack, 1904, 164 Ind. 21, 72 N.E. 879, between a public and a private nuisance in this respect has nothing to recommend it, and was rejected in City of Mansfield v. Brister, 1907, 76 Ohio St. 270, 81 N. E. 631, and Mitchell Realty Co. v. City of West Allis, 1924, 184 Wis. 352, 199 N.W. 390.

8. Woodyear v. Schaefer, 1881, 57 Md. 1 (pollution); Woodland v. Portneuf-Marsh Valley Irr. Co., 1915, 26 Idaho 789, 146 P. 1106 (flooding); Sloggy v. Dilworth, 1888, 38 Minn. 179, 36 N.W. 451 (flooding); Harley v. Merrill Brick Co., 1891, 83 Iowa 73, 48 N.W. 1000 (smoke); Warren v. Parkhurst, 1904, 45 Misc. 466, 92 N.Y.S. 725.

9. Supra, p. 322.

10. See Sadler v. Great Western R. Co., [1895] L.R. 2 Q.B. 688; Woodyear v. Schaefer, 1881, 57 Md. 1; Lambton v. Mellish, [1894] 2 Ch. 163. Cf. Parker v. American Woolen Co., 1907, 195 Mass. 591, 81 N.E. 468; Weidman Silk Dyeing Co. v. East Jersey Water Co., N.J.Sup.1914, 91 A. 338.

11. Joyce, Nuisances, 1906, § 45; Winfield, Nuisance as a Tort, 1931, 4 Camb.L.J. 189, 200; Winfield, Law of Tort, 1937, 501; Shearman and Redfield, Negligence, 6th Ed.1913, § 157.

12. Niagara Oil Co. v. Ogle, 1911, 177 Ind. 292, 98 N. E. 60; Town of Gilmer v. Pickett, Tex.Civ.App.1921, 228 S.W. 347; Worth v. Dunn, 1922, 98 Conn. 51, 118 A. 467; Risher v. Acken Coal Co., 1910, 147 Iowa 459, 124 N.W. 764; Higginbotham v. Kearse, 1931, 111 W.Va. 264, 161 S.E. 37.

13. See supra, p. 426.

14. Hanson v. Hall, 1938, 202 Minn. 381, 279 N.W. 227.

a general rule, and often is merely deceptive, and a source of bad law.[15]

In the first place, there are many nuisances which rest upon nothing more than negligence on the part of the defendant. If a city fails to repair a defective sidewalk [16] or to remove snow and ice from it,[17] or an individual fails to discover and remedy a condition existing on his land when he bought it.[18] or leaves an excavation unguarded,[19] or blows a whistle which frightens a horse,[20] his conduct is not removed from the field of ordinary negligence by calling it a nuisance, and the plaintiff's lack of care for his own protection is as much a defense as in any other negligence case. The failure to recognize this obvious fact has led some courts into considerable confusion.

Even where the principle is recognized, the dividing line between intent and negligence has not always proved easy to draw. This has been true especially where the defendant intentionally creates a public nuisance, as by obstructing the highway, but does not intend the damages, such as personal injury from running into the obstruction, which result to the plaintiff.[21] As to such an injury the defendant has created only a risk, and with respect to the particular damages his invasion cannot be called anything more than negligence. The question is, how the combination of intent as to the public right and negligence as to the private one are to be dealt with.

There have been courts, such as Connecticut,[22] New York,[23] and formerly New Jersey,[24] which have held that since the nuisance itself is an intentional, or "absolute" one, contributory negligence cannot be a defense to the plaintiff's action founded on it. In the better reasoned cases,[25] this has been

---

15. Seavey, Nuisance: Contributory Negligence and Other Mysteries, 1952, 65 Harv.L.Rev. 984; Notes, 1935, 29 Ill.L.Rev. 372; 1937, 36 Mich.L.Rev. 684; 1940, 38 Mich.L.Rev. 1337; 1935, 23 Cal.L.Rev. 427; 1949, 24 Ind.L.J. 402; 1961, 28 Tenn.L.Rev. 561.

16. McFarlane v. City of Niagara Falls, 1928, 247 N. Y. 340, 160 N.E. 391; Llewellyn v. City of Knoxville, 1950, 33 Tenn.App. 632, 232 S.W.2d 568. Cf. Denny v. Garavaglia, 1952, 333 Mich. 317, 52 N.W. 2d 521 (heavy equipment damaging highway); Johnson v. City of Alcoa, 1940, 24 Tenn.App. 422, 145 S.W.2d 796 (pipe in swimming pool); Terrell v. Alabama Water Service Co., 1943, 245 Ala. 68, 15 So.2d 727 (pipe leaking water onto highway).

17. Mayor of Baltimore v. Marriott, 1850, 9 Md. 160.

18. Crommelin v. Coxe & Co., 1857, 30 Ala. 318.

19. Smith v. Smith, 1824, 2 Pick., Mass., 621; Irwin v. Sprigg, 1847, 6 Gill., Md., 200. Cf. Calder v. City and County of San Francisco, 1942, 50 Cal.App.2d 837, 123 P.2d 897; Town of Kirklin v. Everman, Ind.App.1940, 24 N.E.2d 412, affirmed on other grounds, 1940, 217 Ind. 683, 28 N.E.2d 73.

20. Parker v. Union Woolen Co., 1872, 42 Conn. 399; cf. McEniry v. Tri-City R. Co., 1912, 254 Ill. 99, 98 N.E. 227 (negligent operation of unlicensed street car); Brown v. Alter, 1936, 251 Mass. 223, 146 N.E. 691 (unlicensed automobile a "nuisance on the highway").

21. See Seavey, Nuisance: Contributory Negligence and Other Mysteries, 1952, 65 Harv.L.Rev. 984; Werner, Public Nuisance in Personal Injury Actions in Connecticut, 1941, 15 Conn.Bar J. 199; James, Chief Justice Maltbie and the Law of Negligence, 1950, 24 Conn.Bar J. 61, 73ff.; Prosser, Private Action for Public Nuisance, 1966, 52 Va.L.Rev. 997, 1023–1027; Notes, 1934, 29 Ill.L.Rev. 372; 1949, 24 Ind.L.J. 402; 1961, 28 Tenn.L.Rev. 561.

22. De Lahunta v. City of Waterbury, 1948, 134 Conn. 630, 59 A.2d 800; Beckwith v. Town of Stratford, 1942, 129 Conn. 506, 29 A.2d 775; Warren v. City of Bridgeport, 1942, 129 Conn. 355, 28 A.2d 1. Contra: Carabetta v. City of Meriden, 1958, 145 Conn. 338, 142 A.2d 727; Hill v. Way, 1933, 117 Conn. 359, 168 A. 1.

23. Delaney v. Philhern Realty Holding Corp., 1939, 280 N.Y. 461, 21 N.E.2d 507; Clifford v. Dam, 1880, 81 N.Y. 52; Linzey v. American Ice Co., 1910, 131 App.Div. 333, 115 N.Y.S. 767, affirmed 197 N.Y. 605, 91 N.E. 1116. Contra, Kelly v. Doody, 1889, 116 N. Y. 575, 22 N.E. 1084; Drake v. Corning Bldg. Co., 1934, 241 App.Div. 586, 272 N.Y.S. 726.

Accord: Flaherty v. Great Northern R. Co., 1944, 218 Minn. 488, 16 N.W.2d 553; Baker v. City of Wheeling, 1936, 117 W.Va. 362, 185 S.E. 842.

24. Hammond v. Monmouth County, 1936, 117 N.J.L. 11, 186 A. 452; Thompson v. Petrozzello, 1927, 5 N. J.Misc.R. 645, 137 A. 835. These cases have been overruled by Hartman v. Brigantine, 1957, 23 N.J. 530, 129 A.2d 876.

25. Hartman v. Brigantine, 1957, 23 N.J. 530, 129 A. 2d 876; Runnells v. Maine Cent. R. Co., 1963, 159 Me. 200, 190 A.2d 739; Deane v. Johnston, Fla.1958, 104 So.2d 3; Calder v. City & County of San Fran-

rejected, and it has been recognized that so far as the tort liability is concerned, the defendant has created only a risk, and that with respect to the resulting damage his conduct cannot be called anything more than negligence; and hence that contributory negligence is a valid defense. It may be surmised that the decisions barring the defense have rested in reality upon a dislike of it; but the way to get rid of it is scarcely by resort to fictions transforming negligence into intent.

In the second place, even if the nuisance is a matter of intent, or of some abnormally dangerous activity, the kind of contributory negligence which consists of voluntarily encountering a known danger, and often is called assumption of risk, may still be a defense. The plaintiff is not free to run recklessly into a known obstruction in the street,[26] skate on a pond from which he knows the ice has been cut,[27] or walk into the midst of visible dynamiting operations,[28] and still hold the defendant responsible for his damages. In such cases there is a consent to take the risk, or such an element of wilful misconduct on the part of the plaintiff that he is barred from recovery in nuisance as in the case of any other tort.

Again, notwithstanding considerable authority to the contrary,[29] the greater number of the courts have recognized that the damages rule of avoidable consequences is applicable even to the case of an intentional nuisance. The plaintiff is not required to protect himself in advance against a mere threat of future inconvenience, or the declared purpose of the defendant to create a nuisance.[30] But once the nuisance is established and the interference with his rights is begun, he may be required to take reasonable steps to guard against further harm. The possibility that he may so avoid the consequences not only has a bearing upon the reasonableness of the defendant's conduct and the existence of a nuisance in the first instance,[31] but may prevent liability for a part[32] of the damages even where there is clearly a nuisance. Thus the plaintiff may not allow his livestock to drink poisoned water,[33] or stand idly by and permit the flooding of his premises[34] or the

---

cisco, 1942, 50 Cal.App.2d 837, 123 P.2d 897; McKenna v. Andreassi, 1935, 292 Mass. 213, 197 N.E. 879.

26. See McFarlane v. City of Niagara Falls, 1928, 247 N.Y. 340, 160 N.E. 391; Hammond v. Monmouth County, 1936, 117 N.J.L. 11, 186 A. 452; Hill v. Way, 1933, 117 Conn. 359, 168 A. 1; Thompson v. Petrozzello, 1927, 5 N.J.Misc. 645, 137 A. 835; Schiro v. Oriental Realty Co., 1959, 7 Wis.2d 556, 97 N. W.2d 385 (walking into obvious declivity with insecure footing).

This was held even in a jurisdiction refusing to recognize ordinary contributory negligence in the case of an intentional public nuisance. Jacko v. City of Bridgeport, 1965, 26 Conn.Sup. 73, 213 A.2d 452.

27. Linzey v. American Ice Co., 1909, 131 App.Div. 333, 115 N.Y.S. 767. Cf. Hoffman v. Bristol, 1931, 113 Conn. 386, 155 A. 499 (using unsafe diving board).

28. Worth v. Dunn, 1922, 98 Conn. 51, 62, 118 A. 467, 471; Wells v. Knight, 1911, 32 R.I. 432, 80 A. 16. Cf. Murphy v. Ossola, 1938, 124 Conn. 366, 199 A. 648 (stored dynamite caps).

29. Johnston v. City of Galva, 1925, 316 Ill. 598, 147 N.E. 453 (divide farm by fence); Champa v. Washington Compressed Gas Co., 1927, 146 Wash. 190, 262 P. 228 (move away); American Smelting & Refining Co. v. Riverside Dairy & Stock Farm, 9 Cir. 1916, 236 F. 510 (shut down business). It should be noted that in most of the cases where the generalization has been made no reasonable method of avoiding consequences was open to the plaintiff under the circumstances. McCormick, Damages, 1935, 139.

30. Plummer v. Penobscot Lumbering Ass'n, 1877, 67 Me. 363.

31. See supra, p. 597.

32. Recovery is not defeated, but the damages are reduced. Baltimore & S. P. R. Co. v. Hackett, 1898, 87 Md. 224, 39 A. 510; Carroll Springs Distilling Co. v. Schnepfe, 1909, 111 Md. 420, 74 A. 828.

33. Sherman v. Fall River Iron Works Co., 1861, 2 Allen, Mass., 524; Indiana Pipe Line Co. v. Christensen, 1924, 195 Ind. 106, 143 N.E. 596; Gulf, C. & S. F. R. Co. v. Reed, Tex.Civ.App.1893, 22 S.W. 283.

34. Carroll Springs Distilling Co. v. Schnepfe, 1909, 111 Md. 420, 74 A. 828; Mobile & O. R. Co. v. Red Feather Coal Co., 1928, 218 Ala. 582, 119 So. 606; Atchison, T. & S. F. R. Co. v. Jones, 1903, 110 Ill. App. 626; Southern R. Co. v. Poetker, 1910, 46 Ind.App. 295, 91 N.E. 610; Louisville & N. R. Co. v. Moore, 1907, 101 S.W. 934, 31 Ky.Law Rep. 141.

continuation of a stench from an unburied calf,[35] and still hold the defendant for the ensuing damages when with slight labor, expense and inconvenience he might have prevented them.

The plaintiff never is required to do more than to act reasonably under the circumstances. He need not plant a hopeless crop in a field swept by sulphur fumes,[36] or commit a trespass upon the defendant's land to abate the nuisance.[37] In particular, he need not move away, or surrender a valuable use of his property merely because the defendant has chosen to deprive him of it.[38]

The question frequently arises, whether the plaintiff assumes the risk and is barred from recovery by the fact that he has "come to the nuisance" by purchasing land and moving in next to it after it is already in existence or operation.[39] The prevailing rule is that in the absence of a prescriptive right[40] the defendant cannot condemn the surrounding premises to endure the nuisance, and that the purchaser is entitled to the reasonable use and enjoyment of his land to the

same extent as any other owner,[41] so long as he buys in good faith and not for the sole purpose of a vexatious lawsuit.[42] This is true in particular, for obvious reasons, of public nuisances,[43] and of those private ones which the defendant could abate at any reasonable cost.[44] There are cases, however, which have held that the plaintiff is barred by his voluntary choice of a place to live,[45] particularly where the defendant's activity is one in which the public has a major interest;[46] and the safer and more accurate statement would appear to be that "coming to the nuisance" is merely one factor, although clearly not the most important one, to be weighed in the scale along with the other elements which bear upon the question of "reasonable use."[47]

Finally, mention should be made of occasional cases in which the plaintiff engages in conduct similar to that of the defendant, and causes similar inconvenience to himself, as where both parties pollute the same

35. Central of Ga. R. Co. v. Steverson, 1911, 3 Ala. App. 313, 57 So. 494.

36. United Verde Extension Mining Co. v. Ralston, 1931, 37 Ariz. 554, 296 P. 262. See also the cases cited supra, p. 424.

37. White v. Chapin, 1869, 102 Mass. 138; Missouri, K. & T. R. Co. v. Burt, Tex.Civ.App.1894, 27 S.W. 948; Missouri Pac. R. Co. v. Baker, 1933, 188 Ark. 143, 64 S.W.2d 321.

38. In Garfield Box Co. v. Clifton Paper Board Co., 1941, 125 N.J.L. 603, 17 A.2d 588, this was carried to the length of holding that plaintiff could not be required to keep his doors closed.

39. See Notes, 1943, 17 Temp.L.Q. 449; 1953, 41 Cal. L.Rev. 148; 1953, 32 Or.L.Rev. 264; 1952, 4 Baylor L.Rev. 382.

40. There is no prescriptive right until the nuisance has done actual damage for the required period. Campbell v. Seaman, 1876, 63 N.Y. 568; United Verde Copper Co. v. Ralston, 9 Cir. 1931, 46 F.2d 1. In Anneberg v. Kurtz, 1944, 197 Ga. 188, 28 S.E.2d 769, pollution of a stream for twenty years was held sufficient.

41. Campbell v. Seaman, 1876, 63 N.Y. 568; Ensign v. Walls, 1948, 323 Mich. 49, 34 N.W.2d 549; Lawrence v. Eastern Air Lines, Fla.1955, 81 So.2d 632; Forbes v. City of Durant, 1950, 209 Miss. 246, 46 So.2d 551; Mahone v. Autry, 1951, 55 N.M. 111, 227 P.2d 623.

42. Thus in Edwards v. Allouez Mining Co., 1879, 38 Mich. 46, an injunction was denied for this reason. Cf. Abdella v. Smith, 1967, 34 Wis.2d 393, 149 N.W. 2d 537.

43. People v. Detroit White Lead Works, 1890, 82 Mich. 471, 46 N.W. 735.

44. Guarina v. Bogart, 1962, 407 Pa. 307, 180 A.2d 557.

45. McClung v. Louisville & N. R. Co., 1951, 255 Ala. 302, 51 So.2d 371; Oetjen v. Goff Kirby Co., Ohio App.1942, 49 N.E.2d 95, appeal dismissed 140 Ohio St. 544, 45 N.E.2d 607.

46. East St. Johns Shingle Co. v. City of Portland, 1952, 195 Or. 505, 246 P.2d 554; Powell v. Superior Portland Cement, 1942, 15 Wash.2d 14, 129 P.2d 536.

47. Hartung v. County of Milwaukee, 1958, 2 Wis.2d 269, 86 N.W.2d 475, 87 N.W.2d 799; Hall v. Budde, 1943, 293 Ky. 436, 169 S.W.2d 33; Schott v. Appleton Brewery Co., Mo.App.1947, 205 S.W.2d 917; McIntosh v. Brimmer, 1924, 68 Cal.App. 770, 230 P. 203.

stream[48] or flood the plaintiff's land.[49] In such cases, without regard to any question of contributory negligence, the damage caused may be apportioned between the two, as a matter merely of the harm which each has caused.

It should therefore be clear that in a great many cases the plaintiff's own misconduct is a factor of great importance, and that there is nothing inherent in the nature of nuisance to distinguish it from any other tort.

48.   Randolf v. Town of Bloomfield, 1889, 77 Iowa 50, 41 N.W. 562; Bowman v. Humphrey, 1906, 132 Iowa 234, 109 N.W. 714; cf. Walters v. Prairie Oil & Gas Co., 1922, 85 Okl. 77, 204 P. 906.

49.   Philadelphia & R. R. Co. v. Smith, 3 Cir. 1894, 64 F. 679. Cf. Thomas v. Kenyon, 1861, 1 Daly, N.Y., 132; Gould v. McKenna, 1878, 86 Pa. 297.

CHAPTER 16

TORT AND CONTRACT

92. RELATION BETWEEN THE ACTIONS

The fundamental difference between tort and contract lies in the nature of the interests protected. Tort actions are created to protect the interest in freedom from various kinds of harm. The duties of conduct which give rise to them are imposed by the law, and are based primarily upon social policy, and not necessarily upon the will or intention of the parties. They may be owed to all those within the range of harm, or to some considerable class of people. Contract actions are created to protect the interest in having promises performed. Contract obligations are imposed because of conduct of the parties manifesting consent, and are owed only to the specific individuals named in the contract.[1] Even as to these individuals, the damages recoverable for a breach of the contract duty are limited to those reasonably within the contemplation of the defendant when the contract was made,[2] while in a tort action a much broader measure of damages is applied.[3]

If the defendant undertakes, for a consideration, to pay money to X, and fails to do what he has promised, there is an actionable wrong, not because the law obliges people to make such payments in general, but because he has manifested his consent to assume the obligation, toward X alone. The action in such a case is in contract. But if A negligently runs B down with his automobile, a cause of action arises, not because of any promise to refrain from the commission of the act, but because the law imposes upon A a duty, owed to anyone in his path, to refrain from inflicting such injuries. The remedy in such a case is in tort.

Where a physician has contracted to treat a family for a year, and refuses to attend when sent for, the cause of action has been held to be for breach of contract only,[4] since the law recognizes no obligation upon a doctor to come when he is called for, in the absence of such a promise. But if he does attend, and renders his services negligently, he is liable in tort, even in the absence of a contract, because he is regarded as having assumed the duty, and he is required by law to exercise proper care as to every one whom he treats, even though he does so gratuitously.[5] On the same basis, where the defendants agreed with the plaintiff to prepare something for shipment by a certain train, but failed to do so, it was held that the action lay only on the contract, since there was no duty, apart from the contract, to perform

---

1. Winfield, Province of the Law of Tort, 1931, 40; Pollock, Law of Torts, 13th Ed. 1929, 2, 3.

2. McCormick, The Contemplation Rule as a Limitation Upon Damages for Breach of Contract, 1935, 19 Minn.L.Rev. 497, reprinted in McCormick, Damages, 1935, ch. 22.

3. See supra, § 43.

4. Randolph's Adm'r v. Snyder, 1910, 139 Ky. 159, 129 S.W. 562. See Miller, The Contractual Liability of Physicians and Surgeons, [1953] Wash.U.L.Q. 413. As to the possible effect of reliance on the promise, see supra, p. 347.

5. Du Bois v. Decker, 1891, 130 N.Y. 325, 29 N.E. 313; McNevins v. Lowe, 1866, 40 Ill. 209; Napier v. Greenzweig, 2 Cir. 1919, 256 F. 196.

such acts; [6] but any one who negligently damaged the goods before shipment would of course be liable in tort, without regard to any contract; and if the goods were shipped, and damaged by the carrier in transit, the plaintiff might have his choice of either remedy.[7]

Nonfeasance

The relation between the remedies in contract and tort presents a very confusing, field,[8] still in process of development, in which few courts have made any attempt to chart a path. The earliest cases arising in the borderland were those of negligence on the part of persons engaged in a public trade or calling, as where a ferryman overloaded his boat and drowned the plaintiff's horses,[9] or a smith lamed a horse while shoeing it.[10] The action was on the case, and the underlying theory seems to have been at first one of pure tort. In the course of time the defendant's "assumpsit," or undertaking, came to be regarded as the real foundation of the action; [11] and with the development of the action of assumpsit and the idea of consideration,[12] the obligation of the contract became

recognized as in itself a basis of liability. The tort remedy survived, however, in the situations where it had already existed; and the more or less inevitable efforts of lawyers [13] to turn every breach of contract into a tort forced the English courts to find some line of demarcation.

The line of division which developed quite early [14] was that between "nonfeasance," which meant not doing the thing at all, and "misfeasance," which meant doing it improperly. Much scorn has been poured on the distinction, but it does draw a valid line between the complete non-performance of a promise, which in the ordinary case is a breach of contract only, and a defective performance, which may also be a matter of tort. In general the courts have adhered to the line thus drawn; and a failure even to begin or attempt performance of an agreement to lend money,[15] to employ the plaintiff,[16] to furnish transportation,[17] to deliver

---

6. Newton v. Brook, 1902, 134 Ala. 269, 32 So. 722.

7. Turner v. Stallibrass, [1898] 1 Q.B. 56; Sumsion v. Streator-Smith, 1943, 103 Utah 44, 132 P.2d 680; Quaker Worsted Mills v. Howard Trucking Corp., 1938, 131 Pa.Super. 1, 198 A. 691; Ellis v. Taylor, 1931, 172 Ga. 830, 159 S.E. 266.

8. See Prosser, The Borderland of Tort and Contract, in Prosser, Selected Topics on the Law of Torts, 1954, 380; Guest, Tort or Contract? 3 Univ.Malaya L.Rev. 191; Poulton, Tort or Contract, 1966, 82 L.Q.Rev. 346; Winfield, Province of the Law of Tort, 1931; Thornton, The Elastic Concept of Tort and Contract as Applied by the Courts of New York, 1948, 14 Brook.L.Rev. 196; Note, 1954, 27 So.Cal.L.Rev. 216.

9. 1348, Y.B. 22 Lib.Ass. 94, pl. 41.

10. 1372, Y.B. 46 Edw. III, f. 19, pl. 19. See **Fifoot**, History and Sources of the Common Law, Tort and Contract, 1949, c. 2, 4, 6, 9; Kiraffy, The Action on the Case, 1951, 137–150.

11. 3 Street, Foundations of Legal Liability, 1906, 173.

12. Ames, The History of Assumpsit, 1888, 2 Harv. L.Rev. 1.

13. See for example Courtenay v. Earle, 1850, 10 C. B. 73, 138 Eng.Rep. 30, where the attempt was made to turn the non-payment of a bill of exchange into a tort.

14. The distinction appears to have originated in Watton v. Brinth, 1400, Y.B. 2 Hen. IV, f. 3, pl. 9, where it was pleaded that the defendant had undertaken to rebuild houses within a certain time and had failed to do so. Lord Holt approved the case in Coggs v. Bernard, 1703, 2 Ld.Raym. 909, 92 Eng. Rep. 107; and when the identical situation was repeated in Elsee v. Gatward, 1793, 5 Term Rep. 143, 101 Eng.Rep. 82, it was held that a tort action would lie only on a second count pleading that the defendant had in fact repaired the house with the wrong materials.

15. Farabee-Treadwell Co. v. Union & Planters Bank & Trust Co., 1916, 135 Tenn. 208, 186 S.W. 92; John Deere Co. of St. Louis v. Short, Mo.1964, 378 S.W.2d 496.

16. Braham v. Honolulu Amusement Co., 1913, 21 Hawaii 583. Or to continue to employ him. W. B. Davis & Son v. Ruple, 1930, 222 Ala. 52, 130 So. 772; Manley v. Exposition Cotton Mills, 1933, 47 Ga.App. 496, 170 S.E. 711; May v. Tidewater Power Co., 1939, 216 N.C. 439, 5 S.E.2d 308.

17. Louisville & N. R. Co. v. Spinks, 1898, 104 Ga. 692, 30 S.E. 968.

goods ordered,[18] to furnish light for a room,[19] to obtain the dissolution of an injunction and permit the plaintiff to proceed with the construction of a road,[20] or to attend as a physician,[21] all are held to amount to mere breaches of contract, for which no tort action will lie.

There are, however, a few situations in which failure to perform a contract may amount to a tort. One notable instance is the survival of the old tort duty to serve all comers which arose as to common callings before the idea of contract had developed.[22] Under modern law this duty to serve exists only as to public officers,[23] common carriers,[24] innkeepers,[25] public warehousemen,[26]

and public utilities,[27] who become liable in tort for nonperformance of their contracts, or even for refusal to enter into a contract at all. No such obligation rests today upon ordinary citizens engaged in other activities; and in the absence of legislation a physician,[28] a restaurant[29] or a racetrack[30] will not be liable for turning people away, for any reason or none. This is subject to the qualification that civil rights statutes, prohibiting under criminal penalty discrimination against any person on the ground of race or color are commonly interpreted as intended to provide a tort action as a remedy.[31]

Another type of exception arises where the contract results in or accompanies some relation between the parties which the law recognizes as giving rise to a duty of affirmative care. The typical case is that of a bail-

---

18. Dawson Cotton Oil Co. v. Kenan, McKay & Speir, 1918, 21 Ga.App. 688, 94 S.E. 1037. Cf. Mulvey v. Staab, 1887, 4 N.M. 172, 12 P. 699 (to supply goods if plaintiff opened a store); Ketcham v. Miller, 1922, 104 Ohio St. 372, 136 N.E. 145 (refusal to turn over premises under lease).

19. Stone v. Johnson, 1938, 89 N.H. 329, 197 A. 713, affirmed in 1939, 90 N.H. 311, 8 A.2d 743.

20. Chase v. Clinton County, 1928, 241 Mich. 478, 217 N.W. 565.

21. Randolph's Adm'r v. Snyder, 1910, 139 Ky. 159, 129 S.W. 562. See, generally, Note, 1932, 45 Harv. L.Rev. 164.

22. See Arterburn, The Origin and First Test of Public Callings, 1927, 75 U.Pa.L.Rev. 411; Burdick, The Origin of the Peculiar Duties of Public Service Companies, 1911, 11 Col.L.Rev. 514.

23. Horner v. Terpin, 1934, 63 S.D. 309, 258 N.W. 140; Moffitt v. Davis, 1934, 205 N.C. 565, 172 S.E. 317; Hupe v. Sommer, 1913, 88 Kan. 561, 129 P. 136.

24. Beck & Gregg Hardware Co. v. Associated Transport, Inc., 1954, 210 Ga. 545, 81 S.E.2d 515 (refusal to receive goods); Pittsburgh, C. & St. L. R. Co. v. Morton, 1878, 61 Ind. 539 (failure to furnish cars); Williams v. Carolina & N. W. R. Co., 1907, 144 N.C. 498, 57 S.E. 216 (failure to stop train); Nevin v. Pullman Palace Car Co., 1883, 106 Ill. 222 (failure to provide Pullman berth); Zabron v. Cunard S. S. Co., 1911, 151 Iowa 345, 131 N.W. 18 (failure to deliver ticket).

25. Jackson v. Virginia Hot Springs Co., 4 Cir. 1914, 213 F. 969; Atwater v. Sawyer, 1884, 76 Me. 539; Odom v. East Ave. Corp., 1942, 178 Misc. 363, 34 N.Y.S.2d 312, affirmed, 1942, 264 App.Div. 985, 37 N.Y.S.2d 491.

26. Nash v. Page & Co., 1882, 80 Ky. 539; Gray v. Central Warehouse Co., 1921, 181 N.C. 166, 106 S.E. 657.

27. Oklahoma Natural Gas Co. v. Graham, 1941, 188 Okl. 521, 111 P.2d 173 (gas); Ashelford v. Illinois Northern Utilities Co., 1936, 284 Ill.App. 655, 4 N.E.2d 397 (electricity); Alabama Water Co. v. Knowles, 1929, 220 Ala. 61, 124 So. 96 (water); Masterson v. Chesapeake & Potomac Tel Co., 1923, 52 U.S.App.D.C. 23, 299 F. 890 (telephone).

But even the public utility is liable only for breach of its public duty. Thus a telephone company, while it may be liable for failure to complete a call, is not required to deliver a message. Mentzer v. New England Tel. & Tel. Co., 1931, 276 Mass. 478, 177 N.E. 549; Bess v. Citizens Tel. Co., 1926, 315 Mo. 1056, 287 S.W. 466.

28. Hurley v. Eddingfield, 1901, 156 Ind. 416, 59 N.E. 1058; see Randolph's Adm'r v. Snyder, 1910, 139 Ky. 159, 129 S.W. 562.

29. Nance v. Mayflower Tavern, 1933, 106 Utah 517, 150 P.2d 773.

30. Madden v. Queens County Jockey Club, 1947, 296 N.Y. 249, 72 N.E.2d 697; Garifine v. Monmouth Park Jockey Club, 1959, 29 N.J. 47, 148 A.2d 1.

31. Crawford v. Kent, 1960, 341 Mass. 125, 167 N.E.2d 620 (dancing school); Odom v. East Ave. Corp., 1942, 178 Misc. 363, 34 N.Y.S.2d 312, affirmed 264 App.Div. 985, 37 N.Y.S.2d 491 (restaurant); Bolden v. Grand Rapids Operating Corp., 1927, 239 Mich. 318, 214 N.W. 241; Anderson v. Pantages Theatre Co., 1921, 114 Wash.2d 24, 194 P. 813 (theatre); Orloff v. Los Angeles Turf Club, 1947, 30 Cal.2d 110, 180 P.2d 321 (race track).

ment, where the bare fact that the defendant has possession of the plaintiff's property is enough to create the duty,[32] and it would exist if there were no contract at all and the goods were found on the highway.[33] The tort liability is limited to the scope of the recognized tort duty. A bailee may be liable in tort for failure to take ordinary precautions against the destruction of the goods by fire,[34] but the breach of an agreement to keep a horse in a separate stall [35] or to store butter at a definite temperature [36] is a matter of contract only. Likewise an employer may be liable in tort for a failure to furnish a safe place to work [37] or proper tools,[38] but an agreement to provide special facilities [39] or medical attention [40] must be enforced by a contract action. Mention already has been made [41] of the controversy as to whether a landlord's covenant to repair sets up a relation which is the basis of a tort duty to the tenant.

Another important exception to the nonliability for nonfeasance is the holding that a promise made without intent to perform it may be fraud, for which a tort action in deceit will lie.[42]

Misfeasance

Where the defendant has done something more than remain inactive, and is to be charged with "misfeasance," the possibility of recovery in tort is considerably increased. The older liability has carried over, and a carrier remains liable in tort, as well as on the contract, for negligent injury to a passenger [43] or for carrying him past his station,[44] for negligent loss or damage to goods shipped,[45] or for delay in their delivery.[46] Here

---

32. Turner v. Stallibrass, [1898] L.R. 1 Q.B. 56; Springfield Crystallized Egg Co. v. Springfield Ice & Refrigeration Co., 1914, 259 Mo. 664, 168 S.W. 772.

33. Ryan v. Chown, 1910, 160 Mich. 204, 125 N.W. 46. Cf. Weeg v. Iowa Mut. Ins. Co., 1966, 82 S.D. 104, 141 N.W.2d 913 (contract to maintain fence in safe condition).

34. Aircraft Sales & Service, Inc. v. Bramlett, 1950, 254 Ala. 588, 49 So.2d 144. Cf. Pinnix v. Toomey, 1955, 242 N.C. 358, 87 S.E.2d 893, holding that an owner of a building who brought a tort action against a plumbing contractor for negligently damaging his building could rely only on the common law standard of care, and contract provisions calling for a higher standard were not applicable.

35. Legge v. Tucker, 1856, 1 H. & N. 500, 156 Eng. Rep. 1298.

36. Kings Laboratories v. Yucaipa Valley Fruit Co., 1936, 18 Cal.2d 47, 62 P.2d 1054. Cf. Jacobs, Malcolm & Burtt v. Northern Pac. R. Co., 1925, 71 Cal. App. 42, 234 P. 328 (ventilation of car).

37. Denning v. State, 1899, 123 Cal. 316, 55 P. 1000; Kinnare v. City of Chicago, 1897, 70 Ill.App. 106.

38. Obanhein v. Arbuckle, 1905, 80 App.Div. 465, 81 N.Y.S. 133.

39. Stone v. Johnson, 1938, 89 N.H. 329, 197 A. 713, affirmed, 1939, 90 N.H. 311, 8 A.2d 743.

40. Willey v. Alaska Packers' Ass'n, N.D.Cal.1926, 9 F.2d 937; Galveston, H. & S. A. R. Co. v. Hennigan, Tex.Civ.App.1903, 76 S.W. 452. But in Mueller v. Winston Bros. Co., 1931, 165 Wash. 130, 4 P.2d 854, the duty to provide a qualified physician was held to arise as a matter of the relation, and the tort action was sustained.

41. See supra, p. 408.

42. See infra, p. 729.

43. Kelly v. Metropolitan St. R. Co., [1895] 1 Q.B. 944; Williamson v. Pacific Greyhound Lines, 1945, 67 Cal.App.2d 250, 153 P.2d 990; Webber v. Herkimer & M. St. R. Co., 1888, 109 N.Y. 311, 16 N.E. 358; Herron v. Miller, 1923, 96 Okl. 59, 220 P. 36; Baltimore City Passenger R. Co. v. Kemp, 1883, 61 Md. 619. See Feldman, Actions in Contract Resulting from Aircraft Crashes, 1963, 12 Cleve.Marsh.L.Rev. 472.

44. Seals v. Augusta Southern R. Co., 1898, 102 Ga. 817, 29 S.E. 116; McKeon v. Chicago, M. & St. P. R. Co., 1896, 94 Wis. 477, 69 N.W. 175. Or for putting him off at the wrong station. Wilkes v. Chicago, R. I. & P. R. Co., 1924, 197 Iowa 832, 198 N. W. 44, 36 A.L.R. 1012; Forrester v. Southern Pac. Co., 1913, 36 Nev. 247, 134 P. 753, rehearing denied 1913, 36 Nev. 245, 136 P. 705. Or letting him down at an improper and dangerous place. Vines v. Crescent Transit Co., 1955, 264 Ala. 114, 85 So.2d 436.

45. Turner v. Stallibrass, [1898] 1 Q.B. 56; Sumsion v. Streator-Smith, Inc., 1943, 103 Utah 44, 132 P.2d 680; Ellis v. Taylor, 1931, 172 Ga. 830, 159 S.E. 266; Quaker Worsted Mills Corp. v. Howard Trucking Corp., 1938, 131 Pa.Super. 1, 198 A. 691.

46. Virginia-Carolina Peanut Co. v. Atlantic C. L. R. Co., 1911, 135 N.C. 148, 71 S.E. 71; Owens Bros. v. Chicago, R. I. & P. R. Co., 1908, 139 Iowa 538, 117

again the duty is an incident of the relation rather than the contract, and the carrier would be liable if the passenger were carried free.[47]

Beyond this the American courts [48] have extended the tort liability for misfeasance to virtually every type of contract where defective performance may injure the promisee. An attorney [49] or an abstractor [50] examining a title, a physician treating a patient,[51] a surveyor,[52] an agent collecting a note [53] or lending money [54] or settling a claim,[55] or a liability insurer defending a

suit,[56] all have been held liable in tort for their negligence. The same is true of contractors employed to build a structure,[57] to transport people or goods,[58] to install a windmill [59] or a lightning rod,[60] or to shoot an oil well,[61] or a beauty shop giving a permanent wave; [62] of suppliers of chattels,[63] and of many others.[64] The principle which seems to have emerged from the decisions in the United States is that there will be liability in tort for misperformance of a contract whenever there would be liability for gratuitous performance without the contract—[65] which

---

N.W. 762; Texas & Pac. R. Co. v. Bufkin, Tex.Civ. App.1932, 46 S.W.2d 714.

47. Flint & Pere Marquette R. Co. v. Weir, 1877, 37 Mich. 111; Littlejohn v. Fitchburg R. Co., 1889, 148 Mass. 478, 20 N.E. 103; Pittsburgh, C. C. & St. L. R. Co. v. Higgs, 1905, 165 Ind. 694, 76 N.E. 299.

48. The later English decisions have been much more reluctant to find tort liability. See Groom v. Crocker, [1939] 1 K.B. 194 (attorney); Steljes v. Ingram, 1903, 19 T.L.R. 534 (architect); Jarvis v. Moy, Davies, Smith, Vanderwell & Co., [1936] 1 K. B. 399. But an injured servant has been permitted to sue the master in contract. Matthews v. Kuwait Bechtel Corp., [1959] 2 Q.B. 57.

49. Trimboli v. Kinkel, 1919, 226 N.Y. 147, 123 N.E. 205 (title search); Sullivan v. Stout, 1938, 120 N.J. L. 304, 199 A. 1 (same); Ramage v. Cohn, 1937, 124 Pa.Super. 525, 189 A. 496 (surrender of check); O'Neill v. Gray, 2 Cir. 1929, 30 F.2d 776 (delay in suit). See Coggin, Attorney Negligence—A Suit Within a Suit, 1958, 60 W.Va.L.Rev. 225; Note, 1951, 37 Va.L.Rev. 429.

50. Dorr v. Massachusetts Title Ins. Co., 1921, 238 Mass. 490, 131 N.E. 191; Ehmer v. Title Guarantee & Trust Co., 1898, 156 N.Y. 10, 50 N.E. 420.

51. Huysman v. Kirsch, 1936, 6 Cal.2d 302, 57 P.2d 908; McDonald v. Camas Prairie R. Co., 1935, 180 Wash. 555, 38 P.2d 515; Cochran v. Laton, 1918, 78 N.H. 562, 103 A. 658; Gillette v. Tucker, 1902, 67 Ohio St. 106, 65 N.E. 865.

52. Ferrie v. Sperry, 1912, 85 Conn. 337, 82 A. 577. Cf. Gagne v. Bertran, 1954, 43 Cal.2d 481, 275 P.2d 15 (test hole driller).

53. Robinson v. Threadgill, 1851, 35 N.C. 39. Cf. Adams v. Robinson, 1880, 65 Ala. 586 (renting premises to an insolvent).

54. Shipherd v. Field, 1873, 70 Ill. 438.

55. Thuringer v. Bonner, 1924, 74 Colo. 539, 222 P. 1118.

56. Attleboro Mfg. Co. v. Frankfort Marine A. & P. G. Ins. Co., C.C.Mass.1909, 171 F. 495, affirmed, 1 Cir. 1917, 240 F. 573; Wynnewood Lumber Co. v. Travelers Ins. Co., 1917, 173 N.C. 269, 91 S.E. 946. See Note, 1959, 34 N.Y.U.L.Rev. 783.

57. Lord Elec. Co. v. Barber Asphalt Paving Co., 1919, 226 N.Y. 427, 123 N.E. 756; E. & M. Const. Co. v. Bob, 1967, 115 Ga.App. 127, 153 S.E.2d 641 (repair). Cf. Pinnix v. Toomey, 1955, 242 N.C. 358, 87 S.E.2d 893.

58. McClure v. Johnson, 1937, 50 Ariz. 76, 69 P.2d 573. Cf. Compton v. Evans, 1939, 200 Wash. 125, 93 P.2d 341 (employer).

59. Flint & Walling Mfg. Co. v. Beckett, 1906, 167 Ind. 491, 79 N.E. 503. Cf. Olesen v. Beckanstin, 1919, 93 Conn. 614, 107 A. 514 (hot water system).

60. Holmes v. Schnoebelen, 1935, 87 N.H. 272, 178 A. 258; Whittle v. Miller Lightning Rod Co., 1918, 110 S.C. 557, 96 S.E. 907.

61. Jackson v. Central Torpedo Co., 1926, 117 Okl. 245, 246 P. 426.

62. Banfield v. Addington, 1932, 104 Fla. 661, 140 So. 893.

63. See infra, § 95.

64. See for example Winchester v. O'Brien, 1929, 266 Mass. 33, 164 N.E. 807 (breach of landlord's covenant of quiet enjoyment by making noise); Smith v. Weber, 1944, 70 S.D. 232, 16 N.W.2d 537 (landlord burning rubbish and turning off lights); De Mirjian v. Ideal Heating Corp., 1949, 91 Cal.App.2d 905, 206 P.2d 20 (tenant damaging premises); Eads v. Marks, 1952, 39 Cal.2d 807, 249 P.2d 257 (negligence in leaving milk bottle); Mauldin v. Sheffer, 1966, 113 Ga.App. 874, 150 S.E.2d 150 (negligence of engineer in furnishing plans).

65. "If a defendant may be held liable for the neglect of a duty imposed on him, independently of any contract, by operation of law, a fortiori ought he to be liable when he has come under an obligation to use care as the result of an undertaking

is to say, whenever such misperformance involves a foreseeable, unreasonable risk of harm to the interests of the plaintiff.

There has been little consideration of the problem of just where inaction ceases and "misfeasance" begins. It is clear that it is not always a question of action or inaction as to the particular act or omission which has caused the damage. Failure to blow a whistle [66] or to shut off steam [67] is readily treated as negligent operation of a train, and the omission to repair a gas pipe is regarded as negligent distribution of gas.[68] On the other hand the affirmative act of discharging an employee is uniformly considered to be no more than non-performance of the agreement to continue employment,[69] and the same

conclusion has been reached as to the revocation of a theatre ticket and the expulsion of the patron.[70] The question appears to be rather whether the defendant's performance, as distinct from his promise or his preparation, has gone so far that it has begun to affect the interests of the plaintiff beyond the expected benefits of the contract itself,[71] and is to be regarded, by analogy to the cases of gratuitous undertaking,[72] as a positive act assuming the obligation.

Election and Gravamen

Where on the facts either an action in contract or one in tort is open to the plaintiff, his choice may have important consequences. Some considerations may lead the plaintiff to prefer action on the contract. A contract may lead to strict liability for failure to perform, as in the case of a physician's undertaking to cure his patient,[73] where the tort action would require proof of negligence or some other wrongful conduct. A shorter statute of limitations may bar the tort action,[74] or it may not survive the death of

---

founded on a consideration. Where the duty has its roots in contract, the undertaking to observe due care may be implied from the relationship, and should it be the fact that a breach of the agreement also constitutes such a failure to exercise care as amounts to a tort, the plaintiff may elect, as the common-law authorities have it, to sue in case or in assumpsit." Flint & Walling Mfg. Co. v. Beckett, 1906, 167 Ind. 491, 498, 79 N.E. 503, 505.

Cf. Coss v. Spaulding, 1912, 41 Utah 447, 126 P. 468, where defendant was a physician hired by a motorist who had run over a boy, to give him medical treatment.

66. Southern R. Co. v. Grizzle, 1906, 124 Ga. 735, 53 S.E. 244.

67. Kelly v. Metropolitan R. Co. [1895] 1 Q.B. 944.

68. Consolidated Gas Co. v. Connor, 1911, 114 Md. 140, 78 A. 725. Cf. Osborne v. Morgan, 1881, 130 Mass. 102; Horner v. Lawrence, 1874, 37 N.J.L. 46; Lottman v. Barnett, 1876, 62 Mo. 159.

69. Addis v. Gramophone Co., Ltd., [1909] A.C. 488; May v. Tidewater Power Co., 1939, 216 N.C. 439, 5 S.E.2d 308; W. B. Davis & Son v. Ruple, 1930, 222 Ala. 52, 130 So. 772; Manley v. Exposition Cotton Mills, 1933, 47 Ga.App. 496, 170 S.E. 711; United Protective Workers v. Ford Motor Co., 7 Cir. 1955, 223 F.2d 49. Cf. Hart v. Ludwig, 1956, 347 Mich. 559, 79 N.W.2d 895, where discontinuance of work on a contract for care and maintenance of an orchard was held to be no more than failure to complete a contract.

On the other hand a physician who starts in to treat a patient and abandons him has been held liable in tort. Mehigan v. Sheehan, 1947, 94 N.H. 274, 51 A. 2d 632.

70. Marrone v. Washington Jockey Club, 1913, 227 U.S. 633; Horney v. Nixon, 1905, 213 Pa. 20, 61 A. 1088; Shubert v. Nixon Amusement Co., 1912, 83 N.J.L. 101, 83 A. 369; Boswell v. Barnum & Bailey, 1916, 135 Tenn. 35, 185 S.W. 692.

71. See the language of Cardozo, C. J., in H. R. Moch Co. v. Rensselaer Water Co., 1928, 247 N.Y. 160, 159 N.E. 896, 898.

72. See supra, p. 343.

73. Frankel v. Wolper, 1918, 181 App.Div. 485, 169 N.Y.S. 15, affirmed 1919, 228 N.Y. 582, 127 N.E. 913; Schuster v. Sutherland, 1916, 92 Wash. 135, 158 P. 730; Robins v. Firestone, 1955, 308 N.Y. 543, 127 N.E.2d 330. Cf. Noel v. Proud, 1961, 189 Kan. 6, 367 P.2d 61 (plaintiff's condition to be made no worse); Johnston v. Rodis, D.C.Cir. 1958, 251 F. 917 (treatment perfectly safe); Camposano v. Claiborn, 1963, 2 Conn.Cir. 135, 196 A.2d 129 (warranty against scars). See Miller, The Contractual Liability of Physicians and Surgeons, [1953] Wash.U.L.Q. 413.

74. Whitaker v. Poston, 1907, 120 Tenn. 207, 110 S. W. 1019; Lipman, Wolfe & Co. v. Phoenix Assur. Co., 9 Cir. 1919, 258 F. 544; Manning v. 1234 Corp., 1940, 174 Misc. 36, 20 N.Y.S.2d 121, affirmed, 1941, 260 App.Div. 914, 24 N.Y.S.2d 302, appeal denied,

one of the parties.[75] Some immunities, such as those of municipal corporations [76] or charities [77] may prevent recovery in tort, but not in contract. The damages recoverable on the contract may sometimes be greater, to the extent that they give the plaintiff the benefit of the bargain made, rather than compensation for a loss.[78] A contract claim may be assignable where a tort claim is not,[79] or an inferior court may have jurisdiction over it,[80] or the venue may offer more latitude,[81] or the contract suit may open the way to remedies such as attachment [82] or summary judg-

ment,[83] or be available as a set-off [84] or counterclaim,[85] where the other remedy would not. Finally, the plaintiff may by his own conduct so far have accepted and affirmed the contract as to be bound by it, to the exclusion of tort remedies he might otherwise have had.[86]

Generally speaking, the tort remedy is likely to be more advantageous to the injured party in the greater number of cases, if only because it will so often permit the recovery of greater damages. Under the rule of Hadley v. Baxendale,[87] the damages recoverable for breach of contract are limited to those within the contemplation of the defendant at the time the contract was made,[88] and in some jurisdictions, at least, to those for which the defendant has tacitly agreed to assume responsibility.[89] They may be fur-

---

1941, 261 App.Div. 804, 25 N.Y.S.2d 780; McCoy v. Wesley Hospital & Nurse Training School, 1961, 188 Kan. 325, 362 P.2d 841; Stanley v. Chastek, 1962, 34 Ill.App.2d 220, 180 N.E.2d 512.

75. See infra, § 126.

76. Harlan County v. Cole, 1927, 218 Ky. 819, 292 S. W. 501; City of Hazard v. Eversole, 1931, 237 Ky. 242, 35 S.W.2d 313; Schilling v. Carl Township, 1931, 60 N.D. 480, 235 N.W. 126; Kerns v. Couch, 1932, 141 Or. 147, 12 P.2d 1011, 17 P.2d 323. See Note, 1932, 31 Mich.L.Rev. 864.

77. Ward v. St. Vincent's Hospital, 1899, 39 App.Div. 624, 57 N.Y.S. 784.

78. Particularly in cases of fraud, in jurisdictions which adopt the out-of-pocket measure of damages for deceit. See infra, § 110.
Even in quasi-contract the unjust enrichment of the defendant may exceed the damages which the plaintiff has suffered. Gilmore v. Wilbur, Mass.1831, 12 Pick. 120; cf. Galvin v. Mac Mining & Milling Co., 1894, 14 Mont. 508, 37 P. 366.

79. Vogel v. Cobb, 1943, 193 Okl. 64, 141 P.2d 276. Likewise a contract action may carry interest, where a tort action does not. Miller v. Foltis Fisher, Inc., 1934, 152 Misc. 24, 272 N.Y.S. 712.

80. White v. Ely, 1907, 145 N.C. 36, 58 S.E. 437; Chudnovski v. Eckels, 1908, 232 Ill. 312, 83 N.E. 846; Busch v. Interborough Rapid Transit Co., 1907, 110 App.Div. 705, 96 N.Y.S. 747, affirmed, 1907, 187 N.Y. 388, 80 N.E. 197.

81. Bufkin v. Grisham, 1930, 157 Miss. 746, 128 So. 563; Wright v. Southern R. Co., 1910, 7 Ga.App. 542, 67 S.E. 272.

82. Thuringer v. Bonner, 1924, 74 Colo. 539, 222 P. 1118; De Mirjian v. Ideal Heating Corp., 1949, 91 Cal.App.2d 905, 206 P.2d 20; First Nat. Bank of Nashua v. Van Voorhis, 1895, 6 S.D. 548, 62 N.W. 378.

83. Garfunkel v. Pennsylvania R. Co., 1932, 148 Misc. 810, 266 N.Y.S. 35; Bishop v. Specter, 1932, 150 Misc. 360, 269 N.Y.S. 76.

84. John A. Eck Co. v. Pennsylvania R. Co., 1931, 261 Ill.App. 43; Ellis v. Taylor, 1931, 172 Ga. 830, 159 S.E. 266.

85. Manhattan Egg Co. v. Seaboard Term. & Refrig. Co., 1930, 137 Misc. 14, 242 N.Y.S. 189; Farmers & Merchants' Nat. Bank v. Huckaby, 1923, 89 Okl. 214, 215 P. 429; Casner v. Hoskins, 1913, 64 Or. 254, 128 P. 841, 130 P. 55.

86. Cf. Schmidt v. Mesmer, 1897, 116 Cal. 267, 48 P. 54; Timmerman v. Gurnsey, 1928, 206 Iowa 35, 217 N.W. 879; Simon v. Goodyear Metallic Rubber Shoe Co., 6 Cir., 1900, 105 F. 573; cf. Pohl v. Johnson, 1930, 179 Minn. 398, 229 N.W. 555 (delay in cashing a bad check).

87. 1854, 9 Ex. 341, 156 Eng.Rep. 145. See McCormick, Damages, 1935, ch. 22; Bauer, Consequential Damages in Contract, 1932, 80 U.Pa.L.Rev. 687.

88. Dice's Adm'r v. Zweigart's Adm'r, 1914, 161 Ky. 646, 171 S.W. 195; Timmons v. Williams Wood Products Corp., 1932, 164 S.C. 361, 162 S.E. 329; Korach v. Loeffel, 1912, 168 Mo.App. 414, 151 S.W. 790. In Trammell v. Eastern Air Lines, W.D.S. C.1955, 136 F.Supp. 75, the contract measure was applied where an air line refused to allow plaintiff to board a plane for which he had a ticket. Cf. Edd v. Western Union Tel. Co., 1928, 127 Or. 500, 272 P. 895 (telegraph transmission of money).

89. Globe Refining Co. v. Landa Cotton Oil Co., 1903, 190 U.S. 540; Armstrong Rubber Co. v. Griffith, 2 Cir. 1930, 43 F.2d 689; Givens v. North Augusta

ther limited by the contract itself,[90] where a tort action might avoid the limitation.[91] In contract actions, other than those for breach of promise to marry, punitive damages are not allowed,[92] and there can ordinarily be no recovery for mental suffering.[93] In the tort action the only limitations are those of "proximate cause," [94] and the policy which denies recovery to certain types of interests themselves.[95]

The tort action may offer other advantages. It may permit recovery for wrongful death,[96] for which a contract action normally will not lie. It may be open where the contract fails for lack of proof,[97] for uncertainty,[98] for illegality,[99] for want of consideration,[1] or because of the statute of frauds [2] or the parol evidence rule.[3] It may sometimes avoid some defenses, such as infancy [4] or a discharge in bankruptcy; [5] and it may avoid some counterclaims.[6] It may avoid the necessity of joining several defendants,[7]

Elec. & Imp. Co., 1912, 91 S.C. 417, 74 S.E. 1067. Contra, McKibbin v. Pierce, Tex.Civ.App.1917, 190 S.W. 1149.

90. Hart v. Pennsylvania R. Co., 1884, 112 U.S. 331; Libby v. St. Louis, I. M. & S. R. Co., 1909, 137 Mo. App. 276, 117 S.W. 659; Merchants' & Miners' Transp. Co. v. Moore & Co., 1905, 124 Ga. 482, 52 S.E. 802.

91. Cf. Woodruff & Sons v. Brown, 5 Cir. 1958, 256 F.2d 391; Danann Realty Corp. v. Harris, 1959, 5 N.Y.2d 317, 184 N.Y.S.2d 599, 157 N.E.2d 597. See Note, 1959, 59 Col.L.Rev. 525.

92. McCormick, Damages, 1935, 289, 290. Thus it has been held that punitive damages cannot be awarded where the action is on the contract, although the defendant's conduct constituted a tort. Trout v. Watkins Livery & Undertaking Co., 1910, 148 Mo.App. 621, 130 S.W. 136; Ketcham v. Miller, 1922, 104 Ohio St. 372, 136 N.E. 145; Southwestern Telegraph & Telephone Co. v. Luckett, 1910, 60 Tex.Civ.App. 117, 127 S.W. 856. Contra, Williams v. Carolina & N. W. R. Co., 1907, 144 N.C. 498, 57 S.E. 216.

93. Western Union Tel. Co. v. Speight, 1920, 254 U.S. 17; Morton v. Western Union Tel. Co., 1895, 53 Ohio St. 431, 41 N.E. 689; Western Union Tel. Co. v. Choteau, 1911, 28 Okl. 664, 115 P. 879. In Stewart v. Rudner, 1957, 349 Mich. 459, 84 N.W.2d 816, where there was a contract action for a surgeon's failure to perform a Caesarian operation, the court broke away from the rule, and allowed the damages.

94. See supra, ch. 7.

95. For example, negligent interference with contract relations, infra, p. 938. Or mental suffering at injury or peril to a third person, supra, p. 333.

96. Keiper v. Anderson, 1917, 138 Minn. 392, 165 N. W. 237; Greco v. S. S. Kresge Co., 1938, 277 N.Y. 26, 12 N.E.2d 557; Gosling v. Nichols, 1943, 59 Cal. App.2d 442, 139 P.2d 86; Rodwell v. Camel City Coach Co., 1933, 205 N.C. 292, 171 S.E. 100.

97. Pittsburgh, C., C. & St. L. R. Co. v. Higgs, 1905, 165 Ind. 694, 76 N.E. 299; Corry v. Pennsylvania R. Co., 1900, 194 Pa. 516, 45 A. 341; Jacksonville St. R. Co. v. Chappell, 1886, 22 Fla. 616, 1 So. 10.

98. Richey & Gilbert Co. v. Northern Pac. R. Co., 1910, 110 Minn. 347, 125 N.W. 897.

99. Costello v. Ten Eyck, 1891, 86 Mich. 348, 49 N.W. 152.

1. Daniel v. Daniel, 1921, 190 Ky. 210, 226 S.W. 1070; Pease & Elliman v. Wegeman, 1928, 223 App. Div. 682, 229 N.Y.S. 398.

2. Burgdorfer v. Thielemann, 1936, 153 Or. 354, 55 P.2d 1122; Kinkaid v. Rossa, 1913, 31 S.D. 559, 141 N.W. 969; McNaughton v. Smith, 1904, 136 Mich. 368, 99 N.W. 382.

3. New England Foundation Co. v. Elliott A. Watrous, Inc., 1940, 306 Mass. 177, 27 N.E.2d 756; Duholm v. Chicago, M. & St. P. R. Co., 1920, 146 Minn. 1, 177 N.W. 72; McNeill v. Wabash R. Co., 1921, 207 Mo.App. 161, 231 S.W. 649.

4. Vermont Acceptance Corp. v. Wiltshire, 1931, 103 Vt. 219, 153 A. 199; Wisconsin Loan & Fin. Corp. v. Goodnough, 1931, 201 Wis. 101, 228 N.W. 484; Patterson v. Kasper, 1914, 182 Mich. 281, 148 N.W. 690.

5. The National Bankruptcy Act, 11 U.S.C.A. § 33, excepts from discharge liabilities for obtaining money by false pretenses or false representations, and for wilful and malicious injuries to the person or property of another. See Joslin, Torts and Bankruptcy—A Synthesis, 1960, 1 Bos.Coll.Ind. & Comm.L.Rev. 185; Gleick, Tort Liabilities: To What Extent Are They Dischargeable by Bankruptcy, 1964, 19 Bus.L.Rev. 339; Note, 1939, 23 Minn.L. Rev. 958.

6. Zapfe v. Werner, 1923, 120 Misc. 326, 199 N.Y.S. 293; Sattler v. Neiderkorn, 1926, 190 Wis. 464, 209 N.W. 607.

7. See Clark, Code Pleading, 1928, 257, 260; Keller v. Blasdel, 1865, 1 Nev. 491 (contract); Elliott v. Hayden, 1870, 104 Mass. 180 (tort). It has been held that an action in quasi-contract, the tort being "waived," is several. City Nat. Bank v. National Park Bank, 1884, 32 Hun, N.Y., 105.

or permit successive actions for multiple breaches of a single contract,[8] or the application of a favorable rule under the conflict of laws.[9]

Frequently, where either tort or contract will lie and inconsistent rules of law apply to the two actions, the question arises whether the plaintiff may elect freely which he will bring, or whether the court must itself decide that on the facts pleaded and proved the "gist" or "gravamen" of his cause of action is one or the other. As to this the decisions are in considerable confusion,[10] and it is difficult to generalize.

Where the particular point at issue is one of adjective law only, affecting the suit or its procedure, but not the merits of the cause of action, the courts have tended to be quite liberal in giving the plaintiff his freedom of choice, and have upheld his action of tort or contract as he has seen fit to bring it.[11] Likewise where the point is one affecting substantive rights, but the claim is one for damages to property or to pecuniary interests only, the tendency has been, with some occasional dissent,[12] to allow the election.[13] But

when the claim is one for personal injury, the decision usually [14] has been that the gravamen of the action is the misconduct and the damage, and that it is essentially one of tort, which the plaintiff cannot alter by his pleading.[15] This has the odd result that the negligence of an attorney will survive the death of his client,[16] while that of a physician is oft interred with his patient's bones.[17] Actually the courts appear to have

Better Food Markets v. American Dist. Tel. Co., 1953, 40 Cal.2d 179, 253 P.2d 10 (liquidated damages clause in contract to install burglar alarm).

13. Micheletti v. Moidel, 1934, 94 Colo. 587, 32 P.2d 266 (survival); Southern Pac. R. Co. of Mexico v. Gonzales, 1936, 48 Ariz. 260, 61 P.2d 377 (statute of limitations); Schleifer v. Worcester North Sav. Inst., 1940, 306 Mass. 226, 27 N.E.2d 992 (statute of frauds); Burgdorfer v. Thielemann, 1936, 153 Or. 354, 55 P.2d 1122 (same); Mid-West Chevrolet Corp. v. Noah, 1935, 173 Okl. 198, 48 P.2d 283 (parol evidence).

14. Again there has been occasional disagreement, as in Forrester v. Southern Pac. R. Co., 1913, 36 Nev. 247, 134 P. 753, rehearing denied, 1913, 36 Nev. 247, 136 P. 705 (survival). Particularly as to the election of the contract action to avoid a short tort statute of limitations. Doughty v. Maine Central Transp. Co., 1944, 141 Me. 124, 39 A.2d 758; Williams v. Illinois Central R. Co., 1950, 360 Mo. 501, 229 S.W.2d 1; Stanley v. Chastek, 1962, 34 Ill.App. 2d 220, 180 N.E.2d 512; Stitt v. Gold, 1962, 33 Misc.2d 273, 225 N.Y.S.2d 536, affirmed, 1962, 17 App.Div. 642, 230 N.Y.S.2d 677. See Lillich, The Malpractice Statute of Limitations in New York, 1962, 47 Corn.L.Q. 339.

Compare, where plaintiff sues as a third party beneficiary of the contract: Thompson v. Harry C. Erb Co., 3 Cir. 1957, 240 F.2d 452; Keefer v. Lombardi, 1954, 376 Pa. 367, 102 A.2d 695, cert. denied 347 U.S. 1016.

15. McClure v. Johnson, 1937, 50 Ariz. 76, 69 P.2d 573 (survival; good discussion); Kozan v. Comstock, 5 Cir. 1959, 270 F.2d 839 (statute of limitations); Oklahoma Nat. Gas Co. v. Pack, 1939, 186 Okl. 330, 97 P.2d 768 (measure of damages); Rubino v. Utah Canning Co., 1954, 123 Cal.App.2d 18, 266 P.2d 163 (warranty).

16. Knights v. Quarles, 1820, 2 Brod. & B. 102, 129 Eng.Rep. 896; Stimpson v. Sprague, 1830, 6 Me. 470. Or permit a longer statute of limitations. Schirmer v. Nethercutt, 1930, 157 Wash. 172, 288 P. 265.

17. Huysman v. Kirsch, 1936, 6 Cal.2d 302, 57 P.2d 908; Cochran v. Laton, 1918, 78 N.H. 562, 103 A.

8. Lloyd v. Farmers Coop. Store, 1936, 197 Minn. 387, 267 N.W. 204.

9. Quaker Worsted Mills Corp. v. Howard Trucking Corp., 1938, 131 Pa.Super. 1, 198 A. 691; Schmitt v. Postal Tel. Co., 1914, 164 Iowa 654, 146 N.W. 467; Pittsburgh, C., C. & St. L. R. Co. v. Grom, 1911, 142 Ky. 51, 133 S.W. 977.

10. See Prosser, The Borderland of Tort and Contract, in Prosser, Selected Topics on the Law of Torts, 1954, 380, 429–450; Thornton, The Elastic Concept of Tort and Contract as Applied by the Courts of New York, 1948, 14 Brook.L.Rev. 196.

11. Busch v. International Rapid Transit Co., 1907, 187 N.Y. 388, 80 N.E. 197 (jurisdiction of court); Bufkin v. Grisham, 1930, 157 Miss. 746, 128 So. 563 (venue); Atlantic & Pac. R. Co. v. Laird, 1896, 164 U.S. 393 (joinder of parties); Felder v. Reeth, 8 Cir. 1929, 34 F.2d 744 (counterclaim); Oil Well Core Drilling Co. v. Barnhart, 1937, 20 Cal.App.2d 677, 67 P.2d 696 (attachment).

12. See for example Jackson v. Central Torpedo Co., 1926, 117 Okl. 245, 246 P. 426 (statute of limitations); Cassidy v. Kraft-Phenix Cheese Co., 1938, 285 Mich. 426, 280 N.W. 814 (statute of frauds);

preserved a great deal of flexibility, and to have been influenced in their decisions by their attitude toward the rule of law in question.

93. LIABILITY TO THIRD PARTIES

The responsibility of a contracting party to a third person with whom he has made no contract has a long history, and has presented problems of greater difficulty than those surrounding the relations of the immediate parties to the contract. The first obstacle which arises is the fact that there has been no direct transaction between the plaintiff and the defendant, which usually is expressed by saying that they are not in "privity" of contract. There is thus no logical basis upon which the one may be required to perform the contract for the other, unless the contract has been made expressly for the benefit of the plaintiff, or it has been assigned to him.[18]

In other words, the absence of "privity" between the parties makes it difficult to found any duty to the plaintiff upon the contract itself. But by entering into a contract with A, the defendant may place himself in such a relation toward B that the law will impose upon him an obligation, sounding in tort and not in contract, to act in such a way that B will not be injured. The incidental fact of the existence of the contract with A does not negative the responsibility of the actor when he enters upon a course of affirmative conduct which may be expected to affect the interests of another person.[19]

This idea was slow to find recognition in the courts. In 1842, in Winterbottom v. Wright,[20] the Court of Exchequer held that the breach of a contract to keep a mailcoach in repair after it was sold could give no cause of action to a passenger in the coach who was injured when it collapsed. The decision held only that no action could be maintained on the contract itself; but certain dicta of the judges, and particularly the words of Lord Abinger, who foresaw "the most absurd and outrageous consequences, to which I can see no limit," [21] "unless we confine the operation of such contracts as this to the parties who entered into them," were taken to mean that there could be no action even in tort, and that this was true of any misperformance of a contract, including even the sale of a defective coach in the first instance.[22] The error of this interpretation of the case has been exposed long since; [23] but from it there developed a general rule, which prevailed into the twentieth century, that there was no liability of a contracting party to one with whom he was not in "privity." [24]

The development of the law away from this position in the case of the seller of products has been spectacular in the extreme, and remains to be considered at a later point.[25] As

broken his contract, none can sue him but a party to it, but if he has violated a duty to others, he is liable to them." Peters v. Johnson, 1902, 50 W.Va. 644, 41 S.E. 190.

20. 1842, 10 M. & W. 109, 152 Eng.Rep. 402. See also Langridge v. Levy, 1842, 2 M. & W. 519, 150 Eng.Rep. 863.

21. The source of a most amusing bit, "The Most Outrageous Consequences," in James Reid Parker, Attorneys at Law, 1941, 87–96.

22. See for example Huset v. J. I. Case Threshing Mach. Co., 8 Cir. 1903, 120 F. 865; Earl v. Lubbock, [1905] 1 K.B. 253.

23. Bohlen, The Basis of Affirmative Obligations in the Law of Tort, 1905, 44 Am.L.Reg.,N.S., 209, 280–285, 289–310; and see Lord Atkin, in Donoghue v. Stevenson, [1932] A.C. 562, 588–589.

24. Bohlen, Fifty Years of Torts, 1937, 50 Harv.L. Rev. 1225, 1232.

25. See infra, ch. 17.

658; Mullane v. Crump, 1947, 272 App.Div. 922, 71 N.Y.S.2d 40, affirmed memo. 272 App.Div. 934, 72 N.Y.S.2d 417. Or be barred by the tort statute of limitations. Wilder v. Haworth, 1949, 187 Or. 688, 213 P.2d 797; Trimming v. Howard, 1932, 52 Idaho 412, 15 P.2d 661; Howard v. Middlesborough Hospital, 1932, 242 Ky. 602, 47 S.W.2d 77.

18. Two of the classic statements of this proposition are found in Winterbottom v. Wright, 1842, 10 M. & W. 109, 152 Eng.Rep. 402, and National Sav. Bank v. Ward, 1879, 100 U.S. 195.

19. "The question is: Has the defendant broken a duty apart from the contract? If he has merely

to other contracting parties, such as those who undertake to furnish labor or services, the development has on the whole not kept pace with that as to the seller. Strict liability has gained almost no foothold at all, except as the contract itself may be extended to cover a restricted group of third party beneficiaries; [26] and as to negligence, the law has tended to lag some twenty or thirty years behind. The fetish of "privity of contract" has remained more of an obstacle; [27] and while "the assault upon the citadel of privity is proceeding these days apace," [28] the fear of burdening the defendants with a crushing responsibility, which has largely disappeared from the field of sales, still tends to lead many courts to deny liability in cases which fall behind the general progress.[29]

Nonfeasance

The refusal to find any liability to third persons has been most definite where the defendant's misconduct is found to have consisted merely of a failure to perform the contract at all. Such "nonfeasance" ordinarily leads to no tort liability even to the promisee, whose remedy must be on the contract itself; [30] and it follows that a third person, no party to the contract, has no better claim in tort.[31] Thus it is quite generally agreed that if the defendant contracts to accept employment with A, in work which will affect the safety of B, and then entirely fails to appear for work and never enters upon the employment, he may be liable to A for breach of his contract, but he will have no liability in contract or in tort to B.[32]

However, as we have seen,[33] there are situations in which the making of the contract creates a relation between the defendant and the promisee, which is sufficient to impose a tort duty of reasonable care. By the same token, there are situations in which the making of a contract with A may create a relation between the defendant and B, which will create a similar duty toward B, and may result in liability for failure to act. Perhaps the most obvious illustration is the sending of a telegram. As a result of its contract with the sender, the telegraph company incurs the obligation of a public utility toward the addressee, and becomes liable to him in tort when it fails to transmit the message.[34]

---

26. See 2 Williston, Contracts, Rev.Ed.1936, ch. 14.

27. Bohlen, Fifty Years of Torts, 1937, 50 Harv.L. Rev. 1225, 1232.

28. Cardozo, C. J., in Ultramares Corp. v. Touche, Niven & Co., 1931, 255 N.Y. 170, 174 N.E. 441.

29. See for example Scott v. Huffman, 10 Cir. 1956, 237 F.2d 396 (train conductor); Miller v. Davis & Averill, 1948, 137 N.J.L. 671, 61 A.2d 253 (building contractor); Zamecki v. Hartford Acc. & Ind. Co., 1953, 202 Md. 54, 95 A.2d 302 (inspection of grandstand); Norwood v. Carolina Power & Light Co., E.D.S.C.1947, 74 F.Supp. 483 (manager and foreman).

30. See supra, p. 345.

31. See for example Olsness v. State, 1929, 58 N.D. 20, 224 N.W. 913 (bank negligently forwarding checks to drawee not liable to surety); Gardner v. Huie, Ohio C.P.1946, 68 N.E.2d 397 (contract to support mother; not liable to son-in-law); Mears v.

Crocker First Nat. Bank of San Francisco, 1950, 97 Cal.App.2d 482, 218 P.2d 91 (stock transfer agent not liable to owner for delay); Standard Iron Works v. Southern Bell Tel. Co., W.D.S.C.1917, 256 F. 548 (nonsubscriber using telephone); Baca v. Britt, 1963, 73 N.M. 1, 385 P.2d 61 (failure to repair traffic light).

32. See Waters v. Anthony, 1949, 252 Ala. 244, 40 So.2d 316; Franklin v. May Department Stores, E. D.Miss.1938, 25 F.Supp. 735; Landreth v. Phillips Petroleum Co., W.D.Mo.1947, 74 F.Supp. 801; Sloss-Sheffield Steel & Iron Co. v. Wilkes, 1936, 231 Ala. 511, 165 So. 764; Osborne v. Morgan, 1881, 130 Mass. 102.

See also Hanson v. Blackwell Motor Co., 1927, 143 Wash. 547, 255 P. 939, where defendant did not perform its promise to repair an automobile. The misrepresentation, however, should have led to a different conclusion, as in Moody v. Martin Motor Co., 1948, 76 Ga.App. 456, 46 S.E.2d 197.

33. Supra, p. 622.

34. So Relle v. Western Union Tel. Co., 1881, 55 Tex. 308; Mentzer v. Western Union Tel. Co., 1895, 93 Iowa 752, 62 N.W. 1; Edd v. Western Union Tel. Co., 1928, 127 Or. 500, 272 P. 895; Postal Telegraph-Cable Co. v. Kaler, 1941, 65 Ga.App. 641, 16 S.E.2d 77.

Mention already has been made [35] of the cases holding that a landlord's covenant with his tenant to repair the premises creates a relation of responsibility or "control" which makes him responsible to third persons entering in the right of the tenant for his failure to do so.

There are a few other situations in which such a relation has been found. Where an agent or servant has accepted the control of property under a contract with his principal, and under circumstances where there is an obvious risk of harm to outsiders if he does not use reasonable care, the obligation of affirmative conduct has been imposed upon him.[36] The same is true where he has taken custody or control of people.[37] While there are cases to the contrary,[38] the prevailing view now recognizes the same responsibility where the agent or servant has in fact entered upon his employment, and undertaken to be responsible for the performance of a duty [39] which the employer owes to others, as where, for example, a construction superintendent is hired to inspect scaffolding to be used by employees,[40] or a track walker to inspect poles adjoining the public highway.[41]

This is all the clearer when the defendant's omission to perform his contract has led to harm to a third person, suffered because of reliance upon the performance—as where a railroad crossing watchman, hired to give notice of the approach of a train, goes to sleep and fails to do so.[42] On the same basis a company which enters upon a contract to inspect, maintain or repair a boiler,[43] or an elevator [44] may become liable when the employer relies upon its performance, and as a result a third person is injured. The duty may be limited by the contract,[45] but does

35. Supra, p. 408.

36. The obvious case is that of a manager or superintendent taking over the care of a building. Lough v. John Davis & Co., 1902, 30 Wash. 204, 70 P. 491; Tippecanoe Land & Trust Co. v. Jester, 1913, 180 Ind. 357, 101 N.E. 915; Lambert v. Jones, 1936, 339 Mo. 677, 98 S.W.2d 752; Restatement of Agency, Second, § 355.

37. Hagerty v. Montana Ore Purchasing Co., 1908, 38 Mont. 69, 98 P. 643 (mine superintendent); Osborne v. Morgan, 1884, 130 Mass. 102 (factory superintendent); Greenberg v. Whitcomb Lumber Co., 1895, 90 Wis. 225, 63 N.W. 93. See Restatement of Agency, Second, §§ 351, 356.

38. Scott v. Huffman, 10 Cir. 1956, 237 F.2d 396; Davis v. St. Louis & S. F. R. Co., N.D.Okl.1934, 8 F.Supp. 519; Knight v. Atlantic Coast Line R. Co., 5 Cir. 1934, 73 F.2d 76; Kelly v. Robinson, E.D.Mo. 1920, 262 F. 695; Norwood v. Carolina Power & Light Co., E.D.S.C.1947, 74 F.Supp. 483.

39. Otherwise where the work he is employed to do does not involve such a duty. Miller v. Muscarelle, 1961, 67 N.J.Super. 305, 170 A.2d 437; cf. Southeastern Greyhound Lines v. Callahan, 1943, 244 Ala. 449, 13 So.2d 660.

40. Mayer v. Thompson-Hutchison Bldg. Co., 1894, 104 Ala. 611, 16 So. 670. Accord: Sloss-Sheffield Steel & Iron Co. v. Wilkes, 1936, 231 Ala. 511, 165 So. 764; West Kentucky Coal Co. v. Hazel's Adm'x, 1939, 279 Ky. 5, 129 S.W.2d 1000; Stanolind Oil & Gas Co. v. Bunce, 1936, 51 Wyo. 1, 62 P.2d 1297; Devine v. Kroger Groc. & Bak. Co., 1942, 349 Mo. 621, 162 S.W.2d 813.

41. Murray v. Cowherd, 1932, 148 Ky. 591, 147 S.W. 6. Cf. Hill v. James Walker Memorial Hospital, 4 Cir. 1969, 407 F.2d 1036 (contract with hospital to exterminate rats).

42. Wachovia Bank & Trust Co. v. Southern R. Co., 1936, 209 N.C. 304, 183 S.E. 620; Burrichter v. Chicago, M. & St. P. R. Co., D.Minn.1925, 10 F.2d 165; Albertson v. Wabash R. Co., 1952, 363 Mo. 696, 253 S.W.2d 184. Cf. McDonnell v. Wasenmiller, 8 Cir. 1934, 74 F.2d 320 (engineering firm supervising construction); Perrone v. Pennsylvania R. Co., 2 Cir. 1943, 136 F.2d 941 (de-energizing electric wires). See Seavey, The Liability of an Agent in Tort, 1916, 1 So.L.Q. 16; Note, 1948, 26 N.C.L.Rev. 390.

43. Van Winkle v. American Steam Boiler Ins. Co., 1899, 52 N.J.L. 240, 19 A. 472, American Mut. Liab. Ins. Co. v. St. Paul Fire & Marine Ins. Co., Wis. 1970, 179 N.W.2d 864. Cf. Gimino v. Sears, Roebuck & Co., 1944, 308 Mich. 666, 14 N.W.2d 536 (kerosene stove).

44. Durham v. Warner Elevator Mfg. Co., 1956, 166 Ohio St. 31, 139 N.E.2d 10; Dickerson v. Shepard Warner Elevator Co., 6 Cir. 1961, 287 F.2d 255; Otis Elevator Co. v. Robinson, 5 Cir. 1961, 287 F.2d 62; Evans v. Otis Elevator Co., 1961, 403 Pa. 13, 168 A.2d 573; Wroblewski v. Otis Elevator Co., 1959, 9 App.Div.2d 294, 193 N.Y.S.2d 855.

45. Wolfmeyer v. Otis Elevator Co., Mo.1953, 262 S.W.2d 18 (maintaining elevator involves no duty as to structural plan); Otis Elevator Co. v. Embert to Use of South St. Corp., 1951, 198 Md. 585, 84 A.2d

not depend upon it, and it may arise even where the undertaking is a gratuitous one.[46] In all such cases on which liability has been found, there has been something in the nature of entering upon performance, such as a partial inspection,[47] or making an initial one,[48] so that a duty has been assumed by conduct, and it may fairly be said that there is something in the nature of "misfeasance" rather than "nonfeasance";[49] and undoubtedly most of the decisions are to be explained on this basis.[50] Where there has been only complete nonperformance of the contract, without even an initial action, recovery has been denied.[51]

The "nonfeasance" line has been drawn most sharply in a large number of cases holding that a company which contracts with a city to supply water to the public is not liable to a private citizen when the service fails at a critical moment and his house is destroyed by fire as a result [52]—although if contaminated water is in fact supplied, there is no difficulty in finding liability for misfeasance.[53] The usual explanation of the fire cases has been that the defendant, by entering upon the supplying of water for other purposes, has not begun an undertaking to extinguish fires.[54] These decisions sometimes have been attributed to the fact that most city property carries fire insurance, and the reluctance of the courts to give the insurers a windfall in the way of subrogation claims;[55] but the same rule has been applied to a failure to provide gas and electricity,[56] where no insurance would appear to be involved.

In these cases, which writers have denounced for years,[57] the fear of a catastroph-

---

876 (maintenance involves no duty as to operation); Ulwelling v. Crown Coach Corp., 1962, 206 Cal.App. 2d 96, 23 Cal.Rptr. 631, 651 (inspection for insurance purposes only).

46. Hill v. United States Fidelity & Guaranty Co., 5 Cir. 1970, 428 F.2d 112; Sheridan v. Aetna Cas. & Surety Co., 1940, 3 Wash.2d 423, 100 P.2d 1024; Fabricius v. Montgomery Elevator Co., 1963, 254 Iowa 319, 121 N.W.2d 361; Smith v. American Employer's Ins. Co., 1960, 102 N.H. 530, 163 A.2d 564; Bollin v. Elevator Const. & Repair Co., 1949, 361 Pa. 7, 63 A.2d 19. Cf. Cain v. Meade County, 1929, 54 S.D. 540, 223 N.W. 734 (county agreeing with state to maintain highway).

47. For example Hoppendietzel v. Wade, 1941, 66 Ga.App. 132, 17 S.E.2d 239.

48. Pilinko v. Marlau, 1958, 10 Misc.2d 63, 171 N.Y. S.2d 718, reversed on other grounds 7 App.Div. 617, 179 N.Y.S.2d 136 (liable "once it enters upon its contractual obligations with the owner"); Evans v. Otis Elevator Co., 1961, 403 Pa. 13, 168 A.2d 573 (contract for periodic inspections, complete failure to make one).

49. See supra, p. 614.

50. See Franklin v. May Department Stores Co., E. D.Mo.1938, 25 F.Supp. 735; E. N. Emery Co. v. American Refrigerator Transit Co., 1922, 194 Iowa 926, 189 N.W. 824; Brown v. T. W. Phillips Gas & Oil Co., 3 Cir. 1952, 195 F.2d 643 (maintenance of gas facilities).

51. Rosenbaum v. Branster Realty Corp., 1949, 276 App.Div. 167, 93 N.Y.S.2d 209.

52. H. R. Moch Co. v. Rensselaer Water Co., 1928, 247 N.Y. 160, 159 N.E. 896; Reimann v. Monmouth Consol. Water Co., 1952, 9 N.J. 134, 87 A.2d 325; Earl E. Roher Transfer & Storage Co. v. Hutchinson Water Co., 1958, 182 Kan. 546, 322 P.2d 810; Cole v. Arizona Edison Co., 1939, 53 Ariz. 141, 86 P.2d 946; Consolidated Biscuit Co. v. Illinois Power Co., 1939, 303 Ill.App. 80, 24 N.E.2d 582. See Note, 1952, 26 Temp.L.Q. 214.

53. Hayes v. Torrington Water Co., 1914, 88 Conn. 609, 92 A. 406.

54. An interesting comparison is McClendon v. T. L. James & Co., 5 Cir. 1956, 231 F.2d 802, where a contractor which had begun work under a contract to repair a highway was held to have no responsibility to post a warning of a bad condition six miles further on.

55. Such decisions as Town of Ukiah City v. Ukiah Water & Imp. Co., 1904, 142 Cal. 173, 75 P. 773, and Inhabitants of Milford v. Bangor Ry. & Elec. Co., 1909, 106 Me. 316, 76 A. 696, denying recovery where the property destroyed by fire was that of the city which had the contract, indicate that the basis of the rule is the type of loss, and not lack of privity of contract.

56. Accord, as to gas, City of Jamestown v. Pennsylvania Gas Co., 2 Cir. 1924, 1 F.2d 871. Accord, as to lighting streets, East Coast Freight Lines v. Consolidated Gas, E. L. & P. Co., 1946, 187 Md. 385, 50 A.2d 246; Cochran v. Public Service Elec. Co., 1922, 97 N.J.L. 480, 117 A. 620; Tollison v. Georgia Power Co., 1936, 53 Ga.App. 795, 187 S.E. 181. Cf. Baca v. Britt, 1963, 73 N.M. 1, 385 P.2d 61 (failure to repair traffic light).

57. Sunderland, Liability of Water Companies for Fire Losses, 1905, 3 Mich.L.Rev. 442; Corbin, Lia-

ic burden upon the defendant has bulked unduly large, and appears to offer the only explanation. Three arguments appear to demolish the decisions beyond repair. The defendant has in fact entered upon performance of the undertaking and supplied water, so that there is misfeasance, and not nonfeasance at all.[58] By doing so, it has taken on the status of a public utility, and has entered into a relation with individual members of the public which imposes the duty.[59] By its undertaking, and performance, it has induced the city, and the plaintiff, to rely upon it, and to forego opportunities for other protection to which they might have resorted.[60] But these arguments have had little effect upon the courts; and only Florida,[61] Kentucky,[62] North Carolina,[63] and Pennsylvania [64] have recognized a tort duty of the water company.

Misfeasance

Where the defendant has in fact misperformed his contract, and is to be charged with "misfeasance" resulting in injury to a third person, it is to be expected that liability to third persons will be found more readily; and in general this has been true. Even here, however, the great obstacle has been the notion of the necessity of "privity of contract" inherited from the misinterpretation of Winterbottom v. Wright.[65] As late as 1905 an English court [66] was holding that one who negligently repaired a vehicle owed no duty to a third person whom it might injure; and the same approach was carried over into Washington [67] in 1927, with a quotation of most of the opinion of Lord Abinger. All this is now ancient history. The analogy of the seller has prevailed, and the late decisions are agreed that the man who negligently repairs a vehicle [68] or any other chattel [69] is liable to others who may be injured because of that negligence, to the same

bility of Water Companies for Losses by Fire, 1910, 19 Yale L.J. 425; Seavey, Mr. Justice Cardozo and the Law of Torts, 1939, 52 Harv.L.Rev. 372, 48 Yale L.J. 390, 39 Col.L.Rev. 20; Seavey, Reliance Upon Gratuitous Promises or Other Conduct, 1951, 64 Harv.L.Rev. 913; Note, 1953, 26 Temple L.Q. 214.

The only kind word ever said for the cases is in Kales, Liability of Water Companies for Fire Losses, 1905, 3 Mich.L.Rev. 501.

58. See supra, p. 616. Cf. Brown v. T. W. Phillips Gas & Oil Co., 3 Cir. 1952, 195 F.2d 643 (maintenance of gas facilities).

59. Cf. Alabama Water Co. v. Knowles, 1929, 280 Ala. 61, 124 So. 96; Oklahoma Natural Gas Co. v. Graham, 1941, 188 Okl. 521, 111 P.2d 173; Doherty v. Mississippi Power Co., 1937, 178 Miss. 204, 173 So. 287; Masterson v. Chesapeake & Potomac Tel. Co., 1923, 52 U.S.App.D.C. 23, 299 F. 890.

60. See supra, p. 345.

61. Mugge v. Tampa Water Works Co., 1906, 52 Fla. 371, 42 So. 81; Woodbury v. Tampa Water Works Co., 1909, 57 Fla. 243, 49 So. 556.

62. Harlan Water Co. v. Carter, 1927, 220 Ky. 493, 295 S.W. 426; Tobin v. Frankfort Water Co., 1914, 158 Ky. 348, 164 S.W. 956.

63. Fisher v. Greensboro Water Supply Co., 1901, 128 N.C. 375, 38 S.E. 912; Potter v. Carolina Water Co., 1960, 253 N.C. 112, 116 S.E.2d 374.

64. Doyle v. South Pittsburgh Water Co., 1964, 414 Pa. 199, 199 A.2d 875.

65. Supra, p. 622.

66. Earl v. Lubbock, [1905] 1 K.B. 253, 74 L.J.K.B. 121.

67. Hanson v. Blackwell Motor Co., 1927, 143 Wash. 547, 255 P. 939. Here the defendant did not repair at all, but returned the automobile to the owner with a statement that he had done so.

68. Barnhart v. Freeman Equipment Co., Okl.1968, 441 P.2d 993; General Motors Corp. v. Jenkins, 1966, 114 Ga.App. 873, 152 S.E.2d 796; Zierer v. Daniels, 1956, 40 N.J.Super. 130, 122 A.2d 377; Central & So. Truck Lines v. Westfall GMC Truck, Inc., Mo.App.1958, 317 S.W.2d 841; Jewell v. Dell, Ky.1955, 284 S.W.2d 92. Cf. Woodrick v. Smith Gas Service, Inc., 1967, 87 Ill.App.2d 88, 230 N.E.2d 508 (installing part).

69. Dahms v. General Elevator Co., 1932, 214 Cal. 733, 7 P.2d 1013; Vrooman v. Beech Aircraft Corp., 10 Cir. 1950, 183 F.2d 479; Fish v. Kirlin-Gray Elec. Co., 1904, 18 S.D. 122, 99 N.W. 1092; Williams v. Charles Stores Co., 1936, 209 N.C. 591, 184 S.E. 496; Restatement of Torts, § 404.

Notice of a danger or defect will normally relieve the defendant of responsibility. Wissman v. General Tire Co. of Philadelphia, 1937, 327 Pa. 215, 192 A. 633. And lapse of time may prevent the inference that the work was defective. Luongo v. Courtney's Locks, Inc., N.Y.City Ct.1954, 131 N.Y.S.2d 684.

extent as if he had made and sold the chattel in the first instance. The same, broadly and generally speaking, is true of the misperformance of any other contract [70] made with one person, where the interests of another may be expected to be affected; and one who so much as delivers a milk bottle to a customer may be required to leave it where it is not likely to injure somebody's child.[71]

The liability of building contractors, which bears a close analogy to that of the manufacturer of products, is more appropriately considered in the next chapter.[72]

94. ELECTION TO SUE FOR RESTITUTION

The interrelation of tort and contract was further complicated when the common law courts, late in the seventeenth century, began to take over into the law some of the principles and remedies of equity. The judges, becoming conscious of their shortcomings and jealous of the expanding powers of the chancery courts, sought to broaden their own jurisdiction into equity fields, and found a means ready to their hand in the action of assumpsit.[73] By a series of ingenious fictions it was held first, that assumpsit would lie where a debt existed and a promise to pay it could be inferred, as a fact, from the circumstances of the case; then that the promise would be "implied" by the law from the mere existence of a debt which the defendant ought to pay, although there was nothing to show that the promise was really made; and finally, that the law would "imply" both the debt and the promise whenever one had received or used something for which "natural justice" [74] would require that he compensate another.

The assumpsit action was held to lie at first where the defendant had received the emoluments of a public office to which the plaintiff was entitled; [75] and then where he had converted and sold the plaintiff's goods.[76] It was soon held to include the case where money or property was obtained by misrepresentation,[77] and the plaintiff was permitted to rescind the transaction of his own motion and recover the value of what he had parted with. In later cases the principle was even extended to allow the plaintiff to rescind and maintain a property action of replevin [78] or conversion [79] for specific goods which he had

---

70. Oklahoma Natural Gas Co. v. Courtney, 1938, 182 Okl. 582, 79 P.2d 235 (turning on gas without testing mains); Southern R. Co. v. Grizzle, 1906, 124 Ga. 735, 53 S.E. 244 (running train without blowing whistle); Pittsfield Cottonware Mfg. Co. v. Pittsfield Shoe Co., 1902, 71 N.H. 522, 53 A. 807 (failure to provide heat is negligent operation of a boiler); Consolidated Gas Co. v. Connor, 1911, 114 Md. 140, 78 A. 725 (failure to inspect mains is negligent distribution of gas); Norton v. Hamilton, 1955, 92 Ga.App. 727, 89 S.E.2d 809 (physician treating wife under contract with husband).

On this basis one who negligently draws a will for a testator has been held liable to an intended beneficiary who suffers loss as a result. Biakanja v. Irving, 1958, 49 Cal.2d 647, 320 P.2d 16; Heyer v. Flaig, 1969, 70 Cal.2d 232, 74 Cal.Rptr. 225, 449 P.2d 161. See Notes, 1962, 75 Harv.L.Rev. 620; 1961, 28 Brook.L.Rev. 99; 1961, 30 Ford.L.Rev. 369; 1962, 34 Rocky Mt.L.Rev. 388; 1958, 46 Cal.L.Rev. 851; 1962, 42 Bos.U.L.Rev. 256.

71. Eads v. Marks, 1952, 39 Cal.2d 807, 249 P.2d 257.

72. See infra, p. 680.

73. See Winfield, Province of the Law of Tort, 1931, ch. vii; Restatement of Restitution, Introductory Note to Part I.

74. Mansfield, L. J., in Moses v. Macferlan, 1760, 2 Burr. 1005, 97 Eng.Rep. 676.

75. Woodward v. Ashton, 1676, 2 Mod.Rep. 95, 86 Eng.Rep. 961.

76. Lamine v. Dorrell, 1705, 2 Ld.Raym. 1216, 92 Eng.Rep. 303. See Ames, History of Assumpsit, 1888, 2 Harv.L.Rev. 1, 53, 67.

77. Hill v. Perrott, 1810, 3 Taunt. 274, 128 Eng.Rep. 109; Roth v. Palmer, 1858, 27 Barb., N.Y., 652; Crown Cycle Co. v. Brown, 1901, 39 Or. 285, 64 P. 451; Dashaway Ass'n v. Rogers, 1889, 79 Cal. 211, 21 P. 742; Western Assur. Co. v. Towle, 1886, 65 Wis. 247, 26 N.W. 104.

78. John V. Farwell Co. v. Hilton, D.Wis.1897, 84 F. 293; Furber v. Stephens, C.C.Mo.1888, 35 F. 17; Pearson v. Wallace, 1919, 204 Mich. 643, 171 N.W. 402.

79. Thurston v. Blanchard, 1839, 22 Pick., Mass., 18; Holland v. Bishop, 1895, 60 Minn. 23, 61 N.W. 681;

surrendered to the defendant. The assumpsit action avoided so many of the technical difficulties of pleading which surrounded the older tort actions [80] that it became a popular substitute for them; and its survival and greatly increased use undoubtedly has been due to the genuine advantages which a contract action sometimes offers today.[81] With the disappearance of the form of action of assumpsit, the unblushing fiction of the implied promise has generally been discarded, and the remedy has acquired the name of quasi-contract, or restitution.

Out of this common law procedure there has developed the doctrine that where the commission of a tort results in the unjust enrichment of the defendant at the plaintiff's expense, the plaintiff may disregard, or "waive" [82] the tort action, and sue instead on a theoretical and fictitious contract for restitution of the benefits which the defendant has so received.[83] "Waiver" of the tort is an unfortunate term, since the quasi-contract action itself is still based on the tort, and there is merely an election between alternative, co-existing remedies,[84] and the unsuccessful pursuit of the "implied" contract will not bar a later action for the tort itself.[85]

The ordinary delictual action for a tort usually is not concerned with restitution, since it seeks to compensate the injured person for his loss, irrespective of the receipt of anything by the defendant. Even those tort actions which demand the return of specific property, such as replevin or ejectment, are in theory, at least, seeking to restore the plaintiff to his prior position, although they may often have the incidental effect of giving him the benefit of the increased value of the property. Restitution in quasi-contract, on the other hand, looks to what the defendant has received which in good conscience should belong to the plaintiff; and this may be either more or less [86] than the amount of the plaintiff's actual loss.

The election to sue for restitution is by no means allowed in all tort cases. It is not permitted where the defendant has merely damaged the plaintiff, negligently [87] or otherwise,[88] without benefit to himself; and the plaintiff may not, merely by declaring that

Yeager v. Wallace, 1868, 57 Pa. 365; Baird v. Howard, 1894, 51 Ohio St. 57, 36 N.E. 732. See supra, p. 85.

80. Winfield, Province of the Law of Tort, 1931, 141–146.

81. See supra, p. 618. Also House, Unjust Enrichment: The Applicable Statute of Limitations, 1950, 35 Corn.L.Q. 797; Note, 1950, 25 N.Y.U.L.Rev. 655.

82. "Thoughts much too deep for tears subdue the court
When I assumpsit bring, and god-like waive a tort."
—Adolphus, The Circuiteers, an Eclogue, 1885, 1 L.Q.Rev. 232.
There seems to be some unwritten rule that this must be quoted by anyone who discusses this remedy. The writer is not one to depart from the tradition, although he must confess that the peculiar merit of the jingle escapes him.

83. See Corbin, Waiver of Tort and Suit in Assumpsit, 1910, 19 Yale L.J. 221; Keener, Waiver of Tort, 1893, 6 Harv.L.Rev. 223, 269; Teller, Restitution as an Alternative Remedy, 1956, 2 N.Y.Law Forum 40; Note, 1927, 11 Minn.L.Rev. 532.

84. Keener, Quasi-Contracts, 1893, 159, 160.

85. Gibbs v. Jones, 1868, 46 Ill. 319; Bains v. Price, 1922, 207 Ala. 337, 92 So. 447; Kirkman v. Philips' Heirs, 1871, 7 Heisk., Tenn., 222. But cf. Terry v. Munger, 1890, 121 N.Y. 161, 24 N.E. 272.

86. Felder v. Reeth, 8 Cir. 1929, 34 F.2d 744; Heinze v. McKinnon, 1913, 123 C.C.A. 492, 205 F. 366; In re Baker, 1932, 5 W.W.Harr., Del., 198, 162 A. 356; Galvin v. Mac Min. & Milling Co., 1894, 14 Mont. 508, 37 P. 366; Huganir v. Cotter, 1899, 102 Wis. 323, 78 N.W. 423.

87. Altpeter v. Virgil State Bank, 1952, 345 Ill.App. 585, 104 N.E.2d 334; New York Central R. Co. v. State, 1936, 242 App.Div. 421, 287 N.Y.S. 850; Kyle v. Chester, 1911, 42 Mont. 522, 113 P. 749.

88. Erickson v. Borchardt, 1929, 177 Minn. 381, 225 N.W. 145 (fraud); Howard v. Swift & Co., 1934, 356 Ill. 80, 190 N.E. 102 (directors buying stock for corporation); Burleson v. Langdon, 1928, 174 Minn. 264, 219 N.W. 155 (conversion); Soderlin v. Marquette Nat. Bank, 1943, 214 Minn. 408, 8 N.W.2d 331 (bank paying check on forgery).

he "waives" the tort, create any implied promise to pay in such a case.[89] Restitution is restricted to those cases in which the common counts in the old action of general assumpsit could be used—that is to say, those in which the wrongdoer has been unjustly enriched by his tort, and "is under an obligation from the ties of natural justice to refund," so that "the law implies a debt and gives this action, founded in the equity of the plaintiff's case, as it were upon a contract." [90]

Thus where the defendant has appropriated the plaintiff's money,[91] or has taken his property and sold it,[92] a quasi-contract count will lie for money had and received to the plaintiff's use, through the fiction of an implied promise to repay. If the property has not been sold, but the defendant has retained it, the courts are not in agreement as to whether the owner may sue on an implied contract of sale to the wrongdoer. Some decisions, restricting the doctrine to its original form, where the assumpsit count used was that for money had and received to the de-

fendant's use, have held that it does not apply where the goods have not been exchanged for money.[93] The better reasoning, now followed by the great majority of the courts, is that restitution will be allowed, for so long as the entire doctrine is based on a fiction created by the law there is no reason to draw any distinction between unjust enrichment through the proceeds of a sale of goods and through the goods themselves.[94] On the same basis, it has been held that one who has converted goods and used them, and subsequently has returned them to the owner, may be liable in quasi-contract, on the fiction of a hiring and an obligation to pay value for it.[95] The principle also has been extended to cases where the defendant has tortiously obtained labor or services from the plain-

---

89. Patterson v. Prior, 1862, 18 Ind. 440; Tightmeyer v. Mongold, 1878, 20 Kan. 90; Minor v. Baldridge, 1898, 123 Cal. 187, 55 P. 783; Patterson v. Kasper, 1914, 182 Mich. 281, 148 N.W. 690; Parkersburg & Marietta Sand Co. v. Smith, 1915, 76 W.Va. 246, 85 S.E. 516.

90. Lord Mansfield, in Moses v. Macferlan, 1760, 2 Burr. 1005, 1008, 97 Eng.Rep. 676. See Corbin, Waiver of Tort and Suit in Assumpsit, 1910, 19 Yale L.J. 221; Note, 1927, 11 Minn.L.Rev. 532.

91. Billig v. Goodrich, 1917, 199 Mich. 423, 165 N.W. 647; Craig v. Craig's Estate, 1914, 167 Iowa 340, 149 N.W. 454; Burgoyne v. McKillip, 8 Cir. 1910, 182 F. 452; Humbird v. Davis, 1904, 210 Pa. 311, 59 A. 1082; Guernsey v. Davis, 1903, 67 Kan. 378, 73 P. 101.

92. McDonald v. First Nat. Bank of McKeesport, 1945, 353 Pa. 29, 44 A.2d 265; Taylor Motor Car Co. v. Hansen, 1929, 75 Utah 80, 282 P. 1040; Dallas v. H. J. Koehler Sporting Goods Co., 1914, 86 N.J.L. 651, 92 A. 356; Heinze v. McKinnon, 2 Cir. 1913, 205 F. 366; Smith Lumber Co. v. Scott County Garbage Reducing & Fuel Co., 1910, 149 Iowa 272, 128 N.W. 389.

93. Janiszewski v. Behrmann, 1956, 345 Mich. 8, 75 N.W.2d 77; Anderson Equipment Co. v. Findley, 1944, 350 Pa. 399, 39 A.2d 520; Cox v. Awtry, 1924, 211 Ala. 356, 100 So. 337; Lyon v. Clark, 1902, 129 Mich. 381, 88 N.W. 1046; Woodruff v. Zaban & Son, 1909, 133 Ga. 24, 65 S.E. 123.

See Corbin, Waiver of Tort and Suit in Assumpsit, 1910, 19 Yale L.J. 221, 229; Teller, Restitution as an Alternative Remedy, 1956, 2 N.Y.Law Forum 40; Notes, 1927, 11 Minn.L.Rev. 532, 538; 1948, 20 Rocky Mt.L.Rev. 300.

Some of these courts rather inconsistently allow suit in quasi-contract where the property was acquired rightfully, as under a bailment, and later converted by the defendant, though he did not sell it. Ford & Co. v. Atlantic Compress Co., 1912, 138 Ga. 496, 75 S.E. 609; Brown v. Foster, 1904, 137 Mich. 35, 100 N.W. 167. "For the reason that the relation of the parties, out of which the duty violated grew, had its inception in contract." Tuttle v. Campbell, 1889, 74 Mich. 652, 42 N.W. 384.

94. Downs v. Finnegan, 1894, 58 Minn. 112, 59 N.W. 981; Daniels v. Foster & Kleiser, 1920, 95 Or. 502, 187 P. 627; Garrity v. State Board of A.E.I., 1917, 99 Kan. 695, 162 P. 1167; School Board of Lipps Dist. No. 4 v. Saxon Lime & Lumber Co., 1917, 121 Va. 594, 93 S.E. 579; Heber v. Heber's Estate, 1909, 139 Wis. 472, 121 N.W. 328.

95. Olwell v. Nye & Nissen Co., 1947, 26 Wash.2d 282, 173 P.2d 652; Fanson v. Linsley, 1878, 20 Kan. 235; Stockett v. Watkins' Adm'rs, 1830, 2 Gill & J., Md., 326; Jones v. Randall, 1774, 1 Cowp. 37, 98 Eng.Rep. 954. Cf. Paar v. City of Prescott, 1942, 59 Ariz. 497, 130 P.2d 40 (using water system).

tiff,[96] or has wrongfully manufactured and sold the plaintiff's invention.[97]

The wrongful use and occupation of real property, by one who is not a tenant, was not considered by the earlier cases [98] to be sufficient ground to invoke the quasi-contract action. The explanation lay in the historical reason that the assumpsit count for use and occupation of land would lie only where there was a tenancy,[99] and perhaps in a number of cases in which the defendant was claiming some rights in the land, and the court was unwilling to litigate the title indirectly.[1] This is perhaps still the prevailing rule. Again, however, in the realm of fiction, there is no visible reason to distinguish between unjust enrichment derived from real and that from personal property.[2] The later tendency has been to allow the action in quasi-contract, where, for example, a corporation having the power of eminent domain has taken possession of land without

complying with the statutory procedure; [3] where a valuable part of the soil has been removed; [4] where cattle have been grazed upon the land, irrespective of any damage done to it; [5] and even, in a few cases, where there has been outright occupation and use by a trespasser.[6]

The quasi-contract action is particularly applicable to those torts in which money or property is obtained by fraudulent misrepresentation,[7] as where the defendant induces a sale of goods by misrepresenting his intention to pay or the state of his credit. In such a case the plaintiff may have a choice of a number of remedies, which are considered in a later chapter.[8]

---

96. Patterson v. Prior, 1862, 18 Ind. 440; Abbott v. Town of Fremont, 1857, 34 N.H. 432; Boardman v. Ward, 1889, 40 Minn. 399, 42 N.W. 202. Contra, Thompson v. Bronk, 1901, 126 Mich. 455, 85 N.W. 1084.

Accord, as to plaintiff's child, Smith v. Gilbert, 1906, 80 Ark. 525, 98 S.W. 115; Illinois Central R. Co. v. Sanders, 1913, 104 Miss. 257, 61 So. 309.

97. Eckert v. Braun, 7 Cir. 1946, 155 F.2d 517. Cf. Caskie v. Philadelphia Rapid Transit Co., 1936, 321 Pa. 157, 184 A. 17 (interference with contract).

98. Rogers v. Libbey, 1853, 35 Me. 200; Lloyd v. Hough, 1843, 1 How. (U.S.) 153; Hurley v. Lameraux, 1882, 29 Minn. 138, 12 N.W. 447; Ackerman v. Lyman, 1866, 20 Wis. 454; National Oil Ref. Co. v. Bush, 1879, 88 Pa. 335.

99. See Ames, Assumpsit for Use or Occupation, 1889, 2 Harv.L.Rev. 377; Note, 1932, 30 Mich.L.Rev. 1087; Atlanta, K. & N. R. Co. v. McHan, 1900, 110 Ga. 543, 35 S.E. 634; Hurley v. Lameraux, 1882, 29 Minn. 138, 12 N.W. 447 (" * * * a trespasser cannot be converted into a tenant without his consent.")

1. See Halleck v. Mixer, 1860, 16 Cal. 574; Parks v. Morris, Layfield & Co., 1907, 63 W.Va. 51, 59 S.E. 753; City of Boston v. Binney, 1831, 11 Pick., Mass., 1.

2. "The trespasser is unjustly enriched, and the plaintiff has as much need of a remedy in assump-

sit as in the case of any other tort enriching the tort feasor." Corbin, Waiver of Tort and Suit in Assumpsit, 1910, 19 Yale L.J. 221, 232; Note, 1932, 30 Mich.L.Rev. 1087.

3. Snowden v. Fort Lyon Canal Co., 8 Cir. 1916, 238 F. 495; Wayne County v. Elk Spring Valley Turnpike Co., 1930, 233 Ky. 741, 26 S.W.2d 1049; Efird v. City of Winston-Salem, 1930, 199 N.C. 33, 153 S. E. 632; Mayer v. Studer & Manion Co., 1935, 66 N. D. 190, 262 N.W. 925; cf. Kerns v. Couch, 1932, 141 Or. 147, 12 P.2d 1011, 17 P.2d 323.

4. Shell Petroleum Corp. v. Scully, 5 Cir. 1934, 71 F. 2d 772; West v. McClure, 1904, 85 Miss. 296, 37 So. 752; Franks v. Lockwood, 1959, 146 Conn. 273, 150 A.2d 215; Frankfort Land Co. v. Hughett, 1917, 137 Tenn. 32, 191 S.W. 530; Hudson v. Iguano Land & Min. Co., 1912, 71 W.Va. 402, 76 S.E. 797.

5. Norden v. Jones, 1873, 33 Wis. 600; Lazarus v. Phelps, 1894, 152 U.S. 81; Tsuboi v. Cohn, 1924, 40 Idaho 102, 231 P. 708; Simmonds v. Richards, 1906, 74 Kan. 311, 86 P. 452; Baldwin v. Bohl, 1909, 23 S.D. 395, 122 N.W. 247.

6. Raven Red Ash Coal Co. v. Ball, 1946, 185 Va. 534, 39 S.E.2d 231; West St. Auto Service, Inc. v. Schmidt, 1966, 26 App.Div.2d 662, 272 N.Y.S.2d 615; Edwards v. Lee's Adm'r, 1936, 265 Ky. 418, 96 S.W. 2d 1028; Taggart v. Shepherd, 1932, 122 Cal.App. 755, 10 P.2d 808; Parkinson v. Shew, 1899, 12 S.D. 171, 80 N.W. 189.

7. Tabor v. Universal Exploration Co., 8 Cir. 1931, 48 F.2d 1047; Philpott v. Superior Court, 1934, 1 Cal. 2d 512, 36 P.2d 635; Wallace v. Perry, 1953, 74 Idaho 86, 257 P.2d 231; Heilbronn v. Herzog, 1900, 165 N.Y. 98, 58 N.E. 759. Cf. Chandler v. Sanger, 1874, 114 Mass. 364 (duress).

8. See infra, ch. 18.

The common law courts recognized that they were invading the province of equity,[9] and the relief which they granted by way of restitution has continued to be subject to equitable rules. Unless he is excused by special circumstances, the plaintiff must restore what he has himself received,[10] and his right to restitution is lost by any conduct affirming the transaction,[11] or even by inaction for an unreasonable length of time after discovery of the facts.[12] The measure of his recovery is determined on the equitable basis of the unjust enrichment of the defendant,[13] rather than the tort basis of the plaintiff's loss. Thus a purchaser defrauded in the sale of a horse who seeks a remedy by way of restitution ordinarily must return the horse, and may recover the price he has paid, regardless of the extent of his loss on the transaction. The recovery may be defeated by a subsequent change in the defendant's position which destroys his unjust enrichment.[14]

95. DIRECT SUPPLIERS OF CHATTELS

A somewhat complicated body of law, which still is undergoing a very evident process of development and transition, has grown up about the liability of those who supply chattels for the use of others. Here tort and contract are closely interrelated; and no other group of cases affords so striking an illustration of the historical sweep of the common law, and the constant change which it undergoes by slow degrees. The problems which confront the courts have revolved around two major distinctions, which must be made at the outset: (a) the distinction between the defendant's liability to the person directly supplied and his liability to a third person; and (b) that between liability based on negligence and strict liability, which in this field has become associated with the term "warranty."

The problem of the person directly supplied, which is relatively more simple, may be considered first.

Negligence

In the case of the sale of chattels, both the English and the American law have broken almost entirely away from the ancient rule

9. Moses v. Macferlan, 1760, 2 Burr. 1005, 97 Eng. Rep. 676 ("founded in the equity of the plaintiff's case"); Clarke v. Shee, 1774, 1 Cowp. 197, 98 Eng. Rep. 1041 ("liberal action in the nature of a bill in equity"); Straton v. Rastall, 1788, 2 Term Rep. 366, 100 Eng.Rep. 197 ("must shew that he has equity and conscience on his side, and that he could recover it in a court of equity"); Mason v. Madson, 1931, 90 Mont. 489, 4 P.2d 475. But see Hanbury, The Recovery of Money, 1924, 40 L.Q.Rev. 31, stressing the legal nature of the action, and the vagueness of the "equity" involved.

10. Byard v. Holmes, 1868, 33 N.J.L. 119; Houghton v. Nash, 1874, 64 Me. 477; Adam, Meldrum & Anderson Co. v. Stewart, 1901, 157 Ind. 678, 61 N.E. 1002; James Music Co. v. Bridge, 1908, 134 Wis. 510, 114 N.W. 1108. See Note, 1929, 29 Col.L.Rev. 791.

11. Brennan v. National Equitable Inv. Co., 1928, 247 N.Y. 486, 160 N.E. 924; Samples v. Guyer, 1898, 120 Ala. 611, 24 So. 942; Sherwood v. Walker, 1887, 66 Mich. 568, 33 N.W. 919; Bayer v. Winton Motor Car Co., 1916, 194 Mich. 222, 160 N.W. 642. Cf. Maki v. St. Luke's Hospital Ass'n, 1913, 122 Minn. 444, 142 N.W. 705.

12. Wilbur v. Flood, 1867, 16 Mich. 40; Grant v. Lovekin, 1926, 285 Pa. 257, 132 A. 342; Long v. International Vending Mach. Co., 1911, 158 Mo.App. 662, 139 S.W. 819; Everson v. J. L. Owens Mfg. Co., 1920, 145 Minn. 199, 176 N.W. 505.

13. Seneca Wire & Mfg. Co. v. A. B. Leach & Co., 1928, 247 N.Y. 1, 159 N.E. 700; Note, 1934, 32 Mich.L.Rev. 968. Cf. Houser & Haines Mfg. Co. v. McKay, 1909, 53 Wash. 337, 101 P. 894; Pfeiffer v. Independent Plumbing & Heating Supply Co., Mo. App.1934, 72 S.W.2d 138 (rescission for breach of warranty); and see Rogge, Damages upon Rescission for Breach of Warranty, 1929, 28 Mich.L.Rev. 26.

The relief granted on this theory is of course capable of considerable variation. Thus a defrauded seller ordinarily does not restore anything, or recover what he has given, but recovers the reasonable value of what he has sold, subject to deduction of any payment already received.

14. See Cohen, Change of Position in Quasi-Contracts, 1932, 45 Harv.L.Rev. 1333; Langmaid, Quasi-Contract—Change of Position by Receipt of Money in Satisfaction of a Preëxisting Obligation, 1933, 21 Cal.L.Rev. 311; Woodward, Quasi-Contracts, 1913, §§ 25, 27; Keener, Quasi-Contracts, 1893, 61–67.

of *caveat emptor*, that the buyer must make his own inspection, rely upon his own judgment and assume the risk of any defects in what he buys, which still is applied to sales of real property. When goods are sold by one person to another, it is now well established that the seller is under a duty to exercise the care of a reasonable man of ordinary prudence to see that the goods do no harm to the buyer. This duty, while it arises out of the relation created by the contract, is not identical with the contract obligation, but is merely a part of the general responsibility, sounding in tort, which is placed by the law upon anyone who stands in such a relation that his affirmative conduct will affect the interests of another.[15] In other words, the duty of the seller is founded upon the same basis as that of a physician who contracts to treat a patient, or any other contractor. The liability for negligence, which today usually is more or less submerged by the buyer's cause of action for breach of warranty, may exist parallel with it,[16] and becomes particularly important when for any reason a warranty cannot be found.[17]

The seller's negligence may take a number of forms. It may consist of a misrepresentation of the character of the goods,[18] or of their fitness for a particular use.[19] It may consist of a failure to disclose to the buyer facts of which the seller has knowledge which make the goods dangerous for the buyer's purpose.[20] It may take the form of a sale to a person obviously incompetent to deal with the goods, as in the case of an explosive sold to a child.[21]

Most frequently, it consists merely in failure to exercise reasonable care to inspect the goods to discover defects, or in preparing them for sale.[22] When the action is one for negligence, it is of course agreed that the care required of the seller is only that of a reasonable man under the circumstances. There has been a dispute [23] as to whether the

---

Occasionally, where the misrepresentation is intentional, the action is treated as one of deceit; but where injuries to person or property are concerned, it seems preferable to regard the question as one of negligence. See infra, p. 684.

19. Rulane Gas Co. v. Montgomery Ward & Co., 1949, 231 N.C. 270, 56 S.E.2d 689; Cunningham v. C. R. Pease House Furnishing Co., 1908, 74 N.H. 435, 69 A. 120; Pearlman v. Garrod Shoe Co., 1937, 276 N.Y. 172, 11 N.E.2d 718; J. C. Penny Co. v. Morris, 1935, 173 Miss. 710, 163 So. 124; Ebbert v. Philadelphia Elec. Co., 1937, 126 Pa.Super. 351, 191 A. 384, affirmed 1938, 330 Pa. 257, 198 A. 323.

20. Sterchi Bros. Stores v. Castleberry, 1938, 236 Ala. 349, 182 So. 474; Clarke v. Army and Navy Coop. Soc., [1903] 1 K.B. 155.

21. Burbee v. McFarland, 1931, 114 Conn. 56, 157 A. 538; McEldon v. Drew, 1908, 138 Iowa 390, 116 N. W. 147; Bosserman v. Smith, 1920, 205 Mo.App. 657, 226 S.W. 608; Henry v. Crook, 1922, 202 App. Div. 19, 195 N.Y.S. 642; Indian Ref. Co. v. Summerland, 1930, 92 Ind.App. 429, 173 N.E. 269. But there is no negligence where the goods sold cannot reasonably be expected to be dangerous to the child, Schmidt v. Capital Candy Co., 1918, 139 Minn. 378, 166 N.W. 502, or where he puts them to an unexpected use, as by eating fireworks. Victory Sparkler & Specialty Co. v. Price, 1927, 146 Miss. 192, 111 So. 437.

22. Ellis v. Lindmark, 1929, 177 Minn. 390, 225 N.W. 395; Grant v. Graham Chero-Cola Bottling Co., 1918, 176 N.C. 256, 97 S.E. 27; Davis v. Williams, 1938, 58 Ga.App. 274, 198 S.E. 357; Kraft-Phenix Cheese Corp. v. Spelce, 1938, 195 Ark. 407, 113 S.W.2d 476; Highland Pharmacy v. White, 1926, 144 Va. 106, 131 S.E. 198.

23. See the discussion in Eldredge, Vendor's Tort Liability, 1941, 89 U.Pa.L.Rev. 306; Farage, Must a

---

15. See supra, p. 626.

16. Gilbert v. Louis Pizitz Dry Goods Co., 1939, 237 Ala. 249, 186 So. 179; Kapp v. Bob Sullivan Chevrolet Co., 1960, 232 Ark. 266, 335 S.W.2d 819; and see Burkhardt v. Armour & Co., 1932, 115 Conn. 249, 161 A. 385; Pearlman v. Garrod Shoe Co., 1937, 276 N.Y. 172, 11 N.E.2d 718; Cornelius v. B. Filippone & Co., 1938, 119 N.J.L. 540, 197 A. 647.

17. See Fricke, Personal Injury Damages in Products Liability, 1960, 6 Villanova L.Rev. 1, 126–142, listing situations where other remedies against both the retailer and the manufacturer may prove ineffective, and the plaintiff will want to fall back on a negligence action against the retailer.

18. Waters-Pierce Oil Co. v. Deselms, 1909, 212 U.S. 159; Russell v. First Nat. Stores, 1951, 96 N.H. 471, 79 A.2d 573; Model Drug Co. v. Patton, 1925, 208 Ky. 112, 270 S.W. 998; Wright v. Howe, 1915, 46 Utah 588, 150 P. 956; Edelstein v. Cook, 1923, 108 Ohio St. 346, 140 N.E. 765.

retailer of goods manufactured by another is under a "duty" to inspect them before sale, to discover defects of which he does not know. It may be suggested that the dispute has been addressed to the wrong question. It can scarcely be denied that there is a duty to exercise reasonable care for the protection of the buyer—which is to say, the care of a reasonable man under like circumstances; and the problem is simply one of whether the reasonable man would make such an examination.[24] This will be entirely a matter of the circumstances of the particular case.

In the absence of some special reason to suspect that something is wrong, it is clear that the obligation of the dealer does not extend to the opening of sealed containers,[25] or to taking the goods apart,[26] or to making mechanical or chemical tests; [27] and

it is entirely possible that reasonable precaution will require no inspection at all where the goods are purchased from a reputable manufacturer, there appears to be no occasion for it, and it would normally be regarded as unnecessary.[28] Certainly much less is required of the dealer than of the manufacturer.[29] But the dealer normally handles the goods, if only to put them on his shelves; and he can scarcely be absolved from the obligation of such cursory examination as reasonably accompanies the process.[30] In any case where the nature of the goods themselves makes it more likely that defects will lead to serious injury—as for example on the sale of an automobile—something more careful than such casual examination will be required,[31] and if there is any special reason to believe that the particular product may be defective, very thorough inspection may be required before it is sold.[32] The existence of any special

Vendor Inspect Chattels Before Their Sale—An Answer, 1941, 45 Dick.L.Rev. 159; Eldredge, Vendor's "Duty" to Inspect Chattels—A Reply, 1941, 45 Dick.L.Rev. 469; Farage, Vendor's Duty to Inspect Chattels—A Rejoinder, 1941, 45 Dick.L.Rev. 282; Leidy, Tort Liability of Suppliers of Defective Chattels, 1942, 40 Mich.L.Rev. 679; Fricke, Personal Injury Damages in Products Liability, 1960, 6 Villanova L.Rev. 1, 129–147. The Eldredge articles are reprinted in Eldredge, Modern Tort Problems, 1941, 243–285.

Eldredge had the better of the argument, to the extent that, as Reporter for the 1948 Supplement to the Restatement of Torts, he succeeded in carrying through the American Law Institute a change in § 402, declaring that the retailer is under no duty to inspect.

24. Well dealt with in Kirk v. Stineway Drug Store Co., 1963, 38 Ill.App.2d 415, 187 N.E.2d 307.

25. Kratz v. American Stores Co., 1948, 359 Pa. 335, 59 A.2d 138; Tourte v. Horton Mfg. Co., 1930, 108 Cal.App. 22, 290 P. 919; West v. Emanuel, 1900, 198 Pa. 180, 47 A. 965; Outwater v. Miller, 1956, 3 Misc.2d 47, 153 N.Y.S.2d 708, adhered to, 1956, 3 Misc.2d 47, 155 N.Y.S.2d 357. The last named case was reversed in 3 App.Div.2d 670, 158 N.Y.S.2d 562, on the ground of a duty to inspect goods supplied by an unknown maker or one of dubious reputation.

26. Zesch v. Abrasive Co. of Philadelphia, 1944, 353 Mo. 558, 183 S.W.2d 140; Odum v. Gulf Tire & Supply Co., N.D.Fla.1961, 196 F.Supp. 35; see McKinney v. Frodsham, 1960, 57 Wash.2d 126, 356 P.2d 100, amended, 1961, 360 P.2d 576.

27. Simmons v. Richardson Variety Stores, 1957, 1 Storey, Del., 80, 137 A.2d 747; Levis v. Zapolitz,

1962, 72 N.J.Super. 168, 178 A.2d 44; Guyton v. S. H. Kress & Co., 1939, 191 S.C. 530, 5 S.E.2d 295; Burgess v. Montgomery Ward & Co., 10 Cir. 1959, 264 F.2d 495.

28. Sears, Roebuck & Co. v. Marhenke, 9 Cir. 1941, 121 F.2d 598; Camden Fire Ins. Co. v. Peterman, 1937, 278 Mich. 615, 270 N.W. 807; Meyer v. Rich's, Inc., 1940, 63 Ga.App. 896, 12 S.E.2d 123; Isbell v. Biederman Furniture Co., Mo.App.1938, 115 S.W.2d 46; Belcher v. Goff Bros., 1926, 145 Va. 448, 134 S. E. 588. Cf. Willey v. Fyrogas Co., 1952, 363 Mo. 406, 251 S.W.2d 635 (wholesaler).

29. See Shroder v. Barron-Dady Motor Co., Mo.1937, 111 S.W.2d 66; Washburn Storage Co. v. General Motors Corp., 1954, 90 Ga.App. 380, 83 S.E.2d 26; Zesch v. Abrasive Co. of Philadelphia, 1944, 353 Mo. 558, 183 S.W.2d 140.

30. See McKinney v. Frodsham, 1960, 57 Wash.2d 126, 356 P.2d 100, amended, 1961, 360 P.2d 576; Kirk v. Stineway Drug Store Co., 1963, 38 Ill.App. 2d 415, 187 N.E.2d 307.

31. Bower v. Corbell, Okl.1965, 408 P.2d 307 (assembling power saw); Ebbert v. Philadelphia Elec. Co., 1938, 330 Pa. 257, 196 A. 323; Witt Ice & Gas Co. v. Bedway, 1951, 72 Ariz. 152, 231 P.2d 952; McKinney v. Frodsham, 1960, 57 Wash.2d 126, 356 P.2d 100, amended 360 P.2d 576; Kirk v. Stineway Drug Store Co., 1963, 38 Ill.App.2d 415, 187 N.E.2d 307.

32. Kroger v. Goodhew, 1968, 281 Ala. 637, 206 So.2d 882 (knew goods sometimes delivered in wet condition); Davis v. Williams, 1938, 58 Ga.App. 274, 198 S.E. 357; Albany Coca Cola Bottling Co. v. Shiver,

likelihood of danger, the ease of detection of the defect, the seller's maintenance of sales and service departments, the custom of the business as to such products, the special competence of the seller and his superior position to discover defects, are all factors to be taken into account.[33]

A similar duty of care rests upon other persons who deliver goods in return for a consideration. One who rents out a horse or an automobile,[34] for example, or any other bailor for hire, or otherwise for his own economic advantage,[35] is required not only to disclose to the bailee defects of which he has knowledge, but also to exercise affirmative care to inspect and prepare the chattel, so that it is safe for its intended use. The same obligation is imposed upon a restaurant serving food to customers,[36] and a shipper turning goods over to a carrier for transportation.[37] A gratuitous bailor or donor, how-

ever, assumes no such responsibility. As in the case of a licensee entering upon land,[38] the donee must take the goods as they are given to him, and assume the risk of unknown defects. He is not entitled to demand any care to make them safe for his use,[39] but only that the donor disclose to him any dangers of which he has knowledge.[40]

Strict Liability

The liability of the seller to the buyer for negligence is now very largely superseded by strict liability for breach of warranty, by which the seller insures, to some extent at least, the quality and safe condition of the goods. The seller's warranty is a curious hybrid, born of the illicit intercourse of tort and contract, unique in the law.[41] In its inception the liability was based on tort, and the action was on the case;[42] and it was not until 1778 that the first decision[43] was re-

---

1940, 63 Ga.App. 755, 12 S.E.2d 114. Cf. Blitzstein v. Ford Motor Co., 5 Cir. 1961, 288 F.2d 738 (distributor from long experience should have been aware of defect in design of car).

33. See Fricke, Personal Injury Damages in Products Liability, 1960, 6 Villanova L.Rev. 1, 142–147. As to indemnity over against the manufacturer, see supra, § 51.

34. Swann v. Ashton, 10 Cir. 1964, 327 F.2d 105, modified on other grounds, 330 F.2d 995; Price Boiler & Welding Co. v. Gordon, E.D.Mich.1956, 138 F. Supp. 43; McNeal v. Greenberg, 1953, 40 Cal.2d 740, 255 P.2d 810; Aircraft Sales & Service, Inc. v. Gantt, 1951, 255 Ala. 508, 52 So.2d 388; Doughnut Machine Corp. v. Bibbey, 1 Cir. 1933, 65 F.2d 634.

35. Tierstein v. Licht, 1959, 174 Cal.App.2d 835, 345 P.2d 341; Minicozzi v. Atlantic Refining Co., 1956, 143 Conn. 226, 120 A.2d 924; Hillcary v. Bromley, 1946, 146 Ohio St. 212, 64 N.E.2d 832. Including, for example, an owner turning the chattel over to a repairman. King v. National Oil Co., 1899, 81 Mo. App. 155; Boak v. Kuder, 1939, 336 Pa. 260, 9 A.2d 415.

36. Travis v. Louisville & N. R. Co., 1913, 183 Ala. 415, 62 So. 851; Gannon v. S. S. Kresge Co., 1931, 114 Conn. 36, 157 A. 54; Roseberry v. Wachter, 1925, 3 W.W.Harr. 253, 138 A. 273; Rickner v. Ritz Restaurant Co. of Passaic, 1935, 13 N.J.Misc. 818, 181 A. 398. See Note, 1936, 20 Minn.L.Rev. 527. As to implied warranty, see infra, § 104.

37. Cf. Banfield v. Goole & Sheffield Transport Co., [1910] 2 K.B. 94, 79 L.J.K.B. 1070; Great Northern

R. Co. v. L. E. P. Transport Co., [1922] 2 K.B. 742, 91 L.J.K.B. 807; International Mercantile Marine Co. v. Fels, 2 Cir. 1909, 170 F. 275; see Rixford v. Smith, 1872, 52 N.H. 355.

38. See supra, § 60.

39. Gagnon v. Dana, 1897, 69 N.H. 264, 39 A. 982; Johnson v. H. M. Bullard Co., 1920, 95 Conn. 251, 111 A. 70; Dickason v. Dickason, 1929, 84 Mont. 52, 274 P. 145; Clark v. Granby Mining & Smelting Co., Mo.App.1916, 183 S.W. 1099; Ruth v. Hutchinson Gas Co., 1941, 209 Minn. 248, 296 N.W. 136.

40. Blom v. McNeal, 1937, 199 Minn. 506, 272 N.W. 599; Gibbs v. Gaimel, 1962, 257 N.C. 650, 127 S.E. 2d 271; Blakemore v. Bristol & Exeter R. Co., 1858, 8 El. & Bl. 1035, 120 Eng.Rep. 385; Note, 1930, 78 U.Pa.L.Rev. 413.

41. "A more notable example of legal miscegenation could hardly be cited than that which produced the modern action for breach of warranty. Originally sounding in tort, yet arising out of the warrantor's consent to be bound, it later ceased necessarily to be consensual, and at the same time came to lie mainly in contract." Note, 1929, 42 Harv.L.Rev. 414.

42. Ames, History of Assumpsit, 1888, 2 Harv.L.Rev. 1, 8. The earliest reported case appears to be in 1383, Fitz. Ab. Monst. de Faits, pl. 160. Originally the seller was bound only by express words of warranty. Chandelor v. Lopus, 1603, Cro.Jac. 4, 79 Eng.Rep. 3.

43. Stuart v. Wilkins, 1778, 1 Dougl. 18, 99 Eng.Rep. 15. Even then assumpsit appears to have been re-

ported in which the plaintiff proceeded upon a contract theory. Thereafter the warranty gradually came to be regarded as a term of the contract of sale, express or implied, for which the normal remedy is a contract action. But the obligation is imposed upon the seller, not because he has assumed it voluntarily, but because the law attaches such consequences to his conduct irrespective of any agreement; [44] and in many cases, at least, to hold that a warranty "is a contract is to speak the language of pure fiction." [45]

Unlike other elements of a contract, warranty never has lost entirely its original tort character.[46] The old tort form of action on the case is still very much alive, and there are many cases [47] which have held that it may still be maintained for a breach of warranty, without any proof of either intentional misrepresentation or negligence. Nor is this a mere technical matter of procedure, since there are many decisions that have held, regardless of the form of the action, that the tort aspects of warranty call for the application of a tort rather than a contract rule in various respects, such as the survival of actions,[48] or the statute of limitations,[49]

or the more liberal tort rule as to damages,[50] or even allowing recovery for wrongful death.[51] It has served as a strong argument for the courts which have extended warranties from the producer to the ultimate consumer, in the absence of any "privity of contract" between the two.[52]

---

49. Jones v. Boggs & Buhl, 1946, 355 Pa. 242, 49 A.2d 379; Rubino v. Utah Canning Co., 1954, 123 Cal. App.2d 18, 266 P.2d 163; Finck v. Albers Super Markets, 6 Cir. 1943, 136 F.2d 191; Zellmer v. Acme Brewing Co., 1950, 184 F.2d 940.

50. See for example Despatch Oven Co. v. Rauenhorst, 1949, 229 Minn. 436, 40 N.W.2d 73; Berg v. Rapid Motor Vehicle Co., 1910, 78 N.J.L. 724, 75 A. 933; Madeiros v. Coca-Cola Bottling Co., 1943, 57 Cal.App.2d 707, 135 P.2d 676; Naumann v. Wehle Brewing Co., 1940, 127 Conn. 44, 5 A.2d 181.

Other courts have accomplished the same result by treating personal injury to the buyer as within the contemplation rule as to damages for breach of contract. Ryan v. Progressive Grocery Stores, 1931, 255 N.Y. 388, 175 N.E. 105; Stonebrink v. Highland Motors, 1943, 171 Or. 418, 137 P.2d 986; Royal Paper Box Co. v. Munro & Church Co., 1934, 284 Mass. 446, 188 N.E. 223; Ebbert v. Philadelphia Elec. Co., 1937, 126 Pa.Super. 351, 191 A. 384, affirmed, 1938, 330 Pa. 257, 198 A. 323.

See Amram and Goodman, Some Problems in the Law of Implied Warranty, 1952, 3 Syr.L.Rev. 259.

51. Greco v. S. S. Kresge Co., 1938, 277 N.Y. 26, 12 N.E.2d 557; Greenwood v. John R. Thompson Co., 1919, 213 Ill.App. 371; Schuler v. Union News Co., 1936, 295 Mass. 350, 4 N.E.2d 465; B. F. Goodrich Co. v. Hammond, 10 Cir. 1959, 269 F.2d 501; Kelley v. Volkswagen Aktiengesellschaft, N.H.1970, 268 A. 2d 837 (overruling prior cases). See Notes, 1966, 51 Iowa L.Rev. 1010; 1966, 39 Temp.L.Q. 352; 1966, 51 Iowa L.Rev. 1010.

Many cases formerly held to the contrary, on the ground that the gist of warranty had become contract, and was not included within the wrongful death statutes. Wadleigh v. Howson, 1937, 88 N.H. 365, 189 A. 865; Goodwin v. Misticos, 1949, 207 Miss. 361, 42 So.2d 397; Whiteley v. Webb's City, Fla.1951, 55 So.2d 730; Sugai v. General Motors Corp., D.Idaho 1955, 130 F.Supp. 101; Frankel v. Styer, E.D.Pa.1962, 201 F.Supp. 726.

A late case so holding is Kecktas v. General Motors Corp., Pontiac Division, 1970, —— Mass. ——, 259 N. E.2d 234.

52. See Jacob E. Decker & Sons v. Capps, 1942, 139 Tex. 609, 164 S.W.2d 828; Challis v. Hartloff, 1933, 136 Kan. 823, 18 P.2d 199; Davis v. Van Camp Packing Co., 1920, 189 Iowa 775, 176 N.W. 382;

---

sorted to only for the procedural convenience of joining money counts to recover the price paid. See Williamson v. Allison, 1802, 2 East 446, 102 Eng.Rep. 439.

44. See Bekkevold v. Potts, 1927, 173 Minn. 87, 216 N.W. 790; Hoe v. Sanborn, 1860, 21 N.Y. 552, 564; Lee v. Cohrt, 1930, 57 S.D. 387, 232 N.W. 900; 1 Williston, Sales, 2d Ed.1924, § 197.

45. Williston, Liability for Honest Misrepresentations, 1911, 24 Harv.L.Rev. 415, 420; Smith, Surviving Fictions, 1917, 27 Yale L.J. 147, 317, 326.

46. See Note, 1955, 43 Cal.L.Rev. 381.

47. Greenwood v. John R. Thompson Co., 1919, 213 Ill.App. 371; Wells v. Oldsmobile Co. of Oregon, 1934, 147 Or. 687, 35 P.2d 232; McLachlan v. Wilmington Dry Goods Co., 1940, 2 Terry, Del., 378, 22 A.2d 851; Spillane v. Corey, 1949, 323 Mass. 673, 84 N.E.2d 5; Burgess v. Sanitary Meat Market, 1939, 121 W.Va. 605, 5 S.E.2d 785. See the discussion in Nichols v. Nold, 1953, 174 Kan. 613, 258 P.2d 317.

48. Gosling v. Nichols, 1943, 59 Cal.App.2d 442, 139 P.2d 86; Bernstein v. Queens County Jockey Club, 1927, 222 App.Div. 191, 225 N.Y.S. 449.

Whether it be tort or contract, a breach of warranty gives rise to strict liability, which does not depend upon any knowledge of defects on the part of the seller,[53] or any negligence.[54] The early warranty cases involved express representations as to the character or quality of the goods, on which the buyer relied in making his purchase, and for which the seller was held strictly responsible.[55]

Early in the nineteenth century [56] the slow growth of a business practice by which reputable sellers stood behind their goods,[57] and a changing social viewpoint toward the seller's responsibility,[58] led to the development of "implied" warranties of quality, which were attached by the law to certain types of sales,

and which in effect made the seller an insurer of his goods.

Detailed consideration of these warranties must be left to texts on the law of sales.[59] So far as the remedy between buyer and seller is concerned, the law as it stands today is very largely statutory, with the developments of the common law crystalized, first in the provisions of the Uniform Sales Act,[60] and later in those of the Uniform Commercial Code.[61] Under these statutes any affirmation of fact made by the seller concerning the goods, including any description of them, and any promise relating to them, becomes an express warranty if it is relied on by the buyer as part of the bargain. The implied warranties of quality are reduced to two: a warranty that the goods are fit for the particular purpose of the buyer, when that purpose is made known to the seller, and the latter knows that the buyer is relying upon his skill or judgment to select and furnish suitable goods; [62] and a warranty that the goods are of merchantable quality, when they are bought from one who deals in goods of that description.[63]

It is essential to a warranty that the buyer shall rely on the seller's express or implied assurance. There is no recovery where the defects in the goods are known [64] to the buyer

Mazetti v. Armour & Co., 1913, 75 Wash. 622, 135 P. 633.

53. Pietrus v. Watkins Co., 1949, 229 Minn. 179, 38 N.W.2d 799; Canadian Fire Ins. Co. v. Wild, 1956, 81 Ariz. 252, 304 P.2d 390; Tremeroli v. Austin Trailer Equipment Co., 1951, 102 Cal.App.2d 464, 227 P.2d 923; Great A. & P. Tea Co. v. Eiseman, 1935, 259 Ky. 103, 81 S.W.2d 900; Frank R. Jelleff, Inc. v. Braden, 1956, 98 U.S.App.D.C. 180, 233 F.2d 671.

54. Simon v. Graham Bakery, 1954, 31 N.J.Super. 117, 105 A.2d 877, reversed on other grounds, 1955, 17 N.J. 525, 111 A.2d 884; Ireland v. Louis K. Liggett Co., 1922, 243 Mass. 243, 137 N.E. 371; Keyser v. O'Meara, 1933, 116 Conn. 579, 165 A. 793; Norris v. Parker, 1896, 15 Tex.Civ.App. 117, 38 S.W. 259. Thus the seller may be held liable even though there is no practical way of discovering the defect. Holt v. Mann, 1936, 294 Mass. 21, 200 N.E. 403; Ver Steegh v. Flaugh, 1960, 251 Iowa 1011, 103 N. W.2d 718.

55. 1 Williston, Sales, Rev.Ed.1948, §§ 195, 196. "Any affirmation of fact or any promise by the seller relating to the goods is an express warranty if the natural tendency of such affirmation or promise is to induce the buyer to purchase the goods, and if the buyer purchases the goods relying thereon." Uniform Sales Act, § 12.

56. The development is traced in Prosser, The Implied Warranty of Merchantable Quality, 1943, 27 Minn.L.Rev. 117.

57. See Bogert and Fink, Business Practices Regarding Warranties in the Sale of Goods, 1931, 21 Ill.L. Rev. 400, 415.

58. See Llewellyn, Of Warranty of Quality and Society, 1936, 36 Col.L.Rev. 699, 1937, 37 Col.L.Rev. 404.

59. See 1 Williston, Sales, Rev.Ed.1948, ch. 9; Vold, Sales, 2d Ed.1959, §§ 84-95. Also Frumer and Friedman, Products Liability, 1961, §§ 19-19.08.

60. §§ 12 (express warranty); 14 (sale by description); 15 (implied warranties of quality). See 1 and 1A Uniform Laws Ann.

61. §§ 2-313 (express warranties); 2-314 (implied warranty of merchantability); 2-315 (implied warranty of fitness for the purpose). See Cudahy, Limitations of Warranty Under the Uniform Commercial Code, 1963, 47 Marq.L.Rev. 127; Note, 1963, 38 Ind.L.J. 648.

62. See Corman, Implied Sales Warranty of Fitness for Particular Purpose, [1958] Wis.L.Rev. 219.

63. See Prosser, The Implied Warranty of Merchantable Quality, 1943, 27 Minn.L.Rev. 117; Notes, 1956, 5 De Paul L.Rev. 273; 1962, 48 Va.L.Rev. 152.

64. Wavra v. Karr, 1919, 142 Minn. 248, 172 N.W. 118; Brooks v. Camak, 1908, 130 Ga. 213, 60 S.E.

or obvious to him;[65] or where he elects to make his own inspection and rely solely on it.[66] There was formerly a long-continued controversy over the question of an implied warranty on the part of a retail dealer who sells products manufactured by another, particularly in a sealed container.[67] It was contended[68] that the buyer could not reasonably rely upon any supposed assurance of the seller in such a case, and that no policy demanded strict liability on the part of the innocent seller. The number of courts which continue to take this position has dwindled to a bare handful.[69] Elsewhere the battle has been won for the buyer, with the great majority of the decisions[70] implying the warranty. Sufficient reliance is found upon the seller's undertaking to deliver merchantable goods, according to the description, which will be resonably fit for the general purpose for which such goods are to be used. So far as questions of policy are concerned, the consumer is given the protection in the public interest, and the retailer is regarded as the proper party to litigate any issue as to deficiencies against the manufacturer.

There remains, however, an astonishing little argument over whether the warranty of the product includes the safety of the container in which it is sold. There are courts[71] which formerly held that the one does not include the other, and that there are in effect distinct transactions. Since the container and the contents are sold, and bought, as an integrated whole, and the buyer would not buy one without the other even if he could, this metaphysical distinction between them appears rather amazing; and it is not surprising that the later cases all have held that the one warranty covers both.[72]

456; Cochord Machinery Co. v. Loy-Wilson Foundry & Mach. Co., 1908, 131 Mo.App. 540, 110 S.W. 630.

65. Rosenbush v. Learned, 1922, 242 Mass. 297, 136 N.E. 341; Colitz & Co. v. Davis, 1936, 177 Okl. 607, 62 P.2d 67; American Waste Co. v. St. Mary, 1924, 210 App.Div. 383, 206 N.Y.S. 316; Lowry Coffee Co. v. Andresen-Ryan Co., 1922, 153 Minn. 498, 190 N.W. 985.

66. Barnard v. Kellogg, 1870, 10 Wall., U.S., 383, 19 L.Ed. 987; Cudahy Packing Co. v. Narzisenfeld, 2 Cir. 1924, 3 F.2d 567; Hyde Const. Co. v. Stevenson, 1937, 181 Okl. 8, 72 P.2d 354.

67. Where the goods were open to inspection, the warranty was more readily found. Burgess v. Sanitary Meat Market, 1939, 121 W.Va. 605, 5 S.E.2d 785, 6 S.E.2d 254; Rinaldi v. Mohican Co., 1918, 225 N.Y. 70, 121 N.E. 471; Hazelton v. First Nat. Stores, 1937, 88 N.H. 409, 190 A. 280; Great A. & P. Tea Co. v. Eiseman, 1935, 259 Ky. 103, 81 S.W.2d 900; Keenan v. Cherry & Webb, 1925, 47 R.I. 125, 131 A. 309.

68. Waite, Retail Responsibility and Judicial Law-Making, 1936, 34 Mich.L.Rev. 494; Waite, Retail Responsibility—A Reply, 1939, 23 Minn.L.Rev. 612.

69. Mucauley v. Manda Bros. Provisions Co., La. App.1967, 202 So.2d 492, affirmed, 1968, 252 La. 528, 211 So.2d 637; Postell v. Boykin Tool & Supply Co., 1952, 86 Ga.App. 400, 61 S.E.2d 783; Wilkes v. Memphis Groc. Co., 1939, 23 Tenn.App. 550, 134 S.W.2d 929, rehearing denied 24 Tenn.App. 36, 139 S.W.2d 416; Carter v. Hector Supply Co., Fla.1961, 128 So.2d 390.

70. Vinyard v. Duck, 1965, 278 Ala. 687, 180 So.2d 522; Sams v. Ezy-Way Foodliner Co., 1961, 157 Me. 10, 170 A.2d 160; John A. Brown Co. v. Shelton, Okl.1964, 391 P.2d 259; Gonzales v. Safeway Stores, Inc., 1961, 147 Colo. 358, 363 P.2d 667; Higbee v. Giant Food Shopping Center, E.D.Va.1952, 106 F.Supp. 586.

See Brown, The Liability of Retail Dealers for Defective Food Products, 1939, 23 Minn.L.Rev. 585; Notes, 1950, 3 U.Fla.L.Rev. 380; 1941, 26 Iowa L. Rev. 423; 1939, 23 Minn.L.Rev. 585.

71. Crandall v. Stop & Shop, 1937, 288 Ill.App. 543, 6 N.E.2d 685; Poplar v. Hochschild, Kohn & Co., 1942, 180 Md. 389, 24 A.2d 783; Atwell v. Pepsi-Cola Bottling Co., Mun.App.D.C.1959, 152 A.2d 196; Prince v. Smith, 1961, 254 N.C. 768, 119 S.E.2d 923.

Accord, as to warranty to third parties: Soter v. Griesedieck Western Brewery Co., 1948, 200 Okl. 302, 193 P.2d 575; Anheuser-Busch, Inc. v. Butler, Tex.Civ.App.1944, 180 S.W.2d 996.

72. Renninger v. Foremost Dairies, Inc., Fla.App. 1965, 171 So.2d 602; Naumann v. Wehle Brewing Co., 1940, 127 Conn. 44, 15 A.2d 181; Mead v. Coca Cola Bottling Co., 1952, 329 Mass. 440, 108 N.E.2d 757; Haller v. Rudmann, 1937, 249 App.Div. 831, 292 N.Y.S. 586; Pettella v. Corp. Bros., Inc., R.I. 1970, 268 A.2d 699. Cf. Hadley v. Hillcrest Dairy, Inc., 1961, 341 Mass. 624, 171 N.E.2d 293 (loan of container).

See Pound, The Problem of the Exploding Bottle, 1960, 40 Bos.U.L.Rev. 167.

There was also a dispute of long standing as to the liability of a restaurant serving defective food. A small number of courts continued to cling to the notion, inherited from the days of innkeepers when the guest paid a lump sum for lodging, meals, and a stable for his horse, that such a service was not a sale, and no warranty was to be implied.[73] It is obvious that such a theory is entirely unsuited to modern restaurants, with "orders" of definite quantity served at fixed prices; and here again the great majority of the courts have imposed strict liability upon the restaurant owner, finding that the food is sold, and that there is obvious reliance upon the seller's implied assurance.[74]

There are other situations in which the absence of a technical sale has been held to prevent the existence of any implied warranty. This has been true, for example, of the furnishing of blood plasma in connection with a transfusion,[75] and of the supplying of materials incidental to contracts for work and labor.[76] There are, however, indica-tions of a definite tendency to extend the strict liability of an implied warranty beyond cases involving the sale of goods.[77] It frequently is said that the bailor of a chattel for hire impliedly warrants its fitness for the bailee's use. In some cases this apparently has meant no more than an assurance that reasonable care has been used, which will make the bailor liable for negligence.[78] But in others the bailor clearly is held liable without any negligence.[79] A similar warranty has been found in the case of a shipper delivering goods to a carrier,[80] a processor doing work on goods delivered to him,[81] and a landlord leasing a furnished apartment

73. McCarley v. Wood Drugs, Inc., 1934, 228 Ala. 226, 153 So. 446; Pappa v. F. W. Woolworth Co., 1943, 3 Terry, Del., 358, 33 A.2d 310; Yeo v. Pig & Whistle Sandwich Shops, 1950, 83 Ga.App. 91, 62 S. E.2d 668; Childs Dining Hall Co. v. Swingler, 1938, 173 Md. 490, 197 A. 105; Walton v. Guthrie, 1962, 50 Tenn.App. 383, 362 S.W.2d 41.

74. Levy v. Paul, 1966, 207 Va. 100, 147 S.E.2d 722; Cushing v. Rodman, 1936, 65 U.S.App.D.C. 258, 82 F.2d 864; Arnaud's Restaurant v. Cotter, 5 Cir. 1954, 212 F.2d 883, cert. denied 348 U.S. 915 (Louisiana law); Cliett v. Lauderdale Biltmore Corp., Fla.1949, 39 So.2d 476; Zorinsky v. American Legion Omaha Post No. 1, 1956, 163 Neb. 212, 79 N.W.2d 172. See Notes, 1965, 16 West.Res.L.Rev. 454; [1961] Wis.L.Rev. 141; 1950, 35 Iowa L.Rev. 724.

75. Perlmutter v. Beth David Hospital, 1954, 308 N. Y. 100, 123 N.E.2d 792; Dibblee v. Dr. W. H. Groves Latter-Day Saints Hospital, 1961, 12 Utah 2d 241, 364 P.2d 1085; Gile v. Kennewick Pub. Hosp. Dist., 1956, 48 Wash.2d 774, 296 P.2d 662; Sloneker v. St. Joseph's Hospital, D.Colo.1964, 233 F.Supp. 105. Contra, Hoffman v. Misericordia Hospital of Philadelphia, Pa.1970, 267 A.2d 869. See note, 1970, 21 Sw.L.J. 305.

76. Stammer v. Mulvaney, 1953, 264 Wis. 244, 58 N. W.2d 671; Foley Corp. v. Dove, Mun.App.D.C.1954, 101 A.2d 841.

77. See Farnsworth, Implied Warranties of Quality in Non-Sales Cases, 1957, 57 Col.L.Rev. 653; Note, 1956, 31 Ind.L.J. 367. Cf. Barni v. Kutner, 1950, 6 Terry, Del., 550, 76 A.2d 801 (delivery of car, with title not to pass until payment). As to the effect of the vending machine, see Ruud, The Vendor's Responsibility for Quality in the Automated Retail Sale, 1960, 9 Kan.L.Rev. 139.

78. Dam v. Lake Aliso Riding School, 1936, 6 Cal.2d 395, 57 P.2d 1315; Baty v. Wolff, 1956, 162 Neb. 1, 74 N.W.2d 913; Smith v. Pabst, 1939, 233 Wis. 489, 288 N.W. 780; Artificial Ice & Cold Storage Co. v. Martin, 1935, 102 Ind.App. 74, 198 N.E. 446.

79. Covello v. State, 1959, 17 Misc.2d 637, 187 N.Y.S. 2d 396; Hoisting Engine Sales Co. v. Hart, 1923, 237 N.Y. 30, 142 N.E. 342; Marcos v. Texas Co., 1952, 75 Ariz. 45, 251 P.2d 647; General Talking Pictures Corp. v. Shea, 1933, 187 Ark. 568, 61 S.W. 2d 430; Milwaukee Tank Works v. Metals Coating Co., 1928, 196 Wis. 191, 218 N.W. 835. Cf. Electrical Advertising, Inc. v. Sakato, 1963, 94 Ariz. 68, 381 P.2d 755 (lease). See Farnsworth, Implied Warranties of Quality in Non-Sales Cases, 1957, 57 Col.L.Rev. 653; Brown, Rights and Duties of Bailor and Bailee Under the Law of Pennsylvania, 1944, 18 Temple L.Q. 199, 216; Notes, 1933, 17 Minn.L.Rev. 210; 1949, 2 Vand.L.Rev. 675; 1967, 4 Willam.L.Rev. 421.

80. Bamfield v. Goole & Sheffield Transp. Co., [1910] 2 K.B. 94; Eastern Motor Express v. A. Maschmeijer, Jr., Inc., 2 Cir. 1957, 247 F.2d 826, cert. denied, 355 U.S. 959.

81. Debby Junior Coat & Suit Co. v. Wollman Mills, 1954, 207 Misc. 330, 137 N.Y.S.2d 703; Locks Laboratories v. Bloomfield Molding Co., 1955, 35 N.J.Super. 422, 114 A.2d 457. Also a civil engineering firm furnishing services, plans and specifications. Broyles v. Brown Eng. Co., 1963, 275 Ala. 35, 151 So.2d 767.

for a short term.[82] No reason suggests itself to prevent the ultimate extension of such liability, subject to all of the limitations now found in the case of sales, to any person who furnishes goods under a contract.[83]

When a warranty is found, there is still no liability unless there has been a breach of it. There are a good many questions which arise as to the direct warranty of the seller to his immediate buyer, which are more conveniently considered at a later point in connection with his liability to third parties. Among them are the effect of disclaimers,[84] abnormal use of the product[85] and abnormal users,[86] contributory negligence and assumption of risk,[87] the damages recoverable,[88] and the extension of the strict liability of the seller to related fields.[89]

Vendors and Lessors of Land

The liability for negligence of vendors and lessors of buildings and other real property has already been considered. Strict liability was late in making its appearance as to either, in large part because of the presence of a written deed or lease, which was considered to embody the entire agreement of the parties, and to exclude parol obligations. But in the case of the builder-vendor who sold his own product, the analogy of the manufacturer of chattels[90] finally began to prevail.[91]

Colorado led off[92] in 1964 with Carpenter v. Donohoe,[93] holding that the builder of a new house who sold it to an initial buyer was liable to him on implied warranties that the dwelling conformed to statutory requirements, and was built in a workmanlike manner and fit for habitation. This small beginning led to a sudden flood of decisions[94] finding similar warranties. While there are still courts that have held back,[95] the acceptance of the strict liability has been so rapid and extensive that it now appears that it is destined soon to become the prevailing rule. California has even applied it to the financer of the construction.[96] There is, however, as yet no case applying the strict liability to any vendor who has not constructed the building; and it appears unlikely that there

82. Ingalls v. Hobbs, 1892, 156 Mass. 348, 31 N.E. 286; Morgenthau v. Ehrich, 1912, 77 Misc. 139, 136 N.Y.S. 140.

83. Cf. Bark v. Dixson, 1911, 115 Minn. 172, 131 N.W. 1078, where an employee was furnished food as a part of his compensation. Also Strika v. Netherlands Ministry of Traffic, D.C.Cir.1950, 185 F.2d 555, where a longshoreman was furnished a ship to work on. Thus even if the service of food in a restaurant is not regarded as a sale, there may still be an implied warranty that it is fit to eat. Stanfield v. F. W. Woolworth Co., 1936, 143 Kan. 117, 53 P.2d 878. See Note, 1964, 39 Notre Dame L. 680.

84. See infra, p. 84.

85. See infra, § 102.

86. See infra, § 102.

87. See infra, p. 667.

88. See infra, § 101.

89. See infra, § 104.

90. See infra, § 97.

91. See Dunham, Vendor's Obligation as to Fitness of Land for a Particular Purpose, 1953, 37 Minn.L. Rev. 108; Haskell, Case for an Implied Warranty of Quality in Sales of Real Property, 1965, 53 Geo. L.J. 633; Bearman, Caveat Emptor in Sales of Realty, 1961, 14 Vand.L.Rev. 541; Notes, 1965, 26 U.Pitt.L.Rev. 862; 1967, 28 Ohio St.L.J. 343; 1967, 18 West.Res.L.Rev. 706; 1969, 48 Or.L.Rev. 411; 1969, 47 N.C.L.Rev. 989.

92. There had been prior decisions in Louisiana, based on a statute borrowed from the French Civil Code. For example, Foreman v. Jordan, La.App. 1961, 131 So.2d 796; Glynn v. Delcuze, La.App.1963, 149 So.2d 667.

93. 1964, 154 Colo. 78, 388 P.2d 399.

94. Bethlahmy v. Bechtel, 1966, 91 Idaho 55, 415 P. 2d 698; Waggoner v. Midwestern Development, Inc., S.D.1967, 154 N.W.2d 803; Humber v. Morton, Tex.1968, 426 S.W.2d 554; House v. Thornton, 1969, 76 Wash.2d 428, 457 P.2d 199; Crawley v. Terhune, Ky.1969, 437 S.W.2d 743; Rothberg v. Olenik, 1970, — Vt. —, 262 A.2d 461; Wawak v. Stewart, 1970, — Ark. —, 449 S.W.2d 922.

95. Mitchem v. Johnson, 1966, 7 Ohio St.2d 66, 218 N.E.2d 594; Dooley v. Berkner, 1966, 113 Ga.App. 162, 147 S.E.2d 685.

96. Connor v. Great Western Sav. & Loan Ass'n, 1968, 69 Cal.2d 850, 73 Cal.Rptr. 369, 447 P.2d 609, noted in 1969, 10 W. & M. L. Rev. 1000. Cf. Avner v. Longridge Estates, 1969, 272 A.C.A. 695, 77 Cal. Rptr. 633 (manufacturer of lot).

will be one, for the reason that he is not engaged in the business of selling.

A similar development as to lessors may perhaps be imminent,[97] but it has not yet occurred, at least on any such broad scale. There are older decisions in England [98] and Massachusetts,[99] that one who lets a furnished house or lodging for a short term warrants that the premises and furniture are fit for habitation. There are decisions in a few other jurisdictions [1] finding a "constructive eviction" when any leased premises are not habitable; and in some of them there has been talk of an "implied warranty." But thus far the only complete application of the analogy of the builder-vendor has been in very late cases in Hawaii, New Jersey and the District of Columbia,[2] in which the court rejected the fiction of constructive eviction, and held that a dwelling infested with rats was a breach of an implied warranty of habitability. Whether this is the start of a further expansion is, at the time of publication, a matter of speculation.

97. See Skillern, Implied Warranties in Leases: The Need for Change, 1967, 44 Denv.L.J. 387; Levine, The Warranty of Habitability, 1969, 2 Conn.L.Rev. 61; Schloshinski, Remedies of the Indigent Tenant, 1966, 54 Geo.L.J. 519; Lesar, Landlord and Tenant Reform, 1960, 35 N.Y.U.L.Rev. 1279; Notes, 1970, 21 Hast.L.J. 458; [1968] Wash.U.L.Q. 461.

98. Collins v. Hopkins, [1923] 2 K.B. 617.

99. Ingalls v. Hobbs, 1892, 156 Mass. 348, 31 N.E. 286; Hacker v. Nitschke, 1942, 310 Mass. 754, 39 N.E.2d 644. See Note, 1949, 23 St. Johns L.Rev. 357.

1. Pines v. Perssion, 1961, 14 Wis.2d 590, 111 N.W.2d 409; Reste Realty Corp. v. Cooper, 1969, 53 N.J. 444, 251 A.2d 268; see Buckner v. Azulai, 1967, 251 Cal.App.2d Supp. 1013, 59 Cal.Rptr. 806.

2. Lemle v. Breeden, 1969, 51 Haw. 426, 462 P.2d 470; Reste Realty Corp. v. Cooper, 1969, 53 H.J. 444, 251 A.2d 268; Javins v. First Nat. Realty Corp., D.C.Cir. 1970, 428 F.2d 1071.

CHAPTER 17

PRODUCTS LIABILITY

Products liability is the name currently given to the area of case law involving the liability of sellers [1] of chattels [2] to third persons with whom they are not in privity of contract. It may, infrequently, rest upon intent; [3] but except in rare instances, it is a matter of negligence, or of strict liability.

96. NEGLIGENCE

The law of products liability began with the case of Winterbottom v. Wright, which has been dealt with above, [4] and which has been described as a fishbone in the throat of the law. That case, with the broad language of Lord Abinger, was taken to mean that there could be no action, even in tort, for the misperformance of a contract of sale of a chattel in the first instance. [5] It was not until 1905 that the error of this interpretation of the case was pointed out in a noted article

by Professor Bohlen; [6] and in the meantime the nineteenth century had firmly established the general rule that the original seller of goods was not liable for damages caused by their defects to anyone except his immediate buyer, or one in privity with him. [7]

Various reasons were given in support of this rule. [8] One was that the seller's misconduct was not the cause of the damage to the consumer in a legal sense, because no such harm was to be anticipated from any defects in the goods, and there was an intervening resale by a responsible party, which "insulated" the negligence of the manufacturer. This argument of course has been exploded long since: if goods are sold to a dealer, nothing is more foreseeable than that they will be resold to a consumer, or, if they are dangerously defective, that he will be injured by them; and the case falls well within the limits of legal causation. A second reason,

---

1. Or possibly other suppliers. See infra, § 104.

2. There is also the analogous situation of the builder-vendor of a dwelling. See infra, p. 682.

3. Usually such cases are dealt with in an action of deceit. See for example Benoit v. Perkins, 1918, 79 N.H. 11, 104 A. 254; Langridge v. Levy, 1837, 2 M. & W. 519, 150 Eng.Rep. 863; Kuelling v. Roderick Lean Mfg. Co., 1905, 183 N.Y. 78, 75 N.E. 1098.

4. See supra, p. 622.

5. See for example Huset v. J. I. Case Threshing Mach. Co., 1903, 57 C.C.A. 237, 120 F. 865; Earl v. Lubbock, [1905] 1 K.B. 253.

6. Bohlen, The Basis of Affirmative Obligations in the Law of Tort, 1905, 44 Am.L.Reg.,N.S., 209, 280–285, 289–310. See also Lord Atkin, in Donoghue v. Stevenson, [1932] A.C. 562, 588–589.

7. Hasbrouck v. Armour & Co., 1909, 139 Wis. 357, 121 N.W. 157; Lebourdais v. Vitrified Wheel Co., 1907, 194 Mass. 341, 80 N.E. 482; Burkett v. Studebaker Bros. Mfg. Co., 1912, 126 Tenn. 467, 150 S.W. 421; Stone v. Van Noy Ry. News Co., 1913, 153 Ky. 240, 154 S.W. 1092; Liggett & Myers Tobacco Co. v. Cannon, 1915, 132 Tenn. 419, 178 S.W. 1009.

8. Particularly in Huset v. J. I. Case Threshing Mach. Co., 8 Cir. 1903, 120 F. 865.

which was typical of the social viewpoint of the nineteenth century, was that it would place too heavy a burden upon manufacturers and sellers to hold them responsible to hundreds of persons at a distance whose identity they could not even know, and that it was better to let the consumer suffer. As to this, at least, there has been a definite change in our social philosophy. It is now generally recognized that a manufacturer or even a dealer has a responsibility to the ultimate consumer, based upon nothing more than the sufficient fact that he has so dealt with the goods that they are likely to come into the hands of another, and to do harm if they are defective.[9] The existence of a contract with the buyer of course does not prevent the existence of a tort duty to a third person who will be affected by the seller's conduct.[10] The battle over liability for negligence has been fought and won by the plaintiff, both in England [11] and in the United States,[12] and the scene of combat is now being shifted to the field of strict liability.[13]

The courts began by the usual process of recognizing several exceptions, which whittled down the general rule derived from the supposed holding of Winterbottom v. Wright. These are now largely of purely historical interest. The most important of them held the seller liable to a third person for negligence in the preparation or sale of an article "imminently" or "inherently" dangerous to human safety.[14] This originated in a New York case [15] in 1852; and for more than half a century the category remained vague and imperfectly defined. There was much rather pointless dispute, for example, as to how such products as soap,[16] chewing tobacco,[17] or the container of a beverage [18] were to be classified.

Finally, in 1916 in the famous case of MacPherson v. Buick Motor Co.,[19] the problem fell into the hands of Judge Cardozo, in connection with the liability of a manufacturer of an automobile with a defective wheel, bought from a dealer by an ultimate purchaser, who was injured by its collapse. Cardozo's opinion struck through the fog of the "general rule" and its various exceptions, and held the maker liable for negligence. On its face the decision purported merely to extend the class of "inherently dangerous" articles to include anything which would be dangerous if negligently made.[20] But its ef-

9. See Bohlen, Liability of Manufacturers to Persons Other than Their Immediate Vendees, 1929, 45 L.Q. Rev. 343; Feezer, Tort Liability of Manufacturers and Vendors, 1925, 10 Minn.L.Rev. 1; Feezer, Tort Liability of Manufacturers, 1935, 19 Minn.L.Rev. 752; Russell, Manufacturers' Liability to the Ultimate Consumer, 1933, 21 Ky.L.J. 388; Jeanblanc, Manufacturers' Liability to Persons Other than Their Immediate Vendees, 1937, 24 Va.L.Rev. 134.

10. Labatt, Negligence in Relation to Privity of Contract, 1900, 16 L.Q.Rev. 168; Bohlen, The Basis of Affirmative Obligations in the Law of Tort, 1905, 44 Am.L.Reg.,N.S., 209, 280–285, 289–310.

11. Donoghue v. Stevenson, [1932] A.C. 562; Grant v. Australian Knitting Mills, [1936] A.C. 85. See Fleming, Law of Torts, 2d Ed.1961, ch. 21.

12. See Wilson, Products Liability, 1955, 43 Cal.L. Rev. 614, 809; James, Products Liability, 1955, 34 Tex.L.Rev. 192; Noel, Products Liability of a Manufacturer in Tennessee, 1953, 22 Tenn.L.Rev. 985. Also Gillam, Products Liability in a Nutshell, 1958, 37 Or.L.Rev. 119, 128–30, listing more than two solid pages of books and articles.

13. See infra, §§ 97, 98.

14. Or, as it was put in Huset v. J. I. Case Threshing Mach. Co., 8 Cir. 1903, 120 F. 865, "intended to preserve, destroy, or affect human life."

15. Thomas v. Winchester, 1852, 6 N.Y. 397.

16. Compare Armstrong Packing Co. v. Clem, Tex. Civ.App.1912, 151 S.W. 576, with Hasbrouck v. Armour & Co., 1909, 139 Wis. 357, 121 N.W. 157.

17. Liggett & Myers Tobacco Co. v. Cannon, 1915, 132 Tenn. 419, 178 S.W. 1009 (no); Pillars v. R. J. Reynolds Tobacco Co., (1918) 117 Miss. 490, 78 So. 365 (yes).

18. Stone v. Van Noy R. News Co., 1913, 153 Ky. 240, 154 S.W. 1092 (no); Coca Cola Bottling Works v. Shelton, 1926, 214 Ky. 118, 282 S.W. 778 (yes).

19. 1916, 217 N.Y. 382, 111 N.E. 1050. The story of the case is told, with sidelights, in Peck, Decision at Law, 1961, 38–69.

20. "If the nature of a thing is such that it is reasonably certain to place life and limb in peril when negligently made, it is then a thing of danger. Its

fect was to make the exception swallow up the rule; and its reasoning and its fundamental philosophy were clearly that the manufacturer, by placing the car upon the market, assumed a responsibility to the consumer, resting not upon the contract but upon the relation arising from his purchase, together with the foreseeability of harm if proper care were not used. Legal writers [21] were quick to supply the justification that the manufacturer derives an economic benefit from the sale and the subsequent use of the chattel, and his duty is therefore analogous to that of a possessor of land toward his business visitor; and there has been added some notion of a representation of safety in the mere act of offering the goods for sale, which, because of the original buyer's reliance upon it, deprives the consumer of possible protection at his hands. Such rationalization adds little, however, to the conclusion that the duty is one imposed by the law because of the defendant's affirmative conduct, which he must know to be likely to affect the interests of another.

This decision found immediate acceptance,[22] and at the end of some forty years is universal law in the United States, with Mississippi the last state to fall into line [23] in

1966. Massachusetts, which was one of the later jurisdictions to capitulate, has said that "The MacPherson case caused the exception to swallow the asserted general rule of non-liability, leaving nothing upon which that rule could operate." [24] Some of the courts continued for a time to speak the language of "inherent danger," [25] but it now seems clear that this means nothing more than that substantial harm is to be anticipated if the chattel should be defective.[26] The rule was presently extended to include physical harm to property,[27] and even to negligence in the sale of goods, such as animal food, which involve no recognizable risk of personal injury, and are foreseeably dangerous only to property.[28] The rule that has finally emerged is that the seller is liable for negligence in the manufacture or sale of any product which may reasonably be expected to be capable of inflicting substantial harm if it is defective.[29]

---

nature gives warning of the consequences to be expected. If to the element of danger there is added knowledge that the thing will be used by persons other than the purchaser and used without new tests, then, irrespective of contract, the manufacturer of this thing of danger is under a duty to make it carefully. That is as far as we are required to go for the decision of this case." MacPherson v. Buick Motor Co., 1916, 217 N.Y. 382, 389, 111 N.E. 1050.

21. Particularly Bohlen, Liability of Manufacturers to Persons Other than Their Immediate Vendees, 1929, 45 L.Q.Rev. 343.

22. Johnson v. Cadillac Motor Car Co., 2 Cir. 1919, 261 F. 878, reversing 2 Cir. 1915, 221 F. 801.

23. Actually the Mississippi court never has expressly accepted the MacPherson decision, but leaped over it to strict liability in State Stove Mfg. Co. v. Hodges, Miss.1966, 189 So.2d 113, cert. denied 386 U.S. 912. Federal courts, purporting to apply Mississippi law, have concluded that the case has been accepted. Necaise v. Chrysler Corp., 5 Cir. 1964,

335 F.2d 562; Grey v. Hayes-Sammons Chem. Co., 5 Cir. 1962, 310 F.2d 291.

24. Carter v. Yardley & Co., 1946, 319 Mass. 92, 64 N.E.2d 693, 700. See Peairs, The God in the Machine, 1949, 29 Boston U.L.Rev. 37.

25. See for example Kalash v. Los Angeles Ladder Co., 1934, 1 Cal.2d 229, 34 P.2d 481; Crane Co. v. Sears, 1934, 168 Okl. 603, 35 P.2d 916. New York, in particular, took a very narrow view as to what is to be considered "dangerous if negligently made," and denied liability for such things as a bed, Field v. Empire Case Goods Co., 1917, 179 App.Div. 253, 166 N.Y.S. 509, or a can with a key, in Boyd v. American Can Co., 1936, 249 App.Div. 644, 291 N.Y. S. 205, affirmed 274 N.Y. 526, 10 N.E.2d 532. See Davis, a Reexamination of the Doctrine of MacPherson v. Buick, 1955, 24 Ford.L.Rev. 204; Note, 1948, 14 Brook.L.Rev. 126.

26. Restatement of Torts, § 395.

27. See infra, § 101.

28. Cohan v. Associated Fur Farms, 1952, 261 Wis. 584, 53 N.W.2d 788; Dunn v. Ralston Purina Co., 1954, 38 Tenn.App. 229, 272 S.W.2d 479; Brown v. Bigelow, 1949, 325 Mass. 4, 88 N.E.2d 542; Ellis v. Lindmark, 1929, 177 Minn. 390, 225 N.W. 395; Pine Grove Poultry Farm v. Newtown By-Products Mfg. Co., 1928, 248 N.Y. 293, 162 N.E. 84.

29. See Pitts v. Basile, 1965, 55 Ill.App.2d 37, 204 N. E.2d 43, reversed on other grounds, 1966, 35 Ill.2d 49, 219 N.E.2d 472 (child's dart); Sheward v. Virtue, 1942, 20 Cal.2d 410, 126 P.2d 345 (chair);

Since the liability is to be based on negligence, the defendant is required to exercise the care of a reasonable man under the circumstances.[30] His negligence may be found over an area quite as broad as his whole activity in preparing and selling the product.[31] He may for example, be negligent in failing to inspect or test his materials, or the work itself,[32] or the finished product,[33] to discover possible defects, or dangerous propensities;[34] and in doing so he is held to the standard of an expert in the field.[35] At the other extreme, he must use reasonable care in his methods of advertising and sale, to avoid misrepresentation of the product,[36] and to disclose defects and dangers of which he knows.[37] In between lies the entire process of manufacture and sale.

The development and recognition of strict liability[38] has had a natural tendency to reduce the number of actions founded on negligence; but it continues to have a great deal of importance, if only because counsel for the plaintiff, for reasons readily understandable,[39] have continued to plead and endeavor to prove it. There are, in addition, two particular areas in which the liability of the manufacturer, even though it may occasionally be called strict,[40] appears to rest primarily upon a departure from proper standards of care, so that the tort is essentially a matter of negligence.

One of these involves the design of the product,[41] which includes plan, structure,

---

Smith v. S. S. Kresge Co., 8 Cir. 1935, 79 F.2d 361 (hair combs); Carter v. Yardley & Co., 1946, 319 Mass. 92, 64 N.E.2d 693 (perfume); Simmons Co. v. Hardin, 1947, 75 Ga.App. 420, 43 S.E.2d 553 (sofa bed).

30. Considered in the light of the probability of defects, the magnitude of the possible harm, the cost of effective inspection, and the customs of the business. Marsh Wood Products Co. v. Babcock & Wilcox Co., 1932, 207 Wis. 209, 240 N.W. 392; Kalash v. Los Angeles Ladder Co., 1934, 1 Cal.2d 229, 34 P. 2d 481; Smith v. Peerless Glass Co., 1932, 259 N.Y. 292, 181 N.E. 576; Grant v. Graham Chero-Cola Bottling Co., 1918, 176 N.C. 256, 97 S.E. 27. Hence ordinarily a question for the jury.

31. See Noel, Manufacturers' Liability for Negligence, 1966, 33 Tenn.L.Rev. 444; Noel, Products Liability of a Manufacturer in Tennessee, 1953, 22 Tenn.L.Rev. 985; James, Products Liability, 1955, 34 Tex.L.Rev. 192; Wilson, Products Liability: The Protection of the Injured Person, 1955, 43 Cal.L. Rev. 614.

32. Trowbridge v. Abrasive Co., 3 Cir.1951, 190 F.2d 825; Pierce v. Ford Motor Co., 4 Cir.1951, 190 F.2d 910, cert. denied, 1951, 342 U.S. 887; Willey v. Fyrogas Co., 1952, 363 Mo. 406, 251 S.W.2d 635; Ford Motor Co. v. Zahn, 8 Cir.1959, 265 F.2d 729; Sitta v. American Steel & Wire Division, 6 Cir.1058, 254 F.2d 12.

33. Kross v. Kelsey Hayes Co., 1968, 29 App.Div.2d 901, 287 N.Y.S.2d 926.

34. Walton v. Sherwin-Williams Co., 8 Cir.1951, 191 F.2d 277; Chapman Chemical Co. v. Taylor, 1949, 215 Ark. 630, 222 S.W.2d 820; Ebers v. General Chemical Co., 1945, 310 Mich. 261, 17 N.W.2d 176; Zesch v. Abrasive Co. of Philadelphia, 1944, 353 Mo. 558, 183 S.W.2d 140. See Dillard and Hart, Product Liability: Directions for Use and Duty to Warn, 1955, 41 Va.L.Rev. 145, 159; Note, 1950, 3 Vand.L. Rev. 341.

35. Seward v. Natural Gas Co., 1950, 11 N.J.Super. 144, 78 A.2d 129, reversed on other grounds, 1951,

8 N.J. 45, 83 A.2d 716; Cornbrooks v. Terminal Barber Shops, 1940, 282 N.Y. 217, 26 N.E.2d 25, conformed to 259 App.Div. 375, 19 N.Y.S.2d 390; Trowbridge v. Abrasive Co., 3 Cir. 1951, 190 F.2d 825.

36. Hoskins v. Jackson Grain Co., Fla.1953, 63 So.2d 514; La Plant v. E. I. Dupont de Nemours & Co., Mo.App.1961, 346 S.W.2d 231; Peterson v. Standard Oil Co., 1910, 55 Or. 511, 106 P. 337; Wise v. Hayes, 1961, 58 Wash.2d 106, 361 P.2d 171; Waters-Pierce Oil Co. v. Deselms, 1909, 212 U.S. 159.

37. Schubert v. J. R. Clark Co., 1892, 49 Minn. 331, 51 N.W. 1103; Lewis v. Terry, 1896, 111 Cal. 39, 43 P. 398; Huset v. J. I. Case Threshing Mach. Co., 1903, 57 C.C.A. 237, 120 F. 865; Sterchi Bros. Stores v. Castleberry, 1938, 236 Ala. 349, 182 So. 474. See, as to warning and directions, infra, p. 648.

38. See infra, §§ 97, 98.

39. One is the relative unfamiliarity of counsel with the strict liability, and the rules to be applied to it, so that they tend to fall back upon a second string to the bow. The other is the possible effect upon the jury of evidence of negligence, in determining the size of the verdict.

40. See infra, p. 659.

41. See Noel, Negligence of Design or Directions for Use of a Product, 1962, 71 Yale L.J. 816; Noel, Recent Trends in Manufacturers' Negligence as to Design, Instructions or Warnings, 1965, 19 Sw.L.J. 43;

choice of materials,[42] and specifications. There is no doubt whatever that the manufacturer is under a duty to use reasonable care to design a product that is reasonably safe for its intended use,[43] and for other uses which are foreseeably probable.[44] The question turns on what is reasonable care and what is reasonable safety. The maker is not required to design the best possible product, or one as good as others make, or a better product than the one he has, so long as it is reasonably safe.[45] But the fact that others are making similar product with a safer design may be important evidence bearing upon the defendant's reasonable care.[46] Likewise the fact that others make use of the same design is evidence for the defendant,[47] although it is not always conclusive.[48] The duty of the manufacturer to protect the user against an unsafe design may arise even after the purchase, if the danger is then first discovered.[49]

A good many of the cases dealing with design have involved the automobile.[50] Although it was originally held [51] that the manufacturer was under no duty as to the brake system of a car beyond building it with proper care according to the design of its own engineers, and there have been occasional cases [52] finding that no unreasonable danger was involved, it is no longer seriously disputed that where there is such danger the duty exists.[53]

Notes, 1967, 52 Iowa L.Rev. 953; 1967, 42 Wash.L. Rev. 601.

42. Goullon v. Ford Motor Co., 6 Cir.1930, 44 F.2d 310; Heise v. J. R. Clark Co., 1955, 245 Minn. 179, 71 N.W.2d 818; Gittelson v. Gotham Pressed Steel Corp., 1943, 266 App.Div. 866, 42 N.Y.S.2d 341; Bowles v. Zimmer Mfg. Co., 7 Cir.1960, 277 F.2d 868; Wallace v. Herman Body Co., Mo.1942, 163 S. W.2d 923.

43. Carpini v. Pittsburgh & Weirton Bus Co., 3 Cir. 1954, 216 F.2d 404 (petcock on bus too close to ground); McCormack v. Hankscraft Co., 1967, 278 Minn. 322, 154 N.W.2d 488 (vaporizer); Rooney v. S. A. Healy Co., 1967, 20 N.Y.2d 42, 281 N.Y.S.2d 321, 228 N.E.2d 383 (gas mask); Boeing Airplane Co. v. Brown, 9 Cir.1961, 291 F.2d 310 (alternator drive in jet plane); Swaney v. Peden Steel Co., 1963, 259 N.C. 531, 131 S.E.2d 601 (steel trusses).

44. Wolcho v. Arthur J. Rosenbluth & Co., 1908, 81 Conn. 358, 71 A. 566; Clement v. Crosby & Co., 1907, 148 Mich. 293, 111 N.W. 745; Farley v. Edward E. Tower & Co., 1930, 271 Mass. 230, 171 N.E. 639; Phillips v. Ogle Aluminum Furniture, 1951, 106 Cal.App.2d 650, 235 P.2d 857; Smith v. Hobart Mfg. Co., E.D.Pa.1960, 185 F.Supp. 751, affirmed E. D.Pa.1961, 194 F.Supp. 530.

45. Watts v. Bacon & Van Buskirk Glass Co., 1959, 18 Ill.2d 226, 163 N.E.2d 425; Gossett v. Chrysler Corp., 6 Cir.1966, 359 F.2d 84; Marker v. Universal Oil Prod. Co., 10 Cir.1957, 250 F.2d 603; Brown v. General Motors Corp., 4 Cir.1966, 355 F.2d 814, cert. denied 386 U.S. 1036; Shanklin v. Allis-Chalmers Mfg. Co., S.D.W.Va.1966, 254 F.Supp. 223, affirmed 4 Cir.1967, 383 F.2d 819.

46. Darling v. Caterpillar Tractor Co., 1959, 171 Cal. App.2d 713, 341 P.2d 23; Muller v. A. B. Kirschbaum Co., 1930, 298 Pa. 560, 148 A. 851; Clark v. Zuzich Truck Lines, Mo.App.1961, 344 S.W.2d 304; Garbutt v. Schechter, 1959, 167 Cal.App.2d 396, 334 P.2d 225.

47. Watts v. Bacon & Van Buskirk Glass Co., 1959, 18 Ill.2d 226, 163 N.E.2d 425; Stevens v. Allis-Chalmers Mfg. Co., 1940, 151 Kan. 638, 100 P.2d 723; Blissenbach v. Yanko, 1951, 90 Ohio App. 557, 107 N.E.2d 409; Amason v. Ford Motor Co., 5 Cir.1935, 80 F.2d 265; Lopez v. Heezen, 1961, 69 N.M. 206, 365 P.2d 448.

48. Northwest Airlines, Inc. v. Glenn L. Martin Co., 6 Cir.1955, 224 F.2d 120, cert. denied 350 U.S. 937, rehearing denied 6 Cir., 229 F.2d 434, rehearing denied, 1956, 350 U.S. 976. As to the effect of what is customary in general, see supra, § 33.

49. Noel v. United Aircraft Corp., 3 Cir.1966, 359 F. 2d 671; Comstock v. General Motors Corp., 1959, 358 Mich. 163, 99 N.W.2d 627. See Note, 1966, 27 Ohio St.L.J. 746.

50. See, generally, Katz, Liability of Automobile Manufacturers for Unsafe Design of Passenger Cars, 1956, 69 Harv.L.Rev. 863; Nader and Page, Automobile Design and the Judicial Process, 1967, 55 Cal.L.Rev. 645; Note, 1967, 53 Iowa L.Rev. 953.

51. Dillingham v. Chevrolet Motor Co., W.D.Okl.1936, 17 F.Supp. 615.

52. Schneider v. Chrysler Motors Corp., 8 Cir.1968, 401 F.2d 549 (eye coming in contact with edge of window); Amason v. Ford Motor Co., 5 Cir.1935, 80 F.2d 265 (door hinged at the back); Hatch v. Ford Motor Co., 1958, 163 Cal.App.2d 393, 329 P.2d 605 (child ran into radiator ornament, which pierced his eye); Kahn v. Chrysler Corp., S.D.Tex.1963, 221 F. Supp. 677 (riding bicycle into tail fin).

53. Noonan v. Buick Co., Fla.1968, 211 So.2d 54. See cases cited infra, note 57.

The current lively controversy over automobile design is over whether the maker is under a duty to make the car "crashworthy," or in other words, to prevent injury from what has been called the "second collision," when the plaintiff comes in contact with some part of the automobile after the crash.[54] The greater number of decisions [55] have denied any duty to protect against the consequences of collisions, on the rather specious ground that collision is not the intended use of the car, but is an abnormal use [56] which relieves the maker of responsibility. It is, however, clearly a foreseeable danger arising out of the intended use; and it cannot be expected that this reasoning will continue to hold. In a small number of late decisions,[57] the duty

has been recognized, and the driver or passenger has been allowed to recover.

It may be significant that the cases that have denied recovery have tended to be those in which protection of the plaintiff would have required an extensive, and costly, redesign of the entire automobile, while those allowing it would have tended to call for only minor and inexpensive changes in detail. It seems clear that cost cannot be entirely disregarded in considering the problem. No doubt any automobile could be made safer by redesigning it along the lines of a tank, and the same might even be true of a motorcycle, which is surely the most unsafe thing on the highway. But who would buy it?

The second area in which negligence appears to predominate is that of warning of the dangers involved in use of the product,[58] and, where called for, directions for its use.[59] There is no dispute that the seller is under a duty to give adequate [60] warning of unrea-

54. See Katz, Liability of Automobile Manufacturers for Unsafe Design of Passenger Cars, (1956) 69 Harv.L.Rev. 863; Katz, Negligence in Design: A Current Look, [1965] Ins.L.J. 5; Nader and Page, Automobile Design and the Judicial Process, 1967, 55 Cal.L.Rev. 645; Notes, 1969, 21 S.C.L.Rev. 451; 1967, 52 Iowa L.Rev. 1213; 1967, 52 Corn.L.Q. 444; 1967, 80 Harv.L.Rev. 688; [1966] Utah L.Rev. 698; [1969] U.Ill.L.F. 396.

55. Evans v. General Motors Corp., 7 Cir. 1966, 359 F.2d 822, cert. denied 385 U.S. 836 (X frame instead of perimeter frame; collision from the side at high speed); Shumard v. General Motors Corp., S.D.Ohio 1967, 270 F.Supp. 311 (rear-end collision, location of gasoline tank); Willis v. Chrysler Corp., S.D.Tex. 1967, 264 F.Supp. 1010 (car splitting in two in head-on collision); Walton v. Chrysler Motor Corp., Miss.1970, 229 So.2d 568 (collapse of seat back); Friend v. General Motors Corp., 1968, 118 Ga.App. 763, 165 S.E.2d 734, cert. dismissed 225 Ga. 290, 167 S.E.2d 926.
See also Schemel v. General Motors Corp., 7 Cir. 1967, 384 F.2d 802, cert. denied 390 U.S. 945 (car without governor capable of speed of 115 miles an hour).

56. See infra, § 102.

57. Larsen v. General Motors Corp., 8 Cir. 1968, 391 F.2d 495 (plaintiff impaled on steering shaft); Mickle v. Blackmon, 1969, 252 S.C. 202, 166 S.E.2d 173 (knob on gearshift lever cracked, plaintiff impaled); Ford Motor Co. v. Zahn, 8 Cir. 1959, 265 F.2d 729 (plaintiff thrown against sharp edge of ashtray); Dyson v. General Motors Corp., E.D.Pa.1969, 298 F. Supp. 1064 (car overturned, roof not constructed to stand up); Grundmanis v. British Motor Corp., E. D.Wis.1970, 308 F.Supp. 303 (gas tank hit from rear); Storey v. Exhaust Specialties & Parts, Inc., 1970, —— Or. ——, 464 P.2d 831 (wheel collapsing under impact). Badorek v. General Motors Corp.,

1970, —— Cal.App.3d ——, 90 Cal.Rptr. 305 (gasoline tank ruptured by rear-end collision).
Compare, as to failure to provide seat belts, Mortenson v. Southern Pacific Co., 1966, 245 Cal.App.2d 241, 53 Cal.Rptr. 851; Greyhound Lines, Inc. v. Superior Court, 1970, 3 Cal.App.3d 356, 83 Cal.Rptr. 343. It appears quite probable that this would be applied to car manufacturers.

58. See, Generally, Dillard and Hart, Directions for Use and Duty to Warn, 1955, 41 Va.L.Rev. 145; Noel, Recent Trends in Manufacturers' Negligence as to Design, Instructions or Warnings, 1965, 19 Sw.L.J. 256; Noel, Products Defective Because of Inadequate Directions or Warnings, 1969, 23 Sw.L. J. 256; Notes, 1967 Wash.U.L.Q. 206; 1967, 52 Iowa L.Rev. 1213 (prescription drugs).

59. Directions for use do not in themselves constitute adequate warning of dangers, unless they are specifically pointed out. McCully v. Fuller Brush Co., 1966, 68 Wash.2d 675, 415 P.2d 7; McClanahan v. California Spray-Chemical Corp., 1953, 194 Va. 842, 75 S.E.2d 712; Bean v. Ross Mfg. Co., Mo.1961, 344 S.W.2d 18; Panther Oil & Grease Mfg. Co. v. Segerstrom, 9 Cir.1955, 224 F.2d 216; Miller v. International Harvester Co., 1920, 193 App.Div. 258, 184 N.Y.S. 91.

60. A warning may be inadequate if it is not sufficiently prominent on the label. Maize v. Atlantic Refining Co., 1945, 352 Pa. 51, 41 A.2d 850. Or if it is not sufficiently emphatic. Tampa Drug Co. v.

sonable dangers [61] involved in the use of which he knows,[62] or should know.[63] The duty extends not only to dangers arising from improper design or other negligence in manufacture, but also to dangers inseparable from a properly made product of the particular kind.[64] The warning must be sufficient to protect third persons who may reasonably be expected to come in contact with the product and be harmed by it;[65] and where it is not practical to reach all such people, the seller must do what is reasonable in the way of labels, literature to be distributed, or warnings to those who can be expected to pass them on.[66] The duty continues even after the sale, when the seller first discovers that the product is dangerous.[67]

This is not, however, to be narrowly applied; and a normal, foreseeable use may include such relatively uncommon ones as standing on a chair,[68] eating coffee,[69] test-

Wait, Fla.1958, 103 So.2d 603. Or if it is not calculated to reach those likely to use the product. Petzold v. Roux Laboratories, 1939, 256 App.Div. 1096, 11 N.Y.S.2d 565. Or if it is not intelligible to the ordinary user. Haberly v. Reardon Co., Mo.1958, 319 S.W.2d 859. Or if it does not cover the particular danger. Bean v. Ross Mfg. Co., Mo.1961, 344 S. W.2d 18 (full discussion). Or does not make it clear. McLaughlin v. Mine Safety Appliances Co., 1962, 11 N.Y.2d 62, 226 N.Y.S.2d 407, 181 N.E.2d 430.

61. There is no duty to warn of an unlikely danger which could be expected to lead to only slight injury. Jamieson v. Woodward & Lothrop, 1957, 101 U.S.App.D.C. 32, 247 F.2d 23, cert. denied 355 U.S. 855; Tingey v. E. F. Houghton & Co., 1947, 30 Cal. 2d 97, 179 P.2d 807; Braun v. Roux Dist. Co., Mo. 1958, 312 S.W.2d 758.

62. Boyl v. California Chem. Co., D.Or.1963, 221 F. Supp. 669 (weed killer containing long-lasting poison); Hubbard-Hall Chem. Co. v. Silverman, 1 Cir. 1965, 340 F.2d 402 (poisonous insecticide); High Voltage Eng. Corp. v. Pierce, 10 Cir. 1966, 359 F.2d 33 ("dark current" phenomenon in electron accelerator); Harp v. Montgomery Ward & Co., 9 Cir. 1964, 336 F.2d 255 (necessity of ground for electric clothes drier installed in bathroom); Rumsey v. Freeway Manor Minimax, Tex.Civ.App.1968, 423 S. W.2d 387 (no known antidote for roach poison).

63. Blitzstein v. Ford Motor Co., 5 Cir. 1961, 288 F. 2d 738; Imperial v. Central Concrete Co., 1957, 2 N.Y.2d 939, 162 N.Y.S.2d 35, 142 N.E.2d 209; Maize v. Atlantic Refining Co., 1945, 352 Pa. 51, 41 A.2d 850; Hopkins v. E. I. DuPont de Nemours & Co., 3 Cir. 1952, 199 F.2d 930; Thornhill v. Carpenter-Morton Co., 1915, 220 Mass. 593, 108 N.E. 474. The manufacturer is required to possess the knowledge of an expert, and to keep abreast of scientific discoveries relating to his type of product. Boyl v. California Chem. Co., D.Or.1963, 221 F.Supp. 669; Braun v. Roux Dist. Co., Mo.1958, 312 S.W.2d 758.

It is at least arguable that the liability is not for failure to warn of what defendant does not know, but for failure to find out. Oakes v. Geigy Agr. Chemicals, 1969, 272 Cal.App.2d 645, 77 Cal.Rptr. 709.

64. Martin v. Bengue, Inc., 1957, 25 N.J. 359, 136 A. 2d 626; Mealey v. Super Curline Hair Wave Corp., 1961, 342 Mass. 303, 173 N.E.2d 84; Tomao v. A. P. De Sanno & Son, 3 Cir.1954, 209 F.2d 544; Lovejoy

v. Minneapolis Moline Power Imp. Co., 1956, 248 Minn. 319, 79 N.W.2d 688; McClanahan v. California Spray-Chemical Corp., 1953, 194 Va. 842, 75 S. E.2d 712.

65. Spruill, Adm'r v. Boyle-Midway Inc., 4 Cir. 1962, 308 F.2d 79 (child drinking furniture polish); Gall v. Union Ice Co., 1952, 108 Cal.App.2d 303, 239 P.2d 48 (unlabeled drum of sulphuric acid); Rosenbusch v. Ambrosia Milk Corp., 1917, 181 App.Div. 97, 168 N.Y.S. 505. But not those who will not foreseeably be endangered. Scurfield v. Federal Laboratories, 1939, 335 Pa. 145, 6 A.2d 559; Harper v. Remington Arms Co., 1935, 156 Misc. 53, 280 N.Y.S. 862, affirmed 1936, 248 App.Div. 713, 290 N.Y.S. 130.

66. See McLaughlin v. Mine Safety Appliance Co., 1962, 11 N.Y.2d 62, 226 N.Y.S.2d 407, 181 N.E.2d 430; Walton v. Sherwin-Williams Co., 8 Cir. 1951, 191 F.2d 277; Johnston v. Upjohn Co., Mo.App.1969, 442 S.W.2d 93; Younger v. Dow Corning Corp., 1969, 202 Kan. 674, 451 P.2d 177; Brown v. General Motors Corp., 4 Cir. 1966, 355 F.2d 814, cert. denied, 1967, 386 U.S. 1036.

But a warning to one who cannot reasonably be relied on to pass it on may not be sufficient. Davis v. Wyeth Laboratories, 9 Cir. 1968, 399 F.2d 121; Montesano v. Patent Scaffolding Co., W.D.Pa.1962, 213 F.Supp. 141; Orr v. Shell Oil Co., 1943, 352 Mo. 288, 177 S.W.2d 608. And in Love v. Wolf, 1964, 226 Cal.App.2d 378, 38 Cal.Rptr. 183, a warning to the medical profession was held to be counteracted by overpromotion and puffing of the drug in question.

67. Comstock v. General Motors Corp., 1959, 358 Mich. 163, 99 N.W.2d 627; Nishida v. E. I. Du Pont de Nemours & Co., 5 Cir. 1957, 245 F.2d 768, cert. denied, 1958, 355 U.S. 915, 78 S.Ct. 342, 2 L. Ed.2d 275; Ward v. Morehead City Sea Food Co., 1916, 171 N.C. 33, 87 S.E. 958; Noel v. United Aircraft Corp., 3 Cir.1966, 359 F.2d 671.

68. Phillips v. Ogle Aluminum Furniture, Inc., 1951, 106 Cal.App.2d 650, 235 P.2d 857.

69. Maddox Coffee Co. v. Collins, 1932, 46 Ga.App. 220, 167 S.E. 306.

ing heating fixtures,[70] or wearing a cocktail robe in proximity to the kitchen stove.[71] The seller of pork usually has been held to be entitled to expect that it will be cooked to kill trichinae;[72] but where the question has arisen, it has been held that there is a normal use where the pork is cooked to an extent which the buyer erroneously believes to be sufficient.[73]

In the ordinary case the seller may also assume a normal user of the product; and he is not liable where the injury is due to some susceptibility or idiosyncrasy which is peculiar to the plaintiff.[74]

A large number of cases have involved the problem of warning to users of the product who are, or may be, allergic to it.[75] Here the problem is complicated by the fact that most

of those who are subject to the common allergies, as for example toward milk proteins or citrus fruits, are fully aware of their susceptibility, and quite able to protect themselves against it; and the risk of what is likely to be at most a trivial injury is not sufficiently serious to require even a warning to such purchasers. The situation may be quite different where there is an allergy, more serious in character, to some chemical of which the ordinary man in the street has never heard. The question becomes the familiar one of balancing the probability and gravity of the harm against the value of the product and the inconvenience of precautions. Where the allergy is so extremely rare as to amount to almost a personal idiosyncrasy,[76] or where it is a very infrequent one, found in only an insignificant percentage of the population, and the threatened harm is not very serious, the tendency has been to hold that the seller need not give warning.[77] But if it is one common to any substantial, even though relatively small, number of possible users, and the consequences are more serious, the courts have tended to require the warning, and without it to find negligence.[78]

70. Nathan v. Electriglass Corp., 1955, 37 N.J.Super. 494, 117 A.2d 620.

71. Ringstad v. I. Magnin & Co., 1952, 39 Wash.2d 923, 239 P.2d 848. Cf. Chapman v. Brown, D.Hawaii 1961, 198 F.Supp. 78, affirmed in Brown v. Chapman, 9 Cir. 1962, 304 F.2d 149 (hula skirt coming in contact with lighted cigarette); Martin v. Bengue, Inc., 1957, 25 N.J. 359, 136 A.2d 626 (lighting cigarette after use of ointment with inflammable vapor).

72. Adams v. Scheib, 1962, 408 Pa. 452, 184 A.2d 700; Cheli v. Cudahy Bros. Co., 1934, 267 Mich. 690, 255 N.W. 414; Vaccarino v. Cozzubo, 1943, 181 Md. 614, 31 A.2d 316; Silverman v. Swift & Co., 1954, 141 Conn. 450, 107 A.2d 277; Eisenbach v. Gimbel Bros., 1939, 281 N.Y. 474, 24 N.E.2d 131.

73. McSpedon v. Kunz, 1936, 271 N.Y. 131, 2 N.E.2d 513; Holt v. Mann, 1926, 294 Mass. 21, 200 N.E. 403. See Notes, 1941, 16 Temp.L.Q. 80; 1943, 8 Md.L.Rev. 61.

74. Jacquot v. Wm. Filene's Sons Co., 1958, 337 Mass. 312, 149 N.E.2d 635; Cleary v. John M. Maris Co., 1940, 173 Misc. 954, 19 N.Y.S.2d 5; Briggs v. National Industries, 1949, 92 Cal.App.2d 542, 207 P. 2d 110 (regarded by the court as unique); Ross v. Porteous, Mitchell & Braun Co., 1939, 136 Me. 118, 3 A.2d 650; Barrett v. S. S. Kresge Co., 1941, 144 Pa.Super. 516, 19 A.2d 502; Stanton v. Sears, Roebuck & Co., 1942, 312 Ill.App. 496, 38 N.E.2d 801.

75. See Noel, The Duty to Warn Allergic Users of Products, 1959, 12 Vand.L.Rev. 331; Freedman, Allergy and Products Liability Today, 1963, 24 Ohio St.L.J. 431; Freedman, A Hatband and a Tube of Lipstick, 1966, 43 U.Det.L.Rev. 355; Whitmore, Allergies and Other Reactions Due to Drugs and Cosmetics, 1965, 19 Sw.L.J. 76; Barasch, Allergies and the Law, 1941, 10 Brook.L.Rev. 363; Notes, 1965, 37 U.Colo.L.Rev. 305; 1961, 46 Corn.L.Q. 465; 1952, 5 Bayl.L.Rev. 97; 1950, 49 Mich.L.Rev. 253.

76. Kaempfe v. Lehn & Fink Products Corp., 1964, 21 App.Div.2d 197, 249 N.Y.S.2d 840; Howard v. Avon Products, Inc., 1964, 155 Colo. 444, 395 P.2d 1007; Gran v. Procter & Gamble Co., 5 Cir. 1963, 324 F.2d 309.

77. Bonowski v. Revlon, Inc., 1959, 251 Iowa 141, 100 N.W.2d 5 (1 in 5 million); Bennett v. Pilot Products Co., 1951, 120 Utah 474, 235 P.2d 525 (1 in 1,000); Casagrande v. F. W. Woolworth Co., 1960, 340 Mass. 552, 165 N.E.2d 109 (1 in 2,000); Walstrom Optical Co. v. Miller, Tex.Civ.App.1933, 59 S.W.2d 895 ("most unusual"); Merrill v. Beaute Vues Corp., 10 Cir. 1956, 235 F.2d 893 (500,000,000 products sold with "only rare" ill effects).

78. Zirpola v. Adam Hat Stores, 1939, 122 N.J.L. 21, 4 A.2d 73 (4 to 5 per cent); Bianchi v. Denholm & McKay Co., 1939, 302 Mass. 469, 19 N.E.2d 697 (un-

It would, however, be an oversimplification to reduce all this merely to the percentage of those who might be affected, and to ignore the seriousness of the harm to be expected, and the expert knowledge which the defendant has or should have of the dangers. Quite rare side effects of drugs and the like have been included within the duty to warn; [79] and the most extreme case of all required a warning as to the possible dangers of oral vaccine for poliomyelitis, where the evidence was that the risk was only to one person in a million.[80] The allergy cases have tended to reject any exclusively quantitative standard, and to look instead to the overall danger.[81]

Obvious Dangers

One limitation commonly placed upon the duty to warn, or for that matter the seller's entire liability, is that he is not liable for dangers that are known to the user,[82] or are obvious to him,[83] or are so commonly known that it can reasonably be assumed that the user will be familiar with them.[84] Thus there is certainly no usual duty to warn the purchaser that a knife or an axe will cut, a match will take fire, dynamite will explode, or a hammer may mash a finger.[85] There is a close analogy here to the rule that the possessor of land is not liable to an invitee for similar dangers.[86]

But, as in the cases of the condition of land, there are exceptional situations, where, for example, the danger is observable only upon a close inspection which the user is not likely to make,[87] or the danger is one not likely to be appreciated,[88] or to be regarded as trivial,

specified class); Taylor v. Newcomb Baking Co., 1945, 317 Mass. 609, 59 N.E.2d 293 ("quite a percentage of people"); Braun v. Roux Distributing Co., Mo.1958, 312 S.W.2d 758 (3 to 4 per cent); Crotty v. Shartenberg's-New Haven, Inc., 1960, 147 Conn. 460, 162 A.2d 513 ("an appreciable number of people, though fewer in number than the number of normal buyers").

79. Sterling Drug Co. v. Yarrow, 8 Cir. 1969, 408 F. 2d 978; Sterling Drug, Inc. v. Cornish, 8 Cir. 1966, 370 F.2d 82.

80. Davis v. Wyeth Laboratories, Inc., 9 Cir. 1968, 399 F.2d 121.

81. Wright v. Carter Products, 2 Cir. 1957, 244 F.2d 53, is an especially good opinion rejecting the exclusively quantitative standard. See also Hungerholt v. Land O'Lakes Creameries, D.Minn.1962, 209 F. Supp. 177, finding a duty to warn users of the product of a risk of allergy, known to the defendant, no matter how small the group may be. See also Braun v. Roux Distributing Co., Mo.1958, 312 S.W.2d 758; Arnold v. May Department Stores Co., 1935, 337 Mo. 727, 85 S.W.2d 748 (notice of susceptibility of particular plaintiff).

82. Stevens v. Durbin-Durco, Inc., Mo.1964, 377 S.W. 2d 343; Parker v. Heasler Plumbing & Heating Co., Wyo.1964, 388 P.2d 516; Ford Motor Co. v. Atcher, Ky.1957, 310 S.W.2d 510; Stout v. Madden, 1956, 208 Or. 294, 300 P.2d 461; Hickert v. Wright, 1957, 182 Kan. 100, 319 P.2d 152.

83. Jamieson v. Woodward & Lothrop, 1957, 101 U. S.App.D.C. 32, 247 F.2d 23, cert. denied 355 U.S. 855 (exerciser rope slipped off of foot); Kientz v. Carlton, 1957, 245 N.C. 236, 96 S.E.2d 14 (obvious lack of safety features in power mower); Murphy v. Cory Pump & Supply Co., 1964, 47 Ill.App.2d 382, 197 N.E.2d 849 (same); Harrist v. Spencer-Harris Tool Co., 1962, 244 Miss. 84, 140 So.2d 558 (defect in oil rig); Morris v. Toy Box, 1962, 204 Cal.App.2d 468, 22 Cal.Rptr. 572.

One case much criticized in this connection is Campo v. Scofield, 1950, 301 N.Y. 468, 95 N.E.2d 802, where the defendant sold an onion-topping machine without a guard. Cf. Yaun v. Allis-Chalmers Mfg. Co., 1948, 253 Wis. 558, 34 N.W.2d 853. In each case there was clear foreseeability that the employee using the machine might momentarily forget the absence of the guard.

84. Gibson v. Torbert, 1901, 115 Iowa 163, 88 N.W. 443 (inflammable nature of phosphorus); Dempsey v. Virginia Dare Stores, 1945, 239 Mo.App. 355, 186 S.W.2d 217 (same as to fuzzy lounging robe); Sawyer v. Pine Oil Sales Co., 5 Cir. 1946, 155 F.2d 855 (splashing cleaning fluid into eye); Katz v. Arundel-Brooks Concrete Co., 1959, 220 Md. 200, 151 A.2d 731 (bringing hands in contact with ready-mix concrete); Simmons v. Rhodes & Jamieson, 1956, 46 Cal.2d 190, 293 P.2d 26 (same).

85. See Jamieson v. Woodward & Lothrop, 1957, 101 U.S.App.D.C. 32, 247 F.2d 23, cert. denied 355 U.S. 855; Dempsey v. Virginia Dare Stores, 1945, 239 Mo.App. 355, 186 S.W.2d 217.

86. See supra, p. 394.

87. Calkins v. Sandven, 1964, 256 Iowa 682, 129 N. W.2d 1.

88. Hopkins v. E. I. DuPont de Nemours & Co., 3 Cir. 1952, 199 F.2d 930 (dynamite inserted in warm

in which it has been held that its obvious character does not absolve the seller of the obligation to give proper warning.

97. WARRANTY

With the liability of the seller of chattels to the ultimate consumer once established on the basis of negligence, it was to be expected that some attempt would be made to carry his responsibility even further, and to find some ground for strict liability which would make him in effect an insurer of the safety of the product, even though he had exercised all reasonable care. Beginning about 1905, as a part of a prolonged and violent national agitation over the marketing of defective food,[89] this movement made slow but comparatively steady headway in the one limited area of food and drink, until shortly before 1960, when new decisions extended it to other fields, and gave it a sudden and almost explosive impetus. It met with the approval of the great majority of the legal writers who discussed it.[90] Its advocates pointed

primarily to the difficulty which the plaintiff sometimes encounters in proving negligence,[91] together with the fact that in most sales by wholesale and retail dealers there is simply no negligence to prove.[92] Various arguments have been advanced, such as the supposed incentive which strict liability would provide toward the highest care and safety,[93] the fact that it has become the practice of reputable manufacturers and merchants to stand behind their goods as sound business policy,[94] and the contention that the burden of accidental injuries caused by defective chattels should be placed upon the seller because he is best able to distribute the more or less inevitable losses to the general public by means of liability insurance, treated as a part of his costs, and included in his prices.[95] These arguments were but little reflected in the decisions. Those which have proved convincing to the courts which have accepted the strict liability can be condensed to three:[96]

Freedman, The Three-Pronged Sword of Damocles, Defense Research Institute, 1961.

91. See Llewellyn, Cases on Sales, 1930, 341; Ashe, So You're Going to Try a Products Liability Case, 1961, 13 Hast.L.J. 66.

92. See supra, p. 633.

93. A skeptic may well question whether the callous manufacturer, unmoved by the prospect of negligence liability plus harm to the reputation of his goods, will really be stimulated to any additional precautions by the relatively slight increase in liability. See Plant, Strict Liability of Manufacturers for Injuries Caused by Defects in Products—An Opposing View, 1957, 24 Tenn.L.Rev. 938, 945.

94. See Bogert and Fink, Business Practice Regarding Warranties in the Sale of Goods, 1930, 25 Ill.L. Rev. 400. Undoubtedly the practice exists, on a large scale; but it is limited, on the part of almost all sellers, to replacement, repair, or return of the purchase price to make good the original bargain; and it does not extend to compensation for injuries to the person of the buyer, or his other property.

95. See Patterson, The Apportionment of Business Risks Through Legal Devices, 1924, 24 Col.L.Rev. 335, 337; Notes, 1933, 33 Col.L.Rev. 868; 1935, 23 Cal.L.Rev. 77. Well stated in the concurring opinion of Traynor, J., in Escola v. Coca Cola Bottling Co., 1944, 24 Cal.2d 453, 150 P.2d 436.

96. Perhaps the best over-all statement is in Jacob E. Decker & Sons v. Capps, 1942, 139 Tex. 609, **164**

hole); Haberly v. Reardon Co., Mo.1968, 319 S.W.2d 859 (paint into eye of child); Spruill v. Boyle-Midway, Inc., 4 Cir. 1962, 308 F.2d 79 (child swallowing floor wax); Hardy v. Proctor (sic) & Gamble Mfg. Co., 5 Cir. 1954, 209 F.2d 124 (detergent into eye); La Plant v. E. I. du Pont de Nemours & Co., Mo. App.1961, 346 S.W.2d 231 (dangerous consequences of weed killer). See Notes, 1960, 38 Tex.L.Rev. 342, 1960, 28 Ford.L.Rev. 776.

89. Narrated in Regier, The Struggle for Federal Food and Drugs Legislation, 1933, 1 Law & Con. Prob. 3.

90. Jeanblanc, Manufacturers' Liability to Persons Other than Their Immediate Vendees, 1937, 24 Va. L.Rev. 134; Feezer, Manufacturer's Liability for Injuries Caused by his Product, 1938, 37 Mich.L. Rev. 1; Spruill, Privity of Contract as a Requisite for Recovery on a Warranty, 1941, 19 N.C.L.Rev. 551; James, Products Liability, 1955, 34 Tex.L.Rev. 192; Wilson, Products Liability, 1955, 43 Cal.L.Rev. 614, 809; Noel, Manufacturers of Products—The Drift Toward Strict Liability, 1957, 24 Tenn.L.Rev. 963; Prosser, The Assault Upon the Citadel, 1960, 69 Yale L.J. 1099.

Opposed were Peairs, The God in the Machine, 1949, 29 Bos.U.L.Rev. 37; Plant, Strict Liability of Manufacturers for Injuries Caused by Defects in Products—An Opposing View, 1957, 24 Tenn.L.Rev. 938;

1.   The public interest in human life and safety demands the maximum possible protection that the law can give against dangerous defects in products which consumers must buy, and against which they are helpless to protect themselves; and it justifies the imposition, upon all suppliers of such products, of full responsibility for the harm they cause, even though the supplier has done his best.   This argument, which in the last analysis rests upon public sentiment, has had its greatest force in the cases of food, where there was once popular outcry against an evil industry, injuries and actions have multiplied, and public feeling is most obvious.   It is now advanced as to other products, such as automobiles.

2.   The maker, by placing the goods upon the market, represents to the public that they are suitable and safe for use; and by packaging, advertising or otherwise, he does everything that he can to induce that belief. He intends and expects that the product will be purchased and used in reliance upon this assurance of safety; and it is in fact so purchased and used.   The middleman is no more than a conduit, a mere mechanical device, through whom the thing sold is to reach the ultimate user.   The supplier has invited and solicited the use; and when it leads to disaster, he should not be permitted to avoid the responsibility by saying that he has made no contract with the consumer.

3.   It is already possible to enforce strict liability by resort to a series of actions, in which the retailer is first held liable on a warranty to his purchaser, and indemnity on a warranty is then sought successively from other suppliers, until the manufacturer finally pays the damages, with the added costs of repeated litigation.[97]   This is an expensive,

time-consuming, and wasteful process, and it may be interrupted by insolvency, lack of jurisdiction, disclaimers, or the statute of limitations, anywhere along the line.[98]   What is called for is a direct action which will afford a short cut.

Express Representations

Although it was not the earliest to be recognized, the simplest form of strict liability to the consumer rests upon express representations made to him about the product.   This originated in Baxter v. Ford Motor Co.[99] in 1932, when the Washington court held that a statement, in literature distributed by the manufacturer of an automobile, that the glass in its windshield was "shatterproof" made it liable, without knowledge of falsity or negligence, to one who bought the car from a dealer, and was injured when a pebble struck the glass and shattered it.   The theory first adopted was that of an express warranty to the plaintiff; but on a second appeal[1] the court shifted its ground to one of strict liability, in the nature of deceit, for innocent misrepresentation.

The case was followed elsewhere, and is now generally accepted law.[2]   The courts, in

---

er ultimately paid the consumer's damages, plus a much larger sum covering the heavy costs of the entire litigation.   A similar case is Sheftman v. Balfour Housing Corp., 1962, 37 Misc.2d 468, 234 N. Y.S.2d 791.

98.   To some extent the difficulty could be avoided in many jurisdictions by joining a warranty count against the retailer with one in negligence against the manufacturer.   See for example Burkhardt v. Armour & Co., 1932, 115 Conn. 249, 161 A. 385, 90 A.L.R. 1260; Harward v. General Motors Corp., E. D.N.C.1950, 89 F.Supp. 170; Dobrenski v. Blatz Brewing Co., W.D.Mich.1941, 41 F.Supp. 291.

99.   1932, 168 Wash. 456, 12 P.2d 409, affirmed on rehearing 15 P.2d 1118.

1.   Baxter v. Ford Motor Co., 1934, 179 Wash. 123, 35 P.2d 1090.

2.   See Noel, Manufacturers of Products—The Drift Toward Strict Liability, 1957, 24 Tenn.L.Rev. 963, 999–1009; Notes, 1932, 46 Harv.L.Rev. 161; 1932, 81 U.Pa.L.Rev. 94; 1933, 18 Corn.L.Q. 445; 1937, 22 Wash.U.L.Q. 406; 1958, 19 Ohio St.L.J. 733; 1958,

---

S.W.2d 828.   See also Henningsen v. Bloomfield Motors, 1960, 32 N.J. 358, 161 A.2d 69.

97.   See for example Tri-City Fur Foods v. Ammerman, 1959, 7 Wis.2d 149, 96 N.W.2d 495.   In this connection, there is frequent mention of Kasler & Cohen v. Slavouski, [1928] 1 K.B. 78, where there was a series of five recoveries, and the manufactur-

general, have agreed with the first opinion, and have talked of express warranty; but occasionally, when obstacles have arisen in the way of existing warranty rules, they have reverted to the theory of misrepresentation.[3] There is strict liability for statements that prove to be false when they are made to the public in labels on the goods themselves,[4] or in the seller's advertising,[5] or his disseminated literature.[6] After the Baxter Case, decisions to the contrary have been amazingly few;[7] and this branch of the strict liability appears by now to be firmly established.

Its limitations are also fairly clear. There must be something which is reasonably understood to be a positive assertion of fact, which covers the injurious defect in the goods sold.[8] The assertion must be made by the defendant, or chargeable against him,[9] and it must be addressed to the public,[10] or at least be intended to be passed on to the particular plaintiff,[11] and he can recover only if he does in fact learn of it, and is injured as a result of his reliance upon it.[12] The Washington court, which started the whole development, has held that the principle does not apply to pecuniary loss, as distinguished from tangible damage to person or proper-

11 Vand.L.Rev. 1459; 1958, 58 Col.L.Rev. 1092; 1966, 18 Syr.L.Rev. 127.

3. Thus Ford Motor Co. v. Lonon, 1966, 217 Tenn. 400, 398 S.W.2d 240, where the court did not wish to overrule Kyker v. General Motors Corp., 1964, 214 Tenn. 521, 381 S.W.2d 884. Also Cooper v. R. J. Reynolds Tobacco Co., 1 Cir. 1956, 234 F.2d 170.

The innocent misrepresentation ground was adopted by the Second Restatement of Torts, 402B, where the draftsmen found themselves involved with the complexity of warranty rules under the Uniform Sales Act and the Uniform Commercial Code.

4. Maecherlein v. Sealy Mattress Co., 1956, 145 Cal. App.2d 275, 302 P.2d 331 (mattress; plaintiff stabbed by a spring in her "gluteal prominence"); Worley v. Procter & Gamble Mfg. Co., 1952, 241 Mo.App. 1114, 253 S.W.2d 532 (washing powder); Bonker v. Ingersoll Products Co., D.Mass.1955, 132 F.Supp. 5 ("boneless chicken"); Wise v. Hayes, 1961, 58 Wash.2d 106, 361 P.2d 171 (insecticide); Hoskins v. Jackson Grain Co., Fla.1953, 63 So.2d 514 (watermelon seed).

5. Hamon v. Digliani, 1961, 148 Conn. 710, 174 A.2d 294 (household cleaner); Pritchard v. Liggett & Myers Tobacco Co., 3 Cir. 1961, 295 F.2d 292 (cigarettes); Hansen v. Firestone Tire & Rubber Co., 6 Cir. 1960, 276 F.2d 254 (tubeless tires); Lane v. C. A. Swanson & Sons, 1955, 130 Cal.App.2d 210, 278 P.2d 723 ("boned chicken"); Rogers v. Toni Home Permanent Co., 1958, 167 Ohio St. 244, 147 N.E.2d 612 (home permanent wave solution).

6. Bahlman v. Hudson Motor Car Co., 1939, 290 Mich. 683, 288 N.W. 309 (safety of steel top of automobile); Studebaker Corp. v. Nail, 1950, 82 Ga.App. 779, 62 S.E.2d 198 ("service policy" on automobile); Beck v. Spindler, 1959, 256 Minn. 543, 99 N.W.2d 670 (same); Mannsz v. Macwhyte Co., 3 Cir. 1946, 155 F.2d 445 (wire rope, manufacturer's manuel); Hansen v. Firestone Tire & Rubber Co., 6 Cir. 1960, 276 F.2d 254 (tire).

7. The only two found, almost certainly overruled, are Chanin v. Chevrolet Motor Co., 7 Cir. 1937, 89 F.2d

889, 1235, and Rachlin v. Libby-Owens-Ford Glass Co., 2 Cir. 1938, 96 F.2d 597, both rejecting the Baxter Case on similar facts.

8. Thus "pure and nutritious" was held not to cover a nail in a loaf of bread in Newhall v. Ward Baking Co., 1922, 240 Mass. 434, 134 N.E. 625; and in Murphy v. Plymouth Motor Corp., 1940, 3 Wash.2d 180, 100 P.2d 30, pictures of an automobile being turned over at sixty miles an hour, and of a freight car resting on top of it, as well as descriptions of safety glass, were held to state nothing that was actually false. Cf. Alpine v. Friend Bros., 1923, 244 Mass. 164, 138 N.E. 553; Lambert v. Sistrunk, Fla. 1952, 58 So.2d 434.

9. Thus the wholesaler was held not to have adopted the maker's warranty in Cochran v. McDonald, 1945, 23 Wash.2d 348, 161 P.2d 305.

10. Express warranties to individuals were held not to extend to third persons, in Senter v. B. F. Goodrich Co., D.Colo.1954, 127 F.Supp. 705; Silverman v. Samuel Mallinger Co., 1953, 375 Pa. 422, 100 A.2d 715; Barni v. Kutner, 1950, 6 Terry 550, 76 A.2d 801; Hermanson v. Hermanson, 1954, 19 Conn.Sup. 479, 117 A.2d 840. In all these cases, however, the plaintiff never knew of the representation, and did not rely on it.

11. Cf. Jeffery v. Hanson, 1952, 39 Wash.2d 855, 239 P.2d 346; Lindroth v. Walgreen Co., 1946, 329 Ill. App. 105, 67 N.E.2d 595. In Hayman v. Shoemake, 1962, 203 Cal.App.2d 140, 21 Cal.Rptr. 519, personal statements by defendant's salesman to the plaintiff were held to be enough.

12. Randall v. Goodrich-Gamble Co., 1952, 238 Minn. 10, 54 N.W.2d 769; Dobbin v. Pacific Coast Coal Co., 1946, 25 Wash.2d 190, 170 P.2d 642. In Connolly v. Hagi, 1963, 24 Conn.Sup. 198, 188 A.2d 884, a garage repairman was held entitled to rely upon advertising concerning the safety and fitness of an automobile, addressed to the general public.

ty;[13] but a late decision in New York has not agreed.[14]

The limitations upon the liability appear also to be fairly clear. There must be a misrepresentation of fact, and not mere "puffing" or sales talk.[15] But broad general assertions of quality, and particularly those of safety, as for example that a power tool is "rugged,"[16] that a detergent is "kind to the hands,"[17] or that cigarettes are "harmless" or "safe to smoke,"[18] may readily be found by the jury to include a representation that there is nothing to make the product unsafe. The representation must be made by the defendant, or fairly chargeable against him.[19] It must be made with the intention, or at least the expectation, that it will reach the plaintiff,[20] or a class of persons which includes him; and where there is no such intention or expectation the general rule [21] that liability for misrepresentation does not extend to unexpected third parties applies to bar the recovery.[22] Finally, the plaintiff must rely upon the representation,[23] not necessarily in making his purchase,[24] but at least in using the product.

Food and Drink

The recognition of an "implied" strict liability preceded the "express warranty" by some twenty years. As has been said, the first cases dealt with the sellers of bad food, who had always been subject to a special, but quite undefined, responsibility at common law.[25] The first case, on the heels of a prolonged agitation over food and drink, which discarded the requirement of a contract was Mazetti v. Armour & Co.,[26] in Washington in 1913. It was followed, rapidly and then slowly, over almost half a century, by other courts which found the strict liability as to defective food and drink, until by 1960 the majority of the American courts had made it an established rule. The movement ran considerably ahead of any legal justification to support it.

13. Dimoff v. Ernie Majer, Inc., 1960, 55 Wash.2d 385, 347 P.2d 1056.

14. Randy Knitware, Inc. v. American Cyanamid Co., 1962, 11 N.Y.2d 5, 226 N.Y.S.2d 363, 181 N.E.2d 399.

15. See Lambert v. Sistrunk, Fla.1952, 58 So.2d 434; Topeka Mill & Elev. Co. v. Triplett, 1950, 168 Kan. 428, 213 P.2d 964; Brown v. Globe Labs, Inc., 1957, 165 Neb. 138, 84 N.W.2d 151; Ralston Purina Mills v. Iiams, 1943, 143 Neb. 588, 10 N.W.2d 452; Maupin v. Nutrena Mills, Okl.1963, 385 P.2d 504.

16. Greenman v. Yuba Power Products, Inc., 1963, 59 Cal.2d 57, 27 Cal.Rptr. 697, 377 P.2d 897.

17. Worley v. Procter & Gamble Mfg. Co., 1952, 241 Mo.App. 1114, 253 S.W.2d 532.

18. Pritchard v. Liggett & Myers Tobacco Co., 3 Cir. 1961, 295 F.2d 292. Cf. Hansen v. Firestone Tire & Rubber Co., 6 Cir. 1960, 276 F.2d 254 (tires "safe" within stated limits); Arfons v. E. I. DuPont De Nemours & Co., 2 Cir. 1958, 261 F.2d 434 (dynamite "safe" for the purpose); Hamon v. Digliani, 1961, 148 Conn. 710, 174 A.2d 294 (detergent "safe for household tasks"); Rogers v. Toni Home Permanent Co., 1958, 167 Ohio St. 244, 147 N.E.2d 612 (permanent wave solution "safe and harmless.")

19. Thus the wholesaler was held not to have adopted the maker's warranty in Cochran v. McDonald, 1945, 23 Wash.2d 348, 161 P.2d 305. But in Scovil v. Chilcoat, Okl.1967, 424 P.2d 87, a dealer's statement that the car was "guaranteed" was held to be sufficient to charge him.

20. Cf. Jeffery v. Hanson, 1952, 39 Wash.2d 855, 239 P.2d 346; Lindroth v. Walgreen Co., 1946, 329 Ill. App. 105, 67 N.E.2d 595; Odell v. Frueh, 1956, 146 Cal.App.2d 504, 304 P.2d 45.

21. See infra, p. 704.

22. Collum v. Pope & Talbot, Inc., 1955, 135 Cal. App.2d 653, 288 P.2d 75; Hermanson v. Hermanson, 1954, 19 Conn.Sup. 479, 117 A.2d 840; Barni v. Kutner, 1950, 6 Terry (46 Del.) 550, 76 A.2d 801; Silverman v. Samuel Mallinger Co., 1953, 375 Pa. 422, 100 A.2d 715; Senter v. B. F. Goodrich Co., D.Colo. 1954, 127 F.Supp. 705.

23. Torpey v. Red Owl Stores, 8 Cir. 1955, 228 F.2d 117; Sears, Roebuck & Co. v. Marhenke, 9 Cir. 1941, 121 F.2d 598; Randall v. Goodrich Gamble Co., 1952, 238 Minn. 10, 54 N.W.2d 769; Kepling v. Schlueter Mfg. Co., 6 Cir. 1967, 378 F.2d 5; Dobbin v. Pacific Coast Coal Co., 1946, 25 Wash.2d 190, 170 P.2d 642.

24. Thus in Connolly v. Hagi, 1963, 24 Conn.Sup. 198, 188 A.2d 884, the plaintiff was not a purchaser at all, but a filling station attendant doing work on an automobile.

25. See Dickerson, Products Liability and the Food Consumer, 1951, 26; Melick, The Sale of Food and Drink, 1936, 10; Perkins, Unwholesome Food as a Source of Liability, 1919, 5 Iowa L.Bull. 6, 8–9.

26. 1913, 75 Wash. 622, 135 P. 633.

For a time there was resort to various highly ingenious and patently fictitious devices, such as a postulated agency of the dealer to sell for the manufacturer, or to buy for the consumer, or a third-party beneficiary contract for the benefit of the latter.[27] In 1927 the Mississippi court[28] came up with the device of a warranty running from the manufacturer to the consumer, by analogy to a covenant running with the land; and from then until 1963 all of the decisions imposing the strict liability without privity of contract talked the language of warranty.[29]

This was encouraged by the history of warranty, which in its origin was a tort, and which has never entirely lost its tort character,[30] and the argument that if warranty is a tort, there should be no necessity that it rest upon a contract between the parties. It soon became agreed, however, that the warranty to the consumer was not the one made on the original sale to the dealer, and did not run with the goods, but was a new and independent one made directly to the consumer;[31] and that it did not arise out of or depend upon any contract, but was imposed by law in tort, as a matter of policy.[32]

Beyond Food

The extension of the implied warranty beyond food and drink for human consumption began with animal food,[33] and what might be called products for intimate bodily use, such as cosmetics.[34] The real break to other products came in 1958, with Spence v. Three Rivers Builders & Masonry Supply, Inc.,[35] where the Michigan court found a warranty, without privity and without negligence, of cinder building blocks when the user's home collapsed. The decision was followed in half a dozen other jurisdictions, until in 1960 there came, in New Jersey, what is now commonly regarded as the leading case, Henningsen v. Bloomfield Motors, Inc.[36] It held both the manufacturer of an automobile and the dealer who sold it to the wife of the purchaser who was driving the car, on an implied warranty of safety carried over from the food cases.

What followed was the most rapid and altogether spectacular overturn of an established rule in the entire history of the law of torts.

27. See Gillam, Products Liability in a Nutshell, 1958, 37 Or.L.Rev. 119, 152–55, collecting no less than twenty-nine methods by which the court accomplished the result.

28. In Coca-Cola Bottling Works v. Lyons, 1927, 145 Miss. 876, 111 So. 305.

29. The development is narrated in Prosser, The Assault Upon the Citadel, 1960, 69 Yale L.J. 1099. See also James, Products Liability, 1955, 34 Tex.L. Rev. 192; Wilson, Products Liability, 1955, 43 Cal. L.Rev. 614, 809; Noel, Manufacturers of Products—The Drift Toward Strict Liability, 1957, 24 Tenn. L.Rev. 963; Roberts, Implied Warranties—The Privity Rule and Strict Liability, 1962, 27 Mo.L. Rev. 194; Jaeger, Privity of Warranty: Has the Tocsin Sounded? 1963, 1 Duq.L.Rev. 1.

30. See supra, p. 635.

31. Madouros v. Kansas City Coca-Cola Bottling Co., 1936, 230 Mo.App. 275, 90 S.W.2d 445; Markovich v. McKesson & Robbins, Inc., 1958, 106 Ohio App. 265, 149 N.E.2d 181; Le Blanc v. Louisiana Coca Cola Bottling Co., 1952, 221 La. 919, 60 So.2d 873; B. F. Goodrich Co. v. Hammond, 10 Cir. 1959, 269 F.2d 501; See Worley v. Procter & Gamble Mfg. Co., 1952, 241 Mo.App. 1114, 253 S.W.2d 532.

32. Jacob E. Decker & Sons, Inc. v. Capps, 1942, 139 Tex. 609, 164 S.W.2d 828; La Hue v. Coca-Cola Bottling, Inc., 1957, 50 Wash.2d 645, 314 P.2d 421; Graham v. Bottenfield's, Inc., 1954, 176 Kan. 68, 269 P.2d 413; Crystal Coca-Cola Bottling Co. v. Cathey, 1957, 83 Ariz. 163, 317 P.2d 1094; Patargias v. Coca-Cola Bottling Co., 1947, 74 N.E.2d 1094.

33. McAfee v. Cargill, Inc., S.D.Cal.1954, 121 F.Supp. 5; Midwest Game Co. v. M.F.A. Milling Co., Mo. 1059, 320 S.W.2d 547.

34. Graham v. Bottenfield's Inc., 1954, 176 Kan. 68, 269 P.2d 413 (hair dye); Rogers v. Toni Home Permanent Co., 1958, 167 Ohio St. 244, 147 N.E.2d 612 (permanent wave solution); Worley v. Procter & Gamble Mfg. Co., 1952, 241 Mo.App. 1114, 253 S.W. 2d 532.

35. 1958, 353 Mich. 120, 90 N.W.2d 873. This was, appropriately enough from the point of view of the defendants, an opinion of Justice Voelker, author of the popular best seller, Anatomy of a Murder, which became a motion picture.

36. 1960, 32 N.J. 358, 161 A.2d 69. The development is narrated in Prosser, The Fall of the Citadel, 1966, 50 Minn.L.Rev. 791.

There was a deluge of cases in other jurisdictions following the lead of New Jersey, and finding an implied warranty of safety as to a wide assortment of products.[37] So rapid and complete has been the overthrow, that at the time of publication of this edition there are only eight states that still insist upon privity of contract for the strict liability. They are Georgia, Idaho, Maine, Maryland, Massachusetts, New Mexico, Utah, and West Virginia.[38] In several of these jurisdictions the last decisions are old ones, not overruled, which appear likely to topple when the question arises. It is quite clear that the "citadel of privity" has fallen.

The earlier cases in this avalanche proceeded on the basis of an "implied warranty" made directly to the user or consumer. Even in the food cases, however, it had already become apparent that "warranty" was attended by numerous difficulties. The term had become so closely identified with contract in the minds of most courts and lawyers that contract rules were assumed necessarily to apply to it; and this presented a serious problem where there was no contract. Traditionally "warranty" required that the plaintiff

should act in reliance upon some express or implied representation or assurance, or some promise or undertaking, on the part of the defendant; and this was sometimes impossible to make out, as where, for example, the consumer did not even know the name of the maker. Warranties on the sale of goods were governed in most states by the Uniform Sales Act, and then by its successor, the Uniform Commercial Code; and neither of these statutes had been drawn with anything in mind but a contract between a "seller" and his immediate "buyer."[39]

Two problems in particular gave considerable trouble. Both the Sales Act and the Commercial Code contain provisions which prevent the buyer from recovering on a warranty unless he gives notice to the seller within a reasonable time after he knows or should know of the breach.[40] As between the immediate parties to the sale, this is a sound commercial rule, designed to protect the seller against unduly delayed claims for damages. As applied to personal injuries, and notice to a remote seller, it becomes a booby-trap for the unwary. The injured consumer is seldom "steeped in the business practice which justifies the rule,"[41] and at least until he has legal advice it will not occur to him to give notice to one with whom he has had no dealings. In order to circumvent the statute, the courts were forced to resort to rather transparent devices, holding that a long delay is "reasonable,"[42] or that the provision was not

---

37. Picker X-Ray Corp. v. General Motors Corp., Mun.App.D.C.1962, 185 A.2d 919 (automobile); B. F. Goodrich Co. v. Hammond, 10 Cir. 1959, 269 F.2d 501 (tire); Goldberg v. Kollsman Instrument Corp., 1963, 12 N.Y.2d 432, 240 N.Y.S.2d 592, 191 N.E.2d 81 (airplane); Simpson v. Powered Products of Michigan, Inc., 1963, 24 Conn.Supp. 409, 192 A.2d 555 (power golf cart); Deveny v. Rheem Mfg. Co., 2 Cir. 1963, 319 F.2d 124 (water heater, Vermont law); McQuaide v. Bridgeport Brass Co., D.Conn. 1960, 190 F.Supp. 252 (insecticide, Pennsylvania law).

38. Within the last three years the parade has been joined by New Hampshire, in Buttrick v. Arthur Lessard & Sons, Inc., 1969, —— N.H. ——, 260 A.2d 111; North Carolina, in Tedder v. Pepsi-Cola Bottling Co. of Raleigh, 1967, 270 N.C. 301, 154 S.E.2d 337 (limited to advertised products); and Rhode Island, in Klimas v. International Tel. & Tel. Co., D. R.I.1969, 297 F.Supp. 937 (federal decision construing state case).

Most of the jurisdictions listed have adopted the Uniform Commercial Code, 2–318 of which provides for extension of the seller's warranty to members of the buyer's family and household, and his guests.

39. As to the various difficulties arising in connection with "warranty," see Prosser, The Assault Upon the Citadel, 1960, 69 Yale L.J. 1099, 1127–1133.

40. Uniform Sales Act, § 49, carried over into U.C.C. § 2–607(3).

41. James, Products Liability, 1955, 34 Tex.L.Rev. 44, 192, 197.

42. Bonker v. Ingersoll Products Co., D.Mass.1955, 132 F.Supp. 5; Whitfield v. Jessup, 1948, 31 Cal.2d 826, 193 P.2d 1; Brown v. Chapman, 9 Cir. 1962, 304 F.2d 149; Pritchard v. Liggett & Myers Tobacco Co., 3 Cir. 1961, 295 F.2d 292; Hampton v. Gebhardt's Chili Powder Co., 9 Cir. 1961, 294 F.2d 172.

intended to apply to personal injuries.[43] A few took the obvious way out by holding that it was entirely inapplicable as between parties who had not dealt with one another.[44]

The other provision of the statutes is that sanctioning disclaimers by the seller, which will defeat the warranty.[45] This means that he is free to insert in his contract of sale an effective agreement that he does not warrant at all, or that he warrants only against certain consequences or defects, or that his liability shall be limited to particular remedies, such as replacement, repair, or return of the purchase price.[46] Commercially this may not be at all an unreasonable thing, particularly where the seller does not know the quality of what he is selling, and the buyer is really willing to take his chances. Commercial buyers usually are quite able to protect themselves. It is another thing entirely to say that the consumer who buys at retail is to be bound by a disclaimer which he has never seen, and to which he would certainly not have agreed if he had known of it, but which defeats a duty imposed by the law for his protection. And if the opportunity is to remain open to the seller to frustrate that policy completely by the mere addition to the label on the package of such words as "Not Warranted in Any Way," it may be assumed that there will be those who will avail themselves of it. The courts have displayed no

very favorable attitude toward disclaimers, construing them away, or finding that they were not adequately brought home to the plaintiff.[47] There are now a good many of the strict liability cases[48] which have held disclaimers to the consumer to be entirely invalid, either as adhesion contracts with no equality of bargaining position, or outright as unconscionable and contrary to the policy of the law.

These difficulties ultimately led, in many jurisdictions, to the jettison of "warranty" in favor of a simpler rule of strict liability, which remains to be considered in the next Section.

98. STRICT LIABILITY IN TORT

For the reasons set forth in the preceding Section,[49] it gradually became apparent that "warranty," as a device for the justification of strict liability to the consumer, carries far too much luggage in the way of undesirable complications, and is more trouble than it is worth. The suggestion was therefore a sufficiently obvious one, that we get rid of the word, which was originally adopted only because it provided a theory ready to hand to accomplish the desired result.[50]

---

43. Silverstein v. R. H. Macy & Co., 1943, 266 App. Div. 5, 40 N.Y.S.2d 916; Wright Bachman, Inc. v. Hodnett, 1956, 235 Ind. 307, 133 N.E.2d 713.

44. La Hue v. Coca Cola Bottling, Inc., 1957, 50 Wash.2d 645, 314 P.2d 421; Ruderman v. Warner-Lambert Pharmaceutical Co., 1962, 23 Conn. 416, 184 A.2d 63; Hampton v. Gebhardt's Chili Powder Co., 9 Cir. 1961, 294 F.2d 172.

45. Uniform Sales Act, 71, considerably modified in U.C.C. § 2–316.

46. See Notes, 1961, 109 U.Pa.L.Rev. 453; 1963, 11 Kan.L.Rev. 574; 1963, 51 Cal.L.Rev. 586; James, Products Liability, 1955, 34 Tex.L.Rev. 44, 192, 210–212; Wilson, Products Liability, 1955, 43 Cal. L.Rev. 614, 809, 835–840; Prosser, The Implied Warranty of Merchantable Quality, 1943, 27 Minn. L.Rev. 117, 157–167; Keeton, Assumption of Risk in Products Liability Cases, 1961, 22 La.L.Rev. 122.

47. Cases are collected in Prosser, The Assault Upon the Citadel, 1960, 69 Yale L.J. 1099, 1132. See also Note, 1963, 77 Harv.L.Rev. 318; De Chaine, Products Liability and the Disclaimer, 1967, 4 Willam.L. Rev. 364.

48. In Henningsen v. Bloomfield Motors, Inc., 1960, 32 N.J. 358, 161 A.2d 69, the court threw out a "standard automobile warranty," in reality a disclaimer of almost all liability of consequences. See in accord State Farm Mut. Ins. Co. v. Anderson-Weber, Inc., 1961, 252 Iowa 1289, 110 N.W.2d 449; Ford Motor Co. v. Tritt, 1968, 244 Ark. 883, 430 S. W.2d 778; Crown v. Cecil Holland Ford, Inc., Fla. App.1968, 207 So.2d 67; Walsh v. Ford Motor Co., 1969, 59 Misc.2d 241, 298 N.Y.S.2d 538; Vandermark v. Ford Motor Co., 1963, 61 Cal.2d 256, 37 Cal. Rptr. 896, 391 P.2d 168.

49. Supra, p. 655.

50. "All this is pernicious and unnecessary. No one doubts that, unless there is privity, liability to the consumer must be in tort and not in contract. There is no need to borrow a concept from the contract law of sales; and it is 'only by some violent

The proposal fell upon receptive ears when the drafting group of the Second Restatement of Torts encountered great difficulty in stating a new Section,[51] without running afoul of the statutory limitations on "warranty." They therefore discarded the term, and offered a Section as follows:

402A. Special Liability of Seller of Product for Physical Harm to User or Consumer.

(1) One who sells any product in a defective condition unreasonably dangerous to the user or consumer or to his property is subject to liability for physical harm thereby caused to the ultimate user or consumer, or to his property, if

(a) the seller is engaged in the business of selling such a product, and

(b) it is expected to and does reach the user or consumer without substantial change in the condition in which it is sold.

(2) The rule stated in Subsection (1) applies although

(a) the seller has exercised all possible care in the preparation and sale of his product, and

(b) the user or consumer has not bought the product from or entered into any contractual relation with the seller.

This was accompanied by a Comment [52] saying that if anyone wished to treat this as a "warranty," there was nothing to prevent it; but if so, it should be recognized that the "warranty" was a very different kind of warranty from those usually found in the sale of goods, and that it is not subject to the various contract rules which have grown up to surround such sales.

This Section was approved by the American Law Institute. The first case to apply it was Greenman v. Yuba Power Products, Inc.,[53] in California in 1963. The plaintiff was injured when a combination power tool, in use as a wood lathe, proved to be defective, and let fly a piece of wood, which struck him in the head. When he brought action against the manufacturer of the tool, from whom he had not bought it, there stood in his way not only the California cases refusing to extend the "warranty" without privity beyond food, but also his failure to give timely notice of the breach as required by the Uniform Sales Act. Justice Traynor met these difficulties by saying that this was not really a matter of warranty at all, but simply of strict liability in tort.

This decision was immediately seized by courts in other jurisdictions,[54] who found in it the solution of their difficulties with warranties. In turn it swept the country, as the Henningsen case [55] had done, until at the present writing the simple ground of "strict

---

pounding and twisting' that 'warranty' can be made to serve the purpose at all. Why talk of it? If there is to be strict liability in tort, let there be strict liability in tort, declared outright, without any illusory contract mask. Such strict liability is familiar enough in the law of animals, abnormally dangerous activities, nuisance, workmen's compensation, and respondeat superior. There is nothing so shocking about it today that it cannot be accepted and stand on its own feet in this new and additional field, provided always that public sentiment, public demand, and 'public policy' have reached the point where the change is called for." Prosser, The Assault Upon the Citadel, 1960, 69 Yale L.J. 1099, 1134.

51. The change in the law was so rapid that the Section was actually drawn three times. As first submitted to the American Law Institute, it was limited to food and drink. It was then extended to "products for intimate bodily use," and finally to all products.

52. Comment *m*.

53. 1963, 59 Cal.2d 57, 27 Cal.Rptr. 697, 377 P.2d 897.

54. Putnam v. Erie City Mfg. Co., 5 Cir. 1964, 338 F.2d 911; Garthwait v. Burgio, 1965, 153 Conn. 284, 216 A.2d 189; Suvada v. White Motor Co., 1965, 32 Ill.2d 612, 210 N.E.2d 182; Dealers Transp. Co. v. Battery Distrib. Co., Ky.1965, 402 S.W.2d 441; Wights v. Staff Jennings, Inc., 1965, 241 Or. 301, 405 P.2d 624.

See Wade, Strict Tort Liability of Manufacturers, 1965, 19 Sw.L.J. 5; Keeton, Products Liability— The Nature and Extent of Strict Liability, [1964] U.Ill.L.F. 693; Note, 1967, 55 Geo.L.J. 286; 1966, 27 U.Pitt.L.Rev. 683.

55. Supra, p. 654.

liability in tort" is accepted and applied by some two-thirds of the courts.[56] It would be easy to over-estimate the importance of the change. It is warranty only that has gone overboard, and with it all idea that the plaintiff's recovery is founded on a contract, as well as the statutory provisions. In particular it is the contract defenses, such as lack of notice to the seller and disclaimers, which are out of the window.[57] The cases of warranty, whether on a direct sale between the parties or to the consumer without privity, are still important precedents in determining what the seller has undertaken to deliver.[58]

On the face of it, it would appear that "warranty" without privity is on its way to the ashcan. Some doubt, however, may arise from the fact that the draftsmen of the Uniform Commercial Code, who initially failed entirely to sense the trend of the case law, have now offered an amendment to a section [59] extending the seller's warranty to all persons who may foreseeably be expected to be injured by the product, and providing that the liability cannot be disclaimed. This has been adopted in a few states. While it may have the effect of restoring warranty as an alternative ground of liability, it does not appear likely that it will succeed in halting the avalanche of strict liability in tort. Once the step has been taken of declaring that this is not a matter of warranty at all, and that the statute does not govern, it is difficult to see how any warranty provision in the Code can be controlling.[60]

99. UNSAFE PRODUCTS

There is today no doubt at all that the seller's liability for negligence extends to and includes any kind of product that is sold.[61] Likewise, since the break through the barrier beyond food, there is no question that the strict liability, whether it is called warranty or declared outright in tort, extends to any kind of product which is recognizably dangerous to those who may come in contact with it. The decisions range from automobiles [62] and airplanes [63] to cinder building blocks,[64]

---

56. Late cases which have swung into line are Hawkeye-Security Ins. Co. v. Ford Motor Co., 1970, — Iowa —, 174 N.W.2d 672; Buttrick v. Arthur Lessard & Sons, Inc., 1969, — N.H. —, 260 A.2d 111; Ulmer v. Ford Motor Co., 1969, 75 Wash.2d 522, 452 P.2d 729; Olney v. Beaman Bottling Co., 1967, 220 Tenn. 459, 418 S.W.2d 430; Helene Curtis Industries v. Pruitt, 5 Cir. 1967, 385 F.2d 841, cert. denied 391 U.S. 913 (Texas and Oklahoma law); McCormack v. Hankscraft Co., 1967, 278 Minn. 322, 154 N.W.2d 488.

57. Strict liability in tort is "hardly more than what exists under implied warranty when stripped of the contract doctrines of privity, disclaimer, requirements of notice of defect, and limitation through inconsistencies with express warranties." Greeno v. Clark Equipment Co., N.D.Ind.1965, 237 F.Supp. 427, 429. See also Dippel v. Sciano, 1967, 37 Wis.2d 443, 155 N.W.2d 55; Ilnicki v. Montgomery Ward & Co., 7 Cir. 1966, 371 F.2d 195.

58. "Although the rules of warranty frustrate rational compensation for physical injury, they function well in a commercial setting . . . These rules determine the quality of the product the manufacturer promises, and thereby determine the quality he must deliver." Traynor, C. J., in Seely v. White Motor Co., 1965, 63 Cal.2d 9, 16, 45 Cal.Rptr. 17, 22, 403 P.2d 145, 150.

59. § 2–318.

60. As to the relation between strict liability in tort and the Uniform Commercial Code, see Speidel, The Virginia "Anti-Privity" Statute: Strict Products Liability Under the Uniform Commercial Code, 1965, 51 Va.L.Rev. 804; Donovan, Recent Developments in Products Liability in New England, 1969, 19 Me.L.Rev. 181; Donnelly, After the Fall of the Citadel, 1967, 19 Syr.L.Rev. 1; Notes, 1965, 31 Brook.L.Rev. 367; 1965, 13 Kan.L.Rev. 411; 1966, 42 Wash.L.Rev. 253; Titus, Restatement (Second) Torts, Section 402A and the Uniform Commercial Code, 1970, 22 Stan.L.Rev. 713.

In Wachtel v. Rosol, 1970, — Conn. —, 271 A.2d 84, a Code provision extending warranty was held not to affect strict liability in tort.

61. See supra, p. 643.

62. Henningsen v. Bloomfield Motors, Inc., 1960, 32 N.J. 358, 161 A.2d 69; State Farm Mut. Auto. Ins. Co. v. Anderson-Weber, Inc., 1961, 252 Iowa 1289, 110 N.W.2d 449; Vandermark v. Ford Motor Co., 1964, 61 Cal.2d 256, 37 Cal.Rptr. 896, 391 P.2d 168.

63. Goldberg v. Kollsman Instrument Corp., 1963, 12 N.Y.2d 432, 240 N.Y.S.2d 592, 191 N.E.2d 81.

64. Spence v. Three Rivers Builders & Masonry Supply, Inc., 1958, 353 Mich. 120, 90 N.W.2d 873.

glass doors,[65] and paper cups.[66] The tide of decisions has swept away the highly metaphysical distinction between the product and the container in which it is sold, which used to perplex some courts in the food cases.[67] The two are sold as an integrated whole, and it is inconceivable that anyone would buy one without the other. When a bottle of beer explodes and puts out the eye of the man about to drink it, surely nothing should be less material than whether the explosion is due to a flaw in the glass of the bottle or to overcharged contents.[68]

There must, however, be something wrong with the product which makes it unreasonably dangerous to those who come in contact with it. An ordinary pair of shoes does not become unreasonably unsafe merely because the soles become somewhat slippery when wet; [69] nor is there unreasonable danger in a hammer merely because it can mash a thumb. Knives and axes would be quite useless if they did not cut.

The question of when a product is unreasonably unsafe has occupied a good many writers.[70] The language of the Second Re-

statement of Torts in dealing with it is that for strict liability the product must be "in a defective condition unreasonably dangerous to the user or consumer or to his property." [71] This terminology may perhaps leave something to be desired, since it is clear that the "defect" need not be a matter of errors in manufacture, and that a product is "defective" when it is properly made according to an unreasonably dangerous design,[72] or when it is not accompanied by adequate instructions and warning of the dangers attending its use.[73]

The prevailing interpretation of "defective" is that the product does not meet the reasonable expectations of the ordinary consumer as to its safety.[74] It has been said that

---

65. Gutierrez v. Superior Court, 1966, 243 Cal.App.2d 710, 52 Cal.Rptr. 592.

66. Bernstein v. Lily-Tulip Cup Corp., Fla.1966, 181 So.2d 641.

67. See for example McIntyre v. Coca-Cola Bottling Co., W.D.Mo.1949, 85 F.Supp. 708; Soter v. Griesedieck Brewery Co., 1948, 200 Okl. 302, 193 P.2d 575.

68. Kroger Co. v. Bowman, Ky.1967, 411 S.W.2d 339; Vallis v. Canada Dry Ginger Ale, Inc., 1960, 190 Cal.App.2d 35, 11 Cal.Rptr. 823; Renninger, Inc. v. Foremost Dairies, Inc., Fla.App.1965, 171 So.2d 602; Addeo v. Metropolitan Bottling Co., 1963, 39 Misc.2d 474, 241 N.Y.S.2d 120, affirmed 20 App.Div.2d 967, 251 N.Y.S.2d 412; Nichols v. Nold, 1953, 174 Kan. 613, 258 P.2d 317.

69. Fanning v. Le May, 1967, 38 Ill.2d 209, 230 N.E. 2d 182. Cf. Flippo v. Mode O'Day Frock Shops of Hollywood, 1970, — Ark. —, 449 S.W.2d 692 (slacks not defective merely because poisonous spider could crawl into them).

70. See for example Keeton, Products Liability: Liability Without Fault and the Requirement of a Defect, 1963, 41 Tex.L.Rev. 855; Dickerson, Products Liability: How Good Does a Product Have to be,

1967, 42 Ind.L.J. 301; Traynor, The Ways and Meanings of Defective Products and Strict Liability, 1965, 32 Tenn.L.Rev. 363.

71. § 402A.

72. Dyson v. General Motors Corp., E.D.Pa.1969, 298 F.Supp. 1064; Wright v. Massey-Harris, Inc., 1966, 68 Ill.App.2d 70, 215 N.E.2d 465; Bowles v. Zimmer Mfg. Co., 7 Cir. 1960, 277 F.2d 868; Pike v. Frank G. Hough Co., 1970, — Cal.2d —, 85 Cal.Rptr. 629, 467 P.2d 229; Stephan v. Sears, Roebuck & Co., N.H.1970, 266 A.2d 855; Pizza Inn, Inc. v. Tiffany, Tex.Civ.App.1970, 454 S.W.2d 420.

Since proper design is a matter of reasonable fitness, the strict liability adds little or nothing to negligence on the part of the manufacturer; but it becomes more important in the case of a dealer who does not design the product.

73. Canifax v. Hercules Powder Co., 1965, 237 Cal. App.2d 44, 46 Cal.Rptr. 552; Crane v. Sears, Roebuck & Co., 1963, 218 Cal.App.2d 855, 32 Cal.Rptr. 754; Davis v. Wyeth Laboratories, Inc., 9 Cir. 1968, 399 F.2d 121.

Again, in the case of the manufacturer, the strict liability adds little or nothing to negligence; but where the sale is by a dealer, who does not know the danger, it becomes important.

74. One of the best cases on this is Dunham v. Vaughn & Bushnell Mfg. Co., 1969, 42 Ill.2d 339, 247 N.E.2d 401. See also Second Restatement of Torts, 402A, Comment *g*; Keeton, Products Liability: Liability Without Fault and the Requirement of a Defect, 1963, 41 Tex.L.Rev. 855; Traynor, The Ways and Meanings of Defective Products and Strict Liability, 1965, 32 Tenn.L.Rev. 363; Freedman, "Defect" in the Product: The Necessary Basis for Products Liability, 1966, 33 Tenn.L.Rev. 323;

this amounts to saying that if the seller knew of the condition he would be negligent in marketing the product.[75] This is borne out by the cases of conditions "natural" to food, such as a fish bone in a plate of chowder, or a cherry pit in cherry pie, which the ordinary consumer would expect to encounter, and against which he would normally take his own precautions.[76]

There are still two areas in which it is difficult to state any definite conclusions as to the law. One of these concerns products which are expected to be processed, or otherwise altered, after they have left the seller and before they have reached the consumer.[77] The seller of raw pork, which is expected to be cooked before it is made into sausage, is certainly not to be held liable when it is packed half raw into the casings.[78] On the other hand, if poisoned coffee beans are sold to a buyer who is to do no more than roast, grind and pack them, it cannot be supposed that the seller will escape liability. The question is one of whether the responsibility is

shifted to the intermediate handler,[79] which will turn upon the nature of the defect and the degree of danger, as well as the relation of the parties. The maker of an automobile with a defective steering gear, or a leak in the hydraulic brake line, can surely have no hope of relief from his responsibility by reason of the fact that the car is sold to a dealer who is expected to service it before it is ready for use.[80]

The second, and more important, question concerns products that in the present state of human skill and knowledge are unavoidably dangerous, and cannot be made safe.[81] Where, as in the case of whiskey, the danger of their use is generally known, it seems clear that the product cannot be regarded as unreasonably unsafe merely because it is capable of doing harm. Although all of the few decisions have not agreed,[82] it is quite possible that cigarettes are to be placed in this category, even though they may cause lung cancer.[83] But where, as in the case of

---

Rheingold, What Are the Consumer's "Reasonable Expectations," 1967, 22 Bus.Law. 589; Dickerson, Products Liability: How Good Does a Product Have to Be, 1967, 42 Ind.L.J. 301.

75. Wade, Strict Tort Liability of Manufacturers, 1965, 19 Sw.L.Rev. 5.

76. Webster v. Blue Ship Tea Room, Inc., 1964, 347 Mass. 421, 198 N.E.2d 309 (fish bone in chowder); Hunt v. Ferguson-Paulus Enterprises, 1966, 243 Or. 546, 415 P.2d 13 (cherry pit in pie); Musso v. Picadilly Cafeterias, Inc., La.App.1965, 178 So.2d 421, application denied 248 La. 468, 179 So.2d 641 (same); Adams v. Great A. & P. Tea Co., 1960, 251 N.C. 565, 112 S.E.2d 92 (crystallized grain of corn in corn flakes); Allen v. Grafton, 1960, 170 Ohio St. 249, 164 N.E.2d 167 (small bit of shell in fried oyster).

It is not the fact that the defect is a natural one which is important, but the fact that the ordinary consumer would expect that he might encounter it. Zabner v. Howard Johnson's, Inc., Fla.App.1967, 201 So.2d 824 (piece of walnut shell in maple walnut ice cream).

77. Because of the dearth of cases the Second Restatement of Torts, 402A, Caveat (2), has expressed no opinion on this subject.

78. Schneider v. Suhrmann, 1958, 8 Utah 2d 35, 327 P.2d 822.

79. See supra, p. 176.

80. See Vandermark v. Ford Motor Co., 1964, 61 Cal. 2d 256, 37 Cal.Rptr. 896, 391 P.2d 168.

81. See Connolly, Liability of a Manufacturer for Unknowable Hazards Inherent in His Product, 1965, 32 Ins.Couns.J. 305.

82. In Pritchard v. Liggett & Myers Tobacco Co., 3 Cir. 1961, 295 F.2d 292, it was held by a 2–1 vote that there was an implied warranty to the consumer that cigarettes were safe to smoke. In Green v. American Tobacco Co., beginning in 5 Cir. 1962, 304 F.2d 70, the federal court first put the wrong question as to Florida law to the supreme court of Florida, Fla.1963, 154 So.2d 169; and then, assuming what has since proved to be the wrong answer to the right question, left the implied warranty to the jury, 5 Cir. 1963, 325 F.2d 673. The jury returned a verdict for the defendant, which was set aside on appeal, and an implied warranty found as a matter of law, 5 Cir. 1968, 391 F.2d 97; but the entire Circuit, sitting in banc, reversed this decision and entered judgment for the defendant, 5 Cir. 1969, 409 F.2d 1166. The whole comedy of errors inspires no confidence in any of the opinions.

83. Lartigue v. R. J. Reynolds Tobacco Co., 5 Cir. 1963, 317 F.2d 19, cert. denied 375 U.S. 865 (followed in Hudson v. R. J. Reynolds Tobacco Co., 5 Cir. 1970, 427 F.2d 541); Ross v. Philip Morris & Co., 8 Cir. 1964, 328 F.2d 3 (both on the ground that

the vaccine for the Pasteur treatment for rabies,[84] there is no such common knowledge, the question becomes one of whether there is to be liability for marketing such a product at all. The whole pharmacopeia is full of drugs which are not safe, and at present cannot be made safe.[85]

Where only negligence liability is in question, the answer as to such products is usually a simple one. The utility and social value of the thing sold normally outweighs the known, and all the more so the unknown risk, and there is no negligence in selling it, provided always that proper warning and directions are given.[86] But strict liability, whether on warranty or in tort, does not require negligence; and the question becomes one of whether the defendant is to be held liable for marketing the thing at all. The argument that industries producing potentially dangerous products should make good the harm, distribute it by liability insurance, and add the cost to the price of the product,[87] encounters reason for pause, when we consider that two of the greatest medical boons to the human race, penicillin and cortisone, both have their dangerous side effects, and that drug companies might well have been deterred from producing and selling them.

Thus far the courts have tended to hold the manufacturer to a high standard of care in

preparing and testing drugs of unknown potentiality and in giving warning;[88] but in the absence of evidence that this standard has not been met, they have refused to hold the maker liable for the unforeseeable harm.[89] One important group of cases involved the drug known as MER/29,[90] which was effective in reducing cholesterol in the blood, but was found after it was marketed to have dangerous side effects, including causing cataracts on the eyes of the user. The initial cases refused to find strict liability, on the ground that the maker could not reasonably have been expected to know of such effects;[91] but later decisions in the mass litigation which followed allowed recovery, on the basis of evidence that the defendant had had sufficient warning, and had misrepresented its experiments to the Food and Drug Administration in order to obtain the privilege of marketing.[92]

There are a number of cases involving hepatitis resulting from blood transfusions. So far as the transfusion itself is concerned, it

at the time of sale by the defendant the danger could not have been known).

See Wegman, Cigarettes and Health, 1966, 51 Corn.L. Q. 678; Siler, Legal Liability in Tobacco Products Cases, 1965, 53 Ky.L.J. 712; Notes, 1964, 17 Vand. L.Rev. 315; 1966, 11 Vill.L.Rev. 546; 1964, 6 Ariz. L.Rev. 82.

84. In Carmen v. Eli Lilly & Co., 1941, 109 Ind.App. 76, 32 N.E.2d 729, the plaintiff was informed of the risk, and was held to have assumed it.

85. See Spangenberg, Aspects of Warranties Relating to Defective Prescription Drugs, 1965, 37 U.Colo.L. Rev. 194; Notes, 1967, 46 Or.L.Rev. 235; 1966, 28 U.Pitt.L.Rev. 37; 1965, 16 West.Res.L.Rev. 392.

86. See supra, p. 646.

87. See James, The Untoward Effects of Cigarettes and Drugs: Reflections on Enterprise Liability, 1966, 54 Cal.L.Rev. 1550.

88. See for example Stromsodt v. Parke-Davis & Co., D.N.D.1966, 257 F.Supp. 991, affirmed 8 Cir. 1969, 411 F.2d 1390; Tinnerholm v. Parke Davis & Co., S.D.N.Y.1968, 285 F.Supp. 432, affirmed 2 Cir. 1969, 411 F.2d 48; Love v. Wolf, 1964, 226 Cal.App.2d 378, 38 Cal.Rptr. 183.

89. Cochran v. Brooke, 1966, 243 Or. 89, 409 P.2d 904.

90. The story of the mass litigation over this drug is narrated in Rheingold, The MER/29 Story—An Instance of Successful Mass Disaster Litigation, 1968, 56 Cal.L.Rev. 116. See also Keeton, Some Observations About the Strict Liability of the Maker of Prescription Drugs, 1968, 56 Cal.L.Rev. 149.

As to the story of the tranquilizer thalidomide, see Mellin and Katzenstein, The Saga of Thalidomide, 1962, 267 J.A.M.A. 1184, 1187–90, 1238; Bennett, Liability of the Manufacturers of Thalidomide to the Affected Children, 1965, 39 Aust.L.J. 256.

91. Cudmore v. Richardson-Merrell, Inc., Tex.Civ. App.1965, 398 S.W.2d 640, refused n. r. e., cert. denied, 1967, 385 U.S. 1003; Lewis v. Baker, 1966, 243 Or. 317, 413 P.2d 400; McLeod v. W. S. Merrell Co., Fla.1965, 174 So.2d 736.

92. Typical cases are Roginsky v. Richardson-Merrell, Inc., S.D.N.Y.1966, 254 F.Supp. 430, affirmed in part, reversed in part on other grounds, 2 Cir. 1967, 378 F.2d 832; Toole v. Richardson-Merrell, Inc., 1967, 251 Cal.App.2d 689, 60 Cal.Rptr. 398.

has been regarded by most courts as a service, and not a sale, so that in the absence of negligence [93] there is no liability of the hospital which gives it.[94] But a blood bank which supplies the blood is certainly to be regarded as a seller; and the general refusal to hold it strictly liable has gone on the basis of the unavoidability of the danger.[95] When any evidence can be produced that it might have been avoided, it becomes a question for the jury, and may lead to liability.[96]

100. PARTIES

The MacPherson decision [97] did not carry the liability of the seller for negligence beyond the ultimate purchaser himself. It was, however, soon expanded to other users and consumers of the product, and then to those who were "in the vicinity of the chattel's probable use," [98] or, as it is now put by the Second Restatement,[99] "those whom he should expect to be endangered by its probable use." There is no longer any doubt that the negligence liability extends to any law-

ful [1] user of the thing supplied, as well as to a mere bystander,[2] or a pedestrian in the path of a car.[3] For negligence, in other words, there is liability to any foreseeable plaintiff.

Perhaps because the early decisions were grounded on a theory of warranty, the strict liability of the seller was at first limited to "users" or "consumers" of the product. Both terms were, however, applied in a very broad sense. Passengers in automobiles [4] and airplanes [5] were held to be users; and so were a customer in a beauty shop whose hair was treated with the defendant's dye,[6] a shopper in a self-service store who had not yet bought,[7] a wife preparing rabbits for her husband's dinner,[8] a filling station mechanic do-

---

93. In Fischer v. Wilmington General Hospital, 1959, 1 Storey, Del., 554, 149 A.2d 749, it was held that there was no negligence in ordering the transfusion itself, since the utility outweighed the risk.

94. See supra, p. 638.

95. Balkowitsch v. Minneapolis War Memorial Blood Bank, 1965, 270 Minn. 151, 132 N.W.2d 805; Koenig v. Milwaukee Blood Center, Inc., 1964, 23 Wis.2d 324, 127 N.W.2d 50; Whitehursh v. American Nat. Red Cross, 1965, 1 Ariz.App. 326, 402 P.2d 584; Jackson v. Muhlenberg Hospital, 1967, 96 N.J.Super. 314, 232 A.2d 879, reversed on other grounds 1969, 53 N.J. 138, 249 A.2d 65; Community Blood Bank, Inc. v. Russell, Fla.1967, 196 So.2d 115.

See Notes, 1966, 21 U.Miami L.Rev. 479; 1966, 50 Minn.L.Rev. 535; 1966, 15 Cleve.Marsh.L.Rev. 497; 1970, 24 Sw.L.J. 305.

96. Community Blood Bank, Inc. v. Russell, Fla.1967, 196 So.2d 115; Hoder v. Sayet, Fla.App.1967, 196 So. 2d 205; Jackson v. Muhlenberg Hospital, 1967, 96 N.J.Super. 314, 232 A.2d 879, reversed on other grounds, 1969, 53 N.J. 138, 249 A.2d 65;

97. Supra, p. 642.

98. First Restatement of Torts, § 395.

99. Second Restatement of Torts, § 395.

---

1. No decision has been found as to any unlawful user, such as a thief or a trespasser. It appears unlikely that any liability would be found.

2. Gall v. Union Ice Co., 1951, 108 Cal.App.2d 303, 239 P.2d 48; McLeod v. Linde Air Products Co., 1927, 318 Mo. 397, 1 S.W.2d 122; Hopper v. Charles Cooper & Co., 1927, 104 N.J.L. 93, 139 A. 19; Benton v. Sloss, 1952, 38 Cal.2d 399, 240 P.2d 575 (passenger in colliding car).

3. Gaidry Motors v. Brannon, Ky.1954, 268 S.W.2d 627; Flies v. Fox Bros. Buick Co., 1928, 196 Wis. 196, 218 N.W. 855; cf. Ford Motor Co. v. Zahn, 8 Cir. 1959, 265 F.2d 729; Carpini v. Pittsburgh & Weirton Bus Co., 3 Cir. 1954, 216 F.2d 404 (passenger in bus); Greyhound Corp. v. Brown, 1959, 269 Ala. 520, 113 So.2d 916 (same).

4. Thompson v. Reedman, E.D.Pa.1961, 199 F.Supp. 120; Hacker v. Rector, D.C.Mo.1966, 250 F.Supp. 300.

5. Hinton v. Republic Aviation Corp., S.D.N.Y.1959, 180 F.Supp. 31; Ewing v. Lockheed Aircraft Corp., D.Minn.1962, 202 F.Supp. 216; King v. Douglas Aircraft Co., Fla.App.1963, 159 So.2d 108; Goldberg v. Kollsman Instrument Corp., 1963, 12 N.Y.2d 432, 240 N.Y.S.2d 592, 191 N.E.2d 81.

6. Graham v. Bottenfield's Inc., 1954, 176 Kan. 68, 269 P.2d 413; Garthwait v. Burgio, 1965, 153 Conn. 284, 216 A.2d 189.

7. Rogers v. Karem, Ky.1966, 405 S.W.2d 741; Faucette v. Lucky Stores, Inc., 1963, 219 Cal.App.2d 196, 33 Cal.Rptr. 215. Cf. Delaney v. Towmotor Corp., 2 Cir. 1964, 339 F.2d 4 (trying out product); Matthews v. Lawnlite Co., Fla.1956, 88 So.2d 299 (same).

8. Haut v. Kleene, 1943, 320 Ill.App. 273, 50 N.E.2d 855.

ing work on a car,[9] and even one who tried to walk through an invisible glass door.[10] But one who was making no use at all of the product except to be injured by it, as in the case of a pedestrian hit by an automobile,[11] or a bystander injured by the explosion of a beer bottle,[12] were denied recovery in the absence of negligence, on the ground that they were not within the class of persons whom the seller had been seeking to reach in marketing the product, and they had not relied in any way upon his implied representation of safety. Their only qualification for recovery was that they were there when the accident happened, which is a thing not uncommon in plaintiffs.

The break away from these decisions came in Michigan [13] in 1965, when a bystander was injured by the explosion of a shotgun. The case was followed by a few other courts.[14]

The first real discussion of the basis of liability was in Elmore v. American Motors Corp.,[15] in California in 1969, when an automobile veered across the center line of the highway and collided head-on with the plaintiff. Justice Peters said that the purpose of the strict liability in tort was to make the industry responsible for all of the foreseeable harm done by its defective products, with the expectation that the losses would be distributed to the public through liability insurance added to the cost; and that the bystander was as much entitled to protection as the consumer, and more in need of it. Other jurisdictions have agreed with this decision,[16] until it is by now the rule of a slight majority of the courts. Its effect is obviously to put the strict liability on the same footing as negligence, as to all foreseeable injuries.

Defendants

So far as liability for negligence is concerned, there is no longer any doubt that it attaches to any seller of a product, including the maker of a component part of the final product,[17] and an assembler of parts sup-

9. Connolly v. Hagi, 1963, 24 Conn.Sup.198, 188 A.2d 884. Cf. Keener v. Dayton Elec. Mfg. Co., Mo. 1969, 445 S.W.2d 362 (lifting sump pump in aiding friend to clear water from basement); Cottom v. McGuire Funeral Service, Inc., D.C.App.1970, 262 A.2d 807 (pallbearer carrying casket). In Guarino v. Mine Safety Appliance Co., 1969, 25 N.Y.2d 460, 306 N.Y.S.2d 942, 255 N.E.2d 173, the court found strict liability to a rescuer of a user of a safety mask for miners.

10. Gutierrez v. Superior Court, 1966, 243 Cal.App.2d 710, 52 Cal.Rptr. 592.

11. Mull v. Ford Motor Co., 2 Cir. 1967, 368 F.2d 713; Hahn v. Ford Motor Co., 1964, 256 Iowa 27, 126 N.W.2d 350 (driver of colliding car); Berzon v. Don Allen Motors, Inc., 1965, 23 App.Div.2d 530, 256 N.Y.S.2d 643 (passenger in colliding car); Davidson v. Leadingham, E.D.Ky.1968, 294 F.Supp. 155 (occupants of colliding car); Schneider v. Chrysler Motors Corp., 8 Cir. 1968, 401 F.2d 549.

12. Kasey v. Suburban Gas Heat, Inc., 1962, 60 Wash.2d 468, 374 P.2d 549 (cafe wrecked by explosion of propane gas). Cf. Torpey v. Red Owl Stores, 8 Cir. 1955, 228 F.2d 117 (guest opening glass jar); Rodriguez v. Shell's City, Inc., Fla.App. 1962, 141 So.2d 590 (bystander injured by disintegration of sanding kit); and see Alexander Funeral Homes, Inc. v. Pride, 1964, 261 N.C. 723, 136 S.E. 2d 120 (building run into by car).

13. Piercefield v. Remington Arms Co., 1965, 375 Mich. 85, 133 N.W.2d 129.

14. Trojan Boat Co. v. Lutz, 5 Cir. 1966, 358 F.2d 299 (cabin cruiser blew up and set fire to other

boats in the vicinity); Mitchell v. Miller, 1965, 26 Conn.Supp. 142, 214 A.2d 694 (driver of colliding car); Webb v. Zern, 1966, 422 Pa. 424, 220 A.2d 853 (bystander injured by explosion of beer keg); Toombs v. Fort Pierce Gas Co., Fla.1968, 208 So.2d 615 (bystander injured by explosion of tank of propane gas). See also Ford Motor Co. v. Cockrell, Miss.1968, 211 So.2d 833.

15. 1969, 70 Cal.2d 578, 75 Cal.Rptr. 652, 451 P.2d 84. Followed in Johnson v. Standard Brands Paint Co., 1969, 274 Cal.App.2d 369, 79 Cal.Rptr. 194; Preissman v. D'Ornellas, 1969, 1 Cal.App.3d 841, 82 Cal. Rptr. 108.

16. Darryl v. Ford Motor Co., Tex.1969, 440 S.W.2d 630 (driver of colliding car); Caruth v. Mariani, 1970, 11 Ariz.App. 188, 463 P.2d 83 (same); Sills v. Massey-Ferguson, Inc., N.D.Ind.1969, 296 F.Supp. 776 (bystander hit by object thrown 150 feet by power mower); Wasik v. Borg, 2 Cir. 1970, 423 F. 2d 44 (Vermont law); Pike v. Frank O. Hough Co., 1970, 85 Cal.Rptr. 629, 467 P.2d 229.

See Notes, 1964, 64 Col.L.Rev. 916; 1969, 2 Creight. L.Rev. 295.

17. Smith v. Peerless Glass Co., 1932, 259 N.Y. 292, 181 N.E. 576, motion denied 259 N.Y. 664, 182 N.E. 225; Spencer v. Madsen, 10 Cir. 1944, 142 F.2d 820;

plied by others,[18] or even a mere processor under contract with the maker.[19] It applies to dealers, whether at wholesale or retail,[20] and to a second-hand dealer who reconditions automobiles for sale.[21] It is obvious that less in the way of care may be required of some of these sellers than of others;[22] but if reasonable care has not been exercised, there may be liability.

In a number of cases it has been held that one who labels a product with his own name, or otherwise represents it to be his own,[23] is to be treated on the same basis as if he had manufactured it, and so is liable for any negligence on the part of the actual maker.[24]

The courts have talked occasionally of an "estoppel" on the part of the seller to deny that the negligence is his own; but this is quite difficult to make out where, as is often enough the case, the injured plaintiff never heard of either seller. The basis of liability appears to be nothing more than the fact that the defendant has vouched for the product, and so made the responsibility his own.

As to strict liability, whether on warranty or in tort, no case has been found in any jurisdiction in which it has been imposed upon anyone who was not engaged in the business of supplying goods of the particular kind. The Second Restatement of Torts[25] has so limited the liability. When a housewife, on one occasion, sells a jar of jam to her neighbor, or the owner of an automobile trades it in to a dealer,[26] the undertaking to the public and the justifiable reliance upon that undertaking on the part of the ultimate consumer, which are the basis of the strict liability, are conspicuously lacking.

There is no dispute that the strict liability applies to the manufacturer of the product, including the maker of a component part,[27]

State for Use of Woodzell v. Garzell Plastics Industries, E.D.Mich.1957, 152 F.Supp. 483; Fredericks v. American Export Lines, 2 Cir. 1955, 227 F.2d 450, cert. denied 350 U.S. 989; Willey v. Fyrogas Co., 1952, 363 Mo. 406, 251 S.W.2d 635.

18. Sheward v. Virtue, 1942, 20 Cal.2d 410, 126 P.2d 345; Rauch v. American Radiator & Standard San, Corp., 1960, 252 Iowa 1, 104 N.W.2d 607; Alexander v. Nash-Kelvinator Corp., 2 Cir. 1958, 261 F.2d 187; Spencer v. Madsen, 10 Cir. 1944, 142 F.2d 820; Comstock v. General Motors Corp., 1959, 358 Mich. 163, 99 N.W.2d 627.

19. Block v. Urban, E.D.Mich.1958, 166 F.Supp. 19.

20. Jones v. Burgermeister Brewing Corp., 1961, 198 Cal.App. 198, 18 Cal.Rptr. 311; Ellis v. Lindmark, 1929, 177 Minn. 390, 225 N.W. 395; Egan Chevrolet Co. v. Bruner, 8 Cir. 1939, 102 F.2d 373; Stout v. Madden, 1956, 208 Or. 294, 300 P.2d 461; Gall v. Union Ice Co., 1951, 108 Cal.App.2d 303, 239 P.2d 48.

21. Flies v. Fox Bros. Buick Co., 1928, 196 Wis. 196, 218 N.W. 855; Gaidry Motors v. Brannon, Ky.1952, 268 S.W.2d 327; Bock v. Truck & Tractor, Inc., 1943, 18 Wash.2d 458, 139 P.2d 706; Jones v. Raney Chevrolet Co., 1940, 217 N.C. 693, 9 S.E.2d 395.

22. See, as to the dealer, supra, p. 631.

23. Where the goods are merely labeled with the seller's name as distributor, it is held that he is not responsible for the maker's negligence. Degouveia v. H. D. Lee Merc. Co., 1937, 231 Mo.App. 447, 100 S.W.2d 336; Fleetwood v. Swift & Co., 1921, 27 Ga. App. 502, 108 S.E. 909; Second Restatement of Torts, § 400, Comment d.

24. Smith v. Regina Mfg. Corp., 4 Cir. 1968, 396 F.2d 826; Penn v. Inferno Mfg. Corp., La.App.1967, 199 So.2d 210; Standard Motor Co. v. Blood, Tex.Civ. App.1964, 380 S.W.2d 651; Swift & Co. v. Blackwell, 4 Cir. 1936, 84 F.2d 130; Sears, Roebuck & Co. v. Morris, 1961, 273 Ala. 218, 136 So.2d 883.

25. § 402A, and Comment f.

26. In Thrash v. U-Drive-It Co., 1953, 158 Ohio St. 465, 110 N.E.2d 419, an owner trading a car "as is" to a second-hand dealer was held not even to be under a duty of reasonable care. See also Wagner v. Coronet Hotel, 1969, 10 Ariz.App. 296, 458 P.2d 390; Magrine v. Krasnica, 1967, 94 N.J.Super. 228, 227 A.2d 539, affirmed in Magrine v. Spector, 1967, 100 N.J.Super. 223, 241 A.2d 637; Southwest Forest Industries, Inc. v. Westinghouse Elec. Corp., 9 Cir. 1970, 422 F.2d 1013; Freitas v. Twin City Fishermen's Coop. Assn., Tex.Civ.App.1970, 452 S.W.2d 931.

27. Deveny v. Rheem Mfg. Co., 2 Cir. 1963, 319 F.2d 124 (Vermont law); McKee v. Brunswick Corp., 7 Cir. 1965, 354 F.2d 577; Putman v. Erie City Mfg. Co., 5 Cir. 1964, 338 F.2d 911; Suvada v. White Motor Co., 1965, 32 Ill.2d 612, 210 N.E.2d 182; Rosenau v. City of New Brunswick, 1968, 51 N.J. 130, 238 A.2d 169.

In Goldberg v. Kollsman Instrument Corp., 1963, 12 N.Y.2d 432, 240 N.Y.S.2d 592, 191 N.E.2d 81, the court refused to hold the maker of an airplane altimeter to strict liability, on the rather unusual ground that the plaintiff had sufficient remedy against the maker of the plane.

and an assembler of parts,[28] as well as one who vouches for manufacturer by another by selling the product as his own.[29] Except in a state or two,[30] there is now general agreement that it applies to a wholesale dealer,[31] and to one at retail.[32] All of the valid arguments supporting the strict liability would appear to have no less force in the case of the dealers; and there are enough cases in which the manufacturer is beyond the jurisdiction,[33] or even unknown to the injured plaintiff,[34] to justify giving the consumer the maximum of protection, and requiring the dealer to argue out with the manufacturer any questions as to their respective liability. Particularly today, when the large wholesale supply house, or even the retail chain, is actually the prime mover in marketing the goods, and the manufacturer is only a small concern which feeds it, it is unrealistic to draw any distinction between different kinds of sellers.

101. INTERESTS PROTECTED

There can be no doubt that the seller's liability for negligence covers any kind of physical harm, including not only personal injuries, but also property damage to the defective chattel itself, as where an automobile is wrecked by reason of its own bad brakes,[35] as well as damage to any other property in the vicinity.[36] But where there is no accident, and no physical damage, and the only loss is a pecuniary one, through loss of the value or use of the thing sold, or the cost of repairing it, the courts have adhered to the rule, to be encountered later,[37] that purely economic interests are not entitled to protection against mere negligence, and so have denied the recovery.[38]

28. Putman v. Erie City Mfg. Co., 5 Cir. 1964, 338 F. 2d 911; Ford Motor Co. v. Mathis, 5 Cir. 1963, 332 F.2d 267; King v. Douglas Aircraft Co., Fla.App. 1963, 159 So.2d 108; Courtois v. General Motors Corp., 1962, 37 N.J. 525, 182 A.2d 545; Holman v. Ford Motor Co., Fla.App.1970, 239 So.2d 40.

29. Schwartz v. Macrose Lumber & Trim Co., 1966, 50 Misc.2d 547, 270 N.Y.S.2d 875, motion denied 50 Misc.2d 1055, 272 N.Y.S.2d 227, reversed on other grounds, 29 App.Div.2d 781, 287 N.Y.S.2d 706, affirmed 24 N.Y.2d 856, 301 N.Y.S.2d 91, 248 N.E.2d 920.

30. The only certain one is Florida, where the dealer is held strictly liable for food, but not for other products. Food Fair Stores of Florida v. Macurda, Fla.1957, 93 So.2d 860 (food); Carter v. Hector Supply Co., Fla.1961, 128 So.2d 390 (no as to other products).

In Howard v. General Motors Corp., D.Miss.1968, 287 F.Supp. 646, and Picker X-Ray Corp. v. Frerker, 8 Cir. 1969, 405 F.2d 916, the federal courts concluded that the former rules in Mississippi and Missouri no longer applied, and the dealers were liable.

31. Barth v. B. F. Goodrich Tire Co., 1968, 265 Cal. App.2d 228, 71 Cal.Rptr. 306; Dunham v. Vaughan & Bushnell Mfg. Co., 1969, 42 Ill.2d 339, 247 N.E.2d 401; Chandler v. Anchor Serum Co., 1967, 198 Kan. 571, 426 P.2d 82; Nelson v. West Coast Dairy Co., 1940, 5 Wash.2d 284, 105 P.2d 76; Pimm v. Graybar Elec. Co., 1967, 27 App.Div.2d 309, 278 N.Y.S.2d 913. See Note, 1967, 19 Me.L.Rev. 92.

32. Housman v. C. A. Dawson & Co., 1969, 106 Ill. App.2d 225, 245 N.E.2d 886; Read v. Safeway Stores, 1968, 264 Cal.App.2d 404, 70 Cal.Rptr. 454; Dealers Transport Co. v. Battery Dist. Co., Ky.1965, 402 S.W.2d 441; Browne v. Fenestra, Inc., 1965, 375 Mich. 566, 134 N.W.2d 730; Henningsen v. Bloomfield Motors, Inc., 1960, 32 N.J. 358, 161 A.2d 69.

33. Cf. Burkhardt v. Armour & Co., 1932, 115 Conn. 249, 161 A. 385, where the actual packer of corned beef was in Argentina, the first buyer a subsidiary corporation in Argentina, the primary distributor who put its name on the can in Illinois, and the retailer, the buyer at retail, and the injured consumer in Connecticut.

34. Baum v. Murray, 1945, 23 Wash.2d 890, 162 P.2d 801; Comarow v. Levy, Sup.Ct.1952, 115 N.Y.S.2d 873.

35. International Harvester Co. v. Sharoff, 10 Cir. 1953, 202 F.2d 52; Quackenbush v. Ford Motor Co., 1915, 167 App.Div. 433, 153 N.Y.S. 131; C. D. Herme, Inc. v. R. C. Tway Co., Ky.1956, 294 S.W.2d 534; Fentress v. Van Etta Motors, 1958, 157 Cal. App.2d 863, 323 P.2d 227.

36. Rose v. Buffalo Air Service, 1960, 170 Neb. 806, 104 N.W.2d 431; Gosnell v. Zink, Okl.1958, 325 P.2d 965; Todd Shipyards Corp. v. United States, D. Me.1947, 69 F.Supp. 609; Marsh Wood Products Co. v. Babcock & Wilcox Co., 1932, 207 Wis. 209, 240 N.W. 392; Genesee County Patrons Fire Relief Ass'n v. L. Sonneborn Sons, 1934, 263 N.Y. 463, 189 N.E. 551.

37. See infra, p. ——.

38. Wyatt v. Cadillac Motor Car Division, 1956, 145 Cal.App.2d 423, 302 P.2d 665; Trans World Air-

Personal injury has long dominated the strict liability cases, if only because it is the obvious consequence of bad food. Recognition that warranty without privity of contract must be a matter of tort, and the development of strict liability in tort, have finally laid to rest the former controversy [39] over whether an action for wrongful death will lie; and the recovery is now generally allowed.[40] With the extension of the strict liability beyond food, and in particular to products likely to cause harm only to property, such as animal food,[41] physical harm to property began to be included; and there is now general agreement that there may be recovery not only for damage to the defective chattel itself,[42] or to other products made from it,[43]

but also to other property in the vicinity, as where a building is wrecked by the explosion of a gasoline stove.[44]

Pecuniary loss, mere pocketbook damage, has offered greater difficulties, if only because it has always been recoverable on a direct warranty from the seller to his immediate buyer. There is nothing inherent in the character of such loss to prevent its compensation; and the very first case [45] in which the Washington court declared the strict liability without privity as to food allowed recovery for loss of goodwill when a restaurant served bad food to its customers. Liability has readily been found by way of indemnity when the purchaser incurs liability to another party by reason of the defective product.[46]

The troublesome question concerns the liability of the manufacturer for mere loss on the bargain—which is to say that the thing the plaintiff has purchased has less value than it was supposed to have.[47] The difficulty is

lines, Inc. v. Curtiss-Wright Corp., 1955, 1 Misc.2d 477, 148 N.Y.S.2d 284; Inglis v. American Motors Corp., 1965, 3 Ohio St.2d 132, 209 N.E.2d 583; Amodeo v. Autocraft Hudson, Inc., Misc.1959, 195 N.Y. S.2d 711, affirmed, 1960, 12 App.Div.2d 499, 207 N. Y.S.2d 101.

Cf. Karl's Shoe Stores v. United Shoe Mach. Corp., D.Mass.1956, 145 F.Supp. 376; Donovan Const. Co. v. General Elec. Co., D.Minn.1955, 133 F.Supp. 870; A. J. P. Contr. Corp. v. Brooklyn Builders Supply Co., 1939, 171 Misc. 157, 11 N.Y.S.2d 662, affirmed memo. 258 App.Div. 747, 15 N.Y.S.2d 424, affirmed memo. 283 N.Y. 692, 28 N.E.2d 412.

39. See supra, p. 635.

40. Dagley v. Armstrong Rubber Co., 7 Cir. 1965, 344 F.2d 245; DiBelardino v. Lemmon Pharmacal Co., 1965, 416 Pa. 580, 208 A.2d 283; B. F. Goodrich Co. v. Hammond, 10 Cir. 1959, 269 F.2d 501; Goldberg v. Kollsman Instrument Corp., 1963, 12 N.Y.2d 432, 240 N.Y.S.2d 592, 191 N.E.2d 81; Kelley v. Volkswagen Aktiengesellschaft, N.H.1970, 268 A.2d 837. See Note, 1966, 51 Iowa L.Rev. 1010.

41. McMillen Feeds, Inc. of Texas v. Harlow, Tex. Civ.App.1966, 405 S.W.2d 123, ref. n. r. e.; Kassab v. Central Soya, 1968, 432 Pa. 217, 246 A.2d 848; O. M. Franklin Serum Co. v. C. A. Hoover & Son, Tex. 1967, 418 S.W.2d 482, second appeal, C. A. Hoover & Son v. O. M. Franklin Serum Co., Tex.1969, 444 S. W.2d 596 (animal serum); McAfee v. Cargill, Inc., S.D.Cal.1954, 121 F.Supp. 5; Midwest Game Co. v. M. F. A. Milling Co., Mo.1959, 320 S.W.2d 547.

42. Simpson v. Logan Motor Co., D.C.App.1963, 192 A.2d 122; State Farm Mut. Auto. Ins. Co. v. Anderson-Weber, Inc., 1961, 252 Iowa 1289, 110 N.W.2d

449; Jarnot v. Ford Motor Co., 1959, 191 Pa.Super. 422, 156 A.2d 568.

43. Gladiola Biscuit Co. v. Southern Ice Co., 5 Cir. 1959, 267 F.2d 138 (batch of dough ruined by glass in ice); Spence v. Three Rivers Builders & Masonry Supply, Inc., 1958, 353 Mich. 120, 90 N.W.2d 873 (building blocks used in house); Southland Mill Co. v. Vege Fat, Inc., E.D.Ill.1965, 248 F.Supp. 482 (toxic liquid vegetable fat used in egg product); Hayman v. Shoemake, 1962, 203 Cal.App.2d 140, 21 Cal. 519 (crop grown from seed). Cf. Randy Knitwear, Inc. v. American Cyanamid Co., 1962, 11 N.Y.2d 5, 226 N.Y.S.2d 363, 181 N.E.2d 399 (fabrics made into garments, express warranty).

44. Morrow v. Caloric Appliance Corp., Mo.1963, 372 S.W.2d 41; Rasmus v. A. O. Smith Corp., N.D.Iowa 1958, 158 F.Supp. 70; Burrus Feed Mills, Inc. v. Reeder, Tex.Civ.App.1965, 391 S.W.2d 121. See also the cases cited supra, note 35.

45. Mazetti v. Armour & Co., 1913, 75 Wash. 622, 135 P. 633.

46. Suvada v. White Motor Co., 1965, 32 Ill.2d 612, 210 N.E.2d 182; Di Gregorio v. Champlain Valley Fruit Co., Inc., 1969, — Vt. —, 255 A.2d 183. See Note, [1965] U.Ill.L.F. 144.

47. See Franklin, When Worlds Collide, 1966, 18 Stan.L.Rev. 974; Notes, 1965, 19 Rut.L.Rev. 715; 1966, 66 Col.L.Rev. 917; 1966, 79 Harv.L.Rev. 1315;

that the existence, and the extent of any loss on the bargain must depend on what the bargain is; and the bargain is made with the dealer from whom the plaintiff buys, and not with the manufacturer. If the plaintiff trades in his old automobile on a new one, and is given an inadequate allowance by the dealer, is his loss on the bargain to be charged to the manufacturer, even if the new car has its defects? Such arguments might be persuasive to the effect that loss on the bargain is a matter to be determined in the first instance between the plaintiff and the dealer; and that if the manufacturer is to be liable, it should be to the dealer.

Where the liability rests upon express warranty without privity,[48] or upon innocent misrepresentation,[49] so that the manufacturer can be regarded as having assumed responsibility for more than the safety of the product, pecuniary loss on the bargain has uniformly been held to be recoverable. As to implied warranty, or strict liability in tort, the courts have not agreed. A few of them have allowed the recovery;[50] but in about an equal number it has been denied.[51] The best discus-

sion is probably to be found in the majority and dissenting opinions in Seely v. White Motor Co. in California in 1965.

102. ABNORMAL USE AND CONTRIBUTORY NEGLIGENCE

The effect, as a matter of "proximate cause," of negligence on the part of an intermediate buyer of the product, has arisen in several cases. There is general agreement that the seller may reasonably anticipate that the buyer may fail to inspect the goods and discover their defects before he delivers them to the plaintiff, and that this[52] or any other foreseeable negligence of the buyer,[53] or of his employees,[54] or indeed of any other person,[55] will not relieve the seller of liability.

On the other hand, it is ordinarily not reasonably to be expected that one who knows that a chattel is dangerous will pass it on to another without a warning. Where the buyer is notified of the danger,[56] or discovers

---

1966, 19 Vand.L.Rev. 214; 1966, 17 Hast.L.J. 385; 1966, 52 Va.L.Rev. 509; 1966, 114 U.Pa.L.Rev. 539; 1967, 19 Me.L.Rev. 92; 1967, 4 William.L.Rev. 402.

48. Posey v. Ford Motor Co., Fla.App.1961, 128 So.2d 149; Inglis v. American Motors Corp., 1965, 3 Ohio St.2d 132, 209 N.E.2d 583; Beck v. Spindler, 1959, 256 Minn. 543, 99 N.W.2d 670; Seely v. White Motor Co., 1965, 63 Cal.2d 9, 45 Cal.Rptr. 17, 403 P.2d 145; Ford Motor Co. v. Lemieux Lumber Co., Tex. Civ.App.1967, 418 S.W.2d 909.

49. Ford Motor Co. v. Lonon, 1966, 217 Tenn. 400, 398 S.W.2d 240.

50. Santor v. A & M Karagheusian, Inc., 1965, 44 N. J. 52, 207 A.2d 305; Lang v. General Motors Corp., N.D.1965, 136 N.W.2d 805; Manheim v. Ford Motor Co., Fla.1967, 201 So.2d 440; see Beck v. Spindler, 1959, 256 Minn. 543, 99 N.W.2d 670.

51. Seely v. White Motor Co., 1965, 63 Cal.2d 9, 45 Cal.Rptr. 17, 403 P.2d 145; Dennis v. Willys-Overland Motors, Inc., W.D.Mo.1953, 111 F.Supp. 875; Inglis v. American Motors Corp., (Ohio App.1964) 197 N.E.2d 921, affirmed on other grounds, 3 Ohio St.2d 132, 209 N.E.2d 583; Price v. Gatlin, 1965, 241 Or. 315, 405 P.2d 502. Cf. Kyker v. General Motors Corp., 1964, 214 Tenn. 521, 381 S.W.2d 884.

52. Boeing Airplane Co. v. Brown, 9 Cir. 1961, 291 F.2d 310; Alexander v. Nash-Kelvinator Co., 2 Cir. 1958, 261 F.2d 187; Ellis v. Lindmark, 1929, 177 Minn. 390, 225 N.W. 395; Pierce v. Ford Motor Co., 1951, 190 F.2d 910, cert. denied 342 U.S. 887; Beebe v. Highland Tank & Mfg. Co., 3 Cir. 1967, 373 F.2d 886, cert. denied 388 U.S. 911.

53. Burk v. Creamery Package Mfg. Co., 1905, 126 Iowa 730, 102 N.W. 793 (leaving unlabeled jug of sulphuric acid accessible); Moehlenbrock v. Parke Davis & Co., 1918, 141 Minn. 154, 169 N.W. 541 (surgeons using impure ether); Colvin v. John Powell & Co., 1956, 163 Neb. 112, 77 N.W.2d 900 (filling barrels containing poison with molasses, and selling them).

54. Steele v. Rapp, 1958, 183 Kan. 371, 327 P.2d 1053 (dropping jug full of nail polish remover); Smith v. Hobart Mfg. Co., E.D.Pa.1961, 194 F.Supp. 530 (removing guard from meat grinder).

55. Ford Motor Co. v. Zahn, 8 Cir. 1959, 265 F.2d 729 (sudden swerve by driver of car to avoid collision); Parkinson v. California Co., 10 Cir. 1956, 233 F.2d 432 (workman lighting match); Farrell v. G. O. Miller Co., 1920, 147 Minn. 52, 179 N.W. 566 (placing unlabeled gasoline beside kerosene).

56. Foster v. Ford Motor Co., 1926, 139 Wash. 341, 246 P. 945; Ford Motor Co. v. Wagoner, 1946, 183 Tenn. 392, 192 S.W.2d 840; Nishida v. E. I. Du Pont de Nemours & Co., 5 Cir. 1957, 245 F.2d 768, cert. denied 355 U.S. 915; Trust Co. of Chicago v.

it for himself,[57] and delivers the product without warning, it usually has been held that the responsibility is shifted to him,[58] and that his negligence supersedes the liability of the seller. This must, however, be qualified by the holdings in a few cases,[59] that there are some products which are so highly dangerous, and so utterly unsuited for their intended use, that the responsibility cannot be shifted; and that even such discovery and deliberate failure to disclose will not relieve the seller. There are also decisions [60] holding that where there is appreciable likelihood that the buyer will pass on the product without warning, and that any notice to him will not reach the ultimate user, there is liability for placing the product in his hands for marketing, even with such notice.

Although there have been few decisions,[61] there is every reason to expect that the same conclusions, in general, will be reached when strict liability is in question. One striking decision is Vandermark v. Ford Motor Co.,[62] in California in 1964, in which it was held that the obligation of the manufacturer of an automobile to the ultimate user was such that it could not delegate to its dealer responsibility for the final inspections, corrections and adjustments necessary to make the car ready for use, and that it could not escape responsibility on the ground that the defect in the delivered car was caused by something that the dealer did or failed to do.

A related rule, which developed in the negligence cases, and also turns on proximate cause, is that the seller is entitled to expect a normal use of his product, and is not liable when it is put to an abnormal one.[63] This too has been carried over to strict liability. On either basis, the seller is not liable when the product is materially altered before use,[64] or is combined with another product which

---

Lewis Auto Sales, 1940, 306 Ill.App. 132, 28 N.E.2d 300; E. I. Du Pont de Nemours & Co. v. Ladner, 1954, 221 Miss. 378, 73 So.2d 249.

57. Stultz v. Benson Lumber Co., 1936, 6 Cal.2d 688, 59 P.2d 100; Olds Motor Works v. Shaffer, 1911, 145 Ky. 616, 140 S.W. 1047; Catlin v. Union Oil Co. of Cal., 1916, 31 Cal.App. 597, 161 P. 29; Kapp v. E. I. Du Pont de Nemours & Co., E.D.Mich.1944, 57 F.Supp. 32.

Cf. Drazen v. Otis Elev. Co., 1963, 96 R.I. 114, 189 A.2d 693; McLaughlin v. Mine Safety Appliances Co., 1962, 11 N.Y.2d 62, 226 N.Y.S.2d 407, 181 N.E.2d 430; Whitehead v. Republic Gear Co., 9 Cir. 1939, 102 F.2d 84.

58. See supra, p. 176.

59. Kentucky Independent Oil Co. v. Schnitzler, 1925, 208 Ky. 507, 271 S.W. 570 (gasoline mixed with kerosene); Clement v. Crosby & Co., 1907, 148 Mich. 293, 111 N.W. 745 (explosive stove polish); Farley v. Edward E. Tower & Co., 1930, 271 Mass. 230, 171 N.E. 639 (inflammable combs for beauty shops); Warner v. Santa Catalina Island Co., 1955, 44 Cal. 2d 310, 282 P.2d 12 (high power cartridges for shooting gallery).

60. Comstock v. General Motors Corp., 1959, 358 Mich. 163, 99 N.W.2d 627; United States v. Lobb, D.Ky.1961, 192 F.Supp. 461.

61. Duckworth v. Ford Motor Co., E.D.Pa.1962, 211 F.Supp. 888, affirmed in part, remanded, reversed in part on other grounds, 320 F.2d 130 (dealer's fail-

ure to discover defect); Pabon v. Hackensack Auto Sales, Inc., 1960, 63 N.J.Super. 476, 164 A.2d 773 (same); Jarnot v. Ford Motor Co., 1959, 191 Pa. Super. 422, 156 A.2d 568 (same); Suvada v. White Motor Co., 1964, 51 Ill.App.2d 318, 201 N.E.2d 313, affirmed 32 Ill.2d 612, 210 N.E.2d 182 (failure to discover bad brakes); Halpern v. Jad Const. Corp., 1960, 27 Misc.2d 675, 202 N.Y.S.2d 945 (discovery of the danger).

62. 1964, 61 Cal.2d 256, 37 Cal.Rptr. 896, 391 P.2d 168. This might perhaps be justified on the basis of the somewhat peculiar relation between automobile manufacturers and their dealers; but in Alvarez v. Felker Mfg. Co., 1964, 230 Cal.App.2d 987, 41 Cal.Rptr. 514, it was applied to the maker of a concrete cutting machine, where no vestige of an agency relation could be found.

63. See Dale and Hilton, Use of the Product—When is it Abnormal? 1967, 4 William.L.Rev. 350; Note, 1967, 42 N.Y.U.L.Rev. 381.

64. Young v. Aeroil Prods. Co., 9 Cir. 1957, 248 F.2d 185; Martinez v. Nichols Conveyor & Eng. Co., 1966, 243 Cal.App.2d 795, 52 Cal.Rptr. 842; State Stove Mfg. Co. v. Hodges, Miss.1966, 189 So.2d 113, certiorari den. 386 U.S. 912; O. S. Stapley Co. v. Miller, 1968, 103 Ariz. 556, 447 P.2d 248; Westerberg v. School Dist. No. 792, 1967, 276 Minn. 1, 148 N.W.2d 312.

makes it dangerous,[65] or is mishandled,[66] or used in some unusual and unforeseeable way, as when a wall decorating compound is stirred with the finger,[67] or nail polish is set on fire,[68] or an obstinate lady insists on wearing shoes two sizes too small.[69] The seller is entitled to have his due warnings and instructions followed; and when they are disregarded, and injury results, he is not liable.[70]

At the same time, there are some relatively unusual uses of a product, such as standing on a chair,[71] or wearing a cocktail robe in proximity to the flame of a kitchen stove,[72] or cooking pork to an inadequate extent believed to be sufficient,[73] or using barbecue briquets as an indoor fuel,[74] which the seller may reasonably be expected to foresee and guard against; and he may have reason to know of an otherwise unforeseeable use made by those whom the product will reach,[75] and so be required to take precautions. Likewise, even in the case of normal uses, there may be a recognizable danger that the product will get into the hands of children or other wrong people,[76] which will call for steps to guard

65. Pabellon v. Grace Line, Inc., S.D.N.Y.1950, 94 F. Supp. 989, reversed on other grounds, 191 F.2d 169, certiorari denied 342 U.S. 893 (cleaning fluid mixed with other chemical); Newton v. Rockwood & Co., D.Mass.1966, 261 F.Supp. 485, affirmed 378 F.2d 315 (unit added to milking system).

66. Zesch v. Abrasive Co. of Philadelphia, 1946, 354 Mo. 1147, 193 S.W.2d 581 (grinding wheel subjected to side pressure); Waterman v. Liederman, 1936, 16 Cal.App.2d 483, 60 P.2d 881, hearing denied 16 Cal. App.2d 483, 62 P.2d 142 (wild driving on defective tire); Gilbride v. James Leffel & Co., Ohio App. 1942, 47 N.E.2d 1015 (operation of a boiler); Meche v. Farmers Drier & Storage Co., La.App.1967, 193 So.2d 807, writ refused 250 La. 369, 195 So.2d 644 (elevator improperly installed); Despatch Oven Co. v. Rauenhorst, 1949, 229 Minn. 436, 40 N.W.2d 73 (corn dryer operated at excessive heat).

67. Schfranek v. Benjamin Moore & Co., D.N.Y.1931, 54 F.2d 76.

68. Lawson v. Benjamin Ansehl Co., Mo.App.1944, 180 S.W.2d 751. Cf. Neusus v. Sponholtz, 7 Cir. 1966, 369 F.2d 259 (climbing fire truck ladder without lowering it); McCready v. United Iron & Steel Co., 10 Cir. 1959, 272 F.2d 700 (casements for use as window frames used as ladders); Vincent v. Nicholas E. Tsiknas Co., 1958, 337 Mass. 726, 151 N.E.2d 263 (beer can opener used to pry open glass jar); Cohagan v. Laclede Steel Co., Mo.1958, 317 S.W.2d 452 (wire binder used as handle in lifting steel with crane).

69. Dubbs v. Zak Bros. Co., 1931, 38 Ohio App. 299, 175 N.E. 626. Cf. Odekirk v. Sears, Roebuck & Co., 7 Cir. 1960, 274 F.2d 441, cert. denied 362 U.S. 974 (hammers struck together); Stevens v. Allis-Chalmers Mfg. Co., 1940, 151 Kan. 638, 100 P.2d 723 (dangerous method of controlling agricultural implement); Marker v. Universal Oil Prods. Co., 10 Cir. 1957, 250 F.2d 603 (hot catalyst used in refining unit).

70. Power Ski Co. of Florida, Inc. v. Allied Chemical Corp., Fla.App.1966, 188 So.2d 13 (substance used to fill skis improperly compounded); Procter & Gamble Mfg. Co. v. Langley, Tex.Civ.App.1967, 422 S.W. 2d 773, error dismissed (home permanent hair waving preparation); Taylor v. Jacobson, 1958, 336 Mass. 709, 147 N.E.2d 770 (hair dye used without

patch test); Kaspirowitz v. Schering Corp., 1961, 70 N.J.Super. 397, 175 A.2d 658 (drug sold and used without prescription); Fredendall v. Abraham & Straus, Inc., 1938, 279 N.Y. 146, 18 N.E.2d 11 (carbon tetrachloride used in enclosed space).

71. Phillips v. Ogle Aluminum Furniture, Inc., 1951, 106 Cal.App.2d 650, 235 P.2d 857.

72. Ringstad v. I. Magnin & Co., 1952, 39 Wash.2d 923, 239 P.2d 848. Cf. Brown v. Chapman, 9 Cir. 1962, 304 F.2d 149 (dancing in hula skirt).

73. McSpedon v. Kunz, 1936, 271 N.Y. 131, 2 N.E.2d 513; Holt v. Mann, 1936, 294 Mass. 21, 200 N.E. 403.

74. Alfieri v. Cabot Corp., 1963, 13 App.Div.2d 1027, 245 N.Y.S.2d 600, 195 N.E.2d 310. Cf. Lovejoy v. Minneapolis-Moline Power Imp. Co., 1956, 248 Minn. 319, 79 N.W.2d 688 (tractor operated downhill, using engine compression as brake); Nathan v. Electriglas Corp., 1955, 37 N.J.Super. 494, 117 A.2d 620 (testing electric fixture); Dunham v. Vaughan & Bushnell Mfg. Co., 1967, 86 Ill.App.2d 915, 229 N.E. 2d 684, affirmed in 42 Ill.2d 339, 247 N.E.2d 401 (claw hammer used to pound pin).

75. Swaney v. Peden Steel Co., 1963, 259 N.C. 531, 131 S.E.2d 601 (custom of workers to ride the load on steel truss); Simpson Timber Co. v. Parks, 9 Cir. 1966, 369 F.2d 324, reversed in 388 U.S. 459, conformed to in 390 F.2d 353, cert. denied 393 U.S. 858 (custom of stevedores to walk on covering of window openings). The case last cited makes it clear that it is not a question of what the seller does anticipate, but of what he should. See also Dunham v. Vaughan & Bushnell Mfg. Co., 1967, 86 Ill.App.2d 315, 229 N.E.2d 684, affirmed in 42 Ill.2d 339, 247 N.E.2d 401.

76. Estabrook v. J. C. Penney Co., 1969, 10 Ariz.App. 545, 456 P.2d 960 (child poking finger into escalator); Spruill, Adm'r v. Boyle-Midway, Inc., 4 Cir.

against it. In such cases the seller is not relieved.

In the ordinary case the seller may also expect a normal user of the product; and he is not liable where the injury is due to some susceptibility or idiosyncrasy which is peculiar to the plaintiff.[77] Where, however, the peculiarity is one common to a substantial, even though relatively small, number of possible users, he may be required to give warning; and without it there may be negligence or strict liability.[78]

Contributory Negligence

Contributory negligence is not the same thing as abnormal use; and although the two frequently coincide, one may exist without the other.[79] There is no doubt that where the plaintiff's action is founded on negligence, his contributory negligence will bar his recovery to the same extent as in any other negligence case.[80] But so far as strict liability is concerned, the decisions are ostensibly in a state of flat contradiction as to whether contributory negligence is available as a defense.[81]

Nearly all of the decisions have involved warranty, either on a direct sale or without privity. It has been said very often that contributory negligence is never a defense to the strict liability. It has been said somewhat more often that it is always a defense. The disagreement, however, is a superficial one of language only, and is merely part of the general murk that has surrounded "warranty." If the substance of the cases is looked to, with due regard to their facts, they fall into an entirely consistent pattern.

If the plaintiff's negligence consists only in a failure to discover the danger involved in the product,[82] or to take precautions against the possibility of its existence, as in the case of negligent driving on a defective tire,[83] it is quite clear that it is no defense

1962, 308 F.2d 79 (child drinking furniture polish); Haberly v. Reardon Co., Mo.1958, 319 S.W.2d 859 (eye of child coming in contact with paint brush); Hardman v. Helene Curtis Industries, Inc., 1964, 48 Ill.App.2d 42, 198 N.E.2d 681 (child and inflammable hair spray).

77. Jacquot v. Wm. Filene's Sons Co., 1958, 337 Mass. 312, 149 N.E.2d 635; Briggs v. National Industries, 1949, 92 Cal.App.2d 542, 207 P.2d 110; Ross v. Porteous, Mitchell & Braun Co., 1939, 136 Me. 118, 3 A.2d 650; Barrett v. S. S. Kresge Co., 1941, 144 Pa.Super. 516, 19 A.2d 502; Stanton v. Sears, Roebuck & Co., 1942, 312 Ill.App. 496, 38 N. E.2d 801.

78. See, as to allergies, supra, p. 648.

79. The distinction is well brought out in Swain v. Boeing Airplane Co., 2 Cir. 1964, 337 F.2d 940, cert. denied 380 U.S. 951, where defendant withdrew the defense of contributory negligence because it could not prove which decedent was flying the plane, but the question of abnormal use by improper flying was held to be still in the case. Other good cases on it are Preston v. Up-Right, Inc., 1966, 243 Cal. App.2d 636, 52 Cal.Rptr. 679; McDevitt v. Standard Oil Co. of Texas, 5 Cir. 1968, 391 F.2d 364; See also Rasmus v. A. O. Smith Corp., N.D.Iowa 1958, 158 F.Supp. 70; Gardner v. Coca-Cola Bottling Co., 1964, 267 Minn. 505, 127 N.W.2d 557.

80. See for example Pinto v. Clairol, Inc., 6 Cir. 1963, 324 F.2d 608; Siemer v. Midwest Mower

Corp., 8 Cir. 1961, 286 F.2d 381; Barbe v. Barbe, Okl.1963, 378 P.2d 314; Saeter v. Harley-Davidson Motor Co., 1960, 186 Cal.App.2d 248, 8 Cal.Rptr. 747; Scalzo v. Marsh, 1961, 13 Wis.2d 126, 108 N. W.2d 163 (comparative negligence statute).

81. See Levine, Buyer's Conduct as Affecting the Extent of Manufacturer's Liability in Warranty, 1968, 52 Minn.L.Rev. 627; Epstein, Products Liability: Defenses Based on Plaintiff's Conduct, [1968] Utah L.Rev. 267; Notes, 1966, 39 Temp.L.Q. 361; 1966, 33 Tenn.L.Rev. 464; 1969, 20 Syr.L.Rev. 924.

82. Pritchard v. Liggett & Myers Tobacco Co., 3 Cir. 1965, 35 F.2d 479, cert. denied 382 U.S. 987, amended 370 F.2d 95, cert. denied 386 U.S. 1009 (smoking cigarettes in ignorance of danger of lung cancer); Simmons v. Wichita Coca-Cola Bottling Co., 1957, 181 Kan. 35, 309 P.2d 633 (failure to discover matches in beverage); Brockett v. Harrell Bros., 1965, 206 Va. 457, 143 S.E.2d 897 (failure to discover shot in ham); Shamrock Fuel & Oil Sales Co. v. Tunks, Tex.Civ.App.1966, 406 S.W.2d 483 (failure to test kerosene); De Felice v. Ford Motor Co., 1969, 28 Conn.Sup. 164, 255 A.2d 636 (operating automobile without knowledge gasoline tank would explode in collision).

83. Dagley v. Armstrong Rubber Co., 7 Cir. 1965, 344 F.2d 245; Hansen v. Firestone Tire & Rubber Co., 6 Cir. 1960, 276 F.2d 254. Cf. Wendt v. Balletto, 1966, 26 Conn.Sup. 367, 224 A.2d 561 (minor making potassium chlorate bomb); Bahlman v. Hudson

to the strict liability. Thus if the plaintiff drinks a beverage without discovering that it is full of broken glass,[84] his failure to exercise due care in doing so does not relieve the defendant. On the other hand the kind of negligence which consists of proceeding voluntarily to encounter a known unreasonable danger and which tends to overlap the defense of assumption of risk, will relieve the defendant of liability.[85] If the plaintiff continues to operate a washing machine after discovery that the wringer is dangerously defective,[86] or negligently drives on a tire that he knows to be unsafe,[87] he cannot recover. These rules are quite consistent with those that have been worked out for other strict liability for animals and for abnormally dangerous activities.[88] Several cases have recognized the distinction,[89] and it is quite clear that it is made in fact.

Assumption of risk without contributory negligence, which turns upon consent of the plaintiff to relieve the defendant of his obligation, has seldom appeared in products liability cases;[90] but there can be no doubt that the defense is valid in a proper case. Thus when the plaintiff, bitten by a mad dog, consented to inoculation with the defendant's vaccine, with full knowledge of the risk involved, it was held that there was no liability for his death.[91]

103. PROOF

The proof required of a plaintiff seeking to recover for injuries from an unsafe product is very largely the same, whether his cause of action rests upon negligence, warranty, or strict liability in tort.[92]

On any of the three bases of liability, the plaintiff has the initial burden of establishing three things. The first is that he has been injured by the product. It is not enough to show that he ate the defendant's food and became ill, when he ate other things which

---

Motor Co., 1939, 290 Mich. 683, 288 N.W. 309 (express warranty of top of car, negligent driving).

See also Keener v. Dayton Elec. Mfg. Co., Mo.1969, 445 S.W.2d 362; McKisson v. Sales Affiliates, Tex. 1967, 416 S.W.2d 787; O. S. Stapley Co. v. Miller, 1969, 103 Ariz. 556, 447 P.2d 248.

84. Barefield v. La Salle Coca Cola Bottling Co., 1963, 370 Mich. 1, 120 N.W.2d 786.

85. Dippel v. Sciano, 1967, 37 Wis.2d 443, 155 N.W.2d 55; Topeka Mill & Elev. Co. v. Triplett, 1950, 168 Kan. 428, 213 P.2d 964 (feed known to be injuring chickens); Nelson v. Anderson, 1955, 245 Minn. 445, 72 N.W.2d 861 (oil burner known not to be functioning properly); Maiorino v. Weco Prods. Co., 1965, 45 N.J. 570, 214 A.2d 18 (opening glass toothbrush container with pressure); Dallison v. Sears, Roebuck & Co., 10 Cir. 1962, 313 F.2d 343 (smoking in bed).

86. Gutelius v. General Elec. Co., 1940, 37 Cal.App.2d 455, 99 P.2d 682, motion denied 39 Cal.App.2d 292, 102 P.2d 1108. Cf. Missouri Bag Co. v. Chemical Delinting Co., 1952, 214 Miss. 13, 58 So.2d 71 (use of bags known to be defective); Tex-Tube, Inc. v. Rockwall Corp., Tex.Civ.App.1964, 379 S.W.2d 405 (failure to shut off pump after discovery of leak in pipe); Finks v. Viking Refrigerators, Inc., 1941, 235 Mo.App. 679, 147 S.W.2d 124 (refrigerated meat showcase discovered to be unfit).

87. Youtz v. Thompson Tire Co., 1941, 46 Cal.App.2d 672, 116 P.2d 636. Cf. Cintrone v. Hertz Truck Leasing & Rental Service, 1965, 45 N.J. 434, 212 A. 2d 769 (bad brakes); Buttrick v. Arthur Lessard & Sons, Inc., 1969, —— N.H. ——, 260 A.2d 111 (lights); Ferraro v. Ford Motor Co., 1966, 423 Pa. 324, 223 A.2d 746 (wheels locking on left turns).

88. See supra, p. 522.

89. Cedar Rapids & Iowa City Ry. & Light Co. v. Sprague Elec. Co., 1917, 280 Ill. 386, 117 N.E. 461, 462; Pauls Valley Milling Co. v. Gabbert, 1938, 182 Okl. 500, 78 P.2d 685; Chapman v. Brown, D.Hawaii 1961, 198 F.Supp. 78, affirmed 9 Cir. 1962, 304 F.2d 149. See Notes, 1962, 15 U.Fla.L.Rev. 85; 1963, 36 So.Cal.L.Rev. 490.

90. There is a good discussion in Keeton, Assumption of Risk in Products Liability Cases, 1961, 22 La.L.Rev. 122.

91. Carmen v. Eli Lilly Co., 1941, 109 Ind.App. 76, 32 N.E.2d 729.

92. See Keeton, Products Liability—Proof of the Manufacturer's Negligence, 1963, 49 Va.L.Rev. 675; Keeton, Products Liability—Problems Pertaining to Proof of Negligence, 1965, 19 Sw.L.J. 26; Keeton, Products Liability—Inadequacy of Information, 1970, 48 Tex.L.Rev. 398; Emroch, Pleading and Proof in a Strict Products Liability Case [1966] Ins.L.J. 581; Notes, 1966, 45 Neb.L.Rev. 189; 1969, 21 Stan.L.Rev. 1777; 1969, 22 Me.L.Rev. 189.

might just as easily have been responsible.[93] The second is that the injury occurred because the product was defective, unreasonably unsafe. Proof that an airplane has crashed does not make out a case against a seller, where there is no evidence to show that it was not due to negligent flying.[94] The third is that the defect existed when the product left the hands of the particular defendant. When meat has been exposed to the air for a considerable time by a dealer, and might have spoiled in the process, the burden of proof against the original seller of the meat is not sustained.[95]

Once the plaintiff has proved all three, all trial lawyers know that the plaintiff will usually recover against the manufacturer for negligence. This is because the doctrine of res ipsa loquitur [96] ordinarily allows the case to go to the jury, and the jury is permitted to, and usually does, infer that some negligence of the defendant was responsible for the defect. There have been occasional cases in which the defect has been such that res ipsa loquitur has not been applied to aid the plaintiff in his proof of negligence,[97] and there have been a few in which the defendant's evidence of his own due care has been held to entitle him to a directed verdict,[98] and fewer still in which the jury has found that there is no negligence.[99] The total of these has, however, been so small as to be almost negligible; and by and large, once the proof reaches this point, the jury is permitted to and does find for the plaintiff.

Strict liability has eliminated any question of negligence, and in the ordinary case has made evidence of the defendant's due care immaterial.[1] So far as the manufacturer is concerned, the importance of this is probably slight; but when the action is against a dealer, who is not held to the same duty of care as the manufacturer,[2] and is as a matter of fact frequently not negligent at all,[3] there may be substantial increase in liability.

The difficult problems are those of proof by circumstantial evidence. Strictly speaking, since proof of negligence is not in issue, res ipsa loquitur has no application to strict liability; but the inferences which are the

---

93. Geisness v. Scow Bay Packing Co., 1942, 16 Wash.2d 1, 132 P.2d 740. Accord, English v. Louisiana Creamery, Inc., La.App.1965, 181 So.2d 800; John Morrell & Co. v. Shultz, Miss.1968, 208 So.2d 906. Cf. Landers v. Safeway Stores, 1943, 172 Or. 116, 139 P.2d 788.

94. Hurley v. Beech Aircraft Corp., 7 Cir. 1966, 355 F.2d 517, cert. denied 385 U.S. 821; Swain v. Boeing Airplane Co., 2 Cir. 1964, 337 F.2d 940, cert. denied 380 U.S. 951. Accord: Elliott v. Lachance, 1969, 109 N.H. 481, 256 A.2d 153; Delta Oxygen Co. v. Scott, 1964, 238 Ark. 534, 383 S.W.2d 885; Gardner v. Coca-Cola Bottling Co., 1964, 267 Minn. 505, 127 N.W.2d 557; Scientific Supply Co. v. Zelinger, 1959, 139 Colo. 568, 341 P.2d 897.

95. Tiffin v. Great A. & P. Tea Co., 1959, 18 Ill.2d 48, 162 N.W.2d 406; Cudahy Packing Co. v. Baskin, 1934, 170 Miss. 834, 155 So. 217. Cf. Eversmeyer v. Chrysler Corp., La.App.1966, 192 So.2d 845.

96. See supra, § 39. For applications of the principle to products liability, see Liggett & Myers Tobacco Co. v. De Lape, 9 Cir. 1940, 109 F.2d 598 (explosive cigarette); Zentz v. Coca-Cola Bottling Co., 1952, 39 Cal.2d 436, 247 P.2d 344 (exploding bottle); Woodworkers Tool Works v. Byrne, 9 Cir. 1951, 191 F.2d 667 (disintegration of panel hood on shaper); Peterson v. Minnesota Power & Light Co., (1940) 207 Minn. 387, 291 N.W. 705; Killian v. Logan, 1932, 115 Conn. 437, 162 A. 30.

97. H. J. Heinz Co. v. Duke, 1938, 196 Ark. 180, 116 S.W.2d 1039; Sheffers v. Willoughby (contaminated oysters); O'Brien v. Louis K. Liggett Co., 1926, 255 Mass. 553, 152 N.E. 57; Crocker v. Baltimore Dairy Lunch, 1913, 214 Mass. 177, 100 N.E. 1078.

98. For example Nichols v. Continental Baking Co., 3 Cir. 1929, 34 F.2d 141; Swenson v. Purity Baking Co., 1931, 183 Minn. 289, 236 N.W. 310; Smith v. Salem Coca-Cola Bottling Co., 1942, 92 N.H. 97, 25 A.2d 125.

99. See for example Weggeman v. Seven-Up Bottling Co., 1959, 5 Wis.2d 503, 93 N.W.2d 467, rehearing denied, amended 94 N.W.2d 645.

1. Pulley v. Pacific Coca-Cola Bottling Co., 1966, 68 Wash.2d 778, 415 P.2d 636.

2. See supra, § 95.

3. For example, where the defect is latent, and not discoverable by any inspection the dealer is required to make. Lipari v. National Grocery Co., 1938, 120 N.J.L. 97, 198 A. 393; Miller v. Steinfeld, 1916, 174 App.Div. 337, 160 N.Y.S. 800; Stone v. Van Noy R. News Co., 1913, 153 Ky. 240, 154 N.Y.S. 1092.

core of the doctrine remain, and are no less applicable.[4] The plaintiff is not required to eliminate all other possibilities, and so prove his case beyond a reasonable doubt. As on other issues in civil actions, it is enough that he makes out a preponderance of probability. It is enough that the court cannot say that reasonable men on the jury could not find it more likely than not that the fact is true.[5]

The mere fact of an accident, standing alone, as where an automobile goes into the ditch, does not make out a case that the product was defective,[6] nor does the fact that it was found in a defective condition after the event, where it appears equally likely that it was caused by the accident itself.[7] But the addition of other facts tending to show that the defect existed before the accident,[8] such

as its occurrence within a short time after sale,[9] or proof of the malfunction of a part for which the manufacturer alone could be responsible,[10] may make out a sufficient case, and so may expert testimony.[11] So likewise may proof that other similar products made by the defendant met with similar misfortunes,[12] or the elimination of other likely causes by satisfactory evidence.[13] In addition, there are some accidents, as where a bev-

---

4. Kroger Co. v. Bowman, Ky.1967, 411 S.W.2d 339; State Farm Mut. Auto. Ins. Co. v. Anderson-Weber, Inc., 1961, 252 Iowa 1289, 110 N.W.2d 449. See also Falstaff Brewing Corp. v. Williams, Miss.1967, 234 So.2d 620.

5. Vandagriff v. J. C. Penney Co., 1964, 228 Cal.App. 2d 579, 39 Cal.Rptr. 671.

6. Payne v. Valley Motor Sales, Inc., 1962, 146 W.Va. 1063, 124 S.E.2d 622; McNamara v. American Motors Corp., 5 Cir. 1957, 247 F.2d 445 (backing car shot forward); Smith v. General Motors Corp., 5 Cir. 1955, 227 F.2d 210 (car leaving road); Herrin's Adm'x v. Jackson, Ky.1954, 265 S.W.2d 775 (door of car coming open); Shramek v. General Motors Corp., 1966, 69 Ill.App.2d 72, 216 N.E.2d 244 (blowout).

7. Davis v. Firestone Tire & Rubber Co., N.D.Cal. 1961, 196 F.Supp. 407 (tread separated from tire); General Motors Corp. v. Wolverine Ins. Co., 6 Cir. 1958, 255 F.2d 8 (wheel off of car); Lovas v. General Motors Corp., 6 Cir. 1954, 212 F.2d 805 (steering wheel off of shaft); Hupp Motor Car Corp. v. Wadsworth, 6 Cir. 1940, 113 F.2d 827 (tire deflated); Fisher v. Sheppard, 1951, 366 Pa. 347, 77 A.2d 417 (broken sleeve in differential).

8. State Farm Mut. Auto. Ins. Co. v. Anderson-Weber, Inc., 1961, 252 Iowa 1289, 110 N.W.2d 449 (localized smell of burning); Clark v. Zuzich Truck Lines, Mo.App.1961, 344 S.W.2d 304 (car out of control before leaving road); Knapp v. Willys-Ardmore, Inc., 1958, 174 Pa.Super. 90, 100 A.2d 105 (broken tie rod, from wheel seen to turn); Jones v. Burger-

meister Brewing Corp., 1961, 198 Cal.App.2d 198, 18 Cal.Rptr. 311 (abrasion or scuff mark on bottle).

In Redman v. Ford Motor Co., 1969, — S.C. —, 170 S.E.2d 207, the improbability that a dangling wheel and axle could have been caused by the accident was held to make out a case.

9. Gherna v. Ford Motor Co., 1966, 246 Cal.App.2d 639, 55 Cal.Rptr. 94 (fire in automobile engine driven 1600 miles); Jacobson v. Broadway Motors, Inc., Mo.App.1968, 430 S.W.2d 602 (same, 1100 miles); Bailey v. Montgomery Ward & Co., 1967, 6 Ariz. App. 213, 431 P.2d 108 (pogo stick broke after short use); Henningsen v. Bloomfield Motors, Inc., 1960, 32 N.J. 358, 161 A.2d 69 (new car veering from road); M. Dietz & Sons v. Miller, 1957, 43 N.J.Super. 334, 128 A.2d 719 (brake failure, car driven 50 miles).

10. MacDougall v. Ford Motor Co., 1969, 214 Pa.Super. 384, 257 A.2d 676 (steering gear); Kridler v. Ford Motor Co., 3 Cir. 1970, 422 F.2d 1182 (same); Le Blanc v. Ford Motor Co., 1963, 346 Mass. 225, 191 N.E.2d 301 (car went into gear with shift lever in neutral); Smith v. Hencir-Nichols, Inc., 1967, 276 Minn. 390, 150 N.W.2d 556 (steering gear). Cf. Greco v. Bucciconi Eng. Co., W.D.Pa.1968, 283 F. Supp. 978, affirmed C.A., 407 F.2d 87.

11. Kuzma v. United States Rubber Co., 3 Cir. 1963, 323 F.2d 657; Smith v. Hencir-Nichols, Inc., 1967, 276 Minn. 390, 150 N.W.2d 556; Vandermark v. Ford Motor Co., 1964, 61 Cal.2d 256, 37 Cal.Rptr. 896, 391 P.2d 168; Simpson v. Logan Motor Co., D.C.App.1963, 192 A.2d 122. Cf. Buffums' v. City of Long Beach, 1931, 111 Cal.App. 327, 295 P.2d 540 (water main broke).

12. Coca-Cola Bottling Works v. Shelton, 1926, 214 Ky. 118, 282 S.W. 778; Boyd v. Marion Coca-Cola Bottling Co., 1962, 240 S.C. 383, 126 S.E.2d 178; cf. Ashkenazi v. Nehi Bottling Co., 1940, 217 N.C. 552, 8 S.E.2d 818.

13. Vaccarezza v. Sanguinetti, 1945, 71 Cal.App.2d 687, 163 P.2d 470; Patterson v. George H. Weyer, Inc., 1962, 189 Kan. 501, 370 P.2d 116.

erage bottle explodes [14] or even breaks [15] under normal handling, as to which there is common experience that they do not ordinarily occur without a defect; and this permits the inference.

Tracing the defect in the product into the hands of the defendant confronts the plaintiff with greater difficulties.[16] There is first of all the question of lapse of time and long continued use. This in itself will never prevent recovery where there is satisfactory proof of an original defect; [17] but when there is no such definite evidence, and it is only a matter of inference from the fact that something broke or gave way, the continued use usually prevents the inference that more probably than not the product was defective when it was sold.[18] It has been said many times

that the seller does not undertake to provide a product that will not wear out.[19] Several jurisdictions, however, have drawn a distinction between moving and stationary parts, which are not so likely to fail with wear, and have permitted the inference as to the latter.[20]

With continued use eliminated as an obstacle, the plaintiff must further eliminate his own improper conduct as an equally probable cause of the injury.[21] When he has done this, and has accounted for other reasonably probable causes, he has made out a sufficient case of strict liability against the dealer who last sold the product. But the very presence of the latter in the picture means that he too must be eliminated before the case is established against the manufacturer. When on the evidence it appears equally probable that the defect has developed in the hands of the dealer, the plaintiff has not made out a case of strict liability, or even negligence, against any prior party.[22]

This has meant, in a good many cases, that when a beverage bottle breaks or explodes the case against the manufacturer is not established until the intermediate handling has

---

14. Zentz v. Coca Cola Bottling Co., 1952, 39 Cal.2d 436, 247 P.2d 344; Nichols v. Nold, 1953, 174 Kan. 613, 258 P.2d 317; Johnson v. Louisiana Coca-Cola Bottling Co., La.App.1953, 63 So.2d 459; Canada Dry Bottling Co. v. Shaw, Fla.App.1960, 118 So.2d 840; Addeo v. Metropolitan Bottling Co., 1963, 39 Misc.2d 474, 241 N.Y.S.2d 120, affirmed 20 App.Div.2d 967, 251 N.Y.S.2d 412. See Spangenberg, Exploding Bottles, 1963, 24 Ohio St.L.J. 431; Bishop, Trouble in a Bottle, 1964, 16 Bay.L.Rev. 337.

15. Vassallo v. Sabatte Land Co., 1963, 212 Cal.App. 2d 11, 27 Cal.Rptr. 814; Renninger v. Foremost Dairies, Inc., Fla.App.1965, 171 So.2d 602.

16. This must be pleaded and proved even in cases of strict liability. Olney v. Beaman Bottling Co., 1967, 220 Tenn. 459, 418 S.W.2d 430; Rossignol v. Danbury School of Aeronautics, 1967, 154 Conn. 549, 227 A.2d 418; see Bailey v. Montgomery Ward & Co., 1967, 6 Ariz.App. 213, 431 P.2d 108.

17. Mickle v. Blackmon, 1969, 252 S.C. 202, 166 S.E. 2d 173 (13 years); Burns v. Pennsylvania Rubber & Supply Co., 1961, 117 Ohio App.2d 12, 189 N.E.2d 645 (12 years); Pryor v. Lee C. Moore Corp., 10 Cir. 1958, 262 F.2d 673, cert. denied 360 U.S. 902 (15 years); International Derrick & Equip. Co. v. Croix, 5 Cir. 1957, 241 F.2d 216, cert. denied 354 U. S. 910 (7 years); Tucker v. Unit Crane & Shovel Corp., 1970, —— Or. ——, 473 P.2d 862 (9 years); Rosenau v. City of New Brunswick, 1968, 51 N.J. 130, 238 A.2d 169 ("prolonged safe use"). See Note, 1967, 4 Willam L.Rev. 394.

18. Courtois v. General Motors Corp., 1962, 37 N.J. 525, 182 A.2d 545; United States Rubber Co. v. Bauer, 8 Cir. 1963, 319 F.2d 463; Kapp v. Sullivan Chevrolet Co., 1962, 234 Ark. 395, 353 S.W.2d 5; Solomon v. White Motor Co., W.D.Pa.1957, 153 F.

Supp. 917; D'Allesandro v. Edgar Murray Supply Co., La.App.1966, 185 So.2d 34.

19. Triplett v. American Creosote Works, 1965, 251 Miss. 727, 171 So.2d 342; Jakubowski v. Minnesota Min. & Mfg. Co., 1964, 42 N.J. 177, 199 A.2d 826; Gomez v. E. W. Bliss Co., 1961, 27 Misc.2d 649, 211 N.Y.S.2d 246.

20. Darling v. Caterpillar Tractor Co., 1959, 171 Cal. App.2d 713, 341 P.2d 23; Carney v. Sears, Roebuck & Co., 4 Cir. 1962, 309 F.2d 300; Beadles v. Servel, Inc., 1951, 344 Ill.App. 133, 100 N.E.2d 405; Parker v. Ford Motor Co., Mo.1956, 296 S.W.2d 35.

21. Honea v. City Dairy, Inc., 1943, 22 Cal.2d 614, 140 P.2d 369.

22. Tiffin v. Great A. & P. Tea Co., 1959, 18 Ill.2d 48, 162 N.E.2d 406 (opened meat); Cudahy Packing Co. v. Baskin, 1934, 170 Miss. 834, 155 So. 217 (same); Kerr v. Corning Glass Works, 1969, 284 Minn. 115, 169 N.W.2d 587 (glass dish might have been dropped); Alexander v. Davis, Tex.Civ.App. 1954, 383 S.W.2d 822, ref. n. r. e. (contaminated beans); Huggins v. John Morrell & Co., 1964, 176 Ohio St. 171, 198 N.E.2d 448 (explosion of pigs' feet, several intermediate handlers).

been accounted for.[23] There need not be conclusive proof, and only enough is required to permit a finding of the greater probability.[24] Since the plaintiff nearly always finds it difficult to obtain evidence as to what has happened to the bottle along the way, the courts have been quite lenient in finding the evidence sufficient. He is not required to do the impossible by accounting for every moment of the bottle's existence since it left the defendant;[25] and it is enough that he produces sufficient evidence of careful handling in general, and of the absence of unusual incidents, to permit reasonable men to draw the conclusion.[26]

If the product reaches the plaintiff in a sealed container, with the defect on the inside, the inference against the manufacturer is easily drawn, and may even be conclusive.[27] The typical case is that of the foreign object in the bottle.[28] There may still be the possibility of intentional tampering; and there are decisions which have held that the plaintiff must disprove it, particularly where the bottle has been exposed to meddling by irresponsible persons,[29] or a charged beverage is found to be "flat" when opened.[30] But in the absence of any such special reason to look for it, the considerable majority of the later cases have held that intentional tampering is so unusual, and so unlikely, that the probabilities are all against it, and the plaintiff is not required to prove that it did not occur.[31]

There have been sporadic attempts to aid the plaintiff in his difficulty of proof in cases where multiple defendants were joined. Kansas,[32] Pennsylvania,[33] and Washington[34] have shifted the burden of proof as to tracing the defect onto the shoulders of the manufacturer and the dealer. The reasoning of these cases, which find "exclusive control" where it is quite obviously not exclusive as to either defendant, is not very convincing. They are quite evidently deliberate decisions of policy, seeking to compensate the plaintiff first, and to leave the defendants to

---

23. Trust v. Arden Farms Co., 1958, 50 Cal.2d 217, 324 P.2d 583; Joffre v. Canada Dry Ginger Ale, Inc., 1960, 222 Md. 1, 158 A.2d 631; Johnson v. Coca-Cola Bottling Co., 1952, 235 Minn. 471, 51 N. W.2d 573; Miami Coca-Cola Bottling Co. v. Reisinger, Fla.1953, 68 So.2d 589; Smith v. Coca-Cola Bottling Co., 1952, 97 N.H. 522, 92 A.2d 658.

24. Gordon v. Aztec Brewing Co., 1949, 33 Cal.2d 514, 203 P.2d 522; Honea v. Coca-Cola Bottling Co., 1944, 143 Tex. 272, 183 S.W.2d 968.

25. Macon Coca-Cola Bottling Co. v. Chancey, 1960, 101 Ga.App. 166, 112 S.E.2d 811, affirmed 216 Ga. 61, 114 S.E.2d 517; Zarling v. La Salle Coca Cola Bottling Co., 1958, 2 Wis.2d 596, 87 N.W.2d 263.

26. Lafleur v. Coca-Cola Bottling Co. of Lake Charles, La.App.1966, 195 So.2d 419, writ refused 250 La. 488, 196 So.2d 802; Gordon v. Aztec Brewing Co., 1949, 33 Cal.2d 514, 203 P.2d 522; Ryan v. Adam Scheidt Brewing Co., 3 Cir. 1952, 197 F.2d 614; Groves v. Florida Coca-Cola Bottling Co., Fla. 1949, 40 So.2d 128; Coca Cola Bottling Works v. Crow, 1956, 200 Tenn. 161, 291 S.W.2d 589.

27. Dryden v. Continental Baking Co., 1938, 11 Cal.2d 33, 77 P.2d 833 (glass baked in bread).

28. Heimsoth v. Falstaff Brewing Corp., 1953, 1 Ill. App.2d 28, 116 N.E.2d 193; Le Blanc v. Louisiana Coca Cola Bottling Co., 1952, 221 La. 919, 60 So.2d 873; Manzoni v. Detroit Coca Cola Bottling Co., 1961, 363 Mich. 235, 109 N.W.2d 918; Keller v. Coca Cola Bottling Co., 1958, 214 Or. 654, 330 P.2d 346; Tafoya v. Las Cruces Coca-Cola Bottling Co., 1955, 59 N.M. 43, 278 P.2d 575.

29. Williams v. Paducah Coca Cola Bottling Co., 1951, 343 Ill.App. 1, 98 N.E.2d 164; Williams v. Coca-Cola Bottling Co., Mo.App.1955, 285 S.W.2d 53; Cunningham v. Coca-Cola Bottling Co., 1948, 87 Cal.App.2d 106, 198 P.2d 333.

30. Sharpe v. Danville Coca-Cola Bottling Co., 1956, 9 Ill.App.2d 175, 132 N.E.2d 442.

31. Coca-Cola Bottling Co. v. Negron Torres, 1 Cir. 1958, 255 F.2d 149; Miami Coca Cola Bottling Co. v. Todd, Fla.1958, 101 So.2d 34; Le Blanc v. Louisiana Coca Cola Bottling Co., 1952, 221 La. 919, 60 So.2d 873; Keller v. Coca-Cola Bottling Co., 1958, 214 Or. 654, 330 P.2d 346.

Particularly when the beverage foams or effervesces when it is opened. Heimsoth v. Falstaff Brewing Corp., 1953, 1 Ill.App.2d 28, 116 N.E.2d 193; Rozumailski v. Philadelphia Coca-Cola Bottling Co., 1929, 296 Pa. 114, 145 A. 700; Wichita Coca-Cola Bottling Co. v. Tyler, Tex.Civ.App.1956, 288 S.W.2d 903, ref. n. r. e.

32. Nichols v. Nold, 1953, 174 Kan. 613, 258 P.2d 317.

33. Loch v. Confair, 1953, 372 Pa. 212, 93 A.2d 451.

34. Pulley v. Pacific Coca-Cola Bottling Co., 1966, 68 Wash.2d 778, 415 P.2d 636.

fight out the question of responsibility among themselves. The same is to be said of a federal case out of Texas,[35] where the burden was shifted to the maker of dynamite and the maker of the cap attached to it, on the ground that they were cooperating in turning out the final product, and one from New York,[36] where the same thing was done as to the maker of an altimeter and the manufacturer of a plane in which it was installed. Other courts have thus far refused to follow along these lines.[37]

104. OTHER SUPPLIERS

As to defendants other than sellers, who supply chattels under contract, there has been much the same development in the law of negligence as in the case of sellers. The lessor of an automobile, or any other bailor for hire, is liable to a guest in the vehicle, or a person run down by it on the highway, not only if he knows that the car is dangerously defective at the time he turns it over,[38] or that the person entrusted with it is incompetent to handle it,[39] but also if he merely fails to make reasonable inspection to discover possible defects before turning it over.[40] The

same responsibility has been imposed upon a caterer serving food to the plaintiff under contract with another,[41] and upon a shipper of goods where a servant of the carrier or the consignee is injured while unloading a defective vehicle which the shipper has furnished for transportation.[42] Although there are old cases to the contrary,[43] the modern view is definitely that the obligation of a railway company to make reasonable inspection and repair of its cars before supplying them extends to the employees of a shipper,[44] of a consignee,[45] and of a connecting carrier.[46] In such a case, however, it has been held that the responsibility does not extend beyond the use of the car in accordance with the original contract, and that a reconsignment by a connecting carrier terminates the liability.[47] A

---

35. Dement v. Olin-Mathieson Chem. Corp., 5 Cir. 1960, 282 F.2d 76.

36. Becker v. American Airlines, Inc., S.D.N.Y.1961, 200 F.Supp. 839.

37. See Gobin v. Avenue Food Mart, 1960, 178 Cal. App.2d 345, 2 Cal.Rptr. 822; Vandermark v. Ford Motor Co., 1964, 61 Cal.2d 256, 37 Cal.Rptr. 896, 391 P.2d 168.

38. Broome v. Budget Rent-A-Car of Jax, Inc., Fla. App.1966, 182 So.2d 26; Lynch v. Richardson, 1895, 163 Mass. 160, 39 N.E. 801; Trusty v. Patterson, 1930, 299 Pa. 469, 149 A. 717; Ferraro v. Taylor, 1936, 197 Minn. 5, 265 N.W. 829. Cf. Bryson v. Hines, 4 Cir. 1920, 268 F. 290.

39. See infra, p. 678.

40. Hinson v. Phoenix Pie Co., 1966, 3 Ariz.App. 523, 416 P.2d 202; Ikeda v. Okada Trucking Co., 1964, 47 Haw. 588, 393 P.2d 171; Austin v. Austin, 1960, 252 N.C. 283, 113 S.E.2d 553; Scharf v. Gardner Cartage Co., 1953, 95 Ohio App. 153, 113 N.E.2d 717; Mitchell v. Lonergan, 1934, 285 Mass. 266, 189 N.E. 39.

41. Bishop v. Weber, 1885, 139 Mass. 411, 1 N.E. 154. Cf. Hayes v. Torrington Water Co., 1914, 88 Conn. 609, 92 A. 406 (water supplied under contract with city).

42. Elliott v. Hall, 1885, 15 Q.B.D. 315; Standard Oil Co. v. Wakefield's Adm'r, 1904, 102 Va. 824, 47 S.E. 830; Gaston v. Wabash R. Co., Mo.1959, 322 S.W.2d 865; Fouraker v. Hill & Morton, 1958, 162 Cal. App.2d 668, 328 P.2d 527; Yandell v. National Fireproofing Corp., 1953, 239 N.C. 1, 79 S.E.2d 223. See Note, 1966, 54 Geo.L.J. 1439.

43. Roddy v. Missouri Pac. R. Co., 1891, 104 Mo. 234, 15 S.W. 1112; Missouri, K. & T. R. Co. v. Merrill, 1902, 65 Kan. 436, 70 P. 358; Glynn v. Central R. Co., 1900, 175 Mass. 510, 56 N.E. 698.

44. Chicago, R. I. & P. R. Co. v. Williams, 8 Cir. 1957, 245 F.2d 397, cert. denied 355 U.S. 855; Bierzynski v. New York Cent. R. Co., 1969, 31 App.Div.2d 294, 297 N.Y.S.2d 457, on remand 59 Misc.2d 315, 298 N.Y.S.2d 584; Missouri Pac. R. Co. v. Burks, 1939, 199 Ark. 189, 133 S.W.2d 9; Peneff v. Duluth, M. & N. R. Co., 1925, 164 Minn. 6, 204 N.W. 524; Chicago, I. & L. R. v. Pritchard, 1906, 168 Ind. 398, 81 N.E. 78.

45. D'Almeida v. Boston & Me. R. Co., 1911, 209 Mass. 81, 95 N.E. 398; Wabash R. Co. v. Hartog, 8 Cir. 1958, 257 F.2d 401; Brehmer v. Chicago & N. W. R. Co., 1955, 269 Wis. 383, 69 N.W.2d 565; Erie R. Co. v. Murphy, 6 Cir. 1940, 108 F.2d 817, 126 A. L.R. 1093; Chicago, R. I. & P. R. Co. v. Sampson, 1940, 200 Ark. 906, 142 S.W.2d 221.

46. Moon v. Northern Pac. R. Co., 1891, 46 Minn. 106, 48 N.W. 679; Pennsylvania R. Co. v. Snyder, 1896, 55 Ohio St. 342, 45 N.E. 559.

47. Sawyer v. Minneapolis & St. L. R. Co., 1888, 38 Minn. 103, 35 N.W. 671; Demers v. Illinois Central

similar duty of reasonable care has been imposed upon owners of premises [48] and contractors [49] who supply chattels for use by employees of others in connection with work to be done under a contract. The conclusion seems to be that any person furnishing a chattel for a use in which he has a business interest may be liable for his negligence to anyone who may reasonably be expected to be in the vicinity of its probable use.[50]

Occasionally in such cases it has been held that the duty of the person supplied to inspect the chattel himself relieves the supplier of liability, because there is "superseding negligence." [51] But as in the case of a seller, most courts have held that his failure to make such inspection is within the foreseeable risk, and does not excuse the supplier.[52] When the defect is disclosed to the one supplied, or is in fact discovered by him, the supplier usually is relieved of responsibility; [53] but in a few cases of extreme danger, as where an

automobile unfit to be driven on the highway is delivered to one who may be expected to use it nevertheless, the supplier has been held liable to a third person notwithstanding such discovery.[54]

The cases which have dealt with gratuitous lenders and bailors have held that there is no greater obligation toward a third person than to the immediate bailee. The bailor is therefore under no duty to inspect the chattel before delivering it,[55] and the bailee assumes the full responsibility for its condition. There is liability only for a failure to disclose defects of which the bailor has knowledge which may render it dangerous to others.[56] In all such cases, however, the bailor may be liable if he entrusts the chattel to a person whom he knows or should know [57] to

---

R. Co., 1959, 339 Mass. 247, 158 N.E.2d 672; cf. Caledonian R. Co. v. Mulholland, [1898] A.C. 216.

48. Heaven v. Pender, 1883, 11 Q.B.D. 503; Coughtry v. Globe Woolen Co., 1874, 56 N.Y. 124; Johnson v. Spear, 1889, 76 Mich. 139, 42 N.W. 1092; The Student, 4 Cir. 1917, 243 F. 807.

49. See infra, p. 680.

50. Second Restatement of Torts, § 392. See for example Perfection Paint & Color Co. v. Kouduris, Ind.App.1970, 258 N.E.2d 681.

51. Risque's Adm'r v. Chesapeake & O. R. Co., 1905, 104 Va. 476, 51 S.E. 730; Louisville & N. R. Co. v. Weldon, 1915, 165 Ky. 654, 177 S.W. 459; Missouri, K. & T. R. Co. v. Merrill, 1902, 65 Kan. 436, 70 P. 358.

52. Gaston v. Wabash R. Co., Mo.1959, 322 S.W.2d 865; Yandell v. National Fireproofing Corp., 1953, 239 N.C. 1, 79 S.E.2d 223; D'Almeida v. Boston & Me. R. Co., 1911, 209 Mass. 81, 95 N.E. 398; Chicago, I. & L. R. Co. v. Pritchard, 1906, 168 Ind. 398, 81 N.E. 78; Peneff v. Duluth, M. & N. R. Co., 1925, 164 Minn. 6, 204 N.W. 524; Second Restatement of Torts, § 393.

53. American Mut. Liability Ins. Co. of Boston v. Chain Belt Co., 1937, 224 Wis. 155, 271 N.W. 828; McCallon v. Missouri Pac. R. Co., 1906, 74 Kan. 785, 88 P. 50; Dominices v. Monongahela Connecting R. Co., 1937, 328 Pa. 203, 195 A. 747; Moore v. Ellis, Tex.Civ.App.1964, 385 S.W.2d 261.

54. Trusty v. Patterson, 1930, 299 Pa. 469, 149 A. 717; Ferraro v. Taylor, 1936, 197 Minn. 5, 265 N.W. 829; Mitchell v. Lonergan, 1934, 285 Mass. 266, 189 N.E. 39.

55. Johnson v. H. M. Bullard Co., 1920, 95 Conn. 251, 111 A. 70; Hill v. Lyons Plumbing & Heating Co., Ky.1970, 457 S.W.2d 503; Davis v. Sanderman, 1938, 225 Iowa 1001, 282 N.W. 717; Ruth v. Hutchinson Gas Co., 1941, 209 Minn. 248, 296 N.W. 136; Nelson v. Fruehauf Trailer Co., 1952, 20 N.J.Super. 445, 89 A.2d 445, affirmed, 1953, 11 N.J. 413, 94 A.2d 655.

Since the bailee may reasonably assume in many cases that the chattel is in good condition, this may leave the plaintiff with no remedy. Where the bailor knows that an automobile will be driven without inspection, it seems reasonable to impose the duty. See Kaplan v. Stern, 1951, 198 Md. 414, 84 A.2d 81; Marsh, The Liability of the Gratuitous Transferor; A Comparative Study, 1950, 66 L.Q. Rev. 39; Note, 1944, 48 Dick.L.Rev. 103.

56. See cases cited in note 55. Also Russell Const. Co. v. Ponder, 1945, 143 Tex. 412, 186 S.W.2d 233; Sturtevant v. Pagel, 1939, 134 Tex. 46, 130 S.W.2d 1017; Clancy v. R. O'Brien & Co., 1963, 345 Mass. 772, 187 N.E.2d 865; Pereza v. Mark, 2 Cir. 1970, 423 F.2d 149, and cf. Pease v. Sinclair Refining Co., 2 Cir. 1939, 104 F.2d 183.

There is, however, no duty to warn the bailee of an obvious condition. Villanueva v. Nowlin, 1966, 77 N.M. 174, 420 P.2d 764.

57. See Saunders Drive-It-Yourself Co. v. Walker, 1926, 215 Ky. 267, 284 S.W. 1088; White v. Holmes, 1925, 89 Fla. 251, 103 So. 623; Neubrand v. Kraft, 1915, 169 Iowa 444, 151 N.W. 455; Restatement of Torts, § 390; see Note, 1927, 13 Va.L.Rev. 564. Cf.

be incompetent to use it safely. Thus even a gratuitous lender of an automobile may be liable to one who is struck on the highway through the negligence of an inexperienced,[58] unlicensed,[59] immature,[60] intoxicated [61] or habitually careless [62] driver, if such characteristics were apparent when the car was turned over.

There are cases,[63] such as the one in Kentucky [64] in which a fond mother gave an automobile to her son knowing that he was an alcoholic and a drug addict, which have held that the donor in such a case is not liable to an injured third person, on the ground that the passage of title makes all the difference. Such decisions have been severely criticized,[65] and look definitely wrong. Even a seller who delivers a dangerous thing to one whom he should know to be unfit to handle it has been held liable for the harm which results to others—as where, for example, a gun is sold to a child,[66] or an automobile to a known incompetent driver.[67] There are by now a good many cases of so-called "common law dramshop" liability, in which a seller has been held liable to third parties for the sale of intoxicating liquor to a minor,[68] or to an intoxicated person.[69] It is the negligent en-

Green v. Hatcher, 1958, 236 Miss. 830, 105 So.2d (garage for repairs).

58. Lorts v. McDonald, 1958, 17 Ill.App.2d 278, 149 N.E.2d 768; Harris v. Smith, 1969, 119 Ga.App. 306, 167 S.E.2d 198; Rounds v. Phillips, 1933, 166 Md. 151, 170 A. 532, second appeal, 1935, 168 Md. 120, 177 A. 174; Hopkins v. Droppers, 1924, 184 Wis. 400, 198 N.W. 738; Elliott v. Harding, 1923, 107 Ohio St. 501, 140 N.E. 338. See Woods, Negligent Entrustment, 1966, 20 Ark.L.Rev. 101; Notes, 1963, 30 Tenn.L.Rev. 658; 1967, 19 Bay.L.Rev. 75.

Cf. Syah v. Johnson, 1966, 247 Cal.App.2d 534, 55 Cal.Rptr. 741 (epileptic).

59. This was held conclusive as to incompetence in Gordon v. Bedard, 1929, 265 Mass. 408, 164 N.E. 374; Roark v. Stone, 1930, 224 Mo.App. 554, 30 S. W.2d 647; Wery v. Seff, 1940, 136 Ohio St. 307, 25 N.E.2d 692. In Canzoneri v. Hickert, 1936, 223 Wis. 25, 269 N.W. 716, it was held merely to create a presumption. Cf. Toole v. Morris-Webb Motor Co., La.App.1938, 180 So. 431 (entrusting license plates).

60. La Faso v. La Faso, 1966, 126 Vt. 90, 223 A.2d 814; McBerry v. Ivie, 1967, 116 Ga.App. 808, 159 S. E.2d 108; Miles v. Harrison, 1967, 115 Ga.App. 143, 154 S.E.2d 377, reversed on other grounds, 223 Ga. 352, 155 S.E.2d 6, conformed to 115 Ga.App. 821, 155 S.E.2d 864.

61. Deck v. Sherlock, 1956, 162 Neb. 86, 75 N.W.2d 99; Harrison v. Carroll, 4 Cir. 1943, 139 F.2d 427; Pennington v. Davis-Child Motor Co., 1936, 143 Kan. 753, 57 P.2d 428; Owensboro Undertaking & Livery Ass'n v. Henderson, 1938, 273 Ky. 112, 115 S.W.2d 563; Alspach v. McLaughlin, 1969, —— Ind. App. ——, 247 N.E.2d 840.

Or one who may reasonably be expected to become intoxicated. Powell v. Langford, 1941, 58 Ariz. 281, 119 P.2d 230 (dipsomaniac); State of Maryland for Use of Weaver v. O'Brien, D.Md.1956, 140 F.Supp. 306 (history of drinking); Mitchell v. Churches, 1922, 119 Wash. 547, 206 P. 6 (declared intention); Crowell v. Duncan, 1926, 145 Va. 480, 134 S.E. 576.

62. Frasier v. Pierce, Tex.Civ.App.1965, 398 S.W.2d 955; Fogo v. Steele, 1956, 180 Kan. 326, 304 P.2d 451; Dinkins v. Booe, 1960, 252 N.C. 731, 114 S.E. 2d 672; Chaney v. Duncan, 1937, 194 Ark. 1076, 110 S.W.2d 21; Tyree v. Tudor, 1922, 183 N.C. 340, 111 S.E. 714. Cf. Roberts v. Williams, N.D.Miss.1969, 302 F.Supp. 972 (shotgun entrusted to prisoner known to be violent).

63. Brown v. Harkleroad, 1955, 39 Tenn.App. 657, 287 S.W.2d 92 (gift of car to son known to be reckless, incompetent and drinking driver); Shipp v. Davis, 1932, 25 Ala.App. 104, 141 So. 366 (drinking). Cf. Rush v. Smitherman, Tex.Civ.App.1956, 294 S.W.2d 873, error refused (sale of car to unlicensed driver); Smith's Adm'r v. Corder, Ky.1956, 286 S.W.2d 512 (gun entrusted to known heavy drinker with violent disposition).

64. Estes v. Gibson, Ky.1953, 257 S.W.2d 604 (4–3 decision).

65. See Notes, 1954, 32 Chicago-Kent L.Rev. 479; 1954, 43 Ky.L.J. 178; 1954, 2 Kan.L.Rev. 311; 1953, 33 Bos.U.L.Rev. 538; 1954, 29 N.Y.U.L.Rev. 530.

66. Anderson v. Settergren, 1907, 100 Minn. 294, 111 N.W. 279; Semeniuk v. Chentis, 1954, 1 Ill.App.2d 508, 117 N.E.2d 883. Cf. Neff Lumber Co. v. First Nat. Bank, 1930, 122 Ohio St. 302, 171 N.E. 327; Stone v. Shaw Supply Co., 1934, 148 Or. 416, 36 P. 2d 606; Bosserman v. Smith, 1920, 205 Mo.App. 657, 226 S.W. 608.

67. Johnson v. Casetta, 1961, 197 Cal.App.2d 272, 17 Cal.Rptr. 81.

68. Elder v. Fisher, 1966, 247 Ind. 598, 217 N.E.2d 847; Rappaport v. Nichols, 1959, 31 N.J. 188, 156 A.2d 1.

69. Jardine v. Upper Darby Lodge Co. 1964, 413 Pa. 626, 198 A.2d 550; Galvin v. Jennings, 3 Cir. 1961, 289 F.2d 15; Berkeley v. Park, 1965, 47 Misc.

trusting which creates the unreasonable risk; and this is none the less when the goods are conveyed. There are decisions the other way, which appear to be preferred.[70]

As has already been noted,[71] strict liability of the supplier who does not sell has made its appearance in a number of cases of direct warranty between the immediate parties to transactions of rental or bailment for hire.[72] Extension of the liability to third parties was long delayed. The first case to adopt it was Cintrone v. Hertz Truck Leasing & Rental Service Co.,[73] in New Jersey in 1965, where the implied warranty on the lease of a truck was extended to an employee who was driving it. The case has been followed in California [74] and in Florida, New York and Hawaii; [75] and

since there is no visible reason for any distinction between those engaged in the businesses [76] of selling and renting, it appears inevitable that such strict liability with rapidly meet with general acceptance.

Services

It is no longer in dispute that one who renders services to another is under a duty to exercise reasonable care in doing so, and that he is liable for any negligence to anyone who may foreseeably be expected to be injured as a result.[77] This applies in particular to the testing of products, by those who do not supply them.[78]

Thus far efforts to find strict liability as to the services themselves have entirely failed.[79] Even when a product is used or supplied in the course of and as an incident to the service, strict liability has usually been denied. This has been true as to the prescription, fitting and sale of contact lenses, not in themselves defective; [80] a defective surgical pin insert-

---

2d 381, 262 N.Y.S.2d 290; Adamian v. Three Sons, Inc., 1968, 353 Mass. 498, 233 N.E.2d 18; Colligan v. Cousar, 1963, 38 Ill.App.2d 392, 187 N.E.2d 292. See Cahn, New Common Law Dramshop Rule, 1960, 9 Cleve.Marsh.L.Rev. 302; Note, 1966, 18 West.Res. L.Rev. 251.

70. Liability was found in Golembe v. Blumberg, 1941, 262 App.Div. 759, 27 N.Y.S.2d 692, where a father bought a car for his epileptic son. Also in Bugle v. McMahon, Sup.Ct.1942, 35 N.Y.S.2d 193 (alcoholic).

71. Supra, p. 638.

72. Thompson v. Reily, Miss.1968, 211 So.2d 537 (washing machine in laundromat); Smith v. Alexandria Arena, Inc., E.D.Va.1969, 294 F.Supp. 695 (roller skates); Hoisting Engine Sales Co. v. Hart, 1923, 237 N.Y. 30, 142 N.E. 342; Electrical Advertising, Inc. v. Sakato, 1963, 94 Ariz. 68, 381 P.2d 755. See Note, 1970, 31 Ohio St.L.J. 140.

73. 1965, 43 N.J. 434, 212 A.2d 769. Recovery was denied, however, because of contributory negligence of the plaintiff in driving with knowledge that the brakes were bad. The case was followed in Ettin v. Ava Truck Leasing, Inc., 1968, 100 N.J.Super. 515, 242 A.2d 663, affirmed in part, reversed in part 53 N.J. 463, 251 A.2d 278.

74. The case was first followed in McClaflin v. Bayshore Equipment Rental Co., 1969, 274 Cal.App.2d 487, 79 Cal.Rptr. 337, a case of strict liability in tort upon a rental by defendant to plaintiff. This was extended to a third party in Price v. Shell Oil Co., 1970, 2 Cal.3d 245, 85 Cal.Rptr. 178, 466 P.2d 722. Cf. Garcia v. Halsett, 1970, 3 Cal.App.3d 319, 82 Cal.Rptr. 420.

75. W. E. Johnson Equipment Co. v. United Airlines, Inc., Fla.1970, 238 So.2d 98; Accelerated Trucking

Corp. v. McLean Trucking Co., 1967, 53 Misc.2d 321, 278 N.Y.S.2d 516; Stewart v. Budget Rent-A-Car Corp., 1970, —— Haw. ——, 470 P.2d 240.

Contra: Speyer, Inc. v. Humble Oil & Ref. Co., D.Pa. 1968, 275 F.Supp. 861, affirmed, 3 Cir. 1968, 403 F.2d 766, cert. denied 394 U.S. 1015; Lechuga, Inc. v. Montgomery, 1970, 12 Ariz.App. 32, 467 P.2d 256.

76. All of the decisions have laid stress upon the requirement that the defendant be engaged in the business of supplying such chattels.

77. See for example Kalinowski v. Truck Equipment Co., 1933, 237 App.Div. 472, 261 N.Y.S. 657; Zierer v. Daniels, 1956, 40 N.J.Super. 130, 122 A.2d 377; Central & Southern Truck Lines v. Westfall G.M.C. Truck, Inc., Mo.App.1958, 317 S.W.2d 841.

78. Hanberry v. Hearst Corp., 1969, 276 Cal.App.2d 820, 81 Cal.Rptr. 519 (Good Housekeeping certification as to shoes); Hempstead v. General Fire Extinguisher Corp., D.Del.1967, 269 F.Supp. 109 (testing and prescribing standards for fire extinguishers); Buszta v. Souther, 1967, 102 R.I. 609, 232 A. 2d 396 (motor vehicle inspection station).

79. See for example La Rossa v. Scientific Design Co., 3 Cir. 1968, 402 F.2d 937; and see Farnsworth, Warranty of Quality in Non-Sales Cases, 1957, 57 Col.L.Rev. 653.

80. Barbee v. Rogers, 1968, 425 S.W.2d 342.

ed in the course of an operation;[81] a bath mat supplied with a hotel room;[82] and the use of a dentist's hypodermic needle which broke in the plaintiff's jaw.[83] There is, however, a late New Jersey decision[84] in which a beauty parlor applied a lotion to the plaintiff's hair, and the court found both a service and a sale, refusing to distinguish the case in which the product was sold for the plaintiff herself to apply.

Builders

The liability of building contractors[85] has tended to follow the same general path of development as that of suppliers of chattels, but to lag behind it by some twenty years. This was a field in which the ghost of Winterbottom v. Wright[86] died very hard. Initially it was held that, while the contractor would be liable for any injury resulting from his negligence before his work was completed,[87] his responsibility was terminated, and he was not liable to any third person once the struc-

ture was completed and accepted by the owner.[88]

As in the case of sellers of goods, the change which has occurred began with inroads upon the general rule with a long list of exceptions. The earliest to develop held the contractor liable for "something like fraud" if he turned the work over knowing that it was dangerously defective.[89] Some courts attempted to discover something resembling "privity" of contract in the fact that use by the individual plaintiff was intended or to be anticipated.[90] Still other cases relied on the analogy of the seller of goods, and found a duty to use care where the product of the work could be regarded as "inherently" or "imminently" dangerous.[91] Where there was an interference with the rights of the public,[92] or with the use or enjoyment of adjoining land,[93] the contractor was held liable for

81. Cheshire v. Southampton Hospital Ass'n, 1967, 53 Misc.2d 355, 278 N.Y.S.2d 531. As to blood transfusions, see supra, p. 638.

82. Wagner v. Coronet Hotel, 1969, 10 Ariz.App. 296, 458 P.2d 390.

83. Magrine v. Krasnica, 1967, 94 N.J.Super. 228, 227 A.2d 539, affirmed in Magrine v. Spector, 1967, 100 N.J.Super. 223, 241 A.2d 637. See, generally, Note, 1969, 30 U.Pitt.L.Rev. 508.

84. Newmark v. Gimbel's, Inc., 1969, 54 N.J. 585, 258 A.2d 697. The court, however, reaffirmed the Magrine case, supra note 83.

85. See Tucker and Kuhn, The Decline of the Privity Rule in Tort Liability, 1950, 11 U.Pitts.L.Rev. 236; Eldredge, The Liability of Manufacturers and Contractors to Persons Not in Privity of Contract With Them, 1934, 6 Pa.Bar A.Q. 154, reprinted in Eldredge, Modern Tort Problems, 1941, 103; Notes, 1938, 22 Minn.L.Rev. 709; 1949, 24 Ind.L.J. 286; 1954, 14 Md.L.Rev. 77; 1956, 44 Geo.L.J. 534; 1957, 42 Corn.L.Q. 441; 1957, 4 St. Louis U.L.Rev. 344; 1958, 19 La.L.Rev. 221.

86. See supra, p. 622.

87. Mann v. Leake & Nelson Co., 1945, 132 Conn. 251, 43 A.2d 161; S. Blickman, Inc. v. Chilton, Tex.Civ. App.1938, 114 S.W.2d 646; Bacak v. Hogya, 1950, 4 N.J. 417, 73 A.2d 167; Steers v. Marshall, 1952, 207 Okl. 218, 248 P.2d 1047.

88. Curtin v. Somerset, 1891, 140 Pa. 70, 21 A. 244; Daugherty v. Herzog, 1896, 145 Ind. 255, 44 N.E. 457; Galbraith v. Illinois Steel Co., 7 Cir. 1904, 133 F. 485, certiorari denied, 1906, 201 U.S. 643, 26 S.Ct. 759, 50 L.Ed. 902; Young v. Smith & Kelly Co., 1905, 124 Ga. 475, 52 S.E. 765; Ford v. Sturgis, 1926, 56 App.D.C. 361, 14 F.2d 253, 619.

89. Pennsylvania Steel Co. v. Elmore & Hamilton Contracting Co., D.N.Y.1909, 175 F. 176; O'Brien v. American Bridge Co., 1910, 110 Minn. 364, 125 N.W. 1012; Lechman v. Hooper, 1890, 52 N.J.L. 253, 19 A. 215; Ryan v. St. Louis Transit Co., 1905, 190 Mo. 621, 89 S.W. 865; Bryson v. Hines, 4 Cir. 1920, 268 F. 290; Bray v. Cross, 1958, 98 Ga.App. 612, 106 S.E.2d 315.

90. Grodstein v. McGivern, 1931, 303 Pa. 555, 154 A. 794; McGuire v. Dalton Co., La.App.1939, 191 So. 168; cf. Barabe v. Duhrkop Oven Co., 1919, 231 Mass. 466, 121 N.E. 415.

91. Holland Furnace Co. v. Nauracaj, 1938, 105 Ind. App. 574, 14 N.E.2d 339; McCloud v. Leavitt Corp., E.D.Ill.1948, 79 F.Supp. 286; Johnston v. Long, 1943, 56 Cal.App.2d 834, 133 P.2d 409; Foley v. Pittsburgh-Des Moines Co., 1949, 363 Pa. 1, 68 A.2d 517; Cox v. Ray M. Lee Co., 1959, 100 Ga.App. 333, 111 S.E.2d 246, followed, 1959, 100 Ga.App. 340, 111 S.E.2d 251.

92. Schumacher v. Carl G. Neumann Dredging & Imp. Co., 1931, 206 Wis. 220, 239 N.W. 459; see Delancy v. Supreme Inv. Co., 1947, 251 Wis. 374, 29 N.W.2d 754.

93. Thompson v. Gibson, 1841, 7 M. & W. 456, 151 Eng.Rep. 845; Ackerman v. Ellis, 1911, 81 N.J.L. 1,

creating a nuisance; and where his misconduct could be found to go entirely beyond and outside of the contract, the question was treated as one of ordinary negligence liability.[94]

As in the case of the seller of chattels, the exceptions tended gradually to swallow up the prevailing rule, until the analogy of MacPherson v. Buick Motor Co.[95] was persuasive, and was finally accepted. It is now the almost universal rule that the contractor is liable to all those who may foreseeably be injured by the structure, not only when he fails to disclose dangerous conditions known to him,[96] but also when the work is negligently done.[97] This applies not only to contractors doing original work,[98] but also to those who make repairs,[99] or install parts,[1] as well as supervising architects and engineers.[2] There may be liability for negligent design,[3] as well as for negligent construction.

One important limitation recognized in several cases is that the contractor is not liable if he has merely carried out carefully the plans, specifications and directions given him, since in that case the responsibility is assumed by the employer, at least where the plans are not so obviously defective and dangerous that no reasonable man would follow them.[4] Where this is the case, there appears to be no doubt that there will be liability.[5] It seems clear, by analogy to the case of the supplier of chattels, that the owner's failure to discover the danger, even though it may be negligent, will not relieve the contractor of liability to another.[6] If he does discover it,[7] or it is obvious to him,[8] and he fails to rem-

---

79 A. 883; cf. Davey v. Turner, 1937, 55 Ga.App. 786, 191 S.E. 382.

94. Konskier v. B. Goodman, Ltd., [1928] 1 K.B. 421 (continuing trespass); Van Alstyne v. Rochester Tel. Corp., 1937, 163 Misc. 258, 296 N.Y.S. 726 (same). Cf. Oestrike v. Neifert, 1934, 267 Mich. 462, 255 N.W. 226; Littell v. Argus Production Co., 10 Cir. 1935, 78 F.2d 955.

95. Supra, p. 642.

96. Gasteiger v. Gillenwater, 1966, 57 Tenn.App. 206, 417 S.W.2d 568; Rogers v. Scyphers, 1968, 251 S.C. 128, 161 S.E.2d 81.

97. Kapalczynski v. Globe Const. Co., 1969, 19 Mich. App. 396, 172 N.W.2d 852; Moran v. Pittsburgh-Des Moines Steel Co., 3 Cir. 1948, 166 F.2d 908, cert. denied 334 U.S. 846; Hale v. Depaoli, 1948, 33 Cal.2d 228, 201 P.2d 1; Hunter v. Quality Homes, 1949, 6 Terry, Del., 100, 68 A.2d 620; Wright v. Holland Furnace Co., 1932, 186 Minn. 265, 243 N.W. 387. See Notes, 1949, 24 Ind.L.J. 286; 1958, 19 La.L.Rev. 221; 1945, 62 Harv.L.Rev. 145.

98. Fisher v. Simon, 1961, 15 Wis.2d 207, 112 N.W.2d 705; Cosgriff Neon Co. v. Matthews, 1962, 78 Nev. 281, 371 P.2d 819; Thompson v. Burke Engineering Sales Co., 1960, 252 Iowa 146, 106 N.W.2d 351; Leigh v. Wadsworth, Okl.1961, 361 P.2d 849; Krisovich v. John Booth, 1956, 181 Pa.Super. 5, 121 A.2d 890.

99. Colton v. Foulkes, 1951, 295 Wis. 142, 47 N.W.2d 901; Hanna v. Fletcher, 1956, 97 U.S.App.D.C. 246, 231 F.2d 469, cert. denied, 359 U.S. 912.

1. Dow v. Holly Mfg. Co., 1958, 49 Cal.2d 720, 321 P. 2d 736 (elevator); Banaghan v. Dewey, 1959, 340 Mass. 73, 162 N.E.2d 807 (same); Marine Ins. Co. v. Strecker, 1957, 234 La. 522, 100 So.2d 493 (cabinet).

2. United States for Use and Benefit of Los Angeles Testing Laboratory v. Rogers & Rogers, S.D.Cal. 1958, 161 F.Supp. 132; Paxton v. Alameda County, 1953, 119 Cal.App.2d 393, 259 P.2d 934; Harley v. Blodgett Eng. & Tool Co., 1925, 230 Mich. 510, 202 N.W. 953; McDonnell v. Wasenmiller, 8 Cir. 1934, 74 F.2d 320; Pastorelli v. Associated Engineers, D. C.R.I.1959, 176 F.Supp. 159. See Bell, Professional Negligence of Architects and Engineers, 1959, 12 Vand.L.Rev. 711; Witherspoon, When is an Architect Liable? 1960, 32 Miss.L.J. 40.

3. Cross v. M. C. Carlisle & Co., 1 Cir. 1966, 368 F.2d 947; Hunt v. Star Photo Finishing Co., 1967, 115 Ga.App. 1, 153 S.E.2d 602.

4. Leininger v. Stearns-Roger Mfg. Co., 1965, 17 Utah 2d 37, 404 P.2d 33; Johnson v. City of San Leandro, 1960, 179 Cal.App.2d 794, 4 Cal.Rptr. 404; Davis v. Henderlong Lumber Co., N.D.Ind.1963, 221 F.Supp. 129; Person v. Cauldwell-Wingate Co., 2 Cir. 1951, 187 F.2d 832, cert. denied 341 U.S. 936; Lydecker v. Board of Chosen Freeholders of Passaic County, 1918, 91 N.J.L. 622, 103 A. 251.

5. See Belk v. Jones Const. Co., 6 Cir. 1959, 272 F.2d 394; Trustees of First Baptist Church v. McElroy, 1955, 223 Miss. 327, 78 So.2d 138; Loesch v. R. P. Farnsworth & Co., La.App.1943, 12 So.2d 222.

6. Foley v. Pittsburgh-Des Moines Co., 1949, 363 Pa. 1, 68 A.2d 517.

7. Leininger v. Stearns-Roger Mfg. Co., 1965, 17 Utah 2d 37, 404 P.2d 33; Miner v. McNamara, 1909, 81 Conn. 690, 72 A. 138.

8. Inman v. Binghamton Housing Authority, 1957, 3 N.Y.2d 137, 164 N.Y.S.2d 699, 143 N.E.2d 895; Price

edy it, it has been held that his responsibility supersedes that of the contractor. It would appear, however, that this has no bearing upon the contractor's duty of care, and goes only to the issue of "proximate cause," in the form of a responsibility taken over by the owner.[9]

Reference has already been made [10] to the direct "warranty" of the builder of a new house to the initial buyer to whom he sells it. The analogy of the manufacturer of chattels led more or less inevitably to the extension of this strict liability to third persons. In 1965, in Schipper v. Levitt & Sons, Inc.,[11]

New Jersey again led off by holding that the warranty protected a child of the lessee of the buyer, injured by a defective water heating apparatus. The decision has since been followed in California,[12] Florida,[13] and Mississippi,[14] with dicta in two or three other jurisdictions approving it.[15] Again the prediction is easily made, that this too is rapidly to become the prevailing rule.

v. Johnston Cotton Co. of Wendell, 1946, 226 N.C. 758, 40 S.E.2d 344; Howard v. Reinhart & Donovan Co., 1946, 196 Okl. 506, 166 P.2d 110.

9. Strakos v. Gehring, Tex.1962, 360 S.W.2d 787.

10. Supra, p. 639.

11. 1965, 44 N.J. 70, 207 A.2d 314.

12. Kriegler v. Eichler Homes, Inc., 1969, 269 Cal. App.2d 224, 74 Cal.Rptr. 749. This was followed, as to the land itself, in Avner v. Longridge Estates, 1969, 272 Cal.App.2d 695, 77 Cal.Rptr. 633.

13. Calvera v. Green Springs, Inc., Fla.App.1969, 220 So.2d 414.

14. State Stove Mfg. Co. v. Hodges, Miss.1966, 189 So.2d 113, cert. denied 386 U.S. 912.

15. See Bethlahmy v. Bechtel, 1966, 91 Idaho 55, 415 P.2d 698; Humber v. Morton, Tex.1968, 426 S.W.2d 554.

CHAPTER 18

MISREPRESENTATION

105. REMEDIES FOR MISREPRESENTATION

Misrepresentation runs all through the law of torts, as a method of accomplishing various types of tortious conduct which, for reasons of historical development or as a matter of convenience, usually are grouped under categories of their own. Thus a battery may be committed by feeding the plaintiff poisoned chocolates,[1] or by inducing his consent to a physical contact by misrepresenting its character;[2] false imprisonment may result from a pretense of authority to make an arrest,[3] a trespass to land from fraudulent statements inducing another to enter,[4] or a conversion from obtaining possession of goods by false representations;[5] and a malicious lie may give rise to a cause of action for the intentional infliction of mental suffering.[6] A great many of the common and familiar forms of negligent conduct, resulting in invasions of tangible interests of person or property, are in their essence nothing more than misrepresentation,[7] from a misleading signal by a driver of an automobile about to make a turn, or an assurance that a danger does not exist,[8] to false statements[9] concerning a chattel sold, or non-disclosure of a latent defect by one who is under a duty to give warning.[10] In addition, misrepresentation may play an important part in the invasion of intangible interests, in such torts as defamation,[11] malicious prosecution,[12] or interference with contrac-

1. Commonwealth v. Stratton, 1873, 114 Mass. 303; State v. Monroe, 1897, 121 N.C. 677, 28 S.E. 547.

2. Bartell v. State, 1900, 106 Wis. 342, 82 N.W. 142; De May v. Roberts, 1861, 46 Mich. 160, 9 N.W. 146; Crowell v. Crowell, 1920, 180 N.C. 516, 105 S.E. 206, rehearing denied, 1921, 181 N.C. 66, 106 S.E. 149.

3. Whitman v. Atchison, T. & S. F. R. Co., 1911, 85 Kan. 150, 116 P. 234; Hebrew v. Pulis, 1906, 73 N.J.L. 621, 64 A. 121.

4. Donovan v. Consolidated Coal Co., 1900, 187 Ill. 28, 58 N.E. 290; Hendrix v. Black, 1918, 132 Ark. 473, 201 S.W. 283; Murrell v. Goodwill, 1925, 159 La. 1057, 106 So. 564.

5. Holland v. Bishop, 1895, 60 Minn. 23, 61 N.W. 681; Hagar v. Norton, 1905, 188 Mass. 47, 73 N.E. 1073; Baird v. Howard, 1894, 51 Ohio St. 57, 36 N.E. 732.

6. Wilkinson v. Downton, [1897] 2 Q.B. 57, 66 L.J. Q.B. 493; cf. Nickerson v. Hodges, 1920, 146 La. 735, 84 So. 37.

7. See supra, p. 177.

8. Skillings v. Allen, 1919, 143 Minn. 323, 173 N.W. 663; Washington & Berkeley Bridge Co. v. Pennsylvania Steel Co., 4 Cir. 1915, 226 F. 169; Valz v. Goodykoontz, 1911, 112 Va. 853, 72 S.E. 730; Virginia Dare Stores v. Schuman, 1938, 175 Md. 287, 1 A.2d 897.

9. Cunningham v. C. R. Pease House Furnishing Co., 1908, 74 N.H. 435, 69 A. 120; Ahrens v. Moore, 1944, 206 Ark. 1035, 178 S.W.2d 256; Andreotalla v. Gaeta, 1927, 260 Mass. 105, 156 N.E. 731; Dalrymple v. Sinkoe, 1949, 230 N.C. 453, 53 S.E.2d 437.

10. Huset v. J. I. Case Threshing Mach. Co., 8 Cir. 1903, 120 F. 865 (seller of chattel and third person); Benson v. Dean, 1921, 232 N.Y. 52, 133 N.E. 125 (surgeon and patient); Cowen v. Sunderland, 1887, 145 Mass. 365, 14 N.E. 117 (landlord and tenant); Campbell v. Boyd, 1883, 88 N.C. 129 (possessor of premises and licensee).

11. See infra, ch. 19.

12. See infra, ch. 22.

tual relations.[13] In all such cases the particular form which the defendant's conduct has taken has become relatively unimportant, and misrepresentation has been merged to such an extent with other kinds of misconduct that neither the courts nor legal writers have found any occasion to regard it as a separate basis of liability.

So far as misrepresentation has been treated as giving rise in and of itself to a distinct cause of action in tort, it has been identified with the common law action of deceit. The reasons for the separate development of this action, and for its peculiar limitations, are in part historical, and in part connected with the fact that in the great majority of the cases which have come before the courts the misrepresentations have been made in the course of a bargaining transaction between the parties.[14] Consequently the action has been colored to a considerable extent by the ethics of bargaining between distrustful adversaries. Its separate recognition has been confined in practice very largely to the invasion of interests of a financial or commercial character, in the course of business dealings. There is no essential reason to prevent a deceit action from being maintained, for intentional misstatements at least, where other types of interests are invaded; and there are a few cases in which it has been held to lie for personal injuries,[15] for tricking the plaintiff into an invalid marriage [16] or marriage with one who is physically unfit,[17] or for inducing the plaintiff to leave a husband,[18] or to incur criminal penalties.[19] In general, however, other theories of action have been sufficient to deal with non-pecuniary damage, and the somewhat narrower theory of deceit is not called into question. The typical case of deceit is one in which the plaintiff has parted with money, or property of value, in reliance upon the defendant's representations.

The law of misrepresentation is thus considerably broader than the action for deceit. Liability in damages for misrepresentation, in one form or another, falls into the three familiar divisions with which we have dealt throughout this text—it may be based upon intent to deceive, upon negligence, or upon a policy which requires the defendant to be strictly responsible for his statements without either. For the most part, the courts have limited deceit to those cases where there is an intent to mislead, and have left negligence and strict liability to be dealt with in some other type of action.[20] There has been a good deal of overlapping of theories,[21] and no little confusion, which has been increased by the indiscriminate use of the word "fraud," a term so vague that it requires definition in nearly every case. Further difficulty has been added by a failure to distinguish the requisites of the action in tort at

---

13. See infra, § 129.

14. See Restatement of Torts, Scope Note to chapter 22, preceding § 525.

15. Benoit v. Perkins, 1918, 79 N.H. 11, 104 A. 254; Langridge v. Levy, 1837, 2 M. & W. 519, 150 Eng. Rep. 863; Kuelling v. Roderick Lean Mfg. Co., 1905, 183 N.Y. 78, 75 N.E. 1098. Cf. Graham v. John R. Watts & Son, 1931, 238 Ky. 96, 36 S.W.2d 859 (damage to property). "The injury to one's person by the fraud of another is quite as serious as an injury to one's pocketbook." Start, C. J., in Flaherty v. Till, 1912, 119 Minn. 191, 137 N.W. 815.

16. Sham marriage: Jekshewitz v. Groswald, 1929, 265 Mass. 413, 164 N.E. 609; Tuck v. Tuck, 1964, 14 N.Y.2d 341, 251 N.Y.S.2d 653, 200 N.E.2d 554. Bigamy: Morris v. MacNab, 1957, 25 N.J. 271, 135 A.2d 657; Humphreys v. Baird, 1956, 197 Va. 667, 90 S.

E.2d 796; Wolf v. Fox, 1922, 178 Wis. 369, 190 N. W. 90.

17. Kujok v. Goldman, 1896, 150 N.Y. 176, 44 N.E. 773; Leventhal v. Liberman, 1933, 262 N.Y. 209, 186 N.E. 675.

18. Work v. Campbell, 1912, 164 Cal. 343, 128 P. 943.

19. Burrows v. Rhodes, [1899] 1 Q.B. 816. Cf. Stryk v. Mnichowicz, 1918, 167 Wis. 265, 167 N.W. 246, (false statements by parent as to child's age inducing plaintiff to employ child, with resulting tort liability for violation of statute when child was injured).

20. See infra, § 107.

21. See Green, Deceit, 1930, 16 Va.L.Rev. 749, contending that the resulting flexibility is a desirable thing, and a great advantage to the courts in dealing with varying types of cases.

law from those of equitable remedies, and to distinguish the different forms of misrepresentation from one another, and misrepresentation itself from mere mistake.[22] Any attempt to bring order out of the resulting chaos must be at best a tentative one, with the qualification that many courts do not agree.

Deceit

The action of deceit is of very ancient origin. There was an old writ of deceit known as early as 1201, which lay only against a person who had misused legal procedure for the purpose of swindling someone.[23] At a later period this writ was superseded by an action on the case in the nature of deceit, which became the general common law remedy for fraudulent or even non-fraudulent misrepresentation resulting in actual damage.[24] In particular, it was extended to afford a remedy for many wrongs which we should now regard as breaches of contract, such as false warranties in the sale of goods.[25] Its use was limited almost entirely to cases of direct transactions between the parties, and it came to be regarded as inseparable from some contractual relation.[26] It was not until 1789, in Pasley v. Freeman,[27] which is the parent of the modern law of deceit, that the action was held to lie where the plaintiff had had no dealings with the defendant, but had been induced by his misrepresentation to deal with a third person. After that date deceit was recognized as purely a tort action, and not necessarily founded upon a contract. At about the same time,[28] the remedy for a breach of warranty was taken over into the action of assumpsit, and it was thus established that it had a contract character. Thereafter the two lines of recovery slowly diverged, although some vestiges of confusion between the two still remain in many courts, particularly as to the measure of damages.[29] The distinction was made clear in the English courts by decisions holding that the tort action of deceit requires something in the way of knowledge of the falsity of the statement and an intention to mislead,[30] while the contract action on a warranty does not.[31]

The elements of the tort cause of action in deceit which at last emerged from this process of development frequently have been stated[32] as follows:

1. A false representation[33] made by the defendant. In the ordinary case, this representation must be one of fact.[34]

2. Knowledge or belief on the part of the defendant that the representation is false— or, what is regarded as equivalent, that he has not a sufficient basis of information to

---

22. See infra, p. 687.

23. 1 Street, Foundations of Legal Liability, 1906, 375; Winfield, History of Conspiracy, 1921, 33.

24. 1 Street, Foundations of Legal Liability, 1906, 376; Winfield, Province of the Law of Tort, 1931, 13–14.

25. 3 Holdsworth, History of English Law, 4th Ed. 1935, 428–434; 1 Street, Foundations of Legal Liability, 1906, 377–382; Ames, History of Assumpsit, 1888, 2 Harv.L.Rev. 1, 8 ff.

26. As late as Roswel v. Vaughan, 1607, Cro.Jac. 196, 79 Eng.Rep. 171.

27. 1789, 3 Term Rep. 51, 100 Eng.Rep. 450. "The Court in Pasley v. Freeman were convinced that they were creating a new tort. In fact, it was the novelty of it that frightened Grose, J. (a very conservative judge) into dissent." Winfield, Law of Tort, 1937, 400n.

28. Stuart v. Wilkins, 1778, 1 Dougl. 18, 99 Eng.Rep. 15.

29. See infra, § 110.

30. Derry v. Peek, 1888, 14 A.C. 337. See infra, p. 700.

31. Williamson v. Allen, 1802, 2 East 446, 102 Eng. Rep. 439.

32. Restatement of Torts, 525; Suburban Properties Managment v. Johnson, 1964, 236 Md. 455, 204 A.2d 326; Broberg v. Mann, 1965, 66 Ill.App.2d 134, 213 N.E.2d 89; Traylor Eng. & Mfg. Co. v. National Container Corp., 1949, 6 Terry, Del. 143, 70 A.2d 9; Safety Inv. Corp. v. State Land Office Board, 1944, 308 Mich. 246, 13 N.W.2d 278; McKay v. Anheuser-Busch, Inc., 1942, 199 S.C. 335, 19 S.E.2d 457.

33. See infra, § 106.

34. See infra, § 109.

make it. This element often is given the technical name of "scienter." [35]

3. An intention to induce the plaintiff to act or to refrain from action in reliance upon the misrepresentation.[36]

4. Justifiable reliance upon the representation on the part of the plaintiff, in taking action or refraining from it.[37]

5. Damage to the plaintiff, resulting from such reliance.[38]

As will be seen, some of these elements have undergone modification or qualification in some jurisdictions. In addition, it must be repeated that such an action of deceit is only one of several possible remedies for various forms of misrepresentation, even where there is only pecuniary loss. Before proceeding to consider the elements of the cause of action in deceit, it is desirable to distinguish other theories upon which relief may be granted, the proximity of which has been a fertile source of the general confusion and uncertainty surrounding the deceit action itself.

Distinguished from Warranty and Negligence

The divorce of warranty from deceit was completed by about the beginning of the nineteenth century. By that time warranty had become identified, at least in lawyers' usage, with the existence of a contract between the parties. Although the original tort form of the action still survives as a possible procedural alternative, and the tort theory may have important consequences,[39] there are only a limited number of cases, and those entirely concerned with the liability of a seller of goods to the ultimate consumer,[40] in which a warranty has been found without

a contract. Deceit, on the other hand, is essentially a tort action, and does not require the existence of any contract, although of course the tort itself may often coincide with one. Furthermore, because of its contract character, warranty has become a matter of strict liability, without any wrongful intent or negligence on the part of the defendant, while deceit, as it developed in the law of England, is to be classified as an intentional tort, requiring knowledge or belief of falsity or conscious ignorance of the truth, and hence something of an intent to mislead. In the American courts, this distinction is not always clearly drawn, and it has been obscured or abandoned in many jurisdictions by decisions which in effect have taken over the strict liability of warranty and adopted it in the deceit form of action.[41]

The same intentional element distinguished deceit, as it is defined by the English courts and by many American jurisdictions, from negligence. In finding the necessary "knowledge" as to the falsity of the representation, these courts have stopped short of the situation where the defendant honestly believes that he knows and that his statement is true, but is negligent in not obtaining accurate information. There is nothing, however, to prevent an ordinary negligence action for the use of language in such a case; and while such an action is most often brought where the damage which results is a personal injury,[42] it has been extended, with a somewhat restricted scope,[43] to cases involving financial or commercial loss.[44]

In some jurisdictions, then, the distinction as to the actions for deceit, negligence and warranty coincides in general with that as to intent, negligence and strict liability. In many courts, however, these lines have been blurred or obliterated by an extension of the

---

35. See infra, p. 700.

36. See infra, p. 703.

37. See infra, § 108.

38. See infra, § 110.

39. See supra, p. 635.

40. See supra, § 97.

41. See infra, p. 710.

42. See supra, note 15.

43. See infra, p. 706.

44. See infra, p. 706.

deceit action to cover all three types of liability. The dispute over the proper form of action frequently has obscured the real question of whether the defendant should be held liable in the particular case. With the declining importance of the form and theory of the action under modern code pleading,[45] it is the latter which is the really important problem, with which we must chiefly be concerned; and the discussion which is to follow looks to the nature of the defendant's conduct rather than the form of his recovery.

In addition, in England and in several American courts, the tort action carries a measure of damages based on the extent to which the plaintiff is out of pocket as a result of the misrepresentation, while the contract action of warranty gives him the benefit of what he was promised. But here again the distinction has been obscured in many jurisdictions by an adoption of the contract measure of damages in actions for deceit.[46]

Equitable Relief

To the difficulties arising from the existence of these three strictly legal remedies, there must be added the further confusion resulting from the possibility of equitable relief. Misrepresentation was recognized very early as a basis for the jurisdiction of courts of equity, at a time when the existing forms of action at law were inadequate to deal with the injustices which resulted. When the law courts later developed remedies for such cases, the equity courts refused to surrender their jurisdiction, saying that the nature of the "fraud" made it peculiarly a matter for their interference.[47] The particular form of

relief granted by equity might be almost anything appropriate to the particular case;[48] but the most common remedies for misrepresentation were rescission or reformation of a contract between the parties, or requiring a defendant who had been unjustly enriched to hold the money or property he had received subject to a constructive trust, or an equitable lien.

The equity courts were not bound by rules adopted at law, and proceeded to evolve their own definition of the "fraud" which would justify relief. Since they did not take jurisdiction for the purpose of giving the plaintiff damages, they were more concerned with the injustice of allowing the defendant to retain what he had received through the plaintiff's erroneous belief in the truth of his statement than with any question of the wrongfulness of his own conduct. Hence they gave a remedy for innocent misrepresentation,[49] without the element of intent which became necessary for the tort action of deceit. Even beyond this, mere mistake, without any misrepresentation at all, was recognized from a very early date as a basis for equitable relief. The tangle of rules surrounding mistake in equity [50] is beyond the scope of this book;

Many courts, however, deny relief by a suit in equity, where the remedy at law is adequate. Buzard v. Houston, 1886, 119 U.S. 347; Des Moines Life Ins. Co. v. Seifert, 1904, 210 Ill. 157, 71 N.E. 349; Johnson v. Swanke, 1906, 128 Wis. 68, 107 N.W. 481; McClintock, Equity, 2d Ed.1948, § 50.

48. Thus denial of specific performance of a contract. Restatement of Contracts, § 471. Or subrogation to the claim of another. Restatement of Restitution, § 162. See Pomeroy, Equity Jurisprudence, 5th Ed.1941, § 910.

49. Redgrave v. Hurd, 1881, 20 Ch.Div. 1; Jacobson v. Chicago, M. & St. P. R. Co., 1916, 132 Minn. 181, 156 N.W. 251; Bloomquist v. Farson, 1918, 222 N.Y. 375, 118 N.E. 855; Woods-Faulkner & Co. v. Michelson, 8 Cir. 1933, 63 F.2d 569; Lorenzen v. Langman, 1927, 204 Iowa 1096, 216 N.W. 768. See Keeton, Actionable Misrepresentation: Legal Fault as a Requirement—Rescission, 1949, 2 Okl.L.Rev. 56; 2 Pomeroy, Equity Jurisprudence, 5th Ed.1941, § 888; McClintock, Equity, 2d Ed.1948, § 80.

50. See Abbot, Mistake of Fact as a Ground for Affirmative Equitable Relief, 1910, 23 Harv.L.Rev.

---

45. See for example Baxter v. Ford Motor Co., 1932, 168 Wash. 456, 12 P.2d 409, 15 P.2d 1118, 88 A.L.R. 521, second appeal, 1934, 179 Wash. 123, 35 P.2d 1090 where it is almost impossible to say which of the three theories the court has adopted.

46. See infra, § 110.

47. Colt v. Woollaston, 1723, 2 P.Wms. 154, 24 Eng. Rep. 579; Evans v. Bicknell, 1801, 6 Ves. 174, 31 Eng.Rep. 908; Bacon v. Bronson, 1823, 7 Johns.Ch., N.Y., 194, 11 Am.Dec. 449; Eggers v. Anderson, 1901, 63 N.J.Eq. 264, 49 A. 578.

but it may be said, in general, that relief would be granted where the mistake was a mutual one as to a basic fact,[51] or where it was a unilateral one of which the adverse party knew and took advantage.[52] The line between misrepresentation and mistake never was very clearly drawn in equity, and the whole matter was obscured by the use of the word "fraud" in several different senses.[53] This of course made for considerable uncertainty when the same term was used in actions at law.

Equitable relief, when it was granted, was subject to restrictions peculiar to equity. The plaintiff must himself do equity by restoring whatever he had received,[54] unless excused by special circumstances; and he must do nothing inconsistent with the relief demanded, so that the right to rescind a sale, for example, would be lost by any conduct affirming the transaction,[55] or even by non-action for an unreasonable length of time after discovery of the facts.[56] These restrictions, of course, had no application to actions at law.

Restitution at Law

The confusion arising from the co-existence of these legal and equitable remedies was not lessened when a considerable part of the relief afforded by equity was taken over into actions at law. Reference has already been made [57] to the process by which the idea of "quasi-contract" became engrafted upon the action of assumpsit, to permit the plaintiff to rescind a transaction of his own motion and recover the value of what he had parted with, without resort to a court of equity.

In granting such relief, the common law courts recognized that they were invading the province of equity, and retained the equity rules. Thus, so far as misrepresentation is concerned, most courts [58] have held that it is unnecessary to establish for restitution the mental element of knowledge commonly required in the tort action of deceit, and it is sufficient to show an honest misrepresenta-

---

608; Patterson, Equitable Relief for Unilateral Mistakes, 1928, 28 Col.L.Rev. 859; Lubbell, Unilateral Palpable and Impalpable Mistake in Construction Contracts, 1932, 16 Minn.L.Rev. 137; Thayer, Unilateral Mistake and Unjust Enrichment as a Ground for the Avoidance of Legal Transactions, Harvard Legal Essays, 1934, 467.

51. Virginia Iron, Coal & Coke Co. v. Graham, 1919, 124 Va. 692, 98 S.E. 659; Bluestone Coal Co. v. Bell, 1893, 38 W.Va. 297, 18 S.E. 493; Hoops v. Fitzgerald, 1903, 204 Ill. 325, 68 N.E. 430; Merriam v. Leeper, 1921, 192 Iowa 587, 185 N.W. 134; Hannah v. Steinman, 1911, 159 Cal. 142, 112 P. 1094.

52. Nadeau v. Maryland Casualty Co., 1927, 170 Minn. 326, 212 N.W. 595; Shelton & Co. v. Ellis, 1883, 70 Ga. 297; Nelson v. Pederson, 1922, 305 Ill. 606, 137 N.E. 486; Bell v. Carroll, 1925, 212 Ky. 231, 278 S.W. 541.

53. Thus "constructive fraud," defined as "any act of omission or commission which is contrary to legal or equitable duty, or trust or confidence justly reposed, and which is contrary to good conscience and operates to the injury of another." 1 Black, Rescission and Cancellation, 2d Ed. 1929, § 18; Nocton v. Lord Ashburton, [1914] A.C. 932; City of Clay Center v. Myers, 1893, 52 Kan. 363, 35 P. 25; Haas v. Sternbach, 1894, 156 Ill. 44, 41 N.E. 51.

54. Hunt v. Silk, 1804, 5 East 449, 102 Eng.Rep. 1142; De Montague v. Bacharach, 1902, 181 Mass. 256, 63 N.E. 435; Fay v. Oliver, 1848, 20 Vt. 118.

55. Parsons v. McKinley, 1894, 56 Minn. 464, 57 N.W. 1134 (affirmance); Day v. Fort Scott Inv. & Imp. Co., 1894, 153 Ill. 293, 38 N.E. 567 (affirmance); Bell v. Keepers, 1888, 39 Kan. 105, 17 P. 785 (continued payments); In re Warner's Estate, 1914, 168 Cal. 771, 145 P. 504 (accepting payments); Romanoff Land & Mining Co. v. Cameron, 1902, 137 Ala. 214, 33 So. 864 (use). See Yerkes, Election of Remedies in Cases of Fraudulent Misrepresentation, 1953, 26 So.Cal.L.Rev. 157.

56. Howie v. North Birmingham Land Co., 1891, 95 Ala. 389, 11 So. 15; Litchfield v. Browne, 8 Cir. 1895, 70 F. 141; Clampitt v. Doyle, 1907, 73 N.J.Eq. 678, 70 A. 129; Wilbur v. Flood, 1867, 16 Mich. 40. See Friedman, Delay as a Bar to Rescission, 1941, 26 Corn.L.Q. 426.

57. Supra, § 94.

58. Occasional decisions, such as New York Title & Mortgage Co. v. Hutton, 1934, 63 App.D.C. 266, 71 F.2d 989, and Ebbs v. St. Louis Union Trust Co., 1930, 199 N.C. 242, 153 S.E. 858, have lost sight of history, and required scienter for rescission.

tion,[59] or even, in some cases, a mere mistake.[60] Likewise, unless he is excused by special circumstances, the plaintiff must restore what he has himself received,[61] and his action is lost by any conduct affirming the transaction,[62] or even by nonaction for an unreasonable length of time,[63] after discovery of the facts. Furthermore, the measure of his recovery is determined on the equitable basis of the unjust enrichment of the defendant,[64] rather than the tort basis of the

plaintiff's loss. Thus a purchaser defrauded in the sale of a horse who seeks a remedy by way of restitution ordinarily must return the horse, and may recover the price he has paid, regardless of the extent of his loss on the transaction.

Misrepresentation as a Defense

Further complications arise when there is added the possibility that misrepresentation may be set up as a defense to an action brought by the adverse party, as where one who is sued on a contract claims that he was induced by false statements to enter into it. The common law courts, apparently recognized at a very early date the kind of misrepresentation which went to the existence of the contract itself, as where a man who could not read was induced to sign an instrument, such as a promissory note, which was represented to be of a different character, as a mere receipt. Such misrepresentation, which was called fraud in the factum, or in the essence of the contract, could be shown as a defense under a plea denying that there was a contract at all.[65] But at least in the case of sealed instruments, misrepresentation going merely to the inducement or the consideration of the contract was not available as a defense at law, and the defrauded party was compelled to resort to equity for affirmative relief setting the transaction aside.[66] As the law courts invaded equity fields, the "equitable" defense of fraud in the inducement gradually filtered into the common law

59. Flight v. Booth, 1834, 1 Bing.N.C. 370, 131 Eng. Rep. 1160; Seneca Wire & Mfg. Co. v. A. B. Leach & Co., 1928, 247 N.Y. 1, 159 N.E. 700; Agricultural Bond & Credit Corp. v. August Brandt Co., 1931, 204 Wis. 48, 234 N.W. 369; Henry v. Kopf, 1925, 104 Conn. 73, 131 A. 412; Joslyn v. Cadillac Automobile Co., 6 Cir. 1910, 177 F. 863. See Keeton, Actionable Misrepresentation: Legal Fault as a Requirement, 1948, 1 Okl.L.Rev. 21, 1949, 2 Okl. L.Rev. 56; Note, 1928, 37 Yale L.J. 1141.

60. Grand Lodge, A. O. U. W. of Minnesota, v. Towne, 1917, 136 Minn. 72, 161 N.W. 403; Ketchum v. Catlin, 1849, 21 Vt. 191; Strauss v. Hensey, 1896, 9 App.D.C. 541; De Wolff v. Howe, 1906, 112 App. Div. 104, 98 N.Y.S. 262; Ex parte Richard & Thalheimer, 1913, 180 Ala. 580, 61 So. 819.

61. Byard v. Holmes, 1868, 33 N.J.L. 119; Houghton v. Nash, 1874, 64 Me. 477; Adam, Meldrum & Anderson Co. v. Stewart, 1901, 157 Ind. 678, 61 N.E. 1002; James Music Co. v. Bridge, 1908, 134 Wis. 510, 114 N.W. 1108. See Note, 1929, 29 Col.L.Rev. 791.

62. Brennan v. National Equitable Inv. Co., 1928, 247 N.Y. 486, 160 N.E. 924, reargument denied 248 N.Y. 560, 162 N.E. 524; Samples v. Guyer, 1898, 120 Ala. 611, 24 So. 942; Bayer v. Winton Motor Car Co., 1916, 194 Mich. 222, 160 N.W. 642. Cf. Maki v. St. Luke's Hospital Ass'n, 1913, 122 Minn. 444, 142 N. W. 705. See Deinard and Deinard, Election of Remedies, 1922, 6 Minn.L.Rev. 341, 480; Yerkes, Election of Remedies in Fraudulent Misrepresentation, 1953, 26 So.Cal.L.Rev. 157; Notes, 1949, 2 U. Fla.L.Rev. 142.

63. Wilbur v. Flood, 1867, 16 Mich. 40; Grant v. Lovekin, 1926, 285 Pa. 257, 132 A. 342; Long v. International Vending Mach. Co., 1911, 158 Mo.App. 662, 139 S.W. 819; Everson v. J. L. Owens Mfg. Co., 1920, 145 Minn. 199, 176 N.W. 505. See Friedman, Delay as a Bar to Recission, 1941, 26 Corn.L. Q. 426.

64. Seneca Wire & Mfg. Co. v. A. B. Leach & Co., 1928, 247 N.Y. 1, 159 N.E. 700; Note, 1934, 32 Mich.L.Rev. 968. Cf. Houser & Haines Mfg. Co. v. McKay, 1909, 53 Wash. 337, 101 P. 894; Pfeiffer v.

Independent Plumbing & Heating Supply Co., Mo. App.1934, 72 S.W.2d 138 (rescission for breach of warranty); and see Rogge, Damages Upon Rescission for Breach of Warranty, 1929, 28 Mich.L.Rev. 26.

65. Thoroughgood's Case, 1584, 2 Co.Rep. 9a, 76 Eng. Rep. 408; Stone v. Compton, 1838, 5 Bing.N.C. 142, 132 Eng.Rep. 1059; see Smith v. Ryan, 1908, 191 N.Y. 452, 84 N.E. 402; Ames, Specialty Contracts and Equitable Defenses, 1895, 9 Harv.L.Rev. 49, 51.

66. 1 Holdsworth, History of English Law, 5th Ed. 1931, 576. The reason being that covenant, upon a sealed instrument, was the only contract action originally available.

actions,[67] although it was held as late as 1854 in England,[68] and still later in the United States,[69] particularly in the federal courts,[70] that it was not available. Modern procedure codes, which have terminated the separate existence of equity courts, and permit equitable defenses to be pleaded in actions at law,[71] have very largely obliterated the distinction; and except as to matters of pleading,[72] the

right to a jury trial,[73] and questions arising as to whether the transaction is to be considered as void or merely voidable, the American courts have treated the two kinds of "fraud" upon the same footing.

The fusion of law and equity under modern procedure, and the hybrid character of the "equitable" defense where it had been recognized earlier at law, have resulted in a great deal of uncertainty as to its nature. Some courts have regarded it as a form of rescission in equity, permitting the defendant to set up innocent misrepresentation[74] or even mere mistake,[75] requiring him to act promptly and restore what he has received,[76] and holding that the defense is lost by any act affirming the transaction.[77] Others have considered it as something analogous to a tort action of deceit, set up by way of defense to avoid circuity of action,[78] and have required knowledge of the falsity of the statements,

67. Fitzherbert v. Mather, 1785, 1 Term Rep. 12, 99 Eng.Rep. 944; Grew v. Beaven, 1822, 3 Stark. 134, 171 Eng.Rep. 798; Raphael v. Goodman, 1838, 8 Ad. & El. 565, 112 Eng.Rep. 952; Hazard v. Irwin, 1836, 18 Pick., Mass., 95. See Abbot, Fraud as a Defence at Law in the Federal Courts, 1915, 15 Col.L.Rev. 489, 504–505.

68. Mason v. Ditchbourne, 1835, 1 Mood. & Rob. 460, 174 Eng.Rep. 158; Feret v. Hill, 1854, 15 C.B. 207, 139 Eng.Rep. 400. The rule was altered by the Common Law Procedure Act of 1854, permitting the pleading of equitable defenses at law.

69. Dyer v. Day, 1871, 61 Ill. 336; Eaton v. Eaton, 1874, 37 N.J.L. 108; McArthur v. Johnson, 1867, 61 N.C. 317; Richelieu Hotel Co. v. International Military Encampment Co., 1892, 140 Ill. 248, 29 N.E. 1044.

70. Hartshorn v. Day, 1856, 19 How., U.S., 211, 15 L.Ed. 605; George v. Tate, 1880, 102 U.S. 564. The rule was abandoned as to instruments not under seal, if it ever applied to them. American Sign Co. v. Electro-Lens Sign Co., D.Cal.1913, 211 F. 196. See Abbot, Fraud as a Defence at Law in the Federal Courts, 1915, 15 Col.L.Rev. 489; McBaine, Equitable Defenses to Actions at Law in the Federal Courts, 1929, 17 Cal.L.Rev. 591. It was finally abrogated by a statute in 1915, permitting the pleading of equitable defenses at law, and terminated by the Federal Rules of Civil Procedure, uniting law and equity practice, in 1938.

71. See Clark, Code Pleading, 2d Ed. 1947, § 98; Hinton, Equitable Defenses Under Modern Codes, 1920, 18 Mich.L.Rev. 716; Cook, Equitable Defenses, 1923, 32 Yale L.J. 645; Moreland, Equitable Defenses, 1940, 1 Wash. & Lee L.Rev. 153.

72. Fraud in the factum negatives the existence of the contract, and may be shown under a denial of the obligation. Boxberger v. New York, N. H. & H. R. Co., 1923, 237 N.Y. 75, 142 N.E. 357; Walton Plow Co. v. Campbell, 1892, 35 Neb. 173, 52 N.W. 883; Christianson v. Chicago, St. P., M. & O. Ry. Co., 1895, 61 Minn. 249, 63 N.W. 639. Fraud in the inducement must be pleaded specially. Burlington Grocery Co. v. Lines, 1923, 96 Vt. 405, 120 A. 169; Daly v. Ploetz, 1874, 20 Minn. 411; cf. Whipple v. Brown Bros. Co., 1919, 225 N.Y. 237, 121 N.E. 748.

73. Thus it has been held that fraud in the factum is a legal defense, to be determined by the jury, while fraud in the inducement is equitable and hence for the court. Pringle v. Storrow, D.Mass. 1925, 9 F.2d 464; Hoad v. New York Cent. R. Co., D.N.Y.1934, 6 F.Supp. 565. See Note, 1931, 15 Minn.L.Rev. 805.

74. Evans v. Edmonds, 1853, 13 C.B. 777, 138 Eng. Rep. 1407; Frenzel v. Miller, 1871, 37 Ind. 1; New York Life Ins. Co. v. Marotta, 3 Cir. 1932, 57 F.2d 1038; Taylor v. Burr Printing Co., 2 Cir. 1928, 26 F.2d 331, cert. denied 278 U.S. 641; Standard Mfg. Co. v. Slot, 1904, 121 Wis. 14, 98 N.W. 923.

75. Crary v. Goodman, 1855, 12 N.Y. 266; Leach v. Leach, 1925, 162 Minn. 159, 202 N.W. 448.

76. Bwlch-Y-Plwn Lead Min. Co. v. Baynes, 1867, L. R. 2 Ex. 324; Clough v. London & N. W. R. Co., 1871, L.R. 7 Ex. 26; Heaton v. Knowlton, 1876, 53 Ind. 357; cf. Harris v. Equitable Life Assur. Soc. of United States, 1876, 64 N.Y. 196. See 1 Bigelow, Fraud, 1888, 79.

77. Bell v. Baker, 1890, 43 Minn. 86, 44 N.W. 676; Marks v. Stein, 1916, 61 Okl. 59, 160 P. 318.

78. Peck v. Brewer, 1868, 48 Ill. 54; Piper v. Menifee, 1851, 12 B.Mon., Ky., 465; Gillespie v. Torrance, 1862, 25 N.Y. 306. Cf. Byers v. Lemay Bank & Trust Co., 1955, 365 Mo. 341, 282 S.W.2d 512 ("set-off" of equitable character). A fortiori, a counterclaim for damages under code procedure is clearly the equivalent of a tort action for deceit.

or at least conscious ignorance of the truth,[79] and have permitted the defendant to retain what he has received and recoup his damages when he is sued, usually on the theory of a failure of the consideration promised him.[80]

The nature of the defense is seldom discussed and nowhere definitively established, and seems to be poorly comprehended by the courts. The logic of the matter would seem to be, that when the defense takes the form of avoidance of the transaction sued upon, or seeks relief by way of restitution, it is an equitable remedy, and the defendant should be permitted to set up innocent misrepresentation or even mere mistake; he should be required to act promptly and to restore what he has received, and should be held to have lost the defense by any act affirming the transaction, to the same extent as though he were suing for rescission or restitution as a plaintiff. Where the defense is set up by way of recoupment, or by way of affirmative counterclaim, it in no way operates in avoidance of the transaction, but seeks relief analogous to that afforded by a tort action of deceit, and therefore should be governed by the requirements of that action. Most courts have arrived at a result similar to that achieved in the case of breach of warranty in the sale of goods,[81] allowing the defendant the option of rescission and recovery of what he has paid, or affirmance and recoupment of his damages, but without very clearly distinguishing the grounds for the two.

This uncertainty has had its effect in turn upon the affirmative tort action for deceit itself.

Estoppel

Still another form in which misrepresentation may play an important part in the law of torts is that of estoppel. An estoppel is a rule which precludes a party from taking a particular legal position because of some impediment or bar recognized by the law.[82] It was applied originally to prevent a party from challenging the validity of a legal record, or his own deed; but the equity courts developed it later as a general principle, used as a means of preventing him from taking an inequitable advantage of a predicament in which his own conduct had placed his adversary. It was taken over in turn by the common law judges, as a device to enable them to lengthen their arm, and afford a relief which equity had always offered.[83] Such equitable estoppel, or as it is often called, estoppel in pais, has been defined as "an impediment or bar, by which a man is precluded from alleging, or denying, a fact, in consequence of his own previous act, allegation or denial to the contrary." [84]

For obvious reasons, it appears most frequently as a defense to an action brought by the party to be estopped; but, while it never has been recognized as a cause of action in itself, it may serve as an important, or even the

---

79. Public Motor Service Co. v. Standard Oil Co. of N. J., 1938, 69 App.D.C. 89, 99 F.2d 124; Schlossman's, Inc. v. Niewinske, 1951, 12 N.J.Super. 500, 79 A.2d 870; Weintrob v. New York Life Ins. Co., 3 Cir. 1936, 85 F.2d 158; Latta v. Robinson Erection Co., 1952, 363 Mo. 47, 248 S.W.2d 569; Hodgens v. Jennings, 1912, 148 App.Div. 879, 133 N.Y.S. 584.

80. Williston, Contracts, Rev. Ed. 1937, § 1524; American Sign Co. v. Electro-Lens Sign Co., D.C. Cal.1913, 211 F. 196; Peck v. Brewer, 1868, 48 Ill. 54; Sharp v. Ponce, 1883, 74 Me. 470; Huber Mfg. Co. v. Hunter, 1903, 99 Mo.App. 46, 72 S.W. 484.

81. See Uniform Sales Act, § 69(1); Uniform Commercial Code, § 2–601; 2 Williston, Sales, Rev.Ed. 1948, §§ 604, 605, 605a, 608.

82. " 'Estoppel' cometh of the French word *estoupe*, from whence the English word *stopped*; and it is called an estoppel, or conclusion, because a man's own act, or acceptance, stoppeth or closeth up his mouth to allege or plead the truth." Co.Litt. 352a. It was at one time regarded as a rule of pleading, or of evidence; but since it goes to the position taken upon the merits, it is clearly a rule of substantive law. Williston, Liability for Honest Misrepresentation, 1911, 24 Harv.L.Rev. 415, 425.

83. Bacon, V. C., in Keate v. Phillips, 1881, 18 Ch. Div. 560, 577. The leading case in which the principle of estoppel is fully recognized at law is Pickard v. Sears, 1837, 6 Ad. & El. 469, 112 Eng.Rep. 179.

84. 2 Jacob, Law Dictionary, 1811, 439; Ewart, Principles of Estoppel, 1900, 4.

sole, aid to the plaintiff.[85] Thus a warehouse-man, who represents that he holds goods for another in response to an inquiry by an intending purchaser from that other,[86] or one who informs such a purchaser that his signature forged to a negotiable instrument is genuine,[87] may be estopped to deny the truth of his statement if the purchase is made in reliance upon it; or a corporation which fails to require surrender of an old stock certificate when a new one is issued may find itself estopped as against a holder for value of the old certificate.[88] In such cases the plaintiff prevails, not on the theory that the defendant's misrepresentation is tortious in itself, but because the defendant is not allowed to assert the truth, which would otherwise be a defense to some other action. Estoppel, of course, is not confined to tort cases, and runs throughout the entire field of law.

Such equitable estoppel may be separated into two branches. The first is based upon some definite misrepresentation of fact, made with reason to believe that another will rely upon it, upon which the other does rely in changing his position to his prejudice.[89] Perhaps because of the equity origin of the doctine, such misrepresentation has not been identified with that required for the action of deceit, but rather with that necessary for equitable relief. Although there are occasional decisions [90] to the effect that estoppel cannot arise unless the party estopped had knowledge of the falsity of his statement, or was at least negligent in making it, it seems to be quite clearly established that entirely innocent misrepresentation may be sufficient.[91] It is the inequity of seeking to take advantage of another's position resulting from a misleading statement which is the basis of the relief.

The second branch does not depend upon positive misrepresentation, but is based upon a mere failure to take action. It arises where the party "stands by" and allows another to deal with his property, or to incur some liability toward him, without informing the other of his mistake.[92] Thus he may not remain silent when he sees his goods sold to a stranger,[93] or improvements made upon his land,[94]

---

85. Restatement of Torts, § 872; Williston, Liability for Honest Misrepresentation, 1911, 24 Harv.L.Rev. 415, 425; Weisiger, Basis of Liability for Misrepresentation, 1930, 24 Ill.Rev. 866, 867–869; Harper and McNeely, A Synthesis of the Law of Misrepresentation, 1938, 22 Minn.L.Rev. 938, 971, 972.

86. Commercial Nat. Bank v. Nacogdoches Compress & Warehouse Co., 5 Cir.1904, 133 F. 501; Tradesmen's Nat. Bank v. Indiana Bicycle Co., 1895, 166 Pa. 554, 31 A. 337. Cf. Burrowes v. Lock, 1805, 10 Ves.Jr. 470, 32 Eng.Rep. 927; Low v. Bouverie, [1891] 3 Ch. 82 (trustee making false statements as to extent of cestui's interest to prospective purchaser).

87. Wolfe v. First Nat. Bank, 1922, 140 Md. 479, 117 A. 898; Corner Stone Bank v. Rhodes, 1904, 5 Ind. T. 256, 82 S.W. 739; Furst & Thomas v. Smith, 1939, 280 Ky. 601, 133 S.W.2d 941.

88. Joslyn v. St. Paul Distilling Co., 1890, 44 Minn. 183, 46 N.W. 337; Jarvis v. Manhattan Beach Co., 1896, 148 N.Y. 652, 43 N.E. 68. Cf. also Nickerson v. Massachusetts Title Ins. Co., 1901, 178 Mass. 308, 59 N.E. 814 (title company certifying title as unencumbered when it held a mortgage, estopped to assert its lien against purchaser); Fry v. Smellie, [1912] 3 K.B. 282, and many cases of apparent authority of an agent.

89. Restatement of Torts, §§ 872, 894(1).

90. For example Eaton v. Wilkins, 1912, 163 Cal. 742, 127 P. 71; Brian v. Bonvillain, 1902, 111 La. 441, 35 So. 632; Bishop v. Minton, 1893, 112 N.C. 524, 17 S.E. 436.

91. McLaren v. Hill, 1931, 276 Mass. 519, 177 N.E. 617; Kelly v. Richards, 1938, 95 Utah 560, 83 P.2d 731; Dill v. Widman, 1953, 413 Ill. 448, 109 N.E.2d 765; Chambers v. Bookman, 1903, 67 S.C. 432, 46 S.E. 39; Two Rivers Mfg. Co. v. Day, 1899, 102 Wis. 328, 78 N.W. 440. See Restatement of Torts, § 894, Comment b; Williston, Liability for Honest Misrepresentation, 1911, 24 Harv.L.Rev. 415, 423–426; Ewart, Principles of Estoppel, 1900, 83–88.

92. Restatement of Torts, § 894(2); Ewart, Principles of Estoppel, 1900, 88–94.

93. Pickard v. Sears, 1837, 6 Ad. & El. 469, 112 Eng. Rep. 179; Milligan v. Miller, 1912, 253 Ill. 511, 97 N.E. 1054; Helwig v. Fogelsong, 1914, 166 Iowa 715, 148 N.W. 990; Craig v. Crossman, 1920, 209 Mich. 462, 177 N.W. 400; McNamara v. Feihe, 1921, 139 Md. 516, 115 A. 753.

94. Logan v. Gardner, 1890, 136 Pa. 588, 20 A. 625; Martin v. Maine Cent. R. Co., 1890, 83 Me. 100, 21

and still enforce his rights against the innocent wrongdoer. The law of estoppel creates a duty to speak, under penalty of loss of the right to assert the truth at a later time. Since in such a case there is no active misleading of the other party, who has misled himself, the courts have insisted upon some fault in connection with the conduct of the one to be estopped. There is no estoppel where he has remained silent reasonably and in good faith; he must be aware of his rights,[95] and must realize that the other is about to act under a mistaken belief.[96] Thus this branch of estoppel requires either an intent to mislead or unreasonable conduct amounting to negligence in failing to act,[97] rather than the strict responsibility imposed in estoppel by misrepresentation.

These two branches of equitable estoppel not only have been confounded with one another, but have added their contribution to the uncertainty in which the whole subject of misrepresentation has at times been lost.

Summary

Let it be supposed that A buys a horse and a cow from B, relying upon B's statement that he owns both animals. A pays one-third of the purchase price at the time of sale, and contracts to pay the balance at a later time. When it develops that the cow is in fact owned by C, A may have the possibility of no less than eight different reme-

dies based upon some form of misrepresentation. These are:

1. A tort action for damages for deceit. In many jurisdictions this requires proof that B knew that his statement was false, or at least was consciously ignorant of the truth. In others, it has been extended to include negligence, or even strict liability.

2. A tort action for damages for negligence, upon proof that B made the statement without reasonable care to learn the truth.

3. A contract action for damages for breach of warranty, which regards the statement as a part of the contract, and therefore requires only proof that it was made and relied on.

4. In some jurisdictions, at least,[98] a suit in equity to rescind the sale, by which A seeks to return both animals and recover the payment made. This also will lie where the statement was an innocent one.

5. A restitution action at law, on the theory that A rescinds the sale of his own motion, is willing to return both animals, and seeks to recover the payment made. This also will lie where the statement was innocent.

6. If B brings an action for the balance of the purchase price, A may set up the misrepresentation as a defense, upon the theory that he rescinds the sale and is willing to return both animals, and defeat all recovery. This remedy is likewise available, in most jurisdictions, for innocent misrepresentation.

7. In B's action for the balance of the price, A may retain the horse and set up the misrepresentation as a defense, claiming recoupment of his damages by reducing the amount of B's recovery to any excess value the horse may have over the amount paid. There is still considerable uncertainty as to

A. 740; Bastrup v. Prendergast, 1899, 179 Ill. 553, 53 N.E. 995; Macomber v. Kinney, 1910, 114 Minn. 146, 130 N.W. 851. See also the forgery cases supra, note 87.

95. Titus v. Morse, 1855, 40 Me. 348; Formby v. Hood, 1898, 119 Ala. 231, 24 So. 359; Starr v. Bartz, 1909, 219 Mo. 47, 117 S.W. 1125; Milburn v. Michel, 1921, 137 Md. 415, 112 A. 581.

96. Beechley v. Beechley, 1906, 134 Iowa 75, 108 N. W. 762; Scharman v. Scharman, 1893, 38 Neb. 39, 56 N.W. 704; Allen v. Shaw, 1881, 61 N.H. 95; Sullivan v. Moore, 1909, 84 S.C. 426, 65 S.E. 561.

97. Restatement of Torts, § 894(2); Terrell Hills Baptist Church v. Pawel, Tex.Civ.App.1956, 286 S. W.2d 204.

98. As noted supra, p. 687, note 47, some courts refuse to allow this remedy, upon the ground that there is an adequate remedy at law, in the form of a restitution action (No. 5 in the text).

whether this remedy is available for innocent misstatements.[99]

8. If C claims the cow from A, A may set up by way of estoppel the fact that C actively misrepresented to him that B was its owner, or that C stood by knowing that A was about to purchase from B, and failed to assert his claim.

One has only to consider the variety of these remedies to understand why the law of misrepresentation has not been clarified by the courts. Considering them by the numbers given, 1, 2, 3, 7 and 8 proceed upon the theory of affirmance of the transaction and retention of what has been received; 4, 5 and 6 upon the theory of disaffirmance and rescission. Number 1 is based by some courts upon wrongful intent, by others upon negligence or strict liability; 2 is a matter of negligence; 3, 4, 5 and 6 of strict responsibility; 8 falls into two branches, one based on strict liability, the other on negligence; while 7 has been assigned by various courts to each of the three theories.

Our chief concern is of course with the tort action of deceit. But any discussion of that action obviously would be incomplete without reference to the divergent rules which have developed as to the other remedies, and the disturbing effect which they have had upon the deceit action itself.

106. REPRESENTATION AND NON-DISCLOSURE

The representation[1] which will serve as a basis for an action of deceit, as well as other forms of relief, usually consists, of course, of oral or written words; but it is not necessarily so limited. The exhibition of a document,[2] turning back the odometer of an automobile offered for sale,[3] drawing a check without funds,[4] or a wide variety of other conduct calculated to convey a misleading impression under the circumstances of the case,[5] may be sufficient. Merely by entering into some transactions at all, the defendant may reasonably be taken to represent that some things are true—as, for example, that a bank which receives deposits is solvent,[6] or that a stock certificate sold is a valid one,[7] and he has a permit to sell it.[8] It is trite

action in tort, on the same basis as misrepresentation. This is scanty authority. It usually is held that the duress merely invalidates the plaintiff's consent, leaving open to him any action, such as conversion, which would have been open to him if it had not been given. Grainger v. Hill, 1838, 4 Bing.N.C. 212, 132 Eng.Rep. 769; General Motors Acceptance Corp. v. Davis, 1931, 151 Okl. 255, 7 P. 2d 157; Saunders v. Mullinix, 1950, 195 Md. 235, 72 A.2d 720; Murphy v. Hobbs, 1884, 8 Colo. 17, 5 P. 637, rehearing denied, 1886, 8 Colo. 130, 11 P. 55.

2. Baker v. Hallam, 1897, 103 Iowa 43, 72 N.W. 419; Leonard v. Springer, 1902, 197 Ill. 532, 64 N.E. 299; McCall v. Davis, 1867, 56 Pa. 431.

3. Osborn v. Gene Teague Chevrolet Co., 1969, —— Or. ——, 459 P.2d 988; District Motor Co. v. Rodill, Mun.App.D.C.1952, 88 A.2d 489; Chapman v. Zakzaska, 1956, 273 Wis. 64, 76 N.W.2d 537; Sarwark Motor Sales, Inc. v. Husband, 1967, 5 Ariz.App. 304, 426 P.2d 404; Boise Dodge, Inc. v. Clark, 1969, 92 Idaho 902, 453 P.2d 551. Cf. Lindberg Cadillac Co. v. Aron, Mo.App.1963, 371 S.W.2d 651 (trading in car with cracked engine block, painted over).

4. Eastern Trust & Banking Co. v. Cunningham, 1908, 103 Me. 455, 70 A. 17; Sieling v. Clark, 1896, 18 Misc. 464, 41 N.Y.S. 982; cf. City Nat. Bank v. Burns, 1880, 68 Ala. 267.

5. Such as stacking aluminum sheets to conceal corroded ones in the middle. Salzman v. Maldaver, 1946, 315 Mich. 403, 24 N.W.2d 161.

6. Cassidy v. Uhlmann, 1902, 170 N.Y. 505, 63 N.E. 554.

7. Hutchings v. Tipsword, Mo.App.1962, 363 S.W.2d 40; MacDonald v. Reich & Lievre, 1929, 100 Cal. App. 736, 281 P. 106.

8. Pennebaker v. Kimble, 1928, 126 Or. 317, 269 P. 981.

99. See supra, p. 689. In the case supposed, of course, the statement might amount to a warranty, for which recoupment would be allowed even if it were innocently made. See Uniform Sales Act, § 69(1).

1. Mention should be made also of Neibuhr v. Gage, 1906, 99 Minn. 149, 108 N.W. 884, affirmed, 1906, 99 Minn. 149, 109 N.W. 1; Smith v. Blakesburg Sav. Bank, 1917, 182 Iowa 1190, 164 N.W. 762; and Woodham v. Allen, 1900, 130 Cal. 194, 62 P. 398, all of which say that duress provides a basis for an

to say in such cases that "actions may speak louder than words."

The significance to be assigned to such words or conduct will be determined according to the effect they would produce, under the circumstances, upon the ordinary mind.[9] Ambiguous statements, which are reasonably capable of both a true and a false meaning, will amount to misrepresentation if the false meaning is accepted, and is intended [10] or known [11] to be accepted—although if the true meaning is intended and believed to be understood, it would seem that any liability would be in negligence rather than deceit.[12] Likewise, misrepresentation may be found in statements which are literally true, but which create a false impression in the mind of the hearer,[13] as is sometimes the case where a complicated financial statement is issued by a seller of securities. "A fraud may be as

effectually perpetrated by telling the truth as a falsehood; by calling things by their right names as by their wrong names." [14]

In addition to such representations by word or conduct, which might be called definite or positive, deceit, as well as other remedies, may be based upon an active concealment of the truth.[15] Any words or acts which create a false impression covering up the truth,[16] or which remove an opportunity that might otherwise have led to the discovery of a material fact—as by floating a ship to conceal the defects in her bottom,[17] sending one who is in search of information in a direction where it cannot be obtained,[18] or even a false denial of knowledge by one in possession of the facts—[19] are classed as misrepresentation, no less than a verbal assurance that the fact is not true.

Nondisclosure

A much more difficult problem arises as to whether mere silence, or a passive failure to disclose facts of which the defendant has knowledge, can serve as the foundation of a deceit action.[20] It has commonly been stated

---

9. Downey v. Finucane, 1912, 205 N.Y. 251, 98 N.E. 391; Windram v. French, 1890, 151 Mass. 547, 24 N.E. 914; Miles v. Stevens, 1846, 3 Pa. 21; Davis v. Louisville Trust Co., 6 Cir. 1910, 181 F. 10.

10. "If they palter with him in a double sense, it may be that they lie like truth; but I think they lie, and it is a fraud. Indeed, as a question of casuistry, I am inclined to think the fraud is aggravated by a shabby attempt to get the benefit of a fraud, without incurring the responsibility." Lord Blackburn, in Smith v. Chadwick, 1884, L.R. 9 A.C. 187.

11. Busch v. Wilcox, 1890, 82 Mich. 315, 46 N.W. 940, affirmed 82 Mich. 336, 47 N.W. 328; Degman v. Mason County, 1874, 15 Ky.L.Abs. 876; Angus v. Clifford, [1891] 2 Ch.Div. 449, 472. See Terry, Intent to Defraud, 1915, 25 Yale L.J. 87, 94.

12. Nash v. Minnesota Title Ins. & Trust Co., 1895, 163 Mass. 574, 40 N.E. 1039; Slater Trust Co. v. Gardiner, 2 Cir. 1910, 183 F. 268; Restatement of Torts, § 528. See Smith v. Chadwick, 1884, L.R. 9 A.C. 187; Angus v. Clifford, [1891] 2 Ch.Div. 449, 472.

13. Cahill v. Readon, 1929, 85 Colo. 9, 273 P. 653 (rent values had "become stabilized"—at zero). Cf. Lomerson v. Johnston, 1890, 47 N.J.Eq. 312, 20 A. 675; Downey v. Finucane, 1912, 205 N.Y. 251, 98 N.E. 391; Wolfe v. A. E. Kusterer & Co., 1934, 269 Mich. 424, 257 N.W. 729; Atwood v. Chapman, 1877, 68 Me. 38. See the language of Baron Alderson in Moens v. Heyworth, 1842, 10 M. & W. 147, 152 Eng.Rep. 418.

14. Mulligan v. Bailey, 1859, 28 Ga. 507.

15. See Keeton, Fraud—Concealment and Non-Disclosure, 1936, 15 Tex.L.Rev. 1, 2–5; Wilson, Concealment or Silence as a Form of Fraud, 1895, 5 Counsellor 230.

16. Croyle v. Moses, 1879, 90 Pa. 250 (cribbing horse offered for sale tied up short); Kuelling v. Roderick Lean Mfg. Co., 1905, 183 N.Y. 78, 75 N.E. 1098 (defects in road roller concealed with putty and paint); Ten-Cate v. First Nat. Bank, Tex.Civ.App. 1932, 52 S.W.2d 323 (portion of contract omitted in reading it). Cf. Pickering v. Dowson, 1813, 4 Taunt. 779, 128 Eng.Rep. 537 (defects in house covered with plaster and paint); Weikel v. Sterns, 1911, 142 Ky. 513, 134 S.W. 908.

17. Schneider v. Heath, 1813, 3 Camp. 505, 170 Eng. Rep. 1462.

18. Chisolm v. Gadsden, 1847, 1 Strob., S.C., 220; Stewart v. Wyoming Cattle Ranch Co., 1888, 128 U.S. 383. Cf. Griffiths v. Thrasher, 1953, 95 Mont. 210, 26 P.2d 995 (staffing hotel with confederates).

19. Smith v. Beatty, 1843, 37 N.C. 456, 2 Ired.Eq. 456.

20. See Keeton, Fraud—Concealment and Non-Disclosure, 1936, 15 Tex.L.Rev. 1; Notes, 1942, 22 Bos.

as a general rule,[21] particularly in the older cases, that the action will not lie for such tacit nondisclosure.[22] This rule of course reflected the dubious business ethics of the bargaining transactions with which deceit was at first concerned, together with a touch of the old tort notion that there can be no liability for nonfeasance, or merely doing nothing.[23] It finds proper application in cases where the fact undisclosed is patent,[24] or the plaintiff has equal opportunities for obtaining information which he may be expected to utilize,[25] or the defendant has no reason to think that he is acting under any misapprehension.[26] There are, however, occasional modern cases which have held that so long as one adversary does not actively mislead another, he is perfectly free to take advantage, no matter how unfair, of ignorance; and that the owner of a dwelling which he knows to be riddled with termites can un-

load it with impunity upon a buyer unaware, and go on his way rejoicing.[27] These are surely singularly unappetizing cases.

To this general rule, if such it be, the courts have developed a number of exceptions, some of which are as yet very ill defined, and have no very definite boundaries. The most obvious one is that if the defendant does speak, he must disclose enough to prevent his words from being misleading,[28] and that there is fraud in a statement as to the rental of property which does not mention that it is illegal,[29] or as to the income of an amusement center which does not disclose that there has been a police raid which is likely to affect it,[30] or in the disclosure of the existence of one graveyard on premises without disclosing another.[31] In other words, half of the truth may obviously amount to a lie, if it is understood to be the whole. Again, one who has made a statement, and subsequently acquires new information which makes it untrue or misleading, must disclose such information to anyone whom he knows to be still acting on the basis of the original

---

U.L.Rev. 607; 1948, 21 Temple L.Q. 368; 1956, 29 So.Cal.L.Rev. 378.

21. Derived originally from the language of Lord Cairns in Peek v. Gurney, 1873, L.R. 6 H.L. 377. See Bower, Actionable Nondisclosure, 1915, 134; and cf. Beachey v. Brown, 1860, El.Bl. & El. 796, 120 Eng.Rep. 706.

22. Keates v. Earl of Cardogan, 1851, 10 C.B. 591, 138 Eng.Rep. 234; Crowell v. Jackson, 1891, 53 N. J.L. 656, 23 A. 426; Boileau v. Records & Breen, 1913, 165 Iowa 134, 144 N.W. 336; Iron City Nat. Bank v. Anderson, Du Puy & Co., 1899, 194 Pa. 205, 44 A. 1066; Windram Mfg. Co. v. Boston Blacking Co., 1921, 239 Mass. 123, 131 N.E. 454.

23. See supra, § 56.

24. Riley v. White, Mo.App.1950, 231 S.W.2d 291; Schnader v. Brooks, 1926, 150 Md. 52, 132 A. 381; cf. Gibson v. Mendenhall, 1950, 203 Okl. 558, 224 P. 2d 251 (generally known); Kapiloff v. Abington Plaza Corp., Mun.App.D.C.1948, 59 A.2d 516 (act of Congress).

25. Phillips v. Homestake Consol. Placer Mines Co., 1929, 51 Nev. 226, 273 P. 657; Oates v. Taylor, 1948, 31 Wash.2d 898, 199 P.2d 924.

26. Haddad v. Clark, 1945, 132 Conn. 229, 43 A.2d 221; Egan v. Hudson Nut Products, Inc., 1955, 142 Conn. 344, 114 A.2d 213; Industrial Bank of Commerce v. Selling, 1952, 203 Misc. 154, 116 N.Y.S.2d 274; Blair v. National Security Ins. Co., 3 Cir. 1942, 126 F.2d 955. Cf. Lindquist v. Dilkes, 3 Cir. 1942, 127 F.2d 21.

27. Swinton v. Whitinsville Sav. Bank, 1942, 311 Mass. 677, 42 N.E.2d 808; Fegeas v. Sherrill, 1958, 218 Md. 472, 147 A.2d 223; Hendrick v. Lynn, 1958, 37 Del.Ch. 402, 144 A.2d 147.

28. Smith v. Pope, 1961, 103 N.H. 555, 176 A.2d 321; Newell v. Randall, 1884, 32 Minn. 171, 19 N.W. 972; Noved Realty Corp. v. A. A. P. Co., 1937, 250 App.Div. 1, 293 N.Y.S. 336; Berry v. Stevens, 1934, 168 Okl. 124, 31 P.2d 950; Dennis v. Thomson, 1931, 240 Ky. 727, 43 S.W.2d 18.

Otherwise where the statement does not purport to tell the whole truth. Potts v. Chapin, 1882, 133 Mass. 276.

29. Palmeter v. Hackett, 1919, 95 Or. 12, 185 P. 1105, 186 P. 581; Tucker v. Beasley, Mun.App.D.C.1948, 57 A.2d 191; Cf. Kraft v. Lowe, Mun.App.D.C. 1950, 77 A.2d 554 (statement that plumbing is all right, without disclosing septic tank). Otherwise where the defendant honestly believes that the rental is legal. Ceferatti v. Boisvert, 1950, 137 Conn. 280, 77 A.2d 82.

30. Dyke v. Zaiser, 1947, 80 Cal.App.2d 639, 182 P.2d 344.

31. Elsey v. Lamkin, 1914, 156 Ky. 836, 162 S.W. 106; Junius Const. Co. v. Cohen, 1931, 257 N.Y. 393, 178 N.E. 672 (streets).

statement—as, for example, where there is a serious decline in the profits of a business pending its sale.[32]

Another exception is found where the parties stand in some confidential or fiduciary relation to one another, such as that of principal and agent,[33] executor and beneficiary of an estate,[34] bank and investing depositor,[35] majority and minority stockholders,[36] old friends,[37] or numerous others where special trust and confidence is reposed.[38] In addi-

tion, certain types of contracts, such as those of suretyship or guaranty,[39] insurance,[40] partnership and joint adventure,[41] are recognized as creating something in the nature of a confidential relation, and hence as requiring the utmost good faith, and full and fair disclosure of all material facts.

Beyond this, there has been a rather amorphous tendency on the part of most courts to find a duty of disclosure in cases where the defendant has special knowledge, or means of knowledge, not open to the plaintiff, and is aware that the plaintiff is acting under a misapprehension as to facts which would be of importance to him, and would probably affect his decision.[42] This tendency, which has gone far to whittle away the "general rule," has been most manifest in cases involving latent dangerous physical conditions of land[43] or chattels,[44] or defects in the title,[45]

---

32. With v. O'Flanagan, [1936] 1 Ch. 575; Loewer v. Harris, 2 Cir. 1893, 57 F. 368; Guastella v. Wardell, Miss.1967, 198 So.2d 227; Fischer v. Kletz, S. D.N.Y.1967, 266 F.Supp. 180; Restatement of Torts, § 551(2). Cf. Equitable Life Ins. Co. of Iowa v. Halsey, Stuart & Co., 1941, 312 U.S. 410; Hush v. Reaugh, E.D.Ill.1938, 23 F.Supp. 646. See Note, 1968, 116 U.Pa.L.Rev. 500.

Cf. Pilmore v. Hood, 1838, 5 Bing.N.C. 97, 132 Eng. Rep. 1042 (statement made without intent that plaintiff should rely on it must be corrected when reliance is discovered).

33. McDonough v. Williams, 1905, 77 Ark. 261, 92 S. W. 783.

34. Foreman v. Henry, 1922, 87 Okl. 272, 210 P. 1026; Murphy v. Cartwright, 5 Cir. 1953, 202 F.2d 71.

35. Brasher v. First Nat. Bank, 1936, 232 Ala. 340, 168 So. 42.

36. Speed v. Transamerica Corp., D.C.Del.1951, 99 F. Supp. 808, supplemented 100 F.Supp. 461, petition denied 100 F.Supp. 463.

37. Feist v. Roesler, Tex.Civ.App.1953, 86 S.W.2d 787. Cf. In re Estate of Enyart, 1916, 100 Neb. 337, 160 N.W. 120, overruled in part Kingsley v. Noble, 1935, 129 Neb. 808, 263 N.W. 222 (affianced).

38. Edward Barron Estate Co. v. Woodruff Co., 1912, 163 Cal. 561, 126 P. 351. " * * * for instance, the relations of trustee and cestui que trust, principal and agent, attorney and client, physician and patient, priest and parishioner, partners, tenants in common, husband and wife, parent and child, guardian and ward, and many others of like character." Farmers State Bank of Newport v. Lamon, 1925, 132 Wash. 369, 231 P. 952, 42 A.L.R. 1072. There is dispute as to the confidential nature of certain relations. Thus tenants in common, Phillips v. Homestake Consol. Placer Mines Co., 1929, 51 Nev. 226, 273 P. 657; Neill v. Shamburg, 1893, 158 Pa. 263, 27 A. 992, and corporate directors purchasing stock from stockholders. Crowell v. Jackson, 1891, 53 N.J.L. 656, 23 A. 426; Goodwin v. Agassiz, 1933, 283 Mass. 358, 186 N.E. 659, have been held to be under no duty to make disclosure.

As to the latter, see Note, 1930, 14 Minn.L.Rev. 530, and the numerous articles there cited.

39. Cf. Connecticut Gen. Life Ins. Co. v. Chase, 1900, 72 Vt. 176, 47 A. 825; Atlantic Trust & Deposit Co. v. Union Trust & Title Corp., 1909, 110 Va. 286, 67 S.E. 182; Arant, Suretyship, 1931, 77–81.

40. See Vance, Insurance, 2d Ed. 1930, §§ 96–98; Note, 1928, 14 Corn.L.Q. 91.

41. Cf. Noble v. Fox, 1912, 35 Okl. 70, 128 P. 102.

42. Cf. Tone v. Halsey, Stuart & Co., 1936, 286 Ill. App. 169, 3 N.E.2d 142; Strong v. Repide, 1909, 213 U.S. 419; Rothmiller v. Stein, 1894, 143 N.Y. 581, 38 N.E. 718; Edward Malley Co. v. Button, 1905, 77 Conn. 571, 60 A. 125.

43. Weikel v. Sterns, 1911, 142 Ky. 513, 134 S.W. 908 (concealed cesspool); Southern v. Floyd, 1954, 89 Ga.App. 602, 80 S.E.2d 490 (defect in furnace boiler); Cutter v. Hamlen, 1888, 147 Mass. 471, 18 N.E. 397 (premises infected with disease); Herzog v. Capital Co., 1945, 27 Cal.2d 349, 164 P.2d 8 (leaky house); Mincy v. Crisler, 1923, 132 Miss. 223, 96 So. 162. Compare, as to lessors, supra, p. 401.

44. Marsh v. Webber, 1868, 13 Minn. 109 (diseased sheep); Puls v. Hornbeck, 1909, 24 Okl. 288, 103 P. 665 (diseased cattle); Grigsby v. Stapleton, 1888, 94 Mo. 423, 7 S.W. 421 (same); French v. Vining, 1869, 102 Mass. 132 (poisoned hay); Morriss-Buick Co. v. Huss, Tex.Civ.App.1935, 84 S.W.2d 264, reversed on other grounds, 1938, 113 S.W.2d 891 (wrecked and repaired car).

45. Corry v. Sylvia Capitol Cia, 1915, 192 Ala. 550, 68 So. 891; Newell Bros. v. Hanson, 1924, 97 Vt.

where the plaintiff has acted upon the reasonable assumption that such conditions do not exist. This has now generally been extended to any facts or conditions basic to the transaction, even though they are of a kind likely to cause only pecuniary loss.[46] Thus when the seller of a house fails to disclose to the buyer the fact that it is infested with termites,[47] or built on improperly compacted filled ground,[48] the modern law is definitely that he will be liable for the pecuniary loss sustained.

There seems to be no corresponding tendency in the case of special information in the hands of one who buys rather than sells. The buyer is permitted to reap the advantage which his industry in discovering the facts,

and his business acumen, can bring him.[49] It may therefore perhaps be suggested that the courts which are requiring such disclosure from a seller are pursuing a policy rather similar in its purpose to that which imposes implied warranties of quality or title.[50] In a number of recent decisions, however, the same duty of disclosure has been found in other types of business transactions, where one party remains silent as to a fact which he knows to be of importance to the other.[51] The law appears to be working toward the ultimate conclusion that full disclosure of all material facts must be made whenever elementary fair conduct demands it.[52]

When the plaintiff seeks relief of an equitable character, as by rescission of the transaction and recovery of what he has parted with, a more liberal rule usually is applied. Mutual mistake as to a material fact ordi-

297, 123 A. 208; Dirks Trust & Title Co. v. Koch, 1913, 32 S.D. 551, 143 N.W. 952; Hall v. Carter, Ky.1959, 324 S.W.2d 410; Kallgren v. Steele, 1955, 131 Cal.App.2d 43, 279 P.2d 1027; cf. Curran v. Heslop, 1953, 115 Cal.App.2d 476, 252 P.2d 378 (porch enclosed without a permit in violation of building code).

46. Chandler v. Butler, Tex.Civ.App.1955, 284 S.W.2d 388 (numerous facts affecting market value of stock sold); Boonstra v. Stevens-Norton, Inc., 1964, 64 Wash.2d 621, 393 P.2d 287 (facts which made loan unsafe); Edward Malley Co. v. Button, 1905, 77 Conn. 571, 60 A. 125 (married woman obtaining goods on credit when separated from her husband); Dyke v. Zaiser, 1947, 80 Cal.App.2d 639, 182 P.2d 344 (police raid on amusement center sold); Neuman v. Corn Exchange Nat. Bank & Trust Co., 1947, 356 Pa. 442, 51 A.2d 759, supplemented 52 A. 2d 177 (tie-in agreement affecting value of stock).

See Berger and Hirsch, Pennsylvania Tort Liability for Concealment and Nondisclosure in Business Transactions, 1948, 21 Temple L.Q. 368; Goldfarb, Fraud and Nondisclosure in the Vendor-Purchaser Relation, 1956, 8 West.Res.L.Rev. 5; Note, 1942, 22 Bos.U.L.Rev. 607; Keeton, Rights of Disappointed Purchasers, 1953, 32 Tex.L.Rev. 1.

47. Obde v. Schlemeyer, 1960, 56 Wash.2d 449, 353 P. 2d 672; Williams v. Benson, 1966, 3 Mich.App. 9, 141 N.W.2d 650.

48. Loghry v. Capel, 1965, 257 Iowa 285, 132 N.W.2d 417; Brooks v. Ervin Const. Co., 1960, 253 N.C. 214, 116 S.E.2d 454; Rothstein v. Janss Inv. Corp., 1941, 45 Cal.App.2d 64, 113 P.2d 465. Cf. Kaze v. Compton, Ky.1955, 283 S.W.2d 204 (drain under house); Jenkins v. McCormick, 1959, 184 Kan. 842, 339 P.2d 8 (defect in floor); Dargue v. Chaput, 1958, 166 Neb. 69, 88 N.W.2d 148 (inadequate drainage).

49. Laidlaw v. Organ, 1817, 2 Wheat., U.S., 178, 4 L. Ed. 214; Pratt Land & Imp. Co. v. McClain, 1902, 135 Ala. 452, 33 So. 185; James v. Anderson, 1927, 149 Va. 113, 140 S.E. 264; Hays v. Meyers, 1908, 139 Ky. 440, 107 S.W. 287; Holly Hill Lumber Co. v. McCoy, 1942, 201 S.C. 427, 23 S.E.2d 372. See Goldfarb, Fraud and Nondisclosure in the Vendor-Purchaser Relation, 1956, 8 West.Res.L.Rev. 5.

50. Implied warranties do not require knowledge of the truth on the part of the defendant, but arise as part of the contract of sale, or a legal consequence of it. There may, however, be liability in deceit for failure to disclose known defects, where no implied warranty would arise. See Barton v. Dowis, 1926, 315 Mo. 226, 285 S.W. 988; Downing v. Wimble, 1924, 97 Vt. 390, 123 A. 433.

51. Fuller v. De Paul University, 1938, 293 Ill.App. 261, 12 N.E.2d 213 (married apostate priest employed at Catholic institution); D'Alessandra v. Manufacturers' Cas. Ins. Co., Sp. Term 1951, 106 N.Y.S.2d 564 (indemnity agreement to obtain release of prisoner; non-disclosure of release on bail); Ainscough v. O'Shaughnessy, 1956, 346 Mich. 307, 78 N.W.2d 209 (penciled notation in contract reducing allowance for car traded in); Musgrave v. Lucas, 1951, 193 Or. 401, 238 P.2d 780 (threat of government litigation affecting value of business); Highland Motor Transfer Co. v. Heyburn Bldg. Co., 1931, 237 Ky. 337, 35 S.W.2d 521 (swimming pool not disclosed to building contractor).

52. See Keeton, Fraud—Concealment and Non-Disclosure, 1936, 15 Tex.L.Rev. 1, 31–40; Note, 1965, 2 Idaho L.Rev. 112.

narily is sufficient ground for such relief; and when the plaintiff is proceeding under a material mistake, the defendant's position can scarcely be improved if he stands by with knowledge of the error, fails to make disclosure, and takes advantage of the situation.[53] Likewise, as has previously been mentioned,[54] there is one branch of estoppel in pais which is based upon a failure to take action, or to disclose the truth, where a reasonable man would not fail to do so. The greater liberality found as to such remedies is probably due to the fact that they are primarily concerned with preventing the defendant from obtaining an unfair advantage of his own, while the action of deceit requires him to go further, and compensate the plaintiff for the loss he has sustained.

107. BASIS OF RESPONSIBILITY

Misrepresentation, as has been said before,[55] may be separated into the three familiar tort classifications of intent, negligence, and strict responsibility. The earlier cases made little or no attempt to distinguish the three, no doubt because there had been no occasion to distinguish the possible remedies. The actions for deceit and for breach of warranty, with their common origin in the action on the case, were not yet clearly recognized as separate,[56] and it was assumed, by the text writers at least,[57] that negligent misrepresen-

tation would find a remedy in deceit. It was not until as late as 1889 that the House of Lords, in the leading case of Derry v. Peek,[58] clearly identified the deceit action with intentional misrepresentation, and left negligence and strict responsibility to be dealt with by other remedies.

In that case the defendants, who were directors of a tramway corporation, issued a prospectus to induce the public to subscribe for stock, which contained the unqualified statement that " * * * the company has the right to use steam, or mechanical motive power, instead of horses. * * * " In fact, the company had no such right. The plaintiff, who had purchased stock on the faith of the statement, brought an action of deceit. The court took an extremely charitable view of the evidence, and concluded that the defendants had honestly believed the statement to be true, although they had no reasonable ground for any such belief. It was held that the action could not be maintained, since nothing more than negligence was shown. For deceit there must be proof "that a false representation has been made (1) knowingly, or (2) without belief in its truth, or (3) recklessly, careless whether it be true or false." [59]

This decision, which excluded from the action of deceit any misrepresentation that is innocent, or merely negligent, has been something of a storm center ever since. It has been condemned as a backward step in the law, and in cases where there is a contract between the parties a substantial minority group of the American courts flatly refuse to follow it.[60] The majority purport to accept it as sound law,[61] but a great many of them

---

53. Hill v. Gray, 1816, 1 Starkie 434, 171 Eng.Rep. 521; Simmons v. Evans, 1927, 185 Tenn. 282, 206 S.W.2d 295; Salmonson v. Horswill, 1917, 39 S.D. 402, 164 N.W. 973; Tyra v. Cheney, 1915, 129 Minn. 428, 152 N.W. 835; Clauser v. Taylor, 1941, 44 Cal. App.2d 453, 112 P.2d 661. See Note, 1918, 27 Yale L.J. 691.

54. Supra, p. 691.

55. Supra, p. 686.

56. See, slowly working out the distinction, Williamson v. Allison, 1802, 2 East 446, 102 Eng.Rep. 439; Vail v. Strong, 1838, 10 Vt. 457; Mahurin v. Harding, 1853, 28 N.H. 128; Pierce v. Carey, 1875, 37 Wis. 232.

57. See Beven, Negligence, 2d Ed., 1474; 1 Bigelow, Fraud, 1st Ed. 1888, 509, 516, 517; 2 Pomeroy, Equity Jurisprudence, 1st Ed. 1882, § 884.

58. 1889, 14 A.C. 337.

59. Per Lord Herschell, 14 A.C. 374.

60. See infra, pp. 705, 710.

61. Lambert v. Smith, 1964, 235 Md. 284, 201 A.2d 491; Kountze v. Kennedy, 1895, 147 N.Y. 124, 41 N. E. 414; Wishnick v. Frye, 1952, 111 Cal.App.2d 926, 245 P.2d 532; Dundee Land Co. v. Simmons, 1948, 204 Ga. 248, 49 S.E.2d 488; Sledge & Norfleet Co. v. Mann, 1937, 193 Ark. 884, 103 S.W.2d 630.

have devised various more or less ingenious fictions and formulae [62] which permit them to render lip service to Derry v. Peek, and yet allow recovery in deceit for misrepresentation which falls short of actual intent to deceive. If one looks to the facts of the cases rather than the formulae adopted by the courts, it is by no means clear that Derry v. Peek is supported by the weight of American authority. The controversy which has raged about the case [63] has been concerned more with the question of the form of action which should be available, rather than with the substantive law of liability. It may be suggested that it is the latter which is of primary importance,[64] and that once it is determined that liability is to be imposed, it is a comparatively easy matter to find an appropriate remedy in deceit, negligence or warranty. The problem may be approached as one of the basis of liability, with only incidental regard for the form of the remedy.

Scienter—Intent to Deceive

The intent which underlies an intentional misrepresentation is a more complex matter

than the relatively simple intention in the case of assault and battery.[65] It involves the intent that a representation shall be made, that it shall be directed to a particular person or class of persons,[66] that it shall convey a certain meaning,[67] that it shall be believed, and that it shall be acted upon in a certain way.[68] In the usual case, all of this is present beyond dispute. In addition, there is the intent to accomplish an ultimate purpose, as to benefit the speaker, or to cause harm to the one addressed. It is well settled that, except as to the issue of punitive damages,[69] this last is of no importance. The fact that the defendant was disinterested,[70] that he had the best of motives, and that he thought he was doing the plaintiff a kindness,[71] will not absolve him from liability, so long as he did in fact intend to mislead.

So far as culpability is concerned, none of these intentions is controlling. The intent which becomes important is the intent to deceive, to mislead, to convey a false impression. Obviously this intent, which has been given the name of "scienter" by the courts, must be a matter of belief, or of absence of belief, that the representation is true; and it was this element which was so strongly emphasized in Derry v. Peek. The state of the speaker's mind, notwithstanding its elusiveness as a matter of psychology and its diffi-

---

62. See infra, p. 705. Green, Deceit, 1930, 16 Va. L.Rev. 749, considers the resulting flexibility desirable, since it enables the courts to accomplish substantial justice and still preserve the appearance of a fixed rule. There is, of course, not so much to be said for the resulting unpredictability of decisions.

63. See Smith, Liability for Negligent Language, 1909, 14 Harv.L.Rev. 184; Williston, Liability for Honest Misrepresentation, 1911, 24 Harv.L.Rev. 415; Bohlen, Misrepresentation as Deceit, Negligence or Warranty, 1929, 42 Harv.L.Rev. 733; Carpenter, Responsibility for Intentional, Negligent and Innocent Misrepresentation, 1930, 24 Ill.L.Rev. 749; Weisiger, Basis of Liability for Misrepresentation, 1930, 24 Ill.L.Rev. 866; Green, Deceit, 1930, 16 Va. L.Rev. 749, 750–762; Morris, Liability for Innocent Misrepresentation, 1930, 64 U.S.L.Rev. 121; Bohlen, Should Negligent Misrepresentations Be Treated as Negligence or Fraud, 1932, 18 Va.L.Rev. 703; Green, Innocent Misrepresentation, 1933, 19 Va.L. Rev. 742; Keeton, Fraud: The Necessity for an Intent to Deceive, 1958, 5 U.C.L.A.L.Rev. 583; Notes, 1927, 12 Corn.L.Q. 539; 1928, 28 Col.L.Rev. 216; 1928, 37 Yale L.J. 1141; 1931, 26 Ill.L.Rev. 49; 1937, 21 Minn.L.Rev. 434.

64. See Harper and McNeely, A Synthesis of the Law of Misrepresentation, 1939, 22 Minn.L.Rev. 939.

65. See Terry, Intent to Defraud, 1915, 25 Yale L.J. 87.

66. As to this, see infra, p. 702.

67. As to intent or negligence in the case of ambiguous statements, see supra, p. 695.

68. As to this, see infra, p. 702.

69. Thompson v. Modern School of Business and Correspondence, 1920, 183 Cal. 112, 190 P. 451; Laughlin v. Hopkinson, 1920, 292 Ill. 80, 126 N.E. 591; Kluge v. Ries, 1917, 66 Ind.App. 610, 117 N.E. 262.

70. Foster v. Charles, 1830, 7 Bing. 105, 131 Eng.Rep. 40; Holloway v. Forsyth, 1917, 226 Mass. 358, 115 N.E. 483; Endsley v. Johns, 1887, 120 Ill. 469, 12 N.E. 247; Wilson v. Jones, Tex.Com.App.1932, 45 S.W.2d 572.

71. Polhill v. Walter, 1832, 3 B. & Ad. 114, 110 Eng. Rep. 43; Boyd's Ex'rs v. Browne, 1847, 6 Pa. 310; Smith v. Chadwick, 1884, L.R. 9 A.C. 187.

culty of proof, must be looked to in determining whether the action of deceit can be maintained.

There is of course no difficulty in finding the required intent to mislead where it appears that the speaker believes his statement to be false.[72] Likewise there is general agreement that it is present when the representation is made without any belief as to its truth,[73] or with reckless disregard whether it be true or false.[74] Further than this, it appears that all courts have extended it to include representations made by one who is conscious that he has no sufficient basis of information to justify them.[75] A defendant who asserts a fact as of his own knowledge, or so positively as to imply that he has knowledge,[76] under circumstances where he is aware that he will be so understood [77] when

he knows that he does not in fact know whether what he says is true, is found to have the intent to deceive, not so much as to the fact itself, but rather as to the extent of his information. Since the state of his mind may be inferred from the circumstances, and in the absence of satisfactory evidence to the contrary it may sometimes be quite reasonable to infer that he must have known that he did not know,[78] there is a certain amount of leeway in the direction of holding the defendant to something like a reasonable standard of judgment.

Apparently it is at this point that the line is to be drawn between an intent to mislead and mere negligence. An honest belief, however unreasonable, that the representation is true and the speaker has information to justify it, was held in Derry v. Peek [79] to be no sufficient basis for deceit. It is of course clear that the very unreasonableness of such a belief may be strong evidence that it does not in fact exist; and where this conclusion is reached as an inference of fact,[80] or even through a presumption capable of being re-

72. See for example Howard v. Gould, 1856, 28 Vt. 523.

73. Shackett v. Bickford, 1906, 74 N.H. 57, 65 A. 252; Griswold v. Gebbie, 1889, 126 Pa. 353, 17 A. 673. See Derry v. Peek, 1889, 14 A.C. 337; Restatement of Torts, § 526(b).

74. Rosenberg v. Howle, Mun.App.D.C.1948, 56 A.2d 709; Atkinson v. Charlotte Builders, 1950, 232 N.C. 67, 59 S.E.2d 1; Otis & Co. v. Grimes, 1935, 97 Colo. 219, 48 P.2d 788; Richards v. Foss, 1927, 126 Me. 413, 139 A. 231; Zager v. Setzer, 1955, 242 N.C. 493, 88 S.E.2d 94.

75. Hadcock v. Osmer, 1897, 153 N.Y. 604, 47 N.E. 923; Sovereign Pocohontas Co. v. Bond, 1941, 74 U.S.App.D.C. 175, 120 F.2d 39; Fausett & Co. v. Bullard, 1950, 217 Ark. 176, 229 S.W.2d 490; Zager v. Setzer, 1955, 242 N.C. 493, 88 S.E.2d 94; Hollerman v. F. H. Peavey & Co., 1964, 269 Minn. 221, 130 N.W.2d 534.

As to the distinction between knowledge of falsity and conscious ignorance, see Jos. Greenspon's Son Pipe Corp. v. Hyman-Michaels Co., Mo.App.1939, 133 S.W.2d 426.

76. An unqualified assertion of fact is regarded as made as of the speaker's own knowledge. Bullitt v. Farrar, 1889, 42 Minn. 8, 43 N.W. 566; Schlossman's v. Niewinski, 1951, 12 N.J.Super. 500, 79 A.2d 870; Kirkpatrick v. Reeves, 1889, 121 Ind. 280, 22 N.E. 139; First Nat. Bank of Tigerton v. Hackett, 1914, 159 Wis. 113, 149 N.W. 703; Pumphrey v. Quillen, 1956, 165 Ohio St. 343, 135 N.E.2d 328.

77. Thus where the matter is clearly susceptible of knowledge. Wiley v. Simons, 1927, 259 Mass. 159,

156 N.E. 23. Otherwise where it is clear to the plaintiff that it is not, or that the defendant is not asserting knowledge. Harris v. Delco Products Co., 1940, 305 Mass. 362, 25 N.E.2d 740; Smith v. Badlam, 1941, 112 Vt. 143, 22 A.2d 161; cf. Duryea v. Zimmerman, 1907, 121 App.Div. 560, 106 N.Y.S. 237.

78. Coman v. Williams, N.D.1954, 65 N.W.2d 377; Trebelhorn v. Bartlett, 1951, 154 Neb. 113, 47 N.W. 2d 374; Clark v. Haggard, 1954, 141 Conn. 668, 109 A.2d 358; Mayfield Motor Co. v. Parker, 1954, 222 Miss. 152, 75 So.2d 435; Pumphrey v. Quillen, 1956, 165 Ohio St. 343, 135 N.E.2d 328. See Keeton, Fraud: The Necessity for an Intent to Deceive, 1958, 5 U.C.L.A.L.Rev. 583.

79. See supra, p. 700. Accord: Boddy v. Henry, 1901, 113 Iowa 462, 85 N.W. 771; Donnelly v. Baltimore Trust & Guarantee Co., 1905, 102 Md. 1, 61 A. 301; and cases cited supra, p. 700.

80. Kimber v. Young, 8 Cir.1905, 137 F. 744; Ultramares Corp. v. Touche, 1931, 255 N.Y. 170, 174 N.E. 441; State Street Trust Co. v. Ernst, 1938, 278 N.Y. 104, 15 N.E.2d 416; see People's Nat. Bank v. Central Trust Co. of Kansas City, 1904, 179 Mo. 648, 78 S.W. 618; Schaffner v. National Supply Co., 1917, 80 W.Va. 111, 92 S.E. 580.

butted,[81] there is nothing inconsistent with a basis of intent. But the courts which go further and adopt arbitrary rules as to when an honest belief does not exist[82] would appear to cross the boundaries of intent, and to impose liability upon another basis.

Thus far attention has been directed to the action of deceit. Other remedies for misrepresentation are more liberal in their scope; and it has never been disputed that the "scienter" or intent which is a basis for deceit is sufficient to justify relief in equity, restitution at law, the defense of fraud, or estoppel.

Once the intent to mislead is established, troublesome questions arise as to the persons to whom the representor will be liable.[83]

In the leading English case of Peek v. Gurney,[84] in which the directors of a corporation issued a prospectus for the purpose of inducing the public to purchase stock from the company itself, it was held that there was no liability to an investor who bought his stock on the market from a stockholder. The court limited responsibility to those whom the defendants had desired to influence, in the manner which had occasioned the damage.[85]

The doctrine of transferred intent,[86] which has been applied in the case of personal violence intended for one person which injures another, was thus rejected in the case of misrepresentation, for the obvious reason[87] of policy that the class of persons who may conceivably learn of a misstatement and be influenced by it is so enormous that an impossible burden, likely to be out of all proportion to the fault involved, might be cast upon anyone who makes a false assertion. This decision, which has been accepted by the Restatement of Torts,[88] has been followed by numerous American courts, in cases involving, for example, similar remote investors,[89] an assignee[90] or a subpurchaser[91] from the one originally dealt with, a casual bystander who overhears but is not expected to take action,[92] and others who were not intended to

---

81. See Vincent v. Corbitt, 1908, 94 Miss. 46, 47 So. 641 (defendant made false statement as of his own knowledge, where facts were available to him; presumption that he knew it was false, which he must rebut).

82. See infra, p. 705.

83. See Keeton, The Ambit of a Fraudulent Representor's Responsibility, 1938, 17 Tex.L.Rev. 1; Prosser, Misrepresentation and Third Persons, 1966, 19 Vand.L.Rev. 231.

84. 1873, L.R. 6 Eng. & Ir.App. 377.

85. Where there is a sale or contract between the parties, and the representation occurs during the preliminary bargaining between them, the desire is conclusively presumed. See Brady v. Finn, 1894, 162 Mass. 260, 38 N.E. 506; Hadley v. Clinton County Importing Co., 1862, 13 Ohio St. 502; Boddy v. Henry, 1904, 126 Iowa 31, 101 N.W. 447.

86. See supra, p. 32.

87. See 2 Cooley, Torts, 3d Ed. 1906, 940–942; Keeton, The Ambit of a Fraudulent Representor's Responsibility, 1938, 17 Tex.L.Rev. 1, 7, 8. The latter author, however, suggests that a broader rule would impose no liability upon any honest man, and that the total *amount* of damages would seldom be increased. Also that the true reason for the limitation may be the ease with which reliance upon the representation may be claimed, and the difficulty of disproving it.

88. § 531, as qualified by § 532 (document or other thing) and § 536 (information required by statute).

89. Cheney v. Dickinson, 7 Cir. 1909, 172 F. 109; Greenville Nat. Bank v. National Hardwood Co., 1928, 241 Mich. 524, 217 N.W. 786; Gillespie v. Hunt, 1923, 276 Pa. 119 A. 815, cert. denied 261 U.S. 622; New York Title & Mortgage Co. v. Hutton, 1934, 63 U.S.App.D.C. 266, 71 F.2d 989, cert. denied 293 U.S. 605; Wheelwright v. Vanderbilt, 1914, 69 Or. 326, 138 P. 857.

90. Butterfield v. Barber, 1897, 20 R.I. 99, 37 A. 532; Puffer v. Welch, 1911, 144 Wis. 506, 129 N.W. 525; Pamela Amusement Co. v. Scott Jewelry Co., D.Mass.1960, 190 F.Supp. 465; Nearpark Realty Corp. v. City Investing Co., Sup.Ct.1952, 112 N.Y. S.2d 816.

91. Abel v. Paterno, 1935, 245 App.Div. 285, 281 N.Y. S. 58; Cohen v. Citizens Nat. Trust & Sav. Bank, 1956, 143 Cal.App.2d 480, 300 P.2d 14; Bechtel v. Bohannon, 1930, 198 N.C. 730, 153 S.E. 316; Ellis v. Hale, 1962, 13 Utah 2d 279, 373 P.2d 382; Nash v. Minnesota Title Ins. & Trust Co., 1893, 159 Mass. 437, 34 N.E. 625.

92. Westcliff Co. v. Wall, 1954, 153 Tex. 271, 267 S. W.2d 544. Otherwise where defendant knows that such a person is interested, and may be expected to

be affected by the representation, with no special reason to expect them to act upon it.[93] The same has been true in cases where the transaction which resulted was of a type different from that originally intended, as where one to whom statements were made in his capacity as agent for another buys for himself.[94]

The limitation thus imposed must, however, be qualified to a considerable extent. The class of persons whom the speaker desires to influence may of course be a very large one, as where he publishes a statement in a newspaper intending to reach a whole class of purchasers or investors,[95] or furnishes information to a credit agency in the expectation that it will be passed on to those with whom he may deal,[96] or where a man-

ufacturer advertises his goods to possible consumers.[97] A statement may be intended to be directed to others in addition to the immediate recipient,[98] as where an auditor's report is prepared to be exhibited to the plaintiff,[99] or information is given to a promoter for the purpose of inducing action by the corporation to be formed.[1]

But apart from such cases, there is a very definite tendency to depart from the old position, and to extend liability to those whom there is no desire to influence, but whose reliance upon the representation there is some special reason to anticipate. This has been almost a matter of necessity where the representation is embodied in a document, such as a negotiable instrument,[2] a bill of lading,[3]

act in reliance on the representation. Southern States Fire & Cas. Co. v. Cromartie, 1913, 181 Ala. 295, 61 So. 907.

93. McCracken v. West, 1842, 17 Ohio 16 (letter intended to be shown to A used to induce B to act). Williamson v. Patterson, Tex.Civ.App.1937, 106 S. W.2d 753, error dismissed (statement to A before he became the agent of B); Lembeck v. Gerken, 1916, 88 N.J.L. 329, 96 A. 577.

94. Wells v. Cook, 1865, 16 Ohio St. 67; Walker v. Choate, 1929, 228 Ky. 101, 14 S.W.2d 406; McCane v. Wokoun, 1920, 189 Iowa 1010, 179 N.W. 332; Butterfield v. Barber, 1897, 20 R.I. 99, 37 A. 532. Cf. Wollenberger v. Hoover, 1931, 346 Ill. 511, 179 N.E. 42 (purchase of land instead of bonds).

95. Holloway v. Forsyth, 1917, 226 Mass. 358, 115 N. E. 483; Willcox v. Harriman Securities Corp., S.D. N.Y.1933, 10 F.Supp. 532; cf. Sims v. Tigrett, 1934, 229 Ala. 486, 158 So. 326; Diel v. Kellogg, 1910, 163 Mich. 162, 128 N.W. 420 (letter written to be shown to investors).

96. Tindle v. Birkett, 1902, 171 N.Y. 520, 64 N.E. 210; Hulsey v. M. C. Kiser Co., 1925, 21 Ala.App. 123, 105 So. 913; Reliance Shoe Co. v. Manly, 4 Cir. 1928, 25 F.2d 381; Forbes v. Auerbach, Fla. 1952, 56 So.2d 895; Manly v. Ohio Shoe Co., 4 Cir. 1928, 25 F.2d 384.

In Davis v. Louisville Trust Co., 6 Cir. 1910, 181 F. 10, and Jamestown Iron & Metal Co. v. Knofsky, 1927, 291 Pa. 60, 139 A. 611, plaintiffs, who were not even subscribers, were allowed to recover, where there was reason to expect that the information would reach them.

97. Baxter v. Ford Motor Co., 1932, 168 Wash. 456, 12 P.2d 409, 15 P.2d 1118, second appeal in 1934, 179 Wash. 123, 35 P.2d 1090.

98. Henry v. Dennis, 1901, 95 Me. 24, 49 A. 58 (business associate); Iowa Economic Heater Co. v. American Economic Heater Co., C.C.Ill.1887, 32 F. 735; Harold v. Pugh, 1959, 174 Cal.App.2d 603, 345 P.2d 112.

99. American Indemnity Co. v. Ernst & Ernst, Tex. Civ.App.1937, 106 S.W.2d 763 error refused. Accord: Wice v. Schilling, 1954, 124 Cal.App.2d 735, 269 P.2d 231 (exterminator certifying for vendor that premises were free from vermin held liable to purchaser); Reservoir Manor Corp. v. Lumbermen's Mut. Ins. Cas. Co., 1957, 334 Mass. 620, 137 N.E.2d 912 (report of boiler inspection).

1. Scholfield Gear & Pulley Co. v. Scholfield, 1898, 71 Conn. 1, 40 A. 1046. Accord, Crystal Pier Amusement Co. v. Cannon, 1933, 219 Cal. 184, 25 P.2d 839, 91 A.L.R. 1357; E. M. Fleischmann Lbr. Corp. v. Resources Corp. International, D.Del.1952, 105 F. Supp. 681.

Cf. Mullen v. Eastern Trust & Sav. Bank, 1911, 108 Me. 498, 81 A. 948 (trustee certifying overissue of bonds, to induce the public to buy); Taylor v. Thomas, 1907, 55 Misc. 411, 106 N.Y.S. 538, modified and affirmed 124 App.Div. 53, 108 N.Y.S. 454, affirmed 195 N.Y. 590, 89 N.E. 1113, affirmed 224 U.S. 73 (false report by bank officer).

2. Peoples Nat. Bank v. Dixwell, 1914, 217 Mass. 436, 105 N.E. 435; National Shawmut Bank of Boston v. Johnson, 1945, 317 Mass. 485, 58 N.E.2d 849.

3. National Bank of Savannah v. Kershaw Oil Mill, 4 Cir.1912, 202 F. 90.

a deed,[4] or a stock certificate,[5] or even an article of commerce [6] of a kind customarily relied upon by third persons; and likewise, of course, where a statute enacted for the protection of a particular class of persons [7] requires the information to be published or filed.[8] Beyond this, the same result sometimes has been reached by finding that that was "intended" which was merely specially foreseeable; [9] and in a few cases by holding outright that it is enough that the defendant should have contemplated the plaintiff's reliance.[10] The limitation to a "desire" to influence the plaintiff seems clearly too narrow, and there is much merit in the contention [11] that, while the defendant is not required to investigate or otherwise guard against the possibility that his statements may come into the hands of strangers and affect their conduct, his responsibility should at least extend to those who might reasonably be expected to assume from appearances that the representation was intended to reach them.

Negligence

A representation made with an honest belief in its truth may still be negligent, because of lack of reasonable care in ascertaining the facts,[12] or in the manner of expression,[13] or absence of the skill and competence required by a particular business or profession.[14] As has been repeated above,[15] misrepresentation frequently occurs in ordinary negligence actions for personal injuries or property damage, in the form of misleading words or acts, or non-disclosure of known facts, and the courts have not found it necessary to distinguish it in any way from any other negligence. It is only where intangible economic interests are invaded that they have become alarmed at possible liability of unknown or virtually unlimited extent,[16] and

4. Baker v. Hallam, 1897, 103 Iowa 43, 72 N.W. 419. Cf. Leonard v. Springer, 1902, 197 Ill. 532, 64 N.E. 299 (fictitious deed recorded).

5. Merchants' Nat. Bank v. Robison, 1892, 8 Utah 256, 30 P. 985; Bruff v. Mali, 1867, 36 N.Y. 200, 24 How.Prac. 338; Bank of Montreal v. Thayer, C.C. Iowa 1881, 7 F. 622, 2 McCrary 1 (receiver's certificate); Stickel v. Atwood, 1903, 25 R.I. 456, 56 A. 687 (bond).

6. Graham v. John R. Watts & Son, 1931, 238 Ky. 96, 36 S.W.2d 859 (mislabeled sack of seed).

7. Otherwise where the statute is construed to be for the benefit of the state only. Ashuelot Sav. Bank v. Albee, 1884, 63 N.H. 152; Hunnewell v. Duxbury, 1891, 154 Mass. 286, 28 N.E. 267; Utley v. Hill, 1900, 155 Mo. 232, 55 S.W. 1091; Hindman v. First Nat. Bank, 6 Cir. 1902, 112 F. 931, cert. denied 186 U.S. 483.

8. Mason v. Moore, 1906, 73 Ohio St. 275, 76 N.E. 932; Gerner v. Mosher, 1899, 58 Neb. 135, 78 N.W. 384; Warfield v. Clark, 1902, 118 Iowa 69, 91 N.W. 833; Ver Wys v. Vander Mey, 1919, 206 Mich. 499, 173 N.W. 504. See Restatement of Torts, § 536.

Compare the cases where a false statement was made to rent control authorities for the purpose of evicting plaintiff as a tenant. Lyster v. Berberich, 1949, 3 N.J.Super. 78, 65 A.2d 632; Alabiso v. Schuster, 1948, 273 App.Div. 655, 80 N.Y.S.2d 314. See Note, 1949, 33 Minn.L.Rev. 194.

9. Cf. New York Title & Mortgage Co. v. Hutton, 1934, 63 App.D.C. 266, 71 F.2d 989; Southern States Fire & Casualty Ins. Co. v. Cromartie, 1913, 181 Ala. 295, 61 So. 907.

10. Davis v. Louisville Trust Co., 6 Cir. 1910, 181 F. 10; Ultramares Corp. v. Touche, Niven & Co., 1931, 255 N.Y. 170, 174 N.E. 441; State Street Trust Co. v. Ernst, 1938, 278 N.Y. 104, 15 N.E.2d 416; Fidelity & Deposit Co. of Md. v. Atherton, 1944, 47 N.M. 443, 144 P.2d 157.

11. Keeton, The Ambit of a Fraudulent Representor's Responsibility, 1938, 17 Tex.L.Rev. 1, 11; Seavey, Mr. Justice Cardozo and the Law of Torts, 1939, 52 Harv.L.Rev. 372, 404, 48 Yale L.J. 390, 39 Col.L. Rev. 20.

12. International Products Co. v. Erie R. Co., 1927, 244 N.Y. 331, 155 N.E. 662, cert. denied 275 U.S. 527; Houston v. Thornton, 1898, 122 N.C. 365, 29 S. E. 827; Maxwell Ice Co. v. Brackett, Shaw & Lunt Co., 1921, 80 N.H. 236, 116 A. 34.

13. See Nash v. Minnesota Title Ins. & Trust Co., 1895, 163 Mass. 574, 40 N.E. 1039; Slater Trust Co. v. Gardiner, 2 Cir. 1910, 183 F. 268; Angus v. Clifford, 1891, 2 Ch.Div. 449, 472; Restatement of Torts, § 528.

14. Dickel v. Nashville Abstract Co., 1890, 89 Tenn. 431, 14 S.W. 896; Brown v. Sims, 1899, 22 Ind.App. 317, 53 N.E. 779. See Rouse, Legal Liability of the Public Accountant, 1934, 23 Ky.L.J. 3.

15. Supra, p. 683.

16. "If liability for negligence exists, a thoughtless slip or blunder, the failure to detect a theft or for-

have developed a more restricted rule. This has taken the form of limitation of the group of persons to whom the defendant may be liable, short of the foreseeability of possible harm.[17]

After the decision in Derry v. Peek [18] excluded negligent misrepresentation from the action of deceit, the English courts concluded, and continued to hold until 1963, that no other action was available, and that the wrong was without a remedy,[19] except where tangible harm resulted, in which case the misrepresentation was assimilated to other negligent conduct.[20] In that year the House of Lords abruptly overthrew the existing law, and extended the liability for negligence to pecuniary loss in any case where some "special relation" between the parties could be

found.[21] The decision has left a good many unsolved problems for the English courts, as to the third persons to whom this liability may extend.[22]

A minority of the American courts have refused to accept Derry v. Peek, and have held that deceit will lie for negligent statements—either declaring outright that the fault is equally great and the reliance of the plaintiff equally justified, or adopting the rather obvious fiction that a duty to learn the facts or not to speak without knowing them is the full equivalent of knowledge.[23] Several other courts, recognizing the essential basis of the liability, have carried over the negligence action itself from tangible injuries to economic loss, and have allowed recovery in such an action.[24] This position has prevailed, and the negligence action is now generally allowed for negligent misrepresentation, even though it causes only pecuniary harm. Two conclusions seem obvious: first, that the negligence action is quite as appro-

gery beneath the cover of deceptive entries, may expose accountants to a liability in an indeterminate amount for an indeterminate time to an indeterminate class. The hazards of a business conducted on these terms are so extreme as to enkindle doubt whether a flaw may not exist in the implication of a duty that exposes to these consequences." Cardozo, C. J., in Ultramares Corp. v. Touche, Niven & Co., 1931, 255 N.Y. 170, 174 N.E. 441. See also Smith, Liability for Negligent Language, 1909, 14 Harv.L.Rev. 184, 195; Seavey, Mr. Justice Cardozo and the Law of Torts, 1939, 52 Harv.L.Rev. 372, 400, 48 Yale L.J. 390, 39 Col.L.Rev. 20; Note, 1934, 8 Temple L.Q. 404.

17. See infra, p. 708.

18. Supra, p. 700.

19. Le Lievre v. Gould, [1893] 1 Q.B. 491, 62 L.J.Q.B. 353; Old Gate Estates v. Toplis, [1939] 3 All Eng. Rep. 209; Candler v. Crane, Christmas & Co., [1951] 1 All Eng.Rep. 406 [1951] 2 K.B. 164. See Morison, Liability in Negligence for False Statements, 1951, 67 L.Q.Rev. 212; Seavey, Candler v. Crane, Christmas & Co.; Negligent Misrepresentation by Accountants, 1951, 67 L.Q.Rev. 466; Paton, Liability in Tort for Negligent Statements, 1947, 25 Can.Bar.Rev. 123; Fullagar, Liability for Representations at Common Law, 1951, 25 Aust.L.J. 278; Goodhart, Liability for Negligent Misstatements, 1962, 78 L.Q.Rev. 107.

20. The Apollo, [1891] A.C. 499; Clayton v. Woodman & Son, [1962] 2 Q.B. 533; Watson v. Buckley, [1940] 1 All Eng. Rep. 174; Sharp v. Avery, [1938] 4 All Eng.Rep. 85.

21. Hedley Byrne & Co. v. Heller & Partners, [1964] A.C. 465.

22. See Goodhart, Liability for Innocent but Negligent Misrepresentations, 1964, 74 Yale L.J. 286; Stevens, Hedley Byrne v. Heller, 1964, 27 Mod.L. Rev. 121; Gordon, Hedley Byrne v. Heller in the House of Lords, 1965, 2 U.B.C.L.Rev. 113; Payne, Hedley Byrne & Co. v. Heller & Partners, 1964, 6 U.West.Aust.L.Rev. 467; Glasbeek, Limited Liability for Negligent Misstatement, 1968, Studies in Canadian Tort Law 115; Notes, 1965, 50 Corn.L.Q. 331; 1964, 3 West.Ont.L.Rev. 104.

23. Anderson v. Tway, 6 Cir. 1944, 143 F.2d 95, cert. denied, 324 U.S. 861; Vincent v. Corbitt, 1908, 94 Miss. 46, 47 So. 641; Scholfield Gear & Pulley Co. v. Scholfield, 1898, 71 Conn. 1, 40 A. 1046; Mullen v. Eastern Trust & Banking Co., 1911, 108 Me. 449, 81 A. 948; Watson v. Jones, 1899, 41 Fla. 241, 25 So. 678. Many of the cases which talk of a "duty to know" and appear to impose strict liability (infra, p. 711) may perhaps have had negligence in mind.

24. Weston v. Brown, 1925, 82 N.H. 157, 131 A. 141; International Products Co. v. Erie R. Co., 1927, 244 N.Y. 331, 155 N.E. 662, cert. denied 275 U.S. 527; Brown v. Underwriters at Lloyd's, 1958, 53 Wash.2d. 142, 332 P.2d 228; Gediman v. Anheuser Busch, Inc., 2 Cir. 1962, 299 F.2d 537; Sult v. Scandrett, 1947, 119 Mont. 570, 178 P.2d 405.

priate to the one type of damage as to the other,[25] and second, that apart from outmoded theories of pleading no particular disadvantage can result if the remedy for negligent misrepresentation is incorporated in the action of deceit.

Except for procedural technicalities, therefore, it is probably of little importance whether the form of the action is negligence or deceit, so long as a remedy is provided.[26] It is, however, clearly important, so far as the nature of the defendant's conduct is concerned, that the theory of the liability is one of negligence rather than of intent to mislead. Furthermore, negligence requires a duty of care. A gratuitous statement, made by one who derives no benefit from giving the information, will result in liability when it is intentionally false; [27] but when it is merely negligent, there is an analogy to the gift or loan of chattels,[28] where the recipient is not justified in relying upon any care on the part of the donor.[29] An attorney or a physician

who gives curbstone advice when it is requested by one who is not a client or a patient, is required only to give an honest answer.[30] But where the representation, although itself gratuitous, is made in the course of the defendant's business or professional relations, the duty is usually found.[31]

Again, if the representation is intended to deceive, contributory negligence of the plaintiff in relying on it will be no defense,[32] but there is no apparent reason for distinguishing negligent misrepresentation from any other negligence in this respect, and the few decisions [33] are agreed that the defense is good.

The problem of the persons to whom the defendant may be liable, already difficult in the case of intentional misrepresentation,[34] becomes still more acute where it is merely negligent.[35] Any human words, written or

---

25. Green, The Duty to Give Accurate Information, 1965, 12 UCLA L.Rev. 464; Goodhart, Liability for Innocent but Negligent Misrepresentation, 1964, 74 Yale L.J. 286; Wiener, Negligent Misrepresentation: Fraud or Negligence, 1964, 13 Cleve.Marsh L.Rev. 250; Smith, Liability for Negligent Language, 1909, 14 Harv.L.Rev. 184; Bohlen, Misrepresentation as Deceit Negligence or Warranty, 1929, 42 Harv.L.Rev. 733; Bohlen, Should Negligent Misrepresentations be Treated as Negligence or Fraud, 1932, 18 Va.L.Rev. 703.

26. See Green, Deceit, 1930, 16 Va.L.Rev. 749, arguing for deceit as the more flexible action, and Bohlen, Should Negligent Misrepresentations be Treated as Negligence or Fraud, 1932, 18 Va.L.Rev. 703, arguing for negligence in reply. Also, in turn, Green, Innocent Misrepresentations, 1933, 19 Va.L. Rev. 742.

27. Endsley v. Johns, 1887, 120 Ill. 469, 12 N.E. 247; Foster v. Charles, 1830, 7 Bing. 105, 131 Eng.Rep. 40; Beatrice Creamery Co. v. Goldman, 1935, 175 Okl. 300, 52 P.2d 1033.

28. Supra, p. 677.

29. Renn v. Provident Trust Co. of Philadelphia, 1938, 328 Pa. 481, 196 A. 2; Holt v. Kolker, 1948, 189 Md. 636, 57 A.2d 287; Webb v. Cerasoli, 1949, 275 App.Div. 45, 87 N.Y.S.2d 884, affirmed 300 N.Y. 603, 90 N.E.2d 64; Vartan Garapedian, Inc. v. An-

derson, 1943, 92 N.H. 390, 31 A.2d 371; Restatement of Torts, § 552, Comment c.

See, however, the cases, supra, p. ——, of information volunteered, where the defendant was held to have assumed a duty of care by his affirmative conduct.

30. Fish v. Kelly, 1864, 17 C.B.,N.S. 194, 144 Eng. Rep. 78; Buttersworth v. Swint, 1936, 53 Ga.App. 602, 186 S.E. 770.

31. Washington & Berkeley Bridge Co. v. Pennsylvania Steel Co., 4 Cir. 1915, 226 F. 169; Virginia Dare Stores v. Schuman, 1938, 175 Md. 287, 1 A.2d 897; Manock v. Amos D. Bridge's Sons, Inc., 1934, 86 N.H. 411, 169 A. 881; Robb v. Gylock Corp., 1956, 384 Pa. 209, 120 A.2d 174; Valz v. Goodykoontz, 1911, 112 Va. 853, 72 S.E. 730.

32. See infra, p. 711.

33. Gould v. Flato, 1939, 170 Misc. 378, 10 N.Y.S.2d 361; Vartan Garapedian, Inc. v. Anderson, 1943, 92 N.H. 390, 31 A.2d 371; see Maxwell Ice Co. v. Brackett, Shaw & Lunt Co., 1921, 80 N.H. 236, 116 A. 34; Bohlen, Misrepresentation as Deceit, Negligence or Warranty, 1929, 42 Harv.L.Rev. 733, 739; Bohlen, Should Negligent Misrepresentations be Treated as Negligent Misrepresentations be Treated as Negligence or Fraud, 1932, 18 Va.L.Rev. 703, 709.

34. See supra, p. 702.

35. See Ultramares Corp. v Touche, Niven & Co., 1931, 255 N.Y. 170, 174 N.E. 441; Seavey, Mr. Justice Cardozo and the Law of Torts, 1939, 52 Harv. L.Rev. 372, 400, 48 Yale L.J. 390, 39 Col.L.Rev. 20; Notes, 1931, 26 Ill.L.Rev. 49; 1934, 8 Temple L.Q. 404.

oral, are capable of being repeated and passed on indefinitely, so that, in a very general sense, it is always foreseeable that they may come into the hands of any number of third persons. An extreme illustration is the Tennessee case [36] where the plaintiff, in 1958, bought land in reliance upon a survey and description negligently made by the defendant in 1934. The courts have become genuinely disturbed at the prospect of "a liability in an indeterminate amount for an indeterminate time to an indeterminate class." [37] and the prospect of a huge and crushing burden of liability out of all proportion to the magnitude of the defendant's fault. But the point of limitation has been a subject of considerable discussion. [38]

When the representation is made directly to the plaintiff, in the course of his dealings with the defendant, [39] or is exhibited to him by the defendant with knowledge that he intends to rely upon it, [40] or even where he is an unidentified member of a group or class all of whom the defendant is seeking to influence, [41] there has been no difficulty in finding a duty of reasonable care; and the same duty has been found where it is made to a third person with knowledge that he intends to communicate it to the specific individual plaintiff for the purpose of inducing him to act. This has been held to be true as to the certifications of public weighers, [42] accountants, [43] abstractors of title, [44] an appraiser, [45] an auditor, [46] a boiler inspector, [47] and an architect. [48]

This is the point at which most of the courts have drawn the line, holding that

bonds); Mullen v. Eastern Trust & Banking Co., 1911, 108 Me. 498, 81 A. 948 (same).

42. Glanzer v. Shepard, 1922, 233 N.Y. 236, 135 N.E. 275. Cf. First Nat. Bank, Henrietta v. Small Business Adm'n, 5 Cir. 1970, 429 F.2d 280; Lesser v. Wm. Holliday Cord Ass'n Inc., 8 Cir. 1965, 349 F.2d 490. Tartera v. Palumbo, 1970, — Tenn. —, 453 S.W.2d 780.

43. Ryan v. Kanne, 1969, — Iowa —, 170 N.W.2d 395; Rusch Factors, Inc. v. Levin, D.R.I.1968, 284 F.Supp. 85; Duro Sportswear v. Cogen, Sup.Ct. 1954, 131 N.Y.S.2d 20, motion denied 132 N.Y.S.2d 51, affirmed memo. 285 App.Div. 867, 137 N.Y.S.2d 829.

In Fischer v. Kletz, S.D.N.Y.1967, 266 F.Supp. 180, this was held to extend to the correction of previous information now known to be false.

44. Anderson v. Spriestersbach, 1912, 69 Wash. 393, 125 P. 166; Dickel v. Nashville Abstract Co., 1890, 89 Tenn. 431, 14 S.W. 896; Western Loan & Sav. Co. v. Silver Bow Abstract Co., 1904, 31 Mont. 448, 78 P. 774; Beckovsky v. Burton Abstract & Title Co., 1919, 208 Mich. 224, 175 N.W. 235, affirmed 208 Mich. 224, 178 N.W. 238; see Phoenix Title & Trust Co. v. Continental Oil Co., 1934, 43 Ariz. 219, 29 P. 2d 1065.

45. United States v. Neustadt, 4 Cir. 1960, 281 F.2d 596, reversed on other grounds, 1961, 366 U.S. 696.

46. American Ind. Co. v. Ernst & Ernst, Tex.Civ.App. 1937, 106 S.W.2d 763, error refused.

47. Du Rite Laundry v. Washington Elec. Co., 1942, 263 App.Div. 396, 33 N.Y.S.2d 925.

48. United States v. Rogers & Rogers, S.D.Cal.1958, 161 F.Supp. 132. Cf. Robitscher v. United Clay Products Co., Mun.App.D.C.1958, 143 A.2d 99 (layout for air conditioning); Craig v. Everett M. Brooks Co., 1967, 351 Mass. 497, 222 N.E.2d 752 (engineer laying out stakes to guide contractor in work). Cf. Massei v. Lettunich, 1967, 248 Cal.App. 2d 68, 56 Cal.Rptr. 232 (failure to disclose land improperly filled).

36. Howell v. Betts, 1962, 211 Tenn. 134, 362 S.W.2d 924.

37. Ultramares Corp. v Touche, Niven & Co., 1931, 255 N.Y. 170, 179, 174 N.E. 441, 444.

38. See Keeton, The Ambit of a Fraudulent Representor's Responsibility, 1938, 17 Tex.L.Rev. 1; Prosser, Misrepresentation and Third Persons, 1966, 19 Vand.L.Rev. 231; Notes, 1951, 36 Iowa L.Rev. 319; 1962, 48 Va.L.Rev. 1476.

39. International Products Co. v. Erie R. Co., 1927, 244 N.Y. 331, 155 N.E. 662, cert. denied 275 U.S. 527; Morin v. Divide County Abstract Co., 1921, 48 N.D. 214, 183 N.W. 1006; Wacek v. Frink, 1892, 51 Minn. 282, 53 N.W. 633; De Zemplen v. Home Federal Sav. & Loan Ass'n, 1963, 221 Cal.App.2d 197, 34 Cal.Rptr. 334.

40. Decatur, Land, Loan & Abstract Co. v. Rutland, Tex.Civ.App.1916, 185 S.W. 1064.

41. Granberg v. Turnham, 1958, 166 Cal.App.2d 390, 333 P.2d 423 (information to a real estate board, to be included in its multiple listing sent out to many prospective buyers); Durham v. Wichita Mill & Elev. Co., Tex.Civ.App.1918, 202 S.W. 138, error refused (negligent report to mercantile credit agency); Doyle v. Chatham & Phoenix Nat. Bank, 1930, 253 N.Y. 369, 171 N.E. 574 (trustee certifying

mere reasonable anticipation that the statement will be communicated to others whose identity is unknown to the defendant, or even knowledge that the recipient intends to make some commercial use of it in dealing with unspecified third parties, is not sufficient to create a duty of care toward them. The spectre of unlimited liability, with claims devastating in number and amount crushing the defendant because of a momentary lapse from proper care, has haunted the courts. Thus attorneys,[49] abstractors of title,[50] inspectors of goods,[51] accountants,[52] surveyors,[53] the operator of a ticker service,[54] and a bank dealing with a non-depositor's check [55] all have been held to be under no obligation to third parties.

The difficult questions are those involving the question of whether the defendant has some special reason to anticipate the reliance of the plaintiff. The outstanding case is Ultramares Corporation v. Touche, Niven & Co.,[56] in which a firm of accountants negligently certified a corporation's balance sheet, with the expectation that it would be used as a basis for some kind of unspecified financial dealings, but without notice of the nature of such dealings, or the persons who might be influenced. They were held liable in deceit, upon the ground that their neglect was so great as to justify a finding of conscious ignorance; but the liability in negligence was rejected. The case has been followed by two other decisions.[57]

But what if the defendant is informed that his representation is to be passed on to some more limited group, as a basis for action on the part of some one or more of them? There is a California case [58] in which an engineering company was hired to prepare a soil report, knowing that it was intended to be made available to all bidders for work on a sewer system, and to be used by the successful bidder to do the work. It prepared the report negligently, and the bidder lost money; accordingly, it was held liable for negligent misrepresentation. On the other hand, on quite similar facts, a federal case arising in

---

49. Rosenberg v. Cyrowski, 1924, 227 Mich. 508, 198 N.W. 905; Savings Bank v. Ward, 1879, 100 U.S. 195, 25 L.Ed. 621 (abstract). See Averill, Attorney's Liability to Third Person for Negligent Malpractice, 2 Land & Water Rev. 379.

50. Talpey v. Wright, 1895, 61 Ark. 275, 32 S.W. 1072 (not liable to assignee); Thomas v. Guarantee Title & Trust Co., 1910, 81 Ohio St. 432, 91 N.E. 183; Ohmart v. Citizens Sav. & Trust Co., 1924, 82 Ind. App. 219, 145 N.E. 577; Peterson v. Gales, 1926, 191 Wis. 137, 210 N.W. 407; Phoenix Title & Trust Co. v. Continental Oil Co., 1934, 43 Ariz. 219, 29 P.2d 1065.

51. National Iron & Steel Co. v. Hunt, 1924, 312 Ill. 245, 143 N.E. 833; see Anglo-American & Overseas Corp. v. United States, S.D.N.Y.1956, 144 F.Supp. 635, affirmed, 1957, 242 F.2d 236.

52. Ultramares Corp. v. Touche, Niven & Co., 1931, 255 N.Y. 170, 174 N.E. 441; Landell v. Lybrand, 1919, 264 Pa. 406, 107 A. 783; O'Connor v. Ludlam, 2 Cir. 1937, 92 F.2d 50, cert. denied 302 U.S. 758; Blank v. Kaitz, 1966, 350 Mass. 779, 216 N.E.2d 110.

53. Howell v. Betts, 1962, 211 Tenn. 134, 362 S.W.2d 924. Cf. Le Lievre v. Gould, [1891] 1 Q.B. 491 (reporting on progress of building).

54. Jaillet v. Cashman, 1923, 235 N.Y. 511, 139 N.E. 714. Cf. MacKown v. Illinois Pub. & Printing Co., 1937, 289 Ill. 59, 6 N.E.2d 526 (newspaper).

55. Cohen v. Tradesmen's Nat. Bank, 1918, 262 Pa. 76, 105 A. 43. Cf. Courteen Seed Co. v. Hong Kong & Shanghai Banking Corp., 1927, 245 N.Y. 377, 157 N.E. 272.

56. 1931, 255 N.Y. 170, 174 N.E. 441.

57. O'Connor v. Ludlam, 2 Cir. 1937, 92 F.2d 50, cert denied 302 U.S. 758; Landell v. Lybrand, 1919, 264 Pa. 406, 107 A. 783. See Rouse, Legal Liability of the Public Accountant, 1934, 23 Ky.L.J. 3; Meek, Liability of the Accountant to Parties Other than His Employer for Negligent Misrepresentation; Katsoris, Accountant's Third Party Liability—How Far Do We Go? 1967, 36 Ford.L.Rev. 191; Anote, Accountant's Liability for False and Misleading Financial Statements, 1967, 67 Col.L.Rev. 1437; Levitin, Accountants' Scope of Liability for Defective Financial Reports, 1964, 15 Hast.L.J. 436; Notes, 1951, 36 Iowa L.Rev. 319; 1962, 48 Va.L.Rev. 1476; 1967, 9 B.C.Ind. & Comm.L.Rev. 90; 1967, 67 Col.L. Rev. 1437; 1968, 23 U.Miami L.Rev. 256; 1968, 18 De Paul L.Rev. 56; 1969, 53 Minn.L.Rev. 1375.

58. M. Miller Co. v. Central Contra Costa Sanitary Dist., 1961, 198 Cal.App.2d 305, 18 Cal.Rptr. 13.

Tennessee denied the recovery,[59] although it laid considerable stress upon a disclaimer of accuracy and responsibility contained in the report itself. Finally, there is a late Illinois case [60] in which a surveyor was held liable, in part on the basis of an "express guarantee for accuracy," for the pecuniary loss sustained by a purchaser of a lot in a real estate development, when the boundary lines proved to be erroneous.

Other cases will no doubt have to resolve the problem; but where the group affected is a sufficiently small one, and particularly, as in the case of the successful bidder, only one person can be expected to suffer loss, the guess may be hazarded that the recovery will be allowed. Certificates of expert examination are intended to be exhibited, not hidden under a bushel; and a rule which denies recovery because the defendant who has provided one for such a purpose does not know the plaintiff's name, or the particulars of the transaction, has a very artificial aspect.

Statutes in several states [61] have imposed a liability to third persons upon title abstractors and similar businesses; and in the case of public officers, such as notaries,[62] re-cording clerks,[63] and food inspectors,[64] those who rely upon certificates have been permitted to recover upon the ground that an official duty to them has been assumed. There are also statutes requiring information to be filed for public record, or to be published, which have been held to create a similar duty to members of the public who may foreseeably be expected to rely on it.[65] Such cases, no doubt, are to be distinguished on the basis of the public responsibility of the defendants.

Where tort liability is not in question, there has been little reluctance to grant relief for negligent misrepresentations. Since restitution, either in equity or at law, is permitted for representations which are entirely innocent,[66] it is allowed almost without discussion of the question where there is an absence of reasonable care; and the same is true, in general, of the defense of fraud where it takes the form of rescission. One branch of estoppel, involving active misrepresentation, likewise extends to strict responsibility, and hence will include negligence; [67] while the other, arising in cases of "standing by" while another acts to his prejudice, apparently must be based upon some elements of unreasonable conduct, which sel-

59. Texas Tunneling Co. v. City of Chattanooga. Recovery was first allowed in E.D.Tenn.1962, 204 F.Supp. 821, but the Court of Appeals reversed and denied it, in 6 Cir. 1964, 329 F.2d 402. The last opinion is weakened by a misconstruction of the Ultramares case as limiting liability to a specifically foreseeable plaintiff, and by reliance upon a Tennessee case in which there was no special reason to expect the plaintiff's reliance.

60. Rozny v. Marnul, 1969, 43 Ill.2d 54, 250 N.E.2d 656. See also the dicta in Rusch Factors, Inc. v. Levin, D.R.I.1968, 284 F.Supp. 85. See Note, 1970, 1 Loy.Chi. 176.

61. Arnold & Co. v. Barner, 1914, 91 Kan. 768, 139 P. 404; Gate City Abstract Co. v. Post, 1898, 55 Neb. 742, 76 N.W. 471; Sackett v. Rose, 1916, 55 Okl. 398, 154 P. 1177; Goldberg v. Sisseton Loan & Title Co., 1909, 24 S.D. 49, 123 N.W. 266.

62. Figuers v. Fly, 1917, 137 Tenn. 358, 193 S.W. 117; Clapp v. Miller, 1916, 56 Okl. 29, 156 P. 210; State ex rel. Gardner v. Webber, 1914, 177 Mo.App. 60, 164 S.W. 184; Anderson v. Aronsohn, 1919, 181 Cal. 294, 184 P. 12; Erie County United Bank v. Berk, 1943, 73 Ohio App. 314, 56 N.E.2d 285.

63. Mulroy v. Wright, 1931, 185 Minn. 84, 240 N.W. 116; Commonwealth, for Use of Green v. Johnson, 1906, 123 Ky. 437, 96 S.W. 801; Cole v. Vincent, 1930, 229 App.Div. 520, 242 N.Y.S. 644.

64. Pearson v. Purkett, 1834, 15 Pick., 32 Mass. 264; Nickerson v. Thompson, 1851, 33 Me. 433. In some instances recovery has been denied on the ground that the certification was no part of the officer's public duties. Kahl v. Love, 1874, 37 N.J.L. 5; Houseman v. Girard Mut. Bldg. & Loan Ass'n, 1876, 81 Pa. 256.

65. Ver Wys v. Vander Mey, 1919, 206 Mich. 499, 173 N.W. 504; Vandewater & Lapp v. Sacks Builders, Inc., 1959, 20 Misc.2d 677, 186 N.Y.S.2d 103; Mason v. Moore, 1906, 73 Ohio St. 275, 76 N.E. 932; Warfield v. Clark, 1902, 118 Iowa 69, 91 N.W. 833; Coughlin v. State Bank, 1926, 117 Ore. 83, 243 P. 78.

66. See infra, p. 711.

67. See supra, p. 691; Ewart, Principles of Estoppel, 1900, 101–102; Burrowes v. Lock, 1805, 10 Ves. 470.

dom is called negligence but amounts to the same thing.[68]

Strict Responsibility

Strict responsibility for innocent misrepresentation is long familiar in equitable remedies, such as rescission of a transaction.[69] At law it first appeared at a very early date in connection with the sale of goods; and it was not until a very much later period that it was called "warranty." [70] When, shortly before the beginning of the nineteenth century, deceit took separate form as a tort action requiring no contract between the parties,[71] warranty remained behind as something identified with or accompanying a contract, and capable of being remedied by a contract action. When Derry v. Peek made it clear in English law that deceit must be based upon an intent to mislead, it had been established for nearly two centuries [72] that a warranty might be an entirely innocent misrepresentation. At a later date it was held that there need not be even an intention to be bound, and that any affirmation of fact relating to goods sold is a warranty if its natural tendency is to induce a purchase, and if the purchase is made in reliance upon

it.[73] This, together with the fact that implied warranties were imposed by law because of the conduct of the parties where nothing was said,[74] indicates that the action for breach of warranty has a definite tort character, analogous to other strict tort liabilities —which is borne out by the survival, in many jurisdictions, of the original tort form of the action.[75]

For reasons that remain rather obscure, the notion of warranty, that an assertion of fact made to induce a bargain becomes part of the contract, was confined quite strictly to the sale, or other furnishing [76] of tangible chattels. It has not been extended, for example, to the sale of corporate securities.[77] The explanation must be that there was no demand for its extension into other fields until it had become crystallized as a doctrine peculiar to the sale of goods. One notable exception is that of an agent's representation, express or implied, that he has authority to act for his principal—which whether it be founded upon a theory of contract [78] or tort,[79] is a form of strict liability, and is called "warranty."

68. Ewart, Principles of Estoppel, 1900, 103–108. Cf. Snyder v. Corn Exch. Nat. Bank, 1908, 221 Pa. 599, 70 A. 876; Timbel v. Garfield Nat. Bank, 1907, 121 App.Div. 870, 106 N.Y.S. 497; Morgan v. United States Mortgage & Trust Co., 1913, 208 N.Y. 218, 101 N.E. 871; Thomson v. Shelton, 1896, 49 Neb. 644, 68 N.W. 1055.

69. See supra, p. 688; De Joseph v. Zambelli, 1958, 392 Pa. 24, 139 A.2d 644; Fields v. Haupert, 1958, 213 Or. 179, 323 P.2d 332; Equitable Life Assur. Society v. New Horizons, Inc., 1958, 28 N.J. 307, 146 A.2d 466; Halpert v. Rosenthal, 1970, — R.I. —, 267 A.2d 730. Compare, as to equitable estoppel, Kantor v. Cohn, 1917, 98 Misc. 355, 164 N.Y.S. 383, affirmed, 1918, 181 App.Div. 400, 168 N.Y.S. 846; Blygh v. Samson, 1890, 137 Pa. 368, 20 A. 996.

70. Hamilton, The Ancient Maxim Caveat Emptor, 1931, 40 Yale L.J. 1133.

71. See supra, p. 685.

72. Cross v. Gardner, 1689, 3 Mod.Rep. 261, 87 Eng. Rep. 172; Medina v. Stoughton, 1700, 1 Ld.Raym. 593, 91 Eng.Rep. 1297.

73. Uniform Sales Act, § 12; McClintock v. Emick, 1888, 87 Ky. 160, 7 S.W. 903; Fairbank Canning Co. v. Metzger, 1890, 118 N.Y. 260, 23 N.E. 372; Herron v. Dibrell, 1891, 87 Va. 289, 12 S.E. 674.

74. Uniform Sales Act, §§ 13–16; Bekkevold v. Potts, 1927, 173 Minn. 87, 216 N.W. 790; Hoe v. Sanborn, 1860, 21 N.Y. 552; Lee v. Cohrt, 1930, 57 S.D. 387, 232 N.W. 900.

75. See supra, p. 635.

76. See supra, p. 676.

77. Heilbut, Symons & Co. v. Buckleton, [1913] A.C. 30; Henderson v. Plymouth Oil Co., D.C.Pa.1926, 13 F.2d 932; Goodwyn v. Folds, 1923, 30 Ga.App. 204, 117 S.E. 335; Burwash v. Ballou, 1907, 230 Ill. 34, 82 N.E. 355. Contra: Iler v. Jennings, 1910, 87 S.C. 87, 68 S.E. 1041.

78. Collen v. Wright, 1857, 8 El. & Bl. 647, 120 Eng. Rep. 241; Lasater v. Crutchfield, 1909, 92 Ark. 535, 123 S.W. 394; Mendelsohn v. Holton, 1925, 253 Mass. 362, 149 N.E. 38.

79. See Young v. Toynbee, [1910] 1 K.B. 215; Chieppo v. Chieppo, 1914, 88 Conn. 233, 90 A. 940; Outagamie County Bank of Appleton v. Tesch, 1920, 171 Wis. 249, 177 N.W. 6.

Any demand for the application of the principle to other transactions found the concept of warranty rigidly defined, the door of deceit barred by the requirement of intent to mislead, and equity partitioned off as applicable only to a special group of remedies, which did not include any tort action for damages. Nevertheless, a large group of the American courts have succeeded in prying open the door, and extending strict liability to express representations made in the course of other commercial dealings, such as the sale of land, securities, or patent rights.[80] Until quite recent years the process has been rather a haphazard one, and ill defined. In the beginning there was a resort to fictions, which was facilitated by the ease with which, on the basis of circumstantial evidence, the defendant could be found to have had the wrong state of mind.[81] Some courts then found that the defendant was under a "duty to know" the truth of his statements,[82] which was more than a duty to use care to find out; or they extended the rule as to conscious ignorance [83] by treating a false representation made as of the defendant's own knowledge as necessarily meaning that he knew that he did not know.[84] This process was aided, of course, by the nebulous and uncertain distinctions between various states of mind.

Still other courts resorted to presumptions of knowledge,[85] apparently incapable of being rebutted, which must obviously result in strict liability, or to an "imputed knowledge" [86] amounting to the same thing.

As might be expected, the outcome was that a good many courts finally discarded these rather transparent devices, and declared outright that at law, as in equity, a cause of action could be founded upon quite innocent misrepresentation, with neither scienter nor negligence, if it was made to induce a business transaction, and relied upon by the plaintiff to his damage. The first step in this direction was taken in 1888 in Michigan, in a case [87] which uterly confused the tort action for damages with the equity relief in rescission, and appeared never to have heard of any distinction between the two. But in 1929 it was held in Virginia [88] that there was just as much reason to afford the relief in the one as in the other, since nothing new was being added in the way of liability, and it was only an additional remedy which was made available. The definite advantage to the plaintiff of being allowed to keep what he has received and recover damages, in cases where, for example he has made improvements, or has lost the rescission remedy by delay or election, or for other reasons finds it desirable to keep what he has received rather than to return it, has carried the day.

Although there are isolated cases in other jurisdictions which look in this direction, the strict liability appears thus far clearly to have been accepted by some eighteen courts,

80. Harper and McNeely, A Synthesis of the Law of Misrepresentation, 1938, 22 Minn.L.Rev. 939, 955–978; Morris, Liability for Innocent Misrepresentation, 1939, 64 U.S.L.Rev. 121, 129–132; Green, Deceit, 1930, 16 Va.L.Rev. 749, 750–762; Notes, 1928, 37 Yale L.J. 1141; 1937, 21 Minn.L.Rev. 434.

81. See supra, p. 705.

82. Chitty v. Horne-Wilson, Inc., 1955, 92 Ga.App. 716, 89 S.E.2d 816; Davis v. Central Land Co., 1913, 162 Iowa 269, 143 N.W. 1073; Horton v. Tyree, 1927, 104 W.Va. 238, 139 S.E. 737; Becker v. McKinnie, 1920, 106 Kan. 426, 186 P. 496; Thompson v. Walker, 1931, 253 Mich. 126, 234 N.W. 144.

83. See supra, p. 701.

84. Chatham Furnace Co. v. Moffatt, 1888, 147 Mass. 403, 18 N.E. 168; Clark v. Haggard, 1954, 141 Conn. 668, 109 A.2d 358; Peterson v. Schaberg, 1928, 116 Neb. 346, 217 N.W. 586; National Bank of Pawnee v. Hamilton, 1916, 202 Ill.App. 516; Gagne v. Bertran, 1954, 43 Cal.2d 481, 275 P.2d 15.

85. Watson v. Jones, 1899, 41 Fla. 241, 25 So. 678; Lehigh Zinc & Iron Co. v. Bamford, 1893, 150 U.S. 665; Edwards v. Sergi, 1934, 137 Cal.App. 369, 30 P.2d 541.

86. Becker v. McKinnie, 1920, 106 Kan. 426, 186 P. 496; Clarke Auto Co. v. Reynolds, 1949, 119 Ind. App. 586, 88 N.E.2d 775.

87. Holcomb v. Noble, 1888, 69 Mich. 396, 37 N.W. 497.

88. Trust Co. of Norfolk v. Fletcher, 1929, 152 Va. 868, 148 S.E. 785 (sale of stock).

with the number increasing every year. Most of the cases, naturally enough, have involved sales of land [89] or chattels; [90] but there is no visible reason to limit the rule to such transactions, and several have applied it to other types of business dealings.[91] Statutes in a few other states have achieved the same result in some specific types of cases.[92] Others appear to be struggling toward the same conclusion, and there is often considerable confusion in a particular jurisdiction.[93]

It was at one time a matter of dispute whether the result toward which the law was obviously tending should be brought about by opening the action of deceit to innocent misrepresentation,[94] or by broadening the

law of warranty.[95] It would be easy to dismiss the question as a relatively unimportant one of the choice of a form of action, were it not for the parol evidence rule, which usually is held to bar proof of oral warranties,[96] but not of fraudulent statements,[97] and which might easily be evaded by a warranty sued in deceit.[98] But whatever the merits of the dispute, the trend of the later cases has rather definitely settled the question in favor of an action which, in form at least, is one of deceit.

The courts which impose the strict liability have not as yet stated its limits very definitely. It seems clear that, as in other cases of strict responsibility, there is a more or less conscious policy of placing the loss upon the innocent defendant rather than the innocent plaintiff who has been misled, in cases where public opinion seems to call for such a result. Thus far this has been done only where the representation is made as of the defendant's own knowledge, concerning a matter as to which he purports to have knowledge,[99]

89. Ham v. Hart, 1954, 58 N.M. 550, 273 P.2d 748; Lanning v. Sprague, 1951, 71 Idaho 138, 227 P.2d 347; Moulton v. Norton, 1931, 184 Minn. 343, 238 N.W. 686; Dargue v. Chaput, 1958, 166 Neb. 69, 88 N.W.2d 148; Pratt v. Thompson, 1925, 133 Wash. 218, 233 P. 637.

90. Stein v. Treger, 1949, 86 U.S.App.D.C. 400, 182 F.2d 696 (whiskey); New England Foundation Co. v. Elliott A. Watrous Co., 1940, 306 Mass. 177, 27 N.E.2d 756; Irwin v. Carlton, 1963, 369 Mich. 92, 119 N.W.2d 617 (hogs); Clarke Auto Co. v. Reynolds, 1949, 119 Ind.App. 586, 88 N.E.2d 775; Helvetia Copper Co. v. Hart-Parr Co., 1917, 137 Minn. 321, 163 N.W. 665.

91. Essenburg v. Russell, 1956, 346 Mich. 319, 78 N.W.2d 136 (sale of grocery business); Jacquot v. Farmers' Straw Gas Producer Co., 1926, 140 Wash. 482, 249 P. 984 (sale of patent rights); Gulf Elec. Co. v. Fried, 1928, 218 Ala. 684, 119 So. 685 (lease of building); Baker v. Moody, 5 Cir. 1955, 219 F.2d 368 (inducing investment); Fidelity & Cas. Co. of New York v. J. D. Pittman Tractor Co., 1943, 244 Ala. 354, 13 So.2d 669 (liability insurance policy).

92. See for example Cartwright v. Braly, 1928, 218 Ala. 49, 117 So. 477; Welge v. Thompson, 1924, 103 Okl. 114, 229 P. 271; Speer v. Pool, Tex.Civ.App. 1948, 210 S.W.2d 423. As to the provisions of the Federal Securities Act, see Shulman, Civil Liability and the Securities Act, 1933, 43 Yale L.J. 227; Notes, 1940, 50 Yale L.J. 90; 1941, 36 Ill.L.Rev. 117.

93. See for example Miller, Innocent Misrepresentations as the Basis of an Action for Deceit, 1928, 6 Tex.L.Rev. 151; Note, 1951, 36 Iowa L.Rev. 648.

94. Advocated by Williston, Liability for Honest Misrepresentation, 1911, 24 Harv.L.Rev. 415; Green, Deceit, 1930, 16 Va.L.Rev. 749.

95. Advocated by Bohlen, Misrepresentation as Deceit, Negligence or Warranty, 1929, 42 Harv.L.Rev. 733; Carpenter, Responsibility for Intentional, Negligent and Innocent Misrepresentation, 1930, 24 Ill. L.Rev. 749. See Wimple v. Patterson, Tex.Civ.App. 1909, 117 S.W. 1034.

96. O'Hara v. Hartford Oil Heating Co., 1927, 106 Conn. 468, 138 A. 438; Bennett v. Thomson, 1920, 235 Mass. 463, 126 N.E. 795; Meyer v. Packard Cleveland Motor Co., 1922, 106 Ohio St. 328, 140 N.E. 118; See Mechem, Implied and Oral Warranties and the Parol Evidence Rule, 1928, 12 Minn.L.Rev. 209; Strahorn, The Parol Evidence Rule and Warranties of Goods Sold, 1935, 19 Minn.L.Rev. 725.

97. Bareham & McFarland v. Kane, 1930, 228 App. Div. 396, 240 N.Y.S. 123; Blecher v. Schmidt, 1931, 211 Iowa 1063, 235 N.W. 34; J. B. Colt Co. v. Brown, 1928, 224 Ky. 438, 6 S.W.2d 473.

98. As was done in Duholm v. Chicago, M. & St. P. R. Co., 1920, 146 Minn. 1, 177 N.W. 772; New England Foundation Co. v. Elliott A. Watrous, Inc., 1940, 306 Mass. 177, 27 N.E.2d 756.

99. Tucker v. White, 1878, 125 Mass. 344; Krause v. Cook, 1906, 144 Mich. 365, 108 N.W. 81; and compare New England Foundation Co. v. Elliott A. Watrous, Inc., 1940, 306 Mass. 343, 27 N.E.2d 756, with Harris v. Delco Products Co., 1940, 305 Mass. 362,

so that he may be taken to have assumed responsibility as in the case of a warranty. It is clear, however, that the warranty requirement of a contract between the parties is not carried over into the tort action; [1] but thus far it has been held that the defendant must have some economic interest in the transaction into which the plaintiff enters, and expect to derive some direct or indirect benefit from it, so that the information is not given entirely gratuitously.[2] Agents negotiating for others have been held strictly liable [3] or not,[4] according to the interest which they are found to have in seeing that the contract is made; but corporate officers, directors and promoters,[5] whose interest is sufficiently obvious, are held responsible for statements made to induce dealings with the corporation. The problem of the persons to whom

the defendant may be liable has received little consideration; [6] but responsibility may be expected to be more narrow than in the case of intentional or even negligent misrepresentation, and no case has been found holding that anyone may recover unless he is within the class of persons whom the representation was in fact intended to influence.[7]

The development of strict liability in a tort action has been encouraged [8] by the analogy of strict responsibility in equity. The equity courts, concerned with the restitution of unjust enrichment of the defendant rather than compensation of the plaintiff's damages, have permitted rescission or other equitable relief [9] for innocent misrepresentation, frequently under the name of mutual mistake as to a material fact.[10] When rescission is granted in an action at law, such as one of quasi-contract, the equity rule has been followed, and the defendant's innocence has not prevented relief.[11]

Reference already has been made [12] to the confusion which surrounds the defense of "fraud" to an action brought by the adverse party; but where that defense takes the form of rescission of the contract, the equity rule is

---

25 N.E.2d 740. See Harper and McNeely, A Synthesis of the Law of Misrepresentation, 1938, 22 Minn.L.Rev. 939, 955–971.

Thus far the rule has been limited to business transactions. In Christensen v. Thornby, 1934, 192 Minn. 123, 255 N.W. 620, the court refused to find strict liability in the case of a surgeon's representation that a sterilization operation performed on the plaintiff was effective.

1. See for example Baxter v. Ford Motor Co., 1932, 168 Wash. 456, 12 P.2d 409, affirmed 168 Wash. 456, 15 P.2d 1118, second appeal 1934, 179 Wash. 123, 35 P.2d 1090; Cooper v. R. J. Reynolds Tobacco Co., 1 Cir. 1956, 234 F.2d 170; Ford Motor Co. v. Lonon, 1966, 217 Tenn. 400, 398 S.W.2d 240.

2. Rosenberg v. Cyrowski, 1924, 227 Mich. 508, 198 N.W. 905; Kolinsky v. Reichstein, 1942, 303 Mich. 710, 7 N.W.2d 117; Neelund v. Hansen, 1919, 144 Minn. 228, 175 N.W. 538; Noble v. Libby, 1911, 144 Wis. 632, 129 N.W. 791. But see Lahay v. City Nat. Bank, 1890, 15 Colo. 339, 25 P. 704; National Bank of Pawnee v. Hamilton, 1916, 202 Ill.App. 516.

3. Krause v. Cook, 1906, 144 Mich. 365, 108 N.W. 81 (commission); Tischer v. Bardin, 1923, 155 Minn. 361, 194 N.W. 3 (commission).

4. Aldrich v. Scribner, 1908, 154 Mich. 23, 117 N.W. 581; Wimple v. Patterson, Tex.Civ.App.1909, 117 S. W. 1034; Williamson v. Hannan, 1918, 200 Mich. 658, 166 N.W. 829.

5. Giddings v. Baker, 1891, 80 Tex. 308, 16 S.W. 33; Osborne v. Holt, 1922, 92 W.Va. 410, 114 S.E. 801; Huntress v. Blodgett, 1910, 206 Mass. 318, 92 N.E. 427; Kuehl v. Parmenter, 1923, 195 Iowa 497, 192 N.W. 429.

6. In Rosenberg v. Cyrowski, 1924, 227 Mich. 508, 198 N.W. 905, and Kolinsky v. Reichstein, 1942, 303 Mich. 710, 7 N.W.2d 117, it was held that there was no strict liability to a third person where the defendant derived no benefit from the transaction. In Russo v. Merck & Co., D.R.I.1956, 138 F.Supp. 147, a case of a sale of blood plasma, it was held that there was no strict liability in deceit to one with whom there was no privity of contract.

7. Which, as for example in the case of false statements in advertising, may still be a large class of persons. See cases cited supra, note 703.

8. See for example Trust Co. of Norfolk v. Fletcher, 1929, 152 Va. 868, 148 S.E. 785.

9. For example, reformation. McDonald v. Mullins, 1944, 197 Ga. 511, 29 S.E.2d 507; Rhyne v. Ganimal, 1952, 215 Miss. 68, 60 So.2d 500.

10. See for example Ross v. Harding, 1964, 64 Wash. 2d 231, 391 P.2d 526.

11. See cases cited supra, p. 688.

12. See supra, p. 689.

properly adopted,[13] and the courts which permit the tort action where the defendant is innocent will of course allow recoupment upon the same basis.[14] The branch of estoppel which rests upon active misrepresentation does not, according to the prevailing view, require either intent or negligence on the part of the one estopped,[15] although when it is based upon mere inaction or "standing by," some unreasonable conduct amounting to negligence seems to be required.[16]

It thus appears that strict responsibility for innocent misrepresentation is common to all of these remedies except the action of deceit,[17] which is in a process of gradual invasion that may be expecting to continue. The foregoing analysis gives no hint of the uncertainty which exists in many jurisdictions, and the variety of views which have been adopted in a single state. If attention were directed to the essential problem of substantive liability, rather than the procedural one of the form of the action, it would be much more easy for any court to reach a conclusion as to the rule to be followed.

108. RELIANCE

The causal connection between the wrongful conduct and the resulting damage, essential throughout the law of torts, takes in cases of misrepresentation the form of inducement of the plaintiff to act, or to refrain from acting,[18] to his detriment. The false representation must have played a material and substantial part in leading the plaintiff to adopt his particular course; and when he was unaware of it at the time that he acted,[19] or it is clear that he was not in any way influenced by it, and would have done the same thing without it for other reasons,[20] his loss is not attributed to the defendant.

In order to be influenced by the representation, the plaintiff must of course have relied upon it, and believed it to be true. If it appears that he knew the facts,[21] or believed the statement to be false,[22] or that he was in fact so skeptical as to its truth that he reposed no confidence in it,[23] it cannot be regarded as a substantial cause of his conduct. If, after hearing the defendant's words, he makes an investigation of his own, and acts upon the basis of the information so obtained, he may be found not to have relied on the defendant,[24] since the fact that he was unwilling to

Watkins, 1871, 13 Wall., U.S., 456, 20 L.Ed. 629; Ross v. W. D. Cleveland & Sons, Tex.Civ.App.1910, 133 S.W. 315; Stern Bros. v. New York Edison Co., 1937, 251 App.Div. 379, 296 N.Y.S. 857.

19. Brackett v. Griswold, 1889, 112 N.Y. 454, 20 N.E. 376; Burnett v. Hensley, 1902, 118 Iowa 575, 92 N. W. 678; Chemical Bank v. Lyons, C.C.Pa.1905, 137 F. 976.

20. McIntyre v. Lyon, 1949, 325 Mich. 167, 37 N.W.2d 903; Tsang v. Kan, 1947, 78 Cal.App.2d 275, 177 P. 2d 630; Wann v. Scullin, 1908, 210 Mo. 429, 109 S. W. 688. It is on this basis that a specific disclaimer of reliance upon representations, brought home to the plaintiff, is held to bar an action in deceit. Danann Realty Corp. v. Harris, 1959, 5 N.Y.S.2d 317, 184 N.Y.S.2d 599, 157 N.E.2d 597.

21. Cox v. Johnson, 1946, 227 N.C. 69, 40 S.E.2d 418; Williams v. Bisson, 1946, 142 Me. 83, 46 A.2d 708; Tyler v. Turner Center System, 1929, 102 Vt. 202, 147 A. 287.

22. Edwards v. Hudson, 1938, 214 Ind. 120, 14 N.E.2d 705; Wegefarth v. Wiessner, 1919, 134 Md. 555, 107 A. 364; Lilienthal v. Suffolk Brewing Co., 1891, 154 Mass. 185, 28 N.E. 151; Hooper v. Whitaker, 1900, 130 Ala. 324, 30 So. 355.

23. Proctor v. McCoid, 1882, 60 Iowa 153, 14 N.W. 208; Humphrey v. Merriam, 1884, 32 Minn. 197, 20 N.W. 138; McIntyre v. Lyon, 1949, 325 Mich. 167, 37 N.W.2d 903; Williams v. Bisson, 1947, 142 Me. 83, 46 A.2d 708.

24. McNabb v. Thomas, 1951, 88 App.D.C. 379, 190 F.2d 608; Sacramento Suburban Fruit Lands Co. v.

13. Frenzel v. Miller, 1871, 37 Ind. 1; Johnson v. Gulick, 1890, 46 Neb. 817, 65 N.W. 883; Standard Mfg. Co. v. Slot, 1904, 121 Wis. 14, 98 N.W. 923; Foulks Accelerating Air Motor Co. v. Thies, 1901, 26 Nev. 158, 65 P. 373. Contra: Security Sav. Bank of Wellman v. Smith, 1909, 144 Iowa 203, 122 N.W. 825; Griswold v. Sabin, 1871, 51 N.H. 167.

14. Baughman v. Gould, 1881, 45 Mich. 481, 8 N.W. 73.

15. See cases cited supra, p. 692.

16. See cases cited supra, p. 692.

17. Williston, Liability for Honest Misrepresentation, 1911, 24 Harv.L.Rev. 415.

18. Fottler v. Moseley, 1901, 179 Mass. 295, 60 N.E. 788, 1904, 185 Mass. 563, 70 N.E. 1040; Butler v.

accept the statement without verification is evidence that he did not believe it.[25]

However, here as elsewhere,[26] it is not required that the defendant shall have been the sole cause of the damage; and indeed it is seldom, if ever, that the plaintiff is not influenced to some extent by many other factors, most of which are not connected with the defendant at all. It is enough that the representation has had a material influence [27] upon the plaintiff's conduct, and been a substantial factor [28] in bringing about his action. It is not necessary that the representation be the paramount, or the decisive, inducement which tipped the scales, so long as it plays a substantial part in affecting the plaintiff's decision.[29] Each of two or more liars may play a significant part in leading him to his final conclusion; [30] and the mere fact that he has made inquiries, or obtained additional information from other sources, does not neces-

sarily mean that he has disregarded what the defendant told him.[31] An independent investigation, which fails to discover the truth, may not be enough to preclude reliance upon the defendant's statement.[32] Thus inspection of property by a purchaser will not always prevent his reliance upon an assurance against latent defects.[33] The question becomes one of fact, as to whether substantial weight was given to the representation, and it usually is for the jury.[34]

Justifiable Reliance

Not only must there be reliance, but the reliance must be found to be justifiable under the circumstances. The plaintiff's conduct must not be so utterly unreasonable, in the light of the information open to him, that the law may properly say that his loss is his own responsibility. In some cases, of course, the unreasonableness of his conduct has been regarded as sufficient evidence that he did not in fact rely upon the representation—he may testify to his reliance,[35] but the court or

---

Klaffenbach, 9 Cir. 1930, 40 F.2d 899; Imperial Assur. Co. of New York v. Joseph Supornick & Son, 1950, 214 Ind. 120, 14 N.E.2d 705; Davis v. Bayne, 1932, 171 Wash. 1, 17 P.2d 618; Meland v. Youngberg, 1914, 124 Minn. 446, 145 N.W. 167.

25. Thus in Enfield v. Colburn, 1884, 63 N.H. 218, and Wheelwright v. Vanderbilt, 1914, 69 Or. 326, 138 P. 857, it was held that the plaintiffs could not recover for expenses of their investigation, since "if they relied upon the representations, they did not investigate them; if they investigated them they did not rely upon them. It is a perversion of language to say they did both."

26. See supra, p. 239.

27. Howard v. Barnstable County Nat. Bank of Hyannis, 1935, 291 Mass. 131, 197 N.E. 40; Household Finance Corp. v. Christian, 1959, 8 Wis.2d 53, 98 N.W.2d 390.

28. Anderson v. Handley, 1957, 149 Cal.App.2d 184, 308 P.2d 368.

29. Matthews v. Bliss, 1839, 22 Pick., Mass., 48; Neuman v. Corn Exchange Nat. Bank & Trust Co., 1947, 356 Pa. 442, 51 A.2d 759, supplemented 52 A.2d 177; Maxwell Ice Co. v. Brackett, Shaw & Lunt Co., 1921, 80 N.H. 236, 116 A. 34; Mullin v. Gano, 1930, 299 Pa. 251, 149 A. 488 ("material").

30. Addington v. Allen, 1833, 11 Wend., N.Y., 374; Strong v. Strong, 1886, 102 N.Y. 69, 5 N.E. 799; Safford v. Grout, 1876, 120 Mass. 20; Shaw v. Gilbert, 1901, 111 Wis. 165, 86 N.W. 188.

31. John Hancock Mut. Life Ins. Co. of Boston v. Cronin, 1947, 139 N.J.Eq. 392, 51 A.2d 2; Fausett & Co. v. Bullard, 1950, 217 Ark. 176, 229 S.W.2d 490; Schmidt v. Thompson, 1918, 140 Minn. 180, 167 N.W. 543; Nichols v. Lane, 1919, 93 Vt. 87, 106 A. 592; Jones v. Elliott, 1920, 111 Wash. 138, 189 P. 1007.

32. Provident Life & Accident Ins. Co. v. Hawley, 4 Cir. 1942, 123 F.2d 479; Garrett v. Perry, 1959, 53 Cal.2d 178, 346 P.2d 758; Sult v. Bolenbach, 1958, 84 Ariz. 351, 327 P.2d 1023. Christy v. Heil, 1963, 255 Iowa 602, 123 N.W.2d 408.

33. Lobdell v. Miller, 1953, 114 Cal.App.2d 328, 250 P.2d 357; Loehr v. Manning, 1954, 44 Wash.2d 908, 272 P.2d 133; Wolf v. Kansas City Tire & Service Co., Mo.App.1953, 257 S.W.2d 408; Milmoe v. Dixon, 1950, 101 Cal.App.2d 257, 225 P.2d 273; Groening v. Opsata, 1948, 323 Mich. 73, 34 N.W.2d 560.

As to patent defects, however, it may be found that inspection precludes reliance. Carpenter v. Hamilton, 1936, 18 Cal.App.2d 69, 62 P.2d 1397; Follingstad v. Syverson, 1926, 166 Minn. 457, 208 N.W. 200.

34. Wagner v. Binder, Mo.1916, 187 S.W. 1128; Fottler v. Moseley, 1904, 185 Mass. 563, 70 N.E. 1040; Hall v. Johnson, 1879, 41 Mich. 286, 2 N.W. 55.

35. Pease v. Brown, 1870, 104 Mass. 291; Weaver v. Cone, 1896, 174 Pa. 104, 34 A. 551; Continental Coal, Land & Timber Co. v. Kilpatrick, 1916, 172 App.Div. 541, 158 N.Y.S. 1056.

the jury is not compelled to believe him.[36] But in some cases where the plaintiff's reliance in fact, and his good faith, are unquestioned, it may still be held that his conduct was so foolish as to bar his recovery. If he is a person of normal intelligence, experience and education, he may not put faith in representations which any such normal person would recognize at once as preposterous, as, for example, that glasses, once fitted, will alter shape and adapt themselves to the eye,[37] or which are shown by facts within his observation to be so patently and obviously false that he must have closed his eyes to avoid discovery of the truth,[38] and still compel the defendant to be responsible for his loss.

There have been cases [39] in which it was said that such reliance is contributory negligence, and that the plaintiff must exercise the care of a reasonably prudent man for his own protection. Undoubtedly such language is appropriate if the defendant's misrepresentation itself is merely negligent; [40] but where there is an intent to mislead, it is clearly inconsistent with the general rule [41] that mere

negligence of the plaintiff is not a defense to an intentional tort. The better reasoned cases [42] have rejected contributory negligence as a defense applicable to intentional deceit, taking account of the effect which the representation is intended to have upon the plaintiff's mind.[43]

It is a sufficient indication that the person deceived is not held to the standard of precaution, or of minimum knowledge, or of intelligent judgment, of the hypothetical reasonable man, that people who are exceptionally gullible,[44] superstitious,[45] ignorant, stupid, dim-witted,[46] or illiterate,[47] have been al-

---

36. "It may be that the mis-statement is trivial— so trivial as that the Court will be of opinion that it could not have affected the plaintiff's mind at all, or induced him to enter into the contract." Smith v. Chadwick, 1882, 20 Ch.Div. 27, 45. Accord: Bond v. Ramsey, 1878, 89 Ill. 29.

37. H. Hirschberg Optical Co. v. Michaelson, 1901, 1 Neb., Unof., 137, 95 N.W. 461. Accord: Bishop v. Small, 1874, 63 Me. 12; and see that foremost classic of legal humor, the sad but remarkable tale of the Land of Shalam, in Ellis v. Newbrough, 1891, 6 N.M. 181, 27 P. 490.

38. Williams v. Rank & Son Buick, Inc., 1969, 44 Wis.2d 239, 170 N.W.2d 807; Narup v. Benson, 1929, 154 Wash. 646, 283 P. 179; Security Trust Co. v. O'Hair, 1936, 103 Ind.App. 56, 197 N.E. 694, rehearing denied 103 Ind.App. 56, 199 N.E. 602; Kaiser v. Nummerdor, 1904, 120 Wis. 234, 97 N.W. 932; Long v. Warren, 1877, 68 N.Y. 426.

39. For example, Dunn v. White, 1876, 63 Mo. 181; Osborne v. Missouri Pac. R. Co., 1904, 71 Neb. 180, 98 N.W. 685.

40. See cases cited supra, p. 704.

41. See supra, p. 426.
As to strict responsibility for innocent misrepresentation cf. Rogers v. Portland & B. St. R. Co., 1905,

100 Me. 86, 60 A. 713 (estoppel), in accord with the view generally accepted that contributory negligence is no defense to strict liability.

42. Seeger v. Odell, 1941, 18 Cal.2d 400, 115 P.2d 977; Butler v. Olshan, 1966, 280 Ala. 181, 191 So.2d 7; Roda v. Berko, 1948, 401 Ill. 335, 81 N.E.2d 912; Knox v. Anderson, D.Haw.1958, 159 F.Supp. 795, supplemented 162 F.Supp. 338; Pelkey v. Norton, 1953, 149 Me. 247, 99 A.2d 918. See Seavey, Caveat Emptor as of 1960, 1960, 38 Tex.L.Rev. 439.

43. "He has a right to retort upon his objector, 'You, at least, who have stated what is untrue, or have concealed the truth, for the purpose of drawing me into a contract, cannot accuse me of want of caution because I relied implicitly upon your fairness and honesty.'" Lord Chelmsford, in Central R. Co. of Venezuela v. Kisch, 1867, L.R. 2 H.L. 99. Accord: Cottrill v. Crum, 1890, 100 Mo. 397, 13 S.W. 753; Crompton v. Beedle & Thomas, 1910, 83 Vt. 287, 75 A. 331.
Likewise, where strict liability is imposed, the general rule of policy that contributory negligence is not a defense (supra, § 79) has been followed in cases of misrepresentation. Bahlman v. Hudson Motor Car Co., 1939, 290 Mich. 683, 288 N.W. 309; Challis v. Hartloff, 1933, 136 Kan. 823, 18 P.2d 199 (implied warranty).

44. Adan v. Steinbrecher, 1911, 116 Minn. 174, 133 N.W. 477; Sutton v. Greiner, 1916, 177 Iowa 532, 159 N.W. 268.

45. Hyma v. Lee, 1953, 338 Mich. 31, 60 N.W.2d 920 (belief in spiritualism).

46. Teter v. Shultz, 1942, 110 Ind.App. 541, 39 N.E. 2d 802; Jenness v. Moses Lake Development Co., 1951, 39 Wash.2d 151, 234 P.2d 865; Kempf v. Ranger, 1916, 132 Minn. 64, 155 N.W. 1059; King v. Livingston Mfg. Co., 1912, 180 Ala. 118, 60 So. 143; Porter v. United Rys. Co. of St. Louis, 1912, 165 Mo.App. 619, 148 S.W. 162.

47. Weatherford v. Home Finance Co., 1954, 225 S. C. 313, 82 S.E.2d 196; Soltan v. Shahboz, 1956, 383

lowed to recover when the defendant knew it, and deliberately took advantage of it. "The design of the law is to protect the weak and credulous from the wiles and stratagems of the artful and cunning, as well as those whose vigilance and security enable them to protect themselves,"[48] and "no rogue should enjoy his ill-gotten plunder for the simple reason that his victim is by chance a fool."[49]

Rather than contributory negligence, the matter seems to turn upon an individual standard of the plaintiff's own capacity and the knowledge which he has, or which may fairly be charged against him from the facts within his observation in the light of his individual case, and so comes closer to the rules which are associated with assumption of risk.[50] "More succinctly stated, the rule is that one cannot be heard to say he relied upon a statement so patently ridiculous as to be unbelievable on its face, unless he happens to be that special object of the affections of a court of Equity, an idiot."[51] The other side of the shield is that one who has special knowledge, experience and competence may not be permitted to rely on statements for which the ordinary man might recover,[52] and that one who has acquired expert knowledge concerning the matter dealt with may be required to form his own judgment, rather than take the word of the defendant.[53]

The last half-century has seen a marked change in the attitude of the courts toward the question of justifiable reliance. Earlier decisions, under the influence of the prevalent doctrine of "caveat emptor," laid great stress upon the plaintiff's "duty" to protect himself and distrust his antagonist, and held that he was not entitled to rely even upon positive assertions of fact made by one with whom he was dealing at arm's length.[54] It was assumed that any one may be expected to overreach another in a bargain if he can, and that only a fool will expect common honesty. Therefore the plaintiff must make a reasonable investigation, and form his own judgment. The recognition of a new standard of business ethics, demanding that statements of fact be at least honestly and carefully made,[55] and in many cases that they be warranted to be true,[56] has led to an almost complete shift in this point of view.[57]

It is now held that assertions of fact as to the quantity[58] or quality[59] of land or goods[60]

Pa. 485, 119 A.2d 242 ; Pimpinello v. Swift & Co., 1930, 253 N.Y. 159, 170 N.E. 530.

48. Ingalls v. Miller, 1889, 121 Ind. 188, 191, 22 N.E. 995.

49. Chamberlin v. Fuller, 1887, 59 Vt. 247, 256, 9 A. 832, 836.

50. See Frenzel v. Miller, 1897, 37 Ind. 1 ; Green, Deceit, 1930, 16 Va.L.Rev. 749, 763.

51. Obiter Dicta, 1956, 25 Ford.L.Rev. 395, 397.

52. Graff v. Geisel, 1951, 39 Wash.2d 131, 234 P.2d 884 ; Hanson v. Acceptance Finance Corp., Mo.App. 1954, 270 S.W.2d 143 ; Babb v. Bolyard, 1950, 194 Md. 603, 72 A.2d 13.

53. Puget Sound Nat. Bank v. McMahon, 1958, 53 Wash.2d 51, 330 P.2d 559 ; Schmidt v. Landfield, 1960, 20 Ill.2d 89, 169 N.E.2d 229 ; Poe v. Voss, 1955, 196 Va. 821, 86 S.E.2d 47.

54. Sherwood v. Salmon, 1805, 2 Day, Conn., 128 ; Page v. Parker, 1861, 43 N.H. 363 ; Graffenstein v. E. Epstein & Co., 1880, 23 Kan. 443 ; Schwabacker v. Riddle, 1891, 99 Ill. 343 ; Mabardy v. McHugh, 1909, 202 Mass. 148, 88 N.E. 894.

55. "And, generally speaking, until there be written into the law some precept or rule to the effect that the heart of a man is as prone to wickedness as is the smoke to go upward, and that every man must deal with his fellow man as if he was a thief and a robber, it ought not to be held that trust cannot be put in a positive assertion of a material fact, known to the speaker and unknown to the hearer, and intended to be relied upon." Lamm, J., in Judd v. Walker, 1908, 215 Mo. 312, 114 S.W. 979.

56. See supra, § 97.

57. See Harper and McNeely, A Synthesis of the Law of Misrepresentation, 1938, 22 Minn.L.Rev. 939, 957–960 ; Restatement of Torts, §§ 538(3), 540.

58. Lanning v. Sprague, 1951, 71 Idaho 138, 227 P. 2d 347 ; Judd v. Walker, 1908, 215 Mo. 312, 114 S.W. 979 ; George v. Kurdy, 1916, 92 Wash. 277, 158 P. 965 ; Antle v. Sexton, 1891, 137 Ill. 410, 27 N.E. 691.

59. Erickson v. Midgarden, 1948, 226 Minn. 55, 31 N.W.2d 918 ; Ashburn v. Miller, 1958, 161 Cal.App. 2d 71, 326 P.2d 229 ; Blackman v. Howes, 1947, 82 Cal.App.2d 275, 185 P.2d 1019 ; Warne v. Finseth, 1923, 50 N.D. 347, 195 N.W. 573 ; McGuffin v. Smith, 1926, 215 Ky. 606, 286 S.W. 884.

60. Lunnie v. Gadapee, 1950, 116 Vt. 261, 73 A.2d 312 ; Morrow v. Bonebrake, 1911, 84 Kan. 724, 115

sold, the financial status of corporations,[61] and similar matters [62] inducing commercial transactions, may justifiably be relied on without investigation, not only where such investigation would be burdensome or difficult, as where land which is sold lies at a distance,[63] but likewise where the falsity of the representation might be discovered with little effort by means easily at hand.[64] The plaintiff is not required, for example, to examine public records to ascertain the true state of the title claimed by the defendant.[65]

P. 585; Graves v. Haynes, Tex.Civ.App.1921, 231 S.W. 383; Stewart v. Stearns, 1884, 63 N.H. 99.

61. Fargo Gas & Coke Co. v. Fargo Gas & Electric Co., 1894, 4 N.D. 219, 59 N.W. 1066; Buckley v. Buckley, 1925, 230 Mich. 504, 202 N.W. 955; Gallon v. Burns, 1917, 92 Conn. 39, 101 A. 504; cf. Hise v. Thomas, 1917, 181 Iowa 700, 165 N.W. 38; Russell v. Industrial Transp. Co., 1923, 113 Tex. 441, 251 S.W. 1034, 258 S.W. 462.

62. Bishop v. E. A. Strout Realty Agency, 4 Cir. 1950, 182 F.2d 503 (depth of water); Champneys v. Irwin, 1919, 106 Wash. 438, 180 P. 405 (amount of rental); Werline v. Aldred, 1916, 57 Okl. 391, 157 P. 305 (value and rental); Roda v. Berko, 1948, 401 Ill. 335, 81 N.E.2d 912; Twin State Fruit Corp. v. Kansas, 1932, 104 Vt. 154, 157 A. 831 (buyer representing he was the owner of a business).

63. Haskell v. Starbird, 1890, 152 Mass. 117, 142 N.E. 695; Ladner v. Balsley, 1897, 103 Iowa 674, 72 N.W. 787; Brees v. Anderson, 1922, 154 Minn. 123, 191 N.W. 266; Gridley v. Ross, 1926, 37 Idaho 693, 217 P. 989. Cf. Warne v. Finseth, 1923, 50 N.D. 347, 195 N.W. 573; Christensen v. Jauron, Iowa 1919, 174 N.W. 499.

64. Buckley v. Buckley, 1925, 230 Mich. 504, 202 N. W. 955; Gallon v. Burns, 1917, 92 Conn. 39, 101 A. 504; Currie v. Malloy, 1923, 185 N.C. 206, 116 S.E. 564; King v. Livingston Mfg. Co., 1912, 180 Ala. 118, 60 So. 143; Board of Public Instruction of Dade County v. Everett W. Martin & Sons, Fla. 1957, 97 So.2d 21. There are still occasional cases to the contrary, such as Taylor v. Arneill, 1954, 129 Colo. 185, 268 P.2d 695. See Seavey, Caveat Emptor as of 1960, 1960, 38 Tex.L.Rev. 439.

65. Citizens Sav. & Loan Ass'n v. Fischer, 1966, 67 Ill.App.2d 315, 214 N.E.2d 612; Linch v. Carlson, 1952, 156 Neb. 308, 56 N.W.2d 101; Pattridge v. Youmans, 1941, 107 Colo. 122, 109 P.2d 646; Cowles' Ex'r v. Johnson, 1944, 297 Ky. 454, 179 S.W.2d 674; Campanelli v. Vescera, 1949, 75 R.I. 71, 63 A.2d 722. See Seavey, Actions for Economic Harm—A Comment, 1957, 32 N.Y.U.L.Rev. 1242.

It is only where, under the circumstances, the facts should be apparent to one of his knowledge and intelligence from a cursory glance,[66] or he has discovered something which should serve as a warning that he is being deceived,[67] that he is required to make an investigation of his own. The comparative availability of information to the parties may, however, be of considerable importance in determining whether the representation is to be regarded as an assurance of fact, or merely as a statement of opinion.[68]

Materiality

The party deceived must not only be justified in his belief that the representation is true, but he must also be justified in taking action on that basis. This usually is expressed by saying that the fact represented must be a material one. There are misstatements which are so trivial, or so far unrelated to anything of real importance in the transaction, that the plaintiff will not be heard to

Constructive notice under recording acts does not apply to misrepresentations. Schoedel v. State Bank of Newburg, 1944, 245 Wis. 74, 13 N.W.2d 534.

66. Duckworth v. Walker, 1854, 46 N.C. 507; Kaiser v. Nummerdor, 1904, 120 Wis. 234, 97 N.W. 932; Dalhoff Const. Co. v. Block, 8 Cir. 1907, 157 F. 227; Security Trust Co. v. O'Hair, 1936, 103 Ind.App. 56, 197 N.E. 694; Id., 103 Ind.App. 56, 199 N.E. 602. Accord: Dunham Lumber Co. v. Holt, 1898, 123 Ala. 336, 26 So. 663 (intelligent person, able to read and not prevented by defendant's conduct, signing document without reading it).

As to the distinction between that which is obvious to the senses and that which requires the effort of investigation, see Frenzel v. Miller, 1871, 37 Ind. 1; Robertson v. Smith, Mo.App.1918, 204 S.W. 413; Gallon v. Burns, 1917, 92 Conn. 39, 101 A. 504.

67. Feak v. Marion Steam Shovel Co., 9 Cir. 1936, 84 F.2d 670, cert. denied 299 U.S. 604; Carpenter v. Hamilton, 1936, 18 Cal.App.2d 69, 62 P.2d 1397; Dillman v. Nadlehoffer, 1886, 119 Ill. 567, 7 N.E. 88; Godfrey v. Navratil, 1966, 3 Ariz.App. 47, 411 P.2d 470 (written warning of falsity). But the reliance may still be reasonable if the defendant allays the plaintiff's suspicions. Forsyth v. Dow, 1914, 81 Wash. 137, 142 P. 490; cf. Moncrief v. Wilkinson, 1890, 93 Ala. 373, 9 So. 159.

68. Harper and McNeely, A Synthesis of the Law of Misrepresentation, 1938, 22 Minn.L.Rev. 939, 960. See infra, § 109.

say that they substantially affected his decision. Necessarily the test must be an objective one,[69] and it cannot be stated in the form of any definite rule, but must depend upon the circumstances of the transaction itself. The most cogent reason for the requirement of materiality is that of promoting stability in commercial transactions. It has been described as "some assurance that the representee is not merely using the misrepresentation as a pretext for escaping a bargain that he is dissatisfied with on other grounds."[70]

Thus, in particular cases, matters entirely collateral to a contract, and apparently of no significance to any reasonable man under the circumstances, have been held to be immaterial: the defendant's social, political and religious associations;[71] his motive or purpose in entering into the bargain;[72] the details of a seller's title, where good title is still conveyed;[73] a false financial statement which still gives an accurate picture;[74] the identity of the party for whom a purchase is made;[75] and many other items of similar nature.[76]

On the other hand facts to which a reasonable man might be expected to attach importance in making his choice of action, such as the identity of an individual[77] or the directors of a corporation[78] with whom he is dealing, the character of stock sold as treasury stock,[79] the age, horsepower and capacity of an automobile,[80] or the fact that it is a used car,[81] the train service to a suburb,[82] the solvency of purchasers,[83] the limited number of persons whose biographies are to be published in a book,[84] or the number of places where the seller's goods are made,[85] have been held to be material. The question is frequently for the jury[86] whether the statement made might justifiably induce the action taken.

Blewett v. McRae, 1894, 88 Wis. 280, 60 N.W. 258 (commission of agent); Kaplan v. Suher, 1926, 254 Mass. 180, 150 N.E. 9 (length of time facts known); Blair v. Buttolph, 1887, 72 Iowa 31, 33 N.W. 349 (funds to build railway beyond certain point); Stufflebean v. Peaveler, Mo.App.1925, 274 S.W. 926 (person from whom seller bought); Greenawalt v. Rogers, 1907, 151 Cal. 630, 91 P. 526 (trivial assets where insolvency represented).

69. Babb v. Bolyard, 1950, 194 Md. 603, 72 A.2d 13; Hall v. Johnson, 1879, 41 Mich. 286, 2 N.W. 55; Davis v. Davis, 1893, 97 Mich. 419, 56 N.W. 774; Bower, Actionable Misrepresentation, 2d Ed. 1927, ch. 11; Note 1951, 29 Tex.L.Rev. 644.

70. Keeton, Actionable Misrepresentation, 1949, 2 Okl. L.Rev. 56, 59.

71. Farnsworth v. Duffner, 1891, 142 U.S. 43.

72. Byrd v. Rautman, 1897, 85 Md. 414, 36 A. 1099; Lucas v. Long, 1915, 125 Md. 420, 94 A. 12.

73. Provident Loan Trust Co. v. McIntosh, 1904, 68 Kan. 452, 75 P. 498; Saxby v. Southern Land Co., 1909, 109 Va. 196, 63 S.E. 423. Cf. Kevorkian v. Bemis, 1927, 258 Mass. 456, 155 N.E. 452 (land owned by other corporation of which defendant held all the shares).

74. Gerner v. Yates, 1900, 61 Neb. 100, 84 N.W. 596.

75. Haverland v. Lane, 1916, 89 Wash. 557, 154 P. 1118; Cowan v. Fairbrother, 1896, 118 N.C. 406, 24 S.E. 212; O'Brien v. Luques, 1888, 81 Me. 46, 16 A. 304. Otherwise where a hostile interest is involved. Wann v. Scullin, 1907, 210 Mo. 429, 109 S.W. 688.

76. Babb v. Bolyard, 1950, 194 Md. 603, 72 A.2d 13 (price at which other dealers are selling cars);

77. Gordon v. Street, [1899] 2 Q.B. 641. Saxton v. Harris, Alaska, 1964, 395 P.2d 71.

78. Hedden v. Griffin, 1884, 136 Mass. 229; Penn Mut. Life Ins. Co. v. Crane, 1883, 134 Mass. 56.

79. Caswell v. Hunton, 1895, 87 Me. 277, 32 A. 899; Stillwell v. Rankin, 1918, 55 Mont. 130, 174 P. 186.

80. Smithpeter v. Mid-State Motor Co., Mo.App.1934, 74 S.W.2d 47; Fosberg v. Couture, 1923, 126 Wash. 181, 217 P. 1001; Halff Co. v. Jones, Tex.Civ.App. 1914, 169 S.W. 906; Angerosa v. White Co., 1936, 248 App.Div. 425, 290 N.Y.S. 204.

81. Friendly Irishman, Inc. v. Ronnow, 1958, 74 Nev. 316, 330 P.2d 497.

82. Holst v. Stewart, 1894, 161 Mass. 516, 37 N.E. 755.

83. Oswego Starch Factory v. Lendrum, 1881, 57 Iowa 573, 10 N.W. 900. Cf. Dezero v. Turner, 1941, 112 Vt. 194, 122 A.2d 173 (buyer represented he has just received money from an estate).

84. Greenleaf v. Gerald, 1900, 94 Me. 91, 46 A. 799.

85. Porter v. Stone, 1883, 62 Iowa 442, 17 N.W. 654.

86. Ochs v. Woods, 1917, 221 N.Y. 335, 117 N.E. 305; Davis v. Davis, 1893, 97 Mich. 419, 56 N.W. 774; Montgomery v. Jacob Bros. Co., 1931, 5 W.W.Harr. Del., 112, 159 A. 374.

One distinction that seems to have been made, however, is that where the representation is intended to deceive, it will be regarded as material if the maker knows that the recipient is peculiarly disposed to regard it as important, even though the standard reasonable man would not do so.[87] An individual may be known to attach importance to considerations which the normal man would disregard as trivial. He may send his daughter to a school because it has been attended by her former classmates,[88] give money to a college because it is to be named after a certain person,[89] buy pictures because his wife likes them,[90] lay in a stock of goods because another merchant carries them,[91] or do other things for similar personal reasons.[92] One who deliberately practices upon such known idiosyncracies cannot complain if he is held liable when he is successful, and the understanding of the parties themselves makes the statement "material." On the other hand, when the representation is an innocent one and strict responsibility is in question, the courts have tended to adhere rather closely to an objective standard, and to deny relief if the fact is so trivial that only personal peculiarity could regard it as important.[93]

109. OPINION AND INTENTION

A statement of opinion is one which either indicates some doubt as to the speaker's belief in the existence of a state of facts, as where he says, "I think this is true, but I am not sure," or merely expresses his judgment on some matter of judgment connected with the facts, such as quality, value, authenticity and the like, as where he says, "This is a very fine picture."[94] It is not, however, the form of the statement which is important or controlling, but the sense in which it is reasonably understood. Statements very positive in form, asserting facts without qualification, may be held to be only those of opinion, where the recipient is aware that the speaker has no sufficient information or knowledge as to what he asserts;[95] and, as will be seen,[96] there are numerous circumstances in which statements which are in form only of opinion will be held to convey the assertion of accompanying facts.

It is stated very often as a fundamental rule in connection with all of the various remedies for misrepresentation, that they will not lie for misstatements of opinion, as distinguished from those of fact. The usual explanation is that an opinion is merely an assertion of one man's belief as to a fact, of which another should not be heard to complain, since opinions are a matter "of which many men will be of many minds, and which is often governed by whim and caprice. Judg-

---

87. Restatement of Torts, § 538(1) (b).

88. Brown v. Search, 1907, 131 Wis. 109, 111 N.W. 210.

89. Collinson v. Jeffries, 1899, 21 Tex.Civ.App. 653, 54 S.W. 28.

90. Washington Post Co. v. Sorrells, 1910, 7 Ga.App. 774, 68 S.E. 337; J. I. Case Threshing Mach. Co. v. Webb, Tex.Civ.App.1916, 181 S.W. 853 (automobile).

91. Roebuck v. Wick, 1906, 98 Minn. 130, 107 N.W. 1054; National Novelty Import Co. v. Reed, 1921, 105 Neb. 697, 181 N.W. 654.

92. See Stuart v. Lester, 1888, 49 Hun 58, 17 St.R. 248, 1 N.Y.S. 699; Valton v. National Fund Life Assur. Co., 1859, 20 N.Y. 32, 37; Cooper v. Fort Smith & W. R. Co., 1909, 23 Okl. 139, 99 P. 785, 790; Hester v. Shuster, Tex.Civ.App.1921, 234 S.W. 713, error dismissed. Similarly, the transaction itself may show that a fact which normally would be material is regarded as immaterial. Nounnan v. Sutter County Land Co., 1889, 81 Cal. 1, 22 P. 515.

93. See Restatement of Restitution, § 9, Comment b.

94. See Keeton, Fraud—Misrepresentations of Opinion, 1937, 21 Minn.L.Rev. 643.

95. Batchelder v. Birchard Motors, 1958, 120 Vt. 429, 144 A.2d 298 (statements by seller of car assembled to order for plaintiff); Harris v. Delco Products, 1940, 305 Mass. 362, 25 N.E.2d 740 (well dug on land would find water); Saxby v. Southern Land Co., 1909, 109 Va. 196, 63 S.E. 423 (acres of land in timber).

96. See infra, p. 721.

ment and opinion, in such case, implies no knowledge." [97]

But this explanation is scarcely adequate, since an expression of opinion is itself always a statement of at least one fact—the fact of the belief, the existing state of mind, of the one who asserts it. The true reason lies rather in the highly individualistic attitude of the common law toward the bargaining transactions with which the law of deceit has developed. The parties are expected to deal at arm's length and to beware of one another, and each is supposed to be competent to look after his own interests, and to draw his own conclusions. So long as he has not been misled by positive statements of fact, he has no right to rely upon the judgment of his opponent. Justifiable reliance, of course, is essential to any form of relief for misrepresentation.[98] It is more correct to say, therefore, that a statement of opinion is a representation of a fact, but of an immaterial fact, on which the law will not permit the opposing party to rely.[99] When, for any reason, such reliance is regarded as reasonable and permissible, a misstatement of opinion may be a sufficient basis for relief.[1]

In the absence, then of special circumstances affording some reason to the contrary, a representation which purports to be one of opinion only is not a sufficient foundation for the action of deceit.[2] There can be no recovery, for example, for a statement that the plaintiff is being offered an exceptionally good bargain,[3] that he would be foolish not to take advantage of the offer,[4] that his present holdings are a poor investment,[5] that there is water under land,[6] or that a building will withstand earthquakes,[7] where it is clear that these are no more than expressions of opinion. The same rule is carried over into other forms of relief. Thus statements of opinion are not regarded as warranties in contracts for the sale of goods,[8] nor do they afford a basis for estoppel.[9] When the plaintiff seeks equitable relief, as by rescission of a transaction, the equity courts usually have been willing to follow the law in saying that the plaintiff must form his own opinions, and is not entitled to rely upon those of his adversary.[10] But, since equity is concerned primarily with the unjust enrichment of the defendant, they have shown some tendency to be more liberal as to what is a

---

97. Buller, J., in Pasley v. Freeman, 1789, 3 Term Rep. 51, 57.

98. See supra, p. 715.

99. Keeton, Fraud—Misrepresentations of Opinion, 1937, 21 Minn.L.Rev. 643, 644, 650–651; Keeler v. Fred T. Ley & Co., 1 Cir. 1933, 65 F.2d 499; Ouilette v. Theobald, 1918, 78 N.H. 547, 103 A. 306.

1. See infra, p. 726.

2. Saxby v. Southern Land Co., 1909, 109 Va. 196, 63 S.E. 423; Wilson v. Mason, 1970, 78 N.M. 27, 426 P. 2d 789; Sorrells v. Clifford, 1922, 23 Ariz. 448, 204 P. 1013; Penney v. Pederson, 1927, 146 Wash. 31, 261 P. 636; Welch Veterinary Supply Co. v. Martin, Tex.Civ.App.1958, 313 S.W.2d 111, refused n. r. e.

3. Henning v. Kyle, 1949, 190 Va. 247, 56 S.E.2d 67.

4. Tampa Union Terminal Co. v. Richards, 1933, 108 Fla. 516, 146 So. 591.

5. Blakeslee v. Wallace, 6 Cir. 1930, 45 F.2d 347.

6. Harris v. Delco Products, 1940, 305 Mass. 362, 25 N.E.2d 740.

7. Finch v. McKee, 1936, 18 Cal.App.2d 90, 62 P.2d 1380. Cf. Han v. Horwitz, 1965, 2 Ariz.App. 245, 407 P.2d 786.

8. Mantle Lamp Co. v. Rucker, 1924, 202 Ky. 777, 261 S.W. 263; Seitz v. Brewer's Refrigerating Mach. Co., 1891, 141 U.S. 510; Van Horn v. Stautz, 1921, 297 Ill. 530, 131 N.E. 153; Boston Consol. Gas Co. v. Folsom, 1921, 237 Mass. 565, 130 N.E. 197. "No affirmation of the value of the goods, nor any statement purporting to be a statement of the seller's opinion only shall be construed as a warranty." Uniform Sales Act, § 12.

9. The Belle of the Sea, 1874, 87 U.S. (20 Wall.) 421, 22 L.Ed. 362; Intermountain Building & Loan Assn. v. Casper Mut. Building & Loan Assn., 1934, 46 Wyo. 394, 28 P.2d 103; Hammerslough v. Kansas City Building, Loan & Sav. Ass'n, 1883, 79 Mo. 80; Aunt Jemima Mills Co. v. Rigney & Co., 2 Cir. 1917, 247 F. 407, cert. denied, 1918, 245 U.S. 672.

10. Southern Development Co. v. Silva, 1888, 125 U. S. 247; Culton v. Asher, 1912, 149 Ky. 659, 149 S. W. 946; Hart v. Marbury, 1921, 82 Fla. 317, 90 So. 173; Vian v. Hilberg, 1923, 111 Neb. 232, 196 N.W. 153; Seymour v. Chicago & N. W. R. Co., 1917, 181 Iowa 218, 164 N.W. 352.

"material" representation,[11] and more willingness to find some reason for holding reliance on an opinion to be justified, particularly where the statement of the opinion itself is an intentional lie.[12] Also, of course, rescission is allowed for a mutual mistake which is basic to the transaction; and such a mistake frequently can be found where the defendant has stated, and the plaintiff has relied upon, an entirely honest opinion.[13]

An opinion may take the form of a statement of quality, of more or less indefinite content. One common application of the opinion rule is in the case of loose general statements made by sellers in commending their wares. No action lies against a dealer who describes the automobile he is selling as a "dandy," a "bearcat," a "good little car," and a "sweet job;"[14] or as the "pride of our line" and the "best in the American market;"[15] or who merely makes use of broad, and vague, commendatory language comparing his goods favorably with others,[16] or praising them as "good," "proper," "sufficient," and the like.[17]

Such sales talk, or puffing, as it is commonly called, is considered to be offered and understood as an expression of the seller's opinion only, which is to be discounted as such by the buyer, and on which no reasonable man would rely. "A statement that a cigarette is made from the purest tobaccos grown, that an automobile is the most economical car on the market, that a stock is the safest investment in the world, that a machine is 100 per cent efficient, that a household device is absolutely perfect, that a real estate investment will insure a handsome profit, that an article is the greatest bargain ever offered, and similar claims are intended and understood to be merely emphatic methods of urging a sale. * * * These things, then, the buyer must disregard in forming a sober judgment as to his conduct in the transaction. If he succumbs to such persistent solicitation, he must take the risk of any loss attributable to a disparity between the exaggerated opinion of the purchaser and a reasonable or accurate judgment of the value of the article."[18] "The

---

11. See supra, p. 718.

12. "There is a growing unwillingness on the part of the courts to allow statements to be made without liability, which are calculated to induce, and do induce, action on the part of the hearer. Where a statement is made with fraudulent intent, there is still more reason for regarding it as a ground of liability, even though couched in the form of an opinion, or though it relates to a matter as to which certainty is impossible." Schmitt v. Ornes Esswein & Co., 1921, 149 Minn. 370, 183 N.W. 840. Cf. Restatement of Contracts, § 474; Restatement of Restitution, § 8, Comment d.

13. Cf. Daniel v. Mitchell, C.C.Me.1840, Fed.Cas.No. 3,562, 1 Story 172; Thwing v. Hall & Ducey Lumber Co., 1889, 40 Minn. 184, 41 N.W. 815.

14. Bertram v. Reed Automobile Co., Tex.Civ.App. 1932, 49 S.W.2d 517: "Common experience and observation causes one to marvel at the moderation of the selling expert in making his trade talk to appellant. * * * These are relative terms, they may mean anything the orator or the listener wants, and neither one may be penalized if the one exaggerates or the other is disappointed. There may be something more definite in the representations that the car had been well taken care of, had good rubber on it, had been driven but 19,000 miles, had not been mistreated, that mechanics had found it in perfect condition."

Cf. Buckingham v. Thompson, Tex.Civ.App.1911, 135 S.W. 652, where a Texas realtor let himself go; and see the fun with the case in Obiter Dicta, 1957, 25 Ford.L.Rev. 395. Also Keating v. De Arment, Fla.App.1967, 193 So.2d 694 ("This vessel is in perfect shape, and she is my pride and joy").

15. Prince v. Brackett, Shaw & Lunt Co., 1925, 125 Me. 31, 130 A. 509. Accord: Nichols v. Lane, 1919, 93 Vt. 87, 106 A. 592 ("no better land in Vermont"); Gleason v. McPherson, 1917, 175 Cal. 594, 166 P. 332 ("giltedge" bonds); Thorpe v. Cooley, 1917, 138 Minn. 431, 165 N.W. 265 (bonds "as good as gold").

16. McHargue v. Fayette Coal & Feed Co., Ky.1955, 283 S.W.2d 170; Thomas v. Mississippi Valley Gas Co., 1959, 237 Miss. 100, 113 So.2d 535; Hayes Const. Co. v. Silverthorn, 1955, 343 Mich. 421, 72 N. W.2d 190.

17. Poley v. Bender, 1959, 87 Ariz. 35, 347 P.2d 696; cf. John A. Frye Shoe Co. v. Williams, 1942, 312 Mass. 656, 46 N.E.2d 1.

18. Harper and McNeely, A Synthesis of the Law of Misrepresentation, 1938, 22 Minn.L.Rev. 939, 1004. Accord: Nichols v. Lane, 1919, 93 Vt. 87, 106 A. 592 ("no better land in Vermont"); Miller v. Protrka, 1951, 193 Or. 585, 238 P.2d 753 ("hardly ever a va-

law recognizes the fact that men will naturally overstate the value and qualities of the articles which they have to sell. All men know this, and a buyer has no right to rely upon such statements," [19] whether the remedy sought be deceit, warranty,[20] or rescission.[21] Although the question seldom has arisen, the same probably is true of the disparaging words of a buyer seeking to obtain a favorable price.[22]

The "puffing" rule amounts to a seller's privilege to lie his head off, so long as he says nothing specific, on the theory that no reasonable man would believe him, or that no reasonable man would be influenced by such talk. It is not surprising, therefore, that the rule has not been a favored one; and that whenever it can be found under the circumstances that the buyer reasonably understood that he was receiving something in the way of assurance as to specific facts, the question of actionable misrepresentation has been left to the jury.[23]

Statements of value, in general, as well as predictions as to profits to be made from the thing sold,[24] fall into the same class of statements not to be relied on. The value, or financial worth, of property is regarded as a matter of opinion, on which each party must form his own judgment, without trusting to his adversary, and as to which "puffing" and exaggeration are normally to be expected.[25] Very little, however, is required to transform a statement of opinion as to value into one of fact. Thus a representation as to the price paid for the property by the defendant himself is regarded as one of fact,[26] as is also a

---

cancy" in motel); Lambert v. Sistrunk, Fla.1952, 58 So.2d 434 (stepladder "strong; will last a lifetime and never break"); American Laundry Machinery Co. v. Skinner, 1945, 225 N.C. 285, 34 S.E.2d 190 (machine "will do better work, cheaper and with less labor" than one buyer has); James Spear Stove & Heating Co. v. General Electric Co., D.Pa. 1934, 12 F.Supp. 977 (prospectus advertising).

19. Kimball v. Bangs, 1887, 144 Mass. 321, 11 N.E. 113. "There are some kinds of talk which no sensible man takes seriously, and if he does he suffers from his credulity. If we were all scrupulously honest, it would not be so; but, as it is, neither party usually believes what the seller says about his own opinions and each knows it. Such statements, like the claims of campaign managers before election, are rather designed to allay the suspicion which would attend their absence than to be understood as having any relation to objective truth." Learned Hand, J., in Vulcan Metals Co. v. Simmons Mfg. Co., 2 Cir. 1918, 248 F. 853.

"The rule of law is hardly to be regretted, when it is considered how easily and insensibly words of hope or expectation are converted by an interested memory into statements of quality or value when the expectation has been disappointed." Holmes, J., in Deming v. Darling, 1889, 148 Mass. 504, 20 N.E. 107.

20. Ireland v. Louis K. Liggett Co., 1922, 243 Mass. 243, 137 N.E. 371; Rowe Mfg. Co. v. Curtis-Straub Co., 1937, 223 Iowa 858, 273 N.W. 895; Michelin Tire Co. v. Schulz, 1929, 295 Pa. 140, 145 A. 67; Keenan v. Cherry & Webb, 1925, 47 R.I. 125, 131 A. 309.

21. Black v. Irvin, 1915, 76 Or. 561, 149 P. 540; Hunter v. McLaughlin, 1873, 43 Ind. 38; French v. Griffin, 1867, 18 N.J.Eq. 279; Rendell v. Scott, 1886, 70 Cal. 514, 11 P. 779.

22. Fisher v. Budlong, 1873, 10 R.I. 525; Smith v. Boothe, 1918, 90 Or. 360, 176 P. 793; Mathews v. Hogueland, 1916, 98 Kan. 342, 157 P. 1179. "It is naught, it is naught, saith the buyer; but when he is gone his way, then he boasteth." Prov. 20:14.

23. Maxwell Ice Co. v. Brackett, Shaw & Lunt Co., 1921, 80 N.H. 236, 116 A. 34 (capacity of machine); Holland Furnace Co. v. Korth, 1953, 43 Wash.2d 618, 262 P.2d 772, 1166 (capacity of furnace); Herzog v. Capital Co., 1945, 27 Cal.2d 349, 164 P.2d 8 (house "in perfect condition"); Glock v. Carpenter, E.D.Ky.1960, 184 F.Supp. 829, affirmed in 6 Cir. 1961, 286 F.2d 431, cert. denied 366 U.S. 930 ("pure, sweet, premium gas"); Traylor Engineering & Mfg. Co. v. National Container Corp., 1949, 6 Terry, Del., 143, 70 A.2d 9 (capacity and qualities of machine).

24. Kulesza v. Wyhowski, 1921, 213 Mich. 189, 182 N.W. 53; Jewell v. Shell Oil Co., 1933, 172 Wash. 603, 21 P.2d 243; Penfield v. Bennett Film Laboratories, 1935, 4 Cal.App.2d 306, 40 P.2d 587; Lloyd v. Junkin, Tex.Civ.App.1934, 75 S.W.2d 712; Law v. Sidney, 1936, 47 Ariz. 1, 53 P.2d 64.

25. Tetreault v. Campbell, 1948, 115 Vt. 369, 61 A.2d 591; Byers v. Federal Land Co., 8 Cir. 1924, 3 F.2d 9; Sacramento Suburban Fruit Lands Co. v. Melin, 9 Cir. 1929, 36 F.2d 907; Reeder v. Guaranteed Foods, Inc., 1965, 194 Kan. 386, 399 P.2d 822; Rothermel v. Phillips, 1928, 292 Pa. 371, 141 A. 241. See Note, 1953, 7 Ark.L.Rev. 154.

26. Fairchild v. McMahon, 1893, 139 N.Y. 290, 34 N. E. 779; Dorr v. Cory, 1899, 108 Iowa 725, 78 N.W. 682; Kohl v. Taylor, 1911, 62 Wash. 678, 114 P.

statement as to the price at which similar property is selling,[27] the amount of an offer made by a third person,[28] the state of the market,[29] or even the lowest price at which a purchase can be made from another.[30] There is a very noticeable tendency to find such additional elements wherever possible, and to give relief by treating statements of value as covering something more than mere opinion.

Misrepresentations of Law

Statements of law likewise are commonly said to be mere assertions of opinion, which are insufficient as a basis for deceit,[31] estop-

pel,[32] or equitable relief.[33] There may ordinarily be no recovery, for example, for a statement that a divorce will be valid,[34] that a writing will have the legal effect of a guaranty,[35] that particular conduct will or will not lead to legal liability,[36] or that the plaintiff will have the legal right to sell liquor.[37] In explanation, two reasons have been repeated, sometimes in the same decision: first, that every man is presumed to know the law, and hence the plaintiff cannot be heard to say that he reasonably believed the statement made to him; [38] and second, that no man, at

874; Knopfler v. Flynn, 1917, 135 Minn. 333, 160 N.W. 860; Stoney Creek Woolen Co. v. Smalley, 1896, 111 Mich. 321, 69 N.W. 722. A few cases have held that the fact is immaterial and the reliance unreasonable. Bishop v. Small, 1874, 63 Me. 12; Cooper v. Lovering, 1870, 106 Mass. 77.

27. Gray v. Wikstrom Motors, 1942, 14 Wash.2d 448, 128 P.2d 490; Brody v. Foster, 1916, 134 Minn. 91, 158 N.W. 824; Weaver v. Cone, 1896, 174 Pa. 104, 34 A. 551; Conlan v. Roemer, 1889, 52 N.J.L. 53, 18 A. 858. Contra, Babb v. Bolyard, 1950, 194 Md. 603, 72 A.2d 13.

28. Kabatchnick v. Hanover-Elm Bldg. Corp., 1952, 328 Mass. 341, 103 N.E.2d 692; Baloyan v. Furniture Exhibition Bldg. Co., 1932, 258 Mich. 244, 241 N.W. 886; Seaman v. Becar, 1896, 15 Misc. 616, 38 N.Y.S. 69; Strickland v. Graybill, 1899, 97 Va. 602, 34 S.E. 675; Smith, Kline & French Co. v. Smith, 1895, 166 Pa. 563, 31 A. 343. See Notes, 1953, 2 De Paul L.Rev. 107; [1952] Wash.U.L.Q. 593; 1953, 7 Ala.L.Rev. 163.

29. Zimmern v. Blount, 5 Cir. 1917, 238 F. 740; Stoll v. Wellborn, N.J.Eq.1903, 56 A. 894; American Hardwood Lumber Co. v. Dent, 1907, 121 Mo.App. 108, 98 S.W. 14; McDonald v. Lastinger, Tex.Civ.App. 1919, 214 S.W. 829.

30. As by a broker to a prospective customer. Hokanson v. Oatman, 1911, 165 Mich. 512, 131 N.W. 111; Estes v. Crosby, 1920, 171 Wis. 73, 175 N.W. 933, amendment of mandate denied 171 Wis. 73, 177 N.W. 512. Contra: Bradley v. Oviatt, 1912, 86 Conn. 63, 84 A. 321; Ripy v. Cronan, 1909, 131 Ky. 631, 115 S.W. 791. In Duvall v. Walton, 1932, 107 Fla. 60, 144 So. 318, the principal was held not liable, on the ground that he would not have been liable if he had made such a representation himself.

31. Gormely v. Gymnastic Ass'n, 1882, 55 Wis. 350, 13 N.W. 242; Metzger v. Baker, 1933, 93 Colo. 165, 24 P.2d 748; Meacham v. Halley, 5 Cir. 1939, 103

F.2d 967; Unckles v. Hentz, 1896, 18 Misc. 644, 43 N.Y.S. 749; Yappel v. Mozina, 1929, 33 Ohio App. 371, 169 N.E. 315. It is possible to warrant the law expressly, Municipal Metallic Bed Mfg. Corporation v. Dobbs, 1930, 253 N.Y. 313, 171 N.E. 75, but certainly the intent to warrant must be made clear.

32. Sturm v. Boker, 1893, 150 U.S. 312; Aunt Jemima Mills Co. v. Rigney & Co., 2 Cir., 1917, 247 F. 407, cert. denied, 245 U.S. 672; Shapley v. Abbott, 1870, 42 N.Y. 443.

33. Adkins v. Hoskins, 1928, 176 Ark. 565, 3 S.W.2d 322; Dillman v. Nadlehoffer, 1886, 119 Ill. 567, 7 N.E. 88; Champion v. Woods, 1889, 79 Cal. 17, 21 P. 534; Abbott v. Treat, 1886, 78 Me. 121, 3 A. 44. Cf. Jaggar v. Winslow, 1883, 30 Minn. 263, 15 N.W. 242 (defense of fraud); McFarland v. Hueners, 1920, 96 Or. 579, 190 P. 584 (same).

34. Christopher v. Whitmire, 1945, 199 Ga. 200, 34 S.E.2d 100.

35. Ackerman v. Bramwell Inv. Co., 1932, 80 Utah 52, 12 P.2d 623.

36. Williams v. Dougherty County, 1960, 101 Ga.App. 193, 113 S.E.2d 168; Goodspeed v. MacNaughton, Greenawalt & Co., 1939, 288 Mich. 1, 284 N.W. 621.

37. Ad. Dernehl & Sons Co. v. Detert, 1925, 186 Wis. 113, 202 N.W. 207. Cf. Metzger v. Baker, 1933, 93 Colo. 165, 24 P.2d 748 (zoning ordinance will prevent another drug store); McDonald v. Goodman, Ky.1951, 239 S.W.2d 97 (law requires an autopsy); Vokal v. United States, 9 Cir. 1949, 177 F.2d 619 (plaintiffs subject to renegotiation statute).

38. See Beall v. McGehee, 1876, 57 Ala. 438; Abbott v. Treat, 1886, 78 Me. 121, 3 A. 44; Burt v. Bowles, 1879, 69 Ind. 1. It has, of course, been pointed out many times that there is never a "presumption" that any man knows the law. The proper statement is that, in many situations, ignorance of the law is no excuse—a very different thing. See Broom's Legal Maxims, 9th Ed. 1924, 178–188.

Abbott, C.J.: "No attorney is bound to know all the law. God forbid that it should be imagined that an

least without special training, can be expected to know the law, and so the plaintiff must have understood that the defendant was giving him nothing more than an opinion.[39] The contradiction is sufficiently obvious; and both reasons are challenged in turn by the contrast of the generally accepted holding that statements as to the law of a foreign state are to be regarded as representations of fact, on which the plaintiff may reasonably rely.[40] The general rule seems to have arisen rather out of a deliberate policy requiring the parties to a bargain to deal at arm's length with respect to the law, and not to rely upon one another.

The present tendency is strongly in favor of eliminating the distinction between law and fact as "useless duffle of an older and more arbitrary day," [41] and recognizing that a statement as to the law, like a statement as to anything else, may be intended and understood either as one of fact or one of opinion only, according to the circumstances of the case.[42] Most courts still render lip service to the older rule, but they have been inclined whenever possible to find statements of fact

"implied" in representations as to the law. Thus an assertion that a company has the legal right to do business in a state carries an assurance that it has, as a matter of fact, been duly qualified; [43] a representation that certain lands may be obtained by patent free from mineral reservations amounts to saying that the government does not classify them as mineral lands; [44] and statements as to the title to land,[45] the priority of a particular lien,[46] or the validity of a note,[47] as well as many similar legal conclusions,[48] have been held to convey similar implications of fact. Since it is obvious that representations of law almost never are made in such a vacuum that supporting facts are not to be "implied," [49] it would seem that very little can be left of the "general rule" in the face of a series of such decisions.

attorney, or a counsel, or even a judge, is bound to know all the law." Montriou v. Jeffries, 1825, 2 C & P. 116, 172 Eng.Rep. 51.

39. See Champion v. Woods, 1889, 79 Cal. 17, 21 P. 534; Thompson v. Phoenix Ins. Co., 1883, 72 Me. 55; Fish v. Cleland, 1864, 33 Ill. 238.

40. Wood v. Roeder, 1897, 50 Neb. 476, 70 N.W. 21; Schneider v. Schneider, 1904, 125 Iowa 1, 98 N.W. 159; Hembry v. Parreco, Mun.App.D.C.1951, 81 A. 2d 77. This has been explained on the basis of a supposed analogy to the rule that courts will not take judicial notice of foreign law, which must be proved as a fact. Bethell v. Bethell, 1883, 92 Ind. 318; Epp v. Hinton, 1914, 91 Kan. 513, 138 P. 576. The explanation seems a highly artificial one, where the real question is one of reasonable reliance.

41. Peterson v. First Nat. Bank, 1925, 162 Minn. 369, 375, 203 N.W. 53.

42. Fainardi v. Pausata, R.I.1924, 126 A. 865; Restatement of Restitution, § 55(a), and cases cited in the Supplement, Reporters' Notes to § 55; Restatement of Torts, § 545; Keeton, Fraud—Misrepresentations of Law, 1937, 15 Tex.L.Rev. 409; Notes, 1943, 22 Tex.L.Rev. 102; 1932, 32 Col.L.Rev. 1018; 1925, 73 U.Pa.L.Rev. 307; 1929, 14 Iowa L.Rev. 453.

43. Miller v. Osterlund, 1923, 154 Minn. 495, 191 N.W. 919. Accord: Myers v. Lowery, 1920, 46 Cal.App. 682, 189 P. 793 (accredited hospital); Harris-Emery Co. v. Pitcairn, 1904, 122 Iowa 595, 98 N.W. 476 (powers of insurance company); Kerr v. Shurtluff, 1914, 218 Mass. 167, 105 N.E. 871 (power of college to grant medical degree).

44. Pieh v. Flitton, 1927, 170 Minn. 29, 211 N.W. 964; Moreland v. Atchison, 1857, 19 Tex. 303.

45. Motherway v. Wall, 1897, 168 Mass. 333, 47 N.E. 135; Barnett v. Kunkle, 8 Cir. 1919, 256 F. 644, appeal dismissed Harjo v. Kunkle, 1921, 254 U.S. 620; Baldock v. Johnson, 1887, 14 Or. 542, 13 P. 434. See Note, 1942, 30 Cal.L.Rev. 197.

46. Kehl v. Abram, 1904, 210 Ill. 218, 71 N.E. 347; Faust v. Hosford, 1903, 119 Iowa 97, 93 N.W. 58.

47. Brown v. Rice's Adm'r, 1875, 26 Grat.,Va., 467.

48. Westervelt v. Demarest, 1884, 46 N.J.L. 37 (liability of directors); Commercial Sav. Bank v. Kietges, 1928, 206 Iowa 90, 219 N.W. 44 (same); Kathan v. Comstock, 1909, 140 Wis. 427, 122 N.W. 1044 (legal effect of tax deeds); Unger v. Eagle Fish Co., 1945, 185 Misc. 134, 56 N.Y.S.2d 265, affirmed 269 App.Div. 950, 58 N.Y.S.2d 332 (no price ceiling on frozen fish); Sorenson v. Gardner, 1959, 215 Or. 255, 334 P.2d 471 (compliance of house with state building code).

49. See Eaglesfield v. Marquis of Londonderry, 1877, L.R. 4 Ch. 693; West London Commercial Bank v. Kitson, 1884, 13 Q.B.D. 360. See also the discussion as to what is "law" in the Note, 1932, 32 Col.L.Rev. 1018, 1028–1030.

Justifiable Reliance on Opinion

The courts have developed numerous exceptions to the rule that misrepresentations of opinion are not a basis for relief. Apparently all of these may be summed up by saying that they involve situations where special circumstances make it very reasonable or probable that the plaintiff should accept the defendant's opinion and act upon it, and so justify a relaxation of the distrust which is considered admirable between bargaining opponents.[50] Thus where the parties stand in a relation of trust and confidence, as in the case of members of the same family,[51] partners,[52] attorney and client,[53] executor and beneficiary of an estate,[54] principal and agent,[55] insurer and insured,[56] close friendship,[57] and the like,[58] it is held that reliance upon an opinion, whether it be as to a fact or a matter of law, is justifiable, and relief is granted.

Further than this, it has been recognized very often that the expression of an opinion may carry with it an implied assertion, not only that the speaker knows no facts which would preclude such an opinion,[59] but that he does know facts which justify it.[60] There is quite general agreement that such an assertion is to be implied where the defendant holds himself out [61] or is understood as having special knowledge of the matter which is not available to the plaintiff, so that his opinion becomes in effect an assertion summarizing his knowledge. Thus the ordinary man is free to deal in reliance upon the opinion of an expert jeweler as to the value of a diamond,[62] of an attorney upon a point of law,[63]

---

50. See Keeton, Fraud—Misrepresentations of Opinion, 1937, 21 Minn.L.Rev. 643; Notes, 1948, 28 Bos. U.L.Rev. 352; 1928, 13 Corn.L.Q. 140; 1932, 32 Col. L.Rev. 1018; 1929, 14 Iowa L.Rev. 453; 1938, 38 Col.L.Rev. 1110.

51. Sims v. Ferrill, 1872, 45 Ga. 585; Baldock v. Johnson, 1887, 14 Or. 542, 13 P. 434; Collins v. Lindsay, Mo.1930, 25 S.W.2d 84; cf. Jekshewitz v. Groswald, 1929, 265 Mass. 413, 164 N.E. 609 (affianced).

52. Teachout v. Van Hoesen, 1878, 76 Iowa 113, 40 N.W. 96.

53. Ward v. Arnold, 1958, 52 Wash.2d 581, 328 P.2d 164 (law); Rice v. Press, 1953, 117 Vt. 442, 94 A. 2d 397 (legal right to fee); Benson v. Bunting, 1900, 127 Cal. 532, 59 P. 991; Allen v. Frawley, 1900, 106 Wis. 638, 82 N.W. 593; Hicks v. Deemer, 1899, 87 Ill.App. 384. Cf. Squyres v. Christan, Tex.Civ.App. 1951, 242 S.W.2d 786, error dismissed (accountant).

54. Stephens v. Collison, 1911, 249 Ill. 225, 94 N.W. 664; Schuttler v. Brandfass, 1895, 41 W.Va. 201, 23 S.E. 808; Tompkins v. Hollister, 1886, 60 Mich. 470, 27 N.W. 651.

55. Rogers v. Brummet, 1923, 92 Okl. 216, 220 P. 362; Cheney v. Gleason, 1873, 125 Mass. 166.

56. Colby v. Life Indemnity & Inv. Co., 1894, 57 Minn. 510, 59 N.W. 539; Knox v. Anderson, D.Hawaii 1958, 159 F.Supp. 795, supplemented 162 F.Supp. 338; Stark v. Equitable Life Assur. Soc., 1939, 205 Minn. 138, 285 N.W. 466.

57. Erickson v. Frazier, 1926, 169 Minn. 118, 210 N.W. 868; Spiess v. Brandt, 1950, 230 Minn. 246, 41 N.W. 2d 561; Casper v. Bankers' Life Ins. Co. of Lincoln, 1927, 238 Mich. 300, 212 N.W. 970.

58. Rowe v. Phillips, 1919, 214 Ill.App. 582 (banker and investor); Hassman v. First State Bank, 1931,

183 Minn. 453, 236 N.W. 921 (confidence reposed for ten years); Pulliam v. Gentry, 1925, 206 Ky. 763, 268 S.W. 557 (past business association); Dombrowski v. Tomasino, 1965, 27 Wis.2d 378, 134 N.W.2d 420 (past reliance); Emily v. Bayne, Mo.App.1963, 371 S.W.2d 663 (law).

59. Zingale v. Mills Novelty Co., 1943, 244 Wis. 144, 11 N.W.2d 644.

60. Shepherd v. Kendrick, 1938, 236 Ala. 289, 181 So. 782. Cf. Ward v. Jenson, 1918, 87 Or. 314, 170 P. 538, where the opinion was "so blended with statements of fact supporting it" as to carry an inference that it was itself a statement of fact.

61. Lambach v. Lundberg, 1934, 177 Wash. 568, 33 P.2d 105 (express assertion); Eno Brick Corp. v. Barber-Greene Co., 1968, 109 N.H. 156, 245 A.2d 545.

62. Picard v. McCormick, 1862, 11 Mich. 68. Accord: Carruth v. Harris, 1894, 41 Neb. 789, 60 N.W. 106 (corporate officer to purchaser of stock); Fourth Nat. Bank in Wichita v. Webb, 1930, 131 Kan. 167, 290 P. 1 (bank dealing in oil stock to inexperienced farmers); Haserot v. Keller, 1924, 67 Cal.App. 659, 228 P. 383 (inventor to co-owner of patent); Warwick v. Corbett, 1919, 106 Wash. 554, 180 P. 928 (owner of business representing profits to be made).

63. Sainsbury v. Pennsylvania Greyhound Lines, 3 Cir. 1950, 183 F.2d 548; Security Sav. Bank v. Kellams, 1928, 321 Mo. 1, 9 S.W.2d 967; Rosenberg v. Cyrowski, 1924, 227 Mich. 508, 198 N.W. 905; Bowman v. Payne, 1921, 55 Cal.App. 789, 204 P. 406; Regus v. Schartkoff, 1957, 156 Cal.App.2d 382, 319 P.2d 721.

of a physician upon a matter of health,[64] of a banker upon the validity of a signature,[65] or the owner of land at a distance as to its worth,[66] even though the opinion is that of his antagonist in a bargaining transaction. On the same basis it has been held that statements by a seller as to the capacity of the thing sold,[67] or the condition of land,[68] or other matters,[69] which on the part of one without special knowledge would be regarded as mere opinion, may be relied on as statements of fact.

Notwithstanding the finding of an implied assertion of fact, the true reason for these holdings appears to be that when the parties do not purport to be dealing on an equal footing as to available information, the basis for the individualistic approach of the common law is destroyed.[70] This is borne out by the fact that the plaintiff is allowed to recover when the disparity of knowledge arises, not from any special information on the part of the defendant, but from the ignorance or illiteracy of the plaintiff.[71] Consistent with this is the further exception which allows recovery where the defendant, after expressing his opinion, makes use of artifice or trickery to prevent further investigation, and so deprives the plaintiff of other sources of information.[72] And for the same reason, where the opinion is that of one who purports to be a disinterested person, not involved in any dealing with the plaintiff, it is generally agreed that there may be reasonable reliance upon it.[73]

64. Hedin v. Minneapolis Medical & Surgical Institute, 1895, 62 Minn. 146, 64 N.W. 158; St. Louis & S. F. R. Co. v. Reed, 1913, 37 Okl. 350, 132 P. 355; Brown v. Ocean Accident & Guarantee Corp., 1913, 153 Wis. 196, 140 N.W. 1112. Accord: Rodee v. Seaman, 1914, 33 S.D. 184, 145 N.W. 441 (real estate expert); Board of Water Com'rs v. Robbins & Potter, 1910, 82 Conn. 623, 74 A. 938 (engineer); Vilett v. Moler, 1900, 82 Minn. 12, 84 N.W. 452 (expert barber school); Powell v. Fletcher, N.Y.C.P. 1892, 18 N.Y.S. 451 (violin expert); McDonald v. Lastinger, Tex.Civ.App.1919, 214 S.W. 829 (stockbroker selling bonds).

65. Wilson v. Jones, Tex.Comm.App.1932, 45 S.W.2d 572. Accord, Sparks v. Guaranty State Bank, 1956, 179 Kan. 236, 293 P.2d 1017 (credit of drawer of a check).

66. Scott v. Burnight, 1906, 131 Iowa 507, 107 N.W. 422; Heal v. Stoll, 1922, 176 Wis. 137, 185 N.W. 242; Bonnarjee v. Pike, 1919, 43 Cal.App. 502, 185 P. 479; Long v. Freeman, 1934, 228 Mo.App. 1002, 69 S.W.2d 973. Cf. Smith v. Land & House Prop. Corp., 1884, L.R. 28 Ch.Div. 7 (statement by landlord as to his tenant).

67. F. B. Connelly Co. v. Schleuter Bros., 1923, 69 Mont. 65, 220 P. 163; Schmitt v. Ornes Esswein & Co., 1921, 149 Minn. 370, 183 N.W. 840; Burroughs Adding Mach. Co. v. Scandinavian-American Bank, D.Wash.1917, 239 F. 179; Pitney Bowes, Inc. v. Sirkle, Ky.1952, 248 S.W.2d 920.

68. Doran v. Milland Development Co., 1958, 159 Cal. App.2d 322, 323 P.2d 792.

69. Aldrich v. Worley, 1925, 200 Iowa 1009, 205 N. W. 851 (suitability of land for raising rice); F. H. Smith Co. v. Low, 1927, 57 App.D.C. 167, 18 F.2d 817 (value of property sold); Coleman v. Night Commander Lighting Co., 1928, 218 Ala. 196, 118 So. 377 (expected carbide consumption of lighting plant); Mears v. Accomac Banking Co., 1933, 160 Va. 311, 168 S.E. 740 (bonds as good investment); Bankers Bond Co. v. Cox, 1936, 263 Ky. 481, 92 S. W.2d 790 (seller's bonds better than buyer's); Sluss v. Brown-Crummer Inv. Co., 1936, 143 Kar. 14, 53 P.2d 900 (bonds "gilt edge," "safe and sound").

70. Shepherd v. Woodson, Mo.1959, 328 S.W.2d 1; Gugel v. Neitzel, 1929, 248 Mich. 312, 226 N.W. 869; cf. Gable v. Niles Holding Co., 1941, 209 Minn. 445, 296 N.W. 525.

Compare Powell v. Fletcher, 1892, 45 N.Y. 294, 18 N.Y.S. 451 (violin expert to layman) and Plimpton v. Friedberg, 1933, 110 N.J.L. 427, 166 A. 295 (art expert to layman), with Banner v. Lyon & Healy Co., 1937, 249 App.Div. 569, 293 N.Y.S. 236, affirmed, 1938, 277 N.Y. 570, 13 N.E.2d 774 (violin expert to experienced violinist); Smith v. Zimbalist, 1934, 2 Cal.App.2d 324, 38 P.2d 170 (same).

71. Benedict v. Heirs of Dickens, 1935, 119 Conn. 541, 177 A. 715; Crofford v. Bowden, Tex.Civ.App.1958, 311 S.W.2d 954, error refused; Ellis v. Gordon, 1930, 202 Wis. 134, 231 N.W. 585; Hoptowit v. Brown, 1921, 115 Wash. 661, 198 P. 370; Kraus v. National Bank of Commerce, 1918, 140 Minn. 108, 167 N.W. 353.

72. Adan v. Steinbrecher, 1911, 116 Minn. 174, 133 N.W. 477; Crompton v. Beedle & Thomas, 1910, 83 Vt. 287, 75 A. 331; Owens v. Norwood-White Coal Co., 1919, 188 Iowa 1092, 174 N.W. 851. Cf. Mattauch v. Walsh Bros. & Miller, 1907, 136 Iowa 225, 113 N.W. 818; Scheele v. Union Loan & Finance Co., 1937, 200 Minn. 554, 274 N.W. 673.

73. Medbury v. Watson, 1843, 6 Metc., Mass., 246; Batchelder v. Stephenson, 1921, 150 Minn. 215, 184 N.W. 852; Melgreen v. McGuire, 1958, 214 Or. 128,

Prediction and Intention

Ordinarily a prediction as to events to occur in the future is to be regarded as a statement of opinion only, on which the adverse party has no right to rely.[74] It was said very early that "one cannot warrant a thing which will happen in the future,"[75] and where the statement is that prices will remain unchanged,[76] that taxes will be reduced,[77] that cattle will reach a given weight within a specified time,[78] that the plaintiff will be able to obtain a position,[79] or that he will have profitable building lots next to a highway,[80] the law has required him to form his own conclusions. Such prophecy does, however, always carry an implied representation that the speaker knows of no facts which will prevent it from being accomplished;[81] and as

in the case of any other opinion, it has been held that there may be reasonable reliance upon the assertion where the speaker purports to have special knowledge of facts which would justify the expectations he is raising.[82]

On the other hand statements of intention, whether of the speaker himself or of another,[83] usually are regarded as statements of fact.[84] "The state of a man's mind," said Lord Bowen[85] in 1882, "is as much a fact as the state of his digestion;" and this catch phrase has been repeated ever since in explanation of the distinction between prediction and intention. But any statement of an opinion is at least as much an assertion of the fact of a present state of mind; and the justification of the distinction must be that the intention is regarded as a material fact, by which the adverse party may reasonably be expected to govern his conduct.[86] A promise, which carries an implied representation that there is a present intention to carry it out,[87] is recognized everywhere as a proper basis for reliance; and assertions of intention which are not promissory in form

---

327 P.2d 1114; Kenner v. Harding, 1877, 85 Ill. 264; Samp v. Long, 1926, 50 S.D. 492, 210 N.W. 733.

74. Sawyer v. Prickett, 1875, 19 Wall., U.S., 146, 22 L.Ed. 105; McElrath v. Electric Inv. Co., 1911, 114 Minn. 358, 131 N.W. 380; Farwell v. Colonial Trust Co., 8 Cir. 1906, 147 F. 480; Henry v. Continental Bldg. & Loan Assn., 1909, 156 Cal. 667, 105 P. 960; Davis v. Reynolds, 1910, 107 Me. 61, 77 A. 409.

75. Choke, J., in Y.B. 11 Edw. IV, 6.

76. Coe v. Ware, 1930, 271 Mass. 570, 171 N.E. 732; Hilgendorf v. Shuman, 1939, 232 Wis. 625, 288 N.W. 184.

77. 3700 S. Kedzie Bldg. Corp. v. Chicago Steel Foundry Co., 1959, 20 Ill.App.2d 483, 156 N.E.2d 618.

78. Wright v. Couch, Tex.Civ.App.1932, 54 S.W.2d 207. Cf. Kennedy v. Flo-Tronics, Inc., 1966, 274 Minn. 327, 143 N.W.2d 827 (stock would triple in value within a year); Ashalter v. Peterson, 1927, 240 Mich. 64, 214 N.W. 964 (black foxes to be born in particular year).

79. Schwetters v. Des Moines Commercial College, 1925, 199 Iowa 1058, 203 N.W. 265. Cf. Moser v. New York Life Ins. Co., 9 Cir. 1945, 151 F.2d 396 (future earnings).

80. Campbell County v. Braun, 1943, 295 Ky. 96, 174 S.W.2d 1. Cf. Leece v. Griffin, Colo.1962, 371 P.2d 264 (predicted income); Alropa Corp. v. Flatley, 1938, 226 Wis. 561, 277 N.W. 108 (canal to be constructed).

81. Hill v. Stewart, 1956, 93 Ga.App. 792, 92 S.E.2d 829; Patterson v. Correll, 1955, 92 Ga.App. 214, 88 S.E.2d 327, appeal transferred 211 Ga. 372, 86 S.E. 2d 113; Rochester Civic Theater, Inc. v. Ramsey, 8 Cir. 1966, 368 F.2d 748.

82. Claus v. Farmers & Stockgrowers State Bank, 1936, 51 Wyo. 45, 63 P.2d 781; Eastern States Petroleum Co. v. Universal Oil Products Co., 1939, 24 Del.Ch. 11, 3 A.2d 768; Potter v. Crawford, 1934, 106 Vt. 517, 175 A. 229; Freggens v. Clark, 1927, 100 N.J.Eq. 389, 135 A. 681; Russell v. Industrial Transp. Co., 1924, 113 Tex. 441, 251 S.W. 1034, affirmed 258 S.W. 462.

83. Cofield v. Griffin, 1953, 238 N.C. 377, 78 S.E.2d 131; McElrath v. Electric Inv. Co., 1911, 114 Minn. 358, 131 N.W. 380; Jeck v. O'Meara, 1938, 341 Mo. 419, 107 S.W.2d 782; City Deposit Bank v. Green, 1908, 138 Iowa 156, 115 N.W. 893; Shaffer v. Rhyne, Tex.Civ.App.1934, 75 S.W.2d 133. See Note, 1942, 20 Tex.L.Rev. 625.

84. Keeton, Fraud—Statements of Intention, 1937, 15 Tex.L.Rev. 185; Restatement of Torts, § 544; Notes, 1938, 38 Col.L.Rev. 1461; 1945, 24 N.C.L.Rev. 49; 1949, 2 Okl.L.Rev. 365.

85. In Edgington v. Fitzmaurice, 1882, L.R. 29 Chi. Div. 359.

86. See Keeton, Fraud—Statements of Intention, 1937, 15 Tex.L.Rev. 185; Restatement of Torts, § 544.

87. Church v. Swetland, 2 Cir. 1917, 243 F. 289; Feldman v. Witmark, 1926, 254 Mass. 480, 150 N.E. 329;

may be, although they are not always,[88] quite as material and persuasive.[89] All but a few courts[90] regard a misstatement of a present intention as a misrepresentation of a material fact;[91] and a promise made without the intent to perform it[92] is held to be a suffi-

cient basis for an action of deceit,[93] or for restitution or other equitable relief.[94] A very common illustration is the purchase of goods with a preconceived intention not to pay for them.[95] The door is thus opened to a tort remedy which may offer important advantages over any action on the contract itself,[96] including the possibility of the recovery of specific goods surrendered in the course of the transaction.[97] The question frequently arises, whether the action for misrepresentation can be maintained when the promise itself cannot be enforced—as where it is without consideration,[98] is illegal,[99] is barred by the statute of frauds,[1] or

---

Hobaica v. Byrne, 1924, 123 Misc. 107, 205 N.Y.S. 7; Foster v. Dwire, 1924, 51 N.D. 581, 199 N.W. 1017; Maguire v. Maguire, 1927, 171 Minn. 492, 214 N.W. 666.

88. Assertions of a collateral intention, not reasonably understood as a binding obligation, obviously offer less justification for reliance, and occasionally are held not to be enough for an action founded on misrepresentation. Marlin v. Drury, 1951, 124 Mont. 576, 228 P.2d 803; Adams v. Gillig, 1910, 199 N.Y. 314, 92 N.E. 670; Reed v. Cooke, 1932, 331 Mo. 507, 55 S.W.2d 275. See Restatement of Contracts, § 473.

89. Edgington v. Fitzmaurice, 1882, L.R. 29 Ch.Div. 459; Rorer Iron Co. v. Trout, 1887, 83 Va. 397, 2 S.E. 713; Bedell v. Daugherty, 1951, 362 Mo. 598, 242 S.W.2d 572. And a prediction may be made in such terms as to imply an intention to bring it about. McElrath v. Electric Inv. Co., 1911, 114 Minn. 358, 131 N.W. 380.

90. Illinois and Indiana flatly reject the doctrine. Brodsky v. Frank, 1930, 342 Ill. 110, 173 N.E. 775; Sachs v. Blewett, 1933, 206 Ind. 151, 185 N.E. 856. Missouri makes a rather incomprehensible distinction between the intention contained in a promise, which is not actionable in tort, and a collateral intention, for which the action will lie. Younger v. Hoge, 1908, 211 Mo. 444, 111 S.W. 20; Metropolitan Paving Co. v. Brown-Crummer Inv. Co., 1925, 309 Mo. 638, 274 S.W. 815; Ashton v. Buchholz, 1949, 359 Mo. 296, 221 S.W.2d 496. Apparently the same distinction is made in Vermont. Compare, Woods v. Scott, 1935, 107 Vt. 249, 178 A. 886, with Comstock v. Shannon, 1950, 116 Vt. 245, 73 A.2d 111.

See, applying Illinois and Missouri law, Gass v. National Container Corp., S.D.Ill.1959, 171 F.Supp. 441, appeal dismissed 271 F.2d 231.

91. See Sallies v. Johnson, 1911, 85 Conn. 77, 81 A. 974; Adams v. Gillig, 1910, 199 N.Y. 314, 92 N.E. 670; Feldman v. Witmark, 1926, 254 Mass. 480, 150 N.E. 329. See Burdick, Deceit by False Statement of Intent, 1918, 3 So.L.Q. 118; Keeton, Fraud—Statements of Intention, 1937, 15 Tex.L.Rev. 185; Note, 1938, 38 Col.L.Rev. 1461.

92. In Elk Refining Co. v. Daniel, 4 Cir. 1952, 199 F. 2d 479, under West Virginia Law, it was held that the mere absence of an intent to perform is enough, and that a positive intent not to perform is not required.

The same is true when the defendant knows that the promise cannot be carried out. Taylor v. Court, 1962, 20 App.Div.2d 699, 246 N.Y.S.2d 962.

93. Sweet v. Kimball, 1896, 166 Mass. 332, 44 N.E. 243; Sabo v. Delman, 1957, 3 N.Y.2d 155, 164 N.Y. S.2d 714, 143 N.E.2d 906; Hunt v. Goodimate Co., 1947, 94 N.H. 421, 55 A.2d 75; Page v. Pilot Life Ins. Co., 1939, 197 S.C. 88, 14 S.E.2d 625; Kauffman v. Bobo & Wood, 1950, 99 Cal.App.2d 322, 221 P.2d 750.

94. Morgan v. Morgan, 1946, 94 N.H. 116, 47 A.2d 569; Waddell v. White, 1940, 56 Ariz. 420, 108 P. 2d 565, 109 P.2d 843; Brittingham v. Huyler's, 1935, 118 N.J.Eq. 352, 179 A. 275; Daniel v. Daniel, 1921, 190 Ky. 210, 226 S.W. 1070; Nelson v. Berkner, 1918, 139 Minn. 301, 166 N.W. 347.

95. Swift v. Rounds, 1896, 19 R.I. 527, 35 A. 45; Burrill v. Stevens, 1882, 73 Me. 395; Donovan v. Clifford, 1917, 225 Mass. 435, 114 N.E. 681; Syracuse Knitting Co. v. Blanchard, 1898, 69 N.H. 447, 43 A. 637.

96. See supra, p. 619.

97. See Dow v. Sanborn, 1861, 3 Allen, Mass., 181; Hotchkin v. Third Nat. Bank, 1891, 127 N.Y. 329, 27 N.E. 1050.

98. Maintainable: Lampesis v. Comolli, 1958, 101 N. H. 279, 140 A.2d 561; Daniel v. Daniel, 1921, 190 Ky. 210, 226 S.W. 1070; Pease & Elliman v. Wegeman, 1928, 223 App.Div. 682, 229 N.Y.S. 398. Contra: Rankin v. Burnham, 1929, 150 Wash. 615, 274 P. 98; Restatement of Contracts, § 473, Comment d.

99. See Keeton, Fraud—Statements of Intention, 1937, 15 Tex.L.Rev. 185, 213–216, concluding that "the parties are never in pari delicto where the promisor does not intend to perform his bargain from the time he made it, and a tort action in deceit should lie, although it is admitted that the opposite conclusion could be supported by a strong argument."

As to infancy of the promisor, see infra, p. 997.

1. See note 1 on page 730.

the statute of limitations,[2] or falls within the parol evidence rule,[3] or a disclaimer of representations.[4]

One group of cases, undoubtedly in the minority, have held that it cannot, arguing that to allow the action would be to permit an evasion of the particular rule of law which makes the promise unenforceable, or that the promisee must be deemed to know the law,

and must be held not to have been deceived by such a promise. The prevailing view, however, permits the action to be maintained, considering that the policy which invalidates the promise is not directed at cases of dishonesty in making it, and that it may still reasonably be relied on even where it cannot be enforced. Obviously the conclusion will depend upon the favor with which the particular rule of law is regarded by the court under the circumstances of the case; but the tendency is clearly to treat the misrepresentation action as a separate matter from the contract.

Unless the present state of mind is misstated, there is of course no misrepresentation. When a promise is made in good faith, with the expectation of carrying it out, the fact that it subsequently is broken gives rise to no cause of action, either for deceit,[5] or for equitable relief.[6] Otherwise any breach of contract would call for such a remedy.[7] The mere breach of a promise is never enough in itself to establish the fraudulent intent.[8] It

1. Maintainable: Burgdorfer v. Thielemann, 1936, 153 Or. 354, 55 P.2d 1122; Channel Master Corp. v. Aluminum Ltd. Sales, Inc., 1958, 4 N.Y.2d 403, 176 N.Y.S.2d 259, 151 N.E.2d 833; Pao Chen Lee v. Gregoriou, 1958, 50 Cal.2d 502, 326 P.2d 135; Charpentier v. Socony-Vacuum Oil Co., 1940, 91 N.H. 38, 13 A.2d 141; Kinkaid v. Rossa, 1913, 31 S.D. 559, 141 N.W. 969.

Contra: Cassidy v. Kraft-Phenix Cheese Corp., 1938, 285 Mich. 426, 280 N.W. 814; Dawe v. Morris, 1889, 149 Mass. 188, 21 N.E. 313; Sachs v. Blewett, 1933, 206 Ind. 151, 185 N.E. 856, rehearing denied, 1934, 206 Ind. 151, 188 N.E. 674. See General Corp. v. General Motors Corp., D.C.Minn.1960, 184 F.Supp. 231, saying that there should be no bar only where tort damages are claimed. See Note, 1958, 7 Buffalo L.Rev. 332.

2. Maintainable: Redgrave v. Hurd, 1881, L.R. 20 Ch.Div. 1; Fidelity-Philadelphia Trust Co. v. Simpson, 1928, 293 Pa. 577, 143 A. 202. Contra: Brick v. Cohn-Hall-Marx, 1937, 276 N.Y. 259, 11 N.E.2d 902.

3. Maintainable: Gifford v. Wichita Falls & S. R. Co., 5 Cir. 1954, 211 F.2d 494; Thomas & Howard Co. v. Fowler, 1954, 225 S.C. 354, 82 S.E.2d 454; Sharkey v. Burlingame Co., 1929, 131 Or. 185, 282 P. 546; Palmetto Bank & Trust Co. v. Grimsley, 1926, 134 S.C. 493, 133 S.E. 437; Kett v. Graeser, 1966, 241 Cal.App.2d 571, 50 Cal.Rptr. 727.

Contra: Beers v. Atlas Assur. Co., 1934, 215 Wis. 165, 253 N.W. 584; McCreight v. Davey Tree Expert Co., 1934, 191 Minn. 489, 254 N.W. 623. See Sweet, Promissory Fraud and the Parol Evidence Rule, 1961, 49 Cal.L.Rev. 877.

4. Maintainable ("fraud vitiates everything it touches"): Nyquist v. Foster, 1954, 44 Wash.2d 465, 268 P.2d 442; Miller v. Troy Laundry Machinery Co., 1936, 178 Okl. 313, 62 P.2d 975; S. Pearson & Son v. Lord Mayor of Dublin, [1907] A.C. 351; Katz v. Dunn, 1934, 285 Mass. 340, 189 N.E. 54.

Contra: Abbot v. Stevens, 1955, 133 Cal.App.2d 242, 284 P.2d 159; Danann Realty Corp. v. Harris, 1959, 5 N.Y.2d 317, 184 N.Y.S.2d 599, 157 N.E.2d 597; cf. Billington v. Vest, Tex.Civ.App.1954, 268 S.W.2d 705.

5. Ford v. C. E. Wilson & Co., 2 Cir. 1942, 129 F.2d 614; Kirk v. Vaccaro, 1955, 344 Mich. 226, 73 N.W. 2d 871; Sparks v. Rudy Fick, Inc., Mo.App.1958, 309 S.W.2d 687; Beach v. Fleming, 1958, 214 Ga. 303, 104 S.E.2d 427; Hills Transp. Co. v. Southwest Forest Industries, 1968, 266 Cal.App.2d 702, 72 Cal. Rptr. 441. And when the defendant has an option to do one of two things, an intent not to do one is not enough. Blake v. Paramount Pictures, S.D.Cal. 1938, 22 F.Supp. 249.

6. Bigelow v. Barnes, 1913, 121 Minn. 148, 140 N.W. 1032; Stewart v. Larkin, 1913, 74 Wash. 681, 134 P. 186; Farwell v. Colonial Trust Co., 8 Cir. 1906, 147 F. 480.

7. See Brooks v. Pitts, 1919, 24 Ga.App. 386, 100 S.E. 776. As to a broken promise as a possible basis for action in tort, see supra, § 92.

8. Justheim Petroleum Co. v. Hammond, 10 Cir. 1955, 227 F.2d 629; Galotti v. United States Trust Co., 1957, 335 Mass. 496, 140 N.E.2d 449; Conzelmann v. Northwest Poultry & Dairy Products Co., 1950, 190 Or. 332, 225 P.2d 757; Fanger v. Leeder, 1951, 327 Mass. 501, 99 N.E.2d 533; Janssen v. Carolina Lumber Co., 1952, 137 W.Va. 561, 73 S.E.2d 12.

Cf. Pybus v. Grasso, 1945, 317 Mass. 716, 59 N.E.2d 289 (promise to convey land which defendant did not own, but might still acquire); Lowe v. Kohn,

may, however, be inferred from the circumstances, such as the defendant's insolvency [9] or other reason to know that he cannot pay,[10] or his repudiation of the promise soon after it is made, with no intervening change in the situation,[11] or his failure even to attempt any performance,[12] or his continued assurances after it is clear that he will not do so.[13]

So far as estoppel is concerned, the courts have gone to considerable lengths to avoid the injustice which may result from reliance on a broken promise, by developing a doctrine of "promissory estoppel," [14] whose chief function has been to provide a substitute for consideration in enforcing contract liability. Discussion of that doctrine is necessarily beyond the scope of this text.

110. DAMAGES

Since the modern action of deceit is a descendant of the older action on the case, it

carries over the requirement that the plaintiff must have suffered substantial damage before the cause of action can arise.[15] Nominal damages are not awarded in deceit,[16] and there can be no recovery if the plaintiff is none the worse off for the misrepresentation, however flagrant it may have been, as where for example he receives all the value that he has been promised and has paid for,[17] or is induced to do only what his legal duty would require him to do in any event.[18] The same is undoubtedly true of any negligence action for misrepresentation.[19] The damages must be established with reasonable certainty, and must not be speculative or contingent,[20] although a loss reasonably certain to occur in the future, such as an established liability to a third person, may be compensated.[21] Much the same rule is applied to estoppel, where the party misled must have changed his po-

1941, 128 Conn. 45, 20 A.2d 407 ("promise" that third party would guarantee plaintiff against loss).

9. City of Southport v. Williams, E.D.N.C.1923, 290 F. 488, affirmed, 4 Cir. 1924, 298 F. 1023; Gillespie v. Piles, 8 Cir. 1910, 178 F. 886; In re Barnet Mfg. Co., D.Mass.1926, 11 F.2d 873. See Note, 1950, 11 U.Pitts.L.Rev. 666.

10. Evola Realty Co. v. Westerfield, Ky.1952, 251 S. W.2d 298; California Conserving Co. v. D'Avanzo, 2 Cir. 1933, 62 F.2d 528; Watson v. Silsby, 1896, 166 Mass. 57, 43 N.E. 1117; In re Whitewater Lumber Co., D.Ala.1925, 7 F.2d 410.

11. Guy T. Bisbee Co. v. Granite City Inv. Co., 1924, 159 Minn. 238, 109 N.W. 14; Dowd v. Tucker, 1874, 41 Conn. 197.

12. Law v. Sidney, 1936, 47 Ariz. 1, 53 P.2d 64; Foster v. Dwire, 1924, 51 N.D. 581, 199 N.W. 1017; Chicago, T. & M. C. R. Co. v. Titterington, 1892, 84 Tex. 218, 19 S.W. 472.

13. Charpentier v. Socony-Vacuum Oil Co., 1940, 91 N.H. 38, 13 A.2d 141.

14. See 1 Williston, Contracts, Rev.Ed.1936, §§ 139, 140; Restatement of Contracts, § 90; Boyer, Promissory Estoppel: Requirements and Limitations of the Doctrine, 1950, 98 U.Pa.L.Rev. 459; Fuller and Perdue, The Reliance Interest in Contract Damages, 1937, 46 Yale L.J. 52, 373; Snyder, Promissory Estoppel as Tort, 1949, 35 Iowa L.Rev. 28; Notes, 1938, 22 Minn.L.Rev. 843; 1939, 48 Yale L.J. 1036.

15. Casey v. Welch, Fla.1951, 50 So.2d 124; Tsang v. Kan, 1947, 78 Cal.App.2d 275, 177 P.2d 630; Castleman v. Stryker, 1923, 107 Or. 48, 213 P. 436; Benson v. Garrett Inv. Co., 1955, 135 Cal.App.2d 853, 287 P.2d 405; Dilworth v. Lauritzen, 1967, 18 Utah 2d 386, 424 P.2d 136.

16. Alden v. Wright, 1891, 47 Minn. 225, 49 N.W. 767; Bailey v. Oatis, 1911, 85 Kan. 339, 116 P. 830; Castelli v. Abramo, Mun.Ct.N.Y.1956, 12 Misc.2d 145, 176 N.Y.S.2d 525; and cases cited immediately above in note 15. They may, however, be awarded where there is proof that actual damage has occurred, but no proof as to the amount. Oates v. Glover, 1934, 228 Ala. 656, 154 So. 786.

17. See infra, p. 734.

18. Musconetcong Iron Works v. Delaware, L. & W. R. Co., 1909, 78 N.J.L. 717, 76 A. 971; Story v. Conger, 1867, 36 N.Y. 673.

19. See supra, p. 704. Cf. Heyer v. Flaig, 1969, 70 Cal.2d 223, 74 Cal.Rptr. 225, 449 P.2d 161.

20. Ansley v. Bank of Piedmont, 1896, 113 Ala. 467, 21 So. 59; Fitzsimmons v. Chapman, 1877, 37 Mich. 139, 26 Am.Rep. 508 (speculative); Freeman v. Venner, 1876, 120 Mass. 424; Dunn & McCarthy v. Bishop, R.I.1914, 90 A. 1073 (contingent).

21. Hoffman v. Toft, 1914, 70 Or. 488, 142 P. 365; Ely v. Stannard, 1878, 46 Conn. 124; Luetzke v. Roberts, 1906, 130 Wis. 97, 109 N.W. 949. Cf. Briggs v. Brushaber, 1880, 43 Mich. 330, 5 N.W. 383 (loan on poor security); Currier v. Poor, 1898, 155 N.Y. 344, 49 N.E. 937.

sition substantially [22] to his prejudice; [23] but, since the purpose of the principle is to prevent the one estopped from taking inequitable advantage, it is sufficient that there will be prejudice if the estoppel is denied.[24]

Furthermore, the damage upon which a deceit action rests must have been "proximately caused" by the misrepresentation. So far as the fact of causation is concerned, any loss which follows upon a transaction into which the misstatement induces the plaintiff to enter may be said to be caused by it; but the same considerations which limit liability in cases of tangible harm [25] have operated here. In general, with only a few exceptions,[26] the courts have restricted recovery to those damages which might foreseeably be expected to follow from the character of the misrepresentation itself.[27] Thus if the plaintiff stores his goods in a warehouse represented to him to be fireproof, and they are destroyed when it burns down, he can recover; [28] and likewise where he invests in an automobile agency after false assurances of profits made by similar agencies, and goes bankrupt.[29] But if false statements are made

in connection with the sale of corporate stock, losses due to a subsequent decline of the market, or insolvency of the corporation, brought about by business conditions or other factors in no way related to the representations, will not afford any basis for recovery.[30] It is only where the fact misstated was of a nature calculated to bring about such a result [31] that damages for it can be recovered. Sometimes this has been expressed by saying that the representation in such a case is "immaterial" to the result; but the conclusion is reached even though the plaintiff has in fact relied, and justifiably so, upon what he has been told.

When restitution is sought, either in equity or at law,[32] a much more liberal policy has been adopted.[33] Since the purpose is not to compensate the plaintiff's loss, but to restore what the defendant has received, the courts look to the inequity of allowing him to retain it, rather than to the damage which the plaintiff has sustained. It is often repeated that damage must be shown for rescission, and recovery has been denied on that basis; [34]

22. Hardin's Adm'rs v. Hardin, 1923, 201 Ky. 310, 256 S.W. 417; Ashwander v. Tennessee Valley Authority, 1936, 297 U.S. 288; Third Nat. Bank v. Merchants' Nat. Bank, 1894, 76 Hun 475, 27 N.Y.S. 1070.

23. Boone v. Citizens Bank & Trust Co., 1926, 154 Tenn. 241, 290 S.W. 39; Farley v. Scherno, 1913, 208 N.Y. 269, 101 N.E. 891; Houseman-Spitzley Corporation v. American State Bank, 1919, 205 Mich. 268, 171 N.W. 543; Lindenthal v. Northwest State Bank, 1921, 221 Ill.App. 145.

24. Queen Ins. Co. of America v. Baker, 1935, 174 Okl. 273, 50 P.2d 371.

25. See supra, ch. 7.

26. Fottler v. Moseley, 1901, 179 Mass. 295, 60 N.E. 788; affirmed, 1904, 185 Mass. 563, 70 N.E. 1040. Accord: David v. Belmont, 1935, 291 Mass. 450, 197 N.E. 83.

27. See Note, 1955, 43 Cal.L.Rev. 356.

28. Rosenblatt v. John F. Ivory Storage Co., 1933, 262 Mich. 513, 247 N.W. 733. See also Mortimer v. Otto, 1912, 206 N.Y. 89, 99 N.E. 189; The Normannia, S.D.N.Y.1894, 62 F. 469.

29. Hanson v. Ford Motor Co., 8 Cir. 1960, 278 F.2d 586. A particularly good opinion.

30. Waddell v. White, 1940, 46 Ariz. 420, 108 P.2d 565, 109 P.2d 843; Morrell v. Wiley, 1935, 119 Conn. 578, 178 A. 121; Boatmen's National Co. v. M. W. Elkins & Co., 8 Cir. 1933, 63 F.2d 214; Beare v. Wright, 1905, 14 N.D. 26, 103 N.W. 632; Morgan v. Hodge, 1911, 145 Wis. 143, 129 N.W. 1083.

Cf. Ward Cook, Inc. v. Davenport, 1966, 243 Or. 301, 413 P.2d 387 (embezzlement).

31. Haentze v. Loehr, 1940, 233 Wis. 583, 290 N.W. 163. In Hotaling v. A. B. Leach Co., 1928, 247 N.Y. 84, 159 N.E. 870, where bonds were bought for investment and "weakness inherent in the investment" was covered by the misrepresentations, recovery was allowed for a collapse during a subsequent financial crisis. But in People v. S. W. Straus & Co., 1935, 156 Misc. 642, 282 N.Y.S. 972, it was denied where the loss was found to be due entirely to external economic conditions.

32. Seneca Wire & Mfg. Co. v. A. B. Leach & Co., 1928, 247 N.Y. 1, 159 N.E. 700.

33. McCleary, Damage as Requisite to Rescission for Misrepresentation, 1937, 36 Mich.L.Rev. 1, 227; Notes, 1935, 48 Harv.L.Rev. 480; 1934, 32 Mich.L. Rev. 968.

34. Jakway v. Proudfit, 1906, 76 Neb. 62, 106 N.W. 1039, 109 N.W. 388; Russell v. Industrial Transp.

but the assertion is so far honored in the breach that it has little or no validity.[35] The plaintiff will not be permitted to rescind where he has received substantially what he bargained for,[36] or where subsequent events have made the representation good.[37] But sufficient "damage" has been found, or dispensed with, where the plaintiff has received property of a different character or condition than he was promised, although of equal value,[38] where the transaction proves to be less advantageous than as represented, although there is no actual loss; [39] and where the false statement was important to the

plaintiff for reasons personal to himself, not affecting any financial value or profit.[40] It seems correct to say rather that damage is not essential to rescission, but that it is merely one factor to be considered in determining whether it is equitable to allow the transaction to stand.[41]

Where misrepresentation is set up as a defense to an action brought by the adverse party, the prevailing confusion as to the character of the defense has obscured the distinction between legal and equitable relief. It is obvious that damage, proximately caused, is necessary where the claim is one of recoupment of a loss by reduction of the amount due; [42] but if the defense takes the form of rescission of the bargain, with restoration of what has been received, no more damage should be required than in any other case of rescission.[43]

Measure of Damages

The proximity of other forms of relief has been reflected in the conflicting rules which have been adopted as to the normal measure of damages in the action of deceit.[44] The American courts are divided over two standards of measurement. One of these, the so-called "out of pocket" rule, looks to the loss which the plaintiff has suffered in the trans-

---

Co., 1923, 113 Tex. 441, 251 S.W. 1034, affirmed, 1924, 258 S.W. 462; Ziegler v. Stinson, 1924, 111 Or. 243, 224 P. 641; Hewlett v. Saratoga Carlsbad Spring Co., 1895, 84 Hun 248, 32 N.Y.S. 697.

35. Restatement of Contracts, § 476, Comment *c*; McCleary, Damage as Requisite to Rescission for Misrepresentation, 1937, 36 Mich.L.Rev. 1, 227; Note, 1935, 48 Harv.L.Rev. 480.

36. Mason v. Madson, 1931, 90 Mont. 489, 4 P.2d 475; Bomar v. Rosser, 1901, 131 Ala. 215, 31 So. 430; Struve v. Tatge, 1918, 285 Ill. 103, 120 N.E. 549; Aultman, Miller & Co. v. Nilson, 1900, 112 Iowa 634, 84 N.W. 692; Hays v. Hays, 1897, 179 Pa. 277, 36 A. 311. It frequently is held in such cases that the representation is "immaterial," and could not justifiably have induced reliance. See Ziegler v. Stinson, 1924, 111 Or. 243, 224 P. 641; Ryals v. Livingston, 1932, 45 Ga.App. 43, 163 S.E. 286; American Building & Loan Ass'n v. Bear, 1896, 48 Neb. 455, 67 N.W. 500; McCleary, Damage as Requisite to Rescission for Misrepresentation, 1937, 36 Mich.L. Rev. 1, 254.

37. Billingsley v. Benefield, 1908, 87 Ark. 128, 112 S. W. 188; Farwell v. Colonial Trust Co., 8 Cir. 1906, 147 F. 480; National Leather Co. v. Roberts, 6 Cir. 1915, 221 F. 922; Smith v. Johns, 1925, 113 Or. 351, 232 P. 786.

38. Tonkovich v. South Florida Citrus Industries, Inc., Fla.App.1966, 185 So.2d 710, cause remanded 196 So.2d 438, on remand 202 So.2d 579; Mosely v. Johnson, 1954, 90 Ga.App. 165, 82 S.E.2d 163; Nance v. McClellan, 1936, 126 Tex. 580, 89 S.W.2d 774; Dimond v. Peace River Land & Dev. Co., 1918, 182 Iowa 400, 165 N.W. 1032; Hirschman v. Healy, 1925, 162 Minn. 328, 202 N.W. 734.

39. In jurisdictions which adopt the out-of-pocket measure of damages (infra, note 47): King v. Lamborn, 9 Cir. 1911, 186 F. 21; Ludowese v. Amidon, 1914, 124 Minn. 288, 144 N.W. 965; Stillwell v. Rankin, 1918, 55 Mont. 130, 174 P. 186.

40. Brett v. Cooney, 1902, 75 Conn. 338, 53 A. 729, 1124; Williams v. Kerr, 1893, 152 Pa. 560, 25 A. 618; Rice v. Gilbreath, 1898, 119 Ala. 424, 24 So. 421; Thompson v. Barry, 1903, 184 Mass. 429, 68 N.E. 674.

41. Cf. La Bar v. Lindstrom, 1924, 158 Minn. 453, 197 N.W. 756; Baker v. Combs, 1930, 232 Ky. 73, 22 S. W.2d 442; Murphy v. Sheftel, 1932, 121 Cal.App. 533, 9 P.2d 568.

42. Hammatt v. Emerson, 1847, 27 Me. 308.

43. Stuart v. Lester, 1888, 49 Hun 58, 1 N.Y.S. 699, 17 N.Y.St.Rep. 248; Metropolitan Life Ins. Co. v. James, 1935, 231 Ala. 295, 164 So. 377.

44. See McCormick, Damages, 1935, ch. 18; Hannigan, The Measure of Damages in Tort for Deceit, 1938, 18 Bos.U.L.Rev. 681; Rossen and Fairweather, Damages in Fraud Actions, 1964, 13 Cleve. Marsh.L.Rev. 288; Notes, 1964, 11 U.C.L.A.L.Rev. 876; 1939, 23 Minn.L.Rev. 205; 1961, 47 Va.L.Rev. 1209.

action, and gives him the difference between the value of what he has parted with and the value of what he has received. If what he received was worth what he paid for it, he has not been damaged, and there can be no recovery.[45] This rule is followed in deceit actions by the English courts,[46] and by a minority of perhaps a dozen American jurisdictions.[47] It is always adopted as to a defense in the nature of recoupment,[48] and is of course the practical result reached by rescission, where each party is restored to his original position. The other measurement, called the "loss-of-bargain" rule, gives the plaintiff the benefit of what he was promised, and allows recovery of the difference between the actual value of what he has received and the value that it would have had if it had been as represented. This, of course, is the rule applied in contract actions for breach of warranty,[49] and it is consistent with the result in cases of estoppel. It has been adopted by some two-thirds of the courts which have considered the question in actions of deceit.[50] There is the same con-

flict where the recovery is based on negligent misrepresentation.[51]

As a matter of the strict logic of the form of action, the first of these two rules is more consistent with the purpose of tort remedies, which is to compensate the plaintiff for a loss sustained, rather than to give him the benefit of any contract bargain.[52] Also, it must of necessity be adopted where the defendant is a third party who has made no contract with the plaintiff,[53] and it has been contended that the presence of a contract should not change the damages where the action is not on the contract itself.[54] On the other hand, it is urged in support of the majority rule that the form of the action should be of little importance, that in an action in the form of tort for breach of warranty the plaintiff is given the benefit of his bargain and the addition of an allegation of intent to deceive should certainly not decrease his recovery, and that in many cases the out-of-pocket measure will permit the fraudulent defendant to escape all liability and have a chance

45. Urtz v. New York Cent. & H. R. R. Co., 1911, 202 N.Y. 170, 95 N.E. 711; Alden v. Wright, 1891, 47 Minn. 225, 49 N.W. 767; Doyle v. Union Bank & Trust Co., 1936, 102 Mont. 563, 59 P.2d 1171.

46. Peek v. Derry, 1887, L.R. 37 Ch.Div. 541.

47. Beardmore v. T. D. Burgess Co., 1967, 245 Md. 387, 226 A.2d 329; Reno v. Bull, 1919, 226 N.Y. 546, 124 N.E. 144, rearg. denied 227 N.Y. 591, 125 N.E. 924; Heidegger v. Burg, 1917, 137 Minn. 53, 162 N. W. 889; Browning v. Rodman, 1920, 268 Pa. 575, 111 A. 877.

This was formerly the rule of the federal courts. Smith v. Bolles, 1889, 132 U.S. 125.

48. This is true even in warranty cases. Impervious Products Co. v. Gray, 1915, 127 Md. 64, 96 A. 1; Hunter v. Finnerty, 1922, 119 Misc. 724, 197 N.Y.S. 215; Hirschl v. Richards, 1927, 28 Ohio App. 38, 162 N.E. 616.

49. Cf. Uniform Sales Act, § 69(7).

50. Dempsey v. Marshall, Ky.1961, 344 S.W.2d 606; Polley v. Boehck Equipment Co., 1956, 273 Wis. 432, 78 N.W.2d 737; Nelson v. Leo's Auto Sales, Inc., 1962, 158 Me. 368, 185 A.2d 121; Yoder v. Nu-Enamel Corp., 8 Cir. 1944, 145 F.2d 420 (Nebraska

law); Brown v. Ohman, Miss.1949, 42 So.2d 209, suggestion of error overruled, 1950, 43 So.2d 727.

Where this measure is adopted, it has been held to preclude allowance for loss of plaintiff's time, or other out-of-pocket losses. Salter v. Heiser, 1951, 39 Wash.2d 826, 239 P.2d 327.

51. See Morin v. Divide County Abstract Co., 1921, 48 N.D. 214, 183 N.W. 1006 (out of pocket); Williams v. Spazier, Cal.App.1933, 21 P.2d 470 (same); Long v. Douthitt, 1911, 142 Ky. 427, 134 S.W. 453 (loss of bargain); Spreckels v. Gorrill, 1907, 152 Cal. 383, 92 P. 1011 (same); Hartwell Corp. v. Bumb, 9 Cir. 1965, 345 F.2d 453, cert. denied 382 U. S. 891 (same).

52. See Restatement of Torts, § 549; 2 Sedgwick, Measure of Damages, 9th Ed.1912, §§ 780, 781.

53. Macdonald v. Roeth, 1918, 179 Cal. 194, 176 P. 38; Sorensen v. Gardner, 1959, 215 Or. 255, 334 P. 2d 471. Cf. Morin v. Divide County Abstract Co., 1921, 48 N.D. 214, 183 N.W. 1006.

54. See 2 Sedgwick, Measure of Damages, 9th Ed. 1912, 1628. But see Harper and McNeely, A Synthesis of the Law of Misrepresentation, 1938, 22 Minn.L.Rev. 939, 964, 990, 1000, supporting a different rule in the two types of cases.

to profit by the transaction if he can get away with it.[55]

Few courts have followed either rule with entire consistency,[56] and various proposals have been made to introduce some flexibility into the measure of damages. Thus it has been suggested that the loss-of-bargain rule should be applied in cases of intentional misrepresentation, the out-of-pocket rule where it is innocent;[57] that the plaintiff be given the option of either rule,[58] or that the court should adopt the rule which best fits the certainty of the damages proved, and so avoid the possibility that a plaintiff who has suffered a real damage may be denied recovery because he is unable to prove values.[59] A leading Oregon decision,[60] which seems to have given more careful consideration to the problem than any other and now has been followed in a few other jurisdictions,[61] reduces the matter to four rules, as follows:

1. If the defrauded party is content with the recovery of only the amount he has actually lost, his damages will always be measured under that rule.

2. If the fraudulent transaction also amounted to a warranty, he may recover for loss of the bargain, because a fraud accompanied by a broken promise should cost the wrongdoer as much as the breach of promise alone.

3. Where the circumstances disclosed by the proof are so vague as to cast virtually no light upon the value of the property had it conformed to the representations, damages will be awarded equal to the loss sustained, and

4. Where the damages under the benefit-of-bargain rule are proved with reasonable certainty, that rule will be employed.

In addition to such a normal measure of damages under whatever rule the court may adopt, the plaintiff may recover for consequential damages, such as personal injuries,[62] damage to other property,[63] or expenses to which he has been put,[64] provided that they are regarded as "proximate" results of the misrepresentation.[65] If the deception is

---

55. 5 Williston, Contracts, Rev.Ed.1936, §§ 1391, 1392; Hannigan, The Measure of Damages in Tort for Deceit, 1938, 18 Bos.U.L.Rev. 681.

56. See cases collected in the annotation, 1940, 124 A.L.R. 37; Note, 1930, 34 Dick.L.Rev. 181. As to the New York history, see Note, 1942, 55 Harv.L. Rev. 1019.

57. See McCormick, Damages, 1935, 453, 454, pointing out that the possibility of punitive damages may be a sufficient differentiation as to intentional fraud. The distinction was made, however, in Williams v. Spazier, Cal.App.1933, 21 P.2d 470.

58. See Harper and McNeely, A Synthesis of the Law of Misrepresentation, 1938, 22 Minn.L.Rev. 939, 964, 990, 1000.

59. McCormick, Damages, 1935, 454. This seems in effect to be the result reached by a number of courts. Hines v. Brode, 1914, 168 Cal. 507, 143 P. 729; Jammie v. Robinson, 1921, 114 Wash. 275, 195 P. 6; Monsanto Chemical Works v. American Zinc, Lead & Smelting Co., Mo.1923, 253 S.W. 1006. In the case of the sale of corporate securities, a similar flexibility has been achieved in some cases by looking to the value of the securities at a time after the purchase. See Hotaling v. A. B. Leach & Co., 1928, 247 N.Y. 84, 159 N.E. 870; David v. Belmont, 1935, 291 Mass. 450, 197 N.E. 83; Cartwright v. Hughes, 1933, 226 Ala. 464, 147 So. 399. As to the provisions of the Federal Securities Act, see Shulman, Civil Liability and the Securities Act, 1933, 43 Yale L.J. 227, 244–248.

60. Selman v. Shirley, 1938, 161 Or. 582, 85 P.2d 384, 91 P.2d 312.

61. Weitzel v. Jukich, 1942, 73 Idaho 301, 251 P.2d 542; Zeliff v. Sabatino, 1954, 15 N.J. 70, 104 P.2d 54; United States v. Ben Grunstein & Sons Co., D. N.J.1955, 137 F.Supp. 197; Rice v. Price, 1960, 340 Mass. 502, 164 N.E.2d 891; Salter v. Heiser, 1951, 39 Wash.2d 826, 239 P.2d 327.

62. Vezina v. Souliere, 1931, 103 Vt. 190, 152 A. 798.

63. Sampson v. Penney, 1922, 151 Minn. 411, 187 N. W. 135; Economy Hog & Cattle Powder Co. v. Compton, 1922, 192 Ind. 222, 135 N.E. 1.

64. Edward Barron Estate v. Woodruff Co., 1912, 163 Cal. 561, 126 P. 351; Snyder v. Markham, 1912, 172 Mich. 693, 138 N.W. 234; Commonwealth Fuel Co. v. McNeil, 1925, 103 Conn. 390, 130 A. 794; Garrett v. Perry, 1959, 53 Cal.2d 178, 346 P.2d 758; Cole v. Gerhart, 1967, 5 Ariz.App. 24, 423 P.2d 100; cf. Lowrey v. Dingmann, 1957, 251 Minn. 124, 86 N.W. 2d 499 (loss of other sales, harm to reputation as dealer).

65. Cf. Foster v. De Paolo, 1923, 236 N.Y. 132, 140 N.E. 220.

found to have been deliberate or wanton, punitive damages may be recovered, as in the case of other torts of similar character.[66]

Any act amounting to affirmance of the transaction after the plaintiff has discovered the fraud will preclude the remedy of rescission.[67] But, since the tort action for damages is based on an acceptance of the contract, it is not barred by mere acts of affirmance.[68] If, however, the plaintiff discovers the truth while the contract is still entirely executory,[69] or almost entirely so,[70] and then

performs his part of it, he has been denied recovery for the resulting damages upon the ground that they are self-inflicted, without reliance upon the representation. If he has executed a substantial part of his performance before discovery, it is generally recognized that it is too late to require him to rescind, and that his continued performance is merely affirmance, and not a waiver of his action for damages.[71] He must, however, deal at arm's length and comply with the terms of the contract, asking no modifications,[72] favors or concessions,[73] or he will be held to have surrendered his claim in return for what is in effect a new agreement, replacing the old one.

66. Thompson v. Modern School of Business and Correspondence, 1920, 183 Cal. 112, 190 P. 451; Laughlin v. Hopkinson, 1920, 292 Ill. 80, 126 N.E. 591; Kluge v. Ries, 1917, 66 Ind.App. 610, 117 N.E. 262.

67. Maki v. St. Luke's Hospital Ass'n, 1913, 122 Minn. 444, 142 N.W. 705; Marks v. Stein, 1916, 61 Okl. 59, 160 P. 318 (defense).

68. Van Vliet Fletcher Automobile Co. v. Crowell, 1914, 171 Iowa 64, 149 N.W. 861; Engen v. Merchants' & Mfrs' State Bank, 1925, 164 Minn. 293, 204 N.W. 963.

69. Thompson v. Libby, 1886, 36 Minn. 287, 31 N.W. 52; McDonough v. Williams, 1905, 77 Ark. 261, 92 S.W. 783; Minnesota Thresher Mfg. Co. v. Gruben, 1897, 6 Kan.App. 665, 50 P. 67. See Notes, 1936, 34 Mich.L.Rev. 384; 1930, 14 Minn.L.Rev. 299.

70. Thus where the performance before discovery has been so slight as to be negligible. Simon v. Goodyear Metallic Rubber Shoe Co., 6 Cir. 1900, 105 F. 573; Kingman & Co. v. Stoddard, 7 Cir. 1898, 85 F. 740; Ponder v. Altura Farms Co., 1914, 57 Colo. 519, 143 P. 570.

71. Elson v. Harris, 1959, 356 Mich. 175, 96 N.W.2d 767; Forsberg v. Baker, 1941, 211 Minn. 59, 300 N.W. 371; Weckert v. Wentworth & Irwin, 1920, 129 Or. 342, 277 P. 815; Pryor v. Foster, 1891, 130 N.Y. 171, 29 N.E. 123; Van Natta v. Snyder, 1916, 98 Kan. 102, 157 P. 432.

72. Fryar v. Forrest, Tex.Civ.App.1941, 155 S.W.2d 679; Timmerman v. Gurnsey, 1928, 205 Iowa 35, 217 N.W. 879; Burne v. Lee, 1909, 156 Cal. 221, 104 P. 438; Kintz v. Galvin, 1922, 219 Mich. 48, 188 N.W. 408; Franklin Motor Car Co. v. Hilkert, 1925, 82 Ind.App. 513, 146 N.E. 825.

73. Schmidt v. Mesmer, 1897, 116 Cal. 267, 48 P. 54; Schagun v. Scott Mfg. Co., 8 Cir. 1908, 162 F. 209; Tuttle v. Stovall, 1910, 134 Ga. 325, 67 S.E. 806; Humphrey v. Sievers, 1917, 137 Minn. 373, 163 N.W. 737. See Note, 1930, 14 Minn.L.Rev. 299.

CHAPTER 19

DEFAMATION

111. DEFAMATION

Defamation is made up of the twin torts of libel and slander—the one being, in general, written, while the other in general is oral, with somewhat different rules applicable to each, as will be explained later. In either form, defamation is an invasion of the interest in reputation and good name. This is a "relational" interest,[1] since it involves the opinion which others in the community may have, or tend to have, of the plaintiff. Consequently defamation requires that something be communicated to a third person that may affect that opinion. Derogatory words and insults directed to the plaintiff himself may afford ground for an action for the intentional infliction of mental suffering,[2] but unless they are communicated to another the action cannot be one for defamation,[3] no matter how harrowing they may be to the feelings. Defamation is not concerned with the plaintiff's own humiliation, wrath or sorrow, except as an element of "parasitic" damages attached to an independent cause of action.[4]

It must be confessed at the beginning that there is a great deal of the law of defamation which makes no sense. It contains anomalies and absurdities for which no legal writer ever has had a kind word,[5] and it is a curious compound of a strict liability imposed upon innocent defendants, as rigid and extreme as anything found in the law, with a blind and almost perverse refusal to compensate the plaintiff for real and very serious harm. The explanation is in part one of historical accident and survival, in part one of the conflict of opposing ideas of policy in which our traditional notions of freedom of expression have collided violently with sympathy for the victim traduced and indignation at the maligning tongue.

The actions for defamation developed according to no particular aim or plan.[6] Originally the common law courts took no jurisdiction, leaving defamatory utterances to be dealt with by the local seigniorial courts. When these began to fall into decay, the ecclesiastical courts stepped in, regarding defamation as a sin, and punishing it with penance. As these courts in turn lost their power, there was in the sixteenth century a slow infiltration of tort actions for slander into the common law courts. For a

---

1. Green, Relational Interests, 1936, 31 Ill.L.Rev. 35.

2. See supra, § 12.

3. See infra, p. 766.

4. See infra, p. 761.

5. "No branch of the law has been more fertile of litigation than this (whether plaintiffs be more moved by a keen sense of honour, or by the delight of carrying on personal controversies under the protection and with the solemnities of civil justice), nor has any been more perplexed with minute and barren distinctions. * * * The law went wrong from the beginning in making the damage and not the insult the cause of action." Pollock, Law of Torts, 13th Ed. 1929, 243, 249. See also 1 Street, Foundations of Legal Liability, 1906, 273 ("marred in the making"); Winfield, Law of Tort, 5th Ed. 1950, 244; Veeder, History and Theory of the Law of Defamation, 1904, 4 Col.L.Rev. 33; Carr, The English Law of Defamation, 1902, 18 L.Q.Rev. 255, 388; Courtney, Absurdities of the Law of Slander and Libel, 1902, 36 Am.L.Rev. 552.

considerable length of time there were conflicts over jurisdiction between the two sets of tribunals, which led the common law courts to hold that unless "temporal" damage could be proved, defamation was a "spiritual" matter which should be left to the Church.[7] When the common law jurisdiction was once established, an unexpected flood of actions was let loose upon the judges, who seem to have been annoyed and dismayed by it, and so proceeded to hedge the remedy about with rigid restrictions, some of which still survive.[8]

Later, about the beginning of the seventeenth century, the Court of Star Chamber, of infamous memory, began quite independently to punish the crime of political libel, in order to suppress the seditious publications which had come with the spread of printing. Originating strictly as a crime, and a form of sedition, this was later extended to non-political libels. Later still, tort damages were awarded to the person defamed, probably in order to provide a legal substitute for the duel when it was forbidden. With the abolition of the Star Chamber, jurisdiction over libel in turn passed to the common law courts. They continued, however, to recognize the difference between libel, which was

criminal as well as tortious, and the earlier action for slander, which was not.

One heritage of this haphazard development is the present distinction between libel and slander, to be considered below.[9] Another is the set of arbitrary and illogical rules which surround both, but particularly the latter. Still further difficulties arose when the law of defamation encountered the rising tide of sentiment in favor of freedom of speech and of the press, which, together with hatred of the memory of the Star Chamber, made the action an unpopular one, and the courts somewhat timid in dealing with it.[10] It is to this that we owe the general rule that defamation will not be enjoined,[11] unless it is incident to some other tort,[12] and more indirectly the holding of the Supreme Court of the United States that a statute authorizing injunctions against defamatory publications is an unconstitutional denial of the guaranty of freedom of the press.[13] The late nineteenth century found something of a swing of the pendulum back

---

6. See Veeder, History and Theory of the Law of Defamation, 1903, 3 Col.L.Rev. 546, 1904, 4 Col.L. Rev. 33; Donnelly, History of Defamation, [1949] Wis.L.Rev. 99; Holdsworth, Defamation in the Sixteenth and Seventeenth Centuries, 1924, 40 L.Q.Rev. 302, 397, 1925, 41 L.Q.Rev. 13; Green, Slander and Libel, 1872, 6 Am.L.Rev. 592; Carr, The English Law of Defamation, 1902, 18 L.Q.Rev. 255, 388; 1 Street, Foundations of Legal Liability, 1906, c. XIX; Kelly, Criminal Libel and Free Speech, 1958, 6 Kan.L.Rev. 295. Restatement of Torts, § 568, Comment *b*.

7. See Ogden v. Turner, 1703, 6 Mod.Rep. 104, 87 Eng.Rep. 862; Regina v. Read, 1708, Fortescue 98, 92 Eng.Rep. 777. The common law courts required proof of "temporal" damage. Palmer v. Thorpe, 1883, 4 Co.Rep. 20a, 76 Eng.Rep. 909; Davies v. Gardiner, 1593, Popham 36, 79 Eng.Rep. 1155; Matthew v. Crass, 1614, Cro.Jac. 323, 79 Eng.Rep. 276.

8. See Lovell, The Reception of Defamation by the Common Law, 1962, 15 Vand.L.Rev. 1051.

9. See infra, § 112.

10. See Pound, Eqquitable Relief Against Defamation and Injuries to Personality, 1916, 29 Harv.L. Rev. 640; Shientag, From Seditious Libel to Freedom of the Press, 1942, 11 Brook.L.Rev. 125; Leflar, Legal Liability for the Exercise of Free Speech, 1956, 10 Ark.L.Rev. 155; Leflar, The Free-ness of Free Speech, 1962, 15 Vand.L.Rev. 1073; Sedler, Injunctive Relief and Personal Integrity, 1964, 9 St. L.L.Rev. 147.

11. Kwass v. Kersey, 1954, 139 W.Va. 497, 81 S.E.2d 237; Krebiozen Research Foundation v. Beacon Press, 1956, 334 Mass. 86, 134 N.E.2d 1, cert. denied, 1956, 352 U.S. 848; Montgomery Ward & Co. v. United Retail, Wholesale & Dept. Store Employees, 1948, 400 Ill. 38, 79 N.E.2d 46; Kuhn v. Warner Bros. Pictures, S.D.N.Y.1939, 29 F.Supp. 800; Howell v. Bee Pub. Co., 1916, 100 Neb. 39, 158 N.W. 358. See Note, 1954, 33 Tex.L.Rev. 265; Leflar, Legal Remedies for Defamation, 1952, 6 Ark.L.Rev. 423.

12. Cf. Gompers v. Buck's Stove & Range Co., 1911, 221 U.S. 418; Lawrence Trust Co. v. Sun-America Pub. Co., 1923, 245 Mass. 262, 139 N.E. 655; American Malting Co. v. Keitel, D.N.Y.1914, 217 F. 672. See McClintock, Equity, 2d Ed. 1948, §§ 151, 154.

13. Near v. Minnesota ex rel. Olson, 1931, 283 U.S. 697.

in the direction of no disfavor for defamation,[14] as the courts became more tender of reputations injured by the modern newspaper; but in recent years, if one were to hazard a guess, it would be that the trend is again toward a more restricted liability.[15] No very comprehensive attempt ever has been made to overhaul and untangle this entire field of law,[16] and, unhappily, there seems to be none in prospect.

Definition

While the general idea of defamation is sufficiently well understood, the courts have not been altogether in harmony in dealing with it, so that very often a particular rule or holding is peculiar to a small number of jurisdictions. A defamatory communication usually has been defined as one which tends to hold the plaintiff up to hatred, contempt or ridicule, or to cause him to be shunned or avoided.[17] This definition is certainly too narrow, since an imputation of insanity,[18] or

poverty,[19] or an assertion that a woman has been raped,[20] which would be likely to arouse only pity or sympathy in the minds of all decent people, have been held to be defamatory. Defamation is rather that which tends to injure "reputation" in the popular sense; to diminish the esteem, respect, goodwill or confidence in which the plaintiff is held,[21] or to excite adverse, derogatory or unpleasant feelings or opinions against him.[22] It necessarily, however, involves the idea of disgrace; and while a statement that a man is a Republican may very possibly arouse adverse feelings against him in the minds of many Democrats, and even diminish him in their esteem, it cannot be found in itself to be defamatory, since no reasonable man could consider that it reflects upon his character.[23]

In the absence of special circumstances which add another meaning to the words, it is not defamatory to say that a man is dead,[24] that he is overly cautious with money,[25] that he has refused to abate his fees [26] or made

---

14. See the instructions to the jury, approved in Lewis v. Williams, 1916, 105 S.C. 165, 89 S.E. 647, that slander suits are proper, are frequent in civilized countries, and are better than taking the law into one's own hands.

15. See Wettach, Recent Developments in Newspaper Libel, 1928, 13 Minn.L.Rev. 21; infra. ch. 21.

16. See, however, the reforms made by the English Defamation Act of 1952, noted in 1953, 16 Mod.L. Rev. 198; 1953, 66 Harv.L.Rev. 476; and see Paton, Reform and the English Law of Defamation, 1939, 33 Ill.L.Rev. 669.

17. "Words which tend to expose one to public hatred, shame, obloquy, contumely, odium, contempt, ridicule, aversion, ostracism, degradation or disgrace, or to induce an evil opinion of one in the minds of right-thinking persons, and to deprive one of their confidence and friendly intercourse in society." Kimmerle v. New York Evening Journal, 1933, 262 N.Y. 99, 186 N.E. 217. The definition appears to have originated with Baron Parke in Parmiter v. Coupland, 1840, 6 M. & W. 105, 151 Eng. Rep. 340.

18. Kenney v. Hatfield, 1958, 351 Mich. 498, 88 N.W. 2d 535; Cowper v. Vannier, 1959, 20 Ill.App.2d 499, 156 N.E.2d 761; Seip v. Deshler, 1895, 170 Pa. 334, 32 A. 1032; Totten v. Sun Printing & Pub. Ass'n, C.C.N.Y.1901, 109 F. 289; Moore v. Francis, 1890, 121 N.Y. 199, 23 N.E. 1127. Cf. Miles v. Record

Pub. Co., 1926, 134 S.C. 462, 133 S.E. 99 (typhoid carrier).

19. Katapodis v. Brooklyn Spectator, 1941, 287 N.Y. 17, 38 N.E.2d 112. See Notes, 1942, 27 Iowa L.Rev. 656; 1942, 26 Minn.L.Rev. 563.

20. Youssoupoff v. Metro-Goldwyn-Mayer Pictures, 1934, 50 T.L.R. 581, 51 L.Q.Rev. 281.

21. Bower, Actionable Defamation, 2d Ed. 1923, 4; Restatement of Torts, § 559.

22. Salmond, Law of Torts, 8th Ed. 1934, 398.

23. Cf. Frinzi v. Hanson, 1966, 30 Wis.2d 271, 140 N.W.2d 259; Steinman v. Di Roberts, 1965, 23 App. Div.2d 693, 257 N.Y.S.2d 695 ("liberal"); Haas v. Evening Democrat, 1961, 252 Iowa 517, 107 N.W.2d 444 (conservative).

Similarly, a charge of a single act of negligence does not reflect on the plaintiff's character. Cowan v. Time, Inc., 1963, 41 Misc.2d 198, 245 N.Y.S.2d 723.

24. Cohen v. New York Times Co., 1912, 153 App.Div. 242, 138 N.Y.S. 206; Lemmer v. The Tribune, 1915, 50 Mont. 559, 148 P. 338; O'Neil v. Edmonds, E.D. Va.1958, 157 F.Supp. 649; Cardiff v. Brooklyn Eagle, 1947, 190 Misc. 730, 75 N.Y.S.2d 222.

25. Kelly v. Partington, 1833, 5 B. & Ad. 645, 110 Eng.Rep. 929.

26. De Pasquale v. Westchester Newspapers, 1938, 170 Misc. 268, 8 N.Y.S.2d 829; Gang v. Hughes, 9 Cir. 1954, 218 F.2d 432.

a charge for cashing poor relief checks,[27] that he has refused to make concessions to a union,[28] that he has led an eventful life,[29] that he has no known permanent address;[30] that he has no export license,[31] that he is not entitled to communion in a particular church,[32] that he is a labor agitator,[33] that he left his employment during a strike,[34] that he has taken advantage of his legal rights,[35] that construction work he is performing is unduly delayed,[36] that itinerant solicitors have sold space in his newspaper at higher cost than he sold it himself,[37] that he has possession of the goods of another and owes him money,[38] or that he "figured quite prom-

inently in some of the squatter riots."[39] Such language, if it is false and malicious, may afford a basis for another type of tort action for any special damage resulting,[40] but it lacks the element of personal disgrace necessary for defamation; and the fact that the plaintiff finds it unpleasant and offensive is not enough.[41]

On the other hand it is defamatory upon its face to say that the plaintiff has attempted suicide,[42] that he refuses to pay his just debts,[43] that he is immoral or unchaste,[44] or "queer," [45] or has made improper advances to women,[46] or is having "wife trouble," and

---

27. Lynch v. Lyons, 1939, 303 Mass. 116, 20 N.E.2d 953.

28. Montgomery Ward & Co. v. McGraw-Hill Pub. Co., 7 Cir. 1944, 146 F.2d 171.

29. Harriman v. New Nonpareil Co., 1906, 132 Iowa 616, 110 N.W. 33. Cf. Kimmerle v. New York Evening Journal, 1933, 262 N.Y. 99, 186 N.E. 217 (woman "courted by a murderer"); Pogany v. Chambers, Sup.Ct.1954, 134 N.Y.S.2d 691 (brother of a Communist).

30. Kamsler v. Chicago American Pub. Co., 1967, 82 Ill.App.2d 86, 225 N.E.2d 434.

31. Frawley Chemical Corp. v. A. P. Larson Co., 1949, 274 App.Div. 643, 86 N.Y.S.2d 710.

32. Cf. Carter v. Papineau, 1916, 222 Mass. 464, 111 N.E. 358. In Nichols v. Item Publishers, 1956, 309 N.Y. 596, 132 N.E.2d 860, a statement that a pastor had been removed from his office in a church by a meeting which was deemed illegal by a jury was held, by a vote of 4 to 2, not to be defamatory.

33. Vallen v. Fanjo Taxi Corp., Sup.Ct.1947, 73 N.Y. S.2d 23; Wabash R. Co. v Young, 1904, 162 Ind. 102, 69 N.E. 1003; Chicago, R. I. & P. R. Co. v. Medley, 1916, 55 Okl. 145, 155 P. 211.

34. Kansas City, M. & B. R. Co. v. Delaney, 1899, 102 Tenn. 289, 52 S.W. 151.

35. Hollenbeck v. Hall, 1897, 103 Iowa 214, 72 N.W. 518; Fey v. King, 1922, 194 Iowa 835, 190 N.W. 519; Homer v. Engelhardt, 1875, 117 Mass. 539; Foot v. Pitt, 1903, 83 App.Div. 76, 82 N.Y.S. 464.

36. Grande & Son v. Chace, 1955, 333 Mass. 166, 129 N.E.2d 898.

37. Digest Pub. Co. v. Perry Pub. Co., Ky.1955, 284 S.W.2d 832.

38. Sim v. Stretch, [1936] 2 All Eng.Rep. 1237.

39. Clarke v. Fitch, 1871, 41 Cal. 472.

40. See infra, § 12.

41. Gang v. Hughes, S.D.Cal.1953, 111 F.Supp. 27, affirmed, 9 Cir. 1954, 218 F.2d 432.

42. Wandt v. Hearst's Chicago American, 1900, 129 Wis. 419, 109 N.W. 70. Cf. Quinn v. Sun Printing & Pub. Co., 1907, 55 Misc. 572, 105 N.Y.S. 1092, affirmed, 1908, 125 App.Div. 900, 109 N.Y.S. 1143 (found dead under disgraceful circumstances).

43. Neaton v. Lewis Apparel Stores, 1944, 267 App. Div. 728, 48 N.Y.S.2d 492, appeal granted, 1944, 268 App.Div. 834, 50 N.Y.S.2d 463; Sheppard v. Dun & Bradstreet, S.D.N.Y.1947, 71 F.Supp. 942; Thompson v. Adelberg & Berman, 1918, 181 Ky. 487, 205 S.W. 558; Turner v. Brien, 1918, 184 Iowa 320, 167 N.W. 584; Muetze v. Tuteur, 1890, 77 Wis. 236, 46 N.W. 123.

But not to say merely that one has debts, or is unable to pay them, unless he is engaged in business (see infra, p. 757). Hollenbeck v. Hall, 1897, 103 Iowa 214, 72 N.W. 518; Harrison v. Burger, 1925, 212 Ala. 670, 103 So. 842.

44. Hall v. Hall, 1920, 179 N.C. 571, 103 S.E. 136; More v. Bennett, 1872, 48 N.Y. 472; Flues v. New Nonpareil Co., 1912, 155 Iowa 290, 135 N.W. 1083; Collins v. Dispatch Pub. Co., 1893, 152 Pa. 187, 25 A. 546. Cf. Sydney v. McFadden Newspaper Pub. Corp., 1926, 242 N.Y. 208, 151 N.E. 209 (married woman the "lady love" of a man); Martin v. Johnson Pub. Co., Sup.Ct.1956, 157 N.Y.S.2d 409 ("man hungry" woman); White v. Birmingham Post Co., 1937, 233 Ala. 547, 172 So. 649 (Arab sheik wanted to buy American girl for his harem).

45. Buck v. Savage, Tex.Civ.App.1959, 323 S.W.2d 363, ref. n.r.e.

46. Jamison v. Rebenson, 1959, 21 Ill.App.2d 364, 158 N.E.2d 82.

is about to be divorced;[47] that he is a coward,[48] a drunkard,[49] a hypocrite,[50] a liar,[51] a scoundrel,[52] a crook,[53] a scandal-monger,[54] an anarchist,[55] a skunk,[56] a bastard,[57] a eunuch,[58] or a "rotten egg;"[59] that he is "unfair" to labor,[60] or that he has done a thing which is oppressive or dishonorable,[61] or heartless,[62] because all of these things obviously tend to affect the esteem in which he is held by his neighbors.

The defamatory character of the statement may arise from and affect a particular characteristic or activity of the plaintiff, as where a kosher meat dealer is accused of selling bacon,[63] an amateur golfer is called a professional,[64] an actor of standing is said to have stooped below his class of entertainment,[65] a physician is reported to have advertised,[66] or the incumbent of a public office for which only citizens are eligible is said not to be a citizen.[67] The form of the statement is not important, so long as the defamatory meaning is conveyed; and it may be merely a report of "rumors and whispers,"[68] or even conditional, so long as the condition is known to the hearer to be satisfied.[69]

The courts have, however, attempted to make something like the distinction found in

---

47. Gersten v. Newark Morning Ledger Co., 1958, 52 N.J.Super. 152, 145 A.2d 56; Lyman v. New England Newspaper Pub. Co., 1934, 286 Mass. 258, 190 N.E. 542.

48. Price v. Whitley, 1872, 50 Mo. 439; Byrne v. Funk, 1905, 38 Wash. 506, 80 P. 772.

49. Buck v. Hersey, 1850, 31 Me. 558; Hay v. Reid, 1891, 85 Mich. 296, 48 N.W. 507; Holmes v. Jones, 1895, 147 N.Y. 59, 41 N.E. 409; Dawkins v. Billingsley, 1918, 69 Okl. 259, 172 P. 69.

50. Knox v. Meehan, 1896, 64 Minn. 280, 66 N.W. 1149; Newby v. Times-Mirror Co., 1916, 173 Cal. 387, 160 P. 233; Overstreet v. New Nonpareil Co., 1918, 184 Iowa 485, 167 N.W. 669.

51. Prewitt v. Wilson, 1905, 128 Iowa 198, 103 N.W. 365; Smith v. Lyons, 1918, 142 La. 975, 77 So. 896; Paxton v. Woodward, 1904, 31 Mont. 195, 78 P. 215; Colvard v. Black, 1900, 110 Ga. 642, 36 S.E. 80; Murphy v. Harty, 1964, 238 Or. 228, 393 P.2d 206.

52. Upton v. Hume, 1893, 24 Or. 420, 33 P. 810; Crocker v. Hadley, 1885, 102 Ind. 416, 1 N.E. 734 ("hoary-headed filcher"); Candrian v. Miller, 1898, 98 Wis. 164, 73 N.W. 1004 ("smooth swindler"); Bell v. Stone, 1798, 1 Bos. & P. 331, 126 Eng.Rep. 933 ("villain").

53. Pandolfo v. Bank of Benson, 9 Cir. 1921, 273 F. 48. Accord: Stevens v. Snow, 1923, 191 Cal. 58, 214 P. 968 ("crooked methods"); Peterson v. Western Union Tel. Co., 1896, 65 Minn. 18, 67 N.W. 646; Thompson v. Upton, 1958, 218 Md. 433, 146 A.2d 880 (engaged in a "racket").

54. Patton v. Cruce, 1904, 72 Ark. 421, 81 S.W. 380.

55. Cerveny v. Chicago Daily News Co., 1891, 139 Ill. 345, 28 N.E. 692; Lewis v. Daily News Co., 1895, 81 Md. 466, 32 A. 246 ("would be an anarchist if he thought it would pay").

56. Massuere v. Dickens, 1887, 70 Wis. 83, 35 N.W. 349; Solverson v. Peterson, 1885, 64 Wis. 198, 25 N. W. 14 ("swine").

57. Shelby v. Sun Printing & Pub. Ass'n, 1886, 38 Hun, N.Y., 474; Harris v. Nashville Trust Co., 1914, 128 Tenn. 573, 162 S.W. 584.

58. Eckert v. Van Pelt, 1904, 69 Kan. 357, 76 P. 909.

59. Pfitzinger v. Dubs, 7 Cir. 1894, 64 F. 696.

60. Paducah Newspapers v. Wise, Ky.App.1951, 247 S.W.2d 989, cert. denied, 1952, 343 U.S. 942. This may, however, be privileged. See infra, § 115.

61. Clement v. Chivis, 1829, 9 B. & C. 172, 109 Eng. Rep. 64; Snyder v. Fulton, 1871, 34 Md. 128.

62. MacRae v. Afro-American Co., E.D.Pa.1959, 172 F.Supp. 184, affirmed, 3 Cir. 1960, 274 F.2d 287 (mother responsible for daughter's suicide); Brown v. Du Frey, 1956, 1 N.Y.2d 190, 151 N.Y.S.2d 649, 134 N.E.2d 469 (husband had neglected wife, treated her with indifference, failed to support her).

63. Braun v. Armour & Co., 1939, 254 N.Y. 514, 173 N.E. 845.

64. Tolley v. J. S. Fry & Sons, Ltd., [1931] A.C. 333.

65. Lahr v. Adell Chemical Co., 1 Cir. 1962, 300 F.2d 256; Louka v. Park Entertainments, 1936, 294 Mass. 268, 1 N.E.2d 41. Cf. Clevenger v. Baker Voorhis & Co., 1960, 8 N.Y.2d 187, 203 N.Y.S.2d 812, 168 N.E.2d 643 (book revised by plaintiff said to be full of errors).

66. Gershwin v. Ethical Pub. Co., 1937, 166 Misc. 39, 1 N.Y.S.2d 904.

67. MacInnis v. National Herald Printing Co., 1918, 140 Minn. 171, 167 N.W. 550.

68. MacRae v. Afro-American Co., E.D.Pa.1959, 172 F.Supp. 184, affirmed, 3 Cir. 1960, 274 F.2d 287.

69. Clarke v. Zettick, 1891, 153 Mass. 1, 26 N.E. 234; Ruble v. Bunting, 1903, 31 Ind.App. 654, 68 N. E. 1041; American Life Ins. Co. v. Shell, 1956, 265 Ala. 306, 90 So.2d 719.

the law of misrepresentation,[70] between assertions of fact and those of opinion, and have held [71] that mere words of abuse, indicating that the defendant dislikes the plaintiff and has a low opinion of him, but without suggesting any specific charge against him, are not to be treated as defamatory. A certain amount of vulgar name-calling is tolerated, on the theory that it will necessarily be understood to amount to nothing more. It may be significant that most of the cases have involved slander, which would not have been actionable in any event without proof of special damage; [72] but there are occasional decisions in which what would otherwise be clearly defamatory has been dismissed as only hasty, ill-tempered abuse.[73] There has been, however, more willingness than in the case of misrepresentation to find that an

opinion carries with it assertions of fact; [74] and even when the facts are fully known to the hearer, an unprivileged [75] comment or opinion is now generally regarded as sufficiently defamatory in itself.[76]

One common form of defamation is ridicule. It has been held to be defamatory to publish humorous articles,[77] verses,[78] cartoons or caricatures [79] making fun of the plaintiff, to heap ironical praise upon his head,[80] to print his picture in juxtaposition with an article on evolution and a photograph of a gorilla,[81] or with an optical illusion of

---

70. See supra, § 109.

71. The distinction is an old one. See Penfold v. Westcote, 1806, 2 Bos. & P. N. R. 335, 127 Eng.Rep. 636; Barnett v. Allen, 3 H. & N. 376, 157 Eng.Rep. 516; Rice v. Simmons, 1841, 2 Har., Del. 309, 417; Robbins v. Treadway, 1829, 2 J.J.Marsh., Ky., 540. All on the ground that the words must have been understood as mere bad temper.

72. Crozman v. Callahan, W.D.Okl.1955, 136 F.Supp. 466 (obscene language from military official to enlisted man); Durr v. Smith, La.App.1956, 90 So.2d 147 ("invective epithet which deleteriously reflected upon the validity of his parentage"); Notarmuzzi v. Shevack, Sup.Ct.1951, 108 N.Y.S.2d 172 ("You are a bleached blond bastard, a God damn son of a bitch and a bum and a tramp; get the hell out of here"); Halliday v. Cienkowski, 1939, 333 Pa. 123, 3 A.2d 372; Mann v. Roosevelt Shop, Fla.1949, 41 So.2d 894.

But in White v. Valenta, 1965, 234 Cal.App.2d 243, 44 Cal.Rptr. 241, "son of a bitch" was held under the circumstances to impute unfair business dealing.

73. Tomakian v. Fritz, 1949, 75 R.I. 496, 67 A.2d 834 ("drunken driver"); Curtis Pub. Co. v. Birdsong, 5 Cir. 1966, 360 F.2d 344 ("bastards"); Cowan v. Time, Inc., 1963, 41 Misc.2d 198, 245 N.Y.S.2d 723 ("idiot"); Morrissette v. Beatte, 1941, 66 R.I. 73, 17 A.2d 464 (sodomy); Hansen v. Dethridge, City Ct. N.Y.1946, 67 N.Y.S.2d 168.

In extreme cases abuse may be actionable as the intentional infliction of mental disturbance. See supra, § 12.

74. Cf. Cole v. Millspaugh, 1910, 111 Minn. 159, 126 N.W. 626 ("I would not touch him with a ten foot pole"); Eikhoff v. Gilbert, 1900, 124 Mich. 353, 83 N.W. 110; Davis & Sons v. Shepstone, 1886, 11 App.Cas. 187.

75. Statements of opinion may be privileged in some cases where statements of fact are not. See infra, § 115.

76. Thomas v. Bradbury, Agnew & Co., [1906] 2 K.B. 627; Woolston v. Montana Free Press, 1931, 90 Mont. 299, 2 P.2d 1020; Professional & B. M. Life Ins. Co. v. Bankers Life Co., D.Mont.1958, 163 F. Supp. 274; Goldwater v. Ginzburg, S.D.N.Y.1966, 261 F.Supp. 784.

77. Triggs v. Sun Printing & Pub. Ass'n, 1904, 179 N.Y. 144, 71 N.E. 739 (parody of Romeo and Juliet ridiculing English professor); Snyder v. New York Press Co., 1910, 137 App.Div. 291, 121 N.Y.S. 944 (report plaintiff was served with process in the bathtub); Pignatelli v. New York Tribune, 1921, 117 Misc. 466, 192 N.Y.S. 605 (saying foreign nobleman was trying to avoid work); Megarry v. Norton, 1955, 137 Cal.App.2d 581, 290 P.2d 571 (sign, "Nuts to You—You Old Witch"); Powers v. Durgin-Snow Pub. Co., 1958, 154 Me. 108, 144 A.2d 294 (making own funeral casket, will next dig his own hole for it). See Naughton and Gilbertson, Libelous Ridicule by Journalists, 1969, 18 Cleve.Marsh.L.Rev. 450.

78. Villers v. Monsley, 1769, 2 Wils.K.B. 403, 95 Eng. Rep. 886; Levi v. Milne, 1827, 4 Bing. 195, 130 Eng.Rep. 743.

79. Brown v. Harrington, 1911, 208 Mass. 600, 95 N. E. 655; Dunlop v. Dunlop Rubber Co., [1920] 1 Ir. Ch. 280.

80. Buckstaff v. Viall, 1893, 84 Wis. 129, 54 N.W. 111. Cf. Martin v. The Picayune, 1906, 115 La. 979, 40 So. 376.

81. Zbyszko v. New York American, 1930, 228 App. Div. 277, 239 N.Y.S. 411. Cf. Louka v. Park Entertainments, 1936, 294 Mass. 268, 1 N.E.2d 41 (picture

an obscene and ludicrous deformity, readily detected at second glance.[82] It is of course possible that humor may be understood by all who hear or read it as good-natured fun, not to be taken seriously or in any defamatory sense;[83] but when it carries a sting and causes adverse rather than sympathetic or neutral merriment, it becomes defamatory. Thus a speech made after dinner, understood by all present as a harmless joke, may amount to libel when it is published in a newspaper and reaches those who do not understand the circumstances.[84]

The question of the standard by which defamation is to be determined has given rise to some difficulty.[85] It has been held in England [86] that the communication must tend to defame the plaintiff in the eyes of the community in general, or at least of a reasonable man,[87] rather than in the opinion of any particular group or class. The American courts have taken a more realistic view, recognizing that the plaintiff may suffer real damage if he is lowered in the esteem of any substantial and respectable group,[88] even though it may be quite a small minority.[89] It has sometimes been said that these must be "right-thinking people;" but this seems clearly wrong, since the court cannot be called upon to make a definitive pronouncement upon whether the views of different segments of the community are right or wrong, sound, or morally justifiable.[90] Thus, without regard to whether such opinions are "right-thinking," the publication of the plaintiff's picture in connection with a whiskey advertisement,[91] the statement that he is about to be divorced,[92] the insinuation that a white man

---

of Greek tragedy actress exhibited in front of burlesque show).

82. Burton v. Crowell Pub. Co., 2 Cir. 1936, 82 F.2d 154. See Notes, 1936, 21 Corn.L.Q. 665; 1936, 49 Harv.L.Rev. 840. Cf. Dall v. Time, Inc., 1937, 252 App.Div. 636, 300 N.Y.S. 680, affirmed, 1938, 278 N. Y. 635, 16 N.E.2d 297, reargument denied, 1938, 278 N.Y. 718, 17 N.E.2d 138 (obvious fiction), discuss in Note, 1938, 7 Ford.L.Rev. 271.

83. Hanson v. Feuling, 1915, 160 Wis. 511, 152 N.W. 287; Berry v. City of New York Ins. Co., 1923, 210 Ala. 369, 98 So. 290. Cf. Lamberti v. Sun Printing & Pub. Ass'n, 1906, 111 App.Div. 437, 97 N.Y.S. 694 (report of trivial practical joke); Cheatham v. Westchester County Publishers, Sup.Ct.1947, 73 N. Y.S.2d 173 (humorous account of event in fact occurring, which was funny in itself); McCullagh v. Houston Chronicle Pub. Co., 5 Cir. 1954, 211 F.2d 4, cert. denied, 348 U.S. 827 (same); Blake v. Hearst Publications, 1946, 75 Cal.App.2d 6, 170 P.2d 100 (cartoons of plaintiff in assumed role of counterspy); Arno v. Stewart, (1966) 245 Cal.App.2d 955, 54 Cal. Rptr. 392 (television comedian—"the singing member from the Mafia").

84. Dolby v. Newnes, 1887, 3 T.L.R. 393. Cf. Cook v. Ward, 1830, 6 Bing. 409, 130 Eng.Rep. 1338 (publication of joke told by plaintiff on himself).

85. See Notes, 1939, 24 Corn.L.Q. 258; 1949, 58 Yale L.J. 1387.

86. Clay v. Roberts, 1863, 8 L.T. 397; Miller v. David, 1874, L.R. 9 C.P. 118; Myroft v. Sleight [1921] 90 L.J.K.B. 853.

87. See Tolley v. J. S. Fry & Sons, [1930] 1 K.B. 467, [1931] A.C. 333 (holding it libel to call an amateur golfer a professional).

88. Restatement of Torts, § 559 Comment e. Accord: Munden v. Harris, 1910, 153 Mo.App. 652, 134 S.W. 1076 (infant defamed only in eyes of infants); Foster-Milburn Co. v. Chinn, 1909, 134 Ky. 424, 120 S.W. 364; Morley v. Post Printing & Publishing Co., 1928, 84 Colo. 41, 268 P. 540; Reiman v. Pacific Development Soc., 1930, 132 Or. 82, 284 P. 575; Brauer v. Globe Newspaper Co., 1966, 351 Mass. 53, 217 N.E.2d 736. See Note, 1970, 34 Alb. L.Rev. 634.

89. Thus in Ben-Oliel v. Press Pub. Co., 1929, 251 N. Y. 250, 167 N.E. 432, it was held that plaintiff was defamed by attributing to him the authorship of a bad book on the culture of Palestine, although only a few experts in that field would recognize that it was a bad one.

90. Grant v. Reader's Digest Ass'n, 2 Cir. 1945, 151 F.2d 733, cert. denied 326 U.S. 797; Herrmann v. Newark Morning Ledger Co., 1958, 49 N.J.Super. 551, 140 A.2d 529; Ingalls v. Hastings & Sons Pub. Co., 1939, 304 Mass. 31, 22 N.E.2d 657.

91. Peck v. Tribune Co., 1909, 214 U.S. 185 (Holmes, J.: "Liability is not a question of majority vote").

92. Gersten v. Newark Morning Ledger Co., 1958, 52 N.J.Super. 152, 145 A.2d 56. Cf. Geriepy v. Pearson, 1953, 92 U.S.App.D.C. 337, 207 F.2d 15 (alienation of plaintiff's affections); Brown v. Du Frey, 1956, 1 N.Y.2d 190, 151 N.Y.S.2d 649, 134 N.E.2d 469 (marital discord). See Note, 1956, 23 Brook.L.Rev. 156.

is a Negro,[93] that a business man is a price-cutter[94] or a kosher meat dealer sells bacon,[95] that the plaintiff is anti-Semitic,[96] or the daughter of a murderer,[97] may be defamatory even though it be assumed that all adverse opinions are wrong, and that the majority of the community will think none the worse. The line is drawn, however, when the group who will be unfavorably impressed becomes so small as to be negligible,[98] or one whose standards are so clearly anti-social that the court may not properly consider them.[99] The state of mind of the particular community must of course be taken into account,[1] as well as its fluctuations over a period of time; and the accusation of membership in the Communist party, or of Communist affiliation or sympathy,[2] which has led to varying conclusions over the last two decades,[3] is at present all but universally regarded as clearly defamatory.[4]

Who May be Defamed

Any living person may be defamed. The civil action is personal to the plaintiff, and cannot be founded on the defamation of another;[5] but it is of course possible that two persons may stand in such a relation that defamation of one will be found to reflect upon the reputation of the other—as where, for example, it is said that the plaintiff's mother was not married to his father; and where

---

93. Natchez Times Pub. Co. v. Dunigan, 1954, 221 Miss. 320, 72 So.2d 681; Bowen v. Independent Pub. Co., 1957, 230 S.C. 509, 96 S.E.2d 564; Jones v. R. L. Polk & Co., 1915, 190 Ala. 243, 67 So. 577; Spencer v. Looney, 1914, 116 Va. 767, 82 S.E. 745; Upton v. Times-Democrat Pub. Co., 1900, 104 La. 141, 28 So. 970.

94. Meyerson v. Hurlbut, 1938, 68 App.D.C. 360, 98 F.2d 232, cert. denied, 1938, 305 U.S. 610.

95. Braun v. Armour & Co., 1930, 254 N.Y. 514, 173 N.E. 845.

96. Sweeney v. Schenectady Union Pub. Co., 2 Cir. 1941, 122 F.2d 288, affirmed 1942, 316 U.S. 642, rehearing denied 316 U.S. 710.

97. Van Wiginton v. Pulitzer Pub. Co., 8 Cir. 1914, 218 F. 795.

98. Restatement of Torts, § 559, Comment *e.* Cf. Galveston Tribune v. Guisti, Tex.Civ.App.1911, 134 S. W. 239.

99. Thus the criminal's dislike of informers. Mawe v. Piggott, 1869, Ir.Rep. 4 C.L. 54; Connelly v. McKay, 1941, 176 Misc. 685, 28 N.Y.S.2d 327; Rose v. Borenstein, City Ct.N.Y.1953, 119 N.Y.S.2d 288. See also, the classic opinion of Minturn, J., In the Matter of Kirk, 1925, 101 N.J.L. 450, 130 A. 569, dealing with popular esteem of the bootlegger.

1. Oles v. Pittsburg Times, 1896, 2 Pa.Super. 130 ("witch" in community believing in witchcraft); Larean v. La. Compagnie d'Imprimerie de la Minerve, Quebec 1883, 27 L.C.J. 336 ("freemason" in Catholic community).

2. Grant v. Reader's Digest Ass'n, 2 Cir. 1945, 151 F.2d 733, cert. denied, 326 U.S. 797; Utah State Farm Bureau Federation v. National Farmers Union Serv. Corp., 10 Cir. 1952, 198 F.2d 20; Mosler v. Whelen, 1958, 48 N.J.Super. 491, 138 A.2d 559, reversed as question of fact, 1959, 28 N.J. 397, 147 A. 2d 7; MacLeod v. Tribune Pub. Co., 1959, 52 Cal.2d 536, 343 P.2d 36.

3. Toomey v. Jones, 1926, 124 Okl. 167, 254 P. 736 ("red;" defamatory); Garriga v. Richfield, 1940, 174 Misc. 315, 20 N.Y.S.2d 544 (not defamatory); Levy v. Gelber, 1941, 175 Misc. 745, 25 N.Y.S.2d 148 (Russia allied with Germany; defamatory); Mencher v. Chesley, 1946, 270 App.Div. 1040, 63 N. Y.S.2d 108, reversed in 1947, 297 N.Y. 94, 75 N.E.2d 257 (Russia allied with United States; defamatory only in relation to business or office); McAndrew v. Scranton Republican Pub. Co., 1950, 364 Pa. 504, 72 A.2d 780 (not defamatory).

See Notes, 1947, 45 Mich.L.Rev. 518; 1950, 50 Col.L. Rev. 526; 1953, 29 N.D.L.Rev. 296; 1954, 19 Mo.L. Rev. 91; [1953] Wash.U.L.Q. 331.

4. Spanel v. Pegler, 2 Cir. 1947, 160 F.2d 619; Toomey v. Farley, 1956, 2 N.Y.2d 71, 138 N.E.2d 221; Ward v. League for Justice, Ohio App.1950, 93 N.E. 2d 723; Joopanenko v. Gavagan, Fla.1953, 67 So.2d 434; Herrmann v. Newark Morning Ledger Co., 1958, 48 N.J.Super. 420, 138 A.2d 61, second appeal, 1958, 49 N.J.Super. 551, 140 A.2d 529.

As to whether the accusation is slander per se, see infra, p. 759.

5. Ryan v. Hearst Publications, 1940, 3 Wash.2d 128, 100 P.2d 24 (family); Alfone v. Newark Umbrella Frame Co., 1951, 13 N.J.Super. 526, 80 A.2d 589 (wife); Security Sales Agency v. A. S. Abell Co., D.Md.1913, 205 F. 941; Child v. Emerson, 1894, 102 Mich. 38, 60 N.W. 292; Pogany v. Chambers, 1954, 206 Misc. 933, 134 N.Y.S.2d 691, affirmed, 1955, 285 App.Div. 866, 137 N.Y.S.2d 828, appeal denied, 1955, 285 App.Div. 934, 139 N.Y.S.2d 887 (brother of a Communist).

such is the case, the plaintiff may have an action in his own right.[6] Likewise, no civil action will lie for the defamation of one who is dead,[7] unless there is a reflection upon those still living, who are themselves defamed.[8] Statutes in several states have made defamation of the dead a crime, but they have been construed as intended only to protect the public interest and the memory of the deceased, and so to afford no civil action to the surviving relatives.[9]

A corporation is regarded as having no reputation in any personal sense, so that it cannot be defamed by words, such as those imputing unchastity, which would affect the purely personal repute of an individual.[10] But it has prestige and standing in the business in which it is engaged, and language which casts

an aspersion upon its honesty,[11] credit,[12] efficiency or other business character may be actionable.[13] The same is true of a partnership,[14] or an unincorporated association.[15] Non-trading organizations, such as those formed for benevolent or charitable purposes, may still be dependent upon the donations or support of the public, and so may still be defamed by attacks which would tend to decrease contributions.[16] An organization is not defamed by words directed at its officers,

---

6. Merrill v. Post Pub. Co., 1908, 197 Mass. 185, 83 N. E. 419. Accord: Vicars v. Worth, 1722, 1 Stra. 471, 93 Eng.Rep. 641; Hodgkins v. Corbett, 1723, 1 Stra. 545, 93 Eng.Rep. 690; Ryalls v. Leader, 1866, L.R. 1 Ex. 296; Huckle v. Reynolds, 1859, 7 C.B., N.S., 114; Restatement of Torts, § 564, Comment *e.*

7. Gruschus v. Curtis Pub. Co., 10 Cir. 1965, 342 F.2d 775; Bello v. Random House, Inc., Mo.1968, 422 S. W.2d 339; Mahaffey v. Official Detective Stories, Inc., W.D.La.1962, 210 F.Supp. 251, affirmed 5 Cir. 1968, 389 F.2d 525; Kelly v. Johnson Pub. Co., 1958, 160 Cal.App.2d 718, 325 P.2d 659; Insull v. New York World Tel. Corp., N.D.Ill.1959, 172 F.Supp. 615, aff'd, 1960, 273 F.2d 166, cert. denied 362 U.S. 942.

See Notes, 1940, 26 Corn.L.Q. 372; 1940, 40 Col.L.Rev. 1267; 1941, 10 Ford.L.Rev. 319.

8. See Eagles v. Liberty Weekly, 1930, 137 Misc. 575, 244 N.Y.S. 430; Walton, Libel upon the Dead and The Bath Club Case, 1927, 9 J.Comp.Leg. & Int.Law 1; Restatement of Torts, § 560. But cf. Rose v. Daily Mirror, 1940, 284 N.Y. 335, 31 N.E.2d 182.

9. Saucer v. Giroux, 1921, 54 Cal.App. 732, 202 P. 887; Renfro Drug Co. v. Lawson, 1942, 138 Tex. 434, 160 S.W.2d 246. See Armstrong, Nothing But Good of the Dead, 1932, 18 A.B.A.J. 5229.

10. Reporters' Ass'n of America v. Sun Printing & Pub. Ass'n, 1906, 186 N.Y. 437, 79 N.E. 710; People's United States Bank v. Goodwin, 1912, 167 Mo. App. 211, 149 S.W. 1148; Adirondack Record v. Lawrence, 1922, 202 App.Div. 251, 195 N.Y.S. 627; see Axton-Fisher Tobacco Co. v. Evening Post Co., 1916, 169 Ky. 64, 183 S.W. 269.

11. Den Norske Ameriekalinje Actiesselskabet v. Sun Printing & Pub. Co., 1919, 226 N.Y. 17, 122 N.E. 463; Pullman Standard Car Mfg. Co. v. Local Union No. 2928, 7 Cir. 1945, 152 F.2d 493.

12. Aetna Life Ins. Co. v. Mutual Benefit Health & Acc. Ass'n, 8 Cir. 1936, 82 F.2d 115; Maytag Co. v. Meadows Mfg. Co., 7 Cir. 1930, 45 F.2d 299, cert. denied, 283 U.S. 843; Wayne Works v. Hicks Body Co., 1944, 115 Ind.App. 10, 55 N.E.2d 382; Brayton v. Crowell-Collier Pub. Co., 2 Cir. 1953, 205 F.2d 644.

13. Axton-Fisher Tobacco Co. v. Evening Post Co., 1916, 169 Ky. 64, 183 S.W. 269; Gross Coal Co. v. Rose, 1905, 126 Wis. 24, 105 N.W. 225; Di Giorgio Fruit Corp. v. American Federation of Labor, etc., 1963, 215 Cal.App.2d 560, 30 Cal.Rptr. 350; Utah State Farm Bureau Federation v. National Farmers Union Serv. Corp., 10 Cir. 1952, 198 F.2d 20; R. H. Bouligny, Inc. v. United Steelworkers of America, 1967, 270 N.C. 160, 154 S.E.2d 344.

14. Both the partnership and individual partners may be defamed. Vogel v. Bushnell, 1920, 203 Mo. App. 623, 221 S.W. 819; Constitution Pub. Co. v. Way, 1894, 94 Ga. 120, 21 S.E. 139; Donaghue v. Caffey, 1885, 53 Conn. 43, 2 A. 397; Stone v. Textile Examiners & Shrinkers Employers' Ass'n, 1910, 137 App.Div. 655, 122 N.Y.S. 460.

15. Kirkman v. Westchester Newspapers, 1942, 287 N.Y. 373, 39 N.E.2d 919; Daniels v. Sanitarium Ass'n, 1963, 59 Cal.2d 602, 30 Cal.Rptr. 828, 381 P. 2d 652; Di Giorgio Fruit Co. v. American Federation of Labor, 1963, 215 Cal.App.2d 560, 30 Cal.Rptr. 350; Calore v. Powell-Savory Corp., 1964, 21 App. Div.2d 877, 251 N.Y.S.2d 732.

16. New York Society for Suppression of Vice v. McFadden Publications, 1927, 129 Misc. 408, 221 N. Y.S. 563, affirmed, 1928, 222 App.Div. 739, 226 N.Y. S. 870; Finnish Temperance Society Sovittaja v. Finnish Socialistic Pub. Co., 1921, 238 Mass. 345, 130 N.E. 845; Aetna Life Ins. Co. v. Mutual Benefit Health & Acc. Ass'n, 8 Cir. 1936, 82 F.2d 115; Boston Nutrition Society Inc. v. Stare, 1961, 342 Mass. 439, 173 N.E.2d 812; Americans for Democratic Action v. Meade, 1950, 72 Pa.D. & C. 306.

stockholders or employees,[17] nor are they defamed by words directed at it,[18] unless the words are such, in the light of the connection between them, as to defame both.[19] It has been held in three cases,[20] that a municipal corporation can not maintain an action for defamation; but the decisions have turned upon the particular facts and questions of privilege, and have been criticized.[21]

Interpretation: Inducement, Innuendo, and Colloquium

In order that the defendant's words may be defamatory, they must be understood in a defamatory sense. It is not necessary that anyone believe them to be true,[22] since the fact that such words are in circulation at all concerning the plaintiff must be to some extent injurious to his reputation—although obviously the absence of belief will bear upon the amount of the damages. There must be, however, a defamatory meaning conveyed. Thus it is always open to the defendant to show that the words were not understood at all,[23] that they were taken entirely in jest,[24] or that some meaning other than the obvious one was attached by all who heard or read.[25] The form of the language used is not controlling, and there may be defamation by means of a question,[26] an indirect insinuation,[27] an expression of belief or opinion,[28] or sarcasm or irony.[29] The imputation may be

17. Life Printing & Pub. Co. v. Field, 1946, 327 Ill. App. 486, 64 N.E.2d 383; Hapgoods v. Crawford, 1908, 125 App.Div. 856, 110 N.Y.S. 122; People's United States Bank v. Goodwin, 1912, 167 Mo.App. 211, 149 S.W. 1148; Brayton v. Cleveland Special Police Co., 1900, 63 Ohio St. 83, 57 N.E. 1085; Novick v. Hearst Corp., D.Md.1968, 278 F.Supp. 277.

Cf. Gilbert v. Crystal Fountain Lodge, 1887, 80 Ga. 284, 4 S.E. 905 (Bleckley, C. J.: "The venereal disease was not a partnership malady. That was individual property.")

18. Gilbert Shoe Co. v. Rumpf Pub. Co., D.Mass.1953, 112 F.Supp. 228 (president); McBride v. Crowell-Collier Pub. Co., 5 Cir. 1952, 196 F.2d 187 (stockholder).

19. Brayton v. Crowell-Collier Pub. Co., 2 Cir. 1953, 205 F.2d 644 (individual identified with corporation); De Mankowski v. Ship Channel Development Co., Tex.Civ.App.1927, 300 S.W. 118 (officers "a bunch of crooks"); Neiman-Marcus Co. v. Lait, S. D.N.Y.1952, 107 F.Supp. 96 (employees); Axton-Fisher Tobacco Co. v. Evening Post Co., 1916, 169 Ky. 64, 183 S.W. 269. See Note 1953, 51 Mich.L. Rev. 611.

20. Mayor of Manchester v. Williams, [1891] 1 Q.B. 94, 63 L.T. 805; City of Chicago v. Chicago Tribune Co., 1923, 307 Ill. 595, 139 N.E. 86; City of Albany v. Meyer, 1929, 99 Cal.App. 651, 279 P. 213.

21. Bower, Actionable Defamation, 2d Ed.1923, 245; 1924, 9 Corn.L.Q. 211. The Restatement of Torts, § 561, Caveat, expresses no opinion.

22. Knight v. Gibbs, 1834, 1 Ad. & El. 43, 110 Eng. Rep. 1124; Gillett v. Bullivant, 1846, 7 L.T., O.S., 490; Marble v. Chapin, 1882, 132 Mass. 225; see Modisette & Adams v. Lorenze, 1927, 163 La. 505, 112 So. 397; Dall v. Time, Inc., 1937, 252 App.Div. 636, 300 N.Y.S. 680, affirmed 1938, 278 N.Y. 635, 16

N.E.2d 297, reargument denied 1938, 278 N.Y. 718, 17 N.E.2d 138.

23. Thus in the case of words spoken in a foreign language. Price v. Jenkins, 1601, Cro.Eliz. 805, 78 Eng.Rep. 1091; Rich v. Scalio, 1904, 115 Ill.App. 166; Mielenz v. Quasdorf, 1886, 68 Iowa 726, 28 N. W. 41; Economopoulos v. A. G. Pollard Co., 1914, 218 Mass. 294, 105 N.E. 896.

24. See cases cited supra, p. 743.

25. Ayers v. Grider, 1853, 15 Ill. 37; Fawsett v. Clark, 1878, 48 Md. 494; Brown v. Myers, 1883, 40 Ohio St. 99; Line v. Spies, 1905, 139 Mich. 484, 102 N.W. 993; Insurance Research Service v. Associates Finance Co., M.D.Tenn.1955, 134 F.Supp. 54. But where the words are open only to one defamatory meaning under the circumstances, a witness will not be permitted to testify that he understood them in a different sense. Smith v. Smith, 1940, 194 S.C. 247, 9 S.E.2d 584.

26. State v. Norton, 1896, 89 Me. 290, 36 A. 394; Goodrich v. Davis, 1846, 11 Metc., Mass., 473; Meaney v. Loew's Hotels, Inc., 1968, 29 App.Div.2d 850, 288 N.Y.S.2d 217.

27. Merrill v. Post Pub. Co., 1908, 197 Mass. 185, 83 N.E. 419; Gendron v. St. Pierre, 1905, 73 N.H. 419, 62 A. 966; Palmerlee v. Nottage, 1912, 119 Minn. 351, 138 N.W. 312; Sherin v. Eastwood, 1922, 46 S. D. 24, 190 N.W. 320.

See Spiegel, Defamation by Implication—in the Confidential Manner, 1956, 29 So.Cal.L.Rev. 306.

28. Nye v. Otis, 1811, 8 Mass. 122; Gendron v. St. Pierre, 1905, 73 N.H. 419, 62 A. 966; Prewitt v. Wilson, 1905, 128 Iowa 198, 103 N.W. 365.

29. Boydell v. Jones, 1838, 4 M. & W. 36, 150 Eng. Rep. 1333; Diener v. Star-Chronicle Pub. Co., 1910, 230 Mo. 613, 132 S.W. 1143; Buckstaff v. Viall, 1893, 84 Wis. 129, 54 N.W. 111.

carried quite indirectly, as where the plaintiff's name is signed as author to a false [30] or very bad [31] piece of writing, or the plaintiff is made to appear willing to publish a love affair to the world.[32]

The reluctance with which the common law courts at first entertained actions for defamation led them to hold that words must be interpreted in the best possible sense, and that the plaintiff must entirely negative any possible nondefamatory meaning. The result was a set of artificial and absurd rules of pleading and proof, by which "Thou art as arrant a thief any is in England" was not actionable until it was pleaded that there were thieves in England,[33] and "Thou art a murderer, for thou art the fellow that didst kill Mr. Sydnam's man" required an averment that any man of Mr. Sydnam's had in fact been murdered.[34] This triumph of technicality, some traces of which still remain,[35] has long since largely been buried in the past, and it is now held that words are to be taken in the sense in which they are reasonably understood under the circumstances, and are to be presumed to have the meaning ordinarily attached to them by those familiar with the language used.[36] Thus Horace Greeley's well-known words concerning James Fenimore Cooper, "He will not bring the action in New York, for we are known here, nor in Otsego, for he is known there" were held to carry the imputation of bad repute in Otsego.[37] On the other hand, no artificial and unreasonable construction placed upon innocent words by the evil-minded can add a defamatory meaning not fairly to be found in the light of the circumstances.[38] If there are listeners who reasonably understand the words in a defamatory sense, the fact that most of those who hear them will give them an innocent meaning will not prevent defamation.[39]

It is for the court in the first instance to determine whether the words are reasonably capable of a particular interpretation, or whether they are necessarily so; [40] it is then

30. Locke v. Benton & Bowles, 1937, 165 Misc. 631, 1 N.Y.S.2d 240; Ben-Oliel v. Press Pub. Co., 1929, 251 N.Y. 250, 167 N.E. 432.

31. D'Altomonte v. New York Herald Co., 1913, 154 App.Div. 453, 139 N.Y.S. 200, aff'd, 1913, 208 N.Y. 596, 102 N.E. 1101; Sperry Rand Corp. v. Hill, 1 Cir. 1966, 356 F.2d 181, cert. denied 384 U.S. 973. Cf. Carroll v. Paramount Pictures, S.D.N.Y.1943, 3 F. R.D. 47 (bad motion picture); Gardella v. Log Cabin Prods. Co., 2 Cir. 1937, 89 F.2d 891 (impersonation and inferior performance).

32. Karjavainean v. MacFadden Publications, 1940, 305 Mass. 573, 26 N.E.2d 538.

33. Foster v. Browning, 1625, Cro.Jac. 688, 79 Eng. Rep. 596.

34. Barrons v. Ball, 1614, Cro.Jac. 331, 79 Eng.Rep. 282; cf. Lacy v. Reynolds, 1591, Cro.Eliz. 215, 78 Eng.Rep. 471; Holt v. Astgrigg, 1611, Cro.Jac. 184, 79 Eng.Rep. 161; Ball v. Roane, 1593, Cro.Eliz. 308, 78 Eng.Rep. 559.

35. See for example Davis v. Niederhof, 1965, 246 S. C. 192, 143 S.E.2d 367.

36. World Pub. Co. v. Mullen, 1894, 43 Neb. 126, 61 N.W. 108; Boyer v. Pitt Pub. Co., 1936, 324 Pa. 154, 188 A. 203; Lorentz v. R. K. O. Radio Pictures, 9 Cir. 1946, 155 F.2d 84, cert. denied 329 U.S. 727; Budd v. J. Y. Gooch Co., 1948, 157 Fla. 716, 27 So.2d 172; McRae v. Afro-American Co., E.D.Pa. 1959, 172 F.Supp. 184, affirmed, 3 Cir. 1960, 274 F.2d 287; Restatement of Torts, § 563. California abandoned the old position in MacLeod v. Tribune Pub. Co., 1959, 52 Cal.2d 536, 343 P.2d 36.

37. Cooper v. Greeley, 1845, 1 Denio, N.Y., 347.

38. Phillips v. Union Indemnity Co., 4 Cir. 1928, 28 F.2d 701; Marshall v. National Police Gazette Corp., 8 Cir. 1952, 195 F.2d 993; Lorentz v. R. K. O. Radio Pictures, 9 Cir. 1946, 155 F.2d 84, cert. denied 329 U.S. 727; Campbell v. Post Pub. Co., 1933, 94 Mont. 12, 20 P.2d 1063; Kluender v. Semann, 1927, 203 Iowa 68, 212 N.W. 326.

39. Ervin v. Record Pub. Co., 1908, 154 Cal. 79, 97 P. 21; cf. Wandt v. Hearst's Chicago American, 1906, 129 Wis. 419, 109 N.W. 70; Van Wiginton v. Pulitzer Pub. Co., 8 Cir. 1914, 218 F. 795; Fetler v. Houghton Mifflin Co., 2 Cir. 1966, 364 F.2d 650.

40. Hays v. American Defense Society, 1929, 252 N.Y. 266, 169 N.E. 380; Davis v. R. K. O. Radio Pictures, 8 Cir. 1951, 191 F.2d 901; Lane v. Washington Daily News, 1936, 66 App.D.C. 245, 85 F.2d 822; Smith v. Smith, 1940, 194 S.C. 247, 9 S.E.2d 584; Morrissette v. Beatte, 1941, 66 R.I. 73, 17 A.2d 464.

Constitutional and statutory provisions in many states, modeled after Fox's Libel Act, 1792, 32 Geo. III, ch. 60, that the jury shall determine the law in libel cases, have been construed to mean merely that the jury shall apply the law as instructed by

for the jury to say whether they were in fact so understood.[41] If the language used is open to two meanings, as in the case of the French word "cocotte," which, according to one court, signifies either a prostitute or a poached egg, it is for the jury to determine whether the defamatory sense was the one conveyed.[42] One obvious rule of limitation is that an entire writing, conversation or motion picture,[43] must be construed as a whole. The plaintiff may not lift words out of their context, and the defamation contained in one line may be negatived or explained away by what appears elsewhere.[44] It is clear, however, that an undue emphasis may be given a part of the publication, as in the case of headlines, which may convey a meaning which the remainder does not remedy.[45]

A publication may be defamatory upon its face; or it may carry a defamatory meaning only by reason of extrinsic circumstances. The distinction is not the same as that between defamation which is actionable of itself and that which requires proof of special damage, which is considered below.[46] There has been no little confusion as to this, sometimes with unfortunate results.[47] If the defamatory meaning arises only from facts not apparent upon the face of the publication, the plaintiff has the burden of pleading and proving such facts, by way of what is called "inducement."[48] Likewise, he must establish the defamatory sense of the publication with reference to such facts, or the "innuendo."[49] Thus a statement that the plaintiff has burned his own barn is not defamatory on its face, since he was free to do so; but when it is pleaded as inducement that he had insured his barn, and as innuendo that the words were understood to mean that he was defrauding the insurance company, a charge of the crime of arson is made

the court. State v. Heacock, 1898, 106 Iowa 191, 76 N.W. 654 (court may instruct); People v. McDowell, 1886, 71 Cal. 194, 11 P. 868 (jury may not disregard existing law); Paxton v. Woodward, 1904, 31 Mont. 195, 78 P. 215 (erroneous instruction). But it has been held that the court can not set aside a verdict once rendered. Harrington v. Butte Miner Co., 1914, 48 Mont. 550, 139 P. 451; State v. Zimmerman, 1883, 31 Kan. 85, 1 P. 257. See Note, 1927, 11 Minn.L.Rev. 472.

41. Washington Post Co. v. Chaloner, 1919, 250 U.S. 290; Gariepy v. Pearson, D.C.Cir. 1953, 207 F.2d 15, cert. denied 346 U.S. 909; Linehan v. Nelson, 1910, 197 N.Y. 482, 90 N.E. 1114; Alderson v. Kahle, 1914, 73 W.Va. 690, 80 S.E. 1109; Clark v. Pearson, D.D.C. 1965, 248 F.Supp. 188; Restatement of Torts, § 614.

42. Rovira v. Boget, 1925, 240 N.Y. 314, 148 N.E. 534. Accord, Clark v. Pearson, D.D.C.1965, 248 F.Supp. 188; Eadie v. Pole, 1966, 91 N.J.Super. 504, 221 A. 2d 547; MacDonough v. A. S. Beck Shoe Corp., 1939, 1 Terry, Del., 318, 10 A.2d 510 (man "intimate" with girl employees); Nettles v. MacMillan Petroleum Corp., 1947, 210 S.C. 200, 42 S.E.2d 57.

43. Houston v. Interstate Circuit, Tex.Civ.App.1939, 132 S.W.2d 903.

44. Ledger-Enquirer Co. v. Grimes, 1958, 214 Ga. 422, 105 S.E.2d 229; Helton v. Joplin, Ky.1955, 281 S. W.2d 917; Yakavicke v. Valentukevicius, 1911, 84 Conn. 350, 80 A. 94; Macurda v. Lewiston Journal Co., 1912, 109 Me. 53, 82 A. 438; First Nat. Bank of Waverly v. Winters, 1918, 225 N.Y. 47, 121 N.E. 459. See Note, 1946, 95 U.Pa.L.Rev. 98.

45. Brown v. Ledger-Enquirer Co., 1958, 97 Ga.App. 595, 105 S.E.2d 616, reversed as matter of interpre-

tation, 1958, 214 Ga. 422, 105 S.E.2d 229; Shubert v. Variety, Inc., 1926, 128 Misc. 428, 219 N.Y.S. 233, affirmed, 1927, 221 App.Div. 856, 224 N.Y.S. 913. Cf. Landon v. Watkins, 1895, 61 Minn. 137, 63 N.W. 615; Gustin v. Evening Press Co., 1912, 172 Mich. 311, 137 N.W. 674. See Note, 1942, 7 Mo.Rev. 80.

46. See infra, pp. 754–761.

47. See infra, p. 762. The distinction is illustrated by Bowie v. Evening News, 1925, 148 Md. 569, 129 A. 797; Woolston v. Montana Free Press, 1931, 90 Mont. 299, 2 P.2d 1020. As the terms "defamation per se" and "defamation per quod" are used indiscriminately in both senses, they are avoided throughout the text.

48. McLaughlin v. Fisher, 1890, 136 Ill. 111, 24 N.E. 60; McNamara v. Goldan, 1909, 194 N.Y. 315, 87 N. E. 440; Penry v. Dozier, 1909, 161 Ala. 292, 49 So. 909; Kee v. Armstrong, Byrd & Co., 1919, 75 Okl. 84, 182 P. 494; Ten Broeck v. Journal Printing Co., 1926, 166 Minn. 173, 207 N.W. 497.

49. Pfeifly v. Henry, 1921, 269 Pa. 533, 112 A. 768; Kee v. Armstrong, Byrd & Co., 1919, 75 Okl. 84, 182 P. 494; Penry v. Dozier, 1909, 161 Ala. 292, 49 So. 909. No innuendo need be pleaded, however, where the publication is clearly defamatory in the light of the inducement. Sharpe v. Larson, 1897, 70 Minn. 209, 72 N.W. 961.

out, which is defamatory.[50] Or, in the case of words spoken in a foreign language, or in an unusual sense, the inducement would consist of the fact that there were those present who had reason to understand them to have a defamatory meaning, and the innuendo of the meaning itself.[51] The technical rules of common law pleading in such cases became so artificial and intricate that justice was often "smothered in her own robes,"[52] but somewhat less technicality is required under the codes.[53]

The function of the innuendo is merely to explain the words in the light of the facts. No mere claim of the plaintiff can add a defamatory meaning where none is apparent from the publication itself in the light of the inducement;[54] and it remains a question for the court whether the meaning claimed might reasonably be conveyed,[55] and for the jury whether it was so understood.[56]

Reference to Plaintiff: Colloquium

A publication may clearly be defamatory as to somebody, and yet on its face make no reference to the individual plaintiff. In such a case the plaintiff must sustain the burden of pleading and proof, by way of "colloquium," that the defamatory meaning attached to him. If he fails to do so, he has not made out his case.[57] He need not, of course, be named, and the reference may be an indirect one, with the identification depending upon circumstances known to the hearers,[58] and it is not necessary that every listener understand it, so long as there are some who reasonably do;[59] but the understanding that the plaintiff is meant must be a reasonable one,[60] and if it arises from extrinsic facts, it must be shown that these were known to those who heard.[61]

Two or more persons may of course be defamed by the same publication.[62] But diffi-

---

50. Bloss v. Tobey, 1824, 2 Pick., Mass., 320. Cf. Arne v. Johnson, 1712, 10 Mod. 111, 88 Eng.Rep. 651 ("You are a soldier," when it was the practice for tradesmen to protect themselves against their creditors by counterfeit enlistment); Cassidy v. Daily Mirror Newspapers, [1929] 2 K.B. 331, 69 A.L.R. 720; Traynor v. Seiloff, 1895, 62 Minn. 420, 64 N. W. 915.

51. Cf. Price v. Jenkings, 1601, Cro.Eliz. 805, 78 Eng.Rep. 1091; Pelzer v. Benish, 1886, 67 Wis. 291, 30 N.W. 366; Acker v. McCullough, 1875, 50 Ind. 447; Wimer v. Allbaugh, 1889, 78 Iowa 79, 42 N.W. 587.

52. Harris v. Zanone, 1892, 93 Cal. 59, 28 P. 845.

53. Clark, Code Pleading, 2d Ed. 1947, 315.

54. Grice v. Holk, 1959, 268 Ala. 500, 108 So.2d 359; Sarkees v. Warner-West Corp., 1944, 349 Pa. 365, 37 A.2d 544; Marshall v. National Police Gazette Corp., 8 Cir. 1952, 195 F.2d 993; Lorentz v. R. K. O. Radio Pictures, 9 Cir. 1946, 155 F.2d 84, cert. denied 329 U.S. 727; Carey v. Evening Call Pub. Co., 1948, 74 R.I. 473, 62 A.2d 327.

55. Cleary v. Webster, 1927, 170 Minn. 420, 212 N.W. 898; Herrick v. Tribune Co., 1903, 108 Ill.App. 244; Naulty v. Bulletin Co., 1903, 206 Pa. 128, 55 A. 862; Kilgour v. Evening Star Newspaper Co., 1902, 96 Md. 16, 53 A. 716; Davis v. R. K. O. Radio Pictures, 8 Cir. 1951, 191 F.2d 901.

56. Linehan v. Nelson, 1910, 197 N.Y. 482, 90 N.E. 1114; Holmes v. Clisby, 1904, 121 Ga. 241, 48 S.E.

934; Cassidy v. Gannett Co., 1940, 173 Misc. 634, 18 N.Y.S.2d 729.

57. Gnapinsky v. Goldyn, 1957, 23 N.J. 243, 128 A.2d 697; Brodsky v. Journal Pub. Co., 1950, 73 S.D. 343, 42 N.W.2d 855; Helmicks v. Stevlingson, 1933, 212 Wis. 614, 250 N.W. 402; Weidman v. Ketcham, 1938, 278 N.Y. 129, 15 N.E.2d 426; Ryan v. Hearst Publications, 1940, 3 Wash.2d 128, 100 P.2d 24. See Yankwich, Certainty in the Law of Defamation, 1954, 1 U.C.L.A.L.Rev. 163; Note, 1947, 12 Mo.L. Rev. 365.

58. Mothersill v. Voliva, 1910, 158 Ill.App. 16; Overstreet v. New Nonpareil Co., 1918, 184 Iowa 485, 167 N.W. 669; Brown v. Journal Newspaper Co., 1914, 219 Mass. 486, 107 N.E. 358; Connell v. A. C. L. Haase & Sons Fish Co., 1923, 302 Mo. 48, 257 S. W. 760; Cosgrove Studio & Camera Shop, Inc. v. Pane, 1962, 408 Pa. 314, 182 A.2d 751.

59. Colvard v. Black, 1900, 110 Ga. 642, 36 S.E. 80; Fitzpatrick v. Age-Herald Pub. Co., 1913, 184 Ala. 510, 63 So. 980; Youssoupoff v. Metro-Goldwyn-Mayer Pictures, 1934, 50 T.L.R. 581, 99 A.L.R. 864.

60. Davis v. R. K. O. Pictures, 8 Cir. 1951, 191 F.2d 901.

61. Gnapinsky v. Goldyn, 1957, 23 N.J. 243, 128 A.2d 697.

62. Constitution Pub. Co. v. Way, 1894, 94 Ga. 120, 21 S.E. 139; Robinett v. McDonald, 1884, 65 Cal. 611, 4 P. 651; Ellis v. Kimball, 1834, 16 Pick., Mass., 132.

culties arise when the defamatory words are directed at a group or class of persons rather than an individual.[63] The plaintiff must first of all show that he is in fact a member of the class defamed.[64] Beyond this, he must establish some reasonable personal application of the words to himself. If the group is a very large one, as in the case of such words as "all lawyers are shysters," [65] they are considered to have no application to anyone in particular, since one might as well defame all mankind. Not only does the group as such have no acton, but the plaintiff does not establish any personal reference to himself.[66] But if the plaintiff is the only lawyer present, or for some other reason the words are reasonably understood by the hearers to be directed individually at him, the personal application may be made to appear, by pleading

and proof of the special circumstances by way of inducement, and the innuendo.[67]

The rule has been applied quite uniformly to comparatively large groups or classes of a definite number, exceeding, say twenty-five persons.[68] When the group becomes smaller than that,[69] as in the case of a jury,[70] a family,[71] an election board,[72] or the four officers of an association,[73] the courts have been will-

---

63. See Tanenhaus, Group Libel, 1950, 35 Corn.L.Q. 261; Wittenberg, Individual Recovery for Defamation of a Group, 1954, 15 Ohio St.L.J. 273; Riesman, Democracy and Defamation: Control of Group Libel, 1942, 42 Col.L.Rev. 727, 1085; Beth, Group Libel and Free Speech, 1954, 39 Minn.L.Rev. 167; Belton, The Control of Group Defamation, 1960, 34 Tulane L.Rev. 300; Lewis, The Individual's Right to Recover for a Defamation Leveled at the Group, 1963, 17 U.Miami L.Rev. 519; Symposium, 1964, 13 Cleve.Marsh.L.Rev.; Notes, 1951, 1 Duke Bar J. 218; 1952, 61 Yale L.J. 252; 1953, 41 Cal.L.Rev. 144; 1953, 28 N.Y.U.L.Rev. 220; 1950, 98 U.Pa.L.Rev. 865; 1951, 24 So.Cal.L.Rev. 213; 1963, 35 U.Colo.L.Rev. 616.

64. Dunlap v. Sundberg, 1909, 55 Wash. 609, 104 P. 830; Ewell v. Boutwell, 1924, 138 Va. 402, 121 S.E. 912; Blaser v. Krattiger, 1921, 99 Or. 392, 195 P. 359 (plaintiff must prove that "he belongs to that class whose ancestry is ascribed to a canine of the female sex.")

65. Cf. Schutzman & Schutzman v. News Syndicate Co., 1969, 60 Misc.2d 827, 304 N.Y.S.2d 167.

66. Hospital Care Corp. v. Commercial Cas. Ins. Co., 1940, 194 S.C. 370, 9 S.E.2d 796 (small insurance companies); Service Parking Corp. v. Washington Times Co., 1937, 67 App.D.C. 351, 92 F.2d 502 (parking lot owners in Washington); Watts-Wagner Co. v. General Motors Corp., S.D.N.Y.1945, 64 F.Supp. 506 (sellers of battery compounds); Oma v. Hillman Periodicals, 1953, 281 App.Div. 240, 118 N.Y.S. 2d 720 (persons connected with pugilism); Golden North Airways v. Tanana Pub. Co., 9 Cir. 1955, 218 F.2d 612 (nonscheduled air carriers).

67. Marr v. Putnam, 1952, 196 Or. 1, 246 P.2d 509, second appeal, 1958, 213 Or. 17, 321 P.2d 1061. Cf. M'Clean v. New York Press Co., 1892, 64 Hun 639, 19 N.Y.S. 262. See Note, 1953, 28 N.Y.U.L.Rev. 220.

68. Noral v. Hearst Publications, 1940, 40 Cal.App.2d 348, 104 P.2d 860 (162 officials of Workers Alliance); Macaulay v. Bryan, 1959, 75 Nev. 278, 339 P.2d 377 (United Freeway Association, number unspecified); Louisville Times v. Stivers, 1934, 252 Ky. 843, 68 S.W.2d 411 ("Stivers clan"); Fowler v. Curtis Pub. Co., D.C.Cir. 1950, 86 U.S.App.D.C. 349, 182 F.2d 377 (60 cab drivers employed by one company); Comes v. Cruce, 1908, 85 Ark. 79, 107 S.W. 185 ("wine joint owners" in the community).

69. The largest group as to which the possibility of recovery has been recognized under the common law consisted of the "sixty or seventy" members of the University of Oklahoma football team, in Fawcett Publications, Inc. v. Morris, Okl.1962, 377 P.2d 42, where, however, there appears to have been a direct accusation that *all* of the team took drugs. The second largest is the group of 25 salesmen employed by one store in Neiman-Marcus Co. v. Lait, S.D.N.Y.1952, 13 F.R.D. 311. The third is the 17 men "that helped to murther Henry Farrer", in Foxcraft v. Lary, 1613, Hobart 89a, 80 Eng.Rep. 239.

In Ortenberg v. Plamondon, 1914, 35 Can.L.T. 262, Ann.Cas.1915C, 347, under the civil law, recovery was allowed for defamation of 75 Jewish families in the city of Quebec.

70. Byers v. Martin, 1875, 2 Colo. 605. Accord, Bornmann v. Star Co., 1903, 174 N.Y. 212, 66 N.E. 723 (12 doctors at a hospital). Contra, Smallwood v. York, 1915, 163 Ky. 139, 173 S.W. 380 (jury).

71. Fenstermacher v. Tribune Pub. Co., 1896, 13 Utah 552, 45 P. 1097; Gidney v. Blake, 1814, 11 Johns., N.Y. 54.

72. Reilly v. Curtiss, 1912, 83 N.J.L. 77, 84 A. 199. Accord: Swearingen v. Parkersburg Sentinel Co., 1943, 125 W.Va. 731, 26 S.E.2d 209 (city council of 4); Wofford v. Meeks, 1900, 129 Ala. 349, 30 So. 625 (commissioners); Palmerlee v. Nottage, 1913, 119 Minn. 136, 143 N.W. 260 (same).

73. De Witte v. Kearney & Treaker Corp., 1953, 265 Wis. 184, 60 N.W.2d 748. Accord: Schomberg v.

ing to permit the conclusion that the finger of defamation is pointed at each individual. There is more difficulty, however, when the words purport to refer only to a part of such a smaller group, as in the case of "some of A's children are thieves." Usually, in such a case, the plaintiff has been denied recovery, since all are not defamed, and those who are are not identified.[74] There are, however, cases [75] which have taken the more realistic view that the jury can find that suspicion thus cast upon the entire group has reached and defamed every member of it, so that all are entitled to maintain the action. Certainly this is possible; but it may well be affected by numbers. A statement that "all but one" of twelve are corrupt would seem clearly to affect the entire dozen,[76] where the conclusion scarcely seems justifiable as to one out of twenty.[77]

Group defamation has been a fertile and dangerous weapon of attack on various racial, religious and political minorities,[78] and

has led to the enactment of criminal statutes in a number of states.[79] Thus far any civil remedy for such broadside defamation has been lacking.

112. LIBEL AND SLANDER

The erratic and anomalous historical development of the law of defamation [80] has led to the survival until the present day of two forms of action for defamatory publications. One is libel, which originally concerned written or printed words; the other slander, which might be, and usually was, of an oral character. Libel was criminal in its origin, and it has remained a common law crime; [81] while slander was never criminal in itself, and could become so only when the words amounted to some other offense, such as sedition, blasphemy, or a breach of the peace.[82] When the two at last met in the common law courts, they tended to become separate rather than united; and since libel was already established as the greater wrong, greater responsibility continued to be attached to it.[83] There is some reason to believe that this was in part at least a conscious effort to rescue a portion of the law of defamation from the morass into which the law of

Walker, 1901, 132 Cal. 224, 64 P. 290 (3 trustees); Goldsborough v. Orem & Johnson, 1906, 103 Md. 671, 64 A. 36 (church vestry).

74. Ball v. White, 1966, 3 Mich.App. 579, 143 N.W.2d 188 (one of five); Fowler v. Curtis Pub. Co., D.D.C.1950, 182 F.2d 377 (one of three); Latimer v. Chicago Daily News, 1947, 330 Ill.App. 295, 71 N.E.2d 553 ("some" of 23 lawyers); Cohn v. Brecher, 1959, 20 Misc.2d 329, 192 N.Y.S.2d 877 (one of three); Kenworthy v. Journal Co., 1906, 117 Mo.App. 327, 93 S.W. 882 ("two or three" out of seven).

75. Forbes v. Johnson, 1850, 50 Ky. 48 (note altered by one of two); Hardy v. Williamson, 1891, 86 Ga. 551, 12 S.E. 874 ("some" of 11 engineers employed by one company); Neiman-Marcus Co. v. Lait, S.D. N.Y.1952, 13 F.R.D. 311 (25 salesmen; "most of the sales staff are fairies"); Farrell v. Triangle Publications, 1960, 399 Pa. 102, 159 A.2d 734 ("a number" of the township commissioners); American Broadcasting-Paramount Theatres, Inc. v. Simpson, 1962, 106 Ga.App. 230, 126 S.E.2d 873 (one of two).

76. Gross v. Cantor, 1936, 270 N.Y. 93, 200 N.E. 592.

77. Blaser v. Krattiger, 1921, 99 Or. 392, 195 P. 359; cf. Zanker v. Lackey, 1924, 2 W.W.Harr., Del., 588, 128 A. 373.

78. See Riesman, Democracy and Defamation: Control of Group Libel, 1942, 42 Col.L.Rev. 727; Tanenhaus, Group Libel, 1950, 35 Corn.L.Q. 261.

79. See Scott, Criminal Sanctions for Group Libel: Feasibility and Constitutionality, 1951, 1 Duke B.J. 218; Beth, Group Libel and Free Speech, 1955, 39 Minn.L.Rev. 167; Notes, 1947, 42 Col.L.Rev. 727; 1952, 32 Bos.U.L.Rev. 414; 1952, 61 Yale L.J. 252; 1953, 33 Or.L.Rev. 360.
The Illinois statute was held constitutional in Beauharnais v. Illinois, 1952, 342 U.S. 250.

80. See supra, § 111.

81. See Kelly, Criminal Libel and Free Speech, 1958, 6 Kan.L.Rev. 295; Leflar, The Social Utility of the Criminal Law of Defamation, 1956, 34 Tex.L.Rev. 984.

82. 1 Russell, Crimes, 8th Ed.1923, 983. Some slanderous words, such as those imputing unchastity to a woman, are now made criminal by special statutes in various jurisdictions.

83. Holdsworth, Defamation in the Sixteenth and Seventeenth Centuries, 1925, 41 L.Q.Rev. 13, 16; Kelly, Criminal Libel and Free Speech, 1958, 6 Kan.L.Rev. 295; Note, 1955, 25 U.Chi.L.Rev. 132.

slander had fallen; [84] and no doubt it was encouraged by the reverence of an illiterate nation for the printed word, and its correspondingly greater potentialities for harm. It was accordingly held that some kinds of defamatory words might be actionable without proof of any actual damage to the plaintiff if they were written, where such damage must be proved if they were spoken.[85] This remains the chief importance of the distinction. As early as 1812 [86] Sir James Mansfield condemned it as indefensible in principle, but held it to be too well established to be repudiated.

Distinction

The distinction itself between libel and slander is not free from difficulty and uncertainty. As it took form in the seventeenth century, it was one between written and oral words. But later on libel was extended to include pictures,[87] signs,[88] statues,[89] motion pictures,[90] and even conduct carrying a defamatory imputation, such as hanging the plaintiff in effigy,[91] erecting a gallows before

his door,[92] dishonoring his valid check drawn upon the defendant's bank,[93] or even, in one Wisconsin case, following him over a considerable period in a conspicuous manner.[94] From this it has been concluded that libel is that which is communicated by the sense of sight, or perhaps also by touch or smell,[95] while slander is that which is conveyed by the sense of hearing. But this certainly does not fit all of the cases, since it seems to be agreed that defamatory gestures or the signals of a deaf-mute are to be regarded as slander only,[96] while matter communicated by sound to be reduced to writing afterwards, as in the case of a telegraph message,[97] or dicta-

---

84. 1 Street, Foundations of Legal Liability, 1906, 292.

85. King v. Lake, 1670, Hardres 470, 145 Eng.Rep. 552; Austin v. Culpepper, 1633, 2 Show.K.B. 313, 89 Eng.Rep. 960; Cillers v. Monsley, 1799, 2 Wils.K.B. 403, 95 Eng.Rep. 886.

86. Thorley v. Lord Kerry, 1812, 4 Taunt. 355, 128 Eng.Rep. 367.

87. Du Bost v. Beresford, 1810, 2 Camp. 511, 170 Eng.Rep. 1235; Francis Mazzera's Case, 1817, 2 N. Y. City Hall Recorder 113; Thayer v. Worcester Post Co., 1933, 284 Mass. 160, 187 N.E. 292; Burton v. Crowell Pub. Co., 2 Cir. 1936, 82 F.2d 154; Dunlop v. Dunlop Rubber Co., [1920] 1 Ir.Rep. 280. See Note, 1938, 33 Ill.L.Rev. 87.

88. See Tarpley v. Blabey, 1836, 2 Bing.N.C. 437, 132 Eng.Rep. 171; Haylock v. Sparke, 1853, 1 El. & Bl. 471, 118 Eng.Rep. 512.

89. Monson v. Tussauds, [1894] 1 Q.B. 671.

90. Merle v. Sociological Research Film Corp., 1915, 166 App.Div. 376, 152 N.Y.S. 829.

91. Eyre v. Garlick, 1878, 42 J.P. 68; Johnson v. Commonwealth, 1888, 14 A. 425, 22 Wkly.Notes Cas., Pa., 68.

92. De Libellis Famosis, 1605, 5 Co.Rep. 125a, 77 Eng.Rep. 250; cf. Jefferies v. Duncombe, 1809, 11 East 226, 103 Eng.Rep. 991 (lantern indicating bawdy house); Thompson v. Adelberg & Berman, 1918, 181 Ky. 487, 205 S.W. 558 (collector has called).

93. Svendsen v. State Bank of Duluth, 1896, 64 Minn. 40, 65 N.W. 1086; Cox v. National Loan & Exchange Bank, 1927, 138 S.C. 381, 136 S.E. 637; Gatley, Libel and Slander, 2d Ed.1929, 19. See, 1930, 9 North Car.L.Rev. 94.

94. Schultz v. Frankfort Marine, Acc. & P. G. Ins. Co., 1913, 151 Wis. 537, 139 N.W. 386. See Note, 1920, 5 Corn.L.Q. 340. Accord, Varner v. Morton, 1919, 53 Nova Scotia 180, 10 B.R.C. 218 (charivari). Contra, under statute, Collins v. Oklahoma State Hospital, 1919, 76 Okl. 229, 184 P. 946 (placing white person in colored ward). Cf. Molt v. Public Indemnity Co., 1940, 10 N.J.Misc. 879, 161 A. 346 (insurance investigation held to be "continuing slander").

95. As in the case of a blind man reading Braille, or feeling a defamatory statue? Or one spraying the plaintiff with a malodorous liquid, with a defamatory imputation?

96. Bennett v. Norban, 1959, 396 Pa. 94, 151 A.2d 476 (searching pockets on the street); Lonardo v. Quaranta, 1964, 99 R.I. 70, 205 A.2d 837 (omitting name of daughter from obituary notice). See Lord Abinger, in Gustole v. Mathers, 1836, 1 M. & W. 495, 501, 150 Eng.Rep. 530; Lord Ellenborough, in Cook v. Cox, 1814, 3 M. & S. 110, 114, 105 Eng.Rep. 552; Bower, Actionable Defamation, 2d Ed.1923, 20–21; Restatement of Torts, § 568, Comment *d*.

97. Peterson v. Western Union Tel. Co., 1896, 65 Minn. 18, 67 N.W. 646; 1898, 72 Minn. 41, 74 N.W. 1022; 1899, 75 Minn. 368, 77 N.W. 985. See Smith, Liability of a Telegraph Company for Transmitting a Defamatory Message, 1920, 20 Col.L.Rev. 30, 44– 46.

tion to a stenographer,[98] or even an interview given to a reporter,[99] is considered libel. Furthermore, it is generally held that it is a publication of a libel to read a defamatory writing aloud.[1] This might suggest that the distinction is one of embodiment in some more or less permanent physical form, and frequently it is so stated. There has been semihumorous speculation as to a phonograph record, or words taught to a parrot,[2] but the cases have not arisen.

The unexpected advent of new methods of communication has left the courts struggling with the distinction. They have found no difficulty in holding that the sound in a "talking" picture is libel, since it accompanies and is identified with the film itself.[3] Defamation by radio and television is, however, still a subject of violent debate.[4] It has been considered by comparatively few courts, and held by some to be libel,[5] by one slan-

der,[6] by others to be libel if the broadcaster reads from a script,[7] but slander if he does not; while still others apparently have regarded it as having special characteristics half way between the two,[8] and one court has even coined a barbarous new word, "defamacast," to avoid calling it either.[9] Television obviously will follow radio,[10] wherever radio may be going, rather than an analogy to motion pictures.

The dispute rages between those who believe that radio and television broadcasting, because of the extensive damage it may inflict, should incur all of the responsibilities of newspaper publication,[11] and those who

98. See infra, p. 767.

99. Valentine v. Gonzales, 1920, 190 App.Div. 490, 179 N.Y.S. 711.

1. See infra, p. 768.

2. 1935, 51 L.Q.Rev. 281–283, 573, 574; Winfield, Law of Tort, 1937, 259. See A. P. Herbert, Uncommon Law, 1936, 43–48 ("the law is clear"—but owing to the sudden demise of Lord Goat, it is not clear in what direction it is clear).

3. Youssoupoff v. Metro-Goldwyn-Mayer Pictures, 1934, 50 T.L.R. 581, 51 L.Q.Rev. 281; Brown v. Paramount-Publix Corp., 1934, 240 App.Div. 520, 270 N.Y.S. 544; Kelly v. Loew's, D.Mass.1948, 76 F. Supp. 473.

4. See Donnelly, Defamation by Radio: A Reconsideration, 1948, 34 Iowa L.Rev. 12; Yankwich, Trends in the Law Affecting Media of Communication, 1954, 15 F.R.D. 291; Notes, 1935, 51 L.Q.Rev. 573; 1938, 23 Wash.U.L.Q. 262; 1938, 26 Geo.L.J. 475; 1941, 39 Mich.L.Rev. 1002; 1942, 25 Chicago-Kent L.Rev. 142; 1947, 33 Va.L.Rev. 612; 1957, 43 Corn.L.Q. 320; 1961, 33 Miss.L.J. 33; 1964, 2 Houst.L.Rev. 238; 1964, 15 Mercer L.Rev. 450.

5. Sorensen v. Wood, 1932, 123 Neb. 348, 243 N.W. 82; Coffey v. Midland Broadcasting Co., D.Mo.1934, 8 F.Supp. 889; Wanamaker v. Lewis, D.C.D.C.1959, 173 F.Supp. 126; Shor v. Billingsley, Sup.Ct.1956, 158 N.Y.S.2d 476, affirmed without opinion, 1957, 4 App.Div.2d 1017, 169 N.Y.S.2d 416. The English Defamation Act of 1952, 15 & 16 Geo. 6 & 1 Eliz. 2, ch. 66, cl. 1–2, makes such defamation libel.

6. Meldrum v. Australian Broadcasting Co., [1932] Vict.L.Rep. 425, [1932] Aust.L.Rep. 452.

7. Hartmann v. Winchell, 1947, 296 N.Y. 296, 73 N. E.2d 30; Hryhorijiv v. Winchell, 1943, 180 Misc. 574, 45 N.Y.S.2d 31, affirmed, 1944, 267 App.Div. 817, 47 N.Y.S.2d 102; Gibler v. Houston Post Co., Tex.Civ.App.1958, 310 S.W.2d 377, ref. n. r. e.; Charles Parker Co. v. Silver City Crystal Co., 1955, 142 Conn. 605, 116 A.2d 440. Cf. Weglein v. Golder, 1935, 317 Pa. 437, 177 A. 47 (script sent to newspapers).

The distinction makes no great amount of sense, when the listener does not know whether there is a script. See the vigorous concurring opinion of Fuld, J., in Hartmann v. Winchell, supra. What if the defendant falsely says "I am reading you a letter," etc.?

8. Summit Hotel Co. v. National Broadcasting Co., 1939, 336 Pa. 182, 8 A.2d 302; Kelly v. Hoffman, 1948, 137 N.J.L. 695, 61 A.2d 143; Irwin v. Ashurst, 1938, 158 Or. 61, 74 P.2d 1127. See Newhouse, Defamation by Radio: A New Tort, 1938, 17 Or.L.Rev. 314; Note, 1933, 12 Or.L.Rev. 149.

Other courts have avoided the issue, as in Lynch v. Lyons, 1939, 303 Mass. 116, 20 N.E.2d 953; Miles v. Louis Wasmer, Inc., 172 Wash. 466, 20 P.2d 847; Singler v. Journal Co., 1935, 218 Wis. 263, 260 N.W. 431.

9. American Broadcasting-Paramount Theatres, Inc. v. Simpson, 1962, 106 Ga.App. 230, 126 S.E.2d 873. The defendant was held liable, however, as if there were libel.

10. Remington v. Bentley, S.D.N.Y.1949, 88 F.Supp. 166 (held to be slander in the absence of a script); Landau v. Columbia Broadcasting System, 1954, 205 Misc. 357, 128 N.Y.S.2d 254 (libel with a script).

11. Vold, The Basis for Liability for Defamation by Radio, 1935, 19 Minn.L.Rev. 611; Vold, Defamation

think that it should be favored by the law.[12] Since it obviously does not fit at all into the rather senseless distinctions inherited from the sixteenth century, there was originally some hope [13] that its development might lead to a complete overhauling of the law, and a reorganization of the rules of defamation upon some other basis. The matter is now rapidly being regulated by statutes, adopted in most jurisdictions.[14] Unfortunately the statutes began by exhibiting the same disagreement, some of them treating the defamation as libel,[15] others as slander,[16] and others with blissful complacency, as both.[17] The recent trend, thanks to the industrious lobbying of the broadcasting companies, has been strongly in the direction of holding such defamation to be slander; and that is now the rule in the considerable majority of the jurisdictions which have any law on the matter.

Slander Actionable Without Proof of Damage

The reluctance with which the common law courts at first received the action of

slander, and their fear of invading the province of ecclesiastical law, led them to hold that the action would not lie without proof of "temporal" damage. From this there developed the rule that slander, in general, is not actionable unless actual damage is proved. To this the courts very early established certain specific exceptions: the imputation of crime, of a loathsome disease, and those affecting the plaintiff in his business, trade, profession, office or calling—which required no proof of damage. The exact origin of these exceptions is in some doubt, but probably it was nothing more unusual than a recognition that by their nature such words were especially likely to cause pecuniary, or "temporal" rather than "spiritual" loss.[18] Modern statutes and decisions have added a fourth category, the imputation of unchastity to a woman. For these four kinds of slander, no proof of any actual harm to reputation or any other damage is required for the recovery of either nominal [19] or substantial [20] damages. Otherwise stated, proof of the defamation itself is considered to establish the existence of some damages, and the jury are permitted, without other evidence, to estimate their amount.

1. *Crime.* The original basis of the exception as to words imputing crime seems to have been that the plaintiff was thereby

by Radio, 1932, 2 J.Radio Law 673; Vold, Defamatory Interpolations in Radio Broadcasts, 1940, 88 U.Pa.L.Rev. 249; Haley, The Law on Radio Programs, 1937, 5 Geo.Wash.L.Rev. 157, 184–185; Farnum, Radio Defamation and the American Law Institute, 1936, 16 Bos.U.L.Rev. 1; Notes, 1933, 11 Neb.L.B. 325; 1957, 43 Corn.L.Q. 320.

12. Davis, Law of Radio Communication, 1927, 160–162; Guider, Liability for Defamation in Political Broadcasts, 1932, 2 J.Radio Law 708; Sprague, Freedom of the Air, 1937, 8 Air L.Rev. 30; Notes, 1932, 46 Harv.L.Rev. 133; 1935, 8 So.Cal.L.Rev. 359.

13. See 1926, 70 Sol.J. 213; Bohlen, Fifty Years of Torts, 1937, 50 Harv.L.Rev. 725, 729–731; Graham, Defamation and Radio, 1937, 12 Wash.L.Rev. 282, 290; 1939, 24 Minn.L.Rev. 118.

14. See Remmers, Recent Legislative Trends in Defamation by Radio, 1951, 64 Harv.L.Rev. 727.

15. Illinois—S.H.A. ch. 38, §§ 404.1 to 404.4; Wash. Rev.Stat.Ann., Remington Supp.1940, §§ 2424, 2427.

16. California—Civ.Code, § 46; North Dakota—NDRC 1943, 12–2815.

17. Florida—F.S.A. § 770.03; Ind.Stat., Burns' Ann. St. § 2.518; Mont.Rev.Code, 1939, Supp., c. 3A, § 5694.1.

18. Holdsworth, Defamation in the Sixteenth and Seventeenth Centuries, 1924, 40 L.Q.Rev. 302, 397, 398–401. Thus as late as 1851 the Exchequer was still talking of "spiritual" damage, and denying recovery for slander of a clergyman on the ground that no "temporal" damage was proved. Gallwey v. Marshall, 1851, 9 Ex. 294, 156 Eng.Rep. 126.

19. Mayo v. Goldman, 1909, 57 Tex.Civ.App. 475, 122 S.W. 499; Wilson v. Sun Pub. Co., 1915, 85 Wash. 503, 148 P. 774.

20. Taylor v. Gumpert, 1910, 96 Ark. 354, 131 S.W. 968; Ventresca v. Kissner, 1927, 105 Conn. 533, 136 A. 90. Even evidence that no actual damage was suffered goes only to mitigate the damages recovered. First Nat. Bank of Forrest City v. N. R. McFall & Co., 1920, 144 Ark. 149, 222 S.W. 40.

placed in danger of criminal prosecution.[21] Hence the rule that accusations of the mere intent to commit a crime are not sufficient,[22] and that crimes not recognized by the law, as in the case of larceny of land,[23] are not included. With the passage of time, the emphasis shifted to the social ostracism involved, and it was held that the action lay without proof of damage although the words made it clear that the plaintiff had been punished [24] or pardoned,[25] or could not be punished,[26] or that prosecution was barred by the statute of limitations.[27]

With the extension of criminal punishment to many minor offenses, it was obviously necessary to make some distinction as to the character of the crime, since a charge of a traffic violation, for example, would not exclude a man from society, and today would do little, if any, harm to his reputation at all. The English courts arrived at the rule that the crime must be one subject to corporal punishment, which in practice now means death or imprisonment.[28] The American jurisdictions, in general, began by adding the requirement that it must be subject to indictment, either at common law or by statute.[29] This is obviously a poor test, since it makes the decision turn upon the eccentricities of the criminal procedure provided by the legislature; and with the general modern tendency to substitute the information for the indictment, it has now very largely passed from the picture. Other courts, following an early New York case,[30] have required that, even though indictable, the offense must be one that involves an "infamous" or "disgraceful" punishment.[31] The vagaries of criminal punishments have made this too unreliable. The formula upon which most courts are now agreed is that the crime must be one which involves "moral turpitude." [32] A number of courts require this alone, without the possibility of an indictment or infamous punishment; [33] the greater number, however, state it as an alternative to one or the other.[34] Neither infamous punishment

21. Heming v. Power, 1842, 10 M. & W. 564, 569, 152 Eng.Rep. 595; 1 Street, Foundations of Legal Liability, 1906, 279.

22. Fanning v. Chace, 1891, 17 R.I. 388, 22 A. 275. Cf. Stees v. Kemble, 1858, 27 Pa. 112; Stokes v. Arey, 1860, 53 N.C.(8 Jones) 66.

23. Ogden v. Riley, 1833, 14 N.J.L. 186; Jackson v. Adams, 1835, 2 Bing.N.C. 402, 132 Eng.Rep. 158; Lemon v. Simmons, 1888, 57 L.J.Q.B. 260; Barnes v. Crawford, 1894, 115 N.C. 76, 20 S.E. 386. This although the speaker intends to charge the commission of a crime, and is understood to do so. Such a statement, if in writing, may be libel. Dooley v. Press Pub. Co., 1915, 170 App.Div. 492, 156 N.Y.S. 381, affirmed, 1954, 224 N.Y. 640, 121 N.E. 865; Note, 1916, 29 Harv.L.Rev. 857.

24. Fowler v. Dowdney, 1838, 2 Moo. & Rob. 119, 174 Eng.Rep. 234; Krebs v. Oliver, 1858, 12 Gray, 78 Mass., 239; Wiley v. Campbell, 1827, 5 T.B.Mon., 21 Ky. 396; Smith v. Stewart, 1847, 5 Pa. 372.

25. Shipp v. McCraw, 1858, 7 N.C. 463.

26. Thus as to infancy, Stewart v. Howe, 1855, 17 Ill. 71; Chambers v. White, 1855, 47 N.C., 2 Jones, 383.

27. Van Ankin v. Westfall, 1817, 14 Johns., N.Y., 233; Brightman v. Davies, 1925, 3 N.J.Misc. 113, 127 A. 327. Cf. French v. Creath, 1820, 1 Ill. 31 (statute creating offense repealed); Tenney v. Clement, 1838, 10 N.H. 52 (person asserted to have been murdered alive).

28. Hellwig v. Mitchell, [1910] 1 K.B. 609.

29. Brooker v. Coffin, 1809, 5 Johns., N.Y., 188; Birch v. Benton, 1858, 26 Mo. 153; Tharpe v. Nolan, 1905, 119 Ky. 870, 74 S.W. 1168; Herzog v. Campbell, 1896, 47 Neb. 370, 66 N.W. 424; Cullen v. Stough, 1917, 258 Pa. 196, 101 A. 937.

30. Brooker v. Coffin, 1809, 5 Johns., N.Y., 188.

31. Blake v. Smith, 1896, 19 R.I. 476, 34 A. 995; Deese v. Collins, 1926, 191 N.C. 749, 133 S.E. 92; McKee v. Wilson, 1882, 87 N.C. 300; Stevens v. Wilber, 1931, 136 Or. 599, 300 P. 329.

32. Wooten v. Martin, 1910, 140 Ky. 781, 131 S.W. 783; Morris v. Evans, 1918, 22 Ga.App. 11, 95 S.E. 385; Ranger v. Goodrich, 1863, 17 Wis. 78; Murray v. McAllister, 1856, 38 Vt. 167; Walker v. Tucker, 1927, 220 Ky. 363, 295 S.W. 138, 53 A.L.R. 547.

33. Larson v. R. B. Wrigley Co., 1931, 183 Minn. 28, 235 N.W. 393; Brown v. Nickerson, 1855, 5 Gray, Mass., 1; Halley v. Gregg, 1888, 74 Iowa 563, 38 N.W. 416; Kelly v. Flaherty, 1888, 16 R.I. 234, 14 A. 876.

34. Amick v. Montross, 1928, 206 Iowa 51, 220 N.W. 51; Woodville v. Pizatti, 1919, 119 Miss. 85, 80 So. 491; Shaw v. Killingsworth, 1925, 213 Ala. 655, 106

nor moral turpitude has received more than the vaguest definition; the former seems to mean death or imprisonment,[35] while the latter is said to refer to "inherent baseness or vileness of principle in the human heart." [36] It seems clear that it is not always the crime, but rather the character of the act charged, which will be determinative. It is not every trivial assault or battery which involves "moral turpitude," but an accusation that the plaintiff beat his mother necessarily does so.[37]

The idea toward which the courts obviously have been struggling is that the imputation is to be actionable without proof of damages only if it involves a major social disgrace, which might very well be the ultimate test. On this basis, it has been held that the character of the crime is to be determined by the law of the place where the defamatory statement is heard, rather than where the crime is alleged to have been committed.[38]

If these requirements are met, no particular form of language is necessary to liability.

Technical precision as to the particular crime is not called for,[39] and "thief" is enough,[40] as are slang synonyms, such as "pimp" [41] or "bootlegger." [42] It is not even necessary that the commission of any particular crime be charged at all, so long as it is said that the defendant has done something which meets the test; and a "deed without a name," such as "I know enough to put him in jail" [43] will be sufficient.

2. *Loathsome disease.* The basis of the exception as to the imputation of a loathsome disease seems originally to have been the exclusion from society which would result.[44] From the beginning it was limited to cases of venereal disease,[45] with a few instances

So. 138; Barnett v. Phelps, 1920, 97 Or. 242, 191 P. 502; Cline v. Holdredge, 1931, 122 Neb. 151, 239 N. W. 639.

35. See Earley v. Winn, 1906, 129 Wis. 291, 109 N.W. 633; Mackin v. United States, 1886, 117 U.S. 348; Geary v. Bennett, 1881, 53 Wis. 444, 10 N.W. 602; Note, 1922, 8 Corn.L.Q. 50.

36. Hughey v. Bradrick, 1931, 39 Ohio App. 486, 177 N.E. 911; Sipp v. Coleman, D.N.J.1910, 179 F. 997; Amick v. Montross, 1928, 206 Iowa 51, 220 N.W. 51; In re Henry, 1909, 15 Idaho 755, 99 P. 1054; In re Hopkins, 1909, 54 Wash. 569, 103 P. 805; Note, 1928, 12 Minn.L.Rev. 172.

As to particular crimes, see Hughey v. Bradrick, 1931, 39 Ohio App. 486, 177 N.E. 911 (theft); Pett-Morgan v. Kennedy, 1895, 62 Minn. 348, 64 N.W. 912 (habitual drunkenness); Le Moine v. Spicer, 1941, 146 Fla. 758, 1 So.2d 730 (same); Stevens v. Wilber, 1931, 136 Or. 599, 300 P. 329 ("bootlegger"); but cf. Bartos v. United States District Court, 8 Cir. 1927, 19 F.2d 722 (violation of National Prohibition Act).

37. Sipp v. Coleman, D.N.J.1910, 179 F. 997.

38. Klumph v. Dunn, 1870, 66 Pa. 141; Shipp v. McCraw, 1819, 7 N.C. 463. Contra: Dufresne v. Weise, 1879, 46 Wis. 290, 1 N.W. 59; Kinney v. Hosea, 1839, 3 Harr., Del., 77.

39. Bihler v. Gockley, 1886, 18 Ill.App. 496; Garrett v. Dickerson, 1863, 19 Md. 418; Seller v. Jenkins, 1884, 97 Ind. 430; Payne v. Tancil, 1900, 98 Va. 262, 35 S.E. 725.

40. O'Cana v. Espinosa, 1960, 141 Colo. 371, 347 P.2d 1118; Robins v. Franks, 1601, Cro.Eliz. 857, 78 Eng.Rep. 1083; cf. Tennyson v. Werthman, 1958, 167 Neb. 208, 92 N.W.2d 559 ("kidnaper").

41. Lander v. Wald, 1926, 218 App.Div. 514, 219 N.Y. S. 57, affirmed, 1927, 245 N.Y. 590, 157 N.E. 870. Cf. Toal v. Zito, 1958, 11 Misc.2d 260, 171 N.Y.S.2d 393 ("confidence man").

42. Kammerer v. Sachs, 1928, 131 Misc. 640, 227 N. Y.S. 641; Stevens v. Wilber, 1931, 136 Or. 599, 300 P. 329.

43. Webb v. Beaven, 1883, 11 Q.B.D. 699; Johnson v. Shields, 1855, 25 N.J.L. 116. Accord (and doubtful): Munafo v. Helfand, S.D.N.Y.1956, 140 F.Supp. 234 ("a known criminal"). Cf. Lorillard v. Field Enterprises, Inc., 1965, 65 Ill.App.2d 65, 213 N.E.2d 1 (suit against plaintiff for bigamy).

On the other hand, "You should be jailed" was held insufficient in Tex Smith, The Harmonica Man, v. Godfrey, 1951, 198 Misc. 1006, 102 N.Y.S.2d 251. And "You have a criminal record" was obviously insufficient in Riley v. Baddour, Sup.Ct.1947, 73 N. Y.S.2d 140.

44. See Crittal v. Horner, 1619, Hob. 219, 80 Eng. Rep. 366; Taylor v. Hall, 1743, 2 Stra. 1189, 93 Eng.Rep. 1118; Carlslake v. Mapledoram, 1788, 2 Term Rep. 473, 100 Eng.Rep. 255.

45. Crittal v. Horner, 1619, Hob. 219, 80 Eng.Rep. 366; Smith v. Hobson, 1647, Style 112, 82 Eng.Rep. 571; Kaucher v. Blinn, 1875, 29 Ohio St. 62; McDonald v. Nugent, 1904, 122 Iowa 651, 98 N.W. 506; Sally v. Brown, 1927, 220 Ky. 576, 295 S.W. 890.

of leprosy,[46] and it was not applied to more contagious and equally repugnant disorders such as smallpox.[47] The basis of the distinction was in all probability the fact that syphilis and leprosy were regarded originally as permanent, lingering and incurable, while from smallpox one either recovered or died in short order. The advance of medical science tended to keep the exception within its original limits; and today accusations of insanity [48] or of tuberculosis [49] or other communicable diseases [50] are not included. Furthermore, since there would not be the same social avoidance of one who had recovered, it is well established that the imputation that the plaintiff has had even a venereal disease in the past is not sufficient without proof of damage.[51]

3. *Business, trade, profession or office.* "The law has always been very tender of the reputation of tradesmen, and therefore words spoken of them in the way of their trade will bear an action that will not be actionable in the case of another person." [52] The likelihood of "temporal" damage in such a case is sufficiently obvious; and the rule was soon extended to cover anyone engaged in a business[53] or profession, or holding a public[54] or even a private office.[55] Any calling is included, "be it ever so base," [56] but it must be a legal one, entitled to such a sanction.[57] Furthermore, since the object of the exception is to protect the plaintiff in his office or calling, it was decided quite early that it must appear that he held or was engaged in it,

---

46. Taylor v. Perkins, 1607, Cro.Jac. 144, 79 Eng.Rep. 126; Lewis v. Hayes, 1913, 165 Cal. 527, 132 P. 1022; Simpson v. Press Pub. Co., 1900, 33 Misc. 228, 67 N.Y.S. 401. There is occasional mention in the decisions of the plague, but no case seems to have been reported.

47. James v. Rutledge, 1599, Moore 573, 4 Co.Rep. 17a, 76 Eng.Rep. 900.

48. Count Joannes v. Burt, 1863, 6 Allen, Mass., 236. As to the history of that extraordinary litigant, the "Count" Joannes, see Browne, Count Johannes, 1896, 8 Green Bag 435. Cf. Barry v. Baugh, 1965, 111 Ga.App. 813, 143 S.E.2d 489 ("crazy").

49. Rade v. Press Pub. Co., 1902, 37 Misc. 254, 75 N. Y.S. 298; Kassowitz v. Sentinel Co., 1938, 226 Wis. 468, 277 N.W. 177. Contra, under statute, Brown v. McCann, 1927, 36 Ga.App. 812, 138 S.E. 247; and cf. Kirby v. Smith, 1929, 54 S.D. 608, 224 N.W. 230 (affecting employment).

50. Lowe v. De Hoog, Mo.App.1917, 193 S.W. 969 ("a bad" communicable disease). Cf. Cobb v. Tinsley, 1922, 195 Ky. 781, 243 S.W. 1009 (bed wetting). In Miles v. Record Pub. Co., 1926, 134 S.C. 462, 133 S. E. 99, a statement that plaintiff was a typhoid carrier was held to be libel per se; but this was in part on the basis of interference with plaintiff's business.

51. Smith's Case, 1604, Noy 151, 74 Eng.Rep. 1112; Taylor v. Hall, 1743, 2 Stra. 1189, 93 Eng.Rep. 1118; Bruce v. Soule, 1879, 69 Me. 562; Nichols v. Guy, 1850, 2 Ind. 82; Halls v. Mitchell, [1927] 1 Dom.L.Rep. 163.

52. Harman v. Delany, 1731, 2 Strange 898, 93 Eng. Rep. 925. See, generally, Lawson, The Slander of a Person in His Calling, 1881, 15 Am.L.Rev. 573.

53. In Carter v. Sterling Finance Co., Fla.App.1961, 132 So.2d 430, an allegation of interference with "business relations" was held to be sufficient, without specifying the business.

54. Foley v. Hoffman, 1947, 188 Md. 273, 52 A.2d 476; Correia v. Santos, 1961, 191 Cal.App.2d 844, 13 Cal.Rptr. 132. See Note, 1942, 51 Yale L.J. 693.

55. It has been held in England that the mere imputation of lack of ability in connection with an honorary office, as distinguished from one of profit, is not actionable without proof of damage. Alexander v. Jenkins, [1892] 1 Q.B. 797. Otherwise as to misconduct in office. Booth v. Arnold, [1895] 1 Q.B. 571. The American cases apparently have not distinguished in any way between offices of honor and of profit. Doherty v. Lynett, C.C.Pa.1907, 155 F. 681; Fitzgerald v. Piette, 1923, 180 Wis. 625, 193 N.W. 86; Maidman v. Jewish Publications, 1960, 54 Cal.2d 643, 7 Cal.Rptr. 617, 355 P.2d 265; Correia v. Santos, 1961, 191 Cal.App.2d 844, 13 Cal.Rptr. 132; Dietrich v. Hauser, 1965, 45 Misc.2d 805, 257 N.Y.S.2d 716.

56. Terry v. Hooper, 1663, 1 Lev. 115, 83 Eng.Rep. 325. Accord: Fitzgerald v. Redfield, 1868, 51 Barb., N.Y., 484 (mason); Burtch v. Nickerson, 1819, 17 Johns., N.Y., 217 (blacksmith); Lloyd v. Harris, 1923, 156 Minn. 85, 194 N.W. 101 (tenant farmer); cf. Hoeppner v. Dunkirk Printing Co., 1930, 254 N. Y. 95, 172 N.E. 139 (football coach).

57. Hunt v. Bell, 1822, 1 Bing. 1, 130 Eng.Rep. 1; Hargan v. Purdy, 1892, 93 Ky. 424, 20 S.W. 432; Williams v. New York Herald Co., 1914, 165 App. Div. 529, 150 N.Y.S. 838, dismissed 1916, 218 N.Y. 625, 112 N.E. 1079; Weltmer v. Bishop, 1902, 171 Mo. 110, 71 S.W. 167, dismissed, 191 U.S. 560.

or at least about to be so engaged, when the words complained of were published.[58]

For the same reason, the exception was limited to defamation of a kind incompatible with the proper conduct of the business, trade, profession or office itself. The statement must be made with reference to a matter of significance and importance for that purpose, rather than a more general reflection upon the plaintiff's character or qualities, where such special significance is lacking.[59] Thus it is actionable without proof of damage to say of a physician that he is a butcher and the speaker would not have him for a dog,[60] of an attorney that he is a shyster,[61] of a school teacher that he has been guilty of improper conduct as to his pupils,[62] of a clergyman that he is the subject of scandalous rumors,[63] of a chauffeur that he is habitually drinking,[64] of a merchant that his credit is bad[65] or that he sells adulterated goods,[66] of a public officer that he has accepted a bribe or has used his office for corrupt purposes,[67] or that he is a Communist,[68] or of any of these that he is dishonest,[69] incompetent,[70] or insane [71]—since these things obviously discredit him in his chosen calling.

On the other hand it has been held not to be actionable without proof of damage to say

58. Collis v. Malin, 1632, Cro.Car. 282, 79 Eng.Rep. 847; Gallwey v. Marshall, 1851, 9 Ex. 294, 156 Eng.Rep. 126; Forward v. Adams, 1831, 7 Wend., N.Y., 204.

59. See Restatement of Torts, § 573; Ireland v. McGarvish, 1847, 3 N.Y.Super., 1 Sandf., 155. Thus in Bruno v. Schukart, 1958, 12 Misc.2d 383, 177 N. Y.S.2d 51, "liar" and "no-good crook" were held not to meet the test, in the absence of some showing that they would affect the plaintiff's business.

60. Cruikshank v. Gordon, 1890, 118 N.Y. 178, 23 N. E. 457. Accord: Crane v. Darling, 1899, 71 Vt. 295, 44 A. 359; Depew v. Robinson, 1883, 95 Ind. 109; Elmergreen v. Horn, 1902, 115 Wis. 385, 91 N.W. 973.

61. Rush v. Cavenaugh, 1845, 2 Pa. 187; Nolan v. Standard Pub. Co., 1923, 67 Mont. 212, 216 P. 571; Kraushaar v. Levin, 1943, 181 Misc. 508, 42 N.Y.S. 2d 857 ("unethical"). Accord: Mains v. Whiting, 1891, 87 Mich. 172, 49 N.W. 559; Patangall v. Mooers, 1915, 113 Me. 412, 94 A. 561.

62. Thompson v. Bridges, 1925, 209 Ky. 710, 273 S.W. 529. Accord: Bray v. Callihan, 1900, 155 Mo. 43, 55 S.W. 865; Wertz v. Lawrence, 1919, 66 Colo. 55, 179 P. 813; Cavarnos v. Kokkinak, 1959, 338 Mass. 355, 155 N.E.2d 185 (introducing Communist literature into school).

63. Cobbs v. Chicago Defender, 1941, 308 Ill.App. 55, 31 N.E.2d 323.

64. Louisville Taxicab & Transfer Co. v. Ingle, 1929, 229 Ky. 518, 17 S.W.2d 709.

65. Jones v. Littler, 1841, 7 M. & W. 423, 151 Eng. Rep. 831; Fred v. Traylor, 1903, 115 Ky. 94, 72 S. W. 768; Phillips v. Hoefer, 1845, 1 Pa. 62; Walter v. Duncan, Sup.Ct.1956, 153 N.Y.S.2d 916 ("You never pay your bills"); Meyerson v. Hurlbut, 1938, 68 App.D.C. 360, 98 F.2d 232, cert. denied 305 U.S. 610.

66. Mowry v. Raabe, 1891, 89 Cal. 606, 27 P. 157; Blumhardt v. Rohr, 1889, 70 Md. 328, 17 A. 266; Singer v. Bender, 1885, 64 Wis. 169, 24 N.W. 903. As to the distinction between defamation of the person and disparagement of the goods, see Wham, Disparagement of Property, 1926, 21 Ill.L.Rev. 26; Hibschman, Defamation or Disparagement, 1940, 24 Minn.L.Rev. 625; infra, § 108.

67. Earle v. Johnson, 1900, 81 Minn. 472, 84 N.W. 332; Heller v. Duff, 1898, 62 N.J.L. 101, 40 A. 691; Gottbheut v. Hubachek, 1875, 36 Wis. 515; Reilly v. Curtiss, 1912, 83 N.J.L. 77, 84 A. 199; Jarman v. Rea, 1902, 137 Cal. 339, 70 P. 216.

68. Remington v. Bentley, S.D.N.Y.1949, 88 F.Supp. 166.

69. Correia v. Santos, 1961, 191 Cal.App.2d 844, 13 Cal.Rptr. 132 (private office); Lendino v. Fiorenza, 1952, 203 Misc. 115, 115 N.Y.S.2d 160 (attorney); Badame v. Lampke, 1955, 242 N.C. 755, 89 S.E.2d 466 (business man) Fitzgerald v. Piette, 1923, 180 Wis. 625, 193 N.W. 86 (trustee of church); Wallace v. Jameson, 1897, 179 Pa. 98, 36 A. 142; Noeninger v. Vogt, 1886, 88 Mo. 589.

70. Stevens v. Morse, 1925, 185 Wis. 500, 201 N.W. 815 (farm labor organizer said to be utterly ignorant of farming); MacInnis v. National Herald Printing Co., 1918, 140 Minn. 171, 167 N.W. 550 (office holder said not to be a citizen, where this necessary to eligibility); Foley v. Hoffman, 1947, 188 Md. 273, 52 A.2d 476 (incapacity for office held); Fitzgerald v. Redfield, 1868, 51 Barb., N.Y., 484; Hellstern v. Katzer, 1899, 103 Wis. 391, 79 N.W. 429.

71. Fitzgerald v. Young, 1911, 89 Neb. 693, 132 N.W. 127; Wertz v. Lawrence, 1919, 66 Colo. 55, 179 P. 813; Clifford v. Cochrane, 1882, 10 Ill.App. 570; Lynott v. Pearson, 1910, 138 App.Div. 306, 122 N.Y. S. 986.

of a gas company clerk that he has been consorting with prostitutes,[72] since he might still be a satisfactory clerk; or of a stenographer that she does not pay her bills,[73] since she might still be a good stenographer; or of a physician that he has committed adultery,[74] of a dancing teacher that he has been drunk,[75] of an attorney that he has lost thousands,[76] or of an engineer that he is a Communist,[77] or of a Congressman that he is anti-Semitic.[78] Sometimes this has been carried to ridiculous lengths, as in the case of the decision [79] that an attorney is not defamed in his profession by being called a "bum in a gin mill." The effect of a charge that the plaintiff is insolvent, illiterate, a coward or has been seen drunk, may depend upon whether he is a merchant, a professor, a soldier, or a clergyman.[80] An accusation

of a single act of misconduct may not be sufficient, since one mistake does not amount to incompetence,[81] but if it fairly imputes either habitual conduct or a lack of qualities which the public has a right to expect of the plaintiff in his calling, it may be actionable.[82]

4. *Unchastity.* An accusation of unchastity was at first regarded as purely a "spiritual matter"—that is, a sin—and so was not actionable without proof of "temporal" damage, such as the loss of a particular marriage.[83] This remained the law of England until 1891, when it was remedied, as to the female sex, by the Slander of Women Act.[84] Similar statutory changes of the common law rule have been made in a number of American states,[85] and several courts have accomplished much the same result by holding that an imputation of unchastity to either sex is equivalent to a charge of the crime of adultery or fornication, which involves an infamous punishment or moral turpitude.[86] In some jurisdictions cases following the older rule have not yet been over-

---

72. Lumby v. Allday, 1831, 1 C. & J. 301, 148 Eng. Rep. 1434. See also Buck v. Savage, Tex.Civ.App. 1959, 323 S.W.2d 363, ref. n. r. e. (homosexuality attributed to druggist).

73. Liebel v. Montgomery Ward & Co., 1936, 103 Mont. 370, 62 P.2d 667.

74. Ayre v. Craven, 1834, 2 Ad. & El. 2, 111 Eng.Rep. 1. Accord: Jones v. Jones, [1916] 2 A.C. 481. Cf. Ireland v. McGarvish, 1847, 3 N.Y.Super. 155; Redway v. Gray, 1859, 31 Vt. 292; Dallavo v. Snider, 1906, 143 Mich. 542, 107 N.W. 271; Vinson v. O'Malley, 1923, 25 Ariz. 552, 220 P. 393.

75. Buck v. Hersey, 1850, 31 Me. 558.

76. Dauncey v. Holloway, [1901] 2 K.B. 441. Cf. Doyley v. Roberts, 1837, 3 Bing.N.C. 835, 132 Eng. Rep. 632 (defrauded his creditors and was horsewhipped off the course at Doncaster).

77. Gurtler v. Union Parts Mfg. Co., 1955, 285 App. Div. 643, 140 N.Y.S.2d 254, motion dismissed, 1955, 286 App.Div. 832, 143 N.Y.S.2d 627, affirmed, 1956, 1 N.Y.2d 5, 150 N.Y.S.2d 4, 132 N.E.2d 889.

78. Sweeney v. Philadelphia Record Co., 3 Cir. 1942, 126 F.2d 53; Sweeney v. Patterson, D.C.Cir. 1942, 128 F.2d 457, cert. denied 317 U.S. 678.

79. Weidberg v. La Guardia, 1939, 170 Misc. 374, 10 N.Y.S.2d 445.

80. Cf. Winsette v. Hunt, 1899, 53 S.W. 522, 21 Ky. Law Rep. 922; Darling v. Clement, 1897, 69 Vt. 292, 37 A. 779; Hayner v. Cowden, 1875, 27 Ohio St. 292; Boling v. Clinton Cotton Mills, 1932, 163

S.C. 13, 161 S.E. 195; Cobbs v. Chicago Defender, 1941, 308 Ill.App. 55, 31 N.E.2d 323.

81. Camp v. Martin, 1854, 23 Conn. 86; Foot v. Brown, 1811, 8 Johns., N.Y., 64.

82. Secor v. Harris, 1854, 18 Barb., N.Y., 425; Sumner v. Utley, 1829, 7 Conn. 257; Amick v. Montross, 1928, 206 Iowa 51, 220 N.W. 51. Charges of repeated misconduct nearly always have been held sufficient, as in High v. Supreme Lodge of the World, 1943, 214 Minn. 164, 7 N.W.2d 675; Dickey v. Brannon, 1968, 118 Ga.App. 33, 162 S.E.2d 827.

83. Davies v. Gardiner, 1593, Popham 36, 79 Eng. Rep. 1155; Oxford v. Cross, 1599, 4 Co.Rep. 18, 76 Eng.Rep. 902; Matthew v. Crass, 1614, Cro.Jac. 323, 79 Eng.Rep. 276.

84. 1891, 54 & 55 Vict. ch. 51.

85. See Richter v. Stolze, 1909, 158 Mich. 594, 123 N. W. 13; Vanloon v. Vanloon, 1911, 159 Mo.App. 255, 140 S.W. 631; Pink v. Catanich, 1876, 51 Cal. 420; Smith v. Gaffard, 1857, 31 Ala. 45.

86. Davis v. Sladden, 1889, 17 Or. 259, 21 P. 140; Kelley v. Flaherty, 1888, 16 R.I. 234, 14 A. 867; Zeliff v. Jennings, 1884, 61 Tex. 458; Reitan v. Goebel, 1885, 33 Minn. 151, 122 N.W. 291.

ruled,[87] although it does not appear very likely that they will be followed today. Most courts, however, have now rebelled at the reproach to the law involved in such a result, and have held that an oral imputation of unchastity to a woman is actionable without proof of damage without regard to whether it charges a crime.[88] Such a rule never has been applied to a man, since the damage to his reputation is assumed not to be as great.[89] Although the question has arisen in only one case,[90] it appears very likely, in view of popular feeling on the matter, that the imputation of homosexuality to either sex would be held to constitute a fifth category, actionable without proof of damage.

Special Damage

All other slanderous words, no matter how grossly defamatory or insulting they may be, which cannot be fitted into the arbitrary categories listed above, are actionable only upon proof of "special" damage—special in the sense that it must be supported by specific proof, as distinct from the damage assumed to follow in the case of libel or the kinds of slander already considered.[91] This is true, for example, of the accusation that the plaintiff is a bastard,[92] or the related im-

putation of canine ancestry,[93] or that he is a crook,[94] a damn liar,[95] or a Communist [96] where none of the exceptional rules is applicable;[97] or that he does not pay his debts,[98] or is dirty,[99] or wets the bed.[1]

This was in all conscience bad enough; but since "temporal" damage was necessary, the courts made matters worse by requiring that the special damage be pecuniary in its nature. Thus, while the loss of customers or

Paysse, 1915, 84 Wash. 351, 146 P. 840; Mishkin v. Roreck, 1952, 202 Misc. 653, 115 N.Y.S.2d 269.

93. Ringgold v. Land, 1937, 212 N.C. 369, 193 S.E. 267; Martin v. Sutter, 1922, 60 Cal.App. 8, 212 P. 60; Torres v. Huner, 1912, 150 App.Div. 798, 135 N.Y.S. 332. Cf. Dalton v. Woodward, 1938, 134 Neb. 915, 280 N.W. 215.

94. Nelson v. Rosenberg, 1938, 135 Neb. 34, 280 N.W. 229; Mishkin v. Roreck, 1952, 202 Misc. 653, 115 N.Y.S.2d 269; Hofstadter v. Bienstock, 1925, 213 App.Div. 807, 208 N.Y.S. 453; Eggleston v. Whitlock, 1927, 242 Ill.App. 379; Gaare v. Melbostad, 1932, 186 Minn. 96, 242 N.W. 466 ("If Joe had not been a crooked son-of-a-bitch that bank would never have gone broke").

95. Shipe v. Schenk, Mun.App.D.C.1960, 158 A.2d 910.

96. Johnson v. Nielsen, N.D.1958, 92 N.W.2d 66; Gurtler v. Union Parts Mfg. Co., 1956, 1 N.Y.2d 5, 150 N.Y.S.2d 4, 132 N.E.2d 889; Ward v. Forest Preserve District, 1957, 13 Ill.App.2d 257, 141 N.E. 2d 753; Pecyk v. Semoncheck, Ohio App.1952, 105 N.E.2d 61. See Booker, The Accusation of Communism as Slander Per Se, 1954, 4 Duke Bar J. 1.

97. In some jurisdictions the accusation has been held to charge a crime. Grein v. La Poma, 1959, 54 Wash.2d 844, 340 P.2d 766; Joopanenko v. Gavagan, Fla.1953, 67 So.2d 434; Lightfoot v. Jennings, 1953, 363 Mo. 878, 254 S.W.2d 596; Solosko v. Paxton, 1956, 383 Pa. 419, 119 A.2d 230. See Note, 1959, 33 So.Cal.L.Rev. 104.

98. Urban v. Hartford Gas Co., 1952, 139 Conn. 301, 93 A.2d 292; Patton v. Jacobs, 1948, 118 Ind.App. 358, 78 N.E.2d 789; Hudson v. Pioneer Service Co., 1959, 218 Or. 561, 346 P.2d 123; cf. Shipe v. Schenk, Mun.App.D.C.1960, 158 A.2d 910 ("deadbeat"); Loyd v. Pearse, 1618, Cro.Jac. 424, 79 Eng.Rep. 362 ("bankrupt rogue").

99. Larson v. R. B. Wrigley Co., 1931, 183 Minn. 28, 235 N.W. 393. Cf. Newman v. Ligo Operating Co., Sup.Ct.1955, 142 N.Y.S.2d 821 ("bum").

1. Cobb v. Tinsley, 1922, 195 Ky. 781, 243 S.W. 1009.

87. Pollard v. Lyons, 1875, 91 U.S. 225, 23 L.Ed. 308; Barnett v. Phelps, 1920, 97 Or. 242, 191 P. 502; Ledlie v. Wallen, 1895, 17 Mont. 150, 42 P. 289; Douglas v. Douglas, 1895, 4 Idaho 293, 38 P. 934.

88. Biggerstaff v. Zimmerman, 1941, 108 Colo. 194, 114 P.2d 1098; Hollman v. Brady, 1956, 16 Alaska 308, 233 F.2d 877 (Alaska law); Gnapinsky v. Goldyn, 1952, 23 N.J. 243, 128 A.2d 697; Crellin v. Thomas, 1952, 122 Utah 122, 247 P.2d 264; Cooper v. Seaverns, 1909, 81 Kan. 267, 105 P. 509.

89. Terwilliger v. Wands, 1858, 25 Barb. 313, 17 N.Y. 54; Hickerson v. Masters, 1921, 190 Ky. 168, 226 S. W. 1072; Marion v. Davis, 1927, 217 Ala. 16, 114 So. 357.

90. Nowark v. Maguire, 1964, 22 App.Div.2d 901, 255 N.Y.S.2d 318. In Buck v. Savage, Tex.Civ.App.1959, 323 S.W.2d 363, ref. n. r. e., this was held to be slander per se because it charged a crime.

91. McCormick, Damages, 1935, 442.

92. Walker v. Tucker, 1927, 220 Ky. 363, 295 S.W. 138; Hoar v. Ward, 1875, 47 Vt. 657; Paysse v.

business,[2] or a particular contract[3] or employment,[4] or of an advantageous marriage,[5] will be sufficient to make the slander actionable, it is not enough that the plaintiff has lost the society of his friends and associates,[6] unless their hospitality or assistance was such that it could be considered a pecuniary benefit;[7] or that he has suffered acute mental distress and serious physical illness as a result of the defamation,[8] or has been put to expense to refute it.[9]

On the other hand, once the cause of action is established, either by the character of the defamation itself or by the proof of pecuniary loss, the bars are lowered, and "general" damages may be recovered for the injury to the plaintiff's reputation,[10] his wounded feelings and humiliation,[11] and resulting physical illness and pain,[12] as well as estimated future damages of the same kind.[13] In other words, such damages are insufficient in themselves to make the slander actionable, but once the cause of action is made out without them, they may be tacked on as "parasitic" to it.[14] The tendency has been to leave the amount to be awarded, within very wide limits, to the jury; and there has been a wide range of variation, running from six cents to $1,000,000 in compensatory damages with an additional $1,250,000 in punitive damages.[15]

2. Evans v. Harries, 1856, 1 H. & N. 251, 156 Eng. Rep. 1197; Brooks v. Harison, 1883, 91 N.Y. 83; Ross v. Fitch, 1882, 58 Tex. 148; Schoen v. Washington Post, D.C.Cir. 1957, 246 F.2d 670; Morasse v. Brochu, 1890, 151 Mass. 567, 25 N.E. 74. It was formerly the rule, and still is in some states that these must be pleaded and proved "with particularity." Life Printing & Pub. Co. v. Field, 1944, 324 Ill.App. 254, 58 N.E.2d 307. The prevailing rule today is that a general allegation, with proof of a general decline in business and the elimination of other causes, is sufficient where it is impossible to be more specific. Ellsworth v. Martindale-Hubbell Law Directory, 1938, 68 N.D. 425, 280 N.W. 879. See infra, p. 923.

3. Storey v. Challands, 1837, 8 C. & P. 234, 173 Eng. Rep. 475. Cf. Prettyman v. Shockley, 1890, 4 Har. Del., 112 (loss of credit).

4. Dixon v. Smith, 1860, 5 H. & N. 450, 157 Eng.Rep. 1257; Hartley v. Herring, 1799, 8 Term Rep. 130, 101 Eng.Rep. 1305; Wilson v. Cotterman, 1886, 65 Md. 190, 3 A. 890; Lombard v. Lennox, 1891, 155 Mass. 70, 28 N.E. 1125.

5. Matthew v. Crass, 1614, Cro.Jac. 323, 79 Eng.Rep. 276; Moody v. Baker, 1826, 5 Cow., N.Y., 351.

6. Allsop v. Allsop, 1860, 5 H. & N. 534, 157 Eng.Rep. 431; Roberts v. Roberts, 1864, 5 B. & S. 384, 122 Eng.Rep. 874; Beach v. Ranney, 1842, 2 Hill, N.Y., 309; Williams v. Riddle, 1911, 145 Ky. 459, 140 S. W. 661; Clark v. Morrison, 1916, 80 Or. 240, 156 P. 429.

7. Moore v. Meagher, 1807, 1 Taunt. 39, 127 Eng. Rep. 745; Davies v. Solomon, 1871, 7 Q.B. 112, 115 Eng.Rep. 431; Corcoran v. Corcoran, 1857, 7 Ir.C. L.Rep. 272; Pettibone v. Simpson, 1873, 66 Barb., N.Y. 492.

8. Allsop v. Allsop, 1860, 5 H. & N. 534, 157 Eng.Rep. 1292; Terwilliger v. Wands, 1858, 17 N.Y. 54; Harrison v. Burger, 1925, 212 Ala. 670, 103 So. 842; Clark v. Morrison, 1916, 80 Or. 240, 156 P. 429; Scott v. Harrison, 1939, 215 N.C. 427, 2 S.E.2d 1. See Day, Mental Suffering as an Element of Damages in Defamation Cases, 1966, 15 Cleve.Marsh.L. Rev. 26.

9. Bigelow v. Brumley, 1941, 138 Ohio St. 514, 37 N. E.2d 584.

10. Craney v. Donovan, 1917, 92 Conn. 236, 102 A. 640.

11. Pion v. Caron, 1921, 237 Mass. 107, 129 N.E. 369; Viss v. Calligan, 1916, 91 Wash. 673, 158 P. 1012; Baker v. Winslow, 1922, 184 N.C. 1, 113 S.E. 570; Finger v. Pollack, 1905, 188 Mass. 208, 74 N.E. 317; Poleski v. Polish-American Pub. Co., 1931, 254 Mich. 15, 235 N.W. 841. See Day, Mental Suffering as an Element of Damages in Defamation Cases, 1966, 15 Cleve.Marsh.L.Rev. 26.

It usually is held, however, that "reflex' mental suffering caused by the mental distress of the plaintiff's family over the defamation is not recoverable. Bishop v. New York Times Co., 1922, 233 N.Y. 446, 135 N.E. 845; Dennison v. Daily News Pub. Co., 1903, 82 Neb. 675, 118 N.W. 568. See Note, 1922, 8 Corn.L.Q. 65.

12. Sweet v. Post Pub. Co., 1913, 215 Mass. 450, 102 N.E. 660; Garrison v. Sun Printing & Pub. Assn., 1912, 207 N.Y. 1, 100 N.E. 430. Contra, holding it "too remote," Butler v. Hoboken Printing & Pub. Co., 1905, 73 N.J.L. 45, 62 A. 272.

13. Craney v. Donovan, 1917, 92 Conn. 236, 102 A. 640; Elms v. Crane, 1919, 118 Me. 261, 107 A. 852.

14. Compare supra, § 54.

15. In Faulk v. Aware, Inc., Sup.Ct.1962, 231 N.Y.S. 2d 270 (accusation of communism, causing plaintiff to be blacklisted). See McCormick, Damages, 1935, 444–445, listing various cases with amounts. Also Gregory and Kalven, Cases and Materials on Torts, 1959, 925–926.

So far as "proximate cause" is concerned, recovery has been limited very definitely to those damages which are regarded as reasonably foreseeable or normal consequences of the defamation.[16] Formerly it was held that the original defamer was liable only for the damages caused by his own publication, and was not responsible for repetition by others, on the theory that the "last human wrongdoer" must be responsible, and there is still some authority to this effect;[17] but there has been the same broadening of "proximate cause" as in other fields of liability, and the prevailing view now appears to be that there is liability for damages due to such a repetition when it was authorized or intended, or when the circumstances were such that it might reasonably have been anticipated.[18]

Libel

Any defamatory imputation may of course be conveyed in libelous form. By the beginning of the nineteenth century it was well established that any libel, as distinct from the same imputation in the form of slander,

was actionable without the necessity of pleading or proving that the plaintiff had in fact suffered any damage as a result of it.[19] In other words, the existence of damage was conclusively assumed from the publication of the libel itself, without other evidence that there was any damage at all. The practical result is that the jury may award not only nominal damages,[20] but substantial sums in compensation of the supposed harm to the plaintiff's reputation,[21] without any proof that it has in fact occurred. This is the accepted rule in England,[22] and it is still the law in a small minority of the American jurisdictions, not only as to publications which are defamatory on their face,[23] but also to those which require resort to extrinsic facts by way of "inducement" to establish the defamatory meaning.[24] Until quite lately this position was clearly taken by only one New York decision,[25] on which some doubt was

---

16. Lynch v. Knight, 1861, 9 H.L.C. 577, 11 Eng.Rep. 854; Anonymous, 1875, 60 N.Y. 262; Georgia v. Kepford, 1876, 45 Iowa 48; Field v. Colson, 1892, 93 Ky. 347, 20 S.W. 264.

17. Vicars v. Wilcocks, 1806, 8 East 1, 103 Eng.Rep. 244; Lehner v. Kelley, 1934, 215 Wis. 265, 254 N.W. 634; Hastings v. Stetson, 1879, 126 Mass. 329; Maytag v. Cummins, 8 Cir. 1919, 260 F. 74; Age-Herald Pub. Co. v. Waterman, 1914, 188 Ala. 272, 66 So. 16.

18. Zier v. Hofflin, 1885, 33 Minn. 66, 21 N.W. 862; Sawyer v. Gilmers, Inc., 1925, 189 N.C. 7, 126 S.E. 183; Southwestern Tel. & Tel. Co. v. Long, Tex. Civ.App.1915, 183 S.W. 421; Elms v. Crane, 1919, 118 Me. 261, 107 A. 852; Fitzgerald v. Young, 1911, 89 Neb. 693, 132 N.W. 127. See Restatement of Torts, § 576. Apparently damage due to repetition alone is sufficient to make slander actionable. Cf. Gillett v. Bullivant, 1846, 7 L.T.,O.S., 490; Derry v. Handley, 1867, 16 L.T.,N.S., 263; cf. Weaver v. Beneficial Finance Co., 1957, 199 Va. 196, 98 S.E.2d 687.

There is, however, still no liability for a republication which could not reasonably have been anticipated. Waite v. Stockgrowers' Credit Corp., 1933, 63 N.D. 763, 249 N.W. 910.

19. Thorley v. Lord Kerry, 1812, 4 Taunt. 355, 128 Eng.Rep. 367.

20. Jones v. Register & Leader Co., 1916, 177 Iowa 144, 158 N.W. 571; Godin v. Niebuhr, 1920, 236 Mass. 350, 128 N.E. 406.

21. Youssoupoff v. Metro-Goldwyn-Mayer Pictures, 1934, 50 T.L.R. 581, 99 A.L.R. 864 (£25,000); Lewis v. Hayes, 1918, 177 Cal. 587, 171 P. 293; Oklahoma Pub. Co. v. Givens, 10 Cir. 1933, 67 F.2d 62; Starks v. Comer, 1914, 190 Ala. 245, 67 So. 440. Even positive evidence that there was in fact no damage to the plaintiff's reputation does not go to defeat the action, but only to mitigate damages. First Nat. Bank v. N. R. McFall & Co., 1920, 144 Ark. 149, 222 S.W. 40.

22. Cassidy v. Daily Mirror Newspapers, [1929] 2 K. B. 331; Youssoupoff v. Metro-Goldwyn-Mayer Pictures, 1934, 50 T.L.R. 581, 99 A.L.R. 864.

23. See supra, p. 746. See for example Cowper v. Vannier, 1959, 20 Ill.App.2d 499, 156 N.E.2d 761 (charge of "mental illness"); Brauer v. Globe Newspaper Co., 1966, 351 Mass. 53, 217 N.E.2d 736 ("mentally retarded").

24. See supra, p. 746.

25. Sydney v. MacFadden Newspaper Pub. Corp., 1926, 242 N.Y. 208, 151 N.E. 209.

Obviously to be distinguished are such cases as Upton v. Times-Democrat Pub. Co., 1900, 104 La. 141, 28 So. 970, and Bowen v. Independent Pub. Co., 1957, 230 S.C. 509, 96 S.E.2d 564, where an identified in-

cast by other New York cases. But after an article [26] which provoked extended discussion in the law reviews,[27] the rule was reaffirmed in New York,[28] and clearly adopted in four or five other jurisdictions.[29]

The great majority, of some thirty-five other courts, have agreed where the publication is defamatory upon its face. They have disagreed, however, where extrinsic facts are necessary to make out the defamatory meaning conveyed; and they have held that such libel "per quod" [30] is to be treated like slander. If the imputation falls into one of the four special slander categories,[31] it is action-

able without proof of special damage.[32] If it does not, there can be no recovery unless special damage is pleaded and proved.[33]

This peculiar departure from the common law appears [34] to have resulted originally from a confusion of the two meanings of defamation "per se," which may signify either that the words are defamatory on their face or that they are actionable without proof of damage. The persistence of the rule appears, however, to represent a deliberate retreat from the rigors of the common law of libel; [35] and in at least one state [36] the legislature has made the change by statute. Its justification must be that when extrinsic facts must be resorted to the libel, as a libel, is incomplete. Whether the reason for the more stringent liability for libel is veneration for the written or printed word, or the likeli-

---

dividual was called a Negro. Here the defamatory imputation is clear from the face of the publication, and the fact that the plaintiff was a white man only goes to its falsity.

26. Prosser, Libel Per Quod, 1960, 46 Va.L.Rev. 839.

27. Eldredge, The Spurious Rule of Libel Per Quod, 1966, 79 Harv.L.Rev. 733; Prosser, More Libel Per Quod, 1966, 79 Harv.L.Rev. 1629; Henn, "Libel-by-Extrinsic-Fact, 1961, 47 Corn.L.Q. 14; Samore, New York Libel Per Quod: Enigma Still? 1967, 31 Alb.L.Rev. 250; Notes, 1962, 30 Ford.L. Rev. 463; 1967, 45 N.C.L.Rev. 241; 1964, 4 Nat. Res.J. 590; 1967, 16 Buff.L.Rev. 502; 1967, 51 Minn.L.Rev. 775; 1967, 33 Brook.L.Rev. 373; 1967, 24 Wash. & Lee L.Rev. 139.

28. Hinsdale v. Orange County Publications, Inc., 1966, 17 N.Y.2d 284, 270 N.Y.S.2d 592, 217 N.E.2d 650.

29. Herrmann v. Newark Morning Ledger Co., 1958, 48 N.J.Super. 420, 138 A.2d 61, aff'd on rehearing, 49 N.J.Super. 551, 140 A.2d 529; Pitts v. Spokane Chronicle Co., 1964, 63 Wash.2d 763, 388 P.2d 976; Martin v. Outboard Marine Corp., 1962, 15 Wis.2d 452, 113 N.W.2d 135; Hinkle v. Alexander, 1966, 244 Or. 267, 417 P.2d 586.

30. This was the phrase formerly used to precede the portion of the declaration alleging special damage, in the old common law pleading. Black's Law Dictionary, 4th Ed. 1951, 1293. See, as to the distinction between libel per se and per quod, Thompson v. Upton, 1958, 218 Md. 453, 146 A.2d 880. The classic case of libel per quod is Morrison v. Ritchie & Co. [1902] 4 Fraser, Sess.Cas., 645, 39 Scot.L.Rep. 432, where defendant's newspaper published a report that the plaintiff had given birth to twins. There were readers who knew that she had been married only one month.

31. See supra, p. 754.

32. Broking v. Phoenix Newspapers, 1953, 76 Ariz. 334, 264 P.2d 413; Creekmore v. Runnels, 1949, 359 Mo. 1020, 224 S.W.2d 1007; Rachels v. Deener, 1930, 182 Ark. 931, 33 S.W.2d 39; Foley v. Hoffman, 1947, 188 Md. 273, 52 A.2d 476; Wegner v. Rodeo Cowboys Ass'n, 10 Cir. 1960, 417 F.2d 881, cert. denied 398 U.S. 903.

33. Piver v. Hoberman, Fla.App.1969, 220 So.2d 408; Ilitzky v. Goodman, 1941, 57 Ariz. 216, 112 P.2d 860; Karrigan v. Valentine, 1959, 184 Kan. 783, 339 P.2d 52; Electric Furnace Corp. v. Deering Milliken Research Corp., 6 Cir. 1963, 325 F.2d 761; Chase v. New Mexico Pub. Co., 1949, 53 N.M. 145, 203 P.2d 594; Barrett v. Barrett, R.I.1970, 271 A.2d 825.

Virginia has gone even further, and has held that all libel is to be treated like slander, even though defamatory upon its face. M. Rosenberg & Sons v. Cerf, 1944, 182 Va. 512, 29 S.E.2d 375; Weaver v. Beneficial Finance Co., 1959, 200 Va. 572, 106 S.E. 2d 620; Carwile v. Richmond Newspapers, 1954, 196 Va. 1, 82 S.E.2d 588.

34. The best account of its origin is in the Note, 1960, 13 Vand.L.Rev. 730. See also McCormick, Damages, 1935, 415–419; Carpenter, Defamation— Libel and Special Damages, 1928, 7 Or.L.Rev. 353; Green, Relational Interests, 1936, 31 Ill.L.Rev. 35, 47–48; Notes, 1925, 14 Cal.L.Rev. 61; 1938, 26 Geo.L.J. 469; 1939, 38 Mich.L.Rev. 253.

35. See MacLeod v. Tribune Pub. Co., 1959, 52 Cal.2d 536, 343 P.2d 36, regarding it as a protection of the defendant against liability for defamation arising from facts of which he was ignorant.

36. California—Civ.Code, § 45a.

hood of wider dissemination or circulation, or the reduction to permanent form, still, as to all three, the facts do not go with the writing. They may be expected to be known to relatively few people, and not to reach the general public with the newspaper. Therefore, as to those relatively less serious imputations which, if they are slander, are not actionable without special damage, the same rule is applied to libel. Not all writers have accepted this; but the state of the cases leaves little doubt that the courts have done so. The effect is of course to blur still further the wavering distinction between libel and slander, and to add "an additional complexity to a subject already overburdened with rules which are holding over long after the judicial rivalries which have produced them have been forgotten." [37]

In 1966 the American Law Institute [38] tentatively proposed a compromise position, under which the defendant would be liable without special damages if he knew or should have known of the extrinsic facts which supplied the defamatory imputation, but not otherwise. The relegation of the topic of defamation to the foot of the Restatement calendar pending clarification of constitutional privilege by the Supreme Court called a temporary halt to any further consideration. As of the date of publication, only the New Mexico court [39] has adopted the compromise position.

Reform of the Law

The distinctions of libel and slander are those by which it is actionable to write that the plaintiff is a damned liar on a postcard, which is read by a single third person, but it may not be actionable to say the same thing in a speech to an audience of a thousand people; and by which, in some states, there may be recovery for a line in a newspaper to the effect that a woman wears a funny hat, or an oral assertion that she is a poor stenographer, but not for an oral accusation that she has given birth to a bastard child. [40] For upwards of a century and a half no one has defended these absurdities. The reasons that have been given for them have been offered in explanation rather than in justification. It used to be said that libel was capable of wider circulation, which obviously is not true; and that writing or print required forethought, and so showed greater malignity —which is a poor reason when liability does not rest upon any intent to defame. [41] These arguments were exploded by Sir James Mansfield as long ago as 1812. [42] Nothing but historical survival of the relics of forgotten jurisdictional conflicts accounts for a state of affairs peculiar to the common law, and unknown elsewhere in the civilized world. [43] Nowhere is the layman's criticism and the cry, "kill all the lawyers first," more thoroughly justified. Undoubtedly the ingenuity of the judge and the good sense of the jury often will introduce some degree of flexibility, [44] but more often they are quite helpless before rigid and arbitrary categories.

In addition to an almost incredible judicial inertia, one reason that the law has remained as it stands is that there is violent dispute as to the direction in which it should move. Assuming that the distinction between libel and slander is a thing without reason and to be abandoned, at least four proposals have been made [45] as to the basis on which the two might be united:

---

37. McCormick, Damages, 1935, 418.

38. [1966] Proceedings Am.Law.Inst. 460.

39. Reed v. Melnick, 1970, 81 N.M. 608, 471 P.2d 178.

40. Burch, J., in Cooper v. Seaverns, 1909, 81 Kan. 267, 105 P. 509.

41. See infra, p. 772.

42. In Thorley v. Lord Kerry, 1812, 4 Taunt. 355, 128 Eng.Rep. 367.

43. Carr, The English Law of Defamation, 1902, 18 L.Q.Rev. 255, 256–257.

44. See Green, Relational Interests, 1936, 31 Ill.L. Rev. 35.

45. See Donnelly, The Law of Defamation: Proposals for Reform, 1949, 33 Minn.L.Rev. 600.

1. To require, in all cases, proof of actual damage as essential to the existence of a cause of action.[46] This suggestion, of course, has been a popular one with publishers. It undoubtedly would go far to do away with the genuine evils of the petty spite suit for trivial utterances, and the serious abuse of the action of defamation as a weapon of extortion. But it will probably never be adopted, because it is clear that proof of actual damage will be impossible in a great many cases where, from the character of the defamatory words and the circumstances of publication, it is all but certain that serious harm has resulted in fact.

2. To make all defamation, oral or written, actionable without proof of damage.[47] This, in substance, is the present law of Louisiana,[48] and perhaps Washington,[49] and of Scotland,[50] and it has been adopted in some jurisdictions in Australia and New Zealand, and embodied in the Canadian Uniform Act, enacted in Alberta and Manitoba.[51] It seems to be administered in these jurisdictions without undue difficulty. Opposed to it is the obvious argument that much defamatory language, particularly in the case of hasty spoken words, is utterly trivial, harmless, and unworthy of redress; that the existing opportunities for extortion would be considerably increased; that in the interest of freedom of speech some safety-valve should be left open for the expression of unflattering views; and that if recovery is to be permitted in every case of defamation, it can only be kept within reasonable bounds by a degree of control over jury verdicts which our courts are no longer accustomed to exercise.

3. To distinguish between major and minor defamatory imputations, having regard to all extrinsic facts, and to make only the former actionable without proof of damage. This was the tenor of the English Press Union Bill of 1938, which failed of passage.[52] There is of course a very evident difference between calling a man a liar and accusing him of rape. But the fixed and arbitrary classifications now found in the law of slander have not been so outstandingly successful as to lead anyone to recommend their retention; and if they are not to be preserved, there must be in each case an individual determination of the question of degree, with a great deal of latitude left to the trial court in determining the seriousness of each charge upon the particular facts. While this does not appeal to those who distrust trial judges, the courts do appear to be dealing quite successfully with such questions of degree in the closely related tort of the intentional infliction of mental distress by extreme and outrageous conduct;[53] and it may be that there is no insuperable reason, other than sheer judicial reluctance to undertake the task, to working it out in defamation.

4. Finally, to distinguish upon the basis of the manner and extent of publication. Thus really "public" defamation, in the sense of publicity given in a newspaper, over television, or in a public address, might well be held actionable without proof of damage, because of its greater potentialities for harm and the impossibility of determining how far it has affected reputation, where a private

---

46. Advocated by Courtney, Absurdities of the Law of Slander and Libel, 1902, 36 Am.L.Rev. 552.

47. Advocated by Carr, The English Law of Defamation, 1902, 18 L.Q.Rev. 255, 388; Veeder, The History and Theory of the Law of Defamation, 1904, 4 Col.L.Rev. 33, 54–56; Paton, Reform and the English Law of Defamation, 1939, 33 Ill.L.Rev. 669.

48. Miller v. Holstein, 1839, 16 La. 389; Spotorno v. Fourichon, 1888, 40 La.Ann. 423, 4 So. 71; Fellman v. Dreyfous, 1895, 47 La.Ann. 907, 17 So. 422.

49. See the dictum in Grein v. La Poma, 1959, 54 Wash.2d 844, 340 P.2d 766.

50. Normand, The Law of Defamation in Scotland, 1938, 6 Camb.L.J. 327.

51. See Fleming, Law of Torts, 2d Ed. 1961, 488.

52. See Paton, Reform and the English Law of Defamation, 1939, 33 Ill.L.Rev. 669; Note, 1938, 85 L.J. 440.

53. See supra, § 12.

letter or conversation would not. This, at least, seems to make a great deal more sense than any arbitrary line drawn between written and oral communication.

If one were now approaching the question for the first time, without the dead weight of four centuries of precedent, some combination of the last two possibilities might appear to offer the most satisfactory solution, with only publicity given to major defamatory imputations made actionable without proof of special damage. This might, however, require also some relaxation of the rule, left over from the days of "spiritual" and "temporal" harm, that the special damage which will support an action must be pecuniary in its nature.

The difficulties of reform are obviously great; and the Porter Committee in England,[54] which studied the matter for nine years, finally came to the conclusion that the present law, absurd as it was admitted to be, afforded as good a compromise as any. As a result the English Defamation Act of 1952 made only minor changes.[55]

113.　BASIS OF LIABILITY

Publication

Since the interest protected is that of reputation, it is essential to tort liability for either libel or slander that the defamation be communicated to some one other than the person defamed.[56] This element of communication is given the technical name of "publication," but this does not mean that it must be printed or written; it may be oral, or conveyed by means of gestures, or the exhibition of a picture or statue.[57] Where there is no communication to any one but the plaintiff there may be criminal responsibility,[58] or a possible action for the intentional infliction of mental suffering,[59] but no tort action can be maintained upon the theory of defamation.[60] It is not enough that the words are uttered in the presence of others unless they are in fact overheard;[61] nor, although there is some authority to the contrary,[62] is it usually regarded as sufficient that they were sent through the mail on a

54.　Committee on the Law of Defamation, Report Cmd. No. 7536. See Lloyd, Reform of the Law of Libel, 1952, Curr.Leg.Prob. 168; Wade, Defamation, 1950, 66 L.Q.Rev. 348; Williams, Committee on the Law of Defamation: The Porter Report, 1949, 12 Mod.L.Rev. 217.

55.　Chiefly in making all radio defamation libel. See Todd, The Defamation Act, 1952, 1953, 16 Mod. L.Rev. 198; Note, 1953, 66 Harv.L.Rev. 476.

56.　Thus failure of the complaint to allege when, where and to whom the defamation was published is a fatal omission on demurrer. McGuire v. Adkins, 1969, 284 Ala. 602, 226 So.2d 659.

57.　Cf. Hird v. Wood, 1894, 38 Sol.J. 234 (pointing at sign); Schultz v. Frankfort Marine, Accident & Plate Glass Ins. Co., 1913, 151 Wis. 537, 139 N.W. 386 (shadowing); Louka v. Park Entertainments, 1936, 294 Mass. 268, 1 N.E.2d 41 (picture); Monson v. Tussauds, [1894] 1 Q.B. 671 (statue).

58.　Since it tends to a breach of the peace. Regina v. Brooke, 1857, 7 Cox C.C. 251; Regina v. Adams, 1886, 22 Q.B.D. 66. In Jacobs v. Transcontinental & Western Air, Mo.App.1947, 205 S.W.2d 887, a criminal statute was held to support a civil action. This was criticized in Notes, 1948, 13 Mo.L.Rev. 235; 1948, 32 Minn.L.Rev. 841, and reversed on other grounds in 1948, 358 Mo. 674, 216 S.W.2d 523. The court refused to follow it in Insurance Research Service v. Associates Finance Corp., M.D. Tenn.1955, 134 F.Supp. 54.

59.　See supra, § 12.

60.　Yousling v. Dare, 1904, 122 Iowa 539, 98 N.W. 371; Fry v. McCord Bros., 1895, 95 Tenn. 678, 33 S.W. 568; Busby v. First Christian Church, 1923, 153 La. 377, 95 So. 869; Insurance Research Service v. Associates Finance Corp., M.D.Tenn.1955, 134 F.Supp. 54; Almy v. Kvamme, 1963, 63 Wash.2d 326, 387 P.2d 372 (over telephone).

61.　Tocker v. Great A. & P. Tea Co., D.C.Cir. 1963, 190 A.2d 822; Sheffill v. Van Deusen, 1859, 13 Gray, Mass., 304; Gelhaus v. Eastern Air Lines, 5 Cir. 1952, 194 F.2d 774; Davidson v. Walter, 1958, 214 Ga. 187, 104 S.E.2d 113, conformed to 97 Ga. App. 728, 104 S.E.2d 337.

This may, however, be proved by circumstantial evidence, that there were those nearby who probably heard. Gaudette v. Carter, 1965, 100 R.I. 259, 214 A.2d 197.

62.　Ostro v. Safir, 1937, 165 Misc. 647, 1 N.Y.S.2d 377. See Robinson v. Jones, 1879, 4 L.R.Ir. 391; Huth v. Huth, [1915] 3 K.B. 32; Logan v. Hodges, 1907, 146 N.C. 38, 59 S.E. 349.

postcard,[63] or in an unsealed letter,[64] unless it is proved that a third person read them. Furthermore, since it is the defamatory meaning which must be communicated, it must be shown that the utterance was understood in that sense.[65] Thus words spoken in a foreign tongue are not actionable unless they are heard by one who understands the language.[66] In the case of publication in a newspaper, however, even in a foreign language, it is presumed that there are readers familiar with the ordinary meaning of the words.[67]

There may be publication to any third person. It may be made to a member of the plaintiff's family, including his wife,[68] or to the plaintiff's agent or employee.[69]

It may be made to the defendant's own agent, employee or officer, even where the defendant is a corporation.[70] The dictation of defamatory matter to a stenographer generally is regarded as sufficient publication,[71] although it may be privileged.[72] A few courts, with a tendency to confuse the question of publication with that of privilege, have held that it is not, regarding dictation as an indispensable method in modern business transactions, and therefore merely equivalent to the defendant's own writing.[73]

---

63. McKeel v. Latham, 1932, 202 N.C. 318, 162 S.E. 747; Steele v. Edwards, 1897, 15 Ohio Cir.Ct. 52, 8 Ohio Dec. 161. Cf. Continental Nat. Bank v. Dowdre, 1893, 92 Tenn. 723, 23 S.W. 131. See Note, 1916, 64 U.Pa.L.Rev. 193.

64. Huth v. Huth, [1915] 3 K.B. 32. Cf. Renfro Drug Co. v. Lawson, 1942, 138 Tex. 434, 160 S.W.2d 246 (exhibition of magazine for sale not enough without proof that it was sold or read). Cf. Neeley v. Winn-Dixie Greenville, Inc., S.C.1971, 178 S.E. 2d 662.

65. See supra, p. 746. See for example Geraghty v. Suburban Trust Co., 1965, 238 Md. 197, 208 A.2d 606.

66. Mielenz v. Quasdorf, 1886, 68 Iowa 726, 28 N.W. 41; Economopoulos v. A. G. Pollard Co., 1914, 218 Mass. 294, 105 N.E. 896; Pouchan v. Godeau, 1914, 167 Cal. 692, 140 P. 952; Rich v. Scalio, 1904, 115 Ill.App. 166. Cf. Sullivan v. Sullivan, 1892, 48 Ill. App. 435 (too young).

67. Steketee v. Kimm, 1882, 48 Mich. 322, 12 N.W. 177.

68. Wenman v. Ash, 1853, 13 C.B. 836, 138 Eng.Rep. 1432; Theaker v. Richardson, [1962] 1 All Eng. 229; Schenck v. Schenck, 1843, 20 N.J.L. 208; Luick v. Driscoll, 1895, 13 Ind.App. 279, 41 N.E. 463; Bonkowski v. Arlan's Dept. Store, 1970, 383 Mich. 90, 174 N.W.2d 755.

As to publication by one spouse to the other, see infra, p. 785.

69. Duke of Brunswick v. Harmer, 1849, 14 Q.B.D. 185, 53 L.J.Q.B. 20; Brown v. Elm City Lumber Co., 1914, 167 N.C. 9, 82 S.E. 961. There have been occasional cases which, apparently confusing publication with privilege, have held the contrary, as in Patrick v. Thomas, Okl.1962, 376 P.2d 250.

70. Fulton v. Atlantic Coast Line R. Co., 1951, 220 S.C. 287, 67 S.E.2d 425; Bacon v. Michigan Cent. R. Co., 1884, 55 Mich. 224, 21 N.W. 324; Kennedy v. James Butler, Inc., 1927, 245 N.Y. 204, 156 N.E. 666; Cochran v. Sears, Roebuck & Co., 1945, 72 Ga.App. 458, 34 S.E.2d 296.

There is some authority to the contrary, apparently as a result of confusing publication with privilege. Prins v. Holland-North America Mortgage Co., 1919, 107 Wash. 206, 181 P. 680; Chalkley v. Atlantic Coast Line R. Co., 1928, 150 Va. 301, 143 S.E. 631; Burney v. Southern R. Co., 1964, 276 Ala. 637, 165 So.2d 726. In Walter v. Davidson, 1958, 214 Ga. 187, 104 S.E.2d 113, conformed to 97 Ga.App. 728, 104 S.E.2d 337, this was carried to the length of holding that there was no publication in a communication between two members of a college faculty.

See Note, 1952, 38 Va.L.Rev. 400.

71. Pullman v. Walter Hill & Co., [1891] 1 Q.B. 524, 60 L.J.Q.B. 209; Rickbeil v. Grafton Deaconess Hospital, 1946, 74 N.D. 525, 23 N.W.2d 247, 166 A. L.R. 99; Ostrowe v. Lee, 1931, 256 N.Y. 36, 175 N. E. 505; Arvey Corp. v. Peterson, E.D.Pa.1959, 178 F.Supp. 132; Gambrill v. Schooley, 1901, 93 Md. 48, 48 A. 730; Berry v. City of New York Ins. Co., 1923, 210 Ala. 369, 98 So. 290. See Notes, 1954, 27 So.Cal.L.Rev. 229; 1954, 27 Temple L.Q. 127; 1950, 2 S.Car.L.Q. 290; 1964, 17 Ala.L.Rev. 176.

Some of these courts have held that there is publication only by the individual dictating, and not by the corporation employing both. Mims v. Metropolitan Life Ins. Co., 5 Cir. 1952, 200 F.2d 800; Owen v. Ogilvie Pub. Co., 1898, 32 App.Div. 465, 53 N.Y.S. 1033; Prins v. Holland-North America Mortgage Co., 1919, 107 Wash. 206, 181 P. 680.

72. See infra, p. 793. This seems to be much the better position. Suppose the defendant seizes the occasion to dictate to the stenographer an unprivileged letter to her fiancé, which defames him? Is there no publication?

73. Watson v. Wannamaker, 1950, 216 S.C. 295, 57 S.E.2d 477; Cartwright-Caps Co. v. Fischel & Kaufman, 1917, 113 Miss. 359, 74 So. 278; Satterfield v.

Where the matter is actually transcribed by the stenographer, the publication has been held to be one of libel rather than of slander.[74] The same is true of the delivery of a message to a telegraph office,[75] and the transmission of the message itself by one agent of the telegraph company to another.[76] On much the same basis of the existence of a permanent record, it is uniformly held that the reading of written defamation aloud is the publication of a libel, even though it is conveyed by sound.[77]

Every repetition of the defamation is a publication in itself,[78] even though the re-peater states the source,[79] or resorts to the customary newspaper evasion "it is alleged,"[80] or makes it clear that he does not himself believe the imputation.[81] The courts have said many times that the last utterance may do no less harm than the first, and that the wrong of another cannot serve as an excuse to the defendant.[82] Likewise every one who takes part in the publication, as in the case of the owner,[83] editor,[84] printer,[85] vendor,[86] or even carrier [87] of a newspaper is

McLellan Stores Co., 1939, 215 N.C. 582, 2 S.E.2d 709; Insurance Research Service v. Associates Finance Corp., M.D.Tenn. 1955, 134 F.Supp. 54.

74. Ostrowe v. Lee, 1931, 256 N.Y. 36, 175 N.E. 505; Gambrill v. Schooley, 1901, 93 Md. 48, 48 A. 730; Nelson v. Whitten, D.N.Y.1921, 272 F. 135; cf. Adams v. Lawson, 1867, 17 Grat., Va., 250. Contra: Osborn v. Thomas Boulter & Son, [1930] 2 K.B. 226; Angelini v. Antico, 1912, 31 N.Z.L.Rep. 141.

75. Williamson v. Freer, 1874, L.R. 9 C.P. 393; Monson v. Lathrop, 1897, 96 Wis. 386, 71 N.W. 596; Robinson v. Robinson, 1897, 13 T.L.R. 564.

76. Peterson v. Western Union Tel. Co., 1896, 65 Minn. 18, 67 N.W. 646; Id., 1898, 72 Minn. 41, 74 N.W. 1022. Contra, Western Union Tel. Co. v. Lesesne, 4 Cir. 1952, 198 F.2d 154, cert. denied, 344 U.S. 896 (South Carolina law). See Smith, Liability of a Telegraph Company for Transmitting a Defamatory Message, 1920, 20 Col.L.Rev. 30, 369; Note, 1930, 5 Wis.L.Rev. 297.

77. Bander v. Metropolitan Life Ins. Co., 1943, 313 Mass. 337, 47 N.E.2d 595; Ohio Pub. Serv. Co. v. Myers, 1934, 54 Ohio App. 40, 6 N.E.2d 29; Miller v. Donovan, 1896, 16 Misc. 453, 39 N.Y.S. 820; McCoombs v. Tuttle, 1840, 5 Blackf., Ind., 431; Adams v. Lawson, 1867, 17 Grat., Va., 250. Cf. Hartmann v. Winchell, 1947, 296 N.Y. 296, 73 N.E.2d 30.

78. Nance v. Flaugh, 1952, 221 Ark. 352, 253 S.W.2d 207; Lubore v. Pittsburgh Courier Pub. Co., D.D.C. 1951, 101 F.Supp. 234, affirmed, D.C.Cir. 1952, 200 F.2d 255; Folwell v. Providence Journal Co., 1896, 19 R.I. 551, 37 A. 6. See Painter, Republication Problems in the Law of Defamation, 1961, 47 Va.L. Rev. 1131; Notes, 1958, 26 Ford L.Rev. 713; 1957, 43 Va.L.Rev. 1132. In Weaver v. Beneficial Finance Co., 1957, 199 Va. 196, 98 S.E.2d 687, a foreseeable republication by a third person after the lapse of a year was held to afford a new cause of action against the original publisher, which started a new limitations period running.

79. McPherson v. Daniels, 1829, 10 B. & C. 263, 109 Eng.Rep. 448; Haines v. Campbell, 1891, 74 Md. 158, 21 A. 702; Vanover v. Wells, 1936, 264 Ky. 461, 94 S.W.2d 999; Times Pub. Co. v. Carlisle, 8 Cir. 1899, 94 F. 762; Lorillard v. Field Enterprises, Inc., 1965, 65 Ill.App.2d 65, 213 N.E.2d 1.

In MacFadden v. Anthony, Sup.Ct.1952, 117 N.Y.S.2d 520, a mere reference to the existence of an article, without repeating its contents, was held not to be a publication.

80. Lundin v. Post Pub. Co., 1914, 217 Mass. 213, 104 N.E. 480; Lancour v. Herald & Globe Ass'n, 1941, 111 Vt. 371, 17 A.2d 253; Maloof v. Post Pub. Co., 1940, 306 Mass. 279, 28 N.E.2d 458; Cobbs v. Chicago Defender, 1941, 308 Ill.App. 55, 31 N.E.2d 323 (it is rumored).

81. Branstetter v. Dorrough, 1882, 81 Ind. 527; Morse v. Times-Republican Print. Co., 1904, 124 Iowa 707, 100 N.W. 867; Cobbs v. Chicago Defender, 1941, 308 Ill.App. 55, 31 N.E.2d 323; Bishop v. Journal Newspaper Co., 1897, 168 Mass. 327, 47 N. E. 119.

82. "Talebearers are as bad as talemakers." Cavalier v. Original Club Forest, La.App.1952, 59 So.2d 489.

83. Crane v. Bennett, 1904, 177 N.Y. 106, 69 N.E. 274; Davis v. Hearst, 1911, 160 Cal. 143, 116 P. 530; Wahlheimer v. Hardenbergh, 1914, 160 App. Div. 190, 145 N.Y.S. 161, reversed on other grounds, 1916, 217 N.Y. 264, 111 N.E. 826.

84. Smith v. Utley, 1896, 92 Wis. 133, 65 N.W. 744; World Pub. Co. v. Minahan, 1918, 70 Okl. 107, 173 P. 815.

85. Baldwin v. Elphinstone, 1775, W.Bl. 1037; cf. Youmans v. Smith, 1897, 153 N.Y. 214, 219, 47 N.E. 265, 266. In Rex v. Clerk, 1728, 1 Barn. 304, 94 Eng.Rep. 207, a servant of the printer "whose business was only to clap down the press" was convicted of criminal libel.

86. Staub v. Van Benthuysen, 1884, 36 La.Ann. 467; Vizetelly v. Mudie's Select Library, [1900] 2 K.B. 170, 69 L.J.Q.B. 654; see Bigelow v. Sprague, 1886, 140 Mass. 425, 5 N.E. 144.

87. Cf. Arnold v. Ingram, 1912, 151 Wis. 438, 138 N.W. 111; Paton v. Great Northwestern Tel. Co. of

charged with publication, although so far as strict liability is concerned the responsibility of some of these has been somewhat relaxed.[88]

The English rule [89] has been that every sale or delivery of each single copy of a newspaper is a distinct publication, and a separate basis for a cause of action. This rule has received the unqualified acceptance of the Restatement of Torts,[90] and there are American jurisdictions in which it is still the last word of the courts.[91] The majority of the American courts, however, have developed, in cases involving venue [92] or the statute of limitations,[93] a "single publica-tion" rule,[94] under which an entire edition [95] of a newspaper, magazine or book [96] is treated as only one publication, and the plaintiff is permitted to plead and prove merely a general distribution of the libel [97] and show the extent of the circulation as evidence bearing on the damages.[98] Under this rule the publication has been treated as complete when "the finished product was released by the publisher for sale in accord with trade practice." [99] This rule has been adopted by the Commissioners on Uniform State Laws in the Uniform Single Publication Act.[100] It was formerly held by several courts [1] that

---

Canada, 1919, 141 Minn. 430, 170 N.W. 511 (telegraph company).

88. See infra, p. 775.

89. Duke of Brunswick v. Harmer, 1849, 14 Q.B. 185, 117 Eng.Rep. 75.

90. § 578, Comment *b*. The context makes it clear, however, that the language is directed at the liability of those who repeat defamation, and that no thought was given to the problem of separate sales or communications by the same defendant.

91. Staub v. Van Benthuysen, 1848, 36 La.Ann. 467; Renfro Drug Co. v. Lawson, 1942, 138 Tex. 434, 160 S.W.2d 246; Louisville Press Co. v. Tenelly, 1899, 105 Ky. 365, 49 S.W. 15; Holden v. American News Co., E.D.Wash.1943, 52 F.Supp. 24, dismissed 144 F. 2d 249; Hartmann v. American News Co., W.D. Wis.1947, 69 F.Supp. 736, affirmed, 7 Cir. 1948, 171 F.2d 581. Georgia abandoned this position in Rives v. Atlanta Newspapers, Inc., 1964, 110 Ga.App. 184, 138 S.E.2d 100.

92. Julian v. Kansas City Star Co., 1908, 209 Mo. 35, 107 S.W. 496; Age-Herald Pub. Co. v. Huddleston, 1921, 207 Ala. 40, 92 So. 193; O'Malley v. Statesman Printing Co., 1939, 60 Idaho 326, 91 P.2d 357; Forman v. Mississippi Publishers Corp., 1943, 195 Miss. 90, 14 So.2d 344. See, however, Firstamerica Develop. Corp. v. Daytona Beach-N.J. Corp., Fla. 1967, 196 So.2d 97.

93. The subsequent mailing of late copies, or sales from stock, is regarded as a part of the original publication, and will not extend the statute. Stephenson v. Triangle Publications, S.D.Tex.1952, 104 F.Supp. 215; McGlue v. Weekly Publications, Inc., D.Mass.1946, 63 F.Supp. 744; Winrod v. Time, Inc., 1948, 334 Ill.App. 59, 78 N.E.2d 708; Gregoire v. G. P. Putnam's Sons, 1948, 298 N.Y. 119, 81 N.E.2d 45, motion denied 298 N.Y. 119, 81 N.E.2d 152; Wolfson v. Syracuse Newspapers, 1938, 254 App.Div. 211,

4 N.Y.S.2d 640, affirmed, 1939, 279 N.Y. 716, 18 N. E.2d 676, reargument denied 280 N.Y. 572, 20 N.E.2d 21 (reading in defendant's files).

94. See Prosser, Interstate Publication, 1953, 51 Mich.L.Rev. 959, reprinted in Prosser, Selected Topics on the Law of Torts, 1954, 70; Leflar, The Single Publication Rule, 1953, 25 Rocky Mt.L.Rev. 263; notes, 1949, 62 Harv.L.Rev. 1041; 1957, 19 U.Pitt. L.Rev. 98; 1962, 56 Northwestern U.L.Rev. 823; 1956, 32 N.D.L.Rev. 120; 1957, 35 N.C.L.Rev. 535.

95. Each edition is a separate publication. Wheeler v. Dell Pub. Co., 7 Cir. 1962, 300 F.2d 372; Fisher v. New Yorker Staats-Zeitung, 1906, 114 App.Div. 824, 100 N.Y.S. 185; Gordon v. Journal Pub. Co., 1908, 81 Vt. 237, 69 A. 742; Backus v. Look, Inc., S.D.N.Y.1941, 39 F.Supp. 662.

96. Gregoire v. G. P. Putnam's Sons, 1948, 298 N.Y. 119, 81 N.E.2d 45; Ogden v. Association of the United States Army, D.D.C.1959, 177 F.Supp. 498.

97. Bigelow v. Sprague, 1886, 140 Mass. 425, 5 N.E. 144; Palmer v. Mahin, 8 Cir. 1903, 120 F. 737; Brian v. Harper, 1919, 144 La. 585, 80 So. 885; Fried, Mendelson & Co. v. Edmund Halstead, Ltd., 1922, 203 App.Div. 113, 196 N.Y.S. 285.

98. Fry v. Bennet, 1863, 28 N.Y. 324; Bigelow v. Sprague, 1886, 140 Mass. 425, 5 N.E. 144; Palmer v. Mahin, 8 Cir. 1903, 120 F. 737.

99. Cassius v. Mortimer, S.D.N.Y.1957, 161 F.Supp. 74. Accord: Osmers v. Parade Publications, Inc., S.D.N.Y.1964, 234 F.Supp. 924; Zuck v. Interstate Pub. Corp., 2 Cir. 1963, 317 F.2d 727; Sorge v. Parade Publications, Inc., 1964, 20 App.Div.2d 338, 247 N.Y.S.2d 317; Brush-Moore Newspapers v. Pollitt, 1959, 220 Md. 132, 151 A.2d 530.

100. See Leflar, The Single Publication Rule, 1953, 25 Rocky Mt.L.Rev. 263; Notes, 1958, 15 Wash. & Lee L.Rev. 321; 1956, 44 Cal.L.Rev. 146.

1. O'Reilly v. Curtis Pub. Co., D.Mass.1940, 31 F. Supp. 364; Hartmann v. American News Co., W.D.

the single publication rule could not cross a state line, so that there must be at least as many separate causes of action as there were states involved. The later cases [2] have held that it can do so; but the resulting problems of the conflict of laws,[3] which lie beyond the scope of this book, become extremely complex and difficult.

There may be responsibility for publication by another, as in the case of defamation published by an agent within the scope of his authority,[4] or an express or implied authorization to publish, as where a statement is made to a newspaper reporter.[5] It has even been held, in a few cases,[6] that there

may be an affirmative duty to remove a publication made by another, where for example the defendant's bulletin board is used for the purpose.

The probate of defamatory wills has presented a good many problems.[7] Since the executor is under a duty to probate the will, any defamation can scarcely be charged against him;[8] and since the publication has occurred after the death of the testator, there are logical difficulties in the way of holding his estate, including the generally accepted rule that liability for defamation dies with the defamer.[9] For such reasons two American decisions have refused to find any liability at all.[10] Four others have held the estate liable, more or less frankly recognizing that the recovery, whether or not it fits very well into common law principles, is necessary as a matter of policy for the protection of those who would otherwise be

Wis.1947, 69 F.Supp. 736; Sheldon-Claire Co. v. Judson Roberts Co., S.D.N.Y.1949, 88 F.Supp. 120; Sidis v. F–R Pub. Co., 2 Cir. 1940, 113 F.2d 806; Donahue v. Warner Bros. Pictures, 10 Cir. 1952, 194 F.2d 6.

2. Hartmann v. Time, Inc., 3 Cir. 1948, 166 F.2d 127, cert. denied 334 U.S. 838; Kilian v. Stackpole Sons, Inc., M.D.Pa.1951, 98 F.Supp. 500; Insull v. New York World-Telegram Corp., N.D.Ill.1959, 172 F. Supp. 615, aff'd in 273 F.2d 166, cert. denied 362 U. S. 942; Palmisano v. News Syndicate Co., S.D.N.Y. 1955, 130 F.Supp. 17; Anderson v. Hearst Pub. Co., S.D.Cal.1954, 120 F.Supp. 850.

3. See Prosser, Interstate Publication, 1953, 51 Mich. L.Rev. 959, reprinted in Prosser, Selected Topics on the Law of Torts, 1954, 70; Notes, 1957, 35 N.C.L. Rev. 535; 1956, 32 N.D.L.Rev. 120; 1962, 56 Northwestern U.L.Rev. 823; 1957, 19 U.Pitt.L.Rev. 98; 1949, 35 Va.L.Rev. 627; 1953, 28 N.Y.U.L.Rev. 1006; 1953, 14 Ohio St.L.J. 96; 1963, 32 U.Cin.L.Rev. 520; 1964, 77 Harv.L.Rev. 1463.

4. Draper v. Hellman Commercial Trust & Sav. Bank, 1928, 203 Cal. 26, 263 P. 240; Aetna Life Ins. Co. v. Brewer, 1926, 56 App.D.C. 283, 12 F.2d 818; Manion v. Jewel Tea Co., 1916, 135 Minn. 250, 160 N.W. 767. See Note, 1936, 20 Minn.L.Rev. 805.

5. Bond v. Douglas, 1836, 7 C. & P. 626, 173 Eng.Rep. 275; Valentine v. Gonzalez, 1929, 190 App.Div. 490, 179 N.Y.S. 711; Taylor v. Kinston Free Press, 1953, 237 N.C. 551, 75 S.E.2d 528; Storch v. Gordon, 1960, 23 Misc.2d 477, 197 N.Y.S.2d 309, reargument 23 Misc.2d 477, 202 N.Y.S.2d 43; Commonwealth v. Pratt, 1911, 208 Mass. 553, 95 N.E. 105. Otherwise if no authorization can be found. Schoepflin v. Coffey, 1900, 162 N.Y. 12, 56 N.E. 502; Henry v. Pittsburgh & L. E. R. Co., 1891, 139 Pa. 289, 21 A. 157.

6. Byrne v. Dean, [1937] 1 K.B. 818. Accord: Fogg v. Boston & Lynn R. Co., 1889, 148 Mass. 513, 20 N.

E. 109; Woodling v. Knickerbocker, 1883, 31 Minn. 268, 17 N.W. 387; Tidmore v. Mills, 1947, 33 Ala. App. 243, 32 So.2d 769, cert. denied 249 Ala. 648, 32 So.2d 782; Hellar v. Bianco, 1952, 111 Cal.App.2d 424, 244 P.2d 757. Contra, Scott v. Hull, 1970, 22 Ohio App.2d 141, 259 N.E.2d 160. See Notes, 1952, 40 Cal.L.Rev. 625; 1952, 31 N.C.L.Rev. 130; 1953, 5 Stan.L.Rev. 363.

7. See Freifield, Libel by Will, 1933, 19 A.B.A.J. 301; Di Falco, Libel in Wills, 1962, 8 N.Y.Law Forum 405; Notes, 1955, 24 Ford.L.Rev. 417; 1955, 12 Wash. & Lee L.Rev. 288; 1949, 6 Wash. & Lee L. Rev. 247; 1954, 1 U.C.L.A.L.Rev. 575; [1950] Wash.U.L.Rev. 122; 1949, 48 Mich.L.Rev. 220; 1945, 32 Va.L.Rev. 189; 1954, 33 N.C.L.Rev. 146; 1937, 21 Minn.L.Rev. 870.

8. Brown v. Mack, 1945, 185 Misc. 368, 56 N.Y.S.2d 910; See Harris v. Nashville Trust Co., 1913, 128 Tenn. 573, 162 S.W. 584; Carver v. Morrow, 1948, 213 S.C. 199, 48 S.E.2d 814.

9. See infra, § 126.

10. Carver v. Morrow, 1948, 213 S.C. 199, 48 S.E.2d 814; Citizens & Southern Nat. Bank v. Hendricks, 1933, 176 Ga. 692, 168 S.E. 313.

In Nagle v. Nagle, 1934, 316 Pa. 507, 175 A. 487, the will was held to be privileged, by analogy to pleadings filed in an action. The case does not make it clear whether the privilege is absolute or qualified; and in Kleinschmidt v. Matthieu, 1954, 201 Or. 406, 266 P.2d 686, it was interpreted to mean the latter.

helpless against the malice of the dead.[11] One possible solution may be for the probate court to strike the defamatory matter from the copy of the will admitted to probate.[12]

Ordinarily the defendant is not liable for any publication made to others by the plaintiff himself, even though it was to be expected that he might publish it.[13] There are, however, a few cases in which, because of the plaintiff's blindness or immaturity,[14] or because of some necessity he was under to communicate the matter to others,[15] it was reasonably to be anticipated that he would do so, and the writer has been held to be responsible.

Intention and Malice

As in the case of deceit, the intention underlying a defamatory publication may involve a number of elements. The publisher may intend one or more of the following things:

1. He may intend, by words or conduct, to make a particular statement.

2. He may intend to communicate it to a person other than the plaintiff.

3. He may intend that it shall be understood to refer to the plaintiff.

4. He may intend it to convey a defamatory meaning.

5. He may intend that the meaning shall be false. In other words, he may intend to lie—the element which in deceit is known as "scienter."

6. He may intend to cause damage to the plaintiff's reputation.

As to any or all of these the defendant, instead of intending the particular result, may be merely negligent, in failing to anticipate it or to take the precautions of a reasonable man against it; or his conduct may be entirely innocent and reasonable, without any wrongful intent or negligence. The present state of the law may be stated very simply. As to all of the above elements except the second, that of publication to a third person, the defendant is held strictly responsible for innocent conduct, without proof that he intended the consequences or was at all negligent with respect to them.[16]

At one stage of development[17] of the law of defamation, at least, a contrary view prevailed. It was held that the plaintiff must plead and prove not only that the defendant intended to defame him, but that he was inspired by malice, in the sense of spite or an

11. Kleinschmidt v. Matthieu, 1954, 201 Or. 406, 266 P.2d 686; Harris v. Nashville Trust Co., 1913, 128 Tenn. 573, 162 S.W. 584; Brown v. Mack, 1945, 185 Misc. 368, 56 N.Y.S.2d 910; In re Gallagher's Estate, 1901, 10 Pa.Dist. 733; Brown v. Du Frey, 1956, 1 N.Y.2d 190, 151 N.Y.S.2d 649, 134 N.E.2d 469.

12. In re Estate of White, [1914] P. 153, 83 L.J.P. 67; In re Draske's Will, 1936, 160 Misc. 587, 290 N.Y.S. 581. See Notes, 1937, 21 Minn.L.Rev. 870; 1945, 32 Va.L.Rev. 189. The solution is not a complete one, since defamatory words which are an inseparable part of dispositive clauses obviously cannot be expunged.

13. Lyle v. Waddle, 1945, 144 Tex. 90, 188 S.W.2d 770; Wilcox v. Moon, 1892, 64 Vt. 450, 24 A. 244; Lyon v. Lash, 1906, 74 Kan. 745, 88 P. 262; Konkle v. Haven, 1905, 140 Mich. 472, 103 N.W. 850; cf. Olson v. Molland, 1930, 181 Minn. 364, 232 N.W. 625 (negligence of plaintiff).

14. Lane v. Schilling, 1929, 130 Or. 119, 279 P. 267; Hedgepeth v. Coleman, 1922, 183 N.C. 309, 111 S.E. 517; Davis v. Askin's Retail Stores, 1937, 211 N.C. 551, 191 S.E. 33. Cf. Stevens v. Haering's Grocetorium, 1923, 125 Wash. 404, 216 P. 870 (hysterical Plaintiff).

But in Riley v. Askin & Marine Co., 1926, 134 S.C. 198, 132 S.E. 584, a more mature minor was held not to be expected to make the publication.

15. Colonial Stores v. Barrett, 1946, 73 Ga.App. 839, 38 S.E.2d 306 (wartime certificate of availability which plaintiff was required to exhibit); Grist v. Upjohn Co., 1969, 16 Mich.App. 452, 168 N.W.2d 389 (inquiry of prospective employer); Bretz v. Mayer, 1963, 1 Ohio Misc. 59, 203 N.E.2d 665 (letter to pastor containing very real threat to existence of church).

16. See Restatement of Torts, §§ 579, 580.

17. Apparently the early law imposed strict liability, as in the case of other torts. See Holdsworth, Defamation in the Sixteenth and Seventeenth Centuries, 1925, 41 L.Q.Rev. 13, 24–26.

improper motive.[18] But the pleading of "malice" tended more and more to become a pure formality, until in 1825 it was held [19] that "malice" would be implied by the law from an intentional publication of a defamatory character, even though the defendant harbored no ill will toward the plaintiff, and honestly believed what he said to be true. In any such sense as this, "malice" becomes a bare fiction.[20] The existence of actual ill will or the absence of honest belief remains important where the exercise of a qualified privilege is in question,[21] and it may affect the measure of damages to be imposed, particularly as to punitive damages,[22] but it is not at all essential to liability in the first instance.

Strict Liability

In 1910, in the celebrated case of Hulton & Co. v. Jones,[23] the English courts carried this to its logical conclusion. The defendants published in their newspaper a story from their Paris correspondent to the effect that one Artemus Jones, a person whom they intended and believed to be entirely fictitious, had been seen at Dieppe with a woman not his wife. Out of the wilds of North Wales appeared a real Artemus Jones—incidentally a lawyer—claiming that the story had been understood by his neighbors to refer to him. The House of Lords affirmed a decision in his favor, holding, to the extent of £1,750 in damages, that the defendant's innocence did not excuse him from liability.

Following the rule laid down by the English decisions, the defendant has been held liable, without regard to any question of negligence, in a series of cases where he did not intend to make the particular statement at all, as where a typographical error has changed "cultured gentleman" into "colored gentleman;" [24] where he did not intend to refer to the plaintiff or was ignorant of his existence,[25] as in the case of a mistake as to the name, photograph or address,[26] or the use of a name believed to be fictitious,[27] or where the statement was true of one of two persons of the same name but not as to the oth-

18. Parson Prick's Case, cited in Cro.Jac. 91, 79 Eng.Rep. 78; Crawford v. Middleton, 1674, 1 Lev. 82, 83 Eng.Rep. 308. Apparently this was carried over from the ecclesiastical law, which was concerned with the moral sin, and from that of criminal libel, where the allegation of a malicious intent was required. Green, Slander and Libel, 1872, 6 Am.L.Rev. 593, 596–597, 609–611; Veeder, History and Theory of the Law of Defamation, 1904, 4 Col. L.Rev. 33, 35–37; Holdsworth, Defamation in the Sixteenth and Seventeenth Centuries, 1925, 41 L.Q. Rev. 13, 24–26.

19. Bromage v. Prosser, 1825, 4 B. & C. 247, 107 Eng.Rep. 1051. Accord, Times Pub. Co. v. Carlisle, 8 Cir. 1899, 94 F. 762; McDonald v. Nugent, 1904, 122 Iowa 651, 98 N.W. 506; King v. Patterson, 1887, 49 N.J.L. 417, 9 A. 705; Hoffman v. Trenton Times, 1939, 17 N.J.Misc. 339, 8 A.2d 837. See Holdsworth, A Chapter of Accidents in the Law of Libel, 1941, 57 L.Q.Rev. 74.

20. See Burch, J., in Coleman v. MacLennan, 1908, 78 Kan. 711, 98 P. 281.

21. See infra, § 115.

22. See Scott v. Times-Mirror Co., 1919, 181 Cal. 345, 184 P. 672; Corrigan v. Bobbs-Merrill Co., 1920, 228 N.Y. 58, 126 N.E. 260; Fields v. Bynum, 1911, 156 N.C. 413, 72 S.E. 449. The "presumed" malice does not entitle the plaintiff to punitive damages. Devoy v. Irish World & American Industrial Liberator Co., 1924, 208 App.Div. 319, 203 N.Y.S. 369.

23. [1909] 2 K.B. 44, affirmed, [1910] A.C. 20. See Holdsworth, A Chapter of Accidents in the Law of

Libel, 1941, 57 L.Q.Rev. 74; Smith, Jones v. Hulton: Three Conflicting Views as to Defamation, 1912, 60 U.Pa.L.Rev. 364, 461.

24. Upton v. Times-Democrat Pub. Co., 1900, 104 La. 141, 28 So. 970; Taylor v. Hearst, 1896, 107 Cal. 262, 40 P. 392; Id., 1897, 118 Cal. 366, 50 P. 541. Cf. Burton v. Crowell Pub. Co., 2 Cir. 1936, 82 F.2d 154 (obscene optical illusion in photograph).

25. Switzer v. Anthony, 1922, 71 Colo. 291, 206 P. 391.

26. Laudati v. Stea, 1922, 44 R.I. 303, 117 A. 422 ("The question is not who was aimed at, but who was hit"); Walker v. Bee-News Pub. Co., 1932, 122 Neb. 511, 240 N.W. 579; Hatfield v. Gazette Printing Co., 1918, 103 Kan. 513, 175 P. 382; Whitcomb v. Hearst Corp., 1952, 329 Mass. 193, 107 N.E.2d 295; Petransky v. Repository Printing Co., 1935, 51 Ohio App. 306, 200 N.E. 647.

27. Hulton & Co. v. Jones, [1909] 2 K.B. 44, affirmed [1910] A.C. 20; Corrigan v. Bobbs-Merrill Co., 1920, 228 N.Y. 58, 126 N.E. 260.

er;[28] where he did not expect the words to be understood in any defamatory sense,[29] or the meaning was attached solely by extrinsic facts of which he was quite unaware—as in the Scottish case [30] in which the plaintiff who was stated to have given birth to twins had been married only one month; where the defendant honestly and reasonably believed his statement to be true, and was repeating it on good authority;[31] where he intended to praise the plaintiff rather than to defame him;[32] where he believed in good faith that he was exercising a privilege which did not exist,[33] and where he was drunk at the time and did not know what he was saying.[34]

The only limitation placed upon the liability is that the defamatory meaning and the reference to the plaintiff must be reasonably conveyed to and understood by others;[35] and in the case of the use of a name for an obviously fictitious character in a book, it has been held that there is no liability where no sensible man would understand that it is intended to depict the plaintiff.[36]

The effect of this strict liability is to place the printed, written or spoken word in the same class with the use of explosives or the keeping of dangerous animals. If a defamatory meaning, which is false, is reasonably understood, the defendant publishes at his peril, and there is no possible defense except the rather narrow one of privilege. The rule has not gone without criticism.[37] In the interest of our traditional freedom of expression, it is not clear that the losses due to innocently inflicted harm to reputation should be borne by the publishing industry, or a fortiori by the individual speaker—particularly if libel, and some forms of slander, are to be actionable without proof that harm has occurred. The opportunity for extortionate suits is great, and it is an open secret that plaintiffs frequently take advantage of it; and while the law of libel provides a useful restraint upon irresponsible journalism, it is achieved at the expense of a heavy burden

28. Washington Post Co. v. Kennedy, 1925, 55 App. D.C. 162, 3 F.2d 207; Newstead v. London Express Newspapers, [1940] 1 K.B. 377; Lee v. Wilson and MacKinnon, 1934, 51 Comm.L.Rep., Aust., 276. See Notes, 1935, 51 L.Q.Rev. 572; 1941, 89 U.Pa.L.Rev. 676.

Otherwise where there are accompanying words indicating the other person. Carter Publications v. Fleming, 1937, 129 Tex. 667, 106 S.W.2d 672 ("father of the accused").

29. Hankinson v. Bilby, 1847, 16 M. & W. 442, 153 Eng.Rep. 1262; Barr v. Birkner, 1895, 44 Neb. 197, 62 N.W. 494; Nash v. Fisher, 1917, 24 Wyo. 535, 162 P. 933; Ladwig v. Heyer, 1907, 136 Iowa 196, 113 N.W. 767; Milam v. Railway Express Agency, 1937, 185 S.C. 194, 193 S.E. 324.

30. Morrison v. Ritchie & Co., 1904, 4 Fraser, Sess. Cas., 645, 39 Scot.L.Rep. 432. Accord: Cassidy v. Daily Mirror Newspapers, [1929] 2 K.B. 331.

31. Bromage v. Prosser, 1825, 4 B. & C. 247, 107 Eng.Rep. 1051; Barnes v. Campbell, 1879, 59 N.H. 128; Oklahoma Pub. Co. v. Givens, 10 Cir. 1933, 67 F.2d 62; Szalay v. New York American, 1938, 254 App.Div. 249, 4 N.Y.S.2d 620; Kelly v. Independent Pub. Co., 1912, 45 Mont. 127, 122 P. 735.

32. Martin v. The Picayune, 1906, 115 La. 979, 40 So. 376. Cf. Triggs v. Sun Printing & Pub. Ass'n, 1904, 179 N.Y. 144, 71 N.E. 739 (jest); Dall v. Time, Inc., 1937, 252 App.Div. 636, 300 N.Y.S. 680, affirmed, 1938, 278 N.Y. 635, 16 N.E.2d 297, reargument denied 278 N.Y. 718, 17 N.E.2d 138 (intended as fiction).

33. See Stuart v. Bell, [1891] 2 Q.B. 341; Hebditch v. MacIlwaine, [1894] 2 Q.B. 54. The defendant's good faith belief, however, may bear upon the existence of the privilege itself. See infra, § 115.

34. Reed v. Harper, 1868, 25 Iowa 87.

35. Macfadden's Publications v. Turner, Tex.Civ. App.1936, 95 S.W.2d 1027.

36. Clare v. Farrell, D.Minn.1947, 70 F.Supp. 276. Accord: Nebb v. Bell Syndicate, D.N.Y.1941, 41 F. Supp. 929 (comic strip character); Landau v. Columbia Broadcasting System, 1954, 205 Misc. 357, 128 N.Y.S.2d 254 (name on door in television broadcast); Newton v. Grubb, 1918, 155 Ky. 479, 159 S. W. 994 (rumor identifying woman not named by defendant).

37. See Notes, 1941, 25 Minn.L.Rev. 495; 1947, 25 Cal.L.Rev. 462; 1909, 25 L.Q.Rev. 341; 1912, 32 Can.L.T. 621; 1916, 29 Harv.L.Rev. 533; 1925, 38 Harv.L.Rev. 1100; 1925, 10 Corn.L.Q. 527. The rule is defended, however, by Smith, Jones v. Hulton: Three Conflicting Views as to a Question of Defamation, 1912, 60 U.Pa.L.Rev. 365, 461; Morris, Inadvertent Newspaper Libel and Retraction, 1937, 32 Ill.L.Rev. 36.

upon innocent and careful publishers. It is not at all certain that liability for negligence, coupled with a high standard of care and a presumption that defamatory publications are made negligently, would not provide all the protection that is really desirable.[38] There has been something of an undercurrent of rebellion against the strict liability rule, and a tendency to hold that at least negligence is essential to the cause of action.[39]

Liability Based on Negligence

The chief relaxation of strict liability, however, has been in connection with publication. It is difficult to see any reason for distinguishing between that which is intentionally or negligently published but accidentally defamatory, and that which is intentionally defamatory but accidentally published; but that is the present state of the law. There is no liability for publication which the defendant did not intend and could not reasonably anticipate, as in the case of words spoken with no reason to suppose that anyone but the plaintiff would overhear them,[40] or a sealed letter sent to the plaintiff himself which is unexpectedly opened and read by another.[41]

On the other hand, if the defendant speaks in a loud voice with reason to expect that he will be overheard,[42] or if he has reason to believe, from past experience or special information, that his letter will be read by the plaintiff's wife or clerk,[43] or if he knows that the plaintiff is blind, illiterate, or immature,[44] there is liability, which seems to be based on negligence. The same is true of a letter mailed to a third person by mistake,[45] a message on a postcard,[46] or a defamatory document dropped in the street.[47]

38. It should be noted that many of the cases cited above, involving typographical errors, mistakes as to the identity of the person, or the interpretation of the words used, might have reached the same conclusion on the basis of negligence. Other examples of careless reporting: Thorson v. Albert Lea Pub. Co., 1933, 190 Minn. 200, 251 N.W. 177, 90 A. L.R. 1169; Park v. Detroit Free Press Co., 1888, 72 Mich. 560, 40 N.W. 731; Coffman v. Spokane Chronicle Pub. Co., 1911, 65 Wash. 1, 117 P. 596; Turton v. New York Recorder Co., 1894, 144 N.Y. 144, 38 N.E. 1009; Turner v. Hearst, 1896, 115 Cal. 394, 47 P. 129.

39. Hanson v. Globe Newspaper Co., 1893, 159 Mass. 293, 34 N.E. 462 (mistake in name; discredited, however, in Sweet v. Post Pub. Co., 1913, 215 Mass. 450, 102 N.E. 660); Jones v. R. L. Polk & Co., 1915, 190 Ala. 243, 67 So. 577 (typographical error); Memphis Commercial Appeal v. Johnson, 6 Cir. 1938, 96 F.2d 672 (identity of person). Cf. Layne v. Tribune Co., 1933, 108 Fla. 177, 146 So. 234 (honest and reasonable republication); Summit Hotel Co. v. National Broadcasting Co., 1939, 336 Pa. 182, 8 A.2d 302 (interpolation in radio broadcast).

40. See Hall v. Balkind, [1918] N.Z.L.Rep. 740; McNichol v. Grandy, [1931] Can.S.C.Rep. 696. Cf. Weir v. Hoss, 1844, 6 Ala. 881 (document copied and published without consent of defendant).

41. Yousling v. Dare, 1904, 122 Iowa 539, 98 N.W. 371; Riley v. Askin & Marine Co., 1926, 134 S.C. 198, 132 S.E. 584; Fordson Coal Co. v. Carter, 1937, 269 Ky. 805, 108 S.W.2d 1007; Olson v. Molland, 1930, 181 Minn. 364, 232 N.W. 625; Weidman v. Ketcham, 1938, 278 N.Y. 129, 15 N.E.2d 426.

The mere fact that defendant thought it possible that some third person might open the letter was held not sufficient for publication, where he had no special reason to expect it. Barnes v. Clayton House Motel, Tex.Civ.App.1968, 435 S.W.2d 616.

42. McNichol v. Grandy, [1931] Can.S.C.Rep. 696; Hall v. Balkind, [1918] N.Z.L.Rep. 740.

43. Rumney v. Worthley, 1904, 186 Mass. 144, 71 N.E. 316; Roberts v. English Mfg. Co., 1908, 155 Ala. 414, 46 So. 752; Kramer v. Perkins, 1907, 102 Minn. 455, 113 N.W. 1062; cf. Theaker v. Richardson, [1962] 1 All Eng.Rep. 229.

A fortiori where unsealed letters are sent with the expectation that they will be opened by others. Cyran v. Finlay Straus, Inc., 1951, 302 N.Y. 486, 99 N.E.2d 298.

44. Lane v. Schilling, 1929, 130 Or. 119, 279 P. 267; Allen v. Wortham, 1890, 89 Ky. 485, 13 S.W. 73; Hedgepeth v. Coleman, 1922, 183 N.C. 309, 111 S.E. 517; Davis v. Askin's Retail Stores, 1937, 211 N.C. 551, 191 S.E. 33. Cf. Stevens v. Haering's Grocetorium, 1923, 125 Wash. 404, 216 P. 870.

45. Fox v. Broderick, 1864, 14 Ir.C.L.Rep. 453; cf. Tompson v. Dashwood, 1883, 11 Q.B.D. 43.

46. Ostro v. Safir, 1937, 165 Misc. 647, 1 N.Y.S.2d 377; Freeman v. Busch Jewelry Co., N.D.Ga.1951, 98 F.Supp. 963; see Sadgrove v. Hole, [1901] 2 K.B. 1; Logan v. Hodges, 1907, 146 N.C. 38, 59 S.E. 349.

47. See Weld-Blundell v. Stephens, [1920] A.C. 956, 971.

Where written or printed matter is intentionally delivered in ignorance of its defamatory content, those who are primarily responsible for the publication, such as the owner or managing editor of a newspaper,[48] or apparently even the printer,[49] cannot escape liability on the ground of innocence. But one who merely plays a secondary part in disseminating information published by another, as in the case of libraries,[50] news vendors[51] and distributors,[52] or carriers,[53] may avoid liability[54] by showing that he had

no reason to believe it to be a libel. This has been applied to the transmission by a telegraph company of a message innocent on its face.[55] A Florida case[56] extended the principle to the publication by a newspaper of an Associated Press dispatch, but other jurisdictions[57] have rejected the decision.

There is still a lively dispute over defamation by radio, which has turned chiefly on whether broadcasting companies are to be held primarily responsible, like a newspaper, for their cooperation in publishing defamation originating with others,[58] or only secondarily so, by analogy to the telegraph company and the news vendor.[59] Six deci-

---

48. Corrigan v. Bobbs-Merrill Co., 1920, 228 N.Y. 58, 126 N.E. 260; Smith v. Utley, 1896, 92 Wis. 133, 65 N.W. 744; World Pub. Co. v. Minahan, 1918, 70 Okl. 107, 173 P. 815; People v. Fuller, 1909, 238 Ill. 116, 87 N.E. 336.

But cf. Sakamu v. Zellerbach Paper Co., 1938, 25 Cal. App.2d 309, 77 P. 313 (business manager of Japanese paper not understanding Japanese); Folwell v. Miller, 2 Cir. 1906, 145 F. 495 (editor not on active duty).

49. Rex v. Clerk, 1728, 1 Barn. 304, 94 Eng.Rep. 207; Watts v. Fraser, 1835, 7 C. & P. 369, 173 Eng.Rep. 164; see Youmans v. Smith, 1897, 153 N.Y. 214, 47 N.E. 265.

In McDonald v. R. L. Polk & Co., 1940, 346 Mo. 615, 142 S.W.2d 635, and Edwards v. Nulsen, 1941, 347 Mo. 1077, 152 S.W.2d 28, the same rule was applied to mail advertising agencies sending out circulars supplied by customers.

50. Martin v. British Museum Trustees, 1894, 10 T. L.R. 338; Vizetelly v. Mudie's Select Library, [1900] 2 Q.B. 170.

51. Balabanoff v. Fossani, 1948, 192 Misc. 615, 81 N. Y.S.2d 732; Emmons v. Pottle, 1885, 16 Q.B.D. 354; Weldon v. Times Book Co., 1911, 28 T.L.R. 143.

52. Bottomley v. F. W. Woolworth & Co., Ct.App. 1932, 48 T.L.R. 521; Sexton v. American News Co., N.D.Fla.1955, 133 F.Supp. 591. See Hartmann v. American News Co., W.D.Wis.1947, 69 F.Supp. 736; Hartmann v. American News Co., 7 Cir. 1949, 171 F.2d 581, cert. denied 337 U.S. 907.

53. Day v. Bream, 1837, 2 Moo. & R. 54, 174 Eng. Rep. 212 (porter distributing handbills). Accord: Layton v. Harris, 1842, 3 Har.,Del., 406; see Arnold v. Ingram, 1912, 151 Wis. 438, 138 N.W. 111. Cf. McLeod v. St. Aubyn, [1899] A.C. 549 (private lending of newspaper).

54. The burden of proof is on the defendant. Vizetelly v. Mudie's Select Library, [1900] 2 Q.B. 170, 69 L.J.Q.B. 154; Staub v. Van Benthuysen, 1884, 36 La.Ann. 467; Street v. Johnson, 1891, 80 Wis. 455, 50 N.W. 395.

55. Nye v. Western Union Tel. Co., C.C.Minn.1900, 104 F. 628; Stockman v. Western Union Tel. Co., 1900, 10 Kan.App. 580, 63 P. 658; Grisham v. Western Union Tel. Co., 1911, 238 Mo. 480, 142 S.W. 271; see Lesesne v. Willingham, E.D.S.C.1949, 83 F.Supp. 918. See Smith, Liability of a Telegraph Company for Transmitting a Defamatory Message, 1920, 20 Col.L.Rev. 30, 369; Notes, 1930, 5 Wis.L.Rev. 297; 1930, 78 U.Pa.L.Rev. 252; 1950, 28 Tex.L.Rev. 601.

56. Layne v. Tribune Co., 1933, 108 Fla. 177, 146 So. 234. See, 1939, 27 Mich.L.Rev. 495; 1933, 17 Minn. L.Rev. 820.

57. Oklahoma Pub. Co. v. Givens, 10 Cir. 1933, 67 F. 2d 62; Szalay v. New York American, 1938, 254 App.Div. 249, 4 N.Y.S.2d 620; Wood v. Constitution Pub. Co., 1937, 57 Ga.App. 123, 194 S.E. 760; Kelly v. Independent Pub. Co., 1912, 45 Mont. 127, 122 P. 735.

58. See Vold, The Basis of Liability for Defamation by Radio, 1935, 19 Minn.L.Rev. 611; Vold, Defamation by Radio, 1932, 2 J.Radio Law 673; Vold, Defamatory Interpolations in Radio Broadcasts, 1940, 88 U.Pa.L.Rev. 249; Donnelly, Defamation by Radio: A Reconsideration, 1948, 34 Iowa L.Rev. 212; Remmers, Recent Trends in Defamation by Radio, 1951, 64 Harv.L.Rev. 727; Leflar, Radio and TV Defamation: Fault or Strict Liability? 1954, 15 Ohio St.L.J. 252; Notes, 1933, 11 Neb.L.B. 325; 1932, 81 U.Pa.L.Rev. 249; 1941, 39 Mich.L.Rev. 1002; 1964, 2 Houst.L.Rev. 238; 1964, 15 Mercer L.Rev. 450.

59. See Bohlen, Fifty Years of Torts, 1937, 50 Harv. L.Rev. 725, 729–31; Sprague, Freedom of the Air, 1937, 8 Air L.Rev. 30; Sprague, More Freedom of the Air, 1940, 11 Air L.Rev. 17; Farnham, Defamation by Radio and the American Law Institute, 1936, 16 Bos.U.L.Rev. 1; Haley, The Law on Radio Programs, 1937, 5 Geo.Wash.L.Rev. 157; Guider, Liability for Defamation in Political Broadcasts,

sions have dealt with the question, and three of them have held the station strictly liable,[60] while the other three have held that it is not liable in the absence of intent or negligence.[61] Statutes in a number of states, urged by the National Broadcasting Association, have adopted the latter position.[62] On the other hand the English Defamation Act of 1952 imposed strict liability.[63] In view of its enormous potentialities for harm, there seems to be little reason to distinguish the radio from the newspaper; and so long as strict liability remains in the law of libel, it is at least arguable that the radio beyond all other media should be subject to it.

114. ABSOLUTE PRIVILEGE

In an action for defamation, the plaintiff's prima facie case is made out when he has established a publication to a third person for which the defendant is responsible, the recipient's understanding of the defamatory meaning, and its actionable character.[64] It is then open to the defendant to set up various defenses, which to some extent have moderated the rigors of the law of libel and slander. Two of these—privilege and truth

—are complete defenses, avoiding all liability when they are established. Others, such as retraction, bad reputation of the plaintiff, and honest belief or proper motive on the part of the defendant, go merely to reduce the damages to be recovered. These remain to be considered.

Privilege

The defense of privilege,[65] or immunity,[66] in cases of defamation does not differ essentially from the privileges, such as those of self-defense, protection of property, or legal authority, available as to assault and battery.[67] It rests upon the same idea, that conduct which otherwise would be actionable is to escape liability because the defendant is acting in furtherance of some interest of social importance, which is entitled to protection even at the expense of uncompensated harm to the plaintiff's reputation.[68] The interest thus favored may be one of the defendant himself, of a third person, or of the general public. If it is one of paramount importance, considerations of policy may require that the defendant's immunity for false statements be absolute, without regard to his purpose or motive, or the reasonableness of his conduct. If it has relatively less

1932, 2 J.Radio Law 728; Seitz, Responsibility of Radio Stations for Extemporaneous Defamation, 1940, 24 Marq.L.Rev. 117.

60. Sorenson v. Wood, 1932, 123 Neb. 348, 243 N.W. 82; Miles v. Louis Wasmer, Inc., 1933, 172 Wash. 466, 20 P.2d 847; Coffey v. Midland Broadcasting Co., D.Mo.1934, 8 F.Supp. 889. See also Irwin v. Ashurst, 1938, 158 Or. 61, 67, 74 P.2d 1127, 1130.

61. Summit Hotel Co. v. National Broadcasting Co., 1939, 336 Pa. 182, 8 A.2d 302; Kelly v. Hoffman, 1948, 137 N.J.L. 695, 61 A.2d 143; Josephson v. Knickerbocker Broadcasting Co., 1942, 179 Misc. 787, 38 N.Y.S.2d 985.

62. See Remmers, Recent Legislative Trends in Defamation by Radio, 1951, 64 Harv.L.Rev. 727; Leflar, Radio and TV Defamation: Fault or Strict Liability, 1954, 15 Ohio St.L.J. 252; Note, 1956, 9 Okla.L.Rev. 103.

63. See Williams, Committee on the Law of Defamation: The Porter Report, 1949, 12 Mod.L.Rev. 217; Todd, The Defamation Act, 1952, 1953, 16 Mod.L. Rev. 476; Note, 1953, 66 Harv.L.Rev. 476.

64. Restatement of Torts, § 613.

65. Many courts and writers have limited "privilege" to the *occasion* on which the defendant may speak with immunity, as distinguished from questions of the "fairness" of comment or criticism. See for example Wagner v. Retail Credit Co., 7 Cir. 1964, 338 F.2d 598; infra, § 115. As no difference in principle is apparent, the term is used in the text to include both. Cf. Restatement of Torts, § 606.

66. Certainly the more accurate term, although the courts have not adopted it. See Bower, Actionable Defamation, 2d Ed. 1923, Appendix VIII; Green, Relational Interests, 1935, 30 Ill.L.Rev. 314; Green, The Right to Communicate, 1960, 35 N.Y.U.L.Rev. 903; Evans, Legal Immunity for Defamation, 1940, 24 Minn.L.Rev. 607, 613.

67. See supra, § 16.

68. See Note, 1954, 15 Ohio St.L.J. 330; Holmes Privilege, Malice and Intent, 1894, 8 Harv.L.Rev. 1; Harper, Privileged Defamation, 1936, 22 Va.L.Rev. 642; Veeder, Absolute Immunity in Defamation, 1909, 9 Col.L.Rev. 463; Veeder, Freedom of Public Discussion, 1910, 23 Harv.L.Rev. 413.

weight from a social point of view, the immunity may be qualified,[69] and conditioned upon good motives and reasonable behavior. The defendant's belief in the truth of what he says, the purpose for which he says it, and the manner of publication, all of which are immaterial when no question of privilege is involved,[70] may determine the issue when he enters the defense of such a conditional privilege.

Absolute immunity has been confined to a very few situations where there is an obvious policy in favor of permitting complete freedom of expression, without any inquiry as to the defendant's motives. By general agreement, it is limited to the following situations:

Absolute Immunity

1. *Judicial Proceedings.* The judge on the bench must be free to administer the law under the protection of the law, independently and freely, without fear of consequences. No such independence could exist if he were in daily apprehension of having an action brought against him, and his administration of justice submitted to the opinion of a jury.[71] As in the case of other acts in his judicial capacity,[72] therefore, the judge is absolutely privileged as to any defamation he may utter, even though he knows it to be false and is motivated by personal ill will toward the plaintiff.[73] The privilege extends

to the official publication of his judicial opinions.[74] For the same reason, a similar absolute immunity is conferred upon grand [75] and petit [76] jurors in the performance of their functions. It likewise has been conferred upon witnesses,[77] whether they testi-

---

v. Bowles, 1963, 369 Mich. 680, 120 N.W.2d 842; Mundy v. McDonald, 1921, 216 Mich. 444, 185 N.W. 877; Karelas v. Baldwin, 1932, 237 App.Div. 265, 261 N.Y.S. 518 (justice of the peace).

74. Hanft v. Heller, Sup.Ct.1970, 316 N.Y.S.2d 255 (both judge and publisher). The only remedy is to strike the defamatory opinion from the record. Nadeau v. Texas Co., 1937, 104 Mont. 558, 69 P.2d 586.

In Murray v. Brancato, 1943, 290 N.Y. 52, 48 N.E.2d 257 it was held that there was only a qualified privilege to publish unofficially in the New York Law Journal and the New York Supplement Reports. See Note, 1943, 12 Ford.L.Rev. 193. But in Garfield v. Palmieri, S.D.N.Y.1961, 193 F.Supp. 137, publication in the Federal Supplement was held to be absolutely privileged, where there was no official published report, and no other way of letting the bar know of the opinion.

75. Hayslip v. Wellford, 1953, 195 Tenn. 621, 263 S. W.2d 136, cert. denied 346 U.S. 911; Ryon v. Shaw, Fla.1955, 77 So.2d 455; O'Regan v. Schermerhorn, 1946, 25 N.J.Misc. 1, 50 A.2d 10; Griffith v. Slinkard, 1896, 146 Ind. 117, 44 N.E. 1001; Engelke v. Chouteau, 1889, 98 Mo. 629, 12 S.W. 358. See Notes, 1937, 31 Minn.L.Rev. 500; 1955, 8 U.Fla.L. Rev. 342.

A report not followed by indictment was held to go outside of the grand jury's functions, and to be only qualifiedly privileged, in Bennett v. Stockwell, 1916, 197 Mich. 50, 163 N.W. 482; Rich v. Eason, Tex.Civ.App.1915, 180 S.W. 303; Rector v. Smith, 1860, 11 Iowa 302. Contra, Greenfield v. Courier Journal & Louisville Times Co., Ky.1955, 283 S.W. 2d 839.

76. Dunham v. Powers, 1868, 42 Vt. 1; Irwin v. Murphy, 1933, 129 Cal.App. 713, 19 P.2d 292; see Hoosac Tunnel Dock & Elevator Co. v. O'Brien, 1874, 137 Mass. 424.

77. Seaman v. Netherclift, 1876, L.R. 2 C.P. 53, 46 L. J.C.P. 128; Massey v. Jones, 1944, 182 Va. 200, 28 S.E.2d 623; Veazey v. Blair, 1952, 86 Ga.App. 721, 72 S.E.2d 481; Johnston v. Dover, 1940, 201 Ark. 175, 143 S.W.2d 1112; Taplin-Rice-Clerkin Co. v. Hower, 1931, 124 Ohio St. 123, 177 N.E. 203. Even where the testimony is perjured and malicious. Feltz v. Paradise, 1942, 178 Tenn. 427, 158 S.W.2d 727; Kinter v. Kinter, 1949, 84 Ohio App. 399, 87 N.E.2d 379; Buchanan v. Miami Herald Pub. Co., Fla.App.1968, 206 So.2d 465.

---

69. Bower, Actionable Defamation, 2d Ed. 1923, Appendix VIII, prefers to call it a "defeasible" immunity.

70. See supra, p. 772.

71. Scott v. Stansfield, 1868, L.R. 3 Ex. 220; Veeder, Absolute Immunity in Defamation, 1909, 9 Col.L. Rev. 463, 474. Otherwise "no man but a beggar or a fool would be a judge." Lord Stair, in Miller v. Hope, 1824, 2 Shaw, Sc.App.Cas., 125.

Louisiana, operating under a civil law heritage, rejects the absolute privilege in judicial proceedings entirely. There is a qualified privilege only. Oakes v. Alexander, La.App.1961, 135 So.2d 513.

72. See infra, § 132.

73. Scott v. Stansfield, 1868, L.R. 3 Ex. 220; Irwin v. Ashurst, 1938, 158 Or. 61, 74 P.2d 1127; Ginger

fy voluntarily [78] or not, and even though their testimony is by affidavit or deposition.[79] The resulting lack of any really effective civil remedy against perjurers [80] is simply part of the price that is paid for witnesses who are free from intimidation by the possibility of civil liability for what they say. Likewise the privilege extends to counsel in the conduct of the case;[81] and, since there is an obvious public interest in affording to everyone the utmost freedom of access to the courts, it extends also to the parties [82] to private litigation,[83] as well as to defendants and instigators of prosecution in criminal cases.[84] The privilege covers anything that

may be said in relation to the matter at issue, whether it be in the pleadings,[85] in affidavits,[86] or in open court.[87]

It is the rule in England that the immunity exists as to any utterance arising out of the judicial proceeding and having any reasonable relation to it, although it is quite irrelevant to any issue involved.[88] Nearly all of the American courts, alarmed at the idea that a court of justice might become a place where extraneous defamation may be published with complete freedom, have said that there is no immunity unless the particular statement is in some way "relevant" or "pertinent" to some issue in the case.[89] On this basis defendants have been held liable, for example, for entirely foreign and irrelevant defamation of a person in no way in-

---

78. Beggs v. McCrea, 1901, 62 App.Div. 39, 70 N.Y.S. 864; Buschbaum v. Heriot, 1909, 5 Ga.App. 521, 63 S.E. 645; Ginsburg v. Halpern, 1955, 383 Pa. 178, 118 A.2d 201. Cf. Weil v. Lynds, 1919, 105 Kan. 440, 185 P. 51 (volunteered statement in court).

79. Dunbar v. Greenlaw, 1956, 152 Me. 270, 128 A.2d 218; Dyer v. Dyer, 1941, 178 Tenn. 234, 156 S.W.2d 445; Mezullo v. Maletz, 1954, 331 Mass. 233, 118 N.E.2d 356; Jarman v. Offutt, 1954, 239 N.C. 468, 80 S.E.2d 248. Cf. Thornton v. Rhoden, 1966, 245 Cal. App.2d 80, 53 Cal.Rptr. 706, (making transcript). This does not, however, extend to one who improperly procures the affidavit to be made. Bailey v. McGill, 1957, 247 N.C. 286, 100 S.E.2d 860. See Note, 1958, 36 N.C.L.Rev. 552.

As to other documents filed in the proceeding, cf. Soter v. Christoforacos, 1964, 53 Ill.App.2d 133, 202 N.E.2d 847.

80. See Note, 1960, 2 Osgoode Hall L.J. 154; McClintock, What Happens to Perjurors, 1940, 24 Minn.L.Rev. 747; Ginsburg v. Halpern, 1955, 383 Pa. 178, 118 A.2d 201. See Note, 1966, 19 Ark.L. Rev. 386.

81. Munster v. Lamb, 1883, 11 Q.B.D. 588; Irwin v. Ashurst, 1938, 158 Or. 61, 74 P.2d 1127; Ginsburg v. Black, 7 Cir. 1951, 192 F.2d 823, cert. denied, 343 U.S. 934, rehearing denied 343 U.S. 958; Carpenter v. Ashley, 1906, 148 Cal. 422, 83 P. 444; McDavitt v. Boyer, 1897, 169 Ill. 475, 48 N.E. 317. See Note, 1957, 35 N.C.L.Rev. 541.

82. In Laun v. Union Elec. Co. of Missouri, 1943, 350 Mo. 572, 166 S.W.2d 1065, the privilege was held not to extend to one not a party or counsel in the case who inserted defamatory matter in a pleading.

83. Lann v. Third Nat. Bank in Nashville, 1955, 198 Tenn. 70, 277 S.W.2d 439.

84. Boulton v. Clapham, 1640, W. Jones 431, 82 Eng. Rep. 227; Trotman v. Dunn, 1915, 4 Camp. 211, 66 Eng.Rep. 297; Restatement of Torts, § 587.

85. Di Blasio v. Kolodner, 1964, 233 Md. 512, 197 A. 2d 245; Taliaferro v. Sims, 5 Cir. 1951, 187 F.2d 6; Fletcher v. Maupin, 4 Cir. 1943, 138 F.2d 742, cert. denied, 322 U.S. 750; McClure v. Stretch, 1944, 20 Wash.2d 460, 147 P.2d 935; Greenberg v. Aetna Ins. Co., 1967, 427 Pa. 511, 235 A.2d 576 (answer).

86. Sacks v. Stecker, 2 Cir. 1932, 60 F.2d 73; Hager v. Major, 1945, 353 Mo. 1166, 186 S.W.2d 564; Stone v. Hutchinson Daily News, 1928, 125 Kan. 715, 266 P. 78; Keeley v. Great Northern R. Co., 1914, 156 Wis. 181, 145 N.W. 664; Tonkonogy v. Jaffin, 1963, 41 Misc.2d 155, 244 N.Y.S.2d 840, appeal dismissed 21 App.Div.2d 264, 249 N.Y.S.2d 934. Cf. Richeson v. Kessler, 1953, 73 Idaho 548, 255 P.2d 707 (counsel's letter to judge on substitution of attorneys).

87. Wells v. Carter, 1932, 164 Tenn. 400, 50 S.W.2d 228; Nissen v. Cramer, 1889, 104 N.C. 574, 10 S.E. 676; Clemmons v. Danforth, 1895, 67 Vt. 617, 32 A. 626; McDavitt v. Boyer, 1897, 169 Ill. 475, 48 N.E. 317.

88. Munster v. Lamb, 1883, 11 Q.B.D. 588, 52 L.J.Q.B. 726; Seaman v. Netherclift, 1876, L.R. 2 C.P. 53, 46 L.J.C.P. 128; Bower, Actionable Defamation, 2d Ed. 1923, 91, 92.

89. Adams v. Alabama Lime & Stone Corp., 1932, 225 Ala. 174, 142 So. 424; La Porta v. Leonard, 1916, 88 N.J.L. 663, 97 A. 251; Magelo v. Roundup Coal Min. Co., 1939, 109 Mont. 293, 96 P.2d 932; Penick v. Ratcliffe, 1927, 149 Va. 618, 140 S.E. 664; Laing v. Mitten, 1904, 185 Mass. 233, 70 N.E. 128. In Stahl v. Kincade, 1963, 135 Ind.App. 699, 192 N.E.2d 493, it was held that a counterclaim entirely irrelevant and in no way pertinent to the complaint was not absolutely privileged.

volved in the suit.[90] But it is generally agreed that "relevancy" does not mean that the statement must come within the technical rules of evidence,[91] since a witness should not be required to determine at his peril whether his testimony may safely be given, or deterred by fear of suit from what he believes to be proper,[92] and if he is asked a question, he may reasonably be expected to reply with anything reasonably responsive to it.[93] Most of our courts have adopted what appears to be a standard of good faith,[94] requiring only that the statement have some reasonable relation or reference to the subject of inquiry,[95] or be one that "may possibly be pertinent,"[96] with all doubts resolved in favor of the defendant—a conclusion

which seems in effect to adopt the English rule.[97]

The "judicial proceeding" to which the immunity attaches has not been defined very exactly. It includes any hearing before a tribunal which performs a judicial function,[98] ex parte[99] or otherwise, and whether the hearing is public or not.[1] It includes, for example, lunacy,[2] bankruptcy,[3] or naturalization[4] proceedings, and an election contest.[5] It extends also to the proceedings of many administrative officers, such as boards

---

90. Anonymous v. Trenkman, 2 Cir. 1931, 48 F.2d 571; Wels v. Rubin, 1939, 280 N.Y. 233, 20 N.E.2d 737. Cf. Dayton v. Drumheller, 1919, 32 Idaho 283, 182 P.2d 102 (old evidence on motion for new trial); Harshaw v. Harshaw, 1941, 220 N.C. 145, 16 S.E.2d 666 (evidence whose falsity defendant was estopped to deny); McLaughlin v. Cowley, 1879, 127 Mass. 316 (extraneous allegation of murder and adultery in pleading); Dodge v. Gilman, 1913, 122 Minn. 177, 142 N.W. 147; Barnett v. Loud, 1917, 226 Mass. 447, 115 N.E. 767.

91. Taliaferro v. Sims, 5 Cir. 1951, 187 F.2d 1; Brown v. Shimabukuro, 1940, 73 U.S.App.D.C. 194, 118 F.2d 17; Johnston v. Schlarb, 1941, 7 Wash.2d 528, 110 P.2d 190.

92. See Veeder, Absolute Immunity in Defamation, 1909, 9 Col.L.Rev. 463, 600, 608; Bussewitz v. Wisconsin Teachers' Ass'n, 1925, 188 Wis. 121, 205 N.W. 808.

93. Greenberg v. Ackerman, 1956, 41 N.J.Super. 146, 124 A.2d 313; Aborn v. Lipson, 1970, —— Mass. ——, 256 N.E.2d 442.

94. Johnston v. Dover, 1940, 201 Ark. 175, 143 S.W.2d 1112 (an honest belief that the statement is pertinent is enough). Tonkonogy v. Jaffin, 1963, 41 Misc.2d 155, 244 N.Y.S.2d 840 (enough that defendant "believed that the language would have a tendency to move the court's discretion.").

95. Ginsburg v. Black, 7 Cir. 1951, 192 F.2d 823, cert. denied 343 U.S. 934 rehearing denied 343 U.S. 958; Johnston v. Schlarb, 1941, 7 Wash.2d 528, 110 P.2d 190; Matthis v. Kennedy, 1954, 243 Minn. 219, 67 N.W.2d 413.

96. Bleecker v. Drury, 2 Cir. 1945, 149 F.2d 770; Andrews v. Gardiner, 1918, 224 N.Y. 440, 121 N.E.2d 341; McKinney v. Cooper, 1940, 163 Or. 512, 98 P.2d 711; Young v. Young, 1927, 57 App.D.C. 157,

18 F.2d 807; Seltzer v. Fields, 1963, 20 App.Div.2d 60, 244 N.Y.S.2d 792, affirmed 14 N.Y.2d 624, 249 N.Y.S.2d 174, 198 N.E.2d 368.

The fact that the language used is unduly extreme will not defeat the privilege. Parker v. Kirkland, 1939, 298 Ill.App. 340, 18 N.E.2d 709; Irwin v. Ashurst, 1938, 158 Or. 61, 74 P.2d 1127.

A litigant may be allowed more latitude than his counsel. Compare, as to interjections in court, Wells v. Carter, 1932, 164 Tenn. 400, 50 S.W.2d 278, with Breeding v. Napier, 1929, 230 Ky. 85, 18 S.W. 2d 872.

97. Kemper v. Fort, 1907, 219 Pa. 85, 67 A. 991; Myers v. Hodges, 1907, 53 Fla. 197, 44 So. 357; Harlow v. Carroll, 1895, 6 App.D.C. 128; Greenberg v. Aetna Ins. Co., 1967, 427 Pa. 511, 235 A.2d 576.

98. See Note, 1948, 13 Mo.L.Rev. 320.

99. Gunter v. Reeves, 1945, 198 Miss. 31, 21 So.2d 468 (search warrant); Stone v. Hutchinson Daily News, 1928, 125 Kan. 715, 266 P. 78 (same); Beiser v. Scripps-McRae Pub. Co., 1902, 113 Ky. 383, 68 S.W. 457.

1. Schultz v. Strauss, 1906, 127 Wis. 325, 106 N.W. 1066 (grand jury); Sands v. Robison, 1849, 12 Smedes & M. 704, 20 Miss. 704 (same); Taafe v. Downes, 1812, 3 Moo.P.C. 36 (in chambers).

2. Corcoran v. Jerrel, 1919, 185 Iowa 532, 170 N.W. 776; Dunbar v. Greenlaw, 1956, 152 Me. 270, 128 A. 2d 218; Mezullo v. Maletz, 1954, 331 Mass. 233, 118 N.E.2d 356; Jarman v. Offutt, 1954, 239 N.C. 468, 80 S.E.2d 248; Dyer v. Dyer, 1941, 178 Tenn. 234, 156 S.W.2d 445.

3. Rogers v. Thompson, 1916, 89 N.J.L. 639, 99 A. 389; Abrams v. Crompton-Richmond Co., 1957, 7 Misc.2d 461, 164 N.Y.S.2d 124, affirmed, 1958, 5 App.Div.2d 811, 170 N.Y.S.2d 981.

4. Nickovich v. Mollart, 1929, 51 Nev. 306, 274 P. 809.

5. Penick v. Ratcliffe, 1927, 149 Va. 618, 140 S.E. 664. See also Youmans v. Smith, 1893, 153 N.Y. 214, 47 N.E. 265 (disbarment); Note, 1938, 23 Iowa L.Rev. 83 (same); Talley v. Alton Box Board Co.,

and commissions,[6] so far as they have powers of discretion in applying the law to the facts which are regarded as judicial, or "quasi-judicial," in character. Thus the ordinary administrative proceeding to revoke a license [7] is held to lie within the privilege. On the other hand, of course, the mere fact that an officer must make a decision or determine the existence of a fact does not make his function a judicial one,[8] and the powers and procedure of such agencies vary so greatly that no very definite classifications can be made.[9] There are frequent dicta to the effect that the tribunal must have jurisdiction, or power to act in the situation

presented;[10] but this would compel everyone concerned to decide the question of jurisdiction at his peril, and it seems clear that the correct rule is that a mere color of jurisdiction, in fact assumed, is sufficient.[11]

The immunity extends to every step in the proceeding [12] until final disposition,[13] although it does not cover publications made before commencement [14] or after termination.[15] Conversations preliminary to the proceeding have given some difficulty. Although there is some authority to the con-

1962, 37 Ill.App.2d 137, 185 N.E.2d 349 (proceeding to recover attorney's fees); Jenson v. Olson, 1966, 273 Minn. 390, 141 N.W.2d 488 (civil service hearing).

6. Bleecker v. Drury, 2 Cir. 1945, 149 F.2d 770 (industrial board); Parker v. Kirkland, 1939, 298 Ill. App. 340, 18 N.E.2d 709 (tax board of appeals); White v. United Mills Co., 1948, 240 Mo.App. 443, 208 S.W.2d 893 (state labor commissioners, separation notice); Reagan v. Guardian Life Ins. Co., 1942, 140 Tex. 105, 166 S.W.2d 909 (insurance commission); Loudin v. Mohawk Airlines, Inc., 1964, 44 Misc.2d 926, 255 N.Y.S.2d 302 modified on other grounds, 24 App.Div.2d 447, 260 N.Y.S.2d 899 (Civil Aeronautics Board).

7. Lininger v. Knight, 1951, 123 Colo. 213, 226 P.2d 809 (liquor); Rainier's Dairies v. Raitan Valley Farms, 1955, 19 N.J. 552, 117 A.2d 889 (dairymen); Robertson v. Industrial Ins. Co., Fla.1954, 75 So.2d 198, 45 A.L.R.2d 1292 (insurance agent).

Compare, as to complaints to grievance committee of integrated state bar association, Ramstead v. Morgan, 1959, 219 Or. 338, 347 P.2d 594; Wiener v. Weintraub, 1968, 22 N.Y.2d 330, 292 N.Y.S.2d 667, 239 N.E.2d 540; McAfee v. Feller, Tex.Civ.App. 1970, 452 S.W.2d 56.

8. Fedderwitz v. Lamb, 1943, 195 Ga. 691, 25 S.E.2d 414 (state revenue commission); Johnson v. Independent Life & Acc. Ins. Co., E.D.S.C.1951, 94 F. Supp. 959 (insurance commission); Longo v. Tauriello, 1951, 201 Misc. 35, 107 N.Y.S.2d 361 (state housing rent commission); Blakeslee v. Carroll, 1894, 64 Conn. 223, 29 A. 473 (investigating committee of aldermen); Elder v. Holland, 1967, 208 Va. 15, 155 S.E.2d 369 (departmental hearing before police superintendent).

9. See Meyer v. Parr, 1941, 69 Ohio App. 344, 37 N. E.2d 637 (board of embalmers and funeral directors); Grubb v. Johnson, 1955, 205 Or. 624, 289 P.2d 1067 (revocation of insurance license); Ellish v.

Goldman, Sup.Ct.1952, 117 N.Y.S.2d 867 (zoning board of appeals).

10. See Johnson v. Brown, 1878, 13 W.Va. 71; Jones v. Brownlee, 1901, 161 Mo. 258, 61 S.W. 795; Ball v. Rawles, 1892, 93 Cal. 222, 28 P. 937.

11. Lake v. King, 1680, 2 Keb. 832, 84 Eng.Rep. 526; Allen v. Crofoot, 1829, 2 Wend., N.Y., 515, 20 Am. Dec. 647. In the case of the immunity of the judge, however, it would seem that he must at least have sufficient color of jurisdiction so that it can be said that he is acting as a court.

As to the general privilege of officers acting without jurisdiction, see infra, p. 991.

12. McKinney v. Cooper, 1940, 163 Or. 512, 98 P.2d 711 (objection to final account); Glasson v. Bowen, 1928, 84 Colo. 57, 267 P. 1066 (change of venue); Stone v. Hutchinson Daily News, 1928, 125 Kan. 715, 266 P. 78 (application for search warrant); Simon v. Stim, 1958, 11 Misc.2d 653, 176 N.Y.S.2d 475, affirmed, 1959, 10 App.Div.2d 647, 199 N.Y.S.2d 405 (pleading, and letter to judge concerning it); Spoehr v. Mittelstadt, 1967, 34 Wis.2d 653, 150 N.W. 2d 502 (pre-trial conference).

13. Jones v. Trice, 1962, 210 Tenn. 535, 360 S.W.2d 48 (motion for new trial); Hager v. Major, 1945, 350 Mo. 1166, 186 S.W.2d 564 (same); Brown v. Shimabukuro, 1941, 73 App.D.C. 194, 118 F.2d 17 (motion for rehearing); Hammett v. Hunter, 1941, 189 Okl. 455, 117 P.2d 511 (modification of decree); Petty v. General Acc., F. & L. Assur. Corp., 3 Cir. 1966, 365 F.2d 419 (settlement in open court, entered in the record).

14. Gould v. Hulme, 1829, 3 C. & P. 625, 172 Eng. Rep. 574; Koehler v. Dubose, Tex.Civ.App.1918, 200 S.W. 238, error refused; Timmis v. Bennett, 1958, 352 Mich. 355, 89 N.W.2d 748 (attorney writing letter concerning contemplated lawsuit); Johnston v. Cartwright, 8 Cir. 1966, 355 F.2d 32.

15. Burlingame v. Burlingame, 1828, 8 Cow., N.Y., 141; Paris v. Levy, 1860, 9 C.B.,N.S., 342, 142 Eng. Rep. 135. Cf. Bigner v. Hodges, 1903, 82 Miss. 215, 33 So. 980 (statement to person not concerned in case).

trary,[16] the better view seems to be that an informal complaint to a prosecuting attorney or a magistrate is to be regarded as an initial step in a judicial proceeding, and so entitled to an absolute, rather than a qualified immunity.[17] On the other hand preliminary communications between an interested party and his own attorney [18] usually have been regarded as something apart from the proceeding itself, and so at best conditionally privileged, although an interview of the attorney with a prospective witness [19] has been considered a necessary step in taking legal action, and the immunity has been held to be absolute. It is clear, however, that statements given to the newspapers concerning the case are no part of a judicial proceeding, and are not absolutely privileged.[20]

2. *Legislative Proceedings.* A long struggle between crown and parliament [21] established by the time of the English revolution the immunity, indispensable in any

system of free democratic government, of members of legislative bodies for acts in the performance of their duties. An absolute immunity was recognized at common law as to defamatory statements made by legislators in the course of any of their functions as such,[22] whether it be in debate, voting, reports, or work in committee.[23] The common law immunity was subject to the limitation that the defamation must have some relation to the business of the legislature;[24] but in this country federal [25] and state [26] constitutional provisions generally have extended it to anything whatever that is said in the course of legislative proceedings themselves. The privilege includes the official publication of what is said, as for example in the Congressional Record;[27] but it has been held that no absolute immunity is attached to republication, as by unofficial distribution of reprints from the Record, outside of the legislature.[28]

Witnesses in legislative hearings are given the same protection as in judicial proceedings,[29] and there is some rather doubtful

---

16. Magness v. Pledger, Okl.1959, 334 P.2d 792; Pecue v. West, 1921, 233 N.Y. 316, 135 N.E. 515; Marshall v. Gunter, 1853, 6 Rich. (S.C.) 419; Miller v. Nuckolls, 1905, 77 Ark. 64, 91 S.W. 759; Hathaway v. Bruggink, 1919, 168 Wis. 390, 170 N.W. 244.

17. Vogel v. Gruaz, 1884, 110 U.S. 311; Gabriel v. McMullin, 1905, 127 Iowa 426, 103 N.W. 355; Hott v. Yarbrough, 1922, 112 Tex. 179, 245 S.W. 676; Wells v. Toogood, 1911, 165 Mich. 677, 131 N.W. 124; Schultz v. Strauss, 1906, 127 Wis. 325, 106 N.W. 1066.

18. Lapetina v. Santangelo, 1908, 124 App.Div. 519, 108 N.Y.S. 975; Kruse v. Rabe, 1910, 80 N.J.L. 378, 79 A. 316. Contra, More v. Weaver, [1928] 2 K.B. 520.

19. Watson v. M'Ewan, [1905] A.C. 480, 74 L.J.P.C. 151; Beresford v. White, 1914, 30 T.L.R. 591; Youmans v. Smith, 1897, 153 N.Y. 214, 47 N.E. 265; Beggs v. McCrea, 1901, 62 App.Div. 39, 70 N.Y.S. 864.

Contra, Robinson v. Home Fire & Marine Ins. Co., 1953, 244 Iowa 1084, 59 N.W.2d 776 (qualified privilege only).

20. Kennedy v. Cannon, 1962, 229 Md. 92, 182 A.2d 54.

21. Veeder, Absolute Immunity in Defamation, 1910, 10 Col.L.Rev. 130–134; Yankwich, The Immunity of Congressional Speech—Its Origin, Meaning and

Scope, 1951, 99 U.Pa.L.Rev. 960; Field, The Constitutional Privilege of Legislators, 1925, 9 Minn. L.Rev. 442. See also Hynes, Defamation During Congressional Investigations: A Proposed Statute, 1966, 39 U.Colo.L.Rev. 48; Note, 1949, 16 U.Chi. L.Rev. 544.

22. Ex parte Wason, 1869, L.R. 4 Q.B. 73; Dillon v. Balfour, 1887, 20 L.R.Ir. 600; see Coffin v. Coffin, 1808, 4 Mass. 1.

23. See Coffin v. Coffin, 1808, 4 Mass. 1.

24. Coffin v. Coffin, 1808, 4 Mass. 1.

25. See Cochran v. Couzens, 1930, 59 App.D.C. 374, 42 F.2d 783, cert. denied 282 U.S. 874; Kilbourn v. Thompson, 1880, 103 U.S. 168.

26. See Cole v. Richards, 1932, 108 N.J.L. 356, 158 A. 466; Field, The Constitutional Privileges of Legislators, 1925, 9 Minn.L.Rev. 442.

27. Methodist Federation for Social Action v. Eastland, D.D.C.1956, 141 F.Supp. 729.

28. Rex v. Abingdon, 1795, 1 Esp. 226, 170 Eng.Rep. 337; Rex v. Creevy, 1813, 1 M. & S. 273, 105 Eng. Rep. 102; Cole v. Richards, 1932, 108 N.J.L. 356, 158 A. 466; Long v. Ansell, 1934, 293 U.S. 76; McGovern v. Martz, D.C.D.C.1960, 182 F.Supp. 343.

authority [30] that petitions addressed to legislatures, under the constitutional guaranty, enjoy an absolute immunity. There has been disagreement over whether the absolute privilege extends to the proceedings of subordinate bodies performing a legislative function, such as municipal councils. A substantial number of cases [31] have held that it does; [32] but a scant majority have held that such proceedings are not within the policy underlying the immunity, and that the members of such bodies are sufficiently protected by a qualified privilege in the exercise of good faith. [33]

3. *Executive Communications.* Under the same policy, the protection of absolute immunity also is extended to certain executive officers, at least, of the government in the discharge of their duties. [34]

The doctrine originated in 1895, with two decisions in England [35] and the Supreme Court of the United States, [36] both of which involved members of the cabinet, and held that the immunity was essential in order that the administration of government should not be hampered by the fear of lawsuits against such officers. In England the rule has been quite strictly limited to those on the highest level, whose conduct constitutes an "act of state." [37] In this country it was extended to other superior officers of the executive departments and branches of the federal, [38] and in a few cases, of the state [39] governments. Originally the line

---

29. Kelly v. Daro, 1941, 47 Cal.App.2d 418, 118 P.2d 37; Logan's Super Markets v. McCalla, 1961, 208 Tenn. 68, 343 S.W.2d 892; Wright v. Lathrop, 1889, 149 Mass. 385, 21 N.E. 963; Sheppard v. Bryant, 1906, 191 Mass. 591, 78 N.E. 394; Terry v. Fellows, 1869, 21 La.Ann. 375; see Notes, 1962, 29 Tenn.L. Rev. 314; 1942, 15 So.Cal.L.Rev. 276. In Fiore v. Rogero, Fla.App.1962, 144 So.2d 99, it was held that volunteered testimony was only qualifiedly privileged.

30. Lake v. King, 1680, 1 Lev. 240, 83 Eng.Rep. 387; Harris v. Huntington, 1802, 2 Tyler (Vt.) 129; see Cook v. Hill, 1849, 3 Sandf. (N.Y.) 341; Veeder, Absolute Immunity in Defamation, 1910, 10 Col.L. Rev. 131, 138.

In Bigelow v. Brumley, 1941, 138 Ohio St. 574, 37 N.E. 584, a statement to the electorate in connection with an initiative proposal for a constitutional amendment was held to be part of the legislative process.

31. Bolton v. Walker, 1917, 197 Mich. 699, 164 N.W. 420; Tanner v. Gault, 1925, 20 Ohio App. 243, 153 N.E. 124; McNayr v. Kelly, Fla.1966, 184 So.2d 428 conformed to 185 So.2d 194; Larson v. Doner, 1961, 32 Ill.App.2d 471, 178 N.E.2d 399; Carter v. Jackson, 1960, 10 Utah 2d 284, 351 P.2d 957 (under statute).

32. McClendon v. Coverdale, Del.Super.1964, 203 A. 2d 815; Mills v. Denny, 1954, 245 Iowa 584, 63 N.W.2d 222; Ivie v. Minton, 1915, 75 Or. 483, 147 P. 395; Burch v. Bernard, 1909, 107 Minn. 210, 120 N.W. 33; McGaw v. Hamilton, 1898, 184 Pa. 108, 39 A. 4. Accord, Jones v. Monico, 1967, 276 Minn. 371, 150 N.W.2d 213 (board of county commissioners).

Accord, as to town meetings: Smith v. Higgins, 1860, 82 Mass. (16 Gray) 251; Bradford v. Clark, 1897, 90 Me. 298, 38 A. 229.

33. Omitted.

34. Handler and Klein, The Defense of Privilege in Defamation Suits Against Government Executive Officials, 1960, 74 Harv.L.Rev. 44; Becht, The Absolute Privilege of the Executive in Defamation, 1962, 15 Vand.L.Rev. 1127; Gray, Private Wrongs of Public Servants, 1959, 47 Cal.L.Rev. 303; Notes, 1960, 44 Minn.L.Rev. 547; 1960, 55 Northwestern U.L.Rev. 228; 1954, 7 Okl.L.Rev. 105; 1954, 32 N.C. L.Rev. 564; 1953, 20 U.Chi.L.Rev. 677; 1953, 37 Minn.L.Rev. 141; 1952, 38 Iowa L.Rev. 186; 1942, 40 Mich.L.Rev. 919.

35. Chatterton v. Secretary of State for India, [1895] 2 Q.B. 189.

36. Spalding v. Vilas, 1896, 161 U.S. 483 (Postmaster General).

37. Szalatnay-Stacho v. Fink, [1947] 1 K.B. 1; Gibbons v. Duffell, 1932, 47 Comm.L.Rep., Aust., 520, 530; Jackson v. McGrath, 1947, 75 Comm.L.Rep., Aust., 293, 306.

38. Standard Nut Margarine Co. v. Mellon, 1934, 63 U.S.App.D.C. 339, 72 F.2d 557, cert. denied 293 U.S. 605 (Secretary and Assistant Secretary of Treasury); Adams v. Home Owners Loan Corp., 8 Cir. 1939, 107 F.2d 139 (officers of Home Owners Loan Corporation); Pearson v. Wright, D.D.C.1957, 156 F.Supp. 136 (Chairman of Federal Commission on Government Service); Short v. News-Journal Co., Del.1965, 212 A.2d 718 (Director of Internal Revenue).

39. Ryan v. Wilson, 1941, 231 Iowa 33, 300 N.W. 707 (governor); Matson v. Margiotti, 1952, 371 Pa. 188, 88 A.2d 892 (attorney general); Gold Seal Chinchillas, Inc. v. State, 1966, 69 Wash.2d 828, 420 P.2d 698 (same); Hackworth v. Larson, 1969, 83 S.D. 674, 165 N.W.2d 705 (Secretary of State);

was drawn at such superior officers.[40] Over several years, however, a series of decisions in the lower federal courts [41] extended the immunity to lower federal officers and employees as to communications which they are required or authorized to make in connection with the performance of their duties.

In Barr v. Matteo,[42] the Supreme Court not only confirmed the extension to all such federal personnel, but held that it included all publications within the "outer perimeter" of their "line of duty," such as defamatory press releases explaining their actions to the public.[43] While there are a few state court decisions which appear to reach the same conclusion as to subordinate state officers,[44]

such courts in general have refused to accept the extension, and have recognized no absolute privilege on the part of such officers as superintendents of schools,[45] mayors and aldermen,[46] prosecuting attorneys and policemen,[47] state investigators,[48] and the like. Unless such an executive officer can claim immunity on the basis of a quasi-judicial or legislative function,[49] he is held to be subject to a qualified privilege only. It seems to be generally agreed, also, that petitions or complaints of private citizens to executive officers concerning public affairs are likewise only qualifiedly privileged.[50]

Immunity for defamation is only part of a larger problem, of the limits to the responsibility of public officers for torts against private citizens.[51] The argument in favor of Barr v. Matteo is that a qualified privilege would not be adequate protection for the

Hughes v. Bizzell, 1941, 189 Okl. 472, 117 P.2d 763 (president of state university).

40. Maurice v. Worden, 1880, 54 Md. 233; Hemmens v. Nelson, 1893, 138 N.Y. 517, 34 N.E. 342; Peterson v. Steenerson, 1910, 113 Minn. 87, 129 N.W. 147.

41. See for example Miles v. McGrath, D.Md.1933, 4 F.Supp. 603 (naval officer); Taylor v. Glotfelty, 6 Cir. 1952, 201 F.2d 51 (psychiatrist at medical center); United States to Use of Parravicino v. Brunswick, 1934, 63 U.S.App.D.C. 65, 69 F.2d 383 (consul); Lang v. Wood, 1937, 67 U.S.App.D.C. 287, 92 F.2d 211, certiorari denied 302 U.S. 686, 58 S.Ct. 48, 82 L.Ed. 530 (warden of a prison); Harwood v. McMurtry, 1938, 22 F.Supp. 572 (internal revenue agent).

42. 1959, 360 U.S. 564, rehearing denied 361 U.S. 855 (Acting Director of Office of Rent Stabilization). This was a 5–4 decision, with Mr. Justice Black concurring specially. See also Preble v. Johnson, 10 Cir. 1960, 275 F.2d 275 (civil service employees and naval enlisted man).

43. Accord, as to press releases: Glass v. Ickes, 1940, 73 U.S.App.D.C. 3, 117 F.2d 273, cert. denied 311 U.S. 718 (Secretary of the Interior); Ryan v. Wilson, 1941, 231 Iowa 33, 300 N.W. 707 (governor); Matson v. Margiotti, 1952, 371 Pa. 188, 88 A.2d 892 (attorney general); Short v. News-Journal Co., Del. 1965, 212 A.2d 718 (Director of Internal Revenue).

44. Sheridan v. Crisona, 1964, 14 N.Y.2d 108, 249 N.Y.S.2d 161, 198 N.E.2d 359 (borough president); McNayr v. Kelly, Fla.1966, 184 So.2d 428, conformed to 185 So.2d 194 (county manager); Long v. Mertz, 1965, 2 Ariz.App. 215, 407 P.2d 404 (highway department engineer); Montgomery v. City of Philadelphia, 1958, 392 Pa. 178, 140 A.2d 100 (city commissioner of public property and city architect); Schlinkert v. Henderson, 1951, 331 Mich. 284, 49 N.W. 2d 180 (liquor control commissioner).

45. Barry v. McCollom, 1908, 81 Conn. 293, 70 A. 1035; Tanner v. Stevenson, 1910, 138 Ky. 578, 128 S.W. 878; Hemmens v. Nelson, 1893, 138 N.Y. 517, 34 N.E. 342 (principal of state institution for deaf mutes); Collins v. Oklahoma State Hospital, 1916, 76 Okl. 229, 184 P. 946 (superintendent of state asylum); Ranous v. Hughes, 1966, 30 Wis.2d 452, 141 N.W.2d 251 (board of education).

46. Mayo v. Sample, 1865, 18 Iowa 306; Weber v. Lane, 1903, 99 Mo.App. 69, 71 S.W. 1099; Ranous v. Hughes, 1966, 30 Wis.2d 452, 141 N.W.2d 25 (county manager). See Note, 1967, 21 U.Miami L. Rev. 498.

47. Earl v. Winne, 1953, 14 N.J. 119, 101 A.2d 535; Carr v. Watkins, 1962, 227 Md. 578, 177 A.2d 841 (particularly good on difference between federal and state law).

48. Peeples v. State, 1942, 179 Misc. 272, 38 N.Y.S.2d 690 (state examiner of accounts); In re Investigating Commission, 1887, 16 R.I. 751, 11 A. 429 (governor's investigating commission). Cf. Pearce v. Brower, 1884, 72 Ga. 243 (road commissioners).

49. Cf. Larkin v. Noonan, 1865, 19 Wis. 82; McAlister & Co. v. Jenkins, 1926, 214 Ky. 802, 284 S.W. 88; Trebilcock v. Anderson, 1898, 117 Mich. 39, 75 N.W. 129.

50. Licciardi v. Molnar, 1945, 23 N.J.Misc. 361, 44 A. 2d 653; Bingham v. Gaynor, 1911, 203 N.Y. 27, 96 N.E. 84; Maurice v. Worden, 1880, 54 Md. 233; Andrews v. Gardiner, 1918, 224 N.Y. 440, 121 N.E. 341.

51. See infra, § 132.

public officer, since it would necessitate calling him as a witness to deny malice, and so subject him to cross-examination upon his official conduct in a private suit, and would end by submitting it to the eccentric and unreliable judgment of a jury; and that in the public interest no good and worthy public servant should be deterred from accepting office or acting by the fear of such a proceeding. It does not appear, however, that anyone has been deterred in those states where only the qualified privilege is recognized; and the decision has been attacked with vigor [52] as affording a golden opportunity for utterly unscrupulous politicians to abuse their position by inflicting outrageous injury upon the helpless and innocent, for the worst kind of motives, and with no redress. It can scarcely be said that our governments, state or federal, have always been so free of scoundrels as to inspire confidence in such a rule.[53]

One limiting factor, of obvious importance, lies in the general agreement that the publication must at least be found to lie within the defendant's authorized functions. It is no part of the duties of a janitor, or a United States marshal,[54] to issue a press release concerning what he sees and hears, of school district trustees to issue such statements concerning the superintendent or pupils,[55]

of a state conservation commissioner to make dinner speeches attacking other officials,[56] or of a mayor to act as an unofficial censor of art.[57]

4. *Consent of the Plaintiff.* The general social policy of denying recovery for conduct to which the plaintiff has given his consent [58] finds expression in an absolute immunity in cases where consent is given to defamation.[59] One who has himself invited or instigated the publication of defamatory words cannot be heard to complain of the resulting damage to his reputation;[60] and this is true although the publication was procured for the very purpose of decoying the defendant into a lawsuit.[61] At the same time, of course, it is not every request to speak which manifests consent to slander,[62] and an honest in-

---

52. See Handler and Klein, The Defense of Privilege in Defamation Suits Against Government Executive Officials, 1960, 74 Harv.L.Rev. 44; Becht, The Absolute Privilege of the Executive in Defamation, 1962, 15 Vand.L.Rev. 1127; Gray, Private Wrongs of Public Servants, 1959, 47 Cal.L.Rev. 303; Note, 1962, 48 Corn.L.Q. 199.

53. One rather startling, and perhaps alarming, decision is Heine v. Raus, D.Md.1966, 261 F.Supp. 570 on remand 305 F.Supp. 816, holding that an employee of CIA was absolutely privileged in reports he made to third persons. See Note, 1967, 67 Col.L. Rev. 752.

54. Colpoys v. Gates, 1940, 73 U.S.App.D.C. 193, 118 F.2d 16. Cf. Jacobs v. Herlands, Sup.Ct.1940, 17 N.Y.S.2d 711, affirmed 1940, 259 App.Div. 823, 19 N.Y.S.2d 770 (investigator of crime).

55. Lipman v. Brisbane Elementary School Dist., 1961, 55 Cal.2d 224, 359 P.2d 465; Elder v. Ander-

son, 1962, 205 Cal.App.2d 326, 23 Cal.Rptr. 48. Cf. Tanner v. Stevenson, 1910, 138 Ky. 578, 128 S.W. 878 (matters outside of county).

56. Cheatum v. Wehle, 1959, 5 N.Y.2d 585, 186 N.Y.S. 2d 606, 159 N.E.2d 166.

57. Walker v. D'Alesandro, 1957, 212 Md. 163, 129 A. 2d 148.

58. See supra, § 18.

59. Where the plaintiff is uncertain as to just what will be said, but consents to publication which he has reason to believe may be defamatory, the defense would seem properly to be one of assumption of risk. Cf. Chapman v. Ellesmere, [1932] 2 K.B. 431.

60. Shinglemeyer v. Wright, 1900, 124 Mich. 230, 82 N.W. 887; Christopher v. Akin, 1913, 214 Mass. 332, 101 N.E. 971; Burdett v. Hines, 1921, 125 Miss. 66, 87 So. 470; Taylor v. McDaniels, 1929, 139 Okl. 262, 281 P. 967. Cf. Mick v. American Dental Ass'n, 1958, 49 N.J.Super. 262, 139 A.2d 570 (request for opinion); Patrick v. Thomas, Okl.1962, 376 P.2d 250 (plaintiff's agent entered into correspondence). In Mims v. Metropolitan Life Ins. Co., 5 Cir. 1952, 200 F.2d 800, and National Disabled Soldiers' League v. Haan, 1925, 55 App.D.C. 243, 4 F.2d 436, the inquiry of a United States Senator instigated by the plaintiff was held to show consent.

61. Richardson v. Gunby, 1912, 88 Kan. 47, 127 P. 533; Howland v. George F. Blake Mfg. Co., 1892, 156 Mass. 543, 31 N.E. 656; Melcher v. Beeler, 1910, 48 Colo. 233, 110 P. 181; Gordon v. Spencer, 1829, 2 Blackf., Ind., 286; Hellesen v. Knaus Truck Lines, Mo.1963, 370 S.W.2d 341.

62. Nelson v. Whitten, D.N.Y.1921, 272 F. 135 (request for recommendation); Arvey Corp. v. Peter-

quiry as to what is meant,[63] or an investigation in good faith to find out what the defendant has been saying [64] will not bar the action, even though it is made for the ultimate purpose of vindication at law. As in other cases of consent, the privilege is limited by the scope of the assent apparently given, and consent to one form of publication does not confer a license to publish to other persons, or in a different manner.[65]

5. *Husband and Wife.* The few cases which have considered the question [66] have dealt with communications between husband and wife upon the basis that there is no publication, retaining the venerable fiction that man and wife are but one person, and no one can publish to himself. Since this hoary absurdity has long since been discarded elsewhere,[67] and since a third person may publish defamation concerning one spouse to the other,[68] the better explanation is that there is an absolute immunity as to what is said between husband and wife, based upon the very confidential character of the relation.[69]

6. *Political Broadcasts.* The provision of the Federal Communications Act [70] that radio stations shall afford equal opportunities to all political candidates,[71] and that the station shall have no power of censorship over their speeches, has meant that the station may be unable to refuse time on the air, yet powerless to exert any control over what is said. This at first gave rise to a dispute, with a few opinions of lower courts divided,[72] as to whether the statute necessarily carried the implication of absolute immunity on the part of the broadcaster. In 1959 the controversy was finally settled by the Supreme Court of the United States, which held that the publication is absolutely privileged.[73] In all probability the same conclusion would be reached as to any other publication required by law, as in the case of a newspaper required to publish a legal notice.[74]

115. QUALIFIED PRIVILEGE

There remain a group of situations in which the interest which the defendant is seeking to vindicate is regarded as having an

son, E.D.Pa.1959, 178 F.Supp. 132 (request for payment of wages).

63. Smith v. Dunlop Tire & Rubber Co., 1938, 186 S. C. 456, 196 S.E. 174.

64. Thorn v. Moser, 1845, 1 Denio, N.Y., 488; Griffiths v. Lewis, 1846, 7 Q.B. 61, 115 Eng.Rep. 411; Wharton v. Chunn, 1909, 53 Tex.Civ.App. 124, 115 S.W. 887.

65. See Cook v. Ward, 1830, 6 Bing. 409, 130 Eng. Rep. 1338; Luzenberg v. O'Malley, 1906, 116 La. 699, 41 So. 41; Hope v. L'Anson, 1901, 18 T.L.R. 201. But in Sharman v. C. Schmidt & Sons, E.D. Pa.1963, 216 F.Supp. 401, consent to the use of plaintiff's picture in advertising was held to include beer advertising.

66. Wennhak v. Morgan, 1880, 20 Q.B.D. 635, 57 L.J. Q.B. 241; Dyer v. McDougall, E.D.N.Y.1950, 93 F. Supp. 484; Lawler v. Merritt, 1944, 182 Misc. 648, 48 N.Y.S.2d 843, affirmed, 1945, 269 App.Div. 662, 53 N.Y.S.2d 465; Springer v. Swift, 1931, 59 S.D. 208, 239 N.W. 171; Conrad v. Roberts, 1915, 95 Kan. 180, 147 P. 795.

67. See infra, § 122.

68. Wenman v. Ash, 1853, 13 C.B. 836, 138 Eng.Rep. 1432; Schenck v. Schenck, 1843, 20 N.J.L. 208; Luick v. Driscoll, 1895, 13 Ind.App. 279, 41 N.E. 463; Bonkowski v. Arlan's Dept. Store, 1970, 383 Mich. 90, 174 N.W.2d 765.

69. Restatement of Torts, § 592; see Campbell v. Bannister, 1886, 79 Ky. 205, 2 Ky.Law Rep. 72.

70. Federal Communications Act of 1934, 47 U.S.C.A. § 315.

71. Held in Felix v. Westinghouse Radio Stations, 3 Cir. 1950, 106 F.2d 1, not to apply to supporters of candidates.

72. See Snyder, Liability of Station Owners for Defamatory Statements by Political Candidates, 1953, 37 Va.L.Rev. 303; Berry and Goodrich, Political Defamation: Radio's Dilemma, 1948, 1 U.Fla.L.Rev. 343; Notes, 1956, 25 Ford.L.Rev. 385; 1958, 32 So. Cal.L.Rev. 71; 1959, 8 Buff.L.Rev. 275; 1958, 107 U.Pa.L.Rev. 280.

73. Farmers Educational and Co-op. Union of America, No. Dak. Div. v. WDAY, Inc., 1959, 360 U.S. 525.

74. Cf. Becker v. Philco Corp., 4 Cir. 1967, 372 F.2d 771 (employer required by defense contract to report any loss or compromise of classified information).

intermediate degree of importance, so that the immunity conferred is not absolute, but is conditioned upon publication in a reasonable manner and for a proper purpose. The privilege is therefore spoken of as "qualified," "conditional," or "defeasible."[75] It is difficult to reduce these cases to any single statement, and perhaps no better formula can be offered than that of Baron Parke,[76] that the publication is privileged when it is "fairly made by a person in the discharge of some public or private duty, whether legal or moral, or in the conduct of his own affairs, in matters where his interest is concerned."

A considerable segment of the rules formerly applied to qualified privileges under the common law has now been taken over, by decisions of the Supreme Court of the United States, into a broad constitutional privilege under the First Amendment. Since this involves not only defamation, but also invasions of privacy, it is more conveniently dealt with in a later chapter[77] concerned with both.

In so far as constitutional questions are not involved, the types of interests which are protected by a qualified privilege may be classified as follows:

1. *Interest of Publisher.* Roughly similar to the privileges of self-defense or the defense of property[78] is the privilege which attaches to the publication of defamatory matter for the protection or advancement of the defendant's own legitimate interests.

Thus he may publish, in an appropriate manner, anything which reasonably appears to be necessary to defend his own reputation against the defamation of another,[79] including, of course, the allegation that his accuser is an unmitigated liar and the truth is not in him. He will, however, be liable if he adds anything irrelevant and unconnected with the charges made against him, as where he attempts to refute an accusation of immorality by saying that the plaintiff has stolen a horse.[80] A similar privilege extends to the protection of his other interests of any importance. He may make a reasonable effort to recover stolen property[81] or to that end to discover and prosecute the thief,[82] to collect money due him[83] or to prevent

75. See generally Restatement of Torts, §§ 593–612; Bower, Actionable Defamation, 2d Ed. 1923, Appendix VIII; Harper, Privileged Defamation, 1936, 22 Va.L.Rev. 642; Evans, Legal Immunity for Defamation, 1940, 24 Minn.L.Rev. 607; Jones, Interest and Duty in Relation to Qualified Privilege, 1924, 22 Mich.L.Rev. 437; Smith, Conditional Privilege for Mercantile Agencies, 1914, 14 Col.L.Rev. 187, 296; Note, 1963, 30 Tenn.L.Rev. 569.

76. In Toogood v. Spyring, 1834, 1 C. M. & R. 181, 149 Eng.Rep. 1044.

77. See infra, ch. 21.

78. See supra, §§ 19, 21.

79. Haycox v. Dunn, 1958, 200 Va. 212, 104 S.E.2d 800; Shenkman v. O'Malley, 1956, 2 App.Div.2d 567, 157 N.Y.S.2d 290; Preston v. Hobbs, 1914, 161 App. Div. 363, 146 N.Y.S. 419; Duncan v. Record Pub. Co., 1927, 145 S.C. 196, 143 S.E. 31; Craig v. Wright, 1938, 182 Okl. 68, 76 P.2d 248. See Note, 1969, 34 Alb.L.J. 95.

80. Brewer v. Chase, 1899, 121 Mich. 526, 80 N.W. 575; Fish v. St. Louis County Printing & Pub. Co., 1903, 102 Mo.App. 6, 74 S.W. 641; Sternberg Mfg. Co. v. Miller, Du Brul & Peters Mfg. Co., 8 Cir. 1909, 170 F. 298; Ivie v. King, 1914, 167 N.C. 174, 83 S.E. 339, rehearing denied, 1915, 169 N.C. 261, 85 S.E. 413; cf. Conroy v. Fall River Herald News Co., 1940, 306 Mass. 488, 28 N.E.2d 729. As to mitigation of damages because of provocation, see infra, p. 801. Louisiana denies recovery in cases of "mutual vituperation." Bloom v. Crescioni, 1903, 109 La. 667, 33 So. 724; Pellifigue v. Judice, 1923, 154 La. 782, 98 So. 244.

81. Padmore v. Lawrence, 1840, 11 Ad. & El. 380, 113 Eng.Rep. 460; Brow v. Hathaway, 1866, 95 Mass. (13 Allen) 239; Faber v. Byrle, 1951, 171 Kan. 38, 229 P.2d 718; Bavington v. Robinson, 1914, 124 Md. 85, 91 A. 777.
Cf. Ripps v. Herrington, 1941, 241 Ala. 209, 1 So.2d 899 (claim to fidelity insurance company).

82. Ram v. Lamley, 1633, Hut. 113, 123 Eng.Rep. 1139; Klinck v. Colby, 1871, 46 N.Y. 427; Flanagan v. McLane, 1913, 87 Conn. 220, 87 A. 727, 88 A. 96; cf. Ginsberg v. Union Surety & Guaranty Co., 1902, 68 App.Div. 141, 74 N.Y.S. 561.

83. Dickinson v. Hathaway, 1909, 122 La. 644, 48 So. 136. In Miller v. Howe, 1932, 245 Ky. 568, 53 S.W. 2d 938, a mere collecting agent was held to have no interest justifying a privilege.

others from collecting it,[84] to warn his servants against the conduct of the plaintiff, or others of questionable character,[85] to consult an attorney for legal advice,[86] to protest against the mismanagement of a concern in which he has an interest,[87] or to protect his business against unethical competition.[88] In all of these cases the privilege is lost if he says more than reasonably appears to be necessary,[89] or if the publication is made to a person who apparently [90] is in no position to give legitimate assistance, as where complaint is made to an employer that his employee will not pay the defendant a debt.[91]

2. *Interest of Others.* The privilege to use force to protect the safety of another [92] finds a general parallel in the privilege to publish defamation for the protection of the interests of persons other than the publisher. The publication may be made to the individual who is thus protected, as in the case of a warning to a woman not to marry a supposed ex-convict, or it may be made to a third person, as where the warning is given to her father. As in the case of the use of force, the defendant must have reason to believe that the publication is necessary for the purpose, and that the other is unable to protect himself. Thus there is no privilege to refute a libel on behalf of one who is quite able to publish his own denial,[93] although the privilege may exist if he is precluded by army orders from speaking.[94]

The extent of this privilege has been a matter of considerable discussion,[95] and because the fact situations are of infinite variety, it is not possible to reduce them to any formula, other than the general one that the publication must be justified by the importance of the interest served, and it must be called for by a legal or moral "duty," or by generally accepted standards of decent conduct.[96] The privilege is clearest when some definite legal relation exists between the defendant and the person on whose behalf he intervenes. Thus a man may advise a member of his family not to marry one be-

84. Blackham v. Pugh, 1846, 2 C.B. 611, 135 Eng.Rep. 1086; Gassett v. Gilbert, 1856, 72 Mass. (6 Gray) 94; Hatch v. Lane, 1870, 105 Mass. 394; cf. Holmes v. Royal Fraternal Union, 1909, 222 Mo. 556, 121 S.W. 100; Tierney v. Ruppert, 1912, 150 App.Div. 863, 135 N.Y.S. 365 (warning against purchase of mortgaged property).

85. Somerville v. Hawkins, 1851, 10 C.B. 583, 138 Eng.Rep. 231; Nichols v. J. J. Newberry Co., 9 Cir. 1945, 150 F.2d 15; Lawler v. Earle, 1862, 87 Mass. (5 Allen) 22; Hunt v. Great Northern R. Co., [1891] 1 Q.B. 601.
Cf. Conner v. Taylor, 1930, 233 Ky. 706, 26 S.W.2d 561 (effort to keep diseased employee away so that others would work).

86. Lapetina v. Santangelo, 1908, 124 App.Div. 519, 108 N.Y.S. 975; see Kruse v. Rabe, 1910, 80 N.J.L. 378, 79 A. 316.

87. McDougall v. Claridge, 1808, 1 Camp. 267, 170 Eng.Rep. 953.

88. Powell v. Young, 1928, 151 Va. 985, 144 S.E. 624, 145 S.E. 731; cf. John W. Lovell Co. v. Houghton, 1889, 116 N.Y. 520, 22 N.E. 1066; Hovey v. Rubber Tip Pencil Co., 1874, 57 N.Y. 119.

89. Holmes v. Clisby, 1904, 121 Ga. 241, 48 S.E. 934. See infra, p. 795.

90. As to the effect of reasonable belief in the existence of the privilege, see infra, p. 795.

91. Over v. Schiffling, 1885, 102 Ind. 191, 26 N.E. 91; Vail v. Pennsylvania R. Co., 1927, 103 N.J.L. 213, 136 A. 425; cf. Hollenbeck v. Ristine, 1901, 114 Iowa 358, 86 N.W. 377; Brown v. Vanneman, 1893, 85 Wis. 451, 55 N.W. 183; Preston v. Frey, 1891, 91 Cal. 107, 27 P. 533.

92. See supra, § 20.

93. Ritschy v. Garrels, 1916, 195 Mo.App. 670, 187 S.W. 1120.

94. Adam v. Ward, [1917] A.C. 309. Cf. Israel v. Portland News Pub. Co., 1936, 152 Or. 225, 53 P.2d 529 (deceased husband). See Notes, 1936, 20 Minn. L.Rev. 438; 1936, 49 Harv.L.Rev. 839. In Smith v. Levitt, 9 Cir. 1955, 227 F.2d 855, a combination of this privilege and that of fair comment was held to justify defense of a United States Senator by his political friends and supporters.

95. See Jones, Interest and Duty in Relation to Qualified Privilege, 1924, 22 Mich.L.Rev. 437; Smith, Conditional Privilege for Mercantile Agencies, 1914, 14 Col.L.Rev. 187, 296; Harper, Privileged Defamation, 1936, 22 Va.L.Rev. 642; Evans, Legal Immunity for Defamation, 1940, 24 Minn.L.Rev. 607.

96. See Restatement of Torts, § 595.

lieved to be a scoundrel,[97] or protest to school authorities against the students with whom his daughter is brought in contact;[98] or a physician may speak to protect the interest of his patient,[99] an attorney that of his client,[100] or an agent or employee that of his principal or employer.[1]

Beyond this, the courts have recognized in many instances a moral justification, where under ordinary social standards a reasonable man would feel called upon to speak. It is permissible to warn a present[2] or prospective[3] employer of the misconduct or bad character of an employee, to notify an insurance company that it is being swindled by the insured,[4] to inform a landlord that his tenant is undesirable,[5] a creditor that his debtor is insolvent,[6] or one who appears likely to deal with the plaintiff that his credit or character is bad.[7]

A point is reached at which the line must be drawn against officious intermeddling, where a reasonable man would conclude that the matter is none of his affair, and that he would do better to remain silent. Particularly in the case of interference with personal or family matters, such as a word to a husband about the conduct of his wife,[8] or to a woman concerning her prospective husband,[9] the courts have been inclined to say that the tale-bearing "friend" who stirs up domestic discord has no privilege, and must take the chance that his information is wrong. It has proved, however, unusually difficult to draw any definite line as to what is improper. In all such cases, the fact that the defendant has been requested to give information, or

97. Todd v. Hawkins, 1837, 8 C. & P. 88, 173 Eng. Rep. 411; cf. McBride v. Ledoux, 1904, 111 La. 398, 35 So. 615; Kimble v. Kimble, 1896, 14 Wash. 369, 44 P. 866; Harriott v. Plimpton, 1896, 166 Mass. 585, 44 N.E. 992.

98. Hansen v. Hansen, 1914, 126 Minn. 426, 148 N.W. 457. Cf. Kenney v. Gurley, 1923, 208 Ala. 623, 95 So. 34 (school to parent); Coopersmith v. Williams, 1970, —— Colo. ——, 468 P.2d 739.

99. Cameron v. Cockran, 1895, 2 Marv., Del., 166, 42 A. 454; Cash Drug Store v. Cannon, Tex.Civ.App. 1932, 47 S.W.2d 861. Cf. Thornburg v. Long, 1919, 178 N.C. 589, 101 S.E. 99 (one physician to another).

100. Kruse v. Rabe, 1910, 80 N.J.L. 378, 79 A. 316.

1. Scarll v. Dixon, 1864, 4 F. & F. 250, 176 Eng.Rep. 552; Lewis v. Chapman, 1857, 16 N.Y. 369; Ritchie v. Arnold, 1898, 79 Ill.App. 406. Accord, as to reporting theft: Bell v. Bank of Abbeville, 1947, 211 S.C. 167, 44 S.E.2d 328; Lee v. Cannon Mills, 4 Cir. 1939, 107 F.2d 109; Snyder v. Fatherly, 1930, 153 Va. 762, 151 S.E. 149.

Accord, as to hired investigators: Combes v. Montgomery Ward & Co., 1951, 119 Utah 407, 228 P.2d 272; Roscoe v. Schoolitz, 1970, 105 Ariz. 310, 464 P.2d 333; Campbell v. Willmark Service System, 3 Cir. 1941, 123 F.2d 204.

2. Coxhead v. Richards, 1846, 2 C.B. 569, 135 Eng. Rep. 1069; Doyle v. Clauss, 1920, 190 App.Div. 838, 180 N.Y.S. 671. Cf. Simonsen v. Swenson, 1920, 104 Neb. 224, 177 N.W. 831 (physician informing hotel owner his employee had syphilis); Leonard v. Wilson, 1942, 150 Fla. 503, 8 So.2d 12 (physician reporting on fitness for work); Cochran v. Sears, Roebuck & Co., 1945, 72 Ga.App. 458, 34 S.E.2d 296 (nurse reporting disease).

3. Fresh v. Cutter, 1890, 73 Md. 87, 20 A. 774; Doane v. Grew, 1915, 220 Mass. 171, 107 N.E. 620; Hoff v. Pure Oil Co., 1920, 147 Minn. 195, 179 N.W. 891; Carroll v. Owen, 1914, 178 Mich. 551, 146 N. W. 168; Zeinfeld v. Hayes Freight Lines, Inc., 1969, 41 Ill.2d 345, 243 N.E.2d 217. In Williams v.

Kansas City Transit, Inc., Mo.1960, 339 S.W.2d 792, a discharging employer, required by statute to give the employee a letter stating the cause for his leaving the service, was held to be conditionally privileged. Accord, Henthorn v. Western Maryland R. Co., 1961, 226 Md. 499, 174 A.2d 175 (hearing required under collective bargaining provisions of Railway Labor Act).

4. Noonan v. Orton, 1873, 32 Wis. 106; Hubbard v. Rutledge, 1879, 57 Miss. 7.

5. Morton v. Knipe, 1908, 128 App.Div. 94, 112 N.Y.S. 451; Rose v. Tholborn, 1910, 153 Mo.App. 408, 134 S.W. 1093.

6. See Ormsby v. Douglass, 1867, 37 N.Y. 477; Lewis v. Chapman, 1857, 16 N.Y. 369; Ritchie v. Arnold, 1898, 79 Ill.App. 406.

7. Melcher v. Beeler, 1910, 48 Colo. 233, 110 P. 181; Richardson v. Gunby, 1912, 88 Kan. 47, 127 P. 533; Fahr v. Hayes, 1888, 50 N.J.L. 275, 13 A. 261; Froslee v. Lund's State Bank, 1915, 131 Minn. 435, 155 N.W. 619; Browne v. Prudden-Winslow Co., 1921, 195 App.Div. 419, 186 N.Y.S. 350 (warning customers against salesman discharged for dishonesty).

8. Watt v. Longsdon, [1930] 1 K.B. 130; Burton v. Mattson, 1917, 50 Utah 133, 166 P. 979.

9. Krebs v. Oliver, 1858, 12 Gray, Mass., 239; Joannes v. Bennett, 1862, 5 Allen, Mass., 169.

to obtain it,[10] becomes quite important, although not conclusive. Such a request on the part of one who has no other apparent interest than that of idle curiosity will not of course create a privilege in itself;[11] but it does indicate that the recipient regards the matter as important to his interests, and if those interests are otherwise apparent it will ordinarily make it reasonable to speak.[12] It has been said that volunteered information is never privileged,[13] and that it is privileged to the same extent as though it has been requested.[14] It seems clear that neither statement is correct, and that while more in the way of good reason to speak may be required of a volunteer, the absence of a request is merely one factor to be considered, along with the importance of the interest to be protected[15] and other elements, in determining the propriety of the defendant's conduct.[16] The same is no doubt true of the fact that the statement is made to a third person, rather than directly to the one for whose protection it is intended.[17]

3. *Common Interest.* A conditional privilege is recognized in many cases where the publisher and the recipient have a common interest, and the communication is of a kind reasonably calculated to protect or further it. Frequently in such cases there is a legal, as well as a moral obligation to speak. This is most obvious, of course, in the case of those who have entered upon or are considering business dealings with one another,[18] or where the parties are members of a group[19] with a common pecuniary interest, as where officers, agents or employees of a business organization communicate with stockholders,[20] or with other employees or branch of-

10. Rude v. Nass, 1891, 79 Wis. 321, 48 N.W. 555.

11. Swift & Co. v. Gray, 9 Cir. 1939, 101 F.2d 976 (customers of discharged truck driver); Byam v. Collins, 1888, 111 N.Y. 143, 19 N.E. 75; Carpenter v. Willey, 1892, 65 Vt. 168, 26 A. 488; Ritchie v. Widdemer, 1896, 59 N.J.L. 290, 35 A. 825.

12. Restatement of Torts, § 595, Comment *i*; Rude v. Nass, 1891, 79 Wis. 321, 48 N.W. 555; Posnett v. Marble, 1889, 62 Vt. 481, 20 A. 813; Rosenbaum v. Roche, 1907, 46 Tex.Civ.App. 237, 101 S.W.2d 1164; Zeinfeld v. Hayes Freight Lines, Inc., 1969, 41 Ill. 2d 345, 243 N.E.2d 217. Cf. Stevenson v. Baltimore Baseball Club, 1968, 250 Md. 482, 243 A.2d 533.

13. Draper v. Hellman Commercial Trust & Savings Bank, 1928, 203 Cal. 26, 263 P. 240; cf. Rosenbaum v. Roche, 1907, 46 Tex.Civ.App. 237, 101 S.W. 1164.

14. See Pattison v. Jones, 1828, 8 B. & C. 578, 108 Eng.Rep. 1157; Fresh v. Cutter, 1890, 73 Md. 87, 20 A. 774.

15. See Samples v. Carnahan, 1898, 21 Ind.App. 55, 51 N.E. 425; Restatement of Torts, § 595, Comment *i*.

16. Thus volunteered information to protect interests of importance was held privileged in Hubbard v. Rutledge, 1879, 57 Miss. 7; Morton v. Knipe, 1908, 128 App.Div. 94, 112 N.Y.S. 451; Rose v. Tholborn, 1910, 153 Mo.App. 408, 134 S.W. 1093; Fahr v. Hayes, 1888, 50 N.J.L. 275, 13 A. 261; Fresh v. Cutter, 1890, 73 Md. 87, 20 A. 774.

17. This may be entirely reasonable, as in Hansen v. Hansen, 1914, 126 Minn. 426, 148 N.W. 457, where a father protested to school authorities against students with whom his daughter was brought in contact. Or it may be found to be totally unnecessary and unjustified, as in Krebs v. Oliver, 1858, 78 Mass. (12 Gray) 239. In Berry v. Moench, 1958, 8 Utah 2d 191, 331 P.2d 814, where a psychiatrist passed on the word that plaintiff was a psychopathic personality to the family doctor of a woman contemplating marriage with him, the question was left to the jury.

18. Johns v. Associated Aviation Underwriters, 5 Cir. 1953, 203 F.2d 208 (insurers to insured); Cook v. Gust, 1914, 155 Wis. 594, 145 N.W. 225 (promoter to prospective investor); Hales v. Commercial Bank of Spanish Fork, 1948, 114 Utah 186, 197 P.2d 910 (bank to payee of forged check); Flowers v. Smith, Tex.Civ.App.1934, 80 S.W.2d 392 (employee of electric company to housewife); West v. People's Banking & Trust Co., 1967, 14 Ohio App.2d 69, 236 N.E.2d 679 (bank and commercial borrower).

19. See Evans, Legal Immunity for Defamation, 1940, 24 Minn.L.Rev. 607, regarding the privilege as attached to the group relation.

20. Philadelphia W. & B. R. Co. v. Quigley, 1858, 21 How., U.S., 202, 16 L.Ed. 73; Montgomery v. Knox, 1887, 23 Fla. 595, 3 So. 211; Garey v. Jackson, 1917, 197 Mo.App. 217, 193 S.W. 920.

Accord, as to communications between stockholders: Chambers v. Leiser, 1906, 43 Wash. 285, 86 P. 627; Ashcroft v. Hammond, 1910, 197 N.Y. 488, 99 N.E. 117; Baker v. Clark, 1920, 186 Ky. 816, 218 S.W. 280. Cf. Loewinthan v. Levine, 1946, 270 App.Div. 512, 60 N.Y.S.2d 433 (hospital trustees to trustees).

fices [21] about the affairs of the organization itself, or taxpayers discuss the management of public funds,[22] or an association of property owners the desirability of a prospective purchaser,[23] or creditors the affairs of a common debtor.[24]

Mutual credit organizations for protection against bad credit risks or delinquent debtors usually are given the privilege,[25] so long as it is exercised in good faith and not as a mere cloak for coercion of payment.[26] Mercantile credit rating agencies were for a considerable time a subject of considerable disagreement. They were denied any privilege in England,[27] on the ground that they were mere business ventures trading for profit in the characters of other people. Although there are American courts which have agreed with this,[28] the great majority of them have recognized that such agencies perform a useful business service for the benefit of those who have a legitimate interest in obtaining the information, and who request the agency to obtain it for them. Such agencies are therefore held to have a qualified privilege,[29] where their inquiries are honestly made and the information is furnished to subscribers in good faith.[30] There is general agreement, however, that the privilege is limited by the extent to which the particular subscriber to whom the publication is made has an apparent, present interest in the report; and that in so far as there is general publication to those without such an interest, the risk of false information is one to be borne by the business.[31]

21. Bander v. Metropolitan Life Ins. Co., 1943, 313 Mass. 337, 47 N.E.2d 595; Miley v. Foster, 1956, 229 Miss. 106, 90 So.2d 172; Peoples Life Ins. Co. of Washington v. Talley, 1936, 166 Va. 464, 186 S.E. 42; Louisiana Oil Corp. v. Renno, 1934, 173 Miss. 609, 157 So. 705; Johnson v. Rudolph Wurlitzer Co., 1928, 197 Wis. 432, 222 N.W. 451.

22. Spencer v. Amerton, 1835, 1 Moo. & Rob. 470, 174 Eng.Rep. 162; Smith v. Higgins, 1860, 82 Mass. (16 Gray) 251.

23. Bufalino v. Maxon Bros., 1962, 368 Mich. 140, 117 N.W.2d 150.

24. Smith Bros. & Co. v. W. C. Agee & Co., 1912, 178 Ala. 627, 59 So. 647. Cf. Edwards v. Kevil, 1909, 133 Ky. 392, 118 S.W. 273 (owners of buildings destroyed by fire); Spielberg v. A. Kuhn & Bro., 1911, 39 Utah 276, 116 P. 1027 (defendants in lawsuits brought by plaintiff); cf. Rodgers v. Wise, 1940, 193 S.C. 5, 7 S.E.2d 517 (attorneys engaged in same suit).

25. Putnal v. Inman, 1918, 76 Fla. 553, 80 So. 316; Woodhouse v. Powles, 1906, 43 Wash. 617, 86 P. 1063; McDonald v. Lee, 1914, 246 Pa. 253, 92 A. 135; Ideal Motor Co. v. Warfield, 1925, 211 Ky. 576, 277 S.W. 862; Pavlovsky v. Board of Trade of San Francisco, 1959, 171 Cal.App.2d 110, 340 P.2d 63.

26. Traynor v. Seiloff, 1895, 62 Minn. 420, 64 N.W. 915; Hartnett v. Goddard, 1900, 176 Mass. 326, 57 N.E. 677; Muetze v. Tuteur, 1890, 77 Wis. 236, 46 N.W. 123.

27. MacIntosh v. Dunn, [1908] A.C. 300.

28. Johnson v. Bradstreet Co., 1886, 77 Ga. 172; Pacific Packing Co. v. Bradstreet Co., 1914, 25 Idaho 696, 139 P. 1007.

29. Altoona Clay Products, Inc. v. Dun & Bradstreet, Inc., W.D.Pa.1968, 286 F.Supp. 899 vacated on other grounds 308 F.Supp. 1068; Retail Credit Co. v. Garraway, 1961, 240 Miss. 230, 126 So.2d 271; A. B. C. Needlecraft Co. v. Dun & Bradstreet, 2 Cir. 1957, 245 F.2d 775; Petition of Retailers Commercial Agency, 1961, 342 Mass. 515, 174 N.E.2d 376; Barker v. Retail Credit Co., 1960, 8 Wis.2d 664, 100 N.W.2d 391.

See Smith, Conditional Privilege for Mercantile Agencies, 1914, 14 Col.L.Rev. 187, 296; Notes, 1953, 2 De Paul L.Rev. 69; 1957, 31 Temple L.Q. 50; 1960, 36 N.Dak.L.Rev. 201.

30. The privilege is lost when the agency acts with conscious indifference and reckless disregard of the plaintiff's rights. Dun & Bradstreet v. Robinson, 1961, 233 Ark. 168, 345 S.W.2d 34. Mere negligence, however, is not enough to defeat the privilege. H. R. Crawford Co. v. Dun & Bradstreet, 4 Cir. 1957, 241 F.2d 387; A. B. C. Needlecraft Co. v. Dun & Bradstreet, 2 Cir. 1957, 245 F.2d 775; Dun and Bradstreet, Inc. v. O'Neil, Tex.1970, 456 S.W.2d 896.

31. King v. Patterson, 1887, 49 N.J.L. 417, 9 A. 705; Pollasky v. Minchener, 1890, 81 Mich. 280, 46 N.W. 5; Sunderlin v. Bradstreet, 1871, 46 N.Y. 188. Mitchell v. Bradstreet Co., 1893, 116 Mo. 226, 22 S. W. 358, 724, motion for rehearing overruled 116 Mo. 226, 22 S.W. 724; Hanschke v. Merchants' Credit Bureau, 1931, 256 Mich. 272, 239 N.W. 318.

The agency is not, however, liable for unauthorized republication by its customers to third parties. Peacock v. Retail Credit Co., N.D.Ga.1969, 302 F. Supp. 418.

The privilege has also been extended to the members of groups with a common interest of a non-pecuniary character, such as religious [32] or professional [33] societies, fraternal,[34] social [35] or educational [36] organizations, families,[37] or labor unions,[38] if the matter communicated is pertinent to the interest of the group. In all such cases, however, the privilege is lost if the defamation goes beyond the group interest,[39] or if publication is made to persons who have no reason to receive the information.[40]

4. *Communications to One Who May Act in the Public Interest.* The interest of the general public, as distinguished from that of any individual, has given rise to two qualified privileges, which often have been confused. One is broad as to what may be said, but narrow as to those to whom it may be communicated; the other is more restricted as to content, but broader as to publication. The first, sometimes called the "public interest" privilege, involves communications made to those who may be expected to take official action of some kind for the protection of some interest of the public. It is on this basis that communications from one public officer to another, in an effort to discharge official duty, are held to be at least qualifiedly privileged,[41] even where no absolute privilege [42] is found. But private citizens likewise are privileged to give information to proper [43] authorities for the prevention or detection of crime,[44] or to complain to them

32. Jarvis v. Hatheway, 1808, 3 Johns. (N.Y.) 180; Slocinski v. Radwan, 1929, 83 N.H. 501, 144 A. 787; Creswell v. Pruitt, Tex.Civ.App.1951, 239 S.W.2d 165; Pinn v. Lawson, 1934, 63 U.S.App.D.C. 370, 72 F.2d 742; Stewart v. Ging, 1958, 64 N.M. 270, 327 P.2d 333.

In Warren v. Pulitzer Pub. Co., 1934, 336 Mo. 184, 78 S.W.2d 404, a hearing before a church tribunal was held to be absolutely privileged. In Van Vliet v. Vander Naald, 1939, 290 Mich. 365, 287 N.W. 564, and Browning v. Gomez, Tex.Civ.App.1960, 332 S. W.2d 588, it was held that there was only a qualified privilege.

33. Barrows v. Bell, 1856, 73 Mass. (7 Gray) 301; McKnight v. Hasbrouck, 1890, 17 R.I. 70, 20 A. 95; Mick v. American Dental Ass'n, 1958, 49 N.J.Super. 262, 139 A.2d 570; Judge v. Rockford Memorial Hospital, 1958, 17 Ill.App.2d 365, 150 N.E.2d 202; Willenbucher v. McCormick, D.Colo.1964, 229 F. Supp. 659 (association of retired army officers).

34. Reininger v. Prickett, 1943, 192 Okl. 486, 137 P.2d 595; Peterson v. Cleaver, 1920, 105 Neb. 438, 181 N.W. 187; Cadle v. McIntosh, 1912, 51 Ind.App. 365, 99 N.E. 779; Bayliss v. Grand Lodge of State of Louisiana, 1912, 131 La. 579, 59 So. 996.

35. Hayden v. Hasbrouck, 1912, 34 R.I. 556, 84 A. 1087; cf. Kersting v. White, 1904, 107 Mo.App. 265, 80 S.W. 730.

36. Gattis v. Kilgo, 1905, 140 N.C. 106, 52 S.E. 249; cf. Clark v. McBaine, 1923, 299 Mo. 77, 252 S.W. 428.

37. Zanley v. Hyde, 1919, 208 Mich. 96, 175 N.W. 261; Brown v. Radebaugh, 1901, 84 Minn. 347, 87 N.W. 937.

38. Bereman v. Power Pub. Co., 1933, 93 Colo. 581, 27 P.2d 749; Ward v. Painters' Local Union No. 300, 1953, 41 Wash.2d 859, 252 P.2d 253; Sheehan v. Tobin, 1950, 326 Mass. 185, 93 N.E.2d 524; Wise v. Brotherhood of Locomotive Firemen and Enginemen, 8 Cir. 1918, 252 F. 961; De Mott v. Amalgamated Meat Cutters & Butchers, 1958, 157 Cal.App. 2d 13, 320 P.2d 50; Manbeck v. Ostrowski, 1967, 128 U.S.App.D.C. 1, 384 F.2d 970, cert. denied 390 U.S. 966.

39. Cf. Smith v. Smith, 1940, 194 S.C. 247, 9 S.E.2d 584; Hocks v. Sprangers, 1901, 113 Wis. 123, 87 N. W. 1101, 89 N.W. 113; Carpenter v. Willey, 1893, 65 Vt. 68, 26 A. 488; York v. Johnson, 1875, 116 Mass. 482; Lovejoy v. Whitcomb, 1899, 174 Mass. 586, 55 N.E. 322.

40. See infra, p. 794.

41. Peterson v. Steenerson, 1910, 113 Minn. 87, 129 N.W. 147; Hemmens v. Nelson, 1893, 138 N.Y. 517, 34 N.E. 342; Greenwood v. Cobbey, 1889, 26 Neb. 449, 42 N.W. 413; Barry v. McCollom, 1908, 81 Conn. 293, 70 A. 1035; Tanner v. Stevenson, 1910, 138 Ky. 578, 128 S.W. 878.

42. See supra, p. 782.

43. As to the effect of a reasonable belief that the authority is the proper one, see infra, p. 793.

44. Foltz v. Moore McCormack Lines, 2 Cir. 1951, 189 F.2d 537, cert. denied 342 U.S. 871; Robinson v. Van Auken, 1906, 190 Mass. 161, 76 N.E. 601; Joseph v. Baars, 1910, 142 Wis. 390, 125 N.W. 913; Taylor v. Chambers, 1907, 2 Ga.App. 178, 58 S.E. 369; Hutchinson v. New England Tel. & Tel. Co., 1966, 350 Mass. 188, 214 N.E.2d 57 (bomb threat). See Notes, 1951, 51 Col.L.Rev. 244; 1952, 30 Tex.L. Rev. 875. In Otten v. Schutt, 1962, 15 Wis.2d 497, 113 N.W.2d 152, a communication to a police officer

about the conduct of public officials and seek their removal from office.[45] Thus, for example, complaints made by members of the public to school boards about the character, competence or conduct of their teachers are subject to a qualified privilege.[46] The privilege includes false statements of fact concerning the plaintiff made in good faith; but, although it is not impossible that communications to other non-official interested persons will be protected,[47] publication to the world at large in a newspaper is not.[48]

5. *Fair Comment on Matters of Public Concern.* A large area of qualified privilege developed at common law to cover what was called "fair comment" on matters of public concern. Since the Supreme Court of the United States has now made this privilege a constitutional one, under the First Amendment, and since the privilege applies also to invasions of the right of privacy, it is more conveniently dealt with in a subsequent chapter [49] covering both defamation and privacy.

6. *Reports of Public Proceedings.* Another area of qualified privilege, formerly recognized at common law, which has now apparently been taken over under the wing of the Constitution, is that of reporting to the public on official or other public proceedings. This too is more conveniently dealt with in connection with other such areas, and is therefore postponed to the later chapter.[50]

Abuse of Qualified Privilege

The condition attached to all such qualified privileges is that they must be exercised in a reasonable manner and for a proper purpose. The immunity is forfeited if the defendant steps outside of the scope of the privilege, or abuses the occasion.[51] Thus qualified privilege does not extend, in any of the above cases, to the publication of irrelevant defamatory matter with no bearing upon the public or private interest which is entitled to protection;[52] nor does it include publication to any person other than those whose hearing of it is reasonably believed to be necessary or useful for the furtherance of that interest.[53] An attorney is not free, for example, to publish in a newspaper a statement that the victim of his client's alleged rape consented to it,[54] nor is the owner of property privileged to accuse the plaintiff of theft of it in the presence of a

accusing the plaintiff of crime was held not to be privileged where it was not made for the bona fide purpose of investigation or prosecution.

45. Nuyen v. Slater, 1964, 372 Mich. 654, 127 N.W.2d 369; Sowder v. Nolan, D.C.Mun.App.1956, 125 A.2d 52; Ponder v. Cobb, 1962, 257 N.C. 281, 126 S.E.2d 67; Dempsky v. Double, 1956, 386 Pa. 542, 126 A.2d 915; Hancock v. Mitchell, 1919, 83 W.Va. 156, 98 S.E. 65.

Cf. Lee v. W. E. Fuetterer Battery & Supplies Co., 1929, 323 Mo. 1204, 23 S.W.2d 45 (complaint to bar association about attorney); Licciardi v. Molnar, 1945, 23 N.J.Misc. 361, 44 A.2d 653 (memorial to officers about conduct of other officers).

46. Bodwell v. Osgood, 1825, 20 Mass., 3 Pick., 379; Wieman v. Mabee, 1881, 45 Mich. 484, 8 N.W. 71; Wakefield v. Smithwick, 1857, 49 N.C. 327; Johnson v. Langley, 1933, 247 Ky. 7, 57 S.W.2d 21; Segall v. Piazza, 1965, 46 Misc.2d 700, 260 N.Y.S.2d 543.

47. Thus in Dempsky v. Double, 1956, 386 Pa. 542, 126 A.2d 915, a copy sent to the League of Women Voters was held to be privileged, on the ground that it was a reputable organization which might cooperate in requesting an investigation.

48. Bingham v. Gaynor, 1911, 203 N.Y. 27, 96 N.E. 84.

49. See infra, ch. 118.

50. See infra, ch. 118.

51. See, generally, Hallen, Excessive Publication in Defamation, 1932, 16 Minn.L.Rev. 160; Hallen, Character of Belief Necessary for the Conditional Privilege in Defamation, 1931, 25 Ill.L.Rev. 865.

52. Huntley v. Ward, 1859, 6 C.B.,N.S., 514, 141 Eng. Rep. 557; Hines v. Shumaker, 1910, 97 Miss. 669, 52 So. 705; Sullivan v. Strahorn-Hutton-Evans Comm. Co., 1899, 152 Mo. 268, 53 S.W. 912; Lathrop v. Sundberg, 1909, 55 Wash. 144, 104 P. 176.

53. Vail v. Pennsylvania R. Co., 1927, 103 N.J.L. 213, 136 A. 425; Over v. Schiffling, 1885, 102 Ind. 191, 26 N.E. 91; Pollasky v. Minchener, 1890, 81 Mich. 280, 46 N.W. 5; Sheftall v. Central of Georgia R. Co., 1905, 123 Ga. 589, 51 S.E. 646; Ramsdell v. Pennsylvania R. Co., 1910, 79 N.J.L. 379, 75 A. 444.

54. Kennedy v. Cannon, 1962, 229 Md. 92, 182 A.2d 54.

third person who has no legitimate interest in the matter.[55] There is authority in England [56] to the effect that a publication made in the mistaken belief that the recipient is a proper person to hear it is not privileged; but the few American cases [57] which have considered the question tend to adopt what seems clearly to be the more desirable rule, that while a misguided notion as to the defendant's moral obligation or justification to make the statement will not exonerate him,[58] he is privileged to publish it to any person who reasonably appears to have a duty, interest or authority in connection with the matter.

Any reasonable and appropriate method of publication may be adopted which fits the purpose of protecting the particular interest. The dictation of a business letter to a stenographer,[59] use of the telegraph where time is important,[60] or publication in a newspaper in order to reach the public or a large number of interested persons [61] may be privileged on a proper occasion. The instruments of communication, such as the newspaper, are themselves privileged to aid in the publication, wherever the privilege in fact exists; [62] and in the case of a public utility, such as the telegraph,[63] which is not in a position to refuse a message or to investigate, the better view seems to be that it is privileged to publish matter which is obviously defamatory, unless it has reason to believe that the sender is not privileged.

In all such cases, the fact that the communication is incidentally read or overheard by a person to whom there is no privilege to publish it will not result in liability, if the method adopted is a reasonable and appro-

55. Sias v. General Motors Corp., 1964, 372 Mich. 542, 127 N.W.2d 357; Southwest Drug Stores of Miss., Inc. v. Garner, Miss.1967, 195 So.2d 837; Williams v. Kroger Grocery & Baking Co., 1940, 337 Pa. 17, 10 A.2d 8; Galvin v. New York, N. H. & H. R. Co., 1960, 341 Mass. 293, 168 N.E.2d 262; Washington Annapolis Hotel Co. v. Riddle, 1948, 83 U.S. App.D.C. 288, 171 F.2d 732.

56. Hebditch v. MacIlwaine, [1894] 2 Q.B. 54.

57. See McKee v. Hughes, 1916, 133 Tenn. 455, 181 S.W. 930; Joseph v. Baars, 1910, 142 Wis. 390, 125 N.W. 913; Popke v. Hoffman, 1926, 21 Ohio App. 454, 153 N.E. 248; Berot v. Porte, 1919, 144 La. 805, 81 So. 323; Finkelstein v. Geismar, 1918, 92 N.J.L. 251, 106 A. 209; Harper, Privileged Defamation, 1936, 22 Va.L.Rev. 642, 651–654; Restatement of Torts, §§ 1037–1041.

58. See Whiteley v. Adams, 1863, 15 C.B.,N.S., 392, 412, 143 Eng.Rep. 838; Stuart v. Bell, [1891] 2 Q.B. 341.

59. Ostrowe v. Lee, 1931, 256 N.Y. 36, 175 N.E. 505; Globe Furniture Co. v. Wright, 1920, 49 App.D.C. 315, 265 F. 873; Montgomery Ward & Co. v. Nance, 1935, 165 Va. 363, 182 S.E. 264; Domchick v. Greenbelt Consumer Services, 1952, 200 Md. 36, 87 A.2d 831; Mick v. American Dental Assn., 1958, 49 N.J.Super. 262, 139 A.2d 570. Apparently contra is Rickbeil v. Grafton Deaconess Hospital, 1946, 74 N. D. 525, 23 N.W.2d 247. See Smith, Liability of a Telegraph Company for Transmitting a Defamatory Message, 1920, 20 Col.L.Rev. 30, 35–46; Notes, 1921, 6 Corn.L.Q. 430, 1930, 16 Corn.L.Q. 103; 1930, 28 Mich.L.Rev. 348.

Some courts have accomplished the same result by holding that there is no publication, which seems erroneous. See supra, p. 767.

60. Edmondson v. Birch & Co., [1907] 1 K.B. 371; Ashcroft v. Hammond, 1910, 197 N.Y. 488, 90 N.E. 1117; Western Union Tel. Co. v. Brown, 8 Cir. 1923, 294 F. 167; Nye v. Western Union Tel. Co., C.C. Minn.1900, 104 F. 628.

61. Coleman v. MacLennan, 1908, 78 Kan. 711, 98 P. 281; Bereman v. Power Pub. Co., 1933, 93 Colo. 581, 27 P.2d 749; Dickins v. International Brotherhood of T. C. W. & H., 1948, 84 U.S.App.D.C. 51, 171 F.2d 21; Arnold v. Ingram, 1913, 151 Wis. 438, 138 N.W. 111.

62. Preston v. Hobbs, 1914, 161 App.Div. 363, 146 N. Y.S. 419; Israel v. Portland News Pub. Co., 1936, 152 Or. 225, 53 P.2d 529.

63. Flynn v. Western Union Tel. Co., 1929, 199 Wis. 124, 225 N.W. 742; Klein v. Western Union Tel. Co., 1939, 257 App.Div. 336, 13 N.Y.S.2d 441; O'Brien v. Western Union Tel. Co., 1 Cir. 1940, 113 F.2d 539; see Smith, Liability of a Telegraph Company for Transmitting a Defamatory Message, 1920, 20 Col.L.Rev. 369; Notes, 1930, 5 Wis.L.Rev. 297; 1930, 78 U.Pa.L.Rev. 252; 1940, 38 Mich.L.Rev. 734; Restatement of Torts, § 612. Other cases indicate such a privilege only if the message is ambiguous, or the operator reasonably believes the sender to be privileged. Paton v. Great Northwestern Tel. Co. of Canada, 1919, 141 Minn. 430, 170 N.W. 511; Nye v. Western Union Tel. Co., C.C.Minn.1900, 104 F. 628.

priate one under the circumstances.[64] Thus the privilege of publication in a newspaper to reach interested parties will not necessarily be defeated by the fact that there are readers who are not concerned.[65] But the fact that there will be such incidental publication to improper persons is itself important in determining whether the method is a reasonable one; and the defendant may be liable if he unnecessarily sends a defamatory message on a postcard [66] or uses the telegraph [67] or a newspaper,[68] or speaks so that he will be overheard,[69] instead of resorting to some adequate but less public alternative.

Furthermore, the qualified privilege will be lost if the defendant publishes the defama-

tion in the wrong state of mind. The word "malice," which has plagued the law of defamation from the beginning, has been much used in this connection, and it frequently is said that the privilege is forfeited if the publication is "malicious." It is clear that this means something more than the fictitious "legal malice" which is "implied" as a disguise for strict liability in any case of unprivileged defamation.[70] On the other hand, it may mean something less than spite, ill will, or a desire to do harm for its own sake; [71] and, while there is authority to the contrary,[72] it is the better and perhaps more generally accepted view that the mere existence of such ill will does not necessarily defeat the privilege. "Malice" in this sense may subject the defendant to punitive damages [73] if he is liable at all; but if the privilege is otherwise established by the occasion and a proper purpose, the addition of the fact that the defendant feels indignation and resentment toward the plaintiff and enjoys defaming him will not always forfeit it.[74] Per-

---

64. Montgomery Ward & Co. v. Watson, 4 Cir. 1932, 55 F.2d 184; Shoemaker v. Friedberg, 1947, 80 Cal. App.2d 911, 183 P.2d 318; McKenzie v. Wm. J. Burns International Detective Agency, 1921, 149 Minn. 311, 183 N.W. 516; New York & Porto Rico S. Co. v. Garcia, 1 Cir. 1926, 16 F.2d 734; Hoover v. Jordan, 1915, 27 Colo.App. 515, 150 P. 333.

Allowance must be made for the exigencies of the occasion. Kroger Grocery & Baking Co. v. Yount, 8 Cir. 1933, 66 F.2d 200; Gust v. Montgomery Ward & Co., 1935, 229 Mo.App. 371, 80 S.W.2d 286.

65. Coleman v. MacLennan, 1908, 78 Kan. 711, 98 P. 281; Dickins v. International Brotherhood of T. C. W. & H., 1948, 84 U.S.App.D.C. 51, 171 F.2d 21; Mertens v. Bee Pub. Co., 1904, 5 Neb.Unof. 592, 99 N.W. 847; Arnold v. Ingram, 1913, 151 Wis. 438, 138 N.W. 111; cf. Burton v. Dickson, 1919, 104 Kan. 594, 180 P. 216, rehearing denied, 1919, 180 P. 775.

66. Logan v. Hodges, 1907, 146 N.C. 38, 59 S.E. 349.

67. Williamson v. Freer, 1874, L.R. 9 C.P. 393, 43 L. J.C.P. 161; Monson v. Lathrop, 1897, 96 Wis. 386, 71 N.W. 596; Williams v. Equitable Credit Co., 1925, 33 Ga.App. 441, 126 S.E. 855.

68. Moyle v. Franz, 1944, 267 App.Div. 423, 46 N.Y. S.2d 667, affirmed, 1944, 293 N.Y. 842, 59 N.E.2d 437; Flynn v. Boglarsky, 1911, 164 Mich. 513, 129 N.W. 674; Lathrop v. Sundberg, 1909, 55 Wash. 144, 104 P. 176. Cf. Sheftall v. Central of Georgia R. Co., 1905, 123 Ga. 589, 51 S.E. 646; Ramsdell v. Pennsylvania R. Co., 1910, 79 N.J.L. 379, 75 A. 444.

69. Montgomery Ward & Co. v. Nance, 1935, 165 Va. 363, 182 S.E. 264; Perry Bros. Variety Stores v. Layton, 1930, 119 Tex. 130, 25 S.W.2d 310, conformed to, 1930, 32 S.W.2d 863; Williams v. Kroger Grocery & Baking Co., 1940, 337 Pa. 17, 10 A.2d 8; Fields v. Bynum, 1911, 156 N.C. 413, 72 S.E. 449; Kruse v. Rabe, 1911, 80 N.J.L. 378, 79 A. 316.

70. See supra, p. 772. As to the distinction, see Cherry v. Des Moines Leader, 1901, 114 Iowa 298, 86 N.W. 323; Kirkpatrick v. Eagle Lodge No. Thirty-Two, 1881, 26 Kan. 384; Gattis v. Kilgo, 1905, 140 N.C. 106, 52 S.E. 249; Iverson v. Frandsen, 10 Cir. 1956, 237 F.2d 898; Jolly v. Valley Pub. Co., 1964, 63 Wash.2d 537, 388 P.2d 139.

71. See Hooper v. Truscott, 1836, 3 Bing.N.C. 457, 132 Eng.Rep. 486; Fahr v. Hayes, 1888, 50 N.J.L. 275, 13 A. 261; Iden v. Evans Model Laundry, 1931, 121 Neb. 184, 236 N.W. 444; Stevens v. Morse, 1925, 185 Wis. 500, 201 N.W. 815; Kennedy v. Mid-Continent Telecasting Co., Inc., 1964, 193 Kan. 544, 394 P.2d 400.

72. Phillips v. Bradshaw, 1910, 167 Ala. 199, 52 So. 662; Gerlach v. Gruett, 1921, 175 Wis. 354, 185 N.W. 195; Tanner v. Stevenson, 1910, 138 Ky. 578, 128 S.W. 878; Hemmens v. Nelson, 1893, 138 N.Y. 517, 34 N.E. 342.

73. Times Pub. Co. v. Carlisle, 8 Cir. 1899, 94 F. 762; Hoffman v. Trenton Times, 1939, 17 N.J.Misc. 339, 8 A.2d 837; Ventresca v. Kissner, 1927, 105 Conn. 533, 136 A. 90; Plecker v. Knottnerus, 1926, 201 Iowa 550, 207 N.W. 574. See Note, 1941, 10 Brook.L.Rev. 292.

74. Fahr v. Hayes, 1888, 50 N.J.L. 275, 13 A. 261; Craig v. Wright, 1938, 182 Okl. 68, 76 P.2d 248; Doane v. Grew, 1915, 220 Mass. 171, 107 N.E. 620;

haps the statement which best fits the decided cases is that the court will look to the primary motive or purpose by which the defendant apparently is inspired. Discarding "malice" as a meaningless and quite unsatisfactory term, it appears that the privilege is lost if the publication is not made primarily for the purpose of furthering the interest which is entitled to protection.[75] If the defendant acts chiefly from motives of ill will,[76] he will certainly be liable; and the vehemence of his language may be evidence against him in this respect.[77] But he will likewise be liable if he publishes his statement to accomplish a distinct objective, which may be legitimate enough in itself but is not within the privilege—as for example, to retain a servant in his employment,[78] to obtain assistance in collecting a debt,[79] or to increase the circulation of a newspaper.[80]

New York & Porto Rico S. S. Co. v. Garcia, 1 Cir. 1926, 16 F.2d 734; Restatement of Torts, § 603. See Purrington, Malice as an Essential Element of Responsibility for Defamation Uttered on a Privileged Occasion, 1898, 57 Albany L.J. 134, 149; Evans, Legal Immunity for Defamation, 1940, 24 Minn.L.Rev. 607, 610.

75. Restatement of Torts, § 603.

76. Brewer v. Second Baptist Church of Los Angeles, 1948, 32 Cal.2d 791, 197 P.2d 713; Mullen v. Lewiston Evening Journal, 1952, 147 Me. 286, 86 A.2d 164; Rosenberg v. Mason, 1931, 157 Va. 215, 160 S. E. 190; Joseph v. Baars, 1910, 142 Wis. 390, 125 N.W. 913.

77. Newark Trust Co. v. Bruwer, 1958, 51 Del. (1 Storey) 188, 141 A.2d 615.

Malice may be inferred from republication after suit. O'Donnell v. Philadelphia Record Co., 1947, 356 Pa. 307, 51 A.2d 775. Or from a refusal to retract, after notice of falsity. Morgan v. Dun & Bradstreet, Inc., 5 Cir. 1970, 421 F.2d 1241.

78. Jackson v. Hopperton, 1864, 16 C.B.,N.S., 829, 143 Eng.Rep. 1352.

79. Hollenbeck v. Ristine, 1901, 114 Iowa 358, 86 N. W. 377; Over v. Schiffling, 1885, 102 Ind. 191, 26 N.E. 91. Cf. Stevens v. Sampson, 1879, 5 Ex.Div. 53, where an attorney in a case sent a report of it to newspapers, with the objective of doing harm to the opposition.

80. Cf. McNally v. Burleigh, 1897, 91 Me. 22, 39 A. 285; Maclean v. Scripps, 1883, 52 Mich. 214, 17 N. W. 815, 18 N.W. 209; Ramsey v. Cheek, 1891, 109

Finally, since there is no social advantage in the publication of a deliberate lie, the privilege is lost if the defendant does not believe what he says.[81] Many courts have gone further, and have said that it is lost if the defamer does not have reasonable grounds, or "probable cause" to believe it to be true,[82] while others have insisted that good faith, no matter how unreasonable the basis, is all that is required.[83] Neither position seems tenable in all cases. Certainly no reasons of policy can be found for conferring immunity upon the foolish and reckless defamer who blasts an innocent reputation without making any attempt to verify his statements; but on the other hand there are occasions on which it

N.C. 270, 13 S.E. 775; Lowry v. Vedder, 1889, 40 Minn. 475, 42 N.W. 542; Doane v. Grew, 1915, 220 Mass. 171, 107 N.E. 620.

81. Russell v. Geis, 1967, 251 Cal.App.2d 560, 50 Cal. Rptr. 569; Caldwell v. Personal Finance Co. of St. Petersburg, Fla.1950, 46 So.2d 726; Froslee v. Lund's State Bank, 1915, 131 Minn. 435, 155 N.W. 619; Lawless v. Muller, 1923, 99 N.J.L. 9, 123 A. 104; Phillips v. Bradshaw, 1910, 167 Ala. 199, 52 So. 662. Cf. Vigil v. Rice, 1964, 74 N.M. 693, 397 P.2d 719 (failure to correct medical report discovered to be false).

82. Ranous v. Hughes, 1966, 30 Wis.2d 452, 141 N.W. 2d 251; Altoona Clay Products, Inc. v. Dun & Bradstreet, Inc., 3 Cir. 1966, 367 F.2d 625; Stationers Corp. v. Dun & Bradstreet, Inc., 1965, 62 Cal.2d 412, 42 Cal.Rptr. 449, 398 P.2d 785; Mulderig v. Wilkes-Barre Times Co., 1906, 215 Pa. 470, 64 A. 636.

83. Clark v. Molyneux, 1877, 3 Q.B.Div. 237; Joseph v. Baars, 1910, 142 Wis. 390, 125 N.W. 913; International & G. N. R. Co. v. Edmundson, Tex. Comm.App.1920, 222 S.W. 181; H. E. Crawford Co. v. Dun & Bradstreet, 4 Cir. 1957, 241 F.2d 387; A. B. C. Needlecraft Co. v. Dun & Bradstreet, 2 Cir. 1957, 245 F.2d 775.

In several cases the influence of the Supreme Court decisions on constitutional privilege (infra, ch. 21) has had its effect, and it has been held that there is "malice" only if the publication is known to be false, or is in reckless disregard of the truth. Phifer v. Foe, Wyo.1968, 443 P.2d 870; Roemer v. Retail Credit Co., 1970, 3 Cal.App.3d 368, 83 Cal. Rptr. 540; Petition of Retailers Commercial Agency, Inc., 1961, 342 Mass. 515, 174 N.E.2d 376; Dun & Bradstreet, Inc. v. O'Neil, Tex.1970, 456 S.W.2d 896. Cf. Hogan v. New York Times Co., 2 Cir. 1963, 313 F.2d 354.

may be entirely proper to give information of a rumor or a mere suspicion, as such, without any belief or any reason to believe that it represents the truth.[84] Probably the best statement of the rule is that the defendant is required to act as a reasonable man under the circumstances, with due regard to the strength of his belief, the grounds that he has to support it, and the importance of conveying the information.[85]

Burden of Proof—Court and Jury

The burden is upon the defendant in the first instance to establish the existence of a privileged occasion for the publication, by proof of a recognized public or private interest which would justify the utterance of the words.[86] Whether the occasion was a privileged one,[87] is a question to be determined by the court as an issue of law, unless of course the facts are in dispute, in which case the jury will be instructed as to the proper rules to apply.[88] Once the existence of the privilege is established, the burden is upon the plaintiff to prove that it has been abused by excessive publication, by use of the occasion for an improper purpose, or by lack of belief or grounds for belief in the truth of what is said.[89] Unless only one conclusion can be drawn from the evidence, the determination of the question whether the privilege has been abused is for the jury.[90] Undoubtedly the very vagueness of the rules as to the public or private interest which will be protected, the "fairness" of comment or criticism, and the "malice" in cases where the privilege is abused, has been of considerable aid to the courts in achieving a degree of flexibility which permits the particular issue to be determined by the court or passed over to the jury, as the particular case seems to demand.[91]

116. OTHER DEFENSES

Truth

The defense that the defamatory statement is true has been given the technical name of justification. Under the common law it was not open to the defendant in prosecutions for criminal libel. That crime, which was originated to suppress sedition, and later extended to prevent breaches of the peace, took no account of any freedom to publish the truth with immunity.[92] since neither sedition nor the provocation to a duel was at

84. See Doane v. Grew, 1915, 220 Mass. 171, 107 N.E. 620; Pecue v. West, 1922, 233 N.Y. 316, 135 N.E. 515; British Ry. Traffic Co. v. C. R. C. Co., [1922] 2 K.B. 260; Billings v. Fairbanks, 1885, 139 Mass. 66, 29 N.E. 544.

85. See Hallen, Character of Belief Necessary for the Conditional Privilege in Defamation, 1931, 25 Ill.L.Rev. 865; Restatement of Torts, §§ 600–602.

86. Hebditch v. MacIlwaine, [1894] 2 Q.B. 54, 63 L.J. Q.B. 587; Howland v. George F. Blake Mfg. Co., 1892, 156 Mass. 543, 31 N.E. 656; Salinger v. Cowles, 1922, 195 Iowa 873, 191 N.W. 167; Savage v. Stover, 1914, 86 N.J.L. 478, 92 A. 284; Peterson v. Rasmussen, 1920, 47 Cal.App. 694, 191 P. 30.

87. Hebditch v. MacIlwaine, [1894] 2 Q.B. 54, 63 L.J. Q.B. 587; Israel v. Portland News Pub. Co., 1936, 152 Or. 225, 53 P.2d 529; Kenney v. Gurley, 1923, 208 Ala. 623, 95 So. 34; Byam v. Collins, 1888, 111 N.Y. 143, 19 N.E. 75; Nichols v. Eaton, 1900, 110 Iowa 509, 81 N.W. 792.

88. Brinsfield v. Howeth, 1908, 107 Md. 278, 68 A. 566; Switzer v. American Ry. Exp. Co., 1922, 119 S.C. 237, 112 S.E. 110; Warner v. Press Pub. Co., 1892, 132 N.Y. 181, 30 N.E. 393; Carpenter v. Ashley, 1906, 148 Cal. 422, 83 P. 444.

89. Cook v. Pulitzer Pub. Co., 1912, 241 Mo. 326, 145 S.W. 480; Hayden v. Hasbrouck, 1912, 34 R.I. 556, 84 A. 1087; Williams Print. Co. v. Saunders, 1912, 113 Va. 156, 73 S.E. 472; Gattis v. Kilgo, 1905, 128 N.C. 402, 38 S.E. 931; Wetherby v. Retail Credit Co., 1964, 235 Md. 237, 201 A.2d 344.

90. Thomas v. Bradbury, Agnew & Co., [1906] 2 K.B. 627; Hamilton v. Eno, 1880, 81 N.Y. 116; Conrad v. Allis-Chalmers Mfg. Co., 1934, 228 Mo.App. 817, 73 S.W.2d 438; Stevenson v. Northington, 1933, 204 N.C. 690, 169 S.E. 622; Williams v. Standard-Examiner Pub. Co., 1933, 83 Utah 31, 27 P.2d 1.

91. See Green, Relational Interests, 1936, 30 Ill.L. Rev. 314, 1936, 31 Ill.L.Rev. 35.

92. De Libellis Famosis, 1605, 5 Co.Rep. 125, 77 Eng.Rep. 250; Franklin's Case, 1731, 9 Hargrave St. Trials 255, 269. See Ray, Truth: A Defense to Libel, 1931, 16 Minn.L.Rev. 43; Harnett and Thornton, The Truth Hurts: A Critique of a Defense to Defamation, 1949, 35 Va.L.Rev. 425.

all lessened because the defamation was true.[93] Hence the criminal courts declared that "the greater the truth the greater the libel." [94] This rule, which later was changed by statute in England,[95] was taken over by the early American decisions [96] along with the rest of the common law of defamation; but it was so obviously incompatible with all public policy in favor of free dissemination of the truth that it has been altered by statute in nearly every state,[97] usually to make truth a complete defense provided that it is published with good motives and for justifiable ends.

The criminal law rule seems never to have been applied in civil actions.[98] Whether the reason was that the delinquent plaintiff was precluded from any standing in court by reason of his own bad character,[99] or that the defendant was considered to have rendered a public service in exposing him,[1] or merely that public policy demands that the truth shall not be fettered by fear of damage

suits,[2] truth was a defense to any civil action for either libel or slander, and it remains so in the great majority of jurisdictions. It is immaterial that the defendant published the facts for no good reason or for the worst possible motives,[3] or even that he did not believe at the time that they were true.[4] The rule has been attacked [5] on the ground that it affords immunity for morally indefensible malevolence and needlessly kicking a man when he is down. There is some indication of a tendency to depart from it. Some ten states have statutory provisions,[6] requiring that the publication must have been made for good motives or for justifiable ends, and New Hampshire [7] has reached the same conclusion without a statute. In 1969 an Illinois decision [8] held that a statute of this type

---

93. Bl.Com. 151; Trial of Jutchin, 1704, 5 Hargrave St. Trials 527, 532.

94. This maxim usually is attributed to Lord Mansfield. Thus:
"Dost know that old Mansfield
Who writes like the Bible,
Says the more 'tis a truth, sir,
The more 'tis a libel?"
         —Burns, "The Reproof."

95. By Lord Campbell's Act, 1843, 6 & 7 Vict., ch. 96, § 6.

96. People v. Croswell, 1804, 3 Johns., N.Y., 337; Commonwealth v. Morris, 1811, 1 Va.Cas. 176; see Commonwealth v. Snelling, 1834, 15 Pick., Mass., 337; State v. Lehre, 1811, 4 S.C.Law 446, 2 Brev. 446.

97. The statutes are collected in Angoff, Handbook of Libel, 1946, passim.

98. Johns v. Gittings, 1590, Cro.Eliz. 230, 78 Eng. Rep. 495; Hilsdon v. Saunders, 1624, Cro.Jac. 677, 79 Eng.Rep. 586; Holdsworth, Defamation in the Sixteenth and Seventeenth Centuries, 1925, 41 L.Q. Rev. 13, 28.

99. Starkie, Slander and Libel, Folkard's Am.Ed. 1858, 692.

1. 3 Bl.Com. 125.

2. See Ray, Truth: A Defense to Libel, 1931, 16 Minn.L.Rev. 43, 56–58; Harnett and Thornton, The Truth Hurts: A Critique of a Defense to Defamation, 1949, 35 Va.L.Rev. 425, 434–437.

3. Cochrane v. Wittbold, 1960, 359 Mich. 402, 102 N. W.2d 459; McCuddin v. Dickinson, 1941, 230 Iowa 1141, 300 N.W. 308; Herald Pub. Co. v. Feltner, 1914, 158 Ky. 35, 164 S.W. 370; Craig v. Wright, 1938, 182 Okl. 68, 76 P.2d 248; Lancaster v. Hamburger, 1904, 70 Ohio St. 156, 71 N.E. 289; Restatement of Torts, § 582, Comment a.

4. Foss v. Hildreth, 1865, 10 Allen, Mass., 76; Restatement of Torts, § 582, Comment g.

5. Ray, Truth: A Defense to Libel, 1931, 16 Minn.L. Rev. 43; Harnett and Thornton, The Truth Hurts: A Critique of a Defense to Defamation, 1949, 35 Va.L.Rev. 425.

6. See for example Perry v. Hearst Corp., 1 Cir. 1964, 334 F.2d 800 (freedom from actual malice); Stanley v. Prince, 1919, 118 Me. 360, 108 A. 328 (good motive); Briggs v. Brown, 1908, 55 Fla. 417, 46 So. 325 (same); Ogren v. Rockford Star Printing Co., 1919, 288 Ill. 405, 123 N.E. 587 (good motive and justifiable ends); Burkhart v. North American Co., 1906, 214 Pa. 39, 63 A. 410 (freedom from malice or negligence, and a proper purpose). See Angoff, Handbook of Libel, 1946, Passim; Note, 1961, 56 Northwestern U.L.Rev. 547.

7. Hutchins v. Page, 1909, 75 N.H. 215, 72 A. 689 (good faith, proper occasion, and justifiable purpose).

8. Farnsworth v. Tribune Co., 1969, 43 Ill.2d 286, 253 N.E.2d 408. See Franklin, The Origins and Constitutionality of Limitations on Truth as a Defense in Tort Law, 1964, 16 Stan.L.Rev. 789.

was unconstitutional, as a violation of the freedom of the press provision of the First Amendment. The recognition by nearly all courts of the right of privacy [9] has afforded a remedy in many cases apart from that of defamation, and may perhaps explain failure to modify the rule.

Out of a tender regard for reputations, the law presumes in the first instance that all defamation is false, and the defendant has the burden of pleading and proving its truth.[10] His justification must be as broad, and as narrow, as the defamatory imputation itself. He may not avoid liability by proving that the imputation was true in part,[11] or, if the charge is one of persistent misconduct, by showing that it was true in a single instance.[12] If the defendant repeats the defamation as reported by another, it will not be enough to prove the fact of the report, without proving the truth of the imputation reported.[13] Specific charges cannot be justified by showing the plaintiff's general bad character;[14] and if the accusation is one of particular misconduct, such as stealing a watch from A, it is not enough to show a different offense, even though it be a more serious one, such as stealing a clock from A,[15] or six watches from B.[16] The courts never have looked with any great favor upon the defense of truth, and formerly these rules were carried to ridiculous extremes,[17] but it is now generally agreed that it is not necessary to prove the literal truth of the accusation in every detail, and that it is sufficient to show that the imputation is substantially true,[18] or, as it is often put, to justify the "gist," the "sting," or the "substantial truth" of the defamation.[19] Thus an accusation that the mayor of a town has wasted

9. See infra, § 112.

10. Atwater v. Morning News Co., 1896, 67 Conn. 504, 34 A. 865; Langton v. Hagerty, 1874, 35 Wis. 150; Bingham v. Gaynor, 1911, 203 N.Y. 27, 96 N.E. 84.

11. Weaver v. Lloyd, 1824, 2 B. & C. 678, 107 Eng. Rep. 535; Shepard v. Merrill, 1816, 13 Johns., N.Y., 475; Register Newspaper Co. v. Stone, 1907, 31 Ky.L.Rep. 458, 102 S.W. 800; White v. White, 1921, 129 Va. 621, 106 S.E. 350. Cf. Stewart v. Enterprise Co., Tex.Civ.App.1965, 393 S.W.2d 372, ref. n. r. e., appeal after remand 439 S.W.2d 674, ref. n. r. e.

If the publication imputes to the plaintiff willingness to publish the defamatory truth, the proof must extend to that. Karjavainean v. MacFadden Publications, 1940, 305 Mass. 573, 26 N.E.2d 538. An assertion of personal observation is not supported by proof that others saw it. Kilian v. Doubleday & Co., 1951, 367 Pa. 117, 79 A.2d 657.

12. Rutherford v. Paddock, 1902, 180 Mass. 289, 62 N.E. 381 ("dirty old whore" not supported by proof of adultery); Crellin v. Thomas, 1952, 122 Utah 122, 247 P.2d 264 ("whore" not supported by career as dance hall girl); Wakley v. Cooke, 1849, 4 Exch. 511, 154 Eng.Rep. 1316.

13. Watkin v. Hall, 1868, L.R. 3 Q.B. 396, 37 L.J.Q.B. 125; Fountain v. West, 1867, 23 Iowa 9; Dement v. Houston Printing Co., 1896, 14 Tex.Civ.App. 391, 37 S.W. 985.

14. Dowie v. Priddle, 1905, 216 Ill. 553, 75 N.E. 243. Cf. Crane v. New York World Telegram Corp., 1955, 308 N.Y. 470, 126 N.E.2d 753 ("under indictment" not justified by "indictment" in a moral sense because plaintiff accused of crime by various people).

15. Hilsden v. Mercer, 1624, Cro.Jac. 677, 79 Eng. Rep. 586; Eastland v. Caldwell, 1810, 2 Bibb, Ky., 21; Downs v. Hawley, 1873, 112 Mass. 237; Sun Printing & Pub. Ass'n v. Schenck, 2 Cir. 1900, 98 F. 925; Kilian v. Doubleday & Co., 1951, 367 Pa. 117, 79 A.2d 657.

16. Gardner v. Self, 1852, 15 Mo. 480; Buckner v. Spaulding, 1891, 127 Ind. 229, 26 N.E. 792; Pallet v. Sargent, 1858, 36 N.H. 496; Haddock v. Naughton, 1893, 74 Hun 390, 26 N.Y.S. 455. Cf. Stewart v. Enterprise Co., Tex.Civ.App.1965, 393 S.W.2d 372, ref. n. r. e., appeal after remand 439 S.W.2d 674, ref. n. r. e. (two accusations, truth of only one proved).

17. See for example Swann v. Rary, 1833, 3 Blackf., Ind., 208 (two hogs and one); Sharpe v. Stephenson, 1851, 12 Ired., N.C., 348 (time and place); cf. Coffin v. Brown, 1901, 94 Md. 190, 50 A. 567 (time and place). See Courtney, Absurdities of the Law of Slander and Libel, 1902, 36 Am.L.Rev. 552, 561–564.

18. Alexander v. North Eastern R. Co., 1865, 6 B. & S. 340, 122 Eng.Rep. 1221; Zoll v. Allen, S.D.N.Y. 1950, 93 F.Supp. 95; Florida Pub. Co. v. Lee, 1918, 76 Fla. 405, 80 So. 245; McGuire v. Vaughan, 1896, 106 Mich. 280, 64 N.W. 44; Skrocki v. Stahl, 1910, 14 Cal.App. 1, 110 P. 957.

19. Edwards v. Bell, 1824, 1 Bing. 403, 130 Eng.Rep. 162; Bell Pub. Co. v. Garrett Eng. Co., Tex.Civ. App.1941, 154 S.W.2d 885.

$80,000 of the taxpayers' money has been held to be justified by proof that he wasted $17,500, since there is no more opprobrium attached to the greater amount.[20] If, however, the defendant adds to the facts stated an opinion or comment of his own, the comment must be justified as a proper one in the light of the facts proved.[21]

The defense of truth frequently is a hazardous venture for the defendant, since if he fails to sustain it the jury may be permitted to find that he has reiterated the defamation, and to consider the fact in aggravation of the damages.[22] The modern cases, however, have tended quite properly to recognize that the defendant is entitled to present an honest defense without being penalized, and have limited such aggravation to cases where it appears that the defense was entered in bad faith, without evidence to support it.[23]

Mitigation of Damages

In addition to the complete defenses of privilege and truth already considered, there are partial defenses open to the defendant, which will not avoid his liability, but will go to reduce the damages recovered by the plaintiff. Perhaps the most important of these is a retraction of the defamatory statement. At common law a retraction does not exonerate the defamer, unless it is made immediately after the defamation, and is so clearly connected with it that in effect it negatives the utterance itself.[24] If it follows so far behind that the words have had time to make an impression and be spread further, the courts refuse to hold that it has entirely repaired the damage.[25] Evidence of a retraction may, however, be admissible for three purposes.[26] It may go to show that the plaintiff has suffered less than he claims in the way of actual damage to his reputation.[27] It may tend to negative the "malice" or outrageous conduct which is a basis for punitive damages.[28] Finally, where privilege is in question, it would seem that it may be evidence of the defendant's good intentions and worthy motives, from which the jury may conclude that the privilege has not been

20. Fort Worth Press Co. v. Davis, Tex.Civ.App.1936, 96 S.W.2d 416. Cf. Smith v. Byrd, 1955, 225 Miss. 331, 83 So.2d 172 (statement that sheriff shot a man justified by proof that sheriff was acting in concert with deputy who shot him).

21. Cooper v. Lawson, 1838, 8 Ad. & El. 746, 112 Eng.Rep. 1020; Commercial Pub. Co. v. Smith, 6 Cir. 1907, 149 F. 704; cf. Morrison v. Harmer, 1837, 3 Bing.N.C. 759, 132 Eng.Rep. 603.

22. Will v. Press Pub. Co., 1932, 309 Pa. 539, 164 A. 621; Coffin v. Brown, 1901, 94 Md. 190, 50 A. 567; Krulic v. Petcoff, 1913, 122 Minn. 517, 142 N.W. 897; Hall v. Edwards, 1942, 138 Me. 231, 23 A.2d 889 (with other evidence of malice). See Note, 1958, 56 Mich.L.Rev. 659.

In Domchick v. Greenbelt Consumer Services, 1952, 200 Md. 36, 87 A.2d 831, it was held that pleading truth makes a prima facie case as to malice. In Shumate v. Johnson Pub. Co., 1956, 139 Cal.App.2d 121, 293 P.2d 531, a publisher who verified a pleading of truth was held subject to punitive damages, although he was out of the state and took no other part.

23. Webb v. Gray, 1913, 181 Ala. 408, 62 So. 194; Fodor v. Fuchs, 1910, 79 N.J.L. 529, 76 A. 1081; Willard v. Press Pub. Co., 1900, 52 App.Div. 448, 65 N.Y.S. 73; Las Vegas Sun, Inc. v. Franklin, 1958, 74 Nev. 282, 329 P.2d 867; Snyder v. Fatherly, 1930, 153 Va. 762, 151 S.E. 149.

24. Trabue v. Mays, 1835, 3 Dana, Ky., 138; Linney v. Maton, 1855, 13 Tex. 449.

25. Lehrer v. Elmore, 1896, 100 Ky. 56, 37 S.W. 292; Dixie Fire Ins. Co. v. Betty, 1912, 101 Miss. 880, 58 So. 705; De Severinus v. Press Pub. Co., 1911, 147 App.Div. 161, 132 N.Y.S. 80; Taylor v. Hearst, 1895, 107 Cal. 262, 40 P. 392.

26. See Note, 1922, 35 Harv.L.Rev. 867. Also the excellent discussion of mitigation of damages and the proper instruction to the jury in Morris, Inadvertent Newspaper Libel and Retraction, 1937, 32 Ill.L. Rev. 36. Also Leflar, Legal Remedies for Defamation, 1952, 6 Ark.L.Rev. 423.

27. Webb v. Call Pub. Co., 1920, 173 Wis. 45, 180 N. W. 263; Turner v. Hearst, 1896, 115 Cal. 394, 47 P. 129; Meyerle v. Pioneer Pub. Co., 1920, 45 N.D. 568, 178 N.W. 792; White v. Sun Pub. Co., 1905, 164 Ind. 426, 73 N.E. 890; O'Connor v. Field, 1943, 266 App.Div. 121, 41 N.Y.S.2d 492.

Contra, Kehoe v. New York Tribune Co., 1930, 229 App.Div. 220, 241 N.Y.S. 676.

28. Fessinger v. El Paso Times Co., Tex.Civ.App. 1913, 154 S.W. 1171, error refused; Meyerle v. Pioneer Pub. Co., 1920, 45 N.D. 568, 178 N.W. 792; O'Connor v. Field, 1943, 266 App.Div. 121, 41 N.Y.S. 2d 492.

abused.[29] By the same token, of course, a refusal to retract when a request has been made may be evidence in favor of the plaintiff, tending to show malevolence or an improper purpose in the original publication.[30]

When the defendant's motives are in issue, any evidence tending to show that he is in a different state of mind about the publication may be admissible. A retraction, as such, however, can be effective only if it is a full [31] and unequivocal one, which does not contain lurking insinuations, hypothetical or hesitant withdrawals, or new calumnies in disguise. It must, in short, be an honest endeavor to repair all of the wrong done by the defamatory imputation, or it will merely aggravate the original offense.[32] A statement that the plaintiff has not the manners of a hog is not corrected by an assertion that he has the manners of a hog.[33] The retraction must in general, be given the same publicity and prominence as the defamation.[34] An offer to make a public apology or retraction, which is refused, will go to mitigate damages; [35] but a mere offer to publish any statement the plaintiff himself cares to make is not an

offer to retract.[36] In a number of states the matter of retraction is covered by statutes, which usually limit the damages recoverable in cases where a proper retraction is made, or is not demanded.[37] Some of these statutes have been declared unconstitutional,[38] while others have been sustained.[39] They usually have been held to call for a specific retraction of the original publication, with reference to it, rather than a mere second explanatory article stating the true facts.[40]

29. See Note, 1922, 35 Harv.L.Rev. 867.

30. Brown v. Fawcett Publications, Fla.App.1967, 196 So.2d 465; Vigil v. Rice, 1964, 71 N.M. 693, 397 P.2d 719; Crane v. Bennett, 1904, 177 N.Y. 106, 69 N.E. 274; Reid v. Nichols, 1915, 166 Ky. 423, 179 S.W. 440; Morgan v. Dun & Bradstreet, Inc., 5 Cir. 1970, 421 F.2d 1241. See Note, 1922, 35 Harv.L.Rev. 867.

31. Luna v. Seattle Times Co., 1936, 186 Wash. 618, 59 P.2d 753; Monaghan v. Globe Newspaper Co., 1906, 190 Mass. 394, 77 N.E. 476; Goolsby v. Forum Printing Co., 1913, 23 N.D. 30, 135 N.W. 661; Gray v. Times Newspaper Co., 1898, 74 Minn. 452, 77 N.W. 204.

32. Hotchkiss v. Oliphant, 1842, 2 Hill, N.Y., 510; Lehrer v. Elmore, 1896, 100 Ky. 56, 37 S.W. 292; Palmer v. Mahin, 8 Cir. 1903, 120 F. 737.

33. Winfield, Law of Tort, 1937, 323.

34. Storey v. Wallace, 1871, 60 Ill. 51; Kent v. Bonzey, 1854, 38 Me. 435; Lafone v. Smith, 1858, 3 H. & N. 735, 157 Eng.Rep. 664.

35. Dinkelspiel v. New York Evening Journal Pub. Co., 1903, 42 Misc. 74, 85 N.Y.S. 570; Dalziel v. Press Pub. Co., 1906, 52 Misc. 207, 102 N.Y.S. 909; Emery v. Cooper & Sons, 1909, 19 Pa.Dist. 509.

36. Coffman v. Spokane Chronicle Pub. Co., 1911, 65 Wash. 1, 117 P. 596; Constitution Pub. Co. v. Way, 1894, 94 Ga. 120, 21 S.E. 139; cf. Williams v. Hicks Printing Co., 1914, 159 Wis. 90, 150 N.W. 183.

37. See Miami Herald Pub. Co. v. Brown, Fla.1953, 66 So.2d 679; White v. Sun Pub. Co., 1905, 164 Ind. 426, 73 N.E. 890; Gray v. Times Newspaper Co., 1898, 74 Minn. 452, 77 N.W. 204; Osborn v. Leach, 1904, 135 N.C. 628, 47 S.E. 811; Comer v. Age Herald Pub. Co., 1907, 151 Ala. 613, 44 So. 673. As to the "mangling" of these statutes by judicial interpretation, see Morris, Inadvertent Newspaper Libel and Retraction, 1937, 32 Ill.L.Rev. 36.

The California statute, which is unique in that it includes intentional, malicious libel, has been held not to apply to publication in magazines, because of a requirement of retraction within three weeks of demand. Morris v. National Federation of the Blind, 1961, 192 Cal.App.2d 162, 13 Cal.Rptr. 336. The New Jersey statute, notwithstanding language limiting recovery to "actual damages proved," has been held to prevent only the recovery of punitive damages. Gersten v. Newark Morning Ledger Co., 1958, 52 N.J.Super. 152, 145 A.2d 56; Bock v. Plainfield Courier-News, 1957, 45 N.J.Super. 302, 132 A.2d 523.

38. Hanson v. Krehbiel, 1889, 68 Kan. 670, 75 P. 1041; Park v. Detroit Free Press, 1888, 72 Mich. 560, 40 N.W. 731; Byers v. Meridian Printing Co., 1911, 84 Ohio St. 408, 95 N.E. 917; Holden v. Pioneer Broadcasting Co., 1961, 228 Or. 405, 365 P.2d 845, appeal dismissed and cert. denied 370 U.S. 157. See Note, 1956, 36 Or.L.Rev. 70.

39. Allen v. Pioneer Press Co., 1889, 40 Minn. 117, 41 N.W. 936; Osborn v. Leach, 1904, 135 N.C. 628, 47 S.E. 811; Werner v. Southern Cal. Assoc. Newspapers, 1950, 35 Cal.2d 121, 216 P.2d 825; Meyerle v. Pioneer Pub. Co., 1920, 45 N.D. 568, 178 N.W. 792. See Note, 1950, 38 Cal.L.Rev. 951.

40. Roth v. Greensboro News Co., 1940, 217 N.C. 13, 6 S.E.2d 882; Brogan v. Passaic Daily News, 1956, 22 N.J. 139, 123 A.2d 473. Cf. Kirby v. Pittsburgh Courier Pub. Co., 2 Cir. 1945, 150 F.2d 480.

Nevada and Mississippi [41] go further, and provide a "right of reply," under which the plaintiff may publish his own version of the matter with the defendant's facilities. This is a common remedy among European countries, and has had numerous advocates in the United States.

Since the plaintiff seeks to recover for harm to his reputation, evidence that that reputation was already bad is admissible in mitigation of damages, as bearing on the value of what has been destroyed.[42] For this purpose, it usually is held that evidence of a rumor or report that the plaintiff has committed the particular act charged is not sufficient,[43] unless it is shown to have been so widely diffused as to affect his general reputation.[44] Proof that the defendant was merely repeating what others had said is, however, held by most courts to be admissible,[45]

along with any other facts tending to show a reasonable belief that his statement was true,[46] for the purpose of proving good faith and absence of "malice." Provocation by the plaintiff, indicating that the defendant uttered the words in the heat of passion or the excitement of the moment caused by the plaintiff's improper conduct, may be admitted for the same purpose.[47] The greater number of courts have held that such evidence to negative "malice" may be considered by the jury only as bearing upon the punitive damages recoverable where the defendant has been motivated by ill will.[48] There is a more realistic minority view that since the humiliation or mental suffering of the plaintiff may be enhanced by the defendant's ill will and outrageous conduct, proof of his good faith is to be considered in reduction of this element of compensatory damages.[49]

41. Nev.Comp. Laws, Hillyer, 1929, § 10506; Miss. Code Ann.1942, § 3175. See Manasco v. Walley, 1953, 216 Miss. 614, 63 So.2d 91; Donnelly, The Right of Reply: An Alternative to an Action for Libel, 1948, 34 Va.L.Rev. 867; Leflar, Legal Remedies for Defamation, 1952, 6 Ark.L.Rev. 423.

42. Sclar v. Resnick, 1921, 192 Iowa 669, 185 N.W. 273; Snively v. Record Pub. Co., 1921, 185 Cal. 565, 198 P. 1; Dodge v. Gilman, 1913, 122 Minn. 177, 142 N.W. 147; Georgia v. Bond, 1897, 114 Mich. 196, 72 N.W. 332.

43. Utah State Farm Bureau Fed. v. National Farmers Union Service Corp., 10 Cir. 1952, 198 F.2d 20; Abell v. Cornwall Industrial Corp., 1925, 241 N.Y. 327, 150 N.E. 132; Mahoney v. Bedford, 1882, 132 Mass. 393; Pease v. Shippen, 1876, 80 Pa. 513. See Note, 1953, 32 Neb.L.Rev. 121. Nor is evidence of other misconduct of the plaintiff admissible, since it shows "not that the plaintiff's reputation is bad, but that it ought to be bad." Sun Printing & Pub. Co. v. Schenck, 2 Cir. 1900, 98 F. 925, 929; Bergstrom v. Ridgway Co., 1910, 138 App.Div. 178, 123 N.Y.S. 29.

44. Blickenstaff v. Perrin, 1867, 27 Ind. 527; Wetherbee v. Marsh, 1847, 20 N.H. 561; Stuart v. News Pub. Co., 1902, 67 N.J.L. 317, 51 A. 709.

45. Broadfoot v. Bird, 1926, 217 App.Div. 325, 216 N.Y.S. 670; Darling v. Mansfield, 1923, 222 Mich. 278, 192 N.W. 595; Pfister v. Milwaukee Free Press Co., 1909, 139 Wis. 627, 121 N.W. 938; Gill v. Ruggles, 1913, 95 S.C. 90, 78 S.E. 536. Contra, Preston v. Frey, 1891, 91 Cal. 107, 27 P. 533.

46. Massee v. Williams, 6 Cir. 1913, 207 F. 222; Scripps v. Foster, 1879, 41 Mich. 742, 3 N.W. 216; Davis v. Hearst, 1911, 160 Cal. 143, 116 P. 530; Gressman v. Morning Journal Ass'n, 1910, 197 N.Y. 474, 90 N.E. 1131. Where truth was not pleaded, and so not admissible as an absolute defense, it has been held that the defendant could still show it on the issue of malice. Schlaf v. State Farm Mut. Auto. Ins. Co., 1957, 15 Ill.App.2d 194, 145 N.E.2d 791.

47. McLeod v. American Pub. Co., 1923, 126 S.C. 363, 120 S.E. 70; Shockey v. McCauley, 1905, 101 Md. 461, 61 A. 583; Ivie v. King, 1914, 167 N.C. 174, 83 S.E. 339. But the mere fact that the words are spoken in the heat of a quarrel is not sufficient, unless it is shown that plaintiff brought on the quarrel. Rohr v. Riedel, 1922, 112 Kan. 130, 210 P. 644.

48. Farrell v. Kramer, 1963, 159 Me. 387, 193 A.2d 560; Palmer v. Mahin, 8 Cir. 1903, 120 F. 737; Callahan v. Ingram, 1894, 122 Mo. 355, 26 S.W. 1020; Garrison v. Robinson, 1911, 81 N.J.L. 497, 79 A. 278.

49. Craney v. Donovan, 1917, 92 Conn. 236, 102 A. 640; Massee v. Williams, 6 Cir. 1913, 207 F. 222; Faxon v. Jones, 1900, 176 Mass. 206, 57 N.E. 359; Conroy v. Fall River Herald News Co., 1940, 306 Mass. 488, 28 N.E.2d 729. It may be suggested that the distinction is almost entirely academic, and that once the evidence is admitted the jury will use it for any purpose they see fit.

CHAPTER 20

PRIVACY

117. RIGHT OF PRIVACY

The recognition and development of the so-called "right of privacy," [1] is perhaps the outstanding illustration of the influence of legal periodicals upon the courts. Prior to the year 1890, no English or American court ever had granted relief expressly based upon the invasion of such a right, although there were cases [2] which in retrospect seem to have been groping in that direction, and Judge Cooley [3] had coined the phrase, "the right to be let alone." In 1890 there appeared in the Harvard Law Review a famous article,[4] by Samuel D. Warren and Louis D. Brandeis, which reviewed a number of cases in which relief had been afforded on the basis of defamation, invasion of some property right,[5] or breach of confidence or an implied contract,[6] and

concluded that they were in reality based upon a broader principle which was entitled to separate recognition. In support of their argument they contended [7] that the growing excesses of the press made a remedy upon such a distinct ground essential to the protection of private individuals against the unjustifiable infliction of mental pain and distress. Although there was at first some hesitation,[8] a host of other legal writers have taken up the theme,[9] and no other tort has

---

1. This term has been difficult of definition. See Davis, What Do We Mean by "Right to Privacy," 1959, 4 S.Dak.L.Rev. 1. It frequently has been misused, by those politically inclined, as a means of begging the question whether an individual may refuse to give information demanded of him by legal authorities. See for example Note, 1962, 40 N. C.L.Rev. 788. In the tort sense, at least, it has no such significance.

2. For example De May v. Roberts, 1881, 46 Mich. 160, 9 N.W. 146 (intrusion upon childbirth); Lord Byron v. Johnston, 1816, 2 Mer. 29, 35 Eng.Rep. 851 (authorship of spurious poem attributed).

3. Cooley, Torts, 2d Ed. 1888, 29.

4. Warren and Brandeis, The Right to Privacy, 1890, 4 Harv.L.Rev. 193.

5. Woolsey v. Judd, 1855, 4 Duer, N.Y., 379, 11 How. Pr. 49 (publication of private letters); Gee v. Pritchard, 1819, 2 Swans. 402, 36 Eng.Rep. 670 (same); Prince Albert v. Strange, 1849, 1 Mach. & G. 25, 41 Eng.Rep. 1171, affirmed 1849, 2 De G. & Sm. 652, 64 Eng.Rep. 293 (exhibition of private etchings and publication of catalogue).

6. Yovatt v. Winyard, 1820, 1 Jac. & W. 394, 37 Eng. Rep. 425 (publication of recipes obtained surreptitiously by employee); Abernathy v. Hutchinson,

1825, 3 L.J.Ch. 209 (publication of lectures delivered to class of which defendant was a member); Pollard v. Photographic Co., 1888, 40 Ch.Div. 345 (publication of plaintiff's picture made by defendant).

7. "The press is overstepping in every direction the obvious bounds of propriety and of decency. Gossip is no longer the resource of the idle and of the vicious, but has become a trade, which is pursued with industry as well as effrontery. To satisfy a prurient taste the details of sexual relations are spread broadcast in the columns of the daily papers. To occupy the indolent, column upon column is filled with idle gossip, which can only be procured by intrusion upon the domestic circle. The intensity and complexity of life, attendant upon advancing civilization, have rendered necessary some retreat from the world, and man, under the refining influence of culture, has become more sensitive to publicity, so that solitude and privacy have become more essential to the individual; but modern enterprise and invention have, through invasions upon his privacy, subjected him to mental pain and distress, far greater than could be inflicted by mere bodily injury." Warren and Brandeis, The Right to Privacy, 1890, 4 Harv.L.Rev. 193, 196.

8. See O'Brien, The Right of Privacy, 1902, 2 Col.L. Rev. 437; Notes, 1902, 2 Col.L.Rev. 486; 1902, 64 Albany L.J. 428. Later dissenting voices are Lisle, The Right of Privacy (A Contra View), 1931, 19 Ky. L.J. 137; Kalven, Privacy in Tort Law—Were Warren and Brandeis Wrong? 1966, 31 Law & Con.Prob. 326; Notes, 1925, 29 Law Notes 64; 1929, 43 Harv.L.Rev. 297; 1931, 26 Ill.L.Rev. 63.

9. Among others Larremore, The Law of Privacy, 1912, 12 Col.L.Rev. 693; Ragland, The Right of Pri-

received such an outpouring of comment in advocacy of its bare existence.

The first state really to come to grips with the doctrine thus advanced was New York. After cases in its lower courts [10] had accepted the existence of the right of privacy proposed by Warren and Brandeis, it fell into the hostile hands of the Court of Appeals in

vacy, 1929, 17 Ky.L.J. 101; Winfield, Privacy, 1931, 47 L.Q.Rev. 23; Green, The Right of Privacy, 1932, 27 Ill.L.Rev. 237; Kacedan, The Right of Privacy, 1932, 12 Bos.U.L.Rev. 353, 600; Dickler, The Right of Privacy, 1936, 70 U.S.L.Rev. 435; Harper and McNeely, A Re-examination of the Basis of Liability for Emotional Distress, [1938] Wis.L.Rev. 436; Nizer, The Right of Privacy, 1941, 39 Mich.L.Rev. 526; Feinberg, Recent Developments in the Law of Privacy, 1948, 48 Col.L.Rev. 713; Ludwig, "Peace of Mind" in 48 Pieces vs. Uniform Right of Privacy, 1948, 32 Minn.L.Rev. 734; Yankwich, The Right of Privacy, 1952, 27 Notre Dame L. 429; Prosser, Privacy, 1960, 48 Cal.L.Rev. 383; Brittan, The Right of Privacy in England and The United States, 1963, 37 Tul.L.Rev. 235; Symposium, 1966, 31 Law & Con.Prob. 251 ff.

Also Notes in 1929, 43 Harv.L.Rev. 297; 1929, 7 N.C. L.Rev. 435; 1931, 26 Ill.L.Rev. 63; 1933, 81 U.Pa. L.Rev. 324; 1938, 33 Ill.L.Rev. 87; 1939, 13 So.Cal. L.Rev. 81; 1941, 15 Temple L.Q. 148; 1941, 25 Minn.L.Rev. 619; 1945, 30 Corn.L.Q. 398; 1948, 48 Col.L.Rev. 713; 1948, 15 U.Chi.L.Rev. 926; 1952, 6 Ark.L.Rev. 459; 1952, 38 Va.L.Rev. 117; 1953, 28 Ind.L.J. 179; 1958, 44 Va.L.Rev. 1303; 1960, 31 Miss.L.J. 191.

The foreign law is discussed in Gutteridge, The Comparative Law of the Right to Privacy, 1931, 47 L. Q.Rev. 203; Walton, The Comparative Law of the Right to Privacy, 1931, 47 L.Q.Rev. 219.

10.   The first case to allow recovery on the independent basis of the right of privacy was an unreported decision of a New York trial judge, where an actress very scandalously appeared on the stage in tights, and the defendant snapped her picture from a box, and was enjoined from publishing it. Manola v. Stevens, N.Y.Sup.Ct.1890, in N. Y. Times, June 15, 18, 21, 1890. This was followed by decisions in New York, and in a Massachusetts federal court, in which the courts appeared to be quite willing to accept the principle. Mackenzie v. Soden Mineral Springs Co., 1891, 27 Abb.N.C. 402, 18 N.Y.S. 240; Marks v. Jaffa, 1893, 6 Misc. 290, 26 N.Y.S. 908; Schuyler v. Curtis, 1895, 147 N.Y. 434, 42 N.E. 22; Corliss v. E. W. Walker Co., D.Mass.1894, 64 F. 280. Michigan, however, flatly rejected the whole idea, in Atkinson v. John E. Doherty & Co., 1899, 121 Mich. 372, 80 N.W. 285, where a brand of cigars was named after a deceased public figure.

Roberson v. Rochester Folding-Box Company,[11] where the defendant made use of the picture of a pulchritudinous young lady to advertise its flour without her consent. In a four-to-three decision, with a vigorous dissent, the court flatly denied the existence of any right to protection against such conduct, because of the lack of precedent, the purely mental character of the injury, the "vast amount of litigation" which might be expected to follow, the difficulty of drawing a distinction between public and private characters, and the fear of undue restriction of liberty of speech and freedom of the press.

The immediate result of the Roberson decision was a storm of public disapproval, which led one of the concurring judges to take the unprecedented step of publishing a law review article in defense of the decision.[12] In consequence the next New York legislature enacted a statute [13] making it both a misdemeanor and a tort to make use of the name, portrait or picture of any person for "advertising purposes or for the purposes of trade" without his written consent. This act remains the law of New York, where there have been upwards of a hundred decisions dealing with it. Except as the statute itself limits the extent of the right, the New York decisions are quite consistent with the common law as it has been worked out in other states, and they are customarily cited in privacy cases throughout the country. Three years later the supreme court of Georgia had essentially the same question presented in Pavesich v. New England Life Ins. Co.,[14] where the defendant's insurance ad-

11.   1902, 171 N.Y. 538, 64 N.E. 442. See the account of the case in Peck, Decision at Law, 1961, 70–96.

12.   O'Brien, The Right of Privacy, 1902, 2 Col.L.Rev. 437.

13.   N.Y.Sess.Laws 1903, ch. 132, §§ 1–2. Now, as amended in 1921, N.Y.Civil Rights Law, §§ 50–51. Held constitutional in Rhodes v. Sperry & Hutchinson Co., 1908, 193 N.Y. 223, 85 N.E. 1097, affirmed, 1911, 220 U.S. 502. See, generally, Hofstadter, The Development of the Right of Privacy in New York, 1954.

14.   1905, 122 Ga. 190, 50 S.E. 68.

vertising made use of the plaintiff's name and picture, as well as a spurious testimonial from him. With the example of New York before it, George in turn rejected the Roberson case, accepted the views of Warren and Brandeis, and recognized the existence of a distinct right of privacy. This became the leading case.

For a time authority was divided, but along in the thirties, with the benediction of the Restatement of Torts,[15] the tide set in strongly in favor of recognition, and the rejecting decisions began to be overruled. In one form of another, the right of privacy is by this time recognized and accepted in all but a very few jurisdictions.[16] It is recognized in a limited form by the New York statute, and by similar acts adopted in Oklahoma, Utah and Virginia. At the time of publication, the right of privacy stands rejected by a 1909 decision in Rhode Island,[17] not yet overruled, and by more recent ones in Nebraska,[18] Texas,[19] and Wisconsin,[20] which have

said that any change in the old common law must be for the legislature, and which have not gone without criticism.

The early cases in all jurisdictions were understandably preoccupied with the question whether the right of privacy existed at all, and gave little or no consideration to what it would amount to if it did. Today, with something over four hundred cases in the books, some rather definite conclusions are possible. What has emerged is no very simple matter. As it has appeared in the cases thus far decided, it is not one tort, but a complex of four. To date the law of privacy comprises four distinct kinds of invasion of four different interests of the plaintiff, which are tied together by the common name, but otherwise have almost nothing in common except that each represents an interference with the right of the plaintiff "to be let alone." Whether there may be invasions of other interests which are properly to be included under the same generic term of "privacy" is a matter to be considered later,[21] after the existing four have been dealt with.

Appropriation

The first form of invasion of privacy to be recognized by the courts consists of the appropriation, for the defendant's benefit or advantages, of the plaintiff's name or likeness.[22] By reason of its early appearance in

15. § 867, approving a cause of action for "unreasonable and serious" interference with privacy.

16. Comparatively recent decisions adding new jurisdictions to the list include Carr v. Watkins, 1962, 227 Md. 578, 177 A.2d 841; Truxes v. Kenco Enterprises, Inc., 1963, 80 S.D. 104, 119 N.W.2d 914; Olan Mills, Inc. of Texas v. Dodd, 1962, 234 Ark. 495, 353 S.W.2d 22; Barbieri v. News-Journal Co., Del.1963, 189 A.2d 773; Korn v. Rennison, 1959, 21 Conn.Sup. 400, 156 A.2d 476; Fergerstrom v. Hawaiian Ocean View Estates, 1968, 50 Haw. 374, 441 P.2d 141.

17. Henry v. Cherry & Webb, 1909, 30 R.I. 13, 73 A. 97.

18. Brunson v. Ranks Army Stores, 1955, 161 Neb. 519, 73 N.W.2d 803. See also Schmieding v. American Farmers Mut. Ins. Co., D.Neb.1955, 138 F.Supp. 167.

19. Milner v. Red River Valley Pub. Co., Tex.Civ. App.1952, 249 S.W.2d 227; McCullagh v. Houston Chronicle Pub. Co., 5 Cir. 1954, 211 F.2d 4, cert. denied 348 U.S. 827. See Seavey, Can Texas Courts Protect Newly Discovered Interests, 1953, 31 Tex.L. Rev. 309.

20. Yoeckel v. Samonig, 1956, 272 Wis. 430, 75 N.W. 2d 925 (truly an appalling decision); Judevine v. Benzies-Montanye Fuel & Warehouse Co., 1936, 222 Wis. 512, 269 N.W. 295; State ex rel. Distenfeld v.

Neelen, 1949, 255 Wis. 214, 38 N.W.2d 703. See Note, [1952] Wis.L.Rev. 507.

21. See infra, p. 816.

22. See Gordon, Right of Property in Name, Likeness, Personality and History, 1961, 55 Northwestern U.L.Rev. 553; Note, 1953, 26 So.Cal.L.Rev. 311. It is not impossible that, in the absence of a limiting statute, there might be invasion of privacy by appropriation of the plaintiff's identity, as by impersonation, without the use of either his name or his likeness. In Carlisle v. Fawcett Publications, 1962, 201 Cal.App.2d 733, 20 Cal.Rptr. 405, the name "John," with accompanying description sufficient to identify the plaintiff, was held to be enough.

On the other hand, in Lahr v. Adell Chemical Co., 1 Cir. 1962, 300 F.2d 256, it was held that the New York statute as to name or likeness did not include appropriation of the plaintiff's distinctive voice.

the Roberson case,[23] and the resulting New York statute, this form of invasion has bulked rather large in the law of privacy. Thus in New York, as well as in many other states, there are a great many decisions in which the plaintiff has recovered when his name [24] or picture,[25] or other likeness,[26] has been used without his consent to advertise the defendant's product, or to accompany an article sold,[27] to add luster to the name of a corporation,[28] or for other business purposes.[29]

The statute in New York and the others patterned after it are limited by their terms to uses for advertising or for "purposes of trade," and the common law of other states may therefore be somewhat broader in its scope; [30] but in general, there has been no very significant difference in the cases.

It is the plaintiff's name as a symbol of his identity that is involved here, and not as a mere name. Unless there is some tortious use made of it, there is no such thing as an exclusive right to the use of a name; and any one can be given or assume any name he likes.[31] It is only when he makes use of the name to pirate the plaintiff's identity for some advantage of his own, as by impersonation to obtain credit or secret information,[32] or by posing as the plaintiff's wife,[33] or providing a father for a child on a birth certificate,[34] that he becomes liable. It is in this

23. Supra, p. 803.

24. Brociner v. Radio Wire Television, 1959, 15 Misc.2d 843, 183 N.Y.S.2d 743; Birmingham Broadcasting Co. v. Bell, 1953, 259 Ala. 656, 68 So.2d 314, later appeal, 1957, 266 Ala. 266, 96 So.2d 263; Kerby v. Hal Roach Studios, 1942, 53 Cal.App.2d 207, 127 P.2d 577; Fairfield v. American Photocopy Equipment Co., 1955, 138 Cal.App.2d 82, 291 P.2d 194; Manger v. Kree Institute of Electrolysis, Inc., 2 Cir. 1956, 233 F.2d 5.

It has been held that the New York statute does not protect a stage or other assumed name. Geisel v. Poynter Products, Inc., S.D.N.Y.1968, 295 F.Supp. 331: On its face this looks foolish; it means that Samuel L. Clemens would have a cause of action, but Mark Twain would not.

25. Flores v. Mosler Safe Co., 1959, 7 N.Y.2d 276, 196 N.Y.S.2d 975, 164 N.E.2d 853; Olan Mills, Inc., of Texas v. Dodd, 1962, 234 Ark. 495, 353 S.W.2d 22; Colgate-Palmolive Co. v. Tullos, 5 Cir. 1955, 219 F. 2d 617 (Georgia law); Eick v. Perk Dog Food Co., 1952, 347 Ill.App. 293, 106 N.E.2d 742; Flake v. Greensboro News Co., 1938, 212 N.C. 780, 195 S.E. 55.

26. Young v. Greneker Studios, 1941, 175 Misc. 1027, 26 N.Y.S.2d 357 (manikin). See Note, 1964, 9 Vill.L. Rev. 274.

27. Lane v. F. W. Woolworth Co., 1939, 171 Misc. 66, 11 N.Y.S.2d 199, affirmed, 1939, 256 App.Div. 1065, 12 N.Y.S.2d 352; Jansen v. Hilo Packing Co., 1952, 202 Misc. 900, 118 N.Y.S.2d 162, affirmed, 1952, 282 App.Div. 935, 125 N.Y.S.2d 648; Miller v. Madison Square Garden Corp., 1941, 176 Misc. 714, 28 N.Y.S. 2d 811; Selsman v. Universal Photo Books, Inc., 1963, 18 App.Div.2d 151, 238 N.Y.S.2d 686.

28. Von Thodorovich v. Franz Josef Beneficial Ass'n, E.D.Pa.1907, 154 F. 911; Edison v. Edison Polyform Mfg. Co., 1907, 73 N.J.Eq. 136, 67 A. 392.

29. Binns v. Vitagraph Co. of America, 1913, 210 N. Y. 51, 103 N.E. 1108 (motion picture); Stryker v. Republic Pictures Corp., 1951, 108 Cal.App.2d 191, 238 P.2d 670 (same); Almind v. Sea Beach Co., 1912, 157 App.Div. 230, 141 N.Y.S. 842; (picture of plaintiff entering and leaving street car used to

teach other passengers how to do it); Selsman v. Universal Photo Books, Inc., 1963, 18 App.Div.2d 151, 238 N.Y.S.2d 686 (motion picture star's photograph used in camera manual).

30. See, as illustrations of possible differences: Cardy v. Maxwell, 1957, 9 Misc.2d 329, 169 N.Y.S.2d 547 (use of name to extort money not commercial use within statute); Hamilton v. Lumbermen's Mut. Cas. Co., La.App.1955, 82 So.2d 61, appeal transferred, 1955, 226 La. 644, 76 So.2d 916 (advertising in name of plaintiff for witnesses of accident); State ex rel. La Follette v. Hinkle, 1924, 131 Wash. 86, 229 P. 317 (use of name as candidate for office by political party); Burns v. Stevens, 1926, 236 Mich. 443, 210 N.W. 482 (posing as plaintiff's wife); Vanderbilt v. Mitchell, 1907, 72 N.J.Eq. 910, 67 A. 97 (providing father for child on birth certificate).

31. Du Boulay v. Du Boulay, 1869, L.R. 2 P.C. 430; Cowley v. Cowley, [1901] A.C. 450; Brown Chemical Co. v. Meyer, 1891, 139 U.S. 540; Smith v. United States Cas. Co., 1910, 197 N.Y. 420, 90 N.E. 947; Baumann v. Baumann, 1929, 250 N.Y. 382, 165 N.E. 819, reargument denied, 1929, 250 N.Y. 612, 166 N.E. 344; Bartholomew v. Workman, 1946, 197 Okl. 267, 169 P.2d 1012.

32. Goodyear Tire & Rubber Co. v. Vandergriff, 1936, 52 Ga.App. 662, 184 S.E. 452. The decision had been predicted in Green, The Right of Privacy, 1932, 27 Ill.L.Rev. 237, 243–44.

33. Burns v. Stevens, 1926, 236 Mich. 443, 210 N.W. 482.

34. Vanderbilt v. Mitchell, 1907, 72 N.J.Eq. 910, 67 A. 97.

sense that "appropriation" must be understood. It is therefore not enough that a name which is the same as the plaintiff's is used in a novel,[35] or the title of a corporation,[36] unless the context or the circumstances [37] indicate that the name is that of the plaintiff. On the other hand, there is no liability for the publication of a picture of his hand, leg or foot,[38] or of his house, his automobile, or his dog,[39] with nothing to indicate whose they are. Nor is there any liability when the plaintiff's character, occupation, and the general outline of his career, with many real incidents in his life, are used as the basis for a figure in a novel who is still clearly a fictional one.[40]

Once the plaintiff is identified, there is the further question whether the defendant has appropriated the name or likeness for his own advantage. Under the statutes the advantage must be a pecuniary one; but the common law is almost certainly not limited in this manner.[41] The New York courts were faced very early with the obvious fact that newspapers and magazines, to say nothing of radio, television and motion pictures, are by no means philanthropic institutions, but are operated for profit. As against the contention that everything published by these agencies must necessarily be "for purposes of trade," they were compelled to hold that there must be some closer and more direct connection, beyond the mere fact that the newspaper itself is sold; and that the presence of advertising matter in adjacent columns,[42] or even the duplication of a news item for the purpose of advertising the publication itself,[43] does not make any difference. Any other conclusion would in all probability have been an unconstitutional in-

35. Harrison v. Smith, 1869, 20 T.L.R.,N.S., 713; Swacker v. Wright, 1935, 154 Misc. 822, 277 N.Y.S. 296; People on Complaint of Maggio v. Charles Scribner's Sons, 1954, 205 Misc. 818, 130 N.Y.S.2d 514. Cf. Nebb v. Bell Syndicate, S.D.N.Y.1941, 41 F.Supp. 929 (comic strip).

36. Pfaudler v. Pfaudler Co., 1920, 114 Misc. 477, 186 N.Y.S. 725.

37. See for example Uproar Co. v. National Broadcasting Co., D.Mass.1934, 8 F.Supp. 358, affirmed as modified, 1 Cir. 1936, 81 F.2d 373; Kerby v. Hal Roach Studios, 1942, 53 Cal.App.2d 207, 127 P.2d 577; Krieger v. Popular Publications, 1938, 167 Misc. 5, 3 N.Y.S.2d 480.

The addition of other elements may make out the reference. Mackenzie v. Soden Mineral Springs Co., 1891, 27 Abb.N.C. 402, 18 N.Y.S. 240 (signature); Orsini v. Eastern Wine Corp., 1947, 190 Misc. 235, 73 N.Y.S.2d 426, affirmed, 1948, 273 App.Div. 947, 78 N.Y.S.2d 224, appeal denied, 1948, 273 App.Div. 996, 79 N.Y.S.2d 870 (coat of arms).

38. Brewer v. Hearst Pub. Co., 1950, 185 F.2d 846. Compare, as to pictures of unidentifiable dead bodies, Sellers v. Henry, Ky.1959, 329 S.W.2d 214; Waters v. Fleetwood, 1956, 212 Ga. 161, 91 S.E.2d 344.

39. Rozhon v. Triangle Publications, 7 Cir. 1956, 230 F.2d 359 (house); Branson v. Fawcett Publications, E.D.Ill.1954, 124 F.Supp. 429 (car); Lawrence v. Ylla, 1945, 184 Misc. 807, 55 N.Y.S.2d 343 (dog).

40. Toscani v. Hersey, 1946, 271 App.Div. 445, 65 N.Y.S.2d 814. Cf. Bernstein v. National Broadcasting Co., D.D.C.1955, 129 F.Supp. 817, affirmed, D.C. Cir. 1956, 98 U.S.App.D.C. 112, 232 F.2d 369; Miller v. National Broadcasting Co., D.Del.1957, 157 F. Supp. 240; Levey v. Warner Bros. Pictures, S.D.N.Y.1944, 57 F.Supp. 40.

41. See for example State ex rel. La Follette v. Hinkle, 1924, 131 Wash. 86, 229 P. 317 (use of name as candidate by political party); Hinish v. Meier & Frank Co., 1941, 166 Or. 482, 113 P.2d 438 (name signed to telegram urging governor to veto a bill); Schwartz v. Edrington, 1913, 133 La. 235, 62 So. 660 (name signed to petition); Hamilton v. Lumbermen's Mut. Cas. Co., La.App.1955, 82 So.2d 61, appeal transferred, 1955, 226 La. 644, 76 So.2d 916 (advertising in name of plaintiff for witnesses of accident); Burns v. Stevens, 1926, 236 Mich. 443, 210 N.W. 482 (posing as plaintiff's common law wife); Vanderbilt v. Mitchell, 1907, 72 N.J.Eq. 910, 67 A. 97 (birth certificate naming plaintiff as father).

42. Colyer v. Richard K. Fox Pub. Co., 1914, 162 App.Div. 297, 146 N.Y.S. 999.

43. Booth v. Curtis Pub. Co., 1962, 15 A.D.2d 343, 223 N.Y.S.2d 737, affirmed, 1962, 11 N.Y.2d 907, 228 N.Y.S.2d 468, 182 N.E.2d 812. See Note, 1962, 31 Ford.L.Rev. 394; cf. Rand v. Hearst Corp., 1969, 31 App.Div.2d 406, 298 N.Y.S.2d 405, affirmed 26 N.Y.2d 806, 309 N.Y.S.2d 348, 257 N.E.2d 895. But in Hill v. Hayes, 1963, 18 App.Div.2d 485, 240 N.Y.S.2d 286, where the revival of past events involving the plaintiff was found to be primarily for the purpose of increasing circulation and advertising a play, plaintiff was allowed to recover.

terference with the freedom of the press.[44] Accordingly, it has been held that the mere incidental mention of the plaintiff's name in a book or a motion picture[45] is not an invasion of his privacy; nor is the publication of a photograph[46] or a newsreel[47] in which he incidentally appears.

Although the element of protection of the plaintiff's personal feelings is obviously not to be ignored in such a case,[48] the effect of the appropriation decisions is to recognize or create an exclusive right in the individual plaintiff to a species of trade name, his own, and a kind of trade mark in his likeness. It seems quite pointless to dispute over whether such a right is to be classified as "property;"[49] it is at least clearly proprietary in

its nature. Once protected by the law, it is a right of value upon which the plaintiff can capitalize by selling licenses. It has been held in the Second Circuit[50] that an exclusive licensee has what has been called a "right of publicity,"[51] which entitles him to enjoin the use of the name or likewise by a third person.

Intrusion

An obviously different form of invasion of privacy consists of intrusion upon the plaintiff's physical solitude or seclusion,[52] as by invading his home[53] or other quarters,[54] or an illegal search of his shopping bag in a store.[55] The principle has, however, been carried beyond such physical intrusion, and extended to eavesdropping upon private conversations by means of wire tapping[56] and micro-

---

44. See Donahue v. Warner Bros. Picture Distributing Corp., 1954, 2 Utah 2d 256, 272 P.2d 177, infra, ch. 21.

45. University of Notre Dame Du Lac v. Twentieth Century-Fox Film Corp., 1965, 22 App.Div.2d 452, 256 N.Y.S.2d 301, affirmed 15 N.Y.2d 940, 259 N.Y. S.2d 832, 207 N.E.2d 508; Shubert v. Columbia Pictures Corp., 1947, 189 Misc. 734, 72 N.Y.S.2d 851, affirmed 274 App.Div. 751, 80 N.Y.S.2d 724, appeal denied 274 App.Div. 80, 83 N.Y.S.2d 233. Compare, as to a commentary on news which is part of an advertisement, Wallach v. Bacharach, 1948, 192 Misc. 979, 80 N.Y.S.2d 37, affirmed 1948, 274 App.Div. 919, 84 N.Y.S.2d 894; and see O'Brien v. Pabst Sales Co., 5 Cir. 1941, 124 F.2d 167, cert. denied 315 U.S. 823.

46. Dallessandro v. Henry Holt & Co., 1957, 4 App. Div.2d 470, 166 N.Y.S.2d 805, appeal dismissed 7 N. Y.2d 735, 193 N.Y.S.2d 635, 162 N.E.2d 726. Cf. Moglen v. Varsity Pajamas, Inc., 1961, 13 App.Div. 2d 114, 213 N.Y.S.2d 999.

47. Humiston v. Universal Film Mfg. Co., 1919, 189 App.Div. 467, 178 N.Y.S. 752; Merle v. Sociological Research Film Corp., 1915, 166 App.Div. 376, 152 N.Y.S. 829.

48. Foster-Milburn Co. v. Chinn, 1909, 134 Ky. 424, 120 S.W. 364.

49. See Rhodes v. Sperry & Hutchinson Co., 1908, 193 N.Y. 223, 85 N.E. 1097, affirmed, 1911, 220 U.S. 502; Gautier v. Pro-Football, Inc., 1952, 304 N.Y. 354, 107 N.E.2d 485; Mau v. Rio Grande Oil, Inc., N.D.Cal. 1939, 28 F.Supp. 845; Hull v. Curtis Pub. Co., 1956, 182 Pa.Super. 86, 125 A.2d 644; Metter v. Los Angeles Examiner, 1939, 35 Cal.App.2d 304, 95 P.2d 491. See Gordon, Right of Property in Name, Likeness, Personality and History, 1961, 55 Nw.L.Rev.

553; Ludwig, "Peace of Mind" in 48 Pieces v. Uniform Right of Privacy, 1948, 32 Minn.L.Rev. 734.

50. Haelan Laboratories v. Topps Chewing Gum, Inc., 2 Cir. 1953, 202 F.2d 866, cert. denied 346 U.S. 816.

51. Nimmer, The Right of Publicity, 1954, 19 Law & Con.Prob. 203; Notes, 1953, 62 Yale L.J. 1123; 1953, 41 Geo.L.J. 583. But see contra, Strickler v. National Broadcasting Co., S.D.Cal.1958, 167 F. Supp. 68.

52. See Ezer, Intrusion on Solitude, 1961, 21 Law in Transition 63.

53. Dietemann v. Time, Inc., D.C.Cal.1968, 284 F. Supp. 925; Young v. Western & A. R. Co., 1929, 39 Ga.App. 761, 148 S.E. 414 (search without warrant); Thompson v. City of Jacksonville, Fla.App.1961, 130 So.2d 105 (same); Walker v. Whittle, 1951, 83 Ga. App. 445, 64 S.E.2d 87 (entry without legal authority to arrest husband); Welsh v. Pritchard, 1952, 125 Mont. 517, 241 P.2d 816 (landlord moving in on tenant). Cf. De May v. Roberts, 1881, 46 Mich. 160, 9 N.W. 146 (intruding on childbirth). In Ford Motor Co. v. Williams, 1963, 108 Ga.App. 21, 132 S. E.2d 206, entry into plaintiff's home was held to be an invasion of his privacy, even though he was not there at the time.

54. Newcomb Hotel Co. v. Corbett, 1921, 27 Ga.App. 365, 108 S.E. 309 (hotel room); Byfield v. Candler, 1924, 33 Ga.App. 275, 125 S.E. 905 (woman's stateroom on steamboat).

55. Sutherland v. Kroger Co., 1959, 144 W.Va. 673, 110 S.E.2d 716.

56. Rhodes v. Graham, 1931, 238 Ky. 225, 37 S.W.2d 46; Le Crone v. Ohio Bell Tel. Co., 1961, 114 Ohio

phones;[57] and there are decisions indicating that it is to be applied to peering into the windows of a home,[58] as well as persistent and unwanted telephone calls.[59] The tort has been found in the case of unauthorized prying into the plaintiff's bank account,[60] and the same principle has been used to invalidate a blanket subpoena duces tecum requiring the production of all his books and documents,[61] and an illegal compulsory blood test.[62]

It is clear, however, that there must be something in the nature of prying or intrusion, and that mere noises which disturb a church congregation,[63] or bad manners, harsh names, and insulting gestures in public,[64] are not enough. It is clear also that the intrusion must be something which would be offensive or objectionable to a reasonable man, and that there is no tort when the landlord stops by on Sunday morning to ask for the rent.[65] It is clear also that the thing into which there is intrusion or prying must be, and be entitled to be, private. The plaintiff has no right to complain when his pretrial testimony is recorded,[66] or when the police, acting within their powers, take his photograph, fingerprints or measurements,[67] or when there is inspection and public disclosure of corporate records which he is required by law to keep and make available.[68] On the public street, or in any other public place, the plaintiff has no legal right to be alone; and it is no invasion of his privacy to do no more than follow him about and watch him there.[69] Neither is it such an invasion

App. 299, 182 N.E.2d 15. Even though no one listens, as in Hamberger v. Eastman, 1964, 106 N.H. 107, 206 A.2d 239; or the information obtained is not disclosed to others. Fowler v. Southern Bell Tel. & Tel. Co., 5 Cir. 1965, 343 F.2d 150. See Sullivan, Wiretapping and Eavesdropping: A Review of the Current Law, 1966, 18 Hast.L.J. 59; Notes, 1965, 2 Houst.L.Rev. 285; 1967, 52 Corn.L.Q. 975; 1969, 36 Tenn.L.Rev. 362.

57. McDaniel v. Atlanta Coca-Cola Bottling Co., 1939, 60 Ga.App. 92, 2 S.E.2d 810; Roach v. Harper, 1958, 143 W.Va. 869, 105 S.E.2d 564. Elson v. Bowen, 1967, 83 Nev. 515, 436 P.2d 12. See Note, 1969, 20 Syr.L.Rev. 601.

58. Souder v. Pendleton Detectives, Inc., La.App.1956, 88 So.2d 716; Moore v. New York Elevated R. Co., 1892, 130 N.Y. 523, 29 N.E. 997; Pritchett v. Board of Commissioners of Knox County, 1908, 42 Ind. App. 3, 85 N.E. 32; cf. Pinkerton Nat. Detective Agency v. Stevens, 1963, 108 Ga.App. 159, 132 S.E. 2d 119.

This topic gave rise to a possible nomination for the all-time prize law review title, in the Note, Crimination of Peeping Toms and Other Men of Vision, 1951, 5 Ark.L.Rev. 388.

59. Housh v. Peth, 1956, 165 Ohio St. 35, 133 N.E.2d 340, affirming, 1955, 99 Ohio App. 485, 135 N.E.2d 440; Harms v. Miami Daily News, Inc., Fla.1961, 127 So.2d 715; Carey v. Statewide Finance Co., 1966, 3 Conn.C.C. 716, 223 A.2d 405.

60. Brex v. Smith, 1929, 104 N.J.Eq. 386, 146 A. 34; Zimmermann v. Wilson, 3 Cir. 1936, 81 F.2d 847.

61. Frey v. Dixon, 1848, 141 N.J.Eq. 481, 58 A.2d 86; State ex rel. Clemens v. Witthaus, 1950, 360 Mo. 274, 228 S.W.2d 4 (court order).

62. Bednarik v. Bednarik, 1940, 18 N.J.Misc. 633, 16 A.2d 80. See Notes, 1967, 14 UCLA L.Rev. 680; 1967, 19 Ala.L.Rev. 174; 1967, 45 N.C.L.Rev. 174; 1967, 28 Ohio St.L.J. 185.

63. Owen v. Henman, 1841, 1 W. & S., Pa., 548.

64. Lisowski v. Jaskiewicz, 1950, 76 Pa.D. & C. 79; Christie v. Greenleaf, 1951, 78 Pa.D. & C. 191.

65. Horstman v. Newman, Ky.1956, 291 S.W.2d 567. Accord, Harms v. Miami Daily News, Inc., Fla.1961, 127 So.2d 715 (for the jury whether telephone calls objectionable to a reasonable man).

66. Gotthelf v. Hillcrest Lumber Co., 1952, 280 App. Div. 668, 116 N.Y.S.2d 873.

67. Voelker v. Tyndall, 1947, 226 Ind. 43, 75 N.E.2d 548; McGovern v. Van Riper, 1947, 140 N.J.Eq. 341, 54 A.2d 469; Norman v. City of Las Vegas, 1947, 64 Nev. 38, 177 P.2d 442; Mabry v. Kettering, 1909, 89 Ark. 551, 117 S.W. 746, second appeal, 1909, 92 Ark. 81, 122 S.W. 115; Hodgeman v. Olsen, 1915, 86 Wash. 615, 150 P. 1122; Walker v. Lamb, 1969, —— Del. ——, 254 A.2d 265. Cf. Herschel v. Dyra, 7 Cir. 1966, 365 F.2d 17, cert. denied 385 U.S. 973 (retaining record of arrest); Kolb v. O'Connor, 1957, 14 Ill.App.2d 81, 142 N.E.2d 818 (same); Anthony v. Anthony, 1950, 9 N.J.Super. 411, 74 A.2d 919 (compulsory blood test in paternity suit).

68. Bowles v. Misle, D.Neb.1946, 64 F.Supp. 835; United States v. Alabama Highway Express Co., D. Ala.1942, 46 F.Supp. 450; Alabama State Federation of Labor v. McAdory, 1944, 246 Ala. 1, 18 So.2d 810, cert. dismissed 325 U.S. 450.

69. Chappell v. Stewart, 1896, 82 Md. 323, 33 A. 542; Forster v. Manchester, 1963, 410 Pa. 192, 189 A.2d

to take his photograph in such a place,[70] since this amounts to nothing more than making a record, not differing essentially from a full written description, of a public sight which anyone would be free to see. On the other hand, when the plaintiff is confined to a hospital bed,[71] and when he is merely in the seclusion of his home,[72] the making of a photograph is an invasion of a private right, of which he is entitled to complain. And even in a public place, there can be some things which are still private, so that a woman who is photographed with her dress unexpectedly blown up in a "fun house" has a right of action.[73]

Public Disclosure of Private Facts

A second group of cases have found a cause of action in publicity, of a highly objectionable kind, given to private information about the plaintiff, even though it is true and no action would lie for defamation. Although there were earlier instances in which other elements were involved,[74] the first real application of this was in a Kentucky case [75] in 1927, in which the defendant put up a notice in the window of his garage announcing to the world that the defendant owed him money and would not pay it. But the decision which became the leading case, largely because of its spectacular facts, was Melvin v. Reid,[76] in California in 1931, where an exhibited motion picture revived the past history and disclosed the present identity of a reformed prostitute who, seven years before, had been the defendant in a notorious murder trial. Other decisions have followed, involving publicity given to the plaintiff's debts,[77] to medical pictures of his more intimate anatomy,[78] and to embarassing details

---

147; see Pinkerton Nat. Detective Agency v. Stevens, 1963, 108 Ga.App. 159, 132 S.E.2d 119. Cf. McKinzie v. Huckaby, W.D.Okl.1953, 112 F.Supp. 642, where defendant, calling at plaintiff's home, brought along a policeman, who remained outside in the car. But in Pinkerton Nat. Detective Agency v. Stevens, 1963, 108 Ga.App. 159, 132 S.E.2d 119, ostentatious shadowing on the street, which drew public attention, was held to be an invasion of privacy.

70. Forster v. Manchester, 1963, 410 Pa. 192, 189 A. 2d 147; Gill v. Hearst Pub. Co., 1953, 40 Cal.2d 224, 253 P.2d 441; Berg v. Minneapolis Star & Tribune Co., D.Minn.1948, 79 F.Supp. 957 (courtroom); Lyles v. State, Okl.Cr.1958, 330 P.2d 734 (television in court). Cf. Gautier v. Pro-Football, Inc., 1953, 304 N.Y. 354, 107 N.E.2d 485. In United States v. Gugel, E.D.Ky.1954, 119 F.Supp. 897, the right to take such pictures was said to be protected by the Constitution of the United States. See Fitzpatrick, Unauthorized Photographs, 1932, 20 Geo.L.J. 134; Note, 1938, 33 Ill.L.Rev. 87.

71. Barber v. Time, Inc., 1942, 348 Mo. 1199, 159 S. W.2d 291. Cf. Clayman v. Bernstein, 1940, 38 Pa. D. & C. 543 (picture of semi-conscious patient taken by physician). Without the intrusion, publication of matters of public interest was held to be privileged in Pearson v. Dodd, 1969, 133 U.S.App.D.C. 279, 410 F.2d 701, cert. denied 395 U.S. 947.

72. Dietemann v. Time, Inc., C.D.Cal.1968, 284 F. Supp. 925.

73. Daily Times Democrat v. Graham, 1964, 276 Ala. 380, 162 So.2d 474.

74. Such as Douglas v. Stokes, 1912, 149 Ky. 506, 149 S.W. 849 (publication of picture by photographer in breach of implied contract).

75. Brents v. Morgan, 1927, 221 Ky. 765, 299 S.W. 867. "Dr. W. R. Morgan owes an account here of $49.67. And if promises would pay an account this account would have been settled long ago. This account will be advertised as long as it remains unpaid."

76. 1931, 112 Cal.App. 285, 297 P. 91. See also, under statute, Nappier v. Jefferson Standard Life Ins. Co., 4 Cir. 1963, 322 F.2d 502 (name of victim of rape).

77. Trammell v. Citizens News Co., 1941, 285 Ky. 529, 148 S.W.2d 708; Biederman's of Springfield, Inc. v. Wright, Mo.1959, 322 S.W.2d 892; Tollefson v. Price, 1967, 247 Or. 398, 430 P.2d 990; cf. Bennett v. Norban, 1959, 396 Pa. 94, 151 A.2d 476. A rather spectacular case is Santiesteban v. Goodyear Tire & Rubber Co., 5 Cir. 1962, 306 F.2d 9, where a creditor stripped the tires off the debtor's car in public, and it was held to be a "demonstrative publication" of the debt. See Note, 1963, 49 Iowa L. Rev. 208.

78. Banks v. King Features Syndicate, S.D.N.Y.1939, 30 F.Supp. 352 (X-rays of woman's pelvic region); Griffin v. Medical Society, Sup.Ct.1939, 11 N.Y.S.2d 109 (deformed nose); Feeney v. Young, 1920, 191 App.Div. 501, 181 N.Y.S. 481 (public exhibition of films of caesarian operation); Lambert v. Dow Chemical Co., La.App.1968, 215 So.2d 673.

of a woman's masculine characteristics and eccentric behavior.[79]

Some limits of this branch of the right of privacy appear to be fairly well marked out. The disclosure of the private facts must be a public disclosure, and not a private one; there must be, in other words, publicity.[80] It is an invasion of his rights to publish in a newspaper that the plaintiff does not pay his debts, or to post a notice to that effect in a window on the public street, or to cry it aloud in the highway,[81] but not to communicate the fact to the plaintiff's employer,[82] or to any other individual, or even to a small group,[83] unless there is some breach of contract, trust or confidential relation which will afford an independent basis for relief.[84] Warren and Brandeis[85] thought that the publica-

tion would have to be written or printed unless some special damage could be shown, and there have been decisions[86] that the action will not lie for oral publicity; but the growth of radio alone has been enough to make this quite obsolete,[87] and there now can be little doubt that writing is not required.[88]

The facts disclosed to the public must be private facts, and not public ones. The plaintiff cannot complain when an occupation in which he publicly engages is called to public attention,[89] or when publicity is given to matters such as the date of his birth or marriage,[90] or his military service record,[91]

79. Cason v. Baskin, 1945, 155 Fla. 198, 20 So.2d 243, second appeal, 1947, 159 Fla. 31, 30 So.2d 635.

80. Santiesteban v. Goodyear Tire & Rubber Co., 5 Cir. 1962, 306 F.2d 9.

81. See cases cited supra, notes 75–77.

82. Household Finance Corp. v. Bridge, 1969, 252 Md. 531, 250 A.2d 878; Timperley v. Chase Collection Service, 1969, 272 Cal.App.2d 697, 77 Cal.Rptr. 782; Harrison v. Humble Oil & Ref. Co., D.C.S.C.1967, 264 F.Supp. 89; Yoder v. Smith, 1962, 253 Iowa 505, 112 N.W.2d 862; Berrier v. Beneficial Finance Co., N.D.Ind.1964, 234 F.Supp. 204. Contra is Pack v. Wise, La.App.1964, 155 So.2d 909, writ refused 245 La. 84, 157 So.2d 231; but the case was limited, in Passman v. Commercial Credit Plan of Hammond, Inc., La.App.1969, 220 So.2d 758, application denied 254 La. 287, 223 So.2d 410, to some attempt at coercion. See Note, 1969, 36 Brook.L.Rev. 95.

83. Gregory v. Bryan-Hunt Co., 1943, 295 Ky. 345, 174 S.W.2d 510 (oral accusation of theft); French v. Safeway Stores, Inc., 1967, 247 Or. 554, 430 P.2d 1021; Schwartz v. Thiele, 1966, 242 Cal.App.2d 799, 51 Cal.Rptr. 767. On the other hand, in Kerby v. Hal Roach Studios, 1942, 53 Cal.App.2d 207, 127 P. 2d 577, the distribution of a letter to a thousand men was held, without discussion, to make it public.

84. Copley v. Northwestern Mut. Life Ins. Co., S.D. W.Va.1968, 295 F.Supp. 93; Peterson v. Idaho First Nat. Bank, 1961, 83 Idaho 578, 367 P.2d 284; Berry v. Moench, 1958, 8 Utah 2d 191, 331 P.2d 814; cf. Simonsen v. Swenson, 1920, 104 Neb. 224, 177 N.W. 831. See Note, 1959, 43 Minn.L.Rev. 943.

85. Warren and Brandeis, The Right to Privacy, 1890, 4 Harv.L.Rev. 193, 217.

86. Martin v. F. I. Y. Theatre Co., 1838, 10 Ohio Op. 338; Gregory v. Bryan-Hunt Co., 1943, 295 Ky. 345, 174 S.W.2d 510; Pangallo v. Murphy, Ky.1951, 243 S.W.2d 496; Lewis v. Physicians & Dentists Credit Bureau, 1947, 27 Wash.2d 267, 177 P.2d 896; Grimes v. Carter, 1966, 241 Cal.App.2d 694, 50 Cal. Rptr. 808.

87. Mau v. Rio Grande Oil, Inc., N.D.Cal.1939, 28 F. Supp. 845; Strickler v. National Broadcasting Co., S.D.Cal.1958, 167 F.Supp. 68; Binns v. Vitagraph Co. of America, 1913, 210 N.Y. 51, 103 N.E. 1108 (motion picture); Donahue v. Warner Bros. Pictures, 10 Cir. 1952, 194 F.2d 6 (same); Ettore v. Philco Television Broadcasting Co., 3 Cir. 1956, 229 F.2d 481, cert. denied, 351 U.S. 926 (motion picture film on television).

88. Carr v. Watkins, 1962, 227 Md. 578, 177 A.2d 841; Bennett v. Norban, 1959, 396 Pa. 94, 151 A.2d 476; Biederman's of Springfield, Inc. v. Wright, Mo.1959, 322 S.W.2d 892; Linehan v. Linehan, 1955, 134 Cal.App.2d 250, 285 P.2d 326; Norris v. Moskin Stores, Inc., 1961, 272 Ala. 174, 132 So.2d 321. Cf. Santiesteban v. Goodyear Tire & Rubber Co., 5 Cir. 1962, 306 F.2d 9 (conduct).

There must, however, be communication to others; and publication to the plaintiff himself is not enough. Zimmerman v. Associates Discount Corp., Mo.1969, 444 S.W.2d 396.

89. Reed v. Orleans Parish Schoolboard, La.App.1945, 21 So.2d 895 (compulsory disclosure of war work and other outside activities on part of schoolteacher).

90. Meetze v. Associated Press, 1956, 230 S.C. 330, 95 S.E.2d 606.

91. Stryker v. Republic Pictures Corp., 1951, 108 Cal.App.2d 191, 238 P.2d 670; Continental Optical Co. v. Reed, 1949, 119 Ind.App. 643, 86 N.E.2d 306, rehearing denied 119 Ind.App. 643, 88 N.E.2d 55. Accord: Thompson v. Curtis Pub. Co., 3 Cir. 1952, 193 F.2d 953 (patent obtained by plaintiff); Lang-

which are a matter of public record, and open to public inspection.[92] It seems to be generally agreed that anything visible in a public place can be recorded and given circulation by means of a photograph, to the same extent as by a written description, since this amounts to nothing more than giving publicity to what is already public and what anyone present would be free to see.[93] The contention[94] that when an individual is thus singled out from the public scene and undue attention is focused upon him, there is an invasion of his private rights, has not been borne out by the decisions.[95] On the other hand, it is clear that when a picture is taken without the plaintiff's consent in a private place,[96] or one already made is stolen,[97] or obtained by bribery or other inducement of breach of trust,[98] the plaintiff's appearance which is thus made public is still a private thing, and there is an invasion of a private right, for which an action will lie.

The final limitation is that the matter made public must be one which would be offensive and objectionable to a reasonable man of ordinary sensibilities.[1] The law is not for the protection of the hypersensitive, and all of us must, to some reasonable extent, lead lives exposed to the public gaze. Anyone who is not a hermit must expect the more or less casual observation of his neighbors and the passing public as to what he is and does, and some reporting of his daily activities. The ordinary reasonable man does not take offense at mention in a newspaper of the fact that he has returned home from a visit, or gone camping in the woods, or given a party at his house for his friends. It is quite a different matter when the details of sexual relations are spread before the public eye,[2] or there is highly personal portrayal

ford v. Vanderbilt University, 1956, 199 Tenn. 389, 287 S.W.2d 32 (pleading filed in lawsuit); Johnson v. Scripps Pub. Co., Ohio Com.Pl.1940, 6 Ohio Supp. 13 (signature on nominating petition).

92. Hubbard v. Journal Pub. Co., 1962, 69 N.M. 473, 368 P.2d 147 (court record); Bell v. Courier-Journal & Louisville Times Co., Ky.1966, 402 S.W.2d 84 (tax delinquency); cf. Rome Sentinel Co. v. Boustedt, 1964, 43 Misc.2d 598, 252 N.Y.S.2d 10 (death certificate); Lamont v. Commissioner of Motor Vehicles, S.D.N.Y.1967, 269 F.Supp. 880, affirmed 386 F.2d 449, cert. denied 391 U.S. 915 (motor vehicle registration records).

Otherwise where the record is not an open one. Maysville Transit Co. v. Ort, 1944, 296 Ky. 524, 177 S.W.2d 369 (income tax returns); Munzer v. Blaisdell, 1944, 183 Misc. 777, 49 N.Y.S.2d 919, affirmed 1945, 269 App.Div. 970, 58 N.Y.S.2d 360 (records of mental institution); Patterson v. Tribune Co., Fla. App.1962, 146 So.2d 623 (progress records of narcotic addict). Cf. Sellers v. Henry, Ky.1959, 329 S.W.2d 214 (police photograph).

93. Gill v. Hearst Pub. Co., 1953, 40 Cal.2d 224, 253 P.2d 441 (plaintiff embracing his wife in market place); Humiston v. Universal Film Mfg. Co., 1919, 189 App.Div. 467, 178 N.Y.S. 752 (street); Berg v. Minneapolis Star & Tribune Co., D.Minn.1948, 79 F.Supp. 957 (courtroom); Gautier v. Pro-Football, Inc., 1952, 304 N.Y. 354, 107 N.E.2d 485 (football game); Jacova v. Southern Radio & Television Co., Fla.1955, 83 So.2d 34 (cigar store raid). The parent case is Sports & General Press Agency v. "Our Dogs" Pub. Co., [1916] 2 K.B. 880.

94. See Note, 1958, 44 Va.L.Rev. 1303.

95. There is one decision to that effect, Blumenthal v. Picture Classics, 1932, 235 App.Div. 570, 257 N. Y.S. 800, affirmed, 1933, 261 N.Y. 504, 185 N.E. 713. It was, however, later explained upon the basis of the introduction of an element of fiction into the accompanying narrative. Sarat Lahiri v. Daily Mirror, 1937, 162 Misc. 776, 295 N.Y.S. 382.

96. Barber v. Time, Inc., 1942, 348 Mo. 1199, 159 S. W.2d 291 (hospital bed); cf. Clayman v. Bernstein, 1940, 38 Pa.D. & C. 543 (picture of semi-conscious patient taken by physician).

97. Peed v. Washington Times, D.C.1927, 55 Wash.L. Rep. 182. This was conceded in Metter v. Los Angeles Examiner, 1939, 35 Cal.App.2d 304, 95 P.2d 491, but the court refused to permit the obvious conclusion from the evidence.

98. Bazemore v. Savannah Hospital, 1930, 171 Ga. 257, 155 S.E. 194; Douglas v. Stokes, 1912, 149 Ky. 506, 149 S.W. 849.

1. Reed v. Real Detective Pub. Co., 1945, 63 Ariz. 294, 162 P.2d 133; Davis v. General Finance & Thrift Corp., 1950, 80 Ga.App. 708, 57 S.E.2d 225; Gill v. Hearst Pub. Co., 1953, 40 Cal.2d 224, 253 P.2d 441; Samuel v. Curtis Pub. Co., N.D.Cal.1954, 122 F.Supp. 327; Meetze v. Associated Press, 1956, 230 S.C. 330, 95 S.E.2d 606. Cf. Hamilton v. Crown Life Ins. Co., 1967, 246 Or. 1, 423 P.2d 771.

2. Garner v. Triangle Publications, S.D.N.Y.1951, 97 F.Supp. 546. Cf. Myers v. U. S. Camera Pub. Corp., 1957, 9 Misc.2d 765, 167 N.Y.S.2d 771; Fee-

of his intimate private characteristics or conduct.[3] The outstanding decision in this area is Sidis v. F–R Pub. Corp.,[4] where a magazine revived the history of a former infant mathematical prodigy, and described his present whereabouts and activities, and it was held that there was nothing in this which would be objectionable to any normal person. The case, when compared with Melvin v. Reid,[5] with its revelation of the past of a prostitute and a murder defendant, suggests something in the nature of a "mores" test,[6] under which there will be liability only for publicity given to those things which the customs and ordinary views of the community would regard as highly objectionable.

False Light in the Public Eye

The third form of invasion of privacy consists of publicity which places the plaintiff in a false light in the public eye.[7] It seems to have made its first appearance in 1816, when Lord Byron succeeded in enjoining the circulation of a bad poem which had been attributed to his pen.[8] Over a good many years the principle made a rather nebulous appearance in a line of decisions[9] in which falsity or fiction was held to defeat the privilege of reporting news or other matters of public interest. It is only in late years that it has begun to receive independent recognition of its own.

One form in which it occasionally appears, as in Byron's case, is that of publicly attributing to the plaintiff some opinion or utterance, such as spurious books or articles,[10] or the unauthorized use of his name on a petition,[11] or as a candidate for office,[12] or to advertise for witnesses to an accident,[13] or the entry of an actor, without his consent, in a popularity contest of an embarrassing kind,[14] or filing suit in the plaintiff's name without authorization.[15]

Another form in which it frequently appears is the use of the plaintiff's picture to illustrate a book or an article with which he has no reasonable connection, with the implication that such a connection exists—as where, for example, the face of an honest taxi driver is used to ornament a story about

ney v. Young, 1920, 191 App.Div. 501, 181 N.Y.S. 481; Banks v. King Features Syndicate, S.D.N.Y. 1939, 30 F.Supp. 352.

3. Cason v. Baskin, 1944, 155 Fla. 198, 20 So.2d 243; second appeal, 1947, 159 Fla. 31, 30 So.2d 635. Cf. Stryker v. Republic Pictures Corp., 1951, 108 Cal. App.2d 191, 238 P.2d 670.

4. 2 Cir. 1940, 113 F.2d 806, affirming S.D.N.Y.1938, 34 F.Supp. 19.

5. 1931, 112 Cal.App. 285, 297 P. 91.

6. Suggested by the lower court in Sidis v. F–R Pub. Corp., S.D.N.Y.1938, 34 F.Supp. 19, affirmed, 2 Cir. 1940, 113 F.2d 806, cert. denied, 311 U.S. 711.

7. See, generally, Wade, Defamation and the Right of Privacy, 1962, 15 Vand.L.Rev. 1093; Note, 1962, 50 Cal.L.Rev. 357.

8. Lord Byron v. Johnston, 1816, 2 Mer. 29, 35 Eng. Rep. 851.

9. See infra, p. 826.

10. D'Altomonte v. New York Herald Co., 1913, 154 App.Div. 453, 139 N.Y.S. 200, modified, as not within the New York statute in 1913, 208 N.Y. 596, 102 N.E. 1101; Goldberg v. Ideal Pub. Corp., Sup.Ct. 1960, 210 N.Y.S.2d 928; Hogan v. A. S. Barnes & Co., Pa.C.P.1957, 114 U.S.P.Q. 314; cf. Kerby v. Hal Roach Studios, 1942, 53 Cal.App.2d 207, 127 P.2d 577. See Wigmore, The Right Against False Attribution of Belief or Utterance, 1916, 4 Ky.L.J.No. 8, p. 3.

Compare, as to the use of fictitious testimonials in advertising, Pavesich v. New England Life Ins. Co., 1905, 122 Ga. 190, 50 S.E. 68; Manger v. Kree Institute of Electrolysis, Inc., 2 Cir. 1956, 233 F.2d 5; Foster-Milburn Co. v. Chinn, 1909, 134 Ky. 424, 120 S.W. 364; Fairfield v. American Photocopy Equipment Co., 1955, 138 Cal.App.2d 82, 291 P.2d 194.

11. Schwartz v. Edrington, 1913, 133 La. 235, 62 So. 660. Accord, Hinish v. Meier & Frank Co., 1941, 166 Or. 482, 113 P.2d 438 (telegram to governor urging him to veto a bill).

12. State ex rel. La Follette v. Hinkle, 1924, 131 Wash. 86, 229 P. 317; Battaglia v. Adams, Fla. 1964, 164 So.2d 195.

13. Hamilton v. Lumbermen's Mut. Cas. Co., La.App. 1955, 82 So.2d 61, appeal transferred, 1955, 226 La. 644, 76 So.2d 916.

14. Marks v. Jaffa, 1893, 6 Misc. 290, 26 N.Y.S. 908.

15. Steding v. Battistoni, 1964, 3 Conn.Cir. 96, 208 A.2d 559.

the cheating propensities of taxi drivers in the city.[16] Still another is the inclusion of the plaintiff's name, photograph or fingerprints in a public "rogue's gallery" of convicted criminals, when he has not in fact been convicted of any crime.[17]

The false light need not necessarily be a defamatory one,[18] although it very often is,[19] so that a defamation action will also lie. It seems clear, however, that it must be something that would be objectionable to the ordinary reasonable man under the circumstances, and that, as in the case of disclosure,[20] the hypersensitive individual will not be pro-

tected.[21]   Thus minor and unimportant errors in an otherwise accurate biography, as to dates and places, and incidents of no significance, do not entitle the subject of the book to recover,[22] nor does the erroneous description of the plaintiff as a cigarette girl when an inquiring photographer interviews her on the street.[23] Again, in all probability, something of a "mores" test must be applied.

There has been a good deal of overlapping of defamation in the false light cases, and it seems clear that either action, or both, will very often lie. The privacy cases do go considerably beyond the narrow limits of defamation, and no doubt have succeeded in affording a needed remedy in a good many instances not covered by the other tort. But the question may well be raised, and is still unanswered, whether this branch of the tort is not capable of swallowing up and engulfing the whole law of defamation; and whether there is any false libel printed, for example, in a newspaper, which cannot be redressed upon the alternative ground. There has as yet been little consideration [24] of how far the

---

16. Peay v. Curtis Pub. Co., D.C.D.C.1948, 78 F.Supp. 305. Accord: Valerni v. Hearst Magazines, Sup. Ct.1949, 99 N.Y.S.2d 866 (similar as to waiters); Leverton v. Curtis Pub. Co., 3 Cir. 1951, 192 F.2d 974 (negligence of children); Gill v. Curtis Pub. Co., 1952, 38 Cal.2d 273, 239 P.2d 630 (profane love); Martin v. Johnson Pub. Co., Sup.Ct.1956, 157 N.Y.S. 2d 409 ("man hungry" women); Metzger v. Dell Pub. Co., 1955, 207 Misc. 182, 136 N.Y.S.2d 888 (juvenile delinquents). As to pertinent and appropriate illustrations, see infra, p. 826.

17. Itzkovitch v. Whitaker, 1950, 115 La. 479, 39 So. 499; see Downs v. Swann, 1909, 111 Md. 53, 73 A. 653; State ex rel. Mavity v. Tyndall, 1946, 224 Ind. 364, 66 N.E.2d 755; Norman v. City of Las Vegas, 1947, 64 Nev. 38, 177 P.2d 442.

Distinguish the use of the picture for identification before trial, or after conviction. Hodgeman v. Olsen, 1915, 86 Wash. 615, 150 P. 1122; Bartletta v. McFeeley, 1930, 107 N.J.Eq. 141, 152 A. 17, affirmed, 1931, 109 N.J.Eq. 241, 156 A. 658; cf. McGovern v. Van Riper, 1945, 136 N.J.Eq. 24, 43 A.2d 514, affirmed, 1946, 137 N.J.Eq. 548, 45 A.2d 842 (fingerprints).

18. See Zolich, Laudatory Invasion of Privacy, 1967, 16 Clev.Marsh.L.Rev. 540.

19. Bennett v. Norban, 1959, 396 Pa. 94, 151 A.2d 476 (public accusation of theft); Linehan v. Linehan, 1955, 134 Cal.App.2d 250, 285 P.2d 326 (public statement plaintiff not a lawful wife); D'Altomonte v. New York Herald Co., 1913, 154 App.Div. 453, 139 N.Y.S. 200, modified, 1913, 208 N.Y. 596, 102 N.E. 1101 (imputing authorship of absurd story); Martin v. Johnson Pub. Co., Sup.Ct.1956, 157 N.Y.S.2d 409 ("man hungry" women); Russell v. Marboro Books, 1959, 18 Misc.2d 166, 183 N.Y.S.2d 8 (picture used in bawdy advertisement).

20. See supra, p. 809.

21. Carlisle v. Fawcett Publications, Inc., 1962, 201 Cal.App.2d 733, 20 Cal.Rptr. 405. In Strickler v. National Broadcasting Co., S.D.Cal.1958, 167 F. Supp. 68, it was left to the jury whether fictitious details of plaintiff's conduct in an airplane crisis, as portrayed in a broadcast, would be objectionable to a reasonable man.

22. Koussevitzky v. Allen, Towne & Heath, 1947, 188 Misc. 479, 68 N.Y.S.2d 779, affirmed, 1947, 272 App. Div. 759, 69 N.Y.S.2d 432. Cf. Carlisle v. Fawcett Publications, Inc., 1962, 201 Cal.App.2d 733, 20 Cal. Rptr. 405.

23. Middleton v. News Syndicate Co., 1937, 162 Misc. 516, 295 N.Y.S. 120. Accord: Molony v. Boy Comics Publishers, 1950, 277 App.Div. 166, 98 N.Y.S.2d 119; Reardon v. News-Journal Co., 1960, 3 Storey, Del., 29, 164 A.2d 263; Werner v. Times-Mirror Co., 1961, 193 Cal.App.2d 111, 14 Cal.Rptr. 208. It would appear, however, that this was carried entirely too far in Jones v. Herald Post Co., 1929, 230 Ky. 227, 18 S.W.2d 972, where in an account of the murder of plaintiff's husband false and sensational statements were attributed to her, that she had fought with the criminals, and would have killed them if she could.

24. Wade, Defamation and the Right of Privacy, 1962, 15 Vand.L.Rev. 1093, is a very thoughtful,

numerous restrictions and limitations which have hedged defamation about for so many years, in part as a matter of historical survival and in part in the interest of freedom of the press and the discouragement of trivial and extortionate claims, can be by-passed by bringing the other action. Certainly this is possible as to the requirement of proof of special damages in cases of libel per quod and most kinds of slander,[25] and apparently as to such matters as the applicable statute of limitations,[26] survival of the action,[27] and a statute requiring the plaintiff to file a bond for costs.[28] On the other hand, it has been held that the single publication rule applies to privacy as well as defamation,[29] and that a retraction statute specifying only defamation applies to both if the matter published is defamatory.[30] The plaintiff cannot, of course, recover double damages for the one publication.[31]

Common Features

It is evident that these four forms of invasion of privacy are distinct, and based on different elements. It is the failure to recognize this which has been responsible for much of the apparent confusion in the decisions.[32] Taking them in order—intrusion disclosure, false light, and appropriation— the first and second require the invasion of something secret, secluded or private pertaining to the plaintiff; the third and fourth do not. The second and third depend upon publicity, while the first does not, nor does the fourth, although it usually involves it. The third requires falsity or fiction; the other three do not. The fourth involves a use for the defendant's advantage, which is not true of the rest.

There has nevertheless been a good deal of consistency in the rules that have been applied to the four disparate torts under the common name. As to any of the four, it is agreed that the plaintiff's right is a personal one, which does not extend to members of his family,[33] unless, as is obviously possible,[34] their own privacy is invaded along with

---

acute and penetrating attempt at analysis and prediction. Thus far it stands alone.

25. Norris v. Moskin Stores, Inc., 1961, 272 Ala. 174, 132 So.2d 321; Sutherland v. Kroger Co., 1959, 144 W.Va. 673, 110 S.E.2d 716; Fairfield v. American Photocopy Equipment Co., 1955, 138 Cal.App.2d 82, 291 P.2d 194; Flake v. Greensboro News Co., 1938, 212 N.C. 780, 195 S.E. 55; Reed v. Real Detective Pub. Co., 1945, 63 Ariz. 294, 162 P.2d 133.

26. Hazlitt v. Fawcett Publications, D.Conn.1953, 116 F.Supp. 538; Annerino v. Dell Pub. Co., 1958, 17 Ill.App.2d 205, 149 N.E.2d 761; Hull v. Curtis Pub. Co., 1956, 182 Pa.Super. 86, 125 A.2d 644. See also Fouts v. Fawcett Publications, Inc., D.Conn.1953, 116 F.Supp. 535; and cf. Frith v. Associated Press, E.D.S.C.1959, 176 F.Supp. 671.

27. Reed v. Real Detective Pub. Co., 1945, 63 Ariz. 294, 162 P.2d 133.

28. Grimes v. Carter, 1966, 241 Cal.App.2d 694, 50 Cal.Rptr. 808.

29. Fouts v. Fawcett Publications, Inc., D.Conn.1953, 116 F.Supp. 535, 537; and see Hazlitt v. Fawcett Publications, D.Conn.1953, 116 F.Supp. 538. The Uniform Single Publications Act by its terms includes privacy as well as defamation actions. See Hull v. Curtis Pub. Co., 1956, 182 Pa.Super. 86, 125 A.2d 644.

30. Werner v. Times-Mirror Co., 1961, 193 Cal.App.2d 111, 14 Cal.Rptr. 208. See also Kapellas v. Kofman, 1969, 1 Cal.3d 20, 81 Cal.Rptr. 360, 459 P.2d 912.

31. Brink v. Griffith, 1964, 65 Wash.2d 253, 396 P.2d 793. See Note, 1966, 41 Wash.L.Rev. 370.

32. See Biggs, J., in Ettore v. Philco Television Broadcasting Co., 3 Cir. 1956, 229 F.2d 481, cert. denied 351 U.S. 926, describing the present state of the law of privacy as "still that of a haystack in a hurricane."

33. Murray v. Gast Lithographic & Engraving Co., 1894, 8 Misc. 36, 28 N.Y.S. 271, affirmed, 1895, 10 Misc. 365, 31 N.Y.S. 17; Rozhon v. Triangle Publications, 7 Cir. 1956, 230 F.2d 359; Waters v. Fleetwood, 1956, 212 Ga. 161, 91 S.E.2d 344; Bremmer v. Journal-Tribune Pub. Co., 1956, 247 Iowa 817, 76 N.W.2d 762; Kelly v. Johnson Pub. Co., 1958, 160 Cal.App.2d 718, 325 P.2d 659. See Note, 1966, 21 Rut.L.Rev. 74.

34. Walker v. Whittle, 1951, 83 Ga.App. 445, 64 S. E.2d 87; see Coverstone v. Davies, 1952, 38 Cal.2d 315, 239 P.2d 876, cert. denied, 1952, Mock v. Davies, 344 U.S. 840; Smith v. Doss, 1948, 251 Ala. 250, 37 So.2d 118; and cf. Bazemore v. Savannah Hospi-

his. The right is not assignable,[35] and while the cause of action may [36] or may not [37] survive after his death, according to the survival rules of the particular state, there is no common law right of action for a publication concerning one who is already dead.[38]

The statutes of Oklahoma, Utah, and Virginia,[39] however, expressly provide for such an action. It seems to be generally agreed that the right of privacy is one pertaining only to individuals, and that a corporation [40] or a partnership [41] cannot claim it as such, although either may have an exclusive right to the use of its name, which may be protected upon some other basis such as that of unfair competition.[42]

So far as damages are concerned, there is general agreement that the plaintiff need not plead or prove special damages,[43] and that in this respect the action resembles one for libel or slander per se. The difficulty of measuring damages is no more reason for denying relief here than in a defamation action.[44] If there is evidence of special damage, such as resulting illness, or unjust enrichment of the defendant,[45] or harm to the plaintiff's own commercial interests,[46] it can be recovered. Punitive damages can be awarded upon the same basis as in other torts, where a wrongful motive or state of mind appears,[47] but not in cases where the defendant has acted innocently, as for example in the belief that the plaintiff has given his consent.[48]

tal, 1930, 171 Ga. 257, 155 S.E. 194; Douglas v. Stokes, 1912, 149 Ky. 506, 149 S.W. 849.

35. Hanna Mfg. Co. v. Hillerich & Bradsby Co., 5 Cir. 1939, 78 F.2d 763; Murray v. Gast Lithographic & Engraving Co., 1894, 8 Misc. 36, 28 N.Y.S. 271; Rhodes v. Sperry & Hutchinson Co., 1908, 193 N.Y. 223, 85 N.E. 1097, affirmed, 1911, 220 U.S. 502; cf. Von Thodorovich v. Franz Josef Beneficial Ass'n, E.D.Pa.1907, 154 F. 911.

36. Reed v. Real Detective Pub. Co., 1945, 63 Ariz. 294, 162 P.2d 133.

37. Wyatt v. Hall's Portrait Studios, Sup.Ct.1911, 71 Misc. 199, 128 N.Y.S. 247; Lunceford v. Wilcox, N.Y.City Ct.1949, 88 N.Y.S.2d 225.

38. Maritote v. Desilu Productions, Inc., 7 Cir. 1965, 345 F.2d 418, cert. denied 382 U.S. 883; Ravellette v. Smith, 7 Cir. 1962, 300 F.2d 854; Bradley v. Cowles Magazines, Inc., 1960, 26 Ill.App.2d 331, 168 N.E.2d 64; Gruschus v. Curtis Pub. Co., 10 Cir. 1965, 342 F.2d 775; Abernethy v. Thornton, 1955, 263 Ala. 496, 83 So.2d 235. See Notes, 1966, 21 Rut. L.Rev. 74; 1966, 51 Iowa L.Rev. 786; 1965, 40 Notre Dame L. 324; 1963, 30 U.Chi.L.Rev. 722.

39. Okla.Stat.Ann.1958, tit. 21, §§ 839–40; Utah Code Ann.1953, §§ 76–4–8 and 76–4–9; Va.Code Ann.1957, § 8–650. See Donahue v. Warner Bros. Pictures, 10 Cir. 1952, 194 F.2d 6; Donahue v. Warner Bros. Pictures Dist. Corp., 1954, 2 Utah 2d 256, 272 P.2d 177.

40. University of Notre Dame du Lac v. Twentieth Century-Fox Film Corp., 1965, 22 App.Div.2d 452, 256 N.Y.S.2d 301; Maysville Transit Co. v. Ort, 1944, 296 Ky. 524, 177 S.W.2d 369; Shubert v. Columbia Pictures Corp., 1947, 189 Misc. 734, 72 N.Y. S.2d 851, affirmed 274 App.Div. 751, 80 N.Y.S.2d 724, appeal denied 274 App.Div. 80, 83 N.Y.S.2d 233.

41. Rosenwasser v. Ogoglia, 1916, 172 App.Div. 107, 158 N.Y.S. 56.

42. Vassar College v. Loose-Wiles Biscuit Co., W.D. Mo.1912, 197 F. 982.

43. Reed v. Real Detective Pub. Co., 1945, 63 Ariz. 294, 162 P.2d 133; Fairfield v. American Photocopy Equipment Co., 1955, 138 Cal.App.2d 82, 291 P.2d 194; Cason v. Baskin, 1945, 155 Fla. 198, 20 So.2d 243; Pavesich v. New England Life Ins. Co., 1905, 122 Ga. 190, 50 S.E. 68; Flake v. Greensboro News Co., 1938, 212 N.C. 780, 195 S.E. 55.

44. Brents v. Morgan, 1927, 221 Ky. 765, 299 S.W. 967; Rhodes v. Graham, 1951, 238 Ky. 225, 37 S.W. 2d 46; Hinish v. Meier & Frank Co., 1941, 166 Or. 482, 113 P.2d 438; Fairfield v. American Photocopy Equipment Co., 1955, 138 Cal.App.2d 82, 291 P.2d 194.

45. Bunnell v. Keystone Varnish Co., 1938, 254 App. Div. 885, 5 N.Y.S.2d 415 (statute).

46. Continental Optical Co. v. Reed, 1949, 119 Ind. App. 643, 86 N.E.2d 306, rehearing denied, 1949, 119 Ind.App. 643, 88 N.E.2d 55; Manger v. Kree Institute of Electrolysis, 2 Cir. 1956, 233 F.2d 5; Hogan v. A. S. Barnes & Co., Pa.C.P.1957, 114 U.S.P.Q. 314.

47. Munden v. Harris, 1911, 153 Mo.App. 652, 134 S. W. 1076; Hinish v. Meier & Frank Co., 1941, 166 Or. 482, 113 P.2d 438; Welsh v. Pritchard, 1952, 125 Mont. 517, 241 P.2d 816.

48. Fisher v. Murray M. Rosenberg, Inc., 1940, 175 Misc. 370, 23 N.Y.S.2d 677; Barber v. Time, Inc., 1942, 348 Mo. 1199, 159 S.W.2d 291.

Possible Expansion

Not long after 1950, the Supreme Court of the United States began, in cases of criminal prosecutions raising the question of improper actions of government officers, to talk of a Constitutional "right of privacy," which protected the individual against such acts.[49] These were cases of what might fairly be called intrusion;[50] but in Griswold v. Connecticut,[51] in 1965, the Court held unconstitutional a statute prohibiting the giving of contraceptive information, on the ground that it deprived married couples of a "right of privacy" guaranteed by the Constitution. The Court never has made any attempt to define this right, or to indicate its limitations, if any; and nothing in the decisions has referred to tort liability. They suggested none the less that the Constitutional right, thus declared to exist, must have some application to tort liability; and that the decisions in four states[52] denying any recognition of the right are to be overruled, as well as the limitation to commercial appropriation contained in the statutes of four other jurisdictions.[53]

The extension to liability in tort has already begun, with two cases,[54] both involving intrusion, where the decision went upon the Constitutional right. But the most significant decision may be that of a trial court in New York,[55] again involving intrusion in several forms, which held that the existence of the Constitutional privilege extended the liability beyond the cases of appropriation specified in the statute. While the appellate courts[56] went out the back door by holding that the case was governed by the law of the District of Columbia, which recognized the liability for intrusion, and therefore did not reach the Constitutional question, the decision in the trial court was not overruled, and may still be followed.

Coupled with the Constitutional issue, which is still obviously quite vague as to its scope and content, there has been discussion of possible expansion at common law, to include anything involving an "affront to human dignity"[57]—a concept sufficiently broad to include almost all personal torts, from assault and battery and false imprisonment through all insults, whether or not amounting to extreme outrage, defamation, and no doubt many others. Thus far no such expansion has occurred; and there is as yet no decided case allowing recovery which does not fall fairly within one of the four categories[58] with which the courts have thus far been concerned. This is not, of course, to say that it will not occur, either soon or at some more remote future date. For the present, all that can be said is that no such development has

49. Although preceded by Wolf v. People of the State of Colorado, 1949, 338 U.S. 25, the leading case of this type is Rochin v. California, 1952, 342 U.S. 165 where a stomach pump was used on a protesting individual accused of crime. See also Tehan v. United States ex rel. Shott, 1966, 382 U.S. 406, rehearing denied 383 U.S. 931; Beaney, The Constitutional Right to Privacy in the Supreme Court, [1962] Sup. Ct.Rev. 212; Long, The Right to Privacy: The Case Against the Government, 1965, 10 St.L.L.Rev. 1.

50. See supra, p. 807.

51. 1965, 381 U.S. 479. See Beaney, The Griswold Case and the Expanding Right to Privacy, [1966] Wis.L.Rev. 979; Symposium, 1965, 64 Mich.L.Rev. 197 Notes, 1966, 38 U.Colo.L.Rev. 267; [1966] Duke L.J. 562.

52. See supra, p. 804.

53. See supra, p. 804.

54. One is York v. Story, 9 Cir. 1963, 324 F.2d 450, cert. denied 376 U.S. 939, where police photographed plaintiff in the nude and circulated the picture. See Notes, 1964, 17 U.Fla.L.Rev. 146; 1966, 60 Nw.L. Rev. 813. The other is Dietemann v. Time, Inc., C.

D.Cal.1968, 284 F.Supp. 925, involving entry into plaintiff's home and unauthorized photographs.

55. Nader v. General Motors Corp., 1968, 57 Misc.2d 301, 292 N.Y.S.2d 514, affirmed 31 App.Div.2d 392, 298 N.Y.S.2d 137, affirmed 25 N.Y.2d 560, 307 N.Y. S.2d 647, 255 N.E.2d 765. See Note, 1969, 2 Creight.L.Rev. 354.

56. Nader v. General Motors Corp., 1969, 31 App. Div.2d 392, 298 N.Y.S.2d 137, affirmed in (1970) 25 N.Y.2d 560, 307 N.Y.S.2d 647, 255 N.E.2d 765.

57. See Bloustein, Privacy as an Aspect of Human Dignity, 1964, 39 N.Y.U.L.Rev. 962.

58. See supra, pp. 804–814.

as yet taken place, under either the Constitution or the common law.

Defenses

The invasion of the field of privacy by the Supreme Court has picked up and absorbed one of the chief defenses to a privacy action available at common law, namely, the privilege to report on and discuss public figures, and news. This is more conveniently considered in the next chapter,[59] in connection with the similar privilege as to defamation. There remain to be considered here a few other defenses at common law.

Chief among these is the plaintiff's consent to the invasion, which will bar his recovery as in the case of any other tort.[60] It may be given expressly or by conduct, such as posing for a picture with knowledge of the purposes for which it is to be used,[61] or industriously seeking publicity of the same kind.[62]

A gratuitous consent can be revoked at any time before the invasion;[63] but if the agreement is a matter of contract, it is normally irrevocable, and there is no liability for any publicity or appropriation within its terms.[64] But if the actual invasion goes beyond the contract, fairly construed, as for example by alteration of the plaintiff's picture,[65] or publicity differing materially in kind or in extent from that contemplated,[66] or exceeding the authorized duration,[67] there is liability. The statutes [68] all require that the consent be given in writing. The defendant's honest belief that he has the plaintiff's consent, when he has not, will go to mitigate punitive damages, but otherwise is not a defense.[69]

Other defenses have appeared only infrequently. Warren and Brandeis [70] thought that the action for invasion of privacy must be subject to any privilege which would justify the publication of libel or slander, reasoning that if there is a privilege to publish matter which is both false and defamatory, there must necessarily be the same privilege

59. See infra, ch. 21.

60. Grossman v. Frederick Bros. Acceptance Corp., Sup.Ct.1942, 34 N.Y.S.2d 785; Jenkins v. Dell Pub. Co., W.D.Pa.1956, 143 F.Supp. 952, affirmed, 3 Cir. 1958, 251 F.2d 447; Reitmeister v. Reitmeister, 2 Cir. 1947, 162 F.2d 691; Tanner-Brice Co. v. Sims, 1931, 174 Ga. 13, 161 S.E. 819; Volk v. Auto-Dine Corp., N.D.1970, 177 N.W.2d 525. This must be pleaded and proved as a defense. Porter v. American Tobacco Co., 1910, 140 App.Div. 871, 125 N.Y.S. 710.

61. Gill v. Hearst Pub. Co., 1953, 40 Cal.2d 224, 253 P.2d 441; Thayer v. Worcester Post Co., 1933, 284 Mass. 160, 187 N.E. 292; Wendell v. Conduit Machine Co., 1911, 74 Misc. 201, 133 N.Y.S. 758; Johnson v. Boeing Airplane Co., 1953, 175 Kan. 275, 262 P.2d 808.

62. O'Brien v. Pabst Sales Co., 5 Cir. 1941, 124 F.2d 167, cert. denied 315 U.S. 823; Gautier v. Pro-Football, Inc., 1952, 304 N.Y. 354, 107 N.E.2d 485. Cf. Schmieding v. American Farmers Mut. Ins. Co., D. Neb.1955, 138 F.Supp. 167 (failure to object).

63. Garden v. Parfumerie Rigaud, 1933, 151 Misc. 692, 271 N.Y.S. 187; State ex rel. La Follette v. Hinkle, 1924, 131 Wash. 86, 229 P. 317.

64. Lillie v. Warner Bros. Pictures, 1934, 139 Cal. App. 724, 34 P.2d 835; Long v. Decca Records, Sup.Ct.1947, 76 N.Y.S.2d 133; Fairbanks v. Winik, 1922, 119 Misc. 809, 198 N.Y.S. 299, reversed on other grounds, 1923, 206 App.Div. 449, 201 N.Y.S. 487; Marek v. Zanol Products Co., 1937, 298 Mass. 1, 9 N.E.2d 393; Johnson v. Boeing Airplane Co., 1953, 175 Kan. 275, 262 P.2d 808.

65. Cf. Manger v. Kree Institute of Electrolysis, 2 Cir. 1956, 233 F.2d 5 (letter); Myers v. Afro-American Pub. Co., 1938, 168 Misc. 429, 5 N.Y.S.2d 223, affirmed, 1938, 255 App.Div. 838, 7 N.Y.S.2d 662.

66. Ettore v. Philco Television Broadcasting Co., 3 Cir. 1956, 229 F.2d 481, cert. denied 351 U.S. 926; Sinclair v. Postal Tel. & Cable Co., Sup.Ct.1935, 72 N.Y.S.2d 841; Russell v. Marboro Books, 1959, 18 Misc.2d 166, 183 N.Y.S.2d 8; Smith v. WGN, Inc., 1964, 47 Ill.App.2d 183, 197 N.E.2d 482. In Sharman v. C. Schmidt & Sons, E.D.Pa.1963, 216 F.Supp. 401, the consent, not restricted, was held to extend to publication in beer advertising.

67. Colgate-Palmolive Co. v. Tullos, 5 Cir. 1955, 219 F.2d 617; McAndrews v. Roy, La.App.1961, 131 So. 2d 256. See Note, 1962, 8 Wayne L.Rev. 348.

68. Supra, p. 804.

69. Fisher v. Murray M. Rosenberg, Inc., 1940, 175 Misc. 370, 23 N.Y.S.2d 677; Barber v. Time, Inc., 1942, 348 Mo. 1199, 159 S.W.2d 291; Wilk v. Andrea Radio Corp., Sup.1960, 200 N.Y.S.2d 522, modified, 1961, 13 App.Div. 745, 216 N.Y.S.2d 662.

70. Warren and Brandeis, The Right to Privacy, 1890, 4 Harv.L.Rev. 193, 216.

to publish what is not defamatory, or true. There is still no reason to doubt this conclusion, since the absolute privilege of a witness,[71] or an executive officer in the performance of his duty,[72] as well as the qualified one to report public proceedings,[73] have been recognized. The qualified privilege of the defendant to protect or further his own legitimate interest has appeared in a few cases, as where a telephone company has been permitted to monitor calls,[74] or the defendant was allowed to make use of the plaintiff's name in insuring his life without his consent.[75] Unquestionably reasonable investigations of credit,[76] or of insurance claims[77] are privileged.

It has been held that where uncopyrighted literature is in the public domain, and the defendant is free to publish it, the name of the plaintiff may be used to indicate its authorship,[78] and that when the plaintiff has designed dresses for the defendant it is no invasion of his privacy to disclose his connection with the product in advertising.[79]

71. Application of Tiene, 1955, 19 N.J. 149, 115 A.2d 543.

72. Carr v. Watkins, 1962, 227 Md. 578, 177 A.2d 841; Sellers v. Henry, Ky.1959, 329 S.W.2d 214.

73. Reardon v. News-Journal Co., 1960, 3 Storey, Del. 29, 164 A.2d 263 (court); cf. Johnson v. Scripps Pub. Co., 1940, 16 Ohio App. 13 (filing nominating petition for office); Langford v. Vanderbilt University, 1956, 199 Tenn. 389, 287 S.W.2d 32 (pleadings in civil suit); Lyles v. State, Okl.Cr.1958, 330 P.2d 734 (television in courtroom); Blount v. T D Pub. Co., 1967, 77 N.M. 384, 423 P.2d 421 (news distributor not liable where no knowledge of the invasion).

74. Schmukler v. Ohio-Bell Tel. Co., Ohio C.P.1953, 116 N.E.2d 819. Accord: Thomas v. General Elec. Co., W.D.Ky.1962, 207 F.Supp. 792 (time and motion studies of employees); People v. Appelbaum, 1950, 277 App.Div. 43, 97 N.Y.S.2d 807, affirmed 301 N.Y. 738, 95 N.E.2d 410 (tapping own telephone to protect own interests); Wheeler v. P. Sorenson Mfg. Co., Ky.1967, 415 S.W.2d 582 (publication of wages and deductions of employees to combat drive by union); City of University Heights v. Conley, 1969, 20 Ohio Misc. 112, 252 N.E.2d 198 (spying on suspected thief).

75. Holloman v. Life Ins. Co. of Va., 1940, 192 S.C. 454, 7 S.E.2d 169.

76. Shorter v. Retail Credit Co., D.C.S.C.1966, 251 F. Supp. 329. See Note, 1969, 57 Geo.L.J. 509.

77. Tucker v. American Employers' Ins. Co., Fla. App.1965, 171 So.2d 437. See Alabama Elec. Co-op., Inc. v. Partridge, 1969, 284 Ala. 442, 225 So.2d 848; Forster v. Manchester, 1963, 410 Pa. 192, 189 A.2d 147; and cf. Bodrey v. Cape, 1970, 120 Ga.App. 859, 172 S.E.2d 643 (father deprived of custody of child investigating wife). See Note, 1964, 17 Vand. L.Rev. 1342.

78. Ellis v. Hurst, 1910, 70 Misc. 122, 128 N.Y.S. 144, affirmed, 1911, 145 App.Div. 918, 130 N.Y.S. 1110; Shostakovitch v. Twentieth-Century Fox Film Corp., 1948, 196 Misc. 67, 80 N.Y.S.2d 575, affirmed, 1949, 275 App.Div. 692, 87 N.Y.S.2d 430.

79. Brociner v. Radio Wire Television, Inc., 1959, 15 Misc.2d 843, 183 N.Y.S.2d 743.

CHAPTER 21

CONSTITUTIONAL PRIVILEGE

118. Constitutional Privilege.

118. CONSTITUTIONAL PRIVILEGE.

Prior to 1964 there had been occasional mention in the cases dealing with both defamation and privacy, of the guarantee of freedom of speech and of the press contained in the First Amendment to the Constitution of the United States. It was usually mentioned as an argument in support of a decision at common law holding that the particular conduct of the defendant was privileged. In 1964, in the famous case of New York Times Co. v. Sullivan,[1] the Supreme Court of the United States introduced something of a bombshell by holding that the First Amendment itself required the privilege. A series of subsequent decisions, in both the federal and the state courts, have resulted in taking over under the aegis of the Constitution a large area of privileges, and in the process considerably broadening them beyond the scope within which they had previously been recognized.[2] This is unquestionably the greatest victory won by the defendants in the modern history of the law of torts.

The background of the Sullivan case lay in the general recognition, at common law, of a qualified privilege in defamation actions, of what was called "fair comment" upon the conduct and qualifications of public officers[3] and public employees.[4] Unlike the privilege of complaint to officials,[5] this broader privilege extended to publication to the public in general of a matter of public concern.

While the existence of this privilege was undisputed, there was disagreement as to whether it was restricted to statements expressing only "comment" or opinion, as distinct from misstatements of fact. Some three-fourths of the state courts which considered the question held that the privilege of public discussion was limited to opinion, criticism and comment, and did not extend to any false assertion of fact.[6] The reason usually given was, that while men in public life must expect to be subjected to public comment, opinion and criticism, they were not to be made the victims of misrepresentation as to the facts without redress, lest de-

1. 1964, 376 U.S. 254, motion denied 376 U.S. 967. A parallel decision as to freedom of religion is Cimijotti v. Paulson, N.D. Iowa 1964, 230 F.Supp. 39, affirmed, 8 Cir. 1964, 340 F.2d 613 holding that the First Amendment confers an absolute privilege as to communications to the Catholic church.

2. See Pedrick, Freedom of the Press and the Law of Libel, 1964, 49 Corn.L.Q. 581; Berney, Libel and the First Amendment—A New Constitutional Privilege, 1965, 51 Va.L.Rev. 1; Meiklejohn, Public Speech and the First Amendment, 1967, 55 Geo.L.J. 234; Notes, 1964, 9 Vill.L.Rev. 534; 1964, 113 U.Pa.L.Rev. 284; 1965, 51 Va.L.Rev. 106; 1965, 12 U.C.L.A.L.Rev. 1420; 1965, 13 Kan.L.Rev. 399; 1965, 30 Mo.L.Rev. 457; 1965, 18 Vand.L.Rev. 1429; 1967, 14 U.C.L.A.L.Rev. 631.

3. Knapp v. Post Printing & Pub. Co., 1943, 111 Colo. 492, 144 P.2d 981; White v. Fletcher, Fla.1956, 90 So.2d 129; Everett v. California Teachers Ass'n, 1962, 208 Cal.App.2d 291, 25 Cal.Rptr. 120; Cartwright v. Herald Pub. Co., 1951, 220 S.C. 492, 68 S.E.2d 415; Morgan v. Bulletin Co., 1952, 369 Pa. 349, 85 A.2d 869.

4. See for example Hoeppner v. Dunkirk Printing Co., 1930, 254 N.Y. 95, 172 N.E. 139 (high school football coach).

5. See supra, p. 791.

6. Owens v. Scott Pub. Co., 1955, 46 Wash.2d 666, 284 P.2d 296, cert. denied 350 U.S. 968; A. S. Abell Co. v. Kirby, 1961, 227 Md. 267, 176 A.2d 340; Mencher v. Chesley, 1947, 297 N.Y. 94, 75 N.E.2d 257; Westropp v. E. W. Scripps Co., 1947, 148 Ohio St. 365, 74 N.E.2d 340; Murphy v. Farmers Ed. & Coop. Union of America, North Dakota Division, N.D.1955, 72 N.W.2d 636.

sirable candidates be deterred from seeking office, and the public interest suffer.[7]

There was a substantial,[8] and vigorous, minority view that even false statements of fact were privileged, if they were made for the public benefit with an honest belief in their truth, because the public interest demanded that those who are in a position to furnish information about public servants be not deterred by fear of suit, with the resulting necessity of proving the truth of what they say in court.[9] The "opinion" limitation proved to be a most unsatisfactory and unreliable one, difficult to draw in practice;[10] and there is nothing in the history of the position of the minority states to indicate that the rule in any way deterred candidates from seeking office.

The Sullivan case[11] arose out of a racial disturbance in Montgomery, Alabama. The New York Times published a paid advertisement, signed by a number of prominent individuals, complaining, among other things,

of the conduct of the police in dealing with the disturbance. Police Commissioner Sullivan brought an action for libel, alleging that he was personally defamed as one of the persons responsible. There were a few minor, and quite insignificant, misstatements of fact in the publication, only two of which[12] in any way reflected on the plaintiff. Alabama, however, was one of the states which limited the privilege of "fair comment" to opinion; and when the jury returned a verdict for the plaintiff in the amount of $500,000, the state supreme court affirmed the verdict and the judgment.

On certiorari the Supreme Court of the United States reversed, holding that the First Amendment conferred a qualified privilege upon the defendants, which was not limited to comment or opinion, and which extended to false statements of fact, provided that they were made without "malice," in the sense of knowledge that they were false, or reckless disregard of the truth. The theory of the decision was that the Constitution proceeds on the basis of free discussion of issues of public concern, and that "right conclusions are more likely to be gathered out of a multitude of tongues, than through any kind of authoritative selection."[13] The Court laid a good deal of stress upon the "pall of fear and timidity imposed upon those who would give voice to public criticism," and the "self-censorship" which would result from any other rule. Three of the Justices concurred,[14] but thought that the privilege should be an absolute one, regardless of "malice" or knowledge of falsity.

---

7. The leading case was probably Post Pub. Co. v. Hallam, 6 Cir. 1893, 59 F. 530. Accord: State Press Co. v. Willett, 1952, 219 Ark. 850, 245 S.W.2d 403; Bell Pub. Co. v. Garrett Eng. Co., 1943, 141 Tex. 51, 170 S.W.2d 197; Hubbard v. Allyn, 1908, 200 Mass. 166, 86 N.E. 356; Sherman v. International Publications, 1925, 214 App.Div. 437, 212 N. Y.S. 478.

8. Noel, Defamation of Public Officers and Candidates, 1949, 49 Col.L.Rev. 875, 896–7, lists twenty-six states with the majority view, and nine with the minority.

9. The leading case is Coleman v. MacLennan, 1908, 78 Kan. 711, 98 P. 281. Accord: Snively v. Record Pub. Co., 1921, 185 Cal. 565, 198 P. 1; Charles Parker Co. v. Silver City Crystal Co., 1955, 142 Conn. 605, 116 A.2d 440; Clancy v. Daily News Corp., 1938, 202 Minn. 1, 277 N.W. 264; Lafferty v. Houlihan, 1923, 81 N.H. 67, 121 A. 92.

10. See Titus, Statement of Fact Versus Statement of Opinion—A Spurious Dispute in Fair Comment, 1962, 15 Vand.L.Rev. 1203; Note, 1949, 62 Harv.L. Rev. 1207.

11. There is a good account of the case in Pierce, The Anatomy of an Historic Decision: New York Times Co. v. Sullivan, 1965, 43 N.C.L.Rev. 315. See also Notes, 1964, 113 U.Pa.L.Rev. 284; 1964, 31 Tenn.L.Rev. 504; 1966, 61 Nw.U.L.Rev. 614.

12. It was said that the police had "ringed" the college campus involved, whereas they were merely deployed near it in large numbers on three occasions. Also that Dr. Martin Luther King had been arrested seven times, whereas he had only been arrested four. The other misstatements of fact concerned the actions of the college authorities and others.

13. This was quoted from Judge Learned Hand, in United States v. Associated Press, S.D.N.Y.1943, 52 F.Supp. 362, 372, affirmed 326 U.S. 1; rehearing denied 326 U.S. 802, 803.

14. Justices Black, Douglas and Goldberg.

In another portion of the opinion, which has largely escaped comment, the Court intimated that finding personal defamation of the Police Commissioner in statements concerning the activities of the police, where there was not even "an oblique reference to him," was in itself an unconstitutional invasion of freedom of the press by the imposition of liability; and this was presently reaffirmed by the Court itself.[15]

The decision was promptly followed, and extended. The Supreme Court immediately applied it to prosecutions for criminal libel.[16] It was held by state courts to apply to candidates for public office,[17] and then to all public employees, no matter how inferior and lowly their station.[18] Two subsequent decisions of the Supreme Court reiterated the new requirement and definition of "malice," holding that actual ill will and a desire to do harm was not sufficient to defeat the privilege,[19] nor was mere negligence in publishing the defamation without verification;[20] and that it could be defeated only by the plaintiff's proof[21] of knowledge of falsity or reckless disregard of the truth.

It is certainly highly unfortunate that the Court chose to cling to the discredited term "malice," which has meant all things to all men,[22] and is here highly misleading. A much better word would have been "scienter," since the state of mind required is obviously the same as in deceit actions for intentional misrepresentation.[23] Where this is proved, there is no doubt that there can still be liability.[24] It can, of course, be proved by the circumstances,[25] as in the case of any other issue; and a failure to distinguish a mere assertion of opinion from others of fact may be sufficient to show reckless disregard of the truth.[26] But the addition of a personal motive is not enough,[27] nor is the use of extravagant language,[28] nor, as the Supreme

15. In Rosenblatt v. Baer, 1966, 383 U.S. 75.

16. Garrison v. Louisiana, 1964, 379 U.S. 64.

17. Noonan v. Rousselot, 1966, 239 Cal.App.2d 447, 48 Cal.Rptr. 817; Dyer v. Davis, La.App.1966, 189 So. 2d 678, writ refused 250 La. 533, 199 So.2d 79; Tilton v. Cowles Pub. Co., 1969, 76 Wash.2d 707, 459 P.2d 8. See Note, 1969, 71 W.Va.L.Rev. 360.

18. Rosenblatt v. Baer, 1966, 383 U.S. 75; Pape v. Time, Inc., 7 Cir. 1965, 354 F.2d 558, cert. denied 384 U.S. 909 (lieutenant of police); Tucker v. Kilgore, Ky.1965, 388 S.W.2d 112 (ordinary patrolman); Gilligan v. King, 1965, 48 Misc.2d 212, 264 N.Y.S.2d 309 (same), affirmed 29 App.Div.2d 935, 290 N.Y.S. 2d 1014; Reaves v. Foster, Miss.1967, 200 So.2d 453 (school principal); Krutech v. Schimmel, 27 App. Div.2d 837, 278 N.Y.S.2d 25 (part-time accountant for public waterworks).

19. Henry v. Collins, 1965, 380 U.S. 356, on remand 176 So.2d 891, two cases, 253 Miss. 34, 62. Accord, Rose v. Koch, 1967, 278 Minn. 235, 154 N.W.2d 409; Tagawa v. Maui Pub. Co., 1968, 50 Haw. 648, 448 P.2d 337.

20. St. Amant v. Thompson, 1968, 390 U.S. 727.

21. Fegley v. Morthimer, 1964, 204 Pa.Super. 54, 202 A.2d 125.

22. See supra, p. 772.

23. See supra, p. 700.

24. Varnish v. Boat Medium Pub. Co., 2 Cir. 1968, 405 F.2d 608, rehearing denied 395 U.S. 930; Fox v. Kahn, 1966, 421 Pa. 563, 221 A.2d 181, cert. denied 385 U.S. 935; see Note, 1969, Utah L.Rev. 118.

25. An important case on this is Goldwater v. Ginzburg, 2 Cir. 1969, 414 F.2d 324, cert. denied 396 U.S. 1049; rehearing denied 397 U.S. 978, where the negligence of the defendant was so gross as to permit an inference of reckless disregard of the truth. Keogh v. Pearson, D.C.D.C.1965, 244 F.Supp. 482 (implication from the face of the defamatory statement). Mahnke v. Northwest Publications, Inc., 1968, 280 Minn. 328, 160 N.W.2d 1 (failure to verify information from one known to have no first-hand knowledge).

26. Ragano v. Time, Inc., N.D.Fla.1969, 302 F.Supp. 1005.

27. Cabin v. Community Newspaper, Inc., 1966, 27 App.Div.2d 543, 275 N.Y.S.2d 396.

28. Chauffeurs, Teamsters and Helpers Local Union No. 795 v. Kansans for Right to Work, 1962, 189 Kan. 115, 368 P.2d 308. Compare, at common law, Brinkley v. Fishbein, 5 Cir. 1940, 110 F.2d 62, cert. denied 311 U.S. 672 ("charlatan"); Grower v. State, 1965, 23 App.Div.2d 506, 255 N.Y.S.2d 135 ("hoodlums"); and see Cherry v. Des Moines Leader, 1901, 114 Iowa 298, 86 N.W. 323 (the classic case of dramatic criticism); Dowling v. Livingstone, 1896, 108 Mich. 321, 66 N.W. 225.
"Mere exaggeration, slight irony or wit, and all those delightful touches of style which go to make an article readable, do not push beyond the limits of fair comment." Briarcliff Lodge Hotel v. Citizen-Sentinel Pub. Co., 1932, 260 N.Y. 106, 183 N.E. 193, 261

Court has explicitly held, mere negligence in making the statement without discovering the truth.[29]

One question upon which there has as yet been little discussion is the common law limitation that "fair comment" extends only to matters bearing upon the official conduct or fitness of the officer or candidate, and not to his purely private life or character as an individual.[30] It is obvious, of course, that in many instances the latter will have an obvious bearing upon the former; [31] but where it did not, it was held that the privilege did not extend to it. The rule appears to be an obviously reasonable one, and it may no doubt be expected to be taken over under the Constitution.

Matters of Public Concern

The common law privilege of "fair comment" in public discussion was not limited to officers and candidates, but extended to other matters of public concern, such as work to be paid for out of public funds,[32]

the admission or disbarment of attorneys,[33] and the management of institutions, such as schools,[34] charities,[35] and churches,[36] in which the public has a legitimate interest. Likewise any private enterprise,[37] to the extent that it begins to affect the general interests of the community, as by the distribution of food,[38] the pollution of the water supply,[39] quack medical services,[40] the promotion of race hatred,[41] the employment of a large

N.Y. 537, 185 N.E. 728. Accord, Cohen v. New York Herald Tribune, Inc., 1970, 63 Misc.2d 87, 310 N.Y. S.2d 709.

29. St. Amant v. Thompson, 1968, 390 U.S. 727; Ross v. News-Journal Co., Del.1967, 228 A.2d 531; Tagawa v. Maui Pub. Co., 1968, 50 Haw. 648, 448 P.2d 337.

30. Commonwealth v. Wardell, 1883, 136 Mass. 164; Post Pub. Co. v. Moloney, 1893, 50 Ohio St. 71, 33 N.E. 921; Sweeney v. Baker, 1878, 13 W.Va. 158. The distinction was apparently recognized in Monitor Patriot Co. v. Roy, 1971, —— U.S. ——, 91 S.Ct. 621.

31. Monitor Patriot Co. v. Roy, 1971, —— U.S. ——, 91 S.Ct. 621; Ocala Star-Banner Co. v. Damron, 1971, —— U.S. ——, 91 S.Ct. 628; State ex rel. Zorn v. Cox, 1927, 318 Mo. 112, 298 S.W. 837; Jones v. Express Pub. Co., 1927, 87 Cal.App. 246, 262 P. 78; Moynahan v. Waterbury Republican, 1918, 92 Conn. 331, 102 A. 653. Cf. Dressler v. Mayer, 1952, 22 N.J. Super. 129, 91 A.2d 650 (political conduct of candidate's wife).

32. Bailey v. Charleston Mail Assn., 1943, 126 W.Va. 292, 27 S.E.2d 837; Holway v. World Pub. Co., 1935, 171 Okl. 306, 44 P.2d 881; Yancey v. Gillespie, 1955, 242 N.C. 227, 87 S.E.2d 210; Grell v. Hoard, 1931, 206 Wis. 187, 239 N.W. 428; Bishop v. Wom-

etco Enterprises, Inc., Fla.App.1970, 235 So.2d 759 (preferential tax treatment).

33. Kennedy v. Item Co., 1941, 197 La. 1050, 3 So.2d 175; Spriggs v. Cheyenne Newspapers, 1947, 63 Wyo. 416, 182 P.2d 801.

34. O'Connor v. Sill, 1886, 60 Mich. 175, 27 N.W. 13, 28 N.W. 162; Clark v. McBaine, 1923, 299 Mo. 77, 252 S.W. 428; Hoeppner v. Dunkirk Printing Co., 1930, 254 N.Y. 95, 172 N.E. 139.

35. Cox v. Feeney, 1863, 4 F. & F. 13, 176 Eng.Rep. 552; Campbell v. Spottiswoode, 1863, 3 B. & S. 769, 122 Eng.Rep. 288.

36. Klos v. Zahorik, 1901, 113 Iowa 161, 84 N.W. 1046; Shurtleff v. Stevens, 1879, 51 Vt. 501; Kelly v. Tinling, 1865, L.R. 1 Q.B. 699.

37. The fact that the business deals with the public was not enough in itself to make it a matter of public concern. Atkinson v. Detroit Free Press Co., 1881, 46 Mich. 341, 9 N.W. 501 (lawyer); Tryon v. Evening News Ass'n, 1878, 39 Mich. 636 (reporter); Baker v. State, 1940, 199 Ark. 1005, 137 S.W.2d 938 (privately owned hospital); Wilson v. Fitch, 1871, 41 Cal. 363.

38. Hubbard v. Allyn, 1908, 200 Mass. 166, 86 N.E. 356; Schwarz Bros. Co. v. Evening News Pub. Co., 1913, 84 N.J.L. 486, 87 A. 148. Accord: Hahnemannian Life Ins. Co. v. Beebe, 1868, 48 Ill. 87 (insurance); Duffy v. New York Evening Post Co., 1905, 109 App.Div. 471, 96 N.Y.S. 629 (political leader); Flanagan v. Nicholson Pub. Co., 1915, 137 La. 588, 68 So. 964 (transfer of exhibition to another city); South Hetton Coal Co. v. North-Eastern News Assn., [1894] 1 Q.B. 133 (sanitary conditions in which two thousand people were housed).

39. Williams v. Standard-Examiner Pub. Co., 1933, 83 Utah 31, 27 P.2d 1. Cf. Mick v. American Dental Assn., 1958, 49 N.J.Super. 262, 139 A.2d 570 (fluoridation).

40. Brinkley v. Fishbein, 5 Cir. 1940, 110 F.2d 62. Cf. Blanchard v. Claremont Eagle, 1949, 95 N.H. 375, 62 A.2d 791 (inability to get medical treatment).

41. Beauharnais v. Pittsburgh Courier Pub. Co., 7 Cir. 1957, 243 F.2d 705.

number of people,[42] or the operation of a railroad,[43] was held to be a proper subject for such privileged comment.

No reason is apparent why the Constitutional privilege should not be extended to include all such matters of public concern; and in a few jurisdictions the expansion is already under way.[44] The outstanding case is a federal one,[45] in which the operation of a mail order clinical testing laboratory was held to affect the public interest; and quack medical service,[46] the operation of a charity,[47] the activities of party politicians,[48] and a national union election campaign [49] all have led to the same conclusion.

Public Figures and News

In 1967, in Time, Inc. v. Hill,[50] the Supreme Court extended the Constitutional privilege to include the tort of invasion of privacy. The background of the decision lay in the general recognition, at common law, of two closely related, and perhaps identical privileges, both founded upon the basic idea of freedom of the press.[51] One was the privilege of giving further publicity to already public figures; the other that of giving publicity to news, and other matters of public interest. The one primarily concerned the person to whom publicity was given; the other the event, fact or subject-matter in which he was involved. They were, however, obviously only different phases of the same thing, and in practice frequently became so merged as to be inseparable.[52]

A public figure has been defined as a person who, by his accomplishments, fame, or mode of living, or by adopting a profession or calling which gives the public a legitimate interest in his doings, his affairs, and his character, has become a "public personage." [53] He is, in other words, a celebrity. Obviously to be included in this category are those who have achieved some degree of reputation by appearing before the public, as in the case of an actor,[54] a professional baseball player,[55] a pugilist,[56] or any other entertainer.[57] The list is, how-

42. Charles Parker Co. v. Silver City Crystal Co., 1955, 142 Conn. 605, 116 A.2d 440.

43. Crane v. Waters, C.C.Mass.1882, 10 F. 619.

44. See Notes, 1966, 17 Hast.L.J. 347; 1966, 20 Rut. L.Rev. 390; 1967, 52 Corn.L.Q. 419.

45. United Medical Laboratories, Inc. v. Columbia Broadcasting System, Inc., 9 Cir. 1968, 404 F.2d 706, cert. denied 394 U.S. 921.

46. Farnsworth v. Tribune Co., 1969, 43 Ill.2d 286, 253 N.E.2d 408.

47. Murphy v. Daytona Beach Humane Society, Inc., Fla.App.1965, 176 So.2d 922.

48. McNabb v. Tennessean Newspapers, Inc., 1965, 55 Tenn.App. 380, 400 S.W.2d 871; News-Journal Co. v. Gallagher, Del.1967, 233 A.2d 166.

49. McKinnon v. Smith, 1966, 52 Misc.2d 349, 275 N. Y.S.2d 900, affirmed 32 App.Div. 615, 300 N.Y.S.2d 520.

50. 1967, 385 U.S. 374. There had been prior discussion of the problem in Franklin, Constitutional Problem in Privacy Protection: Legal Inhibitions on Reporting of Fact, 1963, 16 Stan.L.Rev. 107; Silver, Privacy and the First Amendment, 1966, 34 Ford.L.Rev. 553; Notes, 1967, 67 Col.L.Rev. 926; 1967, 45 Tex.L.Rev. 758.

51. See Note, 1953, 28 Ind.L.J. 180.

52. See for example Elmhurst v. Pearson, 1946, 80 U.S.App.D.C. 372, 153 F.2d 467; Martin v. Dorton, 1951, 210 Miss. 668, 50 So.2d 391; Stryker v. Republic Pictures Corp., 1951, 108 Cal.App.2d 191, 238 P.2d 670; Molony v. Boy Comics Publishers, 1950, 277 App.Div. 166, 98 N.Y.S.2d 119.

53. Cason v. Baskin, 1947, 159 Fla. 31, 30 So.2d 635, 638.

54. Paramount Pictures v. Leader Press, W.D.Okl. 1938, 24 F.Supp. 1004, reversed on other grounds, 10 Cir. 1939, 106 F.2d 229; Chaplin v. National Broadcasting Co., S.D.N.Y.1953, 15 F.R.D. 134.

55. Ruth v. Educational Films, 1920, 194 App.Div. 893, 184 N.Y.S. 948. Cf. O'Brien v. Pabst Sales Co., 5 Cir. 1941, 124 F.2d 167, cert. denied 315 U.S. 823.

56. Jeffries v. New York Evening Journal Pub. Co., 1910, 67 Misc. 570, 124 N.Y.S. 780; Cohen v. Marx, 1950, 94 Cal.App.2d 704, 211 P.2d 320; Oma v. Hillman Periodicals, 1953, 281 App.Div. 240, 118 N.Y.S. 2d 720.

57. Colyer v. Richard K. Fox Pub. Co., 1914, 162 App.Div. 297, 146 N.Y.S. 999 (high diver); Koussevitzky v. Allen, Towne & Heath, 1947, 188 Misc. 479, 68 N.Y.S.2d 779, affirmed, 1947, 272 App.Div. 759,

ever, broader than this. It includes public officers,[58] famous inventors [59] and explorers,[60] war heroes [61] and even ordinary soldiers,[62] an infant prodigy,[63] and no less a personage than the Grand Exalted Ruler of a lodge.[64] It includes, in short, anyone who has arrived at a position where public attention is focused upon him as a person.

Such public figures were held to have lost, to some extent at least, their right of privacy. Three reasons were given, more or less indiscriminately, in the decisions: that they had sought publicity and consented to it, and so could not complain when they received it; that their personalities and their affairs had already become public, and could no longer be regarded as their own private business; and that the press had a privilege, under the Constitution, to inform the public about those who have become legitimate matters of public interest. On one or another of these grounds, and sometimes all, it was held that there was no liability when they were given additional publicity, as to matters legitimately within the scope of the public interest they had aroused.

The privilege of giving publicity to news, and other matters of public interest, was held to arise out of the desire and the right of the public to know what is going on in the world, and the freedom of the press and other agencies of information to tell it. "News" includes all events and items of information which are out of the ordinary humdrum routine, and which have "that indefinable quality of information which arouses public attention." [65] To a very great extent the press, with its experience or instinct as to what its readers will want, has succeeded in making its own definition of news, as a glance at any morning newspaper will sufficiently indicate. It includes homicide [66] and other crimes,[67] arrests [68] and police raids,[69] suicides,[70] marriages [71] and divorces,[72]

69 N.Y.S.2d 432, appeal denied, 1947, 272 App.Div. 794, 71 N.Y.S.2d 712 (symphony conductor); Gavrilov v. Duell, Sloan & Pearce, Sup.Ct.1948, 84 N.Y.S. 2d 320, affirmed, 1950, 276 App.Div. 826, 93 N.Y.S. 2d 715 (dancer); Redmond v. Columbia Pictures Corp., 1938, 277 N.Y. 707, 14 N.E.2d 636 (trick shot golfer).

58. Martin v. Dorton, 1951, 210 Miss. 668, 50 So.2d 391 (sheriff); Hull v. Curtis Pub. Co., 1956, 182 Pa.Super. 86, 125 A.2d 644 (arrest by policeman).

59. Corliss v. E. W. Walker Co., D.Mass.1894, 64 F. 280.

60. Smith v. Suratt, 1926, 7 Alaska 416.

61. Stryker v. Republic Pictures Corp., 1951, 108 Cal.App.2d 191, 238 P.2d 670; cf. Molony v. Boy Comics Publishers, 1950, 277 App.Div. 166, 98 N.Y. S.2d 119 (heroic rescuer).

62. See Continental Optical Co. v. Reed, 1949, 119 Ind.App. 643, 86 N.E.2d 306, rehearing denied, 1949, 119 Ind.App. 643, 88 N.E.2d 55.

63. Sidis v. F–R Pub. Corp., 2 Cir. 1940, 113 F.2d 806, cert. denied 311 U.S. 711.

64. Wilson v. Brown, 1947, 189 Misc. 79, 73 N.Y.S.2d 587.

65. Sweenek v. Pathe News, E.D.N.Y.1936, 16 F.Supp. 746, 747. See Note, 1963, 30 U.Chi.L.Rev. 722.

66. Jones v. Herald Post Co., 1929, 230 Ky. 227, 18 S.W.2d 972; Bremmer v. Journal-Tribune Co., 1956, 247 Iowa 817, 76 N.W.2d 762; Waters v. Fleetwood, 1956, 212 Ga. 161, 91 S.E.2d 344; Jenkins v. Dell Pub. Co., W.D.Pa.1956, 143 F.Supp. 952, affirmed 3 Cir. 1958, 251 F.2d 447, cert. denied 357 U.S. 921; Bernstein v. National Broadcasting Co., D.D.C.1935, 129 F.Supp. 817, affirmed, 1956, 98 U.S.App.D.C. 112, 232 F.2d 369, cert. denied 352 U.S. 945.

67. Elmhurst v. Pearson, 1946, 80 U.S.App.D.C. 372, 153 F.2d 467 (sedition); Miller v. National Broadcasting Co., D.Del.1957, 157 F.Supp. 240 (robbery); Hillman v. Star Pub. Co., 1911, 64 Wash. 691, 117 P. 594 (mail fraud).

68. Frith v. Associated Press, E.D.S.C.1959, 176 F. Supp. 671; Coverstone v. Davies, 1952, 38 Cal.2d 315, 239 P.2d 876, cert. dismissed Mock v. Davies, 344 U.S. 840; Hull v. Curtis Pub. Co., 1956, 182 Pa.Super. 86, 125 A.2d 644.

69. Jacova v. Southern Radio & Television Co., Fla. 1955, 83 So.2d 34; cf. Schnabel v. Meredith, 1956, 378 Pa. 609, 107 A.2d 860.

70. Metter v. Los Angeles Examiner, 1939, 35 Cal. App.2d 304, 95 P.2d 491; Samuel v. Curtis Pub. Co., N.D.Cal.1954, 122 F.Supp. 327 (attempted).

71. Aquino v. Bulletin Co., 1959, 190 Pa.Super. 528, 154 A.2d 422.

72. Berg v. Minneapolis Star & Tribune Co., D.Minn. 1948, 79 F.Supp. 957; Aquino v. Bulletin Co., 1959, 190 Pa.Super. 528, 154 A.2d 422.

accidents,[73] a death from the use of narcotics,[74] a woman with a rare disease,[75] the birth of a child to a twelve year old girl,[76] the reappearance of one supposed to have been murdered years ago,[77] and undoubtedly many other similar matters of genuine, if more or less deplorable popular appeal.[78]

The privilege of enlightening the public was not, however, limited to the dissemination of news in the sense of current events. It extended also to information or education, or even entertainment and amusement,[79] by books, articles, pictures, films and broadcasts concerning interesting phases of human activity in general,[80] as well as the reproduction of the public scene in newsreels and travelogues.[81] In determining where to draw the line the courts were invited to exercise a species of censorship over what the public may be permitted to read; and they were understandably liberal in allowing the benefit of the doubt.

Caught up and entangled in this web of news and public interest were a great many people who had not sought publicity, but indeed, as in the case of any accused criminal, had tried assiduously to avoid it. They had nevertheless lost some part of their right of privacy. The misfortunes of the frantic victim of sexual assault,[82] the woman whose husband was murdered before her eyes,[83] or the innocent bystander who was caught in a raid on a cigar store and mistaken by the police for the proprietor,[84] could be broadcast to the world, and they had no remedy. Such individuals became public figures for a season; and "until they have reverted to the lawful and unexciting life led by the great bulk of the community, they are subject to the privileges which publishers have to satisfy the curiosity of the public as to their leaders, heroes, villains, and victims."[85] The privilege extended even to identification and some reasonable depiction of the individual's family,[86] although there must certainly be

73. Kelley v. Post Pub. Co., 1951, 327 Mass. 275, 98 N.E.2d 286; cf. Strickler v. National Broadcasting Co., S.D.Cal.1958, 167 F.Supp. 68.

74. Rozhon v. Triangle Publications, 7 Cir. 1956, 230 F.2d 359. Cf. Abernethy v. Thornton, 1955, 263 Ala. 496, 83 So.2d 235 (death of criminal paroled for federal offense).

75. See Barber v. Time, Inc., 1942, 348 Mo. 1199, 159 S.W.2d 291.

76. Meetze v. Associated Press, 1956, 230 S.C. 330, 95 S.E.2d 606.

77. Smith v. Doss, 1948, 251 Ala. 250, 37 So.2d 118.

78. Smith v. National Broadcasting Co., 1956, 138 Cal.App.2d 807, 292 P.2d 600 (report to police concerning escape of black panther); Themo v. New England Newspaper Pub. Co., 1940, 306 Mass. 54, 27 N.E.2d 753 (unspecified).

79. Ruth v. Educational Films, 1920, 194 App.Div. 893, 184 N.Y.S. 948 (baseball); Sweenek v. Pathe News, E.D.N.Y.1936, 16 F.Supp. 746 (group of fat women reducing with novel and comical apparatus) and see Jenkins v. Dell Pub. Co., W.D.Pa.1956, 143 F.Supp. 952, affirmed 3 Cir. 1958, 251 F.2d 447, cert. denied 357 U.S. 921.

80. Kline v. Robert M. McBride & Co., 1939, 170 Misc. 974, 11 N.Y.S.2d 674 (strike-breaking); Samuel v. Curtis Pub. Co., N.D.Cal.1954, 122 F.Supp. 327 (suicide); Hogan v. A. S. Barnes Co., Pa.C.P.1957, 114 U.S.P.Q. 314 (golf); Oma v. Hillman Periodicals, 1953, 281 App.Div. 240, 118 N.Y.S.2d 720 (boxing); Delinger v. American News Co., 1958, 6 App. Div.2d 1027, 178 N.Y.S.2d 231 (muscular development and verility).

81. Humiston v. Universal Film Mfg. Co., 1919, 189 App.Div. 467, 178 N.Y.S. 752. Accord: Gill v. Hearst Pub. Co., 1953, 40 Cal.2d 224, 253 P.2d 441; Berg v. Minneapolis Star & Tribune Co., D.Minn. 1948, 79 F.Supp. 957; Lyles v. State, Okl.Cr.1958, 330 P.2d 734.

82. Hubbard v. Journal Pub. Co., 1962, 69 N.M. 473, 368 P.2d 147.

83. Jones v. Herald Post Co., 1929, 230 Ky. 227, 18 S.W.2d 972.

84. Jacova v. Southern Radio & Television Co., Fla. 1955, 83 So.2d 34. Cf. Frith v. Associated Press, E.D.S.C.1959, 176 F.Supp. 671.

85. Restatement of Torts, § 867, Comment f.

86. Smith v. Doss, 1948, 251 Ala. 250, 37 So.2d 118 (family of man who disappeared, was believed murdered, and his body was brought home); Coverstone v. Davies, 1952, 38 Cal.2d 315, 239 P.2d 876, cert. denied Mock v. Davies, 344 U.S. 840 (father of boy arrested for "hot-rod" racing); Kelley v. Post Pub. Co., 1951, 327 Mass. 275, 98 N.E.2d 286 (parents of girl killed in accident); Aquino v. Bulletin Co., 1959, 190 Pa.Super. 528, 154 A.2d 422 (parents of girl secretly married and then divorced);

some limits as to their own private lives into which the publisher could not go.[87]

What was called for was some logical connection between the plaintiff and the matter of public interest. Perhaps the most extreme cases of the privilege were those in which the likeness of an individual were used to illustrate a book or an article on some general topic, rather than any specific event. Where this was appropriate and pertinent, as where the picture of a strike-breaker was used to illustrate a book on strike-breaking,[88] or that of a Hindu illusionist was employed to illustrate an article on the Indian rope trick,[89] it is held that there was no liability, since the public interest justified any invasion of privacy. On the other hand, where the illustration was not pertinent, and a connection was suggested which did not exist, as where the picture of a decent model appear-

ed in connection with an article on "man hungry" women,[90] the plaintiff was placed in a false light, and might recover on that basis.[91]

The Hill case,[92] which threw the privilege into the hands of the Supreme Court, involved the branch of invasion of privacy which consists of placing the plaintiff in a false light in the public eye.[93] The plaintiff's home had been invaded in 1952 by three escaped convicts, and he and his family had been held prisoners for nineteen hours. In 1953 a writer published a novel about the incident, in which he resorted to several elements of pure fiction; and later the novel was made into a play, which contained the same elements of fiction.[94] In 1955 Life Magazine published an article about the play, with pictures from it, which portrayed the play as a re-enactment of the actual experience of the Hill family, who were named. In an action under the New York statute, for invasion of privacy, the New York courts held that there was liability because of the false statements of fact.[95]

On certiorari, the analogy of defamation was manifest and persuasive; and the Supreme Court applied the rule of the Sullivan case, holding the misstatements of fact to be privileged unless it was found that they were made with knowledge of falsity or in reckless

---

Jenkins v. Dell Pub. Co., W.D.Pa.1956, 143 F.Supp. 952, affirmed 3 Cir. 1958, 251 F.2d 447, cert. denied 357 U.S. 921 (family of boy kicked to death by hoodlums).

87. This is indicated in Martin v. New Metropolitan Fiction, 1941, 139 Misc. 290, 248 N.Y.S. 359, affirmed, 1931, 234 App.Div. 904, 254 N.Y.S. 1015 and Shiles v. News Syndicate Co., 1970, —— N.Y.2d ——, 313 N.Y.S.2d 104, 261 N.E.2d 251.

88. People on Complaint of Stern v. Robert R. McBride & Co., 1936, 159 Misc. 5, 288 N.Y.S. 501; Kline v. Robert M. McBride & Co., 1939, 170 Misc. 974, 11 N.Y.S.2d 674. Cf. Klein v. McGraw-Hill, Inc., D.C.D.C.1966, 263 F.Supp. 919 (picture of high school student who had made important contribution used in radio textbook); LaForge v. Fairchild Publications, 1965, 23 App.Div.2d 636, 257 N.Y.S.2d 127 (picture of dressy individual used to illustrate article on current fashions).

89. Sarat Lahiri v. Daily Mirror, 1937, 162 Misc. 776, 295 N.Y.S. 382. Accord: Delinger v. American News Co., 1958, 6 App.Div.2d 1027, 178 N.Y.S.2d 231 (physical training instructor, article on relation between muscular development and virility); Dallessandro v. Henry Holt & Co., 1957, 4 App.Div.2d 470, 166 N.Y.S.2d 805, appeal dismissed 7 N.Y.2d 735, 193 N.Y.S.2d 635, 162 N.E.2d 726 (picture of plaintiff conversing with priest who was subject of the book); Oma v. Hillman Periodicals, 1953, 281 App. Div. 240, 118 N.Y.S.2d 720 (boxer, article on boxing); Gavrilov v. Duell, Sloan & Pierce, Sup.Ct. 1948, 84 N.Y.S.2d 320, affirmed, 1948, 276 App.Div. 826, 93 N.Y.S.2d 715 (dancer, book on dancing).

90. Martin v. Johnson Pub. Co., Sup.Ct.1956, 157 N. Y.S.2d 409. Accord, Peay v. Curtis Pub. Co., D. D.C.1948, 78 F.Supp. 305 (cheating taxi drivers).

91. Cf. Samuel v. Curtis Pub. Co., N.D.Cal.1954, 122 F.Supp. 327 (picture of plaintiff arguing with a would-be suicide on a bridge properly used to illustrate article on suicide), with Metzger v. Dell Pub. Co., 1955, 207 Misc. 182, 136 N.Y.S.2d 888 (picture of boy in slums improperly used to illustrate article on juvenile delinquency).

92. See supra, note 50.

93. See supra, p. 812.

94. Neither the novel nor the play named or in any way identified the Hill family, so that there was no action for invasion of privacy.

95. The last New York decision was Hill v. Hayes, 1965, 15 N.Y.2d 986, 260 N.Y.S.2d 7, 207 N.E.2d 604, amended 16 N.Y.2d 658, 261 N.Y.S.2d 289, 209 N.E. 2d 282, set aside Time, Inc. v. Hill, 385 U.S. 374.

disregard of the truth. By this decision, and others which followed it,[96] the two branches of invasion of privacy which turn on publicity [97] were taken over under the Constitutional privilege. The other two, however, are pretty clearly not. As at common law,[98] the celebrity can still undoubtedly complain of the appropriation of his name or likeness for purposes of advertising or the sale of a product,[99] and so can the man in the news.[1] And the Supreme Court decisions on intrusion [2] have made it clear that either has as much right as anyone else to be free from intrusion into his home or his bank account.[3]

The courts have carried over under the Constitution the rule of the common law,[4] that the "public figure" must have achieved that stature before there can be any privilege arising out of it, and that the defendant, by directing attention to one who is obscure and unknown, cannot himself create a public figure, or make him news.[5]

One troublesome question, upon which none of the cases dealing with the Constitutional privilege has yet touched, is that of the effect of lapse of time, during which the plaintiff has returned to obscurity. There can be no doubt that one quite legitimate function of the press is that of educating or reminding the public as to past history, and that the recall of former public figures, the revival of past events that one were news, can properly be a matter of present public interest. If it is only the event which is recalled, without the use of the plaintiff's name, there seems to be no doubt that even a great lapse of time does not destroy the privilege.[6] Most of the common law decisions have held that even the addition of his name [7] and likeness [8] is not

---

96. Hemingway's Estate v. Random House, Inc., 1966, 49 Misc.2d 726, 268 N.Y.S.2d 531, affirmed 25 App.Div.2d 719, 269 N.Y.S.2d 366; Rosemont Enterprises, Inc. v. Random House, Inc., 1968, 58 Misc.2d 1, 294 N.Y.S.2d 122, affirmed 32 App.Div.2d 892, 301 N.Y.S.2d 948; Cordell v. Detective Publications, Inc., 6 Cir. 1969, 419 F.2d 989; Bon Air Hotel, Inc. v. Time, Inc., S.D.Ga.1969, 295 F.Supp. 704, affirmed 426 F.2d 858; Rosenbloom v. Metromedia, Inc., 3 Cir. 1969, 415 F.2d 892, cert. granted 397 U. S. 904; Lloyds v. United Press International, Inc., 1970, 63 Misc.2d 421, 311 N.Y.S.2d 373.

97. See supra, p. 814.

98. Lane v. F. W. Woolworth Co., 1939, 171 Misc. 66, 11 N.Y.S.2d 190, affirmed 1939, 256 App.Div. 1065, 12 N.Y.S.2d 352; Birmingham Broadcasting Co. v. Bell, 1953, 259 Ala. 656, 68 So.2d 314, later appeal, 1957, 266 Ala. 266, 96 So.2d 263; Continental Optical Co. v. Reed, 1949, 119 Ind.App. 643, 86 N.E.2d 306, rehearing denied 88 N.E.2d 55; Kerby v. Hal Roach Studios, 1942, 53 Cal.App.2d 207, 127 P.2d 577; Jansen v. Hilo Packing Co., 1952, 202 Misc. 900, 118 N.Y.S.2d 162, affirmed 282 App.Div. 935, 125 N.Y.S.2d 648.

In Von Thodorovich v. Franz Josef Beneficial Ass'n, E.D.Pa.1907, 154 F. 911, even the Emperor of Austria was held to have a right to complain when his name was bestowed on an insurance company. Accord, Edison v. Edison Polyform Mfg. Co., 1907, 73 N.J.Eq. 136, 67 A. 392.

99. Palmer v. Schonhorn Enterprises, Inc., 1967, 96 N.J.Super. 72, 232 A.2d 458; Uhlaender v. Henricksen, D.Minn.1970, 316 F.Supp. 1277.

1. Flores v. Mosler Safe Co., 1959, 7 N.Y.2d 276, 196 N.Y.S.2d 975, 164 N.E.2d 853.

2. Supra, p. 819.

3. Cf. Barber v. Time, Inc., 1942, 348 Mo. 1199, 159 S.W.2d 291; Peed v. Washington Times, D.C.1927, 55 Wash.L.Rep. 182; Bazemore v. Savannah Hospital, 1930, 171 Ga. 257, 155 S.E. 194; Douglas v. Stokes, 1912, 149 Ky. 506, 149 S.W. 849.

4. Cason v. Baskin, 1945, 155 Fla. 198, 20 So.2d 943, second appeal, 1947, 159 Fla. 31, 30 So.2d 635.

5. Rosenbloom v. Metromedia, Inc., E.D.Pa.1968, 289 F.Supp. 737, reversed on other grounds, 3 Cir. 1969, 415 F.2d 892, cert. granted 397 U.S. 904; Dietemann v. Time, Inc., C.D.Cal.1968, 284 F.Supp. 925; Arber v. Stahlin, 1969, 382 Mich. 300, 170 N.W.2d 45, 47 note, Afro-American Pub. Co. v. Jaffe, 1966, 125 U.S.App.D.C. 70, 366 F.2d 649.

6. Bernstein v. National Broadcasting Co., D.D.C. 1955, 129 F.Supp. 817, affirmed 98 U.S.App.D.C. 112, 232 F.2d 369, cert. denied 352 U.S. 945; Miller v. National Broadcasting Co., D.Del.1957, 157 F.Supp. 240; Smith v. National Broadcasting Co., 1956, 138 Cal.App.2d 807, 292 P.2d 600.

7. Cohen v. Marx, 1950, 94 Cal.App.2d 704, 211 P.2d 320 (pugilist, 10 years); Sidis v. F–R Pub. Corp., 2 Cir. 1940, 113 F.2d 806, cert. denied 311 U.S. 711 (infant prodigy, 7 years); Barbieri v. News Journal Co., Del.1963, 189 A.2d 773 (whipping post, 9 years); Carlisle v. Fawcett Publications, 1962, 201 Cal.App. 2d 733, 20 Cal.Rptr. 405 (husband of motion picture actress, 18 years); Schnabel v. Meredith, 1954, 378 Pa. 609, 107 A.2d 860 (slot machine found on plaintiff's premises, 6 months).

8. Estill v. Hearst Pub. Co., 7 Cir. 1951, 186 F.2d 1017 (sheriff photographed with criminal, 15

enough to lead to liability. There are, however, two or three decisions [9] indicating that a point may be reached at which a past event is no longer news, and the unnecessary mention of the plaintiff's name in connection with it may afford a cause of action. Thus far none of the decisions dealing with the Constitution has afforded any clue as to whether such a limitation is possible.[9a]

The next step after the Hill case was to carry that decision back to defamation, as applied to "public figures" and "news." Initially the lower federal and state courts [10] had refused to apply the Sullivan rule to one who was not a public officer or employee. But in Associated Press v. Walker,[11] in 1967, the Supreme Court extended the privilege to cover one who had invited public attention by tak-

ing a belligerent controversial position in the public eye; and in the companion case of Curtis Publishing Co. v. Butts,[12] it applied the same privilege to a magazine story about a university football coach who was not a public employee. The result appears to be that so far as defamation and privacy are concerned, the Constitutional privilege is the same in its application to public figures and news.

Picked up and clearly included in the process [13] was the privilege, recognized at common law, of "fair comment" upon anything submitted to the public for its approval, as in the case of books,[14] articles,[15] advertisements,[16] radio and television programs,[17] exhibitions of art,[18] music,[19] acting and similar

years); Jenkins v. Dell Pub. Co., W.D.Pa.1956, 143 F.Supp. 952, affirmed 3 Cir. 1938, 251 F.2d 447, cert. denied 357 U.S. 921 (family of murdered boy, 3 months); cf. Rozhon v. Triangle Publications, 7 Cir. 1956, 230 F.2d 359; Samuel v. Curtis Pub. Co., N.D.Cal.1954, 122 F.Supp. 327, arguing with suicide, 22 months).

9. Melvin v. Reid, 1931, 112 Cal.App. 285, 297 P. 91; Mau v. Rio Grande Oil, Inc., N.D.Cal.1939, 28 F. Supp. 845; Wagner v. Fawcett Publications, 7 Cir. 1962, 307 F.2d 400, cert. denied 372 U.S. 909.

9a. Monitor Patriot Co. v. Roy, 1971, —— U.S. ——, 91 S.Ct. 621, applied the privilege to a charge that the plaintiff had been an old bootlegger in the days of prohibition.

10. Fignole v. Curtis Pub. Co., S.D.N.Y.1965, 247 F. Supp. 595; Dempsey v. Time, Inc., 1964, 43 Misc.2d 754, 252 N.Y.S.2d 186, affirmed 22 App.Div.2d 854, 254 N.Y.S.2d 80; Powell v. Monitor Pub. Co., 1966, 107 N.H. 83, 217 A.2d 193; Clark v. Pearson, D. D.C.1965, 248 F.Supp. 188; Mason v. Sullivan, 1966, 26 App.Div.2d 115, 271 N.Y.S.2d 314.

11. 1967, 388 U.S. 130. Accord, as to the Constitution: Tait v. King Broadcasting Co., 1969, Wash. App., 460 P.2d 307 ("our leading American fascist and Jew-baiter"); Rose v. Koch, 1967, 278 Minn. 235, 154 N.W.2d 409; Pauling v. Globe-Democrat Pub. Co., 8 Cir. 1966, 362 F.2d 188, cert. denied 388 U.S. 909.

See also, at common law: Kellems v. California CIO Council, N.D.Cal.1946, 68 F.Supp. 277; Clark v. McBaine, 1923, 299 Mo. 77, 252 S.W. 428; Berg v. Printer's Ink Pub. Co., S.D.N.Y.1943, 54 F.Supp. 795, affirmed 2 Cir. 1944, 141 F.2d 1022; Brewer v. Hearst Pub. Co., 7 Cir. 1951, 185 F.2d 846; Houston Press Co. v. Smith, Tex.Civ.App.1928, 3 S.W.2d 900, error dismissed.

12. 1967, 388 U.S. 130. Accord, Grayson v. Curtis Pub. Co., 1967, 72 Wash.2d 999, 436 P.2d 756; Davis v. National Broadcasting Co., E.D.La.1970, 320 F. Supp. 1070. See Notes, 1966, 33 Brook.L.Rev. 166; 1966, 35 U.Cin.L.Rev. 685; 1966, 44 N.C.L.Rev. 442; 1967, 16 Buff.L.Rev. 496; 1967, 42 Wash.L.Rev. 654.

13. Cepeda v. Cowles Magazine & Broadcasting Co., 9 Cir. 1968, 392 F.2d 417, cert. denied 393 U.S. 840; Paulsen v. Personality Posters, Inc., 1968, 59 Misc. 2d 444, 299 N.Y.S.2d 501.

14. Carr v. Hodd, 1808, 1 Camp. 355, 170 Eng.Rep. 983; Dowling v. Livingstone, 1896, 108 Mich. 321, 66 N.W. 225.

15. Potts v. Die, D.C.Cir.1942, 132 F.2d 734; Thompson v. Matthiasen, 1912, 150 App.Div. 739, 135 N.Y. S. 796.

16. Paris v. Levy, 1860, 9 C.B., N.S., 342, 142 Eng. Rep. 135; Willis v. O'Connell, D.Ala.1916, 231 F. 1004; cf. Press Co. v. Stewart, 1888, 119 Pa. 584, 14 A. 51.

17. Lyon v. Daily Telegraph, [1943] 1 K.B. 746; McCarthy v. Cincinnati Enquirer, 1956, 101 Ohio App. 297, 136 N.E.2d 393; Rutherford v. Dougherty, 3 Cir. 1937, 91 F.2d 707. Cf. Julian v. American Business Consultants, 1956, 2 N.Y.2d 1, 155 N.Y.S.2d 1, 137 N.E.2d 1 (Communist infiltration of industry).

18. Thompson v. Shackell, 1828, Moo. & Mal. 187, 173 Eng.Rep. 1126; Battersby v. Collier, 1898, 34 App. Div. 347, 54 N.Y.S. 363; Outcault v. New York Herald Co., 1907, 117 App.Div. 534, 102 N.Y.S. 685 (cartoonist); Soane v. Knight, 1827, Moo. & Mal. 74, 173 Eng.Rep. 1086 (architecture).

19. McQuire v. Western Morning News Co., [1903] 2 K.B. 100; cf. Brown v. New York Evening Journal, 1932, 143 Misc. 199, 266 N.Y.S. 403, affirmed, 1932, 235 App.Div. 840, 257 N.Y.S. 903; Man v. Warner Bros., Inc., S.D.N.Y.1970, 317 F.Supp. 50.

entertainments,[20] or sports,[21] scientific discoveries,[22] or projects appealing for support.[23]

One uncertainty as to the Constitutional privilege is as to whether it is limited, as was the common law privilege of fair comment,[24] to those matters which reasonably bear upon what is already public, or whether it extends to the private life and character of the individual in question. It has been held, for example, that while an attack on the merits of a work of art may be privileged, a charge of plagiarism is not;[25] and that defamation of the personal character of the author of a book was not privileged, where it had nothing to do with the book.[26] Nor was a publisher privileged to read treason and sinister influences into the vote of a Congressman on a bill.[27] And as to privacy, while the biographies of celebrities can certainly be written,[28] and their life histories and their characters set forth before the world in unflattering detail,[29] there have been at least indications that the private sex relations of actresses and baseball players, to say nothing of inventors and the victims of automobile accidents, are still not in the public domain.[30] The private letters, even of celebrities cannot be published without their consent;[31] and the good Prince Albert was once held to have an action when his private etchings were exhibited to all comers.[32]

If such a limitation upon the privilege is to be recognized under the Constitution, it appears very probable that there is some rough proportion to be looked for, between the importance of the public figure or the man in the news, and of the occasion for the public interest in him, and the nature of the private facts revealed. Perhaps there is very little in the way of information about the President of the United States, or any candidate

---

20. Cherry v. Des Moines Leader, 1901, 114 Iowa 298, 86 N.W. 323; Cleveland Leader Printing Co. v. Nethersole, 1911, 84 Ohio St. 118, 95 N.E. 735. Cf. Gott v. Pulsifer, 1877, 112 Mass. 235 (the "Cardiff Giant").

21. Cohen v. Cowles Pub. Co., 1954, 45 Wash.2d 262, 273 P.2d 893 (horse racing); Lloyds v. United Press International, Inc., 1970, 63 Misc.2d 421, 311 N.Y.S. 2d 373 (same); Hoeppner v. Dunkirk Printing Co., 1930, 254 N.Y. 95, 172 N.E. 139 (football).

22. Hunter v. Sharpe, 1866, 4 F. & F. 983, 176 Eng. Rep. 875; Dakhyl v. Labouchere, [1908] 2 K.B. 325; cf. Brinkley v. Fishbein, 5 Cir. 1940, 110 F.2d 62.

23. Henwood v. Harrison, 1872, L.R. 7 C.P. 606; Kulesza v. Chicago Daily News, 1941, 311 Ill.App. 117, 35 N.E.2d 517.

24. See supra, p. 819.

25. Fitzgerald v. Hopkins, 1967, 70 Wash.2d 924, 425 P.2d 920.

26. Cooper v. Stone, 1840, 24 Wend. (N.Y.) 434; Triggs v. Sun Printing & Pub. Assn., 1904, 179 N.Y. 144, 71 N.E. 739; Clifton v. Lange, 1899, 108 Iowa 472, 79 N.W. 276; Wood v. Boyle, 1896, 177 Pa. 620, 35 A. 853; Thomas v. Bradbury, Agnew & Co., [1906] 2 K.B. 627. In the case of comments on public officers and candidates, considerable latitude is allowed, since private character obviously may bear upon fitness. Coleman v. MacLennan, 1908, 78 Kan. 711, 98 P. 281.

27. Hall v. Binghamton Press Co., Misc.1941, 29 N.Y. S.2d 760. Cf. Morgan v. Bulletin Co., 1952, 369 Pa. 349, 85 A.2d 869 ("Mata Hari of the parking meters").

28. Jeffries v. New York Evening Journal Co., 1910, 67 Misc. 570, 124 N.Y.S. 780; Koussevitzky v. Allen, Towne & Heath, 1947, 188 Misc. 479, 68 N.Y.S. 2d 779, affirmed, 1947, 272 App.Div. 759, 69 N.Y.S. 2d 432, appeal denied 272 App.Div. 794, 71 N.Y.S.2d 712; cf. Corliss v. E. W. Walker Co., D.Mass.1894, 64 F. 280.

29. Smith v. Suratt, 1926, 7 Alaska 416 (Dr. Cook).

30. Cf. Garner v. Triangle Publications, S.D.N.Y. 1951, 97 F.Supp. 546 (relations, partly fictional, between participants in murder).

31. Pope v. Curl, 1741, 2 Atk. 341, 26 Eng.Rep. 608; Roberts v. McKee, 1859, 29 Ga. 161; Woolsey v. Judd, 1855, 11 N.Y.Super. (4 Duer) 379; Denis v. Leclerc, 1811, 1 Mart.O.S., La., 297; Baker v. Libbie, 1912, 210 Mass. 599, 97 N.E. 109. Usually this has been put upon the ground of a property right in the letter itself, or literary property in its contents. See Note, 1959, 44 Iowa L.Rev. 705.

32. Prince Albert v. Strange, 1848, 1 Mac. & G. 25, 64 Eng.Rep. 293, affirmed, 1849, 2 De G. & Sm. 652, 41 Eng.Rep. 1171. Two state court decisions indicate clearly that only matters bearing upon public life are within the Constitutional privilege. Ocala Star-Banner Co. v. Damron, Fla.App.1969, 221 So.2d 459; Roy v. Monitor Patriot Co., 1969, — N.H. —, 254 A.2d 832.

for that high office,[33] that is not a matter of legitimate public concern; but when a mere member of the armed forces is in question, the line is to be drawn at his military service, and those things that more or less directly bear upon it.[34] And no doubt the defendant in a spectacular murder trial which draws national attention must expect a good deal less in the way of privacy than an ordinary citizen who is arrested for ignoring a parking ticket. But thus far there is very little in the cases to indicate where such lines are to be drawn.

Reports of Public Proceedings

Obviously swept up and included under the Constitution as a part of the general heading of "news" is the common law privilege of reporting on public proceedings.[35] Since it is clearly to the interest of the public that information be made available as to what takes place in public affairs, the qualified privilege was recognized, under which a newspaper or anyone else [36] might make such a report to the public.[37] The privilege rests upon the idea that any member of the public, if he were present, might see and hear for himself, so that the reporter is merely a substitute for

the public eye—this, together with the obvious public interest in having public affairs made known to all. The privilege of reporting extends to all legislative proceedings,[38] including the investigations of committees[39] and the deliberations of municipal councils,[40] and to the acts of executive or administrative officials of the national, state or municipal governments, including their official reports and communications.[41]

There are cases[42] in a few jurisdictions which have extended it further, to include meetings open to the public, at which matters of public concern were discussed. It is clear, however, that there was no common law privilege to report the proceedings of any private

---

33. Witness the disclosure, in the election of 1884, of Grover Cleveland's parentage of an illegitimate child many years before.

34. Stryker v. Republic Pictures Corp., 1951, 108 Cal.App.2d 191, 238 P.2d 670; and see Continental Optical Co. v. Reed, 1949, 119 Ind.App. 643, 86 N.E. 2d 306, rehearing denied 119 Ind.App. 643, 88 N.E.2d 55.

35. Sellers v. United States, 1970, 89 S.Ct. 36; Lulay v. Peoria Journal-Star, Inc., 1966, 34 Ill.2d 112, 214 N.E.2d 746; Nusbaum v. Newark Morning Ledger Co., 1965, 86 N.J.Super. 132, 206 A.2d 185; Pape v. Time, Inc., 7 Cir. 1969, 419 F.2d 980, cert. granted 397 U.S. 1062.

36. Irwin v. Ashurst, 1938, 158 Or. 61, 74 P.2d 1127. A newspaper has no special privilege to publish defamation. It can publish with immunity only that which anyone else could publish. England v. Daily Gazette Co., 1958, 143 W.Va. 700, 104 S.E.2d 306.

37. Barnett, The Privilege of Defamation by Private Report of Public Official Proceedings, 1952, 31 Or. L.Rev. 185; Notes, 1964, 64 Col.L.Rev. 1102; [1953] Wash.U.L.Q. 224.

38. Wason v. Walter, 1868, L.R. 4 Q.B. 573; Garby v. Bennett, 1901, 166 N.Y. 392, 59 N.E. 1117. See Bryan, Publication of Record Libel, 1918, 5 Va.L. Rev. 513.

39. Cresson v. Louisville Courier Journal, 6 Cir. 1924, 299 F. 487 (report of majority of Congressional committee); Terry v. Fellows, 1869, 21 La.Ann. 375. Accord, Coleman v. Newark Morning Ledger Co., 1959, 29 N.J. 357, 149 A.2d 193 (senator's press conference); Bray v. Providence Journal Co., 1966, 101 R.I. 111, 220 A.2d 531 (public meeting of school committee). See Notes, 1959, 59 Col.L.Rev. 521; 1959, 13 Rutgers L.Rev. 723.

40. Swede v. Passaic Daily News, 1959, 30 N.J. 320, 153 A.2d 36; Meteye v. Times-Democrat Pub. Co., 1895, 47 La.Ann. 824, 17 So. 314; Leininger v. New Orleans Item Pub. Co., 1924, 156 La. 1044, 101 So. 411. See Note, 1924, 23 Mich.L.Rev. 420.

41. Brandon v. Gazette Pub. Co., 1961, 234 Ark. 332, 352 S.W.2d 92 (report to governor, of official investigation); Sciandra v. Lynett, 1963, 409 Pa. 595, 187 A.2d 586 (same); Painter v. E. W. Scripps Co., 1957, 104 Ohio App. 237, 148 N.E.2d 503 (order of county coroner); Begley v. Louisville Times Co., 1938, 272 Ky. 805, 115 S.W.2d 345 (adjutant general); Briarcliff Lodge Hotel v. Citizen-Sentinel Pub. Co., 1932, 260 N.Y. 106, 183 N.E. 193, Id., 1932, 261 N.Y. 537, 185 N.E. 728 (water board).

42. Jackson v. Record Pub. Co., 1935, 175 S.C. 211, 178 S.E. 833 (report of words of a candidate at a political rally); Phoenix Newspapers v. Choisser, 1957, 82 Ariz. 271, 312 P.2d 150 (same at Chamber of Commerce "forum"); Pulvermann v. A. S. Abell Co., 4 Cir. 1956, 228 F.2d 797 (report of speech of candidate for President); Borg v. Boas, 9 Cir. 1956, 231 F.2d 788 (report of mass meeting held to urge calling grand jury to investigate local law enforcement); see Hartzog v. United Press Associations, 4

group, such as the stockholders of a corporation,[43] unless the meeting is open to the public, and what is said there itself bears upon the public interest, as "fair comment" or otherwise.[44] With the extension of the Constitutional privilege to include the "news," however, it appears probable that even such private meetings can be reported, to the extent that they are legitimate matters of public interest. There is also no privilege to report the unofficial talk of such officials as policemen,[45] as distinct from their official utterances or acts, such as an arrest.[46] An important field for the privilege is the reporting of any judicial proceeding,[47] no matter how inferior the tribunal,[48] and regardless of its

jurisdiction over the particular matter.[49] The proceeding may be an ex parte one,[50] so long as some official action is taken, even though it is only the holding of a hearing; but a mere contemplated lawsuit, not yet begun is clearly not enough.[51] Because of the opportunity afforded for malicious public defamation and even extortion,[52] through suits begun and promptly discontinued, most courts are agreed that some official action is essential to the privilege. Thus it is the prevailing view, with some few courts to the contrary,[53] that a pleading [54] or a deposition [55] filed in a

Cir. 1953, 202 F.2d 81 (ejection of member at meeting of Republican Executive Committee); Abram v. Odham, Fla.1956, 89 So.2d 334 (speech of candidate for office).

43. Kimball v. Post Pub. Co., 1908, 199 Mass. 248, 85 N.E. 103. Cf. Lewis v. Hayes, 1913, 165 Cal. 527, 132 P. 1022 (casual conversation at social banquet).

44. Barrows v. Bell, 1856, 7 Gray, Mass. 301; cf. Lothrop v. Adams, 1882, 133 Mass. 471; Shurtleff v. Stevens, 1879, 51 Vt. 501; Rabb v. Trevelyan, 1908, 122 La. 174, 47 So. 455.

45. Kelley v. Hearst Corp., 1956, 2 App.Div.2d 480, 157 N.Y.S.2d 498 amended, 1957, 3 App.Div.2d 610, 158 N.Y.S.2d 781, reargument and appeal denied, 1957, 3 App.Div.2d 963, 163 N.Y.S.2d 937; Hornby v. Hunter, Tex.Civ.App.1964, 385 S.W.2d 473; Sorge v. Parade Publications, 1964, 20 App.Div.2d 338, 247 N.Y.S.2d 317.

46. Francois v. Capital City Press, La.App.1964, 166 So.2d 84; Piracci v. Hearst Corp., D.Md.1966, 263 F.Supp. 511, affirmed memorandum 4 Cir. 1966, 371 F.2d 1016; cf. Lotrich v. Life Printing & Pub. Co., 1969, 117 Ill.App.2d 15, 253 N.E.2d 899.

47. Alexandria Gazette Corp. v. West, 1956, 198 Va. 154, 93 S.E.2d 274 (proceeding to disqualify judge); Rhodes v. Star Herald Printing Co., 1962, 173 Neb. 496, 113 N.W.2d 658 (posting bonds); Greenfield v. Courier Journal & Louisville Times Co., Ky.1955, 283 S.W.2d 839 (grand jury report); Grossman v. Globe-Democrat Pub. Co., 1941, 347 Mo. 869, 149 S.W.2d 362; Irwin v. Ashurst, 1938, 158 Or. 61, 74 P.2d 1127.

48. Hahn v. Holum, 1917, 165 Wis. 425, 162 N.W. 432 (justice court); McBee v. Fulton, 1878, 47 Md. 403 (same); Flues v. New Nonpareil Co., 1912, 155 Iowa 290, 135 N.W. 1083 (police court); Parsons v. Age-Herald Co., 1913, 181 Ala. 439, 61 So. 345

(grand jury); Williams v. Journal Co., 1933, 211 Wis. 362, 247 N.W. 435 (same).

49. Lee v. Brooklyn Union Pub. Co., 1913, 209 N.Y. 245, 103 N.E. 155; Hahn v. Holum, 1917, 165 Wis. 425, 162 N.W. 432; Usill v. Hales, 1878, 3 C.P.D. 319. But cf. Trebby v. Transcript Pub. Co., 1898, 74 Minn. 84, 76 N.W. 961 (city council exceeding its powers).

50. Fitch v. Daily News Pub. Co., 1928, 116 Neb. 474, 217 N.W. 947; American Pub. Co. v. Gamble, 1906, 115 Tenn. 663, 90 S.W. 1005; Beiser v. Scripps-McRae Pub. Co., 1902, 113 Ky. 383, 68 S.W. 457; Metcalf v. Times Pub. Co., 1898, 20 R.I. 674, 40 A. 864.

51. Gariepy v. Pearson, 1953, 92 U.S.App.D.C. 337, 207 F.2d 15, cert. denied 346 U.S. 909.

52. See Nadelmann, The Newspaper Privilege and Extortion by Abuse of Legal Process, 1954, 54 Col. L.Rev. 359.

Cf. Williams v. Williams, 1969, 23 N.Y.2d 592, 298 N.Y.S.2d 473, 246 N.E.2d 333, where defendant filed a pleading and then circulated it himself.

53. Langford v. Vanderbilt University, 1956, 199 Tenn. 389, 287 S.W.2d 32; Campbell v. New York Evening Post, 1927, 245 N.Y. 320, 157 N.E. 153; Lybrand v. State Co., 1936, 179 S.C. 208, 184 S.E. 580; Johnson v. Johnson Pub. Co., D.C.App.1970, 271 A.2d 696; American Dist. Tel. Co. v. Brink's Inc., 7 Cir. 1967, 380 F.2d 131.

54. Sanford v. Boston Herald-Traveler Corp., 1945, 318 Mass. 156, 61 N.E.2d 5; Byers v. Meridian Printing Co., 1911, 84 Ohio St. 408, 95 N.E. 917; Nixon v. Dispatch Printing Co., 1907, 101 Minn. 309, 112 N.W. 258; Meeker v. Post Printing & Pub. Co., 1913, 55 Colo. 355, 135 P. 457; Park v. Detroit Free Press Co., 1888, 72 Mich. 560, 40 N.W. 731. See Note, 1946, 44 Mich.L.Rev. 675.

As to the privilege of legal commentators, see Note, 1933, 31 Mich.L.Rev. 255.

55. Mannix v. Portland Telegram, 1933, 144 Or. 172, 23 P.2d 138.

case but not yet acted upon may not be reported under the claim of privilege. Likewise sealed records and documents withheld from the public eye under court order [56] may not be so reported.

The same is of course true of the preliminary statements of police, or any other evidence not yet given.[57] How far all this may be modified or affected by the broad privacy definition of "public figures" and "news" under the Constitution, is as yet anyone's guess.

It is of course essential to the privilege that it covers defamation of those who are not themselves involved in the proceeding in any way.[58] But it has always been held that the report must be a fair and accurate one, and the privilege did not cover false statements of fact as to what has occurred,[59] or mistakes in the names of parties,[60] or the interpolation of defamatory matter, or a one-sided account.[61] Neither did it include garbled [62] or partial [63] reports, although it was obviously not essential that the proceedings be set forth verbatim, and a summary of substantial accuracy was enough.[64] But with the application, under the Constitution, of the rule of the Sullivan case, it seems beyond dispute that even if the report is an inaccurate one, it is privileged unless it is made with knowledge of the falsity or in reckless disregard of its truth.[64a]

There is no privilege attached to the report as such to add comment,[65] or headlines which do not fairly reflect the gist of the text,[66] unless such additions are themselves privileged because the subject of the pro-

56. Danziger v. Hearst Corp., 1952, 304 N.Y. 244, 107 N.E.2d 62, modifying, 1951, 279 App.Div. 560, 107 N.Y.S.2d 423, appeal granted, 1951, 279 App.Div. 644, 107 N.Y.S.2d 1007. Cf. McCurdy v. Hughes, 1933, 63 N.D. 435, 248 N.W. 512 (preliminary inquiry into disbarment).

57. Lubore v. Pittsburgh Courier Pub. Co., D.C.D.C. 1951, 101 F.Supp. 234, affirmed, 1952, 91 U.S.App. D.C. 311, 200 F.2d 355; Houston Chronicle Pub. Co. v. Tiernan, Tex.Civ.App.1914, 171 S.W. 542. Cf. Rogers v. Courier Post Co., 1949, 2 N.J. 393, 66 A.2d 869 (after adjournment).

58. Sherwood v. Evening News Ass'n, 1931, 256 Mich. 318, 239 N.W. 305; Lehner v. Berlin Pub. Co., 1932, 209 Wis. 536, 245 N.W. 685; Mortensen v. Los Angeles Examiner, 1931, 112 Cal.App. 194, 296 P. 297; Schaffran v. Press Pub. Co., 1932, 258 N.Y. 207, 179 N.E. 387.

59. Brush-Moore Newspapers v. Pollitt, 1959, 220 Md. 132, 151 A.2d 530; Carey v. Hearst Publications, 1943, 19 Wash.2d 655, 143 P.2d 857; Bowerman v. Detroit Free Press, 1939, 287 Mich. 443, 283 N.W. 642; Hartzog v. United Press Assn., 4 Cir. 1953, 202 F.2d 81; Atlanta Journal Co. v. Doyal, 1950, 82 Ga.App. 321, 60 S.E.2d 802.

60. Whitcomb v. Hearst Corp., 1952, 329 Mass. 193, 107 N.E.2d 295; Switzer v. Anthony, 1922, 71 Colo. 291, 206 P. 391. But an immaterial mistake, such as an error in stating the age of a victim of forcible rape, does not make the defendant liable. Torski v. Mansfield Journal Co., 1956, 100 Ohio App. 538, 137 N.E.2d 679.

61. Robinson v. Johnson, 8 Cir. 1917, 239 F. 671. Cf. Brown v. Providence Telegram Pub. Co., 1903, 25 R.I. 117, 54 A. 1061; Jones v Pulitzer Pub. Co., 1912, 240 Mo. 200, 144 S.W. 441; Atlanta News Pub. Co. v. Medlock, 1905, 123 Ga. 714, 51 S.E. 756. Cf. Purcell v. Westinghouse Broadcasting Co., 1963, 411 Pa. 167, 191 A.2d 662 (embellishment of account of judicial proceeding with extra-judicial "investigation").

62. Arnold v. Sayings Co., 1898, 76 Mo.App. 159; Thomas v. Croswell, 1810, 7 Johns., N.Y., 264. Cf. Pape v. Time, Inc., 7 Cir. 1963, 318 F.2d 652 (what official document merely stated to be "alleged," newspaper stated as fact); Hogan v. New York Times Co., 2 Cir. 1963, 313 F.2d 354 ("reckless disregard of the truth.")

63. Metcalf v. Times Pub. Co., 1898, 20 R.I. 674, 40 A. 864; Saunders v. Mills, 1829, 6 Bing. 213, 130 Eng.Rep. 1262; Brown v. Publishers: George Knapp & Co., 1908, 213 Mo. 655, 112 S.W. 474.

64. Milissich v. Lloyd's, 1877, 13 Cox C.C. 575, 46 L.J. C.P. 404; Salisbury v. Union & Advertiser Co., 1887, 45 Hun, N.Y. 120, 9 N.Y.St.Rep. 465; Boogher v. Knapp, 1889, 97 Mo. 122, 11 S.W. 45; Lehner v. Berlin Pub. Co., 1932, 209 Wis. 536, 245 N.W. 685.

64a. Time, Inc. v. Pape, 1971, —— U.S. ——, appears to indicate this quite clearly.

65. Scripps v. Reilly, 1878, 38 Mich. 10; Cass v. New Orleans Times, 1875, 27 La.Ann. 214.

66. Brown v. Publishers: George Knapp & Co., 1908, 213 Mo. 655, 112 S.W. 474; Brown v. Globe Printing Co., 1908, 213 Mo. 611, 112 S.W. 462; Ilsley v. Sentinel Co., 1907, 133 Wis. 20, 113 N.W. 425. Otherwise if they are a fair index. Lawyers' Coop. Pub. Co. v. West Pub. Co., 1898, 32 App.Div. 585, 52 N.Y.S. 1120.

ceeding reported is a matter of public concern.[67] It has been held that the report must state the source of what is being reported, and that if it does not there is no privilege.[68]

67. Hibbins v. Lee, 1864, 4 F. & F. 243, 176 Eng.Rep. 549; Andrews v. Chapman, 1853, 3 C. & K. 286, 175 Eng.Rep. 558; Brown v. Publishers: George Knapp & Co., 1908, 213 Mo. 655, 112 S.W. 474.

Prosser Torts 4th Ed. HB—53

68. Hughes v. Washington Daily News, 1952, 90 App.D.C. 155, 193 F.2d 922; Henderson v. Evansville Press, 1957, 127 Ind.App. 592, 142 N.E.2d 920.

CHAPTER 22

MISUSE OF LEGAL PROCEDURE

119. MALICIOUS PROSECUTION

The interest in freedom from unjustifiable litigation receives protection in actions which, for want of a better name, have been called malicious prosecution and abuse of process. Obviously such an interest has much in common with that of reputation.[1] It is evident, for example, that the institution of criminal proceedings by one individual against another amounts to a publication of the charge that he is guilty of the crime for which he is prosecuted; and that this is a form of publication which, above all others, is dangerous to the repute of the person so charged.[2] In the first instance, therefore, such "malicious prosecution" might well have been included as a branch of the law of defamation. There are at least three reasons why it has not been so included, and is regarded by the courts and by legal writers as a separate tort.

One reason is that of historical development. An early form of malicious prosecution preceded defamation in the king's courts by some centuries, appearing as early as the reign of Edward I, in an old writ of conspiracy aimed at combinations to abuse legal procedure.[3] When this fell into decay in the sixteenth century, partly because of its narrow limitation to abuse by two or more persons, it was replaced by an action on the case

in the nature of the conspiracy writ, which, however, would lie against a single defendant.[4] Thus when defamation was taken over from the ecclesiastical courts, malicious prosecution was already established as a distinct cause of action.

The second reason is that both torts had to tread a rather difficult path in overcoming the obvious policy in favor of permitting honest men to bring criminals to justice. The strict liability of defamation, where the plaintiff made out his case by showing nothing more than the publication and its defamatory meaning, proved too drastic, and was defeated by the recognition of a privilege to make formal complaint to the proper authorities.[5] While some courts have held that informal complaints are only qualifiedly privileged, it seems a tenable view that the immunity is absolute in such cases also.[6] Malicious prosecution then remains as a possible remedy, with the burden upon the plaintiff to prove the perversion of legal process to improper ends.

Finally, it appears that the interests protected are not altogether identical.[7] Malicious prosecution covers a somewhat broader field than mere harm to reputation. It may involve an interference with personal integrity, by arrest or confinement of the plain-

---

1. 1 Street, Foundations of Legal Liability, 1906, 326–328; Harper, Malicious Prosecution, False Imprisonment and Defamation, 1937, 15 Tex.L.Rev. 157.

2. 1 Street, Foundations of Legal Liability, 1906, 326.

3. See, generally, Winfield, History of Conspiracy and Abuse of Legal Procedure, 1921.

4. Fuller v. Cook, 1584, 3 Leon. 100, 74 Eng.Rep. 567; Jerom v. Knight, 1587, 1 Leon. 107, 74 Eng. Rep. 99. The real leading case, which put the action on a firm basis, is Savile v. Roberts, 1698, 1 Ld.Raym. 374, 91 Eng.Rep. 1147.

5. See supra, p. 791.

6. See supra, p. 781.

7. Harper, Malicious Prosecution, False Imprisonment and Defamation, 1937, 15 Tex.L.Rev. 157, 160.

tiff, or financial damage in the form of expense to which he is put in defending himself against the criminal charge. Furthermore, it has been extended to interferences with property, as in the case of malicious attachment, and by many courts to ordinary civil suits, where no defamation is involved.[8] It may therefore properly be considered a distinct field of liability, subject to rules of its own.

The elements of a cause of action for malicious prosecution, as it originally developed, frequently have been stated [9] as follows:

1. A criminal [10] proceeding instituted or continued by the defendant against the plaintiff.

2. Termination of the proceeding in favor of the accused.

3. Absence of probable cause for the proceeding.

4. "Malice," or a primary purpose other than that of bringing an offender to justice.

Before considering these elements, some reference must be made again to the distinction between malicious prosecution and the kindred tort of false imprisonment, in cases of arrest and confinement. As has been stated above,[11] the difference is one of the regularity of the legal process under which the plaintiff's interests have been invaded. If he is arrested or confined without a warrant, or legal authority apart from a warrant, malicious prosecution will not lie, since the essence of that tort is the perversion of proper legal procedure,[12] and the remedy is false imprisonment. On the other hand, if there is valid process or due authority apart from

it, the arrest is not "false," and the action must be one of malicious prosecution.[13] Malicious prosecution is the less rigorous of the two remedies. It assumes that the defendant has proceeded under proper legal formalities, and therefore takes into account his good motives and probable cause for his conduct, which are immaterial in false imprisonment,[14] where the tort consists of a departure from due process of law.

Institution of Proceeding

Any proceeding of a criminal character [15] will support an action of malicious prosecution. Although there is some authority to the contrary, most courts have held that it makes no difference that the court or magistrate before whom it is brought has no jurisdiction,[16] or that the indictment or com-

---

8. See infra, § 120.

9. Larocque v. Dorsey, 2 Cir., 1924, 299 F. 556; Glenn v. Lawrence, 1917, 280 Ill. 581, 117 N.E. 757; Wilson v. Lapham, 1923, 196 Iowa 745, 195 N.W. 235; Kennedy v. Burbidge, 1919, 54 Utah 497, 183 P. 325; Pessagno v. Keyes, 1923, 143 Md. 437, 122 A. 651.

10. As to civil proceedings, see, infra, § 120.

11. Supra, p. 49. The distinction is well stated in Sears, Roebuck & Co. v. Alexander, 1949, 252 Ala. 122, 39 So.2d 570.

12. Prince v. Bryant, 1962, 274 Ala. 134, 145 So.2d 837; Lowe v. Turner, 1967, 115 Ga.App. 503, 154 S. E.2d 792 (void warrant). Auerbach v. Freeman, 1915, 43 App.D.C. 176 (no warrant). See Dorsey v. Winters, 1923, 143 Md. 399, 122 A. 257; De Bouchel v. Koss Const. Co., 1933, 177 La. 841, 149 So. 496; American Ry. Exp. Co. v. McDermott, 3 Cir. 1933, 44 F.2d 955.

13. Nesmith v. Alford, 5 Cir. 1963, 318 F.2d 110 (Alabama law); Colter v. Lower, 1871, 35 Ind. 285; Wilson v. Lapham, 1923, 196 Iowa 745, 195 N.W. 235; Rich v. McInerny, 1894, 103 Ala. 345, 15 So. 663; Pandjiris v. Hartman, 1906, 196 Mo. 539, 94 S.W. 270.

14. Diehl v. Friester, 1882, 37 Ohio St. 473; Southern R. Co. v. Shirley, 1906, 121 Ky. 863, 90 S.W. 597; Adair v. Williams, 1922, 24 Ariz. 422, 210 P. 853. The same is true as to the termination of the proceeding in favor of the accused, which is unnecessary to false imprisonment. Boesch v. Kick, 1922, 98 N.J.L. 183, 119 A. 1; Davis v. Johnson, 4 Cir., 1900, 101 F. 952; Barry v. Third Ave. R. Co., 1900, 51 App.Div. 385, 64 N.Y.S. 615.

15. Long v. Rogers, 1850, 17 Ala. 540. As to quasi criminal proceedings, such as bastardy or juvenile delinquency, see infra, p. 851. There must, however, be a judicial proceeding; and a mere investigation by the district attorney is not enough. Losi v. Natalicchio, Sup.Ct.1952, 112 N.Y.S.2d 706.

16. Morris v. Scott, 1839, 21 Wend., N.Y., 281; Sutor v. Wood, 1890, 76 Tex. 403, 13 S.W. 321; Ailstock v Moore Lime Co., 1905, 104 Va. 565, 52 S.E. 213; Kuhnhausen v. Stadelman, 1944, 174 Or. 290, 148 P. 2d 239, 149 P.2d 168 (colorable jurisdiction

plaint upon which the prosecution is based lacks essential particulars,[17] or even that it fails to charge the commission of any offense known to the criminal law.[18] So long as the proceeding is treated by the court as a proper one, the plaintiff's interests have been invaded, his reputation has suffered, and he has been put to the expense of defending himself. He is not to be dismissed from court with the consoling assurance that he never really was prosecuted at all;[19] nor is it any the less a prosecution because it is successfully defended on the law rather than the facts.[20]

The proceeding must, however, have been commenced. It is not enough that a mere complaint has been made to the proper authorities for the purpose of setting prosecution in motion, where no official action ever has been taken,[21] or that evidence has been

presented to a grand jury which refuses to indict.[22] On the other hand, it usually is held to be sufficient that a warrant has been issued for the plaintiff's arrest, although it never has been served.[23] The initial step is of course a matter of the procedure of the particular jurisdiction; and where prosecution is begun by an indictment, or an information filed by the prosecuting attorney, it seems clear that this should be enough,[24] since it constitutes official action and sets the law in motion.

The defendant may be liable either for initiating or for continuing[25] a criminal prosecution without probable cause. But he cannot be held responsible unless he takes some active part in instigating or encouraging the prosecution.[26] He is not liable merely because of his approval or silent acquiescence in the acts of another,[27] nor for appearing as a witness against the accused,[28]

---

enough); Ferraris v. Levy, 1963, 223 Cal.App.2d 408, 36 Cal.Rptr. 30.

Contra: Vinson v. Flynn, 1897, 64 Ark. 453, 43 S.W. 146, 46 S.W. 186; Bixby v. Brundige, 1854, 68 Mass., (2 Gray) 129; Berger v. Saul, 1901, 113 Ga. 869, 39 S.E. 326; and see Weidlich v. Weidlich, 1941, 177 Misc.2d 246, 30 N.Y.S.2d 326.

17. Minneapolis Threshing Mach. Co. v. Regier, 1897, 51 Neb. 402, 70 N.W. 934; Potter v. Gjertsen, 1897, 37 Minn. 386, 34 N.W. 746; Harrington v. Tibbet 1904, 143 Cal. 78, 76 P. 816; McIntosh v. Wales, 1913, 21 Wyo. 397, 134 P. 274; Tobey v. Orr, 1926, 92 Fla. 964, 111 So. 110. Contra, Caudle v. Benbow, 1947, 228 N.C. 482, 45 S.E.2d 361. See Note, 1927, 11 Minn.L.Rev. 678.

18. Tobey v. Orr, 1926, 92 Fla. 964, 111 So. 110; Puutio v. Roman, 1926, 76 Mont. 105, 245 P. 523; Nelson v. Hill, 1924, 30 N.M. 288, 232 P. 526; George v. Williams, 1924, 26 Ariz. 91, 222 P. 410; Finn v. Frink, 1892, 84 Me. 261, 24 A. 851.

Contra: Moser v. Fulk, 1950, 237 N.C. 302, 74 S.E.2d 729; Krause v. Spiegel, 1892, 94 Cal. 370, 29 P. 707; Satilla Mfg. Co. v. Cason, 1895, 98 Ga. 14, 25 S.E. 909.

19. See Shaul v. Brown, 1869, 28 Iowa 37; Dennis v. Ryan, 1875, 65 N.Y. 385; Bell v. Keepers, 1887, 37 Kan. 64, 14 P. 542; Mask v. Rawls, 1879, 57 Miss. 270.

20. Cf. Finn v. Frink, 1892, 84 Me. 261, 24 A. 851.

21. Cooper v. Armour, C.C.N.Y.1893, 42 F. 215; Reach v. Quinn, 1909, 159 Ala. 340, 48 So. 540; Larocque

v. Dorsey, 2 Cir. 1924, 299 F. 556. Cf. Heyward v. Cuthbert, 1827, 4 McCord, S.C., 354.

22. Byne v. Moore, 1813, 5 Taunt. 187, 128 Eng.Rep. 658.

23. Halberstadt v. New York Life Ins. Co., 1909, 194 N.Y. 1, 86 N.E. 801; Coffey v. Myers, 1882, 84 Ind. 105; Haden v. Tinnin, 1915, 170 N.C. 84, 86 S.E. 1017. Cf. Olson v. Haggerty, 1912, 69 Wash. 48, 124 P. 145 (search warrant); Hardin v. Hight, 1911, 106 Ark. 190, 153 S.W. 99 (same); Ballard v. Cash, 1921, 191 Ky. 312, 230 S.W. 48 (same). Contra: Davis v. Sanders, 1901, 133 Ala. 275, 32 So. 499; Mitchell v. Donanski, 1906, 28 R.I. 94, 65 A. 611.

24. See Restatement of Torts § 654, comment a.

25. Lavey v. Glidden Co., 1940, 239 Ala. 396, 194 So. 849; Killen v. Olsen, Fla.1952, 59 So.2d 524; Wenger v. Phillips, 1900, 195 Pa. 214, 45 A. 927; Johnson v Miller, 1884, 63 Iowa 529, 17 N.W. 34.

26. Fertitta v. Herndon, 1939, 175 Md. 560, 3 A.2d 502; Shannon v. Sims, 1906, 146 Ala. 673, 40 So. 574; Bazzell v. Illinois Cent. R. Co., 1924, 203 Ky. 626, 262 S.W. 966; Munday v. Gott, 1912, 146 Ky. 177, 142 S.W. 238.

27. McNamara v. Pabst, 1921, 137 Md. 468, 112 A. 812; Dugan v. Midwest Cap Co., 1931, 213 Iowa 751, 239 N.W. 697; Mark v. Merz, 1894, 53 Ill.App. 458; Marks v. Hastings, 1893, 101 Ala. 165, 13 So. 297.

28. McClarty v. Bickel, 1913, 155 Ky. 254, 159 S.W. 783; Gianitsas v. Mercantile Nat. Bank at Dallas,

even though his testimony is perjured, since the necessities of a free trial demand that witnesses are not to be deterred by fear of tort suits, and shall be immune from liability. On the other hand, if he advises or assists another person to begin the proceeding,[29] ratifies it when it is begun in his behalf,[30] or takes any active part in directing or aiding the conduct of the case,[31] he will be responsible. The question of information laid before prosecuting authorities has arisen in many cases. If the defendant merely states what he believes, leaving the decision to prosecute entirely to the uncontrolled discretion of the officer,[32] or if the officer makes an independent investigation,[33] or prosecutes for an offense other than the one charged by the defendant,[34] the latter is not regarded as having instigated the proceeding; but if it is found that his persuasion was the determining factor in inducing the officer's decision,[35] or that he gave information which he knew to be false and so unduly influenced the authorities,[36] he may be held liable.

Prosecuting attorneys themselves, when they merely conduct proceedings on complaints sworn out by others, are held to be quasi-judicial officers, protected by an absolute privilege, and are not liable for malicious prosecution even when they act in bad faith and without probable cause,[37] or overdo the prosecution.[38] The same immunity is, in general, extended to the police and other

Tex.Civ.App.1967, 410 S.W.2d 848 (under subpoena); King v. Martin, 1928, 150 Va. 122, 142 S.E. 358; Atkinson v. Birmingham, 1922, 44 R.I. 123, 116 A. 205; Taplin-Rice-Clerkin Co. v. Hower, 1931, 124 Ohio St. 123, 177 N.E. 203. The immunity of the witness does not extend to one who suborns him to commit perjury. Rice v. Coolidge, 1876, 121 Mass. 393.

Evidence that the defendant testified as a witness is, however, admissible with other acts and circumstances to show instigation or active encouragement of the prosecution or an improper motive. Fitzjohn v. Mackinder, 1861, 9 C.B.N.S. 505, 142 Eng.Rep. 199; Stansbury v. Fogle, 1873, 37 Md. 369; Dennis v. Ryan, 1875, 65 N.Y. 385; Hall v. Adams, 1917, 128 Ark. 116, 193 S.W. 520; Angelozzi v. Cossentino, 1931, 160 Md. 678, 155 A. 178; Fusario v. Cavallaro, 1928, 108 Conn. 40, 142 A. 391.

29. Meraz v. Valencia, 1922, 28 N.M. 174, 210 P. 225; Cooper v. Electro-Tint Eng. Co., 1918, 70 Pa.Super. 517; Gilbert v. Emmons, 1866, 42 Ill. 143; Mowry v. Miller, 1832, 3 Leigh. Va., 561, 24 Am.Dec. 680.

30. See Grimes v. Greenblatt, 1910, 47 Colo. 495, 107 P. 1111; Shannon v. Sims, 1906, 146 Ala. 673, 40 So. 574.

31. Lemke v. Anders, 1952, 261 Wis. 555, 53 N.W.2d 436; Bair v. Shoultz, 1943, 233 Iowa 980, 7 N.W.2d 904; Russell v. Chamberlain, 1906, 12 Idaho 299, 85 P. 926; Fusario v. Cavallaro, 1928, 108 Conn. 40, 142 A. 391; Gettinger v. McRae, 1899, 89 Md. 513, 43 A. 823.

32. Archer v. Cachat, 1956, 165 Ohio St. 286, 135 N.E.2d 404; Bromund v. Holt, 1964, 24 Wis.2d 336, 129 N.W.2d 149; Wilson v. O'Neal, Fla.App.1960, 118 So.2d 101; American Surety Co. v. Pryor, 1927, 217 Ala. 244, 115 So. 176; King v. Martin, 1928, 150 Va. 122, 142 S.E. 358. Even where the defendant signs a complaint at the officer's direction. Hughes v. Van Bruggen, 1940, 44 N.M. 534, 105 P.2d

494; cf. Charles Stores Co. v. O'Quinn, 4 Cir. 1949, 178 F.2d 372.

33. Cox v. Lauritsen, 1914, 126 Minn. 128, 147 N.W. 1093; Christy v. Rice, 1908, 152 Mich. 563, 116 N.W. 200; Malloy v. Chicago, M. & St. P. R. Co., 1914, 34 S.D. 330, 148 S.W. 598; Dickson v. Young, 1928, 208 Iowa 1, 221 N.W. 820; Caddel v. Brown, 1920, 57 Mont. 266, 187 P. 897.

34. Bennett v. Black, 1828, 1 Stew., Ala., 494; Frankfurter v. Bryan, 1882, 12 Ill.App. 549; Carter v. Sutherland, 1884, 52 Mich. 597, 18 N.W. 375; Hamburg v. Eagleson, 1921, 116 Wash. 616, 200 P. 306.

35. Zenik v. O'Brien, 1951, 137 Conn. 592, 79 A.2d 769. Cf. Mertens v. Mueller, 1913, 119 Md. 525, 87 A. 501; Mertens v. Mueller, 1914, 122 Md. 313, 89 A. 613; Hadley v. Tinnin, 1915, 170 N.C. 84, 86 S.E. 1017; Creelman v. Svenning, 1966, 67 Wash.2d 882, 410 P.2d 606.

36. Dennis v. Ryan, 1875, 65 N.Y. 385; cf. Wilmerton v. Sample, 1891, 42 Ill.App. 254.

37. Gregoire v. Biddle, 2 Cir. 1949, 177 F.2d 579, cert. denied, 339 U.S. 949; Yaselli v. Goff, D.N.Y.1925, 8 F.2d 161, affirmed 2 Cir. 1926, 12 F.2d 396, cert. denied 273 U.S. 677, affirmed, 1928, 275 U.S. 503; Griffith v. Slinkard, 1896, 146 Ind. 117, 44 N.E. 1001; Smith v. Parman, 1917, 101 Kan. 115, 165 P. 663; Watts v. Gerking, 1924, 111 Or. 641, 228 P. 135; Anderson v. Manley, 1935, 181 Wash. 327, 43 P.2d 39.

38. Ostmann v. Bruere, 1910, 141 Mo.App. 240, 124 S.W. 1059.

law enforcement officers [39] acting within the scope of their duties. There is authority, however, which may perhaps reach the right conclusion,[40] that where such an officer himself initiates the complaint,[41] or where he concocts false evidence,[42] he steps outside of his official function, and may be liable. Private attorneys are privileged to the extent of advising their clients as to the law,[43] and representing them in good faith,[44] but may be liable if they swear out complaints themselves without probable cause,[45] or if knowing that there is no sufficient basis for the prosecution, they proceed to assist it.[46]

Termination in Favor of Accused

In order to maintain his action for malicious prosecution, the plaintiff must show not only that the criminal proceeding has terminated,[47] but also that it has terminated in his favor.[48] Two reasons have been suggested for this. One is that a conviction of the accused is sufficient to establish that there was probable cause for the prosecution; [49] the other that in the malicious prosecution action the plaintiff cannot be permitted to make a collateral attack upon the criminal judgment, which would be "blowed off by a sidewind." [50] Hence a conviction is a bar to the action, even though there is an unexercised right of appeal,[51] and, according to decisions which have not gone without criticism,[52] even though the conviction was obtained by perjury or other fraud upon the court.[53] Likewise any disposition of the

---

39. Laughlin v. Garnett, 1943, 78 App.D.C. 194, 138 F.2d 931 (police); Coverstone v. Davies, 1952, 38 Cal.2d 315, 239 P.2d 876 (sheriff); White v. Towers, 1951, 37 Cal.2d 757, 235 P.2d 209 (fish and game investigator); Springfield v. Carter, 8 Cir. 1949, 175 F.2d 914 (building inspector); Adams v. Home Owners' Loan Corp., 8 Cir. 1939, 107 F.2d 139 (forwarding information to department under government regulations). See Note, 1954, 32 N.C.L.Rev. 360.

40. See, 1928, 12 Minn.L.Rev. 665, pointing out that the initiation of proceedings by the prosecuting attorney relieves others of responsibility, and so may leave the plaintiff without a remedy. See, generally, Jennings, Tort Liability of Administrative Officers, 1937, 21 Minn.L.Rev. 263.

41. Leong Yau v. Carden, 1916, 23 Hawaii 362; Prentice v. Bertken, 1942, 50 Cal.App.2d 344, 123 P. 2d 96 (highway patrol officer). Cf. Schneider v. Shepherd, 1916, 192 Mich. 82, 158 N.W. 182 (arrest without sworn complaint; false imprisonment).

42. Carpenter v. Sibley, 1908, 153 Cal. 215, 94 P. 879.

43. See Burnap v. Marsh, 1852, 13 Ill. 535.

44. Bicknell v. Dorion, 1835, 33 Mass., (16 Pick.) 478; Peck v. Chouteau, 1886, 91 Mo. 138, 3 S.W. 577; Stockley v. Hornidge, 1837, 8 C. & P. 11, 173 Eng.Rep. 377.

45. Whitney v. New York Cas. Ins. Ass'n, 1898, 27 App.Div. 320, 50 N.Y.S. 227.

46. Burnap v. Marsh, 1852, 13 Ill. 535; Warfield v. Campbell, 1859, 35 Ala. 349; Staley v. Turner, 1886, 21 Mo.App. 244; Anderson v. Canaday, 1913, 37 Okl. 171, 131 P. 697; Liquid Carbonic Acid Mfg. Co. v. Convert, 1898, 82 Ill.App. 39, affirmed, 1900, 186 Ill. 334, 57 N.E. 1129.

47. "Otherwise he might recover in the action and yet be convicted in the original prosecution." Fisher v. Bristow, 1779, 1 Dougl. 215, 99 Eng.Rep. 140. Accord: Wyatt v. Gridella, 1918, 82 W.Va. 266, 95 S.E. 956; Wilson v. Hale, 1901, 178 Mass. 111, 59 N.E. 632; Bonney v. King, 1903, 201 Ill. 47, 66 N.E. 377; Schaefer v. Cremer, 1905, 19 S.D. 656, 104 N. W. 468.

The statute of limitations does not begin to run until termination of the criminal action in favor of the accused. Sicola v. First Nat. Bank of Altoona, 1961, 404 Pa. 18, 170 A.2d 584.

48. Merritt v. Merritt, 1922, 193 Iowa 899, 188 N.W. 32; cf. Fetterley v. Gibson, 1930, 210 Cal. 282, 291 P. 411; 1937. See cases cited infra, to note 54.

49. Mellor v. Baddeley, 1834, 2 Cr. & M. 675, 149 Eng.Rep. 932; Frisbie v. Morris, 1903, 75 Conn. 637, 55 A. 9; Merritt v. Merritt, 1922, 193 Iowa 899, 188 N.W. 32.

50. Basebe v. Matthews, 1867, L.R. 2 C.P. 684. Accord, Bacon v. Towne, 1839, 4 Cush., Mass., 217.

51. Mellor v. Baddeley, 1834, 2 Cr. & M. 675, 149 Eng.Rep. 932; Luby v. Bennett, 1901, 111 Wis. 613, 87 N.W. 804; cf. Foster v. Denison, 1896, 19 R.I. 351, 36 A. 93 (right to move for a new trial). If an appeal has been taken, it has been said that the malicious prosecution action may be stayed. Marks v. Townsend, 1885, 97 N.Y. 590.

52. See Note, 1931, 25 Ill.L.Rev. 957; Winfield, Law of Tort, 1937, 648.

53. Basebe v. Matthews, 1867, L.R. 2 C.P. 684; Clewley v. Brown, Thomson, Inc., 1935, 120 Conn. 440, 181 A. 531; Turbessi v. Oliver Iron Min. Co., 1930, 250 Mich. 110, 229 N.W. 454; Keithley v. Stevens, 1908, 142 Ill.App. 406, affirmed, 1909, 238 Ill. 199, 87 N.E. 375. Contra, Johnson v. Girdwood, 1894, 7

cause which does not terminate it but permits it to be renewed, as in the case of the refusal of a grand jury to indict which is not followed by discharge,[54] cannot serve as a foundation for the action.

On the other hand, it will be enough that the proceeding is terminated in such a manner that it cannot be revived, and the prosecutor, if he proceeds further, will be put to a new one.[55] This is true, for example, of an acquittal in court,[56] a discharge by a magistrate [57] or a justice of the peace [58] upon preliminary hearing, or by a governor in extradition proceedings,[59] a failure of a grand jury to indict which results in discharge,[60] the quashing of an indictment,[61] the entry of a nolle prosequi [62] or a dismissal,[63] abandon-

ment of the prosecution by the prosecuting attorney or the complaining witness,[64] or continuance beyond a time limit,[65] where any of these things have the effect of ending the particular proceeding and requiring new process or other official action to commence a new prosecution. It may be said generally, that this is true whenever the charges or the proceeding are withdrawn on the initiative of the prosecution. There is, however, authority that when a proceeding is withdrawn merely in order to substitute immediately another one for the same offense, it is to be regarded as one continuous proceeding, which is not terminated.[66]

On the other hand, where charges are withdrawn or the prosecution is terminated at the instigation of the accused himself,[67] or by reason of a compromise into which he

---

Misc. 651, 28 N.Y.S. 151, affirmed, 1895, 143 N.Y. 660, 39 N.E. 21.

54. Knott v. Sargent, 1878, 125 Mass. 95; Stark v. Bindley, 1899, 152 Ind. 182, 52 N.E. 804. Cf. Komar v. City of New York, 1965, 24 App.Div.2d 941, 265 N.Y.S.2d 331 (release on own recognizance); Prentice v. Bertken, 1942, 50 Cal.App.2d 344, 123 P.2d 96 (non-arraignment).

55. See Graves v. Scott, 1905, 104 Va. 372, 51 S.E. 821; Apgar v. Woolston, 1881, 43 N.J.L. 57; Casebeer v. Drahoble, 1885, 13 Neb. 465, 14 N.W. 397; Southern Car & Foundry Co. v. Adams, 1901, 131 Ala. 147, 32 So. 503.

56. Singer Mfg. Co. v. Bryant, 1906, 105 Va. 403, 54 S.E. 320.

57. See v. Gosselin, 1946, 133 Conn. 158, 48 A.2d 560; Jaffe v. Stone, 1941, 18 Cal.2d 146, 114 P.2d 335; Moyle v. Drake, 1886, 141 Mass. 238, 6 N.E. 520; Rider v. Kite, 1897, 61 N.J.L. 8, 38 A. 754; Stewart v. Blair, 1911, 171 Ala. 147, 54 So. 506.

58. Overson v Lynch, 1957, 83 Ariz. 158, 317 P.2d 948.

59. Keller v. Butler, 1927, 246 N.Y. 249, 158 N.E. 510. Contra, Cowan v. Gamble, Mo.1952, 247 S.W.2d 779. See Note, 5 Stan.L.Rev. 560.

60. Kearney v. Mallon Suburban Motors, 1945, 23 N.J.Misc. 83, 41 A.2d 274; Zello v. Glover, Tex.Civ. App.1933, 59 S.W.2d 877; Wells v. Parker, 1905, 76 Ark. 41, 88 S.W. 602; Graves v. Dawson, 1881, 130 Mass. 78; McIver v. Russell, D.Md.1967, 264 F. Supp. 22.

61. Lytton v. Baird, 1883, 95 Ind. 349; Reit v. Meyer, 1914, 160 App.Div. 752, 146 N.Y.S. 75.

62. Taylor v. Hodge, 1948, 229 N.C. 558, 50 S.E.2d 307; Snead v. Jones, 1910, 169 Ala. 143, 53 So.

188; Lamprey v. H. P. Hood & Sons, 1905, 73 N.H. 384, 62 A. 380; De la Riva v. Owl Drug Co., 1967, 253 Cal.App.2d 593, 61 Cal.Rptr. 291; Wilson v. Lapham, 1923, 196 Iowa 745, 195 N.W. 235. Contra, Fogg v. First Nat. Bank, 1929, 268 Mass. 25, 167 N. E. 251.

63. Myhre v. Hessey, 1943, 242 Wis. 638, 9 N.W.2d 106; Green v. Warnock, 1936, 144 Kan. 170, 58 P.2d 1059; Rankin v. Saenger, Tex.Civ.App.1952, 250 S. W.2d 465.

64. Glover v. Heyward, 1917, 108 S.C. 486, 94 S.E. 878; Empire Gas & Fuel Co. v. Wainscott, 1923, 91 Okl. 66, 216 P. 141; Twist v. Mullinix, 1916, 126 Ark. 427, 190 S.W. 851; Manz v. Kippel, 1914, 158 Wis. 557, 149 N.W. 375; McRae v. Brant, 1967, 108 N.H. 177, 230 A.2d 753 (appeal).

65. Winkler v. Lenoir & Blowing Rock Lines, 1928, 195 N.C. 673, 143 S.E. 213.

66. Schippel v. Norton, 1888, 38 Kan. 567, 16 P. 804; Hartshorn v. Smith, 1898, 104 Ga. 235, 30 S.E. 666; Weglein v. Trow Directory P. & B. Co., 1912, 152 App.Div. 705, 137 N.Y.S. 556; Simmons v. Sullivan, 1914, 42 U.S.App.D.C. 523; Bacon v. Towne, 1849, 4 Cush., Mass., 217. The Restatement of Torts, § 660, concludes that there is no sufficient termination whenever new prosecution has been begun for the same offense; but this apparently is not borne out by the decisions. See Reell v Petritz, 1922, 224 Ill. App. 65.

67. This does not include a motion to dismiss for lack of prosecution, where the prosecution has abandoned the case. Gumm v. Heider, 1960, 220 Or. 5, 348 P.2d 455.

has entered voluntarily,[68] there is no sufficient termination in favor of the accused. Sometimes it is said that this is an admission of probable cause; [69] but the better reason seems to be that the accused has consented to a termination which leaves open the question of his guilt and possible conviction, and so cannot take advantage of it,[70] after the prosecutor has voluntarily foregone the opportunity of proving that there was really guilt.[71] If the consent is found to have been given under protest because of "duress," however, the courts have refused to hold that the cause of action is lost.[72] The distinction is at best a vague one, and it may be that the court's opinion as to the probable guilt or innocence of the accused has entered into it. Where the prosecution has terminated by reason of suppression of evidence or other improper conduct on the part of the accused, malicious prosecution will not lie,[73] and the same is true where it was impossible to bring him to trial because he has left the jurisdiction.[74]

A further limitation upon the action of malicious prosecution is that it is always open to the defendant to show that the plaintiff was in fact guilty of the offense with which he was charged.[75] This defense, which is closely analogous to that of truth in actions for defamation,[76] is supported by a similar policy in favor of encouraging exposure of the guilty.[77] It does not depend upon the prosecutor's reasonable belief that the accused was in fact guilty, and it is available even though the criminal proceeding was begun with no such belief at all.[78] As in defamation, the burden of proof of the issue is upon the defendant,[79] and the guilt proved must be substantially equivalent to the charge made.[80] The defense is available notwithstanding an acquittal in the criminal proceeding,[81] and the question of guilt is retried in the malicious prosecution action. The reason for this is that a verdict of not guilty does not necessarily establish innocence, but merely a failure of the prosecu-

68. Freedman v. Chabro Motors, Inc., Fla.App.1967, 199 So.2d 745; Bristol v. Eckhardt, 1949, 254 Wis. 297, 36 N.W.2d 56; Alexander v. Lindsey, 1949, 230 N.C. 663, 55 S.E.2d 470; Leonard v. George, 4 Cir. 1949, 178 F.2d 312, cert. denied 339 U.S. 965; Ellis v. Sinton Savings Ass'n, Tex.Civ.App.1970, 455 S. W.2d 834. See Note, 1950, 3 Vand.L.Rev. 841.

69. Nelson v. National Cas. Co., 1929, 179 Minn. 53, 228 N.W. 437; Saner v. Bowker, 1924, 69 Mont. 463, 222 P. 1056; Ruble v. Cohn, 1918, 212 Ill.App. 563; Forster v. Orr, 1889, 17 Or. 447, 21 P. 440.

70. Restatement of Torts, § 660, Comment b.

71. "If this should be allowed, the defendant would be deceived by the consent, as without that he would certainly have gone on with the action, and might have shown a foundation for it." Wilkinson v. Howell, 1830, M. & M. 495, 173 Eng.Rep. 1236.

72. White v. International Text Book Co., 1912, 156 Iowa 210, 136 N.W. 121; Morton v. Young, 1867, 55 Me. 24; Smith v. Markensohn, 1908, 29 R.I. 55, 69 A. 311; Lyons v. Davy-Pocahontas Coal Co., 1915, 75 W.Va. 739, 84 S.E. 744. An analogy may be suggested to the cases of contracts compounding a felony.

73. See Leyenberger v. Paul, 1890, 40 Ill.App. 516; Halberstadt v. New York Life Ins. Co., 1909, 194 N.Y. 1, 86 N.E. 801; Restatement of Torts, § 660(a).

74. Halberstadt v. New York Life Ins. Co., 1909, 194 N.Y. 1, 86 N.E. 801.

75. Shoemaker v. Selnes, 1960, 220 Or. 573, 349 P.2d 473; Clary v. Hale, 1959, 175 Cal.App.2d 880, 1 Cal.Rptr. 91; Horne v. Bridwell, 1952, 193 Va. 381, 68 S.E.2d 535; Nettleton v. Cook, 1917, 30 Idaho 82, 163 P. 300; Sessoms v. Union Savings & Trust Co., 6 Cir. 1964, 338 F.2d 752 (Ohio law) rehearing denied 342 F.2d 751, cert. denied 382 U.S. 821.

76. See supra, p. 796.

77. Harper, Malicious Prosecution, False Imprisonment and Defamation, 1937, 15 Tex.L.Rev. 157, 174.

78. Mooney v. Mull, 1939, 216 N.C. 410, 5 S.E.2d 122; Newton v. Weaver, 1882, 13 R.I. 616.

79. Shelton v. Southern R. Co., D.Tenn.1918, 255 F. 182; Levin v. Costello, 1919, 214 Ill.App. 505; Magowan v. Rickey, 1900, 64 N.J.L. 402, 45 A. 804.

80. Cf. Nettleton v. Cook, 1917, 30 Idaho 82, 163 P. 300; Sears v. Hathaway, 1859, 12 Cal. 277.

81. Shoemaker v. Selnes, 1960, 220 Or. 573, 349 P.2d 473; Mack v. Sharp, 1904, 138 Mich. 448, 101 N.W. 631; Wiggs v. Farmer, 1964, 205 Va. 149, 135 S.E. 2d 829; Mooney v. Mull, 1939, 216 N.C. 410, 5 S.E. 2d 122; Newton v. Weaver, 1882, 13 R.I. 616.

tion to prove guilt beyond a reasonable doubt; and in the subsequent civil action, where all that is required is a preponderance of the evidence on the issue,[82] a further inquiry may be made before a new jury as to whether the lesser burden of proof can be sustained. Thus, while an unreversed conviction is conclusive as to guilt and bars malicious prosecution, an acquittal is not conclusive as to the plaintiff's innocence.[83]

Probable Cause

Malicious prosecution is an action which runs counter to obvious policies of the law in favor of encouraging proceedings against those who are apparently guilty, and letting finished litigation remain undisturbed and unchallenged.[84] It never has been regarded with any favor by the courts, and it is hedged with restrictions which make it very difficult to maintain.[85] Chief among these is the requirement that the plaintiff must sustain the burden of proof [86] that the criminal proceeding was initiated or continued by the defend-

ant without "probable cause." This is true even though the defendant is found to have acted with "malice," for an improper purpose,[87] since it is the part of a good citizen to bring about the prosecution of those who are reasonably suspected of crime, and the addition of a personal motive should not result in liability for performing a public obligation. The existence of such "malice" does not create even an inference that probable cause was lacking.[88]

Probable cause has been defined as "a reasonable ground of suspicion, supported by circumstances sufficient to warrant an ordinarily prudent man in believing the party is guilty of the offense." [89] It resembles very closely the reasonable conduct under the circumstances which is the fundamental issue in negligence cases.[90] It includes first of all an honest belief in the guilt of the accused,[91] since the reasonable man will not prosecute

---

82. See, generally, Groom, Proof of Crime in a Civil Proceeding, 1929, 13 Minn.L.Rev. 556.

83. Restatement of Torts, § 667.

84. Green, Judge and Jury, 1930, 338–339. There are good discussions of the policy involved in Griswold v. Horne, 1917, 19 Ariz. 56, 165 P. 318; Schubkegel v. Gordino, 1943, 56 Cal.App.2d 667, 133 P.2d 475. Cf. Mayflower Industries v. Thor Corp., 1951, 15 N.J.Super. 139, 83 A.2d 246, affirmed, 1952, 9 N.J. 605, 89 A.2d 242.

85. ". . . indeed it is so much hedged about with restrictions and the burden of proof upon the plaintiff is so heavy that no honest prosecutor is ever likely to be deterred by it from doing his duty. It is notable how rarely an action is brought at all, much less a successful one, for this tort." Winfield, Law of Tort, 1937, 644. "There is no other cause of action which is more carefully guarded." Green, Judge and Jury, 1930, 338.

86. Mitchell v. John Heine & Sons, 1938, 38 N.S.W. 466; Eumont v. Railway Express Agency, 1948, 213 La. 1040, 36 So.2d 30; Garfield v. People's Finance & Thrift Co. of Riverside, 1937, 24 Cal.App.2d 144, 74 P.2d 1061; Noblett v. Bartsch, 1903, 31 Wash. 24, 71 P. 551; Legallee v. Blaisdell, 1883, 134 Mass. 473. Cf. Ferry v. Ferry, 1947, 94 N.H. 395, 54 A.2d 151 (must be pleaded).

87. Foshay v. Ferguson, 1846, 2 Denio (N.Y.) 617; Stewart v. Sonneborn, 1878, 98 U.S. 187; Glenn v. Lawrence, 1917, 280 Ill. 581, 117 N.E. 757; Jordan v. Alabama G. S. R. Co., 1886, 81 Ala. 220, 8 So. 191; Smith v. Pierson, Tex.Civ.App.1912, 151 S.W. 1113. Contra, Curley v. Automobile Finance Co., 1941, 343 Pa. 280, 23 A.2d 48.

88. Stewart v. Sonneborn, 1878, 98 U.S. 187; Plummer v. Collins, 1910, 1 Boyce (Del.) 281, 77 A. 750; Moneyweight Scale Co. v. McCormick, 1909, 109 Md. 170, 72 A. 537; Rouse v. Burnham, 10 Cir. 1931, 51 F.2d 709.

89. Gallucci v. Milavic, Fla.1958, 100 So.2d 375; McAfee v. Los Angeles Gas & Elec. Corp., 1932, 215 Cal. 219, 9 P.2d 212; Hyman v. New York Cent. R. Co., 1925, 240 N.Y. 137, 147 N.E. 613; McGann v. Allen, 1926, 105 Conn. 177, 134 A. 810; Louisville & N. R. Co. v. Sharp, 1940, 282 Ky. 758, 140 S.W.2d 383.

90. Green, Judge and Jury, 1930, 342. Cf. Lee v. Levison, 1916, 173 Cal. 166, 149 P. 438 ("reasonable man"); Miller v. Willis, 1920, 189 Ind. 664, 128 N.E. 831 ("reasonable, prudent and cautious"); Hudson v. Nolen, 1911, 142 Ky. 824, 135 S.W. 414 ("of ordinary judgment and reasonable discretion").

91. Pessagno v. Keyes, 1923, 143 Md. 437, 122 A. 651; Dunlap v. Chesapeake & Ohio R. Co., 1929, 107 W. Va. 186, 148 S.E. 105; Bowie v. Stackpole, 1920, 119 Me. 333, 111 A. 409; Watson v. Cain, 1911, 171 Ala. 151, 54 So. 610; Callahan v. Kelso, 1913, 170 Mo.App. 338, 156 S.W. 716.

another whom he does not believe to be guilty; and this belief must be one as to the fact of guilt, rather than as to the possibility of securing a conviction.[92] While it need not approach absolute certainty as to the facts, and it is not inconsistent with a considerable element of doubt,[93] it must be more than mere conjecture or unfounded suspicion.[94] Beyond this, the belief must be supported by appearances[95] known to the defendant at the time, and a prosecution instituted without probable cause cannot be justified by anything, short of guilt in fact, which comes to the knowledge of the defendant later.[96]

The appearances must be such as to lead a reasonable man to set the criminal proceeding in motion.[97] The defendant is not necessarily required to verify his information, where it appears to be reliable;[98] but where

a reasonable man would investigate further before beginning the prosecution, he may be liable for failure to do so.[99] All such factors as the reliability of the source,[1] the availability of further information[2] and the difficulty of obtaining it,[3] the reputation of the accused,[4] and his opportunity to offer an explanation,[5] and the apparent necessity of prompt action,[6] are to be considered in determining whether it was reasonable to act without seeking verification.

Since probable cause is a matter of the appearances presented to the defendant, a mistake of fact as to the conduct of the accused will of course not prevent its existence. Some courts have held[7] that a mistake of law, as to whether such conduct amounts to a criminal offense, or to the particular offense

---

92. Michael v. Matson, 1909, 81 Kan. 360, 105 P. 537 (belief in guilt but not likelihood of conviction); Schwartz v. Boswell, 1913, 156 Ky. 103, 160 S.W. 748 (same); Connery v. Manning, 1895, 163 Mass. 44, 39 N.E. 558 (vice versa).

93. McAfee v. Los Angeles Gas & Elec. Corp., 1932, 215 Cal. 219, 9 P.2d 212; Knapp v. Chicago, B. & Q. R. Co., 1901, 113 Iowa 532, 85 N.W. 769; Bowen v. W. A. Pollard & Co., 1917, 173 N.C. 129, 91 S.E. 711.

94. Hyman v. New York Cent. R. Co., 1925, 240 N.Y. 137, 147 N.E. 613; Graeter v. Williams, 1876, 55 Ind. 461; Krol v. Plodick, 1915, 77 N.H. 557, 94 A. 261; Stone v. Stevens, 1837, 12 Conn. 219.

95. The fact that the defendant's information was false of course does not prevent his having probable cause. Kennedy v. Burbidge, 1919, 54 Utah 497, 183 P. 325.

96. Smith v. King, 1893, 62 Conn. 515, 26 A. 1059; Galloway v. Stewart, 1874, 49 Ind. 156; Nachtman v. Hammer, 1893, 155 Pa. 200, 26 A. 311.

97. Well stated by Vann, J., in Burt v. Smith, 1905, 181 N.Y. 1, 73 N.E. 495. Accord: Perry v. Hurdle, 1948, 229 N.C. 216, 49 S.E.2d 400; Tucker v. Bartlett, 1916, 97 Kan. 163, 155 P. 1; Alexander v. Emmke, Mo.App.1929, 15 S.W.2d 868; Casavan v. Sage, 1909, 201 Mass. 547, 87 N.E. 893 (a "cautious man"). See Note, 1949, 3 Ark.L.Rev. 445.

98. Campbell v. Yellow Cab. Co., 3 Cir. 1942, 137 F. 2d 918; Brodie v. Huck, 1948, 187 Va. 485, 47 S.E. 2d 310; Johnson v. Southern Pac. Co., 1910, 157 Cal. 333, 107 P. 611; Birdsall v. Smith, 1909, 158 Mich. 390, 122 N.W. 626; Kansas & T. Coal Co. v. Galloway, 1903, 71 Ark. 351, 74 S.W. 521.

99. Hutchinson v. Wenzel, 1900, 155 Ind. 49, 56 N.E. 845; Wilson v. Thurlow, 1912, 156 Iowa 656, 137 N.W. 956; Thompson v. Price, 1894, 100 Mich. 558, 59 N.W. 253; Bechel v. Pacific Exp. Co., 1902, 65 Neb. 826, 91 N.W. 853.

1. Blunk v. Atchison, T. & S. F. R. Co., C.C.Mo.1889, 38 F. 311; Plassau v. Louisiana Lottery Co., 1882, 34 La.Ann. 246; Chapman v. Dunn, 1885, 56 Mich. 31, 22 N.W. 101. Admissions of the accused may provide probable cause. Rawls v. Bennett, 1942, 221 N.C. 127, 19 S.E.2d 126.

2. Lacy v. Mitchell, 1864, 23 Ind. 67; Boyd v. Mendenhall, 1893, 53 Minn. 274, 55 N.W. 45; Sweet v. Smith, 1899, 42 App.Div. 502, 59 N.Y.S. 404; Thompson v. Price, 1894, 100 Mich. 558, 59 N.W. 253.

3. Fisher v. Hamilton, 1874, 49 Ind. 341 (danger); Kansas & T. Coal Co. v. Galloway, 1903, 71 Ark. 351, 74 S.W. 521.

4. Woodworth v. Mills, 61 Wis. 44, 20 N.W. 728; Stubbs v. Mulholland, 1902, 168 Mo. 47, 67 S.W. 650; Hirsch v. Feeney, 1876, 83 Ill. 548.

5. Hutchinson v. Wenzel, 1900, 155 Ind. 49, 56 N.E. 845; Norrell v. Vogel, 1888, 39 Minn. 107, 38 N.W. 705; Bechel v. Pacific Exp. Co., 1902, 65 Neb. 826, 91 N.W. 853; Lacy v. Mitchell, 1864, 23 Ind. 67.

6. Restatement of Torts, § 662, Comment *i.*

7. Gray v. Bennett, 1959, 250 N.C. 707, 110 S.E.2d 324; Dunn v. Alabama Oil & Gas Co., 1956, 42 Tenn.App. 108, 299 S.W.2d 25; Vasser v. Berry, 1952, 85 Ga.App. 435, 69 S.E.2d 701; Brown v. Kisner, 1942, 192 Miss. 746, 6 So.2d 611; Nehr v. Dobbs, 1896, 47 Neb. 863, 66 N.W. 864. See Note, 1958, 25 Tenn.L.Rev. 316.

charged, cannot protect the instigator of prosecution—apparently upon the antique and questionable theory that he is required at his peril to know the law. For the most part such cases appear to have involved mistakes of law so extreme that they would be unreasonable even for a layman to make. What would seem to be much the better view is that supported by a considerable minority of the decisions,[8] that a mistake of law stands upon the same footing as a mistake of fact, and will not preclude probable cause if it is one which it is reasonable for the particular individual to make under the circumstances.

The layman's ignorance of the law has been taken into account, however, in the almost universal[9] holding that probable cause is established where the prosecution was instituted with the advice of counsel.[10] Such advice is properly addressed to the question of probable cause, since it bears upon the defendant's reasonable belief that he has a legal justification for the criminal proceeding; and for this purpose it is effective even though it may be erroneous and not warranted by the facts submitted to counsel.[11] It must, however, be followed,[12] and in good faith, rather than as a mere pretext or cover for the defendant's personal ends.[13] The opinion of an attorney that the defendant has sufficient evidence cannot serve as a substitute for belief in the guilt of the accused, since a reasonable man would not proceed in such a case.[14] Furthermore, the defendant must have made full and fair disclosure to the attorney of everything within his knowledge and information[15] which a reasonable man would regard as material for the attorney to know[16] in order to give a sound opinion; and the failure to disclose any such information,[17] or false statements to the attorney[18] will prevent any justifiable reliance on the advice given. Some courts have gone further, and have required that the defend-

8.   Whipple v. Gorsuch, 1907, 82 Ark. 252, 101 S.W. 735; Nettleton v. Cook, 1917, 30 Idaho 82, 163 P. 300; Vincioni v. Phelps Dodge Corp., 1930, 35 N.M. 81, 290 P. 319; Kuhnhausen v. Stadelman, 1944, 174 Or. 290, 144 P.2d 168; Franklin v. Irvine, 1921, 52 Cal.App. 286, 198 P. 647. Cf. Dunlap v. New Zealand Fire & Marine Ins. Co., 1895, 109 Cal. 365, 42 P. 29 (advice of counsel). Accord, as to unconstitutional statutes: Birdsall v. Smith, 1909, 158 Mich. 390, 122 N.W. 626.

9.   See Preston, Advice of Counsel as a Defense, 1941, 28 Va.L.Rev. 26, 34. A small number of courts have held that advice of counsel is not a complete defense, but only to be considered by the jury on the issue of probable cause. Aland v. Pyle, 1919, 263 Pa. 254, 106 A. 349; Gulf, C. & S. F. R. Co. v. James, 1889, 73 Tex. 12, 10 S.W. 744; Bassinov v. Finkle, 1964, 261 N.C. 109, 134 S.E.2d 130; cf. Gladfelter v. Doemel, 1958, 2 Wis.2d 635, 87 N.W.2d 490 (not conclusive where evidence of malice).

10.   Reid v. True, Ky.1957, 302 S.W.2d 846; Thomas v. Hinton, 1955, 76 Idaho 337, 281 P.2d 1050; Kunz v. Johnson, 1953, 74 S.D. 577, 57 N.W.2d 116; Citizens State Bank of Long Beach v. Hoffman, 1941, 44 Cal.App.2d 854, 113 P.2d 221; White v. Pacific Tel. & Tel. Co., 1939, 162 Or. 270, 90 P.2d 193. See Note, 1937, 21 Minn.L.Rev. 217.

11.   Kompass v. Light, 1899, 122 Mich. 86, 80 N.W. 1008; Steed v. Knowles, 1885, 79 Ala. 446; Chapman v. Anderson, 1925, 55 U.S.App.D.C. 165, 3 F.2d 336; Brodrib v. Doberstein, 1928, 107 Conn. 294, 140 A. 483.

12.   Manning v. Finn, 1888, 23 Neb. 511, 37 N.W. 314.

13.   Adkin v. Pillen, 1904, 136 Mich. 682, 100 N.W. 176; McCarthy v. Kitchen, 1877, 59 Ind. 500; Neufeld v. Rodeminski, 1893, 144 Ill. 83, 32 N.E. 913; Hopkinson v. Lehigh Valley R. Co., 1928, 249 N.Y. 296, 164 N.E. 104.

14.   Vann v. McCreary, 1888, 77 Cal. 434, 19 P. 826; Johnson v. Miller, 1891, 82 Iowa 693, 47 N.W. 903, affirmed 82 Iowa 693, 48 N.W. 1081; Burke v. Watts, 1922, 188 Cal. 118, 204 P. 578; Gurden v. Stevens, 1906, 146 Mich. 489, 109 N.W. 856.

15.   But not, of course, what he does not know. Elmer v. Chicago & N. W. R. Co., 1952, 260 Wis. 567, 51 N.W.2d 707.

16.   But not minor collateral details. Brooks v. Bolde, 1941, 11 Wash.2d 37, 118 P.2d 193.

17.   Southern Farmers Ass'n v. Whitfield, 1964, 238 Ark. 607, 383 S.W.2d 506; Jackson v. Beckham, 1963, 217 Cal.App.2d 264, 31 Cal.Rptr. 739; Galafaro v. Kuenstler, 1958, 53 N.J.Super. 379, 147 A.2d 550; Kirkpatrick v. Hollingsworth, 1952, 207 Okl. 292, 249 P.2d 434; Hubert v. Alta Life Ins. Co., 1939, 136 Pa.Super. 147, 7 A.2d 98. The fact that the attorney would not listen to full disclosure is no excuse. Exchange Nat. Bank of Colorado Springs v. Cullum, 1945, 114 Colo. 26, 161 P.2d 336.

18.   Drakos v. Jones, 1941, 189 Okl. 593, 118 P.2d 388; Smith v. Hensley, 1941, 107 Colo. 180, 109 P.2d 909.

ant use the diligence of a reasonable man to ascertain anything that he does not know before consulting counsel,[19] but the prevailing view, which seems the better one, is that this is unnecessary where he informs the attorney of the state of his information and is assured that he need not seek to learn anything more.[20]

The advice of counsel establishes probable cause only when it is given by an apparently competent attorney, duly admitted to the practice of law within the state where the proceedings are brought,[21] or, if he is admitted to practice elsewhere, apparently qualified to offer a reliable opinion as to the applicable law.[22] The advice of a layman is not sufficient, even though he holds some official position such as that of magistrate or justice of the peace,[23] since whatever dignity

accompanies such an office does not carry with it any assurance of competence to advise a client. The attorney must advise in his professional capacity, and can give no protection when it is clear that he is not speaking as an attorney;[24] but the fact that he is regularly employed by the defendant does not prevent his giving reliable professional advice.[25] Prosecuting attorneys employed by the state are at least as well qualified to give advice on criminal proceedings as any others, and it is agreed everywhere that their advice is sufficient to establish probable cause.[26]

The attorney must be apparently disinterested, and there cannot be justifiable reliance upon his opinion where he is known to have an interest of his own to protect by the prosecution,[27] or to be biased or prejudiced

19.   Jones v. Flaherty, 1917, 139 Minn. 97, 165 N.W. 963; Nelson v. Peterman, 1926, 119 Okl. 125, 249 P. 333; Hendrie v. Perkins, 1931, 240 Ky. 366, 42 S. W.2d 502.

20.   Johnson v. Miller, 1886, 69 Iowa 562, 29 N.W. 743; Scrivani v. Dondero, 1900, 128 Cal. 31, 60 P. 463; Hess v. Oregon German Baking Co., 1897, 31 Or. 503, 49 P. 803; King v. Apple River Power Co., 1907, 131 Wis. 575, 111 N.W. 668.

21.   Competence: Clement v. Major, 1896, 8 Colo.App. 86, 44 P. 776; Stubbs v. Mulholland, 1902, 168 Mo. 47, 67 S.W. 650; Roy v. Goings, 1885, 112 Ill. 656. License for practice: Stanton v. Hart, 1873, 27 Mich. 539; Davis v. Baker, 1899, 88 Ill.App. 251; Murphy v. Larson, 1875, 77 Ill. 172; Anderson v. Fletcher, 1923, 228 Ill.App. 372. In the last two cases it was held that one who consulted a person whom he had reason to believe a qualified attorney was not protected. It is at least open to question whether a layman should be required at his peril to know the membership of the bar.

22.   Truman v. Fidelity & Cas. Co., 1961, 146 W.Va. 707, 123 S.E.2d 59; Closgard Wardrobe Co. v. Normandy, 1932, 158 Va. 50, 163 S.E. 355; Goldstein v. Foulkes, 1896, 19 R.I. 291, 36 A. 9; El Reno Gas & Elec. Co. v. Spurgeon, 1911, 30 Okl. 88, 118 P. 397.

23.   Brown v. Kisner, 1942, 192 Miss. 746, 6 So.2d 711; Jones v. MacConochie, 1948, 162 Pa.Super. 124, 56 A.2d 284; Catzen v. Belcher, 1908, 64 W.Va. 314, 61 S.E. 930; Clinchfield Coal Corp. v. Redd, 1918, 123 Va. 420, 96 S.E. 836.

Accord: Mowell v. Von Moschzisker, 1932, 109 N.J.L. 241, 160 A. 680 (handwriting expert); Groda v. American Stores Co., 1934, 315 Pa. 484, 173 A. 419

(state constabulary); Morin v. Moreau, 1914, 112 Me. 471, 92 A. 527 (clerk of court); Truax v. Pennsylvania R. Co., 1895, 58 N.J.L. 218, 33 A. 278 (court commissioner).

Contra: Monaghan v. Cox, 1892, 155 Mass. 487, 30 N. E. 467; Ball v. Rawles, 1892, 93 Cal. 222, 28 P. 937.

24.   See Marks v. Hastings, 1893, 101 Ala. 165, 174, 13 So. 297, 299; Morin v. Moreau, 1914, 112 Me. 471, 92 A. 527, 528; Mayer v. Goodman, 1923, 94 Okl. 12, 15, 220 P. 656, 659.

25.   Truman v. Fidelity & Cas. Co., 1961, 146 W.Va. 707, 123 S.E.2d 59; Miller v. American Nat. Bank in Little Falls, 1943, 216 Minn. 19, 11 N.W.2d 655; Closgard Wardrobe Co. v. Normandy, 1932, 158 Va. 50, 163 S.E. 355; Bell v. Jewel Tea Co., D.Ky.1955, 135 F.Supp. 745; Ashland v. Lapiner Motor Co., 1956, 247 Iowa 596, 75 N.W.2d 357.

26.   Montgomery Ward & Co. v. Pherson, 1954, 129 Colo. 502, 272 P.2d 643; Modla v. Miller, 1955, 344 Mich. 21, 73 N.W.2d 220; Jones v. Zimmerman, 1957, 180 Kan. 701, 308 P.2d 96; Peasley v. Puget Sound Tug & Barge Co., 1942, 13 Wash.2d 485, 125 P.2d 681; Petrie v. Roberts, 1943, 242 Wis. 539, 8 N.W.2d 355.

27.   White v. Carr, 1880, 71 Me. 555; Union v. United Battery Serv. Co., 1929, 35 Ohio App. 68, 171 N.E. 608; Vinal v. Core, 1881, 18 W.Va. 1; Adkin v. Pillen, 1904, 136 Mich. 682, 100 N.W. 176. Cf. Smith v. Hensley, 1941, 107 Colo. 180, 209 P.2d 909 (counsel husband).

But the fact that the advice was not given in good faith will not affect the defendant where he had no reason to suspect it. Seabridge v. McAdam, 1897, 119 Cal. 460, 51 P. 691; Shea v. Cloquet Lumber Co., 1904, 92 Minn. 348, 100 N.W. 111.

against the plaintiff,[28] or where his fees will depend upon the number of prosecutions brought.[29] Although one attorney, as a defendant, may be protected by the advice of another,[30] it is sufficiently obvious that no man can justify his conduct by reliance upon his own opinion as his own counsel.[31] The ordinary interest which any attorney feels in the affairs of his client, however, even though it be inspired by the prospect of a fee, will not disqualify his advice; and the opinion of a retained counsel, who has represented the defendant in other litigation, has been held to be sufficient.[32]

Considerable controversy has arisen over the effect of the disposition of the criminal proceeding itself as evidence of the existence or absence of probable cause. This necessarily will turn upon how far such a disposition is to be regarded as a determination by those who are legally qualified of the sufficiency of the evidence to justify a reasonable belief in guilt. It is agreed that an acquittal after trial is no evidence of the lack of probable cause, since it amounts only to a decision that the fact of guilt has not been proved beyond a reasonable doubt.[33] On the other hand, a discharge by a magistrate after preliminary hearing, or the refusal of a grand jury to indict, is at least evidence that probable cause was lacking, since it is the function of such individuals to pass upon the sufficiency of the case against the accused to justify prosecution. Although there is authority to the contrary,[34] the prevailing rule is that either is conclusive of the issue [35] unless the defendant explains it, as by showing that the discharge was not upon the merits, or was due to official misconduct, or was based upon testimony offered by the accused at the hearing.[36] A discharge brought about by abandonment of the proceedings by the prosecuting witness [37] or the prosecuting attorney [38] usually is held to afford no evidence

---

28. Perrenoud v. Helm, 1902, 65 Neb. 77, 90 N.W. 980; Smith v. Fields, 1910, 139 Ky. 60, 129 S.W. 325.

29. McGarry v. Missouri Pac. R. Co., 1889, 36 Mo. App. 340.

30. Steadman v. Topham, 1959, 80 Wyo. 63, 338 P.2d 820; Terre Haute & I. R. Co. v. Mason, 1897, 148 Ind. 578, 46 N.E. 332.

31. Epstein v. Berkowsky, 1896, 64 Ill.App. 498; Whipple v. Gorsuch, 1907, 82 Ark. 252, 101 S.W. 735. Cf. Union v. United Battery Serv. Co., 1929, 35 Ohio App. 68, 171 N.E. 608 (officer and director of defendant corporation); but see contra, Charles City Plow & Mfg. Co. v. Jones, 1887, 71 Iowa 234, 32 N.W. 280.

32. Miller v. American Nat. Bank in Little Falls, 1943, 216 Minn. 19, 11 N.W.2d 655; Kroger Groc. & Baking Co. v. Hamlin, 1921, 193 Ky. 116, 235 S.W. 4; Steppuhn v. Railroad, 1918, 199 Mo.App. 571, 204 S.W. 579.

33. Moran Utilities Co. v. Childs, Tex.Civ.App.1965, 392 S.W.2d 536; Conder v. Morrison, 1938, 275 Ky. 360, 121 S.W.2d 930; Boyd v. Hodson, 1947, 117

Ind.App. 296, 72 N.E.2d 46; Meyer v. Nedry, 1938, 159 Or. 62, 78 P.2d 339; Altman v. Standard Refrig. Co., 1934, 315 Pa. 465, 173 A. 411.

34. Glenn v. Lawrence, 1917, 280 Ill. 581, 117 N.E. 757 (no indictment); Apgar v. Woolston, 1881, 43 N.J.L. 57 (same); Davis v. McMillan, 1905, 142 Mich. 391, 105 N.W. 862 (discharge); Chesapeake & Ohio R. Co. v. Faverty, 1925, 212 Ky. 140, 278 S.W. 551 (same); Heldt v. Webster, 1883, 60 Tex. 207 (same).

35. Tucker v. Bartlett, 1916, 97 Kan. 163, 155 P. 1; Eggett v. Allen, 1903, 119 Wis. 625, 96 N.W. 803; Sudnick v. Kohn, 1918, 81 W.Va. 492, 94 S.E. 962 (discharge); Shelton v. Southern R. Co., D.Tenn. 1918, 255 F. 182; Harper v. Harper, 1901, 49 W.Va. 661, 39 S.E. 661 (failure to indict). See Restatement of Torts, §§ 663(1), 664(1).

36. As in Nettleton v. Cook, 1917, 30 Idaho 82, 163 P. 300; Snide v. Smith, 1918, 102 Neb. 448, 167 N.W. 573 (not on merits); Cole v. Curtis, 1881, 16 Minn. 182; Harper v. Harper, 1901, 49 W.Va. 661, 39 S.E. 661 (evidence of accused).

37. Norvell v. Safeway Stores, 1957, 212 Md. 14, 128 A.2d 591; Floyd County Dairies Co. v. Brooks, 1939, 61 Ga.App. 239, 6 S.E.2d 360; Odell v. Hatfield, 1903, 40 Misc. 13, 81 N.Y.S. 158; Western Union Tel. Co. v. Thomasson, 4 Cir. 1918, 251 F. 833; Remington Typewriter Co. v. Nolan, 3 Cir. 1918, 250 F. 685.

38. Smith v. Clark, 1910, 37 Utah 116, 106 P. 653; McIntosh v. Wales, 1913, 21 Wyo. 397, 134 P. 274; Prine v. Singer Sewing Mach. Co., 1913, 176 Mich. 300, 142 N.W. 377; Eckerle v. Higgins, 1911, 159 Mo.App. 177, 140 S.W. 616. See Restatement of Torts, § 665(2).

of lack of probable cause; but here again there are decisions to the contrary.[39]

Conversely, where the accused is committed or held to bail by a magistrate,[40] or indicted by the grand jury,[41] it is evidence that there was probable cause for the prosecution. It is very often said that this establishes a "prima facie" case; but since the plaintiff has the burden of proving lack of probable cause in any case, and is free to do so,[42] this apparently means nothing more than that the commitment is important evidence on the issue.[43] The same effect is given to a commitment where the accused has waived the preliminary examination.[44] A conviction

after trial, even though it is subsequently reversed,[45] obviously presents strong evidence that there was enough of a case to convince a jury, and it usually is held to be conclusive as to the existence of probable cause,[46] in the absence of a showing that the conviction was obtained by fraud, perjury or other corrupt means.[47] There is a considerable minority view which regards the conviction as creating only a presumption, which may be rebutted by any competent evidence showing that probable cause for the prosecution did not in fact exist.[48] Very possibly, however, the practical effect of the two rules is the same, since proceeding without probable cause will ordinarily involve a fraud upon the court.[49]

The courts have always distrusted malicious prosecution actions, and have retained a strong hand over them. For this reason the existence of probable cause, which in-

39. Peasley v. Puget Sound Tug & Barge Co., 1942, 13 Wash.2d 485, 125 P.2d 681; State ex rel. Mann v. Timble, 1921, 290 Mo. 661, 232 S.W. 100; Eagleton v. Kabrich, 1896, 66 Mo.App. 231; Quinlan v. Breslin, 1938, 61 R.I. 327, 200 A. 989; see Restatement of Torts, § 665(1). It is of course clear that such a dismissal, with other facts, may be sufficient. Shoemaker v. Shoemaker, 1951, 11 N.J.Super. 471, 78 A.2d 605.

40. Gallucci v. Milavic, Fla.1958, 100 So.2d 375; Penton v. Canning, 1941, 57 Wyo. 390, 118 P.2d 1002; Mitchem v. National Weaving Co., 1936, 210 N.C. 732, 188 S.E. 329; White v. Pacific Tel. & Tel. Co., 1939, 162 Or. 270, 90 P.2d 193; L. B. Price Mercantile Co. v. Cuilla, 1911, 100 Ark. 316, 141 S.W. 194; Restatement of Torts, § 663(2).

41. Friedes v. Sani-Mode Mfg. Co., 1965, 33 Ill.2d 291, 211 N.E.2d 286; Brown v. Simab Corp., 1963, 20 App.Div.2d 121, 244 N.Y.S.2d 907; Stidham v. Diamond State Brewery, 1941, 41 Del. (2 Terry) 330, 21 A.2d 283; Bowen v. W. A. Pollard Co., 1917, 173 N.C. 129, 91 S.E. 711; Wilkinson v. McGee, 1915, 265 Mo. 574, 178 S.W. 471; Restatement of Torts, § 664(2).

42. Huffstutler v. Coates, Mo.1960, 335 S.W.2d 70; Hryciuk v. Robinson, 1958, 213 Or. 542, 326 P.2d 424; Duckwall v. Davis, 1924, 194 Ind. 670, 142 N.E. 113; Conder v. Morrison, 1938, 275 Ky. 360, 121 S.W.2d 930; Randol v. Kline's, Inc., 1932, 330 Mo. 343, 49 S.W.2d 113.

43. Wells v. Parker, 1905, 76 Ark. 41, 88 S.W. 602; Dean v. Noel, 1902, 70 S.W. 406, 24 Ky.Law Rep. 969; Flackler v. Novak, 1895, 94 Iowa 634, 63 N.W. 348; Raleigh v. Cook, 1883, 60 Tex. 438.

44. Apparently on the theory that the accused has thus confessed the sufficiency of the case against him. Brady v. Stiltner, 1895, 40 W.Va. 289, 21 S.E. 729; Hess v. Oregon German Baking Co., 1897, 31 Or. 503, 49 P. 803; Jones v. Wilmington & W. R.

Co., 1899, 125 N.C. 227, 34 S.E. 398; Jones v. McKesson & Robbins, Inc., D.N.D.1965, 237 F.Supp. 454. In Ferguson v. Reinhart, 1937, 125 Pa.Super. 154, 190 A. 153, the same effect was given to a plea of nolo contendere.

45. If the conviction is unreversed, there is of course no termination in favor of the accused. See supra, p. 838.

46. Tarantino v. Griebel, 1960, 9 Wis.2d 37, 100 N.W.2d 350; Alexander v. Laman, 1955, 225 Ark. 498, 283 S.W.2d 345; Engleman v. Progressive Machinery Corp., D.Mass.1957, 156 F.Supp. 46; Hill v. Day, 1950, 168 Kan. 604, 215 P.2d 219; Broussard v. Great A. & P. Tea Co., 1949, 324 Mass. 323, 86 N.E.2d 439; Restatement of Torts, § 667(1). See Note, 1938, 22 Minn.L.Rev. 740.

47. Taylor v. Nohalty, Ky.1966, 404 S.W.2d 448; Sheffield v. Cantwell, 7 Cir. 1938, 101 F.2d 351; Moore v. Winfield, 1935, 207 N.C. 767, 178 S.E. 605; Desmond v. Fawcett, 1917, 226 Mass. 100, 115 N.E. 280; Randol v. Kline's, Inc., 1932, 330 Mo. 343, 49 S.W.2d 112. Cf. Brown v. Cluley, Del.Super.1962, 179 A.2d 93 (withholding material information).

48. McRae v. Brant, 1967, 108 N.H. 177, 230 A.2d 753; Skeffington v. Eylward, 1906, 97 Minn. 244, 105 N.W. 638; McElroy v. Catholic Press Co., 1912, 254 Ill. 290, 98 N.E. 527; Ex parte Kemp, 1919, 202 Ala. 425, 89 So. 809; Nesmith v. Alford, 5 Cir. 1963, 318 F.2d 110 (Alabama law).

49. See McElroy v. Catholic Press Co., 1912, 254 Ill. 290, 98 N.E. 527.

volves only the conduct of a reasonable man under the circumstances, and does not differ essentially from the determination of negligence, usually is taken out of the hands of the jury, and held to be a matter for decision by the court.[50] That is to say, the court will determine whether upon the appearances presented to the defendant, a reasonable man would have instituted the proceeding.[51] The disingenuous reason sometimes is given, that since the authority to bring criminal prosecutions is derived from the law, it is for the law to determine what will constitute justification for it.[52] If there are questions of fact in dispute, as to what appeared to the defendant or what he did or did not do, they are submitted to the jury for a special verdict, or under instructions declaring the issue of probable cause according to either version of the facts.[53] The question is then a "mixed one of law and fact."[54] In many cases, where other issues are involved under a general verdict, the jury undoubtedly proceeds to determine probable cause to its own satisfaction.[55] A few jurisdictions, par-

ticularly New York, have rejected the rule that probable cause is for the court, and have held that where more than one conclusion may be drawn as to the reasonableness of the defendant's conduct, the question is for the jury.[56]

Malice: Improper Purpose

Second in importance to the issue of probable cause is that of "malice," which has given the action its name. The plaintiff has the burden of proving[57] that the defendant instituted the proceeding "maliciously." This unfortunate word, which has so much vexed the kindred law of defamation,[58] requires no less in the way of definition here. It means something more[59] than the fictitious "malice in law" which has been developed in defamation cases as a cloak for strict liability. There must be "malice in fact."[60] At the same time it does not necessarily mean that the defendant was inspired by hatred, spite or ill will;[61] and there is authority that if his

---

50. Green, Judge and Jury, 1930, 342; Restatement of Torts, § 673(1). It has been said, however, that this is true only as to the question of the reasonableness of the defendant's belief in the guilt of the accused, and that the actual existence of such belief is for the jury. Stewart v. Sonneborn, 1878, 98 U.S. 187.

51. Roblyer v. Hoyt, 1955, 343 Mich. 431, 72 N.W.2d 126; Miller v. Pennsylvania R. Co., 1952, 371 Pa. 308, 89 A.2d 809; Stearns Coal Co. v. Johnson, 1931, 238 Ky. 247, 37 S.W.2d 38; Smith v. Smith, 1944, 296 Ky. 785, 178 S.W.2d 613.

52. Hess v. Oregon Baking Co., 1897, 31 Or. 503, 49 P. 803.

53. Simpson v. Montgomery Ward & Co., 1946, 354 Pa. 87, 46 A.2d 674; Shafer v. Hertzig, 1904, 92 Minn. 171, 99 N.W. 796; Ball v. Rawles, 1892, 93 Cal. 222, 28 P. 937; Lewton v. Hower, 1895, 35 Fla. 58, 16 So. 616; Schattgen v. Holnback, 1894, 149 Ill. 646, 36 N.E. 969.

54. Snathorst v. Williams, 1949, 240 Iowa 561, 36 N. W.2d 739; McNulty v. Walker, 1897, 64 Miss. 198, 1 So. 55; Schattgen v. Holnback, 1894, 149 Ill. 646, 36 N.E. 969.

55. Green, Judge and Jury, 1930, 343; cf. Bennett v. Pillion, 1929, 105 N.J.L. 359, 144 A. 601; Hall v.

American Inv. Co., 1928, 241 Mich. 349, 217 N.W. 18.

56. Heyne v. Blair, 1875, 62 N.Y. 19; Galley v. Brennan, 1915, 216 N.Y. 118, 110 N.E. 179. Cf. Wilson v. Thurlow, 1912, 156 Iowa 656, 137 N.W. 956; Davis v. McMillan, 1905, 142 Mich. 391, 105 N.W. 862.

57. Purcell v. Macnamara, 1808, 9 East 361, 103 Eng.Rep. 610; Gibson v. Chaters, 1800, 2 Bos. & P. 129, 126 Eng.Rep. 1196; Dietz v. Langfitt, 1869, 63 Pa. 234; McKown v. Hunter, 1864, 30 N.Y. 625; Seaboard Oil Co. v. Cunningham, 5 Cir. 1931, 51 F. 2d 321, cert. denied 284 U.S. 657.

58. See supra, p. 771.

59. Mitchell v. Jenkins, 1833, 5 B. & Ad. 588, 110 Eng.Rep. 908; Humphries v. Parker, 1864, 52 Me. 502; Hanowitz v. Great Northern R. Co., 1913, 122 Minn. 241, 142 N.W. 196; Ahrens & Ott Mfg. Co. v. Hoeher, 1899, 106 Ky. 692, 51 S.W. 194; Linitzky v. Gorman, N.Y.City Ct.1914, 146 N.Y.S. 313.

60. Downing v. Stone, 1910, 152 N.C. 525, 68 S.E. 9; Metropolitan Life Ins. Co. v. Miller, 1903, 114 Ky. 754, 71 S.W. 921; Levy v. Brannan, 1870, 39 Cal. 485; Griswold v. Horne, 1917, 19 Ariz. 56, 165 P. 318 ("malice of the evil motive").

61. Pullen v. Glidden, 1877, 66 Me. 202; Foltz v. Buck, 1913, 89 Kan. 381, 131 P. 587; Hammond v. Rowley, 1912, 86 Conn. 6, 84 A. 94; Fleischhauer v. Fabens, 1908, 8 Cal.App. 30, 96 P. 17; Metropolitan

purpose was otherwise a proper one, the addition of the incidental fact that he felt indignation or resentment toward the plaintiff will not make him liable.[62] As in the cases of qualified privilege in defamation,[63] the courts seem to have looked to the primary purpose behind the defendant's action. If he is found to have acted chiefly to give vent to motives of ill will, "malice" is established.[64] But it is found also where his primary purpose was merely something other than the social one of bringing an offender to justice, which alone is recognized as a justification for a criminal proceeding.[65] "Malice" is found when the defendant uses the prosecution as a means to extort money,[66] to collect a debt,[67] to recover property [68] to compel performance of a contract,[69] to "tie up the

mouths" of witnesses in another action,[70] or as an experiment to discover who might have committed the crime.[71] On the other hand, any purpose legitimate in itself will not be "malice" if it is clearly secondary and incidental to the disinterested one of convicting the guilty.[72]

Unlike probable cause, the question of "malice" is to be determined by the jury,[73] unless only one conclusion may reasonably be drawn from the evidence.[74] The defendant's improper purpose usually is proved by circumstantial evidence.[75] The plaintiff must establish malice in addition to the absence of probable cause;[76] but, since there can be no legitimate purpose in a prosecution unless there is an honest belief in the guilt of the accused,[77] it is generally agreed that the

---

Life Ins. Co. v. Miller, 1903, 114 Ky. 754, 71 S.W. 921.

62. Lalor v. Byrne, 1892, 51 Mo.App. 578; Sharp v. Johnston, 1877, 4 Mo.App. 576; Restatement of Torts, § 668, Comment f.

63. See supra, p. 795.

64. Smith v. Kidd, Ky.1952, 246 S.W.2d 155; Thurston v. Wright, 1889, 77 Mich. 96, 43 N.W. 860; Sims v. Kent, 1930, 221 Ala. 589, 130 So. 213; Reed v. Lindley, Tex.Civ.App.1922, 240 S.W. 348.

65. Lounder v. Jacobs, 1949, 119 Colo. 511, 205 P.2d 236 ("any motive other than to bring an offender to justice"); Wenger v. Phillips, 1900, 195 Pa. 214, 45 A. 927; McElroy v. Catholic Press Co., 1912, 254 Ill. 290, 98 N.E. 527; Vinal v. Core, 1881, 18 W.Va. 1, 27; Nesmith v. Alford, 5 Cir. 1963, 318 F.2d 110.

66. Cf. Krug v. Ward, 1875, 77 Ill. 603.

67. Kitchens v. Barlow, Miss.1964, 250 Miss. 121, 164 So.2d 745; Rhodes v. Roberts, 1955, 223 Miss. 580, 78 So.2d 614; Peters v. Hall, 1953, 263 Wis. 450, 57 N.W.2d 723; Curley v. Automobile Finance Co., 1941, 343 Pa. 280, 23 A.2d 48; Peterson v. Reisdorph, 1896, 49 Neb. 529, 68 N.W. 943.

68. Suchey v. Stiles, 1964, 155 Colo. 363, 394 P.2d 739; White v. Apsley Rubber Co., 1907, 194 Mass. 97, 80 N.E. 500; Hall v. American Investment Co., 1928, 241 Mich. 349, 217 N.W. 18; Wadkins v. Digman, 1918, 82 W.Va. 623, 96 S.E. 1916; Underwood Typewriter Co. v. Shouldis, Tex.Civ.App.1923, 253 S.W. 935.

69. Whiteford v. Henthorn, 1893, 10 Ind.App. 97, 37 N.E. 419. Cf. Munson v. Linnick, 1967, 255 Cal. App.2d 589, 63 Cal.Rptr. 340.

70. Haddrick v. Heslop, 1848, 12 Q.B. 267, 116 Eng. Rep. 869. Cf. Hammond v. Rowley, 1912, 86 Conn. 6, 84 A. 94 (to frighten off other trespassers).

71. Johnson v. Ebberts, C.C.Or.1880, 11 F. 129.

72. Thompson v. Beacon Valley Rubber Co., 1888, 56 Conn. 493, 16 A. 554 ("it can hardly be expected that all selfish aims and desires can be eliminated from such prosecutions"); Kelsea v. Swett, 1919, 234 Mass. 79, 125 N.E. 143; Wenger v. Phillips, 1900, 195 Pa. 214, 45 A. 927; Williams v. Kyes, 1896, 9 Colo.App. 220, 47 P. 839.

73. Stearns Coal Co. v. Johnson, 1931, 238 Ky. 247, 37 S.W.2d 38; Stewart v. Sonneborn, 1878, 98 U.S. 187; Bartlett v. Hawley, 1888, 38 Minn. 308, 37 N. W. 580; Torsch v. Dell, 1898, 88 Md. 459, 41 A. 903; Feltzer v. Burlew, 1906, 114 App.Div. 650, 99 N.Y.S. 1100.

74. Atkinson v. Birmingham, 1922, 44 R.I. 123, 116 A. 205; Virginia Elec. & Power Co. v. Wynne, 1928, 149 Va. 882, 141 S.E. 829; Richards v. Jewett Bros. & Co., 1902, 118 Iowa 629, 92 N.W. 689; see Bartlett v. Hawley, 1888, 38 Minn. 308, 37 N.W. 580.

75. Severns v. Brainerd, 1895, 61 Minn. 265, 63 N.W. 477; Thurston v. Wright, 1889, 77 Mich. 96, 43 N. W. 860; Pierce v. Thompson, 1828, 6 Pick., Mass., 193; Holden v. Merritt, 1894, 92 Iowa 707, 61 N.W. 390. It may be inferred from a gross or reckless disregard of the plaintiff's rights. Blunk v. Atchison T. & S. F. R. Co., C.C.Mo.1889, 38 F. 311; Stubbs v. Mulholland, 1902, 168 Mo. 47, 67 S.W. 650.

76. Vanderbilt v. Mathis, 1856, 5 Duer (N.Y.) 304; Dietz v. Langfitt, 1869, 63 Pa. 234; Atkinson v. Birmingham, 1922, 44 R.I. 123, 116 A. 205.

77. Haddrick v. Heslop, 1848, 12 Q.B. 267, 116 Eng. Rep. 869; Griswold v. Horne, 1917, 19 Ariz. 56, 165

lack of probable cause may give rise to an inference of malice, sufficient to carry the question to the jury.[78] Although it has been doubted [79] that good motives may ever coincide with absence of reasonable grounds for suspicion, most courts have recognized that the two are not necessarily inconsistent, and have held that the jury may reject the inference if it sees fit.[80] The advice of counsel is evidence tending to negative malice by proving honest belief and good faith, and may be accepted as sufficient by the jury.[81] The termination of the prosecution in favor of the accused of course affords no evidence that the defendant had an improper purpose in commencing it.[82]

P. 318; Lammers v. Mason, 1913, 123 Minn. 204, 143 N.W. 359; Callahan v. Kelso, 1913, 170 Mo.App. 338, 156 S.W. 716.

78. Giant of Virginia, Inc. v. Pigg, 1967, 207 Va. 679, 152 S.E.2d 271; Azrikan v. O'Brien, Fla.App.1965, 173 So.2d 711; Bailey v. Century Finance Co., 1969, 119 Ga.App. 845, 169 S.E.2d 173; Hendrie v. Perkins, 1931, 240 Ky. 366, 42 S.W.2d 502; Halladay v. State Bank of Fairfield, 1923, 66 Mont. 111, 212 P. 861.

79. Schofield v. Ferrers, 1864, 47 Pa. 194.

80. Engelgau v. Walter, 1947, 181 Or. 481, 182 P.2d 987; Hanowitz v. Great Northern R. Co., 1913, 122 Minn. 241, 142 N.W. 196; Reinhardt v. Reitz, 1917, 176 Cal. 209, 167 P. 865; Pierce v. Doolittle, 1906, 130 Iowa 333, 106 N.W. 751; Atkinson v. Birmingham, 1922, 44 R.I. 123, 116 A. 205, reargument denied 117 A.2d 274.

In Barker v. Waltz, 1952, 40 Wash.2d 866, 246 P.2d 846, it was held that malice was not to be inferred from the "prima facie" want of probable cause shown by a dismissal.

81. Wright v. Hanna, 1884, 98 Ind. 217; Ramsey v. Arrott, 1885, 64 Tex. 320; El Reno Gas & Elec. Co. v. Spurgeon, 1911, 30 Okl. 88, 118 P. 397. Sometimes it is said that advice of counsel removes the inference of malice from lack of probable cause. McClafferty v. Philp, 1892, 151 Pa. 86, 24 A. 1042; Sparling v. Conway, 1882, 75 Mo. 510. It is not conclusive on the issue of malice, which is still for the jury. Le May v. Williams, 1877, 32 Ark. 166; Roy v. Goings, 1885, 112 Ill. 656. It has been held that the advice of a justice of the peace who is not an attorney is evidence to negative malice. Kable v. Carey, 1918, 135 Ark. 137, 204 S.W. 748.

82. Bekkeland v. Lyons, 1903, 96 Tex. 255, 72 S.W. 56; McClafferty v. Philp, 1892, 151 Pa. 86, 24 A. 1042; Malloy v. Chicago, M. & St. P. R. Co., 1914,

Damages

In theory, at least, since malicious prosecution is a descendant of the action on the case, there can be no recovery unless it is proved that the plaintiff has suffered actual damage.[83] But in practice this rule has been almost entirely nullified by the "benevolent fiction" [84] that certain kinds of damage necessarily follow from the wrongful prosecution itself, and so will be assumed by the law to exist, and may be recovered without special pleading [85] or proof. As malicious prosecution involves not only a defamatory charge of crime, which usually is reduced to writing, but likewise process to enforce it, there is an obvious analogy to libel, or the kind of slander which is actionable without proof of damage; and so it is held that there may be recovery without proof for harm to the plaintiff's reputation, standing and credit.[86] The same is true, and upon the same basis, as to humiliation and other mental suffering or injury to his feelings.[87]

34 S.D. 330, 148 N.W. 498. Similarly, commitment by a magistrate is no evidence of lack of malice. Lewton v. Hower, 1895, 35 Fla. 58, 16 So. 616.

83. Byne v. Moore, 1813, 5 Taunt. 187, 128 Eng.Rep. 658; Stanford v. A. F. Messick Grocery Co., 1906, 143 N.C. 419, 55 S.E. 815.

84. McCormick, Damages, 1935, 382.

85. Luby v. Bennett, 1901, 111 Wis. 613, 87 N.W. 804; Davis v. Seeley, 1894, 91 Iowa 583, 60 N.W. 183; Barnes v. Culver, 1921, 192 Ky. 10, 232 S.W. 39; Grorud v. Lossl, 1913, 48 Mont. 274, 136 P. 1069; Restatement of Torts, § 670. Cf. Singleton v. Perry, 1955, 45 Cal.2d 489, 289 P.2d 794 (where prosecution on two charges, one found justified and the other not, plaintiff can recover damages for the false one without proving what damages due to that charge only).

86. Drakos v. Jones, 1941, 189 Okl. 593, 118 P.2d 388; Bernstein v. Simon, 1925, 77 Colo. 193, 235 P. 375; Miles v. Walker, 1902, 66 Neb. 728, 92 N.W. 1014; Wheeler v. Hanson, 1894, 161 Mass. 370, 37 N.E. 382; Daughtry v. Blanket State Bank, Tex.Civ. App.1931, 41 S.W.2d 527 (diminished earning capacity due to loss of reputation).

87. Howarth v. Segal, E.D.Pa.1964, 232 F.Supp. 617; Kirkpatrick v. Hollingsworth, 1952, 207 Okl. 292, 249 P.2d 434; Barnes v. Culver, 1921, 192 Ky. 10, 232 S.W. 39; Black v. Canadian Pac. R. Co., D.N.

Beyond this, there may be recovery of other damages, designated as "special," if there is specific pleading and proof. The plaintiff may recover compensation for any arrest or imprisonment,[88] including damages for discomfort or injury to his health,[89] or loss of time[90] and deprivation of the society of his family.[91] He may recover any reasonable expenses to which he has been put in defending the prosecution and establishing his innocence,[92] including attorney's fees in the criminal proceeding,[93] although such fees in the action for malicious prosecution itself are normally not recoverable.[94] In addition, he

may recover for any specific financial loss, such as the loss of present[95] or prospective[96] employment, which can be proved with reasonable certainty to have been caused[97] by the prosecution, provided that it is regarded as a foreseeable, or normal, consequence of the criminal proceeding.[98] The limitations upon recovery in terms of "proximate cause" are apparently much the same as in cases of defamation.[99] Because of the intentional and outrageous nature of the tort, malicious prosecution is peculiarly adapted to the award of punitive damages, and it is agreed generally that the jury may award them when they find personal ill will or oppressive conduct in the prosecution.[1]

120. WRONGFUL CIVIL PROCEEDINGS

The action of malicious prosecution, which began as a remedy for unjustifiable criminal proceedings, has been undergoing a slow

---

Y.1914, 218 F. 239, affirmed 2 Cir. 1916, 230 F. 798; Grorud v. Lossl, 1913, 48 Mont. 274, 136 P. 1069. See Witte, Damages for Injury to Feelings in Malicious Prosecution and Abuse of Process, 1966, 15 Clev.Marsh.L.Rev. 15.

88. Rich v. Rogers, 1925, 250 Mass. 587, 146 N.E. 246; Wilson v. Bowen, 1887, 64 Mich. 133, 31 N.W. 81.

89. Stoecker v. Nathanson, 1904, 5 Neb.Unof. 435, 98 N.W. 1061; Grimes v. Greenblatt, 1910, 47 Colo. 495, 107 P. 1111; Equitable Life Assur. Soc. v. Lester, Tex.Civ.App.1908, 110 S.W. 499. But see contra, on the ground that bad conditions or bad treatment in the jail are not a normal consequence: Duckwall v. Davis, 1924, 194 Ind. 670, 142 N.E. 113; Seidler v. Burns, 1911, 84 Conn. 111, 79 A. 53; Redman v. Hudson, 1916, 124 Ark. 26, 186 S.W. 312.

90. Helfer v. Hamburg Quarry Co., 1921, 208 Mo. App. 58, 233 S.W. 275; Hunter v. Laurent, 1925, 158 La. 874, 104 So. 747; Jacquemin v. Bunker, 1922, 15 Ohio App. 491; Davis v. Teague, Tex.Civ. App.1923, 256 S.W. 957.

91. Walling v. Fields, 1923, 209 Ala. 389, 96 So. 471; Killebrew v. Carlisle, 1892, 97 Ala. 535, 12 So. 167. Cf. Davis v. Seeley, 1894, 91 Iowa 583, 60 N.W. 183.

92. Seidler v. Burns, 1912, 86 Conn. 249, 85 A. 369; Wheeler v. Hanson, 1894, 161 Mass. 370, 37 N.E. 382; Blazek v. McCartin, 1909, 106 Minn. 461, 119 N.W. 215; Blunk v. Atchison, T. & S. F. R. Co., C. C.Mo.1889, 38 F. 311.

93. Benderach v. Grujicich, 1925, 30 N.M. 331, 233 P. 520; Farris v. Messimore, 1920, 219 Ill.App. 582; Stevens v. Chisholm, 1919, 179 Cal. 557, 178 P. 128; Bernstein v. Simon, 1925, 77 Colo. 193, 235 P. 375; Mitchell v. Davies, 1892, 51 Minn. 168, 53 N.W. 363.

94. Benderach v. Grujicich, 1925, 30 N.M. 331, 233 P. 520; cf. Stewart v. Sonneborn, 1878, 98 U.S. 187; Beckham v. Collins, 1909, 54 Tex.Civ.App.

241, 117 S.W. 431. In Davis v. Tunison, 1957, 153 Ohio Abs. 474, 477, 153 N.E.2d 190, reversed on other grounds, 1959, 168 Ohio St. 471, 155 N.E.2d 904, it was held that there can be recovery where there is "fraud, malice, or willful misconduct."

95. H. S. Leyman Co. v. Short, 1926, 214 Ky. 272, 283 S.W. 96.

96. Stoecker v. Nathanson, 1904, 5 Neb., Unof., 435, 98 N.W. 1061; Davis v. McMillian, 1922, 28 Ga. App. 689, 112 S.E. 913; cf. Long v. Burley State Bank, 1917, 30 Idaho 392, 165 P. 1119 (profits).

97. Cf. Baer v. Chambers, 1912, 67 Wash. 357, 121 P. 843 (cold caught while in prison).

98. Cf. Hanson v. Rhodes-Burford Furn. Co., 1923, 227 Ill.App. 471; Laing v. Mitten, 1904, 185 Mass. 233, 70 N.E. 128; Seidler v. Burns, 1911, 84 Conn. 111, 79 A. 53; Redman v. Hudson, 1916, 124 Ark. 26, 186 S.W. 312; Duckwall v. Davis, 1924, 194 Ind. 670, 142 N.E. 113.

99. Restatement of Torts, § 671, Comment d.

1. Western Union Tel. Co. v. Thomasson, 4 Cir.1918, 251 F. 833; Virginia Elec. & Power Co. v. Wynne, 1928, 149 Va. 882, 141 S.E. 829; cf. Stalker v. Drake, 1913, 91 Kan. 142, 136 P. 912. It has been held that the malice to be inferred from lack of probable cause is not sufficient for punitive damages, and that there must be affirmative proof of a bad motive or oppressive conduct. Sparrow v. Vermont Sav. Bank, 1921, 95 Vt. 29, 112 A. 205; Motsinger v. Sink, 1915, 168 N.C. 548, 84 S.E. 847.

process of extension into the field of the wrongful initiation of civil suits. The common law of England has refused thus far to extend the tort to the ordinary civil action, even though it be instituted for an improper purpose and without probable cause;[2] and this is the position still taken by a large minority of rather less than half of the American courts.[3]

Three reasons, all of questionable validity, have been advanced to justify this refusal. One is that the successful party to a civil litigation is awarded costs, which are intended as full compensation, and hence as an exclusive remedy, for any damages that he has suffered. This may perhaps have been true in earlier days,[4] and is still true to some limited extent in England, where the costs awarded include the fees of the party's attorney—although even there other damages, such as harm to his reputation, remain uncompensated. But in the United States, where the costs are set by statute at trivial amounts, and no attorney's fees are allowed, there can be no pretense at compensation even for the expenses of the litigation itself.[5] As a second reason, it is said that honest litigants are to be encouraged to seek justice and not to be deterred by fear of an action in return, and that the good citizen must endure any resulting expense or damage as an inevitable burden to be borne under his government; and as a third, that litigation must end somewhere, and that if one counter-action may be brought, so may another, and another. But surely there is no policy in favor of vexatious suits known to be groundless, which are a real and often a serious injury; and the heavy burden of proof upon the plaintiff, to establish both lack of probable cause and an improper purpose, should afford sufficient protection to the bona fide litigant and adequate safeguard against a series of actions.

These jurisdictions which refuse the remedy for an ordinary civil suit have given way, however, in a large group of exceptional cases. The most obvious exception is that of civil actions which are recognized as quasi-criminal in character, or which involve an interference with the person, as in the case of proceedings in lunacy,[6] contempt,[7] bastardy,[8] juvenile delinquency,[9] arrest under civil proc-

---

2. Cotterell v. Jones, 1851, 11 C.B. 713, 138 Eng. Rep. 655; Quartz Hill Gold Min. Co. v. Eyre, 1883, 11 Q.B.D. 674.

3. Aalfs v. Aalfs, 1954, 246 Iowa 158, 66 N.W.2d 121; Avco Delta Corp. of Ohio v. Walker, 1969, 22 Ohio App.2d 61, 258 N.E.2d 254; Ring v. Ring, 1967, 102 R.I. 112, 228 A.2d 582; Landavazo v. Credit Bureau of Albuquerque, 1963, 72 N.M. 456, 384 P.2d 891; La Salle Nat. Bank v. 222 East Chestnut St. Corp., 7 Cir. 1959, 267 F.2d 247, cert. denied 361 U.S. 836 (Illinois law).

Even though the proceeding is of the kind which usually results in interference with person or property, where it has not done so in the particular case. Publix Drug Co. v. Breyer Ice Cream Co., 1943, 347 Pa. 346, 32 A.2d 413 (confession of judgment on note); Peckham v. Union Finance Co., 1931, 60 App.D.C. 104, 48 F.2d 1016 (receivership); Perry v. Arsham, 1956, 101 Ohio App. 285, 136 N.E. 2d 141 (forcible entry and unlawful detainer); Vancouver Book & Stationery Co. v. L. C. Smith & Corona Typewriters, 9 Cir. 1943, 138 F.2d 635, cert. denied 321 U.S. 786 (temporary restraining order).

4. See McCormick, Counsel Fees and Other Expenses of Litigation as an Element of Damages, 1931, 15 Minn.L.Rev. 619, reprinted in McCormick, Damages, 1935, ch. 8; Goodhart, Costs, 1929, 38 Yale L.J. 849. The American statutes passed at an early date have not been revised to keep pace with the fall in the value of money.

5. McCormick, Counsel Fees and Other Expenses of Litigation as an Element of Damages, 1931, 15 Minn.L.Rev. 619, reprinted in McCormick, Damages, 1935, ch. 8.

6. Fowle v. Fowle, 1965, 263 N.C. 724, 140 S.E.2d 398; Yelk v. Seefeldt, 1967, 35 Wis.2d 271, 151 N.W.2d 4; Hill v. Carlstrom, 1959, 216 Or. 300, 338 P.2d 645; Lowen v. Hilton, 1960, 142 Colo. 200, 351 P.2d 881; Alexander v. Alexander, 4 Cir. 1956, 229 F.2d 111 (Florida law). See Note, 1918, 16 Mich.L. Rev. 457.

7. Sebring v. Van Aken, 1932, 235 App.Div. 420, 257 N.Y.S. 104; Tavenner v. Morehead, 1895, 41 W.Va. 116, 23 S.E. 673.

8. Coffey v. Myers, 1882, 84 Ind. 105.

9. Lueptow v. Schraeder, 1938, 226 Wis. 437, 277 N. W. 124. See Note, 1938, 22 Minn.L.Rev. 1060.

ess,[10] or binding over to keep the peace.[11] But the extension of the remedy has gone even further, and has included proceedings in which there has been interference with property or business, or damage differing in kind from the ordinary burden of defending a lawsuit,[12] such as attachment,[13] garnishment,[14] replevin,[15] the search of premises under a warrant,[16] injunctions,[17] proceedings in bankruptcy,[18] or for the dissolution of a partnership.[19] Even proceedings before an administrative agency [20] have been held to be sufficient, where they result in similar interference, as in the case of one for the suspension of an officer,[21] or for the revocation of a license to do business.[22]

One English court [23] has recognized the analogy to the "business slander" which is actionable without proof of damage, and it may be that any civil action which involves such slander would be included.[24] Several jurisdictions [25] allow an action of malicious

10. Woodley v. Coker, 1903, 119 Ga. 226, 46 S.E. 89; Collins v. Hayte, 1869, 50 Ill. 353; Lauzon v. Charroux, 1894, 18 R.I. 467, 28 A. 975.

11. Oliver v. Haspil, Fla.App.1963, 152 So.2d 758; Lanterman v. Delaware, L. & W. R. Co., D.N.J.1916, 229 F. 770; Hyde v. Greuch, 1884, 62 Md. 577.

12. As to this requirement, see Petrich v. McDonald, 1954, 44 Wash.2d 211, 266 P.2d 1047; Capitol Elec. Co. v. Cristaldi, D.Md.1958, 157 F.Supp. 646; Luckett v. Cohen, S.D.N.Y.1956, 169 F.Supp. 808. In Aalfs v. Aalfs, 1954, 246 Iowa 158, 66 N.W.2d 121, impaired credit, impaired saleability of property, temporarily clouded title, damaged reputation, humiliation and expense, resulting from an ordinary civil action, were held not to be enough in the way of such special damage.

13. Leeseberg v. Builders Plumbers Supply Co., 1967, 6 Mich.App. 321, 149 N.W.2d 263; Blankenship v. Staton, Ky.1961, 348 S.W.2d 925; Dangel v. Offset Printing Co., 1961, 342 Mass. 170, 172 N.E.2d 610; Morfessis v. Baum, 1960, 108 U.S.App.D.C. 303, 281 F.2d 938; Martin v. Rexford, 1915, 170 N.C. 540, 87 S.E. 352. Cf. Peebler v. Olds, 1945, 71 Cal.App.2d 382, 162 P.2d 953 (action to quiet title, creating lien on property); Chappelle v. Gross, 1966, 26 App. Div.2d 340, 274 N.Y.S.2d 555 (lis pendens filed); Baber v. Fitzgerald, 1949, 311 Ky. 382, 224 S.W.2d 135 (forcible detainer).

14. Gore v. Gorman's, Inc., W.D.Mo.1956, 143 F.Supp. 9; Novick v. Becker, 1958, 4 Wis.2d 432, 90 N.W.2d 620; Atlanta Hub Co. v. Bussey, 1956, 93 Ga.App. 171, 91 S.E.2d 66; King v. Yarbray, 1911, 136 Ga. 212, 71 S.E. 131; Gundermann v. Buschner, 1897, 73 Ill.App. 180.

15. Brounstein v. Sahlein, 1892, 65 Hun 365, 20 N.Y. S. 213.

16. Hollinshed v. Shadrick, 1957, 95 Ga.App. 88, 97 S.E.2d 165, error transferred, 1956, 212 Ga.App. 624, 94 S.E.2d 705; Whitson v. May, 1880, 71 Ind. 269; Shaw v. Moon, 1926, 117 Or. 558, 245 P. 318.

17. Mayflower Industries v. Thor Corp., 1951, 15 N. J.Super. 139, 83 A.2d 246, affirmed, 1952, 9 N.J. 605, 89 A.2d 242; Black v. Judelsohn, 1937, 251 App.Div. 559, 296 N.Y.S. 960; Shute v. Shute, 1920, 180 N.C. 386, 104 S.E. 764.

18. Neumann v. Industrial Sound Engineering, Inc., 1966, 31 Wis.2d 471, 143 N.W.2d 543; Hubbard v. Beatty & Hyde, Inc., 1961, 343 Mass. 258, 178 N.E. 2d 485; Balsiger v. American Steel & Supply Co., 1969, —— Or. ——, 458 P.2d 932; Nassif v. Goodman, 1932, 203 N.C. 451, 166 S.E. 308; Norin v. Scheldt Mfg. Co., 1921, 297 Ill. 521, 130 N.E. 791.

19. Luby v. Bennett, 1901, 111 Wis. 613, 87 N.W. 804.

20. Kauffman v. A. H. Robbins Co., 1969, —— Tenn. ——, 448 S.W.2d 400. See Notes, [1962] Wis.L.Rev. 701; 1957, 31 So.Cal.L.Rev. 105; 1955, 24 Ford.L. Rev. 479.

21. Fulton v. Ingalls, 1914, 165 App.Div. 323, 151 N. Y.S. 130, affirmed, 1914, 214 N.Y. 665, 108 N.E. 1094. Accord, Hardy v. Vial, 1957, 48 Cal.2d 577, 311 P.2d 494 (dismissal of professor at state college).

22. National Surety Co. v. Page, 4 Cir. 1932, 58 F.2d 145, 59 F.2d 370 (insurance agent); Melvin v. Pence, 1942, 76 App.D.C. 154, 130 F.2d 423 (private detective); Dixie Broadcasting Co. v. Rivers, 1952, 209 Ga. 98, 70 S.E.2d 734 (broadcasting station); Carver v. Lykes, 1964, 262 N.C. 345, 137 S.E.2d 139 (real estate broker).

California appears to stand alone in rejecting all such extensions where the proceeding is not considered "judicial." Shigeru Hayashida v. Tsunehachi Kakimoto, 1933, 132 Cal.App. 743, 23 P.2d 311 (detention of alien on admission); Comlich v. Stempel, 1927, 81 Cal.App. 278, 253 P. 344 (revocation of real estate commission license).

23. Quartz Hill Gold Min. Co. v. Eyre, 1883, 11 Q.B. D. 674. Accord, Lockenour v. Sides, 1877, 57 Ind. 360.

24. See Salmond, Law of Torts, 8th Ed.1934, 648, suggesting that naming the party as co-respondent in a divorce suit might be sufficient.

25. Shedd v. Patterson, 1922, 302 Ill. 355, 134 N.E. 705; Soffos v. Eaton, 1945, 80 U.S.App.D.C. 306, 152 F.2d 682; Davis v. Boyle Bros., Mun.App.D.C.

prosecution for any civil suit initiated a second time without ground, where they do not allow it for the first.

The majority of the American courts, however, have ended by throwing over all such restrictions, and permit an action to be founded on any ordinary civil suit, provided that the necessary elements are present and material damage results.[26] Sometimes the tort is called "malicious use of process," [27] by way of distinguishing the criminal proceeding. Colorado has allowed the action even for the unjustifiable filing of a counterclaim,[28] and no doubt the ultimate has been reached in a Florida case [29] founding the action upon a prior one for malicious prosecution. The principle seems by now to be sufficiently well established,[30] and opposition to it definitely on the wane.

1950, 73 A.2d 517; see Perry v. Arsham, 1956, 101 Ohio App. 285, 136 N.E.2d 141; cf. Holt v. Boyle Bros., 1954, 95 U.S.App.D.C. 1, 217 F.2d 16 (unfounded appeal); see Note, 1920, 30 Yale L.J. 1310.

Contra: Carnation Lumber Co. v. McKenney, 1960, 224 Or. 541, 356 P.2d 932; Myhre v. Hessey, 1943, 242 Wis. 638, 9 N.W.2d 106; Pye v. Cardwell, 1920, 110 Tex. 572, 222 S.W. 153, answers conformed to Civ.App., 224 S.W. 542; Rappaport v. Rappaport, 1964, 44 Misc.2d 523, 254 N.Y.S.2d 174, affirmed 24 App.Div.2d 844, 263 N.Y.S.2d 442.

26. Peerson v. Ashcraft Cotton Mills, 1917, 201 Ala. 348, 78 So. 204; Ahring v. White, 1942, 156 Kan. 60, 131 P.2d 669; Rosenblum v. Ginis, 1937, 297 Mass. 493, 9 N.E.2d 525; Shaeffer v. O. K. Tool Co., 1930, 110 Conn. 528, 148 A. 330; Ryerson v. American Surety Co. of New York, 1963, 213 Tenn. 182, 373 S.W.2d 436. See Note, [1941] Wis.L.Rev. 257.

27. Cf. Publix Drug Co. v. Breyer Ice Cream Co., 1943, 347 Pa. 346, 32 A.2d 413; and see Baldwin v. Davis, 1939, 188 Ga. 587, 4 S.E.2d 458.

28. Slee v. Simpson, 1932, 91 Colo. 461, 15 P.2d 1084. See in accord, Potts v. Imlay, 1816, 4 N.J.L. 330; Kolka v. Jones, 1897, 6 N.D. 461, 71 N.W. 558; see Note, 1933, 17 Minn.L.Rev. 553. Contra, Baxter v. Brown, 1910, 83 Kan. 302, 111 P. 430.

29. Hopke v. O'Byrne, Fla.App.1963, 148 So.2d 755.

30. It has been approved by the restatement of Torts, § 674. "As for practical results, the testimonies of the judges in other jurisdictions concur to the effect that this rule has brought no crowd of rashly importunate litigants." Peerson v. Ashcraft Cotton Mills, 1917, 201 Ala. 348, 78 So. 204.

Compared with Malicious Prosecution

Where a cause of action founded upon a civil proceeding is recognized, it usually is called malicious prosecution, although "prosecution" is something of a misnomer. In general, it is governed by the same rules and limitations as the action based upon criminal proceedings; but there are a few significant differences arising out of the type of suit involved.[31]

Ordinarily the plaintiff must prove the termination of the former proceeding in his favor.[32] But there are necessary exceptions where, as in the case of putting a man under bond to keep the peace,[33] the proceeding is an ex parte one and relief is granted without an opportunity for the party against whom it is sought to be heard. This is true also as to proceedings ancillary to a civil suit, such as attachment [34] or arrest under civil process,[35] as to which, if they are themselves unjustified, it is unnecessary to show a favor-

31. See Restatement of Torts, § 674, Comment c.

32. Nichols v. Severtsen, 1951, 39 Wash.2d 836, 239 P.2d 349; Moffett v. Commerce Trust Co., Mo.1955, 283 S.W.2d 591; Martin v. Cedar Lake Ice Co., 1920, 145 Minn. 452, 177 N.W. 631; Dangel v. Offset Printing, Inc., 1961, 342 Mass. 170, 172 N.E.2d 610; Schwartz v. Schwartz, 1938, 25 Cal.App.2d 303, 77 P.2d 260. Thus a default judgment must be set aside. McMahon v. May Dept. Stores Co., Mo. 1964, 374 S.W.2d 82.

The requirement of termination ordinarily makes a counterclaim for malicious prosecution in the original civil action premature. Alexander v. Petty, 1954, 35 Del.Ch. 5, 108 A.2d 575; Baker v. Littman, 1956, 138 Cal.App.2d 510, 292 P.2d 595; Niedringhaus v. Zucker, Mo.1948, 208 S.W.2d 211; Rosemont Enterprises, Inc. v. Random House, Inc., S.D.N.Y. 1966, 261 F.Supp. 691; Metro Chrysler-Plymouth, Inc. v. Pearce, 1970, 121 Ga.App. 835, 175 S.E.2d 910. See Note, 1949, 58 Yale L.J. 490.

33. Steward v. Gromett, 1859, 7 C.B.,N.S., 191, 141 Eng.Rep. 788; Hyde v. Greuch, 1884, 62 Md. 577; Lanterman v. Delaware, L. & W. R. Co., D.N.J.1916, 229 F. 770.

34. Blankenship v. Staton, Ky.1961, 348 S.W.2d 925; McLaughlin v. Davis, 1875, 14 Kan. 168; Zinn v. Rice, 1891, 154 Mass. 1, 27 N.E. 772.

35. Ingram v. Root, 1889, 51 Hun 238, 3 N.Y.S. 858; Hogg v. Pinckney, 1881, 16 S.C. 387.

able termination of the main action. It usually is held, however, with a little authority to the contrary,[36] that if an opportunity has been given to contest the facts,[37] the plaintiff must show a favorable termination of the ancillary proceeding itself.[38] As in the case of criminal proceedings, a termination of the suit by way of compromise and settlement is not sufficient to support the cause of action;[39] but the filing of a bond for the release of property attached is not regarded as such a compromise, since the party acts under compulsion.[40]

The plaintiff must also prove that the proceeding was initiated without probable cause.[41] But obviously less in the way of grounds for belief will be required to justify a reasonable man in bringing a civil rather than a criminal suit. Sometimes this is expressed by saying that want of probable cause must be "very clearly proven,"[42] or "very palpable,"[43] or that "greater latitude" must be allowed than in a criminal case.[44] Apparently what is meant is merely that the instigator need not have the same degree of certainty as to the facts, or even the same belief in the soundness of his case, and that he is justified in bringing a civil suit when he reasonably believes that he has a good chance of establishing it to the satisfaction of the court or the jury.[45] He may, for example, reasonably submit a doubtful issue of law, where it is uncertain which view the court will take.[46] Advice of counsel to the effect that there is a reasonable chance that the claim will be found to be valid is enough to establish probable cause.[47]

---

36.   Fortman v. Rottier, 1858, 8 Ohio St. 548. Brand v. Hinchman, 1888, 68 Mich. 590, 36 N.W. 664. The reason advanced is that damage has been caused immediately on issuance and execution of the writ, which is ex parte.

37.   Otherwise where there was no opportunity to vacate the attachment. Bump v. Betts, 1830, 19 Wend., N.Y., 421. Or where the only method of vacating it does not put in issue the grounds on which it was sued out. Donnell v. Jones, 1848, 13 Ala. 490; Rossiter v. Minnesota Bradner-Smith Paper Co., 1887, 37 Minn. 296, 33 N.W. 855.

38.   Dixon v. Smith-Wallace Shoe Co., 1918, 283 Ill. 234, 119 N.E. 265; Pixley v. Reed, 1879, 26 Minn. 80, 1 N.W. 800; Wright v. Harris, 1912, 160 N.C. 542, 76 S.E. 489; Kassel Poultry Co. v. Sheldon Produce Co., 1925, 3 N.J.Misc. 277, 129 A. 424.

39.   Nolan v. Allstate Home Equipment Co., Mun. App.D.C.1959, 149 A.2d 426; Fenton Storage Co. v. Feinstein, 1937, 129 Pa.Super. 125, 195 A. 176; Paskle v. Williams, 1931, 214 Cal. 482, 6 P.2d 505; Baird v. Aluminum Seal Co., 3 Cir. 1957, 250 F.2d 595; Webb v. Youmans, 1967, 248 Cal.App.2d 851, 57 Cal.Rptr. 11.

40.   Rossiter v. Minnesota Bradner-Smith Paper Co., 1887, 37 Minn. 296, 33 N.W. 855; cf. Slater v. Kimbro, 1892, 91 Ga. 217, 18 S.E. 296; Alexander v. Jacoby, 1872, 23 Ohio St. 358.

41.   See, giving the term the same meaning as in criminal prosecutions: Stewart v. Sonneborn, 1878, 98 U.S. 187; Le Clear v. Perkins, 1894, 103 Mich. 131, 61 N.W. 357; Hill Co. v. Contractors' Supply Co., 1910, 156 Ill.App. 270; Wilcox v. Gilmore, 1928, 320 Mo. 980, 8 S.W.2d 961.

42.   Eickhoff v. Fidelity & Casualty Co., 1898, 74 Minn. 139, 76 N.W. 1030; United States Tire Co. v. Kirk, 1918, 102 Kan. 418, 170 P. 811; see Owens v. Graetzel, 1926, 149 Md. 689, 132 A. 265.

43.   Kasal v. Picha, 1923, 156 Minn. 446, 195 N.W. 280; Brown v. Keyes, 1929, 54 S.D. 598, 223 N.W. 819.

44.   Virtue v. Creamery Package Mfg. Co., 1913, 123 Minn. 17, 142 N.W. 930, reargument denied 123 Minn. 17, 142 N.W. 1136.

45.   Smith v. Smith, 1944, 296 Ky. 785, 178 S.W.2d 613. See Pangburn v. Bull, 1828, 1 Wend., N.Y., 345; Allen v. Codman, 1885, 139 Mass. 136, 29 N.E. 537; Hubbard v. Beatty & Hyde, Inc., 1961, 343 Mass. 285, 178 N.E.2d 485; and cf. Connery v. Manning, 1895, 163 Mass. 44, 39 N.E. 558.

46.   Hoffmann v. Kimmel, 1933, 142 Or. 397, 20 P.2d 393. In Standley v. Western Auto Supply Co., Mo. App.1959, 319 S.W.2d 924, this was carried to the length of holding that there was probable cause when suit was brought on an otherwise valid claim known to be discharged in bankruptcy, since the defense might be waived if the debtor chose not to avail himself of it. But see contra, Gore v. Gorman's Inc., W.D.Mo.1956, 143 F.Supp. 9, noted in 1957, 22 Mo.L.Rev. 215.

47.   Harter v. Lewis Stores, Ky.1951, 240 S.W.2d 86; Dorr Cattle Co. v. Des Moines Nat. Bank, 1904, 127 Iowa 153, 98 N.W. 918, rehearing denied 1905, 127 Iowa 153, 102 N.W. 836. It has been held that in a proper case expert advice may have the same effect. Allen v. Codman, 1885, 139 Mass. 136, 29 N.E. 537 (fire hazard); Bode v. Schmoldt, 1922, 177 Wis. 8, 187 N.W. 648, 1024 (lunacy). But not, of course,

It is generally agreed that the termination of the proceeding in favor of the person against whom it is brought is no evidence that probable cause was lacking, since in a civil action there is no preliminary determination of the sufficiency of the evidence to justify the suit.[48] But such a judgment, if it is on the merits of the controversy, is a final adjudication of the matters then in dispute, and the unsuccessful instigator cannot, as in the case of a criminal proceeding, relitigate his claim in the tort action by setting up the defense that he was right upon the facts.[49] A recovery by the plaintiff in the original action usually is regarded as conclusive evidence of the existence of probable cause,[50] even though it is subsequently reversed,[51] unless it can be shown to have been obtained by fraud or other imposition upon the court.[52]

The plaintiff must also prove "malice" in bringing the former action; but here again somewhat more latitude is permitted than in the case of criminal prosecutions, since the plaintiff in a civil suit is always seeking his own ends. "Malice" may consist of a primary motive of ill will, or a lack of belief in any possible success of the action;[53] but neither is necessary to it. It has been found where the proceeding was begun primarily for a purpose other than the adjudication of the claim in suit, such as preventing an owner from selling his land to another.[54] As in malicious prosecution proper, the jury may infer an improper purpose from the lack of probable cause, although the converse inference may not be drawn.[55]

Finally, in an action founded upon an ordinary civil suit, no damages will be presumed, and the plaintiff must prove actual damages in excess of the costs recoverable in the original action.[56] There may perhaps be an exception in the case of civil suits such as lunacy or bankruptcy proceedings, which would carry defamation of a kind actionable as slander without proof of damage, but for the privilege of a litigant; it has been said that then proof of damage to reputation should not be required.[57] Once actual dam-

where full disclosure is not made. Alexander v. Alexander, 4 Cir. 1956, 229 F.2d 111.

48. Barton v. Woodward, 1919, 32 Idaho 375, 182 P. 916; O'Malley-Kelly Oil & Auto Supply Co. v. Gates Oil Co., 1923, 73 Colo. 140, 214 P. 398; Milner v. Hare, 1926, 125 Me. 460, 134 A. 628; Reichert v. Neacy, 1914, 158 Wis. 657, 149 N.W. 586; Novick v. Becker, 1958, 4 Wis.2d 432, 90 N.W.2d 620.

There are courts which have said that a voluntary dismissal or discontinuance affords evidence that probable cause was lacking. Kolka v. Jones, 1897, 6 N.D. 461, 71 N.W. 558; Wetmore v. Mellinger, 1884, 64 Iowa 741, 18 N.W. 870. Contra; Asevado v. Orr, 1893, 100 Cal. 293, 34 P. 777; Cohn v. Saidel, 1902, 71 N.H. 558, 53 A. 800; Warner v. Gulf Oil Corp., N.D.N.C.1959, 178 F.Supp. 481.

49. Since the parties are the same and the judgment is res judicata as to such issues. Ackerman v. Kaufman, 1932, 41 Ariz. 110, 15 P.2d 966.

50. Rouse v. Twin Pines Sanitarium, 1958, 162 Cal. App.2d 639, 328 P.2d 536; Lancaster & Love Co. v. Mueller Co., Tex.Civ.App.1958, 310 S.W.2d 659, error refused.

51. Goldstein v. Sabella, Fla.1956, 88 So.2d 910; Laughlin v. St. Louis Union Trust Co., 1932, 330 Mo. 523, 50 S.W.2d 92; Overton v. Combs, 1921, 182 N.C. 4, 108 S.E. 357; McBride v. Alles, 1928, 222 Ky. 725, 2 S.W.2d 391; Goldner-Siegel Corp. v. Kraemer Hosiery Co., 1934, 153 Misc. 159, 274 N.Y. S. 681.

52. Lockett & Williams v. Gress Mfg. Co., 1911, 8 Ga.App. 772, 70 S.E. 255; see Palmer v. Avery, 1864, 41 Barb., N.Y., 290.

53. Pangburn v. Bull, 1828, 1 Wend., N.Y., 345; Wills v. Noyes, 1832, 12 Pick. 324, 29 Mass. 324; Southwestern R. Co. v. Mitchell, 1880, 80 Ga. 438, 5 S.E. 490.

54. Malone v. Belcher, 1913, 216 Mass. 209, 103 N.E. 637; Burhans v. Sanford, 1838, 19 Wend., N.Y., 417; Wills v. Noyes, 1832, 12 Pick., Mass., 324; Southwestern R. Co. v. Mitchell, 1880, 80 Ga. 438, 5 S.E. 490. Cf. Johnson v. Mount Ogden Enterprises, Inc., 1969, 23 Utah 2d 169, 460 P.2d 333 (injunction suit to gain time).

55. Stewart v. Sonneborn, 1878, 98 U.S. 187; National Surety Co. v. Page, 4 Cir. 1932, 58 F.2d 145, 59 F.2d 370; Kryszke v. Kamin, 1910, 163 Mich. 290, 128 N.W. 190; Henderson v. Cape Trading Co., 1926, 316 Mo. 384, 289 S.W. 332; Cole v. Neaf, 8 Cir. 1964, 334 F.2d 326.

56. See McCardle v. McGinley, 1882, 86 Ind. 538; Carbondale Inv. Co. v. Burdick, 1903, 67 Kan. 329, 72 P. 781; Lipscomb v. Shofner, 1896, 96 Tenn. 112, 33 S.W. 818.

57. Restatement of Torts, § 681, Comment a.

age of some kind has been shown, however, the recovery may include compensation for any arrest of the person,[58] seizure or interference with property,[59] harm to credit or reputation,[60] expenses incurred in defending the suit,[61] resulting financial loss or injury to business,[62] or even mental suffering [63] of a kind normally to be expected to follow from the action.

121. ABUSE OF PROCESS

The action for malicious prosecution, whether it be permitted for criminal or civil proceedings, has failed to provide a remedy for a group of cases in which legal procedure has been set in motion in proper form, with probable cause, and even with ultimate success, but nevertheless has been perverted to accomplish an ulterior purpose for which it was not designed. In such cases a tort action has been developed for what is called abuse of process.[64] In the leading English case [65]

the defendant had the plaintiff arrested under civil process in order to compel him through duress to surrender the register of a vessel, without which the plaintiff could not go to sea. Although malicious prosecution would not lie because the proceeding had not been terminated, the court refused to permit its process to be misused for such an end, and held the defendant liable. This decision has been widely followed, and the tort is now well established.

Abuse of process differs from malicious prosecution in that the gist of the tort is not commencing an action or causing process to issue without justification, but misusing, or misapplying process justified in itself for an end other than that which it was designed to accomplish.[66] The purpose for which the process is used, once it is issued, is the only thing of importance. Consequently in an action for abuse of process it is unnecessary for the plaintiff to prove that the proceeding has terminated in his favor,[67] or that the process was obtained without probable cause or in the course of a proceeding begun without probable cause.[68] It is often said that proof

---

58. See Closson v. Staples, 1869, 42 Vt. 209.

59. Farrar v. Brackett, 1890, 86 Ga. 463, 12 S.E. 686; Moffatt v. Fisher, 1877, 47 Iowa 473; Boland v. Ballaine, 9 Cir. 1920, 266 F. 22.

60. Malone v. Belcher, 1913, 216 Mass. 209, 103 N.E. 637; Bradford v. Lawrence, 1922, 208 Ala. 248, 94 So. 103; Lord v. Guyot, 1902, 30 Colo. 222, 70 P. 683; Sonsee v. Jones & Green, 1923, 157 Ark. 131, 248 S.W. 289.

61. Slater v. Kimbro, 1892, 91 Ga. 217, 18 S.E. 296; Stevens v. Chisholm, 1919, 179 Cal. 557, 178 P. 128; Connelly v. White, 1904, 122 Iowa 391, 98 N.W. 144; see Scheide v. Home Credit Co., 1932, 107 Pa. Super. 204, 162 A. 321.

62. Slater v. Kimbro, 1892, 91 Ga. 217, 18 S.E. 296; Boland v. Ballaine, 9 Cir. 1920, 266 F. 22; Magmer v. Renk, 1886, 65 Wis. 364, 27 N.W. 26; Munro Hotel Co. v. Brough, 1915, 26 Ohio Cir.Ct.,N.S. 185.

63. Stalker v. Drake, 1913, 91 Kan. 142, 136 P. 912; Cohn v. Saidel, 1902, 71 N.H. 558, 53 A. 800.

64. See Goldoftas, Abuse of Process, 1964, 13 Cleve. Marsh.L.Rev. 163 Notes, 1938, 16 N.C.L.Rev. 277; 1948, 32 Minn.L.Rev. 805; 1937, 7 Brook.L.Rev. 123; Restatement of Torts, § 682. Cf. White v. Scarritt, 1937, 341 Mo. 1004, 111 S.W.2d 18 ("duress").

As to the distinction between malicious prosecution, "malicious use of process" in civil proceedings, and

abuse of process, see Baldwin v. Davis, 1939, 188 Ga. 587, 4 S.E.2d 458.

65. Grainger v. Hill, 1838, 4 Bing.N.C. 212, 132 Eng. Rep. 769.

66. Wood v. Graves, 1887, 144 Mass. 365, 11 N.E. 567; Garland v. Wilson, 1927, 289 Pa. 272, 137 A. 266; Abernethy v. Burns, 1936, 210 N.C. 636, 188 S.E. 97; Glidewell v. Murray-Lacy & Co., 1919, 124 Va. 563, 98 S.E. 665; Assets Collecting Co. v. Myers, 1915, 167 App.Div. 133, 152 N.Y.S. 930.

Regularity or irregularity of the process itself makes no difference. Compare Hall v. Field Enterprises, Mun.App.D.C.1953, 94 A.2d 479, with Hoppe v. Klapperich, 1947, 224 Minn. 224, 28 N.W.2d 780.

67. Lambert v. Breton, 1929, 127 Me. 510, 144 A. 864; Sneeden v. Harris, 1891, 109 N.C. 349, 13 S.E. 920; Brantley v. Rhodes-Haverty Furniture Co., 1908, 131 Ga. 276, 62 S.E. 222; Kool v. Lee, 1913, 43 Utah 394, 134 P. 906; Moore v. Michigan Nat. Bank, 1962, 368 Mich. 71, 117 N.W.2d 105.

68. Mayer v. Walter, 1870, 64 Pa. 283; Grimestad v. Lofgren, 1908, 105 Minn. 286, 117 N.W. 515; Glidewell v. Murray-Lacy & Co., 1919, 124 Va. 563, 98 S.E. 665; Moore v. Michigan Nat. Bank, 1962, 368 Mich. 71, 117 N.W.2d 105. It has been said that

of "malice" is required;[69] but it seems well settled that, except on the issue of punitive damages,[70] this does not mean spite or ill will, or anything other than the improper purpose itself for which the process is used,[71] and that even a pure spite motive is not sufficient where process is used only to accomplish the result for which it was created.[72] Thus if the defendant prosecutes an innocent plaintiff for a crime without reasonable grounds to believe him guilty, it is malicious prosecution; if he prosecutes him with such grounds to extort payment of a debt, it is abuse of process.[73] But the two torts have the common element of an improper purpose in the use of legal process, and there are many cases in which they overlap and either will lie, such as the excessive attachment of property to coerce settlement of a suit,[74] or

indeed any unjustified criminal prosecution or civil action in which legal process is used for an end other than that of the proceeding itself.[75]

The essential elements of abuse of process, as the tort has developed, have been stated to be: first, an ulterior purpose, and second, a wilful act in the use of the process not proper in the regular conduct of the proceeding.[76] Some definite act or threat not authorized by the process, or aimed at an objective not legitimate in the use of the process, is required; and there is no liability where the defendant has done nothing more than carry out the process to its authorized conclusion, even though with bad intentions.[77] The improper purpose usually takes the form of coercion to obtain a collateral advantage, not properly involved in the proceeding itself, such as the surrender of property or the payment of money, by the use of the process as a threat or a club. There is, in other words, a form of extortion, and it is what is done in the course of negotiation, rather than the issuance or any formal use of the process itself, which constitutes the tort. The cases have

there can be no such thing as probable cause for perversion of process. Kool v. Lee, 1913, 43 Utah 394, 134 P. 906.

69. Shaw v. Fulton, 1929, 266 Mass. 189, 165 N.E. 26; Lambert v. Breton, 1929, 127 Me. 510, 144 A. 864.

70. See Blackmon v. Gilmer, 1930, 221 Ala. 554, 130 So. 192; McGann v. Allen, 1926, 105 Conn. 177, 134 A. 810; Sokolowske v. Wilson, 1931, 211 Iowa 1112, 235 N.W. 80; Saliem v. Glovsky, 1934, 132 Me. 402, 172 A. 4; Whelan v. Miller, 1912, 49 Pa.Super. 91, 100.

71. Glidewell v. Murray-Lacy & Co., 1919, 124 Va. 563, 98 S.E. 665; Coplea v. Bybee, 1937, 290 Ill.App. 117, 8 N.E.2d 55; Pittsburg, J. E. & E. R. Co. v. Wakefield Hardware Co., 1906, 143 N.C. 54, 55 S.E. 422; Bourisk v. Derry Lumber Co., 1931, 130 Me. 376, 156 A. 382; Petry v. Childs & Co., 1904, 43 Misc. 108, 88 N.Y.S. 286.

72. Rosemont Enterprises, Inc. v. Random House, Inc., S.D.N.Y.1966, 261 F.Supp. 691; Blackstock v. Tatum, Tex.Civ.App.1965, 396 S.W.2d 463; Bonney v. King, 1903, 201 Ill. 47, 66 N.E. 377; Carpenter, Baggott & Co. v. Hanes, 1914, 167 N.C. 551, 83 S.E. 577; Docter v. Riedel, 1897, 96 Wis. 158, 71 N.W. 119.

73. Hotel Supply Co. v. Reid, 1918, 16 Ala.App. 563, 80 So. 137; Moore v. Michigan Nat. Bank, 1962, 368 Mich. 71, 117 N.W.2d 105; Cardy v. Maxwell, 1957, 9 Misc.2d 329, 169 N.Y.S.2d 547; McClenny v. Inverarity, 1909, 80 Kan. 569, 103 P. 82; Marlatte v. Weickgenant, 1907, 147 Mich. 266, 110 N.W. 1061.

74. State for Use of Little v. United States F. & G. Co., 1953, 217 Miss. 576, 64 So.2d 697 (both). Cf.

Zinn v. Rice, 1891, 154 Mass. 1, 27 N.E. 772; Harris v. Harter, 1926, 29 Cal.App. 190, 249 P. 39 (malicious prosecution) with Saliem v. Glovsky, 1934, 132 Me. 402, 172 A. 4; Pittsburg, J. E. & E. R. Co. v. Wakefield Hardware Co., 1905, 148 N.C. 175, 50 S.E. 571 (abuse of process).

75. See Bond v. Chapin, 1844, 8 Metc., Mass., 31; Antcliff v. June, 1890, 81 Mich. 477, 45 N.W. 1019; Coulter v. Coulter, 1923, 73 Colo. 144, 214 P. 400.

76. Bonney v. King, 1903, 201 Ill. 47, 66 N.E. 377; Hauser v. Bartow, 1937, 273 N.Y. 370, 7 N.E.2d 268; Bourisk v. Derry Lumber Co., 1931, 130 Me. 376, 156 A. 382; Pittsburg, J. E. & E. R. Co. v. Wakefield Hardware Co., 1906, 143 N.C. 54, 55 S.E. 422; Templeton Feed & Grain Co. v. Ralston Purina Co., 1968, 69 Cal.2d 461, 72 Cal.Rptr. 344, 446 P.2d 152.

77. Barnette v. Woody, 1955, 242 N.C. 424, 88 S.E.2d 223; Moffett v. Commerce Trust Co., Mo.1955, 283 S.W.2d 591; Mullins v. Sanders, 1949, 189 Va. 624, 54 S.E.2d 116; Brown v. Robertson, 1950, 120 Ind. App. 434, 92 N.E.2d 856; Elliott v. Warwick Stores, 1952, 329 Mass. 406, 108 N.E.2d 681.

involved such extortion by means of attachment,[78] execution,[79] garnishment,[80] or sequestration[81] proceedings, or arrest of the person,[82] or criminal prosecution,[83] or even such infrequent cases as the use of a subpoena for the collection of a debt.[84] The ulterior motive or purpose may be inferred from what is said or done about the process,[85] but the improper act may not be inferred from the motive.[86] Some actual damage is necessary to the tort, but any completed use of the process which involves an interference with the plaintiff's rights will necessarily involve such damage. Once the tort is proved, the damages recoverable are in general much the same as in cases of malicious prosecution.[87]

78. Saliem v. Glovsky, 1934, 132 Me. 402, 172 A. 4 (excessive attachment, appointment of keeper); Malone v. Belcher, 1913, 216 Mass. 209, 103 N.E. 637; Pittsburg, J. E. & E. R. Co. v. Wakefield Hardware Co., 1905, 138 N.C. 174, 50 S.E. 571.

79. Coplea v. Bybee, 1937, 290 Ill.App. 117, 8 N.E.2d 55 (exacting conditions for surrender); Docter v. Riedel, 1897, 96 Wis. 158, 71 N.W. 119; Antcliff v. June, 1890, 81 Mich. 477, 45 N.W. 1019; Little v. Sowers, 1949, 167 Kan. 72, 204 P.2d 605 (execution on void judgment).

80. Buckenhizer v. Times Pub. Co., 1934, 267 Mich. 393, 255 N.W. 213 (assignment of claim to avoid garnishment offset); see Williams v. Adelman, 1930, 41 Ga.App. 424, 153 S.E. 224.

81. Casey v. Hanrick, 1887, 69 Tex. 44, 6 S.W. 405. Cf. Ludwick v. Penny, 1911, 158 N.C. 104, 73 S.E. 228 (claim and delivery).

82. Brantley v. Rhodes-Haverty Furniture Co., 1908, 131 Ga. 276, 62 S.E. 222; Lockhart v. Bear, 1895, 117 N.C. 298, 23 S.E. 484; Ash v. Cohn, 1937, 119 N.J.L. 54, 194 A. 174.

83. Ellis v. Wellons, 1944, 224 N.C. 269, 29 S.E.2d 884; Lader v. Benkowitz, 1946, 188 Misc. 906, 66 N.Y.S.2d 713; Glidewell v. Murray-Lacy & Co., 1919, 124 Va. 563, 98 S.E. 665; Jackson v. American Telephone & Telegraph Co., 1905, 139 N.C. 347, 51 S.E. 1015; Marlatte v. Weickgenant, 1907, 147 Mich. 266, 110 N.W. 1061.

84. Dishaw v. Wadleigh, 1897, 15 App.Div. 205, 44 N.Y.S. 207. Cf. Dean v. Kochendorfer, 1924, 237 N.Y. 384, 143 N.E. 229 (abuse by magistrate issuing process); Bond v. Chapin, 1844, 8 Metc., Mass., 31 (bringing civil suit in name of another without authority); Cardy v. Maxwell, 1957, 9 Misc.2d 329, 169 N.Y.S.2d 547 (deceit action to force payment of money in order to avoid adverse publicity).

85. Kool v. Lee, 1913, 43 Utah 394, 134 P. 906; Glidewell v. Murray-Lacy & Co., 1919, 124 Va. 563, 98 S.E. 665; Tranchina v. Arcinas, 1947, 78 Cal.App.2d 522, 178 P.2d 65.

86. Jeffery v. Robbins, 1897, 73 Ill.App. 353; Bartlett v. Christhilf, 1888, 69 Md. 219, 14 A. 518; Saliem v. Glovsky, 1934, 132 Me. 402, 172 A. 4.

87. See McCormick, Damages, 1935, § 109. Thus there is no cause of action for an abuse of process which does not succeed in its purpose of compelling the plaintiff to pay any part of a debt, and does no other damage. Gore v. Gorman's Inc., W.D.Mo. 1956, 148 F.Supp. 241, appeal dismissed, 244 F.2d 716.

CHAPTER 23

DOMESTIC RELATIONS

122. TORTS IN THE FAMILY

Causes of action founded upon tortious conduct may be affected by the fact that at least one of the persons involved is a member of a family. The tort-feasor, a stranger to the family relation, may injure one who is a party to the relation; the tort-feasor, a party to the relation, may injure a stranger to the relation; one member of a family may injure another. Few topics in the law of torts, in view of modern economic, social and legislative changes, display in their treatment greater inconsistency and more unsatisfactory reasoning. This is true particularly of the third situation named, where the question is as to the civil liability of husband or wife, or of parent or minor child, to one another for acts, which if they were done by one ordinary person to another would be torts. Here there is waged a battle between conflicting conceptions of the family and between idea of individual and relational rights and duties. Here the last few decades have witnessed a great revival of interest, and a shift in the tendencies of the law in the direction of liability where it did not exist before.[1]

Husband and Wife

Any tort action between husband and wife[2] encountered at the outset the common law doctrine of the legal identity of the two. It has been said, whether humorously or not, that at common law husband and wife were one person, and that person was the husband —which is not strictly accurate, since the criminal law, at least, regarded them as separate individuals, and the wife could be named as a party to a civil action, even though her husband must be joined with her, if he were alive when suit was brought. But as to her personal and property rights, the very legal existence of the wife was regarded as suspended for the duration of the marriage,[3] and merged into that of the husband, so that she lost the capacity to contract for herself,[4] or to sue[5] or be sued[6] without joining the

---

Injury Torts Between Spouses, 1959, 4 Villanova L. Rev. 303; Sanford, Personal Torts Within the Family, 1956, 9 Vand.L.Rev. 823; Notes, 1952, 30 Chicago-Kent L.Rev. 343; 1952, 32 Or.L.Rev. 60; 1954, 42 Ky.L.J. 497; 1954, 7 Vand.L.Rev. 717; 1958, 30 So.Cal.L.Rev. 431; 1959, 14 U.Miami L. Rev. 99; 1961, 26 Mo.L.Rev. 152.

3. "By marriage, the husband and wife are one person in law; that is, the very being or legal existence of the woman is suspended during the marriage, or at least is incorporated and consolidated into that of the husband." 1 Bl.Comm. 442; 2 Bl. Comm. 433.

See Williams, The Legal Unity of Husband and Wife, 1947, 10 Mod.L.Rev. 16; Kahn-Freund, Inconsistencies and Injustices in the Law of Husband and Wife, 1952, 15 Mod.L.Rev. 133.

4. 1 Bl.Comm. 443; Norris v. Lantz, 1861, 18 Md. 260; Farrar v. Bessey, 1852, 24 Vt. 89; Ross v. Singleton, 1821, 1 Del.Ch. 149; Butler v. Buckingham, 1813, 5 Day, Conn., 492.

5. Dengate v. Gardiner, 1838, 4 M. & W. 5, 150 Eng. Rep. 1320; Laughlin v. Eaton, 1866, 54 Me. 156; see Rogers v. Smith, 1861, 17 Ind. 323.

6. Head v. Briscoe, 1833, 5 C. & P. 484, 172 Eng.Rep. 1064; Stockton v. Farley, 1877, 10 W.Va. 171.

---

1. The paragraph is paraphrased from McCurdy, Torts Between Persons in Domestic Relations, 1930, 43 Harv.L.Rev. 1030. See also, generally, as to tort actions within the family, Sanford, Personal Torts Within the Family, 1956, 9 Vand.L.Rev. 823; Note, 1961, 26 Mo.L.Rev. 152.

2. See McCurdy, Property Torts Between Spouses, 1957, 2 Villanova L.Rev. 447; McCurdy, Personal,

husband as a plaintiff or defendant. The husband acquired the right to possession and use of his wife's real [7] and personal [8] property, and he was entitled to all of her choses in action, provided that he "reduced them to possession" during marriage by some act by which he appropriated them to himself, such as collecting the money or obtaining judgment in a suit in his own name.[9] In turn he became liable for the torts of his wife, committed either before or during the marriage.[10]

It is perhaps idle to speculate at this late date as to how far the historical basis of these rules is a mixture of the Bible and mediaeval metaphysics, the position of the father of the family in Roman law, the natural law concept of the family as an informal unit of government with the physically stronger person at the head, or the property law of feudalism.[11]

A combination of all these incidents made it impossible to maintain a tort action between husband and wife. If the man were the tort-feasor, the woman's right would be a chose in action which the husband would have the right to reduce to possession, and he must be joined as a plaintiff against himself and the proceeds recovered must be paid to him; and if the tort involved property, the wife had no right of possession to support the action. If the wife committed the tort,

the husband would be liable to himself for it, and must be joined as a defendant in his own action. As a result, it was held that neither spouse could maintain an action against the other for either a personal [12] or a property [13] tort, whether it was committed before [14] or during marriage; and the action was not maintainable even after divorce,[15] which came late in the English law, after these rules were well established. The wife received some limited protection from the criminal law, which refused to stand on the identity of the persons,[16] except as to crimes involving the right to possession of property; [17] and some intentional torts committed between husband and wife were recognized as a ground for separation or divorce.[18] Likewise the

---

7. Clapp v. Inhabitants of Stoughton, 1829, 10 Pick., Mass., 463; Jones v. Patterson, 1852, 11 Barb., N. Y., 572; Burleigh v. Coffin, 1850, 22 N.H. 118; Payne v. Parker, 1833, 10 Me. 178.

8. Lamphir v. Creed, 1803, 8 Ves.Jr. 599, 32 Eng.Rep. 488; Kensington v. Dolland, 1834, 2 My. & K. 184, 39 Eng.Rep. 914; Ellington v. Harris, 1906, 127 Ga. 85, 56 S.E. 134; Morgan v. Thames Bank, 1840, 14 Conn. 99; Snyder v. Jett, 1917, 138 Tenn. 211, 197 S.W. 488.

9. Little v. Marsh, 1841, 37 N.C. 18; Searing v. Searing, 1841, 9 Paige, N.Y., 283; Howard v. Bryant, 1857, 9 Gray, Mass., 239; Tritt's Adm'r v. Colwell's Adm'r, 1858, 31 Pa. 228.

10. See infra, § 123.

11. See Bryce, Studies in History and Jurisprudence, 1901, 819; 2 Pollock and Maitland, History of English Law, 2d Ed.1923, 399–436.

12. Thompson v. Thompson, 1910, 218 U.S. 611; Freethy v. Freethy, 1865, 42 Barb., N.Y. 641; Libby v. Berry, 1883, 74 Me. 286; Peters v. Peters, 1875, 42 Iowa 182; Nickerson v. Nickerson, 1886, 65 Tex. 281.

13. See Kelley v. Kelley, 1931, 51 R.I. 173, 153 A. 314; Plotkin v. Plotkin, 1924, 2 W.W.Harr., Del., 455, 125 A. 455; Smith v. Gorman, 1856, 41 Me. 405; Howe v. Blanden, 1849, 21 Vt. 315.

14. See Buckeye v. Buckeye, 1931, 203 Wis. 248, 234 N.W. 342; Newton v. Weber, 1922, 119 Misc. 240, 196 N.Y.S. 113; Spector v. Weisman, 1930, 59 App. D.C. 280, 40 F.2d 792; Scales v. Scales, 1934, 168 Miss. 439, 151 So. 551.

15. Phillips v. Barnet, 1876, 1 Q.B.D. 436; Abbott v. Abbott, 1877, 67 Me. 304; Strom v. Strom, 1906, 98 Minn. 427, 107 N.W. 1047.

16. Commonwealth v. McAfee, 1871, 108 Mass. 458 (homicide); State v. Lankford, 1917, 6 Boyce, Del., 594, 102 A. 63 (battery); Fulgham v. State, 1871, 46 Ala. 143 (battery); State v. Fulton, 1908, 149 N.C. 485, 63 S.E. 145 (slander).

17. Rex v. Willis, 1833, 1 Moody C.C. 375, 168 Eng. Rep. 1309 (larceny); Thomas v. Thomas, 1869, 51 Ill. 162 (same); State v. Phillips, 1912, 85 Ohio St. 317, 97 N.E. 976 (same); State v. Arnold, 1931, 182 Minn. 313, 235 N.W. 373 (same); Snyder v. People, 1872, 26 Mich. 106 (arson). The survival of this rule into modern times has resulted in many states in the anomaly that for injuries to property there may be civil but not criminal liability and for injuries to the person criminal but not civil—a result which scarcely commends itself to common sense. See Notes, 1931, 15 Minn.L.Rev. 589; 1932, 30 Mich.L.Rev. 622.

18. E.g., cruel and inhuman treatment.

equity courts disregarded questions of identity and protected the wife in any separate trust estate she might have, against the tortious conduct of the husband.[19]

All this state of affairs belonged to a social order which has been dead for more than a century. Beginning about 1844 statutes known as Married Women's Acts, or Emancipation Acts were passed in all American jurisdictions, which were designed primarily to secure to a married woman a separate legal identity and a separate legal estate in her own property. The statutes differ widely in their language, and still more so as they have been construed by the courts, which received them in the beginning with no great enthusiasm, but have tended to deal with them more liberally in recent years. Reference must of course be made to the statutes of each jurisdiction.[20] It may be said that with very rare exceptions,[21] they confer upon married women the separate ownership and control of their own property, including their choses in action, and the capacity to sue or be sued without joinder of the husband; and that the wife is made separately responsible for her own torts.

Since the primary object of these statutes was to free the wife from the husband's control of her property, the courts have generally agreed[22] that they enable her to maintain an action against him for any tort against her property interests. Thus she may recover from him for conversion[23] or detention of chattels,[24] for fraud,[25] for trespass to land,[26] for waste,[27] for negligent damage to property,[28] or in an action of ejectment[29] or unlawful detainer.[30] Likewise, since the statutes destroy the unity of the persons and place them upon an equality, it is held that the husband may recover from the wife for similar torts as to his property.[31]

So far as personal torts are concerned, however, rather less than half of the courts

---

19. See Garner v. Lankford, 1917, 147 Ga. 235, 93 S. E. 411; Dicey, Law and Public Opinion in England, 1914, 375–379; Snell, Principles of Equity, 19th Ed. 1925, 364.

20. The statutes are collected in 3 Vernier, American Family Laws, 1935, §§ 167, 179, 180.

21. See for example Gregg v. Gregg, 1952, 199 Md. 662, 87 A.2d 581, holding that the wife has no right to sue the husband to recover her expenditures for necessaries.

22. See McCurdy, Property Torts Between Spouses, 1957, 2 Villanova L.Rev. 447. A very few of the statutes were held only to create a separate estate, with rights enforceable in equity. Smith v. Coggan, 1928, 263 Mass. 248, 160 N.E. 799; Metzler v. Metzler, 1930, 8 N.J.Misc. 821, 151 A. 847; cf. Plotkin v. Plotkin, 1924, 2 W.W.Harr., Del., 455, 125 A. 455; Howe v. Blanden, 1849, 21 Vt. 315; Smith v. Gorman, 1856, 41 Me. 405.

23. Hamilton v Hamilton, 1950, 255 Ala. 284, 51 So. 2d 13; Madget v. Madget, 1949, 85 Ohio App. 18, 87 N.E.2d 918; Eddleman v. Eddleman, 1937, 183 Ga. 766, 189 S.E. 833, conformed to 55 Ga.App. 333; Carpenter v. Carpenter, 1908, 154 Mich. 100, 117 N. W. 598.

24. Good v. Good, 1894, 39 W.Va. 357, 19 S.E. 382; Easterly v. Wildman, 1924, 87 Fla. 73, 99 So. 359; Notes v. Snyder, 1925, 55 App.D.C. 233, 4 F.2d 426; White v. White, 1885, 58 Mich. 546, 25 N.W. 490; Bruner v. Hart, 1936, 178 Okl. 222, 62 P.2d 513.

25. Langley v. Schumacker, 1956, 46 Cal.2d 601, 297 P.2d 977; Adams v. Adams, 1883, 51 Conn. 135; Whiting v. Whiting, 1916, 114 Me. 382, 96 A. 500; Heckman v. Heckman, 1906, 215 Pa. 203, 64 A. 425; Moreau v. Moreau, 1924, 250 Mass. 110, 145 N.E. 43; see Keen v. Coleman, 1861, 39 Pa. 299; Note, 1956, 4 U.C.L.A. L.Rev. 114. See Note, 1963, 38 Wash.L.Rev. 371.

26. Weldon v. De Bathe, 1884, 14 Q.B.D. 339; Larison v. Larison, 1881, 9 Ill.App. 27.

27. Freiler v. Kear, 1889, 126 Pa. 470, 17 A. 668, 906, 1890, 133 Pa. 40, 19 A. 310; Borton v. Borton, Tex. Civ.App.1916, 190 S.W. 192, error refused.

28. Hubbard v. Ruff, 1958, 97 Ga.App. 251, 103 S.E. 2d 134; cf. Vigilant Ins. Co. v. Bennett, 1955, 197 Va. 216, 89 S.E.2d 69.

29. Crater v. Crater, 1888, 118 Ind. 521, 21 N.E. 290; Cook v. Cook, 1899, 125 Ala. 583, 27 So. 918; Edmonds v. Edmonds, 1924, 139 Va. 652, 124 S.E. 415. Cf. Caudill v. Caudill, 1935, 39 N.M. 248, 44 P.2d 724 (action to quiet title).

30. Hall v. Hall, 1951, 193 Tenn. 74, 241 S.W.2d 919; Walker v. Walker, 1926, 215 Ky. 154, 284 S.W. 1042.

31. Mason v. Mason, 1892, 66 Hun 386, 21 N.Y.S. 306 (conversion); Shewalter v. Wood, Mo.App.1916, 183 S.W. 1127 (same); Lombard v. Morse, 1891, 155 Mass. 136, 29 N.E. 205 (fraud); Hedlund v. Hedlund, 1930, 87 Colo. 607, 290 P. 285 (replevin); Vigilant Ins. Co. v. Bennett, 1955, 197 Va. 216, 89 S.E.2d 69 (negligence).

which have considered the question have refused, and still refuse, to construe the statutes to alter the common law rule, and to permit any action for any personal tort between the spouses. This means that neither spouse can maintain an action against the other for assault and battery,[32] false imprisonment,[33] malicious prosecution,[34] defamation,[35] or injuries resulting from negligence.[36] And this is true even though the tort was committed [37] and the action was begun [38] before the marriage of the parties, or where the action is brought after the marriage relation has been terminated by separation,[39] divorce,[40] or even annulment,[41] or

by the death of one spouse or even both.[42] In some states this construction no doubt has been compelled by the language of the statute itself;[43] but in by far the greater number it has been read into a statute which is silent on the subject of actions for personal torts.

The courts which follow this majority view have buttressed their conclusion by inventing new arguments, not found in the early cases, for denying the remedy.[44] Apart from stare decisis or judicial inertia, and the policy of strict construction of statutes changing the common law, it has been said that each spouse has remedy enough in the criminal and divorce laws—which obviously is untrue, since neither compensates for the damage done, or covers all the torts that may be com-

32. Thompson v. Thompson, 1910, 218 U.S. 611; Strom v. Strom, 1906, 98 Minn. 427, 107 N.W. 1047; Bandfield v. Bandfield, 1898, 117 Mich. 80, 75 N.W. 287; Lillienkamp v. Rippetoe, 1915, 133 Tenn. 57, 179 S.W. 628; Fisher v. Toler, 1965, 194 Kan. 701, 401 P.2d 1012.

33. Nickerson v. Nickerson, 1886, 65 Tex. 281; Rogers v. Rogers, 1915, 265 Mo. 200, 177 S.W. 382.

34. Holman v. Holman, 1945, 73 Ga.App. 205, 35 S.E. 2d 923.

35. Ewald v. Lane, 1939, 70 App.D.C. 89, 104 F.2d 222, cert. denied 308 U.S. 568; Faris v. Hope, 8 Cir. 1924, 298 F. 727.

36. Rubalcava v. Gisseman, 1963, 14 Utah 2d 344, 384 P.2d 389; Rodgers v. Galindo, 1961, 68 N.M. 215, 360 P.2d 400; Campbell v. Campbell, 1960, 145 W. Va. 245, 114 S.E.2d 406; Prince v. Prince, 1959, 205 Tenn. 451, 326 S.W.2d 908; Koplik v. C. P. Trucking Corp., 1958, 27 N.J. 1, 141 A.2d 34.

37. Monk v. Ramsey, 1969, —— Tenn. ——, 443 S.W. 2d 653; Thomas v. Herron, 1969, 20 Ohio St.2d 62, 253 N.E.2d 772; Taylor v. Vezzani, 1964, 109 Ga. App. 167, 135 S.E.2d 522; Greenberg v. Owens, 1960, 31 N.J. 402, 157 A.2d 689; Latiolais v. Latiolais, Tex.Civ.App.1962, 361 S.W.2d 252; Note, 1960, 36 N.Dak.L.Rev. 206.

38. Spector v. Weisman, 1930, 59 U.S.App.D.C. 280, 40 F.2d 792; Wolfer v. Oehlers, 1950, 8 N.J.Super. 434, 73 A.2d 95; Patenaude v. Patenaude, 1935, 195 Minn. 523, 263 N.W. 546; Lubowitz v. Taines, 1936, 293 Mass. 39, 198 N.E. 320; Newton v. Weber, 1922, 119 Misc. 240, 196 N.Y.S. 113.

39. Taibi v. De Gennaro, 1961, 65 N.J.Super. 294, 167 A.2d 667; Holman v. Holman, 1945, 73 Ga.App. 205, 35 S.E.2d 923; Mountjoy v. Mountjoy, D.C.Cir. 1965, 347 F.2d 811.

40. Ensminger v. Campbell, 1961, 242 Miss. 519, 134 So.2d 728; Strom v. Strom, 1906, 98 Minn. 427, 107

N.W. 1047; Schultz v. Christopher, 1911, 65 Wash. 496, 118 P. 629; Lillienkamp v. Rippetoe, 1915, 133 Tenn. 57, 179 S.W. 628; Fisher v. Toler, 1965, 194 Kan. 701, 401 P.2d 1012.

41. Gordon v. Pollard, 1960, 207 Tenn. 45, 336 S.W.2d 25; Callow v. Thomas, 1948, 322 Mass. 550, 78 N. E.2d 637; Lunt v. Lunt, Tex.Civ.App.1938, 121 S. W.2d 445 error dismissed. See Note, 1948, 48 Col. L.Rev. 961.

42. Saunders v. Hill, Del.1964, 202 A.2d 807. Wright v. Davis, 1949, 132 W.Va. 722, 53 S.E.2d 335 (separated, husband murdered wife and killed himself—surely a disrupted marriage); Levlock v. Spanos, 1957, 101 N.H. 22, 131 A.2d 319; Castellucci v. Castellucci, 1963, 96 R.I. 34, 188 A.2d 467; Heckendorn v. First Nat. Bank of Ottawa, 1960, 19 Ill.2d 190, 166 N.E.2d 571, cert. denied 364 U.S. 882.

43. See Hindman v. Holmes, 1955, 4 Ill.App.2d 279, 124 N.E.2d 344; Edwards v. Royal Indemnity Co., 1936, 182 La. 171, 161 So. 191. Examples are the absurd results formerly reached in North Carolina and Wisconsin, but now changed in both states by statute, by which the wife could sue the husband for a personal tort, but the husband could not sue the wife. See Scholtens v. Scholtens, 1949, 230 N.C. 149, 52 S.E.2d 350; Singer v. Singer, 1944, 245 Wis. 191, 14 N.W.2d 43.

44. See McCurdy, Torts Between Persons in Domestic Relations, 1930, 43 Harv.L.Rev. 1030, 1050–1056; Herskowitz, Tort Liability Between Husband and Wife, 1966, 21 U.Miami L.Rev. 423; Notes, 1969, 21 U.Fla.L.Rev. 484; 1967, 21 Rut.L.Rev. 491; 1966, 27 Ohio St.L.J. 550; 1966, 79 Harv.L.Rev. 1650; 1954, 42 Ky.L.J. 497.

mitted.[45] Stress has been laid upon the danger of fictitious and fraudulent claims,[46] on the very dubious assumption that a wife's love for her husband is such that she is more likely to bring a false suit against him than a genuine one; and likewise the possibility of trivial actions for minor annoyances,[47] which might well be taken care of by finding consent to all ordinary frictions of wedlock— [48] or at least assumption of risk! The chief reason relied upon by all these courts, however, is that personal tort actions between husband and wife would disrupt and destroy the peace and harmony of the home, which is against the policy of the law. This is on the bald theory that after a husband has beaten his wife, there is a state of peace and harmony left to be disturbed; and that if she is sufficiently injured or angry to sue him for it, she will be soothed and deterred from reprisals by denying her the legal remedy— and this even though she has left him [49] or divorced him [50] for that very ground, and

although the same courts refuse to find any disruption of domestic tranquillity if she sues him for a tort to her property, or brings a criminal prosecution against him. If this reasoning appeals to the reader, let him by all means adopt it.[51]

Any such precarious structure, subjected to this type of long-continued critical hammering, is likely sooner or later to develop cracks. In some sixteen states one or more "exceptions" have been recognized to the general rule of complete immunity between husband and wife, where for one reason or another the considerations of policy supposed to underlie it have been held not to apply. The entering wedge is recognition that there is a tort, but disability to sue for it; and that when the reasons for the disability fail, the tort becomes actionable. Thus recovery has been permitted for intentional physical attacks,[52] on the ground that "the peace and harmony of the home has been so damaged that there is no danger that it will be further impaired." The same conclusion has been reached where the marriage has been terminated by separation,[53] divorce,[54] or an-

---

45. Ordinary negligent injury, for example, is nowhere a crime, or a ground for divorce.

46. ". . . and this would add a new method by which estates could be plundered." Abbott v. Abbott, 1877, 67 Me. 304. No wife would want to sue her husband for a negligent tort except as a "raid on an insurance company." Newton v. Weber, 1922, 119 Misc. 240, 196 N.Y.S. 113. As to collusion in connection with liability insurance, see infra, p. 868.

47. Cf. Drake v. Drake, 1920, 145 Minn. 388, 177 N. W. 624, denying an injunction against nagging; and the dissenting opinion of Eschweiler, J., on the excessively kissed wife, in Wait v. Pierce, 1926, 191 Wis. 202, 209 N.W. 475, affirmed 210 N.W. 822.

48. See McCurdy, Torts Between Persons in Domestic Relations, 1930, 43 Harv.L.Rev. 1030, 1053; McCurdy, Personal Injury Torts Between Spouses, 1959, 4 Villanova L.Rev. 303; Note, 1961, 59 Mich. L.Rev. 1263.

49. Clark v. Clark, D.N.Y.1925, 11 F.2d 871.

50. See cases cited supra, note 40. Compare with these the violent language in Ritter v. Ritter, 1858, 31 Pa. 396: "The flames which litigation would kindle on the domestic hearth would consume in an instant the conjugal bond, and bring on a new era indeed—an era of universal discord, of unchastity, of bastardy, of dissoluteness, of violence, cruelty, and murders."

51. "Whether a man has laid open his wife's head with a bludgeon, put out her eye, broken her arm, or poisoned her body, he is no longer exempt from liability to her on the ground that he vowed at the altar to 'love, cherish, and protect' her. We have progressed that far in civilization and justice." Bogen v. Bogen, 1941, 219 N.C. 51, 53, 12 S.E.2d 649, 651.

52. Apitz v. Dames, 1955, 205 Or. 242, 287 P.2d 585; Self v. Self, 1962, 58 Cal.2d 632, 26 Cal.Rptr. 97, 376 P.2d 65. Accord, although decided on other elements: Goode v. Martinis, 1961, 58 Wash.2d 229, 361 P.2d 941 (separation); Taylor v. Patten, 1954, 2 Utah 2d 404, 275 P.2d 696 (same, semble); Brown v. Selby, 1960, 206 Tenn. 71, 332 S.W.2d 166 (death); Johnson v. Ottomeier, 1954, 45 Wash.2d 419, 275 P.2d 723 (death); Shiver v. Sessions, Fla. 1955, 80 So.2d 905 (death). Compare the cases as to parent and child, cited infra, p. 864.

53. Goode v. Martinis, 1961, 58 Wash.2d 229, 361 P.2d 941; Taylor v. Patten, 1954, 2 Utah 2d 404, 275 P. 2d 696 (semble); Le Crone v. Ohio Bell Tel. Co., 1963, 120 Ohio App.2d 129, 201 N.E.2d 533.

54. Steele v. Steele, D.D.C.1946, 65 F.Supp. 329; Gremillion v. Caffey, La.App.1954, 71 So.2d 670;

nulment,[55] or by the death of one or both spouses, whether the action is brought under a wrongful death act [56] or a survival statute.[57] There is also considerable authority that the action can be maintained for an antenuptial tort,[58] upon the theory that the cause of action is a separate property right, preserved to the injured spouse by the statutes. It is difficult not to regard these decisions as bites at the cherry, which will ultimately succeed in nibbling it away.

This is fully borne out by the fact that several jurisdictions, with the unanimous approval of legal writers,[59] have followed the lead of a noted dissenting opinion of Mr. Justice Harlan,[60] have rejected all ar-

guments in justification of the immunity as specious, have thrown it completely overboard, and have construed the Married Women's Acts to authorize an action by either spouse for a personal tort committed by the other, whether it be intentional or negligent in character. There are now some nineteen such jurisdictions; [61] and the number has been increasing at an accelerated pace in recent years. The list of such jurisdictions has been increasing in recent years; and this has been claimed to be due to the presence or availability of liability insurance in automobile cases.[62] The devastating attack on the old rule found in a number of recent decisions seems to leave no possible justification for it except that of historical survival.

Parent and Child

The common law had no similar conception of unity of legal identity in the case of a parent and his minor child. Although the parent was given custody of the child, the latter remained a separate legal person, entitled to the benefits of his own property and to the enforcement of his own choses in action,[63] including those in tort, and was liable in turn as an individual for his own torts. Consequently there were no such theoretical difficulties, no emancipation acts similar to the Married Women's Acts were necessary, and statutory construction has not entered into

---

Lorang v. Hays, 1949, 69 Idaho 440, 209 P.2d 733; Sanchez v. Olivarez, 1967, 94 N.J.Super. 61, 226 A. 2d 752; Gaston v. Pittman, 5 Cir. 1969, 413 F.2d 1031. See Note, 1969, 23 U.Miami L.Rev. 626.

55. Henneger v. Lomas, 1896, 145 Ind. 287, 44 N.E. 462.

56. Jones v. Pledger, 1966, 124 U.S.App.D.C. 254, 363 F.2d 986; First Union Bank of N. C. v. Hackney, 1965, 266 N.C. 17, 145 S.E.2d 352; Shiver v. Sessions, Fla.1955, 80 So.2d 905; Shumway v. Nelson, 1961, 259 Minn. 319, 107 N.W.2d 531; Logan v. Reaves, 1962, 209 Tenn. 631, 354 S.W.2d 789. See Notes, 1952, 5 Vand.L.Rev. 855; 1955, 30 Wash.L. Rev. 184; 1956, 9 U.Fla.L.Rev. 110.
Compare the cases as to parent and child, infra, p. 864.

57. Long v. Landy, 1961, 35 N.J. 44, 171 A.2d 1; Johnson v. Peoples First Nat. Bank & Trust Co., 1958, 394 Pa. 116, 145 A.2d 716; Ennis v. Truhitte, Mo.1957, 306 S.W.2d 549; Pelowski v. Frederickson, 1962, 263 Minn. 371, 116 N.W.2d 701; Poepping v. Lindemann, 1964, 268 Minn. 30, 127 N.W.2d 512. See Note, 1958, 23 Mo.L.Rev. 366. Compare the cases as to parent and child, infra, p. 864.

58. Brandt v. Keller, 1952, 413 Ill. 503, 109 N.E.2d 729; Foote v. Foote, 1959, 170 Cal.App.2d 435, 339 P.2d 188; Morin v. Letourneau, 1955, 102 N.H. 309, 156 A.2d 131; Berry v. Harmon, Mo.1959, 329 S.W. 2d 784; O. Grady v. Potts, 1964, 193 Kan. 644, 396 P.2d 285. In Juaire v. Juaire, 1969, —— Vt. ——, 259 A.2d 786, the court got around the obstacle by holding the wife could sue in equity. See Note, 1957, 22 Mo.L.Rev. 216.

59. See supra, note 2.

60. In Thompson v. Thompson, 1910, 218 U.S. 611, with Holmes and Hughes, JJ., joining in the dissent.

61. Currently the list includes Alabama, Alaska, Arizona, Arkansas, California, Colorado, Connecticut, Idaho, Kentucky, Louisiana, Minnesota, New Hampshire, New Jersey, New York, North Carolina, North Dakota, South Carolina, South Dakota, and Wisconsin.

62. See infra, p. 868.

63. Wilton v. Middlesex R. Co., 1878, 125 Mass. 130; Donahoe v. Richards, 1854, 38 Me. 376. Normally any action is brought on behalf of the child by the parent as natural guardian; but where his interests are adverse to those of the child, another person is appointed guardian ad litem. As to the child's liability for his own torts, see infra, § 134.

the question of tort liability between parent and child.

In matters affecting property, causes of action seems always to have been freely recognized, on the part of either the parent [64] or the child.[65] Although there were no old decisions, the speculation on the matter has been that there is no good reason to think that the English law would not permit actions for personal torts as well,[66] subject always to the parent's privilege to enforce reasonable discipline against the child; [67] and there are decisions in Canada [68] and Scotland [69] holding that such an action will lie. But beginning in 1891 with Hewlett v. George,[70] a Mississippi case of false imprisonment which cited no authorities, the American courts adopted a general rule refusing to allow actions between parent and minor child for personal torts, whether they are intentional [71] or negligent [72] in character. For

reasons that are not altogether clear, however, and perhaps are to be explained only on the basis of an initial retreat from the general rule,[73] the action nearly always has been permitted against one who is not a parent but merely stands in the place of one, such as a stepfather, or another relative who has custody of the child.[74]

The courts which deny the action have relied heavily on the analogy of husband and wife, which seems quite inapplicable because of the difference in the common law concept of the relations, and the absence of statutes to be construed.[75] In addition, they have invented much the same variety of unconvincing reasons as in the case of the marital relation.[76] The danger of "fraud" has been

---

64. Young v. Wiley, 1914, 183 Ind. 449, 107 N.E. 278; McKern v. Beck, 1920, 73 Ind.App. 92, 126 N.E. 641; McCall v. McCall, 1873, 1 Tenn.Ch. 500.

65. During minority: Roberts v. Roberts, 1657, Hard. 96, 145 Eng.Rep. 399; Alston v. Alston, 1859, 34 Ala. 15; Lamb v. Lamb, 1895, 146 N.Y. 317, 41 N.E. 26; Preston v. Preston, 1925, 102 Conn. 96, 128 A. 292. After majority for acts occurring during minority: Thomas v. Thomas, 1855, 2 K. & J. 79, 69 Eng.Rep. 701; McLain v. McLain, 1921, 80 Okl. 113, 194 P. 894.

66. See Reeve, Domestic Relations, 1816, 287; Eversley, Domestic Relations, 3d Ed. 1906, 578; Dunlap v. Dunlap, 1930, 84 N.H. 352, 150 A. 905.

67. See supra, § 27.

68. Deziel v. Deziel, [1953] 1 Dom.L.Rep. 651.

69. Young v. Rankin, [1934] Sess.Cass. 499.

70. 1891, 68 Miss. 703, 9 So. 885. This is the name of the case in the official reports. It is often miscited as Hewellette v. George.

71. McKelvey v. McKelvey, 1903, 111 Tenn. 388, 77 S.W. 664; Roller v. Roller, 1905, 37 Wash. 242, 79 P. 788; Cook v. Cook, 1939, 232 Mo.App. 994, 124 S.W.2d 675; Miller v. Pelzer, 1924, 159 Minn. 375, 199 N.W. 97 (deceit); Smith v. Smith, 1924, 81 Ind. App. 566, 142 N.E. 128 (action after majority for assault during minority).

72. Villaret v. Villaret, 1948, 83 U.S.App.D.C. 311, 169 F.2d 677 (Maryland law); Stevens v. Murphy,

1966, 69 Wash.2d 939, 421 P.2d 668; Chaffin v. Chaffin, 1964, 239 Or. 374, 397 P.2d 771; Hastings v. Hastings, 1961, 33 N.J. 247, 163 A.2d 147; Ownby v. Kleyhammer, 1952, 194 Tenn. 109, 250 S.W.2d 37.

73. Brown v. Cole, 1939, 198 Ark. 417, 129 S.W.2d 245 (stepfather poisoning stepson); Treschman v. Treschman, 1901, 28 Ind.App. 206, 61 N.E. 961; Clasen v. Pruhs, 1903, 69 Neb. 789, 95 N.W. 640; Steber v. Norris, 1925, 188 Wis. 266, 206 N.W. 173; Dix v. Martin, 1913, 171 Mo.App. 266, 157 S.W. 133. On their reasoning these cases appear to contradict the explanations offered for the rule as to parents.

74. Bricault v. Deveau, 1960, 21 Conn.Sup. 486, 157 A.2d 604 (stepfather); Brown v. Cole, 1939, 198 Ark. 417, 129 S.W.2d 245 (adoptive parent); Wilkins v. Kane, 1962, 74 N.J.Super. 414, 181 A.2d 417 (grandparent); Cwik v. Zylstra, 1959, 58 N.J.Super. 29, 155 A.2d 277 (grandparent). Contra, Wooden v. Hale, Okl.1967, 426 P.2d 679.

75. The height of inconsistency is reached by some courts which permit action by the wife but deny it to the child. Redding v. Redding, 1952, 235 N.C. 638, 70 S.E.2d 676; Mesite v. Kirchstein, 1929, 109 Conn. 77, 145 A. 753; Wick v. Wick, 1927, 192 Wis. 260, 212 N.W. 787; Rambo v. Rambo, 1938, 195 Ark. 832, 114 S.W.2d 468.

76. Discussed at length in McCurdy, Torts Between Persons in Domestic Relations, 1930, 43 Harv.L. Rev. 1030, 1072–1077; McCurdy, Torts Between Parent and Child, 1960, 5 Villanova L.Rev. 521; Sanford, Personal Torts Within the Family, 1956, 9 Vand.L.Rev. 823; Notes, 1951, 26 Ind.L.J. 465; 1951, 12 Md.L.Rev. 202; [1952] Wash.U.L.Q. 151; 1953, 38 Corn.L.Q. 462; 1953, 2 DePaul L.Rev. 119; 1956, 34 Chicago-Kent L.Rev. 333; 1959, 26 Tenn.L. Rev. 561; 1961, 23 Mo.L.Rev. 152; 1963, 48 Iowa

stressed, although it is difficult to see why it is any greater, as between the parties themselves, than in any other tort action involving an infant; [77] and likewise the possibility that the defendant might inherit the amount recovered in case of the plaintiff's death, or that the family exchequer might be depleted at the expense of other children—neither of which reasons seems to outweigh the desirability of compensating the injured one for his damage. But again, as in the case of husband and wife, the chief reason offered is that domestic tranquillity and parental discipline and control would be disturbed by the action—and again on the theory that an uncompensated tort makes for peace in the family and respect for the parent, even though it be rape [78] or a brutal beating, [79] and even though the relation itself has been terminated by death before the suit. [80] But none of these arguments has been held sufficient to bar an action by or against an unemancipated minor for a tort against property, although they are all quite obviously equally applicable in such a case. Nor, by common agreement, have they been sufficient to prevent an action for a personal tort between minor brothers and sisters, which uniformly has been allowed. [81]

Although it would appear that no shadow of a difference in principle or policy is to be discovered, the retreat from the common law as to parent and child has lagged behind that as to husband and wife, apparently for no better reason than the absence of statutes such as the Married Women's Acts. It is, however, under way. As in the case of husband and wife, the courts began by recognizing a series of exceptions which have whittled the immunity down. The first of these, generally accepted but quite difficult to justify in principle, is that the action has been allowed where the child has been "emancipated" by the parent's surrender of the right to his earnings and services, and to parental control. [82] Another, which in all honesty can be supported only upon the basis of the greater culpability involved, allows recovery when personal injuries are inflicted intentionally; [83] and several courts have extended this to include "wilful or wanton," or in other words reckless misconduct, [84] sometimes on the manufactured ground that such con-

L.Rev. 748; 1966, 44 N.C.L.Rev. 1169. The only kind word spoken for the immunity is in Cooperrider, Child v. Parent in Tort: A Case for the Jury, 1958, 43 Minn.L.Rev. 73.

77. Except as to liability insurance; see infra, p. 868.

78. Roller v. Roller, 1905, 37 Wash. 242, 79 P. 788.

79. Cook v. Cook, 1939, 232 Mo.App. 994, 124 S.W.2d 675; McKelvey v. McKelvey, 1903, 111 Tenn. 388, 77 S.W. 664; cf. Hewlett v. George, 1891, 68 Miss. 703, 9 So. 885 (imprisonment in insane asylum).

80. Lasecki v. Kabara, 1940, 235 Wis. 645, 294 N.W. 33; Harralson v. Thomas, Ky.1954, 269 S.W.2d 276; Shaker v. Shaker, 1942, 129 Conn. 518, 29 A.2d 765; Damiano v. Damiano, 1928, 6 N.J.Misc. 849, 143 A. 3 (both parent and child dead).

81. Midkiff v. Midkiff, 1960, 201 Va. 829, 113 S.E.2d 875; Herrell v. Haney, 1960, 207 Tenn. 532, 341 S. W.2d 574; Overlock v. Ruedemann, 1960, 147 Conn. 649, 165 A.2d 335; Emery v. Emery, 1955, 45 Cal.2d 421, 289 P.2d 218; Tucker v. Tucker, Okl.1964, 395

P.2d 67. See Notes, 1939, 37 Mich.L.Rev. 658; 1940, 38 Mich.L.Rev. 743; 1939, 23 Minn.L.Rev. 838; 1961, 28 Tenn.L.Rev. 419.

82. Weinberg v. Underwood, 1968, 101 N.J.Super. 448, 244 A.2d 538; Fitzgerald v. Valdez, 1967, 77 N.M. 769, 427 P.2d 655; Carricato v. Carricato, Ky.1964, 384 S.W.2d 85; Tucker v. Tucker, Okl.1964, 395 P. 2d 67; Logan v. Reaves, 1962, 209 Tenn. 631, 354 S.W.2d 789. As to what constitutes emancipation, see Gillikin v. Burbage, 1965, 263 N.C. 317, 139 S.E. 2d 753.

83. Treschman v. Treschman, 1901, 28 Ind.App. 206, 61 N.E. 961; Gillett v. Gillett, 1959, 168 Cal.App.2d 102, 335 P.2d 736; Brown v. Cole, 1939, 198 Ark. 417, 129 S.W.2d 245; Mahnke v. Moore, 1951, 197 Md. 61, 77 A.2d 923. See also Brown v. Selby, 1960, 206 Tenn. 71, 332 S.W.2d 166; Meyer v. Ritterbush, 1949, 196 Misc. 551, 92 N.Y.S.2d 595.

84. Emery v. Emery, 1955, 45 Cal.2d 421, 289 P.2d 218; Wright v. Wright, 1952, 85 Ga.App. 721, 70 S. E.2d 152; Nudd v. Matsoukas, 1956, 7 Ill.2d 608, 131 N.E.2d 525; Henderson v. Henderson, 1957, 11 Misc.2d 449, 169 N.Y.S.2d 106; Cowgill v. Brock, 1950, 189 Or. 282, 218 P.2d 445.

See as to recklessness, Hoffman v. Tracy, 1965, 67 Wash.2d 31, 406 P.2d 323; See Notes, 1958, 50 Col.L.Rev. 576; 1957, 41 Marq.L.Rev. 188; 1966, 15 DePaul L.Rev. 229.

duct terminates or "forfeits" the relationship, and steps outside of it.

As in the case of husband and wife, some courts have allowed recovery when the relation has been terminated by the death of either parent or child, and the action is brought under a wrongful death [85] or a survival [86] act. Even this has been extended to permit an action between parent and child for the wrongful death of the other parent [87] or loss of services of another child,[88] on the ground that these are derivative actions, turning primarily upon the possibility of suit by another. Finally, there are half a dozen courts which have allowed recovery where the child is injured in the course of a business, rather than a personal, activity of the parent,[89] making an artificial separation

of vocational from personal capacity, which suggests a dislike of the immunity more than anything else.

Finally, in 1963, Wisconsin took the lead in declaring that the parent-child immunity was abrogated entirely in that jurisdiction,[90] except as to exercises of parental control and authority, or parental discretion with respect to such matters as food and care.[91] The decision set off something of a long-overdue landslide; and at the present writing it has been followed in Alaska,[92] Arizona,[93] California,[93a] Hawaii,[94] Illinois,[95] Kentucky,[95a] Louisiana,[96] Minnesota,[97] New

85. Hale v. Hale, 1950, 312 Ky. 867, 230 S.W.2d 610; Oliveria v. Oliveria, 1940, 305 Mass. 297, 25 N.E.2d 766; Morgan v. Leuck, 1952, 137 W.Va. 546, 72 S.E.2d 825; Logan v. Reaves, 1962, 209 Tenn. 631, 354 S.W.2d 789; Harlan Nat. Bank v. Gross, Ky.1961, 346 S.W.2d 482. See Note, 1964, 16 U.Me. L.Rev. 238.

86. Thurman v. Etherton, Ky.1970, 459 S.W.2d 402; Palcsey v. Tepper, 1962, 71 N.J.Super. 294, 176 A.2d 818; Krause v. Home Mut. Ins. Co., 1961, 14 Wis.2d 666, 112 N.W.2d 134; Brinks v. Chesapeake & Ohio R. Co., W.D.Mich.1969, 295 F.Supp. 1318; Union Bank & Trust Co. of Mt. Holley, N. J. v. First Nat. Bank & Trust Co. of Waynesboro, Pa., 5 Cir. 1966, 362 F.2d 311, appeal after remand 396 F.2d 795.

87. Shiver v. Sessions, Fla.1955, 80 So.2d 905; Fowler v. Fowler, 1963, 242 S.C. 252, 130 S.E.2d 568; Johnson v. Ottemeier, 1954, 45 Wash.2d 419, 275 P. 2d 723; Brown v. Selby, 1960, 206 Tenn. 71, 332 S. W.2d 166; Minkin v. Minkin, 1939, 336 Pa. 49, 7 A. 2d 461.

Accord, as to the death of another child: Munsert v. Farmers Mut. Auto. Ins. Co., 1938, 229 Wis. 581, 281 N.W. 671. Contra: Durham v. Durham, 1956, 227 Miss. 76, 85 So.2d 807; Wright v. Davis, 1949, 132 W.Va. 722, 53 S.E.2d 335; Heyman v. Gordon, 1963, 40 N.J. 52, 190 A.2d 670.

88. Becker v. Rieck, 1959, 19 Misc.2d 104, 188 N.Y.S. 2d 724.

89. Dunlap v. Dunlap, 1930, 84 N.H. 352, 150 A. 905; Lusk v. Lusk, 1932, 113 W.Va. 17, 166 S.E. 538; Signs v. Signs, 1952, 156 Ohio St. 566, 103 N.E.2d 743; Borst v. Borst, 1952, 41 Wash.2d 642, 251 P.2d 149; Trevarton v. Trevarton, 1963, 151 Colo. 418,

378 P.2d 640. Cf. Worrell v. Worrell, 1939, 174 Va. 11, 4 S.E.2d 343 (under compulsory insurance statute).

90. Goller v. White, 1963, 20 Wis.2d 402, 122 N.W.2d 193. Followed in Ertl v. Ertl, 1966, 30 Wis.2d 372, 141 N.W.2d 208.

91. The same exceptions were stated in Balts v. Balts, 1966, 273 Minn. 419, 142 N.W.2d 66. The first appears to be only a matter of the privilege of parental discipline (see supra, § 27), and the second a matter of discretionary conduct, so that there is simply no tort in either case. In Schenk v. Schenk, 1968, 100 Ill.App.2d 199, 241 N.E.2d 12, the court made a somewhat broader statement, limiting the immunity to torts arising out of the parental relation. This may be intended to mean the same thing.

92. Hebel v. Hebel, 1967, — Alaska —, 435 P.2d 8.

93. Streenz v. Streenz, 106 Ariz. 86, 471 P.2d 282.

93a. Gibson v. Gibson, 1971, — Cal.3d —, 92 Cal. Rptr. 288, 479 P.2d 648.

94. Tamashiro v. De Gama, 1969, 51 Haw. 74, 450 P.2d 998.

95. Schenk v. Schenk, 1968, 100 Ill.App.2d 199, 241 N.E.2d 12.

95a. Rigdon v. Rigdon, Ky.1971, — S.W.2d —.

96. Rouley v. State Farm Mut. Auto. Ins. Co., W.D. La.1964, 235 F.Supp. 786, relying on Smith v. Southern Farm Bureau Cas. Ins. Co., La.App.1964, 164 So.2d 647, amended 247 La. 695, 174 So.2d 122 as to husband and wife.

97. Balts v. Balts, 1966, 273 Minn. 419, 142 N.W.2d 66; Silesky v. Kelman, 1968, 281 Minn. 431, 161 N. W.2d 631.

98. Briere v. Briere, 1966, 107 N.H. 432, 224 A.2d 588.

99. France v. A.P.A. Transport Corp., 1970, 56 N.J. 500, 267 A.2d 490.

Hampshire,[98] New Jersey,[99] New York,[1] and North Dakota.[2] The prediction is easy to make that the number of such jurisdictions will henceforth be rapidly on the increase.

Liability Insurance

The effect which liability insurance has thus far had upon the family immunities is not very easy to evaluate. Where there is such insurance, it becomes still more difficult to maintain most of the stock arguments against allowing recovery. Since the defendant will not have to pay out of his own pocket, it is obvious that the family exchequer will not be diminished, and that domestic harmony will not be disrupted so much by allowing the action as by denying it; and since the party really interested in the defense is the liability insurer, any conception of family unity and sanctity can scarcely extend to or protect him. And where insurance is readily available, there is no great need to be tender of defendants who do not have it, since decisions imposing liability may be expected to lead to its purchase. On the other hand, of course, the danger of collusion between the injured person and the insured, always present in liability insurance cases, is not at all lessened, but in fact considerably increased, by the family relation;[3] and if the far from negligible cost of the insurance premium is to be imposed upon family defendants, they will in the aggregate bear all but an inconsiderable part of the liability.

Most of the courts which have mentioned the matter at all, instead of deciding the

question as one of policy, have gone off on the narrow technical ground that liability insurance does not create liability, but only recompenses it when it otherwise exists. On this basis, it is still undoubtedly the general holding that the fact that the particular defendant has insurance does not change the rule denying a remedy to either spouse,[4] or to parent or child;[5] and that, if anything, the danger of collusion against the insurer affords a reason for not abrogating the immunity.[6]

Liability of Third Parties

In the jurisdictions which deny the action where only members of the family are concerned, further dispute has arisen as to the liability of third parties. Under the Married Women's Acts, there is general agreement that an agent of one spouse may be liable to the other for a tort committed within the scope of his employment,[7] and also that a conspirator or other joint tort-feasor will be liable for his own tortious conduct notwithstanding the immunity of the spouse who joins with him.[8] But as to liability

---

1. Gelbman v. Gelbman, 1969, 23 N.Y.2d 434, 297 N. Y.S.2d 529, 245 N.E.2d 192; Howell v. Perri, 1969, 60 Misc.2d 871, 304 N.Y.S.2d 156.

2. Nuelle v. Wells, N.D.1967, 154 N.W.2d 364.

See, generally, Notes, 1966, 51 Minn.L.Rev. 370; 1967, 12 S.D.L.Rev. 364.

3. See Hastings v. Hastings, 1960, 33 N.J. 247, 163 A.2d 147; Villaret v. Villaret, 1948, 83 U.S.App.D.C. 311, 169 F.2d 677; Luster v. Luster, 1938, 299 Mass. 480, 13 N.E.2d 438; Parks v. Parks, 1957, 390 Pa. 287, 135 A.2d 65; Turner v. Carter, 1935, 169 Tenn. 553, 89 S.W.2d 751.

4. Prince v. Prince, 1959, 205 Tenn. 451, 326 S.W.2d 908; Hamilton v. Fulkerson, Mo.1955, 285 S.W.2d 642; Fehr v. General Accident, F. & L. Assur. Corp., 1944, 246 Wis. 228, 16 N.W.2d 787; Boisvert v. Boisvert, 1947, 94 N.H. 357, 53 A.2d 515 (Massachusetts law). Cf. McKinney v. McKinney, 1943, 59 Wyo. 204, 135 P.2d 940, where the court divided three ways over the question.

5. Schwenkoff v. Farmers Mut. Auto. Ins. Co., 1959, 6 Wis.2d 44, 93 N.W.2d 867; Levesque v. Levesque, 1954, 99 N.H. 147, 106 A.2d 563; Harralson v. Thomas, Ky.1954, 269 S.W.2d 276; Parker v. Parker, 1956, 230 S.C. 28, 94 S.E.2d 12; Ball v. Ball, 1954, 73 Wyo. 29, 269 P.2d 302. See Note, 1955, 29 Temp.L.Q. 112.

6. See cases cited supra, note 3. See Note, 1966, 11 S.D.L.Rev. 144.

7. Pepper v. Morrill, 1 Cir. 1928, 24 F.2d 320; Burns v. Kirkpatrick, 1892, 91 Mich. 364, 51 N.W. 893.

8. Ewald v. Lane, 1939, 70 U.S.App.D.C. 89, 104 F.2d 222, cert. denied 308 U.S. 568; Lorang v. Hays, 1949, 69 Idaho 440, 209 P.2d 733; Rogers v. Rogers, 1915, 265 Mo. 200, 177 S.W. 382; Kimatian v. New England Tel. & Tel. Co., 1928, 49 R.I. 146, 141 A. 331; Smith v. Smith, 1889, 73 Mich. 445, 41 N.W.

which is purely vicarious, such as that of an employer of a husband or father for injury to the wife or child, the courts were for a long time divided. The older, but now almost entirely obsolete view denied recovery in such a case,[9] arguing first that since the master's liability is founded on the servant's tort, he should not be liable where the servant is not; and second, that the master's right of indemnity against the servant would circumvent the domestic immunity, and defeat it by throwing the ultimate loss upon the servant. The first argument confuses immunity from suit with lack of responsibility—the servant has committed a tort which by ordinary rules of law should make the master liable, and there is no reason to include the latter within the purely personal immunity of the family. The second misses the point that the master's recovery over against the servant is not based upon any continuation of the original domestic claim, but upon the servant's independent duty of care for the protection of the master's interests;[10] and that if protection of the servant is still the sine qua non, it can always be accomplished merely by denying the indemnity.[11]

Accordingly the overwhelming majority of the courts now hold that the employer is liable even though the servant is immune from suit.[12] A similar conclusion has been reached as to the vicarious liability of partnerships[13] and associations[14] of which the person immune is a member, and as to that of an automobile owner for the negligence of one whom he allows to operate his car.[15]

123. VICARIOUS LIABILITY FOR TORTS OF FAMILY

As one of the incidents of marriage at common law, a husband became liable for the

---

499. Contra, Graham v. Miller, 1945, 182 Tenn. 434, 187 S.W.2d 622.

See Notes, 1940, 25 Corn.L.Q. 312; 1940, 38 Mich.L. Rev. 745.

9. Myers v. Tranquility Irr. Dist., 1938, 26 Cal.App. 2d 385, 79 P.2d 419; Maine v. James Maine & Sons Co., 1924, 198 Iowa 1278, 201 N.W. 20; Sacknoff v. Sacknoff, 1932, 131 Me. 280, 161 A. 669; Emerson v. Western Seed & Irr. Co., 1927, 116 Neb. 180, 216 N.W. 297. A late example is Pinette v. Pinette, 1965, 106 N.H. 345, 211 A.2d 403 (Maine law).

10. See Jones v. Kinney, W.D.Mo.1953, 113 F.Supp. 923; Hudson v. Gas Consumers' Ass'n, 1939, 123 N. J.L. 252, 8 A.2d 337; Schubert v. August Schubert Wagon Co., 1928, 249 N.Y. 253, 164 N.E. 42; and see Notes, 1928, 23 Ill.L.Rev. 174; 1927, 13 Corn.L. Q. 106; 1928, 6 N.Y.U.L.Rev. 53; 1940, 25 Corn.L.Q 312.

11. Cf. American Auto Ins. Co. v. Molling, 1953, 239 Minn. 74, 57 N.W.2d 847; Yellow Cab Co. of D.C. v. Dreslin, 1950, 86 U.S.App.D.C. 231, 181 F.2d 626.

12. Fields v. Synthetic Ropes, Inc., Del.1965, 215 A.2d 427, on remand 219 A.2d 374; Radelicki v. Travis, 1956, 39 N.J.Super. 263, 120 A.2d 774; Kowaleski v. Kowaleski, 1961, 227 Or. 45, 361 P.2d 64; May v. Palm Beach Chemical Co., Fla.1955, 77 So.2d 468; Wright v. Wright, 1948, 229 N.C. 503, 50 S.E.2d 540; Restatement of Agency, § 217, Comment b. See Green, Master's Liability for Acts of Servant Causing Bodily Injury to Servant's Wife, 1929, 23 Ill.L.Rev. 174; Notes, 1946, 46 Col.L.Rev. 148; 1942, 6 Md.L.Rev. 173; 1954, 1 U.C.L.A.L.Rev. 633; 1957, 30 Temp.L.Q. 215.

13. Eule v. Eule Motor Sales, 1961; 34 N.J. 537, 170 A.2d 241; Cody v. J. A. Dodds & Sons, 1961, 252 Iowa 1394, 110 N.W.2d 255; cf. Tobin v. Hoffman, 1953, 202 Md. 382, 96 A.2d 597 (other partner sued individually). See also Rosefield v. Rosefield, 1963, 221 Cal.App.2d 431, 34 Cal.Rptr. 479 (third person conniving with parent to abduct child.) See Gerdes, Right of a Wife Against Her Husband's Partners for Partnership Torts, 1936, 5 Brook.L.Rev. 174; Notes, 1961, 47 Va.L.Rev. 1450; 1936, 21 Corn.L.Q. 157.

Contra: Caplan v. Caplan, 1935, 268 N.Y. 445, 198 N.E. 23; Karalis v. Karalis, 1942, 213 Minn. 31, 4 N.W.2d 632; Aboussie v. Aboussie, Tex.Civ.App. 1954, 270 S.W.2d 636.

14. Damm v. Elyria Lodge No. 465, 1952, 158 Ohio St. 107, 107 N.E.2d 337; Hary v. Arney, 1957, 128 Ind.App. 174, 145 N.E.2d 575. See Note, 1953, 22 U.Cin.L.Rev. 122.

15. Silverman v. Silverman, 1958, 145 Conn. 663, 145 A.2d 826; May v. Palm Beach Chemical Co., Fla. 1955, 77 So.2d 468; Winnick v. Kupperman Const. Co., 1968, 29 App.Div.2d 261, 287 N.Y.S.2d 329; Davis v. Harrod, 1969, 132 U.S.App.D.C. 345, 407 F. 2d 1280; Broaddus v. Wilkenson, 1940, 281 Ky. 601, 136 S.W.2d 1052. Cf. Freeland v. Freeland, 1968, 152 W.Va. 332, 162 S.E.2d 922 (family car doctrine).

Contra: Raines v. Mercer, 1932, 165 Tenn. 415, 55 S. W.2d 263; Riser v. Riser, 1927, 240 Mich. 402, 215 N.W. 290; Ownby v. Kleyhammer, 1952, 194 Tenn. 109, 250 S.W.2d 37.

torts of his wife,[16] even though they occurred without his knowledge[17] or consent,[18] and out of his presence,[19] or even while the wife was living separate and apart.[20] Various reasons were given for this liability: the wife was incapable of being sued alone, so that the husband must necessarily be joined with her; he was given control of all her property and earnings, so that a judgment against her would be practically worthless, and it was only fair that he should pay instead; he was supposed to exercise his authority over her to keep her in good behavior and see that she did not commit torts.

Curiously enough, the wife herself was not absolved from responsibility, but remained liable for her own torts, and must be joined with her husband as a defendant.[21] By analogy to the criminal law, an exception was recognized where she acted in his presence and by his direction, since the law then assumed that she was coerced by fear of him or his authority, and so held that the tort

was his alone and not hers.[22] Added to this was the presumption, which might be rebutted,[23] that any act done in his presence was done by his direction, so that in the absence of evidence of the wife's independent conduct the husband only was liable.[24]

These common law rules, which of course make no sense whatever in the light of modern ideas of the social and legal position of married women, are now almost entirely abrogated by statute.[25] In about two-thirds of the states there are specific provisions making the wife fully responsible for her own torts, and doing away with the husband's liability for them.[26] Nearly all of the remaining jurisdictions have arrived at the same result by construction of the ordinary Married Women's Acts giving the wife capacity to be sued alone, and control over her own property.[27] Even the common law, of course, nev-

16.   Henley v. Wilson, 1902, 137 Cal. 273, 70 P. 21; Missio v. Williams, 1914, 129 Tenn. 504, 167 S.W. 473; Atwood v. Higgins, 1884, 76 Me. 423.

Even though the tort was committed before marriage. Hawk v. Harman, 1812, 5 Bin., Pa., 43; Phillips v. Richardson, 1830, 4 J.J.Marsh., 27 Ky. 212.

17.   Roberts v. Lisenbee, 1882, 86 N.C. 136.

18.   Baker v. Young, 1867, 44 Ill. 42; Edwards v. Wessinger, 1902, 65 S.C. 161, 43 S.E. 518.

19.   Edwards v. Wessinger, 1902, 65 S.C. 161, 43 S.E. 518; Sargeant v. Fedor, 1925, 3 N.J.Misc. 832, 130 A. 207.

20.   Head v. Briscoe, 1833, 5 C. & P. 484, 172 Eng. Rep. 1064. See, generally, Miller, Liability of a Husband for Wife's Torts, 1932, 18 Iowa L.Rev. 30; Harbison, Family Responsibility in Tort, 1956, 9 Vand.L.Rev. 809; Notes, 1925, 34 Yale L.J. 543; 1926, 2 Camb.L.J. 250; 1926, 74 U.Pa.L.Rev. 305; 1936, 41 Dick.L.Rev. 55.

21.   Smith v. Taylor, 1852, 11 Ga. 20; Baker v. Young, 1867, 44 Ill. 42; Heckle v. Lurvey, 1869, 101 Mass. 344; Crawford v. Doggett, 1891, 82 Tex. 139, 17 S.W. 929; Sargeant v. Fedor, 1925, 3 N.J.Misc. 832, 130 A. 207; see Gill v. State, 1894, 39 W.Va. 479, 20 S.E. 568.

22.   McKeown v. Johnson, 1822, 1 McCord, S.C., 578; McElroy v. Capron, 1902, 24 R.I. 561, 54 A. 44; Thayer v. Spear, 1885, 58 Vt. 327, 2 A. 161.

23.   Miller v. Sweitzer, 1871, 22 Mich. 391; Wagener v. Bill, 1855, 19 Barb., N.Y., 321; Smith v. Schoene, 1896, 67 Mo.App. 604; McElroy v. Capron, 1902, 24 R.I. 561, 54 A. 44; Hildreth v. Camp, 1879, 41 N.J. L. 306.

"If the law supposes that," said Mr. Bumble, "the law is a ass—a idiot. If that's the eye of the law, the law is a bachelor; and the worst I wish the law is, that his eye may be opened by experience—by experience." Dickens, Oliver Twist, ch. 51.

24.   Brazil v. Moran, 1863, 8 Minn. 236; Marshall v. Oakes, 1864, 51 Me. 308; Kosminski v. Goldberg, 1884, 44 Ark. 401; Emmons v. Stevane, 1906, 73 N. J.L. 349, 64 A. 1014. This was rejected in Hux v. Butler, 6 Cir. 1964, 339 F.2d 696.

25.   See Harbison, Family Responsibility in Tort, 1956, 9 Vand.L.Rev. 809; Note, 1966, 17 Bay.L.Rev. 177.

26.   These are collected in the Note, 1950, 3 U.Fla.L. Rev. 206. See Strouse v. Leipf, 1893, 101 Ala. 433, 14 So. 667; Christensen v. Johnston, 1917, 207 Ill. App. 209; Moore v. Doerr, 1918, 199 Mo.App. 428, 203 S.W. 672; McElroy v. Capron, 1902, 24 R.I. 561, 54 A. 44.

27.   Hageman v. Vanderdoes, 1914, 15 Ariz. 312, 138 P. 1053; Bourland v. Baker, 1919, 141 Ark. 280, 216 S.W. 707; Curtis v. Ashworth, 1928, 165 Ga. 782, 142 S.E. 111, conformed to, 1928, 38 Ga.App. 220,

er went to the length of making the wife liable for the tort of her husband.[28] In all probability the dying gasp of the old rule was a Florida decision[29] in 1949, which was promptly changed by statute;[30] and henceforth the vicarious liability of one spouse, as such, for the torts of the other is to be of purely historical interest.

Since the relation of parent and child involved no such fusion of legal identity as in the case of husband and wife, the common law, unlike that of the civil law countries,[31] never has made the parent vicariously liable as such for the conduct of the child. The infant, as a separate legal individual, has been held liable for his own torts,[32] and the parent has, at common law, no legal responsibility for them.[33] With the child usually quite ir-

responsible financially, and the parent not liable at all, the result has been a rather serious problem of uncompensated juvenile depredation, which in recent years has led to the adoption, in some nineteen states,[34] of statutes imposing vicarious liability upon the parent. These statutes have varied considerably in their provisions, as to whether personal injury is to be covered as well as property damage, and as to the financial limits of the liability, which usually has been set in the vicinity of $300.[35]

Apart from any basis of the family relation itself, one member of the family may of course be held responsible for the torts of another to the same extent as for those of any other person. Thus a father may be liable for the tortious act of his son if he has directed[36] or encouraged[37] it, or has ratified

143 S.E. 463; Caplan v. Caplan, 1928, 83 N.H. 318, 142 A. 121; Claxton v. Pool, Mo.1917, 197 S.W. 349. See Notes, 1953, 2 De Paul L.Rev. 345; 1950, 4 U. Miami L.Q. 358.

28. See Vanneman v. Powers, 1874, 56 N.Y. 39; Blake v. Smith, 1896, 19 R.I. 476, 34 A. 995; Scott v. Chambers, 1886, 62 Mich. 532, 29 N.W. 94; Bice v. Brown, 1917, 98 Wash. 416, 167 P. 1097.

29. Rogers v. Newby, Fla.1949, 41 So.2d 451. There are jurisdictions, such as Connecticut and Wyoming, in which statutes do not clearly abrogate the liability, and there are no decisions.

30. Fla.Stats.1961, § 741.23, enacted in 1951.

31. See Takayanagi, Liability Without Fault in the Modern Civil and Common Law, 1921, 16 Ill.L.Rev. 163, 291; Note, 1934, 19 Corn.L.Q. 643; Toca v. Rojas, 1922, 152 La. 317, 93 So. 108; Hudson v. Von Hamm, 1927, 85 Cal.App. 323, 259 P. 374.

32. See infra, § 134.

33. White v. Seitz, 1931, 342 Ill. 266, 174 N.E. 371; Zeeb v. Bahnmaier, 1918, 103 Kan. 599, 176 P. 326, rehearing denied, 1919, 103 Kan. 895, 176 P. 643; Steinberg v. Cauchois, 1937, 249 App.Div. 518, 293 N.Y.S. 147; Chastain v. Johns, 1904, 120 Ga. 977, 48 S.E. 343; Lane v. Chatham, 1959, 251 N.C. 400, 111 S.E.2d 598.

See Greenhood, Liability of a Parent for the Torts of His Minor Child, 1884, 18 Cent.L.J. 3; Wigmore, Parent's Liability for Child's Torts, 1924, 19 Ill.L. Rev. 202; Jordan, Liability of Parent for Child's Tort, 1926, 11 Va.L.Reg.,N.S., 734; Waller, Visiting the Sins of the Children, 1963, 4 Melbourne L.Rev. 17; Freer, Parental Liability for Torts of Children, 1964, 53 Ky.L.J. 254; Notes, 1941, 19 N.C.L.Rev.

605; 1961, 28 U.Kan.City L.Rev. 183; 1934, 32 Mich.L.Rev. 872; 1944, 22 N.C.L.Rev. 333; 1954, 28 Tul.L.Rev. 503; 1932, 17 Corn.L.Q. 178; 1965, 16 U.Toronto L.Rev. 165.

34. The statutes up to 1957 are collected in the Note, 1957, 55 Mich.L.Rev. 1205. As of that date the list included Arizona, California, Connecticut, Florida, Georgia, Idaho, Indiana, Louisiana, Michigan, Montana, Nebraska, Nevada, New Mexico, North Dakota, Rhode Island, South Dakota, Tennessee, Texas, and West Virginia. See also Notes, 1945, 6 La.L. Rev. 478; 1955, 43 Cal.L.Rev. 874; 1959, 37 Tex.L. Rev. 924; 39 Temp.L.Q. 177. Also Stone, Liability for Damage Caused by Minors: A Comparative Study, 1952, 5 Ala.L.Rev. 1; Freer, Parental Liability for Torts of Children, 1965, 53 Ky.L.J. 254; City of Milford v. Swarbrick, 1963, 24 Conn.Sup. 320, 190 A.2d 493.

35. As to constitutionality, see General Ins. Co. of America v. Faulkner, 1963, 259 N.C. 317, 130 S.E.2d 645; Mahaney v. Hunter Enterprises, Inc., 1967, —— Wyo. ——, 426 P.2d 442.

36. Trahan v. Smith, Tex.Civ.App.1922, 239 S.W. 345; Harrington v. Hall, 1906, 6 Pennewill, Del., 72, 63 A. 875; Smith v. Jordan, 1912, 211 Mass. 269, 97 S.E. 761.

37. Stewart v. Swartz, 1914, 57 Ind.App. 249, 106 N. E. 719; Condel v. Savo, 1944, 350 Pa. 350, 39 A.2d 51; Ryley v. Lafferty, D.Idaho 1930, 45 F.2d 641; Sharpe v. Williams, 1889, 41 Kan. 56, 20 P. 497; cf. Knott v. Litton, La.App.1955, 81 So.2d 124 (husband inciting wife to attack plaintiff). But cf. Bowen v. Mewborn, 1940, 218 N.C. 423, 11 S.E.2d 372 (encouragement to illicit intercourse does not include rape).

it by accepting its benefits.[38] Also, of course, the son may act as the agent or servant of the father, and to the extent that the tort is committed within the scope of the agency [39] the parent may be liable.[40] Because of the usual lack of financial responsibility on the part of children, and even of married women, some courts have gone to considerable lengths to find an agency in the case of family relations.[41] One notable instance is the "family car" doctrine previously discussed,[42] which proceeds upon the rather unconvincing theory that the owner of an automobile who permits a member of his family to drive it makes the family affairs or pleasure his "business," and the driver his servant. This doctrine, which obviously is little more than a deliberately fictitious instrument of policy, is rejected by about half of the jurisdictions, and has been replaced in some others by automobile "consent" statutes making the owner responsible for the negligence of anyone whom he allows to drive the car.[43]

Finally, of course, liability for the torts of the family may be based upon the negligence of the defendant himself.[44] A parent, for example, like anyone else, may be negligent in entrusting to a child a dangerous instrument such as a gun,[45] or a thing which he has shown a propensity to misuse, such as matches,[46] or an automobile,[47] or in leaving such a thing where it is accessible to him.[48] But beyond this, the parent has a special power of control over the conduct of the child, which he is under a duty to exercise reasonably for the protection of others.[49] He may thus be liable for a failure to take the gun away from the child when he finds him with it,[50] or to

L.Rev. 333; 1954, 28 Tul.L.Rev. 503; 1929, 23 Ill. L.Rev. 830; 1967, 19 Ala.L.Rev. 123; 1964, 31 Tenn.L.Rev. 553.

45. Vallency v. Rigillio, 1918, 91 N.J.L. 307, 102 A. 348; Souza v. Irome, 1914, 219 Mass. 273, 106 N.E. 998; Dickens v. Barnham, 1920, 69 Colo. 349, 194 P. 356; Carmona v. Padilla, 1957, 4 App.Div.2d 181, 163 N.Y.S.2d 741, affirmed, 1958, 4 N.Y.2d 767, 172 N.Y.S.2d 820, 149 N.E.2d 337 (grandmother giving child bow and arrow); Harvey v. Shaver, 1969, —— Ark. ——, 444 S.W.2d 256 (access to fireworks).

46. Thibodeau v. Cleff [1911] 24 Ont.L.Rep. 211; Gudziewski v. Stemplesky, 1928, 263 Mass. 103, 160 N.E. 334; Johnson v. Glidden, 1898, 11 S.D. 237, 76 N.W. 933; Jarboe v. Edwards, 1966, 26 Conn.Sup. 350, 223 A.2d 402. Cf. May v. Goulding, 1961, 365 Mich. 143, 111 N.W.2d 862 (mentally ill child with semi-automatic rifle); Davis v. Gavalas, 1927, 37 Ga.App. 242, 139 S.E. 577 (velocipede); Zuckerberg v. Munzer, 1950, 277 App.Div. 1061, 100 N.Y.S.2d 910 (baseball bat). But the parent must know of the tendency. Lane v. Chatham, 1959, 251 N.C. 400, 111 S.E.2d 598 (mother, who knew, liable; father, who did not, not liable).

47. Rocca v. Steinmetz, 1923, 61 Cal.App. 102, 214 P. 257; Hopkins v. Droppers, 1924, 184 Wis. 400, 198 N.W. 738; Gardiner v. Solomon, 1917, 200 Ala. 115, 75 So. 621; Allen v. Bland, Tex.Civ.App.1914, 168 S.W. 35.

Cf. Gossett v. Van Egmond, 1945, 176 Or. 134, 155 P. 2d 304 (mental defective driving car).

48. Williams v. Davidson, 1966, 241 Ark. 699, 409 S. W.2d 311 (air gun); Whalen v. Bennett, 1966, 4 Mich.App. 81, 143 N.W.2d 797 (same); Seabrook v. Taylor, Fla.App.1967, 199 So.2d 315.

49. See Harper and Kime, The Duty to Control the Conduct of Another, 1934, 43 Yale L.J. 886.

50. Johnson v. Glidden, 1898, 11 S.D. 237, 76 N.W. 933; Gudziewski v. Stemplesky, 1928, 263 Mass. 103, 160 N.E. 334; Kuchlik v. Feuer, 1933, 239 App.Div. 338, 267 N.Y.S. 256, affirmed, 1934, 264 N. Y. 542, 191 N.E. 555; Salisbury v. Crudale, 1918, 41 R.I. 33, 102 A. 731.

38. Hower v. Ulrich, 1893, 156 Pa. 410, 27 A. 37; Howell v. Norton, 1924, 134 Miss. 616, 99 So. 440.

39. Cf. Hagerty v. Powers, 1885, 66 Cal. 368, 5 P. 622; Smith v. Jordan, 1912, 211 Mass. 269, 97 N.E. 761.

40. Broadstreet v. Hall, 1907, 168 Ind. 192, 80 N.E. 145; Napier v. Patterson, 1923, 198 Iowa 257, 196 N.W. 73; Elms v. Flick, 1919, 100 Ohio St. 186, 126 N.E. 66.

41. Cf. Hiroux v. Baum, 1908, 137 Wis. 197, 118 N.W. 533; Zeidler v. Goelzer, 1926, 191 Wis. 378, 211 N. W. 140; Graham v. Page, 1921, 300 Ill. 40, 132 N.E. 817; Smith v. Jordan, 1912, 211 Mass. 269, 97 N.E. 761; McCrossen v. Moorhead, 1922, 202 App.Div. 560, 195 N.Y.S. 164, 1923, 205 App.Div. 497, 200 N. Y.S. 581, appeal dismissed, 1924, 236 N.Y. 614, 142 N.E. 318. See Lattin, Vicarious Liability and the Family Automobile, 1928, 26 Mich.L.Rev. 846.

42. Supra, p. 483.

43. See supra, p. 486.

44. See Wigmore, Parent's Liability for Child's Torts, 1924, 19 Ill.L.Rev. 202; Jordan, Liability of Parent for Child's Tort, 1926, 11 Va.L.Reg.,N.S., 734; Notes, 1941, 19 N.C.L.Rev. 605; 1944, 22 N.C.

make reasonable efforts to restrain and correct him when he manifests a tendency to beat other children with a stick,[51] or to shoot at horses in the street.[52] Probably, however, the effect of the decided cases is that there is no liability upon the parent unless he has notice of a specific type [53] of harmful conduct, and an opportunity to interfere with it. It has been said [54] that it would be extending the hardships of harassed and exasperated parents too far to hold them liable for general incorrigibility, a bad education and upbringing, or the fact that the child turns out to have a nasty disposition. The parent may, however, be under a duty to warn others who may suffer from such characteristics; [55] and it is undoubtedly true that the parent must take these factors into account in what he does once specific dangerous tendencies have been manifested.[56]

124. INTERFERENCE WITH FAMILY RELATIONS

As has been explained above,[57] the law of torts is concerned not only with the protection of interests of personality and of property, tangible or intangible, but also with what may be called "relational" interests,[58] founded upon the relation in which the plaintiff stands toward one or more third persons. An interference with the continuance of the relation, unimpaired, may be redressed by a tort action; and of this the relations of the family are a conspicuous example.[59] In this field the law is "rather ragged in form," with a certain amount of dead timber to be cleared away before it becomes very intelligible.[60] It developed in the beginning as an offshoot of the action for enticing away a servant and depriving the master of the quasi-proprietary interest in his services.[61] Since the status of a wife, as well as that of minor children, under the early common law was that of more or less valuable superior servants of the husband and father, that action was extended to include the deprivation of their services;[62] and thus the loss of such services became the gist of the action, and remained indispensable to it until comparatively recent years. There has been a gradual shift of emphasis away from "services" and toward a recognition of more intangible elements in the domestic relations, such as companionship and affection.[63] This has progressed further at some points than at

51. Norton v. Payne, 1929, 154 Wash. 241, 281 P. 991; Bieker v. Owens, 1961, 234 Ark. 97, 350 S.W. 2d 522; Polk v. Trinity Universal Ins. Co., La.App. 1959, 115 So.2d 399; Bocock v. Rose, 1963, 213 Tenn. 195, 373 S.W.2d 441; Linder v. Bidner, 1966, 50 Misc.2d 320, 270 N.Y.S.2d 427.

52. Hoverson v. Noker, 1884, 60 Wis. 511, 19 N.W. 382.

53. This need not be precise; knowledge of a tendency to attack others is enough. Caldwell v. Zaher, 1962, 344 Mass. 590, 183 N.E.2d 706.

54. Capps v. Carpenter, 1930, 129 Kan. 462, 283 P. 655; Gissin v. Goodwill, Fla.1955, 80 So.2d 701; Corby v. Foster [1913] 29 Ont.L.Rep. 83; Paul v. Hummel, 1868, 43 Mo. 119.

55. Ellis v. D'Angelo, 1953, 116 Cal.App.2d 310, 243 P.2d 675 (baby sitter); Zuckerberg v. Munzer, 1950, 277 App.Div. 1061, 100 N.Y.S.2d 910.

56. See Paul v. Hummel, 1868, 43 Mo. 119; Cluthe v. Svendsen, 1885, 9 Ohio Dec. 458; Salisbury v. Crudale, 1918, 41 R.I. 33, 102 A. 731; Haunert v. Speier, 1926, 214 Ky. 46, 281 S.W. 998. See Note, 1930, 78 U.Pa.L.Rev. 1032.

57. Supra, p. 737.

58. Green, Relational Interests, 1935, 29 Ill.L.Rev. 460; Foster, Relational Interests of the Family, [1962] U.Ill.L.Forum 493.

59. See Pound, Individual Interests in the Domestic Relations, 1916, 14 Mich.L.Rev. 177; Green, Relational Interests, 1935, 29 Ill.L.Rev. 460; Lippman, The Breakdown of Consortium, 1930, 30 Col.L.Rev. 651.

60. Winfield, Law of Tort, 5th Ed. 1950, 231.

61. See infra, p. 929.

62. See Guy v. Livesey, 1619, Cro.Jac. 501, 79 Eng. Rep. 428; Hyde v. Scyssor, 1620, Cro.Jac. 538, 79 Eng.Rep. 462; Galizard v. Rigault, 1702, 2 Salk. 552, 91 Eng.Rep. 467; 8 Holdsworth, History of English Law, 2d Ed. 1937, 427–430; 1 Street, Foundations of Legal Liability, 1906, 262, 267; Wigmore, Interference with Social Relations, 1887, 21 Am.L. Rev. 764.

63. See Holbrook, The Change in the Meaning of Consortium, 1923, 22 Mich.L.Rev. 1; Lippman, The Breakdown of Consortium, 1930, 30 Col.L.Rev. 651.

others; and on many questions the courts are still in flat disagreement.

In so confused a field, perhaps the simplest approach is to consider the interests of each member of the family, and the extent to which they have received protection.

Husband

The relation of husband and wife must of course be based upon some form of marriage recognized by law. A mere engagement to marry does not entitle the parties to the legal protection afforded to spouses,[64] and a marriage which is entirely void is equally ineffective.[65] But a common law marriage,[66] or a marriage which is merely voidable because of lack of statutory age of one of the parties,[67] has been held to be sufficient.

The husband's interest in his relation with his wife first received recognition as a matter of her services to him as a servant. Over a period of some centuries it took form as something considerably broader than this, which was given the name of "consortium." Consortium was said to be made up of a bundle of legal rights to the alliterative trio of the services, society and sexual intercourse of the wife. To these elements the modern law has added a fourth, that of conjugal affection. The rights of the husband extend to all four; and while it is seldom that the defendant's conduct interferes with only one of them, it now seems clear in nearly all

jurisdictions that such interference with any one will be sufficient as a foundation for the action. The loss of services, essential at the beginning, no longer is indispensable,[68] and is now only one element upon which the action may be based.

Types of interference. One type of interference with the husband's interests is variously called abduction, enticement or harboring of the wife. There was a very early writ "of ravishment" which listed the wife with the husband's chattels, and was available to him when she was taken away forcibly or eloped with another.[69] In time this was replaced by the action of trespass for depriving him of a servant. Since there is an obvious loss of "consortium" when a wife is either compelled or induced to live apart from her husband, all courts are agreed that he may maintain a tort action against anyone who, without justification and for an improper purpose, influences or advises her to do so,[70] or assists her to depart.[71] It was said that the old law was so strict that "if one's wife missed her way upon the road, it was not lawful for another man to take her into his house, unless she was benighted and in danger of being lost or drowned;"[72] but this gentle rule for the encouragement of chivalry is a thing of the

---

64. See Nelson v. Melvin, 1945, 236 Iowa 604, 19 N. W.2d 685; Davis v. Condit, 1914, 124 Minn. 365, 144 N.W. 1089; Homan v. Hall, 1917, 102 Neb. 70, 165 N.W. 881; Conway v. O'Brien, 1929, 269 Mass. 425, 169 N.E. 491; Note, 1926, 10 Corn.L.Q. 259; Restatement of Torts, § 698.

65. See Stark v. Johnson, 1908, 43 Colo. 243, 95 P. 930; Jowett v. Wallace, 1914, 112 Me. 389, 92 A. 321; Hutchins v. Kimmell, 1875, 31 Mich. 126; Jacobson v. Siddal, 1885, 12 Or. 280, 7 P. 108.

66. Hollinghausen v. Ade, 1921, 289 Mo. 362, 233 S. W. 39; Butterfield v. Ennis, 1916, 193 Mo.App. 638, 186 S.W. 1173.

67. Luke v. Hill, 1911, 137 Ga. 159, 73 S.E. 345; Holtz v. Dick, 1884, 42 Ohio St. 23.

68. See Brown, The Action for Alienation of Affections, 1934, 82 U.Pa.L.Rev. 472; Holbrook, The Change in the Meaning of Consortium, 1923, 22 Mich.L.Rev. 1; Lippman, The Breakdown of Consortium, 1930, 30 Col.L.Rev. 651.

69. 1 Street, Foundations of Legal Liability, 1906, 263; Winfield, Law of Tort, 5th Ed. 1950, 234.

70. Boland v. Stanley, 1909, 88 Ark. 562, 115 S.W. 163; Holtz v. Dick, 1884, 42 Ohio St. 23, 51 Am. Rep. 791; Multer v. Knibbs, 1907, 193 Mass. 556, 79 N.E. 762; Allen v. Forsythe, 1912, 160 Mo.App. 262, 142 S.W. 820; Jones v. Monson, 1908, 137 Wis. 478, 119 N.W. 179. As to what is "enticement," see Place v. Searle, [1932] 2 K.B. 497 ("Come on, Gwen. We will go.").

71. Higham v. Vanosdol, 1884, 101 Ind. 160.

72. 3 Bl.Comm. 139. "This does not leave much scope for the energies of a knight-errant whose quest is the relief of distressed wives." Winfield, Law of Tort, 5th Ed. 1950, 232.

past. It may still be a tort against the husband to "harbor" the wife, if it is coupled with persuasion or encouragement not to return to him;[73] but a mere reception in good faith upon grounds of friendship, hospitality or common humanity will not result in liability.[74]

A second form of interference with the interests of the husband is that of adultery with the wife, which in its tort aspects usually is called criminal conversation.[75] For this the husband might maintain an action of trespass,[76] not only where the intercourse was the result of rape,[77] but also even though the wife had consented to it, or was herself the seducer and had invited and procured it,[78] since it was considered that she was no

more capable of giving a consent which would prejudice the husband's interests than was his horse.[79] Although it is often said that there is interference with a "service" which the wife owes exclusively to her husband, even though he is impotent,[80] the real basis of recovery clearly is the defilement of the marriage bed, the blow to family honor, and the suspicion cast upon the legitimacy of the offspring.[81] Consequently it has become unnecessary to prove that the husband has been deprived of intercourse or any other services of the wife,[82] or of any of her affection for him,[83] and recovery has been allowed even though the wife had left him and was living apart.[84] The action for criminal conversation was abolished by statute in England in 1857, and the husband's claim for damages for adultery is now by

---

73. Winsmore v. Greenbank, 1745, Willes 577, 125 Eng.Rep. 1330; see Boland v. Stanley, 1909, 88 Ark. 562, 115 S.W. 163; Barnes v. Allen, 1860, 30 Barb., N.Y., 663, reversed 40 N.Y. 390, 1 Abb.Dec. 111; Powell v. Benthall, 1904, 136 N.C. 145, 48 S.E. 598.

74. Winchester v. Fleming, [1958] 1 Q.B. 259, reversed on other grounds in [1958] 3 All Eng.Rep. 51; Turner v. Estes, 1807, 3 Mass. 317; McGregor v. McGregor, Ky.1909, 115 S.W. 802; Alexander v. Johnson, 1930, 182 Ark. 270, 31 S.W.2d 304; Ridenhour v. Miller, 1945, 225 N.C. 543, 35 S.E.2d 611. See Note, 1958, 21 Mod.L.Rev. 296.

75. "Criminal" because it was an ecclesiastical crime; "conversation" in the sense of intercourse. For the history of the tort, see Lippman, The Breakdown of Consortium, 1930, 30 Col.L.Rev. 651, 654–660.
"In its general and comprehensive sense, the term 'criminal conversation,' is synonymous with 'adultery;' but in its more limited and technical signification, in which it is here to be considered, it may be defined as adultery in the aspect of a tort." Turner v. Heavrin, 1918, 182 Ky. 65, 206 S.W. 23.

76. 3 Bl.Comm. 139–140; Antonelli v. Xenakis, 1949, 363 Pa. 375, 69 A.2d 102.

77. Egbert v. Greenwalt, 1880, 44 Mich. 245, 6 N.W. 654; Bigaouette v. Paulet, 1883, 134 Mass. 123, 45 Am.Rep. 307; Jacobson v. Siddal, 1885, 12 Or. 280, 7 P. 108.

78. Tinker v. Colwell, 1904, 193 U.S. 473; Wales v. Miner, 1883, 89 Ind. 118; Powell v. Strickland, 1913, 163 N.C. 393, 79 S.E. 872; Pierce v. Crisp, 1935, 260 Ky. 519, 86 S.W.2d 293; cf. Hirschy v. Coodley, 1953, 116 Cal.App.2d 102, 253 P.2d 93. "It is but the old cowardly excuse set up by the first man, 'The woman gave me of the tree and I did

eat.' It did not save from the penalty the first defendant, and cannot under the law save this one." Seiber v. Pettitt, 1901, 200 Pa. 58, 49 A. 762.
Tennessee has said, however, that there is no liability where the defendant is not the pursuer, and the wife is "not particular as to her partner." Wilson v. Bryant, 1934, 167 Tenn. 107, 69 S.W.2d 133; Archer v. Archer, 1947, 31 Tenn.App. 657, 219 S.W. 2d 919.

79. 8 Holdsworth, History of English Law, 2d Ed. 1937, 430.

80. Bedan v. Turney, 1893, 99 Cal. 649, 34 P. 442.

81. Bigaouette v. Paulet, 1883, 134 Mass. 123; Stark v. Johnson, 1908, 43 Colo. 243, 95 P. 930; Yundt v. Hartrunft, 1866, 41 Ill. 9; Wood v. Mathews, 1877, 47 Iowa 409; Johnston v. Disbrow, 1881, 47 Mich. 59, 10 N.W. 79.

82. Yundt v. Hartrunft, 1866, 41 Ill. 9; Long v. Booe, 1894, 106 Ala. 570, 17 So. 716; Disch v. Closset, 1926, 118 Or. 111, 244 P. 71; Wood v. Mathews, 1877, 47 Iowa 409; Bigaouette v. Paulet, 1883, 134 Mass. 123.

83. Stark v. Johnson, 1908, 43 Colo. 243, 95 P. 930; Baltrunas v. Baubles, 1926, 23 Ohio App. 104, 154 N.E. 747; Merritt v. Cravens, 1916, 168 Ky. 155, 181 S.W. 970; Watkins v. Lord, 1918, 31 Idaho 352, 171 P. 1133; Rosefield v. Rosefield, 1963, 221 Cal. App.2d 431, 34 Cal.Rptr. 479.

84. Chambers v. Caulfield, 1805, 6 East 244; Browning v. Jones, 1893, 52 Ill.App. 597; Michael v. Dunkle, 1882, 84 Ind. 544; Cross v. Grant, 1883, 62 N. H. 675; Pierce v. Crisp, 1935, 260 Ky. 519, 86 S.W. 2d 293.

way of petition under the Matrimonial Causes Act of 1950, whether accompanied by a petition for divorce or not. The governing principles are in general, however, the same as those for criminal conversation.[85] There are several statutes which have abolished the action in the United States,[86] but otherwise it still lies everywhere.

A third type of interference, which seems to have been recognized first in New York [87] in 1866 and was accepted at common law by all of the states except Louisiana,[88] has been given the name of "alienation of affections." It consists merely in depriving the husband of the affections, which is to say the love, society, companionship and comfort, of his wife. While of course the change in her state of mind toward him must be evidenced by some external conduct,[89] it is not necessary that the wife commit adultery,[90] or that the husband be deprived of any household services,[91] or suffer any pecuniary loss;[92]

nor is it necessary that the wife abandon his home,[93] or that there be more than a partial loss of her affections and attentions.[94] The gist of the tort is thus an interference with the wife's mental attitude toward the husband, and the conjugal kindness of the marital relation,[95] resulting in some actual conduct of hers which materially affects it. As any superficial examination of the cases will reveal, more actions of this kind have been brought against parents than anyone else, and the meddling mother-in-law is more frequently a defendant than the wicked lover.

Criminal conversation, enticement and alienation of affections still are often treated as separate torts,[96] but there is no good reason for distinguishing them. They represent three forms of interference with aspects of the same relational interest, and of course

---

85. The chief difference is that, since the claim is now incidental to a matrimonial proceeding, it is itself defeasible if the petition for a decree fails, as for example by reason of condonation. Bernstein v. Bernstein, [1893] P. 292.

86. See infra, p. 887.

87. Heermance v. James, 1866, 47 Barb., N.Y., 120.

88. Moulin v. Monteleone, 1927, 165 La. 169, 115 So. 447.

Massachusetts, which for a long time held back, now appears to recognize the tort, at least where the husband is deprived of sexual intercourse, or something more than "affection." See Gordon v. Parker, D.Mass.1949, 83 F.Supp. 45, affirmed in Parker v. Gordon, 1 Cir. 1949, 178 F.2d 888.

89. Restatement of Torts, § 683, Comment *d*.

90. Hardison v. Gregory, 1955, 242 N.C. 324, 88 S.E. 2d 96; Georgacopoulos v. Katralis, 1945, 318 Mass. 34, 60 N.E.2d 10; Callis v. Merrieweather, 1903, 98 Md. 361, 57 A. 201; Rinehart v. Bills, 1884, 82 Mo. 534; Ireland v. Ward, 1908, 51 Or. 102, 93 P. 932.

91. Gregg v. Gregg, 1905, 37 Ind.App. 210, 75 N.E. 674; Jenness v. Simpson, 1911, 84 Vt. 127, 78 A. 886.

92. Adams v. Main, 1891, 3 Ind.App. 232, 29 N.E. 792; Woodhouse v. Woodhouse, 1925, 99 Vt. 91, 130 A. 758; Lavigne v. Lavigne, 1923, 80 N.H. 559, 119 A. 869; Woodson v. Bailey, 1924, 210 Ala. 568, 98 So. 809.

93. Remaining with the husband would "rather add the provocation of insult to the keenness of suffering. It would continue before him a present, living, irritating, aggravating, if not consuming source of grief, which even her absence might in a measure relieve." Rinehart v. Bills, 1884, 82 Mo. 534; Heermance v. James, 1866, 47 Barb., N.Y., 120; McGregor v. McGregor, Ky.1939, 115 S.W. 802; Valentine v. Pollak, 1920, 95 Conn. 556, 111 A. 869; Note, 1924, 9 Corn.L.Q. 200.

94. Fratini v. Caslini, 1894, 66 Vt. 273, 29 A. 252.

95. Wright v. Lester, 1961, 105 Ga.App. 107, 123 S.E. 2d 672, affirmed in part, reversed in part, 1962, 218 Ga. 31, 126 S.E.2d 419, on remand 106 Ga.App. 452, 127 S.E.2d 193; Grobart v. Grobart, 1950, 5 N.J. 161, 74 A.2d 294. "There are two primary rights in the case: one is the right of the plaintiff to the body of his wife and the other to her mind, unpolluted." Sullivan v. Valiquette, 1919, 66 Colo. 170, 180 P. 91; Hudima v. Hudyma, 1944, 131 Conn. 281, 39 A.2d 890; Annarina v. Boland, 1920, 136 Md. 365, 111 A. 84; Johnson v. Richards, 1930, 50 Idaho 150, 294 P. 507; Restatement of Torts, § 683.

96. Valentine v. Pollak, 1920, 95 Conn. 556, 111 A. 869; Mission v. Grossman, 1938, 329 Pa. 151, 196 A. 494; Antonelli v. Xenakis, 1949, 363 Pa. 375, 69 A. 2d 102; Gibson v. Gibson, 1966, 240 Ark. 827, 402 S.W.2d 647, appeal after remand 244 Ark. 327, 424 S.W.2d 871; Di Blasio v. Kolodner, 1964, 233 Md. 512, 197 A.2d 245. See Note, 1964, 24 Md.L.Rev. 358.

all three may be present in the same case.[97] When the action is for criminal conversation, proof of enticement or alienation will go to increase the damages,[98] and the converse is likewise true.[99] There is now a decided tendency to confuse the three, or to lump them together, usually under the general name of "alienation of affections," without any attempt to distinguish the possible elements of the tort.

Basis of liability. In order to be held liable for interference with the marriage relation, the defendant must in some way have acted affirmatively. If he has remained entirely passive and indifferent, he cannot be held responsible because the plaintiff's wife has chosen to fall in love with him.[100] But any active participation or encouragement on his part will be sufficient to make him liable even if the initiative comes from her;[101] and since adultery with her obviously meets this description, it usually is held to be no defense to criminal conversation that the wife

was the aggressor and the seducer.[1] In addition, of course, the defendant's conduct must have been a cause of the harm to the marital relation; and if the erring spouse acted entirely of her own volition,[2] or because of the plaintiff's own fault,[3] there is no liability. As in other cases where causation is in issue, however, it is not necessary that the defendant be the sole cause of the loss of consortium, but merely that he be a substantial factor;[4] or, as some courts put it,[5] a "controlling" or "procuring" cause in bringing it about.

Again, there seems to be general agreement that there is no liability in this type of action [6] unless the defendant has acted for the very purpose of affecting the marital relation. Merely negligent conduct which results in the alienation of affections,[7] or even intentional acts directed at another end which the defendant believes will incidentally have that ef-

---

97. As to joinder of counts, see Dodge v. Rush, 1906, 28 App.D.C. 149; Sullivan v. Valiquette, 1919, 66 Colo. 170, 180 P. 91; Murrell v. Culver, 1922, 141 Md. 349, 118 A. 803; Labrie v. Midwood, 1931, 273 Mass. 578, 174 N.E. 214.

98. Hargraves v. Ballou, 1926, 47 R.I. 186, 131 A. 643; Sullivan v. Valiquette, 1919, 66 Colo. 170, 180 P. 91; Bullock v. Maag, 1952, 8 Terry, Del., 519, 94 A.2d 382.

99. Barlow v. Barnes, 1916, 172 Cal. 98, 155 P. 457; Watkins v. Lord, 1918, 31 Idaho 352, 171 P. 1133; Nabors v. Keaton, 1965, 216 Tenn. 637, 393 S.W.2d 382; Joseph v. Naylor, 1917, 257 Pa. 561, 101 A. 846; Hutchinson v. Taylor, 1933, 129 Cal.App. 369, 18 P.2d 722. See Brown, The Action for Alienation of Affections, 1934, 82 U.Pa.L.Rev. 472, 473; Restatement of Torts, § 683, Comment c.

100. McQuarters v. Ducote, Tex.Civ.App.1950, 234 S. W.2d 433, refused n. r. e.; Berger v. Levy, 1935, 5 Cal.App.2d 554, 43 P.2d 610; Curtis v. Miller, 1921, 269 Pa. 509, 112 A. 747; Woodson v. Bailey, 1924, 210 Ala. 568, 98 So. 809; Pederson v. Jirsa, 1963, 267 Minn. 48, 125 N.W.2d 38. Cf. Anderson v. Sturm, 1956, 209 Or. 190, 303 P.2d 509 (at most approval of husband's actions in leaving wife). See Note, 1918, 3 Corn.L.Q. 228.

101. Norris v. Stoneham, Tex.Civ.App.1932, 46 S.W.2d 363.

1. See supra, p. 875.

2. Stefanich v. Kuhns, Ohio App.1950, 96 N.E.2d 318; Curtis v. Miller, 1921, 269 Pa. 509, 112 A. 747; Eklund v. Hackett, 1919, 106 Wash. 287, 179 P. 803. Plaintiff has the burden of pleading and proof that the acts of defendant were "the active controlling cause of the loss of affections." Curry v. Kline, 1860, 187 Kan. 109, 353 P.2d 508.

3. Oyler v. Fenner, 1933, 263 Mich. 119, 248 N.W. 567; Annarina v. Boland, 1920, 136 Md. 365, 111 A. 84.

4. Swearingen v. Vik, 1958, 51 Wash.2d 843, 322 P.2d 876; Lisle v. Lynch, Tex.Civ.App.1958, 318 S.W.2d 763, refused n. r. e.; Booth v. Krouse, 1946, 78 Ohio App. 461, 65 N.E.2d 89; Sargent v. Robertson, 1932, 104 Vt. 412, 160 A. 182; Poulos v. Poulos, 1967, 351 Mass. 603, 222 N.E.2d 887. Restatement of Torts, § 683, Comment i.

5. Hadley v. Heywood, 1876, 121 Mass. 236; Pugsley v. Smyth, 1921, 98 Or. 448, 194 P. 686; Kleber v. Allin, 1922, 153 Minn. 433, 190 N.W. 786; Maahs v. Schultz, 1932, 207 Wis. 624, 242 N.W. 195.

6. As to loss of consortium through negligent personal injuries to the wife, see infra, § 122.

7. Lilegren v. Burns Detective Agency, 1916, 135 Minn. 60, 160 N.W. 203 (detective negligently reporting on wife, with the result that husband accused her of unchastity and her affections were alienated).

fect,[8] will not be sufficient. It is not essential that the defendant be motivated by spite or ill will toward the plaintiff,[9] and the "malice" which sometimes is said to be necessary means, as in cases of defamation,[10] nothing more than an intent to act without justification or excuse.[11] But the tort must at least be an intentional one, directed at the relation itself; and it has been held that there is no liability for alienation of affections where the defendant was ignorant of the existence of the marriage—although the contrary is true where there has been adultery, since the intercourse cannot be lawful and harmless in itself, so that the defendant must take the risk that the woman is married.[12] All this is subject, however, to the obvious qualification that the purpose can be inferred from a course of conduct which would naturally tend toward that result.[13]

Defenses. This type of action is subject to a number of possible defenses. One of the most obvious is that there was no marital relation in existence with which to interfere —or in other words, that there were no "affections" to be alienated. This usually is treated as a matter of defense, on the basis of a presumption that affection always exists between husband and wife.[14] It appears quite logical to hold, as some courts have done,[15] that after a complete and permanent breach of the relation, as by separation, there can be no liability for enticement, harboring or alienation of affections. Other decisions,[16] however, have allowed recovery in such a case for deprivation of whatever chance there might be of reconciliation, and have held that the existing estrangement goes merely to mitigate the damages.[17] The conflict may be more apparent than real, since in the latter group of cases there usually has been reason to believe that a possibility of reconciliation existed,[18] and of course it is

8. Anderson v. McGill Club, 1928, 51 Nev. 16, 266 P. 913 (inducing spouse to spend time and money gambling); Hughes v. Holman, 1924, 110 Or. 415, 223 P. 730 (inviting wife to take part in religious services); Osborn v. Engleman, W.D.Mo.1949, 85 F. Supp. 228 (incidental to employment); Jennings v. Cooper, Mo.App.1921, 230 S.W. 325 (same).

9. Eklund v. Hackett, 1919, 106 Wash. 287, 179 P. 803; Moelleur v. Moelleur, 1918, 55 Mont. 30, 173 P. 419; Hodge v. Brooks, 1922, 153 Ark. 222, 240 S.W. 2; Restatement of Torts, § 683, Comment *h*.

10. See supra, p. 772.

11. Smithhisler v. Dutter, 1952, 157 Ohio St. 454, 105 N.E.2d 868; Harlow v. Harlow, 1928, 152 Va. 910, 143 S.E. 720; Boland v. Stanley, 1909, 88 Ark. 562, 115 S.W. 163; Wallace v. Wallace, 1929, 85 Mont. 492, 279 P. 374. Accord, as to criminal conversation: Tinker v. Colwell, 1903, 193 U.S. 473; Paulson v. Scott, 1951, 260 Wis. 141, 50 N.W.2d 376; Alexander v. Johnson, 1930, 182 Ark. 270, 31 S.W.2d 304.

12. McGrath v. Sullivan, 1939, 303 Mass. 327, 21 N. E.2d 533; see Madison v. Neuberger, 1927, 130 Misc. 650, 224 N.Y.S. 461; Loper v. Askin, 1917, 178 App.Div. 163, 164 N.Y.S. 1036; Restatement of Torts, § 683, Comment 8, § 685, Comment *d*.

13. Swearingen v. Vik, 1958, 51 Wash.2d 843, 322 P. 2d 876; Boyle v. Clark, 1955, 47 Wash.2d 418, 287 P.2d 1006; Martin v. Ball, 1923, 30 Ga.App. 729, 119 S.E. 222; Allen v. Lindeman, 1969, —— Iowa ——, 164 N.W.2d 346; Gibson v. Frowein, Mo.1966, 400 S.W.2d 418.

14. Donnell v. Donnell, 1967, 220 Tenn. 169, 415 S. W.2d 127; Overton v. Overton, 1926, 121 Okl. 1, 246 P. 1095; Weyer v. Vollbrecht, 1929, 208 Iowa 914, 224 N.W. 568; Buckley v. Francis, 1931, 78 Utah 606, 6 P.2d 188; Squire v. Hill, 1937, 100 Colo. 226, 66 P.2d 822. Contra, Curry v. Kline, 1960, 187 Kan. 109, 353 P.2d 508.

15. Fleming v. Fisk, 1936, 66 App.D.C. 350, 87 F.2d 747; Adams v. Carrier, 1948, 214 Ark. 55, 214 S.W. 2d 781; Servis v. Servis, 1902, 172 N.Y. 438, 65 N. E. 270; Smith v. Rice, 1916, 178 Iowa 673, 160 N. W. 6; Cutter v. Cooper, 1924, 234 Mass. 307, 125 N.E. 634.

16. Koenig v. Corcoran, 9 Cir. 1952, 199 F.2d 37; Bryant v. Carrier, 1938, 214 N.C. 191, 198 S.E. 619; Olson v. Erickson, 1929, 152 Wash. 633, 278 P. 692; Sargent v. Robertson, 1932, 104 Vt. 412, 160 A. 182; McNelis v. Bruce, 1961, 90 Ariz. 261, 367 P.2d 625 (defendant did not even meet plaintiff's spouse until after formal separation). See Note, 1963, 4 Ariz.L. Rev. 304.

17. Ruble v. Ruble, 1938, 203 Minn. 399, 281 N.W. 529; Scott v. Bontekoe, 1930, 252 Mich. 185, 233 N. W. 215; Hollingshausen v. Ade, 1921, 289 Mo. 362, 233 S.W. 39; Clark v. Orr, 1937, 127 Fla. 411, 173 So. 155; Amellin v. Leone, 1932, 114 Conn. 478, 159 A. 293.

18. See Brown, The Action for Alienation of Affections, 1934, 82 U.Pa.L.Rev. 472, 488.

not every quarrel or separation that is to be regarded as permanent. As to adultery, however, with its stain upon family honor and the legitimacy of children, it is generally agreed that separation or estrangement of the spouses is not a complete defense and bears only on the question of damages.[19] Consent of the husband to the conduct complained of, whether as alienation [20] or criminal conversation,[21] is a total defense; but his condonation or forgiveness of the wife's offenses after they have occurred does not bar recovery against the interfering defendant,[22] and is considered only in reduction of damages.[23] The same is true of a divorce [24] or a separation [25] occurring after the tort,

even where it is obtained by the alienated wife.[26]

The most important defense, however, is that of privilege. The interest of parents in advising and protecting their children, even after marriage, is recognized by a privilege to alienate the affections of the wife,[27] or to induce her to leave her husband,[28] where it is done to advance what they reasonably believe to be her welfare. The privilege is a qualified or limited one, similar to that found in cases of defamation,[29] and it is forfeited when the primary purpose of the defendant is something other than the benefit of the wife, such as ill will toward the plaintiff [30] or other unworthy motives,[31] or where the interference is reckless, without proper investigation,[32] or "from an ill regulated mind not sufficiently cautious before it occasions the in-

19. Pierce v. Crisp, 1935, 260 Ky. 519, 86 S.W.2d 293; Cross v. Grant, 1883, 62 N.H. 675; Michael v. Dunkle, 1882, 84 Ind. 544; Browning v. Jones, 1893, 52 Ill.App. 597; Fennell v. Littlejohn, 1962, 240 S.C. 189, 125 S.E.2d 408.

20. Nulsen v. Nulsen, 1934, 3 Cal.App.2d 407, 39 P.2d 509; Milewski v. Kurtz, 1908, 77 N.J.L. 132, 71 A. 107; Woldson v. Larson, 9 Cir. 1908, 164 F. 548; Fuller v. Robinson, 1910, 230 Mo. 22, 130 S.W. 343. Passive sufferance may be found to be "connivance." Nadeau v. Dallaire, 1933, 132 Me. 178, 168 A. 778.

21. Hodges v. Windham, 1791, Peake 53, 170 Eng. Rep. 76; Cook v. Wood, 1858, 30 Ga. 891; Morning v. Long, 1899, 109 Iowa 288, 80 N.W. 390; Kohlhoss v. Mobley, 1905, 102 Md. 199, 62 A. 236; Prettyman v. Williamson, 1898, 1 Penn., Del., 224, 39 A. 731.

22. Smith v. Hockenberry, 1904, 138 Mich. 129, 101 N.W. 207; Sikes v. Tippins, 1890, 85 Ga. 231, 11 S.E. 662; Guilbault v. Marcoux, 1921, 121 Me. 568, 115 A. 468; Peak v. Rhyno, 1925, 200 Iowa 864, 205 N.W. 515. Cf. Barker v. Dowdy, 1943, 223 N.C. 151, 25 S.E.2d 404, where the protesting husband continued to live with his wife.

23. Smith v. Hockenberry, 1906, 146 Mich. 7, 109 N.W. 23; Rehling v. Brainard, 1914, 38 Nev. 16, 144 P. 167; Sikes v. Tippins, 1890, 85 Ga. 231, 11 S.E. 662.

24. Vogel v. Sylvester, 1961, 148 Conn. 666, 174 A.2d 122; Sadleir v. Knapton, 1956, 5 Utah 2d 26, 296 P.2d 278; Sickler v. Mannix, 1903, 68 Neb. 21, 93 N.W. 1018; Luick v. Arends, 1911, 21 N.D. 614, 132 N.W. 353; Case v. Case, 1931, 212 Iowa 1213, 238 N.W. 85; Restatement of Torts, § 689(2). See Note, 1957, 42 Iowa L.Rev. 438.

25. Wilson v. Coulter, 1898, 29 App.Div. 85, 51 N.Y.S. 804; Patterson v. Hill, 1920, 212 Mich. 635, 180 N.W. 352.

26. Vogel v. Sylvester, 1961, 148 Conn. 666, 174 A.2d 122; Dunbier v. Mengedoht, 1930, 119 Neb. 706, 230 N.W. 669; Eklund v. Hackett, 1919, 106 Wash. 287, 179 P. 803; Pollard v. Ward, 1921, 289 Mo. 275, 233 S.W. 14; Philpott v. Kirkpatrick, 1912, 171 Mich. 495, 137 N.W. 232.

27. Koehler v. Koehler, 1956, 248 Iowa 144, 79 N.W. 2d 791; Bishop v. Glazener, 1957, 245 N.C. 592, 96 S.E.2d 870; Beckler v. Yates, 1935, 338 Mo. 208, 89 S.W.2d 650; Bradford v. Bradford, 1940, 165 Or. 297, 107 P.2d 106; Pierson v. Pierson, 1935, 133 Me. 367, 178 A. 617.

28. Hutcheson v. Peck, 1809, 5 Johns., N.Y. 196; Beisel v. Gerlach, 1908, 221 Pa. 232, 70 A. 721; Ray v. Parsons, 1915, 183 Ind. 344, 109 N.E. 202; Bourne v. Bourne, 1919, 43 Cal.App. 516, 185 P. 489; Oyler v. Fenner, 1933, 263 Mich. 119, 248 N.W. 567.

29. See supra, § 115.

30. Multer v. Knibbs, 1907, 193 Mass. 556, 79 N.E. 762; Smith v. Smith, 1916, 192 Mich. 566, 159 N.W. 349; Francis v. Outlaw, 1916, 127 Md. 315, 96 A. 517; Woodhouse v. Woodhouse, 1925, 99 Vt. 91, 130 A. 758; Gross v. Gross, 1912, 70 W.Va. 317, 73 N.E. 961.

31. Nelson v. Nelson, 2 Cir., 1924, 296 F. 369; Ramsey v. Ramsey, 1931, 4 W.W.Harr. 576, 34 Del. 576, 156 A. 354; Wallace v. Wallace, 1929, 85 Mont. 492, 279 P. 374; Boland v. Stanley, 1909, 88 Ark. 562, 115 S.W. 163.

32. Brown v. Brown, 1899, 124 N.C. 19, 32 S.E. 320; Biggs v. Biggs, 1926, 78 Colo. 310, 241 P. 539.

jury." [33] In short the parents, while they are not required to be pleasant to the husband,[34] and are aided by a strong inference of proper motives,[35] are privileged to interfere only to the extent that a reasonable man would do so under the circumstances.[36]

The same privilege has been extended to other near relatives, such as brothers and sisters,[37] uncles and aunts,[38] step-parents,[39] guardians,[40] or brothers- and sisters-in-law,[41] with of course similar limitations. A

stranger, however, has no such general privilege of interference for the protection of what he believes to be anyone's welfare.[42]

He is no doubt justified in giving shelter [43] or advice [44] to a wife who asks his help against her husband, where current standards of decent conduct permit it; and there may be relations of a professional, business or social character which justify acts tending to disrupt the marriage relation,[45] but in general the stranger interferes at his peril, regardless of worthy motives.[46]

Equitable relief. One important development in this field is that of equitable relief to prevent interference with the relation of husband and wife.[47] A Texas court [48] led the way by upholding an injunction against association with the plaintiff's wife and other conduct tending to alienate her affections; and similar injunctions have been sustained in a few other cases.[49] The administrative

33. Birchfield v. Birchfield, 1923, 29 N.M. 19, 217 P. 616; Wallace v. Wallace, 1929, 85 Mont. 492, 279 P. 374; Westlake v. Westlake, 1878, 34 Ohio St. 621; Roberts v. Cohen, 1922, 104 Or. 177, 206 P. 293.

34. Smith v. Smith, 1916, 192 Mich. 566, 159 N.W. 349. Still less to support him or permit him to live with them. Beisel v. Gerlach, 1908, 221 Pa. 232, 70 A. 721. But, while they have the legal privilege to disinherit the child, they may not use the threat of disinheritance as a club to break up the marriage. Wallace v. Wallace, 1929, 85 Mont. 492, 279 P. 374; Woodhouse v. Woodhouse, 1925, 99 Vt. 91, 130 A. 758.

35. Worth v. Worth, 1935, 48 Wyo. 441, 49 P.2d 649; Gregg v. Gregg, 1905, 37 Ind.App. 210, 75 N.E. 674; Cornelius v. Cornelius, 1911, 233 Mo. 1, 135 S.W. 65; McLery v. McLery, 1925, 186 Wis. 137, 202 N.W. 156; Miller v. Levine, 1931, 130 Me. 153, 154 A. 174. The effect of the presumption usually is stated to be to increase the burden of proof upon the plaintiff.

36. Restatement of Torts, § 686, Comment *f*. See Poulos v. Poulos, 1967, 351 Mass. 603, 222 N.E.2d 887.

37. Ratcliffe v. Walker, 1915, 117 Va. 569, 85 S.E. 575; Glass v. Bennett, 1891, 89 Tenn. 478, 14 S.W. 1085; Smith v. Smith, 1916, 192 Mich. 566, 159 N.W. 349; Baird v. Carle, 1914, 157 Wis. 565, 147 N.W. 834; Wohlfort v. Wohlfort, 1928, 125 Kan. 234, 263 P. 1062.

38. Falk v. Falk, 1932, 279 Mass. 530, 181 N.E. 715; Cole v. Johnson, 1922, 103 Or. 319, 205 P. 282.

39. Townsend v. Holderby, 1929, 197 N.C. 550, 149 S.E. 855; Brison v. McKellop, 1914, 41 Okl. 374, 138 P. 154. Accord, as to stepchildren: Strader v. Armstrong, 1922, 192 Iowa 1368, 186 N.W. 407; McGregor v. McGregor, Ky.1909, 115 S.W. 802.

40. Trumbull v. Trumbull, 1904, 71 Neb. 186, 98 N.W. 683.

41. Powell v. Benthall, 1904, 136 N.C. 145, 48 S.E. 598. Accord, Turner v. Estes, 1807, 3 Mass. 317 (son-in-law).

42. See Johnson v. Allen, 1888, 100 N.C. 131, 5 S.E. 666; Hartpence v. Rodgers, 1898, 143 Mo. 623, 45 S.W. 650; Modisett v. McPike, 1881, 74 Mo. 636; Alexander v. Johnson, 1930, 182 Ark. 270, 31 S.W.2d 304.

43. Berthon v. Cartwright, 1796, 2 Esp. 480, 170 Eng.Rep. 426; Johnson v. Allen, 1888, 100 N.C. 131, 5 S.E. 666.

44. Modisett v. McPike, 1881, 74 Mo. 636.

45. See Jennings v. Cooper, Mo.App.1921, 230 S.W. 325; Carrieri v. Bush, 1966, 69 Wash.2d 536, 419 P.2d 132 (pastor); Restatement of Torts, § 686, Comment *d*.

46. Grilnberger v. Brotherton, 1933, 173 Wash. 292, 22 P.2d 983; Warren v. Graham, 1916, 174 Iowa 162, 156 N.W. 323.

47. See Moreland, Injunctive Control of Family Relations, 1930, 18 Ky.L.J. 207; Pound, Equitable Relief Against Defamation and Injuries to Personality, 1916, 29 Harv.L.Rev. 640, 674; Long, Equitable Jurisdiction to Protect Personal Rights, 1923, 33 Yale L.J. 115, 126; Notes, 1925, 19 Ill.L.Rev. 587; 1933, 27 Ill.L.Rev. 440.

48. Ex parte Warfield, 1899, 40 Tex.Cr.Rep. 413, 50 S.W. 933. Followed in Witte v. Bauderer, Tex.Civ. App.1923, 255 S.W. 1016; Smith v. Womack, Tex. Civ.App.1925, 271 S.W. 209.

49. Latham v. Karger, 1958, 267 Ala. 433, 103 So.2d 336; Devine v. Devine, 1952, 20 N.J.Super. 523, 90 A.2d 126; Reed v. Carter, 1937, 268 Ky. 1, 103 S.

difficulties standing in the way of enforcement of such injunctions have been enough to deter some of the more conservative courts from granting the relief.[50] While little information is available as to the success of such procedure in operation,[51] the difficulties appear to be inadequate as a reason for denying to family relations the protection given by equity to other recognized interests.

Wife

The wife, at common law, had no actions analogous to those of the husband for interference with the domestic relations. One very good reason was that she had not the capacity to maintain an action of her own against anyone, and the erring husband was scarcely the proper person to be joined with her as a plaintiff.[52] There is one view[53] to the effect that a right existed in the wife to the society, intercourse and affections of her husband, as is indicated by the fact that the ecclesiastical courts gave her a suit against

him for restitution of conjugal rights when he abandoned her,[54] but that the procedural disability prevented her from recovering for interference with it. It is probably idle to speculate upon anything so metaphysical as a legal right with no effective remedy, when obviously the real difficulty was the inferior position of married women, and the feeling that they had no standing to complain, since they were not entitled to any "services" of the husband. This is evidenced by the fact that even after the incapacity to sue was removed by the Married Women's Acts, a few courts[55] still held that the wife had no action; and one immortal opinion[56] held forth at some length upon the purer and nobler nature of wives and their tendency to stay at home and behave themselves, and the temptations, enticements and allurements of the world to which the husband by contrast was exposed, arriving at the conclusion that it was only what she had reason to expect when she married the man.

The altered position of woman in the modern world has swept all this into history, and in virtually all states[57] the wife is now given the same rights and remedies as the husband, either by specific statutes,[58] or by a more liberal interpretation of the Married

W.2d 663; Hall v. Smith, 1913, 80 Misc. 85, 140 N. Y.S. 796; Niver v. Niver, 1951, 200 Misc. 993, 111 N.Y.S.2d 889. Cf. Stark v. Hamilton, 1919, 149 Ga. 227, 99 S.E. 861 (debauching daughter). See Notes, 1932, 27 Ill.L.Rev. 440; 1952, 2 DePaul L.Rev. 75.

50. Snedaker v. King, 1924, 111 Ohio St. 225, 145 N. E. 15; Bank v. Bank, 1942, 180 Md. 254, 23 A.2d 700; White v. Thomson, 1949, 324 Mass. 140, 85 N. E.2d 246; Spitzer v. Spitzer, 1947, 191 Misc. 343, 77 N.Y.S.2d 279, affirmed, 1948, 274 App.Div. 806, 81 N.Y.S.2d 155.

In Knighton v. Knighton, 1949, 252 Ala. 520, 41 So.2d 172, a wife who had left her husband was denied an injunction against his association with another woman.

51. See McClintock, Equity, 2d Ed. 1948, § 162.

52. An attempt to obviate this difficulty by joining the husband as defendant was unsuccessful. See Lynch v. Knight, 1861, 9 H.L.Cas. 577, 11 Eng.Rep. 854.

53. See Note, 1922, 8 Va.L.Rev. 370; Brown, The Action for Alienation of Affections, 1934, 82 U.Pa.L. Rev. 472, 476; Bennett v. Bennett, 1889, 116 N.Y. 584, 23 N.E. 17; Haynes v. Nowlin, 1891, 129 Ind. 581, 29 N.E. 389. See, however, Lippman, The Breakdown of Consortium, 1930, 30 Col.L.Rev. 651, 664, calling this theory incredible "because her very incapacity to sue was due to her inferiority."

54. See Orme v. Orme, 1824, 2 Add.Ec. 382, 2 Eng.Ec. 354; Burroughs v. Burroughs, 1861, 2 Swabey & T. 303, 164 Eng.Rep. 1012; and the noted case of Yelverton v. Yelverton, 1859, 1 Swabey & T. 574, 164 Eng.Rep. 866.

55. Duffies v. Duffies, 1890, 76 Wis. 374, 45 N.W. 522; Hodge v. Wetzler, 1903, 69 N.J.L. 490, 55 A. 49; Doe v. Roe, 1890, 82 Me. 503, 20 A. 83.

56. Duffies v. Duffies, 1890, 76 Wis. 374, 45 N.W. 522. The court also was much perturbed over the possibility of a vast increase in litigation.

57. Maine has construed its specific statute to mean that an action may be maintained against a female defendant but not against a male. Farrell v. Farrell, 1920, 118 Me. 441, 108 A. 648; Howard v. Howard, 1921, 120 Me. 479, 115 A. 259.

58. See for example Sims v. Sims, 1910, 79 N.J.L. 577, 76 A. 1063; Markson v. Shelton, D.Kan.1954, 124 F.Supp. 206 (Wisconsin statute).

Women's Acts in recognition of social changes. The wife may recover for enticement,[59] for criminal conversation,[60] or for mere alienation of affections, even though there is no departure from the home.[61] This is true even though the husband himself was the pursuer or seducer, so long as there was participation or encouragement on the part of the other woman.[62] In other words, so far as intentional interference with the marital relation is concerned the loss of "services" is not necessary to the action, the right of one spouse to the society, sole intercourse and affection of the other is reciprocal, and the law no longer recognizes any inequality of the sexes. Without repeating what has been said as to the husband's action,[63] it may be stated simply that identical rules govern that of the wife, including in particular the necessity that the defendant act for the purpose of affecting the relation,[64] and that he be a substantial factor in causing the aliena-

tion,[65] as well as the privilege of parents and relatives to interfere with proper motives.[66]

Parent

The law has been somewhat more reluctant to protect the relation of parent and child than that of husband and wife. So far as abduction is concerned, there was an old writ giving an action for the taking away of an heir, which apparently was based upon the pecuniary loss to the parent of the heir's marriage prospects, and so did not apply to any other children.[67] When this became obsolete, it was superseded by an action for loss of services of the child, similar to that of any other master.[68] For this some actual loss of services was essential in the beginning, and there could be no recovery when the child was too small to render services,[69] or where they had been contracted away to another.[70] Likewise, while anyone standing in the place of the father might maintain the action,[71] the mother, who had no legal right to the child's services while the father was living

59. Bird v. Ellingsworth, 1937, 156 Or. 103, 65 P.2d 674; Red Eagle v. Free, 1942, 191 Okl. 385, 130 P. 2d 308; Bradstreet v. Wallace, 1926, 254 Mass. 509, 150 N.E. 405; Gross v. Gross, 1912, 70 W.Va. 317, 73 S.E. 961; Wolf v. Frank, 1900, 92 Md. 138, 48 A. 132.

60. Karchner v. Mumie, 1959, 398 Pa. 13, 156 A.2d 537; Knighten v. McClain, 1947, 227 N.C. 682, 44 S.E.2d 79; Woodman v. Goodrich, 1940, 234 Wis. 565, 291 N.W. 768; Newsom v. Fleming, 1935, 165 Va. 89, 181 S.E. 393; Scates v. Nailling, 1954, 196 Tenn. 508, 268 S.W.2d 561.

61. Morey v. Keller, 1957, 77 S.D. 49, 85 N.W.2d 57; Root v. Root, N.D.Cal.1940, 31 F.Supp. 562; Norris v. Stoneham, Tex.Civ.App.1932, 46 S.W.2d 363; Murray v. Murray, 1925, 30 N.M. 557, 240 P. 303; Rott v. Goehring, 1916, 33 N.D. 413, 157 N.W. 294; see Scates v. Nailling, 1954, 196 Tenn. 508, 268 S.W.2d 561.

62. Hart v. Knapp, 1903, 76 Conn. 135, 55 A. 1021; Miller v. Pearce, 1912, 86 Vt. 322, 85 A. 620; Norris v. Stoneham, Tex.Civ.App.1932, 46 S.W.2d 363.

63. Supra, pp. 874–880.

64. Anderson v. McGill Club, 1928, 51 Nev. 16, 266 P. 913; Boden v. Del-Mar Garage, 1933, 205 Ind. 59, 185 N.E. 860.

65. Waldron v. Waldron, C.C.Ill.1890, 45 F. 315; Loper v. Askin, 1917, 178 App.Div. 163, 164 N.Y.S. 1036.

66. Reed v. Reed, 1892, 6 Ind.App. 317, 33 N.E. 638; Melcher v. Melcher, 1918, 102 Neb. 790, 169 N.W. 720.

67. Barham v. Dennis, 1600, Cro.Eliz. 770, 78 Eng. Rep. 1001.

68. Cf. Fores v. Wilson, 1791, 1 Peake 77, 170 Eng. Rep. 85 (enticing and debauching plaintiff's maid servant). See the historical discussion in Pickle v. Page, 1930, 252 N.Y. 474, 169 N.E. 650; and cf. Meredith v. Buster, 1925, 209 Ky. 623, 273 S.W. 454; Oversmith v. Lake, 1940, 295 Mich. 627, 295 N.W. 339.

69. Hall v. Hollander, 1825, 4 B. & C. 660, 107 Eng. Rep. 1206.

70. Dean v. Peel, 1804, 5 East 45, 102 Eng.Rep. 986; Hodges v. Tagg, 1872, L.R. 7 Ex. 283; cf. Terry v. Hutchinson, 1868, L.R. 3 Q.B. 599 (contract terminated by discharge). Contra Bolton v. Miller, 1855, 6 Ind. 262, on the ground that the parent has the power, if not the right, to break the contract and reclaim the child's services.

71. Moritz v. Garnhart, 1838, 7 Watts, Pa., 302; Clark v. Bayer, 1877, 32 Ohio St. 299.

with her, could not do so,[72] unless the child was illegitimate,[73] or the father had died or abandoned it.[74]

From this position the law has moved slowly and incompletely toward a recognition of something like the "consortium" found in the relation of husband and wife. While about half of the courts still appear to require a loss of "services" as the foundation for the action,[75] most of them are willing to find a "constructive" loss whenever the plaintiff has the right to services, although none are being rendered,[76] as in the case of the kidnapping of a child four months old.[77] Once loss of services is established, the parent is allowed to recover damages for deprivation of the child's society, expenses to which he has been put in recovering it, and the wound to his own feelings.[78] A few courts, recognizing that the real cause of action is the interference with the relation have adopted the "modern view"[79] that loss

of services is not essential where a child has been taken from its parent, and that such other damages are a sufficient basis for the action. The two courts which thus far have considered the question[80] have held, however, that no action will lie for the mere alienation of the child's affections, in the absence of either seduction or removal from home.

With these qualifications, the defendant may be liable for abducting the child by force,[81] for enticing it away from its parent,[82] or for "harboring" it in the sense of inducing or encouraging it to remain away from home.[83] The consent of the child is of course no defense to the parent's action.[84] As in the case of husband and wife, the interference with the relation must be a deliberate one, although not necessarily motivated by ill will or anything other than kindness or affection toward the child,[85] and there is no liability for harboring or employing a minor unless there is reason to believe that it is without

72. Pyle v. Waechter, 1926, 202 Iowa 695, 210 N.W. 926; Soper v. Igo, Walker & Co., 1905, 121 Ky. 550, 89 S.W. 538.

73. Illinois Central R. Co. v. Sanders, 1913, 104 Miss. 257, 61 So. 309.

74. Magnuson v. O'Dea, 1913, 75 Wash. 574, 135 P. 640. Cf. Steward v. Gold Medal Shows, 1943, 244 Ala. 583, 14 So.2d 549 (mother entitled to custody); Yost v. Grand Trunk R. Co., 1910, 163 Mich. 564, 128 N.W. 784; Horgan v. Pacific Mills, 1893, 158 Mass. 402, 33 N.E. 581.

75. See Magnuson v. O'Dea, 1913, 75 Wash. 574, 135 P. 640; Clark v. Bayer, 1877, 32 Ohio St. 299; Magee v. Holland, 1858, 27 N.J.L. 86; Hare v. Dean, 1897, 90 Me. 308, 38 A. 227.

76. See Magee v. Holland, 1858, 27 N.J.L. 86; Washburn v. Abrams, 1906, 122 Ky. 53, 90 S.W. 997; Hare v. Dean, 1897, 90 Me. 308, 38 A. 227; Moritz v. Garnhart, 1838, 7 Watts, Pa., 302; Clark v. Bayer, 1877, 32 Ohio St. 299.

77. See Magee v. Holland, 1858, 27 N.J.L. 86.

78. Magee v. Holland, 1858, 27 N.J.L. 86; Little v. Holmes, 1921, 181 N.C. 413, 107 S.E. 577; Meredith v. Buster, 1925, 209 Ky. 623, 273 S.W. 454.

79. So called although it is not particularly recent in its origin. Pickle v. Page, 1930, 252 N.Y. 474, 169 N.E. 650; Steward v. Gold Medal Shows, 1943, 244 Ala. 583, 14 So.2d 549; Montgomery v. Crum, 1928, 199 Ind. 660, 161 N.E. 251; Howell v. Howell, 1913,

162 N.C. 283, 78 S.E. 222; Idleman v. Groves, 1921, 89 W.Va. 91, 108 S.E. 485. See Notes, 1929, 14 Corn.L.Q. 496; 1930, 15 Iowa L.Rev. 505; 1931, 25 Ill.L.Rev. 726.

80. Pyle v. Waechter, 1926, 202 Iowa 695, 210 N.W. 926; Miles v. Cuthbert, Sup.Ct.1909, 122 N.Y.S. 703. See Notes, 1927, 40 Harv.L.Rev. 771; 1927, 27 Col. L.Rev. 604; 1927, 11 Minn.L.Rev. 570; 1927, 25 Mich.L.Rev. 682.

81. Magee v. Holland, 1858, 27 N.J.L. 86; Pickle v. Page, 1930, 252 N.Y. 474, 169 N.E. 650; Howell v. Howell, 1913, 162 N.C. 283, 78 S.E. 222. Cf. Oversmith v. Lake, 1940, 295 Mich. 627, 295 N.W. 339 (false imprisonment and commitment).

82. Evans v. Walton, 1867, L.R. 2 C.P. 615; Armstrong v. McDonald, 1958, 39 Ala.App. 485, 103 So. 2d 818; Horowitz v. Sacks, 1928, 89 Cal.App. 336, 265 P. 281; Selman v. Barnett, 1908, 4 Ga.App. 375, 61 S.E. 501; Hare v. Dean, 1897, 90 Me. 308, 38 A. 227.

83. Everett v. Sherfey, 1855, 1 Iowa 356; Washburn v. Abrams, 1906, 122 Ky. 53, 90 S.W. 997; Sargent v. Mathewson, 1859, 38 N.H. 54; Caughey v. Smith, 1872, 47 N.Y. 244.

84. Fort Wayne, C. & L. R. Co. v. Beyerle, 1887, 110 Ind. 100, 11 N.E. 6; Horowitz v. Sacks, 1928, 89 Cal.App. 336, 265 P. 281.

85. See Restatement of Torts, § 700, Comment *b*.

the parent's consent.[86] No special privilege has been recognized in the other parent, or in any other relative, to interfere with the legal custody of the child, although it would appear that even a stranger might step in to protect the child from physical violence in excess of the parental privilege of discipline.[87]

Seduction. The parent's interests receive the broadest protection in his action for sexual intercourse with his child, which is roughly analogous to the husband's action for criminal conversation with his wife, and involves a similar injury to family honor and reputation and to the feelings incident to the relation. While there probably is no good reason why the action should not lie for intercourse with a male child,[88] it has been limited in practice to the debauching of daughters. The intercourse may be by forcible rape,[89] or more commonly, by seduction with the consent of the girl, which will not defeat the parent's action.[90] The common law rule which makes such consent a bar to any action by a woman for her own seduction[91]

has led the courts to strain every point to provide a remedy at least for the parent, with the result that the action for seduction, like the tort itself, sometimes is supported by very ingenious fictions.

The action developed as trespass[92] or case[93] for loss of services, which was the most convenient device available. The earliest cases were those in which pregnancy or illness deprived the parent of actual services; and it remains the law in England that loss of services is essential to the cause of action,[94] and that it cannot be maintained where the services of the child have been contracted away to another.[95] The American courts, in general, have said in the past that loss of services is the gist of the action, which must fail without it.[96] But once technical loss of services is established, the action has been recognized as one for interference with other aspects of the relation; and

---

86. Kenney v. Baltimore & O. R. Co., 1905, 101 Md. 490, 61 A. 581; Arnold v. St. Louis & S. F. R. Co., 1903, 100 Mo.App. 470, 74 S.W. 5; Butterfield v. Ashley, 1850, 6 Cush., Mass., 249; Caughey v. Smith, 1872, 47 N.Y. 244; see Tavlinsky v. Ringling Bros. Circus Co., 1925, 113 Neb. 632, 204 N.W. 388.

87. See Restatement of Torts, § 700, Comment *e.*

88. "Nor in my judgment does the remedy depend upon the sex of the servant. The debased woman, who lures to her vile embrace an innocent boy and infects him with loathsome disease, is equally liable to this action, if an injury to his master's right to service follow from her crime." Davis, J., in White v. Nellis, 1856, 31 N.Y. 405. No such case has been found.

89. Kennedy v. Shea, 1872, 110 Mass. 147; Lawrence v. Spence, 1885, 99 N.Y. 669, 2 N.E. 145; Lavery v. Crooke, 1881, 52 Wis. 612, 9 N.W. 599; Silva v. Mills, 1926, 47 R.I. 193, 131 A. 695. Cf. Monahan v. Clemons, 1926, 212 Ky. 504, 279 S.W. 974 (statutory rape).

90. Reutkemeier v. Nolte, 1917, 179 Iowa 342, 161 N. W. 290; Simpson v. Grayson, 1891, 54 Ark. 404, 16 S.W. 4.

91. Welsund v. Schueller, 1906, 98 Minn. 475, 108 N. W. 483; Oberlin v. Upson, 1911, 84 Ohio St. 111, 95

N.E. 511; Overhultz v. Row, 1922, 152 La. 9, 92 So. 716. See supra, § 18. It is to be noted that criminal statutes fixing the age of consent are construed to provide a civil action in nearly all jurisdictions, where the plaintiff is below that age.

92. Tullidge v. Wade, 1769, 3 Wils.K.B. 18, 95 Eng. Rep. 909; MacFadzen v. Olivant, 1805, 6 East 387, 102 Eng.Rep. 1335.

93. Norton v. Jason, 1653, Style 398, 82 Eng.Rep. 809; Grinnell v. Wells, 1844, 7 Man. & G. 1033, 135 Eng.Rep. 419. Apparently the writs were concurrent. See McKinney, J., in Parker v. Meek, 1855, 3 Sneed, Tenn., 29.

94. Grinnell v. Wells, 1844, 7 Man. & G. 1033, 135 Eng.Rep. 419; Eager v. Grimwood, 1847, 1 Exch. 61, 154 Eng.Rep. 26; Whitbourne v. Williams, [1901] 2 K.B. 722.

95. Dean v. Peel, 1804, 5 East 45, 102 Eng.Rep. 986; Hedges v. Tagg, 1872, L.R. 7 Ex. 283. Accord Dain v. Wycoff, 1852, 7 N.Y. 191. Cf. Terry v. Hutchinson, 1868, L.R. 3 Q.B. 599 (discharge before seduction). The American courts, however, have tended to hold that the power of the parent to break the agreement and reclaim the child's services is sufficient. Martin v. Payne, 1812, 9 Johns, N.Y., 387; Bolton v. Miller, 1855, 6 Ind. 262.

96. Tittlebaum v. Boehmcke, 1911, 81 N.J.L. 697, 80 A. 323; Blagge v. Ilsley, 1879, 127 Mass. 191; Parker v. Meek, 1855, 3 Sneed, Tenn., 29; Wendt v. Lentz, 1929, 197 Wis. 569, 222 N.W. 798 ("some slight loss of services" necessary).

the plaintiff, who sues as a master, has been permitted to recover as a parent,[97] with damages for medical and other expenses of caring for the daughter,[98] for loss of her society and comfort,[99] for his wounded feelings [1] and his sense of dishonor to himself and his family,[2] and for the evil example to his other children,[3] with punitive damages superimposed.[4]

The tendency, both in England and in America, has been to reduce to a minimum

this element of "services," which obviously is a mere peg on which to hang the real damages. Any services actually rendered, no matter how trivial, such as making a cup of tea for the parent [5] or milking the cows [6] is sufficient. A minor daughter living in her father's home is presumed, without proof, to perform such services,[7] and the fact that she was temporarily absent from home when the seduction occurred will not defeat recovery.[8] From this it has been a comparatively easy step to hold that the right to services is enough, even though none are rendered in fact.[9] A few courts have reached the logical conclusion that the loss of services is an obsolete fiction and is no longer necessary to an action for seduction;[10] and statutes to this effect now have been enacted in approximately a third of the states.[11] Still more striking are decisions in three jurisdictions [12]

97. The plaintiff "comes into court as a master; he goes before the jury as a father." Briggs v. Evans, 1844, 27 N.C. (5 Ired.) 16, 20; Simpson v. Grayson, 1891, 54 Ark. 404, 16 S.W. 4.

98. Middleton v. Nichols, 1898, 62 N.J.L. 636, 43 A. 575; Haeissig v. Decker, 1918, 139 Minn. 422, 166 N.W. 1085; Anderson v. Aupperle, 1908, 51 Or. 556, 95 P. 330. There is no dispute that there may be recovery for the expenses of caring for pregnancy, venereal disease, or other illness resulting directly from the intercourse. White v. Nellis, 1865, 31 N.Y. 405; Manvell v. Thomson, 1826, 2 C. & P. 303, 172 Eng.Rep. 136; Abrahams v. Kidney, 1870, 104 Mass. 222. But there has been considerable reluctance to include illness resulting from fear of exposure or from abandonment by the seducer. Knight v. Wilcox, 1879, 14 N.Y. 413; Boyle v. Brandon, 1845, 13 M. & W. 738, 153 Eng.Rep. 310. Compare the case of demoralization, sexual misconduct and imprisonment in Wendt v. Lentz, 1929, 197 Wis. 569, 222 N.W. 798, and the vigorous attack on the case by Professor Edgerton in 1930, 24 Ill.L.Rev. 232.

99. Bedford v. McKowl, 1800, 3 Esp. 119, 170 Eng. Rep. 560; Milliken v. Long, 1898, 188 Pa. 411, 41 A. 540; Tillotson v. Currin, 1918, 176 N.C. 479, 97 S.E. 395.

1. Andrews v. Askey, 1837, 8 C. & P. 7, 173 Eng.Rep. 376; Dwire v. Stearns, 1919, 44 N.D. 199, 172 N.W. 69; Stevenson v. Belknap, 1858, 6 Iowa 97; Lunt v. Philbrick, 1879, 59 N.H. 59; Barbour v. Stephenson, C.C.Ky.1887, 32 F. 66, affirmed, 1891, 140 U.S. 48.

2. Dwire v. Stearns, 1919, 44 N.D. 199, 172 N.W. 69; Riddle v. McGinnis, 1883, 22 W.Va. 253; Mighell v. Stone, 1893, 175 Ill. 261, 51 N.E. 906.

3. Lavery v. Crooke, 1881, 52 Wis. 612, 9 N.W. 599; Stevenson v. Belknap, 1858, 6 Iowa 97; Bedford v. McKowl, 1800, 3 Esp. 119, 170 Eng.Rep. 560.

4. Lawyer v. Fritcher, 1891, 130 N.Y. 239, 29 N.E. 267; Willeford v. Bailey, 1903, 132 N.C. 402, 43 S.E. 928; Berghammer v. Mayer, 1926, 189 Wis. 197, 207 N.W. 289; Anderson v. Aupperle, 1908, 51 Or. 556, 95 P. 330.

5. Carr v. Clarke, 1818, 2 Chit. 260; Manvell v. Thomson, 1826, 2 C. & P. 303, 172 Eng.Rep. 136; Briggs v. Evans, 1844, 27 N.C. (5 Ired.) 16, 20.

6. See Bennett v. Allcott, 1787, 2 Term Rep. 166, 168, 100 Eng.Rep. 90. Accord: Ball v. Bruce, 1859, 21 Ill. 161; Kendrick v. McCrary, 1852, 11 Ga. 603; Badgley v. Decker, 1865, 44 Barb., N.Y., 577.

7. Jones v. Brown, 1794, 1 Esp. 217, 170 Eng.Rep. 334; Noice v. Brown, 1877, 39 N.J.L. 569.

8. Lipe v. Eisenlerd, 1865, 32 N.Y. 229; Clark v. Fitch, 1829, 2 Wend., N.Y. 459; Ingwaldson v. Skrivseth, 1898, 7 N.D. 388, 75 N.W. 772; Blagge v. Ilsley, 1879, 127 Mass. 191; Hudkins v. Haskins, 1883, 22 W.Va. 645.

9. Bolton v. Miller, 1855, 6 Ind. 262; Martin v. Payne, 1812, 9 Johns., N.Y. 387; Emery v. Gowen, 1826, 4 Greenl., Me., 33; Kennedy v. Shea, 1872, 110 Mass. 147; Reutkemeier v. Nolte, 1917, 179 Iowa 342, 161 N.W. 290.

10. Simpson v. Grayson, 1891, 54 Ark. 404, 16 S.W. 4; Anthony v. Norton, 1899, 60 Kan. 341, 56 P. 529; Dwire v. Stearns, 1919, 44 N.D. 199, 172 N.W. 69; Snider v. Newell, 1903, 132 N.C. 614, 44 S.E. 354; Breining v. Lippincott, 1916, 125 Ark. 77, 187 S.W. 915.

11. See Stoudt v. Shepherd, 1899, 73 Mich. 588, 41 N.W. 696; Schmit v. Mitchell, 1894, 59 Minn. 251, 61 N.W. 140; Graham v. McReynolds, 1891, 90 Tenn. 673, 18 S.W. 272. The statutes are collected in 4 Vernier, American Family Laws, 1936, § 265.

12. Hyatt v. McCoy, 1927, 194 N.C. 25, 138 S.E. 405 (held however, not to apply to an infant female in

which recognize that the parent's action itself is something in the nature of a fiction, as a makeshift device to permit recovery where the daughter could not sue, and accordingly have held that the action may be maintained by the woman herself as the real party in interest. In line with this are statutes in some fourteen states authorizing the woman's action, and so doing away with the common law defense of consent.[13]

The chief importance of "loss of services" at the present time is that it still is necessary for the parent to show that he is a person who would be entitled to the services of the daughter. If the latter has been emancipated, so that the right to her services is lost, the action cannot be maintained.[14] Furthermore, the action is primarily in the father,[15] and it is only after his death[16] or desertion of the family,[17] that it is in the mother, although any third party who stands in the position of a father may be in a po-

sition to sue.[18] It seems to be agreed that the parent's action is not limited to the seduction of minor children, and that it applies to an adult daughter provided that she is rendering actual services to him;[19] but there is a difference of opinion as to whether such services will be presumed from the mere fact of her residence in his house. The prevailing American view seems to be that the presumption does not arise as to an adult.[20] The parent's consent to the intercourse, or conduct inviting it, will of course bar his action.[21]

Child

The older common law gave the child no right to the "services" of a parent, as distinguished from his support. There were no cases dealing with any liability for alienation of the parent's affections. It is only within recent years that the question has even been raised.[22] Since 1923 some eleven courts have held that the child's action will not lie.[23]

Scarlett v. Norwood, 1894, 115 N.C. 284, 20 S.E. 459); Watson v. Watson, 1883, 49 Mich. 540, 14 N.W. 489; Rabeke v. Baer, 1897, 115 Mich. 328, 73 N. W. 242; Johnson v. Harris, 1940, 187 Okl. 239, 102 P.2d 940. See Note, 1928, 12 Minn.L.Rev. 190. Contra, Kirkpatrick v. Parker, 1939, 136 Fla. 689, 187 So. 620.

13. Collected in 4 Vernier, American Family Laws, 1936, § 252.

14. Roberts v. Connelly, 1848, 14 Ala. 235; White v. Murtland, 1874, 71 Ill. 250. In Collis v. Hoskins, 1948, 306 Ky. 391, 208 S.W.2d 70, the emancipated daughter returned home after the seduction and the father was allowed to recover medical expenses of pregnancy.

15. Mulvehall v. Millward, 1854, 11 N.Y. 343; Scarlett v. Norwood, 1894, 115 N.C. 284, 20 S.E. 459; Peters v. Jones, [1914] 2 K.B. 781; Kaufman v. Clark, 1917, 141 La. 316, 75 So. 65.

16. Furman v. Van Sise, 1874, 56 N.Y. 435; Felkner v. Scarlet, 1867, 29 Ind. 154; Gray v. Durland, 1873, 51 N.Y. 424; Coon v. Moffet, 1809, 3 N.J.L. 583.

17. Malone v. Topfer, 1915, 125 Md. 157, 93 A. 397; Badgley v. Decker, 1865, 44 Barb. N.Y. 577; Abbott v. Hancock, 1898, 123 N.C. 99, 31 S.E. 268. The mother of a bastard may recover for seduction. Bunker v. Mains, 1942, 139 Me. 231, 28 A.2d 734.

18. Ball v. Bruce, 1859, 21 Ill. 161 (brother-in-law); Tittlebaum v. Boehmcke, 1911, 81 N.J.L. 697, 80 A. 323 (stepfather); Manvell v. Thomson, 1826, 2 C. & P. 303, 172 Eng.Rep. 136 (uncle); Anderson v. Aupperle, 1908, 51 Or. 556, 95 P. 330 (grandfather).

19. Bennett v. Allcott, 1787, 2 Term Rep. 166, 100 Eng.Rep. 90; Sutton v. Huffman, 1866, 32 N.J.L. 58; Nickleson v. Stryker, 1813, 10 Johns., N.Y., 115; Beaudette v. Gagne, 1895, 87 Me. 534, 33 A. 23; Palmer v. Baum, 1905, 123 Ill.App. 584.

20. Harper v. Luffkin, 1827, 7 B. & C. 387, 108 Eng. Rep. 767; Parker v. Meek, 1855, 3 Sneed, 35 Tenn., 29; Nickleson v. Stryker, 1813, 10 Johns., N.Y., 115. But see Sutton v. Huffman, 1866, 32 N.J.L. 58; Lipe v. Eisenlerd, 1865, 32 N.Y. 229; Stevenson v. Belknap, 1858, 6 Iowa 97.

21. Reddie v. Scoolt, 1794, Peake 240, 170 Eng.Rep. 169; Smith v. Masten, 1836, 15 Wend., N.Y., 270; Vossel v. Cole, 1847, 10 Mo. 634.

22. Coulter v. Coulter, 1923, 73 Colo. 144, 214 P. 400; Cole v. Cole, 1931, 277 Mass. 50, 177 N.E. 810; Morrow v. Yannantuono, 1934, 152 Misc. 134, 273 N.Y.S. 912, all denying liability.

23. Kane v. Quigley, 1964, 1 Ohio St. 1, 203 N.E.2d 338; Whitcomb v. Huffington, 1956, 180 Kan. 340, 304 P.2d 465; Lucas v. Bishop, 1955, 224 Ark. 353, 273 S.W.2d 397; Scholberg v. Itnyre, 1953, 264 Wis. 211, 58 N.W.2d 698; Edler v. MacAlpine-Downie,

No better reasons have been given than the lack of any right to services, the absence of precedent, and the conclusion that any change must be for the legislature. At the time of writing the courts of four jurisdictions[24] have recognized a cause of action in the child analogous to that of the wife for alienation of affections. It has been contended, with obvious reason, that the interest of the child in an undisturbed family life is at least of equal importance with that of either parent, and is entitled to equal consideration and redress;[25] and the prediction may be ventured that the legal remedy will gain ground in the future, and that the protection of the interests of children will not be left entirely to other agencies of social control.

Statutory Abolition of Actions

Those actions for interference with domestic relations which carry an accusation of sexual misbehavior—that is to say, criminal conversation, seduction, and to some extent alienation of affections—have been peculiarly susceptible to abuse. Together with the action for breach of promise to marry, it is notorious that they have afforded a fertile field for blackmail and extortion by means of manufactured suits in which the threat of publicity is used to force a settlement. There is good reason to believe that even genuine actions of this type are brought more frequently than not with purely mercenary or vindictive motives; that it is impossible to compensate for such damage with what has derisively been called "heart balm;" that people of any decent instincts do not bring an action which merely adds to the family disgrace; and that no preventive purpose is served, since such torts seldom are committed with deliberate plan.[26] Added to this is perhaps an increasing notion of personal or even sexual freedom on the part of women, and the feeling, illustrated by the current attitude toward divorce, that a home so easily broken up is not worth maintaining.

The result of all this has been a legislative attack upon the actions named. Statutes abolishing them, which were first proposed by a woman member of the Indiana legislature, have been enacted to date in some ten or twelve states.[27] Their constitutionality has for the most part been upheld against all objections raised.[28] Their desirability is another matter. They reverse abruptly the entire tendency of the law to give increased protection to family interests and the sanctity of the home, and undoubtedly they deny relief in many cases of serious and genuine

---

1950, 86 U.S.App.D.C. 97, 180 F.2d 385; and see cases cited supra, note 22. See Notes, 1965, 34 U. Cin.L.Rev. 545; 1965, 22 Wash. & Lee L.Rev. 247.

In three other courts the action has been held to be barred by the "heart balm" statutes. See infra, p. 888.

24. Daily v. Parker, 7 Cir. 1945, 152 F.2d 174, affirming, N.D.Ill.1945, 61 F.Supp. 701; Miller v. Monson, 1949, 228 Minn. 400, 37 N.W.2d 543; Russick v. Hicks, W.D.Mich.1949, 85 F.Supp. 281; Johnson v. Luhman, 1947, 330 Ill.App. 598, 71 N.E. 2d 810.

25. See Nocca, Should a Child Have a Right of Action Against a Third Person Who Has Enticed One of His Parents Away from the Home, 1956, 2 N.Y. Law Forum 357; Notes, 1951, 39 Cal.L.Rev. 294; 1952, 32 Bos.U.L.Rev. 82; 1953, 6 Vand.L.Rev. 926; 1953, 6 Okl.L.Rev. 500; 1953, 2 St. Louis U.L.J. 305; 1954, 14 La.L.Rev. 713; 1954, 37 Marq.L.Rev. 271; 1956, 8 S.C.L.Q. 477; 1956, 42 Corn.L.Q. 115; 1957, 6 Kan.L.Rev. 95.

26. See, generally, Feinsinger, Legislative Attack on "Heart Balm," 1935, 33 Mich.L.Rev. 979; Feinsinger, Current Legislation Affecting Breach of Promise to Marry, Alienation of Affections and Related Actions, 1935, 10 Wis.L.Rev. 417; Kane, Heart Balm and Public Policy, 1936, 5 Ford.L.Rev. 62; Kingsley, The Anti-Heart Balm Statute, 1939, 13 So.Cal.L.Rev. 37; Notes, 1935, 22 Va.L.Rev. 205; 1936, 5 Brook.L.Rev. 196.

27. See Vernier, American Family Laws, 1938 Supp., §§ 158, 252, 265.

28. Hanfgarn v. Mark, 1937, 274 N.Y. 22, 8 N.E.2d 47, second appeal, 1938, 274 N.Y. 570, 10 N.E.2d 556, appeal dismissed, 302 U.S. 641; Magierowski v. Buckley, 1956, 39 N.J.Super. 534, 121 A.2d 749; Chiyoko Ikuta v. Shunji K. Ikuta, 1950, 97 Cal. App.2d 787, 218 P.2d 854; Rotwein v. Gersten, 1948, 160 Fla. 736, 36 So.2d 419.

wrong.[29] It may be that they do away with spurious suits at too great a price, and that other methods of limitation or control are to be preferred.[30] Perhaps for such reasons the statutes have been construed quite strictly to cover only what their language specifies; and in individual cases injunctions,[31] suits based on fraud,[32] the parent's action for seduction,[33] and an action for criminal conversation,[34] all have been held to be maintainable notwithstanding the statute. It has, however, been held that the legislation has the effect of barring any possibility of the child's action for alienation of the parent's affections, even though no such action had been recognized before the statute was adopted.[35]

125. INJURIES TO MEMBERS OF THE FAMILY

One very obvious manner in which a master may be deprived of the services of a servant is by personal injury to the servant which renders him unfit to perform his duties.[36] Out of this there arose an action given by the common law to a husband for loss of the services of his wife when she was injured by the tort of the defendant,[37] and a similar action of a parent for loss of the services of his child.[38] Any tort resulting in physical injury or incapacity of the wife or child is sufficient to serve as a basis for such an action: assault and battery,[39] malpractice[40] or other negligence,[41] the sale of habit-forming drugs,[42] injuries inflicted by dangerous ani-

29. See for example Lawyer v. Fritcher, 1891, 130 N.Y. 239, 29 N.E. 267; Hope v. Twarling, 1924, 111 Neb. 793, 198 N.W. 161; Richards v. Lorleberg, 1935, 65 U.S.App.D.C. 57, 79 F.2d 413, certiorari denied, 1935, 296 U.S. 642. This is particularly true where the statute destroys the action against parents for alienation. The Michigan statute preserves it. Bean v. McFarland, 1937, 280 Mich. 19, 273 N.W. 332.

30. See Kane, Heart Balm and Public Policy, 1936, 5 Fordham L.Rev. 62; Brown, The Action for Alienation of Affections, 1934, 82 U.Pa.L.Rev. 472, 505; Note, 1936, 30 Ill.L.Rev. 764; and cf. Hibschman, Can "Legal Blackmail" be Legally Outlawed, 1935, 69 U.S.L.Rev. 474.

31. Devine v. Devine, 1952, 20 N.J.Super. 522, 90 A. 2d 126; Henley v. Rockett, 1942, 243 Ala. 172, 8 So.2d 852.

32. Morris v. McNab, 1957, 25 N.J. 271, 135 A.2d 657, (fraudulently inducing plaintiff to enter into bigamous marriage); Tuck v. Tuck, 1964, 14 N.Y.2d 341, 251 N.Y.S.2d 653, 200 N.E.2d 554; see Notes, 1941, 41 Col.L.Rev. 918; 1964, 10 Vill.L.Rev. 189. Cf. Pavlicic v. Vogtsberger, 1957, 390 Pa. 502, 136 A.2d 127 (recovery of gifts, on breach of promise of marriage).

33. Blackman v. Iles, 1950, 4 N.J. 82, 71 A.2d 633; Magierowski v. Buckley, 1956, 39 N.J.Super. 534, 121 A.2d 749; Young v. Young, 1938, 236 Ala. 627, 184 So. 187 (seduction of minor not barred). On the other hand in Aadland v. Flynn, 1961, 27 Misc.2d 833, 211 N.Y.S.2d 221, affirmed, 1961, 14 App.Div. 2d 837, 218 N.Y.S.2d 527 an attempt to maintain a seduction action with an allegation that defendant had "debauched" plaintiff and led her into an immoral life, was unsuccessful.

34. Antonelli v. Xenakis, 1949, 363 Pa. 375, 69 A.2d 102; Di Blasio v. Kolodner, 1964, 233 Md. 512, 197 A.2d 245; Tarquinio v. Pelletier, 1970, 28 Conn.Sup. 487, 266 A.2d 410.

35. Rudley v. Tobias, 1948, 84 Cal.App.2d 454, 190 P. 2d 894; Kleinow v. Ameika, 1952, 19 N.J.Super. 523, 88 A.2d 31; Katz v. Katz, 1950, 197 Misc. 412, 95 N.Y.S.2d 863.

36. See Mary's Case, 1613, 9 Co.Rep. 113a, 77 Eng. Rep. 898; Hodsoll v. Stallebrass, 1840, 11 Ad. & El. 301, 113 Eng.Rep. 429; Woodward v. Washburn, 1846, 3 Denio, N.Y., 369; Ames v. Union R. Co., 1875, 117 Mass. 541.

37. Hyde v. Scyssor, 1620, Cro.Jac. 538, 79 Eng.Rep. 462; Guy v. Livesey, 1629, Cro.Jac. 501, 79 Eng. Rep. 428. As to the present law, see Foster, Relational Interests of the Family [1962] U.Ill.L. Forum 493; Note, 1961, 61 Col.L.Rev. 1341.

38. Norton v. Jason, 1653, Style 398, 82 Eng.Rep. 809; Jones v. Brown, 1794, 1 Esp. 217, 170 Eng. Rep. 334.

39. Berger v. Jacobs, 1870, 21 Mich. 215; Baer v. Hepfinger, 1913, 152 Wis. 558, 140 N.W. 345; Klingman v. Holmes, 1873, 54 Mo. 304.

40. Mewhirter v. Hatten, 1875, 42 Iowa 288; Hoard v. Peck, 1867, 56 Barb., N.Y., 202.

41. Hopkins v. Atlantic & St. L. R. Co., 1857, 36 N.H. 9; Skoglund v. Minneapolis St. R. Co., 1891, 45 Minn. 330, 47 N.W. 1071; Fuller v. Naugatuck R. Co., 1852, 21 Conn. 557; Wilton v. Middlesex R. Co., 1878, 125 Mass. 130.

42. Hoard v. Peck, 1867, 56 Barb., N.Y., 202; Holleman v. Harward, 1896, 119 N.C. 150, 25 S.E. 972; Tidd v. Skinner, 1919, 225 N.Y. 422, 122 N.E. 247.

mals [43] and even false imprisonment and malicious prosecution [44] or libel and slander,[45] when they result in deprivation of services. The action of the husband and parent is entirely distinct from that which may be maintained on behalf of the wife or child for the original tort itself. Thus in his action for loss of services he may not recover damages for the physical or mental suffering of the wife [46] or child,[47] or the harm to the child due to libel,[48] or wrongful exclusion from school,[49] since it is the child alone who is damaged in such a case. In the absence of special statute [50] the actions remain quite separate, and a judgment for or against the plaintiff in one is not binding upon either party to the other; [51] the verdicts need not be consistent; [52] and the husband's action does not abate upon the death of the wife, although his recovery will be limited to the damages he has sustained before her death.[53]

Where the injury is to the wife, the husband recovers for the loss of the same "consortium," consisting of services, society and sexual relations,[54] as in the case of intentional interferences with the relation.[55] The element of "loss of services" has had much the same history here as in the case of direct interference with the family relations. Originally it was indispensable to the cause of action,[56] although the "services" of the wife were defined rather broadly to include her general usefulness, industry, frugality and attentions in the home.[57] Once such a loss was proved, however, recovery soon was ex-

43.   Durden v. Barnett, 1844, 7 Ala. 169; Karr v. Parks, 1872, 44 Cal. 46.

44.   Rogers v. Smith, 1861, 17 Ind. 323.

45.   Garrison v. Sun Printing & Pub. Ass'n, 1912, 207 N.Y. 1, 100 N.E. 430. Cf. Dengate v. Gardiner, 1838, 4 M. & W. 6, 150 Eng.Rep. 1320; Van Vacter v. McKillip, 1845, 7 Blackf., Ind., 578.

46.   Hooper v. Haskell, 1868, 56 Me. 251; Hyatt v. Adams, 1867, 16 Mich. 180; Chicago & M. Elec. R. Co. v. Krempel, 1904, 116 Ill.App. 253.

47.   Pattison v. Gulf Bag Co., 1906, 116 La. 963, 41 So. 224; Kirk v. Middlebrook, 1907, 201 Mo. 245, 100 S.W. 450; Durkee v. Central Pac. R. Co., 1880, 56 Cal. 388; Cuming v. Brooklyn City R. Co., 1888, 109 N.Y. 95, 16 N.E. 65; Tennessee Central R. Co. v. Doak, 1905, 115 Tenn. 720, 92 S.W. 853.

48.   Sorenson v. Balaban, 1896, 11 App.Div. 164, 42 N.Y.S. 654; Atlanta Journal Co. v. Farmer, 1934, 48 Ga.App. 273, 172 S.E. 647. The parent may, however, recover for incidental defamation of himself. See Brown v. Paramount Publix Corporation, 1934, 240 App.Div. 520, 270 N.Y.S. 544.

49.   Boyd v. Blaisdell, 1860, 15 Ind. 73. Cf. Sorrells v. Matthews, 1907, 129 Ga. 319, 58 S.E. 819; Donahoe v. Richards, 1854, 38 Me. 376.

50.   In a few states statutes permit recovery of all damages to both husband and wife in a joint action. Meek v. Pacific Electric R. Co., 1917, 175 Cal. 53, 164 P. 1117; Meese v. City of Fond du Lac, 1879, 48 Wis. 323, 4 N.W. 406. Or the two actions may of course be tried at the same time, with separate judgments rendered. Standen v. Pennsylvania R. Co., 1906, 214 Pa. 189, 63 A. 467.

51.   Wolff v. Du Puis, 1963, 233 Or. 317, 378 P.2d 707; Youngblood v. Taylor, Fla.1956, 89 So.2d 503;

Smittle v. Eberle, Okl.1960, 353 P.2d 121; Trapeni v. Walker, 1958, 120 Vt. 510, 144 A.2d 831; Kleibor v. Rogers, 1965, 265 N.C. 304, 144 S.E.2d 27; Whitehead v. General Tel. Co., 1969, 20 Ohio St.2d 108, 254 N.E.2d 10. See also Russell v. First Nat. Stores, 1951, 96 N.H. 471, 79 A.2d 573 (wife's action founded on warranty, husband's on negligence).

52.   McGilvray v. Powell, 700 North, 7 Cir.1951, 186 F.2d 909; McCray v. Earls, 1937, 267 Ky. 89, 101 S.W.2d 192. Contra, Reilly v. Shapmar Realty Corp., 1943, 267 App.Div. 198, 45 N.Y.S.2d 356.

53.   Long v. Morrison, 1860, 14 Ind. 595; Whitford v. Panama R. Co., 1861, 23 N.Y. 465; Bailey v. Long, 1916, 172 N.C. 661, 90 S.E. 809; Callaghan v. Lake Hopatcong Ice Co., 1903, 69 N.J.L. 100, 54 A. 223; Indianapolis & M. R. T. Co. v. Reeder, 1908, 42 Ind.App. 520, 85 N.E. 1042. See Note, 1932, 9 N.Y. U.L.Q.Rev. 344.

54.   Shreve v. Faris, 1959, 144 W.Va. 819, 111 S.E.2d 169.

55.   See supra, pp. 874–880.

56.   Hall v. Hollander, 1825, 4 B. & C. 660, 107 Eng. Rep. 1206; Dean v. Peel, 1804, 5 East 45, 102 Eng. Rep. 986. In West v. City of San Diego, 1960, 54 Cal.2d 469, 6 Cal.Rptr. 289, 353 P.2d 929, there was a return to this, holding that the husband's recovery could only be for loss of services, as a result of denial of any action to the wife.

57.   Pennsylvania R. Co. v. Goodman, 1869, 62 Pa. 329; Ballard v. Lumbermen's Mut. Cas. Co., 1967, 33 Wis.2d 601, 148 N.W.2d 65; Manders v. Pulice, 1968, 102 Ill.App.2d 468, 242 N.E.2d 617; cf. Price v. H. B. Green Transportation Line, 7 Cir. 1961, 287 F.2d 363.

tended to cover damages for deprivation of the society, fellowship and affectionate relations of the wife or child [58] and the sexual intercourse of the wife,[59] together with any estimated loss in the future.[60] Medical and other expenses actually incurred in caring for the wife or child might also be recovered,[61] although it was considered safer for the protection of the injured person that future medical expenses be left to his own action.[62] The next step taken by the American courts was to reduce the loss of services to a mere technical requirement, and to permit recovery where the child was living apart

from its parent and the only interference was with the bare legal right to services,[63] or where the child was too young to render services and the only deprivation was in the future,[64] with a broad discretion in the trial court and the jury to estimate damages without definite evidence.[65] The logical conclusion has been reached by a number of courts which have held that there may be recovery for medical expenses incurred, without reference to loss of services at all.[66]

As in the case of direct interferences with the relation, the chief importance of loss of services today appears to be that the plaintiff must show that he is the person who would be entitled to such services. Thus no right of action exists in favor of the parent of an emancipated minor,[67] and a total eman-

58. Denver Consol. Tramway Co. v. Riley, 1899, 14 Colo.App. 132, 59 P. 476; Furnish v. Missouri Pac. R. Co., 1890, 102 Mo. 669, 15 S.W. 315; Selleck v. City of Janesville, 1899, 104 Wis. 570, 80 N.W. 944; Gainesville, H. & W. R. Co. v. Lacy, 1893, 86 Tex. 244, 24 S.W. 269; Anderson v. Great Northern R. Co., 1908, 15 Idaho 513, 99 P. 91.

There is still considerable authority to the contrary, as to injuries to children. Gilbert v. Stanton Brewery Co., 1946, 295 N.Y. 270, 67 N.E.2d 155; Quinn v. City of Pittsburgh, 1914, 243 Pa. 521, 90 A. 353.

59. Tunget v. Cook, Mo.App.1936, 94 S.W.2d 921; Price v. H. B. Green Transportation Line, 7 Cir. 1961, 287 F.2d 363; Guevin v. Manchester St. Ry. Co., 1916, 78 N.H. 289, 99 A. 298. Contra, Golden v. R. L. Greene Paper Co., 1922, 44 R.I. 231, 116 A. 579.

60. Kimberly v. Howland, 1906, 143 N.C. 398, 55 S.E. 778; Kirkpatrick v. Metropolitan St. R. Co., 1908, 129 Mo.App. 524, 107 S.W. 1025. In the case of a child, the parent recovers for loss of earnings to be sustained during minority, the child for those lost after majority. Jackiewicz v. United Illuminating Co., 1927, 106 Conn. 310, 138 A. 151; Clarke v. Eighth Ave. R. Co., 1924, 238 N.Y. 246, 144 N.E. 516; Swift & Co. v. Holoubek, 1898, 55 Neb. 228, 75 N.W. 584; Harris v. Crawley, 1910, 161 Mich. 383, 126 N.W. 421.

61. Milde v. Leigh, 1947, 75 N.D. 418, 28 N.W.2d 530; Norton v. United States, N.D.Fla.1953, 110 F.Supp. 94; Travers v. Hartmann, 1914, 5 Boyce 302, 28 Del. 302, 92 A. 855; Chesapeake & O. R. Co. v. De Atley, 1912, 151 Ky. 109, 151 S.W. 363.

62. Cuming v. Brooklyn City R. Co., 1888, 109 N.Y. 95, 16 N.E. 65; Clarke v. Eighth Ave. R. Co., 1924, 238 N.Y. 246, 144 N.E. 516; Karr v. Parks, 1872, 44 Cal. 46; Stone v. Pleasanton, 1924, 115 Kan. 476, 223 P. 303. Contra: Hamlin v. N. H. Bragg & Sons, 1930, 129 Me. 165, 151 A. 197; Bryant v. Kansas City Rys. Co., Mo.App.1920, 217 S.W. 632.

63. Martin v. Payne, 1812, 9 Johns., N.Y., 387; White v. Murtland, 1874, 71 Ill. 250; Ellington v. Ellington, 1872, 47 Miss. 329; Kennedy v. Shea, 1872, 110 Mass. 147.

64. Netherland-American Steam Nav. Co. v. Hollander, 2 Cir. 1894, 59 F. 417; Frick v. St. Louis, K. C. & N. Ry. Co., 1882, 75 Mo. 542; Rice v. Norfolk Southern R. Co., 1914, 167 N.C. 1, 82 S.E. 1034; Sebring v. Bell Tel. Co. of Pennsylvania, 1922, 275 Pa. 131, 118 A. 729; Thompson v. Town of Fort Branch, 1931, 204 Ind. 152, 178 N.E. 440.

65. Jackiewicz v. United Illuminating Co., 1927, 106 Conn. 310, 138 A. 151; Goldberg v. Philadelphia Rapid Transit Co., 1930, 299 Pa. 79, 149 A. 104; Curran v. Lewiston, A. & W. St. R. Co., 1914, 112 Me. 96, 90 A. 973; Stotler v. Chicago & A. R. Co., 1906, 200 Mo. 107, 98 S.W. 509.

66. Dennis v. Clark, 1848, 2 Cush., Mass., 347; Trow v. Thomas, 1898, 70 Vt. 580, 41 A. 652; Sykes v. Lawlor, 1874, 49 Cal. 236; Cuming v. Brooklyn City R. Co., 1888, 109 N.Y. 95, 16 N.E. 65; Williams v. Ward, 1969, 18 Ohio App.2d 37, 246 N.E.2d 780; Contra: Whitaker v. Warren, 1880, 60 N.H. 20; Shields v. Yonge, 1854, 15 Ga. 349.

67. Beebe v. Kansas City, 1929, 223 Mo.App. 642, 17 S.W.2d 608; Memphis Steel Const. Co. v. Lister, 1919, 138 Tenn. 307, 197 S.W. 902; Kuchenmeister v. Los Angeles & S. L. R. Co., 1918, 52 Utah 116, 172 P. 725; Chesapeake & O. R. Co. v. De Atley, 1912, 151 Ky. 109, 151 S.W. 363. Cf. Southern R. Co. v. Flemister, 1904, 120 Ga. 524, 48 S.E. 160 (abandonment of child).

It has been held that the parent may waive his claim and permit the child to recover such elements of damages as medical expenses in his own action.

cipation once conferred cannot be revoked for purposes of suit.[68] The mother of an injured child cannot recover,[69] unless the child is illegitimate, or she has become entitled to its services, through the death or abandonment of the father or a decree giving her custody.[70] In a few states the Married Women's Acts have been interpreted to mean that the wife no longer owes her husband services, and hence that when she is injured he has no action for loss of "consortium," even in its more sentimental aspects of society, sex and affectionate relations,[71] and so his recovery is limited to the expenses he has incurred in caring for her.[72] In two or three others such statutes have been held to do away with the husband's action entirely.[73]

The great majority of the courts have rejected this conclusion and have held that, notwithstanding the altered status of married women, the husband may still recover substantially as at common law,[74] with the exception that the earnings of the wife outside of the home belong to her, and hence any loss of capacity to engage in such outside work must be recovered in her own action.[75]

Defenses

The right of the husband or parent to recover will of course depend upon the existence of tortious conduct on the part of the defendant. Normally this means that there must be a tort for which an action might be maintained by the injured wife, or child. Thus a parent may not recover where the child's injury results from the negligence of an independent contractor [76] or a fellow servant [77] for which the defendant is not responsible, or where the defendant owes the child

National City Development Co. v. McFerran, Mun. App.D.C.1947, 55 A.2d 342; Kentucky Service Co. v. Miracle, 1933, 246 Ky. 797, 56 S.W.2d 521.

68. Memphis Steel Const. Co. v. Lister, 1919, 138 Tenn. 307, 197 S.W. 902, indicating also that the parent may recover where the emancipation is partial, and the minor is permitted to work outside for his own wages, but lives with the family and contributes to its expenses.

69. Keller v. City of St. Louis, 1899, 152 Mo. 596, 54 S.W. 438, laying stress on the correlation between the right to services and the duty to support. See Note, 1928, 42 Harv.L.Rev. 112.

70. Marks v. City of New York, Sup.Ct.1950, 101 N.Y.S.2d 105; Southwestern Gas & Electric Co. v. Denney, 1935, 190 Ark. 934, 82 S.W.2d 17; McGarr v. National & Providence Worsted Mills, 1902, 24 R.I. 447, 53 A. 320; Briscoe v. Price, 1916, 275 Ill. 63, 113 N.E. 881.

71. Whitcomb v. New York, N. H. & H. R. Co., 1913, 215 Mass. 440, 102 N.E. 663; Marri v. Stamford St. R. Co., 1911, 84 Conn. 9, 78 A. 582; Golden v. R. L. Greene Paper Co., 1922, 44 R.I. 231, 116 A. 579, 21 A.L.R. 1514; Blair v. Seitner Dry Goods Co., 1915, 184 Mich. 304, 151 N.W. 724 (allowing recovery, however, for loss of services rendered in fact). These courts have been much influenced by the denial of the wife's action in the leading case of Feneff v. New York Cent. & H. R. R. Co., 1909, 203 Mass. 278, 89 N.E. 436.

72. Bolger v. Boston Elevated R. Co., 1910, 205 Mass. 420, 91 N.E. 389; Erickson v. Buckley, 1918, 230 Mass. 467, 120 N.E. 126.

73. Helmstetler v. Duke Power Co., 1945, 224 N.C. 821, 32 S.E.2d 611; Floyd v. Miller, 1950, 190 Va.

303, 57 S.E.2d 114; Taylor v. S. H. Kress & Co., 1932, 136 Kan. 155, 12 P.2d 808.

74. Hansen v. Costello, 1939, 125 Conn. 386, 5 A.2d 880; Aderhold v. Stewart, 1935, 172 Okl. 77, 46 P.2d 346; Leadbetter v. Glaisyer, 9 Cir. 1930, 44 F.2d 350; Tomme v. Pullman Co., 1922, 207 Ala. 511, 93 So. 462; Brahan v. Meridian Light & R. Co., 1919, 121 Miss. 269, 83 So. 467.

See Holbrook, The Change in the Meaning of Consortium, 1923, 22 Mich.L.Rev. 1; Lippman, The Breakdown of Consortium, 1930, 30 Col.L.Rev. 651; Hannigan, Damages Recoverable by Husband for Injury to Wife, 1916, 16 Col.L.Rev. 122; Warren, Husband's Right to Wife's Services, 1925, 38 Harv.L. Rev. 421.

75. Atchison, T. & S. F. R. Co. v. Dickey, 1895, 1 Kan.App. 770, 41 P. 1070; Gregory v. Oakland Motor Car Co., 1914, 181 Mich. 101, 147 N.W. 614. See Loughrey v. Pennsylvania R. Co., 1925, 284 Pa. 267, 131 A. 260.

76. Regan v. Superb Theater, 1915, 220 Mass. 259, 107 N.E. 984.

77. Zarba v. Lane, 1947, 322 Mass. 132, 16 N.E.2d 318; Harris v. A. J. Spencer Lumber Co., 1914, 185 Ala. 648, 64 So. 557; King v. Floding, 1916, 18 Ga. App. 280, 89 S.E. 451.

no duty of care,[78] or takes all reasonable precautions.[79]

From this the courts generally have concluded, by reasoning which remains rather obscure, that the action of the husband or parent will be defeated by defenses which would bar that of the wife or child. Thus contributory negligence [80] or assumption of risk [81] on the part of the injured person, or a statute of limitations applicable to him [82]

have been held to defeat the recovery. The provisions of some of the workmen's compensation acts taking away the common law action of the injured employee have been construed to have the same effect upon an action for loss of services,[83] and so have the limitations set up in wrongful death actions,[84] although the contrary conclusion has been reached under other statutes.[85] Apart from the threadbare fiction of "imputed" negligence,[86] a variety of highly ingenious reasons have been offered to explain such a result: the cause of action is a "derivative" one, analogous to an assigned contract; [87] or there is only one cause of action, in two parties; [88] or, in one remarkable case,

78. Jones v. Schmidt, 1953, 349 Ill.App. 336, 110 N.E. 2d 688 (landowner); Shiels v. Audette, 1934, 119 Conn. 75, 174 A. 323 (automobile guest); Arritt v. Fisher, 1938, 286 Mich. 419, 282 N.W. 200 (same); Cavanaugh v. First Nat. Stores, 1952, 329 Mass. 179, ¹⁰⁷ N.E.2d 307 (prenatal injury); Stemmer v. Kline, 1942, 128 N.J.L. 455, 26 A.2d 489 (same).

79. Gurll v. Massasoit Greyhound Ass'n, 1949, 325 Mass. 76, 89 N.E.2d 12; Neville v. American Barge Line Co., W.D.Pa.1952, 105 F.Supp. 405; Warrior Mfg. Co. v. Jones, 1908, 155 Ala. 379, 46 So. 456; Savage v. New York, N. H. & H. R. Co., 2 Cir. 1911, 185 F. 778.

80. Wife: Chicago, B. & Q. R. Co. v. Honey, 8 Cir. 1894, 63 F. 39, 26 L.R.A. 42; Jordan v. City of Pittsburgh, 1939, 332 Pa. 230, 3 A.2d 677; Ross v. Cuthbert, 1964, 239 Or. 429, 397 P.2d 529; Cawley v. La Crosse City R. Co., 1900, 106 Wis. 239, 82 N. W. 197; Pioneer Const. Co. v. Bergeron, 1969, —— Colo. ——, 462 P.2d 589.

Child: Brown v. Slentz, 1958, 237 Ind. 497, 147 N.E.2d 239; Callies v. Reliance Laundry Co., 1925, 188 Wis. 376, 206 N.W. 198; Boyett v. Airline Lumber Co., Okl.1954, 277 P.2d 676; Barlow v. Lowery, 1948, 143 Me. 214, 59 A.2d 702; Wineman v. Carter, 1942, 212 Minn. 298, 4 N.W.2d 83. Cf. Nelson v. Busby, 1969, 246 Ark. 243, 437 S.W.2d 799 (comparative negligence statute).

81. No case has been found dealing with this by name; but in many of the contributory negligence cases, the negligence has consisted of proceeding in the face of a known danger, and might well have been called assumption of risk. See Wineman v. Carter, 1942, 212 Minn. 298, 4 N.W.2d 83 (. . . "subject to any defenses that could be urged against the child in whom the whole cause of action, but for the law, would vest").

82. Carter v. Harlan Hospital Ass'n, 1936, 265 Ky. 452, 97 S.W.2d 9; Morgan v. United States, D.N.J. 1956, 143 F.Supp. 580. Cf. Pitrelli v. Cohen, 1938, 169 Misc. 117, 6 N.Y.S.2d 696, reversed 257 App.Div. 845, 12 N.Y.S.2d 71 (parent's action barred although son's not barred). Contra, Corpman v. Boyer, 1960, 171 Ohio St. 233, 169 N.E.2d 14. See Note, 1938, 52 Harv.L.Rev. 169.

83. Novack v. Montgomery Ward & Co., 1924, 158 Minn. 505, 198 N.W. 294; Danek v. Hommer, 1952, 9 N.J. 56, 87 A.2d 5 (wife); Guse v. A. O. Smith Corp., 1952, 260 Wis. 403, 51 N.W.2d 24 (wife); Ellis v. Fallert, 1957, 209 Or. 406, 307 P.2d 283 (wife); Ziegler v. United States Gypsum Co., 1960, 251 Iowa 714, 102 N.W.2d 152 (wife).

Some workmen's compensation acts contain express provisions to this effect. See Hilsinger v. Zimmerman Steel Co., 1922, 193 Iowa 708, 187 N.W. 493; Adkins v. Hope Eng. & Supply Co., 1917, 81 W.Va. 449, 94 S.E. 506. See, 1924, 9 Minn.L.Rev. 80.

The Federal Employers' Liability Act was construed in New York Cent. & H. R. R. Co. v. Tonsellito, 1917, 244 U.S. 360, as expressly intended to do away with the parent's remedy.

84. Lampe v. Lagomarcino-Grupe Co., 1959, 251 Iowa 204, 100 N.W.2d 1; Hoekstra v. Helgeland, 1959, 78 S.D. 82, 98 N.W.2d 669.

85. Workmen's Compensation: Crowder v. Carroll, 1968, 251 S.C. 192, 161 S.E.2d 235; King v. Viscoloid Co., 1914, 219 Mass. 420, 106 N.E. 988; Roxana Petroleum Co. v. Cope, 1928, 132 Okl. 152, 269 P. 1084; Allen v. Trester, 1924, 112 Neb. 515, 199 N.W. 841; Biddle v. Edward Hines Lbr. Co., D.Or.1962, 219 F.Supp. 69; Wrongful death: Alexander v. Botkins, 1959, 231 Ark. 373, 329 S.W.2d 530.

86. See Marbury Lumber Co. v. Westbrook, 1899, 121 Ala. 179, 25 So. 914; Winner v. Oakland Township, 1893, 158 Pa. 405, 27 A. 1110; Gilmore, Imputed Negligence, 1921, 1 Wis.L.Rev. 193, 206; supra, § 73.

87. See Callies v. Reliance Laundry Co., 1925, 188 Wis. 376, 206 N.W. 198; Note, 1933, 13 Boston U.L. Rev. 725.

88. As to this, see the rejection of the theory in Blanken v. Braslow, 1943, 130 N.J.L. 475, 33 A.2d

that the husband has relied on the wife's ability to exercise her own faculties, and must take the consequences of impliedly asserting that she is capable of going abroad alone.[89]

None of this reasoning can be supported, and all of it has been condemned by writers on the subject.[90] There is ample evidence that, historically and at present, the action is an independent one, and is not controlled by the disposition of that of the wife or child. Thus a release[91] or a judgment for the defendant[92] in one action will not operate as a bar to the other, and the death of one plaintiff will not abate the other's action.[93] This is borne out by a number of cases holding that where a person known to be a minor[94] is employed at dangerous work[95] without the consent of the parent, the child's contributory negligence or assumption of risk will not defeat recovery by the parent

for resulting injuries,[96] and that one who sells habit-forming drugs to a wife cannot set up her consent to buy and use them as a defense to the husband's action.[97] It would seem that the denial of recovery can be justified, if at all, only upon the ground that the action for loss of services is itself an historical exception to the rule that one person cannot maintain an action for an injury to another, and hence is limited to cases where the other is free from fault. But there seems to be little or no merit in denying recovery to the plaintiff for damage to his legally protected interests because another person has been negligent, merely upon such historical grounds.

It is of course obvious that the plaintiff's own contributory negligence or assumption

---

742, a case involving jurisdictional amount for removal of causes.

89. Chicago, B. & Q. R. Co. v. Honey, 8 Cir. 1894, 63 F. 39.

90. Gregory, the Contributory Negligence of Plaintiff's Wife or Child in an Action for Loss of Services, 1935, 2 U.Chi.L.Rev. 173; Gregory, Vicarious Responsibility and Contributory Negligence, 1932, 41 Yale L.J. 831; Gilmore, Imputed Negligence, 1921, 1 Wis.L.Rev. 193, 203, 211; James, Imputed Contributory Negligence, 1954, 14 La.L.Rev. 340, 354; Notes, 1926, 21 Mich.L.Rev. 592; 1932, 80 U.Pa.L.Rev. 1128, 1130.

Notwithstanding such criticism, it appears that only Wasney v. Juraszky, [1933] 1 Dom.L.Rep. 616, has reached the contrary conclusion.

91. Leslie v. Proctor & Gamble Mfg. Co., 1917, 102 Kan. 159, 169 P. 193; Missouri Pac. R. Co. v. Lasca, 1909, 79 Kan. 311, 99 P. 616; O'Brien v. Loeb, 1924, 229 Mich. 405, 201 N.W. 488.

92. See supra, note 51.

93. Graham v. Central of Georgia R. Co., 1928, 217 Ala. 658, 117 So. 286; Hyatt v. Adams, 1867, 16 Mich. 180; Trow v. Thomas, 1898, 70 Vt. 580, 41 A. 652.

94. In Ballard v. Smith, 1919, 183 Ky. 705, 210 S.W. 489, and Gulf, C. & S. F. R. Co. v. Redeker, 1886, 67 Tex. 190, 2 S.W. 527, it was held that the rule had no application unless the employer in the exercise of reasonable care should have known of the minority.

95. In Woodward Iron Co. v. Curl, 1907, 153 Ala. 205, 44 So. 974, and Ballard v. Smith, 1919, 183 Ky. 705, 210 S.W. 489, it was held for altogether mysterious reasons that the rule only applies to work which is "dangerous" or "hazardous." But see Meadows v. Du Bose Iron Co., 1924, 212 Ala. 288, 102 So. 431: "The decisions and textbooks in this connection use the words 'hazardous' and 'dangerous' interchangeably and mean a work or business that would ordinarily be dangerous or hazardous taking into consideration the age and experience of the minor. We find nothing in the books requiring that the work or business must be highly dangerous."

96. Marbury Lumber Co. v. Westbrook, 1898, 121 Ala. 179, 25 So. 914; Hendrickson v. Louisville & N. R. Co., 1910, 137 Ky. 562, 126 S.W. 117; Seglinski v. Baltimore Copper Smelting & Rolling Co., 1926, 149 Md. 541, 131 A. 774; Haynie v. North Carolina Elec. Power Co., 1911, 157 N.C. 503, 73 S.E. 198; Boutotte v. Daigle, 1915, 113 Md. 539, 95 A. 213; Texas & Pac. R. Co. v. Brick, 1892, 83 Tex. 526, 18 S.W. 947. These cases also hold that the parent's consent to employment in a non-dangerous occupation will not preclude recovery if the employer sets the child to work in a dangerous one, and he is injured as a result.

97. Hoard v. Peck, 1867, 56 Barb., N.Y., 202; Holleman v. Harward, 1896, 119 N.C. 150, 25 S.E. 972; Morris v. Owen, 1960, 102 Ga.App. 71, 115 S.E.2d 604; cf. Flandermeyer v. Cooper, 1912, 85 Ohio St. 327, 98 N.E. 102; Moberg v. Scott, 1917, 38 S.D. 422, 161 N.W. 998; Pratt v. Daly, 1940, 55 Ariz. 535, 104 P.2d 147. Compare the parent's action for seduction, supra, p. 884.

of risk will defeat his recovery for the resulting injury to his wife or child.[98]

Wife

The common law never recognized any right on the part of the wife to the services of her husband. As the social and legal inferior, she could not require him to work for her, and she had at least no common law remedy for deprivation of his society, intercourse and affections.[99] He was legally bound to provide for her and she was entitled to his support; but any injury to him did not terminate that obligation, and the tortfeasor was liable to the husband himself for any loss of earning power. It followed that there could be no additional recovery on behalf of the wife, even after the Married Women's Acts had removed her procedural disabilities and permitted her to sue in her own name. The development of the remedy for direct attack upon the marital relation by alienation of affections or criminal conversation,[1] which took place toward the close of the nineteenth century, found no parallel where the interference was indirect, through negligent or even intentional[2] injury to the husband. Accordingly it became the settled rule that the wife has no action in such a case for the loss of the various elements of "consortium,"[3] including services, sexual intercourse,[4] society and affectionate relations.

There has been almost universal condemnation of such a result on the part of legal writers.[5] Obviously it can have no other justification than that of history, or the fear of an undue extension of liability of the defendant, or a double recovery by wife and husband for the same damages.[6] The loss of "services" is an outworn fiction, and the

---

98. Contributory negligence: Lowery v. Berry, 1954, 153 Tex. 411, 269 S.W.2d 795; Kimpel v. Moore, 1934, 113 N.J.L. 220, 174 A. 209; Kimball v. Bauckman, 1932, 131 Me. 14, 158 A. 695; Potanko v. Sears, Roebuck & Co., 1951, 368 Pa. 582, 84 A.2d 522; Brennan v. Biber, 1966, 93 N.J.Super. 351, 225 A.2d 742, affirmed 99 N.J.Super. 247, 239 A.2d 261.

Assumption of risk: Sargent v. Williams, 1953, 152 Tex. 413, 258 S.W.2d 787; Beasley v. United States, E.D.S.C.1948, 81 F.Supp. 518; Hale v. Davies, 1952, 86 Ga.App. 130, 70 S.E.2d 923; Sjoberg v. White, 1951, 119 Utah 562, 230 P.2d 331; Wilson v. Newark Smelting & Ref. Co., 1945, 26 N.J.Misc. 51, 56 A.2d 619.

99. See supra, p. 881. " * * * the inferior hath no kind of property in the company, care, or assistance of the superior * * * and therefore can suffer no loss or injury." 3 Bl.Com. 142.

See Cowen, Domestic Relations: Action for Loss of Consortium, 1951, 25 Aust.L.J. 390, 1952, 26 Aust.L. J. 358; Note, 1963, 15 S.C.L.Rev. 810.

1. See supra, p. 883.

2. Nieberg v. Cohen, 1914, 83 Vt. 281, 92 A. 214; Boden v. Del-Mar Garage, 1933, 205 Ind. 59, 185 N. E. 860; Bevers v. Bradstreet, 1926, 170 Ark. 650,

280 S.W. 667. Cf. Anderson v. McGill Club, 1928, 51 Nev. 16, 266 P. 913, certiorari denied 273 U.S. 557.

3. Potter v. Schafter, 1965, 161 Me. 340, 211 A.2d 891; Roseberry v. Starkovich, 1963, 73 N.M. 211, 387 P.2d 321; Hoffman v. Dautel, 1964, 192 Kan. 406, 388 P.2d 615; Baldwin v. State, 1965, 125 Vt. 317, 215 A.2d 492; Rush v. Great American Ins. Co., 1964, 213 Tenn. 506, 376 S.W.2d 454.

4. Best v. Samuel Fox & Co., [1951] 2 K.B. 639, [1951] 2 All.Eng.Rep. 116; Landwehr v. Barbas, 1934, 241 App.Div. 769, 270 N.Y.S. 534.

5. Holbrook, The Change in the Meaning of Consortium, 1923, 22 Mich.L.Rev. 1; Lippman, The Breakdown of Consortium, 1930, 30 Col.L.Rev. 651; Green, Relational Interests, 1934, 29 Ill.L.Rev. 460, 466; Simeone, The Wife's Action for Loss of Consortium—Progress or No? 1957, 4 St. Louis U.L. Rev. 424; Notes, 1951, 29 N.C.L.Rev. 178; 1951, 20 Ford.L.Rev. 342; 1953, 41 Geo.L.J. 443; 1954, 39 Corn.L.Q. 761; 1957, 14 Wash. & Lee L.Rev. 324; 1958, 31 Temp.L.Q. 284; 1958, 13 U.Miami L.Rev. 92; 1960, 20 La.L.Rev. 731; 1962, 50 Ky.L.J. 263. Contra, Thurman, Recovery by Wife for Loss of Consortium of Husband, 1957, 24 Ins.Counsel J. 224; 1969, 18 Buff.L.Rev. 615; 1969, 47 N.C.L.Rev. 1006; 1965, 10 S.D.L.Rev. 120; 1967, 18 West.Res. L.Rev. 621; 1966, 10 St.L.L.Rev. 276.

6. "The reason for not securing the interest of wife or child in these cases seems to be that our modes of trial are such and our mode of assessment of damages by the verdict of a jury is necessarily so crude that if husband and wife were each allowed to sue, instead of each recovering an exact reparation, each would be pretty sure to recover what would repair the injury to both. Moreover, the injury to wife or child is very hard to measure in money. Hence, on a practical balancing of interests the wife is usually denied an action." Pound, Individual Interests in the Domestic Relations, 1913, 14 Mich.L.Rev. 177, 194.

wife's interest in the undisturbed relation with her consort is no less worthy of protection than that of the husband. Nor is any valid reason apparent for allowing her recovery for a direct interference by alienation of affections, and denying it for more indirect harm through personal injury to the husband, where no such distinction is made in his action. There remains of course the important fact that the husband is under the duty to support his wife, so that any compensation for loss of earning power paid to him goes indirectly to benefit her, while the wife is under no such corresponding duty. This must of course be taken into account in any determination of her damages.[7] But such elements of damage as her loss of the husband's society and affection, and in some cases even the expenses to which she has been put in caring for him, remain uncompensated.

All this criticism began at length to have its effect. A few courts began by allowing the wife to recover where there was intentional injury to her husband, as where he was sold narcotics or liquor;[8] and in many states the Dramshop Acts[9] have given her a similar remedy. Other courts have allowed her to recover for medical and funeral expenses for which she has become liable by reason of the injury.[10] The major break came, however, in 1950, in Hitaffer v. Argonne Co.,[11] when the District of Columbia Circuit threw overboard the ancient law, and recognized the wife's cause of action for harm to the marriage relation through mere negligent injury to her husband. The decision encountered strong initial opposition, and was rejected in a number of jurisdictions.[12] Around 1958 something of a current of support for the Hitaffer case set in, and since that date the trend has been definitely in the direction of approval. It now stands accepted, and the wife is allowed her action, in rather more than half of the jurisdictions which have considered the question.[13] Since a considerable number of the courts which have rejected the change have approved it in principle, but have said that it should be for the legislature to make, the prediction is probably justified that the trend will continue, and that public opinion as to the equality of the sexes will have its effect in persuading the courts.

Around 1965 a new argument entered this field, with the contention that the wife was denied the constitutional right to equal protection of the laws when she was not permitted to recover for loss of consortium, while the husband was.[14] Although the Supreme Court of the United States declined to

---

7. See Kotsiris v. Ling, Ky.1970, 451 S.W.2d 411; Manning v. Jones, 8 Cir. 1965, 349 F.2d 992.

8. Flandermeyer v. Cooper, 1912, 85 Ohio St. 327, 98 N.E. 102; Moberg v. Scott, 1917, 38 S.D. 422, 161 N.W. 998; Swanson v. Ball, 1940, 67 S.D. 161, 290 N.W. 482; Pratt v. Daly, 1940, 55 Ariz. 535, 104 P. 2d 147. See Note, 1940, 2 Wash. & Lee L.Rev. 153. Cf. Clark v. Hill, 1897, 69 Mo.App. 541 (husband driven insane).

9. See Benes v. Campion, 1932, 186 Minn. 578, 244 N. W. 72; Wood v. Lentz, 1898, 116 Mich. 275, 74 N.W. 462; Whipple v. Rosenstock, 1915, 99 Neb. 153, 155 N.W. 898.

10. Hansen v. Hayes, 1944, 175 Or. 358, 154 P.2d 202; Follansbee v. Benzenberg, 1954, 122 Cal.App.2d 466, 265 P.2d 183; Thompson v. City of Bushnell, 1952, 346 Ill.App. 352, 105 N.E.2d 311; McDaniel v. Trent Mills, 1929, 197 N.C. 342, 148 S.E. 440.

11. 1950, 87 U.S.App.D.C. 57, 183 F.2d 811, cert. denied 340 U.S. 852.

12. Neuberg v. Bobowicz, 1960, 401 Pa. 146, 162 A.2d 662; Deshotel v. Atchison, T. & S. F. R. Co., 1958, 50 Cal.2d 664, 328 P.2d 449; Page v. Winter, 1962, 240 S.C. 516, 126 S.E.2d 570; Seagraves v. Legg, 1962, 147 W.Va. 331, 127 S.E.2d 605; Simpson v. Poindexter, 1961, 241 Miss. 854, 133 So.2d 286, suggestion of error overruled, 134 So.2d 445.

13. Millington v. Southeastern Elev. Co., 1968, 22 N. Y.2d 498, 293 N.Y.S.2d 305, 239 N.E.2d 897; Fitzgerald v. Meissuer & Hicks, Inc., 1968, 38 Wis.2d 571, 157 N.W.2d 595; Troue v. Mesher, 1969, — Ind. —, 252 N.E.2d 800; Thill v. Modern Erecting Co., 1969, 284 Minn. 508, 170 N.W.2d 865; Clouston v. Remlinger Oldsmobile Cadillac, Inc., 1970, 22 Ohio St.2d 65, 258 N.E.2d 230; Kotsiris v. Ling, Ky.1970, 451 S.W.2d 411.

14. Clem v. Brown, 1965, 3 Ohio Misc. 167, 207 N.E. 2d 398.

pass on this argument,[15] there are enough federal and state court decisions which have approved it to make it at least a makeweight of some consequence.[16]

Some of the courts which have permitted the wife's action have been so far troubled by the possibility of double recovery of the same element of damages,[17] that they have conditioned the action upon joinder with that of the husband for his own injuries, and have said that in the absence of such joinder the wife cannot recover.[18] While the joinder appears eminently desirable in the ordinary case, there will no doubt be enough instances where it is inconvenient or impossible so that it should not be an absolute requirement.[19]

Child

The interest of the child in proper parental care, which has received only scanty recognition in cases of intentional interference,[20] has run into a stone wall where there is merely negligent injury to the parent. The liability has been rejected even in the District of Columbia,[21] which began the recognition of the wife's cause of action; and there has been the same refusal to consider it in half a dozen other jurisdictions.[22] The sole flicker of recognition came from a lower federal court in Hawaii,[23] guessing at Hawaiian law; but after the supreme court of Hawaii [24] itself had held to the contrary, the federal decision had to be reversed on appeal.[25]

It is not easy to understand and appreciate this reluctance to compensate the child who has been deprived of the care, companionship and education of his mother, or for that matter his father, through the defendant's negligence. This is surely a genuine injury, and a serious one, which has received a great deal more sympathy from the legal writers than from the judges.[26] There is of

15. See 386 U.S. 970, denying certiorari in Krohn v. Richardson-Merrell, Inc., 1966, 219 Tenn. 37, 406 S. W.2d 166.

16. Umpleby v. Dorsey, 1967, 10 Ohio Misc. 288, 227 N.E.2d 274; Owen v. Illinois Baking Corp., W.D. Mich.1966, 260 F.Supp. 820; Karczewski v. Baltimore & Ohio R. Co., N.D.Ill.1967, 274 F.Supp. 169; Clouston v. Remlinger Oldsmobile Cadillac, Inc., 1970, 22 Ohio St.2d 65, 258 N.E.2d 230. See Deems v. Western Maryland R. Co., 1967, 247 Md. 95, 231 A.2d 514; Black v. United States, D.Utah 1967, 263 F.Supp. 470; Moran v. Quality Aluminum Casting Co., 1967, 34 Wis.2d 542, 150 N.W.2d 137. See Notes, 1967, 19 Ala.L.Rev. 551, 1968, 54 Iowa L.Rev. 510.

17. See supra, p. 895.

18. Ekalo v. Constructive Service Corp. of America, 1965, 46 N.J. 82, 215 A.2d 1; Deems v. Western Maryland R. Co., 1967, 247 Md. 95, 231 A.2d 514; Moran v. Quality Aluminum Casting Co., 1967, 34 Wis.2d 542, 140 N.W.2d 137; Thill v. Modern Erecting Co., 1969, 284 Minn. 508, 170 N.W.2d 865. See Notes, 1968, 13 Vill.L.Rev. 418; 1967, 27 Md.L.Rev. 403.

19. "Since in New York it is rare, if not unknown, to try a husband's consortium action separately from his wife's negligence action, the fear of duplicative damages is wholly unsupportable. Furthermore if any plaintiff should attempt to exploit the possibility of double recovery by bringing separate actions, motions to consolidate would quickly resolve that difficulty." Millington v. Southeastern Elev. Co., 1968, 22 N.Y.2d 498, 293 N.Y.S.2d 305, 239 N.E.2d 897. See also Kotsiris v. Ling, Ky.1970, 451 S.W.2d 411.

Cf. Manley v. Horton, Mo.1967, 414 S.W.2d 254 (inconsistent verdicts in actions of husband and wife).

20. See supra, p. 886.

21. Hill v. Sibley Memorial Hospital, D.D.C.1952, 108 F.Supp. 729; Pleasant v. Washington Sand & Gravel Co., 1958, 104 U.S.App.D.C. 374, 262 F.2d 471.

22. Jeune v. Del E. Webb Const. Co., 1954, 77 Ariz. 226, 269 P.2d 723; Turner v. Atlantic Coast Line R. Co., N.D.Ga.1958, 159 F.Supp. 590; Hoffman v. Dautel, 1961, 189 Kan. 165, 368 P.2d 57; Erhardt v. Havens, Inc., 1958, 53 Wash.2d 103, 330 P.2d 1010; Hayrynen v. White Pine Copper Co., 1968, 9 Mich. App. 452, 157 N.W.2d 502.

23. Scruggs v. Meredith, D.Hawaii 1955, 134 F.Supp. 868.

24. In Halberg v. Young, 1957, 41 Hawaii 634.

25. Meredith v. Scruggs, 9 Cir. 1957, 244 F.2d 604.

26. See Notes, 1953, 6 Vand.L.Rev. 926; 1953, 2 St. Louis L.Rev. 305; 1962, 11 Kan.L.Rev. 186; 1956, 54 Mich.L.Rev. 1023; 1956, 42 Corn.L.Q. 115; 1956, 8 S.C.L.Q. 477.

course the same problem of preventing double compensation as in the case of the wife's action, since the child will to some extent benefit by any sum recovered by the injured parent; but it is quite evident that this will not and cannot recompense him for all that he has lost. The obstacles in the way of satisfactory limitation of recovery are no greater than in the case of the wife. As has been said even by one court [27] which considered itself forced to deny recovery, it is difficult "on the basis of natural justice to reach the conclusion that this type of action will not lie." It is particularly difficult when recovery is permitted to the wife, but denied to the child.

27. Hill v. Sibley Memorial Hospital, D.D.C.1952, 108 F.Supp. 739.

CHAPTER 24

SURVIVAL AND WRONGFUL DEATH

126. SURVIVAL OF ACTIONS

There are four aspects in which the death of a person connected with a tort may affect the recovery. These are as follows:

1. The death of the tortfeasor may terminate his liability, and prevent an action against his estate or his personal representative.

2. The death of the person injured may terminate an existing cause of action, and prevent any recovery by his estate or his representative.

3. The death of the person injured may itself create a new cause of action in his estate or his representative, or add a new element of damages to a tort action surviving to them.

4. The death of the injured person may create a cause of action in members of his family for loss of the benefits of his relation with them.

Only the last of these, of course, directly concerns the family relation; but the other three at least affect the decedent's estate, and so indirectly the interests of surviving relatives, and there are questions of policy common to all four, so that they may conveniently be dealt with together at this point. A rather tangled history may be summarized briefly by saying that under the common law death gave rise to no causes of action, and terminated all those for personal torts; and that in all four of the above respects statutes now have altered the common law rule to a greater or less extent to authorize recovery. Since these statutes vary greatly in their provisions, the space available will permit only very general statements, and the reader must be referred to the particular acts of each jurisdiction.[1]

The origin of the rule that personal tort actions die with the person of the plaintiff or the defendant is rather obscure [2]—the more so as contract actions which were equally "personal" were held to survive the death of either.[3] The best conjecture on the subject is that it was a result of the development of the tort remedy as an adjunct and incident to criminal punishment in the old appeal of felony and the action of trespass which succeeded it. Since the defendant could not be punished when he was dead, it was natural to regard his demise as terminating the criminal action, and tort liability with it. If it was the plaintiff who died, the early cases usually were those of homicide, for which the crown executed the defendant and confiscated all his property, so that nothing was left for tort compensation; and if not homicide, it was still to be expected that lesser crimes should be redressed by the crown rather than the successors of the deceased.

Whatever the explanation, the rule became settled. Under Edward III it was some-

1. See Oppenheim, The Survival of Tort Claims and the Action for Wrongful Death—A Survey and a Proposal, 1942, 16 Tul.L.Rev. 386.

2. See Winfield, Death as Affecting Liability in Tort, 1929, 29 Col.L.Rev. 239; Smedley, Wrongful Death—Bases of the Common Law Rules, 1960, 13 Vand.L.Rev. 605; 3 Holdsworth, History of English Law, 3d Ed. 1923, 333–336, 576–585, 676–677; Pollock, Law of Torts, 12th Ed. 1923, 66–72; Holdsworth Origin of the Rule in Baker v. Bolton, 1916, 32 L.Q.Rev. 431; Evans, Survival of Claims For and Against Executors and Administrators, 1931, 19 Ky.L.J. 195; Note, 1929, 18 Cal.L.Rev. 44.

3. See 3 Holdsworth, History of English Law, 3d Ed. 1923, 576–585.

what altered by statutes, which were construed to permit only actions for the loss, damage or conversion of personal property to survive to the executor or administrator of the plaintiff.[4] These statutes did not cover torts against land, and made no provision for survival of the death of the defendant;[5] and it was not until 1833 that these were covered by another English statute.[6] The American courts took over the common law as it existed prior to 1833. They recognized the survival of actions for torts affecting personal property to the representative of a deceased plaintiff,[7] but not as against the estate of the decedent,[8] unless the estate was unjustly enriched by the tort so that the action could be maintained as one of quasi-contract restitution.[9] But there was no survival of the death of either in the case of torts against real property, such as trespass,[10] waste,[11] or private nuisance;[12] or those affecting the person, such as assault and battery,[13] false imprisonment,[14] medical malpractice,[15] or other negligent personal injuries,[16] even though the negligence itself was a breach of contract.[17] The same was true as to invasions of the more intangible interests of personality, such as defamation,[18] or malicious prosecution,[19] or personal

4. 4 Edw. III, c. 7; 25 Edw. III, st. 5, c. 5; see Smith v. Colgay, 1595, Cro.Eliz. 384, 78 Eng.Rep. 630; Russell's Case, 1565, 5 Co.Rep. 27a, 77 Eng. Rep. 91.

5. See Hambly v. Trott, 1776, 1 Cowp. 371, 98 Eng. Rep. 1136.

6. 3 & 4 Wm. IV, c. 42. There was no survival of personal injury actions in England until it was provided by the Law Reform Act, 1934, 24 & 25 Geo. V, c. 41.

7. Potter v. Van Vranken, 1867, 36 N.Y. 619; Jenkins v. McConico, 1855, 26 Ala. 213; Reist v. Heilbrenner, 1825, 11 Serg. & R., Pa., 131; Kingsbury's Ex'rs v. Lane's Ex'r, 1855, 21 Mo. 115; see Swartz v. Rosenkrans, 1925, 78 Colo. 167, 240 P. 333.

8. Petts v. Ison, 1852, 11 Ga. 151; Loomis v. Ives, 1834, 15 Pick., Mass., 435; Willard v. Mohn, 1913, 24 N.D. 386, 139 N.W. 981.

9. Patton v. Brady, 1902, 184 U.S. 608; Ex'rs of Middleton v. Robinson, 1787, 1 S.C.Law 58; Coleman v. Woodworth, 1866, 28 Cal. 567; Trust Co. of Norfolk v. Fletcher, 1929, 152 Va. 868, 148 S.E. 785. See United States v. Daniel, 1848, 6 How., U.S., 11, 12 L.Ed. 323.

10. Sims v. Davis, 1904, 70 S.C. 362, 49 S.E. 872; Reed v. Peoria & Oquawka R. Co. 1857, 18 Ill. 403; O'Connor v. Corbitt, 1853, 3 Cal. 370; cf. Johnson v. Elwood, 1880, 82 N.Y. 362 (injunction).

11. Peterson Browne v. Blick, 1819, 7 N.C. 511.

12. Grobart v. North Jersey Dist. Water Supply Comm., 1948, 142 N.J.Eq. 60, 58 A.2d 796 (diversion); Holmes v. Moore, 1827, 5 Pick., Mass., 257 (same); Forist v. Androscoggin River Imp. Co., 1872, 52 N.H. 477 (flowing); Kennedy v. McAfee's Ex'x, 1822, 1 Litt., Ky., 169 (same).

13. Byrd v. Byrd, 1940, 122 W.Va. 115, 7 S.E. 507; Henshaw v. Miller, 1854, 17 How., U. S., 212; Brown v. Wightman, 1915, 47 Utah 31, 151 P. 366; Hadley v. Bryars' Adm'r, 1877, 58 Ala. 185.

14. First Nat. Bank of Portland v. Wall, 1939, 161 Or. 152, 88 P.2d 311; Harker v. Clark, 1881, 57 Cal. 245; Whitten v. Bennert, C.C.Conn.1896, 77 F. 271.

15. Ulvig v. McKennan Hospital, 1930, 56 S.D. 509, 229 N.W. 383; Kuhn v. Brownfield, 1890, 34 W.Va. 252, 12 S.E. 519; Boor v. Lowery, 1885, 103 Ind. 468, 3 N.E. 151; Vittum v. Gilman, 1869, 48 N.H. 416. Actions against attorneys for professional negligence sometimes were held to survive as primarily based on breach of contract. Tichenor v. Hayes, 1879, 41 N.J.L. 193; Miller v. Wilson, 1854, 24 Pa. 114; Stimpson v. Sprague, 1830, 6 Me. 470.

16. Pulling v. Great Eastern R. Co., 1882, L.R. 9 Q. B.D. 110; Herzog v. Stern, 1934, 264 N.Y. 379, 191 N.E. 23, cert. denied, 1934, 293 U.S. 597; Brown v. Stephens, 1932, 165 Tenn. 85, 52 S.W.2d 146; Simons v. Kidd, 1949, 73 S.D. 41, 38 N.W.2d 883; Clark v. Goodwin, 1915, 170 Cal. 527, 150 P. 357.

17. The fact that the action is in form one for breach of contract does not affect the result. McClure v. Johnson, 1937, 50 Ariz. 76, 69 P.2d 573 (private transportation); Compton v. Evans, 1939, 200 Wash. 125, 93 P.2d 341 (same); Gosling v. Nichols, 1943, 59 Cal.App.2d 442, 139 P.2d 86 (same); Tuttle v. Short, 1930, 42 Wyo. 1, 288 P. 524 (injury to prisoner, action on sheriff's bond); Byrd v. Byrd, 1940, 122 W.Va. 115, 7 S.E.2d 507 (same). See supra, p. 618.

18. Begole v. Ferguson, 1941, 299 Mich. 416, 300 N.W. 146; Jones v. Matson, 1940, 4 Wash.2d 659, 104 P. 2d 591; Alles v. Interstate Power Co., 1936, 176 Okl. 252, 55 P.2d 751; Miller v. Nuckolls, 1905, 76 Ark. 485, 89 S.W. 88; Blodgett v. Greenfield, 1929, 101 Cal.App. 399, 281 P. 594; Chiagouris v. Jovan, 1963, 43 Ill.App.2d 213, 193 N.E.2d 205.

19. Meyer v. Peter, 1931, 9 N.J.Misc. 1309, 157 A. 250; Scheirman v. Pemberton, 1932, 180 Okl. 196, 68 P.2d 857; Woodford v. McDaniels, 1914, 73 W. Va. 736, 81 S.E. 544; Lapique v. Dunnigan, 1930,

relations with others, as in alienation of affections,[20] seduction,[21] or loss of services of wife or child.[22] Misrepresentation actions normally did not survive,[23] but quite often it was accomplished by treating them as essentially contractual in their nature,[24] or as a deprivation of property [25] or a suit for the restitution of property;[26] and the same result was sometimes reached as to actions for interference with business relations,[27] or any

other tort action that could be fitted into the desired category.

Apart from historical accident, no rhyme or reason is discernible in these distinctions, and they are now very much altered by statute.[28] All jurisdictions have modified the common law to some extent, if only to provide that causes of action for injuries to all tangible property, personal or real, shall survive the death of both parties.[29] Most of them have gone further, and allow the survival of causes for non-personal injuries, such as deceit. About half of the states permit even personal injury actions to survive the death of either party,[30] and this regardless of the cause of death.[31] In four of these jurisdictions the result was first accomplished by the overthrow of the common law, without the aid of a statute.[32] In only six or seven is the statute construed to cover invasions of intangible interests of person-

210 Cal. 281, 291 P. 184; Shedd v. Patterson, 1924, 312 Ill. 371, 144 N.E. 5.

20. Simmons v. Boston Safe Deposit Co., 1938, 301 Mass. 167, 16 N.E.2d 670; Howard v. Lunaburg, 1927, 192 Wis. 507, 213 N.W. 301; White v. Safe Deposit & Trust Co. of Baltimore, 1922, 140 Md. 593, 118 A. 77; Gross' Adm'r v. Ledford, 1921, 190 Ky. 526, 228 S.W. 24.

21. Brawner v. Sterdevant, 1850, 9 Ga. 69; Shafer v. Grimes, 1867, 23 Iowa 550.

22. State ex rel. National Refining Co. v. Seehorn, 1939, 344 Mo. 547, 127 S.W.2d 418; Gorlitzer v. Wolffberg, 1913, 208 N.Y. 475, 102 N.E. 528; Hey v. Prime, 1908, 197 Mass. 474, 84 N.E. 141; King v. Southern R. Co., 1906, 126 Ga. 794, 55 S.E. 965. See Note, 1932, 9 N.Y.U.L.Q.Rev. 344.

23. Ahern v. McGlinchy, 1914, 112 Me. 58, 90 A. 709; State ex rel. Baeder v. Blake, 1919, 107 Wash. 294, 181 P. 685; Grabow v. Bergeth, 1930, 59 N.D. 214, 229 N.W. 282; Givens v. Powell, 1921, 239 Mass. 110, 131 N.E. 193; Halsey v. Minnesota-South Carolina Land & Timber Co., E.D.S.C.1932, 54 F.2d 933.

Accord, as to actions of tort or contract for breach of warranty: Harkins v. Provenzo, 1921, 116 Misc. 61, 189 N.Y.S. 258; Bernstein v. Queens County Jockey Club, 1927, 222 App.Div. 191, 225 N.Y.S. 449; Singley v. Bigelow, 1930, 108 Cal.App. 436, 291 P. 899.

24. Booth's Adm'r v. Northrop, 1858, 27 Conn. 325; Bryant v. Estate of Rich, 1895, 104 Mich. 124, 62 N.W. 146.

25. Vragnizan v. Savings Union Bank & Trust Co., 1916, 31 Cal.App. 709, 161 P. 507; Reidi v. Heinzl, 1942, 240 Wis. 297, 3 N.W.2d 366; Czako v. Orban, 1938, 133 Ohio St. 148, 13 N.E.2d 121; Trust Co. of Norfolk v. Fletcher, 1929, 152 Va. 868, 148 S.E. 785; Zartner v. Holzhauer, 1931, 204 Wis. 18, 234 N.W. 508.

26. Lufkin v. Cutting, 1917, 225 Mass. 599, 114 N.E. 822; Houston v. Rosborough, 9 Cir. 1924, 295 F. 137; Micheletti v. Moidel, 1934, 94 Colo. 587, 32 P.2d 266.

27. Sullivan v. Associated Billposters and Distributors of United States and Canada, 2 Cir. 1925, 6 F.

2d 1000, 42 A.L.R. 503; Bethlehem Fabricators v. H. D. Watts Co., 1934, 286 Mass. 556, 190 N.E. 828, 93 A.L.R. 1124. Contra: Caillouet v. American Sugar Refining Co., D.La.1917, 250 F. 639; Jones v. Matson, 1940, 4 Wash.2d 659, 104 P.2d 591.

28. See Livingston, Survival of Tort Actions: A Proposal for California Legislation, 1949, 37 Cal.L.Rev. 63; Evans, A Comparative Study of the Statutory Survival of Tort Claims, 1931, 29 Mich.L.Rev. 969; Note, 1935, 48 Harv.L.Rev. 1008; Report of New York Law Revision Commission, Survival of Tort Claims, 1935.

29. An exception is Georgia, where real property actions still do not survive. Davis v. Atlanta Gas Light Co., 1950, 82 Ga.App. 460, 61 S.E. 510.

30. See for example Fitzgerald v. Hale, 1956, 247 Iowa 1194, 78 N.W.2d 509; Posner v. Koplin, 1956, 94 Ga.App. 306, 94 S.E.2d 434; Mohler v. Worley, 1955, 179 Pa.Super. 56, 116 A.2d 342.

31. Prowant v. Kings-X, Inc., 1959, 185 Kan. 602, 347 P.2d 254, reversing 1958, 184 Kan. 413, 337 P.2d 1021.

32. Waller v. First Sav. & Trust Co., 1931, 103 Fla. 1025, 138 So. 780; In re Grainger's Estate, 1931, 121 Neb. 338, 237 N.W. 153; Hunt v. Authier, 1946, 28 Cal.2d 288, 169 P.2d 913 (holding by judicial ingenuity that the family's loss of material benefits through injury to the husband is a "property" right). Cf. McDaniel v. Bullard, 1966, 34 Ill.2d 487, 216 N.E.2d 140 (loss of support held "personal property").

ality, such as defamation; and in a small number only actions pending at the time of death survive. Where survival is permitted as to one party, it usually is allowed as to the other; but this is not always the case.[33] As the title of the plaintiff's administrator to the cause of action is regarded as acquired by transfer, the courts have tended to adopt survival as a criterion of assignability, with the result that the survival statutes have had the incidental effect of broadening the list of actions that are capable of being assigned.[34]

There has been some dispute as to the desirability of broad survival statutes. Opposition to them is based upon the argument that justice does not require a windfall to the plaintiff's heirs by way of compensation for an injury to him when they have suffered none of their own, together with the contention that since one party is dead and the other necessarily not disinterested the truth will be difficult to ascertain in court. The answer to the latter objection is that no serious difficulties have arisen as to contract actions and those torts which now survive. As to the first, the modern trend is definitely toward the view that tort causes of action and liabilities are as fairly a part of the estate of either plaintiff or defendant as contract debts, and that the question is rather one of why a fortuitous event such as death should extinguish a valid action.[35] Accord-

ingly, survival statutes gradually are being extended;[36] and it may be expected that ultimately all tort actions will survive to the same extent as those founded on contract.

127. WRONGFUL DEATH

When the defendant's tort was the responsible cause of the plaintiff's death, the same rather uncertain historical reasons which barred the survival of previous torts arose to prevent any new cause of action in his representative or his estate based on the death itself. If it were conceded that killing the plaintiff was a tort toward him, he was none the less dead, and the tort died with him.[37] It is not so clear, however, that there was ever any adequate reason for denying an action to a third party, still alive, who had lost the services of the plaintiff by reason of his death; and it is possible that such an action might at one time have been maintained.[38] But in 1808 Lord Ellenborough, whose forte was never common sense, held without citing any authority that a husband had no action for loss of his wife's services through her death, and declared in broad terms that "in a civil court the death of a human being could not be complained of as

---

tors and Administrators, 1931, 29 Mich.L.Rev. 969; Notes, 1931, 44 Harv.L.Rev. 980; 1935, 48 Harv.L. Rev. 1008; 1928, 13 Corn.L.Q. 596; 1929, 18 Cal.L. Rev. 44; 1931, 19 Cal.L.Rev. 289; 1936, 24 Cal.L. Rev. 716.

36. Ivey v. Wiggins, 1964, 276 Ala. 106, 159 So.2d 618 (wrongful death action survives death of defendant); Emmanuel v. Bovino, 1966, 26 Conn.Sup. 356, 223 A.2d 541 (alienation of affections).

37. Huggins v. Butcher, 1607, 1 Brown. & Golds. 205, 123 Eng.Rep. 756. See Holdsworth, The Origin of the Rule in Baker v. Bolton, 1916, 32 L.Q.Rev. 431; 3 Holdsworth, History of English Law, 3d Ed. 1923, 331–336; Malone, The Genesis of Wrongful Death, 1965, 17 Stan.L.Rev. 1043; Winfield, Death as Affecting Liability in Tort, 1929, 29 Col.L.Rev. 239; Hay, Death as a Civil Cause of Action in Massachusetts, 1893, 7 Harv.L.Rev. 170; Smedley, Wrongful Death—Bases of the Common Law Rules, 1960, 13 Vand.L.Rev. 605.

38. Winfield, Death as Affecting Liability in Tort, 1929, 29 Col.L.Rev. 239, 252.

---

33. Thus the Minnesota statute provides for survival only of the death of the defendant, and in addition is limited to causes of action for negligence, so that it has been held not to apply to strict liability for a dog bite. Lavalle v. Kaupp, 1953, 240 Minn. 360, 61 N.W.2d 228.

34. McWhirter v. Otis Elevator Co., D.S.C.1941, 40 F.Supp. 11; Saloushin v. Houle, 1931, 82 N.H. 126, 55 A. 47; Tomkovitch v. Mistevitch, 1923, 222 Mich. 425, 192 N.W. 639; Kent v. Chapel, 1897, 67 Minn. 420, 70 N.W. 2; Haymes v. Halliday, 1924, 151 Tenn. 115, 268 S.W. 30. See Notes, 1951, 27 N.Dak. L.Rev. 208; 1934, 18 Minn.L.Rev. 585; 1934, 22 Cal.L.Rev. 456; 1934, 34 Col.L.Rev. 161.

35. See Evans, A Comparative Study of the Statutory Survival of Tort Claims For and Against Execu-

an injury." [39] The decision was accepted and followed, not without dissent, in England,[40] and notwithstanding a good start to the contrary,[41] in the United States.[42]

The result was that it was more profitable for the defendant to kill the plaintiff than to scratch him,[43] and that the most grievous of all injuries left the bereaved family of the victim, who frequently were destitute, without a remedy. Since this was intolerable, it was changed in England by the passage of the Fatal Accidents Act [44] of 1846, otherwise known as Lord Campbell's Act, which has become a generic name for similar statutes. Every American state now has a statutory remedy for wrongful death.[45] Most of the statutes were modeled upon Lord Campbell's Act, which is a "death act," and creates a new cause of action for the death in favor of the decedent's personal representative for the benefit of certain designated persons.

Other states, in the minority, merely have "survival acts," which proceed upon the theory of preserving the cause of action vested in the decedent at the moment of his death and enlarging it to include the damages resulting from his death.[46] One important difference between the two types of statutes may be that where death is instantaneous, or substantially so, there can be no cause of action under the survival acts, since the decedent has had no time to suffer any appreciable damages, and so no cause of action ever has vested in him.[47] This is not, however, a necessary conclusion under such statutes;[48] and in any case recovery does not depend upon consciousness of the injured person before his death.[49] The suddenness of death is of course no bar at all to an action under statutes of the Lord Campbell type.[50]

---

39. Baker v. Bolton, 1808, 1 Camp. 493, 170 Eng.Rep. 1033.

40. Osborn v. Gillett, 1873, L.R. 8 Exch. 88; Clark v. London General Omnibus Co., [1906], 2 K.B. 648; Admiralty Comm'rs v. S. S. Amerika, [1917] A.C. 38.

41. Ford v. Monroe, 1838, 20 Wend., N.Y., 210; Cross v. Guthery, 1794, 2 Root, Conn., 90; Shields v. Yonge, 1854, 15 Ga. 349. See Malone, American Fatal Accident Statutes—The Legislative Birth Pains, [1965] Duke L.J. 673; Hay, Death as a Civil Cause of Action in Massachusetts, 1893, 7 Harv.L.Rev. 170; Signor, Action for Death by Wrongful Act at Common Law and Under the New York Statute, 1905, 67 Albany, L.J. 133.

42. Mobile Life Ins. Co. v. Brame, 1877, 95 U.S. 754; Jackson v. Pittsburgh, C. C. & St. L. R. Co., 1894, 140 Ind. 241, 39 N.E. 663; Major v. Burlington, C. R. & N. R. Co., 1902, 115 Iowa 309, 88 N.W. 815; Kennedy v. Davis, 1911, 171 Ala. 609, 55 So. 104; Perham v. Portland General Elec. Co., 1898, 33 Or. 451, 53 P. 14, 24.

43. Most lawyers are familiar with the legend, quite unfounded, that this was the original reason that passengers in Pullman car berths rode with their heads to the front. Also that the fire axes in railroad coaches were provided to enable the conductor to deal efficiently with those who were merely injured.

44. 9 & 10 Vict. c. 93. See Laughton-Scott, The Fatal Accidents Act, 1954, 9 Ind.L.Q.Rev. 5.

45. An excellent text is Speiser, Recovery for Wrongful Death (1966).

46. The death statutes are classified in Rose, Foreign Enforcement of Actions for Wrongful Death, 1935, 33 Mich.L.Rev. 545; Note, 1954, 39 Iowa L. Rev. 494. See Jamison v. Memphis Transit Management Co., 6 Cir. 1967 (Tennessee statute).

47. Beaven v. Seaboard Air Line R. Co., N.D.Fla. 1951, 100 F.Supp. 336; Micks v. Norton, 1931, 256 Mich. 308, 239 N.W. 512; Royal Indemnity Co. v. Pittsfield Elec. Co., 1935, 293 Mass. 4, 199 N.E. 69; Great Northern R. Co. v. Capital Trust Co., 1916, 242 U.S. 144; Bruck v. Matteo Trucking Corp., 1963, 20 App.Div.2d 521, 245 N.Y.S.2d 232 (death without regaining consciousness). But if there is conscious suffering, its brevity will not prevent recovery. Wiggins v. Lane & Co., E.D.La.1969, 298 F.Supp. 194.

48. To the contrary are Broughel v. Southern New England Tel. Co., 1900, 72 Conn. 617, 45 A. 435; Louisville R. Co. v. Raymond's Adm'r, 1909, 135 Ky. 738, 123 S.W. 281; Justin v. Ketcham, 1941, 297 Mich. 592, 298 N.W. 294.

49. Nelson v. Glover, 1925, 231 Mich. 229, 203 N.W. 840; Farrington v. Stoddard, 1 Cir. 1940, 115 F.2d 96.

50. Coliseum Motor Co. v. Hester, 1931, 43 Wyo. 298, 3 P.2d 105; Grimes v. King, 1945, 311 Mich. 399, 18 N.W.2d 870; Missouri, K. & T. R. Co. v. Elliott, 8 Cir. 1900, 102 F.2d 96, affirmed 184 U.S. 695 (Arkansas statute); Perham v. Portland Elec. Co., 1898, 33 Or. 451, 53 P. 14, rehearing denied 53 P. 24.

Alabama and Massachusetts have statutes which are frankly penal in character, and base the damages upon the culpability of the defendant.[51] Workmen's compensation acts, so far as they apply, have superseded both the death statutes and the common law, with compensation allowances for death arising out of and in the course of employment; and the Federal Employers' Liability Act contains provisions both for survival and for recovery for negligence resulting in death.[52]

The statutes usually provide that the action can be maintained for "any wrongful act, neglect or default" which causes death. They are therefore held to cover intentional, as well as negligent, torts.[53] Strict liability in tort has made its appearance in relatively few cases, but there appears to be no reason to doubt that it is included within the death acts.[54] On the other hand, since under the common law contract actions survived in favor of the plaintiff's representative while tort actions did not, it seems reasonable to suppose that the wrongful death statutes were intended to refer only to torts. Accordingly, there is general agreement that they have no application to any death which results from a pure breach of contract.[55] This,

however, can be somewhat misleading, since it is equally well settled that the acts do apply to the breach of a tort duty arising out of a contract relation, such as that of carrier and passenger;[56] and there is respectable authority that, where this is the case, an action which is in form one for breach of the contract sufficiently alleges a wrongful "default" within the statute.[57]

Reference has already been made[58] to the controversy, in which the courts are now swinging to the affirmative, as to whether the tort character of a breach of warranty is sufficient to include such an action under the wrongful death acts.

Plaintiff and Beneficiaries

Under survival acts the proper plaintiff is of course the executor or administrator of the plaintiff's estate. Under the death acts the action usually is to be brought by such a representative, or by an administrator appointed by the court for the purpose of bringing it, where there is no other estate;[59] but under many of the statutes some one or more of those who are to benefit by recovery may

---

51. See Bonner v. Williams, 5 Cir. 1967, 370 F.2d 301. Note, 1952, 4 Ala.L.Rev. 75.

52. See St. Louis, I. M. & S. R. Co. v. Craft, 1915, 237 U.S. 648; Kansas City Southern R. Co. v. Leslie, 1914, 238 U.S. 599. This was extended in 1926 by 46 U.S.C.A., § 688, to employees of carriers by water engaged in interstate or foreign commerce.

53. Welch v. Creech, 1915, 88 Wash. 429, 153 P. 355; Tucker v. State, 1899, 89 Md. 471, 43 A. 778, 44 A. 1004; Suell v. Derricott, 1909, 161 Ala. 259, 49 So. 895; Howard's Adm'r v. Hunter, 1907, 126 Ky. 685, 104 S.W. 723; Kling v. Torello, 1913, 87 Conn. 301, 87 A. 987.

54. Sullivan v. Dunham, 1900, 161 N.Y. 290, 55 N.E. 923; United States v. Praylou, 4 Cir. 1953, 208 F.2d 291, cert. denied 347 U.S. 934; Mobile, J. & K. C. R. Co. v. Bromberg, 1904, 141 Ala. 258, 37 So. 395; The Tungus v. Skovgaard, 1959, 358 U.S. 588; United N. Y. & N. J. Sandy Hook Pilots Ass'n v. Halecki, 1959, 358 U.S. 613; cf. Kernan v. American Dredging Co., 1958, 355 U.S. 426.

55. Barley's Adm'x v. Clover Spirit Coal Co., 1941, 268 Ky. 218, 150 S.W.2d 670; Willey v. Alaska

Packers' Ass'n, N.D.Cal.1925, 9 F.2d 937; Bloss v. Dr. C. R. Woodson Sanitarium Co., 1928, 319 Mo. 1061, 5 S.W.2d 367; Revell v. Illinois Merchants' Trust Co., 1925, 238 Ill.App. 4, affirmed, Revel v. Butler, 1926, 322 Ill. 337, 153 N.E. 682.

56. Braun v. Riel, Mo.1931, 40 S.W.2d 621, 80 A.L.R. 875; Mueller v. Winston Bros. Co., 1931, 165 Wash. 130, 4 P.2d 854; Pearlman v. Garrod Shoe Co., 1937, 276 N.Y. 172, 11 N.E.2d 718; Thaggard v. Vafes, 1928, 218 Ala. 609, 119 So. 647; Earley v. Pacific Elec. R. Co., 1917, 176 Cal. 79, 167 P. 513.

57. Zostautas v. St. Anthony de Padua Hospital, 1961, 23 Ill.2d 326, 178 N.E.2d 303; Roche v. St. John's Riverside Hospital, 1916, 96 Misc. 289, 160 N.Y.S. 401, affirmed 176 App.Div. 885, 161 N.Y.S. 1143; Calamari v. Mary Immaculate Hospital, 1956, 3 Misc.2d 780, 155 N.Y.S.2d 552; Keiper v. Anderson, 1917, 138 Minn. 392, 165 N.W. 237. See Note, [1962] U.Ill.L.Forum 120.

58. Supra, p. 666.

59. Hartford & N. H. R. Co. v. Andrews, 1869, 36 Conn. 213; Reutenik v. Gibson Packing Co., 1934, 132 Wash. 108, 231 P. 773.

sue.[60] The beneficiaries frequently are designated by the act, in accordance with the purpose of compensating members of the family who might have expected to receive support or assistance from the deceased if he had lived. Lord Campbell's Act, for example, specified that the action was for the benefit of the husband, wife, parent or child, and many of the American acts have limited it to a similar restricted group.[61] Creditors of the deceased can then have no share in the recovery,[62] and it follows that if no such designated beneficiaries are living at the time of the wrongful death, the action fails because there is no one entitled to compensation.[63]

If the sole beneficiary, or all of the specified beneficiaries, die after the decease of the person wrongfully killed but before action is begun,[64] or even after commencement of the action but before judgment,[65] there is considerable authority to the effect that the action does not survive to the beneficiary's estate, on the ground that the compensation is intended to be personal to him. The more reasonable, and probably the prevailing view, is that the cause of action vests in the beneficiary immediately upon the wrongful death, becomes his property, and survives to his representative.[66] There is a similar difference of opinion as to the death or disqualification [67] of all the members of a preferred class of beneficiaries, some courts holding that the action then passes to the members of a secondary deferred class,[68] others that it fails entirely.[69] It is of course undisputed

60. Cummins v. Woody, 1941, 177 Tenn. 636, 152 S. W.2d 246; Stewart v. Louisville & N. R. Co., 1887, 83 Ala. 493, 4 So. 373; Belding v. Black Hills & Ft. P. R. Co., 1892, 3 S.D. 369, 53 N.W. 750. It usually is held, however, that only one action can be brought, and that any claimant not joined is barred. See Muzychuk to Use of Burns v. Yellow Cab Co., 1941, 343 Pa. 335, 22 A.2d 670.

61. In Glona v. American Guarantee & Liability Ins. Co., 1968, 391 U.S. 73, the exclusion of illegitimate children was held to deny equal protection of the laws.

62. State v. Cambria, 1951, 137 Conn. 604, 80 A.2d 516; Lese v. St. Joseph Valley Bank, 1924, 81 Ind. App. 517, 142 N.E. 733; Ghilain v. Couture, 1929, 84 N.H. 48, 146 A. 395; Broadnax v. Broadnax, 1912, 160 N.C. 432, 76 S.E. 216.

63. Chicago & Rock Island R. Co. v. Morris, 1861, 26 Ill. 400; Herro v. Steidl, 1949, 255 Wis. 65, 37 N. W.2d 874; Smith v. Atlantic Coast Line R. Co., 1948, 212 S.C. 332, 47 S.E.2d 725; Nioso v. Aiello, Mun.App.D.C.1949, 69 A.2d 57; Webster v. Norwegian Min. Co., 1902, 137 Cal. 399, 70 P. 276. Cf. Wilder v. Charleston Transit Co., 1938, 120 W.Va. 319, 197 S.E. 814 (no escheat to the state).

64. Danis v. New York Central R. Co., 1954, 160 Ohio St. 474, 117 N.E.2d 39; Hardtner v. Aetna Cas. & Surety Co., La.App.1939, 189 So. 365; Wilcox v. Bierd, 1928, 330 Ill. 571, 162 N.E. 170; Shipley v. Daly, 1939, 106 Ind.App. 443, 20 N.E.2d 653; Freie v. St. Louis-San Francisco R. Co., 1920, 283 Mo. 457, 222 S.W. 824. See Note, 1955, 40 Minn.L. Rev. 94.

65. Schmidt v. Menasha Woodenware Co., 1898, 99 Wis. 300, 74 N.W. 797; Billingsly v. St. Louis, I. M. & S. R. Co., 1907, 84 Ark. 617, 107 S.W. 173; Chivers v. Roger, 1898, 50 La.Ann. 57, 23 So. 100; Doyle v. Baltimore & O. R. Co., 1909, 81 Ohio St. 184, 90 N.E. 165.

66. Gray v. Goodson, 1963, 61 Wash.2d 319, 378 P.2d 413; McDaniel v. Bullard, 1966, 34 Ill.2d 487, 216 N.E.2d 140; Bohannon v. McGowan, Fla.App.1969, 222 So.2d 60; Sharp's Adm'r v. Sharp's Adm'r, Ky. 1955, 284 S.W.2d 673; Williams v. Hoyt, 1917, 117 Me. 61, 102 A. 703. See Note, 1966, 43 Chi.Kent L. Rev. 198.

67. Action maintainable: Missouri-Kansas-Texas R. Co. v. Canada, 1928, 130 Okl. 171, 265 P. 1045 (no pecuniary loss); Notti v. Great Northern R. Co., 1940, 110 Mont. 464, 104 P.2d 7 (same—Federal Employers' Liability Act); Pries v. Ashland Light, Power & Street R. Co., 1910, 143 Wis. 606, 128 N.W. 281 (nonresident aliens); Di Paolo v. Laquin Lumber Co., C.C.Pa.1910, 178 F. 877 (same).

Not maintainable: Logan v. Durham, 1957, 231 Miss. 232, 95 So.2d 227 (family immunity); Cole v. Mayne, C.C.Mo.1901, 122 F. 836 (adulterous wife); Thompson v. Chicago, M. & St. P. R. Co., C.C.Neb. 1900, 104 F. 845 (emancipation); cf. Ross v. Robinson, 1942, 169 Or. 293, 128 P.2d 956 (failure to assert rights).

68. Rushton v. Smith, 1958, 233 S.C. 292, 104 S.E.2d 376; David v. Southwestern R. Co., 1870, 41 Ga. 223; Garrard v. Mahoning Valley R. Co., 1919, 100 Ohio St. 212, 126 N.E. 53; Houston & T. C. R. Co. v. Moore, 1878, 49 Tex. 31.

69. Ondrey v. Shellmar Products Corp., N.D.Ind.1955, 131 F.Supp. 542; Chicago, B. & Q. R. Co. v. Wells-Dickey Trust Co., 1927, 275 U.S. 161; White v. Atchison, T. & S. F. R. Co., 1928, 125 Kan. 537, 265 P. 73; Wilcox v. Warren Const. Co., 1920, 95 Or.

that the death of a beneficiary of a particular class does not affect the rights of others of the same class.[70] Although there is a little authority to the contrary,[71] most courts have arrived at the unfortunate conclusion that actions for wrongful death do not survive the death of the tortfeasor himself, upon the rather dubious ground that they are strictly statutory, and the survival acts are intended to cover only actions at common law.[72]

Other statutes contain broader provisions naming the "heirs" or the "next of kin" of the decedent as beneficiaries.[73] Still others resemble survival acts in that the recovery is merely for the benefit of the decedent's estate, and the proceeds are to be distributed like any inherited sum,[74] usually with a provision that creditors are not to participate.[75] Reference must of course be made to the statutes and decisions of each particular jurisdiction.

Damages

The damages recoverable for death present a large topic, which lies beyond the scope of this text.[76] Brief mention may be made of some of its more salient features. The basis of recovery will of course depend upon the theory of the action, as to those who are to benefit by it. Under the survival acts which have been enlarged to include death, the action is on behalf of the decedent's estate, and the damages will include not only the pain and suffering, medical expenses and loss of earnings of the decedent during his lifetime,[77] but further compensation to the estate itself for loss of prospective economic benefit in the form of future earnings or savings.[78] Under those death acts where the ac-

125, 186 P. 13; Hammond v. Lewiston, A. & W. St. R. Co., 1909, 106 Me. 209, 76 A. 672.

70. Holt v. Stollenwerck, 1911, 174 Ala. 213, 56 So. 912; Fitzgerald v. Edison Electric Illuminating Co., 1903, 207 Pa. 118, 56 A. 350; Heald v. Wallace, 1902, 109 Tenn. 346, 71 S.W. 80; Taylor v. Western Pac. R. Co., 1873, 45 Cal. 323.

71. Meads v. Dibble, 1960, 10 Utah 2d 229, 350 P.2d 853; Fish v. Liley, 1949, 120 Colo. 156, 208 P.2d 930; Kuhnle v. Swedlund, 1945, 220 Minn. 573, 20 N.W.2d 396; Ivey v. Wiggins, 1964, 276 Ala. 106, 159 So.2d 618; Putnam v. Savage, 1923, 244 Mass. 83, 138 N.E. 808. Some states have special provisions for survival. See Evans, Survival of the Action for Death by Wrongful Act, 1933, 1 U.Chi.L. Rev. 102; Notes, 1950, 22 Rocky Mt.L.Rev. 99; 1929, 13 Minn.L.Rev. 632.

72. Mennemeyer v. Hart, 1949, 359 Mo. 423, 221 S. W.2d 960; Burford v. Evans, 1942, 191 Okl. 555, 132 P.2d 653; Ickes v. Brimhall, 1938, 42 N.M. 412, 79 P.2d 942; Tuttle v. Short, 1930, 42 Wyo. 1, 288 P. 524; Carrigan v. Cole, 1913, 35 R.I. 162, 85 A. 934.

73. See for example Chicago & Alton R. Co. v. Shannon, 1867, 43 Ill. 339; Law v. Wynne, 1935, 190 Ark. 1010, 83 S.W.2d 61; Missouri-Kansas-Texas R. Co. v. Canada, 1928, 130 Okl. 171, 265 P. 1045; Grogan v. Denver & R. G. R. Co., 1914, 56 Colo. 450, 138 P. 764.

74. Soreide v. Vilas & Co., 1956, 247 Iowa 1139, 78 N.W.2d 41; Spangler's Adm'r v. City of Middlesboro, 1945, 301 Ky. 237, 191 S.W.2d 414; In re Veanneman's Estate, 1938, 286 Mich. 368, 282 N.W. 180; Cann v. Mann Const. Co., 1952, 8 Terry, Del., 504, 93 A.2d 741; Arizona Binghampton Copper Co.

v. Dickson, 1921, 22 Ariz. 163, 195 P. 538. See Note, 1963, 48 Iowa L.Rev. 666. Thus the action is not barred because the "widow" was not married to decedent, and the children are bastards. Memphis St. R. Co. v. Cooper, 1958, 203 Tenn. 425, 313 S.W 2d 444.

75. Kennedy v. Davis, 1911, 171 Ala. 609, 55 So. 104; Mott v. Central R. Co., 1883, 70 Ga. 680.

76. See Russel, Measure of Damages Under Missouri Wrongful Death Act, 1950, 15 Mo.L.Rev. 31; Duffey, The Maldistribution of Damages in Wrongful Death, 1958, 19 Ohio St.L.J. 264; Duffey, Life Expectancy and Loss of Earning Capacity, 1958, 19 Ohio St.L.J. 314; Bostwick, Wrongful Death and Rightful Damages, 1967, 2 Land & Water Rev. 405; Notes, 1948, 28 Bos.U.L.Rev. 368; 1963, 48 Iowa L. Rev. 666; 1966, 44 N.C.L.Rev. 402; 1967, 19 S.C.L. Rev. 220.

77. Hoke v. Atlantic Greyhound Corp., 1946, 226 N.C. 332, 38 S.E.2d 105.

78. Earning capacity, without deduction of expenses: Mickel v. New England Coal & Coke Co., 1946, 132 Conn. 671, 47 A.2d 187; Spangler's Adm'r v. City of Middlesboro, 1945, 301 Ky. 237, 191 S.W.2d 414; Dmitri v. Peter Cienes & Son, 1918, 41 R.I. 393, 103 A. 1029. Warner v. McCaughan, 1969, —— Wash.2d ——, 460 P.2d 272.

Savings which might have been accumulated, after expenses: Arizona Binghampton Copper Co. v. Dickson, 1921, 22 Ariz. 163, 195 P. 538; Lamm v.

tion is for the benefit of the estate, this last element of damages may sometimes be the sole basis of recovery, since it is the only loss sustained by the estate as such through the death.[79] Under Lord Campbell's Act and the great majority of the death acts, however, the action proceeds on the theory of compensating the individual beneficiaries for loss of the economic benefit which they might reasonably have expected to receive from the decedent in the form of support, services or contributions during the remainder of his lifetime if he had not been killed.[80]

A number of states have both death acts and survival acts.[81] There are then two causes of action, and it usually is held that they may be prosecuted concurrently to successful judgment.[82] The usual method of dealing with the two causes of action has

then been to allocate the pain and suffering, expenses and loss of earnings of the decedent up to the date of his death to the survival action, and hence to the estate,[83] and the loss of benefits of the survivors to the action for wrongful death, and so to the beneficiaries.[84] This has, in the ordinary jurisdiction, the effect of denying all recovery to anyone for the loss of the accumulated savings which the decedent might have been expected to make during the period of his pre-accident life expectancy, or in other words, of the inheritance he might have been expected to leave to his widow and children.[85] A small number of jurisdictions have allowed such damages to the survivors in the death action,[86] or, in the case of Pennsylvania [87] and Hawaii,[88] to the estate as a matter of survival

---

Lorbacher, 1952, 235 N.C. 728, 71 S.E.2d 49; Murray v. Philadelphia Transp. Co., 1948, 359 Pa. 69, 58 A.2d 323; Herzig v. Swift, 2 Cir. 1945, 146 F.2d 444. Cf. O'Toole v. United States, 3 Cir. 1957, 242 F.2d 308.

79. Carlson v. Oregon Short-Line & U. N. Ry. Co., 1892, 21 Or. 450, 28 P. 497; Arizona Binghampton Copper Co. v. Dickson, 1921, 22 Ariz. 163, 195 P. 538; Florida East Coast R. Co. v. Hayes, 1914, 67 Fla. 101, 64 So. 504; Read v. Dunn, 1927, 48 R.I. 437, 138 A. 210. But cf. Michael v. Western & A. R. Co., 1932, 175 Ga. 1, 165 S.E. 37; Lexington Utilities Co. v. Parker's Adm'x, 1915, 166 Ky. 81, 178 S.W. 1173 (gross earnings).

80. Michigan Central R. Co. v. Vreeland, 1912, 227 U.S. 59; Martin v. Mansfeldt, 1950, 100 Cal.App.2d 327, 223 P.2d 501; Thoirs v. Pounsford, 1941, 210 Minn. 462, 299 N.W. 16; Goodyear Yellow Pine Co. v. Anderson, 1934, 171 Miss. 530, 157 So. 700.

It is commonly held that punitive damages can be awarded under a survival statute, but not under a wrongful death act. See Kern v. Kogan, 1967, 93 N.J.Super. 459, 226 A.2d 186.

81. Sometimes with a considerable degree of attendant confusion. See, for example, Alpert, The Florida Death Acts, 1957, 10 U.Fla.L.Rev. 153.

82. Gorman v. Columbus & Southern Ohio Elec. Co., 1945, 144 Ohio St. 593, 60 N.E.2d 700; May Coal Co. v. Robinette, 1929, 120 Ohio St. 110, 165 N.E. 576; Machek v. City of Seattle, 1921, 118 Wash. 42, 203 P. 25; Koehler v. Waukesha Milk Co., 1926, 190 Wis. 52, 208 N.W. 901; Stewart v. United Elec. L. & P. Co., 1906, 104 Md. 332, 65 A. 49.

83. Farrington v. Stoddard, 1 Cir. 1940, 115 F.2d 96; Hindmarsh v. Sulpho Saline Bath Co., 1922, 108 Neb. 168, 187 N.W. 806; O'Leary v. United States Lines Co., D.Mass.1953, 111 F.Supp. 745; Ellis v. Brown, Fla.1955, 77 So.2d 845; Allen v. Burdette, 1942, 139 Ohio St. 208, 39 N.E.2d 153; and see cases cited in the preceding note. See, generally, Schumacher, Rights of Action Under Death and Survival Statutes, 1924, 23 Mich.L.Rev. 114.

84. Patton v. Baltimore & O. R. Co., 3 Cir. 1952, 197 F.2d 732; Farrington v. Stoddard, 1 Cir. 1940, 115 F.2d 96. In Pennsylvania the potential accumulated savings go to the estate. Pezzulli v. D'Ambrosia, 1942, 344 Pa. 643, 26 A.2d 659.

85. See cases cited in the preceding two notes. The entire problem is discussed at length in Fleming, The Lost Years: A Problem in the Computation and Distribution of Damages, 1962, 50 Cal.L.Rev. 598.

86. Martin v. Atlantic Coast Line R. Co., 5 Cir. 1959, 268 F.2d 397 (Florida law); National Airlines v. Stiles, 5 Cir. 1959, 268 F.2d 400 (Louisiana law), O'Toole v. United States, 3 Cir. 1957, 242 F.2d 308 (Delaware law); Blumenthal v. United States, E. D.Pa.1960, 189 F.Supp. 439; Esquilin v. Waterman S. S. Corp., D.P.R.1961, 196 F.Supp. 600; see Chester Parke Co. v. Schulte, 1929, 120 Ohio St. 273, 166 N. E. 186.

87. Pezzulli v. D'Ambrosia, 1942, 344 Pa. 643, 26 A. 2d 659; Murray v. Philadelphia Transp. Co., 1948, 359 Pa. 69, 58 A.2d 323; Ferne v. Chadderton, 1949, 363 Pa. 191, 69 A.2d 104.

88. Rohlfing v. Moses Akiona, Ltd., 1961, 45 Hawaii 373, 443, 369 P.2d 96.

of a right lost by the decedent.[89] A decision in 1966 in the Third Circuit [90] allowed recovery for the abbreviation of the life expectancy itself as a compensable element of damages; and this has been received with general approval by most legal writers.[91] If followed, it would solve the problem by allowing the recovery in the survival action.

Where the damages recoverable are based upon the loss to the surviving beneficiaries, it is the general rule that only pecuniary loss is to be considered. The death acts obviously are aimed at protection of the relational interest, and bear a close analogy to the action of the husband or parent for loss of services through injury to the wife or child. But the original English act received a very strict construction at the hands of a court alarmed at the difficulty of evaluating the impalpable injuries to sentiments and affections because of death,[92] which has been followed in interpreting most of the American statutes to limit the recovery to loss of pecuniary benefits.[93] This has meant

that the courts have rejected the contention that no human life can be without value,[94] and that recovery has repeatedly been denied even where there are beneficiaries of the specified class, but they are not shown to have suffered any pecuniary loss.[95] Thus, with a few exceptions, which, however, have been augmented rapidly of late,[96] the courts refuse to allow damages for the grief or mental suffering of the survivors;[97] and many of them still refuse any compensation for the loss of society, comfort, intercourse, protection, and other incidents of family association.[98] Undoubtedly a lively fear of the over-enthusiasm of sympathetic juries has

473; Miller, Dead Men in Torts; Lord Campbell's Act was Not Enough, 1970, 19 Cath.U.L.Rev. 310.

94. This was fought out in Courtney v. Apple, 1956, 345 Mich. 223, 76 N.W.2d 80. It follows that nominal damages cannot be recovered in an action for wrongful death. Armentrout v. Hughes, 1958, 247 N.C. 631, 101 S.E.2d 793. But it has been held that there is a presumption of substantial pecuniary loss in favor of lineal heirs. Ferraro v. Augustine, 1964, 45 Ill.App.2d 295, 196 N.E.2d 16.

95. San Antonio & A. P. R. Co. v. Long, 1894, 87 Tex. 148, 27 S.W. 113; Courtney v. Apple, 1956, 345 Mich. 223, 76 N.W.2d 80; Armentrout v. Hughes, 1958, 247 N.C. 631, 101 S.E.2d 793. The poverty, wealth, or physical helplessness of the survivor is immaterial, except as it may bear upon the probability of contributions from the decedent. See Chicago, Peoria & St. L. R. Co. v. Woolridge, 1898, 174 Ill. 330, 51 N.E. 701.

96. City of Tucson v. Wondergem, 1970, 105 Ariz. 429, 466 P.2d 383; Stamper v. Bannister, 1961, 146 W.Va. 100, 118 S.E.2d 313; Matthews v. Hicks, 1955, 197 Va. 112, 87 S.E.2d 629; Silverman v. Travelers Ins. Co., 5 Cir. 1960, 277 F.2d 257; Johnson v. Charleston & W. C. R. Co., 1959, 234 S.C. 448, 108 S.E.2d 777.

97. Herbertson v. Russell, 1962, 150 Colo. 110, 371 P.2d 422; Hepp v. Ader, 1942, 64 Idaho 240, 130 P.2d 859; Tufty v. Sioux City Transit Co., 1943, 69 S.D. 368, 10 N.W.2d 767; Ferne v. Chadderton, 1949, 363 Pa. 191, 69 A.2d 104; Interurban R. Co. v. Trainer, 1921, 150 Ark. 19, 233 S.W. 816.

98. Ferne v. Chadderton, 1949, 363 Pa. 191, 69 A.2d 104; Archambeault v. Draper, E.D.N.Y.1951, 101 F.Supp. 1004 (New York law); National Tank Co. v. Scott, 1942, 191 Okl. 613, 130 P.2d 316; Kennedy v. Byers, 1923, 107 Ohio St. 90, 140 N.E. 630; Rogers v. Fancy Farm Tel. Co., 1914, 160 Ky. 841, 170 S.W. 178.

89. From the point of view of the plaintiff, this is the more satisfactory solution, if only because it may be available when there are no statutory beneficiaries, or the statute of limitations has run against them. See Kriesak v. Crowe, D.Pa.1941, 36 F.Supp. 127; Kriesak v. Crowe, D.Pa.1942, 44 F.Supp. 636, affirmed, 3 Cir. 1942, 131 F.2d 1023; First Nat. Bank in Greensburg v. M. & G. Convoy, Inc., W.D.Pa.1952, 106 F.Supp. 261.

90. Downie v. United States Lines Co., 3 Cir. 1966, 359 F.2d 344.

91. Leonard, Future Economic Value in Wrongful Death Litigation, 1969, 30 Ohio St.L.J. 502; Notes, 1967, 41 Temp.L.Q. 142; 1967, 21 Rut.L.Rev. 340; 1969, 29 Md.L.Rev. 24; 1967, 51 Minn.L.Rev. 558; 1967, 65 Mich.L.Rev. 786.

92. Blake v. Midland R. Co., 1852, 18 Q.B. 93, 118 Eng.Rep. 42.

93. Karr v. Sixt, 1946, 146 Ohio St. 527, 67 N.E.2d 331; Louisville & N. R. Co. v. Stephens, 1944, 298 Ky. 328, 182 S.W.2d 447; Gaydos v. Domabyl, 1930, 301 Pa. 523, 152 A. 549; Tufty v. Sioux City Transit Co., 1943, 69 S.D. 368, 10 N.W.2d 767; Lehrer v. Lorenzen, 1951, 124 Colo. 17, 233 P.2d 382. See Green, Relational Interests, 1934, 29 Ill.L.Rev. 460,

had a good deal to do with this result. Recent years, however, have brought considerable modification of the rigid common law rules. It has been recognized that even pecuniary loss may extend beyond mere contributions of food, shelter, money or property; and there is now a decided tendency to find that the society, care and attention of the deceased are "services" to the survivor with a financial value, which may be compensated.[99] This has been true, for example, not only where a child has been deprived of a parent, and there is allowance for the value of "substitute mother" care,[1] but also where the parent has lost a child, and substitution is scarcely in the picture.[2]

In general, however, it is still repeated that the measure of recovery is the value of the support, services and contributions which the beneficiary might have expected to receive if death had not intervened.[3] This necessarily

involves a large element of speculation, turning on such matters as life expectancy,[4] income,[5] character, habits and health of the deceased,[6] and his past contributions to his family,[7] together with the vicissitudes of an uncertain future. These difficulties apparently were foreseen by the framers of the acts, most of which give a very wide discretion to the jury[8] and authorize some resort to conjecture rather than any mathematical rules.[9]

This has been particularly necessary in the case of death of a minor child,[10] where the future is in the highest degree speculative and uncertain. As any parent is well aware, any realistic view of the prospects must mean that the cost of rearing the child

---

99. Lockhart v. Besel, 1967, 71 Wash.2d 112, 426 P.2d 605; McPike v. Scheuerman, Wyo.1965, 398 P.2d 71; Gulf Transport Co. v. Allen, 1950, 209 Miss. 206, 46 So.2d 436; Seaboard Air Line R. Co. v. Martin, Fla.1952, 56 So.2d 509; Gardner v. Hobbs, 1949, 69 Idaho 288, 206 P.2d 539.

See Notes, 1946, 25 N.C.L.Rev. 84; 1952, 38 Va.L.Rev. 909; 1966, 35 U.Cin.L.Rev. 104; 1968, 43 Wash.L. Rev. 654.

1. Williams v. McDowell, 1939, 32 Cal.App.2d 49, 89 P.2d 155; Dahl v. North American Creameries, N. D.1953, 61 N.W.2d 916; Merrill v. United Air Lines, S.D.N.Y.1959, 177 F.Supp. 704; Frasier v. Public Service Interstate Transp. Co., 2 Cir. 1957, 244 F.2d 668; Spangler v. Helm's New York-Pittsburgh Motor Express, 1959, 396 Pa. 482, 153 A.2d 490.

2. Van Cleave v. Lynch, 1946, 109 Utah 149, 166 P.2d 244; Checketts v. Bowman, 1950, 70 Idaho 463, 220 P.2d 682; Hall v. Gillins, 1958, 13 Ill.2d 26, 147 N. E.2d 352; Delta Chevrolet Co. v. Waid, 1951, 211 Miss. 256, 51 So.2d 443; Fussner v. Andert, 1961, 261 Minn. 347, 113 N.W.2d 355 ("advice, comfort, assistance and protection").

3. Hertz v. McDowell, 1948, 358 Mo. 383, 214 S.W.2d 546; American Barge Line Co. v. Leatherman's Adm'x, 1947, 306 Ky. 284, 206 S.W.2d 955; Thompson v. Town of Fort Branch, 1931, 204 Ind. 152, 178 N.E. 440; Blackwell v. American Film Co., 1922, 189 Cal. 689, 209 P. 999; Kansas City Southern R. Co. v. Leslie, 1916, 122 Ark. 516, 189 S.W. 171.

4. Gill v. Baltimore & O. R. Co., 1924, 302 Mo. 317, 259 S.W. 93; Gaydos v. Domabyl, 1930, 301 Pa. 523, 152 A. 549. The life expectancy of the beneficiary also limits recovery. Ure v. Maggio Bros. Co., 1938, 24 Cal.App.2d 490, 75 P.2d 534; Goodyear Yellow Pine Co. v. Anderson, 1934, 171 Miss. 530, 157 So. 700.

5. Director General of Railroads v. Platt, 1 Cir. 1920, 265 F. 918; Perry v. Ryback, 1931, 302 Pa. 559, 153 A. 770.

6. Louisville & N. R. Co. v. Scott's Adm'r, 1920, 188 Ky. 99, 220 S.W. 1066; Morton v. Southwestern Tel. & Tel. Co., 1920, 280 Mo. 360, 217 S.W. 831.

7. Rogers v. Hime, 1948, 76 Ga.App. 523, 46 S.E.2d 367; American Barge Line Co. v. Leatherman's Adm'x, 1947, 306 Ky. 284, 206 S.W.2d 955; Director General of Railroads v. Platt, 1 Cir. 1920, 265 F. 918; Austin Gaslight Co. v. Anderson, Tex.Civ. App.1924, 262 S.W. 136, error dismissed.

8. See Kansas Pac. R. Co. v. Cutter, 1877, 19 Kan. 83, 91; Hunt v. Central Vermont R. Co., 1923, 99 Conn. 657, 122 A. 563; True & True Co. v. Woda, 1902, 104 Ill.App. 15, affirmed, 1903, 201 Ill. 315, 66 N.E. 369; Butler v. Townend, 1931, 50 Idaho 542, 298 P. 375.

9. American Motor Car Co. v. Robbins, 1913, 181 Ind. 417, 103 N.E. 641; Bottum v. Kamen, 1921, 43 S.D. 498, 180 N.W. 948; Fisher v. Treser, 1930, 119 Neb. 529, 229 N.W. 901.

10. See Hare, The Rationale of Damages for the Death of a Minor or Other Dependent Person, 1961, 41 Bos.U.L.Rev. 336; Notes, 1932, 16 Minn.L.Rev. 409; 1927, 13 Va.L.Rev. 392; 1936, 25 Cal.L.Rev. 103; 1936, 30 Ill.L.Rev. 243; 1955, 22 U.Chi.L.Rev. 538; 1961, 22 Ohio St.L.J. 442; 1959, 54 Northwestern U.L.Rev. 254.

will far exceed any conceivable pecuniary benefits that might ever be optimistically expected of him; and damages honestly calculated on this basis could never be anything but a minus quantity.[11] Nevertheless, in such cases substantial verdicts have been sustained, where it is very evident that the jury have taken the bull by the horns, and in reality have compensated for the prohibited sentimental aspects of the family relation, with the court benevolently winking at a flagrant violation of the rule it has laid down.[12] There have been similar cases as to aged decedents, already past the hope of future earnings and contributions.[13] Such decisions do not appear very likely to command respect for the administration of justice; but it seems evident that it is the theory which is wrong, and not the result. In addition, there are some courts which have

held that the benefits to be expected from the continued life of a minor must be limited to the period of his minority,[14] which of course makes it all the more difficult to justify any recovery at all. The greater number, however, have considered that, since the sum need not be based upon any legal right to services, but only expectation, it may extend even beyond the majority of the child, notwithstanding the highly speculative elements which must enter into such predictions.[15]

In 1960 something of a bombshell burst upon this scene with the decision of the Michigan court in Wycko v. Gnodtke.[16] The opinion of Justice Talbot Smith, attributing the "wage-profit" formula, of the expected earnings of the child during minority less the cost of raising him, to a child-labor era when all children were expected to earn money for the benefit of their parents, proceeded to discard it entirely. Instead it was held that, conceding that the damages must be based upon "pecuniary" value of the life, this value was to be measured by the functioning value of the human being as a part of a family, taking into account, as in the case of a machine in a factory, the expenses heretofore incurred, and treating the child as a unit in place. This has met with quite general approval and commendation from legal writers; but the decision is still too recent to permit

11. In 1946 Dublin and Lotka, The Money Value of a Man, 55, Table 14, estimated the cost of raising a child to the age of eighteen would be $16,337 for a family with an income of $5,000 to $10,000. On the basis of the change in price levels, as reflected in Pres.Econ.Rep.1959, 184 Table D–38, the 1959 equivalent of this would be $34,483.

In Hoyt v. United States, 5 Cir. 1961, 286 F.2d 356, the court refused to permit the deduction of the cost of upbringing in an action under the Federal Employers' Liability Act, upon the ground that it would nearly always result in a minus quantity, and defeat the evident intention of the act to allow some recovery.

12. Daggett v. Atchison, T. & S F. R. Co., 1957, 48 Cal.2d 655, 313 P.2d 557 ($50,000 for two children aged 3 years and 10 months); National Homeopathic Hospital v. Hord, D.C.Cir. 1953, 204 F.2d 397 ($17,000 for new born baby); Menneti v. Evans Const. Co., 3 Cir. 1958, 259 F.2d 367 ($45,385 for 7 year old); Reed v. Eubanks, 1957, 232 Miss. 27, 98 So.2d 132 ($40,000 for 8 year old); Miner v. McKay, 1958, 145 Conn. 622, 145 A.2d 758 ($36,000 for 9 year old); Checketts v. Bowman, 1950, 70 Idaho 463, 220 P.2d 682 ($20,000 for 4 year old); Boyd v. Sutton, La.App.1960, 120 So.2d 350 ($7,500 to each parent for 19 months old). Many other cases are collected in Lane v. Hatfield, 1943, 173 Or. 79, 143 P.2d 230.

13. Hudnut v. Schmidt, 1944, 324 Ill.App. 548, 58 N.E.2d 929; Barrow v. Lence, 1958, 17 Ill.App.2d 527, 151 N.E.2d 120. Contra, Armentrout v. Hughes, 1958, 247 N.C. 631, 101 S.E.2d 793.

14. Missouri Pac. R. Co. v. Maxwell, 1937, 194 Ark. 938, 109 S.W.2d 1254; Thompson v. Town of Fort Branch, 1931, 204 Ind. 152, 178 N.E. 440; Clevenger v. Kern, 1935, 100 Ind.App. 581, 197 N.E. 731.

15. Immel v. Richards, 1950, 154 Ohio St. 54, 93 N.E.2d 474; Bohrman v. Pennsylvania R. Co., 1952, 23 N.J.Super. 399, 93 A.2d 190; D'Angelo v. Rutland R. L. & P. Co., 1927, 100 Vt. 135, 135 A. 598; Allen v. Denver-Chicago Trucking Co., W.D.Mo. 1963, 221 F.Supp. 217; Thompson v. Ogemaw County Board of Road Comm'rs, 1959, 357 Mich. 482, 98 N.W.2d 620.

16. 1960, 361 Mich. 331, 105 N.W.2d 118. A 5–3 decision. Followed in Currie v. Fiting, 1965, 375 Mich. 440, 134 N.W.2d 611; Fussner v. Andert, 1961, 261 Minn. 247, 113 N.W.2d 355. See Notes, 1966, 19 Vand.L.Rev. 1405; 1966, 21 Ohio St.L.J. 355.

any estimate of its probable effect upon other courts.

Under rather less than one-third of the death acts, the discretion of the jury is at least partly controlled by a maximum limit of recovery on behalf of all beneficiaries for a single death. These amounts, however, vary considerably under the different statutes.

Defenses

Under the survival type of death statute, which merely continues the decedent's own cause of action beyond his death and enhances it with damages for the death, it is of course clear that any defenses which might have been set up against him if he had lived are still available to the defendant.[17] The contrary might perhaps have been expected of the wrongful death acts, which create a separate and independent cause of action, founded upon the death itself, for the benefit of the designated survivors. The original Lord Campbell's Act, however, contained an express provision limiting the death action to those cases where the deceased might have recovered damages if he had lived;[18] and this provision has been carried over into most of the American acts, or has been read into them by implication where it does not expressly appear.[19] It obviously is intended at

least to prevent recovery for death where the decedent could never at any time have maintained an action, as, for example, where there was simply no tortious conduct toward him.[20]

On the same theoretical basis, but with less manifest justification, there has been general agreement denying recovery where the defendant's conduct has been tortious toward the decedent and has caused his death, thus causing loss to the innocent survivors, but the defendant would have had a defense available against the decedent himself. This has been true of contributory negligence,[21] assumption of risk,[22] or consent to the defendant's conduct[23] which defeat recovery for the death, as does the fellow-servant rule

---

17. Motor Transit v. Hutchinson, 1944, 154 Fla. 798, 19 So.2d 57 (contributory negligence); Florida East Coast R. Co. v. Thompson, 1927, 93 Fla. 30, 111 So. 525 (release); Wright v. Davis, 1949, 132 W.Va. 722, 53 S.E.2d 335 (immunity of spouse); Kling v. Torello, 1913, 87 Conn. 301, 87 A. 987; Cogswell v. Boston & Me. R. Co., 1917, 78 N.H. 379, 101 A. 145.

18. 9 & 10 Vict., ch. 93: " . . . That whensoever the Death of a Person shall be caused by wrongful Act, Neglect or Default, and the Act, Neglect or Default is such as would (if Death had not ensued) have entitled the Party injured to maintain an Action and recover Damages in respect thereof, then and in every such Case the Person who would have been liable if Death had not ensued shall be liable to an Action for Damages, notwithstanding the Death of the Person injured."

19. Murphy v. Boston & Me. R. Co., 1913, 216 Mass. 178, 103 N.E. 291; Melville v. Butte-Balaklava Cop-

per Co., 1913, 47 Mont. 1, 130 P. 441; Ostheller v. Spokane & I. E. R. Co., 1919, 107 Wash. 678, 182 P. 630; Hunt v. Los Angeles R. Corp., 1930, 110 Cal. App. 456, 294 P. 745. See Nourse, Is Contributory Negligence of Deceased a Defense to a Wrongful Death Action? 1954, 42 Cal.L.Rev. 310.

20. State to Use of Bond v. Consolidated Gas, E. L. & P. Co., 1924, 146 Md. 390, 126 A. 105; Meyer v. King, 1894, 72 Miss. 1, 16 So. 245; Emery v. Rochester Tel. Corp., 1936, 271 N.Y. 306, 3 N.E.2d 434; Whang v. Houglum, 1955, 206 Or. 125, 290 P.2d 185, hearing denied, 1956, 206 Or. 125, 291 P.2d 720 (automobile guest statute).

21. Sullivan v. Davidson, 1958, 183 Kan. 713, 332 P. 2d 507; Buckley v. Chadwick, 1955, 45 Cal.2d 183, 288 P.2d 12, rehearing denied, 1955, 45 Cal.2d 183, 289 P.2d 242; Purdy v. Kerentoff, 1949, 152 Ohio St. 391, 89 N.E.2d 565; Zabawa v. Eshenroeder, 1946, 313 Mich. 555, 21 N.W.2d 852; Indiana Harbor Belt R. Co. v. Jones, 1941, 220 Ind. 139, 41 N.E. 2d 361. Cf. Tampa Elec. Co. v. Bryant, 1931, 101 Fla. 204, 133 So. 887 (reduction of damages under comparative negligence act). See Note, 1956, 29 So. Cal.L.Rev. 344.

22. Francis v. Southern Pac. Co., 1948, 333 U.S. 445; Marbury Lumber Co. v. Jones, 1921, 206 Ala. 669, 91 So. 623. Cf. Western Union Tel. Co. v. Cochran, 1949, 196 Misc. 122, 91 N.Y.S.2d 792 (agreement to come under workmen's compensation).

23. Miller v. Bennett, 1949, 190 Va. 162, 56 S.E.2d 217; Szadiwicz v. Cantor, 1926, 257 Mass. 518, 154 N.E. 251; Martin v. Morris, 1931, 163 Tenn. 186, 42 S.W.2d 207; Androws v. Coulter, 1931, 163 Wash. 429, 1 P.2d 320; Howlett v. Doglio, 1949, 402 Ill. 311, 83 N.E.2d 708 (Illinois Dramshop Act).

if there is anywhere where it still applies,[24] or justifications such as self-defense [25] or defense of property.[26] Most of the courts which have considered the question have given the same effect to the immunity of one member of a family for torts against another,[27] although there is a strong minority view to the contrary, based upon the theory that death destroys the reason for the immunity,[28] which seems very much to be preferred.

It is not at all clear, however, that such provisions of the death acts ever were intended to prevent recovery where the deceased once had a cause of action, but it has terminated before his death. The more reasonable interpretation would seem to be that they are directed at the necessity of some original tort on the part of the defendant, under circumstances giving rise to liability in the first instance, rather than to subsequent changes in the situation affecting only the interest of the decedent. Nevertheless, the majority of the courts have held that a judgment for [29] or against [30] the decedent

in an action for his injuries commenced during his lifetime, or the compromise and release of such an action,[31] will operate as a bar to any subsequent suit founded upon his death. This has the effect of placing in the decedent's hands the power to sell out the claim of the beneficiaries before it has come into existence. Their action is regarded as "derivative," arising out of and dependent upon the wrong that has been done to him. The courts undoubtedly have been influenced by a fear of a double recovery.[32] This is of course possible in point of law, not only under the survival type of death act,[33] but also in any jurisdiction where the decedent would be allowed to recover for the prospective earnings lost through his diminished life expectancy.[34] Even without this, however, it

24. Senior v. Ward, 1859, 1 El. & El. 385, 120 Eng. Rep. 954; Ohio & Miss. R. Co. v. Tindall, 1859, 13 Ind. 366.

25. Burdon v. Wood, 7 Cir., 1944, 142 F.2d 303; McMurrey Corp. v. Yawn, Tex.Civ.App.1940, 143 S. W.2d 664; Hunt-Berlin Coal Co. v. Paton, 1918, 139 Tenn. 611, 202 S.W. 935. Cf. Harris v. Embry, 1939, 70 App.D.C. 232, 105 F.2d 111 (justifiable homicide).

26. Suell v. Derricott, 1909, 161 Ala. 259, 49 So. 895; Foster v. Shepherd, 1913, 258 Ill. 164, 101 N.E. 411. In Breed v. Atlanta, B. & C. R. Co., 1941, 241 Ala. 640, 4 So.2d 315, the disability of a convict to sue was held not to bar an action for his death.

27. Cronin v. Cronin, 1944, 244 Wis. 372, 12 N.W.2d 677; Dishon's Adm'r v. Dishon's Adm'r, 1920, 187 Ky. 497, 219 S.W. 794; Keister's Adm'r v. Keister's Ex'rs, 1918, 123 Va. 157, 96 S.E. 315; Wilson v. Barton, 1926, 153 Tenn. 250, 283 S.W. 71; Wilson v. Brown, Tex.Civ.App. 1913, 154 S.W. 322.

28. See supra, p. 864.

29. Perry's Adm'r v. Louisville & N. R. Co., 1923, 199 Ky. 396, 251 S.W. 202; Harris v. Illinois Cent. R. Co., 1916, 111 Miss. 623, 71 So. 878; Edwards v. Interstate Chemical Co., 1916, 170 N.C. 551, 87 S.E. 635; Seaboard Air Line R. Co. v. Oliver, 5 Cir. 1919, 261 F. 1.

30. Collins v. Hall, 1934, 117 Fla. 282, 157 So. 646; Frescoln v. Puget Sound Traction, Light & Power Co., D.Wash.1915, 225 F. 441; Brammer's Adm'r v. Norfolk & W. R. Co., 1907, 107 Va. 206, 57 S.E. 593. Occasionally this is based upon the doctrine of res judicata, as in Little v. Blue Goose Motor Coach Co., 1927, 244 Ill.App. 427, where the tort-feasor recovered from the decedent. Since the parties are not the same, this seems to add little to the idea of a substituted cause of action.

31. Mellon v. Goodyear, 1927, 277 U.S. 335 (Federal Employers' Liability Act); Libera v. Whitaker, Clark & Daniels, 1952, 20 N.J.Super. 292, 89 A.2d 734; Crockett v. Missouri Pac. R. Co., 1929, 179 Ark. 527, 165 S.W.2d 989; Harris v. Illinois Cent. R. Co., 1916, 111 Miss. 623, 71 So. 878; Schlavick v. Manhattan Brewing Co., E.D.Ill.1952, 103 F.Supp. 744 (acceptance of workmen's compensation). Cf. Burke v. Burnham, 1952, 97 N.H. 203, 84 A.2d 918 (release to joint tort-feasor; amount received must be credited). See Notes, 1952, 5 Okl.L.Rev. 93; 1963, 16 Okl.L.Rev. 116.

32. See Schumacher, Rights of Action Under Death and Survival Statutes, 1924, 23 Mich.L.Rev. 114; Fleming, The Lost Years: A Problem in the Computation and Distribution of Damages, 1962, 50 Cal.L.Rev. 598; Notes, 1928, 13 Minn.L.Rev. 47; 1932, 80 U.Pa.L.Rev. 993; 1963, 16 Okl.L.Rev. 116.

33. As in Kling v. Torello, 1913, 87 Conn. 301, 87 A. 987; Perry v. Philadelphia, B. & W. R. Co., 1910, 1 Boyce, Del., 399, 77 A. 725; Cogswell v. Boston & Maine R. Co., 1917, 78 N.H. 379, 101 A. 145.

34. As in Prairie Creek Coal Mining Co. v. Kittrell, 1912, 106 Ark. 138, 153 S.W. 89; Louisville Belt & Iron Co. v. Hart, 1905, 122 Ky. 731, 92 S.W. 951; Person v. Sears Roebuck & Co., 1958, 252 Minn. 110,

is undoubtedly possible, as a practical matter, that a settlement made with the decedent will take into account not only his diminished earning capacity while he does live, but also the decrease in his life expectancy, and the earnings he would have made if he had lived out his normal term, out of which any benefits receivable by the beneficiaries would be expected to come. In other words, the settlement may very well have been an estimate and determination of all the damages then expected to follow from the wrong.

Opposed to this possibility is the counter-danger of an improvident settlement by an optimistic individual, confident that he is not going to die, which takes no account of shortened life expectancy, or of the interests of the survivors. Because of this there is a substantial minority view, largely confined to jurisdictions which do not allow the decedent to recover for his own curtailed life, that neither a judgment in his action [35] nor his release of his claim [36] will bar the action for wrongful death. The possibility of double compensation either has been ignored, on the ground that legally it could not arise,[37]

or has been met by a deduction from the award to the death beneficiaries, of the amount found to have been paid to the decedent covering the permanent destruction of his earning capacity,[38] or the suggestion that the expectancy of the survivors be deducted from the probable earnings in the decedent's own action.[39] It should be obvious that as yet no satisfactory systematic solution to the whole problem has been found.[40]

As to the defense of the statute of limitations, which is distinguishable only in that it does not involve the danger of double compensation, the considerable majority of the courts have held that the statute runs against the death action only from the date of death, even though at that time the decedent's own action would have been barred while he was living.[41] Only a few courts

89 N.W.2d 694; Borcherding v. Eklund, 1952, 156 Neb. 196, 55 N.W.2d 643; Littman v. Bell Tel. Co. of Pa., 1934, 315 Pa. 370, 172 A. 687.

35. De Hart v. Ohio Fuel Gas Co., 1948, 84 Ohio App. 62, 85 N.E.2d 586; Blackwell v. American Film Co., 1922, 189 Cal. 689, 209 P. 999; Dougherty v. New Orleans R. & L. Co., 1913, 133 La. 993, 63 So. 493. Accord, as to workmen's compensation claim, Halling v. Industrial Commission, 1927, 71 Utah 112, 263 P. 78.

36. Goodyear v. Davis, 1923, 114 Kan. 557, 220 P. 282, rehearing denied 1923, 115 Kan. 20, 220 P. 1049 (Federal Employers' Liability Act); Earley v. Pacific Elec. R. Co., 1917, 176 Cal. 79, 167 P. 513; Hugh Breeding, Inc. v. Daniel, Okl.1962, 373 P.2d 75; Phillips v. Community Trac. Co., 1933, 46 Ohio App. 483, 189 N.E. 444; Rowe v. Richards, 1915, 35 S.D. 201, 151 N.W. 1001.

Accord, as to release of claim for workmen's compensation: In re Cripp, 1914, 216 Mass. 586, 104 N.E. 565; Milwaukee Coke & Gas Co. v. Industrial Commission, 1915, 160 Wis. 247, 151 N.W. 245; Lewis v. Connolly Contracting Co., 1936, 196 Minn. 108, 264 N.W. 581.

37. See De Hart v. Ohio Fuel Gas Co., 1948, 84 Ohio App. 62, 85 N.E.2d 586; Robinette v. May Coal Co.,

1929, 31 Ohio App. 113, 166 N.E. 818, affirmed 120 Ohio St. 110, 165 N.E. 576; Rowe v. Richards, 1915, 35 S.D. 201, 151 N.W. 1001.

38. Dougherty v. New Orleans Ry. & Light Co., 1913, 133 La. 994, 63 So. 493.

39. Rohlfing v. Moses Akiona, Ltd., 1961, 45 Hawaii 373, 443, 369 P.2d 96.

40. "What emerges fairly from the preceding discussion is that this complex situation, like so many others involving multiple party interests, is singularly taxing to a system of law which is primarily geared to the adversary process and the demands for simplicity in loss administration imposed by the limitations inherent in jury trial. Each of the various solutions to the present problem that have been canvassed as conceivable alternatives falls in some respect short of the ideal due to the irritating intrusion of administrative or procedural restraints, but, in the absence of a much more drastic overhaul of our whole system for adjusting accident losses, nothing more ambitious can probably be realized with the relatively crude tools presently at our disposal." Fleming, The Lost Years: A Problem in the Computation and Distribution of Damages, 1962, 50 Cal.L.Rev. 598.

41. De Hart v. Ohio Fuel Gas Co., 1948, 84 Ohio App. 62, 85 N.E.2d 586 (death after 12 years); Western Union Tel. Co. v. Preston, 3 Cir. 1918, 254 F. 229, cert. denied 248 U.S. 585 (death after 10 years); Smith v. McComb Infirmary Ass'n, Miss. 1967, 196 So.2d 91; Lawlor v. Cloverleaf Memorial Park, Inc., 1968, 101 N.J.Super. 134, 243 A.2d 293. See Note, 1947, 42 Ill.L.Rev. 688.

hold that it runs from the time of the original injury, and consequently that the death action may be lost before it ever has accrued.[42] Equally inconsistent, at least in theory, is the common holding [43] with which few courts have disagreed,[44] that actions may be prosecuted under both death and survival acts, and that recovery or settlement under one does not bar an action under the other.

Defenses available against the beneficiaries themselves offer a still more troublesome problem, on which all courts have not agreed.[45] Where the action is brought under a survival act, it is in theory still on behalf of the decedent, and the contributory negligence of even a sole beneficiary has been held not to prevent recovery.[46] The same

conclusion has been reached under wrongful death acts where the damages are recoverable on behalf of the decedent's estate, on the ground that the estate is distinct from the beneficiary.[47] Under the usual death act the recovery is for the beneficiaries, and the contributory negligence [48] or the consent or assumption of risk [49] of a sole beneficiary or of all beneficiaries generally is held to preclude the action, on the same principle that would bar any other plaintiff in interest. Some few statutes have been construed to the contrary.[50]

Where only one of several beneficiaries is contributorily negligent, the better view, and now the prevailing one, is that the action is

42. Coulter v. New Jersey Pulverizing Co., 1932, 11 N.J.Misc. 5, 163 A. 661; Street v. Consumers Min. Co., 1946, 185 Va. 561, 39 S.E.2d 271; Piukkula v. Pillsbury Astoria Flouring Mills Co., 1935, 150 Or. 304, 42 P.2d 921, rehearing denied 150 Or. 304, 44 P.2d 162. Under a survival type of statute, this conclusion may be compelled. Natseway v. Jojola, 1952, 56 N.M. 793, 251 P.2d 274.

43. Pantazis v. Fidelity & Deposit Co. of Md., 1952, 369 Pa. 221, 85 A.2d 421; Koehler v. Waukesha Milk Co., 1926, 190 Wis. 52, 208 N.W. 901; Hindmarsh v. Sulpho Saline Bath Co., 1922, 108 Neb. 168, 187 N. W. 806; Puget Sound Traction, L. & P. Co. v. Frescoln, 9 Cir. 1917, 245 F. 301; St. Louis & S. F. R. Co. v. Goode, 1914, 42 Okl. 784, 142 P. 1185.

44. Epps v. Railway Express Agency, Fla.1940, 40 So.2d 131; Chesapeake § O. R. Co. v. Bank's Adm'r, 1911, 142 Ky. 746, 135 S.W. 285; Brammer's Adm'r v. Norfolk & W. R. Co., 1907, 107 Va. 206, 57 S.E. 593.

45. See Wettach, Wrongful Death and Contributory Negligence, 1938, 16 N.C.L.Rev. 211; Wigmore, Contributory Negligence of the Beneficiary as a Bar to an Administrator's Action for Death, 1908, 2 Ill.L. Rev. 487; Gilmore, Imputed Negligence, 1921, 1 Wis.L.Rev. 193, 257, 259–273.

46. Mitchell v. Akers, Tex.Civ.App.1966, 401 S.W.2d 907, ref. n. r. e.; Stockton v. Baker, 1948, 213 Ark. 918, 213 S.W.2d 896; Koehler v. Waukesha Milk Co., 1926, 190 Wis. 52, 208 N.W. 901; Love v. Detroit, J. & C. R. Co., 1912, 170 Mich. 1, 135 N.W. 963; Nashville Lumber Co. v. Busbee, 1911, 100 Ark. 76, 139 S.W. 301. See Notes, 1967, 4 Houst.L. Rev. 534; 1967, 19 Bay.L.Rev. 153.

47. O'Connor v. Benson Coal Co., 1938, 301 Mass. 145, 16 N.E.2d 636; Davis v. Margolis, 1929, 108 Conn. 645, 144 A. 665; Bloomquist v. City of La Grande, 1926, 120 Or. 19, 251 P. 252; Consolidated Traction Co. v. Hone, 1896, 59 N.J.L. 275, 35 A. 899, reversed 1897, 60 N.J.L. 444, 38 A. 759. In Pike v. Adams, 1954, 99 N.H. 221, 108 A.2d 55, recovery was even allowed where the negligent defendant was the sole beneficiary. This amounts, of course, to a raid on an insurance company. See Note, 1955, 29 St. Johns L.Rev. 321.

48. Acres v. Hall's Adm'r, Ky.1952, 253 S.W.2d 373; Nichols v. Nashville Housing Authority, 1949, 187 Tenn. 683, 216 S.W.2d 694; Jenson v. Glemaker, 1935, 195 Minn. 556, 263 N.W. 624; Butterfield v. Community Light & Power Co., 1946, 115 Vt. 23, 49 A.2d 415; Womack v. Preach, 1946, 64 Ariz. 61, 165 P.2d 657. Cf. Gilbertson v. Huffman, 1959, 54 Wash. 2d 312, 340 P.2d 559 (last clear chance).

Under particular statutes, other conduct of a beneficiary may be a complete or partial defense. See for example Matthews v. Hicks, 1955, 197 Va. 112, 87 S.E.2d 629 (adultery of wife). As to immunity of the defendant toward a beneficiary, see supra, p. 666.

49. Lee v. New River & Pocahontas Consol. Coal Co., 4 Cir. 1913, 203 F. 644; Dickinson v. Stuart Colliery Co., 1912, 71 W.Va. 325, 76 S.E. 654; Missouri, K. & T. R. Co. of Texas v. Evans, 1897, 16 Tex.Civ. App. 68, 41 S.W. 80; Hodges v. Savannah Kaolin Co., 1923, 155 Ga. 143, 116 S.E. 303, opinion conformed to 30 Ga.App. 294, 117 S.E. 829 (all cases of consent of parent to employment of child in dangerous occupation).

50. McKay v. Syracuse Rapid Transit Co., 1913, 208 N.Y. 359, 101 N.E. 885; Danforth v. Emmons, 1924, 124 Me. 156, 126 A. 821; Bastedo v. Frailey, 1932, 109 N.J.L. 390, 162 A. 621.

not barred as to those who were not negligent, but that recovery is diminished to the extent of the damages of the negligent beneficiary, who is denied all share in the proceeds.[51] The same conclusion has been reached as to assumption of risk.[52] There were formerly a few decisions to the contrary, holding that the entire action was barred;[53] but since the leading decision to this effect has lately been overruled in Illinois,[54] it appears unlikely that these will be followed today. About all that remains of the barred action is the antique rule in a small number of states [55] which "imputes" the negligence of one parent to the other when the action is for the death of a child. Except where it can be justified on the basis that the damages recovered will be commun-

ity property,[56] this, too, has generally been rejected as a senseless survival of a discarded concept of marital unity.[57] Although the death acts usually are construed to provide that only one action may be maintained for the death,[58] it has been held that a release from one beneficiary will not prevent recovery by others,[59] and even that the statute of limitations may run against recovery on behalf of one, but not others.[60]

The impression gained from a survey of the law of wrongful death and survival is that both the statutes and the decisions interpreting them have suffered from a lack of foresight as to the problems which would arise, and an excessive timidity in compensating the bereaved family; and that the entire field would benefit greatly from redrafting along the lines of some model act which would be both comprehensive and consistent.[61]

---

51. Bartholomay v. St. Thomas Lumber Co., N.D. 1967, 148 N.W.2d 278; City of Louisville v. Stuckenborg, Ky.1969, 438 S.W.2d 94; Oviatt v. Camarra, 1957, 210 Or. 445, 311 P.2d 746; Lindley v. Sink, 1940, 218 Ind. 1, 30 N.E.2d 456; Walden v. Coleman, 1962, 105 Ga.App. 435, 124 S.E.2d 695.

The same conclusion is reached when the defendant is one of the beneficiaries. Nosser v. Nosser, 1931, 161 Miss. 636, 137 So. 491; Bays v. Cox' Adm'r, 1950, 312 Ky. 827, 229 S.W.2d 737. See also, as to statutes of limitations, Cross v. Pacific Gas & Elec. Co., 1964, 60 Cal.2d 690, 36 Cal.Rptr. 321, 388 P.2d 353.

52. Kentucky Utilities Co. v. McCarty's Adm'r, 1916, 169 Ky. 38, 183 S.W. 237.

53. Hazel v. Hoopeston-Danville Motor Bus Co., 1923, 310 Ill. 38, 141 N.E. 392; Wilson v. Clarendon County, 1927, 139 S.C. 333, 138 S.E. 33; Darbrinsky v. Pennsylvania Co., 1915, 248 Pa. 503, 94 A. 269. At the other extreme were such cases as Herrell v. St. Louis-San Francisco R. Co., 1929, 324 Mo. 38, 23 S.W.2d 102, refusing even to reduce the damages. Cf. Kokesh v. Price, 1917, 136 Minn. 304, 161 N.W. 715 (reduction not demanded).

54. In Nudd v. Matsoukas, 1956, 7 Ill.2d 608, 131 N.E.2d 525. See also Walden v. Coleman, 1962, 217 Ga. 599, 124 S.E.2d 265, declining to follow prior authority.

55. Klepper v. Breslin, Fla.1955, 83 So.2d 587; Shelton v. Williams, 1959, 204 Tenn. 417, 321 S.W.2d 807; Beasley v. United States, D.C.S.C.1948, 81 F. Supp. 518.

56. Cervantes v. Maco Gas Co., 1960, 177 Cal.App.2d 246, 2 Cal.Rptr. 75; Crevelli v. Chicago, M. & St. P. R. Co., 1917, 98 Wash. 42, 167 P. 66.

57. Reynolds v. Thompson, Mo.1948, 215 S.W.2d 452; Lindley v. Sink, 1940, 218 Ind. 1, 30 N.E.2d 456; Los Angeles & Salt Lake R. Co. v. Umbaugh, 1942, 61 Nev. 214, 123 P.2d 224; Tufty v. Sioux Transit Co., 1945, 70 S.D. 352, 17 N.W.2d 700; Pearson v. National Manufacture & Stores Corp., 1941, 219 N. C. 717, 14 S.E.2d 811.

58. Daubert v. Western Meat Co., 1915, 139 Cal. 480, 69 P. 297, affirmed 139 Cal. 480, 73 P. 244; Gulf & S. I. R. Co. v. Bradley, 1915, 110 Miss. 152, 69 So. 666; Cowan v. Atchison, T. & S. F. R. Co., 1917, 66 Okl. 273, 168 P. 1015; Edwards v. Interstate Chemical Co., 1916, 170 N.C. 551, 87 S.E. 635. But see contra: Nelson v. Galveston, H. & S. A. R. Co., 1890, 78 Tex. 621, 14 S.W. 1021; Eichorn v. New Orleans & C. R. Light & Power Co., 1905, 114 La. 712, 38 So. 526.

59. Kroger Grocery & Baking Co. v. Reddin, 8 Cir. 1942, 128 F.2d 787; McVeigh v. Minneapolis & R. R. R. Co., 1910, 110 Minn. 184, 124 N.W. 971; Pittsburgh, C. C. & St. L. R. Co. v. Moore, 1898, 152 Ind. 345, 53 N.E. 290.

60. East Line & R. R. R. Co. v. Culberson, 1888, 72 Tex. 375, 10 S.W. 706.

61. See Notes, 1935, 48 Harv.L.Rev. 1008; 1931, 44 Harv.L.Rev. 980; Killion, Wrongful Death Actions in California: Some Needed Amendments, 1937, 25 Cal.L.Rev. 170.

CHAPTER 25

ECONOMIC RELATIONS

128. INJURIOUS FALSEHOOD

A considerable body of law has grown up about the subject of interference with commercial or economic relations. Included in the field of such relations are of course existing contracts, and agreements and understandings which are contractual in their nature—and particularly contracts of a business or commercial character, or those of employment; and in addition, the expectation of pecuniary or economic advantage from dealings with others, such as the prospect of obtaining future customers, or of future employment. The relation may exist between the plaintiff and one individual only, as in the case of an existing contract, or it may be a general relation with such members of the public as may be expected to deal with the plaintiff.[1]

The recognition that such relations are entitled to protection against unreasonable interference is on the whole a comparatively recent development. In one respect, however, it is very old. Pecuniary loss inflicted by interference with the plaintiff's personal reputation already has been encountered in defamation.[2] Because of its ancient, left-handed association with defamation, the kind of interference by falsehoods which are not personally defamatory, and yet cause pecuniary loss, has for some centuries been regarded as a more or less distinct tort in itself. Thus far, however, it lacks any very definite name. So far as the courts have given it one of late, it has been called disparagement.[3]

The earliest cases,[4] which arose shortly before 1600, involved oral aspersions cast upon the plaintiff's ownership of land, by which he was prevented from leasing or selling it; and from this the tort acquired the name of "slander of title."[5] From the beginning, however, the action seems to have been recognized as only loosely allied to defamation, and to be rather an action on the case for the special damage resulting from the defendant's interference. In the nineteenth century it was enlarged by slow degrees, first to include written aspersions[6] and the title to property other than land,[7] and then to cover disparagement of the quality of the property,[8] rather than its title. Hence it has variously been called "disparagement of property," "slander of goods,"

3. See the excellent Note, 1953, 63 Yale L.J. 65. Also Wood, Disparagement of Title and Quality, 1942, 20 Can.Bar Rev. 296, 430; Notes, 1945, 33 Geo.L.J. 213; 1945, 19 So.Cal.L.Rev. 45; 1943, 28 Corn.L.Q. 226.

4. Gerrard v. Dickenson, 1588, Cro.Eliz. 196, 78 Eng. Rep. 452; Pennyman v. Rabanks, 1895, Cro.Eliz. 427, 78 Eng.Rep. 668; see Earl of Northumberland v. Byrt, 1606, Cro.Jac. 163, 79 Eng.Rep. 143. See the chronological list of English Cases in Bower, Actionable Defamation, 2d Ed. 1923, 212 note.

5. Bower, Actionable Defamation, 2d Ed. 1923, 210 note, traces this to the use of "slander" as a generic term for injury or depreciation of any kind.

6. See Coley v. Hecker, 1928, 206 Cal. 22, 272 P. 1045; Barkhorn v. Adlib Associates, D. Hawaii 1962, 203 F.Supp. 121.

7. Malachy v. Soper, 1836, 3 Bing.N.C. 371, 132 Eng. Rep. 453.

8. Western Counties Manure Co. v. Lawes Chem. Manure Co., 1874, L.R. 9 Ex. 218.

1. Green, Relational Interests, 1935, 29 Ill.L.Rev. 1041, 30 Ill.L.Rev. 1.

2. See supra, p. 760.

and "trade libel." As a matter of fact, subsequent decisions have shown that the tort is broader in its scope than any of these terms would indicate.

The principle has been applied, for example, to statements injurious to the plaintiff's business but casting no reflection upon either his person or his property, such as the assertion that he has died or gone out of business,[9] or defamatory words concerning his employees.[10] It has even been carried over to interference with non-commercial relations, such as the expectancy of a marriage,[11] or the right to remain in the United States rather than be deported,[12] or the case of an employer falsely reporting payments to an employee which subject him to income tax prosecution,[13] or a forged assignment of

commissions resulting in plaintiff's discharge by his employer,[14] or even solicitation of money in the plaintiff's name without sending the tips on the races promised in return.[15] Undoubtedly the best and most inclusive name for the tort is that of "injurious falsehood," coined by Sir John Salmond,[16] but it cannot be pretended that thus far the courts have seen fit to make any use of it.

Because of the unfortunate association with "slander," a supposed analogy to defamation has hung over the tort like a fog,[17] concealing its real character, and has had great influence upon its development. The plaintiff's title or property seems to have been regarded as somehow personified, and so defamed.[18] One important consequence has been that many courts have applied to disparagement the rule that equity, in the interest of freedom of speech or trial by jury, will not enjoin the publication of libel

9. Ratcliffe v. Evans, [1892] Q.B. 524; Dudley v. Briggs, 1886, 141 Mass. 582, 6 N.E. 717; American Ins. Co. v. France, 1903, 111 Ill.App. 382; Davis v. New England R. Pub. Co., 1909, 203 Mass. 470, 89 N.E. 565. Cf. Sheppard Pub. Co. v. Press Pub. Co., 1905, 10 Ont.L.Rep. 243; House of Directories v. Lane Directory Co., 1918, 182 Ky. 384, 206 S.W. 475; Jarrahdale Timber Co. v. Temperley & Co., 1894, 11 T.L.R. 119 (statement that plaintiff does not import certain wood); and see Balden v. Shorter, [1933] Ch. 427 (statement that plaintiff was employed by defendant, as a result of which he lost commissions).

10. Riding v. Smith, 1876, 1 Ex. 91, 154 Eng.Rep. 38. Cf. Casey v. Arnott, 1876, 2 C.P.D. 24 (statement that plaintiff's ship was unseaworthy, as a result of which the crew refused to go to sea).

11. Shepherd v. Wakeman, 1662, 1 Sid. 79, 82 Eng. Rep. 982. Cf. Freeman v. Busch Jewelry Co., N.D. Ga.1951, 98 F.Supp. 963 (marriage).

12. Al Raschid v. News Syndicate Co., 1934, 265 N.Y. 1, 191 N.E. 713. See Note, 1934, 14 Boston U.L.Rev. 856.

13. Gale v. Ryan, 1941, 263 App.Div. 76, 31 N.Y.S.2d 732; Penn-Ohio Steel Corp. v. Allis-Chalmers Mfg. Co., 1966, 50 Misc.2d 860, 272 N.Y.S.2d 266, reversed on other grounds, 28 App.Div.2d 659, 280 N.Y.S.2d 679, affirmed 21 N.Y.2d 916, 289 N.Y.S.2d 753, 237 N.E.2d 73. Cf. Owens v. Mench, 1952, 81 D. & C., Pa., 314, 24 Leh.L.J. 522 (physician falsely reporting on injury, necessitating suit for workmen's compensation); Felis v. Greenberg, 1966, 51 Misc.2d 441, 273 N.Y.S.2d 288 (physician falsely reporting to insurer); Cooper v. Weissblatt, 1935, 154 Misc. 522, 277 N.Y.S. 709 (deceiving church tribunal, forcing plain-

tiff to defend suit); Morgan v. Graham, 10 Cir. 1956, 228 F.2d 625 (president of liability insurer denying coverage, plaintiff dismissed his action against insured).

14. Bartlett v. Federal Outfitting Co., 1933, 133 Cal. App. 747, 24 P.2d 877.

15. Wise v. Western Union Tel. Co., 1934, 6 W.W. Harr., Del., 155, 172 A. 757. Cf. Kelite Products Inc. v. Binzel, 5 Cir. 1955, 224 F.2d 131 (filing change of address card with post-office, so that plaintiff did not receive business mail).

Cf. Morrison v. National Broadcasting Co., 1965, 24 App.Div.2d 284, 266 N.Y.S.2d 406 reversed on other grounds, 19 N.Y.2d 453, 280 N.Y.S.2d 641, 227 N.E. 2d 572; and see Note, 1966, 35 U.Cin.L.Rev. 523.

16. Salmond, Law of Torts, § 151.

17. Thus, for example, the statute of limitations applicable to defamation is commonly held to apply, as in Norton v. Kanouff, 1957, 165 Neb. 435, 86 N. W.2d 72; Woodard v. Pacific Fruit & Produce Co., 1940, 165 Or. 250, 106 P.2d 1043.

18. " * * * by a sort of figure of speech, in which the title is personified and made subject to many of the rules applicable to personal slander, when the words themselves are not actionable." Kendall v. Stone, 1851, 5 N.Y. 14. Accord: Coley v. Hecker, 1928, 206 Cal. 22, 272 P. 1045; Carroll v. Warner Bros. Pictures, S.D.N.Y.1937, 20 F.Supp. 405.

or slander.[19] The tendency in recent years has been either to recognize that disparagement stands on an entirely different footing,[20] or to find that it is merely a method of unfair competition [21] or of interference with business relations,[22] or a part of a conspiracy to do one or the other,[23] and so to grant the injunction.[24] The theory upon which the plaintiff's complaint is drawn will obviously very often affect the decision.[25] Since in every case the plaintiff must prove special damage, in the form of loss of a present or a prospective advantage,[26] it seems clear that injurious falsehood should be regarded merely as one form of intentional interference with economic relations,[27] rather than as a branch of the more general harm to reputation involved in libel or slander.[28]

It is not always easy to distinguish between personal defamation of the plaintiff and disparagement of his property or business.[29] If the statement made charges the plaintiff with personal misconduct, or imputes to him reprehensible characteristics, it is regarded as libel or slander;[30] and since any such charge concerning his conduct of his business will affect him in that business, the slander is actionable without proof of damage. On the other hand, if the aspersions reflect only upon the quality of what he has to sell,[31] or the character of his business

19. Boston Diatite Co. v. Florence Mfg. Co., 1873, 114 Mass. 69; Marlin Firearms Co. v. Shields, 1902, 171 N.Y. 384, 64 N.E. 163; A. Hollander & Son v. Jos. Hollander, Inc., 1935, 117 N.J.Eq. 578, 177 A. 80; McMorries v. Hudson Sales Corp., Tex.Civ.App.1950, 233 S.W.2d 938; Schmoldt v. Oakley, Okl.1964, 390 P.2d 882.

20. Black & Yates v. Mahogany Ass'n, 3 Cir. 1941, 129 F.2d 226. Cf. Paramount Pictures v. Leader Press, 10 Cir. 1939, 106 F.2d 229; Saxon Motor Sales v. Torino, 1938, 166 Misc. 863, 2 N.Y.S.2d 885 ("more than a mere libel"); and see Montgomery Ward & Co. v. United Retail, W. & D. S. Employees, 1948, 400 Ill. 38, 49–50, 79 N.E.2d 46, 51–52.

21. Dehydro, Inc. v. Tretolite Co., N.D.Okl.1931, 53 F.2d 273; Bourjois, Inc. v. Park Drug Co., 8 Cir. 1936, 82 F.2d 468; Schering & Glatz v. American Pharmaceutical Co., 1933, 261 N.Y. 304, 185 N.E. 109. See Nims, Unfair Competition by False Statements of Disparagement, 1934, 19 Corn.L.Q. 63; Wolff, Unfair Competition by Truthful Disparagement, 1938, 47 Yale L.J. 1304; Note, [1950] U.Ill.L. Forum 675.

22. Pure Milk Producers Ass'n v. Bridges, 1937, 146 Kan. 15, 68 P.2d 658; I. P. Frink, Inc. v. Erickson, D.Mass.1923, 16 F.2d 496; Davis v. New England Ry. Pub. Co., 1909, 203 Mass. 470, 89 N.E. 565; Carter v. Knapp Motor Co., 1943, 243 Ala. 600, 11 So.2d 383; Maytag Co. v. Meadows Mfg. Co., 7 Cir. 1929, 35 F.2d 403, cert. denied, 1930, 281 U.S. 737. As to the close relation between injurious falsehood and such interference, see Note, 1933, 33 Col.L.Rev. 90; Birmingham Broadcasting Co. v. Bell, 1953, 259 Ala. 656, 68 So.2d 314.

23. Bausch & Lomb Optical Co. v. Wahlgren, N.D. Ill.1932, 1 F.Supp. 799, affirmed, 7 Cir. 1932, 68 F. 2d 660; Russell v. Russell, 1940, 127 N.J.Eq. 555, 14 A.2d 540.

24. See Pound, Equitable Relief Against Defamation and Injuries to Personality, 1916, 29 Harv.L.Rev. 640, 668; Notes, 1946, 21 N.Y.U.L.Rev. 518; 1953, 63 Yale L.J. 65, 96–104.

25. See for example Adriance, Platt & Co. v. National Harrow Co., 2 Cir. 1903, 121 F.Supp. 827; Dittgen v. Racine Paper Goods Co., C.C.Wis.1905, 164 F.

84; Lawrence Trust Co. v. Sun-American Pub. Co., 1923, 245 Mass. 262, 139 N.E. 655; Davis v. New England Ry. Pub. Co., 1909, 203 Mass. 470, 89 N.E. 565.

26. See infra, p. 922. Other important differences arise as to the burden of proof. See infra, p. 921.

27. Green, Relational Interest, 1935, 35 Ill.L.Rev. 1, 37.

28. As to the differences between defamation and disparagement, see Smith, Disparagement of Property, 1913, 13 Col.L.Rev. 13, 121.

29. See Wham, Disparagement of Property, 1926, 21 Ill.L.Rev. 26; Hibschman, Defamation or Disparagement, 1940, 24 Minn.L.Rev. 625; Note, 1953, 63 Yale L.J. 65, 69–74.

30. Merle v. Sociological Research Film Corp., 1915, 166 App.Div. 376, 152 N.Y.S. 829 (factory used as place of assignation); Kilpatrick v. Edge, 1913, 85 N.J.L. 7, 88 A. 839 (misconduct in a Turkish bath).

In Dubourcq v. Brouwer, Sup.Ct.1953, 124 N.Y.S.2d 61, affirmed, 1953, 282 App.Div. 861, 124 N.Y.S.2d 842, it was held that where defamation will lie disparagement is excluded. Contra, Hatchard v. Mège, 1887, 18 Q.B.D. 771 (survival).

31. Drug Research Corp. v. Curtis Pub. Co., 1960, 7 N.Y.2d 435, 199 N.Y.S.2d 33, 166 N.E.2d 319; National Dynamics Corp. v. Petersen Pub. Co., S.D.N. Y.1960, 185 F.Supp. 573; Blens Chemicals v. Wyandotte Chemical Corp., 1950, 197 Misc. 1066, 96 N.Y.

as such, it is merely disparagement, and proof of damage is essential to the cause of action.[32] The difficulty lies in the fact that many statements do both. It might be possible to imply some accusation of personal inefficiency or incompetence, at least, in nearly every imputation directed against a business or its product.[33] The courts have gone to some lengths, however, in refusing to do so,[34] particularly where the most that can be made out of the words is a charge of ignorance or negligence.[35] Personal defamation is found only where the imputation fairly implied is that the plaintiff is dishonest or lacking in integrity, or that he is deliberately perpetrating a fraud upon the public by selling a product which he knows to be defective.[36] Such, at least, is the theory of the

cases; yet it is not always easy to find the purported distinction in the actual facts.

Interests Protected

For the most part the injurious falsehood cases have been concerned with aspersions upon the title to property, or its quality. Any type of legally protected [37] property interest that is capable of being sold may be the subject of disparagement, including land,[38] remainders,[39] leases,[40] mineral

S.2d 47; Testing Systems, Inc. v. Magnaflux Corp., E.D.Pa.1966, 251 F.Supp. 286.

32. Fowler v. Curtis Pub. Co., D.C.Cir. 1950, 182 F.2d 377; General Market Co. v. Post-Intelligencer Co., 1917, 96 Wash. 575, 165 P. 482; National Refining Co. v. Benzo Gas Motor Fuel Co., 8 Cir. 1927, 20 F. 2d 763; Dust Sprayer Mfg. Co. v. Western Fruit Grower, 1907, 126 Mo.App. 139, 103 S.W. 566; Cleveland Leader Printing Co. v. Nethersole, 1911, 84 Ohio St. 118, 95 N.E. 735.

33. Cf. Summit Hotel Co. v. National Broadcasting Co., 1939, 336 Pa. 182, 8 A.2d 302 ("rotten hotel" held to reflect on the operators or management).

34. Australian Newspaper Co. v. Bennett, [1894] A.C. 284 ("Ananias"); Nonpareil Cork Mfg. Co. v. Keasbey & Mattison Co., D.Pa.1901, 108 F. 721 (product a "fraud"); Erick Bowman Remedy Co. v. Jensen Salsbery Laboratories, 8 Cir. 1926, 17 F.2d 255 (Barnum was right); Bosi v. New York Herald Co., 1901, 33 Misc. 622, 68 N.Y.S. 898, affirmed, 1901, 58 App.Div. 619, 68 N.Y.S. 1134 (hotel a favorite resort of anarchists).

35. Dooling v. Budget Pub. Co., 1887, 144 Mass. 258, 10 N.E. 809 (poor dinner served by caterer); Marlin Fire Arms Co. v. Shields, 1902, 171 N.Y. 384, 64 N. E. 163 (poor quality firearms); Shaw Cleaners & Dyers v. Des Moines Dress Club, 1932, 215 Iowa 1130, 245 N.W. 231 (garments only "half cleaned"); Adolf Philipp Co. v. New Yorker Staats-Zeitung Co., 1914, 165 App.Div. 377, 150 N.Y.S. 1044 (theatre and play); Hopkins Chemical Co. v. Read Drug & Chemical Co., 1914, 124 Md. 210, 92 A. 478.

36. Harwood Pharmacal Co. v. National Broadcasting Co., 1961, 9 N.Y.2d 460, 214 N.Y.S.2d 725, 174 N.E.2d 602 (product containing habit-forming

drugs); Rosenberg v. J. C. Penney Co., 1939, 30 Cal.App.2d 609, 86 P.2d 696 (shoddy garments); Vitagraph Co. of America v. Ford, S.D.N.Y.1917, 241 F. 681 (false motives and deceptive advertising); Puget Sound Nav. Co. v. Carter, W.D.Wash.1916, 233 F. 832 (exorbitant rates and ruthless competition); Tobin v. Alfred M. Best Co., 1907, 120 App. Div. 387, 105 N.Y.S. 294 ("fake" insurance policy). See Hibschman, Defamation or Disparagement, 1940, 24 Minn.L.Rev. 625.

37. Doubtful titles have been denied protection. Millman v. Pratt, 1824, 2 B. & C. 486, 107 Eng.Rep. 465; Thompson v. White, 1886, 70 Cal. 135, 11 P. 564; Stovall v. Texas Co., Tex.Civ.App.1924, 262 S. W. 152, error denied, 1926, 114 Tex. 582, 278 S.W. 1115; cf. Welsbach Light Co. v. American Incandescent Lamp Co., C.C.N.Y.1899, 99 F. 501. Also a mere expectancy. Nelson v. Staff, 1618, Cro.Jac. 422, 79 Eng.Rep. 360; Humphreys v. Stanfield, 1638, Cro.Car. 469, 79 Eng.Rep. 1005. Massachusetts has refused to protect an equitable interest, Hurley v. Donovan, 1902, 182 Mass. 64, 64 N.E. 685, and Alabama a debt claim. Pickens v. Hal J. Copeland Grocery Co., 1929, 219 Ala. 697, 123 So. 223. Since both are capable of being sold, the last two decisions seem wrong. On the other hand, in L–M Co. v. Blanchard, La.App.1967, 197 So.2d 178, mere adverse possession of land was held to be sufficient.

38. Thus the tort frequently arises out of the assertion of a lien or other claim against land, preventing its sale or lease. Cronkhite v. Chaplin, 10 Cir. 1922, 282 F. 579; Greenlake Inv. Co. v. Swarthout, Mo.1942, 161 S.W.2d 697; Frega v. Northern New Jersey Mortgage Ass'n, 1958, 51 N.J.Super. 331, 143 A.2d 885. Cf. Cawrse v. Signal Oil Co., 1940, 164 Or. 666, 103 P.2d 729; Lehman v. Goldin, 1948, 160 Fla. 710, 36 So.2d 259; Baker v. Kale, 1947, 83 Cal.App.2d 89, 189 P.2d 57. Compare, as to disparagement of quality, Paull v. Halferty, 1869, 63 Pa. St. 46 (iron ore about to run out).

39. Vaughn v. Ellis, 1609, Cro.Jac. 213, 79 Eng.Rep. 185.

40. Hopkins v. Drowne, 1898, 21 R.I. 20, 41 A. 567; Fleming v. McDonald, 1911, 230 Pa. 75, 79 A. 226;

rights,[41] chattels,[42] and intangible interests, such as trade marks,[43] copyrights,[44] patents,[45] corporate shares,[46] or literary property,[47] such as motion pictures.[48]

It seems clear, however, that entirely too much emphasis has been placed upon the property element. The gist of the tort is the interference with the prospect of sale or some other advantageous relation; and it is equally possible to disparge the plaintiff's business by reflecting upon its existence [49] or character,[50] the manner in which it is con-

ducted,[51] its employees,[52] or its customers,[53] without affecting any property. A common illustration is the assertion that the sale of the plaintiff's product infringes the defendant's patent or copyright,[54] which scarcely can be said to disparage the title or quality of the goods themselves. The disparagement itself may be by implication, as where the statement that one portrait of a President is the first one made of him is understood to mean that another is not.[55] As has been suggested above,[56] the cause of action probably is as broad as any injurious falsehood which disturbs prospective advantage, and it is not necessarily confined even to commercial relations.

Elements of Cause of Action

Injurious falsehood, or disparagement, then, may consist of the publication of matter derogatory to the plaintiff's title to his property, or its quality, or to his business in

Brook v. Rawl, 1849, 4 Exch. 521, 154 Eng.Rep. 1320 (assignee of lease).

41. Reynolds v. Villines, 1931, 148 Okl. 191, 298 P. 262.

42. Woodard v. Pacific Fruit & Produce Co., 1940, 165 Or. 250, 106 P.2d 1043 (crop); Miller v. First Nat. Bank of Gladbrook, 1935, 220 Iowa 1066, 264 N.W. 272 (sheep); Youngquist v. American Ry. Express Co., 1926, 49 S.D. 373, 206 N.W. 576 (horses). See also the cases of disparagement of quality of goods, supra, p. 915.

43. Hatchard v. Mège, 1887, 18 Q.B.D. 771; Royal Baking Powder Co. v. Wright, 1900, 18 Reg.Pat.Cas. 95; Herbert Products v. Oxy-Dry Sprayer Corp., 1955, 1 Misc.2d 71, 145 N.Y.S.2d 168.

44. Dicks v. Brooks, 1880, 15 Ch.Div. 22.

45. Hanson v. Hall Mfg. Co., 1922, 194 Iowa 1213, 190 N.W. 967; Andrew v. Deshler, 1881, 43 N.J.L. 16; Croft v. Richardson, 1880, 59 How.Pr., N.Y., 356.

46. Malachy v. Soper, 1836, 3 Bing.N.C. 371, 132 Eng.Rep. 453; Coronado Development Corp. v. Millikin, 1940, 175 Misc. 1, 22 N.Y.S.2d 670, appeal dismissed, 1941, 262 App.Div. 1019, 30 N.Y.S.2d 847.

47. See Hygienic Fleeced Underwear Co. v. Way, 1908, 35 Pa.Super. 229; John W. Lovell Co. v. Houghton, 1889, 116 N.Y. 520, 22 N.E. 1066.

48. Paramount Pictures v. Leader Press, 10 Cir. 1939, 106 F.2d 229; Carroll v. Warner Bros. Pictures, D.N.Y.1937, 20 F.Supp. 405 (title). Cf. Advance Music Corp. v. American Tobacco Co., 1946, 296 N.Y. 79, 70 N.E.2d 401, reversing, 1944, 268 App.Div. 707, 53 N.Y.S.2d 337 (song hit); Pendleton v. Time, Inc., 1949, 339 Ill.App. 188, 89 N.E.2d 435 (portrait of President Truman).

49. See cases cited supra, note 9.

50. Cf. Le Massena v. Storm, 1901, 62 App.Div. 150, 70 N.Y.S. 882 (suitability of newspaper for advertising); Lyne v. Nicholls, 1906, 23 T.L.R. 86 (circulation of newspaper); Braun v. Armour & Co., 1930,

254 N.Y. 514, 173 N.E. 845 (kosher butcher listed as selling bacon).

51. Shaw Cleaners & Dyers v. Des Moines Dress Club, 1932, 215 Iowa 1130, 245 N.W. 231 (garments only half cleaned); Dooling v. Budget Pub. Co., 1887, 144 Mass. 258, 10 N.E. 809 (poor dinner served by caterer); Australian Newspaper Co. v. Bennett, [1894] A.C. 284 (newspaper "Ananias").

52. Cf. Riding v. Smith, 1876, 1 Exch. 91, 154 Eng. Rep. 38.

53. Cf. Kennedy v. Press Pub. Co., 1886, 41 Hun 422, 3 N.Y.St.Rep. 139; Bosi v. New York Herald Co., 1901, 33 Misc. 622, 68 N.Y.S. 898, affirmed, 1901, 58 App.Div. 619, 68 N.Y.S. 1134; Maglio v. New York Herald Co., 1903, 83 App.Div. 44, 82 N.Y.S. 509; Id., 1904, 93 App.Div. 546, 87 N.Y.S. 927.

54. See cases cited supra, notes 44, 45.

55. Pendleton v. Time, Inc., 1949, 339 Ill.App. 188, 89 N.E.2d 435. Cf. Advance Music Corp. v. American Tobacco Co., 1946, 296 N.Y. 79, 70 N.E.2d 401, reversing, 1944, 268 App.Div. 707, 53 N.Y.S.2d 337 (failure to include song hits in "Hit Parade"); Davis v. New England Ry. Pub. Co., 1909, 203 Mass. 470, 89 N.E. 565 (failure to list plaintiff in directory); and cf. National Refining Co. v. Benzo Gas Motor Fuel Co., 8 Cir. 1927, 20 F.2d 763; Paramount Pictures v. Leader Press, 10 Cir. 1939, 106 F.2d 229.

56. Supra, p. 916.

general, or even to some element of his personal affairs, of a kind calculated to prevent others from dealing with him, or otherwise to interfere with his relations with others to his disadvantage.[57] The cause of action founded upon it resembles that for defamation, but differs from it materially in the greater burden of proof resting on the plaintiff, and the necessity for special damage in all cases.[58] The falsehood must be communicated to a third person,[59] since the tort consists of interference with the relation with such persons. But the plaintiff must plead and prove not only the publication and its disparaging innuendo, as in defamation,[60] but something more. There is no presumption, as in the case of personal slander, that the disparaging statement is false, and the plaintiff must establish its falsity as a part of his cause of action.[61] Although it has been contended [62] that there is no essential reason against liability where even the truth is published for the purpose of doing harm, the policy of the courts has been to encourage the publication of the truth, regardless of motive.

In addition, the plaintiff must prove in all cases that the publication has played a material and substantial part [63] in inducing others not to deal with him, and that as a result he has suffered special damage.[64] The analogy is thus to the kind of personal slander which does not charge a crime or loathsome disease, or defame him in his business, profession, or office, and so is not actionable unless damage is proved.[65]

The basis of the defendant's liability for the publication has given considerable difficulty.[66] It is very often said that proof of "malice" on the part of the defendant is essential to the cause of action.[67] But in such cases the question almost invariably has arisen as a matter of what must be pleaded, or the defendant has asserted a conditional privilege,[68] and the "malice" required has been merely such an improper motive as would defeat the privilege. On the other hand, in the absence of privilege many

---

57. This definition is somewhat broader than that given in Bower, Actionable Defamation, 2d Ed. 1923, 210, and the Restatement of Torts, § 629.

As to disparagement under the Uniform Deceptive Practices Act, see Note, 1966, 51 Iowa L.Rev. 1066.

58. See Smith, Disparagement of Property, 1913, 13 Col.L.Rev. 13, 121.

59. Hill v. Ward, 1848, 13 Ala. 310; Potosi Zinc Co. v. Mahoney, 1913, 36 Nev. 390, 135 P. 1078; Womack v. McDonald, 1929, 219 Ala. 75, 121 So. 57; Rhoades v. Bugg, 1910, 148 Mo.App. 707, 129 S.W. 38; Arnold v. Producer's Oil Co., Tex.Civ.App.1917, 196 S.W. 735.

Filing of liens, mortgages and other encumbrances is a sufficient publication to disparage title. Coffman v. Henderson, 1913, 9 Ala.App. 553, 63 So. 808; Moore v. Rolin, 1892, 89 Va. 107, 15 S.E. 520; New England Oil & Pipe Line Co. v. Rogers, 1932, 154 Okl. 285, 7 P.2d 638; Dwelle v. Home Realty & Investment Co., 1932, 134 Kan. 520, 7 P.2d 522; Kelly v. First State Bank, 1920, 145 Minn. 331, 177 N.W. 347.

60. See supra, p. 746.

61. Brinson v. Carter, 1922, 29 Ga.App. 159, 113 S.E. 820; Allis-Chalmers Mfg. Co. v. Lowry, 1927, 124 Kan. 566, 261 P. 828; Fant v. Sullivan, Tex.Civ. App.1913, 152 S.W. 515, error refused; Long v. Rucker, 1912, 166 Mo.App. 572, 149 S.W. 1051; Felt v. Germania Life Ins. Co., 1912, 149 App.Div. 14, 133 N.Y.S. 519. The matter falsified must cause the damage, and there is no action if it does not. Kirsch v. Barnes, N.D.Cal.1957, 153 F.Supp. 260 (false acknowledgment of genuine contract).

62. See Wolff, Unfair Competition by Truthful Disparagement, 1938, 47 Yale L.J. 1304.

63. Fleming v. McDonald, 1911, 230 Pa. 75, 79 A. 226; Neville v. Higbie, 1933, 130 Cal.App. 669, 20 P.2d 348; Farmers' State Bank v. Hintz, 1928, 206 Iowa 911, 221 N.W. 540; Houston Chronicle Pub. Co. v. Martin, Tex.Civ.App.1933, 64 S.W.2d 816; Union Car Adv. Co. v. Collier, 1934, 263 N.Y. 386, 189 N.E. 463.

64. See infra, p. 922.

65. See supra, p. 760.

66. See Prosser, Injurious Falsehood: The Basis of Liability, 1959, 59 Col.L.Rev. 425.

67. Jarrett v. Ross, 1942, 139 Tex. 560, 164 S.W.2d 550; International Visible Systems Corp. v. Remington-Rand, 6 Cir. 1933, 65 F.2d 540; Waterhouse v. McPheeters, 1940, 176 Tenn. 666, 145 S.W. 2d 766; R. Olsen Oil Co. v. Fidler, 10 Cir. 1952, 199 F.2d 868; Local Federal Sav. & Loan Ass'n of Oklahoma City v. Sickles, 1946, 196 Okl. 395, 165 P.2d 328.

68. See infra, p. 922.

courts have said that "malice" will be presumed from the mere fact of the publication,[69] while others have gone to the extreme of saying that it means no more than an intent to publish, with a simple lack of privilege, which is to say without justification, cause or excuse.[70]

From these last statements a well known article by Jeremiah Smith,[71] which seems to have missed the point of the English cases,[72] jumped to the conclusion that if there is no privilege, then no knowledge of falsity, bad purpose, or even intent to affect the plaintiff at all is required—or in other words, that there is strict liability for entirely innocent falsehood, as in defamation.[73] This article was accepted without further analysis by

the Restatement of Torts.[74] The result, if this is the law, is to impose upon any false statement which does pecuniary harm to another the same strict liability for innocence, good intentions, and honest belief, as is found in defamation; [75] and again the old unsound identity is being carried over. The analogy of injurious falsehood is rather to cases of interference with contract, or with prospective benefits,[76] or to pecuniary harm to the plaintiff resulting from his own reliance upon false statements made to another,[77] none of which involves any strict liability at all, and all of which have narrowly restricted any liability even for negligence.

The small number of decisions which have faced the issue with no question of privilege involved do not at all sustain Jeremiah Smith and the Restatement. There is liability when the defendant acts for a spite motive, and out of a desire to do harm for its own sake; [78] and equally so when he acts for the purpose of doing harm to the interests of the plaintiff in a manner in which he is not privileged so to interfere.[79] There is also liabili-

---

69. Andrew v. Deshler, 1883, 45 N.J.L. 167; Kingkade v. Plummer, 1925, 111 Okl. 197, 239 P. 628; New England Oil & Pipe Line Co. v. Rogers, 1932, 154 Okl. 285, 7 P.2d 638; Ontario Ind. Loan Co. v. Lindsay, 1883, 4 Ont. 473.

70. Western Counties Manure Co. v. Lawes Chem. Manure Co., 1874, L.R. 9 Ex. 218 (Baron Pollock: "without legal necessity or occasion"); Royal Baking Powder Co. v. Wright, Crossley & Co., 1900, 18 Rep.Pat.Cas. 95 (Lord Davey: "without just cause or excuse"). See also Gudger v. Manton, 1943, 21 Cal.2d 537, 134 P.2d 217 (malice "implied" from lack of privilege); Continental Supply Co. v. Price, 1952, 126 Mont. 363, 251 P.2d 553 (malice "presumed" in absence of privilege); Gates v. Utsey, Fla.App.1965, 177 So.2d 486.

71. Smith, Disparagement of Property, 1913, 13 Col. L.Rev. 12, 121. In accord are Newark, Malice in Actions on the Case for Words, 1944, 60 L.Q.Rev. 366; Wood, Disparagement of Title and Quality, 1942, 20 Can.Bar Rev. 296, 430–35. Contra: Salmond, Torts, 13th Ed. 1961, 683–4; Fleming, Torts, 2d Ed. 1961, 677–8; Winfield, Torts, 6th Ed. 1954, 738; Clerk & Lindsell, Torts, 11th Ed. 1954, 842–46.

72. They are reviewed at length by McCardie, J., in British Railway Traffic & Elec. Co. v. C.R.C. Co., [1922] 2 K.B. 260, with the conclusion that "The mere absence of just cause or excuse is not itself malice," and "Malice in its proper and accurate sense is a question of motive, intention, or state of mind." Unless the defendant has the wrong state of mind, there can be no liability for injurious falsehood.

73. See supra, p. 772.

74. Restatement of Torts, § 625. The Smith article was cited four times in Preliminary Draft No. 50, Explanatory Notes, p. 66; and the cases cited are those cited by Smith, and in the same order. None of them supports the broad proposition of strict liability for innocent statements laid down by the Section.

75. See supra, p. 791. In Dale System v. General Teleradio, S.D.N.Y.1952, 105 F.Supp. 745, 751–752, the court invoked Chafee, Free Speech in the United States, 1941, 522, as to the dangerously restrictive effect of such a rule upon freedom of speech and of the press.

76. See infra, §§ 129, 130.

77. See supra, § 107.

78. A. B. Farquhar Co. v. National Harrow Co., 3 Cir. 1900, 102 F. 714; Sinclair Refining Co. v. Jones Super Service Station, 1934, 188 Ark. 1075, 70 S.W.2d 562. Cf. Swan v. Tappan, 1849, 5 Cush., Mass., 104.

79. Olsen v. Kidman, 1951, 120 Utah 443, 235 P.2d 510; Gudger v. Manton, 1943, 21 Cal.2d 537, 134 P. 2d 217; First Nat. Bank v. Moore, Tex.Civ.App. 1928, 7 S.W.2d 145; Dowse v. Doris Trust Co., 1949, 116 Utah 106, 208 P.2d 956; Ezmirlian v. Otto, 1934, 139 Cal.App. 486, 34 P.2d 774.

ty when the defendant knows that what he says is false, regardless of whether he has an ill motive or intends to affect the plaintiff at all.[80] The deliberate liar must take the risk that his statement will prove to be economically damaging to others; and there is something like the "scienter" found in an action of deceit.[81] Any of these three is sufficient to constitute "malice" and support the action. But in the absence of any of the three there is no liability, where the defendant has made his utterance in good faith,[82] even though he may have been negligent in failing to ascertain the facts before he made it.[83]

Special Damage

The "special damage" which the plaintiff must always plead and prove as an essential part of his cause of action [84] means a pecuniary loss. Such personal elements of damage as mental suffering, which frequently are recoverable in defamation, have been very strictly excluded from actions for disparagement and injurious falsehood.[85] It would seem sufficiently obvious that the pecuniary loss may consist of the breach by a third person of an existing contract with the plaintiff,[86] notwithstanding the decisions of a majority of the American courts which, rejecting the analogy to interference with contract,[87] have held that the remedy on the contract is sufficient, and the plaintiff is entitled to nothing more.[88] Likewise it would appear obviously to include the expenses of legal proceedings necessary to remove a cloud on the plaintiff's title, or other expenses to counteract the disparagement,[89] al-

80. Sinclair Refining Co. v. Jones Super Service Station, 1934, 188 Ark. 1075, 70 S.W.2d 562; see Ezmirlian v. Otto, 1934, 139 Cal.App. 486, 34 P.2d 774; Bourn v. Beck, 1924, 116 Kan. 231, 226 P. 769; Frega v. Northern New Jersey Mortgage Ass'n, 1958, 51 N.J.Super. 331, 143 A.2d 885; Kingkade v. Plummer, 1925, 111 Okl. 197, 239 P. 628; Hopkins v. Drowne, 1898, 21 R.I. 20, 41 A. 567; cf. Woodard v. Pacific Fruit & Produce Co., 1940, 165 Or. 250, 106 P.2d 1043.

81. See supra, p. 700. Thus in Advance Music Co. v. American Tobacco Co., 1946, 296 N.Y. 79, 70 N.E.2d 401, action "wantonly and without good faith" was held to be enough, where on the facts the defendants had made their statements in conscious ignorance whether they were true. In accord is Manitoba Free Press Co. v. Nagy, 1907, 39 Can.S.C. 340 ("recklessly, without regard to the consequences").

82. Shapiro v. La Morta, Ct.App.1923, 40 T.L.R. 201; Hahn v. Duveen, 1929, 133 Misc. 871, 234 N.Y.S. 185.

83. Balden v. Shorter, [1933] Ch. 427; Advance Music Corp. v. American Tobacco Co., 1944, 183 Misc. 645, 50 N.Y.S.2d 287; same, 1945, 268 App.Div. 707, 53 N.Y.S.2d 337, reversed on other grounds, 1946, 296 N.Y. 79, 70 N.E.2d 401; Remick Music Corp. v. American Tobacco Co., S.D.N.Y.1944, 57 F.Supp. 475; Dale System v. General Teleradio, S.D.N.Y. 1952, 105 F.Supp. 745; Sacco v. Herald Statesman, Inc., 1961, 32 Misc.2d 739, 223 N.Y.S.2d 329. See also Nagy v. Manitoba Free Press, 1907, 16 Man. 619. The only case found to the contrary is Atkins v. Perrin, 1862, 3 F. & F. 179, 176 Eng.Rep. 81.

84. Malachy v. Soper, 1836, 3 Bing.N.C. 371, 132 Eng.Rep. 453; Carroll v. Warner Bros. Pictures, S. D.N.Y.1937, 20 F.Supp. 405; International Visible Systems Corp. v. Remington-Rand, 6 Cir. 1933, 65 F.2d 540; Frawley Chemical Corp. v. A. P. Larson Co., 1949, 274 App.Div. 643, 86 N.Y.S.2d 710; Hayward Farms Co. v. Union Sav. Bank & Trust Co., 1935, 194 Minn. 473, 260 N.W. 868. See Note, 1966, 17 Hast.L.J. 394.

85. Ward v. Gee, Tex.Civ.App.1933, 61 S.W.2d 555; Ebersole v. Fields, 1913, 181 Ala. 421, 62 So. 73. Cf. Fowler v. Curtis Pub. Co., D.C.Cir.1950, 182 F. 2d 377; Eversharp, Inc. v. Pal Blade Co., 2 Cir. 1950, 182 F.2d 779 (good will and business prestige).

86. See Ashford v. Choate, 1870, 20 U.C.C.P. 471; Cardon v. McConnell, 1895, 120 N.C. 461, 27 S.E. 109; Humble Oil & Refining Co. v. McLean, Tex. Civ.App.1925, 268 S.W. 179; Bower, Actionable Defamation, 2d Ed. 1923, art. 13(b); Smith, Disparagement of Property, 1913, 13 Col.L.Rev. 13, 125–126; Notes, 1933, 33 Col.L.Rev. 90; 1929, 38 Yale L.J. 400.

87. See infra, § 129. The result appears to be that if the defendant has committed either disparagement or interference with contract, the plaintiff can recover; if both, he cannot.

88. Rucker v. Burke, 1938, 183 Okl. 639, 84 P.2d 20; Burkett v. Griffith, 1891, 90 Cal. 532, 27 P. 527; Stiles v. Kuriloff, 1928, 6 N.J.Misc. 271, 141 A. 314; Dent v. Balch, 1925, 213 Ala. 311, 104 So. 651; Felt v. Germania Life Ins. Co., 1912, 149 App.Div. 14, 133 N.Y.S. 519.

89. Dowse v. Doris Trust Co., 1949, 116 Utah 106, 208 P.2d 956; Womack v. McDonald, 1929, 219 Ala.

though here again a few courts have held to the contrary.[90]

Usually, however, the damages claimed have consisted of loss of prospective contracts with the plaintiff's customers. Here the remedy has been so hedged about with limitations that its usefulness to the plaintiff has been seriously impaired.[91] Formerly it was nearly always held that it was not enough to show a general decline in business following the publication of the falsehood,[92] even when there was evidence eliminating other causes for it; and that it was only the loss of specific sales to identified persons that could be recovered.[93] This has meant, in the usual case, that the plaintiff must identify the particular purchasers who have refrained from dealing with him, and specify the transactions of which he claims to have been deprived.[94] Where there has been wide

dissemination of the disparagement to persons unknown, this is obviously impossible. Coupled with the equity decisions denying an injunction because of a supposed analogy to defamation,[95] the rule has had the effect of leaving a serious and genuine wrong entirely without any practical remedy.

The whole modern tendency is away from any such arbitrary rule. Starting with a few cases involving goods offered for sale at an auction,[96] and extending to others in which there has been obvious impossibility of any identification of the lost customers,[97] a more liberal rule has been applied, requiring the plaintiff to be particular only where it is reasonable to expect him to do so. It is probably still the law everywhere that he must either offer the names of those who have failed to purchase or explain why it is impossible for him to do so; [98] but where he cannot, the matter is dealt with by analogy to the proof of lost profits resulting from breach of contract.[99] If the possibility that

75, 121 So. 57; Chesebro v. Powers, 1889, 78 Mich. 472, 44 N.W. 290; Maytag Co. v. Meadows Mfg. Co., 7 Cir. 1930, 45 F.2d 299, cert. denied, 1931, 283 U.S. 843; Cooper v. Weissblatt, 1935, 154 Misc. 522, 277 N.Y.S. 709.

90. Cohen v. Minzesheimer, Sup.Ct.1909, 118 N.Y.S. 385; McGuinness v. Hargiss, 1909, 56 Wash. 162, 105 P. 233; Barquin v. Hall Oil Co., 1921, 28 Wyo. 164, 201 P. 352, rehearing denied, 1922, 28 Wyo. 164, 202 P. 1107.

91. See Handler, Unfair Competition, 1936, 21 Iowa L.Rev. 175, 198; Notes, 1950, 18 U.Chi.L.Rev. 114; 1947, 41 Ill.L.Rev. 661; 1953, 63 Yale.L.J. 65, 90–96.

92. Tobias v. Harland, 1830, 4 Wend., N.Y., 537; Shaw Cleaners & Dyers v. Des Moines Dress Club, 1932, 215 Iowa 1130, 245 N.W. 231; Denney v. Northwestern Credit Ass'n, 1909, 55 Wash. 331, 104 P. 769; Ward v. Gee, Tex.Civ.App.1933, 61 S.W.2d 555; Tower v. Crosby, 1925, 214 App.Div. 392, 212 N.Y.S. 219.

93. Hunt Oil Co. v. Berry, 1956, 227 Miss. 234, 86 So.2d 7, corrected, 1956, 227 Miss. 680, 86 So.2d 854; Alcott v. Miller's Karri & Jarrah Forests, [1904] 21 T.L.R. 30, 91 L.T. 722; Stevenson v. Love, C.C.N.J. 1901, 106 F. 466; Denney v. Northwestern Credit Ass'n, 1909, 55 Wash. 331, 104 P. 769.

94. Wilson v. Dubois, 1886, 35 Minn. 471, 29 N.W. 46; Landstrom v. Thorpe, 8 Cir. 1951, 189 F.2d 46; Del Rico Co. v. New Mexican, 1952, 56 N.M. 538, 246 P.2d 206; Barquin v. Hall Oil Co., 1921, 28 Wyo. 164, 201 P. 352; Stevenson v. Love, C.C.N.J.

1901, 106 F. 466; Hubbard v. Scott, 1917, 85 Or. 1, 166 P. 33.

95. See supra, p. 916.

96. Hargrave v. Le Breton, 1769, 4 Burr. 2422, 98 Eng.Rep. 269; Roche v. Meyler, [1896] 2 Ir. 35.

97. Ratcliffe v. Evans, [1892] 2 Q.B. 524; Erick Bowman Remedy Co. v. Jensen Salsbery Laboratories, 8 Cir. 1926, 17 F.2d 255; Houston Chronicle Pub. Co. v. Martin, Tex.Civ.App.1928, 5 S.W.2d 170, modified on second appeal in, Tex.Civ.App.1933, 64 S.W.2d 816; Dale System v. Time, Inc., D.Conn. 1953, 116 F.Supp. 527; Rochester Brewing Co. v. Certa Bottling Works, 1948, 192 Misc. 629, 80 N.Y. S.2d 925. Cf. Trenton Mut. Life & Fire Ins. Co. v. Perrine, 1852, 23 N.J.L. 402; also Craig v. Proctor, 1918, 229 Mass. 339, 118 N.E. 647 (general allegation upheld, but plaintiff may be required to furnish particulars).

In Pendleton v. Time, Inc., 1949, 339 Ill.App. 188, 89 N.E.2d 435, and Advance Music Corp. v. American Tobacco Co., 1946, 296 N.Y. 79, 70 N.E.2d 401, reversing, 1944, 268 App.Div. 707, 53 N.Y.S.2d 337, motions to dismiss the complaint were denied, but there is no indication of what evidence would be required.

98. Barkhorn v. Adlib Associates, D.Hawaii 1962, 203 F.Supp. 121.

99. See McCormick, Damages, 1935, ch. 4.

other factors have caused the loss of the general business is satisfactorily excluded by sufficient evidence,[1] this seems entirely justified by the necessities of the situation.

Privilege

In general, it may be said that injurious falsehood, which is a tort that never has been greatly favored by the law, is subject to all of the privileges recognized both in cases of personal defamation and in those of other types of interference with economic advantage. The question of absolute privilege to disparage in judicial, legislative and executive proceedings [2] has seldom arisen, except in connection with pleadings, motions and the like in the course of litigation,[3] where it has been recognized. Undoubtedly an absolute privilege must exist when the plaintiff consents to the disparagement.[4] The disinterested protection of the interests of third persons, or of the public in general, has been said to confer a privilege to disparage in several cases, involving the acts of an attorney in asserting his client's claim [5] or giving an opinion on an abstract of title,[6] the fair report by a publisher of a judicial proceeding,[7] fair comment on matters of public interest,[8] notice given by a carrier concerning the inspection of diseased cattle,[9] and the attempt by a friend of a decedent to discover his will.[10] As in defamation,[11] however, the privilege in such cases is a qualified or conditional one, and is lost if the publication is excessive, or if the defendant knows that his statement is false, or is actuated by an improper motive.[12]

Usually, however, the privilege is asserted by a defendant who is seeking to protect his own interests. A rival claimant to the property disparaged, in his capacity as such,[13] is recognized as privileged to assert a bona fide claim by any appropriate means of publication.[14] The same is true of one who

---

1. Cf. Fleming v. McDonald, 1911, 230 Pa. 75, 79 A. 226; Neville v. Higbie, 1933, 130 Cal.App. 669, 20 P.2d 348; Farmers' State Bank v. Hintz, 1928, 206 Iowa 911, 221 N.W. 540; Houston Chronicle Pub. Co. v. Martin, Tex.Civ.App.1933, 64 S.W.2d 816.

2. See supra, § 114; Restatement of Torts, §§ 635–642.

3. Maginn v. Schmick, 1907, 127 Mo.App. 411, 105 S.W. 666; Buehrer v. Provident Mut. Life Ins. Co., 1931, 123 Ohio St. 264, 175 N.E. 25; Davis v. Union State Bank, 1933, 137 Kan. 264, 20 P.2d 508; Lann v. Third Nat. Bank in Nashville, 1955, 198 Tenn. 70, 277 S.W.2d 439 (filing lis pendens); Albertson v. Raboff, 1956, 46 Cal.2d 375, 295 P.2d 405 (same), which overruled West Inv. Co. v. Moorhead, 1953, 120 Cal.App.2d 837, 262 P.2d 322. See Notes, 1956, 4 U.C.L.A.L.Rev. 159; 1956, 24 Tenn.L.Rev. 393. Morgan v. Graham, 10 Cir. 1956, 228 F.2d 625, holding a witness liable for perjured testimony, appears definitely wrong.

4. Restatement of Torts, § 646.

5. Watson v. Reynolds, 1826, Moody & M. 1, 173 Eng.Rep. 1059. Cf. Kendall v. Stone, 1848, 2 Sandf., N.Y.Super.Ct., 269, reversed in 1851, 1 Seld. N.Y., 14.

The constitutional privilege in defamation (supra, ch. 21) has apparently not been recognized as to injurious falsehood. See Note, 1967, 80 Harv.L.Rev. 1005, 1027.

6. Hines v. Lumpkin, 1898, 19 Tex.Civ.App. 556, 47 S.W. 818. Cf. Gilchrist House v. Guaranteed Title & Mortgage Co., 1950, 277 App.Div. 788, 97 N.Y.S.2d 226, affirmed, 1951, 302 N.Y. 852, 100 N.E.2d 46 (refusal to insure title).

7. Mack, Miller Candle Co. v. MacMillan Co., 1934, 239 App.Div. 738, 269 N.Y.S. 33; cf. Artloom Corporation v. National Better Business Bureau, D.N.Y. 1931, 48 F.2d 897.

8. Gott v. Pulsifer, 1876, 122 Mass. 235; Browning v. Van Rensselaer, C.C.Pa.1899, 97 F. 531. Cf. Purofied Down Products Corp. v. National Ass'n of Bedding Manufacturers, Sup.Ct.1950, 97 N.Y.S.2d 683 (industry policing of products); Fahey v. Shafer, 1917, 98 Wash. 517, 167 P. 1118.

9. Youngquist v. American Express Co., 1926, 49 S.D. 373, 206 N.W. 576.

10. Atkins v. Perrin, 1862, 3 F. & F. 179, 176 Eng. Rep. 81. Cf. Pater v. Baker, 1847, 3 C.B. 831, 136 Eng.Rep. 333 (warning given by public officer).

11. See supra, § 115.

12. See cases cited supra, notes 78–80. Also Phillips v. Glazer, 1949, 94 Cal.App.2d 673, 211 P.2d 37.

13. There is no privilege to assert a claim in favor of a third person, where the defendant has no reason to protect the other's interests. Pennyman v. Rabanks, 1595, Cro.Eliz. 428, 78 Eng.Rep. 668.

14. Bogosian v. First Nat. Bank of Millburn, 1943, 133 N.J.Eq. 404, 32 A.2d 585; Conway v. Skelly Oil

claims in good faith that the plaintiff is infringing his patent, copyright or trade mark rights by the sale of goods.[15] The privilege is uniformly held, however, to be a qualified one, and it is defeated if the defendant's motive is shown to be solely a desire to do harm,[16] or if it is found that he did not honestly believe his statements to be true,[17] or that the publication of the statement was excessive.[18] A few cases have gone further and have said that he must have reasonable grounds for believing his disparaging words to be the truth;[19] but the better view, which is now more generally accepted, is that a genuine belief in their truth is sufficient, however unfounded or unreasonable it may be.[20] The absence of probable cause for the

belief may permit the jury to infer that it does not exist, but it is not necessarily conclusive;[21] and the advice of counsel, while it is evidence in favor of good faith, is likewise not determinative in itself.[22] When it appears that a privilege exists, the burden is upon the plaintiff to establish the existence of the "malice" which will defeat it.[23]

The privilege of competition for future business, as distinguished from the protection of an existing interest, has been recognized only to a limited extent. False statements of fact disparaging the quality of a competitor's goods, or the conduct of his business, are regarded as "unfair" methods of competition, and are never privileged.[24] The defendant who violates the rules of business ethics against disparaging attacks upon the business of a competitor must be prepared to prove that his assertions are true, and is not protected even by a genuine belief in their validity.[25] On the other hand,

Co., 10 Cir. 1931, 54 F.2d 11; Allison v. Berry, 1942, 316 Ill.App. 261, 44 N.E.2d 929; Miller v. First Nat. Bank of Gladbrook, 1935, 220 Iowa 1266, 264 N.W. 272; Leslie v. Western Steel Co., S.D. Tex.1962, 202 F.Supp. 27.

15. Kemart Corp. v. Printing Arts Research Laboratories, Inc., 9 Cir. 1959, 269 F.2d 375, cert. denied, 361 U.S. 893; McIlhenny Co. v. Gaidry, 5 Cir. 1918, 253 F. 613; Virtue v. Creamery Package Mfg. Co., 8 Cir. 1910, 179 F. 115, affirmed 227 U.S. 8; Oil Conservation Eng. Co. v. Brooks Eng. Co., 6 Cir. 1931, 52 F.2d 783; Alliance Securities Co. v. De Vilbiss, 6 Cir. 1930, 41 F.2d 668.

16. Swan v. Tappan, 1849, 5 Cush., Mass., 104; Sinclair Refining Co. v. Jones Super Service Station, 1934, 188 Ark. 1075, 70 S.W.2d 562; A. B. Farquhar Co. v. National Harrow Co., 3 Cir. 1900, 102 F. 714.

Cf. Diapulse Corp. of America v. Birtcher Corp., 2 Cir. 1966, 362 F.2d 736, cert. dismissed 385 U.S. 801.

17. Donovan v. Wilson Sporting Goods Co., 1 Cir. 1961, 285 F.2d 714; Frega v. Northern New Jersey Mortgage Ass'n, 1958, 51 N.J.Super. 331, 143 A.2d 885; Ezmirlian v. Otto, 1934, 139 Cal.App. 486, 34 P.2d 774; Sinclair Refining Co. v. Jones Super Service Station, 1934, 188 Ark. 1075, 70 S.W.2d 562; Woodard v. Pacific Fruit & Produce Co., 1940, 165 Or. 250, 106 P.2d 1043.

18. Donovan v. Wilson Sporting Goods Co., 1 Cir. 1961, 285 F.2d 714.

19. Carpenter v. Bailey, 1873, 53 N.H. 590; Conroy v. Pittsburgh Times, 1891, 139 Pa. 334, 21 A. 154.

20. Pitt v. Donovan, 1813, 1 M. & S. 639, 105 Eng. Rep. 238; Barry v. McCollum, 1908, 81 Conn. 293, 70 A. 1035; Bays v. Hunt, 1882, 60 Iowa 251, 14 N. W. 785; Hemmens v. Nelson, 1893, 138 N.Y. 517, 34 N.E. 342.

21. Pitt v. Donovan, 1813, 1 M. & S. 639, 105 Eng. Rep. 238; Pater v. Baker, 1847, 3 C.B. 831, 136 Eng.Rep. 333; Coffman v. Henderson, 1913, 9 Ala. App. 553, 63 So. 808; May v. Anderson, 1896, 14 Ind. App. 251, 42 N.E. 946; Bourn v. Beck, 1924, 116 Kan. 231, 226 P. 769.

22. Humble Oil & Ref. Co. v. Luckel, Tex.Civ.App. 1943, 171 S.W.2d 902; Noble v. Johnson, 1937, 180 Okl. 169, 68 P.2d 838; Gent v. Lynch, 1863, 23 Md. 58; Haldeman v. Chambers, 1857, 19 Tex. 1.

23. Long v. Rucker, 1912, 166 Mo.App. 572, 149 S.W. 1051; Briggs v. Coykendall, 1929, 57 N.D. 785, 224 N.W. 202; Fearon v. Fodera, 1915, 169 Cal. 370, 148 P. 200; Henry v. Dufilho, 1839, 14 La. 48; Glieberman v. Fine, 1929, 248 Mich. 8, 226 N.W. 669.

24. Western Counties Manure Co. v. Lawes Chem. Manure Co., 1874, L.R.Ex. 218; Alcott v. Millar's Karri & Jarrah Forests, 1904, 21 T.L.R. 30, 91 L.T. 722; National Refining Co. v. Benzo Gas Motor Fuel Co., 8 Cir. 1927, 20 F.2d 763, cert. denied 275 U.S. 570. Cf. Shaw Cleaners & Dyers v. Des Moines Dress Club, 1932, 215 Iowa 1130, 245 N.W. 231; Hopkins Chemical Co. v. Read Drug & Chemical Co., 1914, 124 Md. 210, 92 A. 478; George v. Blow, 1899, 20 N.S.W. 395. And see the comparison of the plaintiff's beer with another liquid in Dickes v. Fenne, 1640, March 59, Jones W. 444, 82 Eng. Rep. 233.

25. George v. Blow, 1899, 20 N.S.W. 395. Cf. Mowry v. Raabe, 1891, 89 Cal. 606, 27 P. 157; and see

a considerable amount of leeway has been allowed to those engaged in competition, in the form of "puffing," boasting or exaggeration as to the excellence of their own products, which finds a close parallel in the very similar freedom as to misrepresentations made to customers.[26]

Accordingly, it is held that mere general statements of comparison, declaring that the defendant's goods are the best on the market, or are better than the plaintiff's, are privileged so long as they contain no specific assertions of unfavorable facts reflecting upon the rival product.[27] The feeling has been that the practice of sellers to make consciously exaggerated claims for their own goods is so well known that purchasers attach little or no importance to such assertions, and they usually can do no serious harm. They are sometimes said to be mere statements of opinion. No doubt there has been some reluctance to give the plaintiff free advertising in the form of a verdict declaring a rival's claim to superiority to be unfounded. The leading case in the field[28] declares that such general comparisons are merely not disparagement at all, rather than

privileged, so that the defendant's knowledge of their falsity, or his purpose in making them, are not material. The courts quite often have been willing, however, to find disparaging statements of fact buried in general assertions, and to permit recovery on that basis.[29]

Defamation, interference with contract, injurious falsehood and the broader tort of interference with prospective economic relations, are all different phases of the same general wrong of depriving the plaintiff of beneficial relations with others.[30] The refined distinctions which have grown up as to the four causes of action are in part due to the accident of historical development, in part a matter of the weight attached to the importance of the plaintiff's interests. The greatest protection is given to personal reputation,[31] and existing contracts, the least to the competitive interest in future advantage, where the contest is open, and the competitor is required to do no more than refrain from resorting to "dirty tricks."[32] At some distant future day, when separate "torts" have lost their significance in the eyes of the law, the common basis of all four may lead to some comparison and overhauling, which will make them more consistent with one another.

Smith, Disparagement of Property, 1913, 13 Col.L. Rev. 13, 138–140.

26. See supra, p. 722.

27. White v. Mellin [1895] A.C. 154; Hubbock & Sons v. Wilkinson, [1899] 1 Q.B. 86; Johnson v. Hitchcock, 1818, 15 Johns., N.Y., 185; Nonpareil Cork Mfg. Co. v. Keasbey & Mattison Co., C.C.Pa. 1901, 108 F. 721; National Refining Co. v. Benzo Gas Motor Fuel Co., 8 Cir. 1927, 20 F.2d 763. In Young v. Macrae, 1862, 3 B. & S. 264, 122 Eng.Rep. 100, it was said that if the defendant merely alleges what is true of the plaintiff's product and lies about the merits of his own, there can be no action for disparagement. This is in line with the decisions holding that misrepresentations concerning the defendant's own goods are a fraud only upon the public, and not actionable by a competitor. See infra, p. 959.

28. Hubbock & Sons v. Wilkinson, [1899] 1 Q.B. 86, per Linley, M. R. See Smith, Disparagement of Property, 1913, 13 Col.L.Rev. 13, 133; Bower, Actionable Defamation, 2d Ed. 1923, 211.

29. Thus the assertion that the defendant's goods are the only genuine ones on the market is held to imply that the plaintiff's are not genuine. George v. Blow, 1899, 20 N.S.W. 395; Jarrahdale Timber Co. v. Temperley & Co., 1894, 11 T.L.R. 119; Cf. Lyne v. Nicholls, 1906, 23 T.L.R. 86 (defendant's newspaper circulation "20 to 1 of any other weekly paper"); Acme Silver Co. v. Stacy Hardware Co., 1891, 21 Ont.Rep. 261; Griffiths v. Benn, 1911, 27 T.L.R. 346; Testing Systems, Inc. v. Magnaflux Corp., E. D. Pa.1966, 251 F.Supp. 286.

30. See Green, Relational Interests, 1935, 29 Ill.L. Rev. 1041, 30 Ill.L.Rev. 1.

31. "Who steals my purse steals trash * * *" Othello, Act III, sc. 3.

32. Chafee, Unfair Competition, 1940, 53 Harv.L.Rev. 1289.

129. INTERFERENCE WITH CONTRACTUAL RELATIONS

Apart from the liability for injurious falsehood,[33] the recognition that economic relations are entitled to protection against unreasonable interference is on the whole a comparatively recent development. Most of the law has arisen since the beginning of the twentieth century, and it is necessarily a product of the methods and conditions of modern industry and trade. As these have altered more or less rapidly, and our social ideas have changed with them, the law inevitably has passed through a number of successive changes, attended with some confusion, uncertainty and disagreement. In this field, perhaps more obviously than any other, the problem has continuously been one of adjustment of the conflicting claims of different enterprises, industries, classes and groups, where interests are nicely balanced, and decision on the basis of social policy is not an easy matter. It is perhaps inevitable that the accusation should be made, by partisans of particular groups, that the personal prejudices and predilections of the judges have been at work and their opinions have reflected their own social philosophies; and no doubt it occasionally has been true.

Added to this is the fact that many courts have tended in the past to avoid any complete analysis of the problems, and to take refuge wherever possible in a formula. The law of business competition and labor disputes sometimes has been "shrouded in a fog of catchwords and rubber-stamp phrases,"[34] through which it has been difficult to perceive the real basis of the decisions. It frequently has been necessary to look through the language of the court and rationalize the opinion in order to discover what it means. Most of these formulae have turned on the question of the defendant's motive.

The old assertion that "Malicious motives make a bad case worse, but they cannot make that wrong which is in its essence lawful,"[35] is still occasionally repeated, although it is now very generally agreed that a wrongful motive in itself may turn the scale in favor of liability.[36] The statement that the defendant has acted "illegally," "unlawfully," "wrongfully," or "tortiously"[37] has been characterized, when it appears in a pleading, as mere vituperation;[38] and it can scarcely be less so when it is pronounced as the ground of a court's decision. And if we begin with the assumption that the defendant has either exercised or violated a "legal right,"[39] it is difficult to see what more remains to be said.

In actions for interference with economic relations, the defendant's motive or purpose frequently is the determining factor as to liability,[40] and sometimes it is said that bad mo-

---

33. Supra, § 128.

34. Note, 1927, 12 Minn.L.Rev. 147, 149; 1923, 37 Harv.L.Rev. 143. See Jaffin, Theorems in Anglo-American Labor Law, 1931, 31 Col.L.Rev. 1104.

35. See Boulier v. Macauley, 1891, 91 Ky. 135, 15 S.W. 60; Boyson v. Thorn, 1893, 98 Cal. 578, 33 P. 492; Bohn Mfg. Co. v. Hollis, 1893, 54 Minn. 223, 55 N.W. 1119; Glencoe Sand & Gravel Co. v. Hudson Bros. Commission Co., 1897, 138 Mo. 439, 40 S.W. 93; Lancaster v. Hamburger, 1904, 70 Ohio St. 156, 71 N.E. 289. See the defense of this antiquated position in Ormsby, Malice in the Law of Torts, 1892, 8 L.Q.Rev. 140.

36. See supra, § 5.

37. See Haskins v. Royster, 1874, 70 N.C. 601; Bixby v. Dunlap, 1876, 56 N.H. 456; Doremus v. Hennessy, 1898, 176 Ill. 608, 52 N.E. 924, rehearing denied, 1899, 176 Ill. 608, 54 N.E. 524; Prairie Oil & Gas Co. v. Kinney, 1920, 79 Okl. 206, 192 P. 586.

38. 2 Cooley, Torts, 3d Ed. 1505; Bohn Mfg. Co. v. Hollis, 1893, 54 Minn. 223, 55 N.W. 1119. As Sir Frederick Pollock remarked, "We do not need the House of Lords to tell us that a wrongful procurement of a breach of contract is wrongful or that an unlawful act or one without lawful justification is unlawful."

39. Raycroft v. Tayntor, 1896, 68 Vt. 219, 35 A. 53.

40. See Graham v. St. Charles St. R. Co., 1895, 47 La. Ann. 214, 1656, 16 So. 806; Employing Printers' Club v. Dr. Blosser Co., 1905, 122 Ga. 509, 50 S.E. 353; Dunshee v. Standard Oil Co., 1911, 152 Iowa 618, 132 N.W. 371; Hutton v. Watters, 1915, 132 Tenn. 527, 179 S.W. 134.

tive is the gist of the action.[41] Here, as so often elsewhere in the law of torts,[42] the law has been vexed with the unhappy word "malice." Originally, when it was said in this type of action that the defendant's conduct was "malicious," it appears to have been meant in the sense of a desire to injure and do harm for its own sake;[43] but the word has undergone a gradual process of vitiation,[44] until it now has all shades of meaning from active malevolence,[45] through an intent to profit at the expense of the plaintiff,[46] to a mere intent, with knowledge of his interests, to do an act which will have the effect of interfering with them.[47] Obviously such a term is to be avoided for the sake of clarity.[48]

In recent years, however, the real problem underlying the question of motive has emerged as one of balancing the conflicting interests of the parties, and determining whether the defendant's objective shall prevail at the expense of economic harm to the plaintiff. "The ground of the decision really comes down to a proposition of policy of rather a delicate nature concerning the merits of the particular benefit to themselves intended by the defendants, and suggests a doubt whether judges with different economic sympathies might not decide a case differently when brought face to face with the issue." [49] Although in the past few courts were inclined to do more than resort to catchwords, rules of thumb, or undefined terms such as "malice," there is now a very clear tendency to analyze the interests involved, and make a deliberate decision as to which shall prevail.[50] While there are still many doubtful

41. West Virginia Transportation Co. v. Standard Oil Co., 1902, 50 W.Va. 611, 40 S.E. 591; Wheeler-Stenzel Co. v. American Window Glass Co., 1909, 202 Mass. 471, 89 N.E. 28; Globe & Rutgers Fire Ins. Co. v. Firemen's Fund Fire Ins. Co., 1910, 97 Miss. 148, 52 So. 454; S. C. Posner Co. v. Jackson, 1918, 223 N.Y. 325, 119 N.E. 573.

42. As, for example, in defamation, supra, p. 772; or malicious prosecution, supra, p. 847.

43. Lumley v. Gye, 1853, 2 El. & Bl. 216, 118 Eng. Rep. 749; Bowen v. Hall, 1881, 6 Q.B.D. 333.

44. "From what has been said . . . concerning malice, we could conclude that this element is one which, however conspicuous it may be in the early stages of the evolution of any species of wrong, is yet of continually diminishing importance as the true basis of liability comes to be discovered and defined. At first malice is treated as a reserve fund of sufficient weight to fix liability where no general right of action is recognized. Having thus assisted in the generation of new principle, it subsequently recedes more and more from view." 1 Street, Foundations of Legal Liability, 1906, 335.

45. Aikens v. Wisconsin, 1904, 195 U.S. 194; McCann v. Wolff, 1888, 28 Mo.App. 447.

46. Temperton v. Russell, [1893] 1 Q.B. 715, 62 L.J. Q.B. 412. Cf. Schechter v. Friedman, 1948, 141 N. J.Eq. 318, 57 A.2d 251; Carter v. Knapp Motor Co., 1943, 243 Ala. 600, 11 So.2d 383.

47. Russell v. Croteau, 1953, 98 N.H. 68, 94 A.2d 376; Reichman v. Drake, 1951, 89 Ohio App. 222, 100 N. E.2d 533; Meason v. Ralston Purina Co., 1940, 56 Ariz. 291, 107 P.2d 224; Meyer v. Washington Times Co., 1935, 64 App.D.C. 218, 76 F.2d 988; Luke v. Du Pree, 1924, 158 Ga. 390, 124 S.E. 13.

48. "Bearing in mind that malice may or may not be used to denote ill will, and that in legal language, presumptive or implied malice is distinguishable from express malice, it conduces to clearness in discussing such cases as these to drop the word 'malice' altogether, and to substitute for it the meaning which is really intended to be conveyed by it. Its use may be necessary in drawing indictments, but when all that is meant by malice is an intention to commit an unlawful act, without reference to spite or ill-feeling, it is better to drop the word malice, and so avoid all misunderstanding." Lord Lindley, in South Wales Miners' Federation v. Glamorgan Coal Co., [1905] A.C. 239. See also Jaffin, Theorems in Anglo-American Labor Law, 1931, 31 Col.L.Rev. 1104, 1123; Fridman, Malice in the Law of Torts, 1958, 21 Mod.L.Rev. 484; Stoner, The Influence of Social and Economic Ideals in the Law of Malicious Torts, 1910, 8 Mich.L.Rev. 468; Green, Relational Interests, 1935, 29 Ill.L.Rev. 1041; Notes, 1928, 12 Minn.L.Rev. 147; 1927, 12 St. Louis L.Rev. 286; 1923, 9 Corn.L.Q. 78.

49. Holmes, Privilege, Malice and Intent, 1894, 8 Harv.L.Rev. 1. See also the dissenting opinion of Holmes, J., in Vegelahn v. Guntner, 1896, 167 Mass. 92, 44 N.E. 1077.

50. See Holmes, Privilege, Malice and Intent, 1894, 8 Harv.L.Rev. 1; Sayre, Inducing Breach of Contract, 1923, 36 Harv.L.Rev. 696; Stoner, The Influence of Social and Economic Ideals on the Law of Malicious Torts, 1910, 8 Mich.L.Rev. 468; Green, Relational Interests, 1935, 29 Ill.L.Rev. 1041, 30 Ill. L.Rev. 1; Notes, 1923, 9 Corn.L.Q. 78; 1928, 12 Minn.L.Rev. 147; 1927, 12 St. Louis L.Rev. 286; 1932, 17 Corn.L.Q. 509.

questions, it is now possible to classify the cases and make more or less definite statements as to the generally accepted rules.

Interference with Contract

One type of interference with economic relations has been marked out rather definitely by the courts, and regarded as a separate tort, under the name of inducing breach of contract, or interference with contract.[51] Its family tree goes back to very ancient times, when it was not the existence of a contract which was important, but the status, or relation recognized by the law, in which the parties stood toward one another, and with which the defendant interfered. In early Roman law the pater-familias, or head of the household, was permitted to bring an action for violence committed upon his wife, his children, his slaves, or other members of his establishment, or even for insults offered to them, on the theory that they were so far identified with him that the wrong was one to himself. By the thirteenth century this Roman law idea had been taken over by the common law, but had been somewhat altered in the transition, so that it became an action for damages sustained by any master through actual loss of the services of a servant because of violence inflicted upon him. In 1349 an additional remedy was created by statute. The Black Death had left England with a great shortage of labor, and to meet the resulting agricultural crisis the famous Ordinance of Labourers [52] was enacted, by which a system of compulsory labor was introduced. A penalty was provided to keep the laborer from running away, and a remedy was given to the employer against any-

one who received and retained him in his service. The statutory action for enticing or harboring the servant which thus developed, as well as the older one for violence against him, was enforced in trespass. In time the two became intermingled and confused, so that they were no longer distinguished, and at last both were absorbed into the action on the case.[53]

As early as the fifteenth century cases appeared in which a remedy was given for interference with other relations than that of master and servant,[54] and the development of some broader general principle was long foreshadowed, in England and in the United States.[55] It first appeared in definite form in 1853, in the leading modern case of Lumley v. Gye.[56] Miss Johanna Wagner, an opera singer of some distinction, was under contract to the plaintiff to sing exclusively in his theatre for a definite term. The defendant, "knowing the premises, and maliciously intending to injure plaintiff," "enticed and procured" Miss Wagner to refuse to carry out her agreement. Although it was reasonably clear that an operatic artiste was not to be classed as a "servant" within the

---

51. See Sayre, Inducing Breach of Contract, 1923, 36 Harv.L.Rev. 663; Carpenter, Interference with Contract Relations, 1928, 41 Harv.L.Rev. 728, 7 Or.L. Rev. 181, 301; Harper, Interference with Contractual Relations, 1953, 47 N.W.U.L.Rev. 873; Notes, 1953, 32 N.C.L.Rev. 110; 1959, 43 Marq.L.Rev. 231; 1961, 56 N.W.U.L.Rev. 391.

52. 1349, 23 Edw. III, st. 1, administered under the Statute of Labourers, 1350, 25 Edw. III, st. 1.

53. Hart v. Aldridge, 1774, 1 Cowp. 54, 98 Eng.Rep. 964; Blake v. Lanyon, 1795, 6 Term Rep. 221, 101 Eng.Rep. 521. See Sayre, Inducing Breach of Contract, 1923, 36 Harv.L.Rev. 663; Wigmore, Interference with Social Relations, 1887, 21 Am.L.Rev. 764.

54. See infra, p. 930.

55. See Keeble v. Hickeringill, 1706, 11 Mod.Rep. 14, 130, 3 Salk. 9, 103 Eng.Rep. 1127; Tarleton v. McGawley, 1793, Peake N.P. 205, 170 Eng.Rep. 153; Green v. Button, 1835, 2 Cr.M. & R. 707, 150 Eng. Rep. 299; Aldridge v. Stuyvesant, 1828, 1 Hall, N. Y., 210; Marsh v. Billings, 1851, 7 Cush., Mass., 322; Restatement of Torts, § 766, Comment b.

56. 1853, 2 El. & Bl. 216, 118 Eng.Rep. 749. The story of the case is told in Peck, Decision at Law, 1961, 125–144.

See Restatement of Torts, § 766, Comment b, pointing out that "The significance of Lumley v. Gye lies in its extension of the rule of liability to non-tortious methods of inducement. Particularly in view of subsequent interpretations of that case in England, it established no rule peculiar to contracts."

meaning of the Statute of Labourers, it was held by a divided court that the principle should extend to her, and that it was a tort to persuade her to break her contract. Considerable stress was laid upon the "malice" with which it was alleged that the defendant was animated.

The doctrine thus announced, that intentional interference with a contract may be an actionable tort, was received at first with hesitation or disapproval,[57] but it was reaffirmed nearly thirty years later in England,[58] and then by degrees was extended, first to cover contracts other than those for personal services,[59] and later to include interferences in which no ill-will was to be found on the part of the defendant.[60] The present English law gives it full acceptance, as to all intentional interferences with any type of contract.[61] The American courts were reluctant to accept the doctrine in the beginning,[62] and

a few of them rejected it outright as applied to interference with relations other than that of master and servant.[63] Such decisions have for the most part been overruled,[64] and the tort is now recognized virtually everywhere[65] as to any contract, regardless of its character.[66]

Lumley v. Gye and the succeeding cases laid emphasis upon the existence of the contract, as something in the nature of a prop-

---

57. See Pollock, Law of Torts, 8th Ed., 328; Langdell, A Brief Survey of Equity Jurisdiction, 1887, 1 Harv.L.Rev. 55, 57; Schofield, Lumley v. Gye, 1888, 2 Harv.L.Rev. 19.

58. Bowen v. Hall, 1881, 6 Q.B.D. 333, 50 L.J.Q.B. 305.

59. Temperton v. Russell [1893] 1 Q.B. 715, 62 L.J.Q. B. 412.

60. South Wales Miners' Federation v. Glamorgan Coal Co., [1905] A.C. 239.

61. Jasperson v. Dominion Tobacco Co., [1923] A.C. 709; Thomson v. Deakin, [1952] Ch. 646. See Payne, The Tort of Interference With Contract, 1954, 7 Curr.Leg.Prob. 94.

62. The history of the New York decisions is quite typical. The early cases denied any right of action unless the contract was one for personal services. Ashley v. Dixon, 1872, 48 N.Y. 430; Curran v. Galen, 1897, 152 N.Y. 33, 46 N.E. 297. Later recovery still was denied, but the emphasis was shifted to the defendant's "justification" instead of the plaintiff's failure to state a cause of action. National Protective Assn. of Steam Fitters & Helpers v. Cumming, 1902, 170 N.Y. 315, 63 N.E. 369; Roseneau v. Empire Circuit Co., 1909, 131 App.Div. 429, 115 N.Y.S. 511. Still later, the earlier cases were overruled and recovery was permitted. S. C. Posner Co. v. Jackson, 1918, 223 N.Y. 325, 119 N.E. 573; Lamb v. S. Cheney & Sons, 1920, 227 N.Y. 418, 125 N.E. 817; Gonzales v. Kentucky Derby Co., 1921, 197 App.Div. 277, 189 N.Y.S. 783, affirmed,

1922, 233 N.Y. 607, 135 N.E. 938. Finally intentional interference with contract, in the absence of a privilege, was declared actionable without reservation. Campbell v. Gates, 1923, 236 N.Y. 457, 141 N. E. 914.

63. Boyson v. Thorn, 1893, 98 Cal. 578, 33 P. 492; Kline v. Eubanks, 1902, 109 La. 241, 33 So. 211; Glencoe Sand & Gravel Co. v. Hudson Bros. Commission Co., 1897, 138 Mo. 439, 40 S.W. 93; Swain v. Johnson, 1909, 151 N.C. 93, 65 S.E. 619; Sleeper v. Baker, 1911, 22 N.D. 386, 134 N.W. 716.

64. Imperial Ice Co. v. Rossier, 1941, 18 Cal.2d 33, 112 P.2d 631; Downey v. United Weatherproofing Co., 1953, 363 Mo. 852, 253 S.W.2d 976; Bryant v. Barber, 1953, 237 N.C. 480, 75 S.E.2d 410; see Bekken v. Equitable Life Assur. Soc. of U. S., 1940, 70 N.D. 122, 293 N.W. 200. See Note, 1953, 32 N.C.L. Rev. 110.

Louisiana continues to hold that inducing breach of a contract is no tort unless means unlawful in themselves are used. Robert Heard Hale, Inc. v. Gaiennie, La.App.1958, 102 So.2d 324; Cust v. Item Co., 1942, 200 La. 515, 8 So.2d 361; Hartman v. Greene, 1939, 193 La. 234, 190 So. 390, cert. denied 308 U.S. 612. This is apparently the last word from Kentucky. Chambers v. Probst, 1911, 145 Ky. 381, 140 S. W. 572; Brooks v. Patterson, 1930, 234 Ky. 757, 29 S.W.2d 26.

65. Louis Kamm, Inc. v. Flink, 1934, 113 N.J.L. 582, 175 A. 62; Keviczky v. Lorber, 1943, 290 N.Y. 297, 49 N.E.2d 146, motion denied 290 N.Y. 855, 50 N.E. 2d 242; Knickerbocker Ice Co. v. Gardiner Dairy Co., 1908, 107 Md. 556, 69 A. 405; Sorenson v. Chevrolet Motor Co., 1927, 171 Minn. 260, 214 N.W. 754; Beekman v. Marsters, 1907, 195 Mass. 205, 80 N.E. 817.

66. As examples of the application of the doctrine to unusual situations, see: Globe & Rutgers Fire Ins. Co. v. Firemen's Fund Fire Ins. Co., 1910, 97 Miss. 148, 52 So. 454; Cumberland Glass Mfg. Co. v. De Witt, 1913, 120 Md. 381, 87 A. 927; Prairie Oil & Gas Co. v. Kinney, 1920, 79 Okl. 206, 192 P. 586; Luke v. Du Pree, 1924, 158 Ga. 590, 124 S.E. 13; R an W Hat Shop v. Sculley, 1922, 98 Conn. 1, 118 A. 55.

erty interest in the plaintiff, or a right in rem good against the world.[67] The subsequent development of the law has extended the principle to interference with advantageous economic relations even where they have not been cemented by contract;[68] and the liability for inducing breach of contract now is regarded as merely one instance of protection against such unjustified interference.[69] The addition of the element of a definite contract has its importance, since the person induced to break it is then under a legal duty, and the plaintiff has furnished a consideration for the expectancy with which the defendant interferes. It may therefore curtail the defendant's privilege [70] to pursue his own ends at the expense of the plaintiff. Also, it fixes the limits of the plaintiff's interests, and hence of his damages. Essentially, however, no different principle is involved, and it is chiefly as a matter of convenience that the cases of inducing breach of contract are considered as a group.

Nature of Original Contract

Virtually any type of contract is sufficient as the foundation of an action for procuring its breach. It must of course be in force and effect,[71] and not illegal as in restraint of trade,[72] or otherwise opposed to public policy,[73] so that the law will not aid in upholding it. Thus contracts for exclusive dealing tending to stifle competition in the public utility field have been denied the protection,[74] as has the "yellow dog" contract by which an employee agrees with his employer that he will not join a labor union,[75] which is now made unenforceable by federal and much state legislation. The same is true of any contract which requires the breach of a prior contract; and in such a case it is of course the first of the two agreements which will be protected.[76]

Mont. 24, 245 P. 958 (contract declared forfeited); Rizika v. Potter, Sup.Ct.1947, 72 N.Y.S.2d 372 (no contract); Altman v. Casale, 1966, 25 App.Div.2d 877, 270 N.Y.S.2d 509.

72. Ford Motor Co. v. Union Motor Sales Co., 6 Cir. 1917, 244 F. 156; Paramount Pad Co. v. Baumrind, 1948, 4 N.Y.2d 393, 175 N.Y.S.2d 809, 151 N.E.2d 609; Consolidated Packaging Mach. Corp. v. Kelly, 7 Cir. 1958, 253 F.2d 49, cert. denied 357 U.S. 906; Argus Cameras v. Hall of Distributors, 1955, 343 Mich. 54, 72 N.W.2d 152; Sunbeam Corp. v. Hall of Distributors, E.D.Mich.1956, 142 F.Supp. 609.

73. Gunnels v. Atlanta Bar Ass'n, 1940, 191 Ga. 366, 12 S.E.2d 602 (usury); Bailey v. Banister, 10 Cir. 1952, 200 F.2d 683 (purchase of restricted Indian land); Ely v. Donoho, S.D.N.Y.1942, 45 F.Supp. 27 (contract to file reorganization plan); Seitz v. Michel, 1921, 148 Minn. 474, 181 N.W. 106 (life employment in control of corporation); Mindenberg v. Carmel Film Productions, 1955, 132 Cal.App.2d 598, 282 P.2d 1024 (corporation's purchase of own stock).

74. Citizens Light, Heat & Power Co. v. Montgomery Light & Water Power Co., D.Ala.1909, 171 F. 553; Fairbanks, Morse & Co. v. Texas Elec. Serv. Co., 5 Cir., 1933, 63 F.2d 702.

75. Exchange Bakery & Rest. Co. v. Rifkin, 1927, 245 N.Y. 260, 157 N.E. 130; Interborough Rapid Transit Co. v. Lavin, 1928, 247 N.Y. 65, 159 N.E. 863; La France Elec. Const. & Supply Co. v. International Brotherhood of Electrical Workers, 1923, 108 Ohio St. 61, 140 N.E. 899.

76. Reiner v. North American Newspaper Alliance, 1932, 259 N.Y. 250, 181 N.E. 561. Cf. Roberts v. Criss, 2 Cir., 1920, 266 F. 296; Rhoades v. Malta Vita Pure Food Co., 1907, 149 Mich. 235, 112 N.W. 940; Hocking Valley R. Co. v. Barbour, 1920, 190 App.Div. 341, 179 N.Y.S. 810. See Notes, 1913, 27 Harv.L.Rev. 273; 1932, 18 Corn.L.Q. 84; 1933, 17 Minn.L.Rev. 209.

---

67. "It seems to us that where a party has entered into a contract with another to do or not to do a particular act or acts, he has as clear a right to its performance as he has to his property, either real or personal; and that knowingly to induce the other party to violate it is as distinct a wrong as it is to injure or destroy his property." Raymond v. Yarrington, 1903, 96 Tex. 443, 72 S.W. 580, 73 S.W. 800. Accord, S. C. Posner Co. v. Jackson, 1918, 223 N.Y. 325, 119 N.E. 573; cf. Goldman v. Harford Road Bldg. Ass'n, 1926, 150 Md. 677, 133 A. 843; Carolina Overall Corp. v. East Carolina Linen Supply, Inc., 1970, 8 N.C.App. 528, 174 S.E.2d 659.

68. See infra, § 130.

69. Restatement of Torts, § 766, Comment *b*.

70. See infra, p. 942.

71. Said v. Butt, [1920] 3 K.B. 497, 11 B.R.C. 317 (no contract made); Triangle Film Corp. v. Artcraft Pictures Corp., 2 Cir., 1918, 250 F. 981 (conditions terminated); Burden v. Elling State Bank, 1926, 76

The agreement need not, however, be enforceable by the plaintiff as a contract. Even under the old Statute of Labourers, from which the remedy is descended, labor was compulsory, and it was interference with the relation which was the essence of the tort, so that no binding agreement for service was required.[77] The law of course does not object to the voluntary performance of agreements merely because it will not enforce them, and it indulges in the assumption that even unenforceable promises will be carried out if no third person interferes. Accordingly, it usually is held that contracts which are voidable by reason of the statute of frauds,[78] formal defects,[79] lack of consideration,[80] lack of mutuality,[81] or even uncertainty of terms,[82] or harsh and unconscionable

provisions,[83] or conditions precedent to the existence of the obligation,[84] can still afford a basis for a tort action when the defendant interferes with their performance.

There is some authority to the contrary effect as to contracts which the promisor may terminate at will,[85] on the theory that there is really nothing involved but an option on his part to perform or not.[86] However, eminent legal writers[87] to the contrary notwithstanding, the overwhelming majority of the cases have held that interference with employments[88] or other contracts[89] termi-

---

77. Sayre, Inducing Breach of Contract, 1923, 36 Harv.L.Rev. 663, 666.

78. Royal Realty Co. v. Levin, 1955, 244 Minn. 288, 69 N.W.2d 667; Childress v. Abeles, 1954, 240 N.C. 667, 84 S.E.2d 176, rehearing dismissed, 1955, 242 N.C. 123, 86 S.E.2d 916; McCue v. Deppert, 1952, 21 N.J.Super. 591, 91 A.2d 503; Friedman v. Jackson, 1968, 266 Cal.App.2d 517, 72 Cal.Rptr. 129; Hill & Co. v. Wallerich, 1965, 67 Wash.2d 409, 407 P.2d 956.

Contra: Evans v. Mayberry, 1955, 198 Tenn. 187, 278 S.W.2d 691, rehearing denied 198 Tenn. 187, 279 S.W.2d 705; Little v. Childress, Tex.Civ.App.1928, 12 S.W.2d 648, affirmed, 1929, 17 S.W.2d 786; Levy v. Ross, Sup.Ct.1948, 81 N.Y.S.2d 472 (contract void).

79. Salter v. Howard, 1871, 43 Ga. 601.

80. Rich v. New York Cent. & H. R. R. Co., 1882, 87 N.Y. 382. Otherwise with a mere gratuitous promise which does not purport to be a contract. Risenhoff v. Mariam, 1953, 90 App.D.C. 263, 207 F.2d 449.

81. Aalfo Co. v. Kinney, 1929, 105 N.J.L. 345, 144 A. 715; Philadelphia Record Co. v. Leopold, S.D.N.Y. 1941, 40 F.Supp. 346; Moran v. Dunphy, 1901, 177 Mass. 485, 59 N.E. 125; Jackson v. O'Neill, 1957, 181 Kan. 930, 317 P.2d 440; Union Circulation Co. v. Hardel Publishers Service, 1957, 6 Misc.2d 340, 164 N.Y.S.2d 435.

82. Aalfo Co. v. Kinney, 1929, 105 N.J.L. 345, 144 A. 715. See Note, 1928, 28 Mich.L.Rev. 94. In Grimes v. Baumgart, 1951, 121 Ind.App. 626, 96 N.E.2d 915, the combination of uncertainty and lack of mutuality was held to prevent the action.

83. Union Circulation Co. v. Hardel Publishers Service, 1957, 6 Misc.2d 340, 164 N.Y.S.2d 435.

84. For example, the attorney's contract with his client for a contingent fee. Richette v. Solomon, 1963, 410 Pa. 6, 187 A.2d 910; Herron v. State Farm Mut. Ins. Co., 1961, 56 Cal.2d 202, 14 Cal. Rptr. 294, 363 P.2d 310; Employers Liability Assur. Corp. v. Freeman, 10 Cir. 1955, 229 F.2d 547; State Farm Fire Ins. Co. v. Gregory, 4 Cir. 1950, 184 F.2d 447; Keels v. Powell, 1945, 207 S.C. 97, 34 S.E.2d 482; Cf. Mitchell v. Aldrich, 1960, 122 Vt. 19, 163 A.2d 833.

85. Harris v. Hirschfield, 1936, 13 Cal.App.2d 204, 56 P.2d 1252; E. R. Squibb & Sons v. Ira J. Shapiro, Inc., Sup.Ct.1945, 64 N.Y.S.2d 368; McGuire v. Gerstley, 1905, 26 U.S.App.D.C. 193, affirmed, 1907, 204 U.S. 489; Harley & Lund Corp. v. Murray Rubber Co., 2 Cir., 1929, 31 F.2d 932.

Some other cases frequently cited to the same effect, such as Boston Glass Manufactory v. Binney, 1827, 4 Pick., Mass., 425, appear in reality to hold not that there is no prima facie liability, but merely that the defendant was privileged to interfere.

86. Cf. Richardson v. Terry, Tex.Civ.App.1919, 212 S.W. 523, error dismissed; Roberts v. Clark, Tex. Civ.App.1907, 103 S.W. 417; Campbell v. Cooper, 1856, 34 N.H. 49.

87. Smith, Crucial Issues in Labor Litigation, 1907, 20 Harv.L.Rev. 253, 261; Sayre, Inducing Breach of Contract, 1923, 36 Harv.L.Rev. 663, 701; Harper, Law of Torts, 1933, 475.

88. Canuel v. Oskoian, D.R.I.1960, 184 F.Supp. 70; American Surety Co. v. Schottenbauer, 8 Cir. 1958, 257 F.2d 6; Mendelson v. Blatz Brewing Co., 1960, 9 Wis.2d 487, 101 N.W.2d 805; United States F. & G. Co. v. Millonas, 1921, 206 Ala. 147, 89 So. 732; Mays v. Stratton, Fla.App.1966, 183 So.2d 43.

89. Childress v. Abeles, 1954, 240 N.C. 667, 84 S.E.2d 176, rehearing dismissed, 1955, 242 N.C. 123, 86 N. E.2d 916; W. P. Iverson Co. v. Dunham Mfg. Co.,

nable at will is actionable, since until it is terminated the contract is a subsisting relation, of value to the plaintiff, and presumably to continue in effect. The possibility of termination does, however, bear upon the issue of the damages sustained,[90] and it must be taken into account in determining the defendant's privilege to interfere.[91] So much more is allowed in the way of interference to further the defendant's own legitimate interests where the contract is subject to such termination, that contracts terminable at will might very well be placed in an intermediate classification of their own, half way between contracts for a definite term and the mere expectancy of prospective advantage. The courts, however, do not appear to have recognized them as a separate group; and to avoid too much repetition, it seems desirable to consider them with other contracts, with the recognition that they receive much more limited protection.

For reasons that have not been very clearly stated, contracts to marry have received special treatment, and almost without exception[92] the courts have refused to hold

that it is a tort to induce the parties to break them.[93] There is no direct holding in England,[94] and the American decisions are traceable to an unsupported statement of Judge Cooley's, made at a time when the conception of interference with contract was in the formative stage.[95] The arguments advanced in justification have varied from a confusion of the action with the husband's claim for loss of consortium,[96] through dislike of breach of promise suits and a fear that every disappointed suitor might bring an action against his successful rival, to a vague notion that if the engagement is so easily broken, perhaps it is just as well that the marriage is not to occur after all.[97] Probably the real reason is the feeling that the law should have a policy against encouraging the marriage of any person who has decided that the marriage will be a mistake. On the other hand, there is certainly no policy against agreements to marry in general, but quite the contrary; and it is arguable that one with such a contract is as much entitled to

1958, 18 Ill.App.2d 404, 152 N.E.2d 615; General Outdoor Advertising Co. v. Hamilton, 1935, 154 Misc. 871, 278 N.Y.S. 226; Falstaff Brewing Co. v. Iowa Fruit & Produce Co., 8 Cir. 1940, 112 F.2d 101; George Jonas Glass Co. v. Glass Bottle Blowers Ass'n, 1908, 77 N.J.Eq. 219, 79 A. 262; and see cases cited supra, note 85. See Note, 1961, 56 N.W. U.L.Rev. 391.

90. See Berry v. Donovan, 1905, 188 Mass. 353, 74 N. E. 603; Scott v. Prudential Outfitting Co., 1915, 92 Misc. 195, 155 N.Y.S. 497; Evans v. McKay, Tex. Civ.App.1919, 212 S.W. 680, error dismissed (nominal damages); Tye v. Finkelstein, D.Mass.1958, 160 F.Supp. 666; United States F. & G. Co. v. Millonas, 1921, 206 Ala. 147, 89 So. 732.

91. Carpenter, Interference with Contract Relations, 1928, 41 Harv.L.Rev. 728, 754, 7 Or.L.Rev. 181, 301.

See National Oil Co. v. Phillips Petroleum Co., W.D. Wis.1966, 265 F.Supp. 320; infra, p. 946.

92. In Minsky v. Satenstein, 1928, 6 N.J.Misc. 978, 143 A. 512, and Gunn v. Barr, [1926] 1 Dom.L.Rep. 1855, the possibility of a cause of action was recognized, but a privilege to give advice was found on the facts. See also Dora v. Dora, 1958, 392 Pa. 433, 141 A.2d 587 (property settlement between estranged husband and wife).

93. Brown v. Glickstein, 1952, 347 Ill.App. 486, 107 N.E.2d 267; Nelson v. Melvin, 1945, 236 Iowa 604, 19 N.W.2d 685; Clarahan v. Cosper, 1931, 160 Wash. 642, 296 P. 140; Conway v. O'Brien, 1929, 269 Mass. 425, 169 N.E. 491; Ableman v. Holman, 1926, 190 Wis. 112, 208 N.W. 889. See Notes, 1953, 31 Chicago-Kent L.Rev. 175; 1932, 26 Ill.L.Rev. 454; 1931, 25 Ill.L.Rev. 224; 1929, 77 U.Pa.L.Rev. 515; 1932, 5 So.Cal.L.Rev. 150.

94. Shepherd v. Wakeman, 1661, 1 Sid. 79, 82 Eng. Rep. 982, allowed the action, but there was intentional falsehood involved. There is dictum in National Phonograph Co. v. Edison-Bell Phonograph Co., [1907] 1 Ch. 335, 350, 96 L.T. 218, 224, to the effect that no such action could be maintained.

95. Cooley, Torts, 1st Ed. 1878, 236–237. See Note, 1925, 10 Corn.L.Q. 258.

96. Supra, p. 874. See Stiffler v. Boehm, 1924, 124 Misc. 55, 206 N.Y.S. 187.

97. Or, better stated: "Social considerations may warrant this exception to the general rule. Society has a vital interest in having the marriage relation endure and hasty and ill-conceived marriages are undesirable. Hence, activities which may retard such marriages and possibly secure more permanent ones are to be encouraged." Carpenter, Interference with Contract Relations, 1928, 41 Harv.L.Rev. 728, 751.

protection against unjustifiable interference as those for whom another has promised to sing, or to sell and deliver property.[98] With liberal recognition of a privilege in relatives or even friends to give honest advice,[1] for which there is ample precedent in the law of defamation and interference with domestic relations,[2] and perhaps even in a defeated rival to continue his suit without closing the competition at the betrothal,[3] or in an employer to raise his stenographer's salary to retain her in his service, no very satisfactory reason appears for denying the action where no such basis of privilege exists and the defendant's motive has been purely spiteful or otherwise improper.

Manner of Interference

In order to be held liable for interference with a contract, the defendant must be shown to have caused the interference.[4] It is not enough that he merely has reaped the advantages of the broken contract after the contracting party has withdrawn from it of his own motion.[5] Thus acceptance of an of-

fered bargain is not in itself inducement of the breach of a prior inconsistent contract,[6] and it is not enough that the defendant has done no more than enter into one with knowledge of the other,[7] although he may be liable if he has taken an active part in holding forth an incentive, such as the offer of a better price or better terms.[8] The defendant's breach of his own contract with the plaintiff is of course not a basis for the tort.[9] It seems probable, although the question does not appear to have arisen directly, that the mere statement of existing facts, or as-

---

98. Goodrich, Inducing Breach of Contract—Contract to Marry, 1918, 4 Iowa L.B. 210; Salmond, Torts, 13th Ed.1961, 659.

1. Cf. Minsky v. Satenstein, 1928, 6 N.J.Misc. 978, 143 A. 512; Overhultz v. Row, 1922, 152 La. 9, 92 So. 716; Lukas v. Tarpilauskas, 1929, 266 Mass. 498, 165 N.E. 513; Homan v. Hall, 1917, 102 Neb. 70, 165 N.W. 881.

2. See supra, pp. 787, 879.

3. Cf. Ableman v. Holman, 1926, 190 Wis. 112, 208 N.W. 889. "And it certainly is true that the courts do not trouble to explain why they accord greater protection to the disgruntled business man than to the disappointed lover, other than that as to the latter his name may be legion, and that there is a romantic idea that the lover may find greater solace for his woes in poetry than in pleading, and fitter expression in sighs than in suits at law." Note, 1932, 5 So.Cal.L.Rev. 150, 155.

4. Lingard v. Kiraly, Fla.App.1959, 110 So.2d 715; Wahl v. Strous, 1942, 344 Pa. 402, 25 A.2d 820.

5. B. J. Wolf & Sons v. New Orleans Tailor-Made Pants Co., 1904, 113 La. 388, 37 So. 2; Northern Wisconsin Coop. Tobacco Pool v. Bekkedal, 1923, 182 Wis. 571, 197 N.W. 936; Minnesota Wheat Growers' Coop. Marketing Ass'n v. Radke, 1925, 163

Minn. 403, 204 N.W. 314; Emery v. A & B Commercial Finishing Co., Okl.1957, 315 P.2d 950; Fischnaller v. Sumner, 1959, 53 Wash.2d 332, 333 P.2d 636.

6. Stanton v. Texas Co., 5 Cir. 1957, 249 F.2d 344; Sweeney v. Smith, D.Pa.1909, 167 F. 385, affirmed, 3 Cir. 1910, 171 F. 645, cert. denied 215 U.S. 600; B. J. Wolf & Sons v. New Orleans Tailor-Made Pants Co., 1904, 113 La. 388, 37 So. 2.

7. Horth v. North American Aggregates Corp., Ohio 1940, 35 N.E.2d 592; Lamport v. 4175 Broadway, Inc., S.D.N.Y.1934, 6 F.Supp. 923; Caldwell v. Gem Packing Co., 1942, 52 Cal.App.2d 80, 125 P.2d 901; Wolf v. Perry, 1959, 65 N.M. 457, 339 P.2d 679; Restatement of Torts, § 766, Comment *i.* A fortiori where there is no knowledge. Augustine v. Trucco, 1954, 124 Cal.App.2d 229, 268 P.2d 780; Snowden v. Sorensen, 1956, 246 Minn. 526, 75 N.W.2d 795.

Apparently contra are Wade v. Culp, 1939, 107 Ind. App. 503, 23 N.E.2d 615; Howard v. Houck, 1962, 210 Tenn. 549, 360 S.W.2d 55 (under statute).

8. Cumberland Glass Mfg. Co. v. De Witt, 1913, 120 Md. 381, 87 A. 927, affirmed 237 U.S. 447; Westinghouse Elec. & Mfg. Co. v. Diamond State Fibre Co., D.Del.1920, 268 F. 121; S. C. Posner Co. v. Jackson, 1918, 223 N.Y. 325, 119 N.E. 573; Pure Milk Ass'n v. Kraft, 1955, 8 Ill.2d 102, 130 N.E.2d 765. See Note, 1956, 27 Miss.L.J. 254. Cf. Local Dairymen's Coop. Ass'n v. Potvin, 1934, 54 R.I. 430, 173 A. 535 (aiding in breach by furnishing transportation for product hold).

9. Canister Co. v. National Can Corp., D.Del.1951, 96 F.Supp. 273; Rosenkoff v. Finkelstein, 1952, 90 App.D.C. 263, 195 F.2d 203; United States v. Newbury Mfg. Co., D.Mass.1941, 36 F.Supp. 602, motion denied, 1942, 123 F.2d 453; Allison v. American Airlines, N.D.Okl.1953, 112 F.Supp. 37. Not even where defendant is one of two obligors, alleged to have conspired. Moreno v. Marbil Productions, Inc., 2 Cir. 1961, 296 F.2d 543; Kay v. Sussel, 1960, 22 Misc.2d 627, 199 N.Y.S.2d 180.

sembling of information in such a way that the party persuaded recognizes it as a reason for breaking the contract is not enough, so long as the defendant creates no added reason and exerts no other influence or pressure by his conduct.[10]

Some of the earlier decisions denying liability argued that the defendant's conduct can never be a proximate cause of the breach,[11] since there is an intervening voluntary act of the third party promisor; but where that act is intentionally brought about by the defendant's inducement, or is even a part of the foreseeable risk which he has created, it seems clear that the result is well within the limits of the "proximate." [12] It is a question of fact, and so normally for the jury, whether the defendant has played a material and substantial part in causing the plaintiff's loss of the benefits of the contract.[13]

Notwithstanding the name of "inducing breach of contract" which has been conferred on the tort since Lumley v. Gye, it does not require inducement to action as a means or complete repudiation as a result. The earliest form of the action, which was for injuries to a servant depriving the master of his services,[14] may still be maintained, although apparently it has not been extended to injuries disabling other persons who are under contract with the plaintiff.[15] There are, however, many similar situations in which the action has been allowed where the defendant has merely prevented the performance of a contract, or has made the performance more difficult and onerous. Recovery has been permitted, for example, where the defendant has prevented the promisor from supplying the plaintiff with goods by calling a strike among his workmen,[16] or by refusing to carry out his own contract to supply goods to the supplier,[17] and where the defendant's breach of his own agreement to make purchases from another has deprived an agent or a broker of his commission.[18]

It has been allowed also where the defendant, as agent of the promisor, has himself misdirected performance,[19] or where he has

---

10. See Stone, J., dissenting in Sorenson v. Chevrolet Motor Co., 1927, 171 Minn. 260, 214 N.W. 754. Also Jensen v. Lundorff, 1960, 258 Minn. 275, 103 N.W.2d 887 (advice to consult attorney).

11. Chambers v. Baldwin, 1891, 91 Ky. 121, 15 S.W. 57; Glencoe Sand & Gravel Co. v. Hudson Bros. Commission Co., 1897, 138 Mo. 439, 40 S.W. 93; Kline v. Eubanks, 1902, 109 La. 241, 33 So. 211.

12. Bowen v. Hall, 1881, 6 Q.B.D. 333, 50 L.J.Q.B. 305; Doremus v. Hennessy, 1898, 176 Ill. 608, 52 N.E. 924, rehearing denied, 1899, 176 Ill. 608, 54 N.E. 524; Heath v. American Book Co., D.W.Va.1899, 97 F. 533; Tubular Rivet & Stud Co. v. Exeter Boot & Shoe Co., 1 Cir. 1908, 159 F. 824.

13. Doremus v. Hennessy, 1898, 176 Ill. 608, 52 N.E. 924; Chipley v. Atkinson, 1877, 23 Fla. 206, 1 So. 934; Kock v. Burgess, 1916, 176 Iowa 493, 156 N.W. 174, 158 N.W. 534; cf. Johnson v. Aetna Life Ins. Co., 1914, 158 Wis. 56, 147 N.W. 32.

14. See supra, p. 929.

15. See infra, p. 938.

16. Dail-Overland Co. v. Willys-Overland, D.Ohio 1919, 263 F. 171; Vonnegut Machinery Co. v. Toledo Machine & Tool Co., D.Ohio 1929, 263 F. 192; Quinlivan v. Dail-Overland Co., 6 Cir., 1921, 274 F. 56; R an W Hat Shop v. Sculley, 1922, 98 Conn. 1, 118 A. 55; Service Wood Heel Co. v. Mackesy, 1936, 293 Mass. 183, 199 N.E. 400. Cf. Mealey v. Bemidji Lbr. Co., 1912, 118 Minn. 427, 136 N.W. 1090. See Notes, 1918, 31 Harv.L.Rev. 1017; 1923, 32 Yale L.J. 171. These cases would appear, however, to be open to criticism on the ground that the strike was for a legitimate purpose other than that of interference with the plaintiff's interests, and so was privileged.

17. Phez Co. v. Salem Fruit Union, 1922, 103 Or. 514, 201 P. 222, 205 P. 970. Cf. Unity Sheet Metal Works v. Farrell Lines, Sup.Ct.1950, 101 N.Y.S.2d 1000 (refusal to issue engineer's certificate); Atkinson v. Pack, 1894, 114 N.C. 597, 19 S.E. 628; Cavender v. Waddingham, 1876, 2 Mo.App. 551; Wilkinson v. Powe, 1942, 300 Mich. 275, 1 N.W.2d 539 (refusal to accept deliveries).

18. Livermore v. Crane, 1901, 26 Wash. 529, 67 P. 221; Glover v. Lee, Higginson Corp., D.Mass.1950, 95 F.Supp. 504 (misrepresentation); Childress v. Abeles, 1954, 240 N.C. 667, 84 S.E.2d 176, rehearing dismissed, 1955, 242 N.C. 123, 86 N.E.2d 916 (threat to stop orders). Cf. Keels v. Powell, 1945, 207 S.C. 97, 34 S.E.2d 482 (settlement of lawsuit by-passing attorney).

19. Sidney Blumenthal & Co. v. United States, 2 Cir., 1929, 30 F.2d 247. Cf. Carpenter v. Williams,

ousted the plaintiff's tenants,[20] or prevented their payment of rent [21] or a sale of the plaintiff's land [22] by the assertion of an adverse claim; and where he has prevented performance by converting goods which are the subject of a sale.[23] The action has been allowed where it is the plaintiff himself who has been prevented from performing the contract, and so obtaining its benefits, by threats [24] or exclusion from the premises,[25] or even by inducing him to break the contract himself.[26]

It has been allowed where the performance has merely been rendered more expensive or burdensome to the plaintiff, as by deliberate damage to a highway which he is under contract to repair.[27] In all of these cases, it may be important that the defendant has intended the result, rather than being only negligent with respect to it; [28] but when interference with the performance of the contract is intended, the manner of the interference itself is not of great importance.

The means employed may, however, affect the defendant's privilege to interfere. The privilege of intentional invasion of the plaintiff's economic interests is limited to reasonable and proper means, by a restriction not unlike that which limits the defense of property to the use of reasonable force.[29] Methods which are tortious in themselves, such as violence, threats and intimidation,[30] defamation,[31] misrepresentations,[32] the coun-

1930, 41 Ga.App. 685, 154 S.E. 298 (president of corporation preventing its performance). Contra, Osgoodby v. Talmadge, 2 Cir., 1930, 45 F.2d 696.

20. Walden v. Conn, 1886, 84 Ky. 312, 1 S.W. 537; Sandlin v. Coyle, 1918, 143 La. 121, 78 So. 261 (frightening share-cropper off of land).

21. Gore v. Condon, 1898, 87 Md. 368, 39 A. 1042; Twitchell v. Nelson, 1914, 126 Minn. 423, 148 N.W. 451; Twitchell v. Glenwood-Inglewood Co., 1915, 131 Minn. 375, 155 N.W. 621; cf. Martin v. Sterkx, 1920, 146 La. 489, 83 So. 776 (disturbing tenant so he would not farm).

22. Vaught v. Jonathan L. Pettyjohn & Co., 1919, 104 Kan. 174, 178 P. 623; Andrews v. Blakeslee, 1861, 12 Iowa 577; cf. Reichman v. Drake, 1951, 89 Ohio App. 222, 100 N.E.2d 533 (tenant refusing to surrender possession).

23. Newark Hardware & Plumbing Co. v. Stove Manufacturers Corp., 1948, 136 N.J.L. 401, 56 A.2d 605, affirmed 137 N.J.L. 612, 61 A.2d 240; Carpenter v. Williams, 1930, 41 Ga.App. 685, 154 S.E. 298; G. E. K. Ltd. v. Dunlop Rubber Co., K.B.1926, 42 T.L.R. 376 (removing plaintiff's tires from car). Cf. Zarrow v. Hughes, Okl.1955, 282 P.2d 215 (pollution of stream led to breach of pasturage contract).

Cf. American Transp. Co. v. United States Sanitary Specialties, 1954, 2 Ill.App.2d 144, 118 N.E.2d 793 (trespass damaging voting machines stored with plaintiff); Keene Lumber Co. v. Leventhal, 1 Cir., 1948, 165 F.2d 815 (pretended foreclosure sales of security).

24. Sumwalt Ice & Coal Co. v. Knickerbocker Ice Co., 1911, 114 Md. 403, 80 A. 48.

25. White v. Massee, 1927, 202 Iowa 1304, 211 N.W. 839; Bacon v. St. Paul Union Stockyards Co., 1924, 161 Minn. 522, 201 N.W. 326. Cf. Southern R. Co. v. Chambers, 1906, 126 Ga. 404, 55 S.E. 37; Fradus Contracting Co. v. Taylor, 1922, 201 App.Div. 298, 194 N.Y.S. 286.

26. Pacific Typesetters Union v. International Typographical Union, 1923, 125 Wash. 273, 216 P. 258; Yankee Network v. Gibbs, 1936, 295 Mass. 56, 3 N.

E.2d 228. But cf. Stillwell Theatre v. Kaplan, 1932, 259 N.Y. 405, 182 N.E. 63.

27. McNary v. Chamberlain, 1867, 34 Conn. 384; Cue v. Breland, 1901, 78 Miss. 864, 29 So. 850. Cf. Lichter v. Fulcher, 1938, 22 Tenn.App. 670, 125 S.W.2d 501 (labor union induced to break contract with plaintiff); Piedmont Cotton Mills v. H. W. Ivey Const. Co., 1964, 109 Ga.App. 876, 137 S.E.2d 528; Rockaway Blvd. Wrecking & Lbr. Co. v. Raylite Elec. Corp., 1966, 26 App.Div.2d 9, 269 N.Y.S.2d 926.

28. See infra, p. 938.

29. See supra, § 21.

30. Vegelahn v. Guntner, 1896, 167 Mass. 92, 44 N.E. 1077; Sparks v. McCrary, 1908, 156 Ala. 382, 47 So. 332; Minnesota Stove Co. v. Cavanaugh, 1915, 131 Minn. 458, 155 N.W. 638. Cf. Leek v. Brasfield, 1956, 226 Ark. 316, 290 S.W.2d 632 (threat of lawsuit known by defendant to be unjustified).

31. Mason v. Funderburk, 1969, 247 Ark. 521, 446 S.W.2d 543; Loudin v. Mohawk Airlines, Inc., 1964, 44 Misc.2d 926, 255 N.Y.S.2d 302; Max v. Kahn, 1917, 91 N.J.L. 170, 102 A. 737; Woody v. Brush, 1917, 178 App.Div. 698, 165 N.Y.S. 867; Stebbins v. Edwards, 1924, 101 Okl. 188, 224 P. 714. See Note, 1933, 33 Col.L.Rev. 90. As to disparagement of property, see supra, § 122.

32. Green v. Button, 1835, 2 Cr.M. & R. 707, 150 Eng.Rep. 299; Skene v. Carayanis, 1926, 103 Conn. 708, 131 A. 497; Johnson v. Gustafson, 1938, 201 Minn. 629, 277 N.W. 252; Diver v. Miller, 1929, 4

terfeiting of a product,[33] bribery,[34] or the harassing of agents,[35] will not be privileged even where the defendant is acting for a purpose justifiable in itself, while peaceable inducement, or various forms of economic pressure, might be privileged under similar circumstances.[36] The external form of the defendant's conduct of course is not controlling,[37] and in labor cases particularly the courts have been willing, and perhaps excessively so [38] to look through it to what they conceive to be the realities of the situation.

One question over which controversy continues to rage is that of the effect of concerted action by a number of individuals to do what any one of them might be free to do alone.[39] It becomes especially important in cases of collective refusal on the part of labor unions or trade associations to deal with the plaintiff or a third person, resulting in strikes, boycotts, lockouts, blacklists and the like. It is of course logical to say that where any member of the group might without liability withdraw from such dealings, the element of combination adds nothing in itself, and hence that the group may do whatever an individual might do. This position has been taken by a number of courts, particularly in earlier cases.[40] It overlooks, however, the greatly increased potentiality of coercion, intimidation and economic pressure which lies in the hands of a group, not only as against the object of attack, but also toward its own more reluctant members, as well as the greater damage which may result from group action.[41] Accordingly, where such fac-

W.W.Harr., Del.Super., 207, 148 A. 291. Cf. Klauder v. Cregar, 1937, 327 Pa. 1, 192 A. 667; Bartlett v. Federal Outfitting Co., 1933, 133 Cal.App. 747, 24 P.2d 877. See also supra, § 128.

33. George G. Fox Co. v. Hathaway, 1908, 199 Mass. 99, 85 N.E. 417. And see, infra, p. 959.

34. Angle v. Chicago, St. P., M. & O. Ry. Co., 1893, 151 U.S. 1.

35. Evenson v. Spaulding, 8 Cir. 1907, 150 F. 517; Standard Oil Co. v. Doyle, 1904, 118 Ky. 662, 82 S. W. 271. Cf. Downes v. Culbertson, 1934, 153 Misc. 14, 275 N.Y.S. 233 (groundless civil suits); American Mercury v. Chase, D.Mass.1926, 13 F.2d 224; Pratt Food Co. v. Bird, 1907, 148 Mich. 631, 112 N. W. 701 (criminal prosecutions).

36. See Citizens' Light, Heat & Power Co. v. Montgomery Light & Water Power Co., D.Ala.1909, 171 F. 553; Pierce v. Stablemen's Union, 1909, 156 Cal. 70, 103 P. 324; Roddy v. United Mine Workers, 1914, 41 Okl. 621, 139 P. 126. See Smith, Crucial Issues in Labor Litigation, 1906, 20 Harv.L.Rev. 253, 266.

37. "Suppose half a dozen men stop a coach, and one of them politely asks the passengers to hand over their valuables, thoughtfully adding, 'but you need not do so unless you wish.' Would the courtesy displayed prevent the transaction from being considered robbery?" United States v. Kane, D.Colo. 1885, 23 F. 748, 750.

38. See Cooper, The Fiction of Peaceful Picketing, 1936, 35 Mich.L.Rev. 73.

39. See Morris, History of Labor and Conspiracy, 1937, 52 Pol.Sci.Q. 51; Burdick, Conspiracy as a Crime and as a Tort, 1907, 7 Col.L.Rev. 229; Burdick, The Tort of Conspiracy, 1908, 8 Col.L.Rev.

117; Charlesworth, Conspiracy as a Ground of Liability in Tort, 1920, 36 L.Q.Rev. 38; Kales, Coercive and Competitive Methods in Trade and Labor Disputes, 1922, 8 Corn.L.Q. 1, 128; Hale, Prima Facie Torts, Combination and Non-Feasance, 1946, 46 Col.L.Rev. 196; Note, 1951, 45 Ill.L.Rev. 784.

40. Bohn Mfg. Co. v. Hollis, 1893, 54 Minn. 223, 55 N.W. 1119; John D. Park & Sons v. National Wholesale Druggists Ass'n, 1903, 175 N.Y. 1, 67 N. E. 136; J. F. Parkinson Co. v. Building Trades Council, 1908, 154 Cal. 581, 98 P. 1027.

It is not lacking in more recent decisions. Harding v. Ohio Cas. Ins. Co., 1950, 230 Minn. 327, 41 N.W.2d 818; Canister Co. v. National Can Corp., D.Del. 1951, 96 F.Supp. 273; McNeill v. Hall, 1941, 220 N. C. 73, 16 S.E.2d 456; Edwards v. James Stewart & Co., D.C. Cir.1947, 82 U.S.App.D.C. 123, 160 F.2d 935.

41. "First, the harm to individual or social interests which a concerted refusal to deal may cause is ordinarily much greater than that which an individual's refusal threatens. The power of the individual is ordinarily smaller; and there is greater likelihood of neutralization by the action of other individuals. Secondly, it is thought to be a more serious restraint upon personal liberty to require an individual to justify a refusal to deal than to require a combination of persons to justify a concerted refusal. In uniting on a policy, the persons in a combination restrict their liberty by eliminating from their competition one factor with reference to which they would otherwise make independent and probably different decisions. Preventing action by the combination restores that competition. Thirdly, the purpose of a concerted refusal is ordinarily

tors are present, the more modern view is that concerted action may itself amount to a basis of liability, or, more properly, that more in the way of justification is required to establish the privilege of group interference.[42]

Intent and Negligence

Interference with contract, which had its modern inception in "malice," has remained almost entirely an intentional tort; and in general, liability has not been extended to the various forms of negligence by which performance of a contract may be prevented or rendered more burdensome.[43] There is one conspicuous exception. The earlier rule [44] under which one who negligently injured a servant became liable to his master for loss of his services, apparently is still alive and good law; and to the extent that there are services lost, of value, the employer can recover damages.[45] This has, however,

been under considerable attack of late,[46] and clearly is to be quite narrowly confined within its original limits. Thus there has been very general refusal to extend it to injuries disabling other persons who are under contract with the plaintiff, but are not classified as servants,[47] such as soldiers,[48] policemen,[49] and even civil servants.[50] Recovery has also been denied for other damages than the value of the services themselves, as for example payments which the employer is compelled by contract to make to his injured employee,[51] or an increased workmen's com-

---

more definitely ascertainable than that of an individual's refusal." Restatement of Torts, § 765, Comment a.

"A grain of gunpowder is harmless, but a pound may be highly destructive." Lord Brampton, in Quinn v. Leathem, [1901] A.C. 495, 530.

42. Jackson v. Stanfield, 1893, 137 Ind. 592, 36 N.E. 345, 37 N.E. 14; Martell v. White, 1904, 185 Mass. 255, 69 N.E. 1085; Bankers' Fire & Marine Ins. Co. v. Sloan, 1934, 229 Ala. 26, 155 So. 371; Keviczky v. Lorber, 1943, 290 N.Y. 297, 49 N.E.2d 146; Louis Kamm, Inc. v. Flink, 1934, 113 N.J.L. 582, 175 A. 62.

43. See Carpenter, Interference with Contractual Relations, 1928, 41 Harv.L.Rev. 728, 7 Or.L.Rev. 181, 301; Green, Relational Interests, 1935, 29 Ill.L.Rev. 1041, 1042, 30 Ill.L.Rev. 1, 2; Harper, Interference with Contractual Relations, 1953, 47 N.W.U.L.Rev. 873, 884; Notes, 1953, 20 U.Chi.L.Rev. 283; 1948, 36 Ky.L.J. 142; 1935, 23 Cal.L.Rev. 420; 1933, 18 Corn.L.Q. 292; 1964, 16 Stan.L.Rev. 664.

44. See supra, p. 929; Everard v. Hopkins, 1614, 1 Rolle Rep. 124, 80 Eng.Rep. 1164; Hodsoll v. Stallebrass, 1840, 11 Ad. & El. 301, 113 Eng.Rep. 429; Martinez v. Gerber, 1841, 3 Man. & G. 88, 133 Eng. Rep. 1069; Jones, Per Quod Servitium Amisit, 1958, 74 L.Q.Rev. 39.

45. Mineral Industries, Inc. v. George, 1965, 44 Misc. 2d 764, 255 N.Y.S.2d 114; Jones v. Waterman S. S. Corp., 3 Cir. 1946, 155 F.2d 992; Mankin v. Scala

Theodrome Co., [1947] K.B. 257; see Earley v. Pacific Elec. R. Co., 1917, 176 Cal. 79, 167 P. 513; Interstate Tel. & Tel. Co. v. Public Service Elec. Co., 1914, 86 N.J.L. 26, 90 A. 1062.

46. See Seavey, Liability to Master for Negligent Harm to Servant, [1956] Wash.U.L.Q. 309; Guest, Crown Servants, 1956, 34 Can.Bar Rev. 598; Brett, Consortium and Servitium, 1957, 29 Aust.L.J. 321, 389, 428; Cowen, The Consequences of The Commonwealth v. Quince, 1946, 19 Aust.L.J. 2; Fleming, Action Per Quod Servitium Amisit, 1954, 26 Aust.L.J. 122.

47. In Taylor v. Neri, 1795, 1 Esp. 386, 170 Eng.Rep. 393, recovery was denied to a theatre manager where defendant assaulted an actor and disabled him. See also Cain v. Vollmer, 1910, 19 Idaho 163, 112 P. 686 (jockey). In Darmour Productions Corp. v. Herbert M. Baruch Corp., 1933, 135 Cal.App. 351, 27 P.2d 664, in partial reliance upon a statute, the recovery was extended to the services of a star motion picture actress.

48. United States v. Standard Oil Co., 1947, 332 U.S. 301; Commonwealth v. Quince, [1944] Aust.L.Rep. 50, 68 Comm.L.Rep. 227. To the contrary was Attorney-General v. Valle-Jones, [1935] 2 K.B. 207.

49. Attorney-General for New South Wales v. Perpetual Trustee Co., [1955] A.C. 457; Myers v. Hoffman, 1956, 1 Dom.L.Rep.2d 272. To the contrary were Bradford Corp. v. Webster, [1920] 2 K.B. 135; Attorney-General v. Dublin United Tramways Co., [1939] Ir.Rep. 590.

50. Inland Revenue Commissioners v. Hambrook, [1956] 2 Q.B. 641.

51. The Federal No. 2, 2 Cir. 1927, 21 F.2d 313; Chelsea Moving & Trucking Co. v. Ross Towboat Co., 1932, 280 Mass. 282, 182 N.E. 477; Interstate Tel. & Tel. Co. v. Public Service Elec. Co., 1914, 86 N.J.L. 26, 90 A. 1062; City of Philadelphia v. Philadelphia Rapid Transit Co., 1940, 337 Pa. 1, 10 A.2d 434; Houston Belt & Terminal R. Co. v. Burmester, Tex.Civ.App.1957, 309 S.W.2d 271, ref. n. r. e. Con-

pensation insurance premium resulting from the injury.[52]   Now and then there have been courts [53] which have expressed doubt as to whether such an action should be permitted at all.

Likewise insurance companies have been denied recovery for losses due to negligent injury to persons [54] or property [55] which they have insured.   Any remedy in such cases must be through subrogation to the claim of the person directly injured.[56]   On the same basis, there is no action against one who negligently sinks a barge which the plaintiff has contracted to tow,[57] or destroys

goods which he has contracted to buy,[58] or breaks the machinery of another who is furnishing him with power,[59] or pollutes the stream from which a city is supplying him with water,[60] or kills a person with whom he has a contract for his support,[61] or, as an

tra, Jones v. Waterman S. S. Corp., 3 Cir. 1936, 155 F.2d 992.

52. Northern States Contracting Co. v. Oakes, 1934, 191 Minn. 88, 253 N.W. 371; Decker Const. Co. v. Mathis, 1953, 68 Ohio Abs. 280, 122 N.E.2d 38; Crab Orchard Imp. Co. v. Chesapeake & O. R. Co., 4 Cir. 1940, 115 F.2d 277, cert. denied, 1941, 312 U.S. 702. Contra, on the basis of a duty owed directly to the plaintiff, Midvale Coal Co. v. Cardox Corp., 1949, 152 Ohio St. 437, 89 N.E.2d 673, second appeal, 1952, 157 Ohio St. 526, 106 N.E.2d 556.

53. Chelsea Moving & Trucking Co. v. Ross Towboat Co., 1932, 280 Mass. 282, 182 N.E. 477; City of Philadelphia v. Philadelphia Rapid Transit Co., 1940, 337 Pa. 1, 10 A.2d 434; United States v. Atlantic Coast Line R. Co., D.N.C.1946, 64 F.Supp. 289; Employers' Liability Assur. Corp. v. Daley, 1947, 271 App.Div. 662, 67 N.Y.S.2d 233, 68 N.Y.S.2d 743, affirmed, 1947, 297 N.Y. 745, 77 N.E.2d 515. The whole doctrine was rejected in Dotoratos v. Greenidge, 1967, 54 Misc.2d 85, 281 N.Y.S.2d 498.

54. Connecticut Mut. Life Ins. Co. v. New York & N. H. R. Co., 1856, 25 Conn. 265. Cf. Economy Auto Ins. Co. v. Brown, 1948, 334 Ill.App. 579, 79 N.E.2d 854 (liability insurer denied recovery under Illinois Dramshop Act).

55. Peoria Marine & Fire Ins. Co. v. Frost, 1865, 37 Ill. 333; Sinram v. Pennsylvania R. Co., 2 Cir. 1932, 61 F.2d 767.

56. See Travelers' Ins. Co. v. Great Lakes Eng. Works Co., 6 Cir. 1911, 184 F. 426; Hardman, The Common Law Right of Subrogation Under Workmen's Compensation Acts, 1920, 26 W.Va.L.Q. 183; Notes, 1927, 12 Corn.L.Q. 235; 1933, 18 Corn.L.Q. 292; 1925, 38 Harv.L.Rev. 971.

57. La Société Anonyme de Remorquage à Hélice v. Bennetts, [1911] 1 K.B. 243. Accord: Robins Dry Dock & Repair Co. v. Flint, 1927, 275 U.S. 303 (charterer); Cattle v. Stockton Waterworks Co., 1875, L.R. 10 Q.B. 453; Petition of S. C. Loveland

Co., E.D.Pa.1959, 170 F.Supp. 786. Cf. Forcum James Co. v. Duke Transportation Co., 1957, 231 La. 953, 93 So.2d 228 (negligent damage to bridge which plaintiff was under contract to repair and maintain); Louisville & N. R. Co. v. Arrow Transp. Co., N.D.Ala.1959, 170 F.Supp. 597 (bridge which plaintiff has contracted to use).

Charterers of ships have been allowed to recover for negligent injury to the vessel, on the basis of a property interest. Hines v. Saugstad S. S. Co., 1 Cir. 1902, 266 F. 502; The Aquitania, S.D.N.Y.1920, 270 F. 239; Agwilines v. Eagle Oil Co., 2 Cir. 1946, 153 F.2d 869.

58. Dale v. Grant, 1870, 34 N.J.L. 142; Thompson v. Seaboard Air Line R. Co., 1914, 165 N.C. 377, 81 S. E. 315. Cf. Stromer v. Yuba City, 1964, 225 Cal. App.2d 286, 37 Cal.Rptr. 240 (commission on sale); Rockaway Blvd. Wrecking & Lbr. Co. v. Raylite Elec. Corp., 1966, 26 App.Div.2d 9, 269 N.Y.S.2d 926 (extra costs in performing demolition contract).

59. Byrd v. English, 1903, 117 Ga. 191, 43 S.E. 419. Cf. Stevenson v. East Ohio Gas Co., Ohio App.1946, 73 N.E.2d 200, where the negligence damaged a plant and deprived a workman of employment; also Borcich v. Ancich, 9 Cir. 1951, 191 F.2d 392, certiorari denied 342 U.S. 905, where damage to a fishing vessel prevented seamen from receiving their share of fish.

Contrast this narrow position as to purely pecuniary loss with Newlin v. New England Tel. & Tel. Co., 1944, 316 Mass. 234, 54 N.E.2d 929, where defendant's negligence caused a failure of power, and plaintiff recovered for physical damage to his crop of mushrooms.

60. Pure Oil Co. v. Boyle, Tex.Com.App.1930, 26 S. W.2d 161; Zarrow v. Hughes, Okl.1955, 282 P.2d 215.

61. Brink v. Wabash R. Co., 1900, 160 Mo. 87, 60 N. W. 1058; Steffan v. Zernes, Fla.App.1960, 124 So.2d 495 (court decree). Cf. Anthony v. Slaid, 1846, 11 Metc., Mass., 290 (assault on pauper whom plaintiff had contracted to support); Fifield Manor v. Finston, 1960, 54 Cal.2d 632, 7 Cal.Rptr. 377, 354 P.2d 1073 (negligent injury to one whom plaintiff had contracted to provide with medical care); Baruch v. Beech Aircraft Corp., 10 Cir. 1949, 175 F.2d 1, cert. denied 338 U.S. 900 (assisting pilot to violate contract by flying plane while intoxicated); Morse v. Piedmont Hotel Co., 1964, 110 Ga.App. 509, 139 S.E.2d 133 (salesman lost job because of theft from him negligently permitted by defendants).

agent, negligently fails to see that his principal's contract is performed.[62] And when it is the plaintiff himself who suffers personal injury, his loss of contracts may be admitted in evidence only as bearing upon the value of his lost time, or diminished earning capacity.[63]

No very satisfactory reason has been given for this refusal of a remedy in negligence cases.[64] For the most part the courts have talked of "proximate cause," and have said that the consequences were too "remote." In all of the cases denying recovery the defendant had no knowledge of the contractual relation and no reason to foresee any harm to the plaintiff's interests; and this has led some writers [65] to conclude that they do not mean that no negligence action could ever be maintained, but merely that there was no duty to the plaintiff in the particular instance. While this is very persuasive, it seems more likely that the courts are deliberately refusing to protect any contract against negligence, influenced by fear of an undue burden upon freedom of action, the relative severity of the penalty which may be imposed upon mere negligence, the possibility of collusive claims and increased litigation, and the difficulty of apportioning

damages.[66] If this is true, the question may at least be raised whether such a policy is not too narrow, and whether, as in the somewhat analogous case of the liability of the contractor himself to third parties,[67] the law may not be expected to move in the future in the direction of recovery by those whose damages are foreseeable by the actor.

There is actually, however, very little looking even vaguely in this direction. In one or two cases where the defendant had knowledge of the contract, but apparently was merely negligent, recovery has been allowed by calling the interference "wilful." [68] In some cases where a separate tort is found, damages for loss of the benefits of a contract have been added to the loss of tangible property, under the guise of loss of use of it.[69] Telegraph companies have been held liable, without much discussion of the question, for the negligent transmission of messages resulting in the loss of contract benefits.[70]

---

62. Baird v. Chesapeake & Potomac Tel. Co., 1955, 208 Md. 245, 117 A.2d 873. Cf. Donovan Const. Co. v. General Elec. Co., D.Minn.1955, 133 F.Supp. 870 (negligence in supplying generators delayed plaintiff's contract with the Government); Costello v. Wells Fargo Bank, 1968, 258 Cal.App.2d 90, 65 Cal. Rptr. 612.

63. Steitz v. Gifford, 1939, 280 N.Y. 15, 19 N.E.2d 661; Halloran v. New York, N. H. & H. R. Co., 1912, 211 Mass. 132, 97 N.E. 631; Gray v. Boston Elevated R. Co., 1913, 215 Mass. 143, 102 N.E. 71; Ball v. T. J. Pardy Const. Co., 1928, 108 Conn. 549, 143 A. 855.

64. See the articles and notes cited supra, note 44.

65. Carpenter, Interference with Contractual Relations, 1928, 41 Harv.L.Rev. 728, 737–742, 7 Or.L. Rev. 181, 301; Note, 1933, 18 Corn.L.Q. 292. This is the explanation actually given in Sinram v. Pennsylvania R. Co., 2 Cir. 1932, 61 F.2d 767.

66. See Notes, 1918, 31 Harv.L.Rev. 217; 1935, 23 Cal.L.Rev. 420. "To open the door of legal redress to wrongs received through the mere voluntary and factitious relation of a contractor with the immediate subject of the injury, would be to encourage collusion and extravagant contracts between men, by which the death of either through the involuntary default of others, might be made a source of splendid profits to the other, and would also invite a system of litigation more portentous than our jurisprudence has yet known." Connecticut Mut. Life Ins. Co. v. New York & N. H. R. Co., 1856, 25 Conn. 265, 275.

67. See supra, § 93.

68. Cue v. Breland, 1901, 78 Miss. 864, 29 So. 850. Cf. Twitchell v. Glenwood-Inglewood Co., 1915, 131 Minn. 375, 155 N.W. 621.

69. The Argentino, 1889, 14 A.C. 519; The Aurora, E.D.La.1945, 64 F.Supp. 502, aff'd in Loje v. Protich, 5 Cir. 1946, 153 F.2d 224; American Transp. Co. v. U. S. Sanitary Specialties Corp., 1954, 2 Ill. App.2d 144, 118 N.E.2d 793.

70. Western Union Tel. Co. v. Mathis, 1926, 215 Ala. 282, 110 So. 399; McPherson v. Western Union Tel. Co., 1915, 189 Mich. 471, 155 N.W. 557; Barker v. Western Union Tel. Co., 1908, 134 Wis. 147, 114 N. W. 439; Trapp v. Western Union Tel. Co., 1912, 92 S.C. 214, 75 S.E. 210; see Note, 1936, 20 Minn.L. Rev. 837. It will be noted that in these cases liability is extended even to interference with prospective contracts.

There are one or two cases [71] in which the defendant, having gratuitously assumed a duty to make payments for the plaintiff on a contract, has been held liable when his failure to do so has resulted in the loss of the contract. The cases of negligent misrepresentation [72] which causes loss to third parties in business dealings seem to stand upon much the same footing, although the element of justifiable reliance and business custom may perhaps distinguish them. The limitation to specifically foreseeable plaintiffs there imposed may suggest an ultimate solution to the problem. Thus far, however, it remains the general rule that contract interests are not protected against negligent interference.

If intentional interference is to be required, it presupposes knowledge of the plaintiff's interests, or at least of facts which would lead a reasonable man to believe in their existence.[73] Otherwise there can be no liability,[74] even though the defendant has intentionally injured the other party to the contract, as by killing a policy holder whom the plaintiff has insured,[75] or assaulting one

whom he has contracted to care for.[76] Once such knowledge is established, there is of course no difficulty in finding liability where the defendant has acted with the desire and purpose of interfering with the contract,[77] or of appropriating its benefits to himself.[78] A more difficult question, on which there is little agreement, arises where the defendant has merely pursued his own ends, knowing that his conduct is certain, or substantially so, to prevent performance of the contract, but without any desire or primary object of doing so.

One line of cases has concluded that there is liability for such incidental interference, where the defendant has called a strike against an employer who has contracted to deliver goods to the plaintiff,[79] or has broken his own contract upon which the plaintiff's contract depends,[80] or has otherwise prevent-

71. Spiegel v. Metropolitan Life Ins. Co., 1959, 6 N.Y.2d 91, 188 N.Y.S.2d 486, 160 N.E.2d 40; Walker Bank & Trust Co. v. First Security Corp., 1959, 9 Utah 2d 215, 341 P.2d 944. See Notes, 1960, 12 Stan.L.Rev. 509; 1953, 20 U.Chi.L.Rev. 283.

72. Supra, p. 705.

73. See Twitchell v. Nelson, 1914, 126 Minn. 423, 148 N.W. 451; Twitchell v. Glenwood-Inglewood Co., 1915, 131 Minn. 375, 155 N.W. 621; Tenta v. Guraly, 1966, 140 Ind.App. 160, 221 N.E.2d 577.

74. Snowden v. Sorenson, 1956, 246 Minn. 526, 75 N.W.2d 795; Augustine v. Trucco, 1954, 124 Cal.App.2d 229, 268 P.2d 780; Kenworthy v. Kleinberg, 1935, 182 Wash. 425, 47 P.2d 825; Kerr v. Du Pree, 1926, 35 Ga.App. 122, 132 S.E. 393; Thomason v. Sparkman, Tex.Civ.App.1933, 55 S.W.2d 871. See Kelly v. Central Hanover Bank & Trust Co., S.D.N.Y.1935, 11 F.Supp. 497, 513, remanded for finding inter alia on question of knowledge, 2 Cir. 1936, 85 F.2d 61.

75. Mobile Life Ins. Co. v. Brame, 1877, 95 U.S. 754, 24 L.Ed. 580. Accord: Rockingham Mut. Fire Ins. Co. v. Bosher, 1855, 39 Me. 253 (setting fire to insured building); Midland Ins. Co. v. Smith, 1881, L.R. 6 Q.B.D. 561 (same).

76. Anthony v. Slaid, 1846, 11 Met., Mass., 290. But here again actions for loss of services of a servant are an exception. Woodward v. Washburn, 1846, 3 Denio, N.Y., 369; Jones v. Brown, 1794, 1 Esp. 217.

77. St. Johnsbury & Lake Champlain R. Co. v. Hunt, 1882, 55 Vt. 570; McNary v. Chamberlain, 1867, 34 Conn. 384; Southern R. Co. v. Chambers, 1906, 126 Ga. 404, 55 S.E. 37. See infra, p. 943.

78. Carpenter v. Williams, 1930, 41 Ga.App. 685, 154 S.E. 298; Phez Co. v. Salem Fruit Union, 1922, 101 Or. 514, 201 P. 222, Id., 103 Or. 514, 205 P. 970; Lewis v. Bloede, 4 Cir. 1912, 202 F. 7; Bowen v. Speer, Tex.Civ.App.1914, 166 S.W. 1183; cf. Vaught v. Jonathan L. Pettyjohn & Co., 1919, 104 Kan. 174, 178 P. 623; Andrews v. Blakeslee, 1861, 12 Iowa 577.

79. Niles-Bement-Pond Co. v. Iron Molders' Union, Local No. 68, D.Ohio 1917, 246 F. 851, reversed on other grounds, 1919, 258 F. 408, affirmed 254 U.S. 77; Dail-Overland Co. v. Willys-Overland, D.Ohio 1919, 263 F. 171, affirmed, 6 Cir. 1921, 274 F. 56; Vonnegut Mach. Co. v. Toledo Machine & Tool Co., D.Ohio 1920, 263 F. 192, reversed on other grounds, 6 Cir. 1921, 274 F. 66; Quinlivan v. Dail-Overland Co., 6 Cir. 1921, 274 F. 56; cf. R an W Hat Shop v. Sculley, 1922, 98 Conn. 1, 118 A. 55. The result is criticized on the basis of privilege in the Note, 1923, 32 Yale L.J. 171.

80. Livermore v. Crane, 1901, 26 Wash. 529, 67 P. 221; Cavender v. Waddingham, 1876, 2 Mo.App. 551; Atkinson v. Pack, 1894, 114 N.C. 597, 19 S.E. 628; Reichman v. Drake, 1951, 89 Ohio App. 222,

ed performance by the third party.[81]   Another, not easily distinguished, has considered
that in such cases the damage suffered is too
"remote." [82]   There appears to be no discoverable harmony or agreement in these decisions.   It is difficult to reach a conclusion [83]
where no court has fully considered the
problem; but it may be suggested that the
question is not so much one of prima facie
liability as of the defendant's privilege.   Or
in other words, that such interference is to
be regarded as intentional,[84] and hence as
requiring justification, but that its incidental
character is one factor to be considered in

determining whether the defendant is justified in seeking his own advantage at the
plaintiff's expense.   In an interlocking
society, there may be cases where it would
be an undue and undesirable restraint upon
freedom of action to hold anyone responsible
for such indirect injury; and there will be
others where the protection should be extended to the plaintiff.   It cannot be pretended, however, that any respectable number of
decisions have proceeded along these lines.[85]

Purpose and Privilege

Given the intention to interfere with the
contract, liability usually will turn upon the
ultimate purpose or object which the defendant is seeking to advance.   The early cases,[86]
with their emphasis upon "malice," regarded
proof of an improper motive as an essential
part of the plaintiff's cause of action.   As the
tort became more firmly established, there
was a gradual shift of emphasis, until today
it is generally agreed that an intentional interference with the existing contractual relations of another is prima facie sufficient
for liability, and that the burden of proving
that it is "justified" rests upon the defendant.[87]   Otherwise stated, and perhaps more

100 N.E.2d 533 (tenant refusing to vacate in time
for new lease); Glover v. Lee Higginson Corp., D.
Mass.1950, 95 F.Supp. 504.

81.   The Poznan, D.N.Y.1921, 276 F. 418 (owner ordering back ship under contract to plaintiff); Sandlin
v. Coyle, 1918, 143 La. 121, 78 So. 261 (frightening
away tenant); Keene Lumber Co. v. Leventhal, 1
Cir. 1948, 165 F.2d 815 ("fixed" foreclosure sales
bankrupting debtor); Sidney Blumenthal & Co. v.
United States, 2 Cir. 1929, 30 F.2d 247, cert. denied,
1929, Admiral Oriental Line v. U. S., 279 U.S. 847
(routing goods away from plaintiff's line); Keels v.
Powell, 1945, 207 S.C. 97, 34 S.E.2d 482 (settlement
by-passing attorney); Glover v. Lee Higginson
Corp., D.Mass.1950, 95 F.Supp. 504 (same by-passing
broker).   The liability is easily found where the defendant has undertaken a duty to the plaintiff, as
in Walker Bank & Trust Co. v. First Security
Corp., 1959, 9 Utah 2d 215, 341 P.2d 944 (discontinu-
ing payments on insurance).   See Note, 1960, 12
Stan.L.Rev. 509.

82.   Glazer v. Chandler, 1964, 414 Pa. 304, 200 A.2d
416; Wometco Theatres v. United Artists Corp.,
1936, 53 Ga.App. 509, 186 S.E. 572 (breach of contract on which plaintiff's contract depended); Vis-
intine & Co. v. New York, C. & St. L. R. Co., 1960,
169 Ohio St. 505, 160 N.E.2d 311 (same); R. J.
Caldwell v. Fisk Rubber Co., 1 Cir. 1933, 62 F.2d
475 (same, loss of commissions); Isbrandtsen v. Local 1291 of Int. Longshoremen's Assn., 3 Cir. 1953,
204 F.2d 495 (same, action of labor union); Benton
v. Kennedy-Van Saun Mfg. & Eng. Corp., 1955, 2
App.Div.2d 27, 152 N.Y.S.2d 955 (same, government
contracts).

83.   The Restatement of Torts, § 766, Comments *d*
and *k*, indicates that there may be liability, but
leaves the matter in a highly uncertain state, to
say the least.

84.   Compare the cases of physical injury substantially certain to follow, supra, p. 31.

85.   One such case appears to be Gregory v. Brooks,
1838, 35 Conn. 437.   See also the stress laid upon
the absence of justifiable purpose in Sidney Blumenthal & Co. v. United States, 2 Cir. 1929, 30 F.2d
247, cert. denied, 1929, Admiral Oriental Line
v. United States, 279 U.S. 847; Southern R. Co. v.
Chambers, 1906, 126 Ga. 404, 55 S.E. 37.

86.   Lumley v. Gye, 1853, 2 El. & Bl. 216, 118 Eng.
Rep. 749; Bowen v. Hall, 1881, 6 Q.B.D. 333, 50 L.
J.Q.B. 305; Temperton v. Russell, [1893] 1 Q.B. 715,
62 L.J.Q.B. 412.

87.   Mogul S. S. Co. v. McGregor Gow & Co., 1889, L.
R. 23 Q.B.D. 598, aff'd [1892] A.C. 25; Aikins v.
Wisconsin, 1904, 195 U.S. 194; Berry v. Donovan,
1905, 188 Mass. 353, 74 N.E. 603; Connors v. Connolly, 1913, 86 Conn. 641, 86 A. 600; De Minico v.
Craig, 1911, 207 Mass. 593, 94 N.E. 317.   The two
cases last named held the question to be one of law
for the court; but the issue of reasonable conduct
frequently has been left to the jury.   Order of Railway Conductors v. Jones, 1925, 78 Colo. 80, 239 P.
882; Carnes v. St. Paul Union Stockyards Co.,
1925, 164 Minn. 457, 205 N.W. 630, 206 N.W. 396;
Berry v. Donovan, supra.

accurately, the defendant may show that the interference is privileged by reason of the interests furthered by his conduct, but the burden rests upon him to do so.[88] The question of privilege is of course as broad as the catalogue of the possible interests involved, and it must be considered in the light of the means adopted[89] and the relations between the parties.[90] Obviously in a field so vast only very general mention may be made of the types of cases which have arisen.

Since Lumley v. Gye there has been general agreement that a purely "malicious" motive, in the sense of spite and a desire to do harm to the plaintiff for its own sake, will make the defendant liable for interference with a contract.[91] The same is true of mere officious intermeddling for no other reason than a desire to interfere.[92] On the other hand, in the few cases in which the question has arisen, it has been held that where the defendant has a proper purpose in view, the addition of ill will toward the plaintiff will not defeat his privilege.[93] It may be suggested that here, as in the case of mixed motives[94] in the exercise of a privilege in defamation and malicious prosecution,[95] the court may well look to the predominant purpose underlying the defendant's conduct.

In contrast, an impersonal or disinterested motive of a laudable character may protect the defendant in his interference. This is true particularly where he seeks to protect a third person toward whom he stands in a relation of responsibility, as in the case of a mother endeavoring to exclude a diseased person from her child's school,[96] school authorities making regulations for the welfare of their students,[97] an agent protecting the interests of his principal,[98] or an employer

---

88. Restatement of Torts, §§ 766, 767; Freed v. Manchester Service, 1958, 165 Cal.App.2d 186, 331 P.2d 689.

89. See supra, p. 936.
The New York courts frequently have expressed this by saying that intentional interference with the plaintiff's present or prospective contract interests is a "prima facie" tort, for which the defendant is liable unless he shows "justification" for it. See infra, p. 953; Notes, 1958, 10 Syr.L.Rev. 53; 1958, 32 St. Johns L.Rev. 282.

90. Restatement of Torts, § 767. See also Carpenter, Interference with Contract Relations, 1928, 41 Harv.L.Rev. 728, 7 Or.L.Rev. 181, 301; Green, Relational Interests, 1935, 29 Ill.L.Rev. 1; Notes, 1932, 17 Corn.L.Q. 509; 1928, 12 Minn.L.Rev. 147; 1938, 32 Ill.L.Rev. 611; 1941, 27 Corn.L.Q. 139.

91. Employment contracts: Jones v. Leslie, 1910, 61 Wash. 107, 112 P. 81; De Minico v. Craig, 1911, 207 Mass. 593, 94 N.E. 317; Carnes v. St. Paul Union Stockyards Co., 1925, 164 Minn. 457, 205 N.W. 630, rehearing denied 164 Minn. 457, 206 N.W. 396; Wheeler-Stenzel Co. v. American Window Glass Co., 1909, 202 Mass. 471, 89 N.E. 28.
Other contracts: Martens v. Reilly, 1901, 109 Wis. 464, 84 N.W. 840; Wesley v. Native Lumber Co., 1910, 97 Miss. 814, 53 So. 346; Dunshee v. Standard Oil Co., 1911, 152 Iowa 618, 132 N.W. 371; Hutton v. Watters, 1915, 132 Tenn. 527, 179 S.W. 134.

92. Sidney Blumenthal & Co. v. United States, 2 Cir. 1929, 30 F.2d 247. Cf. Russell v. Croteau, 1953, 98 N.H. 68, 94 A.2d 376 (no reason apparent on record).

93. Lancaster v. Hamburger, 1904, 70 Ohio St. 156, 71 N.E. 289; Gregory v. Dealers' Equipment Co., 1927, 156 Tenn. 273, 300 S.W. 563; Bentley v. Teton, 1958, 19 Ill.App.2d 284, 153 N.E.2d 495; Diver v. Miller, 1929, 4 W.W.Harr., Del., 207, 148 A. 291; Stevens v. Siegel, 1963, 18 App.Div.2d 1109, 239 N.Y.S.2d 827; O'Brien v. Western Union Tel. Co., 1911, 62 Wash. 598, 114 P. 441.

94. One question which seems nowhere to have been considered is whether anything so intrinsically psychological as a mixed motive is really susceptible of proof. Since in many cases the defendant himself is uncertain as to his own motives, and some element of ill will is seldom absent, there is all the more reason for holding that the addition of "malice" should not defeat the privilege.

95. See supra, pp. 794, 847.

96. Legris v. Marcotte, 1906, 129 Ill.App. 67.

97. Cf. Gott v. Berea College, 1913, 156 Ky. 376, 161 S.W. 204; Jones v. Cody, 1902, 132 Mich. 13, 92 N.W. 495; Guethler v. Altman, 1901, 26 Ind.App. 587, 60 N.E. 355; Rowan v. Butler, 1908, 171 Ind. 28, 85 N.E. 714 (soldiers' home); Kuryer Pub. Co. v. Messmer, 1916, 162 Wis. 565, 156 N.W. 948 (church). While these are cases of interference with prospective advantage, their language is equally applicable to existing contracts.

98. Said v. Butt, [1920] 3 K.B. 497. Cf. Caverno v. Fellows, 1938, 300 Mass. 331, 15 N.E.2d 483 (high school supervisor, principal and superintendent re-

those of his employee,[99] provided that the steps taken are not unreasonable in view of the harm threatened.[1] There may also be a privilege to protect the public interest, as by removing a danger to public health or morals,[2] or making complaint of the misconduct of an employee of a public utility,[3] or taxpayers objecting to the expenditure of public money.[4] Beyond this, many cases have said that there is a privilege to give bona fide[5] advice to withdraw from a contractual rela-

tion,[6] although so far as appears this may be limited to cases where the advice is requested,[7] or the defendant stands in such a relation as to justify his intervention. The privilege of relatives to induce the breach of a contract to marry sometimes has been placed upon this ground.[8]

Where the defendant acts to further his own advantage, other distinctions have been made. If he has a present, existing economic interest to protect, such as the ownership or condition of property,[9] or a prior contract of his own,[10] or a financial interest in the

---

porting on conduct of teacher); Bentley v. Teton, 1958, 19 Ill.App.2d 284, 153 N.E.2d 495 (civil servant reporting misconduct of nurse to his superior); Terry v. Zachry, Tex.Civ.App.1954, 272 S.W.2d 157 ref. n. r. e. (chairman of board of corporation inducing it to litigate claim); Garcia Sugars Corp. v. New York Coffee & Sugar Exchange, Sup.Ct.1938, 7 N.Y.S.2d 532 (broker obeying orders of exchange).

99. Gregory v. Dealers' Equipment Co., 1927, 156 Tenn. 273, 300 S.W. 563; cf. Heywood v. Tillson, 1883, 75 Me. 225, 46 Am.Rep. 373; Hopper v. Lennen & Mitchell, S.D.Cal.1943, 52 F.Supp. 319, affirmed in part and reversed in part C.A., 146 F.2d 364, 161 A.L.R. 282; Lawless v. Brotherhood of Painters, 1956, 143 Cal.App.2d 474, 300 P.2d 159 (international union and local union).

1. There is no privilege where there is no reasonable belief that any harm is threatened. Hutton v. Watters, 1915, 132 Tenn. 527, 179 S.W. 134.

2. Cf. Brimelow v. Casson, [1924] 1 Ch. 302 (preventing prostitution); Stott v. Gamble, [1916] 2 K.B. 504 (preventing improper public entertainment); Legris v. Marcotte, 1906, 129 Ill.App. 67 (preventing spread of disease). Cf. Porter v. King County Medical Society, 1936, 186 Wash. 410, 58 P.2d 367 (ethical rules of medical association).

Occasionally the interest in increasing employment or improving working conditions is said to be a "public interest." Green v. Samuelson, 1935, 168 Md. 421, 178 A. 109; Radio Station KFH Co. v. Musicians Association Local No. 297, 1950, 169 Kan. 596, 220 P.2d 199; Wholesale Laundry Board of Trade v. Tarrullo, Sup.Ct.1951, 103 N.Y.S.2d 23.

3. Lancaster v. Hamburger, 1904, 70 Ohio St. 156, 71 N.E. 289. Cf. Chicago, R. I. & P. R. Co. v. Armstrong, 1911, 30 Okl. 134, 120 P. 952 (railway protecting public).

4. Middlesex Concrete Products & Excavating Corp. v. Carteret Industrial Ass'n, 1962, 37 N.J. 507, 181 A.2d 774.

5. Otherwise where the advice is given with a spiteful motive. Morgan v. Andrews, 1895, 107 Wash. 33, 64 N.W. 869.

6. Glamorgan Coal Co. v. South Wales Miners' Federation, [1903] 1 K.B. 118, reversed on other grounds in [1905] A.C. 239; Delaware, L. & W. R. Co. v. Switchmen's Union of North America, C.C.N. Y.1907, 158 F. 541. See Northern Wisconsin Co-op. Tobacco Pool v. Bekkedal, 1923, 182 Wis. 571, 197 N.W. 936; Walker v. Cronin, 1871, 107 Mass. 555; Arnold v. Moffitt, 1910, 30 R.I. 310, 75 A. 502; Coakley v. Degner, 1926, 191 Wis. 170, 210 N.W. 359; Holmes, Privilege, Malice and Intent, 1894, 8 Harv.L.Rev. 1, 6.

7. Restatement of Torts, § 772.

8. Overhultz v. Row, 1922, 152 La. 9, 92 So. 716; Minsky v. Satenstein, 1928, 6 N.J.Misc. 978, 143 A. 512; Lukas v. Tarpilauskas, 1929, 266 Mass. 498, 165 N.E. 513.

9. Diver v. Miller, 1929, 4 W.W.Harr., Del., 207, 148 A. 291; O'Brien v. Western Union Tel. Co., 1911, 62 Wash. 598, 114 P. 441; Winters v. University Dist. Bldg. & Loan Ass'n, 1932, 268 Ill.App. 147; Meason v. Ralston Purina Co., 1940, 56 Ariz. 291, 107 P.2d 224 (mortgagee); cf. Watch Tower Bible & Tract Soc. v. Dougherty, 1940, 337 Pa. 286, 11 A.2d 147 (religious publication); Owen v. Williams, 1948, 322 Mass. 356, 77 N.E.2d 318.

10. Tidal Western Oil Corp. v. Shackelford, Tex.Civ. App.1927, 297 S.W. 279; Williams v. Adams, 1937, 250 App.Div. 603, 295 N.Y.S. 86; Quinlivan v. Brown Oil Co., 1934, 96 Mont. 147, 29 P.2d 374; In re Farrell Pub. Corp., S.D.N.Y.1958, 165 F.Supp. 40, affirmed Hendler v. Cuneo Eastern Press, Inc., C.A., 279 F.2d 181; Millers Mut. Cas. Co. v. Insurance Exch. Bldg. Corp., 1920, 218 Ill.App. 12. The holder of the prior contract may even obtain specific performance at the expense of the later one. White Marble Lime Co. v. Consolidated Lumber Co., 1919, 205 Mich. 634, 172 N.W. 603.

But a purpose of terminating the defendant's own contract is not a legitimate justification for inducing breach of the plaintiff's. A. S. Rampell, Inc. v. Hyster Co., 1955, 1 Misc.2d 788, 148 N.Y.S.2d 102,

affairs of the person persuaded,[11] he is privileged to prevent performance of the contract of another which threatens it; and for obvious reasons of policy he is likewise privileged to assert an honest claim, or bring or threaten a suit in good faith,[12] to exercise the right of petition to public authorities,[13] or to settle his own case out of court.[14]

But where his interest is merely one of prospective advantage, not yet realized, he has no such privilege. The typical case is that of business competition. The courts

have held that the sanctity of the existing contract relation takes precedence over any interest in unrestricted competition, and have enforced as law the ethical precept that one competitor must keep his hands off of the contracts of another. This is true of contracts of employment, where workmen are hired away from an employer,[15] as well as competitive business dealings in general; [16] and it has found particular application in cases of offers of better terms to induce the breach of a contract,[17] and of the violation of exclusive agency agreements [18] and the pur-

---

modified 2 A.D.2d 739, 153 N.Y.S.2d 176, appeal denied 2 N.Y.2d 828, 159 N.Y.S.2d 961, 140 N.E.2d 860, affirmed and reversed 3 N.Y.2d 369, 165 N.Y.S.2d 475, 144 N.E.2d 371.

11. Ford v. C. E. Wilson & Co., 2 Cir. 1942, 129 F.2d 614 (taking security from debtor); Knapp v. Penfield, 1932, 143 Misc. 132, 256 N.Y.S. 41; Aalfo Co. v. Kinney, 1929, 105 N.J.L. 345, 144 A. 715; Petit v. Cuneo, 1937, 290 Ill.App. 16, 7 N.E.2d 774; see Note, 1941, 27 Va.L.Rev. 1102.

See also, as to the interest of directors and stockholders in the affairs of a corporation, Griswold v. Heat, Inc., 1967, 108 N.H. 119, 229 A.2d 183; Coronet Development Co. v. F. S. W., Inc., 1967, 379 Mich. 302, 150 N.W.2d 809.

But a stockholder may be liable for interference with the contract of a corporation for ulterior purposes of his own, even though there is financial advantage in them. W. P. Iverson v. Dunham Mfg. Co., 1958, 18 Ill.App.2d 404, 152 N.E.2d 615; Mendelson v. Blatz Brewing Co., 1960, 9 Wis.2d 487, 101 N.W. 2d 805; Morgan v. Andrews, 1895, 107 Mich. 33, 64 N.W. 869. Compare, as to a workmen's compensation insurer obtaining the discharge of a workman with an accident record, American Surety Co. v. Schottenbauer, 8 Cir. 1958, 257 F.2d 6; Harris v. Traders' & General Ins. Co., Tex.Civ.App.1935, 82 S.W.2d 750, error refused.

12. Elvington v. Waccamaw Shingle Co., 1926, 191 N.C. 515, 132 S.E. 274; Hardin v. Majors, Tex.Civ. App.1923, 246 S.W. 100; Swift v. Beaty, 1954, 39 Tenn.App. 292, 282 S.W.2d 655.

13. Cf. McKee v. Hughes, 1915, 133 Tenn. 455, 181 S.W. 930. Otherwise when the motive is a spiteful one. Vanarsdale v. Laverty, 1871, 69 Pa. 103.

14. Krause v. Hartford Acc. & Ind. Co., 1951, 331 Mich. 19, 49 N.W.2d 41; Orr v. Mutual Ben. Health & Acc. Ass'n, 1947, 240 Mo.App. 236, 207 S.W.2d 511; Herbits v. Constitution Ind. Co. of Philadelphia, 1932, 279 Mass. 539, 181 N.E. 723; cf. Williams v. Ashcraft, 1963, 72 N.M. 120, 381 P.2d 55. Contra, Keels v. Powell, 1945, 207 S.C. 97, 34 S.E.2d 482.

15. International Tailoring Co. of N. Y. v. Lukas, Sup.Ct.1946, 64 N.Y.S.2d 879; Walker v. Cronin, 1871, 107 Mass. 555; Prairie Oil & Gas Co. v. Kinney, 1920, 79 Okl. 206, 192 P. 586; S. C. Posner Co. v. Jackson, 1918, 223 N.Y. 325, 119 N.E. 573; Employing Printers' Club v. Doctor Blosser Co., 1905, 122 Ga. 509, 50 S.E. 353.

16. Wade v. Culp, 1939, 107 Ind.App. 503, 23 N.E.2d 615 (marketing patented article); Wilkinson v. Powe, 1942, 300 Mich. 275, 1 N.W.2d 539 (milk delivery contracts); Nulty v. Hart-Bradshaw Lumber & Grain Co., 1924, 116 Kan. 446, 227 P. 254 (grain partnership); Republic Gear Co. v. Borg-Warner Corp., 7 Cir. 1969, 406 F.2d 57, cert. denied 394 U.S. 1000 (licensing contract); Northeast Airlines, Inc. v. World Airways, Inc., D.Mass.1966, 262 F.Supp. 316.

17. Cumberland Glass Mfg. Co. v. De Witt, 1913, 120 Md. 381, 87 A. 927, affirmed 237 U.S. 447 (sale of goods); Friedberg, Inc. v. McClary, 1917, 173 Ky. 579, 191 S.W. 300 (purchase of goods); Westinghouse Elec. & Mfg. Co. v. Diamond State Fibre Co., D.Del.1920, 268 F. 121 (sale of materials); Sperry & Hutchinson Co. v. Louis Weber & Co., C.C.Ill.1908, 161 F. 219 (trading stamps); Automobile Ins. Co. of Hartford v. Guaranty Securities Corp., D.N.Y.1917, 240 F. 222 (insurance).

18. Beekman v. Marsters, 1907, 195 Mass. 205, 80 N. E. 817; Sorenson v. Chevrolet Motor Co., 1927, 171 Minn. 260, 214 N.W. 754; Schechter v. Friedman, 1948, 141 N.J.Eq. 318, 57 A.2d 251; E. L. Husting Co. v. Coca Cola Co., 1931, 205 Wis. 356, 237 N.W. 85, rehearing denied 205 Wis. 356, 238 N.W. 626, cert. denied Wisconsin Coca Cola Bottling Co. v. E. L. Husting Co., 285 U.S. 538.

Accord, as to broker's contracts: Horn v. Seth, Md. 1953, 95 A.2d 312; Louis Schlesinger Co. v. Rice, 1950, 4 N.J. 169, 72 A.2d 197; Johnson v. Gustafson, 1938, 201 Minn. 629, 277 N.W. 252; Franklin v. Brown, Fla.App.1964, 159 So.2d 893; Graff v. Whitehouse, 1966, 71 Ill.App.2d 412, 219 N.E.2d 128.

The addition of a spite motive will of course not improve the defendant's position. S. C. Posner Co. v.

chase of goods in derogation of a contract limiting their resale.[19]

Where the contract interfered with is terminable at will, however, the privilege of competition has been recognized. In such a case there is no contract right to have the relation continued, but only an expectancy, which is similar to the expectancy of a business man that a customer will continue to do business with him. With such an expectancy of future relations, and prospective advantage, there has been no doubt that a competitor has the privilege of interfering to acquire the business for himself.[20] Accordingly, the considerable weight of authority holds that there is a privilege of competition which extends to inducing the termination of agreements terminable at will, whether they concern employment [21] or other relations.[22]

Still less is there any privilege to interfere with the contract where there is no competitive relation, but the object is to put pressure upon the plaintiff and coerce him into complying with the defendant's wishes in some collateral matter—as where an employer is induced to discharge a workman in order to compel him to pay the defendant a debt,[23] prevent him from bringing a suit,[24] or force him to compromise a claim,[25] or for the purpose of extorting money from him.[26] Interference with contractual relations is not a legitimate method of securing such an advantage.

Labor Unions

Interference with contract was formerly a fertile field for the liability of a labor union. As to activities preventing the performance of existing contracts, the unions were quite strictly curtailed by the common law. The courts tended to find an analogy to the cases of business competition, and to consider that labor was competing with the employer for a larger share of the common fund of wealth produced, and so must be limited in the pursuit of its own interests to the same extent as any other competitor.[27] Where there was a definite con-

Jackson, 1918, 223 N.Y. 325, 119 N.E. 573; Globe & Rutgers Fire Ins. Co. v. Firemen's Fund Fire Ins. Co., 1910, 97 Miss. 148, 52 So. 454; Schonwald v. Ragains, 1912, 32 Okl. 22, 122 P. 203; Sorenson v. Chevrolet Motor Co., 1927, 171 Minn. 260, 214 N.W. 754, 84 A.L.R. 35.

19. Bitterman v. Louisville & N. R. Co., 1907, 207 U. S. 205; Singer Sewing Mach. Co. v. Lang, 1925, 186 Wis. 530, 203 N.W. 399; Dr. Miles Medical Co. v. Goldthwaite, C.C.Mass.1904, 133 F. 794; Kirby v. Union Pac. R. Co., 1911, 51 Colo. 509, 119 P. 1042.

20. See infra, p. 954.

21. Triangle Film Corp. v. Artcraft Pictures Corp., 2 Cir. 1918, 250 F. 981; McCluer v. Super Maid Cook-Ware Corp., 10 Cir. 1932, 62 F.2d 426; Coleman & Morris v. Pisciotta, 1951, 279 App.Div. 656, 107 N.Y.S.2d 715; Diodes, Inc. v. Franzen, 1968, 260 Cal.App.2d 244, 67 Cal.Rptr. 19; Vincent Horwitz Co. v. Cooper, 1945, 352 Pa. 7, 41 A.2d 870.

22. Terry v. Dairymen's League Co-op. Ass'n, 1956, 2 App.Div.2d 494, 157 N.Y.S.2d 71; National Oil Co. v. Phillips Petroleum Co., W.D.Wis.1966, 265 F. Supp. 320; Biber Bros. News Co. v. New York Evening Post, 1932, 144 Misc. 405, 258 N.Y.S. 31; Du-Art Film Laboratories v. Consolidated Film Industries, S.D.N.Y.1936, 15 F.Supp. 689; Kingsbery v. Phillips Petroleum Co., Tex.Civ.App.1958, 315 S.W. 2d 561, ref. n. r. e.

See Notes, 1962, 56 Nw.U.L.Rev. 391; 1964, 24 Md.L. Rev. 85; 1958, 25 Brook.L.Rev. 73.

23. Warschauser v. Brooklyn Furniture Co., 1913, 159 App.Div. 81, 144 N.Y.S. 257; Giblan v. National Union, [1903] 2 K.B. 600; cf. Tubular Rivet & Stud Co. v. Exeter Boot & Shoe Co., 1 Cir. 1908, 159 F. 824.

24. Johnson v. Aetna Life Ins. Co., 1914, 158 Wis. 56, 147 N.W. 32. Cf. Mealey v. Bemidji Lumber Co., 1912, 118 Minn. 427, 136 N.W. 1090 (enticing employees to prevent performance of contract with defendant).

25. London Guarantee & Acc. Co. v. Horn, 1904, 206 Ill. 493, 69 N.E. 526; United States F. & G. Co. v. Millonas, 1921, 206 Ala. 147, 89 So. 732; cf. Joyce v. Great Northern R. Co., 1907, 100 Minn. 225, 110 N. W. 975; Palatine Ins. Co. v. Griffin, Tex.Civ.App. 1918, 202 S.W. 1014, reversed, Com.App.1922, 235 S. W. 202, reversal set aside, 238 S.W. 637.

26. Lopes v. Connolly, 1912, 210 Mass. 487, 97 N.E. 80; Hill Groc. Co. v. Carroll, 1931, 223 Ala. 376, 136 So. 789; Doucette v. Sallinger, 1917, 228 Mass. 444, 117 N.E. 897; Scott v. Prudential Outfitting Co., 1915, 92 Misc. 195, 155 N.Y.S. 497; Bowen v. Morris, 1929, 219 Ala. 689, 123 So. 222.

27. See Kales, Coercive and Competitive Methods in Trade and Labor Disputes, 1922, 8 Corn.L.Q. 1, 128;

tract for a term, there was almost no recognition of any privilege of the union to interfere with its performance. Union interests, and those of labor represented, were held insufficient to justify calling out on strike a workman who had agreed to work for a fixed period,[28] or causing his discharge,[29] and one union which had succeeded in obtaining a closed shop contract with an employer, or the employer himself, was held to be entitled to an injunction against a rival union seeking to invade the field.[30]

The common law was carried to the length of protecting the "yellow dog" contract, by which workmen were forced to agree as a condition of employment that they would not join the union itself.[31] Such contracts, which

became a potent weapon in the hands of the employer, are now declared invalid by the federal acts, and by statutes in about three-fourths of the states.[32] Even contracts between employers and third parties for the purchase and sale of goods were protected against the incidental interference resulting from an otherwise justified strike.[33] Carried to its logical conclusion, this result would prevent any strike against any employer doing business under contracts with others. These rules are now quite certainly of historical interest only, and they are not now in force in any American jurisdiction.

The tort liability of labor unions has been quite radically affected by federal legislation, which has imposed upon industries whose labor disputes affect the flow of interstate commerce a system of collective bargaining, with administrative remedies. In the process not only the jurisdiction but also the substantive law of the state courts has been much limited. The existence of a contract, while it may still be a factor entitled to consideration, is no longer of paramount importance. It is therefore convenient to consider the whole matter later, in connec-

Smith, Crucial Issues in Labor Litigation, 1907, 20 Harv.L.Rev. 253, 345, 429; Sayre, Labor and the Courts, 1930, 39 Yale L.J. 682; Eskin, The Legality of "Peaceful Coercion" in Labor Disputes, 1937, 85 U.Pa.L.Rev. 456; Warm, A Study of the Judicial Attitude Toward Trade Unions and Labor Legislation, 1939, 23 Minn.L.Rev. 255; Notes, 1938, 32 Ill. L.Rev. 611, 625; 1921, 34 Harv.L.Rev. 880.

28. South Wales Miners' Federation v. Glamorgan Coal Co., [1905] A.C. 239; Iron Molders' Union No. 125 v. Allis-Chalmers Co., 7 Cir. 1908, 166 F. 45; Rice, Barton & Fales Machine & Iron Foundry Co. v. Willard, 1922, 242 Mass. 566, 136 N.E. 629; Williams v. Sinclair Refining Co., N.D.Tex.1947, 74 F. Supp. 139.

29. Read v. Friendly Society of Operative Stonemasons, [1902] 2 K.B. 88, 732; Crosby v. Rath, 1939, 136 Ohio St. 352, 25 N.E.2d 934; Eddyside Co. v. Seibel, 1940, 142 Pa.Super. 174, 15 A.2d 691. Cf. Schlesinger v. Quinto, 1922, 201 App.Div. 487, 194 N.Y.S. 401 (employers' association inducing employer to break wage contract).

30. Tracey v. Osborne, 1917, 226 Mass. 25, 114 N.E. 959; Goyette v. C. V. Watson Co., 1923, 245 Mass. 577, 140 N.E. 285; Hotel, Restaurant & Soda Fountain Employees Local Union No. 181 v. Miller, 1938, 272 Ky. 466, 114 S.W.2d 501; Mitnick v. Furniture Workers' Union Local No. 166, 1938, 124 N. J.Eq. 147, 200 A. 553, appeal dismissed 125 N.J.Eq. 142, 4 A.2d 277. New York permitted picketing, but not other methods of interference. Stillwell Theatre v. Kaplan, 1932, 259 N.Y. 405, 182 N.E. 63, motions denied 260 N.Y. 563, 184 N.E. 93, cert. denied 288 U.S. 606.

31. Hitchman Coal & Coke Co. v. Mitchell, 1917, 245 U.S. 229 mandate stayed 241 U.S. 644; Cyrus Cur-

rier & Sons v. International Molders' Union of North America, 1921, 93 N.J.Eq. 61, 115 A. 66; Moore Drop Forging Co. v. McCarthy, 1923, 243 Mass. 554, 137 N.E. 919; Kraemer Hosiery Co. v. American Federation of F. F. Hosiery Workers, 1930, 305 Pa. 206, 157 A. 588.

32. See National Labor Relations Board v. Tidewater Exp. Lines, 4 Cir. 1937, 90 F.2d 301; 2 Teller, Labor Disputes and Collective Bargaining, 1940 and 1947 Supp., § 459; Fraenkel, Recent Statutes Affecting Labor Injunctions and Yellow Dog Contracts, 1936, 30 Ill.L.Rev. 854; Witte, Yellow Dog Contracts, 1930, 6 Wis.L.Rev. 21; Tapley, The Anti-Union Contracts, 1936, 11 St.Johns L.Rev. 40.

33. Carroll v. Chesapeake & Ohio Coal Agency Co., 4 Cir. 1903, 124 F. 305; Carter v. Fortney, D.W.Va. 1909, 170 F. 463, affirmed 4 Cir. 1913, 203 F. 454; Dail-Overland Co. v. Willys-Overland, D.Ohio 1919, 263 F. 171 affirmed 274 F. 56; Vonnegut Machinery Co. v. Toledo Machine & Tool Co., D.Ohio 1920, 263 F. 192 reversed on other grounds, 274 F. 66; Quinlivan v. Dail-Overland Co., 6 Cir. 1921, 274 F. 56. See criticism in Note, 1923, 32 Yale L.J. 171.

tion with interference with prospective advantage.[34]

Damages

Interference with contract is commonly a ground for the jurisdiction of equity, since the remedy at law is often inadequate because the damages suffered cannot be compensated with money, or cannot be estimated with any accuracy. The frequency with which an injunction is sought has somewhat obscured the problem of the measure of damages when a tort action is brought at law. On this there is very little agreement.[35]

It is generally agreed that proof that some damage has been sustained is necessary to the action,[36] although when it is clear that there has been damage but its extent cannot be proved, nominal damages may be awarded.[37] Although older cases sometimes held to the contrary,[38] it is now agreed that the fact that there is an available action against the party who breaks the contract [39] is no de-

fense to the one who induces the breach,[40] since the two are joint wrongdoers, and each is liable for the loss. Even a judgment in such an action, returned unsatisfied,[41] is no defense.[42] Where substantial loss has occurred, one line of cases tends to adopt the contract measure of damages, limiting recovery to those damages which were within the contemplation of the parties when the original contract was made.[43] Another,[44] apparently somewhat more uncertain of its ground, has applied a tort measure, but has limited the damages to those which are sufficiently "proximate," with some analogy to the rules

---

34.   See infra, p. 962.

35.   See Notes, 1930, 30 Col.L.Rev. 232; 1966, 7 Santa Clara L.Rev. 140; 1968, 19 Hast.L.J. 1119.

36.   Bigelow, Torts, 8th Ed. 1907, 255, 266; Hodge v. Meyer, 2 Cir. 1918, 252 F. 479; Exchange Tel. Co. v. Gregory & Co., [1896] 1 Q.B. 147. Thus when the claim is for loss of commissions on sales by a broker, he must prove that the sales would have been made and the commissions earned. Myers v. Arcadio, Inc., 1962, 73 N.J.Super. 493, 180 A.2d 329.

37.   Raymond v. Yarrington, 1903, 96 Tex. 443, 73 S. W. 800; Dannerberg v. Ashley, 1894, 10 Ohio C.C. 558; Max Ams Machine Co. v. International Ass'n of Machinists, Bridgeport Lodge, No. 30, 1917, 92 Conn. 297, 102 A. 706.

38.   Chambers v. Baldwin, 1891, 91 Ky. 121, 15 S.W. 57; Glencoe Sand & Gravel Co. v. Hudson Bros. Commission Co., 1897, 138 Mo. 439, 40 S.W. 93; Swain v. Johnson, 1909, 151 N.C. 93, 65 S.E. 619.

39.   In Carmen v. Fox Film Corp., 1923, 204 App.Div. 776, 198 N.Y.S. 766, it was held that the plaintiff owed the tort feasor no duty to mitigate his damages by seeking other employment.

In Gentile Bros. Corp. v. Rowena Homes, Inc., 1967, 352 Mass. 584, 227 N.E.2d 338, it was held that the recovery of damages for inducing breach of contract was not inconsistent with obtaining specific performance of the contract.

40.   Phillips & Benjamin Co. v. Ratner, 2 Cir. 1953, 206 F.2d 372; Horn v. Seth, 1953, 201 Md. 589, 95 A.2d 312; Childress v. Abeles, 1954, 240 N.C. 667, 84 S.E.2d 176, rehearing dismissed 242 N.C. 123, 86 S.E.2d 916; Hornstein v. Podwitz, 1930, 254 N.Y. 443, 173 N.E. 674; Kock v. Burgess, 1914, 167 Iowa 727, 149 N.W. 858. But, again by analogy to the law of joint tortfeasors, a release of one may release the other. Fowler v. Nationwide Ins. Co., 1962, 256 N.C. 555, 124 S.E.2d 520.

Judgment in an action on the contract has been held to be res judicata in the other action. Israel v. Wood Dolson Co., 1956, 1 N.Y.2d 116, 151 N.Y.S.2d 1, 134 N.E.2d 97; Moreno v. Marbil Productions, Inc., 2 Cir. 1961, 296 F.2d 543.

41.   In Bird v. Randall, 1762, 3 Burr. 1345, 97 Eng. Rep. 866, it was held that a satisfied judgment would bar the action. But in Simon v. Noma Elec. Corp., 1944, 293 N.Y. 171, 56 N.E.2d 537, motion denied, 1945, 293 N.Y. 860, 59 N.E.2d 447, and McNutt Oil & Refining Co. v. D'Ascoli, 1955, 79 Ariz. 28, 281 P.2d 966, it was held that the amount recovered must be credited, but that it did not preclude recovery of other damages that could be shown in the tort action.

42.   Angle v. Chicago, St. P., M. & O. R. Co., 1893, 151 U.S. 1; Meason v. Ralston Purina Co., 1940, 56 Ariz. 291, 107 P.2d 224.

43.   Swaney v. Crawley, 1916, 133 Minn. 57, 157 N.W. 910; Kerr v. Du Pree, 1926, 35 Ga.App. 122, 132 S. E. 393; Mahoney v. Roberts, 1908, 86 Ark. 130, 110 S.W. 225; R an W Hat Shop v. Sculley, 1922, 98 Conn. 1, 118 A. 55; McNutt Oil & Refining Co. v. D'Ascoli, 1955, 79 Ariz. 28, 281 P.2d 966.

44.   Anderson v. Moskowitz, 1927, 260 Mass. 523, 157 N.E. 601; Hooker, Corser & Mitchell Co. v. Hooker, 1915, 89 Vt. 383, 95 A. 649; Day v. Hunnicutt, Tex.Civ.App.1913, 160 S.W. 134; Salter v. Howard, 1871, 43 Ga. 601. Cf. McCormick v. Louis Weber & Co., 1914, 187 Ill.App. 290 (no mental suffering).

as to negligent torts.[45]   A third, perhaps the most numerous, has treated the tort as an intentional one, and has allowed recovery for unforeseen expenses,[46] as well as for mental suffering,[47] damage to reputation,[48] and punitive damages,[49] by analogy to the cases of intentional injury to person or property.[50] In the light of the intent and the lack of justification necessary to the tort, this seems the most consistent result.

130.   INTERFERENCE WITH PROSPECTIVE ADVANTAGE

Tort liability for interference with prospective advantage seems to have developed at a very early date in cases having to do with the use of physical violence, or threats of it, to drive away customers from the plaintiff's market,[51] or those who might make dona-

tions to his church;[52] but it seems to have been limited rather definitely to the use of such improper means.[53]   During the seventeenth and eighteenth centuries there were decisions involving threats and violence to frighten away prospective workmen or customers,[54] and later there were others which gave an action for spiteful shooting to scare off the plaintiff's game.[55]   There was even a case in England in 1844 in which an actor was allowed to recover against a defendant who had succeeded in having him hissed off of the stage, as a result of which he was unable to obtain further employment.[56]   The real source of the modern law, however may be said to be the case of Temperton v. Russell,[57] in which the Court of Queen's Bench declared that the principles of liability for interference with contract extended beyond existing contractual relations, and that a similar action would lie for interference with relations which were merely prospective or potential.

Upon this foundation, a rather formidable body of law has been erected, which in general has followed along the lines of interference with contract.[58]   It has been said

---

45. See supra, ch. 7.

46. Vaught v. Jonathan L. Pettyjohn & Co., 1919, 104 Kan. 174, 178 P. 623 ; Martin v. Sterkx, 1920, 146 La. 489, 83 So. 776 ; Horchheimer v. Prewitt, 1928, 33 N.M. 411, 268 P. 1026 ; see Smith v. Goodman, Howell & Co., 1885, 75 Ga. 198. Cf. Blum v. William Goldman Theatres, S.D.Pa.1946, 69 F.Supp. 468 (counsel fees and expenses of litigation in unsuccessful attempt to enforce the contract).

47. Carter v. Oster, 1908, 134 Mo.App. 146, 112 S.W. 995 ; Doucette v. Sallinger, 1917, 228 Mass. 444, 117 N.E. 897 ; Gould v. Kramer, 1925, 253 Mass. 433, 149 N.E. 142 ; United States Fidelity & Guaranty Co. v. Millonas, 1921, 206 Ala. 147, 89 So. 732.

48. De Minico v. Craig, 1911, 207 Mass. 593, 94 N.E. 317.

49. Burgess v. Tucker, 1913, 94 S.C. 309, 77 S.E. 1016 ; Cotton v. Cooper, Tex.Civ.App.1913, 160 S. W. 597, affirmed, Tex.Com.App.1919, 209 S.W. 135 ; Oxner v. Seaboard Air Line R. Co., 1918, 110 S.C. 366, 96 S.E. 559 ; United States F. & G. Co. v. Millonas, 1921, 206 Ala. 147, 89 So. 732 ; McNutt Oil & Refining Co. v. D'Ascoli, 1955, 79 Ariz. 28, 281 P.2d 966.

50. See supra, ch. 2.

51. Y.B., 1410, 11 Hen. IV 47. Cf., 1356, Y.B. 29 Edw. III 18 ; 1368, Y.B. 41 Edw. III 24B. See Holt, J., in Keeble v. Hickeringill, 1707, 11 East 574 note, 11 Mod.Rep. 14, 130, 3 Salk. 9, Holt, 14, 103 Eng.Rep. 1127 ; Wigmore, The Boycott and Kindred Practices as Ground for Damages, 1887, 21 Am.L. Rev. 509, 515ff. There was an earlier writ giving an action for threatening plaintiff's tenants at will

so that they departed. 1494, Y.B. 9 Hen. VII 7 ; 1443, Y.B. 21 Hen. VI 31.

52. See Bellewe, A. sur. C., 1396.

53. Y.B., 1410, 11 Hen. IV 47 ; 1444, Y.B. 22 Hen. VI 14.

54. Garret v. Taylor, 1621, Cro.Jac. 567, 79 Eng.Rep. 485 (threats of mayhem and vexatious suits against customers and workmen) ; Tarleton v. McGawley, 1793, Peake N.P. 270, 170 Eng.Rep. 153 (firing upon African natives about to trade with the plaintiff).

55. Keeble v. Hickeringill, 1707, 11 Mod.Rep. 14, 130, 103 Eng.Rep. 1127 ; Carrington v. Taylor, 1809, 11 East 571, 103 Eng.Rep. 1126 ; Ibottson v. Peat, 1865, 3 H. & C. 644, 159 Eng.Rep. 684.

56. Gregory v. Duke of Brunswick, 1843, 6 M. & G. 205, 134 Eng.Rep. 866, 1178. In Walker v. Cronin, 1871, 107 Mass. 555, a count for persuading prospective employees to refuse to enter service, without justification, was held to state a cause of action.

57. [1893] 1 Q.B. 715. Cf. Quinn v. Leathem, [1901] A.C. 495.

58. See Sarat Basak, Principles of Liability for Interference with Trade, Profession or Calling, 1911,

that "in a civilized community which recognizes the right of private property among its institutions, the notion is intolerable that a man should be protected by the law in the enjoyment of property once it is acquired, but left unprotected by the law in his effort to acquire it;" [59] and that since a large part of what is most valuable in modern life depends upon "probable expectancies," as social and industrial life becomes more complex the courts must do more to discover, define and protect them from undue interference. [60]

For the most part the "expectancies" thus protected have been those of future contractual relations, such as the prospect of obtaining employment [61] or employees, [62] or the opportunity of obtaining customers. [63] In such cases there is a background of business experience on the basis of which it is possible to estimate with some fair amount of success

both the value of what has been lost and the likelihood that the plaintiff would have received it if the defendant had not interfered. The loss of prospective profits is, for example, a familiar element of damages in cases of breach of contract. [64] When the attempt has been made to carry liability for interference beyond such commercial dealings, and into such areas as exclusion from social organizations, [65] or deprivation of the chance of winning a contest, [66] the courts have been disturbed by a feeling that they were embarking upon uncharted seas, and recovery has been denied; and it is significant that the reason usually given is that there is no sufficient degree of certainty that the plaintiff ever would have received the anticipated benefits.

On this basis the earlier cases held that recovery would be denied for interference with an expected gift or a legacy under a will, [67]

---

27 L.Q.Rev. 290, 399, 1912, 28 L.Q.Rev. 52; Kales, Coercive and Competitive Methods in Trade and Labor Disputes, 1922, 8 Corn.L.Q. 1, 128; Green, Relational Interests, 1935, 29 Ill.L.Rev. 1041, 30 Ill.L. Rev. 1; Handler, Unfair Competition, 1936, 21 Iowa L.Rev. 175; Notes, 1922, 22 Col.L.Rev. 665; 1923, 9 Corn.L.Q. 78; 1927, 12 Minn.L.Rev. 147, 162; 1932, 27 Ill.L.Rev. 96; 1932, 6 U.Cin.L.Rev. 322; 1938, 37 Mich.L.Rev. 115; 1947, 56 Yale L.J. 885; 1964, 77 Harv.L.Rev. 888.

59. Brennan v. United Hatters of North America, 1906, 73 N.J.L. 729, 65 A. 165.

60. Jersey City Printing Co. v. Cassidy, 1902, 63 N. J.Eq. 759, 53 A. 230.

61. Huskie v. Griffin, 1909, 75 N.H. 345, 74 A. 595; Bacon v. St. Paul Union Stockyards Co., 1925, 161 Minn. 522, 201 N.W. 326; Willner v. Silverman, 1909, 109 Md. 341, 71 A. 962; see Hundley v. Louisville & N. R. Co., 1903, 105 Ky. 162, 48 S.W. 429.

In Longo v. Reilly, 1955, 35 N.J.Super. 405, 114 A.2d 302, fraudulent conduct resulted in plaintiff's defeat in election to an office. This was treated as wrongful interference with a business or property right.

62. Jersey City Printing Co. v. Cassidy, 1902, 63 N. J.Eq. 759, 53 A. 230; Vegelahn v. Guntner, 1896, 167 Mass. 92, 44 N.E. 1077; Erdman v. Mitchell, 1903, 207 Pa. 79, 56 A. 327.

63. Tuttle v. Buck, 1909, 107 Minn. 145, 119 N.W. 946; Graham v. St. Charles St. R. Co., 1895, 47 La. Ann. 214, 16 So. 806; Boggs v. Duncan-Schell Furniture Co., 1913, 163 Iowa 106, 143 N.W. 482.

64. See McCormick, Damages, 1935, ch. 4.

65. Trautwein v. Harbourt, 1956, 40 N.J.Super. 247, 123 A.2d 30.

66. Collatz v. Fox Wisconsin Amusement Corp., 1941, 239 Wis. 156, 300 N.W. 162; Harrison v. Jones, 1936, 52 Ga.App. 852, 184 S.E. 889; Phillips v. Pantages Theatre Co., 1931, 163 Wash. 303, 300 P. 1048. Cf. Western Union Tel. Co. v. Crall, 1888, 39 Kan. 580, 18 P. 719 (chance of winning horse races); Cain v. Vollmer, 1910, 19 Idaho 163, 112 P. 686 (same as to future races); Smitha v. Gentry, 1898, 20 Ky.L.Rep. 171, 45 S.W. 515 (chance of obtaining reward); Klous v. Hennessey, 1881, 13 R.I. 332 (unsecured creditor's chance of levying upon property fraudulently conveyed). See Notes, 1964, 18 Rut.L. Rev. 875; 1967, 19 Ala.L.Rev. 495.

Compare the cases in which it has been held that it was insufficiently pleaded or proved that plaintiff would have made a contract without the defendant's interference. Wilson v. Loew's, Inc., 1956, 142 Cal.App.2d 183, 298 P.2d 152, cert. dismissed 355 U. S. 597; Goldman v. Feinberg, 1944, 130 Conn. 671, 37 A.2d 355; Union Car Advertising Co. v. Collier, 1934, 263 N.Y. 386, 189 N.E. 463; Debnam v. Simonson, 1914, 124 Md. 354, 92 A. 782.

67. Hutchins v. Hutchins, 1845, 7 Hill, N.Y., 104; Lewis v. Corbin, 1907, 195 Mass. 520, 81 N.E. 248; Cunningham v. Edward, 1936, 52 Ohio App. 61, 3 N.E.2d 58; Hall v. Hall, 1917, 91 Conn. 514, 100 A. 2d 441. Accord, Hoeft v. Supreme Lodge, Knights of Honor, 1896, 113 Cal. 91, 45 P. 185 (beneficiary

even though the defendant's motives were unworthy and he had resorted to fraudulent means, because the testator might have changed his mind. There is no essential reason for refusing to protect such non-commercial expectancies, at least where there is a strong probability that they would have been realized.[68] In cases where this probability has approached something like certainty, as in the case of incompetency of the testator to make a change,[69] or suppression of the will after his death,[70] recovery has commonly been allowed; and there are now a number of cases [71] in which it has been permitted on the basis of other evidence of a high degree of probability that the testator would have made or changed a bequest. Courts of equity have granted relief by imposing a constructive trust in such a situation.[72] There appears to be little doubt that the same principle would apply to the frustration of intestate succession by fraudulently inducing a will,[73] or even to a prospective gift.[74] The problem appears in reality to be one of satisfactory proof that the loss has been suffered, instead of the existence of a ground of tort liability.[75] It is to be noted, however, that all of these cases in which recovery has been permitted, whether in a tort action or under a constructive trust, have involved conduct tortious in itself, such as fraud, duress or defamation. So far as now appears, there still can be no recovery merely upon the basis of intentional interference, without such otherwise tortious conduct.[76]

of insurance policy). See Notes, 1935, 48 Harv.L. Rev. 984; 1937, 23 Va.L.Rev. 614; 1937, 4 U.Chi.L. Rev. 509; 1937, 32 Corn.L.Q. 440; 1936, 5 Ford.L. Rev. 514.

68. Compare the cases awarding damages for loss of the value of a chance attended with a high probability of success: Chaplin v. Hicks, [1911] 2 K.B. 786 (beauty contest); Wachtel v. National Alfalfa Journal, 1920, 190 Iowa 1293, 176 N.W. 801 (prize magazine subscription contest); Kansas City, M. & O. R. Co. of Texas v. Bell, Tex.Civ.App.1917, 197 S. W. 322 (prize at stock show); see McCormick, Damages, 1935, § 31. Cf. McPeek v. Western Union Tel. Co., 1899, 107 Iowa 356, 78 N.W. 63 (reward regarded as sufficiently certain).

69. Cf. Hall v. Hall, 1917, 91 Conn. 514, 100 A. 441; Murphy v. Mitchell, D.N.Y.1917, 245 F. 219, 246 F. 732, 249 F. 499.

70. Creek v. Laski, 1929, 248 Mich. 425, 227 N.W. 817; Allen v. Lowell's Adm'x, 1946, 303 Ky. 238, 197 S.W.2d 424; Dulin v. Bailey, 1916, 172 N.C. 608, 90 S.E. 689; Morton v. Petitt, 1931, 124 Ohio St. 241, 177 N.E. 591. Cf. McGregor v. McGregor, D.Colo.1951, 101 F.Supp. 848 (probate of prior will).

71. Allen v. Leybourne, Fla.App.1966, 190 So.2d 825; Bohannon v. Wachovia Bank & Trust Co., 1936, 210 N.C. 679, 188 S.E. 390; Hegarty v. Hegarty, D. Mass.1943, 52 F.Supp. 296; see Brignati v. Medenwald, 1944, 315 Mass. 636, 53 N.E.2d 673; Axe v. Wilson, 1939, 150 Kan. 794, 96 P.2d 880; Restatement of Torts, § 912, Comment f.

Accord, as to the beneficiary of an insurance policy, Mitchell v. Langley, 1915, 143 Ga. 827, 85 S.E. 1050. Constructive trusts were imposed in Cason v. Owen, 1897, 100 Ga. 142, 28 S.E. 75; Daugherty v. Daugherty, 1913, 152 Ky. 732, 154 S.W. 9; Munroe v. Beggs, 1914, 91 Kan. 701, 139 P. 422.

See Evans, Torts to Expectancies in Decedents' Estates, 1944, 93 U.Pa.L.Rev. 187; Notes, 1951, 19 U. Kan.City L.Rev. 78; 1952, 1 De Paul L.Rev. 253.

Compare Shepherd v. Wakeman, 1662, 1 Sid. 79, 83 Eng.Rep. 931 (interference with prospective marriage by false statement); and the interesting case of Deon v. Kirby Lumber Co., 1926, 162 La. 671, 111 So. 55, where loss of prospective social relations, rather than economic ones, was held compensable.

72. Latham v. Father Divine, 1949, 299 N.Y. 22, 85 N.E.2d 168, reargument denied 299 N.Y. 599, 86 N. E.2d 114; Moneyham v. Hamilton, 1936, 124 Fla. 430, 168 So. 522; Bohannon v. Trotman, 1939, 214 N.C. 706, 200 S.E. 852; Seeds v. Seeds, 1927, 116 Ohio St. 144, 156 N.E. 193; Monach v. Koslowski, 1948, 322 Mass. 466, 78 N.E.2d 49.

73. Hegarty v. Hegarty, D.Mass.1943, 52 F.Supp. 296; Seeds v. Seeds, 1927, 116 Ohio St. 144, 156 N. E. 193.

74. The possible existence of the tort was recognized in Ross v. Wright, 1934, 286 Mass. 269, 190 N.E. 514, but it was held that there was no liability in the absence of tortious conduct.

75. Logically the damages recovered should be the value of the *chance* of benefit rather than the full value of the legacy. On this basis, there might be recovery for loss of prospects falling considerably short of absolute certainty. See McCormick, Damages, 1935, § 31; Note, 1933, 46 Harv.L.Rev. 696.

76. Marshall v. Dehaven, 1904, 209 Pa. 187, 58 A. 141 (inducing testator not to change will); Lowe Foundation v. Northern Trust Co., 1951, 342 Ill.App. 379, 96 N.E.2d 831 (inducing testator to destroy codicil);

Basis of Liability

The cause of action has run parallel to that for interference with existing contracts.[77] Again the tort began with "malice," and it has remained very largely a matter of at least intent to interfere. Cases have been quite infrequent in which even the claim has been advanced that the defendant through his negligence has prevented the plaintiff from obtaining a prospective pecuniary advantage; and the usual statement is that there can be no cause of action in such a case.[78] There are, however, a few situations in which recovery has been permitted, all of them apparently to be justified upon the basis of some special relation between the parties. They include the failure of a telegraph company to deliver a message which would have resulted in the plaintiff obtaining a contract;[79] the failure of a volunteer to continue the performance of a gratuitous promise to obtain insurance and the like for

the plaintiff;[80] delay in acting upon an application for insurance;[81] and two late California cases[82] holding that the negligent preparation of a will results in liability to the intended beneficiaries. In all probability, as in the case of interference with existing contracts,[83] liability for negligence is not impossible, but it must depend upon the existence of some special reason for finding a duty of care. No case has been found in which intended but purely incidental interference resulting from the pursuit of the defendant's own ends by proper means has been held to be actionable.

With intent to interfere the usual basis of the action, the cases have turned almost entirely upon the defendant's motive or purpose, and the means by which he has sought to accomplish it. As in the cases of interference with contract, any manner of intentional invasion of the plaintiff's interests may be sufficient if the purpose is not a privileged one. Apart from this, however, the means adopted may be unlawful in themselves; and violence[84] or intimidation,[85] def-

Ross v. Wright, 1934, 286 Mass. 269, 190 N.E. 514 (refusal to make transfer in completion of gift, where no duty to do so).

77. See supra, § 129.

78. Rickards v. Sun Oil Co., 1945, 23 N.J.Misc. 89, 41 A.2d 267 (destruction of bridge to island, causing business loss to plaintiff); Wooldridge Mfg. Co. v. United States, 1956, 98 U.S.App.D.C. 286, 235 F.2d 513, cert. denied 351 U.S. 989 (chief of engineers negligently delayed report, causing plaintiff to lose contract); Parker v. Brown, 1940, 195 S.C. 35, 10 S.E.2d 625 (failure to issue executions causing loss of commissions to tax collector); Liesbosch Dredger v. S. S. Edison, [1933] A.C. 449 (damage from collision, loss through inability to charter other vessel).

79. Western Union Tel. Co. v. Bowman, 1904, 141 Ala. 175, 37 So. 493; Western Union Tel. Co. v. McKibben, 1887, 114 Ind. 511, 14 N.E. 894; McPherson v. Western Union Tel. Co., 1915, 189 Mich. 471, 155 N.W. 557; Barker v. Western Union Tel. Co., 1908, 134 Wis. 147, 114 N.W. 439; Western Union Tel. Co. v. Mathis, 1926, 215 Ala. 282, 110 So. 399.

But where the undelivered message is a mere inquiry, recovery of substantial damages has been denied. Wilson v. Western Union Tel. Co., 1905, 124 Ga. 131, 52 S.E. 153; McKenry v. Western Union Tel. Co., 1927, 81 Cal.App. 258, 253 P. 333; Davies v. Western Union Tel. Co., 1912, 93 S.C. 318, 76 S.E. 820. See Note, 1936, 20 Minn.L.Rev. 837.

80. Evan L. Reed Mfg. Co. v. Wurts, 1914, 187 Ill. App. 378; Siegel v. Spear & Co., 1923, 234 N.Y. 479, 138 N.E. 414; Carr v. Maine Central R. Co., 1917, 78 N.H. 502, 102 A. 532 (obtaining Interstate Commerce Commission approval of refund); Condon v. Exton-Hall Brokerage & Vessel Agency, 1913, 80 Misc. 369, 142 N.Y.S. 548, reversed on other grounds, 1913, 83 Misc. 130, 144 N.Y.S. 760 (cancelling insurance); Stockmen's Nat. Bank of Casper v. Richardson, 1933, 45 Wyo. 306, 18 P.2d 635 (recording mortgage).

81. See cases cited supra, p. 345.

82. Biakanja v. Irving, 1958, 49 Cal.2d 647, 320 P.2d 16 (notary public, not properly attested); Lucas v. Hamm, 1961, 56 Cal.2d 583, 364 P.2d 685, 15 Cal. Rptr. 821, cert. denied 368 U.S. 987 (attorney, negligent drafting). Accord, Ward v. Arnold, 1958, 52 Wash.2d 581, 328 P.2d 164 (negligent advice of attorney that no will was necessary).

83. See supra, p. 938.

84. Garret v. Taylor, 1621, Cro.Jac. 567, 79 Eng.Rep. 485; Tarleton v. McGawley, 1793, Peake N.P. 270, 170 Eng.Rep. 153. Cf. Hughes v. McDonough, 1881, 43 N.J.L. 459 (loosening shoe on horse shod by plaintiff, to deprive him of a customer).

85. See note 85 on page 953.

amation,[86] injurious falsehood [87] or other fraud,[88] violation of the criminal law,[89] and the institution or threat of groundless civil suits [90] or criminal prosecutions [91] in bad faith, all have been held to result in liability.

Most of the decisions have turned upon the defendant's motive or purpose. Again, as in the case of interference with contract,[92] the defendant will be held liable if the reason underlying his interference is purely a malevolent one, and a desire to do harm to the plaintiff for its own sake.[93] On the other hand, some element of ill will is seldom absent from intentional interference; and if the defendant has a legitimate interest to protect, the addition of a spite motive usually is not regarded as sufficient to result in liability.[94]

Proof of the intentional interference and resulting damage [95] establishes what the New York courts have called a "prima facie tort," [96] casting upon the defendant the burden of avoiding liability by showing that his conduct was privileged.[97] In general, it may be said that any purpose sufficient to create a privilege to disturb existing contractual relations,[98] such as the disinterested protection of the interests of third persons,[99] or

---

85. Guillory v. Godfrey, 1955, 134 Cal.App.2d 628, 286 P.2d 474; Sparks v. McCrary, 1908, 156 Ala. 382, 47 So. 332; International Ticket Co. v. Wendrich, 1937, 122 N.J.Eq. 222, 193 A. 808, affirmed 1937, 123 N.J.Eq. 172, 196 A. 474; Gilly v. Hirsch, 1909, 122 La. 966, 48 So. 422; Evenson v. Spaulding, 9 Cir. 1907, 150 F. 517.

86. Godin v. Niebuhr, 1920, 236 Mass. 350, 128 N.E. 406; Standard Oil Co. v. Doyle, 1904, 118 Ky. 662, 82 S.W. 271; Kendall v. Lively, 1934, 94 Colo. 483, 31 P.2d 343; Morrison-Jewell Filtration Co. v. Lingane, 1895, 19 R.I. 316, 33 A. 452. See Nims, Unfair Competition by False Statements or Disparagement, 1933, 19 Corn.L.Q. 63.

87. Really only one form of interference with pecuniary advantage. See supra, p. 917.

88. Thus Wise v. Western Union Tel. Co., 1934, 36 Del. 155, 172 A. 757 (sending forged telegrams purporting to come from plaintiff). As to misrepresentation to the public in competition, see infra, p. 959.

89. Glover v. Malloska, 1927, 238 Mich. 216, 213 N.W. 107 (lottery).

90. Munson Line v. Green, S.D.N.Y.1946, 6 F.R.D. 14; Maytag Co. v. Meadows Mfg. Co., 7 Cir. 1929, 35 F. 2d 403; Dehydro, Inc. v. Tretolite Co., D.Okl.1931, 53 F.2d 273; Sun-Maid Raisin Growers of Calif. v. Avis, D.Ill.1928, 25 F.2d 303; see Notes, 1932, 10 N.C.L.Rev. 300; 1947, 56 Yale L.J. 885.

91. American Mercury v. Chase, D.Mass.1926, 13 F.2d 224. Cf. People v. Everest, 1889, 51 Hun 19, 3 N.Y. S. 612 (arrest of engineer to delay train); Pratt Food Co. v. Bird, 1907, 148 Mich. 631, 112 N.W. 701.

92. See supra, p. 943.

93. Tuttle v. Buck, 1909, 107 Minn. 145, 119 N.W. 946; Memphis Steam Laundry-Cleaners v. Lindsey, 1941, 192 Miss. 224, 5 So.2d 227; Graham v. St. Charles St. R. Co., 1895, 47 La.Ann. 214, 16 So. 806; Boggs v. Duncan-Schell Furniture Co., 1913, 163 Iowa 106, 143 N.W. 482; United States Aluminum Siding Corp. v. Dun & Bradstreet, S.D.N.Y.1958, 163 F.Supp. 906. Compare the attempt to coerce a set-

tlement with the "white elephant" car in Carter v. Knapp Motor Co., 1943, 243 Ala. 600, 11 So.2d 383. Also the retaliation in National Ass'n A. C. P. v. Overstreet, 1965, 221 Ga. 16, 142 S.E.2d 816, cert. dismissed 384 U.S. 118, rehearing denied 84 U.S. 981. See Note, 1943, 15 Miss.L.J. 213.

94. Holbrook v. Morrison, 1913, 214 Mass. 209, 100 N.E. 1111 (advertising for Negro purchasers for premises). Accord: Beardsley v. Kilmer, 1922, 200 App.Div. 378, 193 N.Y.S. 285, affirmed, 1923, 236 N. Y. 80, 140 N.E. 203; Katz v. Kapper, 1935, 7 Cal. App.2d 1, 44 P.2d 1060; McMaster v. Ford Motor Co., 1921, 122 S.C. 244, 115 S.E. 244; Lewis v. Huie-Hodge Lumber Co., 1908, 121 La. 658, 46 So. 685; West Virginia Transp. Co. v. Standard Oil Co., 1902, 50 W.Va. 611, 40 S.E. 591.

95. No cause of action is made out unless damage is shown. Rager v. McCloskey, 1953, 305 N.Y. 75, 111 N.E.2d 214.

96. See Forkosch, An Analysis of the "Prima Facie Tort" Cause of Action, 1957, 42 Corn.L.Q. 465; Halpern, Intentional Torts and the Restatement, 1957, 7 Buff.L.Rev. 7; Notes, 1956, 41 Corn.L.Q. 507; 1958, 32 St.Johns L.Rev. 282; 1958, 10 Syr. L.Rev. 53.

97. Although there are almost no cases, it appears that the absolute privileges in defamation will be available as a defense here. Thus in Rainier's Dairies v. Raritan Valley Farms, 1955, 19 N.J. 552, 117 A.2d 889, the absolute privilege of a judicial proceeding was applied.

98. See supra, p. 942.

99. Gott v. Berea College, 1913, 156 Ky. 376, 161 S. W. 204; Jones v. Cody, 1902, 132 Mich. 13, 92 N.W. 495; Guethler v. Altman, 1901, 26 Ind.App. 587, 60 N.E. 355; Rowan v. Butler, 1908, 171 Ind. 28, 86 N.E. 714; Kuryer Pub. Co. v. Messmer, 1916, 162 Wis. 565, 156 N.W. 948.

those of the public,[1] or of the defendant's own property or business interests,[2] or the exercise of the right to bring or to threaten a bona fide lawsuit,[3] or to complain or petition to public authorities,[4] will also justify interference with relations which are merely prospective. The chief difference lies in the recognition of more extensive privileges in the latter case.

Competition

Chief among these is the privilege of competition. The policy of the common law has always been in favor of free competition,[5] which proverbially is the life of trade. So long as the plaintiff's contractual relations are merely contemplated or potential, it is considered to be in the interest of the public that any competitor should be free to divert them to himself by all fair and reasonable means. Any other rule would tend to the recognition of trade monopolies. This has been established since an old case [6] in the year books in which it was held that the owner of an established school could not complain when a new school attracted his prospective pupils; and it was emphatically declared in the leading modern case of Mogul Steamship Co. v. McGregor, Gow & Co.,[7] involving competition between steamship companies for the same trade.

In short, it is no tort to beat a business rival to prospective customers. Thus, in the absence of prohibition by statute,[8] illegitimate means, or some other unlawful element, a defendant seeking to increase his own busi-

1. McCann v. New York Stock Exchange, 2 Cir.1940, 107 F.2d 908, cert. denied 60 S.Ct. 807, rehearing denied 309 U.S. 682 (driving unscrupulous person out of business as a stockbroker); Julie Baking Co. v. Graymond, 1934, 152 Misc. 846, 274 N.Y.S. 250 (picketing bakery in protest against high price of bread); New Negro Alliance v. Sanitary Grocery Co., 1938, 303 U.S. 552 (in protest against non-employment of Negroes); Chicago, R. I. & P. Co. v. Armstrong, 1911, 30 Okl. 134, 120 P. 952 (protection of public against bad hauling to railroad station); Harris v. Thomas, Tex.Civ.App.1920, 217 S.W. 1068 (standards of medical association); cf. Thompson v. New South Wales Branch of British Medical Ass'n, [1924] A.C. 764 (same).

Contra: People v. Kopezak 1934, 153 Misc. 187, 274 N.Y.S. 629, affirmed 1934, 266 N.Y. 565, 195 N.E. 202 (picketing in protest against fire-trap conditions); A. S. Beck Shoe Corp. v. Johnson, 1934, 153 Misc. 363, 274 N.Y.S. 946 (in protest against nonemployment of Negroes); National Ass'n for Advancement of Colored People v. Webb's City, Fla.App. 1963, 152 So.2d 179.

2. Zoby v. American Fidelity Co., 4 Cir. 1957, 242 F. 2d 76; National Life & Acc. Ins. Co. v. Wallace, 1933, 162 Okl. 174, 21 P.2d 492; Karges Furniture Co. v. Amalgamated Wood Workers' Local Union No. 131, 1905, 165 Ind. 421, 75 N.E. 877; Falloon v. Schilling, 1883, 29 Kan. 292; Passaic Print Works v. Ely & Walker Dry-Goods Co., 8 Cir. 1900, 105 F. 163, cert. denied 181 U.S. 617. See Note, 1966, 50 Minn.L.Rev. 570.

3. Oil Conservation Engineering Co. v. Brooks Engineering Co., 6 Cir. 1931, 52 F.2d 783; Everybody's Tool & Die Works v. Costa, D.N.Y.1934, 9 F.Supp. 440; Virtue v. Creamery Package Mfg. Co., 8 Cir. 1910, 179 F. 115; cf. Flynn & Emrich Co. v. Federal Trade Commission, 4 Cir. 1931, 52 F.2d 836; Dr. Herman Heuser v. Federal Trade Commission, 7 Cir. 1925, 4 F.2d 632. See Notes, 1932, 10 N.C.L. Rev. 300; 1935, 23 Geo.L.J. 881.

4. McKee v. Hughes, 1916, 133 Tenn. 455, 181 S.W. 930; Kelly v. Morris County Traction Co., 1924, 2 N.J.Misc.R. 802, 126 A. 24. Otherwise where the petition is in bad faith, and the motive is purely spiteful. Vanarsdale v. Laverty, 1871, 69 Pa. 103.

5. See Jones, Historical Development of the Law of Business Competition, 1926, 35 Yale L.J. 905, 36 Yale L.J. 42, 207, 351; Wyman, Competition and the Law, 1902, 15 Harv.L.Rev. 427; Kennedy and Finkelman, The Right to Trade, 1933.

6. 1410, Y.B. 11 Hen. IV, f. 47, pl. 21.

7. 1889, 23 Q.B.D. 598 affirmed [1892] A.C. 25.

8. If a statute is interpreted as intended to protect the plaintiff against the competition, he will be entitled to maintain the action for its violation. Frost v. Corporation Comm. of Oklahoma, 1929, 278 U.S. 515; National Bank of Detroit v. Wayne Oakland Bank, 6 Cir. 1958, 252 F.2d 537; Commercial State Bank v. Gidney, D.D.C.1959, 174 F.Supp. 770, affirmed 108 U.S.App.D.C. 37, 278 F.2d 871; Burden v. Hoover, 1956, 9 Ill.2d 114, 137 N.E.2d 59; Hobson v. Kentucky Trust Co., 1946, 303 Ky. 493, 197 S.W.2d 454. But not if the statute is not so interpreted. Delaware Optometric Corp. v. Sherwood, 1957, 36 Del.Ch. 223, 128 A.2d 812; New Hampshire Board of Reg. in Optometry v. Scott Jewelry Co., 1939, 90 N.H. 368, 9 A.2d 513; MacBeth v. Gerber's, Inc., 1946, 72 R.I. 102, 48 A.2d 366; Mosig v. Jersey Chiropodists, 1937, 122 N.J.Eq. 382, 194 A. 248.

ness may cut rates or prices,[9] allow discounts or rebates,[10] enter into secret negotiations behind the plaintiff's back,[11] refuse to deal with him [12] or threaten to discharge employees who do,[13] or even refuse to deal with third parties unless they cease dealing with the plaintiff,[14] all without incurring liability.

And, since all the members of a group may be free to do what any one of them may do, the addition of the element of combination or agreement of a number of defendants to carry out such policies adds nothing in itself, and will not result in liability.[15] In such cases of group action, however, the possibilities of unprivileged coercion, intimidation, and a monopolistic restraint of trade are vastly increased, and the defendants frequently have been held liable on this basis.[16]

The privilege of competition is limited to bona fide competition. It does not extend to situations where the defendant is not seeking to acquire the business diverted from the plaintiff for himself, but to gratify ill will or further some unrelated interest.[17] Thus it does not extend to cases where there is no genuine competitive interest, but competition is simulated for spiteful ends or ulterior purposes, as where the defendant sets up a rival barber shop [18] or engages in predatory price cutting,[19] not to make profits for him-

9. Mogul S. S. Co. v. McGregor, Gow & Co., 1889, 23 Q.B.D. 598, aff'd, [1892] A.C. 25; Package Closure Corp. v. Seabright Co., 2 Cir. 1944, 141 F.2d 972; Passaic Print Works v. Ely & Walker Dry-Goods Co., 8 Cir. 1900, 105 F. 163, cert. denied 181 U.S. 617; Katz v. Kapper, 1935, 7 Cal.App.2d 1, 44 P.2d 1060; cf. Fleetway, Inc. v. Public Service Interstate Transp. Co., 3 Cir. 1934, 72 F.2d 761 (under Anti-Trust Act).

10. Mogul S. S. Co. v. McGregor, Gow & Co., 1889, 23 Q.B.D. 598, affirmed [1892] A.C. 25; Munhall v. Pennsylvania R. Co., 1879, 92 Pa. 150; Lough v. Outerbridge, 1893, 143 N.Y. 271, 38 N.E. 292.

11. Goldman v. Harford Road Bldg. Ass'n, 1926, 150 Md. 677, 133 A. 843; Debnam v. Simonson, 1914, 124 Md. 354, 92 A. 782; Hansberry v. Holloway, 1928, 332 Ill. 334, 163 N.E. 662; George F. Hewson Co. v. Hopper, 1943, 130 N.J.L. 525, 33 A.2d 889. Otherwise where fraudulent representations are made. Johnson v. Gustafson, 1938, 201 Minn. 629, 277 N.W. 252; Skene v. Carayanis, 1926, 103 Conn. 708, 131 A. 497. Cf. Krigbaum v. Sbarbaro, 1913, 23 Cal.App. 427, 138 P. 364 (intimidation and molestations); Louis Kamm, Inc. v. Flink, 1934, 113 N.J. L. 582, 175 A. 62 (collusion and disclosure of confidential information).

12. Great Atlantic & Pacific Tea Co. v. Cream of Wheat Co., 2 Cir. 1915, 227 F. 46; United States v. Colgate & Co., 1919, 250 U.S. 300; Locker v. American Tobacco Co., 2 Cir. 1914, 218 F. 447; Baran v. Goodyear Tire & Rubber Co., D.N.Y.1919, 256 F. 571. See Brown, The Right to Refuse to Sell, 1916, 25 Yale L.J. 194.

13. Lewis v. Huie-Hodge Lumber Co., 1908, 121 La. 658, 46 So. 685; Robison v. Texas Pine Land Ass'n, Tex.Civ.App.1897, 40 S.W. 843 (compelling employees to trade at defendant's store rather than plaintiff's); cf. Celli & Del Papa v. Galveston Brewing Co., Tex.Com.App.1921, 227 S.W. 941 (tenants).

14. Photographic Imp. & Dist. Co. v. Elgeet Optical Co., 1953, 282 App.Div. 223, 122 N.Y.S.2d 215, affirmed, 1953, 282 App.Div. 836, 124 N.Y.S.2d 341; Staroske v. Pulitzer Pub. Co., 1911, 235 Mo. 67, 138 S.W. 36; Journal of Commerce Pub. Co. v. Tribune Co., 7 Cir. 1922, 286 F. 111; Andrew Jergens Co. v. Woodbury, Inc., D.Del.1920, 271 F. 43; Dye v. Carmichael Produce Co., 1917, 64 Ind.App. 653, 116 N.E. 425.

15. Bohn Mfg. Co. v. Hollis, 1893, 54 Minn. 223, 55 N.W. 1119; Macauley v. Tierney, 1895, 19 R.I. 255, 33 A. 1; John D. Park & Sons Co. v. National Wholesale Druggists' Ass'n, 1903, 175 N.Y. 1, 67 N. E. 136; Montgomery Ward & Co. v. South Dakota Retail Merchants' & Hardware Dealers' Ass'n, C.C. S.D.1907, 150 F. 413; Sorrell v. Smith, [1925] A.C. 700.

16. Jackson v. Stanfield, 1893, 137 Ind. 592, 36 N.E. 345, rehearing denied 137 Ind. 592, 37 N.E. 14. And see infra, p. 961.

17. International & G. N. R. Co. v. Greenwood, 1893, 2 Tex.Civ.App. 76, 21 S.W. 559; Wesley v. Native Lumber Co., 1910, 97 Miss. 814, 53 So. 346; Graham v. St. Charles St. R. Co., 1895, 47 La.Ann. 1656, 18 So. 707; Hanchett v. Chiatovich, 9 Cir. 1900, 101 F. 742; Peek v. Northern Pac. R. Co., 1915, 51 Mont. 295, 152 P. 421.

18. Tuttle v. Buck, 1909, 107 Minn. 145, 119 N.W. 946; Dunshee v. Standard Oil Co., 1911, 152 Iowa 618, 132 N.W. 371.

19. Boggs v. Duncan-Schell Furniture Co., 1913, 163 Iowa 106, 143 N.W. 482; Memphis Steam Laundry-Cleaners v. Lindsey, 1941, 192 Miss. 224, 5 So.2d 227. Cf. Thomsen v. Cayser, 1917, 243 U.S. 66 (under Anti-Trust Act).

It should be noted, however, that price discrimination is now extensively regulated by the federal Robinson-Patman Act, and by many state resale price

self but to drive the plaintiff out of business. Even the fact that he expects to derive an ultimate economic benefit from the elimination of the plaintiff is not regarded as a sufficient justification in such cases since indirect methods of this kind are not considered legitimate in the pursuit of profits.

Though trade warfare may be waged ruthlessly to the bitter end, there are certain rules of combat which must be observed. "The trader has not a free lance. Fight he may, but as a soldier, not as a guerrilla." [20] In the interests of the public and the competitors themselves, boundaries have been set by the law, and numerous practices have been marked out as "unfair" competition, for which, in general, a tort action will lie in favor of the injured competitor,[21] although very often the tort is given some other name. These practices are a full subject for a treatise in themselves,[22] and in the space here

available it is impossible to do more than touch on them, and indicate the lines which the law has followed.

Included in the list are defamation of the competitor,[23] disparagement of his goods and his business methods,[24] intimidation, harassing and annoyance of his customers [25] or his employees,[26] obstruction of the means of access to his place of business,[27] threats of groundless suits,[28] commercial bribery,[29] and inducing employees to commit sabotage.[30]

maintenance statutes, which may afford a basis of tort liability. See for example Elizabeth Arden Sales Corp. v. Gus Blass Co., 8 Cir. 1945, 150 F.2d 988; Calvert Distillers Corp. v. Nussbaum Liquor Store, 1938, 166 Misc. 342, 2 N.Y.S.2d 320; Burstein v. Charline's Cut Rate, 1940, 126 N.J.Eq. 560, 10 A. 2d 646.

20. Hammond, J., in Martell v. White, 1904, 185 Mass. 255, 260, 69 N.E. 1085, 1087, continuing: "The right of competition rests upon the doctrine that the interests of the great public are best subserved by permitting the general and natural laws of business to have their full and free operation, and that this end is best attained when the trader is allowed in his business to make free use of these laws . . . But . . . the weapons used by the trader who relies upon this right for justification must be those furnished by the laws of trade, or at least must not be inconsistent with their free operation. No man can justify an interference with another man's business through fraud or misrepresentation."

21. See Grismore, Are Unfair Methods of Competition Actionable at the Suit of a Competitor, 1935, 33 Mich.L.Rev. 321.

22. See Nims, Law of Unfair Competition and Trade Marks, 4th Ed. 1947; Handler, Unfair Competition, 1936, 21 Iowa L.Rev. 175; Wright, Tort Responsibility for Destruction of Goodwill, 1929, 14 Corn.L. Q. 298; McLaughlin, Legal Control of Competitive Methods, 1926, 21 Iowa L.Rev. 274; Fathchild, Statutory Unfair Competition, 1936, 1 Mo.L.Rev.

20; Callmann, What is Unfair Competition, 1940, 28 Geo.L.J. 585; Callmann, Copyright and Unfair Competition, 1940, 2 La.L.Rev. 648; Chafee, Unfair Competition, 1940, 53 Harv.L.Rev. 1289; Sadtler, Unfair Competition—Past and Present Trends, 1940, 16 Tenn.L.Rev. 400; Bunn, The National Law of Unfair Competition, 1949, 62 Harv.L.Rev. 987; Notes, 1951, 45 U.Ill.L.Rev. 784; [1950] U.Ill.L. Forum 675.

23. Standard Oil Co. v. Doyle, 1904, 118 Ky. 662, 82 S.W. 271; Van Horn v. Van Horn, 1890, 52 N.J.L. 284, 20 A. 485; Landon v. Watkins, 1895, 61 Minn. 137, 63 N.W. 615; Kendall v. Lively, 1934, 94 Colo. 483, 31 P.2d 343. As to the relation between unfair competition, defamation and disparagement, see Green, Relational Interests, 1935, 30 Ill.L.Rev. 1; Nims, Unfair Competition by False Statements or Disparagement, 1933, 19 Corn.L.Q. 63; Note, 1933, 33 Col.L.Rev. 90.

24. See supra, § 128.

25. Tarleton v. McGawley, 1793, Peake N.P. 270, 170 Eng.Rep. 153; Standard Oil Co. v. Doyle, 1904, 118 Ky. 662, 82 S.W. 271; Sparks v. McCrary, 1908, 156 Ala. 382, 47 So. 332; Evenson v. Spaulding, 9 Cir. 1907, 150 F. 517.

26. Evenson v. Spaulding, 9 Cir. 1907, 150 F. 517; Standard Oil Co. v. Doyle, 1904, 118 Ky. 662, 82 S. W. 271.

27. Cf. Gilly v. Hirsh, 1909, 122 La. 966, 48 So. 422; Brown-Brand Realty Co. v. Saks & Co., 1926, 126 Misc. 336, 214 N.Y.S. 230, affirmed 1926, 218 App. Div. 827, 218 N.Y.S. 706.

28. See supra, notes 90, 91, p. 953. But compare the cases of bona fide threats of suit, supra, note 3, p. 954.

29. See International News Service v. Associated Press, 1918, 248 U.S. 215; Kraus v. H. Pacter & Co., 1929, 134 Misc. 247, 234 N.Y.S. 687; cf. Hurst & Son v. Federal Trade Commission, D.Va.1920, 268 F. 874. See Notes, 1928, 28 Col.L.Rev. 799; 1932, 45 Harv.L.Rev. 1248.

30. Cf. King v. Cope, 1719, 1 Stra. 144, 93 Eng.Rep. 438.

A breach of confidence committed or induced in obtaining or using trade secrets [31] has been a frequent ground for relief by injunction, and this has been extended by some courts to other confidential information, such as lists of customers,[32] although the prevailing view is still to the contrary.[33]

One large area of unfair competition is what may be called for lack of a better generic name false marketing, which used to be called "passing off," and still quite often goes by that designation. It consists of the making of some false representation to the public, or to third persons, likely to induce them to believe that the goods or services of another are those of the plaintiff.[34] This

may be done, for example, by counterfeiting or imitating the plaintiff's trade mark [35] or trade name,[36] his wrappers, labels or containers,[37] his vehicles,[38] the badges or uniforms of his employees,[39] or the appearance of his place of business.[40] The test laid down in such cases has been whether the resemblance is so great as to deceive the ordinary

31. Riess v. Sanford, 1941, 47 Cal.App.2d 244, 117 P. 2d 694; Vulcan Detinning Co. v. American Can Co., 1907, 72 N.J.Eq. 387, 67 A. 339; Stone v. Goss, 1903, 65 N.J.Eq. 756, 55 A. 736; Aronson v. Orlov, 1917, 228 Mass. 1, 116 N.E. 951, cert. denied 245 U. S. 662; Macbeth-Evans Glass Co. v. Schnelbach, 1913, 239 Pa. 76, 86 A. 688. See Whitlock, The Law as to Trade Secrets, 1912, 74 Cent.L.J. 83; McClain, Injunctive Relief Against Employees Using Confidential Information, 1935, 23 Ky.L.J. 248; Notes, 1919, 19 Col.L.Rev. 233; 1923, 23 Col.L.Rev. 164; 1928, 42 Harv.L.Rev. 254; 1928, 6 Tex.L.Rev. 502; 1928, 37 Yale L.J. 1154; 1930, 14 Minn.L.Rev. 546.

32. Colonial Laundries v. Henry, 1927, 48 R.I. 332, 138 A. 47; Empire Steam Laundry Co. v. Lozier, 1913, 165 Cal. 95, 130 P. 1180; People's Coat, A. & T. Supply Co. v. Light, 1918, 171 App.Div. 671, 157 N.Y.S. 15, affirmed, 1918, 224 N.Y. 727, 121 N.E. 886; Morrison v. Woodbury, 1919, 105 Kan. 617, 185 P. 735. See McClain, Injunctive Relief Against Employees Using Confidential Information, 1935, 23 Ky.L.J. 248; Hannigan, The Implied Obligation of an Employee, 1929, 77 U.Pa.L.Rev. 970; Kramer, Protection of Customer Lists in California, 1935, 23 Cal.L.Rev. 399.

33. Progress Laundry Co. v. Hamilton, 1925, 208 Ky. 348, 270 S.W. 834; Woolley's Laundry v. Silva, 1939, 304 Mass. 383, 23 N.E.2d 899; Abalene Exterminating Co. v. Elges, 1947, 137 N.J.Eq. 1, 43 A.2d 165; Fulton Grand Laundry Co. v. Johnson, 1922, 140 Md. 359, 117 A. 753; Jewel Tea Co. v. Grissom, 1938, 66 S.D. 146, 279 N.W. 544.

34. See for example Dixi-Cola Laboratories v. Coca-Cola Co., 4 Cir. 1941, 117 F.2d 352, cert. denied 314 U.S. 629; Timken Roller Bearing Co. v. Leterstone Sales Co., N.D.Ill.1939, 27 F.Supp. 736; Standard Brands v. Smidler, 2 Cir. 1945, 151 F.2d 34; American Distilling Co. v. Bellows & Co., 1951, 102 Cal.

App.2d 8, 226 P.2d 751; Smith v. Dental Products Co., 7 Cir. 1944, 140 F.2d 140, cert. denied 322 U.S. 743.

35. Coca-Cola Co. v. Chero-Cola Co., 1921, 57 App.D. C. 27, 273 F. 755; Walter M. Steppacher & Bro. v. Karr, D.Pa.1916, 236 F. 151; Vogue Co. v. Thompson-Hudson Co., 6 Cir. 1924, 300 F. 509, rehearing denied Vogue Co. v. Vogue Hat Co., 12 F.2d 991 and cert. denied Thompson v. Vogue Co., 273 U.S. 706; Manitowoc Malting Co. v. Milwaukee Malting Co., 1903, 119 Wis. 543, 97 N.W. 389; Triangle Publications, Inc. v. Rohrlich, 2 Cir. 1948, 167 F.2d 969. See Nims, The Law of Unfair Competition and Trade Marks, 4th Ed. 1947; Derenberg, Trade-Mark Protection and Unfair Trading, 1936; Callman, The Law of Unfair Competition and Trade Marks, 2d Ed. 1950; Handler and Pickett, Trade-Marks and Trade Names—An Analysis and Synthesis, 1930, 30 Col.L.Rev. 168, 759; Note, 1955, 68 Harv.L.Rev. 814.

36. Sartor v. Schaden, 1904, 125 Iowa 696, 101 N.W. 511; Reddaway v. Banham, [1896] A.C. 199; J. A. Scriven Co. v. Girard Co., 2 Cir. 1906, 148 F. 1019; Barton v. Rex-Oil Co., 3 Cir. 1924, 2 F.2d 402, modified in 29 F.2d 474; Standard Paint Co. v. Rubberoid Roofing Co., 7 Cir. 1915, 224 F. 695; Mayo Clinic v. Mayo's Drug & Cosmetic, Inc., 1962, 262 Minn. 101, 113 N.W.2d 852.

37. Lever Bros. v. Jay's Chemical Corp., E.D.N.Y. 1934, 6 F.Supp. 933; New England Awl & Needle Co. v. Marlboro Awl & Needle Co., 1897, 168 Mass. 154, 46 N.E. 386; Charles E. Hires Co. v. Consumers' Co., 7 Cir. 1900, 100 F. 809; L. P. Larson, Jr. Co. v. Lamont, Corliss & Co., 7 Cir. 1918, 257 F. 270, cert. denied 249 U.S. 603; American Chicle Co. v. Topps Chewing Gum, Inc., 2 Cir. 1953, 208 F.2d 560.

38. Mundon v. Taxicab Co., 1926, 151 Md. 449, 135 A. 177; Yellow Cab Co. v. Becker, 1920, 145 Minn. 152, 176 N.W. 345; Seattle Taxicab Co. v. De Jarlais, 1925, 135 Wash. 60, 236 P. 785; Yellow Cab. Co. of Rhode Island v. Anastasi, 1924, 46 R.I. 49, 124 A. 735.

39. Marsh v. Billings, 1851, 7 Cush., Mass., 322.

40. Weinstock, Lubin & Co. v. Marks, 1895, 109 Cal. 529, 42 P. 142; Charles S. Cash v. Steinbook, 1927, 220 App.Div. 569, 222 N.Y.S. 61, affirmed 1928, 247 N.Y. 531, 161 N.E. 170.

customer acting with the caution usually exercised in such transactions, so that he may mistake one for the other.[41] The older rule was that there must be proof of a fraudulent intent, or conscious deception, before there could be any liability, and this is still occasionally repeated;[42] but the whole trend of the later cases is to hold that it is enough, at least for purposes of injunctive relief, that the defendant's conduct results in a false representation, which is likely to cause confusion or deception, even though he has no such intention.[43]

On the other hand the appropriation of abstract ideas, not yet embodied in any tangible form,[44] of styles [45] or designs,[46] of advertising layouts or schemes,[47] have been held, in the absence of any patent, copyright or deception as to the identity or source, to be privileged, apparently on the theory that the right to compete is the right to imitate, and there can be no monopoly as to such commercial matters. Nevertheless news,[48] radio broadcasts,[49] and other similar literary or musical material,[50] have been protected against piracy where they have been reduced to concrete form, and are no longer in the stage of mere conception or idea.

Some shadow of doubt may, however, be cast upon these last decisions by two cases [51]

41. See Nims, Law of Unfair Competition and Trade Marks, 4th Ed. 1947.

42. See for example Fawcett Publications v. Bronze Publications, 5 Cir. 1949, 173 F.2d 778, rehearing denied 174 F.2d 646, cert. denied 338 U.S. 869; Anheuser-Busch, Inc. v. Du Bois Brewing Co., 3 Cir. 1949, 175 F.2d 370, cert. denied 339 U.S. 934, rehearing denied 339 U.S. 959.

43. Fry v. Layne-Western Co., 8 Cir. 1960, 282 F.2d 97; Lane Bryant, Inc. v. Maternity Lane, Ltd. of Calif., 9 Cir. 1949, 173 F.2d 559; Elastic Stop Nut Corp. of America v. Greer, N.D.Ill.1945, 62 F.Supp. 363; Telechron, Inc. v. Telicon Corp., 3 Cir. 1952, 198 F.2d 903; Howard's Clothes, Inc. v. Howard's Clothes Corp., 1952, 236 Minn. 291, 52 N.W.2d 753.

44. Haskins v. Ryan, 1906, 71 N.J.Eq. 575, 64 A. 436, affirmed 75 N.J.Eq. 623, 73 A. 1118; Alberts v. Remington Rand, 1940, 175 Misc. 486, 23 N.Y.S.2d 892; Lueddecke v. Chevrolet Motor Co., 8 Cir. 1934, 70 F.2d 345; Grombach Productions v. Waring, 1944, 293 N.Y. 609, 59 N.E.2d 425, motion denied 294 N.Y. 697, 60 N.E.2d 846; Affiliated Enterprises v. Gruber, 1 Cir. 1936, 86 F.2d 958. See Logan, Legal Protection of Ideas, 1939, 4 Mo.L.Rev. 239; Callman, He Who Reaps Where He Has Not Sown, 1942, 55 Harv.L.Rev. 595; Havighurst, The Right to Compensation for an Idea, 1954, 49 N.W.U.L.Rev. 295; Callman, Competition in Ideas and Titles, 1954, 42 Cal.L.Rev. 77; Yankwich, Recent Developments in the Law of Creation, Expression and Communication of Ideas, 1953, 48 Nw.U.L.Rev. 543; Notes, 1946, 31 Corn.L.Q. 382; 1934, 47 Harv.L.Rev. 1419.

45. Montegut v. Hickson, 1917, 178 App.Div. 94, 164 N.Y.S. 858. But cf. Margolis v. National Bellas Hess Co., 1931, 139 Misc. 738, 249 N.Y.S. 175.

46. Cheney Bros. v. Doris Silk Corp., 2 Cir. 1929, 35 F.2d 279, cert. denied 281 U.S. 728; Richard J. Cole

v. Manhattan Modes Co., Sup.Ct.1956, 159 N.Y.S.2d 709; Samuel Winston, Inc. v. Charles James Services, Inc., Sup.Ct.1956, 159 N.Y.S.2d 716. See Weikart, Design Piracy, 1944, 19 Ind.L.J. 235; Chafee, Unfair Competition, 1940, 53 Harv.L.Rev. 1289; Wolff, Is Design Piracy Unfair Competition, 1941, 23 J.Pat.Off.Soc. 431; Callman, Style and Design Piracy, 1940, 22 J.Pat.Off.Soc. 557.

47. Westminster Laundry Co. v. Hesse Envelope Co., 1913, 174 Mo.App. 238, 156 S.W. 767; cf. Armstrong Seatag Corp. v. Smith's Island Oyster Co., 4 Cir. 1918, 254 F. 821. See Note, 1932, 45 Harv.L.Rev. 542.

48. International News Service v. Associated Press, 1918, 248 U.S. 215; Associated Press v. KVOS, Inc., 9 Cir. 1935, 80 F.2d 575, cert. granted 298 U.S. 650; Pottstown Daily News Pub. Co. v. Pottstown Broadcasting Co., 1963, 411 Pa. 383, 192 A.2d 657; Veatch v. Wagner, 1953, 14 Alaska 183, 109 F.Supp. 537; Notes, 1935, 44 Yale L.J. 877; 1966, 35 Ford. L.Rev. 385.

49. Pittsburgh Athletic Club v. KQV Broadcasting Co., W.D.Pa.1938, 24 F.Supp. 490; Metropolitan Opera Ass'n v. Wagner-Nichols Recorder Corp., 1950, 199 Misc. 786, 101 N.Y.S.2d 483; Uproar Co. v. National Broadcasting Co., 1 Cir. 1936, 81 F.2d 373, cert. denied 298 U.S. 670; Southwestern Broadcasting Co. v. Oil Center Broadcasting Co., Tex.Civ.App. 1947, 210 S.W.2d 230, ref. n. r. e.; See Nizer, Proprietary Interest in Radio Programs: Recent Developments, 1938, 38 Col.L.Rev. 538; Solinger, Unauthorized Uses of Television Broadcasts, 1948, 48 Col.L.Rev. 848; Notes, 1938, 48 Yale L.J. 288; 1954, 29 Notre Dame L. 456.

50. Waring v. WDAS Broadcasting Station, 1937, 327 Pa. 433, 194 A. 631; Waring v. Dunlea, E.D.N.C. 1939, 26 F.Supp. 338. But cf. RCA Mfg. Co. v. Whiteman, 2 Cir. 1940, 114 F.2d 86.

51. Sears, Roebuck & Co. v. Stiffel Co., 1964, 376 U. S. 225, rehearing denied 376 U.S. 973; Compco

in which the Supreme Court of the United States held that a state court could not impose liability for unfair competition for the copying of the design of an article which was not protected by either a federal patent or by copyright.

Imitation of the physical appearance of the product sold has offered some difficulty. In general, in the absence of some showing of misrepresentation, passing off or confusion,[52] the conclusion has been that there can be no exclusive right to physical appearance, and there is no liability for duplicating it.[53] This is always held where the features in question are "functional," defined as affecting the purpose, action or performance of the goods, or the facility or economy of processing, handling or using them.[54] Nonfunctional features likewise may be duplicated without liability,[55] unless they are found to

have acquired a "secondary" association with the plaintiff,[56] analogous to the "secondary meaning" which attaches to trade marks—which means that it has been used in a manner and to an extent such that it has come in fact to identify the goods or services of the plaintiff in the public eye, and to distinguish them from others.

The earlier decisions displayed a rather surprising reluctance to afford any protection to a competitor against the defendant's misrepresentation, in the form of misdescription, misbranding, or false advertising of his goods, where there was no disparagement of the plaintiff's product, and no passing off or other confusion of source.[57] This was held to be a fraud only upon the public, for which the competitor had no redress at common law, notwithstanding the damage which his own business, or even an entire industry, might suffer as a result of it. It was only where the plaintiff could show, by virtue of some exclusive position or other reason, that any diversion of customers by such misrepresentation must necessarily have damaged him,[58] that his action was permitted. The

Corp. v. Day-Brite Lighting, Inc., 1963, 376 U.S. 234, rehearing denied 377 U.S. 913. See Notes, 1968, 2 U.S.F.L.Rev. 292; 1967, 53 Va.L.Rev. 356; 1965, 40 N.Y.U.L.Rev. 101.

52. Diebold, Inc. v. Record Files, N.D.Ohio 1955, 135 F.Supp. 74, aff'd, 237 F.2d 527; Smith, Kline & French Laboratories v. Waldman, 3 Cir. 1946, 157 F.2d 725, cert. denied 329 U.S. 796, rehearing denied 329 U.S. 834; Neely v. Boland Mfg. Co., 8 Cir. 1960, 274 F.2d 195.

53. Kramer Jewelry Creations v. Capri Jewelry, Inc., S.D.N.Y.1956, 143 F.Supp. 120; Jessar Mfg. Corp. v. Berlin, 1955, 380 Pa. 453, 110 A.2d 396; Squeezit Corp. v. Plastic Dispensers, 1954, 31 N.J.Super. 217, 106 A.2d 322; Winston & Newell Co. v. Piggly Wiggly Northwest, Inc., 1946, 221 Minn. 287, 22 N. W.2d 11; Weeks v. Variety Nut & Date Co., 6 Cir. 1953, 208 F.2d 414.

See Diamond, Product Imitation, 1964, 13 Cleve. Marsh.L.Rev. 280.

54. Restatement of Torts, § 742; West Point Mfg. Co. v. Detroit Stamping Co., 6 Cir. 1955, 222 F.2d 581, cert. denied 350 U.S. 840; Rader v. Derby, 1950, 120 Ind.App. 202, 89 N.E.2d 724; Johnson Gas Appliance Co. v. Reliable Gas Products Co., 1943, 233 Iowa 641, 10 N.W.2d 23; Pagliero v. Wallace China Co., 9 Cir. 1952, 198 F.2d 339; Sylvania Elec. Products Co. v. Dura Elec. Lamp Co., D.N.J.1956, 144 F.Supp. 112, affirmed 3 Cir. 1957, 247 F.2d 730.

55. Hawley Products Co. v. United States Trunk Co., 1 Cir. 1958, 259 F.2d 69; American-Marietta Co. v. Krigsman, 2 Cir. 1960, 275 F.2d 287; American Fork & Hoe Co. v. Stampit Corp., 6 Cir. 1942, 125

F.2d 472; Huston v. Buckeye Bait Corp., S.D.Ohio 1955, 145 F.Supp. 600, affirmed, 6 Cir. 1956, 237 F. 2d 920; Charles D. Briddell, Inc. v. Alglobe Trading Corp., 2 Cir. 1952, 194 F.2d 416.

56. Car-Freshner Corp. v. Marlenn Products Co., D. Md.1960, 183 F.Supp. 20; Mastercrafters Clock & Radio Co. v. Vacheron Constantin-LeCoultre Watches, Inc., 2 Cir. 1955, 221 F.2d 464, cert. denied 350 U.S. 832, rehearing denied 350 U.S. 897. See also the cases cited in the preceding note.

57. American Washboard Co. v. Saginaw Mfg. Co., 6 Cir. 1900, 103 F. 281; Borden's Condensed Milk Co. v. Horlick's Malted Milk Co., E.D.Wis.1913, 206 F. 949; California Apparel Creators v. Wieder of California, 2 Cir. 1947, 162 F.2d 893; Hall v. Duart Sales Co., N.D.Ill.1939, 28 F.Supp. 838. See Handler, False and Misleading Advertising, 1929, 39 Yale L.J. 22; Callmann, False Advertising as a Competitive Tort, 1948, 48 Col.L.Rev. 876; Note, 1951, 64 Harv.L.Rev. 1383.

58. Ely-Norris Safe Co. v. Mosler Safe Co., 2 Cir. 1925, 7 F.2d 603, reversed in Mosler Safe Co. v. Ely-Norris Safe Co., 1927, 273 U.S. 132; Motor Improvements, Inc. v. A. C. Spark Plug Co., 6 Cir. 1935, 80 F.2d 385; Grand Rapids Furniture Co. v.

Federal Trade Commission, which had, by statute, jurisdiction over false advertising, was upheld in many attempts to deal with it.[59] All this was changed by a provision of the Federal Trademark Act [60] of 1946, which gave a remedy to "any person who believes that he is or is likely to be damaged by the use of any such false description or representation," or, in the case of a false designation of geographical origin, to "any person doing business in the locality." The effect of this is to create a federal statutory tort,[61] which does not depend upon the existence of any actual market competition between the plaintiff and the defendant,[62] and justifies at least an injunction whenever it is found that the provisions of the statute have been violated.[63]

A distinct basis for restricting the privilege of competition lies in the policy of the common law against monopoly and undue restraint of trade. In this field, the law has been concerned with the preservation of competition rather than the regulation of it. There is a long history of combinations, contracts and practices in restraint of trade discountenanced by the law, which lies outside of the scope of this book. One practice which must be mentioned, however, is the boycott. This immortalizes the name of a pariah English land agent in Ireland whose neighbors would have nothing to do with him.[64]

A boycott is an organized effort to withdraw from business relations with another, or to induce third persons to do the same. It may be primary, where the defendant himself refuses to deal with the other; or secondary, where he seeks to compel third persons not to do so, by refusing to have dealings with them if they do; or even tertiary, when he refuses to deal with a fourth party if he deals with the third.[65] All of these may

---

Grand Rapids Furniture Co., 7 Cir. 1942, 127 F.2d 245.

59. Federal Trade Commission v. Winsted Hosiery Co., 1922, 258 U.S. 483; Royal Baking Powder Co. v. Federal Trade Commission, 2 Cir. 1922, 281 F. 744; Federal Trade Commission v. Kay, 7 Cir. 1929, 35 F.2d 160; Guarantee Veterinary Co. v. Federal Trade Commission, 2 Cir. 1922, 285 F. 853. See Handler, The Jurisdiction of the Federal Trade Commission over False Advertising, 1931, 31 Col.L. Rev. 527.

60. Now 15 U.S.C. 1125(a).

61. See S. C. Johnson & Son v. Gold Seal Co., D.D. C.1955, 97 U.S.App.D.C. 282, 230 F.2d 832; L'Aiglon Apparel, Inc. v. Lana Lobell, Inc., 3 Cir. 1954, 214 F.2d 649.

62. Maternally Yours v. Your Maternity Shop, 2 Cir. 1956, 234 F.2d 538; Blue Bell Co. v. Frontier Refining Co., 10 Cir. 1954, 213 F.2d 354; Dad's Root Beer Co. v. Doc's Beverages, Inc., 2 Cir. 1951, 193 F.2d 77.

63. Gold Seal Co. v. Weeks, D.D.C.1955, 129 F.Supp. 928, affirmed 1955, 230 F.2d 832, cert. denied 352 U.S. 829; Parkway Baking Co. v. Freihofer Baking Co., 3 Cir. 1960, 255 F.2d 641; American Rolex Watch Corp. v. Jack Laufer & Jan Voort, Inc., E. D.N.Y.1959, 176 F.Supp. 858; Norwich Pharmacal Co. v. Hoffman-La Roche, Inc., D.N.J.1960, 180 F. Supp. 222; Federal-Mogul-Bower Bearings, Inc. v. Azoff, N.D.Ohio 1962, 201 F.Supp. 788. See Note, 1962, 9 U.C.L.A.L.Rev. 719.

64. "Captain Boycott, an Englishman, who was agent of Lord Earne and a farmer of Lough Mask, served notices upon the lord's tenants, and they in turn, with the surrounding population, resolved to have nothing to do with him, and, as far as they could prevent it, not to allow anyone else to have. His life appeared to be in danger, and he had to claim police protection. His servants fled from him, and the awful sentence of excommunication could hardly have rendered him more helplessly alone for a time. No one would work for him, and no one would supply him with food. He and his wife were compelled to work in their own fields with the shadows of armed constabulary ever at their heels; Justin MacCarthy's England under Gladstone." Bouvier's Law Dictionary, summarizing statement in State v. Glidden, 1887, 55 Conn. 46, 8 A. 890. See also Wyman, The Law as to the Boycott, 1903, 15 Green Bag 208.

65. See the elaborate analysis in Kales, Coercive and Competitive Methods in Trade and Labor Disputes, 1922, 8 Corn.L.Q. 1, 128. Also Kovarsky, A Social and Legal Analysis of the Secondary Boycott, 1956, 35 Or.L.Rev. 71, 223; Lesnick, The Gravamen of the Secondary Boycott, 1962, 62 Col.L.Rev. 1363; Notes, 1953, 28 Ind.L.J. 467; 1961, 12 West.Res.L. Rev. 759; 1942, 10 Geo.Wash.L.Rev. 302; 1941, 41 Col.L.Rev. 941.

Tertiary boycotts generally have been held to be illegal. See Carlson v. Carpenter Contractors' Ass'n, 1922, 305 Ill. 331, 137 N.E. 222; Burnham v. Dowd, 1914, 217 Mass. 351, 104 N.E. 841; New England

involve the persuasion or coercion of still other persons to join in the boycott.

Competition in business always has been held to be a sufficient justification for a primary boycott on the part of a single defendant,[66] and likewise for a secondary boycott whose object is the immediate appropriation of the trade or patronage diverted from the other—[67] and this notwithstanding the elements of coercion which usually are present. The individual is regarded as free to acquire business by dealing or refusing to deal with anyone he likes.[68]

When several defendants combine in a boycott, however, a different picture is presented. Unless he has monopolistic power,[69] the individual is limited in the damage he can do by his own capacity for economic pressure or persuasion. A combination has far greater potentialities of coercion,[70] not only of others,

but also of its own more reluctant members; and it may so far restrict and control the trade of an entire industry as to ruin the plaintiff or drive him out of business. It undoubtedly is true that in the absence of statute combinations to refuse to deal are not in themselves and without more unlawful,[71] particularly where their purpose is merely to protect their members against evils which threaten their own business.[72] But in many cases the combination has been found to be intended to insure its members a monopoly of the business in their particular line, and the boycott, primary or secondary, has been enjoined as an illegal restraint of trade.[73] While it is probably impossible to harmonize all of the decisions, the courts seem to have looked at the aggressive purpose of obtaining monopolistic control, as distinguished from the more or less defensive one of preserving an existing state of competition. There has been extensive statutory regulation of combinations in restraint of trade, by

Cement Gun Co. v. McGivern, 1914, 218 Mass. 198, 105 N.E. 885. It will be noted that every tertiary boycott includes a secondary boycott of the third party, which is not justified if the third party is not a competitor. Lehigh Structural Steel Co. v. Atlantic Smelting & Refining Works, 1920, 92 N.J. Eq. 131, 111 A. 376.

66. Great A. & P. Tea Co. v. Cream of Wheat Co., 2 Cir. 1915, 227 F. 46; Barish v. Chrysler Corp., 1942, 141 Neb. 157, 3 N.W.2d 91; Guthrie v. Great American Ins. Co., 4 Cir. 1945, 151 F.2d 738; Green v. Victor Talking Mach. Co., 2 Cir. 1928, 24 F.2d 378; and see cases cited supra, p. 955. See Brown, The Right to Refuse to Sell, 1916, 25 Yale L.J. 194; Note, 1951, 45 Ill.L.Rev. 784.

67. Photographic Importing & Distributing Co. v. Elgeet Optical Co., 1953, 282 App.Div. 223, 122 N.Y.S. 2d 215, appeal denied, 1953, 282 App.Div. 836, 124 N.Y.S.2d 341; Staroske v. Pulitzer Pub. Co., 1911, 235 Mo. 67, 138 S.W. 36; Journal of Commerce Pub. Co. v. Tribune Co., 7 Cir. 1922, 286 F. 111; Andrew Jergens Co. v. Woodbury, Inc., D.Del.1920, 271 F. 43; Dye v. Carmichael Produce Co., 1917, 64 Ind.App. 653, 116 N.E. 425.

See Notes, 1965, 52 Geo.L.J. 392, 406; 1965, 19 Sw.L. J. 567.

68. But compare the cases of spiteful motive or remote advantage, supra, p. 955.

69. Cf. Eastman Kodak Co. of New York v. Southern Photo Materials Co., 1927, 273 U.S. 359.

70. There is a good statement of this in Boutwell v. Marr, 1899, 71 Vt. 1, 42 A. 607.

71. Bohn Mfg. Co. v. Hollis, 1893, 54 Minn. 223, 55 N.W. 1119; Macauley v. Tierney, 1895, 19 R.I. 255, 33 A. 1; John D. Park & Sons v. National Wholesale Druggists' Ass'n, 1903, 175 N.Y. 1, 67 N.E. 136; Montgomery Ward & Co. v. South Dakota Retail Merchants' & Hardware Dealers' Ass'n, C.C.S.D. 1907, 150 F. 413; Rosenau v. Empire Circuit Co., 1909, 131 App.Div. 429, 115 N.Y.S. 511, motion to amend decision denied 132 App.Div. 947, 117 N.Y.S. 1146.

72. Sorrell v. Smith [1925] A.C. 700; Wolfenstein v. Fashion Originators' Guild of America, 1935, 244 App.Div. 656, 280 N.Y.S. 361; Wm. Filene's Sons Co. v. Fashion Originators' Guild of America, 1 Cir. 1937, 90 F.2d 556; Arnold v. Burgess, 1934, 241 App.Div. 364, 272 N.Y.S. 534; Edelstein v. Gillmore, 2 Cir. 1929, 35 F.2d 723; Contra, Millinery Creators' Guild v. Federal Trade Commission, 2 Cir. 1940, 109 F.2d 175; and cf. Fashion Originators' Guild of America v. Federal Trade Commission, 2 Cir. 1940, 114 F.2d 80.

73. Jackson v. Stanfield, 1894, 137 Ind. 592, 36 N.E. 345, rehearing denied 137 Ind. 592, 37 N.E. 14; Grillo v. Board of Realtors of Plainfield Area, 1966, 91 N.J.Super. 202, 219 A.2d 635; Brown v. Jacobs' Pharmacy Co., 1902, 115 Ga. 429, 41 S.E. 553; Klingel's Pharmacy v. Sharp & Dohme, 1906, 104 Md. 218, 64 A. 1029; Martell v. White, 1904, 185 Mass. 255, 69 N.E. 1085. See Note, 1950, 45 Ill.L.Rev. 784.

the Sherman Anti-Trust Act [74] and state acts modeled upon it,[75] as well as other legislation, to which reference must be made in a particular case.

Labor Unions

Violent controversies have raged about the question of the privilege of labor unions to interfere with the interests of employers and others, and it is still a subject of bitter dispute, with the law in a state of confusion, conflict and change. The early attitude of the courts toward the unions was that they were outlaw organizations, and their activities were criminal conspiracies to disrupt the social order.[76] This point of view has long since given way to a recognition that they are legitimate and socially desirable, and they are now protected and favored by much legislation, and to a considerable extent by the courts themselves.

As to interference with existing contracts, the activities of the unions were quite strictly curtailed by the common law. The courts tended to find an analogy to the cases of business competition, and to consider that labor was competing with the employer for a larger share of the common fund of wealth produced, and so must be limited in the pursuit of its own interests to the same extent as any other competitor.[77] Whenever there was a definite contract for a term, there was almost no recognition of any privilege of the union to interfere with its performance.[78]

Where, however, the contractual relation might be terminated at will, as in the case of the ordinary individual employment, the interests of labor prevailed to a much greater extent under the common law. As has been mentioned above,[79] such relations differ from contracts for a term in that the parties are themselves free to withdraw at any time without being charged with any wrongful act, and so are only induced to do what they may legitimately do. Such relations occupy an intermediate position between definite contracts for a term and mere expectancies of future benefits, and perhaps should be placed in a category of their own. Against them, any workman, or any group, were held to be free to withdraw from employment at any time, for any reason or for none; and the right to strike, which is merely that of concerted refusal to serve the employer, was not denied in any jurisdiction.[80] Union officials who called the strike were recognized as the chosen representatives of the workmen for the purpose of protecting any legiti-

74. As to boycotts under the Anti-Trust Act, see Eastern States Retail Lumber Dealers' Ass'n v. United States, 1914, 234 U.S. 600; Binderup v. Pathe Exchange, 1923, 263 U.S. 291; Paramount Famous Lasky Corp. v. United States, 1930, 282 U.S. 30; Fashion Originators' Guild v. Federal Trade Commission, 1941, 312 U.S. 457. See Rahl, Conspiracy and the Antitrust Laws, 1950, 44 Ill.L.Rev. 743; Barber, Refusals to Deal under the Federal Antitrust Laws, 1955, 103 U.Pa.L.Rev. 847.

75. Cf. Retail Lumber Dealers' Ass'n v. State, 1910, 95 Miss. 337, 48 So. 1021, affirmed in Grenada Lumber Co. v. Mississippi, 1910, 217 U.S. 433.

76. See Holdsworth, Industrial Combinations and the Law in the Eighteenth Century, 1936, 20 Minn.L. Rev. 367; Wigmore, Interference with Social Relations, 1887, 21 Am.L.Rev. 764; Morris, History of Labor and Conspiracy, 1937, 52 Pol.Sci.Q. 51; Sayre, Criminal Conspiracy, 1922, 35 Harv.L.Rev. 393; Nelles, The First American Labor Case, 1931, 41 Yale L.J. 165; Burdick, Conspiracy as a Crime and as a Tort, 1907, 7 Col.L.Rev. 229; Burdick, The Tort of Conspiracy, 1908, 8 Col.L.Rev. 117.

77. See Kales, Coercive and Competitive Methods in Trade and Labor Disputes, 1922, 8 Corn.L.Q. 1, 128; Smith, Crucial Issues in Labor Litigation, 1907, 20 Harv.L.Rev. 253, 345, 429; Sayre, Labor and the Courts, 1930, 39 Yale L.J. 682; Eskin, The Legality of "Peaceful Coercion" in Labor Disputes, 1937, 85 U.Pa.L.Rev. 456; Warm, A Study of the Judicial Attitude Toward Trade Unions and Labor Legislation, 1939, 23 Minn.L.Rev. 255; Notes, 1938, 32 Ill. L.Rev. 611, 625; 1924, 34 Harv.L.Rev. 880.

78. See supra, p. 947.

79. See supra, p. 933.

80. See National Protective Ass'n of Steam Fitters & Helpers v. Cumming, 1902, 170 N.Y. 315, 63 N.E. 369; Kemp v. Division No. 241, 1912, 255 Ill. 213, 99 N.E. 389; C. B. Rutan Co. v. Local Union No. 4, Hatters' Union of America, 1925, 97 N.J.Eq. 77, 128 A. 622.

mate interests of the employees.[81] On the other hand the courts found a sufficient element of third-party interference, and persuasion of doubtful workmen, to require some acceptable purpose for their action. The union would be liable if, for example, its object was found to be purely a spiteful one, designed to do harm for its own sake to the employer,[82] or to a particular employee.[83]

In general, it may be said that any objective which tended directly and immediately to benefit the workmen in their employment, such as better wages,[84] shorter hours,[85] or better working conditions,[86] was held to be a legitimate end for a strike. The same was true where the benefit was somewhat more indirect, as in the case of an attempt to compel the employer to bargain collectively with the union,[87] or to prevent him from discriminating against union workmen.[88] The majority of the state courts upheld the efforts of the union to secure a closed shop,[89] even where it involved the discharge of non-union workers and there was no showing that they were not unfairly excluded from the union.[90] A large minority rejected any such privilege,[91] regarding the advantage to the employees in strengthening their organization as too remote an objective, and as concentrating a dangerous power of monopoly of both available work and available labor in the hands of those controlling it. Legislation in a few states, which was held to be constitutional,[92] outlawed the closed shop.

When a strike was privileged, it was held to be privileged only to the extent that the methods adopted were in themselves legal and permissible. A strike for an entirely proper purpose would not authorize a resort

81. See Eskin, The Legality of "Peaceful Coercion" in Labor Disputes, 1937, 85 U.Pa.L.Rev. 456, 459; Lawless v. Brotherhood of Painters, 1956, 143 Cal. App.2d 474, 300 P.2d 159.

82. Walker v. Cronin, 1871, 107 Mass. 555; Thacker Coal & Coke Co. v. Burke, 1906, 59 W.Va. 253, 53 S.E. 161; Haskins v. Royster, 1874, 70 N.C. 601.

83. De Minico v. Craig, 1911, 207 Mass. 593, 94 N.E. 317; Order of Railway Conductors v. Jones, 1925, 78 Colo. 80, 239 P. 882; Kinane v. Fay, 1933, 111 N.J.L. 553, 168 A. 724; Bausbach v. Reiff, 1914, 244 Pa. 559, 91 A. 224. Cf. Barile v. Fisher, 1949, 197 Misc. 493, 94 N.Y.S.2d 346 (retaliation for resignation from union).

84. Pierce v. Stablemen's Union Local No. 8760, 1909, 156 Cal. 70, 103 P. 324; Perfect Laundry Co. v. Marsh, 1936, 120 N.J.Eq. 508, 186 A. 470; American Steel Foundries v. Tri-City Central Trades Council, 1921, 257 U.S. 184.

85. Kemp v. Division No. 241, 1912, 255 Ill. 213, 99 N.E. 389; Everett Waddey Co. v. Richmond Typographical Union No. 90, 1906, 105 Va. 188, 53 S.E. 273; P. Reardon, Inc. v. Caton, 1919, 189 App.Div. 501, 178 N.Y.S. 713, and 189 App.Div. 515, 178 N.Y. S. 722.

86. Minasian v. Osborne, 1911, 210 Mass. 250, 96 N.E. 1036.

87. International Pocketbook Workers' Union v. Orlove, 1930, 158 Md. 496, 148 A. 826; El Paso Electric Co. v. Elliot, D.Tex.1936, 15 F.Supp. 81; Bayonne Textile Corp. v. Amalgamated Federation of Silk Workers, 1933, 114 N.J.Eq. 307, 168 A. 799.

88. George J. Grant Const. Co. v. St. Paul Building Trades Council, 1917, 136 Minn. 167, 161 N.W. 520; Gill Engraving Co. v. Doerr, D.N.Y.1914, 214 F. 111; United Chain Theatres v. Philadelphia Moving Picture Mach. Operators' Union, Local No. 307, D. Pa.1931, 50 F.2d 189; Restful Slipper Co. v. United Shoe & Leather Union, 1934, 116 N.J.Eq. 521, 174 A. 543.

89. Cohn & Roth Elec. Co. v. Bricklayers' M. & P. Local Union No. 1, 1917, 92 Conn. 161, 101 A. 659; Fenske Bros. v. Upholsterers' Int. Union of North America, 1934, 358 Ill. 239, 193 Ill. 112; Wise Shoe Co. v. Lowenthal, 1935, 266 N.Y. 264, 194 N.E. 749; Scofes v. Helmar, 1933, 205 Ind. 596, 187 N.E. 662; Williams v. Quill, 1948, 277 N.Y. 1, 12 N.E.2d 547. See 1 Teller, Labor Disputes and Collective Bargaining, 1940, §§ 97–100.

90. Kemp v. Division No. 241, 1912, 255 Ill. 213, 99 N.E. 389; National Protective Ass'n of Steam Fitters & Helpers v. Cumming, 1902, 170 N.Y. 315, 63 N.E. 369; Roddy v. United Mine Workers, 1914, 41 Okl. 621, 139 P. 126.

91. Colonial Press v. Ellis, 1947, 321 Mass. 495, 74 N.E.2d 1; White Mountain Freezer Co. v. Murphy, 1917, 78 N.H. 398, 101 A. 357; Bausbach v. Reiff, 1914, 244 Pa. 559, 91 A. 224; Starr v. Laundry & D. C. Workers Local Union, 1936, 155 Or. 634, 63 P.2d 1104. As to legislation outlawing the closed shop, see Note, 1949, 23 So.Cal.L.Rev. 57.

92. Lincoln Federal Union No. 19129 v. Northwestern Iron & Metal Co., 1949, 335 U.S. 525.

to violence,[93] or to threats of it which intimidate the employer, his customers or other workmen,[94] or deliberate falsehood or defamation,[95] or an obstruction of the public highway [96] or the means of access to the employer's premises.[97] Some activities even on the premises were also discountenanced, such as the "sit-down" strike in which the workers took over the place of business,[98] or mutiny at sea,[99] or refusal to work overtime.[1]

With respect to prospective economic advantage, the common law accorded the interests of labor considerably less in the way of privilege than the business competitor. This was in part a survival of the old hostility toward organized labor and all its works, and in part because the activities of the unions necessarily involved the element of combination, which always has been regarded with some degree of disfavor and suspicion. While the older law under which the unions were treated as criminal conspiracies in themselves was everywhere dead, cases were not lacking in which union efforts were held to be attempts to obtain a monopoly of the labor market, and hence to amount to an illegal restraint of trade, either at common law or under the anti-trust acts.[2]

A strike is one form of primary boycott. No one disputed that a strike called for a proper purpose was privileged even though it interfered with the employer's prospective business; or that the strikers could carry the boycott to the extent of refusing as a group to buy the employer's product, or to deal with him in any other way.[3] It was when the effort was made to involve other more or less neutral parties in the dispute, by inducing or compelling them not to deal with the employer, that the question became one of unprivileged interference or coercion, or a secondary boycott. For the most part the cases were concerned with picketing and similar forms of persuasion. There was, however, a considerable body of law dealing with the use of means illegal in themselves, such as violence, intimidation, defamation, or obstruction of access to premises,[4] all of which were of course not privileged. Where such means were resorted to, it frequently was held that an injunction would issue against all picketing, on the ground that it had been

---

93. Milk Wagon Drivers Union of Chicago, Local 753, v. Meadowmoor Dairies, 1941, 312 U.S. 287; Minnesota Stove Co. v. Cavanaugh, 1915, 131 Minn. 458, 155 N.W. 638; Maywood Farms Co. v. Milk Wagon Drivers' Union of Chicago, 1942, 316 Ill.App. 47, 43 N.E.2d 700.

94. Vegelahn v. Guntner, 1896, 167 Mass. 92, 44 N.E. 1077; Busch Jewelry Co. v. United Retail Employees Union, 1939, 281 N.Y. 150, 22 N.E.2d 320; Yale Knitting Mills v. Knitgood Workers Union, 1939, 334 Pa. 23, 5 A.2d 323.

95. Gomez v. United Office & Professional Workers, D.D.C.1947, 73 F.Supp. 679; Olympia Operating Co. v. Costello, 1931, 278 Mass. 125, 179 N.E. 804; Weist v. Dirks, 1939, 215 Ind. 568, 20 N.E.2d 969. Compare, as to inducing the discharge of an individual employee, Dukes v. Brotherhood of Painters, D. & P. of America, Local Union No. 437, 1950, 191 Tenn. 495, 235 S.W.2d 7; Strollo v. Jersey Central P. & L. Co., 1942, 20 N.J.Misc. 217, 6 A.2d 559.

96. Hanson v. Hall, 1938, 202 Minn. 381, 279 N.W. 227.

97. Mackall v. Ratchford, C.C.W.Va.1897, 82 F. 41; American Steel & Wire Co. v. Wire Drawers' & Die Makers' Unions, Nos. One and Three, C.C.Ohio 1898, 90 F. 608; In re Heffron, 1913, 179 Mo.App. 639, 162 S.W. 652; Bomes v. Providence Local No. 223 of Motion Picture Machine Operators of U. S. and Canada, 1931, 51 R.I. 499, 155 A. 581.

98. National Labor Relations Board v. Fansteel Metallurgical Corp., 1939, 306 U.S. 240.

99. Southern S. S. Corp. v. National Labor Relations Board, 1942, 316 U.S. 31.

1. C. G. Conn, Ltd. v. National Labor Relations Board, 7 Cir. 1939, 108 F.2d 390.

2. Loewe v. Lawlor, 1908, 208 U.S. 274; Duplex Printing Press Co. v. Deering, 1921, 254 U.S. 443; Coronado Coal Co. v. United Mine Workers of America, 1925, 268 U.S. 295.

3. Pierce v. Stablemen's Union, Local No. 8760, 1909, 156 Cal. 70, 103 P. 324; Mills v. United States Printing Co., 1904, 99 App.Div. 605, 91 N.Y.S. 185, affirmed, 1910, 199 N.Y. 76, 92 N.E. 214; Foster v. Retail Clerks' International Protective Ass'n, 1902, 39 Misc. 48, 78 N.Y.S. 860.

4. See supra, 963; also Cooper, The Fiction of Peaceful Picketing, 1936, 35 Mich.L.Rev. 73.

shown that it could not be conducted properly.[5] There were courts which went even further, and held that any picketing was itself an unlawful method of conducting a labor dispute,[6] because of its supposed inevitable effect in intimidating neutral third parties. This, at least, is no longer the law anywhere.

Prior to 1940 most of the state courts had arrived at the conclusion that "peaceful" picketing was merely a legitimate method of appealing for public support, and that it was only when its objectives were not privileged that it became unlawful.[7] In 1940 the Supreme Court of the United States held that such picketing was an exercise of the right of free speech, protected by the Constitution against blanket state legislation outlawing it,[8] and the injunctions of state courts.[9]

These decisions, which were hailed by organized labor as a triumph, were limited by a number of subsequent cases,[10] to picketing in a lawful manner, and for lawful objectives. Thus it was held that the Constitution did not prevent an injunction against all picketing where there had been a continued course of violence,[11] or against mass picketing involving the element of intimidation.[12] Likewise there was no constitutional prohibition against the injunction where the purpose of the union was found to be a violation of state anti-trust laws,[13] or of a statute outlawing

5. Busch Jewelry Co. v. United Retail Employees Union, 1939, 281 N.Y. 150, 22 N.E.2d 320; Riggs v. Tucker, 1938, 196 Ark. 571, 119 S.W.2d 507; Levy & Devaney v. International Pocketbook Workers Union, 1932, 114 Conn. 319, 158 A. 795; Bomes v. Providence Local No. 223 of Motion Picture Mach. Operators, 1931, 51 R.I. 499, 155 A. 581.

In Milk Wagon Drivers Union of Chicago, Local 753 v. Meadowmoor Dairies, 1941, 312 U.S. 287, the injunction was held not to be unconstitutional as a denial of the right of freedom of speech.

6. Ellis v. Journeyman Barbers' Int. Union of America, 1922, 194 Iowa 1179, 191 N.W. 111; Local Union No. 313 v. Stathakis, 1918, 135 Ark. 86, 205 S.W. 450. See also American Steel Foundaries v. Tri-City Central Trades Council, 1921, 257 U.S. 184, drawing a metaphysical distinction between "pickets" and "missionaries."

7. Steffes v. Motion Picture Mach. Operators Union, 1917, 136 Minn. 200, 161 N.W. 524; Empire Theatre Co. v. Cloke, 1917, 53 Mont. 183, 163 P. 107; La France Elec. Const. & Supply Co. v. International Brotherhood of Elec. Workers, 1923, 108 Ohio St. 61, 140 N.E. 899; Exchange Bakery & Restaurant v. Rifkin, 1927, 245 N.Y. 260, 651, 157 N.E. 130, reargument denied 245 N.Y. 651, 157 N.E. 895. See Tanenhaus, Picketing as a Tort: The Development of the Law of Picketing from 1880 to 1940, 1953, 14 U.Pitt.L.Rev. 170.

8. Thornhill v. Alabama, 1940, 310 U.S. 88; Carlson v. California, 1940, 310 U.S. 106.

9. American Federation of Labor v. Swing, 1941, 312 U.S. 321.

10. See Gregory, Peaceful Picketing and Freedom of Speech, 1940, 26 A.B.A.J. 709; Larson, May Peaceful Picketing Be Enjoined, 1944, 22 Tex.L.Rev. 392; Armstrong, Where Are We Going with Picketing, 1948, 36 Cal.L.Rev. 1; Teller, The Taft-Hartley Act and Government by Injunction, 1949, 1 Labor L.J. 40; Fraenkel, Peaceful Picketing—Constitutionally Protected, 1950, 99 U.Pa.L.Rev. 1; Frantz, Peaceful Picketing, Unlawful Objective, 1950, 28 N.C.L.Rev. 291; Cox, Strikes, Picketing and the Constitution, 1951, 4 Vand.L.Rev. 574; Williams, Picketing and Free Speech—A Texas Primer, 1951, 30 Tex.L.Rev. 206; Weinberg, Thornhill to Hanke—The Picketing Puzzle, 1951, 20 U.Cin.L.Rev. 437; Daykin, Legalized Concerted Activities Under the Taft-Hartley Act, 1952, 3 Labor L.J. 167; Tanenhaus, Picketing as Free Speech; Early Stages in the Growth of the New Law of Picketing, 1953, 14 U.Pitt.L.Rev. 397; Tanenhaus, Picketing—Free Speech: The Growth of the New Law of Picketing from 1940 to 1952, 1953, 38 Corn.L.Q. 1; Price, Picketing—A Legal Cinderella, 1954, 7 U.Fla.L.Rev. 143; Jones, The Right to Picket—Twilight Zone of the Constitution, 1954, 102 U.Pa.L.Rev. 995; Notes, 1946, 59 Harv.L. Rev. 1123; 1948, 34 Corn.L.Q. 81; 1949, 16 U.Chi. L.Rev. 701; 1950, 98 U.Pa.L.Rev. 545.

11. Milk Wagon Drivers Union of Chicago, Local 753, v. Meadowmoor Dairies, 1941, 312 U.S. 287.

12. Allen-Bradley Local No. 1111, United Elec. R. & M. Workers of America v. Wisconsin Employment Relations Board, 1941, 315 U.S. 740. Cf. Westinghouse Elec. Corp. v. United Elec. R. & M. Workers of American Local No. 410, 1946, 139 N.J.Eq. 97, 49 A.2d 896; Carnegie-Illinois Steel Co. v. United Steelworkers of America, 1946, 353 Pa. 420, 45 A.2d 857. See Kletzing, Mass Picketing and Free Speech, 1949, 22 Rocky Mt.L.Rev. 28.

13. Gibboney v. Empire Storage & Ice Co., 1949, 336 U.S. 490. Cf. Saveall v. Demers, 1947, 322 Mass. 70, 76 N.E.2d 12.

the closed shop,[14] or where it was seeking to establish a racial basis for hiring,[15] or to compel a business without employees to conform to a union scale of rates,[16] or where one place of business was picketed to compel employment of union men in another unrelated business.[17] Where the purpose was to compel employees to join the union, the usual state holding was that "organizational" picketing was legitimate,[18] but that the addition of the element of compulsion of the employer to require union membership might be enough to make it a tort.[19]

The secondary boycott, by which the union attempts to put pressure upon third parties by refusing to deal with them and inducing the public not to do so, in order to compel them not to deal with the employer, has always met with little favor in the labor cases.[20] Although the strikers have a legiti-

mate interest to protect, the analogy of business competitors [21] has not been carried over, since the union is not seeking to obtain for itself the particular trade diverted from the employer or the third party. Picketing, and other appeals or threats, directed at those who deal with the employer's customers,[22] or his distributors and suppliers,[23] were condemned at common law by most of the courts as efforts to ruin the business of a neutral in order to involve him in the dispute; and this was often carried to extreme and apparently quite unjustifiable lengths in finding an enjoinable "threat" of such a secondary boycott in mere notices to the customers that the employer is "unfair" to labor, or requests not to buy from him.[24]

14. Lincoln Federal Labor Union No. 19129 v. Northwestern Iron & Metal Co., 1949, 335 U.S. 525. See Note, 1949, 23 So.Cal.L.Rev. 57.

15. Hughes v. Superior Court in and for County of Contra Costa, 1949, 339 U.S. 460.

16. International Brotherhood of Teamsters, C. W. & H. Union, Local 309, v. Hanke, 1950, 339 U.S. 470. See Note, 1950, 3 Okl.L.Rev. 228.

17. Carpenters & Joiners Union of America, Local No. 213, v. Ritter's Cafe, 1942, 315 U.S. 722.

18. Painters & Paperhangers Local 1018 v. Rountree Corp., 1952, 194 Pa. 148, 72 S.E.2d 402.

19. Goodwins v. Hagedorn, 1951, 303 N.Y. 300, 101 N.E.2d 697, reargument denied, 1952, 303 N.Y. 673, 102 N.E.2d 833; Blue Boar Cafeteria Co. v. Hotel & R. E. & B. Int. Union, Ky.1953, 254 S.W.2d 335, cert denied Hotel & Restaurant Emp. & B. Int. Union v. Blue Boar Cafeteria Co., 346 U.S. 834; Bitzer Motor Co. v. Local 604, 1953, 349 Ill.App. 283, 110 N.E.2d 674.

Cf. Building Service Employees Int. Union v. Gazzam, 1950, 339 U.S. 532, explained in Pocahontas Term. Corp. v. Portland Bldg. & Const. Co., D.Me.1950, 93 F.Supp. 217 as not involving interstate commerce.

See Lauritzen, The Organizational Picket Line, 1951, 3 Stan.L.Rev. 413; Tobriner, The Organizational Picket Line, 1951, 3 Stan.L.Rev. 423; Note, 1953, 51 Mich.L.Rev. 1217.

20. Hellerstein, Secondary Boycotts in Labor Disputes, 1938, 47 Yale L.J. 341; Feinberg, Analysis of the New York Law of Secondary Boycott, 1936, 6

Brook.L.Rev. 209; Smith, Coercion of Third Parties in Labor Disputes—the Secondary Boycott, 1939, 1 La.L.Rev. 277; Barnard and Graham, Labor and the Secondary Boycott, 1940, 15 Wash.L.Rev. 137; Kovarsky, A Social and Legal Analysis of the Secondary Boycott, 1956, 35 Ore.L.Rev. 71, 223; Lesnick, The Gravamen of the Secondary Boycott, 1962, 62 Col.L.Rev. 1363; Notes, 1947, 15 Geo. Wash.L.Rev. 327; 1953, 62 Yale L.J. 1111; 1953, 28 Ind.L.J. 467; 1961, 12 West.Res.L.Rev. 759; 1942, 10 Geo.Wash.L.Rev. 302; 1941, 41 Col.L.Rev. 941.

21. Supra, p. 954.

22. Beck v. Railway Teamsters' Protective Union, 1898, 118 Mich. 497, 77 N.W. 13; Barr v. Essex Trades Council, 1894, 53 N.J.Eq. 101, 30 A. 881; Gray v. Building Trades Council, 1903, 91 Minn. 171, 97 N.W. 663, followed Trevor v. Building Trades Council, 91 Minn. 171, 97 N.W. 1118; Auburn Draying Co. v. Wardell, 1919, 227 N.Y. 1, 124 N.E. 97.

23. Fink & Son v. Butchers Union No. 422, 1915, 84 N.J.Eq. 638, 95 A. 182; H. H. Meyer Packing Co. v. Butchers' Union Local No. 232, 1916, 18 Ohio N.P., N.S., 457.

24. Cf. Loewe v. Lawlor, 1908, 208 U.S. 274; American Federation of Labor v. Buck's Stove & Range Co., 1911, 33 App.D.C. 83, appeal dismissed Buck's Stove & Range Co. v. American Federation of Labor, 219 U.S. 581; My Maryland Lodge No. 186 of Machinists v. Adt, 1905, 100 Md. 238, 59 A. 721; Seattle Brewing & Malting Co. v. Hansen, C.C.Colo. 1905, 144 F. 1011; Wilson v. Hey, 1918, 232 Ill. 389, 83 N.E. 928. Contra: Gray v. Building Trades Council, 1903, 91 Minn. 171, 97 N.W. 663, followed Trevor v. Building Trades Council, 1904, 91 Minn. 171, 97 N.W. 1118; Iverson v. Dilno, 1911, 44 Mont. 270, 119 P. 719.

A few courts, recognizing that the third party is often associated in interest with the employer, and is his valuable ally in the bargaining contest, attempted to moderate the rule. New York, for example, has recognized a "unity of interest" between the employer and the distributors of his products,[25] which justifies the boycott. The National Labor Relations Board has recognized [26] the doctrine of a "roving situs" under which the union may follow and picket the employer's trucks when they have no fixed place of business within the state, or may picket work done by his employees upon the premises of another.[27] A few other courts from time to time have displayed a more liberal attitude under special circumstances.[28]

This lengthy review of the common law serves only as a prelude to sweeping change by legislation. In addition to numerous state regulations, there are four federal statutes which are of predominant importance in the field of labor law. The first of these was the Norris-La Guardia Anti-Injunction Act [29] of 1932, which restricted the use of injunctions in labor disputes in the federal courts, and served as a model for a number of state "baby anti-injunction acts." The second was the National Labor Relations Act [30] of 1936, commonly known as the Wagner Act, which imposed upon industries whose labor disputes affect the flow of interstate commerce a system of collective bargaining through elected representatives, and set up the National Labor Relations Board to administer the Act. This in turn served as a model for "little Wagner Acts" in a number of states. In 1947 the Wagner Act was amended by the Labor Management Relations Act,[31] popularly known as the Taft-Hartley Act, which imposed a number of limitations upon the permissible activities of the unions. For some twelve years this act left in considerable doubt the question of federal or state jurisdiction to deal with labor-management relations. In 1959 the Supreme Court, in the Second Garmon Case,[32] declared that, subject to two exceptions, Congress had preempted the regulation of labor law, and there was no state jurisdiction to deal with it. This decision created a "no man's land" in which the National Labor Relations Board might decline to exercise its exclusive jurisdiction, and the state courts could do nothing. To remedy this situation Congress adopted in 1959 the fourth statute, commonly known as the Landrum-Griffin Act,[33] which added a

25. Goldfinger v. Feintuch, 1937, 276 N.Y. 281, 11 N. E.2d 910. See Barnard and Graham, Labor and the Secondary Boycott, 1940, 15 Wash.L.Rev. 137; Smith, Coercion of Third Parties in Labor Disputes—The Secondary Boycott, 1939, 1 La.L.Rev. 277.

26. In re Schultz Refrigerated Service, 1949, 87 N.L. R.B. 92; see National Labor Relations Board v. Service Trade Chauffeurs, 2 Cir. 1951, 191 F.2d 65. In In re Brewery & Beverage Drivers' Union, 1953, 107 N.L.R.B. # 104, it was indicated that the doctrine would be limited to such facts.

27. In re Richfield Oil Corp., 1951, 95 N.L.R.B. 1191.

28. Pierce v. Stablemen's Union, Local No. 8760, 1909, 156 Cal. 70, 103 P. 324; Lindsay & Co. v. Montana Federation of Labor, 1908, 37 Mont. 264, 96 P. 127; Truax v. Bisbee Local No. 380, Cooks' & Waiters' Union, 1918, 19 Ariz. 379, 171 P. 121; Marx & Haas Jeans Clothing Co. v. Watson, 1901, 168 Mo. 133, 67 S.W. 391.

See also the attempt of the Restatement of Torts, §§ 799–807, to state a detailed compromise rule, which probably does not find complete acceptance in the law of any jurisdiction.

29. 29 U.S.C.A. §§ 101–115. See Witte, The Federal Anti-Injunction Act, 1932, 16 Minn.L.Rev. 638; Monkemeyer, Five Years of the Norris-La Guardia Act 1937, 2 Mo.L.Rev. 1.

30. 29 U.S.C.A. §§ 151–166.

31. 29 U.S.C.A. §§ 141–188. The history of the legislation is set out in detail in Forkosch, Treatise on Labor Law, 1953, 571–582. See Note, 1951, 64 Harv.L.Rev. 781.

32. San Diego Building Trades Council v. Garmon, 1959, 359 U.S. 236. This decision is commonly called "Garmon II," to distinguish it from the earlier decision in the same case in 1957, 353 U.S. 26, in which the Court held that the state court had no power to enjoin conduct which might be subject to the federal act, even though the National Labor Relations Board had declined to exercise its jurisdiction over the conduct.

33. More formally, The Labor Management Reporting and Disclosure Act of 1959, now 29 U.S.C. § 164(c) (Supp. III, 1962).

section to the National Labor Relations Act, and authorized the state courts to take jurisdiction over any labor dispute over which the Board might decline to exercise its optional jurisdiction.

This last legislation has still left a considerable number of unsettled problems as to state jurisdiction over labor law, which have not yet been fully worked out.[34]

State jurisdiction, in the main, is synonymous with court and common law liability, as distinguished from the administrative law and remedies of the National Labor Relations Board; and the extent of state jurisdiction will determine the extent to which the common law liabilities, reviewed above, may still survive, even as modified by state statutes.

While it is difficult to be precise, it appears at the time of writing that the state courts have jurisdiction to apply their own law in the following limited group of situations:

1. Those involving violence, mass picketing, or other imminent threat to public order,[35] which traditionally are within the police power of the states, "where the regulated conduct touched interests so deeply rooted in local feeling and responsibility that, in the absence of compelling congressional direction, we could not infer that Congress had deprived the States of the power to act." [36]

2. Those in which the activity regulated "was a merely peripheral concern of the Labor Management Relations Act," [37] as in the case of expulsion from a union,[38] or denial of union membership,[39] where the employment relation is not directly involved.[40] In this category are the repossession of trucks and equipment in the hands of strikers,[41] a libel action against a union,[42] the recovery of damages where an injunction was issued erroneously,[43] and according to one court,[44] actions to recover pay from the employer, which he has paid over to the union.

3. Cases involving actions for damages arising out of secondary boycotts, jurisdic-

---

36. Specifically excepted in the Second Garmon Case.

37. Specifically excepted in the Second Garmon Case.

38. International Ass'n of Machinists v. Gonzales, 1958, 356 U.S. 617, rehearing denied 357 U.S. 944; Allen v. Los Angeles County Dist. Council of Carpenters, 1959, 51 Cal.2d 805, 337 P.2d 457, cert. denied 361 U.S. 936; McDermott v. Jamula, 1958, 338 Mass. 236, 154 N.E.2d 595, 359 U.S. 968; Lowery v. International Brotherhood of Boilermakers, 1961, 241 Miss. 458, 130 So.2d 831; Green v. Folks, 1961, 33 Misc.2d 91, 223 N.Y.S.2d 287, order affirmed 16 App.Div.2d 755, 227 N.Y.S.2d 896; United Ass'n of Journeymen and Apprentices v. Borden, 1959, 160 Tex. 203, 328 S.W.2d 739.

39. See Barlow v. Roche, Mun.App.D.C.1960, 161 A.2d 58; Bailer v. Local 470, Teamsters, 1960, 400 Pa. 188, 161 A.2d 343.

40. Otherwise where the court has felt that the right really to be protected was one under the federal act. Wagner v. Hartnett, 1959, 2 Storey, Del., 122, 153 A.2d 584; Green v. Folks, 1961, 13 App.Div.2d 744, 215 N.Y.S.2d 116; Dempsey v. Great A. & P. Tea Co., 11 App.Div.2d 419, 208 N.Y.S.2d 18; Wax v. International Mailers Union, 1960, 400 Pa. 173, 161 A.2d 603.

41. Hunt v. Phinney, 1960, 177 Cal.App.2d 212, 2 Cal.Rptr. 57.

42. California Dump Truck Owners' Ass'n v. Joint Council of Teamsters, Cal.Super.1962, 49 L.R.R.M. 2932.

43. National Maritime Union v. City of Norfolk, 1961, 202 Va. 672, 119 S.E.2d 307.

44. Kimbrell v. Jolog Sportswear, Inc., 1962, 239 S.C. 415, 123 S.E.2d 524.

34. The latest, and best discussion to date, is McCoid, State Regulation of Labor-Management Relations: The Impact of Garmon and Landrum-Griffin, 1963, 48 Iowa L.Rev. 478. See also McCoid, Notes on a "G-String": A Study of the "No-Man's Land" of Labor Law, 1959, 44 Minn.L.Rev. 205; Cohen, Congress Clears the Labor No Man's Land, 1961, 56 N.W.U.L.Rev. 333; Note, 1961, 26 Mo.L. Rev. 250.

35. Tidewater Oil Co. v. Dedreux, N.Y.Sup.Ct.1962, 50 L.R.R.M. 2950; Jamestown Sterling Corp. v. United Furniture Works, 1961, 31 Misc.2d 969, 222 N.Y.S.2d 160; United M. P. B. Novelty Mfg. Corp. v. Simensky, S.Ct.1961, 219 N.Y.S.2d 729; Spartan of Plainfield v. Retail Employees Union, Wis.Cir. Ct.1961, 49 L.R.R.M. 2338; Buckman v. U. M. W., 1959, 80 Wyo. 199, 339 P.2d 398, rehearing denied 80 Wyo. 216, 342 P.2d 236.

tional strikes, or picketing for recognition in violation of National Labor Relations Board certification. This is specifically provided by the Taft-Hartley Act.[45] There is also some authority, not undisputed, that the state courts have the power to protect property rights by actions such as trespass.[46]

4. Any cases in which the National Labor Relations Board has declined to exercise its jurisdiction. This is provided by the Landrum-Griffin Act.[47]

5. Cases in which it is clear that the Board would have no jurisdiction under the federal acts, as for example where the employer is not engaged in interstate commerce or in an enterprise which affects it,[48] or the dispute involves independent contractors rather than employees.[49] This is, however, subject to the limitation that whenever the activity is "arguably" subject to the federal act, and it is not clear whether it is governed by the Act or outside of it, the determination must be left in the first instance to the National Labor Relations Board.[50] Accordingly the great majority of the state court decisions, where the question is raised in the first instance, have refused to take jurisdiction because the question presented might be considered as involving the federal act.[51]

---

45. § 303(b).

46. Illinois and Wisconsin have indicated that private property rights will be protected by trespass actions, against invasion in labor disputes. People v. Goduto, 1961, 21 Ill.2d 605, 174 N.E.2d 385, cert. denied, 1962, 368 U.S. 927; Moreland Corp. v. Retail Store Employees Union, 1962, 16 Wis.2d 499, 114 N.W.2d 876. To the contrary, considering that this is not a matter for state jurisdiction, are Freeman v. Retail Clerks Union, 1961, 58 Wash.2d 426, 363 P.2d 803; Green v. Retail Store Employees' Union, Pa.C.P.1961, 49 L.R.R.M. 3059.

In International Union, UAW–AFL v. Wisconsin Employment Relations Board, 1949, 336 U.S. 245, rehearing denied 336 U.S. 970, the Supreme Court allowed state prohibition of intermittent work stoppages, and suggested also sit-down strikes, mutiny, or strike in breach of contract. Apparently in accord with this was National Labor Relations Board v. Insurance Agents' Int. Union, 1960, 361 U.S. 477.

47. 29 U.S.C.A. § 164(c).

48. See State Market of Avenal v. Superior Court, 1959, 172 Cal.App.2d 517, 342 P.2d 325; State ex rel. Yellow Cab Co. v. International Brotherhood of Teamsters, 1959, 53 Wash.2d 644, 333 P.2d 924, reversed per curiam, 1960, 361 U.S. 373; Chavez v. Sargent, 1959, 52 Cal.2d 162, 339 P.2d 801.

49. See Alabama Highway Express, Inc. v. Local 612, Teamsters Union, 1959, 268 Ala. 392, 108 So.2d 350; Rackley v. International Nav. Corp., Tex.Civ.App. 1960, 337 S.W.2d 613.

50. San Diego Building Trades Council v. Garmon, 1959, 359 U.S. 236.

51. Taylor v. Bean, 1962, 234 Ark. 932, 355 S.W.2d 602; Booth Broadcasting Co. v. American Federation of Television and Radio Artists, 1962, 366 Mich. 559, 115 N.W.2d 380; Building Const. Trades Council v. American Builders, Inc., 1959, 139 Colo. 236, 337 P.2d 953; Devine Bros. v. International Brotherhood of Teamsters, Local 191, 1958, 145 Conn. 77, 139 A.2d 60; Wood, Wire & Metal Lathers v. Babcock Co., Fla.1961, 132 So.2d 16; Ex parte Dilley, 1960, 160 Tex. 522, 334 S.W.2d 425; McJunkin Corp. v. Bell Lines, 1959, 144 W.Va. 330, 108 S.E.2d 12.

CHAPTER 26

IMMUNITIES

There are a number of classes of defendants upon whom the law, for various reasons of policy, has in the past conferred immunity from tort liability to a greater or less extent. An immunity differs from a privilege, or justification or excuse, although the difference appears to be largely one of degree. The privilege avoids liability for tortious conduct only under particular circumstances, and because these circumstances make it just and reasonable that the liability shall not be imposed, and so go to defeat the existence of the tort itself. An immunity, on the other hand, avoids liability in tort under all circumstances, within the limits of the immunity itself; it is conferred, not because of the particular facts, but because of the status or position of the favored defendant; and it does not deny the tort, but the resulting liability.[1] Such immunity does not mean that conduct which would amount to a tort on the part of other defendants is not still equally tortious in character, but merely that for the protection of the particular defendant, or of interests which he represents, he is given absolution from liability. Two such immunities already have been encountered, in connection with the tort liability of husband and wife, and parent and child.[2] There are others of which some incidental mention

should be made before completion of this book.

131. GOVERNMENTAL IMMUNITY

The first of these immunities, taken as a group, are those of governments.[3] While these may or may not have had their roots in Roman law,[4] the origin of the idea underlying them in the common law seems to have been the theory, allied with the divine right of kings, that "the King can do no wrong," together with the feeling that it was necessarily a contradiction of his sovereignty to allow him to be sued as of right in his own courts.[5] It was not, however, until the six-

---

1. Thus the "absolute privilege" to publish defamation in the course of judicial or legislative proceedings, supra, § 114, is really an immunity of those engaged in such proceedings, conferred because of the public interest in protecting them from suit.

2. Supra, § 122.

3. See, generally, Borchard, Government Liability in Tort, 1924, 34 Yale L.J. 1, 129, 221, 1926, 36 Yale L.J. 1, 757, 1039, 1928, 28 Col.L.Rev. 577, 734; Borchard, Government Liability in Tort, 1948, 26 Can. Bar Rev. 399; Blachly and Oatman, Approaches to Governmental Liability in Tort: A Comparative Survey, 1942, 9 Law & Con.Prob. 181; Braband, Liability in Tort of the Government and Its Employees: A Comparative Analysis with Emphasis on German Law, 1938, 33 N.Y.U.L.Rev. 18; James, Tort Liability of Government Units and Their Officers, 1955, 22 U.Chi.L.Rev. 610; Davis, Tort Liability of Governmental Units, 1956, 40 Minn.L.Rev. 751; Note, 1953, 47 N.W.U.L.Rev. 914.

4. See Parker, The King Does No Wrong—Liability for Misadministration, 1952, 5 Vand.L.Rev. 167; Watkins, The State as a Party Litigant, 1927, 1–4; Goodnow, Comparative Administrative Law, 1893, 149, 169.

5. Borchard, Governmental Responsibility in Tort, 1926, 36 Yale L.J. 1, 35; 3 Holdsworth, History of English Law, 5th Ed. 1942, 458–469; Holdsworth, The History of Remedies Against the Crown, 1922, 38 L.Q.Rev. 380. Jaffe, Suits Against Governments and Officers, 1963, 77 Harv.L.Rev. 1; Lawyer,

teenth century, in the days of quite absolute monarchs, that this became fully established as law, and then it was always coupled with the qualification that for every act of the King some minister was always responsible.[6] When the individual sovereign was replaced by the broader conception of the modern state, the idea was carried over that to allow a suit against a ruling government without its consent was inconsistent with the very idea of supreme executive power.[7] The association of the immunity with the dignity of the sovereign, and through him the state, is indicated by the fact that, as a matter of international comity, a similar immunity is extended to foreign states,[8] whose official heads,[9] their ministers,[10] their agencies,[11] and

their public property,[12] as well as those of the United Nations,[13] all are held to be immune even from the service of process unless they voluntarily accept it.

The United States

Just how this feudal and monarchistic doctrine ever got itself translated into the law of the new and belligerently democratic republic in America is today a bit hard to understand. In 1821 Chief Justice Marshall gave no reasons when he declared that, without its consent, no suit could be commenced or prosecuted against the United States.[14] Following this, it soon became established that the government could not be sued without its consent.[15] Consent, however, was soon forthcoming in the form of legislation; and with the establishment of a Court of Claims to hear contract cases, and various other minor provisions permitting even some actions in tort, a measure of relief was obtainable for those with grievances against the United States.[16]

Birth and Death of Governmental Immunity, 1966, 15 Cleve.Marsh.L.Rev. 529.

6.   3 Holdsworth, History of English Law, 5th Ed. 1942, 463–469; 6 Ibid. 226–267.

7.   Briggs v. Light Boat Upper Cedar Point, 1865, 11 Allen, Mass., 157, 162. See Maier, Sovereign Immunity and Act of State: Correlative or Conflicting Policies, 1966, 35 U.Cin.L.Rev. 556.

8.   French Republic v. Board of Supervisors of Jefferson County, 1923, 200 Ky. 18, 252 S.W. 124. See Hendry, Sovereign Immunities from the Jurisdiction of the Courts, 1958, 36 Can.Bar Rev. 145; Reeves, The Foreign Sovereign Before United States Courts, 1970, 38 Ford.L.Rev. 455; Notes, 1963, 16 Okl.L.Rev. 457; 1965, 51 Va.L.Rev. 316.

9.   Mighell v. Sultan of Johore, [1894] 1 Q.B. 149; Statham v. Statham and the Gaekwar of Baroda, [1912] P. 92; American Banana Co. v. United Fruit Co., 2 Cir. 1908, 166 F. 261, affirmed 213 U.S. 347; Sullivan v. State of Sao Paolo, 2 Cir. 1941, 122 F.2d 355 (state in Brazil); Restatement of Foreign Relations Law of United States, §§ 68, 69. See Notes, 1941, 26 Corn.L.Q. 727; 1942, 40 Mich.L.Rev. 911.

In Underhill v. Hernandez, 1897, 168 U.S. 250, this was held to extend to a revolutionary leader ruling by force.

10.   Bergson v. De Sieyes, 2 Cir. 1948, 170 F.2d 360 (diplomat in transit). See Note, 1949, 22 So.Cal.L. Rev. 491.

11.   Telkes v. Hungarian Nat. Museum, 1942, 265 App.Div. 192, 38 N.Y.S.2d 419; Hannes v. Kingdom of Roumania Monopolies Institute, 1940, 260 App. Div. 189, 20 N.Y.S.2d 825; Baccus S. R. L. v. Servicio Nacional del Trigo, [1957] 1 Q.B. 438. See Notes, 1941, 50 Yale L.J. 1088; 1948, 58 Yale L.J. 176.

12.   Compania Espanola v. The Navemar, 1938, 303 U.S. 68; Berrizzi Bros. v. S. S. Pesaro, 1926, 271 U.S. 562. See Riesenfeld, Sovereign Immunity of Foreign Vessels, 1940, 25 Minn.L.Rev. 1; Note, 1946, 34 Cal.L.Rev. 441. Compare, however, Republic of Mexico v. Hoffman, 1945, 324 U.S. 30. See, generally, Symposium, 1966, 41 N.Y.U.L.Rev. 1.

13.   Tsiang v. Tsiang, 1949, 194 Misc. 259, 86 N.Y.S.2d 556. See Notes, 1949, 47 Mich.L.Rev. 1025; 1951, 49 Mich.L.Rev. 1244.

14.   Cohens v. Virginia, 1821, 19 U.S. 264, 411, 412. See also Hill v. United States, 1850, 50 U.S. 386, 389; United States v. Lee, 1882, 106 U.S. 196, 207. The statement usually quoted is that of Mr. Justice Holmes, in Kawananakoa v. Polyblank, 1907, 205 U.S. 349, 353, that "A sovereign is exempt from suit, not because of any formal conception or obsolete theory, but on the logical and practical ground that there can be no legal right as against the authority that makes the law on which the right depends."

15.   Osborn v. Bank of United States, 1824, 22 U.S. 738.

16.   As to the United States before the Federal Tort Claims Act, see Gottlieb, Tort Claims Against the United States, 1942, 30 Geo.L.J. 462; Holtzoff, The Handling of Tort Claims Against the Federal Government, 1942, 9 Law & Con.Prob. 311; Note, 1940, 14 Temple L.Q. 395.

In 1946 a very important step forward was taken when the United States waived its immunity from liability in tort, and provided for litigation of tort claims against it in the federal courts, by the Federal Tort Claims Act.[17] This Act makes the United States liable under the local law of the place where the tort occurs,[18] for the negligent or wrongful acts or omissions [19] of federal employees within the scope of their employment "in the same manner and to the same extent as a private individual under like circumstances."[20] It has been held to make the government liable where the negligence of some employee is proved, although he is not identified.[21] It has been held to mean that the United States may be impleaded as a joint tortfeasor, and becomes liable for contribu-

tion where the local law permits it;[22] and that it creates liability to insurers on subrogation claims.[23]

The Act provides a number of exceptions to its general rule of tort liability of the United States. Most of these continue the immunity as to certain specific activities of the government,[24] including the combatant activities of military and naval forces in time of war.[25] Two, however, are more comprehensive. One of these provides that the United States shall not be liable for "any claim arising out of assault, battery, false imprisonment, false arrest, malicious prosecution, abuse of process, libel, slander, misrepresentation, deceit, or interference with contract rights."[26] A broad construction of this language has sometimes led to unfortunate results, as where a mistaken surgical operation

---

17. 28 U.S.C.A. §§ 1346, 1402, 1504, 2110, 2401, 2402, 2411, 2412, 2671–2680.

See Wright, the Federal Tort Claims Act, 1957; Gottlieb, The Federal Tort Claims Act—A Statutory Interpretation, 1946, 35 Geo.L.J. 1; Gellhorn and Schenck, Tort Actions Against the Federal Government, 1947, 47 Col.L.Rev. 722; Gellhorn and Lauer, Federal Liability for Personal and Property Damage, 1954, 29 N.Y.U.L.Rev. 1325; Anderson, Recovery from the United States Under the Federal Tort Claims Act, 1947, 31 Minn.L.Rev. 456; Baer, Suing Uncle Sam in Tort, 1948, 26 N.C.L.Rev. 119; Hulen, Suits on Tort Claims Against the United States, 1948, 7 F.R.D. 143; Fisher, The Federal Tort Claims Act After Five Years, 1952, 3 Mercer L.Rev. 263; Gerwig, A Decade of Litigation Under the Federal Tort Claims Act, 1956, 24 Tenn.L.Rev. 301; Gottlieb, The Tort Claims Act Revisited, 1961, 49 Geo.L.J. 539. See Notes, 1949, 20 Miss.L.J. 364; 1954, 38 Minn.L.Rev. 364; 1957, 22 Mo.L.Rev. 48.

18. Thus where the tort occurred in Montana, it was held that the United States had no governmental immunity, although the state of Montana would have it. Big Head v. United States, D.Mont.1958, 166 F.Supp. 510.

19. It has been held that "negligent omission" presupposes a duty to act; and the omission is not negligent when there is no duty. Rayonier, Inc. v. United States, 9 Cir. 1955, 225 F.2d 642, vacated for determination of duty 352 U.S. 315.

20. 28 U.S.C.A. §§ 1346(b), 2674.

21. United States v. Hull, 1 Cir.1952, 195 F.2d 64 (res ipsa loquitur); Williams v. United States, 5 Cir. 1958, 252 F.2d 887 (practice mine fuse found near army camp).

22. United States v. Yellow Cab Co., 1951, 340 U.S. 543.

23. United States v. Aetna Cas. & Surety Co., 1949, 338 U.S. 366; Old Colony Ins. Co. v. United States, 6 Cir. 1948, 168 F.2d 931.

24. Thus the negligent transmission of mail; the assessment or collection of customs duties; acts in administering the Trading with the Enemy Act; the imposition of a quarantine; an injury to a vessel passing through the Panama Canal; the fiscal operation of the Treasury; acts done in foreign countries, and the activities of the Tennessee Valley Authority. Also causes justiciable under the Suits in Admiralty Acts of 1920 and 1925. 28 U.S. C.A., 1952 Supp., § 2680.

25. 28 U.S.C.A. § 2680(j). See Feres v. United States, 1950, 340 U.S. 135; Preferred Ins. Co. v. United States, 9 Cir. 1955, 222 F.2d 942, cert. denied 350 U.S. 837, rehearing denied 351 U.S. 990. The exception does not extend to non-service injuries to a soldier. Brooks v. United States, 1949, 337 U.S. 49. Or to medical treatment of a veteran after discharge. United States v. Brown, 1954, 348 U.S. 110.

See Hitch, The Federal Tort Claims Act and Military Personnel, 1954, 8 Rutgers L.Rev. 316; Notes, 1949, 35 Corn.L.Q. 233; 1948, 58 Yale L.J. 615; 1952, 20 Geo.Wash.L.Rev. 90.

26. 28 U.S.C.A. § 2680(h). "Interference with contract rights" has been held to include interference with prospective pecuniary advantage. Fletcher v. Veterans Administration, D.Mich.1952, 103 F.Supp. 654; Dupree v. United States, 3 Cir. 1959, 264 F.2d 140, rehearing denied, 1959, 266 F.2d 373, cert. denied 361 U.S. 823, rehearing denied, 361 U.S. 921.

on the wrong hip and leg was ruled out as a technical battery,[27] while "false arrest" was held to include negligent maintenance of records which led to plaintiff's arrest as a deserter,[28] and "misrepresentation" to prevent liability for negligent certification that goods complied with the Pure Food Act.[29]

The other exception is even more sweeping. It provides that the government shall not be liable for acts done with due care in the execution of a statute or regulation, even though it is invalid, or for acts or omissions to act which are within the "discretionary function or duty" of any federal agency or employee.[30] In the outstanding case of Dalehite v. United States,[31] this was held to mean

that negligent decisions of government officials in adopting a plan for the export of fertilizer, in controlling its manufacture, in handling and shipment of the product, and in failing to police the shipboard loading, all of which were made at the "planning or policy" level, afforded no basis for liability of the United States. There has been general agreement that high level policy judgments, as for example, as to a change in the course of the Missouri River,[32] measures to protect migratory fowl,[33] to conduct tests of nuclear explosions,[34] or the decision not to operate a seized coal mine,[35] cannot result in liability; and this is true even though the planning level involves the drafting of specifications, schedules and procedures.[36]

Where the decision occurs at the "operational" level of government activity, which is to say, when it is made by one who is actually engaged in carrying out the work in the field, there have been cases [37] which

27. Moos v. United States, D.Minn.1954, 118 F.Supp. 275, affirmed, 8 Cir. 1955, 225 F.2d 705. See Note, 1954, 7 Vand.L.Rev. 283.

Contra, and clearly to be preferred, is Lane v. United States, E.D.Va.1964, 225 F.Supp. 850.

28. Duenges v. United States, S.D.N.Y.1953, 114 F. Supp. 751. Cf. United States v. Wilcox, S.D.N.Y. 1953, 117 F.Supp. 119 (negligent control over insane hospital inmate, who attacked plaintiff: ruled out as arising out of "assault and battery"); contra, Fleishour v. United States, N.D.Ill.1965, 244 F. Supp. 762, affirmed 365 F.2d 126, cert. denied 385 U.S. 987.

29. Anglo-American & Overseas Corp. v. United States, S.D.N.Y.1956, 144 F.Supp. 635, affirmed, 2 Cir. 1957, 242 F.2d 236.

Contra, as to negligent misrepresentation, Bartie v. United States, W.D.La.1963, 216 F.Supp. 10, affirmed 326 F.2d 754, cert. denied 379 U.S. 852; Jordan v. United States, S.D.Ga.1968, 294 F.Supp. 204.

30. 28 U.S.C.A. § 2680(a). See Dalehite v. United States, 1953, 346 U.S. 15; Harris v. United States, 10 Cir. 1953, 205 F.2d 765; Thomas v. United States, W.D.Mo.1949, 81 F.Supp. 881; Somerset Seafood Co. v. United States, 4 Cir. 1951, 193 F.2d 631.

See James, The Federal Tort Claims Act and the "Discretionary Function" Exception, 1957, 10 U. Fla.L.Rev. 184; Peck, The Federal Tort Claims Act —A Proposed Construction of the Discretionary Function Exception, 1956, 31 Wash.L.Rev. 207; Notes, 1962, 48 Va.L.Rev. 1480; 1951, 45 Ill.L.Rev. 791; 1952, 101 U.Pa.L.Rev. 420; 1953, 39 Corn.L.Q. 134; 1953, 3 Buffalo L.Rev. 163; 1953, 32 N.C.L. Rev. 118; 1954, 23 U.Cin.L.Rev. 125; 1954, 52 Mich.L.Rev. 733.

31. 1953, 346 U.S. 15. See Heuser, Dalehite v. United States: A New Approach to the Federal Tort

Claims Act, 1954, 7 Vand.L.Rev. 175; Notes, 1953, 66 Harv.L.Rev. 488; 1953, 45 Ill.L.Rev. 791; 1951, 27 Ind.L.J. 121; 1951, 52 Mich.L.Rev. 733.

32. Coates v. United States, 8 Cir. 1950, 181 F.2d 816.

33. Sickman v. United States, 7 Cir. 1950, 184 F.2d 616, cert. denied 341 U.S. 939, rehearing denied 342 U.S. 843.

34. Bartholomae Corp. v. United States, S.D.Cal. 1955, 135 F.Supp. 651; Bulloch v. United States, D.Utah 1955, 133 F.Supp. 885.

35. Old King Coal Co. v. United States, S.D.Iowa 1949, 88 F.Supp. 124.

36. Dalehite v. United States, 1953 (making and shipping fertilizer); United States v. Ure, 9 Cir. 1955, 225 F.2d 709 (decision not to line canal with concrete); Thomas v. United States, W.D.Mo.1949, 81 F.Supp. 881 (angles of dikes in flood control project); Sisley v. United States, D.Alaska 1962, 202 F.Supp. 273 (design of road crossings and culvert grades for national highway).

37. Denny v. United States, 5 Cir. 1948, 171 F.2d 365 (refusal to extend medical care to wife of serviceman); Fahey v. United States, S.D.N.Y.1957, 153 F.Supp. 878 (refusal to commit mental patient); Brooks v. United States, S.D.N.Y.1957, 152 F.Supp. 535 (district attorney's refusal to prosecute); Olson v. United States, D.N.D.1950, 93 F.Supp. 150 (opening flood gates); Dugan v. United States, D.D.C.

have declared that there is no less involved in the way of opinion, judgment and "discretion," and there can be no liability. There have been as many cases, however, which have held that such "operational" exercises of discretion are not those contemplated by the Act; [38] and this seems definitely indicated as the position of the Supreme Court.[39] Thus, while the decision of the Civil Aeronautics Authority to establish an instrument approach pattern for an airport is "planning," the failure of the pilots to take precautions against frightening horses in landing is "operational;" and while the United States is not liable for the one, it is for the other.[40]

A good case in the Ninth Circuit [41] has summarized some of the distinctions made along these lines, as follows:

"Discretionary to undertake fire-fighting, lighthouse, rescue, or wrecked-ship marking services, but not discretionary to conduct such operations negligently; discretionary to admit a patient to an Army hospital, but not discretionary to treat the patient in a negligent manner; discretionary to establish a

post office at a particular location, but not to negligently fail to establish handrails; discretionary to establish control towers at airports and to undertake air traffic separation, but not to conduct the same negligently; discretionary to reactivate an airbase, but not to construct a drainage and disposal system thereon in a negligent fashion; and discretionary for CAA to conduct a survey in low flying, twin-engine airplane, but not for pilots thereof to fly negligently." [42]

Dalehite v. United States [43] went further. It added a construction of the statutory language, "wrongful act or omission," to mean that the government was not liable unless it was chargeable with some misfeasance or nonfeasance, or in other words, unless it had been at fault, so that there was no strict liability, without intent to do harm or negligence, for such abnormally dangerous activities as the shipment of large quantities of explosives. The Court said briefly that "the statute requires a negligent act," and that the word wrongful "was not added to the jurisdictional grant with any overtones of the absolute liability theory." While this has been very vigorously denounced [44] on the quite reasonable basis that the tortious abnormal conduct which leads to strict liability is no less "wrongful," the position has been reiterated,[45] and the lower federal courts [46] for the most part have accepted it as conclusive. There may perhaps remain some lingering

1956, 147 F.Supp. 674 (hospital ward in which mental patient to be confined); Smart v. United States, 10 Cir. 1953, 207 F.2d 841 (decision to release mental patient.

38. American Exchange Bank v. United States, 7 Cir. 1958, 257 F.2d 938 (decision not to install handrail on stairs); United States v. Union Trust Co., D.C.Cir. 1955, 95 U.S.App.D.C. 189, 221 F.2d 62, affirmed per curiam in Union Trust Co. v. Eastern Air Lines, 350 U.S. 907 (decision of controller of air traffic not to warn aircraft of collision); Friday v. United States, 9 Cir. 1957, 239 F.2d 701 (ordering tired driver to continue on long trip); Fair v. United States, 5 Cir. 1956, 234 F.2d 288 (release of mental patient); White v. United States, 4 Cir. 1963, 317 F.2d 13 (grounds privilege to same).

39. See, in addition to the Dalehite Case, supra, note 31, Indian Towing Co. v. United States, 1955, 350 U.S. 61, where failure of those in charge of a lighthouse to check the electrical system was said to be upon the "operational level," and to involve no "discretion" within the meaning of the Act.

40. Dahlstrom v. United States, 8 Cir. 1956, 228 F.2d 819.

41. United Air Lines, Inc. v. Wiener, 9 Cir. 1964, 335 F.2d 379, 393, cert. dismissed 379 U.S. 951.

42. Citing cases in footnotes, which are here omitted.

43. 1953, 346 U.S. 15.

44. Peck, Absolute Liability and the Federal Tort Claims Act, 1957, 9 Stan.L.Rev. 433; James, The Federal Tort Claims Act and the "Discretionary Function" Exception, 1957, 10 U.Fla.L.Rev. 184.

45. In Harris v. United States, 10 Cir. 1953, 205 F.2d 765.

46. United States v. Taylor, 6 Cir. 1956, 236 F.2d 649; United States v. Ure, 9 Cir. 1955, 225 F.2d 709; Bulloch v. United States, D. Utah 1955, 133 F.Supp. 885; Bartholomae Corp. v. United States, S.D.Cal.1955, 135 F.Supp. 651; Goodwill Industries v. United States, 5 Cir. 1954, 218 F.2d 270; Strangi v. United States, 5 Cir. 1954, 211 F.2d 305; Heale v. United States, 3 Cir. 1953, 207 F.2d 414.

shadow of doubt, in view of the fact that such cases all have involved decisions at the planning level, and there is some scant case law to the effect that there may be strict liability for conduct which is "operational;" [47] but in all probability further legislation will be required before strict liability is imposed upon the United States.

States

The sovereign immunity likewise carried over from the English crown to the several American states.[48] There was one abortive attempt to change the rule; [49] but it led only to the Eleventh Amendment to the federal Constitution, protecting any state from suit by a private citizen in the federal courts.

Thereafter the doctrine became firmly established, that there is no state liability in tort unless consent is given.[50] The immunity is said to rest upon public policy; the absurdity of a wrong committed by an entire people; the idea that whatever the state does must be lawful, which has replaced the king who can do no wrong; the very dubious theory that an agent of the state is always outside of the scope of his authority and employment when he commits any wrongful act; reluctance to divert public funds to compensate for private injuries; and the inconvenience and embarrassment which would descend upon the government if it should be subject to such liability.[51]

In all of the states, however, consent has been given, to a greater or a lesser extent. Usually it has been granted in a limited form by statutes which authorize particular individuals to maintain a suit,[52] or provide for special procedure or create special courts of claims, or authorize actions against the state in its own courts for particular causes of action.[53]

All such legislation has tended, however, to receive a strict and narrow construction

---

47. In United States v. Praylou, 4 Cir. 1953, 208 F.2d 291, plaintiff recovered under a South Carolina statute imposing strict liability for ground damage from an airplane crash. Accord, United States v. Pendergrast, 4 Cir. 1957, 241 F.2d 687; Long v. United States, D.S.C.1965, 241 F.Supp. 286; and cf. Parcell v. United States, S.D.W.Va.1951, 104 F. Supp. 110.

In Rayonier, Inc. v. United States, 9 Cir. 1955, 225 F. 2d 642, the government was held not liable under a Washington statute imposing strict liability for fire. The point was raised on appeal in the briefs of counsel; but without mentioning it the Court, in 1957, 352 U.S. 315, remanded the case for determination of whether a private person would be liable on the facts under Washington law; and it cited United States v. Praylou, supra, in a footnote with apparent approval. See also Adams v. Tennessee Valley Authority, E.D.Tenn.1966, 254 F.Supp. 78.

In Hopson v. United States, W.D.Ark.1956, 136 F. Supp. 804, it was said that liability for the torts of an independent contractor was not the kind of strict liability condemned by the Dalehite Case; but that there must still be an act or omission of a government employee.

See Peck, Absolute Liability and the Federal Tort Claims Act, 1957, 9 Stan.L.Rev. 433.

48. It has been suggested that the heavy public debts of the states and their precarious financial condition during the years immediately after the Revolution played some part in this. Watkins, The State as a Party Litigant, 1927, 52–54; Gellhorn and Schenck, Tort Actions Against the Federal Government, 1947, 47 Col.L.Rev. 722.

49. Chisholm v. Georgia, 1793, 2 U.S. 419, 1 L.Ed. 440.

50. Faber v. State, 1960, 143 Colo. 240, 353 P.2d 609; Lewis v. State, 1884, 96 N.Y. 71.

51. See Poindexter v. Greenhow, 1884, 114 U.S. 270; State v. Hill, 1875, 54 Ala. 67; Bourn v. Hart, 1892, 93 Cal. 321, 28 P. 951.

52. Or even make an outright appropriation for relief. See Nutting, Legislative Practice Regarding Tort Claims Against the State, 1939, 4 Mo.L.Rev. 1; Shumate, Tort Claims Against State Governments, 1942, 9 Law & Con.Prob. 242; Leflar and Kantrowitz, Tort Liability of the States, 1954, 29 N.Y.U.L. Rev. 1363; Note, 1948, 32 Minn.L.Rev. 539; Minnesota Legislative Research Committee, Payment of Claims Against the State, 1952.

53. See Leflar and Kantrowitz, Tort Liability of the States, 1954, 29 N.Y.U.L.Rev. 1363; Maguire, State Liability in Tort, 1916, 20 Harv.L.Rev. 30; Waterman, One Hundred Years of a State's Immunity from Suit, 1936, 14 Tex.L.Rev. 135, 2 Ark.L.Rev. 354; Eckert, Another Decade of State Immunity to Suit, 1948, 2 Ark.L.Rev. 375.

which favors the state.[54] In particular, the mere authorization to maintain a suit against the state, whether under a general or a special statute, has been held not to waive the immunity and make the state liable for its torts, even when they are fully proved;[55] and the statutes, however broad in their terms,[56] have been held not to create liability for the torts of state agents and employees.[57] New Jersey,[58] with a few other courts in vigorous disagreement,[59] has even converted the shield into a sword by holding that the defense of

contributory negligence cannot be set up against the state when it is suing for damage to its own property.

The immunity has been extended also to various state agencies,[60] such as prisons,[61] hospitals,[62] educational institutions,[63] state fairs,[64] highway authorities,[65] and commissions for public works.[66] There is, however, a decided tendency to find a legislative intent in creating the agency, that it shall be subject to liability;[67] and this is quite com-

---

54. See for example, in North Carolina: Jenkins v. North Carolina Dept. of Motor Vehicles, 1956, 244 N.C. 560, 94 S.E.2d 577 (State Tort Claims Act applies only to a "negligent act," not to intentional shooting); Flynn v. North Carolina State Highway Commission, 1956, 244 N.C. 617, 94 S.E.2d 571 (does not apply to negligent omissions); Alliance Co. v. State Hospital at Butner, 1955, 241 N.C. 329, 85 S.E. 2d 386 (prisoner driving state truck not an "employee" of the state). See Note, 1955, 33 N.C.L.Rev. 588.

55. Shear v. State, 1929, 117 Neb. 865, 223 N.W. 130; Miller v. State, 1931, 231 App.Div. 363, 247 N.Y.S. 399; Manion v. State, 1942, 303 Mich. 1, 5 N.W.2d 527; Talley v. Northern San Diego County Hospital Dist., 1953, 41 Cal.2d 33, 257 P.2d 22. See Davis, Tort Liability of Governmental Units, 1956, 40 Minn.L.Rev. 751, 770–773.

56. See Smith v. State, 1920, 227 N.Y. 405, 125 N.E. 841; Thompson v. State, 1921, 4 Ill.Ct.Cl. 26. See Note, 1920, 5 Corn.L.Q. 340, asking whether the claimant is permitted to sue in the Court of Claims merely "to amuse himself."

57. Davis v. State, 1917, 30 Idaho 137, 163 P. 373; Riddoch v. State, 1912, 68 Wash. 329, 123 P. 450; Houston v. State, 1898, 98 Wis. 481, 74 N.W. 111; Murdock Parlor Grate Co. v. Commonwealth, 1893, 152 Mass. 28, 24 N.E. 854.

58. Miller v. Layton, 1945, 133 N.J.L. 323, 44 A.2d 177; Gruschow v. New Jersey State Highway Dept., 1959, 56 N.J.Super. 146, 152 A.2d 150. Both decisions followed City of Paterson v. Erie R. Co., 1909, 78 N.J.L. 592, 75 A. 922, holding the same as to a municipal corporation. See Notes, 1959, 14 Rutgers L.Rev. 211; 1946, 24 Tex.L.Rev. 227.

59. State v. Shinkle, 1962, 231 Or. 528, 373 P.2d 674; Faulk v. City of Tyler, Tex.Civ.App.1965, 389 S.W. 2d 706, ref. n. r. e.; Department of Public Safety v. Parker, Fla.App.1964, 161 So.2d 886; City of Newark v. United States, 3 Cir. 1958, 254 F.2d 93; United States v. Moscow-Idaho Seed Co., 9 Cir. 1937, 92 F.2d 170.

60. See Note, 1961, 74 Harv.L.Rev. 714.

61. Moody v. State's Prison, 1901, 128 N.C. 12, 38 S. E. 131.

62. Jones v. Jones, 1964, 243 S.C. 600, 135 S.E.2d 233; Maia's Adm'r v. Eastern State Hospital, 1899, 97 Va. 507, 34 S.E. 617; White v. Alabama Insane Hospital, 1903, 138 Ala. 479, 35 So. 454; Leavell v. Western Kentucky Asylum for Insane, 1906, 122 Ky. 213, 91 S.W. 671.

63. Abston v. Waldon Academy, 1906, 118 Tenn. 24, 102 S.W. 351; Alabama Girls' Industrial School v. Reynolds, 1905, 143 Ala. 579, 42 So. 114; Oklahoma Agric. & Mech. College v. Willis, 1898, 6 Okl. 593, 52 P. 921.

64. Morrison v. MacLaren, 1915, 160 Wis. 621, 152 N.W. 475; Zoeller v. State Board of Agriculture, 1915, 163 Ky. 446, 173 S.W. 1143; Minear v. State Board of Agriculture, 1913, 259 Ill. 549, 102 N.E. 1082.

65. Hosterman v. Kansas Turnpike Authority, 1958, 183 Kan. 590, 331 P.2d 323; Louisiana Highway Commission v. Giaccone, 1932, 19 La.App. 446, 140 So. 286; Broyles v. State Highway Commission, Mo.App.1931, 48 S.W.2d 78; Rader v. Pennsylvania Turnpike Commission, 1962, 407 Pa. 609, 182 A.2d 199.

66. Cope v. Hastings, 1897, 183 Pa. 300, 38 A. 717; Rice Hope Plantation v. South Carolina Public Service Authority, 1950, 216 S.C. 500, 59 S.E.2d 132.

67. See Keifer & Keifer v. Reconstruction Finance Corp., 1939, 306 U.S. 381; Sloan Shipyards Corp. v. United States Shipping Board Emergency Fleet Corp., 1922, 258 U.S. 549; Pennell v. Home Owners' Loan Corp., D.Me.1937, 21 F.Supp. 497.

In a number of state cases there has been resort to the idea of a "private" or "corporate" function of the agency, as to which it is liable. Scott v. University of Mich. Athletic Ass'n, 1908, 152 Mich. 684, 116 N.W. 624; Green v. State, 1919, 107 Misc. 557, 176 N.Y.S. 681; Schwab v. State, 1921, 4 Ill.Ct.Cl. 77; Ryan v. State, 1921, 4 Ill.Ct.Cl. 57.

mon in the later cases, in many of which a provision that the agency can sue and be sued has been held sufficient to indicate it.[68] It is generally held that the immunity is shared by a public contractor doing work for the state, in so far as he has merely performed his contract,[69] although he may be liable for his own negligence in doing so.[70]

Until quite recent years the chief breach in the immunity of the state arose out of constitutional provisions forbidding the taking, or sometimes also the damaging, of private property for public purposes without compensation. These provisions usually have been held to be self-executing, so that even though the legislature has failed to provide any procedure for prosecuting such claims against the state, resort to the courts is open if only it can be found that there has been a taking, or damaging, within the terms of the constitution.[71]

The federal example has not yet had its anticipated effect in encouraging widespread state action. Many states have individual statutory provisions permitting suit against the state, or some kind of administrative action, in particular types of cases. A small number of them have broad statutes accepting general tort liability, and either authorizing suit in the state's own courts or creating special courts of claims. There is great variation from state to state, and reference must of course be made to the law of each jurisdiction.[72] Since 1957, however, the immunity of the state has become caught up in the tide of abolition which is now setting in, and which remains to be considered below.[73]

Municipal Corporations

Municipal corporations are regarded as having a rather curious dual character, which has given the courts a great deal of difficulty, and has left the law in a tangle of disagreement and confusion. On the one hand they are subdivisions of the state, endowed with governmental powers and charged with governmental functions and responsibilities. On the other they are corporate bodies, capable of much the same acts as private corporations, and having the same special and local interests and relations, not shared by the state at large. They are at one and the same time a corporate entity and a government. The law has attempted to distinguish between the two functions, and to hold that in so far as they represent the state, in their "governmental," "political," or "public" capacity, they share its

68. Taylor v. New Jersey Highway Authority, 1956, 22 N.J. 454, 126 A.2d 313; Petty v. Tennessee-Missouri Bridge Commission, 1959, 359 U.S. 275; Linger v. Pennsylvania Turnpike Commission, W.D.Pa.1958, 158 F.Supp. 900; Muses v. Housing Authority of City & County of San Francisco, 1948, 83 Cal.App.2d 489, 189 P.2d 305; Hoffmeyer v. Ohio Turnpike Commission, Ohio Com.Pl.1960, 166 N.E.2d 543.

69. Benner v. Atlantic Dredging Co., 1892, 134 N.Y. 156, 31 N.E. 328; De Baker v. Southern Cal. Ry. Co., 1895, 106 Cal. 257, 39 P. 610; Fitzgibbon v. Western Dredging Co., 1908, 141 Iowa 328, 117 N.W. 878; Nelson v. McKenzie-Hague Co., 1934, 192 Minn. 180, 256 N.W. 96. See Note, 1934, 19 Minn. L.Rev. 129.

70. Converse v. Portsmouth Cotton Oil Refining Corporation, 4 Cir. 1922, 281 F. 981; Taylor v. Westerfield, 1930, 233 Ky. 619, 26 S.W.2d 557; Boyd, Higgins & Goforth, Inc. v. Mahone, 1925, 142 Va. 690, 128 S.E. 259.

71. Rose v. State, 1942, 19 Cal.2d 713, 123 P.2d 505; Chick Springs Water Co. v. State Highway Dept., 1931, 159 S.C. 481, 157 S.E. 842; Pelt v. Louisiana State Live Stock Sanitary Board, La.App.1938, 178 So. 644; Schmutte v. State, 1946, 147 Neb. 193, 22 N.W.2d 691. See Davis, Tort Liability of Government Units, 1956, 40 Minn.L.Rev. 751, 766–769. As to the federal history, see Abend, Federal Liability for Takings and Torts: An Anomalous Relationship, 1963, 31 Ford.D.Rev. 481.

72. See the exhaustive summary of the statutes and common law of each state in Leflar and Kantrowitz, Tort Liability of the States, 1954, 29 N.Y.U.L. Rev. 1363. Also Nutting, Legislative Practices Regarding Tort Claims Against the State, 1939, 4 Mo. L.Rev. 1; Shumate, Tort Claims Against State Governments, 1942, 9 Law & Con.Prob. 242; Report of Minnesota State Bar Committee, Claims Against the State, 1948, 32 Minn.L.Rev. 539; Kansas Legislative Counsel Report No. 106, Claims Against the State, 1940.

73. See infra, pp. 984–987.

immunity from tort liability, while in their "corporate," "private," or "proprietary" character they may be liable.

The immunity of the state was first extended to a municipality in 1798 in Russell v. Men of Devon,[74] at a time when the idea of the municipal corporate entity was still in a nebulous state, and the action was in effect against the population of a whole county.[75] In addition to lack of precedent and the fear of an infinity of actions, the decision was based on the fact that there were no corporate funds out of which satisfaction could be obtained. Later decisions evolved the additional explanations that the municipality derives no profit from the exercise of governmental functions, which are solely for the public benefit;[76] that in the performance of such duties public officers are agents of the state and not of the corporation, so that the doctrine of respondeat superior does not apply;[77] that cities cannot carry on their governments if money raised by taxation for public use is diverted to making good the torts of employees;[78] and that it is unreasonable to hold the corporation liable for negligence in the performance of duties imposed upon it by the legislature, rather than voluntarily assumed under its general powers.[79]

Virtually all writers have agreed that no one of these reasons for denying liability is sound,[80] and all of them can be found to have been rejected at one time or another in the decided cases. The current of criticism has been that it is better that the losses due to tortious conduct should fall upon the municipality rather than the injured individual, and that the torts of public employees are properly to be regarded, as in other cases of vicarious liability,[81] as a cost of the administration of government, which should be distributed by taxes to the public. Whether as a result of this criticism or not, there has been a marked and steady trend in the direction of an extension of municipal tort liability, either by finding that the particular activity of the defendant is not a "governmental" one, or by discovering special reasons to take it out of the general rule. For many years, however, the courts were so far bound and hogtied by precedent and existing classifications, that it appeared that any real reform of the law must come by statutes.[82] It is only quite recently that any general movement

---

74. 1798, 2 Term Rep. 667, 100 Eng.Rep. 359.

75. See Harno, Tort Immunity of Municipal Corporations, 1921, 4 Ill.L.Q. 28; Barnett, The Foundations of the Distinction Between Public and Private Functions, 1937, 16 Or.L.Rev. 250.

76. Hill v. City of Boston, 1877, 122 Mass. 344; Howard v. City of Worcester, 1891, 153 Mass. 426, 27 N.E. 11; 4 Dillon, Municipal Corporations, 5th Ed. 1911, § 1642.

77. Burrill v. City of Augusta, 1886, 78 Me. 118, 3 A. 177; Everly v. Adams, 1915, 95 Kan. 305, 147 P. 1134; 4 Dillon, Municipal Corporations, 5th Ed. 1911, § 1655.

78. Riddle v. Merrimack River Locks and Canals, 1810, 7 Mass. 169; Coolidge v. Brookline, 1874, 114 Mass. 592; Board Commissioners of Hamilton County v. Mighels, 1857, 7 Ohio St. 109; 3 Abbott, Municipal Corporations, 1906, § 963.

79. City of Freeport v. Isbel, 1877, 83 Ill. 440; Dickinson v. City of Boston, 1905, 188 Mass. 595, 75 N.

E. 68; Evans v. City of Sheboygan, 1913, 153 Wis. 287, 141 N.W. 265; Boise Development Co. v. Boise City, 1917, 30 Idaho 675, 167 P. 1032.

80. See the exhaustive discussion in Borchard, Government Liability in Tort, 1924, 34 Yale L.J. 1, 129, 229, 1926, 36 Yale L.J. 1, 757, 1039, 1928, 28 Col.L. Rev. 577, 734. Also Harno, Tort Immunity of Municipal Corporations, 1921, 4 Ill.L.Q. 28; David, Municipal Liability in Tort in California, 1933, 6 So.Cal.L.Rev. 269, 7 So.Cal.L.Rev. 48, 214, 295, 372; Fuller and Casner, Municipal Tort Liability in Operation, 1941, 54 Harv.L.Rev. 437; Warp, The Law and Administration of Municipal Tort Liability, 1942, 28 Va.L.Rev. 630; Repko, American Legal Commentary on the Doctrines of Municipal Tort Liability, 1942, 9 Law & Con.Prob. 214; Green, Municipal Liability for Torts, 1944, 38 Ill.L.Rev. 355; Smith, Municipal Tort Liability, 1949, 48 Mich.L. Rev. 41; Antieau, The Tort Liability of American Municipalities, 1952, 40 Ky.L.J. 131.

81. See supra, § 69.

82. See Borchard, State and Municipal Liability in Tort—Proposed Statutory Reform, 1934, 20 A.B.A.J. 747; Borchard, Recent Statutory Developments in Municipal Liability in Tort, 1936, 2 Legal Notes on Local Government 89; Tooke, The Extension of Municipal Liability in Tort, 1932, 19 Val.L.Rev. 97.

for alteration of the common law has been initiated.[83]

The distinction between "governmental" and "proprietary" functions, which was first declared by a New York court [84] in 1842, became generally accepted in every jurisdiction except South Carolina,[85] which refused to find any common law liability at all, and Florida,[86] which held that cities under a commission form of government were subject to the same tort liability as private corporations. But the classification of particular functions as governmental or proprietary has proved to be so confused and difficult, and has been the subject of so much disagreement, that little can be said about it here, and the reader must be referred to the detailed consideration in texts on the law of municipal corporations.[87] It has been said that the "rules which courts have sought to establish in solving this problem are as log-

ical as those governing French irregular verbs." [88]

Certain functions and activities, whch can be performed adequately only by the government, are more or less generally agreed to be "governmental" in character, and so immune from tort liability. There is no liability, for example for a failure to make and enforce appropriate laws and regulations,[89] or a failure to take the proper course in the exercise of the legislative or judicial discretion conferred upon the municipality by the state.[90] There is ordinarily [91] no liability for the torts of police officers, even where they commit unjustifiable assault and battery, false arrest, trespass on land or injury to property, or are grossly negligent, and even though the city authorities ratify the act or have themselves been negligent in fail-

83. See infra, p. 984.

84. Bailey v. City of New York, 1842, 3 Hill, N.Y., 531. It had been foreshadowed for some time before. See Barnett, The Foundations of the Distinction Between Public and Private Functions, 1937, 16 Or.L.Rev. 250.

85. Irvine v. Greenwood, 1911, 89 S.C. 511, 72 S.E. 228.

86. City of Tallahassee v. Kaufman, 1924, 87 Fla. 119, 100 So. 150; City of West Palm Beach v. Grimmett, 1931, 102 Fla. 680, 136 So. 320, 137 So. 385; Wolfe v. City of Miami, 1931, 103 Fla. 774, 134 So. 539, 137 So. 892. Ohio abandoned the distinction in Fowler v. City of Cleveland, 1919, 100 Ohio St. 158, 126 N.E. 72, but the decision was overruled by Aldrich v. City of Youngstown, 1922, 106 Ohio St. 342, 140 N.E. 164.

87. See 18 McQuillin, Municipal Corporations, 3d Ed. 1950, §§ 53.23–53.59; Doddridge, Distinction Between Governmental and Proprietary Functions of Municipal Corporations, 1925, 23 Mich.L.Rev. 325; Seasongood, Municipal Corporations: Objections to the Governmental or Proprietary Test, 1936, 22 Va. L.Rev. 910. Also Casner and Fuller, Municipal Tort Liability in Operation, 1941, 54 Harv.L.Rev. 437; Fairweather, Test of Sovereign Immunity for Municipal Corporations, 1964, 13 Cleve.Marsh.L.Rev. 151.

88. Weeks v. City of Newark, 1960, 62 N.J.Super. 166, 162 A.2d 314, affirmed, 1961, 34 N.J. 250, 168 A.2d 11.

89. Bagni v. City of Bristol, 1940, 127 Conn. 38, 14 A.2d 716; Bean v. City of Moberly, 1943, 350 Mo. 975, 169 S.W.2d 393; Fidelity Laboratories v. Oklahoma City, 1942, 191 Okl. 473, 130 P.2d 834; Whittaker v. Village of Franklinsville, 1934, 265 N.Y. 11, 191 N.E. 716, reargument denied 266 N.Y. 505, 195 N.E. 174; Jones v. City of Williamsburg, 1900, 97 Va. 722, 34 S.E. 883.

90. Rochester White Lead Co. v. City of Rochester, 1850, 3 N.Y. 463; Hill v. City of Charlotte, 1875, 72 N.C. 55; Pope v. City of New Haven, 1917, 91 Conn. 79, 99 A. 51.

91. In a few cases liability has been found. Thus McCrink v. City of New York, 1947, 296 N.Y. 99, 71 N.E.2d 429 (retention of policeman known to be unsuited for the work); McAndrew v. Mularchuk, 1959, 56 N.J.Super. 219, 152 A.2d 372, affirmed, 1960, 33 N.J. 172, 162 A.2d 620 (inadequate training of policeman in use of gun); Jones v. Sioux City, 1919, 185 Iowa 1178, 170 N.W. 445 (hauling policemen to patrols); Herron v. City of Pittsburg, 1903, 204 Pa. 509, 54 A. 311 (open cellar door under police station); Shinnick v. City of Marshalltown, 1908, 137 Iowa 72, 114 N.W. 542 (creating "nuisance" in the street). See Shapo, Municipal Liability for Police Torts, 1963, 17 U.Miami L.Rev. 475.

A case which attracted a good deal of attention was Schuster v. City of New York, 1958, 5 N.Y.2d 75, 180 N.Y.S.2d 265, 154 N.E.2d 534, holding that the city was under a duty to furnish protection to police informers. See Note, 1959, 59 Col.L.Rev. 487.

ing to exact a bond from the officer on which the injured person might have sued.[92] Likewise keeping prisoners in jail is regarded as a purely governmental matter.[93] The same immunity has been conferred by most courts on the acts of firemen,[94] even where they have only a remote connection with fire protection;[95] and likewise on measures for the protection of public health, such as the operation of hospitals,[96] or the administration of quarantine or sanitation laws;[97] and also on

the maintenance and operation of public schools and educational institutions,[98] public charities, poor relief, and the care of dependent or defective classes;[99] and even, in most jurisdictions, on the removal of garbage and other refuse from the streets, or from residences along the streets.[100] As to all of these activities there is an undercurrent of opposition, which finds some reason for saying that the function is not "governmental" or for finding liability in the particular case.

On the other hand, when the city performs a service which might as well be provided by a private corporation, and particularly when it collects revenue from it, the function is considered a "proprietary" one, as to which there may be liability for the torts of municipal agents within the scope of their em-

92. Bartlett v. City of Columbus, 1897, 101 Ga. 300, 28 S.E. 599; Lamont v. Stavanaugh, 1915, 129 Minn. 321, 153 N.W. 720; McSheridan v. City of Talladega, 1942, 243 Ala. 162, 8 So.2d 831; Gillmor v. Salt Lake City, 1907, 32 Utah 180, 89 P. 714; Aldrich v. City of Youngstown, 1922, 106 Ohio St. 342, 140 N.E. 164. See Note, 1932, 42 Yale L.J. 241.

93. Grove v. County of San Joaquin, 1958, 156 Cal. App.2d 808, 320 P.2d 161; City of Miami v. Bethel, Fla.1953, 65 So.2d 34; Cushman v. Grafton County, 1951, 97 N.H. 32, 79 A.2d 630; Eddy v. Village of Ellicottville, 1898, 35 App.Div. 256, 54 N.Y.S. 800.

94. Raynor v. City of Arcata, 1938, 11 Cal.2d 113, 77 P.2d 1054; City of Indianapolis v. Butzke, 1940, 217 Ind. 203, 26 N.E.2d 754, rehearing denied 1940, 217 Ind.App. 203, 27 N.E.2d 350; Howard v. City of Stillwater, 1929, 171 Minn. 391, 214 N.W. 656; Powell v. Village of Fenton, 1927, 240 Mich. 94, 214 N.W. 968; Hooper v. City of Childress, Tex.Civ.App. 1932, 34 S.W.2d 907.

95. Manske v. City of Milwaukee, 1904, 123 Wis. 172, 101 N.W. 377 (moving scale used in weighing coal for fire department); Gillespie v. City of Lincoln, 1892, 35 Neb. 34, 52 N.W. 811 (exercising fire horses); Frederick v. City of Columbus, 1898, 58 Ohio St. 538, 51 N.E. 35 (fire tower on exhibition); Smith v. City of Rochester, 1879, 76 N.Y. 506 (parade); O'Daly v. City of Louisville, 1914, 156 Ky. 815, 162 S.W. 79 (flushing street in front of fire house). Contra, Opocensky v. City of South Omaha, 1917, 101 Neb. 336, 163 N.W. 235 (testing apparatus).

96. Butler v. City of Kansas City, 1916, 97 Kan. 239, 155 P. 12; Martinson v. City of Alpena, 1950, 328 Mich. 595, 44 N.W.2d 148; Beakey v. Town of Billerica, 1949, 324 Mass. 290, 85 N.E.2d 620; Hagerman v. City of Seattle, 1937, 189 Wash. 694, 66 P.2d 1152. See Henry, Governmental Immunity of County Hospitals, 1964, 13 Cleve.Marsh.L.Rev. 496.

Contra: City of Miami v. Oates, 1942, 152 Fla. 21, 10 So.2d 721; Browege v. City of Owatonna, 1933, 190 Minn. 394, 251 N.W. 915; City of Okmulgee v. Carlton, 1937, 180 Okl. 605, 71 P.2d 722.

97. Howard v. City of Philadelphia, 1915, 250 Pa. 184, 95 A. 388; Franklin v. City of Seattle, 1920,

112 Wash. 671, 192 P. 1015; Frost v. City of Topeka, 1916, 98 Kan. 636, 161 P. 936; Bruhnke v. City of La Crosse, 1914, 155 Wis. 485, 144 N.W. 1100.

98. Hill v. City of Boston, 1877, 122 Mass. 344; Kinnare v. City of Chicago, 1898, 171 Ill. 332, 39 N.E. 536; Folk v. City of Milwaukee, 1900, 108 Wis. 359, 84 N.W. 420; Daskiewicz v. District Board of Education, 1942, 301 Mich. 212, 3 N.W.2d 71.

See Poe, School Liability for Injuries to Pupils, 1941; Rosenfield, Governmental Immunity from Liability for Torts in School Accidents, 1940, 5 Leg. Notes on Local Government 358; Seitz, School District Responsibility for Negligent Supervision of Pupils, 1941, 25 Marq.L.Rev. 115; Note, 1932, 46 Harv.L. Rev. 305.

99. Summers v. Board of Com'rs of Daviess County, 1886, 103 Ind. 262, 2 N.E. 725; Lefrois v. Monroe County, 1900, 162 N.Y. 563, 57 N.E. 185; Hughes v. Monroe County, 1895, 147 N.Y. 49, 41 N.E. 407; Neff v. Inhabitants of Wellesley, 1889, 148 Mass. 487, 20 N.E. 111; Curran v. City of Boston, 1890, 151 Mass. 505, 24 N.E. 781.

100. Broughton v. City of Cleveland, 1957, 167 Ohio St. 29, 146 N.E.2d 301; James v. City of Charlotte, 1922, 183 N.C. 630, 112 S.E. 423; Scibilia v. City of Philadelphia, 1924, 279 Pa. 549, 124 A. 273, 32 A.L. R. 981; Behrmann v. City of St. Louis, 1918, 273 Mo. 578, 201 S.W. 547; City of Houston v. Allen, Tex.Civ.App.1964, 380 S.W.2d 696, ref. n. r. e.

Contra: Hutton v. Martin, 1953, 41 Wash.2d 780, 252 P.2d 581; City of Houston v. Shilling, 1951, 150 Tex. 387, 240 S.W.2d 1010; Missano v. Mayor of New York, 1899, 160 N.Y. 123, 54 N.E. 744. See Note, 1951, 30 Tex.L.Rev. 266.

ployment. This is true where it supplies water,[101] gas,[102] or electricity,[1] or where it operates a ferry,[2] wharves or docks,[3] an airport,[4] or a public market.[5] City hospitals have been held both governmental [6] and proprietary.[7] Where such a thing as a municipal garage,[8] a housing unit,[9] or an arts and

crafts center [10] is operated for profit, it nearly always has been held to be proprietary; and the same is true of more doubtful institutions such as hospitals.[11]

The use to which a building is put on a particular occasion may determine liability; and the city will not be responsible for the negligence of its employees in cleaning ice and snow off of the roof of a city hall used exclusively for municipal purposes,[12] but will be liable for failure to light a stairway when a room in the same building has been let for a public entertainment.[13]

There are other functions as to which there has been much less agreement. The planning and laying out of streets and highways,[14] or of sewers and drains,[15] usually is regarded as involving legislative or administrative discretion, and so as "governmental;" and the same is true, in general, of the regu-

101. McGinley v. City of Cherryvale, 1935, 141 Kan. 155, 40 P.2d 377; Buono v. City of Boston, 1935, 290 Mass. 59, 194 N.E. 658; Shandrow v. City of Tacoma, 1936, 187 Wash. 389, 62 P.2d 1090; Badten v. City of Stevens Point, 1932, 209 Wis. 379, 245 N. W. 130; Nestman v. South Davis County Water Imp. Dist., 1965, 16 Utah 2d 198, 398 P.2d 203.

102. City of Richmond v. James, 1938, 170 Va. 553, 197 S.E. 416; Brantman v. Canby, 1912, 119 Minn. 396, 138 N.W. 671.

1. Bathke v. Traverse City, 1944, 308 Mich. 1, 13 N. W.2d 184; City of Duncan v. Canan, 1938, 183 Okl. 315, 62 P.2d 663; Cook v. City of Beatrice, 1934, 114 Neb. 305, 207 N.W. 518. Cf. Storti v. Town of Fayal, 1935, 194 Minn. 628, 621 N.W. 463 (telephone).

2. City of Portsmouth v. Ladrey, 1937, 168 Va. 517, 191 S.E. 595; Jacoby v. Chouteau County, 1941, 112 Mont. 70, 112 P.2d 1068.

Accord, as to transportation systems: Karsey v. City and County of San Francisco, 1933, 130 Cal.App. 655, 20 P.2d 751; Tobin v. City of Seattle, 1923, 127 Wash. 664, 221 P. 583.

3. City of Oakland v. American Dredging Co., 1935, 3 Cal.2d 220, 44 P.2d 309; The President Madison, 9 Cir. 1937, 91 F.2d 835; Blue v. City of Union, 1938, 159 Or. 5, 75 P.2d 977.

4. Wendler v. City of Great Bend, 1957, 181 Kan. 753, 316 P.2d 265; Brummett v. City of Jackson, 1951, 211 Miss. 116, 51 So.2d 52; Granite Oil Securities v. Douglas County, 1950, 67 Nev. 388, 219 P. 2d 191.

There has been some authority that this is governmental. See Note, 1946, 32 Corn.L.Q. 272.

5. Buckelew v. City of New Brunswick, 1935, 115 N. J.L. 112, 178 A. 785; Reed v. City of Baltimore, 1936, 171 Md. 115, 188 A. 15. Cf. City of Atlanta v. Rich, 1941, 64 Ga.App. 193, 12 S.E.2d 436 (cemetery).

6. City and County of Denver v. Madison, 1960, 142 Colo. 1, 351 P.2d 826.

7. Stolp v. City of Arkansas City, 1956, 180 Kan. 197, 303 P.2d 123, adhered to 181 Kan. 225, 310 P.2d 888.

8. Dallas v. City of St. Louis, Mo.1960, 338 S.W.2d 39.

9. Knowles v. Housing Authority of City of Columbus, 1956, 212 Ga. 729, 95 S.E.2d 659.

10. Eversole v. City of Columbus, 1959, 169 Ohio St. 205, 158 N.E.2d 515. Cf. Reierson v. City of Minneapolis, 1962, 264 Minn. 153, 118 N.W.2d 223 (sawmill).

11. Hyde v. City of Lakewood, 1961, 87 Ohio App. 444, 175 N.E.2d 323.

12. Kelley v. City of Boston, 1904, 186 Mass. 165, 71 N.E. 299; cf. Snider v. City of St. Paul, 1892, 51 Minn. 466, 53 N.W. 763.

13. Little v. City of Holyoke, 1900, 177 Mass. 114, 58 N.E. 170; cf. Worden v. City of New Bedford, 1881, 131 Mass. 23. The distinction was carried to a refinement of absurdity in Pleasants v. City of Greensboro, 1926, 192 N.C. 820, 135 S.E. 321, holding that there was no liability to a plaintiff entering a combined city hall and opera house because she had gone in to pay her taxes.

See also, as to the use of a motor vehicle, Note, 1935, 10 Temple L.Q. 75.

14. Hoyt v. City of Danbury, 1897, 69 Conn. 341, 37 A. 1051; City Council of Augusta v. Little, 1902, 115 Ga. 124, 41 S.E. 238; Shippy v. Village of Au Sable, 1887, 65 Mich. 494, 32 N.W. 741; Urquhart v. City of Ogdensburg, 1883, 91 N.Y. 67.

15. Wicks v. Town of De Witt, 1880, 54 Iowa 130, 6 N.W. 176; Harrington v. Township of Woodbridge, 1903, 70 N.J.L. 28, 56 A. 141; Johnston v. District of Columbia, 1886, 118 U.S. 19; Cerise v. Fruitvale Water & Sanitation Dist., 1963, 153 Colo. 31, 384 P. 2d 462; Clay v. Jersey City, 1964, 84 N.J.Super. 9, 200 A.2d 787.

lation of traffic.[16] The actual construction of highways,[17] or of other public improvements,[18] on the other hand, is regarded by most courts as a mere "ministerial" act for which a city may be liable in tort, although some have considered it "governmental." [19]

The maintenance and operation of streets [20] and sewers [21] likewise is treated by the greater number of courts as a "proprietary" or "ministerial" function of cities, although they have found it difficult to explain why it is any less "governmental" than others, and some authority is to be found to the contrary.[22] On the part of counties, however, it usually is held that there is no liability for defective highways, even where the city would be liable.[23] Parks, playgrounds, and other recreational facilities, on the other hand, have been considered by the majority of the courts in the past to be governmental,[24] although the definite tendency of the later cases has been to regard them as proprietary, or "corporate." [25] There is little that can be said about such distinctions except that they exist, that they are highly artificial, and that they make no great amount of sense. Obviously this is an area in which the law has sought in vain for some reasonable and logical compromise, and has ended with a pile of jackstraws.

One anomaly is the generally accepted view that the municipality is liable if it can

16. Hammell v. City of Albuquerque, 1958, 63 N.M. 374, 320 P.2d 384; Dorminey v. City of Montgomery, 1936, 232 Ala. 47, 166 So. 689; Auslander v. City of St. Louis, 1933, 332 Mo. 145, 56 S.W.2d 778; Cleveland v. Town of Lancaster, 1933, 239 App.Div. 263, 267 N.Y.S. 673, affirmed, 1934, 264 N.Y. 568, 191 N.E. 568; Vickers v. City of Camden, 1939, 122 N.J.L. 14, 3 A.2d 613. See Murray, Recent Trends in Municipal Tort Liability, 1940, 5 Leg. Notes on Local Government 353; Note, 1937, 21 Minn.L.Rev. 459.

17. Browning v. City of Springfield, 1855, 17 Ill. 143; Barree v. City of Cape Girardeau, 1906, 197 Mo. 382, 95 S.W. 330; McMahon v. City of Dubuque, 1898, 107 Iowa 62, 77 N.W. 517; Engelking v. City of Spokane, 1910, 59 Wash. 446, 110 P. 25.

18. Bean v. City of Moberly, 1932, 350 Mo. 975, 169 S.W.2d 393; Durante v. City of Oakland, 1937, 19 Cal.App.2d 543, 65 P.2d 1326; Ostrander v. City of Lansing, 1897, 111 Mich. 693, 70 N.W. 332; Judd v. City of Hartford, 1899, 72 Conn. 350, 44 A. 510.

19. McManus v. Inhabitants of Weston, 1895, 164 Mass. 263, 41 N.E. 301; Colwell v. City of Waterbury, 1902, 74 Conn. 568, 51 A. 530; Goddard v. Inhabitants of Harpswell, 1892, 84 Me. 499, 24 A. 958; Bates v. Village of Rutland, 1890, 62 Vt. 178, 20 A. 278.

20. Myers v. City of Palmyra, Mo.1962, 355 S.W.2d 17; Loughran v. City of New York, 1948, 298 N.Y. 320, 83 N.E.2d 136; Parker v. City and County of Denver, 1953, 128 Colo. 355, 262 P.2d 553; Bulette v. City of Bremerton, 1949, 34 Wash.2d 834, 210 P. 2d 408; Aaronson v. City of New Haven, 1920, 94 Conn. 690, 110 A. 872; City of Vicksburg v. Harralson, 1924, 136 Miss. 872, 101 So. 713.

21. Barker v. City of Santa Fe, 1943, 47 N.M. 85, 136 P.2d 480; Oklahoma City v. Myers, 1936, 177 Okl. 622, 61 P.2d 653; City of Maysville v. Brooks, 1911, 145 Ky. 526, 140 S.W. 665; Svendsen v. Village of Alden, 1907, 101 Minn. 158, 112 N.W. 10.

22. Niblock v. Salt Lake City, 1941, 100 Utah 573, 111 P.2d 800; Gitcher v. City of Farmersville, 1940, 137 Tex. 12, 151 S.W.2d 565; Erickson v. City of West Salem, 1931, 205 Wis. 107, 236 N.W. 579.

23. White v. Bond County, 1871, 58 Ill. 297; Jones v. Union County, 1912, 63 Or. 566, 127 P. 781; Murray v. Board of Commissioners of Grant County, 1922, 28 N.M. 309, 210 P. 1067; Wilson v. Wapello County, 1905, 129 Iowa 77, 105 N.W. 363; Brabham v. Hinds County, 1877, 54 Miss. 363.

The result is that if a pedestrian falls into a hole, he may recover if it is on the city side of the line, but not if it is on the county side. Cf. Fleming v. City of Memphis, 1912, 126 Tenn. 331, 148 S.W. 1057, with Wood v. Tipton County, 1874, 7 Baxt., Tenn., 112. The rule has been extensively altered by statutes imposing liability upon counties.

24. Baker v. City of Lexington, Ky.1958, 310 S.W.2d 555; Mathis v. City of Dothan, 1957, 266 Ala. 531, 97 So.2d 908; Pohland v. City of Sheboygan, 1947, 251 Wis. 20, 27 N.W.2d 736; Le Pitre v. Chicago Park District, 1940, 374 Ill. 184, 29 N.E.2d 81; Grover v. City of Manhattan, 1967, 198 Kan. 307, 424 P.2d 256.

25. De Simone v. City of Philadelphia, 1955, 380 Pa. 137, 110 A.2d 431; Murphy v. City of Carlsbad, 1960, 66 N.M. 376, 348 P.2d 492; Bucholz v. City of Sioux Falls, 1958, 77 S.D. 322, 91 N.W.2d 606; Flowers v. Board of Commissioners, 1960, 240 Ind. 668, 168 N.E.2d 224; Caldwell v. Village of Island Park, 1952, 304 N.Y. 268, 107 N.E.2d 441.

See Tooke, The Extension of Municipal Liability in Tort, 1932, 19 Va.L.Rev. 97; Notes, 1938, 24 Va.L. Rev. 430; 1943, 28 Corn.L.Q. 372.

be found to have created or maintained a nuisance, even though it be in the course of an otherwise "governmental" function.[26] The origin of this seems to be found in the idea that the creation of a private nuisance amounted to a taking of land without compensation,[27] or that the city, as a landowner, was necessarily a proprietor, and subject to the responsibilities of one toward other landowners.[28] If this was the explanation, it was soon lost to sight when the principal was extended to public nuisances [29] where neither consideration is involved. Since liability for nuisance rests in many cases upon nothing more than negligence,[30] for which in theory

the municipality is not liable, the result has been a rather hopeless attempt to distinguish between the two, which has added confusion to the law of both nuisance and municipal corporations.[31] It seems reasonable to say that there is no sound argument behind the distinction itself, and that resort to the more or less undefined concept of nuisance is merely one method by which the courts have retreated from municipal nonliability.[32]

In a number of states there are statutes which have changed the common law to a greater or less extent by imposing liability upon municipalities. Such statutes as the California Public Liability Act,[33] and the Wisconsin Safe Place Statute,[34] have made the city liable for injuries on public property, and a number of states have statutes making it liable for the negligent operation of its vehicles.[35] The New York statute waiving the immunity of the state has been held to include municipal corporations in at

26. Jeakins v. City of El Dorado, 1936, 143 Kan. 206, 53 P.2d 798; Gaines v. Village of Wyoming, 1947, 147 Ohio St. 491, 72 N.E.2d 369; Robb v. City of Milwaukee, 1943, 241 Wis. 432, 6 N.W.2d 222; Kurtigian v. City of Worcester, 1965, 348 Mass. 284, 203 N.E.2d 692; Lehmkuhl v. Junction City, 1956, 179 Kan. 389, 295 P.2d 621. See Wilbourne, Municipal Liability: A Problem in Characterization, 1964, 38 Conn.Bar J. 51; Notes, 1941, 16 Notre Dame L. 365; [1948] Wis.L.Rev. 116; 1951, 31 Or.L.Rev. 34.

27. Harno, Tort Immunity of Municipal Corporations, 1921, 4 Ill.L.Q. 28, 37; David Municipal Liability in Tort in California, 1934, 7 So.Cal.L.Rev. 215–219; City of Louisville v. Hehemann, 1914, 161 Ky. 523, 171 S.W. 165.

28. Note, 1940, 28 Geo.L.J. 526, 527; Jones v. Inhabitants of Great Barrington, 1930, 273 Mass. 483, 174 N.E. 118.

29. Lehmkuhl v. Junction City, 1956, 179 Kan. 389, 295 P.2d 621; Robb v. City of Milwaukee, 1943, 241 Wis. 432, 6 N.W.2d 222; Hoffman v. City of Bristol, 1931, 113 Conn. 386, 155 A. 499; Miller v. City of Woodburn, 1930, 134 Or. 536, 294 P. 349; City of Hamilton v. Dilley, 1929, 120 Ohio St. 127, 165 N.E. 713.

30. See supra, p. 575. Also Maxwell v. City of Miami, 1924, 87 Fla. 107, 100 So. 147; Rodgers v. Kansas City, Mo.App.1959, 327 S.W.2d 478; Rudibaugh v. City of Niles, 1937, 56 Ohio App. 451, 11 N.E.2d 193.
The magic of the word is indicated by decisions holding the city liable for mere negligence toward trespassing children on the ground of "attractive nuisance," which of course is not nuisance at all. See supra, p. 365. Roman v. City of Leavenworth, 1913, 90 Kan. 379, 133 P.2d 551; Smith v. Iowa City, 1931, 213 Iowa 391, 239 N.W. 29; Stedwell v. City of Chicago, 1921, 297 Ill. 486, 130 N.E. 729; Capp v. City of St. Louis, 1915, 251 Mo. 345, 158 S.W. 616;

DeGarmo v. City of Alcoa, 6 Cir. 1964, 332 F.2d 403. Contra, Smith v. City of Jefferson, 1959, 8 Wis.2d 378, 99 N.W.2d 119.

31. See for example the New York cases, such as: Dubois v. City of Kingston, 1886, 102 N.Y. 219, 6 N.E. 273; Hunt v. Mayor of New York, 1888, 109 N.Y. 134, 16 N.E. 320; Speir v. City of Brooklyn, 1893, 139 N.Y. 6, 34 N.E. 727; Landau v. City of New York, 1904, 180 N.Y. 48, 72 N.E. 631; Melker v. City of New York, 1908, 190 N.Y. 481, 83 N.E. 565; Hayes v. Brooklyn Heights R. Co., 1910, 200 N.Y. 183, 93 N.E. 469; Lyman v. Village of Potsdam, 1920, 228 N.Y. 398, 127 N.E. 312; McFarlane v. City of Niagara Falls, 1928, 247 N.Y. 340, 160 N.E. 391; Khoury v. Saratoga County, 1935, 267 N.Y. 384, 196 N.E. 299.

32. See Note, 1933, 46 Harv.L.Rev. 305.

33. See David, Municipal Liability in Tort in California, 1934, 7 So.Cal.L.Rev. 412–448; Gibson v. County of Mendocino, 1940, 16 Cal.2d 80, 105 P.2d 105.

34. Applied in Heiden v. City of Milwaukee, 1940, 222 Wis. 92, 275 N.W. 922. See Note [1953] Wis.L. Rev. 311.

35. See for example, Miller v. City of New York, 1932, 235 App.Div. 259, 257 N.Y.S. 33; Schumacher v. City of Milwaukee, 1932, 209 Wis. 43, 243 N.W. 756.

least some respects.[36] Reference must of course be made to the statutes of the particular jurisdiction.

Abrogation of Immunity

For well over a century the immunity of both the state and the local governments for their torts has been subjected to vigorous criticism, which at length has begun to have its effect. It has been characterized as "the gaslight of another time," which "must give way to the brightened illumination of today, which chases the shadows and leaves exposed the inadequacy of such a mid-Victorian concept." [37]

Apart from the general erosion through the expansion of the categories of "proprietary" activities, the first major changes were statutory.[38] One major problem which arose at a relatively early date was that of the effect of liability insurance.[39] This was available to either the state or the municipality; and the insurance might, for a full premium, "waive" the immunity, or, for a much lower one, refuse to do so. In practice state agencies seldom carried the insurance; but municipal corporations began to do so, since they were subject to "proprietary" liability. The practice caught on, presently even at the state level, and statutes began to be adopted which authorized it.

In the absence of such specific statutory authority, it has commonly been held to be beyond the power of the governmental agency itself to expend public money by taking out the insurance, so that it becomes ultra vires, and so is held to be without any legal effect whatever upon government immunity.[40] This has been true even where the policy has waived the immunity, and the insurer has collected the full premium for doing so. Where there is statutory authority for the purchase, the statute may expressly waive the immunity of the government entity from suit, or require a clause in the policy by which the insurer agrees that it will not raise the defense; or it may authorize a direct action against the insurer.[41] If it does none of these things, the large majority of the decisions have held that the mere authorization to expend public money is not a waiver of the tort immunity, and that the insurance has no effect upon it,[42] Again this conclusion has been reached even though the insurer has agreed not to raise the defense, and has collected a full premium for doing so.[43]

The effect of this is to defeat an honest effort to protect the plaintiff, on the part of both the legislature and the insured state agency, merely because the insurance car-

---

36. Bernardine v. City of New York, 1945, 294 N.Y. 361, 62 N.E.2d 604; See Lloyd, Le Roi Est Mort— Vive le Roi, 1949, 24 N.Y.U.L.Rev. 38; Note, 1948, 23 St. Johns L.Rev. 117.

See, generally, Antieau, Statutory Expansion of Municipal Tort Liability, 1957, 4 St. Louis U.L.J. 351; Van Alstyne, Governmental Tort Liability: Judicial Lawmaking in a Statutory Milieu, 1963, 15 Stan.L. Rev. 163.

37. Caporossi v. Atlantic City, D. N.J. 1963, 220 F. Supp. 508, affirmed 328 F.2d 620, cert. denied 379 U.S. 825.

38. See supra, p. 975.

39. See Gibbons, Liability Insurance and the Tort Immunity of State and Local Government, [1959] Duke L.J. 588; Notes, 1956, 54 Mich.L.Rev. 404; 1949, 33 Minn.L.Rev. 634; 1964, 66 W.Va.L.Rev. 351; 1964, 43 Or.L.Rev. 267.

40. Hartford Acc. & Indem. Co. v. Wainscott, 1933, 41 Ariz. 439, 19 P.2d 328; Burns v. American Cas. Co., 1954, 127 Cal.App.2d 198, 273 P.2d 605; Adkins v. Western & So. Indem. Co., 1936, 117 W.Va. 451, 186 S.E. 302; see Adams v. City of New Haven, 1945, 131 Conn. 552, 41 A.2d 111.

41. See Aetna Cas. & Surety Co. of Hartford, Conn. v. Brashears, 1956, 226 Ark. 1017, 297 S.W.2d 662; Baker & Co. v. Lagaly, 10 Cir. 1944, 144 F.2d 344.

42. Maffei v. Incorporated Town of Kemmerer, 1959, 80 Wyo. 33, 338 P.2d 808, rehearing denied, 80 Wyo. 33, 340 P.2d 759; Hummer v. School City of Hartford City, 1953, 124 Ind.App. 30, 112 N.E.2d 891; Rittmiller v. School District No. 84, D.Minn.1952, 104 F.Supp. 187; Chambers v. Ideal Pure Milk Co., Ky.1952, 245 S.W.2d 589; Michael v. School District of Lancaster, 1958, 391 Pa. 209, 137 A.2d 456.

43. Hummer v. School City of Hartford City, 1953, 124 Ind.App. 30, 112 N.E.2d 891; Pohland v. City of Sheboygan, 1947, 251 Wis. 20, 27 N.W.2d 736; Jones v. Scofield Bros., D.Md.1947, 73 F.Supp. 395; Arnold v. Walton, 1949, 205 Ga. 606, 54 S.E.2d 424; Stephenson v. City of Raleigh, 1950, 232 N.C. 42, 59 S.E.2d 195.

rier has seen fit to welsh on its agreement; and it scarcely will appeal to anyone who prefers honest dealing. All this, however, is in the process of giving way. All of the late decisions, in a number of jurisdictions,[44] have held that the authorized purchase of the insurance necessarily carries with it a waiver of the immunity, to the extent of the insurance coverage. While this is clearly right, and carries out the real intent and purpose of the legislation, insurance remains at least a partial solution, since the plaintiff's recovery depends upon the statutory authorization.

This indirect approach by way of insurance has lately given way to a more direct frontal attack upon the governmental immunity itself. This began in 1957 with the supreme court of Florida, which always had tended to confine the immunity of municipal corporations within quite narrow limits.[45]

In Hargrove v. Town of Cocoa Beach,[46] the court abruptly held the city liable when a prisoner, left unattended in jail, was suffocated when a fire broke out. It declared that any municipality should have no immunity from tort liability, even in its governmental capacity. "To continue to endow this type of organization with sovereign divinity appears to us to predicate the law of the Twentieth Century upon an Eighteenth Century anachronism." This was followed

two years later by Illinois,[47] holding a school district liable when a child was injured by the negligent operation of a school bus. These examples touched off, during the succeeding four years, a minor avalanche of decisions repudiating municipal immunity, which were led by California[48] and Michigan.[49] At the time of publication, the total of these jurisdictions has reached seventeen.[50] As in the case of prenatal injuries,[51] and strict products liability to the consumer,[52] the sudden eruption of so many cases within so brief a period appears to leave no doubt that there is to be a radical change in the law.

The abolition of the municipal immunity in Arizona,[53] California,[54] Illinois,[55] Indiana,[56] New Jersey,[57] and Wisconsin[58] was held to

---

44. Wilkie v. Henderson County, 1968, 1 N.C.App. 155, 160 S.E.2d 505; Longpre v. Joint School Dist. No. 2, 1968, 151 Mont. 345, 443 P.2d 1; Shermoen v. Lindsay, N.D.1968, 163 N.W.2d 738; Vendrell v. School Dist. 26C, 1961, 226 Or. 263, 360 P.2d 282; Flowers v. Board of Comm'rs of County of Vanderburgh, 1960, 240 Ind. 668, 168 N.E.2d 224.

45. Thus it had been held that cities under a commission form of government were subject to the same tort liability as private corporations. City of Tallahassee v. Kaufman, 1924, 87 Fla. 119, 100 So. 150; City of West Palm Beach v. Grimmett, 1931, 102 Fla. 680, 136 So. 320, rehearing denied, 102 Fla. 680, 137 So. 385; Wolfe v. City of Miami, 1931, 103 Fla. 774, 134 So. 539, affirmed, 103 Fla. 774, 137 So. 892.

46. Fla.1957, 96 So.2d 130. See note, 1962, 16 U.Miami L.Rev. 572.

47. Molitor v. Kaneland Community Unit Dist. No. 302, 1959, 18 Ill.2d 11, 163 N.E.2d 89. See Hickman, Municipal Tort Liability in Illinois, [1961] U.Ill.L. Forum 475.

48. Muskopf v. Corning Hospital District, 1961, 55 Cal.2d 211, 359 P.2d 457. See note, 1961, 49 Cal.L. Rev. 400.

49. Williams v. City of Detroit, 1961, 364 Mich. 231, 111 N.W.2d 1.

50. Alaska, Arizona, Arkansas, California, District of Columbia, Florida, Idaho, Illinois, Indiana, Kentucky, Michigan, Minnesota, Nebraska, Nevada, New Jersey, Rhode Island, Wisconsin.

In addition, municipal immunity has been abrogated by statute in Iowa, Louisiana, New York, Oregon, and Washington, and to some extent in Utah.

See Van Alstyne, Governmental Tort Liability; A Decade of Change, [1966] U.Ill.L.F. 919.

51. See supra, § 55.

52. See supra, § 98.

53. Stone v. Arizona Highway Commission, 1963, 93 Ariz. 384, 381 P.2d 107.

54. Muskopf v. Corning Hospital District, 1961, 55 Cal.2d 211, 359 P.2d 457.

55. Molitor v. Kaneland Community Unit Dist., 1959, 18 Ill.2d 11, 163 N.E.2d 89, cert. denied 362 U. S. 968.

56. Perkins v. State, 1969, —— Ind. ——, 251 N.E.2d 30 (as to proprietary activities). See Note, 1965, 65 Col.L.Rev. 286.

57. Willis v. Department of Conservation & Econ. Div., 1970, 55 N.J. 534, 264 A.2d 34.

A Nevada statute has largely duplicated California's. State v. Silva, 1970, —— Nev. ——, 478 P.2d 591.

58. See note 58 on page 986.

carry with it a similar abrogation of the immunity of the state. There are in addition five jurisdictions [59] in which the state immunity has been largely terminated by statute. In several other states [60] the courts have refused to include the state, on the ground that it has not consented to be sued on the tort claim, and that without such consent the constitution precludes the action. Wisconsin got around even this by holding that the state has no immunity from tort liability, but only immunity from suit, and that it was for the legislature to determine the extent to which that would still be recognized.[61]

The unusual celerity with which the foregoing developments occurred left for a time a good many unsolved problems. In California the legislature rushed to enact a moratorium on governmental liability for two years, to permit the legislature to work out something in the way of a state tort claims act,[62] more or less modeled on the federal Act. In Illinois special interests succeeded in pushing through bills, which were subsequently held unconstitutional,[63] restoring total immunity on the park of park districts, counties, forest preserve districts, and a limited immunity for school districts.[64]

At the outset it was more or less obvious that some vestige of the governmental immunity must be retained. It was, for example, unthinkable that either state of a municipality should be held liable for a wrong decision of its courts,[65] for an erroneous evaluation of property by a tax assessor. In several of the decisions abrogating the immunities, there was language used which reserved the possibility that there might still be immunity as to "legislative" or "judicial" functions,[66] or as to acts or omissions of government employees which were "discretionary." [67] In California the question arose [68] whether the government might be liable where its employee, in the exercise of his discretion, was not; but both the legislature and the last decision of the courts rejected the possibility, and adhered to the rule that the government can be liable only where its officer is.[69]

58. Holytz v. City of Milwaukee, 1962, 17 Wis.2d 26, 115 N.W.2d 618. Since going to press, Idaho has been added, Smith v. Idaho, Idaho 1970, 473 P.2d 937.

59. Iowa, New York, Oregon, Utah, Washington.

60. Shellhorn & Hill, Inc. v. State, 1962, 55 Del. 298, 187 A.2d 71; Foley Const. Co. v. Ward, Ky. 1963, 375 S.W.2d 392; McDowell v. Mackie, 1961, 365 Mich. 268, 112 N.W.2d 491; Spanel v. Mounds View School District, 1962, 264 Minn. 279, 118 N.W.2d 795; Hardgrave v. State, 1964, 80 Nev. 74, 389 P.2d 249; Metropolitan Government v. Allen, 1967, 220 Tenn. 222, 415 S.W.2d 632.

61. Holytz v. City of Milwaukee, 1962, 17 Wis.2d 26, 115 N.W.2d 618. This was rejected in Muskopf v. Corning Hospital District, 1961, 55 Cal.2d 211, 359 P.2d 457.

62. See Corning Hospital District v. Superior Court, 1962, 57 Cal.2d 488, 370 P.2d 325, 20 Cal.Rptr. 621; Thelander v. Superior Court, 1962, 58 Cal.2d 828, 376 P.2d 571, 26 Cal.Rptr. 643. This resulted in extensive legislation in 1963. See Cobey, The New California Governmental Tort Liability Statutes, 1964, 1 Harv.J.Leg. 16.

63. Harvey v. Clyde Park District, 1965, 32 Ill.2d 60, 203 N.E.2d 573; Hutchings v. Kraject, 1966, 34 Ill. 2d 379, 215 N.E.2d 274.

64. Ill.Rev.Stat.1959, c. 105, §§ 12–1, 491, 333.2a; c. 34, § 301.1; c. 57½, § 3a; c. 122, §§ 821–31.

65. See for example Middleton v. City of Fort Walton Beach, Fla.App.1959, 113 So.2d 431.

66. Parish v. Pitts, 1968, 244 Ark. 1239, 429 S.W.2d 45; Urow v. District of Columbia, 1963, 114 U.S. App.D.C. 350, 316 F.2d 351, cert. denied 375 U.S. 826; Thompson v. City of Jacksonville, Fla.App. 1961, 130 So.2d 105; City of Louisville v. Chapman, Ky.1967, 413 S.W.2d 74; Holytz v. City of Milwaukee, 1962, 17 Wis.2d 26, 115 N.W.2d 618.

67. Muskopf v. Corning Hospital District, 1961, 55 Cal.2d 211, 359 P.2d 457; Urow v. District of Columbia, 1963, 114 U.S.App.D.C. 350, 316 F.2d 351; Spanel v. Mounds View School Dist., 1962, 264 Minn. 279, 118 N.W.2d 795; Creelman v. Svenning, 1966, 67 Wash.2d 882, 410 P.2d 606; Parish v. Pitts, 1968, 244 Ark. 1239, 429 S.W.2d 45.

68. In Lipman v. Brisbane Elementary School Dist., 1961, 55 Cal.2d 224, 11 Cal.Rptr. 97, 359 P.2d 465.

69. Cal. State Tort Claims Act, 815 (2) (b); Ne-Vasek v. City of Los Angeles, 1965, 233 Cal.App.2d 131, 43 Cal.Rptr. 294. Also rejected in Creelman v. Svenning, 1966, 67 Wash.2d 882, 410 P.2d 606.

After a great deal of debate,[70] state tort claims acts, modeled more or less on the federal statute, began to be worked out and adopted. Perhaps the most advanced and effective of these has been that of California, where the example of the Federal Tort Claims Act has been closely followed. The "discretionary" acts of public officers have tended to be limited, as in the case of federal officers,[71] to those at the planning or policy level, and not to include decisions at the operational, or ministerial, level.[72]

132. PUBLIC OFFICERS

The immunity of public officers in the performance of their duties has already been mentioned [73] in connection with liability for arrest, the seizure of property under process, and defamation. The policy involved in such cases applies with broader scope to the general problem of the immunity of officers for other torts.[74] No officer, of course, is absolved from liability for his private and personal torts merely because he is an officer,

and the question arises only where he performs, or purports to perform, his official functions.

The complex process of legal administration requires that officers shall be charged with the duty of making decisions, either of law or of fact, and acting in accordance with their determinations. Public servants would be unduly hampered and intimidated in the discharge of their duties, and an impossible burden would fall upon all our agencies of government if the immunity to private liability were not extended, in some reasonable degree, to those who act improperly, or exceed the authority given. The development of a system of administrative law, insuring a reasonable opportunity to be heard before action is taken, and resulting in effect in the creation of a subordinate body of courts, affords a strong argument for the recognition of an immunity in the individual officers concerned.[75]

On this basis judges [76] always have been accorded complete immunity for their judicial acts within the jurisdiction of courts of justice, even when their conduct is corrupt, or malicious and intended to do injury.[77] Even though a cynic might be forgiven for pointing out just who made this rule, the reason is of course not a desire to protect the

---

70. See Van Alstyne, Governmental Tort Liability: A Public Policy Prospectus, 1963, 10 U.C.L.A.L. Rev. 463; Kennedy and Lynch, Some Problems of a Sovereign Without Immunity, 1963, 36 So.Cal.L.Rev. 161; Davis, Tort Liability of Governmental Units, 1956, 40 Minn.L.Rev. 751, 791–813. See also David, Tort Liability of Local Government: Alternatives to Immunity from Liability or Suit, 1959, 6 U.C.L. A.L.Rev. 1.

71. See supra, p. 974.

72. See Elton v. County of Orange, 1970, 3 Cal.App. 3d 1053, 84 Cal.Rptr. 27; Johnson v. State, 1968, 69 Cal.2d 782, 73 Cal.Rptr. 240, 447 P.2d 352; Note, 1966, 39 So.Cal.L.Rev. 466; Rogers v. State, 1969, 51 Haw. 293, 459 P.2d 378.

73. Supra, §§ 25, 114.

74. See Jennings, Tort Liability of Administrative Officers, 1937, 21 Minn.L.Rev. 263; David, The Tort Liability of Public Officers, 1939, 12 So.Cal.L. Rev. 127, 260, 368; Keefe, Personal Tort Liability of Administrative Officers, 1943, 12 Ford.L.Rev. 130; Gray, Private Wrongs of Public Servants, 1959, 47 Cal.L.Rev. 303; Davis, Administrative Officers' Tort Liability, 1956, 55 Mich.L.Rev. 201; Notes, 1951, 21 Tenn.L.Rev. 306; 1948, 9 Ohio St.L. J. 501; 1957, 5 U.C.L.A.L.Rev. 164; 1965, 14 Cleve. Marsh.L.Rev. 365.

75. Jennings, Tort Liability of Administrative Officers, 1937, 21 Minn.L.Rev. 263.

76. Fletcher v. Wheat, 1938, 69 App.D.C. 259, 100 F. 2d 432, cert. denied 307 U.S. 621; Landseidel v. Culeman, 1921, 47 N.D. 275, 181 N.W. 593; Brictson v. Woodrough, 8 Cir. 1947, 164 F.2d 107, cert. denied 334 U.S. 849; Mother Pauline v. Bray, 1959, 168 Cal.App.2d 384, 335 P.2d 1018; Allen v. Holbrook, 1943, 103 Utah 319, 135 P.2d 242, modified 103 Utah 599, 139 P.2d 233. See Thompson, Judicial Immunity and the Protection of Justices, 1958, 21 Mod.L. Rev. 517; Rubinstein, Liability in Tort of Judicial Officers, 1964, 15 U.Toronto L.Rev. 317.

77. Bradley v. Fisher, 1871, 13 Wall., U.S. 335, 20 L.Ed. 646; Sweeney v. Young, 1925, 82 N.H. 159, 131 A. 155; Early v. Fitzpatrick, 1909, 161 Ala. 171, 49 So. 686; Cuiksa v. City of Mansfield, 6 Cir. 1957, 250 F.2d 700, cert. denied 356 U.S. 937; Ginsburg v. Stern, W.D.Pa.1956, 19 F.R.D. 238, affirmed in part, vacated in part, 1957, 242 F.2d 379.

corrupt, malicious or misbehaving official, but rather the necessity of preserving an independent judiciary, who will not be deterred by the fear of vexatious suits and personal liability, together with the manifest unfairness of placing any man in a position where his judgment is required, and at the same time holding him responsible according to the judgment of others.[78] The same absolute protection extends to members of the state and national legislatures,[79] as well as inferior legislative bodies, such as municipal councils,[80] and to the highest executive officers of the federal and state governments,[81] at least so long as they do not clearly exceed the discretion vested in them by law.[82] As in the case of defamation,[83] the federal courts have tended to extend the immunity down the scale to all officers of lower degree so long as they are acting within the scope of their duties,[84] while those of the states have been, with some exceptions,[85] much more disposed to restrict any absolute immunity to the superior officers.[86]

As to such lower administrative officers, however, the whole situation has been much complicated by the drawing of another line of distinction, which in effect achieves a rather uneasy compromise. The courts have set up a finespun and more or less unworkable distinction between acts which are regarded as "discretionary," or "quasi-judicial," in character, requiring personal deliberation, decision and judgment, and those which are merely "ministerial," amounting only to an obedience to orders, or the performance of a duty in which the officer is

---

78. Stewart v. Case, 1893, 53 Minn. 62, 54 N.W. 938; Pratt v. Gardner, 1848, 2 Cush., Mass., 63. Jennings, Tort Liability of Administrative Officers, 1937, 21 Minn.L.Rev. 263, 271–2, lists nine justifications altogether which have been given: saving judges' time, preventing influence on decisions through fear of subsequent suit, removing a discouragement to judicial service, separation of powers, necessity of finality, other opportunities for review of adverse decisions, duty to the public only and not to individuals, judicial self-protection, and unfairness in penalizing honest error. The same reasons, mutatis mutandi, are mentioned and applied as to other public officers.

79. Kilbourn v. Thompson, 1881, 103 U.S. 168.

80. Incorporated Village of Hicksville v. Blakeslee, 1921, 103 Ohio St. 508, 134 N.E. 445; Pawlowski v. Jenks, 1897, 115 Mich. 275, 73 N.W. 238; McHenry v. Sneer, 1881, 56 Iowa 649, 10 N.W. 234; Jones v. Loving, 1877, 55 Miss. 109.

81. Spalding v. Vilas, 1895, 161 U.S. 483; Booth v. Fletcher, 1938, 69 App.D.C. 351, 101 F.2d 676, cert. denied Fletcher v. Booth, 307 U.S. 628; Cooper v. O'Connor, 1938, 69 U.S.App.D.C. 100, 99 F.2d 135, rehearing denied 1939, 305 U.S. 673, rehearing denied 307 U.S. 651; Hatfield v. Graham, 1914, 73 W.Va. 759, 81 S.E. 533; Matson v. Margiotti, 1952, 374 Pa. 188, 88 A.2d 892.

82. Cf. Sterling v. Constantin, 1932, 287 U.S. 378; Hearon v. Calus, 1935, 178 S.C. 381, 183 S.E. 13. But there must be clear proof of abuse of discretion to justify judicial interference. Powers Merc. Co. v. Olson, D.Minn.1934, 7 F.Supp. 865.

83. Supra, § 114.

84. Baker v. Mueller, 7 Cir. 1955, 222 F.2d 180 (town board and building inspector; wrongful condemnation of a building); De Busk v. Harvin, 5 Cir. 1954, 212 F.2d 143 (employees of Veterans Administration, maliciously obtaining discharge of others); Yaselli v. Goff, 2 Cir. 1926, 12 F.2d 396, cert. granted 273 U.S. 677, affirmed 275 U.S. 503 (United States district attorney and special assistant; malicious prosecution); Gibson v. Reynolds, 8 Cir. 1949, 172 F.2d 95, cert. denied 337 U.S. 925 (draft board personnel, wrongful drafting); Papagianakis v. The Samos, 4 Cir. 1950, 186 F.2d 257, cert. denied 341 U.S. 921 (immigration officials, false imprisonment); Springfield v. Carter, 8 Cir. 1949, 175 F.2d 914 (city officials, malicious prosecution).

85. Particularly in California. Hardy v. Vial, 1957, 48 Cal.2d 577, 311 P.2d 494; White v. Towers, 1951, 37 Cal.2d 727, 235 P.2d 209; Coverstone v. Davies, 1952, 38 Cal.2d 315, 239 P.2d 876, cert. dismissed Mock v. Davies, 344 U.S. 840; Dawson v. Martin, 1957, 150 Cal.App.2d 379, 309 P.2d 915. See also Wilson v. Hirst, 1948, 67 Ariz. 197, 193 P.2d 461; Hjorth v. Whittenburg, 1952, 121 Utah 324, 241 P. 2d 907; Sweeney v. Young, 1925, 82 N.H. 159, 131 A. 155.

86. Paoli v. Mason, 1945, 325 Ill.App. 197, 59 N.E.2d 499 (liquor control commissioner; revocation of license); Taulli v. Gregory, 1953, 223 La. 195, 65 So. 2d 312 (mayor, alderman and police officer; malicious prosecution); Motley v. Dugan, Mo.App.1945, 191 S.W.2d 979 (township constable and deputy, same); Meinecke v. McFarland, 1949, 122 Mont. 515, 206 P.2d 1012 (fish and game warden; refusal of license); Schwartz v. Heffernan, 1952, 304 N.Y. 474, 109 N.E.2d 68 (election board, declaring nominating petition invalid).

left no choice of his own.[87] As to the former, an analogy to the judge is recognized, and the officer is given immunity. Thus the acts of a prosecuting attorney in connection with an indictment,[88] an assessor valuing property for taxes,[89] a school board dismissing a pupil,[90] or a superintendent refusing a license to a teacher,[91] as well the letting of a contract to the lowest responsible bidder,[92] the routing of a highway,[93] or the approval of a surety bond,[94] all have been held to be immune so long as they are done honestly and in good faith.[95]

The considerable majority of the state courts take the position that there is no immunity where the inferior officer does not act honestly and in good faith, but maliciously, or for an improper purpose.[96] The argument in favor of this position has been that the qualified privilege is sufficient to protect the honest officer who tries to do his duty; that official immunity should not become a cloak for malicious, corrupt, and otherwise outrageous conduct on the part of those guilty of intentional abuse of power with which they are entrusted by the people; and that the burden and inconvenience to the officer of an inquiry into his motives is far outweighed by the possible evils of the deliberate misconduct.[97] Certainly there appears to be no evidence of any undue restraint of official conduct, or deterrence of good men from seeking office, in the states which do not recognize the absolute immunity on the part of inferior officers.

Other acts, involving less personal judgment, are classified as "ministerial"[98] only,

87. See Note, 1940, 38 Mich.L.Rev. 1344.

88. Yaselli v. Goff, 2 Cir. 1926, 12 F.2d 396, cert. denied 273 U.S. 677, affirmed 275 U.S. 503; Kittler v. Kelsch, 1927, 56 N.D. 227, 216 N.W. 898; Watts v. Gerking, 1924, 111 Or. 641, 222 P. 318, 228 P. 135; Griffith v. Slinkard, 1896, 146 Ind. 117, 44 N.E. 1001; Bauers v. Heisel, 3 Cir. 1966, 361 P.2d 581. See Notes, 1954, 32 N.C.L.Rev. 360; 1928, 12 Minn. L.Rev. 665.

89. Stewart v. Case, 1893, 53 Minn. 62, 54 N.W. 938; Ballerino v. Mason, 1890, 83 Cal. 447, 23 P. 530; Fawcett v. Dole, 1892, 67 N.H. 168, 29 A. 693. Cf. Nadeau v. Marchessault, 1942, 112 Vt. 309, 24 A.2d 352 (overseer of poor); Harmer v. Peterson, 1949, 151 Neb. 412, 37 N.W.2d 511 (road overseer).

90. Sweeney v. Young, 1925, 82 N.H. 159, 131 A. 155. Cf. Gottschalk v. Shepperd, 1935, 65 N.D. 544, 260 N.W. 573 (discharge of teacher); Wilson v. Hirst, 1948, 67 Ariz. 197, 193 P.2d 461 (hospital board discharging employee); Gibson v. Reynolds, 8 Cir. 1949, 172 F.2d 95 (draft board).

91. Branaman v. Hinkle, 1893, 137 Ind. 496, 37 N.E. 546. Cf. Papagianakis v. The Samos, 4 Cir. 1950, 186 F.2d 257 (immigration officer); Pawlowski v. Jenks, 1897, 115 Mich. 275, 73 N.W. 238; Jaffarian v. Murphy, 1932, 280 Mass. 402, 183 N.E. 110; Roerig v. Houghton, 1919, 144 Minn. 231, 175 N.W. 542.

92. East River Gaslight Co. v. Donnelly, 1883, 93 N. Y. 557.

93. Yealy v. Fink, 1862, 43 Pa. 212; Wilbrecht v. Babcock, 1930, 179 Minn. 263, 228 N.W. 916; Wilson v. Spencer, 1912, 91 Neb. 169, 135 N.W. 546. Or its upkeep and repair. See Stevens v. North States Motor, 1925, 161 Minn. 345, 201 N.W. 435.

94. Amperse v. Winslow, 1889, 75 Mich. 234, 42 N.W. 823; Garden City, G. & N. R. Co. v. Nation, 1910, 83 Kan. 237, 109 P. 772 (determining whether municipal bonds should be registered).

95. Roerig v. Houghton, 1919, 144 Minn. 231, 175 N. W. 542; Rehmann v. City of Des Moines, 1927, 204

Iowa 798, 215 N.W. 957; State ex rel. Robertson v. Farmers' State Bank, 1931, 162 Tenn. 499, 39 S.W. 2d 281; Logan City v. Allen, 1935, 86 Utah 375, 44 P.2d 1085; Nelson v. Knox, 6 Cir. 1958, 256 F.2d 312.

96. Kelley v. Dunne, 1 Cir. 1965, 344 F.2d 129; Vickers v. Motte, 1964, 109 Ga.App. 615, 137 S.E.2d 77; Tillotson v. Fair, 1945, 160 Kan. 81, 159 P.2d 471; Schwartz v. Heffernan, 1952, 304 N.Y. 474, 109 N. E.2d 68; Taulli v. Gregory, 1953, 223 La. 195, 65 So.2d 312.

Contra, that there is no liability even for such conduct: Phelps v. Dawson, 8 Cir. 1938, 97 F.2d 339; Laughlin v. Rosenman, 1947, 82 U.S.App.D.C. 164, 163 F.2d 838; Nadeau v. Marchessault, 1942, 112 Vt. 309, 24 A.2d 352; Papagianakis v. The Samos, 4 Cir. 1950, 186 F.2d 257, cert. denied 341 U.S. 921; Linder v. Foster, 1940, 209 Minn. 43, 295 N.W. 299. See Note, 1957, 9 Hast.L.J. 81.

97. See Jennings, Tort Liability of Administrative Officers, 1937, 21 Minn.L.Rev. 263; Gray, Private Wrongs of Public Servants, 1959, 47 Cal.L.Rev. 303; James, Tort Liability of Governmental Units and Their Officers, 1955, 22 U.Chi.L.Rev. 610.

98. "A duty is to be regarded as ministerial when it is a duty that has been positively imposed by law, and its performance required at a time and in a manner, or upon conditions which are specifically

and are done improperly at the officer's peril, regardless of his good faith. Such are the preparation of ballots,[99] the registration of voters,[1] the recording of documents,[2] the filing of papers,[3] the care of prisoners,[4] the driving of vehicles,[5] the repair of highways,[6] the collection of taxes,[7] the signing of licenses once they are authorized,[8] the taking of acknowledgments,[9] and dipping sheep.[10] It seems almost impossible to draw

any clear and definite line, since the distinction, if it exists, can be at most one of degree. "It would be difficult to conceive of any official act, no matter how directly ministerial, that did not admit of some discretion in the manner of its performance, even if it involved only the driving of a nail." [11] It is not surprising that there has been great difficulty in classifying such acts as those of auditors in issuing and paying warrants,[12] or the destruction of diseased animals.[13] Nor does justice or the public interest suggest that the petty official who is honestly trying to obey orders should be liable for a mistake, while those who are charged with decision escape all liability.[14] Still less reason is apparent in the further distinction, made by some courts [15] but rejected by most of the rest,[16] between ministerial "misfeasance"

designated." First Nat. Bank of Key West v. Filer, 1933, 107 Fla. 526, 534, 145 So. 204, 207.

99. Frank v. Eaton, 1928, 225 App.Div. 149, 231 N.Y. S. 477, followed in 1930, 227 App.Div. 829, 237 N.Y. S. 775. Cf. Larson v. Marsh, 1944, 144 Neb. 644, 14 N.W.2d 189 (Secretary of State placing name on ballot).

1. Lincoln v. Hapgood, 1814, 11 Mass. 350; Jeffries v. Ankeny, 1860, 11 Ohio St. 372. But there are cases holding that election officers are given judicial powers, and so they are not liable. Blake v. Brothers, 1907, 79 Conn. 676, 66 A. 501; Bevard v. Hoffman, 1862, 18 Md. 479.

2. Rising v. Dickinson, 1909, 18 N.D. 478, 121 N.W. 616; Richards v. Tynes, 1931, 149 Okl. 235, 300 P. 297 (docketing judgment); Johnson v. Brice, 1899, 102 Wis. 575, 78 N.W. 1086. Cf. Houseman v. Girard Mut. Bldg. & Loan Ass'n, 1876, 81 Pa. 256; Smith v. Holmes, 1884, 54 Mich. 104, 19 N.W. 767.

3. Rosenthal v. Davenport, 1888, 38 Minn. 543, 38 N. W. 618.

4. Winborne v. Mitchell, 1892, 111 N.C. 13, 15 S.E. 882; Clark v. Kelly, 1926, 101 W.Va. 650, 133 S.E. 365; Farmer v. State for Use of Russell, 1955, 224 Miss. 96, 79 So.2d 528. Compare, as to care of school children: Guerrieri v. Tyson, 1942, 147 Pa. Super. 239, 24 A.2d 468 (teacher); Whitt v. Reed, Ky.1951, 239 S.W.2d 489 (school officials).

5. Florio v. Schmolze, 1925, 101 N.J.L. 535, 129 A. 470; Hansley v. Tilton, 1951, 234 N.C. 3, 65 S.E.2d 300; Wynn v. Gandy, 1938, 170 Va. 590, 197 S.E. 527 (bus); cf. Manwaring v. Geisler, 1921, 191 Ky. 532, 230 S.W. 918.

6. Tholkes v. Decock, 1914, 125 Minn. 507, 147 N.W. 648.

7. Raynsford v. Phelps, 1880, 43 Mich. 342, 5 N.W. 403; Blanchard v. Dow, 1851, 32 Me. 557.

8. Grider v. Tally, 1884, 77 Ala. 422.

9. People for Use of Munson v. Bartels, 1891, 138 Ill. 322, 27 N.E. 1091. Cf. Wasson v. Mitchell, 1864, 18 Iowa 153 (accepting surety bond with forged signatures).

10. Bair v. Struck, 1903, 29 Mont. 45, 74 P. 69. Cf. Saya v. Fuller, 1967, 249 Cal.App.2d 281, 57 Cal.

Rptr. 312 (negligent analysis of plant substance; Scruggs v. Haynes, 1967, 252 Cal.App.2d 256, 60 Cal.Rptr. 355 (unreasonable force in making an arrest).

11. Ham v. Los Angeles County, 1920, 46 Cal.App. 148, 162, 189 P. 462, 468. Compare the two views as to a road overseer driving a snow plow in Mower v. Williams, 1948, 334 Ill.App. 16, 78 N.E.2d 529; Id., 1949, 402 Ill. 468, 84 N.E.2d 435.

12. Fergus v. Brady, 1917, 277 Ill. 272, 115 N.E. 393 (purely ministerial); Hicks v. Davis, 1917, 100 Kan. 4, 163 P. 799 (discretionary).

13. See Miller v. Horton, 1891, 152 Mass. 540, 26 N. E. 100; Lowe v. Conroy, 1904, 120 Wis. 151, 97 N. W. 942; Pearson v. Zehr, 1891, 138 Ill. 48, 29 N.E. 854. Cf. Fath v. Koeppel, 1888, 72 Wis. 289, 39 N. W. 539 (fish inspector); McClellan v. Carter, 1923, 30 Ga.App. 150, 117 S.E. 118 (dipping sheep); Beeks v. Dickinson County, 1906, 131 Iowa 244, 108 N.W. 311 (quarantine); Valentine v. Englewood, 1908, 76 N.J.L. 509, 71 A. 344 (same).

14. Jennings, Tort Liability of Administrative Officers, 1937, 21 Minn.L.Rev. 263, 301.

15. Smith v. Iowa City, 1931, 213 Iowa 391, 239 N.W. 29; Stevens v. North State Motor, 1925, 161 Minn. 345, 201 N.W. 435; Carpenter v. Atlanta & C. A. L. R. Co., 1922, 184 N.C. 400, 114 S.E. 693; Antin v. Union High School Dist. No. 2, 1929, 130 Or. 461, 280 P. 664.

16. Hale v. Johnston, 1918, 140 Tenn. 182, 203 S.W. 949; Gage v. Springer, 1904, 211 Ill. 200, 71 N.E. 860; First Nat. Bank of Key West v. Filer, 1933, 107 Fla. 526, 145 So. 204; Ham v. Los Angeles

and "nonfeasance." If there is a clear duty to act at all, liability may be predicated quite as easily upon nonaction as upon action.

Matters are further complicated by an additional distinction, which holds that all officers, including judges,[17] are liable if they act wholly outside of their jurisdiction or official authority, even where the act is a discretionary one.[18] The officer is then regarded as not acting in the capacity of an officer at all. This has led to a further refinement, distinguishing acts which are merely "in excess" of the jurisdiction or authority—meaning that they are within the scope of the general subject-matter over which the officer has power, although he is without jurisdiction in the particular case. As to such acts there is immunity.[19] But such a conception that "nonexistence can be less than nonexistence"[20] is certainly a fiction, and the public duty of any officer necessarily involves the determination of the facts which do or do not give him jurisdiction or authority, which is obviously a judicial or discretionary function. The injury to the plaintiff, or the hardship upon an officer who has

honestly believed that he was acting properly, is the same in either case. Even as to officers acting under an unconstitutional statute, which can confer no jurisdiction at all, the courts are being driven slowly[21] to the view that the officer cannot be required to determine legal questions which would often perplex a court, and that if he has acted in good faith he should not be liable.[22]

For such reasons, some writers[23] have advocated the abandonment, in the case of administrative officers, of the distinctions between "discretionary" and "ministerial" functions, together with those as to jurisdictional facts, and the substitution of the simple test, whether the officer has acted with proper motives and with due care and diligence in the performance of his official duties. He should neither suffer for an honest and reasonable mistake in the effort to carry out his responsibility to the public, nor escape liability for official negligence because he has been charged with that responsibility. A few scattered cases[24] have shown some tendency in this direction.

County, 1920, 46 Cal.App. 148, 189 P. 462; Farmer v. State for Use of Russell, 1955, 224 Miss. 96, 79 So.2d 528.

17. Bradley v. Fisher, 1871, 13 Wall., U.S. 335, 20 L. Ed. 646; Bates v. Kitchel, 1910, 160 Mich. 402, 125 N.W. 684; Joyce v. Hickey, 1958, 337 Mass. 118, 147 N.E.2d 187; Vickrey v. Dunivan, 1955, 59 N.M. 90, 279 P.2d 853; Utley v. City of Independence, 1965, 240 Or. 384, 402 P.2d 91.

18. Stevens v. Black, 1920, 212 Mich. 281, 180 N.W. 503; Thiede v. Town of Scandia Valley, 1944, 217 Minn. 218, 14 N.W.2d 400; Utley v. City of Independence, 1965, 240 Or. 384, 402 P.2d 91; Lowe v. Conroy, 1904, 120 Wis. 151, 97 N.W. 942; Robichaud v. Ronan, 9 Cir. 1965, 351 F.2d 533.

19. Tedford v. McWhorter, Tex.Civ.App.1964, 373 S. W.2d 832, ref. n. r. e.; Broom v. Douglass, 1912, 175 Ala. 268, 57 So. 860; Calhoun v. Little, 1898, 106 Ga. 336, 32 S.E. 86; Rush v. Buckley, 1905, 100 Me. 322, 61 A. 774; Pogue v. Swink, 1955, 365 Mo. 503, 284 S.W.2d 868; cf. National Surety Co. v. Miller, 1929, 155 Miss. 115, 124 So. 251.

20. National Surety Co. v. Miller, 1929, 155 Miss. 115, 127, 124 So. 251, 254.

21. Contra, holding the officer liable: Sumner v. Beeler, 1875, 50 Ind. 341; Campbell v. Sherman, 1874, 35 Wis. 103; Kelly v. Bemis, 1855, 4 Gray, Mass., 83; Dennison Mfg. Co. v. Wright, 1923, 156 Ga. 789, 120 S.E. 120; Smith v. Costello, 1955, 77 Idaho 205, 290 P.2d 742.

22. A large problem, discussion of which is beyond the scope of this text. See Rapacz, Protection of Officers Who Act Under Unconstitutional Statutes, 1927, 11 Minn.L.Rev. 585; Field, The Effect of an Unconstitutional Statute in the Law of Public Officers, 1928, 77 U.Pa.L.Rev. 155; Note, 1936, 22 Va. L.Rev. 316; and see generally Field, The Effect of an Unconstitutional Statute, 1935.

23. Jennings, Tort Liability of Administrative Officers, 1937, 21 Minn.L.Rev. 263; Gellhorn, Administrative Law Cases and Comments, 1940, 402–414; Gray, Private Wrongs of Public Servants, 1959, 47 Cal.L.Rev. 303; Mathes and Jones, Toward a "Scope of Official Duty" Immunity for Police Officers in Damage Actions, 1965, 53 Geo.L.J. 889; Note, 1965, 53 Geo.L.J. 1144.

24. See Tyrell v. Burke, 1933, 110 N.J.L. 225, 164 A. 586; Wallace v. Feehan, Ind.App.1932, 181 N.E. 862; Silva v. MacAuley, 1933, 135 Cal.App. 249, 26 P.2d 887, 27 P.2d 791; Lincoln Bus Co. v. Jersey

At the other extreme is the contention [25] that there should be no liability upon public officers at all, and that the government which they serve should be made liable for all of their torts in their stead. While this may be in accord with modernistic theories of respondeat superior and the distribution of risks, it appears quite unlikely ever to be carried into effect. Apart from reluctance to impose liability upon governments for the discretionary conduct of their officers,[26] it may seriously be questioned whether the removal of the possible deterrent effect of the individual's tort liability, at least for oppressive and outrageous conduct, would be at all a desirable thing. There once was a disreputable character named John Wilkes, whose newspaper was raided and put out of business, his premises illegally searched, and his property seized and confiscated, all for the worst kind of political motives. The tort actions [27] which arose out of this high-handed piece of oppression were long regarded as a major blow struck for the freedom of the individual against the abuse of governmental power; and so long as cheap and conniving politicians continue to abuse that power, they should not be forgotten.

Thus far, at least, the effort to relieve the officer of all liability, and substitute the government, has succeeded only in a few cases [28] in which statutes, such as the Federal Tort Claims Act, have been given the effect of depriving the government of any right of indemnity over against the officer.

Mut. Cas. Ins. Co., 1932, 162 A. 915, 10 N.J.Misc. 1114.

25. Davis, Administrative Officers' Tort Liability, 1956, 55 Mich.L.Rev. 201; 3 Davis, Administrative Law Treatise, 1958, § 26.02.

26. See supra, p. 986.

27. In particular, Wilkes v. Wood, 1763, Lofft 1. See also Huckle v. Money, 1763, 2 Wils.K.B. 205, 95 Eng.Rep. 768.

28. United States v. Gilman, 1954, 347 U.S. 507; Norton v. McShane, 5 Cir. 1964, 332 F.2d 855; Jarrell v. Gordy, La.App.1964, 162 So.2d 577. See Note, 1965, 113 U.Pa.L.Rev. 450.

133. CHARITIES

The immunity which has been conferred upon charitable organizations and enterprises [29] has been justified upon a number of different grounds, all of which have been the subject of severe criticism.[30] A charity of course exists for the benefit of the public, and even the fact that it receives payment for its services from some of its beneficiaries will not affect its character, so long as the money is used for charitable purposes and not for profit.[31] Municipal corporations, when they enter into charitable enterprises, have been held to be engaged in a governmental function and immune from tort lia-

29. Although most of the decisions have involved charities, and in particular charitable hospitals, the immunity has included religious, educational, and other benevolent and eleemosynary institutions not operated for profit. See for example Parks v. Northwestern University, 1905, 218 Ill. 381, 75 N.E. 991; Hamburger v. Cornell University, 1925, 240 N.Y. 328, 148 N.E. 539. In Hooten v. Civil Air Patrol, 7 Cir. 1958, 161 F.Supp. 478, it was held to cover a Civil Air Patrol, organized by Congress and incorporated solely for benevolent non-profit purposes.

The organization usually is incorporated, but the immunity is not limited to corporations. Farrigan v. Pevear, 1906, 193 Mass. 147, 78 N.E. 855.

30. Appleman, The Tort Liability of Charitable Institutions, 1936, 22 A.B.A.J. 48; Feezer, The Tort Liability of Charities, 1928, 77 U.Pa.L.Rev. 191; McCaskill, Respondeat Superior as Applied in New York to Quasi-Public and Eleemosynary Institutions, 1920, 5 Corn.L.Q. 409, 6 Corn.L.Q. 56; Spencer, Ray v. Tucson Medical Center: A Reappraisal of Tort Liability of Charities, 1951, 24 Rocky Mt.L. Rev. 51; Fisch, Charitable Liability for Tort, 1964, 10 Vill.L.Rev. 71; Notes, 1938, 38 Col.L.Rev. 1485; 1938, 48 Yale L.J. 81; 1950, 25 N.Y.U.L.Rev. 612; 1951, 20 U.Cin.L.Rev. 412; 1951, 30 N.C.L.Rev. 67; 1952, 6 Ark.L.Rev. 209; 1953, 32 N.C.L.Rev. 129; 1954, 32 Tex.L.Rev. 376; 1959, 37 N.C.L.Rev. 209; 1957, 19 U.Pitt.L.Rev. 119; 1966, 23 Wash. & Lee L.Rev. 109. See also the Report of the New York Law Revision Commission, 1953, 805–848.

31. Taylor v. Protestant Hospital Ass'n, 1911, 85 Ohio St. 90, 96 N.E. 1089; Duncan v. Nebraska Sanitarium & Benevolent Ass'n, 1912, 92 Neb. 162, 137 N.W. 1120; Parks v. Northwestern University, 1905, 218 Ill. 381, 75 N.E. 991; Enell v. Baptist Hospital, Tex.Civ.App.1932, 45 S.W.2d 395, error refused.

bility.[32] When a private organization enters the same field, there seems to have been a feeling on the part of the courts that it is working for the public good, and is entitled to the same immunity.[33]

In 1846 it was held in an English case [34] that trust funds in the hands of a charity could not be subjected to the payment of tort claims, since they would thus be diverted from the purpose intended by the donor. The decision was later repudiated in England,[35] but it was nevertheless accepted by two American courts,[36] whose decisions initiated the "trust fund" theory as the basis of a general immunity in charity cases.[37] Its weakness lies in the fact that it is contrary to the various decisions which have evolved methods of making other trust funds responsible for torts committed in administering the trust, and that since such funds

would not be exempt in the hands of the donor himself, he can scarcely have the power, even if it were ever true that he had even the intention, to confer such immunity upon the object of his bounty.[38] A further fault in the justification is that it proves too much, and is inconsistent with the numerous decisions which have held charities liable for damages for breach of contract, and for some kinds of negligence.[39] A second theory is that the rule of respondeat superior does not extend to charities, and so they are not liable for the torts of their agents and employees, because they derive no gain or benefit from the service rendered.[40] But the vicarious liability of a master is certainly not limited to profitable businesses, and it rests rather upon his employment of the servant, his direction and control over the act, and the furtherance of an enterprise which he has set in motion.[41] If he derives profit from the enterprise, that might serve as an added reason for making him take the responsibility; but the reason for making him bear the loss in the first instance is complete without the addition.

32. Tollefson v. City of Ottawa, 1907, 228 Ill. 134, 81 N.E. 823; City of Dallas v. Smith, 1937, 130 Tex. 225, 107 S.W.2d 872; Powers v. Massachusetts Homeopathic Hospital, 1 Cir. 1901, 109 F. 294, certiorari denied, 1902, 183 U.S. 695; Noble v. Hahnemann Hospital, 1906, 112 App.Div. 663, 98 N.Y.S. 605. But cf. Borwege v. City of Owatonna, 1933, 190 Minn. 394, 251 N.W. 915; City of Okmulgee v. Carlton, 1937, 180 Okl. 605, 71 P.2d 722 (proprietary).

33. See McCaskill, Respondeat Superior as Applied in New York to Quasi-Public and Eleemosynary Institutions, 1920, 5 Corn.L.Q. 409, 6 Corn.L.Q. 56, pointing out the extent to which the charity decisions have been influenced by the governmental rule.

34. Feoffees of Heriot's Hospital v. Ross, 1846, 12 C. & F. 507, 8 Eng.Rep. 1508.

35. Mersey Docks Trustees v. Gibbs, 1866, 11 H.L. Cas. 686, 11 Eng.Rep. 1500.

36. McDonald v. Massachusetts General Hospital, 1876, 120 Mass. 432; Perry v. House of Refuge, 1885, 63 Md. 20. Both courts were apparently ignorant of the English reversal.

37. Loeffler v. Trustees of Sheppard & Enoch Pratt Hospital, 1917, 130 Md. 265, 100 A. 301; Eads v. Young Women's Christian Ass'n, 1930, 325 Mo. 577, 29 S.W.2d 701; Forrest v. Red Cross Hospital, Ky. 1954, 265 S.W.2d 80; Williams v. Randolph Hospital, 1953, 237 N.C. 387, 75 S.E.2d 303; Fisher v. Ohio Valley General Hospital, 1952, 137 W.Va. 723, 73 S.E.2d 667.

38. See Gregory v. Salem General Hospital, 1944, 175 Or. 464, 153 P.2d 837; Cristini v. Griffin Hospital, 1948, 134 Conn. 282, 57 A.2d 262; Geiger v. Simpson M. E. Church of Minneapolis, 1928, 174 Minn. 389, 219 N.W. 463; Fulda and Pond, Tort Liability of Trust Estates, 1941, 41 Col.L.Rev. 1332; Stone, A Theory of Liability of Trust Estates for the Contracts and Torts of the Trustee, 1922, 22 Col.L.Rev. 527; Lerr, Liability of the Trust Estate for Torts of the Trustee's Servants, 1927, 5 Tex.L.Rev. 368; 2 Scott, Trusts, 1939, §§ 247, 264, 271A(2); 3 Bogert, Trusts and Trustees, 1935, § 732.

39. See President and Directors of Georgetown College v. Hughes, 1942, 76 U.S.App.D.C. 123, 130 F.2d 810; Zollman, Liability of Charitable Institutions, 1921, 19 Mich.L.Rev. 395, 406.

40. Evans v. Lawrence Hospital, 1946, 133 Conn. 311, 50 A.2d 433; Bachman v. Young Women's Christian Ass'n, 1922, 179 Wis. 178, 191 N.W. 751; Emery v. Jewish Hospital Ass'n, 1921, 193 Ky. 400, 236 S.W. 577; Thornton v. Franklin Square House, 1909, 200 Mass. 465, 86 N.E. 909; Fire Ins. Patrol v. Boyd, 1888, 120 Pa. 624, 15 A. 553.

41. See Ray v. Tucson Medical Center, 1951, 72 Ariz. 22, 230 P.2d 220; Wright v. Wright, 1948, 229 N.C. 503, 50 S.E.2d 540.

Still other courts have relied on the theory that the recipient of the benefits of charity accepts them as they are given, assumes the risk of negligence, and by implication agrees to "waive" the liability and assert no tort claim against his benefactor.[42] Coupled with this is the vague and rather sentimental notion that the "good Samaritan" should not be held to undue responsibility for his efforts.[43] But apart from any question whether a sick or injured man is competent to assume such a risk,[44] the "waiver" theory again, in many cases, does violence to the facts. The patient goes to the hospital because he expects better care than he would receive at home, and he certainly does not in reality consent to be treated with negligence;[45] and those who assume to render gratuitous assistance are held in general to a standard of reasonable conduct in doing so.[46]

Finally, there has been resort to ideas of "public policy" against stifling charities by discouraging donors with the fear that their gifts will go to pay tort claims.[47] But with the development of liability insurance, it seems highly unlikely that donors would refuse to recognize it as a legitimate expense of operation;[48] and in any case, the interest of the public in proper care and the compensation of harm done might well outweigh the encouragement of donations.[49] As a matter of fact, the argument appears to have been concocted out of defense counsel's head rather than to have arisen out of any reality of experience. There is not the slightest indication that donations have been in any way discouraged, or charities crippled in states which deny all immunity.[50]

The present state of the law is one of rapid overthrow of the immunity of charities, not yet fully accomplished. In its complete form, it still persists only in Maine,[51] New Mexico[52] and South Carolina.[53] In seven other

---

42. Powers v. Massachusetts Homeopathic Hospital, 1 Cir. 1901, 109 F. 294, cert. denied 183 U.S. 695; Wilcox v. Idaho Falls Latter Day Saints Hospital, 1938, 59 Idaho 350, 82 P.2d 849; Forrest v. Red Cross Hospital, Ky.1954, 265 S.W.2d 80; St. Vincent's Hospital v. Stine, 1924, 195 Ind. 350, 144 N.E. 537; Duncan v. Nebraska Sanitarium & Ben. Ass'n, 1912, 92 Neb. 162, 137 N.W. 1120.

43. Powers v. Massachusetts Homeopathic Hospital, 1 Cir. 1901, 109 F. 294.

44. "A patient entirely unskilled in legal principles, his body racked with pain, his mind distorted with fever, is held to know, by intuition, the principle of law that the courts after years of travail have at last produced." Dissent, in Lindler v. Columbia Hospital, 1914, 98 S.C. 25, 81 S.E. 512. See also Phillips v. Buffalo General Hospital, 1924, 239 N.Y. 188, 146 N.E. 199 (patient unconscious).

45. See Gamble v. Vanderbilt University, 1918, 138 Tenn. 616, 200 S.W. 510; Mississippi Baptist Hospital v. Holmes, 1951, 214 Miss. 906, 55 So.2d 142, 154; Phillips v. Buffalo General Hospital, 1924, 239 N.Y. 188, 146 N.E. 199; Mulliner v. Evangelischer Diakonniessenverein, 1920, 144 Minn. 392, 175 N.W. 699.

46. See supra, § 56.

47. Vermillion v. Woman's College of Due West, 1916, 104 S.C. 197, 88 S.E. 649; Jensen v. Maine Eye & Ear Infirmary, 1910, 107 Me. 408, 78 A. 898; Weston's Adm'x v. Hospital of St. Vincent of Paul, 1921, 131 Va. 587, 107 S.E. 785; D'Amato v. Orange Memorial Hospital, 1925, 101 N.J.L. 61, 127 A. 340; Landgraver v. Emanuel Lutheran Charity Board, 1955, 203 Or. 489, 280 P.2d 301; Taylor v. Flower Deaconess Home and Hospital, 1922, 104 Ohio St. 61, 135 N.E. 287.

48. See Hewett v. Woman's Hospital Aid Ass'n, 1906, 73 N.H. 556, 64 A. 190; Moore v. Moyle, 1950, 405 Ill. 555, 92 N.E.2d 81; Pierce v. Yakima Valley Memorial Hospital Ass'n, 1953, 43 Wash.2d 162, 260 P. 2d 765; Vanderbilt University v. Henderson, 1938, 23 Tenn.App. 135, 127 S.W.2d 284.

49. See Glavin v. Rhode Island Hospital, 1879, 12 R. I. 411; Geiger v. Simpson Methodist-Episcopal Church of Minneapolis, 1928, 174 Minn. 389, 394, 219 N.W. 463, 465; Sheehan v. North Country Community Hospital, 1937, 273 N.Y. 163, 7 N.E.2d 28.

50. See President and Directors of Georgetown College v. Hughes, 1942, 76 U.S.App.D.C. 123, 130 F.2d 810, 823; Cohen v. General Hospital Society, 1931, 113 Conn. 188, 154 A. 435, 436–7.

51. Rhodes v. Aroostook General Hospital, 1967, —— Me. ——, 226 A.2d 630.

52. Deming Ladies' Hosp. Ass'n v. Price, 8 Cir. 1921, 276 F. 668. There are apparently no state cases.

53. Decker v. Bishop of Charleston, 1966, 247 S.C. 317, 147 S.E.2d 264. See Note, 1967, 19 S.C.L.Rev. 191.

states, by statute [54] or without it,[55] liability is imposed where it is apparent that the assets of the charity will not be depleted by the plaintiff's recovery, as where there is liability insurance—although in most jurisdictions the fact that the defendant is insured usually has been held to make no difference.[56] Seven other courts,[57] with more of an emphasis on the "waiver" theory, deny liability to recipients of the benefits of the charity, such as hospital patients or students, but allow recovery by others, such as employees, invitees and strangers. Three more have abolished the immunity as to charitable hospitals, but left it as to religious institutions and other charities.[58]

Even in these jurisdictions which purport, to a greater or less extent, to retain the immunity, there have been various minor limitations upon it, which are generally recognized. Thus the charity is held liable where the negligence is that of an officer or managing agent in selecting the charity's servants,[59] or is in the course of raising money,[60] or the management of property,[61] or the charity is found to have created a nuisance.[62] One exception upon which there has been general agreement is that the charity is to be held liable when it engages in a commercial enterprise or activity, such as operating an office building,[63] a student health insurance plan,[64] a paid parking lot,[65] or a bingo

---

54. See Michael v. St. Paul Mercury Ind. Co., W.D. Ark.1950, 92 F.Supp. 140; State v. Arundel Park Corp., 1959, 218 Md. 484, 147 A.2d 247; D'Antoni v. Sara Mayo Hospital, La.App.1962, 144 So.2d 643.

55. Michard v. Myron Stratton Home, 1960, 144 Colo. 251, 355 P.2d 1078; Morehouse College v. Russell, 1964, 219 Ga. 717, 135 S.E.2d 432, conformed to 109 Ga.App. 301, 136 S.E.2d 179; Myers v. Drozda, 1966, 180 Neb. 183, 141 N.W.2d 852; O'Quin v. Baptist Memorial Hospital, 1947, 184 Tenn. 570, 201 S. W.2d 694.

The usual device by which this conclusion has been reached is to hold that the immunity does not prevent suit and liability, but only execution levied on exempt charitable funds. Thus where the plaintiff can levy on property not used directly for the charitable enterprise, he may satisfy his judgment. Anderson v. Armstrong, 1943, 180 Tenn. 56, 171 S.W.2d 401.

56. Kreuger v. Schmiechen, 1954, 364 Mo. 568, 264 S. W.2d 311; Cristini v. Griffin Hospital, 1948, 134 Conn. 282, 57 A.2d 262; Grant v. Cottage Hospital Corp., 1962, 368 Mich. 77, 117 N.W.2d 90; Siidekum v. Animal Rescue League of Pittsburgh, 1946, 353 Pa. 408, 45 A.2d 59; Enman v. Trustees of Boston University, 1930, 270 Mass. 299, 170 N.E. 43. Even though the insurance policy waives the immunity. Tomlinson v. Trustees of University of Pennsylvania, E.D.Pa.1958, 164 F.Supp. 353, appeal dismissed, 3 Cir. 1959, 266 F.2d 569. See Notes, 1948, 43 Ill.L. Rev. 248; 1948, 5 Wash. & Lee L.Rev. 272.

57. Alabama Baptist Hospital Board v. Carter, 1933, 226 Ala. 109, 145 So. 443; Coolbaugh v. St. Peter's Roman Catholic Church, 1955, 142 Conn. 536, 115 A.2d 662; Williams v. Randolph Hospital, 1953, 237 N.C. 387, 75 S.E.2d 303; Villarreal v. Santa Rosa Medical Center, Tex.Civ.App.1969, 443 S.W.2d 622; Hill v. Leigh Memorial Hospital, 1963, 204 Va. 501, 132 S.E.2d 411.

Currently the list includes Alabama, Connecticut, Louisiana, New Jersey (statute); North Carolina, Rhode Island (statute), Texas, and Virginia.

58. Collopy v. Newark Eye and Ear Infirmary, 1958, 27 N.J. 29, 141 A.2d 276 (statute); Rabon v. Rowan Memorial Hospital, 1967, 269 N.C. 1, 152 S.E.2d 485; Sturdevant v. Youngstown Dist. Girl Scout Council, 1962, 118 Ohio App.2d 489, 195 N.E.2d 914.

59. Roberts v. Ohio Valley General Hospital, 1923, 98 W.Va. 476, 127 S.E. 318; cf. Norfolk Protestant Hospital v. Plunkett, 1934, 162 Va. 151, 173 S.E. 363; Hoke v. Glenn, 1914, 167 N.C. 594, 83 S.E. 807; Schumacher v. Evangelical Deaconess Society, 1935, 218 Wis. 169, 260 N.W. 476.

Before New York abolished the immunity entirely, it had extended this to any "administrative" as distinguished from "professional" negligence in a charitable hospital. Cadicamo v. Long Island College Hospital, 1954, 308 N.Y. 196, 124 N.E.2d 279.

60. Bader v. United Orthodox Synagogue, 1961, 148 Conn. 449, 172 A.2d 192 (structural defect in house used as meeting place).

61. Reavey v. Guild of St. Agnes, 1933, 284 Mass. 300, 187 N.E. 557; Winnemore v. City of Philadelphia, 1902, 18 Pa.Super. 625.

62. Peden v. Furman University, 1930, 155 S.C. 1, 151 S.E. 907; Smith v. Congregation of St. Rose, 1953, 265 Wis. 393, 61 N.W.2d 896.

63. Blatt v. George H. Nettleton Home for Aged Women, Mo.1955, 275 S.W.2d 344. Cf. Bell v. Salvation Army, 1961, 172 Ohio St. 326, 175 N.E.2d 738; McKay v. Morgan Memorial Coop. Industries and Stores, 1930, 272 Mass. 121, 172 N.E. 68.

64. Grueninger v. President & Fellows of Harvard College, 1961, 343 Mass. 338, 178 N.E.2d 917.

65. Eiserhardt v. State Agric. & Mech. Society, 1959, 235 S.C. 305, 111 S.E.2d 568.

game,[66] even though the proceeds are to be added to trust funds and used exclusively for charitable purposes, and payment of any judgment must be out of such funds. It is not easy to find any real justification for such distinctions.

Prior to 1942 only two or three courts had rejected the immunity of charities outright. In that year a devastating opinion [67] of Judge Rutledge in the Court of Appeals of the District of Columbia reviewed all of the arguments in favor of the immunity, and demolished them so completely as to change the whole course of the law. It has been followed by a deluge of decisions holding that there is no immunity at all, and that a charity is liable for its torts to the same extent as any other defendant. As of the date of publication, the number of jurisdictions which have jettisoned the charity's immunity entirely has reached a total of thirty-one; [68] and the list has been increasing rapidly as older decisions have been overruled.[69]

In short, the immunity of charities is clearly in full retreat; and it may be predicted with some confidence that the end of the next two decades will see its virtual disappearance from American law.

134. INFANTS

For the protection of infants against undue advantage that may be taken of them, the law gives them the power of disaffirming their conveyances and contracts, although they will be liable for the reasonable value of necessaries furnished to them.[70] The law of torts, however, has been more concerned with the compensation of the injured party than with the moral guilt of the wrongdoer, and has refused to hold that an infant is immune from tort liability. As Lord Kenyon said in a leading English case,[71] "If an infant commit an assault, or utter slander, God forbid that he should not be answerable for it in a court of justice." Accordingly, infants are held liable for assault and battery,[72] trespass to land,[73] conversion,[74] defa-

66. Blankenship v. Alter, 1960, 171 Ohio St. 65, 167 N.E.2d 922. In Wertheimer v. Frank, E.D.Pa.1962, 206 F.Supp. 681, summary judgment in favor of a charity was refused because it was not shown to be engaged solely in charitable work.

67. President and Directors of Georgetown College v. Hughes, 1942, 76 U.S.App.D.C. 123, 130 F.2d 810. See also the very complete review in the dissent of Brand, J., in Landgraver v. Emanuel Lutheran Charity Board, 1955, 203 Or. 489, 280 P.2d 301. The majority held that any change must be for the legislature.

68. Currently the list includes Alaska, Arizona, California, Delaware, District of Columbia, Florida, Idaho, Illinois, Indiana, Iowa, Kansas, Kentucky, Massachusetts, Michigan, Minnesota, Mississippi, Missouri, Nevada (statute), New Hampshire, New York, North Dakota, Oklahoma, Oregon, Pennsylvania, Puerto Rico, Utah, Vermont, Washington, West Virginia, Wisconsin, and Wyoming.

69. Late decisions are Colby v. Carney Hospital, 1969, — Mass. —, 254 N.E.2d 407; Abernathy v. Sisters of St. Mary's, Mo.1969, 446 S.W.2d 599; Harris v. Young Women's Christian Ass'n, 1968, 250 Ind. 491, 237 N.E.2d 242; Bell v. Presbytery of Boise, 1966, 91 Idaho 374, 421 P.2d 745; Darling v. Charleston Community Mem. Hospital, 1965, 33 Ill. 2d 326, 211 N.E.2d 353, cert. denied 383 U.S. 946; Flagiello v. Pennsylvania Hospital, 1965, 417 Pa.

486, 208 A.2d 193; Adkins v. St. Francis Hospital, 1965, 149 W.Va. 705, 143 S.E.2d 154; Lutheran Hospitals & Homes Soc. of America v. Yepsen, 1970, — Wyo. —, 469 P.2d 409.

70. See Madden, Domestic Relations, 2d Ed. 1931, 527–614.

71. Jennings v. Randall, 1799, 8 Term.Rep. 335, 337, 101 Eng.Rep. 1419.

72. Ellis v. D'Angelo, 1953, 116 Cal.App.2d 310, 253 P.2d 675 (four years old); Singer v. Marx, 1956, 144 Cal.App.2d 637, 301 P.2d 440; Jorgensen v. Nudelman, 1963, 45 Ill.App.2d 350, 195 N.E.2d 422; Watson v. Wrightsman, 1901, 26 Ind.App. 437, 59 N.E. 1064 (same); Garratt v. Dailey, 1955, 46 Wash.2d 197, 279 P.2d 1091, second appeal, 1956, 49 Wash.2d 499, 304 P.2d 681. See Note, 1954, 27 So. Cal.L.Rev. 214.

73. Scott v. Watson, 1859, 46 Me. 362; Huchting v. Engel, 1863, 17 Wis. 230; Brown v. Dellinger, Tex. Civ.App.1962, 355 S.W.2d 742; Cleveland Park Club v. Perry, Mun.App.D.C.1960, 165 A.2d 485.

Also for trespass to chattels. Conklin v. Thompson, 1859, 29 Barb., N.Y., 218.

Accord, as to arson, Unkelsbee v. Homestead Fire Ins. Co. of Baltimore, Mun.App.D.C.1945, 41 A.2d 168; Seaburg v. Williams, 1958, 16 Ill.App.2d 295, 148 N. E.2d 49.

74. Smith v. Moschetti, 1948, 213 Ark. 968, 214 S.W. 2d 73; Shaw v. Coffin, 1870, 58 Me. 254; Pledge v.

mation,[75] seduction,[76] deceit,[77] and negligence.[78] The fact that a tort is committed by an infant under the direction of his parent may render the parent also liable, but it will not excuse the infant.[79]

This general rule denying immunity must, however, be qualified in a number of respects. In many torts, the state of mind of the actor is an important element. For example, an intent to bring about physical contact is necessary to battery, and in most jurisdictions "scienter," or intent to deceive, is said to be essential to deceit. It has been recognized that a child may be of such tender years that he is not an intelligent actor and is incapable of the specific intent required, so that the tort has not been committed, and

the event is to be classed as an unavoidable accident.[80] Likewise, in the case of negligence, children have been recognized as a special group to whom a more or less subjective standard of conduct is to be applied, which will vary according to their age, intelligence and experience, so that in some cases immunity may be conferred in effect by finding merely that there has been no negligence.[81]

A further qualification is that the tort liability must be applied with due regard for the settled doctrine that the infant may not be held liable on his disaffirmed contracts.[82] Where the wrong complained of consists merely in the nonperformance or the improper performance of an agreement, the plaintiff will not be permitted to recover merely by changing the form of the action to one of tort.[83] He cannot, for example, maintain a tort action for breach of warranty,[84] or for failure to perform a duty undertaken by voluntary agreement;[85] and he cannot hold the

Griffith, 1918, 199 Mo.App. 303, 202 S.W. 460; Walker v. Davis, 1854, 1 Gray, Mass., 506.

75. Defries v. Davis, 1835, 1 Bing.N.C. 692, 131 Eng. Rep. 1284; Fears v. Riley, 1899, 148 Mo. 49, 49 S. W. 836; see Munden v. Harris, 1910, 153 Mo.App. 652, 134 S.W. 1076.

76. Lee v. Hefley, 1863, 21 Ind. 98; Fry v. Leslie, 1891, 87 Va. 269, 12 S.E. 671; Becker v. Mason, 1892, 93 Mich. 336, 53 N.W. 361.

77. Butler Bros. v. Snyder, 1924, 81 Ind.App. 44, 142 N.E. 398; Shenkein v. Fuhrman, 1913, 80 Misc. 179, 141 N.Y.S. 909; Wisconsin Loan & Finance Co. v. Goodnough, 1930, 201 Wis. 101, 228 N.W. 484. See Atiyah, The Liability of Infants in Fraud and Restitution, 1959, 22 Mod.L.Rev. 273.

See, generally, Franzke, Infants' Liability for Intentional Torts and Negligence, [1960] Ins.L.J. 771; Weisiger, Tort Liability of Minors and Incompetents, [1951] U.Ill.L.F. 227; Notes, 1958, 19 Ohio St.L.J. 769; 1959, 36 Chicago-Kent L.Rev. 166.

78. Hopkins v. Droppers, 1926, 191 Wis. 334, 210 N. W. 684; Harrison v. Carroll, 4 Cir. 1943, 139 F.2d 427; House v. Fry, 1916, 30 Cal.App. 157, 157 P. 500; Conway v. Reed, 1877, 66 Mo. 346; Cnaeps v. Brown, 1957, 101 N.H. 116, 135 A.2d 721; Midkiff v. Midkiff, 1960, 201 Va. 829, 113 S.E.2d 875.

See, generally, Bohlen, Liability in Tort of Infants and Insane Persons, 1924, 23 Mich.L.Rev. 9; Weisiger, Tort Liability of Minors and Incompetents, [1951] U.Ill.L.Forum 227; Stone, Liability for Damage Caused by Minors: A Comparative Study, 1952, 5 Ala.L.Rev. 1.

79. Scott v. Watson, 1859, 46 Me. 362; Humphrey v. Douglass, 1838, 10 Vt. 71; see O'Leary v. Brooks Elevator Co., 1898, 7 N.D. 554, 75 N.W. 919.

80. See Johnson v. Pye, 1665, 1 Sid. 258, 82 Eng.Rep. 1091; Bullock v. Babcock, 1829, 3 Wend., N.Y., 391; Johnson v. Butterworth, 1934, 180 La. 586, 157 So. 121; Munden v. Harris, 1910, 153 Mo.App. 652, 134 S.W. 1076; 1 Jaggard, Torts, 1895, 160; Bohlen, Liability in Tort of Infants and Insane Persons, 1924, 23 Mich.L.Rev. 9.

But an intent to do an act which invades the plaintiff's rights is enough, without an intent to do any harm. Cleveland Park Club v. Perry, Mun.App.D. C.1960, 165 A.2d 485; Garratt v. Dailey, 1955, 46 Wash.2d 197, 279 P.2d 1091, second appeal, 1956, 49 Wash.2d 499, 304 P.2d 681.

81. See supra, p. 154.

82. "The dominant consideration is not that of liability for their torts, but of protection from their contracts." Slayton v. Barry, 1900, 175 Mass. 513, 515, 56 N.E. 574, 575. See Notes, 1944, 30 Iowa L.Rev. 88; 1956, 36 Bos.U.L.Rev. 600.

83. Jennings v. Randall, 1799, 8 Term Rep. 355, 101 Eng.Rep. 1419; Gilson v. Spear, 1865, 38 Vt. 311; Frank Spangler Co. v. Haupt, 1913, 53 Pa.Super. 545; Garrard v. Henderson, Tex.Civ.App.1948, 209 S.W.2d 225.

84. Collins v. Gifford, 1911, 203 N.Y. 465, 96 N.E. 721; Prescott v. Norris, 1855, 32 N.H. 101.

85. Long v. Patterson, 1945, 198 Miss. 626, 22 So.2d 490.

infant liable for negligent performance of a contract to transport the plaintiff,[86] or to receive and store his goods.[87] On the other hand if the tort can be regarded as a distinct and independent one, as to which liability can be made out without relying on the existence of the contract or in effect enforcing it, the action will lie.[88] As might be expected, considerable difficulty has arisen in applying such a distinction. It has been held, for example, that there can be no recovery for overdriving a rented horse,[89] but that for allowing him to be used in jumping,[90] or driving him beyond the agreed destination,[91] there may be liability. Trover usually is held to lie for goods converted by an infant, even though they are in his possession by virtue of a contract;[92] but when he contracts to thresh wheat and negligently uses

an engine without a spark arrester,[93] it has been held that he is not liable.

Again, since the infant may disaffirm his contractual or consensual appointment of an agent, it is generally agreed that he is not vicariously liable for the torts of his agents or servants[94] or for those with whom he is engaged in a joint enterprise.[95] This usually is held to mean that he is not liable for the negligence of one whom he has allowed to drive his automobile;[96] but some of the automobile consent statutes have been construed to impose liability.[97]

The question of tort frequently arises where the infant has obtained a contract by misrepresentation. Where the representa-

---

86. Brown v. Wood, 1940, 293 Mich. 148, 291 N.W. 255; Tennyson v. Kern, 1956, 76 S.D. 136, 74 N.W. 2d 316. Both cases apparently overruled, in Pokriefka v. Mazur, 1967, 379 Mich. 348, 151 N.W.2d 806; Friedhoff v. Engberg, 1967, 82 S.D. 522, 149 N.W.2d 759.

87. Brunhoelzl v. Brandes, 1917, 90 N.J.L. 31, 100 A. 163; Williams v. Buckler, Ky.1954, 264 S.W.2d 279. The case last cited makes it clear that an intentional departure from the terms of the bailment will make the infant liable.

88. Becker v. Mason, 1892, 93 Mich. 336, 53 N.W. 361 (seduction under promise of marriage); Sawicki v. Slahor, 1933, 11 N.J.Misc. 604, 167 A. 691 (same); Ray v. Tubbs, 1878, 50 Vt. 688; Freeman & Francis v. Boland, 1882, 14 R.I. 39.

89. Young v. Muhling, 1900, 48 App.Div. 617, 63 N.Y. S. 181; Eaton v. Hill, 1870, 50 N.H. 235; Jennings v. Randall, 1799, 8 Term Rep. 335, 101 Eng.Rep. 1419; Wilt v. Welch, 1837, 6 Watts, Pa., 9.

90. Burnard v. Haggis, 1863, 14 C.B.,N.S., 45, 143 Eng.Rep. 360.

91. Homer v. Thwing, 1826, 3 Pick., 20 Mass., 492; Ray v. Tubbs, 1878, 50 Vt. 688; Churchill v. White, 1899, 58 Neb. 22, 78 N.W. 369; cf. Towne & Co. v. Wiley, 1851, 23 Vt. 355 (circuitous route); Vermont Acceptance Corp. v. Wiltshire, 1931, 103 Vt. 219, 153 A. 199 (using car to transport liquor).

92. Smith v. Moschetti, 1948, 213 Ark. 968, 214 S.W. 2d 73; Caswell v. Parker, 1901, 96 Me. 39, 51 A. 238; Dorothy v. Salzberg, 1917, 207 Ill.App. 133; Vasse v. Smith, 1810, 6 Cranch C.C., 10 U.S., 226, 3 L.Ed. 207. See Note, 1967, 12 S.D.L.Rev. 426.

93. Lowery v. Cate, 1901, 108 Tenn. 54, 64 S.W. 1068. See also cases cited supra, notes 90 and 91.

94. Covault v. Nevitt, 1914, 157 Wis. 113, 146 N.W. 1115; Payette v. Fleischmann, 1950, 329 Mich. 160, 45 N.W.2d 16; Burns v. Smith, 1902, 29 Ind.App. 181, 64 N.E. 94; Burnham v. Seaverns, 1869, 101 Mass. 360; Hodge v. Feiner, 1935, 328 Mo. 268, 90 S.W.2d 90. The infant will, however, be liable if he procures the act, or participates in it. Sikes v. Johnson, 1820, 16 Mass. 389.

See Gregory, Infant's Responsibility for His Agent's Torts, 1930, 5 Wis.L.Rev. 453, criticizing the rule at length; Notes, 1944, 28 Minn.L.Rev. 481; 1943, 21 Chicago-Kent L.Rev. 195; 1959, 47 Ky.L.J. 545.

95. Potter v. Florida Motor Lines, S.D.Fla.1932, 57 F.2d 313; Brown v. Wood, 1940, 293 Mich. 148, 291 N.W. 255; Manley v. Horton, Mo.1967, 414 S.W.2d 254.

96. Thompson v. Bell, 6 Cir. 1942, 129 F.2d 211; Hodge v. Feiner, 1935, 338 Mo. 268, 90 S.W.2d 90; Fernandez v. Lewis, Tex.Civ.App.1936, 92 S.W.2d 305; Palmer v. Miller, 1942, 380 Ill. 256, 43 N.E.2d 973.

The infant may, however, be liable for his own negligence in failing to control that of the driver, where he can do so. Harrison v. Carroll, 4 Cir. 1943, 139 F.2d 427; Woodson v. Hare, 1943, 244 Ala. 301, 13 So.2d 172; Haynie v. Jones, 1939, 233 Mo.App. 948, 127 S.W.2d 105.

In Scott v. Schisler, 1931, 107 N.J.L. 397, 153 A. 395, an infant was held liable for the negligence of his agent driver, on the ground that the agency was only voidable, not void, and was not avoided at the time of the accident. This seems quite persuasive.

97. Ridley v. Young, 1944, 64 Cal.App.2d 503, 149 P. 2d 76; Lind v. Eddy, 1942, 232 Iowa 1328, 6 N.W.2d 427.

tions concern a collateral matter inducing the contract, most courts are agreed that the minor is liable in deceit.[98] Where he has misrepresented only his age, there is a great deal of disagreement.[99] The English courts [100] have held in such a case that there is no tort liability, considering that it would amount to an indirect enforcement of the contract, from which the tort is regarded as inseparable. A few courts in the United States have come to the same conclusion.[101] Most of the American courts have allowed the action in deceit, since the plaintiff is not seeking to enforce the contract or obtain its benefits, but only to recover compensation for the damage he has suffered through the fraud.[1] Other courts have found an estoppel against the infant which prevents him from asserting his minority in his affirmative action for rescission,[2] or as a defense when he is sued on the contract,[3] although here there is more authority to the contrary. In a few states there are statutes creating the estoppel,[4] or requiring the infant to make complete restitution as a condition of rescission.[5]

The effect of the decisions refusing to recognize tort liability for misrepresentation is to create a privileged class of liars who are a great trouble to the business world. The decisions seem to rest on a failure to distinguish between a shield and a sword—between the obligation which the infant has agreed to assume and that which the law imposes upon him for the protection of others. The immunity has a legitimate place where the contract is really being enforced under the guise of a tort action developed long since to avoid the stringencies of common law pleading;[6] but where a genuine duty is independently created by the law because of the relation of the parties, the existence of a contract should not prevent the tort liability,

98. Butler Bros. v. Snyder, 1924, 81 Ind.App. 44, 142 N.E. 398; Shenkein v. Fuhrman, 1913, 80 Misc. 179, 141 N.Y.S. 909; cf. Patterson v. Kasper, 1914, 182 Mich. 281, 148 N.W. 690; Beardsley v. Clark, 1940, 229 Iowa 601, 294 N.W. 887.

Even here there is some authority to the contrary. Lesnick v. Pratt, 1951, 78 A.2d 487, reargument denied 116 Vt. 477, 80 A.2d 663.

99. Fully treated in Miller, Fraudulent Misrepresentations of Age as Affecting the Infant's Contract— A Comparative Study, 1953, 15 U.Pitts.L.Rev. 73.

100. Johnson v. Pye, 1665, 1 Sid. 258, 82 Eng.Rep. 1091; Leslie v. Sheill, [1914] 3 K.B. 607, Ann.Cas. 1916C, 992.

101. Slayton v. Barry, 1900, 175 Mass. 513, 56 N.E. 574; Greensboro Morris Plan Co. v. Palmer, 1923, 185 N.C. 109, 116 S.E. 261; Spangler Co. v. Haupt, 1913, 53 Pa.Super. 545; Summit Auto Co. v. Jenkins, 1925, 20 Ohio App. 229, 153 N.E. 153; cf. Tyda v. Reiter-Schmidt, Inc., 1958, 16 Ill.App.2d 370, 147 N. E.2d 690.

1. Wisconsin Loan & Finance Corp. v. Goodnough, 1950, 201 Wis. 101, 228 N.W. 484; Doenges-Long Motors Inc. v. Gillen, 1958, 138 Colo. 31, 328 P.2d 1077; Berryman v. Highway Trailer Co., 1940, 307 Ill.App. 480, 30 N.E.2d 761; Mestetzko v. Elf Motor Co., 1929, 119 Ohio St. 575, 165 N.E. 93; see Byers v. Lemay Bank & Trust Co., 1955, 365 Mo. 341, 282 S.W.2d 512.

2. Lewis v. Van Cleve, 1922, 302 Ill. 413, 134 N.E. 804; Adkins v. Adkins, 1919, 183 Ky. 662, 210 S.W. 462; Tuck v. Payne, 1929, 159 Tenn. 192, 17 S.W.2d

8; Stallard v. Sutherland, 1921, 131 Va. 316, 108 S. E. 568; Grauman, Marx & Cline Co. v. Krienitz, 1910, 142 Wis. 556, 126 N.W. 50.

Contra: McCarty-Greene Motor Co. v. McCluney, 1929, 219 Ala. 211, 121 So. 713; Whitman v. Allen, 1923, 123 Me. 1, 121 A. 160; Steigerwalt v. Woodhead Co., 1932, 186 Minn. 558, 244 N.W. 412; Sternlieb v. Normandie Nat. Securities Corp., 1934, 263 N.Y. 245, 188 N.E. 726.

3. Clemons v. Olshine, 1936, 54 Ga.App. 290, 187 S.E. 711; New Domain Oil & Gas Co. v. McKinney, 1920, 188 Ky. 183, 221 S.W. 245; Klinck v. Reeder, 1921, 107 Neb. 342, 185 N.W. 100; La Rosa v. Nichols, 1918, 92 N.J.L. 375, 105 A. 201; Reggiori v. Forbes, 1942, 128 N.J.L. 391, 26 A.2d 145.

Contra: Arkansas Reo Motor Co. v. Goodlett, 1924, 163 Ark. 35, 258 S.W. 975; Creer v. Active Auto Exchange, 1923, 99 Conn. 266, 121 A. 888; Sawyer Boot & Shoe Co. v. Braverman, 1927, 126 Me. 70, 136 A. 290; Raymond v. General Motorcycle Sales Co., 1918, 230 Mass. 54, 119 N.E. 539; Russell v. Buck, 1949, 116 Vt. 40, 68 A.2d 691.

4. See Friar v. Rae-Chandler Co., 1921, 192 Iowa 427, 185 N.W. 32; Dillon v. Burnham, 1890, 43 Kan. 77, 22 P. 1016; Thosath v. Transport Motor Co., 1925, 136 Wash. 565, 240 P. 921.

5. See Murdock v. Fisher Finance Corp., 1926, 79 Cal.App. 787, 251 P. 319; Stanhope v. Shambow, 1924, 72 Mont. 166, 232 P. 531.

6. As in Yubas v. Wilson, 1930, 95 Pa.Super. 296.

even though the two obligations closely coincide.[7]

135. INSANITY

Lunatics usually have been classed with infants, and held liable for their torts. The rule seems to have originated in a dictum in a case [8] decided in 1616, at a time when the action of trespass still rested upon the older basis of strict liability without regard to the fault of the individual. When the modern law developed to the point of holding the defendant liable only for wrongful intent or negligence, the dictum was still repeated, and there have been numerous decisions in accord with it. Thus an insane person has been held liable in a tort action for assault and battery,[9] wrongful death,[10] false imprisonment,[11] trespass on land,[12] destruction of property,[13] conversion,[14] wrongfully suing out an injunction,[15] alienation of affections,[16] infringement of a patent,[17] and injuries caused by the defective condition of his property.[18]

A number of different explanations have been given for the lunatic's liability, none of which has gone unchallenged.[19] It has been said that "where one of two innocent persons must suffer a loss, it should be borne by the one who occasioned it." [20] So far as this is anything more than an historical survival, it represents a conclusion that it is better that the estate of the lunatic should be taken to give compensation for the damage he has done than that it should remain to be admin-

---

7. See Gregory, Infant's Responsibility for His Agent's Tort, 1940, 5 Wis.L.Rev. 453; Miller, Fraudulent Misrepresentations of Age as Affecting the Infant's Contract—A Comparative Study, 1953, 15 U.Pitts.L.Rev. 73; Notes, 1930, 5 Wis.L.Rev. 434; 1927, 27 Col.L.Rev. 466; 1921, 31 Yale L.J. 201; 1941, 39 Mich.L.Rev. 1417.

8. Weaver v. Ward, 1616, Hob. 134, 80 Eng.Rep. 284.

9. Mullen v. Bruce, 1959, 168 Cal.App.2d 494, 335 P. 2d 945; Van Vooren v. Cook, 1947, 273 App.Div. 88, 75 N.Y.S.2d 362, reargument denied 273 App.Div. 941, 78 N.Y.S.2d 558; McGuire v. Almy, 1937, 297 Mass. 323, 8 N.E.2d 760; Kusah v. McCorkle, 1918, 100 Wash. 318, 170 P. 1023; Bolen v. Howard, Ky.1970, 452 S.W.2d 401.

In Albiocco v. Nicoletto, 1960, 11 App.Div.2d 690, 204 N.Y.S.2d 566, affirmed memo. 1961, 9 N.Y.2d 920, 217 N.Y.S.2d 91, 176 N.E.2d 100, even insanity caused by defendant's provocation and abuse was held not to prevent liability, although it went to mitigate damages.

10. McIntyre v. Sholty, 1887, 121 Ill. 660, 13 N.E. 239; Phillips' Committee v. Ward's Adm'r, 1931, 241 Ky. 25, 43 S.W.2d 331; Jewell v. Colby, 1890, 66 N.H. 399, 24 A. 902; Seals v. Snow, 1927, 123 Kan. 88, 254 P. 348; Bollinger v. Rader, 1910, 153 N.C. 488, 69 S.E. 497. These are all cases of intentional homicide.

11. Krom v. Schoonmaker, 1848, 3 Barb., N.Y., 647.

12. Cathcart v. Matthews, 1916, 105 S.C. 329, 89 S.E. 1021; Amick v. O'Hara, 1843, 6 Blackf., Ind., 258.

13. Morse v. Crawford, 1893, 17 Vt. 499 (killing an ox); Cross v. Kent, 1870, 32 Md. 581; Mutual Fire Ins. Co. v. Showalter, 1897, 3 Pa.Super.Ct. 452; In re Guardianship of Meyer, 1935, 218 Wis. 381, 261 N.W. 211.

14. Morse v. Crawford, 1893, 17 Vt. 499.

15. Behrens v. McKenzie, 1867, 23 Iowa 333.

16. Shedrick v. Lathrop, 1934, 106 Vt. 311, 172 A. 630; Sweeney v. Carter, 1939, 24 Tenn.App. 6, 137 S.W.2d 892.

17. Avery v. Wilson, W.D.N.C.1884, 20 F. 856.

18. Filip v. Gagne, 1962, 104 N.H. 14, 177 A.2d 509; Morain v. Devlin, 1882, 132 Mass. 87; Campbell v. Bradbury, 1918, 179 Cal. 364, 176 P. 685. Contra, Ward v. Rogers, 1906, 51 Misc. 299, 100 N.Y.S. 1058.

19. See Bohlen, Liability in Tort of Infants and Insane Persons, 1924, 23 Mich.L.Rev. 9; Hornblower, Insanity and the Law of Negligence, 1905, 5 Col.L. Rev. 278; Cook, Mental Deficiency in Relation to Tort, 1921, 21 Col.L.Rev. 333; Green, Public Policies Underlying the Law of Mental Incompetency, 1940, 38 Mich.L.Rev. 1189; Wilkinson, Mental Incompetency as a Defense to Tort Liability, 1944, 17 Rocky Mt.L.Rev. 38; Weisiger, Tort Liability of Minors and Incompetents, [1951] U.Ill.L. Forum 227; Ague, The Liability of Insane Persons in Tort Actions, 1956, 60 Dick.L.Rev. 211; Curran, Tort Liability of the Mentally Ill and Mentally Deficient, 1960, 21 Ohio St.L.J. 52; Friedman, Mental Incompetence, Part II, 1964, 80 L.Q.Rev. 84; Notes, 1938, 22 Minn.L.Rev. 853; 1937, 17 Bos.U.L.Rev. 890; 1935, 13 Tex.L.Rev. 246; 1948, 34 Corn.L.Q. 274.

20. See Seals v. Snow, 1927, 123 Kan. 88, 90, 254 P. 348, 349; Beals v. See, 1848, 10 Pa. 56, 61; Williams v. Hays, 1894, 143 N.Y. 442, 447, 38 N.E. 449, 450; Karow v. Continental Ins. Co., 1883, 57 Wis. 56, 64, 15 N.W. 27, 30.

istered by guardians for his own incompetent benefit.[21] It has been said also that if he is held liable, his custodians and those interested in his estate will be stimulated to keep him in order;[22] and that since insanity is easily feigned, there would be too much temptation to pretend it.[23] Coupled with this is perhaps an unexpressed fear of introducing into the law of torts the confusion and unsatisfactory tests attending proof of insanity in criminal cases.[24] Against these arguments there has been advanced only the simple contention that it is unjust to hold a man responsible for a wrong that he is incapable of avoiding.

A lunatic may be capable of having an intent to bring about a specific result, even though the intent is induced by a delusion; and in that respect his acts are to be distinguished from those of an epileptic or a person seized with temporary unconsciousness, which are regarded as involuntary and accidental.[25] If tort liability without fault is to be imposed upon sane persons who make reasonable mistakes,[26] a lunatic who acts under a perpetual mistake, unreasonable in the eyes of the community, may very well be held liable for his intentional torts. It has been recognized, however, that his insanity may be such that he is incapable of entertaining the specific intent necessary for a particular

tort, such as deceit,[27] malicious prosecution,[28] defamation,[29] or even battery,[30] and so he should not be liable simply because he has not committed the tort. This, however, has not always been carried through very effectively. As to defamation, there has been almost a complete failure to distinguish between the "legal malice" implied as a fiction from the intent to publish the defamatory words, and the "malice in fact" which will defeat a qualified privilege.[31] It would appear that the insane person may properly be charged with the former, but not the latter.[32] It seems well settled that insanity may be shown to disprove evil intent and mitigate actual damages,[33] and that where the insanity is notorious, it may disprove special damage because no one believes what is said.[34] Since the lunatic is regarded as incapable of the necessary guilty mind, and admonition to him is obviously futile, punitive damages are never recoverable against him.[35]

21. See McGuire v. Almy, 1937, 297 Mass. 323, 8 N. E.2d 760; Bohlen, Liability in Tort of Infants and Insane Persons, 1924, 23 Mich.L.Rev. 9, 17–18.

22. See McGuire v. Almy, 1937, 297 Mass. 323, 8 N. E.2d 760; McIntyre v. Sholty, 1887, 121 Ill. 660, 13 N.E. 239; Seals v. Snow, 1927, 123 Kan. 88, 254 P. 348; Williams v. Hays, 1894, 143 N.Y. 442, 38 N.E. 449.

23. See Young v. Young, 1910, 141 Ky. 76, 132 S.W. 155, and cases cited in the preceding footnote.

24. See Bohlen, Liability in Tort of Infants and Insane Persons, 1924, 23 Mich.L.Rev. 9; Note, 1938, 22 Minn.L.Rev. 853, 862.

25. See supra, § 29.

26. See supra, § 17.

27. Chaddock v. Chaddock, 1927, 130 Misc. 900, 226 N.Y.S. 152.

28. Beaubeauf v. Reed, 1926, 4 La.App. 344. But cf. Behrens v. McKenzie, 1867, 23 Iowa 333.

29. Irvine v. Gibson, 1904, 117 Ky. 306, 77 S.W. 1106; Bryant v. Jackson, 1845, 6 Humph., Tenn., 199; Horner v. Marshall's Adm'x, 1817, 5 Munf., Va., 466.

30. See Mullen v. Bruce, 1959, 168 Cal.App.2d 494, 335 P.2d 945; also Morriss v. Marsden, [1952] 1 All Eng.Rep. 925, followed in Beal v. Hayward, [1960] N.Z.L.Rep. 131, and Phillips v. Soloway, [1956] 6 Dom.L.Rep.2d 570.

31. See Notes, 1938, 22 Minn.L.Rev. 853, 859–860; 1934, 34 Col.L.Rev. 185.

32. See Gatley, Libel and Slander, 2d Ed. 1929, 430, 437; Ullrich v. New York Press Co., 1898, 23 Misc. 168, 50 N.Y.S. 788.

33. See Yeates v. Reed, 1838, 4 Blackf., Ind., 463; Gates v. Meredith, 1856, 7 Ind. 440; Dickinson v. Barber, 1812, 9 Mass. 225. Cf. Warner v. Lockerby, 1884, 31 Minn. 421, 18 N.W. 145, rehearing denied, 31 Minn. 421, 18 N.W.2d 821 (heat of passion); Alderson v. Kahle, 1914, 73 W.Va. 690, 80 S.E. 1109.

34. Wilson v. Walt, 1933, 138 Kan. 205, 25 P.2d 343; see Dickinson v. Barber, 1812, 9 Mass. 225.

35. Jewell v. Colby, 1890, 66 N.H. 399, 24 A. 902; see Moore v. Horne, 1910, 153 N.C. 413, 69 S.E. 409; Phillips' Committee v. Ward's Adm'r, 1931, 241 Ky.

So far as negligence is concerned, there have been surprisingly few cases,[36] nearly all of which have held the insane person liable for failure to conform to the standard of conduct required of a sane man. One of these, at least, refused to hold the defendant liable where his insanity was brought on, without his fault, by his employment.[37] There has been virtually no discussion in these few decisions of the volitional element of the defendant's conduct. It is difficult to see how any person who is so absolutely devoid of intelligence or reason as to be unable to apprehend apparent danger and do something to avoid it, can be said to be negligent.[38] On this basis, there is good sense in the Canadian case [39] which refused to find negligence when a truck driver, overcome by the insane delusion that his truck was being operated by remote control, sat transfixed and really powerless to do anything about the collision which ensued. It is perhaps going too far to say, as some writers have said,[40] that the insane man should have the same allowance made for him that is made for children,[41] and be held to no higher degree of care than he is capable of exercising; but it is still possible that some more liberal rule might be applied to the more extreme cases. The question may be said to be still an open one in the United States.

25, 31, 43 S.W.2d 331, 334; Feld v. Borodofski, 1905, 87 Miss. 727, 731, 40 So. 816.

36. Williams v. Hays, 1894, 143 N.Y. 442, 38 N.E. 449, qualified in 1899, 157 N.Y. 541, 52 N.E. 589; Sforza v. Green Bus Lines, 1934, 150 Misc. 180, 268 N.Y.S. 446; Shapiro v. Tchernowitz, 1956, 3 Misc.2d 617, 155 N.Y.S.2d 1011; Johnson v. Lambotte, 1961, 147 Colo. 203, 363 P.2d 165; Ellis v. Fixico, 1935, 174 Okl. 116, 50 P.2d 162 (statute). See also Parke v. Dennard, 1928, 218 Ala. 209, 118 So. 396; Jenkins v. Hankins, 1897, 98 Tenn. 545, 41 S.W. 1028; Leary v. Oates, Tex.Civ.App.1935, 84 S.W.2d 486, error dismissed.

37. Williams v. Hays, 1894, 143 N.Y. 442, 38 N.E. 449, qualified in 1899, 157 N.Y. 541, 52 N.E. 589. The case is discussed at length in Hornblower, Insanity and the Law of Negligence, 1905, 5 Col.L. Rev. 278, 284–293. Compare Goldman v. New York R. Co., 1919, 185 App.Div. 739, 173 N.Y.S. 737 (warning of fainting spell); Bushnell v. Bushnell, 1925, 103 Conn. 583, 131 A. 432 (warning of sleep).

38. So stated, as to contributory negligence, in Emory University v. Lee, 1958, 97 Ga.App. 680, 104 S.E. 2d 234; De Martini v. Alexander Sanitarium, 1961, 192 Cal.App.2d 442, 13 Cal.Rptr. 564; Johnson v. Texas & Pac. R. Co., 1931, 16 La.App. 464, 133 So. 517, 135 So. 114; Riesbeck Drug Co. v. Wray, 1942, 111 Ind.App. 467, 39 N.E.2d 776.

39. Buckley & Toronto Transp. Comm'n v. Smith Transport, Ltd., [1946] Ont.L.Rep. 798, [1946] 4 Dom.L.Rep. 721. This was reiterated in Breunig v. American Family Ins. Co., 1970, 45 Wis.2d 536, 173 N.W.2d 619.

40. Hornblower, Insanity and the Law of Negligence, 1905, 5 Col.L.Rev. 278; Bohlen, Liability in Tort of Infants and Insane Persons, 1924, 23 Mich.L.Rev. 9; Cook, Mental Deficiency in Relation to Tort, 1921, 21 Col.L.Rev. 333.

41. See supra, p. 154.

TABLE OF CASES

References are to Pages

E

H

K

Q

INDEX

References are to Pages